May 13-17
Rio de Janeiro

Association for Computing Machinery

Advancing Computing as a Science & Profession

22nd International World Wide Web Conference
13th-17th, May

WWW'13

Proceedings of the 22nd International Conference on
World Wide Web

Sponsored by:
**CGI.BR (Comite Gestor da Internet no Brazil),
NIC.BR (Nucleo de Informatcao e Coordenacao do Ponto BR)**

In cooperation with:
ACM SIGWEB

IW3C3

Copyright © 2013 by the International World Wide Web Conferences Steering Committee (IW3C3). Permission to make digital or hard copies of portions of this work for personal or classroom use is granted without fee provided that copies are not made or distributed for profit or commercial advantage and that copies bear this notice and the full citation on the first page. Copyright for components of this work owned by others than IW3C3 must be honored. Abstracting with credit is permitted. To copy otherwise, to republish, to post on servers or to redistribute to lists, requires prior specific permission and/or a fee.

For other copying of articles that carry a code at the bottom of the first or last page, copying is permitted provided that the per-copy fee indicated in the code is paid.

Notice to Past Authors of IW3C3 Published Articles
ACM intends to create a complete electronic archive of all articles and/or other material previously published by ACM. If you have written a work that has been previously published by ACM in any journal or conference proceedings prior to 1978, or any SIG Newsletter at any time, and you do NOT want this work to appear in the ACM Digital Library, please inform permissions@acm.org, stating the title of the work, the author(s), and where and when published.

ISBN: 978-1-4503-2035-1 (Digital)

ISBN: 978-1-4503-2444-1 (Print)

Printed in the USA

General Chairs' Welcome

It is our great pleasure to welcome you to the *22nd International World Wide Web Conference – WWW 2013*. The WWW Conference series has been held almost since the creation of the WWW itself, having become the premier forum where key researchers, innovators, decision-makers, technologists, businesses, and standards bodies meet to present their latest works and ideas, and discuss their vision for how the WWW will evolve – often as a direct result of their own actions and initiatives. The conference series is organized by the International World Wide Web Conferences Steering Committee (IW3C2) in collaboration with Local Organizing Committees and Technical Program Committees.

This year the conference is being held in Rio de Janeiro, Brazil, for the first time ever in a Latin American country. We are extremely pleased to offer a top quality program, as can be verified by simply perusing these proceedings and its companion volume. The Research and Practice and Experience tracks present 137 papers in 35 track sessions; the Developers track, 10 papers in 4 sessions; the Demos track, 24 demos in 3 sessions; 100 posters in an ongoing poster exhibition; 12 Doctoral Consortium papers; a W3C track reporting on the latest standardization activities in themes such as Web Performance, eGov and Open Data; and an Industry Track with presentations from major players in the WWW on Big Data and on Patents and Innovation. Complementing this, more recent preliminary results are presented in over 150 papers in 21 Workshops, spanning a myriad of exciting new and existing topics. For those seeking to complement their understanding of the major knowledge areas and research topics associated with the WWW, 22 tutorials are being offered. This program is complemented with several parallel events, such as hackathons, panels, and specialized meetings covering a multitude of new subjects.

The WWW conference is a result of the collective work of many individuals; first and foremost, we must thank all the authors and contributors, including panelists and invited speakers, who provide the core content that is responsible for the conference's success. We also thank all the members of this conference's organizing committee and its sponsors, who are spelled out in the succeeding pages in these proceedings. Beyond these, it's worth mentioning the heavy participation of innumerous Web users with whom we have interacted, gathering suggestions and ideas for improvement. In fact, our logo was chosen as the winning entry in a public open contest run on the Web. We also had the help of a host of volunteers, from all over the world.

We must also thank our institutions, Pontificia Universidade Católica do Rio de Janeiro (PUC-Rio); Federal University of Minas Gerais (UFMG); and especially the Comitê Gestor da Internet no Brasil (CGI.br), who hosts this conference, for their support in allowing us to organize this conference.

We hope this quality program will stimulate you, give you new ideas and encourage you to explore new areas, or to continue your research and development in exciting new ways.

Daniel Schwabe
PUC-Rio, Brazil

Virgilio Almeida
UFMG, Brazil

Hartmut Glaser
CGI.br

Programme Chairs' Welcome

It is our great pleasure to present you the technical programme of WWW 2013, that, for the first time, is held in South America. The call for papers attracted a breath-taking number of more than 1250 abstracts that were converted to 831 full paper submissions. A program committee of 661 PC members and 316 supporting reviewers evaluated these papers. Based on almost 3,000 reviews and meta-reviews, that is, 3.6 reviews per paper on average, as well as many discussions held online, plus a two full days meeting with most of the 23 track chairs, we decided upon the final list of accepted full papers. At the end, 125 papers, only 15% of the submissions, could be accommodated in the technical programme.

The submissions came from 50 countries all around the world, with 24 of them represented in the final program. The top 6 paper contributors were USA (297), China (110), Germany (54), United Kingdom (39), India (36), and Brazil (31). However, the top 6 countries with better acceptance rates were Israel (39%), Austria (24%), Italy (24%), Switzerland (24%), United Kingdom (22%), and United States (21%). These papers represent a well-balanced mix over the 12 tracks listed below. Though the different tracks received very different numbers of submissions, our principal selection criterion was quality. That is, we neither enforced a proportional share of acceptances among the tracks, nor did we favor tracks with lower numbers of submissions. The corresponding submission and acceptance numbers per track are the following:

Track	Submitted	Accepted
Behavioral Analysis and Personalization	83	17
Bringing Unstructured and Structured Data Together	41	3
Content Analysis	59	6
Internet Monetization and Incentives	53	10
Search Systems and Applications	78	10
Security, Privacy, Trust, and Abuse	82	15
Semantic Web	59	7
Social Networks and Graph Analysis	145	22
Software Infrastructure and Their Performance, Scalability and Availability	28	4
User Interfaces, Human Factors, and Smart Devices	53	11
Web Engineering	55	8
Web Mining	95	12
Total	831	125

We hope that you will find the resulting program interesting and thought provoking and that the conference will provide you with a valuable opportunity to share ideas with other researchers and practitioners from institutions around the world. Rio de Janeiro should do the rest.

Ricardo Baeza-Yates
WWW 2013 Programme Co-Chair
Yahoo! Labs, Spain & Chile

Sue Moon
WWW 2013 Programme Co-Chair
KAIST, South Korea

Message from the Chair of IW3C2

In the beached margent of the sea ...

On behalf of the International World Wide Web Conference Committee (IW3C2), the steering committee for this conference series, I welcome you to the 22nd conference of our series. As you may already know, the World Wide Web was first conceived in 1989 by Tim Berners-Lee at CERN in Geneva, Switzerland. The first conference of the series, WWW1, was held at CERN in 1994 and organized by Robert Cailliau. The IW3C2 was founded by Joseph Hardin and Robert Cailliau later in 1994 and has been responsible for the conference series ever since. I have personally been lucky enough to be part of this community since WWW2, when I co-authored a poster. After 1994 and 1995 (when two conferences were held each year), WWW became an annual event held in late April or early May.

The location of the conference generally rotates among the Americas, Europe, and Asia/Pacific. In 2001 we changed the conference designator from a number (1 through 10) to the year it is held; i.e., WWW11 became known as WWW2002. You may browse our website http://www.iw3c2.org/ for information on past and future conferences. **WWW2017 is now open for bids,** preferably from a host in Asia/Pacific. We encourage you to point interested parties to the "Host a Conference" section of the IW3C2's web site.

The International WWW Conference series provides the world with a premier forum about the development of the Web, the standardization of its associated technologies, and the Web's impact on society and culture. These conferences bring together researchers, students, developers, users, and vendors – indeed all of you who are passionate about the Web and what it has to offer, now and in the future. Part of what is exciting about this series is the cross boundary and eclectic nature of the topics covered, and the opportunity it provides for exploration of new directions, both technological and social.

We thank CGI.br for co-organizing WWW2013. We appreciate the cooperation of ACM, which makes our conference the best in the Web area. Many thanks to all of our WWW2013 sponsors, who make this event possible.

We are excited about the opportunity to bring the conference series web community to South America for the first time, to Brazil, and to Rio de Janeiro, to share the history, natural beauty, food, and drink of this stunning city with all of you. We thank the general chairs Virgilio Almeida, Daniel Schwabe and Hartmut Glaser for all their hard work. Let us all take this opportunity to learn new things in technology, in culture, and in business, from each other.

Mary Ellen Zurko
Cisco Systems

Table of Contents

General Chairs' Welcome Message iii
Daniel Schwabe
(Pontificia Universidade Católica do Rio de Janeiro), |
Virgilio Fernades Almeida
(Univerdidade Federal de Minas Gerais),
Hartmut Glaser *(Brazilian Internet Steering Committee)*

Programme Chairs' Welcome v
Ricardo Baeza-Yates *(Yahoo! Labs),*
Sue Moon *(Korea Advanced Institute of Science and Technology)*

Message from the Chair of IW3C2 vii
Mary Ellen Zurko *(Cisco Systems)*

Organization List xiii

Sponsor/Supporters xxix

Volume 1

Technical Presentations

Real-Time Recommendation of Diverse Related Articles 1
Sofiane Abbar *(Qatar Computing Research Institute),*
Sihem Amer-Yahia *(CNRS, LIG),*
Piotr Indyk, Sepideh Mahabadi *(MIT)*

Multi-Label Learning with Millions of Labels: Recommending Advertiser Bid Phrases for Web Pages 13
Rahul Agrawal *(Microsoft AdCenter),*
Archit Gupta *(Indian Institute of Technology Delhi),*
Yashoteja Prabhu, Manik Varma *(Micrososft Research)*

Hierarchical Geographical Modeling of User Locations from Social Media Posts 25
Amr Ahmed *(Google),*
Liangjie Hong *(Yahoo! Labs),*
Alex Smola *(Google & Carnegie Mellon University)*

Distributed Large-scale Natural Graph Factorization 37
Amr Ahmed *(Google),*
Nino Shervashidze *(INRIA, ENS),*
Shravan Narayanamurthy *(Microsoft),*
Vanja Josifovski *(Google),*
Alexander J. Smola *(Carnegie Mellon University & Google)*

A CRM System for Social Media: Challenges and Experiences 49
Jitendra Ajmera *(IBM India Research),*
Hyung-iL Ahn, Nagarajan *(IBM Research),*
Ashish Verma, Danish Contractor *(IBM India Research),*
Stephen Dill, Matthew Denesuk *(IBM Research)*

Here's My Cert, So Trust Me, Maybe? Understanding TLS Errors on the Web 59
Devdatta Akhawe *(University of California, Berkeley),*
Bernhard Amann *(International Computer Science Institute),*
Matthias Vallentin *(University of California, Berkeley),*
Robin Sommer *(International Computer Science Institute)*

Towards a Robust Modeling of Temporal Interest Change Patterns for Behavioral Targeting 71
Mohamed Aly *(Seeloz Inc.),* Sandeep Pandey *(Twitter),*
Vanja Josifovski *(Google Inc.),* Kunal Punera *(RelateIQ)*

The Anatomy of LDNS Clusters: Findings and Implications for Web Content Delivery 83
Hussein A. Alzoubi,
Michael Rabinovich *(Case Western Reserve University),*
Oliver Spatscheck *(AT&T Research Labs)*

Steering User Behavior with Badges 95
Ashton Anderson *(Stanford University),*
Daniel Huttenlocher, Jon Kleinberg *(Cornell University),*
Jure Leskovec *(Stanford University)*

Cascading Tree Sheets and Recombinant HTML: Better Encapsulation and Retargeting of Web Content 107
Edward Benson, David R. Karger *(MIT)*

CopyCatch: Stopping Group Attacks by Spotting Lockstep Behavior in Social Networks 119
Alex Beutel *(Carnegie Mellon University),*
Wanhong Xu *(Facebook),*
Venkatesan Guruswami *(Carnegie Mellon University),*
Christopher Palow *(Facebook),*
Christos Faloutsos *(Carnegie Mellon University)*

Inferring the Demographics of Search Users: Social Data Meets Search Queries 131
Bin Bi *(University of California, Los Angeles),*
Milad Shokouhi *(Microsoft Research Cambridge),*
Michal Kosinski *(University of Cambridge),*
Thore Graepel *(Microsoft Research Cambridge)*

Strategyproof Mechanisms for Competitive Influence in Networks 141
Allan Borodin *(University of Toronto),*
Mark Braverman *(Princeton University),*
Brendan Lucier *(Microsoft Research),*
Joel Oren *(University of Toronto)*

Reactive Crowdsourcing 153
Alessandro Bozzon, Marco Brambilla, Stefano Ceri,
Andrea Mauri *(Politecnico di Milano),*

On Participation in Group Chats on Twitter 165
Ceren Budak *(University of California, Santa Barbara),*
Rakesh Agrawal *(Microsoft Research Labs)*

The Role of Web Hosting Providers in Detecting Compromised Websites 177
Davide Canali, Davide Balzarotti,
Aurélien Francillon *(Eurecom)*

Your Browsing Behavior for a Big Mac: Economics of Personal Information Online 189
Juan Pablo Carrascal *(Universitat Pompeu Fabra),*
Christopher Riederer *(Columbia University),*
Vijay Erramilli, Mauro Cherubini,
Rodrigo de Oliveira *(Telefónica Research)*

Is This App Safe for Children? A Comparison Study of Maturity Ratings on Android and IOS Applications . 201
Ying Chen, Heng Xu *(The Pennsylvania State University),*
Yilu Zhou *(George Washington University),*
Sencun Zhu *(The Pennsylvania State University)*

Traveling the Silk Road: A Measurement Analysis of a Large Anonymous Online Marketplace 213
Nicolas Christin *(Carnegie Mellon University)*

Group Chats on Twitter 225
James Cook *(University of California, Berkeley),*
Krishnaram Kenthapadi, Nina Mishra *(Microsoft Research)*

Table of Contents

How to Grow More Pairs: Suggesting Review Targets for Comparison-Friendly Review Ecosystems 237
James Cook *(University of California, Berkeley)*,
Alex Fabrikant, Avinatan Hassidim *(Google Research)*

A Framework for Benchmarking Entity-Annotation Systems 249
Marco Cornolti, Paolo Ferragina *(University of Pisa)*,
Massimiliano Ciaramita *(Google Research)*

A Framework for Learning Web Wrappers from the Crowd 261
Valter Crescenzi *(Università degli Studi Roma Tre)*,
Paolo Merialdo, Qiu *(Università Roma Tre)*

Lightweight Server Support for Browser-Based CSRF Protection 273
Alexei Czeskis *(University of Washington)*,
Alexander Moshchuk *(Microsoft Research)*,
Tadayoshi Kohno *(University of Washington)*,
Helen J. Wang *(Microsoft Research)*

Aggregating Crowdsourced Binary Ratings 285
Nilesh Dalvi *(Facebook, Inc.)*,
Anirban Dasgupta *(Yahoo! Labs)*,
Ravi Kumar, Vibhor Rastogi *(Google)*

Optimal Hashing Schemes for Entity Matching 295
Nilesh Dalvi *(Facebook)*,
Vibhor Rastogi *(Google)*,
Anirban Dasgupta *(Yahoo!)*,
Anish Das Sarma, Tamás Sarlós *(Google)*

No Country for Old Members: User Lifecycle and Linguistic Change in Online Communities 307
Cristian Danescu-Niculescu-Mizil
(Stanford University & Max Planck Institute SWS),
Robert West, Dan Jurafsky, Jure Leskovec,
Christopher Potts *(Stanford University)*

Crowdsourced Judgement Elicitation with Endogenous Proficiency 319
Anirban Dasgupta *(Yahoo! Labs)*,
Arpita Ghosh *(Cornell University)*

Timespent Based Models for Predicting User Retention 331
Kushal Dave *(IIIT - Hyderabad)*,
Vishal Vaingankar, Sumanth Kolar *(StumbleUpon)*,
Vasudeva Varma *(IIIT - Hyderabad)*

Attributing Authorship of Revisioned Content 343
Luca de Alfaro, Michael Shavlovsky *(University of California)*

ClausIE: Clause-Based Open Information Extraction ... 355
Luciano Del Corro,
Rainer Gemulla *(Max-Planck-Institute für Informatik)*

Pick-A-Crowd: Tell Me What You Like, and I'll Tell You What to Do – A Crowdsourcing Platform for Personalized Human Intelligence Task Assignment Based on Social Networks 367
Djellel Eddine Difallah, Gianluca Demartini,
Philippe Cudré-Mauroux *(University of Fribourg)*

Compact Explanation of Data Fusion Decisions 379
Xin Luna Dong *(Google Inc.)*,
Divesh Srivastava *(AT&T Labs-Research)*

From Query to Question in One Click: Suggesting Synthetic Questions to Searchers 391
Gideon Dror, Yoelle Maarek, Avihai Mejer,
Idan Szpektor *(Yahoo! Research)*

Perception and Understanding of Social Annotations in Web Search 403
Jennifer Fernquist, Ed H. Chi *(Google, Inc.)*

AMIE: Association Rule Mining under Incomplete Evidence in Ontological Knowledge Bases 413
Luis Galárraga,
Christina Teflioudi *(Max-Planck Institute for Informatics)*,
Katja Hose *(Aalborg University)*,
Fabian Suchanek *(Max-Planck Institute for Informatics)*

PrefixSolve: Efficiently Solving Multi-Source Multi-Destination Path Queries on RDF Graphs by Sharing Suffix Computations 423
Sidan Gao, Kemafor Anyanwu *(North Carolina State University)*

When Tolerance Causes Weakness: The Case of Injection-Friendly Browsers 435
Yossi Gilad, Herzberg *(Bar-Ilan University)*

Exploiting Innocuous Activity for Correlating Users Across Sites 447
Oana Goga *(UPMC Sorbonne Universites)*,
Howard Lei, Sree Hari Krishnan Parthasarathi *(ICSI)*,
Gerald Friedland *(ICSI & University of California, Berkeley)*,
Robin Sommer *(ICSI & LBNL)*,
Renata Teixeira *(CNRS & UPMC Sorbonne Universites)*

The Cost of Annoying Ads 459
Daniel G. Goldstein *(Microsoft Research)*,
R. Preston McAfee *(Google Strategic Technologies)*,
Siddharth Suri *(Microsoft Research)*

Researcher Homepage Classification Using Unlabeled Data 471
Sujatha Das Gollapalli *(The Pennsylvania State University)*,
Cornelia Caragea *(The University of North Texas)*,
Prasenjit Mitra, C. Lee Giles *(The Pennsylvania State University)*

Google+ or Google-? Dissecting the Evolution of the New OSN in its First Year 483
Roberto Gonzalez,
Ruben Cuevas *(Universidad Carlos III de Madrid)*,
Reza Motamedi, Reza Rejaie *(University of Oregon)*,
Angel Cuevas *(Telecom Sud Paris)*

Probabilistic Group Recommendation via Information Matching 495
Jagadeesh Gorla *(University College London)*,
Neal Lathia *(University of Cambridge)*,
Stephen Robertson *(Microsoft Research)*,
Jun Wang *(University College London)*

WTF: The Who to Follow Service at Twitter 505
Pankaj Gupta, Ashish Goel, Jimmy Lin, Aneesh Sharma,
Dong Wang, Reza Zadeh *(Twitter, Inc.)*

Mining Expertise and Interests from Social Media 515
Ido Guy, Uri Avraham, David Carmel, Sigalit Ur, Michal Jacovi,
Inbal Ronen *(IBM Research)*

Measuring Personalization of Web Search 527
Aniko Hannak *(Northeastern University)*,
Piotr Sapieżyński *(Technical University of Denmark)*,
Arash Molavi Kakhki *(Northeastern University)*,
Balachander Krishnamurthy *(AT&T Labs - Research)*,
David Lazer, Alan Mislove,
Christo Wilson *(Northeastern University)*

Table of Contents

Estimating Clustering Coefficients and Size
of Social Networks via Random Walk 539
Stephen J. Hardiman *(Capital Fund Management)*,
Liran Katzir *(Microsoft Research)*

Exploiting Annotations for the Rapid Development
of Collaborative Web Applications 551
Matthias Heinrich, Franz Josef Grüneberger *(SAP Research)*,
Thomas Springer *(Dresden University of Technology)*,
Martin Gaedke *(Chemnitz University of Technology)*

Web Usage Mining with Semantic Analysis 561
Laura Hollink
(Delft University of Technology & VU University of Amsterdam),
Peter Mika, Roi Blanco *(Yahoo! Research)*

Organizational Overlap on Social Networks
and Its Applications 571
Cho-Jui Hsieh *(University of Texas at Austin)*,
Mitul Tiwari, Deepak Agarwal *(LinkedIn)*,
Xinyi (Lisa) Huang *(University of Waterloo)*,
Sam Shah *(LinkedIn)*

Space-Efficient Data Structures for Top-k
Completion 583
Bo-June (Paul) Hsu *(Microsoft Research)*,
Giuseppe Ottaviano *(Università di Pisa)*

Personalized Recommendation Via Cross-Domain
Triadic Factorization 595
Liang Hu, Jian Cao *(Shanghai Jiaotong University)*,
Guandong Xu, Longbing Cao *(University Technology Sydney)*,
Zhiping Gu
(Shanghai Technical Institute of Electronics & Information),
Can Zhu *(Shanghai Jiaotong University)*

Unsupervised Sentiment Analysis
with Emotional Signals 607
Xia Hu, Jiliang Tang, Huiji Gao,
Huan Liu *(Arizona State University)*

An Analysis of Socware Cascades
in Online Social Networks 619
Ting-Kai Huang, Md Sazzadur Rahman, Harsha V. Madhyastha,
Michalis Faloutsos *(University of California, Riverside)*

Measurement and Analysis of Child Pornography
Trafficking on P2P Networks 631
Ryan Hurley, Swagatika Prusty, Hamed Soroush,
Robert J. Walls *(University of Massachusetts, Amherst)*,
Jeannie Albrecht *(Williams College)*,
Emmanuel Cecchet, Brian Neil Levine, Marc Liberatore,
Brian Lynn *(University of Massachusetts, Amherst)*,
Janis Wolak *(University of New Hampshire)*

HeteroMF: Recommendation in Heterogeneous
Information Networks Using Context Dependent
Factor Models 643
Mohsen Jamali,
Laks V. S. Lakshmanan *(University of British Columbia)*

Interactive Exploratory Search for Multi Page
Search Results 655
Xiaoran Jin, Marc Sloan, Jun Wang *(University College London)*

Spatio-Temporal Dynamics of Online Memes:
A Study of Geo-Tagged Tweets 667
Krishna Y. Kamath, James Caverlee, Kyumin Lee,
Zhiyuan Cheng *(Texas A&M University)*

Accountable Key Infrastructure (AKI):
A Proposal for a Public-Key Validation
Infrastructure 679
Tiffany Hyun-Jin Kim, Lin-Shung Huang, Adrian Perrig,
Collin Jackson, Virgil Gligor *(Carnegie Mellon University)*

DIGTOBI: A Recommendation System for Digg
Articles Using Probabilistic Modeling 691
Younghoon Kim, Yoonjae Park,
Kyuseok Shim *(Seoul National University)*

Understanding Latency Variations
of Black Box Services 703
Darja Krushevskaja *(Rutgers University)*,
Mark Sandler *(Google Inc.)*

Diversified Recommendation on Graphs:
Pitfalls, Measures, and Algorithms 715
Onur Küçüktunç, Erik Saule, Kamer Kaya,
Ümit V. Çatalyürek *(The Ohio State University)*

What Is the Added Value of Negative Links
in Online Social Networks? 727
Jérôme Kunegis, Julia Preusse,
Felix Schwagereit *(University of Koblenz-Landau)*

Voices of Victory: A Computational Focus Group
Framework for Tracking Opinion Shift in Real Time 737
Yu-Ru Lin, Drew Margolin, Brian Keegan,
David Lazer *(Northeastern University)*

Rethinking the Web as a Personal Archive 749
Siân E. Lindley *(Microsoft Research Cambridge)*,
Catherine C. Marshall *(Microsoft Research Silicon Valley)*,
Richard Banks, Abigail Sellen,
Tim Regan *(Microsoft Research Cambridge)*

Expressive Languages for Selecting Groups
from Graph-Structured Data 761
Vitaliy Liptchinsky, Benjamin Satzger, Rostyslav Zabolotnyi,
Schahram Dustdar *(Vienna University of Technology)*

Modeling/Predicting the Evolution Trend of OSN-
Based Applications 771
Han Liu, Atif Nazir *(University of California-Davis)*,
Jinoo Joung *(Sangmyung University)*,
Chen-Nee Chuah *(University of California-Davis)*

SoCo: A Social Network Aided Context-Aware
Recommender System 781
Xin Liu, Karl Aberer *(École Polytechnique Fédérale de Lausanne)*

Using Stranger as Sensors: Temporal and
Geo-Sensitive Question Answering via Social Media .. 803
Yefeng Liu, Todorka Alexandrova,
Tatsuo Nakajima *(Waseda University)*

Imagen: Runtime Migration of Browser Sessions
for JavaScript Web Applications 815
James Lo, Eric Wohlstadter,
Ali Mesbah *(University of British Columbia)*

Gender Swapping and User Behaviors
in Online Social Games 827
Jing-Kai Lou *(National Taiwan University)*,
Kunwoo Park, Meeyoung Cha, Juyong Park
(Korea Advanced Institute of Science and Technology),
Chin-Laung Lei *(National Taiwan University)*,
Kuan-Ta Chen *(Academia Sinica)*

Author Index 836a

Table of Contents

Volume 2

Mining Structural Hole Spanners Through
Information Diffusion in Social Networks 837
Tiancheng Lou *(Google, Inc. & Tsinghua University)*,
Jie Tang *(Tsinghua University)*

On the Evolution of the Internet
Economic Ecosystem 849
Richard T. B. Ma *(National University of Singapore)*,
John C. S. Lui *(The Chinese University of Hong Kong)*,
Vishal Misra *(Columbia University)*

Two Years of Short URLs Internet Measurement:
Security Threats and Countermeasures 861
Federico Maggi, Alessandro Frossi,
Stefano Zanero *(Politecnico di Milano)*,
Gianluca Stringhini, Brett Stone-Gross, Christopher Kruegel,
Giovanni Vigna *(UC Santa Barbara)*

Know Your Personalization: Learning Topic
Level Personalization in Online Services 873
Anirban Majumder, Nisheeth Shrivastava *(Bell Labs Research)*

Saving, Reusing, and Remixing Web Video: Using
Attitudes and Practices to Reveal Social Norms 885
Catherine C. Marshall *(Microsoft Research, Silicon Valley)*,
Frank M. Shipman *(Texas A&M University)*

From Amateurs to Connoisseurs:
Modeling the Evolution of User Expertise
Through Online Reviews 897
Julian McAuley, Jure Leskovec *(Stanford University)*

The FLDA Model for Aspect-Based Opinion
Mining: Addressing the Cold Start Problem 909
Samaneh Moghaddam, Martin Ester *(Simon Fraser University)*

Iolaus: Securing Online Content Rating Systems ... 919
Arash Molavi Kakhki *(Northeastern University)*,
Chloe Kliman-Silver *(Brown University)*,
Alan Mislove *(Northeastern University)*

On Cognition, Emotion, and Interaction Aspects
of Search Tasks with Different Search Intentions .. 931
Yashar Moshfeghi, Joemon M. Jose *(University of Glasgow)*

Ad Impression Forecasting for Sponsored Search .. 943
Abhirup Nath *(Microsoft Research India)*,
Shibnath Mukherjee *(Microsoft adCenter)*,
Prateek Jain, Navin Goyal,
Srivatsan Laxman *(Microsoft Research India)*

Measurement and Modeling of Eye-Mouse Behavior
in the Presence of Nonlinear Page Layouts 953
Vidhya Navalpakkam, LaDawn Jentzsch, Rory Sayres,
Sujith Ravi, Amr Ahmed *(Google)*,
Alex Smola *(Google & Carnegie Mellon University)*

Understanding and Decreasing
the Network Footprint of Catch-up TV 965
Gianfranco Nencioni *(University of Pisa)*,
Nishanth Sastry *(King's College London)*,
Jigna Chandaria *(BBC R&D)*,
Jon Crowcroft *(University of Cambridge)*

Sorry, I Don't Speak SPARQL – Translating
SPARQL Queries into Natural Language 977
Axel-Cyrille Ngonga Ngomo, Bühmann *(Universität Leipzig)*,
Christina Unger *(Bielefeld University)*,
Jens Lehmann, Daniel Gerber *(Universität Leipzig)*

Bitsquatting: Exploiting Bit-flips for Fun, or Profit? ... 989
Nick Nikiforakis, Steven Van Acker *(iMinds-Distrinet, KU Leuven)*,
Wannes Meert *(DTAI, KU Leuven)*,
Lieven Desmet, Frank Piessens,
Wouter Joosen *(iMinds-Distrinet, KU Leuven)*

One-Class Collaborative Filtering with Random
Graphs 999
Ulrich Paquet *(Microsoft Reseach Cambridge)*,
Noam Koenigstein *(Microsoft R&D)*

Latent Credibility Analysis 1009
Jeff Pasternack *(Facebook, Inc.)*,
Dan Roth *(University of Illinois, Urbana-Champaign)*

Predicting Group Stability in Online Social
Networks 1021
Akshay Patil *(Stony Brook University)*,
Juan Liu *(Palo Alto Research Center)*,
Jie Gao *(Stony Brook University)*

Predictive Web Automation Assistant
for People with Vision Impairments 1031
Yury Puzis, Yevgen Borodin *(Charmtech Labs LLC)*,
Rami Puzis *(Ben-Gurion University)*,
I.V. Ramakrishnan *(Charmtech Labs LLC)*

Mining Collective Intelligence in Diverse Groups ... 1041
Guo-Jun Qi *(University of Illinois at Urbana-Champaign)*,
Charu C. Aggarwal *(IBM T.J. Watson Research Center)*,
Jiawei Han,
Thomas Huang *(University of Illinois at Urbana-Champaign)*

Trade Area Analysis Using User Generated
Mobile Location Data 1053
Yan Qu *(PlaceNous.com)*, Jun Zhang *(Pitney Bowes Inc.)*

Psychological Maps 2.0: A Web Engagement
Enterprise Starting in London 1065
Daniele Quercia *(Yahoo! Research)*,
João Paulo Pesce, Virgilio Almeida *(UFMG)*,
Jon Crowcroft *(University of Cambridge)*

Towards Realistic Team Formation
in Social Networks Based on Densest Subgraphs ... 1077
Syama Rangapuram *(Max Planck Institute for Computer Science)*,
Thomas Bühler, Matthias Hein *(Saarland University)*

Efficient Community Detection in Large Networks
Using Content and Links 1089
Yiye Ruan, David Fuhry,
Srinivasan Parthasarathy *(The Ohio State University)*

Learning Joint Query Interpretation
and Response Ranking 1099
Uma Sawant *(IIT Bombay & Yahoo! Labs)*,
Soumen Chakrabarti *(IIT Bombay)*

A Model for Green Design of Online News Media
Services 1111
Daniel Schien, Paul Shabajee *(University of Bristol)*,
Stephen G. Wood *(University of Surrey)*,
Chris Preist *(University of Bristol)*

Potential Networks, Contagious Communities,
and Understanding Social Network Structure 1123
Grant Schoenebeck *(University of Michigan)*,

Table of Contents

Do Social Explanations Work? Studying and Modeling the Effects of Social Explanations in Recommender Systems 1133
Amit Sharma, Dan Cosley *(Cornell University)*

Question Answering on Interlinked Data 1145
Saeedeh Shekarpour, Axel-Cyrille Ngonga Ngomo, Sören Auer *(Leipzig University)*

Pricing Mechanisms for Crowdsourcing Markets 1157
Yaron Singer *(Google Innc)*,
Manas Mittal *(University of California, Berkeley)*

Truthful Incentives in Crowdsourcing Tasks Using Regret Minimization Mechanisms 1167
Adish Singla, Andreas Krause *(ETH Zurich)*

A Predictive Model for Advertiser Value-Per-Click in Sponsored Search 1179
Eric Sodomka *(Brown University)*,
Sébastien Lahaie *(Microsoft Research)*,
Dustin Hillard *(Microsoft Corp.)*

I Know the Shortened URLs You Clicked on Twitter: Inference Attack Using Public Click Analytics and Twitter Metadata 1191
Jonghyuk Song, Sangho Lee, Jong Kim *(POSTECH)*

Exploring and Exploiting User Search Behavior on Mobile and Tablet Devices to Improve Search Relevance 1201
Yang Song, Hao Ma *(Microsoft Research)*,
Hongning Wang *(University of Illinois at Urbana-Champaign)*,
Kuansan Wang *(Microsoft Research)*

Evaluating and Predicting User Engagement Change with Degraded Search Relevance 1213
Yang Song *(Microsoft Research)*,
Xiaolin Shi *(Microsoft Bing)*,
Xin Fu *(LinkedIn Corporation)*

Data-Fu: A Language and an Interpreter for Interaction with Read/Write Linked Data 1225
Steffen Stadtmüller, Sebastian Speiser, Andreas Harth, Rudi Studer *(Karlsruhe Institute of Technology)*

NIFTY: A System for Large Scale Information Flow Tracking and Clustering 1237
Caroline Suen, Sandy Huang, Chantat Eksombatchai, Rok Sosič, Jure Leskovec *(Stanford University)*

When Relevance Is Not Enough: Promoting Diversity and Freshness in Personalized Question Recommendation 1249
Idan Szpektor, Yoelle Maarek, Dan Pelleg *(Yahoo! Research)*

Mining Acronym Expansions and Their Meanings Using Query Click Log 1261
Bilyana Taneva *(Max-Planck Institute for Informatics)*,
Tao Cheng, Kaushik Chakrabarti, Yeye He *(Microsoft Research)*

Groundhog Day: Near-Duplicate Detection on Twitter 1273
Ke Tao *(Delft University of Technology)*,
Fabian Abel *(Delft University of Technology & XING AG)*,
Claudia Hauff, Geert-Jan Houben,
Ujwal Gadiraju *(Delft University of Technology)*,

Uncovering Locally Characterizing Regions within Geotagged Data 1285
Bart Thomee *(Yahoo! Research)*,
Adam Rae *(brandcrumb)*

Spectral Analysis of Communication Networks Using Dirichlet Eigenvalues 1297
Alexander Tsiatas *(University of California, San Diego)*,
Iraj Saniee *(Alcatel-Lucent Bell Labs)*,
Onuttom Narayan *(University of California, Santa Cruz)*,
Matthew Andrews *(Alcatel-Lucent Bell Labs)*

Subgraph Frequencies: Mapping the Empirical and Extremal Geography of Large Graph Collections 1307
Johan Ugander *(Cornell University)*,
Lars Backstrom *(Facebook)*,
Jon Kleinberg *(Cornell University)*

The Self-Feeding Process: A Unifying Model for Communication Dynamics in the Web 1319
Pedro O. S. Vaz de Melo
(Universidade Federal de Minas Gerais),
Christos Faloutsos *(Carnegie Mellon University)*,
Renato Assunção, Antonio A. F. Loureiro
(Universidade Federal de Minas Gerais)

Google+ Ripples: A Native Visualization of Information Flow 1389
Fernanda Viégas, Martin Wattenberg, Jack Hebert,
Geoffrey Borggaard, Alison Cichowlas, Jonathan Feinberg,
Jon Orwant, Christopher R. Wren *(Google, Inc.)*

Whom to Mention: Expand the Diffusion of Tweets by @ Recommendation on Micro-Blogging Systems 1331
Beidou Wang, Can Wang, Jiajun Bu,
Chun Chen *(Zhejiang University)*,
Wei Vivian Zhang *(Microsoft Corporation)*,
Deng Cai, Xiaofei He *(Zhejiang University)*

Wisdom in the Social Crowd: An Analysis of Quora 1341
Gang Wang, Konark Gill, Manish Mohanlal, Haitao Zheng,
Ben Y. Zhao *(UC Santa Barbara)*

Learning to Extract Cross-Session Search Tasks 1353
Hongning Wang *(University of Illinois at Urbana-Champaign)*,
Yang Song, Ming-Wei Chang, Xiaodong He,
Ryen W. White *(Microsoft Research)*,
Wei Chu *(Microsoft Bing)*

Content-Aware Click Modeling 1365
Hongning Wang,
ChengXiang Zhai *(University of Illinois at Urbana-Champaign)*,
Anlei Dong, Yi Chang *(Yahoo! Labs)*

Is It Time for a Career Switch? 1377
Jian Wang, Yi Zhang *(University of California, Santa Cruz)*,
Christian Posse, Anmol Bhasin *(LinkedIn Corp.)*

From Cookies to Cooks: Insights on Dietary Patterns via Analysis of Web Usage Logs 1399
Robert West *(Stanford University)*,
Ryen W. White, Eric Horvitz *(Microsoft Research)*

Enhancing Personalized Search by Mining and Modeling Task Behavior 1411
Ryen W. White *(Microsoft Research)*,
Wei Chu *(Microsoft Bing)*,
Ahmed Hassan, Xiaodong He, Yang Song *(Microsoft Research)*,
Hongning Wang *(University of Illinois at Urbana-Champaign)*

Table of Contents

Inferring Dependency Constraints on Parameters for Web Services 1421
Qian Wu, Ling Wu, Guangtai Liang, Qianxiang Wang (*Peking University*),
Tao Xie (*North Carolina State University*),
Hong Mei (*Peking University*)

Predicting Advertiser Bidding Behaviors in Sponsored Search by Rationality Modeling 1433
Haifeng Xu (*University of Waterloo*),
Bin Gao (*Microsoft Research Asia*),
Diyi Yang (*Shanghai Jiao Tong University*),
Tie-Yan Liu (*Microsoft Research Asia*)

A Biterm Topic Model for Short Texts 1445
Xiaohui Yan, Jiafeng Guo, Yanyan Lan,
Xueqi Cheng (*Institute of Computing Technology, CAS*)

Unified Entity Search in Social Media Community 1457
Ting Yao (*City University of Hong Kong*),
Yuan Liu (*Ricoh Software Research Center Co., Ltd.*),
Chong-Wah Ngo (*City University of Hong Kong*),
Tao Mei (*Microsoft Research Asia*)

MATRI: A Multi-Aspect and Transitive Trust Inference Model 1467
Yuan Yao
(*State Key Laboratory for Novel Software Technology*),
Hanghang Tong (*City College, CUNY*),
Xifeng Yan (*University of California at Santa Barbara*),
Feng Xu, Jian Lu
(*State Key Laboratory for Novel Software Technology*)

Predicting Positive and Negative Links in Signed Social Networks by Transfer Learning 1477
Jihang Ye, Hong Cheng, Zhe Zhu,
Minghua Chen (*The Chinese University of Hong Kong*)

Sparse Online Topic Models 1489
Aonan Zhang, Jun Zhu, Bo Zhang (*Tsinghua University*)

TopRec: Domain-Specific Recommendation Through Community Topic Mining in Social Network 1501
Xi Zhang, Jian Cheng, Ting Yuan, Biao Niu,
Hanqing Lu (*Chinese Academy of Sciences*)

Localized Matrix Factorization for Recommendation Based on Matrix Block Diagonal Forms 1511
Yongfeng Zhang, Min Zhang, Yiqun Liu, Shaoping Ma,
Shi Feng (*Tsinghua University*)

Predicting Purchase Behaviors from Social Media 1521
Yongzheng Zhang, Marco Pennacchiotti (*eBay Inc.*)

Anatomy of a Web-Scale Resale Market: A Data Mining Approach 1533
Yuchen Zhao (*University of Illinois at Chicago*),
Neel Sundaresan, Zeqian Shen (*eBay Research Labs*),
Philip S. Yu
(*University of Illinois at Chicago & King Abdulaziz University*)

Questions about Questions: An Empirical Analysis of Information Needs on Twitter 1545
Zhe Zhao, Qiaozhu Mei (*University of Michigan*)

Which Vertical Search Engines Are Relevant? Understanding Vertical Relevance Assessments for Web Queries 1557
Ke Zhou (*University of Glasgow*),
Ronan Cummins (*University of Greenwich*),
Mounia Lalmas (*Yahoo! Labs*),
Joemon M. Jose (*University of Glasgow*)

Making the Most of Your Triple Store: Query Answering in OWL 2 Using an RL Reasoner 1569
Yujiao Zhou, Bernardo Cuenca Grau,
Ian Horrocks (*University of Oxford*),
Zhe Wu, Jay Banerjee (*Oracle Corporation*)

Security Implications of Password Discretization for Click-Based Graphical Passwords 1581
Bin B. Zhu (*Microsoft Research Asia*),
Dongchen Wei, Maowei Yang (*Sichuan University*),
Jeff Yan (*Newcastle University*)

Author Index 1592

WWW 2013 22nd International World Wide Web Conference

General Chairs: Daniel Schwabe (*PUC-Rio – Brazil*)
Virgílio Almeida (*UFMG – Brazil*)
Hartmut Glaser (*CGI.br – Brazil*)

Research Track: Ricardo Baeza-Yates (*Yahoo! Labs – Spain & Chile*)
Sue Moon (*KAIST – South Korea*)

Practice and Experience Track: Alejandro Jaimes (*Yahoo! Labs – Spain*)
Haixun Wang (*MSR – China*)

Developers Track: Denny Vrandečić (*Wikimedia – Germany*)
Marcus Fontoura (*Google – USA*)

Demos Track: Bernadette F. Lóscio (*UFPE – Brazil*)
Irwin King (*CUHK – Hong Kong*)

W3C Track: Marie-Claire Forgue (*W3C Training, USA*)

Workshops Track: Alberto Laender (*UFMG – Brazil*)
Les Carr (*U. of Southampton – UK*)

Posters Track: Erik Wilde (*EMC – USA*)
Fernanda Lima (*UNB – Brazil*)

Tutorials Track: Bebo White (*SLAC – USA*)
Maria Luiza M. Campos (*UFRJ – Brazil*)

Industry Track: Marden S. Neubert (*UOL – Brazil*)

Proceedings and Metadata Chair: Altigran Soares da Silva (*UFAM - Brazil*)

Local Arrangements Committee: Chair – Hartmut Glaser
Executive Secretary – Vagner Diniz
PCO Liaison – Adriana Góes, Caroline D'Avo, and Renato Costa
Conference Organization Assistant – Selma Morais
International Relations – Caroline Burle
Technology Liaison – Reinaldo Ferraz
UX Designer / Web Developer – Yasodara Córdova, Ariadne Mello
Internet infrastructure - Marcelo Gardini, Felipe Agnelli Barbosa
Administration– Ana Paula Conte, Maria de Lourdes Carvalho,
   Beatriz Iossi, Carla Christiny de Mello
Legal Issues – Kelli Angelini
Press Relations and Social Network – Everton T. Rodrigues,
S2Publicom and EntreNós
PCO – SKL Eventos e Turismo

Student Volunteers Coordination: Wagner Meira (*UFMG*)
Yasodara Córdova (*NIC.br*)
Sebastien Forget (*Canada*)
John Miller (*Australia*) (International Volunteers)

Program Committee Behavioral analysis and personalization
Eugene Agichtein (Emory U), Yoelle Mareek (Yahoo! Labs) – Chairs

Members
Mikhail Ageev, NIVC MGU
Peter Bailey, MSR
Nicolas Belkin, Rutgers University
Paul Bennet, MSR
Edward Bortnikov, Yahoo!
Peter Brusilovsky
Georg Buscher
Nick Craswell, MSR
Fernando Diaz, Microsoft Research
Andy Edmonds
Henry Feild, Umass
Antonio Gulli
Qi Guo, Emory University
Jeff Huang
Rosie Jones
Diane Kelly, UNC
Gueorgi Kossinets
Dmitry Lagun, Emory University
Mounia Lalmas
Ronny Lempel, Yahoo! Labs
Andreas Paepcke, Stanford
Dan Pelleg
Matt Richardson, MSR
Kerry Rodden
Tetsuya Sakai
Mark Smucker, University of Waterloo
Jaime Teevan
Andrew Tomkins, Google
Ingmar Weber
Ryen White, MSR
Yisong Yue
Zijian Zheng, MSR
Dav Zimak

Program Committee - Content analysis

Claire Cardie (Cornell), Evgeniy Gabrilovich (Google) – Chairs

Members

Aris Anagnostopoulos, University of Roma
Azin Ashkan, University of Waterloo
Michael Bendersky, Umass
Misha Bilenko, MSR
Michael Cafarella, Umich
Yunbo Cao, MSR
Carlos Castillo, U. of Chile
Deepayan Chakrabarti, CMU
Brian Davison, Lehigh U.
Doug Downey, Northwestern U.
Gideon Dror,
Hui Fang, U. Del
Dennis Fetterly, MSR
Shantanu Godbole,
Iryna Gurevych
Bo, June Hsu, MSR
Tapas Kanungo
Nick Koudas, U. of Toronto
Georgia Koutrika, HP
Zornitsa Kozareva, USC, ISI
Oren Kurland, Technion
Lillian Lee, Cornell
Chengkai Li, UTA
Hao Ma, MSR
Qiaozhu Mei, Umich

Donald Metzler
Prasenjit Mitra, PSU
Bo Pang
Dmitry Pechyony, Technion
Fuchun Peng, Yahoo!
John Prager, IBM
Kunal Punera, Utexas
Kira Radinsky
Filip Radlinski, Microsoft
Vibhor Rastogi
Sunita Sarawagi, IIT Bombay
Burr Settles, CMU
Stefan Siersdorfer, University of Hannover
Julia Stoyanovich, Upenn
Gerd Stumme, Uni, Kassel
Idan Szpektor, Yahoo!
Partha Talukdar
Xuanhui Wang, Yahoo!
Gerhard Weikum
Elad Yom, Tov
Torsten Zesch, Tu Darmstadt
Hongyuan Zha, GATech
Chengxiang Zhai, UIUC
Dell Zhang, BBK

Program Committee - Software infrastructure and their performance, scalability, and availability

Torsten Suel (PI), Zhi-Li Zhang (UMinnesota) – Chairs

Members

Michele Colajanni, University of Modena
Anja Feldmann, TU Berlin
Daniel Figueiredo, COPPE/UFRJ
Krishna Kant, Intel Corporation
Purushottam Kulkarni, IIT Bombay
John C.S. Lui, The Chinese University of Hong Kong
Grzegorz Malewicz, Facebook
Martin May, Technicolor
Beng Chin Ooi, National University of Singapore
Giovanni Pacifici, IBM Research
Michael Rabinovich, Case Western Reserve University

Pablo Rodriguez, Telefonica Research
Sambit Sahu, IBM Research
Subhabrata Sen, AT&T Research
Alexander Shraer, Google
Ramesh Sitaraman, Department of Computer Science, University of Massachusetts, Amherst
Malgorzata Steinder, IBM Research
Sandeep Uttamchandani,
Jacobus Vandermerwe,
Maja Vukovic, IBM Research
Zhen Xiao, Peking University

Program Committee - Web mining

Tanya Berger-Wolf (UIC), Bing Liu (UIC), Kyuseok Shim (SNU) – Chairs

Members

Charu Aggarwal, IBM
Amr Ahmed, Yahoo! Labs
Roberto Bayardo, Google
Smriti Bhagat, Technicolor
Yun Chi, NEC Laboratories America
Chin, Wan Chung, KAIST
Gao Cong, Nanyang Technological University
David Crandall, Indiana University
Mayur Datar, Google Inc.
Eduard Dragut
Georges Dupret, Yahoo! Labs
Tina Eliassi, Rad, Rutgers University
Martin Ester, Department of Computer Science, Simon Fraser University, Canada
Christos Faloutsos, Carnegie Mellon University
Ronen Feldman, Hebrew University
Michael Gamon, Microsoft Research
C. Lee Giles, Pennsylvania State University
Aristides Gionis, Aalto University
Dimitrios Gunopulos, UoA
Jiawei Han, University of Illinois at Urbana, Champaign
Wook, Shin Han, Kyungpook National University
Shawndra Hill, University of Pennsylvania
Nitin Jindal, Google
Jaewoo Kang, Korea University
U Kang, Carnegie Mellon University
Sang, Wook Kim, Hanyang University
Irwin King, The Chinese University of Hong Kong
Mayank Lahiri, University of Illinois at Chicago
Wai Lam, The Chinese University of Hong Kong
Hady Lauw, Singapore Management University
Dongwon Lee, Penn State University
Sangkeun Lee, Department of Computer Science and Engineering, Korea University
Hang Li, Huawei Noah's Arc Lab
Xiaoli Li, Institute for Infocomm Research
Huan Liu, Arizona State University
Tie, Yan Liu, Microsoft Research Asia
Yue Lu, University of Illinois at Urbana, Champaign
Michael Lyu
Dunja Mladenic, J. Stefan Institute
Bamshad Mobasher, DePaul University
Arjun Mukherjee, University of Illinois--Chicago
Olfa Nasraoui, University of Louisville
Zaiqing Nie, Microsoft Research Asia
Alexandros Ntoulas, Zynga
Srinivasan Parthasarathy, Department of Computer Science and Engineering, The Ohio State University
Jian Pei, Simon Fraser University
Mark Sandler, Google
Dou Shen, Microsoft Adcenter Labs
Myra Spiliopoulou, U. Magdeburg
Jaideep Srivastava, University of Minnesota
Lei Tang, @WalmartLabs
Masashi Toyoda, University of Tokyo
Jianyong Wang, Tsinghua University
Ke Wang, Simon Fraser University
Michael Wurst, TU Dortmund
Hui Xiong, Rutgers University
Hwanjo Yu, POSTECH
Jeffery Xu Yu, Dept. of Systems Engineering & Engineering Mngt, Chinese University of Hong Kong
Philip Yu, UIC
Lei Zhang, University of Illinois at Chicago

Program Committee internet monetization and incentives

Vanja Josifovski (Google), David Pennock (MSR NYC) – Chairs

Members

Ramakrishna Akella, School of Engineering University of California, Santa Cruz
Sugato Basu, Google Research
Ye Chen, Microsoft
Ingemar Cox, University College London
Nikhil Devanur, Microsoft Research
Marcus Fontoura, Google Inc
Arpita Ghosh, Cornell University
Gagan Goel, Google Research
Sreenivas Gollapudi, Microsoft Research
Ronen Gradwohl, Weizmann Institute of Science
Maria Grineva, Yandex
Ralf Herbrich, Facebook
Patrick Hummel
Krishnamurthy Iyer, University of Pennsylvania
Shaili Jain, Yale University
Patrick Jordan, Microsoft
Radu Jurca
Sebastien Lahaie
Ying Li

Benjamin Lubin, Harvard
Vahab Mirrokni, Google Research
S. Muthukrishnan, Rutgers University
Uri Nadav
Hamid Nazerzadeh, USC Marshall School of Business
Mallesh Pai, University of Pennsylvania
Sandeep Pandey, Twitter
Michael Schapira, Yale University & U.C. Berkeley
James G. Shanahan, Independent Consultant (San Francisco)
Jayavel Shanmugasundaram, Google Inc.
Eric Sodomka, Brown University
Jian, Tao Sun, Microsoft Research Asia
Neel Sundaresan, eBay Research Labs
Ankur Teredesai, University of Washington
Siva Viswanathan, University of Maryland
Haifeng Wang, Baidu
Jun Yan, Microsoft Research Asia
M. Yenmez, Carnegie Mellon University
Georgios Zervas, Yale University

Program Committee Search systems and applications
Soumen Chakrabarti (IIT Mumbai), Wei-Ying Ma (MSR Asia) – Chairs

Members

Omar Alonso, Microsoft
Jaime Arguello, University of North Carolina at Chapel Hill
Ching Man Au Yeung, ASTRI
Shenghua Bao, IBM China Research Lab
Behshad Behzadi, Google Inc.
Gloria Bordogna, National Research Council of Italy, CNR
Rui Cai, Microsoft Research, Asia
Yi Chang, Yahoo! Labs
Zheng Chen, Microsoft Research Asia
Hong Cheng, The Chinese University of Hong Kong
Tao Cheng, Microsoft Research Redmond
Xueqi Cheng, Institute of Computing Technology, CAS, P. R. China
Pablo De La Fuente, GRINBD. Universidad de Valladolid
Edleno Silva De Moura, Universidade Federal do Amazonas
Maarten de Rijke, University of Amsterdam
Arjen de Vries, CWI
Hongbo Deng, Yahoo!
Prasad Deshpande, IBM Research India
Debora Donato, Yahoo! LabsBarcelona
Bin Gao, Microsoft Research Asia
Ashutosh Garg,
Marcos Goncalves, Federal University of Minas Gerais
Maxim Gurevich, Google
Djoerd Hiemstra, University of Twente
Steven C.H. Hoi, Nanyang Technological University
Ming Hua, Facebook Inc.
Xuanjing Huang, Fudan University
Jeannette Janssen, Dalhousie University
Glen Jeh
Jaap Kamps, University of Amsterdam
Evangelos Kanoulas, Google, Inc.
Alexander Kotov, Emory University
Kevin Lang, Yahoo! Research
Amy Langville, College of Charleston

Chin Yew Lin, Microsoft Research Asia
Ling Liu, Georgia Tech
Tie Yan Liu, Microsoft Research Asia
Dmitri Loguinov, Texas A&M
David Losada, University of Santiago de Compostela
Massimo Melucci, University of Padua
Sung Hyon Myaeng, Kaist
Jian Yun Nie, Universit de Montral
Iadh Ounis, University of Glasgow
Umut Ozertem, Microsoft
Gabriella Pasi, Universit degli STudi di Milano Bicocca
Simone Paolo Ponzetto, University of Rome
Davood Rafiei, University of Alberta
Sriram Raghavan, IBM Research India
Stefan Rueger, Knowledge Media Institute
Altigran S. Da Silva, Federal University of Amazonas
Ralf Schenkel, Saarland University
Uri Schonfeld, UCLA
Shuming Shi, Microsoft Research Asia
Milad Shokouhi, Microsoft Research
Mário J. Silva, IST/INESC ID
Fabrizio Silvestri, ISTI CNR
D Sivakumar, Yahoo!
Alex Smola, Google
Marina Sokolova,
Panayiotis Tsaparas, University of Ioannina
Michalis Vazirgiannis, Department of Informatics, AUEB
Adriano Veloso, UFMG
Stratis Viglas, University of Edinburgh, School of Informatics
Tao Yang, Ask.com and UCSB
Emine Yilmaz, Microsoft Research Cambridge
Lei Zhang, Microsoft Research Asia
Min Zhang, Tsinghua University
Lidong Zhou, Microsoft Research, SV
Xiaoyan Zhu, Computer Science and Technology Department, Tsinghua University, Beijing, China
Nivio Ziviani, Department of Computer Science, Federal University of Minas Gerais

Program Committee Security, privacy, trust, and abuse

Krishna Gummadi (MPI-SWS) – Chair

Members

Davide Balzarotti,
Bobby Bhattacharjee, Univ. of Maryland, College Park
Elie Bursztein
Juan Caballero, IMDEA
Jon Crowcroft, University of Cambridge
Bryan Ford
Saikat Guha, Microsoft Research India
Hamed Haddadi, QMUL
Christian Hammer, Saarland University
Aniket Kate, Uni Saarland
Yongdae Kim, KAIST
Engin Kirda, Northeastern University
Alek Kolcz, Twitter
Aleksandra Korolova, Google
Christian Kreibich, ICSI
Christopher Kruegel, Univ. of California, Santa Barbara
Ponnurangam Kumaraguru, IIIT Delhi
David Lie, University of Toronto
Ben Livshits, Microsoft Research Redmond
Harsha Madhyastha, UCR
Arvind Narayanan, Princeton University
Cristina Nita Rotaru, Purdue University
Vern Paxson, University of California, Berkeley
Charlie Reis, Google
Elaine Shi, University of Maryland, College Park
Thorsten Strufe, TU Darmstadt
Andrew Warfield
Fang Yu, Microsoft Research Silicon Valley

Program Committee Semantic Web

Deborah McGuinness (RPI), Steffen Staab (U of Koblenz) - Chairs

Members

Hans Akkermans, VU University Amsterdam
Harith Alani, KMi, The Open University
Lora Aroyo, VU University Amsterdam
Christian Bizer, Freie Universität Berlin
Paul Buitelaar, DERI National University of Ireland, Galway
Philipp Cimiano, University of Bielefeld
Philippe Cudré Mauroux, U. of Fribourg
Claudia D'Amato, Computer Science Department University of Bari
Mathieu D'Aquin, Knowledge Media Institute, the Open University
Hasan Davulcu, Arizona State University
Mike Dean, Raytheon BBN Technologies
Li Ding, Rensselaer Polytechnic Institute
Ying Ding, Indiana University
Jérôme Euzenat, INRIA & LIG
Tim Finin, UMBC
Gerd Gröner, University of Koblenz
Claudio Gutierrez, Universidad de Chile
Olaf Hartig, Humboldt Universität zu Berlin
Manfred Hauswirth, Digital Enterprise Research Institute (DERI), Galway
Jeff Heflin, Lehigh University
Pascal Hitzler, Kno.e.sis Center, Wright State University, Dayton, Ohio
Jihie Kim, Information Science Institute
Manolis Koubarakis, National and Kapodistrian University of Athens
Markus Krötzsch, University of Oxford
Boris Motik, University of Oxford
Natasha F. Noy, Stanford University
Jeff Z. Pan, University of Aberdeen
Peter Patel Schneider, Self
Axel Polleres, Siemens AG Österreich / DERI, National University of Ireland, Galway
Daniel Schwabe, Dept. of Informatics, PUC Rio
Luciano Serafini, Fondazione Bruno Kessler
Patrice Seyed,
Elena Simperl, KIT
Markus Strohmaier, Knowledge Management Institute Graz University of Technology
Rudi Studer, Karlsruher Institut für Technologie (KIT)
Thanh Tran, Institute AIFB
Volker Tresp, Siemens AG, CT IC 4, Munich
Evelyne Viegas, Microsoft Research

Program Committee User interfaces, human factors, and smart devices

James Landay (UW), Nuria Oliver (Telefonica R&D) – Chairs

Members

Florian Alt, University of Stuttgart
Michael Bernstein
Jeffrey Bigham, University of Rochester
Susanne Boll, University of Oldenburg
Joel Brandt, Adobe Systems, Inc.
Irene Celino, CEFRIEL
Matthew Chalmers, University of Glasgow
Mike Y. Chen, NTU
Ed H. Chi, PARC
Karen Church, Telefonica Research
Henriette Cramer, Yahoo! Labs
Rodrigo De Oliveira, Telefonica Research
Marco De Sa, Facebook
Emanuele Della Valle, DEI, Politecnico di Milano
Steven Drucker, Microsoft LiveLabs
Darren Edge, Microsoft Research Asia
Patrik Floreen, Helsinki Institute for Information Technology HIIT, University of Helsinki
Yusuke Fukazawa, NTTDOCOMO, Inc.
Krzysztof Gajos, Harvard University
Daniel Gatica Perez, IDIAP Research Institute
Per Olof Hedvall, Lund University

Sepandar Kamvar, Stanford University
Lyndon Kennedy, Yahoo! Research
Ora Lassila, Nokia Services
Tessa Lau
Yang Li
Jalal Mahmud, IBM Research Almaden
Robert Miller, MIT CSAIL
Ingrid Mulder
Jeffrey Nichols, IBM Almaden Research Center
Kenton O'Hara, Microsoft Research
Alex Olwal, KTH
Jerôme Picault, Alcatel Lucent Bell Labs
Martin Pielot
Jeff Pierce, Samsung
Myriam Ribiere, Alcatel Lucent Bell Labs
Enrico Rukzio, Ulm University
Jose San Pedro Wandelmer,
N. Sadat Shami, IBM Research
Stephan Steglich, FhI FOKUS
Bongwon Suh, Adobe
Manas Tungare, Google
Sarita Yardi, Umich

Program Committee Social networks and graph analysis

Ashish Goel (U Stanford), Sharad Goel (MSR NYC), Wolfgang Nejdl (U of Hannover), Ben Zhao (UCSB) – (Chairs)

Members

Lada Adamic, University of Michigan
Yong Yeol Ahn, Indiana University Bloomington
Fabricio Benevenuto, Federal University of Ouro Preto (UFOP)
Paolo Boldi, Universita' degli Studi di Milano
Joseph Bonneau, University of Cambridge
Meeyoung Cha, KAIST
Augustin Chaintreau, Columbia University
Wei Chen, MSR Asia
Flavio Chierichetti, Sapienza University of Rome
Aaron Clauset, Santa Fe Institute
Yafei Dai, PKU
Atish Das Sarma, eBay Research Labs
David De Roure, Oxford e Research Centre, University of Oxford
Gianluca Demartini, University of Fribourg
Lisa Fleischer, Dartmouth
Santo Fortunato, Complex Networks Lagrange Laboratory, ISI Foundation
Norbert Fuhr, University of Duisburg Essen
Sabrina Gaito, Universita' degli Studi di Milano
Brighten Godfrey, University of Illinois at Urbana Champaign
Pankaj Gupta, Twitter, Inc.
Qi He, IBM
Jake Hofman, Microsoft Research
Andreas Hotho, University of Wuerzburg
Stratis Ioannidis, Technicolor
Alejandro Jaimes, Yahoo! Research
Kamal Jain, eBay Research Labs
Yashodhan Kanoria, Stanford University
David Kempe, University of Southern California
Emre Kiciman, Microsoft Research
Tamara Kolda, Sandia National Laboratories
Silvio Lattanzi, Google

Kristina Lerman, USC
Jure Leskovec, Stanford University
David Liben Nowell, Carleton College
Ee Peng Lim, Singapore Management University
Ashwin Machanavajjhala, Duke University
Michael Mahoney, Stanford University
Cecilia Mascolo, University of Cambridge
Winter Mason, Stevens Institute of Technology
Alan Mislove, Northeastern University
Sue Moon, KAIST
Kamesh Munagala, Duke University
Jennifer Neville, Purdue University
Alessandro Panconesi, Sapienza University of Rome
Spiros Papadimitriou, Rutgers University
Paolo Parigi, Stanford University
Krishna Puttaswamy, Bell Labs, Alcatel Lucent
Daniel Romero, Northwestern University
Ant Rowstron, Microsoft Research
Giancarlo Ruffo, Universita' di Torino
Alessandra Sala, Alcatel Lucent Bell Labs
Stefan Saroiu, Microsoft Research
Lars Schmidt Thieme, University of Hildesheim
Rachel Schutt, Google
Haiying Shen, Clemson University
Amit Sheth, Kno.e.sis Center, Wright State University
Michael Sirivianos, Cyprus University of Technology
Jie Tang, Tsinghua University
Eva Tardos, Cornell University
Evimaria Terzi, Boston University
Sergei Vassilvitskii, Google
Sebastiano Vigna, Universita' degli Studi di Milano
Matthew Weber, Rutgers University
Christo Wilson, Northeastern University
Xifeng Yan, University of California at Santa Barbara
Heather Zheng, UCSB

Program Committee Bridging structured and unstructured data

Kevin Chang (UIUC), Peter Mika (Yahoo! Labs) - Chairs

Members

Phillip Bohannon
Oren Etzioni, U. of Washington
Seung Won Hwang
Chen Li, UCI
Yutaka Matsuo, U. Tokyo
Christopher Olston, Google

Marius Pasca
Aamod Sane, Yahoo!
Anish Das Sarma, Stanford
S Sudarshan, IITB
Yufei Tao, CUHK
Kuansan Wang, MSR

Ji Rong Wen, MSR
Xing Xie, MSR
Cong Yu, Umich
Jeffrey Yu, CUHK

Program Committee Web Engineering

Schahram Dustdar (TU Wien), Geert-Jan Houben (TU Delft) - Chairs

Members

Sören Auer, Universität Leipzig
Maria Bielikova, Slovak University of Technology
Alessandro Bozzon, Politecnico di Milano
Marco Brambilla, Politecnico di Milano
Jordi Cabot, INRIA /École des Mines de Nantes
Fabio Casati, University of Trento
Sven Casteleyn, Vrije Universiteit Brussel
Florian Daniel, University of Trento
Paul Dantzig, IBM T.J. Watson Research Center
Oscar Diaz, University of the Basque Country
Peter Dolog, Aalborg University
Flavius Frasincar, Erasmus University Rotterdam
Piero Fraternali, Politecnico di Milano
Martin Gaedke, Chemnitz University of Technology
Dragan Gasevic, Athabasca University
Michael Grossniklaus, U. Konstanz
Simon Harper, University of Manchester

Gerti Kappel, Vienna University of Technology
Frank Leymann, Universität Stuttgart
Santiago Meliá, Universidad de Alicante
Ali Mesbah, University of British Columbia
Luis Olsina, La Pampa National University
Oscar Pastor, Universidad Politecnica de Valencia
Cesare Pautasso, University of Lugano
Maria da Graça Pimentel, University of São Paulo
Iv Ramakrishnan, Stony Brook University
Gustavo Rossi, Universidad Nacional de La Plata
Michael Sheng, University of Adelaide
Stefan Tai, Karlsruhe Institute of Technology
Takehiro Tokuda, Tokyo Institute of Technology
Bebo White, SLAC National Accelerator Laboratory
Erik Wilde, EMC Corporation
Marco Winkler, University Paul Sabatier

Additional Reviewers

Abedelaziz Mohaisen
Adam Doupé, UCSB
Adila A. Krisnadhi
Adish Singla, ETH Zurich
Afroza Sultana, UTA
Alessandro Epasto, Uniroma
Alex Beutel, CMU
Alex Chen, U. of Manchester
Alexander Bergmayr, TUWien
Alexandros Karatzoglou, TID
Ali Pinar, Sandia
Alvaro Barreiro, UDC
Amarnath Gupta, UCSD
Amin Milani Fard, UBC
Amit Joshi, UMN
Amogh Mahapatra
Anand Bhalgat
Andre Carvalho
Andrej Muhic, IJS
Andrej Rapoport
Andrew Newell
Anisio Lacerda, UFMG
Anthony Fader, U. of Washington
Arijit Khan
Arun Iyer
Ashton Anderson, Stanford
Ashutosh Jadhav, Wright St
Asiful Islam, Google
Asim Jamshid, Kaist
Axel Cyrille Ngonga Ngomo, UniLeipzig
Baichuan Li, CUHK
Balaji Palanisamy
Bangyong Liang, NEC
Basheer Hawwash,
Basil Ell, Uni Karslruhe
Behzad Golshan, BU
Bernhard Amann, UCB
Bin Cao, Microsoft
Bin Chen
Bin Li
Bing He, JHSPH
Binh Han, GATech

Bo Adler
Bo Zhao, Microsoft
Bo Zong, UCSB
Bruno Martins
C Seshadri, Sandia
C. Seshadhri, Sandia
Changhu Wang, Microsoft
Chao Zhou, CUHK
Chen Cheng, CUHK
Chenghua Lin, Open University
Chenyi Zhang
Chi Wang, U. of Illinois
Christian von der Weth, DERI
Christoph Fehling, Uni Stuttgart
Christopher Head, UBC
Christos Giatsidis
Chunye Wang, UCSC
Claus Stadler, Uni Leipzig
Cristina Brandt, Stanford
Dan Liu, Google
Danai Koutra, CMU
Daniel Gerber, Uni Leipzig
Daniel Herzig, KIT
Daniel Lobato
Danielle H. Lee
Darshan Santani
David Carral Martínez
Dawei Yin, Lehigh
Dayong Wang, NTU
Dayu Yuan, PSU
Deepak Garg
Delip Rao
Denis Krompass
Dimitris Kontokostas
Dimitris Kotsakos
Diogo Martins
Donghee Choi
Donghyeon Kim
Endadul Hoque
Enpeng Yao, Microsoft
Enpeng Yao, Microsoft
Eren Manavoglu, Microsoft
Erjia Yan, Indiana

Evan Patton, RPI
Evangelos Papalexakis, CMU
Fabio Drucker
Fan Yang, Microsoft
Fangqiu Han, UCSB
Feng Pan, Microsoft
Feng Qian, ATT
Fragkiskos Malliaros, Polytechnique
Francesco Pasquale
Francois Rousseau
Fred Morstatter, ASU
Gabriele Tolomei, Unive
Gang Luo, Microsoft
Georgeta Bordea, DERI
Georgios Valkanas
Guang Ling, CUHK
Guang Xiang, CMU
Günter Ladwig, KIT
Haichuan Shang,
Haiqin Yang, CUHK
Hamid Mahini
Hao Xia
Hemant Purohit, Wright St
Hernan Molina, UNLPAM
Hong Cao
Huiji Gao, ASU
Hung Hsuan Chen
Hyojeong Kim
Hyoungshick Kim, UBC
Hyuk Yoon Kwon
In Joong Kim
Isaac Jones, ASU
Jaafar Ben Abdallah,
Jakub Šimko, STUBA
Jan Hidders, TU Delft
Jan Rupnik, IJS
Janez Brank, IJS
Javier Luis Canovas Izquierdo, INRIA
Javier Parapar, UDC
Jean Sébastien Légaré, UBC
Jennifer Sleeman, UMBC

Additional Reviewers (Continued)

Jens Lehmann, Uni Leipzig
Jens Witkowski
Jialei Wang
Jianhua Yin
Jiao Tao
Jiliang Tang, ASU
Jim McCusker, RPI
Jin Young Kim, Microsoft
Jing Du, UCSC
Jingyu Zhou, SJTU
Jinha Kim, Postech
Jinoh Oh
Joan Isaac Biel
Joerg Unbehauen, Uni Leipzig
Johanna Voelker, Uni Mannheim
Johannes Wettinger, Uni Stuttgart
Jonathan Mortensen, Stanford
Jordi Atserias, Yahoo!
Jose Fernando Rodrigues Junior, USP
Josep Maria Brunetti Fernández,
Josiane Xavier Parreira, DERI
Juan Lang, Google
Juan Pablo Carrascal
Julia Hoxha, KIT
Julian Mcauley,
Junjie Yao
Junkyu Lee
Jürgen Bock, FZI
karla Caballero, UCSC
Karolina Vukojevic, Uni Stuttgart
Karthik Subbian, UMN
Keon Jang, Microsoft
Kisung Lee, GATech
Kyle Williams,
Lei Shi, Baidu
Liang Dai, UCSC
Liangjie Hong, Lehigh
Liaoruo Wang
Lili Jiang
Lu Chen
Luciano Barbosa, ATT
Madian Khabsa,
Man Zhu

Manuel Salvadores
Marco Montali, UniBZ
Marco Ribeiro
Marián Šimko
Martin Junghans, KIT
Martin Scholz, Google
Martina Deplano, UniTO
Martina Seidl, TUWien
Massimiliano Ciaramita, Google
Matthew Lentz, UMD
Mauro Cherubini
Max Tritschler, Fraunhofer
Max Tritschler, Fraunhofer
Maximilian Nickel
Michael Prentice
Michal Barla, STUBA
Michal Kompan, STUBA
Michelle Cheatham
Miguel Martinez Prieto, UVA
Minh Nhut Nguyen
Miriam Fernandez, Open U.
Mitja Trampus, IJS
Mohammad Ali Abbasi, ASU
Mohammadhossein Bateni,
Nan Li, UCSB
Nandish Jayaram,
Naoki Yoshinaga,
Natali Ruchansky, BU
Nathan Hodas
Negar Hariri
Negin Golrezaei, USC
Nicola Fanizzi, UniBA
Nikolaos Laoutaris,
Ning Chen
Ning Yan
Nitish Aggarwal, DERI
Norman Heino, Uni Leipzig
Nuno Lopes, DERI
Oliver Ferschke, TU Darmstadt
Paola Velardi, UniROMA
Pavan Kapanipathi, Wright St
Pável Calado, UTL
Pavel Dmitriev, Cornell
Pengcheng Wu
Peter Cogan, Lucent

Philip Langer, TUWien
Pinar Ozturk, Stevens
Prakhar Biyani,
Pramod Anantharam, Wright St
Prashanth Mohan, UCB
Pritam Gundecha, ASU
Pushkar Tripathi, GATech
Qi Liu
Qing Ke, Indiana
Qiqi Yan
Quan Wang
Quan Yuan, NTU
Rahul Potharaju
Raju Balakrishnan
Rong Hua Li
Sangho Lee, Postech
Sangrak Lim
Sara Tonelli, FBK
Schahram Proxy Dustdar Proxy,
Seongsoon Kim
Shaghayegh Sahebi, Pittsburgh
Shankar Kalyanaraman,
Shenglin Zhao, CUHK
Shengqi Yang, UCSB
Shulong Tan
Smitashree Choudhury, Open U.
Song Feng, Stonybrook
Sotirios Chatzis, CUT
Stamatina Thomaidou
Stefano Soi
Stefano Tranquillini, UniTN
Sumit Bhatia, PSU
Sungchul Kim
Sungjae Hwang, KAIST
Tadej Štajner, IJS
Taehoon Kim, Postech
Theodoros Lappas, BU
Timofey Ermilov, Uni Leipzig
Todd Plantenga, Sandia
Tom Chao Zhou, CUHK
Tom Schimoler
Tomáš Kramár, STUBA
Tommaso Soru, Uni Leipzig
Trinh Minh Tri Do,
Umang Bhaskar,

Additional Reviewers (Continued)

- Umar Syed
- Vana Kalogeraki,
- Veli Bicer, IBM
- Vikas Ganjigunte Ashok, Stonybrook
- Wei Feng, Tsinghua
- Wei Shen
- Wei Zhang
- Wenbo Wang
- William Heavlin, Google
- William West, Lehigh
- Wladmir Brandao, UFMG
- Xiang Ren, Illinois
- Xiao Huang, Microsoft
- Xiaohui Sun, Microsoft
- Xiaozhong Liu,
- Xin Cao, NTU
- Xin Zhao
- Xin Zhao
- Xueyan Jiang
- Yi Huang, Siemens
- Yi Mao, Microsoft
- Ying Wang, Google
- Yinghui Wu
- Yong Ge
- Yongtao Ma
- Yu Wang, Emory
- Yuan Ren, ABDN
- Yuan Fang Li, Monash
- Yung Yi, KAIST
- Yury Puzis, Charmtech
- Yuting Zhao
- Yuzhe Tang, GATech
- Zhen Liu
- Zhenglu Yang
- Zhenning Shangguan,
- Zhicheng Dou, Microsoft
- Zhong Yuan Zhang
- Zhongmou Li
- Zhuo Feng, ASU

Program Committee Practice and Experience Track

Members

Luca Maria Aiello, Yahoo! Research
Mohamed Aly, Yahoo! Research
Denilson Barbosa, University of Alberta
Stefano Ceri, DEI, Politecnico di Milano
Weizhu Chen, Microsoft
Yun Chi, NEC Laboratories America
Ed H. Chi, Google, Inc.
Fred Douglis, EMC
Christos Doulkeridis, Athens University of Economics and Business
Sameh Elnikety, Microsoft Research
Ariel Fuxman, Microsoft Research
Hong Gao, Harbin Institute of Technology
C. Lee Giles, Pennsylvania State University
Wook Shin Han, Kyungpook National University
Xiaofeng He, ECNU
Seungwon Hwang, POSTECH
Jaewoo Kang, Korea University
David Konopnicki, IBM
Hongrae Lee, Google, Inc.
Ping Luo, HP Labs China
Amin Mantrach, Yahoo! Labs
Francesco Saverio Nucci, Engineering Ingegneria Informatica S.p.A.
Beng Chin Ooi, National University of Singapore
Themis Palpanas, University of Trento
Uri Schonfeld, UCLA
Rok Sosic, Computer Science Department, Stanford University
Fabian M. Suchanek, Max Planck Institute for Informatics
Neel Sundaresan, eBay Research Labs
Vincent S. Tseng, National Cheng Kung University
Stratis Viglas, University of Edinburgh, School of Informatics
Yanghua Xiao, Fudan university
Jun Yan, Microsoft Research Asia
Xiaochun Yang, North Eastern University
Kenny Zhu, Shanghai Jiao Tong University

Additional reviewers

Mikalai Tsytsarau, University of Trento
Andresta Setiawan, Korean University
Ashis Saha, Korea University
Bilal Lodhi, Korea University
Davide Mottin, Trento University
Eduardo Graells, Yahoo
Hung-Yu Kao, National Cheng-Kung University
Hyuk-Yoon Kwon, Kyungpook National University
In-Joong Kim, Kyungpook National University
Jaehoon Choi, Korea University
Ja-Hwung Su, National Cheng-Kung University
Jim Jansen, Penn State University
Jinho Lee, Korea University
Jin-Woo Park, POSTECH
Jonatan Taminau, Vrije Universiteit Brussel
Kenny Zhu, Shanghai Jiaotong University
Krishna Gummadi, MPI
Kun-Ta Chuang, National Cheng-Kung University
Lei Zou, Peking University
Matteo Lissandrini, University of Trento
Mikalai Tsytsarau, University of Trento
Minji Jeon, Korea University
Pasquale Andriani, Engineering Ingegneria Informatica SPA
Steven Whang, Google
Sujatha Das, Penn State University
Vincenzo Croce, Università degli Studi di Palermo
Wen Hua, Renmin University of China
Xing Niu, Shanghai Jiaotong University
Yanghua Xiao, Fudan University
Yangqiu Song, HKUST
Yuchen Zhang, UC Berkeley
Zhen Wang, SYSU
Zhen Yu, ECNU
Zihan Zhou, Penn State University

Posters Track

Members

Dirk Ahlers, UNITEC
Rosa Alarcon, Pontificia Universidad Católica de Chile
Mark Baker, Zepheira LLC
Jöran Beel, Docear
Walter Binder, University of Lugano
Joshua Blumenstock, University of California at Berkeley
Marco Brambilla, Politecnico di Milano
Rommel Carvalho, George Mason University
Stefano A. Cerri, LIRMM: University of Montpellier and CNRS
Philippe Cudré Mauroux, U. of Fribourg
Richard Cyganiak, Digital Enterprise Research Institute, NUI Galway
Florian Daniel, University of Trento, Italy
Cornelia Davis, EMC
Peter Dolog, Department of Computer Science, Aalborg University
Nick Doty, UC Berkeley, School of Information
Flavius Frasincar, Erasmus University Rotterdam
Fred Freitas, CIn UFPE
Tim Furche, Oxford University
Martin Gaedke, Chemnitz University of Technology
Fabien Gandon, INRIA
Béla Gipp, UC Berkeley
Luiz Goncalves, Universidade Federal do Rio Grande do Norte
Joe Gregorio, Google
Giancarlo Guizzardi, Ontology and Conceptual Modeling Research Group (NEMO)/Federal University of Espirito Santo (UFES)
Michael Hausenblas, Digital Enterprise Research Institute (DERI), NUI Galway
Vivien Helmut,
Andreas Henrich, University of Bamberg
Laura Hollink, VU University Amsterdam
Seiji Isotani, University of Sao Paulo
Jorn W Janneck, Lund University
Christopher Jones, Cardiff University
Eric Kansa, UC Berkeley, School of Information
Murat Kantarcioglu, University of Texas at Dallas
Puneet Kishor, University of Wisconsin Madison
Agnes Koschmider, Karlsruher Institute of Technology
Markus Lanthaler, Graz University of Technology
Ray Larson, University of California, Berkeley
Arnaud Le Hors, IBM
Dave Lester, University of California, Berkeley
Fernanda Lima, UnB (Universidade de Brasilia)
Olga Liskin, Leibniz Universität Hannover
Yiming Liu, UC Berkeley
Jose Macedo, Federal University of Ceara
Simon Mayer, ETH Zurich
Lionel Medini, LIRIS lab., Université de Lyon / CNRS
Wagner Meira Jr., UFMG
Cesare Pautasso, University of Lugano
Vivien Petras, HU Berlin
Ross Purves, University of Zürich – Irchel
André Santanchè, Universidade de Campinas
Felix Sasaki, FH Potsdam / W3C German Austrian Office
Arno Scharl, MODUL University Vienna, Department of New Media Technology
Patrick Schmitz, University of California Berkeley
Johannes Schöning, Hasselt University
Ryan Shaw
Maria Augusta Silveira Netto Nunes, DCOMP UFS
Stefan Tai, KIT
Giovanni Tummarello, DERI, National University of Ireland galway
Herbert Van De Sompel, Los Alamos National Laboratory, Research Library
Tomas Vitvar, University of Innsbruck
Norman Walsh, Sun Microsystems, Inc.
Erik Wilde, EMC Corporation
Marco Winckler, ICS IRIT, Université Paul Sabtier
Christian Zirpins, University of Karlsruhe (TH)
Ivan Zuzak, School of Electrical Engineering and Computing, University of Zagreb

Demos Track

Members

Nitin Agarwal, UALR
Omar Alonso, University of California
George Anadiotis, University of Patras
Damires Souza, IFPB
Mirella M.Moro, UFMG
Khalid Belhajjame, University of Manchester
Hao Ma, Microsoft
Paolo Manghi, ISTI CNR
Carlos Eduardo Pires, UFCG
Ryan Shaw, University of North Carolina at Chapel Hill
Fabrizio Silvestri, INSTI CNR
Luciano Barbosa, AT&T Labs Research
Fabricio Benevenuto, UFMG
Jim Blomo, UC Berkeley
Olivier Boissier, ENS Mines Saint Etienne
Vinicius Cardoso Garcia, UFPE
Rodrigo Assad, USTO.RE
Irene Celino, CEFRIEL
Jonathan Chan, King Mongkut's University of Technology Thonburi
Yi Chang, Yahoo! Labs
John Chuang, UC Berkeley
Eli Cortez, UFAM
Frederico Araújo Durão, UFBA
Paolo Frasconi, UniFI
Christophe Guéret, Data Archiving and Networked Services (DANS)
Shengbo Guo, Samsung Media Solution Center America
Mark Michael Hall, Sheffield University,
Harry Halpin, W3C
Dominique Hazael Massieux, W3C
Cornelia Hedeler, University of Manchester
Steven Hoi, NTU
Eero Hyvönen, Aalto University and University of Helsinki
Alejandro Jaimes, Yahoo! Research
Kyomin Jung, KAIST
Zoubida Kedad, Université de Versailles
Juanzi Li, Tsinghua, Tsinghua University
Hang Li, Huawei Noah's Ark Lab
Guang Ling, CUHK
Huan Liu, ASU
Tie Yan Liu, Microsoft
Qin Lu, PolyU HK
Dickson Lukose, MIMOS Berhad
Mário Antonio Meireles Teixeira, UFMA
Hye Young Paik, University of New South Wales
Maria Da Graça Pimentel, USP
Marco Antônio Pinheiro de Cristo, UFAM
Lei Tang, WalmartLabs
George Vouros, University of Piraeus
Hui Xiong, Rutgers University
Albert Yeung, Huawei Noah's Ark Lab
Lei Zhang, Microsoft

WWW 2013 Sponsors & Supporters

These sponsors were confirmed at the time these proceedings were published in April 2013. Additional sponsors may have joined after this date

Sponsors

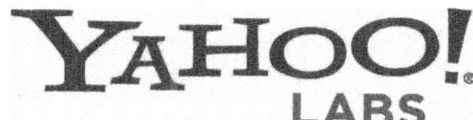 

Institutional supporters

Conference Partners

Organizers

nic.br

cgi.br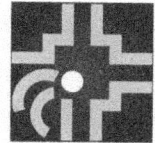

W3C® Brasil

Mining Structural Hole Spanners Through Information Diffusion in Social Networks

Tiancheng Lou[#][†][*] and Jie Tang[†]
[#]Google, Inc., Mountain View, CA 94043, US
[†]Tsinghua University, Beijing 100084, China
acrush@google.com, jietang@tsinghua.edu.cn

ABSTRACT

The theory of *structural holes* [4] suggests that individuals would benefit from filling the "holes" (called as structural hole spanners) between people or groups that are otherwise disconnected. A few empirical studies have verified that structural hole spanners play a key role in the information diffusion. However, there is still lack of a principled methodology to detect structural hole spanners from a given social network.

In this work, we precisely define the problem of mining top-k structural hole spanners in large-scale social networks and provide an objective (quality) function to formalize the problem. Two instantiation models have been developed to implement the objective function. For the first model, we present an exact algorithm to solve it and prove its convergence. As for the second model, the optimization is proved to be NP-hard, and we design an efficient algorithm with provable approximation guarantees.

We test the proposed models on three different networks: Coauthor, Twitter, and Inventor. Our study provides evidence for the theory of structural holes, e.g., 1% of Twitter users who span structural holes control 25% of the information diffusion on Twitter. We compare the proposed models with several alternative methods and the results show that our models clearly outperform the comparison methods. Our experiments also demonstrate that the detected structural hole spanners can help other social network applications, such as community kernel detection and link prediction. To the best of our knowledge, this is the first attempt to address the problem of mining structural hole spanners in large social networks.

Categories and Subject Descriptors

J.4 [**Social and Behavioral Sciences**]: Miscellaneous

General Terms

Algorithms, Experimentation

Keywords

Structural hole, Social network, Information diffusion, Minimal cut

1. INTRODUCTION

In sociology, there are a few well-established ideas on how positions in social networks benefit those people who occupy them [7].

[*]This work was done when the first author was studying in Tsinghua University.

Copyright is held by the International World Wide Web Conference Committee (IW3C2). IW3C2 reserves the right to provide a hyperlink to the author's site if the Material is used in electronic media.
WWW 2013, May 13–17, 2013, Rio de Janeiro, Brazil.
ACM 978-1-4503-2035-1/13/05.

One idea is that positions which act as an intermediary or a bridge between individuals of different groups tend to have access to a richer supply of information and have more control over their network relations. The notion forms the basis for the theory of *structural holes* [4], which suggests that advantages accrue to people who occupy such bridging positions. For example, if a researcher spans a structural hole, he/she could apply ideas and techniques from one group to problems faced by the other, or innovate by synthesizing ideas from different groups.

A series of empirical studies have demonstrated how structural holes positively relate to a wide range of indicators of social success [1, 5, 6, 28]. A few other papers use game theory to model the formation of structural holes in social networks. Goyal and Vega-Redondo [12] propose a model in which a node A potentially benefits from serving as an intermediary between nodes B and C even when it resides on an arbitrarily long B-C path. According to the presented model, the strategic link formation leads to a star network. However, in real world, many networks are not necessarily of the star topology. [7] explicitly models the notion of structural holes using a network formation game. It is based on the idea that A can only benefit from being an intermediary when A is on a length-two path between B and C. Kleinberg et al. [18] study the strategic and dynamic aspect to the theory of structural holes. They extend Burt's work [5] by modeling how social networks change over time if everyone is vying for those bridging positions. However, while much research has focused on studying the correlation between structural hole spanners and their success within an organization (as indicated by salary, reviews, promotion, and other measures), few work systematically investigates the problem in large online social networks.

We address the problem of identifying structural holes spanners: given a social network, who are the top-k users spanning structural holes in the social network, and what are the underlying patterns of these structural hole spanners? The problem could be considered as the reverse process of the study on strategic network formation with structural holes [7, 12, 18]. The latter problem is to design a game-theoretic model to study the evolution of network structure, while our problem is to detect who are likely to span structural holes in social networks based on the network structure.

The Model. We assume a setting in which a set V of n distinct users form l groups $\mathbf{C} = \{C_1, \cdots, C_l\}$ (called communities). A utility function $Q(v, \mathbf{C})$ is defined for each node to measure its degree to span structural holes. Formally, we have the following definition,

Definition 1. Top-k Structural Hole Spanners. Let $G = (V, E)$ denote a social network, where $V = \{v_1, v_2, \cdots, v_n\}$ is a set of n users, and $E \subseteq V \times V$ is a set of undirected social

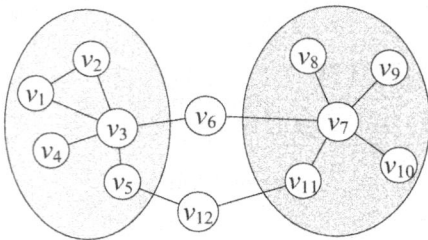

Figure 1: Illustration of structural holes. Nodes in the two ellipses form two communities. v_6 and v_{12} can be considered to span the structural hole between the two communities.

Table 1: Statistics of the three networks. #Articles respectively indicates the number of publications, tweets, and patents in the three networks.

Dataset	#Users	#Relationships	#Articles
Coauthor [31]	815,946	2,792,833	1,572,277
Twitter [15]	112,044	468,238	2,409,768
Inventor [30]	2,445,351	5,841,940	3,880,211

relationships between users. Further assume that the nodes of the social network can be grouped into l (overlapping) communities $\mathbf{C} = \{C_1, \cdots, C_l\}$, with $V = C_1 \cup \cdots \cup C_l$. Then, the top-$k$ structural hole spanners are defined as a subset of k nodes, denoted as V_{SH} in the network, which maximizes the following utility (quality) function:

$$\max_{V_{SH}} Q(V_{SH}, \mathbf{C}), \text{ with } |V_{SH}| = k \quad (1)$$

In the formulation, links can be directed or undirected. The utility function $Q(V_{SH}, \mathbf{C})$ is a general definition, which can be instantiated in different ways. Note that in the definition, we only consider the network information but not the content information. Our goal is to give a theoretical analysis for this problem. Combining the network information and the content information in practical mining algorithms is left as one of our future works.

We develop two instantiation models based on the above objective function. The general idea behind is to measure how a node bridges different communities. In the first model, we consider the importance of those connected nodes for mining the structural hole spanners. That is, if a node connects multiple important nodes (authoritative users), then the node is more likely to be a structural hole spanner. In the second model, we directly measure each node according to the theory of minimal cut on network. The problem is cast as finding k nodes such that after removing these nodes, the *decrease* of minimal cut for communities $\mathbf{C}$ in network G can be maximized. For both models, we provide theoretical analysis and develop efficient algorithms to solve with provable approximation guarantees. As far as we know, it is the first attempt to prove the NP-hardness of maximizing the *decrease* of minimal cut in an unweighted graph.

The problem poses a set of challenges. Figure 1 shows an example of structural holes with two communities. It is easy to see that v_6 and v_{12} can be viewed as structural hole spanners between the two communities. However, there are still several challenging questions: (1) Which node (v_6 or v_{12}) has a higher degree to span structural holes? How to quantify the degree of each node to span structural holes? (2) How to efficiently select top-k nodes to maximize the utility function (Eq. 1)? (3) How the detected structural hole nodes can help other social networking applications?

Results. In this work, we focus on studying the problem of mining top-k structural hole spanners in large-scale networks from both theoretical and empirical aspects. We test the proposed models on three different networks: Coauthor, Twitter, and Inventor. In Coauthor, we try to understand who act as bridges between different research communities; in Twitter, we attempt to detect who act as intermediaries for information diffusion; in Inventor, we study how technologies diffuse across different companies via inventors who span structural holes. Our study presents the following results:

- 1% of Twitter users who span structural holes control 25% of the information diffusion (retweeting). This provides a strong evidence for the theory of structural hole [4, 5].

- We compare the proposed models with several alternative methods for detecting structural hole spanners and the results show that our models clearly outperform (+20-40% for maximizing the information diffusion) the comparison methods.

- We apply the detected structural hole spanners to help communities detection [32] and link prediction [29], two important applications in social networks. Results demonstrate that the structural hole information can significantly improve the quality (+10% in terms of F1-score) of communities detection and improve the performance (+3-4% by F1-score) of predicting the type of relationships in two different networks.

Organization. Section 2 introduces the data sets used in our study and our observations over different networks. Section 3 presents the proposed model and describes the algorithm for solving the model; Section 4 describes potential applications of mining structural hole spanners. Section 5 and Section 6 present the results. Finally, Section 7 discusses related work and Section 8 concludes.

2. DATA AND OBSERVATIONS

Before proceeding, we first engage in some high-level investigation of structural holes in several different social networks.

Data collections. We consider three different types of networks for studying the structural hole problem: Coauthor, Twitter and Inventor. Table 1 gives basic statistics of the three networks.

Coauthor is a network of authors, collected by ArnetMiner[1]. The data set is obtained from [31]. The network consists of 815,946 authors and 2,792,833 coauthorships. For the evaluation purpose, we create a sub-network, which contains coauthorships extracted from papers published at 28 major computer science conferences. These conferences cover six research areas: Artificial Intelligence (AI), Databases (DB), Data Mining (DM), Distributed Parallel Computing (DP), Graphics, Vision and HCI (GV), as well as Networks, Communications and Performance (NC)[2]. Each conference has a group of program committee (PC) members. We extracted the PC member information from respective conference websites from 2008 to 2010. Computer scientists who served as PC members at conferences of different areas are considered as spanning structural

---
[1] http://arnetminer.org, an academic search system.
[2] AI: IJCAI, AAAI, ICML, UAI, UMAP, NIPS, and AAMAS; DB: VLDB, SIGMOD, PODS, ICDE, ICDT, and EDBT; DM: SIGKDD and ICDM; DP: PPoPP, PACT, IPDPS, ICPP, and EuroPar; GV: SIGGRAPH, CVPR, and ICCV; NC: SIGCOMM, PERFORMANCE, SIGMETRICS, INFOCOM, and MOBICOM.

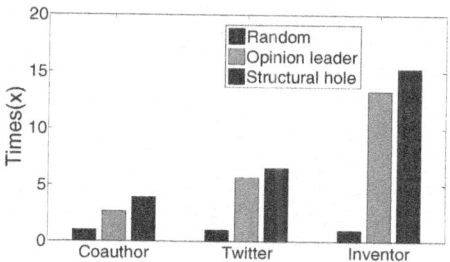

Figure 2: **Structural hole spanners are more likely to connect important nodes than opinion leaders.** Random is the average number of publications/tweets/patents authored by neighborhood nodes of a random user in the respective network. The average number is taken as a unit of measurement and the y-axis indicates the average score of different categories of users under this measurement.

holes across those areas. In total, we extracted 1,718 PC members, among whom 107 PC members span structural holes. Our goal is to identify those PC members who span structural holes from the coauthor network.

Twitter is crawled from Twitter.com, a widely used microblogging system. The data set is obtained from [15, 22]. The subnetwork is comprised of 112,044 users, 468,238 following links among them, and all tweets (2,409,768 tweets) posted by these users. Here, we examine the role of structural hole spanners in the information diffusion process on Twitter.

Inventor is a network of inventors, extracted from a large patent data set from USPTO[3]. The data set is obtain from [30]. The inventor network contains 2,445,351 inventors and 5,841,940 co-inventing relationships. Each company is considered as a community. We study how technologies spread across different companies via inventors who span structural holes.

Observable analysis. We study the different behavior patterns between structural hold spanners and opinion leaders, and the interplay between structural hold spanners and information diffusion. Intuitively, we have the following questions:

- How likely would structural hole spanners connect with "opinion leaders"?

- How likely would structural hole spanners influence the information diffusion?

Structural hole spanner and Opinion leaders. We study the connectivity between opinion leaders and different categories of users (Opinion leaders, Structural holes, and Random). In Coauthor, we take all PC members as opinion leaders and PC members who serve at conferences of different areas as structural holes. In Inventor, we perform PageRank [27] and select the top 1% users with the highest PageRank scores as opinion leaders, and those top users who worked in different companies as structural hole spanners. In Twitter, we also perform PageRank on the following network and select the top 1% users as opinion leaders. We use the $(\alpha - \beta)$ community detection algorithm [14, 24] to find overlapping communities. Then those top users who exist in different communities are treated as structural hole spanners.

Figure 2 shows that structural hole spanners are more likely (+15-50%) to connect important nodes than opinion leaders. In

[3]http://uspto.gov/, the US patent and trademark office.

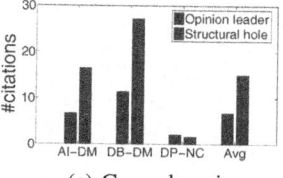 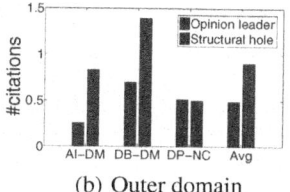

(a) Cross domain (b) Outer domain

Figure 3: **Information diffusion on the Coauthor network.** (a) Average number of cross-domain citations received by structural hole spanners and opinion leaders, e.g., in the AI-DM case, for opinion leaders in AI, only citations from DM are considered. (b) Average number of outer-domain (those domains other than AI and DM) citations received by structural hole spanners and opinion leaders.

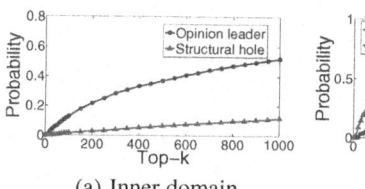 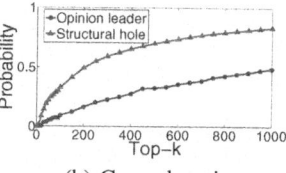

(a) Inner domain (b) Cross domain

Figure 4: **Information diffusion on the Twitter network.** x-axis indicates top k opinion leaders/structural hole spanners; and y-axis indicates the probability of opinion leaders (or structural hole spanners) appearing on a tweet-forwarding path spread within a domain or across different domains.

Figure 2, Random stands for the average number of publications/tweets/patents authored by neighborhood nodes of a random user in the respective network. The average number is taken as a unit of measurement and the y-axis indicates the average score of different categories of users under this measurement. The analysis provides evidence in support of the first proposed model (Cf. §3).

Structural hole spanner and information diffusion. We perform another analysis of information diffusion in the Coauthor and the Twitter networks. In Coauthor, we consider the citation as a type of information diffusion. We count the average numbers of cross-domain citations received by opinion leaders and structural hole spanners. (Within the same domain, opinion leaders receive higher citations than others.) We find a striking phenomenon (Figure 3): contrast to the inner-domain citation, the average number of cross-domain citations received by the structural hole spanners almost doubles the number of opinion leaders. It seems that people from a research community C_1, if they want to follow the work related to community C_2, are more likely to refer (cite) the work of a researcher who spans the structural hole between C_1 and C_2, rather than an opinion leader in community C_2.

For the analysis of information diffusion in Twitter, we estimate the probability of opinion leaders (or structural hole spanners) appearing on a tweet-forwarding path. Figure 4 shows some interesting patterns on Twitter: opinion leaders play a key role in spreading information within a community (Figure 4(a)), while structural hole spanners are more important for spreading information between communities (Figure 4(b)). Another striking phenomenon is that the top 1% ($k = 1,000$) of structural hole spanners control almost 80% of the information diffusion between different communities, and 25% of all the information diffusion on Twitter.

The above observations constitute the intuition behind the following proposed models.

3. MODELS AND ALGORITHMS

We develop two instantiation models for the utility function (Eq. 1). The first model considers the connectivity between opinion leaders and structural hole spanners (Cf. Figure 2). The user's importance (authority) and the degree of spanning structural hole are defined in terms of one another in a mutual recursion. The intuition of the second model is from Figures 3 and 4. The model is defined based on the theory of information flow. We provide theoretical analysis for the two models and prove the NP-hardness for the second model, and develop efficient algorithms to achieve provable approximation guarantees.

3.1 Model One: HIS

The intuition of the first model can be also explained using the two-step information flow theory [16, 20], which suggests that ideas (innovations) usually flow first to opinion leaders, and then from the opinions leaders to a wider population. In this sense, if a user is connected with many "opinion leaders" in different communities, then the user is more likely to span structural holes. For example, in Figure 1, nodes v_3 and v_7 act as opinion leaders respectively in the two communities, thus they have more power to spread information than other nodes (such as v_5 and v_{11}). v_6 and v_{12} can be considered as the bridge to connect the two communities. By comparing v_6 with v_{12}, we see v_6 connects the two opinion leaders of the two communities, while v_{12} only connects two ordinary users. According to the information flow theory, v_6 would have a higher informational advantage (i.e., higher degree to span structural holes) than v_{12}. On the other hand, it would be natural to enhance the power of information spread through the connection to structural hole spanners. Thus, a node is more likely to act as an opinion leader, if it connects with structural hole spanners. Based on this intuition, we develop the first model, referred to as HIS. To begin with, we first give the following definition:

Definition 2. Given a network G, let $\mathbf{C} = \{C_1, \cdots, C_l\}$ denote l communities in the network G; let $I(v, C_i) \in [0, 1]$ be the importance of v in community C_i. Then for each subset of communities S such that $S \subseteq \mathbf{C}$ and $|S| \geq 2$, we define $H(v, S) \in [0, 1]$ as the structural hole score of v in S, i.e., the likelihood of v spanning structural holes across all communities in S.

Here, each node has an importance score in each community and a structural hole score in every possible $S \subseteq \mathbf{C}$ ($|S| \geq 2$). The two types of scores are defined in terms of each other in a mutual recursion as follows:

$$I(v, C_i) = \max_{\substack{e_{uv} \in E, \\ S \subseteq \mathbf{C} \land C_i \in S}} \{I(v, C_i), \alpha_i I(u, C_i) + \beta_S H(u, S)\} \quad (2)$$

$$H(v, S) = \min_{C_i \in S} \{I(v, C_i)\} \quad (3)$$

where α_i and β_S are two tunable parameters. The importance score of user v is computed as the maximal value of the linear combination of v's friend's importance score and the structural hole score. The structural hole score is then defined as the minimal value of user v's importance scores in different communities in S. Essentially, in Eq. 2, the importance score can be explained as the maximal information flow a user can receive from one of her/his friends. Eq. 3 suggests that a structural hole spanner in S should be active in all the communities in S. The two update rules, Eqs. 2 and 3 are the basic approaches by which structural holes and importance (authority) reinforce each other. For initialization, we can use an algorithm such as PageRank [27] or HITS [17] to calculate the authority score $r(v)$ of each node v. Then we initialize the importance score $I(v, C_i)$ in the following ways:

$$\begin{aligned} I(v, C_i) &= r(v), \quad v \in C_i \\ I(v, C_i) &= 0, \quad v \notin C_i \end{aligned} \quad (4)$$

The two update rules Eqs. 2 and 3 run in an alternating fashion until desired equilibrium values for the two scores are reached. Practically, the two scores $I(v, C_i)$ and $H(v, S)$ could be infinitely large without any constraints. We give the following theorem for the condition of the existence of a convergent solution.

Theorem 1. Given α_i and β_S, the two scores $I(v, C_i)$ and $H(v, S)$ always exists for any graph $G = (V, E)$, if and only if,

$$\max_{C_i \in \mathbf{C}, C_i \in S} \{\alpha_i + \beta_S\} \leq 1 \quad (5)$$

PROOF. For the *only if* direction, suppose there exists $C_i \in \mathbf{C}$ and $C_i \in S$ such that $\alpha_i + \beta_S > 1$. We consider two connected nodes v_1 and v_2, with $r(v_1) = r(v_2) = 1$, $v_1 \in \cap_{C_j \in S} C_j$ and $v_2 \in C_i$. Thus, we have $I(v_1, C_i) = 1$. By Eq. 3, we get $H(v_1, S) = \min_{C_j \in S} I(v_1, C_j) = 1$. By Eq. 2, we get $I(v_2, i) \geq \alpha_i I(v_1, C_i) + \beta_S H(v_1, S) = \alpha_i + \beta_S > 1$, which is impossible.

Now we prove the *if* direction, if for each C_i and $C_i \in S$, we have $\alpha_i + \beta_S \leq 1$. We can use induction to prove that, after infinite number of iterations, it satisfies $I(v, C_i) \leq 1$. In the first iteration, we have $I^{(0)}(v, C_i) \leq r(v) \leq 1$. After the k-th iteration, we have $I^{(k)}(v, C_i) \leq r(v) \leq 1$. Hence, in the $(k+1)$-th iteration, for each $C_i \in S$, we have $I^{(k+1)}(v, C_i) \leq \alpha_i I^{(k)}(u, C_i) + \beta_S H^{(k)}(u, S) \leq (\alpha_i + \beta_S) I^{(k)}(u, C_i) \leq I^{(k)}(u, C_i) \leq 1$. □

Algorithm 1 gives the implementation to update Eqs. 2 and 3, which results in a complexity of $O(K2^l|E|)$, where K is the number of iterations. Let us first prove the ϵ-convergence of the algorithm and then discuss its efficiency.

Theorem 2. Algorithm 1 satisfies ϵ-convergence. Denote $\gamma = \max_{C_i \in \mathbf{C}, C_i \in S} \{\alpha_i + \beta_S\}$, we have

$$\max_{v \in V, C_i \in \mathbf{C}} |I^{(k+1)}(v, C_i) - I^{(k)}(v, C_i)| \leq \gamma^k \quad (6)$$

PROOF. Firstly, parameters α_i and β_S satisfy $\gamma = \max_{C_i \in \mathbf{C}, C_i \in S} \{\alpha_i + \beta_S\} \leq 1$. In addition, during the iterations, for any $v \in V$, $C_i \in \mathbf{C}$ and $S \subseteq \mathbf{C}$, the value of $I^{(k)}(v, C_i)$ and $H^{(k)}(v, S)$ are non-decreasing wrt the parameter k.

Now, we use induction to prove

$$\max_{v \in V, C_i \in \mathbf{C}} |I^{(k+1)}(v, C_i) - I^{(k)}(v, C_i)| \leq \gamma^k$$

and

$$\max_{v \in V, S \subseteq \mathbf{C}} |H^{(k+1)}(v, S) - H^{(k)}(v, S)| \leq \gamma^k.$$

When $k = 0$, for each $v \in V$ and $C_i \in \mathbf{C}$, we have $I^{(1)}(v, C_i) \leq 1$, thus $|I^{(1)}(v, C_i) - I^{(0)}(v, C_i)| \leq 1$. And for each $v \in V$ and $S \subseteq \mathbf{C}$, $H^{(1)}(v, S) \leq 1$, thus we also have $|H^{(1)}(v, S) - H^{(0)}(v, S)| \leq 1$.

Input: $G = (V, E)$, parameters α_i, β_S, and convergence threshold ϵ
Output: Importance I and structural hole score H

Initialize $I(v, C_i)$ according to Eq. 4 ;
repeat
  foreach $v \in V$ **do**
    foreach $C_i \in \mathbf{C}$ **do**
      $P(v, C_i) = \max_{S \subseteq \mathbf{C} \wedge C_i \in S} \{\alpha_i I(v, C_i) + \beta_S H(v, S)\}$;
    end
  end
  foreach $v \in V$ **do**
    foreach $C_i \in \mathbf{C}$ **do**
      $I'(v, C_i) = \max\{I(v, C_i), \max_{e_{uv} \in E} P(u, C_i)\}$;
    end
    foreach $S \subseteq \mathbf{C}$ **do**
      $H'(v, S) = \min_{C_i \in S} I'(v, C_i)$;
    end
  end
  Check the ϵ-convergence condition by
$$\max_{v \in V, C_i \in \mathbf{C}} |I'(v, C_i) - I(v, C_i)| \leq \epsilon$$
  Update $I = I'$ and $H = H'$;
until *Convergence*;

Algorithm 1: HIS-algorithm.

Suppose after k iterations, for each $v \in V$ and $C_i \in \mathbf{C}$, we have $|I^{(k+1)}(v, C_i) - I^{(k)}(v, C_i)| \leq \gamma^k$, and for each $v \in V$ and $S \subseteq \mathbf{C}$, $|H^{(k+1)}(v, S) - H^{(k)}(v, S)| \leq \gamma^k$. Hence, in the $(k+1)$-th iteration, for each $v \in V$ and $C_i \in \mathbf{C}$, if $I^{(k+2)}(v, C_i) = I^{(k+1)}(v, C_i)$, then $|I^{(k+2)}(v, C_i) - I^{(k+1)}(v, C_i)| = 0$, otherwise, there exists u, s.t. $e_{uv} \in E$ and $S \subseteq \mathbf{C}$, such that $C_i \in S$ and

$$\begin{aligned} I^{(k+2)}(v, C_i) &= \alpha_i I^{(k+1)}(u, C_i) + \beta_S H^{(k+1)}(u, S) \\ &\leq \alpha_i (I^{(k)}(u, C_i) + \gamma^k) + \beta_S (H^{(k)}(u, S) + \gamma^k) \\ &\leq \alpha_i I^{(k)}(u, C_i) + \beta_S H^{(k)}(u, S) + \gamma^{k+1} \\ &\leq I^{(k+1)}(v, C_i) + \gamma^{k+1} \end{aligned}$$

Thus, we have $|I^{(k+2)}(v, C_i) - I^{(k+1)}(v, C_i)| \leq \gamma^{k+1}$. For each $v \in V$ and $S \subseteq \mathbf{C}$, there exists $C_i \in S$, such that

$$\begin{aligned} H^{(k+1)}(v, S) &= I^{(k+1)}(v, C_i) \\ &\geq I^{(k+2)}(v, C_i) - \gamma^{k+1} \\ &\geq H^{(k+2)}(v, S) - \gamma^{k+1} \end{aligned}$$

Hence $|H^{(k+2)}(v, S) - H^{(k+1)}(v, S)| \leq \gamma^{k+1}$. □

Therefore, when $\gamma = \max_{C_i \in \mathbf{C}, C_i \in S} \{\alpha_i + \beta_S\} < 1 - \delta$, where δ is a small constant, the algorithm is guaranteed to be convergent after a finite number of iterations.

We now discuss the efficiency of the algorithm. The time complexity of the algorithm is $O(2^l |E| / \log \gamma)$, which is insufficient for large networks. We here introduce an improved algorithm. Notice that in the $(k+1)$-th iteration of Algorithm 1, we only need to recompute the values of $I(v, *)$, when one of v's neighbors changes its value in the k-th iteration. We can record the change status of each node in the k-th iteration, and broadcast its change to all neighbors in the next iteration. In this way, we can update Eqs. 2-3 in linear-time on the degree of v and 2^l. In each iteration, we select the node v with the largest updated $I(v, *)$, then broadcast the value to its neighbors. The selection of the node v with the largest updated $I(v, *)$ can be done in time $O(\log |E|) = O(\log |V|)$, by using a priority queue. In § 5, we will give the efficiency performance of the improved algorithm. After running the algorithm, we select k nodes with the highest $\max_{|S| \geq 2}\{\beta_S H(v, S)\}$ as the top-k structural hole spanners.

3.2 Model Two: MaxD

The second model is based on the idea that users who span structural holes play an important role in information diffusion between different communities (confirmed in the observable analysis in § 2). Following this, we formalize the problem of structural hole spanner detection by *minimal cut*.

Definition 3. **Minimal Cut.** Given a network $G = (V, E)$ and l communities $\mathbf{C} = \{C_1, \cdots, C_l\}$, we call $D \subseteq E$ as the minimal cut (denoted as $\text{MC}(G, \mathbf{C})$) of communities $\mathbf{C}$ in G, if D is the minimal number of edges to separate those nodes in each community C_i from the others $\{C_j | j \neq i\}$.

Given this, the structural hole spanner detection problem can be cast as finding top-k nodes such that after removing these nodes, the minimal cut of $\mathbf{C}$ in G will be significantly reduced, i.e., the decrease of the minimal cut after removing will be maximized. The idea is natural, as structural hole spanners play bridging roles between communities. Without these structural hole nodes, the connections between different communities would be minimized. To make the idea precise, we propose the following problem definition:

Definition 4. **Detecting top-k structural hole spanners by minimal cut.** Given a graph $G = (V, E)$, and l communities $\mathbf{C} = \{C_1, \cdots, C_l\}$, the task of detecting top-k structural hole spanners by minimal cut is to find $|V_{SH}| = k$ nodes such that after removing these k nodes, the *decrease* of minimal cut of $\mathbf{C}$ in G should be maximized, i.e.,

$$Q(V_{SH}, \mathbf{C}) = \text{MC}(G, \mathbf{C}) - \text{MC}(G \backslash V_{SH}, \mathbf{C}), \quad |V_{SH}| = k \quad (7)$$

The following theorem shows the hardness of this definition.

Theorem 3. The problem of detecting top-k structural hole spanners by minimal cut is NP-hard, even in the case of $l = 2$.

PROOF. In the case of $l = 2$, the problem can be reduced from the k-DENSEST SUBGRAPH problem, which tries to find a k-node subgraph with the maximum number of edges from a given graph. For the decision version of the problem, it asks whether there exists a k-node subgraph containing at least d edges.

Given an instance $\phi = \{G^* = (V, E), k, d\}$ of the k-DENSEST SUBGRAPH problem, we denote $n = |V|$ and $m = |E|$. We build a graph G consisting of $(n + (n^2 + 1)m + 2)$ nodes, denoted as $\{s, t, x_1, \cdots, x_n, y_{i,1}, \cdots, y_{i,m}\}$, $1 \leq i \leq n^2 + 1$, where $\mathbf{C} = \{C_1, C_2\}$, $C_1 = \{s\}$ and $C_2 = \{t\}$. In the following, we use graphs with polynomially bounded weight (weighted graph for short), and it is straightforward to construct an equivalent un-weighted graph of polynomial size. Graph G contains $(n + (n^2 + 1)(n - 1)m)$ edges. For each $1 \leq j \leq n$, we add one edge between s and x_j with capacity $(n^2 + 1)m$. For each $1 \leq j \leq n$, $1 \leq i \leq n^2 + 1$ and $1 \leq k \leq m$, if node x_j does not appear on the k-th edge (each edge could be regarded as a set of two nodes), we add one edge between x_j and $y_{i,k}$ with capacity

1. For each $1 \leq i \leq n^2 + 1$ and $1 \leq k \leq m$, we add one edge between $y_{i,k}$ and t with capacity 1.

According to the max-flow and min-cut theory, it is easy to see that, $\text{MC}(G, \mathbf{C}) = (n^2 + 1)m$. Now we want to prove that, the k-DENSEST SUBGRAPH instance ϕ is satisfiable, if and only if, there exists a subset $|V_{SH}| = n - k$, such that $\text{MC}(G \setminus V_{SH}, \mathbf{C}) \leq (n^2 + 1)(m - d)$.

For the *only if* direction, suppose the k-DENSEST SUBGRAPH instance ϕ is satisfiable, then we have the subgraph consists of nodes $\{x_{s_j}\}$ and at least d edges. Thus, we can choose $V_{SH} = \{x_j\} \setminus \{x_{s_j}\}$. For the k-th edge e_k in graph G, if e_k exists in the subgraph, for all $1 \leq i \leq n^2 + 1$, node $y_{i,k}$ cannot be reached. Hence, we have $\text{MC}(G \setminus V_{SH}, \mathbf{C}) \leq (n^2 + 1)(m - d)$.

For the *if* direction, if there exists a subset $|V_{SH}| = n - k$ such that $\text{MC}(G \setminus V_{SH}, \mathbf{C}) \leq (n^2 + 1)(m - d)$. Denote $V_{SH}^* = V_{SH} \cap \{x_j\}$, we have $|V_{SH}^*| \leq n - k$, and $\text{MC}(G \setminus V_{SH}^*, \mathbf{C}) \leq (n^2 + 1)(m - d)$. Thus, let the subgraph be the set of corresponding nodes in $\{x_j\} \setminus V_{SH}^*$, there are at least d edges in the graph whose both endpoints are contained in the subgraph. Therefore, the k-DENSEST SUBGRAPH instance ϕ is satisfiable.

Based on the above, we establish the theorem. □

The k-DENSEST SUBGRAPH is hard to approximate, the best known approximation algorithm is $O(n^{1/4+\epsilon})$ [3]. The results in literature [2] indicated the hardness of approximating k-DENSEST SUBGRAPH within $n^{\Omega(1)}$ factors.

Theorem 4. Suppose the k-DENSEST SUBGRAPH is hard to approximate within $n^{\Omega(1)}$, then the problem of detecting top-k structural hole spanners by minimal cut is hard to approximate within $n^{\Omega(1)}$ as well.

PROOF. Suppose there is an approximation algorithm $\mathcal{A}$ for the problem of detecting top-k structural holes by minimal cut with an approximation ratio of $O(f(|G|))$. Given an instance $\phi = \{G^* = (V, E), k, d\}$ of the k-DENSEST SUBGRAPH problem, again we denote $n = |V|$ and $m = |E|$. We continue using the construction in the proof of Theorem 3. Suppose the optimal solution $\{x_{s_j}^*\}$ of ϕ contains d^* edges, then there exists a subset $V_{SH}' = \{x_j\} \setminus \{v_{x_j}^*\}$ such that $|V_{SH}'| = n - k$ and $\text{MC}(G \setminus V_{SH}', \mathbf{C}) \leq (n^2 + 1)(m - d^*)$. We call algorithm $\mathcal{A}$ to compute a subset $|V_{SH}| = n - k$ such that

$$\begin{aligned}\text{MC}(G \setminus V_{SH}, \mathbf{C}) &\leq m(n^2 + 1) - d^*(n^2 + 1)/O(f(n^{C_0})) \\ &= (n^2 + 1)(m - d^*/O(f(n^{C_0})))\end{aligned} \quad (8)$$

where C_0 is a constant. Then denote $V_{SH}^* = V_{SH} \cap \{x_j\}$, we have $|V_{SH}^*| \leq n - k$, and $\text{MC}(G \setminus V_{SH}^*, \mathbf{C}) \leq (n^2 + 1)\lceil m - d^*/O(f(n^{C_0}))\rceil$. Thus, let the subgraph be the set of corresponding nodes in $\{x_j\} \setminus V_{SH}^*$, which contains at least $\lfloor d/O(f(n^{C_0}))\rfloor$ edges. Therefore, the problem of detecting top-k structural holes by minimal cut is also hard to approximate within $n^{\Omega(1)}$. □

Approximate algorithms. Now, we present a polynomial-time algorithm to approximate the problem of structural hole spanners detection by minimal cut.

For any pair of communities, we select $k/\binom{l}{2}$ nodes between them as structural hole spanners using a greedy strategy (referred as MaxD-AL1). In each round, we choose the node which will result in a maximal decrease of the minimal cut when removed it from the network.

Theorem 5. The greedy algorithm can achieve an approximation ratio of $n^{O(1)}$.

Input: $G = (V, E), k, l, \mathbf{C} = \{C_i\}$
Output: Top-k structural hole nodes V_{SH}

Initialize $V_{SH} = \emptyset$;
while $|V_{SH}| < k$ **do**
  Initialize $f(v) = 0$, for each $v \in V$;
  foreach *non empty* $S \subset \{1, \cdots, l\}$ **do**
    $E_S = \cup_{i \in S} C_i$ and $E_T = \cup_{i \notin S} C_i$;
    Compute the maximal flow with source E_S and sink E_T on the induced graph $G \setminus V_{SH}$;
    foreach $v \in V$ **do**
      Add $f(v)$ by the flow though node v ;
    end
  end
  Choose $O(k)$ nodes with the largest f as candidates D;
  Compute $p^* = \arg\max_{p \in D} \text{MC}(G \setminus (V_{SH} \cup \{p\}), \mathbf{C})$;
  Update $V_{SH} = V_{SH} \cup \{p^*\}$
end
return I and H ;

Algorithm 2: MaxD-AL2 Algorithm.

PROOF. Based on the fact that the minimal cut of the graph is bounded by $n^{O(1)}$, the theorem is proved. □

Suppose the time to compute the minimal cut of all communities $\mathbf{C} = \{C_1, \cdots, C_l\}$ in G is $O(T_l(n))$. Thus, the time-complexity of the greedy algorithm is $O(nkT_l(n))$. To scale up the algorithm to large networks, we consider two strategies to improve the efficiency of the algorithm. One idea is to restrict the number of candidates in the greedy algorithm. The first algorithm (MaxD-AL1) only considers $O(k)$ high-degree nodes as candidates, which improves the time-complexity to $O(k^2 T_l(n))$. In the second algorithm (called MaxD-AL2), for each partition E_S and E_T, we call the network-flow algorithm [8, 11] to compute the minimal cut of E_S and E_T. We consider top $O(k)$ nodes with maximal sum of flows through them as candidates. Details can be found in Algorithm 2.

In Algorithm 2, one challenge is to estimate $\text{MC}(G, \mathbf{C})$. As introduced in [10], by a reduction from the 3-DIMENSIONAL MATCHING problem, it is NP-hard to compute the minimal cut between multiple-sets(when $l > 2$). We develop the following algorithm to estimate the minimal cut of communities $\mathbf{C} = \{C_i\}$ in G. The approximation ratio of the algorithm is $O(\log l)$. The idea of the approximation algorithm is as follows. To find the minimal cut of all communities $\mathbf{C} = \{C_i\}$, we try all possible partitions of $\mathbf{C} = \mathbf{C}_1 \cup \mathbf{C}_2$ and find the minimal cut (denoted as D) between $\bigcup_{C_i \in \mathbf{C}_1} C_i$ and $\bigcup_{C_i \in \mathbf{C}_2} C_i$. Then we remove D from the graph G and call sub-tasks on $\mathbf{C}_1$ and $\mathbf{C}_2$ recursively. The time-complexity of the algorithm for computing $\text{MC}(G, \mathbf{C})$ is $O(2^{2l}T_2(n))$.

Theorem 6. The above algorithm for computing $\text{MC}(G, \mathbf{C})$ provides an $O(\log l)$ approximation.

PROOF. The approximation ratio is bounded by the depth of the partition process. There is always a partition whose depth is at most $O(\log l)$. Thus, the approximation ratio is $O(\log l)$. □

4. MODEL APPLICATIONS

Now, we turn to discuss how structural holes can help real social applications. Specifically, we consider detecting community kernels [32] and inferring social ties [29]. The former aims to detect the community structure among influential (kernel) users and the latter is to predict the types of social relationships (can be generally considered as a link prediction task).

4.1 Community Kernel Detection

The community kernel detection problem is defined as: [32] Given a graph $G = (V, E)$, a weight vector $\vec{w}(v) = \{w_1(v), \cdots, w_l(v)\}$ is defined for each node v, with each $w_i(v)$ representing the relative importance of the node wrt the i-th community. Denote s as the size of community kernels. One goal of community kernel detection is to obtain the importance of each node wrt a community. Then those nodes with the highest importance scores are selected as the kernel members. The algorithm proposed in [32] is called WEBA.

Now, we study how to leverage structural hole to help community kernel detection. Our idea is based on the intuition that structural hole spanners may be connected with kernel members in different communities. Following this, we incorporate the output of structural hole analysis into the objective function of WEBA. For HIS, we define

$$p(v) = \max_{S \subseteq \{1,\cdots,l\}} \{\beta_S H(v, S)\} \qquad (9)$$

For MaxD, we first calculate the top-k structural hole spanners V_{SH}. Then we define $p(v) = 1$ if $v \in V_{SH}$, and $p(v) = 0$ otherwise. Given this, we extend the objective function of WEBA, and define the following optimization problem:

$$\max \quad \mathcal{L}(\vec{w}) = \sum_{(u,v) \in E} \vec{w}(u) \cdot \vec{w}(v) + s \sum_{v \in V} \sum_{1 \le i \le l} p(v) w_i(v)$$

$$\text{subject to} \quad \sum_{v \in V} w_i(v) = s, \forall i \in \{1, \cdots, \ell\};$$

$$\sum_{1 \le i \le \ell} w_i(v) \le 1, \forall v \in V;$$

$$w_i(v) \ge 0, \forall v \in V, \forall i \in \{1, \cdots, \ell\}. \qquad (10)$$

We use a similar algorithm as that in [32] to solve the optimization problem in Eq. 10. We still use coauthor data set in [32] to evaluate the performance of community kernel detection in terms of precision, recall, and F1-score.

4.2 Link Prediction

We also apply the results of structural hole analysis to help predict the types of social relationships, an important link prediction task. Specifically, we consider the following data sets used in [29].

Slashdot is a network of friends. Slashdot is a site for sharing technology related news. In Slashdot, users can tag each other as "friends" (like) or "foes" (dislike). The data set is comprised of 77,357 users and 516,575 edges. Our goal is to predict the "friend" relationships between users.

Mobile is a network of mobile users. The data set is from [9]. It consists of the logs of calls, blue-tooth scanning data and cell tower IDs of 107 users during about ten months. If two users communicated (by making a call and sending a text message) with each other or co-occurred in the same place, we create an edge between them. In total, the data contains 5,436 edges. Our goal is to predict whether two users have a friend relationship. For evaluation, all users are required to complete an online survey, in which 157 pairs of users are labeled as friends.

For predicting the types of social relationships on the above data sets, [29] presents a number of algorithms, among which the graphical model PFG (Partially Labeled Factor Graph) achieves the best performance in one single network. We first perform the proposed models to mine structural hole spanners on the two data sets. As for the communities, we use the Newman's algorithm [26]. Then we use the identified structural hole spanners to define correlation features in the PFG algorithm. Specifically, given a structural hole spanner, for any two users who have relationships with the spanner, we create a binary correlation feature. For example, if both users v_i and v_j have a friend relationship with a spanner v_k, then a correlation feature $h(y_{ik} = 1, y_{jk} = 1)$ is defined. For more details about the feature definition, please refer to [29].

5. EXPERIMENTS

In this section, we evaluate the effectiveness and efficiency of our algorithms proposed in Section 3. All data sets and codes used in this work are publicly available.[4]

5.1 Experimental Setup

To quantitatively evaluate the proposed models, we consider the following performance metrics:

- **Accuracy.** In the Coauthor network, we evaluate the proposed models in terms of Precision, Recall, and F1-Measure. In both Twitter and Coauthor networks, we use the maximization of information diffusion to evaluate the proposed models.

- **Case study.** We use several case studies as the anecdotal evidence to further demonstrate the effectiveness of the proposed models.

- **Application improvement.** We apply the detected structural hole nodes to help community kernel detection and link prediction. This will demonstrate how the quantitative measurement of structural holes can benefit other social networking applications.

Comparison Methods We compare the following methods for detecting top-k structural hole spanners.

Pathcount [12]: for each node, the algorithm counts the average number of shortest paths (between each pair of nodes) it lies on, and then selects those nodes with the highest numbers as structural hole spanners.

2-Step Connectivity [29]: for each node, it counts the number of pairs of neighbors who are not directly connected. And then those nodes with the highest numbers are viewed as structural hole spanners.

PageRank: it uses PageRank [27] to estimate the importance of each node and then selects those nodes with the highest PageRank scores as structural hole spanners.

PageRank+: it selects those nodes who have the highest Pagerank scores and appear in more than one communities as structural hole spanners.

HIS: the first proposed model. We empirically set $\alpha_i = 0.3$ and $\beta_S = 0.5 - 0.5^{|S|}$.

MaxD: the second proposed model. By default, we use the MaxD-AL2 algorithm to approximate the model.

In Coauthor, we consider each subject area as a community; in Twitter, we use the $(\alpha - \beta)$ algorithm [24] to find overlapping communities; and in Inventor, we take each company as a community.

All codes are implemented in C++, and all experiments are performed on a PC running Windows 7 with Intel (R) Core (TM) 2 CPU 6600 (2.4GHz) and 4GB memory. Table 2 lists the running time of the comparison algorithms. In general, HIS has a very good efficiency performance and can perform the detection on large network (Inventor) with millions of nodes in 26 seconds. MaxD results in a bit lower efficiency, but is comparable with Pathcount.

---
[4]http://arnetminer.org/structural-hole/

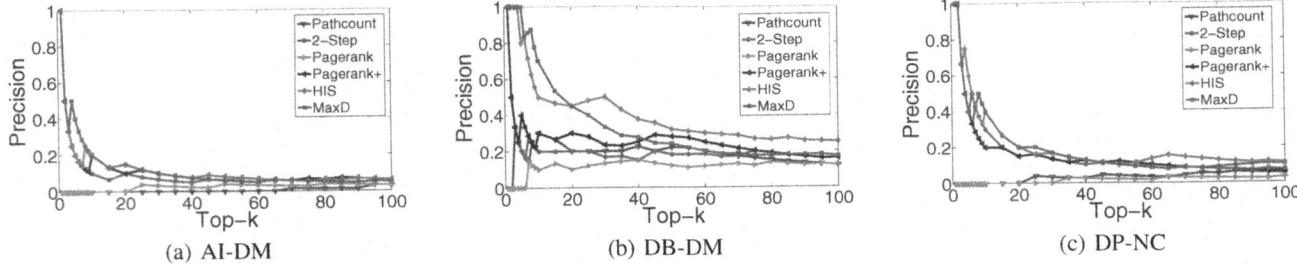

Figure 5: Accuracy performance of different algorithms for detecting top-k structural hole nodes on Coauthor.

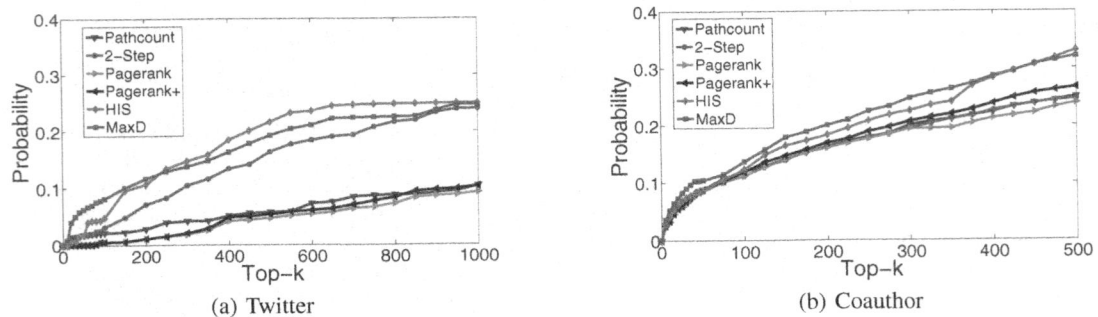

Figure 6: Results of maximization of information diffusion by different algorithms. (a) probability of the detected structural hole nodes appearing on a tweet-forwarding path across different communities; (b) probability of the detected structural hole nodes receiving cross-domain citations.

Table 2: Running time of different algorithms.

Data Set	Pathcount	2-Step	PageRank	HIS	MaxD
Coauthor	350.66s	4.71s	0.20s	0.60s	189.78m
Twitter	32.03m	12.09s	0.67s	3.87s	602.37m
Inventor	494.3 hr	98.96s	3.61s	26.11s	370.8hr

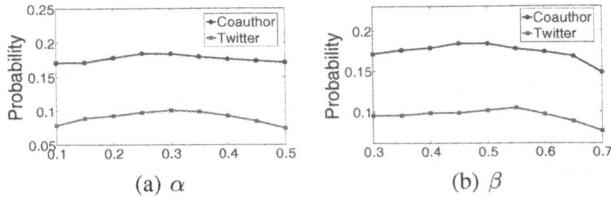

Figure 8: Performance of information spread by HIS with the two parameters α and β varied ($k = 200$).

5.2 Performance Analysis

Accuracy. We first use Coauthor as the benchmark data set to evaluate the proposed models. Figure 5 shows the performance of different algorithms. Both of the proposed models clearly outperform the comparison algorithms by +20-40% at top 20. As expected, choosing important nodes (by PageRank) only is not a good strategy. 2-Step Connectivity and Pathcount achieve a better performance than PageRank. This is because that the objective of PageRank, to find authority nodes, is different from that of finding structural hole spanners. In our first model, HIS, structural hole nodes are determined not only by the bridging positions, but also by the status (e.g., opinion leaders or not) of people connected by the bridging positions. We also note that the two proposed models present different behaviors. Roughly, MaxD performs a bit better at top 20, while HIS outperforms when the number increases to 40-100.

Maximization of information diffusion. Employing Twitter and Coauthor as the basis, we study how the detected structural hole spanners govern the diffusion of information. Specifically, we apply the different algorithms to the Twitter (or the Coauthor) network to detect top-k structural hole spanners. Then we use the tweet-forwarding (or the citation) information to verify the detected results. Figure 6 shows the performance of different algorithms on the two networks. We can see in Twitter the proposed models significantly outperform the comparison algorithms. In Coauthor, the improvements of our models over the comparison algorithms is still clear. We produce sign tests for each result, which confirms that all the improvements of our proposed models over the four methods are statistically significant ($p \ll 0.01$). We can also see that top 100 (0.2%) structural hole users (detected by MaxD) in Twitter influence almost 10% of the forwarding behaviors between different communities. Notice the striking patterns between the two models on the Twitter network. Although MaxD directly models the information diffusion process, HIS clearly outperforms MaxD when the number of k increases up to 200, and by over 20% when $k = 500$. This suggests that there is big a difference between the information network structure and the social network structure. How to combine the two network structures for mining structural hole spanners would be an interesting future work.

Model analysis. We now analyze several properties of the two models. For HIS, we compare the two algorithms described in §3.1

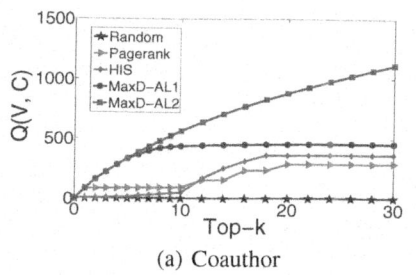 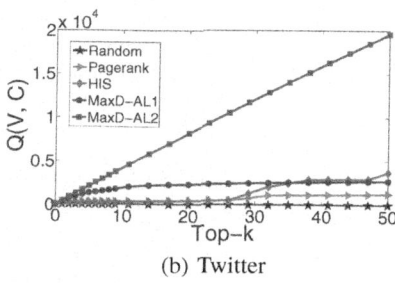 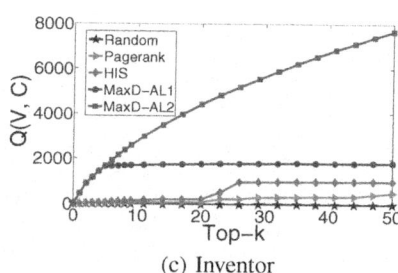

(a) Coauthor (b) Twitter (c) Inventor

Figure 7: Model analysis for MaxD on the three networks.

on the three data-sets. The two algorithms produce the same result, but the improved algorithm achieves an 25× speedup, comparing with the basic algorithm (as shown in Table 2). We further examine how the tunable parameters α and β influence the performance of information spread on the Coauthor and Twitter networks. Figure 8 shows the performance of information diffusion of HIS with the two parameters varied (by fixing $k = 200$). The performance is insensitive to the different parameter settings.

For the MaxD model, we compare different algorithms by the minimal cut described in § 3.2. Figure 7 shows the performance of the different algorithms in Model 2. The MaxD-AL2 algorithm outperforms the other algorithms in terms of $Q(V_{SH}, \mathbf{C})$. This is consistent with the theoretical analysis in §3.2. MaxD-AL1 is close to MaxD-AL2 for a small k ($k < 10$), but the difference quickly becomes wider when increasing the value of k.

5.3 Case study

Now we present a case study on the Inventor network to qualitatively demonstrate the effectiveness of the proposed models. Table 3 lists top-5 structural hole spanners detected by our proposed algorithms from the Inventor network. We find that most of the detected structural hole spanners have been working in more than one job. The exception is T. Kondo and S. Yamazaki. The former is the senior vice president of Sony and holds patents on semiconductor, image processing, and mobile devices. On each topic, he collaborated with people from different companies/universities. S. Yamazaki is the president of SEL (Semiconductor Energy Laboratory). He is a Japanese inventor in the field of computer science and solid-state physics. He holds over 2,680 U.S. utility patents. Part of his patents are in relation to SEL and many others are named individually. Another phenomenon worth mentioning is that HIS seems to select people with the highest PageRank scores, while MaxD tends to select people who have been working on more jobs. This result is consistent with the intuitions behind the two models.

6. APPLICATION IMPROVEMENT

We now turn to evaluate the performance improvement when applying the output of mining structural hole spanners to the two social applications: community kernel detection and link prediction.

Community kernel detection. For fair comparison, we still use the benchmark coauthor network used in [32] to evaluate the performance of community kernel detection in terms of precision, recall, and F1-score. The benchmark network is comprised of authors who have published papers on top conferences in five research areas:[5] Artificial Intelligence (AI), Databases (DB), Distributed and

---
[5]The benchmark network is similar to the Coauthor data set introduced in §2.

Table 3: Top-5 structural hole nodes discovered by our algorithms on the Inventor network. Names with * are inventors with the highest (top-5) PageRank scores.

Inventor	HIS	MaxD	Title
E. Boyden		✓	Professor (MIT Media Lab)
			Associate Professor (MIT McGovern Inst.)
			Group Leader (Synthetic Neurobiology)
A. Czarnik		✓	Founder and Manager (Protia, LLC)
			Visiting Professor (University of Nevada)
			Co-Founder (Chief Scientific Officer)
T. Kondo*	✓	✓	Senior vice president (Sony Corporation)
A. Nishio		✓	Director of Operations (WBI)
			Director of Department Responsible (IDA)
E. Nowak*	✓		Senior vice President (Walt Disney)
			Secretary of Trustees (The New York Eye)
A. Rofougaran	✓		Consultant (various wireless companies)
			Co-founder (Innovent System Corp.)
			Leader (RF-CMOS).
M. Rofougaran	✓	✓	Engineering Director (Broadcom Corp.)
			Co-founder(Iran Today Publications)
S. Yamazaki*	✓		President and majority shareholder (SEL)

Parallel Computing (DP), Graphics, Vision and HCI (GV), and Networks, Communications and Performance (NC). For example, for DB, the conferences include VLDB, SIGMOD, PODS, ICDE, ICDT, and EDBT. The community of program committee (PC) members of those conferences in each area is viewed as the ground truth for quantitatively evaluating the performance of community kernel detection. We empirically set the value of k as 100.

By solving Eq. 10 with the similar algorithms as that in [32], we compare the community detection performance of WEBA with and without the help of structural hole. The performance is shown in Figure 9. Clear improvements on the coauthor data set can be obtained. In terms of F1-score, the average improvement is about 4.5%. HIS performs a bit better than MaxD.

Link prediction. We also apply the discovered structural holes spanners to help link prediction in the two networks: Slashdot and Mobile. Specifically, we first use the Newman's algorithm [26] to discover communities in each network and then use the proposed models to mine top-k structural holes spanners. Then we define correlation features based on the discovered structural hole spanners and add those defined features into the prediction algorithm PFG [29]. We use half of the data for training the PFG algorithm and the rest for testing its prediction performance. Table 4 lists the prediction performance of PFG before and after adding the structural holes-based features. It can be seen that by incorporating the structural holes-based features, the performance of predicting the

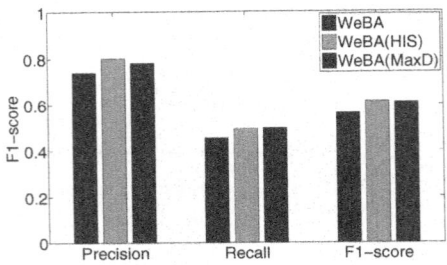

Figure 9: Performance of WEBA for detecting kernel communities with and without the help of structural holes mining.

Table 4: Performance of the PFG algorithm for predicting the type of social relationships before and after combining the structural hole-based features.

Dataset	Algorithm	K	Precision	Recall	F1-score
Mobile	PFG	-	0.9111	0.5694	0.7008
	PFG(HIS)	5	0.8958	0.5972	0.7166
	PFG(HIS)	15	0.8491	0.6250	0.7200
	PFG(HIS)	25	0.8519	**0.6389**	**0.7302**
	PFG(MaxD)	5	**0.9130**	0.5833	0.7118
	PFG(MaxD)	15	0.8776	0.5972	0.7107
	PFG(MaxD)	25	0.8723	0.5972	0.7090
Slashdot	PFG	-	0.6619	0.7281	0.6934
	PFG(HIS)	100	0.6562	0.7965	0.7196
	PFG(HIS)	150	0.6615	**0.8241**	**0.7339**
	PFG(HIS)	200	**0.6788**	0.7886	0.7296
	PFG(MaxD)	100	0.6602	0.7542	0.7041
	PFG(MaxD)	150	0.6667	0.7532	0.7073
	PFG(MaxD)	200	0.6619	0.7775	0.7151

type of social relationships by PFG is clearly improved (+1.4-5.8% by F1-score; t-test, $p < 0.01$). We also evaluate how the performance is affected by the number of k. On the Mobile data, as the network is relatively small, we set k as 5, 15, 25. On the Slashdot data, we set k as 100, 150, 200. The results show that the performance is indeed influenced by different settings of the value for k, but with all the different settings, the performance of link prediction by PFG can be improved. This confirms the effectiveness of the proposed structural hole mining models.

7. RELATED WORK

Structural holes. The concept of structural hole is first introduced in [4] and further elaborated in literature [1, 5, 6]. There have been a few works on mining structural holes from social networks. Goyal and Vega-Redondo [12] propose a model of network formation to study how structural holes are formed in social network. They consider a model in which a node u potentially benefits from serving as an intermediary between nodes v and w even when it resides on an arbitrarily long v-w path. Based on the model, they obtain a star network. However, in real world, many networks are not necessarily of the star topology. Buskens and van de Rijt [7] uses the game theory to model the network formation with structural holes. Kleinberg et al. [18] study the strategic and dynamic aspect to the theory of structural hole. They extend Burt's work [5] by modeling how social networks change over time if everyone is vying for those bridging positions. In this work, we study a novel problem of mining structural hole spanners in social networks, which can be considered as the reverse process of the study of strategic network formation with structural holes [7, 12, 18].

Information diffusion. Our work is also related to a growing body of research on information diffusion. For example, Gruhl et al. [13] study the dynamics of information propagation in environments of low-overhead personal publishing on a web blog data. They apply the theory of infectious diseases to model the "topic" flow on web blogs. Kumar et al. [19] explore the formation of the structure of conversations in social networks and propose a mathematical model to generate the basic structure underlying conversation behaviors. Liben-Nowell and Kleinberg [21] investigate the information spreading processes at a person-to-person level using methods to reconstruct the propagation of massively circulated Internet chain letters. They find the progress of the chain letters proceeds in a narrow but very deep tree-like pattern and propose a probabilistic model based on network clustering and asynchronous response times to produce the tree. Yang et al. [33] analyze how information spread on Twitter via the retweeting behavior and propose a semi-supervised framework to predict users' retweet behaviors. Myers et al. [25] study how the process of information diffusion is influenced by external sources. Matsubara et al. [23] propose a model called SPIKEM to model the rise and fall patterns of influence propagation. However, all these works do not consider how structural holes influence the procedure of information diffusion. To the best of our knowledge, this is the first work to systematically study the problem of mining structural hole spanners in social networks.

8. CONCLUSION

In this paper, we study the novel problem of mining structural hole spanners in large networks. We precisely define the problem of top-k structural hole detection and provide an objective (quality) function to formalize the problem. We develop two instantiation models for the objective function based on the principles of information flow. For both models, we provide theoretical analysis and proofs for their hardness, and develop efficient algorithms to solve with provable approximation guarantees. We validate the effectiveness and efficiency of the proposed models on three different types of networks. We also apply the detected structural hole spanners by the proposed models to help several social networking applications, which further demonstrate its effectiveness.

Structural hole is an important concept in social theory and it relates to a wide range of indicators of social success. As for the future work, it would be intriguing to combine the content information with the user network information and design a unified model for mining structural hole spanners. It is also interesting to further improve the proposed algorithms. For example the MaxD-AL2 algorithm still suffers from the high computational cost (as shown in Table 2) and this HIS model is still lack of a theoretical guarantee. In addition, though the MaxD model uses the information diffusion in the evaluation, but not really uses the process to identify the structural hole spanners. How to elegantly incorporate the information diffusion process into the MaxD model would be a very interesting research topic. Another potential issue is to systematically study how structural holes can help the other social networking applications (e.g., recommendation).

Acknowledgements. We thank Jon Kleinberg for insightful discussions. The work is supported by the Natural Science Foundation of China (No. 61222212, 61073073).

9. REFERENCES

[1] G. Ahuja. Collaboration networks, structural holes, and innovation: A longitudinal study. *Administrative Science Quarterly*, 45(3):425–455, 2000.

[2] A. Bhaskara, M. Charikar, E. Chlamtac, U. Feige, and A. Vijayaraghavan. Detecting high log-densities: an $o(n^{1/4})$ approximation for densest k-subgraph. In *STOC*, pages 201–210, 2010.

[3] A. Bhaskara, M. Charikar, V. Guruswami, A. Vijayaraghavan, and Y. Zhou. Polynomial integrality gaps for strong sdp relaxations of densest k-subgraph. In *SODA*, pages 1395–1408, 2012.

[4] R. S. Burt. *Structural Holes: The Social Structure of Competition*. Harvard University Press, 1992.

[5] R. S. Burt. Structural holes and good ideas. *American Journal of Sociology*, 110:349–399, 2004.

[6] R. S. Burt. Secondhand brokerage: Evidence on the importance of local structure for managers, bankers, and analysts. *Academy of Management Journal*, 50:119–148, 2007.

[7] V. Buskens and A. van de Rijt. Dynamics of networks if everyone strives for structural hole. *American Journal of Sociology*, 114(2):371–407, 2008.

[8] Y. Dinitz. Dinitz' algorithm: The original version and even's version. In *Essays in Memory of Shimon Even*, pages 218–240, 2006.

[9] N. Eagle, A. S. Pentland, and D. Lazer. Inferring social network structure using mobile phone data. *PNAS*, 106(36), 2009.

[10] M. R. Garey and D. S. Johnson. *Computers and Intractability: A Guide to the Theory of NP-Completeness*. W.H. Freeman and Company, 1979.

[11] A. V. Goldberg and S. Rao. Flows in undirected unit capacity networks. *SIAM J. Discrete Math.*, 12(1):1–5, 1999.

[12] S. Goyal and F. Vega-Redondo. Structural holes in social networks. *Journal of Economic Theory*, 137(1):460–492, 2007.

[13] D. Gruhl, R. Guha, D. Liben-Nowell, and A. Tomkins. Information diffusion through blogspace. In *WWW'04*, pages 491–501, 2004.

[14] J. He, J. Hopcroft, H. Liang, S. Suwajanakorn, and L. Wang. Detecting the structure of social networks using (α, β)-communities. In *WAW'11*, 2011.

[15] J. Hopcroft, T. Lou, and J. Tang. Who will follow you back? reciprocal relationship prediction. In *CIKM'11*, pages 1137–1146, 2011.

[16] E. Katz. The two-step flow of communication: an up-to-date report of an hypothesis. *In Enis and Cox(eds.), Marketing Classics*, pages 175–193, 1973.

[17] J. Kleinberg. Authoritative sources in a hyperlinked environment. *Journal of the ACM*, 46(5):604–632, 1999.

[18] J. Kleinberg, S. Suri, E. Tardos, and T. Wexler. Strategic network formation with structural holes. In *EC'08*, pages 284–293, 2008.

[19] R. Kumar, M. Mahdian, and M. McGlohon. Dynamics of conversations. In *KDD'10*, pages 553–562, 2010.

[20] P. F. Lazarsfeld, B. Berelson, and H. Gaudet. *The people's choice: How the voter makes up his mind in a presidential campaign*. Columbia University Press, New York, USA, 1944.

[21] D. Liben-Nowell and J. Kleinberg. Tracing information flow on a global scale using internet chain-letter data. *PNAS*, 105(12):4633–4638, Mar. 2008.

[22] T. Lou, J. Tang, J. Hopcroft, Z. Fang, and X. Ding. Learning to predict reciprocity and triadic closure in social networks. *TKDD*, 2013, (accepted).

[23] Y. Matsubara, Y. Sakurai, B. A. Prakash, L. Li, and C. Faloutsos. Rise and fall patterns of information diffusion: model and implications. In *KDD'12*, pages 6–14, 2012.

[24] N. Mishra, R. Schreiber, I. Stanton, and R. E. Tarjan. Finding strongly-knit clusters in social networks. *Internet Mathematics*, 5(1–2), 2009.

[25] S. A. Myers, C. Zhu, and J. Leskovec. Information diffusion and external influence in networks. In *KDD'12*, pages 33–41, 2012.

[26] M. E. J. Newman. Fast algorithm for detecting community structure in networks. *Phys. Rev. E*, 69(066133), 2004.

[27] L. Page, S. Brin, R. Motwani, and T. Winograd. The pagerank citation ranking: Bringing order to the web. Technical Report SIDL-WP-1999-0120, Stanford University, 1999.

[28] J. M. Podolny and J. N. Baron. Resources and relationships: Social networks and mobility in the workplace. *American Sociological Review*, 62(5):673, 1997.

[29] J. Tang, T. Lou, and J. Kleinberg. Inferring social ties across heterogeneous networks. In *WSDM'12*, pages 743–752, 2012.

[30] J. Tang, B. Wang, Y. Yang, P. Hu, Y. Zhao, X. Yan, B. Gao, M. Huang, P. Xu, W. Li, and A. K. Usadi. Patentminer: Topic-driven patent analysis and mining. In *KDD'2012*, pages 1366–1375, 2012.

[31] J. Tang, J. Zhang, L. Yao, J. Li, L. Zhang, and Z. Su. Arnetminer: Extraction and mining of academic social networks. In *KDD'08*, pages 990–998, 2008.

[32] L. Wang, T. Lou, J. Tang, and J. Hopcroft. Detecting community kernels in large social networks. In *ICDM'11*, pages 784–793, 2011.

[33] Z. Yang, J. Guo, K. Cai, J. Tang, J. Li, L. Zhang, and Z. Su. Understanding retweeting behaviors in social networks. In *CIKM'10*, pages 1633–1636, 2010.

On the Evolution of the Internet Economic Ecosystem

Richard T. B. Ma
ADSC Illinois and National
University of Singapore
tbma@comp.nus.edu.sg

John C. S. Lui
The Chinese University of
Hong Kong
cslui@cse.cuhk.edu.hk

Vishal Misra
Columbia University
misra@cs.columbia.edu

ABSTRACT

The evolution of the Internet has manifested itself in many ways: the traffic characteristics, the interconnection topologies and the business relationships among the autonomous components. It is important to understand why (and how) this evolution came about, and how the interplay of these dynamics may affect future evolution and services. We propose a network aware, macroscopic model that captures the characteristics and interactions of the application and network providers, and show how it leads to a market equilibrium of the ecosystem. By analyzing the driving forces and the dynamics of the market equilibrium, we obtain some fundamental understandings of the cause and effect of the Internet evolution, which explain why some historical and recent evolutions have happened. Furthermore, by projecting the likely future evolutions, our model can help application and network providers to make informed business decisions so as to succeed in this competitive ecosystem.

Categories and Subject Descriptors

C.2.5 [**Computer-Communication Networks**]: Local and Wide-Area Networks—*Internet*; C.4 [**Performance of Systems**]: [Modeling techniques, Performance attributes]

Keywords

Internet Evolution; Economics; IP Transit; Content Delivery

1. INTRODUCTION

The Internet has been and is still changing unexpectedly in many aspects. Started with elastic traffic and applications, e.g., emails and webpage downloading, we have seen significant rise in inelastic traffic, e.g., video and interactive web traffic, across the Internet. According to [19], from 2007 to 2009, web content traffic had increased from 41.68% to 52%, reaching more than half of the total Internet traffic. From a network perspective, the Internet originated from government-owned backbone networks, i.e., the ARPANET, and then evolved to a network of commercial Autonomous Systems (ASes) and Internet Service Providers (ISPs). Meanwhile, ISPs formed a hierarchical structure and were classified by tiers, with higher tier ISPs cover larger geographic regions and provide transit service for smaller/lower tier ISPs. However, recent study [17] has reported that large content providers, e.g., Google and Microsoft, are deploying their own wide-area networks so as to bring content closer to users and bypassing Tier-1 ISPs on many paths. This is known as the *flattening phenomenon* of the Internet topology.

Copyright is held by the International World Wide Web Conference Committee (IW3C2). IW3C2 reserves the right to provide a hyperlink to the author's site if the Material is used in electronic media.
WWW 2013, May 13–17, 2013, Rio de Janeiro, Brazil.
ACM 978-1-4503-2035-1/13/05.

Changes in the content or network topology do not happen independently. Rather, they are driven by the changes in the business relationships among the players in the Internet ecosystem. Not surprisingly, we have observed dramatic changes in the business relationships between the content providers and the ISPs and among the ISPs themselves. Traditionally, ISP settlements were often done bilaterally under either a (zero-dollar) peering or in the form of a customer-provider relationship. Tier-1 ISPs, e.g., Level 3 [5], often charge lower tier ISPs for transit services and connect with each other under settlement-free peering. However, the Tier-1 ISPs do not have any guarantee in their profitability as the Internet evolves. For instance, we have seen exponential decrease (around 20% a year) in IP transit prices [23]. Also, peering disputes happened, e.g., the de-peering between Cogent [3] and Level 3 in 2005, where the lower tier ISPs that are closer to content or users refused to pay for the transit charge. This leads to the recent debate of network neutrality [26], which reflects the ISPs' willingness to provide value-added and differentiated services and potentially charge content providers based on different levels of service quality.

The situation is further complicated by the emergence of new players in the ecosystem: Content Delivery Networks (CDNs), e.g., Akamai [1] and Limelight [6], and high-quality video streaming providers, e.g., Netflix [7]. From content providers' perspective, CDNs can deliver their content faster and more efficiently; from local ISPs' perspective, CDNs can reduce the traffic volume from upstream, saving transit costs from their providers. Very often, ISPs do not charge the CDNs for putting servers in their networks. When the video streaming giant Netflix moved online a few years ago, its traffic surged immediately. Now it accounts for up to 32.7% of peak U.S. downstream traffic [8] and its traffic volume is higher than that of BitTorrent [9] applications. Netflix used Limelight, one of the biggest CDNs, for content delivery, and later, the Tier-1 Level 3 also obtained a contract to deliver Netflix's traffic. Since most of the Netflix customers are based in the U.S., they often use Comcast, the biggest access ISP, as the last-mile access provider. Interestingly, Comcast managed to enter a so-called paid-peering relationship [16] with Level 3 and Limelight, under which the Tier-1 ISP and the CDN have to pay the access ISP for higher bandwidth on the last mile connection. This has totally *reversed* the nominal customer-provider relationship where the Tier-1 ISP was the service provider and should have received payment for connectivity.

It is important to understand how these changes come about, and what the driving factors are behind these changes. In this work, we model the Internet evolution from a macroscopic view that captures the cause and effect of the evolution of the individual players in the ecosystem. Our model expends the traditional view of a single best-effort service model to capture multiple value-added services in the Internet. The main approaches and contributions are as follows.

- We model the preferences and business decisions of the application providers for purchasing Internet services, based on the application characteristics and the price and quality of the transport services (Section 2).

- We characterize the market price and the market share of the Internet transport services by using general equilibrium theory in economics (Section 3).

- We analyze the driving forces of the evolution of the Internet economic ecosystem (Section 4), which provide qualitative answers (Section 4.6) to questions like: *1) Why have the IP transit prices been dropping? 2) Why have the CDNs emerged in the ecosystem? 3) Why has the pricing power shifted to the access ISPs? 4) Why are the large content providers building their own wide-area networks toward users?*

- We incorporate Internet price and capacity data into our model, and quantitatively fit historical prices and project the future evolution of the ecosystem and its price trends (Section 5).

- We demonstrate how our model can help the network providers to make business decisions, e.g., capacity expansion and peering decisions, based on the future price projections under various scenarios (Section 5.3).

Our paper sheds new light on the macroscopic evolution of the Internet economic ecosystem and concretely identifies the driving factors of such an evolution. In particular, our model provides a tool to analyze and project the evolutionary trends of the ecosystem. The fundamental understanding of the preferences of application providers and the market equilibrium of the Internet services will also help the business decisions of the application and network transport providers to succeed in this competitive ecosystem.

2. THE MACROSCOPIC AP-TP MODEL

We start with a macroscopic model of the Internet ecosystem that consists a set of Application Providers (APs) and Transport Providers (TPs). The TPs differ by their service qualities and the prices they charge. We model and analyze the APs' choice of TP based on their own characteristics: how profitable the AP is and how sensitive the AP traffic is to the obtained level of service quality. In essence, this macroscopic model can help us to understand the decision process of these players in the Internet ecosystem and how these decisions may influence their business relationships.

2.1 The Application and Transport Providers

We consider an Internet service market of a geographic region and denote $(\mathcal{M}, \mathcal{N})$ as a macroscopic model of the ecosystem, consisting of a set $\mathcal{M}$ of TPs and a set $\mathcal{N}$ of APs. The APs provide the content/service for the Internet end-users; the TPs provide the network infrastructure for delivering the APs' data to their end-users.

Our notion of an AP broadly includes content providers, e.g., Netflix, online services, e-commerce, and even cloud services, e.g., Amazon EC2 [2]. Our notion of a TP is based on the APs' point of view. In other words, the transport services provided by the TPs are for the APs to reach their customers/users. The scope of a TP is *broader* than an ISP, and it includes CDNs. ISPs, depending on different taxonomies [16, 15, 21], include 1) eyeball/access ISPs that serve the last-mile for end-users, 2) backbone/Tier 1 ISPs that provide transit services for lower tier ISPs, and 3) content ISPs that serve APs and host content servers. A TP can be an ISP of any type. Although access and transit ISPs traditionally do not have business relationships with APs explicitly, with the emergence of video streaming APs, e.g., Netflix, we have seen more and more APs' direct or indirect contracts with the access and transit ISPs. For example, Level 3 contracted with Netflix for content delivery and Comcast managed to charge Level 3 and Limelight via paid-peering contracts (for delivering Netflix's traffic to Comcast's customer base faster) [23]. Although "whether ISPs should be allowed to differentiate services/charges for APs" is hotly debated under the network neutrality [26] argument, legitimate service differentiations will also induce more extensive business relationships among the APs and ISPs. In general, a TP can be any facilitator that delivers content to end-users. An important example of a TP that does not even own network infrastructures in the current Internet ecosystem is Akamai [1], which represents the CDNs.

We characterize each TP $I \in \mathcal{M}$ by its type, denoted as a triple (p_I, q_I, ν_I). p_I denotes the per unit traffic charge for the APs to use TP I. q_I denotes the service quality of TP I, e.g., queueing delay or packet loss probability. Without loss of generality, we assume that $q_I \geq 0$ and smaller values of q_I indicate better quality of services. ν_I denotes the bandwidth capacity of TP I. We characterize each AP $i \in \mathcal{N}$ by its utility function $u_i(\cdot)$. In particular, we define $u_i(p_I, q_I)$ as AP i's utility when it uses TP I, which depends on the service quality q_I and the per unit traffic charge p_I.

Assumption 1. $u_i(\cdot, \cdot)$ *is non-increasing in both arguments.*

Assumption 2. *For any set $\mathcal{M}$ of TPs, each AP $i \in \mathcal{N}$ chooses to use a TP, denoted as $I_i \in \mathcal{M}$, that satisfies*

$$u_i(p_{I_i}, q_{I_i}) \geq u_i(p_I, q_I), \ \forall I \in \mathcal{M}.$$

The above assumes that each AP is rational and chooses a TP that provides the highest utility. Technically, there might exists multiple TPs that provide the same amount of utility for the AP. We assume that every AP has certain preference to break the tie and choose one of the TPs. We further denote $\mathcal{N}_I \subseteq \mathcal{N}$ as the set of APs that choose to use TP I, or the market share of TP I, defined as $\mathcal{N}_I = \{i \in \mathcal{N} : I_i = I\}$. Based on Assumption 1 and 2, if two TPs I, J have the same quality, i.e., $q_I = q_J$, then they have to price equally, i.e., $p_I = p_J$; otherwise, the one with higher price will not obtain any market share. As TPs differ only by price p_I and quality q_I from the APs' perspective, we aggregate the TPs that have the same value pair (p_I, q_I) into a single TP with a capacity that equals the summation of individual TPs' capacity. Similarly, if a TP performs service differentiations, we conceptually treat it as multiple TPs, each with a service class (p_I, q_I) and the corresponding capacity ν_I. More precisely, our abstraction of a TP I models a competitive market segment that provides a quality level q_I and has a total capacity ν_I.

2.2 Throughput and Types of the APs

Although the utility function u_i can be used to model all the characteristics of AP i, the setting does not yet capture the traffic dynamics and the profitability of the APs. We model AP i's profitability by denoting v_i as its per unit traffic revenue. This revenue is related to the AP's core business, e.g., online adverting or e-commerce, and we do not assume how it is generated. We denote $\lambda_i(\cdot)$ as AP i's throughput function, where $\lambda_i(q_I)$ defines the aggregate throughput of AP i toward its consumers under a quality level q_I. Thus, we model any AP i's utility as its total profit (profit margin multiplied by the total throughput rate), defined by

$$u_i(p_I, q_I) = (v_i - p_I)\lambda_i(q_I). \tag{1}$$

Assumption 3. *For any AP $i \in \mathcal{N}$, $\lambda_i(\cdot)$ is a non-increasing function with $\alpha_i = \lim_{q_i \to 0} \lambda_i(q_i)$ and $\lim_{q_i \to \infty} \lambda_i(q_i) = 0$.*

Assumption 3 says that the throughput will not decrease if an AP uses a better service. λ_i reaches a maximum value of α_i when it receives the best quality $q_i = 0$ and decreases to zero if the quality deteriorates infinitely, i.e., q_i tends to $+\infty$. In particular, we consider the following canonical form of the throughput function:

$$\lambda_i(q_I) = \alpha_i e^{-\beta_i q_I}, \quad (2)$$

where AP i's throughput is characterized by a parameter β_i that captures its sensitivity to the received quality q_I.

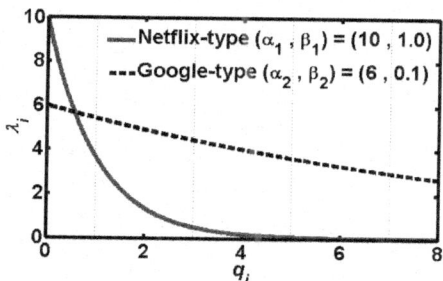

Figure 1: Throughput of different type of APs.

Figure 1 illustrates the throughput of two APs with parameters $(\alpha_1, \beta_1) = (10, 1.0)$ and $(\alpha_2, \beta_2) = (6, 0.1)$ under varying service qualities, interpreted as network delays in this case, along the x-axis. AP 1 represents a Netflix-type of application that is more sensitive to delay and has a high maximum rate $\alpha_1 = 10$ Mbps; however, AP 2 represents a Google-type of query application that is less sensitive to delay. We observe that when delay increases, the throughput of delay-sensitive application decreases sharply, while the delay-insensitive application decreases only mildly.

Because α_i is just a linear scaling factor of the throughput, it does not affect the AP's preference over different TPs. Consequently, APs with the same (β_i, v_i) value pairs will choose the same TP; and therefore, we can conceptually aggregate them as a single AP. Similar to a TP I representing a market segment, each AP i can be interpreted as a group of APs with the same characteristics and α_i represents the aggregate maximum traffic intensity, which depends on the number of APs in the group and the individual traffic intensities. Although α_i does not play a role in the AP's decision of choosing TPs, we will see later that α_i reflects the demand of the APs and affects the market prices of the TPs. In summary, based on our throughput model, we define

$$u_i(p_I, q_I) = (v_i - p_I)\lambda_i(q_I) = \alpha_i(v_i - p_I)e^{-\beta_i q_I}. \quad (3)$$

Similar to each TP I's type (p_I, q_I, ν_I), we can characterize any AP i's type as another triple (α_i, β_i, v_i).

2.3 APs' Choice of Transport Providers

When facing a set $\mathcal{M}$ of TPs, each AP i's best choice I_i depends on the price-quality pairs $\{(p_I, q_I) : I \in \mathcal{M}\}$ and its own characteristics (β_i, v_i). The APs' choices satisfy the following results.

Theorem 1. *For a fixed set $\mathcal{M}$ and any two APs i and j with $\beta_j \geq \beta_i$ and $v_j \geq v_i$, their chosen service qualities satisfy $q_{I_i} \geq q_{I_j}$.*

Theorem 1 says that if an AP j is more profitable and more sensitive to service quality than another AP i, then the chosen quality of AP j will be at least as good as that of AP i. This property holds regardless how the services are priced.

Theorem 2. *For any $\kappa_1, \kappa_2, \kappa_3 > 0$, and system $(\mathcal{M}, \mathcal{N})$, we define a scaled system $(\mathcal{M}', \mathcal{N}')$ as $\mathcal{M}' = \{(\kappa_1 p_I + \kappa_2, q_I/\kappa_3, \nu_I) :$* $I \in \mathcal{M}\}$ and $\mathcal{N}' = \{(\alpha_i, \kappa_3 \beta_i, \kappa_1 v_i + \kappa_2) : i \in \mathcal{N}\}$, then system $(\mathcal{M}', \mathcal{N}')$ satisfies $\mathcal{N}_I(\mathcal{M}', \mathcal{N}') = \mathcal{N}_I(\mathcal{M}, \mathcal{N})$ for all $I \in \mathcal{M}$.

Theorem 2 says that if 1) the AP profitability v_i and the TP price p_I are linearly scaled in the same way, and/or 2) the quality q_I of the TPs and the sensitivity β_i of the APs scale inversely at the same rate, then the APs' choices of TP will not change. This result will help us normalize different systems and make a fair comparison of various solutions.

Theorem 3. *For any $\kappa > 0$ and a fixed set $\mathcal{N}$ of APs, let $\mathcal{M}' = \{(p_I, \kappa q_I, \nu_I) : I \in \mathcal{M}\}$, then for all $i \in \mathcal{N}$, 1) $q_{I'_i} \leq \kappa q_{I_i}$ if $\kappa > 1$ and 2) $q_{I'_i} \geq \kappa q_{I_i}$ if $\kappa < 1$.*

Theorem 3 says that if all the qualities in the market deteriorate ($\kappa > 1$) linearly at the same rate, APs will not use worse quality TPs than before. The opposite is also true: when qualities improve linearly, APs will not use better quality TPs than before.

3. MARKET EQUILIBRIUM

In this section, we start with the definition of a market equilibrium, under which the prices of the TPs are stable and the claimed service qualities can be achieved when APs choose their best TPs. We then proceed to characterize the market equilibrium and calculate the equilibrium prices.

3.1 The Existence of Market Equilibrium

Although any TP I claims to provide service quality q_I, it cannot keep its promise if more APs choose this TP than its capacity can support. We model the achieved quality $Q_I(\lambda_I, \nu_I)$ as a function of the actual throughput λ_I going through I and its capacity ν_I.

Assumption 4. *The achieved quality $Q_I(\lambda_I, \nu_I)$ for any TP $I \in \mathcal{M}$ is non-decreasing in λ_I and non-increasing in ν_I.*

Definition 1. *A set $\mathcal{X} \subseteq \mathcal{N}$ of APs is feasible for TP I with quality q_I, if $Q_I(\lambda_I(\mathcal{X}), \nu_I) \leq q_I$, where $\lambda_I(\mathcal{X}) = \sum_{i \in \mathcal{X}} \lambda_i(q_I)$ defines the induced throughput of the set $\mathcal{X}$ of APs under quality q_I.*

In a market $\mathcal{M}$ of TPs, each TP would adjust its strategies to accommodate its customer APs' traffic demand and keep its service quality promise. For example, if the current capacity of TP I cannot support quality q_I, it might 1) expend its capacity ν_I, 2) increase price p_I, or 3) reduce the quality level q_I. Next, we define a market equilibrium where the APs' demand are *feasible* and the TPs' strategies are *stable*.

Definition 2. *Let p_I^{min} be the cost (or minimum price) of TP I. Let $\mathcal{M}'$ be identical to $\mathcal{M}$ except for $p'_I \neq p_I$ for some $I \in \mathcal{M}$ and $\mathcal{N}'_I$ be the set of APs choosing TP I under $\mathcal{M}'$. A system $(\mathcal{M}, \mathcal{N})$ forms a market equilibrium if 1) all APs' aggregate demands are feasible, i.e., $Q_I(\lambda_I(\mathcal{N}_I), \nu_I) \leq q_I$, $\forall I \in \mathcal{M}$, and 2) each price p_I maximizes the utilization of capacity for acceptable throughput at TP I, i.e., for any $p'_I \geq p_I^{min}$ with the corresponding $\mathcal{N}'_I$ satisfying $Q_I(\lambda_I(\mathcal{N}'_I), \nu_I) \leq q_I, \lambda_I(\mathcal{N}'_I) \leq \lambda_I(\mathcal{N}_I)$.*

One way to understand the above definition of a market equilibrium is that given a set $\mathcal{N}$ of APs and a set $\{q_I : I \in \mathcal{M}\}$ of service qualities for them to choose from, the price p_I and capacity ν_I of each market segment should be consistent in that 1) when the APs make their choices of TP, their expected service quality can be achieved and, 2) the capacities of the TPs are not under-utilized, unless the charge p_I reaches the TP's cost p_I^{min}. If APs' quality expectations are not fulfilled, their choices of TP will change. Furthermore, if capacity ν_I is under-utilized with $p_I > p_I^{min}$, then the market segment I is not correctly priced. That being said, we assume that none of the market segment is controlled by a monopoly, which might want to under-utilize capacity and keep a higher price for profit-maximization. We will summarize and discuss the limitations of our model in Section 5.4. The interesting aspect here is that although p_I, like all other prices, mainly depends on the supply ν_I and the demand $\mathcal{N}_I$ of the APs, all the TPs (or market segments) are correlated, which serve substitutions for the APs.

In practice, the TPs might not have enough capacities to accommodate all APs. As a result, market prices will rise and some APs cannot afford the prices and will not use any of the TPs. However, under Assumption 2, each AP needs to choose a TP even it cannot afford to use any of the TPs, so a market equilibrium might not exist under this assumption. To fix this minor technical issue, we make the following assumption to allow any AP not to use any of the TPs if they all induce negative utilities.

Assumption 5. *There always exists a dummy TP $D \in \mathcal{M}$ with quality $q_D = \infty$ and price $p_D = 0$.*

By Assumption 3, quality q_D always induces zero throughput for any AP, and therefore, the dummy TP guarantees a zero utility and can accommodate as many APs as possible in equilibrium. Effectively, the set $\mathcal{N}_D$ models the APs that cannot afford to use any TP in the market in reality.

Theorem 4. *For any fixed set $\mathcal{N}$ of APs and any set $\mathcal{M}$ of TPs with fixed values of p_I^{min}, q_I and ν_I for all $I \in \mathcal{M}$, there exists a set $\{p_I : I \in \mathcal{M}\}$ of prices that makes $(\mathcal{M}, \mathcal{N})$ a market equilibrium.*

Although TPs might be able to adopt new technologies to improve or differentiate their services, the quality that they can provide is often physically constrained by the nature of the TP, for example, if a TP is a Tier 1 ISP, it cannot guarantee end-to-end delays for the customers unless the access ISP's link is not congested. Similarly, although TPs might execute a long-term capacity planning, the supply of capacity does not change in a small time scale. Compared to service quality and capacity, market prices change more frequently and easily. Theorem 4 says that even in a small time-scale where prices adapt to market conditions, prices might still converge to an equilibrium, which reflects the short-term market structure of the Internet ecosystem.

3.2 Characteristics of a Market Equilibrium

In theory, one might find multiple sets of prices that make $(\mathcal{M}, \mathcal{N})$ a market equilibrium. For example, from any existing equilibrium, one might find a TP I such that with only a small change in p_I, no APs will change their choices. This new price also constitutes a market equilibrium. In practice, these price differences can happen by two reasons. First, even without a monopoly in a market segment, oligopolistic providers might implicitly collude on the price so that they keep a relatively high price simultaneously. When one of them starts to reduce price, the price of that segment will converge to a lower price. Second, the preferences of the APs are quite different so that the price change in one segment might not affect the demand choices of the APs.

Definition 3. *A market equilibrium $(\mathcal{M}, \mathcal{N})$ is competitive if there does not exist any $p_I^{min} \leq p_I' < p_I$ with the corresponding $\mathcal{N}_I'$ satisfying $Q_I(\lambda_I(\mathcal{N}_I'), \nu_I) \leq q_I$.*

If the AP types are very diverse or each market segment consists of many competing providers, one can focus on the above definition of a competitive market equilibrium. Technically, a competitive market equilibrium might not exist, since the minimum price might not exist when all the feasible equilibrium prices form an open set. However, prices in practice have a minimum unit, e.g., one cent, and we can always find such a competitive market equilibrium.

Notice that our model is not limited to competitive market equilibria, i.e., if a segment I is not competitive enough, we can use a higher price for p_I. As a result, competitive equilibrium prices might be biased downward if the real market structure is not perfectly competitive; nevertheless, our qualitative results do not depend on whether the market equilibrium is competitive or not.

Theorem 5. *Let $\mathcal{N}' = \{(\kappa\alpha_i, \beta_i, v_i) : i \in \mathcal{N}\}$ and $\mathcal{M}' = \{(p_I, q_I, \kappa\nu_I) : I \in \mathcal{M}\}$ for some $\kappa > 0$. If $(\mathcal{M}, \mathcal{N})$ is a market equilibrium and the quality function $Q_I(\cdot, \cdot)$s are homogenous of degree 0, i.e., $Q_I(\lambda_I, \nu_I) = Q_I(\kappa\lambda_I, \kappa\nu_I), \forall \kappa > 0, I \in \mathcal{M}$, then $(\mathcal{M}', \mathcal{N}')$ is a market equilibrium too.*

Theorem 5 says that if the quality only depends on the ratio of the incoming traffic rate and the capacity, then when the number of APs (and their traffic intensity) and the capacities scale at the same speed, the original market equilibrium prices will remain in equilibrium. If we consider the queueing delay as the quality metric, because of statistical multiplexing, the average queueing delay reduces when both arrival rate and service rate scales up at the same rate. In this case, Theorem 5 also implies that each TP I can accept more and more traffic for a fixed delay q_I, and as a consequence, the market prices will move downward in a new equilibrium.

3.3 Calculating Market Equilibrium Prices

We denote μ_I as the maximum throughput that TP I can accept when it can still fulfill the quality q_I, defined as

$$\mu_I = \arg\max_{\lambda_I} Q_I(\lambda_I, \nu_I) \leq q_I. \tag{4}$$

For instance, if the quality metric is the average queueing delay under M/G/1 systems and TP I implements a FIFO scheduling policy, by the Pollaczek-Khinchine mean formula, $Q_I(\lambda_I, \nu_I) = \frac{\lambda_I}{\nu_I - \lambda_I} E[R]$, where $E[R]$ denotes the expected residual service time of jobs. If we want λ_I to be feasible, we need $\frac{\lambda_I}{\nu_I - \lambda_I} E[R] \leq q_I \Rightarrow \lambda_I \leq \frac{q_I}{E[R] + q_I} \nu_I = \mu_I$. We define $\eta_I = \mu_I/\nu_I$ as the maximum acceptable throughput per unit capacity, or the conversion factor from raw capacity to achievable throughput. Notice that given a fixed capacity ν_I, the smaller delay TP I wants to provide, the smaller maximum amount of traffic it can accept. For the M/G/1 case, η_I tends to 0 when the required quality q_I tends to 0, which shows a convex cost structure for the TP.

Based on the monotonicity of Q_I (Assumption 4), a market equilibrium can be characterized by using μ_Is as follows.

Definition 4. *A system $(\mathcal{M}, \mathcal{N})$ forms a market equilibrium if for all TP I, 1) $\lambda_I(\mathcal{N}_I) \leq \mu_I$, and 2) there does not exist $p_I' \geq p_I^{min}$ with the corresponding $\mathcal{N}_I'$ satisfying $\lambda_I(\mathcal{N}_I) < \lambda_I(\mathcal{N}_I') \leq \mu_I$.*

Based on the above alternative definition of a market equilibrium, we can calculate the competitive equilibrium prices without evaluating Q_I repeatedly as follows.

Calculate Price Equilibrium$(\mathcal{N}, \{p_I^{min}, q_I, \nu_I : I \in \mathcal{M}\})$
1. Set $p_I = \infty$ for all TP $I \in \mathcal{M}$;
2. Calculate μ_I for all TP $I \in \mathcal{M}$ based on q_I and Q_I;
3. **while** there exists $p_I' \in [p_I^{min}, p_I)$ such that $\lambda_I(\mathcal{N}_I) \leq \lambda_I(\mathcal{N}_I') \leq \mu_I$
4.   **set** $p_I = p_I'$;
5. **return** $\{p_I : I \in \mathcal{M}\}$;

In the above algorithm, we do not restrict which TP I to choose in step 3 if multiple TPs satisfy the condition. However, any sequence of updates will make the price vector converge, because each p_I will only be decreasing monotonically until convergence. Similarly, we can also set $p_I = p_I^{min}$ for all TPs, and the price vector will increase monotonically until convergence.

Based on Theorem 2 and 5, we also have the following result.

Corollary 1. *Let* $\mathcal{N}' = \{(\kappa\alpha_i, \kappa_3\beta_i, \kappa_1 v_i + \kappa_2) : i \in \mathcal{N}\}$ *and* $\mathcal{M}' = \{(\kappa_1 p_I + \kappa_2, q_I/\kappa_3, \nu_I') : I \in \mathcal{M}\}$ *for positive* $\kappa, \kappa_1, \kappa_2, \kappa_3$ *with* $\mu_I' = \kappa\mu_I$ *for all* $I \in \mathcal{M}$. *If* $(\mathcal{M}, \mathcal{N})$ *is a market equilibrium, then* $(\mathcal{M}', \mathcal{N}')$ *is a market equilibrium.*

Although the prices of the TPs influence the APs' choices, which further affect the capacity utilization of the TPs, equilibrium prices are the fixed points in which both the APs' choices and the TPs' prices do not change. However, external factors could move the resulting equilibrium. In the next section, we will study these fundamental driving forces for the evolution of the Internet economic ecosystem. By understanding these factors, we will know why the market prices change and why certain evolutions happen.

4. PRICE DYNAMICS IN EQUILIBRIUM

In this section, we look deeper into the qualitative dynamics of the equilibrium market prices. In particular, we explore how the different characteristics of the APs and the TPs can affect the market prices in equilibrium.

4.1 Evaluation Setting

Each AP i is characterized by three parameters (α_i, β_i, v_i); each TP I is characterized by three parameters (p_I, q_I, ν_I). To make a fair comparison between equilibrium prices under different settings, we carefully normalize the system parameters as follows. We define $v_{max} = \max\{v_i : i \in \mathcal{N}\}$, $\beta_{max} = \max\{\beta_i : i \in \mathcal{N}\}$, and $p_{min} = \min\{p_I^{min} : I \in \mathcal{M}\}$. Based on Theorem 2, we normalize any system $(\mathcal{M}, \mathcal{N})$ by factors $\kappa_1 = 1/(v_{max} - p_{min})$, $\kappa_2 = p_{min}/(v_{max} - p_{min})$, and $\kappa_3 = 1/\beta_{max}$. As a result, we normalize each β_i or v_i within the interval $[0, 1]$ and the equilibrium prices will also be scaled accordingly with $[0, 1]$. If p_I^{scaled} is the derived market equilibrium price in the normalized system, we can recover the real market price p_I as

$$p_I = (v_{max} - p_{min})p_I^{scaled} + p_{min}.$$

When the normalized price p_I^{scaled} tends to 0, it reflects that the real market price p_I goes down to the cost p_{min}; when p_I^{scaled} tends to 1, it reflects that the real market price p_I goes to the maximum AP profitability v_{max}. We describe the TPs' capacity in terms of the maximum acceptable rates μ_Is. We define $\alpha = \sum_{i\in\mathcal{N}}\alpha_i$, $\mu = \sum_{I\in\mathcal{M}}\mu_I$ and the ratio $\rho = \mu/\alpha$. Based on Corollary 1, any price equilibrium sustains when α_is and μ_Is scale at the same rate. Thus, we normalize the APs' aggregate maximum traffic intensity α to be 1. We define $\sigma_I = \mu_I/\mu$ as the capacity share of TP I, and under the normalized system, each TP I has $\mu_I = \sigma_I \rho$.

After the above normalization, we can describe any system by the following four parameters:

1. a set of qualities $\{q_I : I \in \mathcal{M}\}$,

2. the normalized aggregate capacity ρ,

3. the distribution of α_i over the domain $[0, 1]^2$ of (β_i, v_i),

4. the capacity distribution $\{\sigma_I : I \in \mathcal{M}\}$.

We focus on three different quality types: 1) q_A, the highest quality for real-time content delivery, 2) q_B, medium quality, mostly for web applications, and 3) q_C, the best-effort quality, mostly for elastic traffic. As analyzed in [25], IP transit markets will be quite efficient if two tiers of services are provided; thus, q_B and q_C can be considered as the higher and lower tier services of such an IP transit market. To differentiate the three qualities, we set $q_A : q_B : q_C = 1 : 5 : 25$. We vary ρ from 0 to 1, where the system's total capacity varies from extremely scarce to abundant. We discretize the AP domain with 50 levels of v_i and β_i, which forms 2500 types of APs. We assume that APs' profitability and quality-sensitivity follow probability distributions F_v and F_β respectively, and α_i follows the joint distribution of F_v and F_β. We use the various distributions in Figure 2 for F_v and F_β. For instance, when

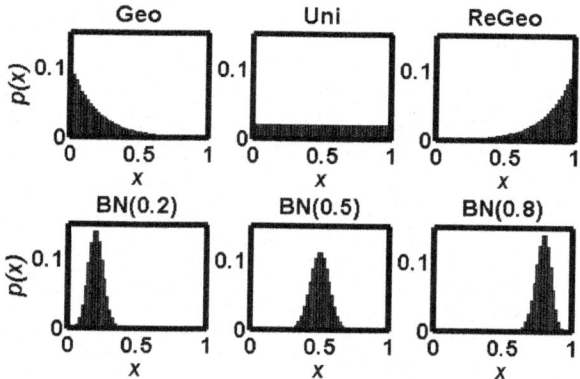

Figure 2: Common distributions: geometric, uniform, reversed geometric, binomial with $p = 0.2, 0.5$ **and** 0.8.

a geometric distribution Geo is used to describe F_β, it models the scenario where most of the AP traffic are elastic and the amount of quality-sensitive traffic decreases exponentially with its sensitivity level β_i. The binomial distributions $BN(p)$ are often used to approximate a normal distribution of the profitability v_i, or quality sensitivity β_i, where p determines the mean value.

4.2 Impact of TP Capacity on Prices

In this subsection, we study how the capacities of the TPs affect the equilibrium prices. We initially set $(q_A, q_B, q_C) = (0.2, 1, 5)$. We will evaluate how the quality may impact the equilibrium prices in the next subsection.

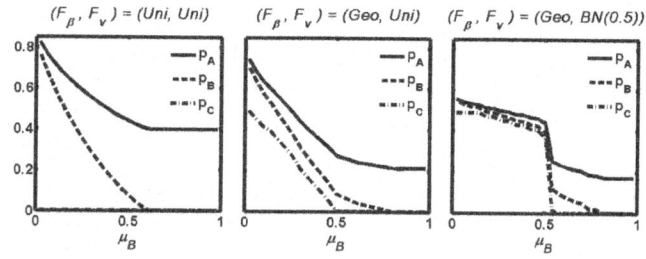

Figure 3: Shift in market prices as μ_B **varies: with** $(q_A, q_B, q_C) = (0.2, 1, 5), \mu_A = 0.05$ **and** $\mu_C = 0.25$.

In Figure 3, we fix $\mu_A = 0.05$, $\mu_C = 0.25$ and vary μ_B from 0 to 1 along the x-axis. The three sub-figures show the equilibrium prices when α_i follows the joint distributions of $(F_\beta, F_v) = (Uni, Uni), (Geo, Uni)$ and $(Geo, BN(0.5))$ respectively. We observe that when μ_B is scarce, equilibrium price p_B is close to (but strictly less than) the price p_A of its upper class TP. When μ_B increases, p_B diverges from p_A and moves to the price p_C of its lower class TP. When μ_B becomes abundant, its market price goes

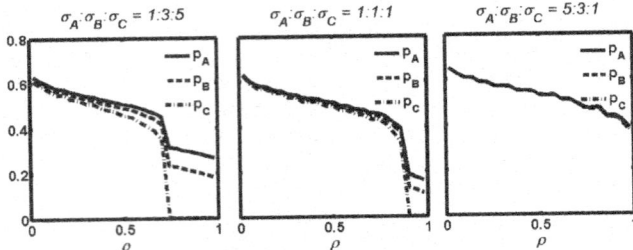

Figure 4: Shift in market prices as ρ varies: with $(q_A, q_B, q_C) = (0.2, 1, 5)$ and $(F_\beta, F_v) = (Geo, Uni)$.

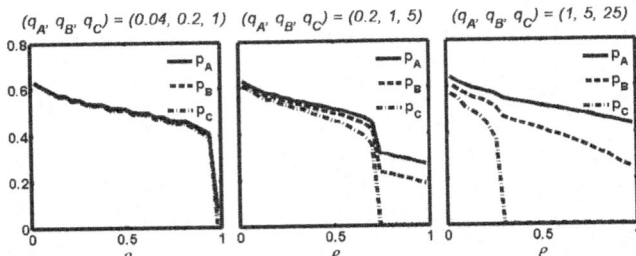

Figure 5: Shift in market prices as ρ varies: with $(q_A, q_B, q_C) = \kappa(0.2, 1, 5)$ where $\kappa = 0.2, 1$ and 5.

down to the minimum price after p_C. In general, when the capacity of a particular TP, i.e., μ_B, increases, it drives all equilibrium prices down; however, the prices of higher quality TPs, e.g., p_A, might not go down to the minimum price.

In the rest of this section, we often use $F_\beta = Geo$, which models the case where more APs were elastic, and $F_v = BN(0.5)$, which approximates that the AP profitability follows a normal distribution centered at $v_i = 0.5$. Note that our qualitative results do not depend on these settings.

In Figure 4, we vary the system capacity ρ from 0 to 1 along the x-axis. α_i follows the joint distribution $(F_\beta, F_v) = (Geo, BN(0.5))$. The sub-figures show the equilibrium prices when the capacity ratio $\sigma_A : \sigma_B : \sigma_C$ equals $1:3:5$, $1:1:1$ and $5:3:1$ respectively. In all three cases, when the total capacity ρ is small, all equilibrium prices are very close and high. When we increase ρ, all market prices drop. By comparing the price curves across the three subfigures, we observe that when the capacity share of the higher class TP is smaller (the left subfigure), 1) the three market prices differ more from each other, 2) p_C drops faster, and 3) all the prices drop to the minimum price faster than the other two cases. Because price differences exist in practice, we will use $\sigma_A : \sigma_B : \sigma_C = 1:3:5$ in the rest of this section.

Lessons (the TP capacity effects on prices) leaned:

- Capacity expansion drives market prices down.

- The capacity expansion of a particular TP I would affect not only its own price p_I, but also other TPs' prices, due to the substitution effect of TP I to other TPs.

- When TP I's capacity share σ_I is small (big), its market price p_I is close to the price of its next higher (lower) class TP.

4.3 Impact of TP Quality on Prices

Let us explore how the quality q_I of the TPs may affect the equilibrium prices. We use the setting that the capacity distribution follows $\sigma_A : \sigma_B : \sigma_C = 1:3:5$ and α_i follows the joint distribution $(F_\beta, F_v) = (Geo, BN(0.5))$.

In Figure 5, we keep the quality ratio $q_A : q_B = q_B : q_C = 1 : 5$ and use $(q_A, q_B, q_C) = \kappa(0.2, 1, 5)$, where κ equals $0.2, 1$ and 5 in the three subfigures. We vary the system capacity ρ from 0 to 1 along the x-axis. We observe that when all the TPs improve their quality by the same ratio, i.e., $\kappa = 0.2$, the market prices of the TPs are very close; when all the TPs degrade their quality by the same ratio, i.e., $\kappa = 5$, the market prices of the TPs diverge greatly. This observation can be explained by Theorem 3. When κ decreases and all qualities are improved, more APs will choose lower class TPs, which move the prices of the lower class TPs upward and the prices of upper class TPs downward. As a result, all TPs prices will move closer. On the other hand, when κ increases and all qualities are

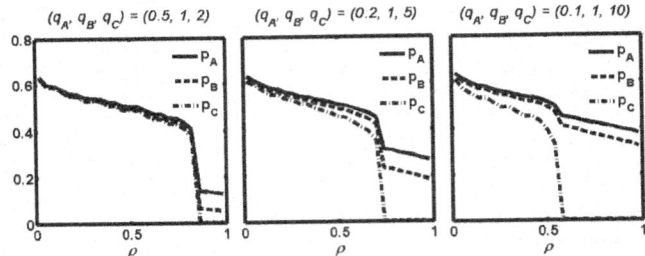

Figure 6: Shift in market prices as ρ varies: with $q_B = 1$, $q_A : q_B = q_B : q_C = 1 : \kappa$ where $\kappa = 2, 5, 100$.

degraded, more APs will choose to upper class TPs, which move the prices of the upper class TPs upward and the prices of lower class TPs downward. This will further diverge the price differences among the TPs with different qualities.

In Figure 6, we keep $q_B = 1$ and vary the quality ratio $q_A : q_B = q_B : q_C = 1 : \kappa$, where κ equals 2, 5 and 10. We observe that the price differences are positively correlated with the quality ratio. In particular, when quality ratio is high, e.g., $\kappa = 10$, the price of the lowest class TP, i.e., p_C, drops earlier and sharper when the total capacity ρ expands. At the same time, higher class TPs can still maintain a non-zero market price even after p_C drops down the minimum price. The general trend is that when the quality ratio keeps increasing, the price curves will move higher and toward the left. In the rest of this section, we will often use the quality ratio $1 : 5$ and $(q_A, q_B, q_C) = (0.2, 1, 5)$ for our evaluations. Again, our qualitative results do not depend on this setting.

Lessons (the TP quality effects on prices) leaned:

- The market prices of the TPs would be close to (far from) one another if the quality ratio is small (big) or/and the overall qualities of the market are high (low).

- In reality, the qualities provided by the TPs are becoming better and better, which implies that market prices for different services might converge.

- High-end market segments can still maintain a price difference if they can differentiate their quality from the lower class TPs substantially.

Next, we will see that the TP price differences also depend on the demand side: the characteristics of the APs.

4.4 Impact of AP Wealth on Prices

Let us explore how the profitability distribution F_v may affect the equilibrium prices. We still keep $\sigma_A : \sigma_B : \sigma_C = 1:3:5$ and

$(q_A, q_B, q_C) = (0.2, 1, 5)$. α_i follows the joint distribution of F_β and F_v, where F_β is distributed as Geo.

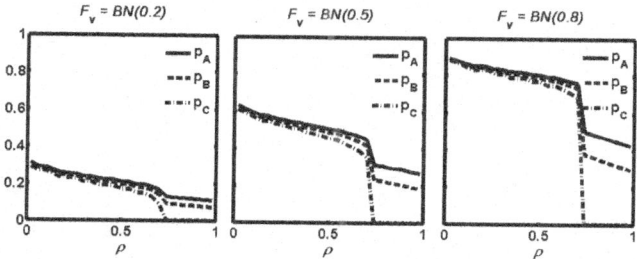

Figure 7: Shift in market prices as ρ varies: $(q_A, q_B, q_C) = (0.2, 1, 5)$, $\sigma_A : \sigma_B : \sigma_C = 1 : 3 : 5$, $F_\beta = Geo$.

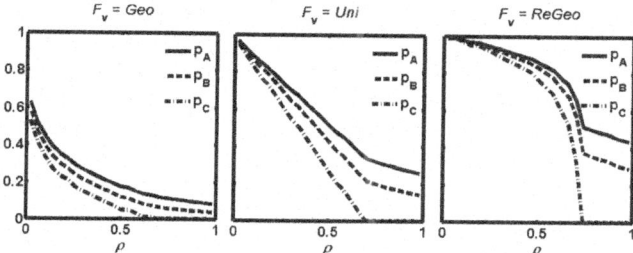

Figure 8: Shift in market prices as ρ varies: $(q_A, q_B, q_C) = (0.2, 1, 5)$, $\sigma_A : \sigma_B : \sigma_C = 1 : 3 : 5$, $F_\beta = Geo$.

In Figure 7, we vary ρ from 0 to 1 along the x-axis and plot the equilibrium prices where the profitability distribution F_v follows a binomial distribution $BN(p)$ parameterized by $p = 0.2, 0.5$ and 0.8 respectively. By doing this, we simulate the normal distributions of the APs' wealth varying the mean value from small to large. We observe that despite the difference in mean profit of the APs, p_C drops to the minimum price at the same time. The price curves in all cases keep the same shape; however, they scale differently on the vertical axis. This indicates that the market prices depend on how much the APs are able to pay for the services, and how they demand for the TPs based on their values of (β_i, v_i).

In Figure 8, we vary F_v to be Geo, Uni and $ReGeo$. We observe that the shapes of the price curves are very different: prices decrease convexly, linearly and concavely in the three subfigures. In general, how fast the prices drop depends on the density of the APs whose profitability are around that price range, and the shape of the curves look like the complimentary cumulative distribution function (CCDF) of F_v.

Lessons (the AP wealth effects on prices) leaned:

- The market prices of the TPs are positively correlated with the mean profitability of the APs.

- At a certain price range where the density of the APs is high (low), more (less) competition among the APs drives the prices close to (far below) their profitability.

4.5 Impact of AP Quality-Sensitivity on Prices

In this subsection, we study how the quality sensitivity distribution F_β affects the equilibrium prices. We set $\sigma_A : \sigma_B : \sigma_C = 1 : 3 : 5$ and $\rho = 0.5$. In the following cases, F_β follows a binomial distribution $BN(p)$, where we vary the parameter p along the x-axis. By doing this, we simulate the cases where the APs become more and more sensitive to quality when the mean sensitivity increases with p.

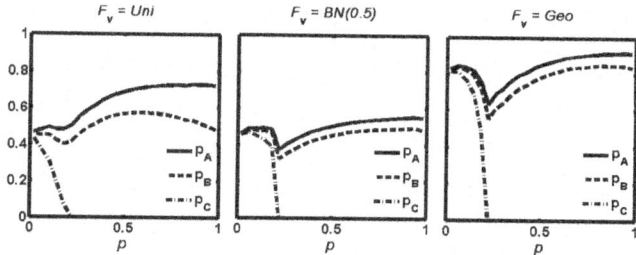

Figure 9: Shift of market prices when we vary AP's sensitivity to quality: with $\sigma_A : \sigma_B : \sigma_C = 1 : 3 : 5$, $\rho = 0.5$, $(q_A, q_B, q_C) = (0.2, 1, 5)$ and $F_\beta = BN(p)$.

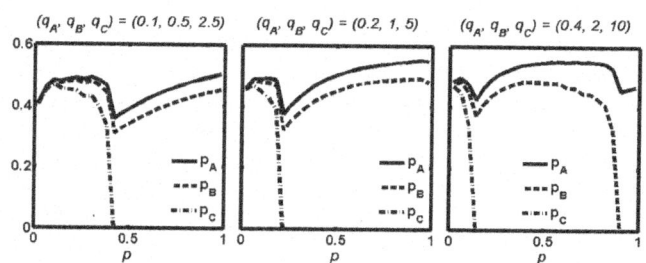

Figure 10: Shift of market prices when we vary AP's sensitivity to quality: with $\sigma_A : \sigma_B : \sigma_C = 1 : 3 : 5$, $\rho = 0.5$, $F_v = BN(0.5)$ and $F_\beta = BN(p)$.

In Figure 9, we fix $(q_A, q_B, q_C) = (0.2, 1, 5)$ and vary F_v to be Uni, $BN(0.5)$ and Geo in the three sub-figures. We observe that although the profitability distribution affect the absolute price values, the shape of the price curves look similar. When the quality sensitivity of the APs increases, the lowest quality service price, i.e., p_C, drops sharply and quickly. Although p_A and p_B drops accordingly with p_C, after p_C reaches the minimum price, both p_A and p_B rebound. With further increase in quality sensitivity, p_B shows a trend to decrease slowly; however, p_A always stays at a high level. When the APs become more sensitive to quality, more and more APs start to move to higher class TPs. As a result, the capacity μ_C becomes under-utilized, which also drives p_C down very quickly. Although p_C's drop pulls down the overall market prices, more APs move to higher class TPs, which make TPs A and B in demand, and therefore, keep p_A and p_B steadier. After p_C reaches the minimum price, p_C stops decreasing. As the APs' quality sensitivity keeps increasing, even the minimum market price of p_C becomes relatively expensive to the APs. This makes even more APs move to TP A and B and drives p_A and p_B upward.

In Figure 10, we fix $F_v = BN(0.5)$ and vary the qualities to be $(q_A, q_B, q_C) = \kappa(0.2, 1, 5)$, where $\kappa = 0.5, 1$ and 2. We observe the same trends as in Figure 9 that p_C drops quickly and sharply to the minimum price as the APs' quality sensitivity increases. As κ increases, all the price curves move to the left and the price drop of lower class TPs becomes quicker and sharper. This also coincides with the observations made in Figure 5 that when the qualities degrade, the price of the lower class TP drops much quicker.

In the above illustrations, we vary the distribution F_β. It is also possible that all the APs' sensitivity increase by $\beta'_i = \xi \beta_i$ for some

$\xi > 1$. By Theorem 2, we can rescale the system by $\kappa_3 = 1/\xi$, as if the APs keep their quality sensitivity constant and all the qualities become poorer. By Theorem 3 and the TP quality effect result in Figure 5, we also conclude that more APs will prefer higher quality TPs and the price of the lower quality TPs will drop sharply.

Lessons (the AP quality-sensitivity effects on prices) leaned:

- When the APs become more sensitive to the service quality, the price of lower class TPs will drop quickly.

- When the price of the lowest quality TP goes down to its cost, the prices of higher quality TPs might increase due to their relatively cheap prices and high demand.

4.6 Internet Evolution: Some Explanations

By understanding the factors that drive the market equilibrium, we reason about the evolution of the Internet ecosystem and reach plausible answers to the questions raised in Section 1. We do not claim that our answers below are exhaustive and the limitations of our model will be discussed in Section 5.4.

1) Why have the IP transit prices been dropping? The capacity effect tells that the price drop can be a consequence of the capacity expansion of the transit providers. Compared to the capacities at the last-miles, the capacity in the backbone grows faster than demand and is abundant [14]. Also, the price drop in better quality services, i.e., CDN prices, will drive the transit prices further down. The quality effect tells that when the transit quality differs a lot from the CDN services, the prices will diverge greatly. The wealth effect tells that since the majority of the elastic APs might not be very profitable, transit providers cannot fully utilize its capacity and charge a high price at the same time. This is also why they are looking for providing value-added and differentiated services. Last, the AP quality-sensitivity effect tells that when AP traffic becomes more and more inelastic, e.g., the surge of Netflix traffic, lower quality service will become less valuable and therefore its price will drop quickly.

2) Why have the CDNs emerged in the ecosystem? The capacity effect tells that when the capacity of higher quality service is small, it can maintain a price difference with the lower quality services. The quality effect tells that if a CDN service's quality differs a lot from the transit services, it can be priced much higher. When the capacity of the transit market was limited and priced high, the demand for even higher quality service drove the price for potential CDN services even higher. This explains why CDNs emerged in the first place. The wealth effect tells that when the APs' profitability is not high, the market prices cannot be high. However, due to the low cost structure of the CDNs, they can still help small APs who could not afford the infrastructure to support large demand. The AP quality-sensitivity effect further tells that with the traffic being more and more sensitive to quality, the price of high quality CDN can sustain at a high level.

3) Why has the pricing power shifted to the access ISPs? This can be partially explained by the AP quality-sensitivity effect and the TP quality effect. When the AP traffic becomes more and more sensitive to service quality, they are more willing to pay for the higher quality services. Because access ISPs are physically closer to the users, their service quality is naturally much better than other providers who have to go through the access ISPs to reach the end-users anyways. Consequently, the difference in service quality makes it possible for the access ISPs to charge services at higher prices. Furthermore, Comcast's monopolistic position in the U.S. market could be another reason, under which its price will be set higher than the competitive market price under Definition 3.

4) Why are the large content providers building their own wide-area networks toward users? Mostly because the APs become more sensitive to service quality, they cannot rely on the transit providers to deliver content. As high quality services are limited and access ISPs would obtain more pricing power, large APs might consider establishing their own networks toward users as a cheaper alternative than paying access ISPs for better services in the future.

5. INTERNET'S ECONOMIC EVOLUTION

Besides understanding how each isolated factor might affect the market prices, we incorporate ground truth data [10, 19, 4, 11], e.g., the historical trends of the TPs' capacity expansion and the APs' characteristics, and project *possible future price dynamics* of the Internet ecosystem. Through this, our model can help the TPs make various long-term business decisions. Let us demonstrate this.

We take a macroscopic view and categorize network services as two types: $\mathcal{M} = \{A, B\}$. B models the IP transit service that provides interconnection based on "best-effort"; A models the CDN or private peering type of service that provides better service quality than B. We categorize the APs as three types: $\mathcal{N} = \{a, b, c\}$. a models the video or realtime interactive applications that are very sensitive to quality. b models the web applications that are elastic but more tolerate to quality than type a applications. c models the inelastic applications, e.g., email and P2P file download.

By Corollary 1, we know that when quality and the sensitivity parameters scale inversely, the equilibrium remains the same; therefore, without loss of generality, we set $q_B = 1$ as the baseline best-effort quality level. We set the quality sensitivity parameters to be $(\beta_a, \beta_b, \beta_c) = (10, 1, 0.1)$. Under this setting, type a APs would only obtain $e^{-10} \approx 4.5^{-5}$ of their maximum throughput under q_B, which implies that the best-effort service cannot support quality sensitive applications. Also, under q_B, a type b AP could get $e^{-1} \approx 37\%$ of its maximum throughput; however, a type c AP could get $e^{-0.1} \approx 90\%$ of its maximum throughput. When measured by delay, the quality of service for realtime applications often require the delay to be at the order of milliseconds [27], compared to the best-effort service delays at the order of seconds. Thus, we choose $q_A = 0.01$ to reflect the same order of magnitude of service difference. As a result, even type a APs would obtain $e^{-0.1} \approx 90\%$ of their maximum throughput under the better quality level q_A.

Next, we try to estimate the capacity of the TPs on the Internet. We take the Equinix Internet Exchange at New York (Equinix-NY) as a reference market and estimate the capacities based on the data provided by PeeringDB [10]. At the end of year 2011, there were 102 ISPs listed on at Equinix New York Exchange in PeeringDB, among which 44 use *Open* peering policy and the remaining 58 use either *Selective* or *Restricted* peering policy. The total capacity was around 21 Tbps, among which the ISPs using Open peering policy contributed 7 Tbps and the remaining ISPs contributed 14 Tbps. Since *Selective* and *Restricted* policies are used for private and often paid-peering agreements, we set ν_A and ν_B to be 14 and 7 Tbps, for the reference time of the year 2011.

From the Global Internet Geography [4] report, between 2007 to 2011, the international Internet capacity increased six-fold and the bandwidth to the U.S. had increased nearly 50 percent per year. To a first approximation, we assume that the capacity ν of the TPs increases 50% per year. We define $\alpha = \alpha_a + \alpha_b + \alpha_c$ and ω_a, ω_b and ω_c as the weight of the throughput upper bound of each application type. Given α and the weight of AP i, we obtain α_i as

$$\alpha_i = \frac{\omega_i}{\omega_a + \omega_b + \omega_c} \alpha, \quad \forall\, i = a, b, c.$$

Based on the observed traffic distribution of various applications in [19], we set $(\omega_a, \omega_b, \omega_c) = (2\%, 75\%, 23\%)$ for the year 2007, and assume that the weight for video (ω_a), web (ω_b) and inelastic applications (ω_c) increase at an annual growth rate of 150%, 50% and 20% respectively. Notice that IP transit prices are often quoted for per Mbps-month, while CDN prices are often quoted for per terabit. If capacity is fully utilized 24/7, $1 per Mbps-month can be translated into $0.386 per terabit. We assume that the maximum per unit traffic revenue for the APs is $10 Mbps-month and the APs' revenue are uniformly distributed.

5.1 A First Approximation Benchmark

We use our macroscopic model to fit the historical prices starting from 2007 and project future Internet prices. In a first approximation, we choose the following parameters.

1. α at year 2007 (denoted as α_{07}) equals 10 Tbps.
2. α increases at an annual growth rate $r_\alpha = 22\%$.
3. $\eta_A = \mu_A/\nu_A = 0.3$ and $\eta_B = \mu_B/\nu_B = 0.9$.

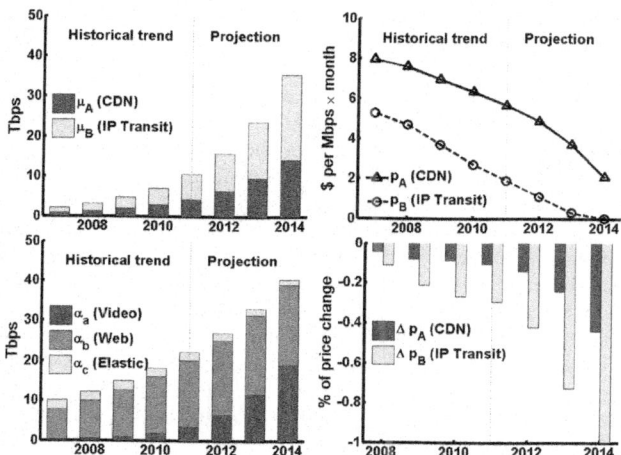

Figure 11: Historical price and future price projection.

In Figure 11, the upper left subfigure plots the achievable throughput for the CDN (μ_A) and IP transit (μ_B) services from 2007 to 2014 and the lower left subfigure plots the maximum demand α_a, α_b and α_c for the same time period. The upper right subfigure plots the price dynamics of both IP transit and CDN services and the lower right subfigure plots the percentage of price change for both services. We observe that average price drop from 2007 to 2011 is approximately 20%, which coincides with the price drop surveyed in the Global Internet Geography [4] report. Also, the price of IP transit is below $2 per Mbps-month, very close to the mean of IP transit prices, where the lowest price fell to $1 per Mbps-month.

Compared to the video delivery pricing [11], our price projection shows that the CDN price drops around 8% annually from 2007 to 2011, and reaches $5.67 per Mbps-month, or $2.18 per terabit. This price is lower than the $7.5 per terabit price for APs with volume of 5PB data and the price drop is slower than the observed 20% price drop in the CDN industry [11]. The difference could come for two reasons: 1) since CDN service charges based on traffic volume, we cannot assume that the APs would always use the capacity 24/7, and therefore, the CDN providers should charge some premium on top of the basic per Mbps per month charge, 2) in contrast to our competitive model for CDN service, the industry might be less competitive and could charge a much higher price; therefore, when the industry becomes more competitive, we expect to see much sharper price drops.

Based on the trend from 2007 to 2011, our model projects that both the IP transit and CDN prices will further drop, at an even faster rate, and IP transit price will drop to its minimum price. Of course, this projection is based on the assumption that the capacity of the TPs will keep expanding at the 50% annual rate. We will further discuss potential trends of future prices in a later subsection.

5.2 Sensitivity of the Benchmark

In this subsection, we show the sensitivity of our price projection with respect to the chosen parameters.

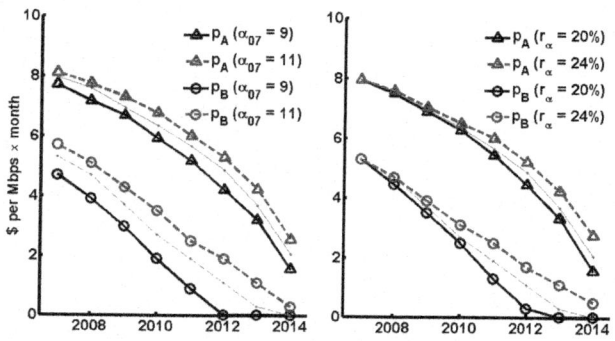

Figure 12: Sensitivity to initial demand α_{07} and rate r_α.

First, we want to see how the demand parameter α affects the price dynamics. Figure 12 shows a projection of service prices when the initial value α_{07} and the growth rate r_α change. In the left subfigure, we vary α_{07} to be 9 and 11 Tbps compared to the benchmark value of 10 Tbps. We observe that the prices are positively correlated with α_{07}. In the right subfigure, we vary the growth rate r_α to be 20% and 24% compared to the benchmark value of 22%. We observe that the prices again are positively correlated with r_α. Both tells that when the demand increases, so do the prices.

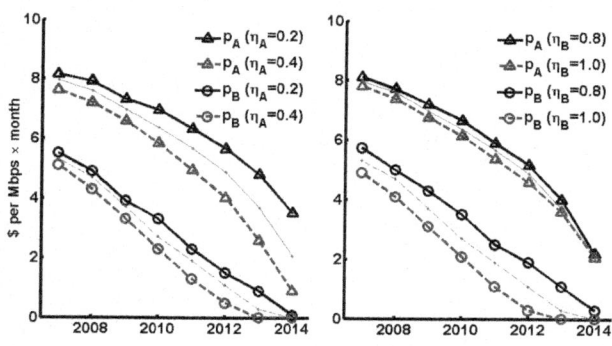

Figure 13: Sensitivity to capacity utilization η_A and η_B.

Second, we want to see how the capacity utilization factor $\eta_I = \mu_I/\nu_I$ affects the price dynamics. Figure 13 shows a projection of Internet service prices when η_A and η_B vary from the benchmark. In the left subfigure, we vary η_A to be 0.2 and 0.4 compared to the benchmark value 0.3. In the right subfigure, we vary η_B to be 0.8 and 1.0 compared to the benchmark value 0.9. We observe that the all prices are negatively correlated with the capacity utilization factors. Also, the IP transit prices are sensitive to both η_A and η_B; while the CDN prices are only sensitive to its utilization factor η_A.

5.3 Price Projection and TP Business Decisions

Now, we demonstrate that by using the price projection from our model, we can help the TPs to make business decisions on 1) how aggressive the TPs should expend their capacity, and 2) whether the TPs should/would tend towards *Open* or *Selective* peering policies.

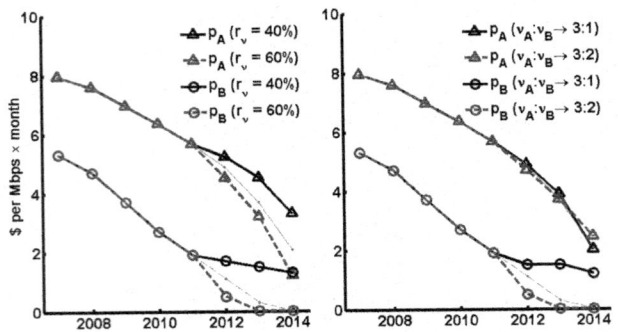

Figure 14: Price projection under various capacity ratios $\nu_A : \nu_B$ and capacity expansion rate r_ν.

To answer the first question, we vary the capacity growth rate of the TPs r_ν to be 40% and 60%, compared to the historical benchmark rate 50% and plot the price projections in the left subfigure of Figure 14. We observe that when the capacity grows at 60% per year, both the CDN and IP transit price drop fast and the IP transit price will down to its cost next year; however, when the growth rate is 40%, the IP transit price will be decreasing at a very slow rate. These observations tell us that the ISPs providing IP transit services might want to slow down their investment in capacity expansion; however, CDN providers and ISPs that sell private-peering and QoS might want to continue to expand their capacity when their profit margins are still above zero. As the price of IP transit drops, we believe that the investment in the transit capacity will slow down, which will also stabilize the price of the IP transit services.

To answer the second question, we vary the capacity ratio $\nu_A : \nu_B$ from the benchmark ratio 2 : 1 (14 Tpbs : 7 Tbps) to 3 : 1 and 3 : 2 for the year 2014 in the right subfigure. These two projections model the scenarios where ISPs will tend to be more *Selective* and more *Open* in their peering policies respectively. We observe that if more ISPs are going to use an *Open* peering policy, the IP transit price will drop to its cost quickly; otherwise, the IP transit price will get closer to the CDN price and be stable. This observation implies that ISPs would have strong incentives to move towards *Selective* peering policies if possible, which coincides with the reality that the access ISP, Comcast, started to use private peering exclusively.

In summary, we predict that although the CDN price will still be dropping, the price of IP transit will be more stable. Furthermore, the capacity expansion will slow down and more ISPs will tend to use *Selective* rather than *Open* peering policies in the near future.

5.4 Limitations of the Model

First of all, our general equilibrium model implicitly assumes that each market segment is competitive. In practice, some market segment could be lack of competition and form a monopolistic or oligopolistic market structure. Thus, the real market prices will be higher than what our model predicts. Second, our equilibrium model does not capture the off-equilibrium and transit dynamics that could happen in practice. Third, our model is in nature macroscopic, and it does not capture detailed information like peering agreement, topology, traffic patterns and etc. Nevertheless, our model does capture the type of different services the TPs provide via implicitly encoding all the relevant information into the quality level q_I. From the APs' point of view, they do care about *quality* rather than other details of the TPs. Fourth, since our focus is on the transit/CDN market, our model does not intend to capture the end-user market aspects. For example, modeling the bundle of access services and other service differentiations are out of scope. Last but not the least, our macroscopic model provides some qualitative reasons for the Internet evolution, which we do not claim to be exhaustive. There might be additional factors/reasons that are not captured by our model, e.g., the lack of competition in the market.

6. RELATED WORK

Many empirical studies have been tracking the evolution of the Internet using measurements and public data sets [19, 15, 17, 24, 12]. Labovitz et al. [19] measured the inter-domain traffic between 2007 and 2009, and observed the changes in traffic patterns as well as the consolidation and disintermediation of the Internet core. Gill et al. [17] collected and analyzed traceroute measurements and showed that large content providers are deploying their own wide-area networks. Dhamdhere et al. [15] confirmed the consolidation of the core of the Internet, that brings the content closer to users. Akella et al. [12] used measurements to identify and characterize non-access bottleneck links in terms of their location, latency and available capacity. At the edge of the Internet, Sundaresan et al. [24] studied the network access link performance measured directly from home gateway devices. We focus on a macroscopic model of the Internet ecosystem that captures the application traffic going through the network transport service providers.

Many works [13, 16, 21, 22, 25, 20, 18] focused on the modeling perspective of the Internet evolution. Chang et al. [13] presents an evolutionary model for the AS topologies. Lodhi et al. [20] used an agent-based model to study the network formation of the Internet. Motiwala et al. [22] used a cost model to study the Internet traffic. Valancius et al. combined models and data to study the pricing [25] structure of the IP transit market. Faratin et al. [16] and Ma et al. [21] studied the evolution of the ISP settlements. In this work, we take a holistic view and analyze the business decisions and evolutions of the APs and TPs altogether.

7. CONCLUSIONS

We proposed a network aware, macroscopic model to explain the evolution of the Internet. Our model captures 1) the business decisions of the APs, 2) the pricing and competition of the TPs, and 3) the resulting market equilibrium of the ecosystem. By analyzing how the AP characteristics (i.e., traffic intensity, profitability and sensitivity to quality), and the TP characteristics (i.e., quality, price and capacity, affect the market equilibrium), we obtain fundamental understanding of why historical and recent evolutions of the Internet have happened. With further estimations of the trends in traffic demand, capacity growth and quality improvements, our model can also project the future evolution of the Internet ecosystem. This model provides a tool for the Internet players to better understand their business and risks, and help them to deal with their business decisions in the complicated and evolving ecosystem.

Acknowledgement

This study is supported by the Human Sixth Sense Programme at the Advanced Digital Sciences Center from Singapore's Agency for Science, Technology and Research (A*STAR), Ministry of Education of Singapore AcRF grant R-252-000-448-133, and the National Science Foundation grants CNS-1017934 and CCF-1139915.

8. REFERENCES

[1] Akamai. http://www.akamai.com/.
[2] Amazon Elastic Compute Cloud (EC2). http://www.amazon.com/ec2.
[3] Cogent Communications, Inc. http://www.cogentco.com.
[4] "Global Internet Geography." Telegeography Research. http://www.telegeography.com/.
[5] Level 3 Communications, Inc. http://www.level3.com.
[6] Limelight Networks. http://www.limelight.com/.
[7] Netflix, Inc. http://www.netflix.com.
[8] Netflix takes up 32.7% of Internet bandwidth, CNN News. http://edition.cnn.com/2011/10/27/tech/web/netflix-internet-bandwith-mashable.
[9] Netflix Traffic Now Bigger Than BitTorrent. Has Hollywood Won? GIGAOM News. http://gigaom.com/broadband/netflix-p2p-traffic/.
[10] PeeringDB. http://www.peeringdb.com/.
[11] Video Delivery Pricing for Q4 2011. http://www.cdnpricing.com/.
[12] A. Akella, S. Seshan, and A. Shaikh. An empirical evaluation of wide-area Internet bottlenecks. In *Proceedings of the ACM conference on Internet measurement (IMC)*, 2003.
[13] H. Chang, S. Jamin, and W. Willinger. To peer or not to peer: Modeling the evolution of the Internet's AS-level topology. In *Proceedings of IEEE Infocom*, Barcelona, Spain, 2006.
[14] C. Courcoubetis and R. Weber. *Pricing Communication Networks: Economics, Technology and Modelling*. John Wiley & Sons Ltd., 2003.
[15] A. Dhamdhere and C. Dovrolis. Ten years in the evolution of the Internet ecosystem. In *Proceedings of the 8th ACM SIGCOMM conference on Internet measurement (IMC 08)*, pages 183–196, Vouliagmeni, Greece, October 2008.
[16] P. Faratin, D. Clark, P. Gilmore, S. Bauer, A. Berger, and W. Lehr. Complexity of Internet interconnections: Technology, incentives and implications for policy. *The 35th Research Conference on Communication, Information and Internet Policy (TPRC)*, 2007.
[17] P. Gill, M. Arlitt, Z. Li, and A. Mahanti. The flattening Internet topology: natural evolution, unsightly barnacles or contrived collapse? In *Proceedings of the 9th international conference on Passive and active network measurement*, 2008.
[18] H. Haddadi, S. Uhlig, A. Moore, R. Mortier, and M. Rio. Modeling Internet topology dynamics. *ACM SIGCOMM Computer Communication Review, Volume 38 Issue 2, April 2008*.
[19] C. Labovitz, D. McPherson, S. Iekel-Johnson, J. Oberheide, and F. Jahanian. Internet inter-domain traffic. In *Proceedings of the ACM SigComm*, New Delhi, India, 2010.
[20] A. Lodhi, A. Dhamdhere, and C. Dovrolis. GENESIS: An agent-based model of interdomain network formation, traffic flow and economics. In *Proceedings of IEEE Infocom*, Miami FL, March 2012.
[21] R. T. B. Ma, D. Chiu, J. C. Lui, V. Misra, and D. Rubenstein. On cooperative settlement between content, transit and eyeball Internet service providers. *IEEE/ACM Transactions on Networking*, 19(3), June 2011.
[22] M. Motiwala, A. Dhamdhere, N. Feamster, and A. Lakhina. Towards a cost model for network traffic. *ACM SIGCOMM Computer Communication Review*, 42(1), January 2012.
[23] W. Norton. *The Internet Peering Playbook: Connecting to the Core of the Internet*. DrPeering Press, 2011.
[24] S. Sundaresan, W. de Donato, N. Feamster, R. Teixeira, S. Crawford, and A. Pescapíí. Broadband Internet performance: A view from the gateway. In *Proceedings of ACM SIGCOMM*, Toronto, Ontario, Canada, August 2011.
[25] V. Valancius, C. Lumezanu, N. Feamster, R. Johari, and V. Vazirani. How many tiers? Pricing in the Internet transit market. In *Proceedings of ACM SIGCOMM*, Toronto, Ontario, Canada, August 2011.
[26] T. Wu. Network neutrality, broadband discrimination. *Journal of Telecommunications and High Technology Law*, 141, 2005.
[27] X. Xiao. *Technical, Commercial and Regulatory Challenges of QoS: An Internet Service Model Perspective*. The Morgan Kaufmann Series in Networking, 2008.

Two Years of Short URLs Internet Measurement: Security Threats and Countermeasures

Federico Maggi, Alessandro Frossi
Stefano Zanero
Politecnico di Milano
{fmaggi, frossi, zanero}@elet.polimi.it

Gianluca Stringhini, Brett Stone-Gross
Christopher Kruegel, Giovanni Vigna
UC Santa Barbara
{gianluca, bstone, chris, vigna}@cs.ucsb.edu

ABSTRACT

URL shortening services have become extremely popular. However, it is still unclear whether they are an effective and reliable tool that can be leveraged to hide malicious URLs, and to what extent these abuses can impact the end users. With these questions in mind, we first analyzed existing countermeasures adopted by popular shortening services. Surprisingly, we found such countermeasures to be ineffective and trivial to bypass. This first measurement motivated us to proceed further with a large-scale collection of the HTTP interactions that originate when web users access live pages that contain short URLs. To this end, we monitored 622 distinct URL shortening services between March 2010 and April 2012, and collected 24,953,881 distinct short URLs. With this large dataset, we studied the abuse of short URLs. Despite short URLs are a significant, new security risk, in accordance with the reports resulting from the observation of the overall phishing and spamming activity, we found that only a relatively small fraction of users ever encountered malicious short URLs. Interestingly, during the second year of measurement, we noticed an increased percentage of short URLs being abused for drive-by download campaigns and a decreased percentage of short URLs being abused for spam campaigns. In addition to these security-related findings, our unique monitoring infrastructure and large dataset allowed us to complement previous research on short URLs and analyze these web services from the user's perspective.

Categories and Subject Descriptors

H.3.5 [**Online Information Services**]: Web-based services; C.2.0 [**Computer Communication Networks**]: General

Keywords

Security; Short URLs; Measurement; Crowdsourcing.

1. INTRODUCTION

Since 2001, a number of URL shortening services have made their appearance on the Web. Users can submit URLs to such services to create aliases (short URLs) that are easier to share than the original URLs. A shortening service will keep an association between the original URL and the alias, and will redirect accesses to the short URL to the original page. Short URLs are commonly used to save valuable characters on services that impose strict length limits (e.g., Twitter). Users have grown accustomed to following a URL that looks like http://bit.ly/1hBa6k, even when the mapped URL may be http://evil.com/attack?id=31337. If it is usually difficult for a user to determine whether a URL is legitimate or not just by looking at it, this is even harder in case of short URLs. As a result, shortening services have been abused by miscreants for masquerading the true URLs of phishing or drive-by-download pages [5, 10, 12]. Large services such as Twitter, Facebook or YouTube have started running their own shortening service, upon which their social networks rely (e.g., t.co, fb.me, youtu.be). Unfortunately, when the hyperlinks of an entire social network rely upon one, single URL "translator", speed and availability also become of concern[1] (similarly to what happens with the DNS service).

To the best of our knowledge, there has never been a large-scale and global measurement study of the *threats to users* introduced by short URLs and the *countermeasures adopted* by shortening services. Previous work highlighted the security and privacy issues related to the rise of short URLs [7, 11], whereas the effectiveness of existing protections adopted by the services was not analyzed. In this work, we first assess whether such countermeasures can substitute blacklist-based protections implemented in current browsers, so that users can actually trust URLs exposed by popular shortening services even when client-side defenses are not in place. According to our experiments, popular services react against attempts of shortening long URLs that expose malicious behavior at the time of submission—by either banning offending URLs or by displaying warning pages; however, from our preliminary experiments we noticed that shortening services do not check existing short URLs periodically (see Tab. 3). Such checks are useful in case the aliased landing pages turn malicious (e.g., after a timeout expiration). The only exception is tinyurl.com, which deleted 1,806 (spam) short URLs that became active *after* the short URLs were created.

In addition, previous work did not consider the *end users* and how they typically access pages containing short URLs. The research described in [2] analyzed the typical referrers, content popularity, geolocalization, and longevity of bit.ly and ow.ly short URLs, collected via Twitter and exhaustive enumeration (i.e., ow.ly/[a-Z0-9]+). We observe the short URL phenomenon from a completely different perspective,

---
[1] http://www.theverge.com/2012/10/9/3477734/twitter-outage-phishing-complaint

which allows us to obtain more detailed information about the usage of short URLs. More precisely, instead of directly crawling short URLs found on web pages, we "crowdsource" the collection to a large pool of real web users. To this end, we developed and deployed a publicly-available web service providing a much-needed feature, that is, a preview of a short URL's landing page. While browsing the Web, our users submitted 24,953,881 distinct short URLs to our servers automatically, via browser add-ons. Although the users in our dataset rarely stumbled upon malicious short URLs, we found some patterns that characterize malicious short URLs: The use of multiple short URLs that point to the same malicious URL is quite common; in contrast, benign URLs are typically aliased less frequently. Also, malicious short URLs remain active longer than benign short URLs. More precisely, we noticed that the difference in time between the first and latest appearance of a malicious short URL—regardless if it migrates intermittently across several pages—is longer than that of benign short URLs.

In summary, this paper makes the following contributions:

- We analyzed the countermeasures adopted by URL shortening services, and show how these are not adequate against pages that expose their malicious content later in time.
- We conduct the first user-centric collection of short URLs that includes the vast majority of shortening services, comprising more than 7,000 real web users.
- To the best of our knowledge, we are the first to broadly analyze the impact of malicious short URLs on users. Thus, our measurements are a complement toward the understanding of how short URLs are used.
- We assess whether there are typical usage patterns that cybercriminals may leverage to drive their campaigns via short URLs. For this, we use our dataset to calculate global rankings and statistics about usage patterns, along with a fine-grained categorization of websites that contain both short and long URLs.

2. CURRENT COUNTERMEASURES

Our first goal is to understand what (if any) measures are taken by shortening services to prevent malicious URLs from being shortened and, if they are shortened, the amount of time it takes for such URLs to be flagged and removed. To this end, we submitted three types of malicious URLs to the most popular short URL services that had a public API. More specifically, we submitted 10,000 URLs (2,000 for each of the five shortening services examined), picked randomly, among those that were recently submitted to Wepawet and that delivered drive-by-download exploits targeted at vulnerabilities in web browsers and browser plugins (e.g., Adobe Flash, Java). In addition, we submitted 10,000 phishing URLs that were online and tracked by PhishTank, and 10,000 URLs that were recently observed in spam emails that we obtained from Spamhaus. The purpose of examining three types of URLs was to determine whether URL shortening services block one or more classes of threats. After submitting the URLs, we first recorded whether the shortening service allowed us to shorten the URL. Then, if the service shortened the URL, we tracked whether the corresponding short URL could be expanded on a daily basis for a four week period.

In addition to the URLs mentioned above, we also submitted 10 URLs of each type that we manually reviewed to ensure that they were actually still delivering live exploits at the time of submission, as it is common that a malicious URL, once discovered, is brought to the attention of a site administrator and removed. We ran the analyses discussed in the remainder of this section on both the large and small set of URLs; as the results we obtained were consistent, we present the results obtained for the larger dataset. An overview of the results of our measurements is shown in Tab. 1. Interestingly, the most popular service, bit.ly, accepted all the malicious URLs we submitted. Among the services that employs countermeasures, is.gd is particularly effective against spam, as it prevented the vast majority of spam URLs that we submitted from being shortened., while migre.me seems to perform some kind of phishing filtering on submitted URLs.

The situation changes significantly when looking at the warnings that are displayed when short URLs are accessed (expanded), as shown in Tab. 2. Overall 2,049 shortened malicious URLs were blacklisted after the submission by these services (about 21.45% of the 9,551 that passed the submission). Here, bit.ly covers a significant fraction of all malicious URLs: It indeed expands a short URL unless it believes the target is malicious. Overall, all services had quite effective spam URL detection systems. We were also rather surprised that goo.gl, in late 2010 when we were able to test it, was not as effective at blocking malware and phishing as (at least) Google's own blacklist.

Summary: bit.ly was the only one that flagged almost all malicious URLs that we shortened, although we recall that they were all accepted for shortening with no checks upon

Service	Malware		Phishing		Spam	
	#	%	#	%	#	%
bit.ly	2,000	100.0	2,000	100.0	2,000	100.0
durl.me	1,999	99.9	1,987	99.4	1,976	98.8
goo.gl*	2000	99.9	994	99.4	1,000	100.0
is.gd	1,854	92.7	1,834	91.7	364	18.2
migre.me	1,738	86.9	1,266	63.3	1,634	81.7
tinyurl.com	1,959	99.5	1,935	96.8	587	29.4
Overall	9,550	95.5	9,022	90.2	6,561	65.6

Table 1: Number and percentage of malicious URLs that were accepted for shortening by the top services. Overall, 25,133 malicious URLs were accepted for shortening, accounting for about 83.78% of the 30,000 submitted.

Service	Malware	Phishing	Spam
bit.ly	0.05	11.3	0.0
durl.me	0.0	0.0	0.0
goo.gl*	66.4	96.9	78.7
is.gd	1.08	2.27	0.8
migre.me	0.86	14.0	0.0
tinyurl.com	0.66	0.7	2.04
Overall	21.45	26.39	31.38

Table 2: Shortened malicious URLs expanded without warnings when accessed. (*) We tested goo.gl in late 2010, whereas the results for the remainder shorteners are up to date (late 2011), when Google introduced a CAPTCHA that prevented automated submissions.

submission. On the other hand, is.gd prevented the majority of malicious URLs from being shortened when submitted—probably using lightweight, blacklist-based checks.

2.1 Deferred Malicious URLs

We measured whether shortening services retroactively analyze malicious URLs, that is, we determined if these services perform any repeated verification of the safety of the long URLs to which their existing short URLs point to. Thus, we set up a web page that served benign HTML content for a period of three days; this page's URL contained 32 random characters to ensure that no legitimate users accidentally stumbled upon the URL. After the third day, we modified our page to redirect to a web site serving non-legitimate content (i.e., malicious, spam or phishing content). We discovered that all the shortening services that we tested did not detect the previously-benign page that we modified to redirect visitors to a malicious site. Surprised by this finding, we set up 3,000 distinct web pages hosted at random domains and URLs and fed each service with all of them, totaling 1,000 distinct short URLs per service for a total of 15,000 short URLs overall. After 72 hours we modified each page so it redirected to a malicious site. More precisely, we used 1,000 unique URLs serving drive-by exploits, 1,000 phishing pages, and 1,000 spam URLs. In other words, after 72 hours, the short URLs became active aliases of the set of 3,000 malicious URLs. We monitored the redirection chain of each short URL on a weekly basis to determine which shortening services displayed an alert or blocked the redirection—as a result of a security check performed *after* the shortening.

From our results in Tab. 3 we notice that only 20% of the malicious URLs were blocked by the shortening service when we accessed them after they became malicious—this 20% is actually due to the fact that durl.me *always* displays a preview for a short URL, regardless of whether the URL is benign or malicious, which is by not a very effective security mechanism. The other services, however, did not block any malicious short URL, neither at submission time nor after they were modified.

Summary: The most popular shortening services verify the URLs only upon submission, and an attacker can evade this check by shortening a benign URL that will begin to redirect to a malicious page a few moments later. As we further elaborate in §7, believe that URL shortening services should periodically sanitize past short URLs, so that benign pages turning malicious can be detected. Clearly, this is not an easy task as it presents the typical challenges of client-side threat analysis (e.g., cloaking, fingerprinting, evasion) [9].

Threat	Shortened	Blocked	Not Blocked
Malware	5,000	20%	80%
Phishing	5,000	20%	80%
Spam	5,000	20%	80%
Overall	15,000	20%	80%

Table 3: Deferred malicious short URLs submitted and percentage of blocked versus not blocked ones. The 20% is simply due to the fact that durl.me displays a default warning for any URL benign or malicious; as a result 1,000 out of 5,000 URLs per threat category are naïvely "blocked" by this mechanism.

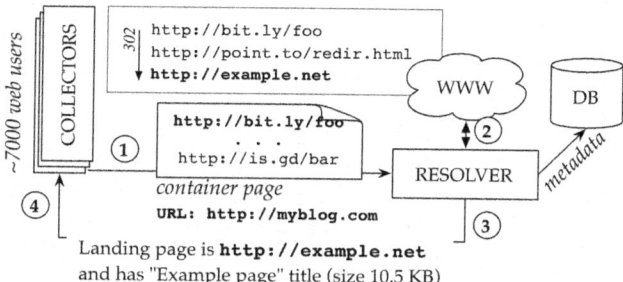

Figure 1: Overview of our collection approach.

We conducted the experiments described in this section in April 2011 and repeated them in April 2012. Alarmingly, we obtained statistically-similar results, showing that none of the shortening services changed their security measures against dangerous short URLs.

3. GOALS & MEASUREMENT APPROACH

Alarmed by our security assessment discussed in Section 2, we wanted to analyze short URLs at a larger scale, to understand how they are used with malicious intents. Unlike previous work, we concentrate on the clients' perspective, so that we can characterize also the usage habits: To this end, we collect short URLs while clients access web pages that contain short URLs. Moreover, we do not limit our analysis to a selection of shortening services (e.g., the most popular ones) nor narrow our attention on short URLs published on a few, specific online social networks and news aggregators (e.g., Twitter). Instead, we cover a wide variety of URL shortening services, up to 622, whose URLs appear in thousands distinct websites.

Our collection system comprises a browser add-on (named "collector") and a centralized short URL resolver. The *collector* analyzes container pages while the user browses the Web. The *container page* is a web page that, when rendered on a browser, displays or contains at least one short URL. Each collector submits short URLs to our resolver, along with a timestamp, URL of the container page, and client IP address. The *resolver* finds the respective *landing page*.

Our add-on works on Google Chrome, Mozilla Firefox, Opera[2], and any browser that support JavaScript-based add-ons. When the browser renders a page, the add-on searches its DOM for short URLs and submits them to our resolver along with the container page URL. The add-on instantiates contextual tooltips associated to each short URL submitted. These tooltips are revealed whenever the mouse cursor hovers on a resolved short URL. The tooltip displays details about the landing page (e.g., URL, size, title, and content type). Users can also contribute by reporting suspicious short URLs by clicking on a "flag as suspicious" link on the tooltip. This action is recorded in our database.

For each short URL received, our resolver obtains the landing page URL, title, size, and content type (e.g., HTML, XML, image), by visiting each short URL with a mechanized browser that follows and tracks redirections. When the re-

---
[2]We released our add-on after approval from the Mozilla community. The code base is the same, although we had to adapt it to the various browsers with minor adjustments.

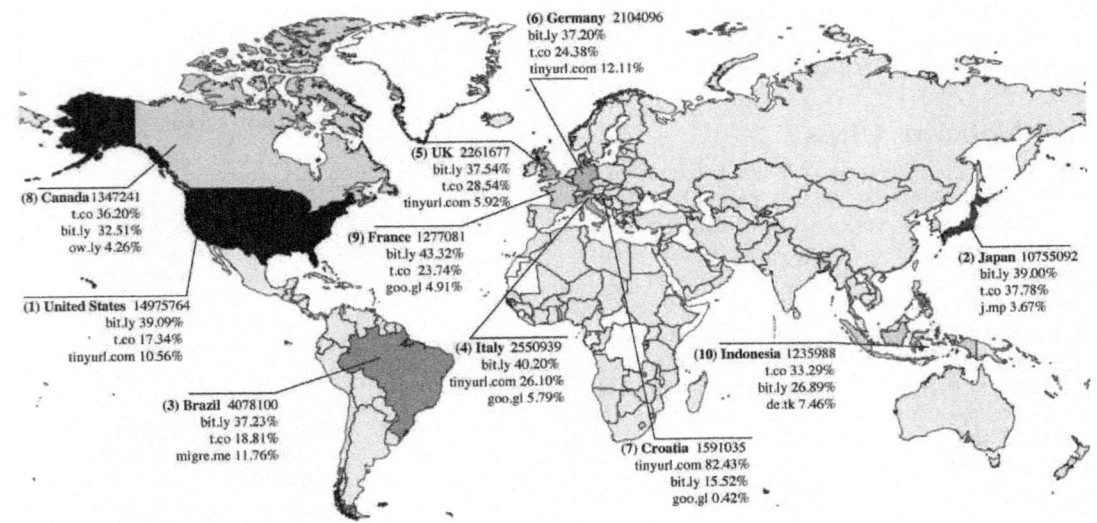

Figure 2: Contributors' geographical location.

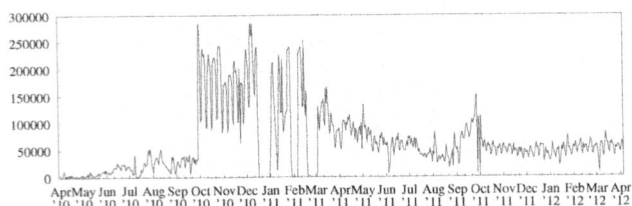

Figure 3: Log entries per day between late March 2010 and April 2012.

Distinct URLs		Log entries	
10,069,846	bit.ly	24,818,239	bit.ly
4,725,125	t.co	12,054,996	t.co
1,418,418	tinyurl.com	5,649,043	tinyurl.com
816,744	ow.ly	2,188,619	goo.gl
800,761	goo.gl	2,053,575	ow.ly
638,483	tumblr.com	1,214,705	j.mp
597,167	fb.me	1,159,536	fb.me
584,377	4sq.com	1,116,514	4sq.com
517,965	j.mp	1,066,325	tumblr.com
464,875	tl.gd	1,045,380	is.gd

Table 4: The 10 most popular services ranked by number of log entries in our database, and number of distinct short URLs collected. Highlighted rows indicate services at the same rank.

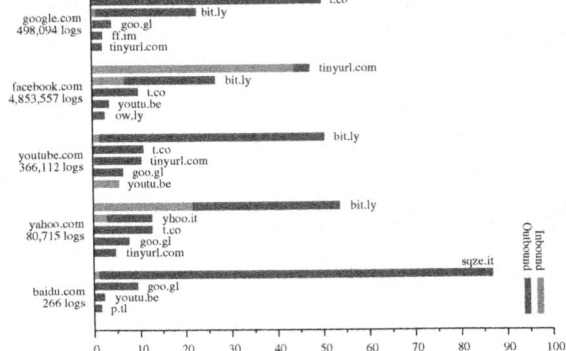

Figure 4: Top 5 services by percentage of log entries of outbound short URLs of **Alexa** top 5 domains. Light gray bars are the portion of logs of outbound short URLs contained that redirect to pages within the same domain (i.e., self loops).

solver receives an HTTP 200 response, it assumes that the landing page has been reached and no further redirections follow. The resolver then extracts the relevant data from the landing page's source code and saves the redirection chain. In addition, we store the collectors' IP addresses for aggregation purposes. The completion of the whole procedure may take up to a few seconds, depending on network conditions and responsiveness of the servers that host the landing and intermediate pages. For this reason, we deployed 100 load-balanced, parallel resolvers along with a caching layer (that stores results for 30 minutes) that ensures short response times. According to the measurements reported in [2], a short URL random suffix, which is its identifier, takes much longer to expire and get recycled. When the cache expires, we retain a snapshot of the log entry (i.e., the history of each short URL).

In summary, our service takes short URLs as input from clients and returns the aliased landing page. These "expansion" services have become useful for previewing the actual websites behind short URLs. The long time span of our measurement and the usefulness of our service—which is free of charge and publicly available through popular browser add-on marketplaces—allowed us to collect a unique, large dataset.

3.1 Measurement

1 We deployed our data collection infrastructure in March 2010 and, as of April 2012, our database contained 24,953,881 unique short URLs. More than 7,000 web users downloaded and installed our browser add-on and submitted short URLs; some users also contacted us and requested that we add support for additional shortening services. Around 100 out of the 622 that are currently supported by our system were

suggested by users. Our collection infrastructure receives data from 500 to 1000 active users every day. We store a record in our database for each short URL submitted. We refer to such records as *log entries*. Each log entry contains the source (geo-localized) IP address, the container page and landing page URLs, and the timestamp. Thus, each log entry corresponds to one short URL found in a given container page, and represents the fact that a user viewed the container page at a given time. We never retain identifying information possibly related to the specific user who submitted a log entry.

3.1.1 Overall Dataset Statistics

Fig. 3 shows the daily number of log entries whereas Fig. 2 shows the contributors' geographical location. Albeit we deployed the system in March 2010, the vast majority of users became active contributors starting from Oct 2010. However, at its humble beginnings our system received 20,000 to 50,000 log entries per day. At steady usage rates, we store an average of 90,000 log entries per day. Each of the 1,649,071 distinct IPs contributed around 37 requests on average, with a standard deviation of 7,157. Distinct IPs may not correspond to distinct users, either because multiple users could share the same sets of IPs (e.g., via NATs) or because of dynamic IP-assignment policies employed by ISPs. Our system experienced three outages due to database failures throughout one year: in late December 2010, in late January 2011, and between late February and March 2011. Nevertheless, we collected a large amount of short URLs useful to conduct the analysis described in the remainder of this paper.

Before analyzing security aspects of short URLs, we describe our dataset through four aggregated statistics: (1) distinct short URLs, (2) log entries in our database, (3) log entries of *inbound* short URLs (distinct short URLs pointing to the sites' pages), and (4) *outbound* short URLs (short URLs that are found in their container pages and that point to both external and internal pages). Shortening services with many distinct short URLs are more popular (i.e., they have become the "shortener of choice" for several users), whereas those characterized by many log entries have their short URLs posted on many popular container pages. As shown in Tab. 3 the top most popular services in our dataset are bit.ly, t.co and tinyurl.com, respectively. As expected, popular shortening services hold a steadily large number of short URLs, whereas site-specific shortening services exhibit a behavior that is typical of content shared through social networks. Fig. 4 shows the ranking of the top websites with respect to inbound and outbound short URLs.

4. RESULTS AND DISCUSSION

Our objective is to assess if malicious short URLs have distinctive features (§4.1) and typical usage patterns (§4.2) that criminals may leverage to target their campaigns.

4.1 Malicious Short URLs

First, we wanted to understand how frequently the users in our database encounter malicious short URLs in a page. For this, we leveraged four datasets: the Spamhaus DBL, a list of DNS domains that are known to host spam pages, Wepawet, a service able to detect drive-by-download exploit pages, Google Safe Browsing, a list of domains known for hosting malware or phishing sites, and PhishTank, a black-

Category	Short URLs	Long URLs	Ratio
Phishing	3,806	920	4.1
Malware	27,203	8,462	3.2
Spam	13,184	10,306	1.2

Blacklist	Phishing	Malware	Spam
Spamhaus	-	-	10,306
PhishTank	7	-	-
Wepawet	-	6,057	-
Safe Browsing	913	2,405	-

Table 5: Number of short and long URLs, respectively, classified as Phishing, Malware, and Spam. The dash '-' indicates that the blacklist in question provides no data about that threat.

list of URLs that are involved in phishing operations. For Spamhaus, we checked the domain against the database. For the other three blacklists, we checked the full URL. We break the landing URLs into three classes: spam, phishing, and malware, according to the dataset they were flagged in: URLs detected by Wepawet are flagged as malware, domains found in Spamhaus are marked as spam, and URLs from PhishTank as phishing. Google Safe Browsing classifies both phishing and malware sites. Tab. 4.1 summarizes the breakdown of malicious short URLs.

We observed 44,932 unique short URLs pointing to 19,216 malicious landing pages. By looking at the referrer, these URLs were hosted on 1,213 different domains. We provide a more detailed analysis on the container pages of malicious URLs in the next section. In total, the malicious URLs in our dataset have been rendered by 1,747 users in their container pages via our browser add-ons: 378 users (about 21.6%) were located in South Korea, 282 (about 16.1%) in the United States, and 98 (about 5.6%) in Germany.

Unsurprisingly, bit.ly is the top most common service, serving 10,392 malicious short URLs, followed by tinyurl.com with 1,389, and ow.ly with 1,327. As a side result, we also measured whether users perceive and report malicious short URLs, and found out that only 2,577 distinct short URLs have been signaled as malicious through our browser add-ons. Only 2 of these URLs were actually malicious according to at least one of the aforementioned blacklists.

4.1.1 Dissemination of Malicious Short URLs

We then analyzed how malicious pages are aliased through short URLs, and whether this trend changed over time. During the first year of our analysis, multiple short URLs were sometimes used to point to the same malicious page, although the average ratio was low. About 2.01 distinct short URLs were used to alias a malicious landing page, whereas we observed an average of 1.3 distinct short URLs per distinct *benign* landing page. Looking at a 2-year span period, however, those average numbers became very similar: about 1.17 unique short URLs per malicious page versus 1.14 unique short URLs per benign page. This comparison is better explained in Fig. 5(a) and Fig. 5(b), which show the empirical cumulative distribution function for the ratio of short URLs per landing page URL of legitimate vs. malicious pages of the two periods. The pattern here is that benign URLs used to have, in general, less short URLs pointing to them when compared to malicious URLs. Interestingly, in the second year of our measurement, the situation changed slightly. In

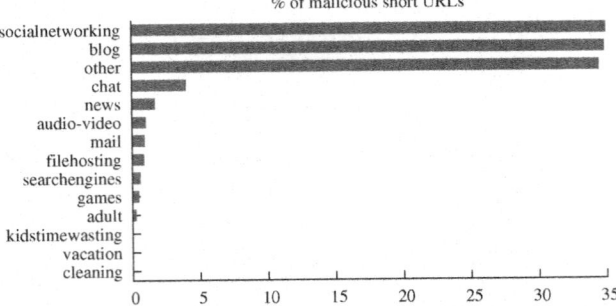

Figure 6: Malicious short URLs: Categories of container page ranked by the amount of short URLs they held. We assigned pages to categories as described in §4.2.

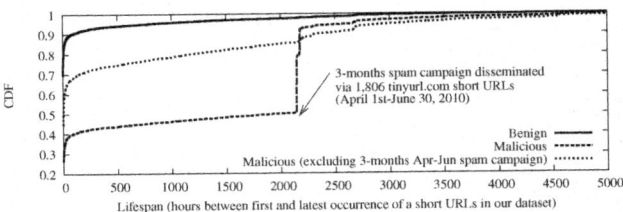

Figure 7: Delta time between first and latest occurrence of malicious versus benign short URLs. The "peak" indicates a high, about 50 %, amount of spam short URLs that lasted about three months. Malicious URLs are usually found on multiple different container pages even for extended periods of time, whereas benign short URLs follow the "one-day-of-fame effect" pattern.

particular, as shown in Fig. 5(b), the practice of using multiple short URLs pointing to the same spamming long URL is less used than in the past (Fig. 5(a)), where the aliasing of spam URLs was more evident.

We then analyzed the frequent container pages abused to publish malicious short URLs through the HTTP requests' `referer` issued while expanding the URLs (9,056 of these had a referrer specified).

As summarized in Fig. 6, the majority of those URLs were found on social networks. More precisely Twitter accounted for 5,881 URLs, 30% of the total. In second position there is Facebook—228 requests, accounting for 1.18% of the total. The third most common referrer is a Belgian news site with 137 requests, accounting for 0.7% of the total. We suspect that this website was victim of massive comment spam. It is also interesting to look at which sites, among those containing malicious short URLs, attracted the most number of users. Twitter is in first position, with 104 potential victims, followed by Facebook with 31, and by a hacking forum with 27 distinct IP addresses visiting it. This forum is probably another example of comment spam. However, these container pages, which are the most targeted ones, do not contain many short URLs, as detailed in Fig. 8: We can argue that the cyber criminals are not considering the "density" of short URLs per container page, but rather its popularity.

4.1.2 Lifespan of Malicious Short URLs

In the previous section we analyzed whether the dissemination of short URLs exhibits different characteristics between malicious and benign content, whereas in this section we compare them by means of timing patterns. We derived the maximum lifespan of each collected URL based on historical access logs to their container pages. We calculated the *maximum lifespan* (or simply lifespan) as the delta time between the first and last occurrence of each short URL in our database. More specifically, our definition of lifespan accounts for the fact that short URLs may disappear from some container pages and reappear after a while on the same or other container pages. Fig. 7 shows the empirical cumulative distribution frequency of the lifespan of malicious versus benign short URLs. About 95% of the benign short URLs have a lifetime around 20 days, whereas 95% of the malicious short URLs lasted about 4 months. For example, we observed a spam campaign spanning between April 1st and June 30th 2010 that involved 1,806 malicious short URLs redirecting to junk landing pages; this campaign lasted about three months until removed by tinyurl.com administrators. The Message-Labs Intelligence Annual Security Report [1] for that year corroborates our findings: The Storm botnet, which made a significant reappearance in April 2010, seems to be the culprit of this massive spam campaign that contains several shortened URLs.

For the sake of clarity, we removed short URLs involved in such spam campaign from the second dashed curve in Fig. 7; nevertheless, we notice that malicious short URLs last longer than benign URLs, in general. Recall that each short URL may have different container pages at the same point in time, and these can vary over time. Also recall that the longevity of short URLs on each container pages is quite low, as observed in [2] by Antoniades et al. A short URL can make its first appearance on a certain page, disappear to make room for new pages, and reappear a few moments later (even) on different container pages. From this observation, we can argue that, from the miscreants' point of view, the lifespan as we calculate it—across different container pages—seems to be of more importance than the lifespan on a single container page. In fact, short URLs that have a longer lifespan—regardless if they migrate intermittently across several pages—have higher chances of receiving visits from a large audience while remaining stealthy even months after publication. However, those URLs that survive on very popular pages only for a few hours may have their one day of fame before disappearing or being deleted by the container page administrators.

As detailed in §5, we do not track clicks on short URLs. Nevertheless, our collection method ensures that short URLs are tracked as soon as they appear the web pages visited by the users in our large pool. This ensures us good visibility

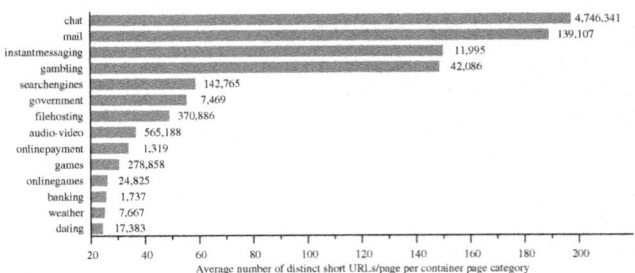

Figure 8: Categories of container page ranked by the average number of short URLs/page they held. The total number of distinct short URLs is also shown.

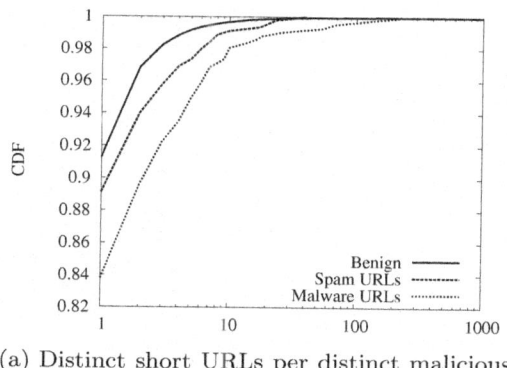
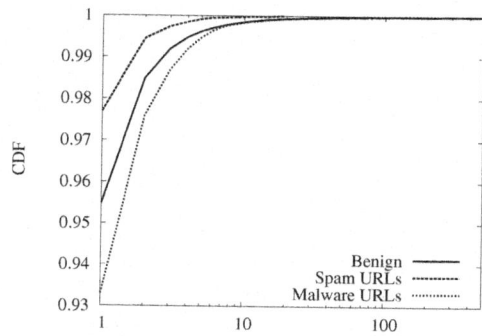

(a) Distinct short URLs per distinct malicious or benign landing URL from April 2010 to April 2011.

(b) Distinct short URLs per distinct malicious or benign landing URL from April 2010 to April 2012.

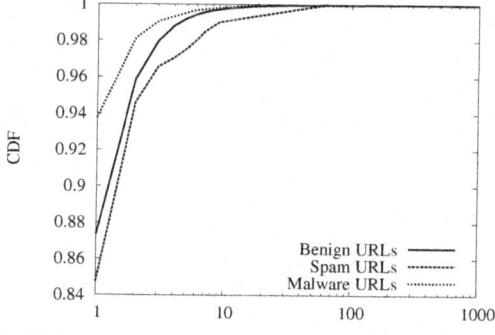
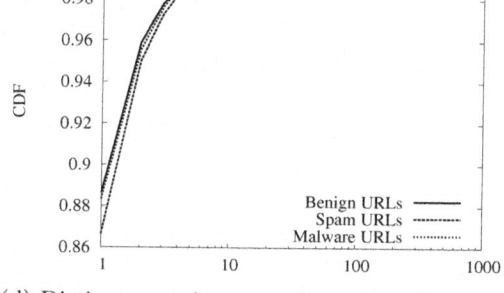

(c) Distinct containers per distinct malicious or benign short URL from April 2010 to April 2011.

(d) Distinct containers per distinct malicious or benign short URL from April 2010 to April 2012.

Figure 5: Comparison of the number of distinct short URLs per unique landing page (a, c) and distinct container page per unique short URL (b, d) after 1 year (a, b) and after 2 years (c, d). The distribution have changed over time: (a) spam pages were generally aliased with a larger number of short URLs than benign pages; (b) in the following year spammers did not to alias their pages as much as before. Also, (c) spam short URLs used to be spread over a larger number of container pages than benign short URLs; however, (c) they now exhibit the same distribution as their benign counterpart. We may argue that short URLs are not seen anymore as a valuable mean of aliasing spam pages.

over their evolution. This is corroborated by the statistics about the abuse of short URLs found in latest three APWG reports [12–14]: After a growing trend, at the beginning of our measurement (2010), the subsequent reports highlight a stable (2011) and decreasing (2012) trend.

4.2 The Short URLs Ecosystem

As part of their research, Antoniades and colleagues in [2] have analyzed the category of the pages to which bit.ly and ow.ly short URLs typically point to, along with the category of the container page, that they had available for bit.ly URLs only. They assigned categories to a selection of URLs. We did a similar yet more comprehensive analysis by characterizing all the short URLs that we collected by means of the categories described in the following.

Categorizing an arbitrary-large number of websites automatically is a problem that has no solution. However, our goal was to obtain a coarse-grained categorization. To this end, we relied on community-maintained directories and blacklists. More precisely, we classified the container pages (about 25,000,000 distinct URLs) and landing pages (about 22,000,000 distinct URLs) using the DMOZ Open Directory Project (http://www.dmoz.org) and URLBlacklist.com. The former is organized in a tree structure and includes 3,883,992 URLs: URLs are associated to nodes, each with localized, regional mirrors. We expanded these nodes by recursively merging the URLs found in these mirrors. The latter complements the DMOZ database with about 1,607,998 URLs and domains metadata. URLBlacklist.com is used by web-filtering tools such as SquidGuard (http://www.squidguard.org) and contains URLs belonging to clean categories (e.g., gardening, news), possibly undesired subjects (e.g., adult sites), and also malicious pages (i.e., 22.6% of the sites categorized as "antispyware", 18.15% of those categorized as "hacking", 8.29% of pages falling within "searchengine" domains, and 5.7% of the sites classified as "onlinepayment" are in this order, the most rogue categories according to an analysis that we run through McAfee SiteAdvisor [3]). Overall, we ended up with 74 categories. For clearer visualization, we selected the 48 most frequent categories. These include, for example, "socialnetworking," "adult," "abortion," "contraception," "chat," etc. We reserved the word "other" for URLs belonging to the less meaningful categories that we removed, or for URLs

---
[3] http://siteadvisor.com/sites/

Service	Most freq.	%	Least frequent	%
bit.ly	News	23.56	Naturism	$8.3 \cdot 10^{-4}$
	Audio-video	10.62	Contraception	$7.7 \cdot 10^{-4}$
	Socialnet	9	Astrology	$1.6 \cdot 10^{-4}$
t.co	Audio-video	29.42	Naturism	$1.07 \cdot 10^{-3}$
	File-hosting	27.43	Anti-spyware	$8.89 \cdot 10^{-4}$
	News	17.48	Contraception	$1.78 \cdot 10^{-4}$
tinyurl	News	24.08	Contraception	$4.5 \cdot 10^{-3}$
	Audio-video	10.61	Naturism	$6.29 \cdot 10^{-4}$
	File-hosting	9.36	Childcare	$2.51 \cdot 10^{-4}$
goo.gl	News	19.10	Gardening	$3.34 \cdot 10^{-3}$
	Audio-video	12.23	Weapons	$1.69 \cdot 10^{-3}$
	Socialnet	11.65	Naturism	$1.69 \cdot 10^{-3}$
ow.ly	News	23.38	Contraception	$2.5 \cdot 10^{-3}$
	Socialnet	12.84	Childcare	$1.32 \cdot 10^{-3}$
	Audio-video	10.03	Naturism	$1.32 \cdot 10^{-3}$

Table 6: Most- and least-popular landing page categories for the top 5 shortening services. There is an overlap between categories, so percentages do not necessarily add up to 100%.

that remained unclassified. Note that each URL can belong to multiple categories.

4.2.1 Frequent and Infrequent Categories

Tab. 4.2.1 details the most and least frequent categories of the landing pages pointed to by short URLs of the top services. We notice that the five most popular services are used to refer to various categories including news, audio-video content, blog, and online social networks. However, the majority of short URLs collected come from user-authored content (e.g., online social networks, blog posts), mainly because these sites are very popular (e.g., Facebook). We also provide a different viewpoint by plotting the number of short URLs *per page* (Fig. 8).

We notice that short URLs are seldom used as aliases of reference, science, and health-related pages. A possible explanation could be that users may have somehow perceived that, as short URLs shall expire sooner or later, they are not reliable for spreading really important content (e.g., health). Secondly, and more importantly, users post short URLs in email and chat messages, weather sites, search-engine pages (including all *.google.com pages), do-it-yourself sites, and news pages. In summary, the majority of short URLs point to content that expires quickly. Therefore, from a security viewpoint, real-time countermeasures against malicious short URLs such as WARNINGBIRD [8] are of paramount importance and much more effective than blacklists. As detailed in Fig. 6, however, the categories that were most targeted by malicious short URLs in 2010–2012 are social networks and blogs.

4.2.2 Content-category Change

To understand how web pages are interconnected through short URLs, we analyzed whether clicking on a short URL brings the user to a landing page of a category that differs from the category of the container page (e.g., from a news website to a file-hosting website).

In Fig. 9, the top 50 shortening services are ranked by the median frequency of category change (plotted as a dot). More precisely, for each service and for each category, we calculated the fraction of short URLs that result in a "change of content category"—such fraction is then normalized by the

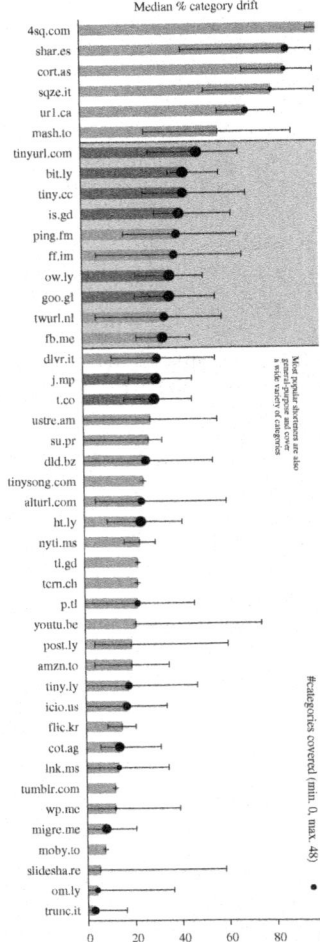

Figure 9: Frequency of change of category (median with 25- and 75-percent quantiles) and number of categories covered (size of black dot) of the top 50 services. The most popular, general-purpose shortening services highlighted are characterized by an ample set of categories (close to 48, which is the maximum) and short URLs that, in 32–48% of the cases, are published on pages having categories different from the landing page category.

total number of unique short URLs. Then, we derived the 25- and 75-percent quantiles to define a confidence interval around the median; this is useful to visually highlight how frequencies are distributed. Values close to 100% are not plotted for the sake of clarity. Services with 0–30% change frequency typically deal with a small set of categories and have short URLs often posted on websites of similar subjects. For example, flic.kr is used exclusively within the Flickr ecosystem; therefore, it covers very few categories and exhibits a very low change frequency, meaning that its short URLs are posted on websites that regard the same subjects, or even on Flickr directly. Another popular example is nyti.ms. On the opposite side, services with values above 50% also cover a small set of categories. However, differently from the first tier (i.e., 0–30%), we notice that the categories of the containers of these short URLs rarely match the categories of their landing pages. This is the case, for example, of 4sq.com

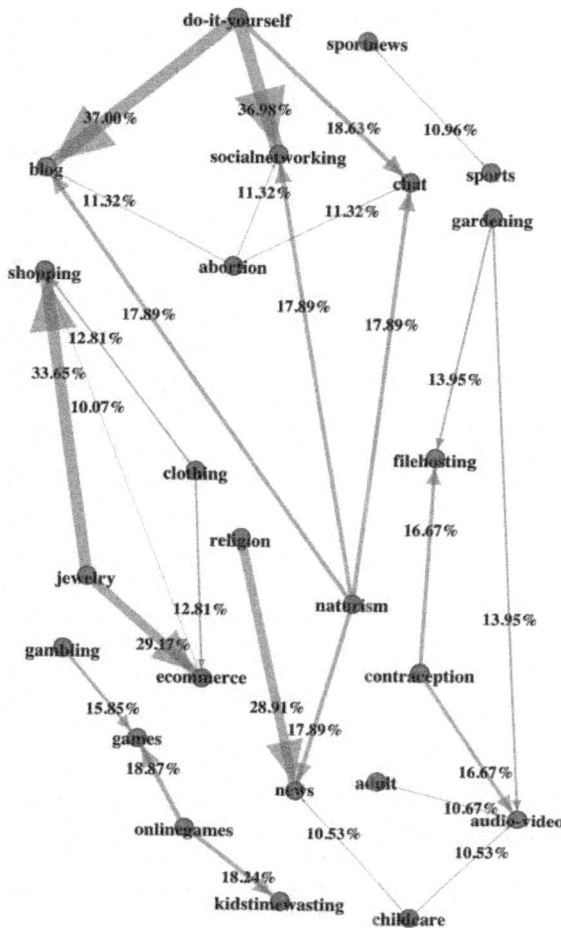

Figure 10: Digraph showing the connections between container- and landing-page categories. The edges' thickness expresses the frequency of finding short URLs between each nodes pair. For the sake of visualization, we removed edges with weight below 10 % and isolated nodes.

ρ	Category	ρ	Category
0.00	abortion	0.07	religion
0.00	antispyware	0.08	personalfinance
0.00	cellphones	0.10	gambling
0.00	childcare	0.14	government
0.00	contraception	0.16	medical
0.00	do-it-yourself	0.16	vacation
0.00	naturism	0.18	onlinegames
0.01	gardening	0.22	onlinepayment
0.01	hacking	0.22	sportnews
0.01	instantmessaging	0.30	searchengines
0.01	jobsearch	0.33	dating
0.01	pets	0.47	kidstimewasting
0.01	weapons	0.55	sports
0.02	artnudes	0.59	adult
0.02	drugs	0.60	games
0.02	jewelry	0.73	ecommerce
0.02	onlineauctions	0.78	shopping
0.02	weather	0.82	blog
0.03	mail	0.82	socialnetworking
0.04	banking	0.83	chat
0.04	cleaning	0.88	news
0.04	clothing	0.90	filehosting
0.06	drinks	0.92	audio-video
0.07	culinary	1.00	astrology

Table 7: Ranking of categories by the ratio of incoming and outgoing connections via short URLs.

(about 100%), whose short URLs always bring from online social-networking sites to pages categorized as "other". The most popular shortening services (e.g., bit.ly, goo.gl, ow.ly) fall into the second tier (i.e., 32–48%), together with those services that cover a wide variety of categories, and typically interconnect pages of different categories. The most general-purpose services are those that are more abused to create aliases of malicious URLs: Here is indeed where we found the vast majority of malicious short URLs. Unfortunately, as we argument in §2, general-purpose shortening services rely on ineffective countermeasures.

4.2.3 Non-obvious Uses of Short URLs

We also analyzed how short URLs interconnect together pages of different categories, to understand whether some categories have a majority of container or landing pages. To this end, we calculated the average frequency of category change from the perspective of the container page and landing page. With this data we created a weighted digraph with 48 nodes, each corresponding to a category. The weights are the frequencies of change, calculated between each pair of categories—and normalized over all the short URLs and pages within each category. We then calculated the average weight of incoming, In(cat), and outgoing, Out(cat), edges for each category cat, and finally derive the ratio $\rho(cat) = \frac{\text{In}(cat)}{\text{In}(cat)+\text{Out}(cat)}$. When $\rho \to 0$, the category has a majority of outgoing short URLs (i.e., many container pages of such category), whereas $\rho \to 1$ indicates that the category has a majority of incoming short URLs (i.e., many landing pages of such categories). The digraph is shown on Fig. 10.

As summarized in Tab. 7, there are clearly categories that exhibit a container-like usage, that is, they typically contain more outgoing short URLs than incoming short URLs. Besides a few extreme cases, which are mostly due to the scarcity of short URLs, container-like categories include, for instance, "onlineauctions," "mail" (web based emails contain outgoing short URLs more often than being referred to by short URLs), and "hacking."

Summary: Categories that we would anecdotally consider as aggregators (i.e., containers) of short URLs are actually more often used as landing pages. The most notable example is "socialnetworking" ($\rho = 0.82$), which we would expect to have many outgoing links as people share lots of resources through them. Instead, it turns out that, from a global viewpoint, this is no longer true. As expected, landing pages of a category with a high ρ (e.g., "socialnetworking", "blog", "audio-video") are the most obvious target of attacks: We indeed found that many short URLs that point to malicious resources have their landing page within these categories.

5. LIMITATIONS AND FUTURE WORK

Some research questions that need further answers include, for instance, to what extent shortening services have a vantage point in predicting trending topics. Indeed, shortening services are the very first services that receive important URLs from users, a few instants before a tweet is actually created.

Another limitation is that we collect short URLs when container pages are visited rather than when short URLs are visited. In addition to privacy concerns, in this initial work we decided to collect short URLs from visited container pages in order to collect a large amount of short URLs. Indeed, we can realistically assume that users follow a subset of the short URLs contained in each page. Therefore, although we do not know exactly what short URLs are clicked by users, such short URLs are always considered in our measurement.

A technical limitation of our current implementation is that the mechanized browser used to resolve the landing page's URL acts as a normal browser would do, except for redirections implemented via (timed) JavaScript or Adobe Flash; these redirection mechanisms are not used by popular shortening services—except for ad-supported ones (e.g., adf.ly)—and are not reliably and efficiently supported by any of the publicly-available, mechanizable browsers. We experimented with scripting libraries such as Watir/webdriver, but they need about ten times the memory resources that our headless solution, which is faster and more reliable than Watir/webdriver.

6. RELATED WORK

We already mentioned the main points of [2] throughout this paper. The authors collected about 8.5M distinct short URLs by periodically crawling for bit.ly URLs on Twitter and by brute-forcing the key space of ow.ly. Although these services are the most popular, part of the statistics analyzed were actually calculated from the data offered by bit.ly, and thus may represent a service-centric view of the overall usage.

In [15] the authors analyzed a corpus of Twitter data (2006–2009) to discover patterns of word-of-mouth propagation of URLs among Internet and social network users. Short URLs were nearly 75% of the URLs on Twitter in 2009, when TinyURL and ow.ly were the top services. Back then, services linked to major social networks (e.g., t.co, fb.me) did not exist yet. Our distribution is consequently very different (see Tab. 3). In addition, they do not enumerate the shortening services, but rely on heuristics to identify them.

In [3] the authors checked how many phishing scams are posted on Twitter, and hidden behind short URLs. They leveraged PhishTank and the bit.ly API to perform their analysis. For this reason, their analysis is limited to a single service (although the biggest one). They found out that most phishing campaigns of this kind target social-network credentials rather than other services.

Klien and Strohmaier in [7] did a geographical analysis of short URLs, yet taking into account only a specific shortening service (qr.cx). Their database, however, as stated by the authors themselves may be biased in terms of location, user preferences and URLs content. Our dataset allowed us to calculate these and other types of aggregated statistics. An advantage of our approach is that we monitor all known shortening services, obtaining therefore less biased results.

In [11] the authors started from a list of shortening services widely used on Twitter and demonstrated that short URLs have implications both in terms of information disclosure (secrecy of the URL being shortened) and security. They assessed the possibility and easiness of enumerating short URLs from widespread shortening services, thus exposing URLs that the users may have wanted to keep secret. The authors also demonstrated that short URLs may also expose the user to security risks, such as hacking of the shortening services to change the redirection chain, or the possibility for the shortening service provider to leverage cookies to track the user. This analysis, however, mainly deals with implications inherent to shortening services design. Our work, instead, is entirely based on the user perspective and analyzes how the short URLs are used and what real security risks they pose.

On a dataset comprising 35 million distinct bit.ly URLs extracted from Twitter in Oct 2009, the authors of [6] observe that the quality of the landing pages is either high or very low. Frequently-tweeted URLs tend to be of very low quality. Although the authors do not detail the method used to detect spam short URLs, their conclusions disagree with our discussion in §4.1.2: According to their measurements, spam short URLs have shorter lifespan than those that point to clean content, whereas we observed the opposite. Recently, the Twitter stream was used as a source of URLs to develop and evaluate WarningBird [8], which analyzes the redirection chain of URLs and finds common "join points" (i.e., URLs that are shared by many redirection chains). The frequency of these join points is leveraged along with other features to train a supervised classifier that can tell malicious and benign URLs apart. The intuition is that these join points are limited in number and thus are easy to spot. This work is related to ours because it concentrates on short URLs, which cover the majority of URLs on Twitter. However, they focus on detecting malicious URLs in general, whereas we focus on assessing the threat level in the short URLs ecosystem. Similarly, [17] also focuses on detection of spam campaigns spread on social networks via (short) URLs. Among the 13 URL features extracted, the redirection chain is one of them (cfr., WarningBird).

Previous work also showed evidence about the abuse of short URLs. In [16] show that most spam campaigns leverage short URLs. Gao et al. in [4] focused on Facebook wall posts and analyzed the activity of about 3.5 million users and detected approximately 200,000 rogue posts (out of 187 million posts) with embedded URLs. The authors found short URLs in 10,041 posts, about 0.005% of the total posts analyzed. Although the authors collected a large amount of data, they concentrated on social networks, whereas our work has a broader viewpoint.

7. CONCLUSIONS

We have observed that, on a global scale, users are seldom exposed, while browsing, to threats spread via short URLs, or at least no more than they are exposed to the same threats spread via long URLs. Although we came across a relatively small number of malicious short URLs in the wild, we were able to evade the security measures currently adopted by the top shortening services to filter dangerous URLs, with a simple time-of-check to time-of-use attack. However, shortening services are not—and should not be—a definitive protection layer between users and malicious resources. In-the-browser defense tools such as blacklists can alert users before visiting malicious URLs, regardless of whether they are short or long URLs. Since it is very inefficient for shortening providers to monitor all their aliases periodically, we believe that this is not necessary when modern browsers are already prepared for counteracting known malicious URLs.

Acknowledgments. The authors are thankful to the reviewers, proofreaders, and to bit.ly, who provided a fast-track access to their API when needed. This work has been supported by the EU Commission through IST-216026-WOMBAT and FP7-ICT-257007 funded by the 7th FP. The opinions expressed in this paper are those of the authors and do not necessarily reflect the views of the EU Commission.

8. REFERENCES

[1] P. W. e. al. MessageLabs Intelligence: 2010 Annual Security Report. Technical report, Symantec, 2010.

[2] D. Antoniades, E. Athanasopoulos, I. Polakis, S. Ioannidis, T. Karagiannis, G. Kontaxis, and E. P. Markatos. we.b: The web of short URLs. In *WWW '11*, 2011.

[3] S. Chhabra, A. Aggarwal, F. Benevenuto, and P. Kumaraguru. Phi.sh/$oCiaL: the phishing landscape through short URLs. In *CEAS '11*. ACM Request Permissions, Sept. 2011.

[4] H. Gao, J. Hu, C. Wilson, Z. Li, Y. Chen, and B. Y. Zhao. Detecting and characterizing social spam campaigns. In *IMC '10*, pages 35–47, New York, NY, USA, 2010. ACM.

[5] C. Grier, K. Thomas, V. Paxson, and M. Zhang. @spam: the underground on 140 characters or less. In *CCS '10*, pages 27–37, New York, NY, USA, 2010. ACM.

[6] V. Kandylas and A. Dasdan. The utility of tweeted URLs for web search. In *WWW '10*, pages 1127–1128, New York, NY, USA, 2010. ACM.

[7] F. Klien and M. Strohmaier. Short links under attack: geographical analysis of spam in a URL shortener network. In *HT '12*. ACM Request Permissions, June 2012.

[8] S. Lee and J. Kim. WarningBird: Detecting Suspicious URLs in Twitter Stream. In *NDSS '12*, 2012.

[9] B. Livshits. Finding malware on a web scale. *Computer Network Security*, 2012.

[10] D. K. McGrath and M. Gupta. Behind phishing: an examination of phisher modi operandi. In *LEET '08*, pages 4:1–4:8, Berkeley, CA, USA, 2008. USENIX Association.

[11] A. Neumann, J. Barnickel, and U. Meyer. Security and Privacy Implications of URL Shortening Services. In *W2SP '11*, 2011.

[12] R. Rasmussen and G. Aaron. Global Phishing Survey: Trends and Domain Name Use in 1H2010. Technical report, APWG, Oct. 2010.

[13] R. Rasmussen and G. Aaron. Global Phishing Survey: Trends and Domain Name Use in 1H2011. Technical report, APWG, Nov. 2011.

[14] R. Rasmussen and G. Aaron. Global Phishing Survey: Trends and Domain Name Use in 1H2012. Technical report, APWG, Oct. 2012.

[15] T. Rodrigues, F. Benevenuto, M. Cha, K. Gummadi, and V. Almeida. On word-of-mouth based discovery of the web. In *Internet Measurement Conference*. ACM Request Permissions, Nov. 2011.

[16] G. Stringhini, C. Kruegel, and G. Vigna. Detecting spammers on social networks. In *Annual Computer Security Applications Conference*, pages 1–9, Austin, TX, USA, Dec. 2010. ACM Request Permissions.

[17] K. Thomas, C. Grier, J. Ma, V. Paxson, and D. Song. Design and evaluation of a real-time url spam filtering service. In *SSP '11*, pages 447–462. IEEE, 2011.

Know Your Personalization: Learning Topic level Personalization in Online Services

Anirban Majumder
Bell Labs Research, Bangalore, India
anirban.majumder@alcatel-lucent.com

Nisheeth Shrivastava
Bell Labs Research, Bangalore, India
nisheeth.shrivastava@alcatel-lucent.com

ABSTRACT

Online service platforms (OSPs), such as search engines, news-websites, ad-providers, etc., serve highly personalized content to the user, based on the *profile* extracted from her history with the OSP. Although personalization (generally) leads to a better user experience, it also raises privacy concerns for the user—she does not know what is present in her profile and more importantly, what is being used to personalize her content. In this paper, we capture OSP's personalization for an user in a new data structure called the *personalization vector* (η), which is a weighted vector over a set of *topics*, and present efficient algorithms to learn it.

Our approach treats OSPs as black-boxes, and extracts η by mining only their *output*, specifically, the *personalized* (for an user) and *vanilla* (without any user information) contents served, and the differences in these content. We believe that such treatment of OSPs is a unique aspect of our work, not just enabling access to (so far hidden) profiles in OSPs, but also providing a novel and practical approach for retrieving information from OSPs by mining differences in their outputs.

We formulate a new model called Latent Topic Personalization (LTP) that captures the personalization vector in a learning framework and present efficient inference algorithms for determining it. We perform extensive experiments targeting search engine personalization, using data from both real Google users and synthetic setup. Our results indicate that LTP achieves high accuracy (R-pre = 84%) in discovering personalized topics. For Google data, our qualitative results demonstrate that the topics determined by LTP for a user correspond well to his ad-categories determined by Google.

Categories and Subject Descriptors

H.2.8 [**Database Management**]: Database Applications—*Data mining*

Keywords

personalization; online service providers; topic model

1. INTRODUCTION

Personalization is being used by most on-line service platforms (OSPs) such as search, advertising, shopping etc. Their goal is to lure users by offering a better service experience customized to their individual interests. A popular trend is to employ profile based personalization, where OSPs build extensive profiles for the user (based on her past interactions such as search queries, browsing history, links shared, etc.) and personalize content using this profile. Several popular services employ such personalization, e.g. search[1], movie recommendations[2], etc.

While OSPs track rich user data in their histories alone, they can infer much more information about them by mining this raw data. Informally speaking, OSPs can determine a user's interests and biases on different categories, which can later be used (along with the history) for personalizing content for her. For example (see [20] for details), Google is shown to have inferred users political affiliations (republican or democratic) and use it to re-rank search results.

For a user, this raises a significant privacy concern—she does not know what was tracked in her history, what has been inferred, and more importantly, is currently being used to personalize her content. Moreover, as both the personalization techniques and the data they operate on are the key differentiators for the OSPs (their *secret sauce*), they do not reveal either of them, making it even harder for an user to understand how personalization is being done (for her).

In this paper, we aim at extracting a user's profile from the OSP. We model this profile as a weighted personalization vector over *topics*, where the weight on a topic indicates her interest in it (higher means more interested). Informally, a topic is any concept or phenomenon that the user could be interested in, e.g. a specific sport, preference over cuisines, favorite author, movie genre, etc.[3]

Our goal is not to reverse-engineer the OSP's inference algorithms. In fact, we treat the OSP as a *black-box* and assume that we only have access to its output, i.e. the (personalized) content served by the OSP to a user on different queries[4]. The central idea in our approach is to get both *personalized content* (served for the user) and *vanilla content* (served for a new/not logged in user) for the same query and analyze their differences. Through careful inspection of

---
[1] http://privacy.microsoft.com/en-us/Bing.mspx; http://support.google.com/websearch/bin/answer.py?answer=1710607.
[2] Netflix: http://www.netflixprize.com
[3] More specifically, we define it as a distribution over bag of words, a common definition in the topic modeling literature (see Section 3).
[4] The query could point to a static page, e.g. reviews and other information on a movie, or dynamically generated, e.g. search results.

these two types of content, we identify the hidden *user profile* (summarized through a weighted set of topics) used by the OSP to serve personalized content.

There is very little concrete information available on the techniques the OSPs use to personalize content. Our paper provides a novel approach to tackle this problem, giving insights into the hidden user profiles without the knowledge of the specific inference techniques used by the OSP or the history of the user. We believe that this idea of comparing the differences in output to extract the hidden personalized topics is a unique aspect of our paper and opens a new direction in privacy research that can be aimed at commercial OSPs.

As an example, consider the case of a search engine. For any search query, we can get the personalized and vanilla results by making the query from a browser with and without logging in, respectively. These results are basically two ranked lists with some urls in the latter moved up or down in the former (i.e. *re-ranked*), based on the user's profile. We study these re-rankings over multiple queries and determine the topics of interest for the user that can best explain these differences.

For the rest of the paper, we focus our attention on search engine personalization. However, our techniques can easily be extended to other services where a) we can observe both vanilla and personalized content and b) the content is offered as ranked lists of items (e.g. urls, movies, products, etc.). For example, we can apply it to movie recommendations by Netflix based on the personalized (and vanilla) ranked list of related movies presented when a user visits a particular movie page.

1.1 Search Personalization and Re-ranking

Although the exact details of personalization for search engines are not publically available, recent works in the web-search community have thrown some light on them [8, 23, 18]. The common underlying theme for these techniques is to first populate the vanilla result using the semantics of the query string and then personalize it by re-arranging the items in this list, using the profile information. Therefore, conceptually, the vanilla and personalized contents are re-ordering of the same set of items. We take advantage of this re-ranking of results to determine the topics present in the user's profile with the OSP.

It is important to observe that the assumption of vanilla and personalized results being re-rankings of same set of urls, does not preclude the generality of our approach. This assumption can easily be lifted by simply adding the extra urls in one list to the end of the other list[5]. The important point is that personalization, by definition, will affect the ranks of the results shown, which is what we use in this paper.

Note that the topics that we learn may not be explicitly maintained by the search engine (or an OSP in general); in fact their profile data could consist of parameters completely unrelated to, and may not even map to, our definition of topics. Our paper hinges on the intuition that a user profile can be succinctly captured by a set of topics that reflects her interests. Any search engine (or OSP) that personalizes results

---

[5]In our experiments with Google, only 15% of personalized results contain any extra result compared to vanilla, and even these contain on average only 14% extra urls (or, 1.4 urls for an avg. result size of 10).

based on her interests must give higher preference to the results matching these topics. Thus our approach of finding topic-level personalization is fairly generic—it can work with OSPs who do not necessarily maintain topic-based profiles of users and without the knowledge of the inference algorithms they use.

An alternate approach to recreate the user profile could be via mining the *inputs* to the search engine (i.e. the user's search query logs, results clicked, browsing history etc.)[8, 23, 22]. However, this approach has several shortcomings compared to us. First of all, it is very hard to catch up to the commercial techniques used by OSPs that are usually more advanced and rapidly evolving. Secondly, due to the proprietary nature of OSPs, it is not clear what algorithm or even what part of the history is being used by them. Finally, in many cases the history information may not be available publicly (i.e. while a Google user's search history is available, past ads served are not), limiting the effectiveness of these approaches. In contrast, our approach is agnostic to OSP's personalization scheme and can work even when the history is not public.

1.2 Our Contributions

The main contributions of the paper are as follows.

- We propose a new direction in privacy research that gives users a glimpse of their profile information being used by commercial OSPs to serve personalized content. We formally capture this information as a personalization vector over topics that provides a concise and accurate summary of the user profile.

- We propose a novel way to compute this personalization vector based on the personalized and vanilla content served by an OSP. This formulation treats the OSP as a *black-box* and hence can work with a variety of on-line services. We believe that this is a unique aspect of our work and can open a new direction for privacy research by enabling access to (so far hidden) profile information in OSPs.

- We present a probabilistic model (named Latent Topic Personalization, or LTP) that captures the intuition behind our approach. LTP is both expressive and leads to computationally efficient inference algorithms (LTP-INF and LTP-EM) that find the personalization vector on real data-sets.

- Our experiments with synthetic data-sets generated by a state-of-the-art personalization engine show that LTP can learn the personalization parameters very accurately, achieving on average 84% precision in learning personalized topics.

- We perform experiments on a novel real-life data-set containing the personalized and vanilla query results collected from 10 Google users. Our qualitative results demonstrate that the personalized topics determined by LTP for a user correspond well to his ad-categories determined by Google.

2. RELATED WORK

Search personalization: A large body of work exists on personalizing search results using user-profiles [8, 23, 18], that collectively give overwhelming evidence of its benefits. More recently, researchers have also explored creating profiles using topic models [22] and other textual information [25]. These works are not competitors of our paper, but rather serve as a motivation for us, as they highlight the existence and importance of profiles in the state-of-the-art in personalization.

Another body of work explores short-term and session based personalization [1, 8], that personalize based on user's current *intention*, based on his recent history or session. While such approaches are not aligned with our idea, there are two important points to note—a) they do no imply profile-based personalization does not happen, rather, they are typically used in conjunction with each other [1, 13], and b) since they are applicable only during a session, it is easy to remove their affect by making sure no coherent session is tracked during our data collection (by doing the queries in a random order or adding sufficient delays).

Researchers have also found that personalization is not always beneficial and have proposed various approaches, such as click-entropy [26, 27], dynamic user interests [13] and query difficulty [31], to filter queries that should not be personalized (irrespective of user's profile). Such filtering is very hard replicate in our approach since the output may not contain any information to model them. We therefore allow for existence of this hidden process in our model via a latent variable deciding (randomly) if personalization happens on a query (see Section 4.1 for details).

In a paper contemporary to ours, Hannak et al. [9], study the parameters (location, demographics, etc.) that effect personalization in Google search. While these parameters give insights on what *inputs* influence personalization in practice, it is very different from the topic-based approach we take to capture the hidden user profiles.

Topics Models: Although topic models are clearly a popular tool for processing textual information and have also been used in personalization, there is no work to our knowledge that models the *differences* in two documents (or two ranked set of documents) as us. A recent work by Bischof et al. [2] comes close—they find exclusive topics (that are sufficiently different from each other) so that the documents can be classified into a non-overlapping hierarchy. While this also involves finding topics which are present in some documents and not in others, it is still very different from our approach of finding a consistent (may not be exclusive) set of personalized topics that can differentiate personalized and vanilla content.

Privacy: Finally, our problem stems from the general area of privacy of user data. Various studies have highlighted problems of privacy in information leaks from OSPs[11, 17, 10]. Korolova et al. [10] showed how targeted ads can pinpoint individual users in Facebook, Mao et al. [17] analyzed tweets to find vacation plans and medical conditions for real users, etc. However, these studies are focused on finding instances of privacy leaks from the entire OSP network and do not help users understand leaks in their own account. Other approaches of privacy preserving personalization aim at building systems from scratch that ensure certain norms are preserved in the personalized output, e.g. grouping user profiles [29, 30] to preserve k-anonymity or making a differentially private recommender system[14]. Recently, Chen et al. [6] presented a more user centric approach that gives user control over fine grained categories (represented as a fixed hierarchical taxonomy) which they want personalization on.

These techniques, however, require the users to switch to these new systems which is not practical.

3. PROBLEM FORMULATION

In this section, we introduce our notations and define the technical problem that we consider in this paper.

3.1 Notation

Let $I = \{i_1, i_2, \cdots\}$ be the universe of all the *items* being present at the personalization server, where, an item might represent a url (for search engines like Google, Bing, etc.), a product web-page (for e-commerce sites like Amazon, Net-Flix, etc.) or an advertisement (for ad servers). For a query q, let π_q and σ_q denote the personalized and vanilla results. In the following discussion, we will often drop the subscript q, when the query is understood from the context.

As mentioned earlier, both π and σ are treated as permutations over a finite set of items $I' \subset I$. Technically, a ranking/permutation[6] is a bijection from a set to itself. For any permutation π, $\pi(i)$ denotes the item assigned at rank (position) i, hence $\pi = (\pi(1), \pi(2), \cdots)$. The notation $\pi^{-1}(d)$ denotes the rank i of an item $d \in I$ in π such that $\pi(i) = d$. For any two permutations π and σ, we use the notation $\sigma^{-1}(\pi(i))$ to denote the rank of the item $\pi(i)$ in σ. Observe that $\pi^{-1}(\pi(i)) = i$. We use S_n to denote the set of all permutation over n items.

We assume that there are T topics $\{\beta_1, \beta_2, \cdots, \beta_T\}$ in our system where each topic β_k is defined as a multinomial distribution over a fixed vocabulary V. For each word $w \in V$, we have a parameter $\beta_{k,w} = \Pr(w \mid \beta_k)$ such that $\sum_{w \in V} \beta_{k,w} = 1$. Each item[7] $i \in I$ is represented by its topic-map θ_i which is a multinomial distribution over the set of topics. By inspecting the components of θ_i, one can infer how related the item is to a particular topic.

We now describe our representation of topic-level user profile information. For each user u and topic $\beta_k \in \beta$, we associate a variable $\eta_{u,k} \in R$. It captures the importance of β_k (more relevant topics have higher values) for serving personalized content to u. The complete profile information (we name it as *latent personalization vector*) is denoted by $\eta_u = (\eta_{u,1}, \eta_{u,2}, \cdots, \eta_{u,T})$. We often drop the subscript u and refer to it simply as η whenever the user is understood from the context.

3.2 Problem

Our strategy to learn the personalization vector η is to repeatedly frame queries to the search engine and observe the difference between its vanilla and personalized results. For a given user u, we first sign-in to her account and submit a query. This gives the search engine an opportunity to personalize the result by using u's profile information and through this process, we obtain the personalized result π. Next, we submit the same query in an anonymized form, by removing all cookies from the http request, thus removing all account details (but keeping all other parameters same such as IP address, User-Agent, etc.). This time the server sends back the vanilla result σ. We expect that as this process is repeated many times, the cumulative difference between these two kinds of results will become statistically signifi-

---
[6]We often use them interchangeably.
[7]Specifically, the textual content or meta-data of the item.

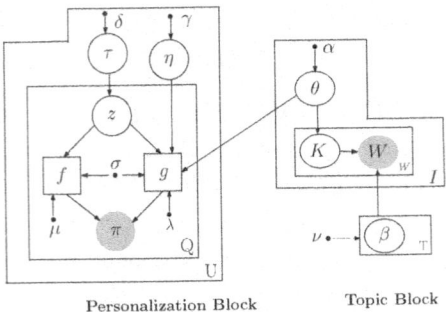

Figure 1: Graphical model representation of LTP.

cant and contain substantial evidence for η. In this paper, we study the following problem: *Given pairs of query results $(\sigma_1, \pi_1), (\sigma_2, \pi_2) \cdots (\sigma_m, \pi_m)$, how do we learn the latent personalization vector η, for a given user?*

Non-profile factors Although personalization normally yields its benefits by presenting more relevant results to the users, it is also known to be less effective and even detrimental in many cases. For example, while personalizing results are known to work well for short and ambiguous queries [24] where user searching same query may be looking for completely different things, for common and specific queries two users with very different profiles are normally looking for the same information and are satisfied with the same (ordering of) results. In such cases, even though user's profile implies re-ranking, the server may decide not to personalize. This creates a problem for our approach as a search engine's decision whether to personalize the result of a search query or not, is influenced not only by the topical content of the query result, but also through other filtering processes that are hidden from us.

We take care of this in our model by introducing a latent parameter that, during training phase, filters out such inexplicable events and reduces the noise in the personalization vector. In our experiments with the Google data-set, we found several instances of queries with results at higher ranks having higher "scores" (see Section 4 for definition of scores) the ones at lower ranks, that were not personalized, while another query with similar scores was personalized. Without this latent parameter, these instances would have reduced the effectiveness of learning η.

4. LTP MODEL

The goal of topic-based personalization learning is to capture the following information: topics on which personalization takes place and a weight vector corresponding to the degree of personalization on these topics. In addition, the approach has to scale with large number of queries. To meet these objectives, we first propose Latent Topical Personalization model (LTP) to study the problem from a Bayesian perspective. Following that, we develop efficient variational inference and estimation techniques for learning the parameters of this model.

4.1 Model Description

We now formally describe the proposed LTP model. LTP models (Figure 1) both topics and personalization. It involves a *topic block* to model the topical content creation of the items and a *personalization block* to model the personalized responses (i.e. $\pi_1, \pi_2, \cdots, \pi_m$).

Topic Block The topic block follows the description of standard topic models (c.f. LDA [3]) and we present it here for the sake of completeness. The generative process for the topic block is as follows

- For each topic $\beta_k, k = 1, 2 \cdots, T$
  1. Sample $\beta_k \sim Dirichlet(\nu)$.
- For each item $i \in I$
  1. Sample its topic-map $\theta_i \sim Gaussian(0, diag(\alpha^2))$.
  2. For each word position $j = 1 \cdots n_i$ for item i
     (a) Sample topic $K_{i,j}$ with $\Pr(K_{i,j} = k) \propto e^{\theta_{i,k}}$.
     (b) Sample word $W_{i,j} \sim Multinomial(\beta_{K_{i,j}})$.

The joint distribution for the topic-block can be written as

$$p(\theta, K, W, \beta \mid \alpha, \nu) = \prod_{i \in I} p(\theta_i \mid \alpha) \cdot \prod_{k=1}^{T} p(\beta_k \mid \nu)$$
$$\prod_{i \in I} \prod_{j=1}^{n_i} p(K_{i,j} \mid \theta_i) \cdot p(W_{i,j} \mid K_{i,j}, \beta_{1\ldots T}) \quad (1)$$

Personalization Block Our design of the personalization block is little more involved. The main difficulty stems from the non-profile based factors, which may lead to no re-ranking of results even when the user profile (i.e. η) indicates personalization should happen. In LTP, we achieve it by introducing a latent switch variable z (refer to Figure 1). Independently, for each query, we sample z, governed by a prior parameter τ and based on its value decide whether to allow topical personalization or not. The parameter τ is user-specific and controls the rate at which topical personalization takes place (for that user).

Based on the value of z, we pick a probability distribution over permutations and sample π from it. Probabilistic models on permutations have recently been applied to solve various problems related to ranking [21]. Probability distributions defined over permutations can be broadly categorized into two types—*distance based* and *score based*. In a distance based model [16], the probability of a permutation is defined according to its distance from a central permutation. They have rich expressive power as they can incorporate a wide variety of distance functions over permutations but are, in general, computationally inefficient.

Score based models [12], on the other hand, are very efficient as they divide permutation construction into stages and assign scores on each stage such that the final probability is a combination (multiplication) of stage-wise scores. However, being defined as a specific function over scores, they have limited expressive power e.g. they can not take into account any central permutation in the generative process. For LTP, we have a central permutation (vanilla list σ) and want to model π as being generated from it. Further, as explained later, we define scores on items as a function η. Therefore, we need a model which combines the notion of distance with scores and is computationally efficient.

The probability distribution f (Figure 1) is a process for generating the personalized response π, and is decomposed

σ	2	3	1
π	3	1	2

Items	1	2	3	π		
1st Stage	e^{-2}	e^0	e^{-1}	3		
2nd Stage	e^{-1}	e^1		3	1	
3rd Stage			1	3	1	2

$$f(\pi \mid \sigma) = 0.03$$

Figure 2: An example illustrating the steps of f. We have assumed $\mu = 1$. At each stage, the actual outcome is marked in blue and the most likely outcome is marked in red.

into sequential stages. Observed that (see Figure 1) this process is activated only if $z = 0$, thereby, implying no topical personalization should happen. In the first stage, we pick the item $\pi(1)$ with probability $\frac{\exp(\mu(1-\sigma^{-1}\pi(1)))}{\sum_{j\geq 1}\exp(\mu(1-\sigma^{-1}\pi(j)))}$. Note that this probability is maximum when the two permutations agree with the first position i.e. $\pi(1) = \sigma(1)$. However, if we happen to pick some other item i.e. $\pi(1) \neq \sigma(1)$, then for the second stage, the most likely outcome is to bring back the item $\sigma(1)$ and put it at the second position of π i.e. $\pi(2) = \sigma(1)$.

In general, in the kth stage, the probability of selecting $\pi(k)$ is $\frac{\exp(\mu(k-\sigma^{-1}\pi(k)))}{\sum_{j\geq k}\exp(\mu(k-\sigma^{-1}\pi(k)))}$. Intuitively, at each stage k, the model determines the items among $\sigma(1), \sigma(2), \cdots, \sigma(k-1)$ which are not yet sampled by f and assigns higher probability on picking them. In Figure 2 gives an example of this sampling process.

Considering all the stages, we obtain the overall probability of sampling π which is given by the following expression

$$f(\pi \mid \sigma, \mu) = \prod_i \left(\frac{\exp(\mu(i-\sigma^{-1}\pi(i)))}{\sum_{j\geq i}\exp(\mu(i-\sigma^{-1}\pi(j)))} \right) \quad (2)$$

It can be shown that f is a valid probability distribution i.e. $f(\pi \mid \sigma, \mu) \geq 0$ for all $\pi \in S_n$ and $\sum_\pi f(\pi \mid \sigma, \mu) = 1$. The parameter μ controls the spread of the distribution i.e. if $\mu \to 0$ then f converges to the uniform distribution over S_n; otherwise, for $\mu > 0$ the distribution is concentrated around σ. We assume $\mu \geq 1$.

We now describe our next permutation model g that captures the topic-level personalization which is invoked only if $z = 1$. Model g is also decomposed into sequential stages and at each stage uses both the central permutation σ and a set of scores, to determine π. Each item $d \in I$ is assigned a score $\eta^T \theta_d$. In the ith stage, g selects the item $\pi(i)$ with probability

$$\frac{\exp(\lambda \eta^T \theta_{\pi(i)} + (1-\lambda)(i - \sigma^{-1}\pi(i)))}{\sum_{j\geq i} \exp(\lambda \eta^T \theta_{\pi(j)} + (1-\lambda)(i - \sigma^{-1}\pi(j)))}$$

The working principle for g is similar to f, except that it now allows for deviations from σ only if it is explained by the scores. Parameter λ is tuned to adjust the relative importance of the scores and the central permutation σ. For example, if $\lambda = 0$ then the scores are ignored and if $\lambda = 1$ then the central permutation does not play any role. We treat $0 \leq \lambda \leq 1$ as a free parameter whose value needs to be

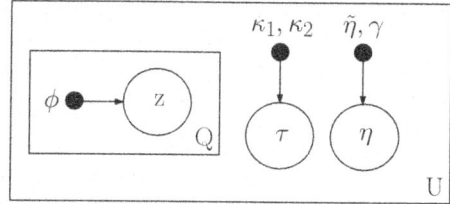

Personalization Block

Figure 3: Variational distribution used for inferring personalization in LTP.

learned from the data. The overall probability of sampling π is given by

$$g(\pi \mid \eta; \sigma, \lambda, \theta) = \prod_i \left(\frac{\exp(\lambda \eta^T \theta_{\pi(i)} + (1-\lambda)(i - \sigma^{-1}\pi(i)))}{\sum_{j\geq i} \exp(\lambda \eta^T \theta_{\pi(j)} + (1-\lambda)(i - \sigma^{-1}\pi(j)))} \right)$$

It can be verified that g is also a valid probability distribution.

The generative process for the personalization block can be described as

- For each user u
  1. Sample $\tau \sim Beta(\delta, \delta)$.
  2. Sample $\eta \sim Gaussian(0, diag(\gamma^2))$
- For each query $q_i, i = 1, 2, \cdots, m$
  1. Sample $z_i \sim Bernoulli(\tau)$ to decide whether to allow topical personalization.
  2. If $z_i = 1$, sample $\pi_i \sim g(\cdot \mid \sigma_i, \lambda, \theta, \eta)$.
  3. Else, sample $\pi_i \sim f(\cdot \mid \sigma_i, \mu)$.

The joint distribution for the personalization block can be written as

$$p(\pi, z, \tau, \eta \mid \theta; \gamma, \delta, \mu, \lambda, \sigma) = p(\eta \mid \gamma) \cdot p(\tau \mid \delta)$$
$$\prod_{i=1}^m p(z_i \mid \tau) \cdot g(\pi_i \mid \sigma_i, \lambda, \theta, \eta)^{z_i} f(\pi_i \mid \sigma_i, \mu)^{1-z_i} \quad (3)$$

Finally, the full joint distribution for LTP can be obtained by multiplying Equations 1 and 3. We treat the parameters $\nu, \alpha, \delta, \gamma$ as constant and do not consider learning them. However, the parameters μ and λ that controls the permutation models need to be learned. We have assumed a Gaussian prior on η. The role of this prior is to set η to zero when we do not observe any *significant* difference between π and σ i.e $\pi_i \approx \sigma_i$.

We first assume that λ and μ are predefined constants and describe the inference (LTP-INF) of the personalization vector η based on these values in Section 4.2. We will then use LTP-INF to also estimate these parameters in Section 4.3.

4.2 Inference of Personalization Vector

The key inferential problem that we study in this work is to obtain the posterior distribution on the latent variables i.e. to determine $p(\theta, K, \beta, z, \tau, \eta \mid \sigma; \lambda, \mu)$. As with simpler topic models, the exact inference is intractable and therefore, we resort to approximate inference techniques. Given the non-conjugacy of π and θ, sampling based techniques are unlikely to be efficient. In this paper, we propose a variational approximation scheme. In a variational inference, one defines a family of simpler distribution over the latent variables to approximate the true posterior distribution. This family of distribution is indexed by additional parameters (called *variational parameters*) which are tuned so as to minimize the KL divergence with the true posterior.

We first simplify the inference by breaking it into two parts. For the first part, we ignore the dependency between the topic and the personalization block. Therefore, our strategy is to first infer the topics and use the inferred topics and the topic-maps of the items to carry out inference for the personalization block. This will simplify the exposition greatly and the ideas that we develop here will carry over naturally to the general case of inferring the blocks jointly. We revisit the inference for the complete model in Section 4.4. Inference for the topic block follows standard techniques (see e.g. [3]) and therefore, we omit the details here. For the rest of this sub-section we assume that the topics have been inferred and develop an inference scheme for the personalization block.

For the personalization block, the key inferential problem is to obtain the posterior distribution $p(z, \tau, \eta \mid \sigma; \lambda, \mu)$. This posterior is approximated with the help of a variational distribution r. Figure 3 illustrates its graphical model representation. The personalization vector η is assumed to be Gaussian with the following density

$$r(\eta \mid \tilde{\eta}) = (2\pi\gamma^2)^{-\frac{T}{2}} \exp\left(-\frac{1}{2\gamma^2}(\eta - \tilde{\eta})' \cdot (\eta - \tilde{\eta})\right)$$

Here, the variational parameter $\tilde{\eta}$ represents the mean of the gaussian and its variance is $\gamma^2 \mathbb{I}$. For query q_i we assume that z_i is sampled from a Bernoulli distribution with parameter $\phi_i \in (0, 1)$. Finally, for user u, we assume that τ is sampled from a beta distribution having the following density function

$$r(\tau \mid \kappa_1, \kappa_2) = \frac{\Gamma(\kappa_1 + \kappa_2)}{\Gamma(\kappa_1)\Gamma(\kappa_2)} \tau^{\kappa_1 - 1}(1 - \tau)^{\kappa_2 - 1}$$

where the parameters $\kappa_1, \kappa_2 > 0$ and $\Gamma(x)$ is the Gamma function. We use the notation $\Psi(x)$ for the digamma function which is defined as $\frac{d}{dx} \ln \Gamma(x)$.

The next step in our variational analysis is to learn the particular value of the parameters $(\phi, \kappa_1, \kappa_2, \tilde{\eta})$ that minimizes the KL divergence between r and the true posterior p. It can be shown[8] that minimizing the KL divergence has the same effect as maximizing the following objective function,

$$\Lambda(\phi, \kappa_1, \kappa_2, \tilde{\eta}) = \mathbb{E}_r[\ln p] + \mathbb{H}(r) \qquad (4)$$

where $\mathbb{H}(r)$ is the entropy and $\mathbb{E}_r$ denotes expectation w.r.t the distribution r.

We use block coordinate-wise ascent to maximize the expression in Equation 4. Intuitively, we perform fixed point iterations by updating one block of parameters at a time, keeping all other parameters fixed to their most recent value. The update rule for parameters $\phi_{1,2,\cdots,m}, \kappa_1, \kappa_2$ are obtained by setting the partial derivatives of Λ to zero. Due to our choice of r, the update rules for ϕ, κ_1, κ_2 are particularly simple and have closed-form expressions.

---
[8]Refer to [3] for the proof.

Algorithm 1 *LTP-INF: Variational Inference Algorithm for LTP*

1: **Input** Training data-set $(\pi, \sigma)_{1,2,\cdots,m}$; values for $\lambda, \gamma, \delta, \mu$;
2: **Output** Values $(\phi'_{1\cdots m}, \kappa'_1, \kappa'_2, \tilde{\eta}')$ that maximize Λ;
3: **Initialization** Randomly initialize to $(\phi^{(0)}_{1\cdots m}, \kappa^{(0)}_1, \kappa^{(0)}_2, \tilde{\eta}^{(0)})$ such that $1 > \phi^{(0)}_{1\cdots m} > 0$ and $\kappa^{(0)}_1, \kappa^{(0)}_2 > 0$;
4: $i \leftarrow 0$; $\Delta^{(0)} \leftarrow \Lambda(\phi^{(0)}_{1\cdots m}, \kappa^{(0)}_1, \kappa^{(0)}_2, \tilde{\eta}^{(0)})$;
5: **while** Δ has not converged **do**
6: $\quad i \leftarrow i + 1$;
7: $\quad \kappa^{(i)}_1 \leftarrow \delta + \sum_{j=1}^{m}(1 - \phi^{(i-1)}_j)$;
8: $\quad \kappa^{(i)}_2 \leftarrow \delta + \sum_{j=1}^{m} \phi^{(i-1)}_j$;
9: $\quad$ **for** $j = 1\ldots m$ **do**
10: $\quad\quad \mu_j \leftarrow \Psi(\kappa^{(i)}_2) - \Psi(\kappa^{(i)}_1) + \ln f(\pi_j \mid \sigma_j, \mu) - \mathbb{E}_r[\ln g(\pi_j \mid \eta; \sigma_j, \theta, \lambda)]$;
11: $\quad\quad \phi^{(i)}_j \leftarrow 1/(1 + e^{\mu_j})$; /* Update ϕ_j */
12: $\quad$ **end for**
13: $\quad \tilde{\eta}^{(i)} \leftarrow \arg\max_{\tilde{\eta}} \Lambda(\phi^{(i)}_{1\cdots m}, \kappa^{(i)}_1, \kappa^{(i)}_2, \tilde{\eta})$; /* Use conjugate gradient to optimize this block */
14: $\quad \Delta^{(i)} \leftarrow \Lambda(\phi^{(i)}_{1\cdots m}, \kappa^{(i)}_1, \kappa^{(i)}_2, \tilde{\eta}^{(i)})$;
15: **end while**
16: **return** $(\phi^{(i)}_{1\cdots m}, \kappa^{(i)}_1, \kappa^{(i)}_2, \tilde{\eta}^{(i)})$

To maximize Λ with respect to $\tilde{\eta}$, we use the conjugate gradient algorithm[9]. The objective function for $\tilde{\eta}$ can be written as

$$L(\tilde{\eta}) = -\frac{1}{2\gamma^2}\tilde{\eta}' \cdot \tilde{\eta} + \sum_i (1 - \phi_i) \cdot \mathbb{E}_r[\ln g(\pi_i \mid \sigma_i, \theta, \lambda)]$$

It can be proved that L is concave (with respect to $\tilde{\eta}$) and therefore, using simple optimizers like conjugate gradient, we will be able to obtain the global maximum [4]. Algorithm 1 summarizes the inference procedure. Due to page limits, we omit the derivations and refer to the full version of the paper [15] for details.

4.3 Parameter Estimation

We now focus our attention at learning λ and μ. We use Maximum Likelihood Estimators (MLE) for this, where one finds the value of the parameters that maximizes the (log) likelihood of the observed data i.e. the following expression

$$\ln p(\pi \mid \lambda, \mu; \sigma) = \sum_{i=1}^{m} \ln p(\pi_i \mid \lambda, \mu; \sigma_i) \qquad (5)$$

However, to calculate the likelihood function, we have to marginalize over the latent variables which is difficult in our model for both real variables (η, τ), as it leads to integrals that are analytically intractable, and discrete variables $(z_{1\cdots m})$, it involves computationally expensive sum over exponential (i.e. 2^m) number of terms.

We use the variational Expectation Maximization (EM) algorithm to circumvent this difficulty. In the E-step, Algorithm 1 approximates the true posterior distribution over the latent variables, using the current estimates of the parameters. The variational parameters learned in this step

---
[9]http://en.wikipedia.org/wiki/Nonlinear_conjugate_gradient_method

Algorithm 2 *LTP-EM: Variational EM Algorithm for LTP*

1: **Input** Training data-set $(\pi, \sigma)_{1,2,\cdots,m}$
2: **Output** Values (λ', μ') that maximize Equation 5
3: **Initialization** Randomly initialize $(\lambda^{(0)}, \mu^{(0)})$ s.t. $0 \leq \lambda^{(0)} \leq 1$ and $\mu^{(0)} > 0$.
4: **while** (λ, μ) have not converged **do**
5:     **E-step**   /* *The variational inference step* */

- $(\phi'_{1\cdots m}, \kappa'_1, \kappa'_2, \tilde{\eta}') \leftarrow \text{LTP-INF}(\sigma, \pi, \lambda^{(i)}, \mu^{(i)})$;

- $\Lambda^{(i)}(\lambda, \mu) \leftarrow \mathbb{E}_{r(\phi', \kappa'_1, \kappa'_2, \tilde{\eta}')}[\ln p]$;

6:     **M-step** /* *Learn new estimates of the parameters* */

- $(\lambda^{(i+1)}, \mu^{(i+1)}) \leftarrow \underset{\substack{\mu > 0 \\ 1 \geq \lambda \geq 0}}{\arg\max} \Lambda^{(i)}(\lambda, \mu)$

7:     $i \leftarrow i + 1$
8: **end while**
9: **return** $(\lambda^{(i)}, \mu^{(i)})$

---

are used in the subsequent M-step to maximize the likelihood function (over the true parameters λ and μ).

Algorithm 2 summarizes the steps of the variational EM. It can be shown [15] that the constraint maximization problem in step 6 is a concave program and therefore, can be solved optimally and efficiently [4].

4.4 Learning Topic Distributions

For inference in the topic block (Figure 1), we augment our variational distribution with additional parameters in the following way. Topic distribution β_k is sampled from a Dirichlet prior with parameters $\{\tilde{\beta}_{k,w} \mid w \in V\}$. The topic assignments $K_{i,j}$ are sampled from a multinomial distribution with parameters $\omega_{i,j,1\cdots T}$ and θ_i is sampled from a normal distribution with mean $\tilde{\theta}_i$ and variance $\alpha^2 \mathbb{I}$. Using the same recipe as in Section 4.2 (c.f. Equation 4), we arrive at the following simple update rule for learning the topic distributions

$$\beta_{k,w} = \nu + \sum_{\substack{i,j \\ W_{i,j} = w}} \omega_{i,j,k}$$

The topic assignments $\omega_{i,j}$ also has a closed form update rule as given by $\omega_{i,j,k} \propto \exp(\mathbb{E}_r[\ln \theta_i] + \mathbb{E}_r[\ln \beta_{k,w_{i,j}}])$.

The main difficulty in learning topic-maps (i.e. θ_i's) stems from the coupling between the personalization and the topic blocks through θ. While determining $\mathbb{E}_r[\ln g(\pi \mid \eta, \theta; \sigma, \lambda)]$ (step 8 of Algorithm 1), we now have to take expectation over θ, in addition to η. However this calculation is analytically tractable due to our assumption of independence and gaussian priors on θ and η. We use gradient descent on θ to solve it. The rest of the calculation remains unchanged.

5. EXPERIMENTS

In this section, we describe a comprehensive set of experiments designed to evaluate the accuracy and effectiveness of our techniques.

5.1 Data-sets

The input to our algorithm consists of a set of queries and the personalized and vanilla results (i.e. π, σ pairs) for them, returned by a search engine. During the training phase, we present these queries to LTP and let it learn the personalization vector η. Once η is learned, the next step is to validate it, by measuring how well it corresponds to the ground truth. However, in practice, such validation schemes are often difficult to design as the search engines do not reveal the actual user profile[10]. We therefore perform our experiments on both real-world data-set comprised of Google search history of a few users, and a large scale synthetic data-set.

5.1.1 Google Search Personalization

We collected search history data from 10 real Google users in Nov 2012. We fetched their past search queries using Google API that returns a sample of about 1000 web queries from her history (it also contains other queries like map, image, etc. that we ignored). We retrieved on average 850 distinct queries for each user.

We issued each distinct query in his history (in a randomized order) to Google both with and without their login credentials to retrieve the search results. For a given query, both the results were fetched at the same time (within a few seconds of each other) and using the identical connection parameters such as user-agent (UA), IP-address, http headers (except cookies), etc. This process removes non-profile based personalizations such as those based on context of the current session (randomized order breaks any coherent context in user's history), IP address or location, time-of-the-day (the whole data collection for a user took only a few minutes), browser or OS type, etc. Hence the differences in results should be only due to user's profile.

We then parsed the result pages and extracted the ranked results. We ignored the paid links (at top and bottom of the page) and any map, image, or other embedded group of results that some queries return. We then used the Mallet [19] toolkit to extract topics from the urls[11] separately for each user. Due to privacy considerations, we then annonymized the entire data set by mapping each url, query and topic to (randomly generated) IDs. Our algorithms were run on this annonymized data.

We found ample evidence of profile based personalization on Google—roughly 30% queries received personalized results, i.e. had differences in the ranks of urls in personalized and vanilla results. We also found that the personalization is much more subtle compared to the impression we get from search personalization literature (and our experiments with AlterEgo server)—most queries ($\approx 70\%$) were not personalized and while there were some queries with fair amount of personalization, on an average, we observed very little difference between the results[12].

5.1.2 AlterEgo

We use an open source search personalization engine called AlterEgo [18] to generate the synthetic dataset. AlterEgo contains implementation of various popular profiling and

---

[10]Google, however, publishes the categories of topics used to serve personalized ads. Unfortunately, this data is not quite helpful as the categories are very high level and do not convey rich enough information.
[11]We used the snippets that Google returns along with the search results to obtain text for the urls.
[12]The avg. EMD (earth mover's distance) over queries with personalization was 5.9 (e.g. the EMD of moving a single url at rank 5 to rank 1 is 4)

personalization techniques; we used their "unique matching" technique for our experiments[13]. In our simulation, we used AlterEgo as a surrogate personalization engine i.e. we obtain the vanilla result from Google and use AlterEgo to personalize it. The benefit of this approach is that we can train AlterEgo on topics of our choice and use this information to validate the model output η. The work-flow and details of the data generation steps are presented below.

Generating Topics We extracted a set of 500 topics by running Mallet on approximately 420k urls obtained from the Delicious dataset[28]. We manually select 50 topics and label them into 10 categories (examples are health, cooking, science, finance, etc.); these topics serve as a ground-truth for us. The selection of these topic categories and urls (used in the next step) is intended to simulate a typical user behavior, where, a user in interested in $\approx$ 10 categories of topics.

Training AlterEgo For each topic, we inspect the topic-maps of the urls and identify the ones which have significant (> 0.2) weight (on this topic). These urls are used to train AlterEgo profile. We generated 10 profiles trained on a subset of 1 to 10 topics (i.e. 10 profile for 1 topic, 10 profile on 2 randomly selected topics, and so on), generating a total of 50 profiles.

Queries We generated 500 queries for each topic by randomly combining the top 10 relevant words from them. This gives us a total of 5k queries (over 10 categories). For each query, we retrieved the vanilla results from Google. Note that, if a query is related to a topic used for training the profile, only then AlterEgo will be able to personalize it. Otherwise, the vanilla and personalized results will be more or less identical.

5.2 Implementation Details

We use JOptimizer [14] - a java based open source optimization package for solving the convex program in Algorithm 2 (step 6) All our experiments are carried out on a Intel Pentium IV machine with 3.0GHz processor and 4GB of RAM.

We use the following values of the hyper-parameters : $\delta = 2.0, \gamma = 1.0$. For computational efficiency, we used Mallet for inference in the topic-block (see Figure 1) and do not use the inference process described in Section 4.4.

5.3 Results with the AlterEgo data-set

In this section, we summarize the result of our experiments with the AlterEgo data-set.

5.3.1 Precision-Recall

Our first set of experiments are designed to evaluate the accuracy of LTP in correctly learning the personalized topics. On each AlterEgo profile, we train LTP and learn the personalization vector η. Next we compare it with the actual list of topics that were used to train this profile (by AlterEgo). Let T_{act} be the true set of personalized topics and T_{inf} be the one inferred by LTP. For this experiment, we measure the precision and recall values, where precision is defined as $\frac{|T_{act} \cap T_{inf}|}{|T_{inf}|}$ i.e. the fraction of reported topics that are actually personalized and recall by $\frac{|T_{act} \cap T_{inf}|}{|T_{act}|}$ i.e.

[13] We also did experiments with their "matching" technique, and got very similar results which are omitted due to lack of space.

[14] http://www.joptimizer.com/

the fraction of the original personalized topics that we are able to identify.

P@1	P@3	P@5	R-pre	P@+1	P@+3	MAP
97.80	84.02	70.60	84.66	70.69	54.44	97.60

Table 1: Performance (in %) of LTP in finding personalized topics (with AlterEgo data-set).

We re-order the topics based on the (decreasing) value of η computed by LTP. For each k, we declare the top-k topics (with maximum η values) as personalized and calculate the precision and recall value for this decision. Table 1 summarizes the precision scores obtained by LTP. Specifically, we evaluate its performance in terms of Precision@1(P@1), P@3, P@5, R-precision (R-pre) and mean average precision (MAP) [5, 7]. Note that the size of actual topics was quite different for different runs (varies from 1-10). Hence, along with the top-k topics, we also study the precision at $|T_{act}+k|$ (denoted as P@+k).

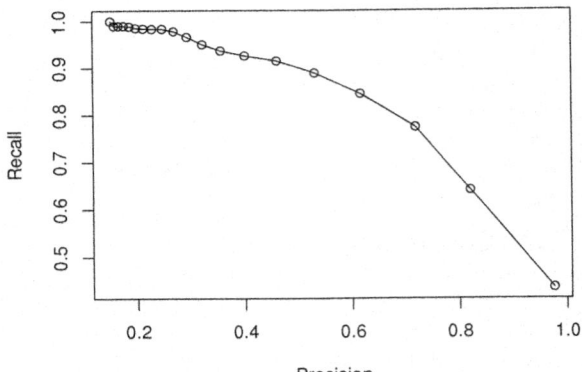

Figure 4: Precision-Recall results for LTP in retrieving the personalized topics (with AlterEgo data-set).

In Figure 4, we illustrate the recall performance of our algorithm. At the expense of low precision (< 0.4), LTP is able to retrieve all the personalized topics (recall ≥ 0.93) and its recall performance is relatively insensitive to precision; however, if we require high precision (> 0.8), the recall drops to ≈ 0.5. As evident from the figure, a typical operating characteristic of LTP is precision ≈ 0.7 and recall ≈ 0.7, which is achieved when we return top-3 topics.

5.3.2 Classification Tests

In this section, we develop two classification tests to evaluate LTP's predictive power. For both these experiments, we randomly split the π, σ list into data-sets D1 (80%), used for training LTP, and D2 (20%), used for testing. We repeat this split with 10 random seeds and report the average number in all the data presented below.

Query Disambiguation In this experiment, while testing on D2, we hide which result is personalized and which one is vanilla and the task of the model is to determine the correct labels.

We proceed with the classification task in the following way. Let η' be the parameter learned by LTP during the training. For input lists l_1 and l_2, LTP calculates the likelihood values $p(l_1 \mid l_2, \eta')$ and $p(l_2 \mid l_1, \eta')$ and whichever likelihood is higher is assigned to the personalized result i.e. if $p(l_1 \mid l_2, \eta') > p(l_2 \mid l_1, \eta')$ then l_1 is declared to be the

#topics	Accuracy ($\mu \pm \sigma$)		Time (secs)	
	LTP-EM	LTP-INF	LTP-EM	LTP-INF
1	.74 ± .09	.72 ± .09	80.7	22.7
2	.72 ± .06	.70 ± .09	154.3	31.5
3	.70 ± .05	.68 ± .06	221.6	42.4
4	.69 ± .04	.67 ± .05	272.2	53.7
5	.69 ± .05	.67 ± .05	336.1	69.8
6	.67 ± .04	.65 ± .05	333.2	70.7
7	.65 ± .04	.65 ± .05	342.5	71.1
8	.63 ± .04	.63 ± .04	348.2	73.6
9	.63 ± .05	.62 ± .05	354.4	76.4
10	.62 ± .02	.62 ± .02	359.2	79.5

Table 2: Summary of results with the AlterEgo dataset

Google Category	Topic in LTP	η
Comics & Animation - Anime & Manga	online read manga kyojin shingeki chapter	0.60
Autos & Vehicles - Vehicle Shopping	car india chrysler price jaguar sport bmw	0.42
Computers - Software Utilities	class import common org public implement	0.15
World Localities - South Asia	seoul citi hotel location shop mall coex	0.13

Table 3: Correlation between personalized topics in LTP and Google categories.

personalized result and vice versa. We name this test as *P-V disambiguation* for a given profile. Over all the test points in D2, the fraction of queries that were labeled correctly is referred to as *disambiguation accuracy*.

Table 2 summarizes the result of this experiment. In summary, we achieve disambiguation accuracy in the range of 62-74%. For each profile, we collect the accuracy values for the 10 different runs and report its mean and standard deviation ($\mu \pm \sigma$). Observe that our accuracy decreases slightly as the AlterEgo profile is trained with more and more topics.

Table 2 also reports the training time of LTP-EM. For profiles trained with many topics, LTP-EM takes more time to converge. We repeat the experiment with LTP-INF with the parameter values fixed to $\lambda = 0.9$ and $\mu = 10.0$. As the results show, LTP-INF is up to 5 times faster to train but achieves slightly lower accuracy. The accuracy however, improves slightly (< 3%) if we increase the amount of training data (D1) from 80% to 90% (not shown in the table).

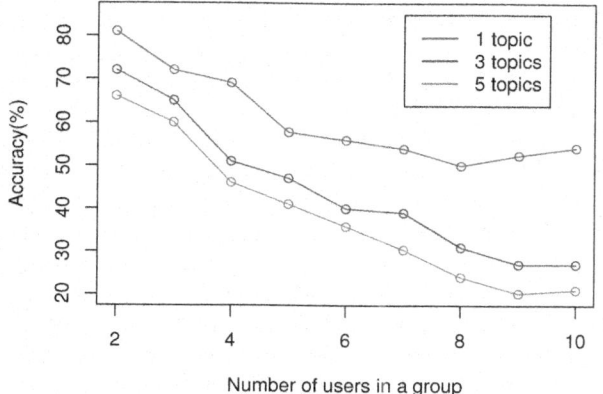

Figure 5: Performance of LTP in user classification (with AlterEgo data-set).

User Classification For this experiment, we consider groups of users (i.e. profiles) and develop a classification test within the group members. We vary the size of the group from 2 to 10 and for each group size, randomly pick 10 groups. For each group G, we present a (π, σ) pair to LTP but do not reveal the user it belongs to. The task of the model is to correctly predict the user.

We again use the likelihood test for this task. Specifically, for each user $u \in G$ and input (π, σ), we calculate $p(\pi \mid \sigma, \eta'_u)$ (η'_u learned during training) and output the user for which the likelihood attains its maximum value.

In Figure 5, we summarize the result of this experiment. There are two parameters in this experiment - the size of the group and the number of topics used to train AlterEgo for each profile in the group. For simplicity, we present here results for the homogeneous case, where we combine profile which are trained on the same number of topics [15]. Observe that the accuracy reported by LTP is significantly higher than a random guess (which is 1/g, g being the group size). The accuracy decreases slightly if profiles are trained with many topics. We believe this reduction in accuracy is also an artifact of our data generation—profiles trained on multiple topics can (and do) have topics in common, that will make it hard to distinguish personalized response on two profile trained on the same topic.

In summary, these results, together with the precision-recall values from last section highlight that our model fits the data well and learns the correct set of personalized topics on synthetic data.

5.4 Results with the Google dataset

In this section we describe the results with the Google data-set. Note that since we do not know the actual personalization on different topics (ground truth) for a real Google user, we cannot perform the precision-recall experiments as with AlterEgo dataset, and resort to only query disambiguation and user classification test described above. However, we also perform some qualitative tests that give ample indication that we have found a good personalization vector.

5.4.1 Qualitative Evidences for Correctness of η

We now present our analysis on finding qualitative correctness of η using *evidences* of personalization. An evidence is an instance of π, σ where results were re-ranked such that the ones with η were moved up. Note that while such evidence have no statistical significance, they are much more helpful for a user's understanding of his profile compared to the personalization vector. Such evidences are a core feature of the privacy toolkit we are building (see Section 6).

Figure 6 shows an example evidence of personalization happening on a user's account. The result for query Q ("how to decide mixing of markov chain") and theta values for two relevant topics T1 (about "Algorithms" defined by words algorithm, design, complexity) and T2 (about "Probability" defined by words probability, distribution) are shown. For

---

[15] We also performed experiments on the general case (e.g. by grouping profiles trained on 3 topics with 5 topics). The results are similar and not repeated here.

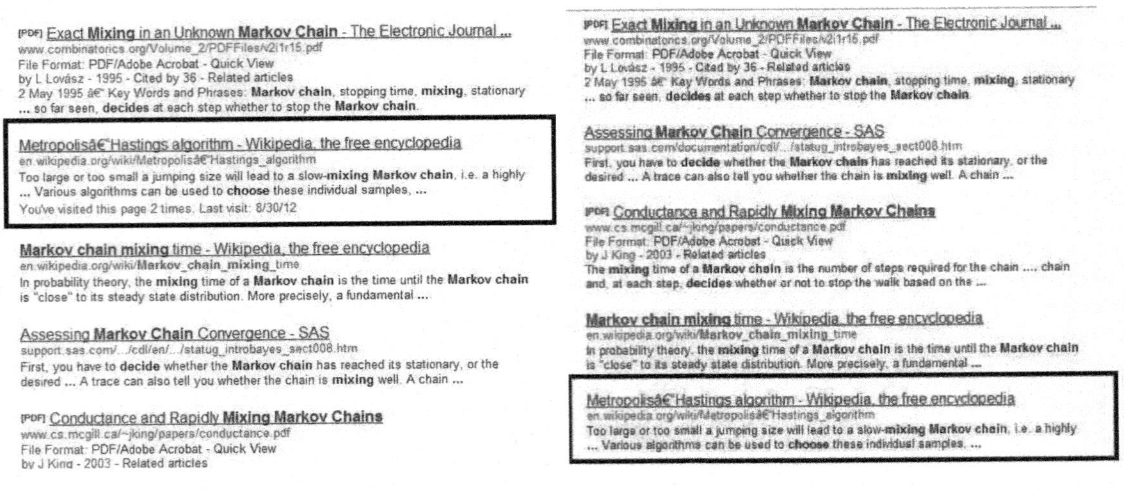

Figure 6: An example to illustrate the difference between personalized (left) and vanilla (right) search results (for a real user) returned by Google.

	Topic	
	T1	T2
η	.90	.40
Q	.01	.30
U1	.15	.10
U2	.01	.25

User Id	15 Topics	20 Topics	50 Topics	100 Topics
1	.74±.05	.70±.05	.70±.06	.73±.04
2	.68±.05	.70±.04	.70±.04	.65±.03
3	.67±.13	.72±.14	.67±.13	.73±.11
4	.54±.08	.51±.06	.55±.06	.59±.07
5	.54±.11	.47±.09	.49±.11	.43±.09
6	.85±.07	.78±.05	.84±.04	.81±.07
7	.73±.04	.70±.05	.71±.06	.73±.06
8	.66±.03	.62±.03	.61±.04	.64±.03
9	.52±.04	.52±.03	.50±.04	.54±.04

Table 4: Accuracy of LTP over 9 Google users.

Group Size	Number of Topics			
	10	20	50	100
2	.59 ± .06	.61 ± .06	.65 ± .04	.58 ± .05
3	.48 ± .04	.53 ± .05	.60 ± .05	.50 ± .06

Table 5: User classification accuracy on Google data.

this user, η value for T1 is very high compared to T2. Observe that the wiki link U1 (in the box), although less relevant to the query, is placed higher in the personalized results. As our analysis shows, U2 is has a high weight on topic T1 compared to U2, which leads to this personalization. The user can therefore see not just his inferred interests (more in "Algorithms" compared to "Probability"), but also *how* it affects his results.

We next move to another qualitative analysis of η by comparing it directly with the categories Google itself associates with a user[16]. We try to match topics with high η (top-k such topics) with the broad categories in Google. Table 3 shows the result of such matching for 3 users. Take for example, the "Anime and Manga" category, that was also assigned a very high $\eta = .6$ (compared to an average value of .004) by LTP.

Such anecdotes show that our techniques have, in fact, learned the personalization vector correctly.

5.4.2 Quantitative Experiments

Query Disambiguation Table 4 summarizes the result of query disambiguation on the Google dataset. We first study the effects of number of topics (T) chosen for the user. We notice that only a few topics 15-50 are enough to get good accuracy for any user. Our accuracy results differ significantly for different users, varying from as low as 54% to 85%. We believe this is because the amount of personalization is different for various users, and this affects the learning accuracy of our techniques.

User Classification Table 5 show that even with 3 users, we are able to get an accuracy of up to 60%. For this experiments, we extracted η values over a common set of topics for each user. These η values learned were also very different for different users (data not shown). This shows that η is in fact learned tailored to the personalization of each user.

6. CONCLUSIONS

In this paper we have presented a novel approach to extract user profile information in the form of personalization vector over topics from commercial OSPs (such as Google search). Our approach treats OSPs as black-boxes, i.e. assumes no knowledge of the personalization algorithms and history of users maintained by them, and works by comparing the personalized and vanilla content served by them.

To the best of our knowledge, this is the first work that tries to extract information based solely on mining the output of OSPs. This approach is unique in not just enabling access to (so far hidden) profiles in OSPs, but also in providing a novel and practical approach for retrieving information from OSPs by mining differences in their outputs.

Our approach also has direct benefits for end users, as for the first time, it enables them to access their (so far hidden) profile information tracked by an OSP. While being an informational tool by itself, this has wider implications to the outlook of user privacy research—it can be used to infer the personalization happening on *sensitive* topics (e.g. financial, medical history, etc.), which a user may not be comfortable with. We believe that this can be used to build an end-user privacy preserving tool and are currently working on a prototype for the same.

---

[16]Shown in Google ads preference manager https://www.google.com/settings/ads/onweb/

7. REFERENCES

[1] P. N. Bennett, R. W. White, W. Chu, S. T. Dumais, P. Bailey, F. Borisyuk, and X. Cui. Modeling the impact of short-and long-term behavior on search personalization. In *SIGIR*, 2012.

[2] J. Bischof and E. Airoldi. Summarizing topical content with word frequency and exclusivity. *ICML*, 2012.

[3] D. M. Blei, A. Y. Ng, and M. I. Jordan. Latent dirichlet allocation. *J. Mach. Learn. Res.*, 2003.

[4] S. Boyd and L. Vandenberghe. *Convex Optimization*. Cambridge University Press, 2004.

[5] C. Buckley and E. M. Voorhees. Retrieval evaluation with incomplete information. In *SIGIR*, 2004.

[6] G. Chen, H. Bai, L. Shou, K. Chen, and Y. Gao. Ups: efficient privacy protection in personalized web search. In *SIGIR*, 2011.

[7] N. Craswell, A. P. de Vries, and I. Soboroff. Overview of the trec-2005 enterprise track. In *TREC*, 2005.

[8] Z. Dou, R. Song, and J. R. Wen. A large-scale evaluation and analysis of personalized search strategies. In *WWW*, 2007.

[9] A. Hannak, P. Sapiezynski, A. M. Kakhki, B. Krishnamurthy, D. Lazer, A. Mislove, and C. Wilson. Measuring personalization of web search. In *WWW*, 2013.

[10] A. Korolova. Privacy violations using microtargeted ads: A case study. In *ICDMW*, 2010.

[11] J. Lindamood, R. Heatherly, M. Kantarcioglu, and B. Thuraisingham. Inferring private information using social network data. In *WWW*, 2009.

[12] R. D. Luce. *Individual choice behavior: A theoretical analysis*. Wiley, 1959.

[13] J. Luxenburger, S. Elbassuoni, and G. Weikum. Matching task profiles and user needs in personalized web search. In *CIKM*, 2008.

[14] A. Machanavajjhala, A. Korolova, and A. D. Sarma. Personalized social recommendations: accurate or private. *VLDB Endowment*, 2011.

[15] A. Majumder and N. Shrivastava. Know your personalization: Learning topic level personalization in online services. *Arxiv*, abs/1212.3390, 2012.

[16] C. L. Mallows. Non-null ranking models. *Biometrika*, 1957.

[17] H. Mao, X. Shuai, and A. Kapadia. Wpes. In *Proc. workshop on Privacy in the electronic society*, 2011.

[18] N. Matthijs and F. Radlinski. Personalizing web search using long term browsing history. In *WSDM*, 2011.

[19] A. K. McCallum. Mallet: A machine learning for language toolkit. http://mallet.cs.umass.edu.

[20] E. Pariser. *The Filter Bubble: What the Internet Is Hiding from You*. Penguin Press, 2011.

[21] T. Qin, X. Geng, and T. Y. Liu. A new probabilistic model for rank aggregation. In *NIPS*, 2010.

[22] D. Sontag, K. Collins-Thompson, P. N. Bennett, R. W. White, S. Dumais, and B. Billerbeck. Probabilistic models for personalizing web search. In *WSDM*, 2012.

[23] B. Tan, X. Shen, and C. X. Zhai. Mining long-term search history to improve search accuracy. In *SIGKDD*, 2006.

[24] J. Teevan, E. Adar, R. Jones, and M. Potts. History repeats itself: repeat queries in yahoo's logs. In *SIGIR*, 2006.

[25] J. Teevan, S. T. Dumais, and E. Horvitz. Personalizing search via automated analysis of interests and activities. In *SIGIR*, 2005.

[26] J. Teevan, S. T. Dumais, and E. Horvitz. Potential for personalization. *TOCHI*, 2010.

[27] J. Teevan, S. T. Dumais, and D. J. Liebling. To personalize or not to personalize: modeling queries with variation in user intent. In *SIGIR*, 2008.

[28] R. Wetzker, C. Zimmermann, and C. Bauckhage. Detecting trends in social bookmarking systems: A del.icio.us endeavor. *IJDWM*, 2010.

[29] Y. Xu, K. Wang, B. Zhang, and Z. Chen. Privacy-enhancing personalized web search. In *WWW*, 2007.

[30] Y. Zhu, L. Xiong, and C. Verdery. Anonymizing user profiles for personalized web search. In *WWW*, 2010.

[31] Z. A. Zhu, W. Chen, T. Wan, C. Zhu, G. Wang, and Z. Chen. To divide and conquer search ranking by learning query difficulty. In *CIKM*, 2009.

Saving, Reusing, and Remixing Web Video: Using Attitudes and Practices to Reveal Social Norms

Catherine C. Marshall
Microsoft Research, Silicon Valley
1065 La Avenida
Mountain View, CA 94043
1-650-693-1308
cathymar@microsoft.com

Frank M. Shipman
Department of Computer Science
Texas A&M University
College Station, TX 77843-3112
1-979-862-3216
shipman@cs.tamu.edu

ABSTRACT
The growth of online videos has spurred a concomitant increase in the storage, reuse, and remix of this content. As we gain more experience with video content, social norms about ownership have evolved accordingly, spelling out what people think is appropriate use of content that is not necessarily their own. We use a series of three studies, each centering on a different genre of recordings, to probe 634 participants' attitudes toward video storage, reuse, and remix; we also question participants about their own experiences with online video. The results allow us to characterize current practice and emerging social norms and to establish the relationship between the two. Hypotheticals borrowed from legal research are used as the primary vehicle for testing attitudes, and for identifying boundaries between socially acceptable and unacceptable behavior.

Categories and Subject Descriptors
H.4.3 [**Information Systems**]: Communications Applications.

General Terms
Design, Experimentation, Human Factors, Legal Aspects.

Keywords
Video reuse, social media, property rights, social norms.

1. INTRODUCTION
The growth and ubiquity of video as an everyday medium raises new issues about its ownership and control. Before the advent of inexpensive digital video production and display tools, video belonged in a handful of distinct realms. On one hand, home movies were used to record special occasions and family events; on the other hand, professional video was the realm of experienced videographers who used the medium primarily for entertainment and education.

The distinction between professional video and amateur video is blurring. Home video producers can purchase sophisticated cameras and video manipulation tools that were once limited to professionals. Although not all home video enthusiasts have the talent and skill to make professional-quality videos, they do have access to the means of production and venues for distribution. A popular amateur video on YouTube or Vimeo may have cost little to produce, and may garner as many views as a movie or TV series that cost millions to make and is available through a for-pay subscription service like Netflix or Hulu. Sites like Funny or Die blur the distinction further, as homemade videos vie with professionally-made web series for audiences' attention; in fact, this blurring is sometimes purposeful, as amateur videos aspire to be mistaken for professional videos and vice-versa.

At the same time, because modern video is a digital medium—and therefore easy to download, copy, republish, and remix--professional video makers (and some amateurs) are nervous about protecting their assets, either via law, technology, or explicit provisions of a service's terms and conditions. It is unusual for video producers and consumers to even be fully aware of the applicable laws, pivotal legal cases, policies, and provisions that restrict copying or (more infrequently) promote reuse. To further complicate matters, social media sites like Facebook and Twitter make it easy to repost videos to reach new audiences.

Many competing interests are at work. Generally video sharing services and file storage sites err on the side of caution: why provoke needless copyright infringement lawsuits? Similarly, professional media production concerns such as Sony and Disney aggressively push forward to protect their assets [27]. Meanwhile, non-professionals may have other concerns: why prohibit distribution if what you're seeking is fame? Amateur video-makers rely on a combination of sharing, remix, and reuse to achieve viral status. At the same time, personal video makers may rely on privacy through obscurity [32].

Given these tensions, developers, service providers, and policy makers are faced with a number of decisions that will influence users' behaviors; concomitantly, as scholars such as Lessig point out [13][14], social norms are emerging that guide peoples' behavior and attitudes. We are interested in characterizing these social norms, and exploring the practice of saving and reusing different recorded genres. We do this by performing three related studies that gather peoples' reactions to a series of hypotheticals (modeled after those used in legal research [24][31]) and the characteristics their video use.

We are specifically interested in three common practices—saving video on personal storage; reusing video as-is in new venues; and remixing video content to create new forms—along with questions introduced by new technologies such as cloud storage and social media as well as questions raised by concepts like permission, attribution, and community-contributed metadata.

To provide background for this study, we first summarize related work. Next we describe our method and characterize the participants and their use of online video. We then present findings about participants' attitudes toward the storage and reuse of recorded media. Finally, we discuss the implications of these findings on design and policy.

2. RELATED WORK

Studies of video sharing have explored how people upload and share content and the communities this activity creates [25]. Two research areas more closely related to our studies investigate (1) the design of systems to support video remix and (2) the automatic identification of reuse/remix in video collections.

Support for Video Reuse. Video reuse relies on existing video content. Most video sharing sites are not designed to support remix. An exception is Metavid.org, an archive of congressional presentations intended as the raw footage that will serve as fodder for remixes [4]. Video remixing also relies on tools for collecting and editing existing video while creating a new video, e.g. [29]. Some tools focused on particular classes of video. For example, Vihavainen et al. [33][34] explore the design and use of tools for remixing videos recorded by audience members at a concert. Looking at the effect of technology design on remix practice, Diakopoulos et al. [5] explore how constraints of a remixing service influence users' creations and how users' values related to authorship affect the design of the service.

Detection of Reuse. Much of the research in the detection of video reuse explores techniques for recognizing the overlap within video collections (e.g. deduplication). A few studies go beyond the identification of reuse and discuss applications of the results of this process. San Pedro et al. [27] describe the application of tags based on identifying remix within YouTube. A more specific study explored how using the results of remix detection to automatically provide attribution compares with human attribution [21]. In their study of identifying video memes through duplicate detection, Xie et al. [35] found a considerable amount of remixed content and that the mix of content from citizen journalists and traditional news media varies depending on the topic.

3. METHOD

We conducted a series of studies to investigate emerging ethical norms and current practice associated with saving and reusing online video content. The studies used crowdsourced questionnaires to elicit this data; each questionnaire was implemented as a Mechanical Turk Human Intelligence Task (HIT) following published best practices [6][11][12]. Participants were solicited from US-based Turkers who had a history of reliable task completion and were self-reported users of the media type and genre in question. By imposing these restrictions, we hoped to ensure a background level of cultural congruity; participants were thus subject to the same legal system and were exposed to many of the same cultural touchstones.

Each of the three questionnaires we discuss was designed around a different media type or genre, and sought to characterize participants in several ways that would afford straightforward triangulation among questions and would give us a reasonably nuanced picture of who they were, what they thought, and what they did. First, we collected some standard demographic information; this information helped us understand what kind of people were filling out the questionnaires. For example, were they students? Was Mechanical Turk their primary income source? How experienced were they as Internet users and content contributors? Second, we set up familiar hypothetical situations—for example, recording a job interview over Skype—coupled with variations of each situation's details to elicit some basic responses that would reflect the participants' attitudes about saving and reusing online content. Finally, we asked participants about their own practices, for example, what kind of video they had shared or watched themselves. Two reading comprehension questions helped ensure that participants were paying adequate attention to the scenario details.

Table 1 summarizes the three studies. The number of acceptable responses is reported along with the total (in parentheses). Length refers to the number of questions in the HIT, including the comprehension questions and a concluding question ("Would you be willing to work on more HITs like this one?") that we used to make sure the Turkers were not unhappy with our approach (reported in the "Other" column). The studies yielded 634 valid responses out of a total of 719 responses. Throughout this paper we use the abbreviations listed in column 1 to refer to the specific studies and to label participant quotes (e.g. PC014 refers to participant 14 in the podcast study).

We approached data quality issues conservatively: we erred on the side of caution and discarded data based on a point system. Unanswered questions, violations of the going-in restrictions (e.g., participant reported themselves to be other than English-speaking), a suspiciously short work time, or wrong answers to the comprehension probes were each worth one point. If participants scored 2 or more points, their data was discarded. We paid participants according to standard Mechanical Turk rates even if we discarded their data. The point system gave us a means to retain data from participants who might have found one or two questions confusing, or who completed HITs prior to accepting the work (a common practice reported in online forums like Turker Nation). In practice, bad responses were easily detected from a participant's answers to the open-ended questions, but the point system allowed us to handle borderline cases consistently.

Our scenarios set up a series of hypothetical situations in which facts were varied to test aspects of participants' attitudes about the ownership and control of online video content. Specifically, we tested the fairness associated with four standard actions: storing video content, sharing video content, republishing video content, and removing video content. The facts characterize standard features of the situation: the type of online content, where it is stored, and the stakeholders who are taking the actions.

For example, we use a series of hypotheticals to vary whether the person taking the action owns the material, is portrayed in the material, or is peripherally involved in the creation of the material; similarly, we use hypotheticals to vary the extent of the content that is affected (e.g. does the action involve all of a work or only a short excerpt?) and to explore other ethical dilemmas having to do with digital content ownership and manipulation, including concepts such as permission, anonymity, and privacy.

We recount the podcast scenarios and hypotheticals in greater depth as an example to show how the hypotheticals work. The podcast scenarios revolve around 4 named characters: two on-air hosts, an engineer who helps them record the weekly show, and a guest who is on the particular podcast in the scenarios. First we vary who saves the podcast to his local hard drive to test the concept of ownership and storage: can any of the people involved in the podcast's production save the podcast? We use a slippery-slope construction to move from one hypothetical situation to the next. Once we have explored aspects of the connection between

Table 1. Study identifiers, focus, number of responses and questionnaire structure

Study	Media type/genre	# responses	Length	Demographic	Hypotheticals	Practice	Other
1 (PC)	Interview podcast	225 (239)	42	12	22	5	3
2 (VC)	Recorded Video	200 (229)	40	12	20	5	3
3 (ED)	Academic lecture	209 (250)	44	12	25	4	3

Table 2. Summary of scenarios used in the studies and the main concepts they test

Study	Description of central scenarios	Concepts tested
1 (PC)	Two comedians host a weekly interview-format podcast; an engineer (who records a podcast of his own) helps them with production. This week's guest, a musician, performs a parody of a popular pop song during his interview. A fan tags the interview, which enables an ex-band member to find the episode and comment on it. The podcast is re-edited and republished under a variety of circumstances.	Ownership, local storage, reuse, remix, excerption, commercial v. non-commercial reuse, permission, removal of social metadata v. removal of primary content.
2 (VC)	A computer programmer's job interview is conducted via Skype. He records the interview and shares it with a friend (to help a friend apply there too). When he is not offered the job, he posts the interview on YouTube in an effort to interest other employers in him. He also republishes it with a commentary track to help others interview better (using only his side of the interview). Finally he turns it into a parody for a comedy website.	Ownership, local storage v. cloud storage, reuse, remix, excerption, parody, educational use, reposting on social media v. publication on a comedy website.
3 (ED)	An astronaut delivers a popular commencement address at a large public university; she talks about the importance of the manned space program. The lecture is published on a free online service that requires special software be installed on the viewer's computer (the service also provides for-pay content via this delivery vehicle). A geologist critical of the manned space program blogs a rebuttal.	Ownership, local storage, transcoding, permission, republication, ownership, storage, republication, and remix of social metadata.

ownership and storage, we test republication (without any further modification of the podcast); this test moves into adding content before the material is republished. Then we switch the participant's attention from the creators to the guest and his actions: can the podcast's guest take the segment he appears in and modify it before republishing it? Can he excerpt a song he performed on the podcast and sell it separately? The situations gradually test the edges of the participants' ethical boundaries.

These types of scenarios and hypotheticals are borrowed from legal theory, where they are used to help legal scholars explain doctrine and explore the moral underpinnings and consequences of legal rules [15][31]. Hypotheticals are used widely in the law [16] and may be used to "present, support and attack positions (e.g., by testing the consequences of a tentative conclusion, pressing an assertion to its limits, and exploring the meaning of a concept)" and to "factor a complex situation into component parts (e.g., by exaggerating strengths, weaknesses or eliminating features)." ([24], p. 168)

Thus we borrow a technique widely used in law schools and in certain oral argument situations (e.g. the US Supreme Court makes extensive use of hypotheticals to decide cases) and apply it to elicit everyday attitudes toward the storage and reuse of digital video content. This enables the participants to reason about the ethical forces involved in the scenarios without requiring that they imagine potentially widely varying details themselves; it also allows us to make meaningful comparisons between their Likert scale responses to the questions. Table 2 summarizes each scenario and the concepts it tests.

4. PARTICIPANTS

Because they are Turkers, participants are likely to be Internet-savvy; we also require that they have some investment in video content (as users). These limitations are imposed by design; we are more interested in people who have actual experience working out ownership and reuse questions for themselves, for example as they repost videos in Facebook or create YouTube videos. They will have grappled at least implicitly with questions like, "will I get caught if I use Dropbox to share this copyrighted movie with my friend?" or "is it okay for me to post a homemade music video based on my favorite band's hit song?" Although it is unlikely participants will have encountered the specific situations we pose in the hypotheticals, they will have less trouble imagining them than someone who has little experience with video.

What type of Turker responds to this sort of questionnaire? As we might expect, the population is dominated by Turkers in their twenties and thirties (born in the 1970s and 1980s); only about 13% were born prior to 1970 and about 13% were born after 1989. Although often this type of research is reported to have an uneven female-male ratio [10], our studies run counter to this trend, attracting a fairly balanced population. 55% of the podcast study participants are male, as are 53% of the videoconferencing study participants and 50% of the educational recordings study participants. They report being well-educated; over 90% said they have attended at least some college and over 60% have a college degree. About 1/3 are currently students. This self-reported characterization is supported by participants' responses to open-ended questions.

Although the participants are completing questionnaires for pay, generally Mechanical Turk is not reported to be a major source of income; rather many participants either have free-lance jobs in the digital economy (e.g. as graphic designers, programmers, IT support, fact-checkers, writers, or editors), or they do other types of work that places them in front of a computer for much of the day (clerical, library, or paralegal work or office management).

5. PRACTICE-RELATED FINDINGS

In past studies, we have found that participants are better able to reflect on specific ethical questions if they have had to address them in their own experience; they are less apt to fall back on hyperbole and apocryphal stories. Thus we asked about video-sharing experience in a number of ways: via a check-box list of online activities (PC,VC,ED), via open-ended questions about online activities and online publishing (PC,VC,ED), via an open-ended question about video-sharing and reuse in the abstract (VC); via a multiple choice question about what they did with the last useful video they had encountered (ED); and via a yes/no question about whether they had ever shared non-music recording (PC). Their answers paint a broad-brush picture of current practice that is useful in interpreting other results and in further understanding the population that the participants represent.

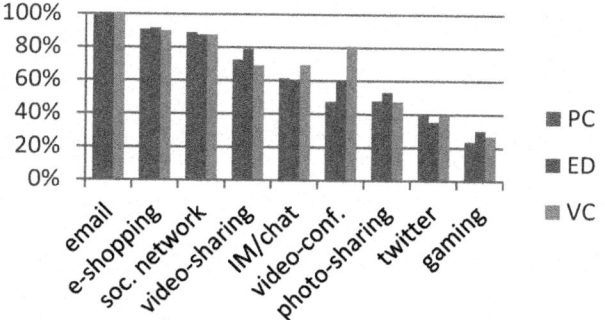

Figure 1. Participants' online activities

First, let's look at the three questions common across studies. Participants were asked to check off their online activities. Figure 1 shows that almost everyone reports using email and social networking. Video-sharing is the fourth most popular activity, more common than photo sharing (at odds with the population at large).

A parallel open-ended question supports this finding. Some participants clarified the activities they picked from the list (e.g. by shopping, they meant bidding on eBay items); others filled in gaps by citing activities we did not list (e.g. finding and listening to music). Many participants reported watching videos, curating the best to share with friends or more broadly on sites like Reddit: "*I upload videos to YouTube & DailyMotion (occasionally)*" [PC089] or "*I've shared video/podcasts/articles on line.*" [ED037] Amateur and professionally produced videos are reported to be a seamless part of an online media diet: "*I use [the Internet] to read up on news, watch TV Shows, upload videos on YouTube, interact with friends on Facebook, shop, and read email.*" [PC125]

As a secondary probe, we asked participants what they publish online; 161 out of 634 participants cited publishing video content. We did not make a bright-line distinction between sharing and publishing. Nor did we distinguish between publishing original content or republishing found media. We wanted to see if participants would make these distinctions themselves, and to see if any ownership and reuse issues arose organically before we presented the hypotheticals. Reports varied. Some referred to profile creation and status sharing as publishing, indistinguishable from other types of sharing; e.g. ED195 reported she publishes "*Various status updates, some profile details such as gender and age, Pictures, videos, funny stuff, informational/education videos or stories.*" Under this rubric, participants said they published personal videos; e.g. ED188 said "*I have a blog about my life and my dogs, I post to Facebook about my life and my dogs, I post videos on YouTube.*" Other participants mentioned creative efforts or cited a mix of genres: "*I have shared/published articles, a few short (self-made) films, and I have re-published videos made by myself or others. I occasionally share photos.*" [PC089] Many participants described republishing multiple content types they had encountered; e.g. PC022 said she published: "*Pictures, Basic information on myself, stories/quotes/videos I have found online.*"

To many, curation is tantamount to publishing. ED207 said "*...I publish any interesting documentary or video related to science. And I published a few instructional videos on software usage.*" He acknowledges the value of his curation of science videos by reporting it in tandem with posting his instructional videos. The distinction between curation and publication may also be enforced by site (e.g. Pinterest v. LinkedIn) and genre (articles v. profiles): "*I share pictures, videos, and articles with friends on Google+ or Pinterest. I have a public profile on Google+ and on LinkedIn which gives personal information about myself and my work history.*" [PC224] Participants feel that certain genres such as comedy and instruction invite republication without concern for content rights, e.g. ED068 said she published both humorous and educational material: "*videos from funny or die or from Youtube - also share videos related to education for nurses (my former career).*" Studies of encountered information (e.g. [17]) have found that sharing published material may have social motivations such as educating friends or keeping in touch: e.g. "*I share videos or articles that I feel my friends would like or should know about...*" [VC190]

Some responses hinted at more subtle ownership and reuse issues. VC027 said he published "*...footage of gameplay from video games.*" The gameplay was his, but the game content was not. Does the subject of a video own sufficient interest to publish it? VC140 reported that he published videos not just *by* him, but also *of* him: "*I usually publish videos of me doing things, like DJ'ing...*" How broadly are rights extended through one's friends and family? PC153 said that he "*Posted video of [his] son's band on youtube...*" Participants also raise a distinction between audio and video tracks; e.g. PC148 said "*...Occasionally I might post a video of something from the travels but generally it's just still images. I am leary [sic] to jump into the world of audio/podcasts, I keep quiet while videotaping.*" We explore the separation of audio and video streams in greater depth via the hypotheticals.

A few responses imposed a linguistic separation between the two terms: one shares what one has found, and one publishes what one has recorded. For example PC141 said he "*Share[s] links to interesting websites and videos. Publish videos of pets. Publish pictures of vacations, home, and garden.*"

Each study included one or two genre-specific practice-oriented questions. We briefly explore these responses with the thought that they reveal the participants' backgrounds, and further contextualize the quantitative portions of the studies.

Keeping podcasts. In the podcast study, we focused on *keeping*, because it is unlikely that participants create or remix podcasts. Thus we asked how many podcasts participants subscribed to and how many they retained after they had listened to them. Out of 225 responses, more than 60% (141) listen to between 1 and 10 podcasts regularly, and about ¼ listen sporadically. Only 11% listen to more than 10 podcasts regularly. Over half (57%) store at least some of podcasts with the intention of permanence. By contrast, 25% delete them after listening and 15% relegate retention to software control. These results show that the storage scenarios represent a familiar decision—can participants intentionally keep content that they've downloaded?

Watching and creating educational videos. In the educational video study, we focused on what participants had watched and whether they had ever created this type of video. Again, we were interested in discovering how far the scenarios were from their own experiences. Most commonly, they had used educational videos occasionally (44%), but it was also fairly common to have used them frequently (28%). Some participants had used them in school (18%), and about 10% had completed entire video courses.

While this made us confident that participants were familiar with educational videos, we wondered if these videos were academic (reflecting the scenario) or practical. We open-coded the responses and identified eight subgenres of instructional videos listed in Table 3, including Humanities and Social Sciences (HSS); Science, Technology, Engineering, and Math (STEM); professional development (e.g. law, EMT, criminal justice, nursing, journalism); how-to tutorials (on practical topics such as auto repair; hobbies; and self-improvement); technology use (how to use hardware, software, and video games); broad topic series (e.g. TED Talks); language-learning; and miscellaneous responses (e.g. "*anything I find interesting*" [ED135]).

Table 3. Genres of instructional videos viewed

Genre	#	%	Genre	#	%
HSS	68	33%	Technology Use	34	16%
STEM	64	31%	Talk Series	22	11%
Professional Dev.	58	28%	Language	14	7%
How-to Tutorials	47	22%	Misc.	10	5%

Finally, we wanted to find out if participants created or recorded educational videos. Almost one-third (31%) had recorded classes; 15% had shared these recordings online. Nearly as many (14%) had created their own educational recordings; 8% had published them on sites like YouTube. Taken together, 22% had published an educational video that they had recorded or created.

Using and recording videoconferences, and sharing videos. In the recorded videoconference study, we wanted to confirm that participants had used Skype or other videoconferencing tools. Exposure to videoconferencing and experience with video-sharing were basic qualifications for understanding the hypotheticals. Only 2% of the participants reported never having used videoconferencing, and 6% had tried it once. Most commonly, participants were occasional (42%) or weekly users (30%). Frequent or daily users made up 20% of study participants.

About two-thirds (133/200) reported that they had shared videos, although we suspect they underreported reuse of copyrighted material, since most reported sharing footage they had recorded themselves.

Table 4 shows the video-sharing breakdown. Open-coding started with a distinction between amateur, found, and professional videos; further distinctions emerged from patterns in the data. Creative efforts are videos participants created or were the subject of, and represent efforts to produce planned artistic works. Everyday documentaries are 'point and shoot' videos that the participant had a hand in creating (as videographer or subject). Found videos are similar to everyday documentaries, except that participants are curators rather than creators, finding the videos and forwarding them to others. Republished videos are professionally made—e.g., TV clips, movie trailers, or music videos—or are recorded from professional performances. The miscellaneous category primarily consists of responses from participants who believe they have not shared the type of videos we are asking about. A few participants justify this as a conscious decision: *"I have not published any video content - the reason is because I know once you put something out there, it's there for good..."* [VC161]

Each category raises different ownership and control issues, issues we anticipate that the participants have become aware of through their own experiences. For example, do subjects or performers have the same rights to content as videographers? Do members of one's social network have more rights than strangers? Do public figures have a reduced expectation of privacy? Does genre have an effect on rights? Does the extent of distribution—or attempts to limit it—matter in determining future rights to reuse? If someone records street performers in a public place (in VC048's case, breakdancers in the subway), does he or she need to obtain the dancers' permission prior to posting the video on YouTube?

Copyright legislation's fair use provisions and existing case law address many of these situations, but it is rare for people to have an accurate picture of what these provisions are, even if they are in professions that rely on fair use. For example, Aufderheide et al. have found that journalists are seldom aware of what fair use provisions dictate, and are indeed more conservative than they need to be [2]. Similarly, we might expect the study participants to reason about the video-sharing instances they report, but we might also expect this reasoning to be based on an emerging notion of fairness and social norms rather than on legal concepts.

Reuse in the abstract. We asked videoconferencing participants about reuse as a general practice. Almost without exception, they

Table 4. Video categories, frequency in data, and use examples

Category	#	Example
Creative effort (e.g. performance, film, sketch comedy)	19	"Srgt. [sic] Richard Cleener was the last video I uploaded to youtube. It was a weekend film challenge and it turned out great!" [VC135]
Everyday documentary (of or by family members)	23	"My son making fart noises with his arm. So that the family could see." [VC128]
Everyday documentary (of or by friends)	19	"I shared a memorial video to a friend who was killed in Iraq." [VC006]
Everyday documentary (vacation/travel footage)	8	"video of vacation to Egypt, to share with family and friends" [VC144]
Everyday documentary (pets)	18	"I took video of my cat rolling around on the floor and eating candy." [VC038]
Everyday documentary (instruction, diagnosis, reviews)	9	"I had shot a video of a positive PPD (Mantoux) on my arm a while ago. I posted it so that others who go through this test will have a rough idea about what will be their end result if at all they take the test." [VC093]
Everyday documentary (business-related)	8	"I produced a small seminar for work, and posted the video via DailyMotion..." [VC044]
Everyday documentary (sports/videogames)	12	"I share video highlights of my basketball team." [VC107]
Found video	12	"It was a dog balancing 36 treats on its nose. Thought it was hilarious, so decided to share." [VC136]
Professional video (specific subgenres)	8	"I shared a video that talks about the SOPA bill..." [VC016]
Professional video (movie and tv clips, commercials, music videos)	8	"The last video I shared was "baby languages" it is a part of an episode from Oprah about 5 sounds that all babies make and what they mean..." [VC047]
Performance video (recording of interview, music, standup, etc.)	7	"It was a brief clip from a sketch comedy show. I shared it because a friend of mine has a thing for Scottish men, and I thought the Glaswegian comedian would brighten her birthday." [VC193]
Miscellaneous negative responses	49	"I have not shared a video - not comfortable with it." [VC080]

interpreted the question in terms of the study's scenarios, which involved publishing a recorded job interview. Thus, in contrast to our other practice-derived findings, participants' answers reflect aspirational beliefs rather normal behavior (similar to what we see happening when privacy questions are pursued [1]).

Recorded videoconferences fall under the rubric of what we're calling 'everyday documentary' (or what Hill and Monroy-Hernandez refer to as functional works [9]). They take the focus off the video's artistic merit or commercial value, and instead explore issues like fairness, privacy, and anonymity. What would participants think were central ideas, preconditions, and issues for the distribution of videoconference content? At one end of the spectrum were participants who felt there should be no publishing restrictions and at the other were participants who felt it was never acceptable. Contrast VC016's response with VC179's:

"I think it is ok at all times. The person is recording something that they are doing on their own so they should have complete rights to the recording. It is originally theirs." [VC016]

"it is almost never a good idea. a videoconference is almost always a "closed door" meeting, and just because it can be recorded doesn't mean that it should..." [VC179]

We open-coded participants' responses and found that they generally reasoned about reuse starting from four situational elements: (1) the content itself and various aspects of the content (e.g. did it reveal confidential, private, or embarrassing information? Was it libelous or malicious?); (2) the production context (e.g. were the people in the videoconference notified beforehand?); (3) the reuse context (e.g. the purpose of publishing the recording); and (4) the legal and technological circumstances (was copyright being infringed?). The dominant concepts we identified within these four overarching categories are shown Table 5. If different concepts appeared in a single response, we coded the response in multiple categories. The counts show the relative frequency of each category.

These themes and other recurring concepts (e.g. minors should be treated differently; credit should always be given; recording can be done for archival purposes) may serve as a bridge to the attitude-related findings we explored through the hypotheticals presented in the next section. As in law, the hypotheticals push participants into stating various boundaries that may not have appeared when they discussed their own practices or their attitudes in the abstract.

6. ATTITUDE-RELATED FINDINGS

Our past studies have shown that experience crucially shapes and refines peoples' attitudes toward ownership [17][19]; it is from this experience that social norms emerge. The results from the practice-oriented questions suggest we thus focus our analysis of the responses to the hypotheticals on the two actions that are common to participants' experience: saving and reusing online video. Table 2 summarizes the three scenarios we used to drive the hypotheticals—a multi-creator comedy podcast, a recorded videoconference of a job interview, and a recorded scientific talk. In this section, we delve into details of individual hypotheticals as we examine aspects of saving and reusing.

The hypotheticals related to *saving* explore four aspects of ownership: (1) the distinction between creator and subject; (2) the difference between local storage and cloud storage; (3) the distinction between primary content (i.e. the recording) and secondary content (e.g. comments and reviews); and (4) the effect of content transformations (e.g. format changes) on perceptions of ownership. Storing content on the cloud provides a venue for probing the boundary between saving and sharing; the cloud potentially exposes the content to external parties, although it is not explicit sharing. Transcoding (converting the video from one format to another) also pushes on the boundary between storage and reuse by posing potential content changes.

Next we explore concepts associated with *reuse*. In the scenarios, reuse appears in its most recognizable form: the video content is taken from one online venue and republished in another. The hypotheticals make a distinction between republication—where content is taken in its entirety and put on a different site or presented to a different audience—and *remix*, where the content is manipulated or excerpted and used in different ways (e.g. the genre may shift from instruction to comedy). Again, we look at issues that arise from reuse of associated secondary content, including social metadata such as comments or tags.

In this group of scenarios we also examine concepts from participants' responses to open-ended questions in past studies, including permission, credit, commercial v. non-commercial use, manipulation and fraud, and changing the mood of the work (e.g. from serious to funny) [18][19].

The results are organized by scenario, so the responses to the successive hypotheticals can be compared.

Table 5. Participants' reactions to reusing recordings

Situational element	Concept	#	Example
content	personal content	35	"...I think it is okay when it is informative information or impersonal items but personal events should be kept private." [VC059]
	confidential content	27	"[It's okay] when it's good for the public interest, as long as it does not violate non-disclosure and/or confidentiality agreements ..." [VC136]
production context	recording notification	40	"...I say you would need ... to let them know ahead of time that it could be shared. I don't think it is ok to post any recording if someone in it is unaware..." [VC171]
	permission or consent	104	"It's ok to share video content if it belongs to you or you get permission from the person that made the videoconference content." [VC071]
	scope	68	"Recording and sharing of videoconference content is OK when all parties have granted permission..." [VC131]
	public space or person	16	"I think it would be okay ... if it is in a public space." [VC095]
	expectation of privacy	15	"It's ok when it is done with permission or when it won't undermine someone else's legitimate expectations." [VC022]
reuse context	personal use	14	"Recording videoconferences I [am] 100% OK with, as long as the recording party intends to keep it for personal use. When publishing and sharing gets involved, things become less simple..." [VC088]
	internal use/ limited distribution	7	"...Meetings can be shared to help people who miss them catch up... Also, there should be some restrictions as to who can access these meetings." [VC189]
	good intentions/ helping others or education	20	"I think it is okay when it is intended as an archive for those who were involved in the videoconference, or for documentation. For example, I have weekly videoconferences as work with employees in other states and countries, and they recorded videos serve as proof of the decisions we made, and as resources for employees..." [VC188]
	misuse	7	"I believe it is only okay when it is for entertaining or informing purposes. I thinks [sic] it is a bad idea when it involves a situation like the one this survey was about because it may allow people to get jobs which they are under-qualified for." [VC091]
	libelous intentions	16	"...It is a bad idea when it is done maliciously or to cause harm by reputation or slander." [VC078]
	imposed anonymity	24	"...If you remove names and specific content and use it as a guide it's ok by me..." [VC078] "...Only the edited down versions where the owner has claim to the video i.e.: his face and voice, should be allowed." [VC125]
legal and technological circumstance	technology dictates use	3	"If the content is publish[ed] one should expect it to be available and searchable by other people." [VC178]
	legally regulated	6	"It should be subject to the same regulations as e-mails: anyone who is a party should be able to do whatever they like with it..." [VC197]
conditional reuse is fine/ control of online content is ultimately impossible		105	"...I like that the internet is still mostly unregulated and am against anything that regulates it like SOPA." [VC191] "Be very careful and be certain it is not anything you care deeply about because once it is out there it is no longer yours to control." [VC056]

6.1 Podcast scenario

In the podcast scenario, we first explored whether it matters who saves the recording: an on-the-air creator of the podcast (host Jordan), a behind-the-scenes creator (engineer Chip), or a podcast guest, Rocky. Figure 2 shows the results. As we have seen in past studies, saving is generally uncontroversial. Participants seem to believe that if you encounter content online, you should be able to save it locally. All three alternatives trend highly positive; there is almost no difference between whether Chip or Jordan can save the podcast. On the other hand, there is mild hesitation about whether the guest (Rocky) should be able to save the recording. The difference between the responses for Rocky and the other two is statistically significant (p<.0001, Wilcoxon signed-rank test).

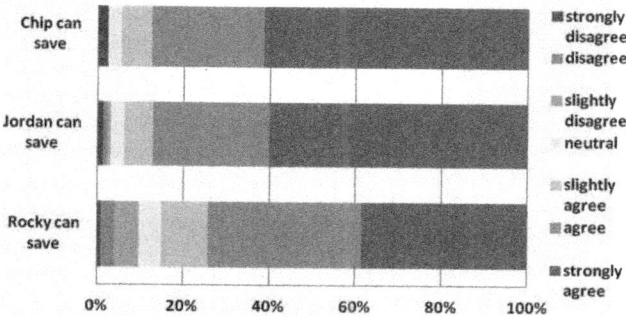

Figure 2. Responses to saving podcast hypotheticals.

A more controversial activity in prior questionnaires has been republishing part or all of an existing work. We explore this through a series of nine hypotheticals. The first six distinguish between republish as is and remix; the final three explore who has the authority to grant permission to republish. Figure 3 shows the results of the first six hypotheticals. The first two hypotheticals posit republication of the recording as-is; the variation is between creator and guest. The third hypothetical looks at partial reuse instead of full republication (Rocky excerpts a song he performed during the original recording). Hypotheticals four and five posit remix (bonus material is added and interview segments are removed). In the final hypothetical, the guest not only remixes the episode, but also republishes the comments along with his remix.

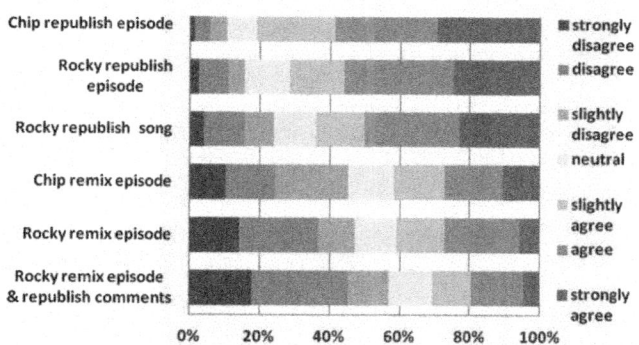

Figure 3. Responses to reusing or remixing podcast.

The results show that republishing the whole episode as-is is more acceptable than the form of remixing we described in the hypotheticals. More participants believed the behind-the-scenes creator (Chip) should be able to republish the episode on his own website than the guest (Rocky) should. This difference was statistically significant (p<.04). Commercial reuse was also explored: guest Rocky excerpted his performance of a new song from the podcast so he could sell it on iTunes. This hypothetical elicited 64% positive and 24% negative responses.

When presented with a hypothetical in which Chip or Rocky published a remixed version of the whole episode, opinions were more sharply divided, with 41-42% positive responses and 45-47% negative responses respectively. The variation in who created the remix did not result in a statistically significant difference in the responses (p<.13). A final hypothetical explored whether Rocky could not only publish a remixed version of the podcast on his own website, but also copy some of the positive user comments attached to the original podcast to promote the remixed version. Not surprisingly, this was viewed most skeptically of all.

6.2 Videoconference

Meetings may be conducted using videoconferencing software that enables the meetings to be recorded. What ownership issues are raised by these recordings? Our second questionnaire uses scenarios in which interviewees Bill and Kyle record Skype-based job interviews.

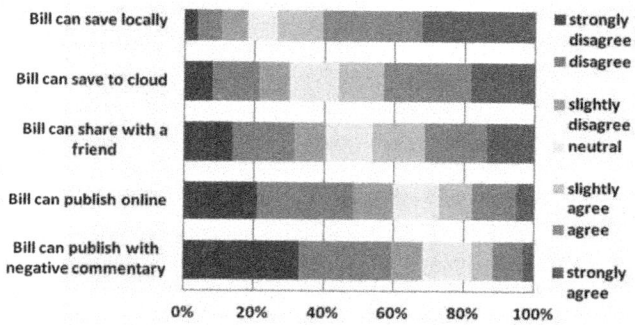

Figure 4. Responses to saving/sharing interview.

In the first set of hypotheticals, Bill records his own job interview with a software company. Saving digital media is normally uncontroversial, but since Bill recorded a conversation, we wondered if saving the recording might raise additional issues. Sure enough, while most of the participants agree that Bill can record the interview for his own use, there are more negative and neutral responses than for any other of our comparable hypotheticals about saving content. We also used this recorded interview to test the difference between saving content locally and storing it in the cloud. From there, we transitioned to a hypothetical in which Bill shares the recording with a friend, then distributes it more broadly online. A final hypothetical finds him overlaying a commentary track about the company's unfair hiring practices. Figure 4 shows the progression of responses to these hypotheticals.

The distinction between saving locally and storing the recording on the cloud provoked a significant drop in agreement (p<.001). Participants may have viewed cloud storage as less secure; they may have found cloud storage as a step closer to sharing; or they may have less understanding of cloud storage's implications.

Only 46% agreed that Bill could share the recorded interview with a friend who was also looking for a job; this agreement dropped to 27% when publication replaced sharing and to 18% when Bill overlaid a commentary track about the company's unfair hiring practices.

But before we assume that there are no widely acceptable uses of the recorded videoconference, we posited two modified versions of the interview video. In the first, Bill remixes the video by extracting his answers to the interview questions so neither the company nor the interviewer's questions are included. He uses these answers to create three videos: one shows off his knowledge in hopes of getting a job, another adds commentary about "Dos and Don'ts" for job interviews, and a third is a self-deprecating comedy video in which he replaces the interviewer's questions with recordings of his brother asking the questions. More than 65% of the participants agreed that Bill could publish or share these remixes. Figure 5 shows that the three most positive responses were elicited by remixes that showed some concern for public good, either by providing lessons or humor for others.

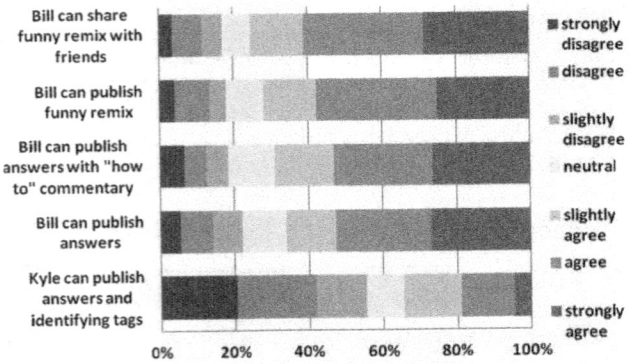

Figure 5. Responses to remixing interview.

In the final hypothetical of the series, Bill publishes his answers to attract another employer; the details are altered to test the effects of anonymization. In this variation, Kyle watches Bill's "How to" video before his own interview. He records the interview and, like Bill, edits out any traces of the company from the recording. He then publishes his new video to "pay it forward," but adds tags that identify the company and specify that it is a job interview. Participants have a significant negative response to the inclusion of the identifying tags. This poses an issue for social media since tags can be added after the content is posted – if someone deduced and tagged the company portrayed in Bill's recording, the same situation would arise.

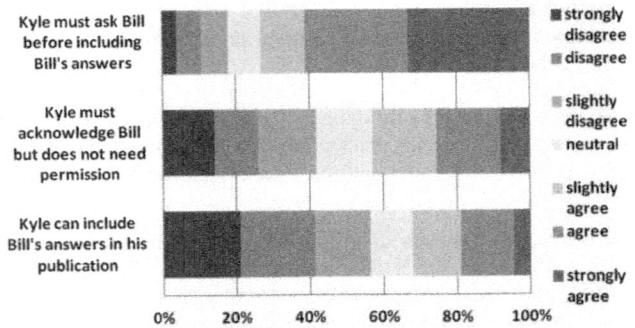

Figure 6. Responses to permission for interview reuse.

Figure 6 shows a last remix episode that explores whether Kyle can use Bill's answers in his new video to create a more valuable "how to interview" video. 73% of the participants believe Kyle must get Bill's permission before he uses the clips. 32% throught Kyle could include Bill's answers as they were already available online, while 43% thought acknowledgement was sufficient. While not all responses are logically consistent, they do provide a relative assessment of participants' beliefs about permission, acknowledgement, and reuse.

6.3 Educational Recordings

Many public and institutional lectures are recorded and published online. These recordings may be of notable speeches or regular class presentations. Because the institutions that collect this content often do not have the infrastructure to provide the content online, they enter into agreements with online services such as iTunes or YouTube. This questionnaire explored the rights of different stakeholders in this situation, including presenters, their peers, institutions, service providers, and viewers.

In the study's primary scenario, an astronaut (Sally) delivers a commencement address on the importance of manned space exploration. A video of the address is captured by the university and is made available through a web service; the video attracts numerous comments, ratings, and tags. A geologist (Cheryl) believes NASA's resources would be better spent on unmanned missions and wants to use the video to provoke discussion.

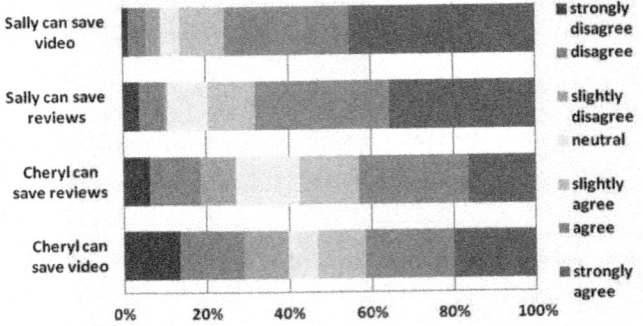

Figure 7. Responses to saving educational video.

We start by exploring different parties' rights to save the video and the associated metadata (comments, tags, etc.). In contrast to hypotheticals in prior studies, saving in this case explicitly involves transcoding the video from the web service's proprietary format to a more common format. Perhaps because of this we see some controversy over saving encountered content. There is general agreement that Sally can save and transcode the video of her own presentation. There is somewhat less agreement that she can save the metadata that has been added by other users of the web service (p<.03). In contrast, there is substantial disagreement about whether Cheryl, Sally's scientific peer, has the same rights. Interestingly, Cheryl's right to save the metadata is seen as greater than her right to save the original video (p<.04). See Figure 7.

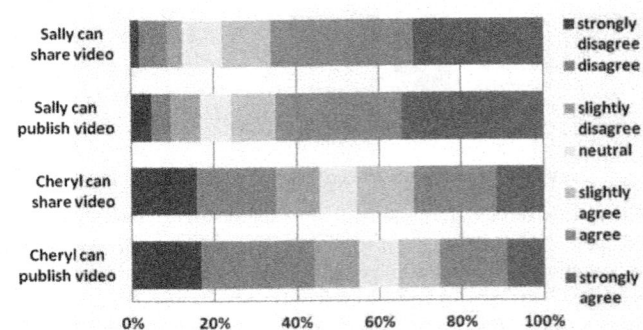

Figure 8. Responses to sharing/republishing educational video.

Beyond saving the video, who can share or republish it? Figure 8 shows that most participants agree that Sally should be able to share the transcoded video with friends via Facebook and to put it on her public website. There was no statistical difference between the responses to these two questions.

Given that Cheryl is seen as having less right to save the video, it is unsurprising that she is also seen as having less rights to share and publish it (p<.0001). Cheryl's right to share the saved video with friends via Facebook is perhaps the most divisive variation; the results are close to symetric around neutral. The majority (55%) of participants feel that Cheryl has a diminished right to republish the video (difference from sharing, p<.0002).

One important characteristic of social media is the community involvement in commenting on, rating, and tagging content. Who owns this secondary content? What rights do the authors of the original content or the added content have? How about the host web service? We explored these issues through a series of hypotheticals about the reuse of reviews and permission for this reuse. Results are shown in Figure 9.

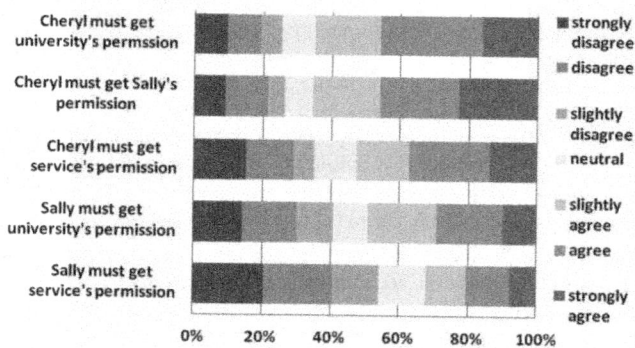

Figure 10. Responses to the concept of permission for educational video reuse.

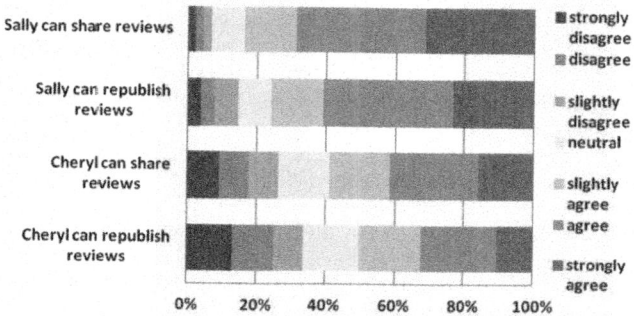

Figure 9. Responses to sharing/publishing reviews of video.

84% of the participants agreed that Sally has a right to share selected reviews of her commencement address via Facebook; 76% believe she should be able to republish selected tags and reviews from the web service when she posts the video to her own web site. The difference between the reactions to sharing and republishing is significant (p<.001).

As we mentioned earlier, Cheryl's rights to the reviews are viewed more positively than her rights to the video itself. 59% agree that Cheryl can share selected reviews from the web service with her friends via Facebook and 50% agree she can republish selected reviews on her own website to help make her point about unmanned space exploration. The difference between her rights and Sally's rights is significant (p<.0001) as is the difference between sharing and publishing (p<.001).

In our earlier studies, authors' permission often arose when participants were asked open-ended questions about appropriate practices for content reuse. The scenario in this study involves a number of stakeholders that might have some say over content reuse. We first asked whether Sally should have to get permission to reuse the video from either the university that recorded the lecture or the web service hosting the video. Figure 10 shows that 49% thought Sally should get the university's permission while only 32% thought it was necessary to seek the service provider's permission. The difference is significant (p<.001).

Because Cheryl has no special claim to the commencement video (she neither delivered the talk nor recorded the video), we explored whether she would need to get permission from Sally, the university, or the web video service provider. Again, the web service provider's permission is the considered the least necessary (difference is significant, p<.001). This is in direct contrast to many interpretations of today's terms-of-use agreements and intellectual property laws. Participants instead thought Cheryl should have to get the university's and Sally's permission (the responses were statistically indistinguishable).

We also asked who needed to give Cheryl permission to republish reviews of the video found on the web service. Nearly half of the participants thought Cheryl should get permission from the review's author and the service. (See Figure 11.) The difference in responses to these two questions were not significant. Only 38% thought Cheryl should get Sally's permission to republish reviews. This is significantly different than the responses to the other two questions (p<.01).

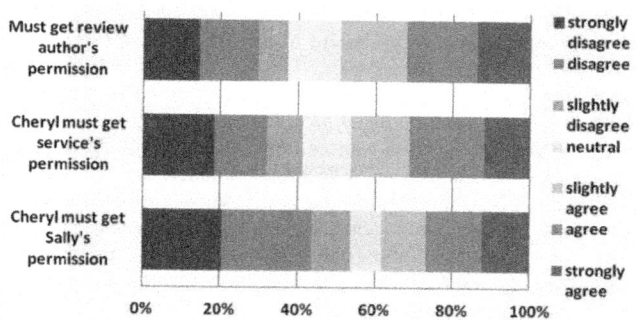

Figure 11. Responses to permission for video review reuse.

While slightly over half of the participants disagreed with the need to get Sally's permission, it is interesting that her claim of authorship (she was the speaker in the video) would extend to the video's comments. Do people view the primary content creator as a proxy for the community's authority? We cannot say from this questionnaire alone, but when we combine these results with those from a similar questionnaire about product reviews [30], it is clear that rights are not limited to the content creator. People apply a more nuanced sense of ownership in such situations.

7. DESIGN IMPLICATIONS

By analyzing data gathered from 634 participants, we are able to characterize emerging social norms and current practices associated with video storage, reuse, and remix. What comes out most strongly is that participants' attitudes and actions are constrained neither by the specific legal provisions that guide reuse, nor the terms and conditions that govern the content on most social media sites, but rather by a nuanced ethos that they have developed though experience. The question, then, is can we design technology and policy that facilitates the constructive aspects of current practice, while satisfying the more restrictive aspirational norms that participants expressed? We observed a very real (and understandable) tension between the two.

First, let's look back at the highlights of what the participants said and did. Through their account of their own experiences, we see that over 70% of the participants report sharing videos (we suspect underreporting, since it is so easy and unremarkable to share a video using a link) and it is likely that even more watch videos; many mention this specifically in an open-ended question about their online activities. The podcast study shows that many participants store downloaded material with an intention of keeping it indefinitely as a personal archive. The educational video study further demonstrates that the recordings represent a range of genres, and span professionally produced material as well as amateur videos. The videoconferencing study shows that many participants have also produced their own videos, including creative efforts, personal footage, and other types of documentary recordings. Finally, also from the videoconferencing study, we learned that participants reason about reuse from different ethical perspectives, including the nature of the content, the conditions of reuse, the details of production, and the technological and legal circumstances that they are aware of. Thus participants are judging the hypotheticals we pose from a vantage point of personal familiarity and are applying their experience.

Next let's look at the hypotheticals. From our previous studies, we believe that downloading primary content and storing it locally is essentially uncontroversial. We tested and confirmed this for online video. But we also introduced three provocative variations (1) the use of cloud storage instead of local storage; (2) the storage of transcoded content instead of duplicate content; and (3) the addition of secondary content to primary content (reviews of videos v. the videos themselves). Cloud storage and transcoding were both situations that blurred boundaries: cloud storage takes the content out of the realm of local control (a service provider is necessarily involved) and transcoding means potentially making changes to the content even if those changes are not directly observable. Secondary content introduces a notion of community ownership, or at the very least, ownership dependencies. Indeed, both cloud storage and transcoding seemed to reduce participants' comfort with saving video. Secondary content proved to be paradoxical; ownership of primary content does not extend to secondary content, but there is a more relaxed attitude toward secondary content in general; it may simply be regarded as less valuable.

Other hypotheticals brought in republishing and remixing. What did we learn there? As we have seen before, ownership comes into play more strongly when a video is shared or republished. In the least controversial case, an owner can fairly freely republish video content, even if there are co-owners. Commercial purposes add complexity, as does remix (especially if it violates abstract notions of fairness by, say, omitting negative reviews, or crossing the boundary into art theft [23]). This echoes some of our earlier findings: participants are sensitive to reuse situations that seem *per se* unfair—a recording that compromises hiring fairness, a satirical video that seems unduly mean-spirited, or not asking permission when it may be advisable.

What are the design and policy implications of what we have seen? The results clearly cannot be taken too literally: participants sometimes favor a permission-based system for reuse when fair use cases establish that none is necessary [26] (not to mention that experience suggests permission will be unobtainable [20]). They also signal certain problems with existing labeling schemes such as Creative Commons [3], because in the abstract, participants seem more sensitive to reuse than they are when confronted with particular instances and reciprocal examples (i.e. when they are the reusers). Nor is all reuse equal in the eyes of content creators and content reusers; the acceptability of reuse depends on circumstantial factors like the nature of the content (e.g., is it personal?), the differential scope of the audience (e.g., is the reused video in the process of going viral or is it now playing to an audience of 10? How different is this scope from the original?), the type of reuse (e.g., has it been included in a clip show? Will the video's original intent be distorted?), and the way the implied (or explicit) social contract between all potential owners of both the original and derived work is handled (e.g., is attribution or anonymity desired?).

Notice that only one of these factors is known at publication time (the nature of the content). Others are contingent on how the content is reused (e.g., changes in genre, audience, or publication venue). Still others are not revealed until time has passed (e.g. the differential scope of the audience). That these factors are crucial to how any labeling scheme is used makes us think that supplemental mechanisms might be desirable (hypothetical scenarios and mixed-initiative dialogs to help content creators envision reuse or decide between attribution or anonymity, or triggers that reveal when the differential scope or audience has changed). Still others depend on, say, the motivations for storing the video (past work tells us that individuals archive work that is not their own just as surely as institutions do [7][19][22]).

Thus ownership-driven questions need to be approached thoughtfully, lest we impose restrictions when none are necessary, or we do not anticipate types of reuse that will trigger the most extreme reactions when these reactions could have been averted. Our future work will continue to explore these questions on a per-genre, per-media basis, using a variety of qualitative and quantitative methods to unpack assumptions, identify social norms, and look forward to an unfolding spectrum of reuse situations.

8. ACKNOWLEDGEMENTS

This work was supported in part by National Science Foundation grants IIS-1049217 and DUE-0938074.

9. REFERENCES

[1] Acquisti, A. and Grossklags, J. Privacy Attitudes and Privacy Behavior, in J. Camp and S. Lewis (Eds.) *The Economics of Information Security*, Kluwer, Boston, pp. 165-178.

[2] Aufderheide, P., Jaszi, P., Boyles, J.L., and Bieze, K. Copyright, Free Speech, and the Public's Right to Know: How Journalists Think about Fair Use, (July 30, 2012). Retrieved from http://dx.doi.org/10.2139/ssrn.2119933

[3] Boyle, J. *The Public Domain: Enclosing the Commons of the Mind*, Yale University Press, New Haven & London, 2008.

[4] Dale, M., Stern, A., Deckert, M. and Sack W.. 2009. Metavid.org: a social website and open archive of congressional video. In *Proc. DGR '09*, 309-310.

[5] Diakopoulos, N., Luther, K., Medynskiy, Y. and Essa, I. The evolution of authorship in a remix society. In *Proc. HT '07*. ACM, New York, NY, USA, 133-136.

[6] Downs, J., Holbrook, M., Sheng, S., and Cranor, L. Are your participants gaming the system?: Screening Mechanical Turk workers. *Proc. of CHI'10*. ACM, 2399-2402.

[7] Greengard, S. Digitally Possessed. *Communications of the ACM*, 55 (5), 2012, 14-16.

[8] Hill, B., Monroy-Hernandez, A., and Olson, K. Responses to Remixing on a Social Media Website. *Proc. AAAI Conference on Weblogs and Social Media*. 2010. 74-81.

[9] Hill, B. and Monroy-Hernandez, A. The Cost of Collaboration for Code and Art: Evidence from a Remixing Community. *Proc. CSCW 2013*. ACM. 1035-1046.

[10] Ipeirotis, P. Analyzing the Amazon Mechanical Turk Marketplace. *ACM XRDS* 17, 2, Winter 2010.

[11] Jakobsson, M. Experimenting on Mechanical Turk: 5 How Tos. *ITWorld*, September 3, 2009.

[12] Kittur, A., Chi, E., and Suh, B. Crowdsourcing User Studies with Mechanical Turk. *Proc. of CHI'08*. ACM, 453-456.

[13] Lessig, L. *Code, Version 2.0*, Basic Books, 2006.

[14] Lessig, L. *Remix: Making Art and Commerce Thrive in the Hybrid Economy*, Penguin, New York, 2008.

[15] Levi, E. *An Introduction to Legal Reasoning*. University of Chicago Press, 1949.

[16] MacCormick D. and Summers, R. (eds.) *Interpreting Precedents*, Ashgate/Dartmouth, 1997, pp. 528-9.

[17] Marshall, C. and Bly, S. Saving and Using Encountered Information: Implications for Electronic Periodicals. *Proc. CHI'05*, ACM, pp. 111-120.

[18] Marshall, C. and Shipman, F. "Social Media Ownership: Using Twitter as a Window onto Current Attitudes and Beliefs", *Proc. of CHI 2011*. ACM. 1081-1090.

[19] Marshall, C. and Shipman, F. "The Ownership and Reuse of Visual Media", *Proc. of JCDL 2011*. ACM. 157-166.

[20] McDonough, J., Olendorf, R., Kirschenbaum, M., Kraus, K., Reside, D., Donahue, R., Phelps, A., Egert, C., Lowood, H., Rojo, S. *Preserving Virtual Worlds Final Report*. 8/ 31/2010.

[21] Monroy-Hernandez, A., Hill, B.M., Gonzalez-Rivero, J. and boyd, d. Computers can't give credit: how automatic attribution falls short in an online remixing community. *Proc CHI '11*. ACM, New York, NY, USA, 3421-3430.

[22] Odom, W. Sellen, A., Harper, R., and Thereska, E. Lost in Translation: Understanding the Possession of Digital Things in the Cloud. *Proc. CHI'12*. ACM. 781-790.

[23] Perkel, D. The Art of Theft: Creativity and Property on deviantART. *Material World Blog*. 2010. Retrieved from http://blogs.nyu.edu/projects/materialworld/2010/07/the_art_of_theft_creativity_an.html.

[24] Rissland, E.L. and Ashley, K. Hypotheticals as Heuristic Device. *Proc. Strategic Computing Natural Language*, Marina del Rey, California, May 1-2, 1986, 165-178.

[25] Rotman, D., and Preece, J. The "WeTube"; in YouTube – creating an online community through video sharing. *Int. J. Web Based Communities* 6, 3 (June 2010), 317-333.

[26] Sag, M. Predicting Fair Use. Ohio State Law Journal, 73 (1), 2012, 47-91.

[27] Samuelson, P. Too Many Copyrights, *CACM* 54, 7 (2011).

[28] San Pedro, J., Siersdorfer, S., and Sanderson, M. Content redundancy in YouTube and its application to video tagging. *ACM TOIS*. 29, 3 (July 2011), Article 13.

[29] Schmitz, P., Shafton, P., Shaw, R., Tripodi, S., Williams, B., and Yang, J. International remix: video editing for the web. *Proc. MM '06*, 797-798.

[30] Shipman, F. and Marshall, C. Are User-contributed Reviews Community Property? Exploring the Beliefs and Practices of Reviewers. *WebSci 2013*. ACM. forthcoming.

[31] Solum, L.B. *Legal Theory Blog*, entry dated July 11, 2010. http://lsolum.typepad.com/legaltheory/2010/07/legal-theory-lexicon-hypotheticals.html.

[32] Stutzman, F. Twitter and the Library of Congress. http://fstutzman.com/2010/04/14/twitter-and-the-library-of-congress/.

[33] Vihavainen, S., Mate, S., Seppälä, L., Cricri, F., & Curcio, I. We want more: human-computer collaboration in mobile social video remixing of music concerts. *CHI '11*, 287-296.

[34] Vihavainen, S., Mate, S., Liikkanen, L. and Curcio, I. Video as memorabilia: user needs for collaborative automatic mobile video production. *Proc CHI '12*. 651-654.

[35] Xie, L., Natsev, A., Kender, J.R., Hill, M., and Smith, J.R. Visual memes in social media: tracking real-world news in YouTube videos. *Proc. ACM MM '11*, 53-62.

From Amateurs to Connoisseurs: Modeling the Evolution of User Expertise through Online Reviews

Julian McAuley
Stanford University
jmcauley@cs.stanford.edu

Jure Leskovec
Stanford University
jure@cs.stanford.edu

ABSTRACT

Recommending products to consumers means not only understanding their *tastes*, but also understanding their level of *experience*. For example, it would be a mistake to recommend the iconic film *Seven Samurai* simply because a user enjoys other action movies; rather, we might conclude that they will *eventually* enjoy it—once they are ready. The same is true for beers, wines, gourmet foods—or any products where users have acquired tastes: the 'best' products may not be the most 'accessible'. Thus our goal in this paper is to recommend products that a user will enjoy *now*, while acknowledging that their tastes may have changed over time, and may change again in the future. We model how tastes change due to the very act of consuming more products—in other words, as users become more *experienced*. We develop a latent factor recommendation system that explicitly accounts for each user's level of experience. We find that such a model not only leads to better recommendations, but also allows us to study the role of user experience and expertise on a novel dataset of fifteen million beer, wine, food, and movie reviews.

Categories and Subject Descriptors

H.3.3 [**Information Search and Retrieval**]: Information Search and Retrieval

Keywords

recommender systems, expertise, user modeling

1. INTRODUCTION

> "Even when experts all agree, they may well be mistaken"
>
> – Bertrand Russell

In order to predict how a user will respond to a product, we must understand the tastes of the user and the properties of the product. We must also understand how these properties change and evolve over time. As an example, consider the *Harry Potter* film series: adults who enjoy the films for their special effects may no longer enjoy them in ten years, once their special effects are obsolete; children who enjoy the films today may simply outgrow them in ten years; *future* children who watch the films in ten years may not enjoy them, once Harry Potter has been supplanted by another wizard.

This example highlights three different mechanisms that cause perceptions of products to change. Firstly, such change may be tied to the age of the *product*. Secondly, it may be tied to the age (or development) of the *user*. Thirdly, it may be tied to the state (or zeitgeist) of the *community* the user belongs to.

These mechanisms motivate different models for temporal dynamics in product recommendation systems. Our goal in this paper is to propose models for such mechanisms, in order to assess which of them best captures the temporal dynamics present in real product rating data.

A variety of existing works have studied the evolution of products and online review communities. The emergence of new products may cause users to change their focus [19]; older movies may be treated more favorably once they are considered 'classics' [20]; and users may be influenced by general trends in the community, or by members of their social networks [26].

However, few works have studied the *personal development* of users, that is, how users' tastes change and evolve as they gain knowledge, maturity, and experience. A user may have to be exposed to many films before they can fully appreciate (by awarding it a high rating) *Citizen Kane*; a user may not appreciate a *Romanée-Conti* (the 'Citizen Kane' of red wine) until they have been exposed to many inferior reds; a user may find a strong cheese, a smokey whiskey, or a bitter ale unpalatable until they have developed a tolerance to such flavors. The very act of consuming products will cause users' tastes to change and evolve. Developing new models that take into account this novel viewpoint of user evolution is one of our main contributions.

We model such 'personal development' through the lens of user *experience*, or *expertise*. Starting with a simple definition, experience is some quality that users gain over time, as they consume, rate, and review additional products. The underlying hypothesis that we aim to model is that users with similar levels of experience will rate products in similar ways, even if their ratings are temporally far apart. In other words, each user evolves on their own 'personal clock'; this differs from other models of temporal dynamics, which model the evolution of user and product parameters on a single timescale [20, 40, 41].

Naturally, some users may already be experienced at the time of their first review, while others may enter many reviews while failing to ever become experienced. By individually learning for each user the rate at which their experience progresses, we are able to account for both types of behavior.

Specifically, we model each user's level of experience using a series of latent parameters that are constrained to be monotonically non-decreasing as a function of time, so that each user becomes more experienced (or stays at least as experienced) as they rate additional products. We learn latent-factor recommender systems for

Copyright is held by the International World Wide Web Conference Committee (IW3C2). IW3C2 reserves the right to provide a hyperlink to the author's site if the Material is used in electronic media.
WWW 2013, May 13–17, 2013, Rio de Janeiro, Brazil.
ACM 978-1-4503-2035-1/13/05.

different experience levels, so that users 'progress' between recommender systems as they gain experience.

'Experience' and 'expertise' are *interpretations* of our model's latent parameters. In our context they simply refer to some unobserved quantity of a user that increases over time as they consume and review more products. Intuitively, our monotonicity requirement constrains users to evolve in the same 'direction', so that what we are really learning is some property of user evolution that is common to all users, regardless of when they arrive in the community. We perform extensive qualitative analysis to argue that 'experience' is a reasonable interpretation of such parameters. In particular, our goal is not to say whether experienced/expert users are 'better' or 'more accurate' at rating products. We simply model the fact that users with the same level of experience/expertise rate products in a *similar* way.

Our experimental findings reveal that modeling the personal evolution of each user is highly fruitful, and often beats alternatives that model evolution at the level of products and communities. Our models of user experience also allow us to study the differences between experienced and novice users, and to discover *acquired tastes* in novel corpora of fifteen million beer, wine, food, and movie reviews.

A Motivating Example

We demonstrate the evolution of user tastes and differences between novices and experts (i.e., experienced users) by considering the beer-rating website *RateBeer*, which consists of around three million beer reviews.

In this data we find a classic example of an acquired taste: hops. The highest-rated beers on the website are typically the hoppiest (American Pale Ales, India Pale Ales, etc.); however, due to their bitterness, such beers may be unpalatable to inexperienced users. Thus we might argue that even if such beers are the *best* (i.e., the highest rated), they will only be *recognized* as the best by the most experienced members of the community.

Figure 1 examines the relationship between product ratings, user experience level, and hoppiness, on *RateBeer* data. Beers of three types are considered (in increasing order of hoppiness): lagers, mild ales, and strong ales. The x-axis shows the average rating of products on the site (out of 5 stars), while the y-axis shows the *difference* between expert and novice ratings. 'Experts' are those users to whom our model assigns the highest values of our latent experience score, while 'novices' are assigned the lowest value; Figure 1 then shows the difference in product bias terms between the two groups.

This simple plot highlights some of our main findings with regard to user evolution: firstly, there is significant variation between the ratings of beginner and expert users, with the two groups differing by up to half a star in either direction. Secondly, there exist entire *genres* of products that are preferred almost entirely by experts or by beginners: beginners give higher ratings to almost all lagers, while experts give higher ratings to almost all strong ales; thus we might conclude that strong ales are an 'acquired taste'.

Finally, we find a strong correlation between the overall popularity of a product, and how much it is preferred by experienced users: experts tend to give the harshest ratings to the lowest-rated products, while they give the most generous ratings to the highest-rated products (continuing our analogy, they have learned to 'fully appreciate' them). Thus while a lager such as *Bud Light* is disliked by everybody, it is *most disliked* by experts; one of the most popular beers in the entire corpus, *Firestone XV*, is liked by everybody, but is *most liked* by experts. We find such observations to be quite general across many datasets that we consider.

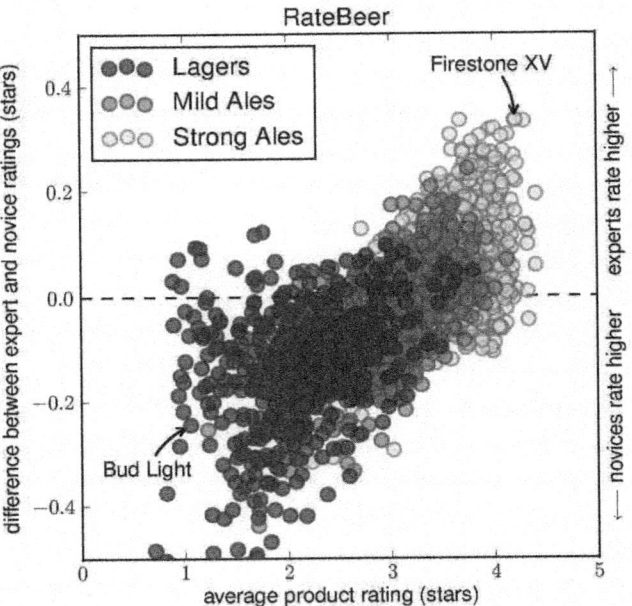

Figure 1: Beloved products are most beloved by experts; hated products are most hated by experts.

Contribution and Findings

We propose a latent-factor model for the evolution of user experience in product recommendation systems, and compare it to other models of user and community evolution. While temporal dynamics and concept drift have been studied in online reviews [13, 20, 29], the critical difference between our model and existing work on temporal dynamics is how we treat experience as a function of time. Existing models for temporal dynamics work under the hypothesis that two users will respond most similarly to a product if they rate the product *at the same time*. In contrast, we model the *personal* evolution of users' tastes over time. We show that two users respond most similarly to a product if they review it *at the same experience level*, even if there is significant separation in time between their reviews. Our model allows us to capture similarities between users, even when their reviews are temporally far apart.

In terms of experiments, we evaluate our model on five product rating websites, using novel corpora consisting of over 15 million reviews. Our ratings come from diverse sources including beers, wines, gourmet foods, and movies.

We find that our model of user *experience* significantly outperforms traditional recommender systems, and similar alternatives that model user evolution at the level of products and communities.

Finally, we find that our latent experience parameters are themselves useful as *features* to facilitate further study of how experts and novices behave. For example, we discover that experienced users rate top products more generously than beginners, and bottom products more harshly (as in Fig. 1); we find that users who fail to gain experience are likely to abandon the community; we find that experts' ratings are easier to predict than those of beginners; and we find that experienced users agree more closely when reviewing the same products. We can also use the notion of experience to discover which products, or categories of products, are preferred by

Community evolution at uniform intervals:

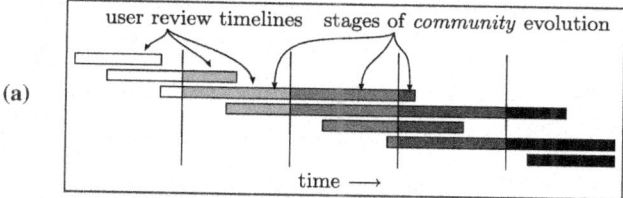

Individual user evolution at uniform intervals:

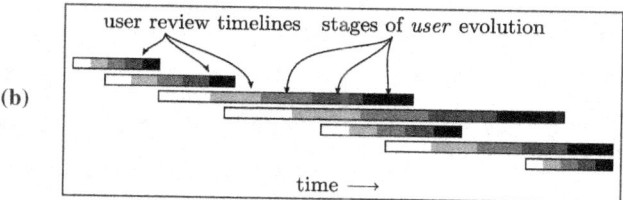

Community evolution at learned intervals:

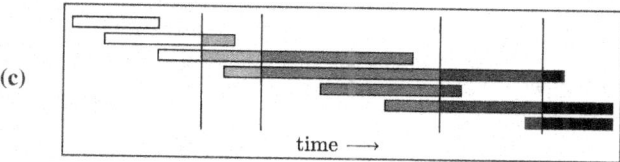

Individual user evolution at learned intervals:

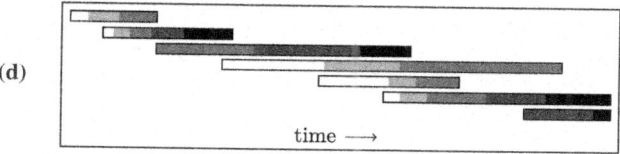

Figure 2: Visualization of the models we consider. Horizontal bars represent user review timelines; colors within each bar represent evolution parameters for each user.

beginners or by experts—that is, we can discover which products are *acquired tastes*.

The rest of this paper is organized as follows: We describe our models for user evolution in Section 2, and we describe how to train these models in Section 3. In Section 4 we describe our novel rating datasets and evaluate our models. In Section 5 we examine the role of our latent experience variables in detail, before reviewing related work in Section 6 and concluding in Section 7.

2. MODELS OF USER EVOLUTION

We design models to evaluate our hypothesis that 'experience' is a critical underlying factor which causes users' ratings to evolve. We do so by considering alternate paradigms of user and community evolution, and determining which of them best fits our data.

Figure 2 visualizes each of the four models we consider. Each horizontal bar represents a single user's review timeline, from their first to their last review; the color within each bar represents the evolution of that user or their community. At each of these stages of evolution, a different recommender system is used to estimate their ratings. Recommender systems for adjacent stages are regularized to be similar, so that transitions between successive stages are smooth.

(a) Community evolution at uniform intervals: First we consider a model where 'stages of evolution' appear at uniform time intervals throughout the history of the community. The model of Figure 2 (a) is in some sense the most similar to existing works [20, 40, 41] that model evolution of users and products using a single global 'clock'. The intuition behind this model is that communities evolve over time, and prefer different products at different time periods.

(b) User evolution at uniform intervals: We extend the idea of community evolution and apply it directly to individual users (Fig. 2 (b)). This model captures the intuition that users go through different life-stages or experience levels and their preferences then depend on their current life stage.

(c) Community evolution at learned intervals: This model extends (a) by *learning* the rates at which communities change over time (Fig. 2 (c)). The model is based on the intuition that a community may not evolve at a uniform rate over time and that it is worth modeling different stages of community evolution.

(d) Individual user evolution at learned intervals: Last, we consider a model where each user individually progresses between experience levels at their own *personal rate* (Fig. 2 (d)). This model is the most expressive of all four and is able to capture interesting phenomena. For example, some users may become experts very quickly while others may never reach the highest level of experience; others may behave like experts from the time they join (e.g. the bottom right user of Fig. 2 (d)). This model is able capture such types of behavior.

Models (a) and (b) are designed to assess whether user evolution is guided by changes at the level of individual users, or by changes in the community at large. We find that, given enough data, both models lead to modest improvements over traditional latent-factor recommender systems, though there is no clear winner between the two. Once we learn the stages at which users and communities evolve, as in (c) and (d), we significantly outperform traditional recommender systems, though the benefit of learning is much higher when we model evolution at the level of each individual user, i.e., when we treat 'evolution' as analogous to 'becoming an expert'.

Put simply, we fit recommender systems for different stages of user evolution, and the models differ only in terms of how users *progress* between stages. Thus the actual recommender systems used by each model have the same number of parameters, though the models of Figure 2 (c) and (d) have additional parameters that control *when* users evolve. The model of Figure 2 (d) is the most expressive, in the sense that it has enough flexibility to represent each of the other models. For example, if no evolution took place at the level of individual users, the model of Figure 2 (d) could learn latent parameters similar to those of Figure 2 (c). In practice, we find that this is not the case; rather we learn dynamics of individual users that are quite different to those at the level of communities.

Model Specification

We shall first describe our most general model, namely that of Figure 2 (d). The other models in Figure 2 can later be treated as special cases.

We start with the 'standard' latent-factor recommender system [33], which predicts ratings for user/item pairs (u, i) according to

$$rec(u, i) = \alpha + \beta_u + \beta_i + \langle \gamma_u, \gamma_i \rangle.$$

Here, α is a global offset, β_u and β_i are user and item biases (respectively), and γ_u and γ_i are latent user and item features.

Although this simple model can capture rich interactions between users and products, it ignores *temporal* information completely, i.e., users' review histories are treated as unordered sets. Even so, such models yield excellent performance in practice [22].

We wish to encode temporal information into such models via the proxy of *user experience*. We do so by designing separate recommender systems for users who have different experience levels. Naturally, a user's experience is not fixed, but rather it evolves over time, as the user consumes (and rates) more and more products.

For each of a user's ratings r_{ui}, let t_{ui} denote the time at which that review was entered (for simplicity we assume that each product is reviewed only once). For each of a user's ratings, we will fit a latent variable, e_{ui}, that represents the 'experience level' of the user u, at the time t_{ui}.

Each user's experience level evolves over time. As a model assumption, we constrain each user's experience level to be a non-decreasing function of time. That is, a user never becomes *less* experienced as they review additional products. We encode this using a simple monotonicity constraint on time and experience:

$$\forall u, i, j \quad t_{ui} \geq t_{uj} \Rightarrow e_{ui} \geq e_{uj}. \quad (1)$$

What this constraint means from a modeling perspective is that different users evolve in similar ways to each other, regardless of the specific time they arrive in the community.

In practice, we model experience as a categorical variable that takes E values, i.e., $e_{ui} \in \{1 \ldots E\}$. Note that it is not required that a user achieves all experience levels: some users may already be experienced at the time of their first review, while others may fail to become experienced even after many reviews.

Assuming for the moment that each experience parameter e_{ui} is observed, we proceed by fitting E separate recommender systems to reviews written at different experience levels. That is, we train $rec_1(u,i) \ldots rec_E(u,i)$ so that each rating r_{ui} is predicted using $rec_{e_{ui}}(u,i)$. As we show in Section 3, we regularize the parameters of each of these recommender systems so that user and product parameters evolve 'smoothly' between experience levels.

In short, each of the parameters of a standard recommender system is replaced by a parameter that is a function of experience:

$$rec(u,i) = rec_{e_{ui}}(u,i)$$
$$= \alpha(e_{ui}) + \beta_u(e_{ui}) + \beta_i(e_{ui}) + \langle \gamma_u(e_{ui}), \gamma_i(e_{ui}) \rangle. \quad (2)$$

Such a model is quite general: rather than assuming that our model parameters evolve gradually over time, as in [20], we assume that they evolve gradually as a function of experience, which is *itself* a function of time, but is learned *per user*. Thus we are capable of learning whether users' 'experience' parameters simply mimic the evolution of the entire community, as in Figure 2 (c), or whether there are patterns of user evolution that occur independently of when they arrive in the community, as in Figure 2 (d).

Because of this generality, all of the models from Figure 2 can be seen as special cases of (eq. 2). Firstly, to model evolution of communities (rather than individual users), we change the monotonicity constraint of (eq. 1) so that it constrains all reviews (rather than all reviews per user):

$$\forall u, v, i, j \quad t_{ui} \geq t_{vj} \Rightarrow e_{ui} \geq e_{vj}. \quad (3)$$

Secondly, the 'learned evolution' models (c, d) and the non-learned models (a, b) differ in terms of how we fit the experience parameters e_{ui}. For the non-learned models, experience parameters are set using a fixed schedule: either they are placed at uniformly spaced time points throughout the entire corpus, as in Figure 2 (a), or they are placed at uniformly spaced time points for each individual user's history, as in Figure 2 (b).

In the next section, we describe how to learn these parameters, i.e., to model the points at which a community or an individual user changes.

3. TRAINING THE MODELS

We wish to optimize our model parameters and latent experience variables so as to minimize the mean-squared-error of predictions on some set of training ratings $r_{ui} \in \mathcal{T}$. Suppose each of our E recommender systems has parameters

$$\Theta_e = (\alpha(e); \beta_u(e); \beta_i(e); \gamma_u(e); \gamma_i(e)),$$

and that the set of all experience parameters e_{ui} is denoted as $\mathcal{E}$. Then we wish to choose the optimal $(\hat{\Theta}, \hat{\mathcal{E}})$ according to the objective

$$(\hat{\Theta}, \hat{\mathcal{E}}) = \underset{\Theta, \mathcal{E}}{\arg\min} \sum_{r_{ui} \in \mathcal{T}} \frac{1}{|\mathcal{T}|}(rec_{e_{ui}}(u,i) - r_{ui})^2 + \lambda \Omega(\Theta)$$
$$\text{s.t. } t_{ui} \geq t_{uj} \Rightarrow e_{ui} \geq e_{uj}. \quad (4)$$

This equation has three parts: the first is the mean-squared-error of predictions, which is the standard objective used to train recommender systems. The second part, $\Omega(\Theta)$, is a regularizer, which penalizes 'complex' models Θ. Assuming that there are U users, I items, E experience levels, and K latent factors, then our model has $(1 + U + I + U \cdot K + I \cdot K) \times E$ parameters, which will lead to overfitting if we are not careful. In practice, similar experience levels should have similar parameters, so we define $\Omega(\Theta)$ using the smoothness function

$$\Omega(\Theta) = \sum_{e=1}^{E-1} \|\Theta_e - \Theta_{e+1}\|_2^2, \quad (5)$$

where $\|\cdot\|_2^2$ is the squared ℓ_2 norm. This penalizes abrupt changes between successive experience levels. λ is a regularization hyperparameter, which 'trades-off' the importance of regularization versus prediction accuracy at training time. We select $\lambda \in 10^0 \ldots 10^5$ by withholding a fraction of our training data for validation, and choosing the value of λ that minimizes the validation error. The third and final part of (eq. 4) is the constraint of (eq. 1), which ensures that our latent experience parameters are monotonically non-decreasing for each user.

Simultaneously optimizing all of the parameters in (eq. 4) is a difficult problem, in particular it is certainly not convex [22]. We settle for a local optimum, and optimize the parameters Θ and $\mathcal{E}$ using coordinate ascent [27]. That is, we alternately optimize (eq. 4) for Θ given $\mathcal{E}$, and for $\mathcal{E}$ given Θ.

Optimizing (eq. 4) for Θ given $\mathcal{E}$, while itself still a non-convex problem, can be approached using standard techniques, since it essentially reduces to optimizing E separate recommender systems. In practice we optimize model parameters during each iteration using L-BFGS [31], a quasi-Newton method for non-linear optimization of problems with many variables.

Alternately, optimizing (eq. 4) for $\mathcal{E}$ given Θ means assigning each of a user's reviews to a particular recommender system, corresponding to that review's experience level. The best assignment is the one that minimizes the mean-squared-error of the predictions, subject to the monotonicity constraint.

Optimizing a sequence of discrete variables subject to a monotonicity constraint can be solved efficiently using dynamic programming: it is related to the *Longest Common Subsequence* problem [4], which admits a solution whose running time (per user) is bilinear in E and the number of ratings in their history.

This procedure is visualized in Figure 3, for $E = 5$ experience levels, and a user with 8 ratings. Rows represent each of the five experience levels, while columns represent each of a particular user's ratings, ordered by time. The optimal non-decreasing set of experience levels is the shortest path from the 'start' to the 'end' of this

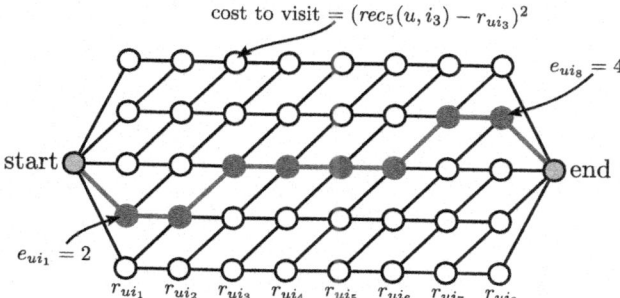

Figure 3: Experience fitting as a dynamic programming problem. Rows represent experience levels, columns represent ratings, ordered by time.

dataset	#users	#items	#ratings
Beer (beeradvocate)	33,387	66,051	1,586,259
Beer (ratebeer)	40,213	110,419	2,924,127
Fine Foods (amazon)	218,418	74,442	568,454
Movies (amazon)	759,899	267,320	7,911,684
Wine (cellartracker)	44,268	485,179	2,025,995
TOTAL	1,096,185	1,003,411	15,016,519

Table 1: Dataset statistics.

graph, where the cost of visiting a node with rating r_{ui} at experience level k is the prediction error $(rec_k(u, i) - r_{ui})^2$.

These two steps are repeated until convergence, that is, until $\mathcal{E}$ does not change between successive iterations. On our largest datasets, all parameters could be optimized in a few hours on a standard desktop machine.

Again, the above procedure refers to the most general version of our model, in which we learn monotonic evolution parameters *per user*, as depicted in Figure 2 (d). Training the community version of our model (Fig. 2 (c)) simply means replacing the monotonicity constraint of (eq. 1) with that of (eq. 3).

4. EXPERIMENTS

Our goal in this section is to evaluate the models described in Figure 2. We compare the following models:

lf: A standard latent-factor recommender system [21].

a: A model whose parameters evolve for the entire community as a function of time (Fig. 2 (a)).

b: A model whose parameters evolve independently for each user (Fig. 2 (b)).

c: A model whose parameters evolve for the entire community as a function of time, where the 'stages' of evolution are learned (Fig. 2 (c)).

d: A model whose parameters evolve independently for each user, where the stages of evolution are learned (Fig. 2 (d)).

The models of Figure 2 (a) and (c) are most similar to existing models for temporal evolution, e.g. [22]: item parameters are shared by ratings made at the same time. We aim to compare this to models where parameters are shared by users at the same experience level, regardless of the specific time they arrive in the community (as in Fig. 2 (d)).

Experimental Setup

To evaluate each method, we report the Mean Squared Error (MSE) on a fraction of our data withheld for testing, that is, for our test set $\mathcal{U}$ we report

$$\text{MSE}(\mathcal{U}) = \frac{1}{|\mathcal{U}|} \sum_{r_{ui} \in \mathcal{U}} (rec_{e_{ui}}(u, i) - r_{ui})^2. \quad (6)$$

We also use a validation set of the same size to choose the hyperparameter λ. Throughout our experiments we set the number of experience levels, and the number of latent product and item dimensions to $E = 5$ and $K = 5$; larger values did not significantly improve performance in our experience.

Since it is unlikely to be fruitful to model the evolution of users who have rated only a few products, we compare our models on users with at least 50 ratings. Users with fewer than 50 ratings are not discarded, but rather their ratings are combined so that they are treated using a single 'background' model; we then model the evolution of this entire group as though it were a single user.

We use two schemes to build our test sets: our first scheme consists of selecting a *random* sample of reviews from each user. This is the standard way of selecting test data for 'flat' models that do not model temporal dynamics. The second scheme we use to build our test set is to consider the *final* reviews for each user.

The latter setting represents how such a system would be used in practice, in the sense that our goal is to predict how users would respond to a product *now*, rather than to make *post hoc* predictions about how they *would have* responded in the past. However, sampling reviews in this way biases our test set towards reviews written by more experienced users; this is no longer the case when we sample reviews randomly.

Of course, we do not fit latent experience parameters for the ratings in our test set. Thus for each rating used for testing, we assign it the experience level of its chronologically nearest training rating.

Datasets

Our choice of rating data reflects a variety of settings where users are likely to have 'acquired tastes'. The datasets we consider are summarized in Table 1. Each of our datasets were obtained from public sources on the web using a crawler, and are made available for others to use.[1] We consider the beer review websites *BeerAdvocate* and *RateBeer*, the wine review website *CellarTracker*, as well as reviews from the *Fine Foods* and *Movies* categories from *Amazon*. In total we obtain over 15 million ratings from these sources. In principle we obtain the *complete* set of reviews from each of these sources; data in each of our corpora spans at least 10 years.

We previously considered *BeerAdvocate* and *RateBeer* data in [28], though not in the context of recommendation. Recommendation on (different) *Amazon* data has been discussed in [15] and [25].

Since each of these rating datasets has a different scale (e.g. beers on *RateBeer* are rated out of 20, wines on *CellarTracker* are rated out of 100, etc.), before computing the MSE we first normalize all ratings to be on the scale $(0, 5]$.

Evaluation

Results in terms of the Mean Squared Error (MSE) are shown in Tables 2 and 3. Table 2 shows the MSE on a test set consisting

---
[1] http://snap.stanford.edu/data/

	BeerAdv. (overall)	BeerAdv. (taste)	BeerAdv. (look)	RateBeer (overall)	Amazon Fine Foods	Amazon Movies	CellarTracker
(lf) latent-factor model	0.452 (.01)	0.442 (.01)	0.313 (.01)	0.496 (.01)	1.582 (.02)	1.379 (.00)	0.055 (.00)
(a) community at uniform rate	0.427 (.01)	0.417 (.01)	0.293 (.01)	0.458 (.01)	1.527 (.02)	1.371 (.01)	0.051 (.00)
(b) user at uniform rate	0.437 (.01)	0.423 (.01)	0.300 (.01)	0.477 (.01)	1.548 (.02)	1.376 (.01)	0.053 (.00)
(c) community at learned rate	0.427 (.01)	0.417 (.01)	0.293 (.01)	0.458 (.01)	1.529 (.02)	1.371 (.01)	0.051 (.00)
(d) user at learned rate	**0.400 (.01)**	**0.399 (.01)**	**0.275 (.01)**	**0.406 (.01)**	**1.475 (.03)**	**1.051 (.01)**	**0.045 (.00)**
benefit of **(d)** over **(lf)**	11.62%	9.73%	12.19%	18.26%	6.79%	23.80%	18.50%
benefit of **(d)** over **(c)**	6.48%	4.12%	6.13%	11.42%	3.53%	23.34%	13.20%

Table 2: Results on users' most recent reviews. MSE and standard error.

	BeerAdv. (overall)	BeerAdv. (taste)	BeerAdv. (look)	RateBeer (overall)	Amazon Fine Foods	Amazon Movies	CellarTracker
(lf) latent-factor model	0.430 (.01)	0.408 (.01)	0.319 (.01)	0.492 (.01)	1.425 (.02)	1.099 (.01)	0.049 (.00)
(a) community at uniform rate	0.415 (.01)	0.387 (.01)	0.298 (.01)	0.463 (.01)	1.382 (.02)	1.082 (.01)	0.048 (.00)
(b) user at uniform rate	0.419 (.01)	0.395 (.01)	0.305 (.01)	0.461 (.01)	1.383 (.02)	1.088 (.01)	0.048 (.00)
(c) community at learned rate	0.415 (.01)	0.386 (.01)	0.298 (.01)	0.461 (.01)	1.374 (.02)	1.082 (.01)	0.048 (.00)
(d) user at learned rate	**0.409 (.01)**	**0.373 (.01)**	**0.276 (.01)**	**0.394 (.01)**	**1.189 (.03)**	**0.711 (.01)**	**0.039 (.00)**
benefit of **(d)** over **(lf)**	5.05%	8.61%	13.45%	19.94%	16.61%	35.31%	20.49%
benefit of **(d)** over **(c)**	1.55%	3.33%	7.20%	14.50%	13.47%	34.32%	18.23%

Table 3: Results on randomly sampled reviews. MSE and standard error.

of the *most recent* reviews for each user, while Table 3 shows the MSE on a *random* subset of users' reviews.

Table 2 shows that our model significantly outperforms alternatives on all datasets. On average, it achieves a 14% reduction in MSE compared to a standard latent factor recommender system, and a 10% reduction compared to its nearest competitor, which models user evolution as a process that takes place at the level of entire communities. Note that due to the large size of our datasets, all reported improvements are significant at the 1% level or better.

By considering only users' most recent reviews, our evaluation may be biased towards reviews written at a high level of experience. To address this possibility, in Table 3 we perform the same evaluation on a *random* subset of reviews for each user. Again, our model significantly outperforms all baselines. Here we reduce the MSE of a standard recommender system by 17%, and the nearest competitor by 13% on average.

Reviews from *BeerAdvocate* and *RateBeer* have multiple dimensions, or 'aspects' to users' evaluations. Specifically, users evaluate beers in terms of their 'taste', 'smell', 'look', and 'feel' in addition to their overall rating [28]. Tables 2 and 3 show results for two such aspects from *BeerAdvocate*, showing that we obtain similar benefits by modeling users' evolution with respect to such aspects. Similar results from *RateBeer* are omitted.

It is perhaps surprising that we gain the most significant benefits on movie data, and the least significant benefits on beer data. However, we should not conclude that movies require more expertise than beer: a more likely explanation is that our movie data has a larger *spectrum* of expertise levels, whereas users who decide to participate on a beer-rating website are likely to already be somewhat 'expert'.

We gain the most significant benefits when considering reviews written at all experience levels (as in Table 3) rather than considering users' most recent reviews (as in Table 2). However we should not conclude from this that experts are unpredictable (indeed in Section 5 we confirm that experts are the *most* predictable). Rather, since inexperienced users are *less* predictable, we gain the most benefit by explicitly modeling them.

We also note that while we obtain significant benefits on *Amazon* data, the mean-squared-errors for this dataset are by far the highest. One reason is that *Amazon* users use a full spectrum of ratings from 1 to 5 stars, whereas *CellarTracker* users (for example) rate wines on a smaller spectrum (after normalizing the ratings, most wines have scores above 4.25); this naturally leads to higher MSEs. Another reason is that our *Amazon* data has many products and users with only a few reviews, so that we cannot do much better than simply modeling their bias terms. As we see in Section 5, bias terms differ significantly between beginners and experts, so that modeling expertise proves extremely beneficial on such data.

5. QUALITATIVE ANALYSIS

So far, we have used our models of user expertise to predict users' ratings, by fitting latent 'experience' parameters to all ratings in our corpora. Now we move on to examine the role of these latent variables in more detail.

Throughout this section we use the term 'expert' to refer to those reviewers (and ratings) that are assigned the highest experience level by our model (i.e., $e_{ui} = E$). We use the term 'beginner' to refer to reviewers and ratings assigned the lowest level (i.e., $e_{ui} = 1$). Again, we acknowledge that 'expertise' is an *interpretation* of our model's latent parameters, and other interpretations may also be valid. However, in this section, we demonstrate that our latent parameters do indeed behave in a way that is consistent with our intuitive notion of expertise.

We begin by examining how a user's experience level impacts our ability to predict their rating behavior. Table 4 compares the prediction accuracy of our model on reviews written at different experience levels. We find in all but one case that users at the highest experience level have the lowest MSE (for *Amazon Movies* they have the second lowest by a small margin). In other words their rating behavior can be most accurately predicted by our model. This is not to say that experts agree with *each other* (which we discuss later); rather, it says that *individual* experts are easier to model than other categories of user. Indeed, one can argue that some notion of

	$e=1$	$e=2$	$e=3$	$e=4$	$e=5$
BeerAdvocate	0.423	0.396	0.471	0.449	**0.358**
RateBeer	0.494	0.469	0.408	0.533	**0.300**
Amazon Fine Foods	1.016	1.914	1.094	2.251	**0.960**
Amazon Movies	0.688	**0.620**	0.685	1.062	0.675
CellarTracker	0.061	0.039	0.041	0.037	**0.028**

Table 4: MSE per experience level e

'predictability' is a necessary condition for such users to be considered 'experts' [12].

While we find that beginners and intermediate users have lower prediction accuracy, it is surprisingly the 'almost experts' ($e_{ui} = E - 1$) who are the *least* predictable; from Table 4 we see that such users have the *highest* MSE in three out of five cases. From this we might argue that users do not become experts via a smooth progression, but rather their evolution consists of several distinct stages.

Experience Progression

Next, we study how users progress through experience levels as a function of time. Figure 4 shows the (cumulative) time taken to progress between experience levels (the final bar represents the entire lifetime of the user, since there is no further level to progress to). The dark blue bars show the progression for those users who progress through all levels of experience, i.e., it ignores those users who arrive to the site already experienced as well as those who never obtain the highest experience levels. The yellow bars show users who reach all but the highest experience level.

How much time is spent at each experience level?

First, we observe that on most datasets, the final experience level is the 'longest', i.e., it covers the longest time period, and includes the largest number of reviews. This makes sense from the modeling perspective, when taken together with our previous finding that experts' ratings are easier to predict: the model is 'finer-grained' during the stages of user evolution that are most difficult to fit accurately. Fewer distinct experience levels are required later on, once users' rating behavior has 'converged'.

Do users who become experts differ from those who don't?

Secondly, Figure 4 compares users who progress through all levels of experience to users who do not. Yellow bars show the progression of users who reach all but the final experience level. Surprisingly, while such users enter roughly the same number of ratings per level (Fig. 4, bottom) as those users who eventually become experts, they do so much slower (Fig. 4, top). Thus it appears as though the *rate* at which users write reviews, and not just the number of reviews they write, is tied to their progression.

Do experts agree with each other?

Thirdly, Figure 5 shows the extent to which users *agree* with each other as they become more experienced. 'Agreement' has been argued to be another necessary condition to define users as experts [12]. To study this, we consider ratings *of the same product, written at the same experience level*. Specifically, for each item i and experience level k, we find the set of users who rated that item at that experience level, i.e., we find all u such that $e_{ui} = k$. We then compute the variance of such ratings for every item and experience level. Our goal is to assess how this quantity changes as a function of users' experience. We do so for all products that were reviewed at least 5 times at the same experience level. Since this limits the amount of data we have to work with, we first linearly interpolate each user's experience function over time (so that their experience function is a piecewise linear function, rather than a step function), and compute this quantity across a sliding window.

Indeed, in Figure 5 we find that users do tend to agree with each other more as they become more experienced, i.e., their ratings have lower variance when they review the same products. This is consistent with our finding that experts' ratings are easier to predict than those of beginners.

User Retention

Next we consider how experience relates to user retention. We want to study how users who leave the community (defined as users who have not entered a review for a period of six months) differ from those who remain in the community. Figure 6 visualizes the experience progression of these two groups. Here we consider the first 10 ratings for all users who have entered at least 10 ratings (Fig. 6, top), and the first 100 ratings for all users who have entered at least 100 ratings (Fig. 6, bottom); this scheme ensures that every datapoint is drawn from the same sample population.

We find that both classes of users *enter* the community at roughly the same level (at the time of their first review, both groups have roughly the same experience on average). However, as the number of reviews increases, users who go on to leave the community have lower experience compared to those who stay. In other words, they gain experience more slowly. This discrepancy is apparent even after their first few reviews. This failure to become experienced may be a factor which causes users to abandon the site, and could be used as a feature in 'churn prediction' problems [11, 18]. We mention the parallel work of [9], which also studies *BeerAdvocate* and *RateBeer* data: there, a user's failure to adopt the *linguistic* norms of a community is considered as a factor that may influence whether they will abandon that community.

Acquired Tastes

In Figure 1, we hinted at the idea that our model could be used to detect *acquired tastes*. More precisely, it can help us to identify products that are preferred by experts over beginners (and *vice versa*).

To do so, we compare the difference in product bias terms between the most expert (experience level 5) and the least expert (experience level 1) users. That is, we compute for each item i the quantity

$$d_i = \beta_i(5) - \beta_i(1).$$

Thus a positive value of d_i indicates that a product is preferred by experts over beginners, while a negative value indicates that a product is preferred by beginners over experts.

How do expert and beginner biases differ?

In Figure 7 we compare the average rating of each product to d_i (for products with at least 50 ratings). Our main finding in this figure is that there exists a positive relationship between products that are highly rated and products that are preferred by experts. In other words, products with high average ratings are rated *more* highly by experts; products with low average ratings are rated more highly by beginners. Recall that in Figure 1 we examined the same relationship on *RateBeer* data in more detail.

One explanation is that the 'best' products tend to be ones that require expertise to enjoy, while novice users may be unable to appreciate them fully. This phenomenon is the most pronounced on

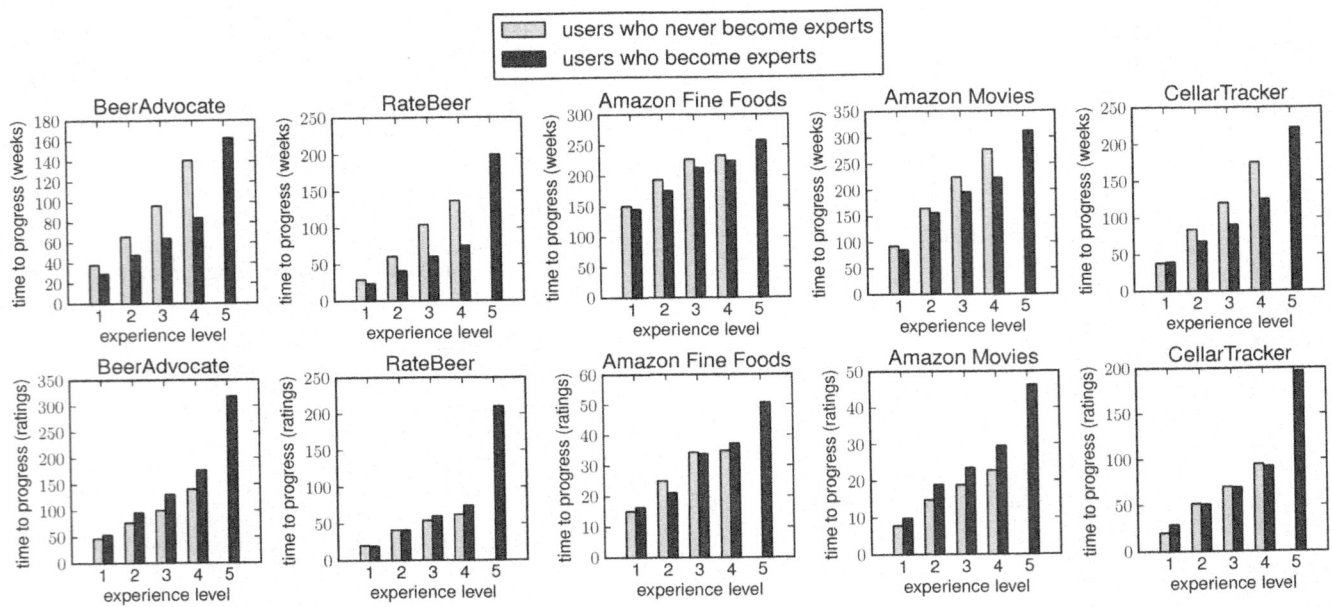

Figure 4: Users who never become 'experts' tend to progress slower than users who do. Cumulative time (top), and number of ratings (bottom), taken to progress between experience levels.

Figure 5: Experienced users agree more about their ratings than beginners. Experience versus rating variance (when rating the same product).

our *Movies* and *RateBeer* data, and exists to a lesser extent on our *BeerAdvocate* and *Fine Foods* data; the phenomenon is absent altogether on our *CellarTracker* data. Again, we should not conclude from this that movies require more 'expertise' than wine, but rather that our *Movies* data has a larger separation between beginners and experts.

Perhaps more surprising is the lack of products that appear in the top left or bottom right quadrants of Figure 7, i.e., products with below average ratings, but positive values of d_i, or products with above average ratings but negative values of d_i. In other words, there are neither products that are disliked by beginners but liked by experts, nor are there products that are liked by beginners but disliked by experts.

It is worth trying to rule out other, more prosaic explanations for this phenomenon: for instance, it could be that beginners give mediocre reviews to all products, while experts have a larger range. We mention two negative results that discount such possibilities: firstly, we found no significant difference between the average ratings given by beginners or experts. Secondly, we did not observe any significant difference in the variance (that is, the variance across all of a user's reviews, not when reviewing the same product as in Figure 5).

Which genres are preferred by experts or beginners?

In Figure 1 we showed that there are entire *genres* of products that tend to be preferred by experts or by beginners. Specifically, we showed that almost all strong ales have positive values of d_i (preferred by experts), while almost all lagers have negative values of d_i (preferred by beginners). Of course, it is not surprising (to a beer drinker) that experts dislike lagers while preferring India Pale Ales (IPAs), though it is more surprising that beginners also have the same polarity with respect to these products—the experts are simply more extreme in their opinions.

Table 5 shows which genres have the lowest and highest values of d_i on average, i.e., which products are most preferred by beginners and experts (respectively). We focus on *BeerAdvocate*, *RateBeer*, and *CellarTracker*, which have the most meaningful genre information. The results are highly consistent across *BeerAdvocate* and *RateBeer*, in spite of the differing product categorizations used by the two sites (Kvass is a form of low-alcohol beer, Kristallweizen is a form of wheat beer, IPA is a form of strong ale, and Gueuze is a type of lambic). Again, there is a clear relationship between products' overall popularity and the extent to which experts prefer them; non-alcoholic beer is naturally not highly rated on a beer rating website, while lambics and IPAs are more in favor.

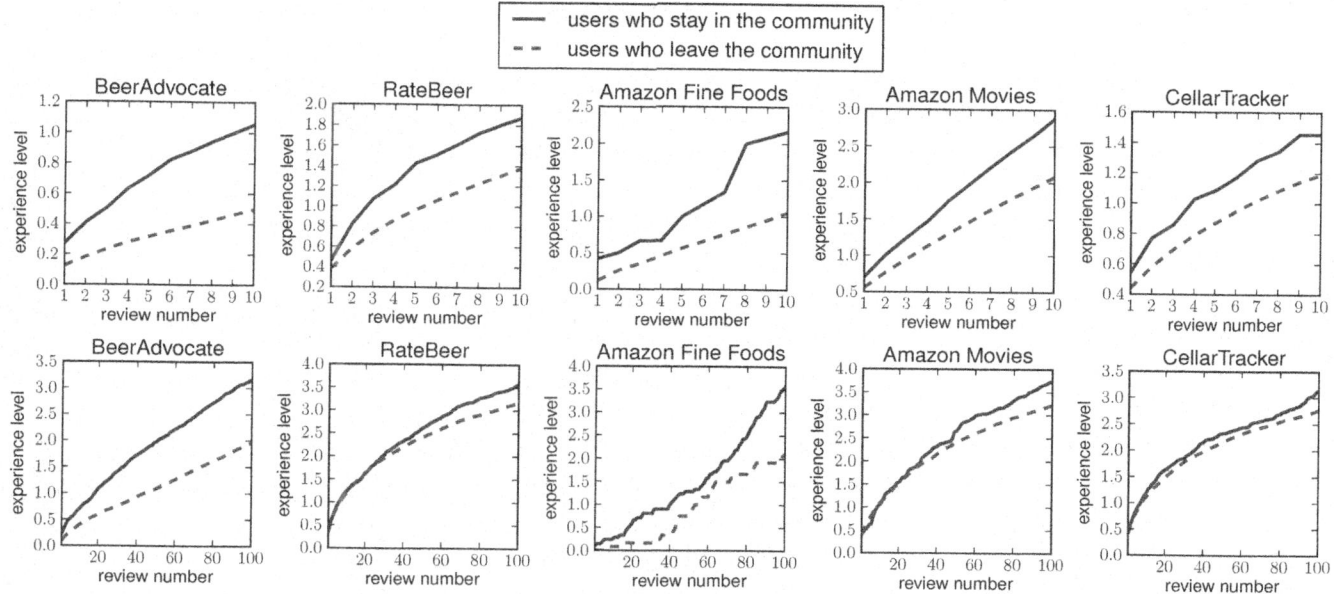

Figure 6: Users whose experience progresses slowly are more likely to abandon the community. First 10 ratings of all users who have at least 10 ratings (top), and first 100 ratings of all users who have at least 100 ratings (bottom).

6. RELATED WORK

Traditional recommender systems treat each user's review history as a series of unordered events, which are simply used to build a model for that user, such as a latent factor model [22]. In spite of the excellent performance of such models in practice, they naturally fail to account for the temporal dynamics involved in recommendation tasks.

Some early works that deal with temporal dynamics do so in terms of *concept drift* [23, 37, 39]. Such models are able to account for short-term temporal effects ('noise'), and long-term changes in user behavior ('drift'), for example due to the presence of new products within a community.

Sophisticated models of such temporal dynamics proved critical in obtaining state-of-the-art performance on the *Netflix* challenge [3], most famously in [20]. As discussed in [20], few previous works had dealt with temporal dynamics, other than a few notable exceptions [2, 10, 35]. Around the same time, 'adaptive neighborhood' models were proposed [24], that address the problem of iteratively training recommender systems whose parameters ought to change over time.

Better performance may be obtained by modeling large-scale global changes at the level of entire communities [41], or by developing separate models for short term changes (e.g. due to external events), and long-term trends [40].

Other works that study temporal dynamics at the level of products and communities include [29], where the authors studied how existing ratings within communities may influence new users, and how community dynamics evolve; and [13], who studied how users are influenced by previous ratings of the same product.

Expertise has been studied in domains other than recommender systems, for example in the literature on education and psychology [5, 34]. One area where 'expertise' has received significant attention is *web search*. The role of expertise with respect to search behavior is a rich and historied topic, whose study predates the emergence of modern search engines [14]. Of particular interest is [38], since the authors study how users *evolve* (with respect to the level of technical content in their queries) as they gain expertise. We also briefly mention the topic of *expertise identification* [1, 6, 16, 32]. This line of work is orthogonal to ours, in that it deals with *discovering experts*, rather than *recommending products based on expertise*; however, such works offer valuable insights, in the sense that like our own work, they attempt to model the behavior of expert users.

7. DISCUSSION AND FUTURE WORK

An interesting finding of our work is that beginners and experts have the same *polarity* in their opinions, but that experts give more 'extreme' ratings: they rate the top products more highly, and the bottom products more harshly. Thus naively, we might conclude that we should simply recommend both groups of users the same products: nobody likes adjunct lagers, so what does it matter if beginners dislike them *less*? The counter to this argument is that in order to *fully* appreciate a product (by giving it the highest rating), a user must first become an expert. Thus perhaps we should focus on *making a user an expert*, rather than simply recommending what they will like *today*.

This viewpoint motivates several novel questions. Can we determine, based only on which products a user reviews, whether they will become an expert? Can we recommend not just products, but *sequences* of products, that will *help* them to become an expert, or maximize their total enjoyment?

Another avenue of research is to study *linguistic* differences between experts and non-experts. 'Expertise' has been studied from the perspective of linguistic development [34], for example in the context of second-language acquisition [8, 36]. Since our rating data comes from *review* corpora, we can use it to study how users' *rating* expertise relates to their *reviewing* expertise. Do experts write longer reviews or use fewer personal pronouns? Are their reviews considered more helpful by others in the community [30]?

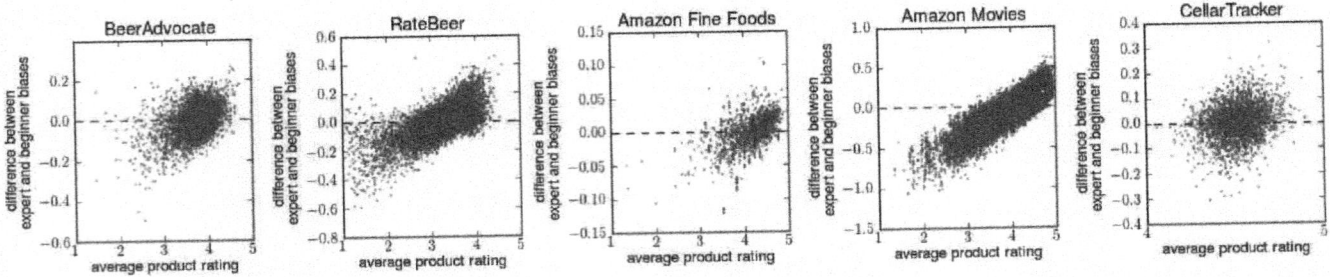

Figure 7: Average product ratings are correlated with the difference between expert and beginner biases. *Seven Samurai* is marked in yellow.

	BeerAdvocate	$\bar{\beta}_i(1)$	$\bar{\beta}_i(5)$	RateBeer	$\bar{\beta}_i(1)$	$\bar{\beta}_i(5)$	CellarTracker	$\bar{\beta}_i(1)$	$\bar{\beta}_i(5)$
Preferred by beginners:	Low Alcohol Beer	-.423	-.534	Low Alcohol	-.581	-.724	Barbera	-.035	-.119
	Kvass	-.316	-.653	Pale Lager	-.519	-.630	Syrah (blend)	-.110	-.182
	Light Lager	-.302	-.487	Premium Lager	-.246	-.290	Cabernet-Syrah	-.048	-.105
	American Adjunct Lager	-.237	-.285	American Dark Lager	-.199	-.287	Zinfandel	-.066	-.111
	European Strong Lager	-.403	-.428	Strong Pale Lager	-.068	-.103	Sémillon	-.092	-.126
	European Pale Lager	-.154	-.216	German Pilsener	-.135	-.202	Syrah	.019	.005
	Japanese Rice Lager	-.144	-.212	Pilsener	-.066	-.095	Port	-.028	-.046
	American Pale Wheat Ale	.033	-.023	Kristallweizen	.060	.016	Grenache (blend)	.011	-.005
	American Blonde Ale	-.047	-.080	Fruit Beer	-.105	-.137	Sauvignon Blanc	-.003	-.020
	English Dark Mild Ale	-.025	-.072	Malt Liquor	-.557	-.675	Gruner Veltliner	.024	.008
Preferred by experts:	Baltic Porter	.091	.128	Strong Porter	.205	.243	Melon de Bourgogne	.261	.412
	English Barleywine	.007	.055	Barley Wine	.216	.248	Champagne	.080	.193
	American Wild Ale	.150	.196	Wild Ale	.197	.261	Cabernet-Syrah (blend)	.083	.173
	English Pale Mild Ale	-.011	.023	American Strong Ale	.203	.227	Petit Verdot	.054	.143
	Flanders Red Ale	.132	.183	Double IPA	.260	.294	Pinot Gris	.118	.206
	Flanders Oud Bruin	.018	.073	Black IPA	.152	.185	Pinotage	.064	.117
	Unblended Lambic	-.019	.028	Unblended Lambic	.135	.240	Grenache	.009	.048
	Gueuze	.160	.223	Saison	.142	.176	Grenache Blanc	.038	.089
	Chile Beer	-.254	-.223	Imperial Stout	.308	.338	Dolcetto	.063	.105
	Rauchbier	-.143	-.095	Quadrupel	.354	.367	Mourvedre Blend	-.031	.007

Table 5: Acquired tastes: products preferred by beginners and products preferred experts. Average beginner and expert item biases are shown.

Do experts use specialized vocabulary (e.g. beer-specific language such as 'lacing' and 'retention'), and do they better conform to the linguistic norms of the community [9]?

Although we argued that gaining expertise is a form of *personal development* that takes place no matter when a user arrives in a community, it is not the *only* such form of development. When a user arrives in a community, they must adopt its norms with respect to rating behavior [29], for example they must learn that while wines are rated on a scale of 1-100, ratings below 85 are seldom used. Like expertise, this form of development is not tied to the user's changing preferences, nor to the changing tastes of the community. Would *BeerAdvocate* 'experts' be considered experts if their ratings were entered on *RateBeer*? Would expert movie reviewers on *Amazon* also be 'experts' gourmet food reviewers? The answers to such questions could help us to determine which forms of personal development are more salient in online communities.

Finally, we believe that our models of expertise may be used to facilitate expert discovery. We identified experts in review systems primarily for the sake of predicting users' ratings, but discovering experts may be useful in its own right. This topic is known as *expert recommendation* [1, 6, 7, 16, 17], and has applications to product ranking and review summarization, among others. For instance, a user may wish to read reviews written by the most expert members of a community, or by members most similar in expertise to themselves.

8. CONCLUSION

Users' tastes and preferences change and evolve over time. Shifting trends in the community, the arrival of new products, and even changes in users' social networks may influence their rating behavior. At the same time, users' tastes may change simply through the act of consuming additional products, as they gain knowledge and experience. Existing models consider temporal effects at the level of products and communities, but neglect the *personal development* of users: users who rate products at the same time may have less in common than users who rate products at *different* times, but who are at the same stage in their personal evolution. We developed models for such notions of user evolution, in order to assess which best captures the dynamics present in product rating data. We found that modeling users' personal evolution, or 'experience', not only helps us to discover 'acquired tastes' in product rating systems, but more importantly, it allows us to discover *when* users acquire them.

Acknowledgements

Thanks to Cristian Danescu-Niculescu-Mizil for help obtaining the data, and to Seth Myers and Dafna Shahaf for proofreading. This research has been supported in part by NSF IIS-1016909, CNS-1010921, CAREER IIS-1149837, IIS-1159679, ARO MURI, Docomo, Boeing, Allyes, Volkswagen, Intel, Okawa Foundation, Alfred P. Sloan Fellowship and the Microsoft Faculty Fellowship.

9. REFERENCES

[1] O. Alonso, P. Devanbu, and M. Gertz. Expertise identification and visualization from CVS. In *Working Conference on Mining Software Repositories*, 2008.

[2] R. Bell and Y. Koren. Scalable collaborative filtering with jointly derived neighborhood interpolation weights. In *ICDM*, 2007.

[3] J. Bennett and S. Lanning. The Netflix prize. In *KDD Cup and Workshop*, 2007.

[4] L. Bergroth, H. Hakonen, and T. Raita. A survey of longest common subsequence algorithms. In *SPIRE*, 2000.

[5] D. Berliner. *The Development of Expertise in Pedagogy*. AACTE Publications, 1988.

[6] J. Bian, Y. Liu, D. Zhou, E. Agichtein, and H. Zha. Learning to recognize reliable users and content in social media with coupled mutual reinforcement. In *WWW*, 2009.

[7] N. Craswell, D. Hawking, A. Vercoustre, and P. Wilkins. P@noptic expert: Searching for experts not just for documents. *Ausweb Poster Proceedings*, 2001.

[8] A. Cumming. Writing expertise and second-language proficiency. *Language learning*, 2006.

[9] C. Danescu-Niculescu-Mizil, R. West, D. Jurafsky, J. Leskovec, and C. Potts. No country for old members: User lifecycle and linguistic change in online communities. In *WWW*, 2013.

[10] Y. Ding and X. Li. Time weight collaborative filtering. In *CIKM*, 2005.

[11] G. Dror, D. Pelleg, O. Rokhlenko, and I. Szpektor. Churn prediction in new users of Yahoo! Answers. In *WWW CQA Workshop*, 2012.

[12] H. Einhorn. Expert judgment: Some necessary conditions and an example. *Journal of Applied Psychology*, 1974.

[13] D. Godes and J. Silva. Sequential and temporal dynamics of online opinion. *Marketing Science*, 2012.

[14] I. Hsieh-Yee. Effects of search experience and subject knowledge on the search tactics of novice and experienced searchers. *Journal of the American Society for Information Science*, 1994.

[15] N. Jindal and B. Liu. Opinion spam and analysis. In *WSDM*, 2008.

[16] P. Jurczyk and E. Agichtein. Discovering authorities in question answer communities by using link analysis. In *CIKM*, 2007.

[17] M. Karimzadehgan, R. White, and M. Richardson. Enhancing expert finding using organizational hierarchies. *Advances in Information Retrieval*, 2009.

[18] M. Karnstedt, T. Hennessy, J. Chan, P. Basuchowdhuri, C. Hayes, and T. Strufe. Churn in social networks. In *Handbook of Social Network Technologies*. Springer, 2010.

[19] J. Kolter and M. Maloof. Dynamic weighted majority: An ensemble method for drifting concepts. *JMLR*, 2007.

[20] Y. Koren. Collaborative filtering with temporal dynamics. *Commun. ACM*, 2010.

[21] Y. Koren and R. Bell. Advances in collaborative filtering. In *Recommender Systems Handbook*. Springer, 2011.

[22] Y. Koren, R. Bell, and C. Volinsky. Matrix factorization techniques for recommender systems. *Computer*, 2009.

[23] L. Kuncheva. Classifier ensembles for changing environments. In *Multiple Classifier Systems*. Springer, 2004.

[24] N. Lathia, S. Hailes, and L. Capra. Temporal collaborative filtering with adaptive neighbourhoods. In *SIGIR*, 2009.

[25] G. Linden, B. Smith, and J. York. Amazon.com recommendations: Item-to-item collaborative filtering. *IEEE Internet Computing*, 2003.

[26] H. Ma, D. Zhou, C. Liu, M. Lyu, and I. King. Recommender systems with social regularization. In *WSDM*, 2011.

[27] D. MacKay. *Information Theory, Inference and Learning Algorithms*. Cambrdige University Press, 2003.

[28] J. McAuley, J. Leskovec, and D. Jurafsky. Learning attitudes and attributes from multi-aspect reviews. In *ICDM*, 2012.

[29] W. Moe and D. Schweidel. Online product opinions: Incidence, evaluation, and evolution. *Marketing Science*, 2012.

[30] D. Nguyen and C. Rosé. Language use as a reflection of socialization in online communities. In *ACL Workshop on Language in Social Media*, 2011.

[31] J. Nocedal. Updating quasi-newton matrices with limited storage. *Mathematics of Computation*, 1980.

[32] A. Pal, R. Farzan, J. Konstan, and R. Kraut. Early detection of potential experts in question answering communities. In *UMAP*, 2011.

[33] F. Ricci, L. Rokach, B. Shapira, and P. Kantor, editors. *Recommender Systems Handbook*. Springer, 2011.

[34] S. Romaine. *The language of children and adolescents: The acquisition of communicative competence*. Wiley, 1984.

[35] K. Sugiyama, K. Hatano, and M. Yoshikawa. Adaptive web search based on user profile constructed without any effort from users. In *WWW*, 2004.

[36] S. Thorne, R. Black, and J. Sykes. Second language use, socialization, and learning in internet interest communities and online gaming. *The Modern Language Journal*, 2009.

[37] A. Tsymbal. The problem of concept drift: Definitions and related work. Technical report, Trinity College Dublin, 2004.

[38] R. White, S. Dumais, and J. Teevan. Characterizing the influence of domain expertise on web search behavior. In *WSDM*, 2009.

[39] G. Widmer and M. Kubat. Learning in the presence of concept drift and hidden contexts. In *Machine Learning*, 1996.

[40] L. Xiang, Q. Yuan, S. Zhao, L. Chen, X. Zhang, Q. Yang, and J. Sun. Temporal recommendation on graphs via long- and short-term preference fusion. In *KDD*, 2010.

[41] L. Xiong, X. Chen, T. Huang, J. Schneider, and J. Carbonell. Temporal collaborative filtering with bayesian probabilistic tensor factorization. In *SDM*, 2010.

The FLDA Model for Aspect-based Opinion Mining: Addressing the Cold Start Problem

Samaneh Moghaddam
School of Computing Science
Simon Fraser University
Burnaby, BC, Canada
sam39@cs.sfu.ca

Martin Ester
School of Computing Science
Simon Fraser University
Burnaby, BC, Canada
ester@cs.sfu.ca

ABSTRACT

Aspect-based opinion mining from online reviews has attracted a lot of attention recently. The main goal of all of the proposed methods is extracting aspects and/or estimating aspect ratings. Recent works, which are often based on Latent Dirichlet Allocation (LDA), consider both tasks simultaneously. These models are normally trained at the item level, i.e., a model is learned for each item separately. Learning a model per item is fine when the item has been reviewed extensively and has enough training data. However, in real-life datasets such as those from Epinions.com and Amazon.com more than 90% of items have less than 10 reviews, so-called *cold start items*. State-of-the-art LDA models for aspect-based opinion mining are trained at the item level and therefore perform poorly for cold start items due to the lack of sufficient training data. In this paper, we propose a probabilistic graphical model based on LDA, called *Factorized LDA (FLDA)*, to address the cold start problem. The underlying assumption of FLDA is that aspects and ratings of a review are influenced not only by the item but also by the reviewer. It further assumes that both items and reviewers can be modeled by a set of latent factors which represent their aspect and rating distributions. Different from state-of-the-art LDA models, FLDA is trained at the category level and learns the latent factors using the reviews of all the items of a category, in particular the non cold start items, and uses them as prior for cold start items. Our experiments on three real-life datasets demonstrate the improved effectiveness of the FLDA model in terms of likelihood of the held-out test set. We also evaluate the accuracy of FLDA based on two application-oriented measures.

Categories and Subject Descriptors

I.7.0 [**Document and Text Processing**]: General; G.3 [**Mathematics of Computing**]: Probability and Statistics—*statistical computing, multivariate statistics*

General Terms

Algorithms, Design, Experimentation

Keywords

aspect-based opinion mining, cold start item, latent dirichlet allocation, aspect identification, rating prediction, user modeling

Copyright is held by the International World Wide Web Conference Committee (IW3C2). IW3C2 reserves the right to provide a hyperlink to the author's site if the Material is used in electronic media.
WWW 2013, May 13–17, 2013, Rio de Janeiro, Brazil.
ACM 978-1-4503-2035-1/13/05.

1. INTRODUCTION

The process of buying a product or selecting a service is usually started with a series of inquires about possible options. Nowadays the Web has become an excellent source of user opinions which answers all of the user's questions by itself. However, the amount of information to be read for decision making is hugely overwhelming. There are now hundreds of Web resources containing user opinions, e.g., reviewing websites, forums, discussion groups, and Blogs, etc. While in most of the reviewing websites, reviewers assigned overall ratings (as stars) to express the overall quality of reviewed items, most of the readers usually need more detailed information than a single rating to make the final decision. For example, in the process of buying a digital camera, one may want to know the quality of zoom, while another may only care about the ease of use. A 4-star rating for a specific camera may convince none of them to purchase it without further review reading.

One of the emerging problems in opinion mining, which attracted a lot of attention recently, is aspect-based opinion mining [17]. Aspect-based opinion mining consists of two main tasks: 1) Extracting major aspects of items from user reviews, and 2) Predicting the rating of each aspect based on the sentiments reviewers used to describe that aspect. Aspects which are attributes or components of items are usually commented on in reviews to give an overview of the item quality. For example, 'zoom', 'LCD' and 'battery life' are some of the aspects of digital cameras. Reviewers express the quality of each aspect using sentiments which are usually adjectives, e.g., 'good zoom', 'blurry LCD' and 'poor battery life'. These sentiments show the level of users' satisfaction regarding the quality of each aspect. To provide a summary of review, aspect-based opinion mining techniques try to interpret sentiments as numerical ratings (usually in the range from 1 to 5) to provide a rated aspect summary of reviews, e.g., 'zoom: 4', 'LCD: 2', and 'battery life: 1'.

In the last decade several latent variable models have been proposed to address the problem of aspect-based opinion mining, e.g., [26, 31, 3, 23, 30, 8, 19, 5, 16, 20]. All of these models are applied at the item level, i.e., they learn one model per item from the reviews of that item. Learning a model per item is logical as the rating of an aspect depends on the aspect quality which usually differs for different items. However, an issue that has been neglected in all of the current works is that latent variable models are not accurate if there is not enough training data. In our recent work [21], we evaluated the impact of the size of the training dataset on models for aspect-based opinion mining. We discussed a series of increasingly sophisticated LDA models representing the essence of the major published methods in the literature. Our comprehensive evaluation of these models on a real-life data set proved that while item level models work well for items with large number of reviews, they perform poorly when the size of the training dataset is small. In fact, the experimental evaluation showed that the basic LDA model outperforms the more complex models for these items. Borrowing a term from the recommender systems literature, we call such items *cold start items*. In real-life data sets such as those from Epinions.com and Amazon.com more than 90% of items are cold start (less than 10 reviews) which indicates there is a great need for accurate opinion mining models for these items.

In this paper, we introduce the problem of identifying aspects and estimating their ratings for cold start items. To address this problem, we propose a probabilistic graphical model based on LDA, called *Factorized LDA (FLDA)*. The underlying assumption of this model is that the aspects and corresponding ratings of reviews are influenced not only by the items but also by the reviewers. It further assumes that both items and reviewers can be modeled by a set of latent factors. Item factors represent the item's probability distribution over aspects and for each aspect its distribution over ratings. In the same way, reviewer factors represent the reviewer's probability distribution over aspects and for each aspect its distribution over ratings. FLDA generates aspects and ratings of reviews by learning the latent factors of items and reviewers.

Different from state-of-the-art LDA models which are learned per item, FLDA is trained at the category level. Note that, a category of items is a set of items sharing common characteristics, e.g., MP3 players, scanners, Bed and Breakfast Inns, etc. FLDA generates each aspect of a review based on both the aspect distribution of the corresponding item and the aspect distribution of the reviewer. It further generates the rating of an aspect depending on that aspect, the rating distribution of that aspect for that item and the rating distribution of that aspect for the reviewer. These distributions are trained using the reviews of all the items of a category, in particular the non cold start items, and serve as prior for the distributions of cold start items that otherwise could not be learned accurately. In other words, for cold start items the aspect distribution is mainly determined by the prior aspect distribution of the category, and the rating distribution of an aspect is mainly determined by the rating distribution of the reviewer or by the prior rating distribution of all reviewers (if the reviewer is cold start, i.e., has written few reviews). On the other hand, for non-cold start items the aspect and rating distributions are mainly determined by the observed reviews of that item.

We report the results of our extensive experiments on three real-life datasets from Epinions, Amazon, and TripAdvisor. The results demonstrate the improved effectiveness of the FLDA model in terms of likelihood of the held-out test set, in particular for cold start items. We also evaluate the accuracy of FLDA based on two application-oriented measures: item categorization and overall rating prediction for reviews. Both applications are performed based on the learned latent factors. We evaluate these applications by comparing the accuracy of the learned classifiers with the state-of-the-art techniques.

The remainder of the paper is organized as follows. The next section is devoted to related work. Section 3 introduces the problem statement and discusses our contribution. Section 4 presents the proposed model, FLDA. Section 5 describes the inference and estimation techniques for FLDA. In Sections 6 and 7, we report the results of our experimental evaluation and discuss two applications of our model. Finally, Section 8 concludes the paper with a summary and the discussion of future work.

2. RELATED WORK

Most of the early works on aspect-based opinion mining are frequency-based approaches [7, 18, 1, 22]. These methods usually mine frequent noun phrases and filter them using certain constraints to identify aspects. These techniques tend to produce too many non-aspects and miss low-frequency aspects [5]. In addition, frequency based approaches require the manual tuning of various parameters which makes them hard to port to another dataset [20]. Addressing these weaknesses, latent variable models automatically learn the model parameters from the data.

While some of the proposed latent variable models are based on Conditional Random Field [14, 4] or Hidden Markov Model [29, 8], most of them are based on Latent Dirichlet Allocation (LDA), e.g., [26, 25, 31, 3, 10, 30, 28, 13, 15, 16, 6]. LDA is a generative probabilistic model of a corpus [2]. The basic idea of this model is that documents are represented as mixtures over latent topics where topics are associated with a distribution over the words of the vocabulary. All of the existing LDA-based opinion mining models are trained at the item level, i.e., from the reviews of a given item. In the following we will discuss the most recent and most important LDA-based models presented in the literature.

The model of [3] assumes that all words in a single sentence are generated from one topic and apply LDA on each sentence to extract topics (as aspects). The authors of [10] further extend the model of [3] to extract sentiments related to each aspect. In this model, each review has a distribution over sentiments and each sentiment has a distribution over aspects. To generate each sentence, a sentiment is first sampled from the review's sentiment distribution and then an aspect is chosen conditioned on the selected sentiment. Each word of the sentence is then generated based on the selected aspect and sentiment.

An LDA-based model for jointly identifying aspects and sentiments is proposed in [31]. This model assumes each review has a distribution over aspects and another distribution over sentiments. The authors further assume there are two types of sentiments in a review: aspect-specific sentiments which are each associated with only a single aspect (e.g., 'tasty' which is associated with 'food'), and general sentiments which are shared across different aspect (e.g., 'great'). They use two indicator variables to distinguish between aspects and sentiments based on their Part-Of-Speech (POS) tags.

The authors of [13] also assume different word distributions for aspects, sentiments, and also background words (other words). The model determines whether the word is an aspect, a sentiment, or a background word, based on the POS tag of that word and the POS tag of the previous word. This model generates each word of a review by first choosing an aspect and a sentiment from the corresponding distributions. Then a word is generated conditioned on both aspect and sentiment. The rating of each sentiment is also computed using a normal linear model learned by the overall rating of review.

In [28] an LDA model is proposed to identify aspects, their ratings, and the weight placed on each aspect by the reviewer. This model takes the overall ratings assigned by reviewers to that product as input. It first samples an aspect from the learned distribution and selects a word conditioned on the that aspect. Then the sampled word and the aspect together generate the rating of the aspect. Finally, the aspect weights are sampled from a normal distribution and the overall rating of review is generated based on the weighted sum of all the aspect ratings.

The model proposed in [26] considers two types of topics for each review: global topics and local topics. Global topics correspond to global properties of the product (e.g., product brand) and local topics are related to the product aspects. The model uses an indicator variable to select the type of topic for generating each word of a review. An existing ranking algorithm is used to estimate the rating of aspects based the learned variables. This model is further extended in [25] to find the correspondence between the extracted topics and the product aspects.

The authors of [30] propose a model generating opinion phrases (pairs of candidate aspect and related sentiment). They first apply a set of predefined POS patterns on the review text to extract nouns and related adjectives as opinion phrases. Then the basic LDA model is applied on each sentence to cluster opinion phrases into k groups. Similar to [30], in [20] an LDA model, called ILDA, is proposed to learn from opinion phrases. To identify opinion phrases, a set of POS patterns are first mined using a seed set of aspects and related sentiments. These patterns are then applied on reviews to extract opinion phrases. ILDA assumes the dependency between aspects and ratings. To generate each opinion phrase, an aspect is first chosen from a Dirichlet distribution and then a rating is selected conditioned on the chosen aspect. An opinion phrase is finally generated based on the selected aspect and rating.

In our recent work [21], we present a set of guidelines for designing LDA-based models by comparing a series of increasingly sophisticated probabilistic graphical models based on LDA. We start with the basic LDA model and then gradually extend the model by adding latent and observed variables as well as dependencies. We argue that these models represent the essence of the major published methods and allow us to tease apart the impact of various design decisions. In addition to design choices, we further evaluate the impact of the size of the training dataset and the performance of different techniques for extracting opinion phrases. We conduct extensive experiments on a very large real-life dataset from Epinions.com and compare the performance of different models in terms of the likelihood of the held-out test set. Based on our experimental results, we find out while for items with many reviews, the model learning aspects and ratings from opinion phrases with dependency assumption (D-PLDA) performs best, for items with few reviews (cold start items) the basic LDA model outperforms the more complex models. We also conclude that using dependency patterns consistently achieves the best performance for extracting opinion phrases.

3. PROBLEM STATEMENT AND CONTRIBUTION

In the opinion mining literature, an *aspect* refers to an attribute or component of an item that has been commented on in a review, e.g., 'sleep quality', 'internet connection', and 'room service' for a hotel. Expressing the *rating* of an aspect by a sentiment, an opinion phrase is a pair of <*head term, modifier*> where head term refers to an aspect and modifier is the related sentiment, e.g. < room service, great >, < screen, inaccurate > [19]. Most of the reviewing websites ask reviewers to express an *overall rating* (as stars) for the reviewed item in addition to the review text.

A *category* of items is defined as a set of items sharing common characteristics. Categorizations can be performed according to different criteria and are typically available in online reviewing websites. For example, hotels may be categorized based on price, location, price & location, etc. Products can be categorized at high level, e.g., electronics, toys, sport, etc. or at more specialized level, e.g., outdoor recreation, team sports, water sports, etc.

Providing aspects and the corresponding ratings does not only help users gain more insight into the quality of items, but also enables them to compare different items. The problem of aspect-based opinion mining addresses this need by performing two main tasks:

- Aspect identification: Identifying and extracting aspects from reviews.

- Rating prediction: Estimating the numerical rating of an aspect (usually in the range from 1 to 5).

As discussed in section 2, all of the current opinion mining models are at the item level. However, learning a model at the item level is not accurate for cold start items, i.e., items that have been reviewed by few reviewers. Since a very large portion of items in real-life reviewing websites are cold start, having a proper model for these items is essential. To address the problem of aspect-based opinion mining for cold start items, we propose a probabilistic model based on LDA, called FLDA. This model assumes that both items and reviewers can be modeled by a set of latent factors. Item's/reviewer's factors represent the item/reviewer distribution over aspects and for each aspect its distribution over ratings. Each review in the FLDA model is generated based on the learned factors of the corresponding item and reviewer. It first samples aspects in a review from the aspect distributions of the corresponding item and reviewer, and then generates the rating of each aspect conditioned on that aspect and the rating distributions of that item and reviewer. For cold start items, the aspect and rating distributions are mainly determined by the prior aspect distribution of the category and the rating distribution of the reviewer (or the prior rating distribution of all reviewers), respectively. For non cold start items, the aspect and rating distributions mainly depend on the observed reviews of that item. In the following section, we will elaborate the proposed FLDA model in detail.

4. PROPOSED MODEL

In this paper, we introduce a probabilistic model based on LDA, called Factorized LDA (FLDA), which models not only items but also reviewers. The FLDA model makes the following assumptions:

- A category has a set of aspects which are shared by all items in that category. For example, {zoom, battery life, shutter lag, etc.} is a set of aspects shared by all products in the category 'digital camera'. Note that, probabilities of occurrence of aspects can differ for different items in the category.

- Each item has a distribution over the aspects representing what aspects of its category are mainly commented on in reviews of that item. Each of these aspects is associated with a distribution of ratings.

- Each reviewer has a distribution over the aspects representing what aspects are more commented on by the reviewer. The reviewer is also associated, for each aspect, with a rating distribution.

Based on the above assumptions, to generate a review, aspects are first sampled conditioned on the aspect distributions of the corresponding item and reviewer. The rating of each aspect is then sampled conditioned on the aspect and the rating distributions of the item and the reviewer. Finally, opinion phrases are sampled based on the chosen aspects and ratings. Figure 1 shows the corresponding graphical model. Following the standard graphical model formalism, nodes represent random variables, edges indicate possible dependency, shaded nodes are observed random variables, and unshaded nodes are latent random variables. A box around groups of random variables is a plate which denotes replication. The shaded box represents a review written by a reviewer about some item. P and U denote the number of items and reviewers, respectively. K is the number of aspects and N is the number of opinion phrases in a review. Note that, a random variable is a variable that can take on a set of possible different values, each with an associated probability.

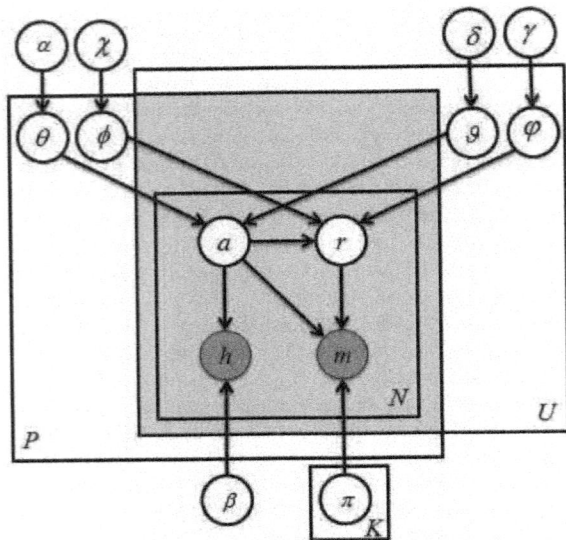

Figure 1: The graphical model for FLDA

As shown in Figure 1, α and δ are the prior aspect distributions and χ and γ are the prior rating distributions for the given category. The basic idea of FLDA is that each item p is represented as random mixtures over latent aspects, θ_p, and latent rating, ϕ_p, and each reviewer u is represented as random mixtures over latent aspect, ϑ_u, and latent ratings, φ_u. The FLDA model assumes the following generative process:

1. For each item $p, p \in \{1, 2, ..., P\}$
   (a) Sample $\theta_p \sim Dir(\alpha)$
   (b) Sample $\phi_p \sim Dir(\chi)$

2. For each reviewer $u, u \in \{1, 2, ..., U\}$
   (a) Sample $\vartheta_u \sim Dir(\delta)$
   (b) Sample $\varphi_u \sim Dir(\gamma)$

3. If there is a review by u about p, then for each opinion phrase $<h_{pun}, m_{pun}>, n \in \{1, 2, ..., N\}$
   (a) Sample $a_{pun} \sim P(a_{pun}|\theta_p, \vartheta_u)$ and sample $r_{pun} \sim P(r_{pun}|a_{pun}, \phi_p, \varphi_u)$
   (b) Sample $h_{pun} \sim P(h_{pun}|a_{pun}, \beta)$ and sample $m_{pun} \sim P(m_{pun}|a_{pun}, r_{pun}, \pi)$

where $P(h_{pun}|a_{pun}, \beta)$ and $P(m_{pun}|a_{pun}, r_{pun}, \pi)$ are multinomial distributions. In the following the resulting joint distribution of the FLDA model is presented:

$$P(a, r, h, m, \theta, \phi, \vartheta, \varphi|\alpha, \chi, \delta, \gamma, \beta, \pi) =$$
$$\prod_{p=1}^{P}[P(\theta_p|\alpha)P(\phi_p|\chi)]\prod_{u=1}^{U}[P(\vartheta_u|\delta)P(\varphi_u|\gamma)]$$
$$\prod_{p=1}^{P}\prod_{u=1}^{U}\epsilon(p,u)\prod_{n=1}^{N}[P(a_{pun}|\theta_p, \vartheta_u)P(r_{pun}|a_{pun}, \phi_p, \varphi_u)$$
$$P(h_{pun}|a_{pun}, \beta)P(m_{pun}|a_{pun}, r_{pun}, \pi)] \quad (1)$$

where $\epsilon(p,u) = 1$ if there is a review written by u about item p, otherwise $\epsilon(p,u) = 0$. The goal is to compute the posterior distribution of the latent variables given a review:

$$P(a, r, \theta, \phi, \vartheta, \varphi|h, m, \alpha, \chi, \delta, \gamma, \beta, \pi) =$$
$$\frac{P(a, r, h, m, \theta, \phi, \vartheta, \varphi|\alpha, \chi, \delta, \gamma, \beta, \pi)}{P(h, m|\alpha, \chi, \delta, \gamma, \beta, \pi)} \quad (2)$$

Similar to the basic LDA, due to the coupling between θ and ϑ with β and also between ϕ and φ with π, the conditional distribution of latent variables given observed data is intractable to compute. A wide variety of approximate inference algorithms have been proposed for LDA models. In this paper, we use variational inference [2] to compute an approximation for the posterior distribution.

5. INFERENCE AND PARAMETER LEARNING

In this section, we describe approximate inference and parameter learning for the FLDA model, adopting a variational method. As computing the posterior distribution of the latent variables for FLDA is intractable, we obtain a tractable lower bound by modifying the graphical model through considering a variational parameters for generating each latent variable. In particular, we simplify FLDA into the graphical model shown in Figure 2.

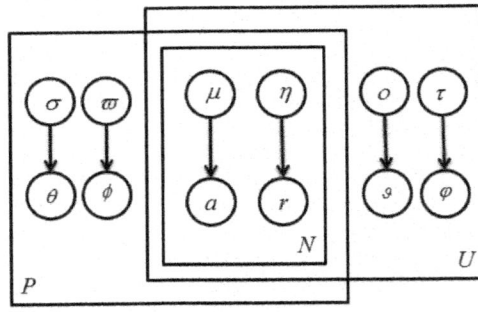

Figure 2: Graphical model representation of variational distribution for FLDA

This model specifies the following variational distribution on the latent variables:

Algorithm 1 E-step of Variational Inference for FLDA

1: initialize $\mu_{puni}^0 = 1/k$ for all p, u, n and i
2: initialize $\eta_{punj}^0 = 1/5$ for all p, u, n and j
3: initialize $\sigma_{pi}^0 = \alpha_i + (N \times U)/k$ for all p and i
4: initialize $\varpi_{pij}^0 = \chi_{ij} + (N \times U)/(k \times 5)$ for all p, i, j
5: initialize $o_{ui}^0 = \delta_i + (N \times P)/k$ for all u and i
6: initialize $\tau_{uij}^0 = \gamma_{ij} + (N \times P)/(k \times 5)$ for all u, i, j
7: **repeat**
8:   **for** $p = 1$ to P **do**
9:     **for** $u = 1$ to U **do**
10:       **if** $\epsilon(p, u) == 1$ **then**
11:         **for** $n = 1$ to N **do**
12:           **for** $i = 1$ to k **do**
13:             $\mu_{puni}^{t+1} = \beta_{ix} \prod_j^5 \pi_{ijy}^{\eta_{punj}^t} \exp(\psi(\sigma_{pi}^t)\psi(o_{ui}^t) + \sum_j^5 \eta_{punj}^t \psi(\tau_{uij}^t)\psi(\varpi_{pij}^t))$
14:           **end for**
15:           normalize μ_{puni}^{t+1} to sum to 1
16:           **for** $j = 1$ to 5 **do**
17:             $\eta_{punj}^{t+1} = \prod_i^K \pi_{ijy}^{\mu_{puni}^t} \exp(\sum_i^K \mu_{puni}^t \psi(\tau_{uij}^t)\psi(\varpi_{pij}^t))$
18:           **end for**
19:           normalize η_{punj}^{t+1} to sum to 1
20:         **end for**
21:       **end if**
22:     **end for**
23:   **end for**
24:   **for** $p = 1$ to P **do**
25:     $\sigma_p^{t+1} = \alpha + \sum_u^U \sum_n^N \mu_{pun}^{t+1} \psi(o_u^{t+1})$
26:     $\varpi_p^{t+1} = \chi + \sum_u^U \sum_n^N \mu_{pun}^{t+1} \eta_{pun}^{t+1} \psi(\tau_u^{t+1})$
27:   **end for**
28:   **for** $u = 1$ to U **do**
29:     $o_u^{t+1} = \delta + \sum_p^P \sum_n^N \mu_{pun}^{t+1} \psi(\sigma_p^{t+1})$
30:     $\tau_u^{t+1} = \gamma + \sum_p^P \sum_n^N \mu_{pun}^{t+1} \eta_{pun}^{t+1} \psi(\varpi_p^{t+1})$
31:   **end for**
32: **until** convergence

Algorithm 2 M-Step of Variational Inference for FLDA

$\beta_{ix} = \sum_p^P \sum_u^U \sum_n^N \mu_{puni}^* h_{pun}^x$
$\pi_{ijy} = \sum_p^P \sum_u^U \sum_n^N \mu_{puni}^* \eta_{punj}^* m_{pun}^y$
$\alpha_{new} = \alpha_{old} - H(\alpha_{old})^{-1} g(\alpha_{old})$
$\chi_{new} = \chi_{old} - H(\chi_{old})^{-1} g(\chi_{old})$
$\delta_{new} = \delta_{old} - H(\delta_{old})^{-1} g(\delta_{old})$
$\gamma_{new} = \gamma_{old} - H(\gamma_{old})^{-1} g(\gamma_{old})$

ence procedure where β_{ix} is $P(h_{pun}^x = 1 | a_{pun}^i = 1)$ for the appropriate x and π_{ijy} is $P(m_{pun}^y = 1 | a_{pun}^i = 1, r_{pun}^j = 1)$ for the appropriate y. Recall that h_{pun} and m_{pun} are vectors with exactly one component equal to one. We can select the unique x and y such that $h_{pun}^x = 1$ and $m_{pun}^y = 1$ [2].

By computing the approximate posterior, we can find a lower bound on the joint probability, $P(\boldsymbol{a}, \boldsymbol{r}, \boldsymbol{\theta}, \boldsymbol{\phi}, \boldsymbol{\vartheta}, \boldsymbol{\varphi})$. Using this lower bound we can find approximate estimates for FLDA parameters via an alternative variational EM procedure [2]. The variational EM algorithm alternates between Expectation (E-step) and Maximization (M-step) steps until the bound on the expected log likelihood converges. The variational EM algorithm for FLDA is as follows[1]:

1. (E-step) For each review, find the optimizing values of the variational parameters σ^*, ϖ^*, o^*, τ^*, μ^*, and η^* (using Algorithm 1).

2. (M-step) Maximize the resulting lower bound on the log likelihood with respect to the model parameters $\alpha, \chi, \delta, \gamma, \beta$, and $\boldsymbol{\pi}$ (using Algorithm 2).

The M-step update for the Dirichlet parameters α, χ, δ and γ are implemented using the Newton-Raphson optimization technique that finds a stationary point of a function by iterating [2]. In Algorithm 2, $H(x)$ and $g(x)$ are the Hessian matrix and gradient respectively at the point x.

Note that, to deal with over fitting, we smooth all the parameters which depend on the observed data by assigning positive probability to all vocabulary terms whether or not they are observed in the training set.

6. EXPERIMENTS

In this section, we first briefly describe the real-life datasets we used for our experiments and then present the results of the experimental evaluation of the FLDA model. We evaluate the performance of the model in terms of likelihood of the held-out test set and also based on two application-oriented measures for categorizing items and predicting reviews overall ratings.

6.1 Datasets

To evaluate the proposed model, we performed experiments on three real-life datasets from Epinions [21], Amazon [9], and TripAdvisor [27]. In each dataset, we select items with at least one review. For preprocessing, we adopt the dependency pattern technique to identify opinion phrases in the form of a pair of head term and modifier. This technique results in the best performance in

$$Q(\boldsymbol{\theta}, \boldsymbol{\phi}, \boldsymbol{\vartheta}, \boldsymbol{\varphi}, \boldsymbol{a}, \boldsymbol{r} | \boldsymbol{\sigma}, \boldsymbol{\varpi}, \boldsymbol{o}, \boldsymbol{\tau}, \boldsymbol{\mu}, \boldsymbol{\eta}) = \prod_{p=1}^P [Q(\theta_p|\sigma_p)Q(\phi_p|\varpi_p)] \prod_{u=1}^U [Q(\vartheta_u|o_u)Q(\varphi_u|\tau_u)] \prod_{p=1}^P \prod_{u=1}^U \epsilon(p,u) \prod_{n=1}^N [Q(a_{pun}|\mu_{pun})Q(r_{pun}|\eta_{pun})] \quad (3)$$

where the Dirichlet parameters σ, ϖ, o and τ, and the multinomial parameters μ and η are free variational parameters. The KL-divergence between the variational distribution and the true posterior should be minimum to have a good approximation. To this end, we set the derivative of the KL-divergence with respect to variational parameters equal to zero, to obtain the update equations. The update equations are invoked repeatedly until the change in KL-divergence is small.

Algorithm 1 presents the pseudo-code of the variational infer-

---
[1]The detailed derivation of the variational EM algorithm is available at http://http://www.sfu.ca/~sam39/FLDA/

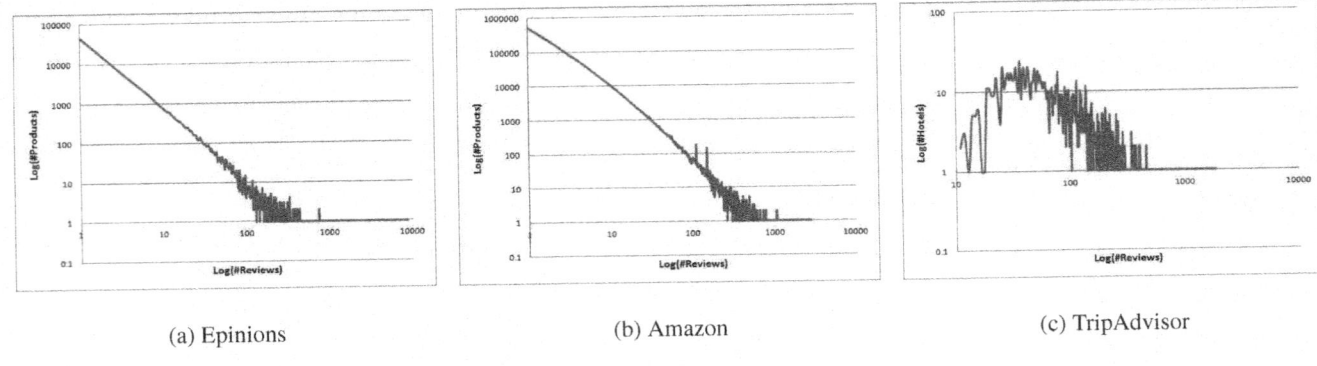

(a) Epinions (b) Amazon (c) TripAdvisor

Figure 3: Log-log plot of #reviews vs. #items

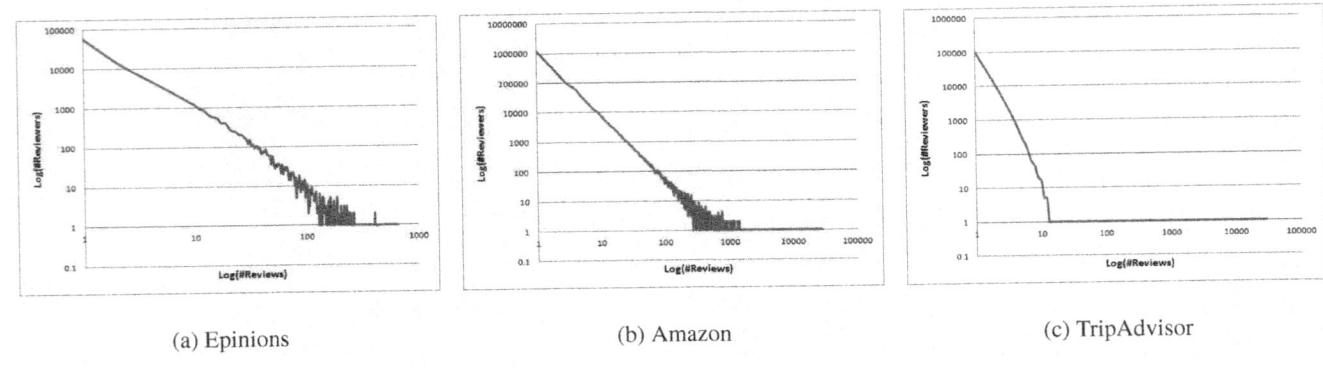

(a) Epinions (b) Amazon (c) TripAdvisor

Figure 4: Log-log plot of #reviews vs. #reviewers

Table 1: General statistics of different datasets

Dataset	Epinions	Amazon	TripAdvisor
#Categories	379	38	5
#Reviews	541,219	5,016,492	181,395
#Reviewers	109,857	1,761,879	117,976
#Items	87,633	1,108,018	1,496

Table 2: Sample categories of each dataset

Dataset	Sample Categories
Epinions	Accessories, Blazers, Dresses, Outerwear, Pants, Shirts, Skirts, ...
Amazon	Apparel, Electronics, Computers, Baby,...
TripAdvisor	1-star, 2-star, 3-star, 4-star, 5-star

compare to other preprocessing techniques according to [21]. In Table 1, general statistics of these datasets are shown.

Regarding item categories, we used the available categorization in each dataset which were mostly at a high level (5 hotel categories based on their number of stars for TripAdvisor, 38 general categories for Amazon, and 379 product categories for Epinions). Table 2 shows some sample categories for each dataset.

All of the current works report only the average number of reviews per item, somehow masking the large percentage of cold start items in real-life datasets. In fact, cold start items are normally ignored in learning latent variable models. In order to show the variance in the numbers of reviews, Figures 3 and 4 show the distributions of #reviews per item and #reviews per reviewer in different datasets, respectively.

Not surprisingly, in the Epinions and Amazon datasets both distributions follow a power law. We can see that a large number of items has only a few reviews, and a few items have a large number of reviews (Figures 3(a) and 3(b)). A similar property can be seen in the log-log plot of the number of reviews vs. the number of reviewers (Figures 4(a) and 4(b)). In the TripAdvisor dataset, the distribution of the number of reviews per reviewer (Figures 4(c)) also follows a power law. However, the relationship between the number of reviews and the number of hotels (Figure 3(c)) is below an ideal straight line for the first few points, since there are surprisingly few hotels with fewer than 50 reviews.

These power law distributions point out substantial diversity among items in real-life review datasets. To analyze the performance of the comparison partners separately on different types of items, we categorize items of each dataset into 5 groups based on the number of reviews. Table 3 shows the percentage of items in each dataset with the specified number of reviews.

Table 3: Percentage of items in each item group

Item Groups	Epinions	Amazon	TripAdvisor
$1 < \#Rev \leq 10$	90%	91%	0%
$10 < \#Rev \leq 50$	8%	7%	31%
$50 < \#Rev \leq 100$	1%	1%	30%
$100 < \#Rev \leq 200$	<1%	<1%	24%
$200 < \#Rev$	<1%	<1%	14%

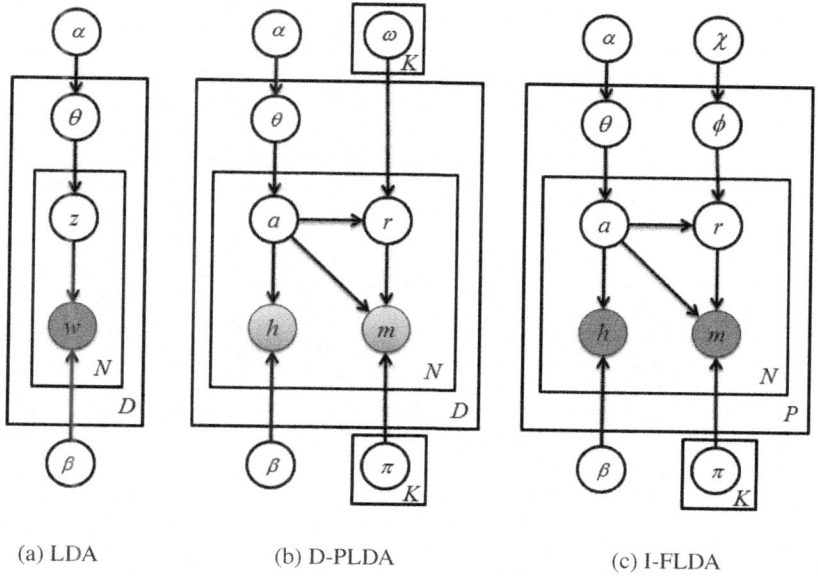

(a) LDA (b) D-PLDA (c) I-FLDA

Figure 5: Comparison partners: LDA and D-PLDA are state-of-the-art models, I-FLDA is a simplified version of FLDA

In the Epinions and Amazon datasets, more than 90% of products have less than 10 reviews which are considered cold start items. The TripAdvisor dataset has larger numbers of reviews per item. However, as Table 3 shows 31% of hotels have been reviewed by less than 50 reviewers which can be considered cold start in this dataset. These statistics clearly indicate that there is a need for opinion mining models with the focus on cold start items.

Table 4 also presents the average number of reviews per item for the defined item groups. It suggests that the average numbers of reviews for cold start items are indeed very small (2 for Epinions and Amazon, 25 for TripAdvisor) which makes it hard to learn an accurate model for these items.

Table 4: Average #reviews per item in each item group

Item Groups	Epinions	Amazon	TripAdvisor
$1 < \#Rev \leq 10$	2	2	0
$10 < \#Rev \leq 50$	16	18	25
$50 < \#Rev \leq 100$	53	62	54
$100 < \#Rev \leq 200$	114	122	107
$200 < \#Rev$	324	338	297

6.2 Comparison Partners

We compare FLDA with the basic LDA model that generates all words of reviews [2] (Figure 5(a)) and the D-PLDA model presented in [21] (Figure 5(b)). We selected these two models as comparison partners since experimental evaluation in [21] showed that the basic LDA performs best for cold start items and D-PLDA outperforms other models for non cold start items. Note that, FLDA adopts the same model for generating opinion phrases as D-PLDA, i.e., they have the same inner plate in the graphical model. Both LDA and D-PLDA are trained at the item level and D is the number of reviews for the given item. To tease apart the impact of the two major changes between D-PLDA and FLDA, we also compare a simplified version of FLDA, called I-FLDA, that does not model reviewers and their parameters but is trained at the category level (Figure 5(c)).

6.3 Quantitative Evaluation

In this section, we evaluate the generalization performance of all comparison partners based on the likelihood of a held-out test set, which is standard in the absence of ground truth. For comparison, we trained all the latent variable models using EM with exactly the same stopping criteria and for various numbers of aspects, $k = \{5, 10, 15, 20, 25\}$. Since the relative results are similar for different values of k, we choose $k = 15$ for our discussion.

In the performance comparison, the goal is achieving high likelihood on a held-out test set. We hold out 10% of the reviews for testing purposes and use the remaining 90% to train models. As is standard for LDA models [2, 30, 20], we computed the perplexity of the held-out test set. A strong correlation of the perplexity and the accuracy (which can be computed only if ground truth is available) of aspect-based opinion mining models is shown in [21]. The perplexity is monotonically decreasing in the likelihood of the test data, and a lower perplexity score indicates better performance. For a test set of N reviews, the perplexity is defined as [2]:

$$perplexity(D_{test}) = exp\{-\frac{\sum_{d=1}^{D} \log P(\boldsymbol{h}_d, \boldsymbol{m}_d)}{\sum_{d=1}^{D} N_d}\} \quad (4)$$

Table 5 and Figure 6 present the perplexity results of FLDA and the comparison partners for different groups of items in different datasets. The first observation, that has already been discussed in [21], is that the D-PLDA model outperforms LDA in all datasets for non cold start items. However, for cold start items it has higher perplexity than LDA, indicating poor performance of the model in the absence of enough training data. We can also observe that I-FLDA, which is trained at the category level but does not model reviewers, achieves lower perplexity than D-PLDA, especially for cold start items. This better performance can be explained by the fact that I-FLDA is trained at the category level and learns the latent factors using the reviews of all the items of a category, in particular the non cold start items, and uses them as prior for cold start items.

Finally, we note that in all datasets and for all item groups, FLDA

Table 5: Perplexity comparison of different item groups in different datasets

Item Groups	LDA	D-PLDA	I-FLDA	FLDA
$1 < \#Rev \leq 10$	4413.65	5413.65	4187.98	3287.98
$10 < \#Rev \leq 50$	2338.67	1975.34	1903.45	1687.67
$50 < \#Rev \leq 100$	1671.23	592.39	588.61	468.12
$100 < \#Rev \leq 200$	1394.72	164.18	153.02	133.90
$200 < \#Rev$	1385.99	142.37	142.16	140.35

(a) Epinions

Item Groups	LDA	D-PLDA	I-FLDA	FLDA
$1 < \#Rev \leq 10$	5019.79	5653.79	4302.45	3494.01
$10 < \#Rev \leq 50$	2434.71	2159.02	1931.34	1833.66
$50 < \#Rev \leq 100$	1183.14	769.77	756.09	744.18
$100 < \#Rev \leq 200$	993.78	339.69	331.45	318.49
$200 < \#Rev$	869.25	177.08	173.15	172.45

(b) Amazon

Item Groups	LDA	D-PLDA	I-FLDA	FLDA
$1 < \#Rev \leq 10$	-	-	-	
$10 < \#Rev \leq 50$	3446.61	3518.95	2898.56	2725.76
$50 < \#Rev \leq 100$	3336.61	2673.19	2394.09	2301.31
$100 < \#Rev \leq 200$	2943.46	1003.09	892.59	843.91
$200 < \#Rev$	1438.59	363.20	362.74	359.03

(c) TripAdvisor

consistently outperforms LDA, D-PLDA and I-FLDA. These findings show that FLDA's assumptions regarding using the category level information for aspect extraction and the user modeling for rating prediction are appropriate. The perplexity gain of FLDA is most notable for cold start items underlining the effectiveness of FLDA in modeling such items. For items with large numbers of reviews, FLDA can slightly improve the performance of I-FLDA by also modeling reviewers. Comparing the results of FLDA, I-FLDA and D-PLDA shows that when there is enough training data (reviews), learning a model at the item level is promising.

7. APPLICATIONS

In the following sections we perform two application-oriented evaluations to demonstrate the gains of FLDA in practice.

7.1 Item Categorization

One of the applications of category-level models is the ability of categorizing new items based on their reviews, e.g., identifying the class of a hotel (1 to 5 star), or type of a book (e.g., children's books, textbooks, audio books, magazines, etc.) based on their reviews. This feature is especially beneficial when working with uncategorized reviews, e.g., forums, Blogs, discussion groups, etc.

In [2], Blei et al. proposed to use the basic LDA model for document classification. In particular, LDA is used as a dimensionality reduction method, as it reduces any document to a vector of real-valued features, i.e., the posterior Dirichlet parameter associated with each document. The parameters of an LDA model are learned using all the documents, without reference to their true class label. The topic distribution provides a low-dimensional representation (feature vector) of a document, and a support vector machine (SVM) is trained on these feature vectors to distinguish the classes.

In our scenario, we can adopt the same approach for item categorization. The FLDA model can be used to produce feature vectors for item categorization as follows. We first estimate the parameters of the FLDA model using all the reviews of all items of all categories. The learned topic distribution σ of an item is used as the feature vector of that item, and an SVM classifier is trained on these feature vectors to classify items into categories (FLDA-SVM). Note that, the topic distribution of an item in this model cannot be interpreted as the aspect distribution of the item.

Since the LDA and D-PLDA models learn topic distributions of reviews, not items, they cannot be directly used as comparison partners for item categorization. However, by applying these models at the category level, we can obtain the topic distribution of items as item feature vectors. These models use all reviews of all items of all categories to learn the feature vectors of items (similar to FLDA-SVM). As a baseline, we also train a classifier on simple bag-of-words features (BOW-SVM). Table 6 shows the accuracy of SVM classifiers for cold start and non cold start items trained on different feature spaces.

Table 6: Average accuracy of SVM classifier trained on different feature sets for item categorization

Dataset	Epinions		Amazon		TripAdvisor	
Item Type	cold	non	cold	non	cold	non
BOW-SVM	64%	88%	62%	88%	68%	91%
LDA-SVM	71%	90%	67%	91%	73%	93%
D-PLDA-SVM	79%	96%	75%	94%	85%	97%
FLDA-SVM	83%	96%	79%	95%	86%	97%

The first observation is that for all feature sets the accuracy of item categorization is higher for non cold start items than for cold start items. This was predictable as there is more training data for non cold start items. Comparing BOW-SVM with LDA-SVM and D-PLDA-SVM, we can see an increase in classification accuracy by using the LDA-based features. This suggests that the topic-based representation provided by LDA can be useful for feature selection in item categorization. We also observe that the classification accuracy is substantially improved by using FLDA features. This suggests that the learned item factors of FLDA can provide a more accurate low-dimensional feature set for item categorization. Note that the LDA-based models ($k = 15$) reduce the feature space of the Epinions, Amazon, and TripAdvisor datasets by 97%, 99%, and 92%, respectively compared to all word features.

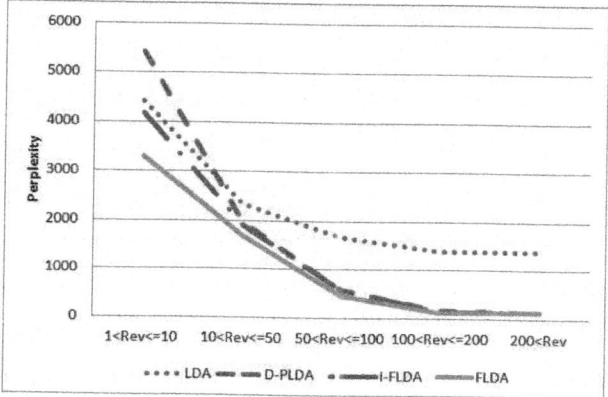

(a) Epinions

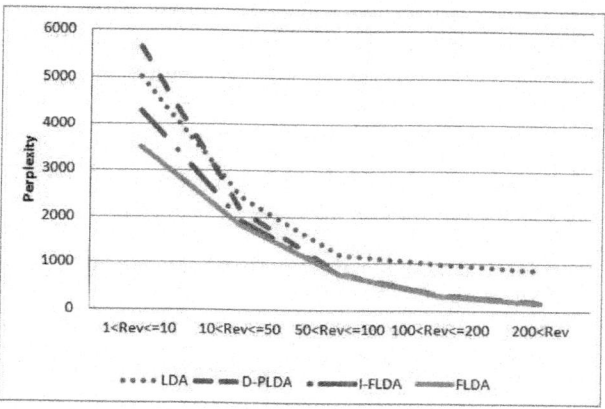

(b) Amazon

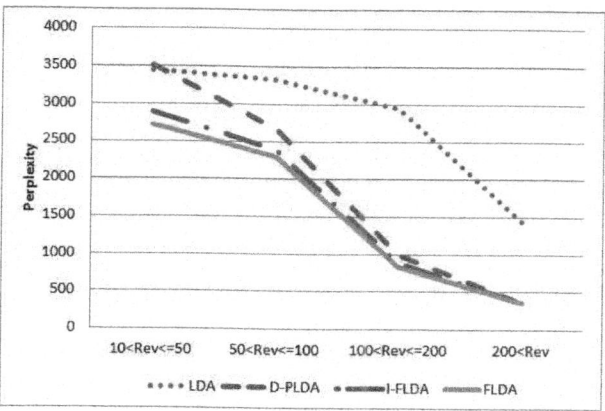

(c) TripAdvisor

Figure 6: Perplexity results of all comparison partners for different datasets

7.2 Overall Rating Prediction for Reviews

In most of the reviewing websites, reviewers are asked to assign an overall rating (as a number in some given range) to express their overall level of satisfaction with the reviewed item. However, in other repositories of reviews, such as forums and Blogs, such overall ratings are not normally provided. One of the applications of FLDA is the ability of predicting the overall rating of a review. As each review is written by a reviewer about an item, the overall rating of a review depends on both item and reviewer factors. The aspect and rating distributions of items and reviewers learned by the FLDA model can be used for computing the overall rating of the review as follows.

In recommender systems, Matrix Factorization (MF) is employed to factorize the $user \times item$ rating matrix to predict the rating of a user for an item [24, 11, 12]. Inspired by this model, we can compute the overall rating of an item by a reviewer using the learned item and reviewer factors. In the FLDA model, the latent aspect distribution of review d_{pu} is determined by the aspect distributions of the corresponding item, p, and reviewer, u, and is denoted by $P(a|\theta_p, \vartheta_u)$. In the same way the latent rating distribution of review d_{pu} is denoted by $P(r|a, \phi_p, \varphi_u)$. According to the probabilistic MF model, the distribution of the overall ratings o_{up} for user u and item p, can be computed as follows:

$$P(o_{up} = r) = \sum_a P(a|\theta_p, \vartheta_u)P(r|a, \phi_p, \varphi_u) \quad (5)$$

Since in the review datasets we used, ratings are chosen from the set $\{1, 2, 3, 4, 5\}$, we define 5 classes of overall ratings. For each item we train an SVM classifier on the distribution of the overall ratings acquired by Equation (5) to classify the overall rating of a given review (FLDA-SVM). As comparison partners, we train two classifiers on the review feature vectors generated by LDA (LDA-SVM) and D-PLDA (D-PLDA-SVM). The review feature vector of LDA is the topic distribution of the review, and the review feature vector of D-PLDA is the distribution of the overall ratings obtained using the probabilistic MF model (similar to Equation (5)). We also train a classifier on simple bag-of-words features (BOW-SVM) as a baseline. Table 7 shows the accuracy of SVM classifiers for cold start and non cold items trained on different feature spaces.

Table 7: Average accuracy of SVM classifier trained on different feature sets for overall rating prediction

Dataset	Epinions		Amazon		TripAdvisor	
Item Type	cold	non	cold	non	cold	non
BOW-SVM	49%	83%	44%	79%	47%	82%
LDA-SVM	56%	85%	53%	80%	59%	85%
D-PLDA-SVM	57%	86%	54%	80%	63%	87%
FLDA-SVM	72%	89%	70%	83%	74%	91%

Again we can see that for all feature sets the accuracy of overall rating prediction for non cold start items is much higher than that of cold start items, and also the accuracy of all LDA-based models is higher than for bag-of-words features. The accuracy of D-PLDA-SVM is slightly higher than that of LDA-SVM as it uses the rating distribution of the item for generating the feature vectors of reviews. Finally, as shown in Table 7, the accuracy of FLDA-SVM for the task of overall rating prediction is much higher than that of the comparison partners. This suggests that for a given review the learned item and user factors can be used as a low-dimensional feature set for predicting its overall rating.

8. CONCLUSION

Aspect-based opinion mining is the problem of automatically extracting aspects and estimating their ratings from reviews. All of the current models are trained at the item level (a model is trained form all reviews of an item) to perform these tasks. In this paper, we argued that while learning a model at the item level is fine for frequently reviewed items, it is ineffective for items with few reviews (cold start items). Note that, more than 90% of products in Epinions and Amazon datasets and 30% of hotels in the TripAdvisor dataset are cold start.

Addressing this need, we introduced the problem of aspect-based opinion mining for cold start items and proposed a probabilistic model based on LDA, called FLDA. Our model assumes that aspects in a review are sampled from the aspect distributions of the corresponding item and reviewer and the rating of each aspect is sampled conditioned on that aspect and the rating distributions of the item and reviewer. For cold start items the aspect distribution is mainly determined by the prior aspect distribution of the category, and the rating distribution of each aspect is mainly determined by the rating distribution of the reviewer (or by the prior rating distribution of all reviewers if the reviewer is cold start). The aspect and rating distributions for non cold start items are mainly determined by the observed reviews of that item.

We conducted extensive experiments on three real-life datasets and compared FLDA against the baseline LDA, the state-of-the-art D-PLDA, and the simplified I-FLDA models. FLDA clearly outperforms all of the comparison partners in terms of likelihood of the test set. For cold start items, the perplexity gain of FLDA is very large. We argued that the major reason for this gain is using the category level information and also modeling reviewers. We further teased apart the impact of modeling reviewers by comparing FLDA with the simplified I-FLDA model showing that modeling reviewers significantly impacts the model performance for cold start items. We also demonstrated the accuracy of FLDA in two applications: categorizing items and predicting the overall rating of reviews based on the learned feature vectors.

This paper suggests several directions for future research. FLDA assumes a given definition of item categories, but there may be alternative options to define them. For example, is it better to categorize hotels based on stars, or location, or price? An item taxonomy is a hierarchical structure of categories and subcategories. For example, the hierarchy for the category 'MP3 Players' could be "Electronics > Audio > Audio Players & Recorders > MP3 Players". In addition, in a scenario with a given item taxonomy, it would be interesting to explore methods to automatically learn the granularity (taxonomy) level that leads to the best model performance.

9. REFERENCES

[1] S. Baccianella, A. Esuli, and F. Sebastiani. Multi-facet rating of product reviews. In *ECIR '09*.

[2] D. M. Blei, A. Y. Ng, and M. I. Jordan. Latent dirichlet allocation. *J. Mach. Learn. Res.*, 2003.

[3] S. Brody and N. Elhadad. An unsupervised aspect-sentiment model for online reviews. In *HLT '10*.

[4] Y. Choi and C. Cardie. Hierarchical sequential learning for extracting opinions and their attributes. In *ACL '10*.

[5] H. Guo, H. Zhu, Z. Guo, X. Zhang, and Z. Su. Product feature categorization with multilevel latent semantic association. In *CIKM '09*.

[6] Y. He, C. Lin, and H. Alani. Automatically extracting polarity-bearing topics for cross-domain sentiment classification. In *HLT '11*.

[7] M. Hu and B. Liu. Mining and summarizing customer reviews. In *KDD '04*.

[8] W. Jin, H. H. Ho, and R. K. Srihari. Opinionminer: a novel machine learning system for web opinion mining and extraction. In *KDD '09*.

[9] N. Jindal and B. Liu. Opinion spam and analysis. In *WSDM '08*.

[10] Y. Jo and A. H. Oh. Aspect and sentiment unification model for online review analysis. In *WSDM '11*.

[11] Y. Koren. Collaborative filtering with temporal dynamics. In *KDD '09*.

[12] Y. Koren, R. Bell, and C. Volinsky. Matrix factorization techniques for recommender systems. *Computer Journal*, 42, 2009.

[13] H. Lakkaraju, C. Bhattacharyya, I. Bhattacharya, and S. Merugu. Exploiting coherence for the simultaneous discovery of latent facets and associated sentiments. In *SDM '11*.

[14] F. Li, C. Han, M. Huang, X. Zhu, Y.-J. Xia, S. Zhang, and H. Yu. Structure-aware review mining and summarization. In *COLING '10*.

[15] F. Li, M. Huang, and X. Zhu. Sentiment analysis with global topics and local dependency. In *AAAI '10*.

[16] C. Lin and Y. He. Joint sentiment/topic model for sentiment analysis. In *CIKM '09*.

[17] B. Liu. *Sentiment Analysis and Opinion Mining*. Morgan & Claypool Publishers, 2012.

[18] B. Liu, M. Hu, and J. Cheng. Opinion observer: analyzing and comparing opinions on the web. In *WWW '05*.

[19] Y. Lu, C. Zhai, and N. Sundaresan. Rated aspect summarization of short comments. In *WWW '09*.

[20] S. Moghaddam and M. Ester. ILDA: interdependent LDA model for learning latent aspects and their ratings from online product reviews. In *SIGIR '11*.

[21] S. Moghaddam and M. Ester. On the design of LDA models for aspect-based opinion mining. In *CIKM '12*.

[22] S. Moghaddam and M. Ester. Opinion Digger: an unsupervised opinion miner from unstructured product reviews. In *CIKM '10*.

[23] A. Mukherjee and B. Liu. Aspect extraction through semi-supervised modeling. In *ACL '12*.

[24] R. Salakhutdinov and A. Mnih. Probabilistic matrix factorization. In *NIPS '07*.

[25] I. Titov and R. McDonald. A joint model of text and aspect ratings for sentiment summarization. In *ACL-HLT '08*.

[26] I. Titov and R. McDonald. Modeling online reviews with multi-grain topic models. In *WWW '08*.

[27] H. Wang, Y. Lu, and C. Zhai. Latent aspect rating analysis on review text data: a rating regression approach. In *KDD '10*.

[28] H. Wang, Y. Lu, and C. Zhai. Latent aspect rating analysis without aspect keyword supervision. In *KDD '11*.

[29] T.-L. Wong, L. Bing, and W. Lam. Normalizing web product attributes and discovering domain ontology with minimal effort. In *WSDM '11*.

[30] T.-J. Zhan and C.-H. Li. Semantic dependent word pairs generative model for fine-grained product feature mining. In *PAKDD '11*.

[31] W. X. Zhao, J. Jiang, H. Yan, and X. Li. Jointly modeling aspects and opinions with a maxent-lda hybrid. In *EMNLP '10*.

Iolaus: Securing Online Content Rating Systems

Arash Molavi Kakhki
Northeastern University
arash@ccs.neu.edu

Chloe Kliman-Silver
Brown University
chloe_kliman-silver@brown.edu

Alan Mislove
Northeastern University
amislove@ccs.neu.edu

ABSTRACT

Online content ratings services allow users to find and share content ranging from news articles (Digg) to videos (YouTube) to businesses (Yelp). Generally, these sites allow users to create accounts, declare friendships, upload and rate content, and locate new content by leveraging the aggregated ratings of others. These services are becoming increasingly popular; Yelp alone has over 33 million reviews. Unfortunately, this popularity is leading to increasing levels of malicious activity, including multiple identity (Sybil) attacks and the "buying" of ratings from users.

In this paper, we present Iolaus, a system that leverages the underlying social network of online content rating systems to defend against such attacks. Iolaus uses two novel techniques: (a) *weighing ratings* to defend against multiple identity attacks and (b) *relative ratings* to mitigate the effect of "bought" ratings. An evaluation of Iolaus using microbenchmarks, synthetic data, and real-world content rating data demonstrates that Iolaus is able to outperform existing approaches and serve as a practical defense against multiple-identity and rating-buying attacks.

Categories and Subject Descriptors

K.4.4 [**Computers and Society**]: Electronic Commerce—*Security*

Keywords

Content rating; Sybil; Vote buying; Social network

1. INTRODUCTION

Online content sharing services are a popular mechanism for users to find and share content; sites exist to share content such as business recommendations (e.g., Yelp, TripAdvisor), news articles (e.g., Digg, reddit), multimedia content (e.g., Flickr, YouTube), apps (e.g., iOS App Store, Google Play), and URLs (e.g., StumbleUpon, del.icio.us). Generally, these sites allow users to create accounts, declare friendships, and upload and rate content. The sites' extreme popularity is evidenced by the massive amounts of content that are uploaded: YouTube receives over 72 hours of new video uploaded every minute [35], and Yelp boasts reviews on over 889,000 businesses worldwide [47]. To locate relevant and trustworthy content from among this massive set of uploaded content, users are encouraged to rate content, with highly rated content receiving more prominent placement. The most highly rated content typically appears on the front page of the site or is listed more highly in search results, garnering significant attention and traffic.

Unfortunately, the increasing popularity of online content sharing sites has made them an attractive target for manipulation. For example, malicious users often attempt to ensure that their content is more highly ranked (or that others' content is more lowly ranked). On certain sites, such manipulation can have significant financial consequences: Recent studies have shown that increasing a business's overall rating on Yelp by one star can lead to 9% increase in revenue [19], explaining the numerous instances of rating manipulation that have been observed [1, 26, 30, 32, 33].

In general, manipulation on content rating sites is enabled by two separate attacks:

- Malicious users can create multiple identities (i.e., Sybils [10]), and use these identities to provide positive ratings on their own content or negative ratings on others' content [30, 32]. This is exacerbated by the fact that accounts are typically free to create, requiring only an email address and a solved CAPTCHA [42].

- Malicious users can "buy" positive or negative ratings from otherwise legitimate users by offering small compensation in exchange for ratings [1,33].[1] This is made worse by the fact that most content only receives a few ratings, making it possible to greatly influence the overall ranking with just a few additional ratings.

Such manipulation is undesirable for the site operator (whose reputation is negatively impacted by successful manipulation) as well as honest end users (who depend on the site to locate relevant and trustworthy content).

In this paper, we present the design and implementation of Iolaus,[2] a system that is designed to be run by the site operator to mitigate the effect of rating manipulation via the creation of multiple identities or the "buying" of ratings. Iolaus works using two techniques: *weighing ratings* and *relative ratings*. First, Iolaus leverages the structure of the

---

[1] This compensation can take multiple forms, depending on the particular site: for example, businesses can offer discounts for Yelp ratings [1], and users can offer reciprocal ratings for Flickr favorites [15].

[2] In Greek mythology, Iolaus was a nephew of Heracles. Iolaus provided essential aid to Heracles by helping to defeat the Hydra, a multi-headed monster who would grow two heads each time an existing head was cut off.

social network to bound the influence over the overall rating that malicious users can achieve via the creation of multiple identities. Iolaus assigns personalized *weights* to each rating, and selects the weights using a multi-commodity max flow formulation. Doing so ensures that the total weight of a single (human) user's ratings is bounded, regardless of the number of identities she creates.

Second, Iolaus uses the fact that most users provide few ratings to reduce the effectiveness of "buying" ratings. Instead of using a single rating directly as a raw score (e.g., content C gets ★★★), Iolaus transforms the user's rating to a ranking relative to all of the user's other ratings (e.g., C is in the top 10% of content). Since most legitimate users provide few ratings, "buying" ratings from random users provides significantly less benefits in Iolaus than it does today.

We demonstrate the effectiveness of Iolaus using three techniques. First, using microbenchmarks, we show that Iolaus has sufficiently low CPU and memory overhead to allow it to be practically deployed to the content sharing sites of today. Second, using synthetically generated simulation data and social network data from YouTube, we demonstrate that Iolaus performs as expected, strictly bounding the influence of malicious users and reducing their ability to "buy" ratings from random legitimate users. Third, we collect a complete dataset of businesses in two cities from Yelp, covering roughly 2M ratings on over 39K businesses provided by 1.5M users. We validate that Iolaus does not adversely affect the rankings for honest users in absence of malicious behavior, and is able to defend against multiple identity and purchased-rating attacks when applied to Yelp.

2. RELATED WORK
We now briefly cover related work, encompassing Sybil attack prevention and fake rating detection.

2.1 Blocking Sybils
Due to the attractive attack vector that free accounts provide, there is significant research interest in mitigating Sybil attacks. Traditional defenses against Sybil attacks rely on either trusted central authorities or tying identities to resources that are hard to obtain, such as social security numbers [5], mobile phones [24], or crypto-puzzles [2, 4, 6].

Recently, researchers have explored analyzing the structure of social networks as a mechanism for locating Sybil identities [9, 20, 29, 37, 44, 45] (a more extensive background is provided in [39]; we review the details relevant to Iolaus here). Unfortunately, there are two drawbacks to using existing Sybil defense schemes in content rating sites. First, existing schemes make the assumption that the honest region of the social network is densely connected with few internal small cuts [41] (formally, that the honest region is fast-mixing [25]). Recent work [18, 21] has cast doubt on this assumption, suggesting that existing Sybil detection schemes may end up accepting many Sybils or preventing honest users from interacting with each other [41]. Second, most pieces of content have few ratings; allowing even a small number of fake identities into the system can allow an attacker to "control" the rating for many items (for reference, SybilLimit [44] accepts $O(\log n)$ Sybils *per attack edge*).

2.2 Tolerating Sybils
Instead of trying to explicitly label identities as Sybil or non-Sybil, other approaches have focused on mitigating Sybil attacks in content rating services. Such systems are known as *Sybil tolerant* systems [39]. For example, DSybil [46] finds trusted users in the network (referred to as *guides*), and has provable optimality guarantees. However, DSybil can only provide recommendations for users who have submitted a sufficient number of ratings, which is often a small fraction of the population in practice. For example, in our Yelp data (fully described in Section 7), only 15% of users have provided more than 5 reviews. Also, DSybil is designed for rating systems where objects can only be either good or bad; Iolaus targets content rating systems that allow users to provide more fine-grained ratings.

SumUp [38] is another Sybil tolerant system that inspired our design. SumUp uses tokens passed over the social network in order to determine whether users' votes will be counted. While SumUp is conceptually similar to Iolaus, SumUp unfortunately has three weaknesses that Iolaus addresses: First, SumUp assumes that the region of the social network surrounding the user requesting the vote (called the *envelope*) is free of malicious users; if a malicious user is nearby, they receive many tokens and can issue many votes. Second, outside of the envelope, SumUp allows manipulation by malicious users: Honest users with multiple links are only allowed to place a single vote, while malicious users who divide their attack links across multiple accounts can potentially place multiple votes. Third, SumUp was not designed to address the "buying" of ratings from otherwise honest users. We demonstrate in Section 7 that Iolaus addresses these drawbacks and outperforms SumUp on real-world data.

2.3 Detecting fake ratings
Additionally, significant research has explored using data-mining techniques to detect and characterize rating manipulation. Systems have been built that use a variety of different inputs, including linguistic characteristics [27], user behavior [16, 17, 23], sets of recommended items [7], and common sets of user-reviewer pairs [43]. While these techniques can detect certain rating manipulation today, they rely on particular characteristics of malicious behavior. Regardless, such techniques could be used in combination with Iolaus.

3. IOLAUS DESIGN
We expect Iolaus to be deployed by the operator of a content rating site, such as Yelp or Flickr; we shall refer to this entity as the *operator*. Iolaus is designed to replace the existing content rating aggregation logic that the operator uses (i.e., instead of taking the average or performing review filtering [49], the operator would instead query Iolaus).

We assume that the operator collects ratings by a set of user accounts (referred to as *identities*) on a set of content objects; a user providing a rating on a given piece of content is referred to as a *rater*. We assume that non-malicious users provide honest ratings, with the exception of a small fraction of "bought" ratings.

We assume that the operator also provides the ability for users to declare "friends" and that friendship requires the approval of both parties; many content rating services (e.g., Yelp, Flickr, YouTube) already have such a social network. Similar to prior work [9, 37, 44, 45], we assume that links to a non-malicious user take effort to form and maintain. In other words, a malicious user cannot obtain an arbitrary number of links to non-malicious users. Note that we make no assumptions about the difficulty of obtaining identities (a single person may have many identities), or the structure or links between the malicious identities. As a result, each (human) user has a cut in the network between identities that she owns and identities owned by other (human) users; while she can create identities and links on her side of the cut, she cannot unilaterally increase the size of her cut.

3.1 Input to Iolaus

We assume that the operator provides input to Iolaus:

- **Social network** Iolaus takes as input the list of social links between the identities. We assume this is represented as an undirected graph $G = (V, E)$, and that this graph is connected.

- **Ratings** Iolaus also takes as input the set of user ratings, represented by $(identity, content, rating)$ tuples. $identity$ represents the user identity, $content$ represents the content being rated, and $rating$ represents the identity's rating.

3.2 System overview

The goal of Iolaus is to aggregate the ratings placed on content while ensuring that malicious users gain little additional influence by creating multiple identities or "buying" ratings. We make three observations that motivate Iolaus's design:

1. **Personalized aggregation** Most existing content rating aggregate schemes provide a single, global, aggregated rating for each piece of content (e.g., a business is ★★★ on Yelp). We take an alternate approach, allowing a personalized aggregated rating for each identity. Such an approach naturally captures legitimate differences of opinion (content ratings are, after all, opinions), and certain sites already provide personalized content ratings (e.g., Digg [36], Netflix [3]). We refer to the identity for whom we are calculating the aggregate rating as the *collector*.

2. **Weighing ratings** Existing approaches generally make a binary choice to either accept or reject each identity's rating when aggregating (e.g., Yelp's distinction between filtered and unfiltered reviews, SumUp's allowing or denying of votes). Instead, we *weigh* each identity's rating, and allow different identities to have different weights.

3. **Relative ratings** Finally, existing approaches view ratings as absolute (e.g., content C gets ★★★). Given that most identities rate few objects, this approach does not consider the amount of information each rater has provided (e.g., an identity who has only rated a single piece of content "counts" the same as an identity who has rated hundreds). In Iolaus, we transform raw ratings into relative ratings before aggregation.

In the following two sections, we describe how Iolaus chooses to weigh and interpret ratings, enabling it to defend against Sybil attacks and the "buying" of ratings.

4. MITIGATING SYBIL ATTACKS

Iolaus defends against multiple identity (Sybil) attacks through the *weighing* of ratings. Consider the set of raters $R \subseteq V$ on a single content object. Instead of taking the

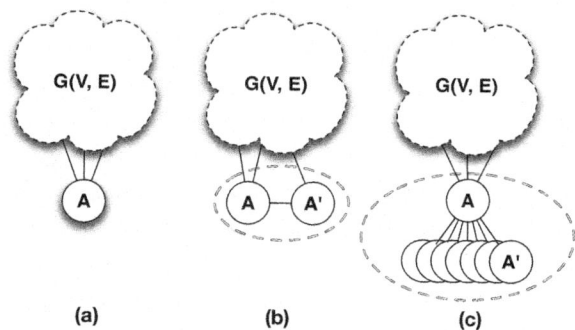

Figure 1: (a) A social graph, (b) malicious user A conducts a Sybil attack by splitting her identity, (c) malicious user A conducts a Sybil attack by creating a Sybil cluster.

average of all ratings to be the aggregate rating, Iolaus uses a *weighting function* $w(r) \to (0, \infty)$ that assigns a positive weight to every rater $r \in R$. The aggregated rating is then simply the weighted average of these ratings

$$\frac{\sum_{r \in R} w(r) \cdot v_r}{\sum_{r \in R} w(r)}$$

where v_r is the rating of rater r. For existing systems which weigh all ratings equally, $w(r) = 1$ for all r.

The key challenge, then, is to select a weighting function that limits the ability for malicious users to gain additional aggregate weight through Sybil attacks (where a user's aggregate weight is the total weight of the subset of her identities in R). We also desire to select a *non-trivial* weighting function, which we define as a weighting function that assigns a non-zero weight to all identities.[3]

Below, we first formally define a Sybil attack in Iolaus's context, before detailing the properties we would like a weighting function to have. Finally, we describe the weighting function in Iolaus.

4.1 Sybil attack

Formally, suppose that a malicious user controls a set of identities $I \subset V$. Consistent with prior work [45], we label the cut $(I, V \setminus I)$ as the *attack cut* (and the links along the cut as *attack links*), as these links signify links between the malicious user and identities controlled by other users. By our assumptions in Section 3, the number of attack links is bounded, but the number of identities in I and the number of links between these identities are unbounded.

As a result, a malicious user is able to perform three actions as part of a Sybil attack, depicted in Figure 1:

1. **Create additional identities** A malicious user is allowed to create any number of identities.

2. **Create links between owned identities** A malicious user is allowed to create links arbitrarily between identities she controls.

---

[3] A non-trivial weighting function is desired as we never actually know if a given rating was placed by a malicious or non-malicious identity; allowing a weighting function to give large numbers of identities 0 weight may discard most of the useful ratings.

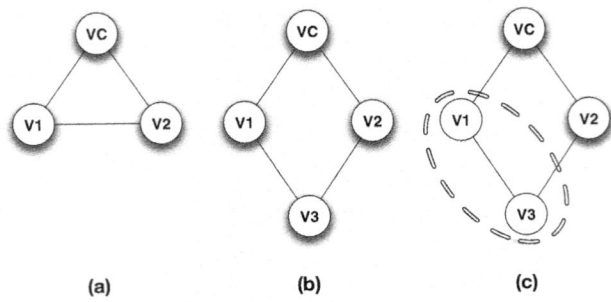

Figure 2: (a) a simple social graph consisting of three nodes a VC and two raters; V1 and V2, (b) same graph, but a new rater, V3, is added to the network, (c) same graph, but now V1 decides to split her identity by creating a new node, V3.

3. **"Split" identities on attack links** A malicious user is allowed to assign her end of her attack links to any of the identities she possesses. For example, if the malicious user possesses malicious identities $A_1 \ldots A_n$, and she has two attack links to non-controlled identities B and C, she can assign any of her A_i identities to be her endpoint of the attack links.

4.2 Sybil-proof

Ideally, we would like to select a weighting function that is *Sybil-proof*, meaning the weighting function ensures that a malicious user can gain no additional aggregate weight by conducting a Sybil attack. Formally, assume we have social networks G and G', where G' is the same as G except that malicious user A has conducted any number of Sybil attack actions (described in Section 4.1). For example, G and G' may be the graphs shown in Figure 1 (a) and Figure 1 (b) or (c). A Sybil-proof rating system would ensure that the aggregate weight assigned to raters that A controls is the same in both G and G'.

Unfortunately, Sybil-proof weighting functions on real-world networks are forced to be trivial, meaning they assign a weight of 0 to all raters that have multiple distinct paths to the collector (which, in practice, is almost all raters). To see why, consider the example shown in Figure 2 (b), where VC is the collector and $V1$, $V2$, and $V3$ are the raters. Consider rater $V3$, who has two distinct paths to VC. $V3$ could be (a) a legitimate, non-malicious identity, (b) part of a Sybil attack by rater $V1$, who splits her identity when linking to $V2$ as shown in Figure 2 (c), or (c) part of a Sybil attack by rater $V2$, who splits her identity when linking to $V1$. In either of the latter cases, each of $V1$ and $V2$ should get the same (aggregate) weight as in the network shown in Figure 2 (a). Thus, any weighting function that is Sybil-proof must assign $V3$ a weight of 0.

As a result, requiring a weighting function to be Sybil-proof precludes non-trivial weighting functions in practice. Instead, we must relax our requirements.

4.3 Sybil-bounded

We relax the requirement of our weighting function from being Sybil-proof to being *Sybil-bounded*. A Sybil-bounded weighting function is one where, given a social network G and malicious user A, there exists a bound $B_A > 0$ such that under any Sybil attack by A, the aggregate weight received by A's raters is always less than B_A. In other words, a malicious user may be able to get some additional weight through Sybil attacks, but there exists a bound on the total weight the malicious user will be able to receive, regardless of the number of identities A creates.

Compared to a Sybil-proof weighting function, a Sybil-bounded weighting function is strictly weaker (as malicious users can gain additional weight via Sybil attacks). However, we demonstrate below that (a) we can construct Sybil-bounded weighting functions that are non-trivial, and (b) we can select a weighting function that has tight bounds (leaving little additional weight to be gained via Sybil attacks).

4.4 Using max flow

Our goal now is to ensure that the weighting function is Sybil-bounded (i.e., that aggregate weight of the identities that the malicious user controls is bounded, regardless of how the malicious user conducts a Sybil attack). To do so, Iolaus expresses the problem of assigning weights as a multi-commodity max flow [11] problem,[4] viewing the social network as a graph with all links having unit capacity, and with the raters each sourcing a different flow, and with the collector serving as all flows' sink. We take the amount of flow that each rater is able to source as that rater's weight.

We choose multi-commodity max flow as it naturally has the Sybil-bounded property that we desire [34]. To see why, recall that the maximum flow between any two sets of nodes is defined by the minimum cut in the graph between the source and sink [13]. The attack links represent such a cut,[5] implying that the total flow—and therefore total weight—of the attacker is bounded, since the size of the attack cut is bounded by our assumptions in Section 3. Thus, regardless of how the malicious user conducts a Sybil attack, the aggregate weight of the attacker's ratings is bounded.

Moreover, using multi-commodity max flow also ensures that multiple malicious users gain no benefit from collusion. To see how, suppose that there are two malicious users. Without collusion, the two are each bounded by their respective set of attack links; should they collude, they are bounded by the union of their attack links.[6]

4.5 Ensuring tight bounds

Ensuring the presence of bounds limits the potential impact of a Sybil attack, but to be useful in practice, we would like to ensure the bounds are *tight*. Formally, we would like to minimize the difference between the assigned weights and the bound; doing so ensures that the malicious users can gain the least amount of weight by creating additional identities.

Ideally, we would like to solve the multi-commodity max flow problem using a linear solver such as CPLEX [8] or GLPK [14]. Unfortunately, expressing the problem *solely* as a linear maximization problem does not provide any guarantees about the tightness of the bounds to the assigned weights: to the linear solver, *any* solution which maximizes

---

[4]In brief, multi-commodity max flow maximizes the total aggregate flow between multiple source/sink pairs, with flows competing with each other for links' capacity.

[5]Of course, there may be additional, smaller, cuts between the attacker's identities and the sink.

[6]In fact, collusion may result in a lower aggregate bound, as the two users may have attack links to each other that become internal once they collude.

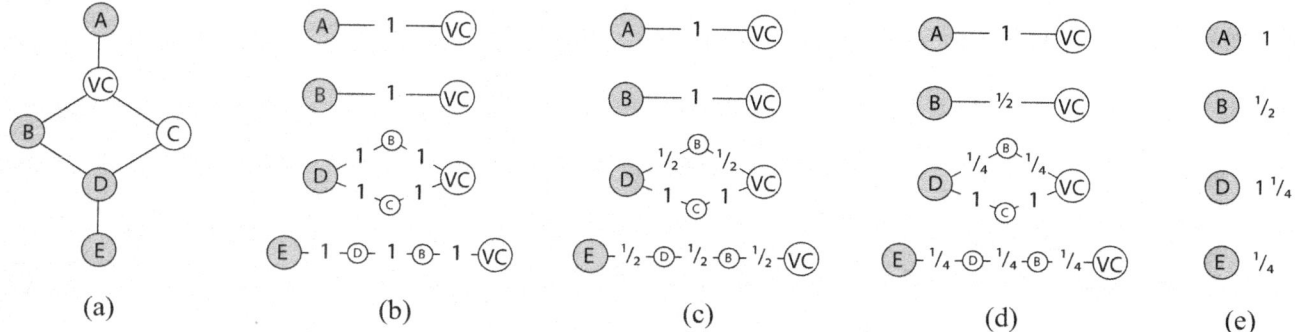

Figure 3: Example of determining weights in Iolaus. Shown are (a) the social network with collector VC and raters A, B, D and E (shaded), (b) paths selected for each rater, (c) resulting weights after normalizing $D-B$ link, (d) weights after then normalizing $B-VC$ link, and (e) final weights for each rater.

the total flow throughput is sufficient. As a result, such a solver may output solutions that have a very uneven distribution of the total weight across sources. For example, in the graph in Figure 2 (a), the solver may give $V2$ weight 2 (along its two paths to VC) while giving $V1$ weight 0.

Instead, Iolaus uses an approximation of max flow which results in more even distribution of capacity between raters and provides tight bounds on Sybil attacks, described below.

4.5.1 Determining weights

For each rater $r \in R$, Iolaus determines the max flow between r and the collector (ignoring all other raters), and derives a set of non-intersecting paths P_r for this flow. When multiple options for P_r exist, Iolaus selects arbitrarily between them. Next, Iolaus considers the graph where all raters attempt to send 1 unit of flow along each of their paths (i.e., for all r in R, each path in P_r is initially assigned weight 1). Since all links have unit capacity, there may be certain links that are over capacity (i.e., multiple raters have paths using that link). To resolve these situations, Iolaus *normalizes* the flow along these links by reducing the amount of flow proportionally. Formally, if a link is used by raters $\{r_1, r_2, ...r_n\}$ with weights $\{w_1, w_2, ...w_n\}$, each w_i is normalized with

$$w'_i = \frac{w_i}{\sum_{j=1}^{n} w_j}$$

where w'_i represents the value of w_i after normalization.

Iolaus normalizes links from the least-overcapacity to the most-overcapacity. Doing so ensures that malicious users are first bottlenecked at their attack cut before affecting any non-malicious users. To see why, recall that all of the paths begin at a rater but end at the single collector. Thus, the highest bottlenecks occur around the collector; links away from the rater are less likely to be over capacity.

4.5.2 Example

As an example of Iolaus's weighting in practice, consider the social network shown in Figure 3 (a), with collector VC and raters A, B, D, and E (C exists in the social network but has not given a rating). Iolaus first determines a set of non-intersecting paths with maximum flow for each rater; these are shown in Figure 3 (b). At this point, there are two links that are over-capacity: $B-VC$ has total weight 3 and $D-B$ has total weight 2. Thus, Iolaus first normalizes $D-B$ (reducing one of D's paths and E's single path to weight $\frac{1}{2}$); this is shown in Figure 3 (c). Then, Iolaus normalizes $B-VC$ (reducing B's path to $\frac{1}{2}$ and both of the previously reduced paths to $\frac{1}{4}$); this is shown in Figure 3 (d). At this point, all links are at or below capacity; the total weight of each rater's path is the weight for that rater (Figure 3 (e)).

4.5.3 Discussion

We observe that this weighting function provides Iolaus's Sybil resilience by providing a Sybil-bounded weighting system. For example, if node A in Figure 3 (a) were to attempt a Sybil attack, she would not be able to increase her aggregate weight beyond 1, regardless of the number of identities, or links between these identities, that she creates. She is always bounded by her attack cut of 1.

5. MITIGATING "BUYING" OF RATINGS

So far, we have described how Iolaus defends against multiple identity attacks; we now detail how Iolaus defends against the "buying" of ratings. Preventing the "buying" of ratings is one of the most difficult challenges facing content rating systems today: Since there is no cost for placing a rating, it is extremely hard to determine if a particular rating was indeed legitimate or the result of some form of out-of-band compensation. This challenge becomes worse by the fact that most content only receives a few ratings, making it possible to greatly influence the overall ranking with just a few additional ratings. The fact that being placed highly on certain content rating sites (e.g., Yelp, TripAdvisor) can have positive financial consequences [19] only further encourages compensation for positive ratings. To the best of our knowledge, no previous work has directly addressed the issue of dishonest ratings by legitimate users.

5.1 Relative ratings

Since placing a rating costs nothing to the identity, there is little to dis-incentivize the identity from doing so. In Iolaus, we add a virtual cost to placing a rating through the use of *relative ratings*. At a high level, relative ratings consider how content relates to other content the identity has rated.

To transform an identity's raw rating to a relative rating, we first consider all of that identity's ratings on other content objects. The relative rating is then simply the ranked score (between 0 and 1) relative to all of the identity's other ratings. For example, consider an identity who has provided ratings ★★★★★ for content object c_1 and ★★ for content objects c_2 and c_3. We observe that the identity ranked c_1 higher than two other content objects; it is therefore in the "top third" of content objects for this identity. The relative rating for c_1 is therefore the midpoint of the top third of objects: 0.833 (the midpoint of [0.66,1]). Similarly, we observe that the identity ranked content objects c_2 and c_3 in the "bottom two-thirds" of content objects, but we do not know their order. Thus, the relative rating of c_2 and c_3 are both assigned to 0.333 (the midpoint of [0,0.66]).

Formally, suppose that the identity provided raw ratings $\{r_1, r_2, ... r_n\}$ on content objects $\{c_1, c_2, ... c_n\}$. For simplicity, assume these are sorted by r_i. Each content object c_i, then, is assigned the relative rating

$$\frac{i - 0.5}{n}$$

with the exception that any set of content objects that have the same raw rating are then assigned the average of all relative ratings with the same raw rating. Examples of converting raw to relative ratings for three different users are shown in Table 1. Note that all of user U_3's raw ratings are the same, so all end up with the same relative rating.

5.2 Discounting "bought" ratings

We now turn to examine how using relative ratings reduces the impact of "buying" of ratings. Consider an identity who is about to give a positive rating on a content object. Without relative ratings, the identity's positive rating would be viewed just like any other identity's rating, and there is no cost to the identity for providing the positive rating. In fact, without relative ratings, the identity could provide positive ratings on a number of content objects (i.e., "selling" her ratings multiple times) without any impact.

With relative ratings, the impact of "buying" ratings from a large number of identities is dramatically decreased. Since most identities provide few ratings (e.g., the average number of ratings per identity is less than two in our Yelp dataset), buying a positive rating from a random identity is unlikely to result in a high relative rating (as the n for most identities is quite small, meaning the resulting relative rating will be much lower than a similar rating placed by a legitimate identity who has placed more ratings).

Moreover, with relative ratings, placing a new rating causes some of the identity's other ratings to change, since inserting new rating into the ordered list of the identity's ratings affects the number of overall ratings (n), as well as the order of some of the ratings (i). Thus, providing a strongly positive rating of a new content object causes the relative view of other positive ratings to be lowered, ensuring that the identity can not simply repeatedly "sell" her ratings in exchange for compensation while providing the same benefit to all content items. Instead, to have the same effect as a single positive rating today, a user must simultaneously rate a large number of content objects negatively; this makes it much more difficult for malicious users to "buy" ratings from otherwise honest users.

6. DISCUSSION

In summary, the two parts of Iolaus work together to strengthen content rating sites. The use of max flow-based techniques ensures that users gain little benefit from creating multiple identities. The use of relative ratings reduces the effectiveness of "buying" positive ratings from random users, who generally do not have a significant rating history. We now discuss a few deployment issues with Iolaus.

Underlying network As discussed in the design section, Iolaus assumes existence of an underlying social network and will not be applicable to services that lack such network. Fortunately, most services today either directly have the social network or allow users to import their friends from other social networks such as Facebook and Twitter.

Disconnected users In Section 3, we noted that Iolaus assumes that the underlying social network is a connected graph. This assumption is not unique to Iolaus (all social network-based Sybil defense systems make a similar assumption [28, 38, 44, 45]). In order to allow users who are not connected in the social network (e.g., guest users), Iolaus could be modified to create a "virtual" account for the user, with random links placed temporarily to allow rating calculation.

Rating interpretation Due to the use of relative ratings, the final ratings calculated by Iolaus will be a real-valued numbers between 0 and 1 (rather than, say, a number of stars). One potential concern is over how users will interpret such values. This range can trivially be mapped to any desirable range by a simple percentile conversion (e.g., the top 15% of content items receive ★★★★★).

Additionally, the ratings in Iolaus are personalized, meaning different users may see different rankings for the same content object. While this will clearly require an explanation to the users, existing sites such as NetFlix [3] and Digg [36] already provide personalized content ratings (implying that users do accept personalized ratings).

Impact on non-malicious users Another potential concern about using Iolaus is that it may change the current ranking of businesses, potentially for the worse. We evaluate this effect in Section 7, demonstrating that Iolaus does not adversely impact the rankings for non-malicious users.

7. EVALUATION

We now turn to evaluate the performance of Iolaus. We implemented Iolaus in C++ and Python. The implementation is divided into two parts: one that locates paths in the social network, and one that uses those paths and the rating history to calculate the rating.

User	#	Rating Raw	Transformed	Relative
U_1	$r_{1,1}$	★★	0.25	0.25
	$r_{1,2}$	★★★★	0.75	0.75
U_2	$r_{2,1}$	★	0.1	0.1
	$r_{2,2}$	★★	0.3	0.3
	$r_{2,3}$	★★★	0.5	0.5
	$r_{2,4}$	★★★★★	0.7	0.8
	$r_{2,5}$	★★★★★	0.9	0.8
U_3	$r_{3,1}$	★★★★★	0.125	0.5
	$r_{3,2}$	★★★★★	0.375	0.5
	$r_{3,3}$	★★★★★	0.625	0.5
	$r_{3,4}$	★★★★★	0.875	0.5

Table 1: Example of converting raw ratings to relative ratings for three users. Raw ratings are first converted to transformed ratings; any transformed ratings with the same raw rating are then averaged.

Finding multiple, disjoint paths between nodes in a large social network is expensive, and naïve implementations can easily result in poor scalability. To avoid this poor scalability, Iolaus is implemented using Canal [40], a system that approximates credit payments in large credit networks. Canal uses landmark routing-based techniques to efficiently locate disjoint paths in large networks; we modified Canal to disable the credit transactions, and only use Canal to quickly find paths.[7]

The remainder of the Iolaus implementation consists of code that interacts with Canal, calculates weights, and transforms raw ratings into relative ratings. This part is implemented in 2,650 lines of Python.

Network	Nodes	Links	Average degree
YouTube	1.1 M	5.8 M	5.2
Yelp Boston	383 K	890 K	4.3
Yelp San Francisco	1.1 M	3.9 M	4.6
Synthetic 1	10 K	29 K	5.6
Synthetic 2	100 K	280 K	5.8
Synthetic 3	600 K	8.11 M	26.8
Synthetic 4	1 M	12.3 M	24.6

Table 2: Statistics of the social networks used for evaluating Iolaus. The synthetic networks are measurement-calibrated synthetic social networks [31].

7.1 Experimental setup

Social networks In the subsequent evaluation, we use both real-world social networks and synthetic social networks of varying sizes. Table 2 gives the statistics of the networks. The synthetic networks are generated using nearest neighbor method [31], with prescribed number of nodes, probability of adding new nodes, and number of random pairs connected. The resulting networks have been shown [31] to have characteristics close to real-world social networks.

The real-world social networks come from two large content rating sites: YouTube and Yelp. First, we use the social network of YouTube users [22], as originally used in the SumUp evaluation [38]. Unfortunately, the YouTube data set only contains the social network, and does not contain content ratings.

Second, we collect data from Yelp containing both social network information and content ratings from two cities: Boston and San Francisco. Specifically, we first determined the set of all businesses on Yelp located within the each city; this totaled 9,228 businesses in Boston and 30,339 in San Francisco. Then, we collected all ratings on these businesses; this totaled 278,719 ratings from 82,846 users in Boston and 1,655,385 ratings from 340,671 users in San Francisco.[8] Finally, we collected all of the social connections of these users; this resulted in a network of 383,557 users connected together with 888,335 links in Boston and 1,111,254 users and 3,920,553 links in San Francisco.

As Iolaus assumes that the social network is a connected graph, we only consider users located in the largest connected component (LCC) [22] of each Yelp graph. The LCC encompasses the vast majority of the data: In Boston, it covers 327,515 (85.3%) users connected by 883,179 (99.4%) links and providing 190,042 (68.1%) ratings. In San Francisco, it covers 1,303,086 (82.7%) users connected by 3,912,279 (99.8%) links and providing 1,303,086 (78.7%) ratings.

Simulating Sybil attacks Similar to prior studies [38], we simulate Sybil attacks by injecting malicious nodes and adding attack links (links from malicious nodes to non-malicious nodes). We refer to non-malicious nodes who are linked to by malicious users as *attacked nodes*. Inspired by prior work [41] we examine three different attack strategies for selecting attacked nodes:

Random Attacked nodes are chosen randomly.

k-**closest** Attacked nodes are chosen randomly among the k closest nodes (by hop distance) to the collector. This represents a targeted attack on a particular collector.

k-**highest** Attacked nodes are chosen randomly from among the k highest degree nodes in the network. This represents the most effective attack for being "close" for many collectors.

Note that we control the "power" of the attacker by varying k; a smaller k implies that the attacker can better target her attack (e.g., a small k in k-closest implies the attacker is able to obtain attack links very close to the collector).

Simulating "bought" ratings We also simulate the "buying" of ratings by malicious businesses in Yelp. To do so, we select random non-malicious users to provide "bought" ratings; each one of these users is simulated to provide one additional highly positive rating on the Yelp business that is trying to manipulate the ratings.

Comparing against SumUp and Yelp We compare the performance of Iolaus to SumUp [38] and a strawman version of Yelp's rating. For SumUp, we use the original code (obtained from the SumUp authors) and configured to the default values[9] prescribed in the original paper [38].

In practice, Yelp has a review filtering mechanism designed to block attacks, but its design is deliberately obfuscated [48]. As a result, we are unable to compare Iolaus directly against Yelp's filtering mechanism (as we do not know how it would perform when we introduce Sybil and rating-buying attacks).

7.2 Microbenchmarks

We begin by examining the amount of CPU time and memory required to determine an aggregate rating in Iolaus. Iolaus is designed to be parallelized; it can be configured to use multiple cores, and distributed across multiple machines, to

---

[7] In Iolaus, we configure Canal to use 15 2-level universes, three threads for creating universes, and sixteen threads for finding paths.

[8] Yelp divides reviews into unfiltered and filtered reviews; only unfiltered reviews are used by Yelp in determining a business' score. We collected both filtered and unfiltered reviews.

[9] We run SumUp with $\rho = 0.5$ and 20 non-greedy steps. However, since attackers can split identities on attack links (§ 4.1), the link pruning optimization in SumUp will only make it harder for honest users to find paths (Sybils can split their attack links across multiple identities, thereby avoiding the effects of pruning). Hence, we turn off this feature to make the comparison to SumUp fair.

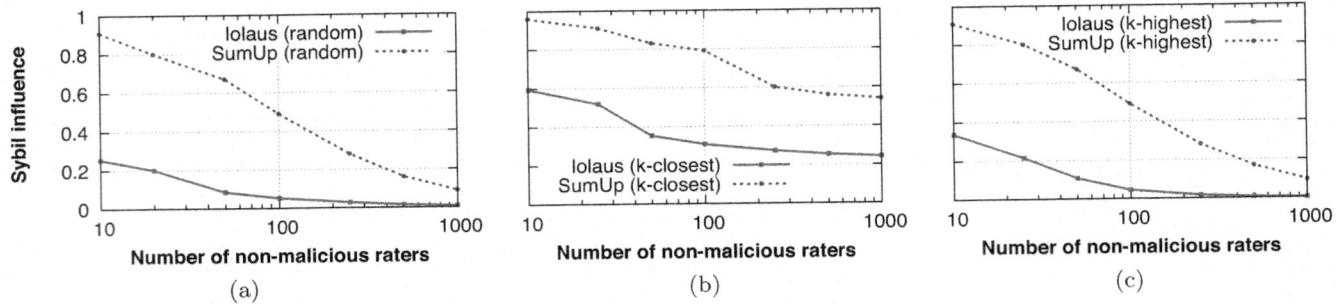

Figure 4: Sybil influence as the number of non-malicious raters is varied, for different attack strategies on the YouTube graph with 100 attack links. The graphs show (a) random attacked nodes, (b) k-closest attacked nodes, and (c) k-highest degree attacked nodes, with $k = 200$.

speed up computation time. We evaluate Iolaus deployed to a single machine with dual 8-core hyper-threaded Intel Xeon 2.1GHz CPUs and 128GB of memory.

Using the different networks, we select a single collector and a variable number of raters randomly from among all nodes. We then measure the time required to determine the aggregate rating, repeating the experiment 20 times and reporting the average. Figure 5 presents the results of this experiment. We observe that even when 100 users place a rating, the time required to determine the aggregate rating is under 5ms in all networks. In practice, most businesses would take substantially less: in our Yelp dataset, only 8% of businesses have more than 100 ratings. Moreover, the site operator could easily cache the calculated ratings, either with a fixed time-out or until a certain number of new ratings are provided.

In Iolaus, Canal stores the social network in memory. As a result, the memory requirements of Iolaus are determined by the memory requirements of Canal. On a similarly configured server to ours, Canal has been shown [40] to scale to networks containing hundreds of millions of links.

7.3 Comparison against SumUp

We now compare Iolaus directly against SumUp. As SumUp was only designed to mitigate the effect of Sybil attacks (and not rating-buying attacks), we only examine Sybil attacks here; in the following section, we examine both Sybil attacks and rating-buying attacks on our Yelp data set. We use the YouTube social network graph that was used in the original evaluation of SumUp [38].

While Iolaus is a weighing system which assigns a weight to every rater, SumUp either accepts or rejects a user's rating outright. Thus, directly comparing the two systems is not immediately straightforward. To make head-to-head comparison, we need a single performance measure which fits both systems. To do so, we consider SumUp also as a weighing system, which assigns weights 0 or 1 to raters that are rejected or accepted, respectively. We then define the metric *Sybil influence* as

$$\text{Sybil influence} = \frac{\text{Aggregate weight of Sybils}}{\text{Aggregate weight of all raters}}$$

representing the fraction of the total weight controlled by the Sybils. Thus, the smaller the Sybil influence value is, the better the system is at mitigating Sybil attacks.

7.3.1 Varying non-malicious raters

We first examine the effect of number of non-malicious raters on Sybil influence when the number of attack links is fixed. As the number of non-malicious raters increases, with a fixed number of attack links, we expect that both SumUp and Iolaus have lower Sybil influence. In this experiment, we select a random collector and 100 attack links, and vary the number of non-malicious raters. We repeat the experiment 20 times and report the average Sybil influence.

Figure 4 presents the results of this experiment when using the random, k-highest degree, and k-closest attack link strategies, with $k = 200$ (note that the k-closest scenario represents a very strong attacker, as there are over 82,000 total users). For all cases, Iolaus outperforms SumUp in reducing the impact of Sybils. The underlying reason is that in SumUp, for the random and k-highest degree attacked nodes, the Sybil raters are able to use each of the 100 attack links to get one rater accepted, allowing the Sybils to have significant influence.

In the case of the k-closest nodes strategy, Sybils are able to be part of SumUp's "envelope" around the collector, enabling them to cast multiple votes per attack link. With Iolaus, the Sybils' 100 attack links are forced to compete with all of the non-malicious raters' links. Sybils in Iolaus still manage to receive significant weight as they are very close to the collector, but have substantially lower influence than SumUp. With most content objects having few ratings, improved performance with few non-malicious raters is extremely important.

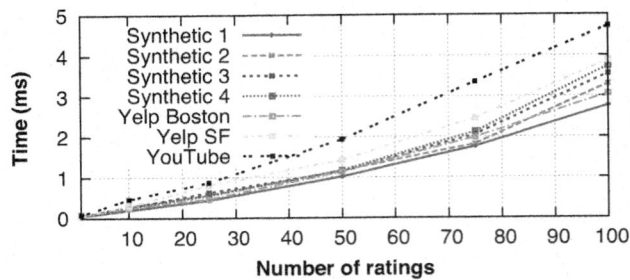

Figure 5: Average Iolaus running time for gathering up to 100 ratings in different networks.

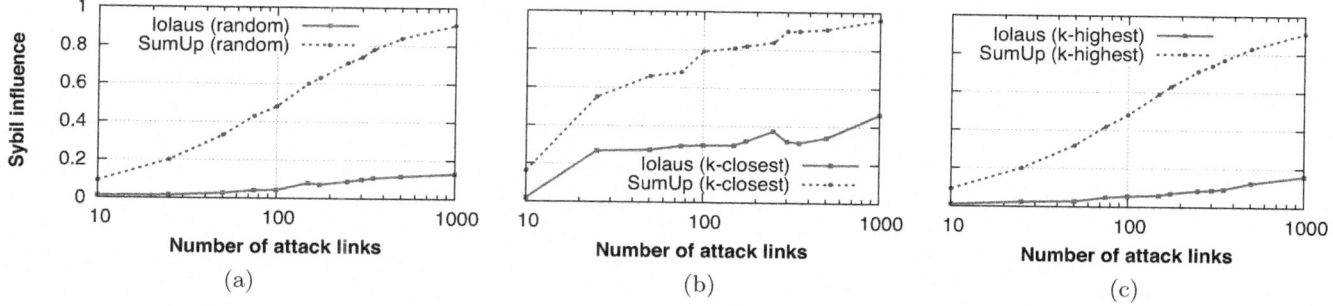

Figure 6: Sybil influence as the number of attack links is varied, for different attack strategies on the YouTube graph with 100 non-malicious raters. The graphs show (a) random attacked nodes, (b) k-closest attacked nodes, and (c) k-highest degree attacked nodes, with $k = 200$.

7.3.2 Varying attack links

We now examine the impact of the number of attack links on the resulting Sybil influence. We expect that as the number of attack links increases, the Sybil influence should increase linearly. In this experiment, we select a random collector, 100 random non-malicious raters, and vary the number of attack links. As before, we repeat the experiment 20 times and report the average.

Figure 6 presents the results of this experiment for all three attack strategies. We observe that Iolaus has lower Sybil influence than SumUp under all three cases. The reason for the superior performance is the same as before: in SumUp, the Sybil raters are able to use each of the attack links to get one rating accepted for random and k-highest attacks, and multiple ratings accepted for the k-closest attack. In Iolaus, the Sybil raters must compete with the aggregate links of the non-malicious raters.

7.4 Iolaus on Yelp

We now evaluate Iolaus on real-world data (including both social network and content ratings), examining Iolaus's resilience to Sybil attacks and rating-buying attacks. In this section, we use the Yelp data sets from Boston and San Francisco, described in Section 7.1.

7.4.1 Ranking performance

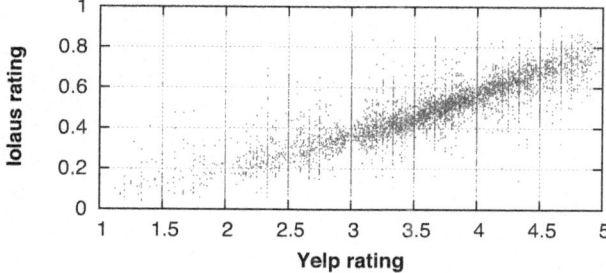

Figure 7: Scatterplot of Iolaus ratings versus Yelp's ratings for all Yelp Boston businesses. For the sake of accuracy, Yelp's ratings are not rounded to half-hops (as they typically are on Yelp's site). A strong agreement between the two ratings is observed.

We begin by examining the impact of using Iolaus on the overall ranking performance. In other words, how much does using Iolaus for aggregating ratings affect objects' rankings, even when Sybil and rating-buying attacks are not occurring? We use two approaches to address this question: First, we examine the global ranking of businesses; we compare these rankings to Yelp's current ranking. Second, we examine the per-collector ranking of businesses by comparing to ground-truth rankings provided by users.

In order to compare two rankings, we use the metric *Area under the Receiver Operating Characteristic (ROC) curve* or A'. In brief, this metric compares two ordered lists and represents the probability that the relative ranking of two items is in the same order in both lists [12]. Therefore, the A' metric takes on values between 0 and 1: A value of 0.5 represents no correlation between the lists, with higher values indicating a better match and 1 representing a perfect match between the two lists.

To examine the global ranking, we first rank all 9,228 Yelp Boston businesses using Iolaus for 10 randomly selected collectors. We then take the average of the Iolaus ranking across these 10 collectors to be the overall ranking of each business. Finally, we compare the order of ranked businesses in Iolaus to Yelp's order. We find that Iolaus's order compares to Yelp's order with an A' of 0.88. This indicates a strong agreement between the two orders, indicating that Iolaus does not significantly impact the ordering when Sybil and rating-buying attacks are not occurring. A scatterplot of the two rankings compared is presented in Figure 7.

Next, we compare the *ranking error* of Yelp, SumUp, and Iolaus. To do so, we first select a set of 500 users who have ranked at least 10 businesses. For each of these users, we calculate the Yelp, SumUp, and Iolaus rating of the businesses that user has rated, excluding the user's own rating. Each of these ratings are essentially *predicted* ratings; we then com-

City	Yelp–Filtered	SumUp	Iolaus
Boston	0.724	0.724	0.702
San Francisco	0.712	0.713	0.703

Table 3: Accuracy (A') of different systems in predicting users' rankings of businesses. All systems perform similarly, showing that Iolaus does not significantly altering the rankings of businesses in Yelp.

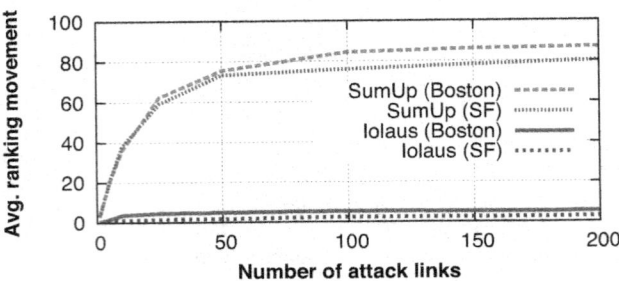
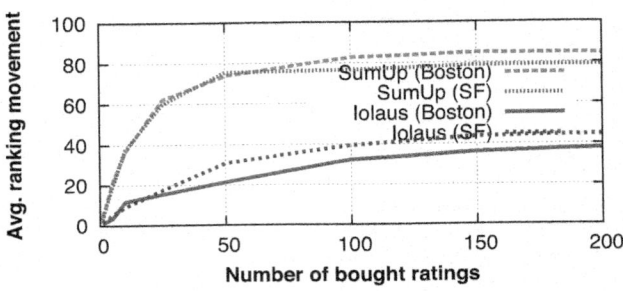

Figure 8: Average ranking movement of Iolaus and SumUp under different numbers of attack links.

Figure 9: Average ranking movement of Iolaus and SumUp under different numbers of "bought" ratings.

pare the predicted ratings to the actual ratings provided by the user, and measure the differences using A'. Table 3 presents the results of this experiment for Yelp data in both Boston and San Francisco. We observe that all three systems are comparable, with Iolaus performing slightly worse. This indicates that Iolaus does not dramatically change the rankings of businesses.

7.4.2 Defending against Sybils

We now investigate Iolaus's performance on the Yelp dataset under Sybil attacks. For these experiments, we simulate Sybils placing highly positive ratings on a target business, and use the k-highest degree attack strategy with $k = 200$. Even though Figures 4 and 6 suggest that k-closest attack is the strongest, this attack is targeted at a particular collector. To influence the ranking for many collectors, Sybils are best served by attacking high-degree nodes.

Unfortunately, we cannot directly compare the SumUp's score with Iolaus's score (recall that SumUp's score is in terms of stars, whereas Iolaus's score is transformed to the unit interval). Thus, we compare the *relative* score of different businesses. To make the results comparable across cities and repetitions of the same experiment, in this section, we only consider businesses with exactly 10 ratings.

To measure the impact of the Sybil attack, we first select a *target business* from the lowest-ranked 25% of businesses with 10 ratings. The target business is the business that is trying to conduct a Sybil attack or "buy" ratings to increase its ranking. We then select a list of businesses to compare the target business against. We select these business with a wide distribution of ranks—up to 20 businesses with an average rating in each $\frac{1}{2}$★ interval—resulting in a list of 111 businesses (not all intervals contain 20 businesses). Finally, we measure the impact rating manipulation by measuring the difference (in terms of the number of places) the target business moves up in the ranking of 111 businesses after manipulation. We refer to this metric as *ranking movement*; lower ranking movement is better (an ideal system, of course, would allow 0 ranking movement).

Figure 8 shows the average ranking movement for 10 target businesses conducting Sybil attacks, averaged across 10 randomly selected collectors. With SumUp, the target business is able to significantly change the ranking, making itself appear much more highly ranked. This manipulation is possible as SumUp allows the Sybils to place an additional rating with each additional attack link. However, Iolaus manages to much more tightly bound the Sybils' influence, allowing significantly less ranking manipulation.

7.4.3 Defending against rating "buying"

Next, we investigate the ability for Iolaus to defend against rating-buying attacks. In these experiments, we do not add any Sybils or attack links, but instead, select a varying number of random non-malicious users to provide "bought" ratings. We simulate the non-malicious users providing highly positive reviews on a business. To evaluate the impact of this attack, we use the same businesses as in 7.4.2, and measure the impact of the attack using ranking movement.

Figure 9 presents the results of this experiment. As before, the results are the average across the same 10 collectors as in 7.4.2. We observe that, without any resistance to rating-buying attacks in SumUp, malicious users are able to greatly influence the overall ranking the business receives. However, with Iolaus, the overall impact on the target business's ranking is much lower, as the relative ratings reduce the impact of the purchased ratings.

Comparing Figures 8 and 9, we observe that rating-buying is a much stronger attack than Sybil attack, and has greater impact on final ratings. This result is expected, as bought ratings come from legitimate users who are likely well-integrated into the social network. However, we can see that Iolaus performs much better against such attacks in comparison to SumUp, which was not designed to protect against rating "buying."

8. CONCLUSION

We have presented Iolaus, a system that is designed to be deployed by the operator of an online content rating site and can defend against multiple-identity (Sybil) attacks and the "buying" of ratings. Iolaus is built using two techniques. First, Iolaus uses the weighing of different ratings to ensure that the total influence that any (human) user can have is bounded, regardless of the number of identities that the user creates. Second, Iolaus converts raw ratings into relative ratings, dramatically reducing the impact of the buying of ratings in practice. An evaluation demonstrated that Iolaus has low overhead and can be applied to the online content rating systems of today.

Acknowledgements

We thank the anonymous reviewers for their helpful comments. We also thank Giorgos Zervas for his assistance with collecting the Yelp data. This research was supported by a Google Faculty Research Award, NSF grant IIS-0964465, and an Amazon Web Services in Education Grant.

9. REFERENCES

[1] K. Ashton. The Not So Secret Business of Fake Yelp Reviews. *Daily Deal Media*, 2012. http://www.dailydealmedia.com/657the-not-so-secret-business-of-fake-yelp-reviews/.

[2] M. Abadi, M. Burrows, M. Manasse, and T. Wobber. Moderately hard, memory-bound functions. *ACM ToIT*, 5(2), 2005.

[3] X. Amatriain and J. Basilico. Netflix Recommendations: Beyond the 5 stars (Part 1). http://techblog.netflix.com/2012/04/netflix-recommendations-beyond-5-stars.html.

[4] N. Borisov. Computational Puzzles as Sybil Defenses. *IEEE P2P*, 2006.

[5] H. Chun, H. Kwak, Y.-H. Eom, Y.-Y. Ahn, S. Moon, and H. Jeong. Comparison of Online Social Relations in Terms of Volume vs. Interaction: A Case Study of Cyworld. *IMC*, 2008.

[6] M. Castro, P. Druschel, A. Ganesh, A. Rowstron, and D. S. Wallach. Secure routing for structured peer-to-peer overlay networks. *OSDI*, 2002.

[7] P.-A. Chirita, W. Nejdl, and C. Zamfir. Preventing shilling attacks in online recommender systems. *WIDM*, 2005.

[8] CPLEX. http://ibm.com/software/integration/optimization/cplex-optimizer.

[9] G. Danezis and P. Mittal. SybilInfer: Detecting Sybil Nodes using Social Networks. *NDSS*, 2009.

[10] J. R. Douceur. The Sybil Attack. *IPTPS*, 2002.

[11] S. Even, A. Itai, and A. Shamir. On the Complexity of Timetable and Multi-Commodity Flow Problems. *FOCS*, 1975.

[12] J. Fogarty, R. S. Baker, and S. E. Hudson. Case studies in the use of ROC curve analysis for sensor-based estimates in human computer interaction. *GI*, 2005.

[13] L. R. Ford and D. R. Fulkerson. Maximal flow through a network. *Can. J. Math.*, 8, 1956.

[14] GLPK. http://www.gnu.org/software/glpk.

[15] L. H. Hwang, P. Damera, L. Brooking, and C. P. Lee. Promoting oneself on Flickr: Users' strategies and attitudes. *GROUP*, 2011.

[16] S. D. Kamvar, M. T. Schlosser, and H. Garcia-Molina. The EigenTrust Algorithm for Reputation Management in P2P Networks. *WWW*, 2003.

[17] E.-P. Lim, V.-A. Nguyen, N. Jindal, B. Liu, and H. W. Lauw. Detecting Product Review Spammers using Rating Behaviors. *CIKM*, 2010.

[18] J. Leskovec, K. J. Lang, and M. W. Mahoney. Empirical Comparison of Algorithms for Network Community Detection. *WWW*, 2010.

[19] M. Luca. Reviews, Reputation, and Revenue: The Case of Yelp.com. *Harvard Business School Working Papers*, 2011. http://www.hbs.edu/research/pdf/12-016.pdf.

[20] C. Lesniewski-Laas and M. F. Kaashoek. Whānau: A Sybil-proof Distributed Hash Table. *NSDI*, 2010.

[21] A. Mohaisen and A. Y. A. Kim. Measuring the mixing time of social graphs. *IMC*, 2010.

[22] A. Mislove, M. Marcon, K. P. Gummadi, P. Druschel, and B. Bhattacharjee. Measurement and Analysis of Online Social Networks. *IMC*, 2007.

[23] A. Mukherjee, B. Liu, and N. Glance. Spotting Fake Reviewer Groups in Consumer Reviews. *WWW*, 2012.

[24] G. Maganis, E. Shi, H. Chen, and D. Song. Opaak: Using Mobile Phones to Limit Anonymous Identities Online. *MobiSys*, 2012.

[25] M. Mitzenmacher and E. Upfal. *Probability and Computing*. Cambridge University Press, 2005.

[26] M. Moyer. Manipulation of the Crowd: How Trustworthy Are Online Ratings? *Scientific American*, volume 303, 2010. http://www.scientificamerican.com/article.cfm?id=manipulation-of-the-crowd.

[27] M. Ott, Y. Choi, C. Cardie, and J. T. Hancock. Finding Deceptive Opinion Spam by Any Stretch of the Imagination. *ACL*, 2011.

[28] A. Post, V. Shah, and A. Mislove. Bazaar: Strengthening user reputations in online marketplaces. *NSDI*, 2011.

[29] D. Quercia and S. Hailes. Sybil Attacks Against Mobile Users: Friends and Foes to the Rescue. *INFOCOM*, 2010.

[30] M. Rose. Microsoft Investigating Claims of Ratings Manipulation in Xbox Live Indie Games. *Indie Games*, 2011. http://indiegames.com/2011/03/microsoft_investigating_claims.html.

[31] A. Sala, L. Cao, C. Wilson, R. Zablit, H. Zheng, and B. Y. Zhao. Measurement-calibrated graph models for social network experiments. *WWW*, 2010.

[32] D. Segal. A Rave, a Pan, or Just a Fake? *The New York Times*, 2011. http://www.nytimes.com/2011/05/22/your-money/22haggler.html.

[33] D. Streitfeld. Ferreting Out Fake Reviews Online. *The New York Times*, 2011. http://nytimes.com/2011/08/20/technology/finding-fake-reviews-online.html.

[34] S. Seuken and D. C. Parkes. On the Sybil-proofness of accounting mechanisms. *NetEcon*, 2011.

[35] Statistics – YouTube. http://www.youtube.com/yt/press/statistics.html.

[36] J. Turner. Personalization and the future of Digg. http://oreil.ly/brZbWK.

[37] N. Tran, J. Li, L. Subramanian, and S. S.M. Chow. Optimal Sybil-resilient node admission control. *INFOCOM*, 2011.

[38] N. Tran, B. Min, J. Li, and L. Subramanian. Sybil-Resilient Online Content Voting. *NSDI*, 2009.

[39] B. Viswanath, M. Mondal, A. Clement, P. Druschel, K. P. Gummadi, A. Mislove, and A. Post. Exploring the design space of social network-based Sybil defense. *COMSNETS*, 2012.

[40] B. Viswanath, M. Mondal, K. P. Gummadi, A. Mislove, and A. Post. Canal: Scaling social network-based Sybil tolerance schemes. *EuroSys*, 2012.

[41] B. Viswanath, A. Post, K. P. Gummadi, and A. Mislove. An Analysis of Social Network-based Sybil Defenses. *SIGCOMM*, 2010.

[42] L. von Ahn, M. Blum, N. Hopper, and J. Langford. CAPTCHA: Using Hard AI Problems for Security. *EuroCrypt*, 2003.

[43] G. Wang, S. Xie, B. Liu, and P. S. Yu. Review Graph based Online Store Review Spammer Detection. *ICDM*, 2011.

[44] H. Yu, P. B. Gibbons, M. Kaminsky, and F. Xiao. SybilLimit: A Near-Optimal Social Network Defense Against Sybil Attacks. *IEEE S&P*, 2008.

[45] H. Yu, M. Kaminsky, P. B. Gibbons, and A. Flaxman. SybilGuard: Defending Against Sybil Attacks via Social Networks. *SIGCOMM*, 2006.

[46] H. Yu, C. Shi, M. Kaminsky, P. B. Gibbons, and F. Xiao. DSybil: Optimal Sybil-Resistance for Recommendation Systems. *IEEE S&P*, 2009.

[47] Yelp 10-Q November 2012 Report. http://www.yelp-ir.com/phoenix.zhtml?c=250809&p=irol-sec.

[48] Yelp Which to Filter. http://www.yelp.com/faq#which_to_filter.

[49] Yelp's Review Filter Explained. http://officialblog.yelp.com/2010/03/yelp-review-filter-explained.html.

On Cognition, Emotion, and Interaction Aspects of Search Tasks with Different Search Intentions

Yashar Moshfeghi
School of Computing Science
University of Glasgow
Glasgow, UK
Yashar.Moshfeghi@glasgow.ac.uk

Joemon M. Jose
School of Computing Science
University of Glasgow
Glasgow, UK
Joemon.Jose@glasgow.ac.uk

ABSTRACT

The complex and dynamic nature of search processes surrounding information seeking have been exhaustively studied. Recent studies have highlighted search processes with different intentions, such as those for entertainment purposes or re-finding a visited information object, are fundamentally different in nature to typical information seeking intentions. Despite the popularity of such search processes on the Web, they have not yet been thoroughly explored. Using a video retrieval system as a use case, we study the characteristics of four different search task types: seeking information, re-finding a particular information object, and two different entertainment intentions (i.e. entertainment by adjusting arousal level, and entertainment by adjusting mood). In particular, we looked at the cognition, emotion and action aspects of these search tasks at different phases of a search process. This follows the common assumption in the information seeking and retrieval community that a complex search process can be broken down into a relatively small number of activity phases. Our experimental results show significant differences in the characteristics of studied search tasks. Furthermore, we investigate whether we can predict these search tasks given user's interaction with the system. Results show that we can learn a model that predicts the search task types with reasonable accuracy. Overall, these findings may help to steer search engines to better satisfy searchers' needs beyond typically assumed information seeking processes.

Categories and Subject Descriptors: H.3.3 Information Storage and Retrieval - *Information Search and Retrieval - Search Process*
General Terms: Experimentation, Human Factors
Keywords: Search Intents, Emotion, Cognition, Interaction, Prediction, Re-finding, Entertainment

1. INTRODUCTION

Recent advances in query log analysis for search engines such as Google, Yahoo! and Bing has shown that Web searchers' intentions[1] do not always fit into the typical taxonomy of informational, navigational or transactional intentions [37]. Although informational (i.e. to acquire information present on one or more sites), navigational (i.e. to reach a particular site) and transactional (i.e. to perform some Web-mediated activity) intentions are all commonly found in query logs [9], there is an increasing body of evidence showing that re-finding and re-retrieving visited information is a regular activity for searchers [37, 12]. In addition, there is also recent interest in the notion of entertainment, where the searchers do not have any particular information need [13] and the prime motivation behind their search is to satisfy an emotion need [28]. The aim of this paper is to study the characteristics of search processes motivated by different intentions, i.e. information seeking, re-finding information and/or entertainment.

Knowledge of the underlying intentions of searchers engaging in a search process on the Web can be very beneficial to better satisfy their needs. Web search engines constantly improve their retrieval effectiveness by mining information from query logs with regards to different aspects of the search processes, including prediction of the search (query) intents. The aim of this paper is to study and compare the seeking activities occurring during search processes with different intents. Through this, we can better quantify searchers' needs, and in turn improve the effectiveness of the recommendation, query suggestion, retrieval, presentation, etc.

As has traditionally been explored, the information seeking process is complex and dynamic [19, 6]. It is complex because it involves a searcher with an information need (IN) initiated by an anomaly in his or her current state of knowledge [7], who is seeking information to resolve the problem, and in turn satisfy the need. This need is usually transformed into a query and submitted to a retrieval system where a set of potentially relevant documents are retrieved and presented. However, the formulated query does not always provide an adequate description necessary to retrieve relevant documents [40] since it is only an approximation of the actual information need [36]. Likewise, it may not adequately define the characteristics of relevant documents, or indeed any relevant information, because of an *ill-defined* information need situation. Therefore, in the majority of cases, searchers are unsatisfied with the results obtained in response to their initial retrieval formulation [38], and must engage in further interaction with the system to resolve their

---
[1]When we say search intention we mean the underlying motivation of the search task. Intent and intention are used interchangeably.

needs. This introduces the dynamic aspect of the information seeking process which we will further examine.

The dynamic aspect of the information seeking process refers to the development and evolution of IN during a search session [35], from an initially vague state to a clear and well-defined one [20]. This change in IN can happen dramatically or gradually [30] as a result of new information a searcher is exposed to, i.e. the perusal of relevant, and even irrelevant documents [40]. This evolution of IN improves the searcher's query statement formulation[4], and changes what they consider relevant at both the early and late stages of the search [31]. However, two important questions emerge. First, whether such characteristics are generalizable to other search scenarios where the motivation is other than seeking information, e.g. re-finding or entertainment. Second, whether these search scenarios can be modelled via such characteristics.

In order to investigate our research questions, we follow a common approach for modelling and explaining information seeking behaviour. In general, it assumes that complex information seeking and retrieval process can be broken down into a relatively small number of activity stages (which we refer to as *phases*) [16] (p. 138) within which user behaviour is investigated. Kuhlthau's *information seeking process* (ISP) model investigated the affect, cognition and action of participants in different phases of an information seeking process [22]. Although Kuhlthau's ISP model was originally proposed for long term information seeking processes, she explains that the concepts of process, uncertainty and complexity emerging from her ISP model can be useful for designing user-centred IR systems [23]. Indeed many researchers follow this approach in information retrieval scenarios, e.g. White et al. [40]. Using an interactive IR framework, we investigate the characteristics of four search processes i.e. information seeking, re-finding, and two different entertainment intentions. In particular, we divide each search process into a small number of phases where the searchers' interactions within each phase is studied. Finally, we investigate the predictability of the search motivation given the interaction history at different phases of the search process.

This paper has three novel contributions. First, based on sociology literature, two simulated search tasks are designed for entertainment-based search processes. Second, the characteristics of search tasks with different intentions are studied using data gathered via questionnaires and interaction history. Finally, the predictability of the search intents is investigated given the interaction history at different points of a search process. The remainder of the paper is organised as follows: related works are presented in Section 2, the experiment methodology is described in Section 3. Results and discussion are presented in Section 4, and finally the paper is concluded in Section 5.

2. RELATED WORK

Seeking Information on the Web: Web search systems such as Google, Bing and Yahoo! are important tools for seeking and accessing information on the World Wide Web (the Web). As we discussed earlier (see Section 1), the information seeking process is complex and dynamic in nature. Many past theories and models have attempted to explain the complexity and dynamic nature of information seeking processes. In general they assume that complex information seeking and retrieval behaviour can be broken down into a relatively small number of activity stages [16] (p. 138). For example, Kuhlthau's *information seeking process* (ISP) model illustrates information seeking activities in six stages, each of which differentiated and determined the cognitive, affective and physical aspects of a searcher. Kuhlthau's model is one of the most popular models to investigate the cognitive, affective and physical aspects of a searcher in an information seeking process. She demonstrated that searchers adopt different information seeking strategies as they move from one stage of the ISP to another. Furthermore, she demonstrated that people's feelings, thoughts and actions interact within the ISP. The fundamental principle behind Kuhlthau's model is the *uncertainty principle* [22]. This refers to the existence of a cognitive state which causes feelings of anxiety and lack of confidence. Feelings of doubt, anxiety and frustration are associated with vague and unclear thoughts. The model shows that during a typical information seeking process, the thoughts of a searcher become clear; consequently, their confidence increases and their feeling of doubt, anxiety and frustration decrease. Following this approach, in this paper we investigate cognition, emotion and interaction aspects of search tasks with different intentions.

The cognitive aspect of the ISP has been an important theme of IR research since the earliest work in the field. Belkin et al. [7] explain that the information need motivating an ISP is derived from searchers' *anomalous state of knowledge* (ASK). The ASK refers to the gap between what searchers know and what they want to know. Taylor [36] explained that query formulation can be a cognitively demanding process, and the searchers' queries are approximate representations of the actual information needs. This query formulation problem can be magnified if searchers are facing a vague or ill-defined information need [35]. On the other hand, Saracevic [31] discussed how the concept of relevance can change for searchers during an ISP as a result of a change or development in their information needs throughout the search. These findings motivated a great deal of past research. However, user activity and expectations on the Web have now expanded well beyond traditionally studied information seeking process. This has led to an emergence of characteristically different search tasks, such as those of entertainment purposes [27]. As such, it is the right time to revisit and verify these findings. This paper is an attempt in this vein of research.

In recent years the emotion aspect of the information seeking process has gained much attention. For example, several works studied the emotional impact of search tasks within the ISP [29, 1, 25]. [29] examined how participants emotion responses are influenced by tasks of different nature. In particular, their results indicate that (i) artificial tasks have higher uncertainty and less sense of ownership than genuine search tasks, and (ii) more complex search tasks have lower positive emotions and more uncertainty before and after searching. Similar findings were earlier reported also by [1] in an information seeking activity. They concluded that users' emotions progressively transit from positive to negative valence as the degree of task difficulty increases. They also found that emotions both interweave with different physiological, psychological and cognitive processes during an information seeking process, and form distinctive patterns according to specific tasks [2]. However, [25] reported no significant relationship between searchers' mood and search tasks due to the complexity involved in such studies. In another study, [18] investigated the relationship between the subjective (e.g. happiness levels, feeling lost during search, etc.) and objective (e.g. search outcomes and search task characteristics, etc.) factors in the ISP. Their results show that "higher happiness levels before the search and during the search correlate with better feelings after the search, but also correlate with worse search outcomes and lower satisfaction, suggesting that, perhaps, it pays off to feel some 'pain' during the search in order to 'gain' quality outcomes" [18]. Despite their valuable insights into various aspects of emotion in the ISP, they do not provide insights into how the trend of emotion varies for search sessions with different search intents. This paper investigates the answer to this research question.

The interaction aspect of the ISP is by far the most studied aspect in both research and practice. One of the important research topics is to understand the intent of search activity. Broder [9] studied Web query logs and categorised the submitted queries into three main search intents: informational, navigational, and transactional. The important outcome of this work was the realisation of the existence of search intents other than the informational intent, which was traditionally assumed to be dominant. In a more recent study, other search intents have been identified, such as re-finding [37] and entertainment [13]. Teevan et al. [37], by analysing Yahoo! Web query logs showed that up to 40% of the submitted queries were re-finding queries. Elsweiler et al. [12], in an empirical study, showed that it is possible to isolate re-finding behaviour in the logs through various qualitative and quantitative analyses. Other researchers investigated the possibility of predicting different search intents from the query log data. For example, Shen et al. [33] proposed a novel model for user intent, leveraging search sessions by learning intermediate hidden-dynamics between intent class labels and user behaviour variables. In general, query intent prediction can be categorised into two methods: context-aware and non-context-aware [33]. Non-context-aware methods learn a model by relying only on the current searchers' behaviours, e.g current submitted query and/or click-though data [24] whereas context-aware methods taken into account both current and past searchers' behaviour throughout the search session [10]. The underlying assumption behind the context-aware methods is that adjacent user behaviour is semantically related and follows the same search intent. It has been shown that context-aware methods outperform the non-context-aware ones [33]. In contrast to previous work, where the main task is to optimise the retrieval results with respect to the query intent, this paper studies search behaviour with different intents and tries to compare their characteristics across sessions.

Seeking Entertainment on the Web: Due to the ubiquity of the emotionally-rich content on the Web (e.g., news, music, movies, etc.), it is important to understand the search behaviour which has an entertainment aspect. It is not controversial to state that entertainment has an important role in human life. The consumable media on the Web, which is particularly easy to access nowadays, provides people with vast varieties of content, making it the most popular type of entertainment. It has therefore been of particular interest to understand its uses and effects on people. Zillmann [39] was instrumental in the development and establishment of a range of theories in this domain. His *mood management* theory explains why and how the audience seeks entertainment.

The underlying speculation of the mood management theory is that hedonistic motivation is a key factor in affecting the entertainment selection process [42]. Zillmann and his colleagues posit that entertainment choices are a reflection of a basic human need to enhance or retain positive states, and to lessen or steer clear of negative ones [28]. They have suggested two possible states in which there may be a need for regulation: physiological arousal and affect. In the case of physiological arousal, mood management theory suggests that users might be over-stimulated (i.e., stress) or under-stimulated (i.e., boredom). An individual experiencing such states will choose their entertainment content according to their expectations of what would lead them back to an optimal state [28]. In the case of affect states, mood management theory suggests that users might be in negative (i.e. dysphoric) or positive (i.e. upbeat) moods. An individual experiencing negative affects will choose entertainment content that helps them to alleviate or diminish the negative mood, and those experiencing positive affects will choose entertainment content that helps them to intensify or prolong their state [28].

Recently, there was an increased effort in the research community in developing IR systems that cope with search processes for entertainment intents. The "Entertain Me" [5] and "Search4FUN" workshops [14] began to explore this area and build resources, such as test collections and evaluation benchmarks. Besides the works published in these workshops, some research has been published that attempts to use emotion in information retrieval. We review this in the remaining part of this section. [13] attempted to understand the needs and motivation underlying leisure-based activities in the context of television viewing. They reported that the nature of the need and motivation are different between leisure-based and work-based situations where most of the needs reported for leisure-based situation are motivated by a desire to change mood, emotion, or arousal level. Another research related to leisure-based activity is the work by [32] which studies pleasure reading behaviour. Their results show that pleasure readers find information without having any prior information need. In addition, [41] and in a more in-depth version, [15], study the characteristics of casual-leisure search as an example of an exploratory search scenario. They reported that in casual search, the motivation is not to resolve an information need but is rather hedonistic, e.g. entertainment driven. Given their results, [15] define a casual-leisure information behaviour model highlighting the key differences between casual-leisure scenarios and typical information behaviour theory. Despite these attempts, our understanding of entertainment-based search processes is still in its infancy. Given the emergence of entertainment seeking intentions on the Web and the unexplored characteristics of them, in this paper we investigate two entertainment seeking tasks: entertainment by adjusting arousal level and entertainment by adjusting mood.

3. EXPERIMENTAL METHODOLOGY

3.1 Experiment Design

This study used a within subject design. The independent variable was the search intents (with four levels: "Information Seeking" (INS), "Information Re-finding" (INF), "Entertainment by adjusting Arousal" (ENA), "Entertainment by adjusting Mood" (ENM)), which was controlled by the simulated search task given to the participants (see Section 3.2). We did not perform any control on the number of relevant and irrelevant results in order to simulate a real search scenario situation as much as possible. The dependent variables are the qualitative (gathered through questionnaire) and quantitative (gathered through system interaction logging) data.

3.2 Tasks

We prepared four search task scenarios, each simulating different search intent. The search tasks were presented using the structural framework of simulated need situations [8]. By doing so, we introduced short cover stories that helped us describe to our participants the source of their information need, the context of the situation and the problem to be solved. This facilitated a better understanding of the search objective and introduced a layer of realism, while preserving well-defined relevance criteria. In the following, each of the search tasks is explained in detail.

3.2.1 INS Task

This search task simulates the information seeking search scenario. Information seeking is the most studied topic in the field. This task is designed as a control group since the majority of cognition and emotion findings in the past were based on a similar search task intent. For this search task, we prepared a number of search topics that covered a variety of contexts in order to capture participants' interests as best as possible. The topics, presented in Table 1, were all checked manually, prior to the experiment, to ensure the availability of relevant documents. The simulated search scenario for INS task was as follows: *"Imagine you have graduated recently and are going to interview for a job in a local company. As part of the interview process, you are asked to explain and expand on the area you will be working on. You feel very enthusiastic about the interview; however, due to your lack of knowledge you would like to find out more about this particular topic before taking part in the interview."* Each participant was then asked to choose one of the topics that they were unfamiliar with but consider interesting. Using the video retrieval system, they had to find as many relevant videos as possible so that they could construct a good knowledge about their selected topic.

Table 1: Search topics for the information seeking task scenario.

Obtaining information regarding contraception methods.
Investigating new knowledge on global warming.
Formulating an opinion about existing social networking sites.

3.2.2 INF Task

This search task simulates the information re-finding search intent. There are two differences between this task and the previous one: (i) there is only one document that can satisfy the information need of the searcher, and (ii) the searcher has seen the relevant documents at some point before initiating the search process and is now attempting to re-find it. The similarity between this task and the previous one is that in both cases searchers have an information need.

For this search task, we prepared a number of videos that covered a variety of contexts in order to capture participants' interests as best as possible. The videos were intentionally selected as they would likely be very hard to find because they lacked textual description. The motivation was to simulate a challenging information re-finding process where the recalled terms are very ambiguous and do not lead directly to the relevant item. This would better represent many realistic re-finding tasks, when the user cannot recall the exact description of the item they are looking for. Of course this only considers one spectrum of re-finding tasks, and more exhaustive studies of such tasks needs to be done in the future. The simulated search scenario for INF task was as follows: *"Imagine you are discussing a video which you have seen few days ago with your friends. They are interested in seeing the video and have asked you to send them a link to it. You can remember the content of the video but you cannot remember its title or any textual information which can help you in retrieving it."* Each participant was then asked to select and watch one of the three videos presented to them (an animal[2], martial arts[3], or a science video[4]) that they are unfamiliar with and consider interesting. Once participants watched the video, they were asked to find it as fast as possible.

3.2.3 ENA Task

This search task simulates the entertainment-based search intent where searchers adjust their arousal level. The main difference between this task and the two tasks before is that the primary need is hedonistic rather than informational. Therefore, to accurately simulate such search processes, we avoid introducing any explicit information need. Thus, for this search task, we did not provide any pre-prepared search topic. This decision is motivated by the literature in sociology [28] and information seeking and retrieval domains on entertainment [13]. To the best of our knowledge, this is the first time that an entertainment-based search task is simulated in this way. The simulated search scenario for ENA task was as follows: *"Imagine you are working in a factory as a night-guard. You have just finished your routine checks and will be taking out more checks shortly. You are tired so you decide to watch some videos to wake yourself up and make yourself ready for your next round of checks."* Each participant was asked to find as many relevant videos as possible that make them feel excited.

3.2.4 ENM Task

This search task simulates the entertainment-based search intent where searchers adjust their mood. Similar to ENA task, searchers engage in such search processes with hedonistic need rather than informational. Therefore, to accurately simulate such search processes, we avoid introducing any explicit information need. Thus, similar to ENA task, we did not prepared any specific search topic. The simulated search scenario for ENM task was as follows: *"Imagine your boyfriend/girlfriend is travelling and communication access is very limited. It is now a few days since he/she has gone and you are missing him/her very much. You are feeling very sad and in order to change your mood, you have decided to watch some videos."* Each participant was asked to

---

[2] www.youtube.com/v/wx7rY11qb0k&showinfo=0
[3] www.youtube.com/v/pEUeP7hx8fs&showinfo=0
[4] www.youtube.com/v/P8Cs2t05w74&showinfo=0

find as many relevant videos as possible that make them feel happy.

3.3 Apparatus

For our experiment we used one desktop computer, equipped with a monitor, keyboard and mouse. The computer provided access to a custom-made search interface which allowed the participants to perform their search tasks. The interface was designed such that it logged participants' desktop actions, such as starting, finishing and elapsed times for interactions, mouse movement, and click-throughs using a common system time. Finally, we used entry, post and exit questionnaires in each session.

3.4 Questionnaires

At the beginning of the experiment, the participants were introduced to an *entry questionnaire*, which gathered background and demographic information, and inquired about previous experience with online videos, in particular, browsing and searching habits including their intentions. At the end of each task, the participants completed a *post-task questionnaire*, to elicit subject's viewpoint on certain aspects of the search process. The questions were divided into three sections that covered the encountered task and the cognition and emotion aspects of the search experience. All of the questions included in these questionnaires were a forced-choice type. Finally, an *exit questionnaire* was introduced at the end of the study. In this questionnaire we gathered information about the encountered system as well as the user study in general: which task they preferred and why, and their general comments about the user study.

3.5 Video Retrieval System

For the completion of the search tasks we used a custom-made search environment (named *VideoHunt*) that was designed to resemble the basic layout of existing search services, while retaining a minimum of graphical elements and distractions. VideoHunt works on top of Bing 2.0 API. For every submitted query it returned a list of fifty results (ten results on each page), stripped of their title, snippet and any other metadata. The title of a video was presented as tooltip by moving the mouse over a particular video. Even though this approach introduced our participants into artificial search situations which differ from real-life experiences, it was a necessary trade-off for capturing the browsing action of the user with the retrieved results.

3.5.1 Search Interface

VideoHunt applies a layered architecture approach, similar to that adopted in [3]. The first layer of the interface is dedicated to supporting any interaction that occurs during the early stages of the search process (such as query formulation and search execution). Any output generated during this phase is presented in the second layer. From there, the participants could easily select and preview any of the retrieved clips. The content of a clip is shown on a separate panel, in the foreground, which corresponds to the third layer of our system. The main reason behind this layered architecture was to isolate the viewed content from all possible actions allowing us to separate the time spent viewing video from other actions such as browsing the retrieved results or formulating queries. Upon viewing the clip, the participants had to explicitly indicate the relevance of the video.

3.5.2 User Tracking and Logging

All user actions were monitored and logged by the search interface including their queries and clicks, as well as the length of time spent watching a clip, expanding the result list and formulating a query. In addition, as it has been shown that mouse movements are correlated with user gaze [17], the system captured mouse events to determine the amount of time the user spent on each retrieved result item. This information was all captured in a log file allowing for easy association of the log information with the corresponding questionnaire responses.

3.6 Procedure

The user study was carried out in the following manner. The formal meeting with the participants took place in the laboratory setting. At the beginning of the session the participants were given an information sheet which explained the conditions of the experiment. They were then asked to sign a Consent Form and were notified about their right to withdraw at any point during the study, without affecting their legal rights or benefits. Then, they were given an Entry Questionnaire to fill in.

The session proceeded with a brief tutorial on the use of the search interface with a short training task. After completion of the training task, each participant had to complete four search tasks (explained in Section 3.2), one for each level of search process intentions (see Section 3.1). To negate the order and fatigue effects we counter-balanced the task distribution using a Graeco-Latin Square design. The subjects were asked every time to provide judgment for any video that they watch, and were given 10 minutes to complete their task, during which they were left unattended to work. At the end of each task, the subjects were asked to complete a post-task questionnaire. Questions in the post-task questionnaire were randomised to avoid the effect of fatigue. Between each task, a cooling-off period was applied to avoid the carry-over effect. An exit questionnaire was administered at the end of the session. Finally, the participants were asked to sign a payment form, prior to receiving the payment of £12.

Each study took approximately 120 minutes to complete; this is from the time they accepted the conditions until they signed the payment receipt. Users could only participate once in the study. The total cost of the evaluation was £348, including the cost of the pilot studies. A user study with the procedure explained above was conduced over a period of 10 days from 16th to 26th of July 2012. The results of these studies are presented in Section 4.

3.6.1 Participants

Participants consisted of 24 healthy participants with equal gender distribution (12 female and 12 male) all under the age of 41, with the largest group between the ages of 18-23 (45.8%) followed by the group between ages of 24-29 (36%). Participants tended to have a high school diploma or equivalent (4.16%), some college degree (4.16%), bachelor (41.66%) or graduate degree (50%). They were primarily students (62.5%), though there were a number of self-employed (16.6%), not employed (4.16%) and employed by a company or organisation (16.6%).

3.6.2 Pilot Studies

Prior to running the actual user study, a pilot study was performed using 5 participants to confirm that the process worked correctly and smoothly. A number of changes were made to the system based on feedback from the pilot study. The changes consisted of modifications to the questionnaires to clarify questions, modifications to the system to improve logging capabilities and improvements to the tasks. After the final pilot, it was determined that the participants were able to complete the user study without problems and that the system was capturing all necessary data. One of the important outcomes of the pilot study was that participants preferred the questions where the search session was broken down into three phases (i.e. beginning, middle, and end), compared to questions where a finer granularity was applied (e.g. broken down into four phases). Therefore, the questionnaire was adapted accordingly. However, for better granularity, the interaction log was divided into four phases.

4. RESULTS AND DISCUSSION

In Section 4.1, we first discuss the task perception expressed in the questionnaire. Following this, we discuss our analysis on the characteristics of the four search tasks outlined in Section 3.2; focusing on the cognition, emotion, and interaction aspects. Finally, we discuss the predictability of search task types based on features derived from the user interaction with the system in Section 4.2.

4.1 Qualitative and Quantitative Analysis

4.1.1 Task Perception

Figures 1 shows the box plots for the qualitative analysis of users' perception of the four tasks (i.e. INS, INF, ENA, and ENM). Each box plot reports data aggregated from 24 participants, along with five key statistics: the minimum, first, second (median), third, and maximum quartiles.[5] We performed an ANOVA test between measures obtained at each phase, across four search tasks for each user to check the significance of the difference among them. The test is suitable for this data as we have four groups of data, therefore we need to compare four means and variances. We use (*) and (**) to denote the fact that a measure had results different across four search tasks with the confidence levels ($p < 0.05$) and ($p < 0.01$), respectively.

In the post-task questionnaire we measured participants' perception of their performed task in terms of the difficulty of the task, the familiarity of the participant with the task, the extent to which they found the task stressful, interesting and clear by asking the following question *"The task we asked you to perform was [easy/stressful/interesting/clear/familiar] (answer: 1: "Strongly Disagree", 2: "Disagree", 3: "Neutral", 4: "Agree", 5: "Strongly Agree")"*. The results shown in Figure 1 indicate that participants found the INF task difficult and stressful, followed by the INS task, whereas they found other two tasks easy and not-stressful (the differences were statistically significant). The difference in the answer provided by the participants for interesting, clear and familiar measures is not statistically significant. In the post-task questionnaire we also asked the opinion of the participants with respect to the following statement *"I had enough time to do an effective search.] (answer: 1:*

---

[5] Further information can be found in [26].

"Strongly Disagree", 2: "Disagree", 3: "Neutral", 4: "Agree", 5: "Strongly Agree")". The results show that they found the given time enough to do an effective search task: INS: M=4.0 SD=0.88; INF: M=3.8 SD=0.96; ENA: M=4.0 SD=0.97; ENM: M=4.3 SD=0.56 (the differences are however not statistically significant across the tasks).

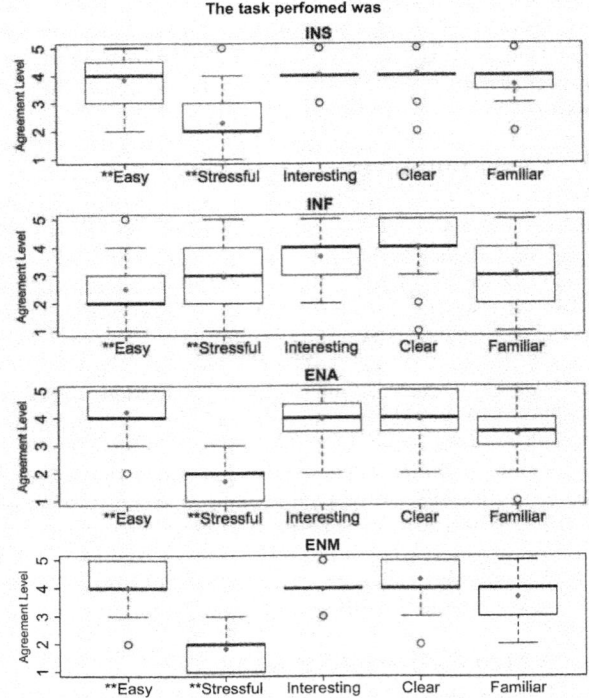

Figure 1: Box plot of the task perception based on the information gathered from 24 participants questionnaire. The diamond represents the mean value. (*) and (**) indicate confidence levels ($p < 0.05$) and ($p < 0.01$) respectively.

4.1.2 Main Results

Figures 2, 3 and 4 show the line plots for the qualitative analysis of users' cognition, emotion, and interaction aspects for the four search tasks (i.e. INS, INF, ENA, and ENM). Each line plot reports the data aggregated from the 24 participants, along with the mean and error bar for three phases of a search process: the beginning, middle and end. We performed the ANOVA test at each phase to check the significance of the difference among the tasks at each phase. We use (*) and (**) to denote the fact that a measure had results different across four search tasks with the confidence levels ($p < 0.05$) and ($p < 0.01$), respectively.

The key finding which emerged from the questionnaire is that search tasks with different intentions have varying characteristics in terms of cognition, emotion, and interaction aspects. From a cognition point of view, the complexity and dynamic concepts associated with an information seeking process do not hold for all four search intents, e.g. not all the search processes have an information need which starts from an ASK. From an emotion point of view, the uncertainty principle of Kuhlthau [22] does not hold (at least for the initiation phase) e.g. not all the search processes start from negative emotions, such as anxiety associated with the realisation of lack of knowledge. However the end of the search process tends to agree with Kuhlthau ISP model [21] since, in the case of a successful search process, participants express satisfaction and in other case anxiety and/or anger. Though Kuhlthau's ISP model is originally proposed for information seeking tasks, it is assumed to hold in IR scenarios [23, 40]. The main result which emerged from interaction analysis is that participants interact differently with the search system throughout the search session when they have different intents. The interaction differences are in terms of the characteristic of the submitted queries and interaction behaviour with the retrieved results. In the remainder of this section we discuss each of these aspects in more details.

4.1.3 Cognition Aspect

To investigate the cognitive aspect of the our search tasks, we study the difficulty of query formulation (associated with complexity of search process), certainty of what to search for and what is relevant (associated with the dynamic concept of search process). Figure 2 presents the results for three questions posed in the post-task questionnaire: *(1) "At the [beginning/Middle/End] of the search session, I was certain about what I was going to search for.", (2) "At the [beginning/Middle/End] of the search session, I had difficulty formulating queries.", and (3) "At the [beginning/Middle/End] of the search session, I didn't have a clear idea what videos would be relevant." (answer: 1: Strongly Disagree, 2: Disagree, 3: Neutral, 4: Agree, 5: Strongly Agree).*

The findings show that for the INS task, at the early stage of the search session participants experience uncertainty of what to search for and have only a vague idea about what videos would be relevant. As they progress through the search session, their uncertainty decreases and their concept of relevant videos becomes more clear. Formulating queries also becomes less difficult as they progress through the search session. The cognitive process reported for the INS task follows the literature in the information seeking and retrieval community such as Belkin et al. [7] and Kuhlthau [22].

In contrast to INS, for the INF task, the findings show that participants at the beginning of the search session experience a high level of certainty, having little problem formulating queries and knowing what video would be relevant. As they progress through the search session, the uncertainty increases, formulating queries became more difficult and what a relevant video would be becomes more vague. Although the cognitive state at the later stage of the INF task is a by-product of the fact that they were unsuccessful in their search task, the cognitive state at the early phase of the search process is contrary to general assumptions in the IR community.

Finally, for the ENM and ENA tasks, the results show a consistent level of certainty throughout the search session. Although the ENA task is similar to INS in terms of answers given to the "difficulty of formulating queries" and "vagueness of the concept of relevance" questions, the ENM task shows consistent behaviour for all three questions across different phases, which indicates yet another cognitive behaviour pattern.

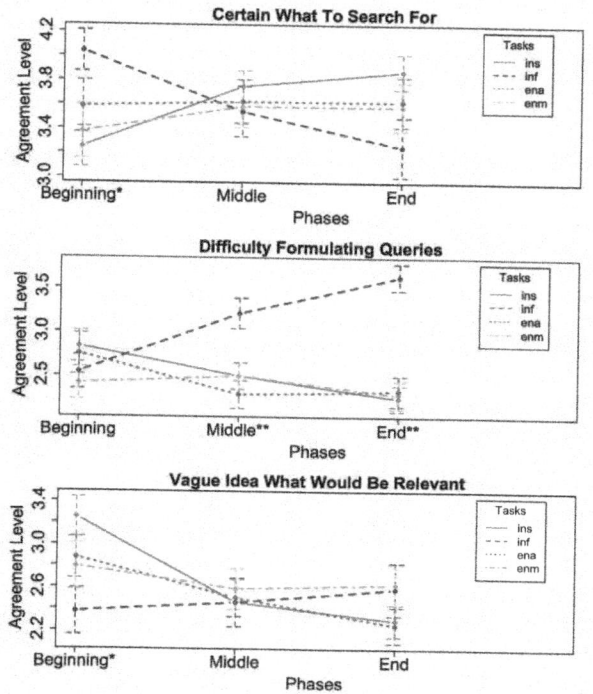

Figure 2: Line plot of the cognitive aspect based on the information gathered from 24 participant questionnaires. (*) and (**) indicate confidence levels ($p < 0.05$) and ($p < 0.01$), respectively.

4.1.4 Emotion Aspect

To investigate the emotion aspect of our search tasks, we study participants' emotion at three stages of the search session using six Ekman emotions [11] plus neutral, anxiety and satisfaction. Figure 3 presents the results for the posed questions in the post-task questionnaire: *(1) "At the [beginning/Middle/End] of the search session I experienced [Sadness/Happiness/Anger/Surprise/ Fear/Disgust/Anxiety/Satisfaction/Neutral]." (answer: 1: Yes, 2: No).*

The results for the INS task show that participants' satisfaction level increases as they progress through the search session. Although this is inline with previous literature (i.e. the increase of the feeling of satisfaction as a result of alleviating ASK), the results for anxiety is not inline with previous work, such as uncertainty principle of Kuhlthau [22]. This is because our findings show that the anxiety level for the INS task at the beginning of the search session is low and remains low throughout the session. Surprisingly, the results show that for this task, the majority of participants are neutral (experiencing no emotion) at the beginning of the search session and as they progress through, they experience emotion (reporting less neutral). In addition, we observe a diverse range of emotion reported at the middle phase of the INS search process (e.g. surprise, fear, disgust, anger) which we assume is a result of the topics and/or watched videos, rather than the search process itself.

For the INF task, the findings show a similar trend for a neutral level, as with what we reported for the INS task. However, we observe that for the INF task, anger constantly increases as the search session progresses, whereas for the

INS task, satisfaction increases instead. Experiencing anger can be a result of the cognitive process participants go through in their search session for this task. As we discussed earlier, the participants did not succeed in completing this task, hence the experience of anger is likely a result of this. In addition, the anxiety level increases as participants progress from the beginning to the middle phase of the search session, but surprisingly, it decreases from the middle to the end of the search session. This can be as a result of transforming anxiety to other negative emotions, e.g. sadness or disgust.

For the ENA and ENM tasks, the results show that fewer participants are neutral at the beginning of the search session compared to INS and INF, and this number further decreases as participants progress through the search session. The findings show that participants' experience of happiness for these two tasks are significantly higher than the INS and INF tasks, indicating the hedonistic meditation underlying such processes. These findings confirm Zillmann theory of mood management [42]. Similar to INS, for both ENA and ENM tasks, participants satisfaction level increases as they progress through the search session, indicating that the underlying need is getting satisfied. The results show that the feeling of satisfaction can also be experienced if the search task does not have a clear IN, which in these tasks relates to a hedonistic need. Another interesting observation is the variety of the emotions experienced at the beginning of the search session for the ENM and ENA tasks. This shows that it is possible that participants begin their search session experiencing emotions other than anxiety or any other negative emotions, as is the case for ENM (e.g. the feeling of sadness) and ENA (e.g. the feeling of surprise). This particular result may be an artefact of our experimental settings and needs to be explored further.

4.1.5 Interaction Aspect

To investigate the interaction aspect of our search tasks, we study a number of features extracted from interaction log data. As the distribution of the search task completion time can be very different, we aggregate the interaction data for each quartile. For each phase, we first calculated general statistics such as the average number of clicked, liked, and disliked videos, as well as the average number of times "Next Page" and "Previous Page" buttons were clicked, the average number of documents the mouse hovered over, and the average number of formulated queries. Then, we calculated the average query formulation time, video viewing time, and mouse hovering duration over the retrieved results. Finally, we calculated the similarity of the submitted queries as well as the similarity of the titles of the viewed videos. The similarity value was calculated using cosine similarity. Figure 4 presents the results for the analysis of the interaction with respect to the features explained above.

The analysis of interaction for the INS task shows that participants at each phase formulate fewer queries in comparison to other tasks, and the number of issued queries and the query formulation time decreases as they progress through the search session. The query formulation time can indicate the cognitive effort required. Therefore, the results obtained for the query formulation time is inline with what we observed from questionnaire results with respect to the cognitive aspect of the INS task where the difficulty of formulating queries decreases as the participants progress through the search session. Another interesting aspect is how they interact with the retrieved results. Participants mainly visited videos present on the first page, and checked a relatively lower number of videos at each phase compared to other tasks. The average video viewing time steadily increases as well as the number of videos judged as relevant.

On the other hand, for the INF task we observe a different interaction behaviour pattern. The number of formulated queries and the similarity between the formulated queries are the highest among the four tasks across all four phases, while the average query formulation time is the lowest. In contrast to the INS task, participants not only visited the retrieved results in the main page but also visited other results pages. They have also checked a larger number of videos at each phase. The time spent viewing selected videos was close to zero, showing that they were certain of what they were looking for and simply wanted to verify the selected video was the correct one. This results holds for difficult re-finding task scenario (see Section 3.2) and may not hold for other spectrum of such a task.

For the ENA and ENM tasks we observe that the number of formulated queries and the average query formulation time are between that of the INS and INF tasks across four phases. The greatest number of submitted queries is in the first phase, however from the second phase onwards the number of formulated queries remains almost static. What distinguishes the formulated queries between the ENA and ENM tasks is the similarity of the formulated queries at each phase. For the ENA task the similarity of formulated queries decreases as the search session progresses, whereas for the ENM task the similarity of formulated queries and the number of formulated queries follows a similar trend across all phases. Another aspect of interaction history which differentiates between the ENA and ENM tasks is the way participants interact with the retrieved results. For the ENA task, similar to the INS task, the visited documents were mainly from the first page across all phases, whereas for the ENM task, participants visited results from other pages as well, in particular during the third phase.

The next question this work addresses is whether we can learn a model from such interactions so that we can accurately predict the search task intentions. Furthermore, to what extent can we accurately predict search task intentions through the search process?

4.2 Prediction of Search Task Intentions

As discussed in Section 1, identification of the intentions behind the search processes can help search engines to better satisfy users' needs. Therefore, in this section, we investigate our second research question on whether the search intents can be modelled to predict given searchers' interaction data with the system. For this purpose, we used the set of features extracted from interaction log data explained in Sections 4.1.5.

For our four search intents, we have a multinomial classification problem where the classes are "INS" (indicating the participant had information seeking), "INF" (indicating the participant had information finding), "ENA" (indicating the participant had emotion need by adjusting arousal level), and "ENM" (indicating the participant had emotion need by adjusting mood). We used SMO, an implementation of SVM in Weka,[6] to discriminate between the four classes

---
[6] http://www.cs.waikato.ac.nz/ml/weka/

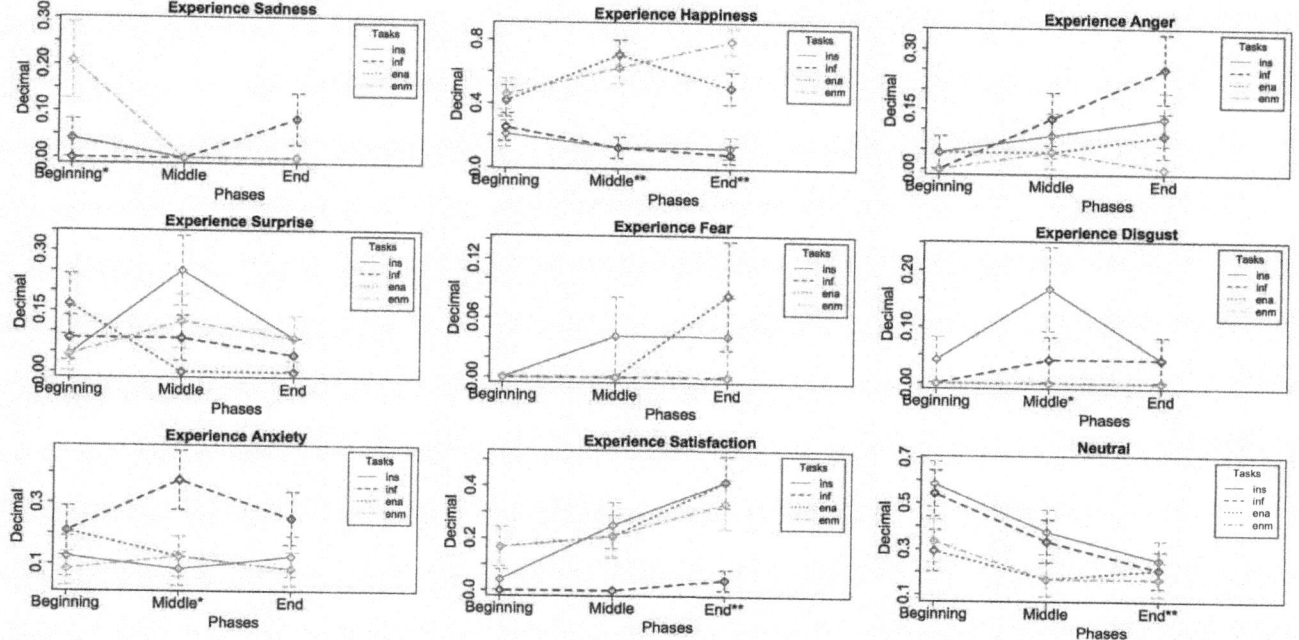

Figure 3: Line plot of the emotion aspect based on the information gathered from 24 participants questionnaire. (*) and (**) indicat confidence levels ($p < 0.05$) and ($p < 0.01$), respectively.

explained above. We trained our models using a normalised polynomial kernel which in the majority of cases outperformed other SVM kernels (e.g. polynomial and radial-basis) based on our analysis, not presented due to the space limits.

Table 2 shows the classification performance averaged over the 24 participants of the study at different phases of the search process. We measured the accuracy of the model (i.e. fraction of items in the test set for which the models' predictions were correct) using 10-fold cross-validation. We obtained more than 100% improvement over a model based on the discrete uniform distribution. The results indicate that at each phase of the search process we are able to successfully predict the search task intentions given the features extracted from interaction logs. The accuracy of the prediction increases as the searcher progresses through the search session. Our findings indicate that it is possible to build effective intention-aware search technologies in which the retrieved results and provided functionality adapt to the needs of the user.

Table 2: The accuracy of the search intent prediction at each phase. Phases are presented as columns. The best performing feature set for each dimension is highlighted in bold.

	Search Process Phases			
	Phase1	Phase2	Phase3	Phase4
Baseline	25%	25%	25%	25%
SVM	51.04%	53.12%	56.25%	57.29%

5. CONCLUSIONS

In this paper we investigated the cognitive, emotion, and interaction aspects of four search tasks namely information seeking (INS), re-finding (INF), entertainment adjusting arousal level (ENA) and entertainment adjusting mood (ENM). In order to do so, we devised four search tasks, each simulating one of these intents. Using a video retrieval system as a use case, we conducted a user study with 24 participants. We analysed the characteristics of each aspect across different phases of the search process. Our findings show differences in cognition, emotion and interaction aspects of search processes for different search tasks. In particular, from a cognition point of view, the complexity and dynamic concepts associated with an information seeking process do not hold for all four search tasks types, e.g. not all the search processes have an information need which starts from an ASK. The cognitive process reported for the INS task shows a parallel with prior findings in the information seeking and retrieval community such as Belkin et al. [7] and Kuhlthau [22]. In contrast, for the INF task, the findings show that participants at the beginning of the search session experience a high level of certainty, having little problem formulating queries and knowing what video would be relevant. Finally, for the ENM and ENA tasks, the results show a consistent level of certainty throughout the search session.

From an emotion point of view, the uncertainty principle of Kuhlthau [22] does not hold (at least for the initiation phase) e.g. not all the search processes start from negative emotions, such as anxiety associated with the realisation of lack of knowledge. However the end of the search process tends to agree with Kuhlthau ISP model [21] since, in the case of a successful search process, participants express satisfaction and in other case anxiety and/or anger. Surprisingly, the results show that for INS task, the majority of participants are neutral (experiencing no emotion) at the beginning of the search session and as they progress through, they experience emotion (reporting less neutral). For the INF task, the findings show a similar trend for a neutral

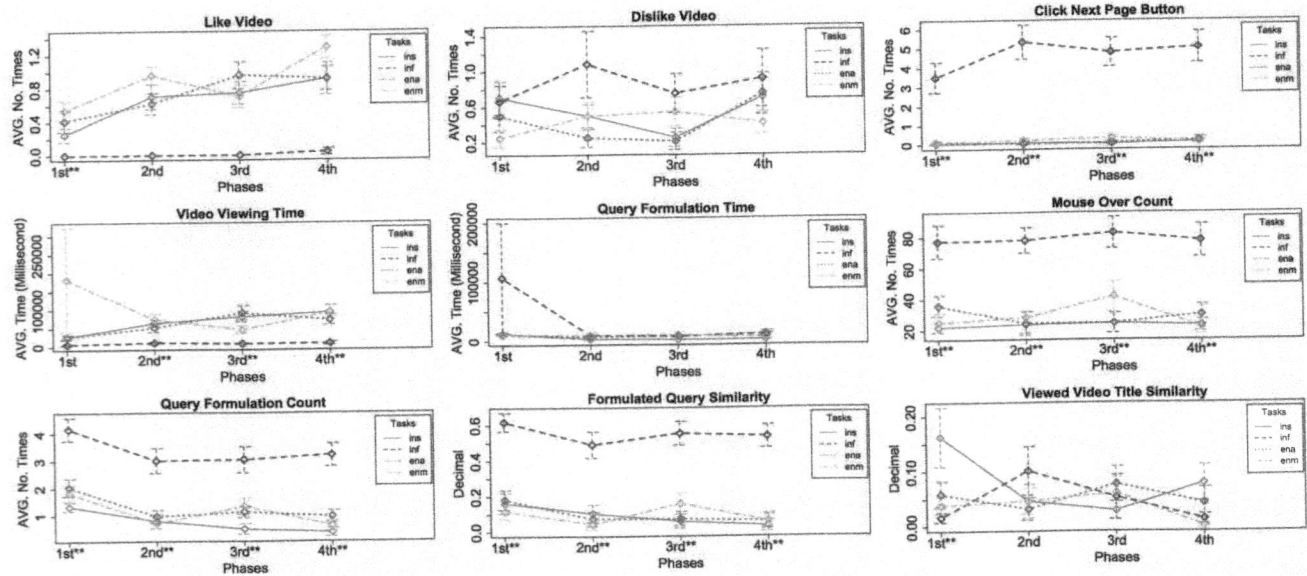

Figure 4: Line plot of the interaction aspect based on the information gathered from 24 participants interaction log data. (*) and (**) indicat confidence levels ($p < 0.05$) and ($p < 0.01$), respectively.

level, as with what we reported for the INS task. For the ENA and ENM tasks, the results show that fewer participants are neutral at the beginning of the search session compared to INS and INF, and this number further decreases as participants progress through the search session.

From an interaction point of view, the main result which emerged from analysis is that participants interact differently with the search system when they have different search tasks. The interaction differences are in terms of the characteristic of the submitted queries and interaction behaviour with the retrieved results. For the INS task, the findings show that participants at each phase formulate fewer queries in comparison to other tasks. Participants also mainly visited videos present on the first page. In contrast to the INS task, for the INF task, the number of formulated queries and the similarity between the formulated queries are the highest among the four tasks across all four phases. In addition, participants not only visited the retrieved results in the main page but also visited other results pages. What distinguishes the formulated queries between these two tasks is the similarity of the formulated queries at each phase.

We further study the possibility of predicting search intents at different phases of a search process, given features extracted from interaction log data. We have achieved more than 100% improvement over our baseline (discrete uniform distribution) on our search intents prediction task, given searchers' interaction data. Discrete uniform distribution is a naïve baseline, however there are no previous studies for comparison. Our prediction accuracy sets the baseline for future studies. The features used for our prediction are computationally inexpensive and easy to calculate. A more exhaustive exploration of features will be studied in future work.

The major implication of our work is in developing effective intent-aware search technologies. Given the fundamental differences in cognition, emotion and interaction aspects of the studied search intents, the next step can be to develop techniques facilitating effective seeking processes and in turn satisfying searchers. In addition, search behaviour characteristics at various phases can be easily detected and exploited for predicting user intents. This may open up avenues for revisiting current intent detection approaches.

Finally, the findings of this paper are limited to the video retrieval domain and we do not generalise it to other domains. Even though significant differences in cognition, emotion and interaction were detected across different search task types, we acknowledge the limitation of a lab-based study. However, our findings motivate the exploration of similar hypotheses in other domains. In future work, we plan to evaluate additional features to improve our prediction accuracy. Further, we want to continue to study how understanding search sessions can be leveraged to improve user satisfaction measures, and possibly build search engines that adapt based on user search process intentions.

6. ACKNOWLEDGEMENT

This work was supported by the EU FP7 LiMoSINe project (288024).

7. REFERENCES

[1] I. Arapakis, J. M. Jose, and P. D. Gray. Affective Feedback: An Investigation into the Role of Emotions in the Information Seeking Process. In *SIGIR*, 395–402, 2008.

[2] I. Arapakis, I. Konstas, and J. M. Jose. Using Facial Expressions and Peripheral Physiological Signals as Implicit Indicators of Topical Relevance. In *MM*, pages 461–470, 2009.

[3] I. Arapakis, Y. Moshfeghi, H. Joho, R. Ren, D. Hannah, and J. M. Jose. Enriching User Profiling with Affective Features for the Improvement of a Multimodal Recommender System. *CIVR*, 2009.

[4] N. Belkin. Helping People Find What They Don't Know. *Communications of the ACM*, 43(8):58–61, 2000.

[5] N. Belkin, C. Clarke, N. Gao, J. Kamps, and J. Karlgren. Report on the SIGIR Workshop on Entertain Me: Supporting Complex Search Tasks. In *ACM SIGIR Forum*, volume 45, 51–59. 2012.

[6] N. Belkin, C. Cool, A. Stein, and U. Thiel. Cases, Scripts, and Information-Seeking Strategies: On the Design of Interactive Information Retrieval Systems. *Expert systems with applications*, 9(3):379–395, 1995.

[7] N. Belkin, R. Oddy, and H. Brooks. Ask for Information Retrieval: Part i. Background and Theory. *Journal of Documentation*, 38(2):61–71, 1982.

[8] P. Borlund and P. Ingwersen. The Development of a Method for the Evaluation of Interactive Information Retrieval Systems. *Journal of Documentation*, 53(3):225–250, 1997.

[9] A. Broder. A Taxonomy of Web Search. In *ACM SIGIR forum*, volume 36, 3–10. 2002.

[10] Z. Cheng, B. Gao, and T.-Y. Liu. Actively Predicting Diverse Search Intent from User Browsing Behaviors. In *WWW*, 221–230. 2010.

[11] P. Ekman and R. J. Davidson. *The Nature of Emotion: Fundamental Questions*. Oxford University Press, 1994.

[12] D. Elsweiler, M. Harvey, and M. Hacker. Understanding Re-finding behavior in Naturalistic Email Interaction Logs. In *SIGIR*, 35–44. 2011.

[13] D. Elsweiler, S. Mandl, and B. Kirkegaard Lunn. Understanding Casual-Leisure Information Needs: a Diary Study in the Context of Television Viewing. In *IIiX*, 25–34, 2010.

[14] D. Elsweiler, M. Wilson, and M. Harvey. Searching4fun. 2012.

[15] D. Elsweiler, M. Wilson, and B. Lunn. Understanding Casual-Leisure Information Behaviour. *Library and Information Science*, 211:241, 2011.

[16] K. E. Fisher, S. Erdelez, and L. McKechnie. *Theories of Information Behavior*. Information Today Inc, 2005.

[17] Q. Guo and E. Agichtein. Towards Predicting Web Searcher Gaze Position from Mouse Movements. In *CHI Extended Abstracts*, 3601–3606, 2010.

[18] J. Gwizdka and I. Lopatovska. The Role of Subjective Factors in the Information Search Process. *JASIST*, 60(12):2452–2464, 2009.

[19] P. Ingwersen. *Information Retrieval Interaction*. Number s 246. Taylor Graham London, 1992.

[20] P. Ingwersen. Polyrepresentation of Information Needs and Semantic Entities: Elements of a Cognitive Theory for Information Retrieval Interaction. In *SIGIR*, 101–110, 1994.

[21] C. Kuhlthau, J. Heinström, and R. Todd. The 'information Search Process' Revisited: Is the Model Still Useful. *Information Research*, 13(4):13–4, 2008.

[22] C. C. Kuhlthau. A Principle of Uncertainty for Information Seeking. *Journal of Documentation*, 49(4):339–355, 1993.

[23] C. C. Kuhlthau. Accommodating the User's Information Search Process: Challenges for Information Retrieval System Designers. *Bulletin of ASIS&T*, 25(3):12–16, 2005.

[24] X. Li, Y. Wang, and A. Acero. Learning Query Intent from Regularized Click Graphs. In *SIGIR*, volume 339, 346. 2008.

[25] I. Lopatovska. Searching for good mood: Examining relationships between search task and mood. *ASIST*, 46(1):1–13, 2009.

[26] R. McGill, J. W. Tukey, and W. A. Larsen. Variations of Box Plots. *American Statistician*, 32(1):12–16, 1978.

[27] Y. Moshfeghi and J. M. Jose. Role of Emotion in Information Retrieval for Entertainment (Position Paper). *Searching4FUN Workshop in ECIR*, 2012.

[28] M. B. Oliver. Mood management and Selective Exposure. *Communication and Emotion: Essays in Honor of Dolf Zillmann*, 85–106, 2003.

[29] A. Poddar and I. Ruthven. The Emotional Impact of Search Tasks. In *IIiX*, 35–44. 2010.

[30] D. Robins. Shifts of Focus in Information Retrieval Interaction. In *ASIST*, volume 34, 123–134, 1997.

[31] T. Saracevic. Relevance: A Review of and a Framework for the Thinking on the Notion in Information Science. *JASIST*, 26(6):321–343, 1975.

[32] C. Sheldrick Ross. Finding without Seeking: The Information Encounter in the Context of Reading for Pleasure. *Information Processing & Management*, 35(6):783–799, 1999.

[33] Y. Shen, J. Yan, S. Yan, L. Ji, N. Liu, and Z. Chen. Sparse Hidden-Dynamics Conditional Random Fields for User Intent Understanding. In *WWW*, 7–16. 2011.

[34] J. A. Singer and P. Salovey. Mood and Memory: Evaluating the Network Theory of Affect. *Clinical Psychology Review*, 1988.

[35] A. Spink, H. Greisdorf, and J. Bateman. From Highly Relevant to Not Relevant: Examining Different Regions of Relevance. *Information Processing & Management*, 34(5):599–621, 1998.

[36] R. Taylor. Question-Negotiation an Information-seeking in Libraries. Technical report, DTIC Document, 1967.

[37] J. Teevan, E. Adar, R. Jones, and M. Potts. Information Re-Retrieval: Repeat Queries in Yahoo's Logs. In *SIGIR*, 151–158. 2007.

[38] C. van Rijsbergen. (Invited Paper) A New Theoretical Framework for Information retrieval. In *SIGIR*, 194–200. 1986.

[39] P. Vorderer. Entertainment theory. *Communication and Emotion: Essays in Honor of Dolf Zillmann*, 131–153, 2003.

[40] R. W. White, J. M. Jose, and I. Ruthven. An Implicit Feedback Approach for Interactive Information Retrieval. *Information processing & management*, 42(1):166–190, 2006.

[41] M. Wilson and D. Elsweiler. Casual-leisure Searching: the Exploratory Search Scenarios that Break our Current Models. In *HCIR*, 28–31, 2010.

[42] D. Zillmann. Mood Management: Using Entertainment to Full Advantage. *In L. Donohew, H.E. Sypher, & E.T. Higgins (Eds.), Communication, social cognition, and affect*, 147–171, 1988.

Ad Impression Forecasting for Sponsored Search

Abhirup Nath[†], Shibnath Mukherjee[‡], Prateek Jain[†], Navin Goyal[†], Srivatsan Laxman[†]
{t-abhin, shibnatm, prajain, navingo, slaxman}@microsoft.com
[†]Microsoft Research, Bangalore, India
[‡]Microsoft adCenter, Bangalore, India

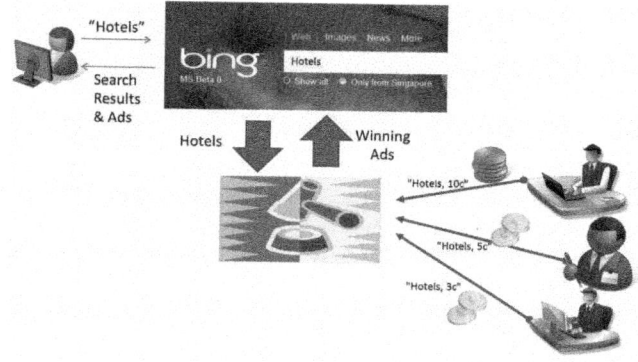

Figure 1: An overview of the sponsored search process: When a user searches for a string say "Hotels", the search engine sends the extracted keyword (from the query string) for an auction between advertisers, who are willing to pay certain amount of money for a click by the user.

ABSTRACT

A typical problem for a search engine (hosting *sponsored* search service) is to provide the advertisers with a forecast of the number of impressions his/her ad is likely to obtain for a given bid. Accurate forecasts have high business value, since they enable advertisers to select bids that lead to better returns on their investment. They also play an important role in services such as automatic campaign optimization. Despite its importance the problem has remained relatively unexplored in literature. Existing methods typically overfit to the training data, leading to inconsistent performance. Furthermore, some of the existing methods cannot provide predictions for new ads, i.e., for ads that are not present in the logs. In this paper, we develop a generative model based approach that addresses these drawbacks. We design a Bayes net to capture inter-dependencies between the query traffic features and the competitors in an auction. Furthermore, we account for variability in the volume of query traffic by using a dynamic linear model. Finally, we implement our approach on a production grade MapReduce framework and conduct extensive large scale experiments on substantial volumes of sponsored search data from Bing. Our experimental results demonstrate significant advantages over existing methods as measured using several accuracy/error criteria, improved ability to provide estimates for new ads and more consistent performance with smaller variance in accuracies. Our method can also be adapted to several other related forecasting problems such as predicting average position of ads or the number of clicks under budget constraints.

General Terms

Algorithms, Economics, Forecasting

Keywords

Sponsored search, Auctions, Bayes net, Dynamic Linear Model

1. INTRODUCTION

Sponsored search has become an important channel of efficient online advertisement and is a multi-billion dollar industry today. It provides value to advertisers and users by providing targeted advertising, and is the major source of revenue for search engines.

Copyright is held by the International World Wide Web Conference Committee (IW3C2). IW3C2 reserves the right to provide a hyperlink to the author's site if the Material is used in electronic media.
WWW 2013, May 13–17, 2013, Rio de Janeiro, Brazil.
ACM 978-1-4503-2035-1/13/05.

Each time a user issues a search query on a web search engine such as Google or Bing, an auction is invoked among advertisers who bid for the search query phrase and the winning ads appear alongside the corresponding 'organic' search results. See Figure 1 for an overview of the sponsored search process.

The auctions are conducted amongst advertisers where winners are determined according to their scores given by: $\text{Score}(L) = \text{bid}(L) \times \text{pclick}(L, Q)$, where $\text{Score}(L)$ is the score of ad L for the auction of query Q, $\text{bid}(L)$ is the bid of L, and $\text{pclick}(L, Q)$ is the predicted Click Through Rate (CTR), i.e., the probability that ad L is clicked when shown to the user in response to query Q. Typically, CTR (or $\text{pclick}(L, Q)$) is estimated by using a learning algorithm such as the one proposed in [5]; these algorithms continuously adjust their estimates of pclick according to the observed click patterns.

Sponsored search is a dynamic process where the set of advertisers and ads change continuously, and the query traffic demonstrate substantial temporal, seasonal and geographic variations (e.g. holiday season, events in news etc. can lead to big fluctuations in traffic volumes of specific queries). This makes it hard for advertisers to set bid values to achieve their objectives (e.g., advertisers may want to maximize the number of impressions/clicks for a given budget). Many advertisers, especially small-scale ones, do not set bids effectively and often end up with left-over budgets. A tool that forecasts the number of impressions, average position and clicks for an ad, given a bid value would therefore be of very useful to advertisers. An estimate of the number of impressions, together with the pclick estimate using methods like [5] would give us an estimate for the number of clicks for the ad. Thus, one of the main challenges that needs be addressed is accurate estimation for the number of impressions of an ad given its bid value. This is the problem we focus on in this paper.

The ad impressions forecasting problem is challenging for the following reasons: (1) Query traffic can be highly variable due to multiple reasons as previously discussed. (2) The set of advertisers and ads changes with time. Advertisers can change their bids; budget pauses and budgets running out are another source of uncertainty. (3) Pclick of an ad varies from auction to auction because of changing query features (e.g. time and location of the query), and also because the pclick estimation algorithm itself can introduce large variations.

Search engines generally have tools that replay past auctions with changing bids and show the result to the advertisers as a proxy for future estimates. This type of past replay makes an inherent simplifying assumption that the auctions in the future are exact replicas of the auctions in the logs. Because of the aforementioned challenges, these assumptions deviate widely in practice leading to errors and inconsistency due to heavy overfitting. There are also a few recent works addressing similar problems, e.g. [1, 3, 8]; we discuss these in some detail in Section 3. These works focus mostly on modeling how advertisers bid in auctions, and do not explicitly model the query traffic. As we show in Section 5 query traffic modeling is a critical component in impression prediction and ignoring it can lead to poor and inconsistent forecast.

In this work, we address the aforementioned challenges by taking a learning-centric view of the problem: our method models auctions by a generative model to avoid overfitting. Specifically, we use a Bayes net to model the query traffic component as well as the minimum score required to win the auction. Since most of the auction features are categorical or can be efficiently discretized, Bayes net can be easily trained and sampled to generate artificial auctions. Furthermore, we parallelize Bayes net training using MapReduce; this parallelization is critical for deployment in real-life large scale systems.

For prediction, we generate artificial auctions using our Bayes net. We then assess win or loss for the ad in each auction to determine the total number of impressions. A crucial issue here is the estimation of the number of samples to be generated from Bayes net. We use a first order dynamic linear model trained on past keyword traffic trends to this end.

We conduct experiments on a substantial portion of traffic from Bing[1] and evaluate performance of our method against two well-known existing methods according to several criteria. Our empirical results demonstrate significantly improved and consistent forecasts on multiple criteria compared to the existing methods. Specifically, our method achieves up to 20% more accuracy than the existing methods and can predict for up to 33% more ads than one of the baseline methods. Furthermore, our method is highly scalable and can be deployed in a real-life system. Our offline training phase takes about four to five hours using standard production architecture, while prediction for advertisers can be provided in real time (online) using pre-computed impression values.

2. PRELIMINARIES AND NOTATION

In this section, we formally introduce the setting of sponsored search auctions.

Following standard terminology, we refer to an ad in sponsored search setting as a listing and denote it by L. Traffic features of a user query are denoted by Q; this includes features such as location, category, and time of the query. $\text{bid}(L)$ denotes the bid value of listing L and $\text{pclick}(L,Q)$ denotes the estimated probability of click on listing L when a user makes query with features Q.

In sponsored search, the ad serving engine conducts an auction for every user query. For each such query phrase, advertisers compete with pre-set bids and the score for each ad L is given by:

$$\text{Score}(L,Q) = \text{bid}(L) \times \text{pclick}(L,Q). \qquad (1)$$

$\text{pclick}(L,Q)$ is estimated using a learning algorithm that uses several features from the query Q such as the traffic features mentioned above and also features from the listing L and the associated advertiser; see [5] for more details.

After computing the score of each listing for a given query, the scores are sorted and at most k listings with highest scores are selected, where k is a parameter set by the search engine and can vary across auctions. Out of these k, only those with scores greater than a reserve score (again a parameter set by the search engine) are selected. There may be additional criteria to further prune this list of ads. If an advertiser's ad is clicked by the user in auction Q, then the advertiser makes a payment to the search engine. This payment is calculated by the GSP method [4]:

$$\text{Payment}(L_i, Q) = \frac{\text{Score}(L_{i+1}, Q)}{\text{pclick}(L_i, Q)},$$

where L_{i+1} is the listing after L_i in the sorted scores list.

3. RELATED WORK

Ads impression forecasting in sponsored search has recently become an important tool, hosted by search engines. The goal is to help advertisers bid appropriately to achieve their return over investment (ROI). Although, the tool is heavily used in practice, there has been little research addressing this problem.

Notable exceptions are the works by Athey and Nekipelov [1] and Pin and Key [8]. Both of these papers assume a probabilistic model on the given ads' competitors' score. They learn parameters of such model using training data and generate and simulate auctions to determine number of impressions. In particular, Pin and Key [8] assume that the "normalized scores" ($ns(L', Q) = \text{bid}(L') \times \text{pclick}(L', Q)/\text{pclick}(L,Q)$) of all the competitor ads L' are sampled i.i.d. from a fixed distribution (where L is the ad for which we are doing the prediction). Now to predict the slot in which L will appear in an auction, we just need to check for how many ads L', we have $\text{bid}(L) < \text{bid}(L') \times \text{pclick}(L', Q)/\text{pclick}(L,Q)$ (which is same as $\text{bid}(L) \times \text{pclick}(L,Q) < \text{bid}(L')\text{pclick}(L', Q)$, i.e., $\text{Score}(L) < \text{Score}(L')$). For a given bid $\text{bid}(L)$, one can then derive the expected number of impressions and clicks. Note, however, that there are issues with the assumptions in this model: For instance, the assumptions that the scores have the same distribution across auctions do not hold in practice. Normalized scores have $\text{pclick}(L,Q)$ in the denominator, and $\text{pclick}(L,Q)$ tends to be highly variable, thus affecting all the normalized scores and introducing correlations.

The Athey and Key [1] model is similar but more involved and detailed and also computationally more demanding. [1] show that the distributional assumptions actually lead to simplification in the set of equilibria (compared to the results in [4, 9]) and can even lead to unique equilibrium under certain conditions. [1, 8] can also infer advertiser's value per click assuming that they bid optimally. In accuracy, [1] does just slightly better.

Duong and Lahaie [3] use discrete choice analysis, a technique developed in econometrics, for the problem of inferring advertiser's

---

[1]Exact percentages are not provided for confidentiality reasons.

value per click. Using the estimated values they can predict how many clicks and impressions an ad will receive in the near future. They, however, require that the ad in question be present in the training week. Their experimental results show accuracy somewhat comparable to [8] in predicting the number of clicks.

Recently, similar problems have also been addressed in the other online advertising paradigms, namely, contextual and display advertising. For contextual ads, Wang et al. [10] propose a method for impression forecasting based on replay of past auctions with the given advertisement. When adapted to sponsored search domain, their approach reduces to *Training Week Replay* (TWR); we empirically evaluate our method against TWR (see Section 5). Also note that, the efficient search strategies proposed by [10] do not apply to our problem as the number of "published" pages are significantly larger for sponsored search than for contextual ads domain.

For display ads, Cui et al. [2] propose a method for impression forecasting based on Gradient Boosted Decision Trees. However, the display ads and sponsored search settings are significantly different: In the display ads setting there are a small number of possible "targettings" for which bid landscape needs to be learned, hence there is enough data to learn a regression model for each parameter setting. In contrast, in sponsored search, the number of possible "parameters" or "targettings" is extremely large (due to large number of query strings and also large number of contexts that give rise to the query strings), hence a reliable regression model cannot be learned for each parameter.

Further pointers to the literature can be found in the above cited papers. In this paper, we will show that our result compare favorably with those of [8]. This will also mean that our results compare favorably with those of [1, 3].

4. METHODOLOGY

In this section, we first describe the problem of ad impression forecasting and then provide our proposed method for this problem.

Ad impression forecasting problem: Given an advertiser A and its advertisement (or listing) L, and a bid value bid(L), the goal of ad impression forecasting is to predict the number of impressions L is likely to obtain in a fixed amount of time in future. For simplicity of exposition and for several practical reasons, we assume that the prediction is made for next 1 week [2]. The training data available for our forecasting problem are auction logs that contain information about all auctions from the recent past, such as, query traffic features, scores of the winners etc.

For the above mentioned problem, our method learns a generative models for auctions, in which the given listing L participates. For modeling, we view an auction (in which the given listing L participates) as a tuple of: 1) features of the query for which the auction is held, 2) competitors' scores, 3) score for the given listing L. Below, we further explain the above mentioned aspects of an auction that we model:

- **Query**: Search engines typically extract several features from a user query. For example, features can include the location where query originated from, time of the query, category of the query, keywords in the query etc. These query traffic features form an important component of auctions because both competitors' score as well as listing L's score depend heavily on these features. For example, suppose listing L got several clicks from users in New York. Hence, if the query originates from New York then the pclick of L would tend to be high, leading to high score for L in those auctions.

---
[2]most of the existing ad impression forecasting tools also forecast for a time period of 1 week

To accurately model auctions for a particular query phrase, we model the query traffic features associated with these auctions. Due to ease of exposition, we focus on queries that contain only a single auction key-phrase[3]. For example, for a query "New York Hotels", only advertisers who bid for "New York Hotels" participate in the auctions.

- **Competitor's score**: We model the scores of "typical" competitors to the given listing L. Note that for predicting the number of impressions, we need to predict whether or not an advertisement will "win" a given auction, i.e., predict the minimum score required to win a given auction. Hence, we model the **minimum score** required to win an auction. The minimum score takes into account various factors such as bids and pclicks of the competitors, the number of winners, as well as the reserve score and other filtering criteria.

As mentioned above, to determine if the given listing L wins a generated auction, we also need to generate the score of L. We would like to stress that we **do not** model pclick. Instead, we compute the score by multiplying the provided bid value and the pclick value estimated using the pclick estimation module in production. However, typically, pclick estimation modules evolve with time. That is, at different time instances, pclick of a listing in an auction for the same query feature set can vary greatly. Hence, we use the pclick values from the latest version of the production modules as a proxy for the real run-time values. Recall that we are not trying to solve the problem of estimating pclick accurately; rather, our focus is on forecasting how a listing will fare under the existing sponsored search engine.

Next, we describe the generative model we use to model auctions in which the given listing L participates. To this end, we use a Bayes net model where each node of Bayes net corresponds to either a query traffic feature or the **minimum score** required to win the auction.

Bayes net is a popular method for modeling a set of correlated random variables or features [6]. Bayes net is represented by a directed acyclic graph (DAG) where every node of the DAG is a random variable or a query feature in our system. Edges between different nodes capture conditional dependencies between different nodes. Specifically, it satisfies the Markovian property that given its parents, a node is independent of all the other nodes that are not its descendants in the Bayes net. That is,

$$Pr(v_i|F_i) = Pr(v_i|G_i),$$

where $F_i = \{v_j | v_i \text{ is a child of } v_j\}$ and $G_i = \{v_k | v_k \text{ is not a descendant of } v_i\}$. Now, any member of the joint distribution can be computed using the above property. Hence, to train a Bayes net, we just need to estimate $Pr(v_i|F_i)$ at each node v_i.

Why Bayes net?: Bayes net is particularly effective for categorical data as the discrete conditional probability tables (CPT) at each node can then be easy formed and manipulated to draw samples or inferences. As all of our query traffic features are categorical, and the **minimum score** can also be discretized easily, we select Bayes net to model auctions. Also, training Bayes net on categorical data is a counting process that can be efficiently implemented on a Map-reduce framework. Further, by restricting the form that joint probability distribution can take, Bayes net helps avoid overfitting to the training data. This is particularly useful for modeling auctions generated from "tail" queries, i.e., queries with a small number of searches.

---
[3]We use the terms key-phrase and keyword interchangeably.

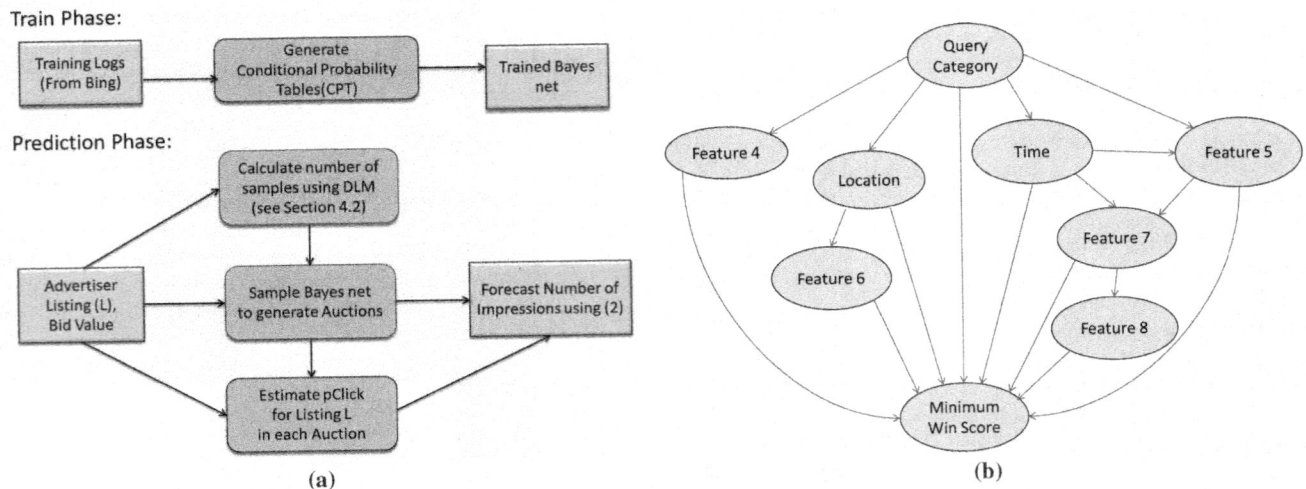

Figure 2: a) Overview of the training as well as prediction phase of our Generative Model based Ad Impression Forecasting Method (GMIF). In training phase, GMIF uses training logs to generate conditional probability tables (CPT) for each node in the Bayes net. During prediction, given a listing L and its bid value, GMIF samples the learned Bayes net to generate auctions. Number of samples required is determined by the DLM module. pclick of L for each generated auction is estimated using latest production module. Using the provided bid value and estimated pclick, GMIF computes score of L in each auction and forecasts number of impressions using (2). b) A sample Bayes net to model Auctions in Sponsored Search

Figure 2 (b) shows a sample Bayes net that we use. We do not reveal query traffic features due to confidentiality reasons. The **Minimum score** of the auction is a child node of each query traffic feature node, implying that the minimum score directly depends on all the traffic features.

As mentioned above, for training Bayes net, we estimate CPT for each node using training logs. We train one Bayes net per keyword. As the number of keywords and volume of auctions is large in a real-life sponsored search system, we use MapReduce framework to efficiently compute CPTs (see Section 4.2).

Next, for forecasting, given a listing L, we use Bayes net trained for its bidded keyword to generate sample auctions. The number of auctions to be sampled is estimated using a Dynamic Linear Model (DLM) based method that we discuss later in Section 4.1.1. After generating the sample auctions, we put listing L in each auction and estimate its pclick value for that auction using the latest production module of pclick generator. Next, using the provided bid value bid(L) we compute Score(L, Q) in each auction and compute the total number of impressions by comparing against minimum win score for the auction.

Formally, let M_L be the estimated number of auctions to be generated for the listing L. Let the set of auctions be: $\mathcal{A} = \{A_1, A_2, \ldots, A_{M_L}\}$, where $A_i = \{Q_i, MS_i\}$, Q_i consists of the query features for the auction A_i and MS_i is the minimum score needed to win A_i. Let the estimated pclick of L in A_i be denoted by pclick(L, Q_i), $\forall 1 \leq i \leq M_L$. Then, the total number of impressions is given by:

$$\text{Impressions}(L) = |\{i \mid \text{bid}(L) \times \text{pclick}(L, Q_i) \geq MS_i\}|. \quad (2)$$

See Figure 2 (a) for an overview of training and prediction phases.

Note that the predicted number of impressions critically depends on M_L, the estimated number of auctions that L will participate in test week. Estimation of M_L is challenging due to two key issues: 1) The number of searches for a given query can vary heavily across different time periods. This effect is especially prominent amongst "tail" queries that are popular for a short amount of time.

For example, queries for a movie name peaks during the week of release and then drops significantly in subsequent weeks. Seasonal trends can also affect volumes of searches for a query, 2) A listing L may not participate in each auction for its bidded keyword due to several reasons. For example, an advertiser might like to target specific segment of users. Also, the sponsored search engine might filter out an ad due to its low relevance for a specific user query or to introduce randomization to do explore-exploit.

4.1 Estimation of The Number of Auctions

In this section, we describe our method for estimation of the number of auctions in which the given listing L is likely to participate in the test week. As mentioned above, prediction of the number of auctions in which L is likely to participate is challenging due to the variability in query traffic and several other factors such as exhaustion of budget, filtering by search engine etc.

To handle these challenges, we decouple the problem into two problems: 1) determine the number of searches in the test week for L's bidded keyword, 2) determine the participation ratio for L, i.e., the fraction of auctions in which L is likely to participate.

For the first problem, our approach is to model the volume of searches for a keyword as a time series and use the first order Dynamic Linear Model (DLM)—a well-known forecasting algorithm—to forecast the next point in the time series. We present details in the next subsection. For the second problem, we estimate participation ratio for each individual listing L using training logs. We present details in Section 4.1.2.

After solving these two problems, i.e., after estimation of the total number of searches and the participation ratio of L, we obtain the number of auctions M_L that L is likely to participate in in the test week using: $M_L = N \times \gamma_L$, where N is the estimated number of searches in the test week for L's bidded keyword, and γ is the estimated participation ratio of L.

4.1.1 Dynamic Linear Model (DLM)

In this section, we describe our method for estimating the number of searches a keyword is likely to obtain in the test week. As mentioned in the previous section, we use the first order DLM over the time series of the number of searches in each week.

Formally, to form the time series, we divide the time axis into bins, each of size one week. Then using logs, we compute the number of searches for each keyword in each week. Let N_t denote the number of searches in the t-th week for the bidded keyword corresponding to listing L. Also, let $1 \leq t \leq T$ where T is the test week for which we want to forecast the number of auctions.

We train the DLM using $\{N_1, \ldots, N_t, \ldots N_{T-1}\}$ and predict the number of searches in the T-th (test) week. Below, we briefly describe the first order DLM based method for time series forecasting; see [11] for more details.

The use of the first order DLMs for prediction of keyword traffic is motivated by the observation that traffic patterns are short lived and DLMs are especially well-suited for such short horizon forecasts. Assuming first order DLM, the number of searches of a particular keyword at time t is given by:

$$N_t = \mu_t + \nu_t, \nu_t \sim \mathcal{N}(0, V),$$
$$\mu_t = \mu_{t-1} + \omega_t, \omega_t \sim \mathcal{N}(0, W), \quad (3)$$

where μ_t is the internal "state" of the series, $V, W > 0$ are constants, and $\mathcal{N}(0, V)$ is the Gaussian distribution with mean 0 and variance V. We assume that $\mu_0 \sim \mathcal{N}(0, C_0)$, where $C_0 > 0$ is a constant.

Now, using the above mentioned model, the following update equations can be easily derived:

$$(N_t | N_1, \ldots, N_{t-1}) \sim \mathcal{N}(m_{t-1}, C_{t-1} + V + W),$$
$$m_t = m_{t-1} + \frac{C_{t-1} + W}{C_{t-1} + W + V}(N_{t-1} - m_{t-1}),$$
$$C_t = \frac{(C_{t-1} + W)V}{C_{t-1} + W + V}, \quad (4)$$

where $m_0 = 0$. N_t is a random variable that corresponds to the number of searches of a given keyword; we abuse notation and denote the t-th observed value also as N_t.

For prediction, we sample $(N_t | N_1, \ldots, N_{t-1})$ using (4), while m_t, C_t are then updated using the observed value for N_t. We fix up the parameters to $W = 20, V = 50, C_0 = 100$; these values are selected using cross-validation over four weeks of data.

4.1.2 Estimation of Participation Ratio

In this section, we describe our method for estimating the participation ratio γ_L of a given listing L which is defined as the ratio of the number of auctions in which L participates in the T-th (test) week to the total number of auctions for L's bidded keyword.

Note that, in real-life systems, a listing typically does not participate in all the auctions (of its bidded keyword) due to several reasons such as budget constraints, advertiser specified targeting constraints, filtering by the sponsored search system etc. For example, if the budget of a listing is finished then it cannot participate in the future auctions for the relevant keyword. Similarly, advertisers can provide certain constraints so as to target a particular group of users only. Consequently, in practice, the participation ratio tends to be very small for several listings. Hence, estimating participation ratio γ_L is a crucial component for our method.

Note that, similar to the previous section, we can try to estimate γ_L, the participation ratio of a listing L, using time series forecasting methods. However, time span of most of the listings is a couple of weeks and hence we cannot train the DLM accurately for this problem.

To handle this problem, we make a simplifying assumption that γ_L remains constant over time; we verify the assumption over multiple weeks of real-life data. Using this assumption, we estimate γ_L by using training logs. That is, we compute the total number of wins for L in the training week and divide it by the total number of auctions that L participates in training week.

Note that the above mentioned method to compute participation ratio of L applies to the existing listings only, i.e, listings present in the logs. This poses a problem for new listings: listings that were not present in the logs in the training week. New listings themselves can be further categorized into: a) new listing by an existing advertiser, b) new listing by a *new* advertiser. Note that for the later category, no information is available to estimate participation ratio. Hence, for these listings we use a constant participation ratio, obtained by cross-validation. However, for existing advertisers, γ_L is set to be mean of the participation ratio existing listings of the same advertiser campaign. That is,

$$\gamma_L = \frac{\sum_{L_A \in \mathcal{L}_A} \gamma_{L_A}}{|\mathcal{L}_A|},$$

where $\mathcal{L}_A$ is the set of all listings in the given campaign by advertiser A which also contains listing L. Now, note that rather than computing γ_L using the above equation, we can use a constant value for γ_L. The later extension to our method, that uses constant γ_L, is referred to as GMIF-Const. For clarity, we call our former method (that uses participation ratios of other listings from the same advertiser) as GMIF-Adv. For a given advertiser campaign, typically targeting and budget allocation are same across all listings. Hence, GMIF-Adv is able to exploit information from other listings from the same campaign. Our empirical results confirm this observation as ad impression forecasts by GMIF-Adv are significantly more accurate than GMIF-Const, which ignores information from other listings of the same advertiser (see Section 5.4.2).

4.2 Large-scale Deployment

In this section, we discuss some of the issues that arise while implementing our methodology in a real-life large scale sponsored search system.

Recall that, our method proceed in two phases: 1) training, 2) prediction. For training, we generate conditional probability distribution for each edge of our Bayes net. Then, for prediction, given a listing, we sample the Bayes net to generate auctions using which we estimate the number of impressions.

Now, while training is offline, it is computationally expensive as cardinalities of some of our features is large leading to large conditional probability distribution tables (CPT). To scale to real-life sponsored search systems, we use MapReduce framework to estimate CPT from raw logs. Specifically, suppose we want to estimate the following CPT: $P(v_i | F_i)$ where $F_i = \{v_j | v_i \text{ is a child of } v_j\}$. First we find out all the unique values each $j \in F_i$ can take. Then, we *Reduce* on each combination of unique values of nodes in F_i and find the probability distribution of v_i using the obtained records. Such a scheme can be implemented easily in any standard MapReduce framework. We then use generated CPTs to construct conditional cumulative distribution functions (CDF) of each node variable. Obtained CDFs simplify and speed up the sampling process.

Next, we consider the the prediction phase of our method. Note that, this step is online, and hence requires real-time response. Consequently, we cannot sample Bayes net online to generate number of impressions. Instead, we pre-compute number of impressions

Table 1: Averaged data statistics for three train-test week combinations.

Statistics	Train	Test	Common
No. of Keywords	38991	37959	33428
No. of Listings	365187	350400	248030
No. of Auctions	6638205	6265138	Not Applicable

at all possible bid values (at small increments). Hence, when an advertiser asks for a forecast, we perform simple look-up to return predicted number of impressions at the supplied bid value. Note that if a listing is not present in the logs, but the advertiser is present. Then, we can pre-compute number of impressions for the *advertiser* at all possible bid values and for all possible keywords. If the advertiser is also, not present, then we simply store pre-computed number of impressions for each *keyword*.

5. EXPERIMENTS

In this section, we present results from large scale experiments conducted over traffic logs obtained from Bing to evaluate our framework. The goal of this section is three-fold: 1) establish that our method outperforms existing methods on several accuracy criteria, 2) demonstrate increase in coverage (% of listings for which prediction is available) over a naive baseline method that replays the training logs, 3) demonstrate scalability of our method on real-life data.

5.1 Experimental Setup and Data Statistics

In this section, we present our experimental setup and some key statistics from the data.

For conducting experiments, we select one week as the unit of time. Our initial experiments showed that the latest weekly data provides more accurate information about trends and patterns in query traffic as well as about advertiser participation as opposed to data from longer or shorter periods. Thus using weekly data leads to best accuracies for all the methods.

For our experiments, we take a randomly sample around 40,000 search queries and select the auctions corresponding to those keywords from the training week logs (around 6.6 million). We select queries with at least 30 impressions in the training week, so that the Bayes net model can be trained with reasonable confidence. We also restrict our focus only on the listings that requires exact match between the bidded keyword and the query.

We call listings appearing in both training and test weeks *existing-listings*, while listings appearing in the test week but were not present in the training week are termed *new-listings*. Table 1 presents a few basic data statistics averaged over three train and test week combinations.

5.2 Implementation Details

In this section, we provide implementation details of our method as well as the existing methods against which we evaluate our method.

As shown in the Table 1, the data that we consider for our experiments is large scale and cannot possibly be processed using stand alone machines. Hence, to evaluate our method, we implemented a production grade prototype of our method as well as existing methods on a proprietary MapReduce platform. We use a total of nine traffic/query related features to construct the Bayes net. While the number of features considered is reasonably small, the cardinality of features tends to be very large with values up to 100,000s.

We generate the conditional probability tables (CPT) using MapReduce framework as explained in Section 4.2. We also use grid to sample the learned Bayes net for testing our method, which we call *Generative Model based Impression Forecasting (GMIF)*.

We evaluate our method against two existing methods: Training Week Replay (TWR), Normalized Bid Model (NBM) [8]. We implemented both the methods on production grid using a proprietary MapReduce platform.

TWR is a baseline method, and for a given listing L with a given bid value, it simply replays relevant auctions from training week logs. That is, it extracts out all the auctions that L participated in training week logs and compute new score for the given listing L using $Score(L, Q) = pclick(L, Q) \times Newbid(L)$, where $Newbid(L)$ is the new bid provided for listing L. TWR then simulates the auctions with new scores, computes total number of winning auctions, and forecasts it as the number of impressions for L. Note that, as TWR replays exact logs from training weeks, the participation and pclick information is not available for new-listings. Hence, this method cannot predict for new listings.

Another method that we use to evaluate our method is an adaptation of the Normalized Bid Model (NBM) by [8]. While there exist a few other approaches in literature, e.g. [1], [3], we select NBM for evaluation as it performs better or similar to the other approaches; see [8] and [3] for comparisons of these approaches. Additionally, NBM is a scalable and easy to implement approach. NBM assumes that competitor listings' "normalized scores" (defined below) are i.i.d. across listings as well as auctions.

$$\text{Normalized Score}(L') = \text{Score}(L')/\text{pclick}(L').$$

In our implementation, we sample this distribution to generate scores for competitors while generating pclick using the prediction module in production.

5.3 Evaluation Metrics

In this section, we describe various evaluation metrics we use to compare different methods. For reporting results, similar to [8], we first bin the listings according to the actual number of impressions obtained in the test week. We form four bins in all and name them as *Bin 1*, *Bin 2*, *Bin 3*, *Bin 4*. The bins are ordered in increasing order of number of impressions, *Bin 1* representing the lowest volumes, *Bin 2* representing the next highest, and so on. We do not disclose exact ranges of these bins due to confidentiality reasons.

We adopt the following metrics to evaluate performance of each method:

Relative Error (RE): Relative error of a listing is given by: $RE = \frac{|predicted-actual|}{actual}$, where $predicted$ is the predicted number of impressions for the listing and $actual$ is the actual number of impressions in the test period. We report average relative error over all the test weeks listings. This is a standard metric in forecasting and was used by [8] and others.

Accuracy: We measure the accuracy of a method for a bin as the number of listings (in the bin considered) that have less than $\tau > 0$ relative error. That is,

$$\text{Accuracy}_\tau = \frac{|\text{Listings s.t. RE} \leq \tau|}{\text{Number of Listings}}. \quad (5)$$

τ is a threshold parameter, where smaller values of τ imply more stringent accuracy measures. We report results for different τ values; default value of τ is 0.5.

Accuracy measures percentage of listings for which the prediction is within a factor τ of the actual prediction. That is, it accounts for the volume of "reasonably good quality forecasts. Note that while using this measure, the very low impression bins will generally show poorer results. This is because of the low values of denominator. For example, assume a listing actually gets 2 impressions while the prediction was 4 for a specific bid value; the RE value for this item will be $+100\%$. The RE number in this case can be misleading since the absolute values are not greatly different. Higher impression bins do not face this problem and give results which are more accurately indicative of the true quality and are important because they belong to bigger advertisers with more budget to spend on their campaigns. Thus while using this measure, though we will provide numbers for both the high and low impression bins, we will specially focus more on the accuracy numbers for the higher impression bins to gain fair insight into the quality of our predictions.

We also report overall accuracy of methods across bins as well as bin-wise averaged accuracies, i.e., average of accuracy obtained in each bin.

F-measure: We report the F-measure to compensate for the deficiencies of the Accuracy metric in lower impression bins. Given the pre-defined bins on actual impressions, we calculate the true positives (predictions in the specific bin and actuals in the same bin too: tp), false positives (predictions fall in the bin but actuals lie in some other bin: fp) and false negatives (predictions made outside of the bin but actuals fall in the specific bin: fn) for each of the bins. The precision and recall for each bin is then calculated as $Pr = \frac{tp}{tp+fp}$ and $Re = \frac{tp}{tp+fn}$ respectively. We also calculate the F-measure which is the harmonic mean of precision and recall: $F = \frac{2Pr \cdot Re}{Pr+Re}$. F-measure is a well known performance measure and is widely used in a number of domains like information retrieval [7].

We also report the additional number of new listings we can predict which did not appear in training week. New listings can be further categorized into: 1) both the advertiser and the keyword were present in the training data but the listing is new to the system, 2) only the corresponding keyword was available in the training data and the advertiser (and so also the listing) is new to the system. We report accuracy and other metrics for both the categories and show that our methods can effectively exploit information available from the advertiser's other listings.

Note that we can measure metrics mentioned in this section for only those listings which do not change their bids in the entire test week window. If a listing changes bid during test week, then it is not clear which bid value to select for forecasting impressions. However, we observe that approximately 80% of the listings do not change bids, hence we can report results over a substantial fraction of listings.

5.4 Results

In this section, we report results of several experiments with multiple weeks of data for evaluating forecasts from our method against existing methods. We use evaluation metrics described in the previous section to compare different methods. Recall that, we name our method as Generative Model based Impression Forecasting (GMIF), a baseline method as Test Week Replay (TWR), and the method by [8] as Normalized Bid Model (NBM). Also, recall that, for reporting results, we bin the listings into four bins: *Bin 1, Bin 2, Bin 3, Bin 4*.

5.4.1 Existing Listings

Here, we report results regarding forecast of impressions for existing listings, i.e., the listings that are present in both training and test week logs. For our experiments, we obtain data from logs of a recent month that shows considerable fluctuations in traffic volume of keywords and distribution of traffic parameters due to reasons such as shopping season surges. As the traffic volume and patterns change week by week, the results clearly bring out the advantages of our method (generative modeling and short horizon time trending) compared to the others.

First, we present average accuracies (see Section 5.1) obtained by all the three methods. Figure 3 compares the average accuracies of the three methods in each of the four bins for $\tau = 0.3, 0.5, 0.6$. The bins are arranged on the axis in order of increasing test week actual impressions. As mentioned earlier, the boundaries of the bins could not be revealed due to confidentiality reasons. Figure 3 also reports the accuracy variances across the multiple test weeks considered. Clearly, our method GMIF outperforms both TWR and NBM in terms of average accuracy for all bins for all threshold values except for Bin 1 with $\tau = 0.3$. GMIF also consistently achieves the lowest variance. NBM approach outperforms TWR in all bins except for the lowest one.

Hence, our method is more accurate as well as more consistent than the existing methods. We believe, low variance is due to our more principled generative model based approach to modeling auctions in comparison to other methods that are prone to overfitting to the training data. Note that although NBM models competitor scores by a simplifying assumption, it assumes exactly the same number of auctions as the past week and uses exactly the same query traffic.

Next, in Table 2, we report the overall accuracy across all the bins (weighted by the number of listings) as well as the accuracy averaged over all the bins (unweighted averaging). Clearly, our method achieves significantly higher accuracy than both TWR and NBM. In term of overall accuracy, GMIF is approximately 7% and 19% more accurate than TWR and NBR, respectively. Similarly, in terms of bin-wise accuracy, GMIF is around 12% and 15% more accurate than TWR and NBM, respectively. Bin-wise accuracy is a widely used metric, but it is particularly useful for the sponsored search scenario as it takes into account the effect of heavy tail distribution of impressions (i.e., many impressions in Bin 1) as well, which is typical to sponsored search.

Method	Overall Accuracy	Bin-wise Accuracy
NBM	0.24	0.35
TWR	0.38	0.38
GMIF	0.45	0.50

Table 2: Overall and bin-wise accuracy ($\tau = 0.5$) for different methods. Our method (GMIF) is at least 7% more accurate (according to overall accuracy) than NBM and TWR.

Now, observe that in Figure 3, the accuracy in the lowest impression bucket (Bin 1) is poor for all the methods. Reason being, in Bin 1, due to small number of actual impressions, the denominator (actual) values in calculating RE are small that leads to large RE. As discussed earlier, this is an inherent drawback of any relative error based metric. To alleviate this problem, we also report F-measure obtained within each bin by the three methods considered. Figure 4 (a) reports the average F-measures for the three methods and also show variance in F-measure for each of the method. Here again, our method (GMIF) consistently outperforms the other methods in all the bins. However, we note that for the F-measure metric, TWR outperforms NBM in all the bins consistently and is closer to GMIF across all the bins.

5.4.2 New Listings

Here, we compare different methods for their predictions on new listings, listings that are present in the test week logs but not in the training week logs. We did similar set of experiments on new listings as on the existing ones and used the same metrics to com-

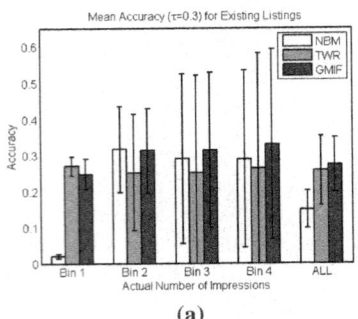 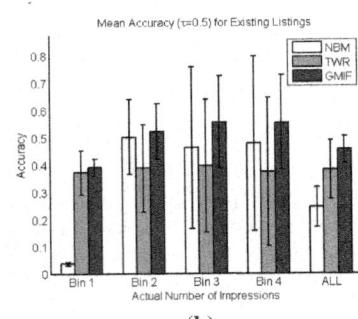 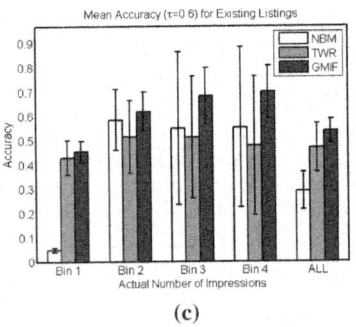

Figure 3: Average accuracy with different thresholds for existing listings: a) $\tau = 0.3$, b) $\tau = 0.5$, c) $\tau = 0.6$. X-axis represents actual number of impressions in test data, and is divided in four bins. Bin "ALL" represents all the listings, irrespective of the number of impressions. Our method (GMIF) consistently obtains higher accuracy than both NBM and TWR, while obtaining smallest variance of the three methods across all bins and all threshold τ values.

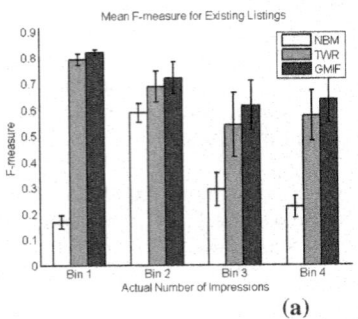 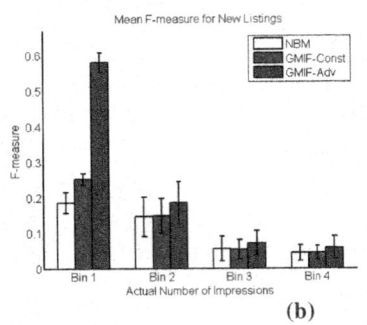

Method	Overall Accuracy	Bin-wise Accuracy
NBM	0.05	0.19
GMIF-Const	0.05	0.21
GMIF-Adv	0.15	0.24

Figure 4: a) Average F-measure for Existing Listings. Our method obtains around 15% higher F-measure than TWR and about 25% higher than NBM, in Bin 2 which forms the torso of the impression range and is one of the most interesting bins for real systems. b) Average F-measure for New Listings. GMIF-Adv obtains 32% higher F-measure than GMIF-Const and 31% higher F-measure than NBM. c) Overall and bin-wise accuracy ($\tau = 0.5$) for different methods for new listings.

pare different approaches. Since the Training Week Replay (TWR) method uses logs to determine pclick as well as participation information, we cannot use it to predict for new listings. However, we can use our adaptation of the NBM method of [8] in this case.

Recall that new listings can be further divided into: 1) listings whose advertiser was present in the past week, 2) listings with new advertisers. As explained in Section 4.1.2, our method can be adapted to both of these categories. We refer to our extension of GMIF method that uses advertiser information as GMIF-Adv, while the GMIF method adaptation that does not use advertiser information is referred to as GMIF-Const.

Figure 5 shows the average accuracy in each bin obtained by NBM as well as our GMIF-Const and GMIF-Adv method for $\tau = 0.3, 0.5, 0.6$. Note that while GMIF-Const and GMIF-Adv perform essentially equally well for the higher impression bins, GMIF-Adv does distinctly better in the lowest bucket which indicates that advertiser specific information plays a significant role in determining the number of impressions for listings with small impression volume (tail listings). The figure also shows that both the GMIF approaches almost always give higher average accuracies and lower variances compared to the NBM approach.

Similar to the previous section, we also report overall accuracies and bin-wise mean accuracies for NBF and our GMIF methods (see Figure 4 (c)). Here again, GMIF-Adv outperforms the other methods in both the measures. The gain in overall accuracy is substantially higher compared to the gain in bin-wise accuracy measure.

Figure 4 (b) shows the corresponding F-measures for the three approaches in different bins. Note that while considering this metric, GMIF-Adv performs consistently better compared to NBM and

Table 3: Decrease in average Relative Error w.r.t. Baseline NBM method.

Method	Bin 1	Bin 2	Bin 3	Bin 4	ALL
GMIF-Const	5.20	11.99	16.54	16.47	5.66
GMIF-Adv	36.38	23.03	18.63	22.04	36.49

GMIF-Const which perform almost similar for the higher impression bins.

For new listings we also report gain in relative error for both the GMIF approaches compared to NBM in each bin (see Table 3). This metric clearly, shows that our methods are significantly better than NBM in each bin and overall. It also corroborates the fact that GMIF-Adv achieves maximum relative gain in the lower bins where we observed that the influence of advertiser campaign information is a crucial factor in predicting impressions (see Section 4.1.2).

5.4.3 Dynamic Linear Model

In this subsection we take a deeper look at the accuracy of our traffic prediction module that is based on first order dynamic linear models. Note that the accuracy of this module in the entire architecture needs special attention since this predicts the number of sample auctions in which a listing will participate in the test period. Inaccuracy in this step should lead to a ripple effect on the error as it magnifies inaccuracies of the overall impression forecasts. As mentioned in Section 4.1.1, we learn a DLM for each keyword using past 6 week traffic volumes as time series points. We then tune the DLM parameters for optimality using cross validation over mul-

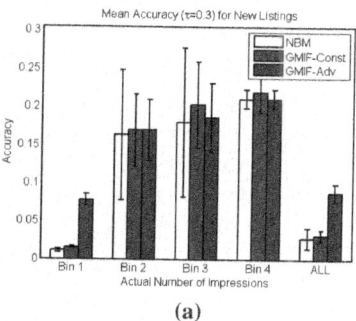 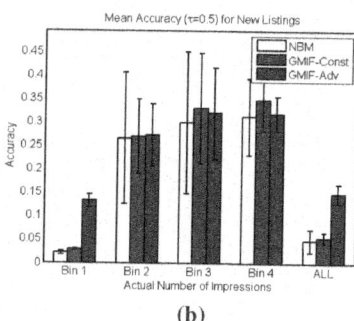 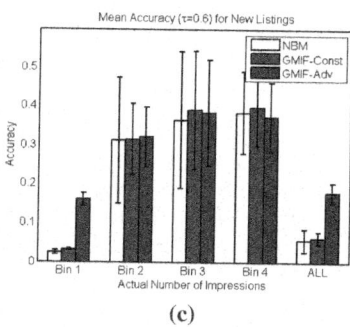

Figure 5: Average accuracy with different thresholds for new listings: a) $\tau = 0.3$, b) $\tau = 0.5$, c) $\tau = 0.6$. GMIF-Const and GMIF-Adv are adaptations of our GMIF method to new listings, with main difference being that GMIF-Adv uses existing advertiser's information, while GMIF-Const ignores that information. Clearly, GMIF-Adv is significantly better than NBM and in Bin 1, outperforms GMIF-Const as well.

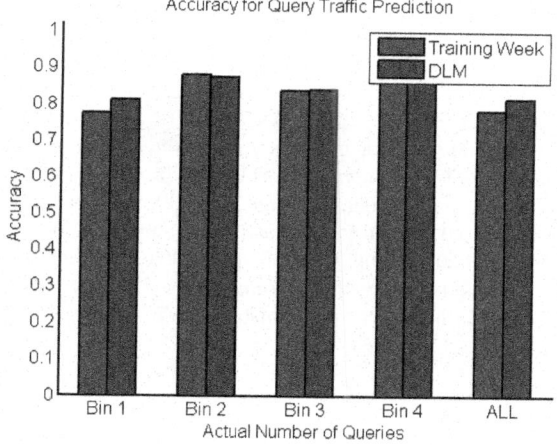

Figure 6: Average accuracy in traffic volume prediction (with $\tau = 0.3$). First order DLM based method achieves significantly higher accuracy than baseline method (using training week traffic volume as approximation to test week traffic volume), especially for Bin1 which constitutes 80% of the traffic.

tiple weeks of learning and use the trained and tuned models for prediction of traffic volumes of keywords. We report relative error/accuracy (defined in Section 5.3) to evaluate gains from using the DLM framework. We compare against a naive but a very effective method in practice: given a keyword assume its last week's traffic volume as the estimate for the next week's traffic volume. Note that both TWR and NBM methods obtain their number of samples using this baseline heuristic. Figure 6 reports the accuracy for the baseline (training week volume) and DLM prediction method with $\tau = 0.3$. We observe similar results for other values of τ. The Bins on the horizontal axis are indicative of real traffic ranges of the test week and are not disclosed for confidentiality reasons. The Bins are arranged in increasing order of test week actual traffic volume from Bin1 to Bin4. It can be observed from Figure 6 that DLM predictions overall show better results compared to the baseline method. Bin1 is of special interest as it represents torso and tail queries and contain around 80% of the total number of keywords. For this bin, our DLM based method is significantly better than baseline method (by 4%). These results show that first order DLMs can learn traffic volume trends reasonably well from only a few points in time series data. This is especially needed in our specific case since most torso and tail keywords have short lifecycles of existence (typically ranging from 6-8 weeks).

5.4.4 Run-times

Finally, in this section we report approximate time required by each step of our approach on a standard proprietary grid platform. For a substantial fraction of production data from Bing, our entire pipeline in offline mode takes approximately 260 mins to run end to end. We provide detailed average time breakups in Table 4

Table 4: Approximate Processing Time

Step	Processing time
Traffic Feature Extraction	192 mins
Train Bayes net	19 mins
DLM based Traffic Volume Prediction	10 mins
Sampling Auctions from Bayes net	12 mins
Simulation on artificial traffic	27 mins

The first row in the above table reports time required to extract query traffic features from raw logs. This time step is most expensive and takes about three hours. Next row shows time required for training the Bayes net. Fourth and fifth row shows the total time required to forecast number of impressions for all the advertisers, which is approximately one hour only. Hence, our method's training as well as pre-computation needed for real-time prediction finishes within only half a day.

6. DISCUSSION AND CONCLUSION

In this paper, we considered the problem of ad impression forecasting, which is critical in helping advertisers optimize their return on invest from sponsored search advertising.

Most of the existing methods view the problem from a game-theoretic point of view, where the goal is to model how competitor's for an ad are going to bid. But they mostly ignore or overfit to the query traffic information which, via pclick, also has a significant impact on the chances of an ad winning an auction. In this paper, we modeled the auctions holistically using a carefully designed Bayes net that captures explicitly the correlation between competitors' scores and query traffic features. Our empirical results corroborate our view that the interplay between the query traffic features and competitors' scores plays a significant role and needs to be captured using a detailed model.

While in this paper we focused on predicting the number of impressions, our method is flexible and allows for various extensions. For example, we can extend our method to estimate other performance indicators such as number of clicks, average position of an ad. Further, our current method is designed assuming that only advertisers who bid for the exact user query can participate in its auctions. However, in real-life systems, a listing can participate in the "related" keywords' auctions as well. For example, a listing that bids on "shoes" can participate in a user query "running shoes". We can extend our method to such cases by forming a mapping between the bidded keywords and user queries for an advertiser by using logs. In future, we plan to conduct rigorous experiments using our method's extension for such listings. Finally, we used a first order DLM to capture trends and momentary peaks in query search volume. However, the DLM ignores information about query traffic features and only focuses on the total number of searches. We plan to address this limitation using dynamic Bayes net, that smoothly vary conditional probability distributions over each edge. Bayes net also allows for feature targeting: For example, if the advertiser has a certain geographical area, or a demographic group to which they would like to advertise, then by fixing the corresponding nodes in the Bayes net, we can generate the traffic corresponding to the targeting.

Acknowledgements

We would like to thank A. Kumaran, Krishna Leela Poola, B. Ashok, and Sayan Pathak for several discussions that helped in shaping core ideas of the paper and also for detailed comments on an initial draft of the paper.

7. REFERENCES

[1] S. Athey and D. Nekipelov. A structural model of sponsored search advertising auctions. In *Technical report, Microsoft Research*, May 2010.

[2] Y. Cui, R. Zhang, W. Li, and J. Mao. Bid landscape forecasting in online ad exchange marketplace. In *KDD*, pages 265–273, 2011.

[3] Q. Duaong and S. Lahaie. Discrete choice models of bidder behavior in sponsored search. In *WINE*, 2011.

[4] B. Edelman, M. Ostrovsky, and M. Schwarz. Internet advertising and the generalized second price auction: Selling billions of dollars worth of keywords. *American Economic Review*, 97(1), March 2007.

[5] T. Graepel, J. Q. Candela, T. Borchert, and R. Herbrich. Web-scale bayesian click-through rate prediction for sponsored search advertising in microsoft's bing search engine. In *ICML*, pages 13–20, 2010.

[6] D. Koller and N. Friedman. *Probabilistic Graphical Models*. MIT Press, 2009.

[7] C. D. Manning, P. Raghavan, and H. Schtze. *Introduction to Information Retrieval*. Cambridge University Press, New York, NY, USA, 2008.

[8] F. Pin and P. Key. Stochastic variability in sponsored search auctions: observations and models. In *ACM Conference on Electronic Commerce*, pages 61–70, 2011.

[9] H. R. Varian. Position auctions. *International Journal of Industrial Organization*, 25 (6):1163–1178, 2007.

[10] X. Wang, A. Z. Broder, M. Fontoura, and V. Josifovski. A search-based method for forecasting ad impression in contextual advertising. In *WWW*, pages 491–500, 2009.

[11] M. West and J. Harrison. *Bayesian Forecasting and Dynamic Models*. Springer Series in Statistics, 1997.

Measurement and Modeling of Eye-mouse Behavior in the Presence of Nonlinear Page Layouts

Vidhya Navalpakkam   LaDawn Jentzsch   Rory Sayres

Sujith Ravi   Amr Ahmed   Alex Smola

{vidhyan,ladawn,sayres,sravi,amra}@google.com, alex@smola.org

ABSTRACT

As search pages are becoming increasingly complex, with images and nonlinear page layouts, understanding how users examine the page is important. We present a lab study on the effect of a rich informational panel to the right of the search result column, on eye and mouse behavior. Using eye and mouse data, we show that the flow of user attention on nonlinear page layouts is different from the widely believed top-down linear examination order of search results. We further demonstrate that the mouse, like the eye, is sensitive to two key attributes of page elements – their position (layout), and their relevance to the user's task. We identify mouse measures that are strongly correlated with eye movements, and develop models to predict user attention (eye gaze) from mouse activity. These findings show that mouse tracking can be used to infer user attention and information flow patterns on search pages. Potential applications include ranking, search page optimization, and UI evaluation.

Categories and Subject Descriptors

H.4.m [**Informations Systems Applications**]: Miscellaneous

General Terms

Design, Experimentation, Human Factors

Keywords

eye, mouse, web search, attention, measurement, prediction

1. INTRODUCTION

A decade ago, search pages were simple, text only and contained a linear listing of documents. Today, search pages are increasingly complex, with interactive elements, images and text in multiple colors, font sizes, and varying indentation; they include new multi-column layouts, and contain various page elements drawn from news, images, documents, maps and facts. *With multiple page elements competing for the user's attention, and attention being a limited resource, understanding which page elements get more or less atten-* *tion is important*, and has applications for ranking, search page optimization, and UI evaluation.

Previous studies of attention on search pages focused on the linear page layout (containing a single column of search results) and showed a Golden Triangle [14] of user attention[1] – where users pay most attention to the top-left of the page, and attention decreases as we move towards the right or bottom of the page. Related studies showed that users tend to scan the search page sequentially from top to bottom, giving rise to popular cascade models and their variants [6, 5]. Given that the search pages have become more complex since (both visually and content-wise), the question of whether the Golden Triangle and other previous findings on attention still hold is open.

Eye tracking has been the favored methodology for studying user attention on the web [9, 8, 7, 2, 3, 20]. It offers rich details on user attention by sampling eye gaze positions every 20ms or more frequently, and providing fairly accurate estimates of user eye gaze (<0.5-1° error, just a few pixels). On the flip side, commercial eye trackers are expensive ($15K upwards per piece), eye tracking is not scalable (typically performed in the lab with 10-30 participants), and it is not clear to what extent findings from eye tracking studies in controlled lab settings can generalize to user attention in the wild.

Recently, researchers have begun exploring whether a user's mouse activity can provide approximations to where the user is looking on the search results page. Previous studies have shown reasonable correlations between the eye and mouse for linear page layouts[2] [22, 12, 15]. In this paper, we conduct a lab study to test whether mouse tracks can be used to infer user attention on complex search pages with nonlinear page layouts. In particular, we test eye-mouse sensitivity to an element's position on the search page, and its relevance to the user's task. The main contributions of this paper are outlined below:

1. We present a lab study to test eye-mouse activity on linear search page layouts (containing one column of search results) and new nonlinear search page layouts

---

[1] in this paper, we use the term "user attention" to refer to those aspects of users' attention that can be *measured by the eye*. Note that attention itself is a more complex, cognitive process.

[2] We ignore ads in this study, and focus only on search results. Thus, linear layout here refers to a single column of search results.

(containing a rich informational panel on the top-right of the page), and demonstrate that the mouse, like the eye, is sensitive to the element's position on the search page in both layouts.
2. We demonstrate that both eye and mouse are sensitive to the element's relevance to the user's task.
3. We identify mouse measures that are most correlated with eye gaze.
4. We develop models that predict users' eye gaze reasonably well from their mouse activity (67% accuracy in predicting the fixated result element, with an error of upto one element).
5. We conclude with limitations of mouse tracking and why it may be a weak proxy for eye tracking, but cannot substitute it.

2. RELATED WORK
2.1 Relationship of eye and mouse signals

The relationship of eye and mouse movements have been explored both in lab studies and at scale. Rodden and colleagues [22] measured eye and mouse movements of 32 users performing search tasks in a lab setting. They identified multiple patterns of eye-mouse coordination, including the mouse following the eye in the x and y directions, marking a result, and remaining stationary while the eye inspected results. They found a general coordination between eye and mouse position, where the distribution of eye/mouse distances centered close to 0 pixels in both x and y directions.

Huang et al [15] extended these findings by examining variations in eye-mouse distance over time. They found that eye-mouse distances peaked around 600 ms after page load and decreased over time, and that the mouse tended to lag gaze by ≈700 ms on average. They classified cursor behaviors into discrete patterns – Inactive, Reading, Action, and Examining – and measured sizeable differences in mouse-cursor position and time spent engaging in different behaviors.

Because mouse-position signals can be collected at scale more readily than eye movements, recent work has focused on relating large-scale mouse signals to eye movements. One approach proposed by Lagun and Agichtein ("ViewSer"; [18]) involves presenting a search result page in which all elements are spatially blurred except the result containing the mouse cursor. The resulting patterns of mouse movement across results were found to correlate with eye tracking results obtained in a lab setting for the same queries.

Other work from Huang, Buscher and colleagues [17, 16, 4] compare eye and mouse tracking results from lab studies to large-scale logs data from a search engine, deployed both internally [17] and on an external sample of users [16, 4]. This work demonstrated that mouse-based data can be used to evaluate search result relevance, distinguish cases of "good" (user need-satisfying) and "bad" abandonment on web pages, and identify clusters of distinct search task strategies.

2.2 Predictive models

Several studies have developed predictive models of user attention, searcher behavior, or both, based on mouse data. Guo and Agichtein [10] collected mouse-movement data from searches at a university library, and were able to discriminate navigational from informational task intent. The authors also built a binary classifier to distinguish whether the mouse was within a specified radius from the eye (varied from 100 to 200 pixels), and showed that this model outperformed a simple baseline model which always guessed the majority category [12]. Huang et al [15] used eye and mouse movement data from a lab study to fit eye positions using a linear model based on extracted mouse interaction features. Their model demonstrated an improved eye gaze prediction (decreased RMS error in mouse-cursor distance in each direction, and Euclidean distance) over mouse data alone.

Mouse behavior has been used to model patterns of user search goals and strategies. Huang et al [16] incorporated mouse data from search logs into a Dynamic Bayesian Network model of searcher activity, using the positions of results that were hovered over but not clicked to provide a more robust measure of which results were evaluated. The searcher model incorporating these signals performed better (lower click perplexity metrics, measuring unexpected click patterns) than models without the signals. Guo and Agichtein [11] used mouse movements to classify hidden states representing searchers' search goals (researching versus conducting a purchase) or ad receptiveness (likely or unlikely to click on a relevant ad) and tested the performance of their model against data extracted from a user study, and user-provided data from a library system. The authors also developed a model of document relevance based on a combination of mouse activity on the search result page, and on subsequent post-search pages [13].

2.3 Differences from our work

To summarize, previous research on attention and eye-mouse behavior in search focused on linear page layouts containing a single column of search results, and demonstrated mouse sensitivity to position on page. Our work differs from previous work in at least 3 ways: 1) In addition to linear page layouts, we explore nonlinear 2-column results layouts, with a rich information panel on the right hand side of the page; 2) Apart from position on page, we test whether the mouse is sensitive to important factors such as element's relevance to user's task; 3) We systematically compare various user-specific, global and hybrid models for predicting user eye gaze based on mouse signals.

3. EXPERIMENT DESIGN

We recruited 31 participants (15 male and 16 female; age range 18-65, with a variety of occupations and self-reported web search expertise). Data from 5 participants was excluded due to calibration problems with the eye tracker.

Participants were given 4 warm-up tasks to familiarize themselves with the testing procedure. They were then asked to describe all of the elements of the search results page to ensure they were aware of all elements on the page, including the relatively new Knowledge Graph (KG) results feature on the top-right of the page.[3] For example, a query on an entity such as a famous celebrity or place triggers a result page with an informational panel (KG) on the right hand side, containing images and facts about that entity.

Participants were provided a list of 24 search tasks. Each task was accompanied by a link to the search results page with a prespecified query (to ensure that all particpants saw

---
[3]http://googleblog.blogspot.com/2012/05/introducing-knowledge-graph-things-not.html

the same page). For consistency in results sets across users, users could not change the queries. Blocks of images and advertisements were suppressed on the results pages.

We used a 2 x 2 within subject design with two factors: (1) KG present or absent, (2) KG relevant or irrelevant to the user's task. We varied task relevance of KG by designing 2 tasks for the same query, one for which the answer was present in KG (e.g., "find the names of Julia Robert's children") and another for which the answer was present in web results, but not KG (e.g. "what does People magazine say about Julia Roberts?"). Each user performed an equal number of tasks with KG present and absent, as well as with KG relevant and irrelevant. The order of tasks, KG presence, and KG task relevance were all randomized within and across users. [4]

For the purposes for this study, we injected custom javascript in search results pages to log mouse activity on search page as users performed their search tasks. In particular, we logged the browser viewport, and sampled mouse x,y positions every 20ms during mouse movements. Eye tracks were simultaneously recorded using a Tobii TX300 eye tracker with 300 Hz tracking frequency and an accuracy of 0.5° visual angle on a 23" monitor (1880 x 1000 browser size). Both eye and mouse tracks were recorded with an origin at the top-left of the document.

We considered data upto the first click on the search page, or until the user terminated the task (by clicking the back-button to revisit the task list). Raw eye and mouse tracks were of the form: <user, task, timestamp, x, y>. The raw eye data was parsed to obtain a sequence of fixations (brief pauses in eye position for around 200-500ms) and saccades (sudden jumps in eye position) using standard algorithms [21, 23]. Eye fixations and their duration are thought to indicate attention and information processing [8]. Thus, our subsequent analysis is performed using eye fixations data. We aligned eye fixation and mouse data using time from page load. Since eye fixations occur every 200-500ms, while mouse movements were logged every 20ms, we aligned them per user, task by assigning the most recently fixated eye position to each mouse event.

4. RESULTS

4.1 Correlations in pixel space

To test eye-mouse correlations in pixel space, we extract the following measures per user, per task: x,y positions of eye and mouse, maximum x, maximum y, minimum x, and minimum y. The scatter plot in figure 1 shows that the maximum y position shows reasonable correlation ($r^2=0.44$). Other pixel measures such as instantaneous x,y positions of eye-mouse, or minimum x, maximum x, and minimum y show poor correlation between eye and mouse ($r^2<0.05$).

4.2 Correlations in Area-of-Interest space

The pixel-level measures described above include eye-mouse activity in white space, and other elements that are not web results (e.g., search bar, navigation menu). Since we mainly care about which result element the user is looking at, we

---

[4] Another example of a query from the study, along with tasks are: For search [hope floats]: "Who directed the movie 'Hope Floats'" (answer in KG); "What does the Hope Floats wellness center do?" (answer not in KG)

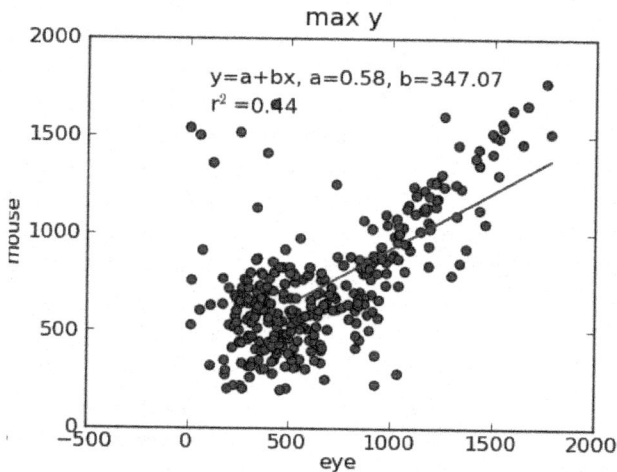

Figure 1: Eye and mouse show correlations in the maximum cursor distance along the vertical axis (y). Each point in the scatter plot denotes a user, task combination.

proceed to analyze the data by defining meaningful areas-of-interest on the search page. We divide the page into Knowledge Graph results (KG), and divide result elements into 3 roughly equal-sized parts (so that their size is similar to KG): Top 3 results (top), middle 3 results (mid), bottom 4 results (bot). In addition, we consider the left navigation menu (left), and group everything else under miscellaneous (misc). Thus, we define 6 areas-of-interest (AoI). The bounding boxes of these AoIs are illustrated in Figure 3, which shows a heatmap visualization of user eye gaze when KG is present and absent.

To analyze the data quantitatively, for each AoI, we extract the following mouse measures: 1) #mouse hovers or visits to the AoI, 2) time to first mouse visit on the AoI (in milliseconds), 3) dwell time (in milliseconds) per mouse position within the AoI, 4) total mouse dwell time (in milliseconds) in the AoI, 5) fraction of page dwell on AoI, 6) fraction of tasks where the last mouse position occurs within the AoI. We also extract corresponding measures for the eye.

Figure 2 shows eye-mouse correlations in AoI space. As seen in the figure, the fraction of page dwell on AoI (dwell time within AoI / total page dwell time) is strongly correlated between the eye and mouse ($r^2=0.89$), followed by dwell per AoI (in seconds, $r^2=0.36$). We believe that the fraction of page dwell time is a more useful measure, as it adjusts for the pace at which users read, while raw dwell times are sensitive to variation in user reading speeds. Interestingly, time-on-page after the eye/mouse visits the AoI is also reasonably well correlated ($r^2=0.45$). We will see later (section 4.5) that this measure is affected by the AoI's relevance (the user spends more time searching on the page after visiting an AoI if the AoI is irrelevant).

We also find strong correlations between the last AoI seen by the eye and mouse before page click or abandonment ($r^2=0.86$), number of eye and mouse visits to an AoI ($r^2=0.83$). In comparison, there is weaker correlation between eye and mouse time to first noticing an AoI ($r^2=0.33$), and no correlation for time per eye/mouse pause ($r^2=0.07$).

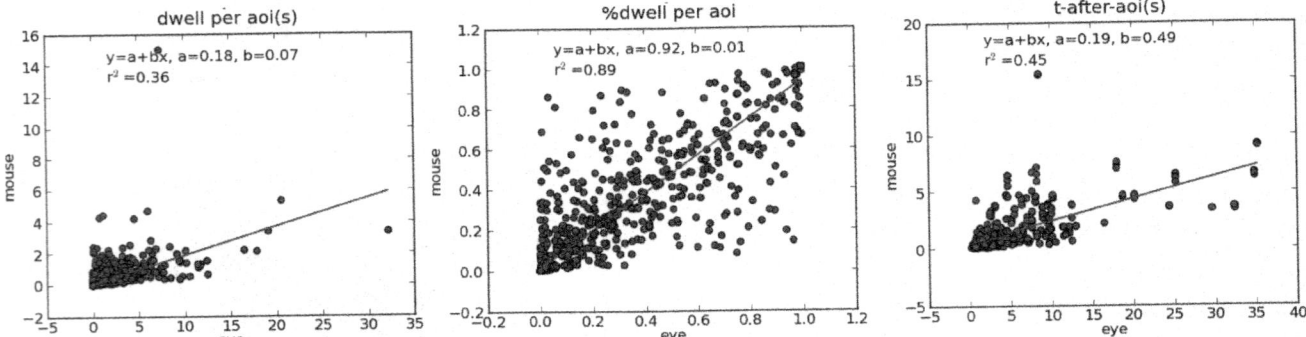

Figure 2: Area of interest (AoI) measures. The measures for eye data are shown in the x axis, and mouse data are shown in the y axis. The left panel shows the dwell time per AoI in seconds, the middle panel shows the fraction of page dwell per AoI, and the right panel shows the time on page after visiting the AoI (in seconds). Each data point reflects one user/task/AoI combination.

4.3 Information flow patterns

Does the different page layout (due to the presence of KG) alter the way users examine the search page? The typical information flow pattern is that users examine the search page linearly from top to bottom (the driving hypothesis behind the popular cascade models of user click behavior on search)[6, 5]. A Markovian analysis of eye tracks shows the following information flow pattern for our study.

- 78% fixations start at the Top (14% on mid, 5.9% on KG and near zero elsewhere), followed by nearly equal probability of switching from top results to KG or middle results.
- majority of incoming fixations on KG come from the top (81%;14% from mid, and 0.7% from bottom)
- majority of outgoing fixations from KG go to the top (78%; 12% to mid, 9.5% to left and 0.4% to bot)

We find strong correlations between eye and mouse-derived transition probabilities across AoIs (r^2=0.73) and the starting distribution (of first AoI visited by eye and mouse; r^2=0.82). This suggests that users' information flow on the page may be reasonably inferred from mouse tracks as well.

4.4 Sensitivity of eye-mouse to position and page layout

Figure 4 shows a visualization of eye and mouse patterns (superimposed) for 2 different experimental conditions, one containing KG (new page layout), and another without (traditional page layout containing one column of results). Eye patterns shown in green, mouse in blue. Each eye/mouse pause is denoted by a circle, whose size is proportional to the duration of the pause. The bigger blue circles and the smaller green circles show that the mouse pause durations are longer (e.g., mouse may be parked idle for a few seconds) compared to eye fixation durations that are typically 200-500ms. This figure shows clearly that the eye and mouse are sensitive to page layouts and KG presence – in this example, both show activity in the right hand side of the page when KG is present, and no activity when KG is absent. Over all users, the fraction of page time spent by the eye increases from <1% when KG is absent to 13% when KG is present.

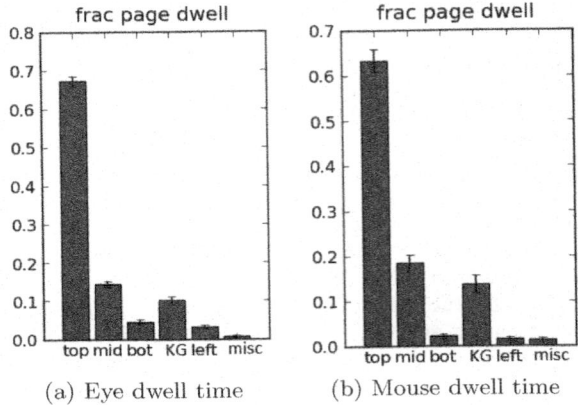

(a) Eye dwell time   (b) Mouse dwell time

Figure 5: Fraction of page dwell in areas of interest is similar for eye and mouse

The mouse shows a similar increase, although to a smaller extent (from 9%[5] to 15%).

Figure 5 further demonstrates sensitivity to position by quantifying the fraction of page dwell by eye (panel a) and mouse (panel b) for different positions on the search page when KG is present. Both the eye and mouse show that the top results dominate by receiving over 60% page dwell, followed by middle results and KG, each receiving between 10-20% page dwell, followed by the bottom results (< 5%; others are negligible).

4.5 Sensitivity of eye-mouse to relevance

Figure 6 shows how KG relevance affects eye attention. While both irrelevant and relevant KGs get around 1s of at-

---

[5]The baseline mouse activity when KG is absent is higher than the corresponding eye activity as some users tend to park their mouse in the whitespace corresponding to the KG area, while scanning nearby result elements. Due to such noise, the magnitude of attention measures may differ between the eye and mouse, however, both the eye and mouse show the same direction of trend – an increase in activity – due to KG presence and relevance.

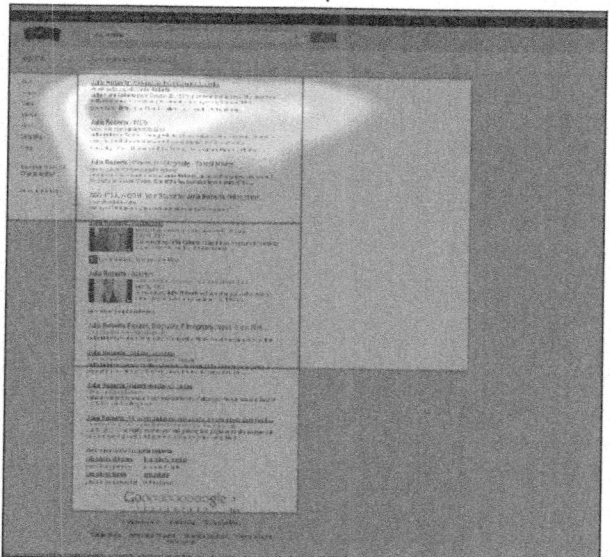 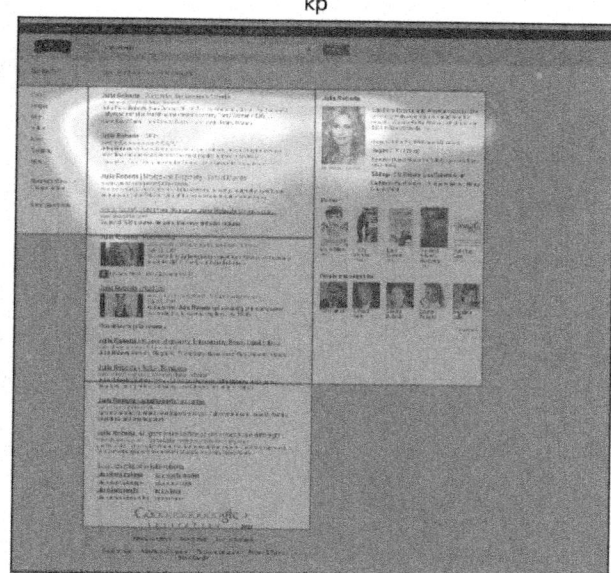

Figure 3: Effect of KG presence on eye gaze heatmaps. Red hotspots indicate where the user spent most time looking. The left panel shows a heatmap of user eye gaze when KG is absent (the shape resembles a Golden Triangle focused on top-left of the page). The right panel shows the corresponding heatmap when KG is present. The search pages have the page areas of interest (AoIs) outlined, and regions outside AoIs dimmed. For the actual result pages presented to users, the AoIs were not visually marked in this way. Note the increased activity near KG, suggesting a potential second Golden Triangle focused on KG.

tention, there are significant differences in other measures: irrelevant KGs slow down the user by 3.5-4s on average (time on page and time on task increase), while relevant KGs speed up the user by around 4s on average (users spend 2-2.5s less on each of the top and mid as the answer is found in KG). Thus, relevant KGs get a higher fraction of page dwell (18%) than irrelevant KGs (8%), and search terminates faster on average after the user visits a relevant KG compared to an irrelevant KG (0.9 vs 2.8s). Clearly, task relevance is an important factor affecting user attention and task performance.

We tested whether mouse activity is sensitive to changes in relevance. We observe similar trends as the eye, but to a smaller extent. Like the eye, the mouse shows that relevant KGs get a higher fraction of page dwell (17%) compared to irrelevant KGs (12%), and search terminates faster on average after the user visits a relevant KG compared to an irrelevant KG (2.9 vs 6.4s). Figure 7a shows sample mouse tracks when KG is relevant – in this example, the task is "when was the sequel to *Toy Story* released?", we find that the user finds the answer in KG, hence search terminates soon after user visits KG. Figure 7b shows sample mouse tracks when KG is irrelevant – in this example, the task is "find more about the *Let's Move* program by Michelle Obama", we find that the user visits KG, and continues searching on the rest of the page [6]. Thus, mouse activity, like eye gaze, is sensitive to relevance.

---

[6]The figure shows two different queries to illustrate more examples of pages with KGs. However, for analysis, we used the same set of queries to compare KG-relevant and KG-irrelevant conditions.

5. PREDICTING EYE FROM MOUSE

Given the observed correlations between eye and mouse activity in some measures, we are motivated to ask the following questions:

- How well can we predict eye gaze from mouse activity?
- Can we achieve higher accuracy by predicting elements of interest on the screen rather than estimating the exact eye gaze coordinates?
- To what extent is the relationship between eye gaze and mouse position user-specific and how far can we generalize to unseen users?

To answer these questions we developed a set of regression and classification models to predict the exact coordinates of the eye gaze and the element of interest on the page, respectively. Before describing these models in detail we need a formal definition of our learning problem: We divided the set of eye-mouse readings into a set of points, where each point $d_i = (y_i, e_i, \mathbf{v_i})$ represents the eye gaze coordinates y_i, a corresponding element of interest on the page e_i, and a covariate vector $\mathbf{v_i}$ comprising of a set of mouse features. We let $D^u = \{d_1^u, \cdots, d_{n_u}^u\}$ be the set of n_u points pertaining to user u, and we let $D = \{D^1, \cdots, D^U\}$ be the set of all data points across all U users.

5.1 Regression to predict the eye position

As a first step consider the problem of estimating the y-coordinate of eye-gaze directly from mouse activity[7]. This

---

[7]Predicting the y coordinate of eye gaze is more interesting than the x coordinate, as it can reveal which result element

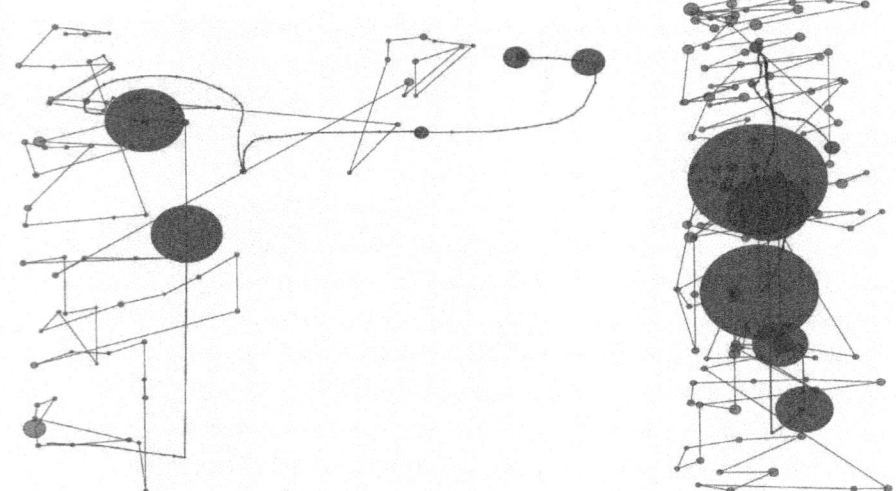

Figure 4: Examples of eye (green) and mouse (blue) tracks when KG is present (left) and absent (right)

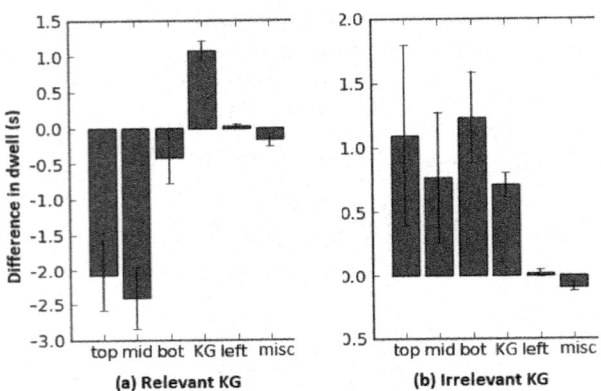

Figure 6: Effect of KG relevance on eye. Consider the left panel. The x axis shows the AoIs, and the y axis shows, for each AoI, the difference in attention (in seconds) when KG is present and relevant vs. when KG is absent (mean ± standard error). Right panel shows the corresponding plot for irrelevant KG.

is a regression problem where we seek to find a function $f : \mathbf{v} \to y$ such that the discrepancy between $f(v)$ and the observed eye position y is minimized.

In the following we use a (generalized) linear model to represent the mapping from attributes to eye positions. That is, we seek to learn a regression function

$$f(\mathbf{v}) = \langle \mathbf{w}, \phi(\mathbf{v}_i) \rangle$$

Here f is parametrized by a weight vector $\mathbf{w}$ that we seek to estimate. When $\phi(\mathbf{v}_i) = \mathbf{v}_i$ we end up with a linear regression function in the input covariate space $\mathbf{v}_i$. When

---

the user is looking at. Thus we focus on y coordinate in this paper.

$\phi(\mathbf{v}_i)$ comprises a nonlinear mapping, we obtain a nonlinear function in the input covariate space.

To assess the impact of a personalized model we compare the following three models: a global model that estimates the parameter $\mathbf{w}$ common for all users. Secondly we infer a user-specific model that provides an upper bound of how accurately the model can estimate eye positions from mouse activity. Finally, we infer a hybrid model that combines global and user-specific components. This allows us to dissociate both parts, thus allowing us to generalize to users where only mouse movements are available while obtaining a more specific model whenever eye tracking is possible. We describe these three approaches below:

Global model: In this setup we learn a global regression function f_g parametrized by a global weight vector $\mathbf{w}_g$. The learning goal is to find $\mathbf{w}_g$ that minimize the average prediction error on the *whole* dataset. More formally, our learning problem for the y-coordinate is:

$$\underset{\mathbf{w}_g}{\text{minimize}} \sum_{d_i \in \mathbf{D}} \|y_i - \langle \mathbf{w}_g, \phi(\mathbf{v}_i) \rangle\|_2^2 + \lambda \|\mathbf{w}_g\|_2^2$$

where λ is a regularization parameter to prevent overfitting. This model tests the hypothesis that eye-mouse correlation is a global phenomenon and does not depend on the specific user behaviour.

User-specific models: In this setup we learn regression functions f_u *independently* for each user u. The learning problem for the y-coordinate is:

$$\underset{\mathbf{w}_u}{\text{minimize}} \sum_{d_i \in \mathbf{D}} \|y_i^u - \langle \mathbf{w}_u, \phi(\mathbf{v}_i^u) \rangle\|_2^2 + \lambda \|\mathbf{w}_u\|_2^2$$

This model tests the hypothesis that eye-mouse correlation is NOT a global phenomenon and depends on the specific user behaviour.

Hierarchical model: In this setup we still learn a per-user regression model, however we decompose each user-specific regression weight additively into a user-dependent part $\mathbf{w}_u$ and a global part $\mathbf{w}_g$. More for-

Relevant KG

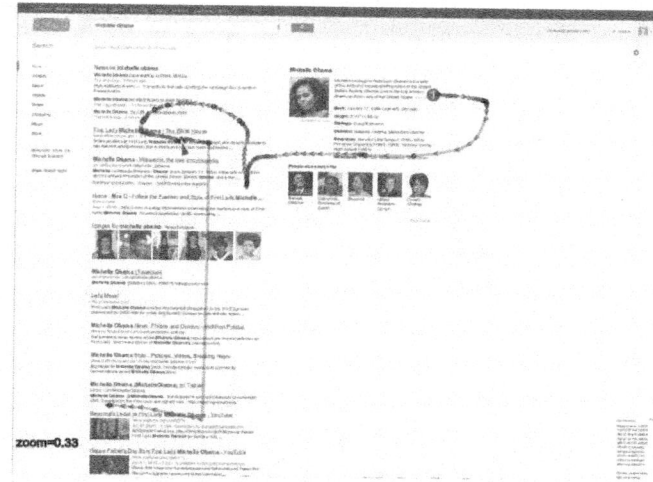
Irrelevant KG

Figure 7: Effect of KG relevance on mouse. Search tends to terminate soon after visiting a relevant KG. For irrelevant KGs the user visits the KG and then continues examining the rest of the page. See footnote 6.

mally, our learning problem for the y-coordinate is:

$$\min_{\mathbf{w}_g, \mathbf{w}_{u_1}, \cdots \mathbf{w}_U} \sum_{u \in U} \sum_{d_i^u \in \mathbf{D}^u} \|y_i^u - \langle \mathbf{w}_u + \mathbf{w}_g, \phi(\mathbf{v}_i^u)\rangle\|_2^2 +$$
$$\lambda \left[\sum_{u \in U} \|\mathbf{w}_u\|_2^2 + \|\mathbf{w}_g\|_2^2\right]$$

This model tests the hypothesis that eye-mouse correlation has some global patterns shared across users, as captured by $\mathbf{w}_g$, in addition to user-specific patterns, as captured by the set $\mathbf{w}_u$ weights.

5.2 Classification for elements of interest

Instead of estimating the absolute position of eye gaze explicitly, one might want to settle for a slightly simpler task — that of estimating which element of interest is being inspected by the user. For this purpose we divide the screen into blocks of pixels that represent special elements on the page (e.g., result element 1,2, etc.). In our experiments, each page is divided into a set of 11 different elements (10 result elements, 1 KG)[8]. The prediction task here involves predicting the particular element that the eye gaze is currently focused on using information from the mouse activity. We treat this as a multi-label classification problem. We use the same terminology from Section 5.1. Our goal is to learn a classification function $h(.,\mathbf{w}) : \phi(\mathbf{v}_i) \to \mathcal{L}$, where $\mathcal{L}$ is the label space. In analogy to Section 5.1, we are interested in the following three cases:

Global model: In this setup we learn a global classification function h_g parametrized by a global weight vector $\mathbf{w}_g$. The learning goal is to find $\mathbf{w}_g$ that minimize the misclassification error on the *whole* dataset:

$$\min_{\mathbf{w}_g} \sum_{d_i \in \mathbf{D}} I\left[e_i \neq h(\phi(\mathbf{v}_i), \mathbf{w}_g)\right] + \lambda \|\mathbf{w}_g\|_2^2$$

---
[8] Note that the 11 elements for classification are different and more fine-grained than the area-of-interest classes mentioned in section 4.

where I is the indicator function, which is 1 iff its argument is evaluated to be true.

User-specific models: In this setup we learn classification function h_u independently for each user u:

$$\min_{\mathbf{w}_u} \sum_{d_i^u \in \mathbf{D}^u} I\left[e_i^u \neq h(\phi(\mathbf{v}_i^u), \mathbf{w}_u)\right] + \lambda \|\mathbf{w}_u\|_2^2$$

Hierarchical models: in this setup we still learn a per-user regression model, however we decompose each user-specific regression weight additively into a user-dependent part $\mathbf{w}_u$ and a global part $\mathbf{w}_g$:

$$\min_{\mathbf{w}_g, \mathbf{w}_{u_1}, \cdots \mathbf{w}_U} \sum_{u \in U} \sum_{d_i^u \in \mathbf{D}^u} I\left[e_i^u \neq h(\phi(\mathbf{v}_i^u), \mathbf{w}_g + \mathbf{w}_u)\right]$$
$$+ \lambda \left(\|\mathbf{w}_g\|_2^2 + \sum_{u \in U} \|\mathbf{w}_u\|_2^2\right)$$

Note that for optimization purposes the indicator function for correct labels is replaced by a differentiable loss function. Alternatively, one may use a reduction to binary approach and solve a sequence of associated cost-sensitive learning problems [1].

5.3 Experimental setup

To be able to test our hypothesis we divided the data into train and test as follows. We randomly sampled 30% of the users and reserved them for test. Then for the remaining 70% users, we randomly sampled 70% of their data points to construct the training data set and added the remaining 30% of their data points to the test set. By that, our test set comprises two kind of users: 1) users unseen during the training, and 2) users partially seen via some of their data points in the training set. This allows us to test the generalizability of our models and test our hypothesis of whether or not mouse-eye correlation is user-specific or user-independent. For all the experiments below, we report accuracy on the whole test set and break it as well into ac-

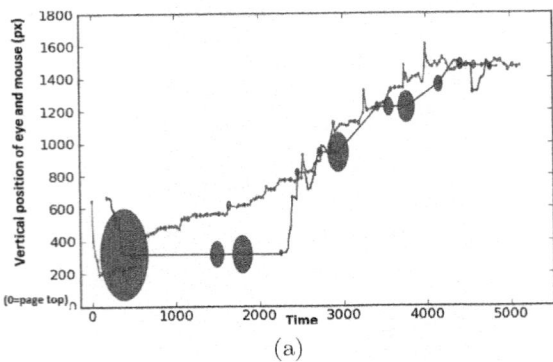
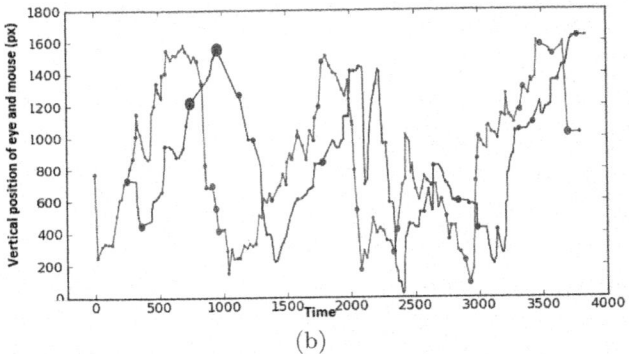

Figure 8: Examples of eye-mouse time course in the y direction. y axis shows the vertical position of eye (green) and mouse (blue) (0 is page-top, and increasing values represent further down the page), and x axis shows time in centiseconds (multiply by 10 to get time in milliseconds). The size of the blue blobs is proportional to the duration of mouse pause at that position. In the example on the left, the mouse is initially parked for around 20 seconds, while the eye examines the nearby elements carefully. The mouse then jumps forward, and then on, correlates better with the eye (task was "Describe the Mozart programming system"). The example on the right shows that the mouse follows eye gaze (with a lag) as the user looks up and down the search page (task was "Describe the koala library for facebook").

curacy on seen user and accuracy on unseen users. [9] We perform prediction as follows based on the model:

Global models: We use the same weight vector $\mathbf{w}_g$ on both seen and unseen users.

User-specific models: If the user was seen before we use his own specific weight $\mathbf{w}_u$. For this model, we do not report results over unseen users.

Hierarchical models: If the user was seen before we use $\mathbf{w}_g + \mathbf{w}_u$, otherwise we use $\mathbf{w}_g$.

We use the following information from mouse activity as features in our prediction models for each time point t:

1. Time from page load (t)
2. Cursor Position (x_t, y_t)
3. Cursor Velocity: magnitude (v_{xt}, v_{yt}), and direction (s_{xt}, s_{yt})
4. Cursor Distance moved (d_{xt}, d_{yt})
5. Area-of-interest in which cursor lies (aoi_t)
6. Corresponding page element (el_{mt})

In addition to computing these features at time t, we consider past and future values of features 2-4. e.g., we consider the future cursor positions, average future velocities, total cursor distance moved, and number of changes in mouse movement direction for time windows $[t, t+k]$ where $k \in \{1, 2, 4, 8, 16\}$; similarly for the past. This gives us a total of 83 features by the above phase space embedding.

5.4 Eye Prediction Results

Next, we show results from various prediction models on different corpora under the various task settings described

---

[9] For seen users, it is possible that adjacent data points from the same user may end up being split across the train and test datasets. However, all the methods compared here are provided with identical train/test distributions and therefore this does not introduce bias for any particular method. In addition (as mentioned earlier), we also report results when predicting on test data from completely unseen users that do not overlap with the train dataset.

above. Following Huang et al. [15], we use a baseline model which predicts that the eye gaze is focused exactly at the mouse position. We use two feature map functions $\phi(\mathbf{v})$: linear where $\phi(\mathbf{v}) = \mathbf{v}$ and nonlinear mapping using Nystrom approximation for Gaussian RBF kernels [24].

Denote by $k(\mathbf{v}, \mathbf{v}') = \exp(-\gamma \|\mathbf{v} - \mathbf{v}'\|^2)$ a Gaussian RBF kernel as it is commonly used in kernel methods. Then this kernel can be approximated by the following feature map:

$$\tilde{k}(\mathbf{v}, \mathbf{v}') = \left\langle \tilde{\phi}(\mathbf{v}), \tilde{\phi}(\mathbf{v}') \right\rangle \text{ where}$$

$$\tilde{\phi}(\mathbf{v}) = K_{nn}^{-\frac{1}{2}} [k(\mathbf{v}_1, \mathbf{v}), \ldots, k(\mathbf{v}_n, \mathbf{v})]$$

Here $\mathbf{v}_1, \ldots, \mathbf{v}_n$ are 1,000 random observations and K_{nn} is an $n \times n$ matrix obtained by forming the inner products $[K_{nn}]_{ij} = k(\mathbf{v}_i, \mathbf{v}_j)$. The advantage of the mapping $\tilde{\phi}(\mathbf{v})$ is that it can be used to learn a linear function in the transformed feature space that is equivalent to learning a nonlinear function in the input space. That is, in both cases we employ the *VW* package [19] to solve all the optimization problems.

Results are shown in Table 1. We draw the following conclusions:

- The observed mouse-eye correlation function is highly nonlinear and that is why nonlinear models outperformed their linear counterparts especially in classification settings. For example, the best results achieved on unseen users using nonlinear features is 62.3% prediction error compared to 80.7% error for the linear counterpart (which amounts to 23% reduction in classification error). This is a natural consequence of the fact that we need to specify nonlinear boundaries in order to distinguish between different blocks in the result set. Here nonlinear basis functions are much more advantageous.

- Our best model (nonlinear hierarchical) provides a 24.3% improvement over the baseline (in RMSE_y for pixel space). In comparison, the best model from Huang et al[15] achieved an improvement of 10.4% over the same baseline.[10]

- The observed mouse-eye correlation function is clearly user-dependent because users exhibit different patterns while navigating the page (for example some users tend to align the mouse with their gaze as their attention shifts around the page, so called mouse readers). From our results, it is clear that the user-specific models overwhelmingly outperform all other models.

- While building a user-specific model is advised whenever abundant training data is available from individual users, it is not a scalable approach. We hypothesized that hierarchical models would help in generalizing eye-gaze prediction to unseen users. As evident from our experiments using a simple additive hierarchical model, the results over unseen users slightly improved compared to the global models. The reason is that additive models separate user-specific patterns (via the $\mathbf{w}_u$ weight vector) from global patterns shared across users (captured via the $\mathbf{w}_g$ vector) which are then used in predicting eye-gaze from mouse activity over unseen users. We believe that this is a promising direction and we plan to investigate further into using more advanced transfer learning approaches for transferring eye-mouse patterns from seen users to unseen users.

- Note that at a first glance, the total classification error over seen and unseen users from our best model seems rather high (nonlinear hierarchical, 60.3% error). However, this impression is misleading: firstly, it amounts to a 14.8% reduction over its counterpart in the baseline (70.8%), and the error reduction is bigger (28%) for user-specific models on seen users. Secondly, the current method of computing error penalizes adjacent elements as much as far away page elements, leading to high values of error (for example, predicting that the user is looking at search result 1 while the ground truth is that he is looking at search result 2 would result in the same classification error as between results 1 and 10). A cost sensitive loss function taking the page layout into account could be used to address this issue. Indeed, we find that the result elements were mostly confused with adjacent result elements, and KG was confused with the first result element. If we ignore errors due to adjacent elements on the page, the total classifier error drops dramatically from 60.3% to 33.1% (nearly halved). For example, the error for the first result element drops from 23 to 12% (91% of this error reduction was from ignoring result 1-2 confusion), the error for the second element drops from 79 to 8% (97% error reduction was from ignoring result 2-1, 2-3 confusion), the error for KG drops from 60 to 12% (75% error reduction was from ignoring KG-result 1 confusion). To summarize, these results suggest that the nonlinear hierarchical model can predict the result element that the user is looking at (with an error of upto one element) at reasonably high accuracy (67%) from mouse tracks only.

6. DISCUSSION

In this paper, we demonstrate through carefully designed experiments in the lab that the mouse, like the eye, is sensitive to two key attributes of page elements – their position on the page, and their relevance to the user's task. Using a 2x2 within subject design, we systematically varied the page layout (2 column content layout – KG present on the top-right of the page, vs. linear 1 column content layout with web results only and KG absent), and relevance (KG either relevant or not to user task). Eye and mouse tracks were recorded simultaneously as users performed the tasks. We discuss the key findings and potential applications.

6.1 Mouse tracking aids layout analysis

Our analysis shows that the eye and mouse are strongly correlated in some measures such as: 1) fraction of page time spent within the area-of-interest, 2) last area-of-interest visited before user clicks/abandons, and 3) transition probabilities between areas of interest. The first measure is particularly interesting as it is sensitive to both the position and relevance of an AoI: comparing different experimental conditions, we observe that like the eye, the fraction of page time on KG as measured by the mouse, is higher when KG is present vs. absent, and higher when KG is relevant vs. irrelevant. In addition, we find that the page time *after* the mouse visits KG is shorter when KG is relevant than when it is irrelevant, suggesting that users terminate search faster after visiting a relevant KG. Together, these mouse measures can provide useful signals about user attention to, and task relevance of, page elements even in the absence of clicks. Potential applications of tracking these mouse measures at scale include ranking, search page optimization and UI evaluation.

The second finding of strong eye-mouse correlations in the last area-of-interest visited before click/abandonment is consistent with Huang et al's finding that eye and mouse are strongly correlated at the time of click (user's decision) than at the beginning of the task (where users tend to explore the page).

As search pages become increasingly complex (visually and content-wise), understanding how users consume the page, or how information flows through the search page is an important question that has applications for ranking and improving user satisfaction (by providing the high quality answers where they are most likely to look at). For example, in linear page layouts containing a single column of search results, the dominant flow pattern is that users scan the page from top to bottom. The corresponding eye gaze heatmaps resemble a Golden triangle with more attention being paid to the top-left of the page, and decreasing attention towards the right or bottom of the page. In contrast, in the new page layout containing 2 columns (one column of search results, and a second column with visually attractive content on the top right of the page corresponding to the Knowledge Graph results), we find that while majority of the users start by viewing the top search results, as a next step, they are equally likely to see the KG on the right, or middle results below. The corresponding eye gaze heatmaps in Figure 3 have 2 Golden triangles, one focused at the top-

---

[10]Huang et al. report results using a slightly different set of features which makes a direct comparison difficult for this particular study. However, we use the same baseline method as theirs and although the feature sets may differ, our global linear model simulates their method. The results presented in this paper indicate that our best approach clearly outperforms these methods and yields a significant improvement in prediction performance for different test settings.

Model		RMSE$_y$ (pixels)			Classification Error (%)		
		Total	Seen users	unseen users	Total	Seen users	unseen users
Baseline	*mouse position*	270.1	276.9	263.9	70.8	72.0	69.7
Linear	Global	218.2	217.0	219.3	77.3	72.4	81.6
	Hierarchical	216.5	215.1	218.2	76.0	71.9	80.7
	User-specific	–	193.8	–	–	55.9	–
Nonlinear	Global	211.7	210.0	213.2	63.9	64.8	63.0
	Hierarchical	204.5	201.3	207.5	60.3	58.7	62.3
	User-specific	–	179.7	–	–	51.8	–

Table 1: Comparison of models for predicting eye gaze from mouse activity. Size of training data $m_{\text{train}} = 20788$, test data $m_{\text{test}} = 19000$ (comprised of 8899 points from previously seen users and 10101 points from new users). Our best model (nonlinear hierarchical) provides a 24.3% improvement over the baseline (in pixel space) and 14.8% improvement in element space.

left of the search results, and a new triangle focused at the top-left of the KG. Our finding of eye-mouse correlations for the starting distribution (first area-of-interest visited by the eye and mouse), and transition probabilities between pairs of area-of-interest suggests that we may reasonably infer user information flow on search pages by analyzing their mouse tracks. This could be potentially useful as search pages evolve to new UIs, layouts, and richer results, which may not be parsed in a conventional linear manner.

There is also reasonable eye-mouse correlation on maximum y distance on the page, which reflects how far down the page did the user visit (with their eye or mouse). This could be useful in inferring which page folds were attended by the user, and how far down the page they read.

6.2 On mouse tracking as a proxy for eye tracking

While mouse tracking is gaining in popularity, it remains a poorly understood science. Future work will involve analyzing mouse usage statistics, understanding how mouse usage behavior varies as a function of users (intent, age, gender, reading fluency), page (UI, images, result quality) and device properties (e.g., trackpad vs. traditional mouse).

In particular, there exists a rich body of statistical literature to analyze models involving partially observed data, such as Hidden Markov Models and Conditional Random Fields. Analysis of users' mouse activity (even in the absence of eye data) can provide information about prototypical mouse behaviors of users (e.g., parking, reading, skimming). In turn, such information can help us estimate eye positions more accurately in spite of the paucity of eye tracking data.

limitations of mouse tracking. Unlike eye gaze patterns, there is wide variability in mouse behavior between and within users. For example, some users read with their mouse, which as Rodden et al. [22] note is a rare event. Other users tend to park their mouse idle while scanning the page with their eye. Some users tend to mark interesting results with their mouse, others simply use their mouse for scrolling and clicking. Given the wide variability and noise in mouse usage behavior, inferring attention from mouse is a hard problem. Further noise in mouse behavior may be introduced depending on the type of mouse device (e.g., a trackpad may involve more scrolling and smooth mouse movements than a linear mouse). Due to the above reasons, we need to rely on aggregate statistics of mouse behavior over several users to infer their attention on page. In contrast, eye tracks from a single user can already reveal a lot about their attention on page.

This leads us to the conclusion that while mouse tracking can offer valuable signals on user attention on areas-of-interest or page elements at an aggregate level, it cannot yet match the millisecond temporal and pixel-level spatial resolution of eye tracking on a per user, per page level. Despite this limitation, mouse tracking has much promise as it offers a scalable methodology to infer user attention on web pages, especially when clicks are absent or few.

7. CONCLUSIONS

We demonstrate through carefully designed lab studies that the mouse, like the eye, is sensitive to 2 key attributes of page elements – their position on page, and their relevance to the user's task – both for linear one-column page layouts and increasingly popular two-column page layouts. Despite the noise in mouse activity due to wide variability in mouse usage behavior within and between users, we find strong eye-mouse correlations in measures such as the fraction of page time on result elements, and transition probabilities between elements, suggesting that one may reasonably infer user attention and information flow over elements on the search page, using mouse tracks. This is further validated by the reasonably high accuracy (67%) in predicting the fixated result element from mouse activity (with an error of upto one element). Potential applications include ranking, search page optimization, and UI evaluation both in the presence, and absence of clicks.

8. REFERENCES

[1] N. Abe, B. Zadrozny, and J. Langford. An iterative method for multi-class cost-sensitive learning. In *KDD*, pages 3–11, 2004.

[2] G. Buscher, E. Cutrell, and M. Morris. What do you see when you're surfing?: using eye tracking to predict salient regions of web pages. In *Proceedings of the 27th international conference on Human factors in computing systems*, pages 21–30. ACM, 2009.

[3] G. Buscher, S. Dumais, and E. Cutrell. The good, the bad, and the random: an eye-tracking study of ad quality in web search. In *Proceeding of the 33rd international ACM SIGIR conference on Research and development in information retrieval*, pages 42–49. ACM, 2010.

[4] G. Buscher, R. W. White, S. Dumais, and J. Huang. Large-scale analysis of individual and task differences in search result page examination strategies. In *Proceedings of the fifth ACM international conference on Web search and data mining*, WSDM '12, pages 373–382, New York, NY, USA, 2012. ACM.

[5] O. Chapelle and Y. Zhang. A dynamic bayesian network click model for web search ranking. In *Proceedings of the 18th international conference on World wide web*, pages 1–10. ACM, 2009.

[6] N. Craswell, O. Zoeter, M. Taylor, and B. Ramsey. An experimental comparison of click position-bias models. In *Proceedings of the international conference on Web search and web data mining*, pages 87–94. ACM, 2008.

[7] E. Cutrell and Z. Guan. What are you looking for?: an eye-tracking study of information usage in web search. In *Proceedings of the SIGCHI conference on Human factors in computing systems*, pages 407–416. ACM, 2007.

[8] A. Duchowski. *Eye tracking methodology: Theory and practice*, volume 373. Springer, 2007.

[9] L. Granka, T. Joachims, and G. Gay. Eye-tracking analysis of user behavior in www search. In *Proceedings of the 27th annual international ACM SIGIR conference on Research and development in information retrieval*, pages 478–479. ACM, 2004.

[10] Q. Guo and E. Agichtein. Exploring mouse movements for inferring query intent. In *Proceedings of the 31st annual international ACM SIGIR conference on Research and development in information retrieval*, SIGIR '08, pages 707–708, New York, NY, USA, 2008. ACM.

[11] Q. Guo and E. Agichtein. Ready to buy or just browsing?: detecting web searcher goals from interaction data. In *Proceedings of the 33rd international ACM SIGIR conference on Research and development in information retrieval*, SIGIR '10, pages 130–137, New York, NY, USA, 2010. ACM.

[12] Q. Guo and E. Agichtein. Towards predicting web searcher gaze position from mouse movements. In *CHI '10 Extended Abstracts on Human Factors in Computing Systems*, CHI EA '10, pages 3601–3606, New York, NY, USA, 2010. ACM.

[13] Q. Guo and E. Agichtein. Beyond dwell time: estimating document relevance from cursor movements and other post-click searcher behavior. In *Proceedings of the 21st international conference on World Wide Web*, WWW '12, pages 569–578, New York, NY, USA, 2012. ACM.

[14] G. Hotchkiss, S. Alston, and G. Edwards. Eye tracking study. *Research white paper, Enquiro Search Solutions Inc*, 2005.

[15] J. Huang, R. White, and G. Buscher. User see, user point: gaze and cursor alignment in web search. In *Proceedings of the SIGCHI Conference on Human Factors in Computing Systems*, CHI '12, pages 1341–1350, New York, NY, USA, 2012. ACM.

[16] J. Huang, R. W. White, G. Buscher, and K. Wang. Improving searcher models using mouse cursor activity. In *Proceedings of the 35th international ACM SIGIR conference on Research and development in information retrieval*, SIGIR '12, pages 195–204, New York, NY, USA, 2012. ACM.

[17] J. Huang, R. W. White, and S. Dumais. No clicks, no problem: using cursor movements to understand and improve search. In *Proceedings of the SIGCHI Conference on Human Factors in Computing Systems*, CHI '11, pages 1225–1234, New York, NY, USA, 2011. ACM.

[18] D. Lagun and E. Agichtein. Viewser: enabling large-scale remote user studies of web search examination and interaction. In *Proceedings of the 34th international ACM SIGIR conference on Research and development in Information Retrieval*, SIGIR '11, pages 365–374, New York, NY, USA, 2011. ACM.

[19] J. Langford, L. Li, and A. Strehl. Vowpal Wabbit, 2007.

[20] J. Nielsen and K. Pernice. *Eyetracking web usability*. New Riders Pub, 2010.

[21] A. Olsen. Tobii i-vt fixation filter - algorithm description white paper. 2012.

[22] K. Rodden, X. Fu, A. Aula, and I. Spiro. Eye-mouse coordination patterns on web search results pages. In *CHI '08 Extended Abstracts on Human Factors in Computing Systems*, CHI EA '08, pages 2997–3002, New York, NY, USA, 2008. ACM.

[23] D. Salvucci and J. Goldberg. Identifying fixations and saccades in eye-tracking protocols. In *Proceedings of the 2000 symposium on Eye tracking research & applications*, pages 71–78. ACM, 2000.

[24] A. J. Smola and B. Schölkopf. Sparse greedy matrix approximation for machine learning. In *ICML*, pages 911–918, 2000.

Understanding and Decreasing the Network Footprint of Catch-up TV

Gianfranco Nencioni
University of Pisa
g.nencioni@iet.unipi.it

Nishanth Sastry
King's College London
nishanth.sastry@kcl.ac.uk

Jigna Chandaria
BBC R&D
jigna@rd.bbc.co.uk

Jon Crowcroft
University of Cambridge
Jon.Crowcroft@cl.cam.ac.uk

ABSTRACT

"Catch-up", or on-demand access of previously broadcast TV content over the public Internet, constitutes a significant fraction of peak time network traffic. This paper analyses consumption patterns of nearly 6 million users of a nationwide deployment of a catch-up TV service, to understand the network support required. We find that catch-up has certain natural scaling properties compared to traditional TV: The on-demand nature spreads load over time, and users have much higher completion rates for content streams than previously reported. Users exhibit strong preferences for serialised content, and for specific genres.

Exploiting this, we design a Speculative Content Offloading and Recording Engine (SCORE) that predictively records a personalised set of shows on user-local storage, and thereby offloads traffic that might result from subsequent catch-up access. Evaluations show that even with a modest storage of 32GB, an oracle with complete knowledge of user consumption can save up to 74% of the energy, and 97% of the peak bandwidth compared to the current IP streaming-based architecture. In the best case, optimising for energy consumption, SCORE can recover more than 60% of the traffic and energy savings achieved by the oracle. Optimising purely for traffic rather than energy can reduce bandwidth by an additional 5%.

Categories and Subject Descriptors

C.2.1 [**Computer-Communication Network**]: Network Architecture and Design; C.4 [**Performance of Systems**]: [Measurement techniques]; H.4.3 [**Information Systems Applications**]: Communications Applications

Keywords

Catch-up TV; OTT content; workload characterization; energy savings; network footprint; traffic offloading.

1. INTRODUCTION

Recently, "Over-the-top" (OTT) Television services – distribution of Television (TV) content on the public Internet, without a dedicated network build out – have emerged as a new and cost-effective option. OTT distribution is especially popular for two kinds of content: streaming of movies (e.g. Netflix), and for providing so-called "catch-up TV" or "replay TV" service, which makes previously broadcast TV content available (typically via IP streaming) for *on-demand* or time-shifted viewing for a limited period after the original broadcast. Examples of catch-up services include Hulu in the USA and BBC iPlayer in the UK.

Unlike push-based traditional or "linear" TV, where programs are broadcast on different channels according to a known schedule, and user choice is limited to watching content showing on a channel at a given time, catch-up follows a pull-based approach, allowing users to choose what to watch and when to watch. Digital Video Recorders (DVRs, also known as Personal Video Recorders or PVRs) also support time-shifted viewing of linear TV by recording the broadcasts on user-local storage. However, users typically need to preprogram the DVR to record their favourite shows. In contrast, catch-up enables on-demand access and does not require users to anticipate what shows they want to have available for viewing later on.

Because of this flexibility, catch-up is becoming increasingly popular as an alternate or supplement to traditional TV in certain countries such as the UK. Ofcom, UK's independent regulator of communications industries, estimates that catch-up services are used by 44% of UK households [18]. According to Sandvine, BBC iPlayer is the most popular long-content streaming application in the UK, and second only to YouTube amongst all streaming video sources [19]. The UK market has several competing catch up TV services in addition to BBC iPlayer, thus the total impact of Catch-up TV on UK's networks is significant.

The traffic impact of Catch-up TV is likely to grow further as new devices such as smart and connected TVs become more prevalent. BBC recently observed over 7 million requests in one month alone from connected TV sets[1], representing an year-on-year increase of over 1000%. Today's accesses to BBC iPlayer are mainly from computer-based systems. Connected TVs, with their much larger screen sizes, will require higher fidelity video streams than required for PC and laptop screens, leading to higher average bit rates and thereby a larger traffic footprint on the network.

Additionally, the trend towards catch-up has increased the carbon footprint of TV content consumption. This is

---
[1] http://www.bbc.co.uk/mediacentre/latestnews/2012/iplayer.html

because broadcast has a fixed carbon cost which can be amortized across its viewers, whereas the carbon footprint of catch-up streaming grows with each additional user. The BBC estimates that for all of its channels except one[2], Digital Terrestrial Television (i.e., broadcast TV) has a smaller per-viewer carbon footprint than catch-up streaming [9].

Using historical access data from nearly 6 million users of the nationwide live deployment of BBC iPlayer in the United Kingdom, this paper seeks to understand how the nature of the catch-up TV workload affects its network footprint, by comparing with traditional linear TV and DVR usage. Our contributions are twofold. First, we show that the pull-based nature of catch-up leads to more manageable network footprint than linear TV, with better network utilisation and scalability. Second, we ask to what extent on-demand access can be converted to the pre-recorded time-shifted viewing model of DVRs by anticipating and predictively recording broadcasts likely to be accessed on catch-up, and show that this can be used to significantly decrease both the traffic and carbon footprint of catch-up TV.

We begin by characterising how people access content on catch-up, and what they access. The workload exhibits the following properties:

- **P1: Load spreading** The support for time-shifted viewing is used extensively: Although content broadcast during TV prime time is also popular on catch-up, accesses are more distributed in time, resulting in a more even spread of peak time load.
- **P2: High engagement** Users show a high engagement: the proportion of short-intervalled catch-up streams (i.e., streams abandoned or stopped after a short period of viewing) is relatively small. This is in contrast with the previously reported high-levels of short-intervalled viewing due to channel surfing in traditional TV.
- **P3: Strong preferences** Users exhibit strong preferences. Shorter content of duration 30 or 60 minutes is more popular than longer duration content such as feature films. Serialised content items (TV shows broadcast as a sequence of episodes, typically one per week) are especially popular, as are certain specific genres.

These properties imply a natural scalability of catch-up that makes it easier to deliver over the public Internet than traditional linear TV. For instance, **P1** indicates that catch-up has better network utilisation than traditional TV, with less pronounced peaks and troughs in diurnal traffic patterns. Users typically finish what they start watching (**P2**), also leading to better network utilisation, with fewer "wasted" streams. Moreover, **P2** suggests that content delivery architectures could consider aggressively prefetching large chunks of content in advance of their view deadlines, when bandwidth and other network resources are available. **P3** can form the basis for choosing which subsets of content to cache, or sophisticated personalised content delivery architectures.

Next, taking advantage of the properties of high engagement and strong user preferences, we design and evaluate the Speculative Content Offloading and Recording Engine (SCORE), which attempts to convert on-demand catch-up accesses to DVR-like recording followed by time-shifted viewing. SCORE decreases the network footprint of catch-up

---
[2]The BBC Parliament channel, which has fewer viewers compared to other channels.

by anticipating on-demand catch-up accesses, automatically recording broadcasts of such items on user-local storage such as DVRs, and then playing the local copy if accessed on-demand, thereby avoiding network usage.

Because the automatic recordings compete with user requested recordings for storage on DVR-like devices, we assume that only a limited storage is available to SCORE. As a baseline we use $S_0 = 32GB$, in line with reserved storage in standards such as YouView [23]. To carefully make use of the limited storage available, we take advantage of the strong affinity of users to certain types of content. SCORE consists of a predictor that assigns a personalised probability of viewing for each content item scheduled to be broadcast, and an optimiser that decides which items to store based on the probabilities and storage space available.

Our evaluations show that given access to just 32GB of storage, an oracle with complete knowledge of users' future accesses could, depending on parameter values of the energy model we use, the bit rate used for streaming, etc., save up to 97% of peak traffic, and up to 74% of the energy. For similar parameter values, SCORE is able to recover more than 60% of the energy and traffic savings obtained by the oracle. Dependency on parameter values is resolved using sensitivity analysis. SCORE is conservative in choosing items to offload because speculative recording of items not watched later increases energy consumption. If traffic is the only consideration, content can be offloaded more aggressively as there is no penalty for being wrong. This can achieve an additional 5% traffic reduction. The difference can be seen as the "price of being green".

The rest of the paper is organised as follows. §2 discusses related work. §3 introduces BBC iPlayer and clarifies TV terminology. §4 characterises properties of the BBC iPlayer workload and their implications for content delivery. §5 introduces SCORE and the details of its design. §6 evaluates the energy and traffic savings of SCORE in relation to the optimal savings achievable by an oracle. §7 concludes by discussing deployability concerns and limitations of our study.

2. RELATED WORK

This paper makes two contributions. The first is an characterisation of the catch-up workload. A number of seminal works [24, 13, 8, 12] have examined different forms of TV and video-on-demand delivery over the Internet. These range from walled garden IPTV architectures to P2P live streaming workloads. We add to this list by examining a catch-up TV workload. An important difference from previous work is that we find "scanning" or "channel zapping" behaviours to be much smaller than previously reported [24, 8], which we conjecture to be a result of the detailed Program Guide Information made available to users in our catch up system before they start streaming.

Our second contribution is the development of a simple algorithm to automatically store content that is likely to be watched by users later on. It has been recognised before that a large amount of savings can be realised by offloading content from the servers [14]. In walled-garden IPTV approaches, when the operator has control over the network, caching at appropriate locations and branch points within the network can be effective [21, 4, 6]. Deployments operating over the public Internet have to rely on end-users, and a popular strategy is to use P2P approaches where users collaboratively download from each other to decrease server load. However, supporting the delivery constraints of streaming in P2P architectures typically introduces complexity such as elaborate mesh/tree topology construction [16, 7], or careful chunk-scheduling strategies [3, 22, 10, 15]. Instead of peers, SCORE exploits the existing *broadcast channel* to decrease server and network load. While this makes the solution specific to catch-up TV, it also makes the design of SCORE very straightforward.

Functionality similar to SCORE is available on some commercially available DVRs, but there are differences. For example, some DVRs, such as TiVo, assist in content discovery by recommending *new* programs to watch [20]. Our goal is similar but with an important difference: we wish to learn the *existing* viewing habits of users and anticipate their usage of catch-up TV. TiVo essentially records as many relevant suggestions as possible, as low priority items to be erased if user-requested recordings require space. SCORE is much more conservative because recording content not watched later on wastes energy. Recent commercial offerings in the USA such as "Primetime Anytime"[3] from DISH, automatically record evening prime time shows for the four major broadcast networks during evening Prime Time. Sky TV in the UK follows a similar approach. The programs recorded by these offerings are expected to be the most popular shows. However, recording all the top-n shows for all users could yield negative energy savings (§6.2.1). For $n = 10$, which yields the best energy savings, the personalised SCORE approach outperforms the one-size-fits-all top-n approach both in energy and traffic savings.

3. PRELIMINARIES

This section introduces the BBC iPlayer, the data set we use, and TV-related terminology used.

3.1 TV content terminology

Television industries in different countries use slightly different terminology, and the same term sometimes has different meanings. Terms are used in this paper as follows:

TV shows, also known as *programs* (*brit.* programmes), are typically serialised into chunks known as *episodes*. Individual episodes, which we interchangeably refer to as *content items*, form the basic unit of broadcast. Usually, one new episode is broadcast per week, although the same episode can sometimes be broadcast at multiple times. A run of several connected episodes is known as a *series* or *season*; some programs can run for several seasons. Although there can be one-off broadcasts of content items (e.g., movies), we treat these as part of a program series with just one episode.

TV shows are assigned to a *channel* owned by the content provider or broadcaster. In traditional broadcast and cable TV, the channel represents the basic unit by which a user may select content for watching. At any time, a channel can only broadcast one content item; this introduces a linear schedule for content items. Thus traditional TV is sometimes known as *linear TV*.

Because the linear schedule is enforced on all users, an extremely important decision for traditional TV is deciding which content items to broadcast when on each channel. Audience numbers dramatically increase during a few hours in the evenings, known as *prime time*. Complex analytics including expected demographics, viewership numbers, their preferred times for viewing etc. may be used to decide which programs to fit into the prime time slots.

The broadcast schedule of a channel for the coming week is typically known in advance and is often available as an Electronic Program Guide (EPG). This information usually classifies the content item into well-known *genres*, such as drama, comedy, factual, and so on. Other information may include the names of actors involved, a blurb or summary describing the content item, etc.

3.2 TV content access in the UK

TV content can be delivered in many ways. To provide context for SCORE, which presupposes access to a DVR, we give a brief overview of common TV-related hardware and service delivery options in the UK: The first delivery mechanism is over-the-air broadcasts. This used to be analog signals, but has shifted to Digital Terrestrial Transmission (DTT) as with many other countries. A popular option to receive DTT broadcasts is using so-called Freeview or YouView boxes. These are sold without the need for a content subscription, and receive many over-the-air transmissions. All but the most basic Freeview model have an integrated hard drive-based Set-Top Box (STB); many can be connected to the Internet. Thus access to high-end DVR storage is available even to users without a cable connection.

Cable and satellite TVs are other common ways to receive content. Cable and satellite connections typically include a set-top box. Many STBs include a hard drive to store programs; this is sufficient for SCORE. Increasingly, an Internet connection is becoming a part of this setup, and is used to access either proprietary content on-demand from the cable/satellite provider or catch-up services from the content provider. Internet-connected TVs and TVs connected to games consoles may also include an iPlayer "app" and typically have local storage available.

3.3 BBC iPlayer

The BBC has a number of local and national TV and radio channels, which broadcast content over the air in the UK. The BBC iPlayer makes this broadcast content available on the iPlayer website for a fixed period of days after the broadcast, depending on content licensing terms and other policies. Thus, the iPlayer provides an alternate "over-the-top" access mechanism for content which is typically broadcast over the air. iPlayer additionally provides live streaming access to content currently being broadcast, but accessing a live video stream requires a TV license to be paid for annually. After the broadcast, the content is available for "catch up" viewing, and may be accessed even without a TV license, for viewers within the UK. Because of the free access after the broadcast, the BBC iPlayer is widely used within the UK as a catch up TV service; and to date has been used by an estimated 40% of online adults in the UK. Both live and catch-up iPlayer are entirely free of advertisements (ads) since the content programming is supported by TV licensing fees; user actions such as program abandonment may be attributed to content rather than ads and ad breaks.

3.4 Dataset

This paper studies a dataset derived from eight weeks of access logs to BBC iPlayer, from 04-Sep-2010 to 31-Oct-2010. Live streams have been filtered out, capturing on-demand or "catch up" access occuring after the broadcast.

---
[3] http://dishuser.org/ptat.php

Catch-up represents the majority of accesses. In September, for example, Live TV viewing represented about 10% of all accesses; catch up constituted the remaining 90%.

One in every four accesses to iPlayer during this period is recorded in the access log, giving a 25% sample of all accesses. This negatively affects our evaluation of the energy and traffic savings achievable by SCORE. We discuss this further in §7.1. However, all the measurements characterising the workload in §4 are percentages or fractions that are expected to be robust against a uniformly sampled workload.

The access logs are time stamps of the start and end of the streaming of one content item to one user. Altogether, the filtered trace consists of 32,691,343 streams from 5,985,458 users. These streams cover 37,728 unique content items (episodes) from 3,518 programs broadcast over 73 channels.

In addition, the BBC maintains web pages about each programme and episode which has been broadcast. By harvesting this data, we are able to augment the historical access logs with broadcast-related information such as the time and channel of broadcast, and the theoretical duration of the content item. We also identify each content item as belonging to one (or more) of eleven genres: kids, drama, learning, factual, music, news, religion and ethics (r&e), sport, weather, comedy and entertainment (entert.).

4. CHARACTERISING CATCH-UP

This section characterises the workload presented by catch-up access in the BBC iPlayer trace, and discusses the implications on designing content delivery architectures for catch-up. We first ask *how* users watch catch-up, and understand this in terms of what is known about linear TV. The main difference arises from the fact that content items may only be watched according to a pre-determined schedule in linear TV, whereas catch-up gives users control over when and what they watch. We then study in more detail *what* people watch, and use this as input to the design of SCORE.

4.1 How users watch catch-up TV

Choosing content to watch on catch-up TV is typically very different from traditional or linear TV. In linear TV, programs are broadcast at pre-determined times, and switching through channels (e.g. using a remote control) is thought to be the main method of choosing what to watch [8]. Although Electronic Program Guide (EPG) information (e.g. genre, duration, summary blurb, actors involved) is usually available, this is off the main content selection process. In contrast, catch-up is a form of video-on-demand; users are in direct control of *when to watch*, and choose *what they are going to watch* from a selection of available content. Further, detailed EPG information is usually available to users before they make their choice.

This section investigates the impact of giving users control over when and what to watch. We find that allowing users the choice of when to watch their content decreases the peak time load and spreads it out more evenly across time. We also find that program abandonment rates are smaller than previously reported for linear TV. We conjecture that this could be a result of users being in control of what they want to watch. Together, these two results imply that catch-up has better network utilisation characteristics than linear TV: fewer streams are wasted as a result of lower abandonment rates; and the network and content delivery servers have to be provisioned for a smaller peak because of load spreading.

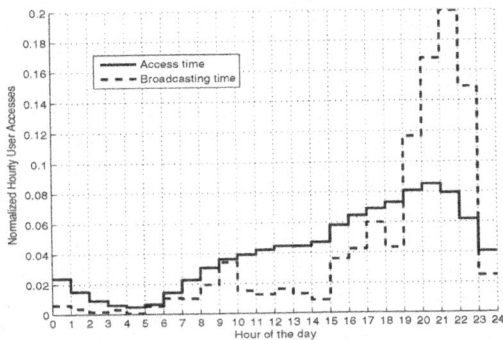

Figure 1: Normalised distributions of access times by hour of day, and the broadcast times of accessed items. Items broadcast during 7-11pm are very popular on catch-up, but the access hour is more evenly distributed.

4.1.1 On-demand access spreads load over time

First, we investigate *when* users access catch-up content, compared to broadcast times (Fig. 1). The dashed line in each time slot depicts the number of accesses (normalised by total number of accesses) to programs broadcast during the given hour of day. This clearly shows that items broadcast during evening hours (corresponding closely to TV "prime time") are much more popular than other content. This can be seen as confirmation that linear TV schedule has chosen the most popular shows for prime time, and that the same shows are popular both on linear and catch-up TV.

The dashed line also indicates the load distribution that would be seen if users were accessing content "live", as it is being broadcast. Instead, the solid line shows the actual (normalised) load distribution observed. This is much more evenly distributed, although a defined peak and trough is still observed, corresponding to users' evening free times and daytime work hours respectively. We conclude that on-demand spreads load over time, resulting in better network utilisation – a catch-up only service just needs to be provisioned for the lower peak, rather than the pronounced peak load that over-the-top live or linear TV needs to handle.

4.1.2 Program abandonment rates are low

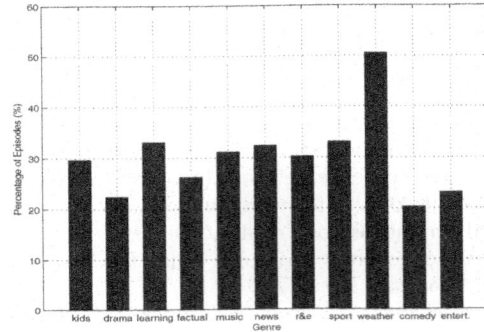

Figure 2: Percentage of items abandoned, by genre, showing relatively low abandonment rates for most, except weather.

In traditional TV setups, it has been shown that users mainly find items to watch by flipping through channels; this results in 60% of channel holding times being less than

10 seconds [8]. In contrast, users explicitly choose *what* to watch on catch-up, and can see a plot summary, actors involved, etc. before streaming. We wish to measure the effect of this on items actually streamed. We define a program stream as being abandoned if the users stops watching it in under five minutes. This threshold is somewhat arbitrary, but has been chosen to be low enough to accommodate most genres (e.g. many kids' programs are only 10 minutes long), and yet give users enough time for losing interest after starting to view an item, or realising that they have already viewed the episode before. On average, we find that ≈25% of catch-up streams are abandoned, much less than the >60% figure reported for linear TV. Fig. 2 shows the percentage of items abandoned, broken down by genre. Across the different categories, abandonment rates are in the region of 20–35%, with popular categories experiencing lower abandonment rates. The exception is weather-related content, which has a high abandonment rate of over 50%. It would seem that users only need the first few minutes of weather-related programs, or may be abandoning such programs for other reasons (e.g. they may skip to the part of the program relevant to their region, or only look for current weather rather than extended forecast).

Low program abandonment has implications for prefetching in different content delivery architectures: caching architectures can prefetch large chunks of content items likely to be watched. In SCORE below, we prefetch entire episodes, by recording them on local storage when they are broadcast. Similarly, progressive download-based streaming architectures, and peer-to-peer live streaming architectures may aggressively prefetch chunks which are due much later.

4.2 What users prefer to watch on catch-up

The previous section discussed the impact of giving users control over their watching pattern. This section asks *what* items they watch when given this control. We consider three axes of choice: duration of content, the type or genre of content, and whether the item is serialised, i.e., whether it belongs to a TV series comprising several episodes in sequence.

In each case, we use the same method to determine user preferences: we first consider the distribution of the parameter (e.g. content duration, genre or serial/non-serial) in the content corpus. Next, we consider a weighted distribution of the same parameter, weighted by the number of accesses. Their relative proportions for a given parameter value indicates user preferences: If a particular value of a parameter is overweighted in the weighted distribution compared to the content corpus, then users prefer that value. If underweighted, users dislike that value.

4.2.1 Users prefer serialised content

As a simple example of the above method, we find that serial content constitutes roughly 53.3% of the content corpus. Yet, in the list of items watched, serial content constitutes nearly 79.5%. Thus, we conclude that users prefer serial content items over non-serialised or one-off items.

4.2.2 Users prefer short duration content

Fig. 3 considers three distributions of content durations, *corpus*, *theoretical* and *actual*. *Corpus* is the distribution of content durations for each item in the catch-up content corpus. *Theoretical* is the distribution of durations obtained by weighting each item by the number of times it is accessed.

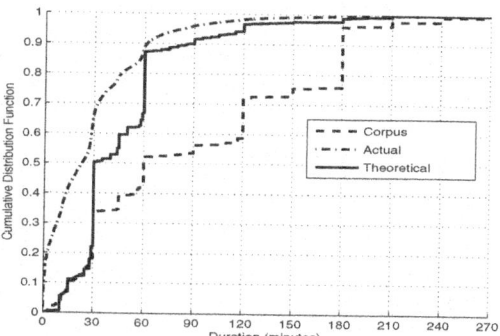

Figure 3: Content length distributions: *Corpus* shows the distribution of durations for all items in the content corpus. *Theoretical* is the distribution of content lengths for items watched. *Actual* shows the observed distribution of stream lengths. The content corpus has the most uniform distribution of content lengths. The theoretical distribution has nearly 90% of its mass under 60 minutes, showing that users prefer content shorter than an hour. Theoretical and actual distributions are close reconfirming low abandonment rates.

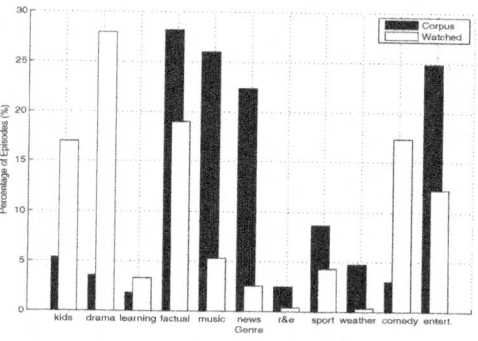

Figure 4: Distribution of episodes genres showing that drama, comedy and kids' programming are overweighted compared to corpus.

Corpus is much more uniformly distributed than *theoretical*, which has most of its mass under one hour. Observe further that the relative mass of *theoretical* increases dramatically at two points: 30 and 60 minutes, which corresponds to standard durations of serialised TV shows. This indicates the relative popularity of these two kinds of content. The third distribution, *actual*, gives the actual durations of streams observed. The difference between *theoretical* and *actual* is an indication of how much of the content is actually watched. This includes the ≈25% of requests abandoned in the first five minutes. Once this is excluded, the two distributions are even closer; suggesting high completion rates.

4.2.3 Users prefer specific genres

Next, in Fig. 4, we consider the relative proportions of different genres in the content corpus compared to their proportions when weighted by the number of accesses. Genres where the watched bar is taller than the corpus are overweighted, and hence preferred by users. This clearly indicates a strong preference for certain genres such as drama, comedy and kids' shows. In contrast, genres such as factual programs, music and news constitute a large proportion of the content corpus but are not watched as much. Thus, although a public service broadcaster might provide a balanced content catalogue, users tend to prefer common kinds of entertainment over other genres.

4.2.4 Summary and Implications

In summary, we find that users overwhelmingly prefer serialised content, and short content of duration 30 or 60 minutes, and have a liking for certain specific genres such as comedy, drama and kids' programming. For content delivery architectures, these attributes can be used to decide which items to cache, if caching selectively. These user preferences can also form the basis for personalised content delivery architectures, as explored in the design of SCORE below (§5).

5. SCORE DESIGN

In this section, we present the design of our Speculative Content Offloading and Recording Engine (SCORE). First, in §5.1 we give an overview of how SCORE fits in, as an additional software element in DVRs. Next, we discuss the components of SCORE, the optimiser which decides the contents to store to minimise wasted energy (§5.2), and the predictor (§5.3), which prioritises content programs for the optimiser, based on expected affinity of the user to the program.

5.1 Overview of operation

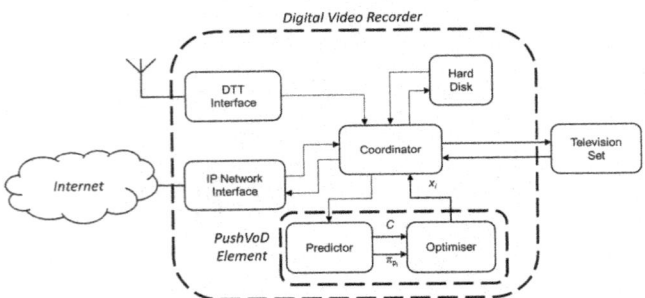

Figure 5: Schematic of a DVR/STB with SCORE

Fig. 5 shows a schematic of a DVR which includes the SCORE element. Content can be acquired either from the DTT interface during broadcast time, or pulled from the IP network interface. For each content item requested by a user, a coordinator decides whether to show the content from (a) the DTT interface (if the content is being broadcast live when the user requests to view), (b) the DVR (if the user had asked the content to be recorded, or if the SCORE element had speculatively stored the content) or (c) via IP streaming from the Catch-up TV servers, if not stored locally.

Apart from user-requested content items, the DVR also stores items speculatively when directed by the SCORE element. The SCORE element consists of a predictor and an optimiser. The predictor calculates weighting factors for each content item based on the program series to which it belongs. The decision on which items will be recorded speculatively is made by an optimiser, which calculates the expected utility of speculatively recording an item, subject to the storage limitations, and the other items that are due to be broadcast. The SCORE optimiser is run at the beginning of every week, using the upcoming broadcast schedule and the user's previous catch-up viewing history as inputs. The output is a schedule of content items to record speculatively. SCORE wakes up the DVR from sleep/stand by at the scheduled broadcast time, records the item, and goes back to sleep.

To avoid making anomalous predictions of items to record (which can waste energy if the recorded items are not watched later on), SCORE runs only after obtaining a sufficient history from the user. Currently, the threshold is set at 25 content items in the previous 3 weeks.

5.2 Optimiser

Speculative recording will never increase network traffic, but recording content not watched later on wastes energy. Although savings from watched items can compensate for unwatched items over a set of recordings, there can be net energy loss. Therefore we conservatively offload only content which is expected to minimise the energy spent in providing catch-up functionality (i.e., on-demand capability).

Deciding which items to record can be formulated as a *binary integer linear programming problem*. Formally, given a set of content items C that are known to be broadcast a given week, and a space constraint that a maximum of S bits can be stored, the task of the optimiser is to compute a binary valued variable $x_i \in \{0,1\}$ for each item $i \in C$. $x_i = 1$ if i is stored in the DVR, 0 otherwise. The decision is based on P^{IP}, the power consumption characteristics of the IP streaming option, P^{DVR}, the power consumed by the DVR for speculative recording, and the characteristics of the content item: the duration τ_i and the bitrate encoding r, which determine the space occupied, and a weighting factor $\pi_{p_i} \in [0,1]$ that encodes the probability that the user will watch item $i \in C$ based on the TV series p_i that i is part of.

Note that we model energy consumed in the Internet in terms of an energy *per bit* figure E^b, following Baliga et al. [5]. Although this model is based on a realistic paper design of a countrywide network, assuming data from commercially deployed networking equipment, there are, as with any such model, several approximations involved. §6.1 provides numerical details and discusses how we resolve the dependency on the E^b value by sensitivity analysis. In practice, for the storage levels we assume, the savings realised are relatively insensitive to E^b, especially for higher bit rates, indicative of future trends.

Speculative recording on the DVR can save energy only if

$$P^{IP} = E^b * r > P^{DVR} \qquad (1)$$

However, speculative recording can still waste energy in either of two ways. First, the optimiser might decide to store an item which is subsequently never watched; thus wasting the energy involved in speculatively storing the item in the DVR. Second, the optimiser can decide not to store a content item which is subsequently streamed by the user.

The function of the optimiser is to minimise wasted energy expenditure while speculatively recording content. This is encoded in the following decision problem:

$$\text{minimize} \sum_{i \in C} \pi_{p_i} \cdot P^{IP} \cdot (1-x_i) + \sum_{i \in C} (1-\pi_{p_i}) \cdot P^{DVR} \cdot x_i \qquad (2)$$

$$\text{subject to} \sum_{i \in C} r \cdot \tau_i \cdot x_i \leq S \qquad (3)$$

The objective function (2) is composed of two addends. The first computes the expected power spent for streaming items which the optimiser decides not to store based on a probability of watching π_{p_i}. The second addend computes the expected power spent speculatively recording content which is not subsequently watched, based on the probability of not watching $1-\pi_{p_i}$. (3) imposes the constraint that the amount of stored contents must to be smaller or equal to the size of the memory S available on the DVR.

In theory, solving this decision problem accurately is NP complete. However, note that we can adopt greedy approach and select content items one by one in descending order of the objective function value (2) until we run out of space S. This works well in practice because most high probability content items are 30 or 60 minute programs; thus, this heuristic fills available storage except for a small slot usually < 60 minutes long.

5.3 Weighting factors

In (2), each program is weighted differently for each user, based on the probability of viewing the content. To be usable in the optimiser, the end requirement from a weighting model M is a weighting factor $0 \leq \pi_p^M(u) \leq 1$ for each user u and program p, with larger π_p^M indicating greater confidence that episodes of p will be watched via IP streaming. We develop different models which obey this convention.

The episodic nature of TV programs and the strong preference of users for serialised content gives a simple but powerful predictor: watching a large fraction of the previous episodes of a program is a good indication that the future episodes will also be watched. Formally, a weighting factor π_p^H can be derived for a user u who has previously watched n_p^u episodes of a program p with n_p episodes, as the frequentist probability of watching that program:

$$\pi_p^H(u) = \frac{n_p^u}{n_p} \quad (4)$$

A second possibility is to weight each program based on the affinity of the user to the genre(s) of the program. Adopting a vector space approach, we assign each user u a vector $\mathbf{g}_u = (g_u^1, g_u^2, \ldots, g_u^m)$, where g_u^j is the number of content items of the jth genre watched by the user. Similarly, each program p is assigned a vector $\mathbf{g}_p = (g_p^1, g_p^2, \ldots, g_p^m)$, where g_p^j is the number of episodes of p tagged with the jth genre. The genre-based weight π_p^G is then calculated as the cosine similarity between the user's genres and program's genres:

$$\pi_p^G(u) = \frac{\mathbf{g}_u \cdot \mathbf{g}_p}{\|\mathbf{g}_u\| \|\mathbf{g}_p\|} \quad (5)$$

We can combine this with the previous predictor as follows:

$$\pi_p^{G+H}(u) = \max(\pi_p^H(u), \pi_p^G(u)) \quad (6)$$

Clearly, more sophisticated predictors can be developed. In particular, we experimented with an item-item collaborative filtering-based predictor, that predicts new accesses based on similar items accessed in the past. However, we did not find any significant improvement over the simple predictors given above, and hence do not present its evaluation.

6. PERFORMANCE ANALYSIS

This section analyses the performance of SCORE using the trace discussed before (§3.4). We compute the aggregate energy and traffic savings achieved when SCORE is run by users in our trace, and present the results as percentage savings. We first discuss the simulation parameters used (§6.1).

Then we assess the energy (§6.2) and traffic (§6.3) savings achieved for the network and the users by SCORE. In each case, we first use an oracle-based approach to compute the theoretical limits of the savings achievable by speculative recording. Next, the savings achieved by SCORE is measured relative to the oracle. Dependence on parameter values assumed is resolved by sensitivity analysis across the range of possible values for all parameter combinations. Finally, we evaluate how SCORE would perform if we optimise purely for traffic rather than energy savings (§6.4).

In computing the list of content items to speculatively record, we focus on weeks 4, 5 and 6 of our eight-week trace. This allows SCORE to work with the previous three weeks of history for the predictor, and at least two weeks after the broadcast for the user to watch the show, allowing a better estimation of achievable savings.

6.1 Parameters for trace-driven simulation

SCORE balances two factors which contribute to energy consumption other than on the content provider servers. The first factor is the energy consumed on DVRs to record the content. We conservatively consider HD double-tuner DVRs, which are the most energy-intensive of the simple Set-Top Boxes under EU regulations. [1] mandates a maximum power consumption of 13W when on or on active standby and to 1W when on passive stand-by for these devices. Therefore, the power consumption *added* by speculatively storing a content in the DVR, P^{DVR}, is conservatively taken as the maximum power difference possible between on and stand by states, i.e., 12W.

The second factor, the energy spent in the IP network to transport the content to the user, is much harder to quantify. Our use case of distributing content from a national broadcaster to audiences within the country over the public Internet closely fits the assumed model of Baliga et al. [5], which is based on a paper design of a national-level network in a broadband-enabled country, and includes a video distribution network for applications such as Video on Demand. The model makes detailed calculations using realistic numbers from various networking equipment currently deployed commercially, and provides a convenient method to calculate energy consumption parameterised in terms of E^b, the average energy per bit transported. However, as with other current energy models for the Internet, this introduces assumptions about the models and technology of networking equipment used, network hops from server to user, network over-provisioning and multiplexing levels, etc. To account for these uncertainties, Baliga et al. derive a range of values possible for this figure, from $E^b = 75\mu J$ for current networks down to $E^b = 2\mu J$, for a future energy-efficient all-optical network. Power consumed can be calculated as $P^{IP} = E^b r$ where r is the bit rate encoding of the content provider.

Given the inherent uncertainty and approximations involved in coming up with these values, we perform a sensitivity analysis over a range of values. The bit rate is varied as $r \in \{480, 800, 1500, 5000\} Kbps$. $r_0 = 800 Kbps$ represents the current default rate[4]; higher rates show currently available, and potential future encoding rates. We experiment with $E^b \in \{\frac{75}{8}, \frac{75}{4}, \frac{75}{2}, 75\}\mu J$, to see the effects over four (bi-

---
[4] http://www.bbc.co.uk/blogs/bbcinternet/2009/04/bbc_iplayer_goes_hd_adds_highe.html. However, when operating in full-screen mode on modern laptops, BBC iPlayer is seen to switch to 1500 Kbps.

nary) orders of magnitude. We do not go down to $E^b = 2\mu J$, the lowest value predicted by Baliga et al. [5], because at that point, for the bit rates we consider, $P^{IP} < P^{DVR}$, making it greener to stream than record on the DVR.

The amount of content that can be offloaded depends on the storage available on individual users' DVRs. Many current DVRs may have a 500GB or 1TB hard disk. Standardised technical specifications such as YouView DVR specify a minimum of 320 GB [23]. We assume that the SCORE element has access to a small fixed size partition in this space. As a baseline, we assume that a storage of $S_0 = 32GB$ is available, similar to the size of "reserved" partitions in architectures such as YouView [23]. We refer to this as the *constant S* case. As the content encoding bitrate increases, fewer content items can be stored in a fixed size partition, leading to decreased gains. Therefore, we also experiment with a *rate-proportional S* case, where the partition size is taken as proportional to the bit rate encoding r as $S = S_0 \frac{r}{r_0}$.

6.2 Understanding energy savings

The energy benefits are quantified by computing the metric *Energy Savings* = $\frac{E^{IP} - E^{SCORE}}{E^{IP}} \cdot 100$, where E^{IP} is the energy consumption of streaming all the contents and E^{SCORE} is the energy consumption using SCORE.

We wish to understand energy savings at two levels. First, we quantify the potential of content offloading. Second, we measure the savings achieved by SCORE. However, we first examine the need for personalisation.

6.2.1 Understanding the need for personalisation

n:	1	10	20	50	100
% savings:	3.3%	4.6%	-5.7%	-38.1%	-99.0%

Table 1: Indiscriminately recording most popular n items for every user leads to negative energy savings ($E^b = 75\mu J$, $r = 800 Kbps$, $S = 32GB$, week 6)

As a baseline, we first study a simple and straightforward approach to content offloading: offloading the most popular content to all users. Table 1 shows that doing so can lead to large numbers of unwatched items; recording items not watched wastes energy, resulting in decreased energy savings as n is increased. We see a net energy loss for $n = 20$ and beyond, motivating the need for a personalised, user-specific solution as developed by SCORE. The best energy savings are for a *top10* approach of saving the most popular 10 items for every user. §6.2.3 and §6.3.2 show that our personalised solution can indeed perform better than this baseline.

6.2.2 Oracle-based savings

To understand the full potential of content offloading, we consider the best-case scenario for a personalised solution: an oracle that has full knowledge of future content consumption decides offloads. Every item stored is guaranteed to be watched by the user. In this scenario, the achievable savings are limited only by the size of the storage available.

Fig. 6 shows the results, for different combinations of parameter settings[5]. The energy savings metric depends on E^b and r, which determine the power consumed by the IP streaming option, and S, which determines the amount of content that can be offloaded. Only those combinations where inequality (1) holds are considered; combinations of

[5]Error bars in all figures show 95% confidence intervals.

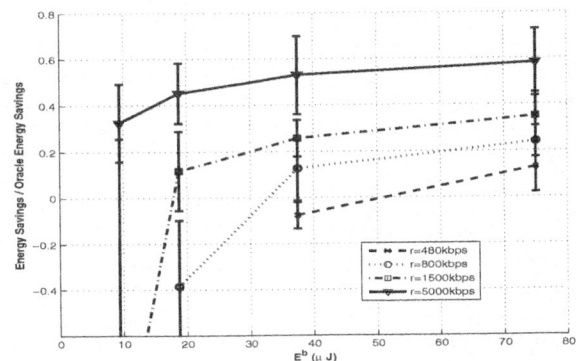

Figure 7: Energy savings of SCORE relative to oracle.

low r and E^b, known to result in negative energy savings, are not shown. In general, as E^b and r increase, IP streaming consumes more energy, and the energy savings are higher. However Fig. 6a shows that for very high bitrates, storage can become a limiting factor: The oracle is not able to store as many items as possible at lower bit rates, resulting in smaller energy savings (e.g. at $E^b = 75\mu J$, the savings from $r = 5000Kbps$ is smaller than savings from lower bit rates). Fig. 6b shows that this limitation is overcome when the storage is proportional to bit rate encoding. Fig. 6c shows the maximum savings achievable, by removing all storage constraints. If every item can be stored locally when broadcast, up to 97% savings can be achieved at high r and E^b. The maximum savings are $\approx 75\%$ considering a constant storage $S_0 = 32GB$, and $\approx 90\%$ considering a rate-proportional S.

6.2.3 Energy savings in SCORE

Next, we study the savings achieved by SCORE, given access to $S_0 = 32GB$[6]. Fig. 7 performs a sensitivity analysis and shows the average energy savings by using SCORE for different combinations of parameter choices. For low values of r and E^b, the achievable energy savings are small, and errors in speculatively recording content which are not watched later can in fact lead to negative energy savings. However, at higher bit rates, savings appear to be relatively insensitive to the assumed values of E^b and SCORE can recover 40-60% of the optimal savings achieved by the oracle.

6.3 Understanding traffic savings

Next we study traffic savings by computing the metric: *Peak bandwidth savings* = $\frac{Q_{95}^{IP} - Q_{95}^{SCORE}}{Q_{95}^{IP}}$, where Q_{95}^{SCORE} and Q_{95}^{IP} are the 95th percentile bandwidth taken across 5 minutes intervals by using SCORE and by streaming all the contents, respectively. This metric is intended to approximate the reductions in operating costs for ISPs, and uses the 95th percentile bandwidth because many ISPs' Service Level Agreements (SLAs) are based on this figure.

6.3.1 Oracle-based savings

Fig. 8 shows the traffic savings obtained using an oracle with complete knowledge of future accesses. Unlike the energy savings computation, the oracle-based traffic savings do not depend on E^b, but only on r, the bit rate encoding,

[6]Due to space constraints, only the more challenging constant S case is presented for SCORE energy & traffic savings.

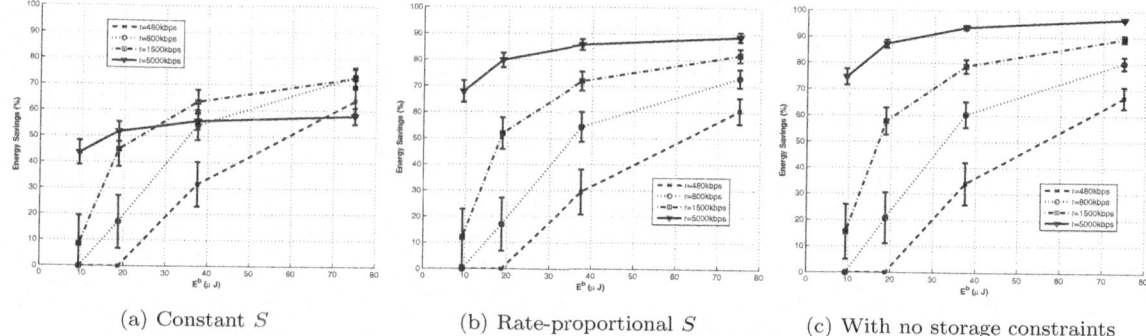

(a) Constant S (b) Rate-proportional S (c) With no storage constraints

Figure 6: Average energy savings (%) with oracle for different E^b, r and S parameter combinations.

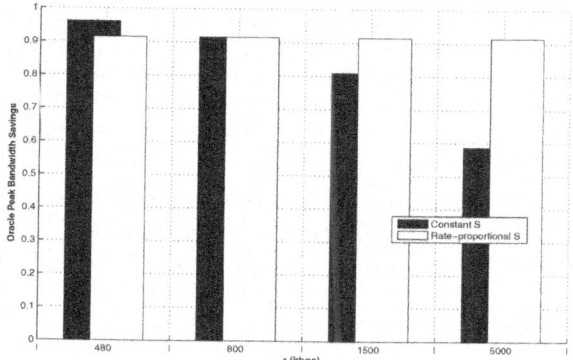

Figure 8: Peak bandwidth savings of oracle.

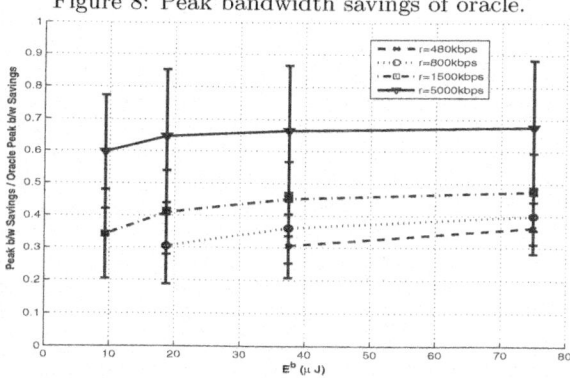

Figure 9: SCORE peak bandwidth savings relative to oracle

which determines the size of the IP flow, and S, the storage available on the DVR, which determines the amount of content which can be offloaded; an oracle with infinite storage can offload *all* the traffic. Therefore we only study the variation in savings for different values of r and finite values of S. The figure highlights that peak bandwidth is insensitive to the bit rate for rate-proportional S, because the memory size per content item remains constant across bit rates. Fig. 8 shows that the peak bandwidth savings can be up to 96% (i.e., peak bandwidth with the oracle can be as low as 4% of the peak without oracle-based offloading), but the peak bandwidth savings rapidly decreases when storage becomes a constraint (constant S scenario, for higher bandwidths).

6.3.2 Traffic benefits from SCORE

Fig. 9 shows a sensitivity analysis of the peak bandwidth

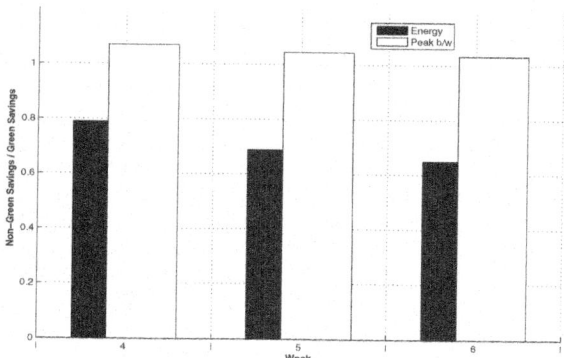

Figure 10: Comparing green or energy-conscious variant of SCORE (Eq. (2)) with the traffic-conscious or non-green version (Eq. (7)) shows that being green achieves 40% more savings in energy at the expense of only 5% more traffic. ($E^b = 75\mu J$, $r = 1500 Kbps$, $S = 32GB$)

savings obtained by SCORE for different parameter settings. Note that unlike the oracle case, the savings with SCORE depend on E^b as well as r and S. This is because the items to download are decided as a *side effect* of saving energy (Eq. (2), also see discussion in §6.4). As with energy, SCORE typically recovers $\approx$ 40–60% of the traffic savings achieved by the oracle, using 32GB storage[6]. These savings are relatively insensitive to assumed values of E^b.

6.4 The price of being green

Eq. (2) decides which items to store speculatively based on their expected *energy* savings. Thus, even if storage is available, our implementation might decide not to save a content item because the expected energy savings may be negative, if our belief that the item will be watched (Eq. (6)) is low enough. If the content item ends up being watched, it represents a missed opportunity to save traffic. We evaluate this "price of being green", by changing the optimiser to the following "non-green" problem, which purely minimises the probability that a recorded content is not watched:

$$\text{minimize} \sum_{i \in C} \pi_{p_i} \cdot (1 - x_i) \quad (7)$$

subject to the memory constraint, Eq. (3).

Fig. 10 shows the impact of greening on the energy and traffic savings in terms of the ratio of the savings achieved in the energy aware or "green" case considered previously (Eq. (2)) to the savings achieved using the "non-green" case (Eq. (7)). The black bars show that the green solution saves up to 40% more energy compared to the non-green solution. The white bars highlight that using energy-unaware SCORE, we could only achieve a traffic savings that is about 1.05 times greater, for the parameter settings indicated. This gap would be bigger if we consider lower values of E^b.

7. DISCUSSION AND CONCLUSIONS

We are currently witnessing the long-predicted convergence of IP and media networks in various forms. While this has offered additional functionality such as catch-up TV—the ability to watch TV programs on-demand, over the public Internet, without a dedicated infrastructure setup—the encroaching of TV content on the IP network can lead to additional network traffic and energy consumption.

Our contributions are twofold. Our first contribution is a characterisation of the catch-up TV workload, showing that catch-up has excellent network utilisation compared to traditional TV because on-demand spreads load over time and because stream abandonment rates are lower. Further, we showed that users prefer content shorter than one hour, and have a strong preference for episodic or serialised content, and certain genres such as comedy, drama and kids' shows.

Our second contribution is a simple approach that leverages the broadcast nature of TV, and the strong user preference for episodic and genre-based content to reduce the energy and traffic footprint of catch-up. The core of our proposal is to speculatively record content as it is being broadcast, using storage local to the user, such as those found on DVRs. Later requests for catch-up viewing can be served locally instead of incurring a network footprint. As a realisation of this concept, we presented the Speculative Content Offloading and Recording Engine (SCORE). For a given user, SCORE selects program episodes to record based on predicted affinity of the user to the program. We suggested simple predictors based on the affinity of users to serialised content and to specific genres.

Our main motivation in developing SCORE was to demonstrate that it is relatively easy to offload catch-up video streams from the Internet, and that significant savings can be obtained as a result. Below, we conclude briefly discuss two aspects that may need to be addressed for wider applicability of SCORE.

7.1 Better predictors for SCORE

Clearly, the performance of SCORE depends on the quality of the predictors used. In this work, we proposed very simple predictors based on episode histories, and genre affinity. We experimented with a more sophisticated item-item collaborative filtering approach, but for entire range of parameter values we assumed, no significant improvement was observed. Hence we present only the simpler alternative.

Our analysis may have been hindered by a few factors: First, other systems such as Netflix and TiVo which recommend items to watch per user can rely on users' ratings for previous content items watched. This information is not available to us. We can only rely on information that a user watched a particular TV show, but we cannot infer *how much* she liked it. Second, we are trying to predict which items will be watched on *catch-up* TV. This is a harder problem than predicting which items will be watched: some episodes may be watched on "catch-up" because the vagaries of a user's schedule might have prevented her from watching the episode as it was broadcast. Since our data only consists of catch-up TV, we will not know that the user regularly watches the TV show. We emphasise that an actual deployment will not have this problem, and can in fact record a show simply based on previous history of watching other episodes. Third, our dataset is sampled. This negatively affects us in two ways – if a historic access is missing due to sampling, we may be unable to predict a future access. On the other hand, we may predict an access that does happen in reality, but gets sampled out of the trace; our trace-based evaluation will not recognise the savings.

Despite these difficulties, we can, depending on parameter settings, recover more than 60% of the traffic and energy savings achieved by an omniscient oracle with full knowledge of a user's future consumption. We conservatively choose to offload only content which can save energy. Optimising purely for traffic can yield an additional 5% traffic savings. Furthermore, especially at higher bit rates which are indicative of present and near future catch-up deployments, these savings appear to be relatively insensitive to the assumptions we make about E^b, the energy per bit transported, the main parameter of the simplified energy model used.

7.2 Deployability and hardware requirements

As described earlier (§5.1), SCORE can operate as a software addition to DVRs. For wide applicability, SCORE needs to be deployable on existing DVRs, and DVRs should be widely available/used. Many DVR specifications include over-the-air or Internet-based software update mechanisms [23, 2]; these can be used to roll out the functionality of SCORE to existing DVRs. As noted in §3.2, many options to obtain TV content include DVR-like storage. Indeed, DVRs have over 50% penetration in major markets such as the US and UK [17, 11]. Thus, we believe SCORE has the potential to be widely deployed. Moreover, SCORE can be deployed independently by users; benefits to the system increase with each additional user, allowing incremental deployability.

The core functionality of SCORE, *offloading* content, requires only a basic DVR with user-local storage and a TV tuner. However, in order to seamlessly switch to IP streaming when the content is not available on local storage, an internet-connected DVR is required. Users with more basic DVRs need to manually switch to an Internet connected device as fallback.

In the current setting, many users who do not own a TV or DVR use the on-demand interface (e.g. Hulu, BBC iPlayer) through their laptop/desktops as their primary means for accessing TV content. For such users, a DVR-based solution may be too cumbersome. In principle, our solution only requires some form of user-local storage and the capability to record broadcasts; thus, SCORE can be deployed for computer-based users using a simple TV tuner attached to a computer. SCORE can operate as a daemon that selectively records content as it is broadcast, onto the computer's hard drive. Alternately, if saving *peak-period* traffic is the only consideration, the concept of SCORE can be used to selectively prefetch content to the laptop/desktop during night time, or other periods when spare bandwidth is available.

Acknowledgements

Jon Crowcroft would like to acknowledge the Engineering and Physical Sciences Research Council, UK, for funding programme grant EP/H040536/1. Gianfranco Nencioni was partially supported by pump-priming funds granted to Nishanth Sastry by King's College London and by the GATE-COM project funded by MIUR (Italian Ministry of Education, University, and Research).

8. REFERENCES

[1] Commission Regulation No 107/2009 of 4 February 2009 implementing Directive 2005/32/EC of the European Parliament and of the Council with regard to ecodesign requirements for simple set-top boxes. *Official Journal of the European Union L36* (2009), 8–14.

[2] Nordig unified requirements for integrated receiver decoders for use in cable, satellite, terrestrial and ip-based networks. Ver. 2.2.1, 2010.

[3] ANNAPUREDDY, S., GUHA, S., GKANTSIDIS, C., GUNAWARDENA, D., AND RODRIGUEZ, P. Is high-quality VoD feasible using P2P swarming? In *Proc. Intl. Conf. on World Wide Web (WWW)* (2007).

[4] APPLEGATE, D., ARCHER, A., GOPALAKRISHNAN, V., LEE, S., AND RAMAKRISHNAN, K. Optimal content placement for a large-scale VoD system. In *Proceedings of the 6th International Conference on Networking EXperiments and Technologies (CoNEXT 2012)* (2010), ACM, p. 4.

[5] BALIGA, J., AYRE, R., HINTON, K., SORIN, W. V., AND TUCKER, R. S. Energy consumption in optical IP networks. *Journal of Lightwave Technology 27*, 13 (Jul 2009), 2391–2403.

[6] BORST, S., GUPTA, V., AND WALID, A. Distributed caching algorithms for content distribution networks. In *Proc. IEEE INFOCOM* (2010).

[7] CASTRO, M., DRUSCHEL, P., KERMARREC, A., NANDI, A., ROWSTRON, A., AND SINGH, A. Splitstream: high-bandwidth multicast in cooperative environments. In *19th ACM Symposium on Operating Systems Principles (SOSP)* (2003).

[8] CHA, M., RODRIGUEZ, P., CROWCROFT, J., MOON, S., AND AMATRIAIN, X. Watching television over an IP network. In *Proceedings of the 8th ACM SIGCOMM conference on Internet measurement (IMC)* (2008), ACM, pp. 71–84.

[9] CHANDARIA, J., HUNTER, J., AND WILLIAMS, A. A comparison of the carbon footprint of digital terrestrial television with video-on-demand. BBC Research Whitepaper 189, March 2011.

[10] CHOE, Y., SCHUFF, D., DYABERI, J., AND PAI, V. Improving VoD server efficiency with bittorrent. In *Proceedings of the 15th international conference on Multimedia* (2007), ACM, pp. 117–126.

[11] DELOITTE. Technology, media & telecom predictions, May 2012.

[12] DOBRIAN, F., AWAN, A., JOSEPH, D., GANJAM, A., ZHAN, J., SEKAR, V., STOICA, I., AND ZHANG, H. Understanding the impact of video quality on user engagement. *SIGCOMM-Computer Communication Review 41*, 4 (2011), 362.

[13] HEI, X., LIANG, C., LIANG, J., LIU, Y., AND ROSS, K. A measurement study of a large-scale P2P IPTV system. *IEEE Transactions on Multimedia 9*, 8 (2007), 1672–1687.

[14] HUANG, C., LI, J., AND ROSS, K. W. Can Internet video-on-demand be profitable? In *Proc. ACM SIGCOMM* (2007).

[15] HUANG, Y., FU, T. Z., CHIU, D.-M., LUI, J. C., AND HUANG, C. Challenges, design and analysis of a large-scale P2P-VoD system. SIGCOMM '08.

[16] KOSTIĆ, D., RODRIGUEZ, A., ALBRECHT, J., AND VAHDAT, A. Bullet: high bandwidth data dissemination using an overlay mesh. In *SOSP* (2003).

[17] NEILSEN. Report: Bigger TVs, DVR and Wi-Fi among Hot U.S. Home Technology Trends, 2010.

[18] OFCOM. Communications market report 2012. Available from http://stakeholders.ofcom.org.uk/binaries/research/cmr/cmr12/CMR_UK_2012.pdf, July 2012.

[19] SANDVINE. Global internet phenomena report, 1h 2012, May 2012.

[20] TIVO. How to find great new shows with TiVo Suggestions. Available from http://www.tivo.com/mytivo/howto/getthemostoftv/howto_use_suggestions.html, Last accessed 25 Apr 2012.

[21] VERHOEYEN, M., DE VLEESCHAUWER, D., AND ROBINSON, D. Content storage architectures for boosted IPTV service. *Bell Labs Tech. J. 13*, 3 (2008), 29–43.

[22] YANG, X., GJOKA, M., CHHABRA, P., MARKOPOULOU, A., AND RODRIGUEZ, P. Kangaroo: video seeking in P2P systems. In *Proc. Intl. Conf. on peer-to-peer Systems* (2009), USENIX Association.

[23] YOUVIEW TV LTD. Youview core technical specification, 2011.

[24] YU, H., ZHENG, D., ZHAO, B., AND ZHENG, W. Understanding user behavior in large-scale video-on-demand systems. *ACM SIGOPS Operating Systems Review 40*, 4 (2006), 333–344.

Sorry, I don't speak SPARQL – Translating SPARQL Queries into Natural Language

Axel-Cyrille Ngonga Ngomo
Universität Leipzig, IFI/AKSW
PO 100920, D-04009 Leipzig
ngonga@informatik.uni-leipzig.de

Lorenz Bühmann
Universität Leipzig, IFI/AKSW
PO 100920, D-04009 Leipzig
buehmann@informatik.uni-leipzig.de

Christina Unger
Bielefeld University, CITEC
Universitätsstraße 21–23,
33615 Bielefeld
cunger@cit-ec.uni-bielefeld.de

Jens Lehmann
Universität Leipzig, IFI/AKSW
PO 100920, D-04009 Leipzig
lehmann@informatik.uni-leipzig.de

Daniel Gerber
Universität Leipzig, IFI/AKSW
PO 100920, D-04009 Leipzig
dgerber@informatik.uni-leipzig.de

ABSTRACT

Over the past years, Semantic Web and Linked Data technologies have reached the backend of a considerable number of applications. Consequently, large amounts of RDF data are constantly being made available across the planet. While experts can easily gather information from this wealth of data by using the W3C standard query language SPARQL, most lay users lack the expertise necessary to proficiently interact with these applications. Consequently, non-expert users usually have to rely on forms, query builders, question answering or keyword search tools to access RDF data. However, these tools have so far been unable to explicate the queries they generate to lay users, making it difficult for these users to i) assess the correctness of the query generated out of their input, and ii) to adapt their queries or iii) to choose in an informed manner between possible interpretations of their input. This paper addresses this drawback by presenting SPARQL2NL, a generic approach that allows verbalizing SPARQL queries, i.e., converting them into natural language. Our framework can be integrated into applications where lay users are required to understand SPARQL or to generate SPARQL queries in a direct (forms, query builders) or an indirect (keyword search, question answering) manner. We evaluate our approach on the DBpedia question set provided by QALD-2 within a survey setting with both SPARQL experts and lay users. The results of the 115 filled surveys show that SPARQL2NL can generate complete and easily understandable natural language descriptions. In addition, our results suggest that even SPARQL experts can process the natural language representation of SPARQL queries computed by our approach more efficiently than the corresponding SPARQL queries. Moreover, non-experts are enabled to reliably understand the content of SPARQL queries.

Copyright is held by the International World Wide Web Conference Committee (IW3C2). IW3C2 reserves the right to provide a hyperlink to the author's site if the Material is used in electronic media.
WWW 2013, May 13–17, 2013, Rio de Janeiro, Brazil.
ACM 978-1-4503-2035-1/13/05.

Categories and Subject Descriptors

H.5.2 [**Information systems**]: User Interfaces—*Natural language, Theory and methods*

General Terms

Algorithms, Experimentation, Theory

Keywords

natural language generation; query verbalization; SPARQL

1. INTRODUCTION

An ever-growing number of applications rely on RDF data as well as on the W3C standard SPARQL for querying this data. While SPARQL has proven to be a powerful tool in the hands of experienced users, it remains difficult to fathom for lay users. To address this drawback, approaches such as question answering [28], keyword search [25] and search by example [18] have been developed with the aim of hiding SPARQL and RDF from the user. Still, these approaches internally construct SPARQL queries to address their data backend, without providing lay users with a possibility to check whether the retrieved answers indeed correspond to the intended information need. Consider for example the natural language question What is the birth date of Li Ling?, for which TBSL [28] returns more than 50 possible interpretations, including the birth date of the pole vaulter Li Ling and the age of the sinologist Li Ling. Since each of the interpretations is realized as a SPARQL query, a lay user cannot pinpoint the set of results that correspond to the person he is actually interested in, nor can he easily detect the source of possible errors. Similar problems occur in keyword-based systems. For example, the keywords Jenny Runacre husbands leads to SINA [25] generating queries for the husbands of Jenny Runacre as well as for the role of Jenny Runacre in the movie "The Husbands". We address this drawback by presenting SPARQL2NL[1], a novel approach

---
[1] http://aksw.org/projects/SPARQL2NL - an open source implementation is available at https://github.com/AKSW/SPARQL2NL

that can verbalize SPARQL queries and therewith bridge the gap between the query language understood by semantic data backends, i.e. SPARQL, and that of the end users, i.e. natural language. Our approach is tailored towards SPARQL constructs typically used in keyword search and question answering, and it consists of four main steps: a *preprocessing* step which normalizes the query and extracts type information for the occurring variables, a *processing* step during which a generic representation of the query is constructed, a *postprocessing* step which applies reduction and replacement rules in order to improve the legibility of the verbalization, and a *realization* step which generates the final natural language representation of the query. As exemplary use cases, we integrated SPARQL2NL into the user interface for the question answering system TBSL[2] as well as into the BioASQ annotation tool[3]. A demo of SPARQL2NL is available at http://sparql2nl.aksw.org/demo.

The rest of this paper is structured as follows: After introducing the notation we employ in this paper, we give an overview of each of the four steps underlying SPARQL2NL. We then evaluate our approach with respect to the *adequacy* and *fluency* [5] of the natural language representations it generates. After a brief review of related work, we conclude with some final remarks. Throughout the rest of the paper, we use the following query shown in Listing 1 as main example[4]. This query retrieves persons that are writers or surfers and were born later than 1950.

```
1  SELECT DISTINCT ?person ?label
2  WHERE { ?person rdf:type dbo:Person.
3          { ?person dbo:occupation res:Writer. }
4          UNION
5          { ?person dbo:occupation res:Surfing. }
6          ?person dbo:birthDate ?date.
7          FILTER(?date > "1950"^^xsd:date) .
8          OPTIONAL {?person rdfs:label ?label
9          FILTER ( lang(?label) = "en" ) } }
```

Listing 1: Running example.

2. PRELIMINARIES AND NOTATION

The goal of our approach is to generate a complete and correct natural language representation of an arbitrary SPARQL query, where completeness means in this context that we aim to represent all information that is necessary for the user to understand the content of the query. In terms of the standard model of natural language generation proposed by Reiter & Dale [24], our preprocessor and processor steps mainly play the role of the document planner, in particular carrying out the task of document structuring, while the postprocessor step corresponds to the micro-planner, with focus on aggregation operations and the lexicalization of referring expressions. In the following, we give a short overview of the notation used throughout this paper to describe our approach. We begin by giving a brief overview of the most important concepts underlying SPARQL queries. Thereafter,

we present our approach to formalizing natural language sentences.

2.1 SPARQL queries and their realization

According to the SPARQL grammar,[5] a SPARQL SELECT query can be regarded as consisting of three parts:

1. a *body section* B, which describes all data that has to be retrieved,

2. an *optional section* O, which describes the data items that can be retrieved by the query if they exist, and

3. a *modifier section* M, which describes all solution sequences, modifiers and aggregates that are to be applied to the result of the previous two sections of the query.

Let Var be the set of all variables that can be used in a SPARQL query. In addition, let R be the set of all resources, P the set of all properties and L the set of all literals contained in the target knowledge base of the SPARQL queries at hand. We call $x \in Var \cup R \cup P \cup L$ an *atom*. The basic components of the body of a SPARQL query are triple patterns $(s, p, o) \in (Var \cup R) \times (Var \cup P) \times (Var \cup R \cup L)$. Let W be the set of all words in the dictionary of our target language. We define the realization function $\rho : Var \cup R \cup P \cup L \to W^*$ as the function which maps each atom to a word or sequence of words from the dictionary. Formally, the goal of this paper is to devise the extension of ρ to all SPARQL constructs. This extension maps all atoms x to their realization $\rho(x)$ and defines how these atomic realizations can be combined. We denote the extension of ρ by the same label ρ for the sake of simplicity. We adopt a rule-based approach to achieve this goal, where the rules extending ρ to all valid SPARQL constructs are expressed in a conjunctive manner. This means that for premises $P_1, \ldots, P_n$ and consequences $K_1, \ldots, K_m$ we write $P_1 \land \ldots \land P_n \Rightarrow K_1 \land \ldots \land K_m$. The premises and consequences are explicated by using an extension of the Stanford dependencies[6]. We rely especially on the constructs explained in Table 1. For example, a possessive dependency between two phrase elements e_1 and e_2 is represented as poss(e_1, e_2). For the sake of simplicity, we slightly deviate from the Stanford vocabulary by not treating the copula to be as an auxiliary, but denoting it as BE. Moreover, we extend the vocabulary by the constructs conj and disj which denote the conjunction resp. disjunction of two phrase elements. In addition, we sometimes reduce the construct subj(y,x) ∧ dobj(y,z) to the triple (x,y,z) $\in W^3$.

3. PREPROCESSING

The goal of the preprocessing step is to normalize the query while extracting central information on projection variables. This is carried out in two steps: *type extraction* and *normalization*.

3.1 Type extraction

Let Q be the input query and C the set of all possible classes from the ontology of the knowledge base to be queried, extended by the classes Resource, Property and Value. The aim of *type extraction* is to assign a combination of types

---

[2] A demo can be found at http://autosparql-tbsl.dl-learner.org.
[3] The tool can be accessed at http://at.bioasq.org
[4] The following prefixes are used:
dbo: <http://dbpedia.org/ontology/>
res: <http://dbpedia.org/resource/>
rdfs: <http://www.w3.org/2000/01/rdf-schema#>
rdf: <http://www.w3.org/1999/02/22-rdf-syntax-ns#>

[5] See http://www.w3.org/TR/sparql11-query/.
[6] For a complete description of the vocabulary, see http://nlp.stanford.edu/software/dependencies_manual.pdf.

Dependency	Explanation
amod	Represents the *adjectival modifier* dependency. For example amod(ROSE,WHITE) stands for white rose.
cc	Stands for the relation between a conjunct and a given conjunction (in most cases and or or). For example in the sentence John eats an apple and a pear, cc(PEAR,AND) holds. We mainly use this construct to specify reduction and replacement rules.
conj*	Used to build the *conjunction* of two phrase elements, e.g. conj(subj(EAT,JOHN),subj(DRINK,MARY)) stands for John eats and Mary drinks. conj is not to be confused with the logical conjunction ∧, which we use to state that two dependencies hold in the same sentence. For example subj(EAT,JOHN) ∧ dobj(EAT,FISH) is to be read as John eats fish.
disj*	Used to build the *disjunction* of two phrase elements, similarly to conj.
dobj	Dependency between a verb and its *direct object*, for example dobj(EAT,APPLE) expresses to eat an/the apple.
nn	The *noun compound modifier* is used to modify a head noun by the means of another noun. For instance nn(FARMER,JOHN) stands for farmer John.
poss	Expresses a possessive dependency between two lexical items, for example poss(JOHN,DOG) express John's dog.
prep_X	Stands for the preposition X, where X can be any preposition, such as via, of, in and between.
prepc_X	Clausal modifier, used to modify verb or noun phrases by a clause introduced by some preposition X, e.g. prepc_suchthat(PEOPLE,c) represents people such that c, where c is some clause, e.g. their year of birth is 1950.
root	Marks the root of a sentence, e.g. the verb. For example ROOT(EAT) ∧ subj(EAT,JOHN) means John eats. The root of the sentence will not always be stated explicitly in our formalization.
subj	Relation between *subject* and verb, for example subj(BE,JOHN) expresses John is.

Table 1: Dependencies used by SPARQL2NL. The dependencies which are part of our extension of the Stanford dependencies are marked with an asterisk.

to each projection variable of the query. To this end, we process the query by finding all graph patterns ?x rdf:type C for each projection variable ?x (with C ∈ C). If none of the statements is part of a UNION statement, we assign the conjunction of all C to ?x. Otherwise we assign to ?x the disjunction of all C that are such that the UNION statements which contain ?x rdf:type C contain no other statements. Consequently, in Example 1, the type dbo:Person is assigned to the variable ?person.

When no explicit type information for a projection variable ?x is found, we try to detect implicit type information by mapping ?x to Resource if ?x is always the subject or the object of an object property, to Property if ?x is always a property, and to Value in all other cases. Thus, ?label is assigned the type Value, as it occurs as the object of a datatype property. Finally, all explicit information that was used to compute type information is deleted from the input query Q. Overall, this preprocessing step alters Example 1 by removing the triple ?person rdf:type dbo:Person and storing it as type information for the variable ?person. In addition, the variable ?label is assigned the type Value.

3.2 Normalization

One SPARQL feature that often leads to queries that are difficult to understand is the nesting of UNION statements. To ensure that we generate easily legible natural language representations of SPARQL queries, we *normalize* the input queries further by transforming any nesting of disjunctions (i.e. UNION statements) into a disjunctive normal form (DNF). We chose to use DNFs because they allow us to make explicit use of conjunctions binding stronger than disjunctions in English. An obvious drawback of this normalization approach is that it can lead to an exponential growth of the number of terms in a query. Yet, this drawback seems to be of minute relevance for practical applications. For example, no query in the benchmark was verbalized in more than 2s.

4. PROCESSING

The goal of the subsequent processing step is to generate a list of dependency trees for an input query. To achieve this goal (and in accordance with formalization introduced in 2.1), the query is subdivided into the three segments *body* (B), *optional* (O) and *modifier* (M), each of which is assigned its own sentence tree. Since ASK queries only possess a subset of these features, they can also be processed by our approach. Therefore, in the following, we only describe how the representation of each of these segments is generated for SELECT queries. As each of these representations relies on the same processors for processing triple patterns, we begin by presenting the processing of simple graph patterns.

4.1 Processing triple patterns

The realization of a triple pattern s p o depends mostly on the verbalization of the predicate p. If p can be realized as a noun phrase, then a possessive clause can be used to express the semantics of s p o, as shown in 1. For example, if p is a relational noun like author, then the verbalization is ?x's author is ?y. In case p's realization is a verb, then the triple can be verbalized as given in 2. For example, if p is the verb write, then the verbalization is ?x writes ?y.

1. $\rho(s\ p\ o) \Rightarrow poss(\rho(p), \rho(s)) \land subj(BE, \rho(p)) \land dobj(BE, \rho(o))$

2. $\rho(\text{s p o}) \Rightarrow \text{subj}(\rho(\text{p}),\rho(\text{s})) \wedge \text{dobj}(\rho(\text{p}),\rho(\text{o}))$

In cases where p is a variable or where our approach fails to recognize the type of the predicate, we rely on the more generic approach in 3 as a fallback, where REL is short for to relate. This representation amounts to s is related to o via p.

3. $\rho(\text{s p o}) \Rightarrow \text{subj}(\text{REL},\rho(\text{s})) \wedge \text{dobj}(\text{REL},\rho(\text{o})) \wedge$
   $\text{prep\_via}(\text{REL},\rho(\text{p}))$

In our running example, verbalizing ?person dbo:birthDate ?date would thus lead to ?person's birth date is ?date, as birth date is a noun.

4.2 Generating the body section

The main effort during the processing step is concerned with representing the body of the query, i.e. the content of the WHERE clause. Our approach begins by transforming the type information retrieved by the preprocessing step described in 3.1 above (either an atomic type y, or a conjunction $y \wedge z$ or disjunction $y \vee z$) into a coordinated phrase element CPE_T, relying on the following rules:

4. $\rho(\text{?x rdf:type y}) \Rightarrow \text{nn}(\rho(\text{y}),\text{?x})$

5. $\rho(y \wedge z) \Rightarrow \text{conj}(\rho(y),\rho(z))$

6. $\rho(y \vee z) \Rightarrow \text{disj}(\rho(y),\rho(z))$

For Example 1, nn(dbo:Person,?person) is generated. DISTINCT is considered an adjective while COUNT is mapped to a noun phrase:

7. $\rho(\text{DISTINCT X}) \Rightarrow \text{amod}(\rho(\text{X}),\text{DISTINCT})$
   (i.e., distinct X)

8. $\rho(\text{COUNT X}) \Rightarrow \text{prep\_of}(\text{NUMBER},\rho(\text{X}))$
   (i.e., number of X)

The processing then continues by converting the content of the WHERE clause into a second coordinated phrase element CPE_W. Within this clause, only group graph patterns GP (i.e., combinations of conjunctions, UNIONs and FILTERs) can be used. The following set of rules deal with conjunctions and disjunctions:

9. $\rho(GP_1,GP_2) \Rightarrow \text{conj}(\rho(GP_1),\rho(GP_2))$

10. $\rho(\text{UNION}(GP_1,GP_2)) \Rightarrow \text{disj}(\rho(GP_1),\rho(GP_2))$

Processing FILTER is more intricate due to the large number of operators and functions that can be used in this construct. Therefore, FILTER leads to a more significant number of rules. In general, most operators OP that can be used in a filter can be expressed by a verbal clause $\rho(\text{OP})$. Binary operators can be translated by the following rule:

11. $\rho(\text{OP}(x,y)) \Rightarrow \text{subj}(\rho(\text{OP}),x) \wedge \text{dobj}(\rho(\text{OP}),y)$

Functional filters (i.e., filters of the form f(x)=y) can be translated into equivalent operators f(x,y) and verbalized as above. The body section B is finally generated by joining CPE_T and CPE_W as follows:

12. $\rho(B) \Rightarrow \text{subj}(\text{RETRIEVE},\text{QUERY}) \wedge$
    $\text{dobj}(\text{RETRIEVE},\rho(CPE_T)) \wedge$
    $\text{prepc\_suchthat}(\rho(CPE_T),\rho(CPE_W))$

This leads to query verbalizations of the general form This query retrieves... such that..., e.g. This query retrieves distinct values ?x such that ?x is Abraham Lincoln's death date.

4.3 Processing the optional section

The SPARQL constructs that can be used in the OPTIONAL section of the query are a subset of the constructs that can be used in the query body. For constructing the representation O of the optional section of the query (if such a section exists) we therefore reuse the same set of rules as those used to generate the body B.

4.4 Processing solution modifiers and aggregates

Solution modifiers alter the order in which the results of the SPARQL query are presented to the user. They include ORDER BY, LIMIT and OFFSET constructs. Translating ORDER BY OG(?x) (where OG is either the empty string, ASC or DESC) follows the rule given in 13, e.g. yielding The results are in descending order.

13. $\rho(\text{ORDER BY OG(?x)}) \Rightarrow \text{subj}(\text{BE},\text{RESULTS}) \wedge$
    $\text{prep\_in}(\text{BE},\text{ORDER}) \wedge$
    $\text{amod}(\text{ORDER},\rho(\text{OG}))$

If no ordering is specified, we assume OG=ASC according to the SPARQL specification. For LIMIT and OFFSET, we use the generic rule in 14, e.g. yielding The query returns results between number 2 and 5.

14. $\rho(\text{OFFSET n LIMIT m}) \Rightarrow \text{subj}(\text{RETURN},\text{QUERY}) \wedge$
    $\text{dobj}(\text{RETURN},\text{RESULTS}) \wedge$
    $\text{prep\_between}(\text{RESULTS},$
    $\text{conj}(\rho(\text{n+1}),\rho(\text{n+m})))$

The sections of this rule are altered depending on whether LIMIT is used without OFFSET and in case the difference between the argument of LIMIT and OFFSET is 1, e.g. in order not to construct The query returns results between number 1 and 1 but rather The query returns the first result. The aggregation constructs are dealt with in a similar fashion.

After the processing step, our Example 1 would be verbalized as follows:

15. This query retrieves distinct people ?person such that ?person's occupation is Surfing or ?person's occupation is Writer, ?person's birth date is ?date and ?date is later than 1950. Additionally, it retrieves distinct values ?string such that ?person's label is ?string and ?string is in English if such exist.

5. POSTPROCESSING

Although the natural language output of the verbalization step just described is a correct description of the content of the SPARQL query, it often sounds very artificial. The general goal of the subsequent postprocessing step is thus to transform the generated description such that it sounds more natural. To this end, we focus on two types of transformation rules (cf. [3]): *aggregation* and *referencing*. Aggregation serves to remove redundancies and collapse information that is too verbose otherwise, for example:

?place is Shakespeare's birth place or ?place is Shakespeare's death place.

$\Rightarrow$?place is Shakespeare's birth place or death place.

Referencing aims at achieving a natural verbalization of noun phrases, in particular avoiding variables wherever possible. For example:

This query retrieves values ?height such that ?height is Claudia Schiffer's height.

⇒ This query retrieves Claudia Schiffer's height.

The input to the postprocessor is the output of the preceding processing step described in Section 4 above, i.e., a set of variables with types (the select clause) and a list of dependency trees describing these variables. In the following, we describe the transformation rules we employ in more detail. The order in which they are applied is: clustering and ordering (5.1), aggregation (5.3), grouping (5.2), referencing (5.4).

5.1 Clustering and ordering rules

The very first aggregation step serves to cluster and order the input sentences. To this end, the variables occurring in the query are ordered with respect to the number of their occurrences, distinguishing projection variables, i.e. variables that occur in the SELECT clause, from all others, and assigning them those input sentences that mention them. In case the most frequent variable is the object of the sentence, the sentence is passivized (presupposed the verb is not an auxiliary or copulative verb such as is or has), in order to maximize the effect of aggregation later on. If, for example, the variable is ?river, then a sentence Brooklyn Bridge crosses ?river is transformed into its passive counterpart ?river is crossed by Brooklyn Bridge. We process the input trees in descending order with respect to the frequency of the variables they contain, starting with the projection variables and only after that turning to other variables. As an example, consider the following query retrieving the youngest player in the Premier League:

```
1  SELECT DISTINCT ?person WHERE {
2    ?person dbo:team ?sportsTeam .
3    ?sportsTeam dbo:league res:Premier_League .
4    ?person dbo:birthDate ?date .
5  }
6  ORDER BY DESC(?date) OFFSET 0 LIMIT 1
```

The only projection variable is ?person (two occurrences), other variables are ?sportsTeam and ?date (one occurrence each). The three triple patterns are verbalized as given in 16a–16c. Clustering and ordering now first takes all sentences containing the primary variable, i.e. 16a and 16b, which are ordered such that copulative sentences (such as ?person is a person) come before other sentences, and then takes all sentences containing the remaining variable ?sportsTeam in 16c (the only occurrence of ?date is already settled with 16b), resulting in a sequence of sentences as in 17.

16. (a) ?person's team is ?sportsTeam.
    (b) ?person's birth date is ?date.
    (c) ?sportsTeam's league is Premier League.

17. ?person's team is ?sportsTeam, ?person's birth date is ?date, and ?sportsTeam's league is Premier League.

5.2 Grouping

Grouping is described by Dalianis & Hovy [3] as a process "collecting clauses with common elements and then collapsing the common elements". The common elements are usually subject noun phrases and verb phrases (verbs together with object noun phrases), leading to subject grouping and object grouping. In order to maximize the grouping effects, we additionally collapse common prefixes and suffixes of sentences, irrespective of whether they are full subject noun phrases or complete verb phrases. In the following we use $X_1, X_2, \ldots$ as variables for the root nodes of the input sentences and Y as variable for the root node of the output sentence. Furthermore, we abbreviate a subject $\mathrm{subj}(X_i, s_i)$ as s_i, an object $\mathrm{dobj}(X_i, o_i)$ as o_i, and a verb $\mathrm{root}(ROOT_i, v_i)$ as v_i.

Object grouping collapses the subjects of two sentences if the realizations of the verbs and objects of the sentences are the same, where the $coord \in \{\mathrm{and}, \mathrm{or}\}$ is the coordination combining the input sentences X_1 and X_2, and $\mathrm{coord} \in \{\mathrm{conj}, \mathrm{disj}\}$ is the corresponding coordination combining the subjects.

18. $\rho(o_1) = \rho(o_2) \land \rho(v_1) = \rho(v_2) \land \mathrm{cc}(v_1, coord)$
    $\Rightarrow \mathrm{root}(Y, \mathrm{PLURAL}(v_1)) \land \mathrm{subj}(v_1, \mathrm{coord}(s_1, s_2)) \land \mathrm{dobj}(v_1, o_1)$

For example, the sentences in 19 share their verb and object, thus they can be collapsed into a single sentence. Note that to this end the singular auxiliary was needs to be transformed into its plural form were. In case the subjects themselves share common elements, the subjects are collapsed as well, as in 20.

19. Benjamin Franklin was born in Boston and Leonard Nimoy was born in Boston. ⇒ Benjamin Franklin and Leonard Nimoy were born in Boston.

20. Abraham Lincoln's birth place is Washington or Abraham Lincoln's death place is Washington. ⇒ Abraham Lincoln's birth place or death place is Washington.

In addition, we remove repetitions that arise when triple pattern verbalizations lead to the same natural language representation. Due to space restrictions, we leave out a presentation of subject grouping, as it works analogously.

A further aggregation rule that removes redundant mentions of variables collapses more generally common suffixes and prefixes, i.e. sentences of form $\mathrm{subj}_1\ \mathrm{verb}_1\ \mathrm{dobj}_1$ with sentences of form $\mathrm{subj}_2\ \mathrm{verb}_2\ \mathrm{dobj}_2$ in case dobj_1 is the same as subj_2 (and if its is a variable, does not occur anywhere else) and either verb_1 or verb_2 is a form of to be. An example is given in 22.

21. (a) $\rho(o_1) = \rho(s_2) \land \rho(v_1) = \mathrm{BE}$
    $\Rightarrow \mathrm{subj}(Y, s_1) \land \mathrm{dobj}(Y, o_2) \land \mathrm{root}(Y, v_2)$
    (b) $\rho(o_1) = \rho(s_2) \land \rho(v_2) = \mathrm{BE}$
    $\Rightarrow \mathrm{subj}(Y, s_1) \land \mathrm{dobj}(Y, o_2) \land \mathrm{root}(Y, v_1)$
    If o_1/s_2 is not a variable occurring anywhere else.

22. ?w's year is ?x. ?x is greater than or equal to 2007.
    ⇒ ?w's year is greater than or equal to 2007.

5.3 Aggregating filters and optional information

The verbalization of filters can be quite verbose, although they often express a simple constraint on a value. Postprocessing thus attaches filter information to the expression they constrain. For example a filter like in 23 is verbalized and then collapsed as in 24.

23. ?person rdfs:label ?name.
    FILTER(regex(?name,'Michelle'))

24. ?person's label is ?name. ?name matches "Michelle".
    ⇒ ?person has the label ?name matching "Michelle".
    ⇒ ?person has a label matching "Michelle".
    (if ?name does not occur anywhere else)

For every sentence, the filter linearizations are checked whether they contain either the subject or object of the sentence, and if they do, they are attached to the it either using a gerund or a relative clause, depending on the filter. A filter construct that is particularly difficult to handle are !BOUND filters as in 25. Postprocessing transforms statements of form X does not exist into the negation of some statement containing X, either negating the verb phrase, as in 26, or by adding the quantifier no, as in This query asks whether there is no entity such that....

25. res:Frank_Herbert dbo:deathDate ?date . FILTER (!BOUND(?date))

26. This query asks whether Frank Herbert's death date is ?date and ?date does not exist. ⇒ This query asks whether Frank Herbert's death date does not exist.

An extensive and careful treatment of all kinds of BOUND filters in SELECT and ASK queries is subject of future work.

Information about the label of a variable and its type (if it is not already part of the SELECT clause) may be part of the filters and is verbalized by the processing step for example as in 27a. In order to collapse these information into something less verbose, the postprocessor collects such sentences based on simple string matching and transforms them into a single sentence as in 27b. In case only the label information is expressed, the result is as in 27c; in case the variable is part of the SELECT clause, the type and label information is attached there, as in 27d.

27. (a) ?uri is of type film. ?uri has label ?string. ?string is in English.
    (b) ?uri is a film with the English label ?string
    (c) ?uri has the English label ?string
    (d) This query retrieves films ?uri and their English label ?string such that...

Content in OPTIONAL statements is expressed as an additional sentence of the form Additionally, it retrieves V such that O if such exists, for some selected entities V and triple patterns O. Postprocessing integrates the information in O into the main body of the natural language description, marking the statements with the modal may, e.g. transforming 27c above into ?uri may have the English label ?string.

5.4 Referencing

Referencing refers to the process of deciding how to verbalize each occurrence of an entity (e.g., as a singular or plural noun phrase or a pronoun). The ultimate aim of the postprocessing step is to collapse and substitute all variable occurrences such that the final output does not contain any variables at all. This goal is achieved for almost all sentences, but proves hard in the case of very complex queries with lots of variables. An easy case is the following: If the input sentence with root X is of the form This query retrieves o such that B, the body B contains a copula statement Y whose subject (resp. object) has the same realization as o, and o does not occur anywhere else, then it is safe to collapse the input sentence into This query retrieves x such that B', where x ist the object (resp. subject) of Y, and B' is B without Y. An example is the following, where the keyword distinct is dropped, as this seems more natural, especially for laymen, although it could be argued that it should be kept for experts:

28. This query retrieves distinct entities ?string such that Angela Merkel's birth name is ?string. ⇒ This query retrieves Angela Merkel's birth name.

In case the verb of the body statement is not a copula, as in the following example, the information is added to the input sentence in form of a relative clause:

29. This query retrieves entities such that ?river is crossed by Brooklyn Bridge. ⇒ This query retrieves entities that are crossed by Brooklyn Bridge.

In addition, the postprocessing step replaces all occurrences of a projection variable, i.e. a variable which occurs in the SELECT clause, by pronouns if this is the only projection variable, e.g. transforming 30 into 31. In case of more variables, this would lead to ambiguities. Also, the first occurrence of remaining non-projecting variables, i.e. those variables which do not occur in the SELECT clause, are replaced by an indefinite (choosing their type as description, if given, e.g. some mountain, or entity otherwise), and all further occurences are replaced by a definite, e.g. further transforming 31 into 32.

30. This query retrieves distinct entities ?uri such that ?uri is ?x's b-side and ?x's musical artist is Ramones.

31. This query retrieves distinct entities such that they are ?x's b-side and ?x's musical artist is Ramones.

32. This query retrieves distinct entities such that they are some entity's b-side and this entity's musical artist is Ramones.

The output of the postprocessor for Example 1 is the following:

33. This query retrieves distinct people and their English label (if it exists) such that their birth date is later than 1950 and their occupation is Writer or Surfing.

Full-fledged referencing still remains a challenging task, especially if a query contains a range of different entities with several occurrences, also because it requires some knowledge about whether it is semantically singular or plural, in order to choose the correct description, e.g. the members of Prodigy (plural) and the father of Queen Elizabeth II (singular), or to decide whether to use the concept name label or name, and whether the entity is animated or not, in order to correctly choose the correct pronoun in the singular case (he/she or it).

6. REALIZATION

The realization of atoms must be able to deal with resources, classes, properties and literals.

6.1 Classes and resources

In general, the realization of classes and resources is carried out as follows: Given a URI u we ask for the English label of u using a SPARQL query.[7] If such a label does not exist, we use either the fragment of u (the string after #) if it exists, else the string after the last occurrence of /. Finally this natural language representation is realized as a noun phrase, and in the case of classes is also pluralized. In our running example, dbo:Person is realized as people (its label).

---
[7]Note that it could be any property which returns a natural language representation of the given URI, see [6].

6.2 Properties

The realization of properties relies on the insight that most property labels are either nouns or verbs. While the mapping of a particular property p can be unambiguous, some property labels are not as easy to categorize. For examples, the label crosses can either be the plural form of the noun cross or the third person singular present form of the verb to cross. In order to automatically determine which realization to use, we relied on the insight that the first and last word of a property label are often the key to determining the type of the property: properties whose label begins with a verb (resp. noun or gerund) are most to be realized as verbs (resp. nouns). We devised a set of rules to capture this behavior, which we omit due to space restrictions. In some cases (such as crosses) none of the rules applied. In these cases, we compare the probability of $P(p|\text{noun})$ and $P(p|\text{verb})$ by measuring

$$P(p|X) = \frac{\sum_{t \in synset(p|X)} \log_2(f(t))}{\sum_{t' \in synset(p)} \log_2(f(t'))}, \quad (1)$$

where $synset(p)$ is the set of all synsets of p, $synset(p|X)$ is the set of all synsets of p that are of the syntactic class $X \in \{\text{noun}, \text{verb}\}$ and $f(t)$ is the frequency of use of p in the sense of the synset t according to WordNet. For

$$\frac{P(p|\text{verb})}{P(p|\text{noun})} \geq \theta, \quad (2)$$

we choose to realize p as a noun; else we realized it as a verb. For $\theta = 1$, for example, dbo:crosses is realized as a verb.

6.3 Literals

The realization of *literals* is carried out by differentiating between plain and typed literals. For plain literals we simply use the lexical form, i.e. omit language tags if they exist. For example, "Albert Einstein"@en is realized as Albert Einstein. For typed literals we further differentiate between built-in and user-defined datatypes. For the former we also use the lexical form, e.g. "123"^^xsd:int $\Rightarrow$ 123. The latter were processed by using the literal value together with the (pluralized) natural language representation of the datatype URI, similarly to the case of classes and resources. Thus, we realize "123"^^<http://dbpedia.org/datatype/squareKilometre> as 123 square kilometres.

7. EXPERIMENTS AND EVALUATION RESULTS

We evaluated SPARQL2NL with respect to i) the realization of atomic graph patterns, ii) the verbalization of whole SPARQL queries, and iii) other approaches, all using the QALD-2 benchmark[8] as basis.

7.1 Realization of atomic graph patterns

Given that the choice for the realization of atomic graph patterns depends on whether the predicate is classified as being a noun phrase or a verb phrase, we measured the accuracy (i.e., the percentage of right classifications) of our approach by realizing all properties occurring in the QALD-2 benchmark. As baseline, we used a simple classifier that

[8] http://www.sc.cit-ec.uni-bielefeld.de/qald-2

classifies every property as a noun. We preferred this classifier over one that classifies every property as a verb, simply because it has a higher accuracy than both the verb classifier and a random classifier. The evaluation was carried out manually by two annotators who assessed the rdfs:label of every property in the QALD-2 benchmark regarding whether it is a noun or a verb. All mismatches were resolved by the same annotators. Note that in rare cases, some properties from the property namespace are used ambiguously within DBpedia. For example, property:design is used to mean designed as, designed in and even designed by. In these cases the annotators evaluated whether our realization mapped the intention of the query as specified in the benchmark.

We evaluated our approach with $\theta = 1$ and $\theta = 2$ by using the accuracy measure, which states the percentage of cases in which the correct classification was achieved across the queries in the benchmark. The results are shown in Table 2. We clearly outperform the baseline in all cases. Especially, setting $\theta = 2$ achieves an overall accuracy of 99.22% and a perfect score on the property from DBpedia namespace contained in the training dataset of QALD-2. Experiments with other values of θ did not lead to better results.

7.2 SPARQL2NL survey

In our second series of experiments, we evaluated the whole SPARQL2NL pipeline, in order to clarify the following two questions:

1. Are the SPARQL2NL verbalizations correct, and are they easy to understand?

2. Do the verbalizations help users that are not familiar with SPARQL, i.e. can they use the verbalizations efficiently and effectively?

7.2.1 Experimental setup

We performed a user study in order to evaluate our verbalizations of SPARQL queries, using the 200 DBpedia queries provided by the QALD-2 benchmark, all of which our approach was able to translate into natural language. We ran a two-phase survey[9]: In the first phase, users were stripped from any communication devices, required to focus on the task at hand and complete the survey swiftly. In the second phase, we ran uncontrolled experiments with users from Semantic Web and NLP mailing lists as well as smaller non-research communities. The survey consists of three different tasks with 10 randomly selected queries each. At the start of the survey users can indicate whether or not they are SPARQL experts. If not, only Task 3 was presented, otherwise they were asked to complete all three tasks.

Task 1 (only for experts):. In this task, the survey participant is presented a SPARQL query and its SPARQL2NL verbalization, and is asked to judge the verbalization regarding fluency and adequacy, following the machine translation standard presented in [5]. Adequacy captures how well the verbalization captures the meaning of the SPARQL query, according to the following six ratings: (6) Perfect. (5) Mostly correct, maybe some expressions don't match the concepts very well. (4) Close, but some information is missing or incorrect. (3) There is significant information missing or

[9] The survey interface can be accessed at http://sparql2nl.aksw.org/eval.

Dataset	Namespace	Frequency	#Verbs	#Nouns	Accuracy in %		
					$\theta = 1$	$\theta = 2$	Baseline
DBpedia-test	property	40	8	25	87.50	**90.00**	75.00
	ontology	97	7	48	91.75	**94.85**	86.60
	Other	99	2	1	**98.99**	**98.99**	32.32
	Overall	236	17	74	94.07	**95.76**	61.86
DBpedia-train	property	41	1	26	**100.00**	**100.00**	80.25
	ontology	81	5	43	95.06	**100.00**	85.37
	Other	135	3	2	**98.51**	**98.51**	42.96
	Overall	257	9	71	97.67	**99.22**	61.48

Table 2: Accuracy of realization of atomic graph patterns. Namespace stands for the namespace of the properties used in a SPARQL query. Frequency denotes the number of times that a property from a given namespace was used, for example property (which stands for http://dbpedia.org/property) or ontology (http://dbpedia.org/ontology). #Verbs (resp. #Nouns) is the number of properties that were classified as verbs (resp. nouns).

incorrect. (2) NL description and SPARQL query are only loosely connected. (1) NL description and SPARQL query are in no conceivable way related. Fluency, on the other hand, captures how good the natural language description is in terms of comprehensibility and readability, according to the following six ratings: (6) Perfectly clear and natural. (5) Sounds a bit artificial, but is clearly comprehensible. (May contain minor grammatical flaws.) (4) Sounds very artificial, but is understandable. (May contain significant grammatical flaws.) (3) Barely comprehensible, but can be understood with some effort. (2) Only a loose and incomplete understanding of the meaning can be obtained. (1) Completely not understandable at all.

Task 2 (only for experts):. In this task, the participant is presented a SPARQL query as well as five different possible answers (variable bindings). From these answers, those which would actually be returned by the query had to be selected. To this end, for each answer a set of triples was offered as explanation, which should be used to judge whether the answer is correct. These triples were generated as follows: We first executed the SPARQL query and randomly selected up to five results from the query answer. For each correct answer, we replaced the return variable (?uri in the case of the QALD-2 SELECT queries) by the URI of the answer, and replaced all other URIs occurring in the query by variables, in order to retrieve all triples relevant for answering the query[10]. For each incorrect answer, we first generalised the SPARQL query by removing a triple pattern, or by replacing a URI by a variable. This procedure is repeated until the query returns results not returned by the original query. This ensures that the incorrect answers are similar to the correct answers in the sense that they are results of a similar SPARQL queries. The formal details of the procedure follow [18].

Task 3 (experts and non-experts):. This task is similar to Task 2, with the difference that the natural language verbalizations of the SPARQL query and a verbalization of the triples were presented, instead of the query and the triples themselves. We also ensured that the queries used

[10]This simple technique does not cover all cases, but we refrain from a full explanation, since it is not necessary to understand the survey.

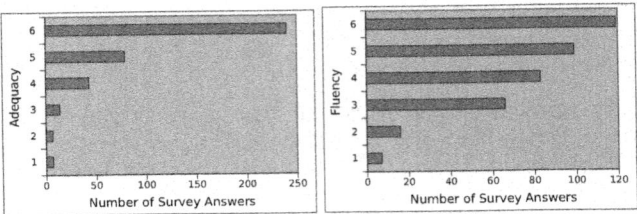

Figure 1: Adequacy and fluency results in survey

were different from those used in Task 2, in order to avoid training effects on particular questions.

7.2.2 Results

The first survey phase was carried out by 10 members of the AKSW and CITEC research groups. As these participants were monitored by one of the authors, we used it for time measurements on the three different tasks. The maximum (minimum) time required was 17 (7) minutes, 13 (6) minutes and 12 (4) minutes for Tasks 1, 2 and 3, respectively. We then ran a public survey, that was announced on Semantic Web and NLP mailing lists as well as to other non-research communities, collecting 115 participants, of which 39 stated they were experts in SPARQL. We used our initial time measurements to filter out those survey participants in the public evaluation who are unlikely to have thoroughly executed the survey or who were likely distracted while executing it. To this end, we decided to admit a time window of 5-18 minutes for Task 1 and 3-15 minutes for Tasks 2 and 3.[11] Although this cannot eliminate all side effects, it reduces the effect of outliers, e.g. people leaving the computer for a long period of time.

The results of the first task showed the fluency of the natural language descriptions to be 4.56 ± 1.29, where in expressions of the form $x \pm y$, x denotes the average value and y denotes the standard deviation. The majority of natural language descriptions were understandable, where 94.1% of the cases achieved a rating of 3 or higher. The adequacy of the verbalizations was judged to be 5.31 ± 1.08, which we consider a positive result. 62% of all verbalizations were

[11]Task 2 and 3 require the same limits in order to avoid a bias when doing cross comparisons between Task 2 and 3.

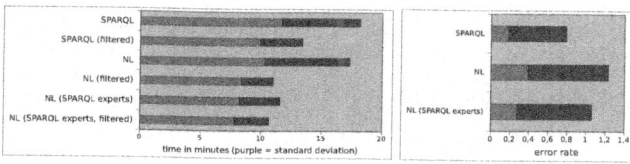

Figure 2: Time and error rate analysis

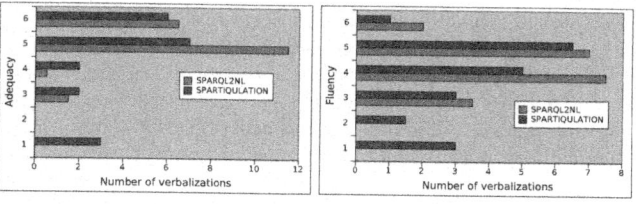

Figure 3: Average adequacy and fluency results for comparison of SPARQL2NL and SPARTIQULATION

judged to be perfectly adequate. Details for the results of Task 1 are depicted in Figure 1.

For Tasks 2 and 3, our main goal was to directly compare the results of users dealing with SPARQL queries against the results of users dealing with natural language descriptions. Here we consider the time required to answer a question as an indicator for efficiency, and the error rate of a user as an indicator for effectiveness. Regarding efficiency, participants required 11.68 ± 6.46 minutes to complete Task 2. Applying the time window mentioned above, the required time drops to 9.89 ± 3.48. For Task 3 we obtained execution times of 10.28 ± 7.03 without filtering, and 8.37 ± 2.63 with time filtering. In general, execution times were in line with what we expected after the first evaluation phase, i.e. most participants swiftly completed the survey. Using a paired t-test with 95% confidence interval, the difference between the time required for Tasks 2 and 3 is statistically significant. Hence, we conclude that the natural language descriptions generated by our approach can be more efficiently read and understood. Note that even the SPARQL experts were faster when being presented the natural language description, with 8.22 ± 3.34 minutes without time window filter and 7.79 ± 2.83 with time window filter. We therefore conclude that the SPARQL2NL translations can be processed efficiently by both experts and non-experts.

Finally we also compared the error rates of participants in Tasks 2 and 3, i.e. the number of incorrect answers per questions, see Figure 2. The error rate in Task 2, i.e. when displaying SPARQL queries and RDF triples, was 0.18 ± 0.61, in contrast to 0.39 ± 0.84 in Task 3, i.e. when displaying natural language descriptions. If we consider only experts in Task 3, i.e. the group of people who did both Task 2 (displaying SPARQL and RDF) and Task 3 (displaying natural language), the error rate was 0.28 ± 0.78. This is a negative result for SPARQL2NL as it appears that non-expert participants made more errors than expert participants; although the overall rate still seems reasonably low. Upon a deeper investigation of this issue, it turned out that almost all errors occurred with two specific queries, both due to bugs in the implementation of SPARQL2NL: one query translation used a passive form incorrectly, and the other one lacked the keyword also indicating that two criteria had to be satisfied.

We fixed these issues in an updated version of SPARQL2NL and ran an internal evaluation again using the new verbalizations. 13 participants from the AKSW and CITEC research groups, excluding the authors, took part in this validation phase. It turned out that the error rate for the natural language expressions in that case is only slightly higher (+0.05) compared to the SPARQL expressions for SPARQL experts. Both error rates were lower than in the public evaluation with 0.12 ± 0.35 and 0.07 ± 0.25 for the natural language and SPARQL part, respectively. The improvements based on the evaluation also led to improved fluency (increased by 0.51 to 5.05 ± 1.01) and adequacy (increased by 0.29 to

5.60 ± 0.85) results. These results strengthen the conclusions made above with respect to the fluency and adequacy of our verbalizations.

7.3 Comparison with other approaches

To the best of our knowledge, SPARTIQULATION [7] is the only other approach that verbalizes SPARQL queries. It relies on detecting a main entity, which is used to subdivide the query graph into subgraphs, that are ordered and matched with pre-defined message types.

We compared SPARQL2NL with SPARTIQULATION on a random sample of 20 queries retrieved from the QALD-2 benchmark within a blind survey: We asked two SPARQL experts to evaluate the adequacy and fluency of the verbalizations achieved by the two approaches. The experts were not involved in the development of any of the two tools and were not aware of which tool produces which verbalization. Of the 20 queries, SPARTIQULATION could only verbalize 17 while SPARQL2NL was able to verbalize all queries. This difference is due to SPARTIQULATION being currently limited to SELECT queries and not covering some important SPARQL features such as UNION and GROUP BY constructs, features which we can deal with as shown above. The results of our comparison show that in average there is a difference of 0.24 resp. 0.27 with respect to adequacy resp. fluency between the two approaches (5.24 resp. 4.41 in adequacy resp. fluency for SPARQL2NL versus 5.0 resp. 4.15 for SPARTIQULATION) when only taking SPARQL queries into consideration queries that SPARTIQULATION was able to process. Note that even in this setting, SPARQL2NL outperforms SPARTIQULATION. When considering all queries in our sample, counting the adequacy and fluency for a query that could not be translated as 1, our approach clearly outperforms SPARTIQULATION, as shown in Figure 3. Most of the verbalizations of SPARQL2NL are scored with 6 or 5 with respect to adequacy by the experts, while a larger amount of verbalizations from SPARTIQULATION are scored with 1–4. Moreover, our verbalizations are most frequently assigned fluency scores between 4 and 5. Overall, SPARQL2NL achieved an average adequacy resp. fluency of 5.15 resp. 4.38 while SPARTIQULATION achieved 4.40 resp. 3.68.

8. RELATED WORK

Although there is a substantial amount of work on translating natural language into database elements or queries (see, e.g., [23]) or even SPARQL [25, 28], the other direction, i.e. verbalizing databases and queries, has started to receive attention only recently [15]. Most of the papers related to this work have been on ontology and RDF verbalization or on reusing such data for the purpose of verbalization. [1] for example combines linguistic and domain-specific ontologies to generate natural-language representations of portions of ontologies required by users. One of the results of this work is that even graphical representations of ontologies are of little help for lay users. This result is the premise for the work by Wilcock [29], who presents a more generic approach for the purpose of verbalizing OWL and DAML+OIL. [14] present an approach for generating paraphrases of the content of OWL ontologies that combines natural-language patterns for expressing the structure of property labels and a verbalization approach for OWL class expression. Works such as [16, 13, 27] use controlled fragments of natural language such as English and Baltic languages to generate textual representation of OWL ontologies. Other works on verbalizing OWL ontologies include [2, 4, 8] and [10].

In addition to the work on OWL, research on textual descriptions of RDF triples is also gaining momentum. For example, [22] elaborates on an approach for transforming RDF into Polish. The authors of [20] argue for relying on the Linked Data Web being created by using to reverse engineer structured data into natural language. The same authors show in [26] how this approach can be used for generating text out of RDF. In newer work, [19] generated natural language out of RDF by relying on the BOA framework [12, 11] with the aim of computing the trustworthiness of RDF triples by using the Web as background knowledge. Other approaches and concepts for verbalizing RDF include [21] and [30]. Moreover, approaches to verbalizing first-order logics [9] are currently being devised.

An approach for translating database queries into natural language text has been provided by, e.g., Koutrika et al. [17], focusing on SQL queries but noting that the same need arises for SPARQL queries. A noteworthy approach is that presented in [15], where the authors apply graph algorithms to an efficient partition and realization of SQL queries. The only work we are aware of that verbalizes SPARQL queries is the aforementioned recent approach by Ell et al. [7].

9. CONCLUSION

In this paper, we presented SPARQL2NL, an approach for verbalizing SPARQL queries. It produces both a direct, literal verbalization of the content of the query and a more natural, aggregated version of the same content. We presented the key steps of our approach and evaluated it with a user survey. Our evaluation showed that the verbalizations generated by our approach are both complete and easily understandable. In addition, our approach allows users not familiar with SPARQL to understand the content of SPARQL queries and also accelerates the understanding of queries by SPARQL experts. Still, our evaluation showed that the legibility of our approach is worse when the queries get more complex. In future work, we will thus improve upon our referencing algorithm so as to further increase the fluency of our approach. Moreover, we will devise a consistency checking algorithm to improve upon the correctness of the natural language generated by our approach. Finally, we will integrate paraphrasing approaches into our system to augment the variety of the formulations used by our system and thus improve the quality of the interaction with the end users. SPARQL2NL represents the first step towards semantic applications that enable lay users to understand the behavior of the applications without any need for technical knowledge. We hope that it will facilitate the acceptance of Semantic Web technologies across domains of application.

Acknowledgement

Parts of the work presented herein were financed by the FP7 Support Action BioASQ under grant agreement no. 318652.

10. REFERENCES

[1] G. Aguado, A. Bañón, John A. Bateman, S. Bernardos, M. Fernández, A. Gómez-Pérez, E. Nieto, A. Olalla, R. Plaza, and A. Sánchez. ONTOGENERATION: Reusing domain and linguistic ontologies for Spanish text generation. In *Workshop on Applications of Ontologies and Problem Solving Methods, ECAI'98*, 1998.

[2] Kalina Bontcheva and Yorick Wilks. Automatic report generation from ontologies: The miakt approach. In *NLDB*, pages 324–335, 2004.

[3] H. Dalianis and E.H. Hovy. Aggregation in natural language generation. In G. Adorni and M. Zock, editors, *Trends in natural language generation: an artificial intelligence perspective*, volume 1036 of *Lecture Notes in Artificial Intelligence*, pages 88–105. Springer, 1996.

[4] Brian Davis, Ahmad Iqbal, Adam Funk, Valentin Tablan, Kalina Bontcheva, Hamish Cunningham, and Siegfried Handschuh. Roundtrip ontology authoring. In *ISWC*, pages 50–65, 2008.

[5] George Doddington. Automatic evaluation of machine translation quality using n-gram co-occurrence statistics. In *Proceedings of HLT*, pages 138–145, 2002.

[6] Basil Ell, Denny Vrandecic, and Elena Paslaru Bontas Simperl. Labels in the web of data. In *Proceedings of ISWC*, volume 7031, pages 162–176. Springer, 2011.

[7] Basil Ell, Denny Vrandečić, and Elena Simperl. SPARTIQULATION – Verbalizing SPARQL queries. In *Proceedings of ILD Workshop, ESWC 2012*, 2012.

[8] Günther Fliedl, Christian Kop, and Jürgen Vöhringer. Guideline based evaluation and verbalization of owl class and property labels. *Data Knowl. Eng.*, 69(4), 2010.

[9] Norbert E. Fuchs. First-order reasoning for attempto controlled english. In *CNL*, pages 73–94, 2010.

[10] Dimitrios Galanis and Ion Androutsopoulos. Generating multilingual descriptions from linguistically annotated owl ontologies: the naturalowl system. In *Proceedings of the Eleventh European Workshop on Natural Language Generation*, ENLG '07, pages 143–146, Stroudsburg, PA, USA, 2007. Association for Computational Linguistics.

[11] Daniel Gerber and Axel-Cyrille Ngonga Ngomo. Extracting multilingual natural-language patterns for rdf predicates. In *EKAW*, pages 87–96, 2012.

[12] Daniel Gerber and Axel-Cyrille Ngonga Ngomo. Bootstrapping the linked data web. In *1st Workshop on Web Scale Knowledge Extraction @ ISWC 2011*, 2011.

[13] Normunds Gruzitis, Gunta Nespore, and Baiba Saulite. Verbalizing ontologies in controlled baltic languages. In Inguna Skadina and Andrejs Vasiljevs, editors, *Baltic HLT*, volume 219 of *Frontiers in Artificial Intelligence and Applications*, pages 187–194. IOS Press, 2010.

[14] Daniel Hewlett, Aditya Kalyanpur, Vladimir Kolovski, and Chris Halaschek-Wiener. Effective natural

language paraphrasing of ontologies on the semantic web. In *Proceedings of the End User Semantic Web Interaction Workshop (ISWC 2005)*, 2005.

[15] Yannis Ioannidis. From databases to natural language: The unusual direction. In E. Kapetanios, V. Sugumaran, and M. Spiliopoulou, editors, *Natural Language and Information Systems*, volume 5039 of *LNCS*, pages 12–16, 2008.

[16] Kaarel Kaljurand and Norbert E. Fuchs. Verbalizing OWL in Attempto Controlled English. In *Proceedings of Third International Workshop on OWL: Experiences and Directions, Innsbruck, Austria (6th–7th June 2007)*, volume 258, 2007.

[17] G. Koutrika, A. Simitsis, and Y.E. Ioannidis. Explaining structured queries in natural language. In *Proceedings of the 26th International Conference on Data Engineering (ICDE)*, pages 333–344, 2010.

[18] Jens Lehmann and Lorenz Bühmann. Autosparql: Let users query your knowledge base. In *Proceedings of ESWC 2011*, 2011.

[19] Jens Lehmann, Daniel Gerber, Mohamed Morsey, and Axel-Cyrille Ngonga Ngomo. Defacto - deep fact validation. In *ISWC*, 2012.

[20] Chris Mellish and Xiantang Sun. The semantic web as a linguistic resource: opportunities for natural language generation. In *Twenty-sixth SGAI International Conference on Innovative Techniques and Applications of Artificial Intelligence*, 2006.

[21] H. Piccinini, M. A. Casanova, A. L. Furtado, and B. P. Nunes. Verbalization of rdf triples with applications. In *ISWC - Outrageous Ideas track*, 2011.

[22] Aleksander Pohl. The polish interface for linked open data. In *Proceedings of the ISWC 2010 Posters & Demonstrations Track*, pages 165–168, 2011.

[23] Ana-Maria Popescu, Oren Etzioni, and Henry Kautz. Towards a theory of natural language interfaces to databases. In *Proceedings of the 8th international conference on Intelligent user interfaces*, IUI '03, pages 149–157, 2003.

[24] Ehud Reiter and Robert Dale. *Building natural language generation systems*. Cambridge University Press, New York, NY, USA, 2000.

[25] Saeedeh Shekarpour, Sören Auer, Axel-Cyrille Ngonga Ngomo, Daniel Gerber, Sebastian Hellmann, and Claus Stadler. Keyword-driven sparql query generation leveraging background knowledge. In *ACM/IEEE WI*, 2011.

[26] Xiantang Sun and Chris Mellish. An experiment on "free generation" from single rdf triples. In *Proceedings of the Eleventh European Workshop on Natural Language Generation*, ENLG '07, pages 105–108, Stroudsburg, PA, USA, 2007. Association for Computational Linguistics.

[27] Allan Third, Sandra Williams, and Richard Power. Owl to english: a tool for generating organised easily-navigated hypertexts from ontologies. In *ISWC Poster and Demo Track*, 2011.

[28] Christina Unger, Lorenz Bühmann, Jens Lehmann, Axel-Cyrille Ngonga Ngomo, Daniel Gerber, and Philipp Cimiano. Template-based question answering over RDF data. In *Proceedings of WWW*, 2012.

[29] Graham Wilcock. Talking OWLs: Towards an Ontology Verbalizer. In *Human Language Technology for the Semantic Web and Web Services, Workshop at ISWC 2003*, pages 109–112, 2003.

[30] Graham Wilcock and Kristiina Jokinen. Generating Responses and Explanations from RDF/XML and DAML+OIL, 2003.

Bitsquatting: Exploiting Bit-flips for Fun, or Profit?

Nick Nikiforakis, Steven Van Acker, Wannes Meert[†], Lieven Desmet, Frank Piessens, Wouter Joosen

iMinds-DistriNet / [†]DTAI, KU Leuven, 3001 Leuven, Belgium
firstname.lastname@cs.kuleuven.be

ABSTRACT

Over the last fifteen years, several types of attacks against domain names and the companies relying on them have been observed. The well-known cybersquatting of domain names gave way to typosquatting, the abuse of a user's mistakes when typing a URL in her browser's address bar. Recently, a new attack against domain names surfaced, namely *bitsquatting*. In bitsquatting, an attacker leverages random bit-errors occurring in the memory of commodity computers and smartphones, to redirect Internet traffic to attacker-controlled domains.

In this paper, we report on a large-scale experiment, measuring the adoption of bitsquatting by the domain-squatting community through the tracking of registrations of bitsquatting domains targeting popular web sites over a 9-month period. We show how new bitsquatting domains are registered daily and how attackers are trying to monetize their domains through the use of ads, abuse of affiliate programs and even malware installations. Lastly, given the discovered prevalence of bitsquatting, we review possible defense measures that companies, software developers and Internet Service Providers can use to protect against it.

Categories and Subject Descriptors

K.6.5 [**Security and Protection**]: Unauthorized access; H.3.5 [**Online Information Services**]: Web-based services; K.4.4 [**Electronic Commerce**]: Security

Keywords

domain name; cybersquatting; bitsquatting; affiliate abuse

1. INTRODUCTION

The Domain Name System plays a crucial role in the world wide web. It transparently converts domain names, i.e., hierarchical user-memorable strings of text, to routable, machine-friendly IP addresses. Users are instructed to trust the domain names shown in their browsers' address bars and to always consult them before divulging sensitive information, making them indicators of the familiarity and legitimacy of any given web site. As with many popular technologies, their ubiquitous nature has made them an attractive target for malicious individuals seeking to exploit users.

In the early days of the web, people would register domain names associated with known companies and trademarks and later sell them back to their rightful owners at a much higher price. This practice was named *cybersquatting*, and it is well-known that cybersquatting pioneers made large profits from buying domains early and selling them when the demand was high [13].

When the web grew in popularity and large companies had already bought the appropriate domains for their business, the cybersquatters based their model on a new type of squatting, namely *typosquatting*. Typosquatting is based on *type-in navigation*, which is the act of a user manually typing a URL in her browser's address bar instead of relying on a hyperlink in an existing site. In the process of typing the URL of a familiar web site, a user may accidentally mistype a character in the desired domain, e.g., paypap.com instead of paypal.com, and have her browser request the page without realizing her mistake. Typosquatters started registering such mistypes of popular authoritative domains and offered them for sale. In the mean-time, the domains were used for displaying ads (even of competing companies), and in some cases, conduct phishing and drive-by download attacks [9]. Even today, the act of typosquatting is so popular that entire companies have been formed, who offer "domain-parking services" and automate the display of relevant ads on a typosquatting domain.

Popular legitimate companies whose domains were typosquatted, in an effort to protect their customers and trademarks, buy common mistypes of their sites and redirect the visiting users back to their main authoritative domains. For instance, the domain microspft.com is owned by Microsoft and redirects users to microsoft.com. Unfortunately, this action exacerbates typosquatting since it drives typosquatters to register even more similar domains in hope that they will be able to sell them to the company for profit.

In 2011, Dinaburg presented a new type of cybersquatting which he named, *bitsquatting* [6]. In bitsquatting, a cybersquatter registers a domain name which has a character that differs for one-bit from the same character in the targeted authoritative domain. Dinaburg postulated that hardware errors could cause a random bit error, specifically a bit-flip, in the bytes of memory storing a domain name and thus route requests towards a different domain, even if the user typed the correct domain. To test this theory, Dinaburg registered 30 bitsquatting domains that were targeting popular authoritative domains, e.g., mic2osoft.com, a bitsquatting domain for microsoft.com. Over a period of eight months, Dinaburg's monitors recorded more than 52,000 requests, originating from all types of operating systems and browsers, even the ones of hand-held gaming devices.

In this paper, we study the influence of Dinaburg's findings on the domain-squatting community. While it would certainly be interesting for researchers to independently verify Dinaburg's claims, we chose not to focus on whether bitsquatting happens but on whether cyber-squatters are *convinced* that it does. Following Dinaburg's report, we construct a crawler for bitsquatting domains which, given a list of authoritative domains, automatically computes all possible bitsquatting domains that are one-bit different from the original domain. For each valid bitsquatting domain, the crawler attempts to resolve its IP address and if it is successful, it then visits and records the HTML code of the bitsquatting domain's main page.

Using our crawler, we track the registration of bitsquatting domains targeting the Alexa top 500 domains for nine months, and discover ample evidence which suggest that bitsquatting is now the newest addition in the arsenal of domain-squatters. In a nine-month period, we recorded a total of 5,366 unique bitsquatting domains, showing a 46% increase from the first day of our experiment. We perform a series of automated and manual experiments on the corpus of the downloaded pages of the bitsquatting domains and discover that, while the majority of them are parked and serving ads, others are abusing affiliate programs of the authoritative sites, launching drive-by download attacks to unsuspecting visitors and attempting to trick users into installing fake antivirus programs [4] and other rogue software.

The main contributions of this paper are the following:

- We present the first large-scale analysis of bitsquatting, covering the Alexa top 500 sites over a nine-month time span
- We provide detailed statistics of the population of discovered domains and categorize the domains according to their usage and their abuse
- We review possible ways of defending against bitsquatting ranging from hardware-based solutions to damage-control and solutions based on legislation

Organization.
The rest of this paper is organized as follows. In Section 2, we briefly define bitsquatting and summarize Dinaburg's findings. In Section 3, we describe our experiment and present our methodology and results for the discovery and categorization of each discovered bitsquatting domain. In Section 4, we provide some details about bitsquatting domains clustering around specific popular web sites, followed by a discussion of possible defenses in Section 5. In Section 6, we review the related work and we conclude in Section 7.

2. BITSQUATTING

In this section, we describe how bitsquatting works and introduce the terminology used in the rest of this paper. We also summarize Dinaburg's empirical validation [6], showing the plausibility of conducting a real-life bitsquatting attack.

2.1 Definition

In July 2011, Dinaburg presented for the first time the notion of bitsquatting [6], i.e., the abuse of random bit-related

1st	2nd	3rd	...	10th	Domain name
1110000	1100001	1111001	...	1101101	paypal.com
1111000	...	...	...	1101101	xaypal.com
1110100	...	...	...	1101101	taypal.com
1110010	...	...	...	1101101	raypal.com
1110001	...	...	...	1101101	qaypal.com
1100000	...	...	...	1101101	0aypal.com

Table 1: All possible and domain-name compatible bit-flips on the first-character byte of paypal.com

errors in the memory of computers, in order to drive traffic to attacker-controlled destinations. Corruption of bits can occur due to faulty hardware, memory present in devices operating outside of the expected temperature range (like smartphones and tablets that are commonly operated outdoors) or even cosmic rays.

While bit-errors (specifically bit-flips) are infrequent on the memory of any given machine, the total amount of RAM available to networked computers and smartphones today is substantial. Moreover, according to Dinaburg, the majority of commodity desktop PCs, laptops and smartphones do not utilize Error-Correcting Code memory (ECC RAM) which could identify and correct erroneous bit-flips. Using conservative assumptions, the researcher calculated the worldwide hourly rate of errors, in devices with non-ECC RAM to 614,400. Even though the majority of these random bit-flips will be of no use to a remote attacker, there is data in memory that could lead to exploitable scenarios. More precisely, the data that could be of use to a remote attacker, is data related to URLs and their resolved IP addresses. This data can be corrupted both at the client and the server-side as well as in-transit. Here we present a few possible scenarios:

- **Cached HTML in server memory** Whenever a web page is requested from a web server, the hardware of the remote server places the page into the server's cache so as to avoid disk I/O in subsequent identical requests. If the random bit-flip occurs in the memory that holds a URL, then the errors will be propagated to clients requesting that specific page.

- **Caches in DNS servers** When a recursive DNS server resolves an unknown domain, bit-flips that happen in the rest of the resolving infrastructure can be populated and stored in the server's cache. These errors are more disastrous than the previous case, since now, all correct requests for a domain name may receive an erroneous cached response.

- **Received HTML on the client** Similarly to web servers, a web page cached in a user's browser can be a victim of bitsquatting, if a bit-flip occurs in URLs of links and remotely-included objects, such as scripts, images, and Cascading Style Sheets.

- **Router memory** Any networking devices between a user and a server are also susceptible to random bit-errors. Thus, bit-flips can be introduced in a page by the routing infrastructure between the client and the server, both in the actual content of the packets relayed as well as the routing decisions.

In all of the above cases, an undetected bit-error in the domain name can cause a user's browser and network-utilizing software to connect to a domain that is one-bit different from the intended, authoritative domain. An attacker who registers these bitsquatting domains, can serve ads, conduct phishing attacks, launch browser exploits or even attempt to steal the cookie-stored credentials of the intended domain in the cases where the bit-flip occured in the DNS infrastructure.

Consider the case of a random bit-error occurring on the first byte of the memory storing the authoritative domain paypal.com, as shown in Table 1. Several observations can be made based on this example. First, not all bit-flips result in characters that are allowed to be part of domain names. Thus, even if a bit-flip takes place in the memory holding a domain name, it may result in an invalid domain and thus not resolve to an IP address. Second, some of the bit-flips result in neighboring characters and thus could be the result of an accidental mistype, (like 0aypal.com). At the same time, other characters are "far-away" from the original characters, essentially ruling out mistypes. We explore the overlap of bitsquatting and typosquatting in Section 3.2.3. Lastly, there is always a chance that the bit-flip will result in a legitimate domain, belonging to another party. In our example with paypal.com, raypal.com is the home page of "Ray Palla", a radio-broadcaster.

In principle, bit-flips can also occur in memory holding IP addresses. While these errors could also divert traffic to attacker-controlled servers, the acquisition of a specific IP address is significantly more complicated than the registration of a bitsquatting domain.

2.2 Empirical validation

In order to discover whether bitsquatting is a real issue, Dinaburg registered 30 domains that were bitsquats of popular domains, such as mic2osoft.com (targeting Microsoft), fbbdn.com (targeting Facebook's content delivery network) and do5bleclick.net (targeting DoubleClick, Google's Ad management platform). In a period of over eight months, his bitsquatting domains received a total of 52,317 requests from 12,949 unique IP addresses with an average of 59 unique IP addresses per day. According to Dinaburg, requests were received from all over the world, by all popular operating systems and browsers, as well as smartphones and gaming consoles with networking capabilities, showing that all systems are potentially vulnerable to a bitsquatting attack. Additionally, Dinaburg found evidence of requests that were definitely not user-initiated, such as automatic update requests from "Windows Update", which could only be generated by misbehaving hardware.

Overall, his study showed that bitsquatting is a real possibility and that companies should protect themselves by e.g., pro-actively registering all bitsquatting domains in the same way as they already do with typosquatting domains [17]. As shown in later sections, attackers are convinced that bitsquatting is a new way to profit, as evidenced by the constant rise of registered bitsquatting domains since Dinaburg's presentation in 2011.

3. ANALYSIS

In this section, we first describe our methodology for gathering data about bitsquatting domains and then provide a detailed analysis of the population of the discovered bitsquatting domains. We study the overlap of bitsquatting with typosquatting and, using a combination of automatic

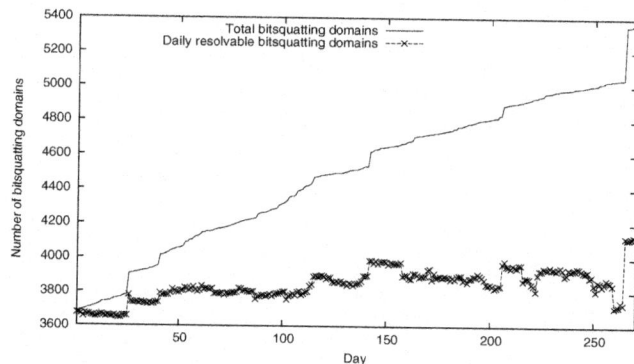

Figure 1: Daily counts of discovered bitsquatting domains

and manual analysis, we categorize the discovered domains based on their content and purpose.

3.1 Experiment

To identify the prevalence of bitsquatting and its evolution over time, we constructed a fully automated crawler capable of discovering and recording bitsquatting domains. For each authoritative domain in a given list, the crawler first computes all possible one-bit text permutations of that domain that adhere to the allowed syntax for domain names. More precisely, a bitsquatting result is considered an allowed domain, if it only contains dots, dashes and alphanumeric characters. For every resulting bitsquatting domain, the crawler attempts to resolve the domain's IP address, and if the resolution is successful, it then requests and records the main page of the site corresponding to that domain. This process is repeated daily, in order to discover new bitsquatting domains and track the disappearing of old ones.

Our crawler was supplied with the list of the Alexa top 500 domains and allowed to execute for 270 days, starting from August 14, 2011.

3.2 Results

3.2.1 Overall growth

In the period of 270 days, we discovered a total of 5,366 different bitsquatting domains targeting 491 out of the Alexa top 500 domains. Moreover, the total number of bitsquatting domains shows a 46% increase from the starting date of our experiment. Figure 1 shows the daily growth of bitsquatting domains over that period. For any given day, the solid line represents all the bitsquatting domains found till that day. The graph shows an obviously increasing trend, which means that as days go by, more and more bitsquatting domains are purchased and made available online. The dotted-line in the same figure, shows the daily number of bitsquatting domains that were resolving to an IP address. The slope of this line is obviously smaller than the slope of the solid line. In addition, there are days where the number of resolving domains is smaller than earlier days showing that, while bitsquatting domains are registered daily, many of them are, willingly or forcefully, taken down. We believe that these domains are taken down after legal action by the authoritative domains who are being bitsquatted. Given, however, the low cost of .com domains, this doesn't stop

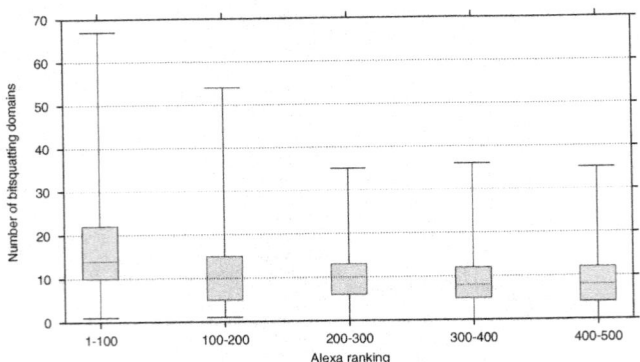

Figure 2: Number of bitsquatting domains per legitimate domain, grouped by Alexa rank

#Domains	QWERTY	AZERTY	QWERTZ	Typo-squatting?
1,301	yes	yes	yes	
6	yes	no	yes	
42	yes	no	no	Possibly yes
118	no	yes	no	
45	no	no	yes	
3,854	no	no	no	Definitely no

Table 2: Number of bitsquatting domains in the experiment that could be confused with typosquatting domains. The last line shows that 3,854 domains can not be a typo-domain according to the given keyboard layouts.

attackers from merely registering new ones, when their old domains become unavailable.

3.2.2 Targeting frequency

Figure 2 shows the number of times, each of the Alexa top 500 domains was targeted by bitsquatters. We use a "box-and-whisker" plot to map the data in quartiles. The graph can be read as follows: The edge of the lower whisker of a box, represents the minimum number of recorded bitsquatting domains for any given authoritative domain, within a specific rank, whereas the edge of the higher whisker represents the maximum number. The dotted line in each box, represents the median number of bitsquatting domains, whereas the box itself is comprised by the median numbers of the groups of data below and above the central median. For example, all sites ranking from one to one hundred were targeted by bitsquatters at least once and at most 67 times. The median number of bitsquatting attacks for all domains of that rank is 14. The small height of all gray boxes in relation to the range of their whiskers, as well as the positions of their median values show that, even though some web sites are attacked much more than the rest, the majority of sites within the Alexa top 500 receive roughly the same number of attacks. From an attacker's point of view, this can be interpreted as follows: most authoritative domains within the Alexa top 500 are equally important and thus most are targeted the same number of times.

3.2.3 Bitsquatting vs. Typosquatting

Before we explore the usage of the discovered bitsquatting domains, we want to focus on the overlap of bitsquatting with typosquatting. Given that typosquatting is known and practiced for over ten years, the question rises of why the domains discovered in our experiment were registered. Were the prospective domain-name owners registering them with typosquatting in mind, or were they considering the newly proposed bitsquatting?

A single bit-flip in a valid DNS character could be interpreted as a typo depending on the keyboard layout used. In fact, the characters resulting from most typos on any keyboard are identical with the characters resulting from a single bit-flip. Of the 38 possible characters (a-z, 0-9, dot and dash) that can be present in a valid domain-name, the binary representation of about 28^1 characters has a Hamming distance of 1 to the binary representation of another character in the valid DNS character set.

We analyzed the bitsquatting domain names in our experiment to determine whether these domains could possibly be typosquatting domains according to any of the popular keyboard-layouts, i.e., QWERTY, AZERTY or QWERTZ. We consider a domain to be a typosquatting domain when it has a "fat-finger" distance of one, from the targeted authoritative domain [14]. The results of this analysis are presented in Table 2 and show that 3,854 or 71.8% of the bitsquatting domains are not typosquatting domains. This indicates that these domains were registered specifically with bitsquatting in mind.

To further support our claim that these domains are registered with bitsquatting in mind we hypothesize that registrations for bitsquatting domains saw a sudden increase when the work of Dinaburg appeared. From the 5,366 discovered bitsquatting domains, we isolated the ones that, given a QWERTY keyboard layout, were not within a "fat-finger" distance of one of the original domain. We limited ourselves to the QWERTY layout since, as shown in Table 2, this layout could be the most responsible for a domain being both a bitsquatting as well as a typosquatting domain. For these domains, we queried their registration dates, which we plot in Figure 3. To prove our hypothesis, we build a linear regression model describing the variation in registrations over time up to the coining of the term *bitsquatting* (no variation $p < 10^{-19}$ and $R = 0.81$). After the coining of the term, we see a sudden increase of registrations which are significantly different from the current trend ($p < 10^{-8}$) and indicates that something has abruptly changed the trend established over multiple years. Intuitively, one can see that while this type of mistyped domains were always registered, the registrations spiked in the second-half of 2011, which is when Dinaburg presented his work at BlackHat [6]. Thus it is reasonable to associate the notion of bitsquatting with the sudden increase in registrations of domains, not commonly associated with typosquatting.

3.2.4 Parked domains

Prior research by Wang et al. [17] has shown that most typosquatting domains are pointing or redirecting their traffic to domain-parking agencies. Domain-parking agencies are Internet advertising companies which specialize in the monetization of domains with no real content. The *modus operandi* of these agencies is the following: A user registers a domain name and forwards all of the received traffic to the domain-parking agency. The agency, using information

---
[1] 28 for QWERTY and QWERTZ layouts, 27 for AZERTY

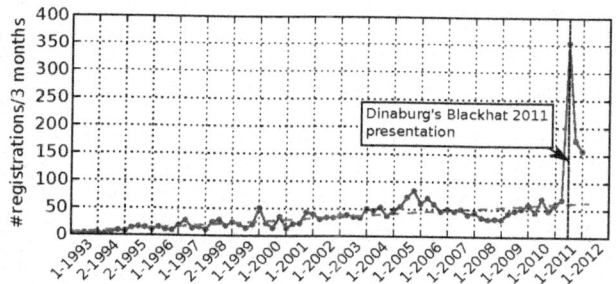

Figure 3: Registrations of bitsquatting domains that are further than a fat-finger distance of one, from the attacked domain

Domain-name-level detection
information.com, domainsponsor.com
oingo.com, sedoparking.com
qsrch.com, netster.com
hitfarm.com
HTML-level detection
perfectnames.com, domainpool.com
siliconalleydomains.com, fabulousdomains.com
googlesyndication.com/apps/domainpark
memorabledomains.co.uk, trafficz.com
revenue.net

Table 3: Domains names utilized for the detection of domain-name parking agencies

Parking methodology	Count
Reverse DNS	1,409
HTTP 302 redirection	108
HTML META-refresh redirection	54
HTML code	1,211
Total parked domains	2,782 (51.8%)

Table 4: Parked domains discovered by each set of heuristics

from both the owner of the domain, as well as the keywords present in the domain name, serves relevant ads to visiting users. Finally, the owner of the domain receives a commission for every click on the displayed ads.

Since domain-parking is prevalent among typosquatters, our hypothesis was that a similar trend would appear for bitsquatting domains. To test this hypothesis, we analyzed the data from all 5,366 bitsquatting domains for evidence of utilizing a domain-parking agency at any point during the 270 days that we were monitoring them.

The redirection of traffic from a domain name towards a domain-parking agency can be done using DNS entries, HTTP status codes, HTML META-refresh tags and client-side scripting languages, like JavaScript. In the first case, the domain owner creates a DNS record which resolves to an IP address controlled by the domain-parking agency. In the case of HTTP redirects, the domain owner needs to setup a web server that issues HTTP 301/302 status messages to forward a visiting user's browser to another website. These status messages are handled by the browser and do not render any information on the page, making the redirection transparent for the user. In the last two cases, a domain owner can setup a web server with a web page containing an HTML META-refresh header or a JavaScript-based redirection. Browsers will then render the page before being redirected to the domain-parking agency.

For redirection through DNS records, our detection method inspects the reverse DNS entry of the IP address to which the bitsquatting domain resolves. For the other three ways of redirecting traffic, our detection method inspects the hostname of the URL being redirected to. If a bitsquatting domain has a reverse DNS entry or redirects to a URL belonging to any known domain-parking agencies, it is flagged as being a "parked domain".

Our list of parking-domain agencies, shown in Table 3 comes from Wang et al. [17]. To account for less known agencies, we also use the occurrence of the word "park" as an indication that the domain is a parking domain, since the word is not frequently used in popular non-domain-parking websites. For instance, in the top 10,000 Alexa domains, there are only ten domains that use the words "park" without being domain parkers. In addition to analysis of the reverse DNS and redirected-to URLs, we also searched the downloaded HTML pages for domains that typically only occur in links embedded on domain-parking agency websites. We obtained these keywords, shown in the second row of Table 3, by preliminary experimentation and analysis of our bitsquatting HTML corpus.

The domain-name-level and HTML-level heuristics for the detection of domains utilizing domain-parking agencies, were used to automatically scan all 5,366 bitsquatting domains and the results are shown in Table 4. The results show that the majority of the discovered domains were indeed trying to capitalize on visiting users through the use of domain parking. At the same time, we discovered that there were some bitsquatting domains that were flagged as a parking domain by our domain-name-level heuristics but not by the HTML-level ones. Although these domains were correctly classified as parking domains, the lack of detection at the HTML-level, meant that our set of heuristics was incomplete, which in turn prompted us to take a closer look at the unclassified data (See Section 3.2.7).

3.2.5 Self-Redirects

As we mentioned in earlier sections, various companies, in an effort to protect their brands and customers from various cybersquatting attacks, register mistypes of their domains. Thus, when a user visits the site corresponding to a mistyped domain, the company will redirect her to the appropriate authoritative domain, usually using an HTTP 302 message. This way, the user ends up on the correct page and also sees the corrected URL (resulting from the redirect) on her browser's address bar.

From the 5,366 bitsquatting domains discovered in our experiment, we recorded 311 domains (5.7%) which redirected, for at least one day, the visiting user back to the correct authoritative domain. We manually inspected the WHOIS records of each bitsquatting domain name and compared the available information, e.g., the name and email address of technical contact and name-servers, to the information listed in the WHOIS records of the corresponding authoritative domain.

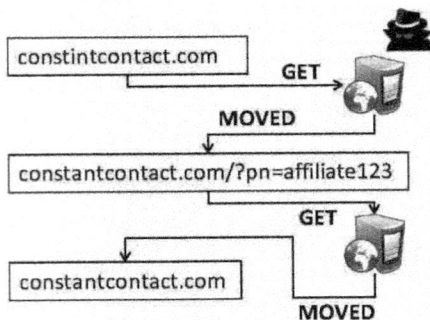

Figure 4: Abuse of bitsquatting in affiliate programs

For 211 bitsquatting domains, we were able to verify that they either belonged to the companies owning the corresponding authoritative domains or they were owned and managed by companies which specialize in brand and trademark protection. By studying the traffic generated upon the visit of the pages of those domains, we saw that the brand- and trade-protecting companies were usually first registering the fact that a user visited the specific bitsquatting domain and then redirected the user back to the appropriate authoritative domain.

From the 100 remaining bitsquatting domains which redirected the user back to the appropriate authoritative domain, we were able to verify that 58 (18.7%) were abusing affiliate programs of the authoritative domains. Affiliate programs are offered by various online companies which pay a commission to their affiliates, for every customer brought to their site, who bought their products or services. These programs usually operate with a unique affiliate identifier embedded in a link, which affiliates are expected to place on their web sites. In the case of bitsquatting, however, the attackers were using the bitsquatting domains to redirect users back to the appropriate authoritative domains with the addition of their affiliate identifiers in the new URLs. Figure 4 shows an example of actual misuse discovered in our data set. When a user requests the bitsquatting domain constintcontact.com, the attacker's web server redirects the user's browser to the affiliate page of constantcontact.com using the attacker's specific affiliate identifier (anonymized as affiliate123). The legitimate web server of constantcontact.com, registers the affiliate's identifier and redirects the user to the main page of the site. At the end of this process, the user is presented with the main page of constantcontact.com without knowing that she has been an unwilling part of an affiliate scheme. The authoritative domains that were targeted by bitsquatting to perform affiliate fraud, were companies offering web hosting, adult content, services, online shopping and travel-booking. Moore et al. [14] have found instances of similar abuse in typosquatting domains.

The remaining 42 bitsquatting domains were redirecting the user to the correct authoritative site and not exploiting the visitor in any obvious way. We theorize, that the owners of these domains fall in the following three categories. First, the domains may be owned by the company owning the corresponding authoritative domain which for some reason lists different details in the WHOIS records. Second, the bitsquatting domains may be registered by researchers who are attempting to recreate Dinaburg's findings. Lastly, the domains may be owned by domain-squatters who have not yet decided on the best way of monetizing their visitors, and forward the traffic back to the original site in an attempt to temporarily avoid unnecessary attention.

3.2.6 Observed bitsquatting experiments

The gathered data also carries evidence of ongoing bitsquatting experiments from third parties. We have recorded a total of 61 bitsquatting domains from 8 authoritative domains that announce that they are part of bitsquatting experiments. These domains were automatically discovered by searching for they keywords "bit," "squatting," and "experiment" in the HTML code of the web pages of all discovered bitsquatting domains.

These experiments are most likely conducted by researchers trying to verify Dinaburg's work [6]. We assume that in these cases, the researchers have no intent of attacking visitors, since attackers experimenting with bitsquatting would have no reason to explicitly announce their work. Examples domains are: iozilla.org and wozdpress.com

3.2.7 Breakdown of domain usage

Figure 5 shows a breakdown of all 5,366 bitsquatting domains in our experiment, by category. After removing 2,782 known parked domains (51.8%), 211 domains that were clearly owned by the companies owning the corresponding authoritative domains (3.9%), 112 domains that were never associated with a web server (2.1%), and 61 domains that were part of other bitsquatting experiments (1.1%), 2,200 domains (41.0%) remain that could not easily be categorized using automated means.

From these 2,200 uncategorized domains, we selected a 10% random sample for a thorough manual analysis. For each domain in the sample, we rendered its page for various days from our logs, inspected its source and whenever necessary checked its WHOIS records and its presence in Google's database of known malicious sites. Our manual inspection resulted in the following categorization:

Legitimately owned (40.0%): These were domains resolving to legitimate web sites that were either not related to the original authoritative domain or were domains with a different TLD of the same company. As demonstrated in Section 2, a random bit-flip in a domain name may result in a different legitimate domain, which is owned by a third-party who has no intent of attacking the authoritative domain, such as androyd.com and raypal.com. There were some cases, however, where the legitimate third-party web site was offering products and services of the same type as the authoritative domain, making it unclear whether it is a double coincidence or whether it is a competitor who is trying to assume the identity of the original authoritative site.

For the latter case, we discovered that some large companies, e.g. Google, own domains that when bitsquatted resolve to new domains, which still belong to the same company but under a different TLD, e.g. a bitsquat of google.com.vn (Google's site in Vietnam), is google.com.tn (Google's site in Tunisia).

Parked (15.4%): These were domains that were serving the same purpose as the ones described in Section 3.2.4 which were not discovered by our set of heuristics.

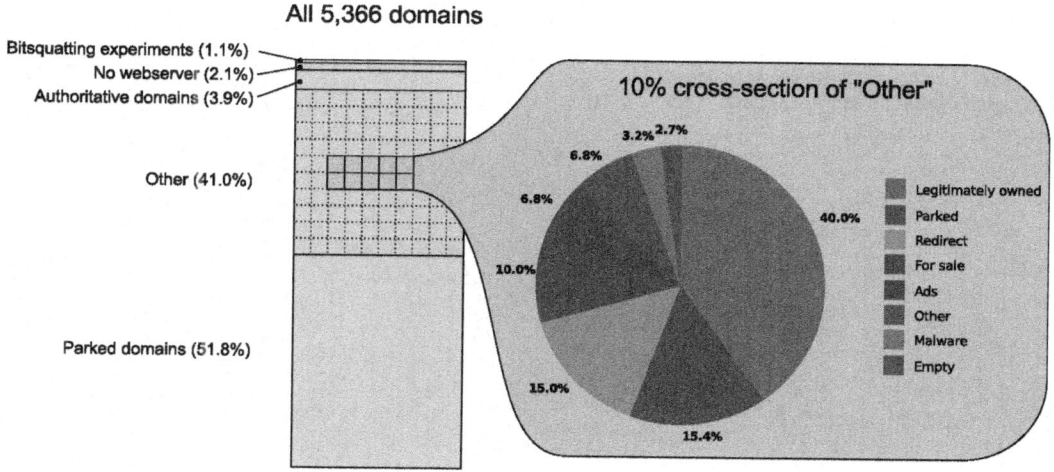

Figure 5: Analysis of bitsquatting domains by category

Among them, we discovered some special cases, such as bitsquatting domains ending in .co.ph. This extension belongs to the Official Domain Registry in the Philippines which resolves all non-existant domains to their own domain-registration web site.

Redirects (15.0%): In this category, the web sites were redirecting the user either to a completely different web site, e.g. that of a competing company, or were redirecting back to the authoritative domains while performing affiliate abuse, as described in Section 3.2.5.

For sale (10.0%): In these cases, the owners of domains were clearly offering their domains for sale and providing means of contacting them.

Ads (6.8%): 6.8% of the sampled domains were showing ads, but were not affiliated to a domain-parking agency. In some cases, the ads were static, specifically targeting the users of the corresponding authoritative domain, revealing the bitsquatter's intent of focusing on specific products and companies.

Search/Under Construction (6.8%) & Empty (2.7%): The domains of this category were generally providing non-useful content, being either empty, or showing an "Under Construction" message. Lastly, some of them were "fronts" for search engines, which merely forwarded a user's query to a popular search engine.

Malware (3.2%): Among the sampled domains, 3.2% of them were serving malware, either through the direct inclusion of a malicious script from a remote host or indirectly through the advertising network with which they collaborated. These script-providing hosts were automatically identified by our web browser, due to their presence in Google's Safe Browsing database.

Overall, our manual analysis, combined with the results of the previous sections leads to the following two observations: First, care must be taken when attempting to characterize a bitsquatting domain, since it may owned by a legitimate third-party. Second, the manual analysis verified that owners of bitsquatting domains are trying to capitalize on visiting users using either adverstising and for-sale listings or in some cases utilizing more intrusive approaches, such as the installation of malware. More precisely, by extrapolating the capitalizing-categories to the entire population of uncategorized results (50.4% of 2,200 uncategorized bitsquatting domains) and including the parking domains from Section 3.2.4, we can conclude that over 73% of the entire set of discovered bitsquatting domains belong to domain-squatters who attempt to profit by exploiting erroneous bit-flips.

4. CASE STUDIES

In this section, we briefly describe two instances of bitsquatting attacks, clustered around specific domains in the list of Alexa top 500 domains.

huffingtonpost.com.
"The Huffington Post", is a popular online newspaper that currently ranks in the top 100 Alexa domains. The newspaper has an unusually long domain name (14 characters excluding the suffix), which provides more bytes of characters that an attacker can squat. In fact, huffingtonpost.com is the host which received the maximum number of bitsquatting attacks, of the 1-100 ranking category, in Figure 2. On the 14th August 2011, when we started our experiment, huffingtonpost.com had 18 bitsquatting domains. This number remained the same till the 8th of September, when overnight, 49 new bitsquatting domains were registered. By manually examining these domains, we found out that for their majority, they were all providing the same page.

As Figure 6 shows, each page was alerting the user that she is there because her hardware was faulty (referring to bit-errors that were responsible for bringing the user to the bitsquatting site) and even warned the user that a malicious individual could have used this opportunity to steal the user's credentials. Subsequently, the owner of the bitsquatting domain, advised the user to buy new hardware from Amazon. More precisely, the bitsquatter was suggesting some Apple products and when clicked, the user would be redirected to Amazon with a specific affiliate identifier, so that if the user did buy a new laptop or smartphone, the bitsquatter would get a commission. Note that this attack instance is different from the affiliate abuse described

Figure 6: Bitsquatting domain for huffingtonpost.com

in Section 3.2.5, in that huffingtonpost.com has no affiliate program of its own and thus the attacker needs to "explain" the transition to amazon.com.

All 49 bitsquatting domains were available till the 29th of April 2012, giving the attacker over seven months to capitalize on visiting users. In addition, we recorded identical pages on bitsquatting domains of zynga.com (a popular game producer), nytimes.com (the New York Times) and reddit.com.

microsoft.com.
In the period of 270 days, we recorded a total of 40 different bitsquatting domains for microsoft.com. While the majority of them were parked or "for sale" domains, we also discovered more intrusive examples. micposoft.com is a domain which used the logo of the Microsoft Corporation and their usual blue-and-white color scheme. The site was supposedly offering multiple downloads, such as a password recovery utility, Internet Explorer 9 and Windows 7, all of which were pointing to the same executable. We downloaded the executable and submitted it to VirusTotal, an online service that scans user-submitted files against the signature databases of popular antivirus software. The executable was flagged as a "packed malware" by 2.3% of the utilized antivirus engines.

Five other domains, e.g., microskft.com and microsogt.com, were redirecting the unsuspecting user to the domain errorfix.com. That site was offering an "Advanced Registry Repair tool", which was flagged as a fake antivirus by 28.6% of VirusTotal's antivirus engines. Lastly, migrosoft.com, was offering products, training and services, abusing the similarity and name of their trademark with Microsoft's.

5. DEFENSES AGAINST BITSQUATTING

In the previous sections, we presented ample evidence showing that cybersquatters are actively bitsquatting popular Internet sites and attempt to monetize, in a variety of ways, the visits of unsuspecting users. In this section, we briefly describe some possible solutions for the protection of users and companies against bitsquatting.

5.1 Hardware-based

Bitsquatting occurs because of hardware problems either on the client-side, the server-side or any of the network infrastructure in between. The most obvious solution therefore, is to address the problem at its root. As Dinaburg suggested, data stored in hardware should include data integrity information to ensure that the data has not suffered unexpected modifications. Such data integrity validation could be accomplished by using ECC memory and CRC checks. Unfortunately, this approach will only ensure that local data is not corrupted. Routers on the network for example, will correctly store and forward any data they receive without corruption, but the corruption might already have occurred. To stop data-corruption in a networked environment, all parties must use hardware-based data integrity validation in order to be effective. Thus, even if all major ISPs and hosting companies would be willing to invest in hardware with error-correction capabilities, a complete migration would require a significant span of time.

5.2 Software-based

Another way to avoid random corruption of critical data, is to validate data integrity more frequently in the software. If the data exchanged between client and server includes data integrity information, then the data integrity can be verified at either end, ensuring that there was no corruption along the way. One option for ensuring data integrity on the DNS level is by using DNS Security Extensions (DNSSEC), which add data integrity information to DNS queries. However, as with all client-server protocols, this approach requires that both the client and the used DNS infrastructure support DNSSEC. While modern operating systems ship with built-in support for DNSSEC, the deployment of the security extensions in the DNS infrastructure is still not complete due to unforeseen obstacles [7, 16]. Another option is to use Transport Layer Security (TLS) or Secure Socket Layer (SSL), to ensure that users at least get a warning about being connected to the wrong endpoint, in case DNS traffic has been corrupted.

5.3 Incentive-removal

In Section 3.2.4, we showed that more than 50% of all registered bitsquatting domains are used to show ads, through the use of dedicated domain-parking agencies. This means, that for their majority, bitsquatters use a relatively simple, non-technical and non-intrusive approach to monetize their newly-purchased domains. Thus, even if there are thousands of individuals purchasing bitsquatting domains, they all eventually cluster to a relatively small number of domain-parking agencies. If legal control would be applied at these companies, i.e., to be forced to deny their services to domains that are obviously bitsquatting domains, then bitsquatters could no longer utilize them. It is worth pointing out that there is already legislation in-place which legally protects companies from cybersquatters and could be straightforwardly extended to cover bitsquatting [1].

If bitsquatters can no longer rely on ads, the only safe alternative for making a profit would be to sell the bitsquatting domain to the company owning the corresponding authoritative domain. While this is still an option, a collective boycott from large companies towards cybersquatters would leave them with useless non-profiting domains. Bitsquatters could of course try to monetize their domains through malware installations, but this assumes significantly more legal risk than the simple hosting of ads.

5.4 Damage-control

A more immediate way for a company to protect its trademark and users, is to accept that data corruption can occur and prevent its exploitation by rogue parties, through the pre-registration of all possible bitsquatting domains when registering the master, authoritative domain. This fix has a substantial cost overhead, as the following example shows:

The most common domain-name length among the top one million Alexa domains, is 9 characters, not counting the top-level domain (TLD); the most common top-level domain is *.com*. Consider a company wishing to register `mycompany.com`, a 9-character domain name under the *.com* TLD, and all the bitsquatting variations of this domain-name to be safe from bitsquatters. In this case, there are 42 *.com* domain names that would need to be registered, including the authoritative `mycompany.com` domain.

For some domains which are not under the *.com* top-level domain, there could be a need to register more domains under a different top-level domain authority. For instance, to register all bit-squatted variations of `mycompany.cn`, requires the registration of all domains in the *.an*, *.bn*, *.cf*, *.cl*, *.co*, *.gn*, *.kn* and *.sn* top-level domains, since a random bit-error can also occur in the TLD part of a domain name. Unfortunately, some of the resulting TLDs may be very expensive or subject to local regulations.

At the same time, Dinaburg pointed out that bitsquatting attacks can be practically exploited only against the companies owning the most popular domains, since these are the ones which get resolved the most and thus have the most chance of a random corruption. These companies are large enough to be able to afford the registration and maintenance of additional domains, especially when it comes to protecting their online identity.

6. RELATED WORK

To the best of our knowledge, our work is the first one that studies the adoption of bitsquatting by the domain-squatting community. Bitsquatting however, is only the latest instantiation of a series of attacks against the Domain Name System and the web sites relying on it. Thus, in this section we review prior domain-squatting attacks and relevant surveys.

6.1 Cybersquatting

Cybersquatting refers to the act of registering domains that are trademarks belonging to other persons and companies. Cybersquatting was popular at the dawn of the world wide web, when there were long-existing brick-and-mortar companies that did not yet have a web presence. Many opportunists registered their trademarks as domain names before them, so that they would sell the domain back to the company for profit [11]. Occasionally, the cybersquatters would host offensive or mocking content on the cybersquatting domains so that they would force the company to buy the domain from them as soon as possible [8].

Today, this type of domain-squatting is not as popular since companies usually register all appropriate domains, well before the company and its trademarks become popular. There are still cases however, where cybersquatters speculate the name of future products and services and register them, before the company marketing the product or service, does [2]. Coull et al. [3] have studied this phenomenon together with other domain registration abuses, such as *domain name tasting* and *domain-name front running*.

6.2 Typosquatting

Cybersquatting later evolved into *typosquatting*, i.e., the act of registering domains that are mistypes of popular authoritative domains, with the intention of capturing the traffic of users that make mistakes while typing a URL in their browsers' address bar. Such mistakes include missing-dot typos, character-omission typos and character-permutation typos. This practice can be traced back to over 13 years, since the 1999 Anticybersquatting Consumer Protection Act (ACPA) already mentions URLs that are "sufficiently similar to a trademark of a person or entity" [1]. In 2003, Edelman reported on 8,800 mistyped and cybersquatting domains that served sexually-explicit content, which he postulated were registered by the same individual [8].

Wang et al. [17] described a system for automatically discovering and analyzing typosquatting by simulating typing errors. The researchers also brought attention to the fact that the majority of the discovered typosquatting domains were pointing to domain-parking agencies, which were used to automatically serve ads related to the mistyped domain name. Banerjee et al. [2] identified that typosquatting extends to the abuse of domain suffixes, such as registering a typosquatting *.org* domain, for an authoritative *.com*.

Moore and Edelman perform a similar experiment to discover typosquatting domains in 2010 [14] and estimated that, at the time, at least 938,000 typosquatting domains targeted the top 3,264 *.com* sites. Interestingly, the authors point out that large advertising networks such as Google Ads, willingly cooperate with typosquatters by showing ads on the mistyped domains and should thus be held equally responsible for the damage against the authoritative domains that are being attacked. Apart from serving ads, there have also been documented cases of typosquatting domains used to serve malware [9]. Nikiforakis et al. [15] recently showed that typosquatting can also occur in remote script inclusions, where developers mistype the domains of remote code providers and thus make their sites susceptible to malicious script injections.

6.3 Homograph attacks

In a domain-homograph attack, an attacker takes advantage of the perceived visual similarity between two or more letters, in order to trick the user into believing that she is interacting with a specific authoritative web site while she is interacting with the attacker's site. This confusion may lead up to the user willingly submitting her credentials or other sensitive information. The main difference between these attacks and the aforementioned domain-squatting attacks, is that the homographed domains are usually spread-out through spam emails and social networks, instead of relying on user mistakes, since their construction cannot usually be achieved by the mistype of a letter for a neighboring one.

Gabrilovich and Gontmakher were the first to bring attention to the possible use of characters from non-Latin character-sets that look like Latin characters and could be substituted to confuse the user of the nature of a given

---

[2] Parked domain with ads - www.iphone6.com

domain [10]. For instance, an attacker could register `paypal.com` using the Cyrillic letter р (lower case "r", Unicode U+0440), which looks almost identical to the Latin letter "p".

Dhamija et al. [5], study the reasons which make phishing work, and make special mention of "visually deceptive text", i.e., domains that substitute characters with lookalikes within the same character-set, such as `paypa1.com` (last letter is the number "one" instead of the letter "l") and `bankofvvest.com` (two "v"s instead of a "w").

Holgers et al. [12] performed a large-scale study of homograph attacks by gathering popular domains and searching for homographed ones by substituting up to three characters of each domain, with their confusable counterparts. They discovered a total of 399 homographed domains, targeting 299 authoritative domains, from a corpus of over 3,000 domains. The majority of the discovered homographed domains were used to display ads to the visiting users. Others were listed for sale and some were even parodies of the authoritative domains that they mimicked. These results suggest that, while homography is used to construct confusable domains, the population of homographed domains is several orders of magnitude less than typosquatting and not exploited as much as it could be.

7. CONCLUSION

The importance of domains has made them an attractive target for malicious individuals. As the web expands, domain names can only become more popular and thus attacks against them are likely to become more frequent and more severe. Even though today, search engines greatly assist users in discovering web sites, domain names are still the de facto symbol of familiarity of any given web page appearing in a user's browser. Bitsquatting is the latest instantiation of attacks against domain names, but differs from its predecessors in that it relies on hardware failure rather than human error.

In this paper, we explored the impact of bitsquatting on the domain-squatting community and showed that domain-squatters have embraced it as the latest way of parasitically profiting on popular web sites. Bitsquatters were found to employ all the known ways of domain-squatters as a way of profiting: parked domains, affiliate abuse and malware installations. We hope that this study, can serve as a reference point for the dangers of bitsquatting and the need for appropriate reaction from companies that wish to protect themselves and their customers.

Acknowledgments: The authors acknowledge the support of EURid, the European Registry of Internet Domain Names. This research was performed with the financial support of the Prevention against Crime Programme of the European Union (B-CCENTRE), the Research Fund KU Leuven and the EU FP7 project NESSoS.

8. REFERENCES

[1] Anticybersquatting Consumer Protection Act (ACPA). http://www.patents.com/acpa.htm, November 1999.

[2] BANERJEE, A., BARMAN, D., FALOUTSOS, M., AND BHUYAN, L. N. Cyber-fraud is one typo away. In *Proceedings of the 27th Conference on Computer Communications, IEEE INFOCOM* (2008).

[3] COULL, S. E., WHITE, A. M., YEN, T.-F., MONROSE, F., AND REITER, M. K. Understanding domain registration abuses. In *Proceedings of the 25th International Information Security Conference (IFIP SEC)* (2010).

[4] COVA, M., LEITA, C., THONNARD, O., KEROMYTIS, A. D., AND DACIER, M. An analysis of rogue AV campaigns. In *Proceedings of the 13th international conference on Recent Advances in Intrusion Detection (RAID)* (2010).

[5] DHAMIJA, R., TYGAR, J. D., AND HEARST, M. Why phishing works. In *Proceedings of the SIGCHI conference on Human Factors in computing systems* (2006), CHI '06, ACM.

[6] DINABURG, A. Bitsquatting: DNS Hijacking without Exploitation. In *Proceedings of BlackHat Security* (July 2011).

[7] EURId Insight: Overview of DNSSEC deployment worldwide, October 2010.

[8] EDELMAN, B. Large-scale registration of domains with typographical errors, September 2003.

[9] F-SECURE. W32/Googkle. http://www.f-secure.com/v-descs/googkle.shtml.

[10] GABRILOVICH, E., AND GONTMAKHER, A. The homograph attack. *Communucations of the ACM 45*, 2 (Feb. 2002), 128.

[11] GOLINVEAUX, J. What's in a domain name: Is cybersquatting trademark dilution? In *University of San Francisco Law Review 33 U.S.F. L. Rev. (1998-1999)*.

[12] HOLGERS, T., WATSON, D. E., AND GRIBBLE, S. D. Cutting through the confusion: a measurement study of homograph attacks. In *Proceedings of the annual conference on USENIX '06 Annual Technical Conference* (Berkeley, CA, USA, 2006), ATEC '06, USENIX Association.

[13] KESMODEL, D. *The Domain Game: How People Get Rich from Internet Domain Names*. Xlibris Corporation, 2008.

[14] MOORE, T., AND EDELMAN, B. Measuring the perpetrators and funders of typosquatting. In *Financial Cryptography and Data Security* (2010), vol. 6052, pp. 175–191.

[15] NIKIFORAKIS, N., INVERNIZZI, L., KAPRAVELOS, A., VAN ACKER, S., JOOSEN, W., KRUEGEL, C., PIESSENS, F., AND VIGNA, G. You Are What You Include: Large-scale Evaluation of Remote JavaScript Inclusions. In *Proceedings of the ACM Conference on Computer and Communications Security (CCS)* (2012).

[16] OSTERWEIL, E., RYAN, M., MASSEY, D., AND ZHANG, L. Quantifying the operational status of the dnssec deployment. In *Proceedings of the 8th ACM SIGCOMM conference on Internet measurement* (New York, NY, USA, 2008), IMC '08, ACM, pp. 231–242.

[17] WANG, Y.-M., BECK, D., WANG, J., VERBOWSKI, C., AND DANIELS, B. Strider typo-patrol: discovery and analysis of systematic typo-squatting. In *Proceedings of the 2nd conference on Steps to Reducing Unwanted Traffic on the Internet - Volume 2* (Berkeley, CA, USA, 2006), SRUTI'06, USENIX Association, pp. 5–5.

One-class Collaborative Filtering with Random Graphs

Ulrich Paquet
Microsoft Reseach Cambridge
ulripa@microsoft.com

Noam Koenigstein
Microsoft R&D, Israel
noamko@microsoft.com

ABSTRACT

The bane of one-class collaborative filtering is interpreting and modelling the latent signal from the missing class. In this paper we present a novel Bayesian generative model for implicit collaborative filtering. It forms a core component of the Xbox Live architecture, and unlike previous approaches, delineates the odds of a user disliking an item from simply being unaware of it. The latent signal is treated as an unobserved random graph connecting users with items they might have encountered. We demonstrate how large-scale distributed learning can be achieved through a combination of stochastic gradient descent and mean field variational inference over random graph samples. A fine-grained comparison is done against a state of the art baseline on real world data.

Categories and Subject Descriptors

G.3 [**Mathematics of computing**]: Probability and statistics

Keywords

One-class collaborative filtering, random graph, variational inference

1. INTRODUCTION

This paper highlights a solution to a very specific problem, the prediction of a "like" or "association" signal from one-class data. One-class or "implicit" data surfaces in many of Xbox's verticals, for example when users watch movies through Xbox Live. In this vertical, we recommend media items to users, drawing on the correlations of their viewing patterns with those of other users. We assume that users don't watch movies that they dislike; therefore the negative class is absent. The problem is equivalent to predicting new connections in a network: given a disjoint user and an item vertex, what is the chance that they should be linked?

We introduce a Bayesian generative process for connecting users and items. It models the "like" probability by interpreting the missing signal as a two-stage process: firstly, by modelling the odds of a user considering an item, and secondly, by eliciting a probability that that item will be viewed or liked. This forms a core component of the Xbox Live architecture, serving recommendations to more than 50 million users worldwide, and replaces an earlier version of our system [10]. The two-stage delineation of popularity and personalization allows systems like ours to trade them off in optimizing user-facing utility functions. The model is simple to interpret, allows us to estimate parameter uncertainty, and most importantly, easily lends itself to large-scale inference procedures.

Interaction patterns on live systems typically follow a power-law distribution, where some users or items are exponentially more active or popular than others. We base our inference on a simple assumption, that the missing signal should have the same power-law degree distribution as the observed user-item graph. Under this assumption, we learn latent parametric descriptions for users and items by computing statistical averages over all plausible "negative graphs".

The challenge for one-class collaborative filtering is to treat the absent signal without incurring a prohibitive algorithmic cost. Unlike its fully binary cousin, which observes "dislike" signals for a selection of user-item pairs, each unobserved user-item pair or edge has a possible negative explanation. For M users and N items, this means that inference algorithms have to consider $\mathcal{O}(MN)$ possible negative observations. In problems considered by Xbox, this amounts to modelling $\mathcal{O}(10^{12})$ latent explanations. The magnitude of real world problems therefore casts a shadow on models that treat each absent observation individually [17].

Thus far, solutions to large-scale one-class problems have been based on one of two main lines of thought. One line formulates the problem as an objective function over all observed and missing data, in which the contribution by the "missing data" drops out in the optimization scheme [7]. It relies on the careful assignment of confidence weights to all edges, but there is no methodical procedure for choosing these confidence weights except an expensive exhaustive search via cross-validation. If a parametric definition of confidence weights is given, a low rank approximation of the weighting scheme can also be included in an objective function [18]. The work presented here differs from these approaches by formulating a probabilistic model rather than an optimization problem, and quantifies our uncertainty about the parameters and predictions.

A second approach is to randomly synthesize negative examples. Our work falls in this camp, for which there already exists a small body of work. The foremost of these is arguably Bayesian Personalized Ranking (BPR), which converts the one-class problem into a ranking problem [21]. In it, it is assumed that the user likes everything that she has seen more than the items that she hasn't seen. This assumption implies a constrained ordering of many unobserved variables, one arising from each item. This user-wise ranking of items facilitates the inference of latent features for each user and item vertex. By design, there is no distinction between missing items in BPR; however, popularity sampling of the unobserved items was employed to give more significance to popular missing items [5]. This approach was effectively utilized by many of the leading solutions in the KDD-Cup'11 competition [4]. An alternative, more expensive approach is to construct an ensemble of solutions, each of which is learned using a different sample of synthesized "negative" edges [19].

We motivate our approach by discussing properties of typical bipartite real world graphs in Section 2. A generative model for collaborative filtering when such graphs are observed is given in Section 3. A component of the model is the hidden graph of edges—items that a user considered, but didn't like. Section 4 addresses the hidden graph as a random graph. Section 5 combines variational inference and stochastic gradient descent to present methods for large scale parallel inference for this probabilistic model. In Section 6, we show state of the art results on two practical problems, a sample of movies viewed by a few million users on Xbox consoles, and a binarized version of the Netflix competition data set.

2. TYPICAL REAL WORLD DATA

The frequency of real-world interactions typically follows some form of power-law. In Xbox Live, we observe a bipartite graph $\mathbf{G}$ of M users and N items, with two (possibly vastly) different degree distributions for the two kinds of vertices. Figure 1 (top) illustrates the degree distribution of a sample of $M = 6.2 \times 10^6$ users that watched $N = 1.2 \times 10^4$ different movies on their Xbox consoles, where an edge appears if a user viewed a movie. Throughout the paper the edges in the observed graph $\mathbf{G}$ will be denoted with the binary variable $g_{mn} \in \{0, 1\}$ for vertices m and n, with a zero value indicating the absence of an edge. We denote the observed degree distributions as $p_{\text{user}}(d)$ and $p_{\text{item}}(d)$. If a user viewed on average μ items, and an item was viewed on average ν times, then $\mathbb{E}_{p_{\text{user}}}[d] = \mu$ and $\mathbb{E}_{p_{\text{item}}}[d] = \nu$, and the constraint

$$\frac{\mu}{N} = \frac{\nu}{M} \qquad (1)$$

should hold [15]. In Figure 1 (top), the empirical distributions satisfy $\mu = 7.1$ and $\nu = 3780$, validating the mean constraint $\mu/N = \nu/M = 0.0006$. We overlay a power law degree distribution to items $p_{\text{item}}(d) \propto d^{-0.77}$. The user distribution exhibits an marked exponential cut-off, with $p_{\text{user}}(d) \propto d^{-1.4} e^{-d/70}$, and shares its form with many scientific collaboration networks [16]. The degree distribution of the publicly available Netflix data set is shown in Figure 1 (bottom). In it, we have $M = 4.8 \times 10^5$ users and $N = 1.8 \times 10^4$ items. We took a positive edge to be present if a user rated an item with four or five stars.

Given $p_{\text{user}}(d)$ and $p_{\text{item}}(d)$, one can sample i.i.d. graphs with the given degree distribution. Firstly, generate vertex degrees for each user and item at random, and calculate their sum. If the sums are unequal, randomly choose one user and item, discard their degrees, and replace them with new degrees of the relevant distributions. This process is repeated until the total user and item degrees are equal, after which vertex pairs are randomly joined up [15].

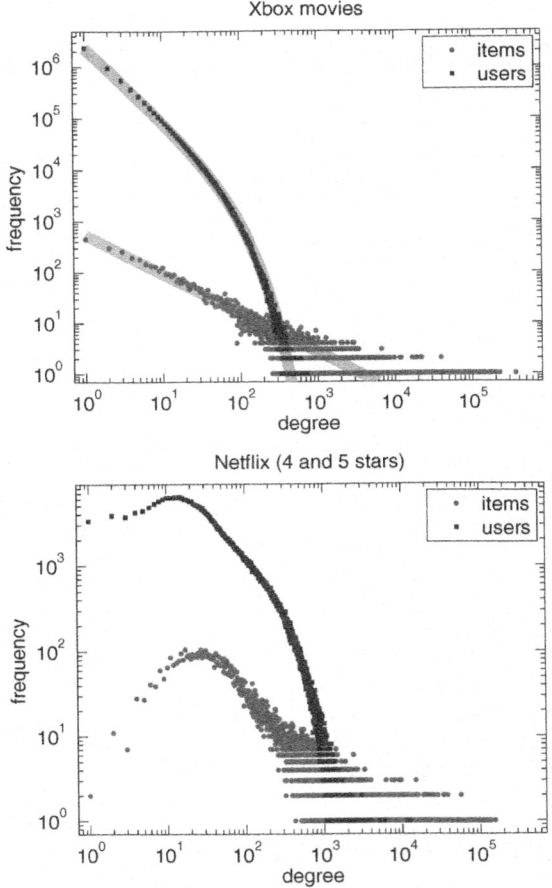

Figure 1: Degree distributions for two bipartite graphs between users and movies: a sample of 4.4×10^7 edges for movies viewed on Xbox (top) and the 5.6×10^7 four and five starred edges in the Netflix prize data set (bottom).

3. COLLABORATIVE FILTERING

Our collaborative filtering model rests on a basic assumption, that if an edge $g_{mn} = 1$ appears $\mathbf{G}$, user m liked item n. However, a user must have considered additional items that she didn't like, even though the dislike or "negative" signals are not observed. This hidden graph with edges $h_{mn} \in \{0, 1\}$ is denoted by $\mathbf{H}$. We say that a user considered an item if and only if $h_{mn} = 1$, and the rule $g_{mn} = 1 \Rightarrow h_{mn} = 1$ holds; namely, a user must have considered all the items that she "liked" in $\mathbf{G}$. The latent signal is necessary in order to avoid trivial solutions, where the interpretation inferred from data tells us that everyone likes everything or that every edge should be present. It strongly depends on our prior beliefs about $\mathbf{H}$, like its degree distribution or power-law characteristics. $\mathbf{G}$ is observed as a subgraph of $\mathbf{H}$, while the rest of the edges of the hidden graph $\mathbf{H}$ form the unobserved "negative" signals.

3.1 The likelihood and its properties

On knowing the hidden graph, we define a bilinear or "matrix factorization" collaborative filtering model. We asso-

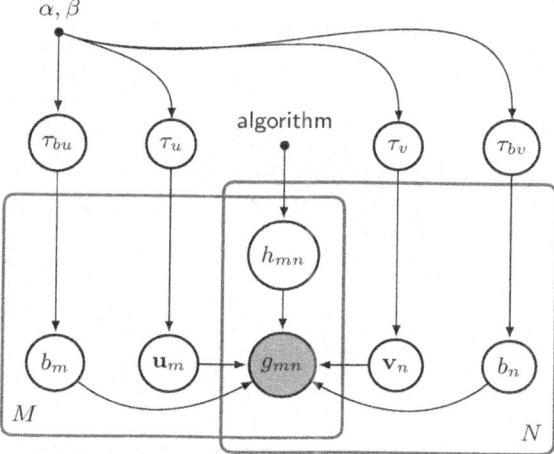

Figure 2: The graphical model for observing graph **G** connecting M user with N item vertices. The prior on the hidden graph **H** is algorithmically determined to resemble the type of the observed graph.

ciate a latent feature $\mathbf{u}_m \in \mathbb{R}^K$ with each user vertex m, and $\mathbf{v}_n \in \mathbb{R}^K$ with each item vertex n. Additionally, we add biases $b_m \in \mathbb{R}$ and $b_n \in \mathbb{R}$ to each user and item vertex. The odds of a user liking or disliking an item under consideration ($h = 1$) is modelled with

$$p(g \mid \mathbf{u}, \mathbf{v}, b, h = 1) = \sigma(\mathbf{u}^T \mathbf{v} + b)^g \left[1 - \sigma(\mathbf{u}^T \mathbf{v} + b)\right]^{1-g}, \quad (2)$$

with the logistic or sigmoid function being $\sigma(a) = 1/(1 + e^{-a})$, with $a \stackrel{\text{def}}{=} \mathbf{u}^T \mathbf{v} + b$. Subscripts m and n are dropped in (2) as they are clear from the context; b denotes the sum of the biases $b_m + b_n$. The likelihood of g for any h is given by the expression

$$p(g \mid a, h) = \left[\sigma(a)^g (1 - \sigma(a))^{1-g}\right]^h \cdot (1 - g)^{1-h}. \quad (3)$$

As $g = 1 \Rightarrow h = 1$ by construction, the last factor can be ignored in (3). If the binary "considered" variable h is marginalized out in (3), we find that

$$p(g = 1 \mid a) = p(h = 1) \sigma(a),$$
$$p(g = 0 \mid a) = p(h = 1)(1 - \sigma(a)) + (1 - p(h = 1)). \quad (4)$$

In other words, the odds of encountering an edge in **G** is the product of two probabilities, separating *popularity* from *personalization*: $p(h = 1)$, the user considering an item, and $\sigma(a)$, the user then liking that item.

3.2 The full model

The probability of **G** depends on the prior distributions of the vertices' hidden features. We choose them to be Gaussian: $p(\mathbf{U}) = \prod_{m=1}^{M} \mathcal{N}(\mathbf{u}_m; \mathbf{0}, \tau_u^{-1}\mathbf{I})$ for the users, where $\mathbf{U} \stackrel{\text{def}}{=} \{\mathbf{u}_m\}_{m=1}^{M}$, with similar Gaussian priors on the parameters governing the item vertices. These are shown in the graphical model in Figure 2. To infer the various scale parameters τ, we place a conjugate Gamma hyperprior on

each, for example

$$\mathcal{G}(\tau_u; \alpha, \beta) = \beta^\alpha / \Gamma(\alpha) \cdot \tau_u^{\alpha-1} e^{-\beta \tau_u}.$$

The only prior beliefs in Figure 2 that do not take an explicit form is that of **H**. It could be parameterized with a particular degree distribution, be it Poisson, exponential, or a power law with an exponential cut-off. However, we would like this to (approximately) be in the same family as the observed data, and determine an algorithm which can generate such graphs. Section 4 elaborates on this, including the closure of the graph family under random sampling of subnetworks.

We collectively denote our parameters by $\boldsymbol{\theta} \stackrel{\text{def}}{=} \{\mathbf{H}, \mathbf{U}, \mathbf{V}, \mathbf{b}, \boldsymbol{\tau}\}$, with $b_{mn} \stackrel{\text{def}}{=} b_m + b_n$ as shorthand notation. The joint density of all the random variables, given the hyperprior parameters α and β, is

$$p(\mathbf{G}, \boldsymbol{\theta}) = \prod_{m=1}^{M} \prod_{n=1}^{N} \overbrace{\sigma(\mathbf{u}_m^T \mathbf{v}_n + b_{mn})^{g_{mn}}}^{\ell_{mn}} \cdots$$
$$\cdots \left[1 - \sigma(\mathbf{u}_m^T \mathbf{v}_n + b_{mn})\right]^{h_{mn}(1-g_{mn})}$$
$$\cdot \prod_{m=1}^{M} \mathcal{N}(\mathbf{u}_m; \mathbf{0}, \tau_u^{-1}\mathbf{I}) \, \mathcal{N}(b_m; 0, \tau_{b_m}^{-1}) \cdot \mathcal{G}(\tau_u; \alpha, \beta)$$
$$\cdot \prod_{n=1}^{N} \mathcal{N}(\mathbf{v}_n; \mathbf{0}, \tau_v^{-1}\mathbf{I}) \, \mathcal{N}(b_n; 0, \tau_{b_n}^{-1}) \cdot \mathcal{G}(\tau_v; \alpha, \beta)$$
$$\cdot \mathcal{G}(\tau_{b_m}; \alpha, \beta) \cdot \mathcal{G}(\tau_{b_n}; \alpha, \beta) \cdot p(\mathbf{H}). \quad (5)$$

The sigmoid product is denoted with ℓ_{mn}, and will later appear in a variational bound in (11). Obtaining a posterior approximation to (5) would follow known literature [20, 25], were it not for the unknown occurrence of edges h_{mn} in **H**. Sections 4 and 5 are devoted to treating **H**.

One might also consider placing Normal-Wishart hyperprior on the means and variances of $\mathbf{u}_m$ and $\mathbf{v}_n$ [20, 23]. In practice, we benefit from additionally using meta-data features in the hyperpriors. They allow us to learn how shared features connect the prior distributions of various items, but is beyond the scope of this paper.

3.3 Factorized approximation

It is analytically intractable to compute the Bayesian averages necessary for marginalization in (5). This hurdle is commonly addressed in one of two ways: Samples from the posterior can be drawn by simulating a Markov chain with the posterior as its stationary distribution, and these samples used for prediction [14]. Alternatively, one might substitute the integration problems required for Bayesian marginalization with an optimization problem, that of finding the best deterministic approximation to the posterior density [9].

We *approximate* the posterior from (5), rather than sample from it, as it allows a compact representation to be serialized to disk. The posterior from (5) is approximated with the fully factorized distribution q,

$$p(\boldsymbol{\theta}|\mathbf{G}) \approx q(\boldsymbol{\theta}) \stackrel{\text{def}}{=} \prod_{m=1}^{M} q(b_m) \prod_{k=1}^{K} q(u_{mk}) \cdot \prod_{n=1}^{N} q(b_n) \prod_{k=1}^{K} q(v_{nk})$$
$$\cdot q(\tau_u) \, q(\tau_v) \, q(\tau_{b_u}) \, q(\tau_{b_v}) \, q(\mathbf{H}). \quad (6)$$

The factors approximating each of the vertex features in **U**, **V**, and **b** are chosen to be a Gaussian, for example

$q(u_{mk}) = \mathcal{N}(u_{mk}; \eta_{mk}, \omega_{mk}^{-1})$. Similarly, the τ's are approximated by Gamma factors in the conjugate exponential family, for example $q(\tau_u) = \mathcal{G}(\tau_u; \phi_u, \varphi_u)$.

The remaining the question is, what to do with $p(\mathbf{H})$, and the posterior marginal approximation $q(\mathbf{H})$?

4. RANDOM GRAPHS

Although an observation $g_{mn} = 1$ implies that $q(h_{mn} = 1) = 1$, we cannot estimate every one of MN $q(h_{mn})$'s, as there are typically $\mathcal{O}(10^{12})$ or more of them. As a recourse, we shall specify q as an algorithm that stochastically generates connections $h_{mn} = 1$, so that $p(\mathbf{H})$ produces (roughly) the same type of graphs as is observed in $\mathbf{G}$.

The graphical model in Figure 2 specifies that every "considered" edge (m, n) in $\mathbf{H}$ contains a "like" probability σ_{mn}. For each edge in $\mathbf{H}$, a coin is flipped, and revealed with probability σ_{mn} to give $\mathbf{G}$. If we assume that the coin is on average unbiased, half the edges will be revealed, and $|\mathbf{H}| \approx 2|\mathbf{G}|$. Alternatively, $\mathbf{G}$ is a subnet of $\mathbf{H}$, containing half (or some rate of) its connections. Working back, we sample graphs $\mathbf{H}$ at this rate, and the family of graphs $\mathbf{H}$ that can be generated this way constitutes our prior. This places no guarantee that the two graphs will always be of the same type, as not all graph types are closed under random sampling. For example, random subnets drawn from exact scale-free networks are not themselves scale-free [26]. However, the practical benefits of this algorithmic simplification outweigh the cost of more exact procedures.

4.1 Sampling $q(\mathbf{H})$

The factor $q(\mathbf{H})$ is defined stochastically, with the criteria that it should not be too expensive to draw random samples $\mathbf{H}$. One approach would be to generate samples, similar to Section 2, by specifying a degree distribution conditioned on the number of degrees d that each user and item vertex in $\mathbf{G}$ has. If the mean of each is $2d$, one can show that a version of (1) will also hold for $\mathbf{H}$. At the cost of many redraws, one can sample half-edges, as in Section 2, and connect them until all half-edges are paired.

We propose a simpler scheme here, which samples $\mathbf{H}$ from $\mathbf{G}$ in $\mathcal{O}(|\mathbf{G}| \log N)$ time. The scheme has the flavour of "sampling by popularity" [5]. We define a multinomial histogram $\mathcal{M}(\pi)$ on the N items, where $\pi_n \geq 0$ for $n = 1, \ldots, N$. This mimics a pseudo degree distribution for missing degrees. Let user m have degree d_m, or have viewed d_m items. For user m, the subset of d_m edges in $\mathbf{H}$ that corresponds to $g_{mn} = 1$ is marked. We then sample d_m random "negative" edges from $\mathcal{M}(\pi)$ *without replacement*—this fills in the remaining values for row m in $\mathbf{H}$, i.e. h_{mn} for $n = 1, \ldots, N$. For user m the sample *without* replacement can be drawn in $\mathcal{O}(\log N)$ time by doing bookkeeping with a weighed binary tree on the items.

There are many ways to define histogram π, one of which is to simply let $\pi_n = d_n$, the number of degrees (or views) of item n. This is effectively a uniform prior: each item should have the same rate of negatives. If we believe that there is some quality bar that drives popular items to be more generally liked, the histogram can be adjusted with

$$\pi_n = d_n^\gamma \qquad (7)$$

so that it obeys a version of the observed power law. A free rate parameter r is introduced, so that the most popular

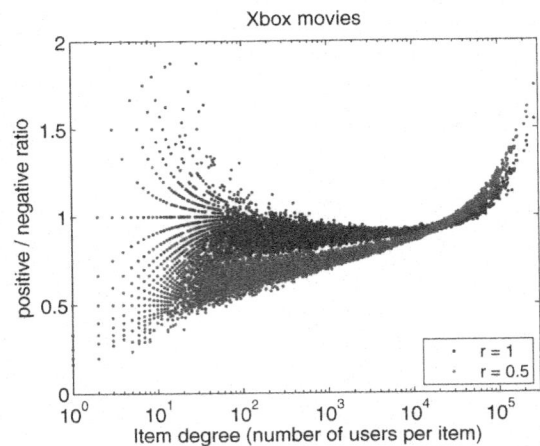

Figure 3: The ratio of positive to negative edges per item, from a single sample from $q(\mathbf{H})$. (The ratio is skewed at the head: sampled edges to more popular items have higher odds to already exist in $\mathbf{G}$. Discarding and resampling them leaves popular items underrepresented in the "negative" set. This can be overcome with another adjustment of π in $\mathcal{M}(\pi)$.)

item with degree $d_{\max} = \max\{d_n\}$ has histogram weight

$$\pi_{\max} = r d_{\max} . \qquad (8)$$

As an example, $r = \frac{1}{2}$ will add half as many unobserved edges to $\mathbf{H}$ for that item. A substitution gives a power

$$\gamma = 1 - \log d_{\max} / \log r \qquad (9)$$

with which the histogram is adjusted in (7).

Figure 3 shows two samples of the edges of $\mathbf{H}$ for two settings of r. For each item, it shows the ratio of "positive" to "negative" edges. A side effect is that at the head, the most popular items are underrepresented in the remainder of $\mathbf{H}$. This is because the items (or edges) sampled from $\mathcal{M}(\pi)$ might already exist in $\mathbf{G}$, and are discarded and another edge sampled.

5. VARIATIONAL INFERENCE

The approximation $q(\boldsymbol{\theta})$ in (6) is found by maximizing a variational lower bound on the partition function of (5), with

$$\log p(\mathbf{G}) \geq \mathcal{L}[q] = \int q(\boldsymbol{\theta}) \log p(\mathbf{G}, \boldsymbol{\theta}) \, \mathrm{d}\boldsymbol{\theta} + \mathcal{H}[q(\boldsymbol{\theta})] . \qquad (10)$$

Here $\mathcal{H}[q]$ is the (continuous) entropy of our choice of q. The expression in (10) is not analytically tractable due to the sigmoids in ℓ_{mn}, which appear in $p(\mathbf{G}, \boldsymbol{\theta})$ in (5), as they are not conjugate with respect to the $q(u_{mk})$'s or any of the other vertex factors. We additionally lower-bound ℓ_{mn} with the logistic or Jaakkola-Jordan bound [8], introducing an additional variational parameter ξ_{mn} on each edge. The logistic bound is

$$\ell \geq \mathrm{e}^{g(\mathbf{u}^T \mathbf{v} + b)} \left[\sigma(\xi) \mathrm{e}^{-\frac{1}{2}(\mathbf{u}^T \mathbf{v} + b + \xi) - \lambda(\xi)((\mathbf{u}^T \mathbf{v} + b)^2 - \xi^2)} \right]^{g + h(1-g)} , \qquad (11)$$

where subscripts m and n that are clear from the context are suppressed. The bound depends on a deterministic function

$\lambda(\xi) \stackrel{\text{def}}{=} \frac{1}{2\xi}[\sigma(\xi) - \frac{1}{2}]$. The substitution of the lower bound in (11) to ℓ_{mn} creates a $p_{\xi}(\mathbf{G}, \boldsymbol{\theta})$ that leaves the bounded likelihood conjugate with respect to its prior. The bound $\mathcal{L}_{\xi}$,

$$\mathcal{L}[q] \geq \mathcal{L}_{\xi}[q] = \int q(\boldsymbol{\theta}) \log p_{\xi}(\mathbf{G}, \boldsymbol{\theta}) \, d\boldsymbol{\theta} + \mathcal{H}[q] \;, \quad (12)$$

is therefore explicitly maximized over both the (variational) distribution q and the additional variational parameters $\boldsymbol{\xi} = \{\xi_{mn}\}$.

5.1 Variational updates

The variational updates for the user factors $q(u_{mk})$ are presented in this section. As the model is bilinear, the gradients of $\mathcal{L}_{\xi}$ with respect to the item factors can be set to zero following a similar pattern. To minimize $\mathcal{L}_{\xi}$ with respect to $q(u_{mk})$, one might take functional derivatives $\partial \mathcal{L}_{\xi}/\partial q(u_{mk})$ with respect to each $q(u_{mk})$, and sequentially equate them to zero. This is slow, as each update will require a loop over all the vertex's edges: for the user, K loops over all the items will be required. The vertex factor can alternatively be updated in bulk, by first equating the gradients of $\mathcal{L}_{\xi}$ with respect to a full Gaussian (not factorized) approximation $\tilde{q}(\mathbf{u}_m)$ to zero. The fully factorized $q(u_{mk})$ can then be recovered from the *intermediate* approximation $\tilde{q}(\mathbf{u}_m)$ as those that minimize the Kullback-Leibler divergence $D_{\text{KL}}(\prod_{k=1}^{K} q(u_{mk}) \| \tilde{q}(\mathbf{u}_m))$: this is achieved when the means of $q(u_{mk})$ match that of $\tilde{q}(\mathbf{u}_m)$, while their *precisions* match the diagonal precision of $\tilde{q}(\mathbf{u}_m)$.

How do we find $\tilde{q}(\mathbf{u}_m)$? The functional derivative $\partial \mathcal{L}_{\xi}/\partial \tilde{q}(\mathbf{u}_m)$ is zero where $\tilde{q}(\mathbf{u}_m)$ has as natural parameters a precision matrix of

$$\mathbf{P}_m = \sum_{n=1}^{N} \mathbb{E}_q[h_{mn}] \cdot 2\lambda(\xi_{mn}) \cdot \mathbb{E}_q[\mathbf{v}_n \mathbf{v}_n^T] + \mathbb{E}_q[\tau_u]\mathbf{I} \quad (13)$$

and mean-times-precision vector $\boldsymbol{\mu}_m \mathbf{P}_m$, which will be stated in (15). Apart from having to average h_{mn} over $q(\mathbf{H})$, which we cannot do analytically, the update in (13) suffers from having a summation over all N item vertices.

The burden of having to determine a sum over a full item catalogue in (13) can be removed with a clever rearrangement of expectations. As h_{mn} is binary,

$$\sum_{n=1}^{N} \mathbb{E}_q[h_{mn}] f(\mathbf{v}_n) = \sum_{\mathbf{H}} q(\mathbf{H}) \sum_{n=1}^{N} h_{mn} f(\mathbf{v}_n)$$
$$= \sum_{\mathbf{H}} q(\mathbf{H}) \sum_{n:h_{mn}=1} f(\mathbf{v}_n) \;. \quad (14)$$

The sum over $\mathbf{H}$ in (14) runs over all 2^{MN} possible instantiations of $\mathbf{H}$. A rearrangement of (13) therefore allows the updates to appear as a *stochastic average*,

$$\mathbf{P}_m = \mathbb{E}_{q(\mathbf{H})}\left[\sum_{n:h_{mn}=1} 2\lambda(\xi_{mn}) \cdot \mathbb{E}_q[\mathbf{v}_n \mathbf{v}_n^T] + \mathbb{E}_q[\tau_u]\mathbf{I}\right]$$

$$\boldsymbol{\mu}_m \mathbf{P}_m = \mathbb{E}_{q(\mathbf{H})}\left[\sum_{n:h_{mn}=1} (g_{mn} - \frac{1}{2} \cdots \right.$$
$$\left. \cdots - 2\lambda(\xi_{mn}) \cdot \mathbb{E}_q[b_m + b_n])\mathbb{E}_q[\mathbf{v}_n]\right] \;. \quad (15)$$

Inside the expectation over $q(\mathbf{H})$, the mean field update in (15) is a quantity specified on the hidden graph $\mathbf{H}$ only, and not all N plausible edges for the user. We are able to sample graphs from $q(\mathbf{H})$ according to Section 4. Retrospectively, this choice now bears fruit, as the update exists as an average amenable to stochastic gradient descent. We remark, too, that the natural parameters in (15) define the *natural gradients* of the variational objective function [1, 24]. The full natural gradient is periodic in the number of vertices and the updates are component-wise, and convergence with such updates can also be achieved using a stochastic gradient algorithm [12].

There are additional variational parameters at play in (15). For the required edges $h_{mn} = 1$ that connect user m with items n, the values ξ_{mn} that maximize $\mathcal{L}_{\xi}$ or $\mathbb{E}_q[\log p_{\xi}(\mathbf{G}, \boldsymbol{\theta})]$ are each given by

$$\xi_{mn}^2 = \mathbb{E}_q\left[(\mathbf{u}_m^T \mathbf{v}_n + b_m + b_n)^2\right] \;, \quad (16)$$

and they are computed and discarded when needed. We take the positive root as ξ_{mn}, and refer the reader to Bishop [2] for a deeper discussion.

Given $\mathbf{P}_m$ and $\boldsymbol{\mu}_m \mathbf{P}_m$ from (15), we have sufficient statistics for $\tilde{q}(\mathbf{u}_m)$, and hence for updating each of the K $q(u_{mk})$'s in bulk. Deriving sufficient statistics for $q(v_{nk})$, $q(b_m)$ and $q(b_n)$ is similar to that presented in (15), and the derivation will not be repeated. Given these, optimization proceeds as follows: At time t, we sample a hidden graph $\mathbf{H}$, over which the user and item vertex factors are updated. Focussing on user m, let $\mathbf{P}_m^{(t-1)}$ be the (diagonal) precision matrix of the factorized distribution $\prod_{k=1}^{K} q(u_{mk})$. We then find $\mathbf{P}_m$ in (15), and now the precision matrix of $\tilde{q}(\mathbf{u}_m)$ will be $\mathbf{P}_m^{(t)}$, found through $\mathbf{P}_m^{(t)} = \epsilon_t \mathbf{P}_m + (1 - \epsilon_t)\mathbf{P}_m^{(t-1)}$, where $\epsilon_t \in [0, 1]$. The factors $q(u_{mk})$ are then recovered from the bulk computation of $\tilde{q}(\mathbf{u}_m)$. The mean-times-precision vector of $\tilde{q}(\mathbf{u}_m)$ is given through a similar stochastic update. The series $\{\epsilon_t\}_{t=1}^{\infty}$ should satisfy $\sum_{t=1}^{\infty} \epsilon_t = \infty$ and $\sum_{t=1}^{\infty} \epsilon_t^2 < \infty$, guarding against premature convergence and infinite oscillation around the minimum [22].

Finally, the marginal approximations for the hyperparameters are updated by setting the functional derivatives, say $\partial \mathcal{L}_{\xi}/\partial q(\tau_u)$, to zero. For instance for $q(\tau_u) = \mathcal{G}(\tau_u; \phi_u, \varphi_u)$ the shape ϕ_u and rate φ_u are

$$\phi_u = \alpha + KM/2$$
$$\varphi_u = \beta + \frac{1}{2}\sum_{m=1}^{M} \mathbb{E}_q[\mathbf{u}_m^T \mathbf{u}_m] \;. \quad (17)$$

As $q(u_{mk})$ is dependent on $\mathbf{H}$, the rate is also stochastically updated as described above.

5.2 Large scale inference

The use of a bipartite graph ensures that variational updates are parallelizable. For instance, by keeping all $q(v_{nk})$, $q(b_n)$ and $q(b_m)$ fixed for the item and user vertices, the gradients $\partial \mathcal{L}_{\xi}/\partial \tilde{q}(\mathbf{u}_m)$, and hence the stochastic updates resulting from (15), have no mutual dependence. Consequently, the loop over user vertex updates $m = 1 \ldots M$ is embarrassingly parallel; the same is true for other updates. This will not hold for more general graphs like those of social networks, though, where more involved logic will be required.

Due to the fact that a variational lower bound is optimized for, optimization can also be distributed across multiple machines, *as long as the bound holds*. For example, one might distribute the graph according to item vertices in blocks $\mathcal{B}_b$, and iteratively optimize one block at a time, or optimize blocks concurrently (with embarrassingly parallel optimization *inside* the blocks, as discussed earlier). In this example the sparse user-item graph (matrix) $\mathbf{G}$ is distributed such that *all* observations for a set $\mathcal{B}_a$ of items are co-located on the same machine. The natural gradients for the users then distribute across machines, and can be written so that the dependence on the data blocks on various machines separates. When optimizing using the item-wise data block $\mathcal{B}_a$ on one machine, we write $\mathbf{P}_m$ in (15) as

$$\mathbf{P}_m = \mathbb{E}_{q(\mathbf{H})}\left[\sum_{\substack{n:h_{mn}=1\\ n\in\mathcal{B}_a}} 2\lambda(\xi_{mn})\cdot\mathbb{E}_q\left[\mathbf{v}_n\mathbf{v}_n^T\right]\cdots\right.$$
$$\left. + \sum_{b\neq a} \overbrace{\sum_{\substack{n:h_{mn}=1\\ n\in\mathcal{B}_b}} 2\lambda(\xi_{mn})\cdot\mathbb{E}_q\left[\mathbf{v}_n\mathbf{v}_n^T\right]}^{\text{block }b\text{'s natural gradient }\mathbf{X}_m^{(b)};\text{ fixed}} + \mathbb{E}_q[\tau_u]\mathbf{I}\right]. \quad (18)$$

Update (18) defines a thin *message interface* between various machines, where each block has to communicate only its *natural gradients* $\mathbf{X}_m^{(b)}$—and similar mean-times-precision gradients—to other blocks.[1] In block $\mathcal{B}_a$ we might iterate between updates (18) and full item updates for all $n\in\mathcal{B}_a$, whilst keeping the incoming messages $\mathbf{X}_m^{(b)}$ from other machines fixed. After a few loops over users and items, one can move to the next block. Similarly, different machines can optimize on all the blocks $\{\mathcal{B}_b\}$ in parallel, as long as the natural gradient messages are periodically communicated to other machines. The scheme presented here generalizes to a further subdivision of user vertices into blocks.

6. RESULTS

Given $\mathbf{G}$, a pivotal task of collaborative filtering is that of accurately predicting the future presence of an edge. This allows online systems to personalize towards a user's taste by recommending items that the user might like.

The collaborative filtering model in Section 3 explicitly separated the probability of a user considering an item from σ, the probability for the user liking the item. The odds of liking an item depends on our inferred certainty of the user and item parameters,[2]

$$p(g=1\,|\,h=1) \approx \iiint \sigma(\mathbf{u}^T\mathbf{v}+b)\,q(\mathbf{u})\,q(\mathbf{v})\,q(b)\,\mathrm{d}\mathbf{u}\,\mathrm{d}\mathbf{v}\,\mathrm{d}b$$
$$\approx \int \sigma(a)\,\mathcal{N}(a\,;\,\mu_a,\sigma_a^2)\,\mathrm{d}a \approx \sigma\left(\mu_a/\sqrt{1+\pi\sigma_a^2/8}\right). \quad (19)$$

The random variable a was defined as $a \stackrel{\text{def}}{=} \mathbf{u}^T\mathbf{v}+b$, with its density approximated with its first two moments under q, i.e. $\mu_a \stackrel{\text{def}}{=} \mathbb{E}_q[\mathbf{u}^T\mathbf{v}+b]$ and $\sigma_a^2 \stackrel{\text{def}}{=} \mathbb{E}_q[(\mathbf{u}^T\mathbf{v}+b-\mu_a)^2]$. The final approximation of a logistic Gaussian integral follows from MacKay [13].

---

[1] The division of data to machines will be dictated by the size of M and N; for $N\ll M$ a user-wise division gives a smaller message interface, as only natural gradients for the items' updates will be required.

[2] We suppress subscripts m and n for clarity, and write $q(\mathbf{u})$ for the diagonal Gaussian $\prod_{k=1}^K q(u_{mk})$.

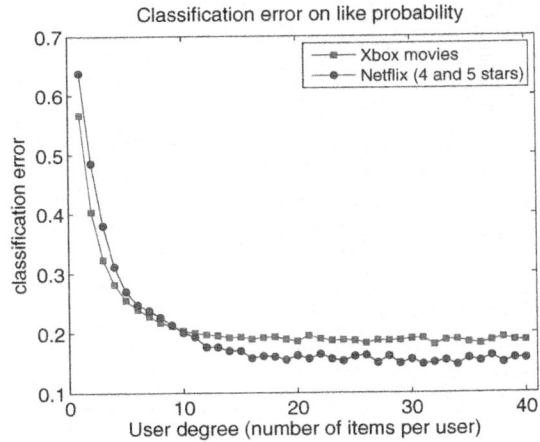

Figure 4: The classification error on $\mathbf{G}_{\text{test}}$, given $h=1$ (the ground truth is $g=1$). The full histograms of probabilities $p(g=1|h=1)$ are presented in Figure 5.

6.1 Evaluation

We evaluated our model by removing a test set from the Xbox movies and Netflix (4 and 5 stars) data sets. The degree distributions for these data sets are presented in Figure 1. The training data $\mathbf{G}_{\text{train}}$ was created by randomly removing one edge (or item) for each user from $\mathbf{G}$; the removed edges formed the test set.

A core challenge of *real world* collaborative filtering algorithms is to find a balance between popular recommendations and personalized content in a structured form. Based on our experience, a criteria of a good recommender is the ability to suggest non-trivial items that the user will like, and surface less popular items in the tail of the item catalogue. In the evaluations we highlight this by grouping results according to item popularity in Figure 6, for example.

Two evaluations are discussed below. Firstly, given that an item is presented to a user with $h_{mn}=1$, we are interested in the classifying $g_{mn}\to\{0,1\}$. This is one of the key contributions that our model brings to the table. As far as we are aware, there are no other algorithms that isolate $p(\text{like})$ in this way. To be able to draw a comparison with a known state-of-the-art algorithm, we consider various forms of a rank-based metric in a second evaluation.

In the tests below, $K=20$ latent dimensions were used. The user biases were clamped at zero, as $q(\mathbf{H})$ was defined to give balanced samples for each user. The rate and shape parameters of the hyperprior were set to $\alpha=\beta=0.01$, giving a hyperprior on the τ's with mean 1 and a flexible variance of 100. The means of the hyperparameter posterior estimates were $\mathbb{E}[\tau_{b_v}]=0.4$, $\mathbb{E}[\tau_v]=3.5$, and $\mathbb{E}[\tau_u]=2.0$. When rounded to one decimal place, these values were similar on both the Netflix (4 and 5 stars) dataset and the Xbox Movies dataset.

6.1.1 The "like" probability

The classification error on the held-out data converges to a stable value as users view between ten and twenty items. Its plot is presented in Figure 4, and has a natural interpre-

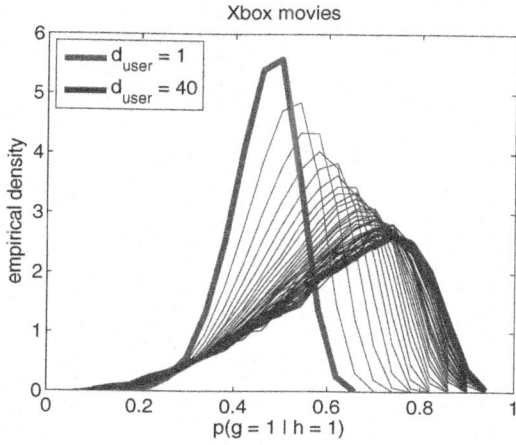

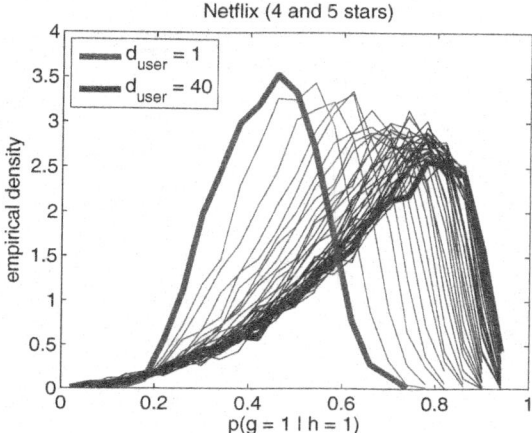

Figure 5: The distribution of $p(g_{mn} = 1 | h_{mn} = 1)$ on the held out items in the evaluation, sliced incrementally according to users connected to $d_{\text{user}} = 1$ to 40 items. The ground truth is $g_{mn} = 1$.

tation. Conventional wisdom dictates that the error rates for explicit ratings-based recommendation systems are typically in the order of 20% of the ratings range. For Netflix's five-star ratings datasets, this error is around one star [11], while an error of around 20 points in the 0-100 scale of the Yahoo! Music dataset is usual [3]. The 16-19% classification error in Figure 4 is therefore in line with the signal to noise ratio in well known explicit ratings datasets. When users viewed only one item, the bulk of the predictive probability mass $p(g = 1 | h = 1)$ is centered around 50%, slightly skewed to being less certain. This is illustrated in Figure 5. As users view more items, the bulk of the predictive probability skews towards being more certain[3].

The probability $p(g = 1 | h = 1)$ is useful in presenting a user with interesting recommendations, as it is agnostic

---

[3] A property of a good probabilistic classification system is that it produces an exact *callibration plot*. For example, we expect 10% of edges to be misclassified for the slice of edges that are predicted with $p(g = 1 | h = 1) = 10\%$. The callibration plot requires a ground truth negative class $g = 0$, which is *latent* in our case. Figures 4 and 5 aim to present an equivalent to a callibration plot.

to each item's popularity. It is therefore possible to define a *utility function* that trades this quantity off with an item's popularity, effectively giving a knob to emphasize exploration or exploitation. Such a utility can be optimized through A/B tests in a flighting framework, but is beyond the scope of this paper.

6.1.2 Average rank

We turn to a ranking task to draw a comparison against known work, as we are unaware of other algorithms that isolate $p(\text{like})$. On seeing $\mathbf{G}_{\text{train}}$, the absent edges (where $g_{mn} = 0$) are ranked for each user m. The ranking is based on various scores s_{mn}:

like the odds of a user liking an item, namely $s_{mn} = p(g_{mn} = 1 | h_{mn} = 1)$ as approximated in (19);

popularity $s_{mn} = \pi_n$;

popularity×like the odds of a user considering *and* liking an item, namely $s_{mn} = \pi_n p(g_{mn} = 1 | h_{mn} = 1)$.

We evaluated models for the two settings of r in (9); a sample from $\mathbf{H}$ for each was shown in Figure 3.

Our metric is computed as follows: If item n' was removed, the rank score counts the position of n' in an ordered prediction list

$$S_{\text{rank}}(m, n') \stackrel{\text{def}}{=} \sum_{n: g_{mn} = 0} \mathbb{I}\Big[s_{mn'} > s_{mn}\Big] \Big/ \sum_{n: g_{mn} = 0} 1 \ . \quad (20)$$

Random guessing would give $S = 0.5$, while $S = 1$ places the held-out item at the head of the list.

As a benchmark, we use the Bayesian Personalized Ranking (BPR) model of Rendle et al. [6, 21]. It has shown state of the art performance on ranking metrics against methods ranging from singular value decompositions and nearest neighbours to weighed regularized matrix factorization [19].

BPR was also used as a key component in many of the leading solutions for the second track of the KDD-Cup'11 competition [4]. The competition was designed to capture the ability of models to personalize recommendations that "fit" specific users regardless of an item's popularity. In that setting, BPR was trained with missing items sampled with probabilities proportional to their popularity as described in [5]. We therefore implemented and trained two BPR models:

BPR-uniform with missing items sampled uniformly;

BPR-popularity with missing items sampled proportional to their popularity.

These two models capture two different aspects of recommender systems. **BPR-uniform** is optimized to learn a userwise ranking of items, where the objective function specifies that items that are liked (i.e. $g_{mn} = 1$) should be ranked above missing items (i.e. $g_{mn} = 0$).

The metric in (20) follows [21]. Because **BPR-uniform** directly optimizes this metric, it should come as no surprise that it will perform better than methods that do not optimize it directly (see Figure 6). However, meaningful insights can still be gleaned from the comparison. **BPR-popularity** is aimed at ranking observed "liked" items above other *popular* items that are missing from the user's history. While two BPR models are required to capture these two different aspects of recommendations, our generative model captures both of these aspects in a structured manner.

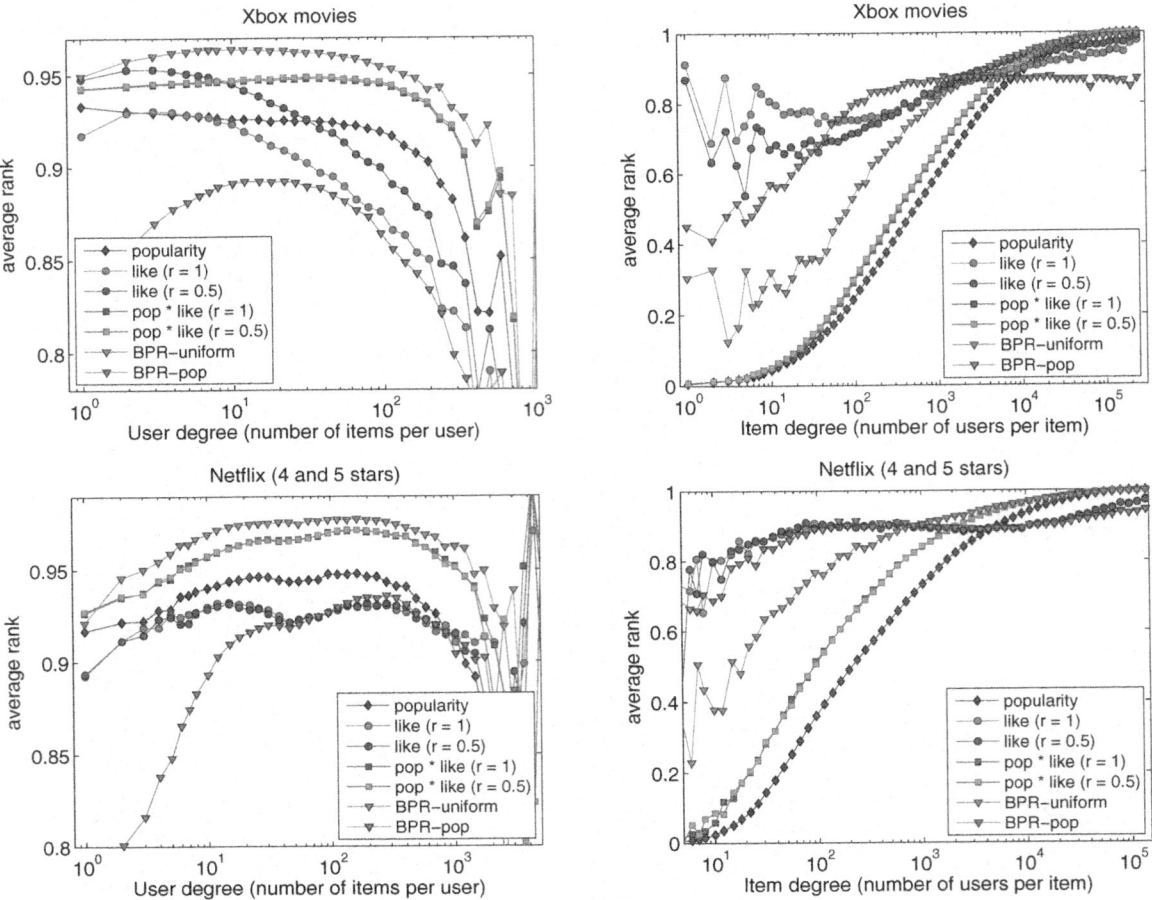

Figure 6: The rank $S_{\text{rank}}(m,n)$ in (20), averaged over users *(left)* and items *(right)*, grouped logarithmically by their degrees. The *top* evaluation is on the Xbox movies sample, while the *bottom* evaluations are on the Netflix set, as given in Figure 1.

Figure 6 illustrates the mean rank scores, grouped logarithmically by user and item degrees. In the plots that are grouped by user degrees, we see improved results for algorithms that prefer popularity, i.e. **popularity×like** and **BPR-uniform**. This is explained by the dominance of popularity biases in both datasets. As expected, **BPR-uniform** show best results as it is optimizes the task at hand directly. The estimates for users with an order of 10^3 to 10^4 degrees are noisy as the data is very sparse (see Figure 1). However, when looking at the per item breakdown, we learn that **BPR-uniform** and the **popularity×like** models perform poorly on less popular items and their superior results are based on recommendations from the short head of the popular items. When it comes to recommending from the long tail of the less familiar items, the **like** models show best results, with **BPR-popularity** just behind. These trends are consistent on both datasets.

The distribution of the ranks over all users (and items) is heavy-tailed, and whilst the average is often reported, the median is much higher than the average reported in Figure 6. Figure 7 shows the *error bars* using the percentiles of the rank scores for tests **like** and **popularity×like** for $r = \frac{1}{2}$. The rank variance decreases as users view a few movies, but increases for heavy users which are harder to model. When popularity is included in the ranking, the error bars get tighter for heavy users, which implies that these users' lists are mostly governed by popularity patterns.

7. CONCLUSIONS

Random graphs can be leveraged to predict the presence of edges in a collaborative filtering model. In this paper we showed how to incorporate such graphs in an inference procedure by rewriting a variational Bayes algorithm in terms of random graph samples. As a result, we were able to explicitly extract a "like" probability that is largely agnostic to the popularity of items. The use of a bipartite graph, central to this exposition, is not a hindrance, as user-user interactions in a general network can be similarity modelled with $\sigma(\mathbf{u}_m^T \mathbf{u}_{m'})$. While scalable parallel inference is not immediately obvious, we believe this to be a worthwhile pursuit. By employing the same machinery on general graphs, one should be able to model connections in social or other similar networks.

The use of a Bayesian graphical model makes it easy to adapt the model to incorporate richer feedback signals. Similarly, both structured and unstructured meta-data can be

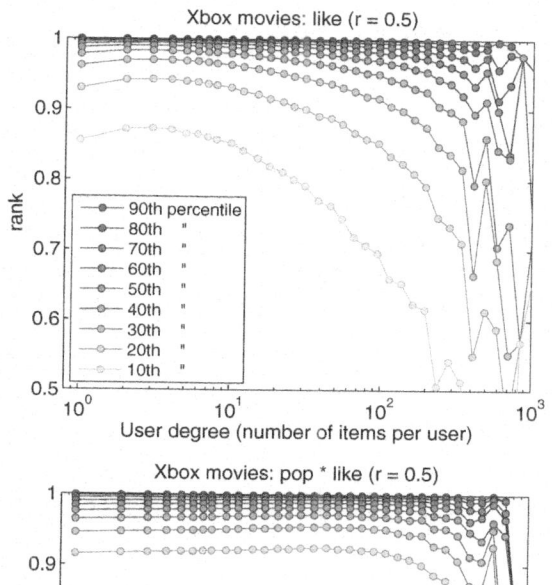

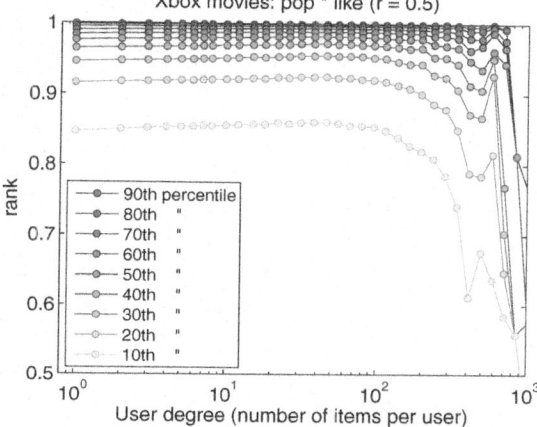

Figure 7: Error bars on the rank tests. The median is much higher than the average rank reported in Figure 6.

plugged into the graphical model. The hidden graph **H** may also be partly observed, for example from system logs. In that case some true negatives exist. Alternatively, we may know *a priori* when a user could never have considered an item, fixing some h at zero. In both these scenarios the process of drawing random hidden graphs **H** can be adjusted accordingly. For the sake of clarity, none of these enhancements were included in this paper.

8. ACKNOWLEDGMENTS

The authors are indebted to Nir Nice, Shahar Keren, and Shimon Shlevich for their invaluable input, management, and stellar engineering skills.

9. REFERENCES

[1] S. Amari. Natural gradient works efficiently in learning. *Neural Computation*, 10(2):251–276, 1998.

[2] C. M. Bishop. *Pattern Recognition and Machine Learning*. Springer, 2006.

[3] G. Dror, N. Koenigstein, and Y. Koren. Yahoo! music recommendations: Modeling music ratings with temporal dynamics and item taxonomy. In *Proc. 5th ACM Conference on Recommender Systems*, 2011.

[4] G. Dror, N. Koenigstein, Y. Koren, and M. Weimer. The Yahoo! music dataset and KDD-Cup'11. *Journal Of Machine Learning Research*, 18:3–18, 2012.

[5] Z. Gantner, L. Drumond, C. Freudenthaler, and L. Schmidt-Thieme. Personalized ranking for non-uniformly sampled items. *Journal of Machine Learning Research*, 18:231–247, 2011.

[6] Z. Gantner, S. Rendle, C. Freudenthaler, and L. Schmidt-Thieme. MyMediaLite: A free recommender system library. In *5th ACM International Conference on Recommender Systems*, 2011.

[7] Y. F. Hu, Y. Koren, and C. Volinsky. Collaborative filtering for implicit feedback datasets. In *IEEE International Conference on Data Mining*, 2008.

[8] T. Jaakkola and M. Jordan. A variational approach to Bayesian logistic regression problems and their extensions. In *Artificial Intelligence and Statistics*, 1996.

[9] M. Jordan, Z. Ghahramani, T. Jaakkola, and L. Saul. An introduction to variational methods for graphical models. *Machine Learning*, 37:183–233, 1999.

[10] N. Koenigstein, N. Nice, U. Paquet, and N. Schleyen. The Xbox recommender system. In *Proc. 6th ACM Conference on Recommender Systems*, 2012.

[11] Y. Koren. The BellKor solution to the Netflix Grand Prize. 2009.

[12] H. J. Kushner and G. G. Yin. *Stochastic Approximation and Recursive Algorithms and Applications*. Springer, 2003.

[13] D. J. C. MacKay. The evidence framework applied to classification networks. *Neural Computation*, 4(5):698–714, 1992.

[14] R. M. Neal. Probabilistic inference using Markov chain Monte Carlo methods. Technical Report CRG-TR-93-1, Dept. of Computer Science, University of Toronto, 1993.

[15] M. E. J. Newman, S. H. Strogatz, and D. J. Watts. Random graphs with arbitrary degree distributions and their applications. *Phys. Rev. E*, 64:026118, 2001.

[16] M. E. J. Newman, D. J. Watts, and S. H. Strogatz. Random graph models of social networks. *Proc. Natl. Acad. Sci. USA*, 99:2566–âĂŞ2572, 2002.

[17] K. Palla, D. A. Knowles, and Z. Ghahramani. An infinite latent attribute model for network data. In *29th International Conference on Machine Learning*, 2012.

[18] R. Pan and M. Scholz. Mind the gaps: Weighting the unknown in large-scale one-class collaborative filtering. In *KDD*, pages 667–675, 2009.

[19] R. Pan, Y. Zhou, B. Cao, N. Liu, R. Lukose, M. Scholz, and Q. Yang. One-class collaborative filtering. In *IEEE International Conference on Data Mining*, pages 502–511, 2008.

[20] U. Paquet, B. Thomson, and O. Winther. A hierarchical model for ordinal matrix factorization. *Statistics and Computing*, 22(4):945–957, 2012.

[21] S. Rendle, C. Freudenthaler, Z. Gantner, and L. Schmidt-Thieme. BPR: Bayesian personalized ranking from implicit feedback. In *Uncertainty in Artificial Intelligence*, pages 452–461, 2009.

[22] H. Robbins and S. Monro. A stochastic approximation method. *The Annals of Mathematical Statistics*, 22(3):400–407, 1951.

[23] R. Salakhutdinov and A. Mnih. Bayesian probabilistic matrix factorization using Markov chain Monte Carlo. In *Proceedings of the 25th International Conference on Machine Learning*, pages 880–887, 2008.

[24] M. Sato. Online model selection based on the variational Bayes. *Neural Computation*, 13(7):1649–1681, 2001.

[25] D. Stern, R. Herbrich, and T. Graepel. Matchbox: Large scale Bayesian recommendations. In *International World Wide Web Conference*, 2009.

[26] M. P. H. Stumpf and C. Wiuf. Sampling properties of random graphs: The degree distribution. *Phys. Rev. E*, 72:036118, 2005.

Latent Credibility Analysis

Jeff Pasternack
Facebook, Inc.
1601 Willow Road
Menlo Park, California 94025
jeffp@fb.com

Dan Roth
University of Illinois, Urbana-Champaign
201 North Goodwin
Champaign, Illinois 61801
danr@illinois.edu

ABSTRACT

A frequent problem when dealing with data gathered from multiple sources on the web (ranging from booksellers to Wikipedia pages to stock analyst predictions) is that these sources *disagree*, and we must decide which of their (often mutually exclusive) claims we should accept. Current state-of-the-art information credibility algorithms known as "fact-finders" are transitive voting systems with rules specifying how votes iteratively flow from sources to claims and then back to sources. While this is quite tractable and often effective, fact-finders also suffer from substantial limitations; in particular, a lack of transparency obfuscates their credibility decisions and makes them difficult to adapt and analyze: knowing the mechanics of how votes are calculated does not readily tell us what those votes *mean*, and finding, for example, that a source has a score of 6 is not informative. We introduce a new approach to information credibility, *Latent Credibility Analysis* (LCA), constructing strongly principled, probabilistic models where the truth of each claim is a latent variable and the credibility of a source is captured by a set of model parameters. This gives LCA models clear semantics and modularity that make extending them to capture additional observed and latent credibility factors straightforward. Experiments over four real-world datasets demonstrate that LCA models can outperform the best fact-finders in both unsupervised and semi-supervised settings.

Categories and Subject Descriptors

H.3.3 [**Information Systems**]: Information Search and Retrieval—*Information filtering*; I.2.m [**Computing Methodologies**]: Artificial Intelligence

General Terms

Algorithms, Experimentation, Measurement, Reliability

Keywords

Credibility, Graphical Models, Trust, Veracity

1. INTRODUCTION

Conflicts among information sources are commonplace: Twitter users debate the effects of healthcare reform, Wikipedia authors provide differing populations for the same city, online retailers offer discordant descriptions of the same product, financial analysts disagree on the future price of securities, and medical blogs prescribe different courses of treatment. Consequently, we need a means of discerning which of the asserted claims are true, especially on the web, where three of our four experimental datasets (from current, real problems in information credibility) originate. Presently this is addressed by simple or weighted voting or, with more sophisticated fact-finder algorithms (e.g. [4, 18, 14]), transitive voting, but these methods tend to be ad hoc and difficult to analyze and extend. Latent Credibility Analysis is a new method of approaching the credibility problem by instead modeling the joint probability of the sources making claims and the unseen (latent) truth of those claims. Finding the probability that a particular claim is true is then performed via inference in a probabilistic graphical model using one of the many extant exact and approximate inference algorithms. Unlike those of fact-finders, the resulting credibility decisions and the parameters capturing the credibility of the sources are distributions and probabilities with clear semantics: for example, in the SimpleLCA model we reason that a claim is likely to be true because the probability that everyone who asserted it was lying (as given by the Honesty parameters of the sources) is relatively small.

This transparency is important both when we need to explain the model's decisions to users (who might otherwise distrust the system itself) and when we adapt an LCA model to real-world problems; in our experiments, we are able to formulate reasonable priors and anticipate (to a degree) the most appropriate, best performing models by understanding the domain. Such clarity is a common trait of probabilistic models, but a substantial improvement over fact-finders, where the closest analog to priors is typically the number of "votes" each claim is initialized with; further, fact-finders in general have few, if any, other tunable parameters that can be adjusted, and where present (like the Investment fact-finder's "growth rate" value [13]) they tend to be both ad hoc and opaque—it is rarely possible to anticipate what values are suitable for a particular problem before evaluating them on labeled data. LCA models are also much simpler to modify on a more substantial level: there is a straightforward path from a "generative story" about why sources assert the claims that they do to the joint distribution, and augmenting this core (e.g. to incorporate the idea that observed attributes of the sources, like academic degrees, influence their credibility) is as simple as finding a product across several independent components. Even in experiments ignorant of such factors and using the fact-finders' standard unsupervised setting, LCA models substantially outperform fact-finders in establishing the credibility of city population, book authorship, stock predictions, and predictions of the Supreme Court of the United States. Perhaps surprisingly, this needn't come at an exorbitant cost: two of our models scale linearly, as fact-finders do, and the remaining two, while not linear time, nonetheless proved tractable even over relatively large (tens of thousands of sources and claims) datasets in our experiments.

In the remainder of this paper we first provide a more detailed description of fact-finders. We subsequently discuss the fundamentals of LCA before introducing, in order of increasing sophistication, four specific LCA models: SimpleLCA, GuessLCA, MistakeLCA, and LieLCA, and then explore the performance of these models in comparison to fact-finders in our experiments.

2. BACKGROUND: FACT-FINDERS

A fact-finder takes as its input a list of assertions of the form "source s asserts claim c" and a list of disjoint *mutual exclusion sets* of claims [14]. Exactly one of the claims in each mutual exclusion set is true, and this is what the fact-finder endeavors to identify. This is done via an iterative transitive voting system: starting from some initial belief score in all the claims, the algorithm calculates the trustworthiness of each information source (e.g. a Wikipedia editor, a financial analyst, a website, a classifier, etc.) based on the claims it makes, and then in turn calculates the belief of the claims based on the trustworthiness of the sources asserting it; this process then repeats for a fixed number of iterations or until convergence.

Fact-finders are differentiated by their various update rules, whereby the trustworthiness of sources and belief in claims is calculated. For example, the "Sums" fact-finder is derived from Hubs and Authorities [9], where source trustworthiness can be considered the "hub" score and claim belief the "authority" score; at each iteration i we calculate the trustworthiness of each source as the sum of the belief in its claims, $T^i(s) = \sum_{c:s \to c} B^{i-1}(c)$, and then the belief score of each claim as the sum of the trustworthiness of the sources asserting it, $B^i(c) = \sum_{s:s \to c} T^i(s)$. Of course, fact-finders can be considerably more complex and varied; in the Investment and PooledInvestment [13] algorithms, sources "invest" their credibility in the claims they make, and claim belief is then non-linearly grown and apportioned back to the sources based on the size of their "investment".

Several fact-finders have probabilistic elements. TruthFinder [19] calculates claim belief as $1 - \prod_{s:s \to c} 1 - T(s)$, with the idea that $T(s)$ is the probability that s tells the truth, so the probability that a claim is wrong is the probability that all the (independent) sources are liars. However, these semantics are problematic: the pseudoprobabilities over all the claims in a mutual exclusion set will not sum to 1 and cannot be readily normalized since the trustworthiness of a source is calculated as the arithmetic mean of those claims it makes. [17] explicitly seeks to create a fact-finder with an (approximate) Bayesian justification, but relies on substantial assumptions, the most important being that $P(s \to c | True(c)) \approx P(s \to c)$, i.e. the probability a source asserts a claim is independent of the truth of that claim (which does not hold in practice). [21] is something of an anomaly, as it, like Latent Credibility Analysis, models the credibility problem as a graphical model (a Bayesian network), but specializes in situations where the truth is a collection of entities (e.g. identify all the authors of a book) and the model has the advantage of reasoning about these directly; other approaches (including LCA) instead simply treat these as binary claims (is "John Smith" an author of "Book" or not?). More importantly, the model makes an implicit assumption (as noted by the authors) that each source is predominately honest, which often does not hold in real data (e.g. vandalism in Wikipedia).

Additionally, some fact-finders have incorporated aspects beyond source trustworthiness and claim belief into their update rules. 3-Estimates [4] adds parameters to attempt to capture the "difficulty" of a claim, an idea also present in our LCA models. Fact-finders have also been applied to instances where the claims are not extracted in a prior step but rather snippets of textual "evidence" are effectively clustered using similarity metrics, as applied by the Apollo system to tweets [10] or to news articles by [16]. AccuVote [3] attempts to identify source dependence (one source copying another) to give greater credence to more "independent" sources, an aspect that is important in certain domains (e.g. blog postings, which are routinely derivative) and could be incorporated in future LCA models, although we do not consider it here.

Finally, frameworks have been created capable of extending any fact-finder. [13] applies declarative prior knowledge (in the form of first-order logic) to fact-finders by using linear programming to constrain claim beliefs; in our experiments, we use this method in an extremely simple form to apply supervision to fact-finders (our constraints are of the type "claim c is true"), which are otherwise wholly unsupervised algorithms. For LCA models, declarative constraints may be enforced by one of several methods for constraining the posterior distributions of probabilistic models, such as Posterior Regularization [5] or Constraint Driven Learning [1]. Further, [14] introduces generalized fact-finders, which adapt the bipartite unweighted graphs of standard fact-finders to weighted, k-partite graphs, allowing such factors as source features (e.g. "source s has a doctorate in a relevant field") and uncertainty in information extraction to be incorporated, essentially changing how votes flow throughout the network. LCA models naturally support these forms of prior knowledge and data in a principled way, as we will discuss shortly, and can incorporate many others (such as priors over the honesty of sources and real-valued features) that generalized fact-finders cannot.

3. LATENT CREDIBILITY ANALYSIS

3.1 Fundamentals

A Latent Credibility Analysis model is a probabilistic model where the true claim $\bar{c}$ in each mutual exclusion set of claims m is a (multinomial) latent variable, y_m. An observed assertion is the probability of c as claimed by s, $b_{s,c}$, typically $\{0,1\}$ (e.g. "John claims Obama was born in Hawaii"), but distributional claims are also possible (e.g. "John is 95% certain Obama was born in Hawaii and 5% certain he was born in Alaska"). Note that $\forall_s, \sum_{c \in m} b_{s,c} = 1$. Every source s also has a $[0, \infty)$ confidence in his assertions over the claims in m, $w_{s,m}$, again typically $\{0,1\}$ (0 if the source makes no assertion about m, 1 if it does), but other values may be used to express degrees of confidence with straightforward seman-

Notation	Description	Examples / Definition
s	An information source	Amazon.com; Dan Rather
c	A claim	President Barack Obama born in 1953
m	A mutually exclusive (ME) set of claims	Claimed Birth Years of Barack Obama
y_m	The true claim in m	President Barack Obama was born in 1961
$b_{s,c}$	The (observed) probability of c asserted by s	0; 1; 0.7
$w_{s,m}$	$[0,\infty)$ confidence of s in the distribution asserted over all $c \in m$	0; 1; 4.5
H_s	The probability s makes an honest, accurate assertion	0.4; 0.9
$D_{g/m/s}$	The probability s knows y_m (global, per-ME set, or per-source)	0.3; 0.7
S	Set of all sources s	$= \{s\}$
C	Set of all claims c	$= \{c\}$
M	Set of all mutual exclusion sets m	$= \{m\}$
B	$|S| \times |C|$ matrix of all observed assertions b	$= \{b_{s,m}\}$
W	$|S| \times |M|$ matrix of all assertion confidences w	$= \{m\}$
Y	Set of all true claims	$= \{y_m : m \in M\}$
Y_U	Set of all latent true claims	$\subseteq Y$
Y_L	Set of all observed true claims (labels)	$\subset Y$
X	Set of all observations (including B)	$= B \cup \{$ all other features $\}$
θ	Set of all latent model parameters	e.g. $\{H_s : s \in S\} \cup \{D_m : m \in M\}$

Table 1: LCA Notation

tics: as can be seen from the joint distributions of our LCA models, a $w_{s,m}$ of 0.5 causes assertions made by s about claims in m to affect the log-likelihood only half as much as sources with $w_{s,m} = 1$, and $w_{s,m} = 2$ is equivalent to making the same assertions twice. This can be useful if, for example, a source expresses abundant or reduced confidence in his assertion, e.g. "John is 50% confident that Obama was born in Hawaii with 95% probability...", comparable in function and purpose to belief and plausibility in Dempster-Shafer theory [20, 15] and uncertainty in subjective logic [8, 7].

Since we are not interested in modeling why a source decides to make an assertion about the claims in a mutual exclusion set (and with what confidence), the confidence matrix $W = \{w_{s,m}\}$ is taken as a given constant rather than an observation. Our observations are the assertion matrix $B = \{b_{s,c}\}$, together with whatever observed features (such as attributes of the sources) are relevant to the particular model; we will collectively refer to these observed variables as X. Similarly, we will refer to our latent variables as $Y = \{y_m\}$, and the model parameters (in the models we describe later these include the honesty of each source and the "difficulty factor" of identifying the true claim) as θ. Finally, when we write the joint probabilities, *we assume all mutual exclusion sets contain at least two claims*; this is a notational convenience, since any uncontested claim must be true (there is no alternative) and the probability of a source asserting it is thus 1 and it does not affect the joint probability.

As an example, consider a problem with two mutual exclusion sets, m_p ="Obama's Birthplace" and m_d ="Obama's Birthdate", where we observe a source s_j = "John" make a single assertion c_h = "Obama was born in Hawaii". Then $b_{s_j, c_h} = 1$, $\forall_{c \in m_p \setminus c_h} b_{s_j, c} = 0$, $w_{s_j, m_p} = 1$, and $w_{s_j, m_d} = 0$ (rendering the values of $\{b_{s_j, c} : c \in m_d\}$ irrelevant). Latent variables y_{m_p} and y_{m_d} are Obama's true birthplace and birthdate, respectively, so y_{m_p} = "Hawaii" and y_{m_d} = "August 4th, 1961".

3.2 Inference

Information credibility problems can be classed as unsupervised or semi-supervised; in the unsupervised case, we are only given observations X and none of the y_m are known, so $Y_U = Y$ and $Y_L = \emptyset$ (Y_U and Y_L are the sets of unlabeled [latent] and labeled [observed] true claims, respectively). Alternatively, when semi-supervised, we know the true claims in some mutual exclusion sets, $Y_L \subset Y$, already and only need to determine the remaining $Y_U = Y \setminus Y_L$. In both cases, our goal is to infer:

$$P(Y_U | X, Y_L) = \frac{\int_\theta P(Y_U, Y_L, X | \theta) P(\theta)}{\sum_{Y_U} \int_\theta P(Y_U, Y_L, X | \theta) P(\theta)}$$

This is the distribution over the possible true claims for each mutual exclusion set where the true claim is not already known, given the observations and true claims already identified. In our experiments we solve this approximately, by using EM [2] to find the maximum a posteriori (MAP) point estimate of the parameters, $\theta^* = \text{argmax}_\theta P(X|\theta) P(\theta)$, and then simply calculating:

$$P(Y_U | X, Y_L, \theta^*) = \frac{P(Y_U, X, Y_L | \theta^*)}{\sum_{Y_U} P(Y_U, X, Y_L | \theta^*)}$$

The expectation and maximization update rules used to find the maximum a posteriori point estimate θ^* are:

Expectation – Step:

$$\forall_m : P(y_m = c | X, \theta^t) = \frac{P(y_m = c, X | \theta^t)}{\sum_{v \in m} P(y_m = v, X | \theta^t)}$$

Maximization – Step:

$$\theta^{t+1} = \underset{\theta}{\text{argmax}}\, \mathbb{E}_{Y|X,\theta^t}[\log(P(X, Y|\theta) P(\theta))]$$

In LCA models, the E-step is always easy, since the y_m values are independent given the observations X and the parameters θ^t at iteration t. The M-step can be more difficult:

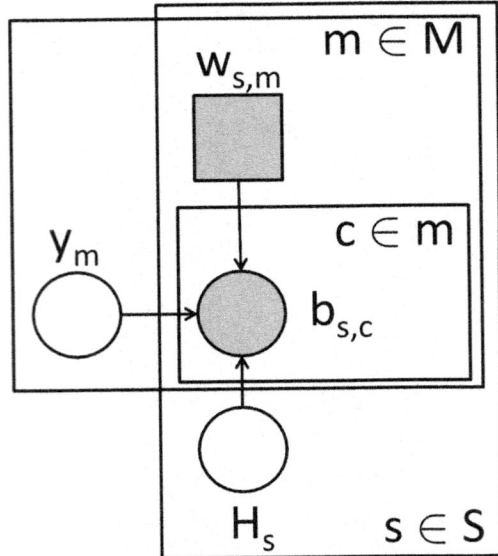

Figure 1: A plate diagram of a basic SimpleLCA model with observed assertions as the sole features ($X = B$).

in SimpleLCA, θ^{t+1} can be calculated in closed form provided that $P(\theta)$ is uniform; otherwise, gradient ascent must be used. Where this can be done parameter-by-parameter, the time required for the M-step scales linearly in the number of parameters; in MistakeLCA and LieLCA, joint gradient ascent requires a number of steps increasing linearly in the number of dimensions [12] (since the Lipschitz constant and squared diameter both increase linearly) while the cost to compute the gradient and the function value also increase linearly (provided the number of assertions per source and claims per mutual exclusion set remains constant), yielding $O(|\theta|^2)$ complexity. However, even on our largest experiments, MistakeLCA and LieLCA took no more than $\sim$ 200 times as long as SimpleLCA and GuessLCA, far less than suggested by this worst case quadratic bound. Exact runtimes varied, but for concreteness LieLCA took approximately 20 minutes on the population dataset, 30 minutes on the stock dataset (per time interval), and from 25-80 minutes on the books dataset (single-threaded on a 3GHz Core 2 Duo E8400); by comparison, GuessLCA was 40 seconds, one minute, and 3-4 minutes, respectively.

3.3 SimpleLCA

SimpleLCA, as with all our models, is a joint distribution that reflects a "story" of how sources decide which claims to assert. For both this and subsequent LCA models, we assume that each $b_{s,c} \in \{0,1\}$ and each $w_{s,m} \in \{0,1\}$; this matches our experimental domains (where sources assert a single claim in a mutual exclusion set with full certainty) and simplifies the equations for the joints by avoiding a cumbersome normalization factor. If these assumptions are relaxed, the joint "distributions" as written will no longer be distributions and must be normalized.

In SimpleLCA, each source s has a probability of being honest, H_s. A source then decides to assert the true claim $\bar{c}$ in mutual exclusion set m with probability H_s; otherwise, it chooses uniformly at random from the other claims in m with probability $\frac{1-H_s}{|m|-1}$. From this intuitive idea, we can immediately derive a joint distribution over y_m and X:

$$P(y_m, X | H_s)$$
$$= P(y_m) \left((H_s)^{b_{s,y_m}} \prod_{c \in m \setminus y_m} \left(\frac{1-H_s}{|m|-1} \right)^{b_{s,c}} \right)^{w_{s,m}}$$
$$= P(y_m) \left((H_s)^{b_{s,y_m}} \left(\frac{1-H_s}{|m|-1} \right)^{(1-b_{s,y_m})} \right)^{w_{s,m}}$$

Here, $P(y_m)$ is our prior probability of y_m being the true claim in m, and $w_{s,m}$ will be 1 if the source asserts (with full certainty) a claim in m, or 0 if the source says nothing about m. In the second equation we have simplified the expression by noting that $\sum_{c \in m} b_{s,c} = 1$, so $\sum_{c \in m \setminus y_m} b_{s,c} = 1 - b_{s,y_m}$.

Observing that all sources make their assertions independently and taking $\theta = \{H_s\}$ we can write the full joint as:

$$P(Y, X | \theta) =$$
$$\prod_m P(y_m) \prod_s \left((H_s)^{b_{s,y_m}} \left(\frac{1-H_s}{|m|-1} \right)^{(1-b_{s,y_m})} \right)^{w_{s,m}}$$

The expected log-likelihood maximized in the M-step is then $\mathbb{E}_{Y|X,\theta^t}[\log(P(X,Y|\theta)P(\theta))] =$

$$\log(P(\theta)) + \sum_Y P(Y|X, \theta^t) \log \left(\prod_m P(y_m) \right.$$
$$\left. \cdot \prod_s \left((H_s)^{b_{s,y_m}} \left(\frac{1-H_s}{|m|-1} \right)^{(1-b_{s,y_m})} \right)^{w_{s,m}} \right)$$

$$= \log(P(\theta)) + \sum_m \sum_{y_m} P(y_m | X, \theta^t) \left(\log(P(y_m)) \right.$$
$$\left. + \sum_s w_{s,m} \left(b_{s,y_m} \log(H_s) + (1-b_{s,y_m}) \log \left(\frac{1-H_s}{|m|-1} \right) \right) \right)$$

Finding the derivative with respect to each $H_s \in \theta$,

$$\frac{\delta}{\delta H_s} \mathbb{E}_{Y|X,\theta^t}[\log(P(X,Y|\theta)P(\theta))] =$$
$$\frac{\delta P(H_s)}{\delta H_s} P(H_s)^{-1}$$
$$+ \frac{\sum_m \sum_{y_m} P(y_m | X, \theta^t) w_{s,m}(b_{s,y_m} - H_s)}{H_s - (H_s)^2}$$

Now we can maximize each H_s independently in our M-step using gradient ascent to find the new, maximizing θ^{t+1}. However, when the priors $P(H_s)$ are uniform (so $\frac{\delta P(H_s)}{\delta H_s} = 0$), the gradient simplifies, allowing us to set it to 0 and solve the resulting equation explicitly for the new maximizing value of H_s at the stationary point:

$$H_s = \frac{\sum_m \sum_{y_m} P(y_m | X, \theta^t) w_{s,m} b_{s,y_m}}{\sum_m w_{s,m}}$$

As we would intuitively expect, we thus estimate the honesty of a source, that is, the probability that it provides the true claim, as essentially the expected proportion of true claims made by the source given our current parameters.

This closed form update rule also means that SimpleLCA with uniform honesty priors is as fast as fact-finders in practice, making it extremely scalable. When alternative priors are used, gradient ascent requires about twice as much time per EM iteration, but even on our largest datasets this was a matter of seconds.

3.4 GuessLCA

SimpleLCA is indeed quite simple. But it's also clear that, for sources, identifying the truth in some mutual exclusion sets is much harder than in others; for example, a source who merely guessed randomly would be assigned an honesty of 0.5 by SimpleLCA if it only made claims in mutual exclusion sets of size 2, and 0.25 if size 4.

In GuessLCA, a source has a probability of knowing and telling the truth, H_s. Thus, with probability H_s, it asserts the true claim. However, with probability $1 - H_s$, it guesses claim c with probability $P_g(c|s)$ (where $\sum_{c \in m} P_g(c|s) = 1$). This gives us the joint probability:

$$P(X, Y|\theta) = \prod_m P(y_m)$$
$$\prod_s (H_s + (1-H_s)P_g(y_m|s))^{b_{s,y_m} w_{s,m}}$$
$$\prod_{c \in m \setminus y_m} ((1-H_s)P_g(c|s))^{b_{s,c} w_{s,m}}$$

This joint can be easily understood by considering the marginal case for each $m \in M$; the probability that the source asserts the true claim ($b_{s,y_m} = 1$) is then just $H_s + (1-H_s)P_g(y_m|s)$, the probability of knowing the truth plus the chance of not knowing the truth and (fortunately) guessing it; $\sum_{c \in m} b_{s,c} = 1 \Rightarrow \forall_{c \neq y_m} b_{s,c} = 0$, so the product $\prod_{c \in m \setminus y_m} (\ldots)^{b_{s,c}} = 1$ is moot. Conversely, the probability of asserting an untrue claim ($b_{s,c \neq y_m} = 1$) can be similarly found as the probability of not knowing the truth and guessing c, $(1-H_s)P_g(c|s)$.

Omitting the intermediate steps for brevity, we find that the gradient of the expected log-likelihood with respect to H_s simplifies to

$$\frac{\delta}{\delta H_s} \mathbb{E}_{Y|X,\theta^t}[\log(P(X,Y|\theta)P(\theta))] =$$
$$\frac{\delta P(H_s)}{\delta H_s} P(H_s)^{-1}$$
$$+ \sum_m \sum_{y_m} P(y_m|X, \theta^t) w_{s,m}$$
$$\cdot \left(\frac{b_{s,y_m}}{H_s + \frac{P_g(y_m|s)}{1 - P_g(y_m|s)}} + \frac{b_{s,y_m} - 1}{1 - H_s} \right)$$

Like SimpleLCA, the gradient with respect to each H_s is independent of the other parameters $\theta \setminus H_s$, allowing us to maximize the expected log-likelihood in the M-step using gradient ascent parameter-by-parameter, which is very fast in practice. The guess distribution $P_g(c|s)$ is provided to the model as a prior; we could, for example, set $P_g(c|s)$ to the distribution of sources asserting the claims in m under the assumption that a guessing source chooses randomly according to the distribution of "votes" it observes at the time. This mitigates sources becoming trusted by asserting obvious or well-known claims: the assessed probability of guessing these will then be high (because a large majority of sources already assert them, and we assume that guessers tend to go with the crowd), so the model is free to set H_s low as the observation can be effectively explained away by $(1-H_s)P_g(y_m|s)$; conversely, a source asserting a true claim with a low probability of being guessed will be attributed to a high H_s. GuessLCA thus rewards getting hard claims right and penalizes getting easy claims wrong.

GuessLCA does require that this "difficulty" information be provided a priori rather than learned by the model, and while in most domains the distribution of guesses is easy to approximate (e.g. if the sources tend to guess with the crowd, probably the most prevalent behavior in practice, we can use the distribution of the number of assertions made by other sources for each alternative within the mutual exclusion set, and if the sources are believed to guess randomly we use a uniform prior over the possibilities) this cannot capture the latent difficulty implied by, for example, the disagreement of two highly honest sources (since honesty itself is latent). More significantly, the model assumes that no source will do worse than guessing—even if $H_s = 0$, a source still has a $P_g(c|s)$ probability of guessing the correct claim c. This assumption is violated when sources are systematically wrong. This may be due to intentional deception, or, more commonly, a recurring mistake: for example, there are multiple ways of defining the population of a city (metro area, city limits, etc.) and some Wikipedia editors consistently use definitions that disagree with the "truth" (census data).

3.5 MistakeLCA

To overcome these problems, MistakeLCA models difficulty explicitly, as the probability of an honest source making a mistake. For a source to assert the true claim it must both intend to tell the truth with probability H_s *and* must know what the truth is with probability D. D may be global (in which case all sources have probability D_g of knowing the truth across all mutual exclusion sets) or tied to each mutual exclusion set (in which case sources have probability D_m of knowing the truth in a particular mutual exclusion set); this results in two variants of the model, which we will refer to as MistakeLCA$_g$ and MistakeLCA$_m$. A source thus asserts the true claim $\bar{c}$ with probability $H_s D$, but otherwise, with probability $1 - H_s D$, chooses another claim $c \in m \setminus \bar{c}$ according to $P_e(c|\bar{c}, s)$. Recall that, in GuessLCA, our guessing probability P_g was not conditioned on the true claim, but P_e specifies the distribution of mistakes a source will make given that $\bar{c}$ is true, with $P_e(\bar{c}|\bar{c}, s) = 0$. Like P_g, P_e is provided as a prior, but conditioning on the true claim means that it can also encode very useful information about similar or easily confused claims; for example, if there are three claims about a person's age, 35, 45, and 46, $P_e(45|46, s)$ and $P_e(46|45, s)$ would both be high.

The joint probability is given by:

$$P(X, Y|\theta) = \prod_m P(y_m)$$
$$\prod_s (H_s D)^{b_{s,y_m} w_{s,m}}$$
$$\prod_{c \in m \setminus y_m} (P_e(c|y_m, s)(1 - H_s D))^{b_{s,c} w_{s,m}}$$

The gradients of the expected log-likelihood are given by:

$$\frac{\delta(\ldots)}{\delta H_s} = \frac{\delta P(H_s)}{\delta H_s} P(H_s)^{-1}$$
$$+ \sum_m \sum_{y_m} P(y_m|X,\theta^t) w_{s,m} \left(\frac{b_{s,y_m} - D_m H_s}{H_s - D_m H_s^2} \right)$$

$$\frac{\delta(\ldots)}{\delta D_m} = \frac{\delta P(D_m)}{\delta D_m} P(D_m)^{-1}$$
$$+ \sum_s \sum_{y_m} P(y_m|X,\theta^t) w_{s,m} \left(\frac{b_{s,y_m} - D_m H_s}{D_m - D_m^2 H_s} \right)$$

The gradient for D_g is identical, except that we sum over all mutual exclusion sets as well as all sources. Since all H_s are linked by D, we must optimize all parameters jointly in the M-step.

3.6 LieLCA

MistakeLCA makes no distinction between intentional lies caused by a lack of honesty and "honest mistakes" that occur with probability $(1-D)$; we can imagine that the former case is governed by a distribution over possible lies, whereas the latter results in guessing. In LieLCA, a source asserts the true claim $\bar{c}$ if it is both honest and knows the answer (with probability $H_s D$). A dishonest source who knows the truth, however, chooses a lie c with probability $(1-H)DP_l(c|\bar{c},s)$, where P_l is the distribution over possible lies given the truth ($P_l(\bar{c}|\bar{c},s) = 0$). Finally, any source who does not know the truth guesses a claim c with probability $(1-D)P_g(c|s)$. The D parameters may be per-source, per-mutual exclusion set, or global, resulting in LieLCA$_s$, LieLCA$_m$, and LieLCA$_g$ variants. The joint probability is thus:

$$P(X,Y|\theta) =$$
$$\prod_m P(y_m)$$
$$\prod_s (H_s D + (1-D)P_g(y_m|s))^{b_{s,y_m} w_{s,m}}$$
$$\prod_{c \in m \setminus y_m} ((1-H_s)DP_l(c|y_m,s) + (1-D)P_g(c|s))^{b_{s,c} w_{s,m}}$$

The gradients of the expected log-likelihood with respect to H_s and D can be found as:

$$\frac{\delta(\ldots)}{\delta H_s} = \frac{\delta P(H_s)}{\delta H_s} P(H_s)^{-1}$$
$$+ \sum_m \sum_{y_m} P(y_m|X,\theta^t) w_{s,m} \left(\frac{b_{s,y_m} D}{(1-D)P_g(y_m|s) + DH_s} \right.$$
$$\left. - \sum_{c \in m \setminus y_m} \frac{b_{s,y_m} DP_l(c|y_m,s)}{(1-D)P_g(c|s) + D(1-H_s)P_l(c|y_m,s)} \right)$$

$$\frac{\delta(\ldots)}{\delta D_g} = \frac{\delta P(D_g)}{\delta D_g} P(D_g)^{-1}$$
$$+ \sum_{m,s} \sum_{y_m} P(y_m|X,\theta^t) w_{s,m} \left(\frac{b_{s,y_m}(H_s - P_g(y_m|s))}{H_s D_g + (1-D_g)P_g(y_m|s)} \right.$$
$$\left. + \sum_{c \in m \setminus y_m} \frac{b_{s,c}((1-H_s)P_l(c|y_m,s) - P_g(c|s))}{(1-D_g)P_g(c|s) + D_g(1-H_s)P_l(c|y_m,s)} \right)$$

Again, the gradients for D_m and D_s are identical, except $\sum_{m,s}$ is replaced by $\sum_s$ and $\sum_m$, respectively. It is interesting to note that LieLCA$_s$ is a special case since each pair of (H_s, D_s) parameters may be optimized independently of the others, with the same linearly scaling complexity as SimpleLCA and GuessLCA; otherwise, like MistakeLCA, the parameters must be optimized jointly.

It is important to note that we are abusing language somewhat here; in LiarLCA, a "lie" is an intentional, incorrect assertion by a source who knows the truth, but it need not imply malice or an intent to deceive. A Wikipedia editor who (perhaps out of ignorance) accurately lists the population of cities by their greater metro area rather than by their city limits when the latter is held to be the true measure would not normally be considered a liar, even though the model considers their assertions to be "lies" (and in this particular case those "lies" may be quite informative since we know they will be drawn from values strictly greater than the true population such that $P_l(c|\bar{c},s) > 0$ iff $c \geq \bar{c}$).

3.7 Discussion

3.7.1 Model Complexity and Semantics

Given that we have presented a series of increasingly complex models it might be tempting to think of these hierarchically along the lines of SimpleLCA $\subset$ GuessLCA $\subset$ MistakeLCA $\subset$ LieLCA. However, this is incorrect: it is easy to see that there are some worlds that SimpleLCA can model (a source with an honesty of 0 who always asserts the wrong claim) that, for example, GuessLCA cannot (at worst a source will still sometimes guess the truth). We can similarly observe that the H_s parameters have subtly different meanings in each model: in SimpleLCA, it is simply the probability that a source asserts the correct claim; in GuessLCA, it is the probability that it both knows and asserts it; and in MistakeLCA and LieLCA, it is the probability the source *intends* to tell the truth. Such distinctions are of practical importance: because each model tells a different story with different semantics, we should not expect, for instance, that the more sophisticated LieLCA will necessarily outperform the SimpleLCA model given sufficient data (as we might if SimpleLCA were indeed subsumed by LieLCA); rather, we expect that relative performance will depend on which model more closely reflects the actual behavior of sources within a particular domain. That said, our experiments showed that, indeed, some models appear to be more plausible than others, and the more complex models are vulnerable to overfitting: in particular, GuessLCA performs substantially better than SimpleLCA overall and is competitive with MistakeLCA and LieLCA, especially where these models overfit (e.g. on the stocks dataset).

3.7.2 Extensions

A key benefit of LCA is its flexibility and transparency relative to fact-finders. Bayesian priors over the parameters, claims, and other phenomena (such as the mistake distribution, P_e) provide a straightforward way of encoding domain knowledge, but many extensions are also possible.

The modularity of LCA can be illustrated by an example: consider a case where we have features X_f (such as the quality of a source's website, his academic degrees, years of experience, etc.) associated with the credibility of our sources. By assuming that these features are independent from the sources' assertions given their credibility, we can create a new model by simply concatenating two joint distributions: $P(X, Y|\theta) = P_{\text{LCA}}(X_b, Y|\theta)P_f(X_f|\theta)$, where $P_{\text{LCA}}(X_b, Y|\theta)$ is an LCA model over observed assertions X_b and $P_f(X_f|\theta)$ is the probability of observing features X_f given the credibility of the sources (captured by parameters θ).

Additionally, LCA models (and fact-finders) will normally only give credibility to claims that are known to exist and asserted by at least one source (an unknown alternative obviously cannot be explicitly considered in the set of possibilities m, and the models infer a distribution over the possible values of $y_m \in m$). However, we can easily create a new "none of the above" claim u and assign it a prior probability $P(u)$; believing one of the known, asserted claims will then depend on the evidence outweighing our prior inclination towards doubt.

4. EXPERIMENTS

We evaluate our models on two unsupervised datasets, book authorship [19] and city populations [13], and two semi-supervised datasets, stock predictions and U.S. Supreme Court decision predictions[1]. Our evaluation compares our four basic LCA models with several top-performing fact-finders found in the literature: TruthFinder [19], Investment, PooledInvestment, and Average-Log [13], Sums [9], 3-Estimates [4], as well as simple voting (choose the claim with the most sources asserting it). For Investment and Pooled-Investment we used the same values for g as [13], 1.2 and 1.4, respectively. We run both the fact-finders and EM (for LCA) until convergence (within 50 iterations in our experiments). Additionally, we supplement our real-world experiments with synthetic data from sampled from SimpleLCA joint distributions to more carefully analyze the relative performance of the LCA models in a controlled context.

4.1 Books

The books dataset [19] is a collection of 14,287 claims of the authorship of various books by 894 websites, with an evaluation set of 605 true claims collected by examining the books' covers. We used uniform priors for the parameters $P(\theta)$. For for the claim priors $P(c)$ and guess priors $P_g(c|s)$ we used "voted" priors corresponding to the distribution of sources asserting each claim relative to the number of sources asserting any claim within the mutual exclusion set: $\frac{|\{t:w_{t,m}=b_{t,c}=1\}|}{\sum_{v \in m}|\{t:w_{t,m}=b_{t,v}=1\}|}$. Finally, the mistake and lie priors $P_e(c|\bar{c}, s)$ were also "voted", computed as $P_l(c|\bar{c}, s) = \frac{|\{t:w_{t,m}=b_{t,c}=1\}|}{\sum_{v \in m\setminus\bar{c}}|\{t:w_{t,m}=b_{t,v}=1\}|}$ [for $c \neq \bar{c}$]; this is the proportion of sources asserting c relative to the total number of sources asserting any claim in m other than $\bar{c}$. For simplicity, the distributions are the same for all sources s. For LieLCA$_s$, LieLCA$_m$, and MistakeLCA$_m$, the D_s or D_m parameters in the model are much more variable than a single global D_g (which tends to be high), resulting in greater emphasis on the voted P_e priors and making voted claim priors $P(c)$ effectively redundant; to correct this, we instead use uniform claim priors on these models.

The results are shown in Table 2; we calculate confidence intervals with the simplifying assumption that the predic-

---

[1]The Supreme Court, city population, and book authorship datasets are available at http://lotho.cs.illinois.edu/data/ Unfortunately, we are unable to release the stock predictions data due to licensing restrictions.

tion over each mutual exclusion set is independent from the others. The only fact-finder to do better than *any* of the LCA models is PooledInvestment, still more than 3% below LieLCA$_s$. The LieLCA$_s$ generative story fits especially well with what we know about online booksellers a priori: some sources will consistently corrupt, abbreviate or omit authors names (in other words, they consistently "lie" with a low H_s), while others "guess" by copying prevailing sources since they tend not to research the information themselves (low D_s).

4.2 Population

The population dataset [13] contains 44,761 claims about the population of a city in a specific year made by 171,171 Wikipedia editors in infoboxes, with an evaluation set of 274 true claims identified from U.S. census data. Our evaluation set is marginally smaller than [13] because when an editor made multiple claims about the population of a city in the same year, we kept only the most recent edit and discarded the rest; this resulted in some true claims becoming uncontested and thus eliminated from the evaluation set. Our priors remained the same as before, except that the claim priors followed the distribution of the number of revisions a claim was present in, rather than the number of sources asserting it, as per [13]. Additionally, we noticed that some models could achieve better results if we knew exactly when to stop them prior to convergence (which is not possible given the unsupervised setting); Investment is the most extreme example of this, as at 20 iterations its accuracy is 86.86%, but it ultimately converges to 75.55%.

There is a wide variance in the the cities in this dataset; some, like Ventura, California are relatively contentious (49 edits asserted a population of 105,000 in 2006, while 68 asserted 106,744), while in others things are more lopsided (in Springfield the split was 202 edits vs. 10). As a consequence, some cities can be considered much "harder" than others, since an overwhelming majority for one option over the others means both that the answer is well-known and that an editor needs only follow the crowd to identify it. Given this, we would expect those models that are capable of capturing this variable difficulty to perform the best, and this matches our experiments exactly: GuessLCA (which attributes greater honesty [H_s] to sources that assert true but hard-to-guess claims and less to those that assert false, easy-to-guess claims) and LieLCA$_m$ and MistakeLCA$_m$ (which model the variable difficulty of each city directly with D_m parameters) are the best performing among the LCA models. TruthFinder also does quite well, but the opaque nature of fact-finders precludes an explanation why, or a prediction of the domains where it might similarly perform well in the future. LieLCA$_m$'s top performance, however, is a result of having both D_m parameters to model latent difficulty (e.g. as demonstrated by incorrect assertions by highly honest sources) and guessing priors to incorporate the more obvious situations of lopsided and even votes where the difficulty is apparent even without having an estimate of the honesty of the sources involved.

4.3 Predicting Stock Returns

We took the set of stocks that were in the S&P 500 Index on January 1st, 2000 (the index changes composition over time) and followed them through February 1st, 2012. Our results average predictive accuracy across 10 dates, at July

Model	Books Unsupervised	Populations Unsupervised	Stocks Semi-Supervised	Supreme Court Semi-Supervised
Voting	84.95 ± 2.85	79.93 ± 4.74	47.14 ± 4.13	54.72 ± 13.40
Sums	82.87 ± 3.00	82.12 ± 4.54	48.93 ± 4.14	56.60 ± 13.34
3-Estimates	85.12 ± 2.84	74.45 ± 5.16	47.14 ± 4.13	52.83 ± 13.44
TruthFinder	86.16 ± 2.75	85.04 ± 4.22	47.14 ± 4.13	58.49 ± 13.27
Average-Log	85.47 ± 2.81	81.02 ± 4.64	46.61 ± 4.13	52.83 ± 13.44
Investment	80.10 ± 3.18	75.55 ± 5.09	51.61 ± 4.14	75.47 ± 11.58
PooledInvestment	87.72 ± 2.62	79.93 ± 4.74	48.93 ± 4.14	77.36 ± 11.27
SimpleLCA	86.51 ± 2.72	82.48 ± 4.50	56.96 ± 4.10	79.25 ± 10.92
GuessLCA	89.10 ± 2.48	83.58 ± 4.39	56.25 ± 4.11	**88.68 ± 8.53**
MistakeLCA$_g$	86.33 ± 2.74	82.12 ± 4.54	55.54 ± 4.12	N/A
MistakeLCA$_m$	88.58 ± 2.53	**86.13 ± 4.09**	50.89 ± 4.14	N/A
LieLCA$_g$	89.62 ± 2.43	81.39 ± 4.61	**57.86 ± 4.09**	N/A
LieLCA$_m$	87.89 ± 2.60	83.94 ± 4.35	51.61 ± 4.14	N/A
LieLCA$_s$	**90.83 ± 2.30**	82.85 ± 4.46	53.39 ± 4.13	N/A

Table 2: Experimental Results (N/A: Not Available).
Values are percent accuracy (proportion of true claims correctly identified) and 95% confidence interval. The best LCA models outperform the best fact-finders with statistical significance in the Books, Stocks and Supreme Court datasets.

1st, 2011 and every two weeks thereafter. We pretend that each of these dates is the present time and interpret stock analysts' buy or sell predictions as claims about whether each stock will yield a return higher or lower than the baseline S&P 500 return over the next 60 days. For example, when we pretend that the date is July 1st, 2011 and are considering Microsoft stock we know the buy or sell recommendations analysts have made over the previous two weeks (in late June), and the latent truth we seek to identify is, of course, whether or not the stock will actually outperform the S&P 500 over the next 60 days. As a technical detail, stocks are assumed to be bought piecemeal over a week, starting on the subsequent day, and then sold piecemeal over a week, starting 60 days later (this reduces the day-to-day price variance). At each of these dates, we also know which recommendations analysts made more 60 days ago were proven true, and this observed truth of whether each stock went up or down is our labeled data. Similarly, the remainder of the predictions (those recommendations made in the last 60 days) are effectively unlabeled data, since we do not know if they will be proven true yet. In total, there are approximately 4K distinct analysts and 80K distinct stock predictions, and our evaluation set consists of 560 true claims about stocks where analysts disagreed.

One thing we can quickly observe is that analysts are, in fact, usually wrong, as reflected by the 47.14% accuracy of voting. We therefore used uniform claim priors, which are a better alternative to the voted priors of our previous experiments; all other priors remain the same. Given the difficulty of the problem (as the oft-cited efficient market hypothesis that consistent risk-adjusted returns relative to the market are impossible would suggest [11]) we would expect no analyst to be especially good (otherwise they would presumably be running a hedge fund) nor any stock to be especially easy to predict; modeling these features, then, would offer little benefit but substantial risk of overfitting, as we observe in LieLCA$_m$, MistakeLCA$_m$, and LieLCA$_s$, the three lowest-performing LCA models. Conversely, LieLCA$_g$, balancing the overall difficulty of stock prediction with each source's ability (captured by H_s), does the best (D_g essentially serves as a latent, universal cap on how accurate any analyst can be at the task). Amusingly, the (aptly-named) Investment is the only fact-finder to do better than 50%, although it surpasses only one LCA model (MistakeLCA$_m$).

Given the practical importance of this domain, a natural question to ask is if these models would work in practice as an investment strategy, given the $\sim 58\%$ accuracy of LieLCA$_g$. It is important to observe, however, that we considered only binary outperform and underperform labels and, critically, not how much would have been gained (or lost) on each stock; overall excess return relative to the market as a whole is likely to be minor. Furthermore, since the market changes over time, there is no guarantee that a strategy that works on historical data would continue to work in the future, nor can we easily quantify this risk (and unexpected, unlikely events can collectively pose a major hazard to any strategy, e.g. the collapse of Long-Term Capital Management [6]).

4.4 Predicting Supreme Court Decisions

Finally, we considered the FantasySCOTUS project; here, 1138 people (largely law students) have made predictions about the outcome of 53 U.S. Supreme Court cases that have already been decided, and 24 that have not been. Using the same priors as the Books experiment (based on voting), we evaluated with 10-fold cross-validation. Within each fold, Investment, PooledInvestment, SimpleLCA and GuessLCA were tuned by nested 4-fold cross-validation. For Investment and PooledInvestment, the growth parameter (from 1 to 2 in increments of .1), was tuned, whereas for SimpleLCA and GuessLCA the parameter priors $P(H_s)$ were tuned over sets of 10 possible Beta distributions. Since the votes for most cases are nearly tied, we concluded that most sources did little better than guessing, and selected Beta distributions biased toward 0 for GuessLCA (such that the prior on the probability of doing better than guessing is low), and biased towards 1/2 for SimpleLCA (such that the prior probability of asserting the truth is near random). The other fact-finders were not tuned because they lacked tunable parameters; LieLCA and MistakeLCA results are omitted because the experiments were not feasible; 10-fold cross-validation with 4-fold nested cross-validated tuning across 10 possible distributions of the priors of $P(H_s)$ and $P(D)$ is 4000 times as expensive as a normal run (and running a greatly reduced cross-validation regimen with just a few alternative priors for each parameter would underestimate performance relative to our other LCA results). This is a tradeoff for the greater sophistication of the LieLCA and MistakeLCA models: not only are there an additional set of parameters (the D's) to select priors for, the M-step requires a substantially more expensive optimization (up to about 200 times as expensive as that for SimpleLCA or GuessLCA as previously discussed; a single, normal run of LieLCA on this dataset takes 20-30 minutes). However, we note that this cross-validated tuning is parallelizable, and a real-world implementation could handle the task by splitting it over a cluster of machines.

4.5 Synthetic Results and Analysis

In our experimental results, our understanding of the domains allowed us to regularly anticipate which models would be most appropriate: in the books domain, the propensity of different booksellers to copy each others' claims ("guessing") or systematically disagree with the truth ("lying", e.g. an idiosyncratic way of abbreviating author names) suggested that $LieLCA_s$ was the best fit. For Wikipedia population claims, $LieLCA_m$ and $MistakeLCA_m$ captured the widely varying difficulty of identifying the true population among the cities. In predicting stocks we could expect $LieLCA_m$ and $MistakeLCA_m$ to *not* work because predicting stocks is more-or-less uniformly challenging across companies and per-company difficulty parameters merely worsens the chance of overfitting. Finally, in the Supreme Court domain, we know that historically some sources have been much more accurate than others, but given the even split of votes in most cases it's clear that other sources (a majority) are more-or-less guessing; here we would expect $LieLCA_m$ (which models both guessing and varying difficulty amongst mutual exclusion sets) to perform best, although it's similarly clear why GuessLCA outperforms SimpleLCA.

However, these are qualitative judgements, and while they certainly help us narrow down the set of potential models, it is not always clear precisely which should be used, particularly when partial supervision is not available to empirically estimate performance; e.g. in city populations it is not obvious why $MistakeLCA_m$ outperforms $LieLCA_m$. Arguably, since both of these models do well (and are presumably both reasonably good approximations to the collection of highly varied processes that sources really do follow in generating claims) we could acknowledge that either would be a satisfactory choice. Still, we also wanted briefly investigate the idea of model fit quantitatively, empirically observing how well these models perform given varying quantities of data and a precise knowledge of how the data were really generated (as opposed to real word datasets, where we are left to speculate using our knowledge of the domain). To do so, we generated data using the SimpleLCA joint distribution with the intent of obtaining a simple underlying process that would allow us to focus on the models' behavior.

4.5.1 SimpleLCA Generation

We ran two sets of experiments using a SimpleLCA model to generate data; SimpleLCA does not incorporate guessing, mistake or lie prior probabilities, so in the first set we give GuessLCA, MistakeLCA and LieLCA uniform probabilities. In the second set, however, we generate these priors randomly[2], with the idea that this will give some insight into the effect of a poor model choice when mixed with a bad (random and independent of reality) priors. In each experiment we had 100 sources and 100 mutual exclusion sets, each containing between 2 and 5 claims (selected uniformly at random). The number of claims made by each source was fixed at 3, 5, 10, or 20, and increasing this effectively increased the amount of data provided to the models. To mitigate statistical noise, every experiment was repeated 100 times with 100 different generated datasets, and the reported accuracies are an average of those runs (and, within each experiment, the same 100 randomly-generated datasets were used to test each model).

The distribution of H_s was $Beta(7,3)$; this prior over H_s was used in all models in both experiment sets, despite H_s having somewhat different semantics in each model (the intent is to observe performance when the models do not fit the data in a well-understood way). The results of our synthetic experiments may be found in Table 3.

There are a number of interesting phenomena that we may observe in these results:

- Surprisingly, with uniform priors, two of the models (GuessLCA and $LieLCA_g$) consistently outperform SimpleLCA on data generated by a SimpleLCA process. In SimpleLCA, the model tends to conclude that, given a disagreement between sources, one is perfectly honest ($H_s = 1$) and the other is constantly wrong ($H_s = 0$). Other models avoid this with guessing, such that even the worst source can always make a lucky guess, which prevents the model from disregarding their claims entirely.

- With sufficient data this overfitting is avoided entirely.

- $MistakeLCA_g$ versus $MistakeLCA_m$: the latter fares quite poorly in all experiments, while the former does quite well, reflecting a substantial difference in the models in practice despite a similar joint distribution. $MistakeLCA_g$'s global D_g parameter controls the frequency sources make mistakes, again creating an alternative explanation for a source's error other than complete dishonesty (since some of their inaccuracy will be attributed to "honest mistakes" rather than dishonesty).

- $MistakeLCA_m$, by contrast, has far more freedom to set its 100 D_m parameters to extreme values (overfitting).

- With randomized priors handicapping the other models, SimpleLCA leads the pack, as expected.

---

[2]We generated these distributions by drawing a [0,1] value uniformly for each claim and then normalizing over the mutual exclusion set for $P_g(c|s)$ and normalizing over the claims in the mutual set excluding y_m for $P_l(c|y_m,s)$ and $P_e(c|y_m,s)$. This results in a rather complex distribution: for example, given two claims A and B, the probability of guessing A is taken as $\frac{a}{a+b}$, where a is the value drawn for claim A, and b is the value drawn for claim B. Marginalizing out b gives $P_g(A) = a(\log(a+1) - \log(a))$.

P_g, P_e, P_l	Uniform				Randomized			
Claims per Source	3	5	10	20	3	5	10	20
SimpleLCA	79.92	87.80	95.83	99.54	79.92	87.80	95.83	99.54
GuessLCA	80.10	88.14	95.96	99.54	77.67	84.73	92.51	96.27
MistakeLCA$_g$	79.90	88.08	96.00	99.52	78.03	86.38	94.52	99.10
MistakeLCA$_m$	75.48	78.08	78.87	80.45	70.53	68.99	60.33	56.60
LieLCA$_g$	80.10	88.06	96.01	99.54	78.83	86.96	95.20	99.28
LieLCA$_m$	79.90	87.92	95.85	99.53	76.14	82.24	89.59	94.51
LieLCA$_s$	78.35	86.89	95.58	99.52	75.23	84.54	94.94	99.29

Table 3: Performance of LCA Models with Synthetic Data from a SimpleLCA Process. Each experiment was run over 100 random datasets and the results averaged.

- With randomized priors, MistakeLCA$_m$ suffers from worsening performance as more assertions are made in each mutual exclusion set, increasing the D_m gradients relative to those of H_s and pushing D_m to lower values (it is easier to "explain away" bad assertions by decreasing the D_m for the mutual exclusion set than decreasing the H_s for many sources). This then places greater weight on the (random) mistake priors.

- The other models prove remarkably robust given their completely incorrect priors, although its clear that this does cap the possible performance of GuessLCA and LieLCA$_m$ a bit, whereas MistakeLCA$_g$ and LieLCA$_g$ can simply set a high D_g, eliminating or reducing their influence, respectively.

In our real-world data, SimpleLCA was often among the least accurate LCA models; the synthetic results here suggest that, indeed, even in an artificial best-case scenario other models are able to perform almost as well. However, SimpleLCA remains easy to implement, easy to understand, and very tractable, and so should not be discounted entirely. It is also apparent that MistakeLCA$_m$ may face severe difficulty in some cases; whereas LieLCA$_m$ can believe a source will assert the correct claim by guessing even if the D_m parameter for the relevant mutual exclusion set is 0, MistakeLCA$_m$ has no "safety valve" of this sort: if D_m is 0, the source must always get the claim wrong (this creates a sort of perverse "anti-vote", whereby the claim with the fewest assertions is likely to be believed). This danger manifests itself in the high variance we see in the model's real-world performance; while the top performer in the population domain, it is also the lowest performer in the stocks domain. Care must therefore be taken to ensure that MistakeLCA$_m$ is a reasonably good fit to the domain, whereas the other models are much more forgiving.

4.5.2 Discussion

Our synthetic experiments are limited in scope, but they do inform our approach to real-world problems. MistakeLCA$_m$ can sometimes yield the best results, but LieLCA$_m$ has a similar generative story and is a less variable choice that can do well in the same domains without MistakeLCA$_m$'s risk of overfitting. A second lesson is that these models can be remarkably resistant to bad priors (when the underlying process generating the data is simple), and uniform priors are a good choice even if the generating process is quite different from the model being applied. GuessLCA in particular does quite well with uniform priors in our synthetic experiments, and, moreover, performs consistently well in the real-world experiments, too. This consistency is partly due to its simplicity (little danger of overfitting) and partly because it manages to at least approximately model the important "difficulty" aspect of claims; not as precisely as the more sophisticated LieLCA or MistakeLCA models, of course, but also without their computational cost. LieLCA and MistakeLCA are, on the other hand, more appropriate where the behavior of sources is well understood (e.g. the books domain) and where partial supervision can be used to avoid overfitting (e.g. the stocks domain).

5. CONCLUSION

Latent Credibility Analysis is a flexible and powerful approach to modeling the information credibility problem; although we have really only begun to explore its potential in our experiments so far, we have nonetheless seen that the performance of LCA models surpasses that of fact-finders on both semi-supervised and unsupervised real-world datasets, often substantially. GuessLCA in particular is promising due to its consistently strong performance and tractability, scaling linearly with the size of the problem as fact-finders do, although other, more expressive (and expensive) LCA models can achieve better results when used judiciously. Future work should extend the LCA framework, capturing phenomena such as source dependency and real-valued claims that will allow it to model an even wider range of domains; for now, however, LCAs are a new approach to credibility that is already both semantically appealing and of substantial practical utility.

6. REFERENCES

[1] M. Chang, L. Ratinov, and D. Roth. Structured Learning with Constrained Conditional Models. *Machine Learning*, 88(3):399–431, 2012.

[2] A. Dempster, N. Laird, and D. Rubin. Maximum likelihood from incomplete data via the EM algorithm. *Journal of the Royal Statistical Society. Series B (Methodological)*, 39(1):1–38, 1977.

This research was sponsored in part by the Army Research Laboratory (ARL) under agreement W911NF-09-2-0053. Any opinions, findings, conclusions or recommendations are those of the authors and do not necessarily reflect the view of the ARL.

[3] X. Dong, L. Berti-Equille, and D. Srivastava. Truth discovery and copying detection in a dynamic world. *VLDB*, 2009.

[4] A. Galland, S. Abiteboul, A. Marian, and P. Senellart. Corroborating information from disagreeing views. In *WSDM*, 2010.

[5] K. Ganchev, J. Graca, J. Gillenwater, and B. Taskar. Posterior Regularization for Structured Latent Variable Models. *Journal of Machine Learning Research*, 2010.

[6] P. Jorion. Risk management lessons from Long-Term Capital Management. *European financial management*, 6(3):277–300, 2000.

[7] A. Josang. Artificial reasoning with subjective logic. *2nd Australian Workshop on Commonsense Reasoning*, 1997.

[8] A. Josang, S. Marsh, and S. Pope. Exploring different types of trust propagation. *Lecture Notes in Computer Science*, 3986:179, 2006.

[9] J. M. Kleinberg. Authoritative sources in a hyperlinked environment. *Journal of the ACM*, 46(5):604–632, 1999.

[10] H. K. Le, J. Pasternack, H. Ahmadi, M. Gupta, Y. Sun, T. Abdelzaher, J. Han, D. Roth, B. Szymanski, and S. Adali. Apollo : Towards Factfinding in Participatory Sensing. *IPSN*, 2011.

[11] B. G. Malkiel. The efficient market hypothesis and its critics. *Journal of Economic Perspectives*, pages 59–82, 2003.

[12] Y. Nesterov and I. U. E. Nesterov. *Introductory lectures on convex optimization: A basic course*, volume 87. Springer, 2004.

[13] J. Pasternack and D. Roth. Knowing What to Believe (when you already know something). In *COLING*, 2010.

[14] J. Pasternack and D. Roth. Making Better Informed Trust Decisions with Generalized Fact-Finding. In *IJCAI*, 2011.

[15] G. Shafer. *A mathematical theory of evidence*. Princeton University Press Princeton, NJ, 1976.

[16] V. G. Vydiswaran, C. X. Zhai, and D. Roth. Content-driven trust propagation framework. In *Proceedings of the 17th ACM SIGKDD international conference on Knowledge discovery and data mining*, pages 974–982. ACM, 2011.

[17] D. Wang, T. Abdelzaher, H. Ahmadi, J. Pasternack, D. Roth, M. Gupta, J. Han, O. Fatemieh, H. Le, and C. Aggarwal. On bayesian interpretation of fact-finding in information networks. *Information Fusion*, 2011.

[18] X. Yin, J. Han, and P. S. Yu. Truth discovery with multiple conflicting information providers on the web. In *Proc. of SIGKDD*, 2007.

[19] X. Yin, P. S. Yu, and J. Han. Truth Discovery with Multiple Conflicting Information Providers on the Web. *IEEE Transactions on Knowledge and Data Engineering*, 20(6):796–808, 2008.

[20] B. Yu and M. P. Singh. Detecting deception in reputation management. *Proceedings of the second international joint conference on Autonomous agents and multiagent systems - AAMAS '03*, page 73, 2003.

[21] B. Zhao, B. I. P. Rubinstein, J. Gemmell, and J. Han. A Bayesian approach to discovering truth from conflicting sources for data integration. *Proceedings of the VLDB Endowment*, 5(6):550–561, 2012.

Predicting Group Stability in Online Social Networks

Akshay Patil
Stony Brook University
Stony Brook, NY
akshay@cs.stonybrook.edu

Juan Liu
Palo Alto Research Center
Palo Alto, CA
Juan.Liu@parc.com

Jie Gao
Stony Brook University
Stony Brook, NY
jgao@cs.stonybrook.edu

ABSTRACT

Social groups often exhibit a high degree of dynamism. Some groups thrive, while many others die over time. Modeling group stability dynamics and understanding whether/when a group will remain stable or shrink over time can be important in a number of social domains. In this paper, we study two different types of social networks as exemplar platforms for modeling and predicting group stability dynamics. We build models to predict if a group is going to remain stable or is likely to shrink over a period of time. We observe that both the level of member diversity and social activities are critical in maintaining the stability of groups. We also find that certain 'prolific' members play a more important role in maintaining the group stability. Our study shows that group stability can be predicted with high accuracy, and feature diversity is critical to prediction performance.

Categories and Subject Descriptors

H.2.8 [**Database Management**]: Database Applications—*Data Mining*; J.4 [**Computer Applications**]: Social and Behavioral Sciences

Keywords

Social Networks, Group Stability, Online Communities

1. INTRODUCTION

Understanding community structures has always been an interesting topic in social sciences. In many social network datasets, a social graph is presented in which nodes represent individuals and edges represent social ties. It is a common experience to observe community structure in such a graph, in the sense that a subset of vertices are well connected within them and less connected to the rest of the graph. For example, communities in a social network often represent social groupings, say by interest or background. Communities in a publication network may represent people who work on similar research problems. Communities of the web graph may suggest pages on related topics. As the complexity of online activity increases, formal group structures have come to play an increasingly important role in the experience and effectiveness of an individual's online life.

Online platforms have provided unprecedented opportunities to study large-scale behavior and dynamics of communities. A lot of studies have focussed on how to define and detect social communities in the network structure and how the groups evolve over time. For the later, the main thrust of such research has been to model the evolution of groups, from the standpoint of growth [6, 27, 19]. A community in these studies always grows. What to be examined is the rate of growth and when the community stops growing. There are two main reasons for this. First, in many online social network settings there is no restriction on the number of groups an individual belongs to. Also, in most cases individuals do *not* quit groups even though they may not be active participants in those particular groups. This often results in groups having a monotonically increasing membership curve throughout their lifetimes. In addition, a practical and commercial motivation for such studies has been to increase the 'stickiness' of an online community, i.e., the capability for it to attract new members. Therefore, a common model in modeling group growth is to consider it as a diffusion process. That is, the social ties that cross group boundaries may influence people not yet in the group to join the group. This observation has been one of the main philosophies in modeling and predicting the growth of online groups. Studies have been performed in examining how diffusion happens and what is the main factor in determining the speed of diffusion. It has been shown using Facebook data [2] that what attracts a new user depends not only on the number of friends on Facebook, but also on the diversity of these friends, as well as the network connectivity structure among them [24].

In this paper, we take a different perspective and study the complementary problem of group stability, i.e., why some groups fall apart and disappear while others thrive. The effectiveness of groups can be undermined when group members depart, taking with them, experience, resources and possibly other group members. The ability to predict the stability of groups is highly desirable, as it offers insights on factors that affect online group effectiveness. It also provides practical guidance to tasks such as risk management and customer retention.

In some online settings an individual can belong to *only* one group at any given point in time. In such settings the group serves as the main engagement platform for the individual. An individual who is not satisfied with his/her group will quit the group and join another one. The reasons for dissatisfaction can be plenty. In such cases the percentage increase/decrease in the number of group members over previous time periods is a good measure in determining whether a group is stable or shrinking. In the settings when users can join multiple groups and probably never quit these groups, the group size always grows. But the growth in group size does not necessarily capture the accurate picture. A group, though accumulating members over time, may still be a shrinking group, if most members do not participate in the group's activities. In addition, most previous studies treat all group members as equals when performing group evolution analysis. We know that groups are often led by a smaller set of leaders who have considerable influence over other group members. In our analysis we take both issues into consideration. For settings that allow multiple group memberships and do not have group quitting events we devise a membership score that will reflect participation level of individual members and prolificness/ranking of individual members.

We perform our analysis on two different types of social networks, a massive multiplayer online role-playing game (World of Warcraft [WoW]) and a large co-authorship network (DBLP). In the first dataset we tackle the scenario of an individual belonging to at most one group (a guild, in WoW terminology) at any given point in time and the second tackles the more general scenario of an individual belonging to multiple groups at any given point in time. Moreover for the second scenario, we also devise a membership score that we believe is more reflective of the stability/growth of a group (as compared to the number of members in the group). This membership score can be easily generalized for a host of social networks. Though the membership score was devised to encapsulate the growth (or lack of) of a group it can also be used to compare groups, as we will demonstrate later. We have built classifiers based on a diverse set of features to predict whether a group will have significant reduction or will remain stable over a period of time.

In our findings regarding the two datasets, we have the following interesting observations:

- We find that the level of diversity has a strong correlation to the stability of the group. In order to keep a group alive, members of the community should vary in terms of expertise, seniority, responsibilities, etc. We also find that the level of activities has a strong predictive power of the group stability. Even when the size of the community stays the same (i.e., not attracting new members), as long as there is a lot of activities within the group the community survives.

- We find that in the case of WoW dataset the age of a community has a strong correlation with the stability of the group — if a guild can sustain itself for a long period of time, it is very likely that the guild does have the essential components necessary for a stable community. On the hand in the DBLP dataset the length of existence does *not* show any correlation with group stability. Whether a conference is old or new does not seem to play a significant role in determining whether it remains stable or shrinks. This observation can be attributed to fact that in WoW there is a lot of churn, whereas in DBLP (or other related social networks) we do not see as much churn.

- For DBLP dataset we observe that the 'average prolificness' feature is important. The correlation shows that groups with more prolific members are more likely to remain stable and groups with more dedicated authors (i.e. authors who continually contribute) are more likely to remain stable. Thus such members play an important role in maintaining the stability of the group.

The paper is organized as follows. We first briefly review literatures on detection of communities and studies of community evolution. We then provide an overview of the datasets, followed by definition of measures used to label groups as stable or shrinking. We then move on to define a range of features that we compute for both datasets. We will also analyze the best set of features that are useful for our prediction task. The later sections present predictive models to predict group stability. We conclude with a discussion of the important factors for predictions and an outline of future work.

2. RELATED WORK

Various methods have been used to detect communities. See the survey paper [21] for a thorough review. Earlier approaches define some measurement of importance of each edges and then define communities by either incrementally adding edges in the order of decreasing importance [25]; or removing edges in the order of increasing importance [14]. This leads to a hierarchical partitioning of the nodes, called a *dendrogram*. Classical clustering techniques are also used here, including k-means clustering, multi-dimensional scaling, principal component analysis, etc. Same for methods that identify clique-like components, or find min-cuts in graphs. In our datasets, community structures are formally defined and explicitly given, hence there is no need to detect them.

When time-stamped data is available it is natural to ask how the communities or groups evolve over time. In the literature the community evolution has been modeled as a diffusion process – ties spanning group boundaries can possibly influence individuals to join the community. Granovetter [15] pointed out that diffusion often benefits from 'weak ties' and indicated that the graph structure may be a critical factor in deciding whether and how fast a community grows. Recent studies, such as by Centola and Macy [10] and from Facebook datasets [24], revealed that one may require multiple contacts within the group to join the community and the diversity of these contacts actually matters. A couple of the analysis using real world datasets show conflicting and intriguing observations that high clustering property inside a community may at the same time both attracts new members and prevents overall growth. A very recent paper by Kairam *et al.* [18] pointed out that new members may join through diffusion (as in the case of being influenced by some friends), or may join the community without having any social ties inside the community, classified as non-diffusion growth. They further point out that in diffusion-based growth, the clustering does help. But groups that only grow through diffusion may not reach large size. Thus non-diffusion growth is important to create large communities.

Most of existing work on community evolution focused on the initial stage of community evolution, when growth is in the dominant form. Our work, on the other hand, mainly looks at the final stage of community evolution, i.e., how a community dies or falls apart. The closest work to ours is the research on group formation in large social networks [6]. They build classifiers based on a range of network-based features to firstly, predict whether an individual will join a community and secondly, to predict the growth of a community. They achieve reasonably good (70 − 75%) accuracy for both prediction tasks. The point to note is that members never quit communities in their model. Thus, for the second prediction task they are predicting from the standpoint of growth. Our work is complementary to their work. In our previous work [20] we have built models to predict if and when an individual is going to quit his/her group, and whether this quitting event will inflict substantial damage on the group. We quantify damage as influencing many of your friends to also quit the group after you do so, thereby leading to a large loss in group membership numbers. In [20] we analyzed quitting from an individual perspective, while this paper addresses the quitting behavior from a group perspective.

3. ANALYSIS ON WORLD OF WARCRAFT

3.1 Dataset

To explore group stability dynamics, we use data from a previous World of Warcraft (WoW) study [13]. WoW is a multiplayer online game in which users interact, collaborate with, or fight against each other. A web-based crawler was deployed to log in-game activities based on the API specified by Blizzard Entertainment, the producer of WoW. The crawler periodically issues "/who" requests every 5 to 15 minutes, depending on server load, to get a list of characters currently being played on a given server. We have data that spans six months, from November 2010 to May 2011. The data is sometimes referred to as the WoW census. Three types of servers are logged: player-vs-environment (PvE), player-vs-player (PvP), and role playing (RP). The servers may present players with different game tasks, but are otherwise identical in terms of game organization and support. In the game there is a social group setting named a 'guild'. Players of the same guild often organize to join battles, gain honors or even monetary returns. In WoW, one player can only join one guild and to join another he/she has to quit the former guild. Overall we observed more than 470,000 unique characters forming over 15000 guilds, scattered on three servers: Eitrigg (a PvE server), Cenarion Circle (a RP server), and Bleeding Hollow (a PvP server).

Social interaction may be an important influencing factor in guild-quitting events. First, we define a friendship network among guild members, where nodes are characters, and edges indicate co-occurrence within gaming zones — if two characters were observed at the same game location (zone in WoW), an edge is added between the corresponding nodes. A gaming zone is a predefined area in the WoW map. A zone can be small or large in size & can contain varying number of characters at any given point in time, depending on several parameters in the game. The underlying assumption is that if characters co-occur in a gaming zone, it is highly likely that the characters are collaborating on a gaming activity. Two possible limitations are noted: (1) there are some gaming zones that are not necessarily associated with any gaming activity, for instance, characters are often left "AFK" (Away from keyboard) in the game's main cities before or at the end of a play session. In this case, the geographic proximity does not necessarily reflect any kind of joint activity. In our data logger, we remove such ambiguous zones from the co-occurrence criteria. (2) Characters may co-occur by chance. This is treated as noise in the social network graph. The basic assumption is that with a large amount of accumulated gaming data, the ties between characters driven by real social interaction will dominate.

Secondly, we add a membership network to indicate the affiliation between characters and guilds. An important point to remember is that a character can belong to only one guild at given point in time. Thus in order to join another guild he/she is required to quit his/her current guild. Nodes fall into two categories: (1) guild nodes, and (2) character nodes. If a character is observed appearing in a guild, an affiliation edge is added. The overall network is the super-imposition of the friendship and the affiliation networks. It is an undirected multi-graph i.e. it allows for multiple edges between any two nodes in the network.

Table 1 lists some statistics in the raw social networks for the three servers. Guild quitting events are fairly common — around 20 − 32% of characters quit from a guild at least once in our observation period. In constructing our social network using the co-occurence heuristic, we eliminate characters that do not join any guilds or collaborate with any other characters (i.e. characters that do not have any social component). Such characters are generally played by new players at initial levels of the game. These characters are uninteresting from the point of view of the problem we seek to tackle and thus can be ignored from our analysis. Similarly we ignore degenerate guilds (i.e. guilds which are observed to have no members over our entire 6 month time-period) from our analysis.

3.2 Gauging Group Stability

It is often of general interest to understand the stability issues of social groups, for instance, the stability of a company, an informal organization, or a user group. In WoW and other MMORGs, as mentioned earlier, guilds have high turn-out rates. In our observation data of over 6 months, some guilds live throughout (188 days), but many other do not survive very long. The average guild lifespan is 82.57 days, with a large standard deviation of 71.25 days. This begs the question, "Why are some guilds more stable than others? In other words, what constitutes a stable guild?"

Guild stability may be related to a variety of factors, some of which have been identified from social psychology studies. In this section, we take a data driven approach — "Can we identify stability or instability patterns from the data?"

It turns out that since a character can only belong to one guild at any given point in time, computing the number of guild members at regular intervals should give us a good idea of how the guild evolves. Futhermore computing the percentage of increase/decrease in the number of members over the previous interval would then give us an accurate idea of whether, (a) the guild is stable (i.e. there is a minimal percentage decrease or a percentage increase in the number of members), or (b) the guild is shrinking (i.e. there is a substantial percentage decrease in the number of members).

To put things more formally, given that a guild G has m_1 members at time snapshot t_1 and m_2 members at time snapshot t_2 ($t_1 < t_2$) the percentage change in membership is defined as $\delta = \frac{m_2}{m_1} - 1$. We could then label a guild as being in the stable or shrinking phase at time t_2 as follows,

$$label = \begin{cases} stable, & \text{if } \delta > -0.15 \\ shrinking, & \text{if } \delta \leq -0.15 \end{cases} \quad (1)$$

Thus we label a guild as shrinking if it loses 15% or more of its members as compared to the previous interval, otherwise the guild is labeled as being stable. In our experiments, we have experimented with several values of δ. Results were comparable when δ ranged between $[0.10, 0.20]$. For $0 < \delta < 0.10$, accuracy was reduced due to addition of noisy/fringe samples to the "shrinking" set. For $\delta > 0.20$, we again observe a drop in accuracy due to vastly fewer "shrinking" samples. Thus, in our experiments, we use a threshold of $\delta = 0.15$ to label whether a guild is stable or shrinking at any given point in time.

3.3 Guild-Level Features

In order to be able to model group stability dynamics, we consider a range of features that span different categories. Almost all of the features are efficient (with linear running time) to compute thereby allowing to compute them at regular intervals & also making our approach scalable to large networks.

Several types of guild-level features may be important in modeling guild stability. We loosely categorize them into three categories: (1) guild composition, (2) game activities aggregated over the guild population, and (3) the structure of social network graph.

Guild composition features reflect diversity or homogeneity of guild members. In WoW, guilds need to have a certain span in skills and roles. For instance, a healthy blend of experts and novices may be important to a guild's long-term survival. Novice players can mature in the game and take over if an expert leaves the guild. In addition, WoW activities are designed to encourage collaboration across roles. Characters are categorized into 10 classes (warriors, paladins, hunters, priests, death knights, etc) with different capabilities (DPSs to cause damage, tanks to contain damage, and healers to heal damage). Coordination among the classes and capabilities is

Statistic	Eitrigg	Bleeding Hollow	Cenarion Circle
Number of Characters	51,224	72,108	47,499
Number of Guilds	2906	3425	2911
Number of Friendship Edges	577,250	937,989	673,502
Number of Membership Edges	1,870,327	2,775,401	2,154,287
Average Collaboration Time (hrs.)	1.73 ± 1.09	1.70 ± 1.10	1.79 ± 1.08
% Characters changing Guild	26.53	32.28	20.69

Table 1: Overall Network Statistics for World of Warcraft

essential to the guild's success. There is a "sweet spot" of diversity, where, a certain degree is desirable, while excessive diversity may be a sign of lack of management and may imply poor guild performance. To investigate the effect on guild stability, we compute the following guild composition features:

- Number of guild members: The size of the guild at time t.

- Length of existence (in days): This feature calculates the number of days since the guild came into existence.

- Average level of guild members: This measures the average level of characters who are members of this guild at time t.

- Standard deviation of character levels of guild members: This feature measures how consistent good/bad characters are across the guild. A smaller standard deviation indicates a bunch of members with equal skill sets and a higher standard deviation indicates a bunch of members with varying skill sets.

- Percentage of character classes present: A character can belong to any one of around 10 character classes. This metric measures whether all character classes are represented amongst its members.

- Entropy of character class distribution: This feature calculates the entropy of the class distribution for the given guild.

- Entropy of character category distribution: There are 3 categories of characters in the game, DPS, Healers and Tanks. Each character class can perform one or more of these category roles. This feature calculates the entropy for category distribution within a guild.

Aggregated game activity features measures the overall game engagement across guild members. We contrast the game activities within the guild and prior to joining the guild. The former is indicative of the devotedness to the guild, while the latter measures the overall engagement in the entire WoW game.

- Average playing time within guild & prior to joining the guild: The features calculate average playing time of all guild members in the current guild and prior to joining the guild respectively.

- Average collaboration time within guild & prior to joining the guild: The features calculate the average collaboration time of all guild members in the current guild and prior to joining the guild respectively.

- Average collaboration coefficient within the guild & prior to joining the guild: The collaboration coefficient for a guild member is defined as the ratio of his/her collaboration time to playing time. These two features compute the average collaboration coefficient across all guild members by considering collaborations within the guild and prior to joining the guild respectively.

We suspect that guild topological structure may have implications on guild stability. Guilds exhibit remarkable diversity in topology, some guilds have a hierarchical structure, where some nodes (typically guild leaders) are of central importance, while other guilds are formed of closely knitted friendship circles, where nodes are more evenly connected. One may speculate that a star topology may be less stable since the removal of the center node may cause the whole graph to fall apart. In the topological features, we measure the average clustering coefficient, which is a metric of degree to which nodes in a graph tends to cluster together. Based on the concept, we compute the following topological features:

- Average clustering coefficient of guild members: We measure the clustering coefficient at each guild member node and then calculate the average of this clustering coefficient across all guild members. The clustering coefficient at each node is also known as the local clustering coefficient [26] and quantifies how close its neighbors are to being a clique.

- Average clustering coefficient of guild members within the guild: The clustering coefficient calculated in this case only takes into consideration the graph induced by all members of the guild.

- Entropy of degree distribution: This feature is a good measure of diversity in node connectivity.

3.3.1 Feature Importance & Correlation

The observation data is organized into temporal snapshots, sampled every 4-day interval. Overall there are about 63000 guild-snapshots. Guild features (composition, game activity, and structural) are computed for each guild-snapshots. Furthermore, we label the data samples as shrinking or stable guilds. If a guild will lose more than 15% of its membership in 4 weeks, the guild at the current time will be labeled as "shrinking", otherwise the guild is labeled as "stable". This simplifies the guild stability problem into binary classification. Thus we are trying to predict 4-weeks into the future as to whether a guild will remain stable or will shrivel.

Random sampling is used for drawing training samples. There are more shrinking guilds in the data than stable guilds, hence an uncontrolled random sampling may cause the classifier to overfit shrinking guilds. We control sampling to produced balanced classes, 2000 samples from each class. We would like to understand which features are important in modeling guild stability. Table 2 reports the correlation coefficient between each feature and the class labels (1 for shrinking, 0 for stable) for Eitrigg. Results for Bleeding Hollow & Cenarion Circle qualitatively agree with these results and hence we omit them for the sake of brevity.

- Among the guild composition features — Large guilds tend to be more stable. Guilds which have survived for longer periods tend to continue to survive. These agree with empirical observations and intuition. Average member level does not seem to matter much, however, diversity seems to play an

Category	Feature	Correlation coefficient
Composition	number of guild members	**-0.1213**
	length of existence	**-0.1501**
	average level of members	0.0037
	standard deviation of member levels	-0.0649
	percentage of character classes present	**-0.1153**
	entropy of character class distribution	-0.0707
	entropy of character category distribution	0.0087
Game stats	average playing time in guild	**-0.1038**
	average playing time prior to guild	0.0053
	average collaboration time in guild	**-0.1025**
	average collaboration time prior to guild	-0.0019
	average collaboration coefficient in guild	**-0.1026**
	average collaboration coefficient prior to guild	0.0067
Structural	average clustering coefficient	**-0.1021**
	average clustering coefficient in guild	**-0.1103**
	entropy of degree distribution	**-0.1288**

Table 2: Correlation coefficient between class labels and feature values. Correlation coefficients with absolute value exceeding 0.10 are marked in bold-face fonts.

important role. For instance, standard deviation of member levels are negatively correlated with guild shrinkage, indicating that diversity seems to help guild stability. Likewise, diversity in character classes is important. Guilds with more number of character classes present survive better.

- Among the game activity features — In-guild activity matters a lot. The more guild members collaborate and play, the more stable the guild is. The activity of guild members prior to joining the guild does not seem to matter at all.

- Among the structural features — All features seems to be very strong features. Balance and diversity in topology helps to improve overall guild stability.

Another common method for assessing the relative importance of features is the mutual information between a feature and the class label. This indicates how informative a feature is. We use Weka [16], a machine learning toolbox. It provides information gain computation and rank the features. In descending order of information gain, the top ten features are listed in Table 3. Compared to correlation coefficient analysis, the information gain ranking is more precise. It does not rely on single-mode distribution, which is an inherent limitation of correlation coefficient. However, the information gain does not reveal the insight that positive/negative correlation reveals. Qualitatively, Tables 2 and 3 are in rough agreement.

3.4 Predicting Guild Stability

Given the feature set and the class labels (stable or shrinking), we want to predict whether a group or community is likely to remain stable or will start shrinking over a period of time. We experiment with a range of supervised learning methods to achieve this.

With the feature set, we are able to predict guild stability with good accuracy. For instance, using guild size feature alone (number of members) and simple classification such as Naive Bayes, we can predict shrinking or stable labels with about 59% accuracy. Using two features for prediction, the number of members and length of existence, Naive Bayes produces a prediction accuracy of roughly 62%.

Table 4 summarizes the result of guild stability prediction using a variety of classification methods. The testing set is balanced, where

Rank	Feature	Category
1	number of members	C
2	entropy of class distribution	C
3	percentage of classes present	C
4	average collaboration time within guild	G
5	length of existence	C
6	average playing time within guild	G
7	entropy of degree distribution	S
8	standard deviation of member levels	C
9	average clustering coefficient within guild	S
10	average clustering coefficient	S

Table 3: Top ten features, ranked in descending order of information gain. In the category column, C stands for composition, G stands for game activity, and S stands for structural.

an equal amount of testing samples from each class are randomly drawn from the observation data. The results are reported after a 10-fold cross validation process.

Classification methods include the following, with the first three methods serving as benchmarks.

- ZeroR baseline: It is a degenerated classifier, always predicting a shrinking guild regardless of the features.

- Naive Bayes: It assumes that all features are independent given the class label, and constructs a probabilistic model for each feature separately. The classifier computes likelihood from all features and chooses the maximum likelihood class label as the classification result.

- Decision stump: It is an one-level decision tree making a prediction with just a single input feature. In our training data, the single feature is average collaboration time within guild. If it is more than 5.002 hours, the guild is predicted to be stable. Despite its simplicity, the prediction accuracy is decent, in the 60 − 70% range.

Method	Classification Accuracy	Precision	Recall	F-measure
ZeroR baseline	50%	0.25	0.5	0.333
Naive Bayes	63.74%	0.682	0.637	0.614
Decision Stump	62.10%	0.651	0.621	0.601
J48 decision tree	78.86%	0.790	0.789	0.789
Bagging	81.98%	0.822	0.821	0.820
Random Forest	84.78%	0.848	0.848	0.848

Table 4: Guild Stability Prediction Results

- J48 tree [22]: It progressively grows a decision tree by identifying the attribute that discriminates the training set most clearly according to an information gain criterion. The tree branch terminates if the training samples at the leave are homogeneous. The prediction accuracy of J48 tree is close to 79%.

- Bagging [7]: Bagging is an ensemble method which improves the classification accuracy through sampling and model averaging. We get an accuracy of close to 82% using Bagging.

- Random Forest [8]: Similar to bagging, random forest is also an ensemble method. It builds a library of decision trees from a set of random samples. Each decision tree is grown by randomly choosing the variables to split data upon. The classifier predicts class label by average voting from the decision trees. This method works well when there is sufficient training data. The accuracy is around 85%.

One hypothesis regarding guild stability is the continuity — if a guild has been shrinking recently, it is anticipated to continue the loosing streak. This hypothesis has been raised in the literature of social network analysis. To validate this hypothesis, we added an additional feature to capture the temporal aspect, i.e., the difference between the guild size in the current snapshot and the previous one. Positive value indicates a growing guild, while negative value indicates a shrinking guild. We have computed this temporal feature for all guild-snapshots. The correlation coefficient with the class label is -0.0382. The negative correlation is expected. Correlation appears very mild, indicating that past history is not a strong indicator of future trend. Furthermore, including this feature in the feature set for classification does not improve accuracy either. Essentially guild stability can be predicted from the guild features listed above (composition, activity, and structure), and temporal continuity seems to provide little additional information. Table 4 gives the detailed prediction results; it can clearly seen that we are able to achieve high accuracy (85%) in predicting guild stability on the Eitrigg server. Similar analysis is performed on Bleeding Hollow, a player-vs-player (PvP) server, and Cenarion Circle, a role playing (RP) server. We achieve qualitatively similar results for the other two servers; for instance, the random forest classifier produces a prediction accuracy of 81% on Bleeding Hollow, and 84.3% on Cenarion Circle.

4. ANALYSIS ON DBLP DATA

4.1 Dataset

DBLP [1], our second dataset provides bibliographic information on major computer science journals and conferences. Each publication is accompanied by its title, list of authors and conference/journal of publication. For the purposes of our study, we view DBLP as a social network of researchers who co-author papers at different conferences or in different journals. Thus the data resembles the social structure of our WoW dataset; the friendship network is defined by linking people that have co-authored a paper and the conferences/journals serve as groups where these friendships are formed. Table 5 show the size of our data and the network that we construct from the raw data. An important distinction between the two datasets is the group membership requirement; in the DBLP network an author can often be a member of multiple groups at any given point in time though with varying commitments.

Statistic for DBLP	
Number of Publications	1,607,524
Number of Authors	1,105,457
Number of Conferences/Journals	7073
Number of Friendship Edges	7,367,343
Number of Membership Edges	5,084,657

Table 5: Overall Network Statistics for DBLP

4.2 Gauging Group Stability

As mentioned earlier there is no concept of an author quitting a group in the DBLP dataset; on the contrary an author is a typically a member of several groups. This is a more commonly occuring scenario in most online social networks as compared to the group membership dynamics of World of Warcraft. The DBLP dataset is also used in [6] to study the formation and evolution of groups. Due to the lack of an explicit quitting action most studies have focussed on evolution from the standpoint of growth. We take a different approach when tackling datasets such as DBLP. Even though an author can belong to multiple groups his activities in individual groups can vary significantly over the course of time. Thus we need a measure that can quantify the involvement of a person in a community. We believe such a measure should encapsulate the following properties,

- A person that contributes frequently to a group should have a higher involvement score as opposed to a person that contributes rarely.

- Recent involvement/activities in a community should be weighted higher than past activities in the community.

- The prolificness of the author should be reflected in the measure of involvement.

Since we have timestamped (year of publication) data detailing the activities (publications) of a person (author) in a community (conference/journal), we can define a measure that reflects all of the above properties by adapting the exponential summarization kernel described in [23]. Let $N_1, N_2 \ldots N_t$ denote the number of publications of an author in a given group at discrete time intervals $t_1, t_2 \ldots t_t$ & $P_{A,t}$ denote the standing/prolificness of the author at time t, the "Involvement Score" of the author A in the given group

G at time t is defined as,

$$I_{A,G,t} = \begin{cases} (1-\theta)I_{A,G,t-1} + \theta N_t P_{A,t} & \text{if } t > t_0 \\ \theta N_t P_{A,t} & \text{if } t = t_0 \end{cases} \quad (2)$$

where t_0 is defined as the initial time and θ controls the rate of decay. The prolificness of an author can be defined in several ways; we define it as the ratio of the total number of publications the author has at time t to the total number of publications the most prolific author has at time t. Prolificness ranges between $[0, 1]$ and serves as a way of determining standing of the author. As mentioned before, the standing can be computed in different ways, for example, total citation count being another effective measure of calculating prolificness. However, the DBLP dataset has no way of determining citation counts, experimenting with other prolificness measures is out of scope of this paper. Table 6 demonstrates the use of the "Involvement Score" measure that we define to uncover trends in publications for prominent authors.

Year	Top-3 Conferences		
1996	STOC	FOCS	SODA
1998	STOC	DM&KD	VLDB
2000	STOC	FOCS	JComputing
2002	JCSS	STOC	JACM
2004	FOCS	JACM	STOC
2006	FOCS	KDD	IPSN
2008	JComputing	KDD	EC
2011	ICWSM	WWW	FOCS
2012	WWW	ICWSM	WSDM

Table 6: Top-3 conferences based on Involvement Score for Jon Kleinberg. One can clearly see a change in the trend, from publishing in Theory conferences (yellow) to publishing in Data Mining conferences (green).

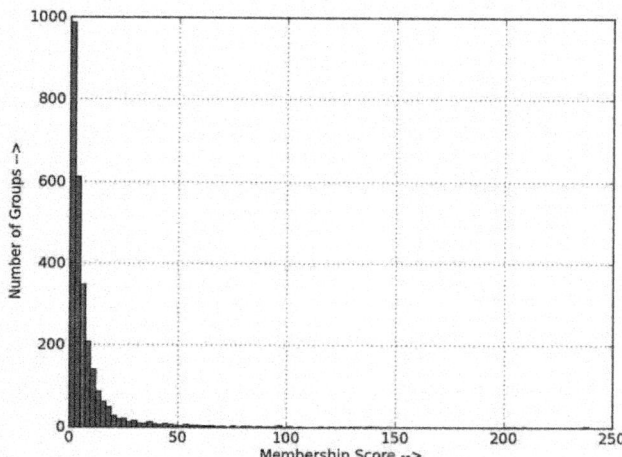

Figure 1: Histogram of membership scores for groups in 2011.

Now that we have defined a measure in Equation 2 to quantify the involvement of a person in a community, we proceed to define "Membership Score" of a group G at time t as the sum of involvement scores for all it's members. Formally,

$$MS_{G,t} = \sum_{A \in G} I_{A,G,t} \quad (3)$$

The membership score that we define has the following desirable properties,

- A group with more number of regularly contributing members has a higher membership score as compared to a group with large number of infrequently active members.

- A group that has more members of repute/standing will have a higher membership score as compared to a group with fewer prolific members.

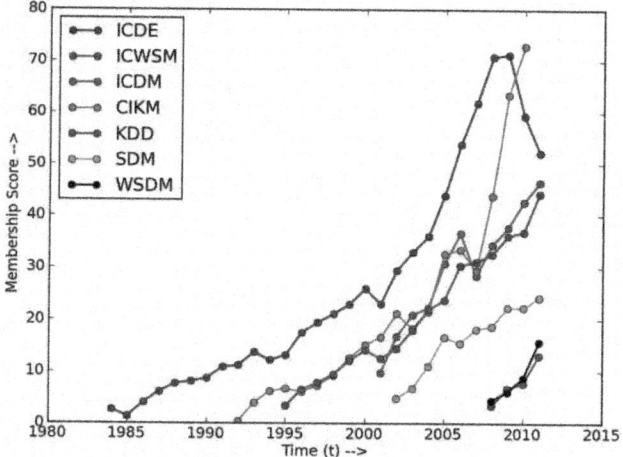

Figure 2: Membership score across time for well-known Data Mining Conferences.

Conference	Publications	H-index	Membership Score
ICDE	1303	35	52.15
KDD	670	30	44.20
CIKM	1348	26	95.81
ICDM	1197	18	46.39
SDM	338	18	24.28
ICWSM	221	18	13.06
WSDM	199	18	15.69

Table 7: Top-7 conferences in Data Mining with their Membership Scores

Figure 2 plots the membership score for 7 well-known conferences in the Data Mining area across the length of their existence. In order to test the efficacy of the membership score, we compute the membership score in 2011 for top-7 conferences in the Data Mining area in the last 5 years (as ranked by H-index [17] using Microsoft Academic Search [4]). Table 7 shows that the two measures are in rough agreement with each other. It is important to point out that we do NOT intend to advocate the membership score as a replacement for H-index (and such related measures). The membership score is able to capture group dynamics and hence can be used to gauge group stability. We compute the membership score for a group at regular time intervals. Thus computing the percentage increase/decrease in the membership score over the previous interval would then give us an accurate idea of whether a group is stable or shrinking. Given that a group G has membership score of ms_1 at time snapshot t_1 and membership score of ms_2 at time snapshot t_2 ($t_1 < t_2$) the percentage change in membership score is defined as $\delta = \frac{ms_2}{ms_1} - 1$. We could then label a group as being in the stable or

Category	Feature	Correlation coefficient
Group	number of group members	**-0.3008**
	length of existence	0.0499
	membership score	**-0.1948**
	average prolificness	**-0.5443**
Activities	average number of collaborations within group	**-0.6202**
	average number of collaborations outside group	**-0.4874**
	total number of collaborations within group	**-0.2293**
	total number of collaborations outside group	**-0.2687**
	average number of publications within group	**-0.7245**
	average number of publications outside group	**-0.5216**
	total number of publications within group	**-0.2670**
	total number of publications outside group	**-0.2732**
	average member loyalty coefficient	**-0.6114**
Structural	average clustering coefficient	**-0.6477**
	average clustering coefficient in group	**-0.6705**
	entropy of degree distribution	**-0.7144**

Table 8: Correlation coefficient between class labels and feature values. Correlation coefficients with absolute value exceeding 0.10 are marked in bold-face fonts.

shrinking phase at time t_2 as defined in equation 1. In our experiments we compute the membership scores at yearly intervals (i.e. $t_2 - t_1 = 1yr$).

4.3 Conference-Level Features

Rank	Feature	Category
1	total number of publications within group	A
2	number of members	G
3	total number of collaborations within group	A
4	average prolificness	G
5	average number of publications within group	A
6	total number of publications outside group	A
7	average number of collaborations within group	A
8	total number of collaborations outside group	A
9	average member loyalty coefficient	A
10	entropy of degree distribution	S

Table 9: Top ten features, ranked in descending order of information gain. In the category column, G stands for group-specific, A stands for activity features, and S stands for structural.

In order to model group stability for the DBLP dataset we consider a range of features that can be broadly classified into three categories: (1) conference/group-specific, (2) publications/activities-specific, and (3) structural features. The following is a list of group specific features,

- Number of members: The size of the group at time t.
- Length of existence (in years): This feature calculates the number of years since the conference/journal came into existence.
- Membership Score: Membership Score of group at time t as defined in 3.

- Average Prolificness: Average Prolificness of group at time t, where prolificness is a measure of standing/repute for an individual. It ranges between $[0, 1]$.

We compute the following list of features to capture the activities of members in a particular group,

- Total & Average Number of Collaborations Within & Outside Group: These features capture the number of collaborations involving the group members. These collaborations can be within the given group or in some other groups.
- Total & Average Number of Publications Within & Outside Group: These features capture the number of publications for group members. Again an individual may have publications within and outside the given group.
- Average Member Loyalty Coefficient: Loyalty Coefficient for a group member is defined as the ratio of the number of publications that member has in the given group to the overall number of publications of the member. It ranges between $[0, 1]$ and is a measure of the loyalty of the member towards a particular group he/she is a member of.

Following is a list of features intended to capture the connectivity information of a group,

- Average clustering coefficient of group members: We measure the clustering coefficient at each group member node and then calculate the average of this clustering coefficient across all group members.
- Average clustering coefficient of group members within the group: The clustering coefficient calculated in this case only takes into consideration the graph induced by all members of the guild.
- Entropy of degree distribution: This feature is a good measure of diversity in node connectivity.

4.3.1 Feature Importance & Correlation

We perform similar analysis as performed on the WoW dataset. We compute features along with class labels (1 for shrinking and 0 for stable) at yearly intervals since most conferences/journals have

Class	Classification Accuracy	Precision	Recall	F-measure
Stable		0.878	0.942	0.909
Shrinking	90.55%	0.937	0.869	0.902
Weighted Average		0.908	0.906	0.905

Table 10: Group Stability Prediction Results using Bagging

an yearly cycle of publication. Thus, we are trying to predict one year into the future as to whether a group will remain stable or not. This results in around 40,000 feature samples; 22.51% of these samples have "shrinking" class labels & 77.49% of the samples have "stable" class labels. In order to avoid overfitting we draw equal number of samples from both classes. Table 8 reports the correlation coefficient between each feature and the class labels (1 for shrinking, 0 for stable) for the DBLP dataset.

Assessing the importance of features by computing the Information Gain, the top ten features are listed in table 9. Tables 8 and 9 are in general agreement about the important features required for the predictiont task.

4.4 Predicting Group Stability

Again, we will use supervised learning techniques and apply them to our feature set to see if we can predict group stability. Due to the unbalanced class problem, we randomly draw equal number of samples from both the classes ($\approx$ 9000 samples per class). Table 10 shows the accuracy achieved by using Bagging (we achieve similar accuracy levels by using Decision Trees and Random Forests). Bagging achieves the best accuracy of 90.55% with a MAE of 0.1402 and a MSE of 0.2601; proof of the fact that our feature based approach produces significantly high accuracy in predicting group stability.

5. INTERNAL CONNECTEDNESS OF FRIENDS

The study of Backstrom et al [6] is amongst the first to comprehensively analyse evolution of groups using real-world social networking data. They demonstrated that the probability of joining increases as the density of linkage increases among the individual's friends in the community. These results are supported by arguments based on social capital [11, 12] that suggest that there is a trust advantage to having friends in a community who know each other. An individual joining such a community is assured of the fact that such a community is a close-knit family of members who know most of the other members.

At the same time Backstrom et al. pointed out that cogent arguments [15, 9] also support the opposite finding; this theory based on weak ties suggested that there is an informational advantage to having loosely connected members. This provides an individual multiple "independent" perspectives; he/she could join based on any one of the ways.

Empirical evidence based on the Live Journal [3] dataset used by Backstrom et al. made them conclude that trust advantage had a stronger effect than informational advantage. Kairam et al. [18] shed further light on the group evolution and growth process. They too touched upon this problem; empirically they came to the same conclusion i.e. probability of joining increases as the density of linkage increases among the individual's friends in the community. They also tried to solve the paradoxical finding of why highly clustered groups tend to have lower growth rates overall. Their findings suggested that some groups grow by appealing to common interests and identities (non-diffusion growth) while other groups grow by virtue of its extra-group connections (diffusion growth). Furthermore they conclude that if a group relies on diffusion growth its scope for growth is limited to the number of ties its members have to non-members. Thus such groups will eventually suffer from lack of new members. Thus, even though high clustering in a group will lead to increased membership it will also lead to diminishing returns (with respect to growth) down the road. In their findings (based on the Ning [5] dataset), they are able to show that groups that grow to small sizes are those that rely on diffusion growth whereas groups that grow to large sizes are those that rely more on non-diffusion growth.

We try to validate the theories and findings put forward in [6, 18] using our datasets as follows,

- WoW Dataset: We compute the correlation between the features "average clustering coefficient in guild" and "number of new members". The "average clustering coefficient in guild" allows us to quantify the density of linkage amongst a guild's members. The correlation coefficient is -0.0584 i.e. weakly negatively correlated which tends to suggest support for informational advantage. This is an interesting finding which hasn't been observed in previous studies. We also compute the correlation between "average clustering coefficient in guild" and "percentage change in number of members over the previous snapshot". This correlation comes in at -0.00959 which indicates that density of linkage does not play any role in determining guild growth.

- DBLP Dataset: Again we compute the correlation between the features "average clustering coefficient in guild" and "number of newly active members". The value of correlation is 0.2530 which shows support for trust advantage over informational advantage. The correlation between "average clustering coefficient in guild" and "percentage change in membership score over the previous snapshot" turns out to be 0.0061 indicating again that density of linkage does not play any role in determining guild growth.

Our findings indicate as far as WoW data is concerned, individuals join guilds due to common interests and identities; thus guilds in WoW are characterized by non-diffusion growth. On the other hand in the DBLP data most of the growth can be characterized as diffusion based growth. These findings are also due to the nature of the social networks. WoW is a multiplayer game where individuals work towards an objective of being successful at playing the game. Gamers are likely to join guilds based on common objectives rather than based on trust factors. On the other hand DBLP data is a co-authorship network where edges indicate collaborations at a particular conference or in a given journal. Thus in this case links amongst an individual's friends indicates stronger endorsement for that group from your peers.

6. CONCLUSION

Our analysis has shown that it is possible to predict group stability with high accuracy using a range of features that describes the group composition, activities within the group & structural aspects of a group. We have experimented with two large social networking datasets and have been able to achieve similar accuracy levels on both datasets. We have also defined an efficient measure of gauging group membership in scenarios where a person is likely a member of several groups. Our analysis can easily be extended to other online social networks and is also scalable to large networks. The study also shows that it is important to choose features from multiple perspectives, in fact combining diverse features is essential to predictor performance.

Acknowledgements

This research is funded in part by DARPA/ADAMS program under contract W911NF-11-C-0216. Any opinions, findings, and conclusions or recommendations in this material are those of the authors and do not necessarily reflect the views of the government funding agencies. We would also like to acknowledge contributions from our colleagues: Nicholas Ducheneaut, Nick Yee, and Oliver Brdiczka (PARC) for providing WoW game census data and insights about game dynamics, and Hossam Sharara (University of Maryland, College Park) for help on processing WoW data and social network analysis.

7. REFERENCES

[1] The dblp computer science bibliography. http://dblp.uni-trier.de.
[2] Facebook. https://www.facebook.com.
[3] Live journal. http://www.livejournal.com.
[4] Microsoft academic search. http://academic.research.microsoft.com.
[5] Ning. http://www.ning.com.
[6] L. Backstrom, D. Huttenlocher, J. Kleinberg, and X. Lan. Group formation in large social networks: membership, growth, and evolution. In *Proceedings of the 12th ACM SIGKDD international conference on Knowledge discovery and data mining*, KDD '06, pages 44–54, New York, NY, USA, 2006. ACM.
[7] L. Breiman. Bagging predictors. *Machine learning*, 24(2):123–140, 1996.
[8] L. Breiman. Random forests. *Machine learning*, 45(1):5–32, 2001.
[9] R. Burt. *Structural holes: The social structure of competition*. Harvard University Press, 1995.
[10] D. Centola and M. Macy. Complex Contagions and the Weakness of Long Ties. *American Journal of Sociology*, 113(3):702–734, Nov. 2007.
[11] J. Coleman. Social capital in the creation of human capital. *American journal of sociology*, pages 95–120, 1988.
[12] J. Coleman. *Foundations of social theory*. Belknap Press, 1994.
[13] N. Ducheneaut, N. Yee, E. Nickell, and R. J. Moore. The life and death of online gaming communities: a look at guilds in world of warcraft. In *Proceedings of the SIGCHI Conference on Human Factors in Computing Systems*, CHI '07, pages 839–848, New York, NY, USA, 2007. ACM.
[14] M. Girvan and M. E. J. Newman. Community structure in social and biological networks. *Proceedings of the National Academy of Sciences*, 99(12):7821–7826, 2002.
[15] M. Granovetter. The strength of weak ties. *American journal of sociology*, pages 1360–1380, 1973.
[16] M. Hall, E. Frank, G. Holmes, B. Pfahringer, P. Reutemann, and I. Witten. The weka data mining software: an update. *ACM SIGKDD Explorations Newsletter*, 11(1):10–18, 2009.
[17] J. Hirsch. An index to quantify an individual's scientific research output. *Proceedings of the National Academy of Sciences of the United states of America*, 102(46):16569, 2005.
[18] S. Kairam, D. Wang, and J. Leskovec. The life and death of online groups: Predicting group growth and longevity. In *Proceedings of the fifth ACM international conference on Web search and data mining*, pages 673–682. ACM, 2012.
[19] A. Mislove, M. Marcon, K. P. Gummadi, P. Druschel, and B. Bhattacharjee. Measurement and analysis of online social networks. In *Proceedings of the 7th ACM SIGCOMM conference on Internet measurement*, IMC '07, pages 29–42, New York, NY, USA, 2007. ACM.
[20] A. Patil, J. Liu, B. Price, H. Sharara, and O. Brdiczka. Modeling destructive group dynamics in on-line gaming communities. In *Proceedings of the 6th International AAAI Conference on Weblogs and Social Media*, ICWSM '12, Dublin, Ireland, June 2012.
[21] M. Porter, J. Onnela, and P. Mucha. Communities in networks. *Notices of the AMS*, 56(9):1082–1097, 2009.
[22] J. R. Quinlan. *C4. 5: programs for machine learning*, volume 1. Morgan kaufmann, 1993.
[23] U. Sharan and J. Neville. Temporal-relational classifiers for prediction in evolving domains. In *ICDM '08. Eighth IEEE International Conference on Data Mining, 2008*, pages 540–549. IEEE, 2008.
[24] J. Ugander, L. Backstrom, C. Marlow, and J. Kleinberg. Structural diversity in social contagion. *Proc. National Academy of Sciences*, 109(16):5962–5966, April 2012.
[25] S. Wasserman and K. Faust. *Social Network Analysis: Methods and Applications*. Cambridge University Press, 1994.
[26] D. Watts and S. Strogatz. Collective dynamics of "small-world" networks. *Nature*, 393(6684):440–442, 1998.
[27] E. Zheleva, H. Sharara, and L. Getoor. Co-evolution of social and affiliation networks. In *Proceedings of the 15th ACM SIGKDD international conference on Knowledge discovery and data mining*, KDD '09, pages 1007–1016, New York, NY, USA, 2009. ACM.

Predictive Web Automation Assistant for People with Vision Impairments

Yury Puzis
Charmtech Labs LLC
CEWIT SBU R&D Park
Stony Brook, NY, USA
yury.puzis@gmail.com

Rami Puzis
Information Systems
Engineering
Ben-Gurion University
Beer-Sheva, Israel
puzis@bgu.ac.il

Yevgen Borodin
Charmtech Labs LLC
CEWIT SBU R&D Park
Stony Brook, NY, USA
borodin@charmtechlabs.com

I.V. Ramakrishnan
Charmtech Labs LLC
CEWIT SBU R&D Park
Stony Brook, NY, USA
ram@charmtechlabs.com

ABSTRACT

The Web is far less usable and accessible for people with vision impairments than it is for sighted people. Web automation, a process of automating browsing actions on behalf of the user, has the potential to bridge the divide between the ways sighted and people with vision impairment access the Web; specifically, it can enable the latter to breeze through web browsing tasks that beforehand were slow, hard, or even impossible to accomplish. Typical web automation requires that the user record a macro, a sequence of browsing steps, so that these steps can be automated in the future by replaying the macro. However, for people with vision impairment, automation with macros is not usable.

In this paper, we propose a novel model-based approach that facilitates web automation without having to either record or replay macros. Using the past browsing history and the current web page as the browsing context, the proposed model can predict the most probable browsing actions that the user can do. The model construction is "unsupervised". More importantly, the model is continuously and incrementally updated as history evolves, thereby, ensuring the predictions are not "outdated".

We also describe a novel interface that lets the user focus on the objects associated with the most probable predicted browsing steps (e.g., clicking links and filling out forms), and facilitates automatic execution of the selected steps. A study with 19 blind participants showed that the proposed approach dramatically reduced the interaction time needed to accomplish typical browsing tasks, and the user interface was perceived to be much more usable than the standard screen-reading interfaces.

Categories and Subject Descriptors

H.5.2 [**Information Interfaces and Presentation**]: User Interfaces;
H.5.4 [**Information Interfaces and Presentation**]: Hypertext / Hypermedia - navigation

Keywords

Web; accessibility; blind; low vision; browser; screen-reader; macro; non-visual; automation; model; prediction; sequence alignment; interface agent; adaptive interface;

1. INTRODUCTION

While browsing, blind users rely on screen-readers [1, 2, 3] which are assistive tools that narrate the screen content. Screen-readers enable sequential navigation over the content and provide numerous shortcuts that can speed up the navigation. In most cases, however, even expert users fall back to the most basic navigation, in which they go through items one by one sequentially. In contrast to sighted users, visually-impaired users cannot just "glance" over a webpage whenever there is a need to quickly find the right button to click or text to read. The sequential mode of interaction with webpages and the inability of screen-reader users to determine whether a piece of content is important before they listen to it often results in high cognitive load that, in turn, impacts users' browsing speed and their overall browsing experience. As a result, visually-impaired users spend significantly more time on seemingly simple online tasks.

Web automation - a process of automating browsing actions on behalf of the user - has the potential to bridge the web accessibility divide between the ways people with and without vision impairments use the Web. The traditional approach to Web automation is via *macros*, pre-recorded sequences of instructions that can automate browsing steps. Macro-based automation tools are finding their way into mainstream technology as part of screen-readers, browser extensions, and browser features (e.g., form filling). The adoption of macro-based Web automation has been stifled by a number of challenges: (a) it requires the user to make an effort to create, manage, and, then, find and replay macros, and (b) it lacks the flexibility necessary to allow the user to deviate from the pre-recorded sequence of steps, or to choose between several options in each step of the macro. Those difficulties make macro-based approaches too limiting to be useful for people with vision impairments; none of our 19 blind participants reported using any kind of web automation technology.

In this paper, we present a novel approach to accessible web automation for people with visual impairments. The salient aspects of the approach, embodied in the prototype system - *Web Automation*

Assistant - are as follows: First, it uses a computational model, based on a modified dynamic programming sequence alignment algorithm, to predict the most probable actions the user can take when browsing. Second, the construction of the model is "unsupervised", continuous, and incremental, i.e., the model is silently updated after every user action. Third, the Assistant uses a novel user interface that focuses the user on the predicted browsing steps and, if necessary, facilitates their automatic execution. This is done by continuously monitoring user activity, and, when requested, guiding the user through browsing tasks step by step, providing relevant contextual suggestions, and enabling the user to confirm each step before the suggestions are executed. The effectiveness of the Assistant was validated in experiments evaluating the prediction accuracy, and in the user study evaluating the Assistant's usability and user experience with 19 blind participants.

It is worthwhile pointing out that the Assistant can be viewed as an *interface agent* [15, 18] - a system that observes user interactions with the UI and interacts with the user or with the UI. This work is also related to *adaptive user interfaces*. Adaptive interface tailors the presentation of functionality to better fit an individual user's tasks, usage patterns, and abilities [14].

2. USE SCENARIO

To illustrate how screen-reader users accomplish browsing tasks, let us consider a simple scenario of finding the "checkout button" to buy some product after adding it to cart. The strategies employed by any given user will depend on the level of expertise of the user and his/her familiarity with the task and/or web page. Beginning users often listen to the content from the top of the page continuously until they hear the button label read to them (if they recognize that it is the button they need). They can also expedite the process by pressing the "Down" key to make the screen-reader skip to the next line. This unfortunately is not much faster because one has to hear at least some of the content before realizing that it is not relevant. More advanced users may employ the search feature to find the button by searching for its label, assuming they know what the label is, and the label is a text string.

Expert users would employ element-specific navigation allowing them to jump back and forth among elements of certain HTML type: buttons, headings, edit fields, etc. Expecting to find a HTML button, they may press "B" to jump only among buttons narrowing down their search space and reducing the amount of information they have to listen to. If they are familiar with the web page, they sometimes find quicker ways to get around, e.g., if the page has many buttons, instead of pressing "B" multiple times to get to the right button, the user may go to the end of the page and go in reverse order, or press "H" to go to next heading, and then "Shift+B" to go to the button that precedes the heading. Unfortunately, if the web page gets a slight make over, or if the user cannot remember the structure of the page, s/he has to fall back to the least efficient navigation with arrows. For instance, the check out button may turn out to be an image-link with the label "Go to Cart", in which case neither pressing "B" nor searching for the label will help.

In contrast, the Web Automation Assistant described in this paper allows the user to examine the most likely action-objects, e.g., a button that needs to be pressed or a form-field to be filled. When the user looks through the suggestions, there may only be the "checkout" and "keep shopping" buttons, because the Assistant will remember that those are the buttons the user usually presses after adding an item to cart. Furthermore, because of the way the actions are recorded in the model, the Assistant is likely to find the button even if its label and/or the position on the page changes. Thus, the Assistant will allow even a novice user to be as efficient as an expert user, while also relieving the expert user from having to remember the web page structure.

In a similar fashion, using the Assistant, the user can just as quickly go through the entire shopping transaction: enter user name and password to log in, select the shipping address, shipping method, billing information, and finally complete the purchase. The Assistant will also help to not only find the form fields to fill, but also enter the values, if necessary. One *could* hypothetically record a macro to help guide the user step by step through the same exact transaction; however, not only does this require some effort on the part of the user, but macros are also a lot less flexible and cannot support the following scenarios: the Assistant lets the user choose from among several possible actions; it can begin guiding from any step of the suggested sequence; it allows the user to diverge from but then continue with the suggested sequence.

3. TECHNICAL PRELIMINARIES

We define the *environment* with which the user and the Assistant interact to be the web browser coupled with the screen-reader. The user, and the Assistant, interact with the environment by executing *browsing actions* ("actions" for brevity). For example, the user can press a keyboard shortcut; the Assistant can simulate a keyboard shortcut press on the user's behalf. In response to the browsing actions, the environment triggers *events*, e.g., browser's JavaScript events, screen-reader's virtual cursor movement, etc.

An *automation instruction* is defined as the instruction that is needed to execute a specific browsing action programmatically on user's behalf. We define 3 types of automation instructions: *Value Change* (change the value of an HTML form field such as textbox, radio button, checkbox, selection list, etc.), *Invocation* (following a link, pressing an on-screen button, except for submit a form), and *Form Submission* (separated for the purpose of combining multiple ways of form submission). Automation instructions are automatically inferred from observed events (e.g., a JavaScript onsubmit event can be used to generate a Form Submission instruction specifying which form needs to be submitted). An action may trigger different events at different times and, hence, may or may not always generate equivalent automation instructions. Similarly, different actions may result in generating equivalent automation instructions. In the remainder of the paper we will use browsing actions and automation instructions interchangeably when there is no confusion in the context.

We define *history* as a sequence of automation instructions that appear in the order in which they were generated from events. An example of history is: < a Value Change for setting the "First Name" textbox to "John", followed by a Value Change for setting the "Last Name" textbox to "Doe", followed by a Form Submission>.

The *query* denotes the set of all suffixes of the browsing history. Observe that suffixes denote recent browsing actions.

4. MODEL-BASED WEB AUTOMATION

4.1 Overview

The basis of our approach is based on the idea that if some subsequence of the history matches the most recent browsing actions, then the action immediately following the matched subsequence can be predicted as the user's next action, and hence it is a possible candidate for suggestion. To illustrate, let

...ABCD...AECE...ACE...ABECF...

be a part of the history capturing prior actions, and let ABC be one of the suffixes in the current query. Each letter represents a single browsing action and the same letters are used for equivalent actions. Then, we can align ABC to every subsequence of the browsing history and predict the next most likely user action (denoted by the ? symbol). In our example we get the following four local sequence alignments:

```
ABCD  AECE  A-CE  ABECF ...
ABC?  ABC?  ABC?  AB-C?
```

First, the suffix may align to more than one subsequence in history. In some cases, different actions may follow each of the aligned subsequences (e.g., D, E, F above). This can be a result of the user executing the same task on a modified webpage, or of the user making different choices within the browsing task, or of the user switching to a different browsing task altogether. Second, the suffix may partially match a subsequence in the history (e.g., AECE, ACE, ABECF), in which case the alignments will have different *edit distances* (minimal number of insertions, deletions, and replacements needed to modify one sequence into another). The larger the edit distance, the smaller is the likelihood that the alignment is useful for making a prediction. However, the ability to find partial matches is very important for the algorithm to be useful whenever the user deviates from historic record.

The time interval between actions in history may have high variance, either due to periods of user inactivity, or because a subsequence of history was deleted (or never recorded). However, it is not obvious that accounting for differences in time intervals will significantly improve the performance of the statistical model, since user's previous actions may be indicative of his/her next action even if they are separated by a large time span. Similarly, a very short (or very typical) time span between two actions is not a guarantee that the user did not make an unpredictable 'switch' to a completely new browsing task. An investigation of usefulness of a sophisticated handling of time intervals may require an in-situ study, and is beyond the scope of this paper.

4.2 Model Construction

The basis of our web automation model (overviewed above) is the Smith-Waterman [30], a dynamic programming sequence alignment algorithm. Smith-Waterman builds a Sequence Alignment Table T of size $m + 1$ columns by $n + 1$ rows. Each row i, and column j in the Sequence Alignment Table corresponds to a single automation instruction q_i, and h_j respectively. The automation instructions in the rows and columns are generated from the user's browsing history. Column m and row n represent the most recent automation instruction. $T[i][j]$ denotes the score of the alignment of two sequences composed of automation instructions from row 0 to i and column 0 to j.

In building the Sequence Alignment Table, we are interested in the alignment of the query to each subsequence of history. Those alignments are represented by the cells in the bottom row of the Sequence Alignment Table. Given a table of $n + 1$ rows, cell $T[n][j-1]$ scores the alignment of the query with the subsequence of history that ends with action h_{j-1}. We say that the subsequent action h_j is predicted by the alignment $j - 1$ with the score of $T[n][j-1]$.

Consider the example in Figure 1, in which we align $V_1 V_2 S_1$ (recent actions) to $\ldots V_1 V_2 I_1 I_2 S_1 V_3 \ldots$ (subsequence of history), where V are Value Change instructions, I are Invocation instructions, S are Form Submission instructions. The score modifier for a match or a mismatch of q_i and h_j is 1 and -1, respectively:

The positive scores in the bottom row indicate that there are three equally likely alignments, each scored 1: (a) rows $V_1 V_2$ match to columns $V_1 V_2$, row S_1 is "deleted", and the predicted action is I_1 (b) rows $V_1 V_2$ match to columns $V_1 V_2$, row S_1 is (mis)matched

	...	V_1	V_2	I_1	I_2	S_1	V_3
	0	0	0	0	0	0	0
V_1	0	1	0	0	0	0	0
V_2	0	0	2	0	0	0	0
S_1	0	0	1	1	0	1	0

Figure 1: Example of a Sequence Alignment Table

with column I_1, and the predicted action is I_2, and (c) row S_1 is matched to column S_1, and the predicted action is V_3.

4.3 Model Optimization

Our sequence alignment is based upon the following definition, drawn from the standard Smith-Waterman algorithm:

$$T_o[i][j] = \max \begin{cases} 0 & \text{case 1} \\ T_o[i-1][j-1] + S_o[i][j] & \text{case 2} \\ T_o[i-1][j] + S_o[i][j] & \text{case 3} \\ T_o[i][j-1] + S_o[i][j] & \text{case 4} \end{cases}$$

Let $\equiv$ denote a match of q_i and h_j, let $\equiv_{vc}$ denote a match of q_i and h_j such that both are Value Change, and have the same value, and let $\not\equiv$ denote a mismatch of q_i and h_j. As already mentioned, Smith-Waterman defines the score modifier, denoted by S_o, as 1 if $q_i \equiv h_j$ and -1 otherwise. We depart from Smith-Waterman by redefining the score modifier as follows:

$$S_o[i][j] = \begin{cases} 1 & \text{if } q_i \equiv h_j \\ 2 & \text{if } q_i \equiv_{vc} h_j \\ P_o[i][j] & \text{if } q_i \not\equiv h_j \end{cases}$$

where P_o is a progressive penalty for a mismatch of two actions, and is defined as follows:

$$P_o[i][j] = \begin{cases} P_o[i-1][j-1] - 1 & \text{if case 2} \\ P_o[i-1][j] - 3 & \text{if case 3} \\ P_o[i][j-1] - 2 & \text{if case 4} \\ 0 & \text{otherwise} \end{cases}$$

Value Change represents a modification to the HTML form fields, and, in some use scenarios, the chosen value of a form field may hint at future user actions. This scenario is accounted for by setting $S_o = 2$ if $q_i \equiv_{vc} h_j$.

The introduction of progressive penalty P_o is done for the following reason. The necessary length of the suffixes in the query is hard to predefine. Ideally, this number should be large enough to include all the actions that can influence the user's choice of the next action, but, at the same time, small enough to exclude the actions that are "irrelevant" when predicting the next action. The local sequence alignment approach taken in this paper allows us to examine the mapping of all possible suffixes to all subsequences of the history simultaneously. For instance, the example in Figure 1 examines the suffixes S_1, $V_2 S_1$, and $V_1 V_2 S_1$; the length of positively scored alignments is 3 for cases (a) and (b) and 1 for case (c). However, this implies that some of the suffixes might be too long (contain "irrelevant" actions). We deal with this by penalizing the mismatch of two actions on a progressive scale, under the assumption that actions become "irrelevant" when they are followed by too many mismatches.

Finally, we want to prioritize case 2 over case 4, and case 4 over case 3. Therefore, the score modifier for aligning mismatching q_i and h_j (case 2) is smaller than the modifier for inserting an item from history (case 4), which is in turn smaller than the modifier for deleting an item from the query (case 3).

4.4 Generation of the Prediction List

As was discussed above, there may be multiple local sequence alignments between the query and the history. Each such alignment can result in a potential prediction. Let the *prediction list* be defined as a list of predicted browsing actions, or, equivalently, automation instructions, ordered by likelihood. The process of inferring a new prediction list is illustrated in Figure 2.

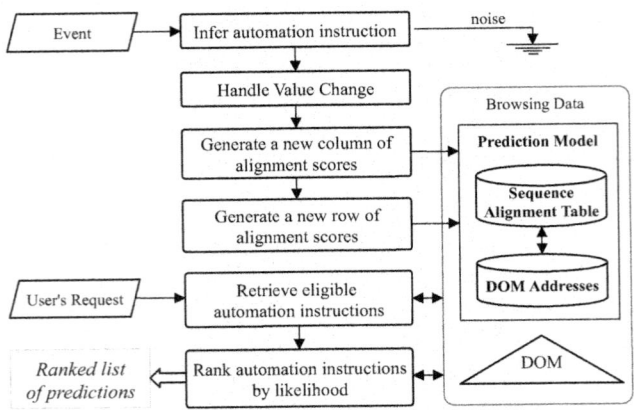

Figure 2: Process Flow for Predicting User Actions

The model is updated on the fly, every time a new environment event is logged. First, unless the event can be ignored (as discussed in Section 4.5), a new automation instruction is inferred. Second, if Value Change was generated, and it has already been executed on the same page since the last page load, then its value is assigned to the first occurrence of the instruction, and the new occurrence is discarded. Third, the model is incrementally updated with the new automation instruction by generating a new column and a new row of alignment scores in the Sequence Alignment Table.

Observe that the model is updated incrementally. This is because the new alignment of the updated query and history is computed by generating a single table row and column (instead of recomputing the Sequence Alignment Table from scratch). This is possible because the Sequence Alignment Table that needs to be computed at step i is a subset of the Sequence Alignment Table that needs to be computed at step $i + 1$. Moreover, adding a new row (column), only involves examining the row above (column to the left), and generation of prediction list only involves the examination of the bottom row. Therefore, only the bottom row and the rightmost column of the Sequence Alignment Table need to be stored (see [22] for further details).

The algorithm generating the prediction list (or, equivalently in this context, automation instructions) is executed upon user's request for suggestions (for example, a shortcut). First, each prediction is evaluated for eligibility to be scored. A prediction is considered non-eligible and is discarded if at least one of the following is true: (a) the targeted webpage element (visual primitive of a webpage) does not exist, (b) it is hidden, (c) it is a disabled or a read-only form field, or (d) the action has been executed since the last page load. For instance, actions I_1 and I_2 in Figure 1 would be discarded if the Form Submission action S_1 triggered a new page load. The hidden, disabled, and read-only form fields are discarded because their value is usually assigned by the webpage itself, as a function of user's interaction with the enabled webpage elements, or factors beyond user's control (e.g., the date).

The eligible predictions are scored as follows. A sliding window of size k is used to collect k top scored, *unique* predictions, i.e., the sliding window always contains k most likely predictions so far. Since predictions need to be unique, each prediction's score is defined as the maximum of scores assigned to it by different alignments. If the scores of two different predictions are equivalent, the prediction with the score provided by the more recent (larger column j index) alignment is ranked higher (discussed in Section 4.5). For instance, the ranking order in Figure 1 would be V_3, I_2, I_1. Furthermore, by ignoring the *number* of predictions for each action, and tie breaking, we aim to minimize the effects of data decay.

The time complexity for updating the model and recomputing the prediction list after each action is $O(m \log k + n)$, where k is the size of the sliding window, $O(m)$ is the time to add a new row, $O(n)$ is the time to add a new column, and $O(m \log k)$ is the time to generate a new prediction list. However, since k is a small constant - providing the user with too many suggestions would be counterproductive - the complexity is $O(m + n)$. The space complexity is also $O(m + n)$.

4.5 Technical Details

Automation instructions are generated from environment events. The mapping between events and instructions is:
- Value Change: triggered by JavaScript *onchange*, or *onreset* events: change of value of an HTML form field such as textbox, radio button, checkbox, selection list, etc.
- Invocation: triggered by (a) JavaScript *onclick* event: a mouse click (except on a form submit button), or (b) JavaScript *keypress* event: a press of the 'enter' key (except in a form field, or a form 'submit' button).
- Form Submission: triggered by a JavaScript *onsubmit* event.

We say that two automation instructions are equivalent if and only if they have the same type and:
- Both are an Invocation of a URI element (e.g., following a link), and refer to the same URI. Otherwise,
- Both refer to the same unique webpage element. The HTML elements can be uniquely identified by an XPath [4] (see [21] for XPath addressing resilient to DOM changes).

When comparing automation instructions, we need to consider the semantics (the actual effect) of the instructions, rather than the specific events from which the instructions were inferred. A mouse click and a press on the 'enter' key are assigned the same type because more often than not the semantics of a mouse click and a press on the 'enter' key is the same (for instance, clicking a link with the mouse, or, focusing on the link and then pressing 'enter'). By not making any assumptions about the specific input device, we make it easier for the model to compare and identify equivalent instructions and ensure that the model created by observing keyboard events will be usable when the user switches to the mouse and vice versa. The mouse can be useful for people with low vision and it can enable sighted people to easily create models for people with vision impairments. This generalization will also enable transparent support for other input modalities (such as Braille devices, touch screens, or speech input) in the future.

A Value Change instruction is parametrized with any input in the corresponding form field, such as entering value into a textbox, (un)checking a checkbox, changing the selection in a combo-box, etc. Value Change is recorded only when the user exits the form field, i.e. the value is final. The value of all the subsequent modifications of the same form field (i.e. if the user comes back to update the value) are stored in the original instruction, i.e. no new instruction is created. For instance, if the user (a) sets "First Name" field to "John", then "Last Name" field to "Smith", and then updated the "First Name" field to "Sam", this generates a sequence of (a) Value

Change "Sam" for "First Name", followed by (b) Value Change "Smith" for "Last Name".

Form submission is always related to the specific form being submitted, and therefore the semantics of submitting a form differs from Invocation. Different Invocation instructions that can be used to submit the same form include pressing 'enter' or clicking the mouse on the form 'submit' button (of which there can be more than one for the same form, including outside the form element, as per HTML5 specification), pressing 'enter' inside a form field, and interacting with a custom form submission mechanism. We want to make sure that the semantically equivalent but otherwise different ways of submitting the same form are considered equal.

However, the general case of comparing instructions by their semantics is not reliable (except form submission, invoking a URI, and possibly other special cases). If a webpage has two controls that cause the same effect (e.g., two buttons that open the same shopping cart) by running custom JavaScript, the corresponding automation instructions will not be equivalent. This is mitigated by the fact that if the user chooses to use both controls interchangeably, the system will learn both variations and so it will provide useful suggestions regardless of user's choice.

5. PUTTING IT ALL TOGETHER

Figure 3 provides a high level overview of Assistants' architecture. The Assistant updates the Sequence Alignment Table by listening to events triggered by browsing actions. The user interacts with the Assistant as follows: (a) while browsing, the user requests suggestions (shortcut); (b) the Assistant exposes a set of suggestions by associating each suggestion with the relevant webpage element; (c) the user examines the suggestions, using a combination of shortcuts provided by the browser, the screen-reader, and the Assistant; the Assistant provides voice feedback where appropriate (supplementing, or replacing the screen-reader feedback); For example, if a textbox is labeled "First name", it has no value, and the suggested value is "John" then the system will announce "Textbox 'First name' blank. Suggestion: John" when the user visits this textbox; (d) the user either confirms automatic execution of one of the suggestions (shortcut), or ignores the suggestions; (e) the user (optionally) verifies that the action was executed correctly by listening to the feedback provided by the Assistant (e.g., voicing the new value of the modified textbox), and/or examining the webpage; (f) the user continues browsing.

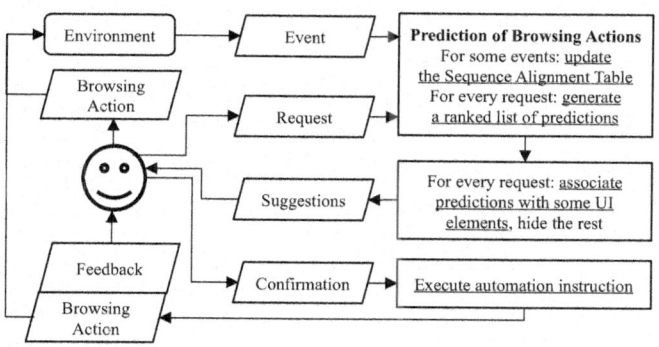

Figure 3: Web Automation Assistant Architecture

There are several important details in this design. First, the user never leaves the webpage to review the suggestions, and the webpage elements are not reordered. Instead, the user is focused on the most important webpage elements and the associated suggested actions. This helps the user to always know the position of the virtual cursor on the webpage, and prevents unexpected context changes. Second, each suggestion is for a *single* action, rather than for a sequence of actions, enabling easy deviation from a scenario after automating one or more actions. Third, confirming one of the suggestions, or interacting with the webpage in any way may automatically refresh the available suggestions, and/or update the model with new data. Fourth, since the system is always monitoring user actions, there is no need to turn it 'on' or 'off'. Fifth, the user is not required to use the Assistant to automate a suggestion s/he finds useful, and can instead use standard screen-reader or browser commands for that purpose: rather than changing his/her workflow, the user can use the Assistant as an "advisor" and, when necessary, an "automator".

6. EVALUATION

We developed a prototype implementation of the Web Automation Assistant. In this section, we describe the evaluation of the model's prediction accuracy, as well as report on the results of a user study with blind participants.

6.1 Model Evaluation

6.1.1 Methodology

The data for model evaluation was collected by observing 8 Firefox users performing 6 different browsing tasks, each associated with a different website. The browsing tasks were chosen to be comparable in difficulty and to be representative use cases for people with vision impairments (according to our accessibility consultants). The 6 chosen tasks were: (1) registering a new website account (ebay.com); (2) searching for and booking a hotel (hilton.com); (3) website registration and product checkout (tigerdirect.com); (4) product checkout (amazon.com); (5) job search (monster.com); and (6) searching for a restaurant and sharing the information with friends (yelp.com).

The data was collected by sighted, rather than blind users, for pragmatic reasons - it takes a blind user on average 5-10 times longer to complete a single task compared to a sighted person, which makes data collection prohibitively expensive. However, as we confirmed in a pilot data collection, the model works the same way for sighted and blind users because they would have to take the same exact steps to complete the tasks. The actions predicted by the model are limited entirely by the functionality of a website; the actions are not specific to non-visual browsing (e.g., movement of the virtual cursor), and are input-modality independent (mouse, keyboard). Hence, the accuracy of the underlying model can be evaluated with sighted, as well as with blind users.

The users generated 5 "noisy" browsing sequences per website by performing a task on each website 5 times, each time varying the browsing actions as they would normally, e.g., choosing a different shipping method while shopping, reviewing product specifications, changing the mind and choosing a different product, filling out form values in different order, re-entering (updating) data in fields, using different methods to submit a form, etc. The users were not constrained by a time limit and completed all the browsing tasks. The resulting dataset contained a total of 240 browsing sequences (30 per person) and 3074 browsing actions (65% Value Changes, 19% Invocations, and 16% Form Submissions).

The goal of the evaluation was to measure the ability of the model to predict a *gold-standard* (minimal) sequences of actions from a noisy browsing history. That is, we considered a scenario in which the user's intention was to complete the remainder of any given browsing task using the Assistant with a minimal number of steps. A gold-standard sequence was independently handcrafted for each of the 6 websites; the resulting sequences contained a total of 51 actions, of which 72% were Value Changes, 17% were Invocations, and 11% were Form Submissions.

The evaluation was done in iterations, where in each iteration $j = 1...6$: 1) the model was updated with randomly selected noisy browsing sequences one by one (from the same website, and the same subject), 2) a new sequence of prediction lists ξ_j was generated, and 3) the accuracy of the prediction was evaluated by comparing the model prediction to the gold standard sequences. That is, on the first iteration, the model contained a single browsing sequence, on the second - two browsing sequences, and so on. The accuracy for each iteration j, denoted μ_j^ξ, is then averaged across all users and websites. The gold-standard sequence was not used to update the model.

Given a gold-standard sequence $h_i \in H$, the prediction list $L_i \in \xi$ was evaluated with the metric *precision at k*, denoted by P@k, and the *mean reciprocal rank* metric, denoted by MRR, of the correct prediction h_{i+1} (sliding window size is unbounded). MRR is defined as follows:

$$MRR(H, \xi) = \frac{1}{|H|-1} \sum_{i=1}^{|H|-1} \psi_i$$

If $h_{i+1} \in L_i \in \xi$ then the utility function $\psi_i = 1/L_i(h_{i+1})$, and $\psi_i = 0$ otherwise; $L_i(h_{i+1})$ is the rank of h_{i+1} in L_i.

It is important to note that the predictions (in form of suggestions) might not be reviewed by the user in the order produced by the ranking algorithm. In a user study with people with vision impairments (Section 6.2), we presented the suggestions in the screen-reading order (preorder DOM traversal) to ease transitions between reviewing suggestions and regular browsing. However, MRR is useful for comparing prediction algorithms, and for producing a rough estimate of a threshold k below which the predictions can be discarded because they are unlikely to be correct. This threshold is the size of the sliding window used to generate the prediction list (see Section 6.2), and is also used for the P@k metric. The smaller is the value of k the more preferable it is for the user, and the less likely it is that a useful prediction will be part of the list made avaliable to the user. In our experiments we set $k = 5$, as a compromise between the two competing considerations, based on empirical obsevations of system results and on a pilot user study.

6.1.2 Results

Table 1 compares the accuracy of 3 methods for gold-standard sequence prediction: (a) $P(h_{j+1}|h_j)$: bigram frequency count, where each bigram represents two consequitive user actions h_j, h_{j+1}, i.e. predict action $j+1$ based on a single most recent action j, (b) $T[i][j]$: the unmodified Smith-Waterman [30], and (c) $T_o[i][j]$: the optimized Smith-Waterman. $S(\cdot)$ denotes discarding of non-eligible predictions (as described in Section 4.4).

Algorithm	P@k μ_1^ξ	P@k μ_6^ξ	MRR μ_1^ξ	MRR μ_6^ξ
$P(h_{j+1}|h_j)$	0.23	0.27	0.19	0.36
$S(P(h_{j+1}|h_j))$	0.43	0.46	0.45	0.30
$T[i][j]$	0.36	0.27	0.17	0.15
$S(T[i][j])$	0.45	0.33	0.27	0.20
$T_o[i][j]$	0.52	0.54	0.35	0.41
$S(T_o[i][j])$	0.62	0.69	0.45	0.49

Table 1: Accuracy of Predicting the Gold-Standard Action Sequence from User-Generated Action Sequences

The results show that (i) looking back at more than one preceeding user action, (ii) optimization of the Smith-Waterman parameters, and (iii) skipping of non-eligible actions all contribute towards better performance; although not shown here, each optimization was also tested independently. Of course, the disadvantages of making predictions just based on a single most recent action will be erased if the user never deviates from his previous steps, but this is a very uncommon scenario in web browsing.

6.2 User Study

We tested the effectiveness of the Assistant in a user study with 19 blind screen-reader users performing tasks on webpages with and without the help of the Assistant. The following hypotheses were formulated:

H1: Visually impaired users can complete tasks significantly faster when using the Assistant (either A or B) than when using a standard screen-reader.

H2: Usability of non-visual browsing is significantly better when using the Assistant (either A or B) than when using a standard screen-reader.

6.2.1 User Interface

In consultation with web accessibility experts, we have designed several versions of the Assistant's interface with two versions making the final cut in a pilot user study. Since even small details of UI design have the potential to influence results, we decided to test both versions of the Assistant UI.

Assistant A. The S and Shift+S keys are used to move the screen-reader's virtual cursor to respectively the next and the previous webpage element for which an action is suggested. This interface is based on the standard screen-reading interface for navigating among webpage elements of a particular type, e.g., B and Shift+B for buttons, A and Shift+A for links.

Assistant B. A single shortcut is used to toggle on/off the "suggestions" mode, in which the user can use standard screen-reader shortcuts, but navigation is only allowed among the suggestions of the Assistant, making the rest of the content "disappear". If the current screen-reader's virtual cursor position is not associated with a suggestion (because the mode was just turned on or the suggestions changed), the cursor position is moved to the suggestion topologically following the current position. If there is no such suggestion, the user is taken to the suggestion topologically preceding the current position. Otherwise, "no suggestions" is voiced.

It is important to note that both Assistant A and B interfaces are designed to coexist in the same system with a screen-reader. If none of the suggestions are useful for the user, he/she can use the standard screen-reader shortcuts to acomplish their immidiate goal, and then continue using the Assistant. Both Assistant A and B interfaces can also coexist in the same system with each other.

For example, imagine that the Assistant is used on a web page containing a large number of elements, of which the 5th one, a textbox, and the 32nd one, a button, are associated with suggestions; the user's current reading position is on the 10th element. With Assistant A, pressing the 'S' key will navigate to the button, while pressing 'Shift+S' will navigate to the textbox. With Assistant B, when the suggestion mode is turned on, the user will be taken to the button, and pressing the 'Up' key will take the user to the textbox. In both interfaces, the content and the suggestions will be read the same way, e.g., "Textbox 'First name' blank, Suggestion: 'John'". Additional shortcuts can be used to iterate over alternative values, if any. Pressing Ctrl+Space will execute the suggestion, voice "Textbox 'First Name' John", and replace the old set of suggestions with a new one. After a suggestion is executed, when using Assistant A, the reading cursor will remain on the same element, and the user will have to press 'S' or 'Shift+S' again or navigate normally. When using Assistant B, the user's position will be automatically moved to the appropriate suggestion; the user will have to exit the suggestion mode to navigate normally. It is notable that .

6.2.2 Subjects and Methodology

The 19 participants of our study consisted of 58% males, and were on average 54 ($\sigma = 12$) years old. The age group represents the typical age of a screen-reader user, as many people lose sight later in life. The participants were White/Caucasian (42%), Black/African-American (26%), Latino/Hispanic (12%), Asian (5%), Indian (5%), Central-American (5%), and 5% declined to respond. The participants rated their level of computer experience at "not comfortable" (0%), "mildly comfortable" (0%), "comfortable" (26%), "very comfortable" (58%), and "expert" (16%). About 90% of the participants used Internet Explorer as their primary browser, 5% use Firefox and another 5% use Safari. About 90% of the participants used JAWS as their primary screen-reader, 5% used ZoomText and 5% VoiceOver. All the participants used JAWS before. The number of hours per week that participants regularly spent using the Web was 1-5h (32%), 6-10h (16%), 11-20h (26%), and more than 20h (26%).

The study was conducted using Capti Web browsing application that a screen-reading interface very similar to the standard screen-readers, with the Firefox browser and IVONA [5] Text-To-Speech (TTS) engine with the voice "Eric", speech rate of 180 words per minute.

In this study, we asked the participants to perform 6 browsing tasks, each associated with a different website. The tasks and the websites were the same as in Section 6.1.1. Subjects were asked to perform the tasks using 3 different systems: the baseline screen-reader without automation (**N-A**), Assistant A (**A-A**), and Assistant B (**A-B**). Each system was evaluated with 2 consecutive tasks. We counterbalanced the task order, the system order, and task-to-system assignment.

Prior to performing the tasks, the participants were explained how to use the system they were about to evaluate, and given an opportunity to practice on a sample web site until they felt comfortable to proceed. Since all the participants had prior experience with the JAWS screen-reader, the interface of our Capti screen-reader, which provides the commonly used features and shortcuts of JAWS, was immediately familiar.

The profiles of the statistical models for the Assistant (same for A-A and A-B) were created in advance, i.e. for each user all initial suggestions contained the correct action that the user was expected to execute, or confirm. During the evaluation, the Assistant updated the model and changed its suggestions based on the subject's behavior when s/he deviated from the initial suggestions. In practice, during the study, the participants ended up with at most 2 suggestions to choose from.

For each task, we measured the completion time, or recorded a time-out if the subject exceeded 10 min. (Table 2). The tasks that timed-out were not included in quantitative results computation. After each system evaluation (2 consecutive tasks) the participants answered the System Usability Scale (SUS) [11] questionnaire. After the completion of all tasks, the participants had to compare the 3 systems (Table 3).

6.2.3 Quantitative Results

Task success. All participants were able to complete all tasks with A-A and A-B within the given time constraint of 10 min. Four participants were not able to complete 1 task in the time allotted (a different task in each case, a total of 4 tasks) using N-A.

Task	A-A μ	A-A σ	A-B μ	A-B σ	N-A μ	N-A σ
1	187	87	**173**	33	448	158
2	**69**	3	92	29	476	55
3	214	67	**193**	49	526	89
4	107	26	**101**	26	342	179
5	**94**	35	112	27	411	164
6	174	36	**171**	48	422	127
AVG	153	71	**142**	52	426	132

Table 2: User Interface Evaluation: Task Completion Time (sec.)

Task completion times are shown in Table 2. One-way ANOVA test ($\alpha = 0.001$) shows statistically significant result ($p < 0.0001$) and Tukey's Multiple Comparison Test showed statistically significant difference between A-A and N-A, as well as between A-B and N-A ($p < 0.0001$). The one-tailed t-test ($\alpha = 0.001$) for all tasks showed that both A-A ($t = 8.9, df = 41$) and A-B ($t = 11, df = 45$) provide statistically significant ($p < 0.0001$) speed improvements when compared to N-A. This corroborates hypothesis **H1**.

Of the 6 websites used in the study, only amazon.com was very familiar to most of the participants - 80% used it on a regular basis (the only other familiar website was ebay.com, with 20%). This resulted in an insignificant improvement in the performance time when using screen-reader without automation (Table 2, task 4, column 5). However, even in this case both A-A and A-B provided statistically significant speedups when compared to N-A. This reinforces hypothesis **H1**.

6.2.4 Post-completion Questionnaire

The SUS questionnaire scores are shown in the first two rows of Table 3. According to Bangor et al. [6] the results for A-B (80), and N-A (78) can be considered "good", while the result for A-A (88) can be considered "excellent".

The ANOVA test between all three systems, as well as the one tailed paired t-test between the A-B and N-A ($p = 0.33, t = 0.44, df = 18$), showed no statistically significant difference. The one tailed paired t-test between the A-A and N-A showed that the improvement was statistically significant ($p = 0.0109 < 0.05, t = 2.5, df = 18$). This corroborates hypothesis **H2**.

After evaluating all three systems, the participants were asked to answer 10 questions comparing the three systems to each other (Table 3). The participants could answer by naming one of the evaluated systems or saying "none of the above". The results show that the A-A was strongly preferred by most participants in all questions (shown in bold: the highest values for positive questions 1,3,5,7,9, and the lowest values for negative questions 2,4,6,8,10). This reinforces the results of the SUS questionnaires. It is notable that the participants scored A-A higher than A-B despite the fact that, in most cases, the participants completed tasks with A-B only marginally faster.

The high deviation values (σ_{SUS}) are, mostly likely, a result of counterbalancing the order of systems, and the fact that SUS questions were asked immediately after each system was evaluated (to ensure the experience was still fresh in the participants' minds). For example, if the subject evaluated A-A before N-A then the latter received much lower scores, reflecting participants' tendency to score each system in the context of prior experience. Likewise,

	A-A	A-B	N-A
μ_{SUS}	**88.16**	80.13	78.03
σ_{SUS}	**11.24**	17.21	22.62
1. Which system would you prefer to use?	**84.2%**	15.8%	0%
2. Which system did you find the most complex?	0%	42.1%	31.6%
3. Which system did you find the easiest to use?	**78.9%**	15.8%	5.3%
4. Which system would need the most support from a technical person?	0%	31.6%	26.3%
5. Which system was the most well integrated?	**63.2%**	21.1%	15.8%
6. Which system was the least consistent?	5.3%	31.6%	15.8%
7. Which system do you imagine most people would learn to use most quickly?	**78.9%**	15.8%	5.3%
8. Which system did you find the most cumbersome to use?	0%	42.1%	21.1%
9. Which system did you feel the most confident using?	**78.9%**	10.5%	10.5%
10. Which system did you feel required you to learn the most before using it?	0%	42.1%	26.3%

* The answer "none of the above" is omitted for brevity
* The questionnaire is a reformulated for comparison SUS

Table 3: User Interface Evaluation: Post-Completion Questionnaire

when N-A was evaluated first, the participants assigned it very high scores because, in this case, they compared it to the screen-reader they were used to the most: JAWS. A possible reason for favorable comparison is that blind users strongly associate a screen-reader with the synthesized voice, and we used IVONA, a high quality voice. In one specific example of contextual scoring, one of the participants, having already given N-A the highest scores possible, expressed her desire to score A-A higher than was permitted by the Likert scale.

6.2.5 Qualitative Results

Our observations show that, when performing tasks using N-A, the participants adopted one of three strategies: (a) moving through the webpage, top down, until finding the element they searched for, or, if not successful after some time, (b) jumping to the end of the webpage and sequentially moving bottom up, or (in about 20% of all cases) (c) using advanced shortcuts such as search or iterating through predefined element types (e.g., buttons, links). When successful, the last strategy provided significant speed improvement; when not, the subject had to fall back to one of the two former strategies.

When using A-A or A-B, the participants initially showed signs of hesitation, often pausing before pressing the next shortcut. However, by the second task the participants were becoming substantially more confident. A common mistake made by the participants when using the A-B was to try to use the "up" and "down" keys to navigate away from the suggested element (this is impossible by design, since those shortcuts only navigate between suggestions when the suggestion mode is on). When using A-A the participants sometimes used those keys to become familiar with the neighborhood of the suggested element before proceeding with the task.

A number of users explicitly stated that they preferred to remain always in the same mode (i.e. not have a special suggestion mode), because this meant they did not need to learn subtle differences between the way the mode behaved. In other words, introduction of multiple states may be increasing cognitive load, and may be the main reason for significantly higher usability scores of the A-A. At the same time, A-B may still be a better choice for power-users, because it after a suggestion is executed, the A-B moves the cursor to the next suggestion, allowing the user to press fewer shortcuts. Also, in case of multiple suggestions, the user could use element-specific navigation shortcuts in the suggestion mode to iterate over suggestions of a particular type. For example, pressing B in suggestion mode will iterate only over suggested buttons.

The participants made a large number of suggestions and provided ideas for improving the Assistant interface. For example, when suggesting to change the state of a checkbox, voicing the suggested value after the current value may be confusing because, in this case, users always listen to the last spoken word to determine checkbox status (the same however was not confusing for other form fields).

6.3 Testimonials

We received no negative comments from the participants about the evaluated user interface. Below are a few quotations that exemplify subject's overall reaction:

"It's like automatic bookmarking on steroids."

"If all what people were doing is browsing the web, this would be perfect."

"I haven't seen anything as unique as this program."

"With one tap it brings you right to where you want to go."

"I hope it is coming soon, many blind people could use it; especially when you go to college it can help students with research."

"Pretty innovative idea... I am wondering why even sighted people wouldn't find this product useful."

7. RELATED WORK

In this overview, we discuss some representative work on web Automation, while a more detailed review of the web automation tools can be found in [27]. The two main approaches to web automation are handcrafting, e.g., [9] and Programming by Demonstration (PBD) [12].

The handcrafting method requires writing a script to customize the behavior of the browser / screen-reader, or hardcoding the automation instructions into a feature in the browser / screen-reader, e.g., JAWS screen-reader has a shortcut to look up a word in an online dictionary. While handcrafting automation instructions is sometimes facilitated by a user interface [21], it typically requires learning to use the tool(s) and the language for creating the automation instructions; for instance, handcrafting scripts for the JAWS screen-reader [1] requires the user to learn to program in a special scripting language and follow the 180+ page macro creation manual, while the instructions for Window-Eyes screen-reader [2] scripting extend to over 1000 pages.

Programming by demonstration (PBD) is a more user-friendly approach that enables the end-user to "demonstrate" to the automation system what actions need to be done and in what order; this is usually accomplished by recording a macro, which can be later replayed to automate the same sequence of steps [17]. To take this further, a recording made for one webpage can sometimes be dynamically adapted to be used for a similar task on a different webpage or even a different website [8]. Typically, to record a macro the system needs to know the beginning and the end of the instruction sequence. This requires that user explicitly start the recording, execute the browsing steps flawlessly, terminate the recording, and save it under a recognizable name, all of which require both manual and mental effort. So, to put the effort into creating the macro, the user has to feel that the it will be very useful and will save a lot of time in the future. Smart Bookmarks [16] tries to make this process a little simpler by automatically guessing the beginning of the macro once the user indicates the end of the sequence. Unfortunately, the approach is not 100% accurate and it still carries most of the previously mentioned disadvantages of macros. Even if the user takes the time to record a macro, it is a fixed sequence of steps, so to automate slight deviations from this sequence, the user has to record multiple macros.

The interface described in this paper can be categorized as PBD, and was inspired by the ideas developed in [24, 25, 26, 27]. In contrast to the standard PBD approaches described above, our approach does not use macros altogether; instead, it uses the history of past browsing actions to predict future actions. Automatic form-filling in modern web browsers is another example of PBD that learns from what the user types into web forms and then helps automate form-filling. The proposed model-based approach, however, subsumes form-filling and even makes it more powerful; specifically, it can propose different values for the same form-fields depending on the browsing context of the user, e.g., if the user enters the first name, the model can predict the related last name(s). Furthermore, the proposed model-based approach can automate other browsing actions such as clicking links and buttons, and, in constrast to macros, it can suggest several possible alternatives at each browsing step.

The feasibility of a step-by-step automation of browsing tasks without macros was also explored in [19, 20, 28], where web automation relied on process models constructed from sequences of actions using machine learning techniques such as clustering, classification, and automata learning. The resulting process models had browsing states as nodes and actions as transitions. However, the approach used to construct the process models was not incremental, requiring that the model be rebuilt in order to accommodate any changes, such as learning new transition (or unlearning old ones). Moreover, the approach implied the system's ability to split clickstreams into sequences corresponding to sessions, cluster similar session sequences into similar groups, and then learn the automata, potentially introducing errors in each of those steps (e.g., it is not clear what is a good indicator of a splitting point, and if one exists at all in our domain). Finally, to predict the next browsing step, this approach required the exact match between the current browsing state and a state in the model (which represents a first-order Markovian process), thus limiting the predicting power of the approach in case of deviations from the process.

The model described in this paper is modeling a higher-order Markovian process, making it possible to predict the next step even if the user deviates from previously learned sequences of browsing actions. Futhermore, the model learns to automate browsing steps incrementally, making it possible to insert new and to remove outdated data on the fly without rebuilding the model. The model takes the history of browsing steps as they are without the need to segment the history into sessions.

Related work on the prediction of user browsing behavior also exists in other application domains such as prefetching [23, 13], e-commerce [29], content personalization [7], etc. These applications are only somewhat related because they pursue different goals, e.g., prefetching files or adjusting web page layout. These applications often construct probability graphs (similar to process models) and tend to do that offline; they do not handle form filling, etc. Notably, in [10], sequence alignment is used to find the next link the user could click in a website directory (e.g., Yahoo!). Apart from the difference in the application domain, the described approach also differs in that it aligns the current user session to multiple past sessions, that were previously clustered and organized into clickstream trees. The ensuing limitations are similar to those of the process-model approach: errors of session segmentation, as well as in clustering, and inefficiency of off-line model construction. In contrast, the approach proposed in this paper avoids the compexity and errors of clustering and segmentation, constructs the model incrementally, automates both form-filling and clicking, indroduces modifications to the alignment algorithm, and, rather than using the final result of sequence alignment, it uses the inner-workings of the algorithm (i.e. alignment table) to predict multiple possible steps the user could take.

8. CONCLUSION AND FUTURE WORK

In this paper, we proposed Web Automation Assistant, an interface agent with an accessible non-visual user interface for step-by-step automation of repetitive web browsing tasks. By combining a very carefully crafted user interface, and a sequence-alignment-based prediction model, we were able to improve significantly the user experience and the usability of web browsing for people with vision impairments. The fact that one of the two evaluated user interfaces turned out to be much more usable than the other serves as a reminder of the importance of attention to detail in interface design in general, and accessible interface design in particular. With further R&D effort, the Assistant has the potential to morph into an eyes-free, voice-controlled system, benefiting people both with and without vision impairments.

The main directions of work that we will pursue next include addressing the need of people with vision impairments to find non-interactive content (e.g., articles), and *silent*, dynamic page modifications (e.g., alerts, error notifications), enabling the model to learn from the browsing history of multiple users, purging the model from decayed data, investigating the possibility of accounting for time intervals, and improving the user interface based on the feedback from the usability study presented in this paper.

9. AKNOWLEDGMENTS

This work was developed under a grant from the Department of Education, NIDRR grants number H133S110023 and H133S120067. However, contents do not represent the policy of the Department of Education, and you should not assume endorsement by the Federal Government. We are also grateful to our Accessibility Consultant, Glenn Dausch, for his insightful feedback.

10. REFERENCES

[1] Freedom Scientific: JAWS screen-reader.
    http://www.freedomscientific.com/.
[2] GW Micro: Window-Eyes screen-reader.
    http://www.gwmicro.com/.
[3] NonVisual Desktop Access: NVDA screen-reader.
    http://www.nvda-project.org/.
[4] World Wide Web consortium (W3C): XML path language (XPath), 1999. http://www.w3.org/TR/xpath.
[5] IVONA software: IVONA multi-lingual speech synthesis system, 2005. http://www.ivona.com/.
[6] Bangor, A., Kortum, P. T., and Miller, J. T. An empirical evaluation of the System Usability Scale. *Int. J. Hum. Comput. Interaction* (2008), 574–594.

[7] Bian, J., Dong, A., He, X., Reddy, S., and Chang, Y. User action interpretation for online content optimization. *Knowledge and Data Engineering, IEEE Transactions on PP*, 99 (2012), 1.

[8] Bigham, J. P., Lau, T., and Nichols, J. Trailblazer: enabling blind users to blaze trails through the web. In *Proceedings of the 14th international conference on Intelligent user interfaces*, IUI '09, ACM (New York, NY, USA, 2009), 177–186.

[9] Bolin, M., Webber, M., Rha, P., Wilson, T., and Miller, R. C. Automation and customization of rendered web pages. In *Proceedings of the 18th annual ACM symposium on User interface software and technology*, UIST '05, ACM (New York, NY, USA, 2005), 163–172.

[10] Bose, A., Beemanapalli, K., Srivastava, J., and Sahar, S. Incorporating concept hierarchies into usage mining based recommendations. In *Proceedings of the 8th Knowledge discovery on the web international conference on Advances in web mining and web usage analysis*, WebKDD'06, Springer-Verlag (Berlin, Heidelberg, 2007), 110–126.

[11] Brooke, J. SUS: A quick and dirty usability scale. In *Usability evaluation in industry*, P. W. Jordan, A. Thomas, B. Weerdmeester, and I. McClelland, Eds., Taylor and Francis (1996).

[12] Cypher, A., Halbert, D. C., Kurlander, D., Lieberman, H., Maulsby, D., Myers, B. A., and Turransky, A., Eds. *Watch what I do: programming by demonstration*. MIT Press, Cambridge, MA, USA, 1993.

[13] Domènech, J., de la Ossa, B., Sahuquillo, J., Gil, J.-A., and Pont, A. A taxonomy of web prediction algorithms. *Expert Syst. Appl. 39*, 9 (2012), 8496–8502.

[14] Findlater, L., and Gajos, K. Z. Design Space and Evaluation Challenges of Adaptive Graphical User Interfaces. *AI Magazine 30*, 4 (2009), 68–73.

[15] Huang, Z., Eliens, A., van Ballegooij, A., and de Bra, P. A taxonomy of web agents. In *Database and Expert Systems Applications, 2000. Proceedings. 11th International Workshop on* (2000), 765–769.

[16] Hupp, D., and Miller, R. C. Smart bookmarks: automatic retroactive macro recording on the web. In *Proceedings of the 20th annual ACM symposium on User interface software and technology*, UIST '07, ACM (New York, NY, USA, 2007), 81–90.

[17] Leshed, G., Haber, E. M., Matthews, T., and Lau, T. Coscripter: automating & sharing how-to knowledge in the enterprise. In *Proceedings of the twenty-sixth annual SIGCHI conference on Human factors in computing systems*, CHI '08, ACM (New York, NY, USA, 2008), 1719–1728.

[18] Lieberman, H. Autonomous interface agents. In *Proceedings of the SIGCHI conference on Human factors in computing systems*, CHI '97, ACM (New York, NY, USA, 1997), 67–74.

[19] Mahmud, J., Borodin, Y., Ramakrishnan, I. V., and Ramakrishnan, C. R. Automated construction of web accessibility models from transaction click-streams. In *Proceedings of the 18th international conference on World Wide Web*, WWW '09, ACM (New York, NY, USA, 2009), 871–880.

[20] Mahmud, J., Sun, Z., Mukherjee, S., and Ramakrishnan, I. Abstract web transactions on handhelds with less tears. In *Proceedings of the Workshop MobEA IV - Empowering the Mobile Web* (2006).

[21] Montoto, P., Pan, A., Raposo, J., Bellas, F., and López, J. Automating navigation sequences in ajax websites. In *Proceedings of the 9th International Conference on Web Engineering*, ICWE '09, Springer-Verlag (Berlin, Heidelberg, 2009), 166–180.

[22] Myers, E. W., and Miller, W. Optimal alignments in linear space. *CABIOS 4* (1988), 11–17.

[23] Padmanabhan, V. N., and Mogul, J. C. Using predictive prefetching to improve World Wide Web latency. *SIGCOMM Comput. Commun. Rev. 26*, 3 (July 1996), 22–36.

[24] Puzis, Y. Accessible web automation interface: a user study. In *Proceedings of the 14th international ACM SIGACCESS conference on Computers and accessibility*, ASSETS '12, ACM (New York, NY, USA, 2012), 291–292.

[25] Puzis, Y. An interface agent for non-visual, accessible web automation. In *Adjunct proceedings of the 25th annual ACM symposium on User interface software and technology*, UIST Adjunct Proceedings '12, ACM (New York, NY, USA, 2012), 55–58.

[26] Puzis, Y., Borodin, E., Ahmed, F., Melnyk, V., and Ramakrishnan, I. V. Guidelines for an accessible web automation interface. In *The proceedings of the 13th international ACM SIGACCESS conference on Computers and accessibility*, ASSETS '11, ACM (New York, NY, USA, 2011), 249–250.

[27] Puzis, Y., Borodin, Y., Ahmed, F., and Ramakrishnan, I. V. An intuitive accessible web automation user interface. In *Proceedings of the International Cross-Disciplinary Conference on Web Accessibility*, W4A '12, ACM (New York, NY, USA, 2012), 41:1–41:4.

[28] Sun, Z., Mahmud, J., Ramakrishnan, I. V., and Mukherjee, S. Model-directed web transactions under constrained modalities. *ACM Trans. Web 1*, 3 (Sept. 2007).

[29] Vanesa Aciar, S., Serarols-Tarres, C., Royo-Vela, M., and De la Rosa i Esteva, J. L. Increasing effectiveness in e-commerce: recommendations applying intelligent agents. *International Journal of Business and Systems Research 1*, 1 (01 2007), 81–97.

[30] Waterman, M. S., and Smith, T. F. Identification of common molecular subsequences. *J. Mol. Biol. 147* (1981), 195–197.

Mining Collective Intelligence in Diverse Groups

Guo-Jun Qi[†], Charu C. Aggarwal[‡], Jiawei Han[†], Thomas Huang[†]

[†]University of Illinois at Urbana-Champaign
{qi4, hanj, t-huang1}@illinois.edu
[‡]IBM T.J. Watson Research Center
charu@us.ibm.com

ABSTRACT

Collective intelligence, which aggregates the shared information from large crowds, is often negatively impacted by unreliable information sources with the low quality data. This becomes a barrier to the effective use of collective intelligence in a variety of applications. In order to address this issue, we propose a probabilistic model to jointly assess the reliability of sources and find the true data. We observe that different sources are often not independent of each other. Instead, sources are prone to be mutually influenced, which makes them dependent when sharing information with each other. High dependency between sources makes collective intelligence vulnerable to the overuse of redundant (and possibly incorrect) information from the dependent sources. Thus, we reveal the latent group structure among dependent sources, and aggregate the information at the group level rather than from individual sources directly. This can prevent the collective intelligence from being inappropriately dominated by dependent sources. We will also explicitly reveal the reliability of groups, and minimize the negative impacts of unreliable groups. Experimental results on real-world data sets show the effectiveness of the proposed approach with respect to existing algorithms.

Categories and Subject Descriptors

H.2.8 [**Database applications**]: Data mining; Statistical databases

Keywords

Collective intelligence; Crowdsourcing; Robust classifier

1. INTRODUCTION

Collective intelligence aggregates contributions from multiple sources in order to collect data for a variety of tasks. For example, voluntary participants collaborate with each other to create a fairly extensive set of entries in *Wikipedia*, or a crowd of paid persons may perform image and news article annotations in *Amazon Mechanical Turk*. These crowdsourced tasks usually involve multiple *objects*, such as Wikipedia entries and images to be annotated. The participating sources collaborate to claim their own *observations*, such as facts and labels, on these objects. Our goal is to aggregate these collective observations to infer the *true values* (e.g., the true fact and image label) for the different objects [18, 14, 5].

We note that an important property of collective intelligence is that different sources are typically not independent of one another.

Copyright is held by the International World Wide Web Conference Committee (IW3C2). IW3C2 reserves the right to provide a hyperlink to the author's site if the Material is used in electronic media.
WWW 2013, May 13–17, 2013, Rio de Janeiro, Brazil.
ACM 978-1-4503-2035-1/13/05.

For example, in the same social community, people often influence each other, where their judgments and opinions are not independent. In addition, task participants may obtain their data and knowledge from the same external information source, and their contributed information will be dependent. Thus, it may not be advisable to treat sources independently and directly aggregate the information from individual sources, when the aggregation process is clearly impacted by such dependencies. In this paper, we will infer the source dependency by revealing latent group structures among involved sources. Dependent sources will be grouped, and their reliability is analyzed at the group level. The incorporation of such dependency analysis in group structures can reduce the risk of overusing the observations made by the dependent sources in the same group, especially when these observations are unreliable. This helps prevent dependent sources from inappropriately dominating collective intelligence especially when these sources are not reliable.

Moreover, we note that groups are not equally reliable, and they may provide incorrect observations which conflict with each other, either unintentionally or maliciously. Thus, it is important to reveal the reliability of each group, and minimize the negative impact of the unreliable groups. For this purpose, we study the *general* reliability of each group, as well as its *specific* reliability on each individual object. These two types of reliability are closely related. General reliability measures the overall performance of a group by aggregating each individual reliability over the entire set of objects. On the other hand, although each object-specific reliability is distinct, it can be better estimated with a prior that a *generally reliable* group is likely to be reliable on an individual object and vice versa. Such prior can reduce the overfitting risk of estimating each object-specific reliability, especially considering that we need to determine the true value of each object at the same time [11, 1].

The remainder of this paper is organized as follows. We review the related work in Section 2. Our problem and notations are formally defined in Section 3. The probabilistic model for the problem is developed in Section 4, followed by a running example that illustrates the impact of group dependency on the model in Section 5. Section 6 presents the model inference and parameter estimation algorithms. Then Section 7 presents the application of the developed model to training classifiers from noisy crowdsourced data. We evaluate the model in Section 8 on real data sets, and summarize the paper with the conclusion in Section 9.

2. RELATED WORK

Aggregating crowdsourced knowledge and information has attracted a lot of research efforts, and yields many insightful discoveries. For example, [16] proposed an iterative truth finder algorithm by simultaneously accessing the trustworthiness of each source and the correctness of claimed facts. [1] developed a probabilistic graphical model by jointly modeling the abilities of participants and the correct answers to questions in an aptitude testing setting. The work in [18] developed a latent truth model to infer the source quality and correct claims by modeling two types of false positive and false negative errors of each source. All of these algorithms estimate the performances of data sources and the impacts on the credibility of their claimed facts.

However, sources are not independent of each other in real world. Instead, their contributions are typically dependent. [16] noted this problem and used a dampening factor to compensate for excessively high confidence due to the copied content between sources. But this method did not explicitly model the dependency between sources, and how the dampening factor can reduce the dependency effect is not clear. On the other hand, [4] studied the relation between the content claimed by sources, and developed a separate weighted voting algorithm by considering the copied content between each other. However, the accuracies are accessed *independently* on the source level, which can make the accuracy of a data source overestimated if many other dependent sources repeat the same false facts.

Moreover, existing models [4, 2, 9, 6] only consider the pairwise relations between sources to their dependency, which completely ignores the higher-order dependency among sources. In contrast, we explicitly group the dependent sources to capture arbitrary orders of dependency among sources. We find that high-order dependency prevails in many real cases, and it is more effective to model them directly rather than decomposing them into separate pairwise relations. For example, sources which obtain the content from the same resource will be assigned to the same group to reflect the high order dependency among them. This yields a more compact representation to jointly assess the reliability of data sources and the correctness of the claimed facts. Moreover, we will see based on the group-level dependency, independent sources from different groups will play more important role than dependent ones in the same group in inferring the true facts. This is a desired property which can properly aggregate collective knowledge in many real world tasks.

Modeling the group dependency can be analogized to the community discovery in social networks. Community structure has been considered as a more effective data structure to capture the social relations among people than the links between pairs of persons [7]. With the similar spirit, the groups can also be more effective than pairwise dependency, and provide deeper insight into the property of high-order dependency among sources and how such property affects the aggregation of collective knowledge. However, it is worth pointing out that the groups defined in our model differ from the communities [3] in social networks. Communities are usually defined as a set of people densely linked in social networks. However, two linked people may not necessarily be influenced by one another when they report the facts and knowledge. Two close friends can express different opinions and claim conflicting truths. Therefore, we will directly investigate the data contributed by sources to find the group structure characterizing their mutual dependency that directly affects the source reliability in our collective intelligence model.

Finally, our model is motivated to explore the objective facts and knowledge. This is in contrast to the inference of individual's preference, which aims to recommend products and services based on user's ratings and opinions [12]. Instead, in this paper we aim at aggregation of collective knowledge to automatically extract the true facts, such as correct answers to questions and true categories for

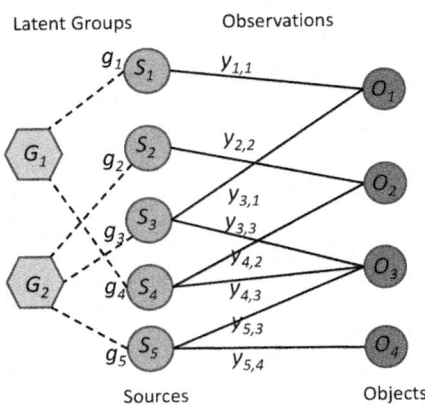

Figure 1: An example illustrating a set of five sources with their observations on four objects.

web pages, which do not depend on the variability of user's subjectivity.

3. PROBLEM DEFINITIONS

We formally define the following Multi-Source Sensing (MSS) model which abstracts the description of collective intelligence. Suppose that we have a set $\mathcal{S} := \{S_1, S_2, \cdots, S_N\}$ of N sources, and a set $\mathcal{O} := \{O_1, O_2, \cdots, O_M\}$ of M objects. Each object O_m takes a value t_m from a domain $\mathcal{X}_m$ which describes one of its attributes. Each source S_n in $\mathcal{S}$ reports its observation $y_{n\,m} \in \mathcal{X}_m$ on an object O_m. Then the goal of the *MSS* model is to infer the true value t_m of each object O_m from the observations made by sources. We introduce some notations, which will be used consistently in this paper. We will use n, m, l and k in the subscript to index sources, objects, groups and values in an object domain, respectively. The variables y, t, u and r denote the observations, true values, group reliability and object-specific reliability respectively.

In this paper, we are particularly interested in categorical domain $\mathcal{X}_m = \{1, \cdots, K_m\}$ with discrete values. For example, in many crowdsourcing applications, we focus on the (binary-valued) assertion correctness in hypothesis test and (multi-valued) categories in classification problem. However, the *MSS* model can be extended to continuous domain with some effort by adopting the corresponding continuous distributions. Due to the space limitation, we leave this extension in the full version of this paper.

Figure 1 illustrates an example, where five sources make their observations on four objects. An object can be an image or a biological molecule, and an annotator or a biochemical expert (as a source) may claim the category (as the value) for each object. Alternatively, an object can be a book, and a book seller web site (as a source) claims the identity of its authors (as the values). In a broader sense, objects are even not concrete objects. They can refer to any crowdsourced tasks, such as questions (e.g., "is Peter a musician?") and assertions (e.g., "George Washington was born on February 22, 1732." and "an animal is present in an image,"), and the observations by sources are the answers to the questions, or binary-valued positive or negative claims on these assertions.

It is worth noting that each source does not need to claim the observations on all objects in $\mathcal{O}$. In many tasks, sources make claims only on small subsets of objects of interest. Thus, for notational convenience, we denote all claimed observations by $\mathbf{y}$ in bold, and use $I = \{(n,m) | \exists\, y_{n\,m} \in \mathbf{y}\}$ to denote all the indices in $\mathbf{y}$. We use the notations $I_{n\,\cdot} = \{m | \exists\,(n,m) \in I\}$ and

$I._m = \{n|\exists (n,m) \in I\}$ to denote the subset of indices that are consistent with the corresponding subscripts n and m.

Meanwhile, in order to model the dependency among sources, we assume that there are a set of latent groups $\{G_1, G_2, \cdots\}$, and each source S_n is assigned to one group G_{g_n} where $g_n \in \{1, 2, \cdots\}$ is a random variable indicating its membership. For example, as illustrated in Figure 1, the five sources are inherently drawn from two latent groups, where each source is linked to the corresponding group by dotted lines. Each latent group contains a set of sources which are influenced by each other and tend to make similar observations on objects. The unseen variables of group membership will be inferred mathematically from the underlying observations. Here, we do not assume any prior knowledge on the number of groups. The composition of these latent groups will be determined with the use of a Bayesian nonparametric approach by stick-breaking construction [15], as to be presented in the next section.

To minimize the negative impact of unreliable groups, we will explicitly model the group-level reliability. Specifically, for each group G_l, we define a group reliability score $u_l \in [0,1]$ in unit interval. This value measures the general reliability of the group over the entire set of objects. A higher value of u_l indicates the greater reliability of the group.

Meanwhile, we also specify the reliability $r_{l\ m} \in \{0,1\}$ of each group G_l on each particular object O_m. When $r_{l\ m} = 1$, group G_l will have reliable performance on O_m, and otherwise it will be unreliable. The reason that we distinguish between reliability u_l and object-specific reliability $r_{l\ m}$ is as follows. While a generally reliable group with a larger value of u_l, provides very useful evidence about the members of the group on a generic basis, there are likely to be natural variations within the group itself. Thus, in our model, a group reliability u_l only measures how likely it will be reliable on object set, and whether it will have a reliable performance on a particular object is given by $r_{l\ m}$. In the next section, we will clarify the relationship between general reliability u_l and object-specific reliability $r_{l\ m}$.

4. MULTI-SOURCE SENSING MODEL

In this section, we present a generative process for the multi-source sensing problem. The output of this model will contain the following three aspects: (1) the group membership of sources which describes their dependency when claiming their observations on a set of objects. (2) the reliability u_l associated with each group and its specific reliability $r_{l\ m}$ on each object. (3) the true values t_m for each object. Our goal is to reveal the connections between these three aspects, especially how the collective observations made by sources can be explained by the latent groups and their reliability in a unified probabilistic framework.

First we define the following generative model for multi-source sensing (MSS) process below, the details of which will be explained shortly.

1. Draw $\boldsymbol{\lambda} \sim \text{GEM}(\kappa)$ (i.e., stick breaking construction with concentration κ).

2. For each source S_n,

    2.1. Draw its group assignment $g_n|\boldsymbol{\lambda} \sim \text{Discrete}(\boldsymbol{\lambda})$;

3. For each object O_m,

    3.1. Draw its true value $t_m \sim \text{Uniform}(\mathcal{X}_m)$;

4. For each group G_l:

    4.1. Draw its group reliability $u_l \sim \text{Beta}(b_1, b_0)$;

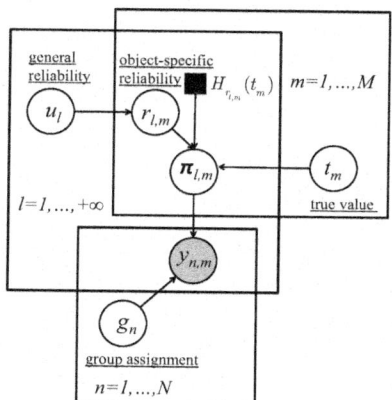

Figure 2: The graphical model for multi-source sensing. The three plates represent group reliability u_l with $l = 1, 2, \cdots$, the true values t_m for each object O_m with $m = 1, \cdots, M$, and the group assignment g_n of each source with $n = 1, \cdots, N$, respectively.

5. For each pair of group G_l and object O_m:

    5.1. Draw reliability indicator $r_{l\ m} \sim \text{Bernoulli}(u_l)$;

    5.2. Draw the observation model parameter
    $$\boldsymbol{\pi}_{l\ m}|r_{l\ m}, t_m = z \sim H_{r_{l,m}}(t_m)$$
    for group G_l on object O_m;

6. For each $(n,m) \in I$:

    6.1. Draw observation $y_{n\ m}|\boldsymbol{\pi}_{l\ m}, g_n \sim F(\boldsymbol{\pi}_{g_n\ m})$;

Here, $g_n|\boldsymbol{\lambda} \sim \text{Discrete}(\boldsymbol{\lambda})$ denotes a discrete distribution, which generates the value $g_n = l$ with probability λ_l; H and F are a pair of conjugate distributions which are determined by the type of data values on objects. For categorical values, these are Dirichlet and Multinomial distributions, respectively. Figure 2 illustrates the generative process in a graphical representation. We will explain the details later.

In Step 1, we adopt the stick-breaking construction $\text{GEM}(\kappa)$ (named after Griffiths, Engen and McCloskey) with concentration parameter $\kappa \in \mathbb{R}^+$ to define the prior distribution of assigning each source S_n to a latent group G_{g_n} [15]. Specifically, in $\text{GEM}(\kappa)$, a set of random variables $\boldsymbol{\rho} = \{\rho_1, \rho_2, \cdots\}$ are independently drawn from the Beta distribution $\rho_i \sim \text{Beta}(1, \kappa)$. They define the mixing weights $\boldsymbol{\lambda}$ of the group membership component such that $p(g_n = l|\boldsymbol{\rho}) = \lambda_l = \rho_l \prod_{i=1}^{l-1}(1 - \rho_i)$. By the aforementioned stick-breaking process, we do not need the prior knowledge of the number of groups. This number will be determined by capturing the degree of dependency between sources.

Clearly, we can see that the parameter κ in the above GEM construction plays the vital role of determining *a priori* the degree of dependency between sources. According to the GEM construction, we can verify that the probability of two sources S_n and S_m being assigned to the same group is given by the following:

$$\begin{aligned} P(g_n = g_m) &= \sum_{l=1}^{+\infty} \mathbb{E}_{\boldsymbol{\lambda}} P(g_n = l|\boldsymbol{\lambda}) P(g_m = l|\boldsymbol{\lambda}) \\ &= \sum_{l=1}^{+\infty} \mathbb{E}_{\lambda_l} \lambda_l^2 = \sum_{l=1}^{+\infty} \frac{2}{(1+\kappa)(2+\kappa)} \left(\frac{\kappa}{2+\kappa}\right)^{l-1} = \frac{1}{1+\kappa} \end{aligned} \quad (1)$$

It is evident that when κ is smaller, sources are more likely to be assigned to the same group where they are dependent and share the same observation model. This will yield higher degree of dependency between sources. As κ increases, the probability that any two sources belong to the same group will decrease. In the extreme case, as $\kappa \to +\infty$, this probability approaches zero. In this case, all sources will be assigned to distinctive groups, yielding complete independence between sources. This shows that the model can flexibly capture the various degrees of dependency between sources by setting an appropriate value of κ.

In Step 3, we adopt the uniform distribution as the prior on the true value t_m of each object over its domain $\mathcal{X}_m$. The uniform distribution sets an unbiased prior so that true values will be completely determined a posteriori given observations in the model inference. In Section 7, we will show how to set a more informative prior when more knowledge about objects is available.

In Step 4, we define a Beta distribution $\text{Beta}(b_1, b_0)$ on the group reliability score u_l, where b_1 and b_0 are the soft counts which specify whether a group is reliable or not a priori, respectively. Then, in Step 5.1, object-specific reliability $r_{l\,m} \in \{0,1\}$ is sampled from the Bernoulli distribution $\text{Bern}(u_l)$ to specify the group reliability on a particular object O_m. The higher the general reliability u_l, the more likely G_l is reliable on a particular object O_m with $r_{l\,m}$ being sampled to be 1. This suggests that a generally more reliable group is more likely to be reliable on a particular object. In this sense, the general reliability serves as a prior to reduce the over-fitting risk of estimating object-specific reliability in the *MSS* model.

In Step 5.2, the model parameter $\pi_{l\,m}$ for each group on a particular object is drawn from the conjugate prior $H_{r_{l,m}}(t_m)$, which depends on the true value t_m and the object-specific group reliability $r_{l\,m}$. Then, given the group membership g_n, each source S_n generates its observation $y_{n\,m}$ according to the corresponding group observation model $F(\pi_{g_n\,m})$ in Step 6. In the next subsection, we will detail the specification of $H_{r_{l,m}}(t_m)$ and $F(\pi_{l\,m})$ in categorical domain.

4.1 Group Observation Models

In this subsection, we discuss the specification of group observation distribution $F(\pi_{l\,m})$ and its conjugate distribution $H_{r_{l,m}}(t_m)$ for categorical values on each object. Here the group observation model on each object depends on two factors: (1) the specific reliability $r_{l\,m}$ on this object, which aims to reveal the differences between reliable and unreliable observations on an object, and (2) the true value t_m for the object.

It is worth noting that although we distinguish each group observation into reliable and unreliable cases in this subsection, it does not mean that two groups are enough to capture the source dependency. These two cases are used to model the performance at the *object* level. However, given more objects, there are many possible combinations of these two cases on different objects. This is why we need more groups to capture the source dependency based on their observations on different objects. In the following, we will discuss the group observations models on each object.

In categorical domains, for each group, we choose the multinomial distribution as its observation model to generate each observation $y_{n\,m}$ for its member sources on each object O_m. Thus, Step 6 in the generative process of *MSS* model becomes the following:

$$y_{n\,m} | \pi_{l\,m}, g_n \sim F(\pi_{g_n\,m}) \triangleq \text{Multinomial}(\pi_{g_n\,m})$$

where $\pi_{l\,m}$ is the parameter of multinomial distribution for group G_l on object O_m. Here, all member sources in the same group share the same observation model to capture their dependency.

The model parameter $\pi_{l\,m}$ is generated by the following:

$$\pi_{l\,m} | r_{l\,m}, t_m = z \sim H_{r_{l,m}}(t_m)$$
$$\triangleq \text{Dir}(\underbrace{\theta^{(r_{l,m})}, \cdots}_{z-1}, \underset{\underset{z^{\text{th}}\,\text{entry}}{\downarrow}}{\eta^{(r_{l,m})}}, \cdots, \theta^{(r_{l,m})})$$

where Dir denotes Dirchlet distribution, and $\theta^{(r_{l,m})}$ and $\eta^{(r_{l,m})}$ are its soft counts for sampling the false and true values under different settings of $r_{l\,m}$.

If group G_l has reliable observations for object O_m (i.e., $r_{l\,m} = 1$), it should be more likely to sample the true value $t_m = z$ as its observation than sampling any other false value. Thus, we should set a larger value for $\eta^{(r_{l,m})}$ than for $\theta^{(r_{l,m})}$.

On the other hand, if group G_l has unreliable observations for object O_m, i.e., $r_{l\,m} = 0$, it should *not* be more likely to claim the true value for the object than claiming the false values. Therefore, the group observation model should have $\eta^{(0)}$ no larger than $\theta^{(0)}$, i.e., $\eta^{(0)} \leq \theta^{(0)}$. Specifically, the mathematical model can distinguish between *uninformative* and *malicious* observations on the target object:

I. **Uninformative observation:** When $\eta^{(0)} = \theta^{(0)}$, sources in group G_l make uninformative observations on object O_m, since false values are equally likely to be claimed as the true value. This can be caused when these sources either carelessly claim their observations at random, or lack the knowledge about the target object.

II. **Malicious observation:** When $\eta^{(0)} < \theta^{(0)}$, it suggests that the group G_l contains malicious sources which tend to claim false values for object O_m. Compared with uninformative observations, these malicious observations can even provide us with some information about the target object by interpreting the observations in a reverse manner. Actually, with $\theta^{(0)} > \eta^{(0)}$, the model gives the unclaimed observation larger weight to be evaluated as the true value.

In summary, depending on $r_{l\,m}$, the sources in group G_l make either reliable (when $r_{l\,m} = 1$) or unreliable (when $r_{l\,m} = 0$) observations on a particular object O_m. Accordingly, the corresponding parameters $\eta^{(r_{l,m})}$ and $\theta^{(r_{l,m})}$ are constrained in different ways. When $r_{l\,m} = 1$, we impose a strict inequality $\eta^{(1)} > \theta^{(1)}$ to enforce that group G_l is more likely to claim the true value. On the contrary, when $r_{l\,m} = 0$, we have $\theta^{(0)} \geq \eta^{(0)}$, representing that G_l will be unreliable in terms of claiming the true value for O_m. In Section 6, we will see how these parameters can be estimated by maximizing the observation likelihood of the *MSS* model subject to these constraints.

By putting together these different pieces, the *MSS* defines a complete distribution

$$p(\mathbf{y}, \mathbf{g}, \mathbf{r}, \mathbf{u}, \mathbf{t}, \boldsymbol{\pi} | \Theta) = \prod_{m=1}^{M} p(t_m) \prod_{l=1}^{L} \prod_{m=1}^{M} p(u_l | b_1, b_0) p(r_{l\,m} | u_l)$$
$$\times p(\pi_{l\,m} | r_{l\,m}, t_m, \eta^{(r_{l,m})}, \theta^{(r_{l,m})})$$
$$\times \prod_{n=1}^{N} p(g_n | \kappa) \prod_{(n\,m) \in I} p(y_{n\,m} | g_n, \pi_{g_n\,m})$$

over $\mathbf{g} = \{g_n\}$, $\mathbf{r} = \{r_{l\,m}\}$, $\mathbf{u} = \{u_l\}$, $\mathbf{t} = \{t_m\}$, $\boldsymbol{\pi} = \{\pi_{l\,m}\}$ and the source observations $\mathbf{y}$ with model parameters $\Theta = \{\eta^{(0)}, \theta^{(0)}, \eta^{(1)}, \theta^{(1)}, b_1, b_0, \kappa\}$. In Section 6, we will present how to infer (1) the true values t_m for each object, (2) group assignment g_n of each source, and (3) the general reliability u_l of each group and its specific reliability $r_{l\,m}$ on each object from the *MSS* model a posteriori given the observations $\mathbf{y}$.

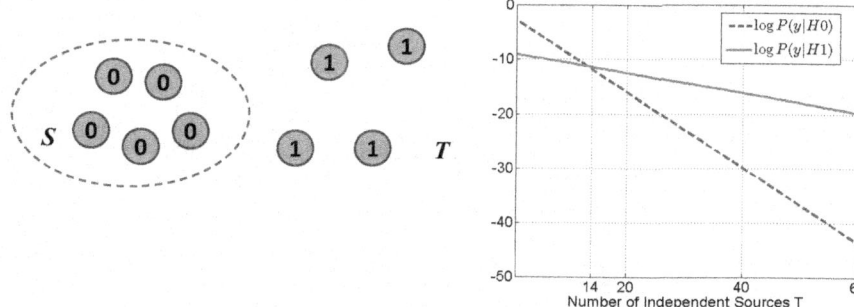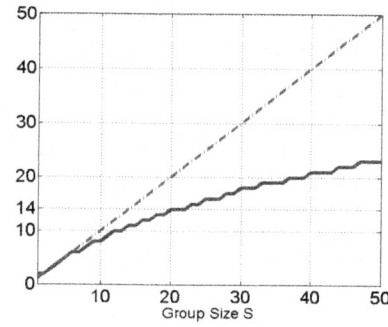

(a) An running example

(b) Likelihoods of two hypotheses

(c) Minimal number of independent sources to overturn the claims by S dependent sources (solid blue curve).

Figure 3: (a) A running example with S dependent sources in the same group and T independent sources. (b) Comparison of the likelihoods of two hypotheses (in Y-axis) versus varying number T of independent sources (in X-axis). The number of dependent sources in the group is fixed to $S = 20$. (c) The minimal number of independent sources (in Y-axis) to overturn the claims made by varying number of dependent sources (in X-axis). The results are obtained with $\eta^{(1)} = 10, \theta^{(1)} = 5$, and $\eta^{(0)} = \theta^{(0)} = 10$.

4.2 Multiple Attributes

In some cases, an object might have multiple attributes. There are many such examples as follows.

- A person can have many attributes. For example, she/he has a hobby of playing piano and takes "software engineer" as her/his vocation. We can consider hobby and vocation as two attributes for each person, and define their values on two different domain sets such as {playing piano, hiking, swimming, traveling $\cdots$} and {software engineer, stock trader, university faculty, $\cdots$} in MSS model, respectively.

- An image can be labeled as "tiger" as well as "forest". We can consider the presence of these two nonexclusive labels as two different attributes, and their values are boolean {Present, Not Present} for an image. In this way, we can allow an image has multiple labels simultaneously.

- A movie can have multiple actors/actresses. We can treat each actor/actress as an attribute, and use a binary value {1,0} to denote whether an actor/actress participates in a particular movie or not.

We can see in these examples, our *MSS* model is much flexible to handle multiple attributes associated with each object. Moreover, we note that different attributes often correlate with each other. For example, image labels "tiger" and "forest" often co-occur in an image, and some actors/actresses may tend to co-star a movie. Exploring these attributes together can improve the accuracy of inferring their true values.

5. DEPENDENCE VS. INDEPENDENCE: A RUNNING EXAMPLE

In this section, we show a running example that demonstrates how group reliability structure captures the dependency between sources when it infers the true value for an object. In Figure 3(a), we show a group of S sources and T independent sources. We consider an ideal case where the S sources in the group make an unanimous claim of the value 0 for an object, while the T independent sources unanimously claims the opposite value 1 for the same object. While the dependent sources in the group and the independent sources claim the different values in this example, we can investigate different values of information contributed by these sources. Especially, we wonder whether independent sources play more important roles than dependent ones in finding the true value for each object in the *MSS* model.

For this purpose, we test the following two hypotheses:

- $H0$: The true value for the object is 0, versus
- $H1$: The true value for the object is 1.

To decide which hypothesis is true, we compare the observation likelihoods given these two hypotheses in the *MSS* model. Figure 3(b) compares the two likelihoods with varying number T of independent sources. The number of dependent sources is fixed to $S = 20$. We can see with more than $T = 14$ independent sources, $H1$ has a larger likelihood than $H0$. In this case, the claims made by independent sources become more credible than that made by dependent sources. This example shows fewer independent sources can overturn the claim made by more dependent sources. This suggests that each dependent source contains less information about the true claim as compared with each independent source.

To make this point more clear, Figure 3(c) illustrates the minimum number of independent sources to ensure $p(\mathbf{y}|H1) > p(\mathbf{y}|H0)$ under varying number of dependent sources S in the group. We can see that usually fewer independent sources is needed to have its claim accepted compared with the same number of dependent sources. This shows that independent sources are more valuable than dependent sources in determining the true value for each object. This is a desired property in our model, since we would like to de-emphasize the excessive impacts of dependent sources in a group.

Of courses, in the real world, sources may not be ideally split into dependent ones in a group, and completely independent ones. The independent sources may not make unanimous claims as in this case. However, this intuitive running example explains how the dependency encoded in group structure will affect the inference of true value on an object, and illustrates the independent claims are generally more valuable than dependent claims in the *MSS* model.

6. MODEL INFERENCE AND PARAMETER ESTIMATION

In this section, we present the inference and learning processes. We wish to infer the tractable posterior $p(\mathbf{g}, \mathbf{r}, \mathbf{u}, \mathbf{t}, \boldsymbol{\pi}|\mathbf{y})$ with a parametric family of variational distributions in the factorized form:

$$q(\mathbf{g}, \mathbf{r}, \mathbf{u}, \mathbf{t}, \boldsymbol{\pi}) = \prod_n q(g_n|\boldsymbol{\varphi}_n) \prod_{l\,m} q(r_{l\,m}|\boldsymbol{\tau}_{l\,m})$$
$$\prod_l q(u_l|\boldsymbol{\beta}_l) \prod_m q(t_m|\boldsymbol{\nu}_m) \prod_{l\,m} q(\pi_{l\,m}|\boldsymbol{\alpha}_{l\,m})$$

with parameters $\boldsymbol{\varphi}_n$, $\boldsymbol{\tau}_{l\,m}$, $\boldsymbol{\beta}_l$, $\boldsymbol{\nu}_m$ and $\boldsymbol{\alpha}_{l\,m}$ for these factors. The distribution and the parameter for each factor can be determined by the variational approach [10]. Specifically, we aim to maximize the lower bound of the log likelihood $\log p(\mathbf{y})$, i.e.,

$$\log p(\mathbf{y}) \geq \mathbb{E} \log p(\mathbf{g}, \mathbf{r}, \mathbf{u}, \mathbf{t}, \boldsymbol{\pi}, \mathbf{y}) - \mathbb{E}(\log q(\mathbf{g}, \mathbf{r}, \mathbf{u}, \mathbf{t}, \boldsymbol{\pi})) \triangleq \mathcal{L}(q)$$

This can obtain the optimal factorized distribution. The lower bound can be maximized over one factor while the others are fixed. This is an approach which is similar to coordinate descent. In each iteration, all the factors are updated sequentially over steps by finding the fixed-point solutions until convergence. The details of these updating steps are provided in Appendix A.

We analyze the computational complexity in one loop of updating all factors. Suppose that we are given N sources, M objects, and obtain L groups by the stick-breaking construction. We also denote by $K_{\max}$ the maximum size of the domain sets among all objects. Then by investigating the updating steps in Appendix A, we can find that the computational complexity is $O(NMLK_{\max})$ for one loop.

On the other hand, the model parameters Θ can be estimated by maximizing the observation likelihood. This can be done by the EM algorithm:

E-Step: Given the current parameters in Θ, apply variational inference to obtain the factorization q and their variational parameters;
M-Step: Given the factorization q, maximize the lower bound $\mathcal{L}(q)$ of the log-likelihood and obtain a new model parameter Θ. (Details of this Maximization step are given in Appendix B.)

These two steps are iterated until convergence. We obtain the variational approximation and the maximum likelihood parameter estimation results simultaneously.

7. CLASSIFICATION PROBLEMS

We are often of particular interest in the classification problem where each object takes a class as its value from a K-class domain $\mathcal{X} = \{1, 2, \cdots, K\}$. Moreover, we might be able to access the feature representations for the objects in $\mathcal{O}$. For example, if the objects are genetic sequences or text documents, we can extract their feature descriptors to describe the genetic structure and document content. Therefore, we wish to impose a more informative prior that aggregates these features into the prior distribution. For this purpose, given a feature vector $\mathbf{x}_m$ for an object, the prior on t_m becomes a conditional distribution on $\mathbf{x}_m$. For greater modeling flexibility, we choose a distribution for this prior. For example, we

can choose an exponential distribution $p(t_m|\mathbf{x}_m, W)$:

$$\mathrm{Exp}(W) := p(t_m|\mathbf{x}_m, W) = \frac{1}{Z} \exp\left\{\sum_{k=1}^K \delta [\![t_m = k]\!] \langle \mathbf{w}_k, \mathbf{x}\rangle\right\} \quad (2)$$

where each coefficient vector is taken from the parameters $W = \{\mathbf{w}_k | k \in \mathcal{X}\}$, $\langle \mathbf{w}_k, \mathbf{x}\rangle$ denotes the inner product between two vectors, and Z is the normalization factor to ensure that the above exponential distribution integrates to unit value.

Accordingly, the model inference in Step A.4 in Appendix A should be changed. Each updated factor $q(t_m)$ in model inference becomes an exponential distribution:

$$q(t_m|\boldsymbol{\nu}_m) := \exp\{\sum_{k=1}^K \delta [\![t_m = k]\!] \nu_{m;k}\} \quad (3)$$

with the parameter $\boldsymbol{\nu}_m$ defined as follows:

$$\nu_{m;k} = \langle \mathbf{w}_k, \mathbf{x}\rangle + \sum_l \sum_{r_l} q(r_l)\{(\eta^{(r_l)} - 1)$$
$$\times \underset{(\pi_{l,m})}{\mathbb{E}} \ln \pi_{l\,m;k} + \sum_{k' \neq k} (\theta^{(r_l)} - 1) \underset{(\pi_{l,m})}{\mathbb{E}} \ln \pi_{l\,m;k'}\}$$

The other updating steps for the model inference in Appendix A stay the same.

Besides the inference, we need to learn the parameter W in $p(t_m|\mathbf{x}_m, W)$. Here, we adopt the variational EM (Expectation-Maximization) algorithm. In each iteration, the E-step (expectation) involves computing the tractable posterior distributions as in the inference step. Then, the maximization step will update W by maximizing the expected log-likelihood over q as follows:

$$\max_W \sum_{m=1}^M \mathbb{E}_{(\,m|\nu_m)} \log p(t_m|\mathbf{x_m}, W) \quad (4)$$

We can adopt any off-the-shelf optimization algorithms to solve the above problem.

The learned parameterized model $p(t_m|\mathbf{x}, W)$, as a byproduct, is a classifier conditional on the input feature vector $\mathbf{x}$. This provides us with a way to train a robust classification model with the noisy crowdsourced labels, compared with typical classifiers trained with the clean labels. On the other hand, the learned classifier enhances the *MSS* model by providing a more discriminative prior of the labeling information on objects through their feature representations. This regularizes the true classes of objects in the feature space, especially when the classes claimed by different sources on an object are too scarce or too inconsistent to make robust estimation of the true classes. In this case, the imposed prior plays a nontrivial role in determining the true class of the object.

8. EXPERIMENTAL RESULTS

In this section, we compare our approach with other existing algorithms and demonstrate its effectiveness for inferring source reliability together with the true values of objects. The comparison is performed on a book author data set from online book stores, and a user tagging data set from the online image sharing web site `Flickr.com`.

8.1 Online Book Store Data Set

The first data set is the book author data set prepared in [16]. The data set is obtained by crawling 1,263 computer science books on *AbeBooks.com*. For each book, *AbeBooks.com* returns the book information extracted from a set of online book stores. This data set contains a total of 877 book stores (sources), and 24,364 listings of books (objects) and their author lists (object values) reported by these book stores. Note that each book has a different categorical domain that contains all the authors claimed by sources. Our goal is to predict the true authors for each book.

Author names are normalized by preserving the first and last names, and ignoring the middle name of each author. For evaluation purposes, the authors of 100 books are manually collected from scanned book covers [16]. We compare the returned results of each model with the ground truth author lists on this test set and report the accuracy.

We compare the proposed algorithm *MSS* with the following baselines: (1) the naive voting algorithm which counts the top voted author list for each book as the truth; (2) *TruthFinder* [16]; (3) *Accu* [4] which considers the dependency between sources; (4) *2-Estimates* as described in [5] with the highest accuracy among all the models in [5].

Table 3 compares the results of the different algorithms on the book author data set in terms of the accuracy. The *MSS* model achieves the best accuracy among all the compared models. We note that the proposed *MSS* model is an unsupervised algorithm which does not involve any training data. In other words, we do not use any true values in the *MSS* algorithm in order to produce the reliability ranking as well as other true values. Even compared with the accuracy of 0.91 of the Semi-Supervised Truth Finder (SST-F) [17] using extra training data with known true values on some objects, the *MSS* model still achieves the highest accuracy of 0.95.

Figure 4(a) illustrates the scatter plot between the predicted reliability u_l for each group and its test accuracy. From this figure, it is evident that the group reliability obtained from the *MSS* model is a good predictor of the true accuracy for each group. Meanwhile, we also report three example groups in Table 1. It is evident that within each group, the member sources have much consistent reliability as they make dependent claims. Therefore, by accurately predicting reliability of groups, the proposed *MSS* model can appropriately aggregate the contributions from differen groups based on their performances and gain the competitive accuracy as shown above.

Moreover, to compare the reliability between sources, we can define the reliability of each source S_n by the expected reliability score of its assigned groups as follows:

$$\text{Reliability}(S_n) = \sum_l q(g_n = l) \mathop{\mathbb{E}}_{(u_l|\beta_l)}[u_l]$$

where

$$\mathop{\mathbb{E}}_{(u_l|\beta_l)}[u_l] = \frac{\beta_{l\,1}}{\beta_{l\,1} + \beta_{l\,2}}$$

Then, sources can be ranked based on such source reliability. In Table 2, we rank the top-10 and bottom-10 book stores in this way.

In order to show the extent to which this ranking list is consistent with the real source reliability, we provide the accuracy of these bookstores on test data sets. Note that each individual bookstore may only claim on a subset of books in the test set, and the accuracy is computed based on the claimed books. From the table, we can see that the obtained rank of data sources is consistent with the rank of their accuracies on the test set. On the contrary, the accuracy of the bottom-10 bookstores is much worse compared to that of the top-10 book stores on the test set. This also partially explains the better performance of the *MSS* model.

Since κ influences the dependency modeling between sources, we study the sensitivity of the model accuracy versus κ in Figure 3. We know that when $\kappa = 0$, all sources are completely dependent, and assigned to the same group. At this point, the model has a much

Table 4: The rounds used before convergence and computing time for each model.

Model	Bookstore		User Tagging	
	Rounds	Time(s)	Rounds	Time (s)
Voting	1	0.2	1	0.5
2-Estimates	29	21.2	32	628.1
TruthFinder	8	11.6	11	435.0
Accu	22	185.8	23	3339.7
MSS	9	10.3	12	366.2

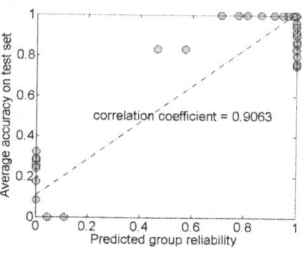
(a) Book author data set

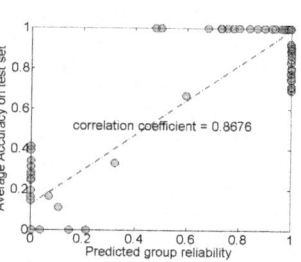
(b) Flickr data set

Figure 4: Scatter plots on two data sets. The horizontal axis represents the predicted group reliability by u_l and the vertical axis represents the average accuracy of the member sources on the test set. The slope of each red line in the scatter is the correlation coefficient which shows the statistical correlation between u_l and the average accuracy.

lower accuracy, since all sources are tied to the same level of reliability within a single group. As κ increases, the accuracy achieves the peak at $\kappa = 5.0$. After that point, it deteriorates as the model gradually stops capturing the source dependency with increased κ. This demonstrates the importance of modeling the source dependency, and the capability of the *MSS* model in capturing such dependencies with κ.

8.2 Flickr Image Tagging Data Set

We also evaluate the algorithm on a user tagging data set from an online image sharing web site *Flickr.com*. This data set contains 13,528 users (data sources) who annotate 36,280 images (data objects) with their own tags. We consider 12 tags - "balloon," "bird," "box," "car," "cat," "child," "dog," "flower," "snow leopard," "waterfall," "guitar," "pumpkin" for evaluation purposes. Each tag is associated with a binary value 1/0 to represent its presence or not in an image. This forms a multi-attribute model with these 12 tags to find whether they are present on each image as described in Section 4.2. Different from the book author data set, we apply the extended classification model in Section 7, where the visual content of each image is represented by a 8,000 dimensional hierarchical gaussian [19] feature vector.

Figure 4 illustrates some image examples in this data set and the tags annotated by users. It is evident that some images are wrongly tagged by users. The *MSS* model aims to correct these errors and yield accurate annotations on these images. To test accuracy, we manually annotate these 12 tags on a subset of 1,816 images.

We follow the same experimental setup as on the book author data set. For the sake of fair comparison, we adopt the variants in [8] to incorporate visual features to enhance the original algorithms for comparison by inferring the true values based on object clusters in

Table 1: Three example groups among all 33 groups discovered by the *MSS* model on book author data set. The parenthesis after the name of each bookstore is its accuracy on test set.

Group I	Group II	Group III
FREE U.S. AIR SHIPPING (0.3750)	The Book Depository (0.3043)	DVD Legacy (0.5833)
TheBookCom (0.3556)	textbookxdotcom (0.4444)	Englishbookservice.com (0.5500)
Browns Books (0.3438)	Caiman (0.3855)	Henry's Biz Books (0.6000)
Mellon's Books (0.4000)	Bobs Books (0.4615)	Blackwell Online (0.6579)
	Books Down Under (0.4750)	Morgenstundt Buch & Kunst (0.6207)
	Limelight Bookshop (0.3896)	
	Powell's Books (0.3810)	

Table 2: Top-10 and bottom-10 book stores ranked by their posterior probability of belonging to a reliable group. We also report the accuracy of these bookstores on the test set.

top-10 bookstore	accuracy	bottom-10 bookstore	accuracy
International Books	1	textbooksNow	0.0476
happybook	1	Gunter Koppon	0.225
eCampus.com	0.9375	www.textbooksrus.com	0.3333
COBU GmbH & Co. KG	0.875	Gunars Store	0.2308
HTBOOK	1	Indoo.com	0.3846
AlphaCraze.com	0.8462	Bobs Books	0.4615
Cobain LLC	1	OPOE-ABE Books	0
Book Lovers USA	0.8667	The Book Depository	0.3043
Versandantiquariat Robert A. Mueller	0.8158	Limelight Bookshop	0.3896
THESAINTBOOKSTORE	0.8214	textbookxdotcom	0.4444

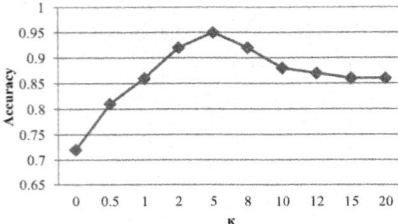

Figure 5: Parametric Sensitivity: model accuracy versus different κ on book author data set.

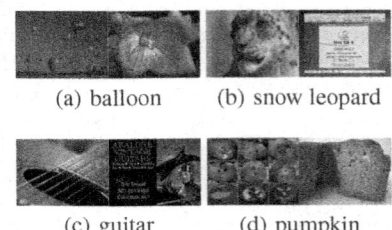

(a) balloon   (b) snow leopard
(c) guitar   (d) pumpkin

Figure 6: Examples of image and the associated user tags in Flickr data set. In each subfigure the left image is correctly tagged by users, while the right one is wrongly tagged.

the feature space. It has shown better accuracy compared with the original algorithms [8]. Table 3 shows the average precision and recall on the 12 tags by the compared algorithms. We can see that *MSS* still performs the best among these compared algorithms. The Figure 4(b) illustrates the scatter plot between the predicted reliability of each group and the average accuracy of its member sources on the test set. It is evident that the obtained group reliability is still a good predictor of the true accuracy with strong correlation coefficient 0.8676. This guarantees a competitive performance of the *MSS* model on this *Flickr* data set as on the book author data set.

We also compare the computational time used by different algorithms in Table 4. The experiments are conducted on a personal computer with Intel Core i7-2600 3.40 GHz CPU, 8 GB physical memory and Windows 7 operating system. We can see that compared with most of other algorithms, *MSS* model can converge in fewer rounds with less computational cost.

9. CONCLUSION

In this paper, we propose an integrated true value inference and group reliability approach. Dependent sources which are grouped together, and their (general and specific) reliability is assessed at the group level. The true data values are extracted from the reliable groups so that the risk of overusing the observations from dependent sources can be minimized. The overall approach is described by a probabilistic multi-source sensing model, based on which we jointly infer group reliability as well as the true values for objects *a posterior* given the observations from sources. The key to the success of this model is to capture the dependency between sources, and aggregate the collective knowledge at the group granularity. We present experimental results on two real data sets, which demonstrate the effectiveness of the proposed model over other existing algorithms.

Acknowledgements

Research was sponsored by the Army Research Laboratory and National Science Foundation and was accomplished under Cooperative Agreement Number W911NF-09-2-0053 and Grant IIS-1144111. The views and conclusions contained in this document are those of the authors and should not be interpreted as representing the official policies, either expressed or implied, of the Army Research Laboratory or the U.S. Government. The U.S. Government is au-

Table 3: Comparison of different algorithms on book author and Flickr data set. On book author data set, the algorithms are compared by their accuracies. On Flickr data set, the algorithms are compared by their average precisions and recalls on 12 tags.

Model	book author data set accuracy	Flickr data set precision	Flickr data set recall
Voting[4]	0.71	0.8499	0.8511
2-Estimates[5]	0.73	0.8545	0.8602
TruthFinder[17]	0.83	0.8637	0.8649
Accu[4]	0.87	0.8731	0.8743
MSS	**0.95**	**0.9176**	**0.9212**

thorized to reproduce and distribute reprints for Government purposes notwithstanding any copyright notation here on. The first author was also in part supported by an IBM Fellowship and National Natural Science Foundation of China under Grant 61272214.

Appendix A: Model Inference

In this Appendix, we derive the variational inference for the proposed *MSS* model, and give the detail steps to update the variational parameters in each factor.

A.1: Update each factor $q(\pi_{l\ m}|\alpha_{l\ m})$ for the group observation parameter $\pi_{l\ m}$.

By variational approach, we can verify that the optimal $q(\pi_{l\ m}|\alpha_{l\ m})$ has the form

$$q(\pi_{l\ m}|\alpha_{l\ m}) \propto \exp\{ \mathbb{E}_{(r_{l,m})\ (m)} \ln p(\pi_{l\ m}|r_{l\ m}, t_m)$$
$$+ \sum_{n \in I_{\cdot,m}} \mathbb{E}_{(g_n)} \ln p(y_{n\ m}|\pi_{l\ m}, g_n)\}$$
$$\propto \prod_{k \in \mathcal{X}} \pi_{l\ m;k}^{\alpha_{l,m;k}-1}$$

It still has Dirichlet distribution with the parameters

$$\alpha_{l\ m;k} = \sum_{n \in I_{\cdot,m}} q(g_n = l)\delta[\![y_{n\ m} = k]\!]$$
$$+ \sum_{r_{l,m} \in \{0\ 1\}} q(r_{l\ m})[(\eta^{(r_{l,m})} - 1)q(t_m = k)$$
$$+ (\theta^{(r_{l,m})} - 1)(1 - q(t_m = k))] + 1$$

for each $k \in \mathcal{X}_m$, where $\delta[\![A]\!]$ is the indicator function which outputs 1 if A holds, and 0 otherwise. Here we index the element in $\alpha_{l\ m}$ and $\pi_{l\ m}$ by k after the colon. We will follow this notation convention to index the element in vectors in this paper.

A.2: Update each factor $q(u_l|\beta_l)$ for general group reliability u_l.

We have

$$\ln q(u_l|\beta_l) \propto \sum_m \mathbb{E}_{(r_{l,m})} \ln p(r_{l\ m}|u_l) + \ln p(u_l|b_1, b_0)$$
$$= (\sum_m q_1(r_{l\ m}) + b_1 - 1) \ln u_l$$
$$+ (\sum_m q_0(r_{l\ m}) + b_0 - 1) \ln(1 - u_l)$$

where $q_i(r_{l\ m})$ is short for $q(r_{l\ m} = i)$ for $i = 0, 1$, respectively. It is evident the posterior of u_l still has Beta distribution as Beta(β_l) with parameter

$$\beta_l = [\sum_m q_1(r_{l\ m}) + b_1, \sum_m q_0(r_{l\ m}) + b_0].$$

It is evident that the above updated parameter sums up the posterior reliability $q_1(r_{l\ m})$ and $q_0(r_{l\ m})$ over all objects. This corresponds to the intuition that the general reliability is the sum of the reliability on individual objects.

A.3: Update each factor $q(r_{l\ m}|\tau_{l\ m})$ for the object-specific reliability $r_{l\ m}$ of group G_l on O_m:

$$\ln q(r_{l\ m}|\tau_{l\ m}) \propto \mathbb{E}_{(m)\ (\pi_{l,m})} \ln p(\pi_{l\ m}|r_{l\ m}, t_m)$$
$$+ \mathbb{E}_{(u_l)} \ln p(r_{l\ m}|u_l) \quad (5)$$

Thus, we have

$$\ln q(r_{l\ m}|\tau_{l\ m})$$
$$\propto \sum_{k \in \mathcal{X}_m} q(t_m = k)[(\eta^{(r_{l,m})} - 1) \mathbb{E}_{(\pi_{l,m})} \ln \pi_{l\ m;k}$$
$$+ (\theta^{(r_{l,m})} - 1) \sum_{j \neq k} \mathbb{E}_{(\pi_{l,m})} \ln \pi_{l\ m;j}] \quad (6)$$
$$+ r_{l\ m} \mathbb{E}_{(u_l)} \ln u_l + (1 - r_{l\ m}) \mathbb{E}_{(u_l)} \ln(1 - u_l)$$

for $r_{l\ m} \in \{0, 1\}$, respectively. Here we compute the expectation of the logarithmic Dirichlet variable as

$$\mathbb{E}_{(\pi_{l,m})} \ln \pi_{l\ m;k} = \psi(\alpha_{l\ m;k}) - \psi(\sum_i \alpha_{l\ m;i})$$

with the digamma function $\psi(\cdot)$; the expectation of the logarithmic Beta variables

$$\mathbb{E}_{(u_l)} \ln u_l = \psi(\beta_{l;1}) - \psi(\beta_{l;1} + \beta_{l;2})$$

and

$$\mathbb{E}_{(u_l)} \ln(1 - u_l) = \psi(\beta_{l;2}) - \psi(\beta_{l;1} + \beta_{l;2}).$$

Finally, the updated values of $q(r_{l\ m})$ are normalized to be valid probabilities.

The last line of Eq. (6) reflects how the general reliability u_l affects the estimation of the object-specific reliability. This embodies the idea that a generally reliable group is likely to be reliable on a particular object and vice versa. This can reduce the overfitting risk of estimating $r_{l\ m}$ especially considering that $q(t_m)$ in the second line also needs to be estimated simultaneously in the *MSS* model as in the next step.

A.4: Update each factor $q(t_m|\nu_m)$ for the true value.

We have

$$\ln q(t_m = k|\nu_m) \propto \ln p(t_m = k)$$
$$+ \sum_l \sum_{r_{l,m} \in \{0\ 1\}} q(r_{l\ m}) \mathbb{E}_{(\pi_{l,m})} \ln p(\pi_{l\ m}|t_m = k, r_{l\ m})$$

This suggests that

$$\ln q(t_m = k|\boldsymbol{\nu_m})$$
$$\propto \sum_l \sum_{r_{l\,m}} q(r_{l\,m})\{(\eta^{(r_{l,m})} - 1) \underset{(\boldsymbol{\pi}_{l,m})}{\mathbb{E}} \ln \pi_{l\,m;k}$$
$$+ \sum_{k' \neq k} (\theta^{(r_{l,m})} - 1) \underset{(\boldsymbol{\pi}_{l,m})}{\mathbb{E}} \ln \pi_{l\,m;k'}\}$$

All $q(t_m = k), k \in \mathcal{X}_m$ are normalized to ensure they are validate probabilities.

A.5: Update each factor $q(g_n|\boldsymbol{\varphi}_n)$ for the group assignment of each source.

We can derive

$$\ln q(g_n = l|\boldsymbol{\varphi}_n)$$
$$\propto \underset{(\boldsymbol{\rho})}{\mathbb{E}} \ln p(g_n = l|\boldsymbol{\rho}) + \sum_{m \in I_{n,\cdot}} \underset{(\boldsymbol{\pi}_{l,m})}{\mathbb{E}} \ln p(y_{n\,m}|\boldsymbol{\pi}_{l\,m}, g_n = l)$$
$$= \underset{(\boldsymbol{\rho})}{\mathbb{E}} \ln p(g_n = l|\boldsymbol{\rho}) + \sum_{m \in I_{n,\cdot}} \underset{(\boldsymbol{\pi}_{l,m})}{\mathbb{E}} \ln \pi_{l\,m;\,n,m}$$

This shows that $q(g_n = l|\boldsymbol{\varphi}_n)$ is a multinomial distribution with its parameter as

$$\varphi_{n;l} = q(g_n = l|\boldsymbol{\varphi}_n) = \frac{\exp(U_{n\,l})}{\sum_{l=1}^{\infty} \exp(U_{n\,l})} \quad (7)$$

where

$$U_{n\,l} = \underset{(\boldsymbol{\rho})}{\mathbb{E}} \ln p(g_n = l|\boldsymbol{\rho}) + \sum_{m \in I_{n,\cdot}} \underset{(\boldsymbol{\pi}_{l,m})}{\mathbb{E}} \ln \pi_{l\,m;\,n,m}$$

As in [13], we truncate after L groups: the posterior distribution $q(\rho_i)$ after the level L is set to be its prior $p(\rho_i)$ from Beta$(1, \kappa)$; and all the expectations $\underset{(\boldsymbol{\pi}_{l,m})}{\mathbb{E}} \ln \pi_{l\,m;k}$ after L are set to:

$$\underset{(\boldsymbol{\pi}_{l,m})}{\mathbb{E}} \ln \pi_{l\,m;k} = \underset{(\,m)}{\mathbb{E}} \underset{p(r_{l,m})}{\,} \{\mathbb{E}[\ln \pi_{l\,m;k}|r_{l\,m}, t_m]\}$$

with the prior distribution $p(r_{l\,m})$ defined as Section 4 for all $l > L$, respectively. The inner conditional expectation in the above is taken with respect to the probability of $\pi_{l\,m}$ conditional on $r_{l\,m}$ and t_m. Similar to the family of nested Dirichlet process mixture in [13], this will form a family of nested priors indexed by L for the MSS model. Thus, we can compute the infinite sum in the denominator of Eq. (7) as:

$$\sum_{l=L+1}^{\infty} \exp(U_{n\,l}) = \frac{\exp(U_{n\,L+1})}{1 - \exp(\underset{\rho_i \sim \text{Beta}(1\,\kappa)}{\mathbb{E}} \ln(1 - \rho_i))}$$

A.6: Update $q(\rho_i)$ in GEM construction.

Before the truncation level L, the posterior distribution $q(\rho_i) \sim$ Beta$(\phi_{i\,1}, \phi_{i\,2})$ is updated as

$$\phi_{i\,1} = 1 + \sum_{n=1}^{N} q(g_n = i), \quad \phi_{i\,2} = \kappa + \sum_{n=1}^{N} \sum_{j=i+1}^{\infty} q(g_n = j)$$

Appendix B: Parameter Estimation

The model parameters $\Theta = \{\eta^{(0)}, \theta^{(0)}, \eta^{(1)}, \theta^{(1)}, b_1, b_0, \kappa\}$ can be estimated by maximizing the log-likelihood $\log \mathcal{L}(q)$ by the obtained factorization q with the constraints $\eta^{(1)} > \theta^{(1)}$ and $\eta^{(0)} \leq \theta^{(0)}$. Since we require $\eta^{(1)} > \theta^{(1)}$ strictly holds, we usually impose $\eta^{(1)} \geq (1+\epsilon)\theta^{(1)}$ with a positive value of ϵ, i.e., $\eta^{(1)}$ is larger than $\theta^{(1)}$ with a margin ϵ. This ensures the strict inequality and improves numerical stability. In the algorithm, we set $\epsilon = 0.5$. Then, the parameter estimation problem becomes the following:

$$\Theta^{\star} = \arg\max_{\Theta} \mathcal{L}(q)$$
$$s.t., 0 \leq \eta^{(0)} \leq \theta^{(0)}, \eta^{(1)} \geq (1+\varepsilon)\theta^{(1)} \geq 0,$$
$$b_1, b_0, \kappa \geq 0$$

This constrained optimization problem can be solved by many off-the-shelf gradient-based constrained optimization solvers with the following gradients:

$$\frac{\partial \mathcal{L}}{\partial \eta^{(r)}} = \sum_{l\,m} \sum_{k \in \mathcal{X}_m} \{\psi(\eta^{(r)} + (K_m - 1)\theta^{(r)}) - \psi(\eta^{(r)})$$
$$+ \psi(\alpha_{l\,m;k}) - \psi(\sum_i \alpha_{l\,m;i})\}$$

$$\frac{\partial \mathcal{L}}{\partial \theta^{(r)}} = \sum_{k \in \mathcal{X}_m} \{\psi(\eta^{(r)} + (K_m - 1)\theta^{(r)}) - (K_m - 1)\psi(\theta^{(r)})$$
$$+ \sum_{k'} \psi(\alpha_{l\,m;k'}) - (K_m - 1)\psi(\sum_i \alpha_{l\,m;i})\}$$

for $r \in \{0, 1\}$.

$$\frac{\partial \mathcal{L}}{\partial b_1} = \sum_l \psi(b_1 + b_0) - \psi(b_1) + \psi(\beta_{l\,1}) - \psi(\beta_{l\,1} + \beta_{l\,2})$$

$$\frac{\partial \mathcal{L}}{\partial b_0} = \sum_l \psi(b_1 + b_0) - \psi(b_0) + \psi(\beta_{l\,2}) - \psi(\beta_{l\,1} + \beta_{l\,2})$$

$$\frac{\partial \mathcal{L}}{\partial \kappa} = \sum_i \psi(1 + \kappa) - \psi(\kappa) + \psi(\phi_{i\,1} + \phi_{i\,2}) - \psi(\phi_{i\,2})$$

10. REFERENCES

[1] Y. Bachrach, T. Minka, J. Guiver, and T. Graepel. How to grade a test without knowing the answers - a bayesian graphical model for adaptive crowdsourcing and aptitude testing. In *Proc. of International Conference on Machine Learning*, 2012.

[2] M. Bilgic, G. Namata, and L. Getoor. Combining collective classification and link prediction. In *Workshop on Mining Graphs and Complex Structures (at ICDM)*, 2007.

[3] A. Clauset, M. E. J. Newman, and C. Moore. Finding community structure in very large networks. *Physical Review E*, 70:066111, 2004.

[4] X. L. Dong, L. Berti-Equille, and D. Srivastava. Integrating conflicting data: The role of source dependence. In *Proc. of International Conference on Very Large Databases*, August 2009.

[5] A. Galland, S. Abiteboul, A. Marian, and P. Senellart. Corroborating information from disagreeing views. In *Proc. of ACM International Conference on Web Search and Data Mining*, February 2010.

[6] L. Getoor, N. Friedman, D. Koller, and B. Taskar. Learning probabilistic models of link structure. *Journal of Machine Learning Research*, (3):679–707, 2002.

[7] M. Girvan and M. Newman. Community structure in social and biological networks. *Proceedings of the National Academy of Sciences*, 99(12):7821–7826, June 2002.

[8] M. Gupta, Y. Sun, and J. Han. Trust analysis with clustering. In *Proc. of International World Wide Web Conference*, April 2011.

[9] O. Hassanzadeh and et al. A framework for semantic link discovery over relational data. In *CIKM*, 2009.

[10] M. Jordan, Z. Ghahramani, T. Jaakkola, and L. Saul. Introduction to variational methods for graphical models. *Machine Learning*, 37:183–233, 1999.

[11] G. Kasneci, J. V. Gael, D. Stern, and T. Graepel. Cobayes: Bayesian knowledge corroboration with assessors of unknown areas of expertise. In *Proc. of ACM International Conference on Web Search and Data Mining*, 2011.

[12] Y. Koren, R. Bell, and C. Volinsky. Matrix factorization techniques for recommender systems. *Computer*, 42(8):30–37, August 2009.

[13] K. Kurihara, M. Welling, and N. Vlassis. Accelerated variational dirichlet process mixtures. In *NIPS*, 2006.

[14] J. Pasternack and D. Roth. Knowing what to believe (when you already know something). In *Proc. of International Conference on Computational Linguistics*, August 2010.

[15] J. Sethuraman. A constructive definition of dirichlet priors. *Statistica Sinica*, 4:639–650, 1994.

[16] X. Yin, J. Han, and P. S. Yu. Truth discovery with multiple conflicting information providers on the web. In *Proc. of ACM SIGKDD conference on Knowledge Discovery and Data Mining*, August 2007.

[17] X. Yin and W. Tan. Semi-supervised truth discovery. In *Proc. of International World Wide Web Conference*, March 28-April 1 2011.

[18] B. Zhao, B. I. P. Rubinstein, J. Gemmell, and J. Han. A bayesian approach to discovering truth from conflicting sources for data integration. In *Proc. of International Conference on Very Large Databases*, 2012.

[19] X. Zhou, N. Cui, Z. Li, F. Liang, and T. Huang. Hierarchical gaussianization for image classification, 2009.

Trade Area Analysis using User Generated Mobile Location Data

Yan Qu
PlaceNous.com
yan.qu@acm.org

Jun Zhang
Pitney Bowes Inc.
jun.zhang@pb.com

ABSTRACT
In this paper, we illustrate how User Generated Mobile Location Data (UGMLD) like Foursquare check-ins can be used in Trade Area Analysis (TAA) by introducing a new framework and corresponding analytic methods. Three key processes were created: identifying the activity center of a mobile user, profiling users based on their location history, and modeling users' preference probability. Extensions to traditional TAA are introduced, including customer-centric distance decay analysis and check-in sequence analysis. Adopting the rich content and context of UGMLD, these methods introduce new dimensions to modeling and delineating trade areas. Analyzing customers' visits to a business in the context of their daily life sheds new light on the nature and performance of the venue. This work has important business implications in the field of mobile computing.

Categories and Subject Descriptors
H.1.2 [**Models and Principles**]: User/Machine Systems

General Terms
Human Factors, Measurement

Keywords
Trade Area Analysis, Mobile marketing, Location based marketing

1. INTRODUCTION
One of the defining characteristics of mobile computing is user mobility. Various applications and services have been developed to make use of location information from people's smart phones, ranging from simple apps like WeatherChannel, to location based guides like Yelp, context aware assistants like GoogleNow, and location based social networking services like Foursquare. These new apps and services were widely adopted and as a result, location data from millions of users has been captured. This data, although anonymized, records users' locations and movements over time. Thus, it has great potential in the study of location related behavior.

Significant research has been done using location data of mobile users. Some were fundamental research such as Song et al.'s work on identifying patterns of human mobility [31]. Some focused on building new services that may have great public or business potentials [35], such as modeling city living neighborhood [6] and recommending friends and locations [38]. The business value of the location data of mobile users has generated a lot of attention in research and industry circles. For example, Baccelli and Bolot [1] modeled the economic value of this data. Companies have started mining such data for location based marketing purposes, such as user profiling (e.g. SenseNetworks.com) and location based advertising (e.g. placecast.com).

This work explores a new business application area for location data of mobile users: studying the interactions between customers and local stores. Specifically, we looked to answer critical questions in business marketing management: What is the trade area of a business? Where are its customers from? What are the characteristics of these customers? Answers to these questions are vital for understanding consumer behavior and effectively allocating limited resources [27].

Our work builds on the traditional Trade Area Analysis (TAA) model that has been used in industry for more than 90 years [15][28]. We propose a new framework and corresponding analytic methods to accommodate mobile location data which has a very different nature from data used in traditional TAA. For instance, location data of mobile users usually does not contain users' home address information, which is required in the traditional TAA. At the same time, mobile location data adds new dimensions to TAA process as it has much richer content and context of people's location history. Using a mobile location dataset of Foursquare check-ins, we illustrate the value and challenges of our TAA process in the era of mobile computing.

In summary, this paper makes three primary contributions:

- To the best of our knowledge, it is the first work to apply Trade Area Analysis to location data of mobile users, opening a new business application area.
- It provides a new analytic framework based on the traditional TAA model. This paper focuses on demonstrating the process of applying this framework to mobile location data rather than analyzing the results gleaned from a special dataset (i.e. Foursquare check-ins).
- It presents new analytic methods within the TAA framework to model customer mobility, create customer profiles and preferences, and examine interactions between customers and stores.

The paper is organized as follows: First, we describe the nature and limitations of location data of mobile users, as well as the Foursquare check-in dataset used in this paper; second, we describe the TAA processes using this new data; third, we discuss novel analyses beyond the traditional TAA process; and last, we discuss related works, review the implications of our findings, and make overall conclusions.

2. USER GENERATED MOBILE LOCATION DATA (UGMLD) AND ITS LIMITATIONS
2.1 Location Data of Mobile Users
There are different types of location data of mobile users with varying methods of collection and degree of granularities. We first exclude several types of data that were not applicable to our

proposed analyses so they will not confuse readers. The most widely used mobile location data in academic research is Call Detail Records (CDR) [31]. It records the closest cell phone tower location when the phone is used and can only be collected by mobile service carriers. Mobility research often uses CDR because it has low user bias and better time coverage [9][31]. However, the location precision of CDR is about 3 square kilometers on average – the range of cell phone tower coverage [9]. Thus, CDR can only draw conclusions at the area level. Similarly, IP address based location data is collected by websites by checking the location associated with the IP address of its visitors. Neither of these two types of data provide the location precision required for our analyses and therefore they were excluded from discussion. Another type of mobile location data we excluded is collected by in-store sensors (e.g. Bluetooth, WIFI, or ultra sound sensing). Such data is limited to a store's boundary and thus inapplicable in our analyses.

Two types of location data of mobile users can be used in our analyses: the first collected by social networking services (e.g. Foursquare) [16] and the second collected by various apps that record users' locations with their permission (Figure 1.a). Such location data has high precision, usually at the store level. Because they need users' active participation or permission to be collected, we called them User Generated Mobile Location Data (UGMLD).

The UGMLD from location based social networking services is well-known in academic circles because it is easy for researchers to access. For instance, [4] reports that about 20% of Foursquare users automatically publish their Foursquare check-ins on Twitter. Several research groups have used this data source to study location behaviors and population dynamics [4][5][13][22]. Their works indicate that although self-selected user location data is limited and biased, it can be used to identify valuable patterns about individuals and places.

The UGMLD collected by various mobile apps is less well-known in academia but widely used in industry by app developers and third parties like mobile ad networks. For instance, Macy's can collect users' location history in its mobile app if the location feature is enabled (Figure 1.a). Mobile ad networks merge user location data from multiple apps into a more complete location history and then display a location related banner in the app (e.g. Figure 1.b: a banner showing the location of a nearby Wells Fargo Bank.). Note that these apps only record latitude/longitude information. High precision reverse geocoding technology [36] is needed to find venue information.

(a) Macy's   (b) WeatherChannel

Figure 1. Two mobile app examples

However, UGMLD has its limitations, including sparse time coverage of location histories and the likelihood to be biased.

When a person uses a mobile application, a piece of data is created with the user's current location and a timestamp. This data is generated at a rate ranging from several times a day to once in several months. Therefore, only small fractions of a user's location history are represented, not to mention the complete reconstruction of the trajectories. There are some applications (e.g. Aloha.com) that run in the background and track a user's complete location trajectory, but they have not been widely adopted.

The nature and frequency of app usage depends on its type and user preferences. For instance, searching for a hotel on Priceline happens less frequently than checking in on a social network service like Foursquare. Even for the same app, a person who wants to share his locations with friends will use it differently than one looking for check-in based discounts [33]. Therefore, UGMLD cannot be treated as a simple location history. We must carefully examine how incentives, users' preferences and habits, and contexts will affect the dataset.

Lastly, location privacy is becoming an important topic in research, industry, and government policy making circles [14][18]. In this paper, we used the publicly available datasets and focused on the technical process instead of privacy policies. However, we hope our work will help others become more aware of the related privacy implications of location information.

2.2 Foursquare Check-in as UGMLD

In this paper, we use a set of publically available UGMLD from Foursquare to conduct our Trade Area Analysis (TAA). Note these analyses can also be applied to mobile app data. In this section, we describe the data set and discuss the challenges of using it in TAA.

2.2.1 Our Dataset

Check-ins from Foursquare is frequently used UGMLD by researchers because of its relatively large size and easy access. Our dataset contains automatically published check-in tweets on Twitter from linked Foursquare accounts. It covers a ten month period in 2012 from January 1st to November 1st. It was collected using a similar method described in [4]. There are total 31,554,516 check-ins at 980,686 distinct places from 1,016,181 unique users. The data includes latitude, longitude, time of the check-in, place name, place category, and related information like tips and shouts.

Although the dataset appears large, it is only a small portion of the total data on Foursquare. For instance, while the Foursquare page of the Whole Foods store at Union Square, New York City shows 16,678 unique visitors, our dataset only contains 682 (about 4%) of them. Still, this number is larger than the number of customer participants in many traditional TAA surveys. It is important to note that, people who publish their check-ins on Twitter might be less privacy sensitive than general users and this fact is likely to bias our results. That said, this is the best dataset we can find to illustrate the potential of using UGMLD for Trade Area Analysis.

Aware of the limitations of our dataset, we are very cautious when interpreting results, focusing instead on illustrating novel methods and new directions for further research. Our methods should be more reliable and applicable to a variety of businesses if conducted by those who have access to larger UGMLD datasets, such as Foursquare or mobile ad networks.

2.2.2 Uneven Business Category Distribution

In our dataset, the numbers of check-in by business category are unbalanced. Figure 2 shows the top 80 frequently visited categories from our data set. "Grocery or Supermarket",

"Restaurant", and "Coffee Shop" were very popular, while others like "Doctor's office" and "Bank" were much less common. There are several reasons that might explain this skewed distribution. Firstly, as Lindqvist et al. [17] found in their study, people have different motivations for checking in or not based on the location in question. For instance, they may check-in at a coffee shop to "signal availability" or "coordinate with friends", or at places like a gym as "a form of presentation of self". Lindqvist et al. found that Foursquare users do not want to check in at Fast food places because "It's embarrassing to be seen there". Secondly, Foursquare users are technology savvy, and are more likely go to technology-oriented locations than the general public. Finally, the adoption of Foursquare is geographically uneven with most users living in big cities like New York City. Therefore, the places they visit are more common in big cities.

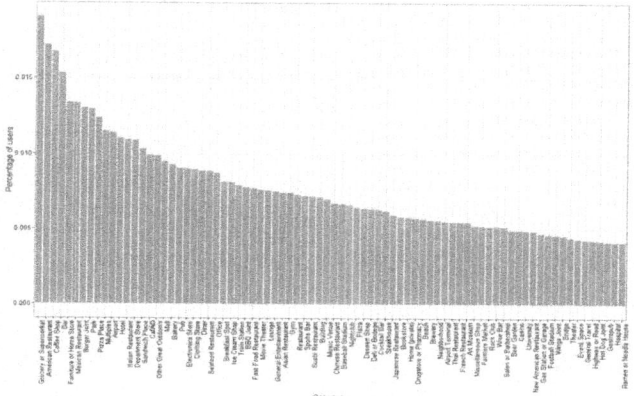

Figure 2. Top 80 check-in categories

Given the skewed distribution by category, the Foursquare data will be more reliable for TAA in the popular categories, not only because there is more data, but also because self-selected data is less biased when the population is larger.

Note: Foursquare also supports none-place check-ins to events. For instance, the most popular "place" in New York in 2011 was a weather event "Snowpocalypse" [32] that could be checked in from any location. These kinds of check-ins were excluded during our collection process.

2.2.3 Skewed User Check-in Distribution

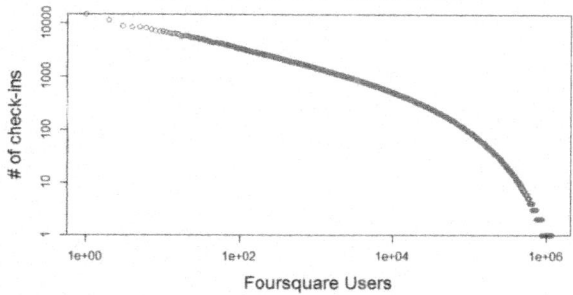

Figure 3. Check-in distribution of Foursquare users

Not surprisingly, the check-in frequency per user is also highly skewed (Figure 3). The number of check-ins range from 1 to 14406 with the median being 5. 25.6% of the users only had one check-in. They might have only tried Foursquare once or they stopped sharing their check-ins on Twitter. There were two users with more than 10,000 check-ins. A detailed review revealed that both were software robots that publish local news. These outliers indicate that we should be very cautious when using check-in data

to infer user behavior. In this study, we interpret the results carefully, well aware of potential biases introduced by these skewed distributions.

3. TRADE AREA ANALYSIS USING FOURSQUARE DATA

3.1 General TAA Process

Trade Area analysis gives a business information about where its customers are from, how far they travel to the store, and their demographics and household information. Thus, marketing activities such as direct mail campaigns can be tailored accordingly.

General Trade Area Analysis typically contains the following steps:

1. Collect basic information about the store to be modeled, such as location and store type, both of which have a large impact on the store's trade area.
2. Select a sample of current customers and collect related customer information, especially where they are from (usually their home address) and their spending in the store.
3. Derive the travel distance polygon to identify the geographic boundary of the customers' locations.
4. Identify the user block group and related information. Create customer profiles, such as block group "Psyte" profiles [19] that represent people's demographic information and income levels, so the business can better understand its customer type.
5. Incorporate other factors like competitors and sister stores.

In following sections, we explore whether we can generate trade areas using Foursquare check-in data, and discuss the challenges of using this type of data. Our analysis roughly follows the same steps of the general TAA process.

3.2 Our Store Samples

The trade area of a store is shaped by many factors, including but not limited to business type, customer population (e.g. students, local residents, daytime employees), geographic settlement context (e.g. urban vs. suburb), underlying road network, and competition. For instance, in traditional TAA, convenience stores that provide products needed on a regular basis (e.g. grocery stores and coffee shops) are treated differently than destination stores that provide major products such as furniture or appliances.

Table 1: selected stores

Store Name	Category	Location	# Checkin Customers
Whole Foods	Grocery store	Union Sq., NYC	682
IKEA	Furniture store	Canton, MI	380
Starbucks	Coffee shop	Union Sq. NYC	420
Macy's	Department store	Downtown, SF	120

To incorporate a variety of the major factors in TAA, we choose four stores of different types and locations as samples, shown in table 1. Most of our analyses that involve store comparison use the Whole Foods in NYC and the IKEA in Canton, MI because they differ in store type and location demographic: the first is a grocery store in an dense urban setting serving residents and daytime employees; the second store is a furniture store in a suburban area that mostly serves residential customers. We also used the other two stores to highlight some interesting observations. Please note: we limited our sample selection to stores with at least 100 unique users in our dataset (a traditional

TAA practice). Thus, our sample is biased towards popular stores in big cities.

3.3 Check-ins as Customer Visitation Data

In traditional TAA, businesses gather customer data from transaction records of current customers, membership information, and surveys of nearby areas. All these methods have their limitations. It is difficult for a business to get its customers' home or office address unless it is a delivery business or requires a registered membership. Business usually only get zip code level information from credit card transactions due to government regulations. Surveys or focus groups are regularly used but expensive and time consuming. They also have issues with self-reporting bias. Although the check-in data differs from actual customer visits, it is relatively easy to get and offers valuable insights into customer behavior, particularly for businesses who want to reach their customers or potential customers with mobile or online marketing.

Below are examples of the check-in data. Note that the latitude/longitude data we retrieved from Twitter is Foursquare normalized store location instead of the real GPS location sent to Foursquare originally.

```
[user_id], [checkin_time], [latitude], [longitude], [store_id]
196514, 2010-07-24 13:45:06, 53.364811914, -2.2723465833, store21
245677, 2010-07-24 13:44:58, 53.364811914, -2.2723465833, store21
....
196514, 2010-07-25 11:21:43, 53.364811914, -2.2723465833, store21
```

In our data, some users checked in at the same store multiple times while many only checked in once. Figure 4 shows the uneven check-in distribution of the four stores with varying degrees of skewness. The top 20% of Starbucks' customers made about 70% of Starbucks' check-ins, while the top 20% of IEKA's customers made only about 41% of IKEA's check-ins, indicating that IKEA has a relatively even user check-in distribution.

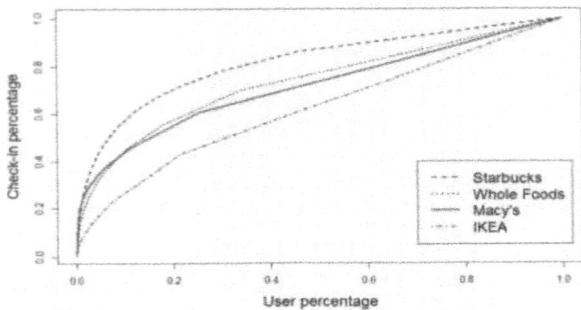

Figure 4. Store check-in distribution

Although there are Foursquare-specific reasons that can lead to this uneven distribution, such as small number of people aggressively checking in to fight for the mayor-ship of a store, these results still reflect customer-store visiting patterns. Stores have loyal customers who visit the store regularly and random customers who rarely visit. Starbucks is a convenience venue thus it is more likely to have customers who visit everyday, while IKEA is a destination venue and therefore likely to have fewer daily visitors.

Furthermore, considering people's check-in behaviors, there are much less false positives (a person checked-in but did not visit) than false negatives (a person visited but did not check in). Therefore, frequent check-ins are likely to indicate a frequent customer, but frequent customers may not check-in frequently. Thus, the check-in distribution is the lower bound of the actual visit distribution. However, we cannot tell if the actual visit distribution is flatter or more skewed.

The important question is how the skewness in data will affect the Trade Area Analysis. For some analysis, the skewness will not bias the results. For example, when drawing trade area polygons, we estimate one activity center for each sampled customer, thus the process is indifferent to the skewness of personal check-ins. However, the skewness will bias the results for certain analysis. For example, in sequence analysis, we want to know where people usually visit before their visit to a specific venue. If the data is highly skewed toward a small group of frequent customers, their behavior pattern will dominate the results. Therefore, in our analysis, we identify such frequent customers and sample only a small number of sequences from them. Throughout this paper, we will adjust the data according to the nature of the analysis and explain our rational.

In our work, to counter the impact of over aggressive check-ins by some users, we removed duplicated check-ins at a venue at the same day. That is, for one customer, we considered at most 1 check-in at one venue in one day. We call such check-in the venue-day check-in (VD check-ins). This is a more truthful indicator of how important a venue is in the person's daily life. The following analyses were only made on VD check-ins.

3.4 Derive Trade Area Boundary using Check-ins

One of the basic questions TAA tries to answer is "Where do my customers come from?" Traditionally, home addresses are collected from a sample of existing customers and used to generate a polygon that includes the majority of customer's households.

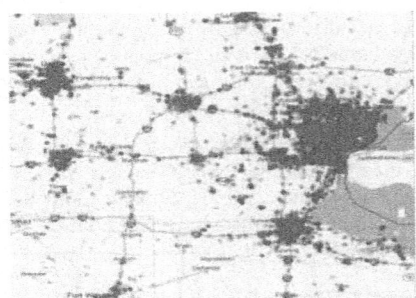

Figure 5. Check-in locations of IKEA customers

However, there is no explicit home address information in our check-in data. Instead, we have a list of customers' check-in locations. Figure 5 shows the spatial distribution of check-in places from customers of the IKEA store at Canton, MI. The picture was generated following two steps: we first identified all the customers who checked in at the IKEA store (the green dot). Then we identified all other places these users checked in and posit them on the map (red dots). Instead of explicitly telling us where the customers are from, this map tells us the areas the customers frequent. According to the basic geographic law of distance decay: interaction between two locales decreases as the distance between them increases, most check-ins a person made should be close to important places in his life, such as his home or office [12]. Therefore, this map provides a rough image of where these important places may be located for this group of IKEA customers.

However, because of the high skewness of the check-in distribution, the patterns shown in Figure 5 may be biased toward those customers with many check-ins. To present the trade area more faithfully, we need to estimate the important places for each customer.

3.4.1 Identifying Users' Activity Centers

In our approach, instead of identifying a customer's home, we identify important places or areas in a customer's life using his check-in location histories.

Previous research based on CDR and UGMLD [4][9][12][25][31] indicates that people's check-ins and activities exhibit both place and area regularity. First, there are places people regularly frequent [9][12][37]: besides their home and office, this might be a gym, grocery store, or library. Second, there are regularly visited areas even if no specific store or location in that area is regularly visited [25]. As an example, figure 6a shows the check-in location heat map of a person who voluntarily shared his Foursquare check-ins and related location information. From the map, we can see that the majority of check-ins falls in three clustered areas. The largest one on the top is the person's "work cluster". The hottest zone with red color in this cluster is around the person's office. The stripe shape of this large cluster is formed by a large number of check-ins along a main street close to his office where he usually has lunch. The bottom right cluster is around the person's home. The cluster in the middle is a popular shopping area. Figure 6b shows the trajectory network of the same user's check-in sequences. It is generated by linking any two consecutive check-in places that happened in the same day. From this figure, we can see there are several check-in hubs with high network degrees. Naturally, the hubs are located in the clustered area in the heat map, which means that frequently visited areas have both spatial importance and sequential significance.

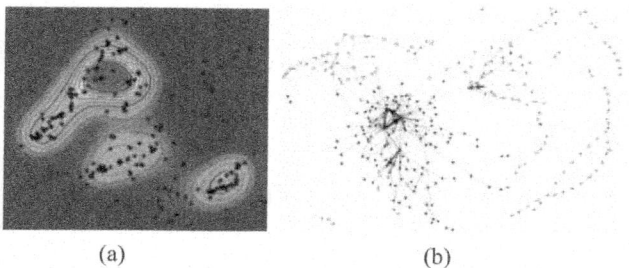

(a) (b)

Figure 6. Check-in heat map and trajectory network from a same person

Place and area regularities allow us to extract locations where there is a high probability that a user will show up in the surrounding area. We call these locations activity centers.

For the purpose of TAA, activity centers are a valid substitute for home location for the following reasons. First, home locations are used to identify target marketing areas. With mobile marketing technologies, knowing where a customer is and where he is likely to show up is more important than only knowing where to mail advertisements. Activity centers serve this purpose better than traditional home location. It is important to note that a person may have multiple activity centers (e.g. home and office). Businesses have a better chance of attracting a customer when they are located close to any one of the customer's activity centers. Second, home locations are used to determine community level demographics or economic data to create customer profiles in traditional TAA. Extracting multiple activity centers, we have a good chance of locating one close to the customer's home (see below for details). Therefore, we can still make coarse community level inferences. Moreover, we propose new methods of creating customer profiles using UGMLD (section 3.5), which generate useful customer information that was never available before.

Previous works such as Isaacman et al. [12] indicate that it is possible to identify important places like home or office area using CDRs. Building on previous works, we propose four methods to identify activity centers using UGMLD and then conduct a limited test.

- Center of Mass: It locates the spatial center of all check-in locations of a person, weighted by the number of check-ins in each place. Note that this method may result in a location in between several check-in clusters.
- Most frequently checked-in location: Intuitively, a customer may be more likely to show up in an area close to this location than other areas.
- Location with the highest check-in density. This method tries to find the hottest spot in a check-in heat map.
- Center of mass of the most frequently visited location cluster. This method firstly identifies a person's regularly visited areas - clusters in the heat map, then extracts the mass center of the most frequently visited cluster. We used the popular density based clustering algorithm DBSCAN [8] with certain prefix density threshold (i.e. there must be at least 5 check-ins in a 1km radius over a period of 30 days to become a potential cluster center). More important is an extension of this method: selecting mass centers of multiple most active areas and then choosing the activity center from them accordingly in TAA. This method heeds the fact that people usually have multiple regular activities areas (e.g. home area and office area). Different TAA tasks may use different activity areas. For example, we can pick the closest activity area rather than the home location when doing a mobile targeting analysis (e.g. for stores whose customers are mainly office workers).

We conducted a simple test to explore the relationship among the activity centers extracted by the above methods and the actual home location. We identified all users who have explicitly checked in at home and have more than 200 check-ins during the 10 month period in our data set, which resulted in 466 users. Figure 7 shows the distance from the identified activity centers and a person's home. The method "cluster – 1" selects the mass center of the most active location cluster. The method "cluster – 3" selects the mass center closest to home from the top 3 active location clusters. Clearly, when we take the top 3 most active clusters, it is very likely that one of them is close to the home location. In our test, 293 (64%) out of the 466 persons live within 2 miles one of the cluster centers. We use this method in the rest of paper.

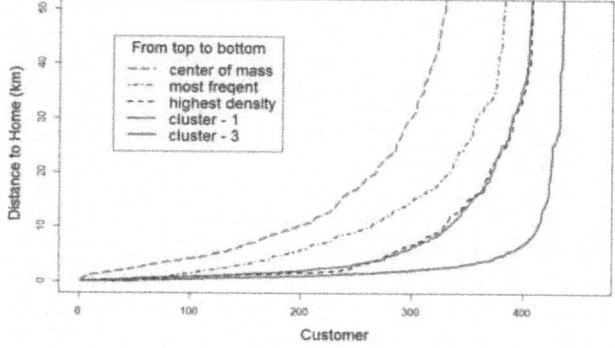

Figure 7. Performance of different activity center identification algorithms

We are aware that this analysis is heavily biased toward people who shared their home locations and these people may have different check-in patterns than others. However, the focus of this paper is not to develop a home prediction algorithm, but rather to demonstrate the added benefits of using activity centers in TAA. Although highly correlated to home locations, activity centers have their own characteristics and meaning within TAA. Many proposed analyses in this paper can be applied to both home location and activity centers. Again, we must emphasize that the results are only valid and valuable if the analysts know how to correctly interpret the data.

3.4.2 Drive Distance based Trade Area Boundary

There are several ways to derive the trade area boundary of a store. Common methods include drive-time/distance polygon, data driven rings, and density clusters [15]. In this paper, we used the drive-time/distance polygon because it is more accurate than the data driven rings and it is less data demanding than the density cluster method which requires large number of user samples to stable the clustering results.

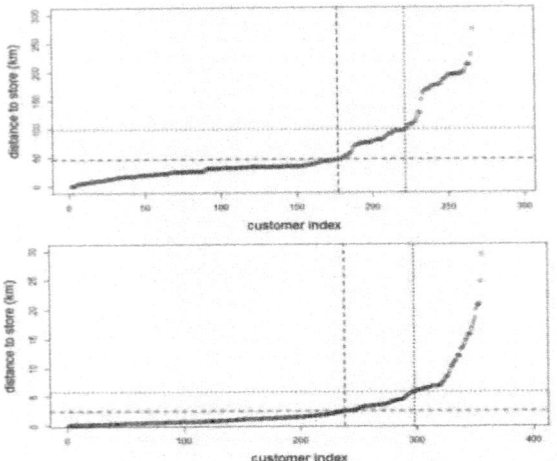

Figure 8. The distance decay of the IKEA (top) and Whole Foods (bottom)

The construction of drive-time/distance polygons starts with distance decay analysis. Distance decay is a geographical term that refers to the decrease of cultural or social interactions as distance increases. In TAA, the most obvious distance decay is the decrease of the number of customers' households or activities centers as the distance to the store increases. Figure 8 illustrates the distance decay effect using the IKEA and Whole Foods stores as examples. The x-axis is the customer index. The y-axis is the distance between the store and the closest activity center of each user. Traditionally, the primary trade area is defined as containing 60% or 75% of the customer population. In our examples, about 60% of the MI IKEA's customers are within 50KM (red line) distance and 75% customers are within 100KM (black line) distance. The Whole Foods at NYC has a much faster distance decay, thus it has a much smaller trade area. 60% of its customers are within 2.5KM and 75% are within 5.8KM.

Figure 9 shows the visualization of the primary trade area polygons containing 60% and 75% customer population of the two stores. The red dots are identified activity centers of customers who have checked in at the store. In the IKEA map, we used the drive-time polygon because people's movement is highly influenced by the road network like high-ways in the suburbs. In the NYC Whole Foods map, we used the drive-distance polygon because it is short ranged and the road speed differences are unpredictable.

Figure 9. Drive distance/time polygons of two stores (left: IKEA, right: Whole Foods)

These two maps and related analyses reveal a lot of information to businesses and can help them with location related decisions. For instance, these stores now know where their customers are from and how long it takes for then to get to the store. The MI IKEA store may want to purchase mobile ad banner space for people who are active in their trade areas such as "Livonia, Detroit, Ann Arbor" while the NYC Whole Food may focus their marketing at lower and midtown Manhattan.

Furthermore, although we did not directly compare the drive-time/distance polygons generated using check-in data to the ones generated using real customer visits, we talked with several trade area experts in industry and their feedback was that the trade areas we created for these stores made great sense and the drive distance patterns were similar to those found using traditional TAA at similar stores.

The trade areas generated here might be biased due to the self-selective nature of UGMLD and our limited data sample. Nonetheless, this method is still very valuable while other data is hard to get. The bias will be less of an issue if analysis is limited to populations similar to the sampled customers' or when researchers have access to more robust UGMLD.

3.5 Location-based User Profiling

Generating the drive-time/distance polygon is not the final step of TAA. In practice, businesses want to know more about current and prospective customers such as their shopping habits and demographic background. Transaction histories and membership information collected by stores are often used to profile customers. However, such detailed personal information is not always available. A less satisfactory approach is Geo-profiling [15][19] – a commonly used method to approximate user characteristics based on neighborhood demographic data (within a 0.3-2 miles range). Its precision is limited but it is very useful when better information is unavailable. However, this method may not be applicable to our dataset, which contains no home address information (activity centers may be too far away to generate similar demographic data.).

To demonstrate new possibilities of user profiling using UGMLD, we choose to characterize users' check-in patterns using the place category information. This new profile feature will tell us what types of places a person like to visit, which is valuable for mobile marketing purpose.

An easy solution is simply count the frequency of one's check-ins within each category. However, we found that almost all users checked in under popular categories like coffee shops. Therefore, this method cannot efficiently distinguish different check-in patterns. Moreover, Foursquare has a hierarchical category structure which includes 9 top categories and 410 sub-categories.

Sub-categories are more valuable in user profiling as they separate a person who likes "Italian food" from another one who likes "Korean food". However, the high dimension of the 410 subcategories presents a challenge.

To address these issues, we chose the Latent Dirichlet Allocation (LDA) [3] method to identify hidden check-in patterns and to profile users based on the identified patterns. LDA is widely adopted in document topic modeling. It assumes that each document contains a mixture of topics and each topic has certain probability of mentioning a word. LDA identifies topics and calculates the proportion of different topics in each document by examining word distributions in the documents. In our work, we treat each person as a "document", each place category as a "word". The "topics" are hidden check-in patterns in the population. LDA requires a pre-determined number of topics. After testing different numbers, we choose 6 that gives intuitively meaningful results.

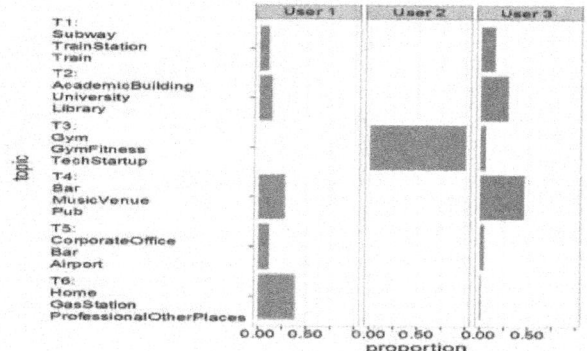

Figure 10. LDA "topics" and user profile

Figure 10 shows the 6 topics (T1 – T6) identified in our dataset, reflecting different check-in patterns. Each topic is labeled by three location category words that have the highest latent factor weight for that topic. T1 is daily commute; T2 is life at school; T3 is the gym and fitness; T4 is night-life; T5 is corporate life and travel; and T6 is the home, driving, and work. We then profile users using these topics. Figure 10 also displays three sample user profiles. We can easily distinguish User 2 from User 1 and User 3 as he only checked in under T3. From his profile, we may guess that he had a gym membership or might work at a startup. The difference between User 1 and User 3 is more subtle. Both had an active night life and traveled to locations on a campus, but User 3 is more likely to be a student in the city than User 1 because he was more active in T2 but almost had no activities in T6. Note that popular categories such as coffee shops may not show up in the LDA results, because they are not helpful when trying to distinguish different groups of users. LDA also addresses the high dimension problem by grouping subcategories into topics.

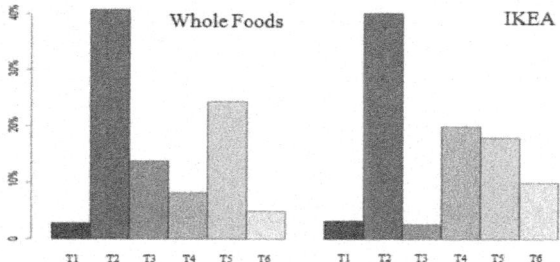

Figure 11. User profile comparison

Next, we compare users' profiles for different stores. To make the comparison easier, we profile each user by the topic with the highest score. Figure 11 shows the profile distributions for Whole Foods and IKEA. Both stores have a significant portion of T2 users (probably college students). The biggest point of difference is at T4 (night life goers).

Our profiling method can be further improved. A more sophisticated method is described in [13]. Our limited goal in this section is to show that the location history based profiling is a promising alternative to traditional profiling methods in TAA.

3.6 Competition and Gravity Models

Competitor stores have a large impact on Trade Area Analysis. Gravity models such as Reilly's Law of Retail Gravitation [28] and Huff's Law of Shopper Attraction [11] are usually adopted in competitor analysis. They are essentially benefit-cost analyses: how frequently a customer visits a business depends on the benefit received by visiting and the cost to visit that location. However, there is a lack of empirical studies modeling a business's attractiveness and the customer's benefit-cost decision making process, which calls into question the validity of those gravity models. Traditionally, there was almost no way for a business to know whether their customers visit competitor stores except expensive surveys. Fortunately, the rise of UGMLD mitigates this concern by providing needed information at little cost. It opens a new window to model customer's preferences in competitor analysis.

In UGMLD, we have information of many customers' visits to many business venues. Formally, for a customer $C_1 \sim C_n$ and a group of competitor venues $V_1 \sim V_m$, we have

$$\begin{array}{cccc} & C_1 & \cdots & C_n \\ V_1 & a_{11} & \cdots & a_{1n} \\ \vdots & \vdots & \ddots & \vdots \\ V_m & a_{m1} & \cdots & a_{1mn} \end{array}$$

Where a_{ij} is the number of visit of customer C_i to store V_j.

What we want to know in competitor analysis is customer's individual and aggregated preferences among competitor stores:

- $P(V_j)$: among all similar business venues $V_1 \sim V_m$ what is the probability of venue V_j being visited;
- $P(V_j|C_i)$: for a customer C_i, what is the probability of visiting venue V_j among all similar places.

Using UGMLD, we can easily estimate customer's preference:

$$P(V_j|C_i) = \frac{a_{ij}}{\sum_{j=1}^{m} a_{ij}}$$

$$P(V_j) = \frac{\sum_{i=1}^{n} a_{ij}}{\sum_{i=1}^{n} \sum_{j=1}^{m} a_{ij}}$$

Such estimations are not possible in traditional TAA when data is limited to a single store (i.e. one row in the above matrix).

We use Whole Foods as an example to illustrate the estimation of customer preferences under the influence of competitor stores. In practice, the competitor stores are manually picked using knowledge about the store, region, and customer segmentation. We didn't have this knowledge about the NYC Whole Foods store, so we simply used the category information provided by Foursquare and treated all stores in the "Grocery and Supermarket" category as potential competitors. For each Whole Foods customer, we counted their check-ins at the store and total check-ins in the category of "Grocery and Supermarket". We estimated $P(V_j|C_i)$ as the number of Whole Foods' check-ins from customer C_i divided by the number of grocery store or supermarket check-ins from C_l. We call $P(V_j|C_i)$ the loyalty index because it reflects how likely a customer will visit this store among all competitors. Note: the Foursquare data may be biased because Whole Foods is not a regular grocery store.

Figure 12 shows a map of the Whole Foods customers with their loyalty index. In the figure, the black dot in the center is the store location. Each colored dot represents a customer. The location of a colored dot is a customer's activity center (we used 5 check-ins in a 0.5km radius area within 30 days as the density threshold in our clustering algorithm). The size of a dot is in proportion to a customer's total grocery or supermarket check-ins. The color of a dot represents the loyalty index of a customer, from 0 (blue) to 1 (red).

Figure 12. Loyalty index of Whole Foods Customers

This loyalty index will not make sense if a customer seldom visits the store or its competitors. In an extreme case, if a customer has only visited the Whole Foods once and has never visited another grocery store or supermarket, then he will have a very high loyalty index (=1), even if he never returned to the Whole Foods again. Therefore, in practice, we suggest a high threshold for the number of visits. In this paper, in order to present the spectrum of different users, we set a relatively low threshold of 3 visits to "Grocery and Supermarket" stores.

Among the 682 Whole Foods customers, there are 171 who have 3 or more visits to Grocery or Supermarket stores. Their loyalty indexes range from 0.01 to 1, with the media of 0.25. From the map we can see the activity centers of our customers are cluttered around the Whole Foods store. Actually 104 (61%) customers have their activity centers closer than 1 km to the store. All the customers with high loyalty index (>0.5) are within 1.45 km distance to the store. However, our data shows no correlation between the loyalty index and the distance between activity centers and the store. Interestingly, customers with a high loyalty index (red or orange dots) are less frequent grocery shoppers than those who have lower loyalty index (blue dots). One possible reason is that when a customer does a lot of grocery shopping, he is more likely to explore more stores. This map provides a visual representation of the trade area under the influence of competitor stores, giving us a rough idea about how likely customers will visit this Whole Foods store among all of its competitors. With more data, this method will provide a more accurate estimation of shopping probabilities, which can be used to inform business strategies or used as the ground truth for testing competing trade area models.

4. BEYOND TRADITIONAL TRADE AREA ANALYSIS

One of the most promising aspects of UGMLD is that it provides a rich and dynamic context of location-based activities that is not included in traditional TAA. In traditional TAA, the business can only get limited transaction information and some customers' home addresses with related demographic characteristics. UGMLD contains much richer information, such as whether a user visited multiple stores in the same area on the same trip, or where he went before and after the visit to a store, which can be used to infer location trajectories. In this section, we explore how to parse this rich information.

4.1 Distance Decay of Customer's Activity

With UGMLD, we can examine the trade area of a store in the context of customers' daily life. In traditional TAA, we study a store's distance decay and where a customer's household is located within the trade area (e.g. in the center or on the fringe). Taking a customer-centric perspective, we examine the distance decay of each customer's shopping activities and ask the question: where is the store located on its customers' activity areas? This gives us a peek into the role a store plays in its customer's daily life.

For each customer, we calculate the Distance Decay Percentage (DDP): percentage of activities within the r radius area to a customer's activity center, where r is the distance between the customer's activity center and the store location. A high DDP (close to 1) means that the store is on the fringe of the customer's activity area. A low DDP (close to 0) means that the store is close to the center of the customer's activity area.

Figure 13 shows the histogram of DDP from all customers of two different stores: Whole Foods and IKEA. X-axis is the activity DDP. Y-axis is the number of customers falling into each bucket. The difference between the two stores is obvious: for most of its customers, the Whole Foods is close to their activity center. On the contrary, IKEA is located on the activity fringe for a large portion of its customers. This implies that Whole Foods is a neighborhood store with most of its customers living nearby, whereas IKEA is a destination store with many of its customers traveling outside of their major activity area.

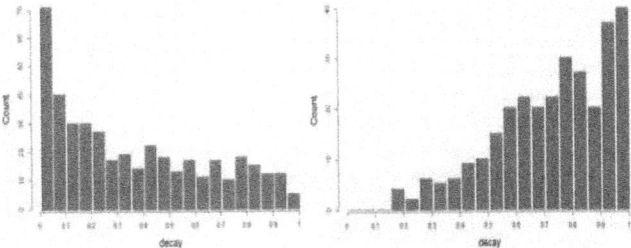

Figure 13. DDP histogram, Whole Foods (left) and Ikea (right)

To further understand the DDP distribution, we draw the scatter plot of DDP vs. distance between store and activity center. In Figure 14, we have plots for Whole Foods and IKEA. Each red dot on the plot is a customer. The size of the dot is in proportion to the log of the total number of check-ins from that customer. The x-axis is the distance between a customer's activity center and the store. The y-axis is the DDP of that customer.

Again, these two plots show two distinct patterns. For Whole Foods, there are a large group of customers with an activity center within 1 km of the store and a relatively low DDP, which means the store is very close to the center of their activity area. When the distance move from about 1km to about 10km, the plot shows a strong correlation between DDP and the distance, which means as customers' activity centers move further away from the store, DDP increases about proportionally. The cluster of dots on the top right corner is customers with activity centers hundreds of miles away from Whole Foods. Understandably their DDP is high, which means the store is on the fringe of their activity area.

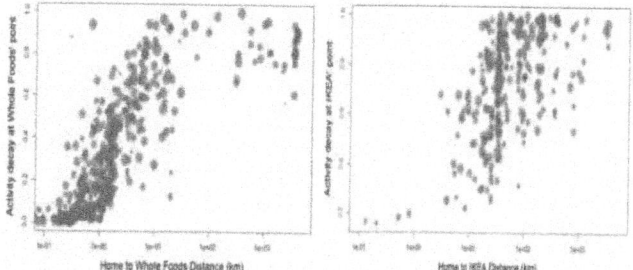

Figure 14. DDP vs. Distance plot, Whole Foods (left) and IKEA (right)

Compared to the plot for Whole Foods, the IKEA has few customers with activity centers within a 5km radius of the store. There is a large group of customers whose activity centers are 10km to 100km away. The almost vertical pattern in the plots indicates a large variety of DDPs at a similar distance, implying a significant difference in customers' mobility (i.e. some customers have a much larger activity area than others). There are also more dots with a high distance but moderately low DDP (0.5~0.8), which are customers who live far away but have very large activity areas, and with the store closer to their activity center than the fringe.

This example analysis shows how a customer-centric perspective can shed light onto hidden patterns of store customer interactions. Above all, we can see that the customer-centric perspective puts the store and purchase transactions in a context of customer's life and helps us understand the intrinsic relationships between customers and stores. This will ultimately help businesses market their products or services and identify potential customers.

4.2 Check-in Sequences Analysis & Use
4.2.1 Analyzing Check-in sequences
Reexamining customers' visits to a particular store in the context of shopping trips can reveal trajectory patterns and provide valuable marketing information. In this section, we explore how to extract and use people's shopping trip information from the check-in data.

To identify shopping trips associated with a particular venue, we extract check-in sequences by sequentially linking the check-ins from a customer during the day he checked in at that business venue.

Next, we analyze the spatial and temporal characteristics of these trips. We use Starbucks to explain what kind of insights can be gained from check-in sequence analysis. We extract 237 sequences with a median number of stops of 3, a median distance span of 2.6km, and a median time span of 5.8 hours.

We draw a bar plot (Figure 15) to illustrate detailed spatial-temporal distribution of check-ins in those sequences. To make the plot readable, we only take check-ins within a 10km distance and ± 10 hour time difference, resulting in 938 (84%) of the Starbucks check-ins in the sequences. In the bar plot, the x-axis is the distance between a check-in in a sequence and the store check-in in the same sequence (before: negative, after: positive), the y axis is the count of check-ins in the corresponding distance range. The colors in the bar indicate the time difference between a check-in and the store check-in, ranging from -10 hours (red) to 10 hours (blue).

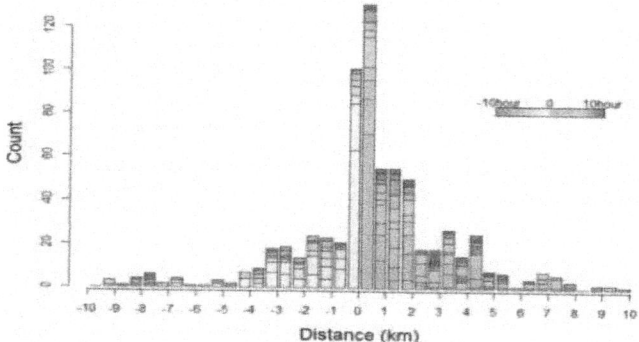

Figure 15. Sequence Check-in distributions (Starbucks)

Several interesting observations can be made from this figure.

First, the highest bars are near to "0" on distance axis within 0.5km, which means many check-ins in the sequence are located very close to the store. Looking at the time segments in those bars, we can see that most of those check-ins are within ±1 hour of the store check-in. This indicates that people check-in at nearby places right before or after they visit a store.

Second, there are more check-ins after the Starbucks check-in than before it, probably because Starbucks is an early destination where people start their trip before moving on to other places. We can infer that people are likely to go to Starbucks to start their day or before other activities.

The check-in sequence analysis provides another example of examining customer-business interactions from a customer-centric perceptive. A business with this knowledge can adjust their marketing strategies accordingly. Data driven geo-fencing is a good example.

4.2.2 Geo-fencing using check-in sequence data
Geo-fencing is a new and exponentially growing mobile marketing technique. The general idea is to target opt-in consumers while they are within a predetermined fence around the store and send them messages or special offers to attract them to walk into the store and make a purchase [20][21]. A key step in the process is setting up the fence. Most current solutions either create a pre-determined radius ring based on store type and location, or use available mall boundaries. The check-in sequence analysis suggests that we can use the check-in data to derive a data driven polygon for Geo-fencing.

Figure 16. Geo-fencing using check-in sequence data

Figure 16 shows a geo-fence created for Whole Foods using check-in data. We used the location a user checked in right before he visited the store. We used the similar distance decay analysis in TAA to determine the drive distance. The red boundary is 0.9km from the store and covers 60% of locations the store's customers visited before they checked in at the store. The blue boundary is 1.8km from the store and covers 75% of such locations. We believe that this fence is more likely to be reliable than a predetermined radius ring, especially when there is no real consumer feedback data in the early stage of geo-fencing marketing.

Alternative geo-fencing methods using check-in sequence may include using all points in the sequence or clustering the points into zones. But we will leave that discussion for a future work.

5. RELATED WORK

Our work builds on industry practices and previous academic research on Trade Area Analysis. Although 90 years old, the pioneering work by Reilly et al. about Laws of Retail Gravitation model is still used in practice to this day. Other classic early work includes Huff's development of probability based analysis of trade area [11] and similar works such as [7][27][29][30]. Our work also greatly benefited from consulting internal subject matter experts and white papers. That said, we have not found any other publications that apply Trade Area Analysis to mobile location data. We hope this paper will draw more attention to this powerful approach.

Our work is inspired by related work in geo-fencing and mobile marketing [2][20][21][26]. Greenwald et al. [10] discussed geo-fencing solutions that can be deployed to large population and used for mobile proximity marketing or social networking services. Ye et al. [34] demonstrated that it is possible to recommend locations based on people's Foursquare check-in histories. Provost et al. proposed a method of geo-social network targeting for mobile advertising [24]. Many of these findings have already been commercialized. Provost et al.'s work has been used in mobile marketing by EveryScreenMedia.com and similar ideas to Ye et al.'s have been used by SenseNetworks.com. Lastly, Partridge and Begole surveyed existing targeting advertising technologies [23] and described the benefits of activity based marketing. They argued that consumers and advertisers' interests are not necessarily at odds, and a balanced privacy and location context sharing can benefit both parties. We agree with this view and think UGMLD-based TAA fits into this vision.

Our work also benefited from excellent works analyzing and making use of UGMLD and human mobility research. Several of our processes were built on methods developed in these works. The details of these linkages are discussed in the previous sections so we will not cover them here again.

6. DISCUSSIONS

In this paper, we open a new application area for User Generated Mobile Location Data (UGMLD): modeling trade areas and consumer-store interactions. Although the dataset has limitations, we demonstrate that it is possible to build meaningful trade areas based on it, including creating drive distance/time boundaries, generating customer profiles, and weighing competitive factors.

This work has immediate business implications. The most promising application is location based mobile advertising. UGMLD-based TAA can inform businesses about the areas their customers visit. Location histories with rich contextual information can be used to model customer behavior, which is likely to outperform existing geographic block based approaches. Moreover, geo-fences created using the dynamic information in UGMLD will more accurately target potential customers than current geo-fencing practices.

Our work outlines a new framework and corresponding analytic methods for UGMLD based Trade Area Analysis. The unique features of UGMLD makes direct adoption of traditional TAA methods impossible. Three key processes were created as a result of this work: identifying activity centers of users, profiling users based on their location history, and modeling users' preference probability. The identification of activity centers is particularly exciting because it proposes a new location concept that is more suitable to mobile TAA analysis than home location. We also extended traditional TAA by adding new types of analysis such as customer oriented distance decay analysis and check-in sequences analysis. This new customer-centric perspective will provide more insights into the relationship between stores and their customers.

Our paper has several limitations: First, our dataset is limited and could be biased. We discussed its bias in detail as well as the steps we took to minimize it. Second, we limited our trade area analysis to four specific business venues and only provide details of two in this paper due to space limitations. Therefore, caution is needed when interpreting or extrapolating these results. Third, we wished to explore each step of the TAA analysis more deeply, but as the first work covering these new topics, we tried to first and foremost to establish the conceptual framework.

Finally, we wish that we can connect to privacy research more closely in the future, because people's privacy preferences, government regulation, and industry practice directly affect how we tweak and use the processes proposed here. For instance, our process for identifying activity centers could be viewed as intrusive or sensitive to privacy concerns depending how it is applied.

In conclusion, despite the limitations of this paper, we believe this conceptual framework and corresponding analytic methods make important theoretical contributions and provide valuable insights to businesses in fields related to mobile computing.

7. REFERENCES

[1] Baccelli, F., and Bolot, J., "Modeling the Economic Value of the Location Data of Mobile Users." *In 2011 Proceedings of IEEE INFOCOM*, 1467 -1475, 2011.

[2] Benita, R., and Subash, G. V., "Design and Implementation of Location Based Ad Delivery System." *Int. J. on Recent Trends in Engineering & Technology* 5, no. 01 (2011).

[3] Blei, D. M., Ng, A. Y., & Jordan, M. I. (2003). Latent dirichlet allocation. *the Journal of machine Learning research*, 3, 993-1022.

[4] Cheng, Z., Caverlee, J., Lee, K., and Sui, D. Z., "Exploring Millions of Footprints in Location Sharing Services." In *Proceedings of AAAI ICWSM 2011*.

[5] Chon, Y., Lane, N. D, Li, F., Cha, H. and Zhao, F., "Automatically Characterizing Places with Opportunistic CrowdSensing Using Smartphones." In *Proceeding of UbiComp 2012*. ACM, 2012.

[6] Cranshaw, J., Schwartz, R., Hong, J. I, and Sadeh, N., "The Livehoods Project: Utilizing Social Media to Understand the Dynamics of a City." In *Proceedings of ICWSM 2012*, 2012.

[7] Donthu, N. "Comparing Market Areas Using Kernel Density Estimation." *Journal of the Academy of Marketing Science* 19, no. 4 (1991): 323-332.

[8] Ester, M., Kriegel, H. P., Sander, J., & Xu, X. "A density-based algorithm for discovering clusters in large spatial databases with noise". In *Proceedings of KDD 1996*, 226-231. AAAI Press.

[9] González, M.C., Hidalgo, C.A., and Barabási, AL. "Understanding Individual Human Mobility Patterns." *Nature* 458, no. 7235 (March 12, 2009): 238-238.

[10] Greenwald, A., Hampel, G., Phadke, C., and Poosala, V., "An Economically Viable Solution to Geofencing for Mass-market Applications." *Bell Labs Technical Journal* 16, no. 2 (2011): 21-38.

[11] Huff, D. L. "A Probabilistic Analysis of Shopping Center Trade Areas." *Land Economics* (1963): 81-90.

[12] Isaacman, S., Becker, R., Cáceres, R., Kobourov, S., Martonosi, M., Rowland, J., and Varshavsky, A. "Identifying Important Places in People's Lives from Cellular Network Data." *Pervasive Computing (2011)*: 133-151.

[13] Joseph, K., Tan, C. H, Afek, Y., Li, M. and Niu, K., "Beyond 'Local','Categories' and 'Friends': Clustering Users Based on Latent 'topics'", in *Proceedings of Ubicomp 2012*, 919-926

[14] Khoshgozaran, A., Shahabi, C. and Shirani-Mehr, H. "Location Privacy: Going Beyond K-anonymity, Cloaking and Anonymizers." *Knowledge and Information Systems* 26, no. 3 (2011): 435-465.

[15] Kures, M. Pinkovitz, Ryan, B., "Downtown and business district market analysis", http://fyi.uwex.edu/downtown-market-analysis/files/2011/02/Trade_Area_Analysis033011.pdf

[16] Li, N., and Chen, G. "Sharing Location in Online Social Networks." *Network*, IEEE 24, no. 5 (2010): 20-25.

[17] Lindqvist, J., Cranshaw, J., Wiese, J., Hong, J., and Zimmerman, J. "I'm the Mayor of My House: Examining Why People Use Foursquare - a Social-driven Location Sharing Application." In *Proceedings of CHI2011*, 2409-2418. ACM, 2011.

[18] Liu, Z., Bonazzi, R., Fritscher, B., and Pigneur, Y. "Privacy-Friendly Business Models for Location-Based Mobile Services." *Journal of Theoretical and Applied Electronic Commerce Research* 6, no. 2 (August 2011): 90-107.

[19] MapInfo, Psyte U.S. Advantage. http://resource.mapinfo.com/static/files/document/1074655820383/psyte_brochure_us.pdf

[20] Martin, D., Alzua, A., and Lamsfus, C. "A Contextual Geofencing Mobile Tourism Service." *Information and Communication Technologies in Tourism* 201, 191-202.

[21] Munson, J. P., and Gupta, V. K. "Location-based Notification as a General-purpose Service." In *Proceedings of the 2nd International Workshop on Mobile Commerce*, 40-44, 2002.

[22] Noulas, A., Scellato, S., Mascolo, C., and Pontil, M. "An Empirical Study of Geographic User Activity Patterns in Foursquare." In *Proceedings of ICWSM'11* (2011).

[23] Partridge, K., and Begole, B. "Activity-Based Advertising." In *Pervasive Advertising*, edited by Jörg Müller, Florian Alt, and Daniel Michelis, 83-101. Human-Computer Interaction Series. Springer London, 2011.

[24] Provost, F., Martens, D. and Murray, A. "Finding similar users with a privacy-friendly geo-social design", http://www.everyscreenmedia.com/esmtwo/wp-content/uploads/2012/11/Finding_Similar_Users.pdf

[25] Qu, Y. and Zhang, J. "Regularly Visited Patches in Human Mobility", to appear in *Proceedings of CHI 2013*, ACM

[26] Quercia, D., Lorenzo, G.D., Calabrese, F., and Ratti, C. "Mobile Phones and Outdoor Advertising: Measurable Advertising." *Pervasive Computing*, no. 99 (2011): 1-1.

[27] Reilly, W. J., *Methods for the Study of Retail Relationships*. University of Texas, Bureau of Business Research, 1929.

[28] Reilly, W.J. *The Laws of Retail Gravitation*, New York, Knickerbocker Press, 1931

[29] Roger, P. "Description of Consumer Spatial Behaviors: a New Approach." *International Journal of Research in Marketing* 1, no. 3 (1984): 171-181.

[30] Sliwinski, A. "Spatial Point Pattern Analysis for Targeting Prospective New Customers: Bringing GIS Functionality into Direct Marketing." *Journal of Geographic Information and Decision Analysis* 6, no. 1 (2002): 31-48.

[31] Song, C., Qu, Z., Blumm, N., and Barabási, AL. "Limits of Predictability in Human Mobility." *Science* 327, no. 5968 (2010): 1018-1021.

[32] Sun, A., Valention, J. and Seward, Z., A week on Foursquare http://graphicsweb.wsj.com/documents/FOURSQUAREWEEK1104/

[33] Tang, K.P., Lin, J., Hong, J., Siewiorek, D.P., and Sadeh, N. "Rethinking Location Sharing: Exploring the Implications of Social-driven Vs. Purpose-driven Location Sharing." In *Proceedings of Ubicomp 2010*, 85-94, ACM, 2010

[34] Ye, M., Yin, P., and Lee, W.C. "Location Recommendation for Location-based Social Networks." In *Proceedings of the 18th SIGSPATIAL International Conference on Advances in Geographic Information Systems*, 458-461, 2010.

[35] Zhang, D., Guo, B., Li, B., and Yu, Z. "Extracting Social and Community Intelligence from Digital Footprints: An Emerging Research Area." *Ubiquitous Intelligence and Computing* (2010): 4-18.

[36] Zhang, J., "Parcel-based high precision reverse geocoding", technical report, Pitney Bowes.

[37] Zhang, J., Qu, Y., and Teng, C.Y., "Understanding User Spatial Behaviors", in *Proceedings of SRS 2013*, Rio, Brazil

[38] Zheng, Y., Zhang, L., Ma, Z., Xie, X., and Ma, W. Y. "Recommending Friends and Locations Based on Individual Location History." *ACM Transactions on the Web* (TWEB) 5, no. 1 (2011): 5.

Psychological Maps 2.0: A Web Engagement Enterprise Starting in London

Daniele Quercia
Yahoo! Research, Barcelona
dquercia@yahoo-inc.com

João Paulo Pesce
UFMG, Brazil
jpesce@dcc.ufmg.br

Virgilio Almeida
UFMG, Brazil
virgilio@dcc.ufmg.br

Jon Crowcroft
University of Cambridge, UK
jon.crowcroft@cl.cam.ac.uk

ABSTRACT

Planners and social psychologists have suggested that the recognizability of the urban environment is linked to people's socio-economic well-being. We build a web game that puts the recognizability of London's streets to the test. It follows as closely as possible one experiment done by Stanley Milgram in 1972. The game picks up random locations from Google Street View and tests users to see if they can judge the location in terms of closest subway station, borough, or region. Each participant dedicates only few minutes to the task (as opposed to 90 minutes in Milgram's). We collect data from 2,255 participants (one order of magnitude a larger sample) and build a recognizability map of London based on their responses. We find that some boroughs have little cognitive representation; that recognizability of an area is explained partly by its exposure to Flickr and Foursquare users and mostly by its exposure to subway passengers; and that areas with low recognizability do not fare any worse on the *economic* indicators of income, education, and employment, but they do significantly suffer from *social* problems of housing deprivation, poor living conditions, and crime. These results could not have been produced without analyzing life off- and online: that is, without considering the interactions between urban places in the physical world and their virtual presence on platforms such as Flickr and Foursquare. This line of work is at the crossroad of two emerging themes in computing research - a crossroad where "web science" meets the "smart city" agenda.

Categories and Subject Descriptors

H.4 [**Information Systems Applications**]: Miscellaneous

Keywords

Social Media, Web Science, Urban Informatics

1. INTRODUCTION

A geographic map of a city consists of, say, streets and buildings and reflects an *objective* representation of the city. By contrast, a psychological map is a *subjective* representation that each city dweller carries around in his/her head. Tourists in a strange city start with few reference points (e.g., hotels, main streets) and then expand the representation in their minds - they slowly begin to build a picture. To see how these subjective representation matter, consider London. Every Londoner has had long attachment with some parts of the city, which brings to mind a flood of associations. Over the years, London has been built and maintained in a way that it is imaginable, i.e., that mental maps of the city are clear and economical of mental effort. That is because, starting from Kevin Lynch's seminal book "The Image of the City" in 1960, studies have posited that good imaginability allows city dwellers to feel at home and increase their community well-being [13]. People generally feel at home in cities whose neighborhoods are recognizable. Comfort resulting from little effort, the argument goes, would impact individual and ultimately collective well-being.

The good news is that the concept of imaginability is *quantifiable*, and it is so using psychological maps (Section 2). Since Stanley Milgram's work in New York and Paris [17, 16], researchers (including HCI ones) have drawn recognizability maps by recruiting city dwellers, showing them scenes of their city, and testing whether they could recognize where those scenes were: depending on which places are correctly recognized, one could draw a collective psychological map of the city. The problem is that such an experiment takes time (in Milgram's, each participant spent 90 minutes for the recognition task), is costly (because of paid participants), and cannot be conducted at scale (so far the largest one had 200 participants). That is why the link between recognizability of a place and well-being of its residents has been hypothesized, qualitatively shown, but has never been quantitatively tested at scale.

To test whether the recognizability of a place makes it a more desirable part of the city to live, we make the following contributions:

First, we build a crowdsourcing web game that puts the recognizability of London's streets to the test (Section 3). It picks up random locations from Google Street View and tests users to see if they can determine in which subway location (or borough or region) the scene is. In the last five months, we have collected data from 2,255 users, have built a collective recognizability map of London based on their responses, and quantified the recognizability of different parts of the city.

Second, by analyzing the recognizability of London regions (Section 4), we find that the general conclusions drawn by Milgram for New York hold for London with impressive consistency, suggesting external validity of our results. Central London is the most recognizable region, while South London has little cognitive coverage. Londoners would answer "West London" when unsure, making the most incorrect guesses for that region - hence a West London response bias. We also find that the mental map of London changes depending on where respondents are from - London, UK, or rest of the world.

Third, we test to which extent an area's recognizability is explained by the area's exposure to people (Section 5). In particular, we study exposure to users of three social media services and to underground passengers. By collecting 1.2M Twitter messages, 224K Foursquare check-ins, 76.6M underground trips, and 1.3M Flickr pictures in London, we find that, the more a social media platform's content is geographically salient (e.g., Flickr's), the better proxy it offers for recognizability.

Finally, upon census data showing the extent to which areas are socially deprived or not, we test whether recognizability of an area is negatively related with the area's socio-economic deprivation (Section 6). We find that recognizability is indeed low in areas that suffer from housing deprivation, poor living conditions, and crime.

This work is at the crossroad of two emerging themes in computing research - web science and smart cities. The combination of the two opens up notable opportunities for future research (Section 7).

2. BACKGROUND

Psychological maps from drawing one's version of the city. In his 1960 "The Image of the City", Kevin Lynch created a psychological map of Boston by interviewing Bostonians. Based on hand-drawn maps of what participants' "versions of Boston" looked like, he found that few central areas were know to almost all Bostonians, while vast parts of the city were unknown to its dwellers. More than ten years later, Stanley Milgram repeated the same experiment and did so in a variety of other cities (e.g., Paris, New York). Milgram was an American social psychologist who conducted various studies, including a controversial study on obedience to authority and the original small world (six degree of separation) experiment [15]. Milgram was interested in understanding mental models of the city, and he turned to Paris to study them: his participants drew maps of what "their versions of Paris" looked like, and these maps were combined to identify the intelligible and recognizable parts of the city. Since then, researchers have collected people's opinions about neighborhoods in the form of hand-drawn maps in different cities, including (more recently) San Francisco [1] and Chicago [3].

Psychological maps from recognizing city scenes. The problem with the mental map experiment is that it takes time and it is not clear how to aggregate the variety of

Figure 1: Google Street View Scene.

unique configurations of answers that are bound to appear. One way of fixing that problem is to place a number of constraints on the participants when externalizing their maps. In this vein, before his experience with Paris, Milgram constrained the experiment so much so to reduce it to a simple question: "If an individual is placed at random at a point in the city, how likely is he to know where he is?" [17]. The idea is that one can measure the relative "imaginability" of cities by finding the proportion of residents who recognize sampled geographic points. That simply translates into showing participants scenes of their city and testing whether they can recognize where the scenes are. Milgram did setup and successfully run such an experiment in lecture theaters. Each participant usually spent 90 minutes on the task, and he collected responses from as many as 200 participants for New York. Hitherto the experimental setup in which maps are drawn has been widely replicated [1, 3], while that in which scenes are recognized has received far less attention. Next, we try to re-create the latter experimental setup at scale by building an online crowdsourcing platform in which each participant plays a one-minute game, a game with a purpose [23].

3. PSYCHOLOGICAL MAPS 2.0

We have created an online game that asks users to identify Google Street View (Panorama) scenes of London. The project aims to learn how its players mentally map different locations around the city, ultimately creating a London-wide map of recognizability.

How it works. For each round, the game shows a player a randomly-selected scene in London and ask him/her to guess the nearest subway station, or generally what section of the city (borough/region) (s)he is seeing. Answers should be easy, and that is why we choose the finest-grained answer to be subway stations as those are the most widely-used point of references among Londoners and visitors alike. To avoid sparsity problems (too few answers per picture), a random scene is selected within a 300-meter radius from a tube station but not next to it (to avoid easing recognizability). The idea is that, by collecting a large number of responses across a large number of participants, we can determine which areas are recognizable. By testing which places are remarkable and unmistakable and which places represent faceless sprawl, we are able to draw the recognizability map of London.

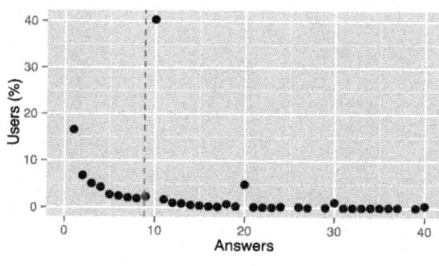
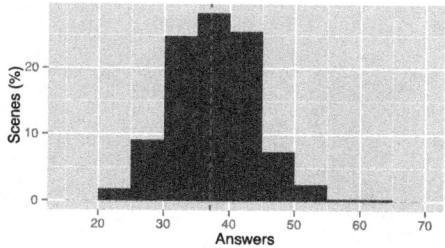

(a) Number of Answers per User (b) Number of Answers per Scene

Figure 2: Number of Answers for Each User/Scene. *(a)* Each game round consists of 10 pictures - that is why outliers are multiples of 10. The analysis considers the 40% of users who have completed one round. *(b)* The number of answers each scene has received is normally distributed thanks to randomization.

Engagement strategies. The strategies we implemented include:

Giving Points. "One of the most direct methods for motivating players in games is to grant points for each instance of successful output produced. Using points increases motivation by providing a clear connection among effort in the game, performance, and outcomes" [23]. When playing the game, each player receives a score that increases with the number of correct guesses of where a given picture was taken. To enhance the gaming experience, we reward not only strictly correct guesses (which are the only ones considered for experimental sake) but also "geographically close" ones by awarding points based on the Euclidian distance d between a user's guess and the correct answer. The idea is that guesses within a radius of 300 meters still amount to reasonable scores, while those outside it are severely and increasingly penalized depending on how far they are from the correct answer. To reduce the number of random guesses, we allow for an "I Don't Know" answer, which still rewards players with 15 points. After being presented with 10 pictures, the player has completed one round and (s)he can share the resulting score on Facebook or Twitter with only one click. The score is supposed to facilitate the player's assessment of his/her performance against previous game rounds or against other players [23]. From the distribution of number answers for each player (Figure 2(a)), we find multiples of 10 to be outliers, suggesting that players do tend to complete at least one round. After the first round, each player is also shown a small questionnaire (e.g., age, gender, location) (s)he is asked to complete. Participants engaging in multiple rounds are identified through browser cookies, which uniquely identify users [1].

Social Media Integration. Players can post their scores on the two social media platforms of Facebook and Twitter after each round with a default message of the form "How well do you know London? My score ...". The goal of such a message is to make Facebook and Twitter users aware of the game.

Randomness. "Games with a purpose should incorporate randomness. For example, inputs for a particular game session are typically selected at random from the set of all possible inputs. Because inputs are randomly selected, their difficulty varies, thus keeping the game interesting and engaging for expert and novice players alike." [23]. In our game, pictures are chosen randomly with the hope of creating a sense of freshness and increasing replay value. In addition, randomizing the selection of picture is a good idea for experimental sake. Randomization reduces spatial biases and leads to reliable results, producing a distribution of answers for each picture that is not skewed. In our analysis, such a distribution will turn out to be distributed around a mean of 37.11 (Figure 2(b)), and no picture has less than 20 answers.

Overall, by providing a clear sense of progression and goals that are challenging enough to maintain interest but not so hard as to put players off, we hope to capture a sense of engagement.

From beta to final version. We build a working prototype featuring those desirable engagement properties and ascertain the extent to which it works in a controlled beta test involving more than 45 urban planners, architects, and computer scientists. We receive four main feedbacks:

Ease. The game is found to be difficult and, as such, frustrating to play. That is because random pictures from every (remote) part of London are shown. One player said: "I've been living in London for the past 35 years and I felt like a tourist. There were so many places I had no clue where they were. It is frustrating to get a score of 200 [out of 1000]! ". To fix this problem, we manually add pictures of easily recognizable places (e.g., spots that are touristic or close to subway stations) and show them together with the randomly selected places from time to time. For the purpose of study, these "fake" pictures are ignored - they are just meant to improve the gaming experience and retention rate.

Feedbacks. The beta version does not show any feedback about which are the correct answers. A large number of testers feel that the game could be an opportunity to learn more about London. That is why, for each incorrect guess, the final version of the game also shows the right answer.

Sense of purpose. The site does not contain any explanation about the research aims behind the game. Yet, our testers feel that providing a sense of purpose to players was essential. The final version contains a short explanation of how the game is designed for purposes beyond pure entertainment, and how it might be used to promote urban interventions where needed.

---

[1] Unless two users use the same computer and the same username on it. This situation should represent a minority of cases though.

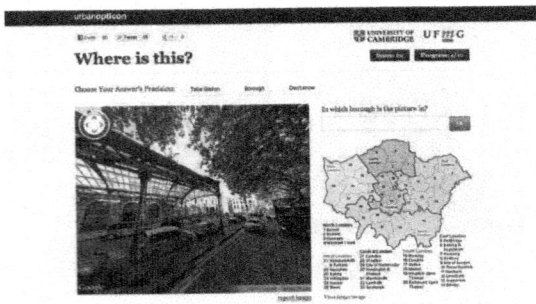

Figure 3: Screenshot of the Crowdsourcing Game. The city scene is on the left, and the answer box on the right.

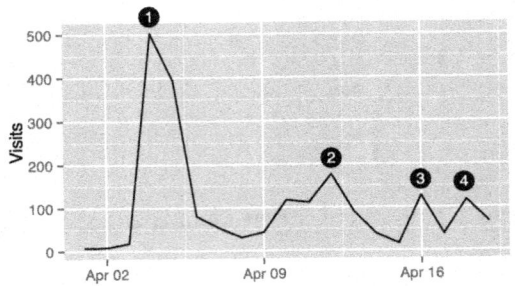

Figure 4: Initial Visitors on the Site. Peaks are registered for: (1) Cambridge press release; (2) The Independent article; (3) New Scientist article; and (4) residual sharing activity on Facebook and Twitter.

	London	UK	World	Total
Answers	7,238	8,705	3,972	19,915
Users	739	973	543	2,255
Gender (%)				
Male	59.1	64.3	46.5	59.6
Female	40.9	35.7	53.5	40.4
Age (%)				
<18	0.9	0.8	0.0	0.7
18-24	16.5	24.8	9.3	19.2
25-34	41.8	38.9	51.2	41.8
35-44	16.5	13.9	20.9	16.0
45-54	13.9	13.9	7.0	12.9
55-64	5.2	6.2	9.3	6.3
65+	5.2	1.5	2.3	3.1
Mean (years)	36.4	33.9	34.5	35.0

Table 1: Statistics of Participants. Gender and age are available for those 287 participants (13%) who have been willing to provide personal details.

Beyond one type of answer. The game asks players to guess the correct subway station. Many testers feel the need for coarser-grained answers. "I know this is Westminster [a borough in London], but I have no idea of the exact tube station!", says one player. The final version thus allows for multiple types of answers: not only subway stations but also boroughs (50 points) or regions such as Central London and South London (25 points).

To sum up, the final version of the game works by giving a player ten (random plus morale boosting) images in Greater London (Figure 3). The player can either guess the tube station, borough, region, or click "Don't know" to move ahead. At the end of the round, the player is given a total score based on the fraction of correct answers. The score can be automatically shared on Facebook or Twitter, and the player is presented with a survey that asks for personal details like birth location, place of employment, and familiarity with the city itself.

Launching the crowdsourcing game. We have made the final version of the game publicly available and have issued a press release in April 2012 (Figure 4). Shortly after that, the game has been featured in major newspapers, including The Independent (UK national newspaper) and New Scientist. After 5 months, we have collected data from as many as 2,255 participants: 739 connecting from London (IP addresses), 973 from the rest of UK, and 543 outside UK. A fraction of those participants (287) specified their personal details. The percentage of male-female participants overall is 60%-40% and slightly changes depending on one's location: it stays 60%-40% in London but changes to 65%-35% in UK and 45%-55% outside it. Also, across locations, average age does not differ from London's, which is 36.4 years old. As for geographic distribution of respondents, we find a strong correlation between London population and number of respondents across regions ($r = 0.82$). Having this data at hand, we are now ready to analyze it.

4. RELATIVE RECOGNIZABILITY

The goal of this project is to *quantify* the relative recognizability of different parts of London. Since familiarity with different parts of the city might depend on place of residence, we filter away participants outside London and consider Londoners first. According to the Greater London Authority's division, London is divided into five different city (sub) regions. Thus, our first research question is to determine which proportion of the Google Street View scenes from each region were correctly attributed to the region. Since users were asked to name either the borough of each scene or the subway station closest to it, we consider an answer to be correct, if the region of the scene is the same as the region of the answered borough/subway station. For each of the five regions, we compute the region's percentage *recognizability* by summing the number of correct answers and then dividing by the total number of answers. Figure 5 reports the results. Clearly, Central London emerges as the most recognizable of the five regions, with about two and a half as many correct placements as the others. Conventional wisdom holds that Central London is better known than other parts of the city, as it hosts the main squares, major railway and subway stations, and most popular touristic attractions and night-life "hotspots". Interestingly, the East Region is twice as recognizable than the North Region. It is difficult to draw conclusions on why this is. However, the three most likely explanations are:

Sample Bias. It might depend on the distribution of the home and work addresses of our participants. However, that

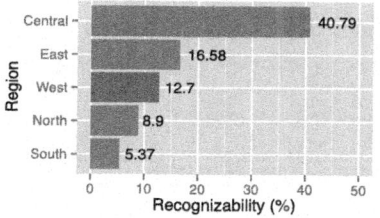 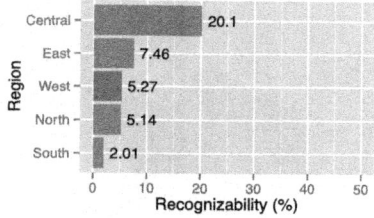 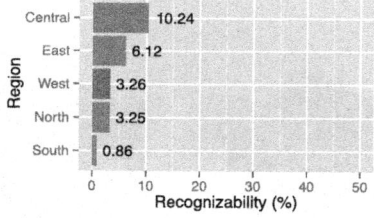

(a) *Region*-level recognizability (b) *Borough*-level recognizability (c) *Subway station*-level

Figure 5: Recognizability Across London Regions. This is computed based on whether scenes are recognized at: *(a)* region level; *(b)* borough level; or *(c)* subway station level.

is unlikely, as the correlation between London population across regions and number of participants who answered the survey is as high as $r = 0.82$. Despite that correlation, we cannot fully rule out the sampling bias though.

Large volume of visitors. High recognizability for the East part of the city can be explained by an experiential effect. Large numbers of people are expected to visit that part of the city: workers at Canary Wharf, visitors to Olympic Park, Excel, City airport, and O2 arena. A recent study of Londoners' whereabouts on Foursquare found them to be skewed towards mostly Central London and partly East London - especially the central east part [2]. The north parts are unlikely to have been visited by similar volumes of people. In Section 5, we will see that there is a significant correlation between recognizability of an area and the area's exposure to specific subgroups of individuals. For example, we will see that the more passengers use an area's subway station, the more recognizable the area ($r = 0.45$).

Distinctiveness of the built environment. The East region includes most of the City and Canary Wharf (financial area with skyscrapers), as well as the O2 arena and Docklands region, all more visually recognizable areas than comparable parts of the North region. Also, East London has been affected by large homogeneous post-war housing projects that make the area quite distinctive [9].

Next, we adopt a more stringent criterion of recognition, that is, we determine what proportion of the scenes in each of the five regions were placed in the correct *borough*. By analyzing the answers at borough-level, we find substantial differences (Figure 5(b)). A scene placed in Central London is almost three times more likely to be placed in the correct borough than a scene in East London, and are four times more likely than a scene in West or North London.

When we then apply even a more stringent criterion of recognition (subway station), the correct guesses are drastically reduced (Figure 5(c)), as one expects. Interestingly, the information value of Central London is less pronounced. Central London scenes are only one and a half time more likely to be associated with the correct subway station than a scene in East London. Guessing the correct subway stations is hard, the more so in the central part of the city where stations are close to each other. During post-game interviews, one participants noted: "Perhaps people know where places are, but have difficulty identifying which of the [subway stations] it is actually close to." Despite these differences, the *relative* recognizability (ranked recognizability of the five regions) does not change. Figure 6 shows the

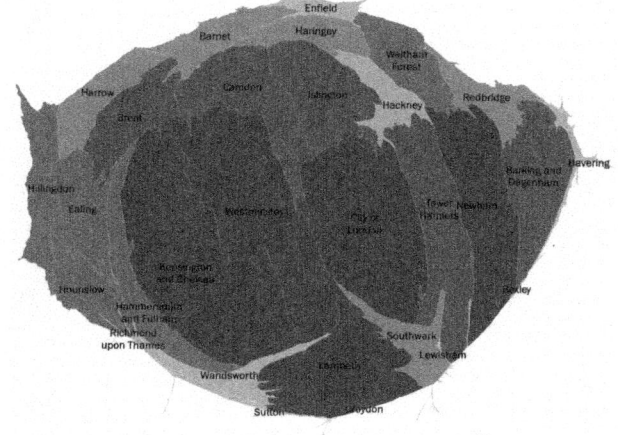

Figure 6: Cartogram of London Boroughs. The geographic area is distorted based on borough's recognizability.

cartogram of London boroughs. The geometry of the map is distorted based on recognizability scores. Central London dominates, while South London is relegated at the bottom.

Another aspect to consider is that one is likely to recognize areas closer to where one lives or works. Based on our survey respondents, we find that there is no relationship between recognizability of a scene and a respondent's self-reported home location. On the contrary, participants are more likely to recognize scenes in Central London rather than scenes in their own boroughs.

The recognizability of each region does not change depending on which parts of the city Londoners live, but does change depending on whether participants are in UK or not. Based on our participants' IP addresses [2], we infer the cities where they are connecting from, and compute aggregate correct guesses by respondent location - that is, by whether participants connect from London, from the rest of UK, or outside UK (Figure 7). As expected, the number of correct guesses drastically decreases for participants outside London - but with two exceptions. First, scenes of South London are more recognizable for participants in the rest of UK than for Londoners themselves. That is because Londoners tend

---

[2]There might be cases of misclassification of cities and of people who use VPNs. However, at the three coarse-grained levels of London *vs.* rest of UK *vs.* rest of the world, misclassification should have a negligible effect.

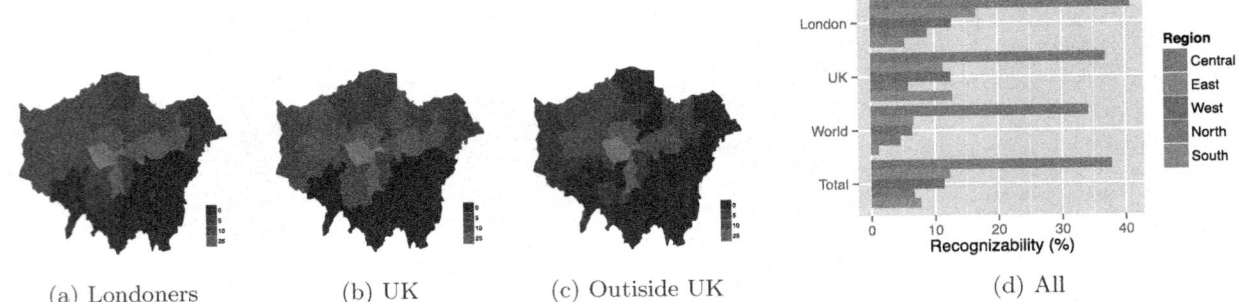

(a) Londoners   (b) UK   (c) Outside UK   (d) All

Figure 7: Recognizability Across London Regions by Respondent Location. On the maps, lighter colors correspond to more recognizable places.

Region actually is	But identified as					Combined Errors	Don't Know
	C	E	W	N	S		
Central	**40.79**	4.52	4.33	1.03	2.13	12.02	47.19
East	6.97	**16.58**	6.80	6.30	7.46	27.53	55.89
West	10.10	6.42	**12.70**	5.77	5.92	28.21	59.09
North	6.85	4.79	12.67	**8.90**	7.53	31.85	59.25
South	6.04	5.37	11.41	3.36	**5.37**	26.17	68.46
Response Bias*	29.96	21.1	**35.21**	16.46	23.04		

* popular among wrong guesses

Table 2: Matrix of Correct Classifications and Misclassifications.

to know Southfields (known as "The Grid", which a series of parallel roads that consist almost entirely of Edwardian terrace houses), while people in the rest of UK recognize scenes not only in Southfields, but also in Clapham South, Balham, South Wimbledon, and Tooting Broadway in that order. Second, recognizability of Central London remains the same across participants from all over: participants outside UK are as good as those inside it at recognizing scenes in Central London. Hosting the most popular tourist attractions in the world, Central London is vividly present in the world's collective psychological map.

So far we have focused on correct guesses. Now we turn to errors that respondent often make, looking for widely-shared sources of confusion. We wish to know in which regions (e.g., North, South) a scene from, say, East London is often misplaced. To this end, Table 2 shows a matrix reporting both the percentage of correct guesses and that of wrong ones for each region. Central London is pre-eminent in Londoners' shared psychological maps as it is hardly confused with any other region. At times, instead, South and North London are thought to be West. It seems that, if respondents do not know where to place a scene, they would preferentially opt for West London. Indeed, the West part of the city is the most popular answer for those who end up guessing wrongly (last row in Table 2). We found a *West London response bias*, as Milgram would put it [3].

Summary. Taken together, the results suggest two generalizable principles on why people recognize an area. They do so because they are exposed to it (Central London attracts

---

[3] Milgram found that New Yorkers would opt for answering "Queens" when unsure - hence he referred to a "Queens response bias" [17]

dwellers from all over the city), and because the area offers a distinctive architecture (e.g., stadium, tower building) or cultural life (as the central part of East London notoriously does). Milgram found the very same two principles to hold for New York as well in 1972. So much so that Milgram hypothesized that the extent to which a scene will be recognized can be described by $R = f(C \cdot D)$, where R is recognition (our recognizability), C centrality of population flow (in the next section, we will see how to compute flow of subway passengers), and D is the social or architectural distinctiveness. It follows that, with simplifying assumptions (e.g., f is a linear relationship), one could derive an area's social or architectural distinctiveness by simply dividing recognizability by subway passenger flow. Since we are interested in the *relative* recognizability and flow, we take the rank values for these two quantities, compute their ratio, and report the results in Table 3. The most distinctive area is Blackfriars. It should be no coincidence that its older parts happen to "have regularly been used as a filming location in film and television, particularly for modern films and serials set in Victorian times, notably Sherlock Holmes and David Copperfield"[4]. In line with Milgram's experiment with New Yorkers [17], we find that the acquisition of a mental map is not necessarily a direct process but can also be indirect through, for example, movies. The following quote from one of our participants is telling: "I've done the quiz 3 or 4 times in the last couple of days, and am surprised how well I am doing - not just because I live in New Zealand, many thousands of kilometres from London (although I did live there for 10 years), but mainly because I am getting good scores on parts of London I have never been to. North and Eastern boroughs like Brent and Haringey seem to be recognisable, even though I have never knowingly gone there. Possibly some recognition from TV programs, or just - could it be - that there is something intrinsically North London about certain types of houses? "

5. RECOGNIZABILITY AND EXPOSURE

5.1 Digital Data for Exposure

The goal of the game is to quantify the recognizability of the different parts of the city. It has been shown that New Yorkers are able to recognize an area partly because they were exposed to it [17]. Thus, to quantify the extent

---

[4] http://en.wikipedia.org/wiki/Blackfriars,_London

name	R	C	r_R	r_C	D
Blackfriars	9.09	4583	30	2	15.00
Park Royal	20.00	13119	61	5	12.20
Pinner	10.00	13823	37	6	6.17
Royal Oak	10.00	16681	37	8	4.63
Westbourne Park	16.66	24593	54	13	4.15
Hornchurch	7.14	11988	16	4	4.00
Essex Road	5.55	2027	4	1	4.00
Oakwood	11.11	22321	41	11	3.73
Hillingdon	6.67	9482	11	3	3.67
Acton Town	40.00	33022	73	22	3.32

Table 3: Subway Stations of Socially/Architecturally Distinctive Areas. For each area, R is the recognizability, C is the flow centrality (number of unique subway passengers), r_R and r_C are the corresponding ranked values, and D is the normalized distinctiveness.

to which it is so in London, we measure the exposure that an area receives by computing the number of overall unique individuals who happen to be in the area. These individuals are of four subgroups: those who post Twitter messages while in the area, those who visit locations (e.g., restaurants, bars) and say so on Foursquare, those who take pictures of the area and post them on Flickr, and those who catch a train in the closest subway station. We are thus able to associate the recognizability of an area with the area's exposure to these four subgroups.

Twitter geo-enabled users. Our goal is to retrieve as large and unbiased a sample of geo-referenced tweets as possible. To do this, we use the public streamer API, which connects to a continuous feed of a random sample of all ever shared tweets, and crawl geo-referenced tweets within the bounding box of Greater London. During the period that goes from December 25th 2011 to January 12th 2012, we retrieve 1,238,339 geo-referenced tweets posted by 57,615 different users.

Foursquare users. *Gowalla, Facebook Places*, and *Foursquare* are popular mobile social-networking applications with which users share their whereabouts with friends. In this work, we consider the most used social-networking site in London - Foursquare [2]. Users can check-in to locations (e.g., restaurants) and share their whereabouts. We consider the geo-referenced tweets collected by Cheng *et al.* [4]. They collected Twitter updates (single tweets) that report Foursquare check-ins all over the world. We take the 224,533 check-ins that fall into Greater London. Those check-ins are posted by 8,735 users.

Flickr users. We collect photo metadata from Flickr.com using the site's public search API. To collect all publicly available geo-referenced pictures in the Greater London area, we divide the area into 30K cells, search for photos in each of them, and retrieve metadata (e.g., tags, number of comments, and annotations). The final dataset contains metadata for 1,319,545 London pictures geo-tagged by 37,928 users. This reflects a complete snapshot of all pictures in the city as of December 21st 2011.

Subway passengers. In 2003, the public transportation authority in London introduced an RFID-based technology, known as Oyster card, which replaced traditional paper-based magnetic stripe tickets. We obtain an anonymized dataset containing a record of every journey taken on the London rail network (including the London Underground) using an Oyster card in the whole month of March 2010. A record registers that a traveler did a trip from station a at time t_a, to station b at time t_b. In total, the dataset contains 76.6 million journeys made by 5.2 million users, and is available upon request from the public transportation authority.

Demographics of the individuals under study. Activity analyzed in this paper clearly relates only to certain social groups, and the exclusionary aspect of certain segments of the population should be acknowledged. It would be thus interesting to compare the demographics of the different types of individuals we are studying here. From a recent Ignite report on social media [10], global demographics of Foursquare and Twitter show a pronounced skew towards university educated 25-34 year old women (66% women for Foursquare and 61% for Twitter), while those of Flickr show a pronounced skew towards university educated 35-44 year old women (54% women). The demographics of subway passengers is by far the most representative but is also slightly skewed towards male with above-average income in the two age groups of 25-44 and 45-59 [21]. Instead, demographics of our London gamers show a skew towards 25-34 year old men (60% men). Thus, compared to social media users, our gamers reflect similar age groups but are more likely to be men. This demographic comparison should inform the interpretation of our results.

5.2 Recognizability and Exposure

After computing each area's exposure to people of four subgroups[5] (i.e., to users of the three main social media sites and to underground passengers), we are now ready to relate the area's exposure to its recognizability. We compute the Pearson's product-moment correlation between recognizability and exposure, for all four classes of individuals. Pearson's correlation $r \in [-1, 1]$ is a measure of the linear relationship between two variables. We expect that the more a given class of individuals is representative of the general population, the higher its correlation with recognizability. When computing the correlation, if necessary (e.g., because of skewness), variables undergo a logarithmic transformation. Figure 8 shows the relationship between recognizability and exposure to the four classes of individuals, with corresponding correlation coefficients (which are all significant at level $p < 0.001$). To put results into context, we should say that the exposure measures derived from the three social media sites all show very similar pair-wise correlations with exposure to subway passengers ($r \approx 0.60$), yet their correlations with recognizability show telling differences. Given that subway passengers are slightly more representative of the general population than social media users [21], it comes as no surprise that they show the highest correlation ($r = 0.40$). Both Flickr and Foursquare users are also associated with robust correlations ($r = 0.36$

---
[5]By area, we mean UK census area also known as Lower Super Output Area, which we will introduce in Section 6.

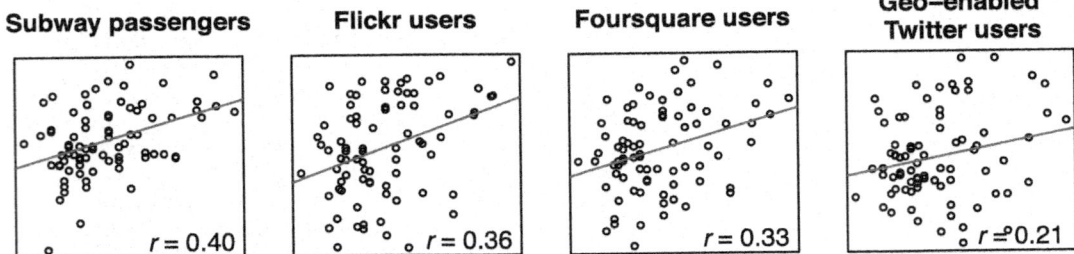

Figure 8: Area recognizability vs. Exposure to Four Classes of Individuals. Correlations are computed at *borough* level.

Exposure	Central	East	West	North	London
Subway	0.87	0.65	0.63	0.95	0.73
Flickr	0.62	0.50	0.27	0.89	0.63
Foursquare	0.72	0.36	0.22	0.97	0.58
Twitter	0.56	0.28	0.11	0.97	0.52

Table 4: Correlations between recognizability and Exposure by Region. Correlations are computed at *region* level. South London does not have enough subway stations to attain statistically significant correlations.

and $r = 0.33$). By contrast, having the least geographically salient content, Twitter shows a moderate correlation ($r = 0.21$). If we break the results down to regions (Table 4) and show which regions' recognizability is easy to predict from exposure and which not, we see that exposure to *any* subgroup of individuals would predict the recognizability of North London ($r = 0.95$). By contrast, the social media subgroup whose exposure correlates with recognizability the most in Central London is Foursquare ($r = 0.72$), and in East London is Flickr' ($r = 0.50$). That is largely because Foursquare activity is skewed towards Central London.

6. RECOGNIZABILITY AND WELL-BEING

As already mentioned in the introduction, Kevin Lynch outlined a theory connecting urban recognizability to a person's well-being [13]. To test this theory, we now gather census data on an area's socio-economic well-being and relate it to the area's recognizability.

Facets of Socio-economic Well-being. Since 2000, the UK Office for National Statistics has published, every three or four years, the Indices of Multiple Deprivation (IMD), a set of indicators which measure deprivation of small census areas in England known as Lower-layer Super Output Areas [14]. These census areas were designed to have a roughly uniform population distribution so that a fine-grained *relative* comparison of different parts of England is possible. As per formulation of IMD, deprivation is defined in such a way that it captures the effects of several different factors. More specifically, IMD consists of seven components: 1. *Income* deprivation (e.g., number of people claiming income support, child tax credits or asylum); 2. *Employment* deprivation (e.g., number of claimants of jobseeker's allowance or incapacity benefit); 3. *Health* deprivation (e.g., includ-

ing a standard measure of premature death, rate of adults suffering mood and anxiety disorders); 4. *Education* deprivation (e.g., education level attainment, proportion of working adults with no qualifications); 5. barriers to *Housing* and services (e.g., homelessness, overcrowding, distance to essential services); 6. *Crime* (e.g., rates of different kinds of criminal act); 7. *Living* Environment Deprivation (e.g., housing condition, air quality, rate of road traffic accidents); and finally a composite measure known as IMD which is the weighted mean of the seven domains.

Recognizability and Well-being. We start at borough level, correlate each transformed facet of deprivation [6] with recognizability, and obtain the results shown in Figure 9(a). We find that the composite score IMD does not correlate with recognizability at all. Neither does income, education, or (un)employment. What correlates are aspects less related to economic well-being and more related to social well-being: boroughs with low recognizability tend to suffer from housing deprivation ($r = 0.64$) and poor living environment ($r = 0.62$). Given the strong correlations [7], one could easily predict which boroughs suffer from housing deprivation and poor living conditions based on relative recognizability scores.

One might now wonder whether that would also be possible from social media data. We correlate each of the deprivation facets with exposure to the four subgroups (subway passengers plus users of three social media). For housing, we see that data on recognizability is hardly replaceable by social media data. Boroughs not suffering from housing deprivation (as per log-transformed score) are more recognizable ($r = 0.64$), and yet do not seem to be more exposed to our subgroups - all correlations between housing deprivation and exposure are not statistically significant. Instead, for living environment, we see that data on recognizability can be replaced by social media data. Boroughs with good living conditions are more recognizable ($r = 0.61$), and do tend to be more exposed to subway passengers ($r = 0.56$),

---

[6] To ease the interpretation of the correlation coefficients, we transformed (inverted) the deprivation scores, in that, the higher they are (e.g., high crime index), the better it is (e.g., low-crime area). We would thus expect the correlations between transformed deprivation scores and recognizability to be generally positive.

[7] Unless otherwise noted all correlations are significant at level $p < 0.001$.

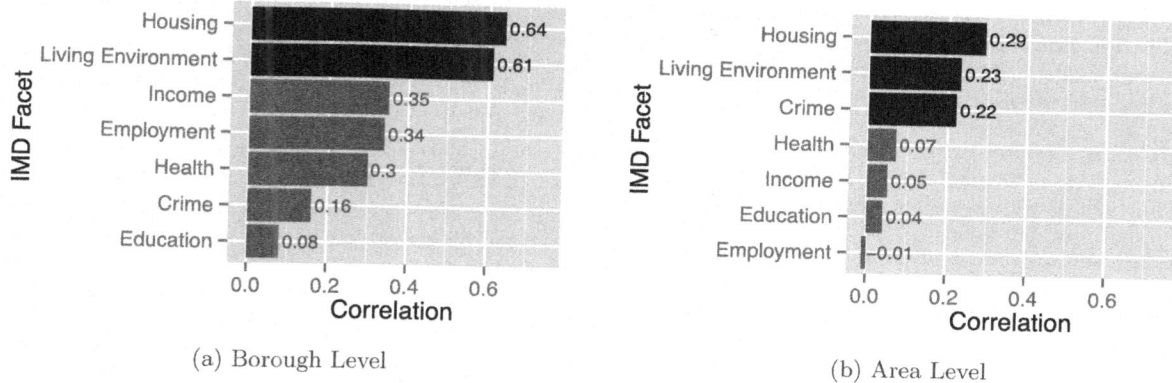

(a) Borough Level (b) Area Level

Figure 9: Correlation between recognizability and Deprivation at the Level of *(a)* Borough or *(b)* Area. For both, the composite index IMD is not shown as it does not correlate. Also, correlations significant at level $p < 0.001$ are shown with black (as opposed to grey) bars.

Flickr users ($r = 0.57$), Foursquare users ($r = 0.52$), and Twitter users ($r = 0.46$, $p < 0.01$).

Here we are not claiming that each census area in a borough is the same. If we were to say that, we would commit an ecological fallacy. For indicators that show high variability within a borough, however, there is a danger of committing such a fallacy. We therefore investigate correlations at the lower geographic level of census area. We correlate each facet of deprivation with recognizability and obtain the results shown in Figure 9(b). Again, the composite score IMD does not correlate with recognizability, while housing, living environment, and crime all do: areas with low recognizability tend to suffer from housing deprivation ($r = 0.29$), poor living environment ($r = 0.23$), and crime ($r = 0.22$). Crime has been added to the list of indicators associated with recognizability, and that is because crime is one of the deprivation facets that varies the most within a borough among the seven.

To sum up, from the previous results, we might say that, based on recognizability scores of *areas*, we could predict *whether* an area suffers from crime or not. Instead, based on recognizability scores of *boroughs*, one could predict not only *whether* but also *to which extent* a borough suffers from poor living conditions and housing deprivation. By contrast, social media data could only be used to identify boroughs with poor living conditions.

7. DISCUSSION

This work is deeply rooted in early urban studies but also taps into recent computing research, especially research on "games with a purpose", whereby one outsources certain activities (e.g., labeling images) to humans in an entertaining way [23]; research on large-scale urban dynamics [6, 7, 18]; and research on how location-based services affect people's behavior [3, 5, 12]. Initially, with this study, we were aiming at informing social media research in the urban context by establishing which social media data could be used as proxy for recognizability and exposure (key aspects in studies of urban dynamics). It turns out that the answer is complex, suggesting a word of caution on researchers not to take social media data at face value. However, there is one generalizable finding: the more the content is geographically salient (e.g., Foursquare's whereabouts *vs.* Twitter messages), the more it is fit for purpose.

7.1 Limitations

Control Variables. To increase response rate, we kept the survey as short as possible. It asks a minimum number of questions from which controlled variables are derived. However, this choice has drawbacks. For example, the survey asks for home location but does not ask for any other information about one's urban recognizability reach (the parts of the city one better knows visually). The problem is that one would know better (apart from the area one lives) also areas near work and on the way back home. We acknowledge this limitation but also stress that these differences are likely to cancel themselves out in a big sample like ours because of randomization.

Information Value of Scenes. Some pictures might be more revealing than others. The game has two kinds of pictures. The fake pictures (excluded from the analysis) are meant to increase retention rate and, as such, are easy to recognize - they depict touristic locations or well-known stations. The real pictures (included in the analysis) are instead less informative as they have been vetted by us. However, they might still contain clues that make them recognizable. We are currently discovering which visual cues tend to be associated with highly recognizable images (e.g., landmarks, memorable horrible buildings). We do so by automatically extracting image features, in a vein similar to an exploration recently proposed by Doersch et al. [8]. We are also discovering which visual cues tend to be associated with beautiful, quiet, and happy urban sceneries [19].

7.2 Smart Cities Meet Web Science

The share of the world's population living in cities has recently surpassed 50 percent. By 2025, we will see another 1.2 billion people living in cities. The world is in the midst of an immense population shift from rural areas to cities, not least because urbanization is powered by the potential for enormous economic benefits. Those benefits will be only realized, however, if we are able to manage the increased complexity that comes with larger cities. The 'smart city' agenda is about the use of technological advances in physical and computing infrastructure to manage that complexity and create better cities. We will now discuss the ways in which this work suggests that the future of web scientists is charged with great potentials.

Planning urban interventions. We have shown that the relationship between recognizability and specific aspects of socio-economic deprivation is strong enough to identify boroughs suffering from high housing deprivation and poor living conditions, and also areas affected by crime. There is strong demand for making cities smarter, and the ability to identify areas in need could provide real-time information to, for example, local authorities. They could receive early warnings and identify areas of high deprivation quickly and at little cost, which is beneficial for cash-strapped city councils when planning renewal initiatives. However, before making any policy recommendation, recognizability data (based on a convenience sample) needs to be supplemented by other types of data - for example, by underground data [11, 20].

Making experiments on the web. By turning the execution of the experiment into a game, we have applied principles from games to a serious task and and have been consequently able to harness thousands of human brains. This might be fascinating to social science researchers, who must usually pay people to participate in their experiments. The game we have presented inverts that rule: players will happily fork out time for the privilege of being allowed to test their knowledge of London. Indeed, participants were rewarded with being able to test how well they knew London. One participant added: "Yesterday we had few friends over for dinner. I started to play the game on my laptop, and that escalated into a ridiculous competition among all of us that left my husband - the only Londoner in the room - quite injured, so to speak".

Rewarding schemes. We should design and test alternative engagement strategies. For now, we have focused on intrinsic (as opposed to extrinsic) rewards [24]. That is because recent psychological experiments (summarized in Werbach's latest book "For the Win" [24]) have suggested that "intrinsic rewards (the enjoyment of a task for its own sake) are the best motivators, whereas extrinsic rewards, such as badges, levels, points or even in some circumstances money, can be counter-productive" [22]. In this vein, it might be beneficial to build a similar game on crowdsourcing platforms where participants are paid (e.g., on Mechanical Turk) and test how different reward schemes affect the externalization of the mental map. Finally, more research has to go into determining which incentives make engagement sustainable.

Beyond London. Comforted by the encouraging results, we are starting to bring the game to other cities in the world. With their recent "smart city" initiatives, Rio de Janeiro and São Paulo are fit for purpose and are thus next on the list. At the moment, when rolling the platform out, the coverage of Google street view is required, and, being not automatic, two main aspects need to be customized: 1) selection of the geographic landmarks users need to recognize - subway stations might not work equally well in all cities; and 2) selection of seed easy-to-guess locations to avoid player frustration - one could make this step automatic by selecting popular city locations from, e.g., Wikipedia. We are currently working on an open-source platform in which those aspects are made automatic. In the short term, to encourage other researchers to join in and allow for research reproducibility, we make the aggregate statistics and the platform's source code publicly available [8].

8. CONCLUSION

In the sixties, scholars started to design experiments that captured the psychological representations that dwellers had of their cities. In mid-2012, we have translated their experimental setup into a 1-minute web game with a purpose, and have began with a deployment in London. We have gained insights into the differing perceptions of London that are held by not only Londoners but also people in UK and the rest of the world. The pre-eminence of Central London in the world's collective psychological map speaks to the popularity of its landmarks and touristic locations. The acquisition of a mental map is a slow process that does not necessarily come from direct experience but might be indirectly learned from, for example, atlases or movies. It comes as no surprise that Blackfriars, having being often used as a filming location, turned out to be the most socially/architecturally distinctive area - that is, an area whose recognizability is explained less by exposure to people and more by its distinctiveness. We have been able to quantitatively show the extent to which Londoners' collective psychological map tallies with the socio-economic indicators of housing deprivation, living environment conditions, and crime. By then comparing different social media platforms, we have suggested that a platform's demographics and geographic saliency determine whether its content is fit for urban studies similar to ours or not. This is a preliminary yet useful guideline for the web community who has recently turned to the study of large-scale urban dynamics derived from social media data. In the long term, having our design suggestions and source code at hand, researchers around the world might well seize the opportunity to take psychological maps to other cities.

Acknowledgement. This research has been guided from nonsense to sense by a large number of individuals. We are eager to spread some credits (while of course remaining accountable for all blame) to Mike Batty, Henriette Cramer, Tim Harris, Tom Kirk, Daniel Lewis, Ed Manley, Amin Mantrach, Guy Marriage, Yiorgios Papamanousakis, Alan Penn, Kerstin Sailer, Chris Smith, and the members of the two mailing lists Space Syntax and Cambridge NetOS. This research was partially supported by RCUK through the Horizon Digital Economy Research grant (EP/G065802/1) and by the EU SocialSensor FP7 project (contract no. 287975).

9. REFERENCES

[1] R. Annechino and Y.-S. Cheng. Visualizing Mental Maps of San Francisco. *School of Information, UC Berkeley*, 2011.

[2] A. Bawa-Cavia. Sensing The Urban: Using location-based social network data in urban analysis. In *Pervasive Urban Applications (PURBA)*, 2011.

[3] F. Bentley, H. Cramer, W. Hamilton, and S. Basapur. Drawing the city: differing perceptions of the urban

---

[8] http://profzero.org/urbanopticon/

environment. In *Proceedings of ACM Conference on Human Factors in Computing Systems (CHI)*, 2012.

[4] Z. Cheng, J. Caverlee, and K. Lee. Exploring millions of footprints in location sharing services. In *Proceedings of the AAAI International Conference on Webblogs and Social Media (ICWSM)*, 2011.

[5] H. Cramer, M. Rost, and L. E. Holmquist. Performing a check-in: emerging practices, norms and 'conflicts' in location-sharing using foursquare. In *Proceedings of ACM International Conference on Human Computer Interaction with Mobile Devices and Services (MobileHCI)*, 2011.

[6] D. J. Crandall, L. Backstrom, D. Huttenlocher, and J. Kleinberg. Mapping the world's photos. In *Proceedings of ACM International Conference on World Wide Web (WWW)*, 2009.

[7] J. Cranshaw, R. Schwartz, J. Hong, and N. Sadeh. The Livehoods Project: Utilizing Social Media to Understand the Dynamics of a City. In *International AAAI Conference on Weblogs and Social Media (ICWSM)*, 2012.

[8] C. Doersch, S. Singh, A. Gupta, J. Sivic, and A. A. Efros. What Makes Paris Look like Paris? *ACM Transactions on Graphics (SIGGRAPH)*, 2012.

[9] P. Glendinning and S. Muthesius. *Tower Block: Modern Public Housing in England, Scotland, Wales, and Northern Ireland*. Yale University Press, 1994.

[10] Ignite. 2012 Social Network Analysis Report. In *Social Media*, 2012.

[11] N. Lathia, D. Quercia, and J. Crowcroft. The Hidden Image of the City : Sensing Community Well-Being from Urban Mobility. In *Proceedings of the International Conference on Pervasive Computing*, 2012.

[12] J. Lindqvist, J. Cranshaw, J. Wiese, J. Hong, and J. Zimmerman. I'm the mayor of my house: examining why people use foursquare - a social-driven location sharing application. In *Proceedings of ACM Conference on Human Factors in Computing Systems (CHI)*, 2011.

[13] K. Lynch. *The Image of the City*. Urban Studies. MIT Press, 1960.

[14] D. Mclennan, H. Barnes, M. Noble, J. Davies, and E. Garratt. *The English Indices of Deprivation 2010*. UK Office for National Statistics, 2011.

[15] S. Milgram. *The individual in a social world: essays and experiments*. Addison-Wesley, 1977.

[16] S. Milgram and D. Jodelet. Psychological maps of Paris. *Environmental Psychology*, 1976.

[17] S. Milgram, S. Kessler, and W. McKenna. A Psychological Map of New York City. *American Scientist*, 1972.

[18] A. Noulas, S. Scellato, R. Lambiotte, M. Pontil, and C. Mascolo. A Tale of Many Cities: Universal Patterns in Human Urban Mobility. *PLoS ONE*, 2012.

[19] D. Quercia, N. Ohare, and H. Cramer. Aesthetic Capital: What Makes London Look Beautiful, Quiet, and Happy? 2013.

[20] C. Smith, D. Quercia, and L. Capra. Finger On The Pulse: Identifying Deprivation Using Transit Flow Analysis. In *Proceedings of ACM International Conference on Computer-Supported Cooperative Work (CSCW)*, 2013.

[21] TfL. London Travel Demand Survey (LTDS). *Transport for London*, 2011.

[22] TheEconomist. More than just a game: Video games are behind the latest fad in management. November 2012.

[23] L. von Ahn and L. Dabbish. Designing games with a purpose. *Communications of ACM*, 2008.

[24] K. Werbach. *For the Win: How Game Thinking Can Revolutionize Your Business*. Wharton Press, 2012.

Towards Realistic Team Formation in Social Networks based on Densest Subgraphs

Syama Rangapuram
Max Planck Institute for
Computer Science
Saarbrücken, Germany
srangapu@mpi-
inf.mpg.de

Thomas Bühler
Faculty of Mathematics
and Computer Science
Saarland University
Saarbrücken, Germany
tb@cs.uni-saarland.de

Matthias Hein
Faculty of Mathematics
and Computer Science
Saarland University
Saarbrücken, Germany
hein@cs.uni-saarland.de

ABSTRACT

Given a task $\mathcal{T}$, a set of experts V with multiple skills and a social network $G(V, W)$ reflecting the compatibility among the experts, *team formation* is the problem of identifying a team $C \subseteq V$ that is both competent in performing the task $\mathcal{T}$ and compatible in working together. Existing methods for this problem make too restrictive assumptions and thus cannot model practical scenarios. The goal of this paper is to consider the team formation problem in a realistic setting and present a novel formulation based on densest subgraphs. Our formulation allows modeling of many natural requirements such as (i) inclusion of a designated team leader and/or a group of given experts, (ii) restriction of the size or more generally cost of the team (iii) enforcing *locality* of the team, e.g., in a geographical sense or social sense, etc. The proposed formulation leads to a generalized version of the classical densest subgraph problem with cardinality constraints (DSP), which is an NP hard problem and has many applications in social network analysis. In this paper, we present a new method for (approximately) solving the generalized DSP (GDSP). Our method, **FORTE**, is based on solving an *equivalent* continuous relaxation of GDSP. The solution found by our method has a quality guarantee and always satisfies the constraints of GDSP. Experiments show that the proposed formulation (GDSP) is useful in modeling a broader range of team formation problems and that our method produces more coherent and compact teams of high quality. We also show, with the help of an LP relaxation of GDSP, that our method gives close to optimal solutions to GDSP.

Categories and Subject Descriptors

H.2.8 [**Database Management**]: Database Applications—*Data mining*; G.2.2 [**Discrete Mathematics**]: Graph Theory—*Graph algorithms*

General Terms

Algorithms, Experimentation, Theory

Keywords

Team formation, Social networks, Densest subgraphs

Copyright is held by the International World Wide Web Conference Committee (IW3C2). IW3C2 reserves the right to provide a hyperlink to the author's site if the Material is used in electronic media.
WWW 2013, May 13–17, 2013, Rio de Janeiro, Brazil.
ACM 978-1-4503-2035-1/13/05.

1. INTRODUCTION

Given a set of skill requirements (called task $\mathcal{T}$), a set of experts who have expertise in one or more skill, along with a social or professional network of the experts, the team formation problem is to identify a competent and highly collaborative team. This problem in the context of a social network was first introduced by [18] and has attracted recent interest in the data mining community [15, 2, 12]. A closely related and well-studied problem in operations research is the assignment problem. Here, given a set of agents and a set of tasks, the goal is to find an agent-task assignment minimizing the cost of the assignment such that exactly one agent is assigned to a task and every task is assigned to some agent. This problem can be modeled as a maximum weight matching problem in a weighted bipartite graph. In contrast to the assignment problem, the team formation problem considers the underlying social network, which for example models the previous collaborations among the experts, while forming teams. The advantage of using such a social network is that the teams that have worked together previously are expected to have less communication overhead and work more effectively as a team.

The criteria explored in the literature so far for measuring the effectiveness of teams are based on the shortest path distances, density, and the cost of the minimum spanning tree of the subgraph induced by the team. Here the density of a subgraph is defined as the ratio of the total weight of the edges within the subgraph over the size of the subgraph. Teams that are well connected have high density values. Methods based on minimizing diameter (largest shortest path between any two vertices) or cost of the spanning tree have the main advantage that the teams they yield are always connected (provided the underlying social network is connected). However, diameter or spanning tree based objectives are not robust to the changes (addition/deletion of edges) in the social network. As demonstrated in [12] using various performance measures, the density based objective performs better in identifying well connected teams. On the other hand, maximizing density may give a team whose subgraph is disconnected. This happens especially when there are small groups of people who are highly connected with each other but are sparsely connected to the rest of the graph.

Existing methods make either strong assumptions on the problem that do not hold in practice or are not capable of incorporating more intuitive constraints such as bounding the total size of the team. The goal of this paper is to consider the team formation problem in a more realistic setting and present a novel formulation based on a generalization of the densest subgraph problem. Our formulation allows modeling of many realistic requirements such as (i) inclusion of a designated team leader and/or a group of given experts, (ii) restriction on the size or more generally cost of the team (iii) enforcing *locality* of the team, e.g., in a geographical sense or social sense, etc. In fact most of the future directions pointed out by [12] are covered in our formulation.

2. RELATED WORK

The first work [18] in the team formation problem in the presence of a social network presents greedy algorithms for minimizing the diameter and the cost of the minimum spanning tree (MST) induced by the team. While the greedy algorithm for minimizing the diameter has an approximation guarantee of two, no guarantee is proven for the MST algorithm. However, [18] impose the strong assumption that a skill requirement of a task can be fulfilled by a single person; thus a more natural requirement such as "at least k experts of skill s are needed for the task" cannot be handled by their method. This shortcoming has been addressed in [12], which presents a 2-approximation algorithm for a slightly more general problem that can accommodate the above requirement. However, both algorithms cannot handle an upper bound constraint on the team size. On the other hand, the solutions obtained by all these algorithms (including the MST algorithm) can be shown to be connected subgraphs if the underlying social graph is connected.

Two new formulations are proposed in [15] based on the shortest path distances between the nodes of the graph. The first formulation assumes that experts from each skill have to communicate with every expert from the other skill and thus minimizes the sum of the pairwise shortest path distances between experts belonging to different skills. They prove that this problem is NP-hard and provide a greedy algorithm with an approximation guarantee of two. The second formulation, solvable optimally in polynomial time, assumes that there is a designated team leader who has to communicate with every expert in the team and minimizes the sum of the distances only to the leader. The main shortcoming of this work is its restrictive assumption that *exactly* one expert is sufficient for each skill, which implies that the size of the found teams is always upper bounded by the number of skills in the given task, noting that an expert is allowed to have multiple skills. They exploit this assumption and (are the first to) produce top-k teams that can perform the given task. However, although based on the shortest path distances, neither of the two formulations does guarantee that the solution obtained is connected.

In contrast to the distance or diameter based cost functions, [12] explore the usefulness of the density based objective in finding strongly connected teams. Using various performance measures, the superiority of the density based objective function over the diameter objective is demonstrated. The setting considered in [12] is the most general one until now but the resulting problem is shown to be NP hard. The greedy algorithms that they propose have approximation guarantees (of factor 3) for two special cases. The teams found by their algorithms are often quite large and it is not straightforward to modify their algorithms to integrate an additional upper bound constraint on the team size. Another disadvantage is that subgraphs that maximize the density under the given constraints need not necessarily be connected.

Recently [2] considered an *online* team formation problem where tasks arrive in a sequential manner and teams have to be formed minimizing the (maximum) load on any expert across the tasks while bounding the coordination cost (a free parameter) within a team for any given task. Approximation algorithms are provided for two variants of coordinate costs: diameter cost and Steiner cost (cost of the minimum Steiner tree where the team members are the terminal nodes). While this work focusses more on the load balancing aspect, it also makes the strong assumption that a skill is covered by the team if there exists at least one expert having that skill.

All of the above methods allow only binary skill level, i.e., an expert has a skill level of either one or zero.

We point out that many methods have been developed in the operations research community for the team formation problem, [5, 9, 21, 20], but none of them explicitly considers the underlying social or professional connections among the experts. There is also literature discussing the social aspects of the team formation [10] and their influence on the evolution of communities, e.g., [4].

3. REALISTIC TEAM FORMATION IN SOCIAL NETWORKS

Now we formally define the *Team Formation* problem that we address in this paper. Let V be the set of n experts and $G(V, W)$ be the weighted, undirected graph reflecting the relationship or previous collaboration of the experts V. Then non-negative, symmetric weight $w_{ij} \in W$ connecting two experts i and j reflects the level of compatibility between them. The set of skills is given by $\mathcal{A} = \{a_1, \ldots, a_p\}$. Each expert is assumed to possess one or more skills. The non-negative matrix $M \in \mathbb{R}^{n \times p}$ specifies the skill levels of all experts in each skill. Note that we define the skill level on a continuous scale. If an expert i does not have skill j, then $M_{ij} = 0$. Moreover, we use the notation $M_j \in \mathbb{R}^{n \times 1}$ for the j-th column of M, i.e. the vector of skill levels corresponding to skill j. A task $\mathcal{T}$ is given by the set of triples $\{(a_j, \kappa_j, \iota_j)\}_{j=1}^{p}$, where $a_j \in \mathcal{A}$, specifying that at least κ_j and at most ι_j of skill a_j is required to finish the given task.

Generalized team formation problem. Given a task $\mathcal{T}$, the generalized team formation problem is defined as finding a team $C \subseteq V$ of experts maximizing the *collaborative compatibility* and satisfying the following constraints:

- **Inclusion of a specified group:** a predetermined group of experts $S \subset V$ should be in C.
- **Skill requirement:** at least κ_j and at most ι_j of skill a_j is required to finish the task $\mathcal{T}$.
- **Bound on the team size:** the size of the team should be smaller than or equal to b, i.e., $|C| \leq b$.
- **Budget constraint:** total budget for finishing the task is bounded by B, i.e., $\sum_{i \in C} c_i \leq B$, where $c_i \in \mathbb{R}_+$ is the cost incurred on expert i.
- **Distance based constraint:** the distance (measured according to some non-negative, symmetric function, dist) between any pair of experts in C should not be larger than d_0, i.e., $\text{dist}(u, v) \leq d_0, \forall u, v \in C$.

Discussion of our generalized constraints. In contrast to existing methods, we also allow an upper bound on each skill and on the total team size. If the skill matrix is only allowed to be binary as in previous work, this translates into upper and lower bounds on the number of experts required for each skill. Using vertex weights, we can in fact encode more generic constraints, e.g., having a limit on the total budget of the team. It is not straightforward to extend existing methods to include any upper bound constraints. Up to our knowledge we are the first to integrate upper bound constraints, in particular on the size of the team, into the team formation problem. We think that the latter constraint is essential for realistic team formation.

Our general setting also allows a group of experts around whom the team has to be formed. This constraint often applies as the team leader is usually fixed before forming the team. Another important generalization is the inclusion of *distance* constraints for any general distance function[1]. Such a constraint can be used to enforce locality of the team e.g. in a geographical sense (the distance could be travel time) or social sense (distance in the network). Another potential application are mutual incompatibilities of team members e.g. on a personal level, which can be addressed by assigning a high distance to experts who are mutually incompatible and thus should not be put together in the same team.

We emphasize that all constraints considered in the literature are special instances of the above constraint set.

Measure of collaborative compatiblity. In this paper we use as a measure of collaborative compatibility a generalized form of the density of subgraphs, defined as

$$\text{density}(C) := \frac{\text{assoc}(C)}{\text{vol}_g(C)} = \frac{\sum_{i,j \in C} w_{ij}}{\sum_{i \in C} g_i}, \quad (1)$$

where w_{ij} is the non-negative weight of the edge between i and j and $\text{vol}_g(C)$ is defined as $\sum_{i \in C} g_i$, with g_i being the positive weight of the vertex i. We recover the original density formulation, via $g_i = 1, \forall i \in V$. We use the relation, $\text{assoc}(C) = \text{vol}_d(C) - \text{cut}(C, V \backslash C)$, where $d_i = \sum_{j=1}^{n} w_{ij}$ is the degree of vertex i and $\text{cut}(A, B) := \sum_{i \in A, j \in B} w_{ij}$.

Discussion of density based objective. As pointed out in [12], the density based objective possesses useful properties like strict monotonicity and robustness. In case of the density based objective, if an edge gets added (because of a new collaboration) or deleted (because of newly found incompatibility) the density of the subgraphs involving this edge necessarily increases resp. decreases, which is not true for the diameter based objective. In contrast to density based objective, the impact of small changes in graph structure is more severe in the case of diameter objective [12].

The generalized density that we use here leads to further modeling freedom as it enables to give weights to the experts according to their expertise. By giving smaller weight to those with high expertise one can obtain solutions that not only satisfy the given skill requirements but also give preference to the more competent team members (i.e. the ones having smaller weights)

---
[1]The distance function need not satisfy the triangle inequality.

Problem Formulation. Using the notation introduced above, an instance of the team formation problem based on the generalized density can be formulated as

$$\max_{C \subseteq V} \frac{\text{assoc}(C)}{\text{vol}_g(C)} \quad (2)$$

$$\text{subject to}: S \subseteq C$$
$$\kappa_j \leq \text{vol}_{M_j}(C) \leq \iota_j, \quad \forall j \in \{1, \ldots, p\}$$
$$|C| \leq b$$
$$\text{vol}_c(C) \leq B$$
$$\text{dist}(u, v) \leq d_0, \quad \forall u, v \in C,$$

Note that the upper bound constraints on the team size and the budget can be rewritten as skill constraints and can be incorporated into the skill matrix M accordingly. Thus, without loss of generality, we omit the budget and size constraints from now on, for the sake of brevity. Moreover, since S is required to be part of the solution, we can assume that $\text{dist}(u, v) \leq d_0, \forall u, v \in S$, otherwise the above problem is infeasible. The distance constraint also implies that any $u \in V$ for which $\text{dist}(u, s) > d_0$, for some $s \in S$, cannot be a part of the solution. Thus, we again assume wlog that there is no such $u \in V$; otherwise such vertices can be eliminated without changing the solution of problem (2).

Our formulation (2) is a generalized version of the classical densest subgraph problem (DSP), which has many applications in graph analysis, e.g., see [19]. The simplest version of DSP is the problem of finding a densest subgraph (without any constraints on the solution), which can be solved optimally in polynomial time [13]. The densest-k-subgraph problem, which requires the solution to contain exactly k vertices, is a notoriously hard problem in this class and has been shown not to admit a polynomial time approximation scheme [16]. Recently, it has been shown that the densest subgraph problem with an upper bound on the size is as hard as the densest-k-subgraph problem [17]. However, the densest subgraph problem with a lower bound constraint has a 2-approximation algorithm [17]. It is based on solving a sequence of unconstrained densest subgraph problems. They also show that there exists a linear programming relaxation for this problem achieving the same approximation guarantee.

Recently [12] considered the following generalized version of the densest subgraph problem with lower bound constraints in the context of team formation problem:

$$\max_{C \subseteq V} \frac{\text{assoc}(C)}{\text{vol}_g(C)} \quad (3)$$

$$\text{subject to}: \text{vol}_{M_j}(C) \geq \kappa_j, \quad \forall j \in \{1, \ldots, p\}$$

where M is the *binary* skill matrix. They extend the greedy method of [17] and show that it achieves a 3-approximation guarantee for some special cases of this problem. [8] recently improved the approximation guarantee of the greedy algorithm of [12] for problem (3) to a factor 2. The time complexity of this greedy algorithm is $O(kn^3)$, where n is the number of experts and $k := \sum_{j=1}^{m} k_j$ is the minimum number of experts required.

Direct integration of subset constraint. The subset constraint can be integrated into the objective by directly working on the subgraph G' induced by the vertex set $V' =$

$V \setminus S$. Note that any $C \subset V$ that contains S can be written as $C = A \cup S$, for $A \subset V'$. We now reformulate the team formation problem on the subgraph G'. We introduce the notation $m = |V'|$, and we assume wlog that the first m entries of V are the ones in V'.

The terms in problem (2) can be rewritten as

$$\begin{aligned}\operatorname{assoc}(C) &= \operatorname{assoc}(A) + \operatorname{assoc}(S) + 2\operatorname{cut}(A, S),\\ &= \operatorname{vol}_d(A) - \operatorname{cut}(A, V \setminus A) + \operatorname{assoc}(S) + 2\operatorname{cut}(A, S)\\ &= \operatorname{vol}_d(A) - \operatorname{cut}(A, V' \setminus A) + \operatorname{assoc}(S) + \operatorname{cut}(A, S)\\ \operatorname{vol}_g(C) &= \operatorname{vol}_g(A) + \operatorname{vol}_g(S)\end{aligned}$$

Moreover, note that we can write: $\operatorname{cut}(A, S) = \operatorname{vol}_{d^S}(A)$, where $d_i^S = \sum_{j \in S} w_{ij}$ denotes the degree of vertex i restricted to the subset S in the original graph. Using the abbreviations, $\mu_S = \operatorname{assoc}(S)$, $\nu_S = \operatorname{vol}_g(S)$, $\operatorname{assoc}_S(A) = \operatorname{vol}_d(A) - \operatorname{cut}(A, V' \setminus A) + \mu_S + \operatorname{vol}_{d^S}(A)$, we rewrite the team formation problem (2) as

$$\max_{A \subseteq V', A \neq \emptyset} \frac{\operatorname{assoc}_S(A)}{\operatorname{vol}_g(A) + \nu_S} \quad \text{(GDSP)}$$

$$\text{subject to}: k_j \leq \operatorname{vol}_{M_j}(A) \leq l_j, \quad \forall j \in \{1, \ldots, p\}$$

$$\operatorname{dist}(u, v) \leq d_0, \quad \forall u, v \in A,$$

where for all $j = 1, \ldots, p$, the bounds were updated as $k_j = \kappa_j - \operatorname{vol}_{M_j}(S)$, $l_j = \iota_j - \operatorname{vol}_{M_j}(S)$. Note that here we already used the assumption: $\operatorname{dist}(u, s) \leq d_0, \forall u \in V, \forall s \in S$. The constraint, $A \neq \emptyset$, has been introduced for technical reasons required for the formulation of the continuous problem in Section 4.2. The equivalence of problem (GDSP) to (2) follows by considering either S (if feasible) or the set $A^* \cup S$, where A^* is an optimal solution of (GDSP), depending on whichever has higher density.

To the best of our knowledge there is no greedy algorithm with an approximation guarantee to solve problem (GDSP). Instead of designing a greedy approximation algorithm for this discrete optimization problem, we derive an *equivalent* continuous optimization problem in Section 4. That is, we reformulate the discrete problem in continuous space while preserving the optimality of the solutions of the discrete problem. The rationale behind this approach is that the continuous formulation is more flexible and allows us to choose from a larger set of methods for its solution than for the discrete one. Although the resulting continuous problem is as hard as the original discrete problem, recent progress in continuous optimization [14] allow us to find a locally optimal solution very efficiently.

4. DERIVATION OF FORTE

In this section we present our method, *Formation Of Realistic Teams* (**FORTE**, for short) to solve the team formation problem, which is rewritten as (GDSP), using the continuous relaxation. We derive **FORTE** in three steps:

i. Derive an equivalent unconstrained discrete problem (4) of the team formation problem (GDSP) via an *exact penalty* approach.

ii. Derive an equivalent continuous relaxation (6) of the unconstrained problem (4) by using the concept of *Lovasz extensions*.

iii. Compute the solution of the continuous problem (6) using the recent method RatioDCA from *fractional programming*.

4.1 Equivalent Unconstrained Problem

A general technique in constrained optimization is to transform the constrained problem into an equivalent unconstrained problem by adding to the objective a penalty term, which is controlled by a parameter $\gamma \geq 0$. The penalty term is zero if the constraints are satisfied at the given input and strictly positive otherwise. The choice of the regularization parameter γ influences the tradeoff between satisfying the constraints and having a low objective value. Large values of γ tend to enforce the satisfaction of constraints. In the following we show that for the team formation problem (GDSP) there exists a value of γ that guarantees the satisfaction of all constraints.

Let us define the penalty term for constraints of the team formation problem (GDSP) as

$$\operatorname{pen}(A) := \begin{cases} \sum_{j=1}^p \max\{0, \operatorname{vol}_{M_j}(A) - l_j\} \\ + \sum_{j=1}^p \max\{0, k_j - \operatorname{vol}_{M_j}(A)\} \\ + \sum_{u,v \in A} \max\{0, \operatorname{dist}(u, v) - d_0\} & A \neq \emptyset \\ 0 & A = \emptyset. \end{cases}$$

Note that the above penalty function is zero only when A satisfies the constraints; otherwise it is strictly positive and increases with increasing infeasibility. The special treatment of the empty set is again a technicality required later for the Lovasz extensions, see Section 4.2. For the same reason, we also replace the constant terms μ_S and ν_S in (GDSP) by $\mu_S \operatorname{unit}(A)$ and $\nu_S \operatorname{unit}(A)$ respectively, where $\operatorname{unit}(A) := 1, A \neq \emptyset$ and $\operatorname{unit}(\emptyset) = 0$.

The following theorem shows that there exists an unconstrained problem equivalent to the constrained optimization problem (GDSP).

THEOREM 1. *The constrained problem (GDSP) is equivalent to the unconstrained problem*

$$\min_{\emptyset \neq A \subseteq V} \frac{\operatorname{vol}_g(A) + \nu_S \operatorname{unit}(A) + \gamma \operatorname{pen}(A)}{\operatorname{assoc}_S(A)} \quad (4)$$

for $\gamma > \frac{\operatorname{vol}_d(V)}{\theta} \frac{\operatorname{vol}_g(A_0) + \nu_S}{\operatorname{assoc}_S(A_0)}$, where A_0 is any feasible set of problem (GDSP) such that $\operatorname{assoc}_S(A_0) > 0$ and θ is the minimum value of infeasibility, i.e., $\operatorname{pen}(A) \geq \theta$, if A is infeasible.

PROOF. We define $\operatorname{spvol}(A) := \frac{\operatorname{vol}_g(A) + \nu_S \operatorname{unit}(A)}{\operatorname{assoc}_S(A)}$. Note that maximizing (GDSP) is the same as minimizing $\operatorname{spvol}(A)$ subject to the constraints of (GDSP). For any feasible subset A, the objective of (4) is equal to $\operatorname{spvol}(A)$, since the penalty term is zero. Thus, if we show that all minimizers of (4) satisfy the constraints then the equivalence follows. Suppose, for the sake of contradiction, that $A^* (\neq \emptyset$, if $S = \emptyset$) is a minimizer of (4) and that A^* is infeasible for problem (GDSP). Since $\nu_S \geq 0$ and $g_i > 0, \forall i$, we have under the given condition on γ,

$$\frac{\operatorname{vol}_g(A^*) + \nu_S + \gamma \operatorname{pen}(A^*)}{\operatorname{assoc}_S(A^*)} > \frac{\gamma \operatorname{pen}(A^*)}{\operatorname{assoc}_S(A^*)}$$

$$\geq \frac{\gamma \theta}{\max_{A \subseteq V} \operatorname{assoc}_S(A)} \geq \frac{\gamma \theta}{\operatorname{vol}_d(V)} > \frac{\operatorname{vol}_g(A_0) + \nu_S}{\operatorname{assoc}_S(A_0)},$$

which leads to a contradiction because the last term is the objective value of (4) at A_0. □

4.2 Equivalent Continuous Problem

We will now derive a tight continuous relaxation of problem (4). This will lead us to a minimization problem over $\mathbb{R}^m$, which then can be handled more easily than the original discrete problem. The connection between the discrete and the continuous space is achieved via thresholding. Given a vector $f \in \mathbb{R}^m$, one can define the sets

$$A_i := \{j \in V | f_j \geq f_i\}, \tag{5}$$

by thresholding f at the value f_i. In order to go from functions on sets to functions on continuous space, we make use of the concept of Lovasz extensions.

DEFINITION 1. *(Lovasz extension) Let $R : 2^V \to \mathbb{R}$ be a set function with $R(\emptyset) = 0$, and let $f \in \mathbb{R}^m$ be ordered in ascending order $f_1 \leq f_2 \leq \cdots \leq f_m$. The Lovasz extension $R^L : \mathbb{R}^m \to \mathbb{R}$ of R is defined by*

$$R^L(f) = \sum_{i=1}^{m-1} R(A_{i+1})(f_{i+1} - f_i) + R(V)f_1.$$

Note that $R^L(\mathbf{1}_A) = R(A)$ for all $A \subset V$, i.e. R^L is indeed an extension of R from 2^V to $\mathbb{R}^V$ ($|V| = m$). In the following, given a set function R, we will denote its Lovasz extension by R^L. The explicit forms of the Lovasz extensions used in the derivation will be dealt with in Section 4.3.

In the following theorem we show the equivalence for GDSP. A more general result showing equivalence for fractional set programs can be found in [7].

THEOREM 2. *The unconstrained discrete problem (4) is equivalent to the continuous problem*

$$\min_{f \in \mathbb{R}_+^{V'}} \frac{\mathrm{vol}_g^L(f) + \nu_S \,\mathrm{unit}^L(A) + \gamma \,\mathrm{pen}^L(f)}{\mathrm{assoc}_S^L(f)} \tag{6}$$

for any $\gamma \geq 0$. Moreover, optimal thresholding of a minimizer $f^* \in \mathbb{R}_+^m$,

$$A^* := \min_{A_i = \{j \in V' | f_j^* \geq f_i^*\}, i=1,\ldots,m} \frac{\mathrm{vol}_g(A_i) + \nu_S + \gamma \,\mathrm{pen}(A_i)}{\mathrm{assoc}_S(A_i)},$$

yields a set A^* that is optimal for problem (4).

PROOF. Let $R(A) = \mathrm{vol}_g(A) + \nu_S \,\mathrm{unit}(A) + \gamma \,\mathrm{pen}(A)$. Then we have

$$\min_{A \subset V'} \frac{R(A)}{\mathrm{assoc}_S(A)} = \min_{A \subset V'} \frac{R^L(\mathbf{1}_A)}{\mathrm{assoc}_S^L(\mathbf{1}_A)} \geq \min_{f \in \mathbb{R}_+^{V'}} \frac{R^L(f)}{\mathrm{assoc}_S^L(f)},$$

where in the first step we used the fact that $R^L(f)$ and $\mathrm{assoc}^L(f)$ are extensions of $R(A)$ and $\mathrm{assoc}(A)$, respectively. Below we first show that the above inequality also holds in the other direction, which then establishes that the optimum values of both problems are the same. The proof of the reverse direction will also imply that a set minimizer of the problem (4) can be obtained from any minimizer f^* of (6) via optimal thresholding.

We first show that the optimal thresholding of any $f \in \mathbb{R}_+^m$ yields a set A such that $\mathbf{1}_A$ has an objective value at least as good as the one of f. This holds because

$$R^L(f) = \sum_{i=1}^{m-1} R(A_{i+1})(f_{i+1} - f_i) + f_1 R(V')$$

$$= \sum_{i=1}^{m-1} \frac{R(A_{i+1})}{\mathrm{assoc}_S(A_{i+1})} \mathrm{assoc}_S(A_{i+1})(f_{i+1} - f_i)$$

$$\quad + \frac{R(V')}{\mathrm{assoc}_S(V')} \mathrm{assoc}_S(V')f_1$$

$$\geq \min_{j=1,\ldots m} \frac{R(A_j)}{\mathrm{assoc}_S(A_j)}$$

$$\quad \Big(\sum_{i=1}^{m-1} \mathrm{assoc}_S(A_{i+1})(f_{i+1}-f_i) + \mathrm{assoc}_S(V')f_1\Big)$$

$$= \min_{j=1,\ldots m} \frac{R(A_j)}{\mathrm{assoc}_S(A_j)} \mathrm{assoc}_S^L(f)$$

The third step follows from the fact that f is non-negative ($f_1 \geq 0$) and ordered in ascending order, i.e., $f_{i+1} - f_i \geq 0, \forall i = 1, \ldots, m-1$. Since $\mathrm{assoc}_S^L(f)$ is non-negative, the final step implies that

$$\frac{R^L(f)}{\mathrm{assoc}_S^L(f)} \geq \min_{j=1,\ldots m} \frac{R(A_j)}{\mathrm{assoc}_S(A_j)}. \tag{7}$$

Thus we have

$$\min_{f \in \mathbb{R}_+^{V'}} \frac{R^L(f)}{\mathrm{assoc}_S^L(f)} \geq \min_{A \subset V'} \frac{R(A)}{\mathrm{assoc}_S(A)}.$$

From inequality (7), it follows that optimal thresholding of f^* yields a set that is a minimizer of problem (4). □

COROLLARY 1. *The team formation problem (GDSP) is equivalent to the problem (6) if γ is chosen according to the condition given in Theorem 1.*

PROOF. This directly follows from Theorems 1 and 2. □

While the continuous problem is as hard as the original discrete problem, recent ideas from continuous optimization [14] allow us to derive in the next section an algorithm for obtaining locally optimal solutions very efficiently.

4.3 Algorithm for the Continuous Problem

We now describe an algorithm for (approximately) solving the continuous optimization problem (6). The idea is to make use of the fact that the fractional optimization problem (6) has a special structure: as we will show in this section, it can be written as a special ratio of difference of convex (d.c.) functions, i.e. it has the form

$$\min_{f \in \mathbb{R}_+^V} \frac{R_1(f) - R_2(f)}{S_1(f) - S_2(f)} := Q(f), \tag{8}$$

where the functions R_1, R_2, S_1 and S_2 are positively one-homogeneous convex functions[2] and numerator and denominator are nonnegative. This reformulation then allows us to use a recent first order method called RatioDCA [14, 7].

In order to find the explicit form of the convex functions, we first need to rewrite the penalty term as $\mathrm{pen}(A) =$

---

[2]A function f is said to be positively one-homogeneous if $f(\alpha x) = \alpha f(x), \alpha \geq 0$.

$\text{pen}_1(A) - \text{pen}_2(A)$, where

$$\text{pen}_1(A) = \sum_{j=1}^p \text{vol}_{M_j}(A) + \sum_{j=1}^p k_j\, \text{unit}(A),$$
$$\text{pen}_2(A) = \sum_{j=1}^p \min\{l_j, \text{vol}_{M_j}(A)\} + \sum_{j=1}^p \min\{k_j, \text{vol}_{M_j}(A)\}$$
$$- \sum_{u,v \in A} \max\{0,\, \text{dist}(u,v) - d_0\}.$$

Using this decomposition of $\text{pen}(A)$, we can now write down the functions R_1, R_2, S_1 and S_2 as

$$R_1(f) = \text{vol}_\rho^L(f) + \sigma \max_i \{f_i\}$$
$$R_2(f) = \gamma\, \text{pen}_2^L(f)$$
$$S_1(f) = \text{vol}_d^L(f) + \text{vol}_{d^S}^L(f) + \mu_S \max_i \{f_i\}$$
$$S_2(f) = \text{cut}^L(f).$$

where $\rho := g + \gamma \sum_{j=1}^p M_j$, $\sigma := \nu_S + \gamma \sum_{j=1}^p k_j$, $\text{pen}_2^L(f)$ denotes the Lovasz extension of $\text{pen}_2(A)$, and

$$\text{vol}_h^L(f) = \langle (h_i)_{i=1}^m, f \rangle, \text{ where } h \in \mathbb{R}^n,$$
$$\text{cut}^L(f) = \tfrac{1}{2} \sum_{i,j=1}^m w_{ij} |f_i - f_j|.$$

LEMMA 1. *Using the functions R_1, R_2, S_1 and S_2 defined above, the problem (6) can be rewritten in the form (8). The functions R_1, R_2, S_1 and S_2 are convex and positively one-homogeneous, and $R_1 - R_2$ and $S_1 - S_2$ are nonnegative.*

PROOF. The denominator of (6) is given as $\text{assoc}_S^L(f) = \text{vol}_d^L(f) - \text{cut}^L(f) + \text{vol}_{d^S}^L(f) + \mu_S \text{unit}^L(f)$, and the numerator is given as $\text{vol}_g^L(f) + \nu_S \text{unit}^L(A) + \gamma\, \text{pen}^L(f)$. Using Prop.2.1 in [3] and the decomposition of $\text{pen}(A)$ introduced earlier in this section, we can decompose $\text{pen}^L(f) = \text{pen}_1^L(f) - \text{pen}_2^L(f)$. The Lovasz extension of $\text{pen}_1(A)$ is given as $\text{pen}_1^L(f) = \sum_{j=1}^p \text{vol}_{M_j}^L(f) + \sum_{j=1}^p k_j \max_i\{f_i\}$, and let $\text{pen}_2^L(f)$ denote the Lovasz extension of $\text{pen}_2(A)$ (an explicit form is not necessary, as shown later in this section). The equality between (6) and (8) then follows by simple rearranging of the terms.

The nonnegativity of the functions $R_1 - R_2$ and $S_1 - S_2$ follows from the nonnegativity of denominator and numerator of (6) and the definition of the Lovasz extension. Moreover, the Lovasz extensions of any set function is positively one-homogeneous [3].

Finally, the convexity of R_1 and S_1 follows as they are a non-negative combination of the convex functions $\max_i\{f_i\}$ and $\langle (h_i)_{i=1}^m, f \rangle$ for some $h \in \mathbb{R}^n$. The function $S_2(f) = \text{cut}^L(f)$ is well-known to be convex [3]. To show the convexity of R_2, we will show that the function $\text{pen}_2(A)$ is submodular[3]. The convexity then follows from the fact that a set function is submodular if and only if its Lovasz extension is convex [3]. For the proof of the submodularity of the first two sums one uses the fact that the pointwise minimum of a constant and a increasing submodular function is again submodular. Writing $D_{uv} := \max\{0, \text{dist}(u,v) - d_0\}$, the last sum can be written as $-\sum_{u,v \in A} D_{uv} = -\sum_{u \in A, v \in V'} D_{uv} + \sum_{u \in A, v \in V' \setminus A} D_{uv}$. Using $(d_D)_i = \sum_j D_{ij}$, we can write its Lovasz extension as $-\text{vol}_{d_D}(f) + \frac{1}{2} \sum_{i,j \in V'} D_{ij} |f_i - f_j|$, which is a sum of a linear term and a convex term. □

The reformulation of the problem in the form (8) enables us to apply a modification of the recently proposed

---

[3] A set function $R : 2^V \to \mathbb{R}$ is submodular if for all $A, B \subset V$, $R(A \cup B) + R(A \cap B) \leq R(A) + R(B)$.

RatioDCA [14, 7], a method for the *local* minimization of objectives of the form (8) on the whole $\mathbb{R}^m$. Given an

---

RatioDCA [14] Minimization of a non-negative ratio of one-homogeneous d.c functions over $\mathbb{R}_+^m$

1: **Initialization:** $f^0 \in \mathbb{R}_+^m$, $\lambda^0 = Q(f^0)$
2: **repeat**
3: $\quad f^{l+1} = \arg\min_{u \in \mathbb{R}_+^m,\, \|u\|_2 \leq 1} R_1(u) + \lambda^l S_2(u) - \langle u, r_2(f^l) + \lambda^l s_1(f^l) \rangle$
$\quad$ where $r_2(f^l) \in \partial R_2(f^l)$, $s_1(f^l) \in \partial S_1(f^l)$
4: $\quad \lambda^{l+1} = Q(f^{l+1})$
5: **until** $\frac{|\lambda^{l+1} - \lambda^l|}{\lambda^l} < \epsilon$

---

initialization f_0, the above algorithm solves a sequence of convex optimization problems (line 3). Note that we do not need an explicit description of the terms $S_1(f)$ and $R_2(f)$, but only elements of their subdifferential $s_1(f) \in \partial S_1(f)$ resp. $r_2(f) \in \partial R_2(f)$. The explicit forms of the subgradients are given in the appendix. The convex problem (line 3) then has the form

$$\min_{f \in \mathbb{R}_+^m} \frac{\lambda^l}{2} \sum_{i,j=1}^m w_{ij}|f_i - f_j| + \langle f, c \rangle + \sigma \max_i\{f_i\}, \quad (9)$$

where $c = \rho - r_2(f^l) - \lambda^l s_1(f^l)$. Note that (9) is a *non-smooth* problem. However, there exists an equivalent smooth dual problem, which we give below.

LEMMA 2. *The problem (9) is equivalent to*

$$\min_{\substack{\|\alpha\|_\infty \leq 1 \\ \alpha_{ij} = -\alpha_{ji}}} \min_{v \in S_m} \frac{1}{2} \left\| P_{\mathbb{R}_+^m}\left(-c - \frac{\lambda^l}{2} A\alpha - \sigma v\right) \right\|_2^2,$$

where $A : \mathbb{R}^E \mapsto \mathbb{R}^V$ with $(A\alpha)_i := \sum_j w_{ij}(\alpha_{ij} - \alpha_{ji})$, $P_{\mathbb{R}_+^m}$ denotes the projection on the positive orthant and S_m is the simplex $S_m = \{v \in \mathbb{R}^m \mid v_i \geq 0, \sum_{i=1}^m v_i = 1\}$.

PROOF. First we use the homogenity of the objective in the inner problem to eliminate the norm constraint. This yields the equivalent problem

$$\min_{u \in \mathbb{R}_+^n} \sigma \max_i u_i + \frac{1}{2}\|u\|_2^2 + \langle u, c \rangle + \frac{\lambda^l}{2} \sum_{i,j=1}^n w_{ij}|u_i - u_j|.$$

We derive the dual problem as follows:

$$\min_{u \in \mathbb{R}_+^n} \frac{\lambda^l}{2} \sum_{i,j=1}^n w_{ij}|u_i - u_j| + \sigma \max_i u_i + \frac{1}{2}\|u\|_2^2 + \langle u, c \rangle$$
$$= \min_{u \in \mathbb{R}_+^n} \Bigg\{ \max_{\substack{\|\alpha\|_\infty \leq 1 \\ \alpha_{ij} = -\alpha_{ji}}} \frac{\lambda^l}{2} \sum_{i,j=1}^n w_{ij}(u_i - u_j)\alpha_{ij}$$
$$\qquad + \max_{v \in S_n} \sigma \langle u, v \rangle + \frac{1}{2}\|u\|_2^2 + \langle u, c \rangle \Bigg\}$$
$$= \max_{\substack{\|\alpha\|_\infty \leq 1 \\ \alpha_{ij} = -\alpha_{ji} \\ v \in S_n}} \min_{u \in \mathbb{R}_+^n} \frac{1}{2}\|u\|_2^2 + \left\langle u, c + \frac{\lambda^l}{2} A\alpha + \sigma v \right\rangle,$$

where $(A\alpha)_i := \sum_j w_{ij}(\alpha_{ij} - \alpha_{ji})$. The optimization over u has the solution $u = P_{\mathbb{R}_+^n}(-c - \frac{\lambda^l}{2}A\alpha - \sigma v)$. Plugging u into the objective and using that $\langle P_{\mathbb{R}_+^n}(x), x \rangle = \|P_{\mathbb{R}_+^n}(x)\|_2^2$, we obtain the result. □

The smooth dual problem can be solved very efficiently using recent scalable first order methods like FISTA [6], which has a guaranteed convergence rate of $O(\frac{1}{k^2})$, where k is the number of steps done in FISTA. The main part in the calculation of FISTA consists of a matrix-vector multiplication. As the social network is typically sparse, this operation costs $O(m)$, where m is the number of non-zeros of W.

RatioDCA [14], produces a strictly decreasing sequence f^l, i.e., $Q(f^{l+1}) < Q(f^l)$, or terminates. This is a typical property of fast local methods in non-convex optimization. Moreover, the convex problem need not be solved to full accuracy; we can terminate the convex problem early, if the current f^l produces already sufficent descent in Q. As the number of required steps in the RatioDCA typically ranges between 5-20, the full method scales to large networks. Note that convergence to the global optimum of (8) cannot be guaranteed due to the non-convex nature of the problem. However, we have the following quality guarantee for the team formation problem.

THEOREM 3. *Let A_0 be a feasible set for the problem (GDSP) and γ is chosen as in Theorem 1. Let f^* denote the result of RatioDCA after initializing with the vector $\mathbf{1}_{A_0}$, and let A_{f^*} denote the set found by optimal thresholding of f^*. Either RatioDCA terminates after one iteration, or produces A_{f^*} which satisfies all the constraints of the team formation problem (GDSP) and*

$$\frac{\mathrm{assoc}_S(A_{f^*})}{\mathrm{vol}_g(A_{f^*}) + \nu_S} > \frac{\mathrm{assoc}_S(A_0)}{\mathrm{vol}_g(A_0) + \nu_S}.$$

PROOF. *RatioDCA generates a decreasing sequence $\{f^l\}$ such that $Q(f^{l+1}) < Q(f^l)$ until it terminates [14]. We have $Q(f^1) < Q(\mathbf{1}_{A_0})$, if the algorithm does not stop in one step. As shown in Theorem (2) optimal thresholding of f^1 yields a set A_f that achieves smaller objective on the corresponding set function. Since the chosen value of γ guarantees the satisfaction of the constraints, A_f has to be feasible.* □

5. LP RELAXATION OF GDSP

Recall that our team formation problem based on the density objective is rewritten as the following GDSP after integrating the subset constraint:

$$\max_{A \subseteq V'} \frac{\mathrm{assoc}_S(A)}{\mathrm{vol}_g(A) + \nu_S} \quad (10)$$

$$\text{subject to}: k_j \leq \mathrm{vol}_{M_j}(A) \leq l_j, \quad \forall j \in \{1, \ldots, p\}$$
$$\mathrm{dist}(u,v) \leq d_0, \quad \forall u,v \in A.$$

Note that here we do not require the additional constraint, $A \neq \emptyset$, that we added to (GDSP). In this section we show that there exists a Linear programming (LP) relaxation for this problem. The LP relaxation can be solved optimally in polynomial time and provides an upper bound on the optimum value of GDSP. In practice such an upper bound is useful to check the quality of the solutions found by approximation algorithms.

THEOREM 4. *The following LP is a relaxation of the Generalized Densest Subgraph Problem (10).*

$$\max_{t \in \mathbb{R}, \, f \in \mathbb{R}^{V'}, \, \alpha \in \mathbb{R}^{E'}} \sum_{i,j=1}^m w_{ij}\alpha_{ij} + 2\left\langle d^S, f \right\rangle + t\mu_S \quad (11)$$

$$\text{subject to}: tk_j \leq \langle M_j, f \rangle \leq tl_j, \quad \forall j \in \{1,\ldots,p\}$$
$$f_u + f_v \leq t, \quad \forall u,v: \mathrm{dist}(u,v) > d_0$$
$$t \geq 0, \quad \alpha_{ij} \leq f_i, \; \alpha_{ij} \leq f_j, \; \forall (i,j) \in E'$$
$$0 \leq f_i \leq t, \; \forall i \in V', \; \alpha_{ij} \geq 0, \; \forall (i,j) \in E'$$
$$\langle g, f \rangle + t\nu_S = 1.$$

where $V' = V \backslash S$, E' is the set of edges induced by V'.

PROOF. *The following problem is equivalent to (10), because (i) for every feasible set A of (10), there exist corresponding feasible y, X given by $y = \mathbf{1}_A$, $X_{ij} = \min\{y_i, y_j\}$, with the same objective value and (ii) an optimal solution of the following problem always satisfies $X^*_{ij} = \min\{y^*_i, y^*_j\}$.*

$$\max_{y \in \{0,1\}^{V'}, \, X \in \{0,1\}^{E'}} \frac{2\sum_{i<j} w_{ij}X_{ij} + 2\langle d^S, y \rangle + \mu_S}{\langle g, y \rangle + \nu_S}$$

$$\text{subject to}: k_j \leq \langle M_j, y \rangle \leq l_j, \quad \forall j \in \{1,\ldots,p\}$$
$$y_u + y_v \leq 1, \quad \forall u,v: \mathrm{dist}(u,v) > d_0$$
$$X_{ij} \leq y_i, \quad X_{ij} \leq y_j, \quad \forall (i,j) \in E'$$

Relaxing the integrality constraints and using the substitution, $X_{ij} = \frac{\alpha_{ij}}{t}$ and $y_i = \frac{f_i}{t}$, we obtain the relaxation:

$$\max_{t \in \mathbb{R}, \, f \in \mathbb{R}^{V'}, \, \alpha \in \mathbb{R}^{E'}} \frac{2\sum_{i<j} w_{ij}\alpha_{ij} + 2\langle d^S, f \rangle + t\mu_S}{\langle g, f \rangle + t\nu_S}$$

$$\text{subject to}: tk_j \leq \langle M_j, f \rangle \leq tl_j, \quad \forall j \in \{1,\ldots,p\}$$
$$f_u + f_v \leq t, \quad \forall u,v: \mathrm{dist}(u,v) > d_0$$
$$t \geq 0, \quad \alpha_{ij} \leq f_i, \; \alpha_{ij} \leq f_j, \; \forall (i,j) \in E'$$
$$0 \leq f_i \leq t, \; \forall i \in V', \; \alpha_{ij} \geq 0, \; \forall (i,j) \in E'$$

Since this problem is invariant under scaling, we can fix the scale by setting the denominator to 1, which yields the equivalent LP stated in the theorem. □

Note that the solution f^* of the LP (11) is, in general, not integral, i.e., $f^* \notin \{0,1\}^{V'}$. One can use standard techniques of randomized rounding or optimal thresholding to derive an integral solution from f^*. However, the resulting integral solution may not necessarily give a subset that satisfies the constraints of (10). In the special case when there are only lower bound constraints, i.e., problem (3), one can obtain a feasible set A for problem (3) by thresholding f^* (see (5)) according to the objective of (10). This is possible in this special case because there is always a threshold f^*_i which yields a non-empty subset A_i (in the worst case the full set V') satisfying all the lower bound constraints. In our experiments on problem (3), we derived a feasible set from the solution of LP in this fashion by choosing the threshold that yields a subset that satisfies the constraints and has the highest objective value.

Note that the LP relaxation (11) is vacuous with respect to upper bound constraints in the sense that given $f \in \mathbb{R}^m$ that does not satisfy the upper bound constraints of the LP (11) one can construct $\tilde{f}$, feasible for the LP by rescaling f without changing the objective of the LP. This implies that one can always transform the solution of the unconstrained problem into a feasible solution when there are *only* upper bound constraints. However, in the presence of lower bound or subset constraints, such a rescaling does not yield a feasible solution and hence the LP relaxation is useful on the instances of (10) with at least one lower bound or a subset constraint (i.e., $\nu_S > 0$).

6. EXPERIMENTS

We now empirically show that **FORTE** consistently produces high quality compact teams. We also show that the quality guarantee given by Theorem 3 is useful in practice as our method often improves a given sub-optimal solution.

6.1 Experimental Setup

Since we are not aware of any publicly available real world datasets for the team formation problem, we use, as in [12], a scientific collaboration network extracted from the DBLP database. Similar to [12], we restrict ourselves to four fields of computer science: Databases (DB), Theory (T), Data Mining (DM), Artificial Intelligence (AI). Conferences that we consider for each field are given as follows: DB = {SIGMOD, VLDB, ICDE, ICDT, PODS}, T = {SODA, FOCS, STOC, STACS, ICALP, ESA}, DM = {WWW, KDD, SDM, PKDD, ICDM, WSDM}, AI = {IJCAI, NIPS, ICML, COLT, UAI, CVPR}.

For our team formation problem, the skill set is given by $\mathcal{A}$ ={DB, T, DM, AI}. Any author who has at least three publications in any of the above 23 conferences is considered to be an expert. In our DBLP co-author graph, a vertex corresponds to an expert and an edge between two experts indicates prior collaboration between them. The weight of the edge is the number of shared publications. Since the resulting co-author graph is disconnected, we take its largest connected component (of size 9264) for our experiments.

Directly solving the non-convex problem (6) for the value of γ given in Theorem 1 often yields poor results. Hence in our implementation of **FORTE** we adopt the following strategy. We first solve the unconstrained version of problem (6) (i.e., $\gamma = 0$) and then iteratively solve (6) for increasing values of γ until all constraints are satisfied. In each iteration, we increase γ only for those constraints which were infeasible in the previous iteration; in this way, each penalty term is regulated by different value of γ. Moreover, the solution obtained in the previous iteration of γ is used as the starting point for the current iteration.

6.2 Quantitative Evaluation

In this section we perform a quantitative evaluation of our method in the special case of the team formation problem with lower bound constraints and $g_i = 1 \, \forall i$ (problem (3)). We evaluate the performance of our method against the greedy method proposed in [12], refered to as **mdAlk**. Similar to the experiments of [12], an expert is defined to have a skill level of 1 in skill j, if he/she has a publication in any of the conferences corresponding to the skill j. As done in [12], we create random tasks for different values of skill size, $k = \{3, 8, 13, 18, 23, 28\}$. For each value of k we sample k skills with replacement from the skill set $\mathcal{A} = \{DB, T, DM, AI\}$. For example if $k = 3$, a sample might contain {DB, DB, T}, which means that the random task requires at least two experts from the skill DB and one expert from the skill T.

In Figure 1, we show for each method the densities, sizes and runtimes for the different skill sizes k, averaged over 10 random runs. In the first plot, we also show the optimal values of the LP relaxation in (11). Note that this provides an upper bound on the optimal value of (GDSP). We can obtain feasible solutions from the LP relaxation of (GDSP) via thresholding (see Section 5), which are shown in the plot as **LPfeas**. Furthermore, the plots contain the results obtained when the solutions of **LPfeas** and **mdAlk** are used as the initializations for **FORTE** (in each of the γ iteration).

The plots show that **FORTE** always produces teams of higher densities and smaller sizes compared to **mdAlk** and **LPfeas**. Furthermore, **LPfeas** produces better results than the greedy method in several cases in terms of densities and sizes of the obtained teams. The results of **mdAlk+FORTE** and **LPfeas+FORTE** further show that our method is able improve the sub-optimal solutions of **mdAlk** and **LPfeas** significantly and achieves almost similar results as that of **FORTE** which was started with the unconstrained solution of (6). Under the worst-case assumption that the upper bound on (GDSP) computed using the LP is the optimal value, the solution of **FORTE** is 94% − 99% optimal (depending on k).

6.3 Qualitative Evaluation

In this experiment, we assess the quality of the teams obtained for several tasks with different skill requirements. Here we consider the team formation problem (GDSP) in its more general setting. We use the generalized density objective of (1) where each vertex is given a rank r_i, which we define based on the number of publications of the corresponding expert. For each skill, we rank the experts according to the number of his/her publications in the conferences corresponding to the skill. In this way each expert gets four different rankings; the total rank of an expert is then the minimum of these four ranks. The main advantage of such a ranking is that the experts that have higher skill are given preference, thus producing more competent teams. Note that we choose a relative measure like rank as the vertex weights instead of an absolute quantity like number of publications, since the distribution of the number of publications varies between different fields. In practice such a ranking is always available and hence, in our opinion, should be incorporated.

Furthermore, in order to identify the main area of expertise of each expert, we consider his/her relative number of publications. Each expert is defined to have a skill level of 1 in skill j if he has more than 25% of his/her publications in the conferences corresponding to skill j. As a distance function between authors, we use the shortest path on the *unweighted version* of the DBLP graph, i.e. two experts are at a distance of two, if the shortest path between the corresponding vertices in the unweighted DBLP graph contains two edges. Note that in general the distance function can come from other general sources beyond the input graph, but here we had to rely on the graph distance because of lack of other information.

In order to assess the *competence* of the found teams, we use the list of the 10000 most cited authors of Citeseer [1]. Note that in contrast to the skill-based ranking discussed above, this list is only used in the evaluation and *not* in the construction of the graph. We compute the average inverse rank as in [12] as $AIR := 1000 \cdot \sum_{i=1}^{k} \frac{1}{R_i}$, where k is the size of the team and R_i is the rank of expert i on the Citeseer list of 10000 most cited authors. For authors not contained

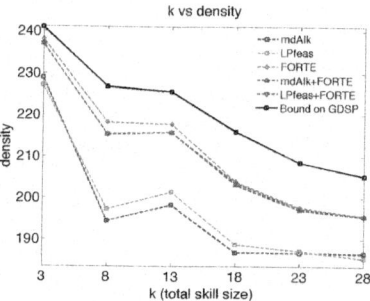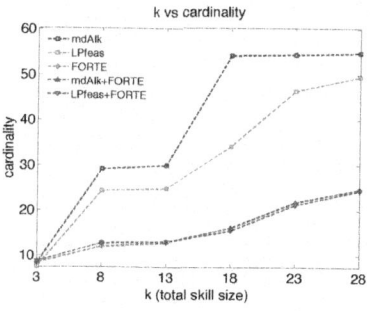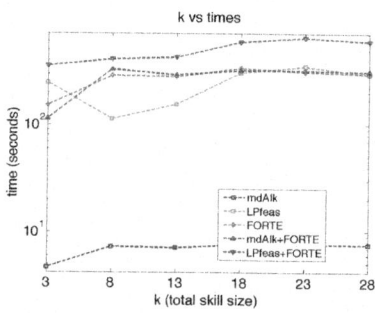

Figure 1: Densities, team sizes and runtimes of mdAlk, our method (FORTE), a feasible point constructed from the LP (LPfeas), and FORTE initialized with LPfeas and mdAlk, averaged over 10 trials. All versions of (FORTE) significantly outperform mdAlk, and LPfeas both in terms of densities and sizes of the teams found. The densities of FORTE are close to the upper bound on the optimum of the GDSP given by the LP.

on the list we set $R_i = 10001$. We also report the densities of the teams found in order to assess their *compatibility*.

We create several tasks with various constraints and compare the teams produced by **FORTE**, **mdAlk** and **LPfeas** (feasible solution derived from the LP relaxation). Note that in our implementation we extended the **mdAlk** algorithm of [12] to incorporate general vertex weights, using Dinkelbach's method from fractional programming [11]. The results for these tasks are shown in Table 1. We report the upper bound given by the LP relaxation, density value, AIR as well as number and sizes of the connected components. Furthermore, we give the names and the Citeseer ranks of the team members who have rank at most 1000. Note that **mdAlk** could only be applied to some of the tasks and **LPfeas** failed to find a feasible team in several cases.

As a first task we show the unconstrained solution where we maximize density without any constraints. Note that this problem is optimally solvable in polynomial time and all methods find the optimal solution. The second task asks for at least three experts with skill DB. Here again all methods return the same team, which is indeed optimal since the LP bound agrees with the density of the obtained team.

Next we illustrate the usefulness of the additional modeling freedom of our formulation by giving an example task where obtaining meaningful, connected teams is not possible with the lower bound constraints alone. Consider a task where we need at least four experts having skill AI (Task 3). For this, all methods return the same disconnected team of size seven where only four members have the skill AI. The other three experts possess skills DB and DM and are densely connected among themselves. One can see from the LP bound that this team is again optimal. This example illustrates the major drawback of the density based objective which while preferring higher density subgraphs compromises on the connectivity of the solution. Our further experiments revealed that the subgraph corresponding to the skill AI is less densely connected (relative to the other skills) and forming coherent teams in this case is difficult without specifying additional requirements. With the help of subset and distance based constraints supported by **FORTE**, we can now impose the team requirements more precisely and obtain meaningful teams. In Task 4, we require that Andrew Y. Ng is the team leader and that all experts of the team should be within a distance of two from each other in terms of the underlying co-author graph. The result of our method is a densely connected and highly ranked team of size four with a density of 3.89. Note that this is very close to the LP bound of 3.91. The feasible solution obtained by **LPfeas** is worse than our result both in terms of density and AIR. The greedy method **mdAlk** cannot be applied to this task because of the distance constraint. In Task 5 we choose Bernhard Schoelkopf as the team leader while keeping the constraints from the previous task. Out of the three methods, only **FORTE** can solve this problem. It produces a large disconnected team, many members of which are highly skilled experts from the skill DM and have strong connections among themselves. To filter these densely connected members of high expertise, we introduce a budget constraint in Task 6, where we define the cost of the team as the total number of publications of its members. Again this task can be solved only by **FORTE** which produces a compact team of four well-known AI experts. A slightly better solution is obtained when **FORTE** is initialized with the infeasible solution of the LP relaxation as shown (only in this task). This is an indication that on more difficult instances of (GDSP), it pays off to run **FORTE** with more than one starting point to get the best results. The solution of the LP, possibly infeasible, is a good starting point apart from the unconstrained solution of (6).

Tasks 7, 8 and 9 provide some additional teams found by **FORTE** for other tasks involving upper and lower bound constraints on different skills. As noted in Section 5 the LP bound is loose in the presence of upper bound constraints and this is also the reason why it was not possible to derive a feasible solution from the LP relaxation in these cases. In fact the LP bounds for these tasks remain the same even if the upper bound constraints are dropped from these tasks.

7. CONCLUSIONS

By incorporating various realistic constraints we have made a step forward towards a realistic formulation of the team formation problem. Our method finds qualitatively better teams that are more compact and have higher densities than those found by the greedy method [12]. Our linear programming relaxation not only allows us to check the solution quality but also provides a good starting point for our non-convex method. However, arguably, a potential downside of a density-based approach is that it does not guarantee connected components. A further extension of our approach could aim at incorporating "connectedness" or a relaxed version of it as an additional constraint.

Task	FORTE	mdAlk	LPfeas
Task 1: Unconstrained (LP bound: 32.7)	#Comps: 1 (2) Density: 32.7 AIR: 11.1 Jiawei Han (54), Philip S. Yu (279)	#Comps: 1 (2) Density: 32.7 AIR: 11.1 Jiawei Han (54), Philip S. Yu (279)	#Comps: 1 (2) Density: 32.7 AIR: 11.1 Jiawei Han (54), Philip S. Yu (279)
Task 2: DB$\geq$3 (LP bound: 29.8)	#Comps: 1 (3) Density: 29.8 AIR: 7.56 Jiawei Han (54), Philip S. Yu (279) (+1)	#Comps: 1 (3) Density: 29.8 AIR: 7.56 Jiawei Han (54), Philip S. Yu (279) (+1)	#Comps: 1 (3) Density: 29.8 AIR: 7.56 Jiawei Han (54), Philip S. Yu (279) (+1)
Task 3: AI$\geq$4 (LP bound: 16.6)	#Comps: 3 (1,3,3) Density: 16.6 AIR: 10.3 Michael I. Jordan (28), *Jiawei Han (54)*, Daphne Koller (127), *Philip S. Yu (279)*, Andrew Y. Ng (345), Bernhard Schoelkopf (364) (+1)	#Comps: 3 (1,3,3) Density: 16.6 AIR: 10.3 Michael I. Jordan (28), *Jiawei Han (54)*, Daphne Koller (127), *Philip S. Yu (279)*, Andrew Y. Ng (345), Bernhard Schoelkopf (364) (+1)	#Comps: 3 (1,3,3) Density: 16.6 AIR: 10.3 Michael I. Jordan (28), *Jiawei Han (54)*, Daphne Koller (127), *Philip S. Yu (279)*, Andrew Y. Ng (345), Bernhard Schoelkopf (364) (+1)
Task 4: AI$\geq$4, $dist_G(u,v) \leq 2$, S={Andrew Ng} (LP bound: 3.91)	#Comps: 1 (4) Density: 3.89 AIR: 14.2 Michael I. Jordan (28), Sebastian Thrun (97), Daphne Koller (127), Andrew Y. Ng (345)		#Comps: 1 (6) Density: 3.5 AIR: 12.5 Michael I. Jordan (28), Geoffrey E. Hinton (61), Sebastian Thrun (97), Daphne Koller (127), Andrew Y. Ng (345), Zoubin Ghahramani (577)
Task 5: AI$\geq$4, $dist_G(u,v) \leq 2$, S={B.Schoelkopf} (LP bound: 6.11)	#Comps: 2 (11,1) Density: 3.54 AIR: 3.94 *Jiawei Han (54)*, Christos Faloutsos (140), Thomas S. Huang (146), *Philip S. Yu (279)*, *Zheng Chen (308)*, Bernhard Schoelkopf (364), *Wei-Ying Ma (523)*, *Ke Wang (580)* (+4)		
Task 6: AI$\geq$4, $dist_G(u,v) \leq 2$, S={B.Schoelkopf}, $\sum_i c_i \leq 255$ (LP bound: 2.06)	#Comps: 1 (4) Density: 1.24 AIR: 1.82 Alex J. Smola (335), Bernhard Schoelkopf (364) (+2) LP+FORTE: #Comps: 2 (2,2) Density: 1.77 AIR: 2.73 Robert E. Schapire (293), Alex J. Smola (335), Bernhard Schoelkopf (364), Yoram Singer (568)		
Task 7: 3$\leq$DB$\leq$6, DM$\geq$10, (LP bound: 11.3)	#Comps: 1 (10) Density: 9.52 AIR: 4.96 Haixun Wang (50), Jiawei Han (54), Philip S. Yu (279), Zheng Chen (308), Ke Wang (580) (+5)		
Task 8: 2$\leq$DB$\leq$5, 10$\leq$DM$\leq$15, 5$\leq$AI$\leq$10 (LP bound: 10.7)	#Comps: 3 (1,12,3) Density: 7.4 AIR: 5.06 Michael I. Jordan (28), Jiawei Han (54), Daphne Koller (127), Philip S. Yu (279), Zheng Chen (308), Andrew Y. Ng (345), Bernhard Schoelkopf (364), Wei-Ying Ma (523), Divyakant Agrawal (591) (+7)		
Task 9: AI$\leq$2, T$\geq$2, $|C|\leq$6 (LP bound: 19)	#Comps: 3 (2,2,2) Density: 6.17 AIR: 1.53 Didier Dubois (426), Micha Sharir (447), *Divyakant Agrawal (591)*, Henri Prade (713), Pankaj K. Agarwal (770) (+1)		

Table 1: Teams formed by FORTE, mdAlk and LPfeas for various tasks. We list the number and sizes of the found components, the (generalized) maximum density as well as the average inverse rank (AIR) based on the Citeseer list. Finally, we give name and rank of each team member with rank at most 1000. Experts who do not have the skill required by the task but are still included in the team are shown in *italic font*.

Acknowledgements

We gratefully acknowledge support from the Excellence Cluster MMCI at Saarland University funded by the German Research Foundation (DFG) and the project NOLEPRO funded by the European Research Council (ERC).

APPENDIX

The subgradient of $S_1(f)$ is given by $s_1(f) = d + d^S + \mu_S I_{max}(f)$, where $I_{max}(f)$ is the indicator function of the largest entry of f. For the subgradient of R_2, using Prop. 2.2. in [3], we obtain for the subgradient $t_{(l_j, M_j)}$ of the terms of the form $\min\{l_j, \text{vol}_{M_j}(A)\}$,

$$(t_{(l_j,M_j)}(f))_i = \begin{cases} 0 & \text{vol}_{M_j}(A_{i+1}) > l_j \\ l_j - \text{vol}_{M_j}(A_{i+1}) & \text{vol}_{M_j}(A_i) \geq l_j, \\ & \text{vol}_{M_j}(A_{i+1}) \leq l_j \\ M_{ij} & \text{vol}_{M_j}(A_i) < l_j \end{cases}$$

Defining $D_{uv} := \max\{0, \text{dist}(u,v) - d_0\}$, an element of the subgradient of the second term of R_2 is given as $d_D - p(f)$, where $(d_D)_i = \sum_j D_{ij}$ and $p(f)_i \in \left\{\sum_{j=1}^m D_{ij} u_{ij} \mid u_{ij} = -u_{ji}, u_{ij} \in \text{sign}(f_i - f_j)\right\}$, where $\text{sgn}(x) := +1$, if $x > 0$; -1 if $x < 0$; $[-1,1]$, if $x = 0$. In total, we obtain for the subgradient $r_2(f)$ of $R_2(f)$,

$$r_2(f) = \gamma \sum_{j=1}^p t_{(l_j,M_j)}(f) + \gamma \sum_{j=1}^p t_{(k_j,M_j)}(f) + \gamma(p(f) - d_D).$$

1. REFERENCES

[1] Citeseer statistics – Most cited authors in computer science. `http://citeseerx.ist.psu.edu/stats/authors?all=true`.

[2] A. Anagnostopoulos, L. Becchetti, C. Castillo, A. Gionis, and S. Leonardi. Online team formation in social networks. In *WWW*, pages 839–848, 2012.

[3] F. Bach. Learning with submodular functions: A convex optimization perspective. *CoRR*, abs/1111.6453, 2011.

[4] L. Backstrom, D. Huttenlocher, J. Kleinberg, and X. Lan. Group formation in large social networks: membership, growth, and evolution. In *KDD*, pages 44–54, 2006.

[5] A. Baykasoglu, T. Dereli, and S. Das. Project team selection using fuzzy optimization approach. *Cybern. Syst.*, 38(2):155–185, 2007.

[6] A. Beck and M. Teboulle. Fast gradient-based algorithms for constrained total variation image denoising and deblurring problems. *IEEE Trans. Image Processing*, 18(11):2419–2434, 2009.

[7] T. Bühler, S. Rangapuram, M. Hein, and S. Setzer. Constrained fractional set programs and their application in local clustering and community detection. In *ICML*, pages 624–632, 2013.

[8] V. T. Chakaravarthy, N. Modani, S. R. Natarajan, S. Roy, and Y. Sabharwal. Density functions subject to a co-matroid constraint. In *FSTTCS*, pages 236–248, 2012.

[9] S. J. Chen and L. Lin. Modeling team member characteristics for the formation of a multifunctional team in concurrent engineering. *IEEE Trans. Engineering Management*, 51(2):111–124, 2004.

[10] N. Contractor. Some assembly required: leveraging web science to understand and enable team assembly. *Physical and Engineering Sciences*, 371(1987), 2013.

[11] W. Dinkelbach. On nonlinear fractional programming. *Management Science*, 13(7):492–498, 1967.

[12] A. Gajewar and A. D. Sarma. Multi-skill collaborative teams based on densest subgraphs. In *SDM*, pages 165–176, 2012.

[13] A. V. Goldberg. Finding a maximum density subgraph. Technical Report UCB/CSD-84-171, EECS Department, University of California, Berkeley, 1984.

[14] M. Hein and S. Setzer. Beyond spectral clustering - tight relaxations of balanced graph cuts. In *NIPS*, pages 2366–2374, 2011.

[15] M. Kargar and A. An. Discovering top-k teams of experts with/without a leader in social networks. In *CIKM*, pages 985–994, 2011.

[16] S. Khot. Ruling out ptas for graph min-bisection, dense k-subgraph, and bipartite clique. *SIAM J. Comput.*, 36(4), 2006.

[17] S. Khuller and B. Saha. On finding dense subgraphs. In *ICALP*, pages 597–608, 2009.

[18] T. Lappas, K. Liu, and E. Terzi. Finding a team of experts in social networks. In *KDD*, pages 467–476, 2009.

[19] B. Saha, A. Hoch, S. Khuller, L. Raschid, and X.-N. Zhang. Dense subgraphs with restrictions and applications to gene annotation graphs. In *RECOMB*, pages 456–472, 2010.

[20] H. Wi, S. Oh, J. Mun, and M. Jung. A team formation model based on knowledge and collaboration. *Expert Syst. Appl.*, 36(5):9121–9134, 2009.

[21] A. Zzkarian and A. Kusiak. Forming teams: an analytic approach. *IIE Trans.*, 31(1):85–97, 2004.

Efficient Community Detection in Large Networks using Content and Links

Yiye Ruan, David Fuhry, Srinivasan Parthasarathy
Department of Computer Science and Engineering
The Ohio State University
{ruan,fuhry,srini}@cse.ohio-state.edu

ABSTRACT

In this paper we discuss a very simple approach of combining content and link information in graph structures for the purpose of community discovery, a fundamental task in network analysis. Our approach hinges on the basic intuition that many networks contain noise in the link structure and that content information can help strengthen the community signal. This enables ones to eliminate the impact of noise (false positives and false negatives), which is particularly prevalent in online social networks and Web-scale information networks.

Specifically we introduce a measure of signal strength between two nodes in the network by fusing their link strength with content similarity. Link strength is estimated based on whether the link is likely (with high probability) to reside within a community. Content similarity is estimated through cosine similarity or Jaccard coefficient. We discuss a simple mechanism for fusing content and link similarity. We then present a biased edge sampling procedure which retains edges that are locally relevant for each graph node. The resulting backbone graph can be clustered using standard community discovery algorithms such as Metis and Markov clustering.

Through extensive experiments on multiple real-world datasets (Flickr, Wikipedia and CiteSeer) with varying sizes and characteristics, we demonstrate the effectiveness and efficiency of our methods over state-of-the-art learning and mining approaches several of which also attempt to combine link and content analysis for the purposes of community discovery. Specifically we always find a qualitative benefit when combining content with link analysis. Additionally our biased graph sampling approach realizes a quantitative benefit in that it is typically several orders of magnitude faster than competing approaches.

Categories and Subject Descriptors

H.2.8 [**Database Management**]: Database Applications—*Data mining*

Keywords

Web mining, graph clustering, content analysis

1. INTRODUCTION

An increasing number of applications on the World Wide Web rely on combining link and content analysis (in different ways) for subsequent analysis and inference. For example, search engines, like Google, Bing and Yahoo! typically use content and link information to index, retrieve and rank web pages. Social networking sites like Twitter, Flickr and Facebook, as well as the aforementioned search engines, are increasingly relying on fusing content (pictures, tags, text) and link information (friends, followers, and users) for deriving actionable knowledge (e.g. marketing and advertising).

In this article we limit our discussion to a fundamental inference problem — that of combining link and content information for the purposes of inferring clusters or communities of interest. The challenges are manifold. The topological characteristics of such problems (graphs induced from the natural link structure) makes identifying community structure difficult. Further complicating the issue is the presence of noise (incorrect links (false positives) and missing links (false negatives). Determining how to fuse this link structure with content information efficiently and effectively is unclear. Finally, underpinning these challenges, is the issue of scalability as many of these graphs are extremely large running into millions of nodes and billions of edges, if not larger.

Given the fundamental nature of this problem, a number of solutions have emerged in the literature. Broadly these can be classified as: i) those that ignore content information (a large majority) and focus on addressing the topological and scalability challenges, and ii) those that account for both content and topological information. From a qualitative standpoint the latter presumes to improve on the former (since the null hypothesis is that content should help improve the quality of the inferred communities) but often at a prohibitive cost to scalability.

In this article we present CODICIL[1], a family of highly efficient graph simplification algorithms leveraging both content and graph topology to identify and retain important edges in a network. Our approach relies on fusing content and topological (link) information in a natural manner. The output of CODICIL is a transformed variant of the original graph (with content information), which can then be clustered by any fast content-insensitive graph clustering algorithm such as METIS or Markov clustering. Through extensive experiments on real-world datasets drawn from Flickr, Wikipedia, and CiteSeer, and across several graph clustering algorithms, we demonstrate the effectiveness and efficiency of our methods. We find that CODICIL runs several orders of magnitude faster than those state-of-the-art approaches and often identifies communities of comparable or superior quality on these datasets.

This paper is arranged as follows. In Section 2 we discuss existent research efforts pertaining to our work. The algorithm of CODICIL, along with implementation details, is presented in Section 3. We report quantitative experiment results in Section 4, and

---

[1]COmmunity Discovery Inferred from Content Information and Link-structure

demonstrate the qualitative benefits brought by CODICIL via case studies in Section 5. We finally conclude the paper in Section 6.

2. RELATED WORK

Community Discovery using Topology (and Content): Graph clustering/partitioning for community discovery has been studied for more than five decades, and a vast number of algorithms (exemplars include Metis [15], Graclus [6] and Markov clustering [27]) have been proposed and widely used in fields including social network analytics, document clustering, bioinformatics and others. Most of those methods, however, discard content information associated with graph elements. Due to space limitations, we suppress detailed discussions and refer interested readers to recent surveys (e.g. [9]) for a more comprehensive picture. Leskovec et al. compared a multitude of community discovery algorithms based on conductance score, and discovered the trade-off between clustering objective and community compactness [16].

Various approaches have been taken to utilize content information for community discovery. One of them is generative probabilistic modeling which considers both contents and links as being dependent on one or more latent variables, and then estimates the conditional distributions to find community assignments. PLSA-PHITS [5], Community-User-Topic model [29] and Link-PLSA-LDA [20] are three representatives in this category. They mainly focus on studies of citation and email communication networks. Link-PLSA-LDA, for instance, was motivated for finding latent topics in text and citations and assumes different generative processes on citing documents, cited documents as well as citations themselves. Text generation is following the LDA approach, and link creation from a citing document to a cited document is controlled by another topic-specific multinomial distribution.

Yang et al. [28] introduced an alternative discriminative probabilistic model, PCL-DC, to incorporate content information in the conditional link model and estimate the community membership directly. In this model, link probability between two nodes is decided by nodes' *popularity* as well as community membership, which is in turn decided by content terms. A two-stage EM algorithm is proposed to optimize community membership probabilities and content weights alternately. Upon convergence, each graph node is assigned to the community with maximum membership probability.

Researchers have also explored ways to augment the underlying network to take into account the content information. The SA-Cluster-Inc algorithm proposed by Zhou et al. [30], for example, inserts virtual *attribute nodes* and *attribute edges* into the graph and computes all-pair random walk distances on the new *attribute-augmented graph*. K-means clustering is then used on original graph nodes to assign them to different groups. Weights associated with attributes are updated after each k-means iteration according to their clustering tendencies. The algorithm iterates until convergence.

Ester et al. [8] proposed an heuristic algorithm to solve the *Connected k-Center* problem where both connectedness and radius constraints need to be satisfied. The complexity of this method is dependent on the longest distance between any pair of nodes in the feature space, making it susceptible to outliers. Biologists have studied methods [13, 26] to find functional modules using network topology and gene expression data. Those methods, however, bear domain-specific assumptions on data and are therefore not directly applicable in general.

Recently Günnemann et al. [12] introduced a subspace clustering algorithm on graphs with feature vectors, which shares some similarity with our topic. Although their method could run on the full feature space, the search space of their algorithm is confined by the intersection, instead of union, of the epsilon-neighborhood and the density-based combined cluster. Furthermore, the construction of both neighborhoods are sensitive to their multiple parameters.

While decent performance can be achieved on small and medium graphs using those methods, it often comes at the cost of model complexity and lack of scalability. Some of them take time proportional to the number of values in each attribute. Others take time and space proportional to the number of clusters to find, which is often unacceptable. Our method, in contrast, is more lightweight and scalable.

Clustering/Learning Multiple Graphs: Content-aware clustering is also related to multiple-view clustering, as content information and link structure can be treated as two views of the data. Strehl and Ghose [23] discussed three consensus functions (cluster-wise similarity partitioning, hyper-graph partitioning and meta-clustering) to implement cluster ensembles, in which the availability of each individual view's clustering is assumed. Tang et al. [24] proposed a linked matrix factorization method, where each graph's adjacency matrix is decomposed into a "characteristic" matrix and a common factor matrix shared among all graphs. The purpose of factorization is to represent each vertex by a lower-dimensional vector and then cluster the vertices using corresponding feature vectors. Their method, while applicable to small-scale problems, is not designed for web-scale networks.

Graph Sampling for Fast Clustering: Graph sampling (also known as "sparsification" or "filtering") has attracted more and more focus in recent years due to the explosive growth of network data. If a graph's structure can be preserved using fewer nodes and/or edges, community discovery algorithms can obtain similar results using less time and memory storage. Maiya and Berger-Wolf [17] introduced an algorithm which greedily identifies the node that leads to the greatest *expansion* in each iteration until the user-specified node count is reached. By doing so, an expander-like node-induced subgraph is constructed. After clustering the subgraph, the unsampled nodes can be labeled by using collective inference or other transductive learning methods. This extra post-processing step, however, operates on the original graph as a whole and easily becomes the scalability bottleneck on larger networks.

Satuluri et al. [22] proposed an edge sampling method to preferentially retain edges that connect two similar nodes. The localized strategy ensures that edges in the relatively sparse areas will not be over-pruned. Their method, however, does not consider content information either.

Edge sampling has also been applied to other graph tasks. Karger [14] studied the impact of random edge sampling on original graph's cuts, and proposed randomized algorithms to find graph's minimum cut and maximum flow. Aggarwal et al. [1] proposed using edging sampling to maintain structural properties and detect outliers in graph streams. The goals of those work are not to preserve community structure in graphs, though.

3. METHODOLOGY

We begin by defining the notations used in the rest of our paper. Let $\mathcal{G}_t = (\mathcal{V}, \mathcal{E}_t, \mathcal{T})$ be an undirected graph with n vertices $\mathcal{V} = v_1, \ldots, v_n$, edges $\mathcal{E}_t$, and a collection of n corresponding term vectors $\mathcal{T} = t_1, \ldots, t_n$. We use the terms "graph" and "network" interchangeably as well as the terms "vertex" and "node". Elements in each term vector t_i are basic content units which can be single words, tags or n-grams, etc., depending on the context of underlying network. For each graph node $v_i \in \mathcal{V}$, let its term vector be t_i.

Our goal is to generate a simplified, edge-sampled graph $\mathcal{G}_{sample} =$

($\mathcal{V}, \mathcal{E}_{sample}$) and then use $\mathcal{G}_{sample}$ to find communities with coherent content and link structure. $\mathcal{G}_{sample}$ should possess the following properties:

- $\mathcal{G}_{sample}$ has the same vertex set as $\mathcal{G}_t$. That is, no node in the network is added or removed during the simplification process.
- $|\mathcal{E}_{sample}| \ll |\mathcal{E}_t|$, as this enables both better runtime performance and lower memory usage in the subsequent clustering stage.
- Informally put, the resultant edge set $\mathcal{E}_{sample}$ would connect node pairs which are both structure-wise and content-wise similar. As a result, it is possible for our method to add edges which were absent from $\mathcal{E}_t$ since the content similarity was overlooked.

3.1 Key Intuitions

The main steps of the CODICIL algorithm are:

1. Create content edges.
2. Sample the union of content edges and topological edges with bias, retaining only edges that are relevant in local neighborhoods.
3. Partition the simplified graph into clusters.

The constructed content graph and simplified graph have the same vertices as the input graph (vertices are never added or removed), so the essential operations of the algorithm are constructing, combining edges and then sampling with bias. Figure 1 illustrates the work flow of CODICIL.

From the term vectors $\mathcal{T}$, content edges $\mathcal{E}_c$ are constructed. Those content edges and the input topological edges $\mathcal{E}_t$ are combined as $\mathcal{E}_u$ which is then sampled with bias to form a smaller edge set $\mathcal{E}_{sample}$ where the most relevant edges are preserved. The graph composed of these sampled edges is passed to the graph clustering algorithm which partitions the vertices into a given number of clusters.

3.2 Basic Framework

The pseudo-code of CODICIL is given in Algorithm 1. CODICIL takes as input 1) $\mathcal{G}_t$, the original graph consisting of vertices V, edges $\mathcal{E}_t$ and term vectors $\mathcal{T}$ where t_i is the content term vector for vertex v_i, $1 \leq i \leq |\mathcal{V}| = |\mathcal{T}|$, 2) k, the number of nearest content neighbors to find for each vertex, 3) $normalize(x)$, a function that normalizes a vector x, 4) α, an optional parameter that specifies the weights of topology and content similarities, 5) l, the number of output clusters desired, 6) $clusteralgo(\mathcal{G}, l)$, an algorithm that partitions a graph $\mathcal{G}$ into l clusters and 7) $similarity(x, y)$ to compute similarity between x and y. Note that any content-insensitive graph clustering algorithm can be plugged in the CODICIL framework, providing great flexibility for applications.

3.2.1 Creating Content Edges

Lines 2 through 7 detail how content edges are created. For each vertex v_i, its k most content-similar neighbors are computed[2]. For each of v_i's top-k neighbors v_j, an edge (v_i, v_j) is added to content edges $\mathcal{E}_c$. In our experiments we implemented the $TopK$ sub-routine by calculating the cosine similarity of t_i's TF-IDF vector and each other term vector's TF-IDF vector. For a content unit

---
[2] Besides top-k criteria, we also investigated using all-pairs similarity above a given global threshold, but this tended to produce highly imbalanced degree distributions.

Algorithm 1 CODICIL

Input: $\mathcal{G}_t = (\mathcal{V}, \mathcal{E}_t, \mathcal{T})$, k, $normalize(\cdot)$, $\alpha \in [0, 1]$, l, $clusteralgo(\cdot, \cdot)$, $similarity(\cdot, \cdot)$
Returns: $\mathcal{C}$ (a disjoint clustering of $\mathcal{V}$)
1: \\Create content edges $\mathcal{E}_c$
2: $\mathcal{E}_c \leftarrow \emptyset$
3: **for** $i = 1$ to $|\mathcal{V}|$ **do**
4:   **foreach** $v_j \in TopK(v_i, k, \mathcal{T})$ **do**
5:     $\mathcal{E}_c \leftarrow \mathcal{E}_c \cup (v_i, v_j)$
6:   **end for**
7: **end for**
8: \\Combine $\mathcal{E}_t$ and $\mathcal{E}_c$. Retain edges with a bias towards locally relevant ones
9: $\mathcal{E}_u \leftarrow \mathcal{E}_t \cup \mathcal{E}_c$
10: $\mathcal{E}_{sample} \leftarrow \emptyset$
11: **for** $i = 1$ to $|\mathcal{V}|$ **do**
12:   \\Γ_i contains v_i's neighbors in the edge union
13:   $\Gamma_i \leftarrow ngbr(v_i, \mathcal{E}_u)$
14:   **for** $j = 1$ to $|\Gamma_i|$ **do** $sim^t_{ij} \leftarrow similarity(ngbr(v_i, \mathcal{E}_t), ngbr(\gamma_j, \mathcal{E}_t))$
15:   $simnorm^t_i \leftarrow normalize(sim^t_i)$
16:   **for** $j = 1$ to $|\Gamma_i|$ **do** $sim^c_{ij} \leftarrow similarity(t_i, t_{\gamma_j})$
17:   $simnorm^c_i \leftarrow normalize(sim^c_i)$
18:   **for** $j = 1$ to $|\Gamma_i|$ **do** $sim_{ij} \leftarrow \alpha \cdot simnorm^t_{ij} + (1 - \alpha) \cdot simnorm^c_{ij}$
19:   \\Sort similarity values in descending order. Store the corresponding node IDs in idx_i
20:   $[val_i, idx_i] \leftarrow descsort(sim_i)$
21:   **for** $j = 1$ to $\lceil \sqrt{|\Gamma_i|} \rceil$ **do**
22:     $\mathcal{E}_{sample} \leftarrow \mathcal{E}_{sample} \cup (v_i, v_{idx_{ij}})$
23:   **end for**
24: **end for**
25: $\mathcal{G}_{sample} \leftarrow (\mathcal{V}, \mathcal{E}_{sample})$
26: $\mathcal{C} \leftarrow clusteralgo(\mathcal{G}_{sample}, l)$ \\Partition into l clusters
27: **return** $\mathcal{C}$

---

c, its TF-IDF value in a term vector t_i is computed as

$$tf\text{-}idf(c, t_i) = \sqrt{tf(c, t_i)} \cdot \log\left(1 + \frac{|\mathcal{T}|}{\sum_{j=1}^{|\mathcal{T}|} tf(c, t_j)}\right). \quad (1)$$

The cosine similarity of two vectors x and y is

$$cosine(x, y) = \frac{x \cdot y}{\|x\|_2 \cdot \|y\|_2}. \quad (2)$$

The k vertices corresponding to the k highest TF-IDF vector cosine similarity values with v_i are selected as the top-k neighbors of v_i.

3.2.2 Local Ranking of Edges and Graph Simplification

Line 9 takes the union of the newly-created content edge set $\mathcal{E}_c$ and the original topological edge set $\mathcal{E}_t$. In lines 10 through 24, a sampled edge set $\mathcal{E}_{sample}$ is constructed by retaining the most relevant edges from the edge union $\mathcal{E}_u$. For each vertex v_i, the edges to retain are selected from its local neighborhood in $\mathcal{E}_u$ (line 13). We compute the topological similarity (line 14) between node v_i and its neighbor γ_j as the relative overlap of their respective topological neighbor sets, $I = ngbr(v_i, \mathcal{E}_t)$ and $J = ngbr(\gamma_j, \mathcal{E}_t)$, using $similarity$ (either cosine similarity as in Equation 2 or Jaccard

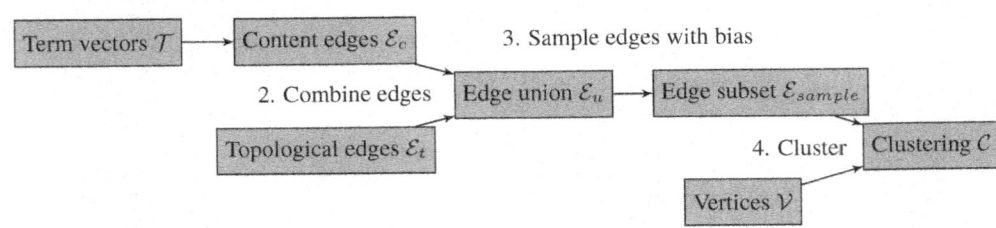

Figure 1: Work flow of CODICIL

coefficient as defined below):

$$jaccard(I, J) = \frac{|I \cap J|}{|I \cup J|} \ . \quad (3)$$

After the computation of the topological similarity vector $sim^t{}_i$ finishes, it is normalized by $normalize$ (line 15). In our experiments we implemented $normalize$ with either $zero\text{-}one$, which simply rescales the vector to $[0, 1]$:

$$zero\text{-}one(\vec{x}) = (x_i - min(\vec{x}))/(max(\vec{x}) - min(\vec{x})) \quad (4)$$

or $z\text{-}norm^3$, which centers and normalizes values to zero mean and unit variance:

$$z\text{-}norm(\vec{x}) = \frac{x_i - \hat{\mu}}{\hat{\sigma}}, \hat{\mu} = \frac{\sum_{i=1}^{|\vec{x}|} x_i}{|\vec{x}|}, \hat{\sigma}^2 = \frac{1}{|\vec{x}| - 1} \sum_{i=1}^{|\vec{x}|} (x_i - \hat{\mu})^2 \ . \quad (5)$$

Likewise, we compute v_i's content similarity to its neighbor γ_j by applying $similarity$ on term vectors t_i and t_{γ_j} and normalize those similarities (lines 16 and 17). The topological and content similarities of each edge are then aggregated with the weight specified by α (line 18).

In lines 20 through 23, the edges with highest similarity values are retained. As stated in our desiderata, we want $|\mathcal{E}_{sample}| \ll |\mathcal{E}_t|$ and therefore need to retain fewer than $|\Gamma_i|$ edges. Inspired by [22], we choose to keep $\lceil \sqrt{|\Gamma_i|} \rceil$ edges. This form has the following properties: 1) every vertex v_i will be incident to at least one edge, therefore the sparsification process does not generate new singleton, 2) concavity and monotonicity ensure that larger-degree vertices will retain no fewer edges than smaller-degree vertices, and 3) sublinearity ensures that smaller-degree vertices will have a larger fraction of their edges retained than larger-degree vertices.

3.2.3 Partitioning the Sampled Graph

Finally in lines 25 through 27 the sampled graph $\mathcal{G}_{sample}$ is formed with the retained edges, and the graph clustering algorithm $clusteralgo$ partitions $\mathcal{G}_{sample}$ into l clusters.

3.2.4 Extension to Support Complex Graphs

The proposed CODICIL framework can also be easily extended to support community detection from other types of graph. If an input graph has weighted edges, we can modify the formula in line 18 so that sim_{ij} becomes the product of combined similarity and original edge weight. Support of attribute graph is also straightforward, as attribute assignment of a node can be represented by an indicator vector, which is in the same form of a text vector.

---

[3] Montague and Aslam [19] pointed out that $z\text{-}norm$ has the advantage of being both shift and scale invariant as well as outlier insensitive. They experimentally found it best among six simple combination schemes discussed in [10].

3.3 Key Speedup Optimizations

3.3.1 *TopK* Implementation

When computing cosine similarities across term vectors $t_1, \ldots, t_{|\mathcal{T}|}$, one can truncate the TF-IDF vectors by only keeping m elements with the highest TF-IDF values and set other elements to 0. When m is set to a small value, TF-IDF vectors are sparser and therefore the similarity calculation becomes more efficient with little loss in accuracy.

We may also be interested in constraining content edges to be within a topological neighborhood of each node v_i, such that the search space of $TopK$ algorithm can be greatly reduced. Two straightforward choices are 1) "1-hop" graph in which the content edges from v_i are restricted to be in v_i's direct topological neighborhood, and 2) "2-hop" graph in which content edges can connect v_i and its neighbors' neighbors.

Many contemporary text search systems make use of inverted indices to speed up the operation of finding the k term vectors (documents) with the largest values of Equation 2 given a query vector t_i. We used the implementation from Apache Lucene for the largest dataset.

3.3.2 Fast Jaccard Similarity Estimation

To avoid expensive computation of the exact Jaccard similarity, we estimate it by using minwise hashing [3]. An unbiased estimator of sets A and B's Jaccard similarity can be obtained by

$$\hat{jaccard}(A, B) = \frac{1}{h} \sum_{i=1}^{h} I(\min(\pi_i(A)) = \min(\pi_i(B))) \ , \quad (6)$$

where $\pi_1, \pi_2, \cdots, \pi_h$ are h permutations drawn randomly from a family of minwise independent permutations defined on the universe A and B belong to, and I is the identity function. After hashing each element once using each permutation, the cost for similarity estimation is only $O(h)$ where h is usually chosen to be less than $|A|$ and $|B|$.

3.3.3 Fast Cosine Similarity Estimation

Similar to Jaccard coefficient, we can apply random projection method for fast estimate of cosine similarity [4]. In this method, each hash signature for a d-dimensional vector x is $h(x) = \text{sgn}(x, r)$, where $r \in \{0, 1\}^d$ is drawn randomly. For two vectors x and y, the following holds:

$$Pr[h(x) = h(y)] = 1 - \frac{\arccos(cosine(x, y))}{\pi} \ . \quad (7)$$

3.4 Performance Analysis

Lines 3–7 of CODICIL are a preprocessing step which compute for each vertex its top-k most similar vertices. Results of this one-time computation can be reused for any $k' \leq k$. Its complexity depends on the implementation of the $TopK$ operation. On our largest dataset Wikipedia this step completed within a few hours.

We now consider the loop in lines 11–24 where CODICIL loops through each vertex. For lines 14 and 16 we use the Jaccard estimator from Section 3.3.2 for which runs in $O(h)$ with a constant number of hashes h. The normalizations in lines 15 and 17 are $O(|\Gamma_i|)$ and the inner loop in lines 21–23 is $O(\sqrt{|\Gamma_i|})$. Sorting edges by weight in line 20 is $O(|\Gamma_i|\log|\Gamma_i|)$. The size of Γ_i, the union of topology and content neighbors, is at most n but on average much smaller in real world graphs. Thus the loop in lines 11–24 runs in $O(n^2 \log n)$.

The overall runtime of CODICIL is the edge preprocessing time, plus $O(n^2 \log n)$ for the loop, plus the algorithm-dependent time taken by *clusteralgo*.

4. EXPERIMENTS

We are interested in empirically answering the following questions:

- **Do the proposed content-aware clustering methods lead to better clustering than using graph topology only?**
- **How do our methods compare to existing content-aware clustering methods?**
- **How scalable are our methods when the data size grows?**

4.1 Datasets

Three publicly-available datasets with varying scale and characteristic are used. Their domains cover document network as well as social network. Each dataset is described below, and Table 1 follows, listing basic statistics of them.

4.1.1 CiteSeer

A citation network of computer science publications[4], each of which labeled as one of six sub-fields. In our graph, nodes stand for publications and undirected edges indicate citation relationships. The content information is stemmed words from research papers, represented as one binary vector for each document. Observe that the density of this network (average degree 2.74) is significantly lower than normally expected for a citation network.

4.1.2 Wikipedia

The static dump of English Wikipedia pages (October 2011). Only regular pages belonging to at least one category are included, each of which becomes one node. Page links are extracted. Cleaned bi-grams from title and text are used to represent each document's content. We use categories that a page belongs to as the page's class labels. Note that a page can be contained in more than one category, thus ground truth categories are overlapping.

4.1.3 Flickr

From a dataset of tagged photos[5] we removed infrequent tags and users associated with only few tags. Each graph node stands for a user, and an edge exists if one user is in another's contact list. Tags that users added to uploaded photos are used as content information. Flickr user groups are collected as ground truth. Similar to Wikipedia categories, Flickr user groups are also overlapping.

4.2 Baseline Methods

[4] http://www.cs.umd.edu/projects/linqs/projects/lbc/index.html
[5] http://staff.science.uva.nl/~xirong/index.php?n=DataSet.Flickr3m

In terms of strawman methods, we compare the CODICIL methods with three existing content-aware graph clustering algorithms, SA-Cluster-Inc [30], PCL-DC [28] and Link-PLSA-LDA (L-P-LDA) [20]. Their methodologies have been briefly introduced in Section 2. When applying SA-Cluster-Inc, we treat each term in $\mathcal{T}$ as a binary-valued attribute, i.e. for each graph node i every attribute value indicates whether the corresponding term is present in t_i or not. For L-P-LDA, since it does not assume a distinct distribution over topics for each cited document individually, only citing documents' topic distributions are estimated. As a result, there are 2313 citing documents in CiteSeer dataset and we report the F-score on those documents using their corresponding ground-truth assignments.

Previously SA-Cluster-Inc has been shown to outperform k-SNAP [25] and PCL-DC to outperform methods including PLSA-PHITS [5], LDA-Link-Word [7] and Link-Content-Factorization [31]. Therefore we do not compare with those algorithms.

Two content-insensitive clustering algorithms are included in the experiments as well. The first method, "Original Topo", clusters the original network directly. The second method samples edges solely based on structural similarity and then clusters the sampled graph [22], and we refer to it as "Sampled Topo" hereafter.

Finally, we also adapt LDA and K-means[6] algorithm to cluster graph nodes using content information only. When applying LDA, we treat each term vector t_i as a document, and one product of LDA's estimation procedure is the distribution over latent topics, θ_{t_i}, for each t_i (more details can be found at the original paper by Blei et al. [2]). Therefore, we treat each latent topic as a cluster and assign each graph node to the cluster that corresponds to the topic of largest probability. We use GibbsLDA++[7], a C++ implementation of LDA using Gibbs sampling [11] which is faster than the variational method proposed originally. Results of this method are denoted as "LDA".

4.3 Experiment Setup

4.3.1 Parameter Selection

There are several tunable parameters in the CODICIL framework, first of which is k, the number of content neighbors in the $TopK$ sub-routine. We propose the following heuristic to decide a proper value for k: the value of k should let $|\mathcal{E}_c| \approx |\mathcal{E}_t|$. As a result, k is set to 50 for both Wikipedia ($|\mathcal{E}_c| = 150,955,014$) and Flickr ($|\mathcal{E}_c| = 722,928$). For CiteSeer, we experiment with two relatively higher k values (50, $|\mathcal{E}_c| = 103,080$ and 70, $|\mathcal{E}_c| = 143,575$) in order to compensate the extreme sparsity in the original network. Though simplistic, this heuristic leads to decent clustering quality, as shown in Section 4.5, and avoids extra effort for tuning.

Another parameter of interest is α, which determines the weights for structural and content similarities. We set α to 0.5 unless otherwise specified, as in Section 4.7. The number of hashes (h) used for minwise hashing (Jaccard coefficient) is 30, and 512 for random projection (cosine similarity). Experiments with both choices of *similarity* function are performed. As for m, the number of non-zero elements in term vectors, we let $m = 10$ for Wikipedia and Flickr. This optional step is omitted for CiteSeer since the speedup is insignificant.

4.3.2 Clustering Algorithm

We combine the CODICIL framework with two different clus-

[6] We do not report running time of K-means as it is not implemented in C or C++.
[7] http://gibbslda.sourceforge.net/

	$|\mathcal{V}|$	$|\mathcal{E}_t|$	# CC	$|CC_{max}|$	# Uniq. Content Unit	Avg $|t_i|$	# Class
Wikipedia	3,580,013	162,085,383	10	3,579,995	1,459,335	202	595,355
Flickr	16,710	716,063	4	16,704	1,156	44	184,334
CiteSeer	3,312	4,536	438	2,110	3,703	32	6

Table 1: Basic statistics of datasets. # CC: number of connected components. $|CC_{max}|$: size of the largest connected component. Avg $|t_i|$: average number of non-zero elements in term vectors. # Class: number of (overlapping) ground truth classes.

tering algorithms, Metis[8] [15] and Multi-level Regularized Markov Clustering (MLR-MCL)[9] [21]. Both clustering algorithms are also applied on strawman methods.

4.4 Effect of Simplification on Graph Structure

In this section we investigate the impact of topological simplification (or sampling) on the spectrum of the graph. For both CiteSeer and Flickr (results for Wikipedia are similar to that of Flickr) we compute the Laplacian of the graph and then examine the top part of its eigenspectrum (first 2000 eigenvectors). Specifically, in Figure 2 we order the eigenvectors from the smallest one to the largest one (on the X axis) and plot corresponding eigenvalues (on the Y axis).

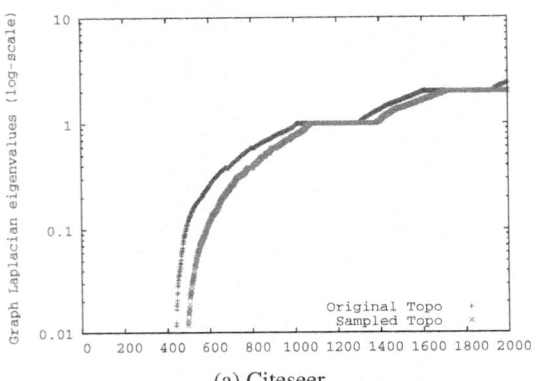

(a) Citeseer

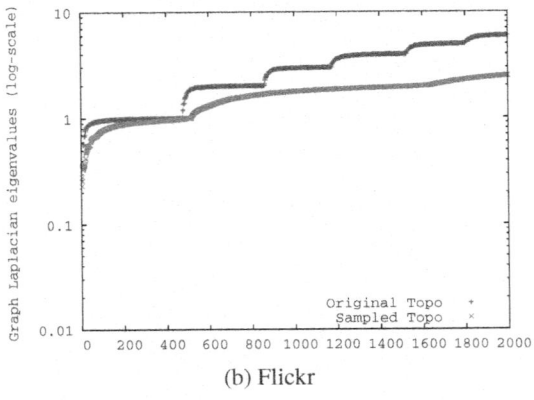

(b) Flickr

Figure 2: Eigenvalues of graph Laplacian before and after simplification

The multiplicity of 0 as an eigenvalue in such a plot corresponds

---
[8] http://glaros.dtc.umn.edu/gkhome/metis/metis/download
[9] http://www.cse.ohio-state.edu/~satuluri/research.html

to the number of independent components within the graph [18]. For CiteSeer we see an increase in the number of components as a result of topological simplification whereas for Flickr (similarly for Wikipedia) the number of components is unchanged. Our hypothesis is that for datasets like CiteSeer this will have a negative impact on the quality of the resulting clustering. We further hypothesize that our content-based enhancements will help in overcoming this shortfall.

Note that the sum of eigenvalues for the complete spectrum is proportional to the number of edges in the graph [18] so this explains why the plots for the original graphs are slightly above those for the simplified graph even though the overall trends (e.g. spectral gap, relative changes in eigenvalues), except for the number of components, are quite similar for both datasets.

4.5 Clustering Quality

We are interested in comparison between the predicted clustering and the real community structure since group/category information is available for all three datasets. Later in Section 5 we will evaluate CODICIL's performance qualitatively. While it is tempting to use conductance or other cut-based objectives to evaluate the quality of clustering, they only value the structural cohesiveness but not the content cohesiveness of resultant clustering, which is exactly the motivation of content-aware clustering algorithm. Instead, we use average F-score with regard to the ground truth as the clustering quality measure, as it takes content grouping into consideration and ensures a fair comparison among different clusterings. Given a predicted cluster p and with reference to a ground truth cluster g (both in the form of node set), we define the precision rate as $\frac{|p \cap g|}{|p|}$ and the recall rate as $\frac{|p \cap g|}{|g|}$. The F-score of p on g, denoted as $F(p, g)$, is the harmonic mean of precision and recall rates.

For a predicted cluster p, we compute its F-score on each g in the ground truth clustering G and define the maximal obtained as p's F-score on G. That is:

$$F(p, G) = \max_{g \in G} F(p, g) \ . \qquad (8)$$

The final F-score of the predicted clustering P on the ground truth clustering G is then calculated as the weighted (by cluster size) average of each predicted cluster's F-score:

$$F(P, G) = \sum_{p \in P} \frac{|p|}{|\mathcal{V}|} F(p, G) \ . \qquad (9)$$

This effectively penalizes the predicted clustering that is not well-aligned with the ground truth, and we use it as the quality measure of all methods on all datasets.

4.5.1 CiteSeer

In Figure 3 we show the experiment results on CiteSeer. Since it is known that the network has six communities (i.e. sub-fields in computer science), there is no need to vary l, the number of desired clusters. We report results using Metis (similar numbers were observed with Markov clustering). For PCL-DC, we set the parameter λ to 5 as suggested in the original paper, yielding an F-score of

0.570. The F-scores of SA-Cluster-Inc and L-P-LDA are 0.348 and 0.458, respectively. As we can see clearly in the bar chart, clustering based on topology alone results in a performance well below the state-of-the-art content-aware clustering methods. This is not surprising as the input graph has 438 connected components and therefore most small components were randomly assigned a prediction label. Although such approach has no impact on topology-based measures (e.g. normalized cut or conductance), it greatly spoils the F-score measure against the ground truth. Moreover, topology-based simplification further deteriorates the clustering performance as it creates even more connected components, as we projected in Section 4.4. Neither is LDA able to provide a competitive result, as it is oblivious to link structure embedded in the dataset. Surprisingly though, K-means only manages to produce a very unbalanced clustering (the largest cluster always contains more than 90% of all papers) even after 50 iterations, and its F-score (averaged over five runs) is only 0.336.

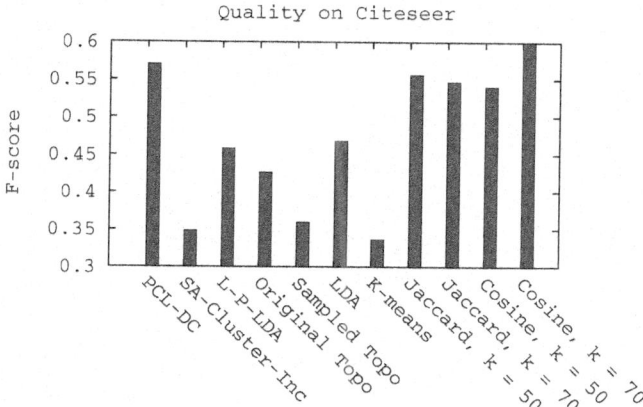

Figure 3: F-score of Metis on CiteSeer

On the other hand, our content-aware approaches (using Metis as the clustering method) were able to handle the issue of disconnection as they also include content-similar edges. For both similarity measures, the F-scores are within 90% range of PCL-DC, and it outperforms PCL-DC when k increases to 70.

While achieving the quality that is comparable with existing methods, the CODICIL series are significantly faster. PCL-DC takes 234 seconds on this dataset and SA-Cluster-Inc requires 306 seconds. LDA finishes in 40 seconds. In contrast, the sum of CODICIL's edge sampling and clustering time never exceeds 1 second. Therefore, the CODICIL methods are at least one order of magnitude faster than state-of-the-art algorithms.

4.5.2 Wikipedia

For the Wikipedia dataset, we were unable to run the experiment on SA-Cluster-Inc, PCL-DC, L-P-LDA, LDA and K-means as their memory and/or running time requirement became prohibitive on this million-node network. For example, storing 10,000 centroids alone in K-means requires 54 GBs).

Figures 4a and 4c plot the performances using MLR-MCL and Metis, respectively. Since category assignments as the ground truth are overlapping, there is no gold standard for the number of clusters. We therefore varied l in both clustering algorithms. Our content-aware clustering algorithms constantly outperforms Sampled Topo by a large margin, indicating that CODICIL methods are able to simplify the network and recover community structure at the same time. CODICIL methods' F-scores are also on par or better than those of Original Topo.

4.5.3 Flickr

Figure 5a shows the performances of various methods with MLR-MCL on Flickr, where SA-Cluster-Inc, PCL-DC, LDA and K-means can also finish in a reasonable time (L-P-LDA still takes more than 30 hours). Again, l was varied for the clustering algorithm. Similar to results on CiteSeer, CODICIL methods again lead the baselines by a considerable margin. The F-scores of SA-Cluster-Inc, LDA, and K-means never exceed 0.2, whereas CODICIL methods' F-scores are often higher, together with Original & Sampled Topo.

Readers may have noticed that for PCL-DC only three data points ($l = 50, 75, 100$) are obtained. That is because its excessive memory consumption crashed our workstation after using up 16 GBs of RAM for larger l values. We also observe that while PCL-DC generates a group membership distribution over l groups for each vertex, fewer than l communities are discovered. That is, there exist groups of which no vertex is a prominent member. Furthermore, the number of communities discovered is decreasing as l increases (45, 43 and 39 communities for $l = 50, 75, 100$), which is opposite to other methods' trends. All three clusterings' F-scores are less than 0.25. Similarly, multiple runs of K-means (K is set to 400, 800, 1200, and 1600) can only identity roughly 200 communities.

4.6 Scalability

The running time on CiteSeer has already been discussed, and here we focus on Flickr and Wikipedia. For CODICIL methods, the running time includes both edge sampling and clustering stage. The plots' Y-axes (running time) are in log scale.

4.6.1 Flickr

We first report scalability results on Flickr (see Figure 5b). For SA-Cluster-Inc, the value of l (the desired output cluster count), ranging from 100 to 5000, does not affect its running time as it always stays between 1 and 1.25 hours with memory usage around 12GB. The running time of LDA appears, to a large extent, linear in the number of latent topics (i.e. l) specified, climbing up from 2.56 hours ($l = 200$) to 15.88 hours ($l = 1600$). For PCL-DC, the running time with three l values (50, 75, 100) is 0.5, 2.0 and 2.8 hours, respectively.

As for our content-aware clustering algorithms, running them on Flickr requires less than 8 seconds, which is three to four orders of magnitude faster than SA-Cluster-Inc, PCL-DC and LDA. Original Topo takes more than 10 seconds, and Sampled Topo runs slightly faster than CODICIL methods.

4.6.2 Wikipedia

Original Topo, Sampled Topo and all CODICIL methods finished successfully. The running time is plotted in Figures 4b and 4d. When clustering using MLR-MCL, our methods are at least one order of magnitude faster than clustering based on network topology alone. For Metis, CODICIL is also more than four times faster. The trend lines suggest our methods have promising scalability for analysis on even larger networks.

4.7 Effect of Varying α on F-score

So far all experiments performed fix α at 0.5, meaning equal weights of structural and content similarities. In this sub-section we track how the clustering quality changes when the value of α is varied from 0.1 to 0.9 with a step length of 0.1.

On Wikipedia (Figure 6a) and Citeseer (Figure 6b), F-scores are greatest around $\alpha = 0.5$, supporting the decision of assigning

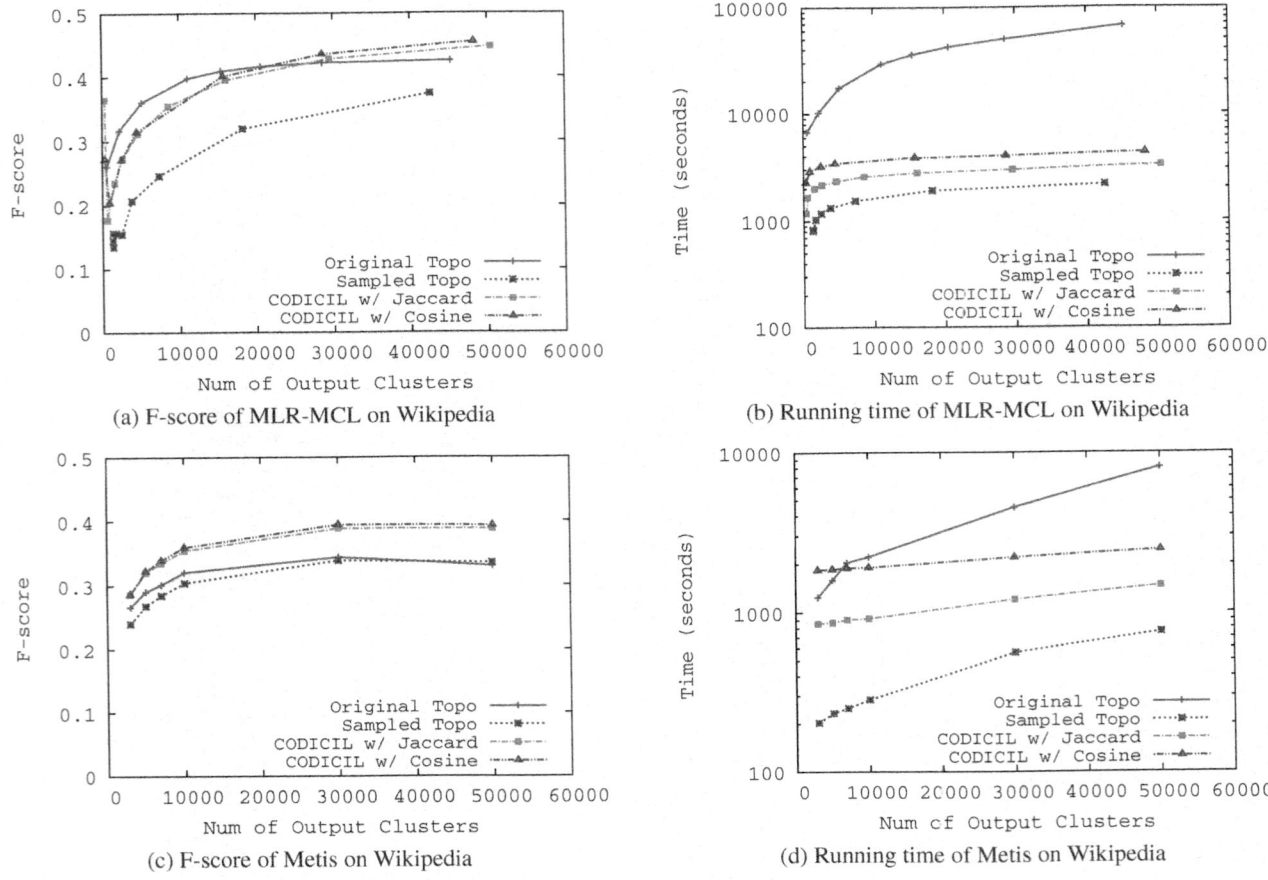

Figure 4: Experiment Results on Wikipedia

equal weights to structural and content similarities. Results differ on Flickr where F-score is constantly improving when α increases (i.e. more weight assigned to topological similarity).

4.8 Effect of $\mathcal{E}_c$ Constraint on F-score

In Section 3.3.1 we discuss the possibility of constraining content edges within a topological neighborhood for each node v_i. Here we provide a brief review on how the qualities of resultant clusterings are impacted by such constraint. For the sake of space, we focus on the F-scores on Wikipedia and Flickr.

Figures 7a and 7b show F-scores achieved on Wikipedia, using different $\mathcal{E}_c$ constraints. *Full* means no constraint and *TopK* subroutine searches the whole vertex set $\mathcal{V}$, whereas *1-hop* constrains the search to within a one-hop neighborhood, and likewise for *2-hop*. Plots of *full* and *2-hop* almost overlap with each other, suggesting that searching within the 2-hop neighborhood can provide sufficiently strong content signals on this dataset. For Flickr (Figures 7c and 7d), interestingly *2-hop* and *1-hop* have a slight lead over *full*. This may be an indication that in online social networks, compared with information networks, content similarity between two closely connected users emits stronger community signals.

4.9 Discussions

An interesting observation on the biased edge sampling is that it always results in an improvement in running time. However, sampling just the topology graph results in a clear loss in accuracy whereas content-conscious sampling is much more effective with accuracies that are on par with the best performing methods at a fraction of the cost to compute. We observe this for all three datasets.

We also find that for probabilistic-model-based methods (PCL-DC, L-P-LDA and LDA) as well as K-means, their running time is at least linear in l, the desired number of output clusters, which becomes a critical drawback in face of large-scale workloads. As the network grows, the number of clusters also increases naturally. Plots on CODICIL methods' running time, on the other hand, suggest a logarithmic increase with regard to the number of clusters, which is more affordable.

5. CASE STUDIES

In this section, we demonstrate the benefits of leveraging content information on two Wikipedia pages: "Machine Learning" and "Graph (Mathematics)".

In the original network, "machine learning" has a total degree of 637, and many of its neighbors (including "1-2-AX working memory task", "Wayne State University Computer Science Department", "Chou-Fasman method", etc.) are at best peripheral to the context. When we sample the graph according to its link structure only, 119 neighbors are retained for "machine learning". Although this eliminates some noise, many others, including the three entries above, are still preserved. Moreover, it also removes during the process many neighbors which should have been kept, e.g. "naive Bayes classifier", "support vector machine", and so on.

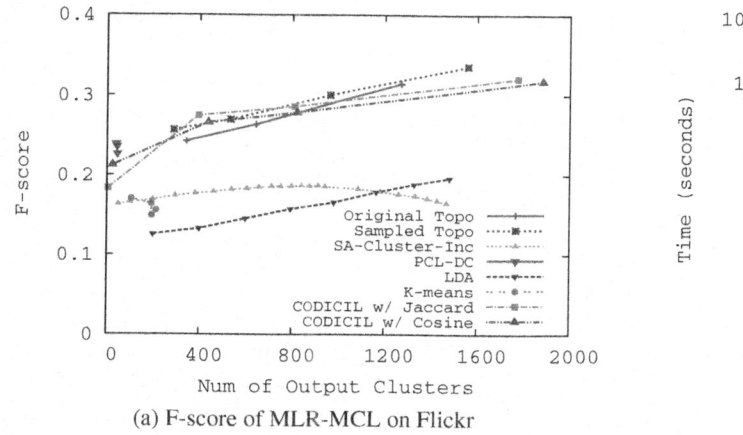
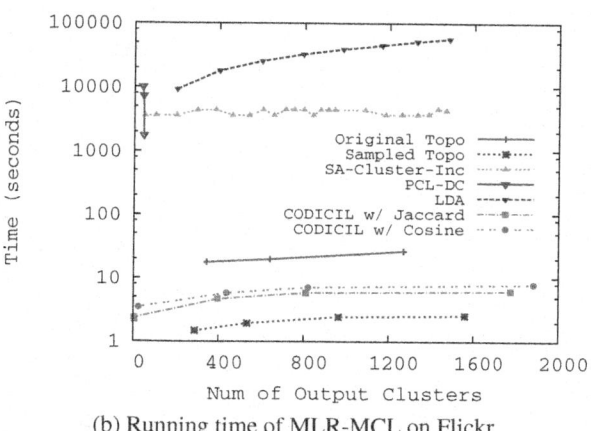

(a) F-score of MLR-MCL on Flickr

(b) Running time of MLR-MCL on Flickr

Figure 5: Experiment Results on Flickr

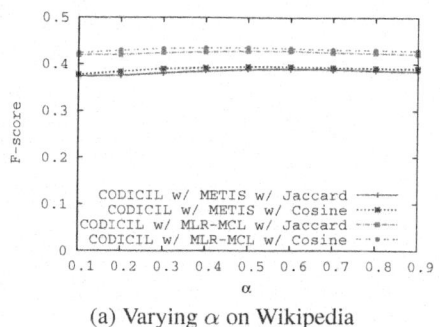
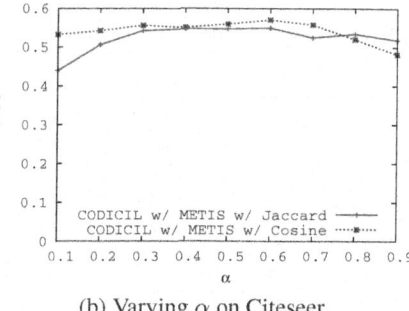
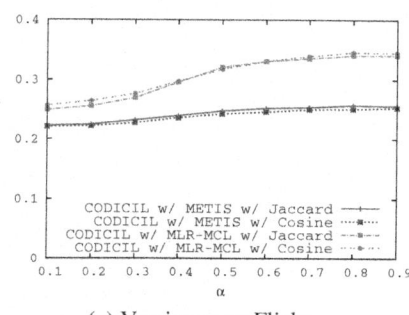

(a) Varying α on Wikipedia

(b) Varying α on Citeseer

(c) Varying α on Flickr

Figure 6: Effect of Varying α on F-score (Avg. # Clusters for Wikipedia: 29,414, Avg. # Clusters for Flickr: 1,911)

The CODICIL framework, in contrast, alleviates both problems. Apart from removing noisy edges, it also keeps the most relevant ones. For example, "AdaBoost", "ensemble learning", "pattern recognition" all appear in "machine learning"'s neighborhood in the sampled edge set $\mathcal{E}_{sample}$. Perhaps more interestingly, we find that CODICIL adds "neural network", an edge absent from the original network, into $\mathcal{E}_{sample}$ (recall that it is possible for CODICIL to include an edge even it is not in the original graph, given its content similarity is sufficiently high). This again illustrates the core philosophy of CODICIL: to complement the original network with content information so as to better recover the community structure.

Similar observations can be made on the "Graph (Mathematics)" page. For example, CODICIL removes entries including "Eric W. Weisstein", "gadget (computer science)" and "interval chromatic number of an ordered graph". It also keeps "clique (graph theory)", "Hamiltonian path", "connectivity (graph theory)" and others, which would otherwise be removed if we sample the graph using link structure alone.

6. CONCLUSION

We have presented an efficient and extremely simple algorithm for community identification in large-scale graphs by fusing content and link similarity. Our algorithm, CODICIL, selectively retains edges of high relevancy within local neighborhoods from the fused graph, and subsequently clusters this backbone graph with any content-agnostic graph clustering algorithm.

Our experiments demonstrate that CODICIL outperforms state-of-the-art methods in clustering quality while running orders of magnitude faster for moderately-sized datasets, and can efficiently handle large graphs with millions of nodes and hundreds of millions of edges. While simplification can be applied to the original topology alone with a small loss of clustering quality, it is particularly potent when combined with content edges, delivering superior clustering quality with excellent runtime performance.

7. ACKNOWLEDGEMENTS

This work is sponsored by NSF Award #1111118 "SoCS: Collaborative Research: Social Media Enhanced Organizational Sensemaking in Emergency Response" and NSF Award #1240651 "CCF: EAGER: Collaborative Research: Scalable Graph Mining and Clustering on Desktop Supercomputers".

8. REFERENCES

[1] C. Aggarwal, Y. Zhao, and P. Yu. Outlier detection in graph streams. In *Data Engineering (ICDE), 2011 IEEE 27th International Conference on*, pages 399–409. IEEE, 2011.

[2] D. Blei, A. Ng, and M. Jordan. Latent dirichlet allocation. *JMLR*, 3:993–1022, 2003.

[3] A. Broder, M. Charikar, A. Frieze, and M. Mitzenmacher. Min-wise independent permutations. In *STOC'98*, pages 327–336. ACM, 1998.

[4] M. Charikar. Similarity estimation techniques from rounding algorithms. In *STOC'02*, pages 380–388. ACM, 2002.

[5] D. Cohn and T. Hofmann. The missing link-a probabilistic model of document

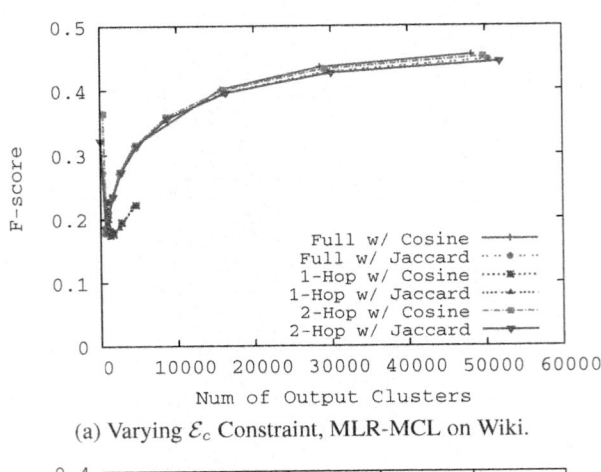
(a) Varying $\mathcal{E}_c$ Constraint, MLR-MCL on Wiki.

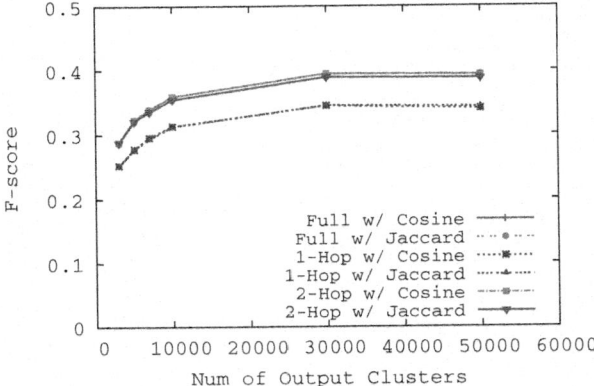
(b) Varying $\mathcal{E}_c$ Constraint, METIS on Wiki.

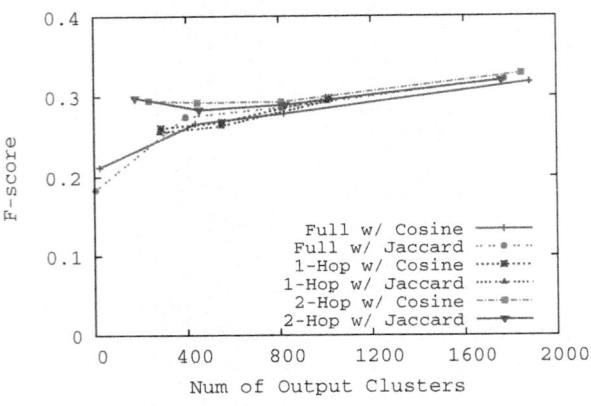
(c) Varying $\mathcal{E}_c$ Constraint, MLR-MCL on Flickr

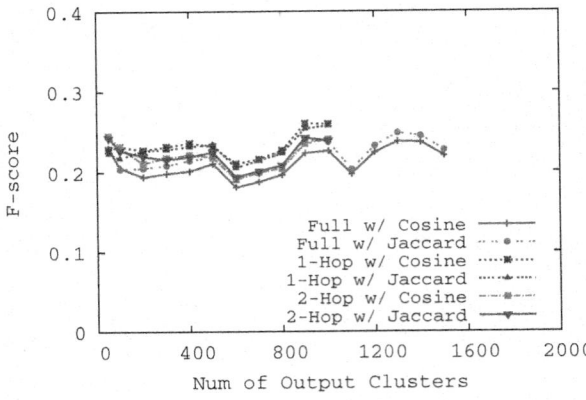
(d) Varying $\mathcal{E}_c$ Constraint, METIS on Flickr

Figure 7: Effect of $\mathcal{E}_c$ Constraint on F-score

content and hypertext connectivity. In *NIPS'01*, volume 13, page 430. The MIT Press, 2001.

[6] I. Dhillon, Y. Guan, and B. Kulis. Kernel k-means: spectral clustering and normalized cuts. In *SIGKDD'04*, pages 551–556. ACM, 2004.

[7] E. Erosheva, S. Fienberg, and J. Lafferty. Mixed-membership models of scientific publications. *PNAS*, 101(Suppl 1):5220, 2004.

[8] M. Ester, R. Ge, B. Gao, Z. Hu, and B. Ben-Moshe. Joint cluster analysis of attribute data and relationship data: the connected k-center problem. In *SDM'06*, pages 25–46, 2006.

[9] S. Fortunato. Community detection in graphs. *Physics Reports*, 486(3-5):75–174, 2010.

[10] E. Fox and J. Shaw. Combination of multiple searches. *NIST SPECIAL PUBLICATION SP*, pages 243–243, 1994.

[11] T. Griffiths and M. Steyvers. Finding scientific topics. *PNAS*, 101(Suppl 1):5228, 2004.

[12] S. Günnemann, B. Boden, and T. Seidl. Db-csc: a density-based approach for subspace clustering in graphs with feature vectors. In *PKDD 2011*, pages 565–580. Springer-Verlag, 2011.

[13] D. Hanisch, A. Zien, R. Zimmer, and T. Lengauer. Co-clustering of biological networks and gene expression data. *Bioinformatics*, 18(suppl 1):S145–S154, 2002.

[14] D. Karger. Random sampling in cut, flow, and network design problems. *Mathematics of Operations Research*, 24(2):383–413, 1999.

[15] G. Karypis and V. Kumar. A fast and high quality multilevel scheme for partitioning irregular graphs. *SIAM Journal on Scientific Computing*, 20(1):359–392, 1998.

[16] J. Leskovec, K. Lang, and M. Mahoney. Empirical comparison of algorithms for network community detection. In *Proceedings of the 19th international conference on World wide web*, pages 631–640. ACM, 2010.

[17] A. Maiya and T. Berger-Wolf. Sampling community structure. In *WWW 2010*, pages 701–710. ACM, 2010.

[18] B. Mohar. The laplacian spectrum of graphs. *Graph theory, combinatorics, and applications*, 2:871–898, 1991.

[19] M. Montague and J. Aslam. Relevance score normalization for metasearch. In *CIKM'01*, pages 427–433. ACM, 2001.

[20] R. Nallapati, A. Ahmed, E. Xing, and W. Cohen. Joint latent topic models for text and citations. In *SIGKDD'08*, pages 542–550. ACM, 2008.

[21] V. Satuluri and S. Parthasarathy. Scalable graph clustering using stochastic flows: applications to community discovery. In *SIGKDD'09*, pages 737–746. ACM, 2009.

[22] V. Satuluri, S. Parthasarathy, and Y. Ruan. Local graph sparsification for scalable clustering. In *SIGMOD 2011*, pages 721–732. ACM, 2011.

[23] A. Strehl and J. Ghosh. Cluster ensembles—a knowledge reuse framework for combining multiple partitions. *The Journal of Machine Learning Research*, 3:583–617, 2003.

[24] W. Tang, Z. Lu, and I. Dhillon. Clustering with multiple graphs. In *ICDM'09*, pages 1016–1021. IEEE, 2009.

[25] Y. Tian, R. A. Hankins, and J. M. Patel. Efficient aggregation for graph summarization. In *SIGMOD'08*, pages 567–580, 2008.

[26] I. Ulitsky and R. Shamir. Identification of functional modules using network topology and high-throughput data. *BMC Systems Biology*, 1(1):8, 2007.

[27] S. van Dongen. Graph clustering by flow simulation. *PhD Thesis*, 2000.

[28] T. Yang, R. Jin, Y. Chi, and S. Zhu. Combining link and content for community detection: a discriminative approach. In *SIGKDD'09*, pages 927–936. ACM, 2009.

[29] D. Zhou, E. Manavoglu, J. Li, C. Giles, and H. Zha. Probabilistic models for discovering e-communities. In *WWW'06*, pages 173–182. ACM, 2006.

[30] Y. Zhou, H. Cheng, and J. Yu. Clustering large attributed graphs: An efficient incremental approach. In *ICDM 2010*, pages 689–698. IEEE, 2010.

[31] S. Zhu, K. Yu, Y. Chi, and Y. Gong. Combining content and link for classification using matrix factorization. In *SIGIR'07*, pages 487–494. ACM, 2007.

Learning Joint Query Interpretation and Response Ranking

Uma Sawant
IIT Bombay, Yahoo! Labs
uma@cse.iitb.ac.in

Soumen Chakrabarti
IIT Bombay
soumen@cse.iitb.ac.in

ABSTRACT

Thanks to information extraction and semantic Web efforts, search on unstructured text is increasingly refined using semantic annotations and structured knowledge bases. However, most users cannot become familiar with the schema of knowledge bases and ask structured queries. Interpreting free-format queries into a more structured representation is of much current interest. The dominant paradigm is to segment or partition query tokens by purpose (references to types, entities, attribute names, attribute values, relations) and then launch the interpreted query on structured knowledge bases. Given that structured knowledge extraction is never complete, here we choose a less trodden path: a data representation that retains the unstructured text corpus, along with structured annotations (mentions of entities and relationships) on it. We propose two new, natural formulations for joint query interpretation and response ranking that exploit bidirectional flow of information between the knowledge base and the corpus. One, inspired by probabilistic language models, computes expected response scores over the uncertainties of query interpretation. The other is based on max-margin discriminative learning, with latent variables representing those uncertainties. In the context of typed entity search, both formulations bridge a considerable part of the accuracy gap between a generic query that does not constrain the type at all, and the upper bound where the "perfect" target entity type of each query is provided by humans. Our formulations are also superior to a two-stage approach of first choosing a target type using recent query type prediction techniques, and then launching a type-restricted entity search query.

Categories and Subject Descriptors

H.3.3 [**Information Storage and Retrieval**]: Information Search and Retrieval

Keywords

Query interpretation; Entity search

1. INTRODUCTION

Web information representation is getting more sophisticated, thanks to information extraction and semantic Web efforts. Much structured and semistructured data now supplements unstructured, free-format textual pages. In verticals such as e-commerce, the structured data can be accessed through forms and faceted search. However, a large number of free-format queries remain outside the scope of verticals. As we shall review in Section 2, there is much recent research on analyzing and annotating them.

Here we focus on a specific kind of entity search query: some words (called *selectors*) in the query are meant to occur literally in a response document (as in traditional text search), but other words *hint* at the type of entity sought by the query. Unlike prior work on translating well-formed sentences or questions to structured queries using deep NLP, we are interested in handling "telegraphic" queries that are typically sent to search engines. Each response entity must be a member of the hinted type.

Note that this problem is quite different from finding answers to well-formed natural language questions (e.g., in Wolfram Alpha) from structured knowledge bases (perhaps curated through information extraction). Also observe that we do not restrict ourselves to queries that seek entities by attribute values or attributes of a given entity (both are valuable query templates for e-commerce and have been researched). In our setup, some responses may only be collected from diverse, open-domain, free-format text sources. E.g., typical driving *time* between Paris and Nice (the target type is time duration), or *cricketers* who scored centuries at Lords (the target type is cricketers).

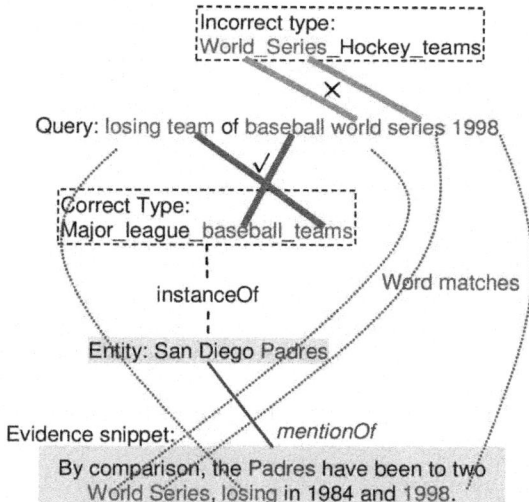

Figure 1: Example of a collective, joint query interpretation and entity ranking problem; includes a query containing different possible hint and selector words, partially matching types with member entities and corpus snippets

The target type (or a more general supertype, such as *sportsperson* in place of *cricketer*) may be instantiated in a *catalog*, but the typical user has no knowledge of the catalog or its schema. Large catalogs like Wikipedia or Freebase evolve "organically". They are not designed by linguists, and they are not minimal or canonical in any sense. Types have overlaps and redundancies. The query interpreter should take advantage of specialized types whenever available, but otherwise gracefully back off to broader types.

Figure 1 shows a query that has at least two plausible hint word sets: {team, baseball} (correct) and {world, series} (incorrect). Hint words partially match descriptions of types in a catalog, which lead to member entities. Potential response entities are mentioned in document snippets (one shown), which in turn partially match selector words (world, series, losing, 1998). Given a limited number of types to choose from, a human will find it trivial to pick the best. However, a program will find it very challenging to decide *which subset* of query words are type hints, and, even after that, to select the *best type(s)* from a large type catalog. This *query interpretation* task is one part of our goal.

We posit that *corpus statistics provide critical signals* for query interpretation. For example, we might benefit from knowing that `San_Diego_Padres` rarely co-occurs with the word "hockey", which can be known only from the corpus. Query interpretation should ideally be done *jointly* with ranking entities from the corpus, because it involves a *delicate combinatorial balance* between the hint-selector split, and the (rather noisy) signals from the quality of matches between type descriptions and hint words, snippets and other words, and mentions of entities in said snippets.

Although query typing has been investigated before [38, 5], to the best of our knowledge this is the first work on combining type interpretation with learning to rank [21]. In Section 4, we present a natural, generative formulation for the task using probabilistic language models. In Section 5 we present a more flexible and powerful max-margin discriminative approach [19, 7].

In Section 6, we report on experiments involving 709 queries, over 200,000 types, 1.5 million entities, and 380 million evidence snippets collected from over 500 million Web pages. The entity ranking accuracy of a reasonable query interpreter will be between the "lower bound" of a generic system that makes no effort to identify the target type (i.e., all catalog entities are candidates), and the upper bound of an unrealistic "perfect" system that knows the target type by magic. Our salient experimental observations are:

- The generative language model approach improves entity ranking accuracy significantly beyond the lower bound wrt MAP, MRR and NDCG.
- The discriminative approach is superior to generative; e.g., it bridges 43% of the MAP gap between the lower and upper bounds.
- In fact, if we discard the entity ranks output from our system, use it only as a target type predictor, and issue a query with the predicted type, entity ranking accuracy *drops*.
- Our discriminative approach beats a recent target type prediction algorithm by significant margins.
- NLP-heavy techniques are not robust to telegraphic queries.

Our data and code will be made publicly available at http://www.cse.iitb.ac.in/~soumen/doc/CSAW/.

2. RELATED WORK

Interpreting a free-format query into a structured form has been explored extensively in the information retrieval (IR) and Web search communities, with several recent dedicated workshops[1]. A preliminary but critical structuring step is to demarcate phrases [6] in free-format queries. There is also a large literature on topic-independent intent discovery [10, 18] as well as topic-dependent facet [30] or template [1] inference.

The problem of *disambiguating named entities* mentioned in queries is superficially similar to ours, but is technically quite different. In Figure 2, query word *ymca* may refer to different entities, but additional query word *lyrics* hints at type *music*, whereas *address* hints at type *organization*. Note that the query text directly embeds a mention of an *entity*, not a type. Disambiguating the entity (usually) amounts to disambiguating the type—contrast Figure 2 with Figure 1. A given mention usually refers to only a few entities. In contrast, misinterpreting the hint often pollutes the entity response list beyond redemption. Delaying a hard choice of the target type, or avoiding it entirely, is likely to help.

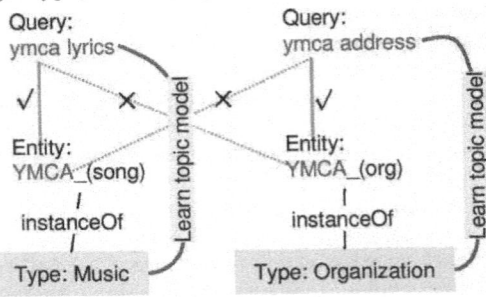

Figure 2: **Disambiguating named entities in queries.**

For entity disambiguation, Guo *et al.* [15] proposed a probabilistic language model through weak supervision that learns to associate, e.g., lyrics with music and address with organization. Pantel *et al.* [25, 26] pushed this farther by exploiting clicks and modeling intent. Hu *et al.* [17] addressed a similar problem. None gave a discriminative max-margin formulation, or unified the framework with learning to rank.

Given that the database community uses SQL and XQuery as unambiguous, structured representations of information needs, and that the NLP community seeks to parse sentences to a well-defined meaning, there also exists convergent database and NLP literature on interpreting free-format (source) queries into a suitable target "query language". Naturally, much of this work seeks to identify types, entities, attributes, and relations in queries. Although the theoretical problem is challenging [14], a common underlying theme is that each token in the query may be an expression of schema elements, entities, or relationships: this leads to a general assignment problem, which is solved approximately using various techniques, summarized below.

Sarkas *et al.* [33] annotated e-commerce queries using schema and data in a structured product catalog. In the context of Web-extracted knowledge bases such as YAGO [35], Pound *et al.* [29, 28] set up a collective assignment problem with a cost model that reflects syntactic similarity between query fragments and their assigned concepts, as well as semantic coherence between concepts [20]. Sarkas, Pound and others, like us, handle "telegraphic queries" that may not be well-formed sentences. DEANNA [39] solved the collective assignment problem using an integer program. It is capable of parsing queries as complex as "which director has won the Academy Award for best director and is married to an actress that has won the Academy Award for best ac-

---

[1] ciir.cs.umass.edu/sigir2010/qru
ciir.cs.umass.edu/sigir2011/qru
strataconf.com/stratany2011/public/schedule/detail/21413
sysrun.haifa.il.ibm.com/hrl/smer2011

km.aifb.kit.edu/ws/jiwes2012

tress?" As might be expected, DEANNA is rather sensitive to query syntax and often fails on telegraphic queries. All these systems interpret the query with the help of a fairly clean, structured knowledge base. [33, 29, 28, 39] do not give discriminative learning-to-rank algorithms that jointly disambiguate the query and ranks responses. IBM's Watson [24] identifies candidate entities first, and then scores them for compatibility with likely target types.

In this work, we do not assume that a knowledge base has been curated ahead of time from a text corpus. Instead we assume entities and types have been annotated on spans of unstructured text. Accordingly, we step back from sophisticated target schemata, settling for three basic relations (*instanceOf*, *subTypeOf*, and *mentionOf*, see Figure 1) that link a structured entity catalog with an unstructured text corpus (such as the Web). On the other hand, we take the first step toward integrating learning-to-rank [21] techniques with query interpretation.

Closest to our goal are those of Vallet and Zaragoza [38] and Balog and Neumayer (B&N) [5]. Vallet and Zaragoza first collected a ranked list of entities by launching a query without any type constraints. Each entity belongs to a hierarchy of types. They accrued a score in favor of a type from every entity as a function of its rank, and ranked types by decreasing total score. B&N investigated two techniques. In the first, descriptions of all entities e belonging to each type t were concatenated into a super document for t, and turned into a language model. In the second (similar in spirit to Vallet and Zaragoza), the score of t was calculated as a weighted average of probabilities of entity description language models generating the query, for $e \in t$.

These approaches [5, 31] use long entity descriptions, such as found on the Wikipedia page representing an entity, but not a corpus where entity mentions are annotated. The corpus documents may well not be definitional, and yet remarkably improve entity ranking accuracy, as we shall see. None of [38, 5, 31] attempt a segmentation of query words by purpose (target type vs. literal matches).

3. BACKGROUND AND NOTATION

3.1 "Telegraphic" queries

A "telegraphic" entity search query q expresses an information need that is satisfied by one or more *entities*. Query q is a sequence of $|q|$ *words*. The jth word of query q is denoted $w_{q,j}$, where $j = 1, \ldots, |q|$, and subscript q in $w_{q,j}$ is omitted if clear from context. We will interchangeably use q (as a query identifier) and $\vec{q}$ (to highlight that it is a sequence of words). Unlike full, well-formed, grammatical sentences or questions, telegraphic queries resemble short Web search queries having no clear subject-verb-object or other complex clausal structure. Some examples of natural telegraphic entity search queries and possible natural language "translations" are shown in Figure 3. $\mathcal{Q}$ denotes a set of queries.

3.2 The entity and type catalog

The *catalog* $(\mathcal{T}, \mathcal{E}, \subseteq^+, \in^+)$, is a directed acyclic graph of *type* nodes $t \in \mathcal{T}$, with edges representing the "is-subtype-of" transitive binary relation $\subseteq^+$. Each type t is described by one or more *lemmas* (descriptive phrases) $L(t)$, e.g., Austrian physicists.

Q1	Woodrow Wilson was president of which university?	woodrow wilson <u>president</u> <u>university</u>
Q2	Which Chinese cities have many international companies?	chinese <u>city</u> many international <u>companies</u>
Q3	What cathedral is in Claude Monet's paintings?	<u>cathedral</u> claude monet paintings
Q4	Along the banks of what river is the Hermitage Museum located?	hermitage <u>museum</u> <u>banks</u> of <u>river</u>
Q5	At what institute was Dolly cloned?	dolly <u>clone</u> <u>institute</u>
Q6	Who made the first airplane?	first <u>airplane</u> <u>inventor</u>

Figure 3: Natural language queries and typical telegraphic forms, with potential type description matches underlined.

Each entity e in the catalog is also represented by a node connected by "is-instance-of" edge(s) to one or more *most specific* type nodes, and transitively belongs to all supertypes; this relation is represented as $\in^+$. An entity e may be a *candidate* for a query q. The set of candidate entities for query q is called $\mathcal{E}_q \subseteq \mathcal{E}$. In training data, an entity e may be labeled relevant (denoted e_+) or irrelevant (denoted e_-) for q. $\mathcal{E}_q$ is accordingly partitioned into $\mathcal{E}_q^+, \mathcal{E}_q^-$.

3.3 Annotated corpus and snippets

The corpus is a set of free-format text documents. Each document is modeled as a sequence of words. Entity e is *mentioned* at some places in an unstructured text corpus. A "mention" is a token span (e.g., *Big Apple*) that gives evidence of reference to e (e.g., New_York_City). The mention span, together with a suitable window of context words around it, is called a *snippet*. The set of snippets mentioning e is called $\mathcal{S}_e$. $c \in \mathcal{S}_e$ is one snippet context *supporting* e.

In the Wikipedia corpus, most mentions are annotated manually as wiki hyperlinks. For Web text, statistical learning techniques [20, 16] are used for high-quality annotations. Here we assume mentions to be correct and deterministic. Extending our work to noisy mentions is left for future work.

4. GENERATIVE FORMULATION

Given the success of generative techniques in corpus modeling [8], IR [41] and entity ranking [3, 4], it is natural to propose a generative language model approach to joint query interpretation and response ranking.

As is common in generative language models, we will fix an entity e and generate the query words, by taking the following steps:

1. Choose a type from $\{t : e \in^+ t\}$;
2. Describe that type using one or more query words, which will be called *hint* words;
3. Collect snippets that mention e; and
4. Generate the remainder of the query by sampling words from these snippets.

Our goal is to rank entities by probability given the query, by taking the expectation over possible types and hints.

4.1 Choosing a type given e

Given entity e, we first pick a type t such that $e \in^+ t$, and describe t in the query (with the expectation that the system will infer t, then instantiate it to e as a response). So the basic question looks like: "if the answer is Albert

Einstein, what type (among scientist, person, organism, etc.) is likely to be mentioned in the query, *before* we inspect the query?" (*After* we see the query, our beliefs will change, e.g., depending on whether the query asks "*who* discovered general relativity?" vs. "which *physicist* discovered general relativity?") So we need to design the prior distribution $\Pr(t|e)$.

Recall that there may be hundreds of thousands of ts, and tens of millions of es, so fitting the prior for each e separately is out of the question. On the other hand, the prior is just a mild guidance mechanism to discourage obscure or low-recall types like "Austrian Physicists who died in 1972". Therefore, we propose the following crude but efficient estimate. From a query log with ground truth (i.e., each query accompanied with a t provided by a human), accumulate a hit count N_t for each type t. At query time, given a candidate e, we calculate

$$\Pr(t|e) = \begin{cases} \dfrac{N_t + \gamma}{\sum_{t': e \in^+ t'}(N_{t'} + \gamma)}, & e \in^+ t \\ 0, & \text{otherwise} \end{cases}, \quad (1)$$

where $\gamma \in (0,1)$ is a tuned constant.

4.2 Query word switch variables

Suppose the query is the word sequence $(w_j, j = 1, \ldots, |q|)$. For each position j, we posit a binary switch variable $z_j \in \{h, s\}$. Each z_j will be generated iid from a Bernoulli distribution with tuned parameter $\delta \in (0,1)$. If $z_j = h$, then word w_j is intended as a *hint* to the target type. Otherwise w_j is a *selector* sampled from snippets mentioning entity e. The vector of switch variables is called $\vec{z}$.

The number of possible partitions of query words into hints and selectors is $2^{|q|}$. By definition, telegraphic queries are short, so $2^{|q|}$ is manageable. One can also reduce this search space by asserting additional constraints, without compromising quality in practice. E.g., we can restrict the type hint to a contiguous span with at most three tokens.

Given $\vec{q}$ and a proposed partition $\vec{z}$, we define two helper functions, overloading symbols s and h:

$$\text{Hint words of } q: \quad h(\vec{q}, \vec{z}) = \{w_{q,j} : z_j = h\} \quad (2)$$
$$\text{Selector words of } q: \quad s(\vec{q}, \vec{z}) = \{w_{q,j} : z_j = s\}. \quad (3)$$

With these definitions, in the exhaustive hint-selector partition case, $\vec{z}$ is the result of $|q|$ Bernoulli trials with hint probability $\delta \in (0,1)$ for each word, so we have

$$\Pr(\vec{z}) = \delta^{|h(\vec{q},\vec{z})|}(1-\delta)^{|s(\vec{q},\vec{z})|}. \quad (4)$$

δ is tuned using training data.

In this paper we will consider strict partitions of query words between hints and selectors, but it is not difficult to generalize to words that may be both hints and selectors. Assuming each query word has a purpose, the full space grows to $3^{|q|}$, but assuming contiguity of the hint segment again reduces the space to essentially $O(|q|)$.

4.3 Type description language model

Globally across queries, the textual description of each type t induces a language model. We can define the exact form of the model in any number of ways, but, to keep implementations efficient, we will make the commonly used assumption that hint words are conditionally independent of each other given the type. Each type t is described by one or more *lemmas* (descriptive phrases) $L(t)$, e.g., Austrian physicists. Because lemmas are very short, words are rarely repeated, so we can use the multivariate Bernoulli [23] distribution derived from lemma ℓ:

$$\widehat{\Pr}(w|\ell) = \begin{cases} 1, & \text{if } w \text{ appears in } \ell, \\ 0, & \text{otherwise} \end{cases} \quad (5)$$

Following usual smoothing policies [41], we interpolate the smoothed distribution above with a background language model created from all types:

$$\widehat{\Pr}(w|\mathcal{T}) = \frac{\sum_{t \in \mathcal{T}} [\![w \text{ appears in } \ell \,;\, \ell \in L(t)]\!]}{|\mathcal{T}|}; \quad (6)$$

in words, the fraction of all types that contain w. $[\![B]\!]$ is 1 if Boolean condition B is true, and 0 otherwise. We splice together (5) and (6) using parameter $\beta \in (0,1)$:

$$\Pr(w|\ell) = (1-\beta)\widehat{\Pr}(w|\ell) + \beta\widehat{\Pr}(w|\mathcal{T}). \quad (7)$$

The probability of generating exactly the hint words in the query is

$$\Pr(h(\vec{q},\vec{z})|\ell) = \prod_{w \in h(\vec{q},\vec{z})} \Pr(w|\ell) \prod_{w \notin h(\vec{q},\vec{z})} (1 - \Pr(w|\ell)), \quad (8)$$

where w ranges over the entire vocabulary of type descriptions. In case of multiple lemmas describing a type,

$$\Pr(\cdot|t) = \max_{\ell \in L(t)} \Pr(\cdot|\ell); \quad (9)$$

i.e., use the most favorable lemma. All fitted parameters in the distribution $\Pr(w|\ell)$ are collectively called φ.

4.4 Entity snippet language model

The selector part of the query, $s(\vec{q}, \vec{z})$, is generated from a language model derived from $\mathcal{S}_e$, the set of snippets that mention candidate entity e. For simplicity we use the same kind of smoothed multivariate Bernoulli distribution to build the language model as we did for the type descriptions. Note that words that appear in snippets but not in the query are of no concern in a language model that seeks to generate the query from distributions associated with the snippets. Suppose $corpusCount(e)$ is the number of mentions of e in the corpus $\mathcal{C}$, and $corpusCount(e, w)$ be the number of mentions of e where w also occurs within a specified snippet window width. The unsmoothed probability of generating a query word w from the snippets of e is

$$\widehat{\Pr}(w|e) = \frac{corpusCount(e,w)}{corpusCount(e)} = \frac{|\{s \in \mathcal{S}_e : w \in s\}|}{corpusCount(e)}. \quad (10)$$

As before, we will smooth the above estimate using an corpus-level, entity-independent background word distribution estimate:

$$\widehat{\Pr}(w|\mathcal{C}) = \frac{1}{|\mathcal{C}|}(\text{number of documents containing } w). \quad (11)$$

And now we use the interpolation

$$\Pr(w|e) = (1-\alpha)\widehat{\Pr}(w|e) + \alpha\widehat{\Pr}(w|\mathcal{C}), \quad (12)$$

where $\alpha \in (0,1)$ is a suitable smoothing parameter. The fitted parameters of the $\Pr(w|e)$ distribution are collectively called θ. Similar to (8), the selector part of the query is

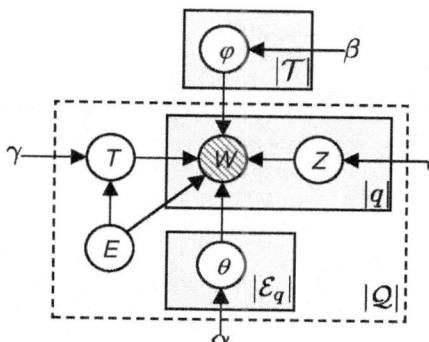

Figure 4: Plate diagram for generating a query q from a candidate entity e. Only $(w_{q,j} : j = 1, \ldots, |q|)$ are observed variables. φ represents the type description language model and θ represents the entity mention snippets language model. $(z_{q,j} : j = 1, \ldots, |q|)$ are the hidden switch variables. T is the hidden type variable.

generated with probability

$$\Pr(s(\vec{q}, \vec{z})|e) = \prod_{w \in s(\vec{q}, \vec{z})} \Pr(w|e) \prod_{w \notin s(\vec{q}, \vec{z})} (1 - \Pr(w|e)), \quad (13)$$

except here w ranges over all query words.

4.5 Putting the pieces together

A plate diagram for the process generating a query $\vec{q}$ is shown in Figure 4. Vertices are marked with random variables E, T, Z, W whose instantiations are specific values $e, t, \vec{z}, w \in q$.

The hidden variables of interest are the binary $Z \in \{h, s\}$, for selecting between type hint (h) and selector (s) words; and T, the type of one query. Each query picks one hidden value t, and a vector of $|q|$ size for Z, denoted $\vec{z}$. The only observed variables are the $|q|$ query words ($w_j : j = 1, \ldots, |q|$). Also, $\alpha, \beta, \gamma, \delta$ are hyper-parameters tuned globally across queries.

In the end we are interested in $\arg\max_e \Pr(e|\vec{q})$, where

$$\Pr(e|\vec{q}) \propto \Pr(e, \vec{q}) = \Pr(e) \Pr(\vec{q}|e) = \Pr(e) \sum_{t, \vec{z}} \Pr(\vec{q}, t, \vec{z}|e)$$

$$= \Pr(e) \sum_{t, \vec{z}} \Pr(t|e) \underline{\Pr(\vec{z}|e, t)} \Pr(\vec{q}|e, t, \vec{z}) \quad (14)$$

$$\approx \Pr(e) \sum_{t, \vec{z}} \Pr(t|e) \underline{\Pr(\vec{z})} \Pr(\vec{q}|e, t, \vec{z}) \quad (15)$$

$$= \Pr(e) \sum_{t, \vec{z}} \underbrace{\Pr(t|e)}_{(4)} \Pr(\vec{z}) \underbrace{\Pr(h(\vec{q}, \vec{z})|t)}_{(9)} \underbrace{\Pr(s(\vec{q}, \vec{z})|e)}_{(13)}.$$

To get from (14) to (15) we make the simplifying assumption that the density of hint words in queries is independent of the candidate entity and type. As mentioned before, adding over $t, \vec{z}$ is feasible for telegraphic queries because they are short. The prior $\Pr(e)$ may be uninformative (i.e., uniform), or set proportional to $|S_e|$ [22], or use shrunk estimates from answer types in the past. We use $\Pr(e) = |S_e|/\sum_{e'} |S_{e'}|$.

If we allow a query word to represent both a type hint and a selector, the clean separation after (15) no longer works, but it is possible to extend the framework using a soft-OR expression. We omit details owing to space constraints.

4.6 Explaining a top-ranking entity

In standard text search, top-ranking URLs are accompanied by a summary with matching query words highlighted. In our system, top-ranking entities need to be justified by explaining to the user how the query was interpreted. Specifically, we need to show the user the inferred type, and the inferred purpose (hint or selector) of each query word.

$$\Pr(t, \vec{z}|e, \vec{q}) \propto \Pr(e, t, \vec{q}, \vec{z})$$
$$= \Pr(e) \Pr(t|e) \underline{\Pr(\vec{z}|e, t)} \Pr(\vec{q}|e, t, \vec{z})$$
$$\approx \Pr(e) \Pr(t|e) \underline{\Pr(\vec{z})} \Pr(\vec{q}|e, t, \vec{z}) \quad (16)$$

approximating $\Pr(\vec{z}|e, t) \approx \Pr(\vec{z})$ as before. Now we can report $\arg\max_{t, \vec{z}} \Pr(t, \vec{z}|e, \vec{q})$ as the explanation for e. It is also possible to report marginals such as $\Pr(t|e, \vec{q})$ or $\Pr(z_j|e, \vec{q})$ this way.

4.7 Potential pitfalls

As often happens, a generative formulation starts out feeling natural, but is soon mired in a number of questionable assumptions and tuned hyper parameters. In recent times, this story has played out in many problems, such as information extraction [32] and learning to rank [21], where generative language models were proposed earlier, but the latest algorithms are all discriminatively trained. The above formulation has several potential shortcomings:

- The modeling of $\Pr(t|e)$ is necessarily a compromise.
- $\Pr(z_j)$ is assumed to be independent of q and e, and iid. These assumptions may not be the best.
- In the interest of computational feasibility, the language models for both types and snippets are simplistic. Phrase and exact matches are difficult to capture.
- Hyper parameters $\alpha, \beta, \gamma, \delta$ can only be tuned by sweeping ranges; no effective learning technique is obvious.
- As often happens with complex generative models, the scales of probabilities being multiplied (15) are diverse and hard to balance.

5. DISCRIMINATIVE FORMULATION

Instead of designing conditional distributions as in Section 4, here we will design feature functions, and learn weights corresponding to them by using relevant and (samples of) irrelevant entity sets $\mathcal{E}_q^+, \mathcal{E}_q^-$ associated with each query q, as is standard in learning to rank [21]. The benefit is that it is much safer to incrementally add highly informative but strongly correlated features (such as exact phrase match, match with and without stemming, etc.) to discriminative formulations.

Standard notation used in structured max-margin learning uses $\phi(x, y) \in \mathbb{R}^d$ as the feature map, where x is an observation and y is the label to be predicted. A *model* $\lambda \in \mathbb{R}^d$ is fitted so that $\lambda \cdot \phi(x, y_{\text{correct}}) > \lambda \cdot \phi(x, y_{\text{incorrect}})$. Once λ gets fixed via training, given a new text instance x_{test}, *inference* is the process of finding $\arg\max_y \lambda \cdot \phi(x_{\text{test}}, y)$.

In our case, we use the notation $\phi(q, e, t, \vec{z})$ for the feature map. q gives us access to the sequence of words in the query, and is the analog of x above. e gives us access to the snippets S_e that support e, and is the analog of y above. t and $\vec{z}$ are *latent variable* [40] inputs to the feature map whose role will be explained shortly.

Guided by the generative formulation in Section 4, we partition the feature vector as follows:

$$\phi(q,e,t,\vec{z}) = \big(\phi_1(q,e), \phi_2(t,e), \phi_3(q,\vec{z},t), \phi_4(q,\vec{z},e)\big), \quad (17)$$

where
- $\phi_1(q,e)$ models the prior for e.
- $\phi_2(t,e)$ models the prior $\Pr(t|e)$.
- $\phi_3(q,\vec{z},t)$ models the compatibility between the type hint part of query words and the proposed type t.
- $\phi_4(q,\vec{z},e)$ models the compatibility between the selector part of query words and $\mathcal{S}_e$.

5.1 Features ϕ_1 modeling entity prior

In Section 4.5 we used $\Pr(e) = |\mathcal{S}_e|/\sum_{e'} |\mathcal{S}_{e'}|$ as a prior probability for e. It is natural to make this one element in ϕ_1. But the discriminative setup allows us to introduce other powerful features.

$|\mathcal{S}_e|$ does not distinguish between snippets that match the query well vs. poorly. Let $\mathrm{IDF}(w)$ be the inverse document frequency [2] of query word w, and $\mathrm{IDF}(q) = \sum_{w \in q} \mathrm{IDF}(w)$. $c \cap q$ is the set of query words found in snippet c, with total $\mathrm{IDF}(c \cap q) = \sum_{w \in c \cap q} \mathrm{IDF}(w)$. Then the match-quality-weighted snippet support for e is characterized as

$$\phi_1(q,e)[\cdot] = \frac{1}{2^{|q|}\mathrm{IDF}(q)} \sum_{c \in \mathcal{S}_e} \mathrm{IDF}(c \cap q), \quad (18)$$

where $2^{|q|}\mathrm{IDF}(q)$ normalizes the feature across diverse queries.

Another feature in ϕ_1 relates to negative evidence. If there are other words present, a query that directly mentions an entity is hardly ever answered correctly by that entity; Tom_Cruise could not be the answer for the query `tom cruise wife`. Another (0/1) element in ϕ_1 is whether a description ("lemma") of e is contained in the query. In our experiments, the model element in λ corresponding to this feature turns out a negative number, as expected.

5.2 Features ϕ_2 modeling type prior

We have already proposed one way to estimate $\Pr(t|e)$ in Section 4.1. This estimate a natural element in ϕ_2. We can also help the learner use the generality or specificity of types, measured as this feature: $|\{e : e \in^+ t\}|/|\mathcal{E}|$. In our experiments, the element of λ corresponding to this feature also got negative values, indicating preference of specific types over generic ones. This corroborates earlier observation regarding the depth of desired types in a hierarchy [5].

5.3 Hint-type compatibility features ϕ_3

Given the input parameters of $\phi_3(\vec{q},\vec{z},t)$, we compute the hint word subsequence $h(\vec{q},\vec{z})$ as in (2). Now we can define any number of features between these hint words and the given type t, which has lemma set $L(t)$.
- A standard feature borrowed from (9) is $\Pr(h(\vec{q},\vec{z})|t)$.
- Unlike in the generative formulation, we can add synthetic features. E.g., a feature that has value 1 if ℓ matches the subsequence $h(\vec{q},\vec{z})$ exactly.
- In Section 4, the size of $h(\vec{q},\vec{z})$ was drawn from a binomial distribution controlled by hyper parameter δ. To model more general distributions, we use binary features of the form

$$\begin{cases} 1, & |h(\vec{q},\vec{z})| < k \\ 0, & \text{otherwise} \end{cases}$$

for $k = 1, \ldots$, to capture the belief that smaller number of hint words is preferable.

5.4 Selector-snippets compatibility features ϕ_4

Now consider q and its selectors $s(\vec{q},\vec{z}) \subseteq q$ as word sets (no duplicates), and the snippets $\mathcal{S}_e$ supporting candidate entity e. $\phi_4(q,\vec{z},e)$ will include feature/s that express the extent of match or compatibility between the selector words and the snippets. We need to characterize and then combine two kinds of signals here:
- The rarity (hence, informativeness) of a subset of $s(\vec{q},\vec{z})$ that match in snippets, and
- The number of supporting snippets [22] that match a given word set.

(A third kind of signal, proximity [27, 37, 36], is favored indirectly, because snippets have limited width. A more refined treatment of proximity is left for future work.)

A snippet $c \in \mathcal{S}_e$, interpreted as a subset of query words q, covers $s(\vec{q},\vec{z})$ if $c \supseteq s(\vec{q},\vec{z})$. Otherwise $c \subset s(\vec{q},\vec{z})$. Recall every snippet c has an $\mathrm{IDF}(c) = \sum_{w \in c \cap q} \mathrm{IDF}(w)$. We propose two features:

$$\frac{1}{2^{|q|}\mathrm{IDF}(q)} \sum_{c \supseteq s(\vec{q},\vec{z})} \mathrm{IDF}(s(\vec{q},\vec{z}))$$

$$= \frac{\mathrm{IDF}(s(\vec{q},\vec{z}))\,|\{c : c \supseteq s(\vec{q},\vec{z})\}|}{2^{|q|}\mathrm{IDF}(q)} \quad (19)$$

and

$$\frac{1}{2^{|q|}\mathrm{IDF}(q)} \sum_{c \subset s(\vec{q},\vec{z})} \mathrm{IDF}(c). \quad (20)$$

We found the separation above to be superior to collapsing covering and non-covering snippets into one sum. Another useful feature was the fraction of snippets c such that $c = q$ (exactly matching all query words).

5.5 Inference and training

With a wrong choice of hint-selector partition $\vec{z}$, or a wrong choice of type t, even a highly relevant response e could score very poorly. Therefore, any reasonable scoring scheme should evaluate e under the *best* choice of $t, \vec{z}$. I.e., the score of e should be

$$\max_{t: e \in^+ t, \vec{z}} \lambda \cdot \phi(q,e,t,\vec{z}). \quad (21)$$

(Note that t ranges over only those types to which e belongs.) In learning to rank [21], three training paradigms are commonly used: itemwise, pairwise and listwise. Because of the added complexity from the latent variables $t, \vec{z}$, here we discuss itemwise and pairwise training. Pairwise linear discrimination [19] remains an effective approach for learning to rank. Listwise training is left for future work, as is the use of nonlinear models like boosted regression trees.

In itemwise training, each response entity e is one item, which can be good (relevant, denoted e_+) or bad (irrelevant, denoted e_-). Following standard max-margin methodology, we want

$$\forall q, e_+: \quad \max_{t,\vec{z}} \lambda \cdot \phi(q,e_+,t,\vec{z}) \geq 1 - \xi_{q,e_+}, \text{ and} \quad (22)$$

$$\forall q, e_-: \quad \max_{t,\vec{z}} \lambda \cdot \phi(q,e_-,t,\vec{z}) \leq 1 + \xi_{q,e_-}, \quad (23)$$

where $\xi_{q,e_+}, \xi_{q,e_-} \geq 0$ are the usual SVM-style slack variables. Constraint (23) is easy to handle by breaking it up into the conjunct:

$$\forall q, e_-, \forall t, \vec{z}: \quad \lambda \cdot \phi(q, e, t, \vec{z}) \leq 1 + \xi_{q,e_-}. \quad (24)$$

However, (22) is a *disjunctive* constraint, as also arises in multiple instance classification or ranking [7]. A common way of dealing with this is to modify constraint (22) into

$$\forall q, e_+: \sum_{t,\vec{z}} u(q, e_+, t, \vec{z}) \lambda \cdot \phi(q, e_+, t, \vec{z}) \geq 1 - \xi_{q,e_+} \quad (25)$$

where $u(q, e, t, \vec{z}) \in \{0, 1\}$ and

$$\forall q, e_+: \quad \sum_{t,\vec{z}} u(q, e_+, t, \vec{z}) = 1.$$

This is an integer program, so the next step is to relax the new variables to $0 \leq u(q, e, t, \vec{z}) \leq 1$ (i.e., the $(t, \vec{z})$-simplex). Unfortunately, owing to the introduction of new variables $u(\cdots)$ and multiplication with old variables λ, the optimization is no longer convex.

Bergeron et al. [7] propose an alternating optimization: holding one of u and λ fixed, optimize the other, and repeat (there are no theoretical guarantees). Note that if λ is fixed, the optimization of u is a simple linear program. If u is fixed, the optimization of λ is comparable to training a standard SVM. The objective would then take the form

$$\tfrac{1}{2}\|\lambda\|^2 + \frac{C}{|\mathcal{Q}|} \sum_{q \in \mathcal{Q}} \frac{\sum_{e_+ \in \mathcal{E}_q^+} \xi_{q,e_+} + \sum_{e_- \in \mathcal{E}_q^-} \xi_{q,e_-}}{|\mathcal{E}_q^+| + |\mathcal{E}_q^-|} \quad (26)$$

Here $C > 0$ is the usual SVM parameter trading off training loss against model complexity. Note that u does not appear in the objective.

In our application, $\phi(q, e, t, \vec{z}) \geq \vec{0}$. Suppose $\lambda \geq \vec{0}$ in some iteration (which easily happens in our application). In that case, to satisfy constraint (25), it suffices to set only one element in u to 1, corresponding to $\arg\max_{t,\vec{z}} \lambda \cdot \phi(q, e, t, \vec{z})$, and the rest to 0s. In other words, a particular $(t, \vec{z})$ is chosen ignoring all others. This severely restricts the search space over u, λ in subsequent iterations and has greater chance of getting stuck in a local minima.

To mitigate this problem, we propose the following annealing protocol. The u distribution collapse reduces entropy suddenly. The remedy is to subtract from the objective (to be minimized) a term related to the entropy of the u distribution:

$$(26) + D \sum_{q,e_+} \sum_{t,\vec{z}} u(q, e_+, t, \vec{z}) \log u(q, e_+, t, \vec{z}). \quad (27)$$

Here $D \geq 0$ is a temperature parameter that is gradually reduced in powers of 10 toward zero with the alternative iterations optimizing u and λ. Note that the objective (27) is convex in u, λ and ξ_*. Moreover, with either u or λ fixed, all constraints are linear inequalities.

1: initialize u to random values on the simplex
2: initialize D to some positive value
3: **while** not reached local optimum **do**
4: fix u and solve quadratic program to get next λ
5: reduce D geometrically
6: fix λ and solve convex program for next u

Figure 5: Pseudocode for discriminative training.

Very little changes if we extend from itemwise to pairwise training, except the optimization gets slower, because of the sheer number of pair constraints of the form:

$$\forall q, e_+, e_-: \max_{t,\vec{z}} \lambda \cdot \phi(q, e_+, t, \vec{z}) - \max_{t,\vec{z}} \lambda \cdot \phi(q, e_-, t, \vec{z})$$
$$\geq 1 - \xi_{q,e_+,e_-}. \quad (28)$$

The itemwise objective in (26) changes to the pairwise objectice

$$\tfrac{1}{2}\|\lambda\|^2 + \frac{C}{|\mathcal{Q}|} \sum_{q \in \mathcal{Q}} \frac{1}{|\mathcal{E}_q^+| |\mathcal{E}_q^-|} \sum_{e_+ \in \mathcal{E}_q^+, e_- \in \mathcal{E}_q^-} \xi_{q,e_+,e_-}. \quad (29)$$

For clarity, first we rewrite (28) as

$$\forall q, e_+, e_-: \quad \max_{t,\vec{z}} \lambda \cdot \phi(q, e_+, t, \vec{z})$$
$$\geq 1 - \xi_{q,e_+,e_-} + \max_{t',\vec{z}'} \lambda \cdot \phi(q, e_-, t', \vec{z}').$$

Then we pull out $t', \vec{z}'$:

$$\forall q, e_+, e_-, t', \vec{z}': \quad \max_{t,\vec{z}} \lambda \cdot \phi(q, e_+, t, \vec{z})$$
$$\geq 1 - \xi_{q,e_+,e_-} + \lambda \cdot \phi(q, e_-, t', \vec{z}').$$

Finally, we use a new set of u variables to convert this to an alternating optimization as before:

$$\forall q, e_+, e_-, t', \vec{z}': \quad \sum_{t,\vec{z}} u(q, e_+, t, \vec{z}) \lambda \cdot \phi(q, e_+, t, \vec{z})$$
$$\geq 1 - \xi_{q,e_+,e_-} + \lambda \cdot \phi(q, e_-, t', \vec{z}'). \quad (30)$$

These enhancements do not change the basic nature of the optimization.

5.6 Implementation details

5.6.1 Reducing computational requirements

The space of $(q, e, t, \vec{z})$ and especially their discriminative constraints can become prohibitively large. To keep RAM and CPU needs practical, we used the following policies; our experimental results are insensitive to them.

- We sampled down bad (irrelevant) entities e_- that were allowed to generate constraint (28).
- For empty $h(\vec{q}, \vec{z}) = \varnothing$, $\phi_3(q, \vec{z}, t)$ provides no signal. In such cases, we allow t to take only one value: the most generic type `Entity`.

5.6.2 Explaining a top-ranking entity

This is even simpler in the discriminative setting than in the generative setting; we can simply use (21) to report $\arg\max_{t,\vec{z}} \lambda \cdot \phi(q, e, t, \vec{z})$.

5.6.3 Implementing a target type predictor

Extending the above scheme, each entity e scores each candidate types t as $score(t|e) = \max_{\vec{z}} \lambda \cdot \phi(\cdot, e, t, \vec{z})$. This induces a ranking over types for each entity. We can choose the overall type predicted by the query as the one whose sum of ranks among the top-k entities is smallest. An apparently crude approximation would be to predict the best type for the single top-ranked entity. But $k > 1$ can stabilize the predicted type, in case the top entity is incorrect. (We may want to predict a single type as a feedback to the user, or to compare with other type prediction systems, but, as we shall see, not for the best quality of entity ranking, which is best done collectively.)

6. EXPERIMENTS

6.1 Testbed

6.1.1 Catalog and annotated corpus

Our type and entity catalog was YAGO [35], with about 200,000 types and 1.9 million entities. An annotator trained on mentions of these entities in Wikipedia[2] was applied [12] over a Web corpus from a commercial search engine, having 500 million spam-free Web pages. This resulted in about 8 billion entity annotations, average 16 annotations per page. These were then indexed [13].

6.1.2 Type constrained entity search

The index supports semistructured queries specified by:
- an answer type t from among the 200,000 YAGO types,
- a bag of words and phrases in a IDF-WAND (weak-and) operator [11], and
- a snippet window width.

A DAAT [11] query processor returns a stream of snippets at most as wide as the given window width limit, that contain a mention of some entity $e \in^+ t$ and satisfies the WAND predicate. In case of phrases in the query, the WAND threshold is computed by adding the IDF of constituent words.

Our query processor is implemented using MG4J [9] in Java, with no index caching. Basic keyword WAND queries take a few seconds over 500 million documents. Setting $t = \texttt{Entity}$, the root type, and asking for a stream of all entities in qualifying snippets, slows down the query by a small factor. A discriminative snippet scoring and aggregation technique [34] achieves entity ranking accuracy superior to recent approaches.

6.2 Queries with ground truth

We use 709 entity search queries collected from many years of TREC and INEX competitions, along with relevant and irrelevant entities. Two paid masters students, familiar with Web search engines, read the full TREC/INEX description of entity search queries and wrote out queries they would naturally issue to a commercial search engine. They also selected the best (as per their judgment) type from YAGO for each query, as ground truth. The distribution of types is heavy-tailed, with 69% of the atypes in this list occurring only once and top four atypes accounting for one third of queries. The atypes towards top are mostly generic (*location*, *person*, etc.), while those toward the bottom are more specific (*Brooklyn_Dodgers_players*, *Dilbert_characters* etc.). This data is publicly available at bit.ly/WSpxvr. Launching the queries with the known types resulted in 380 million snippets supporting candidate entities; these are also available on request. We also performed type prediction (Section 5.6.3) on dataset provided in [5]. Since this dataset does not contain ground truth of relevant entities for each query, we did not test entity ranking.

6.3 Generic and "perfect" baselines

The ranking accuracy of a reasonable query interpreter algorithm in our framework will lie between two baselines:

Generic: The generic baseline assumes zero knowledge of query types, instead using $t = \texttt{Entity}$, the root/s of the type hierarchy in the catalog.

---
[2]Cross validated accuracy on Wikipedia was about 90%.

"Perfect": The "perfect" baseline assumes complete (human-provided) knowledge of the type and uses it in the semistructured query launched over the catalog and annotated corpus.

Of course, even "perfect" may perform poorly in some queries, because of lack of support for relevant entities in the corpus, snippets incorrectly or not annotated (both false positive and negative), incorrect absence of paths between types and entities in the catalog, or some inadequacy of the type-constrained entity ranker. It is also possible for an algorithm (including ours) to perform worse than generic on some queries, by choosing a particularly unfortunate type, but obviously it should do better than generic on average, to be useful.

6.4 Measurements and results

As is standard in entity ranking research, we report NDCG at various ranks, mean reciprocal rank (MRR, not truncated) and mean average precision (MAP) at the entity (not document) level. Space constraints prevent us from defining these; see Liu [21] for details. For Discriminative, C is tuned by 5-fold cross validation at the query level. For Generative, we swept over $\alpha, \beta, \gamma, \delta$ in powers of 10 (e.g. $10^{-5}, 10^{-4}, \ldots, 1$).

	Generic	Generative	Discriminative	Perfect
MAP	0.323↓↓	0.414↓	**0.462**	0.644
MRR	0.332↓↓	0.432↓	**0.481**	0.664

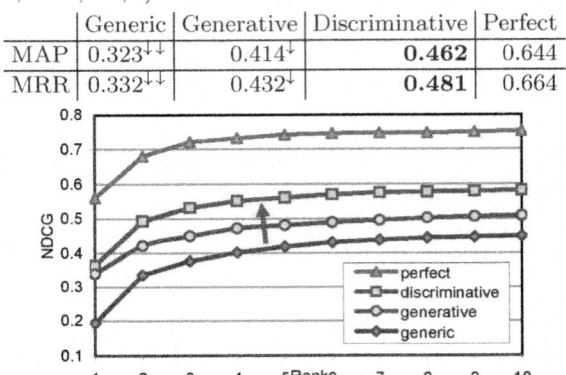

Figure 6: Generic, generative, discriminative and "perfect" accuracies.

6.4.1 Our algorithms vs. generic and perfect

For our techniques to be useful, they must bridge a substantial part of the gap between the generic lower bound and the perfect upper bound. Figure 6 confirms that Generative bridges 28% of the MAP gap between generic and perfect, whereas discriminative is significantly better at 43%. MRR and NDCG follow similar trends. All gaps are statistically significant at 95% confidence level (indicated by ↓).

Figure 6 is aggregated over all queries. Figure 7 focuses on average precision disaggregated into queries, comparing discriminative against generic. While some queries are damaged by discriminative, many more are improved.

Failure analysis revealed residual $(t, \vec{z})$ ambiguity, coupled with lack of $\in^+$ or $\subseteq^+$ paths in an incomplete catalog to be the major reasons for losses on some queries. Even though there is some ground yet to cover to reach "perfect" levels, these results show there is much hope for automatically interpreting even telegraphic queries.

6.4.2 Benefits of annealing optimization

Figure 8 shows that discriminative with our entropy-based annealing protocol performs significantly (marked with "↓")

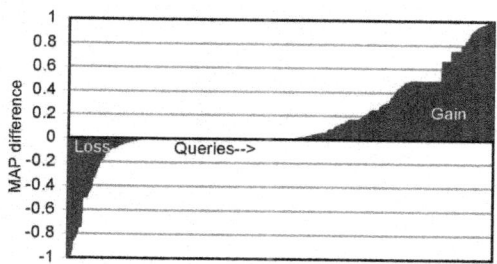

Figure 7: MAP of discriminative minus map of generic, compared query-wise between generic and discriminative. Below zero means discriminative did worse than generic on that query. Queries in (arbitrary) order of discriminative AP gain.

better than the scheme proposed by Bergeron et al.[7]. This may be of independent interest in multiple instance ranking and max-margin learning with latent variables.

	Bergeron (26)	Entropy (27)
MAP	0.416↓	**0.462**
MRR	0.432↓	**0.481**

Figure 8: Benefits of annealing protocol.

6.4.3 Comparison with B&N's type prediction

B&N [5] proposed two models, of which the "entity-centric" model was generally superior. Each entity e was associated with a textual description (e.g., Wikipedia page) which induced a smoothed language model θ_e. B&N estimate the score of type t as

$$\Pr(q|t) = \sum_{e \in +_t} \Pr(q|\theta_e) \Pr(e|t), \qquad (31)$$

where $\Pr(e|t)$ was set to uniform. Note that no corpus (apart from the one of entity descriptions) was used. The output of B&N's algorithm (hereafter, "B&N") is a ranked list of types, not entities. We implemented B&N, and obtained accuracy closely matching their published numbers, using the DBpedia catalog with 358 types, and 258 queries (different from our main query set and testbed).

	B&N	Discr($k=1$)	Discr($k=5$)	Discr($k=10$)
MAP	0.33	0.33	0.384	0.390

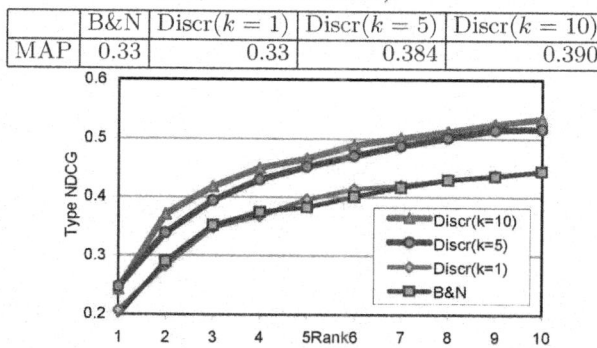

Figure 9: Type prediction by B&N vs. discriminative.

We turned our system into a type predictor (Section 5.6.3), and also used DBpedia like B&N and compared type prediction accuracy on dataset provided in [5]. Results are shown in Figure 9 after including the top k returned types. At $k=1$, our discriminative type prediction matches B&N, and larger k performs better, owing to stabilizing consensus from lower-ranked entities. Coupled with the results in Section 6.4.6, this is strong evidence that our unified formulation is superior, even if the goal is type prediction.

6.4.4 Comparison with B&N-based entity ranking

A type prediction may be less than ideal, and yet entity prediction may be fine. One can take the top type predicted by B&N, and launch an entity query (see Section 6.1.2) with that type restriction. To improve recall, we can also take the union of the top k predicted types. The result is a ranked list of entities, on which we can compute entity-level MAP, MRR, NDCG, as usual. In this setting, both B&N and our algorithm (discriminative) used YAGO as the catalog. Results for our dataset (Section 6.2) are shown in Figure 10.

k	MAP	MRR	%$\mathcal{Q}$ better	%$\mathcal{Q}$ worse
1	0.066	0.068	5.50	88.58
5	0.137	0.144	15.80	76.30
10	0.171	0.180	20.73	69.53
15	0.201	0.211	24.54	63.47
20	0.204	0.215	26.80	60.51
25	0.222	0.233	29.34	56.84
30	0.232	0.244	29.76	55.01
Generic	0.323	0.432	—	—

Figure 10: B&N-driven entity ranking accuracy.

We were surprised to see the low entity ranking accuracy of B&N (which is why we recreated very closely their reported type ranking accuracy on DBpedia). Closer scrutiny revealed that the main reason for lower accuracy was changing the type catalog from DBpedia (358 types) to YAGO (over 200,000 types). Entity ranking accuracy is low because B&N's type prediction accuracy is very low on YAGO: 0.04 MRR, 0.04 MAP, and 0.058 NDCG@10. For comparison, our type prediction accuracy is 0.348 MRR, 0.348 MAP, and 0.475 NDCG@10. This is entirely because of corpus/snippet signal: if we switch off snippet-based features ϕ_4, our accuracy also plummets. The moral seems to be, large organic type catalogs provide enough partial and spurious matches for *any* choice of hints, so it is essential (and rewarding) to exploit corpus signals.

6.4.5 Role of the corpus

A minimally modified B&N that uses the corpus may replace Wikipedia entity descriptions with corpus-driven descriptions, i.e., a pseudo-document made up of all snippets retrieved for a particular entity from the corpus. As we see in Figure 11, ranking accuracy improves marginally. This indicates that in the case of Web-scale entity search, an imperfectly annotated corpus can prove to be more useful than a small human-curated information source.

k	MAP	MRR	%$\mathcal{Q}$ better	%$\mathcal{Q}$ worse
1	0.070	0.078	5.08	88.01
5	0.163	0.170	15.94	73.77
10	0.213	0.222	22.28	63.47
15	0.237	0.246	26.66	55.99
20	0.270	0.279	29.34	49.65
25	0.277	0.287	30.89	45.98
30	0.287	0.299	32.16	42.45
Generic	0.323	0.432	—	—

Figure 11: B&N-driven entity ranking accuracy with corpus-driven entity description.

On an average, B&N type prediction, followed by query launch, seems worse than generic. This is almost entirely because of choosing bad types for many, but not all queries. There *are* queries where B&N shows a (e.g., MAP) lift beyond generic, but they are just too few (Figure 12).

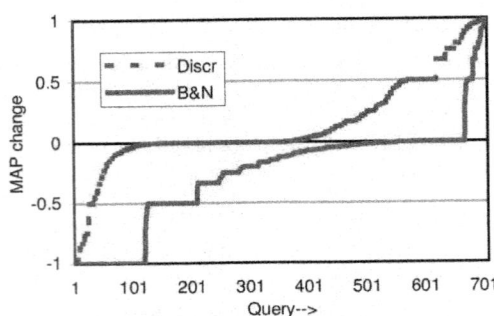

Figure 12: 2-stage entity ranking via B&N does boost accuracy for some queries, but the overall effect is negative. Joint interpretation and ranking also damages some queries but improves many more.

6.4.6 Benefits of joint inference

The beneficial role of the corpus is now established, but is *joint* inference really necessary, if a good query type interpreter were available? To test this in a controlled setting, we run our system, throw away the ranked entity list, and only retain the predicted type (Section 5.6.3), then launch a query restricted to this type (Section 6.1.2) and measure entity ranking accuracy.

	Joint	2-stage ($k=1$)	2-stage ($k=5$)	2-stage ($k=10$)
MAP	**0.462**	0.370↓	0.361↓	0.365↓
MRR	**0.481**	0.384↓	0.375↓	0.377↓

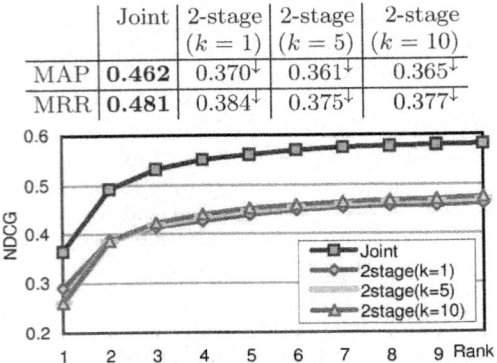

Figure 13: Joint inference improves entity ranking quality compared to 2-stage.

Figure 13 shows that the result is significantly (shown by "↓") less accurate than via joint inference, even after tuning k, which indicates that no *single* inferred type may retain enough information for the best entity ranking, and that *joint* inference is indeed vital.

6.4.7 Coarse DBpedia types with Web corpus

A plausible counter-argument to the above experiments is that, by moving from only 358 DBpedia types to over 20,000 YAGO types, we are making the type prediction problem hopelessly difficult for B&N, and that this level of type refinement is unnecessary for high accuracy in entity search. We modified our system to use types from DBpedia, and correspondingly re-indexed our Web corpus annotations using DBpedia types. As partial confirmation of the above hypothesis, the entity ranking accuracy using B&N did increase substantially. However, as shown in Figure 14, the entity ranking accuracy achieved by our discriminative algorithm remains unbeaten. Also compare with Figure 6 — whereas B&N improves by coarsening the type system, our discriminative algorithm seems to be degraded by this move.

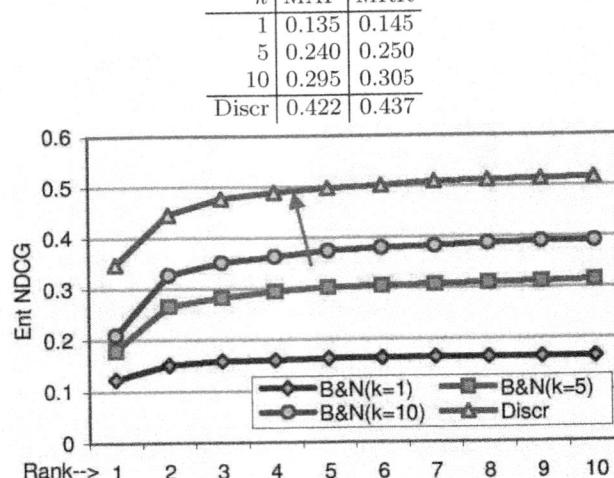

k	MAP	MRR
1	0.135	0.145
5	0.240	0.250
10	0.295	0.305
Discr	0.422	0.437

Figure 14: Entity ranking accuracy using DBpedia types.

6.4.8 DEANNA on telegraphic queries

We also tried to use the Web interface to send a sample of our telegraphic queries and their well-formed sentence counterparts to DEANNA [39] and receive back the interpretation. We manually inspected their output. Some anecdotes are shown in Figure 15. The queries are from Figure 3. None of the telegraphic queries was successfully interpreted. The well-formed questions saw partial success.

QID	Well-formed	Telegraphic
Q1	Missing target type	Empty
Q2	Incorrect, missed Wikipedia type "list of cities in China"	Incorrect fragments
Q3	Incorrect target type (painting)	Empty
Q4	Incorrect fragments	Incorrect fragments
Q5	Incorrect fragments	Empty
Q6	No target type	Empty

Figure 15: DEANNA interpretations of some of our queries.

7. CONCLUSION

We initiated a study of generative and discriminative formulations for joint query interpretation and response ranking, in the context of targeted-type entity search needs expressed in a natural "telegraphic" Web query style. Using 380 million snippets from a Web-scale corpus with 500 million documents annotated at 8 billion places with over 1.5 million entities and 200,000 types from YAGO, we showed experimentally that jointly interpreting target type and ranking responses is superior to a two-phase interpret-then-execute paradigm.

Our work opens up several directions for further research. Our notion of selectors can be readily generalized to allow mentions of entities as literals [15, 26] in the query. More sophisticated training using bundle methods may further improve the discriminative formulation. Finally, modeling listwise [21] losses, and/or exploring more powerful non-linear scoring functions (e.g., via boosting) may also help.

8. REFERENCES

[1] G. Agarwal, G. Kabra, and K. C.-C. Chang. Towards rich query interpretation: walking back and forth for mining query templates. In *WWW Conference*, pages 1–10. ACM, 2010.

[2] R. A. Baeza-Yates and B. Ribeiro-Neto. *Modern Information Retrieval*. Addison-Wesley Longman Publishing Co., Inc., Boston, MA, USA, 1999.

[3] K. Balog, L. Azzopardi, and M. de Rijke. Formal models for expert finding in enterprise corpora. In *SIGIR Conference*, pages 43–50, 2006.

[4] K. Balog, L. Azzopardi, and M. de Rijke. A language modeling framework for expert finding. *Information Processing and Management*, 45(1):1–19, 2009.

[5] K. Balog and R. Neumayer. Hierarchical target type identification for entity-oriented queries. In *CIKM*, pages 2391–2394. ACM, 2012.

[6] M. Bendersky, W. Croft, and D. Smith. Two-stage query segmentation for information retrieval. In *SIGIR Conference*, pages 810–811. ACM, 2009.

[7] C. Bergeron, J. Zaretzki, C. Breneman, and K. P. Bennett. Multiple instance ranking. In *ICML*, pages 48–55. ACM, 2008.

[8] D. M. Blei, A. Y. Ng, and M. I. Jordan. Latent dirichlet allocation. *Journal of Machine Learning Research*, 3:993–1022, 2003.

[9] P. Boldi and S. Vigna. MG4J at TREC 2005. In E. M. Voorhees and L. P. Buckland, editors, *TREC*, number SP 500-266 in Special Publications. NIST, 2005.

[10] A. Broder. A taxonomy of web search. *SIGIR Forum*, 36(2):3–10, 2002.

[11] A. Z. Broder, D. Carmel, M. Herscovici, A. Soffer, and J. Zien. Efficient query evaluation using a two-level retrieval process. In *CIKM*, pages 426–434. ACM, 2003.

[12] S. Chakrabarti, S. Kasturi, B. Balakrishnan, G. Ramakrishnan, and R. Saraf. Compressed data structures for annotated web search. In *WWW Conference*, pages 121–130, 2012.

[13] S. Chakrabarti, D. Sane, and G. Ramakrishnan. Web-scale entity-relation search architecture (poster). In *WWW Conference*, pages 21–22, 2011.

[14] R. Fagin, B. Kimelfeld, Y. Li, S. Raghavan, and S. Vaithyanathan. Understanding queries in a search database system. In *PODS Conference*, pages 273–284. ACM, 2010.

[15] J. Guo, G. Xu, X. Cheng, and H. Li. Named entity recognition in query. In *SIGIR Conference*, pages 267–274. ACM, 2009.

[16] J. Hoffart et al. Robust disambiguation of named entities in text. In *EMNLP Conference*, pages 782–792, Edinburgh, Scotland, UK, July 2011. SIGDAT.

[17] J. Hu, G. Wang, F. Lochovsky, J.-t. Sun, and Z. Chen. Understanding user's query intent with Wikipedia. In *WWW Conference*, pages 471–480. ACM, 2009.

[18] B. J. Jansen, D. L. Booth, and A. Spink. Determining the informational, navigational, and transactional intent of Web queries. *Information Processing and Management*, 44(3):1251–1266, May 2008.

[19] T. Joachims. Optimizing search engines using clickthrough data. In *SIGKDD Conference*, pages 133–142. ACM, 2002.

[20] S. Kulkarni, A. Singh, G. Ramakrishnan, and S. Chakrabarti. Collective annotation of Wikipedia entities in Web text. In *SIGKDD Conference*, pages 457–466, 2009.

[21] T.-Y. Liu. Learning to rank for information retrieval. In *Foundations and Trends in Information Retrieval*, volume 3, pages 225–331. Now Publishers, 2009.

[22] C. Macdonald and I. Ounis. Learning models for ranking aggregates. In *Advances in Information Retrieval*, volume 6611 of *LNCS*, pages 517–529. 2011.

[23] A. McCallum and K. Nigam. A comparison of event models for naive Bayes text classification. In *AAAI/ICML-98 Workshop on Learning for Text Categorization*, pages 41–48. AAAI Press, 1998.

[24] J. W. Murdock, A. Kalyanpur, C. Welty, J. Fan, D. A. Ferrucci, D. C. Gondek, L. Zhang, and H. Kanayama. Typing candidate answers using type coercion. *IBM Journal of Research and Development*, 56(3/4):7:1–7:13, 2012.

[25] P. Pantel and A. Fuxman. Jigs and lures: Associating web queries with structured entities. In *ACL Conference*, pages 83–92, Portland, Oregon, USA, June 2011.

[26] P. Pantel, T. Lin, and M. Gamon. Mining entity types from query logs via user intent modeling. In *ACL Conference*, pages 563–571, Jeju Island, Korea, July 2012.

[27] D. Petkova and W. B. Croft. Proximity-based document representation for named entity retrieval. In *CIKM*, pages 731–740. ACM, 2007.

[28] J. Pound, A. K. Hudek, I. F. Ilyas, and G. Weddell. Interpreting keyword queries over Web knowledge bases. In *CIKM*, 2012.

[29] J. Pound, I. F. Ilyas, and G. Weddell. Expressive and flexible access to Web-extracted data: a keyword-based structured query language. In *SIGMOD Conference*, pages 423–434. ACM, 2010.

[30] J. Pound, S. Paparizos, and P. Tsaparas. Facet discovery for structured Web search: a query-log mining approach. In *SIGMOD Conference*, pages 169–180, 2011.

[31] H. Raviv, D. Carmel, and O. Kurland. A ranking framework for entity oriented search using Markov random fields. In *Joint International Workshop on Entity-Oriented and Semantic Search*, pages 1:1–1:6, Portland, OR, 2012. ACM. Located with SIGIR Conference.

[32] S. Sarawagi. Information extraction. *FnT Databases*, 1(3), 2008.

[33] N. Sarkas, S. Paparizos, and P. Tsaparas. Structured annotations of Web queries. In *SIGMOD Conference*, 2010.

[34] U. Sawant and S. Chakrabarti. Features and aggregators for web-scale entity search. arXiv 1303.3164, 2013.

[35] F. M. Suchanek, G. Kasneci, and G. Weikum. YAGO: A core of semantic knowledge unifying WordNet and Wikipedia. In *WWW Conference*, pages 697–706. ACM Press, 2007.

[36] K. M. Svore, P. H. Kanani, and N. Khan. How good is a span of terms? exploiting proximity to improve Web retrieval. In *SIGIR Conference*, pages 154–161. ACM, 2010.

[37] T. Tao and C. Zhai. An exploration of proximity measures in information retrieval. In *SIGIR Conference*, pages 295–302. ACM, 2007.

[38] D. Vallet and H. Zaragoza. Inferring the most important types of a query: a semantic approach. In *SIGIR Conference*, pages 857–858. ACM, 2008.

[39] M. Yahya, K. Berberich, S. Elbassuoni, M. Ramanath, V. Tresp, and G. Weikum. Natural language questions for the Web of data. In *EMNLP Conference*, pages 379–390, Jeju Island, Korea, July 2012.

[40] C.-N. J. Yu and T. Joachims. Learning structural SVMs with latent variables. In *ICML*, pages 1169–1176. ACM, 2009.

[41] C. Zhai. Statistical language models for information retrieval: A critical review. *Foundations and Trends in Information Retrieval*, 2(3):137–213, Mar. 2008.

A Model for Green Design of Online News Media Services

Daniel Schien*
schien@cs.bris.ac.uk

Paul Shabajee*
paul.shabejee@bristol.ac.uk

Stephen G. Wood[±]
stephen.g.wood@guardian.co.uk

Chris Preist*
cpreist@cs.bris.ac.uk

*Department of Computer Science, University of Bristol, UK
[±]Center for Environmental Strategy, University of Surrey, UK and Guardian News Media, UK

ABSTRACT
The use of information and communication technology and the web-based products it provides is responsible for significant emissions of greenhouse gases. In order to enable the reduction of emissions during the design of such products, it is necessary to estimate as accurately as possible their carbon impact over the entire product system. In this work we describe a new method which combines models of energy consumption during the use of digital media with models of the behavior of the audience. We apply this method to conduct an assessment of the annual carbon emissions for the product suite of a major international news organization. We then demonstrate its use for green design by evaluating the impacts of five different interventions on the product suite. We find that carbon footprint of the online newspaper amounts to approximately 7700 tCO2e per year, of which 75% are caused by the user devices. Among the evaluated scenarios a significant uptake of eReaders in favor of PCs has the greatest reduction potential. Our results also show that even a significant reduction of data volume on a web page would only result in small overall energy savings.

Categories and Subject Descriptors
H.3.4 [**Systems and Software**]: Performance evaluation (efficiency and effectiveness)
C.4 [**Performance of Systems**]: Modeling techniques, Performance attributes

General Terms
Measurement, Design, Economics, Human Factors.

Keywords
Carbon footprinting; digital media; sustainability; green software engineering

1. INTRODUCTION
The use of information and communication technology (ICT) and the software services it provides via the Internet is responsible for significant global energy consumption and the resultant emissions of greenhouse gases often quantified as product energy and carbon footprints. It has been estimated by Malmodin et al. [32] that in the year 2007, such usage was responsible for 710 tera watt-hours (TWh) of electricity consumption – 3.9% of global production, resulting in emissions of 447 million tones carbon dioxide equivalent (tCO_2e).

While many of companies that provide these services consider and optimize the energy efficiency of their data centers, this is often a small part of the total energy consumed compared to other parts of the product system, in particular third-party data centers, networks and user devices such as PCs and tablets (Figure 1).

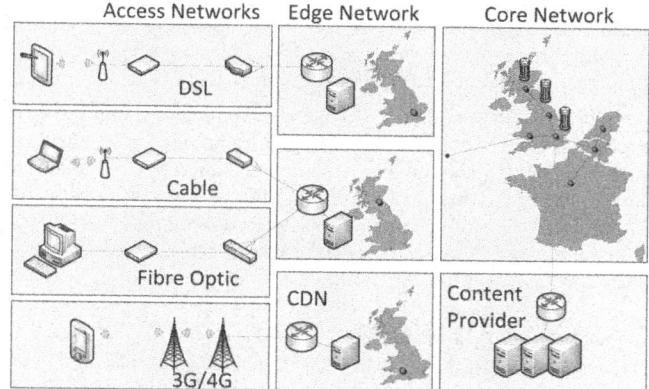

Figure 1 - Illustration of the service system. User devices connect with access network equipment via edge and core networks to the origin servers of the content provider and the CDN servers.

Design decisions by service providers regarding the architecture and use models of digital services can significantly influence their overall environmental impact. Such decisions may be taken explicitly with a view to reducing the overall energy and/or carbon impacts of their digital service, or may be decisions taken for other business reasons. In both cases, having an estimate of their likely resulting environmental impact will allow this factor to be considered alongside others when deciding whether to go ahead, or when considering which of several options to pursue.

The energy consumption by data centers and networks has recently received increasing attention by the engineering community. These efforts are directed to optimize the energy consumption in a single subsystem and can indirectly contribute to reductions of carbon footprints. However, in order to reduce the total energy consumption and avoid shifting burden between

Copyright is held by the International World Wide Web Conference Committee (IW3C2). IW3C2 reserves the right to provide a hyperlink to the author's site if the Material is used in electronic media.
WWW 2013, May 13–17, 2013, Rio de Janeiro, Brazil.
ACM 978-1-4503-2035-1 /13/05.

subsystems, a model of the end-to-end energy consumption is needed. In particular, a quantification of potential savings in subsystems outside the operational control of the service provider is needed to effectively support efforts to reduce energy and carbon footprints.

1.1 Contributions

In this paper, we present an analysis of the suite of digital services offered by Guardian News and Media Ltd (GNM) including the guardian.co.uk website read on PCs, smartphones and tablets and determine the current operational energy and carbon footprint of the end-to-end delivery of these services – that is the energy use required to operate the services at the time of service use. Such delivery involves servers (both at GNM and third parties), network equipment and end-user access equipment. The GNM is an example of a complex media organization providing a mix of digital products and as such the results of this work can be generalized more broadly.

Existing approaches to assessing energy consumption and carbon emissions of digital services use a Life Cycle Assessment (LCA) methodology [20], and adopt a model of an average or prototypical service user. Such an approach provides an estimate of the overall footprint, but is relatively limited when exploring interventions on the service architectural design. We go beyond this state-of-the-art by combining LCA techniques based on a detailed product model with detailed parameters of the behavior of users of the services, and in so doing produce the most accurately modeled assessment of energy use of a digital service conducted to-date. We achieve this by synthesizing models from the engineering disciplines of networks and user devices into an end-to-end model of energy consumption.

We then consider potential design interventions in this system, and quantitatively estimate the change in emissions each enables. We consider six interventions and assess their relative impact on energy use. In doing so, we present the first quantification of carbon reductions of such interventions on a digital service. These interventions are illustrative, and the model can be used to assess other such interventions on a service.

2. RELATED WORK

Our research draws on work in the industrial ecology and computer systems engineering communities. From industrial ecology, we adopt and adapt life cycle modeling techniques used to identify energy use and carbon emissions from the creation and delivery of a given product. Using techniques from computer systems engineering, we integrate these LCAs with models of data flow and energy use across the Internet.

2.1 Carbon and Energy Footprinting of Digital Products

Research in industrial ecology has developed techniques for the environmental assessment of physical products and services, in particular for product life cycle assessment [26]. Recently, work applying these techniques to the carbon and energy footprinting of digital products has been conducted.

These existing studies differ in the level of detail to which they model the digital product systems they consider. Two alternative modeling approaches exist: bottom-up or top-down. A top-down model measures or estimates the total energy use of an entire subsystem, for example 'all data centers' or 'the internet', measures or estimates the total quantity of a given service type provided, for example data transmitted, and divides the former by the latter to give the energy consumption per unit of service. Hence it treats a given subsystem as a black box, and does not model the usage of components within that subsystem by the digital product being assessed.

A bottom-up model on the other hand, includes a model of the subsystem and calculates the energy consumption by measuring or estimating the energy used by each component in delivering the digital product, and combining these figures to give a total. A bottom-up model of the energy consumption for Internet delivery, for example, sums the proportional energy consumption by each network device that plays a role in a typical route between two end points.

Neither approach is intrinsically more accurate than the other. However, only a bottom-up model provides the level of detail needed to assess the impact of a particular design change on the energy footprint of the entire system.

The majority of existing studies use primarily a top-down approach. Taylor and Koomey in [46] develop the most widely referenced top-down model of the energy footprint of data transfer in the Internet, and quantify an estimate of efficiency improvements over time. Due to an overly wide choice of system boundaries (what is included within the 'product system'), they are likely to have overestimated the energy consumption for data transport in the Internet. Weber et al. [49] use an extrapolated value from Taylor and Koomey's model in a comparison of the environmental impact of different methods for delivering music. Moberg et al. [35] also use this, combined with a bottom-up model of the local delivery system, to compare the impact of a printed newspaper and reading news with an e-reader. Teehan et al. [47] also apply Taylor and Koomey's model in conjunction with user behavioral data a study of user behavior by Beauvisage's [6] to estimate the total energy consumption in the US for a variety of digital activities.

A bottom-up model of energy consumption by servers was used by Chandaria et al. to analyze the carbon footprint of digital services at the BBC [11]. Some modeling simplifications, for example, assuming full utilization at nominal throughput rates, mean that they significantly underestimate server energy use. They also assume the energy consumption by networks to be negligible. Williams and Tang use a more realistic bottom-up model for the network although they underestimate the utilization of servers in their assessment of browsing a web shop and downloading a large file [50].

Baliga et al. [5] provide a detailed bottom-up model to estimate energy use of transmitting data through the Internet but exclude servers and end devices, and do not consider carbon emissions.

Our modeling work described below primarily uses a bottom-up approach, and draws on these results, but goes beyond them in several ways. Most notably, all other studies use aggregate data and assumptions regarding an average or prototypical user. We instead use behavioral data derived from web analytics software to estimate far more accurately the spread of behavior and characteristics within the user population, and to calculate energy consumption across this population. This results in a more accurate estimate of the total energy use, and also gives detailed and flexible model which allows the testing of the impact of alternate business and design interventions.

Finally, assessment standards for reporting of emissions by ICT equipment are currently being devised by several international organizations including ITU (International Telecom Union)[27] and GHG (Greenhouse Gas) Protocol [23]. These standards are not directly applicable in support of green design with the goal of reducing total emissions as they firstly, do not mandate the inclusion of scope 3 emissions and secondly suggest top-down modeling approaches which hide the detail required to guide design decision making.

For a more detailed discussion of these approaches, including analysis and critique of the assumptions and methods they use in comparison with our approach, see [42].

2.2 Green Engineering

Our work also draws from recent work on green software and system design in the engineering disciplines extending it through integration into an end-to-end model. It is this work which provides the white box perspective in a bottom-up model of a system.

Significant work already exists on green design of software. According to Nauman et al. [36] green software is that "whose direct and indirect negative impacts on economy, society, human beings, and environment that result from development, deployment, and usage of the software are minimal." They further define green software engineering as "developing software products in a way, so that [...] the negative and positive impacts continuously assessed, documented, and used for a further optimization of the software product". They propose a green software process in which the energy consumption caused from the consumption of a service by a user, its *use phase*, is identified as an impact category, yet they do not propose a method for its assessment.

Some work on the evaluation of green software design exists. Dick et al. in [16] evaluate the energy savings on web servers through several interventions such as reduced image resolution, yet they do not quantify the energy savings over the entire system. Simons in [43] measure the additional power consumption on a PC induced from flash content and find an increase in power consumption by 3.4%. Thiagarajan [48] perform a similar but far more sophisticated experiment on mobile phones and analyze the additional energy consumption induced from rendering individual web elements. They find that they can reduce the energy consumption of mobile phones by 30% by changing the JavaScript contents without impacting the user experience. Other work that does take the energy consumption of software into account was carried out by the human computer interaction community focusing on user devices, for example [34]. They also do not assess the savings across the whole product system but only the user device.

Besides models, several *metrics*, or measurement procedures, to quantify the energy consumption of ICT device have been proposed by both private organizations and academic researchers. The SPEC_power [45] initiative, for instance, provides a standardized protocol to measure the power consumption of servers. EnergyStar develops metrics for many different types energy consuming devices, including servers [19], displays [17] and personal computers (PCs) [13]. While metrics serve to quantify the energy consumption of a particular instance of a system, they cannot provide a *generic estimate* of energy consumption – a role that is fulfilled by models. Additionally, there is no metric which spans all system parts end-to-end. Such a metric is likely to remain infeasible in the near future because subsystems operated by third-party organizations are not open to instrumentation for measurements of energy consumption.

Multiple models have been developed to estimate the energy consumption of all parts of the service system. Examples include user devices [28][14], servers [8], data centers [2] and clouds [22]. Such analytic models and simulations can precisely estimate the device energy consumption from the composition of utilization factors of the device components such as CPU, disc and memory but at present these approaches cannot be used in the evaluation of design interventions directly because such models, firstly, require calibration for each specific device model and additionally - and more importantly - do not include a model of the component utilization that is induced by a particular service. Additionally, these models are currently too complex to be of practical use during software development. We adopt a simplified variant of this approach to estimate the energy consumption on user devices.

Besides these approaches to quantify energy consumption, the vast amount of work on more efficient ICT system design (including of servers [21], data centers [31] and networks [7]) often quantitatively illustrate the potential energy savings which an engineering intervention would provide. However, these savings, firstly, are agnostic of services and do not take an end-to-end perspective and, secondly, are often presented in relative proportions and thus do not allow transfer between subsystems. In some cases, the academic prototype web services used to illustrate potential savings of energy lack the complexity of industrial counterparts and thus further limit the transferability of the results between services. One of the strengths of this work is that the parameters are calculated from measurements of an actual, globally operating news service.

3. METHODOLOGY

In line with current practice of energy and carbon analyses, we adopt methodological principles from Life Cycle Assessment, but adapt them to our specific purpose. Any such assessment must have a clearly defined goal, which helps guide the choice of scope, in particular, the system boundaries which determine what is included or excluded from the analysis.

Our goal is to provide an analysis of the current energy usage and associated greenhouse gas emissions (which we both refer to subsequently as *impacts*) resulting from the use of GNM's digital product suite to its end customers. We wish to do this with sufficient detail to allow what-if analysis of alternative design and business decisions, and to estimate changes in energy and emissions associated with these.

We are interested in the overall impacts associated with this activity, rather than the carbon or energy footprint of an average webpage or an average user. We include within the boundaries all activities within and outside GNM associated with the delivery of the service to the end customer. Specifically, this includes activity by servers within GNM responsible for the dynamic generation of webpage content in response to a user request, activity by third-party servers elsewhere responsible for providing parts of this content (such as images or advertisements), activity within the internet to transfer content between the datacenters and the end users, and activity on end user devices for requesting and downloading the individual resources that constitute the service, and rendering and displaying it during consumption.

As our aim is to provide feedback to software developers, system architects and product managers regarding energy use, we explicitly exclude from our system two impact areas which would be included in a full product carbon assessment for reporting or comparison with alternative products, for a printed newspaper. Firstly, we exclude impacts associated with creation of the product – both journalism for the content (which would be shared with the newspaper), and IT development of the products. Both are straightforward to calculate, and already included in the Guardian News and Media sustainability report [24]. Secondly, we exclude the impacts associated with some share of the manufacture of the IT equipment used. While it is conceptually relatively straightforward in estimation, data availability is poor. Furthermore, these two factors are not impacted by the design of the service delivery.

3.1 Model Structure

To ensure the level of detail necessary to assess design interventions, our model is made up of two parts: a system model and a set of parameter values. Firstly, we use a fully parameterizable model of the service system which can estimate the energy use for an individual user of a digital service based on that presented in [29], which we summarize here. The delivery of a digital service is divided into the following subsystems: user access device; customer premise network devices, access network, edge network, core network, servers/data centers, including both origin data center of the service provider and third-party, such as Content Delivery Networks, ad networks or analytics (see Figure 1). The parameters of the model include user access device (e.g. phone, laptop, tablet, desktop), access network technology (e.g. 3G network, Digital Subscriber Line, Cable Modem, local WiFi, corporate LAN), service choice (web page, video), geographical location and duration of using the service. The model consists of a set of equations and associated data which can be used to determine energy use across the system for a given choice of user access parameters. These equations are presented in detail in [29], and summarized in Figure 2. It illustrates in abstract the structure of the model. For a specific user group, the energy footprint is calculated as the sum of the energy consumption by servers, edge and core networks, access networks (only one variety) and user devices. For example, to calculate the energy consumption by wired access networks, we multiply the power consumption with the duration of the service consumption.

The equation parameters are divided into constants, subsystem variables and service variables. Constants are values which vary only slowly as the internet evolves, such as the energy efficiency of delivery of data across the 3G network. Subsystem variables are those which are also fixed, but are determined by user choice of subsystem, such as the power of the user device or home network setup. Finally, the service variables are those which are determined by the usage of the service itself, such as how much data is transferred and how long the user interacts with it.

Secondly, we segment the user base of the GNM into groups according to service and subsystem variables. This determines for a given (actual or hypothetical) scenario, the number of users from a specific country accessing the service with a specific combination of user and access network devices and includes the number of requests these user groups make to a certain content segment as well as the average duration they spend consuming this content. This population model is generated from detailed data on the behavior of users which is derived from GNM's web analytics tool (Omniture SiteCatalyst). One example of such a group is the set of all users based in the UK who browse the Guardian web site on a specific tablet model via WiFi and DSL together with the average time they spend reading it.

To determine the spread of parameters in the population, we use access data for the month of March 2012, taken as a representative month. It was chosen because nothing unusual, such as the launch of a new digital product was occurring and it does not include significant holiday periods. In order to enable and support comparison with other studies and reporting we scale up all results to give annual equivalent values. Conceptually, we apply the energy model to the parameters of each individual user access, and sum these to determine the overall energy used by the population in accessing the service. In practice, for efficiency purposes, we create batches of similar users within each subsystem to calculate the overall energy used by that subsystem to provide service to the batch of similar users.

As with any such model, there is uncertainty about the data values used. We run a Monte Carlo analysis over 10000 iterations to handle this: we use a spread of values for each equation parameter and randomly sample from this spread repeatedly to obtain a distribution of outcomes.

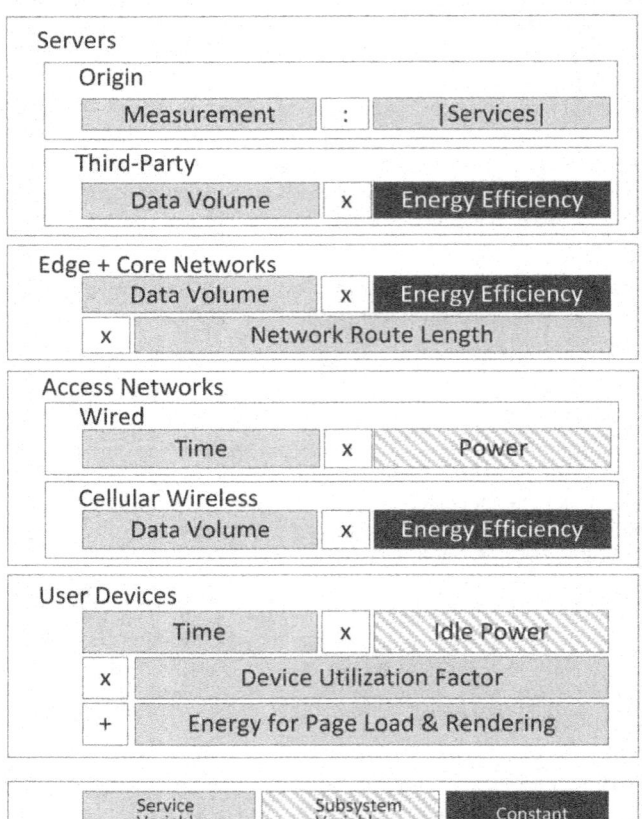

Figure 2- Abstract illustration of the model structure used to calculate the energy consumption per user group. The energy footprint for the service is calculated as the sum over the energy consumption of the relevant subsystems involved in the delivery and consumption.

Having used the data from the GNM's user population to estimate the current actual energy use and associated carbon emissions from the digital service, we then explore alternative design modifications. We do this by adjusting associated parameters in the model and/or user population, followed by a re-running the simulation.

We now turn to each of the subsystems in the model, and discuss how we determine both the equation parameters, and the spread of user behaviors, for each of these. Note, though that the illustration in Figure 2 does not represent the full set of parameters for clarity. For additional detail on the system model, please refer to [42].

3.2 Servers

The servers at GNM are responsible for dynamically generating web page HTML skeletons and text, including comments etc. In the origin datacenter at the GNM the energy consumption of each server and the supporting networking infrastructure and storage devices can be measured directly. We allocate the total monthly energy consumption uniformly between all page requests served during the measurement interval. We include an overhead for cooling and power transformation infrastructure in form of the power utilization effectiveness (PUE) which is a measure of the portion of electrical energy used in computation compared to that used for cooling and power conversion.

Third-party servers are responsible for providing additional content to fill the HTML template. Content Delivery Networks (CDNs) hold image and video caches in servers around the world, allowing data to be provided more locally and therefore faster. Ad Servers provide advertising content. The energy consumption of these servers cannot be measured directly as they are operated outside of the control of the content provider. We estimate the energy consumption of data served to be 3.8 watt-hours per gigabyte (Wh/GB), based on public reports by one of GNM's CDNs – Akamai [1]. We estimate the total energy consumption by multiplying the energy efficiency with the total data volume transferred in the connection to retrieve a specific resource from the CDN server. During the Monte Carlo simulation we use a triangular distribution with a lower and upper bound for this parameter of 0.89 Wh/GB and 29.56 Wh/GB based on estimates by Chandaria [11] and Google [25] respectively. We apply this distribution to all third-party providers.

3.3 Networks

The network used to transfer data between the various servers and the end user devices can be divided into core Internet and more local *edge* and *access* networks. The equipment involved is spread throughout the world among many parties, and so direct energy measurements are not available. Using a combination of industry and academic data we have built a model which, given a traceroute between two IP addresses, can estimate the energy required to transfer a given quantity of data through the core and edge networks [41]. It estimates the likely number of routers and repeaters of different kinds, and uses data regarding their power consumption to estimate this value. We found that the number of network hops in the route between two devices grows proportional with their geographical distance. In particular, this was evident in the connection to the origin servers. We also found that there was little variation in the route lengths to CDN servers and concluded the relative effectiveness in the CDNs in serving the data intensive sections (image, audio, video) from relatively close to the end user. Given that the service provider can very quickly change between CDNs or decide to serve all data locally, we decided to model the energy consumption by core and edge networks by the number of network hops in routes between geographical regions of user location and the average energy consumption per hop. Following the assumptions in above text regarding utilization and energy efficiency of core and edge routers we estimate an average energy efficiency per hop of 1.42 Wh/GB, including a share of electricity for optical equipment. The energy consumption for data transport for a user group is calculated as the product of the proportional volume of each type of data, the average route length to each type of server and the energy efficiency per hop. The average route lengths between continents with the majority of the GNM audience and types of servers are listed in Table 1. These include core and edge network devices. The traceroute servers from which the measurements were made are located in a mix of academic networks, privately hosted servers and ISP's looking glass servers. Thus, these routes include some access network equipment. The average route length is 13.

Table 1 - Average route lengths between regions of GNM readership and server types. 'Other' includes ad and analytics servers and mainly located in the US. Origin servers are located in the UK, CDN relatively local to customers.

	Origin	CDN	Other
Europe	14	9	12
North America	17	8	13
Oceania	21	8	14

During the Monte Carlo simulation, we vary the energy coefficient over a distribution. As an upper bound we assume a value from recent work by Malmodin et al. [33] who found the average energy efficiency of a major Swedish network to be 80 Wh/GB. In order to estimate a per-hop value on this basis, an assumption about the average route lengths in the Swedish network is required. Given that the average route length in our global measurements is 12, on average, routes in the Swedish network are likely to be shorter. We assume a value of 10 hops which results in an energy efficiency of 8 Wh/GB per hop. Given the fivefold difference between both values of per-hop energy efficiency we use those as minimum and maximum values in a triangular distribution during the Monte Carlo simulation and set the mode to the mean of the two at 4.71 Wh/GB.

The energy consumption by the access networks is far more variable. It depends on networking equipment deployed locally to the user, which is more diverse. Broadly, we can divide it into home/small office, institutional/workplace/campus networks, and mobile (3G) access. We categorize users into one of these three categories using user domain data from the web analytics tools. Certain domains are known to be mobile, workplace or domestic/small to medium enterprise Internet Service Providers (ISPs) and can be straightforwardly categorized. To determine unknown domains, we look at the user access patterns from these and compare them with the access patterns of known domains.

Figure 3 gives a smoothed and normalized distribution of page views for a typical Sunday and Monday in March 2012 – this retains the broad qualitative shapes of the distributions but relative numbers of page views and fine detail have been removed for reasons of commercial confidentiality. Page views from three different domains are being displayed: a popular, largely domestic ISP, a typical workplace domain, and a typical academic domain from the UK (ac.uk). The workplace domains have significant daytime peaks around lunchtime, while the domestic domains peak in the evening.

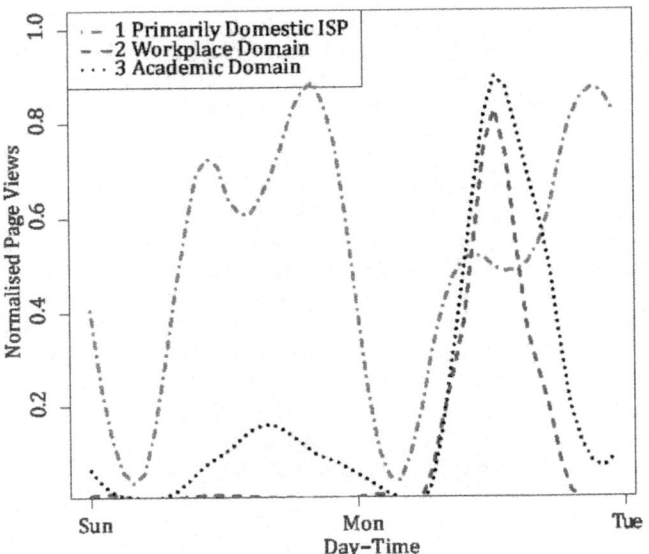

Figure 3 - Variation of number of page views during Sunday and Monday from domestic, commercial and academic ISPs.

Based on our analysis, we adopt a heuristic of classifying an unknown domain based on the ratio of peak access rate in evening to peak access rate in office hours. If the ratio is <20%, we classify a domain as workplace, if it is >200% we classify it as domestic, else we classify it as mixed. Mixed domains are assumed to have a mix of workplace to domestic access based on the overall proportion of accesses in known domains. We explored other approaches, such as the ratio of weekend to weekday daytime traffic, but found this to be the most effective. Based on this distinction, we estimate the energy consumption by wired networks for each batch of users as the product of the service use time and the power consumption per connected user device of each type of access network.

The most common types of access technology for home and small office are ADSL, Cable and Fiber-optic LAN. It is not possible to work out which of these options is being used by a given user based on site analytics data. However, the analytics data does allow us to determine which country users are from, and apportion usage to each technology type based on the relative share according to data from the Organisation for Economic Co-operation and Development (OECD). For instance, the UK has 78% ASDL, 20% Cable and 2% Fiber/LAN while the USA has 36% ASDL, 56% Cable and 7% Fiber/LAN [37].

We assume that those components of Cable, DSL or fiber-optic access network equipment which are shared between multiple subscribers - most commonly those in a neighborhood - consume 19, 2 and 4W per subscriber respectively, derived from Aleksić & Lovrić [3]. Inside of homes, the power consumption varies depending on whether WiFi is deployed, and if so, whether as part of a modem. Based on measurements by Energy Star [44] the power consumption of cable and DSL modems is typically 7W, increasing to 11W if they include a WiFi router. We assume that about 85% of all households use WiFi based on statistics by Ofcom [38]. We follow Lanzisera [30] who assume WiFi routers are built into DSL modems in 80% of subscribers and cable modems in 20% of all subscribers. Remaining WiFi usage is assumed to be a separate device.

Having considered domestic network access, we now turn to workplace campus networks and 3G mobile access. There is relatively little data on energy use in offices. The most widely cited study in is by Roth [40] from 2002 and is now so dated that we believe the use of this data is not justified. In our model, we assume a power figure of 8 W per user, based on averaging results of studies of the LBNL campus [30] and the Stanford Computer Science Department [29].

Models of the power consumption per user of wireless cellular networks still vary widely. Our model is based on third generation networks. Based on our estimates in [42] we assume an average value of 293 Wh/GB. During the Monte Carlo simulation we apply a triangular distribution with a lower bound value of 63 Wh/GB based on a lean component-level model of the most efficient HSPA variant by Deruyck et al. [15]. As an upper bound we apply a value of 729 Wh/GB from the high-use scenario in the system-level model of LTE networks in [18].

3.4 User Devices

The final source of energy consumption is the device used by the user to access the service. The amount of energy consumed will depend both on what the device is, and also what service it is accessing, more specifically web browsing or video content. The service is known from the site visit data. To determine the user device, we use data collected by the web analytics system from the User-Agent string provided by the client and embedded JavaScript in the HTML pages. This provides the operating system of the device, and the screen resolution. This information is sufficient to identify tablets and smartphones devices and there is little variation in power consumption between models. In the case of laptops and desktops with monitors, however, further analysis is required. To do this, we constructed a database containing screen resolution data for laptops and monitors, using information from online stores and other sites. If a screen resolution is only used in the manufacturing of laptop displays, we assume the access is a laptop, and if it only appears as a monitor, we assume it is a desktop in combination with a monitor. If either is possible, we distribute the alternatives across the population of all users with similar parameters according to the relative proportion of laptops and monitors with this resolution in the database.

Our model estimates the energy consumption by user devices as the sum of the base power consumption at active idle and a dynamic portion induced from consuming a service. For web pages from the GNM the dynamic portion is approximated from the sum of the energy for loading and initial rendering. For smartphones, Thiagarajan [48] provide detailed measurements with several different pages and find that the average energy consumption for loading and rendering 20 joules (J). We assume that these findings are representative for tablets, as well. For laptops and desktops, we assume this is 50 J based on our own scoping experiments with a modern EnergyStar-rated laptop. The dynamic portion of power consumption for watching video is assumed to be 15 percent of base power consumption based on the results by [10] for smartphones and our own experiments with a laptop.

To estimate the power consumption of laptop, desktop and monitors, we take power consumption of models as measured by EnergyStar [13], for the one hundred most popular models on Amazon, and calculate the average. This yielded figures of 114W for desktops, 24W for monitors and 27W for laptops. We assume the base power consumption in active idle of smartphones is 1W [10],[48] for smartphones, 3W for tablets [4].

3.5 From Energy to Carbon Footprint

Our model presented so far allows determining the energy footprint of a given user. In order to derive the corresponding carbon footprint we combine this with data about average carbon emissions per unit of energy ($kgCO_2e/kWh$), known as an emissions factor. The emissions factor can vary significantly between countries, as the mix of different energy generation technologies varies. For a given user, the site analytics software can infer their country of origin using their IP address and a geolocation database. We assume electricity use by the end device and access network takes place in this country. We cannot locate the edge and core network components involved with this degree of precision, or most of the CDN servers involved in a given interaction, and so we use the average global emissions factor for OECD countries. Finally, the GNM datacenter is known to be located in the UK, so uses the UK emissions factor. Together, these can be used to convert the various energy consumption figures in the model to provide an overall carbon footprint.

4. RESULTS

Based on our model we calculate the combined end-to-end energy consumption of the service system over on year for the audience of the GNM online news service. We present the annual equivalent values for the operational energy and carbon footprint (in metric tonnes) separately for each subsystem as shown in Table 2.

From our analysis by far the most impactful part of the media subsystem is the user devices which accounts for 74% of all carbon emissions which result from the generation of the consumed electricity. The second most impactful subsystem is the access network equipment which account for 22% of all carbon emissions. Compared to that, the impact of servers and the network is relatively small, however not insignificant, at 3.4%.

The 25th and 75th percentile of the resulting distribution of energy consumption by third-party servers and networks from the Monte Carlo simulation are 7.3% lower and 8.5% higher than the average.

Table 2. Electrical Energy and Carbon Footprint

	Energy [MWh]	Carbon [tCO2e]	% of CO2e
Origin Data Centre	369	199	3%
Shared Networks	111	60	1%
Third Party Servers	29	15	0.2%
Access Networks	3049	1681	22%
Users	10475	5736	75%
Sum	14033	7693	100%

5. ASSESSMENT OF DESIGN INTERVENTIONS

Having used our model to calculate current emissions from GNM digital products, we now turn to assessing six potential interventions on the product. The interventions presented below are a representative sample of interventions we have identified as being of interest to business strategists and sustainability professionals based on interviews and at GNM. Interventions may take place for reasons of business strategy, product improvement, sustainability or a combination of those. Our model is detailed enough to assess the impact of such interventions on carbon emissions, allowing this factor to be included in decisions about whether to go ahead or not.

5.1 Reducing the Data Volume of Web Pages

Preist and Shabajee [39] have identified web pages as a potential source of "digital waste" – transportation of data which is of no value to the end user – suggesting that large web pages could be reduced in size to reduce emissions. We consider a reduction in data volume of 30% in the 1000 most popular pages on GNM. This could be achieved through a combination of reduction of JavaScript (responsible, according to our analysis, for 15-25% of data volume of a web page) through code optimization, and a reduction in the number, size and/or resolution of images. (Note that our original model already accounts for existing caching by browsers, as it uses actual data transferred by CDNs rather than original page size. Caching typically reduces data transfer by an average of 25% of the original page size.)

We assume that the structure of pages remains unchanged. Hence this intervention will not alter energy consumption by the origin servers, responsible for the generation of the HTML template and text content of the page. It will result in energy savings in the CDN servers and core/edge network, and mobile networks due to reduced data transmission.

According to our model, the intervention to reduce the data volume of the most popular web pages by 30% would result in a total reduction of 4,132 $kgCO_2e$, or 0.05% of the overall footprint. This comes from a reduction of 3,332 $kgCO_2e$ (5%) of network emissions, 682 $kgCO_2e$ (4.4%) of third-party server emissions and savings of 118 $kgCO_2e$ in wireless access networks.

5.2 Simplifying Page Rendering

Separately from savings in data volume from optimized JavaScript contents, we also want to evaluate potential reductions on the user devices. In [48] Thiagarajan et al. measure the savings from simplifying the JavaScript contents in a Wikipedia page. They find that a single optimization that does not affect the user experience can realize 30% savings in the energy consumption of loading and rendering the page. We assume this change does not affect the base power consumption.

We evaluate the potential reductions of energy and carbon footprints under the assumption that an optimization could reduce the energy consumption for loading and initial rendering a page by 30% relative to the baseline assumptions between 20 and 50 joules as stated in section 3.4.

Assuming that in this scenario all other system parts are unaffected, we expect a reduction of the carbon footprint by the user devices of 9,344 $kgCO_2e$ (0.16%) or 0.12% of the total carbon footprint.

5.3 Reducing Video Resolution

GNM offers significant amounts of video on its website, and one design option we consider is a reduction in the video quality. The typical bit rate is 1100 kbps and the resolution is 360p. A reduction of the bit rate by circa 50% can be achieved with a change of the resolution to 240p.

The reduced data volume will ease load on the data center of the video CDN and the core and access networks similar to the reduction in page volume but to a greater degree as the data volume per page view is higher. Arguably, the energy consumption of user devices is likely to also be reduced, because less work may be done in rendering lower resolution video, yet a systematic analysis of this effect was out of scope of this analysis and we refrain from speculation and assume no change in their power consumption.

This resulted in a total reduction of 18,595 $kgCO_2e$, or 0.24% of the overall footprint. This comes from a reduction of 9,572 $kgCO_2e$ (14.5%) of core network emissions and 6,341 $kgCO_2e$ (0.37%) reductions in access networks, and 2,682 $kgCO_2e$ (17.3%) in third-party data center emissions. The savings in the energy footprint of the mobile network are equivalent to 47% compared to the corresponding baseline value.

5.4 Disabling CDN Servers

In [41] we found that CDN servers are very effective in reducing the route lengths for data transport to GNM customers. In this scenario we evaluate the impact on energy consumption if delivery of all GNM content, including those parts that are currently served by CDNs, was performed centrally from the origin servers in London. To this effect we modify our model to assume the route length for connections to CDNs is identical to the route length to the origin servers: 14 hops on average from Europe, 17 hops from North America and 21 hops for connections from Australia. We assume that the energy efficiency of servers remains unchanged.

Such a change would result in an increase of the energy footprint of the core and edge networks by 38.04% or 25,130 $kgCO_2e$ (0.3% reductions from total).

5.5 Increasing uptake of E-Readers

GNM provide a number of products targeted at specific devices. We now consider a scenario where a product targeted at passive-display eReaders is actively promoted through a combination of attractive pricing models, exclusive content and user-centric design. In this scenario, we assume this results in an increase in popularity of these devices to 10% of all page views and would displace consumption on PCs to the same degree and uniformly distributed between desktop and laptop. We assume that page volume remains constant. As a result, server and network activity is unchanged, but energy consumption by end-user devices is.

This resulted in a total reduction of 751,761 $kgCO_2e$ (9.77% of the overall footprint).

5.6 Increasing Consumption of Video

We now consider a scenario where the product designers increase the quantity of video content on the site, and actively promote it through means such as high profile banners on the home page, aiming to increase the consumption of video by 10%. We assume that the video quality, and therefore the bit rate, is unchanged.

This will affect the energy consumption of all subsystems: the origin data center will serve additional page requests containing the video, the CDNs will serve additional content, the core and mobile networks will carry increased traffic, and the user devices will be active for the additional period while watching the video.

This resulted in a total increase of 13,304 $kgCO_2e$, or 0.17% of the overall footprint. This comes from an increase of 8,447 $kgCO_2e$ (0.15%) in user device emissions, 1,984 $kgCO_2e$ (3%) in network emissions, 2,216 $kgCO_2e$ (0.13%) increase in emissions from access networks - including a small increase in emissions from mobile networks of 38 $kgCO_2e$ and 551 $kgCO_2e$ (3.56%) in third-party data center emissions. The additional page views would contribute to additional emissions in the origin data center by 103 $kgCO_2e$ (0.05%).

The results of all scenarios are shown graphically in Figure 4.

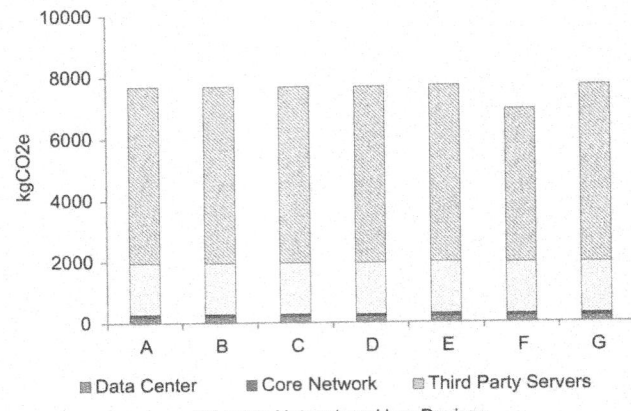

Figure 4 Total Annual Carbon Emissions by Subsystem for Scenarios: A – Baseline Results, B – Reducing the Data Volume of Web Pages, C – Simplifying Page Rendering, D – Reducing Video Resolution, E – Disabling CDN Servers, F – Increasing uptake of E-Readers, G - Increasing Consumption of Video

6. DISCUSSION AND FURTHER WORK

In the previous sections we have presented a methodology for the assessment of carbon emissions by digital services. It combines a detailed model of energy use by subsystems involved in the delivery of a service to a given user with a model of a diversity of behavior in the user population. In this way, it goes beyond the current state of the art which has focused on aggregate measurements and models of an average user. We also provide more detailed and accurate data on energy use by specific subcomponents in the system than has been used in prior studies. We have applied the model to give an accurate assessment of carbon emissions resulting from the delivery of GNM's digital product suite. Unlike prior coarser-grained models of carbon emissions from digital service use, it can be used to assess the impact of design changes on carbon emissions. We have demonstrated this by assessing the impact of six potential interventions on GNM services.

6.1 Intervention Scenarios

Based on the evaluations of interventions presented above we can draw three conclusions about the use of the model for the sustainable design of online news:

Firstly, at current levels of consumptions the displacement of PCs by lower power user devices has by far the highest potential to reduce the total carbon emissions - assuming that the PCs are decommissioned, in sleep mode or turned off instead. Secondly, interventions which significantly reduce the transferred data volume in networks can contribute to a substantial reduction of emission in networks and data centers, although to a much lower degree.

Thirdly, despite mobile networks having a much higher energy consumption per transferred data volume and thus are a risk for the future sustainability of digital media consumption, at the present moment the emissions from use of GNM products over mobile networks are relatively small compared to the emissions of other subsystems, including wired access networks in particular. Thus, the rapid increase of access via mobile networks should not be the central concern of the GNMs sustainability agenda at this time.

6.2 Generality

More broadly the results presented are specific to the product suite and user community of GNM. However, the findings are likely to broadly apply to similar news and media sites and product suites, such as CNN or BBC. The methodology is more broadly applicable than this, and given the availability of appropriate data could be used to assess design interventions on a more video intensive digital product such as YouTube or a social networking service such as Facebook. We would expect the set of potential interventions, and their relative effectiveness, to change with the nature of the digital product.

6.3 Change over Time

One limitation of the work we have presented is that it assumes a steady state of the digital product, based on a snapshot at a given time, when assessing the impact of design interventions. However, it is clear that digital products are in a state of flux, and the web analytics data confirms that the products at GNM are no exception. Changes are resulting both from the uptake of specific new GNM products entering the market, and also because of broader trends such as the increased uptake of tablets. Through the use of web analytics systems our method increases accuracy above others based on annual data. Additionally, close integration of analytic suites significantly reduces the effort to update assessment results in accord to the evolution of the system. Thus, our methodology can be used to closely follow and project the impact of such trends on emissions over an extended period of time. Furthermore, rather than using a snapshot as baseline for assessing design interventions, such a projection can be used as a 'business as usual' baseline to give a longer term assessment of the impact of design interventions against such trends. Additionally, the choice of product design by GNM is co-evolving with such trends: a product may arise in response to a trend, but also will influence the uptake or otherwise of such a trend. Our methodology can support including environmental impacts in the choice of which trends to encourage and which to discourage.

6.4 Limitations

When using an LCA approach, it is important to address issues of data quality and data uncertainty. Comprehensive discussion of this with regard to the underlying energy model is beyond the scope of this paper, but addressed in [42]. Here, we consider these issues with regard to the user behavioral data, which is used to augment the energy model in the methodology presented in this paper. We extract the user data from site user analytics software. There are a range of well-known issues with reliability of such systems, see for example [12]. In our context one specific potential issue with this is the use of cookies and JavaScript to conduct analytics of specific users, meaning that user-based analysis is not reliable if cookies are rejected. We mostly overcome this as our analysis is 'per access', and so a user rejecting cookies will simply appear as multiple accesses. The one exception is in determining time on page. We also place an upper bound of 30mins for time-on-page, to cap cases where a browser is left open on a page, but the user has finished using it and is doing something else.

6.5 Further improving the model

While our model is finer grained than those that have gone before, further improvements would increase its accuracy and allow finer-grained design decisions to be assessed. Firstly, the modeling of the relationship between service type and power use on the end device is relatively simplistic. More sophisticated models of power use by end user devices, based on utilization of CPU, memory, disk and IO could be used to refine this. Secondly, the granularity of data collection by the user analytic software also places limitations on what can be assessed. For example, one design intervention we identified as being of interest but were unable to assess is the effect of 'bounces' - rapid visits to a web page because on arrival the user discovers it isn't really what they want, and is therefore another example of digital waste. This was because the user data did not distinguish rapid (2-3 sec) visits from 15 second visits, where a person may have received some value from the page.

6.6 Extending the model

The model we have presented in the paper is focused on the energy used to deliver a digital service. We have focused on this because it is what is most directly influenced by service design decisions. The scope of the model could be extended to include other carbon emissions that are indirectly associated with the delivery of the service. These would include (a) some share of the emissions associated with the manufacture of IT kit used to deliver and use the service. (b) some share of the energy used by user equipment at times when it is idle or on standby (i.e. not providing any service); (c) some share of energy used (IT equipment, office heating, etc.) by the developers, content providers and maintainers of the service. Such an extension is an area of further work for this model. In particular, questions of accurate allocation (the decision of how to share such emissions between the many services which IT equipment provides) require both further theoretical work and further study of user behavior. Specifically, this will involve analysis of how much time users spend on different services, and how much time devices stay in energy using idle or sleep states

6.8 Short Term, Longer Term and Systemic Impacts of Service Use

In the methodology presented in this paper, in line with standard practice in carbon footprinting, we have adopted an attributional approach. This means sharing out all impacts between the services involved. The disadvantage with this approach is that it does not distinguish between reductions which are immediately realizable and those that are not. For example, using a low power device instead of a higher power device results in an immediately realizable reduction in energy use. Reducing data traffic through a 3G network, on the other hand, may not, as a base station may use nearly as much energy to serve a lower quantity of data. However, such a change does lead to a longer term reduction in impacts if being part of a bigger trend - in that it will decrease the pressure to add new equipment.

There are more subtle long-term systemic trends associated with IT energy use which are notoriously difficult to model. For example, as observed by Blevis [9], the provision of digital services can contribute to the uptake of more digital devices. When making a decision of whether, for example, to promote services on low-power eReaders, organizations such as GNM need to consider the trade-off between the efficiency gains from using such a device against the increase in manufacturing emissions resulting from any increased device purchases motivated by the new service. However, it is very difficult to estimate how much increase in demand for eReaders could be attributed to the new GNM service, and would require modeling and study using econometric techniques. Another broader issue for investigation is the extent to which new services on low power devices displace activity on other higher power devices, and to what extent it results in additional device usage. Our analysis of the eReader intervention assumes that the GNM product does not stimulate new product purchases, and time spent on the eReader correspondingly reduces time using a laptop or desktop. Further work on user behavior is needed to determine if this assumption is appropriate, and if not how best to model these systemic effects.

7. CONCLUSIONS

In this paper, we have presented a methodology that combines user behavior analysis with life cycle analysis to provide the most detailed and extensible carbon and energy footprint of a digital product suite produced to date. The carbon footprinting methodology we have presented is the first that is detailed enough to be able to assess the impact of alternative design decisions in digital products. We demonstrate this by applying it to digital services deployed by GNM, and assess the impact of the current services and potential changes resulting from six alternate interventions. The methodology, and many of the data points we have gathered, can be applied directly to many other digital services with similar delivery architectures, and could be extended to cover services with more complex architectures such as P2P.

The methodology and models we have developed have application in several areas. Firstly, they can be used to support and inform design decisions made by service providers. Secondly, they can be used as an educational tool to make software developers more aware of how design decisions they make impact energy use of the final product. Thirdly, they can be used to guide research in energy-efficient and green design. In particular, the results of our study emphasize the value of work focused on reduction of energy use by services on end user devices.

8. ACKNOWLEDGMENTS

This work was conducted as part of the SYMPACT project, funded by the RCUK Digital Economy and Energy programs (EPSRC EP/I000151/1). The authors would like to acknowledge the contribution of time and data made by Guardian News and Media, particularly Matthew Malthouse, Christopher Hodgson and Jo Confino.

9. REFERENCES

[1] Akamai Environmental Sustainability Initiative Report 2011: 2012. http://www.akamai.com/dl/sustainability/Environmental_Sustainability.pdf. Accessed: 2012-11-22.

[2] Aksanli, B. et al. 2012. Using Datacenter Simulation to Evaluate Green Energy Integration. *Computer*.

[3] Aleksić, S. and Lovrić, A. 2010. Power efficiency in wired access networks. *e & i Elektrotechnik und Informationstechnik*. 127, 11 (2010), 321–326.

[4] Apple - Environment - Reports: 2011. http://www.apple.com/environment/reports/. Accessed: 2011-11-22.

[5] Baliga, J. et al. 2009. Energy Consumption in Optical IP Networks. *Journal of Lightwave Technology*. 27, 13 (Jul. 2009), 2391–2403.

[6] Beauvisage, T. 2009. Computer Usage in Daily Life. *Proceedings of the 27th international conference on Human factors in computing systems* (Boston, MA, 2009), 575–584.

[7] Bianzino, A.P. et al. 2012. A Survey of Green Networking Research. *Communications Surveys & Tutorials, IEEE*. 14, 1 (2012), 3–20.

[8] Bircher, W.L. and John, L.K. 2012. Complete System Power Estimation Using Processor Performance Events. *IEEE Transactions on Computers*. 61, 4 (Apr. 2012), 563–577.

[9] Blevis, E. 2007. Sustainable interaction design: invention & disposal, renewal & reuse. *Proceedings of the SIGCHI conference on Human factors in computing systems* (2007), 503–512.

[10] Carroll, A. and Heiser, G. 2010. An Analysis of Power Consumption in a Smartphone. *USENIX annual technical conference* (Berkeley, CA, 2010), 21–21.

[11] Chandaria, J. et al. 2011. The carbon footprint of watching television, comparing digital terrestrial television with video-on-demand. *Sustainable Systems and Technology (ISSST), 2011 IEEE International Symposium on* (2011), 1–6.

[12] Clifton, B. 2012. *Advanced Web Metrics with Google Analytics*. John Wiley & Sons.

[13] Computers: 2011. http://www.energystar.gov/index.cfm?fuseaction=find_a_product.showProductGroup&pgw_code=CO. Accessed: 2011-11-22.

[14] Da Costa, G. and Hlavacs, H. 2010. Methodology of measurement for energy consumption of applications. *Energy Efficient Grids, Clouds and Clusters Workshop (co-located with Grid)(E2GC2 2010)* (2010).

[15] Deruyck, M. et al. 2010. Comparison of power consumption of mobile WiMAX, HSPA and LTE access networks. *6th Conference on Telecommunication Techno-Economics, 2010. CTTE 2010* (2010), 1–7.

[16] Dick, M. et al. 2012. Green Web Engineering - Measurements and Findings. *EnviroInfo* (2012).

[17] Displays: 2012. http://www.energystar.gov/index.cfm?fuseaction=find_a_product.showProductGroup&pgw_code=MO. Accessed: 2012-05-24.

[18] EARTH Project 2010. *Energy efficiency analysis of the reference systems, areas of improvements and target breakdown*.

[19] Enterprise Servers: 2011. http://www.energystar.gov/index.cfm?fuseaction=find_a_product.showProductGroup&pgw_code=DC. Accessed: 2011-07-21.

[20] European Commission - Joint Research Centre - Institute for Environment and Sustainability 2010. International Reference Life Cycle Data System (ILCD) Handbook - General guide for Life Cycle Assessment - Detailed guidance. Publications Office of the European Union.

[21] Frachtenberg, E. et al. 2011. High-efficiency server design. *Proceedings of 2011 International Conference for High Performance Computing, Networking, Storage and Analysis on - SC '11* (New York, New York, USA, 2011), 1.

[22] Garg, S.K. and Buyya, R. 2011. NetworkCloudSim: Modelling Parallel Applications in Cloud Simulations. *2011 Fourth IEEE International Conference on Utility and Cloud Computing* (Dec. 2011), 105–113.

[23] GHG Protocol Product Life Cycle Accounting and Reporting Standard ICT Sector Guidance: 2012. http://www.ghgprotocol.org/feature/ghg-protocol-product-life-cycle-accounting-and-reporting-standard-ict-sector-guidance. Accessed: 2012-05-30.

[24] GNM Sustainability Report 2011: 2011. http://www.guardian.co.uk/sustainability/series/sustainability-report-2011. Accessed: 2012-09-19.

[25] Google data center efficiency measurements: 2011. http://www.google.com/about/datacenters/inside/efficiency/index.html. Accessed: 2012-07-06.

[26] International Organization For Standardization 2006. ISO 14040: Environmental management — Life cycle assessment — Principles and framework. ISO copyright office.

[27] ITU 2012. *L.1410 - Methodology for environmental impact assessment of information and communication technologies (ICT) goods, networks and services.*

[28] Joulemeter: 2012. http://research.microsoft.com/en-us/downloads/fe9e10c5-5c5b-450c-a674-daf55565f794/. Accessed: 2012-01-24.

[29] Kazandjieva, M. et al. 2012. Green Enterprise Computing Data: Assumptions and Realities. *Proceedings of the Third International Green Computing Conference* (2012).

[30] Lanzisera, S. et al. 2010. Data network equipment energy use and savings potential in buildings. *ACEEE Summer Study on Energy Efficiency in Buildings* (2010), 1–14.

[31] Lin, M. et al. 2011. Dynamic right-sizing for power-proportional data centers. *IEEE INFOCOM* (2011).

[32] Malmodin, J. et al. 2010. Greenhouse Gas Emissions and Operational Electricity Use in the ICT and Entertainment & Media Sectors. *Journal of Industrial Ecology*. 14, 5 (Oct. 2010), 770–790.

[33] Malmodin, J. et al. 2012. LCA of data transmission and IP core networks. *Electronics Goes Green 2012+* (2012), 1–6.

[34] McLachlan, R. and Brewster, S. 2012. Towards new widgets to reduce PC power consumption. *Proceedings of the 2012 ACM annual conference extended abstracts on Human Factors in Computing Systems Extended Abstracts - CHI EA '12* (New York, New York, USA, 2012), 2153.

[35] Moberg, Å. et al. 2010. Printed and tablet e-paper newspaper from an environmental perspective — A screening life cycle assessment. *Environmental Impact Assessment Review*. 30, 3 (Apr. 2010), 177–191.

[36] Naumann, S. et al. 2011. The GREENSOFT Model: A reference model for green and sustainable software and its engineering. *Sustainable Computing: Informatics and Systems*. 1, 4 (Dec. 2011), 294–304.

[37] OECD Broadband Portal: 2011. http://goo.gl/Q30jB. Accessed: 2012-08-27.

[38] Ofcom 2012. *Communications Market Report 2012.*

[39] Preist, C. and Shabajee, P. 2010. Energy Use in the Media Cloud. *2nd IEEE International Conference on Cloud Computing Technology and Science* (Indianapolis, USA, 2010).

[40] Roth, K.W. et al. 2002. Energy Consumption by Commercial Office and Telecommunication Equipment. *2002 ACEEE Summer Study on Energy Efficiency in Buildings* (2002).

[41] Schien, D. et al. 2012. Impact of Location on the Energy Footprint of Digital Media. *IEEE International Symposium on Sustainable Systems and Technology (IEEE ISSST 2012)* (Boston, MA, 2012).

[42] Schien, D. et al. 2013. Modeling and Assessing Variability in Use Phase Energy of Online Multimedia Services. *Journal of Industrial Ecology*. [to appear] (2013).

[43] Simons, R. and Pras, A. 2010. *The Hidden Energy Cost of Web Advertising*. Citeseer.

[44] Small Network Equipment: 2012. http://www.energystar.gov/index.cfm?c=new_specs.small_network_equip. Accessed: 2012-10-09.

[45] SPEC power_ssj2008: 2011. http://www.spec.org/power_ssj2008/. Accessed: 2011-02-09.

[46] Taylor, C. and Koomey, J.G. 2008. Estimating Energy Use and Greenhouse Gas Emissions of Internet Advertising. *Network*. Working paper for IMC2.

[47] Teehan, P. et al. 2010. Estimating the Changing Environmental Impacts of ICT-Based Tasks : A Top-Down Approach. *Sustainable Systems and Technology (ISSST), 2010 IEEE International Symposium on* (2010).

[48] Thiagarajan, N. et al. 2012. Who killed my battery?: analyzing mobile browser energy consumption. *WWW* (2012), 41–50.

[49] Weber, C.L. et al. 2009. *The energy and climate change impacts of different music delivery methods.*

[50] Williams, D.R. and Tang, Y. 2012. A Methodology to Model the Environmental Impacts of Electronic Software Distributions. *Environmental Science and Technology*. 46, 2 (2012), 1087–1095.

Potential Networks, Contagious Communities, and Understanding Social Network Structure

Grant Schoenebeck[*]
University of Michigan
2260 Hayward St.
Ann Arbor, MI, USA
schoeneb@umich.edu

ABSTRACT

In this paper we study how the network of agents adopting a particular technology relates to the structure of the underlying network over which the technology adoption spreads. We develop a model and show that the network of agents adopting a particular technology may have characteristics that differ significantly from the social network of agents over which the technology spreads. For example, the network induced by a cascade may have a heavy-tailed degree distribution even if the original network does not.

This provides evidence that online social networks created by technology adoption over an underlying social network may look fundamentally different from social networks and indicates that using data from many online social networks may mislead us if we try to use it to directly infer the structure of social networks. Our results provide an alternate explanation for certain properties repeatedly observed in data sets, for example: heavy-tailed degree distribution, network densification, shrinking diameter, and network community profile. These properties could be caused by a sort of *sampling bias* rather than by attributes of the underlying social structure. By generating networks using cascades over traditional network models that do not themselves contain these properties, we can nevertheless reliably produce networks that contain all these properties.

An opportunity for interesting future research is developing new methods that correctly infer underlying network structure from data about a network that is generated via a cascade spread over the underlying network.

Categories and Subject Descriptors

G.2.2 [**Discrete Mathematics**]: Graph Theory—*Network problems*; G.3.2 [**Probability and Statistics**]: [Experimental Design]; J.4 [**Social and Behavioral Sciences**]: [Sociology]

General Terms

Theory; Experimentation

---

[*]The author thanks the Simons foundation for their generous support of this research.

Copyright is held by the International World Wide Web Conference Committee (IW3C2). IW3C2 reserves the right to provide a hyperlink to the author's site if the Material is used in electronic media.
WWW 2013, May 13–17, 2013, Rio de Janeiro, Brazil.
ACM 978-1-4503-2035-1/13/05.

Keywords

Social Networks, Community Structure, Random Graphs

1. INTRODUCTION

The advent of Web 2.0 has tremendously enriched researchers' access to data. Instead of observing eighteen monks for months waiting for something interesting to happen [30], researchers now have access to approximately 160 million users' 90 million daily tweets through Twitter's API [1]. While these data tell us what people do online, it is less clear how much these data tell us about people in a broader context.

Social science researchers developed social networks as a methodological tool for understanding social phenomena, such as how individuals' actions affect macro-level features of society, or how an individual's "location" in a network affects his/her opportunities [26, 14]. Sociologists have long distinguished between different types of networks [26]. Some examples are trust networks: from whom would you feel comfortable asking for $1000?; friendship networks: with whom do you want to go out Friday evening; information networks: with whom do you discuss important matters; and self-declared/articulated networks: who do you want the world to believe are your friends?

Social networks are not to be conflated with *online social networks* such as LiveJournal, Epinions, MySpace, Facebook, and Twitter. We will use the terms *contagious networks* to denote networks that grow by adding new members where the new members are often "infected" by their current social ties. The key property of contagious networks is that people often join these networks because they have a friend or acquaintance that is already a member. Contagious networks include most *online social networks* because people are more likely to sign-up for such networks if they already have friends on them. Citation networks, communications networks, collaboration networks, co-authorship networks, product co-purchasing networks may also be considered contagious networks. Contagious networks provide much of the digital data we have about networks. The actions of joining and participating in these networks (e.g. logging into LiveJournal, or coauthoring a paper) are often captured digitally. Hence, contagious networks provide a means for studying social questions pertaining to social networks by providing data.

Because contagious networks are spread over an underlying social network, it is natural to conjecture that these networks share many properties. However, it is difficult to know if this data generalizes past the digital world. The importance of this distinction is indicated by a familiar question, "who in the room is friends with his/her mother on Facebook?" However, even if no one were Facebook friends with his/her mother would this meaningfully affect any large-scale measurements of the data? Does the sheer scale of such data render differences between the contagious networks and social networks to be mere annoyances or do these differences present a substantial obstacle to using data from contagious networks to make inferences about social networks. This is a key question that this paper hopes to address.

1.1 Summary of Results and Implications

We argue that the data from contagious networks is not tantamount to holding up a big mirror to our society; it is more like looking at our society in a fun-house mirror–where things may appear very differently than they are.

Using computer simulations, we illustrate examples where the contagious network and the underlying network have very different properties. Data mining has shown that many contagious networks share a few common features: heavy-tailed degree distributions, shrinking diameters, edge densification, and a particular "network community profile". We show, with computer simulations, that even though certain well-known network models (e.g. the Watts-Strogatz model or a collection of cliques) have none of these properties, if we use these models as an underlying network and grow contagious networks over them in a natural way, then the resulting contagious networks have all of these properties. We investigate various models of transmission and show that these results are robust to changes in the model. We study various parameter regimes to understand when our results hold. We also explore the theoretical mechanisms underlying our experimental results. In the case of degree distribution, we can prove that certain underlying structure will endow the contagious networks with heavy-tailed degree distributions even when the underlying network is regular.

While these models are admittedly stylized, we believe that they are natural, and that these results give strong evidence of important implications, which we summarize here; they are discussed in more detail in Section 5.

(1) These results provide a natural framework for developing generative models for contagious communities which capture the aforementioned four properties: start with a model for an underlying social network and model a contagion spreading over it. (2) These results provide strong intuition that we need different models for social networks and contagious networks. It may be a mistake to import social network intuition into models for contagious networks. Similarly, by datamining contagious networks, one expects to find attributes that are common amongst contagious networks; however, these observations may not apply to the underlying social network. (3) This helps make sense of the counter-intuitive results of Leskovec et al [25] about network structure. These results make intuitive sense in context of contagious communities, but may not apply to other social networks. More speculatively, if we imagine these networks as being a community, it may allow Leskovec et al to give us insight into the structure of communities as well. (4) In a model where social networks are not created *ex nihilo*, but from existing social structures, contagious networks provide a sort of sampling technique for learning the underlying social network. While it may be impossible to directly infer the underlying social structure, more subtle techniques might work. In the Section 6, we pose the question: if contagious network data is akin to looking in a fun-house mirror, then what aspects of reality can we still reliably deduce from looking at this data? After all, if you see feet and a head in a fun-house mirror, you can be fairly certain that there is a body in between.

1.2 Related Work

Technology adoption as a process on a social network has been studied and documented before; however, usually only the size of the cascade is considered. For example, in an experimental study, Centola [6] creates online communities populated with volunteers and studies the spread of joining a health forum network over this strictly enforced underlying network. Centola was mostly concerned with what types of underlying network structures would foster the largest cascade. For more examples, see Chapters 6 and 9 of [16].

Here, we model on-line social network formation as technology adoption, and investigate how the network *structure* of the on-line social network is affected by the underlying social network structure. In fact, we condition on the size and so explicitly remove this variable from study.

This phenomenon of network creation over existing structure extends to many settings beyond on-line communities. Segal [33] observes that the best prediction of who would become friends at a certain police academy was the proximity of their last names in the alphabet (this was presumably due to the frequent placement of the cadets in alphabetical order). Thus the last names indicated a certain underlying social structure over which friendships eventually formed. In another study, also at a police academy, Conti and Doreian [8] show that seating assignments and squad assignments predict friendship ties. In this case, the study tries to manipulate the underlying social structure networks to foster inter-racial camaraderie at the academy.

Our results can be understood as trying to study the sampling bias resulting from the technology adoption process. The same person may interact over many differ types of technology–telephone, text, email, Facebook, Twitter– or without technology. Each technology may be *selectively* used for particular communication needs. Each user may use several distinct instances of the same technology (e.g. a work and home telephone, several email accounts). To use this data to make assertions about social questions, we need to know that the data generalizes past the digital world, at least in the cases that we care about.

A series of work (e.g. [18, 2]) points out a similar sampling bias in context of traceroute sampling. For example, Achlioptas, Clauset, Kempe, and Moore [2] show that traceroute sampling finds power-law degree distributions even in regular random graphs (which are very far from having a power-law degree distribution). A sampling bias caused by using traceroute sampling means a power-law distribution can be measured even when the underlying degree distribution is constant.

However, traceroute sampling is fundamentally different than the cascading processes evaluated here.[1] In particular,

---

[1]Trace-route looks at the degree distribution on a breadth first search tree. In our setting, this would be similar to $RET(n, \alpha = 0, \beta = 1)$–every infected node immediate in-

unlike in the traceroute sampling case, running our models of cascades over Erdös-Rényi random graphs does not yield power-law or heavy-tailed degree distributions. Thus it must be a different mechanism acting in each case.

Terminology.

For expositional convenience and concreteness, throughout this paper we will use off-line friendship interchangeably with social network and as the canonical example of a social network. Likewise, we will use on-line social networks and sometimes Live Journal[2] in particular to be a stand-in for contagious networks. A sharp distinction between contagious and social networks is not always clear, but nonetheless we believe these generalizations are useful. Also, not all online social networks are necessarily contagious communities as membership in some may not be spread primarily via an underlying social structure. While the language of cascades and adoptions is more accurate and traditional to describe the spread of some cultural artifact, we will interchangeably use the notation of a virus and infection because such terminology is it often more concise.

Road Map.

Section 2 describes the models we use to construct the underlying social structure, the processes by which contagious networks spread over this structure, and the properties we are interested in comparing between the original network and the contagious network. The results of simulations over these models are summarized in Section 3. Section 4 presents some theoretical rational for these results. In Section 5 we draw implications of our results. Finally, Section 6 concludes with what we feel is an interesting open question raised by our study as well as a framework with which to approach it.

2. MODELS AND FORMALISMS

In this section we present natural models of underlying social networks and cascades which spread over these networks to create contagious networks. We give examples of properties found across many different network data sets. In subsequent sections we will start with one of these network models, simulate the growth of a contagious network over it, and then compare properties of the contagious network to those of the underlying social network.

2.1 Graph Models

For our underlying social networks, we use simple and traditional generative models which do not exhibit the characteristics we are hoping to capture. The two graphs that we focus on for our potential networks are the Watts-Strogatz model and the Planted Community model. Each is characterized by two properties: 1) "random" short cut paths, and 2) edges that provide a lot of clustering but generally fail to provide shortcut paths.

The *Watts-Strogatz random network model* is defined by three parameters. The undirected $WS(n,d,r)$ ensemble of random graphs–where n is the number of vertices, d is the average degree which is even, and $r \in [0,1]$ is a parameter– are defined by the random process that creates them. This process begins with the graph on n nodes $\{0, 1, \ldots, n-1\}$ where each node is connected to the d closest other nodes so that $E = \{(k, k \pm \ell \mod n) : 1 \leq \ell \leq d/2\}$. With probability r, each edge (u,v) is then "rewired", that is replaced with the edge (u,v') where v' is chosen from the vertices not already connected to u.[3]

The *Planted Community Model* $PC(n,d,r)$ is defined by the same three parameters as the Watts-Strogatz model but here we require that n is a multiple of d. To create such a graph, the vertices are partitioned into n/d equally sized cliques of size d. Each edge (u,v) is then "rewired" with probability r.

Models of Transmission.

In this section we first define four simple models of transmission.

The first, which we call *random edge transmission induced graph*, has one parameter. $RETIG_G(m)$ is defined by starting with the graph $G = (V_G, E_G)$ and initializing the infected set $I \subseteq V_G$ to a single random vertex. A random edge (u,v) is chosen uniformly from $E(I, \bar{I})$ and the vertex v is added to I. This is repeated until $|I| = m$. The resulting infected graph is $G(I)$, the induced subgraph of G on the vertices in I.

The first model includes all the edges in G between vertices that are in I. In the second model, these edges must also be discovered. We call the second model *random edge transmission*, and it has three parameters. $RET_G(m, \alpha, \beta)$ is defined by initializing the infected graph $H = (V_H, E_H)$ to the graph $(\{v_0\}, \emptyset)$ where v_0 is a random vertex from the potential graph $G = (V_G, E_G)$. At each step, each edge $(u,v) \in E_G(V_H, V_H) - E_H$ is added to H with probability α and each edge $(u,v) \in E_G(V_H, \overline{V_H})$ is added to H (along with v) with probability β. The process is run until m additional vertices are included.

The third model *random edge transmission with multiple initial vertices* $RETMIV_G(m, \alpha, \beta, s)$ is defined the same way as $RET_G(m, \alpha, \beta)$ but the transmission is started from s random vertices simultaneously.

Note that $RETIG_G(m)$, $RET_G(m, \alpha, \beta)$, and $RETMIV_G(m, \alpha, \beta, s)$ never add edges that are not in G.

We create a more complex model which allows people in "infected" communities to make new friends within the cascade. The *random edge transmission with exploration* $RETWE_G(m, \alpha, \beta, \gamma)$ is defined exactly like the *random edge transmission* except that at each round, for each triple $u, w, v \in V_H$ where $(u,w), (w,v) \in E_H$ the edge (u,v) is added to E_H with probability γ (this edge is added with probability γ for each such triple).

2.2 Properties studied

Heavy-tailed degree distributions.

Previous research has shown that many networks have heavy-tailed degree distributions[3, 4]. By *heavy-tailed degree distributions* we mean that the degree distribution ap-

---

fecting all uninfected neighbors but no internal edges which, as we will see, is outside the parameters that yield our results or that are interesting in our setting.

[2]LiveJournal is an early blogging and social networking community.

[3]The original WS definition is slightly more complicated than this because the order which you consider the edges may matter, see [37] for the details of ordering. We use the implementation in SNAP [20] which ignores these subtleties.

proximates a straight line when plotted with both axes logarithmically scaled, perhaps followed by a drop-off.[4] Power-law distributions, the related Yule distributions, and truncated power-law distributions are all heavy-tailed distributions [9]. Often heavy-tailed degree distributions serve as a contrast to Poisson distributions, which are much more highly concentrated and have a much thinner tail (fewer points far from the average [16]).

Shrinking Diameters and Edge Densification.

Previous research has also shown that, over time, the diameter of contagious networks tends to shrink and that the average degree of vertices tends to increase [23]. This work was based on analyzing four networks: the ArXiv citation graphs (for high-energy physics theory), the U.S. Patent citation graph, the graph of routers of the Internet, and the ArXiv affiliation graph (on certain topics). Note, however, that none of these is actually an online social network in the usual sense.

Network Community Profile.

Another network feature that we are interested in is called the *network community profile* and is described by Leskovec, Lang, Dasgupta, and Mahoney [25]. The authors develop a tool to analyze network structure that they call the "network community profile"-which we will describe shortly. They show that this tool yields similar results when applied to over 70 data sets, such as LiveJournal. In particular, the network community profile on the on-line social networks: LiveJournal, Epinions, LinkedIn, Del.icio.us, and Flickr look nearly identical (see [25] pages 22 and 25). They note that the plot decreases until around 100, then it stays roughly even for a short period, and finally starts to increase. Finally, they show that this tool yields completely different results on virtually all generative models (except for one that they call the Forest-Fire model).

Leskovec et al were interested in studying the community structure on networks. They define a community as a set of nodes with low conductance–many edges within the set compared to the number of edges leaving the set. Even in very large datasets of contagious networks, they found few large communities (over 100 people) that fit this definition. Broadly speaking, they found that the structure of these graphs was composed of "whiskers" and a "core". Whiskers are a set of nodes connected to the rest of the graph by only a one or a few edges. The *core* is a big connected tangle with no subsets of small conductance. The "community" structure that they detect (sets with low conductance) can be almost entirely attributed to collections of whiskers–groups just barely connected to the rest of the graph.

The *conductance* of a set denoted $S \subseteq V$

$$\Phi(S) = \frac{E(S, \bar{S})}{min\{degree(S), degree(\bar{S})\}}$$

is equal to the number of edges leaving a set S divided by the sum of the degree of the vertices in S (or $\bar{S}$, whichever is smaller). Thus, if S is insular and does not have many edges leaving it relative to its total degree, then S has low conductance. The community network profile finds the set of each size $s : 1 \leq s \leq |V|/2$ with the lowest conductance and then plots this graph. I.e $f_G(x) = \min_{S:|S|=x} \Phi(S)$.

The network community profile is closely related to isoperimetric inequalities which are a mathematical subject concerned with minimizing the boundary for a given volume (such as the circle in the plane), and thus showing that a large volume implies a certain sized boundary. Here the "volume" corresponds to the total degree and the "boundary" corresponds to the number of edges leaving.

3. SIMULATION RESULTS

In this section we will describe the results of our simulations. We compare the studied properties on the contagious networks and the underlying networks. Overall, the simulations support our theory that contagious networks look like a cascade across simple network formation models.

Our results mainly apply to the beginning of a cascade. Once the cascade reaches the entire graph, then by definition the underlying graph and cascade look the same.

All simulations were done using the SNAP System [20]. This is particularly important for the network community profile and diameter which are both approximated with heuristics. These heuristics were shown to work well in other graphs (see Section 5 of Leskovec et al [25]), but that is no guarantee that they work well here. [5]

Unless specified otherwise, simulations were run on an underlying graph of 1,000,000 nodes with average degree 100, using a rewiring parameter of 0.1 and the random edge transmission models with $\alpha = 0.7$, $\beta = 0.01$ and $\gamma = 0.001$.

We first describe the results when the Watts-Strogatz model is used as a potential graph. We study four properties of the contagious network: degree distribution, diameter, edge densification, and network community profile.

Degree Distribution.

Even though the degree distribution of the Watts-Strogratz model is highly concentrated, the resulting contagious networks have a degree distribution that resembles a heavy-tailed distribution (see Figure 1). This is especially surprising since the maximum degree of the original graph G (and hence the largest possible degree in H) was slightly over 100 in the trials we ran. Eventually, the degree distribution looks like a truncated heavy-tailed distribution. That is, all the points present are in a straight line, but this tail suddenly stops when the underlying graph has no vertices with degree above a certain value.

After a large fraction of the underlying network becomes infected, we expect this effect to go away because the underlying networks does not have a heavy-tailed degree distribution. These plots hold to approximately straight lines until the cascade reaches 80,000 nodes at which point they started to diverge. After about 1/3 of the graph is infected, these plots begin to diverge substantially from the truncated heavy-tailed distribution. The same behavior was observed for all transmission types. However, if α is made too low, or β too high, then this behavior is not as prevalent. The extreme case where $\alpha = 0$ and $\beta = 1$, is very similar to the trace-route sampling setting. On regular graphs the conta-

---

[4]While this terminology is not standard, we use because it captures the operational definition in many other papers, provides enough precision to describe our results, and avoids the controversy of the term power-law (see discussion on page 60 of [16]).

[5]The computer code used is available on the author's homepage.

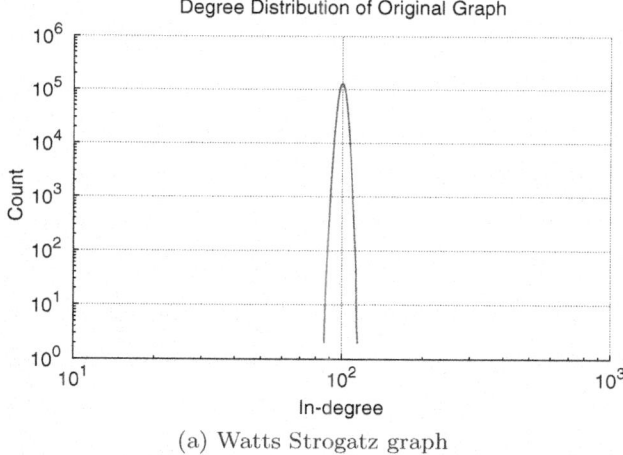
(a) Watts Strogatz graph

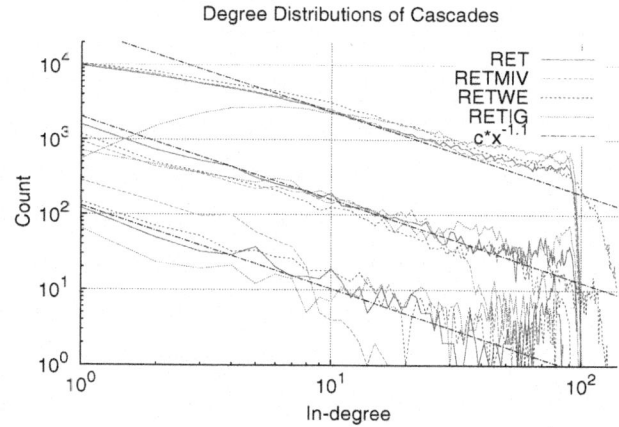
(b) Cascades on Watts Strogatz graph after 625; 5,000; and 80,000 nodes infected. Guidelines indicate a power-law with exponent -1.11

Figure 1: Degree Distribution

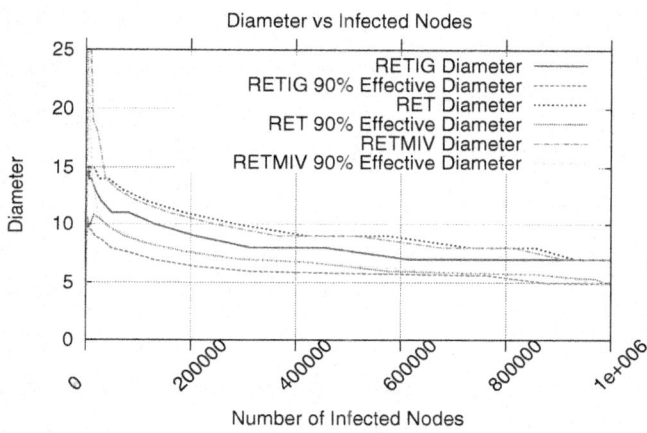

Figure 2: Diameter and 90% effective diameter as a cascade spreads on Watts-Strogatz graph.

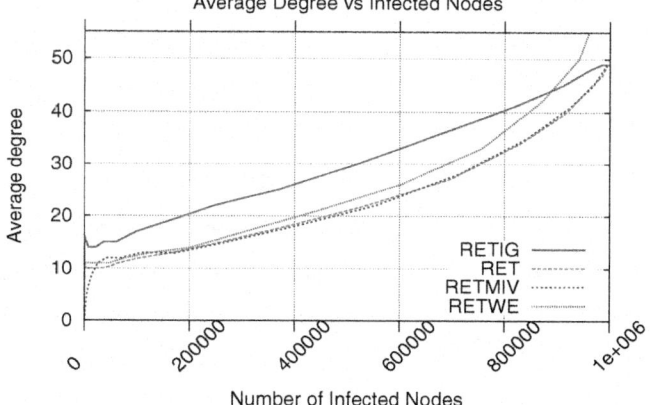

Figure 3: Average degree vs infected Nodes as a cascade spreads on Watts-Strogatz graph.

gious networks limit to a power-law degree distribution [2], but the underlying graphs that we consider do not yield a contagious network with a heavy-tailed degree distribution for these settings of the parameters.

Diameter and Edge density.

We also observe the diameter and average degree of the network. We find the diameter and effective diameter shrink and the average degree increases in accordance with the results of Leskovec, Kleinberg, and Faloutsos [23] (see Figures 2 and 3). Both plots qualitatively match the plots in [23]. The edge density increases approximately linearly, after an initial jump. The diameter, after a large spike and ensuing drop off, decreases gradually.

Network Community Profile.

We found that the network community profile closely matches that of the online social networks that Leskovec et al studied in [25] in all our models of transmission. Figure 4 shows both the original network community profile of the Watts-Strogatz model and the network community profile of a virus spread over the network. This similarity holds up until about 1/3 of the vertices in the graph are infected. Differing the population size and degree does not seem to affect the outcome. However, if the rewiring probability r is made too large ($> .3$) then the shape collapses; the plot never decreases sufficiently. A similar pattern occurs if α is not sufficiently large compared to β; the edges between nodes of the infected graph H fail to fill in and no community structure is detected.

Other Graph Generation Models.

The results for the Planted Community model are nearly identical to those of the Watts-Strogatz model, which implies a certain robustness of these results.

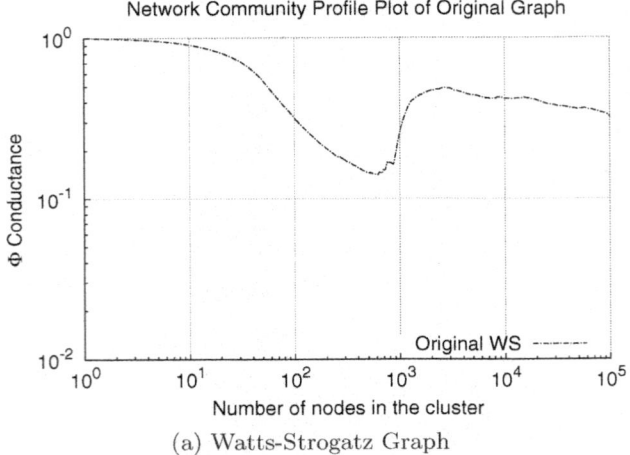
(a) Watts-Strogatz Graph

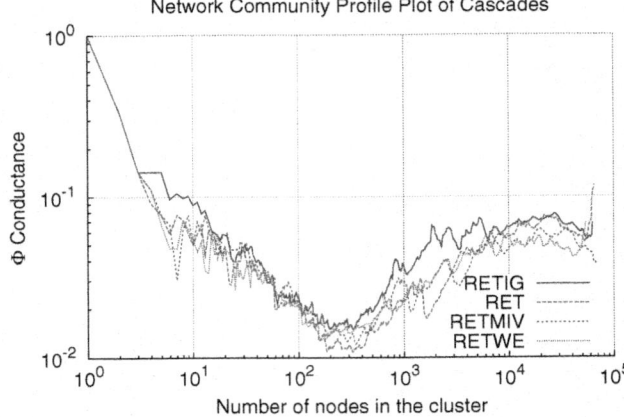
(b) Cascades on Watts-Strogatz Graph after 80,000 nodes infected.

Figure 4: Network Community Profile

Our hypothesis was not confirmed on all graphs. We do not observe all of these behaviors when we run these processes on various graph generation models including Erdös-Rényi random graphs [10], Preferential Attachment networks [4], or complete graphs. We hypothesize that, in the Erdös-Rényi random graphs and the Preferential Attachment model, this is because there is very little clustering to begin with, causing the virus to spread evenly over the graph in a tree like fashion and remain unclustered. Such behavior might not continue if nodes "met" other infected nodes by virtue of being infected and having a common neighbor. To test this hypothesis we embellish the dynamics to artificially add community structure using $RETWE$ as a model of spreading. We find that the network community profile still does not look like the sought after behavior, though it comes closer.

In the complete graph, we hypothesize that the reason contagious communities do not contain all these properties is that there are no "short-cut" edges.

4. THEORETICAL INSIGHTS

In this section, we present mathematical insights that elucidate many of the empirical results of the previous section. In particular, we show that a graph exhibiting both "strong" and "weak" ties should generate contagious networks exhibiting a heavy-tailed degree distribution. This theory accurately predicts the results in the aforementioned section.

The RETIG model is mathematically identical to the model of *first passage percolation*[6] where each edge is equipped with a Poisson clock of unit rate, the number of vertices is conditioned on, and all induced edges are included. First Passage percolation has been studied on Erdös-Rényi random graphs, but to our knowledge, not on graphs with small world properties [35].

While all these properties: degree distribution, diameter, network community profile (referred to as isoperimetric inequalities in this literature), and density have been studied

---

[6]In first passage percolation typically one node starts infected. Each edge is equipped with a clock, and the infection can only travel across each edge when it rings

on certain graphs and even in certain percolation models, we know of no results that apply directly to the situation at hand. In particular, site and bond percolation has been studied (in site percolation each node is present/removed with some independent probability and in bond percolation each edge is present/removed with some independent probability). However, these models differ substantially from the contagion model. Moreover, these results tend to focus on the property of component size, which we fix a priori.

Degree Distribution.

We start with a theorem about a family of graphs closely related to the planted community model.

Definition 1. The *planted clique model* $PCM(n, k, r)$ generates a graph on n nodes by superimposing the edges from a degree rk regular random graph and from partitioning the nodes into n/k cliques of k nodes each.

Next we show that RETIG will produce a power-law degree distribution on such graphs.

Definition 2. A power-law distribution with exponent $-\gamma$ is a distribution on the positive integers where $p(x) \propto L(x)x^{-\gamma}$ such that $\lim_{x\to\infty} L(tx)/L(x) = 1$.

THEOREM 1. *Let G be a family of $PCM(n, \sqrt{n}, r)$ graphs where $0 < r < 1$ is a constant. Then as n increases, the degree distribution of the RETIG on G after infecting $\sqrt[4]{n}$ nodes will limit to a distribution D which is a power-law distribution with exponent $-1 - r$.*

The proof follows from the following more general intuition about the Yule distribution [38, 9, 28]. The Yule distribution was created to model the following situation concerning species and genera: at each time step choose a random species and with probability $1 - \alpha$ the species creates a new species in the same genus, and with probability α the species creates a new species in a new genus. The Yule distribution describes the fraction of genera with a particular number of species in the limit of this process. The tail of this distribution limits to a power-law distribution with exponent $-2 - \frac{\alpha}{1-\alpha}$.

In the PCM graphs, in the limit of n, a $\frac{1}{1+r}$ fraction of each vertices neighbors are *cliquish*–in the same clique–and a $\frac{r}{1+r}$ fraction of its neighbors are *distant*–in different cliques, i.e. neighbors via the random edges. Let $\gamma = \frac{r}{1+r}$. Think of r being small so that γ is close to 0, and consider a cascade over such a network. If we assume that the cliques are sufficiently large, that there are sufficiently many, and that the cascade has not been going too long (so that each vertex has about the same number of non-infected neighbors), then when a new vertex is infected, it is like picking a random vertex in the cascade and infecting a random neighbor. This neighbor has a $1-\gamma$ probability of being cliquish (in the same clique) and a γ probability of being distant (in a different clique). Because of this the number of nodes present in each clique closely follows a Yule distribution with parameter γ, and thus limits to a power-law distribution with exponent $-2 - \frac{\gamma}{1-\gamma} = -2 - r$.

Consider the induced subgraph of the cascade. The degree of each vertex will be equal to the number of cliquish and distant neighbors that are also included. The number of cliquish neighbors of a vertex is simply equal to the number of infected nodes in its clique.

Because the number of infected vertices in each clique limits toward a power-law distribution with exponent $-2 - r$ and a clique with k infected vertices contains k vertices of cliquish degree $k-1$, the degree distribution of cliquish edges limits toward a power-law distribution with exponent about $-2 - r + 1$. Thus the degree distribution will be a power-law with exponent $-1 - r$. It turns out that distant neighbors contribute very little to a vertex's degree in comparison to the cliquish neighbors because the distant neighbors form a random graph. The theorem follows from the above intuition.

Thus in Section 3 we expect that in the RETIG model we have a power-law with exponent ≈ -1.1. We see in Figure 1 of Section 3 that the data fits this well.

Several things break down after the cascade continues to spread. First some vertices in the cascade may have a significant fraction of their neighbors in the cascade. Alternatively, some clusters may have a significant fraction of vertices in the cascade. This means that these vertices (or clusters) are less likely than random to spread to a friend (or gain a new adoptive member). Secondly, as the cascade infects a significant number of nodes in the graph, a random edge may not spread the virus to a new area of the graph, but instead may reach an already infected area.

While the Watts-Strogatz graph with rewire parameter r is not a collection of cliques, it behaves in a similar manner to the above graph. Locally, it looks a lot like a clique. If one imagines several locations of the Watts-Strogatz graph being infected, then each location is "clique-like" in that most vertices in that location are neighbors. When a new vertex is included, with probability r the link will be a rewired link and thus is likely to start a new location of the infection. However, if an original (non-rewired) edge is included, then the new vertex will be in a similar location to previously included vertices (and thus is likely neighbors with most of them).

This argument uses two properties: that networks are locally clique like, and that a fraction of the edges are random. In general, when an underlying network has both high clustering and an α fraction of its edges are "random", we expect the degree distribution of the contagious network to look like a modified Yule distribution for the same reasons.

Edge Densification.

While it seems intuitive that the edges will densify in a cascade, it turns out that the schedule of densification differs between an Erdös-Rényi graph and a graph with clustering.

The edge density of a cascade on an Erdös-Rényi graph will be proportional to the fraction of the network infected by the cascade. Thus, the cascade does not densify until it reaches a constant fraction of the graph. With high probability, all subsets of a small constant fraction, say γn, of nodes in an Erdös-Rényi graph will have average degree less than $2 + \epsilon_\gamma$ where ϵ_γ depends on γ and goes to 0 as γ does. (See, for example, the appendix of [32]). Thus densification cannot happen in a cascade on an Erdös-Rényi random graph with expected constant degree until it infects a significant fraction of nodes. However, as we previously saw, we expect the degree distribution of the cascade in a Watt-Strogatz graph with rewiring probability r to emulate a power-law distribution with exponent $-1-r$ even when only $\sqrt{n}$ vertices have been infected. Thus for $r < 1$ the expected edge density is infinite. Recall that the Yule distribution is what is expected in the limit, so we expect the edge density to grow even before reaching a constant fraction of the vertices.

Forest Fire Model as a Contagious Community.

Leskovec et al found that the Forest Fire model was the one generative model they tested that did replicate the results of the community network profile that they found on the 72 data sets. We note that the exploration component of $RETWE$–that is, adding direct links to neighbors of neighbors–run on a random graph intuitively simulates the Forest Fire model.

The complete Forest Fire model can be found on page 9 of Leskovec, Kleinberg, and Faloutsos [23]. For our purposes, it will suffice to present a slightly simplified undirected version. Our Forest Fire model has one parameter p, the burning probability. The model starts with a single node. At each time step a new node v joins, chooses an existing node u at random, and forms a link with u. For each node w that v links to (starting with u), v also links to k_w of w's neighbors where k_w is chosen from a binomial distribution with mean $(1-p)^{-1}$. This is guaranteed to terminate because v is not allowed to link to any node more than once.

Consider running $RETWE$ on a low degree Erdös-Rényi random graph. When a vertex v joins (if the contagious network has not reached more than a small fraction of the total nodes), then it is very likely that v is attached to exactly one node u of the infected subgraph, H, (the vertex that caused v's infection). The vertex v can add more ties in the infected subgraph H by "exploration" on the infected subgraph through ties of u in H (that is adding direct ties to neighbors of u). Each time that v links to a neighbor w of u in H, the next time step v can add nodes to neighbors of u as well.

The difference between these two models is in the number of neighbors that u finds by exploration. In the forest fire model it is $(1-p)^{-1}$ in expectation, and in the $RETWE$ model it depends on the amount of time the node has been in the network. Also in $RETWE$ a vertex can additionally add ties by infecting neighbors in G that are not yet in H.

Thus it is not surprising that both of these models produce similar though not certainly not identical network community profiles.

5. IMPLICATIONS

We think that there are several important implications from the above models and simulations.

New generative model for contagious networks: This intuition provides us with a new generative model for contagious networks. Start with a social network model, and model a contagion spreading over it. We show that with certain modeling choices (for example Watts-Strogatz with RET adaption) this two-step simulation captures both the intuition of sociology research about social network models–small diameter [27] and local clustering [36]–and the datamining research on contagious networks–shrinking diameter and edge densification [23], heavy-tailed degree distribution [4], and a particular network community profile [21]–all in one simple and intuitive model. We acknowledge that our starting networks (e.g. Watts-Strogatz) are very stylized and not particularly realistic, and we leave it for future work to further develop this framework with more realistic underlying networks and adoption patterns.

Contagious networks and social networks require different models: We show that metrics that appear to test global properties (e.g network community profile) and metrics that appear to test local properties (e.g. degree distribution) may show dramatically different results on contagious networks and the underlying social networks. While this observation has been made before, we provide results that begin to show the scope and scale of the qualitative and quantitative differences.

A long line of work seeks to study network generation models (for examples see [10, 5, 11, 37, 4, 23, 21, 19]). Our results warn that it is unlikely that any one model will serve to generate realistic models for broad class of social networks. This remains true even if we only desire that our models capture fairly basic properties. Indeed, we should not *a priori* expect all properties to be universal, and thus we should not *a priori* expect one generative model. One of the original motivations for sociologists to develop social network theory was to explain how social networks *differ* and to understand the implications of these differences. For example Gans [12] studied how Boston's West End community was unable to form a coalition to fight an "urban renewal" measure that ended up destroying the community, even though other seemingly similar communities were able to organize against and defeat such measures [14] and, moreover, how social structures could have contributed to this outcome.

Distinguishing the two tasks of modeling contagious networks and social networks gives a partial explanation for the difficulty in the task of creating realistic models. By not distinguishing the two tasks, on the one hand, social networks intuition is inadvertently imported into models of contagious networks. However, this intuition is found to be incorrect by datamining contagious communities. On the other hand, the counter-intuitive findings of datamining contagious networks is being advertently brought into social network models, where it makes little intuitive sense.

If indeed social networks and contagious networks are different, this indicates that using data from contagious social networks may mislead us if we try to directly use it to understand social networks. There is selection bias toward datamining contagious networks because data is more easily available for this type of network. Thus, we would expect datamining studies to find attributes that are common amongst contagious networks, but not necessarily present in social networks. Yet, despite the prevalence of certain characteristics (such as heavy tail degree distribution [4]), models without these characteristics may still be valid in a wide variety of interesting settings. In particular, it may be that such characteristics are common to contagious networks, but are not found in many social networks. While we cannot show that contagious networks are necessarily different from social networks on all these metrics, we do remark that if the intuition that guided the first generative models is correct (which do not contain heavy-tailed degree distribution, shrinking diameter [23], edge densification, and a particular network community profile [21]) then such a discrepancy must exist. The counter-intuitive core and whisker structure found by [25] might accurately characterize actual social networks; however, we feel that contagious networks is a more natural explanation of these observations.

At the same time, this distinction frees us from conforming to the intuition of sociologists when modeling contagious communities. Leskovec et al [21], already showed us that contagious networks are not as we would commonly believe them to be. Some doubted the counter-intuitive results. Our experiments provide intuition that supports their observations and show that natural cascades will lead to heavy-tailed degree distributions, edge densification, shrinking diameter, and certain network community profiles in contagious networks.

More speculatively, this gives us an opportunity to *reimagine what a community is and what they look like* through the results of Leskovec et al. These contagious social networks can be seen as a *community* within an underlying social network. That is the nodes of LiveJournal form the "LiveJournal community" which is embedded in society. The LiveJournal network can be viewed both as a network in and of itself, but also as a community in a larger network. We can perhaps use the core/whisker model of Leskovec et al to understand properties of communities.

This model provides an alternate view of community structure compared to that metrics such as modularity [29] and conductance [24]. This view sees communities as gradually adding internal connections and external members who start on the periphery of the group but gradually gradually become more central to the community. Communities are composed of whiskers and a core that has no insular communities.

If dynamics similar to our model exist, then contagious social networks will, with high probability, contain properties for a range of underlying social networks even though these same underlying networks may or may not have these properties. We note that our results only hold when the network is fraction of the total graph. Thus we think they would apply more to LiveJournal than Facebook. Additionally, as we already remarked, not all on-line social networks are necessarily contagious. For example, we do not expect the link structure of anonymous on-line support groups to be generated by a cascade over an underlying social structure.

It would be interesting to go beyond simulation data and attempt to verify this distinction between social networks and contagious networks on real data. However, it is not entirely clear what data set would be a good test. To a certain extent, this is really asking the impossible. How does one accurately measure a "trust" network (even between two people)? However, even in a limited context, it would be interesting to carry out such a study.

5.1 Opportunities

At the same time, these results point toward the opportunities (and challenges) of developing techniques for reconstructing the underlying social network from contagious network data. In a model where social networks are not created *ex nihilo*, but from existing social structures, contagious networks provide a sort of sampling technique for learning the underlying social network.

One future line of inquiry is: what properties can (and what properties cannot) be efficiently recovered? We now suggest how future work could address this question.

6. POTENTIAL NETWORKS

Our model can be conceptualized in a framework that we call "potential networks". Potential networks is a two phase model of social networks. The first phase is the "potential" network. This network may not be directly observed or even exist an any normal manner. The second phase is the "behavioral" network, which is observable. However, the behavior network is realized by running some random process over the potential network which samples vertices and edges from it to produce the behavioral network and in some cases adds additional edges.

The key insight here is that we already have data from contagious networks and the process by which a contagious network grows acts "locally"–ties are added to the community two people at a time. Ethnographic tools could be used to build a model of how a particular technology spreads based on interviewing individuals. Thus, this process may be much easier to observe than the original underlying network. Then, based on this model, the data might be reverse engineered to recover "global" properties of the underlying network.

Of course, real processes are more complicated than the models in this paper. However, we do not think that this formidable challenge is insurmountable. By better modeling how particular contagious networks grow, we may be able to use the vast amounts of data to reconstruct properties of the underlying social network.

Related Work.

Recent work by Gomez-Rodriguez, Leskovec, and Krause [13] creates a model to try to infer a network of influence by looking only at the time sequence of an infectious outbreak (e.g. a news item through the blogosphere). They show via computer simulations that their heuristics for recovering a potential network, given the timing data from a series of outbreaks, can simultaneously give high precision and recall of the original edges. This model requires many cascades to be spread over the same nodes, while in the potential network setting, only one cascade is observed.

Questions similar to this have been looked at before in field of sampling theory, for example see [7] and [31]. However, the techniques for reconstructing graph properties from sampled data is much smaller; see Chapter 5 in [17] for a survey of such results. In fact, graphs have traditionally been hard to sample and this is part of the reason that the newly acquired large-scale data are so welcome.

Work by Handcock and Giles [15] proposes a method of estimating properties from adaptively sampled networks by using maximum likelihood estimates over exponential graph models. Moreover they show that their method does well on real test data. A key observation made here is that simply because the sampled graph data is not representative of the graph, does not mean that key attributes cannot be reconstructed in a more clever way. However this work seems to rely on an assumption that fails in our setting: that which data are observed and which data remain unseen only depends on the observed data. In a cascade, the fact that the cascade does not reach a person, already indicates that the person is likely not tightly connected to many infected nodes.

Finally, there has been recent work on how to sample a network in a way that makes it easy to recover certain properties (e.g. [22, 34]), however, in our framework the way that the network is sampled is fixed.

There are more results in sampling literature, but none seem to apply to the case where the part of the underlying graph that is observed depends on the underlying graph itself in a way that is not explicitly controlled by the sampler.

7. ACKNOWLEDGMENTS

I would like to thank the many people whose help and insights have influenced this paper including Sarita Yardi, Matthew Salganik, Michael Mohoney, Jure Leskovec, and danah boyd. Also, I would like state my appreciation for SNAP the Stanford Network Analysis Platform.

8. REFERENCES

[1] Twitter about page, October 2010. http://www.twitter.com/about.

[2] D. Achlioptas, A. Clauset, D. Kempe, and C. Moore. On the bias of traceroute sampling: or, power-law degree distributions in regular graphs. In *Proceedings of the thirty-seventh annual ACM symposium on Theory of computing*, STOC '05, pages 694–703, New York, NY, USA, 2005. ACM.

[3] L. A. N. Amaral, A. Scala, M. Barthélémy, and H. E. Stanley. Classes of small-world networks. *Proceedings of the National Academy of Sciences of the United States of America*, 97(21):11149–11152, 2000.

[4] A. Barabasi and R. Albert. Emergence of scaling in random networks. *Science*, (286):509–512, 1999.

[5] E. A. Bender and E. R. Canfield. The asymptotic number of labeled graphs with given degree sequences. *Journal of Combinatorial Theory, Series A*, 24(3):296–307, 1978.

[6] D. Centola. The spread of behavior in an online social network experiment. *Science*, 329(5996):1194–1197, 2010.

[7] W. G. Cochran. *Sampling Techniques*. John Wiley, 3rd edition, 1977.

[8] N. Conti and P. Doreian. Social network engineering and race in a police academy: A longitudinal analysis. *Social Networks*, 32(1):30–43, 2010.

[9] M. Draief and L. Massoulié. *Epidemics and Rumours in Complex Networks*. Number 369 in London Mathematical Society Lecture Note Series. Cambridge University Press, 2009.

[10] P. Erdos and A. Renyi. On the evolution of random graphs. In *Publications of the Mathematical Institute of the Hungarian Academy of Sciences*, pages 17–61, 1960.

[11] O. Frank and D. Strauss. Markov graphs. *Journal of the American Statistical Association*, 81(395):832–842, 1986.

[12] H. J. Gans. *The urban villagers: group and class in the life of Italian-Americans*. Free Press (Collier-Macmillan), 1962.

[13] M. Gomez Rodriguez, J. Leskovec, and A. Krause. Inferring networks of diffusion and influence. In *KDD '10: Proceedings of the 16th ACM SIGKDD international conference on Knowledge discovery and data mining*, pages 1019–1028, 2010.

[14] M. Granovetter. The Strength of Weak Ties. *The American Journal of Sociology*, 78(6):1360–1380, 1973.

[15] M. S. Handcock and K. J. Gile. Modeling social networks with sampled data. *The Annals of Applied Statistics*, 4(1):5–25, 2010.

[16] M. O. Jackson. *Social and Economic Networks*. Princeton University Press, 2008.

[17] E. D. Kolaczyk. *Statistical Analysis of Network Data: Methods and Models*. Springer Series in Statistics. Springer, 2009.

[18] A. Lakhina, J. W. Byers, M. Crovella, and P. Xie. Sampling biases in IP topology measurements. In *INFOCOM 2003 Twentysecond Annual Joint Conference of the IEEE Computer and Communications Societies*, volume 1, pages 332–341. Ieee, 2003.

[19] S. Lattanzi and D. Sivakumar. Affiliation networks. In *Proceedings of the 41st annual ACM symposium on Theory of computing*, STOC '09, pages 427–434, 2009.

[20] J. Lescovec. Snap: Stanford network analysis program, 2010.

[21] J. Leskovec, L. Backstrom, R. Kumar, and A. Tomkins. Microscopic evolution of social networks. In *KDD '08: Proceeding of the 14th ACM SIGKDD international conference on Knowledge discovery and data mining*, pages 462–470, New York, NY, USA, 2008. ACM.

[22] J. Leskovec and C. Faloutsos. Sampling from large graphs. *Proceedings of the 12th ACM SIGKDD international conference on Knowledge discovery and data mining KDD 06*, (12):631, 2006.

[23] J. Leskovec, J. Kleinberg, and C. Faloutsos. Graphs over time: densification laws, shrinking diameters and possible explanations. In *KDD '05: Proceedings of the eleventh ACM SIGKDD international conference on Knowledge discovery in data mining*, pages 177–187, New York, NY, USA, 2005. ACM.

[24] J. Leskovec, K. Lang, A. Dasgupta, and M. Mahoney. Statistical properties of community structure in large social and information networks. In *Proceedings of the 17th International World Wide Web Conference*, 2008.

[25] J. Leskovec, K. J. Lang, A. Dasgupta, and M. W. Mahoney. Community structure in large networks: Natural cluster sizes and the absence of large well-defined clusters. *Internet Mathematics*, 6(1):29–123, 2008.

[26] A. Marin and B. Wellman. Social network analysis: An introduction. Book forth-coming, chapter available on-line.

[27] S. Milgram. The small world problem. *Psychology Today*, 1:62–67, 1967.

[28] M. E. J. Newman. Power laws, pareto distributions and zipf's law. *Contemporary Physics*, 46:323–351, 2005.

[29] M. E. J. Newman and M. Girvan. Finding and evaluating community structure in networks. *Phys. Rev. E*, 69(2):026113, 2004.

[30] S. F. Sampson. *Crisis in a cloister*. PhD thesis, Cornell University, 1969.

[31] C. E. Särndal, B. Swensson, and J. Wretman. *Model Assisted Survey Sampling*. Springer Series in Statistics. Springer-Verlag, 1992.

[32] G. Schoenebeck. Linear level Lasserre lower bounds for certain k-CSPs. In *Proceedings of the 49th IEEE Symposium on Foundations of Computer Science*, pages 593–692, 2008.

[33] M. Segal. Alphabet and attraction: An unobtrusive measure of the effect of propinquity in a field setting. *Journal of Personality and Social Psychology*, 30(5):654–657, 1974.

[34] D. Stutzbach, R. Rejaie, N. Duffield, S. Sen, and W. Willinger. On unbiased sampling for unstructured peer-to-peer networks. *IEEE/ACM Transactions on Networking*, 17(2):377–390, 2009.

[35] R. Van Der Hofstad, G. Hooghiemstra, and P. Van Mieghem. First-passage percolation on the random graph. *Probab. Eng. Inf. Sci.*, 15:225–237, April 2001.

[36] D. Watts. Networks, dynamics, and the small world phenomenon. *American Journal of Sociology*, 105(2):493–527, 1999.

[37] D. Watts and S. Strogatz. Collective dynamics of 'small-world' networks. *Nature*, (393):440–442, 1998.

[38] G. U. Yule. A Mathematical Theory of Evolution, Based on the Conclusions of Dr. J. C. Willis, F.R.S. *Royal Society of London Philosophical Transactions Series B*, 213:21–87, 1925.

Do Social Explanations Work? Studying and Modeling the Effects of Social Explanations in Recommender Systems

Amit Sharma
Dept. of Computer Science
Cornell University
Ithaca, NY 14853 USA
asharma@cs.cornell.edu

Dan Cosley
Information Science
Cornell University
Ithaca, NY 14853 USA
danco@cs.cornell.edu

ABSTRACT

Recommender systems associated with social networks often use social explanations (e.g. "X, Y and 2 friends like this") to support the recommendations. We present a study of the effects of these social explanations in a music recommendation context. We start with an experiment with 237 users, in which we show explanations with varying levels of social information and analyze their effect on users' decisions. We distinguish between two key decisions: the likelihood of checking out the recommended artist, and the actual rating of the artist based on listening to several songs. We find that while the explanations do have some influence on the likelihood, there is little correlation between the likelihood and actual (listening) rating for the same artist. Based on these insights, we present a generative probabilistic model that explains the interplay between explanations and background information on music preferences, and how that leads to a final likelihood rating for an artist. Acknowledging the impact of explanations, we discuss a general recommendation framework that models external informational elements in the recommendation interface, in addition to inherent preferences of users.

Categories and Subject Descriptors

H.1.2 [**Models and Principles**]: User/machine systems—*Human Factors*; H.3.3 [**Information Storage and Retrieval**]: Information Search and Retrieval—*Information Filtering*

Keywords

recommender systems, social explanation, influence

1. INTRODUCTION

Theories of social proof and social influence [5] suggest that our preferences are impacted by the actions of those around us. For example, if our friends like a restaurant, we may be tempted to try it out. Many online social networks leverage this notion by supplementing items they recommend with social information about other people who like the item. For example, "N of your friends like this item", or "X and Y recommend this". Figure 1 shows how these bits of information have permeated our online experience.

Copyright is held by the International World Wide Web Conference Committee (IW3C2). IW3C2 reserves the right to provide a hyperlink to the author's site if the Material is used in electronic media.
WWW 2013, May 13–17, 2013, Rio de Janeiro, Brazil.
ACM 978-1-4503-2035-1/13/05.

Depending on the goals of the system, social information may shed light on the underlying algorithm [24] or make recommendations more personal and attractive [11]. This extra social information can be thought of as an *explanation* for a recommendation. These explanations may influence how we think about a recommended item. For instance, social explanations might influence people's willingness to try out an item because a trusted friend has endorsed it or they want to be able to talk about it with their friends. They might influence people's ratings, just as displaying predicted ratings in a recommender system affects people's actual ratings [7]. They might even influence our opinion of the system itself, by making its decision-making more transparent [21].

Although these social explanations are becoming popular, little is known about how they affect decision-making around the recommendations, or how users make sense of this social information. How might different explanations influence our evaluation of a recommended item, and how might particular individuals be more or less susceptible to these explanations? Further, these explanations often involve disclosing others' interests or past activities and may imply endorsement of the recommended items, raising questions about the acceptability of such explanations.

In the present work, we develop a framework for understanding the effect of social explanations on how people make decisions around recommendations. We first distinguish between two phases of evaluation: before and after consuming a recommended item. In the first phase, a user evaluates her *likelihood* of checking out an item. In the second phase, the user evaluates the item itself, based on her *consumption* experience. We can consider these likelihood and consumption ratings as measures of the persuasiveness and informativeness of an explanation: persuasive explanations might increase likelihood ratings, while informative explanations might lead to likelihood ratings that closely align with consumption ratings.

Through a user study in which we recommend musical artists with social explanations and minimal artist information, we find that different kinds of social explanations do have different effects on likelihood ratings. However, it is only a secondary effect, with the dominant influence on most people's likelihood ratings being their inherent expectations of how they will like the item. Further, social explanations are not always persuasive. Users' comments show that a trusted friend's name can increase the credibility of a recommendation, but a friend whose interests are unknown or incompatible negatively influences likelihood ratings. Based on these insights, we present a generative model that ex-

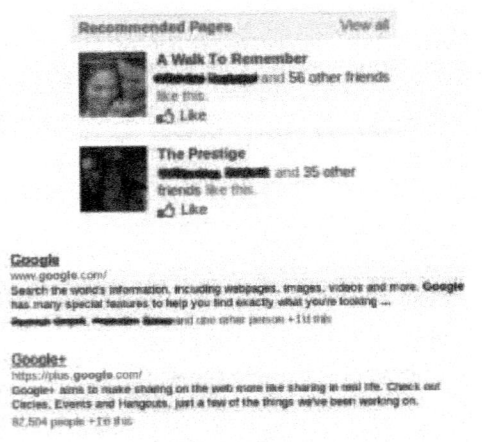

Figure 1: Examples of social explanations typically found on the web. Here we show screenshots from Facebook's page recommender and Google. Names and counts of friends, and number of people who like an item are presented to the user.

plains much of the interplay between social explanations and inherent preferences on likelihood ratings, a model that can be generalized to include other sources of explanation as well. People's comments also revealed that they have quite different strategies for making sense of social explanations, suggesting that personalizing explanations might have real value.

In a second phase of the study, we ask people to return about a week later and listen to music by artists they had rated in the first phase. We find that the effect of different kinds of social explanations does not transfer to the consumption phase. In fact, like Bilgic et al., we find a low correlation between likelihood and consumption ratings people give to the same artist [2]. This suggests that there are different motivations and goals for the two phases, and further, that although explanations are persuasive, they are not very informative and may lead people astray.

These notions of likelihood and consumption have natural parallels to the ideas of click-throughs and purchases in e-commerce. The gap between likelihood and consumption suggests that rather than optimizing one or the other, as most recommender work does, it would be fruitful to model both. We discuss how knowledge of the two phases and their relative characteristics can be used to design recommendation models that consider both the probability of click-throughs and of consumption preferences, helping designers optimize aspects of users' experience to support goals such as serendipity and novelty.

2. RELATED WORK

We build on existing work that shows the value of explaining recommendations in general and the growing trend to use social information in recommender systems for both preference modeling and explanation.

2.1 Explanations in recommender systems

Deciding whether to consume a recommended item is not done in isolation, but in a situated context [14]. Terming rating as a cognitive process, Lueg argues that the ratings are a dynamic result of the interaction of an individual with an "information situation". In our context, an explanation is part of the information presented about a recommendation, and studies show that explanations play an important role in helping a user evaluate a recommendation [23, 26]. In one of the first studies of explanations, Herlocker et al. evaluated 21 types of explanation interfaces for a movie recommender system [11]. They found that a histogram showing the ratings of similar users is the most persuasive for users when asked about their likelihood to see a movie.

However, being persuasive has drawbacks. Another study found that although explanations might persuade a user to try an item, they were not good for accurately estimating the quality of an item [2]. The authors further argue the goal of a recommender should not be to promote a recommendation (which they call *promotion*), but rather enable a user to make a more accurate judgment on the true quality of the item for that person (which they call *satisfaction*).

Besides helping users make an informed choice, explanations may also increase the acceptability of a recommender system overall, by communicating why an item has been recommended to a user [24] and thus helping them understand the system. These explanations and other presentational choices can be designed to increase the system's trustworthiness [18], and a number of real systems incorporate explanations (e.g., Amazon's explanation of "Customers who bought this also bought these", and Netflix's explanation by genres). Tintarev et al. provide a number of desirable attributes of explanations, including transparency, scrutability, trustworthiness, effectiveness, persuasiveness, efficiency, and satisfaction [25].

One outstanding problem it that is not clear how to characterize explanations' influence on either likelihood or consumption ratings. Computing persuasiveness is difficult because people's likelihood decisions are also informed by the merits of the recommended item and by other information presented in the interface. And, though Cosley et al. found that displaying predicted ratings caused people to change their own ratings of movies [7], this was likely a short-term effect caused by displaying the predicted rating at the same time as the user the rated movie. Here, we attempt to tease out persuasiveness through comparing a number of different social explanation strategies and by putting a substantial delay between the likelihood and consumption ratings.

2.2 Social information for recommendation

With the growth of the social web, systems can use the connections people articulate with people in real life as a source of information for both preference modeling and supporting explanation. People prefer the use of known friends to explain recommendations over the use of "similar" neighbors as computed by many recommendation algorithms [3]. This makes sense in the light of literature about how recommendation is a socially embedded process that depends on the relationship and trust between individuals offering and receiving recommendations [14, 17].

Models based on these theories and the availability of social connection information have been proposed to support collaborating filtering algorithms that use social information [12, 15], focusing on preferences in users' immediate social networks [10, 20] and computing trust between people in networks [9] to improve recommendations.

This information can also be used to support social explanation, as with the neighbor-based ratings in Bilgic and

Mooney [2] and aggregate customer behavior in Amazon. Using user-generated tags, based on their popularity and relevance, is another source of social information that has also been studied for explanation [27]. However, despite the appearance in practice of the use of friendship, egocentric networks, and overall popularity information in social explanations, there has been little study of how they influence likelihood and consumption decisions. Our work directly addresses these questions, and we now turn to the particular social explanations we study.

3. SOCIAL EXPLANATIONS IN THE WILD

Facebook is probably the most ubiquitous context in which we see these social explanations, powered by the Like button. Any page on Facebook, or any entity recognized by Facebook's open graph (such as a movie, a URL, or Facebook content such as status updates or comments), can be Liked. Items in Facebook then present information about who else has Liked them. A number of other websites dedicated to social recommendation and discovery (such as Getglue or Hunch[1]) suggest items along with an explanation of who (or how many) watched or rated those items. Even in search, such explanations are starting to be shown (Figure 1).

In general, these social explanations follow a few basic forms that theories of social influence suggest might influence people's decision-making [5]. In Facebook, for instance, many items have information about how many people in general, or how many of a person's own friends, have Liked the item. Such explanations rest on the idea of social proof, that people follow other people's behaviors because they assume that others have reasons for doing those things [6]. Other social explanations provide the names of particular friends who have Liked the item; particularly if the names chosen are good friends, this might tap into the idea that people we like are more persuasive [4, 10]. Finally, the work on trust in recommender systems suggests that recommendations from domain experts are more likely to be persuasive. Social explanations can also combine these kinds of information, for instance, providing both names and counts of others' activity around items.

A fundamental question is whether, and how, these social explanations influence user decisions. In addition, we would like to investigate how different types of social information vary in their impact. We are interested in both the *persuasive* power of such explanations, as well as their *informative* power (whether they lead to satisfying choices). From a recommender systems perspective, this leads to questions of how to choose an appropriate explanation for a recommendation, as well as how to choose the recommendations themselves, given desired goals such as end-user satisfaction. Based on the discussion above, we articulate four high-level research questions:

[**RQ1**]: How do different social explanation strategies influence likelihood ratings?
[**RQ2**]: How do explanations interact with a person's inherent biases or preferences?
[**RQ3**]: How can we model the effect of explanations on likelihood ratings?
[**RQ4**]: How effective are these explanations in directing people to items that receive high consumption ratings?

---
[1]www.getglue.com, www.hunch.com

2,612,211 of Facebook users like this.

Lily Allen
(a) Overall Popularity

7 of your friends like this.

Pink Floyd
(b) Friend Popularity

Amit Sharma likes this.

A.R. Rahman
(c) Good/Random Friend

Amit Sharma and 5 of your friends like this.
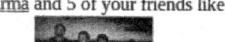

Vampire Weekend
(d) Good Friend & Count

Figure 2: Different explanation strategies used in the experiment, shown along with an artist's name and profile picture. This setup was chosen as a tradeoff between realistic recommendation scenarios (artist information shown) and ideal experiment conditions (no other information).

4. EXPLOREMUSIC: A USER STUDY

We now turn to how we explored these questions through an experiment with 237 users of "ExploreMusic", a web application we created that uses Facebook data to explain a series of music recommendations. We chose music because it is relatively easy to acquire consumption ratings of previously unknown artists (three minutes per song, versus two hours per movie), allowing us to explore whether explanations would influence consumption ratings. We chose Facebook because it has both social network and music preference information already available: Facebook users Like pages associated with musical artists, which both affirms their preferences and makes them publicly visible by default.

4.1 Experiment Design

The experiment took place in two main phases. We initially collect the artists that the participant and her friends Liked. We then show all the artists the participant's friends Like that she hasn't yet Liked and ask her to identify a minimum of 30 that she is not familiar with. We ask for this information to minimize the effects of prior knowledge. To minimize position bias, we ordered artists randomly.

Phase I.

Phase I begins immediately after the initial selection. The experiment is a within-subjects design, where each participant sees the artists they selected, randomly assigned to one of five explanation strategies:

- **Overall Popularity**: The number of Likes by all Facebook users for an artist (*OverallPop*, Figure 2a).

- **Friend Popularity**: The number of friends of a user who Like an artist (*FriendPop*, Figure 2b).

- **Random Friend**: The name of a particular friend, chosen from those that Like an artist (*RandFriend*, Figure 2c).

- **Good Friend**: The name of a "close" friend, chosen from those that Like an artist (*GoodFriend*, Figure 2c).

- **Good Friend & Count** A combination of Good Friend and Friend Popularity (*GoodFrCount*, Figure 2d).

These roughly align with the social explanation strategies described earlier. Given a user and an item, *OverallPop* and *FriendPop* explanations are straightforward to compute using the total number of Facebook users or friends who Like an artist, respectively. For *RandFriend*, we choose a friend at random among all the friends that Like an artist. For *GoodFriend* and *GoodFrCount*, we choose the friend with the highest tie strength who Likes the artist, assuming there exists such a friend with non-zero tie-strength. Using a rough proxy of interaction frequency, loosely inspired by Gilbert and Karahalios' work on predicting tie strength in Facebook [8], we define tie strength between a user and a given friend as the number of interactions (likes, comments, and wall posts) between them among the last 500 interactions involving the user.

For each artist, we show the artist's name, their profile picture on Facebook, and the associated explanation. For *GoodFriend* and *GoodFrCount*, it was often the case that there were no friends with non-zero tie strength who had Liked the item. In these cases, we skipped the item, leading us to show fewer artists in these conditions; we saw this as preferable to assigning artists that random friends had Liked because we were afraid that might dilute the effects of close friendship. For each recommendation, we ask the user how likely is she to check out the recommended artist and how sure is she about her answer. We use a 0-10 (inclusive) Likert scale to collect these answers[2]. To reduce order effects of either artist or explanation strategy, we randomize the order of presentation for artists.

Once all artists are shown, the user fills out a questionnaire that asks about their reaction to the explanations: which ones were more convincing or effective and why, and how she used the information presented to think about the recommended items. We also asked users about how they felt about our using their friends' social information to explain the recommendations, to see if social explanations raised privacy, identity management, or other issues.

Phase II.
In the second phase, users listen to songs by a randomly chosen subset of the artists they had rated in Phase I. Explanations are not shown in this phase. We use Grooveshark[3], a popular music service, to provide the top three songs for a musician, assuming that a musician's best songs are a reasonable representation of the artist. Since each listening task takes 6-9 minutes, we randomly chose two artists from each explanation strategy from Phase I to keep the experiment between 60 and 90 minutes. After listening to the songs, we ask the user to rate how much they liked the artist and their surety about the rating. As before, feedback was collected on a 0-10 Likert scale.

We required participants to wait at least three days between Phase I and Phase II. The goal of this delay, and of not re-showing the social explanation during Phase II, was to

Explanation Strategy	N	Mean	Std. Dev.
FriendPop	1203	2.12	2.42
RandFriend	1225	2.08	2.49
OverallPop	1191	2.36	2.69
GoodFriend	434	2.52	2.69
GoodFrCount	405	2.71	2.90

Table 1: Likelihood ratings for different explanation strategies. Strategies based on good friends have higher ratings.

see whether there was a lasting effect of the explanation on people's consumption ratings [7]. Participants could choose their date for Phase II, with an average delay was 5.2 days.

4.2 Participants and descriptive overview
Participants were drawn from two on-campus experimental subject pools covering undergraduate and graduate students as well as staff at the university. Participants were compensated with either money or with experiment participation credits required by some courses. A total of 237 users took part. Out of these, 175 people completed both phases, while the rest completed only Phase I. The gender ratio was 68% female, 32% male and the average age 20.5 years. We collected a total of 4458 ratings for Phase I and 835 for Phase II.

5. PHASE I: LIKELIHOOD

5.1 Are different social explanations more persuasive on average?
In this section, we address [**RQ1**]: How do different social explanation strategies influence likelihood ratings? Table 1 shows the mean likelihood ratings for different explanation strategies[4]. *GoodFrCount* and *GoodFriend* have relatively high mean ratings, while *FriendPop* and *RandFriend* have relatively low ones, suggesting that good friends are more persuasive than counts or random friends. An ANOVA with repeated measures shows that there is a significant difference between the different explanation strategies ($F(4, 763) = 4.96, p = 0.0006$). A post-hoc Tukey test shows that *GoodFrCount* is significantly higher than *RandFriend* ($p = 0.002$) and *FriendPop* ($p = 0.006$).

Users' qualitative responses give confirmation, explanation, and depth to these differences, showing the importance of good friends and, no matter which explanation strategy, the importance of identifying with the source of the recommendation. Table 2 shows how useful people saw the different information available to them in explanations, based on coding their responses to a question about what aspects of explanations they found most powerful.

Showing the right friends matters.
The most important source of information was the name of the friend who liked the item: *"The best recommendation was the showing which one of my friends liked a song. I didn't really care when I was vaguely told '2 friends'. It was*

---
[2] The initial slider value is 5 and participants usually moved the slider, leading to a relative lack of 5 ratings.
[3] www.grooveshark.com

[4] As a reminder, the good friends-based strategies have fewer ratings because many of the items that were randomly assigned to them hadn't been Liked by a good friend and so were skipped.

Answer Theme	Prevalence (%)
Artist Name and Cover	10
Expert Friends	12
Popular Among Friends	12
Similar Friends	18
Good Friends	26
Overall Popularity	13
None	9

Table 2: Answer themes and their prevalence for the kinds of information participants found most convincing. Some of these were explicitly shown (e.g., overall popularity), while others were raised by participants (e.g., friends having similar taste in music, or perceived to be experts).

Answer Theme	Prevalence (%)
Helped make decision	34
Useful information	40
No use or influence	20
Other	6

Table 3: Answer themes and prevalence for how much participants thought they were influenced by social explanations overall. On balance, people saw them as presenting some useful information, though the amount of influence varied.

important to see names because I know some of my friends' music tastes." [P78]

Good friends were seen as more influential and informative than others: *"I would only be interested in the recommendations based on people who are relatively close to me (compared to random individuals/acquaintances on my friends list)."* [P23]

This is likely because people are better able to think about whether they know and trust good friends' tastes, as suggested by [17]: *"I found it most powerful when I could see what friend likes the artist. I know what kind of music my friends listen to and that helps me know if I would like the artist or not."* [P105]

As Table 2 shows, people also trusted those friends more who were perceived to have similar interests, or a good taste in music: *"Certain friends who I'm close with and have similar interests/music tastes to mine made me feel more likely to listen to a band."* [P141] *"I found the recommendation for Falluah most convincing because it was liked by one of my close friends who has great taste in music."* [P51]

Disagreement, on the other hand, could lead an explanation to be less persuasive: *"Sometimes I judged the artist solely based on which friend liked it. If it was a friend that I did not think I would have similarly music taste too, then I immediately ruled the artist out which may be an incorrect judgment."* [P15]

Popularity only matters if people identify with the crowd.

People were more divided about the efficacy of popularity-based explanations. For some, social proof was clearly an important influence: *"The recommendations that had more 'likes' were most powerful. I assume that there is a reason that so many people like that music."* [P172]

This is particularly true when people see the crowd as providing useful information, as with this person who found recommendations through his friends: *"The recommendations that were most convincing to me were the ones that displayed that a decent number of my friends listened to or liked the artist. I often like to hear my friends' feedback on certain artists and music tastes so that I might get a better idea of what is out there that I might like as well."* [P32]

However, when people don't see their friends as informative for them, they dismissed friend count information: *"Me and my friends' music tastes rarely match up, so I've learned to not care about what music my friends like. Since I mostly listen to mainstream music that means that I would more likely listen to artists with more likes."* [P96]

5.2 How important are social explanations in decision-making?

We have seen that different kinds of social explanations are differently persuasive, and further, that there is variation between individuals in how useful they find different kinds of social explanations. We now look at [**RQ2**]: How do explanations interact with a person's inherent biases or preferences?

People are differently susceptible to social explanation.

Table 3 shows three main groups that emerged when we asked people how they felt about the social explanations and coded their responses. On balance, people felt that social explanations could influence their decisions about artists, but the amount of influence varied quite a bit between people.

As with their reactions to particular kinds of explanation, the differences appear to hinge on whether people expect the social information to be informative: *"I think that it influenced my choice on the degree to which I thought I would search the artist and how confident I felt in that decision. If I knew the person well, trusted them, or was friends with them, or if a lot of my Facebook friends liked that artist, I was definitely more likely to think about researching the artist and feeling confident about it."* [P22]

Social explanation is only part of the story.

Although not cited as important as the social information, the artist's name and photo had an effect too: *"What influenced me the most was the picture associated with the band or artist."* [P66]

For most (Table 2), social explanations were useful, but they were just a part of a story in which other factors also mattered: *"The albums with the most interesting picture, or interesting name, with a lot of likes. If the name struck me, such as 'Formidable Joy', I found myself wondering more. If a lot of my friends liked it, it must be good!"* [P7]

And, as we saw earlier with friends who had incompatible tastes, people would sometimes combine social explanation with artist information in order to reject a recommendation: *"The recommendations didn't really convince me that much. It more mattered what my interests were, not my friends'. If anything, some of the recommendations convinced me not to look up the bands; if the artist looked like a rapper, and the kid who suggested it was a younger boy from my high school who thinks he is cool I was positive that I was not going to look it up."* [P59]

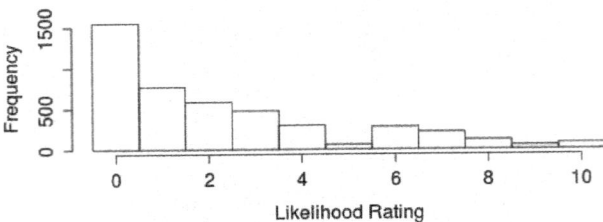

Figure 3: Overall distribution of likelihood ratings across explanation strategies. The mode is 0; frequencies decrease thereafter except for the anomalous 5 and a bump around 6.

Explanation	Fraction > 5
FriendPop	0.137
RandFriend	0.141
OverallPop	0.175
GoodFriend	0.200
GoodFrCount	0.239

Table 4: Fraction of likelihood ratings above 5 (neutral rating) for each explanation strategy. Good friends-based strategies have higher fractions of ratings above 5.

Explanations are a second order effect.
Our final observation is that, based on our data, explanations are a second order effect. The standard deviations for likelihood rating shown in Table 1 were high and the effect size is small (Cohen's $d \approx 0.2$) even between the most and least persuasive social explanation strategies, *GoodFriend* and *RandFriend*. This suggests that other factors play an important role in people's decision-making around recommendations.

Participants' responses comments confirmed that the effect of explanations may depend on pre-conceived notions of quality, or prior information: *"Recommendations of artists that seemed established AND were endorsed by people who I respect were the most powerful. Even if they were endorsed by someone I know and respect, if they seemed to be a garage band, I did not find the recommendation powerful."* [P117] *"I tended to find the most powerful recommendations were the ones whose genre I knew in advance and were liked by my Facebook friends that were closest to me."* [P132]

Further evidence is provided by the distribution of likelihood ratings (Figure 3), which shows that most ratings are below 2. This trend is consistent across explanation strategies, which suggests that in addition to explanation, underlying every rating there is a base decision process, that on average, leans towards rejection.

6. A GENERATIVE MODEL FOR LIKELIHOOD RATINGS

In this section we address [**RQ3**]: How can we model the effect of explanations on likelihood ratings? Figure 4 shows the overall distribution of likelihood ratings, along with the distribution for each social explanation strategy. Although *GoodFrCount* and *GoodFriend* have a higher proportion of likelihood ratings over 5 (see Table 4), it's clear that no matter which explanation strategy is used, people have an underlying model of likelihood that has a stronger influence on their ratings than explanations. This also came out through people's comments in Section 5.2.

Both the graphs and the comments suggest that a mixture model for the ratings might be appropriate, thus, we assume that a person's likelihood rating is derived from a probability distribution that is a mixture of two independent distributions. One represents her inherent likelihood estimate for the item, and the other describes the effect of the social explanation. The density function h for the ratings can be written as:

$$h(x) = af(x) + (1-a)g(x)$$

where $f(x)$ and $g(x)$ are continous density functions representing the inherent preferences and explanations respectively. We model x as a continuous variable, although it is discrete in the data ($x \in \{0, 1, ..., 10\}$). a is a parameter that represents the *rigidness* of the underlying likelihood model, compared to explanations; the higher a is, the less effect explanations have on people's decision-making.

We first specify the base likelihood model, $f(x)$, which in this case includes both a person's base preferences and the effect of showing an artist's name and photo. Note that we are not modeling actual preferences; rather, we are estimating whether the user is likely to try out an artist. Our data shows a large percentage of artists with very low ratings. This is not surprising, since we chose artists that users claimed they knew little about. Thus, we model $f(x)$ as an exponentially decaying function controlled by α, the *discernment* of an individual; discerning individuals tend to give relatively few high ratings.

$$f(x) = \alpha e^{-\alpha x} \quad (1)$$

We now turn to modeling the effect of social explanations, $g(x)$. People described how explanations with specific friends' names had both positive and negative effects, depending on their perception of that friend's usefulness as a source of information. Those who valued popularity-based explanations mentioned how the number of people associated with an explanation helped them decide. It seems plausible that most explanations, whether names or counts, will only be average in their persuasion, as opposed to very convincing ones on either side. Thus we model the effect of explanations by a μ-centered distribution, as shown in equation 2. The center of the distribution gives a sense of the *receptiveness* of an individual, while the standard deviation σ represents how different explanations might affect them differently, the person's *variability*.

$$g(x) = \frac{1}{\sqrt{2\pi}\sigma}e^{-\frac{1}{2}\frac{(x-\mu)^2}{\sigma^2}} \quad (2)$$

Putting things together, we get the following mixture model.

$$h(x) = a(\alpha e^{-\alpha x}) + (1-a)(\frac{1}{\sqrt{2\pi}\sigma}e^{-\frac{1}{2}\frac{(x-\mu)^2}{\sigma^2}}) \quad (3)$$

The mean of density $h(x)$ is given by $a/\alpha + (1-a)\mu$. Constraining the mean to be equal to the mean of the original likelihood distribution (c), we have

$$\alpha = \frac{a}{c - (1-a)\mu}$$

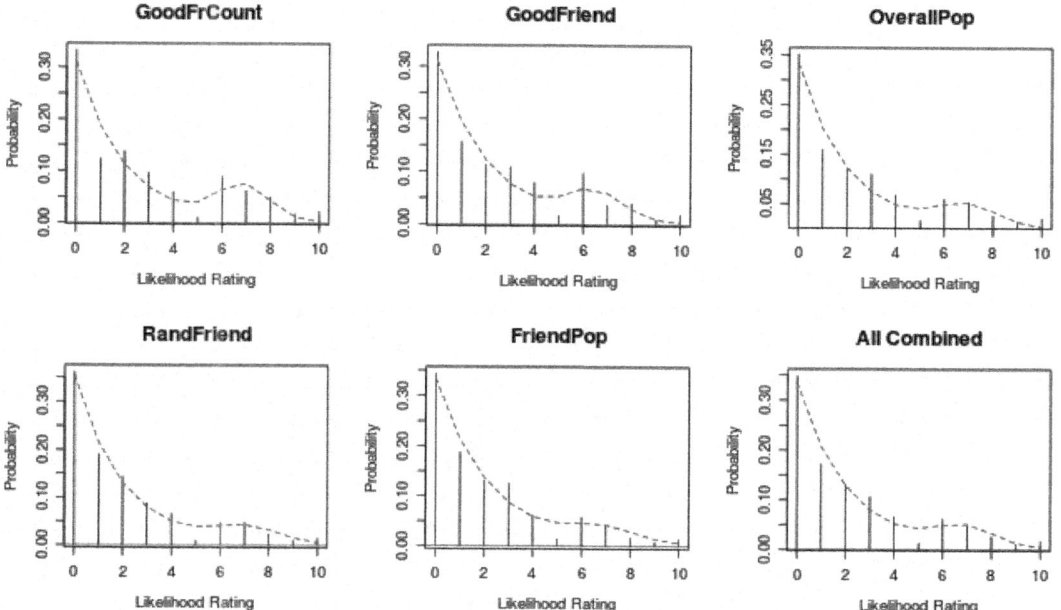

Figure 4: Likelihood densities for different explanation strategies. Note how *GoodFrCount* and *GoodFriend* have higher bumps after 5 than others. The line plot shows the fit of our proposed mixture model.

Thus, the parameters of the model are the receptiveness (μ), the variability (σ), and the rigidness (a) of an individual. Given an artist and an explanation, a user draws her rating from the distribution $h(x)$ as a mixture of her preference and explanation models specified by the triplet (μ, σ, a). Over a set of the user's ratings, the prevalence of a certain rating x can be approximated by $h(x)$.

6.1 Aggregate effects of explanation strategies

We first see how well the model explains the aggregate ratings. For the average user represented by these ratings, we fit the model parameters for ratings from each explanation strategies separately, as well as for the combined case (Figure 4). We evaluate the fits using residual standard error.

Table 5 shows the fitted parameters for the different explanation strategies. First, we observe that values for α are very close to one another for all strategies, giving weight to the assumption of an inherent discernment parameter for the average user that does not depend on explanation strategy. *GoodFrCount* exhibits the lowest value of a, suggesting that explanations of that type influence user ratings more. The receptiveness(μ) and variability(σ) scores together explain how *GoodFrCount* and *GoodFriend* have more ratings above 5, and hence are more consistently persuasive than the others (and giving further support to our earlier findings).

6.2 Different users, different models

Until now, we have analyzed the distribution of the aggregate population. However, as we saw earlier, people are differently affected by explanations; we now look at how we might refine the models by exploiting the differences in susceptibility to explanations demonstrated by Table 3. To do this, we group users into three clusters using a standard

Explanation	Error	α(computed)	μ	σ	a
FriendPop	0.022	0.44	6.85	3.61	0.74
RandFriend	0.018	0.49	7.10	3.57	0.71
OverallPop	0.026	0.49	6.89	3.10	0.66
GoodFriend	0.030	0.46	6.46	2.51	0.66
GoodFrCount	0.034	0.50	6.84	2.26	0.61
Combined	0.022	0.47	6.88	3.05	0.69

Table 5: Fit parameters for likelihood densities of different explanation strategies. *GoodFrCount* has the lowest rigidness (a), which suggests people were more swayed by this explanation strategy.

k-means algorithm, representing users by their mean and variance of ratings. The mean ratings in the three computed clusters are 0.67, 2.44, and 4.89 respectively. Figure 5 shows the distribution of likelihood ratings for the three clusters, and Table 6 shows the fitted parameters (we do not fit for individuals for fear of overfitting, since users have about 30 ratings).

The plots give evidence of these three types of users in the data, with cluster 1 roughly representing the "no use or influence" case, cluster 2 representing "useful information", and cluster 3 representing "helped make decision". Parameter a decreases from cluster 1 to 3, suggesting the decreasing rigidness of individuals towards explanations. Clusters 1 and 3 serve as composing examples of the mixture model: cluster 1 illustrates the dominance of the exponential distribution, while cluster 3 is highly gaussian.

Personalization.

In Section 5.2, we observed how people are differently susceptible to social explanation. The above data provides

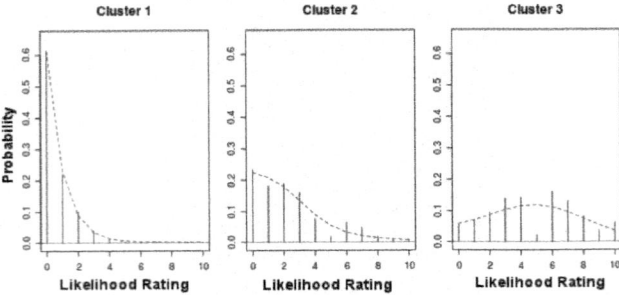

Figure 5: Likelihood rating distributions for three clusters of users. These distributions bring out the three types of users: ones on whom explanations had no effect, those who found them useful and those who relied on them more heavily. As before, the line plots show the fitted mixture models.

Cl#	N	Ratings	Error	μ	σ	a
1	89	1817	0.001	0.05	78.82	0.62
2	84	1610	0.01	1.43	1.98	0.50
3	64	1119	0.04	4.99	3.22	0.08

Table 6: Fitted parameters for three clusters of users. The effect of explanations increases from Cluster 1 to 3, as shown by the values for a.

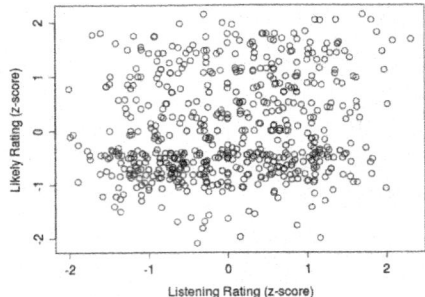

Figure 6: Z-scores of likelihood and listening ratings. The two ratings show little correlation (correlation coeff=0.17)

Explanation	N	Mean	Std. Dev.	Mean-likely
FriendPop	190	4.14	2.85	2.12
RandFriend	192	4.57	3.09	2.08
OverallPop	198	4.86	2.92	2.36
GoodFriend	133	4.57	2.86	2.52
GoodFrCount	122	4.63	2.84	2.71

Table 7: Listening ratings for artists, binned by explanation strategy. *OverallPop* performs the best in Phase II, but we found no significant difference between the ratings.

weight to that observation, and opens up opportunities for personalization of explanations. In a practical system, this could be done in multiple stages. When users first join the system, they can be assigned population averages for these parameters for each explanation strategy. As they encounter explanations, their preferences can be either explicitly captured (e.g., through rating whether an explanation is helpful, as with Amazon reviews) or implicitly inferred based on their reaction to the explained recommendation. As we build up data, we can compare them to cluster models such as those described here to see whether explanations are helpful at all, or have individual models for each user. Eventually, we can infer which types of explanations are the most appropriate for an individual user and prefer showing them when possible.

7. PHASE II: CONSUMPTION

Having analyzed likelihood ratings, we now focus on [**RQ4**]: How effective are these explanations in directing people to items that receive high consumption ratings? First, we study how the different explanation strategies shown in Phase I affected consumption ratings in Phase II. We then contrast the overall consumption ratings with likelihood ratings.

7.1 Do explanations affect consumption ratings?

Table 7 shows the consumption ratings for different explanation strategies. We note that the means for consumption are higher than for likelihood. While *GoodFrCount* performed best for likelihood, we find that *OverallPop* records the highest mean for consumption. However, we must be careful with making conclusions since (except for *FriendPop*), the means for different strategies are quite close, and an ANOVA with repeated measures confirms the differences are not significant ($F(4, 378) = 1.64, p = 0.2$).

Since *OverallPop*, *GoodFrCount* and *GoodFriend* all have comparable ratings, this implies that given a delay of a few days, explanations lose their influence on a user's decision. Figure 7 shows how ratings are close to uniformly distributed across the 11-point scale (except very high ratings, > 8 which show a dip, and the anomalous 5). The different explanation strategies exhibit similar distributions.

7.2 Does likelihood predict consumption?

We next look at whether likelihood ratings can predict later consumption ratings. Figure 6 shows how the two compare, z-score adjusted to control for individual biases in numerical ratings. It is apparent that there is little correlation between likelihood and consumption ratings ($r = 0.17$), suggesting that the persuasiveness and informativeness of an explanation are quite different [2]. Later we will discuss ways to increase the informativeness of explanations through presenting other information, and in the limiting case where we provide almost all the information about an item in a recommendation (such as recommending pictures), these ratings should be close together. But our results show that these two ratings can be quite far apart, suggesting that it will be useful to think about the two kinds of rating independently.

7.3 Modeling Likelihood and Consumption

As noted earlier, scenarios of two-phase recommendation are common on the web—for example, clicking a movie recommendation on Netflix and rating it after watching, or clicking a Page recommendation on Facebook and deciding to Like it. In general, current approaches to information filtering assume that the two ratings are correlated (or have access to only one), and hence optimize only one of the rat-

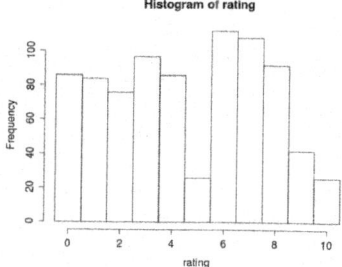

Figure 7: Distribution of consumption ratings for all users. Apart from very high ratings {9,10} and the anomalous 5, ratings are evenly distributed.

ing objectives. For example, recommender systems research focuses mainly on consumption ratings, while ad systems typically optimize click-through rates.

One way we could make use of modeling both likelihood and consumption is by conceptualizing the decision-making as a sequential process. A user proceeds to consume an artist recommendation only after he evaluates a high enough likelihood for liking that artist. Thus we could set up an optimization framework:

$$\text{maximize } R \text{ s.t. } L > \epsilon_u$$

where L and R are the likelihood and consumption ratings for an artist respectively[5]. ϵ can be initialized to a reasonable global value (such as 5 in our case), or a user-specific ϵ_u. Models could iteratively decrement ϵ in case enough recommendations cannot be retrieved, or depending on recommendation goals, may use alternate values for ϵ. For serendipity, one may prefer may prefer to set ϵ lower, for instance. Note that in a domain where R and L are highly correlated, equation reduces to the standard one-phase optimization, maximizing R.

L may depend on the explanation shown, in which case there will be multiple likelihood values for a single item. The models for L and R can be based on standard collaborative filtering models [22] or socially enhanced variants [15].

8. DISCUSSION

We find that social explanations, especially ones involving close friends, are persuasive, though they have secondary effects compared to other sources of informtion about recommended items. However, our data also shows that persuasive explanations may not be informative—that people's ratings of expected liking aren't good proxies of their actual liking of the artists. In this section, we discuss the opportunities and questions that our findings point to, along with the limitations of our study.

Improving expectations of informativeness.

One major finding is that the effect of social explanations is based heavily on a user's expectations of how informative the explanation will be: how they perceive a friend's music tastes to be similar to theirs, or how much they expect to agree with the crowd. Our explanation interfaces were fairly

---

[5]Our formulation is different from multiple objective optimization [1, 19], since the two objectives are sequential.

minimal because, as shown in Section 3, many real social explanation settings—particularly those that present a list of recommended items—convey little additional information beyond a title and a social explanation.

Our results suggest that this might be a mistake, and that systems should design explanation interfaces to increase the informativeness of the explanation. For instance, the interface could show information about similarity to people used in social explanations, either by translating similarity metrics into legible indicators (as with some of the explanation interfaces shown in [11]) or by using representative examples of items liked. It could also show information designed to convey expertise, such as the quantity, diversity, or rarity of items an explainer likes. Based on our results, an effective display of this kind of information might make both individual-based and crowd-based social explanations more useful.

Balancing persuasiveness and informativeness.

Our results also call the difference between persuasiveness and informativeness into sharp focus [2], showing that social explanations along with basic artist information have a limited ability to help people predict their actual liking of a recommended item. Section 7.3 talks about one way to deal with this difference, by modeling persuasiveness and informativeness separately. This approach corresponds to the click-through/purchase distinction in customer behavior in e-commerce sites, and it does have some advantages.

Considering them separately gives designers more freedom to optimize users' experiences and support different recommendation goals [16]. Our initial proposed model suggests that increasing persuasiveness might increase overall user activity and consumption, though at some risk of eroding trust if the system persuades users to consume items they don't actually like. Systems might also effectively support serendipity by increasing the persuasiveness of explanations for items where the consumption model predicts high ratings and the likelihood model predicts low ratings. Tuning the likelihood threshold might also support users who prefer either riskier or more conservative recommendations.

Increasing informativeness of explanations.

An alternative approach to managing the gap between likelihood and consumption ratings would be to enrich explanations in order to close the gap. Our suggestions above about increasing the informativeness of social explanation are one such strategy. However, as we've seen, social explanations are just one part of people's decision-making process. A number of other interface elements have been proposed that might help explain recommendations, including tags associated with the item [27], indicators of the systems's confidence in the recommendation [16], and the predicted rating itself [7].

These interface elements fall into four main classes: tokens of the item itself (such as genres or music clips for music, or trailers, genres, and actors for a movie); data that people attach to the item (ratings, tags, reviews); metadata about those people (similarity information, their ratings); and information about the recommendation system's algorithms (confidence, predicted ratings). Our hypothesis is that item information is more informative, and social and algorithm information are more persuasive, but this is an open question. The space for designing explanations is rich, and more work is needed to explore the effect of these sources of information on both the persuasiveness and the informativeness of explanations of these various types.

Modeling and Personalization.

Our results point towards the merit of personalizing explanation *strategies*, in addition to showing personalized explanations (Section 6.2). Our model may be extended for other explanations, since we make no assumption about the explanations except that they have a gaussian distribution of effects. For instance, in Section 6, we find that some users (cluster 1, Figure 5) do not seem to be affected by social explanations at all, but it is possible they may find other explanations (such as tags, genres) useful. As long as the effects are nearly gaussian, we may use the same model for those explanations too.

There could also be variation within strategies. For example, the relative count of friends who Like an artist, or number of explicit names shown, may impact how a user perceives the explanation (though in our experiments, we did not find a correlation between friend or overall counts and likelihood). Modeling these fine-grained effects can be interesting future work.

Finally, our analysis adds further weight to the importance of *interface elements* such as explanations on how users evaluate a recommendation. Through our model and recommendation framework, we take the first steps towards modeling these effects. In general, it can be useful to augment recommender systems by including these additional signals, either as new item features or through novel models.

Acceptability of social explanation.

Social explanations involve disclosing personal information to friends or even strangers. While we discussed them mainly from the perspective of utility, we have to be mindful of any social norms or privacy expectations these explanations might violate, or personal information they might disclose [13].

At least for the music domain, most participants we surveyed seemed to be comfortable with the idea of sharing Likes: *"Yes, it was just interesting to see which of my friends liked which artists. Depending on how well I knew the person, or what kind of music they listened to, I was more open to listening to the artist."* [P4]

This may be because people are already used to having their information public in online settings: *"While it is off-putting that so much information is online, I do know that this information is accessible whether you show me or not, so I got over it pretty quickly."* [P82]

However, some were still alarmed by the information that can be disclosed. *"No, I was not totally comfortable. Since it could take my friends' information, it could take mine and share it. It felt like a breach of privacy."* [P100]

In particular, social explanations have the potential to misrepresent a person's preferences, taking them out of context by associating him with one or two of his Likes: *"I suppose—I'm not sure that they would be pleased to know that their information appeared in this kind of way. Music preferences are very personal, and this kind of exercise may tend to pull one 'Liked' artist out of context the user's general preferences."* [P128]

Overall, however, participants did not view privacy as a major issue and saw social explanation as a generally useful and acceptable thing to do, at least in this domain. Still, this may not be true for the overall population and for other domains, so exploring design choices that allow users to disable explanation strategies or restrict usage of their data for explanation may be a good idea. This would have little effect on the system's ability to make good explanations in practice but have benefits for people's perceptions of having control over the system.

Limitations.

We want to point out five main factors around our study that readers should bear in mind when applying our results. First, our users are fairly young and primarily drawn from a single university. Older users might have different perceptions of the usefulness and acceptability of social explanations. Second, we focused on the music domain. This was intentional, to support the collection of consumption ratings, but does mean that our results may not apply in domains where consuming items is more costly in terms of money or time. Third, although we took care not to include artists familiar to a user, they were all chosen from her friends' Likes. This might have introduced a selection bias, especially if a few friends Liked most of the artists. Fourth, although we chose a representative sample of social explanation strategies, we did not cover the entire space. Interfaces might show multiple names, or combine other sources of social information. Finally, we focused on explanations in recommendation list interfaces that show relatively little information. Exploring how people make sense of an Amazon or Best Buy product page (with richer information including detailed item information and explanations such as rating histograms) is a largely open, but interesting, question.

9. CONCLUSION

Still, our results add to knowledge around the effects of social explanations on user preferences, both before and after consumption of a recommendation. Based on our findings, we presented a generative model that explains much of the variation in likelihood ratings and that can be personalized. The low correlation between likelihood and consumption ratings highlights another facet of how users make sense of explanations, that persuasiveness and informativeness of an explanation are largely independent. This suggests that modeling one may not be sufficient, and we proposed an optimization framework that can be useful for thinking about both likelihood and consumption ratings.

Going forward, we believe that explanations, and other external informational elements, influence the evaluation of recommendations in non-trivial ways. They raise interesting questions at the intersection of user interfaces and recommender systems. For example, which types of explanations are both persuasive and informative, and for which users? Explicitly modeling interface elements could provide a basis for design choices at the interface level, as well as help in improving the perceived quality of a recommender system.

10. ACKNOWLEDGMENTS

This work was supported by the National Science Foundation under grants IIS 0910664 and IIS 0845351. Michael Triche helped in developing the experimental system.

11. REFERENCES

[1] G. Adomavicius, N. Manouselis, and Y. Kwon. Multi-criteria recommender systems. In *Recommender Systems Handbook*, pages 769–803. Springer US, 2011.

[2] M. Bilgic and R. Mooney. Explaining recommendations: Satisfaction vs. promotion. In *Proc. Beyond Personalization: A Workshop on the Next Stage of Recommender Systems Research, IUI*, pages 13–18, 2005.

[3] P. Bonhard and M. A. Sasse. 'Knowing me, knowing you' – Using profiles and social networking to improve recommender systems. *BT Technology Journal*, 24(3), July 2006.

[4] N. Christakis and J. Fowler. *Connected: The surprising power of our social networks and how they shape our lives*. Little, Brown, 2009.

[5] R. Cialdini. *Influence: Science and practice*, volume 4. Allyn and Bacon Boston, MA, 2001.

[6] R. Cialdini and M. Trost. Social norms, conformity, and compliance. *The Handbook of Social Psychology: 2-Volume Set*, page 151, 1998.

[7] D. Cosley, S. K. Lam, I. Albert, J. A. Konstan, and J. Riedl. Is seeing believing? How recommender system interfaces affect users' opinions. In *Proc. CHI*, pages 585–592, 2003.

[8] E. Gilbert and K. Karahalios. Predicting tie strength with social media. In *Proc. CHI*, pages 211–220, 2009.

[9] J. Golbeck and J. Hendler. Inferring binary trust relationships in Web-based social networks. *ACM Trans. Internet Technol.*, 6:497–529, November 2006.

[10] I. Guy, N. Zwerdling, D. Carmel, I. Ronen, E. Uziel, S. Yogev, and S. Ofek-Koifman. Personalized recommendation of social software items based on social relations. In *Proc. RecSys*, pages 53–60, 2009.

[11] J. L. Herlocker, J. A. Konstan, and J. Riedl. Explaining collaborative filtering recommendations. In *Proc. CSCW*, pages 241–250, 2000.

[12] I. Konstas, V. Stathopoulos, and J. M. Jose. On social networks and collaborative recommendation. In *Proc. SIGIR*, pages 195–202, 2009.

[13] M. Kosinski, D. Stillwell, and T. Graepel. Private traits and attributes are predictable from digital records of human behavior. *Proceedings of the National Academy of Sciences*, 2013.

[14] C. Lueg. Social filtering and social reality. In *Proc. 5th DELOS Workshop on Filtering and Collaborative Filtering*, pages 10–12. ERCIM Press, 1997.

[15] H. Ma, D. Zhou, C. Liu, M. R. Lyu, and I. King. Recommender systems with social regularization. In *Proc. WSDM*, pages 287–296, 2011.

[16] S. M. McNee, S. K. Lam, C. Guetzlaff, J. Konstan, and J. Riedl. Confidence displays and training in recommender systems. In *INTERACT '03 IFIP TC13 Intl. Conf. on HCI*, pages 176–183, 2003.

[17] S. Perugini, M. A. Gonçalves, and E. A. Fox. Recommender systems research: A connection-centric survey. *J. Intell. Inf. Syst.*, 23(2):107–143, Sept. 2004.

[18] P. Pu and L. Chen. Trust building with explanation interfaces. In *Proc. IUI*, pages 93–100, 2006.

[19] M. Rodriguez, C. Posse, and E. Zhang. Multiple objective optimization in recommender systems. In *Proc. RecSys*, pages 11–18, 2012.

[20] A. Sharma and D. Cosley. Network-centric recommendation: Personalization with and in social networks. In *Proc. IEEE SocialCom*, pages 282–289, 2011.

[21] R. Sinha and K. Swearingen. The role of transparency in recommender systems. In *Proc. CHI Extended Abstracts on Human Factors in Computing Systems*, pages 830–831, 2002.

[22] X. Su and T. M. Khoshgoftaar. A survey of collaborative filtering techniques. *Adv. in Artif. Intell.*, 2009:4:2–4:2, January 2009.

[23] K. Swearingen and R. Sinha. Beyond Algorithms: An HCI Perspective on Recommender Systems. In *ACM SIGIR Workshop on Recommender Systems*, 2001.

[24] P. Symeonidis, A. Nanopoulos, and Y. Manolopoulos. Providing justifications in recommender systems. *IEEE Trans. on Systems, Man and Cybernetics, Part A: Systems and Humans*, 38(6):1262–1272, 2008.

[25] N. Tintarev and J. Masthoff. A survey of explanations in recommender systems. In *Proc. ICDEW*, pages 801–810, 2007.

[26] N. Tintarev and J. Masthoff. Designing and evaluating explanations for recommender systems. In *Recommender Systems Handbook*, pages 479–510. Springer US, 2011.

[27] J. Vig, S. Sen, and J. Riedl. Tagsplanations: explaining recommendations using tags. In *Proc. IUI*, pages 47–56, 2009.

Question Answering on Interlinked Data

Saeedeh Shekarpour
Universität Leipzig, IFI/AKSW
shekarpour@informatik.uni-leipzig.de

Axel-Cyrille Ngonga Ngomo
Universität Leipzig, IFI/AKSW
ngonga@informatik.uni-leipzig.de

Sören Auer
Universität Leipzig, IFI/AKSW
auer@informatik.uni-leipzig.de

ABSTRACT

The Data Web contains a wealth of knowledge on a large number of domains. Question answering over interlinked data sources is challenging due to two inherent characteristics. First, different datasets employ heterogeneous schemas and each one may only contain a part of the answer for a certain question. Second, constructing a federated formal query across different datasets requires exploiting links between the different datasets on both the schema and instance levels. We present a question answering system, which transforms user supplied queries (i.e. natural language sentences or keywords) into conjunctive SPARQL queries over a set of interlinked data sources. The contribution of this paper is two-fold: Firstly, we introduce a novel approach for determining the most suitable resources for a user-supplied query from different datasets (disambiguation). We employ a hidden Markov model, whose parameters were bootstrapped with different distribution functions. Secondly, we present a novel method for constructing a federated formal queries using the disambiguated resources and leveraging the linking structure of the underlying datasets. This approach essentially relies on a combination of domain and range inference as well as a link traversal method for constructing a connected graph which ultimately renders a corresponding SPARQL query. The results of our evaluation with three life-science datasets and 25 benchmark queries demonstrate the effectiveness of our approach.

Categories and Subject Descriptors

I.2.7 [**Artificial intelligence**]:

General Terms

Algorithms, Human Factors

Keywords

Question answering, Hidden Markov Model, Linked Data, RDF, Disambiguation, SPARQL

1. INTRODUCTION

There is a large and increasing quantity of structured data available on the Web. Traditional information retrieval approaches based on keyword search are user-friendly but cannot exploit the internal structure of data due to their bag-of-words semantic. For searching information on the Data Web we need similar user friendly approaches i.e. keyword-base interfaces, which leverage the internal structure of the data. Also, Question Answering is a specialized form of information retrieval. A Question Answering system attempts to extract correct answers to questions posed in natural language. Using the structure of data in retrieval process has two prominent advantages. Firstly, it approaches the information retrieval systems to question answering systems. Secondly, it enables us to easily integrate information from different datasets.

In this paper we present an approach for question answering over a set of interlinked data sources. We have to deal with two challenges: A first challenge is that information for answering a certain question can be spread among different datasets employing heterogeneous schemas. This makes the mapping of the input keywords to resources more challenging when compared to querying a single dataset. The second challenge is constructing a formal query from the matched resources across different datasets by exploiting links between the different datasets on the schema and instance levels.

In order to address these challenges, our approach resembles a horizontal search, where query segments derived from an input query are matched against all available datasets. We employ a Hidden Markov Model (HMM) to obtain the optimal input query segmentation and disambiguation of possible matches in a single step. We test different bootstrapping methods for the HMM parameters using various distributions (Normal, Zipf, Uniform) as well as an algorithm based on Hyperlink-Induced Topic Search (HITS). Our proposed functions for HMM parameters produce the best results for both segmentation and disambiguation. Then, we construct a formal query (expressed in SPARQL) using the disambiguated matches by traversing links in the underlying datasets. By taking links between the matched resources (including owl:sameAs links) into account we obtain the *minimum spanning graph* covering all matches in the different datasets.

As a test bed for evaluating our approach we used the Sider [1], Diseasome [8][2] and Drugbank [31][3] datasets published in RDF. Sider contains information about drugs and their side effects. Diseasome contains information about diseases and genes associated with these diseases. Drugbank

---
[1] http://sideeffects.embl.de/
[2] http://diseasome.kobic.re.kr/
[3] http://www.drugbank.ca/

is a comprehensive knowledge base containing information about drugs, drug target (i.e. protein) information, interactions and enzymes. As it can be seen in Figure 1 the classes representing drugs in Drugbank and Sider are linked using `owl:sameAs` and diseases from Diseasome are linked to drugs in Drugbank using `possible Drug` and `possible Disease target`. Diseases and side effects between Sider and Diseasome are linked using the `owl:sameAs` property. Note that in this figure the dotted arrows represent the properties between classes inside a dataset.

Our approach can answer queries with the following three characteristics:

- **Queries requiring fused information:** An example is the query: "side effects of drugs used for Tuberculosis". Tuberculosis is defined in Diseasome, drugs for curing Tuberculosis are described in Drugbank, while we find their side effects in Sider.

- **Queries targeting combined information:** An example depicted in Figure 2 is the query: "side effect and enzymes of drugs used for ASTHMA". Here the answer to that query can only be obtained by joining data from Sider (side effects) and Drugbank (enzymes, drugs).

- **Query requiring keyword expansion:** An example is the query "side effects of Valdecoxib". Here the drug Valdecoxib can not be found in Sider, however, its synonym Bextra is available via Sider.

To the best of our knowledge our approach is the first approach for answering questions on interlinked datasets by constructing a federated SPARQL query. Our main contributions can be summed up as follows:

- We extend the Hidden Markov Model approach for disambiguating resources from different datasets.

- We present a novel method for constructing formal queries using disambiguated resources and leveraging the interlinking structure of the underlying datasets.

- We developed a benchmark consisting of 25 queries for a testbed in the life-sciences. The evaluation of our implementation demonstrates its feasibility with an f-measure of 90%.

This paper is organized as follows: In the subsequent section, we present the problem at hand in more detail and some of the notations and concepts used in this work. Section 3 presents the proposed disambiguation method in detail along with the evaluation of the bootstrapping. In section 4, we then present the key steps of our algorithm for constructing a conjunctive query. Our evaluation results are presented in the section 5 while related work is reviewed in the section 6. We close with a discussion and future work.

2. PROBLEM AND PRELIMINARIES

In this section, we introduce some crucial notions employed throughout the paper and describe the main challenges that arise when transforming user queries to formal, conjunctive queries on linked data.

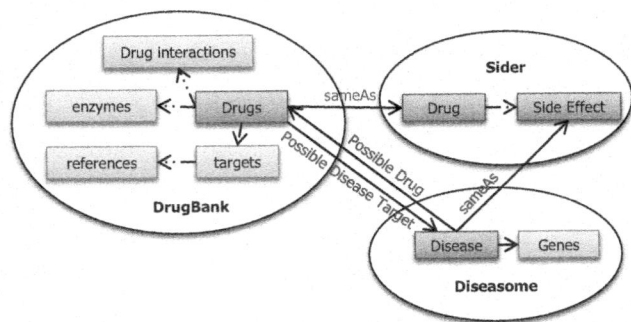

Figure 1: Schema interlinking for three datasets i.e. DrugBank, Sider, Diseasome.

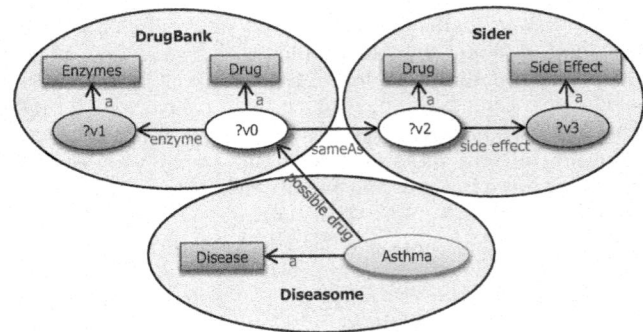

Figure 2: Resources from three different datasets are fused at the instance level in order to exploit information which are spread across diverse datasets.

An RDF knowledge base can be viewed as a directed, labeled graph $G_i = (V_i, E_i)$ where V_i is a set of nodes comprising all entities and literal property values, and E_i is a set of directed edges, i.e. the set of all properties. We define linked data in the context of this paper as a graph $G = (V = \bigcup V_i, E = \bigcup E_i)$ containing a set of RDF knowledge bases, which are linked to each other in the sense, that their sets of nodes overlap, i.e. that $V_i \cap V_j \neq \emptyset$.

In this work we focus on user-supplied queries in natural language, which we transform into an ordered sets of keywords by tokenizing, stop-word removal and lemmatization. Our input query thus is an n-tuple of keywords, i.e. $Q = (k_1, k_2, ..., k_n)$.

Challenge 1: Resource Disambiguation. In the first step, we aim to map the input keywords to a suitable set of entity identifiers, i.e. resources $R = \{r_1, r_2...r_m\}$. Note, that several adjacent keywords can be mapped to a single resource, i.e. $m \leq n$. In order to accomplish this task, the input keywords have to be grouped together to segments. For each segment, a suitable resource is then to be determined. The challenge here is to determine the right segment granularity, so that the most suitable mapping to identifiers in the underlying knowledge base can be retrieved for constructing a conjunctive query answering the input query.

For example, the question *'What is the side effects of drugs used for Tuberculosis?'* is transformed to the 4-keyword tuple *(side, effect, drug, Tuberculosis)*. This tuple can be segmented into *('side effect drug', 'Tuberculosis')* or *('side effect', 'drug', 'Tuberculosis')*. Note that the second segmentation is more likely to lead to a query that contains the results intended by the user. In addition to detecting the right segments for a given input query, we also have to map each of these segments to a suitable resource in the underlying knowledge base. This step is dubbed *entity disambiguation* and is of increasing importance since the size of knowledge bases and schemes heterogeneity on the Linked Data Web grows steadily. In this example, the segment *'drug'* is ambiguous when querying both Sider and Diseasome because it may refer to the resource `diseasome:Tuberculosis` describing the disease Tuberculosis or to the resource `sider:Tuberculosis` being the side effect caused by some drugs.

Challenge 2: Query Construction. Once the segmentation and disambiguation have been completed, adequate SPARQL queries have to be generated based on the detected resources. In order to generate a conjunctive query, a connected subgraph $G' = (V', E')$ of G called the **query graph** has to be determined. The intuition behind constructing such a query graph is that it has to fully cover the set of mapped resources $R = \{r_1, ..., r_m\}$ while comprising a minimal number of vertices and edges ($|V'| + |E'|$). In linked data, mapped resources r_i may belong to different graphs G_i; thus the query construction algorithm must be able to traverse the links between datasets at both schema and instance levels. With respect to the previous example, after applying disambiguation on the identified resources, we would obtain the following resources from different datasets: `sider:sideEffect`, `diseasome:possibleDrug` and `diseasome:1154`. The appropriate conjunctive query contains the following triple patterns:
1. `diseasome:1154    diseasome:possibleDrug    ?v1 .`
2. `?v1              owl:sameAs                ?v2 .`
3. `?v2              sider:sideEffect          ?v3 .`

The second triple pattern bridges between the datasets Drugbank and Sider.

2.1 Resource Disambiguation

In this section, we present the formal notations for addressing the resource disambiguation challenge, aiming at mapping the n-tuple of keywords $Q = (k_1, k_2, ..., k_n)$ to the m-tuple of resources $R = (r_1, ..., r_m)$.

DEFINITION 1 (SEGMENT AND SEGMENTATION). *For a given query $Q = (k_1, k_2, ..., k_n)$, the segment $S_{(i,j)}$ is the sequence of keywords from start position i to end position j, i.e., $S_{(i,j)} = (k_i, k_{i+1}, ..., k_j)$. A query segmentation is an m-tuple of segments $SG(Q) = (S_{(0,i)}, S_{(i+1,j)}, ..., S_{(l,n)})$ with non-overlapping segments arranged in a continuous order, i.e. for two continuous segments $S_x, S_{x+1}: Start(S_{x+1}) = End(S_x) + 1$. The concatenation of segments belonging to a segmentation forms the corresponding input query Q.*

DEFINITION 2 (RESOURCE DISAMBIGUATION). *Let the segmentation $SG' = (S^1_{(0,i)}, S^2_{(i+1,j)}, ..., S^x_{(l,n)})$ be the suitable segmentation for the given query Q. Each segment S^i of SG' is first mapped to a set of candidate resources $R_i = \{r_1, r_2...r_h\}$ from the underlying knowledge base. The aim of the disambiguation step is to detect an m-tuple of resources $(r_1, r_2, ..., r_m) \in R_1 \times R_2 \times ... \times R_m$ from the Cartesian product of the sets of candidate resources for which each r_i*

Valid Segments	Samples of Candidate Resources	
side effect	1. sider:sideEffect	2. sider:side_effects
drug	1. drugbank:drugs	2. class:Offer
	3. sider:drugs	4. diseasome:possibledrug
tuberculosis	1. diseases:1154	2. side_effects:C0041296

Table 1: Generated segments and samples of candidate resources for a given query.

Data: q: n-tuple of keywords, knowledge base
Result: SegmentSet: Set of segments
1 SegmentSet=new list of segments;
2 start=1;
3 **while** $start <= n$ **do**
4      $i = start$;
5   **while** $S_{(start,i)}$ is valid **do**
6         $SegmentSet.add(S_{(start,i)})$;
7   i++;
8   **end**
9   start++;
10 **end**

Algorithm 1: Naive algorithm for determining all valid segments taking the order of keywords into account.

has two important properties: First, it is among the highest ranked candidates for the corresponding segment with respect to the similarity as well as popularity and second it shares a semantic relationship with other resources in the m-tuple. Semantic relationship refers to the existence of a path between resources.

The disambiguated m-tuple is appropriate if a query graph [capable of answering the input query] can be constructed using all resources contained in that m-tuple. The order in which keywords appear in the original query is partially significant for mapping. However, once a mapping from keywords to resources is established the order of the resources does not affect the SPARQL query construction anymore. This is a fact that users will write strongly related keywords together, while the order of only loosely related keywords or keyword segments may vary. When considering the order of keywords, the number of segmentations for a query Q consisting of n keywords is $2^{(n-1)}$. However, not all these segmentations contain valid segments. A *valid segment* is a segment for which at least one matching resource can be found in the underlying knowledge base. Thus, the number of segmentations is reduced by excluding those containing invalid segments.

Algorithm 1 shows a naive approach for finding all valid segments when considering the order of keywords. It starts with the first keyword in the given query as first segment, then adds the next keyword to the current segment and checks whether this addition would render the new segment invalid. This process is repeated until we reach the end of the query. The input query is usually short. The number of keywords is mainly less than 6 [4]; therefore, this algorithm is not expensive. Table 1 shows the set of valid segments along with some samples of the candidate resources computed for the previous example using the naive algorithm. Note that 'side effect drug', 'side', 'effect' are not a valid segments.

---
[4] http://www.keyworddiscovery.com/keyword-stats.html?date=2012-08-01

2.2 Construction of Conjunctive Queries

The second challenge addressed by this paper tackles the problem of generating a federated conjunctive query leveraging the disambiguated resources i.e. $R = (r_1, ..., r_m)$. Herein, we consider conjunctive queries being conjunctions of SPARQL algebra triple patterns[5]. We leverage the disambiguated resources and implicit knowledge about them (i.e. types of resources, interlinked instances and schema as well as domain and range of resources with the type property) to form the triple patterns.

For instance, for the running query which asks for a list of resources (i.e. side effects) which have a specific characteristic in common (i.e. caused by drugs used for Tuberculosis'). Suppose the resources identified during the disambiguation process are: `sider:sideEffect`, `Diseasome:possibleDrug` as well as `Diseasome:1154`. Suitable triple patterns which are formed using the implicit knowledge are:
1. `Diseasome:1154    Diseasome:possibleDrug   ?v1 .`
2. `?v1              owl:sameAs               ?v2 .`
3. `?v2              sider:sideEffect         ?v3 .`

The second triple pattern is formed based on interlinked data information. This triple connects the resources with the type drug in the dataset Drugbank to their equivalent resources with the type drug in the Sider dataset using `owl:sameAs` link. These triple patterns satisfy the information need expressed in the input query. Since most of common queries commonly lack of a quantifier, thus conjunctive queries to a large extend capture the user information need. A conjunctive query is called query graph and formally defined as follows.

DEFINITION 3 (QUERY GRAPH). *Let a set of resources $R = \{r_1, ..., r_n\}$ (from potentially different knowledge bases) be given. A query graph $QG_R = (V', E')$ is a directed, connected multi-graph such that $R \subseteq E' \cup V'$. Each edge $e \in E'$ is a resource that represents a property from the underlying knowledge bases. Two nodes n and $n' \in V'$ can be connected by e if n (resp. n') satisfies the domain (resp. range) restrictions of e. Each query graph built by these means corresponds to a set of triple patterns. i.e. $QG \equiv \{(n, e, n') | (n, n') \in V^2 \wedge e \in E\}$.*

3. RESOURCE DISAMBIGUATION USING HIDDEN MARKOV MODELS

In this section we describe how we use a HMM for the concurrent segmentation of queries and disambiguation of resources. First, we introduce the notation of HMM parameters and then we detail how we bootstrap the parameters of our HMM for solving the query segmentation and entity disambiguation problems.

Hidden Markov Models: Formally, a hidden Markov model (HMM) is a quintuple $\lambda = (X, Y, A, B, \pi)$ where:

- X is a finite set of states. In our case, X is a subset of the resources contained in the underlying graphs.

- Y denotes the set of observations. Herein, Y equals to the valid segments derived from the input n-tuple of keywords.

- $A : X \times X \to [0, 1]$ is the transition matrix of which each entry a_{ij} = is the transition probability $Pr(S_j|S_i)$ from state i to state j;

- $B : X \times Y \to [0, 1]$ represents the emission matrix. Each entry $b_{ih} = Pr(h|S_i)$ is the probability of emitting the symbol h from state i;

- $\pi : X \to [0, 1]$ denotes the initial probability of states.

Commonly, estimating the hidden Markov model parameters is carried out by employing supervised learning. We rely on *bootstrapping*, a technique used to estimate an unknown probability distribution function. Specifically, we bootstrap[6] the parameters of our HMM by using string similarity metrics (i.e., *Levenshtein* and *Jaccard*) for the emission probability distribution and more importantly the topology of the graph for the transition probability. The results of the evaluation show that by using these bootstrapped parameters, we achieve a mean reciprocal rank (MRR) above 84%.

Constructing the State Space: A-priori, the state space should be populated with as many states as there are entities in the knowledge base. The number of states in X is thus potentially large given that X will contain all RDF resources contained in the graph G on which the search is to be carried out, i.e. $X = V \cup E$. For DBpedia, for example, X would contain more than 3 million states. To reduce the number of states, we exclude irrelevant states based on the following observations: (1) A relevant state is a state for which a valid segment can be observed (we described the recognition of valid segments in Section 2.1). (2) A valid segment is observed in a state if the probability of emitting that segment is higher than a given threshold θ. The probability of emitting a segment from a state is computed based on the similarity score which we describe in Section 3.1. Thus, we can prune the state space such that it contains solely the subset of the resources from the knowledge bases for which the emission probability is higher than θ. In addition to these states, we add an **unknown entity state** (UE) which represents all entities that were pruned. Based on this construction of state space, we are now able to detect likely segmentations and disambiguation of resources, the segmentation being the labels emitted by the elements of the most likely sequence of states. The disambiguated resources are the states determined as the most likely sequence of states.

Extension of State Space with reasoning: A further extension of the state space can be carried out by including resources inferred from lightweight `owl:sameAs` reasoning. We precomputed and added the triples inferred from the symmetry and transitivity property of the `owl:sameAs` relation. Consequently, for extending the state space, for each state representing a resource x we just include states for all resources y, which are in an `owl:sameAs` relation with x.

3.1 Bootstrapping the Model Parameters

Our bootstrapping approach for the model parameters A and π is based on the HITS algorithm and semantic relations between resources in the knowledge base. The rationale is that the semantic relatedness of two resources can defined in

---
[5] Throughout the paper, we use the standard notions of the RDF and SPARQL specifications, such as graph pattern, triple pattern and RDF graph.

[6] For the bootstrapping test, we used 11 sample queries from the QALD benchmark 2012 training dataset.

terms of two parameters: the distance between the two resources and the popularity of each of the resources. The distance between two resources is the path length between those resources. The popularity of a resource is simply the connectivity degree of the resource with other resources available in the state space. We use the HITS algorithm for transforming these two values to hub and authority values (as detailed below). An analysis of the bootstrapping shows significant improvement of accuracy due to this transformation. In the following, we first introduce the *HITS* algorithm, since it is employed within the functions for computing the two HMM parameters A and π. Then, we discuss the distribution functions proposed for each parameter. Finally, we compare our bootstrapping method with other well-known distribution functions.

Hub and Authority of States. *Hyperlink-Induced Topic Search* (HITS) is a link analysis algorithm that was developed originally for ranking Web pages [13]. It assigns a hub and authority value to each Web page. The *hub value* estimates the value of links to other pages and the *authority value* estimates the value of the content on a page. Hub and authority values are mutually interdependent and computed in a series of iterations. In each iteration the authority value is updated to the sum of the hub scores of each referring page; and the hub value is updated to the sum of the authority scores of each referring page. After each iteration, hub and authority values are normalized. This normalization process causes these values to converge eventually.

Since RDF data forms a graph of linked entities, we employ a weighted version of the HITS algorithm in order to assign different popularity values to the states based on the distance between states. We compute the distance between states employing weighted edges. For each two states S_i and S_j in the state space, we add an edge if there is a path of maximum length k between the two corresponding resources. Note that we also take **property** resources into account when computing the path length. The weight of the edge between the states S_i and S_j is set to $w_{i,j} = k - pathLength(i,j)$, where $pathLength(i,j)$ is the length of the path between the corresponding resources. The authority of a state can now be computed by: $auth(S_j) = \sum_{S_i} w_{i,j} \times hub(S_i)$. The hub value of a state is given by $hub(S_j) = \sum_{S_i} w_{i,j} \times auth(S_i)$. These definitions of hub and authority for states are the foundation for computing the transition and initial probabilities in the HMM.

Transition Probability. To compute the transition probability between two states, we take both, the connectivity of the whole of space state as well as the weight of the edge between the two states, into account. The transition probability value decreases with increasing distance between states. For example, transitions between entities in the same triple have a higher probability than transitions between entities in triples connected through auxiliary intermediate entities. In addition to edges representing the shortest path between entities, there is an edge between each state and the *unknown entity (UE)* state. The transition probability of state S_j following state S_i is denoted as $a_{ij} = Pr(S_j|S_i)$. Note that the condition $\sum_{S_j} Pr(S_j|S_i) = 1$ holds.

The transition probability from the state S_i to UE is defined as:
$$a_{iUE} = Pr(UE|S_i) = 1 - hub(S_i)$$

Consequently, a good hub has a smaller probability of transition to *UE*. The transition probability from the state S_i to the state S_j is computed by:
$$a_{ij} = Pr(S_j|S_i) = \frac{auth(S_j)}{\sum_{\forall a_{ik}>0} auth(S_k)} \times hub(S_i)$$

Here, the probability from state S_i to the neighboring states are uniformly distributed based on the authority values. Consequently, states with higher authority values are more probable to be met.

Initial Probability. The initial probability $\pi(S_i)$ is the probability that the model assigns to the initial state S_i in the beginning. The initial probabilities fulfill the condition $\sum_{\forall S_i} \pi(S_i) = 1$. We denote states for which the first keyword is observable by *InitialStates*. The initial states are defined as follows:

$$\pi(S_i) = \frac{auth(S_i) + hub(S_i)}{\sum_{\forall S_j \in InitialStates}(auth(S_j) + hub(S_j))}$$

In fact, $\pi(S_i)$ of an initial state is uniformly distributed on both hub and authority values.

Emission Probability. Both the labels of states and the segments contain sets of words. For computing the emission probability of the state S_i and the emitted segment h, we compare the similarity of the label of state S_i with the segment h in two levels, namely string-similarity and set-similarity level:

- The *string-similarity level* measures the string similarity of each word in the segment with the most similar word in the label using the *Levenshtein distance*.

- The *set-similarity level* measures the difference between the label and the segment in terms of the number of words using the *Jaccard similarity*.

Our similarity score is a combination of these two metrics. Consider the segment $h = (k_i, k_{i+1}, ..., k_j)$ and the words from the label l divided into a set of keywords M and stopwords N, i.e. $l = M \cup N$. The total similarity score between keywords of a segment and a label is then computed as follows:

$$b_{ih} = Pr(h|S_i) = \frac{\sum_{t=i}^{j} \text{argmax}_{m_i \in M}(\sigma(m_i, k_t))}{|M \cup h| + 0.1 * |N|}$$

This formula is essentially an extension of the *Jaccard similarity coefficient*. The difference is that we use the sum of the string-similarity score of the intersections in the numerator instead of the cardinality of intersections. As in the Jaccard similarity, the denominator comprises the cardinality of the union of two sets (keywords and stopwords). The difference is that the number of stopwords is down-weighted by the factor 0.1 to reduce their influence since they do not convey much supplementary semantics.

Viterbi Algorithm for the K-best Set of Hidden States. The optimal path through the HMM for a given sequence (i.e. input query keywords) generates disambiguated resources which form a correct segmentation. The *Viterbi algorithm* or *Viterbi path* [28] is a dynamic programming approach for finding the optimal path through a HMM for a given input sequence. It discovers the most likely sequence of underlying hidden states that might have generated a given sequence of observations. This discovered path has the maximum joint emission and transition probability of the involved states. The sub-paths of this most likely path also have the maximum probability for the respective sub sequence of observations. The naive version of this algorithm just keeps track of the most likely path. We extended this algorithm using a tree data structure to store all possible paths generating the observed query keywords. Thus, our implementation can provide a ranked list of all paths generating the observation sequence with the corresponding probability. After running the Viterbi algorithm for our running example, the disambiguated resources are: {$sider:sideEffect$, $diseasome:possibleDrug$, $diseases:1154$} and consequently the detected segmentation is: {$side\ effect,\ drug,\ Tuberculosis$}.

3.2 Evaluation of Bootstrapping

We evaluated the accuracy of our approximation of the transition probability A (which is basically a kind of uniform distribution) in comparison with two other distribution functions, i.e., *Normal* and *Zipfian* distributions. Moreover, to measure the effectiveness of the *hub* and *authority* values, we ran the distribution functions with two different inputs, i.e. *distance* and *connectivity degree* values as well as *hub* and *authority* values. Note that for a given edge the source state is the one from which the edge originates and the sink state is the one where the edge ends. We ran the distribution functions separately with X being defined as the weighted sum of the normalized distance between two states and normalized connectivity degree of the sink state: $X_{ij} = \alpha \times distance_{(S_i-S_j)} + (1-\alpha) \times (1-connectivityDegree_{S_j})$. Similarly, Y was defined as the weighted sum of the hub of the source state and the authority of the sink state: $Y = \alpha \times hub(S_i) + (1-\alpha) \times (1-authority_{s_j})$. In addition, to measuring the effectiveness of *hub* and *authority*, we also measured a similar uniform function with the input parameters *distance* and *connectivity degree* defined as:

$$a_{ij} = \frac{distance(S_i - S_j)}{\sum_{\forall S_k > 0} distance(S_i - S_k)} * connectivitydegree(S_i)$$

Given that the model at hand generates and scores a ranked list of possible tuples of resources, we compared the results obtained with the different distributions by looking at the *mean reciprocal rank* (MRR) [29] they achieve. For each query $q_i \in Q$ in the benchmark, we compare the rank r_i assigned by different algorithms with the correct tuple of resources and set $MRR(\mathcal{A}) = \frac{1}{|Q|} \sum_{q_i} \frac{1}{r_i}$. Note that if the correct tuple of resources was not found, the reciprocal rank was assigned the value 0. We used 11 queries from QALD2-Benchmark 2012 training dataset for bootstrapping[7]. Figure 3 shows the MRR achieved by bootstrapping the transition probability of this model with 3 different distribution functions per query in 14 different settings. Figure 4 compares the average MRR for different functions employed for bootstrapping the transition probability per setting. Our results show clearly that the proposed function is superior to all other settings and achieves an MRR of approximately 81%. A comparison of the MRR achieved

[7] http://www.sc.cit-ec.uni-bielefeld.de/qald-2

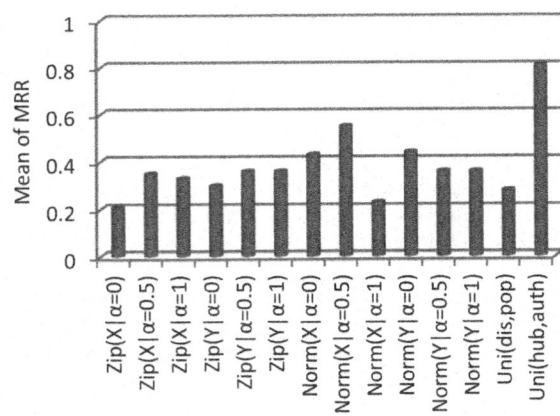

Figure 4: Comparison of different functions and settings for bootstrapping the transition probability. Uni stands for the uniform distribution, while Zip stands for the Zipfian and Norm for the normal distribution.

when using *hub* and *authority* with that obtained when using *distance* and *connectivity degree* reveals that using *hub* and *authority* leads to an 8% improvement on average. This difference is in Zipfian and Normal settings trivial, but very significant in the case of a uniform distribution. Essentially, *HITS* fairly assigns qualification values for the states based on the topology of the graph.

We bootstrapped the emission probability B with two distribution functions based on (1) Levenshtein similarity metric, (2) the proposed similarity metric as a combination of the Jaccard and Levenshtein measures. We observed the MRR achieved by bootstrapping the emission probability of this model employing those two similarity metrics per query in two settings (i.e. natural and reverse order of query keywords). The results show no difference in MRR between these two metrics in the natural order. However, in the reverse order the Levenshtein metric failed for 81% of the queries, while no failure was observed with the combination of Jaccard and Levenshtein. Hence, our combination is robust with regard to change of input keyword order. For bootstrapping the initial probability π, we compared the uniform distribution on both – hub and authority – values with a uniform distribution on the number of states for which the first keyword is observable. The result of this comparison shows a 5% improvement for the proposed function. Figure 5 shows the mean of MRR for different values of the threshold θ employed for prunning the state space. A high value of θ prevents inclusion of some relevant resources and a low value adds irrelevant resources. It can be observed that the optimal value of θ is in the range $[0.6, 0.7]$. Thus, we set θ to 0.7 in the rest of our experiments.

4. QUERY GRAPH CONSTRUCTION

The goal of query graph construction is generating a conjunctive query (i.e. SPARQL query) from a given set of resource identifiers i.e., $R = \{r_1, r_2, ... r_m\}$. The core of SPARQL queries are *basic graph patterns*, which can be viewed as a query graph QG. In this section, we first discuss the formal considerations underlying our query graph

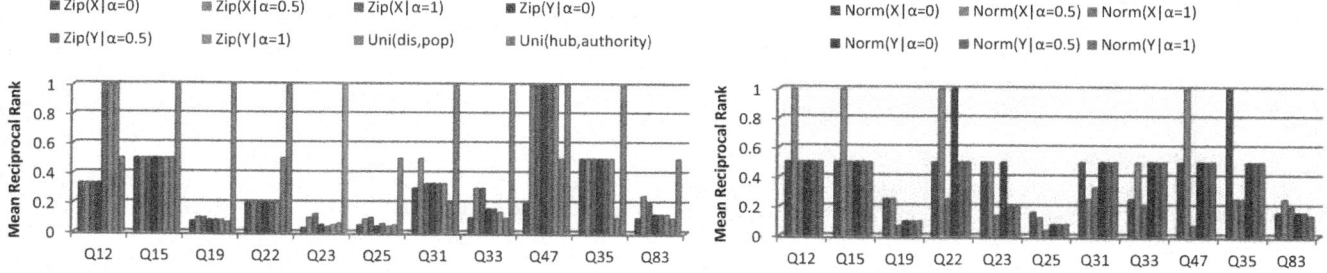

Figure 3: MRR of different distributions per query for bootstrapping the transition probability.

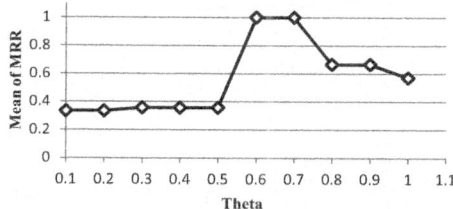

Figure 5: Mean MRR for different values of θ.

generation strategy and then describe our algorithm for generating the query graph. The output of this algorithm is a set of graph templates. Each graph template represents a comprehensive set of query graphs, which are isomorphic regarding edges. A query graph A is isomorphic regarding its edges to a query graph B, if A can be derived from B by changing the labels of edges.

4.1 Formal Considerations

A query graph QG consists of a conjunction of triple patterns denoted by (s_i, p_i, o_i). When the set of resource identifiers R is given, we aim to generate a query graph QG satisfying the *completeness* restriction, i.e., each r_i in R maps to at least one resource in a triple pattern contained in QG. For a given set of resources R, the probability of a generated query graph $\Pr(QG|R)$ being relevant for answering the information need depends on the probability of all corresponding triple patterns to be relevant. We assume that triple patterns are independent with regard to the relevance probability. Thus, we define the relevance probability for a QG as product of the relevance probabilities of the n containing triple patterns. We denote the triple patterns with $(s_i, p_i, o_i)_{i=1...n}$ and their relevance probability with $\Pr(s_i, p_i, o_i)$, thus rendering $\Pr(QG|R) = \prod_{i=1}^{n} \Pr(s_i, p_i, o_i)$. We aim at constructing QG with the highest relevance probability, i.e.
$\arg\max \Pr(QG|R)$. There are two parameters that influence $\Pr(QG|R)$: (1) the number of triple patterns and (2) the number of free variables, i.e. variables in a triple pattern that are not bound to any input resource. Given that $\forall (s_i, p_i, o_i) : \Pr(s_i, p_i, o_i) \leq 1$, a low number of triple patterns increases the relevance probability of QG. Thus, our approach aims at generating small query graphs to maximize the relevance probability. Regarding the second parameter, more free variables increase the uncertainty and consequently cause a decrease in $\Pr(QG|R)$. As a result of these considerations, we devise an algorithm that minimizes the number of both the number of free variables and the number of triple patterns in QG. Note that is each triple pattern, the subject s_i (resp. object o_i) should be included in the domain (resp. range) of the predicate p_i or be a variable. Otherwise, we assume the relevance probability of the given triple pattern to be zero:

$$(s_i \notin domain(p_i)) \vee (o_i \notin range(p_i)) \Rightarrow \Pr(s_i, p_i, o_i) = 0.$$

Forward Chaining. One of the prerequisites of our approach is the inference of implicit knowledge on the types of resources as well as domain and range information of the properties. We define the *comprehensive type* (CT) of a resource r as the set of all super-classes of explicitly stated classes of r (i.e., those classes associated with r via the rdf:type property in the knowledge base). The comprehensive type of a resource can be easily computed using forward chaining on the rdf:type and rdfs:subClassOf statements in the knowledge base. We can apply the same approach to properties to obtain maximal knowledge on their domain and range. We call the extended domain and range of a property p *comprehensive domain* (CD_p) and *comprehensive range* (CR_p). We reduce the task of finding the *comprehensive properties* ($CP_{r-r'}$) which link two resources r and r' to finding properties p such that the comprehensive domain (resp. comprehensive range) of p intersects with the comprehensive type of r resp r' or vice-versa. We call the set OP_r (resp. IP_r) of all properties that can originate from (resp. end with) a resource r the set of outgoing (resp. incoming) properties of r.

4.2 Approach

To construct possible query graphs, we generate in a first step an *incomplete query graph* $IQG(R) = (V'', E'')$ such that the vertices V'' (resp. edges E'') are either equal or subset of the vertices (resp. edges) of the final query graph $V'' \subseteq V'$ (resp. $E'' \subseteq E'$). In fact, an incomplete query graph (IQG) contains a set of disjoint sub-graphs, i.e. there is no vertex or edge in common between the sub-graphs: $IQG = \{g_i(v_i, e_i) | \forall g_i \neq g_j : v_i \cap v_j = \emptyset \wedge e_i \cap e_j = \emptyset\}$. An IQG connects a maximal number of the resources detected beforehand in all possible combinations.

The IQG is the input for the second step of our approach, which transforms the possibly incomplete query graphs into a set of final query graphs QG. Note that for the second step, we use an extension of the minimum spanning tree method that takes subgraphs (and not sets of nodes) as input and generates a minimal spanning graph as output. Since in the second step, the minimum spanning tree does not add any extra intermediate nodes (except nodes connected by owl:sameAs links), it eliminates both the need of keeping an index over the neighborhood of nodes and using exploration for finding paths between nodes.

Generation of IQGs.

After identifying a corresponding set of resources $R = \{r_1, r_2, ...r_m\}$ for the input query, we can construct vertices V' and primary edges of the query graph $E'' \subseteq E'$ in an initial step. Each resource r is processed as follows: (1) If r is an instance, CT of this vertex is equivalent to $CT(r)$ and the label of this vertex is r. (2) If r is a class, CT of this vertex just contains r and the label of this vertex is a new variable.

After the generation of the vertices for all resources that are instances or classes, the remaining resources (i.e., the properties) generate an edge and zero (when connecting existing vertices), one (when connecting an existing with a new vertex) or two vertices. This step uses the sets of incoming and outgoing properties as computed by the forward chaining. For each resource r representing a property we proceed as follows:

- If there is a pair of vertices (v, v') such that r belongs to the intersection of the set of outgoing properties of v and the set of incoming properties of v' (i.e. $r \in OP_v \cap IP_{v'}$), we generate an edge between v and v' and label it with r. Note that in case several pairs (v, v') satisfy this condition, an IQG is generated for each pair.

- Else, if there is a vertex v fulfilling the condition $r \in OP_v$, then we generate a new vertex u with the CT_u being equal to CR_r and an edge labeled with the r between those vertices (v, u). Also, if the condition $r \in IP_v$ for v holds, a new vertex w is generated with CT_w being equal to CD_r as well as an edge between v and w labeled with r.

- If none of the above holds, two vertices are generated, one with CT equal to CD_r and another one with CT equal to CR_r. Also, an edge between these two vertices with label r is created.

This policy for generating vertices keeps the number of free variables at a minimum. Note that whenever a property is connected to a vertex, the associated CT of that vertex is updated to the intersection of the previous CT and CD_p (CR_p respectively) of the property. Also, there may be different options for inserting a property between vertices. In this case, we construct an individual IQG for each possible option. If the output of this step generates an IQG that contains one single graph, we can terminate as there is no need for further edges and nodes.

EXAMPLE 1. *We look at the query:* What is the side effects of drugs used for Tuberculosis?. *Assume the resource disambiguation process has identified the following resources:*

1. diseasome:possibleDrug   (type property)
   CD={diseasome:disease},   CR={drugbank:drugs}
2. diseasome:1154   (type instance)
   CT={diseasome:disease}
3. sider:sideEffect   (type property)
   CD={sider:drug},   CR={sider:sideeffect}

After running the IQGs generation, since we have only one resource with the type class *or* instance, *just one vertice is generated. Thereafter, since only the domain of* possibleDrug *intersects with the CT of the node* 1154, *we generate: (1) a new vertex labeled* ?v0 *with the CT being equal to* $CR =$drugbank:drugs, *and (2) an edge labeled* possibleDrug *from* 1154 *to* ?v0. *Since, there is no matched node for the property* sideEffect *we generate: (1) a new vertex labeled* ?v1 *with the CT being equal to* sider:drug, *(2) a new vertex labeled* ?v2 *with the CT being equal to* sider:sideeffect, *(3) an edge labeled* sideEffect *from* ?v1 *to* ?v2. *Figure 6 shows the constructed IQG, which contains two disjoint graphs.*

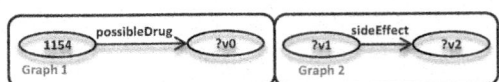

Figure 6: *IQG* **for Example 1.**

Connecting Sub-graphs of an IQG.

Since the query graph QG must be a connected graph, we need to connect the disjoint sub-graphs in each of the $IQGs$. The core idea of our algorithm utilizes the *Minimum Spanning Tree* (MST) approach, which builds a tree over a given graph connecting all the vertices. We use the idea behind Prim's algorithm [3], which starts with all vertices and subsequently incrementally includes edges. However, instead of connecting vertices we connect individual disjoint sub-graphs. Hence, we try to find a minimum set of edges (i.e., properties) to span a set of disjoint graphs so as to obtain a connected graph. Therewith, we can generate a query graph that spans all vertices while keeping the number of vertices and edges at a minimum. Since a single graph may have many different spanning trees, there may be several query graphs that correspond to each IQG. We generate all different spanning graphs because each one may represent a specific interpretation of the user query.

To connect two disjoint graphs we need to obtain edges that qualify for connecting a vertex in one graph with a suitable vertex in the other graph. We obtain these properties by computing the set of comprehensive properties CP (cf. Section 4.1) for each combination of two vertices from different sub-graphs. Note that if two vertices are from different datasets, we have to traverse owl:sameAs links to compute a comprehensive set of properties. This step is crucial for constructing a federated query over interlinked data. In order to do so, we first retrieve the direct properties between two vertices ?v0 ?p ?v1. In case such properties exist, we add an edge between those two vertices to IQG. Then, we retrieve the properties connecting two vertices via an owl:sameAs link. To do that, we employ two graph patterns: (1) ?v0 owl:sameAs ?x. ?x ?p ?v1. (2) ?v0 ?p ?x. ?x owl:sameAs ?v1. The resulting matches to each of these two patterns are added to the IQG. Finally, we obtain properties connecting vertices having owl:sameAs links according to the following pattern:
?v0 owl:sameAs ?x. ?x ?p ?y. ?y owl:sameAs ?v1. Also, matches for this pattern are added to the IQG.

For each connection discovered between a pair of vertices (v, v'), a different IQG is constructed by adding the found edge connecting those vertices to the original IQG. Note that the IQG resulting from this process contains less unconnected graphs than the input IQG. The time complexity in the worst case is $O(|v|^2)$ (with $|v|$ being the number of vertices).

EXAMPLE 2. *To connect two disjoint graphs i.e. Graph 1 and Graph 2 of the IQG shown in Example 1, we need to obtain edges that qualify for connecting either the vertex* 1154 *or* ?v0 *to either vertex* ?v1 *or* ?v2 *in Graph 2. Forward chaining reveals the existence of two* owl:sameAs *connections between two vertices i.e. (1)* 1154 *and* ?v2*, (2)* ?v0 *and* ?v1*. Therefore, we can construct the first query graph template by adding an edge between* 1154 *and* ?v2 *and the second query graph template by adding an edge between* ?v0 *and* ?v1*. The two generated query graph templates are depicted in Figure 7.*

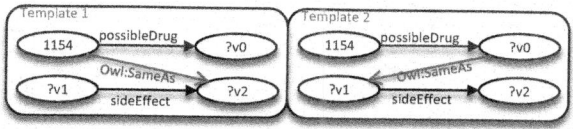

Figure 7: **Generated query graph templates.**

Our approach was implemented as a Java Web application which is publicly available at http://sina-linkeddata.aksw.org. The algorithm is knowledge-base-agnostic and can thus be easily used with other knowledge bases.

5. EVALUATION

Experimental Setup.

The goal of our evaluation was to determine how well (1) our resource disambiguation and (2) our query construction approaches perform. To the best of our knowledge, no benchmark for federated queries over Linked Data has been created so far. Thus, we created a benchmark of 25 queries on the 3 interlinked datasets Drugbank, Sider and Diseasome for the purposes of our evaluation[8]. The benchmark was created by three independent SPARQL experts, which provided us with (1) a natural-language query and (2) the equivalent conjunctive SPARQL query. We selected these three datasets because they are a fragment of the well interlinked biomedical fraction of the Linked Open Data Cloud[9] and thus represent an ideal case for the future structure of Linked Data sources.

We measured the performance of our resource disambiguation approach using the *Mean Reciprocal Rank* (MRR). Moreover, we measured the accuracy of the query construction in terms of precision and recall. To compute the precision, we compared the results returned from the query construction method with the results of the reference query provided by the benchmark. The query construction is initiated with the top-1 tuple returned by the disambiguation approach. All experiments were carried out on a Windows 7 machine with an Intel Core2 Duo (2.66GHz) processor and 4GB of RAM. For testing the statistical significance of our results, we used a Wilcoxon signed ranked test with a significance level of 95%.

---
[8]The benchmark queries are available at http://aksw.org/Projects/lodquery
[9]E.g., 859 owl:sameAs links exists between the 924 drug instances in Sider and the 4772 drug instances in Drugbank

Results.

The detailed results of our evaluation are shown in Figure 9. We ran our approach without and with OWL inferencing during the state space construction. When ran without inferencing, our approach was able to disambiguate 23 out of 25 (i.e. 92%) of the resources contained in the queries without mistakes. For Q9 (resp. Q25), the correct disambiguation was only ranked third (resp. fifth). In the other two cases (i.e. Q10 and Q12), our approach simply failed to retrieve the correct disambiguation. This was due to the path between Doxil and Bextra not being found for Q10 as well as the mapping from disease to side effect not being used in Q12. Overall, we achieve an MRR of 86.1% without inferencing. The MRR was 2% lower (not statistically significant) when including OWL inferencing due to the best resource disambiguation being ranked at the second position for three queries that were disambiguated correctly without inferencing (Q5, Q7 and Q20). This was simply due to the state space being larger and leading to higher transition probabilities for the selected resources. With respect to precision and recall achieved with and without reasoning, there were also no statistically significant differences between the two approaches. The approach without reasoning achieved a precision of 0.91 and a recall of 0.88 while using reasoning led to precision (resp. recall) values of 0.95 (resp. 0.90). Although performance was not (yet) the primary focus of our work, we want to provide evidence, that our approach can be used for real-time querying. Overall the pros and cons of using inferencing are clearly illustrated in the results of our experiments. On Q12, our approach is unable to construct a query without reasoning due to the missing equivalence between the terms disease and side effect. This equivalence is made available by the inference engine, thus making the construction of the SPARQL query possible. On the downside, adding supplementary information through inferencing alters the ranking of queries and can thus lead to poorer recall values as in the case of Q20.

Figure 8 shows the runtime average of disambiguation and query construction with and without inferencing during the state space construction for three runs. As it can be expected, inferencing increases the runtime, especially when the number of input keywords is high. Despite carrying out all computations on-the-fly, disambiguation and query construction terminate in reasonable time, especially for smaller number of keywords. After implementing further performance optimizations (e.g. indexing resource distances), we expect our implementation to terminate in less than 10s also for up to 5 keywords.

6. RELATED WORK

Several **information retrieval** and **question answering** approaches have been developed for the Semantic Web over the past years. Most of these approaches are adaptations of document retrieval approaches. *Swoogle* [5], *Watson* [4] and *Sindice* [24], for example, stick to the document-centric paradigm. Recently, entity-centric approaches, such as *Sig.Ma* [23], *Falcons* [2], *SWSE* [11], have emerged. However, the basis for all these services are keyword indexing and retrieval relying on the matching user keywords and indexed terms. Examples of question answering systems are *PowerAqua* [16] and *OntoNL* [12]. *PowerAqua* can automatically combine information from multiple knowledge bases at runtime. The input is a natural language query

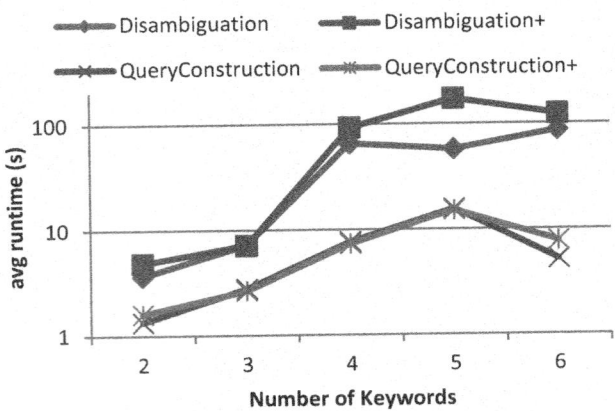

Figure 8: Average runtime of disambiguation and query construction with (+) and without reasoning in the disambiguation phase in logarithmic scale.

and the output is a list of relevant entities. PowerAqua lacks a deep linguistic analysis and can not handle complex queries. *Pythia* [26] is a question answering system that employs deep linguistic analysis. It can handle linguistically complex questions, but is highly dependent on a manually created lexicon. Therefore, it fails with datasets for which the lexicon was not designed. Pythia was recently used as kernel for *TBSL* [25], a more flexible question-answering system that combines Pythia's linguistic analysis and the *BOA framework* [7] for detecting properties to natural language patterns. Exploring schema from anchor points bound to input keywords is another approach discussed in [22]. Querying Linked datasets is addressed with the work mainly treat both the data and queries as bags of words [2, 30]. [10] presents a hybrid solution for querying linked datasets. It run the input query against one particular dataset regarding the structure of data, then for candidate answers, it finds and ranks the linked entities from other datasets. Our approach is a prior work as it queries all the datasets at hand and then according to the structure of the data, it makes a federated query. Furthermore, our approach is independent of any linguistic analysis and does not fail when the input query is an incomplete sentence.

Segmentation and disambiguation are inherent challenges of keyword-based search. Keyword queries are usually short and lead to significant keyword ambiguity [27]. Segmentation has been studied extensively in the natural language processing (NLP) literature e.g., [18]). NLP techniques for chunking such as part-of-speech tagging or name entity recognition cannot achieve high performance when applied to query segmentation. [17] addresses the segmentation problem as well as spelling correction and employs a dynamic programming algorithm based on a scoring function for segmentation and cleaning. An unsupervised approach to query segmentation in Web search is described in [21]. [32] is a supervised method based on Conditional Random Fields (CRF) whose parameters are learned from query logs. For detecting named entities, [9] uses query log data and Latent Dirichlet Allocation. In addition to query logs, various external resources such as Web pages, search result

ID	Query	MRR	Pr	Re	MRR+	Pr+	Re+
1	Which are possible drugs against rickets?	1	1	1	1	1	1
2	Which are the drugs whose side effects are associated with the gene TRPM6?	1	1	1	1	1	1
3	Which diseases are associated with the gene FOXP2?	1	1	1	1	1	1
4	Which are targets of Hydroxocobalamin?	1	1	1	1	1	1
5	Which genes are associated with diseases whose possible drug targets Cubilin?	1	1	1	0.5	1	1
6	Which are possible drugs for diseases associated with the gene ALD?	1	1	1	1	1	1
7	Which are targets for possible drugs for diseases associated with the gene ALD?	1	1	1	0.5	1	1
8	Which are the side effects of Penicillin G?	1	1	1	1	1	1
9	Which drugs have hypertension and vomiting as side effects?	0.33	1	0.2	0.33	1	0.2
10	What are the common side effects of Doxil and Bextra?	0	0	0	0	0	0
11	Which diseases is Cetuximab used for?	1	1	1	1	1	1
12	What are the diseases caused by Valdecoxib?	0	0	0	1	1	1
13	What are the side effects of Valdecoxib?	1	1	1	1	1	1
14	What is the side effects of drugs used for Tuberculosis?	1	0.99	1	1	0.99	1
15	What are enzymes of drugs used for anemia?	1	1	1	1	1	1
16	What are diseases treated by tetracycline?	1	1	1	1	1	1
17	What are side effect and enzymes of drugs used for ASTHMA?	1	0.99	1	1	0.98	1
18	List references of drugs targeting Prothrombin!	1	1	1	1	1	1
19	What are drugs interacting with allopurinol?	1	1	1	1	1	1
20	What are associate genes of diseases treated with Cetuximab?	1	1	1	0.5	1	0.46
21	What is the food interaction of allopurinol?	1	1	1	1	1	1
22	Which drug does have fever as side effect?	1	1	1	1	1	1
23	What is the associated genes of breast cancer?	1	1	1	1	1	1
24	What is the target drug of Vidarabine?	1	1	1	1	1	1
25	Which drugs do target Multidrug resistance protein 1?	0.2	1	1	0.2	1	1

Figure 9: Accuracy results for the benchmark.

snippets, Wikipedia titles and a history of the user activities have been used [19, 21, 1, 20]. Still, the most common approach is using the context for disambiguation [15, 6, 14]. In this work, resource disambiguation is based on the structure of the knowledge at hand as well as semantic relations between the candidate resources mapped to the keywords of the input query.

7. DISCUSSION AND CONCLUSION

We presented a two-step approach for question answering from user-supplied queries over federated RDF data. A main assumption of this work is that some schema information is available for the underlying knowledge base and resources are typed according to the schema. Regarding the disambiguation, the superiority of our model is related to the transition probabilities. We achieved a fair balance between the qualification of states for transiting by reflecting the popularity and distance in the hub and authority values and setting a transition probability to the unknown entity state (depending on the hub value). This resulted in an accuracy of the generated answers of more than 90% for our test-bed with life-science datasets. This work represents a first step in a larger research agenda aiming to make the whole Data Web easily queryable. For scaling the implementation, a first avenue of improvements is related to the performance of the system, which can be improved by several orders of magnitued thorough including better indexing and precomputed forward-chaining.

Acknowledgments

We would like to thank our colleagues from AKSW research group for their helpful comments and inspiring discussions during the development of this approach. This work was supported by a grant from the European Union's 7th Framework Programme provided for the project LOD2 (GA no. 257943).

8. REFERENCES

[1] D. J. Brenes, D. Gayo-Avello, and R. Garcia. On the fly query entity decomposition using snippets. *CoRR*, abs/1005.5516, 2010.

[2] Gong Cheng and Yuzhong Qu. Searching linked objects with falcons: Approach, implementation and evaluation. *Int. J. Semantic Web Inf. Syst.*, 5(3):49–70, 2009.

[3] David R. Cheriton and Robert Endre Tarjan. Finding minimum spanning trees. *SIAM J. Comput.*, 1976.

[4] M. D'aquin, E. Motta, M. Sabou, S. Angeletou, L. Gridinoc, V. Lopez, and D. Guidi. Toward a new generation of semantic web applications. *Intelligent Systems, IEEE*, 23(3):20–28, 2008.

[5] Li Ding, Timothy W. Finin, Anupam Joshi, Rong Pan, R. Scott Cost, Yun Peng, Pavan Reddivari, Vishal Doshi, and Joel Sachs. Swoogle: a search and metadata engine for the semantic web. In *CIKM*. ACM, 2004.

[6] L. Finkelstein, E. Gabrilovich, Y. Matias, E. Rivlin, Z. Solan, G. Wolfman, and E. Ruppin. Placing Search in Context: the Concept Revisited. In *WWW*, 2001.

[7] Daniel Gerber and Axel-Cyrille Ngonga Ngomo. Extracting multilingual natural-language patterns for rdf predicates. In *Proceedings of EKAW*, 2012.

[8] K.I. Goh, M.E. Cusick, D. Valle, B. Childs, M. Vidal, and A.L. Barabási. Human diseasome: A complex network approach of human diseases. In *Abstract Book of the XXIII IUPAP International Conference on Statistical Physics*. 2007.

[9] J. Guo, G. Xu, X. Cheng, and H. Li. Named entity recognition in query. ACM, 2009.

[10] Daniel M. Herzig and Thanh Tran. Heterogeneous web data search using relevance-based on the fly data integration. pages 141–150. ACM, 2012.

[11] Aidan Hogan, Andreas Harth, JÃijrgen Umbrich, Sheila Kinsella, Axel Polleres, and Stefan Decker. Searching and browsing linked data with swse: The semantic web search engine. *J. Web Sem.*, 9(4), 2011.

[12] Anastasia Karanastasi, Alexandros Zotos, and Stavros Christodoulakis. The OntoNL framework for natural language interface generation and a domain-specific application. In *First International DELOS Conference, Pisa, Italy*. 2007.

[13] J. M. Kleinberg. Authoritative sources in a hyperlinked environment. *J. ACM*, 46(5), 1999.

[14] R. Kraft, C. C. Chang, F. Maghoul, and R. Kumar. Searching with context. In *WWW '06*. ACM, 2006.

[15] S. Lawrence. Context in web search. *IEEE Data Eng. Bull.*, 23(3):25–32, 2000.

[16] V. Lopez, Fernandez M., Motta E., and N. Stieler. Poweraqua: Supporting users in querying and exploring the semantic web. In *Journal of Semantic Web*, In press.

[17] K. Q. Pu and X. Yu. Keyword query cleaning. *PVLDB*, 1(1):909–920, 2008.

[18] Lance A. Ramshaw and Mitchell P. Marcus. Text chunking using transformation-based learning. *CoRR*, 1995.

[19] K. M. Risvik, T. Mikolajewski, and P. Boros. Query segmentation for web search. 2003.

[20] A. Shepitsen, J. Gemmell, B. Mobasher, and R. Burke. Personalized recommendation in social tagging systems using hierarchical clustering. ACM, 2008.

[21] B. Tan and F. Peng. Unsupervised query segmentation using generative language models and wikipedia. In *WWW*. ACM, 2008.

[22] Thanh Tran, Haofen Wang, Sebastian Rudolph, and Philipp Cimiano. Top-k exploration of query candidates for efficient keyword search on graph-shaped (rdf) data. In *ICDE*, 2009.

[23] Giovanni Tummarello, Richard Cyganiak, Michele Catasta, Szymon Danielczyk, Renaud Delbru, and Stefan Decker. Sig.ma: Live views on the web of data. *J. Web Sem.*, 8(4):355–364, 2010.

[24] Giovanni Tummarello, Renaud Delbru, and Eyal Oren. Sindice.com: weaving the open linked data. 2007.

[25] Christina Unger, Lorenz Bühmann, Jens Lehmann, Axel-Cyrille Ngonga Ngomo, Daniel Gerber, and Philipp Cimiano. Template-based question answering over rdf data. ACM, 2012.

[26] Christina Unger and Philipp Cimiano. Pythia: compositional meaning construction for ontology-based question answering on the semantic web. In *16th Int. Conf. on NLP and IS*, NLDB'11, pages 153–160, 2011.

[27] A. Uzuner, B. Katz, and D. Yuret. Word sense disambiguation for information retrieval. AAAI Press, 1999.

[28] Andrew J. Viterbi. Error bounds for convolutional codes and an asymptotically optimum decoding algorithm. *IEEE Transactions on Information Theory*, IT-13(2), 1967.

[29] E. Vorhees. The trec-8 question answering track report. In *Proceedings of TREC-8*, 1999.

[30] Haofen Wang, Qiaoling Liu, Thomas Penin, Linyun Fu, Lei Zhang 0007, Thanh Tran, Yong Yu, and Yue Pan. Semplore: A scalable ir approach to search the web of data. *J. Web Sem.*, 2009.

[31] David S. Wishart, Craig Knox, Anchi Guo, Savita Shrivastava, Murtaza Hassanali, Paul Stothard, Zhan Chang, and Jennifer Woolsey. Drugbank: a comprehensive resource for in silico drug discovery and exploration. *Nucleic Acids Research*, 34(Database-Issue), 2006.

[32] X. Yu and H. Shi. Query segmentation using conditional random fields. ACM, 2009.

Pricing Mechanisms for Crowdsourcing Markets *

Yaron Singer
Google, Inc.
Mountain View, CA 94043 USA
yarons@google.com

Manas Mittal
UC Berkeley
Berkeley, CA 94709
mittal@cs.berkeley.edu

ABSTRACT

Every day millions of crowdsourcing tasks are performed in exchange for payments. Despite the important role pricing plays in crowdsourcing campaigns and the complexity of the market, most platforms do not provide requesters appropriate tools for effective pricing and allocation of tasks.

In this paper, we introduce a framework for designing mechanisms with provable guarantees in crowdsourcing markets. The framework enables automating the process of pricing and allocation of tasks for requesters in complex markets like Amazon's Mechanical Turk where workers arrive in an online fashion and requesters face budget constraints and task completion deadlines. We present constant-competitive incentive compatible mechanisms for maximizing the number of tasks under a budget, and for minimizing payments given a fixed number of tasks to complete. To demonstrate the effectiveness of this framework we created a platform that enables applying pricing mechanisms in markets like Mechanical Turk. The platform allows us to show that the mechanisms we present here work well in practice, as well as to give experimental evidence to workers' strategic behavior in absence of appropriate incentive schemes.

Categories and Subject Descriptors

H.0 [**Information Systems**]: General

General Terms

Algorithms, Economics, Human Factors, Theory

Keywords

Crowdsourcing, Mechanism Design, Human Computation, Mechanical Turk, Mechanical Perk

1. INTRODUCTION

The advancement of the internet in the past decade created a platform for a new form of labor markets known as *crowdsourcing markets* where cognitive work can be distributed to hundreds of thousands of geographically disparate workers. In contrast to traditional procurement markets that rely on specialized contractors, requesters in crowdsourcing markets typically outsource large quantities of simple tasks to anonymous, unspecialized workers. Typical examples of crowdsourcing tasks include image labeling, sentiment analysis, content generation, listing verification, image moderation, transcription, and other forms of tasks that are impossible, difficult or too expensive to automate.

There are several crowdsourcing platforms that provide workers with non-monetary incentives like entertainment [9], educational opportunities [5], information [27], and altruism [17] in exchange for their efforts. Despite the success of these platforms, it is often difficult to engineer non-monetary incentive schemes for tedious and repetitive work. Therefore an overwhelming majority of crowdsourcing tasks are performed in exchange for payments [1, 4, 8, 2, 6, 3, 7]. In such markets, implementing a campaign successfully requires pricing and allocating tasks effectively.

Designing effective pricing and allocation schemes presents a challenging problem due to requesters' constraints and the realities of crowdsourcing markets. Requesters often face task completion deadlines and budget constraints, and must account for dramatic elasticity in the workforce supply. Furthermore, there is a large variance in effort required to complete different tasks, which also largely depends on the skills and background of workers who are often based in multiple geographical locations. Despite this difficulty in pricing tasks, most crowdsourcing markets provide requesters surprisingly limited tools for pricing tasks effectively.

In this paper we address the problem of pricing and allocating tasks in crowdsourcing markets. We develop a theoretical framework and design mechanisms that work well in practice and have provable guarantees. In addition, we describe a platform which we implemented that enables requesters to automate the process of pricing in crowdsourcing markets using the mechanisms we present here as well as other pricing schemes. The framework is primarily designed for tasks where the quality of the worker's performance does not yield additional utility to the requester once above a certain quality threshold. Although there are crowdsourcing tasks that do not fall into this category like predicting future events, designing a logo, or writing an introduction to an academic paper, a large fraction of the work in crowdsourcing markets typically fits this criterion. For such tasks requesters often use various methods to ensure the threshold quality is met like injecting gold standards [29], majority voting, and more sophisticated cross-validation methods [31, 36, 30, 35, 28]. Since workers receive payments after requesters' approval in crowdsourcing platforms, we assume

---
*Preliminary results were presented at the *AAAI workshop on Human Computation (HCOMP) 2011*

Copyright is held by the International World Wide Web Conference Committee (IW3C2). IW3C2 reserves the right to provide a hyperlink to the author's site if the Material is used in electronic media.
WWW 2013, May 13–17, 2013, Rio de Janeiro, Brazil.
ACM 978-1-4503-2035-1/13/05.

requesters have access to such verification schemes and focus on efficiently pricing and allocating tasks, independent of their quality.

We take a mechanism design approach to the pricing problem and enable workers to bid on work by expressing their cost for performing tasks and the number of tasks they wish to perform. Although most crowdsourcing platforms do not provide workers such level of expressiveness, existing APIs make this feature easy to integrate into most platforms as we further describe. This relatively minor modification enables designing powerful mechanisms.

The mechanisms we present here are designed for two main objectives: maximizing the number of tasks performed under budget, and minimizing payments for a given number of tasks. We consider requesters that impose a deadline for the completion of tasks and workers who arrive i.i.d. according to some known distribution and can strategically misreport their cost or number of tasks they wish to perform. We therefore design *incentive compatible* mechanisms that ensure that the allocation and pricing are such that it is in every worker's best interest to bid truthfully.

1.1 Related Work

The problem of designing mechanisms for pricing tasks in crowdsourcing markets has been addressed using different models and different techniques, such as bargaining between requesters and workers to minimize work [26] and recently using bandit algorithms to maximize tasks [34]. While both are natural approaches, they leave room for frameworks that allow better theoretical guarantees as used here. In [24] the authors study an orthogonal problem and present an algorithmic framework for matching workers with with requesters based on their skills.

The approach in this paper advocates for eliciting workers costs via incentive compatible protocols. A different approach is that of developing a model for workers' effort and learning its parameters from data as done in [25, 13]. The problem of designing mechanisms for procurement has been extensively studied by the algorithmic game theory community over the past decade. The earlier line of frugality first suggested in [10] focuses on minimizing payments for complex objective functions. Recently, the budget feasibility framework has been initiated in [32], where the goal is to design incentive compatible mechanisms that maximize a requester's objective under a budget. The framework has been adapted to various settings [33, 19, 16, 15, 18] and we follow it in this paper.

In our model we account for the online arrival of workers, which raises a significant challenge. There is substantial literature on online mechanism design where workers arrive according to a given distribution [21, 22, 23, 12, 11]. In our case we consider mechanisms for *buying* items (rather then selling) from strategic agents which requires different machinery. In [14] the authors study online procurement though the emphasis there is on a different model of posted prices.

2. MODEL

In our model we consider a single requester and multiple workers. The requester has a task completion deadline $T \in \mathbb{N}_+$ by which his tasks need to be allocated. Each worker arrives at some time step $t \in \{1, \ldots, T\}$ i.i.d. according to some distribution. Each worker a_i associates a cost $c_i \in \mathbb{R}_+$ for performing a single task posted by the requester and a number of tasks she can complete $v_i \in \mathbb{N}_+$. The requester does not know c_i, v_i, or the total number of workers that will appear by T. We assume the requester knows the distribution of the arrival of workers.[1] The requester either aims to maximize the number of tasks allocated under some budget $B \in \mathbb{R}_+$, or alternatively complete $L \in \mathbb{N}_+$ tasks while minimizing payments, in which case we assume $\sum_{i \in N} v_i \geq 100L$.

One can adversarially assume that the workers know B, L, T and the objective of the requester. When allocated $\bar{w}_i$ tasks at p_i per task, the worker's utility is simply $\bar{w}_i(p_i - c_i)$. We assume that workers are rational in that they wish to maximize their utility.

The protocol. At the time of her arrival, each worker a_i submits a bid indicating her cost per task and the maximal number of tasks she wishes to perform, denoted as b_i and w_i respectively, which do not necessarily correspond to c_i, v_i. The mechanism must decide how many tasks to allocate to the worker and the price for each task upon her arrival, after processing her bid. The bid on the maximal number of tasks is abiding and if a worker completes less than the number of tasks allocated to her, the requester does not pay the worker.

2.1 Design Objectives

Our goal is to design mechanisms that perform well. A mechanism is simply an algorithm that decides how many tasks each worker performs and how she is paid. Since workers may report false costs, we will seek incentive compatible (truthful) mechanisms for which reporting the true costs is a dominant strategy. Formally, a mechanism is *incentive compatible* if for every $a_i \in N$ with cost and limit c_i, v_i and bid b_i, w_i, and every set of bids by $N \setminus \{a_i\}$ we have $x_i(p_i - c_i) \geq x_i'(p_i' - c_i)$, where p_i, p_i' are the payments and x_i, x_i' indicate the number of tasks a_i is allocated, when bidding c_i, v_i and b_i, w_i, respectively. Since an incentive compatible mechanism guarantees that the bids are truthful, its performance over the bids can be compared against a theoretically optimal algorithm that knows workers' true values.

Maximizing Tasks. Under this objective we are given a fixed budget by the requester and seek to maximize the expected number of tasks performed without exceeding the budget, where the expectation is over the random arrival order of the workers and the randomization of the mechanism. This design objective is known as *budget feasiblity* where the mechanism must be designed so that the sum of its payments (and not workers' costs) does not exceed the budget [32]. To quantify the performance of the mechanism we compare its solution with the *optimal offline solution*: the solution that would have been obtainable if all workers' true values were known in advance and we could pay each worker exactly her cost. Note that this is the most demanding benchmark possible. A mechanism is $O(g(n))$-competitive if the ratio between the benchmark and the expected value guaranteed by the mechanism is $O(g(n))$. Ideally, we would like our mechanism to be $O(1)$-competitive.

Minimizing Payments. A complementary objective to maximizing expected number of tasks under budget is that of minimizing expected payments for a given number of tasks. Ideally, we would like the total payments the mechanism makes to be comparable to the minimal cost required

---

[1]For our performance guarantees we actually only need to know the *median* of this distribution.

for performing the task. It is easy to show however that no incentive compatible mechanism can perform well under this benchmark.[2] We therefore set our objective for minimizing payments as follows. Given a fixed number of tasks to perform, L, we say that a mechanism for minimizing payments is α-competitive if it allocates L tasks in expectation and is guaranteed to pay no more than the minimum cost required to complete αL tasks in the offline scenario when all costs are known. Here as well our goal is to design mechanisms that are $O(1)$-competitive.

3. THE PRICING MECHANISMS

The common approach to achieve desirable outcomes in online settings is to observe a fraction of the input and use it as a sample to make an informed decision on the rest of the input. We will use a similar strategy, though rather than rejecting workers whose bids are used as a sample, we will allocate tasks to workers in the sample. When our objective is to maximize the number of tasks performed, our mechanism dynamically learns an appropriate price for a task as it allocates tasks to workers. In the case of minimizing payments, the requester can specify a budget for allocating tasks during the sampling phase.

In essence, both mechanisms sample the input until the median time step – the time step at which each worker appears with probability $1/2$ – and use the sample to estimate a *threshold price*. The mechanisms then use the threshold price to decide which bids to accept or reject. Estimating appropriate threshold prices is an important building block in both mechanisms, and we begin by describing this procedure and its properties.

3.1 Establishing Threshold Prices

Intuitively, the threshold price is the lowest single price we can offer which many workers will accept. The procedure for computing threshold prices presented below is a variant of the proportional share mechanism introduced in [32], which serves as the basis for designing procurement mechanisms under budget [33, 19, 16, 15, 18]. Note that this is an *offline* procedure that has access all bids.

GetThreshold

input: bids $\{(b_1, w_1), \ldots, (b_m, w_m)\}$, Budget B

1. initialize: sort bids s.t. $b_1 \leq b_2 \leq \ldots \leq b_m$; set $i = 1$
2. while $b_i \leq \frac{B}{\sum_{j<i} \bar{w}_j + 1}$
   set: $p = b_i$,
   $\bar{w}_i = \min\{w_i, \lfloor \frac{B}{p} \rfloor - \sum_{j<i} \bar{w}_j\}$,
   $i = i + 1$;

output: p

---

[2]Consider an instance where a single worker can complete all required tasks at some small cost ϵ, while every other workers has some very high costs P. It is not hard to show that any incentive compatible mechanism that completes all required tasks must pay at least P in such a case, thus making the ratio between minimal cost and the total payments of an incentive compatible mechanisms unbounded.

When tasks are priced at $p = b_i$ the remaining budget is $B - p \sum_{j=1}^{i-1} \bar{w}_j$, and therefore the number of tasks she could be allocated at this price without exceeding the total budget is $\bar{w}_i = \min\{w_i, \lfloor \frac{B}{p} \rfloor - \sum_{j<i} \bar{w}_j\}$ as used in the procedure. The desirable property of this threshold price is that it sets a single price which on the one hand is low enough so that it efficiently exhausts the budget and on the other hand is high enough so that enough workers accept. We formalize this in the following lemma. The proof in similar to [32].

LEMMA 3.1. *For a given sample of bids, let L be the maximal number of tasks that can be allocated under a given budget. Then, at least $L/2$ tasks can be allocated under budget at the price computed by the* GetThreshold *procedure.*

PROOF. Let $a_i = (b_i, w_i)$ and $\{a_1, a_2, \ldots, a_k\}$ be the set of bids allocated by the procedure. First, observe that $\bar{w}_i = w_i$ for all $i < k$, as otherwise given an $i < k$ s.t. $w_i > \bar{w}_i = \lfloor \frac{B}{p} \rfloor - \sum_{j=1}^{i-1} \bar{w}_j$ we have:

$$\sum_{j=1}^{i} \bar{w}_j = \sum_{j=1}^{i-1} \bar{w}_j + \left(\lfloor \frac{B}{p} \rfloor - \sum_{j=1}^{i-1} \bar{w}_j\right) = \lfloor \frac{B}{p} \rfloor$$

and thus:

$$b_{i+1} \geq b_i = p > \frac{B}{\lfloor B/p \rfloor + 1} = \frac{B}{\sum_{j<i} \bar{w}_j + 1}$$

which implies that b_{i+1} violates the condition in step 2 of the procedure, in contradiction to the assumption that it was allocated. For the purpose of this analysis, without loss of generality we can assume that $\bar{w}_k = w_k$. This is due to the fact that we can consider an input identical to ours except that a_k is replaced with two bids $a_{k'} = (b_k, \bar{w}_k)$ and $a_{k''} = (b_k, w_k - \bar{w}_k)$. The value over this input is identical to the value obtained over the original input, and $a_{k''}$ is not allocated as it fails to meet condition in step 2 due to the same argument made above.

Given a fixed budget, to achieve the maximal number of tasks one must allocate to lowest bids until exhausting the budget, and thus $\{a_1, \ldots, a_k\}$ are included in the optimal solution. Let $\{a_1 \ldots, a_k, \ldots, a_r\}$ be the optimal solution. Assume for purpose of contraction that $2\sum_{i=1}^{k} w_i < \sum_{i=1}^{r} w_i$. Then, $\sum_{i=1}^{k} w_i < \sum_{i=k+1}^{r} w_i$. By this assumption and the definition of b_{k+1} we have that:

$$b_{k+1} > \frac{B}{\sum_{i=1}^{k+1} w_i + 1} \geq \frac{B}{\sum_{i=k+1}^{r} w_i}$$

which implies:

$$B < b_{k+1} \cdot \left(\sum_{i=k+1}^{r} w_i\right) \leq \sum_{i=k+1}^{r} w_i \cdot b_i$$

but since the optimal solution cannot exceeds the budget, we have a contradiction. □

The above lemma suggests that if we accept all assignments that have cost that is smaller than the threshold price, we will be able to complete at least half of the assignments we would have been able to complete if we paid each worker their cost. As one might imagine, once the sample size is large enough, the threshold prices obtained on the sample will be a good estimate to the real threshold price as if they were computed offline. We formalize this argument and give a rigorous proof in the following section.

3.2 Maximizing Tasks

Given a distribution on the arrival of workers, we can easily compute every 2^i quantile (i.e. the time step t s.t. the probability that a worker arrives before t is 2^{-i}). We therefore assume the mechanism is given $\{q_1, \ldots, q_\ell\}$ where q_ℓ is the first time step $t = 1$. We give a formal description of the mechanism below followed by a brief explanation in plain English. We use $S(t)$ to denote the set of all bids that arrived at and before time step t.

MaximizeTasks

input: Budget B, quantiles $\{q_1, \ldots, q_\ell\}$

1. initialize: $B' = 2^{-(\ell+1)}B, t = 1$;

2. For every quantile $q_j, j = \ell, \ell - 1, \ldots, 1$ do:
    a. at time step $t = q_j$ set:
    $p = \textsc{GetThreshold}(S(t), 2B')$,
    $w^* = \min\{\max_{\{a \in S(t) | c_i \leq p\}} w_i, \lfloor \frac{2B'}{p} \rfloor\}$,
    $B' = 2B', A = \emptyset$;

    b. with probability $1/3$ do:
    while $q_j < t \leq q_{j+1}$:
    for all a_i who arrive at time t s.t. $b_i \leq p$ do:
    allocate $\bar{w}_i = \min\{w_i, \lfloor \frac{B'}{p} \rfloor - \sum_{r \in A} \bar{w}_r\}$ at p,
    set $A = A \cup \{i\}$;

    with probability $2/3$ do:
    for first a_i arriving by q_{j+1} s.t. $w_i \geq w^*$:
    allocate $\bar{w}_i = \min\{w_i, \lfloor \frac{B'}{p} \rfloor\}$ at p;

The mechanism iterates over $q_1, \ldots, q_\ell$ and at every time step q_i it uses a budget of $B/2^i$ to allocate tasks, and decides whether to accept a bid using a threshold price which it computes on bids of all workers that arrived by time step q_i. At every time interval q_i the mechanism randomly selects the procedure it will use on all workers that arrive until q_{i+1}. The first procedure pays each worker the threshold price per task, as long as her cost is below the threshold and the budget has not been exhausted. The second procedure allocates its entire budget to the worker that bid below the threshold price and is willing to perform at least as many tasks as w^*. The randomization between the two procedures handles extreme cases in which only a single worker can complete a large fraction of the tasks at the threshold price. The way which we find the worker that can complete the maximal number of tasks is an incentive compatible variant of Dynkin's celebrated algorithm to the problem of hiring the best secretary [20], tailored to our setting.

LEMMA 3.2. *The mechanism is incentive compatible, i.e. it is in every worker's best interest to bid her true cost for performing an assignment, and the number of assignments she wishes to perform.*

PROOF. Consider a worker a_i with cost of c_i that arrives at some stage for which the threshold price was set to p. If by the time the worker arrives there are no remaining assignments, then the worker's bid will not affect the allocation of the mechanism and thus she cannot benefit by reporting a false cost. Otherwise, assume there are remaining assignments by the time the worker arrives. In case $c_i \leq p$, bidding below p wouldn't make a difference in the worker's allocation and payment and her utility for each assignment would be $p - c_i \geq 0$. Declaring a cost above p would deny the worker from being allocated, and her utility would be 0. In case $c_i > p$, declaring any cost above p would leave the worker unallocated with utility 0. If the worker declares a cost lower than p she will be allocated though her utility will be negative. In the realization where all workers with costs smaller than p are allocated until exhausting the budget, declaring a lower or higher number of tasks does not benefit the worker since her utility is linear. In the realization where we select the first worker with bid smaller than p who will complete at least w^* tasks, if the worker declares $w'_i \geq \min\{w, \lfloor B/p \rfloor\} > w_i$ the worker will be allocated more tasks than she can perform and will be paid 0, and will therefore not benefit. □

LEMMA 3.3. *The mechanism is budget feasible, i.e. the sum of the payments that the mechanism makes to all workers never exceeds the given budget.*

PROOF. At each stage $i = 1, \ldots, \ell$ the mechanism uses a budget of $B' = B/2^i$ and threshold price p computed from the bids of the previous round, and allocates no more than $\lfloor B'/p \rfloor$ tasks. Therefore every iteration is budget feasible and in total $\sum_{i=1}^{\ell} B/2^i < B$. □

LEMMA 3.4. *The MAXIMIZETASKS mechanism is 360 competitive and 120-competitive when using its entire budget in the median time step.*

PROOF. We will analyze the iteration of the mechanism, when the sample consisted of all workers who arrive by the median time step and the budget used for allocation was $B/2$. We will compare the expected number of tasks allocated with the number of tasks that would have been possible to allocate with the same budget on the entire set of workers at a single threshold price.

Let $S(T)$ be the set of all workers who arrive by time step T, and consider running the GETTHRESHOLD procedure on $S(T)$ using a budget of $B' = B/2$; let A be the set of all workers who were allocated by this procedure, $k = |A|$, $W = \sum_{i \in A} \bar{w}_i$, p be the threshold price obtained by running the procedure, and OPT be the maximal number of tasks that can be performed under budget B on $S(T)$. Note that the maximal number of tasks that can be performed under budget $B/2$ is at least $OPT/3$, and therefore from Lemma 3.1 we have that $W \geq OPT/6$.

Assume first that $\max_i w_i \leq W/10$. Consider the median time step t and all workers bids sampled until this time step, $S(t)$. Let $A_1 = S(t) \cap A, A_2 = A \setminus A_1$, and $W_1 = \sum_{i \in A_1} \bar{w}_i, W_2 = \sum_{i \in A_2} \bar{w}_i$. Since each worker $a_i \in A$ arrives before the median with probability $1/2$ we can associate a random variable X_i that takes a value of $\bar{w}_i$ with probability $1/2$ and 0 otherwise. To evaluate the expected value of W_1 and W_2, we can use the following version of the Chernoff bound:

THEOREM 3.5. *(Chernoff Bound) Let $X_1, \ldots, X_k$ be a set of k independent random variables that take values in $[0, w_i]$*

and $\mu = \mathbb{E}[\sum_{i=1}^{k} X_i]$. Then, for any $\delta \in [0,1]$ we have that:

$$Pr\left[\sum_{i=1}^{k} X_i > (1+\delta)\mu\right] \leq \left(\frac{e^{\delta}}{(1+\delta)^{(1+\delta)}}\right)^{\frac{\mu}{\max_i w_i}}$$

$$Pr\left[\sum_{i=1}^{k} X_i < (1-\delta)\mu\right] \leq e^{\frac{-\delta^2 \mu}{2\max_i w_i}}$$

This above bound implies that:

$$Pr\left[W_2 < \frac{1}{4}W\right] = Pr\left[W_1 > \frac{3}{4}W\right] \leq 59/100$$
$$Pr\left[W_1 < \frac{1}{4}W\right] \leq 21/100$$

Therefore, by union bound with probability at least $1/5$ both $W_1, W_2 \geq W/4$. Now, let $p(T), p(t)$ be the thresholds computed using the GETTHRESHOLD procedure over $S(T)$ and the sample $S(t)$, respectively. Since $p(t) \geq p(T)$ as it is computed over a smaller subset, for each worker $a_i \in A_2$ it follows that $c_i \leq p(t)$ and they will be allocated if the budget has not yet been exhausted. If all workers in A_2 were allocated by the mechanism this implies that at least $W/4$ tasks were performed since $W_2 \geq W/4$. If the budget was exhausted before all workers in A_2 arrived, a total of $\lfloor B'/p(t) \rfloor$ were performed. Since

$$p(t) \leq \frac{B'}{W_1} \leq \frac{B'}{W}$$

this implies that at least $W/4$ tasks were performed with probability at least $1/5$. Therefore, since this procedure is realized with probability $1/3$ at least $W/60$ were completed in expectation when $\max_{i \in A} w_i \leq W/10$.

In case $\max_{i \in A} \bar{w}_i > W/10$, let $a = \text{argmax}_{i \in S(T)} w_i$, and $b = \text{argmax}_{i \in S(T) \setminus \{a\}} w_i$. With probability $1/4$, b appears at or before the median time step and a arrives after the median time step, we therefore have at least one worker a_i at stage $t > q_1$ s.t. $w_i \geq w^*$. In this case we have that:

$$\bar{w}_i = \min\{\max_i w_i, \lfloor B/p(t) \rfloor\} \geq W/10$$

since $p' \leq 4B/W$. Since this procedure is realized with probability $2/3$ we have obtain at least:

$$\frac{W}{10} \cdot \frac{1}{4} \cdot \frac{2}{3} = \frac{W}{60}$$

tasks in expectation, as in the previous case. Since $W \geq OPT/6$ the mechanism is 360-competitive. If the entire budget is used in step q_1, $W \geq OPT/2$ and the mechanism is 120-competitive. □

THEOREM 3.6. *The MAXIMIZETASKS mechanism is incentive compatible, budget feasible and $O(1)$-competitive.*

While the constants may seem large, we emphasize that our goal is to show that the mechanisms are indeed $O(1)$-competitive, and thus that their guarantee is independent of the parameters of the problem that can be large (e.g. number of workers, their cost, the number of tasks they are willing to perform, etc.). We will later show that these mechanisms perform well in practice, implying that bounded competitive ratio serves as a good guide for designing such mechanisms.

3.3 Minimizing Payments

The idea behind the mechanism for minimizing payments is based on the following observation. Given a fixed number of tasks L, if we knew the minimal cost for performing $L' = 2L$ tasks, we could use a procedure similar to GETTHRESHOLD with this minimal cost as its budget. From Lemma 3.1 we know that the GETTHRESHOLD procedure finds a price s.t. at least $L'/2 = L$ tasks could be performed. Therefore, such a procedure would be a 2-approximation to the minimal cost in our case. The MINIMIZEPAYMENTS mechanism is based on this idea: we compute the minimal cost for performing a constant blowup of the number of tasks required, and find an appropriate threshold price. We describe the mechanism formally below, followed by a brief description.

MinimizePayments

input: number of tasks L, budget β, price δ, q_1, T

1. For all a_i who arrive at time $t \leq q_1$, if $b_i \leq \delta$ do:
   allocate $\bar{w}_i = \min\{w_i, \lfloor \frac{\beta}{\delta} \rfloor - \sum_{r \in A} \bar{w}_r\}$ at δ,
   set $A = A \cup \{i\}$;

2. At time step $t = q_1$ do:
   set $B = \text{FINDMINCOST}(S(t), 2L)$,
   set $p = \text{GETTHRESHOLD}(S(t), B)$,
   $w^* = \min\{\max_{\{a \in S(t) | c_i \leq p\}} w_i, \lfloor \frac{B}{p} \rfloor\}$

3. with probability $1/4$ do:
   for all a_i who arrive at time $t > q_1$ s.t. $b_i \leq p$ do:
   allocate $\bar{w}_i = \min\{w_i, \lfloor \frac{B}{p} \rfloor - \sum_{r \in A} \bar{w}_r\}$ at p,

   with probability $3/4$ do:
   for first a_i arriving by T s.t. $w_i \geq w^*$:
   allocate $\bar{w}_i = \min\{w_i, \lfloor \frac{B}{p} \rfloor\}$ at p;

The above mechanism has two iterations. The first iteration samples the bids, and uses a given budget of β and price δ specified by the requester to allocate to workers in the sample.[3] After the median time step, the FINDMINCOST$(S(t), 2L)$ procedure finds the minimal cost for performing $2L$ tasks (which can be done by a simple greedy algorithm which sorts workers according to their costs and allocates tasks until reaching the number of tasks required). The threshold price is then computed using the minimal cost as its budget, together with an estimate of the maximal number of tasks a worker can perform. Similarly to the MAXIMIZETASKS mechanism, the mechanism then randomizes between a procedure which allocates tasks to workers with price smaller than p and a procedure that allocates all tasks to a single worker.

The properties of the mechanism can be proven using similar ideas as in the proofs in the previous section. We state the theorem below, and leave the proof to the full version of the paper.

---

[3]In the MAXIMIZETASKS mechanism we automatically used half of the budget for the sampling phase. Here, since we do not a priori know what workers' costs are, we leave β and δ as a design choice to the requester.

THEOREM 3.7. *Given a fixed number of tasks L, the* MINIMIZEPAYMENTS *mechanism is incentive compatible, allocates L tasks in expectation and is $O(1)$-competitive.*

4. EXPERIMENTS

To evaluate the performance of the mechanisms in practice and explore bidding behavior in crowdsourcing markets, we created the *Mechanical Perk* platform which enables us to conduct experiments with workers from Mechanical Turk and to collect real bidding data and observe their behavior.

4.1 Mechanical Perk

To enable implementing various mechanisms on Mechanical Turk (MTurk) we created the Mechanical Perk (MPerk) platform. The platform provides a service for requesters who wish to post Human Intelligence Tasks (HITs) with various automated pricing and incentive mechanisms. The platform receives the HIT from the requester as input and their choice for the mechanism they wish to use, along with additional information like the number of HITs to be posted, budget, expiration date, and other parameters for posting the HIT on MTurk. The platform then posts a HIT on MTurk that serves as a wrapper for the requester's original HITs. The HIT posted by MPerk enables workers to place bids and run a mechanism in the background.

In the Human Intelligence Task (HIT) workers are explained that a mechanism will decide how many assignments, if any, will be allocated to them based on their bid. We explain to workers they would be paid through the Mechanical Turk bonus payment system, which allows a requester to pay workers beyond the fixed price associated with the HIT. To encourage high quality work, we explain to workers they would not be paid if their work will be found unsatisfactory. We also include a screenshot from an example assignment so that workers could assess their cost for performing the assignment prior to bidding. Following the set of instructions, workers need to indicate their cost for performing an assignment and how many assignments they wish to perform. Their bids are collected by a mechanism which decides on their allocation.

A worker that was allocated received assignments to work on, and based on the pricing decided by the mechanism was paid within a few days via the bonus payment system. Each worker that placed a bid was paid for participating in the HIT, independent of the payments made according to the mechanism's decision.

An important fact is that MPerk can use various pricing mechanisms that allow efficient allocation of tasks. In our experiments we used MAXIMIZETASKS as well as other simple pricing schemes to gain insight to bidding behavior in crowdsourcing markets. We describe these in detail in Section 4.5.

4.2 Experiments Objectives

We conducted two main sets of experiments on MPerk. The primary goals were to evaluate the performance of the online mechanism on real bids as well as to test workers' responses to different bidding mechanisms. We implemented the bidding mechanisms through MPerk and for Human Computation tasks, we used a batch of automatically generated assignments.

Performance. We conducted an experiment where we ran the MAXIMIZETASKS on MechanicalPerk with a modest

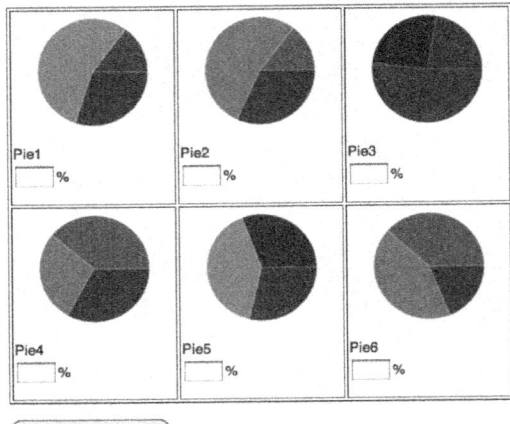

Figure 1: Screenshot of example assignment used in the experiments.

budget. We primarily used this process to collect bids so we can run simulations with different budgets to observe the performance of the mechanism. In general, we found that the mechanism performs very well on real inputs and the threshold prices converge quickly.

Bidding behavior. The main goal in these experiments was to examine workers' responses to various features in the mechanism which could serve as guidelines for future design of mechanisms in crowdsourcing markets. An important guideline in our design is incentive compatibility as we assume workers behave strategically in crowdsourcing platforms. To examine this we observed workers' response to different pricing schemes which suggest that they indeed strategize their bids. Another design principle is to avoid rejecting workers automatically. The main reasoning is that we believe that although rejecting workers automatically to obtain a sample will not hurt the mechanism during its iteration, rejecting bids automatically is not likely to be sustainable in crowdsourcing markets, as workers will avoid tasks that use such mechanisms for pricing. In our experiments we show evidence of this as well.

4.3 Experimental Setup

In the first experiment we ran the MAXIMIZETASKS mechanism described in Section 3 primarily to collect bids that we used to test its performance, and allowed workers to bid only once. In the second experiment we tested workers' responses to four different pricing mechanisms. We allowed workers to bid up to 15 times to observe their responses to various pricing schemes.

We limited the experiment to workers with approval rate on Mechanical Turk higher than 90%. We recorded workers' IP addresses and treated each IP session as a new worker. While this does not guarantee the worker is a different person, we used this as a reasonable proxy. In total we collected 1674 bids, from 764 different workers, allocated 3883 assignments and collected 23298 answers.

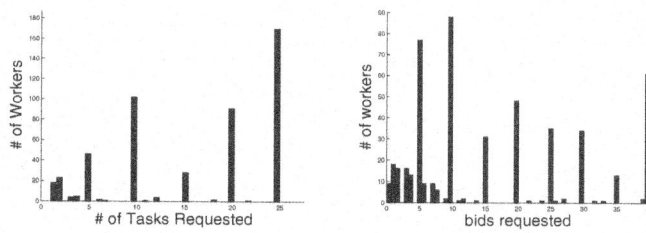

Figure 2: (a) Histogram of price per assignment (0-40 cents) requested by bidders (b) Histogram of number of assignments requested by bidders

The Human Computation Tasks. We used assignments that required workers to estimate area sizes in pie charts. Each assignment included six pie charts, where each pie chart consisted of three colors, one of which was red. In each assignment, the workers were required to estimate the percentage of red color in each one of the six pie charts and these area sizes were randomly generated. The reason for choosing this assignment is that it simulates a human computation task and allows to quantify a worker's performance objectively. We also gave workers an option to send us feedback about their experience. An example assignment is displayed in Figure 1.

4.4 Performance

To collect data for simulations we ran an experiment on Mechanical Perk where MAXIMIZETASKS was used to allocate tasks. To collect a representative data set for the simulations, we allowed workers to bid once in this experiment. The maximal allowed bid was $0.40 and the limit on the number of assignments was set to 25. We collected bids from 391 workers, each providing a single bid which indicates their cost and the number of assignments they wish to perform. The mean bid was 16.33 cents and the mean number of assignments was 16. We plot the distribution of bids and number of assignments in Figure 2.

To test the performance of the MAXIMIZETASKS mechanism, we used the bids collected and compared our mechanism against several benchmarks. Note that in order to show how many assignments can be allocated given a specified budget, we only require the workers' bids, which is a much larger set than the subset of workers that were actually allocated and submitted their answers to the assignments. To simulate a task we use a random permutation of the bids we collected to model the random arrival of workers, and run our mechanism with a specified budget over this ordering.

We compared MAXIMIZETASKS against two benchmarks. The first benchmark is the optimal *offline* algorithm which has *full knowledge* about workers costs. The second benchmark is the GETTHRESHOLD procedure applied offline. This procedure is guaranteed to be within a factor of two of the first benchmark by Lemma 3.1 and is also the optimal incentive compatible solution due to a matching lower bound [32]. This mechanism does not have knowledge about workers' true costs, but it is an offline mechanism, i.e., all workers submit their bids to the mechanism and wait for the mechanism to collect all the bids and decide on an allocation. These benchmarks operate in simpler settings, where all the costs are known *a priori* and will therefore always outperform our mechanism. Ideally, we would be able to compare against other pricing methods such as those used by commercial platforms, though this data is difficult to obtain.

We showed that the mechanism is guaranteed to be, in expectation over the arrival order of the workers, within a constant factor from the optimal offline solution. Our goal in this experiment was to examine this ratio on descriptive inputs. Using the bids provided by workers, we simulated the different algorithms on budgets ranging from $50 to $1000 in increments of $50. In Figure 3 we plot the resulting comparison between our mechanism and the benchmarks.

On the simulated data, the mechanism performs quite well. Analytically, we guarantee that the mechanism has a constant competitive factor in comparison to the optimal offline solution, and the experiments show that this ratio is almost as small as 2. In comparison to the best incentive compatible mechanism, this ratio is substantially smaller, and there is almost no difference in the performance of the two mechanisms. The simulations suggest that the MAXIMIZETASKS has near optimal performance in practice.

To examine the change in the threshold prices as the number of workers increases in the sample, we simulated tasks with various budgets and ran the mechanism. We observed that in all simulations, the threshold prices converged quickly, and typically after running 16 and 32 bids varied by 1 to 2 cents. In Figure 3(a) we plot the value of the threshold price as a function of the stage of the mechanism (the number of workers that submitted their bids) on a logarithmic scale, during a simulation that used a budget of $100. As one can see, the threshold price quickly stabilizes and remains almost constant throughout the run.

4.5 Bidding Behavior

To observe workers' responses to various features in pricing mechanisms we experimented with four simple mechanisms and allowed workers' to bid multiple times in order to observe how features of the mechanisms affect their bidding. All mechanisms required workers to bid how much they wish to be rewarded for each assignment they complete and the number of assignments for this bid. We allowed only 5 assignments to be performed per HIT (where the bid is per assignment), allowed bids no higher than $0.50, and allowed workers to perform 15 HITs.[4] For each HIT performed the workers received a $0.03 fixed reward for participating, even when their bid was rejected. All information was clearly indicated in the instructions. The workers were not notified what the pricing scheme was, and to avoid giving them information about the mechanism, if their bid was accepted, the payment they received was their bid. We used the following pricing schemes:

- **Always Win Mechanism:** This mechanism accepted workers' bids as long as the total payment to the worker did not exceed $3.00. The fact that there is a budget or that it was exceeded was not revealed to the workers. Once meeting their budget workers were allowed to continue bidding but their bids we rejected.

- **Always Lose Mechanism:** This mechanism implements a fixed price mechanism with threshold price of $0, i.e. workers were rejected regardless of their bids.

---
[4]The only exception was the Always Win mechanism described below where the limit on the bid was $0.99 and we set a spending budget on each worker.

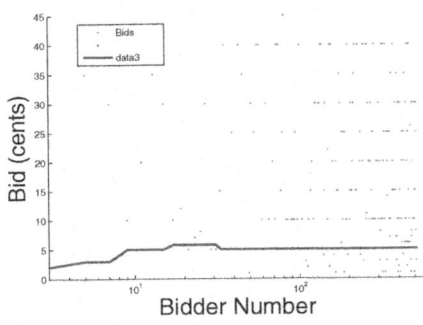
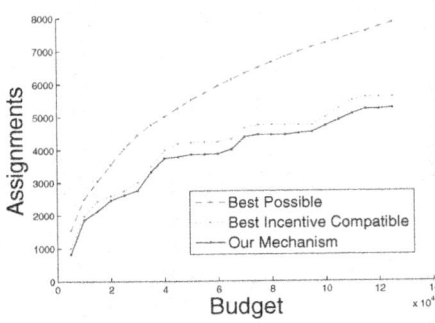

Figure 3: (a) Variation of threshold price (pink line) over time (b) Comparative performance of algorithms

- **Fixed Price Mechanism:** This mechanism uses a fixed threshold price that is not revealed to the workers. Each bid at or below the threshold price was accepted and otherwise rejected. In our experiment we set this threshold price to be $0.04.

- **Random Price Mechanism:** This mechanism randomizes over different threshold prices each time a worker bids. If the bid is below the price the worker was allocated and otherwise their bid was rejected.

We also ran a control mechanism which presented workers with a fixed price of $0.03 per task and required workers to reveal how many assignments they wish to perform. As in the above pricing schemes the limit was set to 5 assignments per HIT, and workers were allowed to perform 15 HITs.

There were 1033 bids (including 138 in the control) from 378 different workers in total (including 66 in control) in this experiment. Each bid consisted of the maximal number of assignments the worker is willing to perform in the bidding round and their cost for performing an assignment. In total, there were 952 valid bids, including 131 in the control (there were 81 *invalid* bids we discarded where the bid cost or number of assignments violated our instructions).

Recall that in this experiment a worker was given a chance to bid 15 times (rounds), and if their bid was accepted they worked on the tasks and received their bid as payment. Figure 4(a) plots the average bid at a given round for each pricing scheme. This figure is complemented by Figure 5 which gives a histogram of the number of workers that remained in each round. In the AlwaysLose pricing scheme, for example, there were only 2 workers after the eighth round, and the average price shown in Figure 4(a) is an average of these two bids. Up until the forth round there were 10 and 11 bidders in AlwaysLose and RandomPrice, respectively, and 16 in both AlwaysWin and FixedPrice. It therefore seems that the majority of the information in Figure 4(a) is the first 5 bids.

Evidence of strategic bidding. To examine whether workers include strategic considerations in their bidding, one can observe the obvious difference between the plots of the different responses to the pricing schemes as shown in Figure 4(a). Bidders in the AlwaysWin scheme, increased their bids as they got accepted (the following drop off is due to the budget constraint we enforced, for methodological reasons). In the AlwaysLose or RandomPrice schemes where workers bids were rejected, bids were lowered. We see this as clear evidence that when given an opportunity workers' will declare false costs if they believe this will increase their profit. We see this as strong support for insisting on *incentive compatible* mechanisms.

Interestingly, although a budget constraint was implemented in the AlwaysWin scheme and workers were automatically rejected, their bids were still significantly higher than those of other pricing schemes.

Effects of rejection. To observe this effect on workers, in Figure 4(b) we plot the mean of the success rate of workers (the number of bids that were accepted) vs. the number of bidding rounds they participated in for the RandomPrice and the FixedPrice mechanisms. [5] Although there seems to be a negative correlation between success and number of rounds, one must remember that there is very little data (in the sixth round there were 12 and 8 workers in the FixedPrice and RandomPrice mechanisms, respectively). Better evidence for whether rejection affects workers can be seen in Figure 5, where we plot the number workers in each bidding round for each pricing scheme. There are evident drop offs in the RandomPrice and AlwaysLose mechanisms, where almost no bidders stayed beyond 6 rounds. Note that this is despite the $0.03 they received simply for placing a bid. This strengthens the claim that workers will avoid a HIT if they know they will be automatically rejected, even if they are paid to bid. Even when there is no monetary loss, there is a price associated with sampling in crowdsourcing platforms which can result in slower completion times for a batch of HITs.

Quality of work. Although the main measure of performance we consider in this paper is the number of assignments that can be performed under the budget, we examined the quality of the work performed as well. Showing that workers perform well on their allocated assignments helps exclude concerns regarding negative effects the bidding method may have. To examine the performance of workers we chose the percentage estimation assignment since it allows us to objectively quantify workers' performance by considering their errors from the true answer. In total, our mechanism allocated to 161 workers who, in aggregate, submitted 10870 answers (we count the number of answers submitted for each pie chart).

---

[5] We only plot the results for these mechanisms as there are no successes in the AlwaysLose mechanism and also in the AlwaysWin mechanism once workers exceeded their budget.

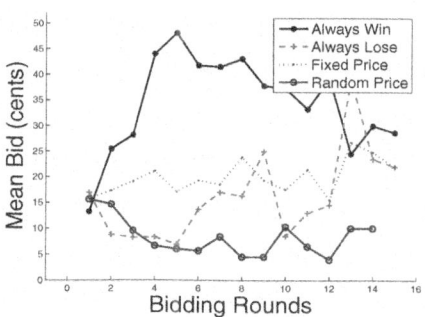
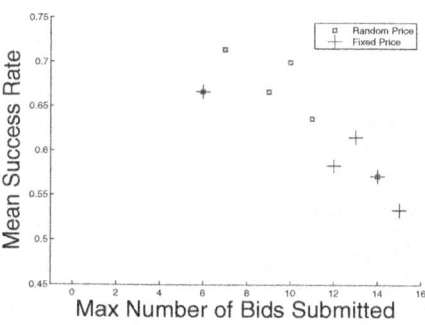

Figure 4: (a) Bids as a function of number of rounds (b) Success rates of workers in Fixed Price and Random mechanisms. All workers who left before the sixth round had all their bids rejected and their success rate of zero is not shown.

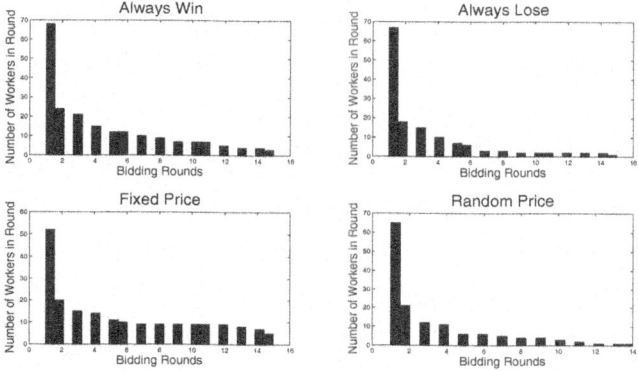

Figure 5: Number of workers in each bidding round.

The error distribution is presented in Figure 6. The error (vertical axis) is the difference between the workers guess and the actual marked percentage of red in the pie chart task. In general, workers performed well on the assignments. The worker mean error was 2.57, and almost all workers who were allocated assignments completed them. This was consistent with the control group of 66 workers who received a fixed price reward, where the mean error was 2.59. This implies that performance is not negatively affected by bidding.

A subject of ongoing debate in the crowdsourcing community is the relationship between performance and monetary incentives. To examine this in our context we compared a worker's mean error on the assignments performed against their bid. The mean error reflects on the quality of work, and the bid indicates the reward the worker expects to receive. We plot the worker's bid against their mean error in Figure 6(b). In our examination we found no significant correlation. We note that the data for this comparison involves 271 workers, since this is the total number of workers who were allocated assignments by the mechanism.

5. DISCUSSION

In this paper we present a framework that enables designing mechanisms for crowdsourcing markets with provable guarantees. The mechanisms we presented are easy to implement, have strong theoretical guarantees, and perform well in practice. From the experimentation on the platform, it seems there is evidence for strategic behavior and negative effects when automatically rejecting workers. We believe this evidence strengthens our model and assumptions and should be taken into account when designing pricing schemes in crowdsourcing markets.

We believe the model provides a good basis for designing pricing mechanisms for crowdsourcing markets, and that it can be further extended. A natural extension of this model could incorporate verification schemes and automatic quality control that could integrate with the pricing mechanisms presented here.

6. ACKNOWLEDGMENTS

We would like to thank Björn Hartmann for valuable discussions and advice. Part of this work was done while the first author was at UC Berkeley and supported by the Microsoft Research fellowship and the Facebook fellowship. We would also like to thank our anonymous reviewers for their thoughtful comments and suggestions.

7. REFERENCES

[1] Amazon mturk https://www.mturk.com.
[2] Clickworker. https://www.crowdflower.com.
[3] CloudCrowd. https://www.cloudcrowd.com.
[4] Crowdflower. https://www.crowdflower.com.
[5] duolingo. http://duolingo.com/.
[6] Microtask. http://microtask.com.
[7] MobileWorks. https://www.mobileworks.com.
[8] oDesk. https://www.odesk.com.
[9] L. v. Ahn. Games with a purpose. *Computer*, 39(6):92–94, June 2006.
[10] A. Archer and É. Tardos. Frugal path mechanisms. In *SODA*, pages 991–999, 2002.
[11] M. Babaioff, N. Immorlica, D. Kempe, and R. Kleinberg. A knapsack secretary problem with applications. In *APPROX-RANDOM*, pages 16–28, 2007.
[12] M. Babaioff, N. Immorlica, D. Kempe, and R. Kleinberg. Online auctions and generalized secretary problems. *SIGecom Exchanges*, 7(2), 2008.

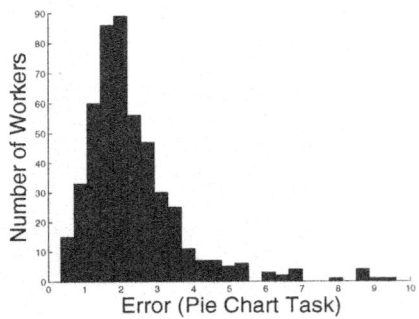 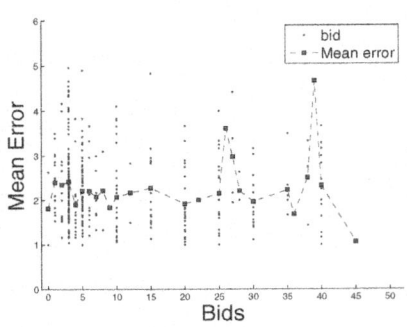

Figure 6: (a) Histogram of errors. (b) Average error (Y) vs bid price in cents (X)

[13] D. F. Bacon, D. C. Parkes, Y. Chen, M. Rao, I. A. Kash, and M. Sridharan. Predicting your own effort. In *AAMAS*, pages 695–702, 2012.

[14] A. Badanidiyuru, R. Kleinberg, and Y. Singer. Learning on a budget: Posted price mechanisms for online procurement. In *ACM Conference on Electronic Commerce*, pages 128–145, 2012.

[15] X. Bei, N. Chen, N. Gravin, and P. Lu. Budget feasible mechanism design via random sampling. *CoRR*, abs/1107.2994, 2011.

[16] N. Chen, N. Gravin, and P. Lu. On the approximability of budget feasible mechanisms. 2011.

[17] S. Cooper, F. Khatib, I. Makedon, H. L§, J. Barbero, D. Baker, J. Fogarty, Z. Popovic, and F. players. Analysis of social gameplay macros in the foldit cookbook. In M. Cavazza, K. Isbister, and C. Rich, editors, *FDG*, pages 9–14. ACM, 2011.

[18] P. Dandekar, N. Fawaz, and S. Ioannidis. Privacy auctions for recommender systems. *WINE*, 2012.

[19] S. Dobzinski, C. Papadimitriou, and Y. Singer. Mechanisms for complement-free procurement. In *EC*, 2011.

[20] E. B. Dynkin. The optimum choice of the instant for stopping a Markov process. *Soviet Math. Dokl*, 4, 1963.

[21] E. J. Friedman and D. C. Parkes. Pricing wifi at starbucks: Issues in online mechanism design. In *ACM Conference on Electronic Commerce*, pages 240–241, 2003.

[22] M. T. Hajiaghayi. Online auctions with re-usable goods. In *Proceedings of the 6th ACM conference on Electronic commerce*, EC '05, pages 165–174, New York, NY, USA, 2005. ACM.

[23] M. T. Hajiaghayi, R. D. Kleinberg, and D. C. Parkes. Adaptive limited-supply online auctions. In *ACM Conference on Electronic Commerce*, pages 71–80, 2004.

[24] C.-J. Ho and J. W. Vaughan. Online task assignment in crowdsourcing markets. In *AAAI*, 2012.

[25] J. J. Horton and L. B. Chilton. The labor economics of paid crowdsourcing. EC '10, pages 209–218, 2010.

[26] J. J. Horton and R. J. Zeckhauser. Algorithmic wage negotiations: Applications to paid crowsourcing. *CrowdConf*, 2010.

[27] S. Jain, Y. Chen, and D. C. Parkes. Designing incentives for online question and answer forums. In *Proceedings of the 10th ACM conference on Electronic commerce*, EC '09, pages 129–138, New York, NY, USA, 2009. ACM.

[28] D. R. Karger, S. Oh, and D. Shah. Iterative learning for reliable crowdsourcing systems. In *NIPS*, pages 1953–1961, 2011.

[29] A. Kittur, E. H. Chi, and B. Suh. Crowdsourcing user studies with mechanical turk. In *Proceeding of the twenty-sixth annual SIGCHI conference on Human factors in computing systems*, CHI '08, pages 453–456, New York, NY, USA, 2008. ACM.

[30] V. C. Raykar, S. Yu, L. H. Zhao, G. H. Valadez, C. Florin, L. Bogoni, and L. Moy. Learning from crowds. *J. Mach. Learn. Res.*, 11:1297–1322, Aug. 2010.

[31] V. S. Sheng, F. J. Provost, and P. G. Ipeirotis. Get another label? improving data quality and data mining using multiple, noisy labelers. In *KDD*, pages 614–622, 2008.

[32] Y. Singer. Budget feasible mechanisms. In *FOCS*, pages 765–774, 2010.

[33] Y. Singer. How to win friends and influence people, truthfully: Influence maximization mechanisms for social networks. In *WSDM*, pages 733–742, 2012.

[34] L. Tran-Thanh, S. Stein, A. Rogers, and N. R. Jennings. Efficient crowdsourcing of unknown experts using multi-armed bandits. In L. D. Raedt, C. Bessiŕre, D. Dubois, P. Doherty, P. Frasconi, F. Heintz, and P. J. F. Lucas, editors, *ECAI*, volume 242 of *Frontiers in Artificial Intelligence and Applications*, pages 768–773. IOS Press, 2012.

[35] P. Welinder, S. Branson, S. Belongie, and P. Perona. The multidimensional wisdom of crowds. In *NIPS*, pages 2424–2432, 2010.

[36] J. Whitehill, P. Ruvolo, T. Wu, J. Bergsma, and J. Movellan. Whose vote should count more: Optimal integration of labels from labelers of unknown expertise. *Advances in Neural Information Processing Systems*, 22:2035–2043, 2009.

Truthful Incentives in Crowdsourcing Tasks using Regret Minimization Mechanisms

Adish Singla
ETH Zurich
Zurich Switzerland
adish.singla@inf.ethz.ch

Andreas Krause
ETH Zurich
Zurich Switzerland
krausea@ethz.ch

ABSTRACT

What price should be offered to a worker for a task in an online labor market? How can one enable workers to express the amount they desire to receive for the task completion? Designing optimal pricing policies and determining the right monetary incentives is central to maximizing requester's utility and workers' profits. Yet, current crowdsourcing platforms only offer a limited capability to the requester in designing the pricing policies and often rules of thumb are used to price tasks. This limitation could result in inefficient use of the requester's budget or workers becoming disinterested in the task.

In this paper, we address these questions and present mechanisms using the approach of regret minimization in online learning. We exploit a link between procurement auctions and multi-armed bandits to design mechanisms that are budget feasible, achieve near-optimal utility for the requester, are incentive compatible (truthful) for workers and make minimal assumptions about the distribution of workers' true costs. Our main contribution is a novel, no-regret posted price mechanism, BP-UCB, for budgeted procurement in stochastic online settings. We prove strong theoretical guarantees about our mechanism, and extensively evaluate it in simulations as well as on real data from the Mechanical Turk platform. Compared to the state of the art, our approach leads to a 180% increase in utility.

Categories and Subject Descriptors

K.4.4 [**Computers and Society**]: Electronic Commerce - Payment schemes; H.2.8 [**Database Management**]: Database applications - Data mining

General Terms

Algorithms, Economics, Experimentation, Human Factors, Theory

Keywords

Crowdsourcing, incentive compatible mechanisms, procurement auctions, posted prices, regret minimization, multi-armed bandits

Copyright is held by the International World Wide Web Conference Committee (IW3C2). IW3C2 reserves the right to provide a hyperlink to the author's site if the Material is used in electronic media.
WWW 2013, May 13–17, 2013, Rio de Janeiro, Brazil.
ACM 978-1-4503-2035-1/13/05.

1. INTRODUCTION

The growth of the Internet has created numerous opportunities for crowdsourcing tasks to online "workers". Specialized marketplaces for crowdsourcing have emerged, including Amazon's Mechanical Turk (henceforth MTurk [1]) and Click Worker[1], enabling "requesters" to post HITs (Human Intelligence Tasks), which can then be carried out by pools of workers available online and suitable for the task. Some of the tasks that are posted on these platforms include image annotation, rating the relevance of web pages for a query in search engines, translation of text or transcription of an audio recording. Similarly, in platforms like social networks, users can be compensated for participation in a viral marketing campaign. The requester generally has a limited budget for the task and needs to come up with a payment scheme for workers in order to maximize the utility derived from the task. For workers, the main goal is to maximize their individual profit by deciding which tasks to perform and at what price.

Monetary incentives in crowdsourcing tasks. One of the central components of these platforms is to design the right incentive structure and pricing policies for workers that maximize the benefits of both requester and the workers. Overpricing the tasks would result in inefficient use of the requester's budget, whereas underpricing could lead to task "starvation" because of unavailability of the workers willing to participate. In this light, how can one design optimal pricing policies? How can workers communicate and negotiate the price with requesters? How would the market behave if workers act strategically by misreporting their costs for their benefit? These are some of the questions that naturally come to mind while studying incentive structures for these online markets, yet they are not well understood.

Pricing models. Current crowdsourcing platforms offer limited capability to the requester in designing the pricing policies, mostly limiting them to a single fixed price ("*fixed price model*"). One way to set prices under such models is to estimate workers' costs via a market analysis and then compute an optimal fixed price which would maximize the utility. However, there are many difficulties in inferring this optimal fixed price, including the high cost of market surveys, the dynamic and online nature of the labor markets, inexperience of the requester and challenges in soliciting true costs from workers because of their self-interest. An alternate approach is to use tools of online procurement auctions where workers can bid on the price they are willing to receive

---
[1] http://www.clickworker.com/

and the requester's mechanism can decide on the allocation and prices to be paid to workers. In this *"bidding model"*, mechanisms need to be truthful: it should be a dominant strategy for rational workers to bid their true cost. However, communicating these true costs to the requester may be challenging in real world settings. The worker may typically not trust the requester and understand the mechanism to reveal their true cost or the cost may not even be known to a worker and perhaps difficult to determine. Instead of soliciting the workers' costs, an often more natural setting is the *"posted price model"* where workers are offered a take-it-or-leave-it price offer. The mechanism interacts with each worker once in a sequential manner and adjusts the offered price from past responses of the workers.

1.1 Our Results

In this paper, we present a novel posted-price mechanism, BP-UCB, for online budgeted procurement, which is guaranteed to be budget feasible, achieve near-optimal utility for the requester, be incentive compatible (truthful) for workers and make minimal assumptions about the distribution of workers' true costs.

On the theoretical side, we present a novel mathematical analysis which exploits a link between procurement auctions and multi-armed bandits – a classical problem in online learning and experimental design – to prove regret bounds for the mechanism. BP-UCB builds on and extends existing mechanisms using multi-armed bandits for online auctions [25, 6] to procurement auctions under budget constraints. However, the mechanisms of [25, 6] are not directly applicable as they optimize a different objective, which leads to a substantially different mathematical analysis. Our analysis further yields insights into an explicit separation of the regret in terms of wasted budget through overpayment and rejected offers through underpayment. Additionally, our BP-UCB approach substantially improves upon the existing mechanisms for procurement auctions which are designed to achieve constant multiplicative approximation ratios [32, 8], which can lead to high additive regret.

We further carry out extensive experiments to compare the performance of BP-UCB with optimal benchmarks, as well as the state of the art mechanism of [8]. To the best of our knowledge, this is the first empirical study of posted-price mechanisms in procurement auctions. Apart from experimenting with simulated workers' cost distributions, we perform experiments using data gathered from an MTurk study to demonstrate the effectiveness of our approach on real world inputs. The results confirm the effectiveness and the practical applicability of using BP-UCB as posted price mechanism on crowdsourcing platforms.

2. RELATED WORK

Understanding incentives in crowdsourcing tasks. There has been growing interest in understanding the right incentives for workers in online labor markets. [21] present a model of workers and introduce methods to estimate workers' appropriate wages. The "hagglebot" of [22] negotiates payment rates for an image-labeling task with workers on MTurk. [28, 29] study other, non-monetary incentives that could improve the quality of workers' performance. [17] applies no-regret learning to better understand prediction markets and improve the results of information aggregation from crowds.

Multi-armed bandits (MAB) & regret minimization. The MAB problem is a natural formalism for studying settings where an agent repeatedly chooses among actions with uncertain rewards, and must trade exploration (gathering information about rewards) and exploitation (maximizing rewards obtained). A primary objective is to design no-regret algorithms which guarantee that the average regret approaches zero asymptotically over time when compared to the single best action in hindsight. MAB and regret minimization algorithms have been studied extensively and [13] gives a good overview. [3] introduces the UCB1 algorithm, which maintains an index (known as Upper Confidence Bound) on the actions and avoids explicit separation of exploration and exploitation by picking the action with the highest index. [24, 4, 10, 33] extend this approach to handle complex (possibly infinite) action spaces. Recently, budgeted variants of the MAB problem, where actions have different known costs, have been considered in [34, 36, 35]. [37] solves the crowdsourcing task whereby the goal is to learn workers' effectiveness as part of exploration. In our setting, in contrast, the costs are unknown and budget is utilized only in rounds when the offer is accepted by the worker – none of the standard approaches apply to this setting.

Learning in online auctions. Competitive online auctions were introduced in [26, 9]. These results were further extended and improved by using insights from regret minimization algorithms in [12, 11, 25]. [16] further extend the online posted price mechanisms for multi-parameter domains. [20, 18] study the auction problem with limited supply in the bidding model under stochastic arrival of the agents. [6] extends these results to the posted price model, by using insights from MAB problems. Our mathematical analysis builds on the results of [6]. However, in contrast, we consider dynamic pricing for procurement (reverse) auctions under a budget constraint. The results from [25, 6] are not applicable to this setting. In fact, straightforward application of the mechanisms of [25, 6] in our setting would simply offer the highest price, as that maximizes the utility of the action (acceptance of the price by the worker), though quickly exhaust the budget (and incur large regret).

Online procurement auctions. Mechanisms for procurement auctions have been extensively studied. Earlier work [2, 23, 14] concerns the frugality of mechanisms with the goal of procuring a feasible solution to a complex problem while minimizing the budget spent. In contrast, we are interested in studying truthful budget feasible mechanisms initiated recently in [30, 31]. Recent research addresses various models of budget constraints including the online knapsack secretary problem [7] and the weighted secretary problem [5]. However these are not directly applicable to truthful procurement mechanisms. [32] and [8] study a problem that is perhaps most similar to ours: they develop mechanisms for budgeted procurement in the stochastic setting for the bidding and posted price model respectively, and prove constant multiplicative bounds. In contrast, our mechanisms use the regret minimization framework, and we prove additive bounds on the regret. We note that mechanisms of constant multiplicative bounds could have arbitrarily poor performance in terms of additive regret. [32, 8] are also used as benchmarks for our experiments and our mechanism BP-UCB shows a substantial improvement over the state of the art mechanism of [8].

3. PROBLEM STATEMENT

We now formalize the problem addressed in this paper.

The requester and workers. There is a principal agent, the "requester", who posts the crowdsourcing task. A task is composed of atomic assignments, which can be performed by individual "workers". The requester has a budget $B > 0$ and a utility function over completed assignments. In this work, we assume that each assignment performed by a worker has unit value, thus the requester wishes to maximize the number of completed assignments subject to the budget constraint. There is a finite pool of workers, denoted by W. Each worker $w_i \in W$ is associated with a private cost $c_i \in \mathbb{R}_{\geq 0}$ for performing an assignment and $b_i \in \mathbb{R}_{\geq 0}$ is their bid or reported cost. We are interested in *truthful* mechanisms where it is a dominant strategy for worker w_i to report $b_i = c_i$. We assume that costs have known bounded support, i.e., $c_i \in [c_{\min}, c_{\max}]$ where $c_{\min}$ and $c_{\max}$ are the parameters of the problem, scaled such that $c_{\min} > 0$ and $c_{\max} \leq 1$. We note that the assumption of bounded costs naturally holds in online crowdsourcing platforms like MTurk, which generally enforce a publicly known minimal and maximal allowed payment for the assignments. We will keep the range of the costs fixed, and consider varying the budget. Also, the number of assignments per worker is normally set to one in MTurk. Furthermore, we assume that there are at least N workers where $N \geq \frac{B}{c_{\min}}$. We note that limiting the pool size to a much smaller number would lead to further constraints in our mechanism design in addition to the budget constraint and is beyond the scope of this work. However, having a very large, essentially infinite pool of workers would make the problem trivial as the mechanism can offer lowest possible prices without any overall loss of utility. We further discuss this issue in Section 6.

Online arrival of workers. We are interested in online settings where workers arrive one at a time. We focus on *stochastic* arrival of workers, where their costs are *i.i.d.* sampled from a distribution f (*i.i.d model*). We let $F : [c_{\min}, c_{\max}] \rightarrow [0, 1]$ denote the cumulative distribution function (CDF) of costs associated with the workers. Note that the stochastic arrival assumption may be violated in real online markets. This could be because of various factors, for example, if the workers' value of service increases over time and hence so does their cost. This non-stochastic setting is often called the *oblivious adversary model*. In our experiments, we empirically evaluate the robustness of our mechanisms in presence of such adversarial noise.

Optimal benchmarks. Consider an (unrealistic) offline mechanism with complete access to the pool of workers' true costs. The maximal utility in this setting can be achieved by sorting the workers by their increasing costs and offering each worker their true cost until the budget is exhausted. We denote this benchmark by OPT-VAR, i.e., the optimal variable price benchmark. An alternate benchmark of interest is a mechanism that is limited to offer a single fixed price to all workers, though this price is computed optimally assuming full knowledge of workers' costs. We denote this by OPT-FIX. Note that these benchmarks are offline, untruthful and assume full knowledge of the workers' costs. It seems natural to compare our online truthful mechanisms to the optimal truthful mechanism in offline settings. The utility of any single priced offline truthful mechanism is bounded by OPT-FIX and [19] shows that the performance of OPT-FIX is close to that of OPT-VAR. Further, recent results in procurement auctions from [30, 8] show that OPT-FIX is only a factor of 2 away from OPT-VAR for modular as well as symmetric submodular functions and this is the best approximation that *any* truthful mechanism can achieve. Therefore we will compare our mechanisms against this benchmark. This optimal offline fixed price denoted by p^*, as illustrated in Figure 1, is given by:

$$p^* = \arg\max_p \min\left\{F(p), \frac{B}{N \cdot p}\right\} \text{ s.t. } p \in [c_{\min} \ldots c_{\max}].$$

Utility and Regret. For a fixed budget B, let $U(M, B)$ denote the expected utility of mechanism M and $U(p, B)$ denote the expected utility of fixed price p. In the regret minimization framework, we are interested in comparing the regret w.r.t. to the best single price p^* offered in hindsight. The expected regret of mechanism M is given by

$$R_M(B) = U(p^*, B) - U(M, B),$$

where $U(p^*, B) = \frac{B}{p^*}$. We write R instead of R_M where the mechanism M is clear from context. Using this notation, our goal is to design mechanisms M where the average regret of the mechanism approaches zero asymptotically, i.e.,

$$\lim_{B \to \infty} \frac{R(B)}{B} = 0.$$

4. MECHANISMS

We begin by describing the high level ideas behind our mechanisms. Then, we design BP-DGREEDY for the bidding model and subsequently extend it to arrive at our main mechanism, BP-UCB, for posted prices. In Section 4.4, we analyze the mechanisms and prove the regret bounds.

4.1 Methodology

Background on classical MAB. In the classical MAB setting [13, 3], there are K independent choices ("arms") associated with unknown reward distributions. A MAB algorithm operates in discrete timesteps (rounds) and pulls an arm in each round to get a stochastic reward associated with that arm. The algorithm needs to "explore" by experimenting with potentially suboptimal arms so as to learn about the optimal arm. Meanwhile, to maximize the reward, it has to "exploit" its learning by pulling the arm that appears best. The goal of the algorithm is to minimize the regret by quickly converging to the optimal arm.

Learning the cost curve and connection to MAB. The main challenge in deciding the payments in our problem is the unknown distribution of the workers' cost ("cost curve"). The mechanism interacts with workers sequentially in discrete timesteps denoted by t, offering a price p^t at each timestep to worker w^t and adjusting the estimates of the cost curve based on observed feedback. In order to cast our problem in the MAB framework, we discretize the prices by creating a set of K price "arms" using a multiplicative factor of $(1 + \alpha)$, where α is a parameter of the mechanism, similar to [12, 6], as illustrated in Figure 1. For these K arms, we maintain F_i^t as an estimate of the CDF of workers' costs for price p_i at time t. The mechanism stops execution when the budget or the pool of workers is exhausted. At each timestep, our mechanisms will pick the arm i^t based on some optimization criterion. Unfortunately, the presence of the budget constraint breaks the standard MAB algorithms: The optimal arm in terms of utility is the one corresponding to the maximal price, though it would quickly exhaust the

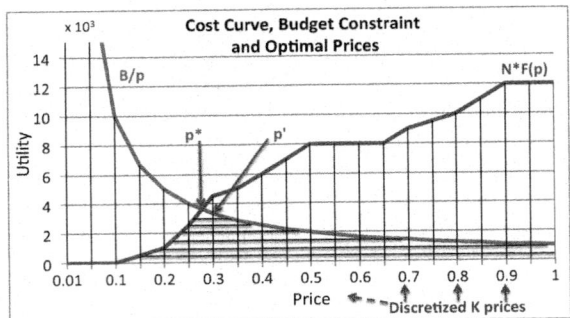

Figure 1: B/p represents the budget constraint, i.e. maximum utility that can be achieved given an infinite pool of workers. $N \cdot F(p)$ represents the utility with unlimited budget. The optimal price p^* lies at the intersection of these two curves. Discretized K prices are used by our mechanism, p' corresponds to the optimal price among these K prices.

Mechanism 1: BP-DGREEDY

1 Parameters: B; N; $\alpha = (0, 1]$; $c_{\min}$; $c_{\max}$;
2 Initialize:
- Prices. $p_0 = c_{\min}$; $p_i = (1+\alpha) \cdot p_{i-1}$; $p_K = c_{\max}$;
- Variables. $time$: $t = 0$; $budget$ $B^t = B$; $utility$: $U = 0$;
- Value estimates. $F_i^t = 0$;

begin
3   while $B^t > c_{\min}$ & $t < N$ do
4 $i^t = \arg\max_i V_i^t$ s.t. $p_i \leq B^t$;
          /* ties broken by picking lowest i */;
5   Offer price $p^t = p_{i^t}$ to worker w^t;
6   Observe bid b^t;
7 $\forall i$, Update $F_i^t = F_i^t + \frac{(S_i^t - F_i^t)}{(t+1)}$;
8   Set $U = U + S_{i^t}^t$; $B^{t+1} = B^t - p^t \cdot S_{i^t}^t$; $t = t + 1$;
        end
end
9 Output: U

---

available budget, leading to diminished utility. Further, we can exploit the fact that the price arms are correlated in our case: Acceptance at an offered price means acceptance for all more "expensive" arms and rejection at an offered price means rejection for all "cheaper" arms.

Additional notation. We need to introduce some more notation in order to describe our mechanisms. Let $i' \in \{1, \ldots, K\}$ denote the index of the optimal price among the K discretized prices, p' denote the corresponding price and F' the value of function $F_{i'} = F(p')$. As illustrated in Figure 1, i' is given by:

$$i' = \arg\max_i \min\left\{F_i, \frac{B}{N \cdot p_i}\right\} \quad \forall i \in [1 \ldots K].$$

We let B^t be the budget remaining at time t, N_i^t be the number of times p_i price has been offered, S_i^t be the indicator random variable indicating $b^t \leq p_i$ and T be the total number of rounds of execution of the mechanism (until the budget is exhausted or all the workers have been seen by the mechanism). Let us define $V_i = \min\left\{F_i, \frac{B}{N \cdot p_i}\right\}$, V_i^t be the estimate of V_i at round t. We further use $\Delta_i = V_{i'} - V_i$.

4.2 BP-DGREEDY for bidding model

We begin by designing a mechanism, BP-DGREEDY (deterministic greedy for budgeted procurement), for the bidding model (see Mechanism 1) in order to gain insights into the problem and develop mathematical foundations for the posted price model. The mechanism solicits the workers' bid b^t about service cost and then offers them a price p^t, based on past observations of workers' bids, which the worker can accept or reject. A natural approach towards ensuring truthful bids is to make the offered price *independent* of the bid of the current worker. Because of this truthfulness, we have $b^t = c^t$, which makes this mechanism resemble online learning with full information (refer [13, 27, 15]). This intuitively means that the mechanism gets to compute response feedback it would have received for any possible action.

We now discuss how to pick the arm i^t to make a price offer p^t independent of b^t. The intuition is simple: BP-DGREEDY just tracks the expected utility V_i^t of the arms based on the estimated F_i^t and offers the price corresponding to the best arm at time t. Based on the observed bid, it updates the estimates of F_i^t for all the arms by simply maintaining the average response of acceptance at arm i.

4.3 BP-UCB for posted price model

Next, we present our main mechanism, BP-UCB (UCB for budgeted procurement, see Mechanism 2) for the posted price model, where we get to see acceptance or rejection feedback only for the price offered. This limited feedback leads to a natural exploration-exploitation tradeoff as in MAB problems. We tackle this problem by modifying BP-DGREEDY, whereby we maintain upper confidence bounds on F_i^t, denoted by $\widetilde{F_i^t}$, which are then used to optimistically estimate the values $\widetilde{V_i^t}$. The mechanism then picks the best arm based on $\widetilde{V_i^t}$ and offers a take-it-or-leave it price p^t. Based on the feedback from the worker, it updates the parameters only for the arm i^t. This approach is inspired from the classical UCB1 algorithm [3]. However, the budget constraints make the analysis of regret bounds non-trivial.

We further exploit the correlation between the arms, as a rejection response actually means rejection for all "cheaper" arms. Similar to [11], we use this correlation to further improve the execution performance of the mechanism by keeping an estimate of the lower bound of the cost curve's support and keeping all the arms (except one) below this estimate as inactive. This modification does not hurt the theoretical guarantees described in Section 4.4.

4.4 Performance Analysis

We now prove regret bounds for our mechanisms BP-DGREEDY and BP-UCB. We begin with the analysis of BP-DGREEDY and develop the mathematical tools that will be useful for the analysis of BP-UCB. A crucial challenge in dealing with the budget constraint lies in the fact that while higher prices are more "effective" since more workers would accept the offer, they would quickly exhaust the budget leading to reduced overall utility.

Components contributing to the regret. There are essentially three components contributing to the regret. The first is the discretization of the prices: Since the mechanism does not have access to the optimal price p^*, p' is the best price available. After accounting for the regret of "discretization", we can consider an alternative mechanism M' which has access to an additional arm corresponding to p^*. Considering M', the second component of the regret is attributed to pulling arms with prices $p_i < p^*$ as cheaper arms are less effective and result in more rejected offers. The third

Mechanism 2: BP-UCB

1 Parameters: B; N; $\alpha = (0,1]$; $c_{\min}$; $c_{\max}$.
2 Initialize:
- **Prices.** $p_0 = c_{\min}$; $p_i = (1+\alpha) \cdot p_{i-1}$; $p_K = c_{\max}$;
- **Variables.** $time$: $t=0$; $budget$ $B^t = B$; $utility$: $U = 0$;
- **Value estimates.** $N_i^t = 0$; $F_i^t = 0$;

begin
3   while $B^t > c_{\min}$ & $t < N$ do
4      $\widetilde{F}_i^t = F_i^t + \sqrt{\frac{2 \cdot \ln(t)}{N_i^t}}$;
5      $\widetilde{V}_i^t = \min\left\{\widetilde{F}_i^t, \frac{B}{N \cdot p_i}\right\}$;
6      $i^t = \arg\max_i \widetilde{V}_i^t$ s.t. $p_i \leq B^t$;
     /* ties broken by picking lowest i */;
7   Offer price $p^t = p_{i^t}$ to worker w^t;
8   Observe acceptance decision y^t;
9   Update $F_{i^t}^t = F_{i^t}^t + \frac{(y^t - F_{i^t}^t)}{(N_{i^t}^t + 1)}$; $N_{i^t}^t = N_{i^t}^t + 1$;
10   Update $U = U + y^t$; $B^{t+1} = B^t - p^t \cdot y^t$; $t = t+1$;
   end
end
11 Output: U

component of the regret is attributed to pulling arms with prices $p_i > p^*$. Though these "expensive" arms are more effective than the price p^*, they overpay and quickly exhaust the budget. We formalize the above discussion in Lemma 1.

Lemma 1. *The expected regret $R_M(B)$ of any mechanism M can be expressed in terms of three components as follows:*

$$R_M(B) < \underbrace{\left(\frac{B}{p^*} - \frac{B}{p'}\right)}_{Discretization} + \underbrace{\sum_{i: p_i < p^*} \mathbb{E}\left[N_i^T\right] \cdot (F^* - F_i)}_{Rejected\ offers}$$

$$+ \underbrace{\sum_{i: p_i > p^*} \frac{\mathbb{E}\left[N_i^T\right] \cdot (p_i \cdot F_i - p^* \cdot F^*)}{p^*} + \frac{c_{\min}}{p^*}}_{Wasted\ budget\ through\ overpayment}$$

The proof is given in Appendix A.

Regret bounds for BP-DGREEDY. To obtain the desired regret bounds for mechanism BP-DGREEDY from Lemma 1, we need to bound N_i^T, as well as the regret of discretization. We bound the N_i^T for an execution of BP-DGREEDY using the Chernoff-Hoeffding concentration inequalities as in [3]. By exploiting the ordering of arms, we are able to separately provide bounds for N_i^T for arms with prices $p_i < p'$ and $p_i > p'$. For our analysis, we consider four separate cases based on whether $F_{i'}^t$ is less or greater than $\frac{B}{N \cdot p'}$ and based on relative ordering of p' compared to p^*. This insight crucially simplifies the analysis, enabling us to use the tools from the original UCB1 analysis in bounding each one of these four cases separately. Theorem 1 provides the desired regret bounds for BP-DGREEDY.

Theorem 1. *The expected regret of mechanism BP-DGREEDY is upper-bounded as follows:*

$$R_{\text{BP-DGREEDY}}(B) < \frac{\alpha \cdot B}{p^*} + \sum_{i: p_i < p^*} \frac{4 \cdot (F^* - F_i)}{\Delta_i^2}$$
$$+ \sum_{i: p_i > p^*} \frac{(p_i \cdot F_i - p^* \cdot F^*)}{2 \cdot \Delta_i^2 \cdot p^*} + \frac{c_{\min}}{p^*}$$

The proof is given in Appendix A.2. Next, we prove the no-regret property of mechanism BP-DGREEDY by using an appropriate choice of the discretization factor α, similar to the choice made for the problem of online auctions with limited supply in [6].

Corollary 1. *The expected average regret of mechanism BP-DGREEDY w.r.t. the budget size B goes to zero asymptotically for appropriate choice of α.*

Proof. By setting α to $\mathcal{O}\left(\frac{\ln(B/c_{\min})}{B}\right)$, the expected average regret of BP-DGREEDY w.r.t. B in the limit $\lim_{B \to \infty}$ is given as:

$$\lim_{B \to \infty} \mathbb{E}\left[\frac{R_{\text{BP-DGREEDY}}(B))}{B}\right] = \lim_{B \to \infty} \frac{\mathcal{O}(\ln(B/c_{\min}))}{B} = 0. \quad \square$$

Regret bounds for BP-UCB. We now extend the analysis of BP-DGREEDY to BP-UCB. Theorem 2 provides the desired regret bounds for BP-UCB.

Theorem 2. *The expected regret of mechanism BP-UCB is upper-bounded as follows:*

$$R_{\text{BP-UCB}}(B) < \frac{\alpha \cdot B}{p^*}$$
$$+ \sum_{i: p_i < p^*} \left(\frac{8 \cdot \ln(B/c_{\min})}{\Delta_i^2} + \frac{\pi^2}{3} + 1\right) \cdot (F^* - F_i)$$
$$+ \sum_{i: p_i > p^*} \frac{\pi^2 \cdot (p_i \cdot F_i - p^* \cdot F^*)}{6 \cdot p^*} + \frac{c_{\min}}{p^*}$$

The proof is given in Appendix A.3. Corollary 2 proves the no-regret property of the mechanism.

Corollary 2. *The expected average of regret of mechanism BP-UCB w.r.t. budget size B goes to zero asymptotically for appropriate choice of α.*

Proof. The proof follows by using exactly the same arguments as in Corollary 1. $\quad \square$

5. EXPERIMENTAL EVALUATION

In this section, we carry out extensive experiments to understand the practical performance of our mechanisms on simulated cost distributions, as well as on costs derived from an actual MTurk study. We begin by describing our benchmarks, metrics and experimental setup.

Benchmarks. We compare our mechanisms against the following benchmarks and state-of-art mechanisms:

- OPT-VAR and OPT-FIX: These are offline, untruthful mechanisms with full information of the workers' true costs as discussed in Section 3.
- MEAN: Another offline mechanism that operates under the bidding model. It offers a fixed price computed as the mean value of the workers' bids. This mechanism serves as a rule of thumb to determine fixed prices for tasks, as possibly used by inexperienced requesters.
- BS'11: We implemented the mechanism for the bidding model based on sampling bids from [32]. This mechanism assumes that workers' arrival order is stochastic *i.i.d.*
- PP'12: This is the online posted price mechanism from [8] designed for the stochastic setting. We found that the recommended parameters used for proving theoretical guarantees did not work in practice. We therefore

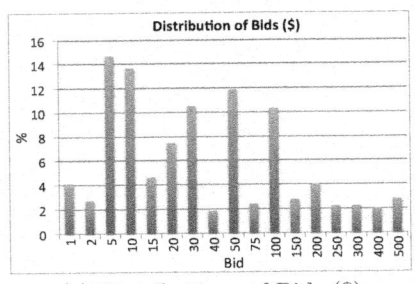 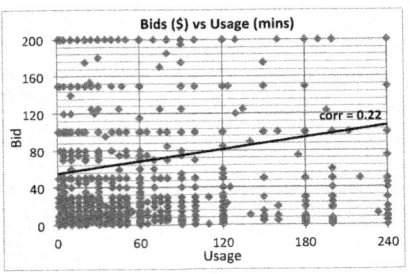 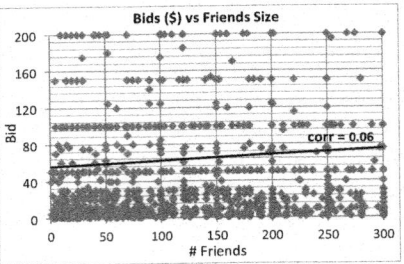

(a) Distributions of Bids ($)   (b) Corr. of Bids ($) vs Usage (mins)   (c) Corr. of Bids ($) vs Friends Size

Figure 2: (a) Distribution of workers' bids, Correlation with (b) usage time and with (c) number of friends online

manually tuned parameters to optimize the performance of this benchmark. Specifically, we ignored the parameter z in determining the price of the highest arm as $\frac{B}{z}$ and instead used $c_{\max}$ as a bound. Also, we used $a = 5$ instead of 4000, which would need an extremely large pool of workers for execution.

Metrics and experiments. The primary metric we track is the utility of the mechanism as we vary the budget B, setting $N = \frac{B}{c_{\min}}$. We also compute the average regret of the mechanism w.r.t. increasing budget to verify its no-regret property. To study the effect of the worker pool size, we also look into varying N for a fixed budget. To gain insight into execution of the mechanisms, we measure their rate of convergence by determining the unique price to which the mechanism converges in the end and measuring the number of times this price has been offered so far with increasing timesteps. Lastly, we evaluate the utility over time to understand the dynamics of how quickly the budget is exhausted.

Parameter choices. We used $c_{\min} = 0.01$ and $c_{\max} = 1$ based on the payment bounds typically seen on MTurk. The price discretization factor α is set to 0.2. We note that setting α to $\mathcal{O}\left(\frac{\ln(B/c_{\min})}{B}\right)$ guarantees asymptotic bounds of $\mathcal{O}\left(\ln(B/c_{\min})\right)$, however smaller values of α would increase the number of arms, leading to slower convergence.

Cost distributions. We considered cost distributions based on simulations as well as gathered from an actual MTurk study. We considered various simulated distributions for analyzing our algorithms, including uniform, normal, exponential and more complex ones including mixture of two uniform or two Gaussian distributions. Also, we considered various settings to simulate the arrival of workers, including ordering by ascending bids to simulate adversarial arrival. To simulate a more realistic non-stochastic setting, we considered groups of two distributions arriving one after another, ordered by their increasing means.

5.1 Mechanical Turk Study

The primary objective of this study was to get cost distributions from a realistic crowdsourcing task, as well as to understand the non-stochastic nature of real inputs that could arise because of the task's temporal nature.

Data Collection. We posted a HIT (Human Intelligent Task) on MTurk in form of a survey, where workers were told about an option to participate in a hypothetical advertisement system for a social networking site. In this hypothetical system, they can opt to use the top of their homepage for banner ads and obtain some monthly payment from the publishers. Workers were asked to bid on the monthly payment they would like to receive, in addition to providing information like years of being active on social networks and time spent there, approximate geographical location, number of friends and optional comments. They were asked to provide this information for different times including July 2012, July 2011 and July 2010. The goal of this survey was twofold. Firstly, we wanted to get the workers' cost distribution for a realistic scenario which fits our procurement auction task. Secondly, we wanted to understand whether the assumption of stochastic costs holds true in real world inputs. A total of 1200 workers participated in our HIT, which was online for one week, restricted to workers with more than 90% approval rate. Workers were paid a fixed amount for participation in the HIT. We did not restrict the workers to any geographical region. Additionally, we made a bonus payment to selected 20 individuals based on their insightful comments about factors affecting their payment choice.

Feature	July10	July11	July12	all
# Active workers	641	833	867	867
# Friends (mean)	165	230	318	242
# Friends (median)	100	160	250	157
Usage mins (mean)	64	73	83	74
Usage mins (median)	30	50	60	50
Bids $ (mean)	55	66	90	71
Bids $ (median)	20	25	30	25

Table 1: Statistics of the data reported for different years

Statistics. The workers represented more than 20 different countries with 44.5% from USA and 44.0% from India. In total 72.25% of the workers agreed to participate in the hypothetical online advertisement system, and we analyze the statistics from these workers below. Workers from USA have lower acceptance rate of participation (59.3%) compared to workers from India (86.1%), which shows interesting dependence on geographical factors in determining the pricing model of the workers. Table 1 shows the mean and median values of various features. The data shows an increase in social activity (in terms of friend count and service usage) as well as the bids reported by workers for their service. Figure 2 shows the distribution of bids collected as well as the correlation with usage time and number of friends. The data is skewed towards lower bids and is discretized because of the tendency of workers to bid at rounded numbers. In total 75.8% of the workers provided subjective feedback in the comments section about the pricing factors. Common themes reported by the workers for the pricing factors were the usage time, friend count and nature of the ads. The statistics related to friend size matches closely with those of publicly available numbers supporting the quality of the data obtained from the workers.

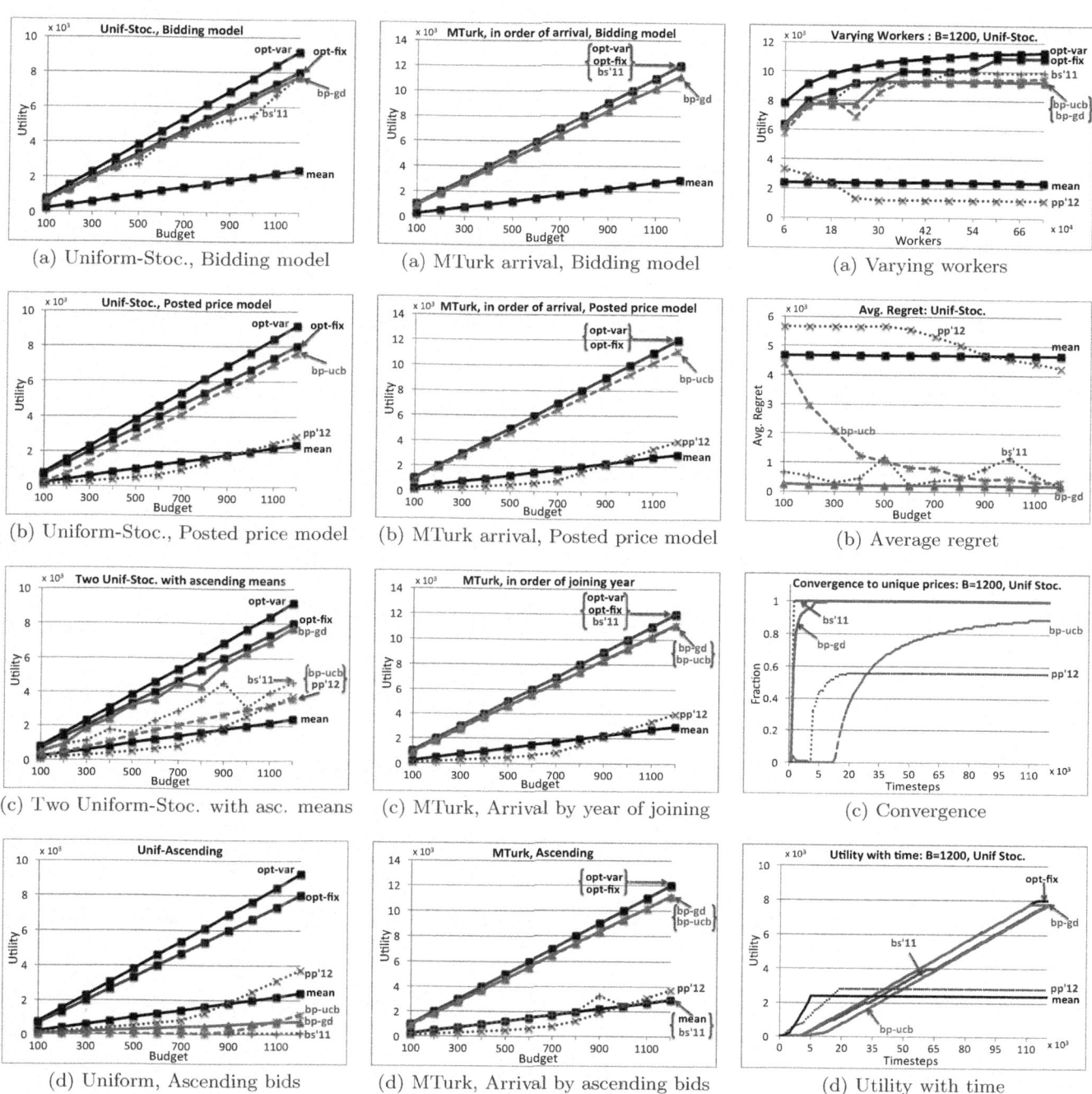

Figure 3 (1st column): Utility for uniform distribution in [0.1, 0.9], varying budget. In **(a)**, BP-UCB outperforms PP'12 by over 150% increase in utility for the stochastic settings. **(c)** uses two uniform distributions in [0.1, 0.5] and [0.5, 0.9].

Figure 4 (2nd column): Utility for MTurk distribution for bids in [10, 100], varying budget. In **(a)**, BP-UCB outperforms PP'12 by over 180% increase in utility. Also, BP-UCB and BP-DGREEDY are robust against all the online settings above.

Figure 5 (3rd column): Uniform distribution in [0.1, 0.9], stochastic settings. In **(b)**, no-regret properties of BP-UCB can be seen as the average regret diminishes with increase in budget. **(c)** shows better convergence rate of BP-UCB compared to PP'12. **(d)** shows that BP-UCB makes low offers in beginning, in contrast to PP'12 which quickly exhausts the budget.

5.2 Results

We now present and discuss the findings from our experiments. In the figures, we denote BP-DGREEDY as *bp-gd*.

Utility for simulated distributions. Figure 3 shows results for costs uniformly distributed in the range [0.1, 0.9], though the results are qualitatively similar for other distributions and ranges. We consider the online setting with stochastic arrival of workers and also assess the robustness of the mechanisms when these assumptions are violated. In Figure 3(a), we can see that the mechanism BP-DGREEDY performs very close to OPT-FIX and slightly outperforms the state of the art mechanism BS'11 for the bidding model.

1173

Somewhat surprisingly, as we can see in Figure 3(b), our mechanism BP-UCB for the posted price model performs as good as BP-DGreedy even though it operates under limited feedback. It clearly outperforms PP'12 by an over 150% increase in utility for all the budgets considered. Mean is much lower compared to both of our mechanisms, suggesting that rules of thumb prices may not be optimal.

We also simulate arrival of the workers in order of ascending bids, violating the stochastic $i.i.d.$ assumptions. In Figure 3(d), we see that all the mechanisms perform quite poorly in this somewhat unrealistic case. Figure 3(c) shows results for a perhaps more meaningful non-stochastic setting where two groups with bids uniformly distributed in $[0.0, 0.5]$ and $[0.5, 0.9]$ respectively arrive after another. Therefore, a natural question is how robust the algorithms are w.r.t. more realistic cost distributions, as we analyze next.

Utility for MTurk distributions. Figure 4 shows results for cost distributions from the MTurk study. We considered bids ranging in $[10\$, 100\$]$, scaled down by 100, although the results are qualitatively similar for other ranges. Note that scaling down the costs is equivalent to scaling up the budget. We sampled with replacement from the bids to generate the entire pool of workers. We considered various online settings to simulate the arrival order of workers: the actual order in which workers arrived on MTurk for completing the task; ordered by their usage time; ordered by number of friends and by the year of joining the social network. Here, we discuss the results for the arguably most natural orderings. For the bidding model, we can see in Figure 4(a) that both OPT-Fix and BS'11 coincide exactly with OPT-Var, in the case of workers arriving according to the actual MTurk ordering. We attribute this to the highly skewed nature of bids at low prices, as the optimal strategy for all these three mechanisms is to offer a single fixed price corresponding to the lowest bid. For the posted price model in Figure 4(b), BP-UCB clearly outperforms PP'12, increasing the utility by over 180% for all the budgets considered.

Figure 4(c) shows results where workers are ordered by the year in which they joined and Figure 4(d) shows the results where workers are ordered by their increasing bids on MTurk. Interestingly, BP-UCB and BP-DGreedy continue to perform well in both the settings, whereas BS'11 degrades in Figure 4(d) and PP'12 performs poorly in both.

Effect of varying N. Apart from varying the budget, it is interesting to compare the impact of workers' pool size on the mechanisms for a fixed budget. Note that the availability of more workers (larger N) shifts the optimal solution towards lower prices. Figure 5(a) shows the impact of varying N. As one would expect, our mechanisms BP-DGreedy and BP-UCB as well as BS'11 show an increase in utility exhibiting diminishing returns. Interestingly, PP'12 shows a decrease in utility as the number of workers increases.

Average regret. Figure 5(b) shows the average regret of the mechanisms with increasing budget. Note that the average regret of BP-UCB decreases at a much faster rate compared to that of PP'12.

Rate of convergence. Here, we look at the rate of convergence of the mechanisms in Figure 5(c), by computing the proportion of times the unique price, to which the mechanism converges in end, has been offered so far with increasing timesteps. BS'11 rapidly converges to the unique price, favorably compared to BP-DGreedy. We can see an initial phase of "exploration" for BP-UCB followed by "exploitation" as the mechanism converges. However, PP'12 stabilizes at 50% convergence as the Markov model used by the mechanism flips back and forth between the equilibrium prices.

Utility with timesteps. Lastly, we study how the mechanisms accrue utility over time (Figure 5(d)). BP-UCB offers very low prices in the initial phase of "exploration", followed by convergence to a unique price, after which the utility increases almost linearly. In contrast, PP'12 quickly exhausts the budget in the beginning by offering high prices, leading to overall reduced utility.

6. CONCLUSIONS AND FUTURE WORK

We designed mechanisms for online budgeted procurement using a regret minimization approach. We started with mechanism BP-DGreedy for the bidding model and then extended it to our main mechanism BP-UCB for the posted price model. These are the first provable no-regret mechanisms for online budgeted procurement. Apart from theoretical guarantees, we prove that they are empirically efficient compared to optimal benchmarks, and dramatically outperform the state of the art posted price mechanism. Our experiments on MTurk further supports the practical applicability of our mechanisms on crowdsourcing platforms. We believe that our results provide an important step towards developing practical, yet theoretically well-founded techniques for increasing the efficiency of crowdsourcing.

There are some natural extensions for future work. Here, we considered a simple additive utility function for the requester. It would be useful to extend our approach to more complex utility functions. Additionally, we assumed a homogeneous pool of workers, although it would be more practical to design mechanisms which can take into account skills and different utility values of the workers.

Our experiments on MTurk suggest that real world inputs may violate stochastic assumptions. While our mechanisms are robust against our study's cost distribution, one can force all the currently available mechanisms to perform poorly by carefully designing (unrealistic) cost distributions. It would be of interest to develop mechanisms that are more robust, and extend to the oblivious adversary model.

We used the knowledge of known bounded support and furthermore discretized the price space. Results from continuous arm bandits in [24, 4, 10, 33] can be applied here by making more realistic assumptions about cost distributions. This would enable learning the support as part of the mechanism itself and remove the regret from discretization.

In this work, we assumed a finite yet large pool of available workers. A perhaps more natural approach is to use time discounted rewards where a mechanism's goal would be *timely* completion of the task. Existing crowdsourcing platforms support only fixed price mechanisms and limited capabilities to design pricing policies. Our experiments show that simple mechanisms like Mean perform quite poorly, although inexperienced requesters may be tempted to use them as rule of thumb. It would be interesting to build applications and conduct studies where we can actually run our mechanisms in real time on crowdsourcing platforms.

Acknowledgments. We'd like to thank Hastagiri Vanchinathan, Yuxin Chen, Brian McWilliams, Patrick Pletscher and Gábor Bartók for helpful discussions. This research was supported in part by SNSF grant 200021_137971, ERC StG 307036 and a Microsoft Research Faculty Fellowship.

APPENDIX
A. PROOFS
A.1 Components contributing to the regret

We begin by expressing the expected utility of a mechanism in terms of N_i^T in Lemma 2. We use I_i^t as indicator variable indicating that price p_i was offered at time t.

Lemma 2. *The expected utility of the mechanism M is given by $U(M, B) = \sum_{i=1}^{K} \mathbb{E}[N_i^T] \cdot F_i$*

Proof. From definition of $S_{i^t}^t$, we have

$$U(M,B) = \mathbb{E}_T\Big[\mathbb{E}\Big[\sum_{t=1}^{T} S_{i^t}^t \mid T\Big]\Big] = \sum_{t=1}^{T}\sum_{i=1}^{K} \mathbb{E}_T\Big[\mathbb{E}\big[I_i^t \cdot S_i^t \mid T\big]\Big]$$

$$= \sum_{t=1}^{T}\sum_{i=1}^{K} \mathbb{E}_T\big[\mathbb{E}[I_i^t \mid T]\big] \cdot \mathbb{E}_T\big[\mathbb{E}[S_i^t]\big] \quad (1)$$

$$= \sum_{i=1}^{K} \mathbb{E}_T\Big[\mathbb{E}\big[\sum_{t=1}^{T} I_i^t \mid T\big]\Big] \cdot F_i = \sum_{i=1}^{K} \mathbb{E}_T\big[\mathbb{E}[N_i^T \mid T]\big] \cdot F_i \quad (2)$$

$$= \sum_{i=1}^{K} \mathbb{E}[N_i^T] \cdot F_i$$

Unlike UCB1, T is a random variable here. Step 1 uses the fact that S_i^t only depends on the order of bids and is therefore independent of the mechanism (i.e., of I_i^t and T). Step 2 follows from definitions of N_i^T and F_i. □

Next, in Lemma 3, we provide a lower bound on the expected timesteps T in the execution of a mechanism, unlike in standard UCB1 where T is fixed. This ensures that the mechanism's regret coming from the component "Wasted budget through overpayment" in Lemma 1 is bounded.

Lemma 3. *The expected number of timesteps T in the execution of the mechanism has lower bound as follows:*

$$\mathbb{E}[T] > \frac{B}{p^* \cdot F^*} - \frac{c_{\min}}{p^* \cdot F^*} - \sum_{i:p_i > p^*} \frac{\mathbb{E}[N_i^T] \cdot (p_i \cdot F_i - p^* \cdot F^*)}{p^* \cdot F^*}$$

Proof. The algorithm terminates when either $i)$ $t > N$ or $ii)$ $B^t < c_{\min}$. In $i)$, $T = N$ and hence bounds in the equation hold trivially since $N \geq \frac{B}{c_{\min}} > \frac{B}{p^*} > \frac{B}{p^* \cdot F^*}$. We will prove the bounds for $ii)$ below by bounding the sum of the prices offered and accepted by workers $\sum_{t=1}^{T} S_{i^t}^t \cdot p^t$.

$$B - c_{\min} < \mathbb{E}_T\Big[\mathbb{E}\Big[\sum_{t=1}^{T} S_{i^t}^t \cdot p^t \mid T\Big]\Big] = \sum_{i=1}^{K} \mathbb{E}[N_i^T] \cdot F_i \cdot p_i \quad (1)$$

$$= \sum_{i=1}^{K} \mathbb{E}[N_i^T] \cdot (F_i \cdot p_i - F^* \cdot p^*) + \sum_{i=1}^{K} \mathbb{E}[N_i^T] \cdot F^* \cdot p^*$$

$$\mathbb{E}[T] \cdot F^* \cdot p^* > B - c_{\min} - \sum_{i:p_i < p^*} \mathbb{E}[N_i^T] \cdot (F_i \cdot p_i - F^* \cdot p^*)$$

$$- \sum_{i:p_i > p^*} \mathbb{E}[N_i^T] \cdot (F_i \cdot p_i - F^* \cdot p^*) \quad (2)$$

Step 1 follows by using the same arguments as in Lemma 2. Step 2 replaces $\sum_i^K N_i^T$ by T and we get the desired bounds by using the fact that $(F_i \cdot p_i - F^* \cdot p^*) < 0$ for $p_i < p^*$. □

We now prove Lemma 1 by using the above results.

Proof of Lemma 1. Consider an alternate mechanism M' which has access to an additional arm corresponding to price p^*. We first analyze the regret of M' below.

$$R_{M'}(B) = U(p^*, B) - U(M', B) = \frac{B}{p^*} - \sum_{i=1}^{K} \mathbb{E}[N_i^T] \cdot F_i$$

$$= \frac{B}{p^*} + \sum_{i=1}^{K} \mathbb{E}[N_i^T] \cdot (F^* - F_i) - \sum_{i=1}^{K} \mathbb{E}[N_i^T] \cdot F^*$$

$$= \frac{B}{p^*} - \mathbb{E}[T] \cdot F^* + \sum_{i:p_i < p^*} \mathbb{E}[N_i^T] \cdot (F^* - F_i)$$

$$+ \sum_{i:p_i > p^*} \mathbb{E}[N_i^T] \cdot (F^* - F_i) \quad (1)$$

$$\leq \frac{B}{p^*} - \mathbb{E}[T] \cdot F^* + \sum_{i:p_i < p^*} \mathbb{E}[N_i^T] \cdot (F^* - F_i) \quad (2)$$

$$< \frac{c_{\min}}{p^*} + \sum_{i:p_i < p^*} \mathbb{E}[N_i^T] \cdot (F^* - F_i)$$

$$+ \sum_{i:p_i > p^*} \frac{\mathbb{E}[N_i^T] \cdot (p_i \cdot F_i - p^* \cdot F^*)}{p^*} \quad (3)$$

Step 1 replaces $\sum_i^K N_i^T$ by T and step 2 uses the fact that $(F^* - F_i) < 0$ for $p_i > p^*$. And, step 3 follows from the results of Lemma 3.

The regret of mechanism M is given by $R_M(B) = R_{M'}(B) + R_{p'}(B)$ where $R_{p'}(B) = \left(\frac{B}{p^*} - \frac{B}{p'}\right)$. Using the value of $R_{M'}$ from above completes the proof. □

A.2 Regret bounds for BP-DGREEDY

In Lemma 4, we show that discretization to a power of $(1 + \alpha)$ results in loss of utility by at most a factor of $(1+\alpha)$, similar to the online auctions as shown in [12, 6].

Lemma 4. *The regret component "discretization" in Lemma 1 is upper-bounded by $R_{p'}(B) \leq \frac{\alpha \cdot B}{p^*}$.*

Proof. Consider price p^h given by:

$$p^h = \inf_{p_i} \{\forall i \in [1 \ldots K] \ s.t. \ p_i \geq p^*\}$$

By the design of discretization, $p^h < (1+\alpha) \cdot p^*$. Now, consider that price p^h is offered to every worker instead of p'.

$$R_{p'}(B) = U(p^*, B) - U(p', B) \leq \frac{B}{p^*} - \frac{B}{p^h} \leq \frac{\alpha \cdot B}{p^*}$$

We use the fact that for $p^h \geq p^*$, $U(p^h; B) = \frac{B}{p^h}$. □

Lemma 5. *$\forall i$ s.t. $p_i < p'$, expected number of times a suboptimal arm i is played is upper-bounded by $\mathbb{E}[N_i^T] \leq \frac{4}{\Delta_i^2}$.*

Proof. A suboptimal arm i is picked at time t when $V_i^t \leq V_{i'}^t$ where $V_j^t = \min\left\{F_i^t, \frac{B}{N \cdot p_j}\right\}$. We consider the following cases:

Case a) $p' \leq p^*$ and $F_{i'}^t \leq \frac{B}{N \cdot p'}$:

$$F_i^t \geq F_{i'}^t$$

$$\left(F_i^t - F_i - \frac{F_{i'} - F_i}{2}\right) + \left(F' - F_{i'}^t - \frac{F_{i'} - F_i}{2}\right) \geq 0$$

$$\left((F_i^t - F_i) - \frac{\Delta_i}{2}\right) + \left((F' - F_{i'}^t) - \frac{\Delta_i}{2}\right) \geq 0 \quad (1)$$

Case b) $p' \leq p^*$ and $F_{i'}^t > \frac{B}{N \cdot p'}$:

$$F_i^t \geq \frac{B}{N \cdot p'} \geq F' \implies F_i^t - F_i \geq \Delta_i \quad (2)$$

Case c) $p' > p^*$ and $F_{i'}^t \leq \frac{B}{N \cdot p'}$:

$$F_i^t \geq F_{i'}^t$$

$$\left(F_i^t - F_i - \frac{\frac{B}{N \cdot p'} - F_i}{2}\right) + \left(\frac{B}{N \cdot p'} - F_{i'}^t - \frac{\frac{B}{N \cdot p'} - F_i}{2}\right) \geq 0$$

$$\left((F_i^t - F_i) - \frac{\Delta_i}{2}\right) + \left((F' - F_{i'}^t) - \frac{\Delta_i}{2}\right) \geq 0 \quad (3)$$

Case d) $p' > p^*$ and $F_{i'}^t > \frac{B}{N \cdot p'}$:

$$F_i^t \geq \frac{B}{N \cdot p'} = \frac{B}{N \cdot p'} + F_i - F_i \implies F_i^t - F_i \geq \Delta_i \quad (4)$$

Using Chernoff-Hoeffding inequality and the fact that $\mathbb{P}(A + B \geq 0) \leq \mathbb{P}(A \geq 0) + \mathbb{P}(B \geq 0)$, we bound step 1 and 3 as:

$$\mathbb{P}\left(\left(F_i^t - F_i - \frac{\Delta_i}{2}\right) + \left(F' - F_{i'}^t - \frac{\Delta_i}{2}\right) \geq 0\right) \leq 2 \cdot e^{-\frac{\Delta_i^2}{2} \cdot t}$$

For step 2 and 4, we have the following bounds:

$$\mathbb{P}\left(F_i^t - F_i \geq \Delta_i\right) \leq e^{-2 \cdot \Delta_i^2 \cdot t} \leq 2 \cdot e^{-\frac{\Delta_i^2}{2} \cdot t}$$

Combining the bounds for above cases, we have:

$$\mathbb{E}\left[N_i^T\right] \leq \sum_{t=1}^T 2 \cdot e^{-\frac{\Delta_i^2}{2} \cdot t} \leq \sum_{t=1}^\infty 2 \cdot e^{-\frac{\Delta_i^2}{2} \cdot t} = \frac{4}{\Delta_i^2} \quad \square$$

Lemma 6. $\forall i$ s.t. $p_i > p'$, expected number of times a suboptimal arm i is played is upper-bounded by $\mathbb{E}[N_i^T] \leq \frac{1}{2 \cdot \Delta_i^2}$.

Proof. A suboptimal arm i is picked at time t when $V_i^t > V_{i'}^t$. We consider the following cases and the conditions that need to hold for picking arm i.

Case a) $p' \leq p^*$:

$$F_{i'}^t < \frac{B}{N \cdot p_i} = F' - \Delta_i \implies F' - F_{i'}^t > \Delta_i \quad (1)$$

Case b) $p' > p^*$:

$$F_{i'}^t < \frac{B}{N \cdot p_i} = \frac{B}{N \cdot p'} - \Delta_i \implies F' - F_{i'}^t > \Delta_i \quad (2)$$

Using Chernoff-Hoeffding inequality, step 1 and step 2 are bounded by $e^{-2 \cdot \Delta_i^2 \cdot t}$. Combining the bounds for above cases, we have:

$$\mathbb{E}\left[N_i^T\right] \leq \sum_{t=1}^T e^{-2 \cdot \Delta_i^2 \cdot t} \leq \sum_{t=1}^\infty e^{-2 \cdot \Delta_i^2 \cdot t} = \frac{1}{2 \cdot \Delta_i^2} \quad \square$$

Proof of Theorem 1. The proof directly follows from the bounds of N_i from Lemmas 5 and 6. By putting in these bounds in Lemma 1 along with the regret of discretization from Lemma 4, we get the desired results. $\square$

A.3 Regret bounds for BP-UCB

Lemma 7. $\forall i$ s.t. $p_i < p'$, expected number of times a suboptimal arm i is played is upper-bounded by

$$\mathbb{E}[N_i^T] \leq \frac{8 \cdot \ln(B/c_{\min})}{\Delta_i^2} + \frac{\pi^2}{3} + 1.$$

Proof. A suboptimal arm i is picked at time t when $\widetilde{V_i^t} \leq \widetilde{V_{i'}^t}$ where $\widetilde{V_j^t} = \min\left\{F_i^t + \sqrt{\frac{2 \cdot \ln(t)}{N_i^t}}, \frac{B}{N \cdot p_j}\right\}$. We consider the following cases:

Case a) $p' \leq p^*$ and $F_{i'}^t + \sqrt{\frac{2 \cdot \ln(t)}{N_{i'}^t}} \leq \frac{B}{N \cdot p'}$:

$$F_i^t + \sqrt{\frac{2 \cdot \ln(t)}{N_i^t}} \geq F_{i'}^t + \sqrt{\frac{2 \cdot \ln(t)}{N_{i'}^t}}$$

$$\left((F_i^t - F_i) - \sqrt{\frac{2 \cdot \ln(t)}{N_i^t}}\right) + \left((F' - F_{i'}^t) - \sqrt{\frac{2 \cdot \ln(t)}{N_{i'}^t}}\right)$$

$$+ \left(2 \cdot \sqrt{\frac{2 \cdot \ln(t)}{N_i^t}} - \Delta_i\right) \geq 0 \quad (1)$$

Case b) $p' \leq p^*$ and $F_{i'}^t + \sqrt{\frac{2 \cdot \ln(t)}{N_{i'}^t}} > \frac{B}{N \cdot p'}$:

$$F_i^t + \sqrt{\frac{2 \cdot \ln(t)}{N_i^t}} \geq \frac{B}{N \cdot p'} \geq F'$$

$$\left((F_i^t - F_i) - \sqrt{\frac{2 \cdot \ln(t)}{N_i^t}}\right) + \left(2 \cdot \sqrt{\frac{2 \cdot \ln(t)}{N_i^t}} - \Delta_i\right) \geq 0 \quad (2)$$

Case c) $p' > p^*$ and $F_{i'}^t + \sqrt{\frac{2 \cdot \ln(t)}{N_{i'}^t}} \leq \frac{B}{N \cdot p'}$:

This case is analogous to (1) in **Case (a)** with some algebraic manipulations.

Case d) $p' > p^*$ and $F_{i'}^t + \sqrt{\frac{2 \cdot \ln(t)}{N_{i'}^t}} > \frac{B}{N \cdot p'}$:

This case is analogous to (2) in **Case (b)** with some algebraic manipulations.

Using the Chernoff-Hoeffding inequality, step 1 and step 2 are bounded by $2 \cdot t^{-4}$ and t^{-4} respectively. Once suboptimal arm i has been played sufficient number of times, given by $N_i^t \geq \left\lceil \frac{8 \cdot \ln(B/c_{\min})}{\Delta_i^2} \right\rceil$, we have:

$$\mathbb{P}\left(2 \cdot \sqrt{\frac{2 \cdot \ln(t)}{N_i^t}} - \Delta_i > 0\right) = 0$$

Combining these together, we have the following:

$$\mathbb{E}[N_i^T] \leq \left\lceil \frac{8 \cdot \ln(B/c_{\min})}{\Delta_i^2} \right\rceil + \sum_{t=1}^T 2 \cdot t^{-4}$$

$$\leq \left\lceil \frac{8 \cdot \ln(B/c_{\min})}{\Delta_i^2} \right\rceil + \sum_{t=1}^\infty 2 \cdot t^{-4} < \frac{8 \cdot \ln(B/c_{\min})}{\Delta_i^2} + \frac{\pi^2}{3} + 1 \quad \square$$

Lemma 8. $\forall i$ s.t. $p_i > p'$, expected number of times a suboptimal arm i is played is upper-bounded by $\mathbb{E}[N_i^T] \leq \frac{\pi^2}{6}$.

Proof. A suboptimal arm i is picked at time t when $\widetilde{V_i^t} > \widetilde{V_{i'}^t}$. Irrespective of the relation between p' and p^*, the following must hold true:

$$F_{i'}^t + \sqrt{\frac{2 \cdot \ln(t)}{N_{i'}^t}} < \frac{B}{N \cdot p_i} < F' \implies F' - F_{i'}^t > \sqrt{\frac{2 \cdot \ln(t)}{N_{i'}^t}}$$

Using Chernoff-Hoeffding inequality, above case is bounded by t^{-4}. We have:

$$\mathbb{E}[N_i^T] \leq \sum_{t=1}^T t^{-4} \leq \sum_{t=1}^\infty t^{-4} < \frac{\pi^2}{6} \quad \square$$

Proof of Theorem 2. The proof follows by using exactly the same arguments as in Theorem 1. $\square$

B. REFERENCES

[1] Mechanical turk platform. https://www.mturk.com/.

[2] A. Archer and E. Tardos. Frugal path mechanisms. In *SODA*, pages 991–999, 2002.

[3] P. Auer, N. Cesa-Bianchi, and P. Fischer. Finite-time analysis of the multiarmed bandit problem. *Machine Learning*, 47(2-3):235–256, 2002.

[4] P. Auer, R. Ortner, and C. Szepesvari. Improved rates for the stochastic continuum-armed bandit problem. In *COLT*, pages 454–468, 2007.

[5] M. Babaioff, M. Dinitz, A. Gupta, N. Immorlica, and K. Tal-war. Secretary problems: weights and discounts. In *SODA*, pages 1245–1254, 2009.

[6] M. Babaioff, S. Dughmi, R. Kleinberg, and A. Slivkins. Dynamic pricing with limited supply. In *EC*, 2012.

[7] M. Babaioff, N. Immorlica, D. Kempe, and R. Kleinberg. A knapsack secretary problem with applications. In *APPROX-RANDOM*, pages 16–28, 2007.

[8] A. Badanidiyuru, R. Kleinberg, and Y. Singer. Learning on a budget: Posted price mechanisms for online procurement. In *EC*, 2012.

[9] Z. Bar-yossef, K. Hildrum, and F. Wu. Incentive-compatible online auctions for digital goods. In *SODA*, pages 964–970, 2002.

[10] O. Besbes and A. Zeevi. Dynamic pricing without knowing the demand function: Risk bounds and near-optimal algorithms. *Operations Research*, 2009.

[11] A. Blum and J. Hartline. Near-optimal online auctions. In *SODA*, 2005.

[12] A. Blum, V. Kumar, A. Rudra, and F. Wu. Online learning in online auctions. In *SODA*, 2003.

[13] A. Blum and Y. Monsour. *Learning, Regret minimization, and Equilibria in Algorithmic Game Theory*. Cambridge University Press, 2007.

[14] M. C. Cary, A. D. Flaxman, J. D. Hartline, and A. R. Karlin. Auctions for structured procurement. In *SODA*, pages 304–313, 2008.

[15] N. Cesa-Bianchi, Y. Freund, D. P. Helmbold, D. Haussler, R. Schapire, , and M. Warmuth. How to use expert advice. *Journal of the ACM*, 44(2):427–485, 1997.

[16] S. Chawla, J. D. Hartline, D. L. Malec, and B. Sivan. Multi-parameter mechanism design and sequential posted pricing. In *EC*, 2010.

[17] Y. Chen and J. W. Vaughan. A new understanding of prediction markets via no-regret learning. In *STOC*, 2010.

[18] N. Devanur and J. Hartline. Limited and online supply and the bayesian foundations of prior-free mechanism design. In *EC*, 2009.

[19] A. Goldberg, J. Hartline, and A. Wright. Competitive auctions and digital goods. In *SODA*, pages 735–744, 2001.

[20] M. T. Hajiaghayi, R. D. Kleinberg, , and D. C. Parkes. Adaptive limited-supply online auctions. In *EC*, 2004.

[21] J. J. Horton and L. B. Chilton. The labor economics of paid crowdsourcing. In *EC*, pages 209–218, 2010.

[22] J. J. Horton and R. J. Zeckhauser. Algorithmic wage negotiations: Applications to paid crowdsourcing. In *CrowdConf*, 2010.

[23] R. Karlin, D. Kempe, and T. Tamir. Beyond vcg: Frugality of truthful mechanisms. In *FOCS*, 2005.

[24] R. Kleinberg. Nearly tight bounds for the continuum-armed bandit problem. In *NIPS*, 2004.

[25] R. D. Kleinberg and F. T. Leighton. The value of knowing a demand curve:bounds on regret for online posted-price auctions. In *FOCS*, 2003.

[26] R. Lavi and N. Nisan. Competitive analysis of incentive compatible on-line auctions. In *EC*, pages 233–241, 2000.

[27] N. Littlestone and M. K. Warmuth. The weighted majority algorithm. *Info and Computation*, 70(2):212–261, 1994.

[28] W. Mason and D. J. Watts. Financial incentives and the performance of crowds. In *SIGKDD Explor. Newsl.*, pages 100–108, 2010.

[29] J. J. Shaw, A. D.; Horton and D. L. Chen. Designing incentives for inexpert human raters. In *CSCW*, pages 275–284, 2011.

[30] Y. Singer. Budget feasible mechanisms. In *FOCS*, pages 765–774, 2010.

[31] Y. Singer. How to win friends and influence people, truthfully: Influence maximization mechanisms for social networks. In *WSDM*, 2011.

[32] Y. Singer and M. Mittal. Pricing tasks in online labor markets. In *Workshop on Human Computation*. ACM, 2011.

[33] N. Srinivas, A. Krause, S. Kakade, and M. Seeger. Gaussian process optimization in the bandit setting: No regret and experimental design. In *ICML*, 2010.

[34] Tran-Thanh, L., C. A., J. E. M. de Cote, A. Rogers, and N. R. Jennings. Epsilon-first policies for budget-limited multi-armed bandits. In *AAAI*, pages 1211–1216, 2010.

[35] L. Tran-Thanh, A. Chapman, A. Rogers, , and N. R. Jennings. Knapsack based optimal policies for budget-limited multi-armed bandits. http://arxiv.org/abs/1204.1909, 2013. Technical report.

[36] L. Tran-Thanh, A. Chapman, A. Rogers, and N. R. Jennings. Knapsack based optimal policies for budget-limited multi-armed bandits. In *AAAI*, 2012.

[37] L. Tran-Thanh, S. Stein, A. Rogers, and N. R. Jennings. Efficient crowdsourcing of unknown experts using multi-armed bandits. In *AAAI*, 2012.

A Predictive Model for Advertiser Value-Per-Click in Sponsored Search

Eric Sodomka*
Brown University
Providence, Rhode Island

Sébastien Lahaie*
Microsoft Research
New York, New York

Dustin Hillard*
Microsoft Corp.
Redmond, Washington

ABSTRACT

Sponsored search is a form of online advertising where advertisers bid for placement next to search engine results for specific keywords. As search engines compete for the growing share of online ad spend, it becomes important for them to understand what keywords advertisers value most, and what characteristics of keywords drive value. In this paper we propose an approach to keyword value prediction that draws on advertiser bidding behavior across the terms and campaigns in an account. We provide original insights into the structure of sponsored search accounts that motivate the use of a hierarchical modeling strategy. We propose an economically meaningful loss function which allows us to implicitly fit a linear model for values given observables such as bids and click-through rates. The model draws on demographic and textual features of keywords and takes advantage of the hierarchical structure of sponsored search accounts. Its predictive quality is evaluated on several high-revenue and high-exposure advertising accounts on a major search engine. Besides the general evaluation of advertiser welfare, our approach has potential applications to keyword and bid suggestion.

Categories and Subject Descriptors

J.4 [**Social and Behavioral Sciences**]: Economics; K.1 [**The Computer Industry**]: Markets

Keywords

Sponsored search; Hierarchical model; Regret loss function

1. INTRODUCTION

Online advertising spend exceeded $100 billion for the first time in 2012, with a significant fraction going to advertising on search engines, a segment known as sponsored search.[1] Sponsored search refers to the practice of displaying ads alongside search results whenever a user issues a query. Advertisers develop campaigns by selecting the keywords they wish to advertise on and setting bids for those keywords, with the placement and cost of ads determined via an auction process [15]. Developing a high-performance online ad campaign is a complicated task. Advertisers must select keywords and bids to optimize returns, and it may require costly experimentation to uncover the keywords that yield the highest profits per click.

This paper proposes a hierarchical linear model to infer an advertiser's value per click on search terms. Our choice of model is based on the hypothesis that keyword values are linked to characteristics such as the demographic profile of users they attract. The growing trend towards geographic, demographic, and even behavioral targeting is evidence that these characteristics can be closely linked to returns [21].

Our model is composed of two key features. First, the regression model uses an *economically meaningful* loss function to determine the regression coefficients. Keyword auctions are not truthful, so bids cannot be taken as proxies for values—independent work has shown that values can be as high as 125% of bids [7]. However, while an advertiser's actual value per click is unobservable, it is possible to fit a model of values such that the advertiser's observed bidding behavior, under the values imputed by the model, is as close to rational as possible in the sense that it minimizes foregone profit, or *regret*. We explain that our regret-based loss function falls in the well-known class of Bregman divergences used in machine learning [2], and therefore allows for efficient convex optimization algorithms to fit the model. To define the loss function on each keyword we need a model of advertiser beliefs about the clicks and costs that are obtained at different bids. For this we draw on the recent work of Pin and Key [16] to develop click and cost function estimates, and in doing so provide an independent evaluation of their approach.

Second, our model exploits the *hierarchical structure* of advertiser accounts to better estimate keyword values. Advertiser accounts consist of various levels of organization, with different decisions (such as demographic targeting or bidding) being made at each level. The advertiser account structure introduces commonality in keyword characteristics, and therefore likely indicates commonality in keyword values. We show that advertiser account structures demonstrate the kind of skew in campaign sizes and bids that motivate hierarchical modeling, and that our hierarchical regression model can improve predictions over a baseline that only takes into account local account structure.

Information about bidder values can inform many aspects of the keyword auction design, including changes to the ranking rules to improve revenue and reserve pricing policies [14]. We see two immediate applications of the value estimates provided by our approach: keyword and bid sugges-

---

*This work was done while the authors were at Yahoo! Inc.
[1] www.emarketer.com/Article.aspx?R=1009592

Copyright is held by the International World Wide Web Conference Committee (IW3C2). IW3C2 reserves the right to provide a hyperlink to the author's site if the Material is used in electronic media.
WWW 2013, May 13–17, 2013, Rio de Janeiro, Brazil.
ACM 978-1-4503-2035-1/13/05.

tion. Search engines typically provide keyword suggestion tools to help advertisers augment their campaigns. The current state of the art provides keyword suggestions based on statistical and semantic similarities using a campaign's initial set of keywords [6], but we have not found any research on how to filter and rank keyword suggestions according to value to the advertiser. The value estimates from our model provide a principled ranking criterion.

The only work on bid generation we are aware of is the recent paper by Broder et al. [5], who use machine learning to directly predict bids based purely on textual features of keywords and ads. While they report good prediction performance, their approach to recommending bids cannot react to changes in opponent bids, and does not provide a criterion for ranking suggestions—high bids may indicate the most competitive keywords, rather than the most valuable. By uncovering the primitives behind advertiser behavior (i.e., values) it becomes possible to automate the complete process of keyword ranking and bidding.

To summarize, our work makes the following four contributions, with the evaluation of our approach being the main contribution.

- Original insights on the structure of sponsored search accounts that motivate hierarchical regression modeling (Section 3).
- A regret-based modeling strategy that allows one to fit a model of unobserved values based on observed bids and click-through rates (Section 4).
- An independent evaluation of the Pin and Key [16] approach to modeling advertiser beliefs on click and cost functions (Section 5).
- An experimental evaluation of our modeling approach using real sponsored search account data (Section 6).

The remainder of this section reviews related work. Section 2 provides the background on sponsored search needed to follow the paper, while Section 7 concludes with directions for improvement and future work.

Related work. Regression models of account performance (e.g., click-through rates) have appeared in the marketing literature for single accounts [11, 13]. Building such models on the search engine side can be an insightful exercise because, while the search engine may not have conversion data, it may have much finer-grained information about the user traffic that visits the ads. The paper of Rutz and Bucklin [17] is most closely related to ours in that it expressly addresses the problem of estimating values, in their case as implied by conversions. Using data from the paid search campaign of a hotel chain, they apply several logit models to predict conversions based on features such as the presence of brand or geographic information.

Our work also connects with the small but influential economic literature on equilibrium models of sponsored search. Edelman et al. [9] introduced the solution concept of envy-free equilibrium, while Varian [20] showed how it could be applied to derive bounds on values per click using bid data from Google. Athey and Nekipelov [1] develop a model that incorporates uncertainty in competitors and quality scores in order to provide more refined bounds and even points estimates. Pin and Key [16] develop a similar method that is much more scalable, and we draw on their work to estimate clicks and cost as functions of bid.

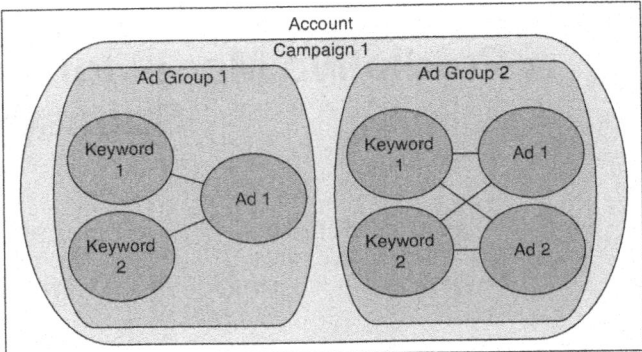

Figure 1: Hierarchical structure of a sponsored search account.

2. SPONSORED SEARCH

We now describe the process of sponsored search and the associated terminology used in this paper. At a high level, the process of bidding in sponsored search proceeds as follows: each advertiser specifies a list of **keywords** (or **terms**), a standing **bid** for each of those keywords, and a specific advertisement (or **creative**) they wish to display for each keyword. When a user issues a query to the search engine, an auction is run among the relevant advertisers to determine which ads appear, in what order on the page they appear, and how much money each advertiser must pay.

The ranking of an ad is determined by a combination of its bid and **quality score**, which is meant to capture the ad's relevance to the keyword; an important ingredient in this score is the search engine's estimate of the ad's probability of being clicked, known as the **click-through rate (CTR)**. By convention, the payment scheme is *per click*, meaning the advertiser only pays when its ads are clicked, not simply when they are shown; the price of a click is often called the **cost per click (CPC)**. Advertisers receive some expected **value per click**, which is private information, and together with the advertiser's estimates of CTR and CPC, drives their decision making.

Advertisers can also make additional decisions beyond what to bid to obtain finer control over who sees their ads. One popular refinement is the choice of **standard** or **advanced** match. For example, if advanced match is enabled for the keyword "sports shoes", the search engine can show the same ad for the related queries "running shoes" or "track shoes" rather than just that exact query. Advertisers can also impose **targeting** settings to specify that their ads should only be shown to users from specific locales or demographics. For example, an advertiser might target their ad to only appear to male searchers in their thirties from California. Finally, advertisers can set **budgets** to limit the amount they spend in a given day; when the advertiser hits its budget, it drops out of the day's auctions. The stochasticity these additional settings create across auctions can be leveraged to obtain models of advertiser beliefs over clicks and costs [1, 16].

Search engines provide advertisers with some organizational structure for their accounts to enable them to apply targeting and budgeting decisions to several keywords at once. Figure 1 illustrates the hierarchical structure of a sponsored search account, which is shared among the leading search engines. Keywords and creatives can are grouped together into **ad groups**; all keywords in the ad group display the same rotation of ads. Advertisers are also able to place a single bid at the ad group level, and all keywords with unspecified bids will default to that ad group bid. Ad groups are grouped into **campaigns**; budgets and targeting options are typically set at the campaign level. The hierarchical structure of these accounts should provide information about an advertiser's keyword values, since keywords in the same ad group or campaign share features as defined by the account hierarchy. This account structure provides partial motivation for hierarchical regression modeling.

3. PRELIMINARY ANALYSIS

Our data set consists of Yahoo's sponsored search logs over one month in the first half of 2010. For each query in the data set, we have information about the *auction, displayed advertisers*, and *user* (who issued the query). Auction information includes the query and the number of ads displayed at the top and to the right of the page. Advertiser information includes each advertiser's bid, whether the ad was displayed via exact or advanced match, the original keyword each advertiser bid on, the displayed creatives, and the predicted CTRs decomposed into position and advertiser effects. User information includes demographics such as predicted age, gender and zip code.

We focus our investigation on 100 advertiser accounts sampled from the set of all accounts. We obtained the total impressions, clicks, and revenue (for Yahoo, or equivalently, advertiser costs) for each account in Yahoo's database and found that, across accounts, impressions and revenue follow lognormal distributions while clicks follow a Pareto distribution (i.e., power law). In particular, the top 10% of accounts by click volume are responsible for over 80% of the monthly clicks, with a similar skew in the distributions for impressions and revenue. Therefore, uniform sampling is inappropriate because the sample would be overwhelmed by accounts with low click volume and revenue.

We found that click volume has a strong (linear) correlation of at least 0.5 with impression volume and revenue. Therefore, we choose to sample accounts proportional to click volume so as to strike a balance between high-revenue and high-exposure accounts. Note that these accounts are not intended to be a representative sample of the entire account space. Rather, they are meant to be a representative sample of the accounts for which it is most worthwhile to provide value estimation services: their high revenue makes them valuable to the search engine, and their high click volume indicates their ads are relevant to users. Our 100 sampled accounts are responsible for hundreds of thousands of clicks throughout the month, and taken together they contain nearly 150K terms. The remainder of this section provides a detailed examination of the structure of the accounts in our sample, which serves to motivate and inform our hierarchical modeling strategy.

3.1 Account Structure

A summary of the basic structure of the sampled accounts is given in Table 1. First, note that even though we sampled proportional to clicks, some accounts are very small: just three terms or one ad group. Further filtering of accounts is needed to restrict our attention to accounts with enough terms to model. An important observation is that the median and mean number of terms per ad group is very small; this makes sense considering the terms in an ad group share the same ads. This suggests that ad groups are very homogeneous, and we would expect clicks from different terms in an ad group to have similar values to the advertiser. Once one moves to the campaign level the number of terms starts to be large enough to support model fitting.

metric	min	median	mean	max
terms per ad group	1	2	6.3	100
terms per campaign	1	30	145.4	4000
ad groups per campaign	1	10	30.9	400
terms per account	3	400	1456.0	10000
ad groups per account	1	300	431.0	8000
campaigns per account	1	20	25.5	100

Table 1: Summary of account structure across the 100 sampled accounts. The min, median, and max have been rounded to one significant figure.

A hierarchical structure to the data alone does not completely motivate hierarchical modeling. The latter is useful when groups have uneven sample sizes and some groups are small. In that case the group intercepts are pulled towards those of larger groups, so that information from large groups is taken into account for predictions within small groups, which otherwise do not have enough data to support inference.

Figure 2 provides plots that describe the distributions of ad group and campaign sizes across the accounts. Recall that skewness is a measure of the asymmetry of a distribution. We see that ad group sizes have a positive skewness for almost all accounts, which indicates a long right tail—there are a few large ad groups and many small ones, rather than the reverse. The kurtosis is a measure of the sharpness of a distribution's peak. Most accounts have ad group sizes whose kurtosis exceeds that of the normal distribution, which means accounts consist mainly of relatively small ad groups. The same pattern holds for campaign sizes, which show a positive skewness and high kurtosis in general, though not to the extent of ad group sizes. This justifies a hierarchical model that includes every level of an account.

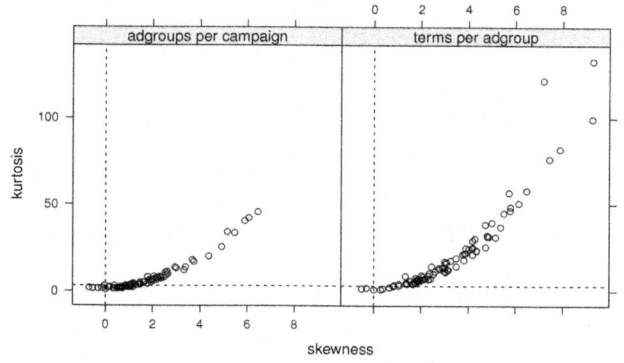

Figure 2: Skewness and kurtosis of group (ad group and campaign) sizes for the 100 accounts. The reference lines show the standard moments of the normal distribution: 0 for skewness and 3 for kurtosis.

3.2 Tail Contribution

Our observations on account structure might lead one to believe that only a few large ad groups matter in an account, but this is incorrect. In aggregate, small ad groups typically make up a substantial fraction of an account's click volume and revenue, so that it remains important to model advertiser value on terms in small ad groups. To confirm this, we examine the tail of the distribution of impressions, clicks, and revenue across the ad groups in an account, where the tail is defined as the bottom 80% of ad groups for the associated metric. We define three regimes: the 'Pareto' regime corresponds to a tail contribution of less than 20% to the total; the 'Long-Tail' regime corresponds to a contribution of at least 50%; and 'Intermediate' lies between the two.

We find that around 30 accounts fall under the Pareto regime for clicks or for revenue; thus, we cannot focus on just the head (top 20%) of ad groups in general. There are 13 accounts that fall under the Long-Tail regime for both clicks and revenue, and 19 accounts that are Long-Tail for at least one of them. Furthermore, the accounts in the Pareto regime are not responsible for much click volume or revenue in our account sample (less than 15%). We conclude that tail ad groups and terms, in aggregate, often generate much of the click volume and revenue in an account, and it is therefore important to develop models of value on all the terms and ad groups.

3.3 Bid Variation

We now examine the bid variation in accounts. We first consider bid changes across time. For each term we counted the number of distinct bids placed on that term throughout the month, and averaged over terms in an account. The numbers are low: the maximum number of distinct bids is 60, or just 2 new bids per day.[2] The relative standard deviation (standard deviation over the mean, expressed in percents) of the bids on a term, averaged over the terms in an account, is also very small: the mean is 3% over the accounts. For these reasons we choose to consider just the average bid across time on a term—a similar simplification was made by Broder et al. [5], who developed regression models of bids in sponsored search.

We next consider bid variation across the terms in an account; we would like to understand at what level (ad group, campaign, account) the variation arises. To decompose the variance among levels we make use of a simple hierarchical model that also serves as a precursor to our later model for values. Let b_i be the bid on term i. We model the bids in ad group j as drawn from a normal distribution with mean b_j. The means b_j of the ad groups in a campaign k are themselves drawn from a normal distribution with mean b_k, and the campaign means are normal with mean b_h:

$$b_i \sim \mathcal{N}(b_j, \sigma_1^2), \quad b_j \sim \mathcal{N}(b_k, \sigma_2^2), \quad b_k \sim \mathcal{N}(b_h, \sigma_3^2).$$

Here it is implied that term i is in ad group j, which is in campaign k. The proportion of variance at the first (i.e., ad group) level is $\sigma_1^2/(\sigma_1^2 + \sigma_2^2 + \sigma_3^2)$, and similarly for the other levels. For each account, the hierarchical model was fit using the lmer function in R. The assumption of normal

---
[2]This does not necessarily mean that no interesting bidding behavior occurs across time—advertisers could be using intricate strategies that cycle through different bids. This has been observed in some early studies [8].

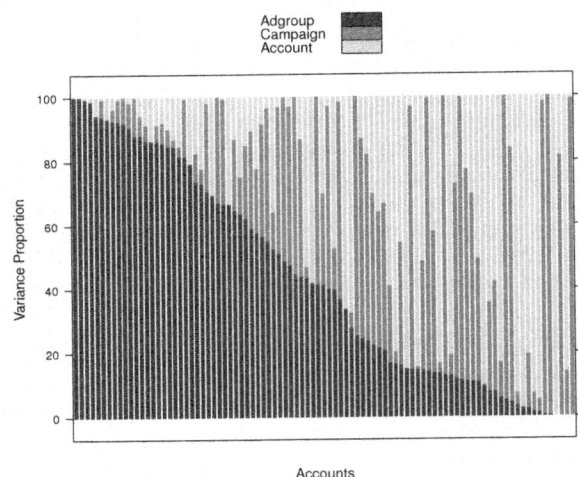

Figure 3: Proportion of bid variance that arises among terms within ad groups, ad groups within campaigns, and campaigns within accounts.

distributions amounts to fitting a model with squared loss. Figure 3 gives the variance proportions for the sampled accounts. We find a wide spectrum of proportions: for some accounts almost all the variance occurs at the ad group level, while for others it is all at the campaign or account level.

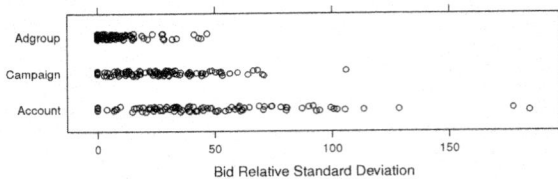

Figure 4: Relative standard deviation of bids. For each account, we take the relative standard deviation of bids within its ad groups, then average these over the ad groups in the account. We do the same for campaigns. The final line lists the relative standard deviation of bids over terms in each account.

The amount of bid variation at each level is also informative. For each account we looked at the relative standard deviation of bids within each ad group, and averaged over ad groups. We did the same looking at bids within campaigns, and within the account. The results are given in Figure 4. We find that relative standard deviation within ad groups is small: the median across accounts is 5%. The median within-campaign and within-account relative standard deviations are 26% and 41% respectively. This seems to suggest that many advertisers make their bidding decisions at the ad group level, and the bids on terms within an ad group do not stray far from their ad group baseline. The most interesting and challenging inference problem in such cases is to predict ad group-level average values rather than term-specific values.

4. HIERARCHICAL MODEL

The basis for our value estimation approach is a simple quasi-linear model of advertiser utility on each term. We focus on an individual advertiser with n terms in its account, with i used to index terms. Let v_i be the advertiser's value per click on term i. Let $c_i : \mathbf{R} \to \mathbf{R} \cup \{+\infty\}$ be an extended real-value function that gives the expected cost per impression $c_i(x_i)$ of obtaining a click-through rate (CTR) x_i on term i. The purpose of introducing $+\infty$ into the range is to implicitly encode the domain of c_i as $\{x_i \in \mathbf{R} : c_i(x_i) < +\infty\}$, following standard conventions in convex analysis. For instance, negative CTRs are infeasible and would have a cost of $+\infty$. We assume that c_i is convex and differentiable.[3] The cost functions estimated later in Section 5 are in fact piece-wise linear, but by selecting a subgradient at the (finite) number of points of non-differentiability, the following applies with minor technical changes.

We assume that the advertiser's utility for clicks on a term is quasi-linear in cost, so that it takes the form

$$u_i(x_i, c_i) = v_i x_i - c_i(x_i). \quad (1)$$

Letting w_i be the search volume for term i, the aggregate utility to the advertiser of obtaining the vector of CTRs $x = (x_1, \ldots, x_n)$ across the terms in its account, given the vector of cost functions $c = (c_1, \ldots, c_n)$, is $u(x, c) = \sum_{i=1}^n w_i u_i(x_i, c_i)$. Our goal is to obtain a regression model of the v_i values, but these are not observable. Instead, we observe the CTRs x_i chosen by the advertiser via its bids on each term, and we can estimate the cost functions c_i.

4.1 Loss Function

A naive approach to developing a regression model of values would be to first estimate the values v_i on each term, and then run a standard regression on top of these (e.g., using least squares). Indeed, from the utility form (1) and our convexity assumptions on c_i, it follows that at the advertiser's observed choice of CTR x_i we must have $v_i = \nabla c_i(x_i)$ under utility-maximizing behavior (where ∇ refers to the first derivative).

The issue with this approach is that typical loss functions like squared error find little justification in economic settings like sponsored search: variance in the estimated values within an ad group may be a result of optimization error on the part of the advertiser, rather than statistical error, and there is no sound basis for optimization errors to be Gaussian [19]. Here we develop an economically meaningful loss function that is also computationally appealing because the problem of model fitting remains convex, as with conventional statistical loss functions. Under our loss function, value estimation occurs in tandem with model fitting, rather than as a preliminary step.

The idea is to draw on the notion of Bregman divergence, which has seen increasing attention in machine learning [2]. First, we need the concept of a convex conjugate. In what follows, we will suppress the term subscript i on values, costs, and CTRs for clarity. The *dual space* $\mathbf{R}^*$ is the vector space of all linear functions on $\mathbf{R}$. Observe that values can be identified with elements of the dual space. The *convex conjugate* $c^* : \mathbf{R}^* \to \mathbf{R}$ of cost function c is defined as

$$c^*(v) = \sup_{x \in \mathbf{R}} \{vx - c(x)\}. \quad (2)$$

Observe that c^* is convex, even if c is not, because is it the supremum of affine functions. A Bregman divergence is defined with respect to a strictly convex, differentiable function, in our case the conjugate cost function c^*. Given c^*, the divergence between two values v and v' in its domain is defined as

$$D_{c^*}(v'||v) = c^*(v') - c^*(v) - \nabla c^*(v) \cdot (v' - v). \quad (3)$$

This is the loss function between values that we propose. Here v' should be viewed as the estimated value, and v the true value (not directly observed).

The following proposition collects some standard facts about Bregman divergence (e.g., see [2]) that serve to motivate this choice of loss and explain how it is evaluated in practice.

PROPOSITION 1. *Let c^* be a convex and differentiable function. The associated Bregman divergence D_{c^*} satisfies the following properties.*

1. *$D_{c^*}(v'||v) \geq 0$ for all v, v' in the domain of c^*, with equality if $v = v'$.*

2. *$D_{c^*}(v'||v)$ is convex in its first argument.*

3. *$D_{c^*}(v'||v) = D_c(x||x')$ where x, x' are such that $v = \nabla c(x)$ and $v' = \nabla c(x')$.*

Property 1 confirms that D_{c^*} is a sensible loss function. Bregman divergence in fact generalizes losses such as squared loss, KL-divergence, and Itakura-Saito distance, which can all be recovered with a suitable choice of convex function c [2]; for example, squared loss corresponds to a quadratic cost function. Property 2 ensures that is it computationally tractable to fit the estimate v'. Finally, Property 3 shows that our loss function can be equivalently viewed as a loss on CTRs, which are observable.

Economic Interpretation

To see the economic motivation for this loss function, let $v' = \nabla c(x')$ be the value for which the choice of CTR x' is optimal. Then by Property 3 loss function (3) evaluates to

$$\begin{aligned} D_c(x||x') &= c(x) - c(x') - \nabla c(x') \cdot (x - x') & (4) \\ &= [v'x' - c(x')] - [v'x - c(x)]. & (5) \end{aligned}$$

This is the *regret* from bidding so that CTR x is received, rather than the optimal choice x' when the advertiser's value is v'. Stated another way, in order to minimize the loss we seek an estimated value v' such that the advertiser's regret from obtaining the observed CTR x under this value is minimized.

Varian [19] has proposed several 'economically meaningful' loss functions of this sort for both parametric and non-parametric models. For parametric models of production analysis, he proposes a loss function which captures the degree to which the observed choice behavior fails to maximize the *estimated* production function, which is precisely the re-

---

[3]Since agent values are linear in CTR, replacing c_i with its convex envelope (the largest convex function it dominates) does not change the agent's utility maximization problem. Therefore, the assumption that c_i is convex is without loss of generality when it comes to analyzing an agent's choice of bid and CTR on a keyword.

gret in (5).[4] In microeconomics the conjugate (2) is known as the *indirect utility function*; intuitively, it gives the maximum utility that an advertiser with value v can achieve. Our loss function is the Bregman divergence associated with indirect utility.

Evaluating Loss

The loss function (3) is defined in terms of unobservable values, whereas its alternate form (4) is defined in terms of the observable CTR and cost function, but does not allow one to incorporate a linear model for value. Instead we will work with the following form for loss. Let x be the optimal choice of clicks when the advertiser's value is v; from (2) and Danskin's theorem [3, p. 717] we have $x = \nabla c^*(v)$. Thus,

$$\begin{aligned} D_{c^*}(v'||v) &= c^*(v') - c^*(v) - \nabla c^*(v) \cdot (v' - v) \\ &= c^*(v') - [vx - c(x)] - x \cdot (v' - v) \\ &= c^*(v') - xv' + c(x). \end{aligned}$$

Now, if we have a linear model for the fitted value, so that $v' = a \cdot \beta$ where a is the feature vector and β are the coefficients, then the loss function can be written as

$$D_{c^*}(v'||v) = c^*(a \cdot \beta) - x(a \cdot \beta) + c(x). \quad (6)$$

This loss is convex in the parameters β and is formulated in terms of the observed chosen CTR x, the cost function c, and its conjugate c^*. The conjugate c^* of a one-dimensional convex cost function can be computed in linear time using elementary convex hull algorithms. Section 5 addresses the problem of estimating the cost function c.

4.2 Levels

We now describe the aggregate loss function across all terms in an account. There are three levels in an account: (1) terms within ad groups, (2) ad groups within campaigns, and (3) campaigns within the account. Our regret-based loss function applies to the first level, while standard squared loss is used at higher levels for regularization. We index the terms, ad groups, and campaigns in the advertiser's account by i, j, and k respectively, and with an abuse of notation write $i \in j$ to denote that term i belongs to ad group j, and $j \in k$ to denote that ad group j belongs to campaign k.

We implicitly observe v_i for each term i via the chosen CTRs x_i. Let a_i be the vector of predictors for term i and let v_j be the intercept for ad group j. Let β_1 be the model coefficients at the ad group level. Writing D_i for the divergence (3) associated with c_i^*, the aggregate loss at the first level is

$$\sum_k \sum_{j \in k} \sum_{i \in j} D_i(v_j + a_i \cdot \beta_1 || v_i). \quad (7)$$

As explained above each term in the summation can be evaluated in practice via (6), and because D_i is convex in its first argument it is also convex in the parameters β_1 and v_j.

Analogous aggregate loss functions could be derived for the second and third levels, but it is unclear whether advertisers reason in terms of regret at those levels. Another

---

[4]Our model of advertiser utility is closer to producer theory than consumer theory. We have surveyed the econometric literature and, despite Varian's convincing arguments, it seems the idea of 'economic' loss functions has not caught on, and standards like squared loss are still in favor. This may be due to computational reasons: not all of Varian's loss functions are convex in the estimated parameters.

problematic aspect of using regret-based loss at higher levels is that parameters appear in the second argument, where convexity is not guaranteed. Because the purpose of higher-level loss is regularization, we therefore use standard squared loss. Again, let a_j be the vector of predictors for ad group j and let v_k be the intercept for campaign k. Let β_2 be the model coefficients at the campaign level. The loss at this level is

$$\sum_k \sum_{j \in k} (v_k + a_j \cdot \beta_2 - v_j)^2. \quad (8)$$

In the ad group-level loss (8), the "observation" v_j is in fact the intercept fit at the lower level in (7).

We use the index h to refer to the intercept at the third level (i.e., account level), where we also use squared loss:

$$\sum_k (v_h + a_k \cdot \beta_3 - v_k)^2. \quad (9)$$

The "observation" v_k here in fact corresponds to the intercept from (8). Finally, the aggregate losses from the three levels are summed up to yield the complete loss used to ultimately fit the model. Again we stress that only the aggregate regret (7) captures the performance of the model; losses at higher levels of the hierarchy are for regularization, as motivated by our observations on account structure in Section 3. Introducing (8) pulls all the v_j ad group intercepts towards a common intercept v_k for the campaign, so that information is shared across ad groups in the campaign, and similarly for (9). This is completely analogous to the motivation for multi-level models with standard losses like least-squares [10].

The aggregate loss combined over all levels is convex in all model parameters, so fitting the model is straightforward via algorithms like stochastic gradient descent. We implemented an incremental subgradient algorithm [3, p. 614] similar to the stochastic gradient descent used in [5] to develop a model of bids. While the implementation details are beyond the scope of this paper, we note that running times to fit the model ranged from under a second to around 25 minutes on the largest account (we did not attempt to optimize the code). The bottleneck is in reading in the account data and setting up the data structures rather than running the algorithm.

5. COST FUNCTION ESTIMATION

The preceding sections developed a linear model for estimating a term i's value-per-click from its features. The proposed method required knowledge of advertiser costs $c_i(x_i)$ for a given observed (implicit) choice of click-through rate x_i; we now describe an approach to estimating this cost function $c_i(x_i)$.

As discussed in Section 2, there are numerous factors that cause variability in the competitive landscape across auctions. These factors make it impossible to compute exact costs for the next upcoming search, making cost functions based on individual auctions (as studied by Edelman et al. [9] and Varian [20]) less realistic for our domain. The observation from Section 3 that advertisers infrequently modify their bids further suggests that advertisers make decisions at a coarser level of granularity than the auction level. Following recent approaches [1, 16], we assume the advertiser creates a stochastic model of costs based on a distribution over the observed competitive landscape.

Specifically, we use a version of the cost function described by Pin and Key [16].[5] The model is from the perspective of a single advertiser, with each term in the advertiser's account treated independently. Each opponent participating in an auction is assumed to stochastically submit a bid i.i.d. from a known probability density function; let $F(b)$ be the corresponding c.d.f. that gives the probability an opponent submits a bid less than b. These bids are assumed to be weighted to adjust for differences in opponent quality score[6]. Variation in $F(b)$ comes from both the variation in these quality scores across searches and from the search-specific set of competing advertisers (determined by standard match, advanced match and targeting settings described in Section 2).

Let k be a possible slot, where $k = 0$ is the top slot. Given the cumulative distribution over opponent bids $F(b)$, an advertiser can compute the probability ϕ of appearing in the kth slot in a single auction when there are n opponents and the advertiser places a bid b:

$$\phi(k, n, b) = \binom{n}{k}(1 - F(b))^k F(b)^{n-k} \quad (10)$$

In words, this computation is the number of ways k opponents could be chosen to appear in slots above the advertiser, times the probability that those k opponents appear in slots above the advertiser, times the probability the remaining $n - k$ opponents appear in slots below the advertiser.

For a given term, let p_n be the probability that n opponents participate in each auction, where n is at most N. Each slot k has a known click-through rate s_k, where $s_k = 0$ if k exceeds the number of available slots. Assuming the advertiser bids above the known reserve price r, the advertiser's expected click-through rate $\hat{x}_i(b)$ as a function of its bid b is computed as follows:

$$\hat{x}_i(b) = \sum_{n=0}^{N} \sum_{k=0}^{n} p_n \phi(k, n, b) s_k \quad (11)$$

Similarly, cost per impression $\hat{c}_i(b)$ is computed as:

$$\hat{c}_i(b) = \sum_{n=0}^{N} \sum_{k=0}^{n} p_n \phi(k, n, b) s_k \underbrace{\left(b - \int_r^b \frac{F(t)^{n-k}}{F(b)^{n-k}} dt \right)} \quad (12)$$

The additional bracketed term is the expected cost per click, given the advertiser appears in the kth slot against n bidders with a bid of b and reserve price r.

A given bid b is thus associated with an expected cost per impression $\hat{c}_i(b)$ and an expected click-through rate $\hat{x}_i(b)$. The expected cost per impression $c_i(x_i)$ as a function of click-through rate x_i is then reconstructed by pairing the calculated $\hat{x}_i(b)$ and $\hat{c}_i(b)$ values for each possible bid b:

$$c_i(x_i) = \hat{c}_i(\hat{x}_i^{-1}(x_i)) \quad (13)$$

---

[5] Pin and Key present several models of increasing complexity; we use their most complex model that does not consider distributions over promoted reserve price (i.e., reserve price for ads shown at the top of the page), since this data was unavailable.

[6] Recall from Section 2 that advertisers are ranked by their bid b times their quality score w. The opponent bid distribution $F(b)$ created by advertiser a gives the probability that advertiser a's weighted bid wb is greater than the opponent's weighted bid $w'b'$.

This version of the Pin and Key model matches our environment closely but not exactly. First, reserve prices are not known exactly and are not necessarily of a fixed value in our domain. Second, the slot click-through rates depend not only on the slot k, but also the number of promoted slots (i.e., shown at the top) and the number of opponents. To extend the model, we take additional summations in Equations (11) and (12) over possible reserve prices r and possible available promoted slots d, and slot click-through rate s_k is instead computed as s_{kdn}, which gives a different slot click-through rate depending on the competitive landscape.

5.1 Distribution Estimation

Thus far we have expressed the cost function $c_i(x_i)$ in terms of other stochastic variables (such as distributions over participants and opponent bids), but we have not specified how these other distributions are obtained. We follow the approaches taken by Athey and Nekipelov [1] and Pin and Key [16], in that distributions are created from actual sponsored search records for the given time period. For each sampled account, we get all actual user searches for which a term in the account appeared, and then get all competing advertiser bids for those searches. For each term, histograms are created of opponent weighted bids, advertiser reserve prices, number of opponents and number of available promoted slots, and slot click-through rates. Bids and reserve prices are discretized by ten cents, which is the minimum bid increment on Yahoo.

5.2 Cost Function Evaluation

We now evaluate the accuracy of our cost function, following the same evaluation technique used by Pin and Key [16] for comparison purposes. For each term i in the 100 sampled accounts, we create predictions of expected CTR $\hat{x}_i(b)$ using the method described above, and evaluate these predictions against two metrics, both based on the actual sponsored search data from individual auctions.

First, we compare against the *expected slot CTR*, given the advertiser's historically realized slots for that term. This quantifies the error associated with making the independence assumptions described above and with assuming a fixed bid (taken to be the average) over the entire duration of the month. Put another way, this gives an idea of how accurately an advertiser might be able to predict CTR, given the limitations of not knowing *a priori* the realized values of stochastic processes. Figure 5(a) shows the relative error in estimating CTR. Each term is a single data point, and terms are sorted on the x-axis by the number of actual clicks received for that term. We observe that the mean and median ratios between predicted and actual expected CTR are 0.99 and 0.97, respectively. As observed by Pin and Key, we also find that the variance in relative error across terms decreases as the number of clicks increases.

Next, we compare our estimates to the *realized slot CTR*. This takes into account the fact that our predictions of an advertiser's CTR may not be perfectly accurate, even if we know exactly the slot that the advertiser appears in. Figure 5(b) shows, for each term, the estimated clicks for placing the bid versus the actual number of clicks. We see a bias in these predictions, as our model is under-predicting the amount of clicks that will occur. This can be explained by our account selection process: since accounts with the most clicks were favored in the sampling, these sampled accounts

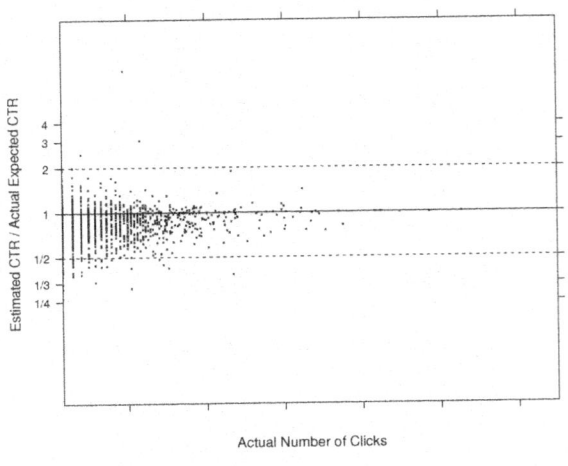
(a) Predicted versus expected CTR.

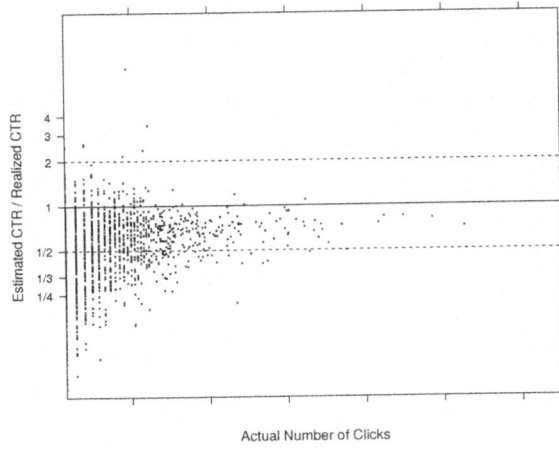
(b) Predicted versus realized CTR.

Figure 5: Accuracy of the cost function's CTR estimates when compared to the expected and realized CTRs from actual sponsored search logs. Plots show a random sub-sampling of 10% of all terms for clarity. Model accuracy is shown with respect to the number of clicks received by each term. The x-axis is on a logarithmic scale and labels ommitted for confidentiality reasons.

are more likely to have received more clicks than expected. Advertisers whose terms experience this bias would likely be unable to predict such a deviation from a learned model of their click-through rate, particularly if the increased amount of clicks is due to stochastic user behavior and not any changes made to the advertiser's ads or keywords.

Despite independence assumptions about the distributions of opponent bids and the number of participants, our results support the findings of Pin and Key [16] that their model estimates click-through rates with accuracy comparable to other methods proposed in the literature. While we use their model because of its computational tractability and similar accuracy to more complex methods, any advertiser cost function could similarly be substituted into Equation (6) to regress on advertiser values-per-click.

6. EXPERIMENTAL EVALUATION

We fit a separate model to each account to allow for the fact that the effect of the features used might vary across accounts. We evaluate the predictive performance of our approach via synthetic leave-out estimates: for each account, some fixed proportion of the terms, ad groups, or campaigns is used for training, and we then record the aggregate *regret* of the fitted model's value predictions on the remaining terms used for testing. The regret on a term is given by (6)—observe that this does not include the squared loss (8–9) at the ad group and campaign levels used for model fitting, which is only for regularization. We considered training-testing splits where 50%, 75%, and 90% of the terms, ad groups, or campaigns are randomly selected for training. For each combination of leave-out and split we did 10 runs and averaged the results over the runs. Because some accounts have too few terms to properly develop a value model, we restricted our attention to the 88 accounts in our sample with at least 40 terms. The remaining accounts on which we trained and made predictions consisted of nearly 150 thousand terms.

As a baseline prediction for a term's value, we used the average value of the other terms in its ad group, as predicted by the Pin and Key approach. Specifically, the value on each other term i is given by $v_i' = \nabla c_i(x_i)$, where c_i is the cost function derived as explained in Section 4.1 and x_i is the observed CTR. The regret on the term is again evaluated using (6). If there are no other terms in the given term's ad group or campaign present in the training set (e.g., when leaving out ad groups or campaigns), we use the average value over terms in the same campaign or over the account, respectively.

6.1 Features

We used the following features to develop our models. Features can arise at the term, ad group, and campaign levels, but there were no obvious features to use at the campaign level so only an intercept is present there for regularization. The following predictors (or categories of predictors) were used at the term level. As indicated, some predictors are logged to account for skew in their distributions. No other transformations were made to these predictors and no interaction effects were introduced.

age five separate predictors indicating the percent of offers to users in their twenties, thirties, etc.

gender three separate predictors indicating the percent of offers to male and female users, or gender unknown.

exact match percent of opponent ads presented due to exact rather than advanced match.

user click propensity (log) mean of a metric quantifying, for each keyword the ad matches to, the propensity of users who search on the keyword to click on ads—see [12].

query length mean word length of the user queries leading to the offer.

north state five separate predictors indicating the percent of searches for the keyword yielding a page with zero, one, two, three, or four ads at the top of the page.

competitors (log) mean number of competitors on the keyword.

The first four features capture aspects of a term that may have inherent value to the advertiser (e.g., the demographic profile of searchers), while the last two capture the level of competition on the term, which may correlate with unseen aspects of the term that drive value. Statistics on gender or age come from the self-reports of searchers who are logged in to their Yahoo account.[7] We next turn to the predictors at the ad group level.

creatives number of creatives in the ad group.

linead length word length of the keyword bid on.

title length word length of the ad title.

These predictors give some indication of the specificity of the advertisement, which may correlate with value. To clarify the difference between 'linead length' and 'query length', the former corresponds to the length of the keyword specified for the ad group, while the latter corresponds to the mean length of the query actually matched to, which can vary in the case of advanced match.

In terms of goodness of fit, we found that the most predictive feature varied across accounts. This result is not surprising, as different accounts do not necessarily represent companies from the same industry and thus could have different levels of importance for different user characteristics.

6.2 Results

When evaluating the model and baseline on the testing set terms we recorded the average regret per term for each and compared them against each other. We consider two comparison metrics:

$$\text{absolute improvement} = \text{baseline regret - model regret}$$
$$\text{relative improvement} = \frac{\text{baseline regret - model regret}}{\text{baseline regret}}$$

A positive value for either indicates that the model outperformed the baseline, and vice-versa. Note however that there is an asymmetry in reporting relative improvement: its maximum value is 1 (regret is always non-negative), or 100%, but it can take on arbitrarily large negative values as the baseline regret approaches zero. As a result, taking the mean of the relative improvement across accounts leads to a misleading assessment of model performance: the result is highly negative for every choice of split and choice of leave-out (i.e., term, ad group, or campaign) due to outliers.

---

[7]Personal account information was not accessed for this study. Anonymized, aggregate statistics on gender and age were already available in the sponsored search logs.

To give a clearer picture of the distribution, Table 2 summarizes for each regime the relative improvement quartiles, which are robust to outliers. Recall that the first quartile cuts off the lowest 25% of the data, the third cuts off the highest 25%, and the second quartile is the median. The interquartile range (difference between third and first quartiles) is a non-parametric analog of standard deviation.

Leave-out	Split	Q_1	Q_2	Q_3	IQR
term	50%	-130.9	-3.9	30.8	161.8
	75%	-103.9	4.1	33.8	137.7
	90%	-121.2	5.5	31.4	152.7
ad group	50%	-107.4	-5.1	29.8	137.2
	75%	-87.5	6.7	36.5	124.1
	90%	-79.3	4.6	40.2	119.6
campaign	50%	-24.6	13.9	38.6	63.2
	75%	-23.1	14.4	43.4	66.5
	90%	-26.9	11.3	45.6	72.5

Table 2: Quartiles of percent relative improvement over the baseline, across accounts, together with interquartile range.

The clearest observation is that the relative performance against the baseline improves as one moves up the leave-out hierarchy from terms to ad groups to campaigns. We attribute this to the fact that model performance remains relatively stable in each case while the baseline necessarily degrades. There is a monotonic improvement in model performance as the size of the training set increases, as expected, but relative improvement is not necessarily monotone because the baseline also improves. We see from the second quartile (median) that the model improves on the baseline for over half the accounts in all regimes except leaving out terms or ad groups with 50% training split.

In Figure 6 we present summaries of the model's absolute improvement over the baseline. Observe that the differences are very small: for many they are just fractions of cents more in profit. To give a sense of the scale, for a 90% split the median improvement was 0.01, 0.14, and 0.23 for terms, ad groups, and campaigns. However, given the click volume of these accounts small differences can translate into substantial increases in monthly profits. In many cases the opportunities for improvement may be limited, for instance when the cost function c_i on a term is almost flat. The same pattern of improvement as earlier can be seen when moving from term to ad group to campaign value prediction, as the right tail of the improvement distribution becomes slightly heavier.

We conclude from this analysis that our modeling approach holds the most promise for predicting advertiser values on newly created ad groups and campaigns, rather than just single terms added to ad groups. In the latter case, the value for the term is likely close to the average value of the ad group, which is expected given the close relationship between terms in an ad group—recall they all share the same creative.

7. CONCLUSIONS

This paper proposed a regret-based hierarchical model for estimating advertiser values per click from keyword char-

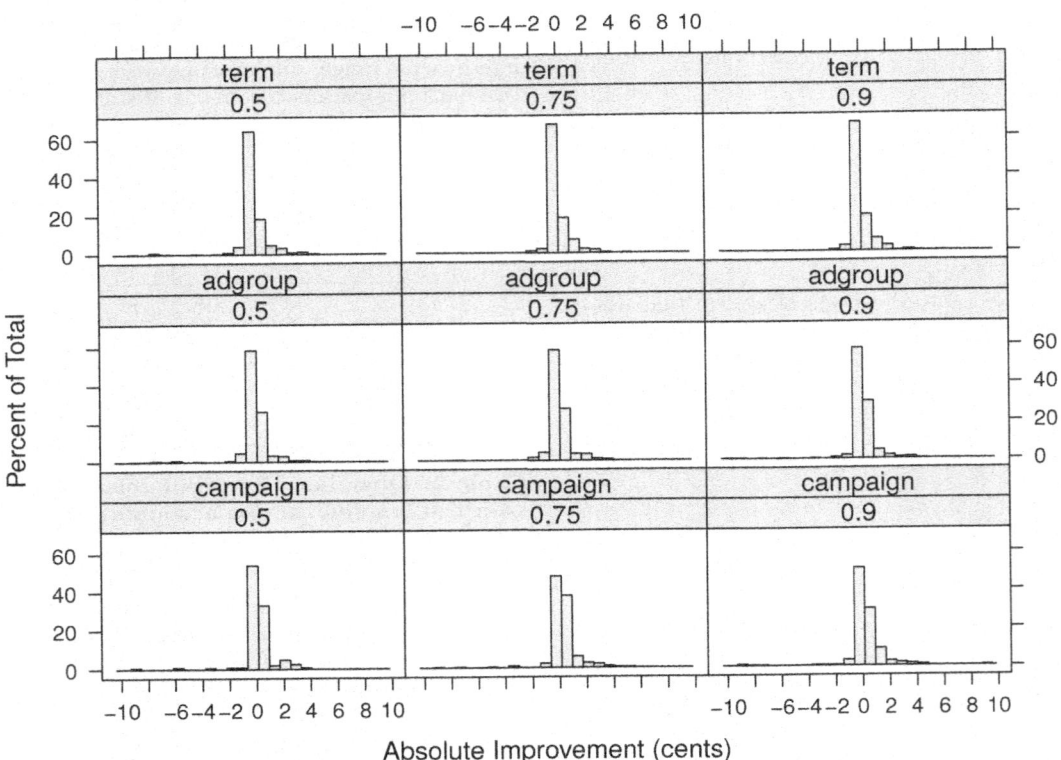

Figure 6: Distribution of the absolute improvement of the model over the baseline. A positive difference indicates the model did better than the baseline.

acteristics, observed costs and click-through rates, and observed advertiser bids. Our modeling strategy was evaluated on nearly 150 thousand terms and outperformed a competitive baseline [16] on the majority of our leave-out experiments. We found that value estimation using this approach is most fruitful when predicting values on new ad groups and campaigns. We also independently validated recently proposed methods for estimating advertiser cost and click beliefs, and provided data-driven insights into the structure of advertisers' sponsored search campaigns.

We see several avenues for improvement and future work. First, there is room for improvement in the prediction performance of our hierarchical model. We chose this kind of model with a view towards interpretation as well as prediction, which can be important if advertisers demand explanations for keyword or bid suggestions. We believe good improvements could be obtained using machine learning algorithms specialized for prediction (e.g, boosting [18]) if that were the sole concern. We also see the need to move beyond ad-hoc feature selection. To this end, we intend to apply techniques such as topic models [4] to uncover conceptual and semantic regularities among campaign terms.

8. ACKNOWLEDGEMENTS

We thank Amy Greenwald and David Pennock for initiating this project, and Eliot Li for bringing the collaborators together. Furcy Pin gave us valuable clarifications on his clicks and cost modeling methodology. We received helpful comments and suggestions from Amy Greenwald, Patrick Jordan, Ashvin Kannan, Prabhakhar Krishnamurthy, Eren Manavoglu, David Pennock, and Michael Schwarz.

References

[1] Susan Athey and Denis Nekipelov. A structural model of sponsored search advertising auctions. Technical report, Microsoft Research, May 2010.

[2] Arindam Banerjee, Srujana Merugu, Inderjit S. Dhillon, and Joydeep Ghosh. Clustering with Bregman divergence. *Journal of Machine Learning Research*, 6:1–48, 2005.

[3] Dimitri P. Bertsekas. *Nonlinear Programming*. Athena Scientific, 1999.

[4] David M. Blei, Andrew Y. Ng, and Michael I. Jordan. Latent Dirichlet allocation. In *Journal of Machine Learning Research*, volume 3, pages 993–1022, March 2003.

[5] Andrei Broder, Evgeniy Gabrilovich, Vanja Josifovski, George Mavromatis, and Alex Smola. Bid generation for advanced match in sponsored search. In

Proceedings of the fourth ACM International Conference on Web Search and Data Mining, pages 515–524, 2011.

[6] Yifan Chen, Gui-Rong Xue, and Yong Yu. Advertising keyword suggestion based on concept hierarchy. In *Proceedings of the International Conference on Web Search and Web Data Mining*, pages 251–260, 2008.

[7] Quang Duong and Sébastien Lahaie. Discrete choice models of bidder behavior in sponsored search. In *Proceedings of the 7th International Workshop on Internet and Network Economics*, 2011.

[8] Benjamin Edelman. Strategic bidder behavior in sponsored search auctions. In *Workshop on Sponsored Search Auctions*, pages 192–198, 2005.

[9] Benjamin Edelman, Michael Ostrovsky, and Michael Schwarz. Internet advertising and the Generalized Second-Price auction: Selling billions of dollars worth of keywords. *American Economic Review*, 97(1), March 2007.

[10] Andrew Gelman and Jennifer Hill. *Data analysis using regression and multilevel/hierarchical models*. Cambridge University Press, 2007.

[11] Anindya Ghose and Sha Yang. An empirical analysis of search engine advertising: Sponsored search in electronic markets. *Management Science*, 55:1605–1622, October 2009.

[12] Dustin Hillard, Stefan Schroedl, Eren Manavoglu, Hema Raghavan, and Chris Leggetter. Improving ad relevance in sponsored search. In *Proceedings of the third ACM international conference on Web Search and Data Mining*, pages 361–370, New York, NY, 2010. ACM.

[13] Bernard J. Jansen and Lauren Solomon. Gender demographic targeting in sponsored search. Working paper, 2010.

[14] Sébastien Lahaie and David M. Pennock. Revenue analysis of a family of ranking rules for keyword auctions. In *Proceedings of the 8th ACM Conference on Electronic Commerce*, pages 50–56, 2007.

[15] Sébastien Lahaie, David M. Pennock, Amin Saberi, and Rakesh V. Vohra. Sponsored search auctions. In Noam Nisan, Tim Roughgarden, Éva Taros, and Vijay V. Vazirani, editors, *Algorithmic Game Theory*, pages 699–716. Cambridge University Press, 2007.

[16] Furcy Pin and Peter Key. Stochastic variability in sponsored search auctions: observations and models. In *Proceedings of the 12th ACM Conference on Electronic Commerce*, pages 61–70, 2011.

[17] Oliver J. Rutz and Randolph E. Bucklin. A model of individual keyword performance in paid search advertising. *SSRN eLibrary*, 2007.

[18] Robert E. Schapire. A brief introduction to boosting. In *Proceedings of the 16th International Joint Conference on Artificial Intelligence*, pages 1401–1406, 1999.

[19] Hal R. Varian. Goodness-of-fit in optimizing models. *Journal of Econometrics*, 46:125–140, 1990.

[20] Hal R. Varian. Position auctions. *International Journal of Industrial Organization*, 25:1163–1178, 2007.

[21] Jun Yan, Ning Liu, Gang Wang, Wen Zhang, Yun Jiang, and Zheng Chen. How much can behavioral targeting help online advertising? In *Proceedings of the 18th International World Wide Web Conference*, pages 261–270, Madrid, Spain, 2009.

I Know the Shortened URLs You Clicked on Twitter: Inference Attack using Public Click Analytics and Twitter Metadata

Jonghyuk Song
Dept. of CSE, POSTECH
Pohang, Republic of Korea
freestar@postech.ac.kr

Sangho Lee
Dept. of CSE, POSTECH
Pohang, Republic of Korea
sangho2@postech.ac.kr

Jong Kim
Div. of ITCE, POSTECH
Pohang, Republic of Korea
jkim@postech.ac.kr

ABSTRACT

Twitter is a popular social network service for sharing messages among friends. Because Twitter restricts the length of messages, many Twitter users use URL shortening services, such as bit.ly and goo.gl, to share long URLs with friends. Some URL shortening services also provide click analytics of the shortened URLs, including the number of clicks, countries, platforms, browsers and referrers. To protect visitors' privacy, they do not reveal identifying information about individual visitors. In this paper, we propose a practical attack technique that can infer who clicks what shortened URLs on Twitter. Unlike the conventional browser history stealing attacks, our attack methods only need publicly available information provided by URL shortening services and Twitter. Evaluation results show that our attack technique can compromise Twitter users' privacy with high accuracy.

Categories and Subject Descriptors

H.3.5 [**Information Storage and Retrieval**]: Online Information Services—*Web-based services*; K.6.5 [**Management of Computing and Information Systems**]: Security and Protection

Keywords

Twitter; URL shortening service; Inference; Privacy leak

1. INTRODUCTION

Twitter is one of the most popular social network services for exchanging messages (tweets) among people. On April 5, 2012, Twitter announced that it has over 140 million active users and that more than 340 million messages are created every day [26]. Another interesting characteristic of Twitter is its ecosystem. On July 11, 2011, Twitter advertised that it has over one million registered applications built by more than 750,000 developers [25]. The third party applications include client applications for various platforms, such as Windows, Mac, iOS, and Android, and web-based applications such as URL shortening services, image-sharing services, and news feeds.

Among the third party services available to Twitter users, URL shortening services are one of the most essential services. Because Twitter restricts the length of a tweet to 140 characters and allows a tweet to contain only text, Twitter might not be able to include their complete thought in a tweet. Therefore, when a user wants to share more complicated information, such as news or multimedia pages, he will include a URL of the web page that contains the information into a tweet. However, when the length of an entire message, including the URL, is greater than 140 characters, the problem still exists. URL shortening services solve this length problem by providing a shortened URL that redirects visitors to the original, longer URL. Moreover, some URL shortening services, such as *bit.ly* and *goo.gl*, publicly publish *click analytics* which include the number of clicks, countries, browsers and referrers of visitors. Anyone can use such data to analyze statistics of visitors of a shortened URL. A curious user or an attacker might even want to obtain specific information about individual visitors of the shortened URL. However, to protect the privacy of visitors, URL shortening services only provide aggregated data; therefore, we cannot distinguish individual visitors using these data only. The main question is whether *we can extract information that can be used to identify individual visitor from the aggregated click analytics*.

Interestingly, Twitter itself provides a set of metadata that can be used to differentiate Twitter users. For instance, if a user, Alice, updates her messages using the official Twitter client application for iPhone, "Twitter for iPhone" will be included in the source field of the metadata of her messages. Using this information, we can determine that Alice is an iPhone user. Moreover, Alice might have disclosed on her profile page that she lives in the USA or she might have activated the location service of a Twitter client application to automatically fill the location field in the metadata. From this information, we can conclude that Alice is in the USA.

Along with the above example, let us consider a simple inference attack conducted by Bob – Alice's boyfriend. Bob posts a tweet with a URL shortened by *goo.gl*, and Alice sees the Bob's URL. If Alice clicks on the shortened URL, then *goo.gl* records {"country": "US", "platform": "iPhone", "referrer": "twitter.com"} in the click analytics of the shortened URL. Otherwise, no information may be added to the click analytics. Later, Bob retrieves the click analytics of the shortened URL to know whether Alice clicked on his URL or not. If the click analytics has not changed or if its changes do not include information about the USA, iPhone, and twitter.com, he could infer that Alice did not click on his URL. Otherwise, he could infer that Alice clicked on his URL. This simple form of inference may include some errors because another Twitter user who also uses "Twitter for iPhone" in the USA could click on Bob's shortened URL. However, the main advantage of this inference attack is that *it is a passive attack relying on public information only*, unlike conventional browser history stealing attacks [3, 8, 10, 11, 14–18].

The goal of history stealing attacks is to know the URLs that a target browser (host or user) visited. However, all of the existing history stealing attacks are active attacks and require some private information. The required information includes Cascading Style Sheet (CSS) visited styles, browser cache, DNS cache and latency. To collect such information, we have to prepare a web page that contains scripts or malware that extract the CSS styles, browser cache or required time to load some pages from a visited browser, or monitor DNS requests to measure the DNS lookup time of a target host. In other words, we need to deceive or compromise a target user or his network to obtain the browsing history.

In this paper, we propose an attack technique to infer whether a specific user clicked on certain shortened URLs on Twitter. As shown in the above simple inference attack, our attack is based on the combination of publicly available information: click analytics from URL shortening services and metadata from Twitter. The goal of the attack is to know which URLs were clicked on by a target user. To perform the attack, we create *monitoring accounts* that monitor messages from all followings of a target user to collect all shortened URLs that the target user might click on. We then monitor the click analytics of those shortened URLs and compare them with the metadata of the target user. Such an attack could be used for targeted marketing, targeted spamming, or cyberstalking. Evaluation results show that our attack can successfully infer the click information with a high degree of probability.

In summary, the main contributions of this paper are as follows:

- We propose novel attack techniques to determine whether a specific user clicks on certain shortened URLs on Twitter. To the best of our knowledge, this is the first study that infers URL visiting history on Twitter.

- We only use public information provided by URL shortening services and Twitter; i.e., click analytics and Twitter metadata. We determine whether a target user visits a shortened URL by correlating the publicly available information. Our approach does not need complicated techniques or assumptions such as script injection, phishing, malware intrusion or DNS monitoring. All we need is publicly available information.

2. URL SHORTENING SERVICES

The first notable URL shortening service is TinyURL, which was launched in 2002. The success of TinyURL influenced the development of many URL shortening services. These services reduce the length of URLs for easy sharing. Shortened URLs are especially convenient for users of Twitter, which imposes a limit on the length of a message. In the past, Twitter used TinyURL and *bit.ly* as the default URL shortening services. As of October 10, 2011, Twitter started using its own URL shortening service, *t.co*, to wrap all URLs in tweets in order to protect Twitter users from malicious URLs [24, 28].

Some URL shortening services provide click analytics about each shortened URLs. Whenever a user clicks on a shortened URL, some information about the user is recorded. The click analytics is usually made public and can be accessed by anyone. Among such URL shortening services, we focus on *bit.ly* and *goo.gl* because they are broadly used and provide meaningful information.

2.1 goo.gl

In December 2009, Google launched a URL shortening service called Google URL Shortener at *goo.gl*. Its click analytics provides information about the visitors as follows:

- Referrers
- Countries
- Browsers
- Platforms

For example, let us assume a user uses a BlackBerry phone and is located in the USA. If he clicks on a shortened URL from *goo.gl* on Twitter, *t.co* is recorded in the Referrers field; *Mobile Safari* in the Browsers field; *US* in the Countries field; and *BlackBerry* in the Platforms field of *goo.gl*'s click analytics. The reason why *t.co* is recorded in the Referrers field is that all links shared on Twitter are wrapped using *t.co* by Twitter from October 10, 2011.

2.2 bit.ly

Bitly company launched a URL shortening service *bit.ly* in 2008. Its click analytics provides information about visitors as follows:

- Referrers
- Countries

bit.ly does not provide information about browsers and platforms. However, its Referrers field has more detailed information than that of *goo.gl*. When a user clicks on a shortened URL on Twitter, only "*t.co*" is recorded in the Referrers field in the *goo.gl* click analytics. However, *bit.ly* records the entire URL of the referrer site in the Referrers field, as "http://t.co/*****". With the information provided by *goo.gl*, we only know whether a visitor of a shortened URL comes from Twitter or not. However, if we use the information provided by *bit.ly*, we can determine the exact URL of the tweet containing the clicked shortened URL. This information makes our inference attack possible even without having information about browsers and platforms.

3. USER MATCHING

Whenever we notice that there is a visitor of the shortened URL by monitoring the click analytics, we compare the information about the visitor and Twitter users. If the shortened URL is *goo.gl*, the information about the visitor consists of four parts: Referrers, Countries, Platforms, and Browsers. If the shortened URL is *bit.ly*, only Referrers and Countries are provided. We regularly monitor the click analytics to check whether the number of clicks on a shortened URL increased, which indicates a new visitor. Information about the visitor can be obtained from the differences between the new and the old click analytics. Figure 1 shows

		#clicks
Referrers	t.co	10
	twitter.com	5
	Unknown/empty	6
	www.facebook.com	2
Countries	US	11
	CA	7
	JP	3
	KR	2
Browsers	Mobile	13
	Mobile Safari	4
	Internet Explorer	5
	Chrome	1
Platforms	iPhone	10
	iPad	1
	BlackBerry	5
	Windows	7
	Chrome	1

→ Δ time

		#clicks
Referrers	t.co	11
	twitter.com	5
	Unknown/empty	6
	www.facebook.com	2
Countries	US	12
	CA	7
	JP	3
	KR	2
Browsers	Mobile	14
	Mobile Safari	4
	Internet Explorer	5
	Chrome	1
Platforms	iPhone	11
	iPad	1
	BlackBerry	5
	Windows	7
	Chrome	1

Figure 1: The proposed system notices that there is a visitor using differences in the click analytics. We can infer that the information of the visitor is {"country": "US", "platform": "iPhone", "referrer": "t.co"} (*goo.gl* case)

the example of the process we used to obtain the information about the visitor. Then we compared the information about the visitor who clicked on the shortened URL with information about the Twitter users whom we were tracking.

Twitter does not officially provide personal information about Twitter users such as country, browsers and platforms. Therefore, we need to infer the information about Twitter users by investigating their timeline and profile pages. Next, we describe how we extract the information from Twitter metadata.

3.1 Referrers

Our goal is to identify whether a known user clicked on a specific shortened URLs on Twitter. We can determine whether the visitor comes from Twitter by using the referrer information. The click analytics of *goo.gl* only records the hostname of the referrer site; therefore, if a visitor comes from Twitter, "*t.co*" or "*twitter.com*" is recorded in the Referrers field. In most cases, "*t.co*" is recorded because all links shared on Twitter are automatically shortened to *t.co* links. *t.co* handles redirections by context and user agents, so Referrer depends on the source of click [27]. In some cases, "*twitter.com*" is recorded because some Twitter applications use original links instead of *t.co* links. Therefore, if the Referrers information of the visitor is "*t.co*" or "*twitter.com*", we regarded the visitor as coming from Twitter.

When a shortened URL is provided by *bit.ly*, we can analyze it in greater detail, because the entire URL of the referrer site is provided in the click analytics of the shortened URL (Table 1). On Twitter, all URLs are converted into different *t.co* URLs. If the target user clicks on the shortened URL, the URL shortening services record the *t.co* URL in the Referrers field. The referrer match is considered successful when the *t.co* URL recorded in the click analytics is the same as the *t.co* URL of the target shortened URL.

		#
Referrers	direct	2
	http://t.co/3slAb	8
	http://t.co/xInA4	4
	https://twitter.com/[UID]/status/[TID]	3
Countries	US	9
	KR	5
	ID	1
	CH	2

Table 1: The examples of *bit.ly* click analytics. UID is a Twitter ID and TID is a numerical ID of each tweet.

3.2 Country

The country information of a Twitter user can be inferred using the location field in the profile page. In many cases, Twitter users fill in the location field with their city or place name. We can determine the user's country by searching GeoNames with the information in the location field of the user's Twitter profile [1]. GeoNames returns the country code that corresponds to the search keywords. The country information provided by the click analytics is also a country code; therefore, we have a successful country match if both country codes are the same.

Some Twitter users, hide their location by leaving the location field empty. Other users fill in the location field with meaningless information, such as "earth" and "in your heart." We cannot obtain accurate location information from these users. In those cases, we do not perform country matching. In our attack experiments, we avoided these problems by selecting only target users who filled in valid location names in the location field. However, even without location information, our attacks are still possible with other information. Location information increases the accuracy of our attacks, but it is optional.

Source	Browsers	Platforms
Twitter for iPhone	Mobile	iPhone
Twitter for iPad	Mobile	iPad
Twitter for Android	Mobile Safari	Linux
Twitter for BlackBerry	Mobile Safari	BlackBerry

Table 2: The examples of Browsers and Platforms corresponding to source

Additionally, we could rely on recent studies, which infer the location of Twitter users based on their posts [7, 13].

3.3 Browsers and Platforms

When our target user clicks a shortened URL provided by *goo.gl*, we can use the browser and platform information of the target user to increase the accuracy of inference because the click analytics of *goo.gl* provide such information unlike *bit.ly*. Twitter does not provide the browser and platform information of Twitter users, but Twitter provides the information what applications are used for posting the tweets. Whenever a Twitter user posts a tweet, the application name is recorded in the Source field of the tweet. For example, if a user uses the official Twitter client application for the iPhone, "via Twitter for iPhone" is recorded in the Source field. We can use this source information to infer the browser and platform used. Table 2 shows an example of the source values corresponding to browsers and platforms. Some values in the Sources field, however, correspond to several browsers and platforms because some applications support multiple platforms. For instance, TweetDeck is a multi-platform application that support the iPhone, Android, Windows, and Mac OS X. If a Twitter user uses a multi-platform application, we assume that the user uses all the platforms that the application supports.

4. INFERENCE ATTACK IN THE SIMULATED ENVIRONMENT

The definite ways that can exactly evaluate our system are asking the target users whether they really visited the shortened URLs or not, or monitoring their browsing activities by using logging software. However, both approaches are restrictive because we cannot survey all of them or require them to install logging software. Therefore, we built a simulated environment where we performed our experiments. Figure 2 shows the overall architecture of the attack in the simulated environment.

In this experiment, we used virtual users instead of Twitter users in the real world. The system tried to infer the shortened URLs clicked on by the virtual users. The processes involved in this attack system are as follows:

1. The system monitors the click analytics of the shortened URLs that are posted by Twitter users.

2. Changes in the shortened URL's click analytics indicate a new visitor, and the system extracts the visitor information from the click analytics.

3. The extracted visitor information is recorded in the simulated click analytics.

4. The system stochastically adds the information about the virtual users to the simulated click analytics to simulate the click of a real Twitter user.

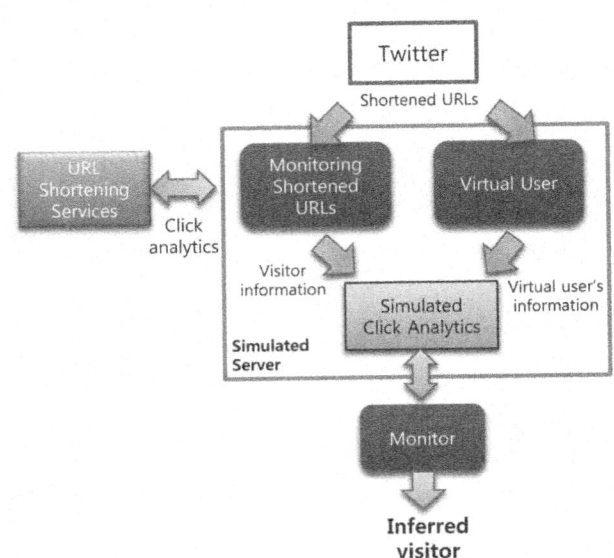

Figure 2: Overall architecture of the attack in the simulated environment

5. Changes in the simulated click analytics indicate a new visitor of the simulated server, an inferred visitor, and the system extracts the information of the inferred visitor from the simulated click analytics.

6. The system compares the inferred visitor and the information about the virtual user. If the information is matched, we infer that the shortened URL was clicked on by the virtual user.

Before the experiment could start, we selected 56 Twitter users who posted *goo.gl* or *bit.ly* URLs regularly. The clicks of virtual users are controlled by the system. Whenever a shortened URL is posted by a Twitter user, the virtual users click on the shortened URL with a probability of 0.7. We correctly know which shortened URLs were clicked on by the virtual users, so we can estimate the performance of the system.

We cannot test all types of Twitter users using the virtual users. Twitter users come from many countries, and they use many different platforms and browsers. Therefore, we had to limit the number of user types for our experiment. We selected six countries: United States (US), Great Britain (GB), Brazil (BR), Japan (JP), Italy (IT), and Rwanda (RW). The first five are among the top 20 countries with the largest number of Twitter accounts [23]. We added Rwanda to learn the effectiveness of the system when the target user lives in a country with only a few Twitter users. We also selected four smartphone platforms: an iPhone, Android, BlackBerry, and a Windows Phone. A combination of six countries and four platforms, gave us 24 types of users for the experiment.

4.1 Data Collection

We collected data by crawling the click analytics of the shortened URLs, using the API methods offered by *goo.gl* and *bit.ly*. *goo.gl* APIs have a rate limit of 1,000,000 queries per day. Similarly, *bit.ly* allows users to create no more than five concurrent connections from one IP address. *bit.ly* also

# of followers	goo.gl	bit.ly
100 - 1k	3	3
1k - 10k	10	5
10k - 100k	9	13
100k - 1M	7	6
total	29	27

Table 3: Twitter users used in the simulated experiment

		Actual value	
		Click	Non click
Prediction	Click	True positive	False positive
Value	Non click	False negative	True negative

Table 4: Confusion matrix

enforces per-hour limits, per-minute limits, and per-IP rate limits for each API method. However, *bit.ly* does not publish the exact number of allowed requests on each limit. In all, we monitored 31,525 *goo.gl* URLs and 24,144 *bit.ly* URLs from September to October 2012. Those shortened URLs were posted by 56 Twitter users (Table 3).

4.2 Evaluation

In this experiment, true positive rate (TPR) is meaningless because false negative is always zero. False negative cases are cases where a virtual user clicks on the shortened URL but the system infers that the virtual user has not click on the URL (Table 4). In the real world, the system is occasionally unable to obtain all information about the target user if he uses several platforms and browsers. In the simulated environment, however, the system knows all information about the virtual users, and the information is not changed during the entire experiment. Therefore, the system always knows what URLs are clicked on by the virtual user by monitoring the simulated click analytics. However, false positive cases are possible because some Twitter users have the same information as the virtual users. If such Twitter users click on the shortened URLs monitored, we get a false positive result. For these reasons, we used two metrics to evaluate the system: precision and false positive rate (FPR).

$$\text{Precision} = \frac{\text{True positive}}{\text{True positive} + \text{False positive}}.$$

$$\text{FPR} = \frac{\text{False positive}}{\text{False positive} + \text{True negative}}.$$

4.2.1 goo.gl

We created a Twitter account and followed 29 Twitter users who posted *goo.gl* URLs regularly. The accuracy of our system depends on the number of the followers of the those users because the shortened URLs posted on Twitter are exposed to the followers of the posting users. With a large number of followers, it is highly likely that many of those followers live in the same country and use the same platform or browser as the target user. Therefore, our system would guess incorrectly because the system misjudges those other users as the target user. We grouped the posting users based on the number of their followers to determine the effect of the number of followers on the results of the experiment.

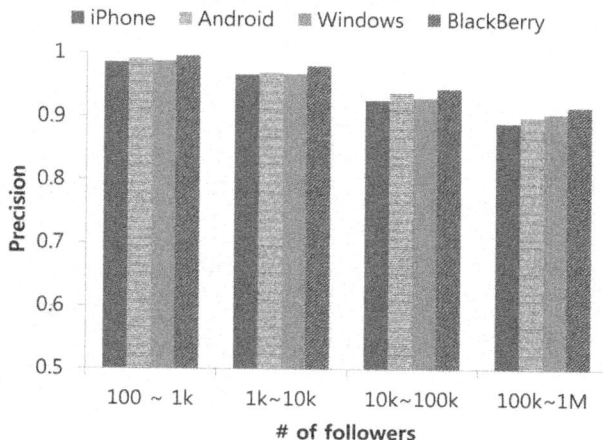

Figure 3: The precision of *goo.gl* URLs in terms of platforms. X axis means the number of followers of the updating users.

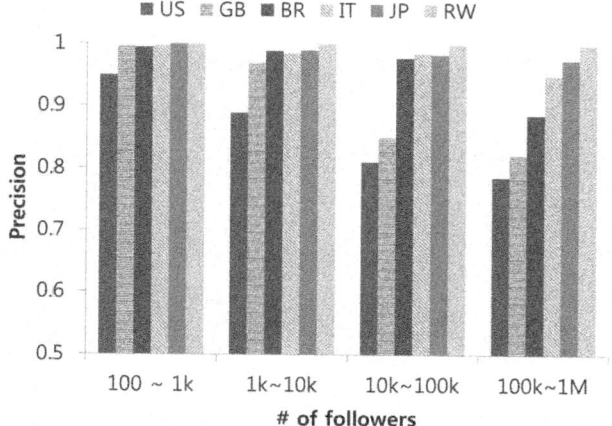

Figure 4: The precision of *goo.gl* URLs in terms of country. X axis means the number of followers of the updating users.

Figure 3 shows the precision of each platform according to the number of followers. We expected to see low precision with iPhone and Android users because of the large number of users on those platforms. As expected, the results showed that our system had the lowest precision with iPhone users; however, the differences among the platforms were minimal. Average precisions of each platform were as follows: iPhone was 0.94, Android was 0.95, Windows Phone 0.95 and BlackBerry was 0.96.

Figure 4 shows the precision of each country according to the number of followers. The result is compared against the number of Twitter accounts in that country. We achieved the lowest precision with US users because they comprise a large percentage of the total number of Twitter accounts [23]. Average precisions of each country were as follows: US was 0.85, GB was 0.90, BR was 0.96, IT was 0.97, JP was 0.98 and RW was 0.99. The total average precision for all countries in our experiment was 0.94.

Both results showed that the precision decreased as the number of followers increased. The average precision was

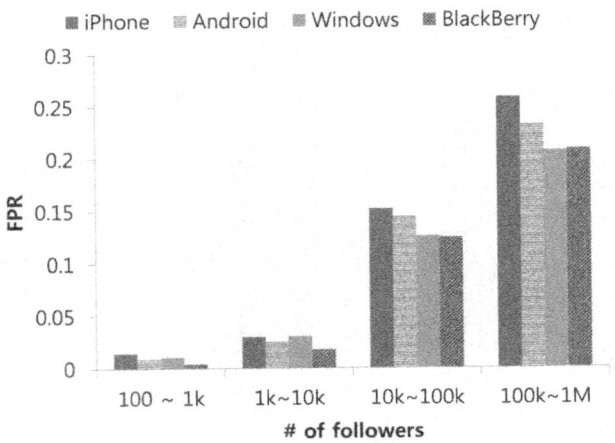

Figure 5: The FPR of *goo.gl* URLs in terms of platforms. X axis means the number of followers of the updating users.

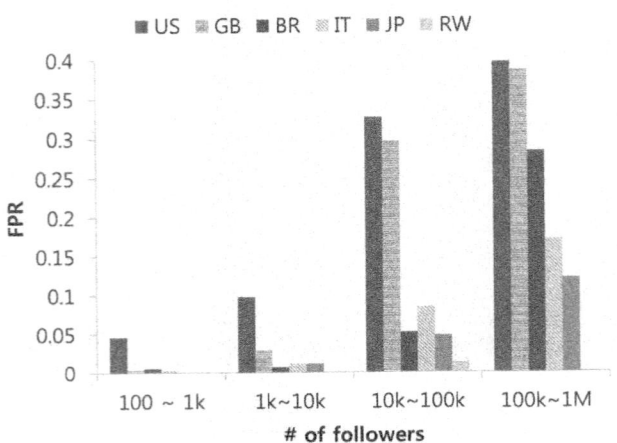

Figure 6: The FPR of *goo.gl* URLs in terms of country. X axis means the number of followers of the updating users.

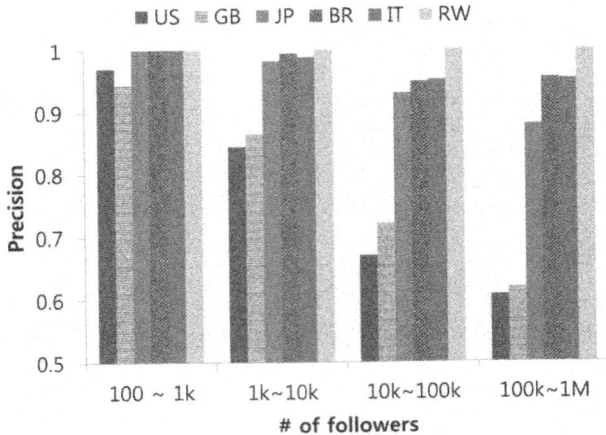

Figure 7: The precision of *bit.ly* URLs in terms of country. X axis means the number of followers of the updating users.

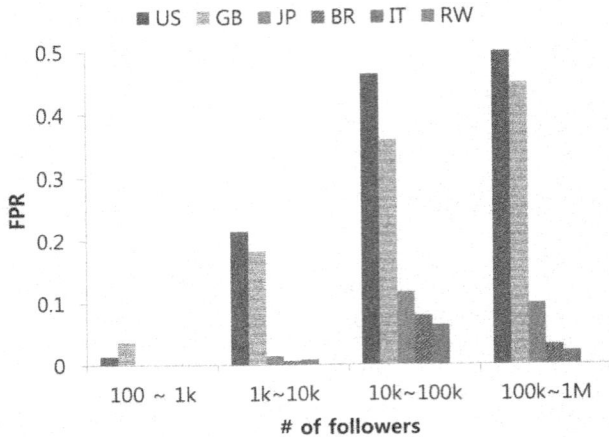

Figure 8: The FPR of *bit.ly* URLs in terms of country. X axis means the number of followers of the updating users.

0.99 when the number of followers was less than 1,000, but the average precision was 0.90 when the number of followers was greater than 100,000.

As shown in Figures 5 and 6, FPR results showed an inverse correlation with the precision results. US and iPhone users had higher FPR than others. The total average FPR was 0.1.

4.2.2 bit.ly

Our monitoring account also followed 27 Twitter users who updated *bit.ly* URLs regularly. Figures 7 and 8 show the results of the *bit.ly* cases, and the results were similar to the *goo.gl* cases. US users also have lower precision and higher FPR than others. The overall accuracy of the system was lower with *bit.ly* cases than with *goo.gl* cases, because *goo.gl* offers four types of information in the click analytics, whereas *bit.ly* offers only two types of information, namely, the Referrers and the Countries, as mentioned in Section 2.2. The system had to infer URL clicks based on less information. The total average precision was 0.87 and the total average FPR was 0.16.

4.2.3 Discussion

The most influential factor that affected the accuracy of the system is the number of followers who follow the same Twitter user and who have the same information as the target user. If no other user had the same information as the target user, the system could infer perfectly regardless of the number of the posting user's followers. In fact, most of the URLs clicked on by the Rwanda users were successfully inferred by the system regardless of the number of followers and platforms. In contrast, the system had the lowest accuracy if the target user lived in the US and used an iPhone. The user who lived in US and used an iPhone had the lowest precision with 0.81 and the highest FPR with 0.28. It means that even in the worst case our system has high performance. In general, the system successfully inferred the URLs clicked on by the target users with a high precision and a low FPR.

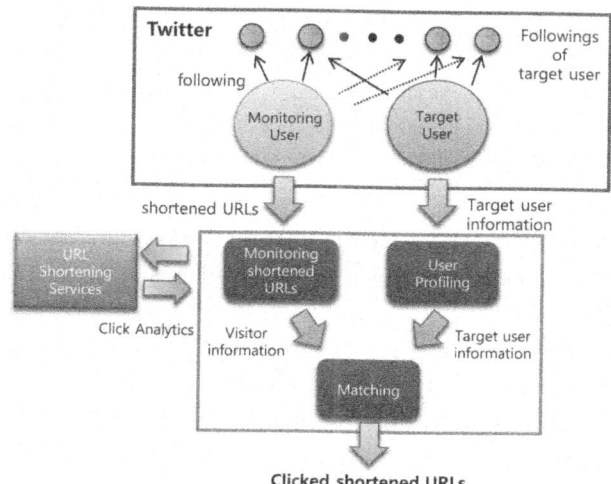

Figure 9: Overall architecture of the attack in the real world

5. INFERENCE ATTACK IN THE REAL WORLD

In this section, we introduce the inference attack in the real world. The system identifies whether a Twitter user clicked a shortened URL that were posted by his or her followings or not.

We selected a number of Twitter users as our target users. Our goal was to identify the shortened URLs that were clicked on by a target user. The result of this attack is a set of URLs that could have been clicked on by a target user. The procedures of this attack system are as follows:

1. The system selects a target Twitter user who follows some accounts that post shortened URLs.

2. The system monitors the click analytics of all shortened URLs that are posted by the followings of the target user.

3. When the system notices changes in the click analytics, which indicates a new visitor to the shortened URL, the system extracts the visitor's information from the click analytics.

4. The system compares the information about the visitor with known information the target user. If both pieces of information match, it infers that the shortened URL was clicked on by the target user.

Figure 9 shows the overall architecture. The architecture consists of three modules: profiling, monitoring, and matching. The profiling module gets the information of the target user from the target user's profile and timeline, as mentioned in Sections 3.2 and 3.3. We created a Twitter user (monitoring user) who followed all the followings of the target user in order to access all tweets that might be viewed by the target user. The monitoring module extracts the shortened URLs from the tweets posted by the followings of the target user and monitors the changes in the click analytics of those shortened URLs. When the monitoring module notices the change, which indicates a new visitor to the shortened URL, the matching module compares the information of the visitor with information about the target user. After the matching procedure, all shortened URLs that were clicked on by visitors with the same information as the target user will be included in a set of candidate URLs.

We identify a set of candidate URLs that could be visited by the target user whenever shortened URLs are clicked. The candidate URLs, however, may not be accurate because other Twitter users who have the same information as the target user could click on the candidate URLs. There are many Twitter users who have received the same shortened URLs seen by the target user. All the followers of that user who has sent the shortened URLs to the target user receive the same shortened URLs. Among them, someone who has the same information with the target user may click on a shortened URL that is being monitored by our system. The system could mistakenly conclude that the shortened URL was clicked on by the target user. However, the probability that the clicks are from the target user was significant.

On the other hand, it is also possible that the candidate set might not include a shortened URL that is clicked on by the target user, particularly if the target user clicks on the shortened URL in an unusual environment that is atypical for that user. For example, if a target user typically uses an iPhone in the USA, our system would only monitor changes of click analytics involving the iPhone and the USA. However, it is possible for the target user to change his smart phone or to use a personal computer for using Twitter. If he clicks on the shortened URLs in such environments, our system cannot notice those events. However, this kind of situation temporarily occurs because if the target user posts a tweet using the new environment at least once, the profiling module will add the new environment into his profile information. Therefore, we can successfully identify the user's information and perform the inference attack with high accuracy.

5.1 Target User Selection

The main goal of the attack is to identify the shortened URLs that are clicked on by a target user. There are a number of criteria used to select target users for our experiments. First, we needed to select the target users whose exact information could be identified by us. Their profile must be public and they must use well-known applications, such as the official Twitter applications for the smartphone. Second, the target user must follow some users who post shortened URLs frequently because we want to obtain enough experimental results. If no shortened URL appears in the timeline of the target user, we cannot attempt an attack. Third, the target users must actively use Twitter. If we select an inactivate user as a target user, we cannot obtain enough experimental data. Our ideal target users are Twitter users who frequently check their timeline and click on URLs on their timeline. Another important condition of a target user is that the user needs to post or retweet a tweet that includes the shortened URLs that he clicked on. We assume that we successfully inferred the click on the shortened URLs if the target user posts a tweet with the shortened URL that is one of the URLs in a candidate set. However, the criteria listed above are used only to obtain enough experimental data and to conduct evaluation, which will be covered later in the Section 5.3. They are not strongly related to the accuracy of the attack. Any Twitter user who can be identified by an attacker could be a target user.

In order to find qualified target users for the experiments, we manually searched *goo.gl* or *bit.ly* strings on Twitter and reviewed the user's timeline.

5.2 Data Collection

First, we crawled Twitter data using two sets of Twitter API methods: Streaming APIs and REST APIs. The Streaming APIs enable us to monitor target users in real time. We used the REST APIs for crawling profile pages, timelines, followers, and followings. However, the REST APIs have a rate limit: a host is permitted 150 requests per hour. In order to overcome the rate limit, we changed the IP address of the crawling servers when the servers exceeded the rate limit. We used 10 servers and 100 IP addresses to crawl Twitter data. Second, we crawled the click analytics of the shortened URLs as mentioned in Section 4.2.

We selected 27 target users and crawled their profiles, timelines, and favorites. We monitored 2,278 *goo.gl* URLs and 25,816 *bit.ly* URLs. The collection lasted for about two months from March to April 2012.

5.3 Evaluation

As mentioned in Section 4, it is difficult to evaluate the system properly. Therefore, we use a different method to evaluate our system. We assume that if a URL is included in the tweets or favorites of a Twitter user, the Twitter user had already visited them. To validate the correctness of our inference that a user visited a URL, we checked whether the user included the same URL in his tweets or favorites in the near future.

To clarify, suppose that our system inferred that Twitter user A visited the shortened URL B. We collect the timeline and the favorites of user A and check whether a tweet containing the shortened URL B exists. If we find the shortened URL B in the timeline or favorites, then we are certain that the system successfully infers the shortened URL visited by the candidates.

We computed three probabilities as follows:

$$\mathbf{P1} = \frac{|\mathbf{U} \cap \mathbf{RT}|}{|\mathbf{U}|},$$

$$\mathbf{P2} = \frac{|\mathbf{C}_{urls} \cap \mathbf{RT}|}{|\mathbf{C}_{urls}|},$$

$$\mathbf{P3} = \frac{|\mathbf{N}_{urls} \cap \mathbf{RT}|}{|\mathbf{N}_{urls}|}.$$

Let $\mathbf{U}$ be a set of all shortened URLs that are posted by followings of the target user. $\mathbf{U}$ is classified into two sets $\mathbf{C}_{urls}$ and $\mathbf{N}_{urls}$ where $\mathbf{C}_{urls}$ is a set of shortened URLs inferred as visited by the target user, candidate URLs set, and $\mathbf{N}_{urls}$ is a set of shortened URLs inferred as unvisited by the target user. $\mathbf{RT}$ is a subset of $\mathbf{U}$ that includes the shortened URLs which are in the target user's timeline including retweeted or favorited by the target user.

The resulting probabilities were as follows: $\mathbf{P1}$ was 0.032, $\mathbf{P2}$ was 0.048, and $\mathbf{P3}$ was 0.003. $\mathbf{P2}$ was 1.5 times higher than $\mathbf{P1}$ and 16 times higher than $\mathbf{P3}$. This implies that we can successfully categorize all shortened URLs into a set of visited URLs and a set of unvisited URLs. The target users normally posted tweets containing shortened URLs that are included in the candidate URLs set. They rarely posted

	# of shortened URLs	RR
goo.gl	2,278	0.584
bit.ly	25,816	0.674
Total	28,094	0.669

Table 5: The monitored shortened URLs and RR for each URL shortening services in the real world attack

tweets with shortened URLs outside the candidate URLs set. According to boyd et al. [4], about 3% of tweets are likely to be retweets. That percentage was similar to our calculation of $\mathbf{P1}$ which was 0.032; therefore, the value of $\mathbf{P1}$ is also trustworthy.

To view the results from a different angle, we also calculated two other metrics.

$$\mathbf{P4} = \frac{|\mathbf{C}_{urls} \cap \mathbf{RT}|}{|\mathbf{RT}|}.$$

$$\mathbf{P5} = \frac{|\mathbf{N}_{urls} \cap \mathbf{RT}|}{|\mathbf{RT}|}.$$

$\mathbf{P4}$ indicates the fraction of candidate URLs that are in $\mathbf{RT}$, and $\mathbf{P5}$ indicates the fraction of non-candidate URLs are in $\mathbf{RT}$. The results were as follows: $\mathbf{P4}$ was 0.952 and $\mathbf{P5}$ was 0.048. We found that $\mathbf{P4}$ was much higher than $\mathbf{P5}$. Most of the shortened URLs that are in the timeline or favorites of the target users were inferred as candidate URLs. Therefore, we can say with confidence that a shortened URL is highly likely to be retweeted or favorited by the target user if it is included in the candidate set.

We also computed the reduction ratio $\mathbf{RR}$, which represents how much we reduced the number of candidate URLs from the number of all shortened URLs posted by the followings of the target user. $\mathbf{RR}$ is computed as follows:

$$\mathbf{RR} = \frac{|\mathbf{C}_{urls}|}{|\mathbf{U}|}.$$

$\mathbf{RR}$ depends on click tendency of the target users. When the target user clicks on all of the shortened URLs in $\mathbf{U}$, $\mathbf{RR}$ becomes 1. Therefore, a higher $\mathbf{RR}$ does not always indicate that the system is performing poorly. Table 5 shows the results for each URL shortening service. The average value of the reduction ratio is 66.9%. This means that our system inferred that the target users clicked on 66.9% of the shortened URLs posted by their followings. The reduction ratio in the *goo.gl* case is lower than in the *bit.ly* case, because *goo.gl* provides more information than *bit.ly* in the click analytics. Since the number of *bit.ly* shortened URLs is fairly larger than that of *goo.gl* on Twitter, we have a larger number of *bit.ly* shortened URLs than that of *goo.gl* shortened URLs.

6. DISCUSSION

6.1 Limitations

Our inference attack method has some limitations due to the restrictions in the given information. We cannot guarantee the correctness of the given location information because some users do not reveal their exact location information on Twitter. Moreover, the given browser and platform information is also restricted because some client applications do not reveal the exact platforms that they use. Even when we are able to identify specific Twitter users, many users have the same information as the identified Twitter users have. Therefore, the results of inference cannot be 100% guaranteed. However, with more information about the target users, the accuracy of our system will improve. For example, if we know when the target user frequently uses Twitter, we can further reduce the number of the candidates. One way to infer this timeframe is by analyzing the time history of the target user's tweets. We will use this time history for future work. Further, if we could obtain information about a target user from different channels (e.g., if we are personally acquainted with the target), we could increase the probability of succeeding with our inference attack.

6.2 Countermeasures

We only need public information provided by Twitter and the URL shortening services. Therefore, the published information must be changed to prevent our inference attacks. A simple measure of prevention is by delaying the update to the click analytics of shortened URLs. If the click analytics is updated every minute or every tens of minutes, the changes of the click analytics would more likely include a larger number of click events, so that inference attacks would have difficulties in differentiating an individual from the group of click events. In addition, providers could add noise information to the click analytics in order to prevent exact inference, as the differential privacy does [9].

6.3 Applications

Using our inference attack method, attackers can determine the URLs that the target user visited. Based on the visited URLs, the attackers could infer the target user's preferences, such as music interests, political inclination, or favorite products. This information could be used for targeted marketing or targeted spamming. Moreover, we discovered that it is very easy to cyber-stalk on Twitter. Anyone can stalk a target user by creating a Twitter account that follows everyone whom the target user follows (if the target user is not a private user). This way, the attacker receives the same tweets that appear in the target user's timeline.

Some active inference attacks are also possible. We did inference attacks after we identified the information of the target user. On the contrary, we can use our inference attacks to obtain information about the target user. If an attacker creates a shortened URL and sends the shortened URL to the target user, who then clicks on the shortened URL, the attacker can obtain information, such as the target user's current location and platform, from the click analytics.

7. RELATED WORK

7.1 Browser History Stealing

There are several types of history stealing attacks. First, the cached data of the browser was used for sniffing browser history [10, 14, 15]. There is a time difference between retrieving cached resources and retrieving non-cached resources. The attackers can know which pages were visited by analyzing the differences in latency. DNS cache was also used for history stealing attacks [10, 11, 18]. In general, most of the history stealing attacks are based on Cascading Style Sheet (CSS) visited styles [3, 8, 16, 17]. They use the fact that browsers display visited links differently from unvisited links. These history stealing attacks assume that victims visit a malicious web page or that victims are infected by malware. However, our inference attacks do not need to make these assumptions. The inference attacks only use the combinations of publicly available information. Therefore, anyone can be an attacker, and anyone can also be a victim.

7.2 Privacy Leaks from Public Information

Many previous studies proposed attack techniques that cause privacy leaks in social networks, such as inferring private attributes or de-anonymizing users. Most of these studies used public information to infer hidden information. Some studies combined information from several different data sets. First, there are studies introducing de-anonymzing attacks in social networks. Backstrom et al. [2] tried to identify edge existence in anonymized network and Narayanan and Shmatikov [21] identified Netflix records of known users using only a little bit of data about the users. Furthermore, they combined their results with IMDb data and inferred user's political preferences or religious view. Narayanan and Shmatikov [22] also proved that users who have accounts in both Twitter and Flickr can be recognized in the anonymous Twitter graph. Wondracek et al. [29] proposed the de-anonymized attack using group membership information obtained by browser history stealing attack. There are also studies inferring private attributes of users in the social networks. He et al. [12] and Lindamood et al. [19] built a Bayesian network to predict undisclosed personal attributes. Zheleva and Getoor [30] showed how an attacker can exploit a mixture of private and public data to predict private attributes of a target user. Similarly, Mislove et al. [20] inferred the attributes of a target user by using a combination of attributes of the user's friends and other users who are loosely (not directly) connected to the target user. Calandrino et al. [5] proposed algorithms inferring customer's transactions in the recommender systems, such as Amazon and Hunch. They combined public data of the recommender systems and some of the transactions of a target user in order to infer the target user's unknown transactions. Chaabane et al. [6] proposed an inference attack to predict undisclosed attributes by using only music interests. They derived semantics using Wikipedia ontology and measured the similarity between users.

8. CONCLUSION

In this paper, we proposed an inference attack that infers shortened URLs that are clicked on by the target user. All the information needed in our attack is public information; that is, the click analytics of URL shortening services and Twitter metadata. Both information are public and can be accessed by anyone. We combined two pieces of public information with inferred candidates. To evaluate our system, we crawled and monitored the click analytics of URL shortening services and Twitter data. Throughout the experiments, we have shown that our attack can infer the candidates in the majority of cases. To the best of our knowledge, this is the first study that infers URL visiting history on Twitter. We also proved that if an attacker knows some information about the target user, he could determine whether the target user clicks on the shortened URL.

9. ACKNOWLEDGEMENTS

This research was supported by World Class University program funded by the Ministry of Education, Science and Technology through the National Research Foundation of Korea (R31-10100). Also, this research was supported by the MKE(The Ministry of Knowledge Economy), Korea, under the ITRC(Information Technology Research Center) support program supervised by the NIPA(National IT Industry Promotion Agency). (NIPA-2012-H0301-12-3002)

10. REFERENCES

[1] geonames. http://www.geonames.org/export/client-libraries.html.

[2] L. Backstrom, C. Dwork, and J. Kleinberg. Wherefore art thou r3579x? anonymized social networks, hidden patterns, and structural steganography. In *WWW*, 2007.

[3] D. Baron. :visited support allows queries into global history, 2002. https://bugzilla.mozilla.org/show_bug.cgi?id=147777.

[4] D. boyd, S. Golder, and G. Lotan. Tweet, tweet, retweet: Conversational aspects of retweeting on twitter. In *HICSS*, 2010.

[5] J. A. Calandrino, A. Kilzer, A. Narayanan, E. W. Felten, and V. Shmatikov. "you might also like:" privacy risks of collaborative filtering. In *IEEE Security and Privacy*, 2011.

[6] A. Chaabane, G. Acs, and M. A. Kaafar. You are what you like! information leakage through users' interests. In *NDSS*, 2012.

[7] Z. Cheng, J. Caverlee, and K. Lee. You are where you tweet: A content-based approach to geo-locating twitter users. In *ACM CIKM*, 2010.

[8] A. Clover. Css visited pages disclosure, 2002. http://seclists.org/bugtraq/2002/Feb/271.

[9] C. Dwork. Differential privacy. In *ICALP*, 2006.

[10] E. W. Felten and M. A. Schneider. Timing attacks on web privacy. In *ACM CCS*, 2000.

[11] L. Grangeia. Dns cache snooping or snooping the cache for fun and profit. In *SideStep Seguranca Digitial, Technical Report*, 2004.

[12] J. He, W. W. Chu, and Z. V. Liu. Inferring privacy information from social networks. In *ISI*, 2006.

[13] B. Hecht, L. Hong, B. Suh, and E. H. Chi. Tweets from justin bieber's heart: The dynamics of the location field in user profiles. In *ACM CHI*, 2011.

[14] C. Jackson, A. Bortz, D. Boneh, and J. C. Mitchell. Protecting browser state from web privacy attacks. In *WWW*, 2006.

[15] M. Jakobsson and S. Stamm. Invasive browser sniffing and countermeasures. In *WWW*, 2006.

[16] A. Janc and L. Olejnik. Feasibility and real-world implications of web browser history detection. In *W2SP*, 2010.

[17] A. Janc and L. Olejnik. Web browser history detection as a real-world privacy threat. In *ESORICS*, 2010.

[18] S. Krishnan and F. Monrose. Dns prefetching and its privacy implications: When good things go bad. In *USENIX LEET*, 2010.

[19] J. Lindamood, R. Heatherly, M. Kantarcioglu, and B. Thuraisingham. Inferring private information using social network data. In *WWW*, 2009.

[20] A. Mislove, B. Viswanath, K. P. Gummadi, and P. Druschel. You are who you know: Inferring user profiles in online social networks. In *WSDM*, 2010.

[21] A. Narayanan and V. Shmatikov. Robust de-anonymization of large sparse dataset. In *IEEE Security and Privacy*, 2008.

[22] A. Narayanan and V. Shmatikov. De-anonymizing social networks. In *IEEE Security and Privacy*, 2009.

[23] Semiocast. Twitter reaches half a billion accounts more than 140 millions in the u.s., 2012. http://semiocast.com/publications/2012_07_30_Twitter_reaches_half_a_billion_accounts_140m_in_the_US.

[24] Twitter blog. Links and twitter: Length should't matter, 2010. http://blog.twitter.com/2010/06/links-and-twitter-length-shouldnt.html.

[25] Twitter blog. One million registered twitter apps, 2011. http://blog.twitter.com/2011/07/one-million-registered-twitter-apps.html.

[26] Twitter blog. Shutting down spammers, 2012. http://blog.twitter.com/2012/04/shutting-down-spammers.html.

[27] Twitter developers. t.co redirection behavior, 2012. https://dev.twitter.com/docs/tco-redirection-behavior.

[28] Twitter developers. The t.co url wrapper, 2012. https://dev.twitter.com/docs/tco-url-wrapper.

[29] G. Wondracek, T. Holz, E. Kirda, and C. Kruegel. A practical attack to de-anonymize social network users. In *IEEE Security and Privacy*, 2010.

[30] E. Zheleva and L. Getoor. To join or not to join: The illusion of privacy in social networks with mixed public and private user profiles. In *WWW*, 2009.

Exploring and Exploiting User Search Behavior on Mobile and Tablet Devices to Improve Search Relevance

[1]Yang Song, [1]Hao Ma, [2]Hongning Wang, [1]Kuansan Wang

[1]Microsoft Research,
One Microsoft Way,
Redmond, WA 98052, USA

[2]Department of Computer Science
University of Illinois at Urbana-Champaign
Urbana IL, 61801 USA

ABSTRACT

In this paper, we present a log-based study on user search behavior comparisons on three different platforms: desktop, mobile and tablet. We use three-month search logs in 2012 from a commercial search engine for our study. Our objective is to better understand how and to what extent mobile and tablet searchers behave differently than desktop users. Our study spans a variety of aspects including query categorization, query length, search time distribution, search location distribution, user click patterns and so on. From our data set, we reveal that there are significant differences between user search patterns in these three platforms, and therefore use the same ranking system is not an optimal solution for all of them. Consequently, we propose a framework that leverages a set of domain-specific features, along with the training data from desktop search, to further improve the search relevance for mobile and tablet platforms. Experimental results demonstrate that by transferring knowledge from desktop search, search relevance on mobile and tablet can be greatly improved.

Categories and Subject Descriptors

H.3.3 [**Information Storage and Retrieval**]: Information Search and Retrieval—*Internet search*; H.3.0 [**Information Storage and Retrieval**]: General—*Web search*

General Terms

Measurement,Experimentation

Keywords

mobile search, tablet search, user behavior analysis, search result ranking

1. INTRODUCTION

With the prevalence of smart phones and tablet PCs in the past few years, we have all witnessed an evolution in the search engine industry where the user search activities have shifted from desktop to mobile devices at an incredibly fast pace. According to a recent report [1], the year-on-year growth of mobile search volumes have more than doubled from 2011 to 2012, while the search volumes on all platforms have merely increased by 11% over the year. Therefore, it is quite evident that understanding user search behavior on mobile devices has become more and more crucial to the IR community as well as the success of search engine companies. Particularly, what do users search? How do users formulate/reformulate queries? More importantly, what are the differences between desktop search and mobile search?

Google and Yahoo! released their statistics regarding mobile search usages [24, 14], in 2008 and 2009, respectively. The report from Google revealed that iPhone users bear lots of similarities with desktop users in terms of query length and query type distribution, while other mobile phones have shown different search patterns. On the other hand, Yahoo!'s findings disclosed that the US mobile query categorization is noticeably different from those of international mobile queries, where US users often issue longer and more complicated queries. At a high level, both reports have shown that users exhibit different search intent on mobile than desktop. For example, personal entertainment is the most popular category on mobile.

While much has been revealed from the aforementioned reports, we still believe that it is valuable to re-visit this problem with the latest data. As suggested in the Yahoo! report [24], the authors discovered that mobile search pattern is still evolving, in terms of query distribution they studied. One reason to support that is the query length: Yahoo! reported an average of 3.05 query length on mobile in 2008, which turns out to be 2.93 (for iPhone) and 2.44 (for mobile) in Google's 2009 report, indicating that users continue to change their search and reformulation behavior.

Moreover, at the time the above reports were written, tablet PCs were not so popular. However, with the debut of Apple's iPad in 2010, the usage of tablets for search has soared drastically in the past three years. It is reported that as of March 2012, over 30% of US users have one or more tablets [2]. Therefore, in this paper, we also analyze the behavior of tablet searchers in order to update the mobile search picture with this important missing piece.

Specifically, we make the following contributions:
• We collect search engine logs with over 1 million users for a period of three months (August 2012 to October 2012) from Bing desktop and mobile search engine, where we restrict our study to be English queries in the en-US search market. The mobile search logs include cell-phone users while desktop logs contain both desktop and tablet users.
• We perform a series of thorough and rigorous analysis

on mobile search behavior, in terms of time distribution, search locality, query categories, click patterns, browse patterns and so on, where we also compare with previous studies.

• Based on the results which revealed noticeable differences in mobile and tablet search patterns, we propose a novel knowledge transfer framework to train new rankers for mobile and tablet search results by leveraging a set of novel device-specific features, as well as incorporating the training labels from desktop data to improve the search relevance.

2. RELATED WORK

In this section, we review the literature of mobile search behavior in recent years. Although there has been many related work on mobile search [17, 5, 9, 19, 10, 11, 20, 18], we decided to primarily focus on the study after 2007 since the screen of smart phones have drastically changed after the appearance of iPhone in January 2007, which is one of the primary devices we analyze in this paper.

Kamvar and Baluja were among one of the earliest to report a large-scale study of mobile search statistics using over 1 million randomly sample queries from Google's mobile log in early 2007 [13]. They explicitly compared the search behavior in 2007 to those of 2005, and found out that users tended to enter a query faster in 2007 due to the availability of high-end devices. They discovered that query length increased from 2.3 in 2005 to 2.6 in 2007. They also found out that, surprisingly, the click through rate, i.e., percentage of queries that had one or more clicks, had dramatically increased from less than 10% to over 50%. Their study also revealed more tail queries issued during 2007, as well as a larger portion of adult queries in mobile devices.

In 2008, Church et al. [8] reported a study on European mobile search logs, using 6 million queries from 260,000 search engine users over a period of 7 days. In their study, query length appeared to be similar for both desktop and mobile searchers, who also exhibited similar click patterns via focusing on top-ranked results. The query categories, or topics, however, appeared to be quite different, where adult queries consisted of over 60% of all queries, followed by email-related queries and personal entertainment queries. Their data also demonstrated a larger portion of navigational and transactional queries in mobile logs, consisted of 60.4% and 29.4%, respectively.

In [24], the authors studied Yahoo! mobile search logs during a period of 2 months in the second half of 2007, containing both US searchers and international searchers. They explicitly studied three user interfaces of mobile applications: Yahoo! oneSearch XHTML/WAP interface, Yahoo! Go for Mobile, and Yahoo! SMS Search. The authors have observed that personal entertainment was the most popular query category, after filtering out adult and spam queries. Comparatively, US searchers often issue longer queries with more words than international searchers, resulting more tail queries in the US search logs. At the same time, international searchers have larger diversity in terms of search intent, as indicated by the query topical distributions. Finally, the authors concluded that mobile search was still evolving, based on the inconsistency observed from a variety of studies.

The study in [14] by Kamvar, Kellar, Patel and Xu was among the first to make explicit comparison between iPhone users and other mobile users. They used the data from Google mobile logs with a period of 35 days in the summer of 2008, which contains over 100,000 queries issued by over 10,000 searchers. Their study revealed several interesting aspects. First, queries issued by iPhone users had similar length with desktop searchers (2.93), but significantly shorter for other mobile searchers (2.44). Second, iPhone searchers also exhibited similar query categories with desktop users, both of which were more diverse than mobile searchers. In terms of session statistics, the authors discovered that desktop users have the most queries per session, followed by iPhone then mobile users, indicating a possibility that the information needs were more diverse on desktop and iPhone, whereas mobile users were more likely to issue simple navigational queries with a more focused intent.

The authors in [15] studied user behavior in terms of abandoned queries in both mobile and PC search. The objective of the study was to approximate the prevalence of good abandonment, i.e., queries that lead to satisfied user information need without clicks. In three locales, US, JP and CN, the authors discovered that on mobile the portion of good abandonment is significantly higher than PC search. In particular, for the US search market, the highest rate of good abandoned queries were primarily from local, answer and stock search, which was different from the other two markets. The study suggested that query abandonment should not be treated as negative signal uniformly, instead both the locale and modality should be considered when categorizing abandoned queries into good and bad.

More recently, Teevan et.al [23] addressed the issue of local search on mobile devices, in which they conducted a survey on 929 mobile searchers. The authors claimed that the mobile local search experience differed a lot from desktop due to the limitation of the device, and therefore affected user search behavior for local-related information. Particularly, location (geographic features) and time (temporal aspects) played an important contextual rule in user's search behavior. Users are more likely to search for locations that are close to their relative locations. Besides, users are more likely to initiate a local search during a specific time period.

Nevertheless, among all the aforementioned work we covered, none of them had studied the search behavior on tablet PCs such as iPad. In what follows, we will analyze the differences between mobile phone users and tablet users in a variety of aspects, as well as comparing to desktop searchers.

3. DEVICE AND DATA SET

Due to the availability of different types of mobile devices in terms of screen size and network capacity, it becomes difficult to study user behavior across different platforms. Thus we are unable to draw conclusions that are applicable to all types of devices. Consequently, we restrict our study by focusing on two devices that are most popular on the market, i.e., iPhone and iPad. The other reason is due to the consistent screen size of iPhone, which has not changed since its first generation[1], neither has iPad. Therefore, it is much more convenient and reliable to study the user search experience on these two devices.

In this paper, the data we use is from two different sources of Bing search logs. iPhone users who visit Bing are presented with Bing mobile search interface (http://m.bing.com), while iPad users are experiencing the same search interface

---

[1] For iPhone 5, users see the same number of search results as other iPhone users but two more extrac lines.

	Mobile (iPhone)	Tablet (iPad)	Desktop
Total Queries	9,732,938	8,423,111	13,928,038
Total Users	1,233,720	1,153,270	1,181,000

Table 1: The data sets used in this paper. The first row represents total query volume and the second row are number of unique users.

	Mobile	Tablet	Desktop
Number of words	3.05	2.88	2.73
Number of characters	18.93	18.02	17.44

Table 2: Average Query Length.

Category	Mobile	Tablet	Desktop
Adult	23.5%	5.6%	5.0%
Autos	2.4%	2.7%	2.1%
Celebrity	8.3%	4.5%	3.0%
Commerce	8.6%	11.6%	7.7%
Finance	0.4%	1.0%	1.0%
Health	1.7%	2.3%	1.7%
Image	42.0%	25.8%	19.9%
Local	10.3%	11.5%	9.1%
Maps	0.1%	0.3%	0.3%
Movie	1.6%	0.9%	0.8%
Music	3.4%	2.3%	2.3%
Name	7.3%	4.8%	3.6%
Sports	5.7%	4.8%	3.8%
Navigational	15.4%	32.6%	36.9%

Table 3: Query Categorization Distribution.

as desktop searchers (http://www.bing.com) but on a smaller screen. We distinguish iPhone and iPad users from other mobile users by filtering based on the request agent and the platform. We extract a sample of three months search logs in the United States search market, during August 2012 to October 2012 for iPhone, iPad and desktop users, respectively. We then sub-sample roughly 1,000,000 users for each of the logs based on their unique user id string. Finally, we filter out non-English queries and consider only sessions that start from the Web vertical. Table 1 presents the overall statistics.

Note that from now on, "mobile" explicitly means "mobile phones" in our description, as to be distinguished from "tablet". We will also be using terms "mobile" and "iPhone", "tablet" and "iPad", interchangeably.

4. USER BEHAVIOR ON MOBILE & TABLET

In this section, we analyze the differences between mobile and tablet searchers in a variety of aspects, including search time, location, query categorization, clicks and etc.

4.1 Query Distributions

In this section, we provide query statistics including query length, query categorization and etc for the three platforms.

4.1.1 Query Length

Table 2 summarizes the query length in terms of words and characters for mobile, tablet and desktop, respectively. We observe that mobile users in general issue longer queries than tablet and desktop users. The average number of words for mobile is 3.05, which is identical to Yahoo!'s report [24] and slightly larger than Google's report (2.93) [14]. The length of tablet queries is shorter than mobile but longer than desktop, an average of 2.88 words and 18.02 characters per query.

The inconsistency of query length among various reports can be attributed to many reasons. e.g., the evolving of user typing behavior, the diversity of query intent on different platforms and so on. Among all these aspects, we believe that query auto-suggestion plays an important role. We discover that in our data set, query reformulation rate is almost identical on three platforms. However, mobile users are more likely to rely on auto-suggestion for query reformulation, perhaps due to the difficulty of typing [14], where often longer queries are suggested by the Bing search engine. On the other hand, since tablet users experience the same search interface as desktop users, it is hence not surprising to see the query length to be similar on these two platforms.

4.1.2 Query Categorization

To analyze the query categorization for each device, we use a multiple-class classifier which categorizes a query into over 80 different categories. Our classifier works slightly different than previous ones [24, 14] in the sense that we use a different taxonomy than others, e.g., we do not have an "Entertainment" category but similar ones like "Celebrity" or "Game". Additionally, our classifier also allows one query to be classified into more than one categories, e.g., query "Michael Jackson" is categorized into both "Celebrity" and "Name" categories.

Table 3 lists the top-14 categories and their corresponding query distributions. Different from previous reports [14], we see a significant difference in iPhone categories than desktop categories, while the difference between iPad and desktop is much less comparatively.

In general, mobile users are much more likely (23.5%) to issue adult-content queries than tablet and desktop users, which aligns with the fact found previously. Mobile users are also over two times more likely to search for celebrity. Also, 42% of the queries on mobile contain image-intent, where those queries trigger image answers on search result pages. Noticeably, desktop only consists of 19.9% image-intent queries. The most surprising finding for mobile queries, however, is the percentage of navigational queries, i.e., 15.4%, which is much less than iPad (32.6%) and desktop (36.9%). This discovery is interesting and also truth-telling. Our hypothesis is that, after digging into the data, for the iPhone platform which has a quite mature app market, developers have already released corresponding apps for those navigational queries such as the facebook app for query "facebook" and amazon app "amazon". As a consequence, with those free and powerful apps in hand, iPhone users are more likely to directly use the apps for their tasks, instead of resorting to search engines to find the corresponding sites. Since navigational queries are in general shorter than informational queries, this further explains why iPhone users have longer query length as shown in Table 2.

On the other hand, iPad users exhibit different query category distributions than desktop in primarily two classes: local and commerce. First, our data confirms the findings

	Mobile	Tablet	Desktop
Mobile	/	58	47
Tablet	58	/	63
Desktop	47	63	/

Table 4: Top-100 Query Overlap on three platforms.

in [14] that for local-intent queries, only 1.2% more local queries were issued from iPhone users than desktop computers (1.7% in previous report). Surprisingly, iPad users have the largest percentage of local queries (11.5%) among all three, which could attribute to the fact that they use the map application more often than iPad and computer users [14]. Secondly, we observe that iPad users exhibit noticeably stronger shopping intent by searching for more commerce-related topics (11.6%) than the other two platforms.

Quantitatively, by normalizing the overall probability distribution to sum up to 1 and calculating the Kullback–Leibler (KL) divergence, we observe that desktop and mobile have the largest divergence in query distribution with a score of 0.31, followed by the score between tablet and mobile of 0.21. Tablet and desktop in overall exhibit quite similar query distributions with a KL score of 0.07.

Additionally, we list in Table 4 the number of overlapped queries for the three platforms, by comparing the top-100 most frequent queries from each of them. Comparatively, mobile and desktop share only 47 common queries, the least among all three pairs, while tablet and desktop have overlapping on 63 top queries. These statistics are consistent with the KL divergence score listed above.

4.2 Usage Time Distribution

So what time of the day do users use their mobile phones and tablets for search? Figure 1 illustrates the query volumes as a distribution of the time of the day. Not surprisingly, the majority of desktop search occurs during normal working hours from 8AM to 5PM. Meanwhile, as we can see, mobile search volume continues to rise starting from 5AM till 10PM of the day, and then declines during midnights. On the other hand, tablet usage shows a fairly different pattern. The search volume of iPad maintains relatively low during normal business hours, i.e., from 7AM to 5PM. It then rises sharply from 6PM to 10PM, which peaks at 7PM with over 9% of the traffic of the day. It is interesting to see that the increase of iPad search activities during the night compensates for the steep decline of the desktop search volume at the same time period.

Furthermore, we are interested in the distribution of query categorization at different time of the day. To do so, we separate one day into four groups with each group of 6-hour duration. Table 5 lists the top-3 query categories for each platform during the day. We omitted the *night group* (1AM to 6 AM) here since the search volume is not significant to draw a distribution. Overall, mobile searchers exhibit much diversified information need at different time of the day. While showing image and navigational-related intent during the mornings, mobile searchers are more likely to issue local queries in the afternoons, adult and music queries during the evenings. For tablet users, local queries have been observed as one of the top-3 categories throughout the day, whereas commerce-related queries start to emerge in the afternoon and evening groups. In contrast, desktop searchers

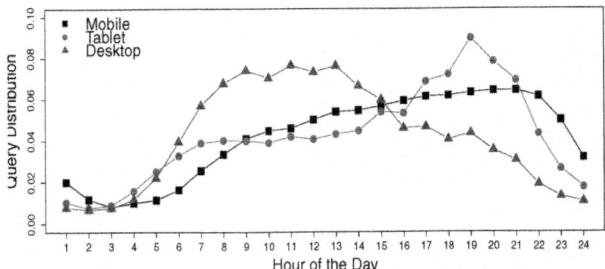

Figure 1: The time distribution of usage in terms of search volumes for three platforms.

	Mobile	Tablet	Desktop
Morning (7-12)	Image	Navigational	Navigational
	Navigational	Image	Image
	Name	Local	Local
Afternoon (13-18)	Local	Local	Navigational
	Celebrities	Commerce	Local
	Image/Name	Image	Name
Evening (19-24)	Adult	Navigational	Navigational
	Music	Commerce	Local
	Sports	Local	Commerce

Table 5: Break down of top query categorization by time of the day.

are always more interested in issuing navigational queries than the other two platform users, and exhibit a fairly stable information need throughout the day.

4.3 Location of Usage

Next, we analyze the location where search activities happen for mobile and tablets. As previous reports indicated, tablets are mostly used on couches and beds [3]. Therefore, we hypothesize that in terms of *mobility*, iPad users do not move as frequently as iPhone users, who can basically perform search at any location they go to during the day. To validate our assumption, we sub-select a sample of 2,000 users from the data sets in the Seattle area. For the mobile and tablet logs, we were able to extract the longitude and latitude of the location where the user query was issued. Each of the geo-location is mapped to its nearest city as well, e.g., "Redmond, WA", "Bellevue, WA" etc.

Table 6 lists some statistics regarding location changes during the three-month logs we collected. Overall, mobile users searched from 4.52 different cities on average, while table users only traveled to an average of 1.79 cities. Note, it does not mean that on average a mobile user only appeared at 4.52 different places when performing search, since multiple geo-locations can be mapped to the same city name. Instead, the second row of the table shows how much distance (in miles) users traveled: on average mobile searchers were recorded to travel over 118 miles while tablet users only traveled for less than 50 miles. The percentage of users who never traveled, i.e., all search requests came from the same city, also shows significant difference between two types of devices. For mobile, less than 10% of users stay in one city, while the number is 3.7 times more for tablet users. Since

	Mobile	Tablet
Cities Visited	4.52	1.79
Distance Traveled (mi)	118.75	49.91
% users never traveled	9.54%	37.23%
% queries issued at home	43%	79%

Table 6: Statistics on location changes.

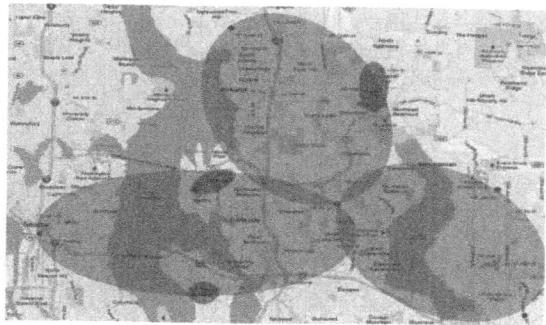

Figure 2: The locations where users performed search. Blue eclipses correspond to mobile searchers while red eclipses mean tablet searchers.

	Mobile	Tablet	Desktop
Number of queries in Session	1.48	1.94	1.89
Session Duration(min)	7.62	9.32	8.61
(Filtered) Session Duration(min)	8.25	12.78	10.22
Daily Number of Sessions	1.79	1.42	1.95

Table 7: Session statistics. Filter sessions are sessions without abandoned queries.

	Mobile	Tablet
SERP DwellTime (sec)	−20.54	+87.35
Avg Click Position	+0.54	−0.04
Answer CTR	+0.07	+0.02
Algo CTR	−0.20	−0.08
Click Entropy	+0.14	−0.05

Table 8: Click statistics are shown as relative numbers comparing to the desktop search numbers.

we do not know exactly where the "home" of a user locates, we simply treat the city that most queries were issued for that user as his/her home. By doing that, we observe that mobile users indeed issued queries at many more different locations than tablet users: 43% of queries issued at home versus 79%, which nearly doubled.

Figure 2 illustrates an example of three mobile users and three tablet users, respectively. We use eclipses to approximate the perimeters that cover the cities in which users traveled, where blue corresponds to mobile and red to tablet users. Clearly, the eclipses for mobile users cover much larger diameters than tablet users, who merely traveled to very nearby locations around their home.

4.4 Sessions and Clicks

In this section we analyze user session and click characteristics. We use the conventional definition of sessions in our analysis: a session contains user activities including query, query reformulation, URL clicks and so on. Sessions are grouped based on user IDs which are unique for each user. A session ends if there is no user activity for 30 minutes or longer. Each session is also assigned with a unique ID. The duration of a session is defined as the difference of timestamps between the last and first activity.

4.4.1 Session Duration and Engagement

Table 7 shows several basic statistics of sessions. Since a large portion of the sessions contain only abandoned queries, i.e., sessions with only one query but no clicks [15], we want to distinguish these sessions from others so we report numbers with and without these sessions. We first observe that mobile sessions contain the least number of queries (1.48), and therefore the shortest session duration of 7.62 minutes (8.25 filtered) among all three. iPad users, however, spent longer time than desktop and iPhone users with an overall 1.94 queries per session and 9.32 minutes (12.78 filtered) in each session. Despite longer session time, iPad users have in general the least number of sessions in a day (1.42). This could be explained by the fact, as also shown in Figure 1, that most iPad search happened during night time between 7PM and 9PM so that the queries issued during that time are more likely to be in the same sessions. Comparatively, desktop users have more search sessions in a day than mobile and tablet which is expected since desktop still has the largest search volume.

4.4.2 Click Distributions

Next, we examine the differences in search result clicks. Note that our data is collected from Web vertical only. However, since Web vertical sometimes also shows image, video or local results, we group these non-algorithmic clicks to be *answer clicks* in our analysis.

In Table 8, we illustrate basic click statistics. Due to the sensitivity of the click data, we decide to report relative numbers here which use the number from desktop search as baseline comparison. Our first observation comes from SERP dwell time, where mobile searchers spent 20 less seconds examining the result page than desktop searchers. Meanwhile, tablet users exhibited much stronger interests in examining the SERP, 87 seconds more than desktop searchers. These numbers further confirm our results in Table 7 regarding the overall session duration time. In terms of click position, we observe that mobile searchers are more likely to click results that rank lower, an average increased position of 0.54. Tablet users, however, show no significant difference than desktop with similar click position (-0.04).

The click through rate (CTR) is an important metric used to measure search relevance. We can see from Table 8 that both mobile and tablet searchers are more lean to click on answers rather than algorithmic results (i.e., the ten blue-links). Specifically, mobile users have demonstrated 7% more CTR on answers but 20% less CTR on algo results, whereas tablet searchers are 2% more likely to click answers but 8% less willing to click algo results. Finally, the click entropy scores [22] indicate that on mobile, the clicks are more spread out with a higher entropy score, whereas on tablets clicks are often concentrated on top results, similar to that of desktop clicks.

Mobile	Tablet	Desktop
youtube.com	youtube.com	facebook.com
en.wikipedia.org	en.wikipedia.org	yahoo.com
answers.yahoo.com	amazon.com	en.wikipedia.org
ehow.com	msn.com	youtube.com
imdb.com	ebay.com	walmart.com
amazon.com	imdb.com	ebay.com
wiki.answers.com	ehow.com	amazon.com
chacha.com	facebook.com	mail.google.com
facebook.com	craigslist.org	aol.com
myspace.com	itunes.apple.com	craigslist.org

Table 9: Top-10 click domains.

	CTR for Knowledge Base Sites on		
Query	Mobile	Tablet	Desktop
hotmail	2.5%	0.8%	0.3%
microsoft	16%	11%	2.0%
usa	33%	23%	14%
facebook	3.5%	2.7%	0.2%
louis vuitton	4.3%	1.5%	0.0%

Table 10: CTR for knowledge base sites such as Wikipedia, Yahoo! answers and etc. Mobile and tablet users are much more likely to click on those sites than desktop searchers.

4.4.3 Click Intents

The previous results include user clicks on both answers and algorithmic results. Since we see a significant difference on algo result clicks, we will focus on click patterns only on algorithmic results in this section.

We first list the top-10 most clicked URL domains in Table 9. It is interesting to see that the top-two clicked domains on desktop (i.e., facebook and yahoo), have both been replaced by youtube and wikipedia sites on mobile and tablet. The results again reflect our discovery in Table 3, but from the perspective of clicks, that mobile and tablet both have lower navigational-type queries and therefore users are less likely to click on those sites where iPhone and iPad apps are already available.

Next, we can also clearly observe that on tablet, shopping-related sites such as amazon, ebay and craigslist are ranked much higher than desktop and mobile. This is also consistent with Table 3 where we show that tablet users in general have higher percentage of commerce-related queries.

Perhaps the most interesting discovery in Table 9 is those highly-ranked *knowledge base* sites on tablet and mobile, especially on mobile. In particular, we observe that among the 10 most popular sites on mobile, 6 of them (Wikipedia, Yahoo! answer, ehow, etc.) are knowledge base sites. Consequently, the click distributions of traditional navigational queries have changed accordingly on mobile and tablet platforms. For example, for the query "louis vuitton", desktop searchers clicked on the first result and went to its official site with over 0.7 CTR. However, this number dropped to 0.66 for iPad and 0.54 for iPhone searchers. In turn, iPad and iPhone users clicked more frequently on the Wikipedia page of *Louis Vuitton*, with CTR of 1.5% and 4.3%, respectively, even that the page is ranked at the bottom of the search results. Even for the query "facebook" that has the strongest navigation intent among all queries, mobile and tablet still possess 3.5% and 2.7% CTR on the Wikipedia page, respectively. Table 10 lists some example queries and their CTRs on knowledge base sites for mobile, tablet and desktop respectively. We have noticed that our findings concur with some recent studies as well [21, 7].

5. IMPROVE RANKING ON MOBILE AND TABLET

From the analysis we have performed in the previous section, we have clearly observed different user search behavior on both mobile (iPhone) and tablet (iPad) than desktop users, in terms of query categorization, click intent, time and location of search and etc. Consequently, due to the diversity of search intent, mobile and tablet users have incurred a significantly lower click through rate (CTR) on algorithmic results as shown in Table 8, due to the factor of using a unified ranker on all three platforms.

To further improve the search relevance for mobile and tablet users, we propose to optimize the (algorithmic) search results by (1) incorporating new features that consider a variety of search aspects including time, location, intent and so on, (2) adopting the existing relevance labels from desktop search to train new rankers, as inspired by [4, 6].

5.1 New Features for Mobile and Tablet

Inspired by the analysis in previous section, two sets of features are derived in our framework. Specifically, query attributes features measure the characteristics of the query itself, across three devices and at different time of the day. On the other hand, URL relevance features estimate the importance of URLs given a particular query. Table 11 lists the features and the equations to calculate them.

5.1.1 Query Attributes Features

q-prob(Query|d) and **q-prob**(Query|t) measure the query frequency on a particular device d at time t of the day, where d is the one of the three devices we considered here: mobile, tablet and desktop. t is a numerical value indicating the time windows of the day, which is split into four groups (morning, afternoon, evening and night), similar as shown in Table 5.

q-prob-cross(Query|d) and **q-prob-cross**(Query|t), on the other hand, measure the cross-device and cross-time probability of a query. Comparatively, **q-prob**(Query|d) estimates how important the query is comparing to *all other queries issued on the same device*, whereas **q-prob-cross**(Query|d) judges how likely this query is issued *on that particular device rather than other two devices*. Likewise for t. These four features together demonstrate the overall importance of a query in the entire data set.

CTR(Query|t, d) signals the search intent of users when they are interested in the particular query. The higher the CTR is, the more likely users are clicking on related URLs. The CTR is estimated by averaging over CTRs on all return URLs for the query during time t on device d in the data set.

Entropy(Query|t, d) calculates the entropy of a given query. This is also a signal to measure the popularity of the query during different time of the day, given a particular device d.

5.1.2 URL Relevance Features

KL(Class(Query), Class(U)) measures the topical closeness between the query and the URL. As we mentioned before, our classifier assigns each query (as well as a URL) into one or more of the 80 categories, which is essentially a probability distribution over all topics. The smaller the KL score is, the more likely the query and URL are related.

click-prob(U|Query, t, d, loc) considers the probability a URL gets clicked when a user issues the query at time t on device d and at a specific location loc. We specify the location parameter at two levels: *city* and *state*. To be concrete, we assign each city a unique ID and calculate **click-prob**(U|Query, t, d, city). Likewise for the state level. At these two different granularities, we measure the locality effect of the URL clicks.

Comparatively, **loc-prob**(U|loc) is a query-independent metric that calculates the overall locality effect of a URL. Similarly, **Entropy**(U|loc) also measures how likely the URL gets clicked at location loc. These two features are also parameterized with two different location levels: city and state. Likewise, we also include query-independent features for time and device, which have similar equations and therefore omitted from Table 11.

Since we have discovered that mobile and tablet users are more likely to click on knowledge base sites, we propose a feature to take that into consideration. Specifically, **wiki-prob**(U) calculates the probability of a sites to be knowledge base, according to the frequency the site is clicked. We maintain a list of over 30 knowledge base sites including Wikipedia, Freebase, Yahoo! answers, eHow and etc.

5.2 Improve Ranking via Knowledge Transfer from Desktop Search

With the new features derived in the previous section, we are ready to train a ranking model to improve the relevance on mobile and tablet. One way to achieve this goal is to leverage the learning-to-rank framework [16] by collecting judgement labels for individual query-URL pairs to form a training set, and use the domain-specific features in Table 11 to train a ranker. However, this approach seems suboptimal due to the expensive cost of acquiring human labels. In particular, it is very labor-intensive and cost-ineffective to gather labels on mobile and tablet platforms, especially in our scenario where each query-URL pair can generate multiple labels according to different time, location and device. Consequently, the cost could go exponential to the number of query-URL pairs and make this approach unable to scale.

On the other hand, human judgement labels for desktop search are available in abundance on many benchmark data sets, e.g., TREC, LETOR [16] and etc. These data sets, along with a rich set of textual features such like BM25, term frequency and etc, facilitate the work of training rankers for desktop search using different machine learning methods.

Therefore, our objective is to leverage the labels and content-features from desktop search, combining with a few labels from mobile and tablet as well as their domain-specific features, to train new rankers for the two new domains. Our framework is greatly inspired by the work in [4] and [6]. The general idea is to simultaneously use the source (desktop) and target (mobile and tablet) domain training data during the learning process, where the training data from the target domain is difficult to acquire while the data from source domain is available in abundance. These two domains, however, share certain common features, and therefore we can learn a low-dimensional representation so that the features from both domains can be projected to. In [4], the authors have shown that this problem can be formulated as a 1-norm regularization problem that provides a sparse representation for multiple domains. Furthermore, in [6], the authors have proven that for learning-to-rank, the same problem can be transformed into an optimization framework which can be solved by using Ranking SVM [12], after certain transformation of the training data.

Formally, we are given three sets of training data D_d, D_m and D_t, which correspond to desktop, mobile and tablet respectively. These data sets share the same feature space $w \in \mathbb{R}^d$, which can be broken down into two parts. The first part contains k features $[w_1, ... w_k]$ that are common features available on all domains (e.g., BM25, document length and etc). The second half of features $[w_{k+1}, ..., w_d]$ are domain-specific features which are only available on mobile and tablet domains. The learning objective is to minimize the pair-wise loss on all three domains. Specifically, for each domain, given a set of training data $D = \{x_i\}_1^m$, we form a set of pair-wise preferences $S = \{(x_{i1}, x_{i2})\}_1^n$, where each pair indicates a preference relationship of $x_i \succ x_j$, which can be determined, for example, using human labels. Using Ranking SVM as a learning framework, we can assume the learning function to be linear, e.g., $f(x) = \langle w, s \rangle$, where $s_i = x_{i1} - x_{i2}$ is a new training sample by subtracting the feature values of x_{i2} from x_{i1}. The label y_i of s_i is 1 if $x_i \succ x_j$ and -1 otherwise. This way we form a set of new training data $S' = \{s_i, y_i\}_1^n$ solvable by Ranking SVM.

Algorithm 1 sketches the learning process of how to minimize the pair-wise loss for three domains. Our algorithm is similar to the CLRank algorithm in [6]. The major difference is that we apply the learning to three domains instead of two which was the case in [6]. The general idea is to find a lower-dimensional representation of the three feature vectors, by performing SVD on D, which represents the covariance matrix of the model weights, or how many common features these three domains share.. The training instances are then transformed into this low dimension and trained using Ranking SVM. After training, the original feature weights are updated by transforming back the weights into its original dimension. The matrix D is also updated with the new W. This algorithm runs in iterations and stops when some criteria are met, e.g., the covariance matrix D is no longer showing significant change.

6. EXPERIMENTS ON RANKING

In this section, we conduct rigorous experiments to assess the performance of ranking mobile and tablet algorithmic results using domain-specific features and the CLRank algorithm. The data sets used for ranking is the same as the ones we perform user behavioral analysis, as shown in Table 1. To gather the desktop training data, we ask human assessors to manually label each query-URL pair with 5-point Likert scale: Perfect (5), Excellent (4), Good (3), Fair (2) and Bad (1). Each query-URL pair is given to three human assessors and we apply majority vote to get its final label. Overall, we randomly select 3,500 query-URL pairs from the 1 million queries used in our study for judgement.

On the other hand, as mentioned above, for mobile and tablet, it is difficult to collect human labels because each query-URL pair can have different ratings depending on the

Type	Feature
Query Attributes	**q-prob**(Query|d) = $\frac{cnt(Query\|d)+\lambda_{qd}}{\sum_q cnt(Query\|d)+\lambda_d}$
	q-prob-cross(Query|d) = $\frac{cnt(Query\|d)+\lambda_{qdc}}{\sum_d cnt(Query\|d)+\lambda_{cd}}$
	q-prob(Query|t) = $\frac{cnt(Query\|t)+\lambda_{qt}}{\sum_q cnt(Query\|t)+\lambda_t}$
	q-prob-cross(Query|t) = $\frac{cnt(Query\|t)+\lambda_{qtc}}{\sum_t cnt(Query\|t)+\lambda_{ct}}$
	CTR(Query|t, d) = avg [**CTR**(U|Query, t, d)]
	Entropy(Query|t, d) = -**q-prob**(Query|t, d) $*$ log **q-prob**(Query|t, d)
URL Relevance	**KL**(Class(Query), Class(U)) = $\sum_c \log\left(\frac{P_c(Query)}{P_c(U)}\right) P_c(Query)$
	click-prob(U|Query, t, d, loc) = $\frac{cnt(U\|Query,t,d,loc)+\lambda_{qtdl}}{\sum_{q'}\sum_{t'}\sum_{d'}\sum_{l'} cnt(U\|Query,t,d,loc)+\lambda_{qtdl'}}$
	loc-prob(U|loc) = $\frac{cnt(U\|loc)}{\sum_{l'} cnt(U\|loc)}$
	Entropy(U|loc) = -**loc-prob**(U|loc) $*$ log**loc-prob**(U|loc)
	wiki-prob(U) = $\frac{cnt(U)*\mathbb{I}(\mathbf{IsWiki}(U))}{\sum_{u\in List(wiki)} cnt(u)}$

Table 11: List of query-attribute and URL-relevance features used for ranking. All the λ's are smoothing parameters that are estimated from the data set.

Algorithm 1 The CLRank algorithm

1: **Input**: Three training set converted to Ranking SVM format $S^d = \{s_i^d, y_i^d\}_1^{N_d}$, $S^m = \{s_i^m, y_i^m\}_1^{N_m}$, $S^t = \{s_i^t, y_i^t\}_1^{N_t}$, Parameter γ for Ranking SVM
2: **OUTPUT**: ranking models on original features $W = [w_d, w_m, w_t]$
3: Initialize covariance matrix $D = \frac{I_{d\times d}}{d}$;
4: **while** not converge **do**
5:   **for** $m = 1$ to M
6:   Do SVD on D, so that $D = P^T \Sigma P$;
7:   Multiply all feature vectors in S^d, S^m and S^t with $\Sigma^{\frac{1}{2}} P$, get three new training data sets $S^{d'}$, $S^{m'}$, and $S^{t'}$
8:   Run Ranking SVM on these data sets to get feature weights u_d, u_m and u_t;
9:   Transform $w_d = P^T \Sigma^{\frac{1}{2}} u_d$, $w_m = P^T \Sigma^{\frac{1}{2}} u_m$, $w_t = P^T \Sigma^{\frac{1}{2}} u_t$;
10:   Set $D = \frac{(WW^T)^{1/2}}{trace(WW^T)^{1/2}}$
11: **end while**

---

time, location, device and etc. As a result, we resort to user clicks as *pseudo labels* for mobile and tablet. We count all clicks for each query-URL pair which is parameterized by time, location and device. For each query, we assign the same 5-point labels to URLs according to the descending order of the click counts. Overall, we collect 5,000 such query-URL pairs for mobile and tablet, respectively – a total of 10,000 training examples.

For each training instance, we generate 400 content-based features such like BM25, document length [16], along with the 20 domain-specific features proposed in Table 11.

6.1 Baseline Comparisons and Metrics

To be more convincing, we compare with several baseline methods in order to show the superior of our proposal.

Baseline 1: the default ranking model of mobile and tablet – the same ranker as the desktop search. Here we do not modify anything but just report the default score.

Baseline 2: content-based features plus new domain-specific features. i.e., we train Ranking SVM models for mobile and tablet respectively, using the new 5,000 training instances described in the previous section.

Baseline 3: knowledge transfer without new features. Train CLRank algorithm on three domains with the original 400 content-based features. This model is similar to our final ranker except that it does not leverage the domain-specific features proposed in Table 11.

Note that for both baseline 1 and baseline 2, two separate rankers need to be trained respectively for mobile and tablet. While for baseline 3, as well as our final ranker, only one optimized model will be outputted, i.e., the W matrix on line 2 of Algorithm 1, which contains feature weights for all three domains.

For evaluation, we employ two classic metrics: MAP@K and NDCG@K. MAP calculates the mean of average precision scores on all queries in the test set. NDCG score, on the other hand, takes both the 5-scale relevance score and the position of the relevant documents into consideration. In our experiments, we report results for both $K = 1$ and 3.

6.2 Experimental Results

To report experimental results that are statistically meaningful, we randomly separate the 10,000 labeled data of mobile and tablet into two parts for training and test at 1:1 ratio, where the test set is withheld only for evaluation. We repeat this process 20 times and report the average performance. To determine the optimal value of the only parameter γ in the CLRank algorithm, we perform a 5-fold cross validation on the training set, and find out $\gamma = 0.15$ to be the optimal value.

Table 12 compares the overall performance of the four methods on mobile and tablet, in terms of MAP and NDCG scores respectively. In general, we see that both baseline 2 and baseline 3 make noticeable improvement over the default baseline 1. In comparison, baseline 3, which applies the knowledge transfer framework (CLRank) without new features, slightly outperforms baseline 2 which only uses the new features to train new rankers. As mentioned previously, baseline 3 leverages the CLRank model that jointly optimizes the rankers for all three domains, instead of training separate rankers for each domain as used by baseline 2. This comparative result indicates the potential superiority of using existing labels from other domains to enhance the current ranking system of the target domain.

	Mobile				Tablet			
	MAP@1	MAP@3	NDCG@1	NDCG@3	MAP@1	MAP@3	NDCG@1	NDCG@3
Baseline 1	0.3725	0.3981	0.2988	0.3584	0.2693	0.2986	0.2381	0.2949
Baseline 2	0.3746	0.4082*	0.3074	0.3782*	0.2711	0.3001	0.2579*	0.3183*
Baseline 3	0.3843	0.4123	0.3076	0.3799*	0.2854*	0.3129*	0.2894*	0.3281*
Our Method	0.4226**	0.4526**	0.3412**	0.3985**	0.2973**	0.3285**	0.3189**	0.3498**

Table 12: Overall performance of three baseline methods and our framework in MAP and NDCG. Our method outperforms all baseline methods, where * indicates p-value < 0.05 and ** means p-value < 0.01.

On the other hand, when combining the domain-specific features with the labels from desktop training data, we have observed significant performance improvement of our method comparing with all the baselines, with statistical significance level at p-value < 0.01 for all the metrics. Overall, our framework improves around 5% for both MAP and NDCG on mobile ranking baseline 1, whereas for tablet, the improvement is less (3%) but still quite significant comparing to other baselines.

In previous experiments, we limit the use of desktop training data to be 3,500. It would be helpful to analyze the performance change when that part of data becomes more/less. Consequently, we run a series of experiments by using only a certain portion of the desktop data for knowledge transfer, ranging from 500 to 3,500 instances.

Figure 3 illustrates the MAP and NDCG changes in terms of the training data size. Note that neither baseline 1 nor baseline 2 leverages training data from desktop, their performance is therefore not affected as demonstrated by the horizontal lines. Overall, we observe that for both baseline 3 and our method, more desktop data indeed helps improving the performance. More specifically, for the mobile domain, we see a dramatic increase of MAP and NDCG scores when the data increases from 500 to 1,000. The performance is then stabilized after 2,000 instances and only minor improvement can be observed beyond that. Comparatively, we notice that for the tablet domain, the performance increase is almost linear to the number of desktop training data, where it shows no sign of stopping even when all 3,500 training data has been utilized. Therefore, the tablet domain may potentially benefit more if we can provide more than 3,500 labeled desktop data in this scenario.

Next, we illustrate the performance improvement within different query categories. In Figure 4, we show the improvement in terms of the MAP@3 scores by our method over baseline 1. Among all 14 categories, our algorithm improves mostly on navigational, local and map queries. As we discussed before, for navigational queries, mobile and tablet users tend to click more on the knowledge base sites. Therefore, by leveraging the domain-specific features to improve the ranking of these sites, we successfully increase the MAP score for those navigational queries. Comparatively, we also observe that tablet has less MAP@3 improvement. In particular, queries in adult, movie and name categories benefit little from our algorithm. It could be the reason that these queries are more informational, where user intents are more diversified and therefore more difficult to optimize.

Finally, we also break down the metrics based on the time of the day as discussed in Section 3, as shown in Table 13, which indicates the relative improvement of our CLRank algorithm over the default baseline method. We see that in

	Mobile		Tablet	
	MAP@3	NDCG@3	MAP@3	NDCG@3
Morning	0.082	0.032	0.028	0.053
Afternoon	0.126	0.065	0.021	0.032
Evening	0.097	0.043	0.055	0.074
Night	0.031	0.027	0.015	0.036

Table 13: MAP and NDCG improvement based on the time of day. The numbers mean the absolute difference between our algorithm and baseline 1.

general, mobile gains the most improvement during afternoons and evenings, whereas tablet has the biggest jump in evenings. Since the majority of the search traffic is from afternoons (for mobile) and evenings (for mobile and tablet) as illustrated in Figure 1, we can clearly see the benefit of using our algorithm over the existing systems.

7. DISCUSSIONS AND CONCLUSIONS

The objective of our query analysis study was to reveal the user behavior difference between mobile, tablet and desktop searchers by using the latest log data from a commercial search engine. More importantly, our research aimed at filling the gap between mobile and desktop search by taking tablet user behavior into consideration, which we found missing in the previous studies of mobile search [24, 14]. We provided quantitative statistics on a variety of aspects for mobile and tablet search which were later used to guide the improvement of search result ranking on them. Our study on the three-month Bing mobile and desktop logs disclosed various points that were different from previous studies. The following is a few key discoveries from our study:

- The query length on mobile continues to change. Our study showed an average of 3.05 words per query for mobile and 2.88 for tablet, both of which are longer than desktop. Comparing to the numbers from Yahoo! (3.05) and Google (2.93), this number seems to change all the time. Therefore, we think that the usage patterns are still evolving.

- The distribution of query categories was different between mobile, tablet and desktop in certain categories. Specifically, tablet users were more likely to issue commerce and local queries, while mobile users issued more adult, celebrity and image queries. One important finding in our study was that both mobile and tablet users issued significantly less navigational queries than desktop users, due to the wide availability of mobile apps on these two platforms.

- The distribution of usage time was also different on three platforms. While desktop users performed search mostly during working hours (8AM to 5PM), mobile and tablet

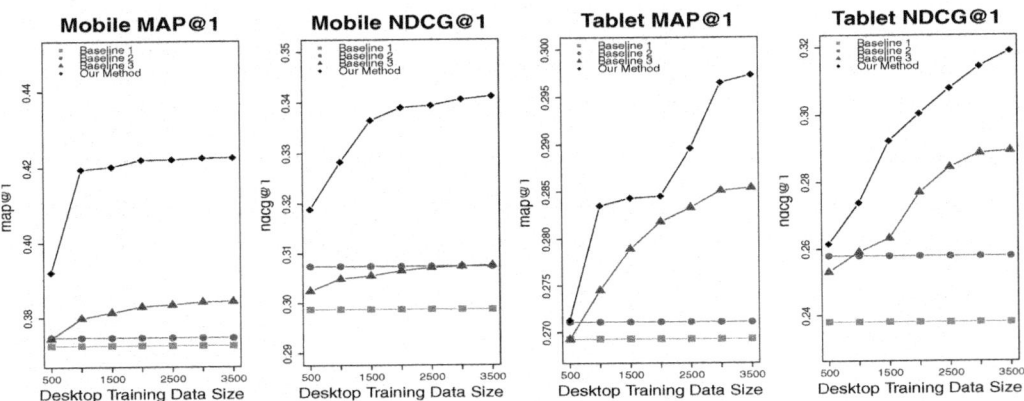

Figure 3: MAP@1 and NDCG@1 change in terms of the desktop training data size, which is used in the knowledge transfer algorithm (CLRank) to boost the performance of mobile and tablet.

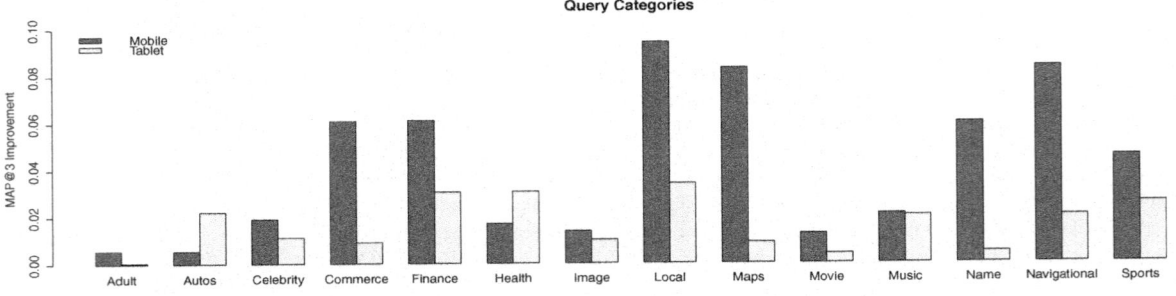

Figure 4: MAP@3 improvement by our algorithm over baseline 1 in 14 query categories.

usages peaked during evenings (6PM to 10PM). We also revealed that during different time of the day, mobile and tablet users had more diverse search intent than desktop, where the latter seldom changed throughout the day.

• The location of usage was quite different between mobile and tablet. Overall, mobile users tended to travel a lot more than tablet users and issued queries at a variety of locations. For tablet users, 79% of queries were issued at home, whereas only 43% mobile users issued queries at their home locations.

• Interestingly, mobile and tablet users tended to click more on knowledge base sites like Wikipedia, even for very top navigational queries such as "facebook" and "hotmail". This discovery can help us better understand user click intent which may eventually lead us to re-train the query classifier for mobile and tablet.

• Merely using traditional content-based features to rank search results on mobile and tablet can lead to suboptimal performance. We observed a significantly lower CTR on these two platforms while using the default ranker from desktop. We therefore proposed a set of domain-specific features to address the limitation of features from desktop. By leveraging a knowledge transfer algorithm (CLRank) that used training data from all three domains simultaneously, we eventually saw a significant performance improvement on mobile and tablet. This study revealed that (1) domain-specific features were important for mobile and tablet relevance. Even with only 20 new features, we have witnessed a 5% and 3% relevance improvement for mobile and tablet, respectively, and (2) human labels from desktop can be leveraged to improve the rankers for other domains as well. A joint optimization on three rankers work better than optimizing rankers for different domains individually, especially when these domains share some common features.

Overall, we have observed that tablet users have distinguished themselves from desktop and mobile users with quite different user behavior and intent. It is therefore suggested that when performing user behavior analysis or designing relevance algorithms, tablet should be treated as a separate device rather than merge it with either desktop or mobile.

There is still a lot left to be done in the future. Our study covered two most widely used mobile and tablet devices (iPhone and iPad) on the market. However, with the choice of smart devices becomes more and diversified nowadays, it is important to take user behavior on all different devices into consideration to get a complete picture to draw unbiased conclusions. In the future, we plan to extend our work to cover more smart devices such as Android tablets, Microsoft Surface, iPad Mini and so on. A comparison between these tablet users may yield different outcomes than what have been observed in this paper. On the other hand, since we have observed that more and more users tend to click on answer results besides the algorithmic results, we will also be interested in extending our knowledge transfer algorithms beyond algorithmic results, by also adopting answers and ads into the framework.

8. REFERENCES

[1] Mobile search volume more than doubles year-on-year. http://www.smartinsights.com/search-engine-optimisation-seo/seo-analytics/mobile-search-volume-more-than-doubles-year-on-year/.

[2] Survey: 31 percent of u.s. internet users own tablets. http://www.pcmag.com/article2/0,2817,2405972,00.asp.

[3] What you need to know about targeting ipad and tablet searchers. http://searchengineland.com/what-you-need-to-know-about-targeting-ipad-tablet-searchers-109685.

[4] A. Argyriou, T. Evgeniou, and M. Pontil. Multi-task feature learning. In *Advances in Neural Information Processing Systems 19*. MIT Press, 2007.

[5] R. Baeza-yates, G. Dupret, and J. Velasco. A study of mobile search queries in japan. In *In Query Log Analysis: Social and Technological Challenges, WWW 2007*, 2007.

[6] D. Chen, Y. Xiong, J. Yan, G.-R. Xue, G. Wang, and Z. Chen. Knowledge transfer for cross domain learning to rank. *Inf. Retr.*, 13(3):236–253, June 2010.

[7] K. Church and N. Oliver. Understanding mobile web and mobile search use in today's dynamic mobile landscape. In *Proceedings of the 13th International Conference on Human Computer Interaction with Mobile Devices and Services*, MobileHCI '11, pages 67–76, New York, NY, USA, 2011. ACM.

[8] K. Church, B. Smyth, K. Bradley, and P. Cotter. A large scale study of european mobile search behaviour. In *MobileHCI 2008*, pages 13–22, New York, NY, USA, 2008.

[9] K. Church, B. Smyth, P. Cotter, and K. Bradley. Mobile information access: A study of emerging search behavior on the mobile internet. *ACM Trans. Web*, 1(1), May 2007.

[10] Y. Cui and V. Roto. How people use the web on mobile devices. In *Proceedings of the 17th international conference on World Wide Web*, WWW '08, pages 905–914, New York, NY, USA, 2008. ACM.

[11] R. Hinman, M. Spasojevic, and P. Isomursu. They call it surfing for a reason: identifying mobile internet needs through pc internet deprivation. In *CHI '08 Extended Abstracts on Human Factors in Computing Systems*, CHI EA '08, pages 2195–2208, New York, NY, USA, 2008. ACM.

[12] T. Joachims. Optimizing search engines using clickthrough data. In *KDD 2002*, pages 133–142, 2002.

[13] M. Kamvar and S. Baluja. Deciphering trends in mobile search. *Computer*, 40(8):58–62, Aug. 2007.

[14] M. Kamvar, M. Kellar, R. Patel, and Y. Xu. Computers and iphones and mobile phones, oh my!: a logs-based comparison of search users on different devices. In *WWW 2009*, pages 801–810, New York, NY, USA, 2009.

[15] J. Li, S. Huffman, and A. Tokuda. Good abandonment in mobile and pc internet search. In *SIGIR 2009*, pages 43–50, New York, NY, USA, 2009.

[16] T.-Y. Liu. Learning to rank for information retrieval. *Found. Trends Inf. Retr.*, 3(3):225–331, Mar. 2009.

[17] Y. Lv, D. Lymberopoulos, and Q. Wu. An exploration of ranking heuristics in mobile local search. In *Proceedings of the 35th international ACM SIGIR conference on Research and development in information retrieval*, SIGIR '12, pages 295–304, New York, NY, USA, 2012. ACM.

[18] H. Mueller, J. L. Gove, and J. S. Webb. Understanding tablet use: A multi-method exploration. In *Proceedings of the 14th Conference on Human-Computer Interaction with Mobile Devices and Services (Mobile HCI 2012)*, 2012.

[19] H. Müller, J. Gove, and J. Webb. Understanding tablet use: a multi-method exploration. In *Proceedings of the 14th international conference on Human-computer interaction with mobile devices and services*, MobileHCI '12, pages 1–10, New York, NY, USA, 2012. ACM.

[20] S. Nylander, T. Lundquist, and A. Brännström. At home and with computer access: why and where people use cell phones to access the internet. In *Proceedings of the SIGCHI Conference on Human Factors in Computing Systems*, CHI '09, pages 1639–1642, New York, NY, USA, 2009. ACM.

[21] C. A. Taylor, O. Anicello, S. Somohano, N. Samuels, L. Whitaker, and J. A. Ramey. A framework for understanding mobile internet motivations and behaviors. In *CHI '08 Extended Abstracts on Human Factors in Computing Systems*, CHI EA '08, pages 2679–2684, New York, NY, USA, 2008. ACM.

[22] J. Teevan, S. T. Dumais, and D. J. Liebling. To personalize or not to personalize: modeling queries with variation in user intent. In *SIGIR 2008*, pages 163–170, 2008.

[23] J. Teevan, A. Karlson, S. Amini, A. J. B. Brush, and J. Krumm. Understanding the importance of location, time, and people in mobile local search behavior. In *MobileHCI 2011*, pages 77–80, New York, NY, USA, 2011.

[24] J. Yi, F. Maghoul, and J. Pedersen. Deciphering mobile search patterns: a study of yahoo! mobile search queries. In *WWW 2008*, pages 257–266, New York, NY, USA, 2008.

Evaluating and Predicting User Engagement Change with Degraded Search Relevance

Yang Song
Microsoft Research
One Microsoft Way
Redmond, WA
yangsong@microsoft.com

Xiaolin Shi
Microsoft Bing
One Microsoft Way
Redmond, WA
xishi@microsoft.com

Xin Fu[*]
LinkedIn Corporation
2029 Stierlin Court
Mountain View, CA
xin.fu.2007@gmail.com

ABSTRACT

User engagement in search refers to the frequency for users (re-)using the search engine to accomplish their tasks. Among factors that affected users' visit frequency, relevance of search results is believed to play a pivotal role. While multiple work in the past has demonstrated the correlation between search success and user engagement based on longitudinal analysis, we examine this problem from a different perspective in this work. Specifically, we carefully designed a large-scale controlled experiment on users of a large commercial Web search engine, in which users were separated into control and treatment groups, where users in treatment group were presented with search results which are deliberate degraded in relevance. We studied users' responses to the relevance degradation through tracking several behavioral metrics (such as query per user, click per session) over an extended period of time both during and following the experiment. By quantifying the relationship between user engagement and search relevance, we observe significant differences between user's short-term search behavior and long-term engagement change. By leveraging some of the key findings from the experiment, we developed a machine learning model to predict the long term impact of relevance degradation on user engagement. Overall, our model achieves over 67% of accuracy in predicting user engagement drop. Besides, our model is also capable of predicting engagement change for low-frequency users with very few user signals. We believe that insights from this study can be leveraged by search engine companies to detect and intervene search relevance degradation and to prevent long term user engagement drop.

Categories and Subject Descriptors

G.3 [**Probability and Statistics/Experimental Design**]: controlled experiments, randomized experiments, A/B testing; H.4.m [**Information Systems**]: Miscellaneous

General Terms

Measurement, Design, Experimentation, Prediction

---

[*]Work done at Microsoft Bing.

Copyright is held by the International World Wide Web Conference Committee (IW3C2). IW3C2 reserves the right to provide a hyperlink to the author's site if the Material is used in electronic media.
WWW 2013, May 13–17, 2013, Rio de Janeiro, Brazil.
ACM 978-1-4503-2035-1/13/05.

Keywords

search quality, search relevance, user engagement, longitudinal analysis

1. INTRODUCTION

As Web search engines have become a necessity in our daily lives, the *relevance* of search engine results has undoubtedly become the deterministic factor for search engines like Google, Bing, Yahoo! and etc. to declare their successes and compete for query market share. For the past decade, researchers and practitioners have never stopped working towards improving search engines' relevance, by leveraging state-of-the-art methods from communities like machine learning, data mining, natural language processing and so on. These restless efforts have brought tremendous success to search engine companies with noticeable advances in search result relevance. According to a recent report by Experian[1], the *search success rate* for Yahoo!, Bing and Google were 81%, 80% and 66%, respectively.

Although it seems to be common sense that the better a search engine's relevance is, the more likely that users will engage with it (i.e., come back to search more often), it has come to our attention that few research effort has been spent to study the relationship between search relevance and user engagement. Until very recently, Hu et al.[6] proposed to characterize the relationship between *search success* and search engine reuse by measuring the correlation between changes in search satisfaction ratio and the rate of return. A positive correlation was identified between these two variables, which truly indicates that search success can lead to higher user engagement rate.

In this paper, we propose to study search relevance and user engagement from a ranking perspective, and in a more controlled environment. Despite the existence of many factors that can potentially influence search relevance, such as snippet quality, domain bias [7], the quality of the ranking algorithm is by far the most dominant component that determines a search engine's relevance score. We therefore isolate ranking from all other factors to better understand the change of user engagement from a longitudinal perspective.

On the other hand, our study tries to look at the correlations between these two variables from a different perspective than previous work [6]: how user engagement changes when the ranking algorithm suddenly becomes *worse than*

---

[1]http://www.experian.com/hitwise/press-release-experian-hitwise-reports-google-share-of-searche.html

before? While most existing research aims at improving the ranking algorithm, and most user engagement analysis is conducted in the environment where users succeeded their search objective, we, however, believe that *search failure* can potentially lead to engagement changes which is more complicated to understand and therefore should not be ignored. The momentum for this study is quite straightforward: search engine companies nowadays make changes to their ranking algorithms on regular basis. Before releasing a new ranking algorithm, it is common sense to first test it on a small portion of user basis, which is widely known as randomized experiments or A/B tests [10]. Apparently, not all changes can lead to an improved ranking algorithm in practice but may possibly hurt user experience and turn users away. It is therefore essential to understand the user behaviors under this scenario and make proper adjustments, e.g., performing early-termination of a bad ranking experiment, promptly.

Specifically, this paper makes the following contributions: We present a longitudinal study on a large amount of users from the logs of a widely-used commercial Web search engine. These users are enrolled in a carefully designed experiment in which the changes were *only* made to the ranking algorithm such that the ranking results look worse than before, while all other elements on the search result page stay the same. We then perform deep analysis on user engagement changes by studying the user behavior data at session-level, user-level as well as query-level to fully understand the root causes of user behavior changes.

Given the user engagement numbers over time, we propose a machine learning model to predict engagement changes, i.e., whether a user will come back more/less often in the future. To be concrete, we leverage a set of features such as the average length of user queries, the portion of queries that has no clicks and so on, and use these features to train an SVM model to make binary predictions for each user's *weekly* engagement change.

The rest of the paper is organized as follows: Section 2 discusses Related Work; Section 3 presents the details of our controlled experiments and the data collected; Section 4 performs deep analysis on the data; Section 5 proposes the model to predict user behavior changes; we conclude our paper and discuss potential future work in Section 6.

2. RELATED WORK

Our study is based on a large-scale controlled experiment of a commercial search engine. In the industry of online services, designing online experiments to test the impact of changes of products or services with large amounts of real users has been an extremely important problem [19]. Among many approaches, online controlled experiments have been widely adopted, as this type of experiments have the advantages of having best scientific design for establishing a causal relationship between changes and their influence on user-observable behavior and providing the first-hard feedback from large volumes of online users directly [10].

There has been extensive study on online user behavior that is related to information seeking and navigation. Most of such study uses recorded user search data [8], which can provide us with rich signals about different aspects of user behavior. For example, by studying clickthrough data, we are able to evaluate and monitor user satisfaction toward the relevance of a search engine [16, 20]. We can also have a good estimation on users intent [8] or how much they are frustrated with their search [5]. Previous research has also found that, by tracking user search behavior over time, such behavior could be well modeled and predicted [3, 15]. Moreover, some longitudinal study on user search behavior suggests that there are two classes of users: navigators and explorers [21]. In this work, we show that user behavior in the virtual world of information search, similar to behavior in many other real-world social and ecology systems [18], is also highly adaptive with regard to the change of this information system.

The main focus of user behavior in our study is user engagement in search, which directly ties to the market share of a search engine. It is believed that in many other forms of products and brands, customer satisfaction has a strong influence on the loyalty and market share [1, 14]. However, only very recently researchers started investigation on the relationship between user engagement and their satisfaction toward the service provided by search engines [6]. One significant difference between the research of user engagement and loyalty in the use of search engines and other products lies in that, it is a complicated problem of defining the usage of a search engine. This is because the frequency of issuing queries is not equal to the frequency of accomplishing tasks in information search, as users may issue multiple queries to accomplish one task [13, 11]. Moreover, we should be aware that, in real business, the long-term user behavior do not always align with short-term behavior, and this problem is particularly prominent in user engagement in search [10]. Thus, unlike [6], which only considers user usage on the query level, we focus more on the task or session level in terms of user engagement in this paper.

3. EXPERIMENT DESIGN AND DATA COLLECTION

In this work, we conducted an A/B testing user experiment on a widely-used commercial Web search engine in the US search market, from Jan 2011 to March 2011 for a total of 47 days. Two randomized buckets of users, of approximately equal size, were chosen as the *control* and *treatment* groups, whereas for the control group, the ranking algorithm remains the same as before. For the treatment group, we deliberately released an inferior ranking algorithm which has shown to have worse relevance scores in terms of NDCG scores [9] – approximately 3-point NDCG loss. To be more concrete, we used an old ranker with a less sophisticated machine-learning model and a different set of features. Almost 100% of queries were affected, i.e., showing different or re-ordered top-10 results between control and treatment. Figure 1 shows an example. For the query "yahoo email", we can clearly observe the differences between control and treatment results. For control, the ideal ranking is preserved where the #1 result is indeed what users look for. However, for users in the treatment group, they suffered from a totally weird list of ranked results: the official yahoo homepage was ranked first, followed by an ehow page and a wikipedia page, both of which are somewhat irrelevant. The fourth result looks like the desired page at the first glance, but unfortunately it turns out to be misleading too. Notice that although here we say that 100% of queries have different top-10 results, what we really mean is that *at least* one result in top-10 are different. Therefore, many of the queries, especially top navigational ones, still show the same top-3 or top-5 results in both control and treatment. In the next section, we shall examine the impact of *truly* degraded queries to users in more details.

Overall, a total of 2.2 million users were enrolled in this experiment. After the finish of the experiment, we collected user session data from the logs. By our definition [6], a user session is a sequence of user search activities, including user queries, clicks on the search results and so on. A session ends when the user becomes inactive for 30 minutes or more. Users are anonymized by given a randomly generated user id for each user.

Let's define a metric named percentage delta, which is used throughout this paper to measure the difference of any metric between treatment and control:

$$\%\Delta(f) = \frac{f(Treatment) - f(Control)}{f(Control)} \times 100\% \quad (1)$$

Here f can be any arbitrary metric, e.g., session per user, click through rate and so on (details in next session). In our study, we notice a significant difference between the number of active days of users in treatment (4.500 days) vs. control (4.515 days) (whose % Δ is -0.335% with p-value 0.004), where a user is defined as active if he/she issued one or more queries on that day. However, there is no significant difference between the range of active days of users in treatment and control (both are around 11 days on average), which is defined as the date difference between user's first active day and last active day. For example, two users u_1 and u_2 are active on days $\{1, 2, 3, 4, 15\}$ and $\{1, 15\}$ of the experiment, respectively. Both of them have 15 as their range of active days, while u_1 has 5 active days but u_2 has only 2. These facts reveal that, the quality change of search engine has effect on the users' frequency of usage; however, we don't see there is a higher rate of abandonment when the search quality gets worse.

4. USER ENGAGEMENT ANALYSIS

We focus on three aspects of user analysis in this section: (1) treatment/control comparison in terms of several key metrics, (2) affected user analysis, i.e., how user engagement changes before and after users were exposed to bad relevance results, and (3) degree of affect analysis: quantifying engagement ratio changes across user groups characterized by the number of bad search results experienced.

4.1 Overall Engagement Changes Over Time

If we consider the search engine as an ecosystem, it is expected to see that users change their behavior accordingly once this ecosystem, i.e. the quality of the search results, changes. In this part, we investigate the overall user search behavior change with regard to the change of the search environment with a deliberate setback. In generally, search related user behavior can be classified into three categories:

a. **Types of queries users issue**. This type of behavior is performed before a user seeing the search result of the current query. Queries can be classified according to different criteria, such as navigational queries vs. informational queries, head queries vs. tail queries and short queries vs. long queries [2, 12].

b. **User's satisfaction toward the search results**. This type of behavior shows users' reaction toward the search result of the current query. Behaviors such as how quick the users click the search results and how soon they issue the next queries are strong signals showing users' satisfaction.

c. **User's engagement in search**. This type of behavior indicates the usage frequency and how frequently users using or reusing the search engine in order to accomplish their search tasks. From the following analysis, we will see that the short-term and long-term engagements are very different.

By studying the three types of user search behaviors, we aim to answer the following two questions: 1, what are the temporal patterns of user search behavior when the search quality changes? 2, how do different search behaviors correlate with each other? Especially, how do other behaviors correlate with the long-term user engagement?

Therefore, we focus on examining the following key metrics in our study (the type in square bracket indicates the type of user behavior mentioned above):

- [c] **Average daily sessions per user (S/U)**: $\frac{\sum_u S(u)}{|u|}$, where $S(u)$ indicates user u's daily session number and $|u|$ is the total number of users on that day.

- [b] **Average unique queries per session (UQ/S)**: $\frac{\sum_s UQ(s)}{|s|}$, where $UQ(s)$ represents the number of unique queries within session s, and $|s|$ the total number of sessions on that day.

- [b] **Average session length per user (SL/U)**: the total number of queries within a session, averaged over each user.

- [a] **Percentage of navigational queries per user (%-Nav-Q/U)**: there exists many methods for this type of classification [2, 12]. We propose a simple method by looking at click positions: if over $n\%$ of all clicks for a query is concentrated on top-3 ranked URLs, this query is considered to be navigational. Otherwise it is treated as informational. Here we empirically set n to be 80.

- [a] **Average query length per user (QL/U)**: the query length measures the number of words in a user query.

- [b] **Average query success rate per user (Q-Success/U**: a user query is said to be successful if the user clicks one or more results and stays at any of them for more than 30 seconds [6].

- [b] **Average query Click Through Rate (CTR)**: the CTR for a query is 1 if there is one or more clicks, otherwise 0.

- [b] **Average query interval per user (QI/U)**: the average time difference between two consecutive user queries within a user session.

While S/U indicates the user engagement ratio, the remaining metrics measure the user satisfaction as well as their effort spent to complete user's search task, and therefore can be categorized as *relevance* metrics.

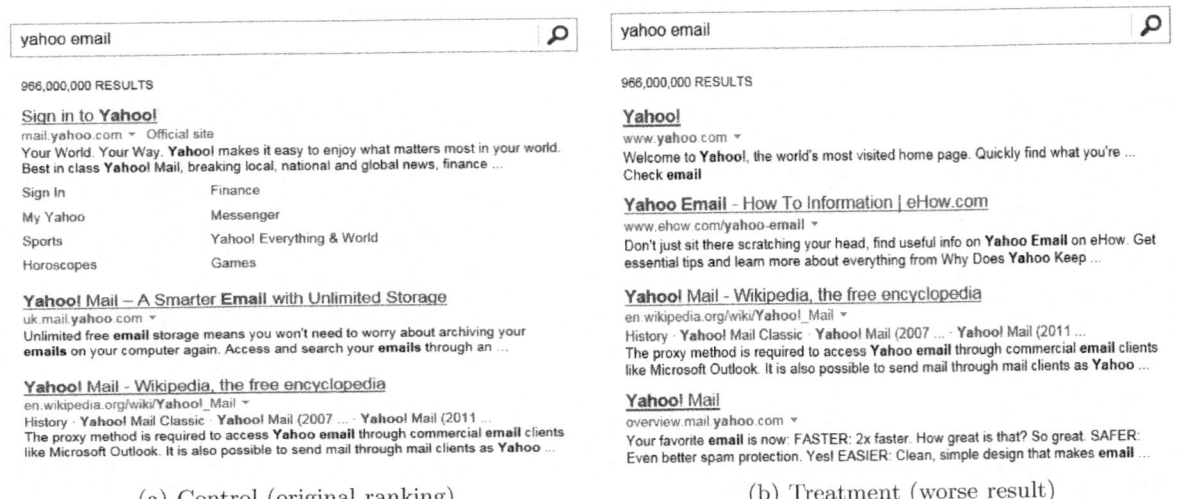

(a) Control (original ranking) (b) Treatment (worse result)

Figure 1: Example query of "yahoo email" and the ranking differences between control and treatment.

We first examine the user engagement change by looking at S/U and UQ/S. Rather than comparing treatment and control groups on a daily basis, we propose to use *accumulated numbers* to better capture the metric changes from a longitudinal perspective. For example, to compare S/U on the K's day since the starting of the experiment, we aggregate user sessions from day 1 to day K for each user, and calculate the difference between treatment and control using unpaired (two sample) t-test.

The accumulated results of these two metrics are shown in Figure 2. With the treatment group having a worse relevance algorithm, we initially expect to see a noticeable drop of S/U in treatment in the first few days, resulting in a dip in t-stat that may reach significance level (t-stat $\leq$ -1.96) very quickly. However, in contrast with common sense, we see that S/U in treatment actually went up quite a bit for the first three days, and then gradually decreased. The t-stat for S/U did not reach significance level until almost two weeks after the experiment. We also observe diminishing returns after two weeks for the rest of days.

On the other hand, UQ/S has shown significance from the very first day of the experiment, with t-stat $>$ 5 for the first few days. We have observed that UQ/S raised over 2% for treatment comparing to control (3.66 vs. 3.57) on day 1, and continue to stay at 1% for the first two weeks. This shows a clear sign that users in treatment group have spent more effort to complete their search tasks than users in control.

Next, we show the (non-accumulative) temporal change of user behavior related to their satisfaction with the search results and engagement in Figure 3. We measure the difference between treatment and control using eq.(1). In Figure 3(a), we see that the average query success rate drops significantly as soon as the search quality degrades, which means that user satisfaction toward their search results is an immediate indication of the change of search quality. Figure 3(b) shows the change of average query intervals. The time interval is also strongly correlated with user satisfaction due to the fact that if users are not satisfied with their current search results, they are very likely to reformulate the original queries within a very short period of time. Similarly, Figure 3(c) shows that after the search results get worse,

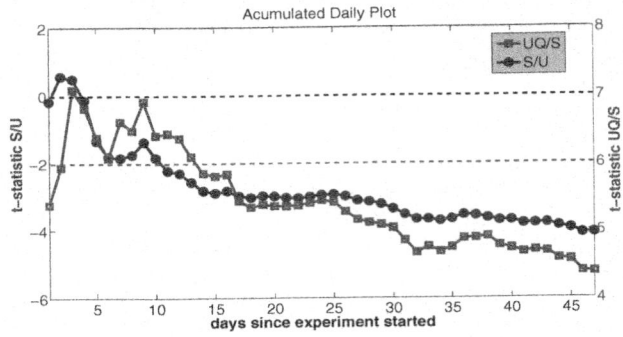

Figure 2: Accumulated daily plots for S/U and UQ/S. T-stats are shown on the left and right y-axis respectively.

the average session length increases. This again tells us that after the search quality gets worse, there are more queries within a session as it requires more efforts from the users to accomplish their search tasks.

Therefore, with user engagement metric S/U going up then down (↑ then ↓), relevance metric UQ/S going up (↑), and average session length going up a little bit (↑), what is really going on underneath these metric changes? There can be a few possible reasons: (1) users indeed come back less frequently, but issue the same type of queries day after day. Due to the deteriorated relevance, users need to formulate more frequently to complete same tasks as before; or (2) users still come back at the same rate as before, but however do not *trust* the search engine any more, and hence give easier tasks to it, e.g., by issuing more navigational queries. For more difficult tasks, users simply find other workarounds for example by switching to another search engine with better relevance results.

To find the exact answer for that, we perform a more fine-grained analysis on *affected* users in the next section.

4.2 Affected User Analysis

What we have observed in the previous section is the s-

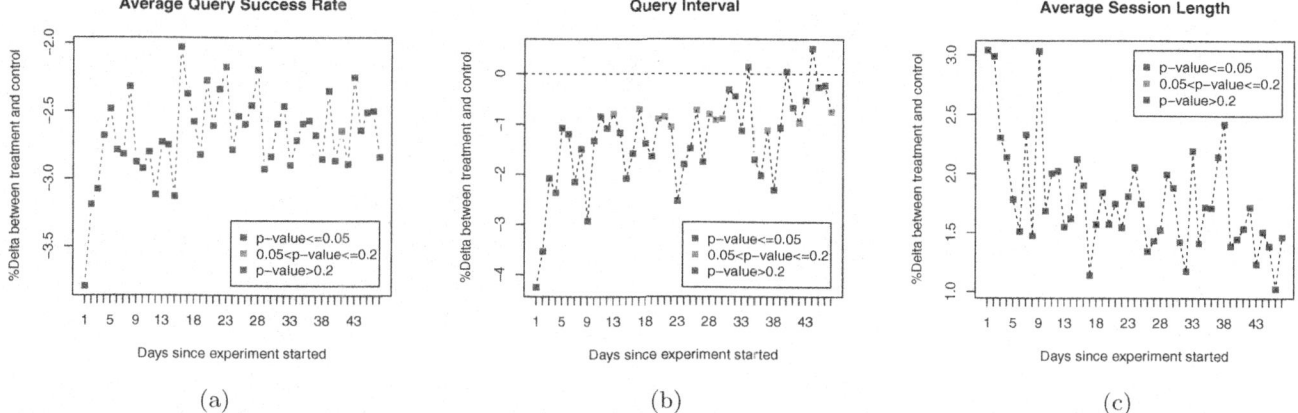

Figure 3: Daily change of behavior related to user satisfaction toward their search results and user engagement with search.

tatistics from overall users in both groups, which gives us some hints in terms of which direction those metrics developed. However, in this experiment we performed (as well as many other relevance-improvement experiments), though we claim that almost 100% of queries had different search results, only a small fraction of queries are *practically* involved, where their top-3 search results got re-ordered. Since most of the time, users are indeed only examine and click top-3 search results. As a result, many users were not truly exposed to results with bad relevance at all and their engagement changes are quite unnoticeable. Therefore, we only aim at studying behavioral changes for the group of affected users in this section.

We define the set of affected queries retrospectively. After the experiment was finished, we collected a set of queries that had been issued by users from both treatment and control groups. Within them, we isolated queries where the rankings of the results were different in treatment and control. We also filtered out queries with very low frequencies to make sure the difference was not caused by server instability. For each of these queries, we gathered top-10 results for treatment and control respectively. We then asked human assessors to evaluate the relevance of each result with respect to that query, in a 5-level Likert scale: Perfect (5), Excellent (4), Good (3), Fair (2) and Bad (1). We employed normalized discounted cumulative gain (NDCG) [9] to assess the relevance of a ranking result, where higher NDCG scores (between 0 and 1) indicate better relevance. With that, the set of affected queries is defined to have at least k difference ($k \in (0,1)$) between control and treatment, with control having higher score. The value of k balances the trade-off between the size of the query set and the discriminative power of the set, where a high value of k results in a smaller set but queries with larger NDCG differences. Note that since we are only interested in truly impacted users, we use NDCG@3 as the metric here.

We then define the set of affected users. A user is said to be affected if he/she issued at least one of the queries in the affected query set. To better interpret user behaviorial changes before and after the user was affected, we select users who were only affected *after* the third week of the experiment. We expect those users to behave similarly as

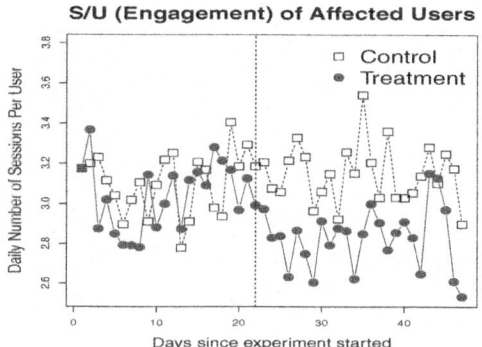

Figure 4: S/U change of the affected users in treatment and control. Users were affected on and after the 21st day of the experiment, indicated by the vertical dash line.

other non-affected users in the first three weeks, while exhibit different usage patterns after they were affected by bad relevance queries.

In our study, we empirically tried a number of k's for the affected query set but due to space limitation only $k = 0.6$ is reported here. We ended up having roughly 450 queries in the set. After filtering, 5,134 and 5,287 users were selected from treatment and control groups, respectively.

Figure 4 illustrates the change of user engagement in terms of S/U over time, where the vertical grey dotted line indicates the affected date[2]. During the first three weeks, no significant difference can be observed for the treated users. Nevertheless, once treated users were affected, we immediately notice substantial drop of engagement rate. The value of $\%\Delta(S/U)$ suggests a 5% drop during the first few affected days, and raises up to as high as 20% at peak.

On the other hand, UQ/U shows a similar pattern as S/U for the first three weeks, as demonstrated in Figure 5. However, as soon as treated users were affected, the number of

---

[2]Due to the sensitivity of data, all the absolute values reported in this paper have been linearly scaled.

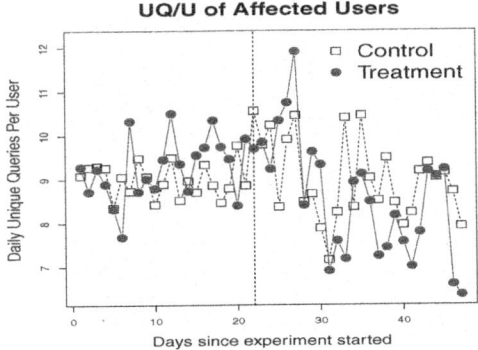

Figure 5: UQ/U change of the affected users in treatment and control. Users were affected on and after the 21st day of the experiment.

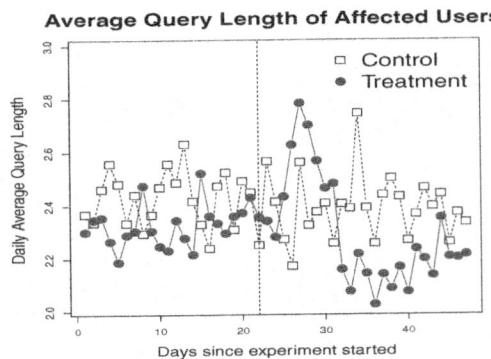

Figure 7: Average daily query length for affected users. Shorter queries are more likely navigational while longer queries are tail/hard queries.

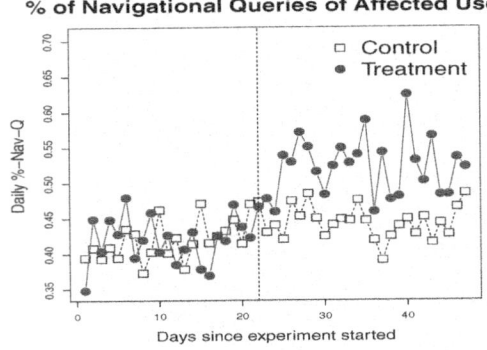

Figure 6: Query distribution change over time. Y-axis indicates the percentage of navigational queries users issued.

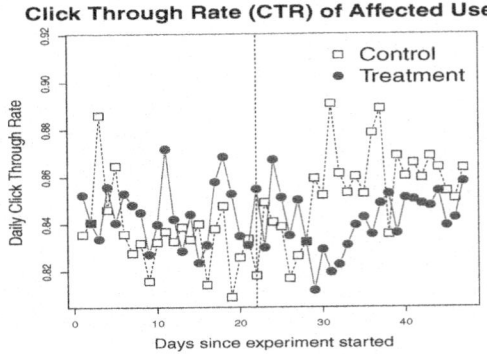

Figure 8: Change of CTR of impacted users. CTR first went up after the 21 day of experiment then suddenly dropped significantly.

unique queries they issued clearly went up for the next 6-7 days, which gradually decreased in the following weeks as UQ/U in treatment became less than that of controlled users. This further confirms the same findings as we found in the previous section: after initially affected by a relevance engine, users spent more effort on refining their queries to complete the same task, but gradually lost confidence so they came back less frequently.

Now that we know that user engagement decreases when exposed to a bad relevance engine, we want to further understand how that influence users' queries and clicks over time. To start with, we classify user queries into either navigational or informational [2, 12] as discussed in previous section. The distribution of query types is depicted in Figure 6. Before affected, both control and treatment users have roughly the same % of navigational queries — around 40% daily. After the affected point, we can clearly observe a soar of navigational queries merely after three days for those who got affected, which raised much as 64% on day 40.

We then examine the change of user query length. Previous research has shown that there is a high correlation between query length and its difficulty [17], i.e., navigational queries are mostly short queries (1 or 2 words), while tail queries are longer than head queries in general. With the relevance getting worse in treatment, we expect user-

s to issue easier queries than before. This assumption is confirmed in Figure 7. After initially affected, users started to reformulate their queries and therefore a sudden increase of query length is observed for the first week after affected. Users then gradually became inpatient and only issued short queries.

Last but certainly not the least, we quantify the changes in user clicks in terms of click through rate (CTR). In general, higher CTRs correspond to better user satisfaction. From Figure 8, we notice that CTR dropped substantially during the first week after treated users were affected, as they began to issue more queries to fight against bad relevance but eventually failed. Later, as those users started to issue more navigational queries, the CTRs gradually increased to a comparable rate to those of the controlled users.

We summarize these five findings for affected users in Table 2. Statistical significance test is conducted where the changes of the five metrics are all significant. Figure 10 also plots the %Δ changes for these five metrics on daily basis. Note that before the affected date, most of the date points are within $[-0.1, 0.1]$ range, meaning there is no big differences between treated and controlled users. On the other hand, after affected, we observe a lot of escalated points: treated users have as much as 40% more navigational

Metric	Before Affect	After Affect	%Δ(f)
S/U	3.0347	2.8238	7.47%*
UQ/U	9.2907	8.4752	9.62%**
% Nav Q	0.4237	0.5247	-19.25%**
Avg Q Len	2.3270	2.2908	1.58%*
CTR	0.8438	0.8356	0.98%*

Table 2: Summary of changes for the 5 metrics discussed before and after affected. Numbers here are for the affected users in the treatment group. *: p-val <0.05. **: p-val <0.01. *Values are linearly scaled due to sensitivity.*

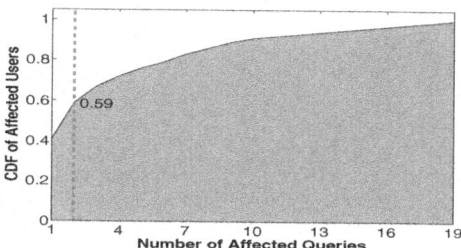

Figure 11: Cumulative Distribution Function of users in terms of affected queries.

Metric	Lightly-Affected	Heavily-Affected
S/U	2.8408	2.8077
*UQ/U	8.4871	8.4421
**% Nav Q	0.4929	0.5713
*Avg Q Len	2.3007	2.2863
*CTR	0.8407	0.8258

Table 3: Breakdown of metrics in two buckets of users based on the degree of affect. Except for S/U, all other metrics show statistical significance.

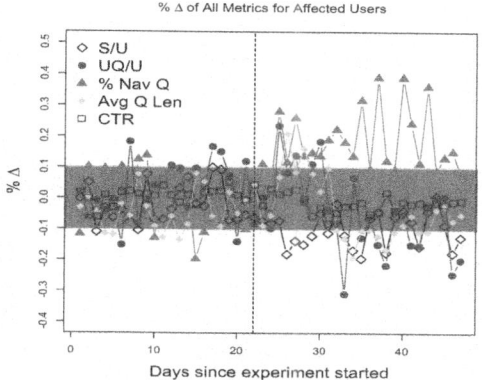

Figure 10: Daily changes for the 5 metrics before and after the affected date. Most metrics are not significant before affected date but turned out to be significant afterwards.

queries, 20% and 30% less daily sessions (S/U) and unique queries (UQ/U), respectively.

Examples of sessions are shown in Table 1 between treated and controlled users, where users started with the same query and ended up clicking on the same result. With these constraints, we assume that users have the same search intent. However, in these examples, we see that users in treatment spent significantly more effort in completing the same tasks, by issuing and reformulating more queries and clicking on more results. Figure 9 illustrates a randomly-chosen individual user whose engagement dropped during the experiment, where the y-axis shows the number of daily sessions. It is obvious that before affected, the user tended to issue more complicated informational queries. After affected, we observe that most of the queries were navigation-only queries. The S/U for that user dropped from 4.3 to 2.2, significantly.

4.3 Degree of Impact Analysis

In this section, we want to further confirm our findings in the previous section by dividing treated users into two buckets: heavily-affected users and lightly-affected users. Our assumption is that users who are exposed more often to bad relevance results should demonstrate stronger signals to the metrics we discussed, than those gently affected.

Figure 11 shows the cumulative distribution function (CDF) for users by affected queries. Since over half of the users were only affected by two or less queries, we use two as our cut-off to separate users into heavily-affected and lightly-affected users, respectively.

The comparative results are shown in Table 3. In general, our assumption is confirmed by the data: heavily-affected users exhibited stronger signals than lightly-affected users, with five metrics all pointing to the correct direction. Except for the S/U metric, the rest are all statistically significant. Specifically, heavily-affected users issued substantially more navigational queries (57.13%) than the other group (49.29%). The CTR of heavily-affected users also dropped from 0.84 to 0.82. Also, heavily-affected users are less likely to issue new queries as indicated by UQ/U (8.44 vs. 8.48).

5. PREDICT USER ENGAGEMENT CHANGE

For search engines, keep the users engaged is the key to their success. Now that we understand how users behave under the circumstance of bad relevance, we want to further leverage these signals to predict the change of user engagement in the future. To start with, we formulate this problem as a binary classification task using machine learning technique. Our primary objective is to quickly detect user session *decrease* in practical large-scale online experiments so that search engines can take actions properly.

5.1 Data Preparation

Specifically, we focus on predicting user *weekly* number of sessions, whether decrease (-) or increase (+). Due to the fact of session differences during weekdays and weekends (i.e., users issue more queries during weekdays than weekends), we decide to aggregate data to weekly level so that this weekday/weekend impact is minimized. However, we believe that our work can be easily adapted to predict daily session changes with the addition of some daily-based user features.

There are various ways to formulate the prediction prob-

Treatment		Control	
query	click	query	click
doc bao bao daily express doc bao express	docbao.com.vn www.express.co.uk **vnexpress.net**	doc bao	**vnexpress.net**
free credit report free annual transunion credit report federal free annual credit report	www.annualcreditreport.com /cra/index.jsp **www.ftc.gov/bcp/edu/ microsites/freereports/**	free credit report	**www.ftc.gov/bcp/edu/ microsites/freereports/**
grammy awards 2011 grammy awards 2011 live performances at grammys 2011 grammys 2011 performers	idolator.com/5766501/grammy- awards-2011-performances **www.grammy.com/news/ grammy-performers**	grammy awards 2011	**www.grammy.com/news/ grammy-performers**

Table 1: Examples of sessions in comparison. Users in treatment spent more effort for the same query intent than controlled users. Bolded URLs are desired pages.

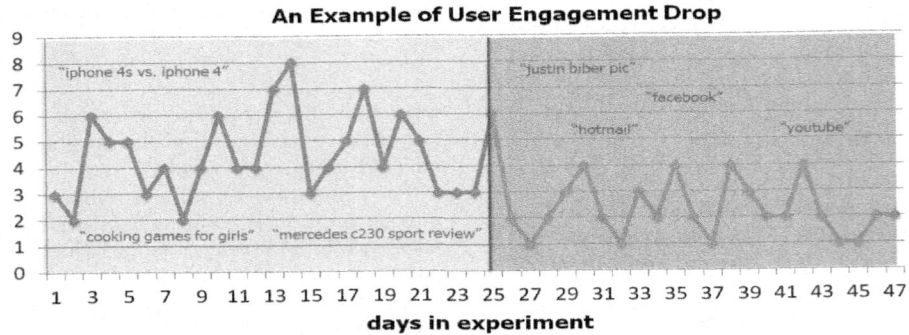

Figure 9: An example of user engagement drop before and after the user was affected in terms of daily session number. It is also clear that the user starts to issue more navigational queries after exposed to a bad relevance engine.

lem. Ideally, we would like to be aware of the engagement change as soon as possible, i.e., during the first week of the experiment. However, from a machine learning perspective of view, this approach is infeasible due to the lack of *training data*. Therefore, to make reasonable predictions, we are required to have at least one week training data to start with so that the best we can do is to predict the second week's engagement given the first week's signals. In what follows, we experiment with different amounts of training data: one with three week's training data and one with one week's training data. Since users who have three week's engagement are usually heavy users while users with one week data are often low-frequency users, these two experiments essentially measure the effect of degraded search relevance to heavy and low-frequency users, respectively.

5.2 Prediction for High-Frequency Users

From the experimental data, we filter users who have at least one activity during week 1, 2, 3 and 4 of the experiment. Data is aggregated to user level as the prediction is per use base. Prediction is made on week 4 by leveraging user data from week 1-3. A positive label is assigned if week 4's total session number is *more than* that of week 3. Otherwise a negative label is assigned. Overall, 77,940 positive instances and 54,470 negative instances are collected.

5.2.1 Classifiers

We experimented with a variety of classification algorithms, including logistic regression, boosted decision trees and linear Support Vector Machines (SVM) [4]. Among them, linear SVM demonstrated the best performance in terms of both classification accuracy and scalability. Therefore, we only report the results from linear SVM in our experiments.

5.2.2 Features

Table 4 summarizes the set of basic features we used, which covers both aspects of engagement and relevance. Some of them are closely related to the features used in the previous section. For example, *numSessions* is the same as S/U on a weekly basis; *numUnqQueries* equals weekly UQ/U; *numNoClickQueries* is correlated with CTR and etc.

We then derive a set of Δ-features based on the basic features. To be concrete, for each basic features, we calculate the Δ differences between each two weeks of week 2 to week

4. For example, for *numClicks*, it has three Δ-features for each pair of weeks: $\Delta W_3 W_2 numClicks$, $\Delta W_3 W_1 numClicks$ and $\Delta W_2 W_1 numClicks$, where

$$\Delta W_i W_j numClicks = \frac{W_i numClicks - W_j numClicks}{W_i numClicks}. \quad (2)$$

We further transform some of the count features into percentile-based features. Features like *maxSessionLength* and *QueryTimeInterval* are un-bounded so that directly apply them to classifiers may not be an optimal choice. Consequently, these features are transformed into percentile and included along with the original count features. As a result, a total of 60 features are used for training the classifier.

5.2.3 Results

Since we have over 50% more training instances in the positive class than the negative class, we perform subsampling from both classes with certain ratio to address the class imbalance issue. To be concrete, we randomly sample 20,000 instances from each class, resulting a total of 40,000 training examples, and then randomly split them on a 50/50 ratio to fit a linear SVM model. This process is repeated 10 times and the average result is reported here. To find the best parameters for the model, we perform a grid search. Overall, the best performance is reached with $s = 2$, i.e., L2-regularized L2-loss support vector classification (primal), and $c = 2$ the cost factor.

We compare to several baselines:

Baseline (Session): baseline that leverages only weekly number of sessions as the predictor.
Baseline (CTR): baseline that uses only weekly click through rate (CTR). $CTR = 1 - \frac{numNoClickQueries}{numQueries}$.
Baseline (Basic): baseline that uses the basic features only, as listed in Table 4.

Figure 12 summarizes the performance of all algorithms in comparison. It can be observed that with only the session feature, the result is almost equal to random guess around 50%, which demonstrates a very poor correlation between users weekly sessions. With the introduction of click features (CTR), the result is substantially improved. This indicates a strong connection between search relevance and user engagement. The performance is further improved by leveraging all basic features, except for a few cases at very low recalls. Finally, by combining basic features with Delta features as well as percentile features, the algorithm achieves the best predictive performance among all. Overall, linear SVM achieves 72.17% of accuracy when using all 60 features. Noticeably, at low levels of recall, by adding the Δ-based features and percentile-based features, the model is capable of improving the precision by 10% to 12% over basic features.

We list the top-15 highest weighted features in Table 5 from the linear SVM model. Overall, *numClicks*, average *avgSessionLength*, and *numNoClickQueries*, as well as their Δ-based features, play the most important roles in the model. We also notice that *numSessions*-related features did not make into this list, which again demonstrates a poor correlation between users weekly session numbers.

5.3 Prediction for Low-frequency Users

Given the fact that user's last weekly features (W_3 in our case) are the most important features as shown in Table 5, here we build another model by leveraging only one week features. A legitimate reason for doing this study is due to the

Basic Features
numSessions: total number of sessions
numQueries: total number of queries
numUnqQueries: total number of unique queries
numNavQueries: total number of Navigational queries
numNoClickQueries: total number of queries without clicks
numClicks: total number of clicked URLs
avgQueryLength: average length of user queries
avgClickPosition: average SERP position of clicks
avgSessionLength: average length of sessions (# of queries)
maxSessionLength: maximum length of sessions
QueryTimeInterval: average time gap between two queries
ClickEntropy: the entropy of the user's all clicks

Table 4: The basic features used in this paper. All features are weekly-based. These features are used to form a total of 60 features used by the classifier.

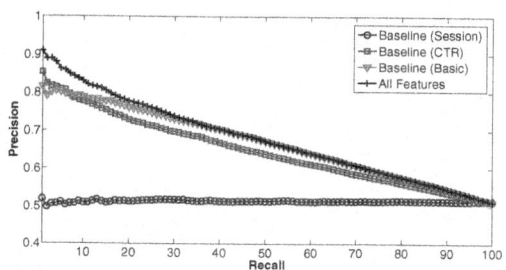

Figure 12: Precision-Recall curve for all algorithms.

fact that lots of search engine users are low-frequency users, whose activities cannot be tracked consistently by search engines for many reasons (e.g., a user who clears its browser cookies will have a new user id). Therefore, we would like to see how our algorithm performs when the data is sparse.

To this end, we extract a list of users from our data who have at least one activity in each of two *consecutive* weeks. We then randomly sample 20,000 users from the list. Features are extracted from the first week to make prediction for the second week. The data is split into 50/50 for training and testing. Note that since we only have one week data, we are unable to construct Δ-based features. Therefore, only basic features and percentile features are used for training.

Figure 13 demonstrates the result of precision-recall curves for using one-week feature, as well as the model that leverages all features for comparison. Comparatively, our algorithm is able achieve 68.59% of accuracy for low-frequency users even with one-week data, which is slightly worse (~4%) than the model using all features.

6. DISCUSSION AND CONCLUSION

From our longitudinal analysis, we have observed that the change of user engagement follows a complex trend that is affected by multiple factors, therefore sometimes counter-intuitive. One would assume that under a deliberate setback of search relevance, user's engagement should immediately drop, which is, however, different from what we have observed. Our analysis indicated that user engagement in a short-term actually increased significantly, due to the fact that users tend to spend more effort by issuing more refor-

Feature Name	Weight
$\Delta W_3 W_2 numClicks$	0.041983
$W_3\_avgSessionLength$	0.034985
$\Delta W_3 W_1 numQueries$	0.025762
$W_3\_numClicks$	0.020579
$\Delta W_3 W_2 numNavQueries$	0.019042
$\Delta W_2 W_1 numQueries$	0.019013
$W_2\_avgQueryLength$	0.015908
$W_2\_numClicks$	0.015897
$\Delta W_3 W_1 numNoClickQueries$	0.014183
$\Delta W_2 W_1 avgSessionLength$	0.014054
$W_1\_avgSessionLength$	0.011007
$W_1\_numNoClickQueries$	0.010058
$\Delta W_3 W_1 avgSessionLength$	0.008692
$W_3\_avgQueryLength$	0.008319
$\Delta W_2 W_1 numNoClickQueries$	0.003609

Table 5: Top 15 highest-weighted features.

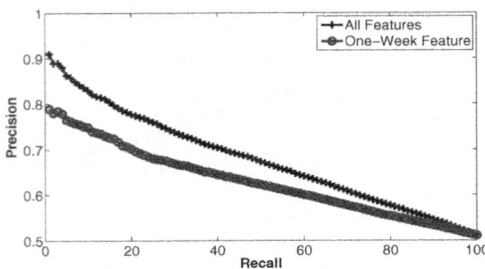

Figure 13: Precision-Recall curve for low-frequency users.

mulation, to accomplish their search tasks. As a result, during the early stage of our experiment, engagement metrics are indeed *negatively correlated* with search relevance. Nevertheless, we did observe that engagement finally dropped after a certain period of time, when users eventually gave up trusting the current search engine. Our further deep-dive analysis demonstrated that after users lost their momentum, they tend to issue more navigational-type queries (e.g., "facebook", "amazon"), and have less queries in a session, as well as a substantial drop of the click through rate.

By isolating affected users from normal users, our time series study focused on a set of core metrics that defines user behavioral change over time. With the help of these user-level and session-level features, we proposed a machine learning framework that predicts user's weekly engagement change. The model achieved over 72% of accuracy for high-frequency users and 66% for low-frequency ones. In practice, predicting user engagement is indeed a difficult task. And therefore, it is reasonable for one to assume that the number of sessions a user is going to issue in the future week is highly correlated to her current week's number, as well as the trend in the past few weeks. However, our model revealed that the highest correlated feature with engagement was in fact the number of clicks, which turns out to be a relevance metric, while the number of sessions did not make into our Top-15 feature list. This finding supports the correlation between search relevance and user engagement in a positive way.

We believe ourselves to be among the first to study the relationship between engagement and relevance under the setting of a deliberate relevance setback. Commercial Web search engine companies like Google and Bing often perform numerous online A/B experiments before they finally decide to ship new features to customers. In terms of search relevance, some new algorithms may indeed improve user satisfaction while others may eventually fail. The ship or no-ship decision is often depend on how well those online metrics perform like the ones we studied in the paper. Our study revealed that even algorithms with bad relevance may still be able to see a positive signal during the early stage of the experiment. Therefore, our advice is *not to celebrate too early* even if the signals look very positive in the first few days. We should consider keeping the experiments running for a fairly reasonable amount of time (e.g., in our case at least for two weeks), until the signals become stable or a clear trend is observed.

Our study in this paper mainly targeted the relevance domain. It would be interesting to see if the same methodology applies to other domains, e.g., User Interface (UI) changes. In the future, we also plan to further improve the accuracy of our prediction model by incorporating more features.

7. ACKNOWLEDGEMENTS

We would like to thank Pavel Dmitriev, Ya Xu, Brian Frasca, Fritz Behr, Bing Data Mining Team and Bing Relevance Team for their numerous support for this project.

8. REFERENCES

[1] E. W. Anderson and M. W. Sullivan. The antecedents and consequences of customer satisfaction for firms. *Marketing Science*, 12(2):125–143, 1993.

[2] A. Broder. A taxonomy of web search. *SIGIR FORUM*, 36(2):3–10, 2002.

[3] B. Carterette, E. Kanoulas, and E. Yilmaz. Simulating simple user behavior for system effectiveness evaluation. In *CIKM '11*, pages 611–620, 2011.

[4] R. E. Fan, K. W. Chang, C. J. Hsieh, X. R. Wang, and C. J. Lin. Liblinear: A library for large linear classification. *The Journal of Machine Learning Research*, 9(6/1/2008):1871–1874, 2008.

[5] H. A. Feild, J. Allan, and R. Jones. Predicting searcher frustration. In *SIGIR '10*, pages 34–41, New York, NY, USA, 2010. ACM.

[6] V. Hu, M. Stone, J. Pedersen, and R. W. White. Effects of search success on search engine re-use. In *CIKM '11*, pages 1841–1846. ACM, 2011.

[7] S. Ieong, N. Mishra, E. Sadikov, and L. Zhang. Domain bias in web search. In *WSDM '12*, pages 413–422, New York, NY, USA, 2012. ACM.

[8] B. J. Jansen, D. L. Booth, and A. Spink. Determining the user intent of web search engine queries. In *WWW '07*, pages 1149–1150. ACM, 2007.

[9] K. Järvelin and J. Kekäläinen. Cumulated gain-based evaluation of ir techniques. *ACM Trans. Inf. Syst.*, 20(4):422–446, Oct. 2002.

[10] R. Kohavi, R. M. Henne, and D. Sommerfield. Practical guide to controlled experiments on the web: listen to your customers not to the hippo. In *KDD '07*, pages 959–967.

[11] Z. Liao, Y. Song, L.-w. He, and Y. Huang. Evaluating the effectiveness of search task trails. In *WWW '12*, pages 489–498, New York, NY, USA, 2012. ACM.

[12] C. D. Manning, P. Raghavan, and H. Schtze. *Introduction to Information Retrieval*. Cambridge University Press, New York, NY, USA, 2008.

[13] M. Meiss, J. Duncan, B. Gonçalves, J. J. Ramasco, and F. Menczer. What's in a session: tracking individual

behavior on the web. In *HT '09*, pages 173–182, 2009.

[14] B. Mittal and W. M. Lassar. Why do customers switch? the dynamics of satisfaction versus loyalty. *Journal of Services Marketing*, 12:177–194, 1998.

[15] K. Radinsky, K. Svore, S. Dumais, J. Teevan, A. Bocharov, and E. Horvitz. Modeling and predicting behavioral dynamics on the web. In *WWW '12*, pages 599–608, 2012.

[16] F. Radlinski, M. Kurup, and T. Joachims. How does clickthrough data reflect retrieval quality? In *CIKM '08*, pages 43–52, New York, NY, USA, 2008. ACM.

[17] Y. Song and L. He. Optimal rare query suggestion with implicit user feedback. In *WWW '10*, pages 901–910, New York, NY, USA, 2010. ACM.

[18] J. E. R. Staddon. *Adaptive Behavior and Learning*. Cambridge University Press, 1983.

[19] D. Tang, A. Agarwal, D. O'Brien, and M. Meyer. Overlapping experiment infrastructure: More, better, faster experimentation. In *CIKM 2010*, pages 17–26.

[20] K. Wang, T. Walker, and Z. Zheng. Pskip: estimating relevance ranking quality from web search clickthrough data. In *KDD '09*, pages 1355–1364, 2009.

[21] R. W. White and S. M. Drucker. Investigating behavioral variability in web search. In *WWW '07*, pages 21–30, New York, NY, USA, 2007. ACM.

Data-Fu: A Language and an Interpreter for Interaction with Read/Write Linked Data

Steffen Stadtmüller
Institutes AIFB, KSRI
Karlsruhe Institute of
Technology (KIT), Germany
steffen.stadtmueller@kit.edu

Sebastian Speiser
Institutes AIFB, KSRI
Karlsruhe Institute of
Technology (KIT), Germany
speiser@kit.edu

Andreas Harth
Institute AIFB
Karlsruhe Institute of
Technology (KIT), Germany
harth@kit.edu

Rudi Studer
Institutes AIFB, KSRI
Karlsruhe Institute of
Technology (KIT), Germany
studer@kit.edu

ABSTRACT

An increasing amount of applications build their functionality on the utilisation and manipulation of web resources. Consequently REST gains popularity with a resource-centric interaction architecture that draws its flexibility from links between resources. Linked Data offers a uniform data model for REST with self-descriptive resources that can be leveraged to avoid a manual ad-hoc development of web-based applications. For declaratively specifying interactions between web resources we introduce *Data-Fu*, a lightweight declarative rule language with state transition systems as formal grounding. Data-Fu enables the development of data-driven applications that facilitate the RESTful manipulation of read/write Linked Data resources. Furthermore, we describe an interpreter for Data-Fu as a general purpose engine that allows to perform described interactions with web resources by orders of magnitude faster than a comparable Linked Data processor.

Categories and Subject Descriptors

H.5.4 [**Hypertext/Hypermedia**]: Architectures

General Terms

Languages, Performance

Keywords

REST; Linked Data; Web Interaction; Rule Language; Interpreter

1. INTRODUCTION

There is a growing offer of functionality via web APIs[1]. Increased value comes from combining data from multiple sources and functionality from multiple providers. The importance of such compositions is reflected in the constant growth of mashups – small programs that combine multiple web APIs [33]. There is a strong movement in the web community toward a resource-oriented model of services based on Representational State Transfer (REST [11]). Flexibility, adaptivity and robustness are the major objectives of REST and are particularly useful for software architectures in distributed data-driven environments such as the web [22]. However, data sources and APIs are published according to different interaction models and with interfaces using non-aligned vocabularies, which makes writing programs that integrate offers from multiple providers a tedious task.

The goal of our work is to provide a declarative means to specify interactions between data and functionality from multiple providers. Such declarative specifications provide a modular way of composing the functionality of multiple APIs. Also, declarative methods allow for automatically optimising a program and parallelising the execution.

In a REST architecture, client and server are supposed to form a contract with content negotiation, not only on the data format but implicitly also on the semantics of the communicated data, i.e., an agreement on how the data have to be interpreted [32]. Since the agreement on the semantics is only implicit, programmers developing client applications have to manually gain a deep understanding of the provided data, often based on natural text descriptions. The combination of RESTful resources originating from different providers suffers particularly from the necessary manual effort to use and combine them. The reliance on natural language descriptions of APIs has led to mashup designs in which programmers are forced to write glue code with little or no automation and to manually consolidate and integrate the exchanged data.

Linked Data unifies a standardised interaction model with the possibility to align vocabularies using RDF, RDFS and OWL. However, the interactions are currently constrained to simple data retrieval. Following the motivation to look beyond the exposure of fixed datasets, the extension of Linked Data with REST technologies has been explored [5, 34] and

---

[1] Alone http://programmableweb.com/ lists 7,991 APIs on November 24th 2012, which is almost twice the number from one year earlier.

Copyright is held by the International World Wide Web Conference Committee (IW3C2). IW3C2 reserves the right to provide a hyperlink to the author's site if the Material is used in electronic media.
WWW 2013, May 13–17, 2013, Rio de Janeiro, Brazil.
ACM 978-1-4503-2035-1/13/05.

led recently to the establishment of the *Linked Data Platform*[2] W3C working group.

Several existing approaches recognise the value of combining RESTful services and Linked Data [17, 26, 30]. In this paper, we go one step further and propose *Data-Fu*, a data- and resource-driven programming approach leveraging the combination of REST with Linked Data. Data-Fu enables the development of applications built on semantic web resources with a declarative rule language. The main goal of Data-Fu is to minimise the manual effort to develop web-based applications and the preservation of loose coupling by

- leveraging links between resources provided by Linked Data, and
- specifying desired interactions dependent on resource states, which is enabled by a uniform state description format, i.e., RDF.

A further requirement for our programming approach in a web-based environment is a fast and scalable execution of the applications. While there has been recent work on extending the Map/Reduce model for data-driven processing [15, 4], these approaches are geared towards deployment in data centers. In contrast, our approach operates on the networked open web.

This paper is based on a previous publication on a data-driven programming model for the web [27] and describes

- how self-descriptive resources can be designed to enable loosely coupled clients (Section 4.1);
- a service model for REST based on state transition systems as formal grounding (Section 4.2);
- the Data-Fu language, a declarative rule-based execution language to allow an intuitive specification of the interaction with resources from different providers (Section 5);
- an execution engine as an artefact to perform the defined interactions in a scalable manner (Section 6).

We provide a motivating scenario in Section 2. We evaluate our approach in two ways: (i) we describe throughout the paper how our motivating scenario can be realised with Data-Fu; and (ii) we conduct performance experiments with the Data-Fu interpreter in Section 7. Section 8 covers existing work. We conclude in Section 9.

2. MOTIVATING SCENARIO

In our scenario, we consider the Acme corporation, a consumer goods producer, that aims at extending their social media activities to a broader range of dissemination channels (for more on multi-channel communication see [7]). Acme's marketing department observes that while the number of potential channels is constantly increasing, the channels can be broadly categorised into micro blog services and social networks. Information about new products, special offers, and other news should be disseminated in the following ways: (i) posts on the company's micro blogs; and (ii) messages to social network users who are followers of the company.

We assume that the dissemination channels offer Linked APIs, i.e., resources are exposed that offer read/write Linked Data functionality.[3]

Table 1: URI prefixes used throughout this paper

Prefix	IRI
acme:	http://acme.example.org/company/
p:	http://acme.example.org/vocabulary/
sna:	http://sna.example.org/lapi/
snb:	http://snb.example.org/rest/
mb:	http://mb.example.org/interface/

The marketing department orders a system from Acme's IT that manages the dissemination channels and automatically disseminates a post to all available channels either as a micro blog entry or as a personal message. Initially the micro blog service MB and the social network SNA have to be supported. Marketing will supply their posts in an Acme-specific vocabulary as so-called InfoItems.

After a while, the marketing department decides to add the new social network SNB as a dissemination channel, which requires two steps: (i) the IT department extends the dissemination system to support the interface of SNB; and (ii) the marketing department adds Acme's identity in SNB to the dissemination channels.

Throughout the paper, we will illustrate our technical contributions by realising bits and pieces of the proposed scenario. When modeling services and interactions, we will use a number of URI prefixes for brevity that are either common[4] or listed in Table 1.

3. BACKGROUND

According to the Richardson maturity model [24] REST is identified as the interaction between a client and a server based on three principles:

- The use of URI-identified resources.
- The use of a constrained set of operations, i.e., the HTTP methods, to access and manipulate resource states.
- The application of hypermedia controls, i.e., the data representing a resource contains links to other resources. Links allow a client to navigate from one resource to another during his interaction.

The idea behind REST is that applications, i.e., clients, using functionalities provided on the web, i.e., APIs, are not based on the call of API-specific operations or procedures but rather on the direct manipulation of exposed resource representations or the creation of new resource representations. A resource can be a real world object or a data object on the web. The representation of a resource details the current state of the resource. A manipulation of the state representation implies that the represented resource is manipulated accordingly. For brevity in this paper we often talk about "the manipulation of a resource", when we actually mean "the manipulation of the state representation of a resource and the subsequent change of the resource itself".

The flexibility of REST results from the idea that client applications do not have to know about all necessary resources. The retrievable representations of some known resources contain links to other resources, that the client can

---

[2] http://www.w3.org/2012/ldp/charter
[3] If there is no Linked API available, the conventional APIs can be easily wrapped to consume and produce RDF, see, e.g., [29, 17]. Wrapping APIs is out of scope of this paper.

[4] See http://prefix.cc/ for their full URIs, accessed on November 22nd 2012.

discover during runtime. Clients can use such discovered resources to perform further interaction steps.

The Linked Data design principles[5] also address the use of URI-identified resources and their interlinkage. However Linked Data is so far only concerned with the provisioning and retrieval of data. In contrast to REST, Linked Data does distinguish explicitly between URI-identified objects (i.e., non-information resources) and their data representation (information resources). An extension of Linked Data with REST to allow for resource manipulation leads to read/write Linked Data, i.e., information resources can be accessed and manipulated. REST furthermore implies that a change of an information resource implies a change in the corresponding non-information resource.

The development of applications in a REST framework is especially challenging, since the links between resources and the resource states can only be determined during runtime, however, programmers have to specify their desired interactions at design time.

Traditional service composition approaches that aim to decrease the manual effort to use web-offered functionality lead to a tight coupling between client and server, i.e., they sacrifice flexibility and are prone to failures due to server-side changes. Traditional composition approaches often fail to leverage links between resources and do not provide straightforward mechanisms to dynamically react to state changes of resources. The reaction on state changes becomes especially important in a distributed programming environment, since a client cannot ex ante predict the influence of other clients on the resources, i.e., REST does not allow a client to make assumptions on resource states.

4. READ/WRITE LINKED DATA

In this section, we describe our approach for modelling of RESTful services based on Linked Data. Our approach has two layers:

- Individual *Read/Write Linked Data Resources* with descriptions that allow predicting the effect of the execution of a functionality before invocation (Section 4.1);
- A formal *REST Service Model*. A single REST service can consist of several resources, potentially spread over different servers. The *service model* is the grounding for describing the interactions that are offered by the individual RESTful Linked Data resources and the overall service (Section 4.2).

4.1 Read/Write Linked Data Resources

In a RESTful interaction with Linked Data resources only the HTTP methods can be applied to the resources. The semantics of the HTTP methods itself is defined by the IETF[6] and do not need to be explicitly described.

Table 2 shows an overview of the most important HTTP methods. We can distinguish between safe and non-safe methods, where safe methods guarantee not to affect the current states of resources. Further, some of the methods require additional input data to be provided for their invocation. The communicated input data can be subject to requirements that need to be described to allow an automated interaction, e.g., the input data can be required to use a specific vocabulary. Furthermore, the effect of a non-

[5]http://www.w3.org/DesignIssues/LinkedData.html
[6]http://www.ietf.org/rfc/rfc2616.txt

Table 2: Overview of HTTP methods

Method	Safe	Input required	Intuition
GET	x		Retrieve the current state of a resource.
OPTIONS	x		Retrieve a description of possible interactions.
DELETE			Delete a resource
PUT		x	Create or overwrite a resource with the submitted input.
POST		x	Send input as subordinate to a resource or submit input to a data-handling process.

safe method on the state of an addressed resource can depend on the input data. The dependency between communicated input and the resulting state of resources also needs to be described. Therefore, only the non-safe HTTP methods that require input data need further description mechanisms. Note, the POST method can also influence the states of not directly addressed resources. The precise effect of a POST depends on the resource, since POST allows to send input data to a data-handling process of a resource.

The state of a Linked Data resource is expressed with RDF. It is sensible to serialise the input data in RDF as well, i.e., data that is submitted to resources to manipulate their state. To convey the resulting state change after application of a HTTP method we use RDF output messages. In previous work [20] we analysed the potential of graph patterns, based on the syntax of SPARQL[7], to describe required input as well as their relation to output messages. The resulting graph pattern descriptions are attached to the resource and can be retrieved via the *OPTIONS* method on the respective resource. Therefore the resources stay self-descriptive, i.e., their current state can be retrieved with *GET*, the possibilities to influence their state with *OPTIONS*.

Example. Acme's IT creates the resource acme:Acme representing Acme. A GET on acme:Acme returns the following initial description: acme:Acme rdf:type p:Company .
The marketing department updates the acme:Acme resource with the dissemination channels SNA and MB by performing a PUT with the following input data:

    acme:Acme   rdf:type   p:Company .
    acme:Acme   p:dissChannel   sna:Acme, mb:Acme .
    sna:Acme   rdf:type   p:SocialNetworkID .
    mb:Acme   rdf:type   p:MicroBlogTimeline .

A subsequent GET on acme:Acme would result in exactly the description that marketing supplied with their PUT request.

A GET on sna:Acme, Acme's identifier in the social network SNA, would result in a description of Acme in SNA's vocabulary including its fans:

    sna:Acme   rdf:type   sna:CommercialOrganisation .
    sna:Acme   sna:founded   "11/20/2012" .
    sna:Acme   sna:hasFan   sna:User1, sna:User2, ...

The resources representing users in the SNA network provide

[7]http://www.w3.org/TR/rdf-sparql-query/#GraphPattern

functionality to send messages to the corresponding users. A POST can be employed to send a message to a user resource (e.g., to `sna:User1`). The input data for the POST contains its `sna:sender` and its `sna:content`, according to the description of the user resource that can be retrieved with an OPTIONS request:

```
INPUT:   ?m  rdf:type       sna:Message .
         ?m  sna:sender     ?s .
         ?m  sioc:content   ?c .
OUTPUT:  ?m  sna:sender     ?s .
         ?m  sioc:content   ?c .
         ?m  sna:receiver   sna:User1 .
```

Acme's timeline `mb:Acme` on the micro blogging service MB also supports the POST operation. Figure 1 illustrates the timeline resource `mb:Acme` of our example, with a set of entries in the current state and the graph pattern that describe how a new entry can be POSTed.

Applying a DELETE on a blog post, e.g., one that advertises an expired sale, does not require input; its effect is inherently defined by the method: the entry is erased.

4.2 REST Service Model

A REST service can be identified with the resources it exposes. An interaction within a REST architecture is based on the manipulation of the states of the exposed resources.

We develop a model, that allows to formalise the functionalities exposed by a REST API based on read/write Linked Data resources. A formal service model serves as rigorous specification of how the use of individual HTTP methods influences resource states and how these state changes are conveyed to interacting clients.

We model a Linked Data-based RESTful service as a REST state transition system (RSTS) similar to a state machine as defined by Lee and Varaiya [18]. The behavior of the clients themselves is not in the scope of this model, it rather formalises all possible interaction paths of a client with the resources.

DEFINITION 1. *A REST state transition system (RSTS) is defined as a 5-tuple $RSTS = \{R, \Sigma, I, O, \delta\}$ with:*

- *A set of resources $R = \{r_1, r_2, ...\}$.*
- *A set of states $\Sigma = \{\sigma_1, ..., \sigma_m\}$. Each state $\sigma_k \in \Sigma$ of the RSTS is defined as the union of the states of all resources: $\sigma_k = \bigcup_{r_i \in R} \overline{r_i^k}$. The state of a single resource $r_i \in R$ in a state σ_k is given by its RDF representation $\overline{r_i^k} \in G$, where G is the set of all possible RDF graphs.*
- *An input alphabet $I = \{(r, \mu, g) : R \times M \times G\}$, where $M = \{GET, DELETE, PUT, POST\}$ is the set of the supported HTTP methods[8].*
- *An output alphabet $O = \{(c, o) : C \times G\}$, where C is the set of all HTTP status codes.*
- *An update function $\delta : \Sigma \times I \to \Sigma \times O$ that returns for a given state and input the resulting state and the output. We decompose δ into a state change function $\delta^s : \Sigma \times I \to \Sigma$ and an output function $\delta^o : \Sigma \times I \to O$, such that $\delta(\sigma, i) = (\delta^s(\sigma, i), \delta^o(\sigma, i))$. We define the*

state change function as

$$\delta^s(\sigma_k, (r_i, \mu, g)) = \begin{cases} \sigma_k, & \text{if } \mu = GET \\ \sigma_k \setminus \{\overline{r_i^k}\}, & \text{if } \mu = DELETE \\ (\sigma_k \setminus \{\overline{r_i^k}\}) \cup g, & \text{if } \mu = PUT \\ \text{post}_i(\sigma_k, g), & \text{if } \mu = POST, \end{cases}$$

where the function post_i encapsulates the resource specific behaviour of a POST request, as described by its INPUT/OUTPUT patterns, which can be obtained via an OPTIONS request on the resource. Let σ_l be the new state as defined by δ^s, we define the output function as

$$\delta^o(\sigma_k, (r_i, \mu, g)) = \begin{cases} (c, \overline{r_i^k}), & \text{if } \mu = GET \\ (c, \emptyset), & \text{if } \mu = DELETE \\ (c, \sigma_l \setminus \sigma_k), & \text{if } \mu = PUT \\ (c, \sigma_l \setminus \sigma_k), & \text{if } \mu = POST. \end{cases}$$

A client interacting with a service modelled by an $RSTS = \{R, \Sigma, I, O, \delta\}$ creates an input $i = (r_i, \mu, g)$ for $RSTS$ by invoking the HTTP method μ on the resource r_i and passing the potentially empty RDF graph g in the request body. Depending on the current state σ_k of the service the following happens:

1. The service transitions into the state $\delta^s(\sigma_k, (r_i, \mu, g))$.
2. The client gets an HTTP response with the HTTP code c and the RDF graph g' in the body, where $(c, g') = \delta^o(\sigma_k, (r_i, \mu, g))$.

Safe methods that do not change any resource states, describe self-transitions, i.e., transitions that start and end in the same state.

The output function in the case of PUT and POST report to the client the effect the invocation of the method had on the state of the RSTS (i.e. $\sigma_l \setminus \sigma_k$).

Resources do not necessarily allow the use of all HTTP methods. Note that all state change functions are defined for every resource, i.e., every resource can be addressed with all methods: If a resource does not allow for the application of a specific method, the state change function describes a self-transition.

The defined service model serves as formal grounding of the execution language described in Section 5. However, the self-descriptive resources provide sufficient information for the interaction with the exposed resources.

- The current state of Linked Data resources – and therefore the state of the RSTS – can be accessed as RDF.
- The possible transitions and the state they result in are independent of the specific resource, except for POST transitions. The effect of POST transitions is declared with graph pattern descriptions (see Section 4.1).

Example. Figure 2 illustrates a state transition in RSTS where an entry is POSTed to `mb:Acme`. Note, that a client could derive the input for the POST method from the states of other resources (e.g., from Acme InfoItems).

5. THE DATA-FU LANGUAGE

In this section, we present Data-Fu[9], an *execution language* to instantiate a concrete interaction between a client

---

[8] For brevity we focus here on the four most important methods. Other methods can be added analougously.

[9] We use the name *Data-Fu* in adaption of the term *google-fu*, which adopts the suffix x*Fu* of from Kung Fu, implying great skill or mastery. Thus Data-Fu hints at the mastery of data interaction that can be achieved with the language.

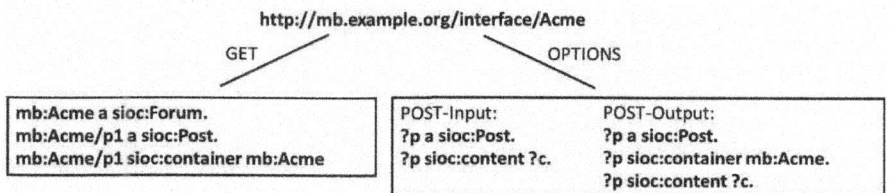

Figure 1: Self-descriptive resource: current state can be accessed with GET, input/output description with OPTIONS

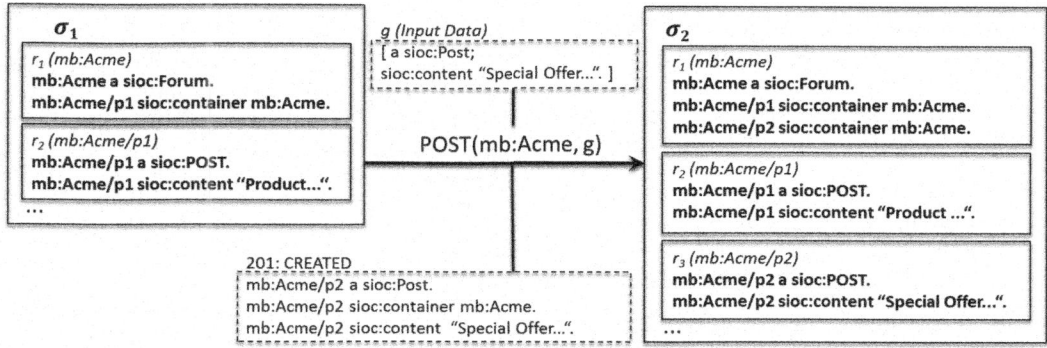

Figure 2: State transition of a RSTS, with excerpts of two states.

and resources, which preserves the adaptability, robustness and flexibility of REST.

In a resource-driven environment, applications retrieve and manipulate resources exposed on the Web. Since the resources can potentially be accessed by a multitude of clients, applications have to react dynamically on the state of the resources. Therefore, an important factor in the development of resource-driven applications is the dependency between the invoked transitions and resource states. The dependency between the invoked state transitions (i.e., applied HTTP methods) and the states of resources is that

1. input data for the transition is derived from RDF detailing the states of resources and/or
2. the transition is only invoked, if resources are in a specified state.

Data-Fu, a declarative rule-based execution language, enables programmers to define their desired state transitions. Data-Fu rules specify the interaction of a client with RESTful Linked Data resources and congruously a path through the RSTS. Further Data-Fu allows to specify the conditions under which a specific transition is to be invoked as subject to the states of resources.

DEFINITION 2. *A rule ρ is of the form $\mu(r,g) \leftarrow q$, where $\mu \in M$ is an HTTP method, $r \in R \cup V$ is a resource or a variable with V the set of all variables, $g \in G \cup P$ is a (potentially empty) RDF graph or graph pattern, and $q \in P$ is a conjunctive query with P the set of all possible RDF graph patterns. If r is a variable, it must be bound in q. If g is a graph pattern, all its variables must be bound in q.*

The head of a rule corresponds to an update function of the RSTS in that it describes an HTTP method that is to be applied to a resource. The rule bodies are conjunctive queries that allow programmers to express their intention under which condition a method is to be applied. Thus, programmers can define an interaction pattern with a set of rules for their client applications.

The use of conjunctive queries is motivated by the idea that clients have to maintain a knowledge space (KS) in which they store their knowledge about the states of the resources they interact with [17, 25]. KS is filled with the RDF data the client receives after applying an HTTP method, as defined by the output functions of the RSTS. The output always informs the client about the current state after the application of the method.

Concretely N3 graph patterns are employed as queries q, which are evaluated over KS. If the evaluation of q is successful, i.e., matches are found in KS, the defined HTTP method μ is applied to r with input g. The query q can also be used to dynamically (i.e., during runtime)

1. derive input data from the states of other resources, as stored in KS and
2. identify the resource to which an HTTP method has to be applied, i.e., leveraging hypermedia controls.

Regarding 1: Instead of specifying the input data g explicitly as RDF graph, a graph pattern can be used. If a match is found for q in KS, the identified bindings for q are used to replace the variables in g to establish the input data for the interaction (with HTTP method μ at resource r). g as graph pattern and q act together similar to a SPARQL *construct* query over KS, where the result of the query is used as input data for the invocation of the method μ.

Regarding 2: To preserve the flexibility provided by REST our execution language has to be able to make use of links in the resource states to other resources. Rather than specifying the addressed resource r of a rule explicitly as URI, a variable can be used. If a match is found for q in KS, an identified binding for a variable q is used for the variable r. r as variable and q act together as a SPARQL *select* query to identify the targeted resources of method μ.

A Data-Fu program terminates when there are no active transitions and no rules can be activated that could trigger new transitions. In general, termination of a program cannot be guaranteed, as every transition can result in data that triggers new transitions. However, the termination of a program is not necessarily intended by a programmer, in the case of applications that are supposed to continuously interact with resources. Furthermore, the deletion and change of resources can lead to applications with a non-deterministic execution behavior. For discussions about properties of rule sets in related languages that guarantee termination and determinism, we refer the reader to [2].

Example. The IT department of Acme creates the dissemination system with four Data-Fu rules. The marketing department has simply to create new InfoItems and the system automatically distributes the information over the dissemination channels of Acme. The rules are defined as follows:

1. Whenever a InfoItem is found, retrieve the resource acme:Acme to get an up-to-date list of the current dissemination channels.
   GET (acme:Acme, {}) ← { ?x rdf:type p:InfoItem }

2. If a p:MicroBlogTimeline is found (from the retrieved dissemination channels), post a new entry to the timeline using the content from the InfoItem.
   POST (?mb, { [] rdf:type   sioc:Post ;
                   sioc:content ?c .   })
   ← { ?x rdf:type p:InfoItem .
       ?x p:content ?c .
       ?mb rdf:type p:MicroBlogTimeline } .

3. If a social network ID of Acme is found (from the retrieved dissemination channels), retrieve the representation of Acme from the social network to get a list of Acme's followers.
   GET (?sid, {})
   ← { ?sid rdf:type p:SocialNetworkID } .

4. Post to every found follower of Acme on SNA a message with the content of the InfoItem.
   POST (?f, { [] rdf:type   sna:Message ;
                  sna:sender sna:Acme ;
                  sna:content ?c .   })
   ← { sna:Acme sna:hasFan ?f .
       ?x   rdf:type   p:InfoItem .
       ?x   p:content ?c   } .

The described rules disseminate new information items automatically to social network SNA and the micro blog MB. IT deploys the dissemination system itself as a read/write Linked Data resource under acme:Dissemination. Marketing uses the dissemination service by POSTing a graph to the dissemination resource that corresponds to the following input pattern:
{ ?x rdf:type p:InfoItem. ?x p:content ?c } .

Other dissemination channels can easily be added to the system, simply by adding corresponding rules in the system. For example, we consider that IT adds support for social network SNB by adding a rule that uses SNB's vocabulary for retrieving followers and sending a message:

POST (?f, { [] rdf:type   snb:PrivateMsg ;
               snb:origin snb:ACME ;
               snb:text   ?c .   })
← { snb:ACME snb:followedBy ?f .
    ?x   rdf:type   p:InfoItem .
    ?x   p:content   ?c   } .

The new dissemination channel is active when marketing PUTs Acme's identifier in SNB's network to acme:Acme.

6. THE DATA-FU INTERPRETER

The Data-Fu interpreter is an execution engine for service interactions specified as a set of Data-Fu rules. The engine implements the KS as well as the functionality to invoke interactions with resources as defined in the rules. In practice, we translate a Data-Fu program into a logical dataflow network, which is then optimised (e.g., re-using triple patterns and joins). The optimised logical network is then transformed into an evaluator plan that actually implements the dataflow network.

We realise the evaluator plan for the Data-Fu engine as a streaming processor that can process several queries in parallel. We implement the processor as a multi-threaded component with one thread evaluating individual triple patterns, and separate threads for each join operator and for each rule head, i.e., the component that performs the state transitions by invoking the corresponding HTTP methods on resources. The joins are implemented as symmetric hash join operators [35]. The implemented dataflow network is similar to a parallel version of the Rete algorithm [12].

To enable a wide variety of applications the engine can include an extension to support the interaction with REST resources that are not based on Linked Data. The engine can store data entities (e.g., binaries, JSON documents) received from such services separately. A triple pointing to a received non-RDF entity can be included in KS, thus the entities can be used in the logic of the execution rules. However, an interaction with such non-RDF entities requires to fall back to a more mashup-like programming approach.

Example. The dataflow network shown in Figure 3 evaluates the plan generated for the Data-Fu program for Acme's dissemination system. We can see that joins (e.g., the join on ?x) are re-used, i.e., have multiple outgoing edges. The triple stream is initialised by the service input, which is sent by the client via a POST request. If the input data contains a description of an information item, it will trigger the rule retrieving Acme's description containing links to its dissemination channels. The social networks will fire a rule, which then retrieves the social network id's of Acme and thus retrieve the corresponding followers. Both social network followers and micro blog timelines will then trigger the corresponding POST actions that will sent the information item in the appropriate vocabulary to the dissemination channels, i.e., as micro blog posts or personal messages to the followers.

7. EVALUATION

To evaluate the scalability of the Data-Fu engine we compared execution times for different numbers of interactions and rules with Cwm[10], a data-processor for the Semantic Web. Cwm uses a local triple store that supports the full N3 language to save data and intermediate results. The local

---
[10]http://www.w3.org/2001/sw/wiki/CWM

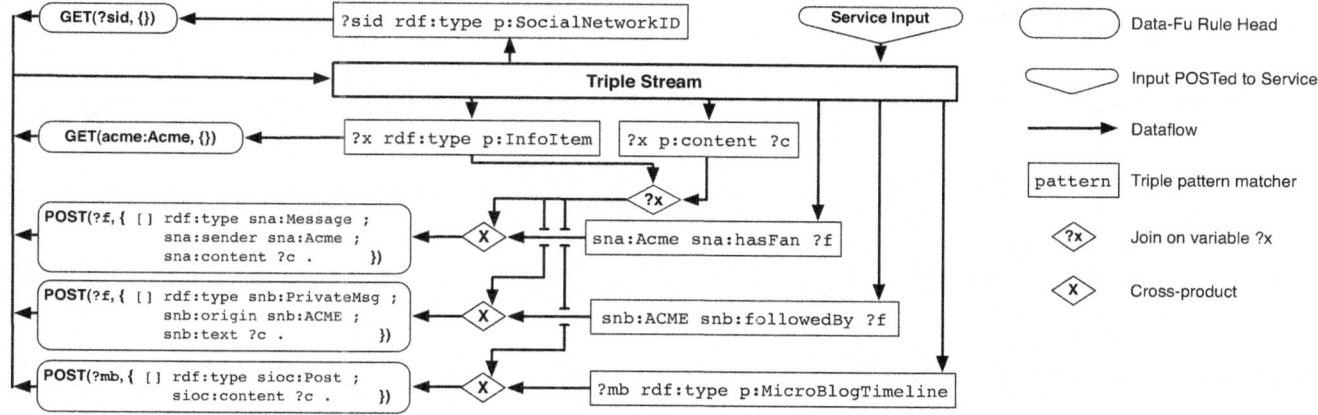

Figure 3: Dataflow network of Acme's dissemination system

triple store of Cwm uses seven indices to allow for a rapid readout of the local data with almost every combination of subject, predicate and object patterns. For inferencing Cwm uses a forward chain reasoner for N3 rules. The pattern matching for the rules is done by recursive search with optimisations, such as identifying an optimal ordering for the evaluation of the rules and patterns.

Cwm is built as a general purpose tool to query, process, filter and manipulate data from the Semantic Web. As such, the motivation behind Cwm is closest to the Data-Fu engine, compared with any other rule engines or reasoning systems, to the best of our knowledge. However, Cwm is not targeted on the direct RESTful manipulation of web resources, but their retrieval and the local manipulation of the data. Therefore to make the systems comparable we limit the evaluated interactions to GET transitions, i.e., we use only rules that retrieve resources, if a match for the rule body is found. Please note that the limitation to GET transitions does not influence the validity of the evaluation: Since additional execution time when using non-safe interactions (e.g., PUT, POST) only results from time required to transmit data to resources and the subsequent time necessary to process this data by the server, where the resource resides. This time overhead caused by non-safe transitions is neither influenced by the Data-Fu engine, nor could it be avoided by any other system that we could use as comparison.

We conducted the experiments on a 2.4 GHz Intel Core 2 Duo with 4 GB of memory (2 GB assigned to Java virtual machine on which the experiments run). Thus we evaluate the Data-Fu engine on commodity hardware with the intent to show the parallelisation-based scalability of the Data-Fu engine not only on high-end industrial machines.

We deploy Linked Data resources used for the interactions locally on an Apache Tomcat[11] server to further minimise execution time variations caused by establishing HTTP connections and retrieving data over the web. In the rules used by the Data-Fu engine and Cwm the resources are addressed with their localhost address. Every deployed resource represents a number. Every number resource is typed as **number** and contains its value as literal and a link to the successor of the number:

```
local:1   rdf:type          local:number.
local:1   local:value       "1".
local:1   local:successor   local:2.
```

We chose this design to easily keep track of the number of performed interactions.

For the evaluation we start with the resource number 0, which we manually inject into the Data-Fu engine and Cwm. We identify and retrieve the successor of the number. The successor of a number yields a new successor to retrieve, and so on. The interactions of this set-up are illustrated in Figure 4.

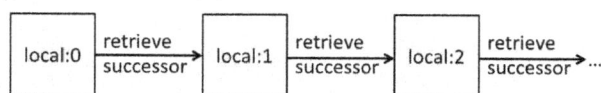

Figure 4: Interactions of evaluation set-up with one rule

We realise the interactions with the Data-Fu Engine and Cwm (for the latter in two different ways) as follows:

- *Data-Fu:* For the Data-Fu engine we use a rule:

$$\text{GET (?suc, \{\})} \leftarrow \{\text{?n rdf:type local:number}\\ \text{?n local:value ?v}\\ \text{?n local:successor ?suc}\}$$

The rule body queries for a resource (variable ?n) that is typed as number, has a value and a successor. If a match is found, a GET transition is triggered at whatever URI is identified to be the successor of the matched number. The Data-Fu engine adds the retrieved representation of the successor to the data flow network, which results in the identification of the next successor to retrieve. Thus, all numbers are iteratively found and retrieved.

- *Cwm direct:* Cwm offers built-in functions to perform web-aware queries in rules. The keyword log:semantics in a query of a rule allows to resolve a URI and bind the retrieved RDF data to a variable as formula. The formula bound to a variable can then be used to construct triples in the rule head. We used the following rule to perform the desired interaction:

---

[11] http://tomcat.apache.org/

```
{{ :n rdf:type local:number.
   :n local:value :v.
   :n local:successor :suc }
       local:is local:known. }
:suc log:semantics :sem.
⇒
   { :sem local:is local:known. }
```

Like in the approach for the Data-Fu engine we query for the successor of a number. The successor is retrieved and bound as formula in subject position to a new triple that is written to the triple store. Since the retrieved representation of the number appears only as formula in triples we have to extend the query in the rule body to search for the successor of a number in a formula in subject position of a triple, thus making the query slightly more complicated than in the case of the Data-Fu engine. Cwm repeatedly applies the rule to the triple store, thus retrieving all numbers.

- *Cwm import:* To compare the performance of Cwm with the Data-Fu engine, where the queries of the rules are equally complex, we implemented the desired retrieval with another approach, with the following rule:

```
{ :n rdf:type local:number.
  :n local:value :v.
  :n local:successor :suc }
⇒
  { :n owl:imports :suc. }
```

We use the same query to identify the successor of a number as for the Data-Fu engine. For every found match we write a triple to the Cwm store, that marks the identified successor with owl:imports. Cwm offers a command to retrieve all resources marked with owl:imports. This allows us to programmatically instruct Cwm to apply the rule and retrieve the successor, as many times as needed. Note, that this implementation of the interaction does not deliver the same functionality as with the Data-Fu engine: We have to manually define how often the rule followed by the retrieve command is to be applied (once for every number), rather then having the engine automatically retrieve all the numbers.

We evaluate the execution time of the interaction with all three setups for sets of 20, 40, 60, 80 and 100 numbers. With the approaches *Data-Fu* and *Cwm direct* the interaction ends when the last number in a set does not refer to a next successor to retrieve. For *Cwm import* we had to decide manually how often the rule is applied and thus how many numbers are retrieved and when the interaction stops. The results are shown in Table 3 and Figure 5. We provide the average execution times from ten runs to reduce variations.

Table 3: Average execution time from ten runs for different evaluation set-ups with one rule

number set size	Data-Fu	Cwm direct	Cwm import
20	342 ms	1549 ms	468 ms
40	371 ms	5144 ms	976 ms
60	500 ms	11272 ms	1595 ms
80	555 ms	21005 ms	2309 ms
100	594 ms	32213 ms	3688 ms

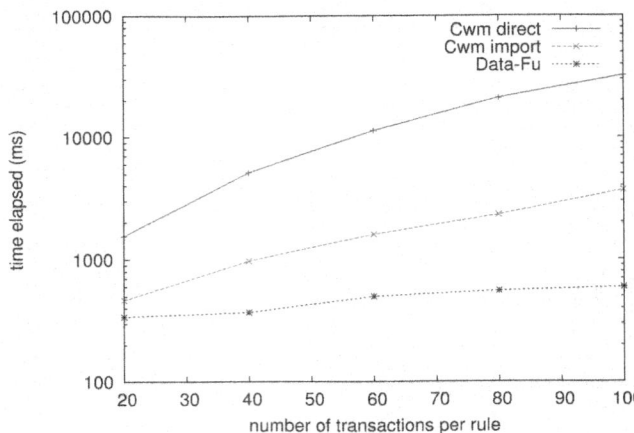

Figure 5: Average execution time from ten runs for different evaluation set-ups with one rule

The Data-Fu engine is able to execute the interaction by orders of magnitude faster than the other two approaches with Cwm. Also the growth-rate of the execution time with the increasing size of number sets is much lower with Data-Fu compared to the Cwm approaches (note the log scale in Figure 5). The Data-Fu engine achieves this time saving by leveraging the data flow network: Data-Fu has just to put the new results after an interaction through the data flow network to find new bindings. Cwm on the other hand has to apply the rules repeatedly over the increasing dataset in its triple store.

To evaluate the capabilities of the Data-Fu engine with regard to parallelisation we run the same interaction of retrieving successors of numbers again, with ten different "kinds" of numbers (A-J) in parallel. The numbers are distinguished by different namespaces. Each of the three evaluation set-ups requires ten rules for the interaction (each addressing another namespace), analog to the previously shown rules. Figure 6 illustrates this evaluation set-up.

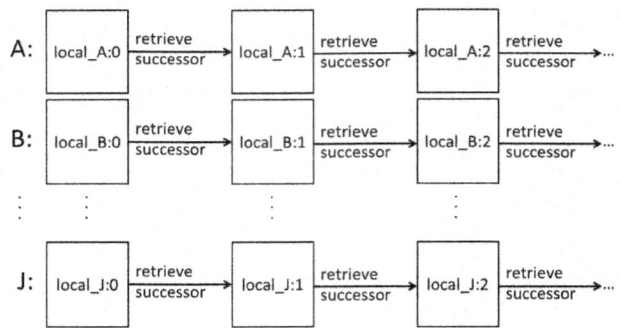

Figure 6: Interactions of evaluation set-up with one rule

The results for the different evaluation set-ups are shown in Table 4 and Figure 7 as average from ten runs. Again Data-Fu executes the interaction significantly faster with a lower growth rate than Cwm in the other set-ups: In the case of the most interactions (10 x 100) *Cwm direct* requires over 17 minutes and *Cwm import* over 32 seconds, the Data-Fu engine handles the same interactions in under 4 seconds.

Table 4: Average execution time from ten runs for different evaluation set-ups with ten rules in parallel

number set size	Data-Fu	Cwm direct	Cwm import
20	1833 ms	22513 ms	2836 ms
40	2421 ms	108421 ms	7067 ms
60	2916 ms	310498 ms	13518 ms
80	3889 ms	621798 ms	21729 ms
100	3944 ms	1038524 ms	32983 ms

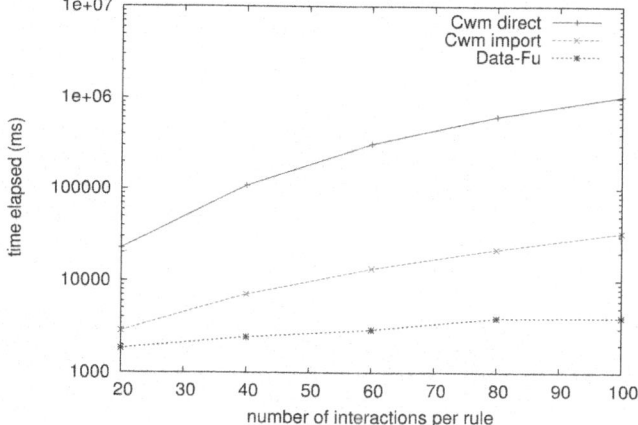

Figure 7: Average execution time from ten runs for different evaluation set-ups with ten rules in parallel

Comparing the results of the interactions with a single rule and the interactions with ten rules in parallel we note, that the Data-Fu engine suffers less than Cwm from the ten times increased workload when executing ten rules in parallel. On average for the individual sizes of number sets

- *Data-Fu* requires 6.2 times longer,
- *Cwm direct* requires 25 times longer,
- *Cwm import* requires 8 times longer,

when running with ten rules compared to one single rule. The reason for this time advantage is the capability of the Data-Fu engine to execute several components of the interaction in parallel, e.g., the evaluation of the triple patterns of the queries and the communication with several web resources. Note, that the theoretically possible speedup due to parallelisation on a dual core system implies that a 10 times increased workload results in a 5 times longer execution time. However, the Data-Fu engine cannot quite reach this optimal speedup, since not all parts in the interaction can be completely parallelised, e.g., the management of the individual threads. These parts of an interaction that cannot be completely parallelised result in a slightly diminished speedup, as stated by Amdahl's Law [3].

Following the results of the evaluation in comparison with Cwm, we devise a final evaluation setting to test the scalability of the Data-Fu engine when performing large amounts of interactions. Similar to the previous evaluation setting we retrieve number resources that are identified during runtime as successor of an already found number. We fix the size of the number sets to 100, i.e., we deploy sets of 100 consecutive number resources that are distinguished with their namespace. Then we retrieve the numbers of every set with a respective rule. We evaluate the runtime of the Data-Fu engine with 20, 40, 60, 80 and 100 rules/number sets, thus performing between 2 000 and 10 000 interactions. Additionally we measure the time needed to calculate the evaluation plan separately to compare it with the total execution time. The results are shown in Table 5 and Figure 8.

Table 5: Average execution time from ten runs of Data-Fu engine with number sets of size 100

rules/number sets	execution time	evaluation plan
20	8357 ms	4 ms
40	17195 ms	6 ms
60	30767 ms	7 ms
80	49430 ms	8 ms
100	75764 ms	9 ms

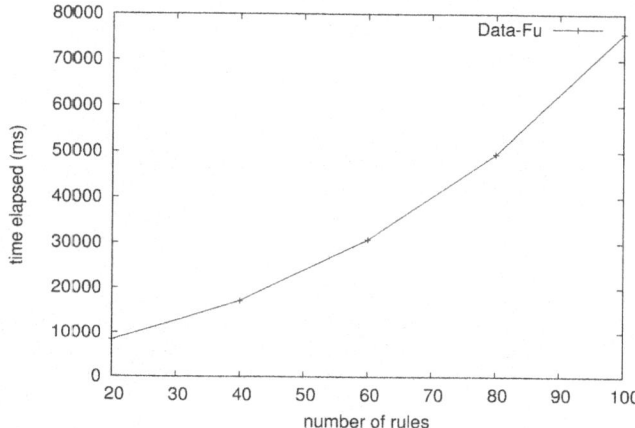

Figure 8: Average execution time from ten runs of Data-Fu engine with number sets of size 100

The results of the evaluation for large amounts of interactions show that the Data-Fu engine scales well up to thousands of interactions even on commodity hardware. The Data-Fu engine is capable of interacting with 10 000 web resources in about 1:15 min. The necessary time required to establish the evaluation plan increases with the number of rules, but remains a very small fraction of the overall execution time and is therefore negligible.

The evaluation shows the advantages of the parallel processing of queries and interactions and provides evidence that the Data-Fu engine is capable of performing rapid interactions with web resources as desired. We did not consider the necessary time to establish HTTP connections on the web and the response time of the servers, where resources are deployed, since these additional time requirements would be the same for any employed interaction system. Note however, that due to its parallel processing nature, the Data-Fu engine could further benefit from longer response times of servers compared to other systems: At the same time as the Data-Fu engine performs the manipulations and retrieval of resources other rules can be evaluated, thus the overall execution time can be minimised.

We provide the data used for the evaluation and an executable jar online[12] to re-run the experiments.

---

[12] http://people.aifb.kit.edu/sts/datafu/evaluation/

8. RELATED WORK

Pautasso introduces an extension to BPEL [21] for a composition of REST and traditional web services. REST services are wrapped in WSDL descriptions to allow for a BPEL composition. Our approach focuses on a native composition of REST services, rather than relying on technologies of traditional web services. For a comparison between RESTful services and "big" services see [23].

There exist several approaches that extend the WS-* stack with semantic capabilities by leveraging ontologies and rule-based descriptions (e.g., [28, 10, 8]) to achieve an increased degree of automation in high level tasks, such as service discovery, composition and mediation. Those approaches extending WS-* became known as Semantic Web Services (SWS). An Approach to combine RESTful services with SWS technologies in particular WSMO-Lite [31] was investigated by Kopecky et al. [16]. In contrast to SWS, REST architectures do not allow to define arbitrary functions, but are constrained to a defined set of methods and are built around another kind of abstraction: the resource. Therefore our approach is more focused on resource/data centric scenarios in distributed environments (e.g., in the Web).

Active XML introduces service calls as XML nodes that are placeholders for new XML documents that can be retrieved from the service [1]. The service calls are comparable to hypermedia links in resource descriptions and the active XML document corresponds to the knowledge space. In contrast to Active XML, our work discovers links to new resources instead of links to function calls. The resource model provides more flexibility, e.g., a Data-Fu program could perform a DELETE on a discovered resource, whereas the Active XML equivalent would be constrained to the predefined operations in the original link.

The scripting language S [6] allows to develop Web resources with a focus on performance due to parallelisation of calculations. Resources can make use of other resources in descriptions, thus also enabling a way of composing REST services. S does not explicitly address the flexibility of REST and has no explicit facilities to leverage hypermedia controls or to infer required operations from resource states.

RESTdesc [30] is an approach in which RESTful Linked Data resources are described in N3-Notation. The composition of resources is based on an N3 reasoner and stipulates manual interventions of users to decide which hypermedia controls should be followed.

Hernandez et al. [14] proposes a model for semantically enabled REST services as a combination of pi-calculus [19] and approaches to triple space computing [9] pioneered by the Linda system [13]. They argue, that the resource states can be seen as triple spaces, where during an interaction triple spaces can be created and destroyed as proposed in an extension of triple space computing by Simperl et al. [25]. Our service model is in contrast to this approach more focused on the composition of data driven interactions.

Similar to the idea of triple spaces is the composition of RESTful resources in a process space, proposed by Krummenacher et al. [17] based on resources described using graph patterns. Speiser and Harth [26] propose similar descriptions for RESTful Linked Data Services. Our approach shares the idea that graph pattern described resources read input from and write output to a shared space. We improve on this approach by providing a service model and a more explicit way of defining the interaction with resources.

9. CONCLUSION

In this paper, we addressed the problem of creating value-added compositions of data and functionalities. As a unifying model for both static data sources and dynamic services, we described how Linked Data Resources can be extended with descriptions for RESTful manipulation. The natural extension of Linked Data with RESTful manipulation of resources enables a framework with uniform semantic resource representations for REST architectures. We have proposed to exploit the advantages resulting from the combination of REST and Linked Data in a programming framework for the Semantic Web. We have introduced Data-Fu, a declarative rule-based execution language with a state transition system as formal grounding, and the challenges we address with this language, i.e., achieving scalability and performance while preserving the flexibility and robustness of REST. Furthermore, we described our implementation of an execution engine for the Data-Fu language.

For future work, we plan to extend our approach in the following directions. First, we will add capabilities to improve handling of failures of resource interactions. Second, we will extend our formal model of Data-Fu to provide clearly defined semantics in the presence of non-deterministic rules. Third, we will integrate support for rule-based reasoning into the execution engine. The rules bring useful expressivity for aligning different vocabularies and can be easily supported in the engine by introducing triple-producing rule heads in addition to the current state transition handlers.

Acknowledgments

This work was partially supported by the PlanetData NoE (FP7:ICT-2009.3.4, #257641) and by the German Ministry of Education and Research (BMBF) within the Software-Campus project framework.

10. REFERENCES

[1] S. Abiteboul, O. Benjelloun, and T. Milo. Positive Active XML. In *Proceedings of the 23rd Symposium on Principles of Database Systems (PODS'04)*, pages 35–45. ACM, 2004.

[2] A. Aiken, J. Widom, and J. M. Hellerstein. Behavior of database production rules: Termination, confluence, and observable determinism. *SIGMOD Record*, 21(2):59–68, 1992.

[3] G. M. Amdahl. Validity of the single processor approach to achieving large scale computing capabilities. In *Proceedings of the 1967 Spring Joint Computer Conference (AFIPS'67)*, pages 483–485, Atlantic City, New Jersey, 1967. ACM.

[4] D. Battré, S. Ewen, F. Hueske, O. Kao, V. Markl, and D. Warneke. Nephele/PACTs: A programming model and execution framework for web-scale analytical processing. In *Proceedings of the 1st ACM Symposium on Cloud Computing (SoCC'10)*, pages 119–130, Indianapolis, Indiana, USA, 2010. ACM.

[5] T. Berners-Lee. *Read-Write Linked Data*. August 2009. Avaiable at http://www.w3.org/DesignIssues/ReadWriteLinkedData.html, accessed 26th November 2012.

[6] D. Bonetta, A. Peternier, C. Pautasso, and W. Binder. S: A scripting language for high-performance RESTful

web services. In *Proceedings of the 17th ACM SIGPLAN Symposium on Principles and Practice of Parallel Programming (PPoPP'12)*, 2012.

[7] C. Brenner, A. Fensel, D. Fensel, A. Gagiu, I. Larizgoitia, B. Leiter, I. Stavrakantonakis, and A. Thalhammer. How to domesticate the multi-channel communication monster. Available at http://oc.sti2.at/sites/default/files/oc_short_handouts.pdf.

[8] J. Cardoso and A. Sheth. *Semantic Web Services, Processes and Applications*. Springer, 2006.

[9] D. Fensel. Triple-space computing: Semantic web services based on persistent publication of information. In *Proceedings of the IFIP International Conference on Intelligence in Communication Systems (INTELLCOMM'04)*, number 3283 in Lecture Notes in Computer Science, pages 43–53, Bangkok, Thailand, 2004. Springer.

[10] D. Fensel, H. Lausen, A. Polleres, J. de Bruijn, M. Stollberg, D. Roman, and J. Domingue. *Enabling Semantic Web Services: The Web Service Modeling Ontology*. Springer, 2006.

[11] R. Fielding. *Architectural Styles and the Design of Network-based Software Architectures*. PhD thesis, University of California, Irvine, 2000.

[12] C. Forgy. Rete: A fast algorithm for the many pattern/many object pattern match problem. *Artificial Intelligence*, 19(1):17–37, 1982.

[13] D. Gelernter. Generative communication in Linda. *ACM Transactions on Programming Languages and Systems (TOPLAS)*, 7:80–112, 1985.

[14] A. G. Hernández and M. N. M. García. A formal definition of RESTful semantic web services. In *Proceedings of the First International Workshop on RESTful Design (WS-REST'10)*, pages 39–45, 2010.

[15] M. Isard, M. Budiu, Y. Yu, A. Birrell, and D. Fetterly. Dryad: Distributed data-parallel programs from sequential building blocks. In *Proceedings of the 2nd ACM SIGOPS/EuroSys European Conference on Computer Systems (EuroSys'07)*, pages 59–72, Lisbon, Portugal, 2007. ACM.

[16] J. Kopecky, T. Vitvar, and D. Fensel. MicroWSMO: Semantic description of RESTful services. Technical report, WSMO Working Group, 2008.

[17] R. Krummenacher, B. Norton, and A. Marte. Towards Linked Open Services. In *Proceedings of the 3rd Future Internet Symposium (FIS'10)*, volume 6369 of *Lecture Notes in Computer Science*, Berlin, Germany, 2010. Springer.

[18] E. A. Lee and P. Varaiya. *Structure and Interpretation of Signals and Systems*. Addison-Wesley, 2011.

[19] R. Milner. *Communicating and Mobile Systems: π-calculus*. Cambridge University Press, Cambridge, UK, 1999.

[20] B. Norton and S. Stadtmüller. Scalable discovery of linked services. In *Proceedings of the 4th International Workshop on REsource Discovery (RED'11)*, 2011.

[21] C. Pautasso. RESTful web service composition with BPEL for REST. *Journal of Data and Knowledge Engineering*, 68(9):851–866, 2009.

[22] C. Pautasso and E. Wilde. Why is the web loosely coupled?: A multi-faceted metric for service design. In *Proceedings of the 18th International Conference on World Wide Web (WWW'09)*, pages 911–920, Madrid, Spain, 2009. ACM.

[23] C. Pautasso, O. Zimmermann, and F. Leymann. Restful web services vs. "big"' web services: making the right architectural decision. In *Proceedings of the 17th International Conference on World Wide Web*, WWW '08, pages 805–814, New York, NY, USA, 2008. ACM.

[24] L. Richardson and S. Ruby. *RESTful Web Services*. O'Reilly Media, 2007.

[25] E. Simperl, R. Krummenacher, and L. Nixon. A coordination model for triplespace computing. In *Proceedings of the 9th International Conference on Coordination Models and Languages (COORDINATION'07)*, 2007.

[26] S. Speiser and A. Harth. Integrating Linked Data and services with Linked Data Services. In *Proceedings of the 8th Extended Semantic Web Conference (ESWC'11) Part I*, volume 6643 of *Lecture Notes in Computer Science*, pages 170–184, Heraklion, Crete, Greece, 2011. Springer.

[27] S. Stadtmüller and A. Harth. Towards data-driven programming for RESTful Linked Data. In *Workshop on Programming the Semantic Web (ISWC'12)*, 2012.

[28] R. Studer, S. Grimm, and Abecker, A. (eds.). *Semantic Web Services: Concepts, Technologies, and Applications*. Springer, 2007.

[29] M. Taheriyan, C. A. Knoblock, P. A. Szekely, and J. L. Ambite. Rapidly integrating services into the Linked Data cloud. In *Proceedings of the 11th International Semantic Web Conference (ISWC'12)*, volume 7649 of *Lecture Notes in Computer Science*, pages 559–574. Springer, 2012.

[30] R. Verborgh, T. Steiner, D. V. Deursen, R. V. de Walle, and J. G. Valls. Efficient runtime service discovery and consumption with hyperlinked RESTdesc. In *Proceedings of the 7th International Conference on Next Generation Web Services Practices (NWeSP'11)*, Salamanca, Spain, 2011.

[31] T. Vitvar, J. Kopecky, M. Zaremba, and D. Fensel. WSMO-Lite: Lightweight semantic descriptions for services on the web. In *Proceedings on the 5th European Conference on Web Services (ECOWS'07)*, pages 77–86, 2007.

[32] J. Webber. *REST in Practice: Hypermedia and Systems Architecture*. O'Reilly, 2010.

[33] M. Weiss and G. R. Gangadharan. Modeling the mashup ecosystem: Structure and growth. *R&D Management*, 40(1):40–49, 2010.

[34] E. Wilde. REST and RDF granularity, 2009. Available at http://dret.typepad.com/dretblog/2009/05/rest-and-rdf-granularity.html.

[35] A. N. Wilschut and P. M. G. Apers. Dataflow query execution in a parallel main-memory environment. In *Proceedings of the 1st International Conference on Parallel and Distributed Information Systems (PDIS'91)*, pages 68–77, Miami Beach, FL, USA, 1991. IEEE Computer Society Press.

NIFTY: A System for Large Scale Information Flow Tracking and Clustering

Caroline Suen,[*] Sandy Huang,[*] Chantat Eksombatchai,[*] Rok Sosič, Jure Leskovec
Stanford University
{csuen, shhuang, chantat, rok, jure}@cs.stanford.edu

ABSTRACT

The real-time information on news sites, blogs and social networking sites changes dynamically and spreads rapidly through the Web. Developing methods for handling such information at a massive scale requires that we think about how information content varies over time, how it is transmitted, and how it mutates as it spreads.

We describe the *News Information Flow Tracking, Yay!* (NIFTY) system for large scale real-time tracking of "memes" — short textual phrases that travel and mutate through the Web. NIFTY is based on a novel highly-scalable incremental meme-clustering algorithm that efficiently extracts and identifies mutational variants of a single meme. NIFTY runs orders of magnitude faster than our previous MEMETRACKER system, while also maintaining better consistency and quality of extracted memes.

We demonstrate the effectiveness of our approach by processing a 20 *terabyte* dataset of 6.1 *billion* blog posts and news articles that we have been continuously collecting for the last four years. NIFTY extracted 2.9 billion unique textual phrases and identified more than 9 million memes. Our meme-tracking algorithm was able to process the entire dataset in less than five days using a single machine. Furthermore, we also provide a live deployment of the NIFTY system that allows users to explore the dynamics of online news in near real-time.

Categories and Subject Descriptors: H.2.8 [Database Management]: Database applications—*Data mining*
General Terms: Algorithms; Experimentation.
Keywords: Networks of diffusion, Information cascades, Blogs, News media, Meme-tracking, Social networks.

1. INTRODUCTION

In less than a decade, the World Wide Web has transformed from a large, static library that people only browse into a vast and dynamic information resource. Today, for example, large media houses and TV stations, small local newspapers, professional online bloggers, as well as casual bloggers and citizen journalists are continuously capturing the pulse of humanity: what we are thinking, what we are doing, and what we know.

Since the early days of the Web, online information content has taken on increasingly dynamic forms, to the extent that the real-time aspect of information has become one of the most pressing concerns in the processing and tracking of Web content. Information on the Web changes rapidly over time due to the rate of production, as well as the ways in which it is transmitted through the network, from website to website. Developing methods for handling such dynamic information at a massive scale poses many challenges. For example, it requires us to think about how content varies and mutates as it is being transmitted over underlying networks. A better understanding of how information spreads on the Web has many practical applications in a wide range of fields, such as social sciences, marketing, and politics.

The goal of this paper is to develop a system that is able to *track information* as it spreads across *billions of documents* on the Web and over time periods spanning *many years*. Studying the spread of online information has been an active research area [1, 3, 15, 21, 39], but reliably tracking the content flow has been extremely challenging [3, 21]. While there has been work on tracking topics [5, 7, 36, 40], tags [13, 24], and keywords [8, 37], scaling difficulties have made it harder to track information across whole websites or across the entire Web.

Additional challenges stem from the fact that for such whole-Web tracking, it is difficult to find the right granularity at which to study the movement of information. For example, entire articles or blog posts (except in rare cases) do not spread and propagate on the scale of the whole-Web [3, 15, 21]. Similarly, terms [16, 18] or topic clusters [7, 36, 40] (e.g. "the presidential election," "the war in Iraq") are generally too broad to truly capture the fine-grained elements of information mutation and diffusion.

In order to study the emergence and the dynamics of Web information, we need to identify the basic units of information that propagate through the Web. We require a level of granularity that is balanced between the coarse-grained structure of whole pages, articles, or posts, and the fine-grained structure of terms, keywords, or topic labels. And even if the basic units of information are successfully identified, the challenge resulting from information that is constantly evolving and mutating as it spreads on the Web remains. Thus it is important to have a robust method to discover and track different mutational variants of the same piece of information.

The sheer volume and time span of Web data requires a system that can process tens of millions of documents per day and billions of documents over several years. Traditional methods for tracking information flow have quadratic time complexity in the number of documents, which makes their running time prohibitively large for practical use over longer time periods. Also, we cannot hope to load all the data in memory, so efficient online incremental algorithms for tracking information flow are needed. And as we would like to run our system over periods spanning several years, a challenge is that our method must not degrade in performance over time.

---
[*]Authors contributed equally to this work.

Copyright is held by the International World Wide Web Conference Committee (IW3C2). IW3C2 reserves the right to provide a hyperlink to the author's site if the Material is used in electronic media.
WWW 2013, May 13–17, 2013, Rio de Janeiro, Brazil.
ACM 978-1-4503-2035-1/13/05.

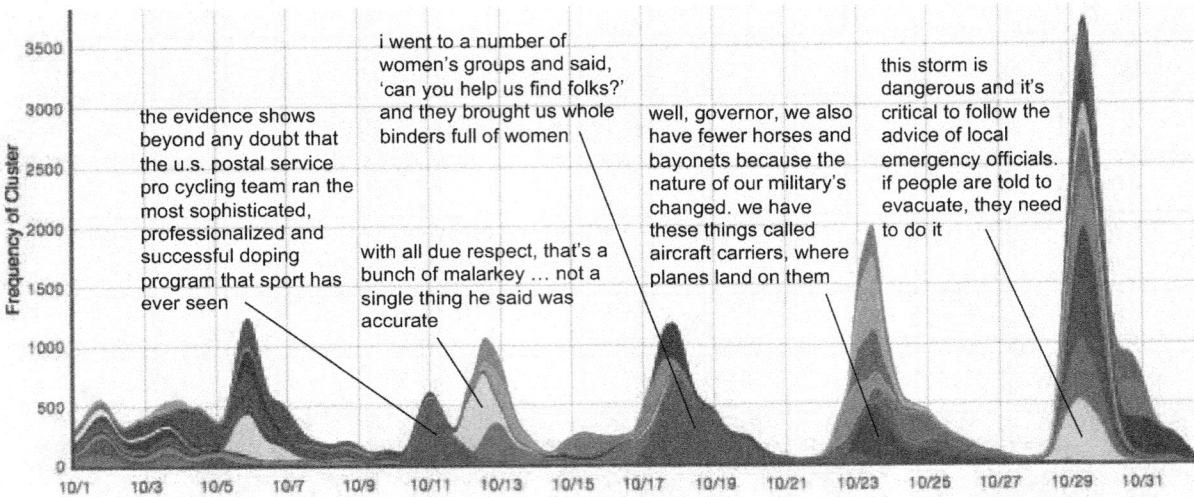

Figure 1: Visualization of the most popular memes in the month of October 2012, with notable memes labeled. Each band represents a meme and the height of the band corresponds to the number of mentions per hour. Real-time visualization is available at http://snap.stanford.edu/nifty.

Overview of results. In this paper we present the *News Information Flow Tracking, Yay!* (NIFTY) system for large scale real-time tracking of new topics, ideas and "memes" across the Web. NIFTY efficiently extracts and traces textual *memes* [20] — short phrases that change, yet remain relatively intact as they propagate from website to website and from blog to blog. NIFTY applies a novel highly-scalable incremental meme-clustering approach for extracting and identifying mutational variants of textual memes. Example output of our system for October 2012 is displayed in Figure 1. NIFTY clearly identified a number of popular memes from that month, such as memes associated with the U.S. presidential election ("binders full of women", "horses and bayonets") as well as memes related to Hurricane Sandy ("this storm is dangerous").

NIFTY builds on our previous MEMETRACKER [20] approach in the sense that it operationalizes the notion of a meme through quotations. Quotations appear in documents as quoted phrases or sentences, operating at a level of granularity between that of individual articles and broad topics. We define memes by combining similar quoted phrases in clusters, each cluster representing one meme.

NIFTY operates as follows. First, we extract quoted phrases from input documents. Once the quoted phrases are extracted, we cluster all the different mutational variants of the same quote to obtain meme clusters. It is challenging to cluster phrases, given that we are working with billions of them. As phrases are short textual fragments containing very little information, traditional bag-of-words representations do not work well. Moreover, we are not interested in simply clustering together all the phrases on the same topic, but rather we want to find all the phrases that evolved through one or more mutational steps from the same original phrase.

Our approach to the problem of identifying meme evolution [20] applies ideas from biological sequence analysis, where we aim to "align" two given phrases using a form of string edit distance and then determine whether one could have evolved from the other. We build a giant *phrase graph* where phrase a has a directed edge to phrase b if there is evidence that a could have evolved from b. We then partition this graph into clusters, such that each cluster is a directed acyclic graph (DAG) with a single root node. The clusters then represent memes, each cluster root node is an original meme phrase and the rest of the cluster nodes are mutational variants of the original phrase. For example, Figure 2 shows a graph of the mutational variants of a meme related to the discovery of the Higgs

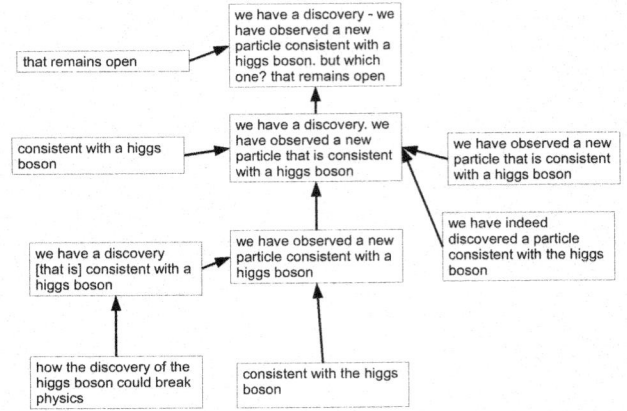

Figure 2: A small subset of mutations of a meme about the discovery of the Higgs boson particle.

boson particle. The advantage of using a graph of phrase variants is that it automatically produces the lineage or ancestry information (as illustrated in Figure 2).

An additional challenge when one works with phrases appearing over longer time periods (e.g., several months or more) is the formation of a "giant component" containing a significant fraction of all phrases. A low distance between two phrases from different, frequently occurring memes can cause their corresponding meme clusters to fuse together, leading to one large cluster over time. As this obscures the structure we are trying to identify, we developed a novel incremental clustering approach to finding mutational variants of a single meme. We keep a dynamic version of the phrase graph and we constantly add new phrases to it. By maintaining the dynamic structure of the phrase graph, we achieve both run time efficiency as well as improved cluster quality. A second essential innovation is that we also continuously remove finalized meme clusters and their corresponding phrases. This means that memes (phrase clusters) that stopped evolving get removed from the graph before a "giant" meme could start swallowing all the phrases.

We demonstrate the effectiveness of our approach by processing a 20 *terabyte* dataset of 6.1 *billion* blog posts and news articles that we have been collecting for the last four years. This dataset essentially represents complete online news coverage during those four years. NIFTY extracted 2.9 billion unique textual phrases and identified more than 9 million unique memes. Our efficient online incremental algorithm was able to process the massive 20TB dataset in less than five days using a single machine and only 60GB of main memory. Incremental meme-clustering has linear runtime in the number of phrases while maintaining cluster consistency and quality provided by MEMETRACKER. Since the input data is processed incrementally, clustering time depends only on the volume of new data, which is practically constant per time unit, and not on the increasing size of the entire dataset as is the case with the offline batch methods. NIFTY thus allows us to quickly process datasets that are beyond the reach of the offline batch methods.

Last, we also deployed our system so that it processes Web documents in near real-time. The system extracts and clusters memes and then employs data visualization and data exploration techniques that allow users to explore the ongoing dynamics of online news. For example, Figure 1 is a screenshot of our interactive data visualization across a one month period, October 2012.

To the best of our knowledge, the present study analyzes one of the largest collections of news media documents and blog posts. In fact, the largest existing study [20] analyzed 90 million documents. Here we increase the scale of the analysis by 60 fold to 6 billion documents, while requiring approximately the same time and hardware resources. More broadly, we believe that our investigations have the potential to transform our understanding of how to manage real-time Web information, as well as our understanding of the evolving landscape of online news and commentary. The contributions of our present work are the following:

- A novel highly-scalable incremental meme-tracking approach for extracting and identifying mutational variants of short textual phrases that spread through the Web.
- A system level implementation of the incremental meme-tracking approach.
- An application of meme-tracking on 6 billion news articles and blog posts that we collected over the past 4 years.
- A live deployment of the NIFTY system to allow users to explore the dynamics of online news in real-time, available at http://snap.stanford.edu/nifty.

Further related work. Taken more broadly, our work here contributes to the growing literature on tracking and studying information dynamics on the Web. Two dominant themes in this work have been the use of algorithmic tools for organizing and filtering news, and the dynamics of online media content. Some of the key research issues concern the filtering and aggregation of online news [6, 12, 14]. While entity based [19, 22] as well as whole-document based [4, 25, 29, 30] approaches have been considered in the past, our work provides a new dimension in which we consider using short textual phrases to track related pieces of information. Another important distinction is that our methods scale to a truly massive dataset, while requiring only modest hardware resources for processing.

Meme-tracking has been successfully applied to other domains and use cases as well. For example, meme-tracking has been used to identify temporal variation of online media news content [10, 28, 39] as well as to reason about the dissemination and mutation of online information [2, 27, 31, 38]. NIFTY complements this line of work as we show that meme-tracking can be efficiently applied to billion-document datasets in order to gain insights about the dynamics of online information.

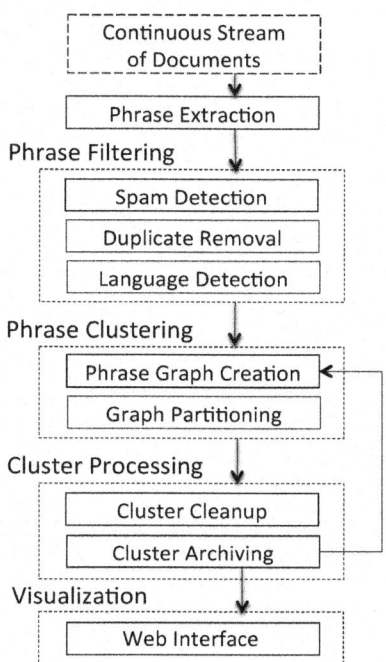

Figure 3: Overview of the NIFTY pipeline.

2. PROPOSED METHOD

NIFTY tracks memes by partitioning quoted phrases from input documents into clusters, such that each cluster represents one meme and the phrases in the cluster are mutational variants of a single original phrase. We now discuss the methods that NIFTY uses to track memes, including our approach to incremental clustering.

NIFTY processes documents through the pipeline of steps illustrated in Figure 3. We start with phrase extraction and proceed with *filtering*, which removes spam and duplicate content. The filtering step is often underappreciated, yet it is crucial for achieving high quality output. Next in the processing pipeline is *phrase clustering*, which groups phrases (i.e., mutational variants) that belong to the same meme. Here, the key challenge is that memes experience significant mutations, so usual text-based distance measures and standard clustering approaches do not work well [20]. The last two steps of the processing pipeline are *cluster processing* and *visualization*. The cluster processing step performs final quality checks of the output, removes old clusters, archives finalized clusters, and provides data updates for incremental clustering. Then, the visualization step uses the finalized cluster archive to present meme clusters via a Web interface.

Next we describe each of these steps in more detail. For ease of exposition we describe the pipeline as if the system operates in a batch setting. Later we discuss how NIFTY extends this batch setting to an incremental, stream based model.

2.1 Phrase Extraction

The input of NIFTY is a set of documents D, where each document in D represents an item from the Web, such as a news report or a blog post. A document contains the document URL, an estimated document publish time, and a list of phrases found in the document.

NIFTY operationalizes the notion of a meme through the extraction of short quoted phrases [20]. Building memes from quotes is natural since quotes are an integral aspect of journalistic practice;

even if a news story is not specifically about a particular quote, quotes are deployed in essentially all stories, and they tend to travel relatively intact through iterations of the story as it evolves [34]. They are also fairly unambiguous and readily identifiable, so that we are studying elements recognizable to consumers of the media, rather than the output of a complex clustering procedure.

2.2 Document and Phrase Filtering

Input documents for NIFTY are crawled off the Web and collected using RSS feeds. Such a data gathering procedure is focused on high coverage and volume. However, this means our data is inundated with spam, duplicates, and irrelevant information. Thus, the task of the filtering step is to clean up the input and select only English phrases, since we want to study only memes in English.

The filtering step passes over data twice. The first pass applies a number of simple heuristics to quickly eliminate as many bad documents and phrases as possible. With fewer documents and phrases, the second pass can use more computationally demanding methods to apply additional filtering criteria.

First pass: Filtering documents and phrases. Documents are eliminated during the first pass, if they are duplicates or their URLs are found on a manually maintained, short blacklist. Phrases are eliminated based on their length and on the portion of ASCII characters.

Phrase length. Intuitively, short phrases do not provide any useful information, while long phrases tend to not be memes. We experimented with different thresholds and found that the best balance between eliminating redundant phrases and preserving useful ones is to discard phrases with less than 3 or more than 30 words.

ASCII characters. As a quick test for English phrases, we apply a simple heuristic that requires at least 50% of the characters in the phrase to be ASCII characters.

Second pass: Advanced phrase filtering. During the second pass, the phrases and their corresponding documents are eliminated based on the phrase frequency, language filtering and URL to domain name ratio.

Infrequent phrases. To further remove noise and spam, we discard all phrases that appear in fewer than 5 distinct documents.

Language filtering. As mentioned, we are interested only in English phrases. To further filter only English documents, we compute for every phrase p the percentage of its words that appear in a list of the 1000 most common English words [35]. After experimenting with a range of values, we found that the best results are obtained by discarding all phrases where the percentage is less than 75%.

URL to domain name ratio. Spam is frequent in our dataset. One property of spam phrases is that they occur frequently but come from a small number of domains. We found the following rule to be our best strategy to remove spam phrases, as most spammers use only a few select domains to publish. If a phrase p appears at more than 20 URLs, we compute a ratio of unique URLs to the number of their unique host names (e.g. "www.cnn.com"). We remove p if this ratio is greater than 6.

Output. At the end of our filtering step we have a sanitized set of documents D, referred to as the **document base**, and a post-filtered set of phrases P, referred to as the **phrase base**. These two sets are used in the subsequent phrase clustering step.

2.3 Phrase Clustering

As memes spread through the Web, they change and mutate. For example, Figure 2 displays a sample of mutational variants of a meme concerning the discovery of the Higgs boson particle. Thus,

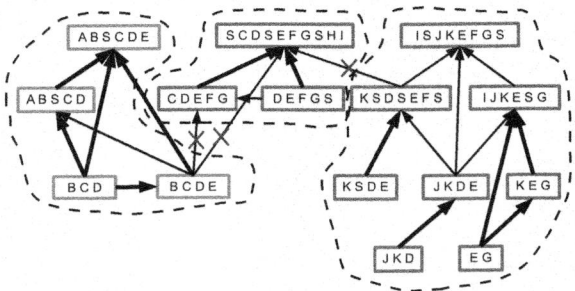

Figure 4: Example phrase graph, in which letters represent words. The letter 'S' indicates a stop word. Directed edges indicate the source phrase is approximately included in the destination phrase. For this example, the edge weight is inversely proportional to the substring edit distance between the two phrases, and is indicated by the thickness of the edge. Deleting the crossed-out edges gives the optimal clustering, shown by the dotted boundaries.

our next goal is to partition the phrase base P into meme clusters, so that the phrases from the same meme are combined into a single cluster. The clustering of phrases requires a non-traditional clustering approach, since two phrases might have only few words in common, yet they could belong to the same meme.

NIFTY extends and heavily improves the phrase clustering algorithm first proposed by MEMETRACKER [20]. The central concept of the algorithm is a phrase graph, which is a directed weighted acyclic graph. Each phrase in the phrase base P is a node in the graph and weighted edges are formed between the nodes based on the textual similarity of the corresponding phrases. After the graph is created, edges are pruned from the graph in order to split the graph into disconnected components with a single root phrase. Each disconnected component then corresponds to a meme where all the nodes (phrases) in the component are meme's mutational variants. In the following, we provide details about the phrase graph creation and partitioning steps.

Phrase graph creation. The purpose of the phrase graph creation step is to construct a directed weighted acyclic graph where phrases are nodes and pairs of similar phrases are connected by directed edges, pointing from shorter phrases to longer ones (Figure 4). The edges capture the intuition that quoted phrases are generally being shortened as they spread over the Web. At the end of this step, every phrase will be connected to a set of its potential "parents", i.e., phrases from which it could have mutated.

In order to create edges between phrases that could have evolved from one another, we apply ideas from biological sequence analysis. We aim to "align" two given phrases using a variant of string edit distance and then determine whether one could have evolved from the other.

Phrase distance. We expand the string edit distance to substrings and determine phrase distances in NIFTY by using what we call *substring edit distance*, an extension of the Levenshtein distance algorithm. Given two strings, we define the substring edit distance to be the minimum number of word insertions, deletions or substitutions needed to transform one string into a *substring* of the other string. We compute the substring edit distance by using a variant of the dynamic programming algorithm for the Levenshtein distance, removing stop words and using stemmed words during this computation.

Algorithm 1 Decision tree to determine if an edge should be created between phrases in the phrase graph

Require: Phrases p_1 and p_2
(1) Set l_p to the minimum number of words in p_1 or p_2.
(2) Compute s_1 and s_2 by stripping the stop words from p_1 and p_2, respectively.
(3) Set l_s to the minimum number of words in s_1 or s_2.
(4) Set d to the substring edit distance between s_1 and s_2.
  if $l_s \geq 2$ and $d = 0$ **then**
    return $True$
  else if $l_p = 4$ and $l_s = 4$ and $d \leq 1$ **then**
    return $True$
  else if $l_p = 5$ and $l_s > 4$ and $d \leq 1$ **then**
    return $True$
  else if $l_p = 6$ and $l_s \geq 5$ and $d \leq 1$ **then**
    return $True$
  else if $l_p > 6$ and $l_s > 3$ and $d \leq 2$ **then**
    return $True$
  else
    return $False$

Edge creation. Next, given a pair of phrases and their substring edit distance, we must determine whether one of them is derived from the other one and thus should be connected by an edge. We hand labeled 1,000 pairs of phrases that are mutational variants of each other as well as 1,000 phrases that are textually similar but are not mutational variants. We then trained a decision tree to distinguish between these two classes of phrases (Algorithm 1). An edge is created between two phrases in the graph, if the decision tree returns $True$.

Speeding up phrase graph creation. A straightforward approach to edge creation performs a pair-wise distance calculation between all the phrases in the phrase base, requiring quadratic number of calculations. This approach is prohibitively slow given the scale of our problem and the size of our dataset.

NIFTY drastically reduces the required number of distance calculations by using locality-sensitive hashing [17] (LSH), an efficient algorithm for identifying candidate pairs of phrases that could potentially be textually similar. LSH uses hash functions to place items into a number of buckets, so that similar items are placed in the same bucket with high probability. Since good locality sensitive hashing functions for substring edit distance are not available, we use shingling [23] with min-hashing [9] (see [26] for an overview) to find candidate pairs of phrases. Although min-hashing is commonly used to identify pairs of phrases with low Jaccard distance, our approach of applying it for substring edit distance makes intuitive sense. We use Jaccard distance as a lower bound for substring edit distance, as high Jaccard distance implies also high edit distance. Our experimental results in Section 3.1 confirm this intuition that LSH with min-hashing works well for substring edit distance and meme clustering.

We create four-character *shingles* from phrases, perform min-hashing by randomly shuffling unique shingles into bands of shingle permutations, and compute phrase signatures. The signature value for each permutation is the index of the first shingle in the permutation that exists in that phrase. Finally, each pair of phrases that have a signature band in common is tested for an edge existence, using the decision tree in Algorithm 1.

Assigning edge weights. Next, edges in the phrase graph are assigned weights based on findings by Yang [39] that most news follow a predictable popularity cycle with two main peaks, one from traditional news reporting and one from blog posts. For an edge from node p_s to p_d, NIFTY uses time and substring edit distance between the nodes and calculates weight for the edge as follows:

$$w(p_s, p_d) = c \cdot \frac{|p_d|}{(D_{edit}(p_s, p_d) + 1) \cdot (T_{peak}(p_s, p_d) + 1)}.$$

$|p_d|$ is the number of documents containing p_d, $D_{edit}(p_s, p_d)$ is the substring edit distance between the phrases, and $T_{peak}(p_s, p_d)$ is the time difference between the first volume peaks for each of the two phrases. We chose this formula so that the edge weight $w(p_s, p_d)$ is proportional to the popularity of p_d and the likelihood that p_s and p_d are mutational variants of the same original meme phrase. Intuitively, if p_s and p_d have a small edit distance and their frequencies first peaked at about the same time, they are more likely to be mutational variants of the same original meme phrase.

At the end, we have a directed acyclic graph $G = (P, E)$ where each phrase $p \in P$ is a node and pairs of similar phrases have weighted edges between them, connecting a phrase to all its potential parents. To obtain clusters, we next partition the phrase graph.

Phrase graph partitioning. Ideally, the creation step produces a phrase graph, such that the connected components of the graph correspond to memes and thus all mutational variants of a single meme are connected together. However, we find that similar phrases may not belong to the same meme and thus the phrase graph needs to be further partitioned.

Traditional graph partitioning criteria (such as the normalized cut or the min cut) are not appropriate here as our aim is to discover all mutational variants of a single meme. With this in mind, our goal can be rephrased as finding clusters in the phrase graph such that each cluster has a single root node. The root node acts as the original phrase from which all other phrases in the cluster evolved through a series of mutations.

Thus more formally, given a weighted directed acyclic graph, our goal is to delete a set of edges with a minimum total weight, so that each of the resulting components is single-rooted. Given that the problem is NP-hard [20], we use the following method.

We partition the phrase graph by repeatedly removing edges from the graph until all outgoing edges for each node belong to the same cluster. This constraint on the outgoing edges follows intuitively from the concept that many phrases are derived from one original phrase, referred to as the *root* phrase. These derived phrases are normally shorter phrase segments that various news sources use. Once all outgoing edges for each node belong to the same cluster, the resulting phrase graph is naturally partitioned into individual meme clusters, where each connected component is considered a meme cluster.

We implement the algorithm by recursively building clusters, starting with a working set that includes all the root phrases, which are nodes in the graph with zero outdegree. At this step, each cluster contains only a single root phrase. Repeatedly, when a node is not in the working set, but all its outgoing neighbors are, we assign the node to a cluster as follows.

For each of the node's neighbors, we find the cluster that the neighbor has been assigned to, then for each cluster found we sum up the edge weights for all the neighbors in this cluster. The node is attached to the cluster with the largest sum and added to the working set; edges to other clusters are removed from the graph. When all the nodes are in the working set, the algorithm terminates (Figure 4).

The final output of our phrase graph partitioning algorithm is a set of clusters, referred to as the **cluster base** C. Clusters have an easily followable acyclic structure that demonstrates how the root phrases branch into different child phrases.

2.4 Cluster Processing

The phrase graph partitioning creates a number of non-meme clusters such as movies, TV shows or song titles currently being promoted in the online media. To address non-memes and any remaining spam clusters, we next describe how the cluster processing step improves the clusters by filtering them by phrase mutations and the number of peaks. Peaks are defined as spikes in the number of phrase mutations within a time period.

Filtering by phrase mutations. This filtering strategy removes all clusters that include a single phrase mutation. Because many movie, TV show and song titles are frequently short and exhibit little to no variation, this strategy removes many non-memes as desired.

Filtering by peaks. As mentioned earlier, most news follow a predictable popularity cycle with at most two main peaks [39]. A cluster that has many peaks is most likely not a meme, so this step removes clusters with more than five peaks.

To identify peaks, our approach is to find points that are 1 standard deviation higher than the average frequency. The point with the highest frequency in each consecutive sequence of such points is marked as a peak. We use a sliding window of 9 days for these calculations.

Filtering by peaks was effective in both removing spam, since it was less likely to follow the news popularity cycle, as well as non-memes (e.g. "The Dark Knight Rises") that otherwise consistently produced large clusters due to active media promotion efforts.

2.5 Incremental Phrase Clustering

So far, we described a batch approach to clustering. Now, we describe how NIFTY extends this batch approach with incremental clustering.

Motivation. We want NIFTY to be able to update the meme clusters with new stories each day and also to process our entire dataset, spanning more than four years. We need NIFTY to be *fast* and *scalable* while maintaining *consistent* meme clusters over time.

To achieve these objectives, we developed an *incremental clustering* approach that quickly and consistently creates clusters over arbitrarily long periods of time. Our incremental clustering approach is based on the phrase graph of the batch approach, however, we extended the phrase graph creation and partitioning steps for incremental operation. We also introduced two new steps, cluster completion and removal.

Algorithm overview. While the batch clustering processes all the input documents together, the incremental clustering processes the documents in small batches, which we call mini-batches. The processing of each mini-batch of documents takes the phrase graph from the previous mini-batch as input and adds the phrases from the current mini-batch to the graph. The resulting phrase graph is saved as input for the next mini-batch of documents. We extended the phrase graph creation and partitioning steps, so that consistent clusters are maintained across mini-batches.

We also expanded the algorithm with cluster completion and removal steps, which make certain that old clusters do not impact cluster quality and are removed from the phrase graph when they stop evolving. These steps are necessary to maintain cluster quality over a large number of mini-batches and to keep the processing resources from growing over time.

A natural choice for the mini-batch size in NIFTY is one day and this is what we use here. The algorithm can be easily used for other mini-batch sizes, if needed. We provide the details of our algorithm next.

Phrase graph creation. Our incremental clustering approach creates daily phrase graphs by building upon the previous day's phrase graph. We attach each newly created phrase to the graph. An important detail here is that we only consider edges between phrases where at least one phrase is new. This constraint guarantees that new edges will not be added between previously existing phrases, which could disrupt the existing cluster structure. Edges for new phrases can be freely added to the graph, since they did not exist the previous day. Besides improving the cluster consistency, this constraint also drastically reduces the number of comparisons needed in comparison to the batch approach and thus speeds up the processing.

Phrase graph partitioning. During the phrase graph partitioning, we want to preserve existing clusters by preserving all edges that existed in the graph the day before. Our partitioning strategy remains the same - edges are removed until all outgoing edges for each node belong to the same cluster. For incremental clustering, we require that an edge is selected over other edges and kept in the graph if both its phrases already existed the day before. Only edges of newly added nodes can thus be removed from the graph. Otherwise, we proceed as before, computing edge weights for all outgoing edges and keeping only the edges from the cluster with the highest edge weight.

This approach guarantees that all edges from the previous day's phrase graph are preserved, which maintains cluster consistency. Furthermore, bypassing the edge weight computation for existing edges allows incremental clustering to further reduce the system run time.

Cluster completion and removal. If incremental clustering is run without ever removing old clusters, the cluster base grows over time, which reduces cluster quality and increases running time. Common but not overly popular phrase clusters (e.g. "I love you") accumulate similar phrases over time, artificially inflating the cluster popularity. To solve this problem, we introduce the concepts of cluster completion and removal, which allow the cluster base to retain only clusters that are alive and active.

NIFTY treats a cluster as *completed* if its average document frequency within the last three days is less than 20% of its frequency at its highest peak. After a cluster is completed, no new phrases are added to the cluster. However, the document frequencies of existing phrases in the cluster are still updated, so that the full lifecycle of the cluster is recorded. As an example, cluster completion prevents phrases such as "a step in the right direction," a commonly used political phrase, from getting mixed in with older and unrelated phrases such as "a move in the right direction," a phrase describing a Christian novel. By the time "a step in the right direction" appears, the cluster with "a move in the right direction" would have fallen past its peak popularity and therefore would be completed, preventing "a step in the right direction" from being incorrectly added to it.

A cluster is *removed* from the phrase graph, if its highest peak is more than seven days old. We consider such clusters final and remove them and their associated phrases and documents from the current cluster base and the phrase graph. Cluster removal helps to maintain a relatively constant and therefore scalable cluster base, which enables NIFTY to be run over datasets with a large time span. It also prevents a previously mentioned problem of inflated cluster popularity from occurring. Clusters that remain after the removal step contain memes that are active and relevant to the present time. If newer phrases are similar to some phrases from a removed cluster, they are either being mentioned due to a new and different event, or are spoken under different contexts. These new phrases should therefore be considered a different meme cluster, which is what NIFTY achieves with cluster removal.

Our final addition of cluster completion and removal to the system allows us to achieve the goal of making NIFTY clustering fast, scalable, and consistent. Incremental clustering can be run over any period of time, which was practically impossible before with batch approaches. Detailed speed and quality experiments and comparisons between MEMETRACKER and NIFTY are given in Section 3.

2.6 Visualization

The last step in NIFTY is to rank the clusters by popularity so that the most popular clusters can be visualized (Figure 1). Each cluster c is assigned a time-based popularity score $S(c)$ based on the number of document mentions and cluster recentness using the following exponential decay formula:

$$S(c) = \sum_{p \in c} \sum_{t=t_p}^{t_c} \exp\left[-\left\lfloor \frac{t_c - t}{48} \right\rfloor\right] \cdot M_p(t)$$

p is a phrase in c, t_p is the time of the earliest mention of phrase p, t_c is the current time, and $M_p(t)$ is the number of document mentions of p at time period t. All time entities have one hour resolution with units being hours, so 48 in the formula corresponds to two days. This score ensures that more recent mentions are weighted more heavily than older mentions.

With a popularity score assigned to each cluster, the visualization step simply sorts the clusters by their popularity score to obtain the top clusters for each day.

3. NIFTY SYSTEM EVALUATION

In the following, we evaluate the NIFTY system performance. We discuss experimental results that establish the performance of NIFTY and evaluate our most important design decisions when constructing the NIFTY system. Then we present a series of experiments where we compare the system performance and resource consumption of NIFTY and MEMETRACKER. We establish that NIFTY runs faster than MEMETRACKER, while simultaneously producing meme clusters of higher quality.

The experimental results were obtained using a dataset that we describe in more detail in Section 4.

3.1 Evaluation of NIFTY

In the following we evaluate particular design decisions we made when building NIFTY. First we demonstrate that locality sensitive hashing speeds up the clustering step by reducing the number of comparisons, while still preserving the structure of the graph as created by using brute force with pairwise comparisons. We then evaluate different methods for phrase graph partitioning and find the best performing one.

Candidate pair creation. The Locality Sensitive Hashing (LSH), used in the phrase clustering step (Sec. 2.3), significantly speeds up the algorithm, but is an approximate method. The balance between the quality of approximation and speed is determined by the band size parameter k and the number of bands n. The band size k determines for one band the number of equal hash results that are required for two phrases to be placed in the same bucket. The number of bands n determines how often the process is repeated,

	baseline	size 1	**size 2**	size 3
#Compares	1.8×10^8	8.7×10^7	**2.6×10^7**	6.4×10^6
Run Time	34m38s	31m28s	**6m56s**	4m01s
Pre Precision	1.00	1.00	**1.00**	1.00
Pre Recall	1.00	0.99	**0.80**	0.57
Pre F1 score	1.00	0.99	**0.91**	0.72
Post Precision	1.00	0.99	**0.96**	0.89
Post Recall	1.00	0.99	**0.95**	0.83
Post F1 score	1.00	0.99	**0.95**	0.86

Table 1: Comparison of LSH band sizes.

once for each band. A smaller k therefore results in more comparisons (increasing running time) but also increases the likelihood of finding all similar edges. A larger n gives two phrases more opportunities to be placed in the same bucket, increasing the quality of approximation and increasing running time.

While fixing the number of bands to 20, we experimented with different band sizes to find the optimal value. These experiments were done over one week of data with 38,000 phrases. Without LSH, these phrases require over 721 million pairwise comparisons. Using LSH, the number of comparisons is reduced to only 26 million.

Table 1 gives detailed results. The baseline performance is based on an index of shingles. We compare each pair of phrases that shares a shingle, which guarantees that all similar phrases are compared. The precision of a phrase graph is calculated as the fraction of edges in the graph that exist also in the baseline graph. The recall is the fraction of edges from the baseline graph found in the phrase graph. The F1 score is computed as the harmonic mean of precision and recall. "Pre" values are calculated before the partitioning step. "Post" values are calculated after the partitioning step has been performed.

The results in Table 1 show that setting the band size k to 2 achieves the optimal balance between speed and quality. Setting k to 1 achieves barely any time gain over the baseline method. On the other hand, k equal to 3 produces clusters of significantly lower quality (low edge recall) than k equal to 2, while time gain is limited.

It is interesting to observe that the final post scores improved significantly after the partitioning step ("Post" scores are generally higher than "Pre" scores). This improvement demonstrates the robustness of our phrase graph partitioning method — even though there is some noise in the graph creation step, the final clusters practically remain unchanged.

Phrase graph partitioning. Next, we investigate different edge selection methods for our phrase graph partitioning algorithm. Starting from the roots of the phrase graph, children repeatedly select a single outgoing edge or a set of edges to determine their parents, and thus the cluster they belong to. We evaluate the following methods for selecting these outgoing edges:

- **Baseline:** Randomly pick an outgoing edge for each node.
- **Method 1:** Pick the outgoing edge with the highest edge weight (break ties arbitrarily).
- **Method 2:** Pick the outgoing edges from the cluster with the most neighbors to the node.
- **Method 3:** Pick the outgoing edges from the cluster whose neighbors of the node have the highest total edge weight.

We compare the methods using two metrics: the fraction of edges in the pre-partitioned graph that connect nodes assigned to the same cluster, and the ratio of the total edge weight of these edges compared to the total edge weight in the pre-partitioned graph. The re-

	% edges kept	% edge weight kept
Baseline	13.41	70.96
Method 1	17.02	95.38
Method 2	23.62	80.60
Method 3	**21.03**	**95.48**

Table 2: Comparison of edge selection methods.

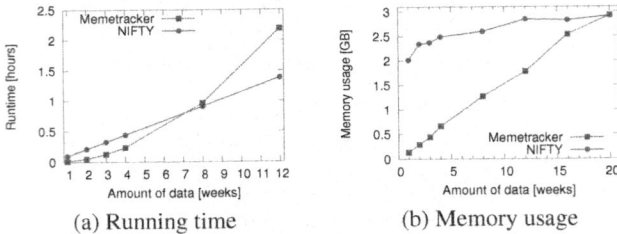

(a) Running time (b) Memory usage

Figure 5: MEMETRACKER and NIFTY resource usage.

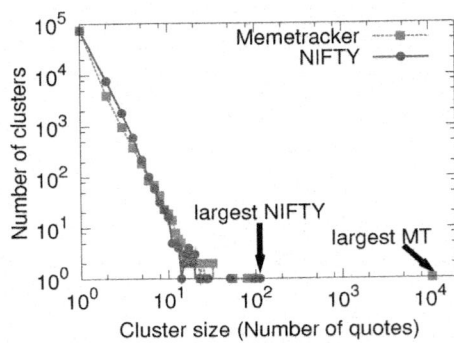

Figure 6: NIFTY vs. MEMETRACKER cluster size distribution. MEMETRACKER produces a giant cluster of 10,000 phrases.

sults are in Table 2. We observe that Method 3 performs best overall. While Method 2 is more successful in retaining edges within clusters, and Method 1 optimizes for the total edge weight, we find Method 3 to give the most balanced performance.

3.2 NIFTY vs. Memetracker

NIFTY builds on MEMETRACKER and we next compare the performance of the two systems. In particular we are interested in comparing resource usage and speed as well as clustering quality.

Resource usage. First in Figure 5 we compare the run time as well as memory usage of the incremental NIFTY algorithm with the batch MEMETRACKER algorithm. Incremental clustering in NIFTY takes on average 1 minute daily to cluster new phrases and documents. As expected, this daily time does not increase over longer time periods, so the total running time increases linearly with the amount of data. Also, because NIFTY archives completed clusters, the amount of memory it requires stabilizes at about 3GB.

On the other hand, MEMETRACKER time complexity and running time is quadratic with respect to the number of days of data that it is processing. Since MEMETRACKER's implementation is less complex than NIFTY's, MEMETRACKER is faster for small datasets. However, we can see that NIFTY is faster once we have at least 8 weeks' worth of data. MEMETRACKER's memory usage is linear with respect to the dataset size because MEMETRACKER must load the whole dataset into memory for clustering.

These results demonstrate that it would be impossible to run MEMETRACKER over our 6 billion document dataset. NIFTY's constant memory usage and linear scaling are the key advantages that allow us to run NIFTY on this large dataset, covering a period of 4 years.

Meme cluster quality. Next we compare the quality of MEMETRACKER and NIFTY clusters. Our first and most important observation is that NIFTY does not suffer from MEMETRACKER's "giant cluster" problem. When MEMETRACKER is run over datasets of non-trivial size, it tends to create a giant cluster that contains a large number of similar phrases that occur over long time periods ("a move in the right direction" vs. "a step in the right direction"). In the giant cluster, multiple phrases are chained together via long and intricate strings of spurious mutations.

For our comparison, we ran NIFTY and MEMETRACKER over the same 1 week input dataset of 102,000 phrases spanning the time period from Jan 1, 2012 to Jan 7, 2012. As shown in Figure 6, MEMETRACKER identified 5,000 nontrivial clusters, but the largest cluster contained more than 10,000 phrases. On the other hand, NIFTY identified 10,000 clusters (twice as many) and the largest NIFTY cluster contained only 112 phrases. MEMETRACKER fused together 10,000 different phrases into a single giant meme cluster, while NIFTY was able to assign those phrases to separate small meme clusters, which is what we want.

We also found that NIFTY and MEMETRACKER produce very similar small clusters except for those that MEMETRACKER folds into the giant cluster. Larger clusters differ more, and a manual inspection shows that MEMETRACKER clusters, when different, combine phrases that do not belong to the same meme. For example, "there is nothing we can do from here" is combined with "we don't care about data or figures, there's nothing we can do about pollution even it exceeds the limit". In conclusion, there are several clustering concerns with MEMETRACKER that we successfully address in NIFTY.

4. PROCESSING 6B DOCUMENTS

Having established the performance of NIFTY we are now ready to run the system over the full 4 year dataset of over 6 billion documents. Here we briefly describe our massive dataset characteristics and give some details of the NIFTY implementation and execution on the dataset.

Data description. Our dataset covers the online media activity since August 1, 2008. It includes posts from the mainstream publishers, blogs, forums and other media sites. At the time of this writing in mid November 2012, the dataset contains over 6.1 billion documents and 2.8 billion unique quoted phrases. Around 3.2 million new documents and 1.5 million unique phrases are added to the dataset daily. The total size of our dataset is 20TB.

We use Spinn3r [33] to obtain new documents. Spinn3r is a service that monitors over 20 million Internet sources, retrieves any new posts and makes them available via an API. The breadth of Spinn3r sources provides essentially complete coverage of online media.

Implementation. The NIFTY pipeline starts with a client that downloads new documents from Spinn3r. The client extracts quoted phrases, which are defined as any string in the document that is enclosed by quotation marks, the URL and an estimated publish time for all new documents. The rest of the pipeline reads the output from the Spinn3r client and implements the methods described in Section 2. The pipeline is initialized with two weeks of data,

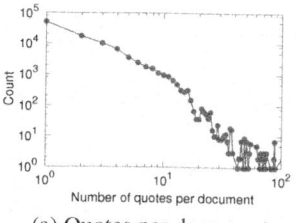
(a) Quotes per document

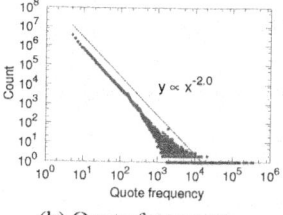
(b) Quote frequency

Figure 7: Basic properties of input data. (a) Number of quotes per document vs. number of such documents. (b) Quote frequency vs. number of such quotes.

processed by our batch clustering algorithm. Afterwards, our incremental clustering algorithm is used to add daily updates.

The entire pipeline is implemented in C++ and uses the open source SNAP software for text and graph manipulation [32]. As part of NIFTY, several novel algorithms were developed. We are in the process of integrating these algorithms in SNAP and making them publicly available as open source.

Execution. Although the main purpose of NIFTY is to process new documents as they become available, its ability to work incrementally allows us to run the pipeline over the entire dataset in our news archive. The processing of 20TB of data with 6.1 billion of documents collected over 4 years took less than five days on a single machine.

Figure 7 shows characteristics of our input data. We note that the distribution over the number of quotes per document (Fig. 7(a)) as well as the quote frequency both exhibit a heavy tailed distribution. While documents contain less than hundred quotes, quotes themselves are heavily popular on the Web and some quotes get mentioned hundreds of thousands of times.

The filtering step (Sec. 2.2) starts with 2.9 billion quoted phrases in 6.1 billion documents. The first filtering pass keeps 0.9 billion unique phrases in 0.5 billion documents. The second filtering pass ultimately selects for further processing 378 million phrases in 133 million documents, which means an average of 2.9 phrases per document. 33 million of those phrases are unique.

The filtering step takes, on average, 7 minutes and 6 GB of memory to filter a day's worth of data. To reduce execution time, we run 10 instances of filtering concurrently on a single multicore machine, which brings the total filtering time for the entire 4 year dataset to 17 hours.

The clustering step (Sec. 2.3) creates 9 million meme clusters from 33 million unique phrases. An average number of phrase mentions for a meme is 42. The clustering step takes four days at a rate of 8.5 million phrases clustered per day, running as a single thread.

5. ANALYSIS OF MEMES

By extracting memes from our massive 6 billion document 20TB dataset spanning 4 years, we also learn interesting facts about the characteristics and dynamics of online memes. We examine some of our findings here.

Properties of meme clusters. We observed several interesting trends illustrated in Figure 8. First, NIFTY outputs between 6 and 10 thousand clusters per day (Fig. 8(a)). While the number of unique extracted quoted phrases varies between 20 and 50 thousand per day, the number of identified meme clusters is about 5 times smaller, which means an average meme has between 3 to 5 mutational variants found on the Web.

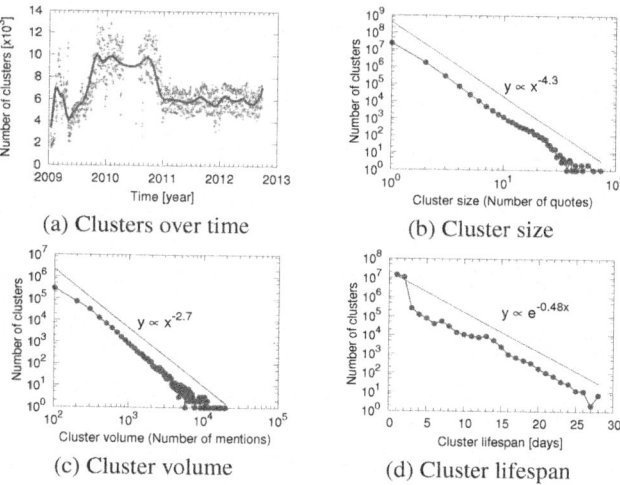

Figure 8: NIFTY meme clusters over a 4 year period.

In terms of the meme cluster size measured in the number of phrases contained in the cluster, we observe a nice heavy tailed distribution with the largest clusters containing slightly fewer than 100 variants (Fig. 8(b)). Similarly, the cluster volume measured as the total number of mentions of all the phrases in the cluster follows a power-law like distribution (Fig. 8(c)). We also observe that the most popular memes on the Web are mentioned tens of thousands of times.

Last, we examine the distribution of meme lifetimes. Here we quantify the lifetime of a cluster simply as the time difference between the 5th and 95th percentile of all mentions of phrases in the cluster. Such a definition is more robust than taking the difference between the time of the first and the time of a last mention of any phrase in the cluster. In Figure 8(d) we note an interesting exponential decay in meme lifetime. While most memes live only for a day or two, long-lasting memes remain for about 1 month. This nicely agrees with previous works on human attention and patterns of temporal variation in online media [39].

Properties of phrases inside clusters. Next we examine how properties of meme clusters vary as a function of the phrases that are part of the same meme cluster. In particular, we characterize every meme cluster in two different ways: by its most mentioned phrase, referred to as the popular phrase, and also by its root phrase (i.e., the root node of the cluster). Figure 9 plots various characteristics of clusters based on the word length of the most popular phrase (left column) as well as the word length of the root phrase (right column).

We observe that most popular phrases as well as root phrases are short in most meme clusters (Figures 9(a),(b)). There is surprisingly little difference between the two distributions. However, we observe an interesting distinction between the length of the root vs. most popular phrase when we compare the cluster sizes (i.e., the number of mutational variants in the cluster). Here we notice memes mutate the most when the most popular phrase is relatively short (Fig. 9(c)) and the root phrase is long (Fig. 9(d)). This is interesting as it suggests that memes that mutate a lot contain short catch phrases that appear in the context of a larger phrase.

We observe similar behavior when investigating meme lifespan. We observe that memes with shorter most popular phrases survive longer (Fig. 9(e)), while memes with short roots diminish sooner (Fig. 9(f)). Such behavior is consistent with our explanation above.

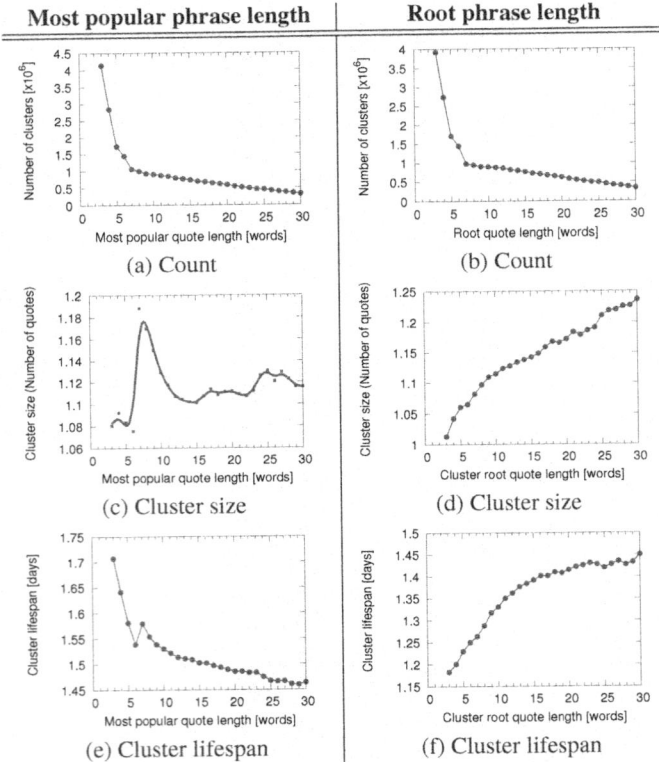

Figure 9: Global characteristics of meme clusters and phrases.

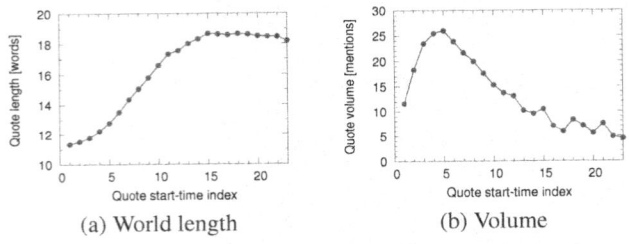

Figure 10: Phrase word length and volume as a function of order of the appearance.

Meme property	Popular	Unpopular
Most popular phrase length	7.49	11.64
Root phrase length	11.46	11.94
#Phrase variants	2.84	1.10
Meme lifespan [days]	8.66	1.33
#Peaks	2.62	1.85

Table 3: Comparison of popular and unpopular meme clusters.

When focusing on the number of mentions a phrase receives as a function of the order of appearance (Figure 10(b)), we notice that a phrase variant that appears 5th tends to be the most popular. The popularity quickly drops off with phrases that appear later in the cluster lifetime receiving less and less attention (i.e., volume).

Comparison of popular and unpopular memes. Last, we also examined the differences between memes that get at least some popularity vs. memes that receive little or no attention. For the purpose of this experiment we call a meme popular if it was mentioned at least 350 times, and we call all other memes unpopular.

Table 3 shows that the average length of the most frequently mentioned phrase in a cluster is significantly shorter in popular clusters in comparison to unpopular ones. On the other hand, the root phrase length does not change excessively. This suggests that popular phrases are significantly more likely to be shortened into more memorable sound bites [11]. The fact that popular clusters contain significantly more phrase variants on average supports this hypothesis. We also noticed that popular memes live significantly longer than unpopular ones on average. This also explains why popular memes exhibit more peaks in their volume, as the temporal dynamics of online media tends to follow a strong daily cycle [39].

6. CONCLUSION

In this paper we have developed NIFTY, a system for tracking short, distinctive textual phrases that travel relatively intact through online text. We presented a highly scalable algorithm for meme-tracking which identifies and clusters mutational variants of textual phrases. Our system scales to a collection of 6 billion articles, which makes the present study one of the largest analyses of online news in terms of data scale. Moreover, we provided a live deployment of the NIFTY system which allows users to explore the dynamics of information dissemination and mutation in mainstream and social media.

Our approach to meme-tracking opens a range of opportunities for future work. For example, how can we understand the dynamics of the mutation of memes over both time and space? Given that our data essentially covers the entire online media landscape over the last four years, it may be possible to more generally identify and model the way in which the essential "core" of a widespread meme emerges and enters popular discourse. Similarly, the long time period that our dataset encompasses may ease studies on the evolution of online media commentary and practices, as well as on the kind of collective behavior that leads directly to the ways in which all of us experience news and its consequences.

Acknowledgements. We thank Hyun Goo Kang, Wonhong Lee, and Hai Wei for their help with the phrase clustering decision tree, Andrej Krevl for his help with the website and Spinn3r for providing the document dataset. This research has been supported in part by NSF IIS-1016909, CNS-1010921, CAREER IIS-1149837, IIS-1159679, ARO MURI, DARPA SMISC, DARPA XDATA, ARL AHPCRC, Brown Institute for Media Innovation, Okawa Foundation, Docomo, Boeing, Allyes, Volkswagen, Intel, Alfred P. Sloan Fellowship and the Microsoft Faculty Fellowship.

Memes with short catch phrases that are parts of longer narratives survive longer and are also more diverse [11].

Properties of phrases. We also compare how properties of phrases change as the memes evolve over time. Here we simply order the phrases belonging to the same meme cluster in order of their first appearance. Figure 10 shows the results, from which we make several interesting observations. We plot the average phrase word length as a function of the order in which the phrases inside the same cluster appear (Figure 10(a)). We observe that phrases that get mentioned first are generally much shorter than phrases that appear later in the meme lifetime. This phenomenon is consistent with the fact that blogs and social media sites react to trends and news quickly, and mention memes before the mainstream media does [20, 39]. Social media sites tend to mention a shorter and more impactful version of the meme. For example, during the 2012 U.S. presidential election campaign, a popular meme "*binders full of women*" emerged. This catchphrase version of the meme was mentioned much before the original long version of the meme which was: "*I went to a number of women's groups and said, can you help us find folks? And they brought us whole binders full of women.*"

7. REFERENCES

[1] L. Adamic and N. Glance. The political blogosphere and the 2004 U.S. election: Divided they blog. In Proc. *LinkKDD '05*, pages 36–43, 2005.

[2] L. Adamic, T. Lento, and A. Fiore. How you met me. In Proc. *ICWSM '12*, pages 371–374, 2012.

[3] E. Adar, L. Zhang, L. A. Adamic, and R. M. Lukose. Implicit structure and the dynamics of blogspace. In *Workshop on the Weblogging Ecosystem*, 2004.

[4] A. Ahmed, Q. Ho, J. Eisenstein, E. Xing, A. Smola, and C. Teo. Unified analysis of streaming news. In Proc. *WWW '11*, pages 267–276, 2011.

[5] J. Allan (editor). *Topic Detection and Tracking: Event-based Information Organization*. Kluwer, 2002.

[6] M. Atkinson and E. Van der Goot. Near real time information mining in multilingual news. In Proc. *WWW '09*, pages 1153–1154, 2009.

[7] D. M. Blei, A. Y. Ng, and M. I. Jordan. Latent dirichlet allocation. In Proc. *NIPS*, pages 601–608, 2001.

[8] K. D. Bollacker, S. Lawrence, and C. L. Giles. A system for automatic personalized tracking of scientific literature on the web. In Proc. *DL '99*, pages 105–113, 1999.

[9] A. Broder, M. Charikar, A. Frieze, and M. Mitzenmacher. Min-wise independent permutations. In Proc. *STOC '98*, pages 327–336, 1998.

[10] J. Cook, A. Das Sarma, A. Fabrikant, and A. Tomkins. Your two weeks of fame and your grandmother's. In Proc. *WWW '12*, pages 919–928, 2012.

[11] C. Danescu-Niculescu-Mizil, J. Cheng, J. Kleinberg, and L. Lee. You had me at hello: How phrasing affects memorability. In Proc. *ACL '12*, pages 892–901, 2012.

[12] A. Das, M. Datar, A. Garg, and S. Rajaram. Google news personalization: scalable online collaborative filtering. In Proc. *WWW '07*, pages 271–280, 2007.

[13] M. Dubinko, R. Kumar, J. Magnani, J. Novak, P. Raghavan, and A. Tomkins. Visualizing tags over time. *ACM Trans. Web*, 1(2):7, 2007.

[14] E. Gabrilovich, S. Dumais, and E. Horvitz. Newsjunkie: Providing personalized newsfeeds via analysis of information novelty. In Proc. *WWW '04*, pages 482–490, 2004.

[15] D. Gruhl, R. Liben-Nowell, R. V. Guha, and A. Tomkins. Information diffusion through blogspace. In Proc. *WWW '04*, 2004.

[16] S. Havre, B. Hetzler, and L. Nowell. ThemeRiver: Visualizing theme changes over time. In Proc. *INFOVIS '00*, 2000.

[17] P. Indyk and R. Motwani. Approximate nearest neighbors: towards removing the curse of dimensionality. In Proc. *STOC '98*, pages 604–613, 1998.

[18] J. Kleinberg. Bursty and hierarchical structure in streams. In Proc. *KDD '02*, pages 91–101, 2002.

[19] M. Krstajic, F. Mansmann, A. Stoffel, M. Atkinson, and D. Keim. Processing online news streams for large-scale semantic analysis. In Proc. *Data Engineering Workshop (ICDEW)*, pages 215–220, 2010.

[20] J. Leskovec, L. Backstrom, and J. Kleinberg. Meme-tracking and the dynamics of the news cycle. In Proc. *KDD '09*, pages 497–506, 2009.

[21] J. Leskovec, M. McGlohon, C. Faloutsos, N. Glance, and M. Hurst. Cascading behavior in large blog graphs. In Proc. *SDM '07*, 2007.

[22] L. Lloyd, D. Kechagias, and S. Skiena. Lydia: A system for large-scale news analysis. In *String Processing and Information Retrieval*, pages 161–166, Springer, 2005.

[23] U. Manber et al. Finding similar files in a large file system. In Proc. *USENIX '94*, pages 1–10, 1994.

[24] C. Marlow, M. Naaman, D. Boyd, and M. Davis. Ht06, tagging paper, taxonomy, flickr, academic article, to read. In Proc. *HYPERTEXT '06*, pages 31–40, 2006.

[25] X. Phan, L. Nguyen, and S. Horiguchi. Learning to classify short and sparse text & web with hidden topics from large-scale data collections. In Proc. *WWW '08*, pages 91–100, 2008.

[26] A. Rajaraman and J. Ullman. *Mining of massive datasets*. Cambridge University Press, 2011.

[27] J. Ratkiewicz, M. Conover, M. Meiss, B. Gonçalves, A. Flammini, and F. Menczer. Detecting and tracking political abuse in social media. In Proc. *ICWSM '11*, 2011.

[28] T. Sakaki, M. Okazaki, and Y. Matsuo. Earthquake shakes twitter users: real-time event detection by social sensors. In Proc. *WWW '10*, pages 851–860, 2010.

[29] D. Shahaf and C. Guestrin. Connecting the dots between news articles. In Proc. *KDD '10*, pages 623–632, 2010.

[30] D. Shahaf, C. Guestrin, and E. Horvitz. Trains of thought: Generating information maps. In Proc. *WWW '12*, pages 899–908, 2012.

[31] M. Simmons, L. Adamic, and E. Adar. Memes online: Extracted, subtracted, injected, and recollected. In Proc. *ICWSM '11*, 2011.

[32] SNAP Software Package. http://snap.stanford.edu. 2012.

[33] Spinn3r API. http://www.spinn3r.com. 2008.

[34] M. L. Stein, S. Paterno, and R. C. Burnett. *Newswriter's Handbook: An Introduction to Journalism*. Blackwell, second edition, 2006.

[35] 1000 Most Common English Words. http://www.perlmonks.org/bare/?node_id=310060. 2003.

[36] C. Wang, D. M. Blei, and D. Heckerman. Continuous time dynamic topic models. In Proc. *UAI '08*, pages 579–586, 2008.

[37] X. Wang, A. McCallum, and X. Wei. Topical n-grams: Phrase and topic discovery, with an application to information retrieval. In Proc. *ICDM '07*, pages 697–702, 2007.

[38] L. Xie, A. Natsev, J. Kender, M. Hill, and J. Smith. Visual memes in social media: tracking real-world news in youtube videos. In Proc. *MULTIMEDIA '11*, pages 53–62, 2011.

[39] J. Yang and J. Leskovec. Patterns of temporal variation in online media. In Proc. *WSDM '11*, pages 177–186, 2011.

[40] L. Yao, D. M. Mimno, and A. McCallum. Efficient methods for topic model inference on streaming document collections. In Proc. *KDD '09*, pages 937–946, 2009.

When Relevance is not Enough: Promoting Diversity and Freshness in Personalized Question Recommendation

Idan Szpektor, Yoelle Maarek, Dan Pelleg
Yahoo! Research
Haifa 31905, Israel
{idan,dpelleg}@yahoo-inc.com, yoelle@ymail.com

ABSTRACT

What makes a good question recommendation system for community question-answering sites? First, to maintain the health of the ecosystem, it needs to be designed around answerers, rather than exclusively for askers. Next, it needs to scale to many questions and users, and be fast enough to route a newly-posted question to potential answerers within the few minutes before the asker's patience runs out. It also needs to show each answerer questions that are relevant to his or her interests. We have designed and built such a system for Yahoo! Answers, but realized, when testing it with live users, that it was not enough.

We found that those drawing-board requirements fail to capture user's interests. The feature that they really missed was diversity. In other words, showing them just the main topics they had previously expressed interest in was simply too dull. Adding the spice of topics slightly outside the core of their past activities significantly improved engagement. We conducted a large-scale online experiment in production in Yahoo! Answers that showed that recommendations driven by relevance alone perform worse than a control group without question recommendations, which is the current behavior. However, an algorithm promoting both diversity and freshness improved the number of answers by 17%, daily session length by 10%, and had a significant positive impact on peripheral activities such as voting.

Categories and Subject Descriptors

H.2.8 [**Database Management**]: Database Apps—*Data Mining*

General Terms

Algorithms, Analysis, Experimentation, Human Factors

Keywords

Recommender Systems, User Models, Community Question Answering

1. INTRODUCTION

Community Question Answering (CQA) websites, such as Yahoo! Answers, Quora, Baidu Zhidao and WikiAnswers,

offer a convenient means for Web users to address needs that Web search engines cannot satisfy. They range from complex, rare or heterogeneous needs, for which content does not exist yet on the Web, to socially oriented needs, for which the asker wants a human to provide a personal subjective opinion. Examples of such needs include homework help, e.g. "*how to integrate e^{-x}?*", opinion seeking, e.g. "*what would be the best kind of pet to have?*", recommendations, e.g. "*best place to hang out in Paris?*", etc. Answerers, in return, help their fellow users mostly for social reward [22], thus creating an askers/answerers ecosystem that all users, active or not, can benefit from.

In order to keep this ecosystem alive, new questions need to be answered constantly. It is therefore crucial for CQA sites to facilitate the answering task. One common way to do so is to recommend questions to potential answerers. Most previous studies on the topic have focused on presenting each question only to the best possible answerers, namely the "experts", so as to satisfy the asker's needs [13, 14, 17, 28]. However, to maintain the ecosystem, it is important to satisfy all potential answerers and not only a limited number of experts. A data analysis we conducted on a sample of 4 million answers from Yahoo! Answers revealed that level-1 users[1], *i.e.* the most junior users in the system (users with less than 250 points) generate almost a third of all answers, as shown in Figure 1. Furthermore, the graph also shows that level-1 and level-2 users together (users with less than 1,000 points) contribute almost 50% of all answers. It would therefore be a major mistake to ignore these "regular" answerers.

A key element to satisfying all types of users is to better understand what types of questions really attract them. The usual approach in question recommendation has been to focus on the relevance of the question to the user, that is, to what degree the question matches the user's tastes [21, 15]. Yet, CQA sites, like most user-generated content sites, are highly dynamic and constantly expose their users to diverse and fresh content originating from other users. Following this observation, we argue here that the engagement of users in CQA sites is driven not only by relevance but also by diversity and freshness needs. These needs were acknowledged in traditional recommender systems [30, 3], as well as in traditional Information Retrieval [8]. However, to the best of our knowledge, they have been ignored in current question recommendation research.

---

[1]See http://answers.yahoo.com/info/scoring_system for more details on levels and points in Yahoo! Answers.

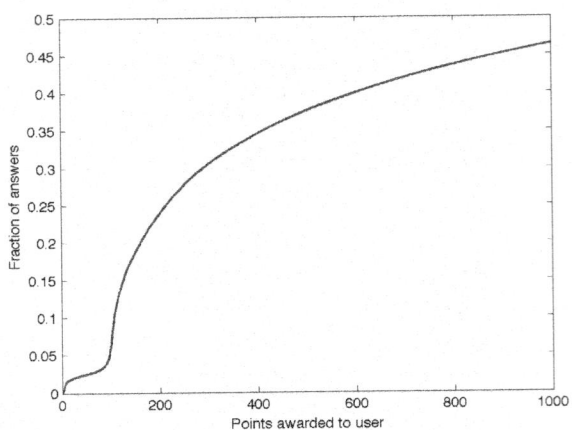

Figure 1: Cumulative rate of answers contribution, by level of activity in Yahoo! Answers

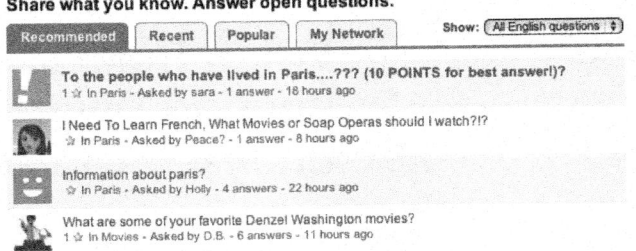

Figure 2: Personalized question recommendation shown in the online experiment in Yahoo! Answers

Following the above motivations, we introduce in this paper a novel question recommendation approach that is designed to meet three requirements: (a) questions need to be recommended for all types of users, from casual with minimal historical data to highly active experts, (b) questions have to be diverse and intriguing in order to keep the potential answerer engaged, and finally (c) recommendations need to be fresh and be served fast. The last requirement refers, among others, to the ability to serve questions as recommendations immediately after they have been posted, as well as to instantly adapting to users' changes in taste as they answer more questions. The above three requirements impose serious scalability constraints on both the serving and learning stages.

In our approach, a user is represented by a *profile* that is instantiated as soon as she answers her first question, allowing even new answerers to receive recommendations. The profile is then incrementally updated and immediately tuned for every new answer the user provides, getting richer with each additional answer. Similarly, profiles for questions are generated right after they are posted. Thus, questions immediately become candidates for recommendation, increasing their chances to be answered fast. Finally, recommendations are selected by relevance to the user, matching question profiles to the user profile. Yet, in addition to identifying personalized relevant questions, we also guarantee diversity by using a novel proactive *topic sampling* algorithm that enforces recommendations to match different topics within the user profile.

We have evaluated our system in production in Yahoo! Answers, launching a "bucket" experiment over a percentage of its users. The users selected in the experiment were exposed to a new tab when visiting the site, labeled "recommended" as shown in Figure 2. In this specific example, the questions were personalized for a user who had answered a few questions in travel in France and in movies. Several configurations of our recommender system were evaluated over a period of two weeks, and the activities of users in each configuration were compared to a control group. The surprising results showed that based only on relevance, the recommender system actually had a negative effect compared to the control group. However, when we added freshness, forcing recommendations to come from recently asked questions, the trend changed, and users answered 4% more when offered personalized *and* fresh questions. But, the highest user activity rates were achieved when diversification was added, even at the cost of reduced freshness. In this configuration, users provided 17% more answers than the control group, and the improvement was observed across all user levels. Furthermore, this successful question recommendation experience had an indirect positive effect on many other user activities. These include, among others, higher asking rates (+5%), voting rates (+19%) and longer dwelling times on the site (+10%).

2. RELATED WORK

With millions of active users, Yahoo! Answers connects between askers and answerers, who interact on a large variety of topics. Askers post questions by providing a title that specifies their core needs, which are often syntactically formulated as a question. They can then optionally add details in a body field. Finally, they assign their question to a specific category within a predefined hierarchy of categories. For example, the question "*how to stop my dog from barking?*" was assigned to the category '*Pets/Dogs*' (*e.g.* the sub-category "Dogs" under the parent "Pets"). Any new question remains "open" for answering for four days, or less if the asker chose a best answer within this period. Users can also rate answers and questions and vote for best answer. Once a question has been answered and a best answer has been chosen, the question is considered resolved.

Today, users in an "answering mood" typically scan a long and dynamic list of all open questions, looking for questions to answer. This list is ranked by recency, with the freshest questions at the top. It is also very diverse, since new questions are asked on different topics all the time. As a result, it is pretty tedious for users to find the questions they like to answer. Consequently, prior work on question recommendation mostly focused on personalizing suggested questions to the user by relevance. The efforts in this direction can be classified into two types, which we refer to as "question routing to experts" and "question recommendation to all".

The first type aims at satisfying first of all the asker, and to this effect attempts to identify the most qualified answerers, or "experts", in order to route questions to them [13, 29, 14, 16, 18, 17, 28, 23]. While this approach does have some benefits, it ignores new and casual users who are essential elements of the ecosystem as discussed before, and represent the majority of users in Yahoo! Answers [11].

The second class of studies, to which this work belongs, aims at satisfying all potential answerers by recommending personalized open questions to them, and include [21, 15, 10]. Most of the existing solutions in this class however suffer from several limitations. First, these algorithms do not scale well to real-time ranking of millions of questions to hundreds of users per second, as required in a large site like Yahoo! Answers. One scalability limitation in these algorithms is the utilization of complex machine learning or time consuming feature construction [15, 10], which hinders fast searching within millions of open questions. Another scalability limitation lies in offline construction of user preferences [21], which prevents real-time response to new questions and answers. Second, the needs of new users with very little historical data are not addressed well. For example, an offline model construction algorithm, such as [21], cannot serve recommendations to brand new users who answer for the first time, since they have no preferences until the next offline construction round. Not only new users but also new questions are not modeled adequately in many cases. For instance, collaborative filtering approaches such as [15] are ineffective for both new users and new questions, as very little information pertaining to questions is available at posting time, as detailed in the next section.

Finally, all prior research on question recommendation focused only on relevance, ignoring the need for diversity in the recommendations as well as their freshness. Yet, research in other recommendation tasks and in Information Retrieval indicates that both diversity [30, 26, 6, 3, 7] and freshness [8, 9] are critical to user engagement and satisfaction. In this paper, we aim at bridging the gap between current question recommendation algorithms and on-line CQA requirements. We propose an algorithm that recommends questions to any user, taking into account relevance, diversification and freshness, as well as scalability and real-time requirements.

We next present our approach, which includes the representation of questions (Section 3) and users (Section 4) followed by the recommendation of questions to users while addressing relevance, diversification and freshness (Section 5).

3. QUESTION PROFILE

We represent each question by a *question profile*, which is the basic building block in our framework. We will discuss in the following section how *user profiles* are derived from question profiles. Thus, questions and users are represented in the same feature space in order to facilitate the matching between open questions and users for personalized recommendations, as done for instance by [13, 18, 10, 23].

We chose not to use a single feature space for all of questions but rather split it according to the 26 top categories in Yahoo! Answers (*Sports, Health, Pets, Travel* etc.), as they usually represent disjoint users' interests. Another advantage of this separation is an implicit word sense disambiguation. We follow Li et al. [17], who showed that language models that incorporate categories are beneficial when modeling answerers, yet we do not go as far as splitting at the category leaf level. Thus, a question posted in the nested category '*Travel/France/Paris*', will be modeled in the feature space associated with the top category level '*Travel*'. Our main rationale is twofold: first, we want to allow matching question and user profiles across leaf cat-

LDA		Lexical		Category	
$topic_5$:	0.6	bark:	0.7	Pets/Dogs:	1.0
$topic_{30}$:	0.3	dog:	0.1		
		stop:	0.2		

Table 1: Example of question profile for "*how to stop my dog from barking?*" posted in top category '*Pets*'

egories, and second, we want to avoid data sparseness in infrequent leaf categories. We do, however, encode the leaf category '*France/Paris*' as a feature in the question profile itself as discussed later.

Since we consider all open questions as recommendation candidates as soon as they are posted, the amount of available information at this time is limited. Indeed, new questions include no information about interactions with answerers, no click data, etc. We note that a consequence of this limited information is that traditional collaborative filtering methods for question recommendation, such as [15], are less appropriate for recommending fresh questions. We decided to take a simplifying approach and to only consider the question textual content (title and body) and its category when building the question profile, ignoring any additional question data that may be added later, as well as the asker id (which is provided at posting time). This is motivated by a previous study conducted by some of the authors of this paper. They showed that the prominent contributors for matching a question to a user are the text and the category of the question, and that user-user interaction does not improve the relevance of question recommendations [10]. We note that this is also the data choice in other studies that considered new questions for recommendation [13, 21, 16, 23]. An additional motivation for utilizing only the initial question data is that it allows for question profiles to be built only once, at posting time, without any updates later. This presents clear benefits in terms of scalability.

Given a freshly posted English question, we first conduct some basic preprocessing on its textual content, before building the actual profile. We concatenate the text and body contents and then apply tokenization, lemmatization, as well as domain-specific stop-word removal[2]. Once the question is preprocessed, we build its profile, which is represented by three vectors: (a) a **Latent Dirichlet Allocation (LDA)** [2] topic vector that represents the latent topics that are related to the question, (b) a **lexical** vector that represents the surface level textual content of the questions, and (c) a **category** vector that represents the category in which the question is posted. Each vector corresponds to a different question model, with its own separate feature space, as illustrated in Table 1.

In the question profile, the relative importance of each vector is left unspecified. Instead, it is tuned in a personalized way for each user in the user profile, as detailed in the next section. In addition, we chose to maintain question profiles under a probabilistic framework, in which each vector represents a question as a probability distribution over the model's feature space. This allows us to have a common comparable ground between models, and facilitates the diversification of recommendations as detailed in Section 5.2.

---

[2]For conciseness, we omit here the details of these stages.

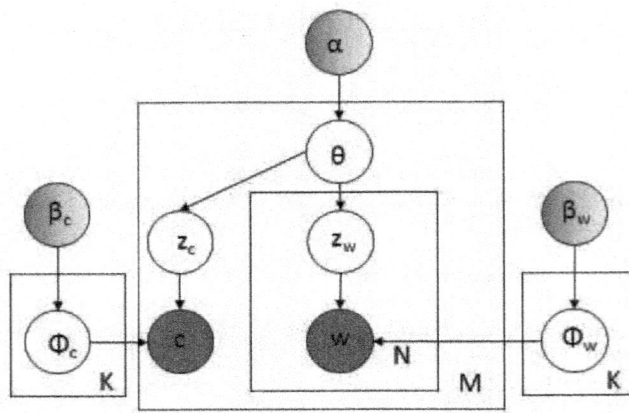

Figure 3: Plate notation of our LDA variant. Categories and words are respectively denoted as c and w. Gradient colored nodes are time-dependent parameters.

3.1 LDA Model

We were inspired by several studies that showed the benefit of utilizing latent topics in various CQA tasks, such as expert finding [13, 18, 23], question recommendation [21] and question retrieval [4, 24]. Following, we employ an LDA variant that explains the textual content of the question as well as its assigned category, as in [13, 4]. We note that the category information is particularly useful for topic inference when there are only few words in the question, as it acts as a constraint over the semantic domain of the question. For longer questions, the effect of the category diminishes. Another particularity of our LDA variant is the incremental time-dependent update of the β and α hyperparameters at training time given new questions, inspired by [1]. This design enables incremental training, and thus supports backward compatibility, since topics are only gradually shifted to include new evidence. As a result, given an incrementally trained model, the only update required in a live system is the reloading of the new LDA models, without the need to construct all question profiles and user profiles from scratch, which would not scale. Our LDA variant is depicted in Figure 3.

Following our top-category split, we learned a separate LDA model for each top category. For each model, we used as initial training set a random sample of up to 2 million resolved questions[3] published in the associated top category between 2010 and 2011. We trained our models using a sparse collapsed Gibbs sampler [25] with 1,000 rounds, learning 200 topics per model. We set β initially to 0.01 and α's sum to 4. After learning the initial model, we evolved it, through incremental learning, to incorporate a random sample of up to half a million questions per top category from the first half of 2012. This allowed us to verify that topics indeed remain stable after a large incremental update, in which each top-category lexicon was enriched by several thousand new words on average. At inference time, we apply 100 burn-in Gibbs rounds and then average 10 rounds with a gap of 10 rounds between each sample.

LDA inference provides a dense topic distribution, in which every topic has a non zero probability due to the Dirichlet smoothing. Even if only topics that were assigned to words are considered, the distribution is not sparse enough due to Gibbs assignment averaging. This is bad news when searching for the best questions that match a user, since many question profiles have to be considered. This is because their topic intersection with the user profile is not empty. Yet, we observed that most questions are short and focus on one theme that represents the asker's need. Therefore, one would expect that most of the probability mass will be assigned to one or two LDA topics. We empirically found it to be the case, and, following this observation, we filter the inferred LDA vector and retain only the topics that were assigned at least 10% of the probability mass. After this filtering, most questions are represented by no more than 3-4 topics that capture the essence of the question, a sparse representation that enables fast matching via an inverted index (see Section 5.1). We note that we do not re-normalize the topic probability after this filtering, but remain with a "discounted" probability distribution (left column of Table 1).

3.2 Lexical Model

We follow prior work in incorporating a unigram bag-of-words representation of a question. This model captures fine-grained word level interests. For example, an answerer may be interested not in haircuts in general, for which there is a specific LDA topic, but in Korean haircuts only. This refinement of the asker's need is addressed by the appearance of the word '*Korean*' in the lexical vector.

To this end, each word in the text of the question is assigned a simple tf·idf score. Note that each top category has its own idf scores, computed over all resolved questions posted in that category between 2010 and 2012. Once the tf·idf scores are calculated, they are $L1$ normalized, resulting in a probability distribution (middle column of Table 1). As for LDA, we support incremental updates to the idf scores.

3.3 Category Model

Finally, the category model is most straightforward as it assigns a probability of 1 to the category in which the question was posted. This model provides a rigid high-level representation of interests, which is useful when encountering fine-grained categories such as '*Paris*', but not as much for more generic leaf categories, such as '*Performing Arts*'.

4. USER PROFILE

In most question recommendation methods, users are represented by their interactions with the questions they answered in the past. More specifically, the user representation is generated by aggregating signals over these questions [13, 29, 21, 15, 16, 18, 17, 10, 28, 23]. We follow this paradigm by deriving *user profiles* from question profiles. In prior work, user profiles might include several models as we do, but the relative weights of models were learned globally, and this unique distribution of weights was applied to all users, as done in [29, 18, 16]. In this work, we take a more personalized approach, learning model weights as well as preferences over top categories for each user separately.

To support this level of personalization, we represent a user profile as a *probability tree*, in which each node consists

---
[3] All questions considered here have been classified as non-spam beforehand by the usual Yahoo! Answers mechanisms.

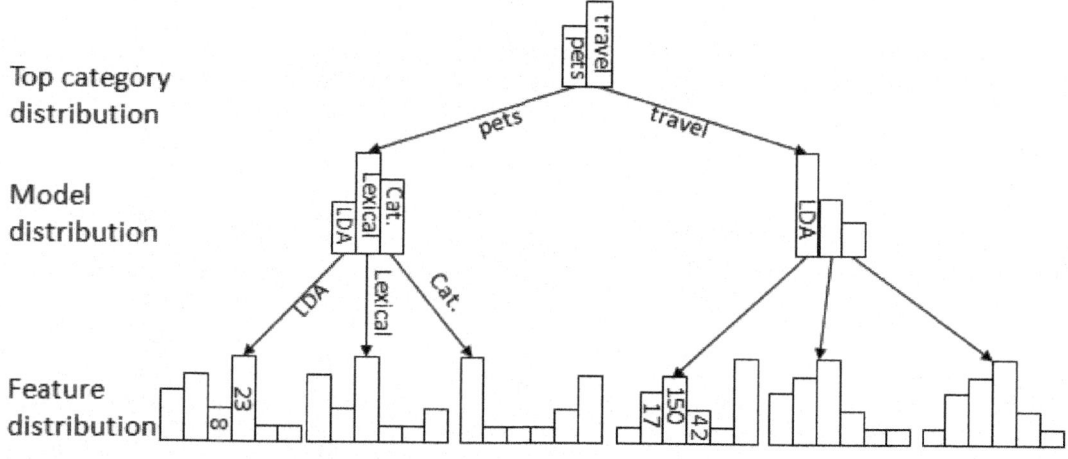

Figure 4: User profile as a probability distribution tree

of a probability distribution that stands over various elements of our question model. Figure 4 exemplifies one such probability tree. There are three levels in each probability tree, defined as follows:

top-category-distribution **level:** The root node consists of a distribution of preference probabilities over top categories. Thus, as illustrated in Figure 4 via histogram-like bars, this specific user has been more active in the '*Travel*' than in the '*Pets*' category and has ignored other categories. For each top category appearing in the root of this user profile, there is an edge (labeled with the top category node in the same Figure) that points to a second-level node.

model-distribution **level:** Each second-level node consists of a distribution of probabilities over the models that define any question profile, namely the LDA, lexical and category models. Each such node points to exactly 3 nodes at the third level of the tree, one for each model.

feature-distribution **level:** The nodes in the third level hold a distribution of probability over features, where features differ for each model. For the nodes reached by an LDA edge, each feature represents a latent topic, for those reached by a lexical edge, each feature is a word, and finally for those reached by a category node, each feature is a leaf category.

We explain next how this data structure is built for each user by aggregating the profiles of the questions the user answered. Specifically, whenever the user answers a question, her user profile is updated with the question profile in a multi-armed bandit fashion. This update changes the probability distributions along the relevant paths in the profile distribution tree that correspond to the question's top category and its models. At the first and third tree levels, representing top-category-distribution and feature-distribution respectively, the updates are rather straightforward, adding each distribution in the question profile to the distribution of the corresponding node in the user profile. One limitation of all prior question recommendation approaches to the best of our knowledge, is that they ignored the fact that users may change their answering tastes. In contrast, we introduce a decaying factor on past questions, reducing their effect on the user profile over time to enable the user to shift their answer tastes more rapidly. We use the following node update formula:

$$p_u = \frac{p_q + \alpha \cdot Z_c \cdot p_c}{1 + \alpha \cdot Z_c}$$
$$Z_u = 1 + \alpha \cdot Z_c$$

where p_q is a distribution in the answered question, p_c is the corresponding current distribution in the user profile, p_u is the updated distribution in the user profile, α is the decaying factor, and Z_c and Z_u are the current and updated normalizing values.

The second level, which represents a distribution over models, cannot be updated in a similar manner, since question profiles do not specify any preference over the LDA, lexical and category models. To overcome this, we first measure the similarity between the feature distribution of each model in the question and the corresponding feature distribution in the user profile. The more similar the vectors, the better this model captures the user's choice of answering this question. The similarity scores are then normalized to a probability distribution, which updates the corresponding second level node in user profile using the same update formula above. Any similarity function is valid, but since we want to promote models that should correlate with future relevant questions, we use here the same similarity function that was chosen also in the recommendation algorithm (see Section 5), which is a dot-product (between two L1-normalized feature vectors).

We discuss next how question and user profiles are used for recommending open questions to potential answerers.

5. QUESTION RECOMMENDATION

We next describe the key elements of personalized question recommendation, namely relevance, diversity and freshness, as captured within our recommendation algorithm.

Pets/LDA/topic$_3$	$\rightarrow$	$(q_7, 0.24), (q_{54}, 0.33), ...$
Travel/Lexical/bag	$\rightarrow$	$(q_2, 0.11), (q_{12}, 0.05), ...$
Travel/Category/France	$\rightarrow$	$(q_3, 0.25), (q_{25}, 0.15), ...$
...	$\rightarrow$	...

Table 2: Inverted index of feature to open questions

5.1 Matching Question and User Profiles

The core idea behind the recommendation algorithm is to return to any user a list of open questions ranked by a relevance score, which is calculated for the pair {*question profile,user profile*}. One important constraint here is to do this in an efficient manner since (1) open questions should be served immediately after having been posted, providing fresh results (this supports "competitive answering", as people prefer to answer fresh questions that have few or no answers), and (2) user profiles should be updated as soon as users post an answer (to support new users who answer for the first time, as well as versatile answerers).

To this effect, we apply an IR-like approach using a traditional vector-space model, in which the questions are seen as documents, and users as queries. To do so, we need to flatten both users and questions profiles into vectors. For question profiles, we first turn the three vectors forming the question profile into a single vector. To be consistent with our probability scheme, we multiply the probability of each feature by $\frac{1}{3}$ before storing it in the index, turning the flattened vector into a proper probability distribution over all features. We then index every question vector and build an inverted index[4], in which the key is the individual feature, namely an LDA topic, a single word from the lexical model or a category. Each key is qualified by a top category and points to a posting list of open question ids together with their adequate feature score, as illustrated in Table 2.

Next we need to turn the user profile into a single vector that can be queried against the inverted index. To do so, we traverse the user profile probability tree and consider as indexing units the individual leaves of the tree, qualified by the path that led to them (top category/model type), similar to the qualified indexed features of the question profile. We associate with each user feature a score that consists of the product of each probability score on the tree path that led to this feature.

Finally for ranking, we experimented with several measures of similarity, and chose a simple dot-product as there was no observed difference between them. We thus have at our disposal a "question retrieval engine" that takes as "query" a user vector u and returns the top ranked open questions $q_1, ..., q_n$ that are the most relevant to the user.

5.2 Proactive Diversification

If we were to simply use our question retrieval engine for recommending questions, a user who answers mostly baseball questions and only occasionally questions about fast food would be offered only baseball questions. The reason is that most of the probability mass in his profile is centered around baseball features. Thus, baseball questions will receive a higher matching score and be ranked higher. Since baseball questions are abundant, they will populate all top ranked positions, from which recommendations are served. To compensate for the imbalance between different user interests, diversification needs to be promoted.

So far, diversification was not addressed in prior work on question recommendation, but it is an active research field in recommender systems. Typically, prior algorithms diversify recommended items as a response to a given recommendation request. Following, such methods either attempt to rerank the retrieved list of recommendations, [30, 26, 12], or apply algorithms for balancing between relevance and item similarity when constructing the recommendation list [3]. Similarly, diversification algorithms in IR attempt to rerank the already retrieved original result-set [5, 27, 6, 7].

In this paper, we propose a different proactive diversification approach, which we call *thematic sampling*. In this approach, for each user vector u, we generate N query vectors $u_1, u_2, ..., u_N$, each with a different constraint that imposes one specific "theme" to be represented in all retrieved questions. These N queries are submitted to the question retrieval engine, and assuming the retrieved ranked lists are disjoined enough (as each is focused on a different theme), blending them together results in a final diverse list that incorporates questions from various themes (see Section 5.3).

We consider here two types of thematic constraints. The first type is a constraint over a specific top category, retrieving only questions that are assigned to categories underneath this top category in the category hierarchy. Since each question is posted in one single top category, the returned lists are disjoint. We randomly select top categories as constraints by sampling without repetition based on their distribution in the root node of the user's probability tree. This allows for diversification while still favoring themes the user typically answers in, since their corresponding top categories will be sampled more.

The second type of constraints is in the form of a specific LDA topic that must appear in all retrieved questions[5]. Since different LDA topics typically represent different interests, and our assignment of topics to questions is sparse (see Section 3.1), the returned ranked lists should have very little overlap. We randomly sample LDA topics without repetition from the user profile by traversing the probability tree based on the distributions in the first and third levels (at the second level we always choose LDA). As in the case of top categories, this allows for diversification while still favoring themes the user typically answers in.

The more queries a system can process per recommendation request the more diverse the results will be. To this end, we found that this stage can be sped up substantially, assuming each constraint relates only to a small subset of questions. This assumption is true for LDA constraints. Following, we maintain for each LDA topic the top (highest probability) questions related to it in a cache. In our implementation, the cache for each topic holds 200 questions. When an LDA topic is sampled, only its top questions are retrieved from the cache and are then reranked based on the complete query u_i. This saves searching over hundred of thousand of questions, resulting in over an order of magnitude speedup in serving time.

---

[4]Since question profiles never change, they are indexed only once and no update is necessary. Resolved questions are flagged for deletion and removed from the index via a lazy deletion process.

[5]This can be viewed as a "+" operator in a free text search, forcing the query term to appear in the retrieved documents.

Top Category	Top topic words	Score
Pets	00th, march, 0th, april, date	0.03
Sports	site, search, website, google	0.11
Games and Recreation	wanna, gonna, yeah, idk, xd	0.18
Environment	term, explain, word	0.42
Society and Culture	watch, movie, tv, film	0.53

Table 3: Examples of non-thematic LDA topics

Top Category	Top topic words	Score
Dining Out	pizza, hut, domino, papa, crust	0.64
Home and Garden	bug, bed, tiny, rid, black	0.82
Science & Math	nuclear, fuel, power, energy	0.95
Arts & Humanities	slave, black, american, african	0.99

Table 4: Examples of thematic LDA topics

5.3 Recommendation Merging

Once we have obtained these N retrieved lists, as described above, we merge them in order to return one single ranked diversified list to the user. We do so by applying a generic *blending algorithm* that takes as input the N lists, each list being associated with a probability score that represents the percentage of recommendations it will contribute to the final recommendation list. One blending step is then performed by sampling an intermediate list, based on the assigned probabilities, and removing one recommendation from the sampled list to be added at the end of the final list. This step is repeated until the final recommendation list is completed.

The blending algorithm does not specify how a recommendation is chosen from each sampled list. One option is to pick the top recommendation, since the lists are ordered. However, in order to increase diversity as well as reduce "question starvation"[6], we sample a question in the list using a mixture of a geometric distribution and a uniform distribution over the ordered items in the list.

The blending algorithm can merge as many intermediate lists as the system can provide. In our implementation we chose 4 latent topic constrained lists, 4 top category constrained lists and 4 top category constrained lists that are also restricted only to questions that were posted in the last 4 hours, to ensure the retrieval of fresh questions. We experienced with different probabilities scores assigned to the lists, in order to test the importance of freshness and diversity on top of relevance (see Section 6.2).

5.4 Non-Thematic LDA Topics

In our thematic sampling algorithm, we assume that each constraint query u_i returns only questions related to a specific theme, which represents one facet of the user's interests. Top categories can indeed be easily mapped into such high level themes. However, we wanted to verify whether this assumption also holds for LDA topics, namely would they all indeed stand for one easily interpretable theme.

Some prior studies that investigated the semantics of LDA topics indeed showed that some generated LDA topics might not be coherent enough [20, 19]. Yet, we observed that there are also coherent LDA topics that still might not be of practical value when identifying user interests. Examples of such topics, as illustrated in Table 3, include style, slang and

---
[6]Question starvation refers to the situation in which a question is not recommended to any user.

(a) Probability that the LDA topic will be assigned to at least one word in a question

(b) Average LDA topic probability within the topic distribution of each question

(c) Average LDA topic probability considering only questions with at least one word assignment for this topic

(d) Histogram Entropy: the entropy of the normalized histogram of leaf category co-occurrence with the topic, constructed by counting the assigned categories of questions that have at least one word assigned to the LDA topic

(e) Entropy over the histogram of the target topic co-occurrence with other topics, constraining that both topics are assigned to words in the question

(f) Bin features: We bucket the topic probability for each question (feature 1) into 10 bins ($0 - 0.1, 0.1 - 0.2$ etc.), counting the number of questions related to each bin. For each bin, we generate features that capture the probability of each bin as well as the average, variance and standard deviation for each range of bins ($1, [1,2], [1,2,3]\ldots[1,..,10]$)

Figure 5: Thematic features generated for each topic

other figure-of-speech lists (third row in Table), clusters of general terms, such as dates or colors (first row), and generic activities within specific top categories (second row). We refer to these LDA topics as "non-thematic topics", and discuss next how to handle them.

In our framework, we learn LDA topics for each top category in Yahoo! Answers separately, ending with 5,200 topics. We discovered that non-thematic topics emerge quite often in all top categories. Identifying them manually would be tedious and not scalable, therefore we decided to build a classifier that would differentiate between thematic and non-thematic topics. One additional requirement was for the classifier to be effective across all top categories, even though they differ in content, corpus size, style etc. This implies that the classification features need to be generic enough to consistently capture thematic behavior across different domains. Our main intuition here is that questions are focused on a narrow theme. Thus, the distribution of LDA topics should be centered around very few topics, which represent the concrete theme of the question (see also Section 3.1). Hence, topics that typically receive few word assignments are the non-thematic ones, as they only help in explaining the style and generic scenario of the question (slang, time, place). Following the same logic, non-thematic topics should co-appear with more leaf categories and other topics than thematic topics. Based on the above intuitions, we extracted the features detailed in Figure 5 for each LDA topic from the training set.

To train the classifier, we labeled 116 topics from 23 top categories, with 13 top categories having 3 or less labeled topics in the training set. This training set consists of 34% non-thematic topics. Obviously, there is redundancy among our features, so we applied forward feature selection. We then learned a logistic regression classifier on the training set, achieving 82% accuracy on 10-fold cross-validation. Examples for topics that are not in our training set, together with their classification scores, are presented in Tables 3 and 4.

We applied this classifier to provide a "thematic" probability to all 5,200 topics, which is then used as a bias during thematic sampling. Specifically, before sampling topics, the user profile is temporarily altered by multiplying each LDA topic probability by its thematic probability. This process promotes thematic topics over non-thematic ones for the sampling task.

6. EXPERIMENTS

To evaluate our question recommendation system, we conducted two experiments. The first experiment is an offline experiment, in which the ground truth is provided by the past questions answered by a sample of users. The closer to these questions our recommendations are, the more effective the algorithm is. While such an offline experiment can provide insights on the differences between algorithms, it still suffers from clear limitations, as we do not know how users would have reacted, had they been exposed to other recommended questions.

As in many other Web systems, a live experiment on a large set of real users provides a more realistic setup for evaluation. Thus, as our main evaluation we conducted a live online experiment comparing the activity of users who are exposed to question recommendations via a new "recommended" tab in the Yahoo! Answers home page, as compared with those who keep the traditional view.

6.1 Offline Experiment

The goal of our offline experiment was to compare the relative performance of each of our relevance models, namely LDA, lexical and category based, as well as their combination, ignoring freshness and diversification altogether. We evaluated their associated algorithms on 8 different top categories, considering both active users and new users.

In each top category we sampled several thousand *active users*, who answered at least 21 questions as of January 2011. We derived their user profiles from the first 20 questions, and then let the algorithm being evaluated rank the "next question" (namely the 21st one) among other open questions. More specifically, the algorithm ranked only the questions in the top category that were open at the time the user answered the 21st question, which typically includes tens of thousands of questions. Similarly, we sampled several thousand *new users*, who answered at least two questions as of January 2011, and conducted the same ranking experiment, now with a user profile derived from only the first question the user answered, and the "next question" to be ranked being the second one.

We used as metric the percentage of users whose "next question" was ranked within the top 100 questions recommended by the algorithm. This 100 cut-off is quite large as we do not expect recall to be high, mostly because we consider many questions that the users were actually not exposed to before choosing their "next questions". Yet, this metric should provide sufficient insight to compare the relative performance of models. The results for both active and new users are shown in Table 5.

As expected, the results for the combination of models (listed in the rightmost column of the Table) systematically outperformed each independent model. In addition, the LDA model did in general better than the lexical model. Interestingly, while both the LDA and lexical models perform better for active users than for new users, the combined algorithm's performance slightly declines for active users. One possible interpretation for this is that active users hold a more diverse set of interests, and thus guessing the topic

	New Users			
	LDA	Lexical	Category	Combined
Beauty and Style	6.1	6.1	0.8	**7.9**
Food and Drink	14.7	13.1	11.2	**22.3**
Health	7.5	6.5	2.5	**10.5**
Home and Garden	16.6	14.3	5.7	**23.0**
Politics	10.2	8.1	5.8	**15.0**
Pets	13.4	14.5	4.9	**19.3**
Social Science	15.1	14.3	11.2	**24.7**
Sports	28.8	18.5	19.2	**37.7**
	Active Users			
	LDA	Lexical	Category	Combined
Beauty and Style	7.6	6.5	0.1	**7.9**
Food and Drink	17.6	15.8	6.3	**20.9**
Health	7.9	7.5	0.1	**9.3**
Home and Garden	21.7	19.0	0.7	**24.2**
Politics	8.3	7.6	0.3	**9.6**
Pets	17.7	16.6	0.5	**18.7**
Social Science	20.0	17.0	0.5	**21.5**
Sports	33.7	24.6	12.4	**35.0**

Table 5: Percentage of users for whom the next question they answer appears in their top 100 recommendations in the offline experiment

of the next question the user would answer becomes harder. This is also reflected in the category model, which is the worst performing model. One possible reason for this is the coarseness of this model, since there are numerous open questions in each category, and the model picks one randomly. For active users, who answered in several categories, the category model performance is poor, which probably influences negatively the combined model. Yet, for new users it provides a good constraint, thus significantly boosting the combination. In future work, we plan to model answering sessions for improving recommendations for users with heterogeneous interests. One possible conclusion might be to lessen the influence of the category model as the user becomes more active.

Given the results of the offline experiment, when considering relevance, we will refer by default to the combined relevance model. This holds in particular for the online experiment that is described next.

6.2 Online Experiment

In our main experiment, we utilized a common inter-subject design known as a controlled experiment (a.k.a. "bucket test" or "A/B test"). Our system ran on production in the live Yahoo! Answers website for the first fifteen days of October 2012, and was exposed in different configurations to a small random sample of US-based users, who visited the site at least once. All configurations were shown under the same treatment, with a new recommended tab (as shown in Figure 2), except for the control group, which was exposed to the regular view. Each sampled user was assigned and exposed to only one of the configurations under evaluation for the duration of the experiment.

The following configurations were compared using four different *buckets* of n users each as follows:

- **Control bucket, CTL** ($n = 25,093$): Users in this bucket are exposed to the regular user interface without recommendations. This bucket plays the role of the control group.

- **Relevance bucket**, **R** ($n = 5,359$): Users are shown in the recommended tab recommended questions ranked only by relevance, as in the offline experiment, without any diversity or freshness considerations.

- **Freshness bucket**, **F** ($n = 46,228$): Users are shown recommendations ranked by relevance, yet with 50% of them originating only from recent questions (opened in the last 4 hours), and 20% of them selected by thematic sampling.

- **Diversity bucket**, **D** ($n = 42,041$): Recommendations are ranked by relevance with 20% of them originating from recent questions, and 50% of them selected by thematic sampling for diversity.

In addition to monitoring the main activity, namely answering, we tracked the indirect influence of question recommendations on asking and more peripheral activities such as rating or voting, as well as dwell time on Yahoo! Answers. Figure 6 shows the results in a relative scale, in which the statistics of the control bucket CTL serve as the 100% reference point and the percentage difference of each bucket as compared to the CTL performance are displayed on the graph. Answering/asking activities are measured in counts (absolute number of answers and questions normalized by the size of the bucket). Dwell time is measured as the average time in minutes from first to last click on the same day. Other peripheral activities (voting, rating, and starring) are measured as the proportion of users who participated in the activity at least once. Note that the most important metric in the figure is the number of answers (represented in the bottom bar), since our main goal is to increase the number of answers.

From these results, we see that users in the Relevance bucket **R**, with recommendations driven purely by relevance, underperformed as compared to those in the control bucket. This confirmed the major conjecture of this work, namely that in question recommendation, relevance is not enough. Our interpretation here is that users found the recommendations more annoying than useful, left the site early and were less engaged, as reflected by a decline in most metrics. Users did voice their frustration in the Yahoo! Answers blog[7] and complained about not wanting to answer four days old questions. Interestingly, they did not complain about the lack of diversity but in our opinion it is mostly because it is more difficult to perceive. It is thus expected that the response to the Freshness bucket **F** is positive, with a 4% increase in number of answers (not significant, $p > 0.05$), and a general increase in all activities by the users in the bucket. This shows that it is important for users to respond quickly to open questions, one of the reasons being the wish to be one of the first answerers.

Yet, the clear winner in this experiment is the Diversity bucket **D**. In this bucket, recency was significantly reduced in favor of diversity. While bucket users did not explicitly state their need for diversification, the results of this bucket show that they significantly prefer more diverse recommendations, not only over best matching ones, but also over recommendation of recent questions. In terms of number of answers, users in bucket **D** contribute 17% more answers on average than those in the control bucket ($p < 10^{-5}$), and a

[7] http://yanswersblog.com/

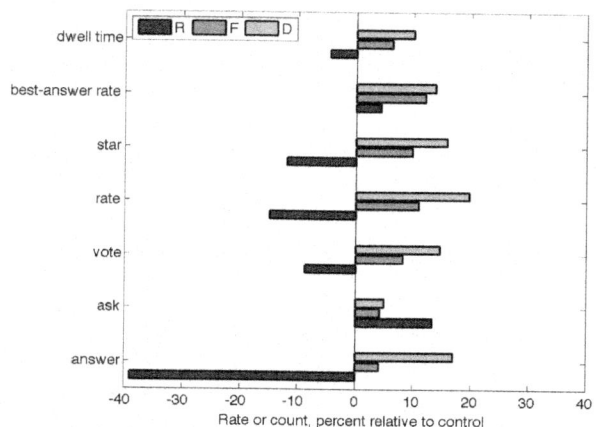

Figure 6: Comparison of user activities in all buckets in percentage, relative to CTL (the 0 median)

relative increase of 12% as compared to Freshness bucket **F** ($p < 10^{-5}$). This is a surprising result that points at the importance of diversification in question recommendation, which was unexplored so far.

Users in the Diversity bucket **D** also significantly increased their peripheral activities as compared to the control group as well as to Freshness bucket **F**, as shown by an improvement in all metrics in Figure 6. For example, users in bucket **D** increase, on average, their daily time spent on the site by 10% compared to CTL ($p < 10^{-6}$), their best-answer rate by 14% ($p < 10^{-5}$), and their rating volume (marking other answers with "thumbs-up" or "thumbs-down") by as much as 20% (not significant, $p > 0.05$). A possible interpretation for this behavior is that many of these activities are correlated and the improved experience in getting personalized questions increases satisfaction, and consequently deepens and prolongs users' engagement.

Taking a closer look at the increase in number of answers, it can be caused either by an increase in number of answers per each individual active user, or (non exclusive or) by a larger number of users contributing answers. This motivated us to go one level deeper and partition our results by the tenure of users on the site. It was shown before that the amount of activity of users on Yahoo! Answers depends on their tenure, [11]. The usual behavior is initial enthusiasm in the first few weeks, which often declines at a later stage, down to churning for a certain percentage of the population.

Figures 7 and 8 respectively show the participation rate and the average number of answers per user split by bucket and user tenure. More specifically, the x-axis refers to the tenure by listing the month on which the user joined Yahoo! Answers, with the "All" category referring to all users independently of tenure. As per the upper part of Figure 7, new users who started in October show low answering participation rates, as expected from users who are just trying out the site. Activity peaks for September users, who, with 2 to 6 weeks seniority, are in their "honeymoon" period with the site. Rates then drop off as the tenure of the user increases. This trend is consistent across all buckets. The lower part of Figure 7 indicates that, overall, the Diversity bucket encourages the highest answering participation rates compared to

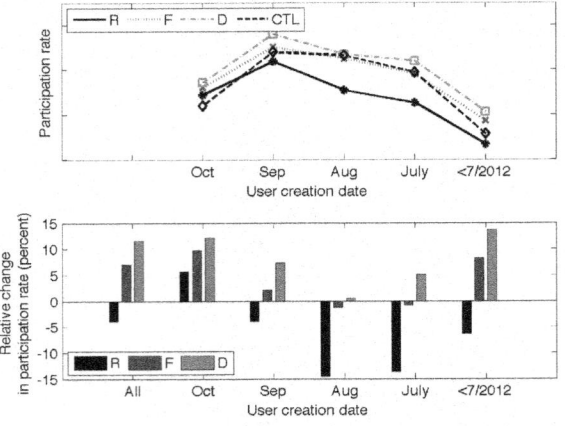

Figure 7: Answering participation rate over time

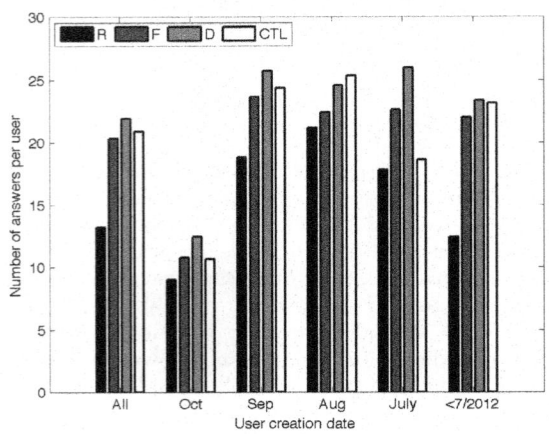

Figure 8: Average number of answers per user by user creation date

all other buckets, with a relative increase of 11% in average participation rate over the control bucket. Yet, it also boasts the highest participation rate for every user tenure group, indicating that diversity is appealing across all types of populations.

Finally, Figure 8 shows that the Diversity bucket also outperforms the other buckets in terms of the number of answers per user, both in the "All" category and at different tenure stages, with the single exception of August. In contrast the Freshness bucket performs better than the control bucket, but only in terms of answering participation rate. It fails do so for the answer rate. It might be interpreted by the fact that users might be attracted by fresh questions for a shorter period of time if they are not diverse enough, hence answering fewer questions.

In conclusion, the online experiment verifies that the Diversity bucket **D**, which promotes diversity spiced with freshness, is the winning bucket, feeding a higher number of overall answers to the site as well as a highest answering participation rate for the different types of users.

7. CONCLUSIONS

In this paper we described a question recommendation approach designed to satisfy all types of answerers in CQA systems. This approach differs from most prior work, which targeted only expert answerers, with the single objective of improving asker satisfaction. The two key novel aspects of our work consist of not being exclusively driven by relevance but also by freshness and diversity. We were motivated by the intuition that CQA systems would follow the same drives that exist in other user-generated content sites. These two additional considerations also imposed further real-time and scalability constraints on our approach, on top of those that are derived from designing a live online recommender system.

We introduced a probabilistic representation of questions and users that incorporates several relevance models of user interests at different levels of granularity. User profiles are derived from the profiles of the questions they answered and are represented as a hierarchical data structure that capture personalized preferences. Each user profile is also incrementally updated as the user keeps answering. We serve question recommendations in an efficient manner using a "question retrieval engine", which given a user profile returns the most relevant questions to answer. Incorporated in our recommendation algorithm is a novel proactive approach for promoting diversity within the returned results, which we coin *thematic sampling*, as well as tunable preferences for fresh results.

We implemented our system for Yahoo! Answers, one of the largest and earliest CQA sites. We conducted an offline experiment to verify the best relevance models for question recommendation and as expected, a combination of three relevance models achieved the highest recall for both active and new users. We then presented our main online experiment on a sample of more than a hundred thousand of Yahoo! Answers users, splitting them into four buckets.

Our online live experiment validated our intuition that relevance was not enough in question recommendation. It even surprised us, as it showed that using only relevance for ranking actually discouraged users from answering questions as compared to the control bucket. In contrast, users answered 4% more questions than the control group when fresh questions were promoted. However, it was the incorporation of diversification that was the most appealing to answerers, even at the cost of reduced freshness. Indeed, users that were shown diverse recommendations answered 17% more questions than the control bucket. Furthermore, we observed indirect benefits to overall user activity, such as an increase in voting (+20%) and longer dwelling times on the site (+10%). These results indicate the importance of integrating diversification and freshness for question recommendation in CQA sites, aspects that were ignored in prior work. The algorithm described in this paper is currently deployed in production on Yahoo! Answers.

Acknowledgments

We wish to thank Gideon Dror for his help in this research and the Yahoo! Answers team at Bangalore for their help in the evaluations.

8. REFERENCES

[1] A. Ahmed, Y. Low, M. Aly, V. Josifovski, and A. J. Smola. Scalable distributed inference of dynamic user interests for behavioral targeting. In *Proceedings of KDD*, 2011.

[2] D. M. Blei, A. Y. Ng, and M. I. Jordan. Latent dirichlet allocation. *J. Mach. Learn. Res.*, 3:993–1022, Mar. 2003.

[3] R. Boim, T. Milo, and S. Novgorodov. Diversification and refinement in collaborative filtering recommender. In *Proceedings CIKM*, 2011.

[4] L. Cai, G. Zhou, K. Liu, and J. Zhao. Learning the latent topics for question retrieval in community qa. In *Proceedings of IJCNLP*, 2011.

[5] J. Carbonell and J. Goldstein. The use of MMR, diversity-based reranking for reordering documents and producing summaries. In *Proceedings of SIGIR*, 1998.

[6] B. Carterette and P. Chandar. Probabilistic models of ranking novel documents for faceted topic retrieval. In *Proceedings of CIKM*, 2009.

[7] V. Dang and W. B. Croft. Diversity by proportionality: an election-based approach to search result diversification. In *Proceedings of SIGIR*, 2012.

[8] A. Dong, Y. Chang, Z. Zheng, G. Mishne, J. Bai, R. Zhang, K. Buchner, C. Liao, and F. Diaz. Towards recency ranking in web search. In *Proceedings of WSDM*, 2010.

[9] A. Dong, R. Zhang, P. Kolari, J. Bai, F. Diaz, Y. Chang, Z. Zheng, and H. Zha. Time is of the essence: improving recency ranking using twitter data. In *Proceedings of WWW*, 2010.

[10] G. Dror, Y. Koren, Y. Maarek, and I. Szpektor. I want to answer; who has a question?: Yahoo! answers recommender system. In *Proceedings of KDD*, 2011.

[11] G. Dror, D. Pelleg, O. Rokhlenko, and I. Szpektor. Churn prediction in new users of Yahoo! answers. In *Proceedings of CQA2012 workshop*, 2012.

[12] M. Drosou and E. Pitoura. Search result diversification. *SIGMOD Rec.*, 39(1):41–47, Sept. 2010.

[13] J. Guo, S. Xu, S. Bao, and Y. Yu. Tapping on the potential of q&a community by recommending answer providers. *Human Factors*, pages 921–930, 2008.

[14] D. Horowitz and S. Kamvar. The anatomy of a large-scale social search engine. In *Proceedings of WWW*, 2010.

[15] Y. Kabutoya, T. Iwata, H. Shiohara, and K. Fujimura. Effective question recommendation based on multiple features for question answering communities. In *Proceedings of ICWSM*, 2010.

[16] B. Li and I. King. Routing questions to appropriate answerers in community question answering services. In *Proceedings of CIKM*, 2010.

[17] B. Li, I. King, and M. R. Lyu. Question routing in community question answering: putting category in its place. In *Proceedings of CIKM*, 2011.

[18] M. Liu, Y. Liu, and Q. Yang. Predicting best answerers for new questions in community question answering. In *Proceedings of WAIM*, 2010.

[19] D. Mimno, H. M. Wallach, E. Talley, M. Leenders, and A. McCallum. Optimizing semantic coherence in topic models. In *Proceedings of EMNLP*, 2011.

[20] D. Newman, J. H. Lau, K. Grieser, and T. Baldwin. Automatic evaluation of topic coherence. In *Proceedings of HLT*, 2010.

[21] M. Qu, G. Qiu, X. He, C. Zhang, H. Wu, J. Bu, and C. Chen. Probabilistic question recommendation for question answering communities. In *Proceedings of WWW*, 2009.

[22] D. Raban. Self-presentation and the value of information in Q&A web sites. *JASIST*, 60(12):2465–2473, 2009.

[23] F. Riahi, Z. Zolaktaf, M. Shafiei, and E. Milios. Finding expert users in community question answering. In *Proceedings of WWW companion*, 2012.

[24] A. Shtok, G. Dror, Y. Maarek, and I. Szpektor. Learning from the past: answering new questions with past answers. In *Proceedings of WWW*, 2012.

[25] L. Yao, D. Mimno, and A. McCallum. Efficient methods for topic model inference on streaming document collections. In *Proceedings of KDD*, 2009.

[26] C. Yu, L. V. S. Lakshmanan, and S. Amer-Yahia. Recommendation diversification using explanations. In *Proceedings of ICDE*, 2009.

[27] C. X. Zhai, W. W. Cohen, and J. Lafferty. Beyond independent relevance: methods and evaluation metrics for subtopic retrieval. In *Proceedings of SIGIR*, 2003.

[28] T. C. Zhou, M. R. Lyu, and I. King. A classification-based approach to question routing in community question answering. In *Proceedings WWW companion*, 2012.

[29] Y. Zhou, G. Cong, B. Cui, C. S. Jensen, and J. Yao. Routing questions to the right users in online communities. In *Proceedings of ICDE*, 2009.

[30] C.-N. Ziegler, S. M. McNee, J. A. Konstan, and G. Lausen. Improving recommendation lists through topic diversification. In *Proceedings of WWW*, 2005.

Mining Acronym Expansions and Their Meanings Using Query Click Log

Bilyana Taneva[1]*, Tao Cheng[2], Kaushik Chakrabarti[2], Yeye He[2]

[1]Max-Planck Institute for Informatics, Saarbrücken, Germany
[2]Microsoft Research, Redmond, WA

[1]btaneva@mpi-inf.mpg.de
[2]{taocheng, kaushik, yeyehe}@microsoft.com

ABSTRACT

Acronyms are abbreviations formed from the initial components of words or phrases. Acronym usage is becoming more common in web searches, email, text messages, tweets, blogs and posts. Acronyms are typically ambiguous and often disambiguated by context words. Given either just an acronym as a query or an acronym with a few context words, it is immensely useful for a search engine to know the most likely intended meanings, ranked by their likelihood. To support such online scenarios, we study the offline mining of acronyms and their meanings in this paper. For each acronym, our goal is to discover all distinct meanings and for each meaning, compute the expanded string, its popularity score and a set of context words that indicate this meaning. Existing approaches are inadequate for this purpose. Our main insight is to leverage "co-clicks" in search engine query click log to mine expansions of acronyms. There are several technical challenges such as ensuring 1:1 mapping between expansions and meanings, handling of "tail meanings" and extracting context words. We present a novel, end-to-end solution that addresses the above challenges. We further describe how web search engines can leverage the mined information for prediction of intended meaning for queries containing acronyms. Our experiments show that our approach (i) discovers the meanings of acronyms with high precision and recall, (ii) significantly complements existing meanings in Wikipedia and (iii) accurately predicts intended meaning for online queries with over 90% precision.

Categories and Subject Descriptors

H.2.8 [**DATABASE MANAGEMENT**]: Database Applications—*Data mining*

Keywords

acronym; acronym expansion; acronym meaning; click log

1. INTRODUCTION

Acronyms are abbreviations formed from the initial components of words or phrases. These components may be individual letters (e.g., "CMU" from "Carnegie Mellon University")

---

*Part of the work was done during employment at Microsoft Research

Copyright is held by the International World Wide Web Conference Committee (IW3C2). IW3C2 reserves the right to provide a hyperlink to the author's site if the Material is used in electronic media.
WWW 2013, May 13–17, 2013, Rio de Janeiro, Brazil.
ACM 978-1-4503-2035-1/13/05.

---

or parts of words (e.g., "HTTP" from "Hypertext Transfer Protocol"). Acronyms are used very commonly in web searches as well as in all forms of electronic communication like email, text messages, tweets, blogs and posts. With the emergence of mobile devices, the usage of acronyms is becoming even more common because typing is difficult in such devices and acronyms provide a succinct way to express information.

One key characteristic of acronyms is that they are typically *ambiguous*, i.e., the same acronym has many different meanings. For example, "CMU" can refer to "Central Michigan University", "Carnegie Mellon University", "Central Methodist University", and many other meanings. Consider a web search scenario: given an acronym as a query, it is immensely useful for the search engine to know all its popular meanings, ranked by their popularity. For example, for "CMU", "Central Michigan University" is the most popular meaning followed by "Carnegie Mellon University" and others. The search engine can either modify the original query with these expansions and retrieve more relevant results [7] or simply show them to users so that they can disambiguate it themselves[1].

A second characteristic of acronyms is that they are typically *disambiguated by context*, i.e., the intended meaning is clear when the user provides a few context words. For example, a user searching for "cmu football" is most likely referring to "Central Michigan University" while the one searching for "cmu computer science" is most likely referring to "Carnegie Mellon University". Given an acronym and one or more context words, it is useful for the web search engine to know the most likely intended meaning (or a few most likely intended meanings, ranked by the likelihood). The search engine can then use query alteration techniques to retrieve more relevant results [7].

To enable the above online scenarios, we study the offline mining of acronyms and their meanings in this paper. For each acronym, we discover its various meanings; for each meaning, we output:

- *Expansion*: The complete expanded string of the acronym for the meaning.
- *Popularity score*: A score reflecting how often people intend this meaning when they use the acronym (e.g., how often web searchers intend it when they use only the acronym as the query).

---

[1]Google has recently started showing the different meanings of a query on the right hand side of search result page for limited queries. The algorithm used by Google has not been published and is hence not publicly known.

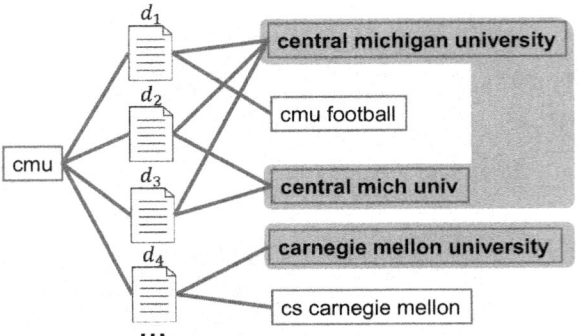

Figure 1: Example illustrating insights.

- *Context words*: A set of words when used in context of the acronym indicates this meaning. Each word has a score reflecting how strongly it indicates this meaning.

For example, for "CMU", we aim to discover the various meanings "Central Michigan University", "Carnegie Mellon University", "Central Methodist University" and so on. The popularity scores should reflect that "Central Michigan University" is more popular compared with the other meanings. Finally, we aim to find context words like "pittsburgh", "computer science", "research", "computing", etc. for the meaning "Carnegie Mellon University". The 1:1 mapping between the output and the meanings is critical to enable the above online scenarios.

There are several efforts in mining expansions of acronyms. We briefly discuss them here; a more detailed discussion can be found in Section 6.

- *Wikipedia*: Wikipedia covers acronyms through its manually edited "disambiguation pages". It has low recall with many meanings not covered. We find from our experiments that roughly two thirds of the meanings of acronyms are not covered in Wikipedia. Furthermore, it does not provide popularity scores.
- *Acronymfinder.com*: Websites such as acronymfinder.com list the possible acronym expansions; this is also manually edited. As in Wikipedia, it does not provide popularity scores. Furthermore, it does not provide any context words for most of the expansions.
- *Automatic Mining*: There has been recent work towards automatic mining of acronym expansions using the Web [6]. The main focus of this work is in finding legitimate expansions of a given acronym. However, there is no 1:1 mapping between the outputted expansions and meanings, no popularity scores and no context words.

Due to the above limitations, it is difficult for web search engines to leverage the above approaches to support the online scenarios discussed above.

Our main insight is that acronyms and their various expansions are captured in a search engine query click log. *While some people use acronyms as queries and click on relevant documents, others use their expanded forms as queries and click on the same documents.* Thus, we can find expansions by observing queries that "co-click" on the same documents as the acronym. As shown in Figure 1, by observing other queries co-clicked with query "cmu", we can find acronym expansions such as "central michigan university", "central mich univ" and "carnegie mellon university".

There are several technical challenges in finding the distinct meanings from the co-clicked queries. First, not all co-clicked queries are expansions (e.g., "cmu football" is not an expansion of "cmu" in Figure 1). How do we identify the ones that are expansions? Second, the co-clicked queries that are expansions do not correspond to the distinct meanings. There are several variants that correspond to the same meaning (e.g., "central michigan university" and "central mich univ" in Figure 1). How do we group them such that there is a 1:1 mapping between groups and meanings? Third, how do we identify context words for each meaning? Fourth, co-clicked queries tend to cover the popular meanings of the acronym (e.g., "Massachusetts Institute of Technology" for "MIT") but not the "tail meanings" (e.g., "Mazandaran Institute of Technology", "Maharashtra Institute of Technology", "Mahakal Institute of Technology", etc.). This is because the first few pages of results returned by a search engine for the query "MIT" do not represent the tail meanings. How do we find such tail meanings?

Our main contributions can be summarized as follows:
- We formulate the offline acronym mining problem. The novelty of our problem formulation is to find the distinct meanings, not just the expansions. This is critical to enable the above online scenarios (Section 2).
- We present a novel, end-to-end solution that leverages the query click log to identify expansions, group them into distinct meanings, compute popularity scores and discover context words (Section 3). We leverage two key insights. First, expansions of the same meaning click on the same set of documents, whereas expansions of different meanings click on different documents. We design similarity functions to leverage this insight and perform clustering to group the expansions. Second, co-clicked queries shed light on the context words of respective meanings. For instance, the fact that "cmu football" and "central michigan university" click on the same document hints the relevance of "football" to "central michigan university". We leverage this insight to discover context words.
- We present a novel enhancement to discover tail meanings in addition to the more popular meanings (Section 3).
- We describe how web search engines can leverage the mined information for prediction of intended meaning for queries containing acronyms (Section 4).
- We perform extensive experiments using a large-scale query click log. Our experiments show that our approach (i) discovers acronym meanings with high precision and recall, (ii) significantly complements existing meanings in Wikipedia and (iii) accurately predicts intended meaning for online queries with over 90% precision (Section 5).

To the best of our knowledge, this is the first work on automatic mining of distinct meanings of acronyms.

2. PROBLEM DEFINITION

In this section, we formally define the offline acronym meaning discovery problem and then present our solution overview.

2.1 Problem Definition

We study the following offline acronym meaning discovery problem.

Definition 1. (**Acronym Meaning Discovery Problem**) Given an input acronym, find the set $\{M_1, \ldots, M_n\}$ of distinct meanings associated to it. For each meaning $M_i = (e, p, C)$, find the canonical expansion $M_i.e$, the popularity score $M_i.p$ and the set $M_i.C$ of context words along with scores.

For any meaning, there can be many variants of the expanded string in the query log. For example, for the meaning "Carnegie Mellon University" of the acronym "CMU", the variants include "Carnegie Mellon University", "Carnegie Mellon Univ" as well as several misspellings. $M_i.e$ is the most representative variant; we refer to it as the *canonical expansion*. The popularity score $M_i.p$ measures how often web searchers intend this meaning when they use the acronym in a query. To easily leverage these scores for online meaning prediction, we compute these scores as probabilities. Finally, the set $M_i.C$ of the context words are the words which when used in context of the acronym in web searches indicate this meaning. For example, for the meaning "Carnegie Mellon University", $M_i.C$ = {"pittsburgh", "research", "cs", "science", etc.}. We associate a score with each context word in $M_i.C$ which measures how strongly the word indicates this meaning. Again, to easily leverage these scores for online meaning prediction, we compute these scores as probabilities.

Notice that our problem formulation assumes that the acronym is given. We assume a separate module that identifies the acronyms commonly used in web searches; this can be used as input to the acronym meaning discovery problem. For example, this module can extract all acronyms listed in Wikipedia. Another approach is to treat all words that are not common English words as acronyms. Our framework will be able to find out the meanings of true acronyms, whereas words which are not actual acronyms will not likely produce any meanings.

2.2 Solution Overview

To discover the different meanings of an acronym, we leverage the query click log of a web search engine. Our solution is based on the following insight: while some searchers use acronyms as queries and click on the relevant documents, others use their expanded forms as queries and click on the same documents. We compute the canonical expansions, popularity scores as well as context words for the different meanings of an acronym by observing the set of queries that click on the same documents as the acronym query. We refer to them as "co-clicked" queries.

Query Click Log: The query click log collects the click behavior of millions of web searchers over a long period of time (say, two years). We assume the query log $\mathcal{Q}$ to contain records of the form (q, d, f) where q is a query string, d is a web document, represented by its unique URI, and f is the number of times d has been clicked by web searchers after posing the query q to the search engine.

It is technically challenging to find the distinct meanings from the co-clicked queries. To address this challenge, we develop a novel, end-to-end solution that consists of the following steps:

- **Candidate Expansion Identification:** We first collect the co-clicked queries for the given acronym. Not all co-clicked queries are valid expansions of the acronym. We identify the valid expansions from the co-clicked queries; we refer to them as *candidate expansions*. For this purpose, we use an *acronym-expansion checking function*, which checks if a query can be considered as the complete expanded string of the acronym.

- **Acronym Expansion Clustering:** The candidate expansions do not correspond to the distinct meanings; there are several variants that correspond to the same meaning. We group the candidate expansions such that each group has unique meaning, and no two groups have the same meaning.

- **Enhancement for Tail Meanings:** We observe that co-clicked queries do not cover the tail meanings. To address this problem, we present a novel extension that considers *supersequence queries*. This approach finds significantly more meanings, especially the tail ones. We refer to this algorithm as *Enhanced Acronym Expansion Clustering*.

- **Canonical Expansion, Popularity Score and Context Words Computation:** We select the canonical expansion for each discovered meaning. We compute the popularity score for each meaning, such that more popular meanings receive higher scores. Finally, we assign a set of context words to each meaning. We also assign a score to each context word.

We describe the above steps in details in Section 3. In Section 4, we describe how we can leverage the discovered meanings to predict the intended meanings of online queries.

3. ACRONYM MEANING DISCOVERY

We explain the four steps in details. The output of each step is the input to the subsequent step. We present the input and output of each step followed by the algorithm.

3.1 Candidate Expansion Identification

Input: The acronym a and the query click log $\mathcal{Q}$.
Output: The set $E(a)$ of candidate expansions of a.

Our main insight is that the expansions corresponding to the different meanings of a are included in the set of co-clicked queries for a. We first compute the co-clicked queries for a. Let $D(q)$ denote the set of documents which users clicked when they searched with the query string q as recorded in the query click log. Furthermore, let $Q(d)$ denote the set of queries for which users clicked on web document d as recorded in the query click log. We first compute from the query click log the set of documents $D(a)$ clicked for acronym a. Then, for each document $d \in D(a)$, we collect the set of queries $Q(d)$ for which d was clicked. We thus obtain the set $\cup_{d \in D(a)} Q(d)$ of co-clicked queries for a.

Not all co-clicked queries are valid expansions for a. To identify the valid expansions in $\cup_{d \in D(a)} Q(d)$, we propose an *acronym-expansion checking function*.

Acronym-Expansion Checking Function: We present a function that checks whether a given string can be considered as the expanded string of a given acronym.

Definition 2. (**Acronym-Expansion Checking Function**) Given a string q and an acronym a, the checking function $IsExp : q \times a \rightarrow \{true, false\}$ returns $true$ if q is a valid expansion of a and $false$ otherwise.

For example, $IsExp$("carnegie mellon university", "cmu") should be true while $IsExp$("cmu football", "cmu") should be false.

It is difficult to develop a set of exact rules for matching acronym letters in a query. For example, a common rule is that acronym letters should be the initial letters of the words in the expansion. However, this rule does not always hold: "<u>H</u>yper<u>t</u>ext <u>T</u>ransfer <u>P</u>rotocol" is expansion for "HTTP". On the other hand, stop words are often skipped when constructing acronyms (e.g. "<u>M</u>aster of <u>B</u>usiness <u>A</u>dministration" is expansion for "MBA"). However, this does not always hold (e.g., "<u>L</u>eague <u>o</u>f <u>L</u>egends" is expansion of "LOL").

We approach the problem by using heuristics based on dynamic programming. We assign weights to the words and letters of the query string, and modify the longest common subsequence algorithm to find the subsequence with highest score [17]. Pseudo-code is shown in Algorithm 1 in the Appendix, along with explanations of the checking function.

Expansion Identification from Co-clicked Queries: A co-clicked query $q \in \cup_{d \in D(a)} Q(d)$ is a valid expansion of acronym a, iff $IsExp(q, a) = true$; we refer to it as a candidate expansion of a. We compute the set $E(a) = \{q | q \in \cup_{d \in D(a)} Q(d), IsExp(q, a) = true\}$ of candidate expansions of a by checking each co-clicked query using the acronym-expansion checking function.

3.2 Acronym Expansion Clustering

Input: The set $E(a)$ of candidate expansions of a and the query click log $\mathcal{Q}$.
Output: Grouping $\mathcal{G}(a) = \{G_1, \ldots, G_n\}$ of candidate expansions $E(a)$.

The set $E(a)$ of candidate expansions output by the previous step does not correspond to the distinct meanings. It contains several variants that correspond to the same meaning. For example, for the meaning "Carnegie Mellon University", the variants include "Carnegie Mellon University", "Carnegie Mellon Univ" as well as misspellings like "Carnegie Melon University". They all pass the acronym-expansion checking function. Given the set $E(a)$ of candidate expansions of a, this step clusters them into a set $\mathcal{G}(a) = \{G_1, \ldots, G_n\}$ of groups such that each group has a unique meaning, and no two groups have the same meaning. These groups correspond the desired set $\{M_1, \ldots, M_n\}$ of distinct meanings. We first discuss the distance metrics between the candidate expansions and then the clustering algorithm.

3.2.1 Distance Metric for Candidate Expansions

Candidate expansions that correspond to the same meaning are typically minor spelling variations of each other (e.g., "Carnegie Mellon University" and "Carnegie Melon University") while those that correspond to different meanings are often far in terms of string distance (e.g., "Carnegie Mellon University" and "Central Michigan University"). One obvious approach is to cluster the candidate expansions based on their string distance, say edit distance. However, there are many cases where expansions corresponding to the same meaning have large string distances. For example, expansions like "Mass Inst Tech" and "Massachusetts Institute of Technology" correspond to the same meaning, but their edit distance is high enough to prevent them from being grouped together. On the other hand, expansions like "Manukau Institute of Technology" and "Manipal Institute of Technology" refer to two different meanings but may incorrectly be grouped together due to their low edit distance.

Our key insight is that each document clicked by any of the expansions in $E(a)$ typically corresponds to a single meaning; hence, *the expansions that correspond to the same meaning will click on the same set of documents, whereas expansions corresponding to different meanings will click on different sets of documents*. We design distance metrics to leverage this insight and perform clustering to group the expansions.

Set Distance (Jaccard Distance): One way to measure the distance between two expansions e_i and e_j in $E(a)$ is by the distance between the corresponding sets $D(e_i)$ and $D(e_j)$ of clicked documents. A common way to measure set distance is Jaccard distance: $dist(e_i, e_j) = 1 - \frac{|D(e_i) \cap D(e_j)|}{|D(e_i) \cup D(e_j)|}$.

However, Jaccard distance has a serious limitation. Click logs are known to be noisy and contain many clicks that users performed by mistake (referred to as "mis-clicks"). For example, documents associated with "Massachusetts Institute of Technology" get significant number of mis-clicks for the query "Michigan Institute of Technology". Jaccard distance is not robust to such mis-clicks.

Distributional Distance (Jensen-Shannon Divergence) Our main insight is to leverage the frequency of clicks. The frequency of mis-clicks is typically much lower compared with frequency of clicks on documents that are consistent with the meaning of the expansion. We consider the *distribution* of documents clicked for a given query instead of the *set* of documents. We use a distributional distance metric, square root of *Jensen-Shannon divergence*, to evaluate distance between expansions. This metric is much more robust to mis-clicks.

Denote by $F(q, d)$ the frequency with which d is clicked by q. The click distribution $\Omega(q)$ of a query q over all possible documents is $Pr(\Omega(q) = d) = \frac{F(q,d)}{\sum_{d \in D(q)} F(q,d)}$.

Given click distributions defined by click frequencies, the Jensen-Shanon divergence between two expansions e_i and e_j in $E(a)$ is:
$JSD(\Omega(e_i)||\Omega(e_j)) = \frac{1}{2} KL(\Omega(e_i)||\Omega(\bar{e})) + \frac{1}{2} KL(\Omega(e_j)||\Omega(\bar{e}))$,
where $\Omega(\bar{e}) = \frac{1}{2}(\Omega(e_i) + \Omega(e_j))$ and $KL(X||Y)$ is the Kullback-Leibler divergence between two distributions:

$$KL(X||Y) = \sum_i Pr(X(i)) \log \frac{Pr(X(i))}{Pr(Y(i))}.$$

Then, $dist(e_i, e_j) = \sqrt{JSD(\Omega(e_i)||\Omega(e_j))}$.

3.2.2 Clustering of Candidate Expansions

We cluster the candidate expansions in $E(a)$ based on the above distance metric. We use the bottom-up, average-link hierarchical clustering [14, 5].

3.3 Enhancement for Tail Meanings

While the set of co-clicked queries for the acronym a covers the popular meanings of a, it does not cover many of the less popular meanings (referred to as "tail meanings"). Consider the acronym "MIT". "Massachusetts Institute of Technology" is the dominating meaning for "MIT"; the first few pages of results returned by the search engine for the query "MIT" are dominated by that meaning. Tail meanings for that acronym (e.g., "Maharashtra Institute of Technology", "Mahakal Institute of Technology", "Mazandaran Institute of Technology" and so on) are not represented in the top results. As a result, the co-clicked queries for "MIT" will not cover these tail meanings. As shown in Figure 2, the co-clicked queries for "MIT" (i.e., "massachusetts institute of technology", "mit boston" and "mass institute of tech") all correspond to the dominating meaning. Hence, the above approach misses the tail meanings.

We leverage the following insight to address this problem. Since users searching for tail meanings do not find the desired documents when they use only the acronym as a query, they use additional words to disambiguate the query. For example, a user searching for the meaning "Maharashtra Institute of Technology" (which is located in Pune, India) will issue the query "mit pune" while the one searching for the

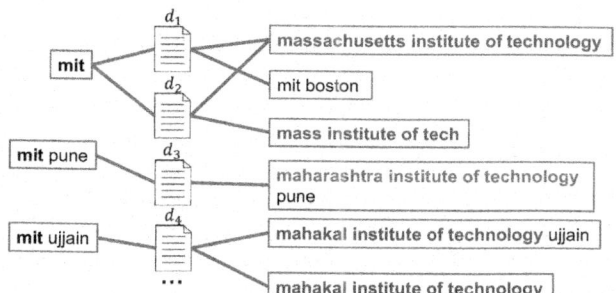

Figure 2: Example illustrating enhancement for tail meanings.

meaning "Mahakal Institute of Technology" (which is located in Ujjain, India) will issue the query "mit ujjain". *Instead of collecting co-clicked queries for the acronym a, we collect co-clicked queries for acronym supersequence queries (ASQ).*

Definition 3. (**Acronym Supersequence Query**) An acronym supersequence query, denoted as $a+s$, for an acronym a is a query in the query click log that contains the string a and an additional sequence of words s either as prefix or as suffix of a.

For example, "mit pune", "mit ujjain" and "mit admission" are ASQs for "mit". Co-clicked queries of ASQs of a contain many more tail meanings of a. As shown in Figure 2, co-clicked of the above ASQs of "mit" cover the tail meanings like "Maharashtra Institute of Technology" and "Mahakal Institute of Technology". We enhance the candidate expansion identification and expansion clustering steps based on the above insight.

Candidate Expansion Identification:
Input: The acronym a and the query click log $\mathcal{Q}$.
Output: The set $E(a)$ of candidate expansions of a.

The goal of this step is to identify the candidate expansions among the co-clicked queries of ASQs of a. However, there is a challenge: unlike in the case of co-clicked queries of a, the candidate expansions may not themselves appear in co-clicked queries of ASQs of a. For example, the co-clicked queries for ASQ "mit pune" does not contain "maharashtra institute of technology". But it contains "maharashtra institute of technology pune". This is because people tend to use acronyms and their expansions interchangeably; so, ASQ $a+s$ may not have co-clicks with e where e is an expansion of a but will have co-clicks with $e+s$. We refer to them as "expansion supersequence queries".

We identify the candidate expansions of a as follows:
1) We first obtain the set $ASQ(a)$ of all ASQs of a. We compute this by scanning the query click log and identifying queries which contain a and a prefix or suffix string. We consider prefix and suffix strings containing zero, one and two words.
2) For each ASQ $a+s \in ASQ(a)$, we collect the set of co-clicked queries $\cup_{d \in D(a+s)} Q(d)$. e is a candidate expansion for a based on ASQ $a+s$ iff (i) the expansion supersequence query has co-clicks with $a+s$, i.e., $e+s \in \cup_{d \in D(a+s)} Q(d)$ and (ii) the acronym-expansion checking function returns true, i.e., $IsExp(e,a) = true$. We formally define the candidate expansion set $E_s(a)$ of a based on ASQ $a+s$:

$$E_s(a) = \{e | e+s \in \cup_{d \in D(a+s)} Q(d) \wedge IsExp(e,a) = true\}$$

3) We obtain the candidate expansion set $E(a)$ of a by unioning the candidate expansion sets based on the ASQs. We formally define the candidate expansion set $E(a)$ of a by $E(a) = \bigcup_{\forall s, a+s \in ASQ(a)} E_s(a)$.

Note that the prefix/suffix can be empty. So, $ASQ(a)$ includes a and hence the above candidate expansion set subsumes the previously defined candidate expansion set. The new candidate expansion set contains strictly more expansions and hence improves coverage.

Acronym Expansion Clustering:
Input: The set $E(a)$ of candidate expansions of a and the query click log $\mathcal{Q}$.
Output: Grouping $\mathcal{G}(a) = \{G_1, \ldots, G_n\}$ of candidate expansions $E(a)$.

The goal is to group the set $E(a)$ of candidate expansions into groups such that each group corresponds to a distinct meaning. The key insight for expansions also holds for expansion supersequence queries: the expansion supersequence queries that correspond to the same meaning will click on the same set of documents, whereas expansion supersequence queries corresponding to different meanings will click on different sets of documents. For example, "massachusetts institute of technology admissions" and "mass inst of tech admissions" will share clicks but "massachusetts institute of technology admissions" and "maharashtra institute of technology admissions" will not. Hence, we can leverage the same general clustering approach based on distributional distance to perform the grouping. However, the same expansions can have multiple corresponding expansion supersequence queries; we need to compute the distance between two expansions by aggregating the distances between the corresponding expansion supersequence queries. There are multiple ways to perform this aggregation; we present two such options:

Distance Aggregation: One option is to compute the distance for each distinct expansion supersequence query (corresponding to a distinct prefix/suffix string) and then aggregate the distances. Let $ASQ(a, e_i, e_j) = \{a+s | a+s \in ASQ(a), e_i+s \in \mathcal{Q}, e_j+s \in \mathcal{Q}\}$ be the subset of ASQ queries for which both e_i+s and e_j+s are valid queries in the query log $\mathcal{Q}$. For each $a+s \in ASQ(a, e_i, e_j)$, denote by $dist_s(e_i, e_j)$ the distance between two candidate expansions e_i and e_j measured over the same supersequence $a+s$, using the distributional distance between queries e_i+s and e_j+s. This can be defined as $dist_s(e_i, e_j) = dist(e_i+s, e_j+s)$. We then aggregate $dist_s(e_i, e_j)$ over all possible $a+s \in ASQ(a, e_i, e_j)$ to obtain the overall distance $dist(e_i, e_j)$ between candidate expansions e_i and e_j. That is $dist(e_i, e_j) = \frac{1}{|ASQ(a, e_i, e_j)|} \sum_{a+s \in ASQ(a, e_i, e_j)} dist_s(e_i, e_j)$.

Click Frequency Aggregation: Another option is to aggregate clicks instead of distance scores. For each pair of candidate expansions, e_i and e_j, we compute the click distribution of expansion e_i by aggregating over all possible expansion supersequence queries in $ASQ(a, e_i, e_j)$. The aggregated click distribution, denoted by $\Omega_{ij}(e_i)$, is:

$$Pr(\Omega_{ij}(e_i) = d) = \frac{\sum_{a+s \in ASQ(a, e_i, e_j)} F(e_i+s, d)}{\sum_{a+s \in ASQ(a, e_i, e_j)} \sum_{d \in D(e_i+s)} F(e_i+s, d)}.$$

We then compute a distributional distance between e_i and e_j based on the aggregated click distribution: $dist(e_i, e_j) = \sqrt{JSD(\Omega_{ij}(e_i) || \Omega_{ij}(e_j))}$.

As we will show later in our experiments, we did not observe noticeable difference between the two aggregation approaches.

We refer to this approach as *Enhanced Acronym Expansion Clustering*; we refer to the approach discussed in Section 3.2 as *Acronym Expansion Clustering*.

3.4 Canonical Expansion, Popularity, Context

Input: Grouping $\mathcal{G}(a) = \{G_1, \ldots, G_n\}$ of candidate expansions $E(a)$ and the query click log $\mathcal{Q}$.
Output: Meanings $\{M_1, \ldots, M_n\}$ with $M_i.e$, $M_i.p$ and $M_i.C$ for each meaning M_i.

The clustering step outputs a set of groups of expansions $\mathcal{G}(a) = \{G_1, \ldots, G_n\}$. These groups correspond to the desired set $\{M_1, \ldots, M_n\}$ of distinct meanings for the acronym a. In this step we compute, for each meaning M_i, canonical expansion $M_i.e$, popularity $M_i.p$, and context words $M_i.C$.

Canonical Expansion: We posit that the canonical expansion of G_i is the most "popular" expansion, because intuitively the canonical acronym expansion should occur more frequently than non-canonical expansions, or expansions with spelling mistakes.

In our click log data, popularity is measured by the number of clicks. If a document d is clicked by acronym a for a total of $F(a, d)$ times, we want to find out how many of those clicks are intended for each expansion $e_k \in G_i$.

Since there is no way for us to know users' real intent, we approximately distribute clicks $F(a, d)$ to each expansion $e_k \in G_i \in \mathcal{G}$ proportionally by the number of clicks between e_k and d, namely, $F(e_k, d)$. The intuition is that if the document d is clicked by a particular expansion e_k a lot, then a significant portion of the clicks $F(a, d)$ should be credited to e_k.

Given a click between a and $d \in D(a)$, the probability that the click is intended for e_k, denoted as $Pr(e_k, d)$, is computed by the total number of clicks between e_k and d, $F(e_k, d)$, divided by the total number of clicks between d and all possible expansions in $\mathcal{G}$. The probability that a click on document $d \in D(a)$ belongs to expansion e_k is thus:

$$Pr(e_k, d) = \frac{F(e_k, d)}{\sum_{G_l \in \mathcal{G}} \sum_{e_j \in G_l} F(e_j, d)}$$

If we only look at acronym a itself (without supersequence tokens), then the probability of an expansion e_k can be computed by aggregating over all possible acronym-document clicks $F(a, d)$:

$$e_k.p = \frac{\sum_{d \in D(a)} F(a, d) Pr(e_k, d)}{\sum_{d \in D(a)} F(a, d)} \quad (1)$$

However, the probability of an expansion should also include cases where the acronym is mentioned in conjunction with supersequence tokens $a + s$, where the meaning of a is intended for that expansion. Conceptually, the meaning probability of a should be counted regardless of whether a is mentioned alone, or with some other tokens. (If we do not account for supersequence queries, on the other hand, then for certain tail expansions discovered via ASQ that have no co-clicks with a, these expansions would get zero-probability, which is intuitively incorrect).

We define $Pr_s(e_k, d)$ for each $a + s \in ASQ(a)$ by:

$$Pr_s(e_k, d) = \frac{F(e_k + s, d)}{\sum_{G_l \in \mathcal{G}} \sum_{e_j \in G_l} F(e_j + s, d)}$$

Then the probability of an expansion e_k, denoted as $e_k.p$, can be computed by aggregating clicks credited to e_k, divided by the total number of query clicks containing a:

$$e_k.p = \frac{\sum_{a+s \in ASQ(a)} \sum_{d \in D(a+s)} F(a+s, d) Pr_s(e_k, d)}{\sum_{a+s \in ASQ(a)} \sum_{d \in D(a+s)} F(a+s, d)} \quad (2)$$

As in our previous notations, $a \in ASQ(a)$ because s can be empty. Notice, Equation (2) is a generalization of Equation (1). If supersequence queries are not considered, then it essentially becomes Equation (1).

With that, the canonical expansion of G_i is simply the expansion with the highest probability:

$$M_i.e = \operatorname*{argmax}_{e_k \in G_i} e_k.p$$

where $e_k.p$ is computed in Equation (2).

Meaning Group Popularity: The second output is the probability of each meaning group $M_i.p$. Since we have already computed $e_k.p$ in Equation (2), we can simply aggregate for all $e_k \in G_i$ to obtain $M_i.p$:

$$M_i.p = \sum_{e_k \in G_i} e_k.p$$

Context Words: Let $D(G_i)$ be the set of documents clicked by expansions in group G_i for meaning M_i. We assign context words to each meaning M_i:
$M_i.C = \{w \mid w \text{ is a word in } q, q \in \cup_{d \in D(G_i)} Q(d)\}$. We assign to each word in $M_i.C$ a probability score, which measures how strongly the word indicates the meaning. Let $F(w, G_i)$ be the frequency of a word w in group G_i, given by $F(w, G_i) = \sum_{w \in q, q \in \cup_{d \in D(G_i)} Q(d), d \in D(G_i)} F(q, d)$. We compute the probability that a word w is indicative for M_i by:

$$Pr(w|M_i) = \frac{F(w, G_i)}{\sum_{w' \in M_i.C} F(w', G_i)}.$$

4. ONLINE MEANING PREDICTION

Acronym queries are very common in Web search. Often users provide some context, in addition to the acronym, which can be one or more other words. In such cases, the user experience can be greatly enhanced if the correct meaning of the acronym can be predicted by the search engine. Then the search results for the query will be more relevant and focused.

We propose a solution to such prediction task: given an acronym and a context, predict the correct meaning of the acronym. We assume that we are given a set of meanings $\{M_1, M_2, \ldots, M_n\}$ for an acronym, found using our offline approach from Section 3. Each meaning M_i is also associated with a set of context words as described in Section 3.4. To predict the correct meaning of an acronym, given context words, we leverage (1) the popularity of each meaning, and (2) the relatedness between each meaning and the context words. In case there are no context words given, to predict the meaning of an acronym, we use only the popularity scores of its meanings, $M_i.p$, as computed in Section 3.4.

For each meaning M_i and context word w, we compute the probability $Pr(M_i|w)$. Applying Bayes' theorem we obtain:

$$Pr(M_i|w) = \frac{Pr(w|M_i) Pr(M_i)}{Pr(w)}$$

Here, $Pr(w|M_i)$ is computed as in Section 3.4, and $Pr(M_i)$ is given by $M_i.p$. $Pr(w)$ can be any dictionary-based probability of the word w. Note that since $Pr(w)$ is the same for all meanings M_i, it is sufficient to consider only the numerator in the above formula.

We compute $Pr(M_i|w)$ for each meaning of the acronym. To predict which is the correct meaning, we consider the meaning with the highest probability score.

This prediction task can be further generalized in case we have more than one context word in addition to the acronym:

$$Pr(M_i|w_1,\ldots,w_k) = \frac{Pr(w_1,\ldots,w_k|M_i)Pr(M_i)}{Pr(w_1,\ldots,w_k)}$$

where $Pr(w_1,\ldots,w_k|M_i) = \prod_j Pr(w_j|M_i)$ by considering that all words are independent and identically distributed. $Pr(w_1,\ldots,w_k)$ is computed analogously.

5. EXPERIMENTS

We present an experimental evaluation of the solution proposed in the paper. The goals of the study are:
- To study the effectiveness of our clustering algorithm and our enhanced clustering algorithm in discovering expansions and grouping expansions into meanings;
- To compare the above algorithms with clusterings based on edit distance and Jaccard distance in terms of cluster quality;
- To compare the meanings available in Wikipedia with those discovered by our clustering algorithm;
- To study the effectiveness of online meaning prediction algorithm for acronym+context queries.

5.1 Experimental Setup

5.1.1 Data

To evaluate the proposed approach of clustering acronym expansions, we randomly sampled 100 pages from Wikipedia disambiguation pages. We filtered out pages which do not represent acronyms (e.g., the disambiguation page about "Jim Gray"), and pages of unambiguous acronyms with a single meaning. This resulted in a set of 64 acronyms, on which we perform our experiments. To collect candidate expansions, we use the query log from Bing from 2010 and 2011[2].

5.1.2 Compared Methods

We compare the following methods, all based on standard bottom-up hierarchical clustering with average link and threshold 0.8:
- **Edit Distance based Clustering (EDC):** Clustering, which uses edit distance between candidate expansions.
- **Jaccard Distance based Clustering (JDC):** Clustering, which uses Jaccard distance between expansions.
- **Acronym Expansion Clustering (AEC):** Our approach from Section 3.2, which uses only acronym queries to collect candidate expansions (no supersequence queries). Square root of Jensen-Shannon divergence is used for distance between expansions.
- **Enhanced Acronym Expansion Clustering (EAEC):** Our enhanced approach from Section 3.3, which uses supersequence queries to collect candidate expansions, square root of Jensen-Shannon divergence as distance, and click frequency based aggregation.

5.1.3 Ground Truth Meanings of Acronyms

We use two sets of ground truth meanings for acronyms:
- **Wikipedia Meanings:** Meanings listed in the Wikipedia disambiguation pages of the acronyms.

[2] Note that due to proprietary and privacy concerns we cannot share more details about the query log.

By analyzing the results from our clustering approach on a set of acronyms, we noticed that the meanings discovered from the query log, and the meanings listed in Wikipedia for the same acronyms, are very different. That is why, in addition to the Wikipedia meanings, we compile a second set of ground truth meanings:
- **Golden Standard Meanings:** We consider for each acronym all queries from the click log, which (1) are legitimate w.r.t the acronym-expansion check (see Section 3.1), and (2) have co-clicks with acronym or acronym supersequence queries. Then, we manually label the different meanings/expansions of the acronym. In the Golden Standard we have one or more different expansions for each distinct meaning. For example, we can have two expansions: "central michigan university" and "central mich univ" referring to the same meaning.

Note that some acronym expansions are not meaningful, even though they are legitimate with respect to our acronym-expansion check. One such example is the expansion "computer processor upgrade" for "CPU", since we speculate people never mean "computer processor upgrade" when they mention "CPU". In our Golden Standard set we do not consider such expansions. Since not all legitimate expansions are included in the ground truth, not all groups from our clustering approaches have specific ground truth meaning. We measured the number of the groups which have ground truth meanings, divided by the total number of groups in the clustering, and on average, 82% of the groups have ground truth meanings.

5.1.4 Evaluation Measures

We use the following measures: *Purity*, *Normalized Mutual Information (NMI)*, and *Recall*.

Our algorithms output a set of groups $\mathcal{G}(a) = \{G_1,\ldots,G_n\}$ which maps to golden standard meanings $\mathcal{M} = \{M_1,\ldots,M_k\}$ for a given acronym a. We map each group of expansions G_i to one or more meanings from $\mathcal{M}$ using the top-5 expansions from G_i, ranked by their probabilities. A group can be mapped to one or more meanings, and multiple groups can be mapped to one meaning. For example, a group with expansions, "carnegie mellon university" and "central michigan university", is mapped to 2 distinct meanings, while a group with expansions, "central michigan university" and "central mich univ", is mapped only to one meaning. By a *group-meaning mapping* we consider a meaning, to which a group can be mapped.

- **Purity:** The Purity measures the accuracy of the group-meaning mappings. Let $N = \sum_{i=1}^{n}\sum_{j=1}^{k}|G_i \cap M_j|$ be the total number of group-meaning mappings. The Purity measure counts the number of groups, which are mapped to some meaning, and divides this number by N:

$$\text{Purity}(\mathcal{G},\mathcal{M}) = \frac{1}{N}\sum_{i=1}^{n}\max_j |G_i \cap M_j|$$

Good clusterings have Purity close to 1, and bad ones – close to 0. Since high Purity is easy to achieve, by simply having all expansions in separate groups, in addition to Purity, we use Normalized Mutual Information, described below.

- **Normalized Mutual Information (NMI):**

$$\text{NMI}(\mathcal{G},\mathcal{M}) = \frac{\text{MI}(\mathcal{G};\mathcal{M})}{[\text{H}(\mathcal{G}) + \text{H}(\mathcal{M})]/2}$$

Here $\text{MI}(\mathcal{G};\mathcal{M}) = \sum_i\sum_j Pr(G_i \cap M_j)\log\frac{Pr(G_i \cap M_j)}{Pr(G_i)Pr(M_j)}$ is the Mutual Information of the clusters and the Golden Stan-

	Purity	NMI
EDC	0.956	0.862
JDC	0.999	0.918
AEC	0.998	0.999

Table 1: Evaluation for EDC, JDC, and AEC.

	Purity	NMI	Recall
AEC	0.993	0.994	0.801
EAEC	0.996	0.995	0.996

Table 2: Evaluation for AEC and EAEC.

N_W	N_{GS}	$|N_W \cap N_{GS}|$	$\frac{|N_W \cap N_{GS}|}{N_W}$	$\frac{|N_W \cap N_{GS}|}{N_{GS}}$
15.859	15.781	4.922	0.351	0.339

Table 4: Number of meanings in Wikipedia (N_W), in the Golden Standard (N_{GS}), and shared ($N_W \cap N_{GS}$).

dard meanings. $H(\mathcal{G}) = -\sum_i Pr(G_i) \log Pr(G_i)$ is the entropy of the clusters, and $H(\mathcal{M})$, computed analogically, is the meanings entropy. NMI is a number between 0 and 1, where good clusterings have NMI close to 1, and bad ones – close to 0. Since, the cluster entropy $H(\mathcal{G})$ increases with the number of groups, clusterings with many groups have low NMI scores. This is why NMI considers the trade-off between the quality of the clusters and their total number.

- **Recall:** We compute Recall only with respect to our ground truth meanings. In practice, it is very difficult to find all possible meanings for a given acronym. The Recall w.r.t our Golden Standard, is the number of meanings, which are found in the clustering, divided by the total number of meanings in the Golden Standard. Furthermore, if a group is mapped to multiple meanings, we consider only one of them, assuming only a single meaning per group.

5.2 Acronym Meaning Discovery Results

We first compare the effectiveness of the Edit Distance based (EDC) and Jaccard Distance based (JDC) clusterings with our Acronym Expansion clustering (AEC) using a subset of 20 acronyms. The results are presented in Table 1.

We notice that both methods, EDC and JDC, have lower cluster quality than AEC, especially in terms of NMI. EDC often fails to cluster expansions by semantic meaning, since expansions with the same meaning can have very large string distance. In such cases, they are incorrectly assigned to different groups. For example "central michigan university", "central mich univ", and "central mi univ" belong to different groups from the EDC clustering. In contrast, the AEC method groups these expansions in a single group, since it does not rely on string distance.

The JDC method has better quality than EDC, but it is still inferior to the AEC method. Since JDC uses set distance between expansions, it is very difficult to find a threshold for similarity. If the threshold is high, then distinct meanings can be easily grouped together due to mis-clicks; if the threshold is low, then identical meanings are not grouped together because sometimes there are not enough clicks. In contrast, the AEC method addresses these problems by using distributional distance metric over click frequencies.

5.2.1 Comparison between AEC and EAEC

To discuss the effectiveness of our clustering approaches, AEC and EAEC, we first present some intuitive examples. In Table 3 we show the top-5 meanings, their probabilities, and a few context words for "CMU", "MBA", and "RISC", using our enhanced clustering EAEC. Each of the three acronyms has one or two dominant meanings, with very high probabilities, and other meanings with much lower probabilities. We also notice that the context words of each meaning are very descriptive. For example, "concrete masonry unit" has context words "cinder", "cement", "construction", etc.

We systematically compare AEC and EAEC in Table 2, using the Golden Standard meanings and our complete data set. We first notice that the quality of the two methods is very good, in terms of both, Purity and NMI. The methods succeed in grouping together expansions referring to the same semantic meaning, even if they have large string distances. Furthermore, due to the choice of distributional distance metric for the clustering, the mis-clicks do not influence the clustering.

From the results we also notice that the Recall improves significantly for the enhanced clustering (EAEC), compared to AEC. Using EAEC with supersequence queries, we discover significantly more new tail meanings. Furthermore, since the enhanced clustering EAEC achieves 0.996 Recall w.r.t the Golden Standard, we succeed to output 99% of the meanings in the Golden Standard to the end users.

In addition to using click frequency based aggregation, we also tried out distance based aggregation as described in Section 3. Distance based aggregation yields a purity of 0.996, NMI of 0.997 and recall of 0.994, which is similar to that of click frequency based aggregation.

5.2.2 Wikipedia vs. Golden Standard Meanings

An important result from our study is the comparison between the Wikipedia meanings and the Golden Standard meanings. First, in Table 5 we present the meanings of "CMU", "RISC" and "MBA" which belong only to Wikipedia, only to the Golden Standard, or are shared by both. We notice, that the amount of shared meanings is relatively small, and that both sets, Wikipedia and Golden Standard meanings have meanings not covered by the other.

In Table 4 we present the average number of meanings in Wikipedia, in the Golden Standard, and their shared meanings. In Figure 3 all acronyms in our data set are presented with their meaning counts from the three meaning sets.

From these results we see that only 35% from the meanings in Wikipedia are found using our clustering aproach. This means that a lot of meanings listed in Wikipedia are typically not used in their abbreviated form. It can be because they are extremely tail meanings, or because they are mostly encyclopedic or domain-specific, e.g., medical or mathematical terms. In such cases there is not enough evidence in the query log that these acronyms refer to the corresponding meanings. For example, for "MBA" our method did not find the meaning "main belt asteroid" (see Table 5), and for "LRA" our method did not find the meaning "leukotriene receptor antagonist".

On the other hand, our acronym mining approach discovers many meanings, currently not present in Wikipedia: in the Golden Standard set only 34% of the meanings belong to Wikipedia. More importantly, we discover acronym meanings which are frequently used by common users. Typically, we discover many company names, associations, universities, events, etc. which are used together with their abbreviated form. By finding such new, valid and widely used acronym

	Meaning	Probability	Context Words
CMU	central michigan university	0.615	michigan, university, athletics, campus, edu, football, chippewas
	carnegie mellon university	0.312	mellon, carnegie, pittsburgh, university, library, computer, engineering
	concrete masonry unit	0.045	block, concrete, cmu, masonry, cinder, cement, construction
	central methodist university	0.017	methodist, university, fayette, central, missouri, baseball
	canton municipal utilities	0.004	canton, court, municipal, docket, case, clerk, records
RISC	reduced instruction set computer	0.737	risc, instruction, set, computer, processor, architecture
	rice insurance services company	0.143	insurance, rice, risceo, services, real, estate
	rna induced silencing complex	0.046	complex, rna, silencing, gene, protein
	reinventing schools coalition	0.037	schools, coalition, inventing, alaska
	recovery industry services company	0.022	recovery, certified, specialist, matrix, educational
MBA	master of business administration	0.868	mba, business, gmat, administration, harvard, programs, degree
	mortgage bankers association	0.069	mortgage, bank, implode, amerisave, bankers, rates
	montgomery bell academy	0.022	bell, montgomery, academy, nashville, mba, school, edu
	metropolitan builders association	0.015	builders, homes, association, wisconsin, milwaukee
	military benefit association	0.006	military, armed, association, benefits, insurance, veterans

Table 3: Top-5 meanings for CMU, RISC, and MBA, ranked by probability, and some of their context words.

	Only Wikipedia Meanings	Only Golden Standard Meanings	Shared Meanings
CMU	caribbean medical university chiang mai university california miramar university colorado mesa university coffman memorial union college music update complete music update communication management unit	central methodist university canton municipal utilities centrul medical unirea case management unit central mindanao university central missouri university	carnegie mellon university central michigan university canadian mennonite university concrete masonry unit couverture maladie universelle
RISC	rural infrastructure service commons research institute for symbolic computation	rice insurance services company reinventing schools coalition recovery industry services company rhode island statewide coalition	reduced instruction set computing rna induced silencing complex
MBA	maldives basketball association marine biological association metropolitan basketball association media bloggers association milwaukee bar association monterey bay aquarium macbook air main belt asteroid market basket analysis miss black america misty's big adventure	metropolitan builders association military benefit association master builders association mississippi basketball association mountain bike action massachusetts bar association mariana bracetti academy missionary baptist association morten beyer agnew mind body awareness memphis business academy	master of business administration mortgage bankers association montgomery bell academy mountain bothy association

Table 5: Meanings from Wikipedia and Golden Standard sets.

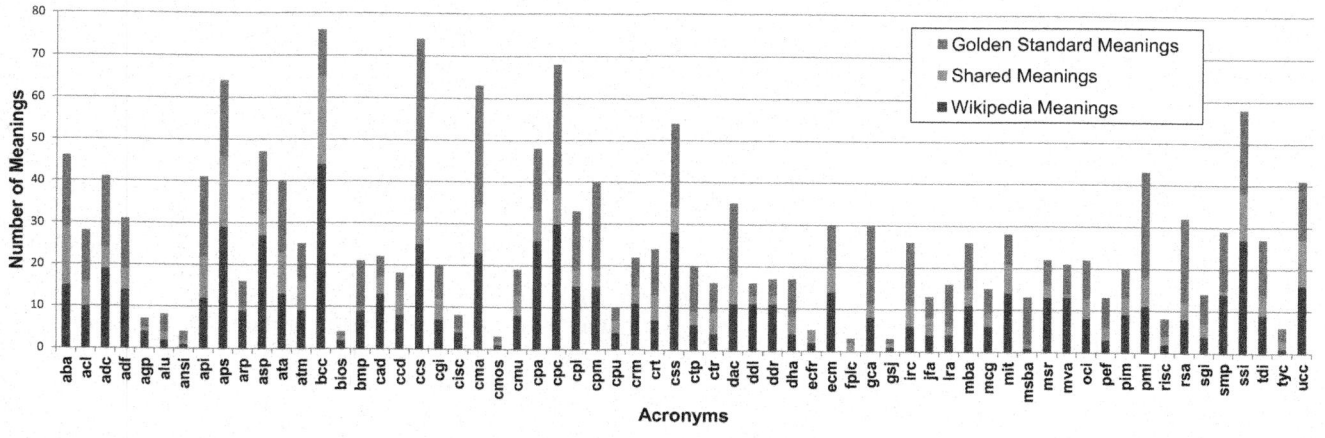

Figure 3: Number of meanings from Wikipedia, from the Golden Standard, and shared between the two sets.

Query	Label
cmu michigan	central michigan university
cmu robotics institute	carnegie mellon university
cmu pittsburgh	carnegie mellon university
cmu fayette missouri	central methodist university

Table 6: Examples for "acronym+context" queries and their labels.

expansions, we can significantly extend the meaning lists in Wikipedia disambiguation pages.

5.3 Online Meaning Prediction Results

Here we consider the online application scenario from Section 4: given acronym+context queries, predict the meaning of the acronym considering the provided context.

We use a set of 7612 acronym+context queries, randomly sampled from the query click log, which refer to the acronyms in our data set. For example, for "CMU" we use queries like "cmu football", "cmu pittsburgh", "cmu robotics institute", etc. Human users label these queries with the meaning they consider most probable, by looking only at the query. For example, "cmu michigan" is labeled by "central michigan university" (see Table 6 for more examples). Queries, for which the additional context does not disambiguate the meaning, are not labeled. For example, "cmu university" can refer to multiple meanings, and hence it is not labeled.

We apply the prediction approach from Section 4 to the labeled queries, without considering their labels. The output is the most probable meaning of the acronym, given the context words in the query.

For each acronym, we compute the number of correctly predicted meanings (by comparing to their labels), divided by the total number of labeled queries for this acronym. The average precision is **0.941**. This means that the assigned context words to each acronym meaning are highly indicative and can be used to predict meanings for online acronym+context queries effectively.

6. RELATED WORKS

While there have been many works and systems available on acronyms, we believe our work has the following unique distinctions compared with the state of art. First, we solve the general acronym meaning discovery problem in a comprehensive way. This is different from other works which either look at domain specific acronyms (e.g., medical domain), or only focus on certain aspects of the problem (e.g., only interested in finding expansions). Second, to the best of our knowledge, this is the first work on acronym expansion and meaning discovery leveraging query click log by exploiting the acronym co-click behaviors. Third, due to the nature of query click analysis, our method is language agnostic. This is different from pattern based discovery in text for instance, where people look for NLP patterns (e.g., "Carnegie Mellon Univeristy, also referred to as CMU, is ...") and therefore the patterns and methods are very language dependent. We now study related works in details.

Wikipedia covers many acronyms and their different meanings through its "disambiguation pages". These pages are manually edited by one or a few editors. First, our experiments show that many meanings are not covered in Wikipedia disambiguation pages; there are almost twice more meanings used in web search queries but not covered in Wikipedia. Second, it does not provide popularity scores. Furthermore, the meanings in Wikipedia are not necessarily the most popular meanings; our experiments show that roughly 65% of the meanings of acronyms on Wikipedia are rarely or never expressed in Web search queries (Section 5). Finally, our work heavily taps into the wisdom of crowds, to discover acronym expansions, understand their meanings and popularity, and mine their corresponding context. Tapping data contributed by millions of end users is a significant and necessary step forward.

Websites such as acronymfinder.com list many possible acronym expansions; this is also manually edited. As in Wikipedia, it does not provide popularity scores. Furthermore, it does not provide any context words for most of the acronym expansions. While it does offer a large number of meanings for a large number of acronyms, our study shows that it suffers significantly from the quality problem: (1) many expansions listed are actually near duplicates ("Reduced Instruction Set Computer" and "Reduced Instruction Set Computing" for "RISC"); (2) many expansions are actually meaningless, in the sense people rarely or never use its acronym form to refer to it (e.g., "More Bad Advice" for "MBA").

Recently, there have been a few works on automatic mining of acronym expansions by leveraging Web data [8, 9, 6]. While some aspects are complementary to ours (e.g., in [6] subsequent queries in query sessions are exploited), our study covers many more aspects, including meaning discovery through clustering analysis, popularity computation and context words mining. Our study heavily relies on query click log, and it is not clear how other works can be adapted to support effective clustering, popularity and context words mining without the help of query click log.

Another line of related work is on mining synonyms [3, 4, 15, 11, 1, 2]. Existing studies on synonyms are mostly focused on unambiguous synonyms. Acronym is a special type of synonym, which is highly ambiguous and context dependent. This work can be regarded as a first attempt at addressing the ambiguity problem in synonyms, with a focus on acronyms only.

There have been many works on acronym expansion discovery in vertical domains (mainly in medical), e.g., [12, 10, 16, 13]. These works mainly rely on text analysis to discover acronym expansions, and tend to be optimized for their respective domains. This is different from both the general acronym mining aspect, as well as the query click log analysis angle of this work.

7. CONCLUSION

In this paper, we introduce the problem of finding distinct meanings of each acronym, along with the canonical expansion, popularity score and context words. We present a novel, end-to-end solution to this problem. We describe how web search engines can leverage the mined information for online acronym and acronym+context queries.

Our work can be extended in multiple directions. There are other ambiguous queries besides acronyms like people and place name queries. For example, the query "Jim Gray" can refer to the computer scientist, the sportscaster in addition to many other less famous Jim Grays. Can our techniques be adapted to find all the distinct meanings of such queries? Furthermore, it will also be interesting to look into data sources other than query click log for the mining task.

8. REFERENCES

[1] S. Chaudhuri, V. Ganti, and D. Xin. Exploiting web search to generate synonyms for entities. In *WWW Conference*, 2009.

[2] S. Chaudhuri, V. Ganti, and D. Xin. Mining document collections to facilitate accurate approximate entity matching. *PVLDB*, 2(1), 2009.

[3] T. Cheng, H. W. Lauw, and S. Paparizos. Fuzzy matching of web queries to structured data. In *ICDE*, 2010.

[4] T. Cheng, H. W. Lauw, and S. Paparizos. Entity synonyms for structured web search. *TKDE*, 2011.

[5] D. Defays. An efficient algorithm for a complete link method. *The Computer Journal*, 20(4):364–366, 1977.

[6] A. Jain, S. Cucerzan, and S. Azzam. Acronym-expansion recognition and ranking on the web. In *Information Reuse and Integration*, 2007.

[7] R. Jones, B. Rey, O. Madani, and W. Greiner. Generating query substitutions. In *WWW*, 2006.

[8] L. S. Larkey, P. Ogilvie, M. A. Price, and B. Tamilio. Acrophile: an automated acronym extractor and server. In *Proceedings of the fifth ACM conference on Digital libraries*, pages 205–214, 2000.

[9] D. Nadeau and P. D. Turney. A supervised learning approach to acronym identification. In *Proceedings of the 18th Canadian Society conference on Advances in Artificial Intelligence*, pages 319–329, 2005.

[10] S. Pakhomov. Semi-supervised maximum entropy based approach to acronym and abbreviation normalization in medical texts. In *Proceedings of the 40th Annual Meeting on Association for Computational Linguistics*, 2002.

[11] P. Pantel, E. Crestan, A. Borkovsky, A.-M. Popescu, and V. Vyas. Web-scale distributional similarity and entity set expansion. In *EMNLP*, 2009.

[12] J. Pustejovsky, J. Castano, B. Cochran, M. Kotecki, and M. Morrell. Automatic extraction of acronym-meaning pairs from medline databases. *Studies in health technology and informatics*, 84(1):371–375, 2001.

[13] J. Pustejovsky, J. Castano, B. Cochran, M. Kotecki, M. Morrell, and A. Rumshisky. Extraction and disambiguation of acronym-meaning pairs in medline. 2004.

[14] R. Sibson. Slink: an optimally efficient algorithm for the single-link cluster method. *The Computer Journal*, 16(1):30–34, 1973.

[15] P. D. Turney. Mining the web for synonyms: Pmi-ir versus lsa on toefl. *CoRR*, cs.LG/0212033, 2002.

[16] J. Wren, H. Garner, et al. Heuristics for identification of acronym-definition patterns within text: towards an automated construction of comprehensive acronym-definition dictionaries. *Methods of information in medicine*, 41(5):426–434, 2002.

[17] M. Zahariev. Efficient acronym-expansion matching for automatic acronym acquisition. In *International Conference on Information and Knowledge Engineering*, 2003.

A. APPENDIX: ACRONYM-EXPANSION CHECKING FUNCTION

Let a and e be an acronym and a query, respectively. The acronym-expansion checking function returns *true* if e is an expansion of a, and *false* otherwise. We modify the longest common subsequence algorithm by assigning weights to the words and letters of the query string. We find the subsequence with the highest score and use heuristics to decide if e is an expansion of a as follows.

To increase the chance of matching an acronym letter at the beginning of a word, we assign weights $w_{ns} = 2$ to the initial letters of normal non-stop words, $w_s = 1$ to the initial letters of stop words, and $w_{ni} = 0.1$ to all other letters (i.e. the non-initial letters of all words). The score s of a match is the sum of the scores of the participating letters (see Line 15). Then we check if $s \geq 0.68 \cdot |a| \cdot w_{ns}$, where $|a|$ denotes the number of letters in the acronym and 0.68 is an empirically set threshold parameter.

A further requirement is that all words in the query contain acronym letters. However, as mentioned earlier, often stop words are not considered when acronyms are formed (e.g., "Master of Business Administration" is an expansion for "MBA"). To solve this we use weights for the non-stop query words ($w_{ns} = 2$) and for the stop words ($w_s = 1$). We use another threshold to check if $s \geq 0.8 \cdot T$, where T is defined in Line 2.

If both conditions in Line 16 are satisfied, the acronym-expansion check returns *true*, and otherwise *false*. For example, the score of "master of business administration" for the acronym "MBA" is 6 and both inequalities in Line 16 are satisfied. The query "master of business administration education" is not expansion of "MBA" as the second inequality is not satisfied ($6 \not\geq 0.8 \cdot 9$). Finally, two initial requirements are that the acronym consists of one word only, and that the query contains at least two words.

Algorithm 1 Acronym-Expansion Checking Function

Input: Acronym a; Query e; Weights $\{w_{ns}, w_s, w_{ni}\}$
Output: True if e is expansion of a, false otherwise

1: **function** IsExpansion($a, e, w_{ns}, w_s, w_{ni}$)
2: $\quad T \leftarrow \sum_{t \in e} w(t), \quad w(t) = \begin{cases} w_{ns}, & t \text{ is non-stop word} \\ w_s, & t \text{ is stop word} \end{cases}$
3: $\quad$ Let R be $(|a|+1) \times (|e|+1)$ array of zeros
4: $\quad$ **for** $i \leftarrow 1$ **to** $|a|$ **do**
5: $\quad\quad$ **for** $j \leftarrow 1$ **to** $|e|$ **do**
6: $\quad\quad\quad p \leftarrow \max(R[i-1, j], R[i, j-1])$
7: $\quad\quad\quad$ **if** $a[i-1] = e[j-1]$ **then**
8: $\quad\quad\quad\quad w \leftarrow \begin{cases} w_{ns}, & \text{non-stop word starts at } j-1 \text{ in } e \\ w_s, & \text{stop word starts at } j-1 \text{ in } e \\ w_{ni}, & \text{else} \end{cases}$
9: $\quad\quad\quad\quad R[i, j] \leftarrow \max(p, R[i-1, j-1] + w)$
10: $\quad\quad\quad$ **else**
11: $\quad\quad\quad\quad R[i, j] \leftarrow p$
12: $\quad\quad\quad$ **end if**
13: $\quad\quad$ **end for**
14: $\quad$ **end for**
15: $\quad s \leftarrow R[|a|, |e|]$ $\quad\quad\quad\triangleright$ Score of the best match
16: $\quad$ **return** $s \geq 0.68 \cdot |a| \cdot w_{ns}$ **and** $s \geq 0.8 \cdot T$
17: **end function**

Groundhog Day: Near-Duplicate Detection on Twitter

Ke Tao[1], Fabian Abel[1,2], Claudia Hauff[1], Geert-Jan Houben[1], Ujwal Gadiraju[1]
[1]TU Delft, Web Information Systems, PO Box 5031, 2600 GA Delft, the Netherlands
wis@st.ewi.tudelft.nl
[2]XING AG, Gänsemarkt 43, 20354 Hamburg, Germany
fabian.abel@xing.com

ABSTRACT

With more than 340 million messages that are posted on Twitter every day, the amount of duplicate content as well as the demand for appropriate duplicate detection mechanisms is increasing tremendously. Yet there exists little research that aims at detecting near-duplicate content on microblogging platforms. We investigate the problem of near-duplicate detection on Twitter and introduce a framework that analyzes the tweets by comparing (i) syntactical characteristics, (ii) semantic similarity, and (iii) contextual information. Our framework provides different duplicate detection strategies that, among others, make use of external Web resources which are referenced from microposts. Machine learning is exploited in order to learn patterns that help identifying duplicate content. We put our duplicate detection framework into practice by integrating it into Twinder, a search engine for Twitter streams. An in-depth analysis shows that it allows Twinder to diversify search results and improve the quality of Twitter search. We conduct extensive experiments in which we (1) evaluate the quality of different strategies for detecting duplicates, (2) analyze the impact of various features on duplicate detection, (3) investigate the quality of strategies that classify to what exact level two microposts can be considered as duplicates and (4) optimize the process of identifying duplicate content on Twitter. Our results prove that semantic features which are extracted by our framework can boost the performance of detecting duplicates.

Categories and Subject Descriptors

H.3.3 [**Information Systems**]: Information Search and Retrieval—*Information filtering*; H.4.m [**Information Systems**]: Miscellaneous

Keywords

Duplicate Detection; Twitter; Diversification; Search

1. INTRODUCTION

On microblogging platforms such as Twitter or Sina Weibo, where the number of messages that are posted per second exceeds several thousands during big events[1], solving the problem of information overload and providing solutions that allow users to access new information efficiently are non-trivial research challenges. The majority of messages on microblogging platforms refer to news, e.g. on Twitter more than 85% of the tweets are news-related [9]. Many of the microposts convey the same information in slightly different forms which puts a burden on users of microblogging services when searching for new content. Teevan et al. [23] revealed that the search behaviour on Twitter differs considerably from the search behaviour that can be observed on regular Web search engines: Twitter users issue repetitively the same query and thus monitor whether there is new content that matches their query.

Traditional Web search engines apply techniques for detecting near-duplicate content [8, 12] and provide diversification mechanisms to maximize the chance of meeting the expectations of their users [19]. However, there exists little research that focuses on techniques for detecting near-duplicate content and diversifying search results on microblogging platforms. The conditions for inferring whether two microposts comprise highly similar information and can thus be considered near-duplicates differ from traditional Web settings. For example, the textual content is limited in length, people frequently use abbreviations or informal words instead of proper vocabulary and the amount of messages that are posted daily is at a different scale (more than 340 million tweets per day[2]).

In this paper, we bridge the gap and explore near-duplicate detection as well as search result diversification in the microblogging sphere. The main contributions of this paper can be summarized as follows[3].

- We conduct an analysis of duplicate content in Twitter search results and infer a model for categorizing different levels of duplicity.

- We develop a near-duplicate detection framework for microposts that provides functionality for analyzing (i) syntactical characteristics, (ii) semantic similarity and (iii) contextual information. The framework also exploits external Web content which is referenced by the microposts.

- Given our duplicate detection framework, we perform extensive evaluations and analyzes of different duplicate detection strategies on a large, standardized Twit-

---
[1]http://blog.twitter.com/2012/02/post-bowl-twitter-analysis.html

[2]http://blog.twitter.com/2012/03/twitter-turns-six.html
[3]We make our framework and datasets publicly available on our supporting website [22].

ter corpus to investigate the quality of (i) detecting duplicates and (ii) categorizing the duplicity level of two tweets.

- We integrate our duplicate detection framework into a Twitter search engine to enable search result diversification and analyze the impact of the diversification on the search quality.

2. RELATED WORK

Since Twitter was launched in 2006 it has attracted a lot of attention both from the general public and research communities. Researchers managed to find patterns in user behaviours on Twitter, including users' interests towards news articles [1], users' behaviour over time [10], and more general habits that users have on Twitter [18]. Previous research also studied the characteristics of emerging network structures [14] and showed that Twitter is rather a news media than a social platform [9]. Another area of interest is event detection in social Web streams [24], for example in the context of natural disasters [20].

The keyword-based search functionality is a generic tool for users to retrieve relevant information. Teevan et al. [23] analyzed the search behaviour on Twitter and found differences with respect to normal Web search. A first benchmark on Twitter data was introduced at TREC[4] 2011 with a track related to search in microblogs[5]. Among the solutions developed by participating researchers are many feature-driven approaches that exploit topic-insensitive features such as "does the tweet contain a URL?" to rank the tweets that match a given keyword query, e.g. [16]. More sophisticated search solutions also extract named entities from tweets in order to analyze the semantic meaning of tweets [21]. Bernstein et al. [5] investigated alternative topic-based browsing interfaces for Twitter while Abel et al. [2] investigated the utility of faceted search for retrieval on Twitter. However, none of the aforementioned research initiatives investigated strategies for near-duplicate detection and search result diversification in microblogs.

Traditional Web search engines benefit from duplicate detection algorithms and diversification strategies that make use of Broder et al.'s [6] shingling algorithm or Charikar's [7] random projection approach. Henzinger conducted a large-scale evaluation to compare these two methods [8] and Manku et al. [12] proposed to use the latter one for near-duplicate detection during Web crawling. To achieve diversification in search results, Agrawal et al. [3] studied the problem of search result diversification in the context of answering ambiguous Web queries and Rafiei et al. [19] suggested a solution to maximize expectations that users have towards the query results. However, to the best of our knowledge, the problem of identifying near-duplicate content has not been studied in the context of microblogs. In this paper, we thus aim to bridge the gap and research near-duplicate detection and search result diversification on Twitter.

3. DUPLICATE CONTENT ON TWITTER

In this section, we provide the outcomes of our study of duplicate content on the Twitter platform. We present a definition of near-duplicate tweets in 5 levels and show concrete examples. We then analyze near-duplicate content in a large Twitter corpus and investigate to what extent near-duplicate content appears in Twitter search results.

All our examples and experiments utilize the Twitter corpus which is provided by TREC [13].

3.1 Different levels of Near-Duplicate tweets

In this paper, we define duplicate tweets as tweets that convey the same information either syntactically or semantically. We distinguish near-duplicates in 5 levels.

Exact copy The duplicates at the level of *exact copy* are identical in terms of characters. An example tweet pair (t_1, t_2) in our Twitter corpus is:
t_1 and t_2: Huge New Toyota Recall Includes 245,000 Lexus GS, IS Sedans - http://newzfor.me/?cuye

Nearly exact copy The duplicates of *nearly exact copy* are identical in terms of characters except for *#hashtags*, *URLs*, or *@mentions*. Consider the following tweet:
t_3: Huge New Toyota Recall Includes 245,000 Lexus GS, IS Sedans - http://bit.ly/ibUoJs
Here, the tweet pair of (t_1, t_3) is a near-duplicate at a level of *nearly exact copy*.

Strong near-duplicate A pair of tweets is *strong near-duplicate* if both tweets contain the same core messages syntactically and semantically, but at least one of them contains more information in form of new statements or hard facts. For example, the tweet pair of (t_4, t_5) is strong near-duplicate:
t_4: Toyota recalls 1.7 million vehicles for fuel leaks: Toyota's latest recalls are mostly in Japan, but they also... http://bit.ly/dHOPmw
t_5: Toyota Recalls 1.7 Million Vehicles For Fuel Leaks http://bit.ly/f1WFWU

Weak near-duplicate Two *weak near-duplicate* tweets either (i) contain the same core messages syntactically and semantically while personal opinions are also included in one or both of them, or (ii) convey semantically the same messages with differing information nuggets. For example, the tweet pair of (t_6, t_7) is a weak near-duplicate:
t_6: The White Stripes broke up. Oh well.
t_7: The White Stripes broke up. That's a bummer for me.

Low-overlapping The *low-overlapping* pairs of tweets semantically contain the same core message, but only have a couple of common words, e.g. the tweet pair of (t_8, t_9):
t_8: Federal Judge rules Obamacare is unconstitutional...
t_9: Our man of the hour: Judge Vinson gave Obamacare its second unconstitutional ruling. http://fb.me/zQsChak9

If a tweet pair does not match any of the above definitions, it is considered as *non-duplicate*.

3.2 Near-Duplicates in Twitter Search Results

In Section 3.1, the example tweets come from the Tweets 2011 corpus [13], which was used in the Microblog track of TREC 2011. The corpus is a representative sample from tweets posted during a period of 2 weeks (January 23rd to February 8th, 2011, inclusive). As the corpus is designed to be a reusable test collection for investigating Twitter search

---
[4]http://trec.nist.gov
[5]http://sites.google.com/site/microblogtrack/

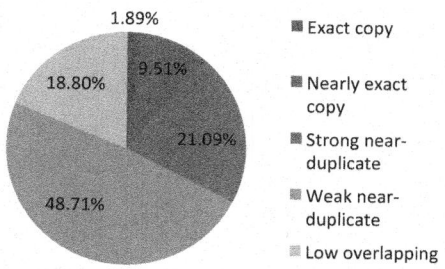

Figure 1: Ratios of near-duplicates in different levels

and ranking, it is used for the experiments of duplicate detection and search result diversification in the rest of the paper. The original corpus consists of 16 million tweets.

Besides the tweets, 49 topics (or queries) were provided for retrieval purposes. Moreover, TREC assessors judged the relevance between 40,855 topic-tweet pairs. A total of 2,825 topic-tweet pairs were judged as relevant. In other words, each topic on average has 57.65 relevant tweets. Employing Named Entity Recognition (NER) services on the content of these relevant tweets and the content of the 1,661 external resources referred by the links mentioned in them results in 6,995 and 56,801 entity extractions respectively when using DBpedia Spotlight [15], or 6,292 and 35,774 entity extractions respectively when using OpenCalais[6]. For each topic, we manually labelled all pairs of relevant tweets according to the levels of near-duplicates that we defined in in Section 3.1. In total, we labelled 55,362 tweet pairs. As a result, we found that 2,745 pairs of tweets are duplicate, 1.89% of them were labelled as exact copy and 48.71% of them were judged as weak near-duplicates (see Figure 1).

For each of the 49 topics, we ranked the tweets according to their relevance to the corresponding topic based on previous work [21] to investigate to what extent the ranked search results contain duplicate items. In the top 10, 20, 50 items and whole range of search results, we find that 19.4%, 22.2%, 22.5%, and 22.3% respectively are duplicates. Given one fifth of the items are duplicates, we consider duplicate detection an important step in the processing pipeline to diversify the search results.

4. DUPLICATE DETECTION FRAMEWORK

We consider the problem of duplicate detection as a classification task that can be performed in two steps: (i) deciding whether a pair of tweets are duplicates or not; and (ii) determining the duplicate level. For both steps, we rely on a collection of features that exploit syntactical elements, the semantics in both tweets and the content of referred Web pages, as well as context information about tweets and users. Finally, we employ logistic regression classifiers to ensemble the characteristics from pairs of tweets into the detection of duplicates and the determination of the levels.

4.1 Features of Tweet Pairs

We now provide an overview of the different features that we extract from tweet pairs for the task of duplicate detection. Given a pair of tweets (t_a, t_b), four sets of features are constructed. In the following sections, we elaborate on the definition of the features and the hypotheses that led us to include them in our strategies.

[6] http://www.opencalais.com

4.1.1 Syntactic Features

We construct syntactical features by matching the tweet pairs with respect to their overlap in letters, words, hashtags and URLs.

Levenshtein distance This feature indicates the number of characters required to change one tweet to the other. Each change can be a deletion, insertion, or substitution. Hence, Levenshtein distance evaluates the difference between a pair of tweets on the basis of differences in the usages of words, phrases, et cetera. As the furthest Levenshtein distance between a pair of tweets is $L_{max} = 140$ (the maximum length of a tweet), we normalize this feature by dividing the original value by L_{max}. Therefore, the final value of this feature is in the range of $[0, 1]$.
Hypothesis H1: The smaller the Levenshtein distance between a pair of tweets, the more likely they are duplicates and the higher the duplicate score.

Overlap in terms This feature compares tweet pairs by words. Although the tweets of near-duplicates use similar sets of words, the ordering of words may differ. Therefore we check the overlap in terms between tweet pairs. In our implementation, this feature is measured by using the Jaccard similarity coefficient as following:

$$overlap(w(t_a), w(t_b)) = \frac{|w(t_a) \cap w(t_b)|}{|w(t_a) \cup w(t_b)|} \quad (1)$$

Here, $w(t_a)$ and $w(t_b)$ are the sets of words that are used in t_a and t_b respectively. As we use the Jaccard similarity coefficient to measure the overlap, the value of this feature is in the range of $[0, 1]$. Similarly, the following features that describe overlap in different aspects are measured by the Jaccard similarity coefficient.
Hypothesis H2: The more overlap in terms we find between a pair of tweets, the higher the duplicate score.

Overlap in hashtags Hashtags are often used by users in tweets to get involved in the discussion about a topic, and also to make their voice easier to be found by others. This feature measures the overlap in hashtags between tweet pairs.
Hypothesis H3: The more common hashtags we find between a pair of tweets, the more likely they are duplicates and the higher the duplicate score.

Overlap in URLs Due to the length limitation of tweets, users often make use of URLs to give pointers to relevant detailed information. Hence we check the overlap of the links contained in the given pair of tweets. If a pair of tweets contain the same URL, they are probably about the same topic and are likely to be duplicates.
Hypothesis H4: The more overlap in URLs we find between a pair of tweets, the more likely they are duplicates and the higher the duplicate score.

Overlap in expanded URLs Various Twitter client applications and sharing functions used by news media sites shorten the URLs in order to give more space for real content [4]. As a result, we may miss some actual overlap in URLs if we only check original URLs. For this reason, we measure the overlap in expanded URLs between tweets. The expanded URLs can be obtained via the redirected locations given in the HTTP responses.
Hypothesis H5: The more common URLs we found between a pair of tweets after expanding the URLs, the more likely they are duplicates and the higher the duplicate score.

Length difference Besides matching letters, words, hashtags, and URLs, we also calculate the difference in length between two tweets and normalize it by L_{max}:

$$length\_difference = \frac{abs(|tweet_a| - |tweet_b|)}{140} \quad (2)$$

Hypothesis H6: The smaller the difference in length between two tweets, the higher the likelihood of them being duplicates and the higher their duplicate score.

4.1.2 Semantic Features

Apart from syntactical features of tweet pairs, semantic information may also be valuable for identifying duplicates, especially when the core messages or important entities in tweets are mentioned in different order. For this reason, we analyze the semantics in both tweets of a pair and construct features that may help with distinguishing duplicate tweets. We utilize NER services like DBpedia Spotlight, OpenCalais as well as the lexical database WordNet to extract the following features.

Overlap in entities Given extracted entities or concepts by employing NER services, we can check the overlap between the sets of entities in tweet pairs. The near-duplicate tweet pairs should contain the same core messages and therefore the same entities should be mentioned.
Hypothesis H7: The tweet pairs with more overlapping entities are more likely to have a high duplicate score.

Overlap in entity types For entities extracted from NER services, the types of the entities can also be retrieved. For example, if t_b contains the entities of type *person* and *location*, t_a should also contain the same type of entities to convey the core messages if they are a near-duplicate tweet pair. Otherwise, more types of entities may indicate it contains more information or less types may suggest only a partial coverage of the core message in t_a. Therefore, we construct features that measure the overlap in entity types between tweet pairs.
Hypothesis H8: The tweet pairs with more overlapping entity types are more likely to have a high duplicate score.

In fact, we found only a slight difference in performance between using DBpedia Spotlight and OpenCalais. In practice, we construct two features and derivative features (introduced later) by using *DBpedia Spotlight* because it yields slightly better results.

Overlap in topics Besides outputting entities with types, OpenCalais can classify the input textual snippets into 18 different categories a.k.a. topics. In this case, each tweet may be assigned more than one topic label or no topic at all. Therefore, it is possible to construct a feature by checking the overlap in topics.
Hypothesis H9: The tweet pairs that share more topics are more likely to have a high duplicate score.

Overlap in WordNet concepts We constructed this feature to compute the overlap based on lexical standards. To achieve this, we make use of the lexical database WordNet [17] to identify the nouns in pairs of tweets and calculate their overlap in these nouns. Practically, we use JWI (MIT Java Wordnet Interface)[7] to find the root concepts of the nouns in the tweets.
Hypothesis H10: The more overlap in WordNet noun concepts we find in a pair of tweets, the more likely they are to be duplicates and the higher their duplicate score.

[7] http://projects.csail.mit.edu/jwi/

Algorithm 1: WordNet similarity of a tweet pair

input : Tweet Pair (t_a, t_b)
output: WordNet similarity of Tweet Pair (t_a, t_b)

acc $\leftarrow$ 0;
if $|t_a| > |t_b|$ **then**
  swap(t_a, t_b);
foreach *WordNet noun concept* c_a *in* t_a **do**
  maximum $\leftarrow$ 0;
  foreach *WordNet noun concept* c_b *in* t_b **do**
    if maximum $<$ *similarity*$_{lin}$ (c_a, c_b) **then**
      maximum $\leftarrow$ *similarity*$_{lin}$ (c_a, c_b);
  acc $\leftarrow$ acc $+$ maximum;
return $\frac{acc}{|W_a|}$;

Overlap in WordNet synset concepts Making use of merely WordNet noun concepts may not fully cover the overlap in information because different tweets may use different words or synonyms to convey the same information. In WordNet, synsets are interlinked by means of conceptual-semantic and lexical relations. We can make use of synsets to include all words with similar meaning for checking the overlap between tweet pairs.
Hypothesis H11: If the concepts in synsets are included for checking overlap between tweet pairs then the overlap feature may have a more positive correlation with the duplicate scores.

WordNet similarity There are several existing algorithms for calculating the semantic relatedness between WordNet concepts, e.g. the method proposed by Lin et al. [11] can measure the semantic relatedness between two concepts with a value between [0, 1]. The WordNet concepts are paired in order to get the highest relatedness. Practically, we follow Algorithm 1 to get this feature for a tweet pair (t_a, t_b). In the description of the algorithm, W_a stands for the set of WordNet noun concepts that appear in t_a.
Hypothesis H12: The higher the WordNet similarity of a tweet pair, the higher the likelihood of the tweets being duplicates and the higher their duplicate score.

4.1.3 Enriched Semantic Features

Due to the length limitation of tweets, 140 characters may not be enough to tell a complete story. Furthermore, some tweets, created by sharing buttons from other news sites for example, may even break the complete message. Thus, we make use of the external resources that are linked from the tweets. This step yields additional information and further enriches the tweets' semantics. Finally, we build a set of so-called *enriched* semantic features.

We construct six enriched semantic features, which are constructed in the same way as semantic features introduced in Section 4.1.2. The only difference is that the source of semantics contains not only the content of the tweets but also the content that we find by retrieving the content of the Web sites that are linked from the tweets.

4.1.4 Contextual Features

Besides analyzing syntactical and semantic aspects, which describe the characteristics of tweet pairs, we also evaluate the effects of the context in which the tweets were published on the duplicate detection. We investigate three types of contextual features: temporal difference of the creation times, similarity of the tweets' authors, and the client application that the authors used.

Temporal difference For several popular events, e.g. UK Royal wedding, Japanese earthquake, and Super Bowl, users have posted thousands of tweets per second. During these events, breaking news are often retweeted not long after being posted. Therefore, it is reasonable to assume that the time difference between duplicate tweets is rather small. We normalize this feature by dividing the original value by the length of the temporal range of the dataset (two weeks in our setup).

Hypothesis H13: The smaller the difference in posting time between a pair of tweets, the higher the likelihood of it being a duplicate pair and the higher the duplicate score.

User similarity Similar users may publish similar content. We measure user similarity in a lightweight fashion by comparing the number of followers and the number of followees. Hence, we extract two features: the differences in #followers and #followees to measure the similarity of the authors of a post. As the absolute values of these two features vary in magnitude, we normalize this feature by applying log-scale and dividing by the largest difference in log-scale, which is 7 in our case.

Hypothesis H14: The higher the similarity of the authors of a pair of tweets, the more likely that the tweets are duplicates.

Same client This is a boolean feature to check whether the pair of tweets were posted via same client application. With authorization, third-party client applications can post tweets on behalf of users. Hence, different Twitter client applications as well as sharing buttons on various Web sites are being used. As the tweets that are posted from the same applications and Web sites may share similar content, provenance information and particularly information about the client application may be used as evidence for duplicate detection.

Hypothesis H15: The tweet pairs that are posted from the same client application tend to be near-duplicates.

4.2 Feature Analysis

As previously stated, we take the Twitter corpus released at TREC (*Tweets2011*) as our Twitter stream sample for the task of duplicate detection. Before we turn to (evaluating) duplicate detection strategies, we first perform an in-depth analysis of this sample with respect to the features that we presented in Section 4.1. We extracted these features for the 55,362 tweet pairs with duplicity judged (see Section 3.2). In Table 1, we list the average values and the standard deviations of the features and the percentages of *true* instances for the boolean feature respectively (*same client*). Moreover, Table 1 shows a comparison between features of duplicate (on all 5 levels) and non-duplicate tweet pairs.

Unsurprisingly, the Levenshtein distances of duplicate tweet pairs are on average 15% shorter than the ones of non-duplicate tweet pairs. Similarly, duplicate tweet pairs share more identical terms than non-duplicate ones: the duplicates have a Jaccard Similarity of 0.2148 in terms, whereas only 0.0571 for the non-duplicates. Hence, these two features which compare the tweets in letters and words may be potentially good indicators for duplicate detection. Although there is a difference in common hashtags between the duplicates and the non-duplicates, the overlap in hashtags does not seem to be a promising feature because of the low absolute value. This may be explained by the low usage of hashtags. The two features that check overlap in hyperlinks show similar characteristics but are slightly better. As expected, we discover more overlap in links by expanding the shortened URLs.

Tweet pairs may convey the same messages with syntactically different but semantically similar words. If this is the case then the syntactical features may fail to detect the duplicate tweets. Therefore, the features that are formulated as overlap in semantics are expected to be larger in absolute values than the syntactical overlap features. Overall, the statistics that are listed in Table 1 are in line with our expectations. We discover more overlap in the duplicates along 3 dimensions, including entities, entity types, and topics, by exploiting semantics with NER services. More distinguishable differences can be found in the features constructed from WordNet. The duplicate tweet pairs have more overlap in WordNet noun concepts or synsets (0.38) than the non-duplicate pairs (0.12). The feature of WordNet similarity is also potentially a good criterion for duplicate detection: the average similarity of duplicate pairs is 0.61 compared to 0.35 for non-duplicate pairs. The comparison of the enriched semantic features shows similar findings to those we observed for the semantic features. Again, the features that compare WordNet-based concepts are more likely to be good indicators for duplicate detection. However the WordNet similarity shows less difference if we consider external resources.

Finally, we attempted to detect the duplicates based on information about the context in which the tweets were posted. Hypothesis H13 (see Section 4.1.4) states that duplicates are more likely to be posted in a short temporal range. The result for the feature of temporal difference in Table 1 supports this hypothesis: the average value of this feature for the duplicate pairs is only 0.0256 (about 8 hours before normalization, see Section 4.1.4) in contrast to 0.2134 (about 3 days) for the non-duplicate ones. With respect to user similarity, we have not discovered an explicit difference between the two classes. Regarding the client applications from which duplicate tweets are posted, we observe the following: 21.1% of the duplicate pairs were posted from the same client applications whereas only 15.8% of the non-duplicate ones show the same characteristic.

4.3 Duplicate Detection Strategies

Having all the features constructed in Section 4.1 and preliminarily analyzed in Section 4.2, we now create different strategies for the task of duplicate detection. In practice, as requirements and limitations may vary in processing time, real-time demands, storage, network bandwidth et cetra, different strategies may be adopted. Given that our models for duplicate detection are derived from logistic regression, we define the following strategies by combining different sets of features, including one *Baseline strategy* and six *Twinder strategies*: *Sy* (only syntactical features), *SySe* (including tweet content-based features), *SyCo* (without semantics), *SySeCo* (without enriched semantics), *SySeEn* (without contextual features), and *SySeEnCo* (all features).

4.3.1 Baseline Strategy

As baseline strategy, Levenshtein distance, which compares tweet pairs in letters, is used to distinguish the duplicate pairs and further the duplicate levels.

Category	Feature	Duplicate	Std. deviation	Non-duplicate	Std. deviation
syntactical	Levenshtein Distance	0.5340	0.2151	0.6805	0.1255
	overlap in terms	0.2148	0.2403	0.0571	0.0606
	overlap in hashtags	0.0054	0.0672	0.0016	0.0337
	overlap in URLs	0.0315	0.1706	0.0002	0.0136
	overlap in expanded URLs	0.0768	0.2626	0.0017	0.0406
	length difference	0.1937	0.1656	0.2254	0.1794
semantics	overlap in entities	0.2291	0.3246	0.1093	0.1966
	overlap in entity types	0.5083	0.4122	0.3504	0.3624
	overlap in topics	0.1872	0.3354	0.0995	0.2309
	overlap in WordNet concepts	0.3808	0.2890	0.1257	0.1142
	overlap in WordNet Synset concepts	0.3876	0.2897	0.1218	0.1241
	WordNet similarity	0.6090	0.2977	0.3511	0.2111
enriched semantics	overlap in entities	0.1717	0.2864	0.0668	0.1230
	overlap in entity types	0.3181	0.3814	0.1727	0.2528
	overlap in topics	0.2768	0.3571	0.1785	0.2800
	overlap in WordNet concepts	0.2641	0.3249	0.0898	0.0987
	overlap in WordNet Synset concepts	0.2712	0.3258	0.0927	0.1046
	WordNet similarity	0.7550	0.2457	0.5963	0.2371
contextual	temporal difference	0.0256	0.0588	0.2134	0.2617
	difference in #followees	0.3975	0.1295	0.4037	0.1174
	difference in #followers	0.4350	0.1302	0.4427	0.1227
	same client	21.13%	40.83%	15.77%	36.45%

Table 1: The comparison of features between duplicate and non-duplicate tweets

4.3.2 Twinder Strategies

The Twinder strategies exploit the sets of features that have been introduced in Section 4.1). In our duplicate detection framework which is integrated in the Twinder search engine for Twitter streams (see Section 6), new strategies can easily be defined by grouping together different features.

Sy The *Sy* strategy is the most basic strategy in Twinder. It includes only *sy*ntactical features that compare tweets on a term level. These features can easily be extracted from the tweets and are expected to have a good performance on the duplicates for the levels of *Exact copy* or *Nearly exact copy*.

SySe This strategy makes use of the features that take the actual content of the tweets into account. Besides the *sy*ntactical features, this strategy makes use of NER services and WordNet to obtain the *se*mantic features.

SyCo The strategy of *SyCo* (without semantics) is formulated to prevent the retrieval of external resources as well as a large amount of semantics extractions that rely on either external Web services or extra computation time. Only *sy*ntactical features and *co*ntextual features are considered by this strategy.

SySeCo Duplicate detection can be configured as applying features without relying on external Web resources. We call the strategy that uses the *sy*tactical features, *se*mantics that are extracted from the content of tweets, and the *co*ntextual informaiton *SySeCo*.

SySeEn The contextual features, especially the ones related to users, may require extra storage and may be recomputed frequently. Therefore, the duplicate detection may work without contextual information by applying the so-called *SySeEn* (without contextual features).

SySeEnCo If enough hardware resources and network bandwidth are available then the strategy that integrates all the features can be applied so that the quality of the duplicate detection can be maximized.

5. EVALUATION OF DUPLICATE DETECTION STRATEGIES

To understand how different features and strategies influence the performance of duplicate detection, we formulated a number of research questions, which can be summarized as follows:

1. How accurately can the different *duplicate detection strategies* identify duplicates?
2. What kind of *features* are of particular *importance* for duplicate detection?
3. How does the accuracy vary for the *different levels* of duplicates?

5.1 Experimental Setup

We employ logistic regression for both steps of the task of duplicate detection: (i) to classify tweet pairs as duplicate or non-duplicate and (ii) to estimate the duplicate level. Due to the limited amount of duplicate pairs (of all 5 levels, 2,745 instances) in the manually labelled dataset (55,362 instances in total, see Section 3.2), we use 5-fold cross-validation to evaluate the learned classification models. At most, we used 22 features as predictor variables (see Table 1). Since the fraction of positive instances is considerably smaller than the negative one, we employed a cost-sensitive classification setup to prevent all the tweet pairs from being classified as non-duplicates. Moreover, because the precision and recall for non-duplicate are over 90%, we use the non-duplicate class as the reference class and focus on the performance of the class of duplicates. We use precision, recall, and F-measure to evaluate the results. Furthermore, since our final objective in this paper is to reduce duplicates in search results, we also point out the fraction of false positives as the indicator of the costs of losing information by applying our framework.

5.2 Influence of Strategies on Duplicate Detection

Table 2 shows the performance of predicting the duplicate tweet pairs by applying the strategies described in Section 4.3. The baseline strategy, which only uses Levensthein distance, leads to a precision and recall of 0.5068 and 0.1913 respectively. It means, for example, if 100 relevant tweets are returned for a certain search query and about 20 tweets (the example ratio of 20% according to the statistics given in Section 3.2) are duplicates that could be removed, the baseline strategy would identify 8 tweets as duplicates. However, only 4 of them are correctly classified while 16 other

Strategies	Precision	Recall	F-measure
Baseline	0.5068	0.1913	0.2777
Sy	0.5982	0.2918	0.3923
SyCo	0.5127	0.3370	0.4067
SySe	0.5333	0.3679	0.4354
SySeEn	0.5297	0.3767	0.4403
SySeCo	0.4816	0.4200	0.4487
SySeEnCo	0.4868	0.4299	0.4566

Table 2: Performance Results of duplicate detection for different sets of features

true duplicates are missed. In order to measure both precision and recall in once, the F-measure is used and for the *Baseline* strategy the value is 0.2777. In contrast, the *Sy* strategy, which is the most basic one for Twinder, leads to a much better performance in terms of all measures, e.g. an F-measure of 0.3923. By combing the contextual features, the *SyCo* strategy achieves a slightly better F-measure of 0.4067. It appears that the contextual features contribute relatively little to the performance.

Subsequently, we leave out the contextual features and check the importance of semantics in the content of the tweets and external resources. The *SySe* (including tweet content-based features) strategy considers not only the syntactical features but also the semantics extracted from the content of the tweets. We find that the semantic features can boost the classifier's effectiveness as the F-measure increased to 0.4354. The enriched semantics extracted from external resources brought little benefit to the result as the *SySeEn* strategy has a performance with F-measure of 0.4403. Overall, we conclude that semantics play an important role as they lead to a performance improvement with respect to F-measure from 0.3923 to 0.4403.

Thus the so-called *SySeCo* strategy excludes the features of enriched semantics but again includes the contextual features. Given this strategy, we observe an F-measure of 0.4487. However, if we adopt the strategy of *SySeEnCo* (all features), the highest F-measure can be achieved. At the same time, we nearly keep the same precision as with the *Baseline* strategy but boost the recall from 0.1913 to 0.4299. This means that more than an additional 20% of duplicates can be found while we keep the accuracy high. In this stage, we will further analyze the impact of the different features in detail as they are used in the strategy of *SySeEnCo*.

In the logistic regression approach, the importance of features can be investigated by considering the absolute value of the coefficients assigned to them. We have listed the details about the model derived for the *SySeEnCo* (all features) strategy in Table 3. The most important features are:

- *Levenshtein distance*: As it is a feature of negative coefficient in the classification model, we infer that a shorter Levenshtein distance indicates a higher probability of being duplicate pairs. Therefore, we confirm our Hypothesis H1 made in Section 4.1.1.

- *overlap in terms*: Another syntactical feature also plays an important role as the coefficient is ranked fourth most indicative in the model. This can be explained by the usage of common words in duplicate tweet pairs. This result supports Hypothesis H2.

- *overlap in WordNet concepts*: The coefficients of semantic and enriched semantic vary in the model. However, the most important feature is overlap in WordNet concepts. It has the largest positive weight which

Performance Measure		Score
precision		0.4868
recall		0.4299
F-measure		0.4566
Category	Feature	Coefficient
syntactical	Levenshtein distance	<u>-2.9387</u>
	overlap in terms	<u>2.6769</u>
	overlap in hashtags	0.4450
	overlap in URLs	1.2648
	overlap in expanded URLs	0.8832
	length difference	1.2820
semantics	overlap in entities	-2.1404
	overlap in entity types	0.9624
	overlap in topics	1.4686
	overlap in WordNet concepts	<u>4.5225</u>
	overlap in WordNet Synset concepts	0.6279
	WordNet similarity	-0.8208
enriched semantics	overlap in entities	-0.8819
	overlap in entity types	0.9578
	overlap in topics	-0.1825
	overlap in WordNet concepts	-2.0867
	overlap in WordNet Synset concepts	<u>2.5496</u>
	WordNet similarity	0.7949
contextual	temporal difference	<u>-12.6370</u>
	difference in #followees	0.4504
	difference in #followers	-0.3757
	same client	-0.1150

Table 3: The coefficients of different features. The five features with the highest absolute coefficients are underlined.

means that pairs of tweets with high overlap in WordNet concepts are more likely to be duplicates, confirming Hypothesis H10 (Section 4.1.2). However, we noticed a contradiction in the feature set of enriched semantics, in which the coefficient for overlap in WordNet concepts is negative (-2.0867) whereas the one the coefficient for the overlap in WordNet synset concept is positive (2.5496). It can be explained by the high correlation between these two features, especially for high coverage of possible words in external resources. For this reason, they counteract each other in the model.

- *temporal difference*: In line with the preliminary analysis, the shorter the temporal difference between a pair of tweets, the more likely that it is a duplicate pair. The highest value of the coefficient is partially due to low average absolute values of this feature. However, we can still conclude that Hypothesis H13 holds (see Section 4.1.4).

Overall, we noticed that the hypotheses that we made for syntactical features can all be confirmed. Although the same conclusion could not be made for all the features constructed based on semantics, some of them can be explained. For example, the overlap of WordNet concepts in the set of enriched semantics is negative. The reason for this may be twofold: (i) more general terms (such as politics, sport, news, mobile) are overlapping if we consider external resources; (ii) the features in the set of enriched semantics may mislead when we extract the features for a pair of tweets from which no external resources can be found or only one tweet contains a URL. The situation for other features, e.g. WordNet similarity, can be explained by the dependencies between some of them. More specifically, the features that are based on WordNet similarity in the sets of semantics and enriched semantics may have positive correlation. Therefore, the coefficients complement each other in values. When we consider only the contextual features, all other three features except the temporal difference do not belong to the most important features. More sophisticated techniques for measuring user similarity might be used to better exploit, for example, the provenance of tweets for the duplicate detection task.

5.3 Influence of Topic Characteristics on Duplicate Detection

In all reported experiments so far, we have considered the entire Twitter sample available to us. In this section, we investigate to what extent certain topic (or query) characteristics play a role for duplicate detection and to what extent those differences lead to a change in the logistic regression models.

Consider the following two topics: *Taco Bell filling lawsuit* (MB020[8]) and *Egyptian protesters attack museum* (MB010). While the former has a business theme and is likely to be mostly of interest to American users, the latter topic belongs into the category of politics and can be considered as being of global interest, as the entire world was watching the events in Egypt unfold. Due to these differences, we defined a number of topic splits. A manual annotator then decided for each split dimension into which category the topic should fall. We investigated four topic splits, three splits with two partitions each and one split with five partitions:

- Popular/unpopular: The topics were split into popular (interesting to many users) and unpopular (interesting to few users) topics. An example of a popular topic is *2022 FIFA soccer* (MB002) – in total we found 24. In contrast, topic *NIST computer security* (MB005) is classified as unpopular (as one of 25 topics).
- Global/local: In this split, we considered the interest for the topic across the globe. The already mentioned topic MB002 is of global interest, since soccer is a highly popular sport in many countries, whereas topic *Cuomo budget cuts* (MB019) is mostly of local interest to users living or working in New York where Andrew Cuomo is the governor. We found 18 topics of global and 31 topics of local interest.
- Persistent/occasional: This split is concerned with the interestingness of the topic over time. Some topics persist for a long time, such as MB002 (the FIFA world cup will be played in 2022), whereas other topics are only of short-term interest, e.g. *Keith Olbermann new job* (MB030). We assigned 28 topics to the persistent and 21 topics to the occasional topic partition.
- Topic themes: The topics were classified as belonging to one of five themes, either business, entertainment, sports, politics or technology. MB002 is, e.g., a sports topic while MB019 is considered to be a political topic.

Our discussion of the results focuses on two aspects: (i) the difference between the models derived for each of the two partitions, and (ii) the difference between these models (denoted $M_{splitName}$) and the model derived over all topics ($M_{allTopics}$) in Table 5. The results for the three binary topic splits are shown in Table 4.

Popularity: A comparison of the most important features of $M_{popular}$ and $M_{unpopular}$ shows few differences with the exception of a single feature: temporal difference. While temporal difference is the most important feature in $M_{popular}$,

[8]The identifiers of the topics correspond to the ones used in the official TREC dataset.

it is ranked fourth in $M_{unpopular}$. We hypothesize that the discussion on popular topics evolve quickly on Twitter, thus the duplicate tweet pairs should have less differences in posting time.

Global vs. local: The most important feature in M_{global}, the overlap in terms, and the second most important feature in M_{local}, Levenshtein distance, do not have a similar significance in each others' models. We consider it as an interesting finding and the possible explanation can lie in the sources of the information. In more detail, on the one hand the duplicate tweets about the local topics may share the same source thus are low in Levenshtein distances; on the other hand, different sources may report on the global topics in their own styles but with the same terms.

Temporal persistence: Comparing the $M_{persistent}$ and the $M_{occasional}$ models, yields to similar conclusions as in the previous two splits: (i) the persistent topics are continuously discussed so that the duplicate pairs are more likely to have short temporal differences, while the temporal differences between tweets on occasional topics are relatively insignificant; (ii) the occasionally discussed topics are often using the same set of words.

Topic Themes: The partial results of the topic split according to the theme of the topic are shown in Table 5 (full results can be found on the supporting website for this paper [22]). Three topics did not fit in one of the five categories. Since the topic set is split into five partitions, the size of some partitions is extremely small, making it difficult to reach conclusive results. Nevertheless, we can detect trends such as the fact that duplicate tweet pairs in sports topics are more likely to contain the same source links (positive coefficient of overlap in original URLs and the opposite of overlap in expanded URLs), while duplicate pairs in entertainment topics contain more shortened links (positive coefficient of overlap in expanded URLs). The overlap in terms has a large impact on all themes but politics. Another interesting observation is that a short temporal difference, is a prominent indicator for the duplicates in the topics of entertainment and politics but not in the other models.

The observation that certain topic splits lead to models that emphasize certain features also offers a natural way forward: if we are able to determine for each topic in advance to which theme or topic characteristic it belongs to, we can select the model that fits the topic best.

5.4 Analysis of Duplicate levels

Having estimated whether a tweet pair is duplicate or not, we now proceed to the second step of the duplicate detection task: determining the exact level of the duplicate tweet pairs. We compare the different strategies (see Section 4.3) in the same way as we have done in Section 5.2. To analyze the performance in general, we used weighted measures, including precision, recall, and F-measure across 5 levels. The results are summarized in Table 6; a similar pattern in performance improvement can be observed. However, it appears that the enriched semantics are more prominent than the contextual features as the so-called *SySeEn* strategy (without contextual features) performs better than *SySeCo* strategy (without enriched semantics).

In Figure 2, we plot the performance of the classification for 5 different levels and the weighted average of them with all the strategies that we have introduced in Section 4.3. The weight of each level depends on the ratio of duplicate instances. The curves for 5 different levels show the simi-

Performance	Measure	popular	unpopular	global	local	persistent	occasional
	#topics	24	25	18	31	28	21
	#samples	32,635	22,727	19,862	35,500	33,474	21,888
	precision	0.4480	0.6756	0.6148	0.4617	0.4826	0.6129
	recall	0.4569	0.6436	0.5294	0.5059	0.5590	0.5041
	F-measure	0.4524	0.6592	0.5689	0.4828	0.5180	0.5532
Category	Feature	popular	unpopular	global	local	persistent	occasional
syntactical	Levenshtein distance	<u>-3.4919</u>	-0.6126	0.1342	<u>-3.5136</u>	<u>-3.5916</u>	-1.2338
	overlap in terms	2.8352	<u>6.0905</u>	<u>6.7126</u>	1.0498	1.3474	<u>5.7705</u>
	overlap in hashtags	0.6234	-2.5868	-1.8751	1.2671	2.2210	-2.7187
	overlap in URLs	-0.1865	<u>5.8130</u>	0.3275	1.6342	3.4323	0.4907
	overlap in expanded URLs	0.5180	2.7594	1.4933	0.6362	1.4936	1.0751
	length difference	1.2459	0.5974	0.5028	1.3236	1.5043	0.3793
semantics	overlap in entities	-2.3460	0.5430	-0.2263	<u>-3.3525</u>	-3.1071	0.5538
	overlap in entity types	1.2612	-1.1651	-0.3301	1.1571	0.8802	-0.8804
	overlap in topics	1.6607	0.7505	1.2147	1.2294	1.3911	0.7848
	overlap in WordNet concepts	<u>5.5288</u>	<u>7.1115</u>	<u>5.8185</u>	2.5319	<u>4.0427</u>	<u>4.6365</u>
	overlap in WordNet Synset concepts	-0.7763	-2.4393	-0.7335	3.0327	1.8752	0.5750
	WordNet similarity	-0.6254	1.8168	1.1355	-0.3909	-0.5141	1.0457
enriched semantics	overlap in entities	-1.3013	0.0583	0.0501	-0.5548	-1.9666	0.8555
	overlap in entity types	0.8997	1.2098	0.1179	0.8132	1.0279	0.3228
	overlap in topics	-0.5470	0.6581	0.0118	-0.1282	0.0292	-0.1884
	overlap in WordNet concepts	-1.8633	-1.2312	-2.3160	-2.4825	-2.5058	-2.1868
	overlap in WordNet Synset concepts	2.4274	1.0336	3.4218	2.6263	3.0461	2.5514
	WordNet similarity	0.7328	0.4342	-1.0359	0.9406	1.0470	-1.1867
contextual	temporal difference	<u>-15.8249</u>	-2.9890	<u>-5.2712</u>	<u>-17.3894</u>	<u>-18.9433</u>	<u>-5.6780</u>
	difference in #followees	0.7026	0.2322	-1.0797	0.5489	0.0659	-1.0473
	difference in #followers	-0.9826	1.1960	-0.3224	0.0048	-0.1281	-0.5178
	same client	-0.1800	0.3851	-0.0272	-0.0692	-0.2641	0.3058

Table 4: Influence comparison of different features among different topic partitions. There are three splits shown here: popular vs. unpopular topics, global vs. local topics and persistent vs. occasional topics. While the performance measures are based on 5-fold cross-validation, the derived feature weights for the logistic regression model were determined across all topics of a split. The total number of topics is 49. For each topic split, the three features with the highest absolute coefficient are underlined.

Performance	Measure	business	entertainment	sports	politics	technology
	#topics	6	12	5	21	2
	#samples	11,445	7,678	1,722	30,037	1,622
	precision	0.6865	0.6844	0.5000	0.4399	0.6383
	recall	0.6615	0.7153	0.6071	0.4713	0.7143
	F-measure	0.6737	0.6995	0.5484	0.4551	0.6742

Table 5: This table shows the comparison of performance when partitioning the topic set according to five broad topic themes. The full results can be found on the supporting website for this paper [22].

Strategies	Precision	Recall	F-measure
Baseline	0.5553	0.5208	0.5375
Sy	0.6599	0.5809	0.6179
SyCo	0.6747	0.5889	0.6289
SySe	0.6708	0.6151	0.6417
SySeEn	0.6694	0.6241	0.6460
SySeCo	0.6852	0.6198	0.6508
SySeEnCo	0.6739	0.6308	0.6516

Table 6: Performance Results of predicting duplicate levels for different sets of features

lar trend with the weighted average of them that indicates the overall performance. We observe that the level of *Weak near duplicate* performs better than average and the reason can be attributed to the large ratio of learning instances (see Figure 1). The classification regarding the level of *Exact copy* is the best because of the decisive influence of the Levensthein distance. However, we see a declining trend in performance as we integrate more other tweets. Hence, further optimization is possible.

5.5 Optimization of Duplicate Detection

To optimize the duplicate detection procedure, we exploit the fact that duplicate pairs of level *Exact copy* can easily

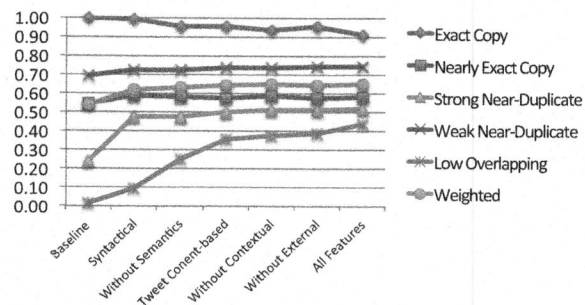

Figure 2: The F-measure of classification for different levels and weighted average by applying different strategies

be detected by their Levenshtein distance of 0. After the removal of mentions, URLs, and hashtags, we can also apply the same rule for *Nearly exact copy*. Therefore, we can optimize the duplicate detection procedure with the following cascade:

1. If the Levensthein distance is zero between a pair of tweets or after removal of mentions, URLs, and hashtags from both of them, they can be classified as *Exact copy* or *Nearly exact copy*;

Strategies	Precision	Recall	F-measure
Baseline	0.9011	0.2856	0.4337
Sy	0.7065	0.4095	0.5185
SyCo	0.6220	0.4550	0.5256
SySe	0.6153	0.4849	0.5424
SySeEn	0.5612	0.5395	0.5501
SySeCo	0.6079	0.4914	0.5435
SySeEnCo	0.5656	0.5512	0.5583

Table 7: Performance Results of duplicate detection using different strategies after optimization

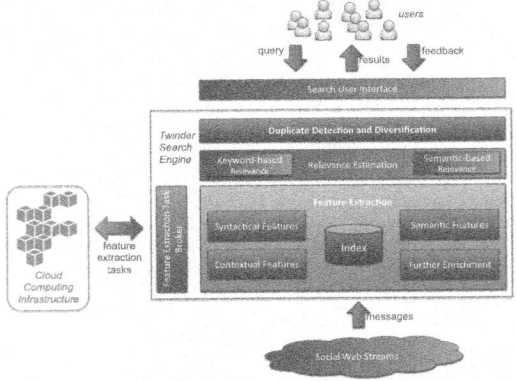

Figure 3: Architecture of the Twinder Search Engine: duplicate detection and diversification based on feature extraction modules.

2. Otherwise, we apply aforementioned strategies to detect duplicity.

After this optimization, we get a performance improvement from 0.45 to 0.55 with respect to the F-measure. The corresponding results are listed in Table 7 (the original results are given in Table 2).

6. SEARCH RESULT DIVERSIFICATION

A core application of near-duplicate detection strategies is the diversification of search results. Therefore, we integrated our duplicate detection framework into the so-called Twinder [21] (*Twitter Finder*) search engine which provides search and ranking functionality for Twitter streams. Figure 3 depicts the architecture of Twinder and highlights the core modules which we designed, developed and analyzed in the context of this paper.

The duplicate detection and diversification is performed after the relevance estimation of the tweets. Hence, given a search query, the engine first ranks the tweets according to their relevance and then iterates over the top k tweets of the search result to remove near-duplicate tweets and diversify the search results. Both, the duplicate detection and the relevance estimation module, benefit from the features that are extracted as part of the indexing step which is performed iteratively as soon as new tweets are monitored.

The lightweight diversification strategy applies the near-duplicate detection functionality as listed in Algorithm 2. It iterates from the top to the bottom of the top k search results. For each tweet i, it removes all tweets at rank j with $i < j$ (i.e. tweet i has a better rank than tweet j) that are near-duplicates of tweet i.

In Section 3.2, we analyzed the ratios of duplicates in the search results. After applying the lightweight diversification strategy proposed above, we again examine the ratios. The results are listed in Table 8 and reveal that the fraction

Algorithm 2: Diversification Strategy

input : Ranking of tweets T, k
output: Diversified top k ranking $T'@k$

$T'@k \leftarrow \emptyset$;
$i \leftarrow 0$;
while $i < k$ and $i < T.length$ do
　$j \leftarrow i+1$;
　while $j < T.length$ do
　　if $T[i]$ and $T[j]$ are duplicates then
　　　remove $T[j]$ from T;
　　else
　　　j++;
　$T'[i] = T[i]$
return $T'@k$;

Range	Top 10	Top 20	Top 50	All
Before diversification	19.4%	22.2%	22.5%	22.3%
After diversification	9.1%	10.5%	12.0%	12.1%
Improvement	53.1%	52.0%	46.7%	45.7%

Table 8: Average ratios of near-duplicates in search results after diversification

of near-duplicate tweets within the top k search results is considerably smaller. For example, without diversification there exists, on average, for 22.2% of the tweets at least one near-duplicate tweet within the top 20 search results. In contrast, the diversification strategy improves the search result quality with respect to duplicate content by more than 50%. Thus there are, on average, less than 11% duplicates in the top 20 search results.

7. CONCLUSIONS

People are confronted with a high fraction of near-duplicate content when searching and exploring information on microblogging platforms such as Twitter. In this paper, we analyzed the problem of near-duplicate content on Twitter and developed a duplicate detection and search result diversification framework for Twitter. Our framework is able to identify near-duplicate tweets with a precision and recall of 48% and 43% respectively by combining (i) syntactical features, (ii) semantic features and (iii) contextual features and by considering information from external Web resources that are linked from the microposts. For certain types of topics such as occasional news events, we even observe performances of more than 61% and 50% with respect to precision and recall. Our experiments show that semantic features such as the overlap of WordNet concepts are of particular importance for detecting near-duplicates. By analyzing a large Twitter sample, we also identified five main levels of duplicity ranging from *exact copies* which can easily be identified by means of syntactic features such as string similarity to *low overlapping duplicates* for which an analysis of the semantics and context is specifically important. Our framework is able to classify the duplicity score on that level with an accuracy of more than 60%. Given our near-duplicate detection strategies, we additionally developed functionality for the diversification of search results. We integrated this functionality into the Twinder search engine and could show that our duplicate detection and diversification framework improves the quality of top k retrieval significantly since we decrease the fraction of duplicate content that is delivered to the users by more than 45%.

Acknowledgements. This work is co-funded by the EU FP7 project ImREAL (http://imreal-project.eu).

8. REFERENCES

[1] F. Abel, Q. Gao, G.-J. Houben, and K. Tao. Analyzing User Modeling on Twitter for Personalized News Recommendations. In *Proceedings of the 19th International Conference on User Modeling, Adaption and Personalization (UMAP)*, pages 1–12. Springer, July 2011.

[2] F. Abel, C. Hauff, G.-J. Houben, R. Stronkman, and K. Tao. Twitcident: Fighting Fire with Information from Social Web Stream. In *Proceedings of the 21st International Conference Companion on World Wide Web (WWW)*, pages 305–308. ACM, April 2012.

[3] R. Agrawal, S. Gollapudi, A. Halverson, and S. Ieong. Diversifying Search Results. In *Proceedings of the 2nd ACM International Conference on Web Search and Data Mining (WSDM)*, pages 5–14. ACM, February 2009.

[4] D. Antoniades, I. Polakis, G. Kontaxis, E. Athanasopoulos, S. Ioannidis, E. P. Markatos, and T. Karagiannis. we.b: The web of Short URLs. In *Proceedings of the 20th International Conference on World Wide Web (WWW)*, pages 715–724. ACM, April 2011.

[5] M. S. Bernstein, B. Suh, L. Hong, J. Chen, S. Kairam, and E. H. Chi. Eddi: Interactive Topic-based Browsing of Social Status Streams. In *Proceedings of the 23rd Annual ACM Symposium on User Interface Software and Technology (UIST)*, pages 303–312. ACM, October 2010.

[6] A. Z. Broder, S. C. Glassman, M. S. Manasse, and G. Zweig. Syntactic Clustering of the Web. In *Selected Papers from the 6th International Conference on World Wide Web (WWW)*, pages 1157–1166. Elsevier Science Publishers Ltd., September 1997.

[7] M. S. Charikar. Similarity Estimation Techniques from Rounding Algorithms. In *Proceedings of the 34th Annual ACM Symposium on Theory of Computing (STOC)*, pages 380–388. ACM, May 2002.

[8] M. Henzinger. Finding Near-Duplicate Web Pages: A Large-Scale Evaluation of Algorithms. In *Proceedings of the 29th Annual International ACM SIGIR Conference on Research and Development in Information Retrieval (SIGIR)*, pages 284–291. ACM, August 2006.

[9] H. Kwak, C. Lee, H. Park, and S. Moon. What is Twitter, a Social Network or a News Media? In *Proceedings of the 19th International Conference on World Wide Web (WWW)*, pages 591–600. ACM, April 2010.

[10] C. Lee, H. Kwak, H. Park, and S. Moon. Finding Influentials Based on the Temporal Order of Information Adoption in Twitter. In *Proceedings of the 19th International Conference on World Wide Web (WWW)*, pages 1137–1138. ACM, April 2010.

[11] D. Lin. An Information-Theoretic Definition of Similarity. In *Proceedings of the 15th International Conference on Machine Learning (ICML)*, pages 296–304. Morgan Kaufmann, July 1998.

[12] G. S. Manku, A. Jain, and A. Das Sarma. Detecting Near-Duplicates for Web Crawling. In *Proceedings of the 16th International Conference on World Wide Web (WWW)*, pages 141–150. ACM, May 2007.

[13] R. McCreadie, I. Soboroff, J. Lin, C. Macdonald, I. Ounis, and D. McCullough. On Building a Reusable Twitter Corpus. In *Proceedings of the 35th International ACM SIGIR Conference on Research and Development in Information Retrieval (SIGIR)*, pages 1113–1114. ACM, August 2012.

[14] B. Meeder, B. Karrer, A. Sayedi, R. Ravi, C. Borgs, and J. Chayes. We Know Who You Followed Last Summer: Inferring Social Link Creation Times In Twitter. In *Proceedings of the 20th International Conference on World Wide Web (WWW)*, pages 517–526. ACM, April 2011.

[15] P. N. Mendes, M. Jakob, A. García-Silva, and C. Bizer. DBpedia Spotlight: Shedding Light on the Web of Documents. In *Proceedings of the 7th International Conference on Semantic Systems (I-SEMANTICS)*, pages 1–8. ACM, September 2011.

[16] D. Metzler and C. Cai. USC/ISI at TREC 2011: Microblog Track. In *Working Notes, The Twentieth Text REtrieval Conference (TREC 2011) Proceedings*. NIST, November 2011.

[17] G. Miller et al. WordNet: A Lexical Database for English. *Communications of the ACM*, 38(11):39–41, November 1995.

[18] M. Pennacchiotti and A.-M. Popescu. A Machine Learning Approach to Twitter User Classification. In *Proceedings of the 5th International AAAI Conference on Weblogs and Social Media (ICWSM)*, pages 281–288. AAAI Press, July 2011.

[19] D. Rafiei, K. Bharat, and A. Shukla. Diversifying Web Search Results. In *Proceedings of the 19th International Conference on World Wide Web (WWW)*, pages 781–790. ACM, April 2010.

[20] T. Sakaki, M. Okazaki, and Y. Matsuo. Earthquake Shakes Twitter Users: Real-time Event Detection by Social Sensors. In *Proceedings of the 19th International Conference on World Wide Web (WWW)*, pages 851–860. ACM, April 2010.

[21] K. Tao, F. Abel, C. Hauff, and G.-J. Houben. Twinder: A Search Engine for Twitter Streams. In *Proceedings of the 12th International Conference on Web Engineering (ICWE)*, pages 153–168. Springer, July 2012.

[22] K. Tao, F. Abel, C. Hauff, G.-J. Houben, and U. Gadiraju. Supporting Website: datasets and additional findings., November 2012. http://wis.ewi.tudelft.nl/duptweet/.

[23] J. Teevan, D. Ramage, and M. R. Morris. #TwitterSearch: A Comparison of Microblog Search and Web Search. In *Proceedings of the 4th International Conference on Web Search and Web Data Mining (WSDM)*, pages 35–44. ACM, February 2011.

[24] J. Weng and B.-S. Lee. Event Detection in Twitter. In *Proceedings of the 5th International AAAI Conference on Weblogs and Social Media (ICWSM)*. AAAI Press, July 2011.

Uncovering Locally Characterizing Regions within Geotagged Data

Bart Thomee
Yahoo! Research
Avinguda Diagonal 177
08018 Barcelona, Spain
bthomee@yahoo-inc.com

Adam Rae
brandcrumb
Carrer de València 352
08009 Barcelona, Spain
adam.rae@brandcrumb.com

ABSTRACT

We propose a novel algorithm for uncovering the colloquial boundaries of locally characterizing regions present in collections of labeled geospatial data. We address the problem by first modeling the data using scale-space theory, allowing us to represent it simultaneously across different scales as a family of increasingly smoothed density distributions. We then derive region boundaries by applying localized label weighting and image processing techniques to the scale-space representation of each label. Important insights into the data can be acquired by visualizing the shape and size of the resulting boundaries for each label at multiple scales. We demonstrate our technique operating at scale by discovering the boundaries of the most geospatially salient tags associated with a large collection of georeferenced photos from Flickr and compare our characterizing regions that emerge from the data with those produced by a recent technique from the research literature.

Categories and Subject Descriptors

H.2.8 [**Database Management**]: Database Applications—*Spatial databases and GIS*; H.3.1 [**Information Storage and Retrieval**]: Content Analysis and Indexing; H.3.3 [**Information Storage and Retrieval**]: Information Search and Retrieval—*Information filtering*

General Terms

Algorithms, Theory, Measurement

Keywords

Geotagged data, spatial analysis, region discovery, scale-space theory, Flickr

1. INTRODUCTION

When considering characteristic geographic areas around the world, there are those that are canonically described in gazetteers (such as cities and states) and there are those that are not, such as the Sahara desert in Africa, the Bordeaux wine region in France and the red light district in Amsterdam. Nonetheless, geographic regions such as the latter are colloquially well-known and there are many others for which official boundaries do not exist or differ from their colloquial boundaries as determined by the consensus of the general populace.

Copyright is held by the International World Wide Web Conference Committee (IW3C2). IW3C2 reserves the right to provide a hyperlink to the author's site if the Material is used in electronic media.
WWW'13, May 13–17, 2013, Rio de Janeiro, Brazil.
ACM 978-1-4503-2035-1/13/05.

In this paper we describe a novel algorithm that automatically uncovers the colloquial boundaries of locally characterizing regions present in collections of labeled geo-referenced data. Our technique uses scale-space theory [47, 27] to detect those geographic areas for which the occurrence of a label is particularly prominent with respect to the other labels occurring in the same area, at a particular scale. Naturally, the set of scales at which characteristic regions can be found for a certain label depends on the nature of the underlying data and the spatial distributions of the labels. The scale-space paradigm is therefore especially suitable, because it represents the data simultaneously across different scales as a family of increasingly smoothed density distributions, allowing us to automatically derive spatially coherent regions by applying image analysis techniques to the scale-space representations of the data for each label and at each scale in a consistent manner, where the regions are generated by applying the exact same sequence of steps at each scale.

In the past, geo-referenced collections have been predominantly analyzed for the extraction of spatial knowledge for a limited number of pre-defined labels or queries, as well as for specific geographic areas. For instance, in the context of online tagged photos – the scenario we primarily focus on in this paper – regions are often specifically restricted to points of interest such as landmarks [7, 34] or they are defined as dense areas of photos from which the most salient tags are discovered [1, 9]. The analyses are further typically performed at a single fixed scale, ignoring the effects of scale on shape and size of the regions, even though intuitively the scale at which any region discovery is performed has a large influence on the final outcome, i.e. coherent regions at a particular scale may not necessarily be coherent at other scales.

To summarize, the main contributions of our work are the following:

- An effective framework for automatically and efficiently discovering the colloquial boundaries of locally characterizing regions present within large collections of labeled geotagged data at multiple scales using scale-space theory and image processing techniques.

- Insights into the effects of scale on the shape, size and quantity of the derived regions and a comparison of the generated regions with those produced by a recent technique from the research literature using a multi-million sample of geo-referenced photos.

Our technique can be applied to any collection of labeled geographic data and is thus not restricted to any particular domain. The regions our technique uncovers can be of benefit to many tasks, for instance monitoring the spread of diseases or discovering trending news topics across the world over time at global and local scales. In the context of multimedia our technique is useful for topics such as tag recommendation and disambiguation [46], content tagging and placing [15, 26], and region summarization [39, 48].

The remainder of this paper is organized as follows. We first discuss related work in Section 2 before presenting our algorithm for boundary discovery using scale-space theory in Section 3. In Section 4 we propose optimizations to handle large-scale data and illustrate our technique by discovering and visualizing the detected tag regions within Flickr photos. We follow with an analysis of the properties of our algorithm in Section 5. We conclude the paper with final remarks and future outlooks in Section 6.

2. RELATED WORK

Discovering geographic regions within georeferenced data has been an active research topic for many years. A variety of methods can be applied to uncover the hidden spatial structures, most notably techniques such as clustering [10], density estimation [17, 21] and neural networks [16]. For example, Hargrove et al. [13] used multivariate clustering to uncover distinct ecoregions based on environmental conditions. In recent years, georeferenced multimedia collections have considerably grown in size, in particular due to the availability of digital cameras with built-in GPS receivers that can automatically attach the geographic location to every photo that is taken. We can therefore find a considerable number of methods in the research literature that try to represent or summarize geographical regions in terms of either the tags associated with the photos in that region [1, 9] or by the photos themselves [39, 7, 23, 19, 48, 8]. For example, language modeling approaches [40, 44, 14] characterize cells that partition the world into discrete units for automatic photo and video geo-localization.

However, the notion of scale is typically not naturally integrated into these techniques, requiring tuning of parameters for each different level of detail at which the data is analyzed. The analyses in the literature are furthermore commonly restricted to a limited set of geographic areas, while the visualizations are restricted to modifying objects of known shape and size by increasing details at small scales and reducing details at large scales. Yet, especially in a geographic context, scale is inherently part of the labeled data and thus should form an integral part of the data modeling, analysis and visualization process. Scale-space theory [47, 27] provides a framework for analyzing the structure of multi-dimensional signals at multiple scales, which has been successfully used within many different fields of research. In the field of computer vision performing analysis at multiple scales benefits many tasks, such as feature detection [32, 5] and object detection [30], while in a geographic context the scale-space framework has been used for analyzing [28, 45] and for visualizing [4, 2] data collections.

In our work, we apply the concept of scale-space theory to labeled data in order to automatically infer regions that are locally characterizing across any area at any scale. While the notion of scale was used in [36, 24] for the detection of photo tags that exhibit significant invariant spatial patterns, we in contrast present a more general approach that focuses on defining the boundaries of the characteristic regions for any label, whether or not it demonstrates spatial invariance. We furthermore do not assume beforehand that labels are related, unlike the authors of [9], who assume that when they are used in close proximity to each other they are therefore semantically related. The most closely related techniques to ours assign localized weights to labels to derive the boundaries of their associated geospatial regions. Nonetheless, these have as drawbacks that the discovered regions can only be elliptical of shape [3], that they have only been applied at very limited scales and geographic areas [22], or that they generate an overwhelming amount of regions [18].

3. ALGORITHM

In our approach we do not focus on the items in a data collection, but instead only focus on the individual instances of their metadata labels (e.g. tags in the case of online photos). We aim to directly discover coherent regions of each label by analyzing their spatial distributions, one at a time. Our technique is thus unlike many of the existing techniques, such as those discussed in the related work section, which first try to discover coherent regions by analyzing how the data is geographically distributed and only afterwards attempt to find the label(s) that most accurately describe each of these regions. Our region discovery approach consists of four main steps, namely:

1. **Data labeling** – Each instance in the collection of geographic data is assigned one or more labels for which ultimately the region boundaries are to be discovered.

2. **Scale-space representation** – The labeled data is represented in a scale-space as a family of increasingly smoothed two-dimensional density distributions.

3. **Region generation** – Two-dimensional regions are generated at multiple scales for each label separately.

4. **Region selection** – The generated regions are validated in order to discard those that are not appropriate at particular scales or do not meet criteria suited to the envisioned use case.

In the following sections we detail each of the aforementioned steps in the algorithm.

3.1 Data labeling

The labels for which we aim to derive their characteristic regions can be simple, e.g. words present in a georeferenced document, or more complex, e.g. visual concepts detected in a georeferenced image. If the data collection is unlabeled, each instance in the collection first needs to be associated with one or more labels before our algorithm can be applied, where the set of labels may be manually specified by a user beforehand or automatically derived from the data. The labeling of an instance is typically done by extracting suitable features and then performing feature analysis and classification to obtain its labels. Whenever an instance or label does not meet pre-defined quality criteria it can be removed from the dataset. To illustrate, a textual document could be considered as an instance and the words it contains as labels, where those labels that are stop words may be discarded.

Given a set of labels Λ, we can define the data collection as $\mathbb{D}_\Lambda = \biguplus \mathbb{D}_\lambda | \lambda \in \Lambda$, where the $\biguplus$ operator performs a union of the data items associated with each label $\mathbb{D}_\lambda$. A data item that has multiple labels will therefore be included as many times in $\mathbb{D}_\Lambda$ as it has labels. We further define $\mathbb{D}_\lambda \triangleq \{d\}$, where d has label λ and is represented by a tuple (l_x, l_y), which contains a geographic location that is expressed by longitude l_x and latitude l_y.

3.2 Scale-space representation

Scale-space theory is predominantly used in image analysis, where an image is represented as a family of images obtained by convolving it using a smoothing kernel parameterized with a scaling factor. Scale-spaces are particularly useful for isolating regions of pixels that exhibit segmentation at certain scales by comparing subsequent increments of smoothing, a notion that techniques such as SIFT [32] and SURF [5] have successfully used for the purpose of extracting scale-invariant features from images. We exploit this property of the scale-space representation in order to uncover regions of sizes appropriate at a given scale. In this work we define a *region* as a closed area on our planet that is bounded by a non-self-intersection polygon, which we refer to as its *contour*.

In order to apply scale-space theory to our data we consider a discretized histogram of label counts to be analogous to a grayscale image. We first represent the data for each label $\mathbb{D}_\lambda$ as a two-dimensional density histogram $f_\lambda(x, y)$, such that

$$|\mathbb{D}_\lambda| = \sum_{x=1}^{w} \sum_{y=1}^{h} f_\lambda(x, y) \quad (1)$$

where w and h are the number of bins along the width and height of the histogram. Even though geographic locations can be represented as a bounded function of continuous longitude and latitude values, they are typically expressed in the discrete domain. In particular, one of the most precise ways of obtaining a geographic location is through the use of digital global positioning systems, which are discrete by nature and yield locations with an accuracy usually in the order of meters, depending on equipment and environmental conditions. We thus represent our data as a two-dimensional histogram along longitude and latitude using finite addressability, where the exact resolution of the histogram depends on the precision of the underlying data as well as on the envisioned use case. For example, for geographic coordinates expressed with up to two decimal places of precision in longitude and latitude, over the whole world the histogram would be of dimensions $w = 36,000$ and $h = 18,000$, ensuring that no cell would be larger than the equivalent of $0.01°$ longitude at the equator, which approximately measures 1km.

Using this data definition, we then define the linear scale-space representation of a family of increasingly smoothed histograms $L_\lambda(x, y; t)$ for a given label λ as a convolution of $f_\lambda(x, y)$ with Gaussian kernels $G(x, y; t)$, as expressed by

$$L_\lambda(x, y; t) = G(x, y; t) * f_\lambda(x, y) \quad (2)$$

where t denotes the variance of the kernel and thus $\sigma = \sqrt{t}$ its standard deviation. At $t = 0$ we obtain the original density distribution of the spatial data for a certain label, whereas for increasing values of t the data is convolved with a kernel of increasing width, so that the density distribution is increasingly smoothed and as a result more and more high frequency details are removed. We exploit this property in the next step to discover the boundaries of the various regions where a label is used across the world at individual scales.

3.3 Region generation

For a given label λ, its scale-space representation L_λ, and a certain scale factor t, we aim to extract a set of locally characterizing regions. These characteristic regions are geographic areas where the occurrence of a particular label is particularly prominent with respect to the other labels occurring in the same area, at the specified scale.

Label prominence

To account for the prominence of a label for a particular point in space at a particular scale, we weight $L_\lambda(x, y; t)$ in proportion to how much it contributes to the overall data density $L_\Lambda(x, y; t)$, such that

$$L'_\lambda(x, y; t) = \frac{(L_\lambda(x, y; t))^2}{L_\Lambda(x, y; t)} \quad (3)$$

Spatial activity isolation

From the resulting histogram we then produce a binary representation that isolates the high frequency spatial activity found in $L_\lambda(x, y; t)$ by removing the lower frequency activity represented in a histogram smoothed at a higher value of t, according to

$$b(x, y; t) = \begin{cases} 1 & \text{if } (L'_\lambda(x, y; t) - L'_\lambda(x, y; t + a) > \epsilon \\ 0 & \text{otherwise} \end{cases} \quad (4)$$

where a is a constant and ϵ is a small threshold applied to the magnitude of the response to suppress noise. When a approaches zero the Difference of Gaussians operation above closely approximates the Laplacian of Gaussian, effectively detecting edges between two areas of uniform but different intensities in the weighted histogram.

By considering t as a continuous variable, each label generates closed contours across one or more ranges of scales [31], provided it is not considered as noise and filtered out. Across scales contours can be formed, cease to exist, merge with other contours or split into multiple contours. By fixing the scale factor t contours are obtained that are appropriate for that scale. We illustrate this in Figure 1.

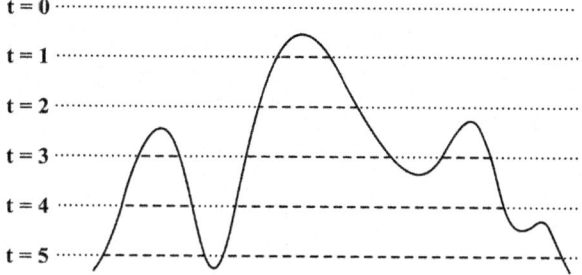

Figure 1: The contours for a certain label across a continuous set of scales undulate, forming peaks and valleys. For visualization purposes we show a two-dimensional view of the three-dimensional plot $b(x, y; t)$ by fixing y. Here, the scale dimension t runs from top to bottom, the spatial dimension x runs from left to right and the spatial dimension y would run from front to back.

At this point we have obtained disjoint contours representing the area where a label is particularly prominent, although depending on the underlying data distribution these may be incoherent. In order to turn this into a set of dis-

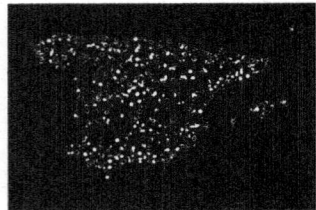 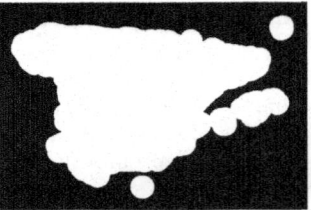  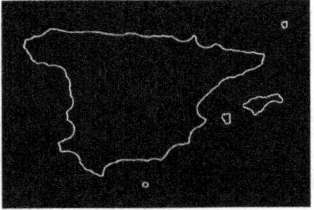

Figure 2: Region generation given a binary representation of the label spain. We first fill all outer contours (left) and then smooth and connect disjoint areas by applying a morphological closing operation that first dilates (middle-left) and then erodes (middle-right) the binary representation, after which the contours are traced (right) to extract the characteristic regions. Here, the label was also prominently used on the Balearic islands (an archipelago of Spain), Melilla (an exclave of Spain) and in a small area in France, causing regions to emerge there as well.

tinct, contiguous regions, we apply three image processing techniques to the binary representation of a label.

Contour filling

We observe that the Difference of Gaussians operation may yield more than one concentric contour for a label for each crossing of the threshold ϵ. To emphasize the full spatial extent of a label rather than its internal density, we apply contour tracing [6] to the binary representation to extract the outermost contours that mark the areas where the label's influence drops below the threshold for the last time. We fill the entire area enclosed by the outer contours, implicitly discarding any inner contours.

Morphological closing

To smooth the contours and to connect disjoint regions that are separated from each other by a small gap, we apply morphological closing to the binary representation after it has been filled. Morphological closing first performs a dilation step followed by an erosion step, where in both steps the same disk-shaped structuring element S is applied to the binary representation, such that

$$b(x,y;t) \bullet S = (b(x,y;t) \oplus S) \ominus S \qquad (5)$$

where the radius ρ of the structuring element can be adjusted to enforce more or less smoothing of a region's contour. The value to use for ρ depends on the envisioned use case, where the parameter can be manually explored or automatically optimized using a particular objective function, e.g. see Section 5.1.

Contour tracing

We again apply contour tracing to the binary representation of each label to extract the outer contours of the locally characterizing regions that have emerged.

We illustrate the image processing operations in Figure 2. Note that these techniques form just one of many ways of generating regions from the binary representation. The contour filling operation could for instance be substituted by applying flood filling that would skip any inner (nested) contours, while the morphological closing operation could be replaced by applying dilate and erode distance transforms [11] to achieve a similar effect. If necessary, the resulting polygon description could even be further simplified, e.g. through iterative end-point fit algorithms [35]. The main motivation for using the image processing techniques we described earlier is because they are mature, well-understood and because efficient implementations exist.

3.4 Region selection

Each binary representation for a label λ at scale t may result in multiple regions emerging at a particular scale. These regions can still vary substantially in their possible sizes, ranging from very small to very large, where their size is primarily determined by the spatial prominence of the label and the magnitude of the signal that remains after the Difference of Gaussians bandpass filter has been applied. Furthermore, the total number of regions generated for all of the labels combined may be too large for effective use. Depending on the envisioned use case further region selection may therefore be necessary. For instance, it may be appropriate to apply a ranking function to only pick a subset of the regions to be shown; the function could be parameterized with characteristics of the regions, such as area size or data density, or alternatively could include constraints to limit the maximal permissible amount of overlap between regions in order to select a disjoint or only partially overlapping set of regions to reduce visual clutter.

3.5 Parameterization

Our technique requires the specification of several parameter values that are, to a certain extent, dependent on the envisioned use case as well as the data itself. For analysis and visualization purposes, one usually focuses on only a limited number of scale levels $s \in \mathbb{N}$ at which the contours are obtained. The distance between consecutive scale levels is not necessarily linear in terms of the scale factor t but in online map-based interfaces, such as Yahoo! Maps, it is often roughly quadrupled so that $t = 4^s$. In addition, the distance between the scale-space representations to which the Difference of Gaussians operation is applied is controlled by the parameter a, which does not necessarily cover the entire range between consecutive scale levels. We illustrate these notions in Figure 3. By adjusting how t is obtained from s, as well as suitably setting a, the amount of smoothing between consecutive scales can be optimized to emphasize certain frequency ranges within the underlying data at certain scales. Finally, the noise threshold ϵ and the default radius ρ of the disk-shaped structuring element used by the morphological closing operation both affect the number, shape and size of the regions that emerge from the data.

If ground truth regions are available it is straightforward to derive the (near-)optimal parameter values by exhaustively comparing the obtained regions with the ground truth across a range of parameters. Multi-parameter learning algorithms [38, 42] can be applied to more efficiently direct the search and thus speed up convergence towards optimality.

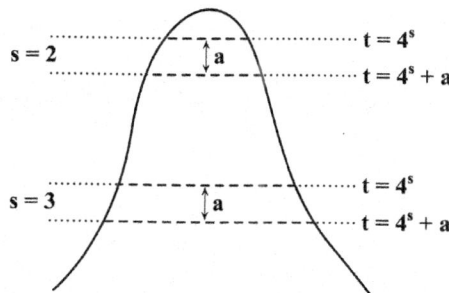

Figure 3: Illustration of the relationship between scale level s, scale factor t and Difference of Gaussians distance a. At scale level $s = 2$ the associated scale factor is $t = 16$, whereas at scale level $s = 3$ the scale factor is $t = 64$. At both locations the underlying density histogram is smoothed using a kernel parameterized by t and a kernel parameterized by $t + a$ after which the difference between them is taken.

3.6 Complexity

In contrast with techniques that process individual labeled instances, such as clustering-based approaches, our technique processes aggregate label counts, which for large quantities of data is much more computationally efficient, since the computational complexity does not increase with the size of the collection once the data has been represented as a histogram. Our approach is furthermore inherently parallelizable. Nonetheless, examining millions of labeled instances in order to assign them to the correct cells within the histograms can still be a time-consuming process – an issue of importance for highly dynamic online datasets – although in preliminary experimentation we observed that for our particular labeled collection the amount of computation could be reduced by subsampling the data without substantially compromising the shape and size of the final regions; however this may not necessarily be the case for other datasets.

4. IMPLEMENTATION

To demonstrate our region discovery technique we envisage a scenario prompted by users wanting to explore and browse large-scale geographically annotated media collections. This kind of scenario is particularly important to address, considering exploration has been shown to be the predominant mode of interaction for users of media systems [20] and exploration and browsing systems that allow the user to gain insight into and support the exploration of media collections are therefore needed [29]. In this section we present details on the implementation of our technique in the context of such a system, where we uncover the regions present within a large collection of labeled georeferenced photographs taken from the online image sharing website Flickr[1]. A preliminary version of our photo exploration and browsing system was presented in earlier work [43]. We emphasize, however, that our region discovery technique can be applied to any kind of labeled dataset of similar nature and not just to visual media; whether (meaningful) regions emerge entirely depends on the characteristics of the dataset. The optimizations we outline below for representing large-scale datasets are generalizable and not specific to our particular dataset.

[1] http://www.flickr.com/

4.1 Dataset

Our Flickr dataset contains a sample of over 56 million georeferenced images uploaded to Flickr before the end of 2010. Each photo is represented by a geographic location, indicated by longitude and latitude, and one or more tags assigned to the photo by the uploading user. We consider each instance of a tag associated with a photo as a label and annotate each label with the location information of its source photo. A single photo may thus generate multiple instances of annotated labels. We perform sanitization on the data by removing all non-latin characters, reducing all remaining latin characters to their lowercase representation and removing all diacritics, so that tags like España and Gaudí become espana and gaudi respectively. We remove tags that refer to years, such as 2006 and 2007, as well as camera manufacturer names, such as canon and nikon, because these at times get automatically added by capture devices or photo applications and thus are not representative for the tagging behavior of users. We additionally remove infrequently used tags by ensuring we have at least 50 instances per tag occurring around the world; while infrequently used tags could certainly yield a locally characterizing region, it was shown in [41] that the tag frequency distribution in photos uploaded to Flickr follows a power law with the very long tail containing the infrequent tags that typically were categorized as incidentally occurring words, making it unlikely such tags will actually generate regions.

4.2 Representation

We aim to compute the regions for all remaining tags in the dataset at several different scales, ranging from street level to world level. At the lowest scale level (i.e. zoomed in) the finest details are captured from the highest frequency components present within the normalized data, while at higher scale levels (i.e. zoomed out) the coarser structure is uncovered from the lower frequency components. This also corresponds well with the paradigm used by typical online systems that show interactive map-based views of the world, where the act of zooming in increases the spatial resolution to reveal more detail, whereas zooming out decreases the spatial resolution and reduces the level of detail.

In order to capture the finest details at the lowest scale the underlying scale-space representation of each tag needs to be of sufficiently high spatial resolution, whereas at higher scales such high resolution is not as necessary; provided that the resolution of the representation is at least high enough to capture the details at each scale level and the Gaussian kernel is correctly adjusted to retain the correct amount of smoothing, our scale-space region derivation technique generates equivalent regions at a reduced resolution at lower computational cost.

We therefore express the difference between two consecutive scales by changing the spatial resolution of the scale-space representation by a factor of two along each dimension, where incrementing the scale level s quarters the spatial resolution u, while decrementing s quadruples it, which also approximates the effects of zooming in and out on the spatial resolution in typical online map-based systems. At the same time we apply the reverse to the scale factor t, where incrementing the scale level s quadruples the scale factor t, while decrementing s quarters it. Since convolving a histogram with a kernel of width σ is analogous to convolving a histogram of quadruple the resolution with a kernel of width

2σ, the inverse relationship between u and t effectively allows us to apply the same Gaussian kernel at each scale level. We illustrate our representation in Figure 4.

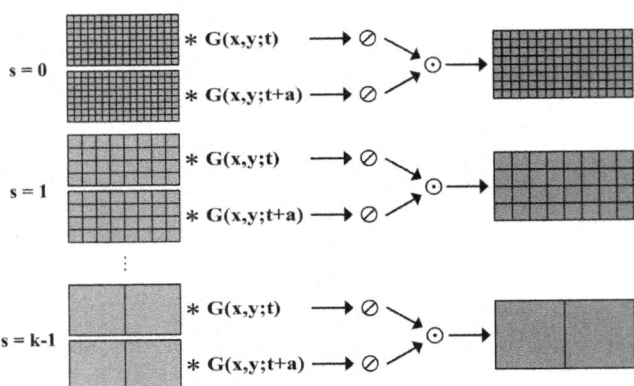

Figure 4: Scale-space representation using variable spatial resolution, where the weighting of the scale-space representation of a label in proportion to how much it contributes to the overall data density is represented by the symbol ⊘ and the difference operation between two scales is represented by the symbol ⊙. The scale-space representation is divided into a varying number of blocks that can be processed in parallel.

As the earth is commonly represented using a cylindrical projection that results in longitude values ranging twice as far as latitude values ($\pm 180°$ versus $\pm 90°$), we found for varying numbers of s that scale-space representations of height $h = r2^{k-s-1}$ and width $w = 2r2^{k-s-1}$ gave results equivalent to those obtained when using representations of the highest resolution at each scale, where k refers to the total number of scale levels being used and r is a constant. In our case we set $k = 12$, which is comparable to the number of scales found in online mapping systems such as Yahoo! Maps, and $r = 1,440$, which for convenience is a power-of-two multiple of the total number of degrees along the longitudinal and latitudinal axes. At street level, where $s = 0$, this effectively results in a scale-space representation of approximately 6 million by 3 million cells, whereas at world level, where $s = k - 1$, the representation measures 2,880 by 1,440 cells; at street level the largest cell is approximately the equivalent of $0.0001°$ longitude at the equator, measuring roughly 13m, while at world level it is the equivalent of $0.25°$ longitude at the equator, or about 28km.

At lower levels of s the representations are typically too large to fit into the memory of a 'standard' personal computer, e.g. at $s = 0$ the scale-space representation for a single tag at a single scale level using 4-byte floating-point values would require 63TB of memory (although admittedly storing the representation in a sparse format would substantially reduce this number). We therefore further optimize the computations by partitioning each histogram into overlapping blocks measuring $o + r + o$ by $o + r + o$ cells and process each of them separately in parallel. Here, r is defined as before and refers to the core area of the block, while o is a sufficiently large border area to avoid the boundary effects otherwise caused by applying the Gaussian kernels or morphological operations to a block containing solely the core area. A labeled data point will thus appear only once in a core area, but may also appear in one or more border areas of its neighboring core areas. Once each block has been processed we then discard the borders, after which we can trivially connect regions spanning across adjacent blocks along their seams.

4.3 Visualization

The final step in our implementation is to integrate all aforementioned aspects into a single system that supports zoomable browsing and exploration of the photos taken across the globe through their tag regions. Our interface, presented in earlier work [43] and shown in Figure 5, initially displays a geographic map of the user's estimated location along with any tag regions for their current map zoom level. The user can explore the regions detected in the world using standard map-based navigation operations such as zooming and panning. A region can be visually browsed by clicking on it, after which our system issues an API call to Flickr to retrieve photos taken within that region that are associated with the region's tag. Our system also supports querying for regions associated with one or more specific places or tags, the latter of which is particularly useful when one wants to visually compare the photos belonging to different regions having the same tag. To provide additional insight into the discovered regions we used the Geonames[2] gazetteer to label tags that refer to place names by matching tags with entries in the gazetteer in order to give the user the ability to show or hide regions based on this property.

Figure 5: A screenshot of our interface showing all tag regions detected in the United States at scale level $s = 10$ and a selection of Flickr photos associated with the tag region colorado. The region colors are derived from the tag using a hash function, thus when a tag generates multiple regions they are assigned the same color.

5. ANALYSIS

In our exploration and browsing scenario, we note that the tags assigned to Flickr photos are user-generated for which no valid ground truth exists against which we can compare the locally characterizing tag regions that emerge from the data. However, we observe that the tags that generate regions often are toponyms, i.e. referring to place names, and a visual inspection of the regions generated for tags that match the name of a country revealed that their shapes and sizes often closely matched the territorial boundaries, which was particularly evident when there was sufficient spatial

---

[2] http://www.geonames.org/

coverage of photos taken in that country. Since countries do have verifiable and canonical boundaries that can be used for evaluation we will therefore first present an exploration of parameters appropriate at country level and then discuss to what degree our parameters are suitably tuned to describe any type of region in general, in particular given that toponym and non-toponym boundaries may not behave in the same manner and that a single set of parameters may not sufficiently account of differences between regions that emerge at different scale levels.

5.1 Parameter exploration

We extracted the polygonal boundaries from OpenStreetMap[3] for all 192 countries in the world (according to the U.N.) and computed the regions of each tag matching the name of one of these countries for an extensive range of parameter values and scales. Our aim was to determine the optimal parameters that would achieve the highest overlap between the Flickr tag regions and the OpenStreetMap regions by only varying the kernel size σ and the morphological disk radius ρ. Since the scale level s is coupled with a scale factor t, which in turn is coupled with the kernel width σ, through our parameter exploration we thus empirically determine the best σ and its associated scale factor t and scale level s.

To get a snapshot of the region contours at a certain scale level s the spacing distance a ideally goes to zero, although this would leave gaps in the scale-space from where we would not obtain any contours. To this end we set our parameter a to cover the entire distance between consecutive scale levels to maximize the signal difference and to capture all contours. At each scale level s we thus applied the Difference of Gaussians operation to the scale-space representations that were spaced a distance of $a = 4^{s+1} - 4^s$ apart. This also had as benefit that the kernel width σ conveniently differed a factor of two between both representations. We suppressed low signal responses resulting from the Difference of Gaussians operation by removing those with magnitudes less than $\epsilon = 0.0005$ by setting them to zero in the binary representation, while all signals above the threshold were set to one.

In order to compare the tag regions with the polygonal boundaries of the countries, we first converted the longitude and latitude coordinates of all points along their exterior paths to an equal-area coordinate system using the Gall-Peters projection [12], allowing us to measure the extent their geographic areas overlap according to

$$overlap(A_{ssr}, A_{osm}; s, \lambda, \sigma, \rho) = \frac{A_{ssr} \bigcap A_{osm}}{A_{ssr} \bigcup A_{osm}} \quad (6)$$

where A_{ssr} refers to the projected area of the scale-space region with tag λ at scale level s generated using a Gaussian kernel of width σ and a morphological disk of radius ρ, whereas A_{osm} refers to the projected area of the OpenStreetMap region of the country with name λ.

We explored the parameter space where σ ranged from 0.2 to 10.0 in steps of 0.2 and ρ ranged from 5 to 75 in steps of 5, where for each parameter combination we retained the highest overlap for each country across all scale levels after which we averaged the overlaps over all countries. The results are shown in Figure 6 in which the lines indicate changes in overlap in steps of 0.02. Our exploration yielded the overall best results with a highest average overlap of 54%

---
[3] http://www.openstreetmap.org/

at $\sigma = 4.8$ and $\rho = 35$. From a practical perspective, given our variable scale-space representation implementation, we can simply smooth the overlapping histogram blocks at each scale level once with a kernel of size $\sigma = 4.8$ and once with a kernel of size $\sigma = 9.6$.

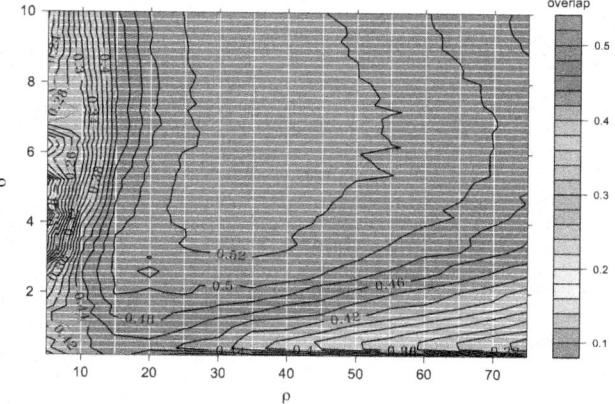

Figure 6: Highest average overlaps across all scales between the areas of Flickr tag regions referring to country names and their matching OpenStreetMap regions shown in a contour plot. Note that the colors do not vary between contour lines and thus do not exactly reflect the actual overlap values.

In Figure 7 we show the countries that emerged from our dataset using the optimal parameter values we established. As can be seen, the generated regions often follow the outline of the countries except in areas where there was little photographic coverage in our Flickr sample, such as in Africa, Russia and the Middle East. Interestingly, we observe several instances where the country regions overlap more than just along the border, e.g. Mexico and the state of Texas in the United States; India that covers Nepal, Bangladesh and Bhutan. Furthermore, we noticed – as expected – that the size of a country did appear to matter at which scale level its best overlap was attained, where larger countries tended to be found at a more global level and smaller ones at a more local level, see Figure 8.

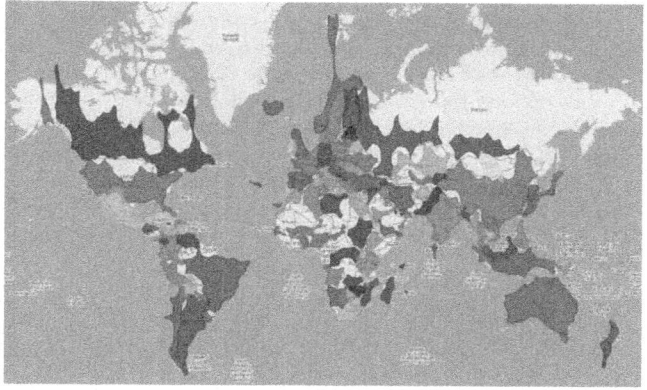

Figure 7: Flickr tag regions referring to country names generated at parameters $\sigma = 4.8$ and $\rho = 35$ extracted at the scales where they had the best overlap.

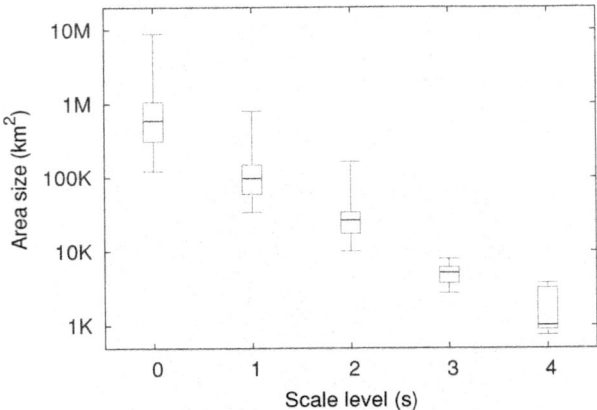

Figure 8: Box and whisker plot showing scale levels 0 to 4 versus area size at which Flickr tag regions referring to country names had the best overlap.

Table 1: Top tags yielding the highest average overlap between their Flickr tag regions referring to country names and their matching OpenStreetMap regions.

	Tag	Overlap
1	germany	84.1%
2	belarus	83.1%
3	poland	83.0%
4	sweden	82.6%
5	cambodia	81.8%
6	south africa	81.6%
7	czech republic	81.3%
8	turkey	80.8%
9	finland	80.0%
10	greece	79.6%

With the best parameter combination for the tag region generated for an individual country we ranked them by their overlap scores, shown in Table 1, demonstrating that with correctly tuned parameters we could achieve overlaps as high as 84.1%. This must be considered with respect to the available coverage of geotagged Flickr photos in each country, as those with poorer coverage across the whole of the territory are likely to give poorer overlap values.

While we acknowledge that we cannot draw any definite conclusions based on our parameter exploration in light of the absence of ground truth beyond country regions, the results suggest that the best parameter values we have obtained for tag regions relating to countries may transfer to other types of regions as well, in particular because the parameters remained stable for regions of varying sizes, while at the same time they were typically obtained at scales appropriate for the region given its size. However, upon closer inspection of local regions, we discovered that the tag regions that were already detected at more global levels were still present at local levels. While the regions emerging at global scales have a large footprint that in principle should be removed at local scales – since the Difference of Gaussians operation acts as a band-pass filter – at street level the coverage of the world in terms of Flickr photos is patchy and they thus still emerge in the form of disjoint smaller regions. One possible solution to this would be to hierarchically connect tag regions by determining superior, inferior and substitution relations between regions [22] and avoid displaying regions at scales substantially lower than the highest scale they have already been found at. This technique would at the same time resolve an issue we observed with near-identical regions emerging that only differ in the language of their associated tags.

5.2 Comparison

As already described in the related work section, alternative techniques for deriving colloquial regions from labeled data can be found in the research literature. In this section we present a comparison between the characteristic regions our technique generates and those obtained using a recently proposed approach that we briefly describe below; our main criteria for choosing this technique was its ability to analyze data at different scales, its applicability to noisy user-generated data on a per-label basis without requiring too many parameters to be tuned and its ability to generate regions of arbitrary shapes. These constraints therefore directly ruled out many other approaches that focus on deriving regions by inspecting the distribution of the georeferenced objects rather than the labels [1, 7, 9, 33], those that focus on the stability of regions across scales rather than the relevance of a region at a particular scale [37], those that can only model regions as elliptical shapes [3], as well as those that do not derive any kind of statistics that measure the influence of a label with respect to all other labels [25], as this would result in regions being generated that can impossibly be locally characterizing. To elaborate on the latter issue, in our preliminary experiments we observed the tag **beach** to be present all over the city center of Barcelona, likely due to users having bulk tagged the photos they took on their holiday trip; with the prominence weighting these tags were voted down at those locations by our algorithm, whereas without such weighting these tags formed a large region that clearly was not locally characterizing.

Crowd-based noise filtering

The objective of the technique of Intagorn and Lerman [18] is the same as ours, namely to derive regions for labels at several scales that are locally special with respect to the use of other labels. However, their approach is different in that it is based on clustering the data relevant for a particular label at a particular scale, after which the polygonal boundaries of the clusters are derived. In addition, the method essentially treats each scale independently from all other scales, unlike our work. Note that the technique is very similar to the approach proposed by Jung et al. [22], although the latter focused on four well-known cities only, whereas the crowd-based noise filtering technique analyzed tags at various scales by varying the parameters and thus fits the context of our comparison better.

To briefly describe the crowd-based noise filtering technique, the underlying algorithm first partitions the world into cells, where for each cell it computes a statistic involving the number of distinct people that used each of the distinct tags in that cell. For each distinct tag the method then assesses whether its occurrence at a certain cell is particularly significant. All cells in which a tag is not used significantly enough are discarded, whereas the remaining cells are clustered by treating them as connected nodes in a graph, in which edges are formed between nodes when they are close enough according to some threshold and disjoint clusters are then identified using connected component analysis. Finally, a polygonal boundary is derived for each resulting cluster by finding a Delauney triangulation that completely subsumes the data within each cluster, where the smoothness of the boundary can be controlled by setting a parameter.

Parameterization

For the evaluation of the colloquial regions generated by both techniques, we focused on nested bounding boxes within the world at different scales corresponding to intuitive geographic areas, where the scales zoom in from the World, to Europe, to Spain, to Catalonia and finally ending in Barcelona, allowing us to investigate the kind of regions that emerge and the nature of their differences.

For our scale-space region derivation technique we used the optimal parameters as determined through our parameter exploration, $\sigma = 4.8$, $\rho = 35$ and $\epsilon = 0.0005$, and as scale levels for the World $s = 0$, Europe $s = 2$, Spain $s = 3$, Catalonia $s = 6$ and Barcelona $s = 10$. As mentioned earlier, while appropriate for a particular scale, our technique can produce regions that may vary substantially in size; considering that a typical computer screen has a resolution on the order of 1440x1440 pixels (hence we had set our block size r to these values), we required that the regions occupied a minimum surface area of 1000 cells and a maximum of 400,000 cells to ensure they are not too large or too small for viewing purposes.

For the crowd-based noise filtering technique we in principle used the parameter values mentioned in the paper at the scale levels that were presented, unless we observed that an adjustment resulted in better results; we used parameters $\alpha = 10$, $k = 1$ and as scale levels for the World $Eps = 500$, Europe $Eps = 100$, Spain $Eps = 50$ and Catalonia $Eps = 10$. Due to the minimum cell size of the world within which the statistics were computed, as specified by α, we could not compute the regions for Barcelona, because this required a finer grid size.

Results

From the quantity of regions obtained at the various scales, shown in Table 2, we can instantly see that the crowd-based noise filtering technique discovers a large number of regions, even after we already limited it by setting a minimum surface area. In contrast, our scale-space region derivation technique finds a small number of regions at world level and larger numbers as the scale level becomes more local. The notion of finding more regions at local scales makes intuitive sense, since at global scales only the regions with large footprints will emerge, of which there are few, while at local scales only the regions with small footprints will be discovered, of which there are many.

Table 2: Number of regions detected by our scale-space region derivation technique (SSR) and by the crowd-based noise filtering technique (CNF) for different areas of the world.

Area	SSR	CNF
World	488	492197
Europe	1274	633193
Spain	3285	663528
Catalonia	6968	617047
Barcelona	9963	—

We illustrate the resulting regions detected within the four geographic areas in Figure 9. As can be seen, both approaches have roughly equivalent coverage of the world, where differences show up at different scale levels. For instance, the crowd-based noise filtering technique is able to cover Africa almost completely and also a larger part of Russia than our scale-space regions approach, and furthermore produces more regions in the Spanish state of Catalonia.

Qualitatively, the scale-space tag regions appear to more closely fit the country regions, whereas the regions produced by the crowd-based noise filtering technique seem to be rather crude; when measuring this quantitatively, by comparing both approaches in terms of overlap with the OpenStreetMap country regions, the scale-space regions approach achieved an average overlap of 56.1%, while the crowd-based noise filtering approach reached an average overlap of 41.9% using the clustering distance threshold of $Eps = 100$ as specified in the paper. Furthermore, due to the scale-space technique generating substantially less regions the interface appears less cluttered than when it is filled with the regions produced by the crowd-based noise filtering approach.

When analyzing the underlying technique of the crowd-based noise filtering approach, it becomes clear why it produces such a large quantity of regions. Namely, once a single labeled data point exceeds the threshold set by the statistic associated with the grid cell the data point is assigned to a region will be generated; the region initially is very small and may get clustered together with other regions, but if not it will remain to exist since the algorithm does not perform any filtering on the produced regions. We can clearly see this in the figures, where even after filtering out small regions and showing a small subset of regions the interface still shows many regions.

6. CONCLUSIONS

In this paper we presented a novel, generalized framework that automatically uncovers locally characterizing regions present within geotagged data using scale-space theory. The regions are generated by applying image analysis techniques to the scale-space representations of each data label. To handle large labeled collections across a wide range of scales we presented optimized implementation techniques to perform the region derivation in an efficient parallel manner. We analyzed the obtained tag regions in terms of the parameterization of the scale-space model at different scales and compared them against the regions produced by a recently proposed technique, showing that our tag regions can closely resemble the polygonal boundaries of the places they refer to. We envisage our technique being used to help users explore labeled geographic data in new ways, allowing them to draw insights in a manner that current interfaces to such data do not yet support. In future work we would like to investigate the implications of a dynamic dataset on the regions produced by our scale-space model and extend our technique to incorporate time as an additional dimension in our scale-space model for the purpose of detecting regions for labeled spatiotemporal data. Furthermore, we would like to use the discovered regions for purposes beyond media exploration, such as supporting spatially-aware and temporally-aware tagging, for instance learning when to suggest certain tags based on the geographic location and the timestamp of a given photo.

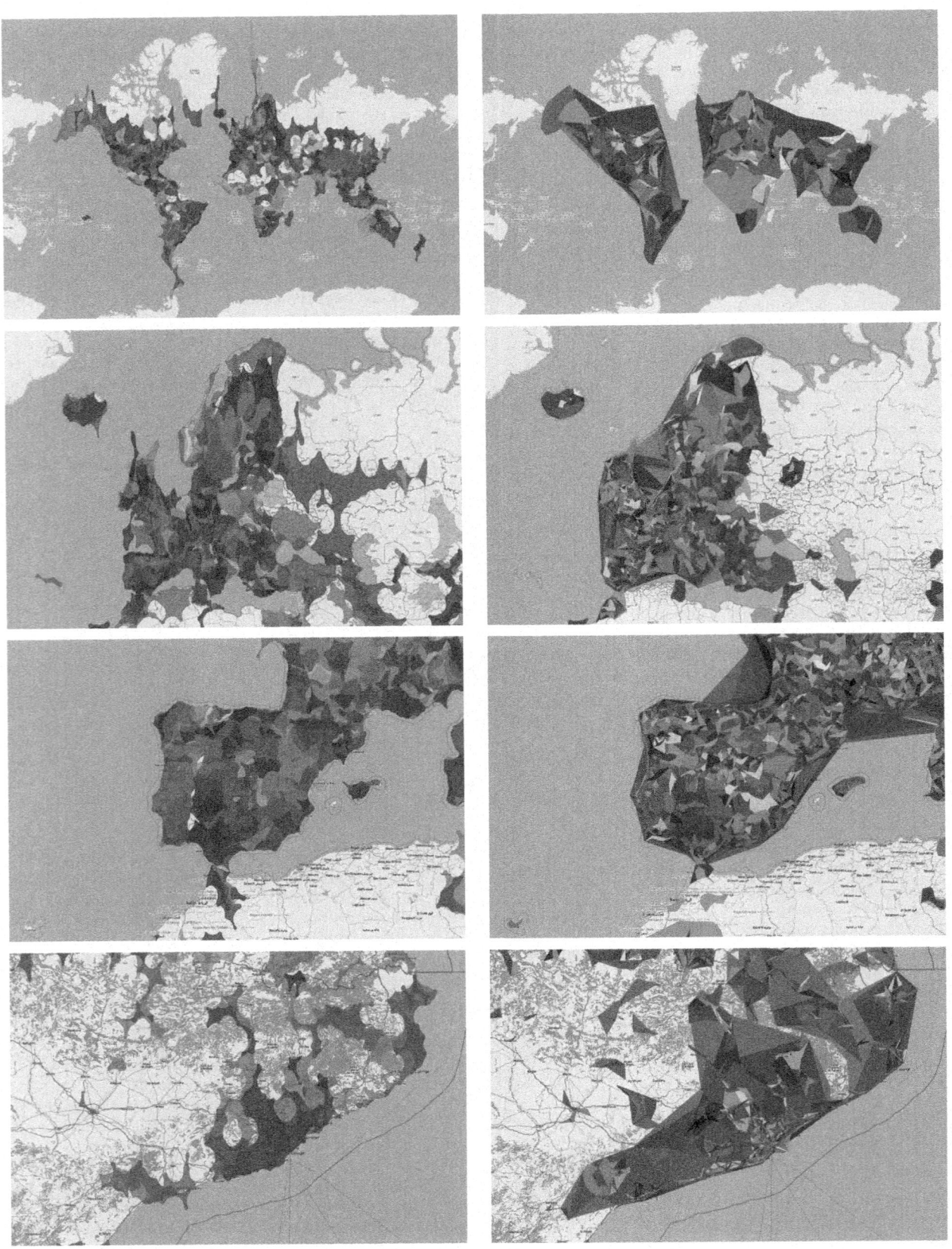

Figure 9: The regions detected by our scale-space region derivation technique (left column) and those by the crowd-based noise filtering technique (right column) for the geographic areas of the World (top), Europe (middle-top), Spain (middle-bottom) and Catalonia (bottom). To avoid excessive numbers of regions to be returned we limited the crowd-based noise filtering to return at most 10,000 regions.

7. REFERENCES

[1] S. Ahern, M. Naaman, R. Nair, and J. Yang. World explorer: visualizing aggregate data from unstructured text in geo-referenced collections. *JDCL*, pp. 1–10, 2007.

[2] T. Ai and J. Li. The lifespan model of GIS data representation over scale space. *GEOINFORMATICS*, pp. 1–6, 2009.

[3] Y. Baba, F. Ishikawa, and S. Honiden. Extraction of places related to Flickr tags. *ECAI*, pp. 523–528, 2010.

[4] T. Barkowsky, L. J. Latecki, and K.-F. Richter. Schematizing maps: simplification of geographic shape by discrete curve evolution. *Spatial Cognition II*, pp. 41–53, 2000.

[5] H. Bay, A. Ess, T. Tuytelaars, and L. van Gool. Speeded-Up Robust Features (SURF). *CVIU*, 110(3):346–359, 2008.

[6] F. Chang, C.-J. Chen, and C.-J. Lu. A linear-time component-labeling algorithm using contour tracing technique. *CVIU*, 93:206–220, 2004.

[7] W.-C. Chen, A. Battestini, N. Gelfand, and V. Setlur. Visual summaries of popular landmarks from community photo collections. *ICMR*, pp. 789–782, 2009.

[8] M. Cristani, A. Perina, U. Castellani, and V. Murino. Content visualization and management of geo-located image databases. *CHI*, pp. 2823–2828, 2008.

[9] D.-P. Deng, T.-R. Chuang, and R. Lemmens. Conceptualization of place via spatial clustering and co-occurrence analysis. *LBSN*, pp. 49–56, 2009.

[10] V. Estivill-Castro and I. Lee. AUTOCLUST: automatic clustering via boundary extraction for mining massive point-data sets. *GeoComputation*, 2001.

[11] P. F. Felzenszwalb and D. P. Huttenlocher. Distance transforms of sampled functions. *Theory of Computing*, 8(1):415–428, 2012.

[12] J. Gall. Use of cylindrical projections for geographical, astronomical, and scientific purposes. *Scottish Geographical Magazine*, 1(4):119–123, 1885.

[13] W. W. Hargrove and F. M. Hoffman. Using multivariate clustering to characterize ecoregion borders. *CiSE*, 1(4):18–25, 1999.

[14] C. Hauff and G.-J. Houben. Geo-location estimation of Flickr images: social web based enrichment. *ECIR*, pp. 85–96, 2012.

[15] J. Hays and A. A. Efros. IM2GPS: estimating geographic information from a single image. *CVPR*, pp. 1–8, 2008.

[16] H. Hotta and M. Hagiwara. A neural-network-based geographic tendency visualization. *WI-IAT*, pp. 817–823, 2008.

[17] H. Hotta and M. Hagiwara. Online geovisualization with fast kernel density estimator. *WI-IAT*, pp. 622–625, 2009.

[18] S. Intagorn and K. Lerman. Learning boundaries of vague places from noisy annotations. *SIGSPATIAL*, pp. 425–428, 2011.

[19] A. Jaffe, M. Naaman, T. Tassa, and M. Davis. Generating summaries and visualization for large collections of geo-referenced photographs. *MIR*, pp. 89–98, 2006.

[20] R. Jain. Experiential computing. *CACM*, 46(7):48–54, 2003.

[21] C. B. Jones, R. S. Purves, P. D. Clough, and H. Joho. Modelling vague places with knowledge from the Web. *IJGIS*, 22(10):1045–1065, 2008.

[22] D. Jung, H. Park, R. Maeng, and S. Han. A geometric pattern-based method to build hierarchies of geo-referenced tags. *SocialCom*, pp. 546–551, 2010.

[23] L. S. Kennedy and M. Naaman. Generating diverse and representative image search results for landmarks. *WWW*, pp. 297–306, 2008.

[24] L. S. Kennedy, M. Naaman, S. Ahern, R. Nair, and T. Rattenbury. How Flickr helps us make sense of the world: context and content in community-contributed media collections. *MM*, pp. 631–640, 2007.

[25] C. Kessler, P. Maué, J. T. Heuer, and T. Bartoschek. Bottom-up gazetteers: learning from the implicit semantics of geotags. *GeoS*, pp. 83–102, 2009.

[26] J. Kleban, E. Moxley, J. Xu, and B. S. Manjunath. Global annotation on georeferenced photographs. *CIVR*, 2009.

[27] J. J. Koenderink. The structure of images. *Biological Cybernetics*, 50:363–370, 1984.

[28] I. Laptev, H. Mayer, T. Lindeberg, W. Eckstein, C. Steger, and A. Baumgartner. Automatic extraction of roads from aerial images based on scale space and snakes. *Machine Vision and Applications*, 12:23–31, 2000.

[29] M. S. Lew, N. Sebe, C. Djeraba, and R. Jain. Content-based multimedia information retrieval: state of the art and challenges. *TOMCCAP*, 2(1):1–19, 2006.

[30] O. Linde and T. Lindeberg. Composed complex-cue histograms: An investigation of the information content in receptive field based image descriptors for object recognition. *CVIU*, 116(4):538–560, 2012.

[31] T. Lindeberg. Detecting salient blob-like image structures and their scales with a scale-space primal sketch: a method for focus of attention. *IJCV*, 11(3):283–318, 1993.

[32] D. G. Lowe. Distinctive image features from scale-invariant keypoints. *IJCV*, 60(2):91–110, 2004.

[33] C.-A. Lu, C.-H. Chen, and P.-J. Cheng. Clustering and visualizing geographic data using geo-tree. *WI-IAT*, pp. 479–482, 2011.

[34] R. Raguram, C. Wu, J.-M. Frahm, and S. Lazebnik. Modeling and recognition of landmark image collections using iconic scene graphs. *IJCV*, 95(3):213–239, 2011.

[35] U. Ramer. An iterative procedure for the polygonal approximation of plane curves. *Computer Graphics and Image Processing*, 1(3):244–256, 1972.

[36] T. Rattenbury, N. Good, and M. Naaman. Towards automatic extraction of event and place semantics from Flickr tags. *SIGIR*, pp. 103–110, 2007.

[37] T. Rattenbury and M. Naaman. Methods for extracting place semantics from Flickr tags. *TWEB*, 3(1):1, 2009.

[38] S. Robertson and H. Zaragoza. The probabilistic relevance framework: BM25 and beyond. *FTIR*, 3(4):333–389, 2009.

[39] S. Rudinac, A. Hanjalic, and M. Larson. Finding representative and diverse community contributed images to create visual summaries of geographic areas. *ICMR*, pp. 1109–1112, 2011.

[40] P. Serdyukov, V. Murdock, and R. van Zwol. Placing Flickr photos on a map. *SIGIR*, pp. 484–491, 2009.

[41] B. Sigurbjornsson and R. v. Zwol. Flickr Tag Recommendation based on Collective Knowledge. *WWW*, pp. 327–336, 2008.

[42] M. Taylor, H. Zaragoza, N. Craswell, S. Robertson, and C. Burges. Optimisation methods for ranking functions with multiple parameters. *CIKM*, pp. 585–593, 2006.

[43] B. Thomee and A. Rae. Exploring and Browsing Photos through Characteristic Geographic Tag Regions. *MM*, pp. 1273–1274, 2012.

[44] O. Van Laere, S. Schockaert, and B. Dhoedt. Finding locations of Flickr resources using language models and similarity search. *ICMR*, article 48, 2011.

[45] F. Wang. Job access and homicide patterns in Chicago: an analysis at multiple geographic levels based on scale-space theory. *JQC*, 21(2):195–217, 2005.

[46] K. Q. Weinberger, M. Slaney, and R. van Zwol. Resolving tag ambiguity. *MM*, pp. 111–120, 2008.

[47] A. Witkin. Scale-space filtering: a new approach to multi-scale description. *ICASSP*, 9:150–153, 1984.

[48] K. Yanai, H. Kawakubo, and B. Qiu. A visual analysis of the relationship between word concepts and geographical locations. *CIVR*, article 13, 2009.

Spectral Analysis of Communication Networks Using Dirichlet Eigenvalues

Alexander Tsiatas[*]
Department of Computer Science and Engineering
University of California, San Diego
9500 Gilman Drive
La Jolla, CA 92093-0404
atsiatas@cs.ucsd.edu

Onuttom Narayan
Department of Physics
University of California, Santa Cruz
1156 High Street
Santa Cruz, CA 95064
narayan@physics.ucsc.edu

Iraj Saniee
Mathematics of Networks
Alcatel-Lucent Bell Labs
600 Mountain Avenue
Murray Hill, NJ 07974
iis@research.bell-labs.com

Matthew Andrews
Mathematics of Networks
Alcatel-Lucent Bell Labs
600 Mountain Avenue
Murray Hill, NJ 07974
andrews@research.bell-labs.com

ABSTRACT

Good clustering can provide critical insight into potential locations where congestion in a network may occur. A natural measure of congestion for a collection of nodes in a graph is its Cheeger ratio, defined as the ratio of the size of its boundary to its volume. Spectral methods provide effective means to estimate the smallest Cheeger ratio via the spectral gap of the graph Laplacian. Here, we compute the spectral gap of the truncated graph Laplacian, with the so-called Dirichlet boundary condition, for the graphs of a dozen communication networks at the IP-layer, which are subgraphs of the much larger global IP-layer network. We show that i) the Dirichlet spectral gap of these networks is substantially larger than the standard spectral gap and is therefore a better indicator of the true expansion properties of the graph, ii) unlike the standard spectral gap, the Dirichlet spectral gaps of progressively larger subgraphs converge to that of the global network, thus allowing properties of the global network to be efficiently obtained from them, and iii) the (first two) eigenvectors of the Dirichlet graph Laplacian can be used for spectral clustering with arguably better results than standard spectral clustering. We first demonstrate these results analytically for finite regular trees. We then perform spectral clustering on the IP-layer networks using Dirichlet eigenvectors and show that it yields cuts near the network core, thus creating genuine single-component clusters. This is much better than traditional spectral clustering where several disjoint fragments near the network periphery are liable to be misleadingly classified as a single cluster. Since congestion in communication networks is known to peak at the core due to large-scale curvature and geometry, identification of core congestion and its localization are important steps in analysis and improved engineering of networks. Thus, spectral clustering with Dirichlet boundary condition is seen to be more effective at finding bona-fide bottlenecks and congestion than standard spectral clustering.

Categories and Subject Descriptors

G.2.2 [**Discrete Mathematics**]: Graph Theory—*network problems*; C.2.1 [**Computer-Communication Networks**]: Network Architecture and Design—*network topology*

Keywords

Spectral clustering, Dirichlet eigenvalues, Communication networks, Cheeger ratio

1. INTRODUCTION

An important problem in network analysis is partitioning nodes, also sometimes known as finding communities. This requires finding clusters of nodes that are inherently well-connected within themselves with sparser connections between clusters; when the clusters do not overlap, they define a partitioning of the graph. This problem is also closely related to finding network bottlenecks; if a graph has bottlenecks, then a good partition is often found by dividing the graph at its bottlenecks. Many real-world networks are truly vast, encompassing hundreds of thousands to billions of nodes and edges; for example, communication, social and biological networks. This scale produces serious computational challenges for detection of bottlenecks and communities: the large majority of algorithms are computationally too intensive to use at this scale on such graphs. Instead, one can study smaller sub-graphs of these networks; for example, the portion of a social network corresponding to one university or the portion of a communication network corresponding to one Internet service provider, and hope to derive properties of the larger graph from those of the smaller subgraphs. In this paper, we show how to define key properties of a graph, its Dirichlet spectral gap and eigenvectors which aid in clustering, and show how these closely relate to the

---

[*]At time of publication, at Google Inc., 1600 Amphitheatre Pkwy, Mountain View, CA 94043.

Copyright is held by the International World Wide Web Conference Committee (IW3C2). IW3C2 reserves the right to provide a hyperlink to the author's site if the Material is used in electronic media.
WWW'13, May 13–17, 2013, Rio de Janeiro, Brazil.
ACM 978-1-4503-2035-1/13/05.

spectral gaps and eigenvectors of its sub-graphs thus making identification of bottlenecks and points of congestion both more effective and scalable.

More precisely, spectral graph theory [3], the study of eigenvalues and eigenvectors of graph-theoretic matrices, is often used to analyze various graph properties. One might hope that the properties of a large sub-graph of a network will be representative of the properties of the entire network. Unfortunately, the properties of an expander graph depend on the conditions imposed at its (large) boundary. For example, the spectral gap of the graph Laplacian on a finite truncation of an infinite regular tree approaches zero as the size of the truncation is increased, even though the spectral gap of its infinite counterpart is non-zero. In this paper we show that, by contrast, if the spectral gap is calculated with *Dirichlet boundary conditions*, it approaches the infinite graph limit as the size of truncation is increased. Computation of a better spectral gap makes it possible to do spectral clustering more effectively thus making identification of bottlenecks and points of congestion more effective.

Motivated by this result, we compute the Dirichlet spectral gap for ten IP-layer communication networks as measured and documented by previous researchers in the Rocketfuel database [18]. We find that the Dirichlet spectral gap is much larger than the traditional spectral gap for these graphs. (Traditional spectral clustering uses the normalized Laplacian matrix $\mathcal{L}$ or some similar matrix; we use the matrix $\mathcal{L}_D$: the Laplacian restricted to the rows and columns corresponding to non-boundary nodes.) Moreover, unlike the traditional spectral gap, it does not trend downwards for larger networks. This indicates that the spectral gap for these networks viewed as sub-graphs of a much larger graph is away from zero.

There are precedents for treating networks essentially as subsets of an an overarching (infinite) graph; many network generation models [2, 6, 21] exhibit unique convergence properties (to power-law degree distributions or otherwise) as the size of the network grows to infinity. We also note that Dirichlet boundary conditions have been shown to be successful at mitigating other boundary-related issues in graph vertex ranking [5].

There is a direct connection between the spectral gap and clustering in networks, through the Cheeger inequality. Spectral graph theory has led to many effective algorithms for finding cuts that result in a small Cheeger ratio, including spectral clustering [15, 17, 16, 20] and local graph partitioning algorithms [1]. These algorithms have been well-studied, both empirically [15, 17] and theoretically [15, 20]. Unfortunately, these algorithms can also exhibit some undesirable behavior. It has been shown empirically [12] that the "best" partitionings of many networks, as measured by the Cheeger ratio, result in cutting off nodes or subtrees near the boundary of the network. The resulting 'clusters' near the boundary actually consist of several disjoint fragments. Especially when viewed as subsets of larger networks, this kind of clustering is not particularly meaningful.

In this paper, we use *Dirichlet spectral clustering* to identify good cuts in the networks in the Rocketfuel database. We use the top two eigenvectors of $\mathcal{L}_D$, the normalized graph Laplacian with Dirichlet boundary conditions, to cut the network into two sections. We demonstrate that, compared to traditional spectral clustering, there is a substantial reduction in the average number of components resulting from the cut, without a significant increase in the Cheeger ratio. Instead of finding cuts near the boundaries of the networks, Dirichlet spectral clustering obtains cuts in the network core.

The Cheeger ratio of a cut is a well known indicator of the congestion across the cut; small Cheeger ratios are likely to be associated with bottlenecks. The emphasis on identifying core bottlenecks becomes more critical in the light of the recent observation that many real-world graphs exhibit large-scale curvature [10, 14]. It has been shown [10, 14] that such global network curvature leads to core bottlenecks with load (or betweenness) asymptotically much worse than flat networks, where "load" means the the maximum total flow through a node assuming unit traffic between every node-pair along shortest paths [14]. As such, it is important to find and characterize bottlenecks at the core rather than the fringes, where they do not matter as much. Our observations, suggest that Dirichlet spectral clustering may be more useful in this regard.

The rest of this paper is structured as follows: in Section 2, we give the theoretical justification for using Dirichlet eigenvalues [4] instead of the traditional spectrum for analyzing and clustering finite portions of much larger graphs. In Section 3, we then compare the spectral gap using Dirichlet eigenvalues to the traditional spectral gap on real, publicly-determined network topologies [18] that represent smaller portions of the wider telecommunications grid. In Section 4, we demonstrate how Dirichlet spectral clustering finds graph partitions that are more indicative of bottlenecks in the network core rather than the fringes.

2. SPECTRUM OF FINITE TREES: MOTIVATION FOR DIRICHLET SPECTRAL CLUSTERING

Throughout this paper, we analyze general undirected connected graphs G by using the normalized graph Laplacian $\mathcal{L}$, defined as in [3]. For two vertices x and y, the corresponding matrix entry is:

$$\mathcal{L}_{xy} = \begin{cases} 1 & \text{if } x = y, \\ -\frac{1}{\sqrt{d_x d_y}} & \text{if } x \text{ and } y \text{ are adjacent, and} \\ 0 & \text{otherwise,} \end{cases}$$

where d_x and d_y are the degrees of x and y. We denote by λ the *spectral gap*, which is simply the smallest nonzero eigenvalue of $\mathcal{L}$.

For any graph G and finite subgraph $S \subset G$, the *Cheeger ratio* $h(S)$ is a measure of the cut induced by S:

$$h(S) = \frac{e(S, \bar{S})}{\min(\text{vol}(S), \text{vol}(\bar{S}))}.$$

We use $e(S, \bar{S})$ to denote the number of edges crossing from S to its complement, and the *volume* $\text{vol}(S)$ is simply the sum of the degrees of all nodes in S. The *Cheeger constant* h is the minimum $h(S)$ over all subsets S. The Cheeger constant and spectral gap are related by the following *Cheeger inequality* [3]:

$$2h \geq \lambda \geq \frac{h^2}{2}.$$

Both λ and h are often used to characterize expansion or bottlenecks in graphs. This inequality shows that they are both good candidates and gives the ability to estimate one based on the other.

For the infinite d-regular tree, the spectral gap and Cheeger constant have both been analytically determined [7, 13]. Using $\mathcal{L}$, the spectral gap is

$$\lambda = 1 - \frac{2}{d}\sqrt{d-1}, \qquad (1)$$

and the Cheeger constant is $h = d - 2$ [9]. Both of these values are nonzero, indicating good expansion. However, the Cheeger ratio for truncated d-regular trees (TdT) – those with all branches of the infinite tree cut off beyond some radius r from the center – approaches zero as the tree gets deeper. By cutting off any one subtree S from the root, there is only one edge connecting S to $\bar{S}$, and as the tree gets deeper, this ratio gets arbitrarily small. Using the Cheeger inequality, it follows that the $\lambda_{TdT} \to 0$ as $r \to \infty$. Thus, the standard spectral properties of finite trees do not approach the infinite case as they get larger; in fact, they suggest the opposite. This is problematic when making qualitative observations about networks and their expansion, necessitating another tool for spectral analysis of networks.

The main reason why the traditional spectral gap does not capture expansion well in large, finite trees is the existence of a boundary. This is also problematic in network partitioning algorithms; often times the "best" partition is a *bag of whiskers* or combination of several smaller cuts near the boundary [12]. In this paper, we will use Dirichlet eigenvalues to eliminate this problem.

Dirichlet eigenvalues are the eigenvalues of a truncated matrix, eliminating the rows and columns that are associated with nodes on the graph boundary. We will use a truncated normalized graph Laplacian, $\mathcal{L}_D$, a submatrix of $\mathcal{L}$. This is different from simply taking the normalized Laplacian of an induced subgraph, as the edges leading to the boundary nodes are still taken into account; it is only the boundary nodes themselves that are ignored. We define the *Dirichlet spectral gap* to be the smallest eigenvalue of $\mathcal{L}_D$. This version of the graph Laplacian was first introduced in [4] to analyze local cuts on graphs.

Using Dirichlet eigenvalues, it is also possible to obtain a *local Cheeger inequality* [4] for the sub-graph S. First, the *local Cheeger ratio* is defined [4] for a set of nodes $T \subset S$ as

$$H(T) = \frac{e(T, \bar{T})}{\text{vol}(T)};$$

because the boundary nodes are excluded from S in the definition of [4], the set T cannot contain any boundary nodes of S. The local Cheeger ratio $H(T)$ is the appropriate quantity when S is a sub-graph of a larger graph. Note that there is no min in the denominator; this is because the local Cheeger ratio is specific to a subgraph, and it does not make sense to take into account the rest of the graph beyond the boundary of that subgraph. The *local Cheeger constant* h_S for S is then defined as the minimum of $H(T)$ for all $T \subset S \setminus \partial(S)$. The local Cheeger inequality obtained in [4] is

$$h_S \geq \lambda_S \geq \frac{h_S^2}{2},$$

where λ_S is the Dirichlet eigenvalue of the normalized Laplacian restricted to the rows and columns corresponding to nodes in S. This inequality indicates a relationship between local expansion and bottlenecks.

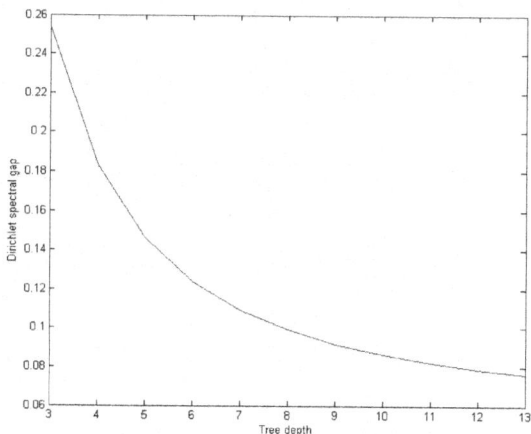

Figure 1: Dirichlet spectral gap for successively larger 3-regular trees, showing convergence to a nonzero value. The limit, as estimated by the Cheeger inequality, is $\lambda \approx 0.057$.

The use of Dirichlet eigenvalues requires that the boundary of the graph S be defined. If S is a tree, the leaf nodes are a natural choice. When S is actually a finite truncation of a larger graph, the boundary can be defined as the set of nodes that connect directly to other nodes outside the truncation; for the Rocketfuel data [18], we will use the nodes with degree 1 which presumably connect outside of the subnetwork.

We first use Dirichlet eigenvalues on d-regular trees as prototypical evidence for their effectiveness in capturing true spectral properties on real-world networks. There is empirical evidence in Figure 1, showing that the Dirichlet spectral gap for 3-regular trees indeed converges to a nonzero value as tree depth increases, contrasting with the traditional spectral gap which converges to zero. This is made rigorous in the following theorem:

THEOREM 1. *For finite d-regular trees of depth L, the Dirichlet spectral gap converges to the true spectral gap (1) of the infinite tree as L approaches infinity.*

PROOF. To derive the Dirichlet spectral gap for finite trees using the leaves as the boundary, we will solve a recurrence that arises from the tree structure and the standard eigenvalue equation

$$\mathcal{L}_d \vec{x} = \lambda \vec{x}. \qquad (2)$$

Let T be a d-regular tree of depth $L + 1$; the $(L + 1)$st level is the boundary. We first consider eigenvectors $\vec{x}$ which have the same value at every node at the same depth within T; these eigenvectors are azimuthally symmetric. We can represent each such eigenvector $\vec{x}$ as a sequence of values $(x_0, x_1, \ldots, x_L)$, where x_i is the uniform value at all nodes at depth i, similar to the analysis of the infinite-tree spectral gap appearing in [7]. Using this eigenvector form for $\vec{x}$ in (2) leads to the recurrence:

$$x_i - \frac{1}{d}x_{i-1} - \frac{d-1}{d}x_{i+1} = \lambda x_i, 2 \leq i \leq L. \qquad (3)$$

At the leaves of the tree, we have the Dirichlet boundary condition:
$$x_{L+1} = 0, \quad (4)$$
and at the root of the tree we have the boundary condition
$$x_0 - x_1 = \lambda x_0. \quad (5)$$
We can solve (3) using the characteristic equation:
$$\frac{d-1}{d}r^2 - (1-\lambda)r + \frac{1}{d} = 0,$$
whose roots can be written as
$$r_{1,2} = \frac{1}{\sqrt{d-1}} e^{\pm i\alpha} \quad (6)$$
with
$$\lambda = 1 - \frac{2}{d}\sqrt{d-1}\cos\alpha. \quad (7)$$
Since λ has to be real, either the real or imaginary part of α must be zero. Substituting the first boundary condition (4) yields a solution to (3) with the form
$$x_n = A(r_1^{n-L-1} - r_2^{n-L-1}). \quad (8)$$
for some constant A and $r_{1,2}$ given in (6). Using (5), the condition for eigenvalues is
$$\frac{\tan\alpha}{\tan(L+1)\alpha} = -\frac{d-2}{d} \quad 0 < \alpha < \pi. \quad (9)$$
Since $\tanh x/\tanh(L+1)x > 0$ for all real x, there are no imaginary solutions to Eq.(9). Therefore all the $L+1$ solutions are real. From Eq.(7), the corresponding $L+1$ eigenvalues are all outside the infinite-tree spectral gap.

We now consider eigenvectors which are zero at all nodes up to the k'th level with $L > k \geq 0$. The eigenvector is non-zero at two daughters of some k'th level node and the descendants thereof. We assume azimuthal symmetry inside both these two sectors. The eigenvalue condition for the parent node at the k'th level forces the eigenvector to be opposite in the two sectors. Inside each sector, (3), (6), (7) (4) and (8) are still valid. However, (5) is replaced by the condition $x_k = 0$, from which $\sin(L+1-k)\alpha = 0$. There are $L-k$ real solutions to this equation, corresponding to eigenvalues that lie outside the infinite-tree spectral gap, each with degeneracy $d^k(d-1)$. The total number of eigenvalues we have found so far is
$$L + 1 + \sum_{k=0}^{L-1} d^k(d-1)(L-k) = \frac{d^{L+1}-1}{d-1} \quad (10)$$
i.e. we have found all the eigenvalues. As L gets larger, the smallest α approaches 0, showing that the Dirichlet spectral gap converges to the spectral gap of the infinite tree (1) as the depth approaches infinity. □

This derivation shows that Dirichlet eigenvalues capture the expansion properties of trees much better than the traditional spectral gap which has been shown to approach zero for large finite trees. This behavior on trees suggests that Dirichlet eigenvalues are a good candidate for use in analyzing real-world networks. Such analysis appears in Section 3.

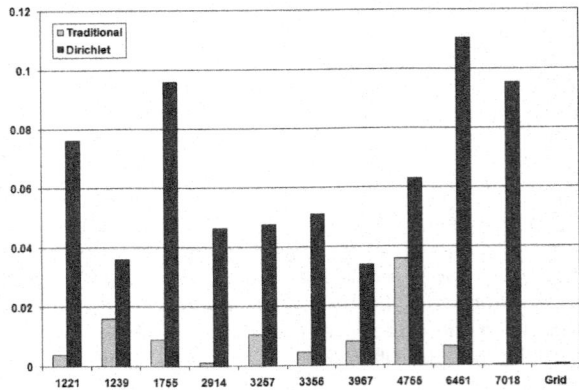

Figure 2: Comparison of traditional and Dirichlet spectral gaps in Rocketfuel data as well as the 2-dimensional Euclidean grid.

3. SPECTRUM OF ROCKETFUEL NETWORKS

Our work is motivated by derivation of scalable methods for clustering of large graphs. As an example, we study clustering of a series of datasets representing portions of network topologies using Rocketfuel [18]. Rocketfuel datasets are publicly-available, created using `traceroute` and other networking tools to determine portions of network topology corresponding to individual Internet service providers. Even though like most measured datasets, the Rocketfuel networks are not free of errors (see for example [19]), they provide valuable connectivity information at the IP-layer of service provider networks across the globe. Because the datasets were created in this manner, they represent only subsets of the much larger Internet; it becomes impossible to determine network topology at certain points. For example, corporate intranets, home networks, other ISP's, and network-address translation cannot be explored. The networks used range in size from 121 to 10,152 nodes.

Because of the method of data collection, the Rocketfuel datasets contain many degree-1 nodes that appear at the edge of the topology. In actuality, the network extends beyond this point, but the datasets are limited to one ISP at a time. As such, for these networks, it makes sense to view these degree-1 nodes as the boundary of a finite subset of a much larger network. Using this boundary definition, we compute the Dirichlet spectral gaps of these graphs and compare with their standard counterparts, as shown in Table 1 and Figure 2. It is apparent that the Dirichlet spectral gaps are much larger than the traditional spectral gaps for all the networks, implying a much higher degree of expansion than one would traditionally obtain. The spectral gaps for a two-dimensional square Euclidean grid are also shown; the grid is known to be a poor expander, and accordingly even the Dirichlet spectral gap is very small.

Figure 3 shows the same data, plotted as a function of the number of nodes N in each network. We see that the traditional spectral gap keeps decreasing as N is increased, whereas the Dirichlet spectral gap does not.

Since Figure 3 compares different networks, possibly with different properties, we confirm the result by computing the

Table 1: Structural and spectral properties of Rocketfuel datasets.

Dataset ID	Nodes	Edges	Traditional spectral gap	Dirichlet spectral gap
1221	2998	3806	0.00386	0.07616
1239	8341	14025	0.01593	0.03585
1755	605	1035	0.00896	0.09585
2914	7102	12291	0.00118	0.04621
3257	855	1173	0.01045	0.04738
3356	3447	9390	0.00449	0.05083
3967	895	2070	0.00799	0.03365
4755	121	228	0.03570	0.06300
6461	2720	3824	0.00639	0.11036
7018	10152	14319	0.00029	0.09531
Grid	10000	19800	0.00025	0.00050

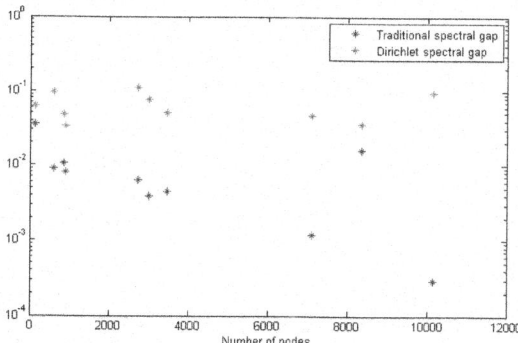

Figure 3: Comparison of traditional and Dirichlet spectral gaps across Rocketfuel networks.

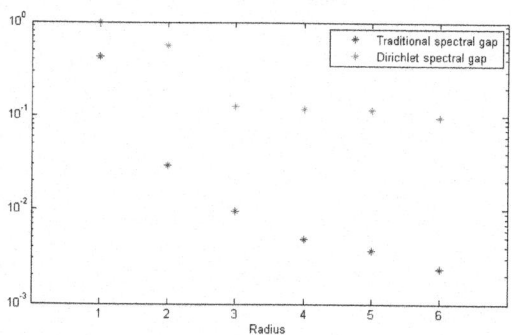

Figure 4: Comparison of traditional and Dirichlet spectral gaps in successively larger subgraphs, grown from the center of mass of dataset 7018.

spectral gap for subgraphs of different sizes drawn from a single network. All the nodes that are within a distance r of the center of mass of a network are included in a subgraph, with r varying between 1 and the maximum possible value for the network. In Fig. 4 shows the results for the largest of the Rocketfuel networks, dataset 7018 containing over 10,000 nodes. For a subgraph of radius r, the boundary is defined as all the nodes which i) have edges connecting them to nodes in the graph that are outside the subgraph or ii) connect to the outside world, i.e. that have degree 1 in the full dataset. As in Fig. 3, in Fig. 4, the traditional spectral gap keeps decreasing as r is increased, but the Dirichlet spectral gap does not.

4. SPECTRAL DECOMPOSITION

One important application of the eigendecomposition of a graph is spectral clustering or partitioning [15, 17]. The problem is to group the nodes into partitions, clusters, or communities that are inherently well-connected within themselves, with sparser connections between clusters. This is closely related to finding bottlenecks; if a graph has a bottleneck, then a good partition is often found by dividing the graph at the bottleneck. See [16] for a general survey of graph clustering.

It is often desirable for a network partition to be balanced, and finding bottlenecks near the core or center of mass of a network is often more useful than simply clipping small subsets of nodes near the boundary. But according to [12], using the Cheeger ratio as a metric on real-world data, the "best" cuts larger than a certain critical size are actually "bags of whiskers" or combinations of numerous smaller cuts. Because many graph clustering algorithms, including spectral clustering, try to optimize for this metric, the resulting partitions often slice numerous smaller cuts off the graph, which is not always useful. For our Rocketfuel data, we know that the boundary of the network is imposed by the method of data collection. Thus, by eliminating the boundary from graph clustering, we can more easily find partitions that are more evenly balanced, and bottlenecks that are closer to the core of the network.

To do this, we use standard spectral clustering techniques from [15], but instead of using the normalized graph Laplacian $\mathcal{L}$, we use the truncated Dirichlet version $\mathcal{L}_D$. The eigenvectors used for clustering will therefore not include components for the degree-1 boundary nodes, but we can assign them to the same side of the partition as their non-boundary neighbor nodes. Specifically, we compute the first two eigenvectors of $\mathcal{L}_D$ and cluster the nodes based on their components in these eigenvectors using k-means. For each node, we compute the distance to both centers and sort the nodes based on the difference. For a partition of size k, we take the top k nodes.

We follow the experiments of Leskovec et al. in [12] by using both traditional spectral clustering and Dirichlet spectral clustering to find cuts of different sizes. Specifically, we find Dirichlet cuts of all possible sizes, and then we find cuts using traditional spectral clustering for those same sizes after adding boundary nodes back in. Thus, for each network of N nodes, we calculate $N - B$ cuts, where B is the number of boundary nodes.

For each cut, we measure the Cheeger ratio h and the number of components c. Ideally, a logical cut would split the network into exactly $c = 2$ components, but as Leskovec et al. demonstrated, as cut size increases, spectral clustering and other algorithms that optimize for h yield cuts with many components. This is precisely the problem we are trying to avoid using Dirichlet clustering, and our results show that Dirichlet clustering is effective in finding cuts with fewer components. Furthermore, even though our algorithm is not specifically optimizing for h, it does not find cuts that have significantly worse values for h while finding cuts with far fewer components.

We outline some aggregate data in Table 2. For several datasets, we count the number of cuts in four different categories, comparing the Dirichlet Cheeger ratio and number of components (h_D and c_D) with traditional spectral clustering (h_T and c_T). It is evident that Dirichlet clustering finds cuts with fewer components than traditional spectral clustering ($c_D \leq c_T$) for most cut sizes, indicating that while spectral clustering optimizes for Cheeger ratio, it often "cheats" by collecting whiskers as one cut. In addition, despite the use of Cheeger ratio optimization, Dirichlet clustering sometimes finds cuts with better Cheeger ratio as well. In the last two columns for each dataset, we give the difference in h and c averaged out over all cut sizes. It turns out that the Cheeger ratios, on average, are not drastically different between the two methods, and Dirichlet clustering gives cuts with far fewer components.

Along with our aggregate data, we illustrate each individual cut for several of our Rocketfuel datasets in Fig. 5. (A few of the datasets were too large for accurate numerical computation and are therefore not shown.) For each cut size, we plot a point corresponding to the difference in Cheeger ratio h and the number of components c between Dirichlet and traditional spectral clustering. It should be clear that for the majority of cut sizes, Dirichlet clustering finds cuts with far fewer components, but there is generally little change in Cheeger ratio. This can be seen in the large variation on the c-axis with much smaller discrepancies on the h-axis. In other words, Dirichlet clustering avoids finding "bags of whiskers" while still maintaining good separation in terms of h, despite not explicitly optimizing for h.

We further visualize Dirichlet spectral clustering for two Rocketfuel data sets, shown in Figures 6 and 7. In both cases, one side of the partition is colored blue, and the other side is colored red. Notice that for these graphs, Dirichlet spectral clustering separates red and blue nodes much better than traditional spectral clustering as expected.

It is clear that using Dirichlet eigenvalues improves the partition by ignoring the boundary, alleviating the tendency to find "bags of whiskers" without drastically changing the Cheeger ratio. Although traditional spectral clustering does not always fail, there is clear evidence that Dirichlet spectral properties are an important tool in the analysis of real-world networks.

5. DISCUSSION

Our results show evidence that eigenvalues of the normalized graph Laplacian can provide rich information about real-world networks when Dirichlet boundary conditions are applied. We find that the Dirichlet spectral gap computed for several IP-layer networks is much larger than the traditional spectral gap, and is likely to go to a finite limit as the size of the network is increased. Rigorous analysis for infinite d-regular trees suggests that this may be the same as the spectral gap of a communication network that is a smaller section of something much larger. Spectral clustering using Dirichlet eigenvalues yields much better clustering than traditional methods.

The spectral decomposition using Dirichlet eigenvalues also suggests a connection to large-scale negative curvature [10, 11, 14] in the Rocketfuel data. Traditional negatively curved graphs such as trees and hyperbolic grids generally exhibit poor connectivity and core congestion. Standard clustering often yields combinations of smaller cuts near the periphery of the graph, but using Dirichlet clustering, we can see that there tend to be bad larger-scale cuts as well in the Rocketfuel datasets, in the graph interior. The presence of these larger-scale cuts is a hallmark of negative curvature or hyperbolicity [8], suggesting that Dirichlet spectral clustering may yield different behavior for hyperbolic and flat networks. The hyperbolic grids themselves are also suitable for further analysis, building from our study of regular trees. Many properties such as the spectral gap remain open questions.

With some evidence of a connection between global negative curvature, the spectral gap, and expansion, it would be interesting to empirically compare the hyperbolicity δ, the Cheeger constant h, and the traditional and Dirichlet spectral gaps of Rocketfuel and other real-world networks as well as well-known network models. From this, it could be possible to classify various networks based on these properties.

6. ACKNOWLEDGMENTS

This work was performed during an internship of A.T. at Bell Labs, Murray Hill, New Jersey and was supported by AFOSR Grants Nos. FA9550-08-1-0064 (for O.N., as a consultant with Bell Labs) and FA9550-11-1-0278.

7. REFERENCES

[1] R. Andersen, F. Chung, and K. Lang. Local graph partitioning using PageRank vectors. In *Proc. IEEE Symposium on Foundations of Computer Science (FOCS'06)*, pages 475–486, Berkeley, California, Oct. 2006.

[2] A.-L. Barabási and R. Albert. Emergence of scaling in random networks. *Science*, 286(5439):509–512, Oct. 1999.

[3] F. Chung. *Spectral Graph Theory*. AMS Press, Providence, RI, 1997.

[4] F. Chung. Random walks and local cuts in graphs. *Linear Algebra Appl.*, 423(1):22–32, May 2007.

[5] F. Chung, A. Tsiatas, and W. Xu. Dirichlet PageRank and trust-based ranking algorithms. In *Proc. Workshop on Algorithms and Models for the Web Graph (WAW'11)*, pages 103–114, Atlanta, Georgia, May 2011.

[6] P. Erdös and A. Rényi. On the evolution of random graphs. *Publ. Math. Inst. Hung. Acad. Sci., Ser. A*, 5:17–61, 1960.

Table 2: Average Cheeger ratios (h) and number of components (c) for Dirichlet and traditional spectral clustering of several Rocketfuel datasets. Extreme values are visible in Fig. 5.

Dataset	Number of cuts in each category:				Avg $c_D - c_T$	Avg $h_D - h_T$	Avg c_T	Avg h_T
	$c_D \leq c_T$ $h_D \leq h_T$	$c_D \leq c_T$ $h_D > h_T$	$c_D > c_T$ $h_D \leq h_T$	$c_D > c_T$ $h_D > h_T$				
1221	49	197	0	6	-28.9	0.0506	36.8	0.0829
1239	538	362	0	30	-75.1	0.0127	83.4	0.1326
1755	32	91	0	14	-4.5	0.0545	7.9	0.1210
2914	224	819	0	323	-107.3	0.0565	125.8	0.1639
3257	49	67	0	35	-12.3	0.0370	20.0	0.1386
3356	182	315	0	41	-34.6	0.0388	45.6	0.1895
3967	24	137	3	129	-3.2	0.1423	9.2	0.1215
4755	15	6	0	6	-12.3	-0.0970	15.4	0.3460
6461	111	199	0	73	-13.4	0.0148	19.7	0.0999
7018	157	465	12	273	-54.3	0.0403	81.4	0.0735

[7] J. Friedman. The spectra of infinite hypertrees. *SIAM J. Comput.*, 20(5):951–961, Oct. 1991.

[8] M. Gromov. Hyperbolic groups. In S. Gersten, editor, *Essays in Group Theory*, pages 75–263. Springer, New York, 1987.

[9] O. Häggström, J. Jonasson, and R. Lyons. Explicit isoperimetric constants and phase transitions in the random-cluster model. *Ann. Probab.*, 30(1):443–473, Jan. 2002.

[10] E. Jonckheere, P. Lohsoonthorn, and F. Bonahon. Scaled Gromov hyperbolic graphs. *J. Graph Theory*, 30(2):157–180, Feb. 2008.

[11] E. Jonckheere, M. Lou, F. Bonahon, and Y. Baryshnikov. Euclidean versus hyperbolic congestion in idealized versus experimental networks. *Internet Math.*, 7(1):1–27, 2011.

[12] J. Leskovec, K. Lang, A. Dasgupta, and M. W. Mahoney. Statistical properties of community structure in large social and information networks. In *Proc. International Conference on the World Wide Web (WWW'08)*, pages 695–704, Beijing, China, Apr. 2008.

[13] B. D. McKay. The expected eigenvalue distribution of a large regular graph. *Linear Algebra Appl.*, 40:203–216, Oct. 1981.

[14] O. Narayan and I. Saniee. Large-scale curvature of networks. *Phys. Rev. E*, 84(6), Dec. 2011.

[15] A. Y. Ng, M. I. Jordan, and Y. Weiss. On spectral clustering: Analysis and an algorithm. In *Advances in Neural Information Processing Systems (NIPS'02)*, pages 849–856, Vancouver, Canada, Dec. 2002.

[16] S. E. Schaeffer. Graph clustering. *Computer Science Review*, 1(1):27–64, Aug. 2007.

[17] J. Shi and J. Malik. Normalized cuts and image segmentation. 22(8):888–905, Aug. 2000.

[18] N. Spring, R. Mahajan, and D. Wetherall. Measuring ISP topologies with Rocketfuel. In *Proc. ACM SIGCOMM Conference (SIGCOMM'02)*, pages 133–145, Pittsburgh, Pennsylvania, Aug. 2002.

[19] R. Teixeira, K. Marzullo, S. Savage, and G. M. Voelker. In search of path diversity in ISP networks. In *Proc. Internet Measurement Conference (IMC'03)*, pages 313–318, Miami, Florida, Oct. 2003.

[20] U. von Luxburg. A tutorial on spectral clustering. *Statist. Comput.*, 17(4):395–416, Dec. 2007.

[21] D. Watts and S. Strogatz. Collective dynamics of 'small-world' networks. *Nature*, 393:440–442, June 1998.

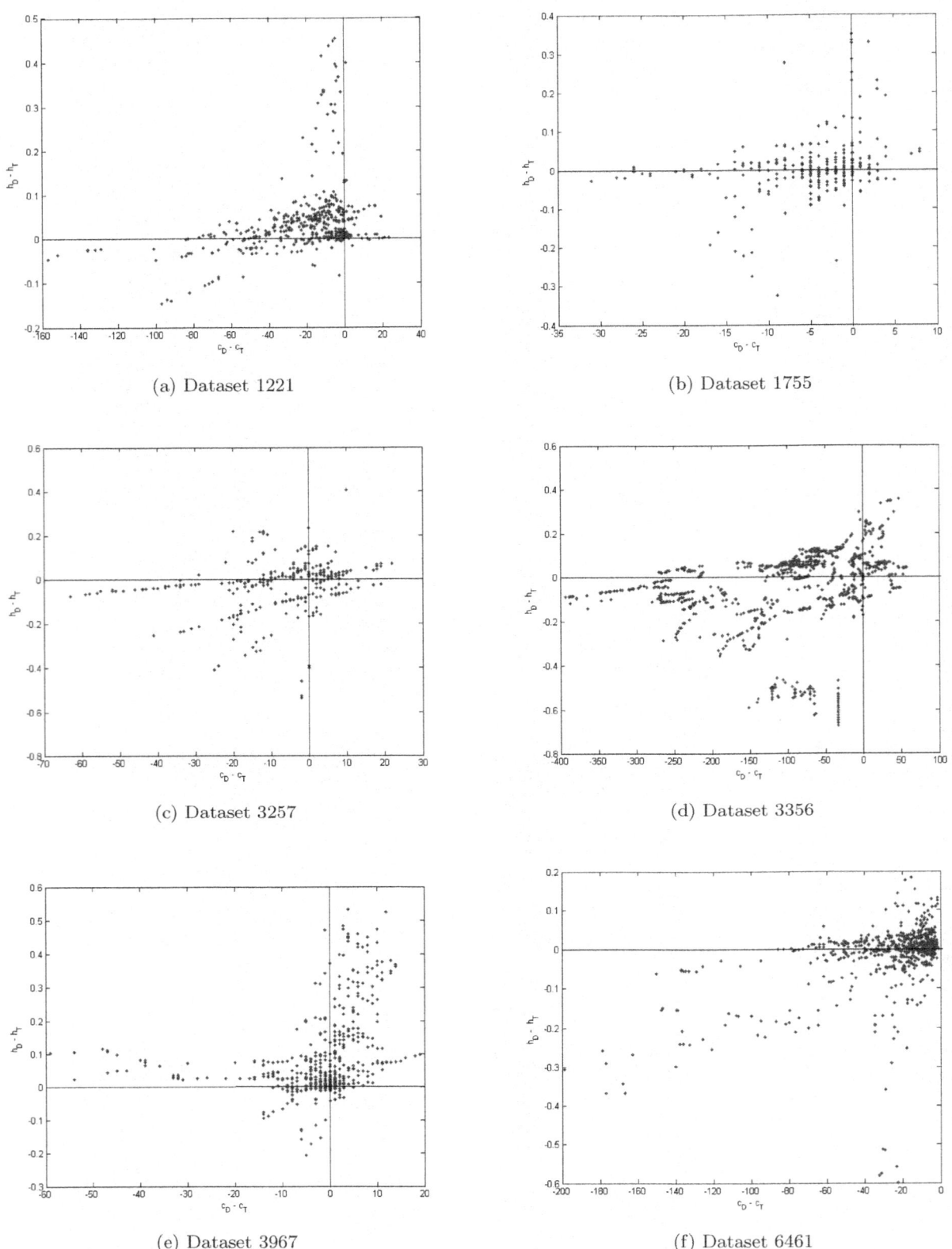

Figure 5: Comparison of Cheeger ratio h and number of components c for cuts for various datasets using Dirichlet (D) and traditional (T) spectral clustering. Each point represents one possible cut size; in general, Dirichlet clustering yields many fewer components without sacrificing much in Cheeger ratio.

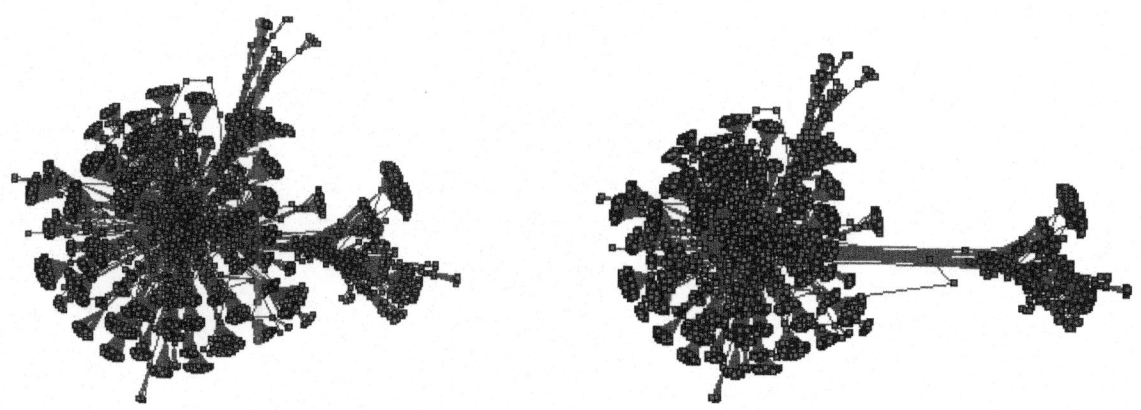

Figure 6: Partition of Rocketfuel dataset 3356 using standard (left) and Dirichlet (right) spectral clustering.

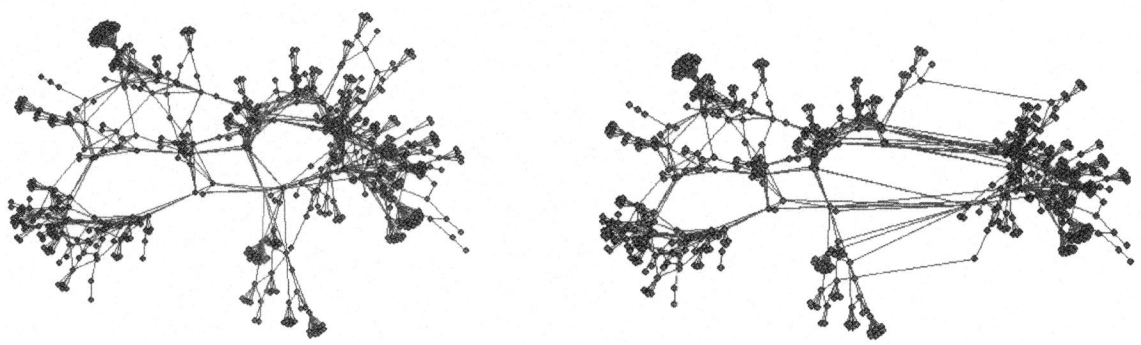

Figure 7: Partition of Rocketfuel dataset 1755 using standard (left) and Dirichlet (right) spectral clustering.

Subgraph Frequencies: Mapping the Empirical and Extremal Geography of Large Graph Collections

Johan Ugander
Cornell University
Ithaca, NY
jhu5@cornell.edu

Lars Backstrom
Facebook
Menlo Park, CA
lars@fb.com

Jon Kleinberg
Cornell University
Ithaca, NY
kleinber@cs.cornell.edu

ABSTRACT

A growing set of on-line applications are generating data that can be viewed as very large collections of small, dense social graphs — these range from sets of social groups, events, or collaboration projects to the vast collection of graph neighborhoods in large social networks. A natural question is how to usefully define a domain-independent 'coordinate system' for such a collection of graphs, so that the set of possible structures can be compactly represented and understood within a common space. In this work, we draw on the theory of graph homomorphisms to formulate and analyze such a representation, based on computing the frequencies of small induced subgraphs within each graph. We find that the space of subgraph frequencies is governed both by its combinatorial properties — based on extremal results that constrain all graphs — as well as by its empirical properties — manifested in the way that real social graphs appear to lie near a simple one-dimensional curve through this space.

We develop flexible frameworks for studying each of these aspects. For capturing empirical properties, we characterize a simple stochastic generative model, a single-parameter extension of Erdős-Rényi random graphs, whose stationary distribution over subgraphs closely tracks the one-dimensional concentration of the real social graph families. For the extremal properties, we develop a tractable linear program for bounding the feasible space of subgraph frequencies by harnessing a toolkit of known extremal graph theory. Together, these two complementary frameworks shed light on a fundamental question pertaining to social graphs: what properties of social graphs are 'social' properties and what properties are 'graph' properties?

We conclude with a brief demonstration of how the coordinate system we examine can also be used to perform classification tasks, distinguishing between structures arising from different types of social graphs.

Categories and Subject Descriptors: H.2.8 [**Database Management**]: Database applications—*Data mining*

Keywords: Social Networks, Triadic Closure, Induced Subgraphs, Subgraph Census, Graph Homomorphisms.

1. INTRODUCTION

The standard approach to modeling a large on-line social network is to treat it as a single graph with an enormous number of nodes and a sparse pattern of connections. Increasingly, however, many of the key problems encountered in managing an on-line social network involve working with large collections of small, dense graphs contained within the network.

On Facebook, for example, the set of people belonging to a group or attending an event determines such a graph, and considering the set of all groups or all events leads to a very large number of such graphs. On any social network, the network neighborhood of each individual — consisting of his or her friends and the links among them — is also generally a small dense graph with a rich structure, on a few hundred nodes or fewer [19]. If we consider the neighborhood of each user as defining a distinct graph, we again obtain an enormous collection of graphs. Indeed, this view of a large underlying social network in terms of its overlapping node neighborhoods suggests a potentially valuable perspective on the analysis of the network: rather than thinking of Facebook, for example, as a single billion-node network, with a global structure that quickly becomes incomprehensible, we argue that it can be useful to think of it as the superposition of a billion small dense graphs — the network neighborhoods, one centered at each user, and each accessible to a closer and more tractable investigation.

Nor is this view limited to a site such as Facebook; one can find collections of small dense graphs in the interactions within a set of discussion forums [7], within a set of collaborative on-line projects [20], and in a range of other settings.

Our focus in the present work is on a fundamental global question about these types of graph collections: given a large set of small dense graphs, can we study this set by defining a meaningful 'coordinate system' on it, so that the graphs it contains can be represented and understood within a common space? With such a coordinate system providing a general-purpose framework for analysis, additional questions become possible. For example, when considering collections of a billion or more social graphs, it may seem as though almost any graph is possible; is that the case, or are there underlying properties guiding the observed structures? And how do these properties relate to more fundamental combinatorial constraints deriving from the extremal limits that govern all graphs? As a further example, we can ask how different graph collections compare to one another; do network neighborhoods differ in some systematic way, for instance, from social graphs induced by other contexts, such as the graphs implicit in social groups, organized events, or other arrangements?

The Present Work. In this paper we develop and analyze such a representation, drawing on the theory of *graph homomorphisms*. Roughly speaking, the coordinate system we examine begins by describing a graph by the frequencies with which all possible small subgraphs occur within it. More precisely, we choose a small number k (e.g. $k = 3$ or 4); then, for each graph G in a collection, we create a vector with a coordinate for each distinct k-node subgraph

H, specifying the fraction of k-tuples of nodes in G that induce a copy of H (in other words, the frequency of H as an induced subgraph of G). For $k = 3$, this description corresponds to what is sometimes referred to as the *triad census* [5, 6, 21].

With each graph in the collection mapped to such a vector, we can ask how the full collection of graphs fills out this space of subgraph frequencies. This turns out to be a subtle issue, because the arrangement of the graphs in this space is governed by two distinct sets of effects: extremal combinatorial constraints showing that certain combinations of subgraph frequencies are genuinely impossible; and empirical properties, which reveal that the bulk of the graphs tend to lie close to a simple one-dimensional curve through the space. We formulate results on both these types of properties, in the former case building on an expanding body of combinatorial theory [4, 11] for bounding the frequencies at which different types of subgraphs can occur in a larger ambient graph.

The fact that the space of subgraph frequencies is constrained in these multiple ways also allows us to concretely address the following type of question: When we see that human social networks do not exhibit a certain type of structure, is that because such a structure is mathematically impossible, or simply because human beings do not create it when they form social connections? In other words, what is a property of graphs and what is a property of people? Although this question is implicit in many studies of social networks, it is hard to separate the two effects without a formal framework such as we have here.

Indeed, our framework offers a direct contribution to one of the most well-known observations about social graphs: the tendency of social relationships to close triangles, and the relative infrequency of what is sometimes called the 'forbidden triad': three people with two social relationships between them, but one absent relationship [14]. There are many sociological theories for why one would expect this subgraph to be underrepresented in empirical social networks [8]. Our framework shows that the frequency of this 'forbidden triad' has a non-trivial upper bound in not just social graphs, but in all graphs. Harnessing our framework more generally, we are in fact able to show that *any* k node subgraph that is not a complete or empty subgraph has a frequency that is bounded away from one. Thus, there is an extent to which almost all subgraphs are mathematically 'forbidden' from occurring beyond a certain frequency.

We aim to separate these mathematical limits of graphs from the complementary empirical properties of real social graphs. The fact that real graph collections have a roughly one-dimensional structure in our coordinate system leads directly to our first main question: is it possible to succinctly characterize the underlying backbone for this one-dimensional structure, and can we use such a characterization to usefully describe graphs within our coordinate system in terms of their deviation from this backbone?

The subgraph frequencies of the standard Erdős-Rényi random graph [3] $G_{n,p}$ produce a one-dimensional curve (parametrized by p) that weakly approximates the layout of the real graphs in the space, but the curve arising from this random graph model systematically deviates from the real graphs in that the random graph contains fewer triangles and more triangle-free subgraphs. This observation is consistent with the sociological principle of *triadic closure* — that triangles tend to form in social networks. As a means of closing this deviation from $G_{n,p}$, we develop a tractable stochastic model of graph generation with a single additional parameter, determining the relative rates of arbitrary edge formation and triangle-closing edge formation. The model exhibits rich behaviors, and for appropriately chosen settings of its single parameter, it produce remarkably close agreement with the subgraph frequencies observed in real data for the suite of all possible 3-node and 4-node subgraphs.

Finally, we use this representation to study how different collections of graphs may differ from one another. This arises as a question of basic interest in the analysis of large social media platforms, where users continuously manage multiple audiences [2] — ranging from their set of friends, to the members of a groups they've joined, to the attendees of events and beyond. Do these audiences differ from each other at a structural level, and if so what are the distinguishing characteristics? Using Facebook data, we identify structural differences between the graphs induced on network neighborhoods, groups, and events. The underlying basis for these differences suggests corresponding distinctions in each user's reaction to these different audiences with whom they interact.

2. DATA DESCRIPTION

Throughout our presentation, we analyze several collections of graphs collected from Facebook's social network. The collections we study are all induced graphs from the Facebook friendship graph, which records friendship connections as undirected edges between users, and thus all our induced graphs are also undirected. The framework we characterize in this work would naturally extend to provide insights about directed graphs, an extension we do not discuss. We do not include edges formed by Facebook 'subscriptions' in our study, nor do we include Facebook 'pages' or connections from users to such pages. All Facebook social graph data was analyzed in an anonymous, aggregated form.

For this work, we extracted three different collections of graphs, around which we organize our discussion:

- **Neighborhoods**: Graphs induced by the friends of a single Facebook user *ego* and the friendship connections among these individuals (excluding the ego).
- **Groups**: Graphs induced by the members of a 'Facebook group', a Facebook feature for organizing focused conversations between a small or moderate-sized set of users.
- **Events**: Graphs induced by the confirmed attendees of 'Facebook events', a Facebook feature for coordinating invitations to calendar events. Users can response 'Yes', 'No', and 'Maybe' to such invitations, and we consider only users who respond 'Yes'.

The neighborhood and groups collections were assembled in October 2012 based on monthly active user egos and current groups, while the events data was collected from all events during 2010 and 2011. For event graphs, only friendship edges formed prior to the date of the event were used. Subgraph frequencies for four-node subgraphs were computed by sampling 11,000 induced subgraphs uniformly with replacement, providing sufficiently precise frequencies without enumeration. The graph collections were targeted at a variety of different graph sizes, as will be discussed in the text.

3. SUBGRAPH SPACE

In this section, we study the space of subgraph frequencies that form the basis of our coordinate system, and the one-dimensional concentration of empirical graphs within this coordinate system. We derive a model capable of accurately identifying the backbone of this empirical concentration using only the basic principle of *triadic closure*, showing how the subgraph frequencies of empirical social graphs are seemingly restricted to the vicinity of a simple one-dimensional structure.

Formally, the subgraph frequency of a k-node graph F in an n-node graph G (where $k \leq n$) is the probability that a random

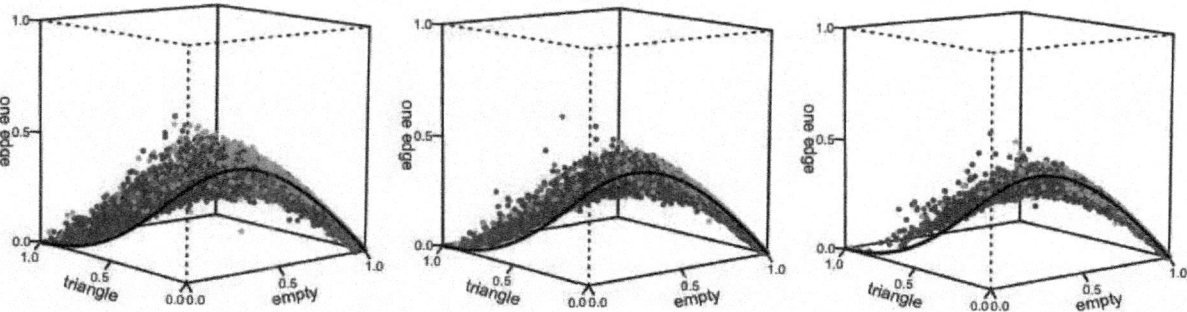

Figure 1: Subgraph frequencies for three node subgraphs for graphs of size 50, 100, and 200 (left to right). The neighborhoods are orange, groups are green, and events are lavender. The black curves illustrate $G_{n,p}$ as a function of p.

k-node subset of G induces a copy of F. It is clear that for any integer k, the subgraph frequencies of all the k-node graphs sum to one, constraining the vector of frequencies to an appropriately dimensioned simplex. In the case of $k = 3$, this vector is simply the relative frequency of induced three-node subgraphs restricted to the 4-simplex; there are just four such subgraphs, with zero, one, two, and three edges respectively. When considering the frequency of larger subgraphs, the dimension of the simplex grows very quickly, and already for $k = 4$, the space of four-node subgraph frequencies lives in an 11-simplex.

Empirical distribution. In Figure 1, the three-node subgraph frequencies of 50-node, 100-node, and 200-node graph collections are shown, with each subplot showing a balanced mixture of 17,000 neighborhood, group and event graphs – the three collections discussed in Section 2, totaling 51,000 graphs at each size. Because these frequency vectors are constrained to the 4-simplex, their distribution can be visualized in $\mathbb{R}^3$ with three of the frequencies as axes.

Notice that these graph collections, induced from disparate contexts, all occupy a sharply concentrated subregion of the unit simplex. The points in the space have been represented simply as an unordered scatterplot, and two striking phenomena already stand out: first, the particular concentrated structure within the simplex that the points follow; and second, the fact that we can already discern a non-uniform distribution of the three contexts (neighborhoods, groups and events) within the space — that is, the different contexts can already be seen to have different structural loci. Notice also that as the sizes of the graphs increases – from 50 to 100 to 200 – the distribution appears to sharpen around the one-dimensional backbone. The vast number of graphs that we are able to consider by studying Facebook data is here illuminating a structure that is simply not discernible in previous examinations of subgraph frequencies [6], since no analysis has previously considered a collection near this scale.

The imagery of Figure 1 directly motivates our work, by visually framing the essence of our investigation: what facets of this curious structure derive from our graphs being social graphs, and what facets are simply universal properties of all graphs? We will find, in particular, that parts of the space of subgraph frequencies are in fact inaccessible to graphs for purely combinatorial reasons — it is mathematically impossible for one of the points in the scatterplot to occupy these parts of the space. But there are other parts of the space that are mathematically possible; it is simply that no real social graphs appear to be located within them. Intuitively, then, we are looking at a population density within an ambient space (the Facebook graphs within the space of subgraph frequencies), and we would like to understand both the geography of the inhabited terrain (what are the properties of the areas where the population

has in fact settled?) and also the properties of the boundaries of the space as a whole (where, in principle, would it be possible for the population to settle?).

Also in Figure 1, we plot the curve for the frequencies for 3 node subgraphs in $G_{n,p}$ as a function of p. The curves are given simply by the probability of obtaining the desired number of edges in a three node graph, $((1 - p)^3, 3p(1 - p)^2, 3p^2(1 - p), p^3)$. This curve closely tracks the empirical density through the space, with a single notable discrepancy: the real world graphs systemically contain more triangles when compared to $G_{n,p}$ at the same edge density. We emphasize that it is not a priori clear why $G_{n,p}$ would at all be a good model of subgraph frequencies in modestly-sized dense social graphs such as the neighborhoods, groups, and events that we have here; we believe the fact that it tracks the data with any fidelity at all is an interesting issue for future work. Beyond $G_{n,p}$, in the following subsection, we present a stochastic model of edge formation and deletion on graphs specifically designed to close the remaining discrepancy. As such, our model provides a means of accurately characterizing the backbone of subgraph frequencies for social graphs.

Stochastic model of edge formation. The classic Erdős-Rényi model of random graphs, $G_{n,p}$, produces a distribution over n-node undirected graphs defined by a simple parameter p, the probability of each edge independently appearing in the graph. We now introduce and analyze a related random graph model, the *Edge Formation Random Walk*, defined as a random walk over the space of all unlabeled n-node graphs. In its simplest form, this model is closely related to $G_{n,p}$, and will we show via detailed balance that the distribution defined by $G_{n,p}$ on n-node graphs is precisely the stationary distribution of this simplest version of the random walk on the space of n-node graphs. We first describe this basic version of the model; we then add a component to the model that captures a triadic closure process, which produces a close fit to the properties we observe in real graphs.

Let $\mathcal{G}_n$ be the space of all unlabeled n-node graphs, and let $X(t)$ be the following continuous time Markov chain on the state space $\mathcal{G}_n$. The transition rates between the graphs in $\mathcal{G}_n$ are defined by random additions and deletions of edges, with all edges having a uniform formation rate $\gamma > 0$ and a uniform deletion rate $\delta > 0$. Thus the single parameter $\nu = \gamma/\delta$, the effective formation rate of edges, completely characterizes the process. Notice that this process is clearly irreducible, since it is possible to transition between any two graphs via edge additions and deletions.

Since $X(t)$ is irreducible, it possesses a unique stationary distribution. The stationary distribution of an irreducible continuous time Markov chain can be found as the unique stable fixed point of the linear dynamical system $X'(t) = Q_n(\nu)X(t)$ that describes the diffusion of probability mass during a random walk on n-node

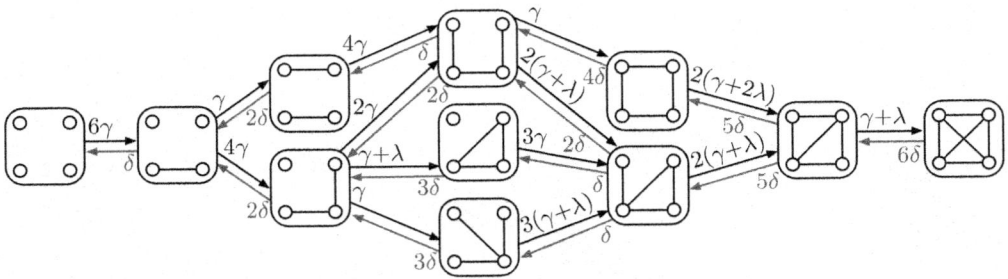

Figure 2: The state transitions diagram for our stochastic graph model with $k = 4$, where γ is the arbitrary edge formation rate, λ is the triadic closure formation rate, and δ is the edge elimination rate.

graphs, where $Q_n(\nu)$ is the generator matrix with transition rates q_{ij} and $q_{ii} = -\sum_{j \neq i} q_{ji}$, all depending only on ν. The stationary distribution π_n then satisfies $Q_n(\nu)\pi_n = 0$.

The following proposition shows the clear relationship between the stationary distribution of this simplest random walk and the frequencies of $G_{n,p}$.

PROPOSITION 3.1. *The probabilities assigned to (unlabeled) graphs by $G_{n,p}$ satisfy the detailed balance condition for the Edge Formation Random Walk with edge formation rate $\nu = p/1 - p$, and thus characterizes the stationary distribution.*

PROOF. We first describe an equivalent Markov chain based on labeled graphs: there is a state for each labeled n-node graph; the transition rate q_{ij} from a labelled graph G_i to a labelled graph G_j is $q_{ij} = \gamma$ if G_j can be obtained from G_i by adding an edge; and $q_{ij} = \delta$ if G_j can be obtained from G_i by removing an edge. All other transition rates are zero. We call this new chain the *labeled chain*, and the original chain the *unlabeled chain*.

Now, suppose there is a transition from unlabeled graph H_a to unlabeled graph H_b in the unlabeled chain, with transition probability $k\gamma$. This means that there are k ways to add an edge to a labeled copy of H_a to produce a graph isomorphic to H_b. Now, let G_i be any graph in the labeled chain that is isomorphic to H_a. In the labeled chain, there are k transitions out of G_i leading to a graph isomorphic to H_b, and each of these has probability γ. Thus, with probability $k\gamma$, a transition out of G_i leads to a graph isomorphic to H_b. A strictly analogous argument can be made for edge deletions, rather than edge additions.

This argument shows that the following describes a Markov chain equivalent to the original unlabeled chain: we draw a sequence of labeled graphs from the labeled chain, and we output the isomorphism classes of these labeled graphs. Hence, to compute the stationary distribution of the original unlabeled chain, which is what we seek, we can compute the stationary distribution of the labeled chain and then sum stationary probabilities in the labeled chain over the isomorphism classes of labeled graphs.

It thus suffices to verify the detailed balance condition for the distribution on the labeled chain that assigns probability $p^{|E(G_i)|}(1-p)^{\binom{n}{2}-|E(G_i)|}$ to each labeled graph G_i. Since every transition of the labeled walk occurs between two labeled graphs G_i and G_j, with $|E(G_i)| = |E(G_j)| + 1$, the only non-trivial detailed balance equations are of the form:

$$\begin{aligned} q_{ij}\Pr[X(t) = G_i] &= q_{ji}\Pr[X(t) = G_j] \\ \Pr[X(t) = G_i] &= \nu\Pr[X(t) = G_j] \\ \Pr[X(t) = G_i] &= \frac{p}{1-p}\Pr[X(t) = G_j]. \end{aligned}$$

Since the probability assigned to the labeled graph G_i by $G_{n,p}$ is simply $p^{|E(G_i)|}(1-p)^{\binom{n}{2}-|E(G_i)|}$, detailed balance is clearly satisfied. □

Incorporating triadic closure. The above modeling framework provides a simple analog of $G_{n,p}$ that notably exposes itself to subtle adjustments. By simply adjusting the transition rates between select graphs, this framework makes it possible to model random graphs where certain types of edge formations or deletions have irregular probabilities of occurring, simply via small perturbations away from the classic $G_{n,p}$ model. Using this principle, we now characterize a random graph model that differs from $G_{n,p}$ by a single parameter, λ, the rate at which 3-node paths in the graph tend to form triangles. We call this model the *Edge Formation Random Walk with Triadic Closure*.

Again let $\mathcal{G}_n$ be the space of all unlabeled n-node graphs, and let $Y(t)$ be a continuous time Markov chain on the state space $\mathcal{G}_n$. As with the ordinary Edge Formation Random Walk, let edges have a uniform formation rate $\gamma > 0$ and a uniform deletion rate $\delta > 0$, but now also add a triadic closure formation rate $\lambda \geq 0$ for every 3-node path that a transition would close. The process is still clearly irreducible, and the stationary distribution obeys the stationary conditions $Q_n(\nu,\lambda)\pi_n = 0$, where the generator matrix Q_n now also depends on λ. We can express the stationary distribution directly in the parameters as $\pi_n(\nu,\lambda) = \{\pi : Q_n(\nu,\lambda)\pi = 0\}$. For $\lambda = 0$ the model reduces to the ordinary Edge Formation Random Walk.

The state transitions of this random graph model are easy to construct for $n = 3$ and $n = 4$, and transitions for the case of $n = 4$ are shown in Figure 2. Proposition 3.1 above tells us that for $\lambda = 0$, the stationary distribution of a random walk on this state space is given by the graph frequencies of $G_{n,p}$. As we increase λ away from zero, we should therefore expect to see a stationary distribution that departs from $G_{n,p}$ precisely by observing more graphs with triangles and less graphs with open triangles.

The framework of our Edge Formation Random Walk makes it possible to model triadic closure precisely; in this sense the model forms an interesting contrast with other models of triangle-closing in graphs that are very challenging to analyze (e.g. [9, 10]). We will now show how the addition of this single parameter makes it possible to describe the subgraph frequencies of empirical social graphs with remarkable accuracy.

Fitting subgraph frequencies. The stationary distribution of an Edge Formation Random Walk model describes the frequency of different graphs, while the coordinate system we are developing focuses on the frequency of k-node subgraphs within n-node graphs. For $G_{n,p}$ these two questions are in fact the same, since the distribution of random induced k-node subgraphs of $G_{n,p}$ is simply $G_{k,p}$. When we introduce $\lambda > 0$, however, our model departs from this symmetry, and the stationary probabilities in a random walk on k node graphs is no longer precisely the frequencies of induced k-node subgraphs in a single n-node graph.

But if we view this as a model for the frequency of small graphs as objects in themselves, rather than as subgraphs of a larger ambient graph, the model provides a highly tractable parameterization

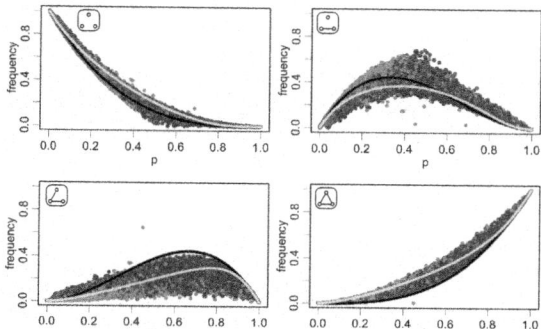

Figure 3: Subgraph frequencies for 3-node subgraphs in 50-node graphs, shown as a function of p. The black curves illustrate $G_{n,p}$, while the yellow curves illustrate the fit model.

that we can use to approximate the structure of subgraph frequencies observed in our families of larger graphs. In doing so, we aim to fit $\pi_k(\nu(p,\lambda),\lambda)$ as a function of p, where $\nu(p,\lambda)$ is the rate parameter ν that produces edge density p for the specific value of λ. For $\lambda = 0$ this relationship is simply $\nu = p/(1-p)$, but for $\lambda > 0$ the relation is not so tidy, and in practice it is easier to fit ν numerically rather than evaluate the expression.

When considering a collection of graph frequencies we can fit λ by minimizing residuals with respect to the model. Given a collection of N graphs, let $y_k^1, \ldots, y_k^N$ be the vectors of k-node subgraph frequencies for each graph and $p^1, \ldots, p^N$ be the edge densities. We can then fit λ as:

$$\lambda_k^{opt} = \arg\min_\lambda \sum_{i=1}^N \|\pi_k(\nu(p^i,\lambda),\lambda) - y_k^i\|_2.$$

In Figure 3 we plot the three-node subgraph frequencies as a function of edge density p, for a collection of 300,000 50-node subgraphs, again a balanced mixture of neighborhoods, groups, and events. In this figure we also plot (in yellow) the curve resulting from fitting our random walk model with triadic closure, $\pi_k(\nu(p,\lambda_k^{opt}),\lambda_k^{opt})$, which is thus parameterized as a function of edge density p. For this mixture of collections and $k = 3$, the optimal fit is $\lambda_3^{opt} = 1.61$. Notice how the yellow line deviates from the black $G_{n,p}$ curve to better represent the backbone of natural graph frequencies. From the figure it is clear that almost all graphs have more triangles than a sample from $G_{n,p}$ of corresponding edge density. When describing extremal bounds in Section 4, we will discuss how $G_{n,p}$ is in fact by no means the extremal lower bound.

As suggested by Figure 2, examining the subgraph frequencies for four-node subgraphs is fully tractable. In Figure 4, we fit λ to the mean subgraph frequencies of our three different collections of graphs separately. Note that the mean of the subgraph frequencies over a set of graphs is not necessarily itself a subgraph frequency corresponding to a graph, but we fit these mean 11-vectors as a demonstration of the model's ability to fit an 'average' graph. The subgraph frequency of $G_{n,p}$ at the edge density corresponding to the data is shown as a black dashed line in each plot — with poor agreement — and gray dashed lines illustrate an incremental transition in λ, starting from zero (when it corresponds to $G_{n,p}$) and ending at λ^{opt}.

The striking agreement between the fit model and the mean of each collection is achieved at the corresponding edge density by fitting only λ. For neighborhood graphs, this agreement deviates measurably on only a single subgraph frequency, the four-node star. The y-axis is plotted on a logarithmic scale, which makes it rather

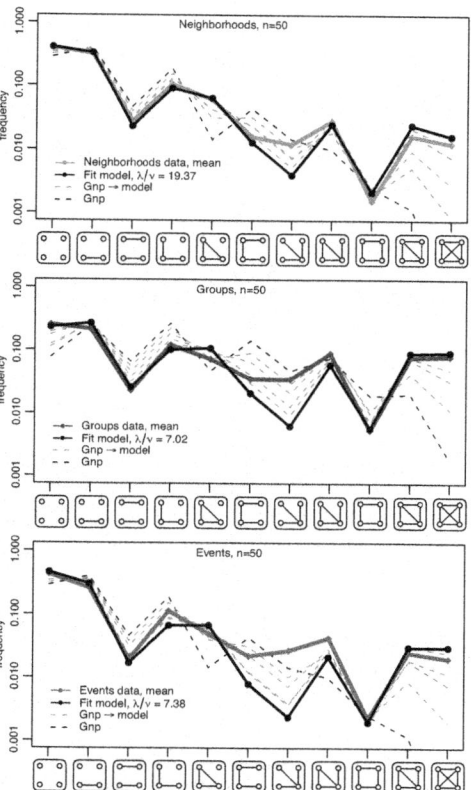

Figure 4: The four-node subgraph frequencies for the means of the 50-node graph collections in Figure 3, and the subgraph frequency of the model, fitting the triadic closure rate λ to the mean vectors. As λ increases from $\lambda = 0$ to $\lambda = \lambda_{opt}$, we see how this single additional parameter provides a striking fit.

remarkable how precisely the model describes the scarcity of the four-node cycle. The scarcity of squares has been previously observed in email neighborhoods on Facebook [18], and our model provides the first intuitive explanation of this scarcity.

The model's ability to characterize the backbone of the empirical graph frequencies suggests that the subgraph frequencies of individual graphs can be usefully studied as deviations from this backbone. In fact, we can interpret the fitting procedure for λ as a variance minimization procedure. Recall that the mean of a set of points in $\mathbb{R}^n$ is the point that minimizes the sum of squared residuals. In this way, the procedure is in fact fitting the 'mean curve' of the model distribution to the empirical subgraph frequencies.

Finally, our model can be used to provide a measure of the triadic closure strength differentially between graph collections, investigating the difference in λ^{opt} for the subgraph frequencies of different graph collections. In Figure 4, the three different graph types resulted in notably different ratios of λ/ν — the ratio of the triadic closure formation rate to the basic process rate — with a significantly higher value for this ratio in neighborhoods. We can interpret this as saying that open triads in neighborhoods are more prone to triadic closure than open triads in groups or events.

4. EXTREMAL BOUNDS

As discussed at the beginning of the previous section, we face two problems in analyzing the subgraph frequencies of real graphs: to characterize the distribution of values we observe in practice, and to understand the combinatorial structure of the overall space in which these empirical subgraph frequencies lie. Having developed stochastic models to address the former question, we now consider the latter question.

Specifically, in this section we characterize extremal bounds on the set of possible subgraph frequencies. Using machinery from the theory of graph homomorphisms, we identify fundamental bounds on the space of subgraph frequencies that are not properties of social graphs, but rather, are universal properties of all graphs. By identifying these bounds, we make apparent large tracts of the feasible region that are theoretically inhabitable but not populated by any of the empirical social graphs we examine.

We first review a body of techniques based in extremal graph theory and the theory of graph homomorphisms [11]. We use these techniques to formulate a set of inequalities on subgraph frequencies; these inequalities are all linear for a fixed edge density, an observation that allows us to cleanly construct a linear program to maximize and minimize each subgraph frequency within the combined constraints. In this manner, we show how it is possible to map outer bounds on the geography of all these structural constraints. We conclude by offering two basic propositions that transcend all edge densities, thus identifying fundamental limits on subgraph frequencies of all sizes.

4.1 Background on subgraph frequency and homomorphism density

In this subsection, we review some background arising from the theory of graph homomorphisms. We will use this homomorphism machinery to develop inequalities governing subgraph frequencies. These inequalities allow us to describe the outlines of the space underlying Figure 1(a) — the first step in understanding which aspects of the distribution of subgraph frequencies in the simplex are the result of empirical properties of human social networks, and which are the consequences of purely combinatorial constraints.

Linear constraints on subgraph frequency. Let $s(F, G)$ denote the subgraph frequency of F in G, as defined in the last section: the probability that a random $|V(F)|$-node subset of G induces a copy of F. Note that since $s(F, G)$ is a probability over outcomes, it is subject to the law of total probability. The law of total probability for subgraph frequencies takes the following form.

PROPOSITION 4.1. *For any graph F and any integer $\ell \geq k$, where $|V(F)| = k$, the subgraph density of F in G, $s(F, G)$ satisfies the equality*

$$s(F, G) = \sum_{\{H : |V(H)| = \ell\}} s(F, H) s(H, G).$$

PROOF. Let H' be a random ℓ-vertex induced subgraph of G. Now, the set of outcomes $\mathcal{H} = \{H : |V(H)| = \ell\}$ form a partition of the sample space, each with probability $s(H, G)$. Furthermore, conditional upon an ℓ-vertex induced subgraph being isomorphic to H, $s(F, H)$ is the probability that a random k-vertex induced subgraph of H is isomorphic to F. □

This proposition characterizes an important property of subgraph frequencies: the vector of subgraph frequencies on k nodes exists in a linear subspace of the vector of subgraph frequencies on $\ell > k$ nodes. Furthermore, this means that any constraint on the frequency of a subgraph F will also constrain the frequency of any subgraph H for which $s(F, H) > 0$ or $s(H, F) > 0$.

Graph homomorphisms. A number of fundamental inequalities on the occurrence of subgraphs are most naturally formulated in terms of *graph homomorphisms*, a notion that is connected to but distinct from the notion of induced subgraphs. In order to describe this machinery, we first review some basic definitions [4]. if F and G are labelled graphs, a map $f : V(F) \to V(G)$ is a *homomorphism* if each edge (v, w) of F maps to an edge $(f(v), f(w))$ of G. We now write $t(F, G)$ for the probability that a random map from $V(F)$ into $V(G)$ is a homomorphism, and we refer to $t(F, G)$ as a *homomorphism density* of F and G.

There are three key differences between the homomorphism density $t(F, G)$ and the subgraph frequency $s(F, G)$ defined earlier in this section. First, $t(F, G)$ is based on mappings of F into G that can be many-to-one — multiple nodes of F can map to the same node of G — while $s(F, G)$ is based on one-to-one mappings. Second, $t(F, G)$ is based on mappings of F into G that must map edges to edges, but impose no condition on pairs of nodes in F that do not form edges: in other words, a homomorphism is allowed to map a pair of unlinked nodes in F to an edge of G. This is not the case for $s(F, G)$, which is based on maps that require non-edges of F to be mapped to non-edges of G. Third, $t(F, G)$ is a frequency among mappings from labeled graphs F to labelled graphs G, while $s(F, G)$ is a frequency among mappings from unlabeled F to unlabeled G.

From these three differences, it is not difficult to write down a basic relationship governing the functions s and t [4]. To do this, it is useful to define the intermediate notion $t_{\text{inj}}(F, G)$, which is the probability that a random *one-to-one* map from $V(F)$ to $V(G)$ is a homomorphism. Since only an $O(1/V(G))$ fraction of all maps from $V(F)$ to $V(G)$ are not one-to-one, we have

$$t(F, G) = t_{\text{inj}}(F, G) + O(1/|V(G)|). \qquad (1)$$

Next, by definition, a one-to-one map f of F into G is a homomorphism if and only if the image $f(F)$, when viewed as an induced subgraph of G, contains all of F's edges and possibly others. Correcting also for the conversion from labelled to unlabeled graphs, we have

$$t_{\text{inj}}(F, G) = \sum_{F' : F \subseteq F'} \frac{\text{ext}(F, F') \cdot \text{aut}(F')}{k!} \cdot s(F', G), \qquad (2)$$

where aut(F') is the number of automorphisms of F' and ext(F, F') is the number of ways that a labelled graph F can be extended (by adding edges) to form a labelled graph H isomorphic to F'.

Homomorphism inequalities. There are a number of non-trivial results bounding the graph homomorphism density, which we now review. By translating these to the language of subgraph frequencies, we can begin to develop bounds on the simplexes in Figure 1.

For complete graphs, the Kruskal-Katona Theorem produces upper bounds on homomorphism density in terms of the edge density while the Moon-Moser Theorem provides lower bounds, also in terms of the edge density.

PROPOSITION 4.2 (KRUSKAL-KATONA [11]). *For a complete graph K_r on r nodes and graph G with edge density $t(K_2, G)$,*

$$t(K_r, G) \leq t(K_2, G)^{r/2}.$$

PROPOSITION 4.3 (MOON-MOSER [12, 16]). *For a complete graph K_r on r nodes and graph G with edge density $t(K_2, G) \in [(k-2)/(k-1), 1]$,*

$$t(K_r, G) \geq \prod_{i=1}^{r-1}(1 - i(1 - t(K_2, G))).$$

The Moon-Moser bound is well known to not be sharp, and Razborov has recently given an impressive sharp lower bound for the homomorphism density of the triangle K_3 [16] using sophisticated machinery [15]. We limit our discussion to the simpler Moon-Moser lower bound which takes the form of a concise polynomial and provides bounds for arbitrary r, not just the triangle ($r = 3$).

Finally, we employ a powerful inequality that is known to lower bound the homomorphism density of any graph F that is either a forest, an even cycle, or a complete bipartite graph. Stated as such, it is the solved special cases of the open *Sidorenko Conjecture*, which posits that the result could be extended to all bipartite graphs F. We will use the following proposition in particular when F is a tree, and will refer to this part of the result as the *Sidorenko tree bound*.

PROPOSITION 4.4 (SIDORENKO [11, 17]). *For a graph F that is a forest, even cycle, or complete bipartite graph, with edge set $E(F)$, and G with edge density $t(K_2, G)$,*

$$t(F, G) \geq t(K_2, G)^{|E(F)|}.$$

Using Equations (1) and (2), we can translate statements about homomorphisms into asymptotic statements about the combined frequency of particular sets of subgraphs. We can also translate statements about frequencies of subgraphs to frequencies of their complements using the following basic fact.

LEMMA 4.5. *If for graphs $F_1, \ldots F_\ell$, coefficients $\alpha_i \in \mathbb{R}$, and a function f,*

$$\alpha_1 s(F_1, G) + \ldots + \alpha_\ell s(F_\ell, G) \geq f(s(K_2, G)), \forall G,$$

then

$$\alpha_1 s(\overline{F_1}, G) + \ldots + \alpha_\ell s(\overline{F_\ell}, G) \geq f(1 - s(K_2, G)), \forall G.$$

PROOF. Note that $s(F, G) = s(\overline{F}, \overline{G})$. Thus if

$$\alpha_1 s(\overline{F_1}, \overline{G}) + \ldots + \alpha_\ell s(\overline{F_\ell}, \overline{G}) \geq f(s(\overline{K_2}, \overline{G})), \forall G,$$

then

$$\alpha_1 s(\overline{F_1}, G) + \ldots + \alpha_\ell s(\overline{F_\ell}, G) \geq f(s(\overline{K_2}, G)), \forall G,$$

where $s(\overline{K_2}, G) = 1 - s(K_2, G)$. □

4.2 An LP for subgraph frequency bounds

In the previous section, we reviewed linear constraints between the frequencies of subgraphs of different sizes, and upper and lower bounds on graph homomorphism densities with applications to subgraph frequencies. We will now use these constraints to assemble a linear program capable to mapping out bounds on the extremal geography of the subgraph space we are considering. To do this, we will maximize and minimize the frequency of each individual subgraph frequency, subject to the constraints we have just catalogued.

We will focus our analysis on the cases $k = 3$, the triad frequencies, and $k = 4$, the quad frequencies. Let x_1, x_2, x_3, x_4 denote the subgraph frequencies $s(\cdot, G)$ of the four possible 3-vertex undirected graphs, ordered by increasing edge count.

PROGRAM 4.6. *The frequency x_i of a 3-node subgraph in any graph G with edge density p is bounded asymptotically (in $|V(G)|$) by $\max / \min x_i$ subject to $x_i \geq 0, \forall i$ and:*

$$x_1 + x_2 + x_3 + x_4 = 1, \qquad \frac{1}{3}x_2 + \frac{2}{3}x_3 + x_4 = p, \quad (3)$$

$$x_4 \leq p^{3/2}, \qquad x_1 \leq (1-p)^{3/2}, \quad (4)$$

$$x_4 \geq p(2p-1) \qquad p \geq 1/2, \quad (5)$$

$$x_1 \geq (1-p)(1-2p) \qquad p \leq 1/2, \quad (6)$$

$$(1/3)x_3 + x_4 \geq p^2, \qquad x_1 + (1/3)x_2 \geq (1-p)^2. \quad (7)$$

Here the equalities in (3) derive from the linear constraints, the constraints in (4) derive from Kruskal-Katona, the constraints (5-6) derive from Moon-Moser, and the constraints in (7) derive from the Sidorenko tree bound. More generally, we obtain the following general linear program that can be used to find nontrivial bounds for any subgraph frequency:

PROGRAM 4.7. *The frequency f_F of a k-node subgraph F in any graph G with edge density p is bounded asymptotically (in $|V(G)|$) by $\max / \min f_F$, subject to $Af_F = b(p), Cf_F \leq d(p)$, appropriately assembled.*

From Program 1 given above it is possible to derive a simple upper bound on the frequency of the 3-node-path (sometimes described in the social networks literature as the "forbidden triad", as mentioned earlier).

PROPOSITION 4.8. *The subgraph frequency of the 3-node-path F obeys $s(F, G) \leq 3/4 + o(1), \forall G$.*

PROOF. Let x_1, x_2, x_3, x_4 again denote the subgraph frequencies $s(\cdot, G)$ of the four possible 3-vertex undirected graphs, ordered by increasing edge count, where x_3 is the frequency of the 3-node-path. By the linear constraints,

$$(1/3)x_2 + (2/3)x_3 + x_4 = p,$$

while by Moon-Moser, $x_4 + O(1/|V(G)|) \geq p(2p-1)$. Combining these two constraints we have:

$$x_3 \leq 3p(1-p) + o(1).$$

The polynomial in p is maximized at $p = 1/2$, giving an upper bound of $3/4 + o(1)$. □

This bound on the "forbidden triad" is immediately apparent from Figure 5 as well, which shows the bounds constructed via linear programs for all 3-node and 4-node subgraph frequencies. In fact, the subgraph frequency of the 'forbidden' 3-node-path in the balanced complete bipartite graph $K_{n/2,n/2}$, which has edge density $p = 1/2$, is exactly $s(F, G) = 3/4$, demonstrating that this bound is asymptotically tight. (In fact, we can perform a more careful analysis showing that it is exactly tight for even n.)

Figure 5 illustrates these bounds for $k = 3$ and $k = 4$. Notice that our empirical distributions of subgraph frequencies fall well within these bounds, leaving large tracts of the bounded area uninhabited by any observed dense social graph. While the bounds do not fully characterize the feasible region of subgraph frequencies, the fact that the bound is asymptotically tight at $p = 1/2$ for the complete bipartite graph $K_{n/2,n/2}$ is important — practically no empirical social graphs come close to the boundary, despite this evidence that it is feasibly approachable. We emphasize that an exact characterization of the feasible space would necessitate machinery at least as sophisticated as that used by Razborov.

In the next subsection we develop two more general observations about the subgraph frequencies of arbitrary graphs, the latter of which illustrates that, with the exception of clique subgraphs and empty subgraphs, it is always possible to be free from a subgraph. This shows that the lower regions of the non-clique non-empty frequency bounds in Figure 5 are always inhabitable, despite the fact that social graphs do not empirically populate these regions.

4.3 Bounding frequencies of arbitrary subgraphs

The upper bound for the frequency of the 3-node-path given in Proposition 4.8 amounted to simply combining appropriate upper bounds for different regions of possible edge densities p. In this

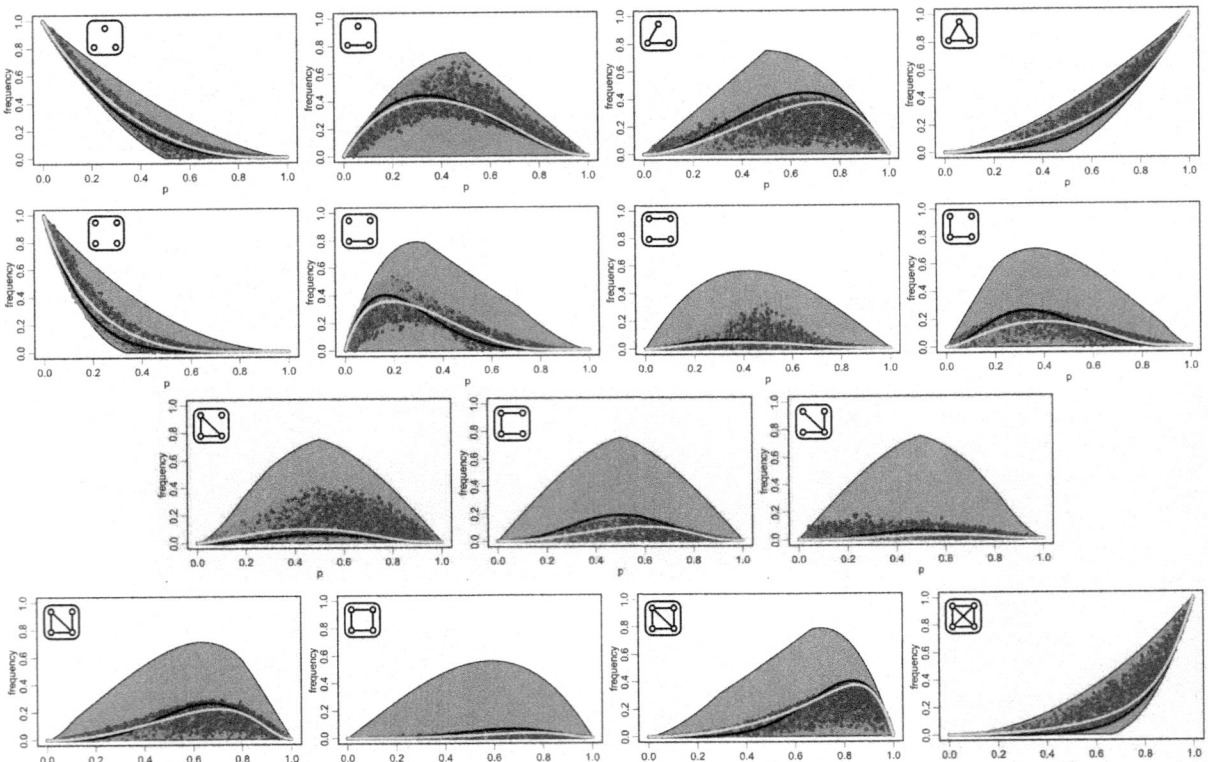

Figure 5: Subgraph frequencies for 3-node and 4-node subgraphs as function of edge density p. The light green regions denote the asymptotically feasible region found via the linear program. The empirical frequencies are as in Figure 3. The black curves illustrate $G_{n,p}$, while the yellow curves illustrate the fit triadic closure model.

section, we provide two general bounds pertaining to the subgraph frequency of an arbitrary subgraph F. First, we show that any subgraph that is not a clique and is not empty must have a subgraph density bounded strictly away from one. Second, we show that for every subgraph F that is not a clique and not empty, it is always possible to construct a family of graphs with any specified asymptotic edge density p that contains no induced copies of F.

With regard to Figures 5, the first of the results in this subsection uses the Sidorenko tree bound to show that in fact no subgraph other than the clique or the empty graph, not even for large values of k, has a feasible region that can reach a frequency of $1 - o(1)$. The second statement demonstrates that it is always possible to be free of any subgraph that is not a clique or an empty graph, even if this does not occur in the real social graphs we observe.

PROPOSITION 4.9. *For every k, there exist constants ε and n_0 such that the following holds. If F is a k-node subgraph that is not a clique and not empty, and G is any graph on $n \geq n_0$ nodes, then $s(F, G) < 1 - \varepsilon$.*

PROOF. Let S_k denote the k-node star — in other words the tree consisting of a single node linked to $k - 1$ leaves. By Equation (1), if G has n nodes, then $t_{\text{inj}}(S_k, G) \geq t(S_k, G) - c/n$ for an absolute constant c. We now state our condition on ε and n_0 in the statement of the proposition: we choose ε small enough and n_0 large enough so that

$$\frac{(1-\varepsilon)^k}{2\binom{k}{2}^{k-1}} > \max\left(\varepsilon, \frac{c}{n}\right). \quad (8)$$

For a k-node graph F, let $\mathcal{P}(F)$ denote the property that for all graphs G on at least n_0 nodes, we have $s(F, G) < 1 - \varepsilon$. Our goal is to show that $\mathcal{P}(F)$ holds for all k-node F that are neither the clique nor the empty graph. We observe that since $s(F, G) = s(\overline{F}, \overline{G})$, the property $\mathcal{P}(F)$ holds if and only if $\mathcal{P}(\overline{F})$ holds.

The basic idea of the proof is to consider any k-node graph F that is neither complete nor empty, and to argue that the star S_k lacks a one-to-one homomorphism into at least one of F or $\overline{F}$ — suppose it is F. The Sidorenko tree bound says that S_k must have a non-trivial number of one-to-one homomorphisms into G; but the images of these homomorphisms must be places where F is not found as an induced subgraph, and this puts an upper bound on the frequency of F.

We now describe this argument in more detail; we start by considering any specific k-node graph F that is neither a clique nor an empty graph. We first claim that there cannot be a one-to-one homomorphism from S_k into both of F and $\overline{F}$. For if there is a one-to-one homomorphism from S_k into F, then F must contain a node of degree $k - 1$; this node would then be isolated in $\overline{F}$, and hence there would be no one-to-one homomorphism from S_k into $\overline{F}$. Now, since it is enough to prove that just one of $\mathcal{P}(F)$ or $\mathcal{P}(\overline{F})$ holds, we choose one of F or $\overline{F}$ for which there is no one-to-one homomorphism from S_k. Renaming if necessary, let us assume it is F.

Suppose by way of contradiction that $s(F, G) \geq 1 - \varepsilon$. Let q denote the edge density of F — that is, $q = |E(F)|/\binom{k}{2}$. The edge density p of G can be written, using Proposition 4.1, as

$$p = s(K_2, G) = \sum_{\{H : |V(H)| = k\}} s(K_2, H) s(H, G)$$
$$\geq s(K_2, F) s(F, G) \geq q(1 - \varepsilon).$$

By a *k-set* of G, we mean a set of k nodes in G. We color the k-sets of G according to the following rule. Let U be a k-set of G: we color U *blue* if $G[U]$ is isomorphic to F, and we color U *red* if there is a one-to-one homomorphism from S_k to $G[U]$. We leave the k-set uncolored if it is neither blue nor red under these rules. We observe that no k-set U can be colored both blue and red, for if it is blue, then $G[U]$ is isomorphic to F, and hence there is no one-to-one homomorphism from S_k into $G[U]$. Also, note that $s(F, G) \geq 1 - \varepsilon$ is equivalent to saying that at least a $(1 - \varepsilon)$ fraction of all k-sets are blue.

Finally, what fraction of k-sets are red? By the Sidorenko tree bound, we have

$$t(S_k, G) \geq p^{k-1} \geq q^k(1-\varepsilon)^k \geq \frac{(1-\varepsilon)^k}{\binom{k}{2}^{k-1}},$$

where the last inequality follows from the fact that F is not the empty graph, and hence $q \geq 1/\binom{k}{2}$. Since $t_{\text{inj}}(S_k, G) \geq t(S_k, G) - c/n$, our condition on n from (8) implies that

$$t_{\text{inj}}(S_k, G) \geq \frac{(1-\varepsilon)^k}{2\binom{k}{2}^{k-1}} > \varepsilon .$$

Now, let $\text{inj}(S_k, G)$ denote the number of one-to-one homomorphisms of S_k into G; by definition,

$$t_{\text{inj}}(S_k, G) = \frac{\text{inj}(S_k, G)}{n(n-1)\cdots(n-k+1)} = \frac{\text{inj}(S_k, G)}{k!\binom{n}{k}},$$

and hence

$$\text{inj}(S_k, G) = k!\binom{n}{k}t_{\text{inj}}(S_k, G) > \varepsilon\, k!\binom{n}{k}.$$

Now, at most $k!$ different one-to-one homomorphisms can map S_k to the same k-set of G, and hence more than $\varepsilon\binom{n}{k}$ many k-sets of G are red. It follows that the fraction of k-sets that are red is $> \varepsilon$; but this contradicts our assumption that at least a $(1-\varepsilon)$ fraction of k-sets are blue, since no k-set can be both blue and red. □

PROPOSITION 4.10. *Assume F is not a clique and not empty. Then for each edge density p there exists a sequence $G_1^p, G_2^p, \ldots$ of asymptotic edge density p for which F does not appear as an induced subgraph in any G_i^p. Equivalently, $s(F, G_i^p) = 0, \forall i$.*

PROOF. We call H a *near-clique* if it has at most one connected component of size greater than one, and this component is a clique. For any $p \in [0, 1]$, it is possible to construct an infinite sequence $H_1^p, H_2^p, \ldots$ of near-cliques with asymptotic density p, by simply taking the non-trivial component of each H_i^p to be a clique of the appropriate size.

Now, fix any $p \in [0, 1]$, and let F be any graph that is neither a clique nor an empty graph. If F is not a near-clique, then the required sequence $G_1^p, G_2^p, \ldots$ is the sequence of near-cliques $H_1^p, H_2^p, \ldots$, since all the induced subgraphs of a near-clique are themselves near-cliques.

On the other hand, if F is a near-clique, then since F is neither a clique nor an empty graph, the complement of F is not a near-clique. It follows that the required sequence $G_1^p, G_2^p, \ldots$ is the sequence of complements of the near-cliques $H_1^{1-p}, H_2^{1-p}, \ldots$. □

Note that it is possible to take an F-free graph with asymptotic density p and append nodes with local edge density p and random (Erdős-Rényi) connections to obtain a graph with any intermediate subgraph frequency between zero and that of $G_{n,p}$. The same blending arguement can be applied to any graph with a subgraph frequency above $G_{n,p}$ to again find graphs with intermediate subgraph frequencies. In this way we see that large tracts of the subgraph frequency simplex are fully feasible for arbitrary graphs, yet by Figure 5 are clearly not inhabited by any real world social graph.

5. CLASSIFICATION OF AUDIENCES

The previous two sections characterize empirical and extremal properties of the space of subgraph frequencies, providing two complementary frameworks for understanding the structure of social graphs. In this section, we conclude our work with a demonstration of how subgraph frequencies can also provide a useful tool for distinguishing between different categories of graphs. The Edge Formation Random Walk model introduced in Section 3 figures notably, providing a meaningful baseline for constructing classification features, contributing to the best overall classification accuracy we are able to produce.

Thus, concretely our classification task is to take a social graph and determine whether it is a node neighborhood, the set of people in a group, or the set of people at an event. This is a specific version of a broader characterization problem that arises generally in social media — namely how social audiences differ in terms of social graph structure [1]. Each of the three graph types we discuss — neighborhoods, groups, and events — define an audience with which a user may choose to converse. The defining feature of such audience decisions has typically been their size — as users choose to share something online, do they want to share it publicly, with their friends, or with a select subgroup of their friends? Products such as Facebook groups exist in part to address this audience problem, enabling the creation of small conversation circles. Our classification task is essentially asking: do audiences differ in meaningful structural ways other than just size?

In Figure 1 and subsequently in Figure 5, we saw how the three types of graphs that we study — neighborhoods, groups, and events — are noticeably clustered around different structural foci in the space of subgraph frequencies. Figure 5 focused on graphs consisting of exactly 50-nodes, where it is visibly apparent that both neighborhoods and events tend to have a lower edge density than groups of that size. Neighborhood edge density — equivalent to the *local clustering coefficient* — is known to generally decrease with graph size [13, 19], but it is not clear that all three of the graph types we consider here should decrease at the same rate.

In Figure 6, we see that in fact the three graph types do not decrease uniformly, with the average edge density of neighborhoods decreasing more slowly than groups or events. Thus, small groups are denser than neighborhoods while large groups are sparser, with the transition occurring at around 400 nodes. Similarly, small event graphs are denser than neighborhoods while large events are much sparser, with the transition occurring already at around 75 nodes.

The two crossing points in Figure 6 suggest a curious challenge: are their structural features of audience graphs that distinguish them from each other even when they exhibit the same edge density? Here we use the language of subgraph frequencies developed in this work to formulate a classification task for classifying audience graphs based on subgraph frequencies. We compare our classification accuracy to the accuracy achieved when also considering a generous vector of much more sophisticated graph features. We approach this classification task using a simple logistic regression model. While more advanced machine learning models capable of learning richer relationships would likely produce better classification accuracies, our goal here is to establish that this vocabulary of features based on subgraph frequencies can produce non-trivial classification results even in conjunction with simple techniques such as logistic regression.

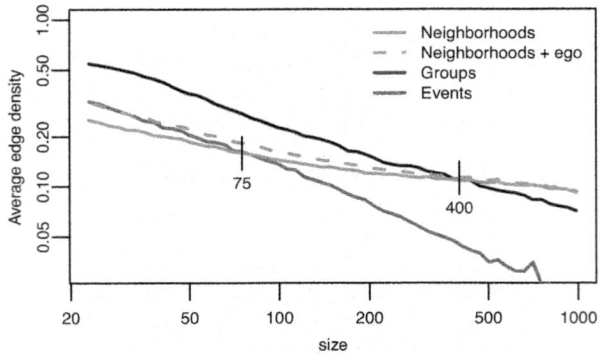

Figure 6: Edge densities of neighborhoods, groups, and events as a function of size, n. When $n < 400$, groups are denser then neighborhoods. When $n < 75$, events are denser then neighborhoods.

When considering neighborhood graphs, recall that we are not including the ego of the neighborhoods as part of the graph, while for groups and events the administrators as members of their graphs. As such, neighborhoods without their ego deviate systematically from analogous audience graphs created as groups or as events. In Figure 6 we also show the average edge density of neighborhoods with their ego, adding one node and $n - 1$ edges, noting that the difference is small for larger graphs.

Classification features. Subgraph frequencies has been the motivating coordinate system for the present work, and will serve as our main feature set. Employing the Edge Formation Random Walk model from Section 3, we additionally describe each graph by its residuals with respect to a backbone — described by the parameter λ — fit to the complete unclassified training set.

Features based on subgraph frequencies are local features, computable by examining only a few local nodes of the graph at a time. Note that the subgraph frequencies of arbitrarily large graphs can be accurately approximated by sampling a small number of induced graphs. Comparatively, it is relevant to ask: can these simple local features do as well as more sophisticated *global* graph features? Perhaps the number of connected components, the size of the largest component, or other global features provide highly informative features for graph classification.

To answer this question, we compare our classification accuracy using subgraph frequencies with the accuracy we are able to achieve using a set of global graph features. We consider:

- Size of the k largest components, for $k = 1, 2$.
- Size of the k-core, for $k = 0, 1, 2, 3$.
- Number of components in the k-core, for $k = 0, 1, 2$.
- Degeneracy, the largest k for which the k-core is non-empty.
- Size of the k-brace [18], for $k = 1, 2, 3$.
- Number of components in the k-brace, for $k = 1, 2, 3$.

These features combine linearly to produce a rich set of graph properties. For example, the number of components in the 1-core minus the number of components in the 0-core yields the number of singletons in the graph.

Classification results. The results of the classification model are shown in Table 1, reported in terms of classification accuracy — the fraction of correct classifications on the test data — measured using five-fold cross-validation on a balanced set of 10,000 instances. The classification tasks were chosen to be thwart classification based solely on edge density, which indeed performs poorly.

Model Features	N vs. E, $n = 75$	N vs. G, $n = 400$
Edges	0.487	0.482
Triads	0.719	0.647
Triads + R_G	0.737	0.673
Triads + R_λ	0.736	0.668
Quads	0.751	0.755
Quads + R_G	0.765	0.769
Quads + R_λ	0.765	0.769
Global + Edges	0.694	0.763
Global + Triads	0.785	0.766
Global + Triads + R_G	0.784	0.766
Global + Triads + R_λ	0.789	0.767
Global + Quads	0.797	0.812
Global + Quads + R_G	0.807	0.815
Global + Quads + R_λ	0.809	0.820

Table 1: Classification accuracy for N(eighborhoods), G(roups), and E(vents) on different sets of features. R_G and R_λ denote the residuals with respect to a $G_{n,p}$ and stochastic graph model baseline, as described in the text.

Using only 4-node subgraph frequencies and residuals, an accuracy of 77% is achieved in both tasks.

In comparison, classification based on a set of global graph features performed worse, achieving just 69% and 76% accuracy for the two tasks. Meanwhile, combining global and subgraph frequency features performed best of all, with a classification accuracy of 81–82%. In each case we also report the accuracy with and without residuals as features. Incorporating residuals with respect to either a $G_{n,p}$ or Edge Formation Random Walk baseline consistently improved classification, and examining residuals with respect to either baseline clearly provides a useful orientation of the subgraph coordinate system for empirical graphs.

6. CONCLUSION

The modern study of social graphs has primarily focused on the examination of the sparse large-scale structure of human relationships. This global perspective has led to fruitful theoretical frameworks for the study of many networked domains, notably the world wide web, computer networks, and biological ecosystems [13]. However, in this work we argue that the locally dense structure of social graphs admit an additional framework for analyzing the structure of social graphs.

In this work, we examine the structure of social graphs through the coordinate system of subgraph frequencies, developing two complementary frameworks that allow us to identify both 'social' structure and 'graph' structure. The framework developed in Section 3 enables us to characterize the apparent social forces guiding graph formation, while the framework developed in Section 4 characterizes fundamental limits of all graphs, delivered through combinatorial constraints. Our coordinate system and frameworks are not only useful for developing intuition, but we also demonstrate how they can be used to accurately classify graph types using only these simple descriptions in terms of subgraph frequency.

Distribution note. Implementations of the Edge Formation Random Walk equilibrium solver and the subgraph frequency extremal bounds optimization program are available from the first author's webpage.

Acknowledgments. This work was supported in part by NSF grants IIS-0910664 and IIS-1016099.

7. REFERENCES

[1] L. Adamic, J. Zhang, E. Bakshy, and M. S. Ackerman. Knowledge sharing and yahoo answers: everyone knows something. In *WWW*, pages 665–674. ACM, 2008.

[2] L. Backstrom, E. Bakshy, J. Kleinberg, T. Lento, and I. Rosenn. Center of attention: How facebook users allocate attention across friends. In *ICWSM*, 2011.

[3] B. Bollobás. *Random Graphs*. Cambridge University Press, second edition, 2001.

[4] C. Borgs, J. T. Chayes, L. Lovasz, V. Sos, B. Szegedy, and K. Vesztergombi. Counting graph homomorphisms. In M. Klazar, J. Kratochvil, M. Loebl, J. Matousek, R. Thomas, and P. Valtr, editors, *Topics in Discrete Mathematics*, pages 315–371. Springer, 2006.

[5] K. Faust. Very local structure in social networks. *Sociological Methodology*, 37(1):209–256, 2007.

[6] K. Faust. A puzzle concerning triads in social networks: Graph constraints and the triad census. *Social Networks*, 32(3):221–233, 2010.

[7] D. Fisher, M. A. Smith, and H. T. Welser. You are who you talk to: Detecting roles in usenet newsgroups. In *HICSS*, 2006.

[8] M. Granovetter. The strength of weak ties. *American Journal of Sociology*, 78:1360–1380, 1973.

[9] E. M. Jin, M. Girvan, and M. E. J. Newman. The structure of growing social networks. *Phys. Rev. E*, 64:046132, 2001.

[10] J. Leskovec, J. Kleinberg, and C. Faloutsos. Graphs over time: densification laws, shrinking diameters and possible explanations. In *KDD*, pages 177–187. ACM, 2005.

[11] L. Lovasz. Very large graphs. In D. Jerison, B. Mazur, T. Mrowka, W. Schmid, R. Stanley, and S. T. Yau, editors, *Current Developments in Mathematics*, pages 67–128. International Press, 2009.

[12] J. W. Moon and L. Moser. On a problem of Turan. *Magyar Tud. Akad. Mat. Kutat Int. Kzl*, 7:283–286, 1962.

[13] M. E. J. Newman. *Networks: An Introduction*. Oxford University Press, 2010.

[14] A. Rapoport. Spread of information through a population with socio-structural bias I: Assumption of transitivity. *Bulletin of Mathematical Biophysics*, 15(4):523–533, December 1953.

[15] A. Razborov. Flag algebras. *Journal of Symbolic Logic*, 72:1239–1282, 2007.

[16] A. Razborov. On the minimal density of triangles in graphs. *Combinatorics, Probability and Computing*, 17:603–618, 2008.

[17] A. Sidorenko. A correlation inequality for bipartite graphs. *Graphs and Combinatorics*, 9:201–204, 1993.

[18] J. Ugander, L. Backstrom, C. Marlow, and J. Kleinberg. Structural diversity in social contagion. *PNAS*, 109(16):5962–5966, 2012.

[19] J. Ugander, B. Karrer, L. Backstrom, and C. Marlow. The anatomy of the facebook social graph. Technical Report cs.SI/1111.4503, arxiv, November 2011.

[20] J. Voss. Measuring Wikipedia. In *ICISSI*, 2005.

[21] S. Wasserman and K. Faust. *Social Network Analysis: Methods and Applications*. Cambridge Univ. Press, 1994.

The Self-Feeding Process: A Unifying Model for Communication Dynamics in the Web

Pedro O.S. Vaz de Melo
Universidade Federal de
Minas Gerais
Belo Horizonte, Brazil
olmo@dcc.ufmg.br

Christos Faloutsos
Carnegie Mellon University
Pittsburgh, USA
christos@cs.cmu.edu

Renato Assunção
Universidade Federal de
Minas Gerais
Belo Horizonte, Brazil
assuncao@dcc.ufmg.br

Antonio A.F. Loureiro
Universidade Federal de
Minas Gerais
Belo Horizonte, Brazil
loureiro@dcc.ufmg.br

ABSTRACT

How often do individuals perform a given communication activity in the Web, such as posting comments on blogs or news? Could we have a generative model to create communication events with realistic inter-event time distributions (IEDs)? Which properties should we strive to match? Current literature has seemingly contradictory results for IED: some studies claim good fits with power laws; others with non-homogeneous Poisson processes. Given these two approaches, we ask: which is the correct one? Can we reconcile them all? We show here that, surprisingly, both approaches are correct, being corner cases of the proposed Self-Feeding Process (SFP). We show that the SFP (a) exhibits a unifying power, which generates power law tails (including the so-called "top-concavity" that real data exhibits), as well as short-term Poisson behavior; (b) avoids the "i.i.d. fallacy", which none of the prevailing models have studied before; and (c) is extremely parsimonious, requiring usually only *one*, and in general, *at most two* parameters. Experiments conducted on eight large, diverse real datasets (e.g., Youtube and blog comments, e-mails, SMSs, etc) reveal that the SFP mimics their properties very well.

Categories and Subject Descriptors

G.3 [**Probability and Statistics**]: [Markov processes, Stochastic processes, Time series analysis, Probabilistic algorithms]; H.4.3 [**Information systems applications**]: [Communication applications]

General Terms

Theory

Keywords

communication dynamics,inter-event times,generative model

1. INTRODUCTION

How long will it take until a next comment arrive on your Youtube[1] video given the past history of comments timestamps? Does the behavior of commenting on Youtube videos differ from the behavior of commenting on web blogs or online news websites? And how different these activities are from writing and receiving e-mails? The current availability of large datasets containing digitalized information about human communication dynamics has made it possible to propose a question that many thought was already answered: what is the timing of human communications[2, 20]? Thus, the focus of this work is to find patterns in inter-event times between real and modern communication activities of humans.

All the aforementioned communication activities are "point processes", and the simplest way to model them is by the Poisson Process (PP) [17]. Unfortunately, this simple and elegant model has proved unsuitable [34, 12, 15, 40], since analysis of real data have shown that humans have very long periods of inactivity and bursts of intense activity [2, 20], in contrast to the PP, where activities occur at a fairly constant rate. Although researches agree that the PP is not suitable, there is no consensus about the right model between two major schools of thought. The first viewpoint [2, 34] states that a power law [13] is an appropriate fit for the Probability Density Function (PDF) of the *inter-event time distribution* (IED), where bursts and heavy-tails in human activities are a consequence of a decision-based queuing process, when tasks are executed according to some perceived priority. The second viewpoint is that the IED is well explained by variations of the PP [25, 32, 31, 30, 23]. They are based on the fact that short-term communication events exhibits a Poissonian behavior [5, 21] and suggest a piecewise Poisson process: the first interval has a constant rate λ; for the next, change the rate, and continue.

Given these two approaches, we ask: which is the correct one? Can we reconcile them all? We show here that, surprisingly, both approaches are correct, being corner cases of the proposed Self-Feeding Process (SFP). The SFP generates a power-law-tail distribution for the inter-event time marginal, like [2], and it behaves as a PP in the short term, like [32]. Moreover, the SFP is also extremely *parsimonious*, requiring at most two parameters.

Additionally, unlike previous studies, we analyze the temporal correlations between inter-event times, illustrating the "i.i.d. fallacy" that has been routinely ignored until recently [22]. We show that, unlike the PP that generates independent and identically distributed (i.i.d.) inter-event times, individual sequences of communications tend to show a high dependence between consecutive inter-arrival times. This is the basis of the SFP model, which uses a Markovian approach to determine that the next inter-event time

---

[1] www.youtube.com

Copyright is held by the International World Wide Web Conference Committee (IW3C2). IW3C2 reserves the right to provide a hyperlink to the author's site if the Material is used in electronic media.
WWW 2013, May 13–17, 2013, Rio de Janeiro, Brazil.
ACM 978-1-4503-2035-1/13/05.

depends solely on the previous one. We validate the SFP model on eight diverse and large datasets from real and modern communication data, that can be divided into two groups. The first group contains five datasets extracted from Web applications in which several users comment on a given topic. The second group contains three datasets in which individuals perform and receive communication events. In summary, the main contributions of the SFP are as follows:

- **Unifying power**. It reconciles existing and contrasting theories in human communication dynamics[2, 32];
- **Temporal correlation**. It shows positive correlation between consecutive inter-event times [22];
- **Parsimony**. It requires usually one and at most two parameters.

Moreover, we would like to point out that our findings open a new perspective in understanding human communication dynamics both at the network (first group) and individual (second group) level. By knowing the typical human behavior, one can leverage a varied number of applications in different areas, such as popularity prediction of videos and news, identification of spammers and other anomalous behavior, resource allocation, among others.

The rest of the paper is organized as follows. In Section 2, we provide a brief survey of the related work that analyzed inter-event times between communications. In Section 3, we describe the eight datasets used in this work. In Section 4, we analyze the IED of individuals from these datasets and we show that the Odds Ratio function of their IEDs is well modeled by a power law. Later, in Section 5, we show that the typical behavior of inter-event sequences shows a positive correlation between consecutive inter-event times. In Section 6, we describe our proposed SFP model that provides an intuitive and simple explanation for the observed data. Then, in Section 7 we show that the SFP model also unifies existing theories on communication dynamics. Finally, we show the conclusions and future research directions in Section 8.

2. RELATED WORK

The accurate understanding of the human dynamics on the Web can benefit a large number of applications, such as query suggestions, crawling policies, advertising, result ranking, recommender systems, anomaly detection, among others. However, the dynamics of humans on the Web is very rich and varied, given the large number of activities one can perform online. For example, in [36] the authors developed methods for modeling the dynamics of the query and click behaviors seen in a large population of Web searchers. In [37], the authors analyzed the tendency a person has to comment on stories in the Web in order to connect users with stories they are likely to comment on. Moreover, [19] analyzed and modeled the temporal behavior of users in social rating networks, what may leverage the prediction of future links, ratings or community structures. Finally, in [27], the authors used stochastic models of user behavior on online news websites to predict the popularity of a given news based on early user reactions to new content. Our work tackle a more general human behavior, i.e., her/his communications activities, which may occur on news websites, online social networks, video channels, directly via e-mail and in many other ways.

The study of the time interval in which events occur in human activity is not new in the literature. The most primitive model is the classic Poisson process [17]. Although the most recent approaches have among themselves significant differences, they all agree that the timing of individuals systematically deviates from this classical approach. The Poisson process predicts that the time interval Δ_t between two consecutive events by the same individual follows an exponential distribution with expected value β and rate $\lambda = 1/\beta$, where

$$\Delta_t = -\beta \times \ln(U(0, 1)), \quad (1)$$

where $U(0, 1)$ is a uniformly random distributed number between $[0, 1]$. While in a Poisson process consecutive events follow each other at a relatively regular time, real data shows that humans have very long periods of inactivity and also bursts of intense activity [2].

Recently, Barabási et. al. [2, 34] proposed that a power law [13] is an appropriate fit for the Probability Density Function (PDF) of the *inter-event time distribution* (IED). They propose that bursts and heavy-tails in human activities are a consequence of a decision-based queuing process, when tasks are executed according to some perceived priority. In this way, most of the tasks would be executed rapidly while some of them may take a very long time. The queuing models generate power law distributions $p(X = x) \approx x^{-\alpha}$ with slopes $\alpha \approx 1$ or $\alpha \approx 1.5$.

The second modern approach claims that the IED is well explained by variations of the PP, such as the Interrupted Poisson [25] (IPP), Non-Homogeneous Poisson Process [32, 31, 30] and Kleinberg's burst model [23]. All these studies are based on the fact that short-term communication events exhibits a Poissonian behavior [5, 21] and suggest a piece-wise Poisson process: the first interval has a constant rate λ; for the next, change the rate (say, to zero, for the IPP, or to double-or-half for Kleinberg's model), and continue. Malmgreen et al. [32, 31, 30] proposes a non-homogeneous Poisson process, where the rate $\lambda(t)$ varies with time, in a periodic fashion (e.g., people answer emails in the morning; then go to lunch; then answer more e-mails, etc). This model explains the data at the cost of requiring several parameters and careful data analysis, being impractical for synthetic data generators, for instance. Later, the authors adapted this model to a more parsimonious version [30], but it still has 9 parameters.

3. DATA DESCRIPTION

In this work we analyze eight datasets that can be divided into two groups. The first group contains five datasets extracted from Web applications in which several users comment on a given topic. The datasets are extracted from five popular websites: Youtube, MetaFilter, MetaTalk, Ask MetaFilter and Digg. The second group contains three datasets in which individuals perform and receive communication events. In this group we have a Short Message Service (SMS), a mobile phone-call and a public e-mail dataset. For simplicity, we use the term "individual" to refer both to topics of the first group and users of the second group.

In the first group, we analyze a public online news dataset, containing a set of stories and comments over each story. More specifically, the data is from the popular social media site Digg and has 1,485 stories and over 7 million comments [11]. The Digg dataset is public for research interests and can be downloaded at http://www.infochimps.com/datasets/diggcom-data-set. We also analyze three publicly available datasets from the *Metafilter Infodump Project*[2], extracted from three discussion forums: MetaFilter[3] (Mefi), MetaTalk[4] (Meta) and Ask MetaFilter[5] (Askme). After

---
[2]downloaded on September 22nd from http://stuff.metafilter.com/infodump/
[3]http://www.metafilter.com/
[4]http://metatalk.metafilter.com/
[5]http://ask.metafilter.com/

disregarding topics which received less than 30 comments, the Mefi dataset has 8,384 topics and 1,471,153 comments, the Meta dataset has 2,484 topics and 503,644 comments and the Askme dataset has 498 topics and 65,950 comments.

Our final dataset from the first group was collected from the Youtube website using the Google's Youtube API[6]. We collected all the comments posted on the videos classified as *trending* by the API[7] from 22/Aug/2012 to 25/Sep/2012. We collected a total of 1,221,390 comments on 989 videos, but we use in our dataset only those videos with more than 30 comments and which the comments span for more than one week, a total of 610 videos and 1,008,511 comments. The full dataset can be downloaded at www.dcc.ufmg.br/~olmo/youtube.zip.

In the second group, the mobile phone calls dataset contains more than 3.1 million customers of a large mobile operator of a large city, with more than 263.6 million phone call records registered during *one month*. From this same operator, we also have a SMS dataset of 300,000 users spanning six months of data, for a total of 8,784,101 records. These datasets from the mobile operator is under Non-Disclosure Agreement (NDA) and belong to the iLab Research at the Heinz College at CMU, but was already used in several papers [38, 39, 1]. We also analyze the public Enron e-mail dataset, consisting of 200,399 messages belonging to 158 users with an average of 757 messages per user [24]. The data is public and can be downloaded at http://www.cs.cmu.edu/enron/.

4. MARGINAL DISTRIBUTION

In this work, we are first interested on the inter-event time distribution IED of the random variable Δ_k representing the time Δ_k between the $k-th$ and the $(k-1)-th$ communication events on a given topic (first group) or of an user (second group). For simplicity, we use the term "individual" to refer both to topics of the first group and users of the second group.

4.1 Odds Ratio Using the Cumulative Distribution Function

In Figure 1, we show the distribution of the time intervals Δ_k between communication events for a typical active user of the SMS dataset, with 44,785 SMS messages sent or received. The histogram is shown in Figure 1-a and, as we observe, this user had a significantly high number of events separated by small periods of time and also long periods of inactivity. Moreover, both the power law fitting, which in the best fit has an exponent of -2, and the exponential fitting, which is generated by a PP, deviates from the real data. The method we use to fit the power law is based on the Maximum likelihood estimation (MLE) described in [7].

In empirical data that spans for several orders of magnitude, which is the case of the IEDs, it is very difficult to identify statistical patterns in the histograms, since the distribution is considerably noisy at its tail [2, 32]. A possible option is to move away from the histogram and analyze the cumulative distributions, i.e., cumulative density function (CDF) and complementary cumulative density function (CCDF), which veil the data sparsity. However, by using the CDF, as we observe in Figure 1-b, we lose information in the tail of the distribution and, on the other hand, by using the CCDF, as we observe in Figure 1-c, we lose information in the head of the distribution.

In order to escape from these drawbacks, we propose the use of the Odds Ratio (OR) function combined with the CDF as it allows for a clean visualization of the distribution behavior both in the

---

[6]https://developers.google.com/youtube/
[7]https://gdata.youtube.com/feeds/api/standardfeeds/on_the_web

head and in the tail. This $OR(k)$ function is commonly used in the survival analysis [3, 29] and measures the ratio between the number of individuals who have not survived by time t and the ones that have survived. Its formula is given by:

$$Odds\ Ratio(t) = OR(t) = \frac{CDF(t)}{1 - CDF(t)}. \quad (2)$$

In this paper, for a set of n inter-event times $\{\Delta_1, \Delta_2, ..., \Delta_n\}$, we calculate the odds ratio for each percentile $P_1, P_2, ..., P_{100}$ of the data. This avoids that minor deviations in the data harms the goodness of fit test we perform, which we explain in Section 4.2.

Thus, in Figure 1-d, we plot the OR for the selected user. From the OR plot, we can clearly see the cumulative behavior in the head and in the tail of the distribution. Also, observe again that both the exponential and the power law significantly deviate from the real data. Moreover, we can also observe that the OR of the inter-event times seems to entirely follow a linear behavior in logarithmic scales, having, then, a power law behavior with OR slope $\rho \approx 1$.

Again, in Figure 2, we plot the OR of a typical individual of each dataset. The OR plots clearly show the cumulative behavior in the head and in the tail of the distribution. Also, we can observe that the OR of the inter-event times seems to follow entirely the same linear behavior in logarithmic scales, having, then, an OR power law behavior. This implies that the marginal distribution of the IEDs is approximately equal to a log-logistic distribution [14], since this distribution shows a OR power law behavior.

4.2 Goodness of Fit

In this section, we check whether the OR of the IEDs of all individuals of our datasets can be explained by a power law. We perform a linear regression using least squares fitting on the OR of the IEDs of all individuals. Since we consider every percentile and the OR is a cumulative distribution, the linear regression is accurate. We performed a Kolmogorov-Smirnov goodness of fit test, but because of digitalization errors and other deviations, this test presented biased results. For instance, it rejects all fittings on distributions where the data is rounded up from seconds to minute values (e.g. 45 seconds to 60 seconds).

Figure 3 shows the histogram of the determination coefficient R^2 of the performed linear regressions. The determination coefficient R^2 is a statistical measure of how well the regression line approximates to the real data points. A $R^2 = 1.0$ indicates that the regression line perfectly fits the data. We observe that for the vast majority of individuals of our eight datasets, the R^2 is close to 1.0. More specifically, for the first group, the R^2 averages 0.97 for the Youtube, Askme and Digg datasets and 0.98 for the Mefi and Meta datasets. For the second group, the R^2 averages 0.99 for the phone dataset, 0.96 for the SMS dataset and 0.97 for the e-mail dataset. This allows us to state that for the vast majority of individuals, the OR of their IEDs is well fitted by a power law.

4.3 Typical Behavior

Since the IED of the majority of individuals is well modeled by an odds ratio power law, then we are able to characterize their behaviors by two values: the slope ρ and the median μ of the fitted OR power law. Observe in Figure 4 the PDF of the slopes ρ_i measured for every individual i of our eight datasets. Except the SMS dataset, the typical ρ_i for the majority of individuals is approximately 1. Moreover, observe in Figure 5 the PDF of the medians μ_i measured for every individual i of our eight datasets. Observe that, while the typical μ_i is around 1 hour for the second group, for the first group it varies from 3 to 8 minutes.

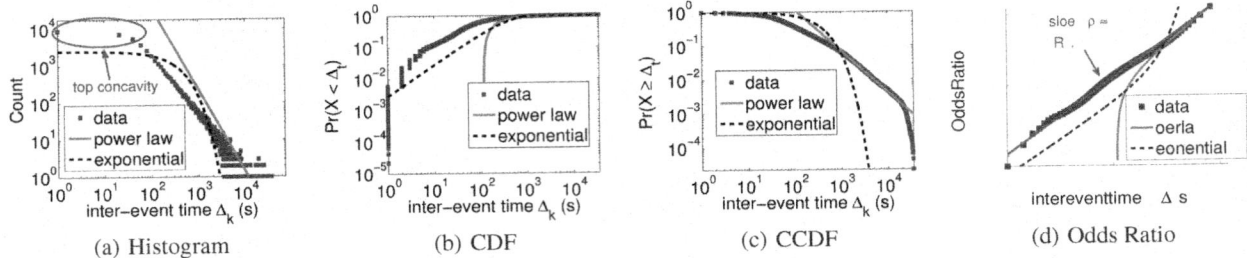

Figure 1: The inter-event times distribution of the most active individual of our eight datasets, with 44,785 SMS messages sent and received. We observe that both the power law fitting (PL fitting) with exponent 2 and the exponential fitting, generated by a PP, deviate from the real data. We also observe that the OR is very well fitted by a straight line with slope ≈ 1.

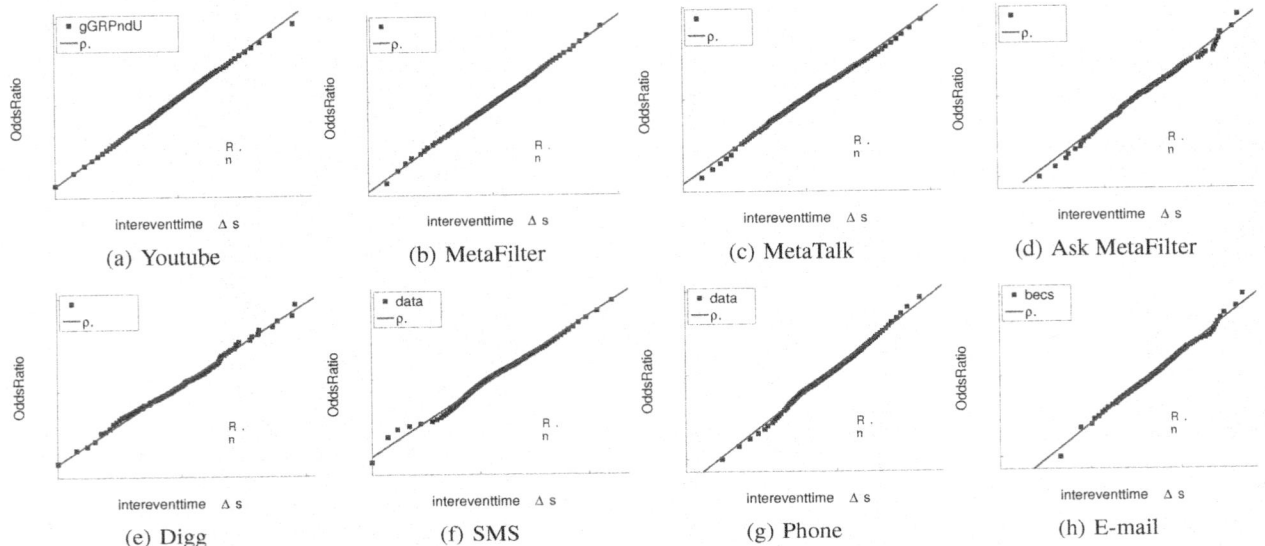

Figure 2: The Odds Ratio plot for one typical active individual of each dataset. Observe that an odds ratio power law, represented by a straight line with slope ρ in a log-log scale, is an appropriate fit for all individuals.

5. TEMPORAL CORRELATION

Although most previous analysis focus solely on the marginal IED, a subtle point is the *correlation* between successive inter-event times (Δ_{k-1} and Δ_k). What we illustrate here is that the independence between Δ_k and Δ_{k-1} does **not** hold for the eight datasets we analyzed in this work.

In Figure 6, we plot, for the same typical users of Figure 2, all the pairs of consecutive inter-event times (Δ_{k-1}, Δ_k). We also show the regression of the data points using the LOWESS smoother [8]. While the PP, as for any other i.i.d. process, the regression is a flat line with slope 0, for the eight typical users Δ_k tends to grow with Δ_{k-1}. This means that if I called you five years ago, my next phone call will be in about five years later. In short, there is a strong, positive dependency between the current inter-event time (Δ_k) and the previous one (Δ_{k-1}), clearly contradicting the independence assumption.

We formally investigate if two consecutive inter-event times are correlated analyzing the autocorrelation [4] of all the time series involving the inter-event times Δ_k of the individuals of our datasets. Autocorrelation refers to the correlation of a time series with its own past and future values. A positive autocorrelation, which is suggested by Figure 6, might be considered a specific form of "persistence", i.e., a tendency for a system to remain in the same state from one observation to the next.

We test if all the Δ_k time series of every individual of our datasets are random or autocorrelated. For this, we define the hypothesis test H_0 that a series $S = \{\Delta_0, \Delta_1, ..., \Delta_n\}$ of inter-event times is random. If S is random, then its autocorrelation coefficient $AC_l \approx 0$ for all lags $l > 0$, where a lag l is used to compare, in this case, values of Δ_k and Δ_{k-l}. More formally, if AC_l is between the 95% confidence interval for S to be random, then we accept H_0 that S is random. As we show in Figure 7, we reject the null hypothesis H_0 that the inter-event times of the individual of Figure 1 is random, since all $AC_l, 1 < l \leq 10$ are outside the confidence interval.

Since we are interested only in the case where the lag $l = 1$, we propose an alternative hypothesis test H_1 that the first-order autocorrelation coefficient AC_1 is greater than 0. If AC_1 is greater than the confidence interval for randomness, then we accept H_1 that the series is not random, i.e., there is a dependence between Δ_k and Δ_{k-1}. In Figure 8, we show the empirical probability $P(H_1)$ of accepting H_1 for individuals with a given number of events n of a given dataset. As we observe, as the number of communication events n grows and becomes significant, the probability of accepting H_1 increases rapidly. This strongly suggests that, on the con-

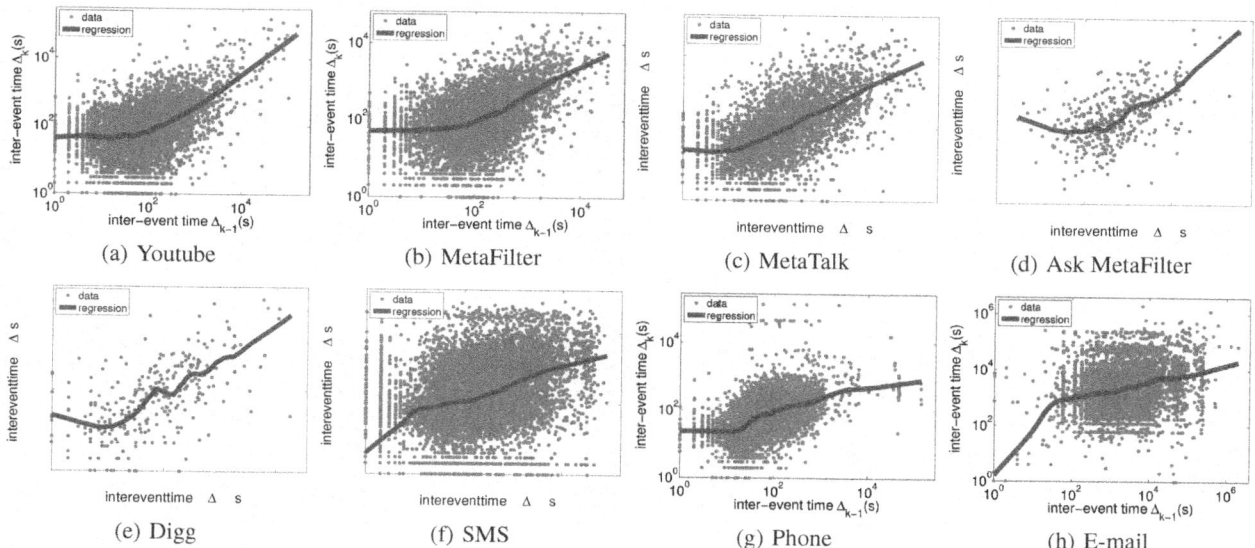

Figure 6: I.i.d. fallacy: dependence between Δ_k and Δ_{k-1}. Each point represents a pair of consecutive inter-event times (Δ_{k-1}, Δ_k) registered for a typical active individual of each dataset. The red line is a regression of the data points using the LOWESS smoother.

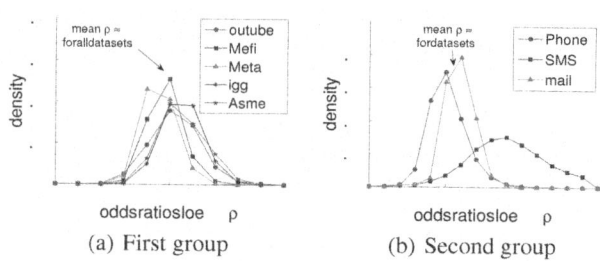

Figure 4: The PDF of the slopes ρ_i measured for every user u_i of our eight datasets. Except the SMS dataset, the typical ρ_i for the majority of individuals is approximately 1.

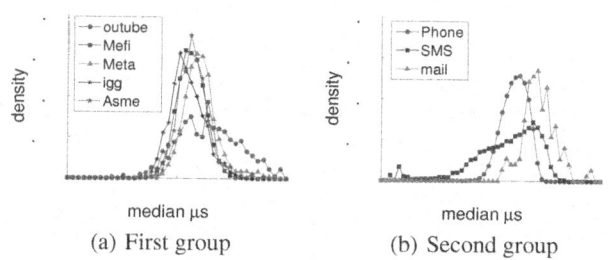

Figure 5: The PDF of the medians μ_i measured for every user of our eight datasets. Observe that the typical μ_i is around 3 and 8 minutes for the first group and around 1 hour for the second group.

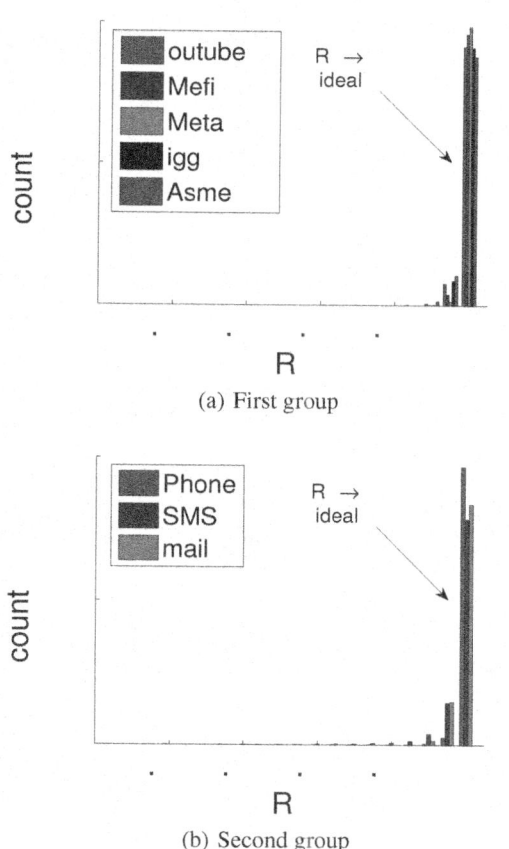

Figure 3: The goodness of fit of our proposed model. We show the histograms of the R^2s measured for every user in the eight datasets. These histograms consider bins of size 0.05. Thus, observe that the R^2 value for the great majority of individuals is located in the last bin, from 0.95 to 1.

trary of what happens with the i.i.d. inter-event times distribution generated by the Poisson Process or simply sampling from a log-logistic distribution, in real data there is a dependence between Δ_k and Δ_{k-1}. This also agrees with a recent work [35], which reports that daily series of calls made by a customer exhibits long memory.

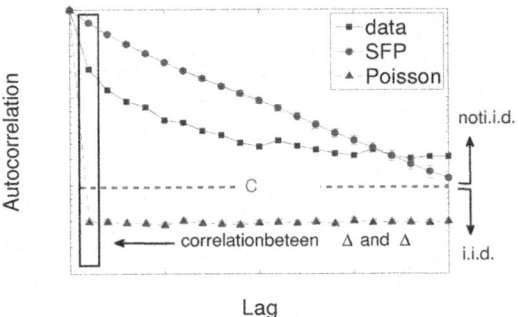

Figure 7: The sample autocorrelation for the same individual of Figure 1 and for synthetic data generated by the SFP and a PP with the same number of communication events and median.

Thus, in summary we can state that

$$E(\Delta_k | \Delta_{k-1}) = f(\Delta_{k-1}) \qquad (3)$$

where f is a function that describes the dependency between Δ_k and Δ_{k-1}.

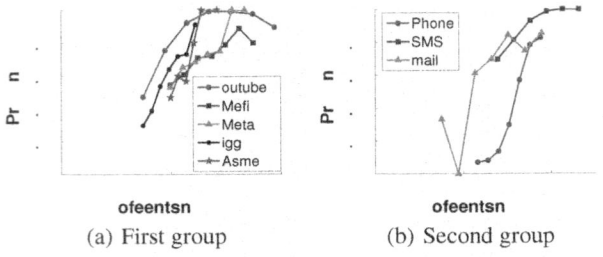

Figure 8: The empirical probability of an individual's inter-event times to be autocorrelated given his/her number of events. Note that as the number of events grows, the probability of having an autocorrelated series increases rapidly for the eight datasets.

6. THE SELF-FEEDING PROCESS

Given all the above evidence (OR power law; i.i.d. fallacy) and all the previous evidence (power law tails by Barabási; short-term regular behavior as the PP), the question is whether can we design a generator which will match all these properties? Our requirements for the ideal generator are the following:

R1: Realism – marginals The model should generate OR power law marginal IED;

R2: Realism – locally-Poisson: The model should behave as a Poisson Process within a short window of time;

R3: Avoid the i.i.d. fallacy Two consecutive inter-event times should be correlated;

R4: Parsimony It should need only few parameters, and ideally, just one or two.

At a high level, our proposal is that the next inter-arrival time will be an exponential random variable, with rate that *depends on the previous* inter-arrival time. It is subtle, but in this way our generator behaves like Poisson in the short term, gives power-law tails in the long term, generates OR power law marginals and is extremely parsimonious: just one parameter, the median μ of the IED. We call this model the *Self-Feeding Process* (SFP).

We propose the generator as follows

MODEL 1. *Self-Feeding Process SFP (μ).*
// μ is the desired median of the marginal PDF

Δ_1	$\leftarrow$	μ
Δ_k	$\leftarrow$	$Exponential\ (mean\ \beta = \Delta_{k-1} + \mu/e)$

where μ is the only parameter of the model, being the desired median of the IED. The part μ/e has to be higher than 0 to avoid Δ_k to converge to 0 and has to be divided by the Euler's number e to make the median of the generated IED around the target median μ (more details in the Appendix A). This type of model is not new in the literature [41, 10] but they have not been extensively studied, perhaps due to the lack of empirical data fitting the implied distribution.

In Figures 9-a and 9-b we compare, respectively, the histogram and the OR of the inter-event times generated by the SFP model, all values rounded up, with the inter-event times of the individual of Figure 1. Notice that the distributions are very similar and both are well fitted by a log-logistic distribution, which looks like a hyperbola, thus addressing both the power-law tail, as well as the "top-concavity" that real data exhibits. For a generalized SFP model, that generates IEDs with different OR slopes, and more details about the log-logistic distribution, please see the Appendix B. Moreover, for an analysis over the temporal correlations generated by the SFP, see the Appendix A.4.

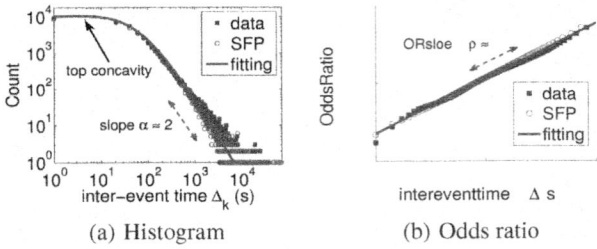

Figure 9: Comparison of the marginal distribution of the inter-event times generated by the SFP model with the inter-event times of the user of Figure 1. Observe that both the histogram (a) and the OR (b) are almost identical.

The SFP model naturally generates an odds ratio power law with slope $\rho = 1$, which is the slope that characterizes the majority of the users of our datasets (see Figure 4). To the best of our knowledge, this is the first work that studies the IED of human communications using such a varied, modern and large collection of data. Despite the fact that the means of communications are intrinsically different, having their own idiosyncrasies, we have observed that the IED of individuals of these systems have the same characteristics, i.e., they follow an odds ratio power law behavior. Moreover, when the OR slope $\rho = 1$, the power law exponent of the PDF is $\alpha = -2$ (see the Appendix B.5 for details). This is the same IED slope α reported in [18, 40] as a result of fluctuations in the execution rate and in particular periodic changes. It has been argued that seasonality can only robustly give rise to heavy-tailed IEDs when the exponent $\alpha = 2$. However, we again point out that the proposed (Generalized) SFP model (see the Appendix A) can generate IEDs with power-law slopes α varying in the range $(-\infty, -1)$, agreeing with all the empirical studies we are aware of. Moreover, we point out that the typical values of the parameters μ and ρ can be easily extracted from the distributions shown in Figures 5 and 4.

7. THE UNIFYING POWER OF THE SFP

Finally, we would like to emphasize the unifying power of the SFP. Several works [21, 32, 31, 30, 25, 23] claim that in the short term, real data behave as regular as a PP. Our model also captures that, since successive inter-event times are exponentially distributed, with similar (but not identical) rates. Thus, one of the major contributions of this work is the unification of the two seemingly-conflicting viewpoints we mentioned earlier. The proposed SFP model unifies both theories by generating Poisson-like traffic in the short term, with smoothly varying rate, like the second viewpoint, and also generates a power-law tail distribution (see the Appendix B.5), even matching the top-concavity that power laws cannot match, like the first modern approach of Barabási [2].

In Figure 10, we explicitly show the SFP's unifying power. We compare synthetic data generated by the SFP model using the same odds ratio slope ρ, median μ and number of events of the user of Figure 1 with the real data from this user. Notice the bursts of activity and also the long periods of inactivity, in the first two columns of Figure 10. Also notice that both synthetic and real traffic significantly deviate from Poisson (sloping lines in Figures 10-b and 10-f) but are similar between themselves. However, in the short term, both real and synthetic data behave like Poisson, being practically on top of the black dashed lines of Figures 10-d and 10-h.

8. CONCLUSIONS

In this paper, we propose the SFP model, which reconciles previous approaches for human communication dynamics. The SFP is a parsimonious generator that requires at most two intuitive parameters, and yet it has several desirable properties:

- Realism: it matches very well the properties of the IEDs of eight large, diverse and real systems, such as online forums, Youtube comments, online news, e-mails, SMSs and phone calls;

- Unification Power: it reconciles seemingly-contradicting theories on human communication dynamics. Our model exhibits power law tail behavior and burstiness in the long term, as well as Poisson-like behavior in the short term;

- It avoids the "i.i.d. fallacy": inter-event times are not independent, i.e., the time needed for the next event to arrive depends on the time the previous event took to arrive. Our model is the first to capture this very subtle point.

Moreover, there are two additional contributions: (i) the proposal to use the so-called "Odds Ratio" function using the cumulative distribution function – most of our real data seems to obey a power-law in their Odds-Ratio function, even when their PDF deviates from a power-law; (ii) the proposal to use the log-logistic distribution, which has power-law tail, but also exhibits the so-called "top-concavity", that real data seem to have.

9. REFERENCES

[1] L. Akoglu, P. O. S. Vaz de Melo, and C. Faloutsos. Quantifying reciprocity in large weighted communication networks. In *Pacific-Asia Conference on Knowledge Discovery and Data Mining (PAKDD), 2012, Kuala Lumpur,* 2012.

[2] A. Barabási. The origin of bursts and heavy tails in human dynamics. *Nature*, 435:207–211, May 2005.

[3] S. Bennett. Log-logistic regression models for survival data. *Journal of the Royal Statistical Society. Series C (Applied Statistics)*, 32(2):165–171, 1983.

[4] G. E. P. Box, G. M. Jenkins, and G. C. Reinsel. *Time Series Analysis, Forecasting, and Control*. Prentice-Hall, Englewood Cliffs, New Jersey, third edition, 1994.

[5] J. Cao, W. S. Cleveland, D. Lin, and D. X. Sun. Internet traffic tends to poisson and independent as the load increases. Technical report, Bell Labs Technical Report, 2001.

[6] F. Chierichetti, R. Kumar, P. Raghavan, and T. Sarlos. Are web users really markovian? In *Proceedings of the 21st international conference on World Wide Web*, WWW '12, pages 609–618, New York, NY, USA, 2012. ACM.

[7] A. Clauset, C. R. Shalizi, and M. E. J. Newman. Power-law distributions in empirical data. *SIAM Review*, 51(4):661+, Feb 2009.

[8] W. S. Cleveland. Robust Locally Weighted Regression and Smoothing Scatterplots. *Journal of the American Statistical Association*, 74(368):829–836, 1979.

[9] D. Cox and V. Isham. *Point Processes*. Monographs on Applied Probability and Statistics. Taylor & Francis, 1980.

[10] D. R. Cox. Some Statistical Methods Connected with Series of Events. *Journal of the Royal Statistical Society. Series B (Methodological)*, 17(2):129–164, 1955.

[11] M. De Choudhury, H. Sundaram, A. John, and D. D. Seligmann. Social synchrony: Predicting mimicry of user actions in online social media. In *Proceedings of the 2009 International Conference on Computational Science and Engineering - Volume 04*, pages 151–158, Washington, DC, USA, 2009. IEEE Computer Society.

[12] J.-P. Eckmann, E. Moses, and D. Sergi. Entropy of dialogues creates coherent structures in e-mail traffic. *Proceedings of the National Academy of Sciences of the United States of America*, 101(40):14333–14337, October 2004.

[13] M. Faloutsos, P. Faloutsos, and C. Faloutsos. On power-law relationships of the internet topology. In *SIGCOMM '99: Proceedings of the conference on Applications, technologies, architectures, and protocols for computer communication*, pages 251–262, New York, NY, USA, 1999. ACM.

[14] P. R. Fisk. The graduation of income distributions. *Econometrica*, 29(2):171–185, 1961.

[15] S. Garriss, M. Kaminsky, M. J. Freedman, B. Karp, D. Mazières, and H. Yu. Re: Reliable email. In *Proceedings of the Third USENIX/ACM Symposium on Networked System Design and Implementation (NSDI'06)*, pages 297–310, 2006.

[16] S. S. Gokhale and K. S. Trivedi. Log-logistic software reliability growth model. In *HASE '98: The 3rd IEEE International Symposium on High-Assurance Systems Engineering*, pages 34–41, Washington, DC, USA, 1998. IEEE Computer Society.

[17] F. A. Haight. *Handbook of the Poisson distribution [by] Frank A. Haight*. Wiley New York,, 1967.

[18] C. A. Hidalgo. Scaling in the inter-event time of random and seasonal systems. *PHYSICA A*, 369:877, 2006.

[19] M. Jamali, G. Haffari, and M. Ester. Modeling the temporal dynamics of social rating networks using bidirectional effects of social relations and rating patterns. In *Proceedings of the*

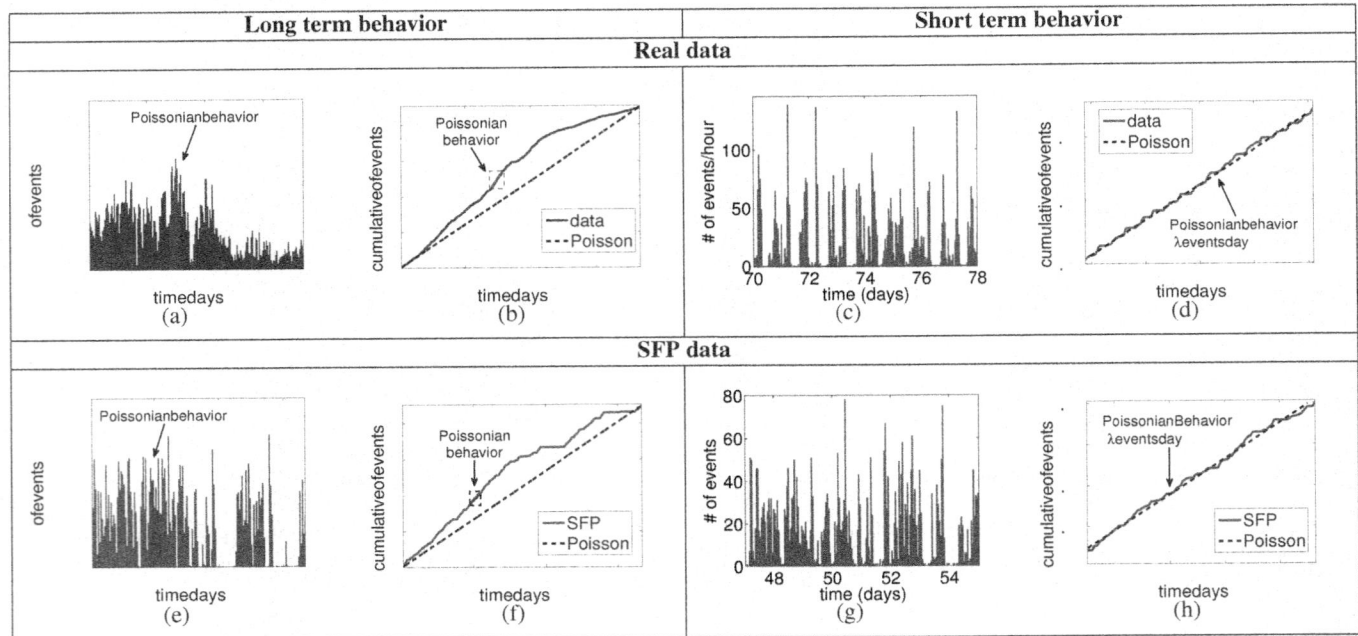

Figure 10: Unification Power of SFP: non-Poisson/bursty in the long term, but Poisson in the short term. Real data: Traffic of the user of Figure 2-1, showing event-count per unit time (a and c) and respective cumulative event-count (b and d). SFP data: synthetic traffic generated by the SFP model (with matching μ, ρ and event-count). Observe that (1) both time series are visually similar; (2) both are bursty in the long run (spikes; inactivity) (3) both are Poisson-like in the short term (last two columns)

20th international conference on World wide web, WWW '11, pages 527–536, New York, NY, USA, 2011. ACM.

[20] H. Jiang and C. Dovrolis. Why is the internet traffic bursty in short time scales? In *Proceedings of the 2005 ACM SIGMETRICS International Conference on Measurement and Modeling of Computer Systems (SIGMETRICS'05)*, pages 241–252, 2005.

[21] T. Karagiannis, M. Molle, M. Faloutsos, and A. Broido. A nonstationary Poisson view of Internet traffic. In *INFOCOM 2004. Twenty-third AnnualJoint Conference of the IEEE Computer and Communications Societies*, volume 3, pages 1558–1569 vol.3, 2004.

[22] M. Karsai, K. Kaski, A.-L. Barabási, and J. Kertész. Universal features of correlated bursty behaviour. *Scientific Reports*, 2, May 2012.

[23] J. Kleinberg. Bursty and hierarchical structure in streams. In *Proceedings of the eighth ACM SIGKDD*, KDD '02, pages 91–101, New York, NY, USA, 2002. ACM.

[24] B. Klimt and Y. Yang. Introducing the enron corpus. In *CEAS'04: The First Conference on Email and Anti-Spam*, 2004.

[25] A. Kuczura. The interrupted poisson process as an overflow process. *The Bell System Technical Journal*, 52:437–448, 1973.

[26] J. F. Lawless and J. F. Lawless. *Statistical Models and Methods for Lifetime Data (Wiley Series in Probability & Mathematical Statistics)*. John Wiley & Sons, January 1982.

[27] K. Lerman and T. Hogg. Using a model of social dynamics to predict popularity of news. In *Proceedings of the 19th international conference on World wide web*, WWW '10, pages 621–630, New York, NY, USA, 2010. ACM.

[28] M. O. Lorenz. Methods of measuring the concentration of wealth. *Publications of the American Statistical Association*, 9:209–219, 1905.

[29] T. Mahmood. Survival of newly founded businesses: A log-logistic model approach. *JournalSmall Business Economics*, 14(3):223–237, 2000.

[30] R. D. Malmgren, J. M. Hofman, L. A. Amaral, and D. J. Watts. Characterizing individual communication patterns. In *Proceedings of the 15th ACM SIGKDD international conference on Knowledge discovery and data mining*, KDD '09, pages 607–616, New York, NY, USA, 2009. ACM.

[31] R. D. Malmgren, D. B. Stouffer, A. S. L. O. Campanharo, and L. A. N. Amaral. On universality in human correspondence activity. *SCIENCE*, 325:1696, 2009.

[32] R. D. Malmgren, D. B. Stouffer, A. E. Motter, and L. A. N. Amaral. A poissonian explanation for heavy tails in e-mail communication. *Proceedings of the National Academy of Sciences*, 105(47):18153–18158, November 2008.

[33] C. S. M.I. Ahmad and A. Werritty. Log-logistic flood frequency analysis. *Journal of Hydrology*, 98:205–224, 1988.

[34] J. G. Oliveira and A.-L. Barabasi. Human dynamics: Darwin and Einstein correspondence patterns. *Nature*, 437(7063):1251, Oct. 2005.

[35] M. Owczarczuk. Long memory in patterns of mobile phone usage. *Physica A: Statistical Mechanics and its Applications*, Oct. 2011.

[36] K. Radinsky, K. Svore, S. Dumais, J. Teevan, A. Bocharov, and E. Horvitz. Modeling and predicting behavioral dynamics on the web. In *Proceedings of the 21st international conference on World Wide Web*, WWW '12, pages 599–608, New York, NY, USA, 2012. ACM.

[37] E. Shmueli, A. Kagian, Y. Koren, and R. Lempel. Care to comment?: recommendations for commenting on news stories. In *Proceedings of the 21st international conference on World Wide Web*, WWW '12, pages 429–438, New York, NY, USA, 2012. ACM.

[38] P. O. S. Vaz de Melo, L. Akoglu, C. Faloutsos, and A. A. F. Loureiro. Surprising patterns for the call duration distribution of mobile phone users. In *The European Conference on Machine Learning and Principles and Practice of Knowledge Discovery in Databases (ECML/PKDD)*, pages 354–369, 2010.

[39] P. O. S. Vaz de Melo, C. Faloutsos, and A. A. Loureiro. Human dynamics in large communication networks. In *SIAM Conference on Data Mining (SDM)*, pages 968–879. SIAM / Omnipress, 2011.

[40] A. Vazquez, J. G. Oliveira, Z. Dezso, K.-I. Goh, I. Kondor, and A.-L. Barabasi. Modeling bursts and heavy tails in human dynamics. *Phys Rev E Stat Nonlin Soft Matter Phys*, 73:036127, 2006.

[41] H. Wold and U. universitet. Statistiska institutionen. *On Stationary Point Processes and Markov Chains*. Selected publications - University of Uppsala, Department of Statistics. Swedish and Danish Actuarial Societies, 1948.

APPENDIX

A. THE GENERALIZED SFP MODEL

A.1 Model Definition

In Figure 4 we showed the slopes ρ of the OR fitting for the IEDs of all individuals of our datasets. It is fascinating that the typical ρ_i for the individuals of seven of our eight datasets is approximately 1, the same slope generated by the SFP model. Several individuals though, mainly from the SMS dataset, have a much higher value of ρ, close to $\rho \approx 2$. To accommodate that and all the variance seen in the data, we introduce our Generalized SFP model, which needs just one parameter more, ρ. Thus, we have:

MODEL 2. *Generalized Self-Feeding Process $SFP(\mu,\rho)$.*

$$\begin{aligned}
\delta_1 &\leftarrow \mu \\
\delta_t &\leftarrow Exponential\ (mean: \beta = \delta_{t-1} + \mu^\rho/e) \\
\Delta_k &\leftarrow \delta_t^{1/\rho}.
\end{aligned}$$

Note the auxiliary variable δ_t, which stores the inter-event times without the influence of ρ.

A.2 Parameters

Before reaching the full SFP model described in the paper, we had a simpler version of it, relying on a different parametrization scheme:

MODEL 3. *Self-Feeding Process SFP (C,a).*

$$\begin{aligned}
\delta_1 &\leftarrow C \\
\delta_t &\leftarrow Poisson\ Process(\beta = \delta_{t-1} + C) \\
\Delta_k &\leftarrow \delta_t^a,
\end{aligned} \quad (4)$$

where C is the location parameter and a is the shape parameter that defines the odds ratio slope ρ. An easy and direct way to define the relationships between this model's parameters and the distribution properties μ and ρ is through simulations.

Thus, the first point we consider is the median μ of the inter-event times generated by the SFP model when $a = 0$. When $OR(x) = 1$, x is the median μ of the distribution. Thus, in Figure 11-a, we plot the OR for different values of C. We observe that changing the value of C changes μ and, consequently, the location of the distribution, but maintains its slope. We also see that μ is close but different than the value of C.

In order to investigate the relationship between C and μ, we run simulations of the model for all integer values of C between [1,10000]. As we observe in Figure 11-b, the median μ of the inter-event times distribution (IED) varies linearly with C according to a slope of ≈ 2.72, that can be approximated by Euler's number e, in a way that $\mu \propto e \times C$. This allows us to generate inter-event times with a determined μ when the slope $\rho = 1$. We ignore the constant factor 3.8 because its 95% confidence interval is $(-8.596, 16.3)$, which contains zero.

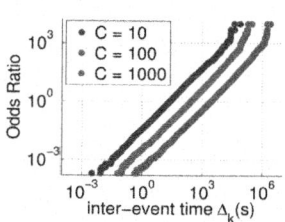 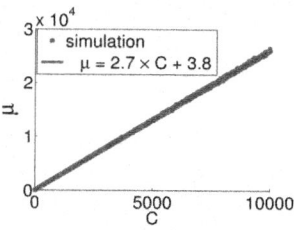

(a) The OR of the IED for different values of C

(b) μ as a function of C

Figure 11: **Changing the value of C changes the location of the distribution. The median of the distribution μ varies linearly with C, $\mu = a \times C + b$, with $a = 2.719$ and $b = 3.8$. The 95% confidence interval for a is $(2.715, 2.723)$ and for b is $(-8.60, 16.3)$. Since the confidence interval for b contains 0, b is not significant.**

Now we know how to generate inter-event times with different medians μ using the parameter $C = \mu/e$ of SFP. The next step is to verify how the SFP model can generate IEDs with a desired slope $\rho \neq 1$. Considering that up to this point the SFP model generates a set of inter-event times I_1 with a slope 1, the idea is to use an exponent a to transform I_1 into I_ρ, which is an IED with a different slope ρ. When we elevate each $\Delta_k \in I_1$ to the power of $a \neq 1$, the resulting slope ρ becomes different than 1, as we see in Figure 12-a. In the same way we did for C, we run simulations of the model for 1000 different values of $a \in [0.1, 2]$. As we observe in Figure 12-b, there is an inverse relationship between a and ρ, i.e., $\rho = a^{-1}$. Moreover, since the median of the distribution is also elevated to the power of a, we have to elevate the parameter μ to the power of $\rho = a^{-1}$ to preserve the median.

A.3 The need for the constant μ/e in SFP

LEMMA 1. *The constant $C = \mu/e > 0$ of Model 3 is needed to assure that the inter-event times generated by the SFP model will not converge to zero.*

PROOF. If we remove the constant C from Model 2, $\Delta_k = (\Delta_{k-1}) \times (-\ln(U(0, 1)))$, or Δ_k will be equal to Δ_{k-1} multiplied by a random number X extracted from the exponential distribution with parameter $\beta = \lambda = 1$. If $(X = \frac{1}{k} \mid k > 1)$, then Δ_k will be equal to Δ_{k-1} divided by k. The probability of X to be $\frac{1}{k}$ is $P(X = \frac{1}{k}) = e^{-\frac{1}{k}} = \frac{1}{\sqrt[k]{e}}$. On the other hand, the probability of multiplying Δ_k by k and, therefore, return Δ_{k+1} to Δ_{k-1} value is $P(X = k) = e^{-k} = \frac{1}{e^k}$. Given

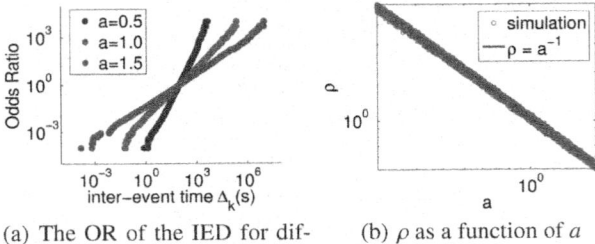

(a) The OR of the IED for different values of a

(b) ρ as a function of a

Figure 12: Changing the value of a changes the slope ρ of the distribution in a way that $\rho = a^{-1}$.

these probabilities, observe that $P(X = \frac{1}{k}) = \frac{1}{\sqrt[k]{e}} > P(X = k) = \frac{1}{e^k}, \forall k > 1$. From this, we conclude that the expected value of Δ_k when $t \to \infty$ is 0. With C in the equation, even when $\Delta_{k-1} = 0$, $\Delta_k = -C \times \ln(U(0, 1))$, that is a classic Poisson process with $\beta = C$, and, obviously, does not converge to 0. □

A.4 Lower Temporal Correlation

The SFP model is build upon a direct dependence between consecutive inter-event times. Because of that, the correlation between consecutive inter-event times is significantly higher than real data. While the average Pearson's correlation coefficient for real data is approximately 0.4, for synthetic data generated by the SFP model it is approximately 0.7. In order to generate more realistic data, we suggest a slight modification of the SFP process. Instead of generating the next inter-event time (Δ_k) based on the immediate previous one (Δ_{k-1}), we propose that it should be generated from a ϵ-th previous one ($\Delta_{k-\epsilon}$). This can be done by extracting ϵ from an exponential distribution with mean $\beta = 1$ and making its ceiling, so the lower bound for ϵ is 1. In summary, the SFP model is changed as follows:

MODEL 4. *Self-Feeding Process* SFP*(μ).*
//μ is the desired median of the marginal PDF

Δ_1	$\leftarrow$	μ
ϵ	$\leftarrow$	$\lceil Exponential\ (mean\ \beta = 1) \rceil$
Δ_k	$\leftarrow$	$Exponential\ (mean\ \beta = \Delta_{k-\epsilon} + \mu/e)$

Observe in Figure 13 that the synthetic data generate by the SFP* has a lower correlation (0.43) between consecutive inter-event times than the original one (0.70). Despite of that, the odds ratio generated by the SFP* is still a power law with slope $\rho \approx 1$.

B. THE SFP STATIONARY DISTRIBUTION

B.1 Analytical Result

The SFP model is within the general class of Wold processes defined as processes with Markov-dependent interevents intervals [41, 10]. These processes have not been extensively studied in the literature, perhaps due to the mathematical difficulties in deriving their probabilistic properties. Consider the existence of a stationary distribution for the generalized SFP model. A stationary PDF $f(x)$

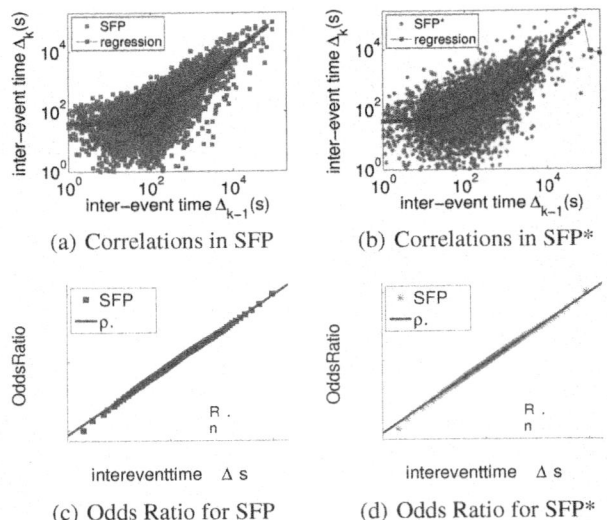

(a) Correlations in SFP

(b) Correlations in SFP*

(c) Odds Ratio for SFP

(d) Odds Ratio for SFP*

Figure 13: Comparison between the synthetic data generated by the SFP and the SFP*. Observe that the synthetic data generate by the SFP* has a lower correlation (0.43) between consecutive inter-event times than the SFP (0.70). Despite of that, the odds ratio generated by the SFP* is still a power law with slope $\rho \approx 1$.

of the Markov chain δ_t must satisfy

$$\begin{aligned} f(x) &= \int_0^\infty f(y \to x) f(y) dy \\ &= \int_0^\infty \frac{1}{y + \mu^\rho/e} \exp(-x/(y + \mu^\rho/e)) f(y) dy \end{aligned}$$

This integral equation has no obvious analytical solution but in the next sections we show via simulations of the point process that $f(x)$ is very well approximated by a log-logistic density. This mathematical difficulty is common in the previous attempts to model data with Wold processes. Even if a consistent density $f(x)$ and a transition kernel $f(y \to x)$ are given, properties are, in general, difficult to obtain [9].

B.2 Fitting Synthetic Data

In Figure 14-a, we plot the histogram of 100,000 time intervals Δ_k generated by the SFP model with $\mu = e$. Moreover, in Figure 14-b, we plot the OR for the same time intervals. While a classic PP generates an exponential distribution, we observe that the generated data by the SFP perfectly fits a distribution with an Odds Ratio function that is a power law with slope $\rho = 1$. Thus, we propose the following conjecture:

CONJECTURE 1. *The SFP model generates a log-logistic distribution with $\rho = \sigma = 1$,*

where σ is the shape parameter of the log-logistic distribution.

We have several and significant evidences that the SFP generates a log-logistic distribution, but at this moment we do not have a formal analytical proof that this is true.

B.3 The SFP Markov Chain

The SFP can be naturally considered as a Markov Chain (MC), since it is a sequence of random variables $\Delta_1, \Delta_2, \Delta_3, \ldots$ with the

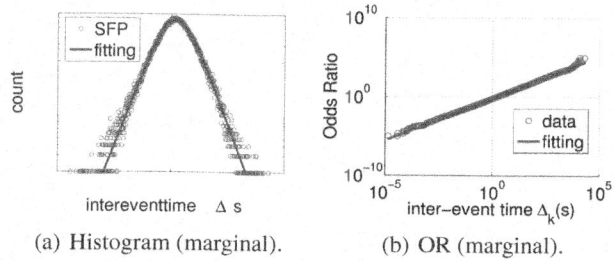

(a) Histogram (marginal). (b) OR (marginal).

Figure 14: Inter-event times Δ_k generated by the SFP. The generated Δ_ks are perfectly fitted by a log-logistic distribution with the slope $\rho = \sigma = 1$.

Markov property, namely that, given the present inter-event time, or state, the future and past inter-event times, or states, are independent. Thus, here we model the SFP as a time-homogeneous Markov chain with a finite state space to give another evidence that the SFP has a stationary distribution and that it is very likely that this distribution is the log-logistic.

Originally, the SFP can be considered as a continuous-time MC, but for simplicity, we build a discrete-time Markov chain in a way that each state $\Delta_i = \{\Delta_1, \Delta_2, \Delta_3, ...\}$ represents the inter-event times with values within the interval $(i - 1, i]$. For instance, considering the granularity in seconds, if the current inter-event time is 3.8 seconds, then the MC is in the state Δ_4. Also for simplicity, we build a finite-state MC with a maximum number of states n, i.e., the states go from Δ_1 to Δ_n. The MC will be in state Δ_n every time the current inter-event time is within the interval (n, ∞).

Thus, considering a n-state MC build from the SFP model, the transitions probabilities $p_{i,j}$ of going from state Δ_i to Δ_j are given in the following way:

$$p_{i,j} = \begin{cases} CDF_{exp}(x{=}j,\beta{=}i{+}C) - CDF_{exp}(x{=}j{-}1,\beta{=}i{+}C) & \text{if } j<n \\ 1 - CDF_{exp}(x{=}j,\beta{=}i{+}C) & \text{if } j=n, \end{cases}$$

where $CDF_{exp}(x, \beta)$ is the cumulative distribution function of the exponential distribution on x with mean β and $C = \mu/e$, given by the SFP (Equation 1). Observe in Figure 15 that the probability density function of the log-logistic is virtually identical to the one of the stationary distribution of the SFP Markov Chain. This is another strong indication that the SFP generates log-logistically distributed data.

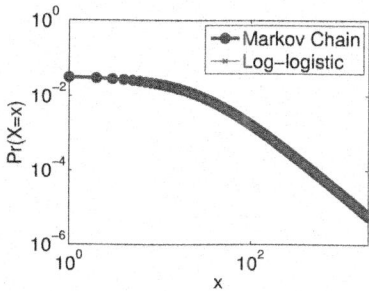

Figure 15: The probability density function of the log-logistic distribution and the stationary distribution of the SFP MC.

It is important to point out that in [6] the authors showed that the behavior of Web users is not Markovian, i.e., a user's next action does not depends only on her/his current state. Our assumption differs from this one because we assume that users have Markovian behavior in communications, while [6] studied whether users have Markovian behavior while navigating on the Web.

B.4 Log-logistic Distribution

The log-logistic distribution was first proposed by Fisk [14] to model income distribution, after observing that the OR plot of real data in log-log scales follows a power law $OR(x) = cx^\rho$. In summary, a random variable is log-logistically distributed if the logarithm of the random variable is logistically distributed. The logistic distribution is very similar to the normal distribution, but it has heavier tails. In the literature, there are examples of the use of the log-logistic distribution in survival analysis [3, 29], distribution of wealth [14], flood frequency analysis [33], software reliability [16] and phone calls duration [38]. A commonly used log-logistic parametrization is [26]:

$$\begin{aligned} PDF_{LLG}(x) &= \frac{e^z}{\sigma x (1+e^z)^2}, \\ CDF_{LLG}(x) &= \frac{1}{1+e^{-z}}, \\ z &= (\ln(x) - \ln(\mu))/\sigma, \end{aligned} \quad (5)$$

where $\sigma = 1/\rho$, the slope of our SFP model, and μ is the same. Moreover, when $\sigma = 1$, it is the same distribution as the Generalized Pareto distribution [28] with shape parameter $\kappa = 1$, scale parameter μ and threshold parameter $\theta = 0$.

B.5 SFP has Power Law Tail

The universality class model proposed by Barabási [2] states that the IED has a power law tail. The proposed SFP model agrees with this model in a way that:

LEMMA 2. *If Conjecture 1 is correct, then the SFP model generates an IED that converges to a power law when $x \to \infty$, i.e., $\lim_{x \to \infty} \frac{PDF_{LLG}(x)}{x^{-\alpha}} = k$, where k is a constant greater than 0.*

PROOF. Considering the Probability Density Function of the log-logistic distribution showed in Equation 5, if we set the location parameter $\mu = 1$ for simplicity, $e^z = x^{1/\sigma}$. Then, $PDF_{LLG}(x)$ can be simplified to

$$PDF_{LLG}(x) = \frac{x^{\frac{1}{\sigma}-1}}{\sigma(1 + x^{\frac{1}{\sigma}})^2}.$$

When $x \to \infty$, the addition of 1 in the denominator can be disregarded, resulting in the following simplification:

$$PDF_{LLG}(x) = \frac{x^{-(1+1/\sigma)}}{\sigma}, x \to \infty.$$

Thus, when $x \to \infty$, the IED generated by the SFP model is a power law with slope

$$\alpha = -(1 + 1/\sigma) = -(1 + \rho). \quad (6)$$

Observe again Figure 14-a and note the power law tail. □

C. SFP CODE

Below we show the *Python* code for the SFP generator.

```
def SFP(n, mu, rho=1):
    #first inter-event time
    deltat = mu
    #list of inter-event times
    Deltat = []
    for i in range(1, n):
        #Poisson Process which Beta=deltat+mu/e
        deltat = -(deltat+(mu**rho)/math.e)
        deltat = deltat * math.log(random.random())
        Deltat.append(deltat**(1/rho))
    return Deltat
```

Whom to Mention: Expand the Diffusion of Tweets by @ Recommendation on Micro-blogging Systems

Beidou Wang[†], Can Wang[†], Jiajun Bu[†], Chun Chen[†], Wei Vivian Zhang[♯], Deng Cai[‡], Xiaofei He[‡]

[†]Zhejiang Provincial Key Laboratory of Service Robot, College of Computer Science, Zhejiang University, China
[♯]Microsoft Corporation, Redmond, WA, USA
[‡]State Key Lab of CAD&CG, College of Computer Science, Zhejiang University, China
[†]{beidou,wcan,bjj,chenc}@zju.edu.cn, [♯]wzha@microsoft.com,
[‡]{dengcai,xiaofeihe}@cad.zju.edu.cn

ABSTRACT

Nowadays, micro-blogging systems like Twitter have become one of the most important ways for information sharing. In Twitter, a user posts a message (tweet) and the others can forward the message (retweet). *Mention* is a new feature in micro-blogging systems. By mentioning users in a tweet, they will receive notifications and their possible retweets may help to initiate large cascade diffusion of the tweet. To enhance a tweet's diffusion by finding the right persons to mention, we propose in this paper a novel recommendation scheme named as *whom-to-mention*. Specifically, we present an in-depth study of *mention* mechanism and propose a recommendation scheme to solve the essential question of whom to mention in a tweet. In this paper, *whom-to-mention* is formulated as a ranking problem and we try to address several new challenges which are not well studied in the traditional information retrieval tasks. By adopting features including user interest match, content-dependent user relationship and user influence, a machine learned ranking function is trained based on newly defined information diffusion based relevance. The extensive evaluation using data gathered from real users demonstrates the advantage of our proposed algorithm compared with the traditional recommendation methods.

Categories and Subject Descriptors

H.3.5 [**Online Information Services**]: Web-based services

General Terms

Theory

Keywords

Micro-blogging Systems; Twitter; Mention; Recommendation; Information Diffusion; Information Retrieval

1. INTRODUCTION

With more than 140 million active users and over 340 million messages posted per day, Twitter has become one of the most influential media for spreading and sharing breaking news, personal updates and spontaneous ideas. In Micro-blogging systems like Twitter, users tweet about any topics within the 140-character limit and follow others to receive their tweets. Furthermore, with *retweeting* (forward a tweet), information can be effectively relayed beyond adjacent neighbors, virtually giving every user the power to spread information broadly.

However, recent studies [2][31][37] show that the diffusion power of tweets from different users varies significantly: 0.05 percent of Twitter users attract almost 50 percent of all attention within Twitter and the spread of a tweet from an ordinary user is rather limited, with an average retweet rate of 0.11. This suggests a very limited diffusion for most tweets.

Fortunately, as a new feature in Micro-blogging systems, *Mention* can help ordinary users to improve the visibility of their tweets and go beyond their immediate reach in social interactions. *Mention* is enabled in a tweet by adding "@username". All the users mentioned by a tweet will receive a mention notification (*e.g.* by an e-mail) and are able to retrieve the tweet from their personal mention tab. By using *Mention*, one can draw attention from a specific user, or highlight a place or organization anytime. Properly using mention can quickly help an ordinary user spreading his tweets:

1. By mentioning a non-follower of the tweet author, the non-follower may retweet it to his followers and spread the tweet to a new group of users, which usually leads to further cascade diffusion.

2. By mentioning a follower of the author, the mention serves as a useful notification, especially when the follower follows a large number of other users and a tweet can be easily swamped in the enormous number of tweets. It's also critical for a tweet to be viewed promptly as 25% replies to a tweet happen within 67 seconds, 75% within 17 minutes and 75% message flow lasts less than an hour [35]. So, without proper notification, a tweet may easily be neglected as one's followers fail to read it in time.

Despite the significance of the mention feature, to the best of our knowledge, *Mention Recommendation* is seldom studied in previous works. To better help an ordinary user spreading their thought in Micro-blogging systems, we propose in this paper a novel Mention Recommendation algorithm named *whom-to-mention*, in which we help a tweet to reach more

Copyright is held by the International World Wide Web Conference Committee (IW3C2). IW3C2 reserves the right to provide a hyperlink to the author's site if the Material is used in electronic media.
WWW 2013, May 13–17, 2013, Rio de Janeiro, Brazil.
ACM 978-1-4503-2035-1/13/05.

people by recommending proper users to be mentioned before publishing it.

The recommendation task can be formulated as a ranking problem. Traditionally, one can rank users based on the similarity between a tweet and a user's profile (e.g. the aggregation of all the tweets posted by a user) and recommend the top ranked users to be mentioned. However, there are several challenges which make the traditional recommendation methods fail:

Information Diffusion Based Relevance: In classic information retrieval tasks (e.g. TREC *adhoc* retrieval tasks), relevance is usually interpreted as topical relevance, which stands for to what extent the topic of a result matches the topic of the query. However, the goal of *mention recommendation* is to find candidates who can help spread a tweet. Instead of topical relevance, the information diffusion power should be considered in the relevance judgement.

Content-dependent User Relationship Model: In traditional social network recommendation, user relationship is usually modeled as a weighted graph with edges indicating the bonds between two users based on explicit social relationship. The interactive functions (e.g. retweet, reply, mention) in micro-blogging systems allow us to adopt the implicit network derived from user's interactive behaviors to achieve more precise user relationship predictions. Moreover, it brings in new features for modeling user relationship, as users' interactions are usually content (topic) related, which makes the user relationship model content-dependent. For instance, a user may selectively retweet sport news from another user while ignoring other contents such as movie comments from the same user. Modeling the content-dependent user relationship based on the implicit network of user interactions thus remains as a challenge.

Recommendation Length Restriction: Due to the strict length restriction of a tweet, only a small number of users can be mentioned in a tweet. Moreover, a tweet mentioning a lot of users is likely to be treated as a spam tweet, which will decrease others' interest in retweeting it. Thus, to accomplish the mention recommendation task, the algorithm needs to be optimized for mentioning only a small number of users.

Recommendation Overload Problem: Traditional recommendation systems such as those used in Amazon may recommend one item to large numbers of users, which results in popular products. However, in the mention recommendation system, a user being recommended too many times will suffer from the severe mention overload problems. Tons of mention notifications will not only interrupt user's daily use of microblogs, but also result in frustration and decrease user's interest in retweeting.

To cope with all the above mentioned challenges, *whom-to-mention* is proposed in this paper. We use a machine learning approach to train a ranking model which consists of three parts: ranking features, relevance and a ranking function [10]:

We adopt a series of new *features* to deliver more precise mention recommendation, including: the match of the given tweet and interest profiles of the recommended users, the user relationship between the recommended users and the author of the tweet, and the influence of the recommended users. Furthermore, we manage to model user relationship based on the implicit network derived from user retweet interactions, which we name as *user social ties* model. We take advantage of the content-dependent feature of user social ties and make use of the content feature of the tweets one user has retweeted from another in a user social tie.

Instead of the classic topical relevance model, the relevance in *whom-to-mention* is redefined as the potential diffusion a user may bring to a tweet, estimating by the expectation user coverage, which will be further explained in section 4.2.

A Support Vector Regression (SVR) based ranking function is then trained to calculate the relevance of a candidate user to a tweet and ranks the most relevant candidates on the top of the recommendation list. Constraints are carefully designed in the ranking process to avoid the recommendation overload problem.

It is worthwhile to highlight the following three aspects of our *whom-to-mention* recommendation scheme in this paper.

1. We present the first in-depth study of mention feature in microblogs by resolving the most essential problem of whom to mention. Instead of passively waiting to be retweeted by others, our novel recommendation scheme allows users to improve the diffusion of their tweets by reaching out to the right person with the help of mention recommendation.

2. We formulate the mention recommendation as a ranking problem and to find the most proper users to be mentioned, a ranking function is learned with a novel information diffusion based relevance, incorporating with new features including user interest match, user social ties and user influence. We model user relationship based on the implicit network derived from user's retweet interactions and take fully exploit of its content-dependent features.

3. Our method is thoroughly evaluated on a real life dataset. *Whom-to-mention* algorithm is proved highly effective compared against a large number of baselines. We analyze how different features affect the recommendation performance with aborative designed comparison experiment. New issues like recommendation length restriction and recommendation overload problem is careful evaluated and discussed.

2. RELATED WORK

2.1 Recommendation Approaches

Using information retrieval approaches to recommend documents, users or items has been a fertile area of research. Content-based recommendation systems like [25][27], recommend items similar to those that a user liked in the past. Though the use of information retrieval on recommendation has been studied for a long time, new studies keep emerging to solve all kinds of new challenges [33]. For instance, Diaz *et al.* make the first in-depth study of information retrieval approaches applied to match-making systems and study unique problems like two-sided and subjective relevance[10]. In our work, the information diffusion based relevance, new features like *user social ties*, new challenges like the recommendation length restriction and overload problem all make our *whom-to-mention* different from previous information retrieval approaches.

Most of the prior work on social network recommendation mainly focuses on recommending interesting users or contents [11]. Hsu et al. address the problem of link recommendation in weblogs and similar social networks by proposing an approach based on collaborative recommendation using the link structure of a social network and content-based recommendation using mutual declared interests [17]. Chen et al. study people recommendations designed to help users find known, offline contacts and discover new friends on social networking sites [7]. Guy et al. study personalized recommendation of social software items and make a comparison between recommendations that are based on the user's familiarity network and his similarity network[13]. None of previous works can be directly applied to *whom-to-mention* task and solve all the new challenges.

2.2 Learning to Rank

Learning to rank has been a popular research area. Existing approaches can be roughly divided into three categories: pointwise approaches[21][26] in which the learning-to-rank problem can be approximated by predicting the score of a single query-document pair and various regression and ordinal regression algorithms can be adopted in this kind of approaches; pairwise approaches [4][5], in which the ranking problem is reduced to pairwise classification and the goal is to minimize average number of inversions in ranking; listwise approaches [28][36], in which the value of the evaluation measures is optimized directly, averaged over all queries in the training data. The ranking algorithm from our work belongs to the pointwise approaches.

2.3 Studies on Micro-blogging Systems

With the launch of Twitter in 2007, microblogs become highly popular and large numbers of researches have been done. Our research is involved with structure and user relationship analysis of microblogs, user interest modeling, recommendation, information diffusion and influential users identification on micro-blogging systems.

The characteristics of network structure and user relationship of microblogs have attracted much attention in the past few years. Kwak et al. make the first quantitative study on the information diffusion on Twitter by studying the topological characteristics of Twitter and provide lots of statistic details of Twitter[20]. Besides the network based on user's explicit following network of Twitter, analysis of the users' interactions in the implicit network of Twitter has been an emerging area [30][18]. Sousa et al. analyze replies of a specific Twitter dataset and a slight tendency for people selectively choosing whom to reply based on the topic of the tweets is found [30]. Jang et al. propose an egocentric semantic social network based on user reply interactions on Twitter, but the strength of user relationship is not considered and user bonds from different user pairs are incomparable[18].

A lot of works have been done on user interest modeling, Michelson et al. discover users' topics of Twitter by categorizing the entities in the tweets and developing a user profile by adopting the categorization result[23]. Hong et al. evaluate how the restricted length of the tweets can limit the potential of traditional topic models and the authors also show that training a topic model on aggregated messages can help to significantly enhance the experiment performance[16].

Information diffusion and influential user identification on Twitter have been extensively studied. Ye et al. first explore the propagation patterns of general messages on Twitter and how to measure social influence on Twitter [35]. Bakshy et al. study the attributes most relevant to the influence of Twitter users [3]. Cha et al. make an in-depth comparison of three measures of influence: indegree, retweets, and mentions and investigate the dynamics of user influence across topics and time [6]. Bakshy et al. find that predictions of which particular user will generate large cascades are relatively unreliable and word-of-mouth diffusion can only be harnessed reliably by targeting large numbers of potential influencers [2]. Romero et al. model the global influence of a node on the rate of diffusion through the network based on a Linear Influence Model [34].

Several researches have focused on recommending who to follow or what to read on Twitter. Hannon et al. recommend Twitter users to follow using content and collaborative filtering approaches [15] and Chen et al. recommend interesting content from information streams on Twitter considering features including content sources, topic interest models for users, and social voting [8]. To the best of our knowledge, recommendation on whom to mention in Twitter has never been studied in previous work.

3. PROBLEM DEFINITION

We formalize *whom-to-mention* into a retrieval scenario consisting of a set of users, U, each of whom maintains a user interest profile and a user influence profile. For a user $u \in U$, a user interest profile r_u, consists of a set of descriptive attributes and tf-idf features extracted from a modified bag of words model used on u's recent tweets. A user influence profile s_u is made up of attributes related to user's influence on Twitter. For users $u, v \in U$, there exists a social tie $tie_{u,v}$ based on the retweeting interactions between u and v, which includes a scalar attribute indicating the strength of bonds between u and v and tf-idf features extracted from the tweets u retweets from v. A query q consists of tf-idf features extracted from a specific tweet.

For each query (tweet) q from user u, we would like to rank all the other users $v \in U - u$ based on features including user interest match, user social ties and user's influence, so that the relevant candidates occur above non-relevant candidates.

4. RECOMMENDING WHOM TO MENTION BY LEARNING A RANKING MODEL

The key of *whom-to-mention* is to rank the candidate users given a specific tweet and we use a machine learning approach to train a ranking model for our recommendation task, which is made up of three parts: ranking features, relevance and a ranking function[10]. Ranking features include all the attributes which may influence the score of a candidate match. Based on our recommendation task, relevance refers to the potential diffusion a user could bring to a specific tweet. A ranking function is a machine learning model which predicts the relevance given observable ranking features. We will discuss the details of the three parts in this section.

4.1 Ranking Features

4.1.1 User Interest Match

The match of a tweet and the candidate's interest is an intuitively important feature for *whom-to-mention*. When mentioning a candidate in a tweet, a candidate interested in it is more likely to retweet it.

To calculate the match, the largest challenge is to generate the user interest model on micro-blogging systems, which differs from traditional user interest models because users' tweets are limited to only 140 characters in length, covering a wide variety of topics, as well as often presented with shorthands and special formats such as hash tags. Moreover, the nature of our recommendation task requires capturing more detailed aspects of interest. For instance, a football fan may be assumed interested in sports based on topic modeling technics like LDA. However, it is not a good interest match, if we mention the football fan in a tweet talking about a basketball match (because the tweet is also considered talking about sports, which makes a match for the tweet and the candidate).

Based on previous studies [16], topic modeling techniques like LDA may not fit the short-length, ambiguous, noisy data feature in Twitter. Consequently, we use a modified bag-of-words model to generate the user interest model.

To begin with, we aggregate a user's recent tweets. For a candidate user u, we define d_u as the set of recent tweets for u; in this work, we will assume that d_u is u's 1000 most recent tweets. We also extract the words from the *hash tag topics*, which we name as h_u and they are important because they are usually used to identify a topic or an event. Besides the tweets, we also consider all the attributes from the user profile page, including user's full name, the location, a short biography and tags. For a user u, we choose the short biography feature f_u and tag feature tag_u for the interest modeling. A user interest profile r_u is then defined as $r_u = \{d_u, h_u, f_u, tag_u\}$ and $R = \{r_u | u \in U\}$. In this way, R provides us the basis for user interest modeling.

To cope with the short noisy text, we first analyze around 50,000 hot short queries (popular words or phrases) based on a latest search engine query log covering a lot of new words and words in short-hand format and we denote these words as *Dict*. In this way, popular phrase like "Big Bang Theory" is considered as a word in *Dict*. We filter the text in R, eliminating all the stop words, only keeping a word if it's either identified as a noun or a word from *Dict*.

The name entity recognition for tweets is conducted with the help of ICTCLAS [1] (a toolkit used for word split and name entity recognition) and the query log is provided by Sogou [2] (a leading search engine company in China).

Given a query (tweet) q_u from user u, we apply the same word parsing strategy as mentioned above and represent q_u and R as tf.idf-based term vectors, which are further used to estimate the user interest match. With the help of Lucene, a proven, robust and scalable indexing and retrieval platform, the match score between a query q_u and a user interest profile r_v can thus be defined as:

$$iscore(q_u, r_v) = coord(q_u, r_v) \cdot queryNorm(q_u) \cdot \sum_{t \in q_u}(tf(t \in r_v) \cdot idf(t)^2 \cdot norm(t, r_v)) \quad (1)$$

The $tf(t \in r_v)$ correlates to the term's frequency:

$$tf(t \in r_v) = \sqrt{n_{t,r_v}} \quad (2)$$

where n_{t,r_v} is the frequency of term t in r_v and normalization of the document length is defined in $norm(t, r_v)$ for efficiency consideration.

$idf(t)$ stands for the *Inverse Documentary Frequency* defined as:

$$idf(t) = 1 + log(\frac{|R|}{|r : t \in r|}) \quad (3)$$

$norm(t, r_v)$ is a normalization factor defined as:

$$norm(t, r_v) = lengthNorm(r_v) \cdot boost(t) \quad (4)$$

where $lengthNorm$ is a length normalization factor which ensures short document contributes more to the score. We also consider boost factors that terms from different sources own different weights (e.g. a term from tag_u is more important than one from d_u). According to evaluation on training data, we set the boost $boost(t)$ as:

$$boost(t) = \begin{cases} 2 & \text{if } t \in h_u, f_u, tag_u \\ 1 & \text{if } t \notin h_u, f_u, tag_u \end{cases} \quad (5)$$

$coord(q_u, r_v)$ is a score factor based on how many query terms are found in document r_v and $queryNorm(q)$ is a normalization factor used to make scores between queries comparable. They are implemented using Lucene's function which details can be found here [3].

4.1.2 User Social Tie Modeling

User relationship plays an important role in *whom-to-mention* task, an acquaintance is usually more likely to retweet compared with a total stranger. Previous studies [20][19] mainly study explicit social connections based on the follow relationship of Twitter. However, according to a study of Facebook [1], people only communicate with a few of their explicit declared friends. So modeling user relationship based on some implicit networks can be better indicators of the actual social relationships between users.

In our work, user relationship model is based on implicit connections derived from users' retweet activities in micro-blogging systems, which we name as *user social tie model*. Though lots of work on retweet behaviors have been done, they are usually in the information diffusion perspective instead of modeling user relationships [2][3][6].

We make two assumptions in modeling user social ties. First, user social ties can be derived from the retweet interactions between two users and frequency of interaction can be used to quantify the strength of a social tie. Second, the social tie between two users is content-dependent. Thus in our model, a user social tie consists of three parts: nodes

---

[1] http://ictclas.org/
[2] http://www.sogou.com/labs/dl/w.html
[3] http://lucene.apache.org/core/old_versioned_docs/versions/3_0_0/api/core/org/apache/lucene/search/Similarity.html

including the two users of a tie, a strength score indicating how strong two users are bonded in a tie and a content vector indicating topics the user interested in retweeting. The details are explained as follows.

For users $u, v \in U$, we define tweet set $rt_{u,v}$ as:

$$rt_{u,v} = \{tw | tw \text{ is a tweet } u \text{ retweets from } v\} \quad (6)$$

We define the social tie strength as $str_{u,v}$

$$str_{u,v} = |rt_{u,v}| \quad (7)$$

We filter $rt_{u,v}$ with the same method mentioned in section 4.1.1 and define user social tie between user u and v as:

$$tie_{u,v} = \{rt_{u,v}, str_{u,v}\} \quad (8)$$

It is important to notice that $tie_{u,v} \neq tie_{v,u}$. Given a query q_u from user u, we can calculate the user relationship score by multiplying the strength of the social tie with the similarity between q_u and $rt_{u,v}$:

$$tscore(q_u, rt_{u,v}) = str_{u,v} \cdot coord(q_u, rt_{u,v}) \cdot queryNorm(q_u)$$
$$\cdot \sum_{t \in q_u} (tf(t \in rt_{u,v}) \cdot idf(t)^2 \cdot norm(t, rt_{u,v}))$$
$$(9)$$

All the factors in formula (9) are defined the same as in formula (1).

4.1.3 User Influence Modeling

Intuitvely, user influence is also important to the performance of our recommendation task. If two users are both likely to retweet the tweet, the more influential one could help it reach more people by initiating a larger cascade of retweet. Given a user u, we summarize a series of statistical indicators which may indicate his influence in Tabel 1.

We can define u's influence profile s_u as:

$$s_u = \{\text{Follower}(u), \text{Avg\_retweet}(u),$$
$$\text{Avg\_reply}(u), \text{Avg\_coverage}(u)\} \quad (10)$$

4.2 Relevance

In traditional text retrieval tasks (*e.g.* search engine retrieval tasks), relevance always refers to the topical match between the query and the document[10]. When interpreted in this way, we can always rely on editors to manually assess the relevance based on their experience and expertise. However, when it comes to our recommendation task, editors have to compare a query (tweet) with user profiles made up of thousands of tweets and analyze hundreds of content-based user relationship bonds, which makes the process time-consuming and result inaccurate.

Instead, we can calculate the relevance based on user behavioral information. Our recommendation scheme aims to spread a tweet to more people by mentioning proper users in it. So we can define the relevance between a query (tweet) and a user as the diffusion the user brings to it. Intuitively, the diffusion can be easily estimated by how many retweets a user initiates by retweeting the tweet. However, for ordinary users, the retweet cascades of their tweets are usually very small. For instance, given a tweet, if one user can results in 3 retweets each by a user with 100 followers and another user brings it 2 retweets each by a user with 1000 followers, the latter user obviously helps it to reach more people (2000

Table 1: Statistical Indicators on Modeling User Influence

Denotation	Explanation
Follower(u)	The number of followers of user u, one of the most popular metrics on estimating a user's influence.
Avg_retweet(u)	The average number of retweets for each tweet from u.
Avg_reply(u)	The average number of replies for each tweet from u.
Avg_coverage(u)	The average number of users a tweet from u can reach. The coverage of a tweet is defined in details in section 4.2.

vs. 300). Thus, it's more accurate to estimate the relevance based on the number of users a candidate helps the tweet to reach, which we name as *coverage*. We denote the relevance of query q and user v as $rel(q, v)$ and define it as:

$$rel(q, v) = \{\sum \text{Follower(u)} | \quad (11)$$
$$u \in \text{the retweet cascades initiate by } v\}$$

4.3 Ranking Function

Many machine learning models can be used as a ranking function for our *whom-to-mention* recommendation task. We adopt a machine learned ranking function based on support vector regression (SVR), because it is a sophisticated proven regression algorithm which is adaptive to complex systems, robust in dealing with corrupted data and with a good generalization ability [32].

Given a query q_u from user u and a candidate match v, we use SVR to compute a score to serve as the relevance $rel(q_u, v)$. We define $x_{q_u,v}$ as the feature vector corresponding to the pair (q_u, v).

$$x_{q_u,v} = \{iscore(q_u, r_v), tscore(q_u, rt_v), s_v\} \quad (12)$$

The set of training data is as $\{(x_1, y_1), ..., (x_n, y_n)\}$, where $x_i \subset R^m$ stands for the feature vector for a pair of query and candidate in which m is the number of feature dimensions, and $y_i \subset R$ stands for the corresponding relevance value.

A generic SVR estimating function is with the form as:

$$f(x) = (w \cdot \phi(x)) + b \quad (13)$$

$w \subset R^m, b \subset R$ and ϕ stands for a nonlinear transformation from R^m to high-dimensional space. The core goal of SVR is to learn the value of w and b to minimize risk of regression.

$$Risk(f) = C \sum_{i=0}^{n} L(f(x_i) - y_i) + \frac{1}{2}||w||^2 \quad (14)$$

$L(\cdot)$ is a loss function and C is a constant used to determine penalties to estimation errors which is determined with grids search and cross-validation techniques. We experiment the performance of different kernel functions and choose kernel function with best performance (RBF kernel). Details of SVR can be found in [29].

4.4 Recommendation Overload Problem

One new issue of our *whom-to-mention* task is that the recommendation may concentrate on a few popular users, which causes mention overload (users get too many mention notifications from the recommendation system). Moreover, different users may respond differently to the overload. For instance, some users may not want to receive any mention notification from the recommender at all, while some others may feel okay even if mentioned 100 times in a day.

In our recommendation framework, we carefully cope with this problem by allowing users to freely set an up-limit of recommended times per day. After ranking phase, all the candidates with recommended times up-limit reached are eliminated and the top k of the remaining candidates are then recommended. In real application, within a day, our recommendation scheme follows a *first publish, first to choose* policy and recommend the next best candidate once a user's recommendation up-limit is reached.

In our evaluation, since our test tweets are published over a period of time, we set the up-limit for mentioning at 25, which as a matter of fact, is a quite strict constraint.

5. EXPERIMENT SETTING

We design the experiment with 4 goals:(1) To evaluate how our proposed algorithm performs compared with other base-line algorithms;(2)To test how different features we considered affect the recommendation performance;(3) To examine how different ranking functions affect the results;(4) To consider how new challenges like the recommendation length restriction and recommendation overload affect the performance of our algorithm.

The key challenge of the experiment design lies in evaluating the information diffusion (coverage of users) resulted by mentioning a user in a tweet. Instead, we make an approximate estimation using the user's retweet behavior. For example, if user A retweets a tweet t and helps t reach 500 people, it's reasonable to assume that A will retweet it if we mention A in t. So in our evaluation, by mentioning A in t, the user coverage A brings to t is 500. If user B has never retweeted t, we assume B will not retweet t when mentioning him in t and the user coverage B brings to t thus is considered to be 0.

5.1 Data Collection

We collected data from Sina Weibo, a Twitter-like microblogging system in China with more than 400 million registered users and over 100 million messages posted per day. Different from Twitter's API, which is restricted in retrieving mention and retweet timelines, Weibo's API allows us to get all the tweets from a user's different timelines. Moreover, we obtained authorizations from over 5000 real Weibo users, who grant us full access to all the authentication-protected user data, including user profiles, tweets, the retweet timeline, the reply and mention timeline, and accurate reply and retweet number for each tweet. We parse 48,000 tweets published by the authorized users, only keeping tweets being retweeted more than 5 times, which leaves us 132,796 retweet records and 7800 tweets to serve as the training and testing tweets.

Based on the retweet records, 52,468 users participate in retweeting and are considered as our recommendation candidates. We collect the most recent 1000 tweets from these users (around 46 million in total) and record their personal information including the full name, the location, user biography *etc*. Average retweet rate and relpy rate for each user are calculated based on the most recent 200 tweets (around 11 million in total). 97,164 user social ties are established based on retweet interactions. In our experiment, we split the parsed tweets into training and testing data set with an 80/20 proportion and cross-validation is used.

5.2 Evaluation Metrics

We evaluate the results using both standard information retrieval metrics[14][9] and metrics featuring on measuring information propogation[35]. In particular, we use the following metrics: precision (P), average precision at K ($AP@K$), retweet times (RT), user coverage (Cov) and normalized user coverage (Cov_N), which are defined as,

$$P = \frac{N_{hit}}{m} \quad (15)$$

$$AP@K = \frac{\sum_{i=1}^{K}(P(i))}{N_{hit}} \quad (16)$$

$$RT = \{\sum_{u \in R} |t| \mid t \in T_{t,u}\} \quad (17)$$

$$Cov = \{\sum_{u \in R} \sum follower(v) | v \in U_{t,u}\} \quad (18)$$

$$Cov\_N = \{arctan(\sum_{u \in R} \sum (follower(v))) | v \in U_{t,u}\} \quad (19)$$

where m is the size of the recommendation list, N_{hit} is the number of users in the recommendation list belonging to the top m relevant matches and $P(k)$ means the precision at cut-off k in the recommendation list. For a user u, a tweet t and the recommendation list R, we define $T_{t,u}$ as all the retweets from the retweet cascades initiated by u retweeting t and $U_{t,u}$ as all the users from the retweet cascades initiated by u retweeting t.

Retweet times stands for the number of hops in a tweet propagation and each hop increases the chance for the tweet to reach more users. User coverage is a more intuitive metric which is the cumulative number of users that a tweet has reached due to the mention recommendation. In the normalized user coverage, we normalize the coverage with an $arctan()$ function, to make the coverage number from different algorithms more comparable.

Due to the length restriction, only a limited number of users can be mentioned in a tweet and thus we set the length of recommendation list as 5 in our evaluations. We also test how the algorithm performs when we only recommend 1∼4 users to mention.

5.3 Comparison Algorithms

To the best of our knowledge, no previous studies have been done on the *whom-to-mention* task. Though the task is with lots of new challenges, we try our best to adapt several classic recommendation algorithms to this new problem to serve as baseline comparison algorithms.

- Content-based Recommendation (**CR**). A content based recommendation algorithm similar to [12] is carefully designed. User profile are based on the content of tweets and attributes from user profile page. A specific tweet is considered as an item, illustrated by its content. Both the user profile and item are modeled as tf.idf-based vectors and we recommend users by ranking the cosine similarity scores of user profile and item.

- Content-boosted Collaborative Filtering Recommendation (**CCFR**). For our task, recommendation is conducted before a tweet is published and there thus exist no user interaction behaviors like retweet and reply to serve as ratings, so the recommender is always in a cold start state. We choose Content-boosted Collaborative Filtering Recommendation[22] which copes with the cold start problem of traditional Collaborative Filtering. A tweet is viewed as an item and a candidate is regarded as a user. When a new item (tweet) needs recommendation, we find 5 most similar items from training data based on content similarity and recommend users by combining the recommendation results from the similar items.

- Bonds-based Recommendation (**BR**). In BR, we recommend candidates to a tweet based on the social bonds between candidates and the tweet author, which means the closer a candidate is linked to the author, the more likely he will be recommended. The social bond is modeled based on users' retweet interactions.

- Influence-based Recommendation (**INFR**). In INFR, we recommend candidates based on their influence, which is a linear combination of influence features mentioned in section 4.1.3. We try to recommend the most influential users to mention given a tweet.

- Random Recommendation (**RR**). In RR, 5 users are randomly chosen from the candidates to generate the recommendation list.

- Whom-to-mention with different Ranking function. To evaluate how different ranking functions affect the recommendation result, we compare the performance of WTM by using three different ranking algorithms as the ranking function, including using Support Vector Regression (**WTM**$_{SVR}$), using Linear Regression (**WTM**$_{LR}$) and using Gradient Boosted Decision Trees [24](**WTM**$_{GBDT}$).

- Twitter and Weibo. Based on statistics from previous studies[2] [37], we get the average retweet rate and coverage of a tweet in Twitter. With the help of the data we collect for user influence modeling (11 million tweets from Weibo), we calculate the average retweet rate and coverage for a tweet from Weibo. These numbers show the general average diffusion of a tweet in a Micro-blogging system.

6. RESULTS AND ANALYSIS

6.1 Algorithm Performance Evaluation

As shown in table 2 and figure 1, our *whom-to-mention* approach (WTM) significantly improves the diffusion of a tweet in all the metrics. We draw the following conclusions from these results.

First, Random Recommendation (RR) barely shows any effect, which makes it clear that simply mentioning some users has little effect in improving the diffusion of a tweet. Second, the poor performance of Influence-based Recommendation (INFR) is because influential users may be neither interested in the tweet, nor share any social ties with

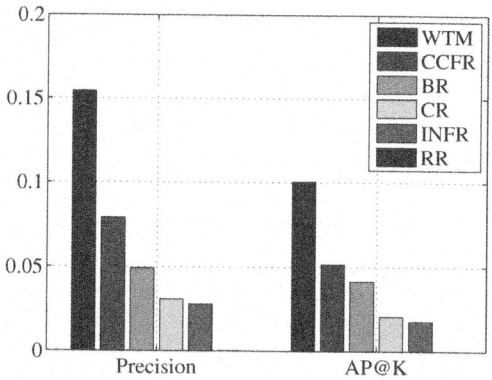
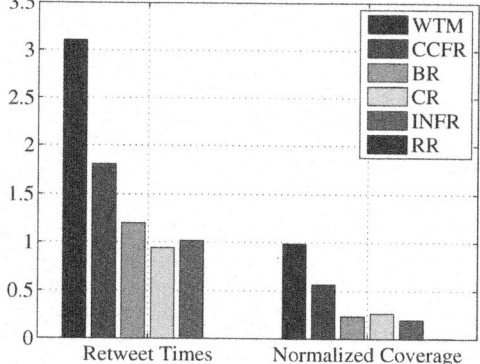

Figure 1: Performance Comparison of WTM and Baseline Algorithms

the author. Moreover, mention notifications may be easily neglected by the influential users since they usually receive thousands of mention notifications per day. Third, Content-based Recommendation (CR), although effective, is not as good as those based on user relationships like BR and CCFR; this is partly attributed to the noise and ambiguity existing in the tweet-based user profiles and item profiles. Fourth, the performance of Bonds-based Recommendation (BR) shows users who share strong social ties with the author are more likely to help him retweet the tweet and it is in accordance with our daily experience. Furthermore, Content-boosted Collaborative Filtering Recommendation (CCFR) shows the best performance in all of our comparison algorithms, owing to both its adoption of sophisticated CF recommendation scheme based on the implicit retweeting interaction network and the incorporation of content-based features during the recommendation.

Finally, our SVR based *whom-to-mention* recommendation (WTM) outperforms all the comparison algorithms. Even comparing with CCFR, it shows 70% increase in precision, a 94% increase in $AP@5$, an 72% increase in retweet rate and a 51% increase in normalized coverage of users. Our algorithm benefits from the exploitation of all the new features, a careful design of relevance model and a ranking function based on machine learning techniques. Moreover, our algorithms results in a 2821% and 389% increase of retweet rate and a 338% and 523% increase of coverage compared with an ordinary tweet from Twitter and Sina Weibo,

Table 2: Result Comparison of WTM and Baseline Algorithms

	WTM	CR	CCFR	BR	INFR	RR	Twitter	Weibo
Precision	**0.1343**	0.0309	0.079	0.0492	0.0279	1.47E-04	-	-
AP@5	**0.1005**	0.0207	0.0515	0.0416	0.0178	4.91E-05	-	-
Retweet Times	**3.1026**	0.9395	1.8058	1.1990	1.0147	0.0015	0.110	0.798
Normalized Coverage	**0.8525**	0.2649	0.5640	0.2349	0.1969	0.0023	-	-

Table 3: Comparison on How Different Features Affect the Performance of WTM

	ALL	NO_Interest	No_Influence	No_Ties	No_ContentInTie	Twitter	Weibo
Precision	**0.1342**	0.1328	0.1319	0.0658	0.1171	-	-
AP@5	0.1005	0.0985	**0.1129**	0.0410	0.0869	-	-
Retweet Times	**3.1026**	3.0559	3.0359	1.7540	2.6770	0.110	0.798
Coverage	**3716**	3643	3592	2185	3239	1100	711

which further confirms the effectiveness of our algorithm on boosting the diffusion of a tweet.

6.2 Feature Importance Evaluation

To analyze how features used in our proposed algorithm contribute to the learned model, we design this contrast experiment by eliminating one feature at a time and observe how the performance of our model changes. Furthermore, since we assume user social ties in micro-blogging systems are content-dependent, we design a contrast algorithm by eliminating all the content information from our user social ties, leaving only the number of interaction times to indicate the strength of social ties. All the results are listed in Table 3.

We note that when eliminating user interest match score (No_Interest), $AP@5$ suffers from a 2.0% decline and the coverage of users suffers from a 2.0% decline. Similar to user interest, the coverage of users decreases 3.4% after excluding user influence features (No_Influence) from our model. When we eliminate the user social ties feature (No_Ties), the model suffers a 60% decline of $AP@5$ and a 41% decline of coverage. This result is in accordance with the results in section 6.1, which shows although user interest match and user influence help to improve the recommendation result, content-dependent user social ties play a much more significant role in the recommendation. It's worth noting that $AP@5$ exhibits the best performance after eliminating the influence features, indicating that not all influential users are interested in the tweet and many pay little attention to mentions since they may receive hundreds, or even thousands per day. However, the influence features do help to expand the retweet rate and user coverage because the influence brought by influential users outweighs the precision loss.

Furthermore, after removing all the content feature from the social ties (No_ContentInTie), a 14% decline in $AP@5$ and a 13% decline in coverage prove that content feature in social ties plays an important part in the recommendation and user social ties are content-dependent.

6.3 Ranking Function Evaluation

Various machine learning models can be used as ranking functions for our task and we explore three most commonly used ones. The result is listed in Table 4. We can see that our SVR based model (WTM_{SVR}) outperforms the linear regression (WTM_{LR}) and GBDT (WTM_{GBDT}) based models

Table 4: WTM with Different Ranking Functions

	WTM_{SVR}	WTM_{LR}	WTM_{GBDT}
Precision	**0.1343**	0.0877	0.0769
AP@5	**0.1005**	0.0613	0.0492
Retweet Times	**3.1026**	2.2342	0.8997
Normalized Coverage	**0.8525**	0.5837	0.7986

Table 5: WTM and CCFR with 1 or 3 Users Recommended

	WTM_1	CCFR_1	WTM_3	CCFR_3
Precision	**0.0988**	0.0358	**0.1263**	0.0718
AP@k (k=1 or 3)	**0.0988**	0.0368	**0.1021**	0.0509
Retweet Times	**1.1313**	0.4945	**2.3307**	1.2913
Normalized Coverage	**0.5003**	0.2569	**0.7224**	0.4587

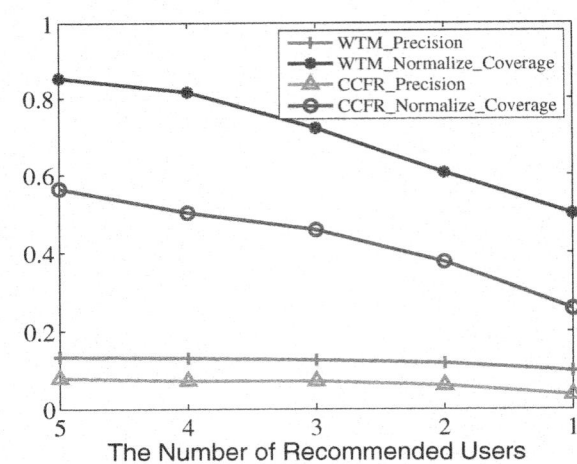

Figure 2: Results with Limited Recommended Users

and we attribute it to the kernel function feature used in SVR which helps us to map the data from the input space into a higher dimensional space.

6.4 Limited Recommended Users

The tweet-length limitation makes it hard to mention many users at the same time and moreover, mention too many users may results in the tweet looking suspicious as a spam tweet. We choose to recommend 5 users in our evaluation

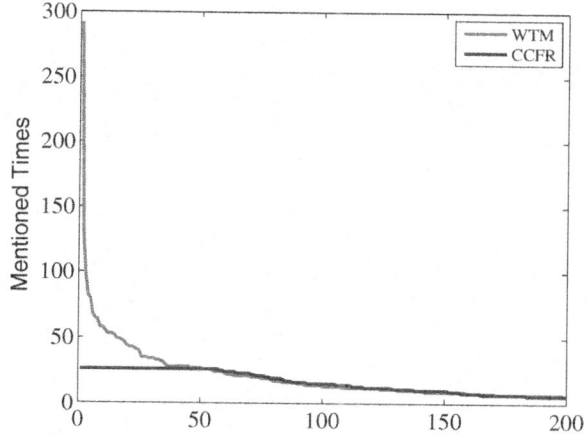

Figure 3: Recommendation Density Comparison Between WTM and CCFR (200 most recommended users)

because we believe 5 is the up-limit of mentioning users in one tweet and in practice use, a user can choose a subset of the 5 users to mention. We also test the performance of our algorithm when only mention 1∼4 users in a tweet and compares it with our best comparison algorithm CCFR, which are shown in table 5 and figure 2.

Our algorithm outperforms CCFR based on all metrics. For instance, when only mentioning one user, our algorithm shows a more than 200% remarkable improvement on all the metrics. Furthermore, compared with CCFR, the performance decline rate of our algorithm is much less than CCFR's when reducing the number of recommended users. For instance based on normalized coverage user metric, the average decline rate of our WTM is 31%, while the average decline rate of CCFR is 51%, which confirms our WTM performs much better when only a few users are recommended.

The precision drops slightly when recommending fewer users, showing that expanding the retweet is a quite difficult task and recommending only few users will incur higher miss rate, leading to the slight precision drop.

6.5 Recommendation Overload Evaluation

If everyone uses the *whom-to-mention* system, recommendation overload may occur and a popular user may receive tons of mention notification from the recommendation system which will result in a severe interruption. We show how many times a user is recommended in our evaluation in a descending order in figure 3. From the figure the recommendation distribution of WTM is more smooth compared with our best comparison algorithm CCFR. It is also worth noting that in CCFR, there exist users recommended hundreds of times which may lead to potential mention overload while our algorithm avoids the overload problem by setting the constraints based on user's free will.

7. DISCUSSION

The experiment results may seem a bit low, which is in accordance with our expectation. On one hand we ascribe it to we performing an off-line evaluation by using user's retweet log to estimate the possible information cascade and a perfect recommendation match in real world may be regarded as a miss in the evaluation as a result of lack of retweet log given the tweet. However, by comparing our algorithm with a set of carefully designed comparison algorithms, we believe our algorithm performs well based on the remarkable improvement on all metrics. On the other hand, attracting others to retweet is not an easy job and comparing with the average retweet rate 0.11 on twitter (0.78 on Weibo), our average 3.1 retweet rate shows a notable improvement.

Based on our comparison evaluation, it shows the content-dependent user social tie feature plays a much more important role compared with user interest match and user influence. We proposes 3 reasons for this phenomenon: First, though with careful pre-processing, the ambiguity and noise in the tweets still decrease the accuracy of user interest match. As a matter of fact, even though both are content features derived from user's tweets to model user's interest, the content feature from user's social ties shows more effectiveness compared with content feature from user's interest model, because the former feature is with less noise (users usually prefer to choose a well written tweet with a clear topic to retweet). Second, though intuitively influential users can lead to a larger diffusion of the tweet, they are usually mentioned by large numbers of people everyday, which makes them more easily to ignore the mention notifications. Third, the content-dependent retweet social tie is a strong indication. A user retweeting another user's tweet usually indicates a close user relationship and people who are close are more likely to retweet a tweet from each other. Moreover, retweet shows a strong interest on the topic of the tweet, so the user will be very likely to retweet the tweet with the same topic again in the future.

8. CONCLUSIONS

We offer the first in-depth study on Mention Recommendation and propose a new recommendation scheme to expand the diffusion of tweets by recommending proper users to mention. We formulate this new problem as a ranking problem and use new features, new relevance and a machine learned ranking function to solve it.

We find that the best performance of the algorithm is achieved when all the new features, including user interest match, user social ties and user influence, are used. A relevance defined by the coverage of users and an SVR based ranking function also help to improve the performance. Based on our comparison experiment, we also find that user relationship based features play a more important role than the content based features. Furthermore, we confirm that the content-dependent feature in user relationships is of high effectiveness in our recommendation model.

Many future works can be further explored. For instance, we use a post-processing step to solve the recommendation overload problem while constrained optimization can be tried to address this issue in the future. It's also interesting to study on how the proportion of strangers and friends in the recommendation list affect the tweet diffusion.

9. ACKNOWLEDGMENTS

This work was supported by the National Basic Research Program of China (973 Program) under Grant 2013CB336500, National Nature Science Foundation of China (Grant Nos: 61173185, 61173186, 61125203, 61222207), National Key Technology R&D Program (Grant Nos: 2012BAI34B01, 2008BAH26B00), Zhejiang Province Key S&T Innovation Group Project (Grant No.2009R50009), Program for New Century Excellent Talents in University (NCET-09-0685).

10. REFERENCES

[1] F. Abel, Q. Gao, G. Houben, and K. Tao. Analyzing user modeling on twitter for personalized news recommendations. *User Modeling, Adaption and Personalization*, pages 1–12, 2011.

[2] E. Bakshy, J. Hofman, W. Mason, and D. Watts. Everyone's an influencer: quantifying influence on twitter. In *Proceedings of WSDM 2011*, pages 65–74, 2011.

[3] E. Bakshy, J. Hofman, W. Mason, and D. Watts. Identifying influencers on twitter. In *WSDM 2011*, 2011.

[4] B. Bartell, G. W. Cottrell, and R. Belew. Learning to retrieve information. In *Proceedings of the Swedish Conference on Connectionism*, 1995.

[5] Y. Cao, J. Xu, T.-Y. Liu, H. Li, Y. Huang, and H.-W. Hon. Adapting ranking svm to document retrieval. In *Proceedings of SIGIR 2006*, pages 186–193, 2006.

[6] M. Cha, H. Haddadi, F. Benevenuto, and K. Gummadi. Measuring user influence in twitter: The million follower fallacy. In *4th International AAAI Conference on Weblogs and Social Media (ICWSM)*, pages 10–17, 2010.

[7] J. Chen, W. Geyer, C. Dugan, M. Muller, and I. Guy. Make new friends, but keep the old: recommending people on social networking sites. In *Proceedings of the 27th international conference on Human factors in computing systems*, pages 201–210, 2009.

[8] J. Chen, R. Nairn, L. Nelson, M. Bernstein, and E. Chi. Short and tweet: experiments on recommending content from information streams. In *Proceedings of the 28th international conference on Human factors in computing systems*, pages 1185–1194, 2010.

[9] M. Chen, J. Han, and P. Yu. Data mining: an overview from a database perspective. *Knowledge and data Engineering, IEEE Transactions on*, pages 866–883, 1996.

[10] F. Diaz, D. Metzler, and S. Amer-Yahia. Relevance and ranking in online dating systems. In *Proceeding of SIGIR2010*, pages 66–73, 2010.

[11] Z. Guan, C. Wang, J. Bu, C. Chen, K. Yang, D. Cai, and X. He. Document recommendation in social tagging services. In *Proceedings of the 19th International Conference on World Wide Web*, pages 391–400, 2010.

[12] I. Guy, I. Ronen, and E. Wilcox. Do you know?: recommending people to invite into your social network. In *Proceedings of the 14th international conference on Intelligent user interfaces*, pages 77–86, 2009.

[13] I. Guy, N. Zwerdling, D. Carmel, I. Ronen, E. Uziel, S. Yogev, and S. Ofek-Koifman. Personalized recommendation of social software items based on social relations. In *Proceedings of the third ACM conference on Recommender systems*, pages 53–60. ACM, 2009.

[14] D. Hand, H. Mannila, and P. Smyth. *Principles of data mining*. The MIT press, 2001.

[15] J. Hannon, M. Bennett, and B. Smyth. Recommending twitter users to follow using content and collaborative filtering approaches. In *Proceedings of the fourth ACM conference on Recommender systems*, pages 199–206, 2010.

[16] L. Hong and B. Davison. Empirical study of topic modeling in twitter. In *Proceedings of the First Workshop on Social Media Analytics*, pages 80–88, 2010.

[17] W. Hsu, A. King, M. Paradesi, T. Pydimarri, and T. Weninger. Collaborative and structural recommendation of friends using weblog-based social network analysis. In *AAAI Spring Symposium Series*, 2006.

[18] J. Jang, J. Choi, G. Jang, and S. Myaeng. Semantic social networks constructed by topical aspects of conversations: An explorative study. In *Sixth International AAAI Conference on Weblogs and Social Media*, 2012.

[19] A. Java, X. Song, T. Finin, and B. Tseng. Why we twitter: understanding microblogging usage and communities. In *Proceedings of the 9th WebKDD*, pages 56–65, 2007.

[20] H. Kwak, C. Lee, H. Park, and S. Moon. What is twitter, a social network or a news media? In *Proceedings of WWW2010*, pages 591–600, 2010.

[21] P. Li, C. J. C. Burges, and Q. Wu. Mcrank: Learning to rank using multiple classification and gradient boosting. In *NIPS'07*, 2007.

[22] P. Melville, R. Mooney, and R. Nagarajan. Content-boosted collaborative filtering for improved recommendations. In *Proceedings of the National Conference on Artificial Intelligence*, pages 187–192, 2002.

[23] M. Michelson and S. Macskassy. Discovering users' topics of interest on twitter: a first look. In *Proceedings of the fourth workshop on Analytics for noisy unstructured text data*, pages 73–80, 2010.

[24] A. Mohan, Z. Chen, and K. Q. Weinberger. Web-search ranking with initialized gradient boosted regression trees. *Journal of Machine Learning Research, Workshop and Conference Proceedings*, 14:77–89, 2011.

[25] R. Mooney and L. Roy. Content-based book recommending using learning for text categorization. In *Proceedings of the fifth ACM conference on Digital libraries*, pages 195–204, 2000.

[26] R. Nallapati. Discriminative models for information retrieval. In *Proceedings of SIGIR 2004*, pages 64–71, 2004.

[27] M. Pazzani and D. Billsus. Learning and revising user profiles: The identification of interesting web sites. *Machine learning*, 27(3):313–331, 1997.

[28] T. Qin, X.-D. Zhang, M.-F. Tsai, D.-S. Wang, T.-Y. Liu, and H. Li. Query-level loss functions for information retrieval. *Information Processing and Management*, 44(2):838–855, 2008.

[29] A. Smola and B. Schölkopf. A tutorial on support vector regression. *Statistics and computing*, 14(3):199–222, 2004.

[30] D. Sousa, L. Sarmento, and E. Mendes Rodrigues. Characterization of the twitter@ replies network: are user ties social or topical? In *Proceedings of SMUC 2010*, pages 63–70, 2010.

[31] S. Wu, J. Hofman, W. Mason, and D. Watts. Who says what to whom on twitter. In *Proceedings of WWW 2011*, pages 705–714, 2011.

[32] X. Wu, V. Kumar, J. Ross Quinlan, J. Ghosh, Q. Yang, H. Motoda, G. McLachlan, A. Ng, B. Liu, P. Yu, et al. Top 10 algorithms in data mining. *Knowledge and Information Systems*, 14:1–37, 2008.

[33] B. Xu, J. Bu, C. Chen, and D. Cai. An exploration of improving collaborative recommender systems via user-item subgroups. In *Proceedings of the 21st international conference on World Wide Web*, 2012.

[34] J. Yang and J. Leskovec. Modeling information diffusion in implicit networks. In *Data Mining, 2010 IEEE 10th International Conference on*, pages 599–608, 2010.

[35] S. Ye and S. Wu. Measuring message propagation and social influence on twitter. com. *Social Informatics*, pages 216–231, 2010.

[36] Y. Yue, T. Finley, F. Radlinski, and T. Joachims. A support vector method for optimizing average precision. In *Proceedings of SIGIR 2007*, pages 271–278, 2007.

[37] W. Zhao, J. Jiang, J. Weng, J. He, E. Lim, H. Yan, and X. Li. Comparing twitter and traditional media using topic models. *Advances in Information Retrieval*, pages 338–349, 2011.

Wisdom in the Social Crowd: an Analysis of Quora

Gang Wang, Konark Gill, Manish Mohanlal, Haitao Zheng and Ben Y. Zhao
Computer Science, UC Santa Barbara, Santa Barbara, CA 93106, USA
{gangw, konarkgill, manish, htzheng, ravenben}@cs.ucsb.edu

ABSTRACT

Efforts such as Wikipedia have shown the ability of user communities to collect, organize and curate information on the Internet. Recently, a number of question and answer (Q&A) sites have successfully built large growing knowledge repositories, each driven by a wide range of questions and answers from its users community. While sites like Yahoo Answers have stalled and begun to shrink, one site still going strong is Quora, a rapidly growing service that augments a regular Q&A system with social links between users. Despite its success, however, little is known about what drives Quora's growth, and how it continues to connect visitors and experts to the right questions as it grows.

In this paper, we present results of a detailed analysis of Quora using measurements. We shed light on the impact of three different connection networks (or graphs) inside Quora, a graph connecting topics to users, a social graph connecting users, and a graph connecting related questions. Our results show that heterogeneity in the user and question graphs are significant contributors to the quality of Quora's knowledge base. One drives the attention and activity of users, and the other directs them to a small set of popular and interesting questions.

Categories and Subject Descriptors

H.3.5 [**Information Storage and Retrieval**]: Online Information Services-Web-based services; J.4 [**Computer Applications**]: Social and Behavioral Sciences

General Terms

Measurement, Management, Design

Keywords

Q&A System, Online Social Networks, Graphs

1. INTRODUCTION

The Internet is a maelstrom of information, most of it real, and much of it false. Efforts such as Wikipedia have shown that collectively, Internet users possess much knowledge on a wide range of subjects, knowledge that can be collated and curated to form valuable information repositories. In the last few years, community question-and-answer (Q&A) sites have provided a new way for users to crowdsource the search for specific detailed information, much of which involves getting first-hand answers of specific questions from domain experts.

While these sites have exploded in popularity, their growth has come at a cost. For example, the first and still largest of these sites, Yahoo Answers, is showing clear signs of stalling user growth and stagnation, with traffic dropping 23% in a span of four months in 2011 [23]. In addition, the Google Answers service launched in 2001 was already shut down by 2006. Why is this the case? One of the prevailing opinions is that as sites grow, a vast number of low-value questions overwhelm the system and make it extremely difficult for users to find useful or interesting content. For example, ridiculous questions and answers are so prevalent on Yahoo Answers that a quick Google search for "Yahoo Answers Fail" turns up more than 8 million results, most of which are sites or blogs dedicated to documenting them.

Bucking the trend thus far is Quora, an innovative Q&A site with a rapidly growing user community that differs from its competitors by integrating a social network into its basic structure. Various estimates of user growth include numbers such as 150% growth in one month, and nearly 900% growth in one year [23]. Despite its short history (Quora exited beta status in January 2010), Quora seems to have achieved where its competitors have failed, *i.e.* successfully drawing the participation of both a rapidly growing user population and specific domain experts that generate invaluable content in response to questions. For example, founders of Instagram and Yelp answered questions about their companies, Stephen Fry and Ashton Kutcher answered questions about actors, and domain-specific answers come from experts such as Navy Seals sharpshooters and San Quentin inmates.

So how does Quora succeed in directing the attention of its users to the appropriate content, either to questions they are uniquely qualified to answer, or to entertaining or informative answers of interest? This is a difficult question to answer, given Quora's own lack of transparency on its inner workings. While it is public knowledge that Quora differs from its competitors in its use of social networks and real identities, few additional details or quantitative measures are known about its operations. A simple search on Quora about how it works produces numerous unanswered questions about Quora's size, mechanisms, algorithms, and user behavior.

In this paper, we perform a detailed measurement study of Quora, and use our analyses to shed light on how its internal structures contribute to its success. To highlight key results, we use comparisons against Stack Overflow, a popular Q&A site without an integrated social network. We seek to answer several key questions:

- What role do traditional question topics play in focusing user attention? How much do followers of a topic contribute to answering its questions?

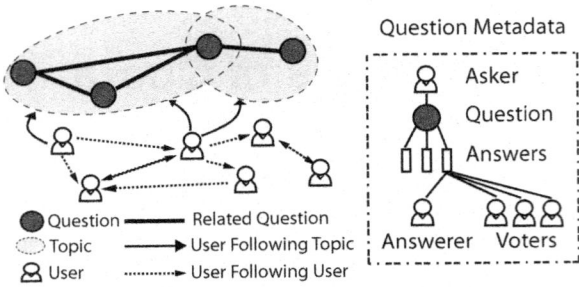

Figure 1: Structure of questions, topics and users in Quora.

Website	Data Since	Total Questions	Total Topics	Total Users	Total Answers
Stack Overflow	Jul. 2008	3.45M	22K	1.3M	6.86M
Quora	Oct. 2009	437K	56K	264K	979K

Table 1: Data Summary.

- What impact do super users have on specific patterns of user activity? Can they generate and focus user attention on individual questions, thus setting them apart from questions on related topics?

- Given the rapid growth of questions on question-and-answer sites, how does Quora help users find the most interesting and valuable questions and avoid spammy or low-value questions? What role do the "related questions" feature play?

Our analysis reveals interesting details about the operations of Quora. We find that while traditional topic-followers generate traffic, social relationships help bring a significant amount of answers to questions, and generally provide much higher quality answers than strangers. Most surprisingly, we find that the related-question graph plays a significant role in funneling user traffic and attention to key questions on a given topic. It exhibits a power-law structure where the degree of a question correlates strongly with the number of views and answers it receives. Finally, we use graph partitioning to identify clusters of related questions in the graph, and find that the large majority of viewers and answers focus on very few questions within each cluster. This further supports our hypothesis that Quora's social graph and question graph have been extremely effective at focusing user attention and input on a small subset of valuable questions.

2. BACKGROUND

Quora is a question and answer site with a fully integrated social network connecting its users. In this section, we introduce Quora, using Stack Overflow as a basis for comparison. We then give details on the key Quora graph structures that connect different components together. Specifically, we describe three types of graphs in Quora: a social graph connecting users, a user-topic following graph and a related question graph.

2.1 Quora and Stack Overflow

Quora. Quora is a question and answer site where users can ask and answer questions and comment on or vote for existing answers. Unlike other Q&A sites where all users exist in a global search space, Quora allows users to follow each other to form a social network. Social connections in Quora are directional like Twitter. A user A can follow user B without explicit permission, and B's actions (new questions, answers, comments and topics) will appear in A's activity stream. We say A is B's *follower* and B is A's *followee*. In addition, users can follow *topics* they are interested in, and receive updates on questions and answers under this topic.

Each Quora user has a *profile* that displays her bio information, previous questions and answers, followed topics, and social connections (followers and followees). Each user has a "Top Stories" page, which displays updates on recent activities and participated questions of their friends (followees), as well as recent questions under the topic they followed. A small subset of registered users are chosen by Quora to be *reviewers* and *admins*, and have the power to flag or remove low quality answers and questions.

Finally, each Quora question has its own page, which includes a list of its answers and a list of related questions. Users can add new answers, and comment, edit and vote on existing answers.

Stack Overflow. Stack Overflow is another successful Q&A site started in 2008. Stack Overflow differs from Quora in two main aspects. First, while Quora covers a broad range of general topics, Stack Overflow focuses specifically on computer programming questions. Second, users in Stack Overflow are fully independent and no social connections exist between users.

2.2 Graph Structures In Quora

The internal structure of question-and-answer sites are often a complex mix of questions, answers, question topics, and users. We summarize the relationships between different entities in Figure 1. Users can follow individual topics and other users for news and events; questions are connected to other "related" questions, and each question can be tagged with multiple topics. Finally, for each question in the system, there is a user who asked that question (the *asker*), users who answered that question (*answerers*), and users who voted on an answer (*voters*).

Quora's internal structure is dominated by three graphs that act as channels that guide user interest and deliver information to users.

1. *User-Topic Graph:* Quora users follow different topics, and receive updates about questions under topics they follow.
2. *Social Graph:* Quora users follow each other to form a Twitter-like social graph. Users receive newsfeed about questions their friends participated in.
3. *Question Graph:* Each question has a list of related questions used by users to browse related questions. The "related" relationship is considered symmetric.

We believe these three graphs are largely responsible for guiding the attention of Quora users. In this paper, we will perform detailed analysis on these graphs to understand how they impact user activities, especially how they help users separate a small subset of interesting questions from the larger number of less interesting questions/answers.

3. DATASET AND PRELIMINARY RESULTS

Before diving into main analytical results of our work, we begin in this section by first describing our data gathering methodology and presenting some preliminary results. Here we describe the properties and limitations of our Quora and Stack Overflow datasets. We also analyze some high level metrics of the Quora data, while using Stack Overflow as a baseline for comparison.

3.1 Data Collection

Our analysis relies on two key datasets. A publicly available dataset periodically released by Stack Overflow, and a dataset crawled

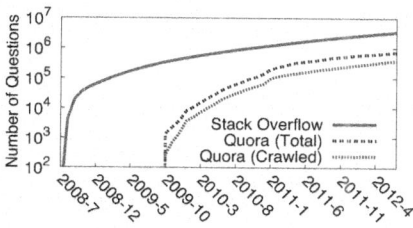
Figure 2: Questions growth.

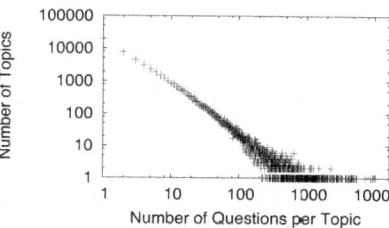
Figure 3: # of Questions per topic.

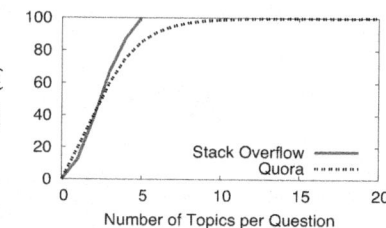
Figure 4: # of Topics per question.

from Quora that contains multiple groups of data on users, questions, topics and votes. We describe details below. The basic statistics of both datasets are shown in Table 1.

Stack Overflow. Stack Overflow periodically releases all of their data to the public. Our site trace was released in August 2012, and covers all activity on Stack Overflow between July 2008 and July 2012.

Quora. We gathered our Quora dataset through web-based crawls between August and early September 2012. We tried to follow crawler-etiquette defined in Quora's `robots.txt`. Limited portions of data were embedded in Ajax calls. We used FireWatir, an open-source Ruby library, to control a FireFox browser object, simulating clicking and scrolling operations to load the full page. We limited these crawls to 10 requests/second to minimize impact on Quora.

Since Quora has no predefined topic structures for its questions (questions can have one or more arbitrary topic "labels"), getting the full set of all questions is difficult. We followed the advice from a Quora data scientist [3] and start our question crawls using 120 randomly selected questions roughly evenly distributed over 19 of the most popular question topics. The crawls follow a BFS pattern through the related questions links for each question. In total, we obtained 437,000+ unique questions. Each question page contains the topics associated to the question, a complete list of answers, and the answerers and voters on each answer. As shown in Table 1, this question-based crawl produced 56,000+ unique topics, 979,000+ answers, and 264,000+ unique users who either asked or answered a question, or voted on an answer.

Our biggest challenge is trying to understand how much of the Quora dataset we were able to gather. The simple answer is we don't know, since there are no official quantitative measures about Quora available. But we found a post by a Quora reviewer [2] that hinted the question ID (or *qid*) in Quora is sequentially assigned. Thus we can infer the total number of questions by inspecting the qid of the newly added questions. To validate this statement, we performed several small experiments where we added small bursts of new (meaningful) questions to Quora. Each burst contains 10 new questions sent seconds apart, and consistently produced 10 sequential qid's. We separated experiments by at least 30 minutes, and observed increments to the qid consistent with the expected number of new questions in the gap between experiments. Finally, we plotted qid values for all questions found by our crawl and correlated them with the estimated date of question creation. The result, discussed below, provides further support that this qid can be used as an estimate of total questions in the system. The largest qid from our crawled questions is 761030, leading us to estimate that Quora had roughly 760K questions at the time of our crawl, and our crawl covered roughly 58% of all questions. Note that not all questions remain on the site, as Quora actively deletes spam and redundant questions [5]. This estimate might provide an upper bound

Topic in Quora	# of Questions	Topic in Stack Overflow	# of Questions
Startups	16.3K	C#	333K
Survey Questions	10.3K	Java	277K
Movies	9.7K	PHP	257K
Medicine / Healthcare	9.3K	Javascript	242K
Food	8.7K	Android	211K
Facebook	7.4K	jquery	207K
Music	5.5K	iPhone	143K
Google	5.4K	C++	139K
Psychology	5.2K	ASP.net	132K
Startup Advice	5.2K	.net	125K

Table 2: Top 10 topics based on number of questions.

of actual number of questions, and our coverage of 58% would be a lower bound.

We also crawled the user profiles for users extracted from the crawled questions. Each user profile contains 6 parts: the list of the user's followers, list of users they follow (followees), their previous answers, their previous questions, their followed topics and boards. Out of the 264K extracted users, we found that roughly 5000 (1.9%) profiles were no longer available, likely deleted either by Quora or the user.

***Qid* Over Time.** Assuming we are correct about the use of qid, we can plot an estimate of the growth of Quora (and Stack Overflow), by plotting qid against time. Since Quora does not show when a question is posted, we estimate the posting time by the timestamp of its earliest answer. For open questions with no answer, we infer the question posting time based on the latest activity timestamp on the question page. Since reading the question does not update this "latest activity" timestamp, this timestamp can estimate posting time for unanswered questions. We estimate the total number of questions in Quora for each month by looking at the largest *qid* of questions posted in that month. For Stack Overflow, we use the timestamp for questions creation in the data trace.

We see in Figure 2 that Stack Overflow is an older site with more questions than Quora. We plot two lines for Quora, a black dashed line for the total number of questions estimated by *qid*, and the blue dashed line is the number of questions we crawled from each month. Both lines increase smoothly without gaps, suggesting that Quora did not reset *qid* in the past and the questions we crawled are not biased to a certain time period. Our estimated number of questions in Quora for June 2012 is 700K, which is consistent with previously reported estimates [24]. As Quora continues to grow, it is clear that helping users easily identify and find the most meaningful and valuable questions and answers is a growing challenge.

3.2 Initial Analysis

Topics. Quora is a general Q&A site with a very broad range of topics. We observed 56K topics in our dataset, which is twice more than that of Stack Overflow, even though Quora is smaller by

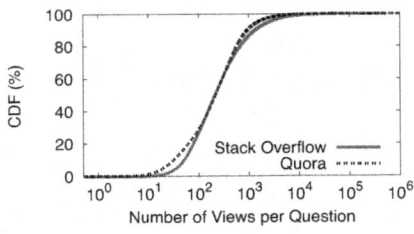
Figure 5: # of User views per question.

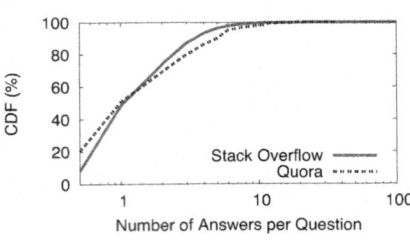
Figure 6: # of Answers per question.

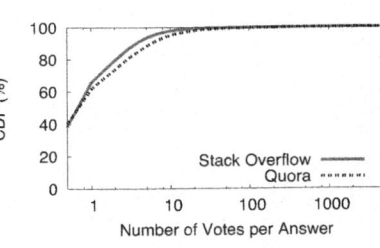
Figure 7: # of Votes per answer.

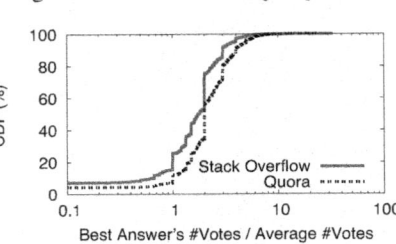
Figure 8: Votes for the best answer vs. the average.

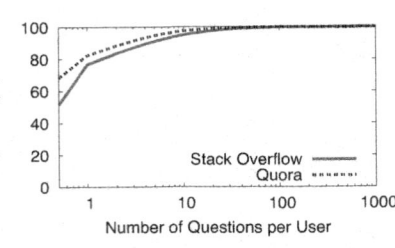
Figure 9: # of Questions per user.

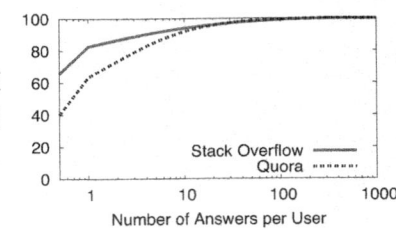
Figure 10: # of Answers per user.

question count. Table 2 lists the top 10 topics with most number of questions in each site. In Quora, the top 10 includes topics in various areas including technology, food, entertainment, health, etc. "Startups" is the most popular one which takes 3.7% of the questions. While all topics in Stack Overflow are different, they are all related to programming. The most popular topic is "C#," which represents roughly 10% of all questions.

Figure 3 plots the distribution of number of questions per topic in Quora in a log-log grid. It shows that for the large majority of topics, each topic contains only a handful of questions, while a few popular topics are responsible for most of all questions. The distribution of number of questions per topic mirrors a power-law distribution. Performing a power-law fitting produces alpha value 2.28 with error 0.03.

Questions and Answers. In both systems, one question can have multiple topics. Figure 4 shows the number of topics per question. Stack Overflow requires a minimum of 1 topic and a maximum of 5 topics per question, and the results are evenly distributed between 1 and 5. Although Quora does not have such requirements, a majority (85%) of questions have no more than 5 topics. Very few (<1%) of questions end up with more than 10 topics, which might be an attempt to draw more attention to the question.

Next, we plot the distribution of views and answers per question in Figure 5 and Figure 6. We are surprised to find that the curves from Stack Overflow and Quora are nearly identical. Although 20% of questions in Quora remain unanswered (10% for Stack Overflow), almost all questions got at least 1 user view. In addition, 99% of questions end up with less than 10 answers, and 20% of all Quora questions managed to collect ≥4 answers. We use this as a minimum threshold for our later analyses on social factors on system performance.

In terms of votes, both Quora and Stack Overflow allow users to upvote and downvote answers. Quora makes visible the list of upvoters, but hides downvoters. Downvotes are processed and only contribute to determining the order answers appear in. Thus in our analysis of Quora, we only refer to upvotes and disregard downvotes. In contrast, Stack Overflow anonymizes all voters and only displays the accumulated number of votes, which can be negative if an answer is poorly received. We plot the distribution of votes per answer in Figure 7. There is still a fairly big portion of answers (about 40% for both sites) that received no votes from users.

Next, we look at how votes impact the order that answers are displayed. Quora uses a proprietary algorithm [1] to rank the answers, where best answers show on the top of the page. In Stack Overflow, the question asker can *accept* one of the answers as the best answer. First, we examine how well votes work to identify the "best answer." We select questions with at least 2 answers, 180K or 40% of all questions in Quora and 1.76M or 51% in Stack Overflow. Figure 8 plots the ratio of the best answer' votes over the average votes per answer under this question. We call this as "best answer vote ratio." Overall, vote count was very effective at identifying the best answers, and the differences between the two sites might be explained by the more concrete (right or wrong) nature of Stack Overflow's questions compared to general questions on Quora. Surprisingly, some of the best answers have less votes than the average answer. 5% of Quora questions ranked answers with fewer upvotes on top, likely due to other features used by Quora's ranking algorithm such as answerer reputation or downvotes. On Stack Overflow, 7% of the answers chosen by the asker had lower votes than average.

Finally, we note that both sites use crowdsourcing to moderate user-generated content. Stack Overflow has administrators who actively flag unqualified questions and close them [4]. Roughly 3% of all questions in Stack Overflow have been closed, and Figure 11 shows the reasons why they were closed. The top two reasons were "not-real," *i.e.* ambiguous, vague, incomplete, overly broad or rhetorical, and redundant questions. In contrast, Quora relies on a total of 43 admins and 140 reviewers chosen from the user population to flag low quality answers and redundant questions [6, 7]. The number of flagged or removed answers and questions is unknown. While it is unclear whether these reviewers are responsible for keeping Quora largely free of fake or scripted accounts (Sybils) [37, 39], recent work has shown that human reviewers can be extremely effective at detecting fake or forged content [36].

Users Activity. Finally, we compare levels of user activity in Quora and Stack Overflow. Figure 9 and Figure 10 show the

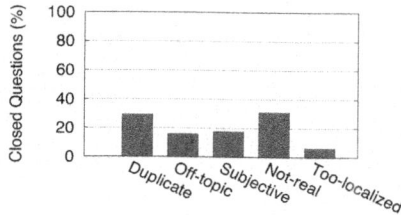

Figure 11: Reasons for deleting questions in Stack Overflow.

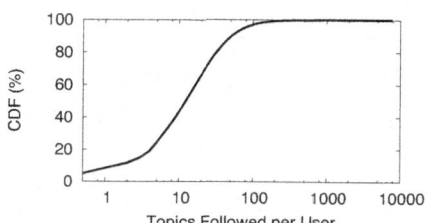

Figure 12: Topics followed per user.

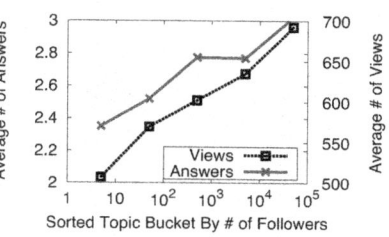

Figure 13: Average views and answers for questions under sorted topic buckets.

total number of questions and answers posted by each user. 60% of Stack Overflow users did not post any questions (or answers), while less than 1% of active users post more than 1000 questions (or answers). We observe similar trends in Quora. 40% of the users in our dataset did not post any answers, and 70% of the users have not asked any questions, indicating that a small portion of users have contributed most of the content.

Summary. Despite their different topics of interest, Quora and Stack Overflow share many similarities in distribution of content and activity. A key observation is that given the broad and growing number of topics in Quora, identifying the most interesting and useful content, *i.e.* separating the wheat from the chaff, is a very difficult problem. Without built-in mechanisms to lead users to useful content, the service will overwhelm users with the sheer volume of its content, much like the Internet itself. This is the focus of the rest of our paper, where we will study different Quora mechanisms to understand which, if any, can keep the site useful by consistently guiding users to valuable information.

4. THE USER-TOPIC GRAPH

Quora allows users to track specific fields by following the corresponding topics, such as "Startups," "Facebook," and "Technology." This also directly connects users to questions (and associated answers). A question, once created or updated under a topic, will be pushed to the newsfeeds of users who follow the topic. In this section, we model the interaction between Quora users and topics using a *user-topic graph*, and examine the impact of such interactions on question answering and viewing activities. Specifically, we seek to understand whether there is a direct correlation between followers of a topic and views and answers to questions, *i.e.* do highly-followed topics draw a large number of views and answers to their questions?

4.1 High-level Statistics

We first examine the number of topics followed by each user[1]. Figure 12 shows the cumulative distribution of the number of topics followed per user. We make three key observations. First, the large majority (95%) of users have followed at least 1 topic. This is because Quora recommends topics during the sign-up process. Second, Quora users each tend to follow a moderate number of topics, *e.g.* more than 50% of users followed at least 10 topics, but 97% of users followed no more than 100 topics. Finally, a very small portion of users (27 or 0.01%) followed more than 1000 topics. We manually checked these users and found that they were legitimate accounts, and come from various backgrounds such as CEOs, co-founders, bloggers, students, and were all very active Quora users.

Topic	# of Followers	Topic	# of Followers
Startups	47,084	Google	18,867
Facebook	25,569	Science	17,669
Twitter	23,034	TechCrunch	13,313
Technology	21,852	Music	13,084
Entrepreneurship	20,661	Venture-Capital	12,863

Table 3: Top 10 topics in Quora based on number of followers.

Next, we rank the topics by the number of followers. Since each Quora user lists the topics she follows in her profile, we estimate the number of followers by examining user profiles in our crawled dataset. Out of 56K topics crawled, 35K topics have at least 1 follower in our dataset. Using these estimates, we list in Table 3 the top 10 topics with the most followers. Clearly, users were highly biased towards certain topics. For example, "Startups" was followed by nearly 18% of users, and "Venture-Capital" by 5% of users. More interestingly, when compared to Table 2 ranking topics by number of questions, only 4 topics ("Startups", "Facebook", "Google", and "Music") are in the top-10 of both rankings. This shows that a high level of interest in a topic, *i.e.* more followers, does not necessarily produce more questions.

4.2 Impact on Question-related Activities

We now examine whether user interest towards certain topics translates into higher level of activities on questions related to those topics. We examine the correlation between the number of views or answers per question, and the number of followers of each topic. Since the number of topics is large (35K), we bucketize topics based on the number of followers in a log scale. For example, topics with number of followers in the range [1, 10] are in one bucket, and topics with number of followers within [10, 100] are in a second bucket. We have a total of 5 buckets. In each bucket, we compute the number of views (answers) per question, averaged over the topics and their questions.

Figure 13 shows the correlation results for both question views and answers. We observe a strong correlation: questions under topics with more followers tend to have a higher number of average page views and answers. This is intuitive: when a user follows a topic, all questions under the topic and their updates show up on the user's newsfeed, thus encouraging page views and answers.

We verify this intuition by examining for each question the percentage of answers that came from followers of the question's topic(s). Unfortunately we could not do the same for question page views, because Quora only reveals the identity of users who answer questions, but not those who browse each question. We focus on questions with some minimum number of user interactions (≥ 4 answers), which filters out all but 87K (20%) questions from our

---
[1] The user-topic interaction is one-way where users can follow multiple topics, but the relation is asymmetric, *i.e.* topics do not follow users.

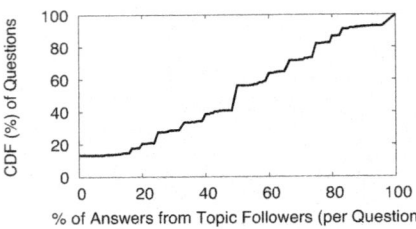
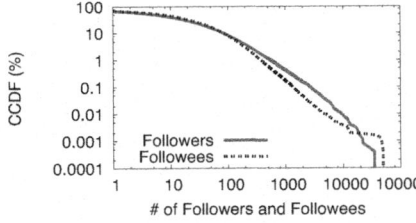
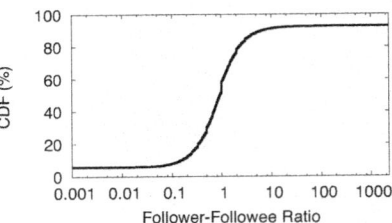

Figure 14: % of Answers added by the followers of the question's topics.

Figure 15: Degree distribution in social graph.

Figure 16: Follower-followee ratio.

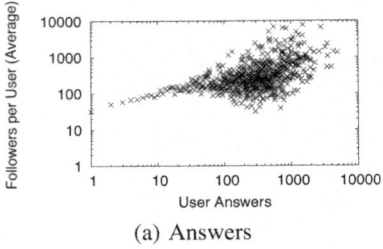
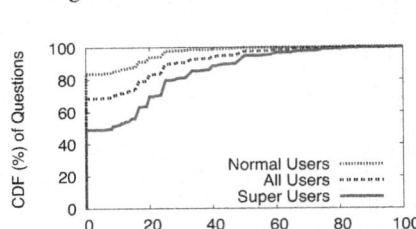

(a) Answers   (b) Received Votes

Figure 17: Correlation between user answers (received votes) and followers per user.

Figure 18: % of Answers written by asker's followers.

dataset. Figure 14 plots the cumulative distribution of the portion of answers contributed by topic followers. It is very close to a uniform distribution with mean of 50%, except for roughly 13% of questions, for which none of the answers were produced by followers of the question's topic(s). At a high level, this suggests that topics are effective ways of guiding users towards questions that are valuable and appealing to them.

Summary. The user-topic interaction has considerable impact on question answering activities in Quora. Not surprisingly, questions under well-followed topics generally draw more answers and views. Following the right topics can introduce users to valuable questions and answers, but is not the only way to access questions.

5. THE SOCIAL GRAPH

In addition to following topics of interest, Quora users also follow each other to form a Twitter-like directed social graph. Questions that a user interact with are disseminated to their followers in the form of events in their newsfeed. Therefore, social relationships clearly affect Q&A activities, and serve as a mechanism to lead users to valuable information.

In this section, we analyze the Quora social graph to understand the interplay between user social ties and Q&A activities. Specifically, we seek to answer three key questions. First, what triggers Quora users to form social ties? Second, does the presence of popular users correlate with high quality questions or answers? That is, do questions raised by "super-users" with many followers receive more and/or better answers from her followers? Finally, do strong social ties contribute to higher ratings on answers to questions? In other words, do questions answered by super-users get more votes because of the sheer number of their followers?

5.1 Social Ties

We begin by examining the follower and followee statistics of Quora users. Figure 15 plots the complementary cumulative distribution function (CCDF) for both the incoming degree (follower) and outgoing degree (followee). As expected, the degree distribution follows the power-law distribution [10]. Specifically, 23% of

users have no followers and 23% do not follow anyone. The vast majority of users (99.6%) have less than 1000 followers, while 23 users have more than 10,000 followers. The exponential fitting parameter α for the incoming degree distribution is 2.49 (with fitting error 0.01). This is very close to that of Twitter (α=2.28), but higher than that of Facebook and Orkut (α=1.5) [38, 26].

Figure 16 plots the distribution of the follower-followee ratio (FFRatio), the ratio of a user's incoming and outgoing degrees. In our data set, 44,091 (17%) of all users have neither followers nor followees (and are thus removed in this particular analysis). For the rest, 6% of users have no followers, and 7% do not follow anyone, representing the two extremes in the FFRatio distribution. Overall, more than half (58%) of all users have more followees than followers. A very small portion (0.1%) have 100 times more followers than followees. Not surprisingly, these are mostly celebrities, e.g. editors, actors and CEOs.

Triggers of Social Ties. To understand how Quora's social network functions, a basic question of interest is how users choose their followees. According to a recent survey of Quora users [31], they tend to follow users who they consider interesting and knowledgeable. Thus our hypothesis is that, outside of the small portion of celebrities who get followers just by their mere presence, the majority of Quora users attract followers by contributing a large number of high-quality answers.

To validate our hypothesis, we examine the correlation between a user's follower count and the quantity and quality of her answers to questions. We approximate the quality of an answer by the number of votes received. We put users with the same number of answers (votes) into a group and compute the average number of followers per user for each group. Figure 17(a) plots the correlation results, which confirm our hypothesis. The correlation is particularly strong for users with less than 100 followers, which account for 91% of the users in our dataset.

5.2 Impact on Question Answering

Quora is unique because it integrates an effective social network (shown above) into a tradition Q&A site. Thus it is important to

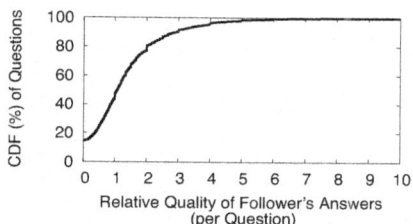
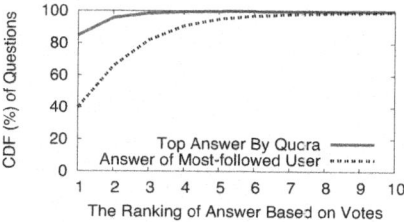
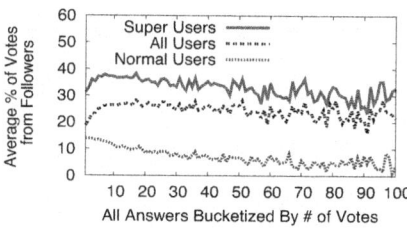

Figure 19: Relative answer quality ratio.

Figure 20: Ranking answers by author popularity vs top answer selected by Quora.

Figure 21: Votes from answerer's followers.

understand how social ties affect Q&A activities. Specifically, we explore whether super users (or users with many followers) draw more and better answers from their followers. To answer this question, we first examine for each question the number of answers, and the portion of answers coming from the asker's followers. We then measure the quality of answers based on votes and explore whether followers provide better answers. We define "Super User" as top 5% of all users by followers. In our dataset, we have 12K super users, each with more 160 followers.

For questions in our dataset, the asker is not shown on the question page. Instead, we match the originator of the question (the "asker") to each question based on user profiles. Each user's profile page contains a list of user's previously asked questions. Using this list, we managed to find the askers for 285K (65%) questions in our question dataset. Since our analysis targets user social activities in the question thread, we do not consider open questions and questions that have not gained enough answers. We only consider questions with known askers and at least 4 answers, which still leaves a large number of questions (59K) for our analysis.

Number of Answers. In Figure 6 we have plotted the distribution of the number of answers received per question across all the questions. We repeat this analysis for both questions raised by super users and non-super users (regardless of the number of answers received), and found that they follow the same distribution (figure omitted due to the space limitations). This shows that users do not get more answers for questions just by having more followers.

Answers by Followers. Next, we examine for each question the portion of answers contributed by the asker's followers. Figure 18 plots the cumulative distribution across all the questions (marked as "All"), across the questions raised by super users ("Super User"), and across the questions raised by non-super users ("Normal").

We make two key observations. First, a big portion of the questions (68% for "All") did not receive answers from the asker's followers. Even half of the questions raised by super users received no answers from their followers. This is likely because users who follow someone tend to seek her (helpful) answers to questions, rather than looking for questions to answer. This also implies that if we build a Q&A site *solely as a social network* that expects answers only from friends (followers), most questions will remain unanswered. Second, compared to normal users, super users do draw more answers from their followers, indicating a moderate level of social influence on question answers.

We also compare the effectiveness of drawing answers using social ties to that of drawing answers from following topics (discussed in Section 4), by comparing the results in Figure 18 and Figure 14. We see that in general, questions received more answers from users who follow the associated topic(s). But neither channel appears to be the primary way of attracting answers, and both channels appear to complement each other in this process.

Answer Quality. We now examine whether answers contributed by the asker's followers have better quality. Again we use the number of votes received to serve as an approximate measure of the quality of an answer. For each question thread, we first compute the average votes per answer for all the answers V_{all} and for all the answers contributed by the asker's followers $V_{follower}$. We define $R = \frac{V_{follower}}{V_{all}}$ as the relative quality of the followers' answers. Thus $R > 1$ indicates that the followers' answers are of higher quality in general.

Figure 19 shows the cumulative distribution of R, where for more than 50% of the questions, answers from the followers were of higher quality, and for 20% of the questions, answers from the followers got more than 2 times the votes than average. This result is consistent with a recent survey study [27] on Q&A behaviors in Facebook, which suggests that close friends have stronger motivation to contribute good answers.

5.3 Impact on Voting

Quora applies a voting system that leverages crowdsourced efforts to promote good answers. By positioning good answers at the top of the questions page, Quora allows users to focus on valuable content. However, the social interaction among Quora users could impact voting in various ways. The key concern is users who have many followers can get their followers to vote for their answers, thus gaining an "unfair advantage" over other users. In the following, we study this issue in detail by exploring two key questions. First, do user votes have a large impact on the ranking of answers in Quora? Second, do super users get more votes, and do these votes mainly come from their followers?

Votes and Ranking. Quora has indicated that the number of votes is the key metric to determine quality of answers [1]. In fact, our results in Figure 8 show that more than 96% of the best answers (ranked 1st by Quora) received more votes than average. Thus our goal is to explicitly examine how much the number of votes matters in Quora's ranking algorithm, and whether social connections give user advantage to gain more votes.

For each question thread, we start by ranking the answers by the number of votes received. Answers with the most votes are ranked first. We then take the best answer (ranked 1st) chosen by Quora's built-in algorithm and study their vote-based ranking. Figure 20 plots the cumulative distribution of these best answers' vote-based ranking. We see that for 85% of the questions, Quora's best answers also ranked the highest in votes, and for 96% of the questions, the best answers from Quora are among the top-2 most votes. This result confirms that the number of votes is the dominating feature for selecting best answers. The same result also implies that potential bias in the voting process could lead to unfair ranking of answers, which we study next.

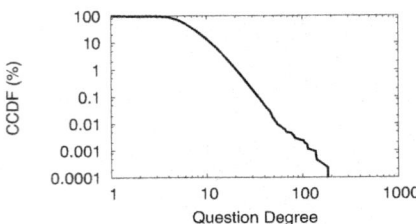
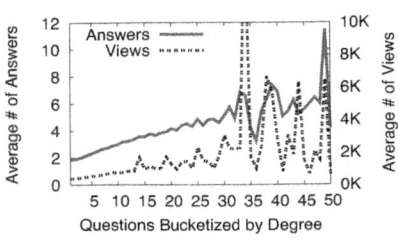
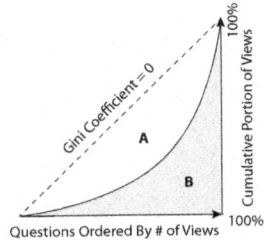

Figure 22: Node degrees in the related question graph.

Figure 23: Question degree versus average views and answers per question.

Figure 24: Gini coefficient, $G = A/(A+B)$.

Votes on Super Users. We repeat the above analysis on answers offered by super users (most followed users). Results in Figure 20 show that for 40% of questions, super users' answers received the highest votes, and for 60% of cases, their answers are among the top-2 most votes. This implies that regardless of the quality of their answers, super users can often get more votes over other users.

To better understand the bias, we examine whether a large portion of votes come from the answerer's followers. For this we gather answers to all the questions and group them by the number of votes received. For each group of answers, we compute the average percentage of votes from the answerer's followers. We also repeat the same process on answers offered by super users and those from non-super users. Figure 21 shows the average percentage of followers' votes across different answer groups. We cut the line at the points where the number of votes reaches 100, which covers 99.9% of all answers (see Figure 7). These results show that answers contributed by super users do receive a large portion of votes (30-40%) from their followers, which is significantly larger than normal users (<10%). This shows that users with more followers tend to get more votes from their followers, which could introduce potential unfairness in answer ranking. For example, an answer contributed by super users gets a much higher rank even though the true quality of the answer is not high.

Summary. In Quora, users who contributed more and good answers tend to have more followers. These well-connected users also gain advantage by having more friends (followers) to answer their questions and upvote for their answers.

6. THE RELATED QUESTIONS GRAPH

One of Quora's core features is the ability to locate questions "related" to a given question. This effectively creates a *related question graph*, where nodes represent questions, and links represent a measure of similarity as determined by Quora. The related question graph provides an easy way for users to browse through Quora's repository of questions with similarity as a distance metric.

In this section, we extract the question graph from our dataset, and seek to determine if the structure of the graph plays a role in helping users to find top questions. Intuitively, a similarity-based question graph would produce large clusters of questions around popular topics, with less popular questions relegated to sparse regions of the graph. Thus users following related question links could encounter popular questions with a higher probability.

6.1 Impact of Degree in the Question Graph

We build the question graph by crawling and extracting related questions links. By default, Quora lists a fixed number (5) of related questions on each question's main page. These are deemed by Quora to be the most related to the question on the current page. Since the "related" relationship is intuitively a bidirectional property, the question graph is a unweighted, bidirectional graph.

Our final question graph has a total of 437K nodes and 1.6M edges. We plot the distribution of question degree in Figure 22. Although each question only has at most 5 outgoing related questions, most questions have incoming connections from other questions, and thus have a total "related" degree greater than 5. However, there are 9% questions with degree less than 5. This is because some of their related questions were not crawled (questions deleted by Quora) and thus are not included as nodes. 99% of the questions have degree less than 50. The distribution shows a distinctive power-law shape, and when we fit the question degree CCDF to the power-law, we get an α value of 3.5 with fitting error 0.048.

Next, we examine the connectivity of the question graph. The question graph is dominated by a single large connected component that covers 98% (430K) of all questions. On closer inspection, we see that the remaining 2% of the questions are either newer questions whose related questions have not yet been computed, or they belong to esoteric topics with very few questions and low user interest.

Stability. One concern we had about the question graph is whether it is stable, *i.e.* does it change on a frequent basis as new questions are added to the system. We test the long-term stability of the related question graph by comparing the related question graph across two snapshots. The first snapshot was taken in our primary measurement period of August 2012. We also took another snapshot in October 2012 (two months after the first snapshot). When we compared the related question set for each question in the system, we found that 60% of all question had no changes in the time between our snapshots, and 30% of the questions have only one new entry (out of five) in its related question list. Thus we can assume that the related question list is relatively stable over moderate time periods, and our snapshots are a reasonable approximation for earlier versions of the question graph.

Question Degree vs. Attention. On each question page, users can browse a series of questions via the related question edges. This leads to the hypothesis that a question with higher question degree can receive more attention, *i.e.* more user views, and potentially more answers as a result.

We validate this hypothesis as follows. We first group all questions based on question degree in the related question graph. Then we compute the average number of answers and views for questions in each group. We plot the results in Figure 23. The dashed line represents the average number of user views across all questions with a given node degree, and the solid red line represents the average number of answers received by all questions with a given degree. There are clear trends in both cases. For questions with higher degree (they are listed as being related to more questions), they are accessible to users via a larger number of incoming

ID	Question Title
459576	What percentage of questions on Quora have no answers?
370857	Can I search Quora only for questions that have been answered?
45022	How many questions have been answered on Quora?
20195	What percentage of Quora questions receive at least one answer?
17363	What percentage of questions on Quora are answerable?
13323	How many questions are on Quora, answered or not?
...	...
Top Topics	Quora, Quora-Usage-Data-and-Analysis, Quora-product

Table 4: A cluster of 43 questions, produced by graph partitioning. The top three tags covers 90% of the questions in the cluster.

links. Hence these high degree questions receive both more page views as well as more answers. The takeaway here is that questions with high degree in the question-relation graph correlates strongly to questions that receive more attention and answers from users.

6.2 Locating Similar Questions

In the question graph, questions on similar topics are clustered together, while irrelevant questions are likely to be "related" to popular questions. Thus they are likely positioned in sparser regions of the graph. In this subsection, we first leverage the graph structure to identify groups of similar questions. We then ask two key questions: do similar questions receive equal attention from users? If not, what are the potential mechanisms that drive users to certain questions while ignoring other similar questions?

Graph Clustering. We first locate similar questions using the question graph. More specifically, we want to generate question clusters where questions within the cluster are more tightly connected than those outside the cluster. This is a simple definition easily characterized by modularity.

We formalize this problem as a graph partition problem, and use the popular graph partitioning tool METIS to perform a multilevel k-way partitioning [18] on our question graph. In this case, we predefine K as the number of clusters we want to generate. We run the graph partitioning algorithm, with K equal to 100, 1000, 10,000 and 100,000. When K is too big, we end up with many small clusters after cutting many edges. On the other hand, when K is too small, we get a small number of big clusters which take in many questions under related topics, but are not truly similar. Since there is no good way to get the ground-truth assessment on how "similar" the questions are, we randomly sample 10 clusters from each run with different K values, and manually inspect questions within each cluster. We find that the best match between semantic clusters and automatically detected clusters occurs when $K = 10,000$.

So we partition the graph into 10,000 clusters of similar sizes. Table 4 shows an example of one generated cluster. This cluster contains 43 questions, and all questions are related to "Quora." We also extract the topics of the questions in the cluster and rank the topics based on how many questions they are associated with. The top 3 topics of the cluster are listed in the table. We see that the three topics are different but all related. In fact, the top three topics cover 90% of the questions in this cluster, which indicates a good cluster focused around a single subject.

Cluster Analysis. Based on the generated clusters, we can now answer the high level question: do similar questions receive equal attention? We answer this question by assessing the distribution of user views and answers between questions in the same cluster. We choose to use *gini coefficient*, a uniformity metric commonly used to evaluate the equality of distributions in economics [11].

We explain how we compute gini coefficient for each question cluster using Figure 24. As an example, the x-axis has the questions sorted by increasing number of views, and the y-axis represents the cumulative portion of the views. So the curve represents y% of contribution (of views) by the bottom x% of questions. By definition, the curve is always at or below the dashed line which represents perfect equality of the distribution. Gini coefficient is defined to quantify how close the curve is to the dashed line: $G = \frac{A}{A+B}$, where A and B represent the corresponding areas above and below the curve. As each axis is normalized to 100%, the gini coefficient G is always within the range of $[0, 1]$, where $G=0$ means perfect equality or uniformity (the dashed line in our example) and $G=1$ means an extremely skewed distribution.

We compute the gini coefficient for the distribution of number of views (and answers) of questions in each cluster. As shown in Figure 25, the solid curve shows the gini coefficient of number of views is highly skewed towards 1. More than 90% of clusters have gini coefficient >0.4. This shows that the numbers of views are extremely uneven among similar questions within each cluster. The same trend applies to answers, as the vast majority of clusters have extremely skewed answer distributions. This means that user attention is tightly focused on a small portion of (valuable) questions within each cluster of similar questions.

Our results suggest that the structure of the related question graph (*e.g.* question degree) is at least partially responsible for focusing user attention and answers on a small subset in each cluster of related questions. Next, we ask whether super users play a role in directing traffic towards specific questions in each cluster of related questions.

Super User Effect. We evaluate whether the skew in the distribution is caused by super user effect. Intuitively, when a user adds new answers or upvotes existing answers on a question, that question will be pushed to all her followers. Thus super users with more followers can disseminate the question to a larger audience. We use the same definition of super users as in previous analysis by taking the top 5% of most followed users. We measure the super user effect by comparing the number of views (answers) of questions involving super users to other questions with no super user involvement. Among all 10000 clusters, only 1 cluster has no super user in any of its questions, and is not considered in the analysis.

Figure 26 shows the scatter plot of average views (and answers) of super user involved questions and normal user questions in each cluster. The X-axes are presented in ascending order of the views (answers) of super user questions, thus the super user question points form a near-continuous line. We first compare the average number of user views in Figure 26(a). In the vast majority of the clusters, the super user questions have more views than that of questions with no super user involvement. There is only a small number of clusters (4%) where normal user questions receive more user views then super user questions.

Figure 26(b) compares the two type of questions with respect to average number of answers per question. The result shows that super user involved questions have significantly more answers than normal user questions. Compared to user views, it shows a even stronger impact of super users on drawing answers. In different clusters, super user questions have an average number of answers ranging from 2 to 10, while questions without super user involvement almost always stays below 2 answers across clusters. Both the number of user views and answers can reflect how much attention each question receives. The result shows choices made by a small number of super users on questions usually affect the focus of attention for the whole community.

Summary. We build the related question graph, and find that it is a relatively stable structure even as new questions are constantly

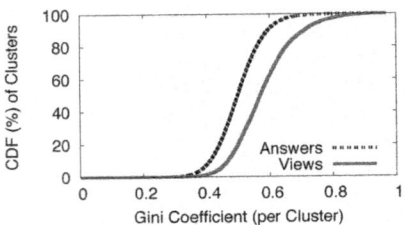
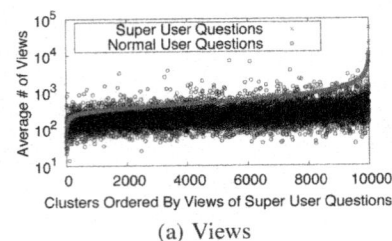
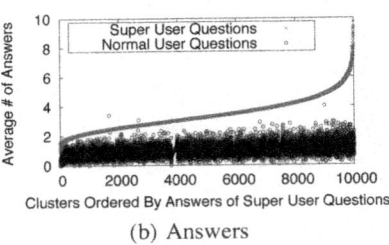

(a) Views (b) Answers

Figure 25: Gini coefficient of view (answer) distribution in each cluster.

Figure 26: Average # of views (answers) of super user questions vs. normal user questions in each cluster.

added to the system. We find that high degree questions generally receive more answers and views compared to others. More specifically, the spread of user views and answers within clusters of related questions is extremely skewed towards a small subset of questions. This bias is likely created by the structure of the question graph, and enhanced by super users, as the questions they interact with receive additional views and answers from their followers.

7. RELATED WORK

Community based Q&A. Researchers have studied community based Q&A (CQA) sites such as Yahoo Answers [13, 8, 12, 25, 33, 34], MSN QnA [15, 32], Stack Overflow [9, 22], Math Overflow [35] from different perspectives. One perspective focuses on managing questions and topics in CQA sites. Some studies look at question archiving and tagging [32]. Others focus on classifying factual questions with conversional questions [12, 25], or reusing the knowledge collected from old questions to answer new similar questions [34]. Finally, others evaluate the quality of user generated content, including answer quality [33, 35, 8, 16] and question quality [9, 20].

A second group of work studies user communities in CQA sites. These projects aim to develop algorithms to identify users with high expertise. One direction is to rank users based on expertise measures generated from user history data (*e.g.* questions, answers, votes) [8, 28, 21]. Another direction is modeling user interaction to design network-based ranking algorithms to identify experts [17, 19, 40]. Finally, other works study user community from perspectives such as answering speed [22] and user incentives in CQA sites [15].

Our work differs from prior art, since we are the first to analyze a social network based Q&A site using large-scale data measurement and analysis. Instead of treating all users as one big community, we explore the impact of a built-in social network as well other graph structures on the Q&A activities. A recent report [31] looks at Quora's reputation system in depth with a small dataset of 5K questions.

Q&A in Social Networks. Studies have also looked into the question and answering behaviors in existing online social networks. Users can ask their friends questions by posting tweets in Twitter [30] or updating status in Facebook [29, 27, 14]. These studies answer high-level questions like what types of questions are suitable to ask in social networks, and whether strong ties (close friends) provide better answers than weak ties.

8. CONCLUSION

Community question and answer sites provide a unique and invaluable service to its users. Yet as these services grow, they face a common challenge of keeping their content relevant, and making it easy for users to "find the signal in the noise," *i.e.* find questions and content that are interesting and valuable, while avoiding an increasing volume of less relevant content.

In this paper, we use a data-driven study to analyze the impact of Quora's internal mechanisms that address this challenge. We find that all three of its internal graphs, a user-topic follow graph, a user-to-user social graph, and a related question graph, serve complementary roles in improving effective content discovery on Quora. While it is difficult to prove causal relationships, our data analysis shows strong correlative relationships between Quora's internal structures and user behavior. Our data suggests that the user-topic follow graph generates user interest in browsing and answering general questions, while the related question graph helps concentrate user attention on the most relevant topics. Finally, the user-to-user social network attracts views, and leverages social ties to encourage votes and additional high quality answers. As Quora and its repository of data continues to grow in size and mature, our results suggest that these unique features will help Quora users continue find valuable and relevant content.

9. ACKNOWLEDGMENTS

We would like to thank the anonymous reviewers for their valuable feedback. This work is supported in part by NSF grant CNS-1224100, DARPA GRAPHS program, and gifts from Cisco and Google. Any opinions, findings, and conclusions or recommendations expressed in this material are those of the authors and do not necessarily reflect the views of the funding agencies.

10. REFERENCES

[1] What is quora algorithm/formula for determining the ordering or ranking of answers on a question? Quora, Feb. 2011. http://www.quora.com/Quora-product/What-is-Quoras-algorithm-formula-for-determining-the-ordering-ranking-of-answers-on-a-question.

[2] How many questions are on quora, answered or not? Quora, Mar. 2012. http://www.quora.com/Quora-Usage-Data-and-Analysis/How-many-questions-are-on-Quora-answered-or-not.

[3] On what topics does quora have the best questions and answers? Quora, Apr. 2012. http://www.quora.com/Lists-of-Top-Quora-Content/On-what-topics-does-Quora-have-the-best-questions-and-answers.

[4] What is a closed question? Stack Overflow, Oct. 2012. http://meta.stackoverflow.com/questions/10582/what-is-a-closed-question.

[5] What is quora's policy on question deletion? Quora, Jun. 2012. http://www.quora.com/Quora-Policies-and-Guidelines/What-is-Quoras-policy-on-question-deletion.

[6] Who are all of the reviewers on quora? Quora, Nov. 2012. http://www.quora.com/Quora-Reviewers/Who-are-all-of-the-reviewers-on-Quora.

[7] Who are the current site admins of quora? Quora, Aug. 2012. http://www.quora.com/Quora-Admins/Who-are-the-current-site-admins-of-Quora.

[8] ADAMIC, L. A., ZHANG, J., BAKSHY, E., AND ACKERMAN, M. S. Knowledge sharing and yahoo answers: everyone knows something. In *Proc. of WWW* (2008).

[9] ANDERSON, A., HUTTENLOCHER, D., KLEINBERG, J., AND LESKOVEC, J. Discovering value from community activity on focused question answering sites: a case study of stack overflow. In *Proc. of SIGKDD* (2012).

[10] BARABASI, A.-L., AND ALBERT, R. Emergence of scaling in random networks. *Science 286* (1999).

[11] DAGUM, C. The Generation and Distribution of Income, the Lorenz Curve and the Gini Ratio. *Economie Applique 33* (1980), 327–367.

[12] HARPER, F. M., MOY, D., AND KONSTAN, J. A. Facts or friends?: distinguishing informational and conversational questions in social Q&A sites. In *Proc. of CHI* (2009).

[13] HARPER, F. M., RABAN, D., RAFAELI, S., AND KONSTAN, J. A. Predictors of answer quality in online Q&A sites. In *Proc. of CHI* (2008).

[14] HOROWITZ, D., AND KAMVAR, S. D. The anatomy of a large-scale social search engine. In *Proc. of WWW* (2010).

[15] HSIEH, G., AND COUNTS, S. mimir: A market-based real-time question and answer service. In *Proc. of CHI* (2009).

[16] JEON, J., CROFT, W. B., LEE, J. H., AND PARK, S. A framework to predict the quality of answers with non-textual features. In *Proc. of SIGIR* (2006).

[17] JURCZYK, P., AND AGICHTEIN, E. Discovering authorities in question answer communities by using link analysis. In *Proc. of CIKM* (2007).

[18] KARYPIS, G., KUMAR, V., AND KUMAR, V. Multilevel k-way partitioning scheme for irregular graphs. *Journal of Parallel and Distributed Computing 48* (1998), 96–129.

[19] LERMAN, K., AND GALSTYAN, A. Analysis of social voting patterns on digg. In *Proc. of WOSN* (2008).

[20] LI, B., JIN, T., LYU, M. R., KING, I., AND MAK, B. Analyzing and predicting question quality in community question answering services. In *Proc. of CQA Workshop (WWW)* (2012).

[21] LI, B., AND KING, I. Routing questions to appropriate answerers in community question answering services. In *Proc. of CIKM* (2010).

[22] MAMYKINA, L., MANOIM, B., MITTAL, M., HRIPCSAK, G., AND HARTMANN, B. Design lessons from the fastest Q&A site in the west. In *Proc. of CHI* (2011).

[23] MCGEE, M. Quora traffic has grown 882% in the last year, but it's still just a fraction of what yahoo answers gets. MarketingLand, Dec. 2011.

[24] MCGEE, M. Yahoo answers hits 300 million questions, but Q&A activity is declining. Search Engine Land, Jul. 2012.

[25] MENDES RODRIGUES, E., AND MILIC-FRAYLING, N. Socializing or knowledge sharing?: characterizing social intent in community question answering. In *Proc. of CIKM* (2009).

[26] MISLOVE, A., MARCON, M., GUMMADI, K. P., DRUSCHEL, P., AND BHATTACHARJE, B. Measurement and analysis of online social networks. In *Proc. of IMC* (2007).

[27] MORRIS, M. R., TEEVAN, J., AND PANOVICH, K. What do people ask their social networks, and why?: a survey study of status message Q&A behavior. In *Proc. of CHI* (2010).

[28] PAL, A., CHANG, S., AND KONSTAN, J. A. Evolution of experts in question answering communities. In *Proc. of ICWSM* (2012).

[29] PANOVICH, K., MILLER, R., AND KARGER, D. Tie strength in question & answer on social network sites. In *Proc. of CSCW* (2012).

[30] PAUL, S. A., HONG, L., AND CHI, E. H. Is twitter a good place for asking questions? a characterization study. In *Proc. of ICWSM* (2011).

[31] PAUL, S. A., HONG, L., AND CHI, E. H. Who is authoritative? understanding reputation mechanisms in quora. In *Proc. of Collective Intelligence* (Cambridge, MA, April 2012).

[32] RODRIGUES, E. M., MILIC-FRAYLING, N., AND FORTUNA, B. Social tagging behaviour in community-driven question answering. In *Proc. of WI-IAT* (2008).

[33] SHAH, C., AND POMERANTZ, J. Evaluating and predicting answer quality in community QA. In *Proc. of SIGIR* (2010).

[34] SHTOK, A., DROR, G., MAAREK, Y., AND SZPEKTOR, I. Learning from the past: answering new questions with past answers. In *Proc. of WWW* (2012).

[35] TAUSCZIK, Y. R., AND PENNEBAKER, J. W. Predicting the perceived quality of online mathematics contributions from users' reputations. In *Proc. of CHI* (2011).

[36] WANG, G., MOHANLAL, M., WILSON, C., WANG, X., METZGER, M., ZHENG, H., AND ZHAO, B. Y. Social turing tests: Crowdsourcing sybil detection. In *Proc. of NDSS* (San Diego, CA, February 2013).

[37] WANG, G., WILSON, C., ZHAO, X., ZHU, Y., MOHANLAL, M., ZHENG, H., AND ZHAO, B. Y. Serf and turf: crowdturfing for fun and profit. In *Proc. of WWW* (Lyon, France, April 2012).

[38] WILSON, C., BOE, B., SALA, A., PUTTASWAMY, K. P. N., AND ZHAO, B. Y. User interactions in social networks and their implications. In *Proc. of EuroSys* (Nuremburg, Germany, April 2009).

[39] YANG, Z., WILSON, C., WANG, X., GAO, T., ZHAO, B. Y., AND DAI, Y. Uncovering social network sybils in the wild. In *Proc. of IMC* (Berlin, Germany, November 2011).

[40] ZHANG, J., ACKERMAN, M. S., AND ADAMIC, L. Expertise networks in online communities: structure and algorithms. In *Proc. of WWW* (2007).

Learning to Extract Cross-Session Search Tasks

Hongning Wang
Department of Computer Science
University of Illinois at Urbana-Champaign
Urbana IL, 61801 USA
wang296@illinois.edu

Yang Song[1], Ming-Wei Chang[1],
Xiaodong He[1], Ryen W. White[1],
Wei Chu[2]
[1]Microsoft Research, Redmond, WA
[2]Microsoft Bing, Bellevue, WA 98004 USA
{yangsong,minchang,xiaohe,ryenw,wechu}
@microsoft.com

ABSTRACT

Search tasks, comprising a series of search queries serving the same information need, have recently been recognized as an accurate atomic unit for modeling user search intent. Most prior research in this area has focused on short-term search tasks within a single search session, and heavily depend on human annotations for supervised classification model learning. In this work, we target the identification of long-term, or *cross-session*, search tasks (transcending session boundaries) by investigating inter-query dependencies learned from users' searching behaviors. A semi-supervised clustering model is proposed based on the latent structural SVM framework, and a set of effective automatic annotation rules are proposed as weak supervision to release the burden of manual annotation. Experimental results based on a large-scale search log collected from Bing.com confirms the effectiveness of the proposed model in identifying cross-session search tasks and the utility of the introduced weak supervision signals. Our learned model enables a more comprehensive understanding of users' search behaviors via search logs and facilitates the development of dedicated search-engine support for long-term tasks.

Categories and Subject Descriptors

H.3.3 [**Information Storage and Retrieval**]: Information Search and Retrieval

General Terms

Algorithms, Experimentation

Keywords

Cross-session search task, query log mining, semi-supervised clustering, weak supervision

1. INTRODUCTION

Search engine users' information needs span a broad spectrum [11, 15]: simple needs, such as homepage finding, can mostly be satisfied via a single query; but users may also issue a series of queries, collect, filter, and synthesize information from multiple sources to solve a complex task, e.g., planning a vacation. To comprehensively and accurately understand these needs from recorded actions in the user query logs, we must segment and associate chronologically-ordered queries into a semantically-coherent structure.

The primary mechanisms for segmenting the logged query streams are *session*-based, where short inactivity timeouts between user actions are applied as a means of demarcating session boundaries [17, 19]. Recently, there has been significant research on identifying *tasks* within these sessions, e.g., Lucchese et al [15] proposed the concept of a "*task-based session*": where a cluster of queries within the same session serves a particular common search intent. However, those methods rely on the accurate identification of the original session boundaries and the empirically-set timeout threshold may not be a valid criterion for identifying the semantic structure among queries: many tasks have been shown to span multiple search sessions [1, 11]. It suggests that there is value in studying and improving task identification methods spanning session boundaries.

Table 1: An example of cross-session search tasks.

Time	Query	SessionID	TaskID
05/29/2012 14:06:04	bank of america	1	1
05/29/2012 14:11:49	sas	1	2
05/29/2012 14:12:01	sas shoes	1	2
05/30/2012 10:19:34	credit union	2	3
05/30/2012 12:25:19	6pm.com	3	4
05/30/2012 12:49:21	coupon for 6pm	3	4

Motivating Example: Consider a real example of search tasks from a single user shown in Table 1, which is extracted from the logs of Bing.com. We manually annotated the in-session tasks in the last column of the table and segmented the sessions using 30-min inactivity threshold. We can observe that the user performed two tasks in the first search session on May 29, 2012, one for personal banking and another for shopping (for shoe-brand San Antonio Shoes). And on the second day, the user performed two individual search sessions, and each session consists of one single task, i.e., banking and shopping (at the online discount merchant 6pm.com) accordingly. However, humans can easily recognize that those four tasks annotated in three different sessions happen to be only two unique tasks: a shopping task including queries of "sas", "sas shoes", "6pm.com" and "coupon for 6pm", and a personal banking task including queries of "bank of america" and "credit union."

Prior work on identifying cross-session tasks has targeted *pairs* of queries, and made predictions about whether they share the same goal or represent the same task [11, 13]. Unfortunately, pairwise predictions alone cannot generate the partition of tasks, and post-processing is needed to obtain the final task partitions [14]. Besides, such pairwise predictions might not be consistent: e.g., predicting query i and j, query i and k to be in the same task, but query j and k are not. As a result, definite decisions have to be made in post-processing; but such decisions are isolated from the classifier training, and are therefore not guaranteed to be optimal. To understand this limitation, taking the search tasks shown in Table 1 as an example. A lexicon-similarity-based classifier can easily recognize the query "6pm.com" and "coupon for 6pm," and "sas" and "sas shoes" belong the same search tasks, because of query overlap; but it can hardly associate "sas" with "6pm.com." Furthermore, the query "sas" is ambiguous: it has other interpretations such as the business analytic software SAS or special air service in British Army. Hence, even the features leveraging external knowledge bases [15] may be unable to assist. But when we consider the temporal juxtaposition of "sas shoes" and "sas," we can confidently infer that the "sas" here refers to "San Antonio Shoes"; and since we know that the queries "6pm.com" and "sas shoes" are both associated with shoe shopping, we can safely conclude that those four different queries are part of the same shopping task. From this example, we can conclude that the queries belonging to the same search task convey rich dependency relationships, which provide us with valuable information to analyze and exploit the search task structure. In contrast, traditional binary classification methods are only optimized for independent predictions and thus cannot explore such in-depth relationships among queries.

Moreover, existing methods for cross-session search task extraction heavily depend on the manual annotation of tasks [11, 13, 14], which is expensive to acquire at scale. Fortunately, we have the opportunity to leverage problem-specific knowledge to assist with model learning, where various informative signals are available for us to identify such knowledge. For example, identical and reformulated queries, e.g., "sas" and "sas shoes" in Table 1, and queries with identical returned URLs should belong to the same search task with high confidence. Such knowledge can be summarized by a set of annotation rules, i.e., must-link and cannot-link [22], and applied at scale to reduce the burden of manual annotation. We refer to such knowledge as *weak supervision*, because it only provides pairwise supervision over a subset of queries; and the quality of such supervision might vary.

The research described in this paper addresses the above challenges and makes the following research contributions:

- Address the cross-session search task extraction problem in a structural learning framework, where we treat a user's entire query log as a whole and explicitly model the dependency among queries in the same task.

- Explore helpful weak supervision from different perspectives to reduce the burden of manual annotation and guide the supervised model learning for cross-session task extraction.

- Provide a detailed analysis of the proposed method whereby we compare it against state-of-the-art cross-session task extraction baselines and demonstrate significant performance gains on a variety of metrics.

2. RELATED WORK

Various methods have been proposed to segment and organize query logs into semantically coherent structures. The most commonly used unit, the search *session*, was often defined based on a timeout criterion, where different thresholds, ranging from 5 to 120 minutes, have been proposed [4, 9, 19]. In addition, Radlinski and Joachims [17] used a 30-minute timeout together with query similarity measures to define sequences of similar queries that combine to form so-called query chains.

Search tasks within the temporally-demarcated session boundaries have also been studied. Spink et al. [20] demonstrated that multi-tasking behavior, whereby multiple tasks are intertwined within the same time period, occurs frequently. Lucchese et al. [15] referred to such sessions as *task-based* sessions (or in-session tasks). Various methods, based on time splitting [2, 9], lexicon similarity [11, 15], and query reformulation patterns [9, 11], have been proposed to identify in-session tasks.

Recently, researchers have realized the necessity of going beyond the session timeout, and several methods have been proposed to tackle the problem by classifying whether two queries share the same search goal, i.e., same-task prediction. Jones et al. [11] claimed that no particular timeout threshold is necessary a valid constraint for identifying task boundaries. They found over 15% of search tasks are performed across time-out based session boundaries in their search log data set. To extract the cross-session tasks (which were defined as mission and goal), they built classifiers to identify task and sub-task boundaries, as well as pairs of queries belonging to the same task. Kotov et al. [13] and Agichtein et al. [1] studied the problem of cross-session task extraction via binary same-task classification, and found different types of tasks demonstrate different life spans.

In this work, although we focus on cross-session tasks, our solution is actually more general than cross-session only. Our only criterion for extracting search tasks is that queries in the same task should serve for the same high-level information need; tasks can be performed in a single session or can span multiple sessions. The major difference between our work and existing cross-session task extraction work is that instead of making a series of binary same-task predictions, we cast this problem as a structural learning problem, which explicitly models the dependency among queries in a search task. As we have discussed in Section 1, independent binary classification cannot capitalize on dependencies between pairs of predictions. In addition, existing classification-based methods heavily depend on manual annotations for model training. This will greatly limit their generalization capability when there is few or no task annotation available. In this work, we explored a variety of informative signals as weak supervision to release the burden of manual annotation and guide model learning.

3. PROBLEM DEFINITION

In this section, we formally define the problem of cross-session search task extraction.

Query log records the interaction behaviors from a set of different users, $\mathcal{U} = \{u_1, u_2, \ldots, u_N\}$, in a search engine. It stores a sequence of queries $\mathcal{Q}_n = \{q_{n1}, q_{n2}, \ldots, q_{nM}\}$ from user u_n, together with the timestamp t_{ni} when the query is submitted and the corresponding list of returned URLs, $\mathcal{URL}_{ni} = \{url_{ni1}, url_{ni2}, \ldots, url_{niL}\}$. Each query q_{ni} is represented as the original string that users submitted to the search engine, and $\mathcal{Q}_n$ is ordered according to query timestamp t_{ni}. Each URL url_{nil} has two attributes: URL string and click timestamp c_{nil} ($c_{nil}=0$ if it was not clicked).

Definition (Session) Given user u_n's search history $\mathcal{Q}_n$ and a fixed time-out threshold τ_{cut}, a session $\mathcal{S}_{nt}$ is a set of consecutive queries from $\mathcal{Q}_n$, such that $\forall q_{ni} \in \mathcal{S}_{nt}, q_{nj} \in \mathcal{S}_{nt}, q_{nl} \notin \mathcal{S}_{nt}, |t_{ni} - t_{nj}| \leq \tau_{cut}$ and $|t_{ni} - t_{nl}| > \tau_{cut}$.

The definition of session implies that $\{\mathcal{S}_{nt}\}_{t=1}^T$ is a set of disjoint partitions of query sequence $\mathcal{Q}_n$, such that $\forall i \neq j$, $\mathcal{S}_{ni} \cap \mathcal{S}_{nj} = \emptyset$ and $\mathcal{Q}_n = \bigcup_i \mathcal{S}_{ni}$. A typical time-out threshold is set to be 30 minutes [13, 15, 17].

Definition (Search Task) Given user u_n's search history $\mathcal{Q}_n$, a search task $\mathcal{T}_{nk}$ is a maximum subset of queries in $\mathcal{Q}_n$, such that all the queries in $\mathcal{T}_{nk}$ correspond to a particular information need.

This definition of search task indicates $\{\mathcal{T}_{nk}\}_{k=1}^K$ is also a set of disjoint partitions of query sequence $\mathcal{Q}_n$: $\forall j \neq k$, $\mathcal{T}_{nj} \cap \mathcal{T}_{nk} = \emptyset$ and $\mathcal{Q}_n = \bigcup_k \mathcal{T}_{nk}$. Therefore, each $\mathcal{T}_{nk}$ is not confined to a particular session $\mathcal{S}_{nt}$; instead they can overlap, or one search task can contain multiple sessions. To emphasize such a difference, we will refer to our definition of search task as *Cross-session Search Task* as opposed to the previous definition of *In-session Search Task* [15, 20].

Based on the above notations and definitions, we define the problem of cross-session search task extraction as,

Definition (Cross-Session Search Task Extraction) Given user u_n's search query log $\mathcal{Q}_n$, partition the sequence into disjoint subsets $\{\mathcal{T}_{n1}, \mathcal{T}_{n2}, \ldots, \mathcal{T}_{nk}\}$, such that the partition is consistent with the user's underlying information need; when explicit task annotation is available, the extracted tasks should be consistent with the annotation.

In particular, such task partition can be uniquely determined by a mapping function $y(q_{ni}) \to \mathcal{T}_{nk}$ from query q_{ni} to its corresponding task partition $\mathcal{T}_{nk}$ for the query sequence $\mathcal{Q}_n$. In addition, we should note that the number of tasks, e.g., K, user u_n can take is not specified in our definition, and therefore the learning method should find the appropriate K for each given $\mathcal{Q}_n$ automatically.

4. SEARCH TASK EXTRACTION WITH LATENT STRUCTURED SVM

We model the cross-session search task extraction as a *supervised clustering problem (SCP)* [6, 8, 22], where given the clustering membership, we need to build up a model which captures the connection between queries.

4.1 Motivation: Best Link vs. All Links

A commonly used assumption in SCP is the *all-link* clustering structure [8, 10], where one needs to associate the queries belonging to the same task together, such that the in-cluster similarity defined by the summation of similarities over all the pairs of instances within a cluster is maximized. However, this objective may not be the most appropriate for our problem: in a task consisting of m queries, many of the $O(m^2)$ pairs are not necessarily similar, or even quite different. Recall the example search tasks shown in Table 1, the query "sas" and "coupon for 6pm" are not directly related under most of similarity metrics, e.g., edit distance or term overlap; putting them into the same task can only hurt the in-cluster similarity. As a result, any algorithm aims at maximizing the *all-link*-based in-cluster similarity can hardly discover this type of task.

A more reasonable way for clustering queries into tasks is to find the *strongest* link between a candidate query and queries in the target cluster, i.e., *bestlink* [10]. For example, after scanning through all the queries listed in Table 1, we can easily infer the relation between "sas" and "coupon for 6pm" based on the decision over the other two queries, "sas shoes" and "6pm.com", which have been recognized as being in the same shoe shopping task.

This motivates us to revise the objective of clustering queries: a query belonging to one particular search task *does not* need to be similar to all the other queries in this task (*all-link*), but there has to be *at least* one query, which is *strongly* associated with this query in that task (*bestlink*). Intuitively, this modeling assumption simulates how a human editor annotates the search tasks in the query log: one might determine if two queries belong to the same task by reasoning transitively over strong connections between queries in the same task.

4.2 Best Link as Latent Structure

Unfortunately, the bestlink structure is *hidden* in the query log, and it is even impossible for the human editors to explicitly annotate, since such structure might not be unique. Therefore, we adopt the structural learning method with latent variables, i.e., latent structural SVMs [5, 24], to realize the bestlink modeling assumption, and utilize the hidden structure to explore the dependency among queries within the same task. We name our method as *bestlink SVM*.

To formalize the idea of bestlink SVM, we denote the hidden best-link structure as h. Before stating clearly the detailed definition of h, it helps to consider h as a graph whose edges connect the "most similar" queries. Given a query sequence $\mathcal{Q} = \{q_1, q_2, \ldots, q_M\}^1$, we define a feature vector for the task partition y specified by the hidden best-link structure h as $\Phi(\mathcal{Q}, y, h)$. And based on $\Phi(\mathcal{Q}, y, h)$, our bestlink SVM is a linear model parameterized by w, and predicts the task partition at testing time by,

$$(\hat{y}, \hat{h}) = \arg\max_{(y,h) \in \mathcal{Y} \times \mathcal{H}} w^\top \Phi(\mathcal{Q}, y, h), \quad (1)$$

where $\mathcal{Y}$ and $\mathcal{H}$ represent the sets of possible structures of y and h respectively. $\hat{y}$ becomes the output for cross-session tasks and $\hat{h}$ is the inferred latent structure. In this paper, we refer to solving Eq (1) as the decoding problem.

The decoding problem of Eq (1) clearly distinguishes the proposed bestlink SVM model from the previous binary-classification-based methods. In bestlink SVM, we model the entire query sequence $\mathcal{Q}$ as a whole, and predict the task membership for all the queries simultaneously; while the previous two-step approaches cannot explore the interactions among queries in the same task, and isolated predictions are made on each pair of queries in those methods.

The definition of h needs to be carefully designed, otherwise the decoding problem (hence the training algorithm as well) can be intractable. We define $h(q_i, q_j) = 1$ if query q_i and q_j are directly connected in h; and otherwise, $h(q_i, q_j) = 0$. To model the first query of a new search task, i.e., the query that does not have a strong connection with any previous queries, we add a dummy query q_0 at the beginning of each user's query log. All the queries connecting to q_0 would be treated as the initial query of a new search task. Besides,

---
[1] In the following discussion, when no ambiguity is invoked, we drop the index n for user u_n to simplify the notations.

we enforce that a query can only link to another query *in the past*, or formally,

$$\sum_{i=0}^{j-1} h(q_i, q_j) = 1, \forall j \geq 1$$

Taking the search tasks shown in Table 1 as an example, we illustrate the idea of bestlink structure in Figure 1. From the figure, we can clearly notice that the bestlink defines a hierarchical tree structure of "strong" connections among the queries: rooted in the dummy query q_0, each subtree of q_0 corresponds to one specific search task in a user's search history. For a new query, it can only belong to a previous search task or be the first query of a new task. Therefore, the temporal order provides us a helpful signal to explore the dependency between queries.

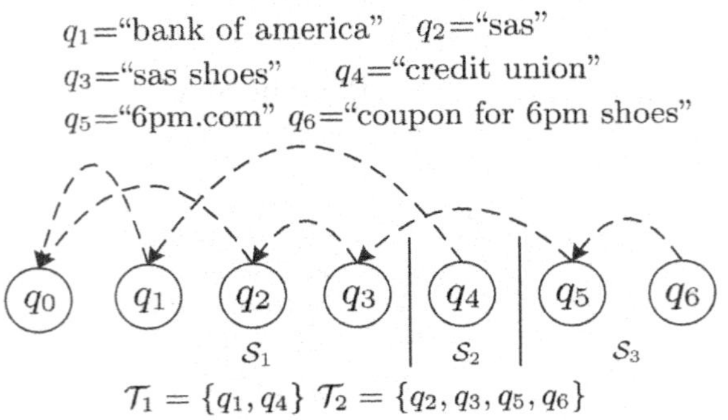

q_1="bank of america" q_2="sas"
q_3="sas shoes" q_4="credit union"
q_5="6pm.com" q_6="coupon for 6pm shoes"

$\mathcal{T}_1 = \{q_1, q_4\}$ $\mathcal{T}_2 = \{q_2, q_3, q_5, q_6\}$

Figure 1: Illustration of hidden search task structure specified in bestlink SVM. $\{\mathcal{S}_1, \mathcal{S}_2, \mathcal{S}_3\}$ **are the sessions segmented by the 30-minutes inactivity threshold,** $\{\mathcal{T}_1, \mathcal{T}_2\}$ **are the search tasks annotated by human editor. The dotted arrows indicate one possible hidden structure identified by bestlink SVM.**

We require h to be consistent with y – that is, $h(q_i, q_j) = 1$ implies $y(q_i) = y(q_j)$; in other words, the task partition y is determined by the connected components in h. As a result, the dependency among the queries belonging to the same task is explicitly encoded by the latent bestlink structure h: as shown in Figure 1, predicting "sas" and "sas shoes", "sas shoes" and "6pm.com" belonging to the same task would immediately lead to the conclusion that all these three queries belong to the same task, even though "sas" and "coupon for 6pm.com" are not directly connected to each other.

Accordingly, our feature vector for a particular task partition y is defined over the links in h as,

$$\Phi(\mathcal{Q}, y, h) = \sum_{i,j} h(q_i, q_j) \sum_{s=1}^{S} \phi_s(q_i, q_j), \quad (2)$$

where a set of symmetric pairwise features $\{\phi_s(\cdot, \cdot)\}_{s=0}^{S}$ is given to characterize the similarity between query q_i and q_j. In particular, to accommodate the dummy query q_0, we set $\phi_0(q_0, \cdot) = 1$ and $\forall s > 0, \phi_s(q_0, \cdot) = 0$.

Based on our feature vector design and the directed linkage structure of h, exact inference can be efficiently calculated for the decoding problem in Eq (1). Algorithm 1 described an incremental implementation to solve the exact inference problem, where we only need the queries appearing before the given query to determine its task membership. This makes bestlink SVM feasible to be deployed in

---

Algorithm 1: Task Partition Prediction

Input: Query sequence $\mathcal{Q} = \{q_1, q_2, \ldots, q_M\}$, pairwise features $\{\phi_k(\cdot, \cdot)\}_{k=0}^{K}$ and linear weight w.
Output: Task partition $\hat{y}$.

//Step 1: Initialize the latent structure $\hat{h}$
$\hat{h}(\cdot, \cdot) = 0$;
//Step 2: Search for the best latent structure $\hat{h}$
for $i = 1 \ldots M$ **do**
$\quad j' = \arg\max_{0 \leq j < i} \sum_{k=1}^{K} w_k^\mathsf{T} \phi_k(q_i, q_j)$;
$\quad \hat{h}(i, j') = 1$;
end
//Step 3: Construct the best task partition $\hat{y}$:
$t = 0$;
for $i = 1 \ldots M$ **do**
$\quad j' = \arg\max_{0 \leq j < i} \hat{h}(i, j)$;
$\quad$ **if** $j' = 0$ **then**
$\quad\quad \hat{y}(i) = t$;
$\quad\quad t = t + 1$;
$\quad$ **end**
$\quad$ **else**
$\quad\quad \hat{y}(i) = \hat{y}(j')$;
$\quad$ **end**
end
return $\hat{y}$

---

the search engine query log system in an online fashion, since the newly arrived queries will not affect the method's prediction on previous queries.

4.3 Solving the bestlink SVM

For a given set of query logs with annotated tasks, $\{(\mathcal{Q}_n, y_n)\}_{n=1}^{N}$, we need to retrieve the optimal weight setting w for the proposed bestlink SVM. Empirically, the optimal weight w should minimize the error between the predicted task partition $\hat{y}_n$ and ground-truth y_n. In addition, w should be also be optimized for good generalization capability, e.g., maximize the margin between ground-truth partition and wrong partitions [21]. This naturally gives rise to the following optimization problem within the latent structural SVMs framework [5, 24]:

$$\min_{w, \xi} \frac{1}{2} ||w||^2 + C \sum_{n=1}^{N} \xi_n^2 \quad (3)$$

$$s.t. \ \forall n, \ \max_{h \in \mathcal{H}} w^\mathsf{T} \Phi(\mathcal{Q}_n, y_n, h) \geq$$
$$\max_{(\hat{y}, \hat{h}) \in \mathcal{Y} \times \mathcal{H}} [w^\mathsf{T} \Phi(\mathcal{Q}_n, \hat{y}, \hat{h}) + \Delta(y_n, \hat{y}, \hat{h})] - \xi_n$$

where $\Delta(y_n, \hat{y}, \hat{h})$ characterizes the distance between the ground-truth partition y_n and predicted partition $\hat{y}$ specified by the latent structure $\hat{h}$, $\{\xi_n\}_{n=1}^{N}$ is a set of slack variables to allow errors in the training set, and C controls the trade-off between empirical loss and model complexity.

Because the ground-truth bestlink structure h_n^* for $\mathcal{Q}_n$ is unobservable in the training data, we cannot measure the distance between (y_n, h_n^*) and $(\hat{y}, \hat{h})$. As a result, we define the margin between the ground-truth task partition y_n and predicted task partition $\hat{y}$ based on the inferred latent structure $\hat{h}$ as,

$$\Delta(y_n, \hat{y}, \hat{h}) = |\mathcal{Q}_n| - |\mathcal{T}_n| - \sum_{i,j} h(i, j) \sigma(y_n, (i, j)) \quad (4)$$

where $|\mathcal{Q}_n|$ is the number of queries in $\mathcal{Q}_n$, $|\mathcal{T}_n|$ is the number of annotated tasks in $\mathcal{Q}_n$, and $\sigma(y, (i, j)) = 1$ if $y(i) =$

Table 2: Pairwise Similarity Features.

Type	Feature	Description
Query -based	Q-COSINE	cosine similarity between the term sets of q_i and q_j
	Q-EDIT	norm edit dist between query strings of q_i and q_j
	Q-JAC	Jaccard coeff between the term sets of q_i and q_j
	Q-TIME	1.0/(absolute time difference in seconds between q_i and q_j)
	Q-DIST	(# of queries in between of q_i and q_j)/$|Q_n|$
	Q-URL-MATCH-SUM	$\sum_{url\in\mathcal{URL}_i}(c(q_j,url)) + \sum_{url\in\mathcal{URL}_j}(c(q_i,url))$
	Q-URL-MATCH-MAX	$\max_{url\in\mathcal{URL}_i}(c(q_j,url)) + \max_{url\in\mathcal{URL}_j}(c(q_i,url))$
	Q-CLICK-URL-MATCH-AVG	$\sum_{url\in\text{clicked }\mathcal{URL}_i}(c(q_j,url)) + \sum_{url\in\text{clicked }\mathcal{URL}_j}(c(q_i,url))$
	Q-CLICK-URL-MATCH-MAX	$\max_{url\in\text{clicked }\mathcal{URL}_i}(c(q_j,url)) + \max_{url\in\text{clicked }\mathcal{URL}_j}(c(q_i,url))$
URL -based	U-EDIT-DOMAIN-MIN	min norm edit dist between domain of $\mathcal{URL}_i$ and domain of $\mathcal{URL}_j$
	U-EDIT-ALL-MIN	min norm edit dist between $\mathcal{URL}_i$ and $\mathcal{URL}_j$
	U-EDIT-ALL-CLICK-MIN	min norm edit dist between clicked $\mathcal{URL}_i$ and clicked $\mathcal{URL}_j$
	U-EDIT-DOMAIN-AVG	avg norm edit dist between domain of $\mathcal{URL}_i$ and domain $\mathcal{URL}_j$
	U-EDIT-ALL-AVG	avg norm edit dist between $\mathcal{URL}_i$ and $\mathcal{URL}_j$
	U-EDIT-ALL-CLICK-AVG	avg norm edit dist between clicked $\mathcal{URL}_i$ and clicked $\mathcal{URL}_j$
	U-JAC-ALL-CLICK	Jaccard coeff between clicked $\mathcal{URL}_i$ and clicked $\mathcal{URL}_j$
	U-JAC-ALL	Jaccard coeff between $\mathcal{URL}_i$ and $\mathcal{URL}_j$
	U-JAC-DOMAIN-CLICK	Jaccard coeff between domain of clicked $\mathcal{URL}_i$ and domain of clicked $\mathcal{URL}_j$
	U-JAC-DOMAIN	Jaccard coeff between domain of $\mathcal{URL}_i$ and domain of $\mathcal{URL}_j$
	U-SIM-CLICK-MAX	max ODP category similarity of clicked $\mathcal{URL}_i$ and clicked $\mathcal{URL}_j$
	U-SIM-CLICK-AVG	avg ODP category similarity of clicked $\mathcal{URL}_i$ and clicked $\mathcal{URL}_j$
	U-SIM-MAX	max ODP category similarity of $\mathcal{URL}_i$ and $\mathcal{URL}_j$
	U-SIM-AVG	avg ODP category similarity of $\mathcal{URL}_i$ and $\mathcal{URL}_j$
Session -based	S-SAME	if q_i and q_j are in the same session
	S-FIRST	if both q_i and q_j are the first query of session
	S-DIST	# queries in between of q_i and q_j

Note: 1) **norm edit dist** is the edit distance between string s and t divided by the maximum length of s and t;
2) $c(q,url)$ is a function counting the number of query terms in q contained in url;
3) **clicked** $\mathcal{URL}$ is a subset of URLs, whose click timestamp $c_{il} > 0$.

$y(j)$, otherwise $\sigma(y,(i,j)) = -1$. It is easy to verify that $\Delta(y_n, \hat{y}, \hat{h})$ is non-negative, and equals to zero if and only if the task partition $\hat{y}$ is the same as y_n.

Since we are minimizing the square hinge loss over the predictions in the training set, the optimization problem introduced in Eq (3) can be efficiently solved by the iterative algorithm proposed in [5]: the optimization procedure minimizes Eq (3) by constructing a sequence of convex problems in each iteration, and each iteration guarantees to decrease the objective function. In the employed optimization algorithm, two types of inference are required: loss-augmented inference, i.e., $\max_{(\hat{y},\hat{h})\in\mathcal{Y}\times\mathcal{H}}[w^\top\Phi(\mathcal{Q}_n,\hat{y},\hat{h})+\Delta(y_n,\hat{y},\hat{h})]$; and latent variable completion inference, i.e., $\max_{h\in\mathcal{H}} w^\top\Phi(\mathcal{Q}_n, y_n, h)$. Since the calculation of $\Delta(y_n, \hat{y}, \hat{h})$ can be decomposed onto the edges in h, loss-augmented inference can be directly solved via Algorithm 1 by adding an additional cost $\sigma(y_n,(i,j))$ into Step 2 when finding the best link for query q_i. And the latent variable completion inference can also be achieved via Algorithm 1 by restricting Step 2 to only search in the queries with the same task label as q_i. Both inference algorithms are exact, which renders us a more precise optimization result for Eq (3). The detailed algorithm is omitted due to the lack of space.

4.4 Pairwise Similarity Features

Our bestlink SVM requires a set of pairwise similarity features as input to characterize the connection between a pair of queries. In this work, we explored a variety of signals, from lexicon similarity to query semantic category similarity, to measure the similarity between a pair of queries.

Our proposed pairwise similarity features are list in Table 2, and categorized into three types: query-based, URL-based and session-based similarities. To analyze the semantic relationships between queries, we assign each URL to a topic distribution over 385 categories from the second level of "Open Directory Project" (ODP, dmoz.org) with a content-based classifier [18]. The inner product of the predicted topic distribution is used to measure the semantic similarity between queries. Besides, to make the features comparable across each other, we normalize them into the range of [0,1] accordingly, e.g., taking reciprocal of the absolute time difference between two queries.

5. IMPROVING THE MODEL WITH WEAK SUPERVISION SIGNALS

The bestlink SVM proposed in Section 4.2 is a supervised clustering algorithm that requires full annotation of tasks in the query log. As we have discussed in Section 1, various types of signals, which can be automatically derived from the query logs, are helpful for identifying the search tasks. In this section, we discuss how to make use of large quantities of unlabeled data with weak supervision signals in the proposed bestlink SVM.

We explore weak supervision signals for the cross-session search task extraction problem from different perspectives, and formalize them in terms of "must-link" and "cannot-link" [22]. Query matching, e.g., identical or reformulated queries, is a strong indication that two queries belong to the same task. Besides, the returned URLs for the given query are also an important source for determining the task membership: because modern search engines have sophisticated query pre-

Table 3: Partial Annotation Rules.

Type	Description
Must-link $(\tilde{y}(i) = \tilde{y}(j))$	$q_i = q_j$ $q_i \subset q_j$ or $q_j \subset q_i$ $\mathcal{URL}_i = \mathcal{URL}_j$ clicked $\mathcal{URL}_i$ = clicked $\mathcal{URL}_j$
Cannot-link $(\tilde{y}(i) \neq \tilde{y}(j))$	$q_i \neq q_j$ AND $\mathcal{URL}_i \cap \mathcal{URL}_j = \emptyset$

processing procedures, e.g., spelling correction [7] and query rewriting [12], when it decides to return identical URLs for two different queries, it is a strong signal that the two queries are related. Table 3 lists four types of must-link and one type of cannot-link we have defined in this work. When there is conflict between the automatically generated must-links and cannot-links, e.g., nontransitive, we will drop the cannot-links to make the annotations consistent.

Though one may treat such signals as features and manually tune the weights to stress their importance, we want emphasize that this approach is sub-optimal for the following two reasons: 1) features are independent in linear models, the knowledge about one feature cannot help the model learn for other features; instead, if we treat such information as supervision, all the features can be adjusted accordingly; 2) it is difficult to manually set the appropriate weights for all the features; while optimizing the objective function defined on both weak supervision and manual annotations would estimate the weights in a systematic way.

Note that when we apply the proposed must-link and cannot-link to the unlabeled user query logs, we can only get partial annotations on those queries given that the coverage of the weak supervision is not perfect. We denote the partial annotation as $\tilde{y}$, and to accommodate such partial annotations in bestlink SVM, we modify the margin defined in Eq (4) as follows,

$$\tilde{\Delta}(\tilde{y}_n, \hat{y}, \hat{h}) = |\mathcal{Q}_n| - |\mathcal{C}_n| - \sum_{i,j} h(i,j)\tilde{\sigma}(y,(i,j)) \quad (5)$$

where $|\mathcal{C}_n|$ is the number of connected components (including singletons) defined by must-links in $\mathcal{Q}_n$, and $\tilde{\sigma}(y,(i,j)) = \lambda^+$ if $\tilde{y}(i) = \tilde{y}(j)$, $\tilde{\sigma}(y,(i,j)) = -\lambda^-$ if $\tilde{y}(i) \neq \tilde{y}(j)$, otherwise $\tilde{\sigma}(y,(i,j)) = 0$ when there is no annotation between query i and j. This modificatoin makes our bestlink SVM a semi-supervised clustering algorithm.

We can easily verify that $\tilde{\Delta}(\tilde{y}_n, \hat{y}, \hat{h})$ is a more general definition of the distance between the given (or partial) task partition and the predicted task partition, in which we count how many edges in $\hat{h}$ are consistent with given annotation (or must-links) in $\tilde{y}$, and how many of them are conflicting with the annotation (or must-/cannot-links). In addition, to distinguish the creditability of the rule-based must-link and cannot-link, we assign them different cost factors, i.e., $\lambda^+ > 0$ and $\lambda^- > 0$, which can be set according to model's performance on a manually annotated held-out set.

6. EXPERIMENT RESULTS

In order to evaluate the proposed method, we performed a series of experiments on a large scale search dataset sampled from the query logs from Bing.com. First, we compared the performance of the proposed bestlink SVM to several state-of-the-art methods for the cross-session search task extraction problem. Then, a set of experiments were conducted to study the effectiveness of using weakly supervised data, which is automatically derived from user query logs, for identifying cross-session search tasks.

6.1 Query Log Dataset

We extracted five days' search logs from Bing.com, from May 27 2012 to May 31 2012, for our experiments. During this period, a subset of users are randomly selected and all their search activities are collected, including the anonymized user ID, query string, timestamp, returned URL sets and the corresponding user clicks. The 30-minutes inactivity threshold is used to segment queries into sessions as pre-processing [14, 23]. Since the focus is identifying cross-session search tasks, we further filtered out the users who submitted less than two queries or had less than two sessions during this period. As a result, we collected 7,628 users with 114,723 queries. The basic statistics of this data set are shown in Table 4.

Table 4: Statistics of evaluation query log data set.

# User	# Session	# Query
7628	37547	114723
Query/User	Session/User	Query/Session
15.1±17.2	4.9±3.5	3.1±1.2

Table 5: Statistics of annotated search tasks.

Single-query Task	Multi-query Task
8044	2283
Multi-session Task	Interleaving Task
1307	709
Task/User	Query/Task*
7.2±10.1	6.6±8.2
Session/Task*	Task duration (mins)*
2.8±2.6	491.1±933.5

*count only in multi-query tasks

In order to evaluate the performance of the proposed method in identifying cross-session search tasks, three editors were recruited to annotate the search tasks. Editors were instructed to group the queries into tasks according to their understanding of users' information needs, and they were encouraged to use external resources, e.g., search for the logged queries and browse the clicked URLs, to infer the relation between queries. The same set of 200 users' query logs are distributed in each editor's annotation assignment to measure their annotation agreement. Cohen's kappa on pairwise annotation of queries showed high inter-annotator agreement, 0.68, 0.73 and 0.77, for the three pairs of editors. After aggregating the three editors' annotations, we got a collection of 10,327 tasks annotated out of 1,436 users' search logs, and the basic statistics of this data set are shown in Table 5.

From Table 5, we observed that in average a user takes 7.2 different tasks during this period, 22.1% of which contain multiple queries, more than 57.2% multi-query tasks span across session boundaries, and 31.1% of them are interleaving. This shows the need of going beyond session boundaries to extract the long-term search tasks. In particular, when we look into those multi-query tasks, they span 6.6 queries, 2.8 sessions and more than 8 hours in average. This indicates that cross-session task extraction is not a trivial problem, and one needs to leverage rich information for identifying the structure of a cross-session search task.

6.2 Search Task Extraction

6.2.1 Baselines

Several methods have been proposed to identify cross-session search tasks based on the idea of same-task classification [11, 13]. However, those methods only provide predictions over pair of queries, and post-processing is needed to obtain the final task partitions. In our experiment, we adapted two best performing clustering methods from Lucchese et al.'s work [15], i.e., QC_wcc and QC_htc, as the post-processing procedure for the baselines. QC_wcc performs clustering by dropping "weak edges" among queries and extracting the connected components as tasks. QC_htc assumes a cluster of queries can be well represented by only the chronologically first and last query in the cluster, and therefore only the similarity among the first and last queries of two clusters is considered in agglomerative clustering. We trained a linear SVM model to classify if two queries are in the same task, treated the predicted positive query pairs as "strong edges," and applied QC_wcc and QC_htc to obtain the final task partition. In this setting, QC_wcc works exactly the same as Liao et al. proposed in [14].

Since our proposed bestlink-SVM can be viewed as a supervised clustering method [6, 8, 22], we also included two state-of-the-art supervised clustering methods, i.e., "adaptive-clustering" [6] and "cluster-svm" [8] as baselines. Adaptive clustering (AdaptClu) performs single-link agglomerative clustering based on binary classification results. To avoid overfitting, it selects a representative subset of all the candidate pairs based on their similarities when training the binary classifier. In our experiment, we used the summation of all the pairwise similarities as defined in Table 2 between two queries (with negative signs for edit-distance-based similarities) for selecting the representative subset of queries. cluster-svm performs correlation clustering by learning a structural SVM model, which simultaneously optimizes the pairwise accuracy and in-cluster similarity defined by *all-link* in one cluster.

To make a fair comparison, all the methods are trained on the same set of pairwise features defined in Table 2.

6.2.2 Performance metrics

A commonly used evaluation metric for search task extraction is pairwise precision/recall [11, 13] defined as,

$$p_{\text{pair}} = \frac{\sum_{i<j} \delta(y(q_i), y(q_j)) \delta(\hat{y}(q_i), \hat{y}(q_j))}{\sum_{i<j} \delta(\hat{y}(q_i), \hat{y}(q_j))} \quad (6)$$

$$r_{\text{pair}} = \frac{\sum_{i<j} \delta(y(q_i), y(q_j)) \delta(\hat{y}(q_i), \hat{y}(q_j))}{\sum_{i<j} \delta(y(q_i), y(q_j))} \quad (7)$$

where p_{pair} evaluates how many pairs of queries predicted in the same task, i.e., $\delta(\hat{y}(q_i), \hat{y}(q_j)) = 1$, are actually annotated as in the same task, i.e., $\delta(y(q_i), y(q_j)) = 1$; and r_{pair} evaluates how many pairs annotated as in the same task are recovered by the algorithm.

However, it is worth noting that these metrics cannot directly measure the clustering quality, and have some limitations: 1) they ignore singleton tasks, since no pairs can be formed from such tasks; 2) they intrinsically favor methods producing fewer tasks [16]. Inspired by the metrics used in the problem of co-reference resolution in natural language processing, we employed the Constrained Entity-Alignment F-Measure ($f1_{\text{CEAF}}$) as proposed in [16] to evaluate the clustering quality. CEAF defines the clustering precision and recall based on the best alignment between the predicted cluster and ground-truth cluster, where the alignment can be measured by any similarity function defined on two sets:

$$p_{\text{CEAF}} = \frac{\sum_i \pi(\hat{\mathcal{T}}_i, g(\hat{\mathcal{T}}_i))}{\sum_i \pi(\hat{\mathcal{T}}_i, \hat{\mathcal{T}}_i)} \quad (8)$$

$$r_{\text{CEAF}} = \frac{\sum_i \pi(\hat{\mathcal{T}}_i, g(\hat{\mathcal{T}}_i))}{\sum_j \pi(\mathcal{T}_j, \mathcal{T}_j)} \quad (9)$$

where $\pi(A, B)$ is a similarity measure between set A and B, which is chosen to be Jaccard coefficient in our evaluation; and $g(\cdot)$ is the optimal mapping between the predicted task partition $\mathcal{T}$ and ground-truth task partition $\hat{\mathcal{T}}$. Then, $f1_{\text{CEAF}}$ can be calculated as,

$$f1_{\text{CEAF}} = \frac{2 \times p_{\text{CEAF}} \times r_{\text{CEAF}}}{p_{\text{CEAF}} + r_{\text{CEAF}}} \quad (10)$$

Furthermore, we also included Normalized Mutual Information (NMI), a standard metric for evaluating the clustering quality, as one of our evaluation metrics. The detailed definition of NMI can be found in [3]. Basically, the higher the NMI score the better clustering performance an automatic system achieves: NMI= 1 if the prediction is identical to the ground-truth; and NMI= 0 if the prediction is independent from the ground-truth.

6.2.3 Evaluation of search task extraction methods

We randomly split the annotated user query logs into a training set with 712 annotated users, and a testing set with the rest 725 annotated users. The parameters in each model, e.g., C in SVM-based models, are tuned by 5-fold cross-validation on the training set (splitting the annotated users into different folds).

We trained all the methods on the manually annotated training set, and compared their task extraction performance in Table 6, where we averaged the performance under each metric over all the testing cases. A paired two-sample t-test is performed to validate the significance of improvement from the best performing method against the runner-up method under each metric.

Table 6: Search Task Extraction Performance.

	p_{pair}	r_{pair}	$f1_{\text{CEAF}}$	NMI
Q_wcc	0.8653	**0.9833***	0.4826	0.4058
Q_htc	0.9213	0.8607	0.5461	0.5636
AdaptClu	0.9059	0.9046	0.5583	0.5466
cluster-svm	0.9232	0.7908	0.5363	0.5602
bestlink SVM	**0.9330***	0.9273	**0.5895***	**0.6046***
AdaptClu$_{\text{all}}$	0.8681	0.4611	0.2880	0.3236
Rule-based	0.8954	0.5570	-	-

* indicates *p-value*<0.01

In Table 6 we first observed that cluster-svm, which is also a structural learning method, performed much worse than bestlink SVM, especially on r_{pair}. The reason is that cluster-svm optimizes the in-cluster similarity defined by *all-link* among the queries; while in bestlink SVM, the in-cluster similarity is only defined on the *bestlink* among the queries, or more precisely, the edges exist in h (as shown in Eq (2)). To validate this hypothesis, we implemented an additional baseline of *all-link*-based adaptive clustering (AdaptClu$_{\text{all}}$).

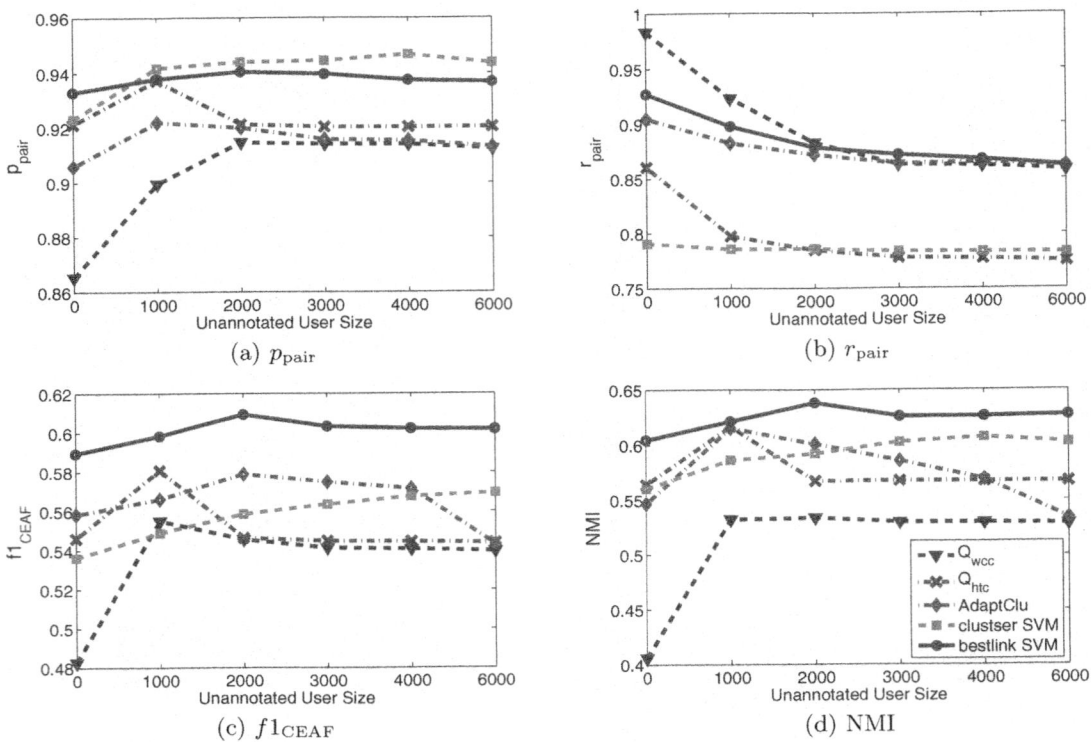

Figure 2: Task extraction performance with increasing volume of weakly supervised data.

In AdaptClu$_{all}$, we changed the original single-link agglomerative clustering to all-link agglomerative clustering, where the in-cluster similarity is defined the same as in cluster-svm. As observed in the result, AdaptClu$_{all}$ performed significantly worse than AdaptClu, especially on r_{pair}. This result validates our basic modeling assumption in the proposed bestlink SVM, i.e., a query belonging to a particular task should have a strong connection with at least another one query rather than all the other queries in the same task.

Besides, as discussed in Section 2, due to the lack of interaction between the binary classifier training and query clustering in post-processing, the two-step approaches are likely to give suboptimal task extraction performance. Q_wcc and Q_htc are based on the same binary classifier's output, but their performance differs because of distinct strategies used in post-processing. Q_wcc tends to connect all the queries together, and results in a high r_{pair}, but poor performance on other metrics. On the other hand, because Q_htc only compares the first and last queries between two different clusters, it gives a relatively lower r_{pair}, but better clustering performance due to a better p_{pair}, as compared to Q_wcc.

In Section 5, we proposed a method for automatically generating weak supervision from search logs in the form of must-link and cannot-link. In Table 6, we also evaluated the quality of such weak supervision. Since the rule-based supervision merely provides pairwise annotations, we only evaluated its p_{pair} and r_{pair}. In general, p_{pair} of these auto-generated annotations is reasonably good, while r_{pair} is relatively poor. This result is expected: the method described in Table 3 uses strong signals for annotation; but the coverage of such signals is limited, since some relations between two distinct queries can only be inferred by reasoning over the whole query sequence by human judges.

6.2.4 Effectiveness of weakly supervised data

To investigate the effectiveness of the weak supervision in helping to train the supervised model, we gradually added the weakly supervised data into our training set. We first obtained the pairwise annotations, as defined in Table 3, for those users who have not been manually annotated; then we gradually added such partially labeled user query logs into the manually-annotated training set. For binary-classification-based baselines, i.e., Q_wcc, Q_htc and AdaptClu, the newly added pairwise annotations are used as regular training supervision; for cluster-svm, the loss function is modified to adopt the partial annotations (similar as Eq (5)). The experimental results are summarized in Figure 2.

From Figure 2 we can study the utility of weakly supervised data on cross-session task extraction. As shown in Figure 2 (c) and (d), the supervised learning methods benefit from a medium volume of weakly supervised data; but when the volume reaches certain limit, the performance stops improving, and even degrades. Figure 2 (a) and (b) help to explain why this happens: all methods' r_{pair} performance drops when adding the weakly supervised data for training, but their p_{pair} performance improves. With the improved p_{pair}, all methods' clustering performance, in terms of $f1_{CEAF}$ and NMI, gets improved. As shown in Table 6, the weakly supervised data has high precision but low recall, adding more such training signals would bias the models toward recognizing the pairs similar to those high-precision must-links. When the volume of weakly supervised data passes a limit, it will overwhelm the signals from human annotations; and therefore hinders further improvement. Figure 2 also shows that, compared to the two-step methods, the structural learning based method, i.e., cluster-svm and bestlink SVM, can utilize more weakly supervised data before the performance saturates. The reason is that structural learning method directly optimizes (or approximates) the clustering metrics during training. The two-step methods perform classification and clustering independently, and there is inconsistency between training objective and evaluation in these two-step methods. As a result, errors in the learned binary classifier cannot be recovered easily in the clustering stage in those methods.

6.2.5 Weakly supervised search task extraction

We are also interested in investigating how well the models could perform when there is only weakly supervised data generated by the proposed must-link and cannot-link. In other words, we want to test if the learning methods' task extraction capability can go beyond the simple annotation rules. In this experiment, we only trained the models on the 6,192 unannotated users with weak supervision, and tested them on the same manually annotated testing set as before. In order to analyze how well the methods generalize from the weakly supervised data, we included a naive baseline Rule-Q_wcc: we adopted Q_wcc by treating the queries connected by the must-links as a task.

Table 7: Task extraction performance when trained only on the weakly supervised data.

	p_{pair}	r_{pair}	$f1_{\text{CEAF}}$	NMI
Rule-Q_wcc	0.9084	0.5136	0.5492	0.5602
Q_wcc	0.9123	0.8582	0.5397	0.5285
Q_htc	0.9204	0.7747	0.5440	0.5669
AdaptClu	0.9131	0.8613*	0.5426	0.5325
cluster-svm	0.9155	0.7565	0.5197	0.4805
bestlinkSVM	0.9334*	0.8161	0.5676*	0.5893*

* indicates $p\text{-}value < 0.01$

As shown in Table 7, all the methods improved p_{pair} and r_{pair} against Rule-Q_wcc, and especially for r_{pair}. However, not all of them can improve the clustering quality metric: besides bestlink SVM, only Q_htc improves NMI metric. We looked into the detailed output of those methods and found that: Rule-Q_wcc generated many singleton tasks because of the low coverage of must-links; the baseline models merged some of the small clusters into larger ones, but they still created too many smaller clusters than ground-truth. bestlink SVM further merged the small clusters correctly, making the number of predicted tasks closest to the ground-truth, and therefore it achieved better clustering performance.

We wanted to further investigate how many "complex tasks," which are not covered by the must-links defined in Table 3, can be extracted by learning from the weak supervision. Specifically, we define the complex task as: $\mathcal{T}^*_{\text{strict}}$, in which no must-link can be applied on any pair of queries in it (strict criterion); or $\mathcal{T}^*_{\text{loose}}$, there exists at least one pair of queries cannot be connected via must-links in it (loose criterion). Based on this notation, we define the coverage of complex task as the proportion of complex tasks which can be perfectly recovered by the automatic methods,

$$c_{\text{loose}} = \frac{\sum_{\mathcal{T}_i \in \hat{\mathcal{T}}} \sum_{\mathcal{T}_j \in \mathcal{T}^*_{\text{loose}}} \delta(\mathcal{T}_i, \mathcal{T}_j)}{|\mathcal{T}^*_{\text{loose}}|} \quad (11)$$

$$c_{\text{strict}} = \frac{\sum_{\mathcal{T}_i \in \hat{\mathcal{T}}} \sum_{\mathcal{T}_j \in \mathcal{T}^*_{\text{strict}}} \delta(\mathcal{T}_i, \mathcal{T}_j)}{|\mathcal{T}^*_{\text{strict}}|} \quad (12)$$

where $\delta(\mathcal{X}, \mathcal{Y}) = 1$ when the set $\mathcal{X}$ and $\mathcal{Y}$ are the same, and otherwise $\delta(\mathcal{X}, \mathcal{Y}) = 0$.

In this experiment, we used all the 1436 annotated users as testing set, where we collected 357 strict complex tasks and 1540 loose complex tasks out of the total 2283 multi-query tasks. All the models are trained on the rest 6192 unannotated users with weak supervision, and the experimental results are list in Table 8, where we used sign-test for validating the improvement over the baselines.

We should note that all those complex tasks cannot be identified by the straight-forward Rule-Q_wcc baseline, so that the newly defined task coverage metric measures how well the learning methods can generalize from the weak supervision. From the results we can notice that bestlink SVM, which achieved the best performance against all the other baselines, can successfully recover about 30% of complex tasks by leveraging the knowledge from weak supervision, which validates the effectiveness of using such signals as supervision for model training.

Table 8: Coverage of complex tasks when trained only on the weakly supervised data.

	c_{loose}	c_{strict}
Q_wcc	0.2914	0.2745
Q_htc	0.2617	0.2761
AdaptClu$_{\text{single}}$	0.2837	0.2717
cluster-svm	0.2883	0.2997
bestlinkSVM	**0.3207***	**0.3501***

* indicates $p\text{-}value < 0.01$

6.3 Feature Weights in bestlink SVM

In order to understand which similarity features are important for the problem of cross-session task extraction, we list the top two positive and top two negative features learned by the proposed bestlink SVM under each category of pairwise similarity features defined in Table 9. To avoid bias introduced by weak supervision, we only demonstrated the weights learned from the manually annotated training set.

Table 9: Top 2 positive and top 2 negative features under each type of pairwise similarity features in bestlink SVM model.

Feature	Weight
Q-COSINE	5.30
Q-JAC	1.51
U-JAC-ALL	4.53
U-SIM-AVG	3.05
S-SAME	1.00
S-DIST	0.60
Q-DIST	-3.38
Q-EDIT	-2.73
U-EDIT-DOMAIN-AVG	-1.39
U-EDIT-ALL-CLICK-AVG	-0.83
S-FIRST	-0.28

As can be noticed in Table 9, Q-COSINE has the largest importance weight for identifying queries belonging to the same task; and U-JAC-ALL is also very informative for recognizing the similar queries. Besides, we found that bestlink SVM assigns relatively low positive weight to S-SAME, and Q-TIME is not the most important feature in the model. The reason is that we already knew 12.7% tasks span cross session boundaries (as shown in Table 5), and placing too large a weight on S-SAME and Q-TIME will forbid the method from identifying those cross-session tasks.

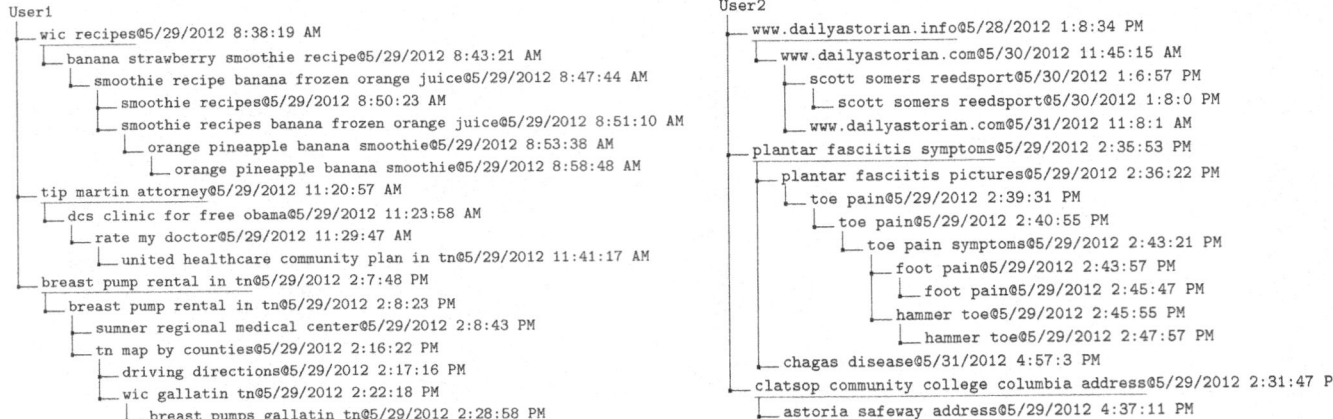

Figure 3: Identified latent search task structure.

6.4 Analysis of Identified Tasks

As we have discussed in Section 4.2, the latent structure h defined in bestlink SVM is a tree formed by strong connections between queries, where each subtree of the dummy query q_0 corresponds to a search task. In Figure 3, we illustrated the latent task structure inferred by our bestlink SVM from two different users' query logs.

Comparing to the flat clustering structure given by the traditional search task extraction methods [13, 15], the hierarchical structure inferred by bestlink SVM provides us with more in-depth details to understand users' search behaviors and their information needs. For example, in Figure 3 we can clearly notice that the identified task structure for User2 is more complex than that for User1: User1 attempted three consecutive tasks on May 29; while User2's two major search tasks, i.e., checking daily news and looking for solutions of her health issue, spanned from May 28 to May 31, and were performed in an interleaved manner. And the subtrees in an identified search task represent finer grained subtasks. For instance, as shown in Figure 3, in User2's second identified task of "plantar fasciitis symptoms," there are two subtasks, one starts with "plantar fasciitis pictures" and another starts with "chagas disease."

At the beginning of Section 6, we listed a brief overview of basic properties of search tasks based on a limited number of human annotations. Now we can get a more comprehensive understanding of user's search behaviors based on the automatically extracted search tasks in our whole query log data set. We listed a set of statistics in Table 10, where we applied a proprietary multi-class classifier to categorize a query into 80 different categories, e.g., navigational, commerce, celebrity and etc., in order to annotate the search intent of queries.

As shown in Table 10, user's search intent in each extracted task is quite concentrated: despite the fact that there are in average 4.41 queries in a task, there are only 1.47 different intents. Particularly, when the user's intent is purely navigational, the task will get mostly simplified: only 1.38 unique queries per task. And more than 25% identified tasks only contain navigational queries. Another interesting phenomenon we found is the transition probability between the navigational and non-navigational queries, which is estimated within the identified tasks, is quite different: the chance a user issues a non-navigational query after a nav-

Table 10: Statistics of extracted search tasks.

Query/Task	UniQuery/Task
4.41±7.48	2.80±4.04
Intent/Task	% of NavTask
1.47±1.20	25.37
Query/NavTask	UniQuery/NavTask
2.45±2.67	1.38±0.80
P(non-nav|nav)	P(nav|non-nav)
0.288	0.124

igational query is much lower than the opposite direction. One possible explanation for this is that when user issues a non-navigational query, they usually do not have a clear sense of where to find the information yet, so they are more likely to keep submitting the questions to the search engine; but when they have specific destination in mind, they would start to issue questions to explore more perspectives of the information they are interested in.

7. CONCLUSIONS

Search tasks frequently span multiple sessions, and thus developing methods to extract these tasks from historic data is central to understanding longitudinal search behaviors and in developing search systems to support users' long-running tasks. In this paper, we have presented a novel method for learning to accurately extract cross-session search tasks from users' historic search activities. We developed a semi-supervised clustering model based on the latent structural SVM framework, which is capable of learning inter-query dependencies from users' searching behaviors. A set of effective automatic annotation rules are proposed as weak supervision to release the burden of manual annotation. Comprehensive experimentation using large-scale search logs from a commercial search engine demonstrated the superior performance of our method in identifying cross-session search tasks versus a number of state-of-the-art algorithms. Importantly, we were able to obtain performance gains while reducing the reliance on costly human annotations via the automatically generated weak supervision. The results are promising and pave the way for a range of future work in this area, including user modeling and long-term task based personalization.

8. REFERENCES

[1] E. Agichtein, R. W. White, S. T. Dumais, and P. N. Bennet. Search, interrupted: understanding and predicting search task continuation. In *Proceedings of the 35th international ACM SIGIR conference on Research and development in information retrieval*, pages 315–324. ACM, 2012.

[2] P. Anick. Using terminological feedback for web search refinement: a log-based study. In *Proceedings of the 26th annual international ACM SIGIR conference on Research and development in informaion retrieval*, pages 88–95. ACM, 2003.

[3] D. Cai, X. He, X. Wang, H. Bao, and J. Han. Locality preserving nonnegative matrix factorization. In *IJCAI'09*, pages 1010–1015, 2009.

[4] L. D. Catledge and J. E. Pitkow. Characterizing browsing strategies in the world-wide web. *Computer Networks and ISDN systems*, 27(6):1065–1073, 1995.

[5] M. Chang, D. Goldwasser, D. Roth, and V. Srikumar. Structured output learning with indirect supervision. In *ICML'10*, 2010.

[6] W. W. Cohen and J. Richman. Learning to match and cluster large high-dimensional data sets for data integration. In *Proceedings of the eighth ACM SIGKDD international conference on Knowledge discovery and data mining*, pages 475–480. ACM, 2002.

[7] S. Cucerzan and E. Brill. Spelling correction as an iterative process that exploits the collective knowledge of web users. In *Proceedings of EMNLP*, volume 4, pages 293–300, 2004.

[8] T. Finley and T. Joachims. Supervised clustering with support vector machines. In *Proceedings of the 22nd international conference on Machine learning*, pages 217–224. ACM, 2005.

[9] D. He, A. Göker, and D. J. Harper. Combining evidence for automatic web session identification. *Information Processing & Management*, 38(5):727–742, 2002.

[10] A. K. Jain, M. N. Murty, and P. J. Flynn. Data clustering: a review. *ACM computing surveys (CSUR)*, 31(3):264–323, 1999.

[11] R. Jones and K. L. Klinkner. Beyond the session timeout: automatic hierarchical segmentation of search topics in query logs. In *Proceedings of the 17th ACM conference on Information and knowledge management*, pages 699–708. ACM, 2008.

[12] R. Jones, B. Rey, O. Madani, and W. Greiner. Generating query substitutions. In *Proceedings of the 15th international conference on World Wide Web*, pages 387–396. ACM, 2006.

[13] A. Kotov, P. N. Bennett, R. W. White, S. T. Dumais, and J. Teevan. Modeling and analysis of cross-session search tasks. *SIGIR'11*, pages 5–14, 2011.

[14] Z. Liao, Y. Song, L.-w. He, and Y. Huang. Evaluating the effectiveness of search task trails. In *Proceedings of the 21st international conference on World Wide Web*, pages 489–498. ACM, 2012.

[15] C. Lucchese, S. Orlando, R. Perego, F. Silvestri, and G. Tolomei. Identifying task-based sessions in search engine query logs. In *Proceedings of the fourth ACM international conference on Web search and data mining*, pages 277–286. ACM, 2011.

[16] X. Luo. On coreference resolution performance metrics. In *Proceedings of the conference on Human Language Technology and Empirical Methods in Natural Language Processing*, pages 25–32. Association for Computational Linguistics, 2005.

[17] F. Radlinski and T. Joachims. Query chains: learning to rank from implicit feedback. In *Proceedings of the eleventh ACM SIGKDD international conference on Knowledge discovery in data mining*, pages 239–248. ACM, 2005.

[18] D. Shen, J.-T. Sun, Q. Yang, and Z. Chen. Building bridges for web query classification. In *Proceedings of the 29th annual international ACM SIGIR conference on Research and development in information retrieval*, pages 131–138. ACM, 2006.

[19] C. Silverstein, H. Marais, M. Henzinger, and M. Moricz. Analysis of a very large web search engine query log. In *ACM SIGIR Forum*, volume 33, pages 6–12. ACM, 1999.

[20] A. Spink, M. Park, B. Jansen, and J. Pedersen. Multitasking during web search sessions. *Information Processing & Management*, 42(1):264–275, 2006.

[21] V. Vapnik. *The nature of statistical learning theory*. springer, 1999.

[22] K. Wagstaff, C. Cardie, S. Rogers, and S. Schrödl. Constrained k-means clustering with background knowledge. In *ICML'01*, pages 577–584, 2001.

[23] R. W. White and S. M. Drucker. Investigating behavioral variability in web search. In *Proceedings of the 16th international conference on World Wide Web*, pages 21–30. ACM, 2007.

[24] C.-N. J. Yu and T. Joachims. Learning structural svms with latent variables. In *Proceedings of the 26th Annual International Conference on Machine Learning*, pages 1169–1176. ACM, 2009.

Content-Aware Click Modeling

Hongning Wang, ChengXiang Zhai
Department of Computer Science
University of Illinois at Urbana-Champaign
Urbana IL, 61801 USA
{wang296,czhai}@illinois.edu

Anlei Dong, Yi Chang
Yahoo! Labs
701 First Avenue, Sunnyvale, CA 94089
{anlei,yichang}@yahoo-inc.com

ABSTRACT

Click models aim at extracting intrinsic relevance of documents to queries from biased user clicks. One basic modeling assumption made in existing work is to treat such intrinsic relevance as an atomic query-document-specific parameter, which is solely estimated from historical clicks without using any content information about a document or relationship among the clicked/skipped documents under the same query. Due to this overly simplified assumption, existing click models can neither fully explore the information about a document's relevance quality nor make predictions of relevance for any unseen documents.

In this work, we proposed a novel Bayesian Sequential State model for modeling the user click behaviors, where the document content and dependencies among the sequential click events within a query are characterized by a set of descriptive features via a probabilistic graphical model. By applying the posterior regularized Expectation Maximization algorithm for parameter learning, we tailor the model to meet specific ranking-oriented properties, e.g., pairwise click preferences, so as to exploit richer information buried in the user clicks. Experiment results on a large set of real click logs demonstrate the effectiveness of the proposed model compared with several state-of-the-art click models.

Categories and Subject Descriptors

H.3.3 [**Information Search and Retrieval**]: Retrieval Models; H.3.5 [**Information Storage and Retrieval**]: Online Information Service

General Terms

Algorithms, Experimentation

Keywords

Click modeling, query log analysis, probabilistic graphical model

1. INTRODUCTION

User click logs provide rich and valuable implicit feedback information and can be used as a proxy for relevance judgments [14] or signals for directly influencing ranking [1].

However, they are also known to be vulnerable to position-bias – documents appearing at higher positions tend to receive more clicks even though they are not relevant to the query [10]. Therefore, properly modeling and interpreting the underlying mechanism that gives rise to user clicks is an important yet challenging research problem.

To fulfill this goal, click models [4, 5, 8, 11, 20] have been proposed for modeling user clicks and extracting intrinsic relevance information from the biased click logs. One fundamental assumption made in click models is the so-called *examination hypothesis*: a user clicks on a returned document *if and only if* that document has been examined by the user and it is relevant to the given query. Based on such an assumption, click models aim to distinguish the relevance-driven clicks from the position-driven clicks by postulating different dependency assumptions between the events of examining a document and clicking on it, e.g., position models [7, 8] and cascade models [4, 11]. Though deviating in various dependency assumptions about the examine and click events, all click models formalize a document's relevance quality to a given query as an *atomic* query-document-specific parameter, e.g., Bernoulli random variable [4, 11], which is solely estimated from multiple occurrences of such specific query-document pair in the click logs.

However, this commonly used modeling approach totally ignores the actual document content, which presumably would directly influence a user's click decision. As a result, the existing click models can neither take advantage of in-depth knowledge about the relevance quality of a document to the query buried in the document content, nor benefit from the semantic relation among the documents under the same query. For example, diversity is an important criterion for satisfying a user's information need [6]. A user would be less likely to click on a near-duplicate document if she has already clicked on a previous one with similar content; but in such a case, her "skip" decision does not necessarily mean that the document is irrelevant to her query. In most of the existing click models, we are only aware of which position is clicked, but the underlying "semantic explanations" for the clicking behavior, e.g., clicked content redundancy and click distance, are completely discarded.

A serious consequence of such an overly simplified assumption of a document's relevance quality to a given query is that the model's generalization capability is limited: one has to collect a large number of such query-document pairs to obtain a confident estimate of relevance. As shown in the previously reported results, only when there is a sufficient number of observations for the given query-document pairs, could the existing click models demonstrate their advantages [4, 8, 11]. In the extreme case, when a new document comes into the search engine, there would be no way for us to accurately infer its relevance to the query immediately by a click model. The situation gets even severer in time-sensitive retrieval tasks, such as news search, where new documents keep emerging and we need timely estimation of their relevance quality to the given query before we could gather large number of user clicks.

In addition, existing click models only target at decomposing the relevance-driven clicks from the position-driven clicks, which boils down to discounting the observed clicks for each document in a *pointwise* manner. However, in a real search scenario, when a user decides to skip one document, it does not necessarily indicate the document is irrelevant to the query, since it is also possible that the previous/next clicked document is more relevant than it. Such property of user behavior has been proved by many real user studies [10, 14]. Therefore, existing click models are not optimized for distinguishing the relative order among the inferred relevance quality.

To the best of our knowledge, no existing work in click modeling attempted to address these two deficiencies, i.e., lack of exploring content information and failing to capture relative relevance preference. In this work, we propose to solve these limitations within a probabilistic generative framework, which naturally incorporates the document content and relative preferences between documents into click modeling. In detail, following the assumptions in cascade models, we propose a Bayesian Sequential State (BSS) model to formalize the generation of the observed clicks under a given query. First, to capture the rich semantic of a document's relevance quality to the query, we introduced a set of descriptive features (e.g., query matching in title and site authority) into query-document relevance modeling. Instead of hard coding the dependency among the click/examine events within a query (e.g., clicked documents must be relevant) [4, 11], we give our model the freedom to learn such relation from data based on the designed features, e.g., a click decision will be affected by the content redundancy between the current and previously clicked documents. Second, ranking-oriented knowledge, e.g., pairwise click preference, is incorporated by regularizing the posterior distribution of clicks, which helps us tailor the proposed probabilistic model and avoid undesirable local maxima.

The proposed model is a general click modeling framework, which covers most of existing models as special cases. On a large set of real click logs, the proposed BSS model outperformed several state-of-the-art click models in terms of relevance estimation quality. Especially when we only have limited size of training samples for a particular query-document pair, BSS model demonstrated its advantage by leveraging the information from ranking-oriented features for accurate relevance estimation. The introduced pairwise click preference renders BSS model better ranking capability in distinguishing the relative order of relevance among the candidate documents. Besides, BSS model provides a principled way of interpreting and modeling user's click behaviors, which is not available in existing click models.

2. BACKGROUND

The main purpose for modeling the user's click behaviors in search engine logs is to fight against the notorious position-bias and extract the document's intrinsic relevance to the query. Richardson et al. [19] attempted to combat position-bias by imposing a multiplicative factor on documents in lower positions to infer their true relevance. This idea was later formalized as the *examination hypothesis* and adopted in the position models [7]. The key assumption in position models is that the user clicks on a document *if and only if* that document has been examined by the user and it is relevant to the query. In addition, the examination event *only* depends on the position. Formally, given a document d displayed at position i, the probability of d being clicked (i.e., $C = 1$) is determined by the latent examination event (i.e., $E = 1$) as,

$$P(C = 1|d, i) = \sum_{e \in \{0,1\}} P(C = 1|d, i, E = e)P(E = e|d, i)$$
$$= P(C = 1|d, E = 1)P(E = 1|i)$$

where $P(C = 1|d, E = 1)$ is specified by a document-specific parameter α_d describing the document's intrinsic relevance quality to the query, and $P(E = 1|i)$ is determined by a position-specific parameter β_i to capture position bias.

However, the pure position models deal with examination event in an isolated manner, i.e., the examination probability $P(E = 1|i)$ is assumed to be independent from the click events. Cascade models are one typical extension to conquer this limitation, which further assume the user will examine the returned documents from top to bottom and make click decisions over each examined document. Once the user stops examining, all the following documents will not be examined. Therefore, a click event in a query session is modeled as,

$$P(C_i = 1) = P(R_i = 1) \prod_{j=1}^{i-1} \left[1 - P(R_j = 1)\right]$$

where $R_i = 1$ is the event that document d at position i is relevant to the given query.

One drawback of the original cascade model is that it can only deal with queries containing one click, later work generalizes it to queries with multiple clicks. Chapelle et al., [4] solved this limitation by distinguishing the perceived and intrinsic relevance of a document: they assumed the perceived relevance controls the click event and the intrinsic relevance determines the user's satisfaction with the current document and her further examination of the following documents.

Our proposed BSS model falls into the category of cascade models: we assume the users would sequentially examine the returned documents from top to bottom for the given query, and a clicked document must be examined beforehand. In addition, by incorporating a set of ranking features, we model a document's relevance quality to a given query in a more general way: we assume the relevance quality of a document to the given query is not only an intrinsic property of the document itself, but also influenced by the displayed document content (e.g., title and abstract). The dependency relation between the examine and click events are flexibly learned from data, e.g., an examined and relevant document may still be skipped. In addition, the proposed method also explores the relationship among the clicked and skipped documents under the same query, e.g., content redundancy, which is not covered by existing click models. In previous work, click decision is only determined by the document's own relevance quality; while in our proposed model, ranking-oriented constraints, e.g., pairwise click preferences, are also incorporated to improve the model's capability of distinguishing the relative order of relevant documents.

3. BAYESIAN SEQUENTIAL STATE MODEL

As discussed earlier, existing click models have two limitations: 1) modeling the relevance of document to the given query as an *atomic* query-document-specific parameter; 2) failing to capture the relative order of estimated relevance between the documents. To break these two limitations and make click models applicable in more search scenarios, we propose a novel Bayesian Sequential State (BSS) model, in which the relevance quality of document to a given query is parameterized by a set of document-specific features, and the dependencies among the click and examine events within the same session are explicitly captured and exploited.

3.1 Basic Generative Assumption

Following the basic modeling assumption in *cascade models*, in our proposed BSS model, we assume that when a user submits a query to the search engine and gets a list of ranked results, she would sequentially examine the returned documents from top to bottom; a document must be examined before she clicks on it; and once she decides to stop examining at current position, she would leave this query session without further interactions. In particular, we assume that when she is examining a document, she would *judge* its relevance according to the displayed document content, e.g., title and abstract, which can be characterized by a set of features, e.g., query term matching in title and abstract; in addition, the user *remembers* her previously examined documents under this query, so that when she moves onto lower positions, her previous click/skip decisions will affect her later choices, e.g., skipping the less relevant documents. In other words, the click/skip events within the same query session are assumed to be dependent with each other.

Formally, assume there are N queries in our collection and for each query there are M ordered documents. Following the notations introduced in Section 2, we use binary variables to denote the relevance status, examine and click events of a document, i.e., $R = \{0,1\}$, $E = \{0,1\}$ and $C = \{0,1\}$. To make the presentation concise, we will ignore the symbol d_i representing the document displayed at position i under a particular query, when no ambiguity is caused. Hence, the generation process of the observed clicks in a collection of query logs defined by the proposed BSS model can be formalized as follows:

- For each query q in the query log:

    - For document d in position i:

        1. Decide whether to examine the current position based on previous examination event E_{i-1} and previous document d_{i-1}'s relevance status R_{i-1}, i.e., $E_i \sim P(E_i|E_{i-1}, R_{i-1}, q)$. If $i = 1$, $E_i = 1$;
        2. If $E_i = 0$, abandon further examination;
        3. Judge d_i's relevance against query q, i.e., $R_i \sim P(R_i|d_i, q)$;
        4. Decide whether to click d_i based on its relevance quality, i.e., $C_i \sim P(C_i|E_i, R_i, q)$.

As a result, the joint probability of random variables $\{E_i, R_i, C_i\}_{i=1}^M$ within a search result page for query q can be formulated as:

$$P(\boldsymbol{E}, \boldsymbol{R}, \boldsymbol{C}|q) = \prod_{i=1}^{M} P(C_i|R_i, E_i, q) P(E_i|R_{i-1}, E_{i-1}, q) P(R_i|d_i, q)$$
(1)

Different from most of the existing click models, where the dependency relation is hard-coded in their conditional probabilities, e.g., an examined and relevant document must be clicked: $E_i = 1, R_i = 1 \Leftrightarrow C_i = 1$ [4, 11], we relax such hard requirement to accommodate noise in clicks [5]. We assume that even an examined document is not relevant, the user might still click on it because of her carelessness, i.e., $P(C_i = 1|E_i = 1, R_i = 0) > 0$; and on the other hand, even if an examined document is relevant, the user might still skip it due to the redundancy or her satisfaction of pervious clicks, i.e., $P(C_i = 0|E_i = 1, R_i = 1) > 0$. In addition, to fully explore the dependency between a click event and the document's relevance status, we assume user's further examination also depends on the current document's relevance quality, i.e., $P(E_i|E_{i-1}, R_{i-1}) \neq P(E_i|E_{i-1})$.

3.2 Conditional Probability Refinement

The generation process introduced in Eq (1) depicts the skeleton of dependencies among the random variables of $\{E_i, R_i, C_i\}_{i=1}^M$ within the search result page for a given query. Next, we will discuss the details of how we can incorporate descriptive features to materialize those dependency relations and exploit rich information conveyed in the users' click behaviors.

To parameterize the dependency, we define the conditional probabilities in BSS model via logistic functions:

1. Relevance probability:

$$P(R_i = 1|d_i, q) = \sigma(w^{R^\top} f_{q,d_i}^R + w_{q,d_i}^R)$$
(2)

2. Click probability:

$$P(C_i = 1|R_i, E_i, q) = \begin{cases} 0 & \text{if } E_i = 0 \\ \sigma(w_{R=0}^{C^\top} f_{q,d_i}^C) & \text{if } E_i = 1, R_i = 0 \\ \sigma(w_{R=1}^{C^\top} f_{q,d_i}^C) & \text{if } E_i = 1, R_i = 1 \end{cases}$$
(3)

3. Examine probability:

$$P(E_i = 1|R_{i-1}, E_{i-1}, q) = \begin{cases} 0 & \text{if } E_{i-1} = 0 \\ \sigma(w_{R=0}^{E^\top} f_{q,d_i}^E) & \text{if } E_{i-1} = 1, R_{i-1} = 0 \\ \sigma(w_{R=1}^{E^\top} f_{q,d_i}^E) & \text{if } E_{i-1} = 1, R_{i-1} = 1 \end{cases}$$
(4)

where $\sigma(x) = \frac{1}{1+\exp(-x)}$, $\{f_{q,d}^R, f_{q,d}^C, f_{q,d}^E\}$ are the features characterizing the conditional probabilities for relevance status, click and examination events of document d_i under query q; and $\Theta = \{w^R, w_{R=0}^C, w_{R=1}^C, w_{R=0}^E, w_{R=0}^E\}$ are the corresponding importance weights for the features.

In particular, to distinguish the intrinsic relevance and perceived relevance, we assume a document's latent relevance status to a given query is determined by the mixture of these two types of relevance, i.e., $P(R_i = 1|q) = \sigma(w^{R^\top} f_{q,d}^R + w_{q,d}^R)$ as defined in Eq (2). In particular, $w_{q,d}^R$ is a scaler factor reflecting the intrinsic relevance quality of a document to the given query, which is assumed to be drawn from a zero mean Normal distribution. And $w^{R^\top} f_{q,d}^R$ is an

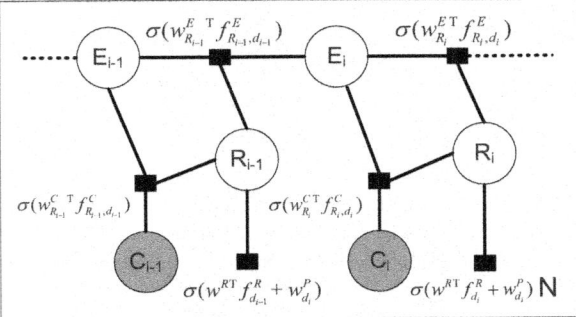

Figure 1: Factor graph representation for the proposed BSS model. Circles denote the random variables and black squares denote the conditional probabilities defined in Eq(2)-(4). Random variable E_i implies whether document d_i is examined, R_i represents d_i's relevance status to the query, and C_i indicates whether d_i is clicked by the user.

estimate of the perceived relevance quality, which is characterized by a weighted combination of relevance-driven features $f_{q,d}^R$, e.g., site authority and query term matching in document title. When we have sufficient observations of the query-document pair (q,d), the estimation of $w_{q,d}^R$ will be close to its true intrinsic relevance; but when we only have limited observations, e.g., for a new document, relevance-driven features $f_{q,d}^R$ will help to identify its perceived relevance, which leads to user clicks.

Using the language of probabilistic graphical models, we summarize the specification of the proposed BSS model by a factor graph representation in Figure 1.

3.3 Feature Instantiation for BSS

Table 1 lists the detailed definition of the proposed features in BSS model, which aim at capturing different factors affecting a user's click decision.

Among the proposed features, $f_{q,d}^R$ is the set of features describing the relevance quality of a document to the given query. This is the core problem for modern information retrieval study, and many effective features have been proposed for this purpose, such as BM25 and PageRank. In this work, we utilized 65 text matching features (e.g., query term matching in document title and abstract) as our relevance features. We should note that the proposed model is general and can potentially accommodate any combination of relevance-driven features.

Though we are aiming to distinguish different effects of the current document's relevance status in examination and click events, it is impossible for us to pre-categorize which set of features would only affect user's click (examine) decision when the current document is relevant and vice versa. We decide to use the same set of features for these two situations, but give them different weights, i.e., $\{w_{R=0}^C, w_{R=1}^C\}$ for click event and $\{w_{R=0}^E, w_{R=1}^E\}$ for examine event, to portray their distinct contributions. In detail, the click-event-related features $f_{q,d}^C$ are used to indicate how the user would behave when an examined document is judged to be relevant ($R=1$) or irrelevant ($R=0$). For example, when the document is irrelevant, a mis-click might be caused by the position of the document (the user trusts more about the top ranked documents); and when the document is relevant,

Table 1: Features for materializing conditional probabilities in BSS model.

Type	Description	Value
f_{q,d_i}^R	65 text matching features e.g., query matching in title, query proximity in abstract	-
f_{q,d_i}^C	position	i
	# clicks	$\sum_{j<i} \mathbf{1}[C_j=1]$
	distance to last click	$i - \arg\max_{j<i}[C_j=1]$
	query length	$\|\|q\|\|$
	clicked content similarity	$\text{AVG}_{j<i,C_j=1} sim(d_i, d_j)$
	skipped content similarity	$\text{AVG}_{j<i,C_j=0}[sim(d_i, d_j)]$
f_{q,d_i}^E	position	i
	# clicks	$\sum_{j<i} \mathbf{1}[C_j=1]$
	distance to last click	$i - \arg\max_{j<i}[C_j=1]$
	avg content similarity	$\text{AVG}_{j<i,k<i}[sim(d_j, d_k)]$
	variance content similarity	$\text{VAR}_{j<i,k<i}[sim(d_j, d_k)]$

(All three types of features also include an additional bias term b accordingly.)

a skip decision may be due to the content redundancy of the clicked documents or her satisfaction of current search result (number of clicks). And the examine-event-related features $f_{q,d}^E$ exploit the factors affecting a user's examine decision on the next position. For example, when the current document is irrelevant ($R=0$) and the user has skipped several documents in a row (e.g., distance to the last click), she would be more likely to give up further examining; and when the current document is relevant ($R=1$) and the clicked documents are quite similar to each other so far (average content similarity), she might be more likely to stop.

3.4 Inference and Model Estimation

When applying the proposed BSS model in the testing phase, we do not need to restrict ourself to the documents ever occurred in the training set (i.e., $w_{q,d}^R$ exists). Since we have formalized the perceived relevance by a set of relevance-driven features, we can directly apply the model to any unseen document by calculating $\sigma(w^{R^\top} f_{q,d}^R)$ as an estimate of its relevance quality to the query (i.e., using mean value of the intrinsic relevance $w_{q,d}^R$ from prior for all the new candidate documents). And for those documents occurred in our training set, we can follow Eq (2) to incorporate the intrinsic relevance of document to the given query learned from the training set.

In model learning phase, because a document's relevance quality and examination status are not observed in the click logs, we appeal to the Expectation Maximization algorithm [18] to estimate the optimal parameter setting, which maximizes the lower bound of the log-likelihood of the observed click events in the training set,

$$L(\mathbf{C}, \mathbf{q}, \Theta) = \sum_{q,i} \log \sum_{E_i, R_i} p(E_i, R_i, C_i|q, \Theta)$$
$$\geq \sum_{q,i} \sum_{E_i, R_i} p(E_i, R_i|C_i, q, \Theta) \log p(E_i, R_i, C_i|q, \Theta) \quad (5)$$

Particularly, in E-Step, we calculate the posterior distribution of $P(\mathbf{E}, \mathbf{R}|\mathbf{C}, q, \Theta^{(t)})$ for the latent variables $(E_i, R_i)_{i=1}^M$

in a query session with respect to the current model $\Theta^{(t)}$. One advantage of the proposed model is that, in the model training phase, since the clicked documents are already known, we can fix them and reduce the maximum clique size in the induced graph structure to 3, i.e., $\{R_{i-1}, E_{i-1}, E_i\}$. As a result, exact inference is tractable and can be efficiently calculated via Belief Propagation [15]. And in M-Step, we obtain the new model parameter $\Theta^{(t+1)}$ by maximizing the expectation of the "complete" log-likelihood under $P(\boldsymbol{E}, \boldsymbol{R}|\boldsymbol{C}, q, \Theta^{(t)})$ as defined in Eq (5), which can be solved by any standard optimization technique (in this work, we used L-BFGS [17]). The E-Step and M-Step are alternatively executed until the relative change of the righthand side of Eq (5) is smaller than a threshold.

3.5 Discussion

There are close connections and clear differences between the proposed BSS model and other existing click models. First, BSS model explicitly encodes a document's relevance quality to a given query as a mix of intrinsic relevance and perceived relevance, which makes it feasible to incorporate richer information conveyed in document content for relevance estimation. Second, BSS model generalizes the dependency between a click event and the corresponding document's examine and relevance status. Most of previous work puts hard constraint over the click event, i.e., $C_i = 1 \Leftrightarrow E_i = 1, R_i = 1$, which fails to recognize noisy clicks and dependency among documents under the same query. Third, the conditional probabilities defined in BSS are no longer simply treated as document- or position-specific parameters; instead, a set of descriptive features are designed to capture rich semantics of users' click behaviors.

If we resume the hard dependency setting and drop most of the newly introduced features, the proposed BSS model can be easily adopted to many existing click models: the examination model proposed in [19] can be treated as a special case of our BSS model if we remove all the examine features except position and assume it is independent of previous relevance status, i.e., $w_{R=0}^E = w_{R=1}^E$. And if we disable the relevance features $f_{q,d}^R$ and only keep $w_{q,d}^R$ for each query-document pair in the logistic function, we will go back to the traditional setting for the click models. Based on this, if we further remove the examination and click features, it reduces to the CCM model proposed in [11]; if we only keep the examine feature of *distance to last click*, it will reduce to the UBM model proposed in [8]; and if we restrict the examine probability to be $E_i = 1 - R_{i-1}$, it will reduce to the original cascade model [7], since the user has to keep examining until the first click.

From the above discussion, we can clearly notice that the proposed BSS model is a more general framework for modeling users' click behaviors: through parameterizations, many informative signals and dependency relation are introduced to help the model explore a document's in-depth relevance quality to the given query from historic clicks.

4. POSTERIOR REGULARIZATION

One potential problem of the current BSS model setting is that the designed structure is too flexible for the learning procedure to identify the "true" parameters, which depict the underlying dependency among the latent variables. One obvious deficiency is that a document's relevance status, $R_i = 1$ or $R_i = 0$, is interchangeable. Since the click/examine events are determined by the same set of features (weights to be learned from data), if we switch the labels of R_i in the whole collection, the model will find another optimal weight setting (switch the weights) to maximize the likelihood, but that is undesirable.

The main reason for this unidentifiable problem is that to capture noise within the click events we did not set hard constraints on the conditional probability of click events, i.e., we allow $P(C_i = 1|E_i = 1, R_i = 0) > 0$ and $P(C_i = 1|E_i = 1, R_i = 1) < 1$; but it gives too much freedom to these two conditional probabilities, such that they can freely exchange their roles and still maximize the likelihood of clicks. Existing click models avoid this unidentifiable problem by hard-coding the click events, i.e., $C_i = 1 \Leftrightarrow E_i = 1, R_i = 1$. In our work, to keep the flexibility of the modeling assumptions and handle the noisy clicks, we decide to regularize the posterior distribution inferred by the model.

Another benefit of posterior regularization is that we can easily incorporate the ranking-oriented knowledge, i.e., pairwise preference, into click modeling, which is hard to be directly encoded in the original conditional probabilities.

4.1 Posterior Regularized EM Algorithm

Posterior Regularization (PR) proposed by Ganchev et al. [9] is a general framework for postulating structural constraints over the latent variable models. The method roots in the block coordinate ascent EM framework [18], and it modifies the E-step of a standard EM algorithm to inject constraints over the posterior distribution of latent variables via the form of expectations. And such regularization will not affect the convergence of original EM algorithm. Taking our problem as an example, we should expect that the number of relevance-driven clicks should be larger than mistaken clicks, e.g., $E[C = 1, E = 1, R = 1] > E[C = 1, E = 1, R = 0]$.

Formally, the regularized E-step in PR framework aims to optimize:

$$\min_{q,\xi} \quad KL(q(Y)||p(Y|X, \Theta^{(t)})) \qquad (6)$$

$$s.t. \quad E_q[\phi(X,Y)] - \mathbf{b} \leq \xi \qquad (7)$$

$$||\xi||_\beta \leq \epsilon$$

where $p(Y|X, \Theta^{(t)})$ is the original posterior distribution of the latent variables Y given the current model $\Theta^{(t)}$ and observation X, $q(Y)$ is the regularized posterior distribution of Y, $\varphi(X, Y)$ is the constraint function defined over (X, Y), and ξ is a slack variable to relax the constraints. In our case, $Y = \{E_i, R_i\}_{i=1}^M$ and $X = \{C_i\}_{i=1}^M$

The convenience of PR framework comes from its dual form: the primal solution $q^*(Y)$ is uniquely determined in terms of the dual solution λ^* by,

$$q^*(Y) = \frac{p_\Theta(Y|X)\exp\{-\lambda^*\phi(X,Y)\}}{Z(\lambda^*)} \qquad (8)$$

and the dual problem is defined as,

$$\max_{\lambda \geq 0} -\mathbf{b}^T\lambda - \log Z(\lambda) - \epsilon||\lambda||_{\beta^*} \qquad (9)$$

where $Z(\lambda)$ is the partition function for Eq(8), and $||\lambda||_{\beta^*}$ is the dual norm of $||\lambda||_\beta$.

Eq (9) can be solved by the projected gradient algorithm [3], and Eq (8) can be effectively computed via Belief Propagation algorithm by factorizing the constraints according to the original factor graph. Intuitively, the PR framework can be thought as regularizing the posterior inference in E-Step of the original EM algorithm, such that the posterior distribution of the latent variables could satisfy some desired properties specified in the expectations.

4.2 Constraints for Posterior Regularization

In this section, we discuss the constraint that we designed to conquer the unidentifiable problem and that to incorporate the search-oriented pairwise constraints into our BSS model. In detail, we choose to relax the posterior constraints by setting ϵ to be a small constant (0.01), and use L2-norm to regularize the slack ξ.

4.2.1 Dampen noisy clicks

As we have discussed before, we need to restrict the influence of the noisy clicks, and we hypothesize that most of the clicks are driven by the relevance quality of the corresponding document. To achieve this, we define the constraint over the click events as:

$$\phi_{noise}(X,Y) = \sum_i \phi_{noise}(X,Y_i) \quad (10)$$

$$= \sum_i \begin{cases} -1 & \text{if } E_i = 1 \text{ and } R_i = C_i \\ c & \text{if } E_i = 1 \text{ and } R_i \neq C_i \\ 0 & \text{otherwise} \end{cases}$$

and set the left-hand side constant **b** to be zero in Eq(6).

The meaning of this constraint is straightforward: we require the ratio between the expectation of relevance-driven clicks ($E_i = 1, R_i = C_i$) and noisy clicks ($E_i = 1, R_i \neq C_i$) under the same query to be below a constant c, i.e., $\mathbf{E}[E_i = 1, R_i = C_i] > c\mathbf{E}[E_i = 1, R_i \neq C_i]$. In other words, we require at least $\frac{c}{c+1}$ clicks should be explained by the relevance quality of the document rather than a mistake.

4.2.2 Reduce mis-ordered pairs

Pairwise click preference can be easily incorporated via the PR framework. In this work, we encoded two frequently employed click heuristics, i.e., *skip above* and *skip next* [14], by the constraints defined below:

$$\phi_{pair}(X,Y) = \sum_i \phi_{pair}(X,Y_i) \quad (11)$$

$$= \sum_i \begin{cases} 0 & \text{if } E_i = 0 \\ 0 & \text{if } E_i = 1, C_i = 1 - C_{i-1}, R_i = C_i, R_{i-1} = C_{i-1} \\ 1 & \text{otherwise} \end{cases}$$

and set the left-hand side constant **b** to be 0 in Eq(6).

The meaning of this constraint is: we only put constraint over the examined documents (i.e., $E_i = 1$) where the user makes different decisions in the adjacent positions (i.e., *skip above* and *skip next*). If the inferred relevance is consistent with the observed click preference (i.e., $R_i = C_i$ and $R_{i-1} = C_{i-1}$), such a constraint is inactive; otherwise, if the inferred relevance preference contradicts the observed click preference, we need to penalize it.

5. EXPERIMENT RESULTS

As we have discussed most of existing click models treat the relevance quality of a document to the given query as a static property, and therefore the evaluation is mostly performed in general web search logs, where the relevance quality of a document to a query is relatively stable. In this work, we are more interested in evaluating the effectiveness of the click models in a more dynamic search environment, i.e., news search, where new documents keep emerging, and existing documents quickly become out-of-date and fall out of the top ranked results. In such a scenario, we cannot expect to collect a large number of clicks for each document before we can make a confident relevance estimation.

5.1 Data Sets

We collected a large set of real user search logs from Yahoo! news search engine[1] in a two months period, from late May to late July 2011. During this period, a subset of queries are randomly selected and all the associated users' search activities are collected, including the anonymized user ID, query string, timestamp, top 10 returned URL sets and the corresponding user clicks. In order to unbiasedly compare the relevance estimation performance among different click modeling approaches, we also set up a random bucket to collect exploration clicks from a small portion of traffic at the same time. In this random bucket, the top four URLs were randomly shuffled and displayed to the real users. By doing such random shuffling, we were able to reduce the noise from position-bias in the collected user click feedback, and such feedback can be used as a reliable proxy on information utility of documents [16]. Therefore, we only collected the top 4 URLs from this random bucket. In addition, we also asked editors to annotate one day's query log on Aug 9, 2011, into five-level relevance labels, e.g., "Bad", "Fair", "Good", "Excellent" and "Perfect", immediately one day after to ensure the annotation quality.

Simple pre-processing is applied on these click data sets: 1) filter out the queries without clicks in the random bucket, since they are useless for testing purpose; 2) discard the queries only appearing once in the whole collection; 3) normalizing the relevance features $f^R_{q,d}$ by their mean and variance estimated on normal click set, i.e., z-score [21]. After these pre-processing steps, we collected 460k queries from the normal click set and 378k queries from the random bucket set. One thing we should note is that because of the way we set up the random bucket, many queries and documents might only appear in the random bucket. Existing click models can hardly estimate the relevance quality of such unseen documents. In order to make a comprehensive comparison, we split the normal click set into two subsets, and ensure each query is evenly distributed in these two subsets. We choose one of them for training purpose and another for testing. The basic statistics of the four data sets used in our experiment are listed in Table 2.

Table 2: Statistics of evaluation corpus.

	# Unique Query	# Query
Normal training clicks	11,701	234,149
Normal testing clicks	6,264	225,452
Random bucket clicks	33,762	378,403
Editorial judgment	1,404	13,091

In order to test the model's generalization capacity, we further split the queries in the normal click testing set and random bucket click testing set into different categories according to their frequencies in the training set. The basic statistics of those categories are shown in Figure 2. As can be clearly noticed in the figure, a large portion of testing

---
[1] http://news.search.yahoo.com/

queries in the random bucket set belong to the less frequent query category (62.92% queries are in the <25 category) comparing to the normal click set (11.49%), which makes the prediction more difficult in the random bucket set.

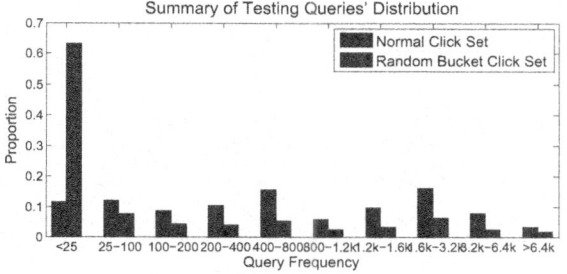

Figure 2: Distribution of testing queries according to their frequencies in training set.

5.2 Quality of Relevance Modeling

The main question to be answered in our experiments is whether the proposed model is more accurate than the existing click models in terms of relevance estimation. To answer this question and evaluate the quality of relevance modeling of the proposed BSS model, we compared it with a set of state-of-the-art click models, including the counting-based models of Dynamic Bayesian Model (DBM) [4] and User Browsing Model (UBM) [8], and feature-based models of Logistic Regression model and Examination Model [19]. Among them, Logistic Regression model and Examination Model are trained on the same set of 65 relevance features $f_{q,d}^R$ as our BSS model.

5.2.1 Evaluation metrics

In previous work [8, 11, 20], perplexity on the testing click set was often used as the metric for comparing different click models, and it is defined as,

$$2^{-\frac{1}{N}\sum_{i=1}^{N} \delta(c_i=1)\log_2 p(c_i=1)+\delta(c_i=0)\log_2 p(c_i=0)}$$

where N is the number of observations in the testing set. The lower perplexity a model can achieve, the closer its prediction is to the observation in the testing set.

However, such evaluation metric is problematic for two major reasons. First, clicks in the testing query log is still position-biased: a less relevant document appears at a higher position would still receive more clicks, such that a model correctly downgrades such a document will even get penalized by the perplexity metric. Second, since perplexity is defined based on the absolute value of the predicted probabilities, it is inherently sensitive to scaling or normalization of these probabilities, making it difficult to interpret the results appropriately.

To examine whether these two concerns are empirically supported, we included a simple baseline for click modeling, Naive Click Model (NCM), which only uses the frequency of clicks on a particular query-document pair observed in the training set as its relevance estimation. In Table 3, we compared NCM's perplexity against other sophisticated click models on normal click testing set. And to compare their relevance estimation quality, we also evaluated their P@1 ranking performance on the random bucket click set, which is proved to be an unbiased proxy of document's rele-

Table 3: Comparison between perplexity metric and ranking metric.

	Examine	UBM	DBN	BSS	NCM
perplexity	3.9534	1.5471	1.5719	1.8213	**1.2925**
P@1	0.3807	0.3603	0.3494	**0.4033**	0.3578

vance quality [16]. Due to space limitation, we did not show the result from Logistic Regress Model.

From Table 3, we can clearly notice that the naive baseline outperforms all the other click models in perplexity on the normal click testing set, but its ranking performance is not the best on the unbiased random bucket click set. Besides, we also observed that the perplexity of Examination Model is significantly larger than the other click models. We looked into the detailed output of Examination Model and found that its predicted click probabilities (with mean 0.78) are much larger than the other models' predictions. Since the probability of a document being clicked in the normal click testing set is generally small (with mean 0.14), Examination Model get seriously penalized by perplexity. However, Examination Model's ranking performance is much better than NCM in the random bucket click set. We thus conclude that the perplexity calculated based on position-biased clicks is not a trustable metric for measuring a click model's capacity of recognizing relevant documents.

A potentially better measure than perplexity is to directly compare different click models' ranking performance based on the estimated relevance of documents. To evaluate ranking performance in a click-based data set, we treat all the clicked documents as relevant and calculate the corresponding *Precision at 1* (P@1), *Precision at 2* (P@2), *Mean Average Precision* (MAP) and *Mean Reciprocal Rank* (MRR). Definitions of these metrics can be found in standard textbooks in information retrieval (e.g., [2]). And in the editorial annotation data set, we treated the grade "Good" and above as relevant for precision-based metrics, and also included the normalized discounted cumulative gain (NDCG) [12] as an evaluation metric. Compared with perplexity metric, such a ranking-based evaluation can better reflect the utility of a click model in estimating the relevance of a document.

We evaluate the quality of relevance estimation of these models from two different perspectives: one is to directly use the estimated relevance from the click models to rank the documents; and another is to treat such relevance estimation as signals for training a learning-to-rank algorithm.

5.2.2 Estimated relevance for ranking

In this approach of evaluation, we ranked the candidate documents with respect to the estimated relevance given by a click model, and compared the ranking result against the logged user clicks. The higher position a click model can put a clicked document on, the better ranking capability it has. We performed the comparison on both random bucket click set and normal testing click set.

We first compared different models' P@1 performance on the random bucket click set in Figure 3 (a), where we illustrated the detailed comparison results under each category of different query frequencies. Li et al. [16] proved that P@1 metric on this random bucket click set can be used as an unbiased proxy to measure the relevance of a document to the given query. And to make a comprehensive comparison, we also performed the same evaluation on the normal click testing set in Figure 3 (b).

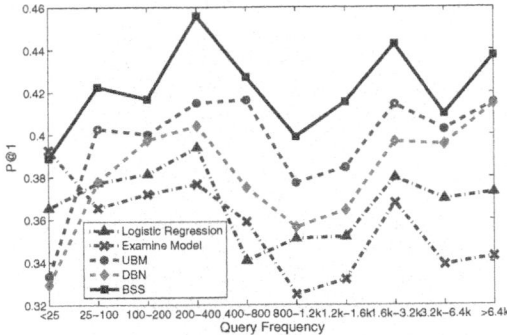
(a) P@1 ranking performance under different query frequency categories on the random bucket click set

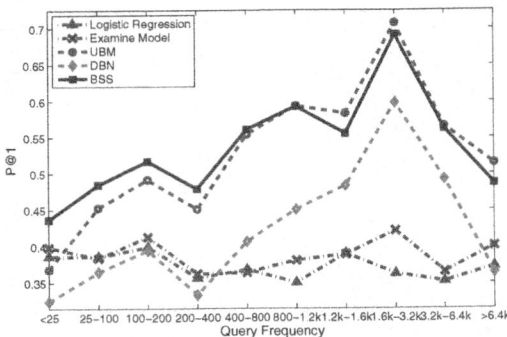
(b) P@1 ranking performance under different query frequency categories on the normal click set

Figure 3: P@1 comparison between different click models over random bucket click set and normal click set.

As shown in Figure 3 (a) and (b), in the low query frequency category (query frequency <25), feature-based models outperformed the counting-based models on both random click set and normal click set. For those less frequent queries, counting-based models do not have enough observations to get a confident estimation of a document's relevance quality; while by leveraging the information across different observations via the same set of relevance-driven features, the feature-based models get a more accurate estimation of relevance for the documents in this category. With more observations available for a particular query, the relevance estimation quality of counting-based methods improves quickly and outperforms the simple feature-based methods on both testing sets. The reason for this slow improvement of simple feature-based methods is also due to the feature sharing: in terms of model complexity, counting-based models have more freedom to tune the parameters for each query-document pair; while feature-based models have to adjust the shared feature weights across all the training samples, such that it cannot arbitrarily fit all the observations. Our BSS model takes advantages of both counting-based and feature-based models by combining the perceived relevance, which is defined by the weighted sum of relevance-driven features as $w^{R\top} f^R_{q,d}$, and the intrinsic relevance, which is modeled as query-document dependent parameters $w^R_{q,d}$, in a principled optimization framework. In BSS model, $w^R_{q,d}$ will be pushed close to zero for the less frequent queries, since there are no sufficient observations to get confident estimations for them, and therefore $w^{R\top} f^R_{q,d}$ plays a more important role in estimating relevance. And when we get more observations for a particular query, $w^R_{q,d}$ is adjusted to further enhance the relevance estimation, which cannot be correctly predicted by the shared relevance features.

In Table 4 and Table 5, we list the ranking performance over all queries in the two testing sets, where a paired two-samples t-test is performed to validate the significance of improvement from the best performing method against the runner-up method under each performance metric. Since a large portion of testing queries in the random bucket click set belong to the less frequent category (only 29.3% queries appeared more than 100 times in the training set) comparing to the normal click set (76.7%), it becomes much more difficult for the purely counting-based methods to make accurate relevance estimation in the random bucket set. As we can ob-

Table 4: Ranking performance on random bucket click set.

	LogisicReg	Examine	UBM	DBN	BSS
P@1	0.3696	0.3807	0.3603	0.3494	**0.4033***
P@2	0.3118	0.3348	0.3239	0.3194	**0.3509***
MAP	0.5628	0.6094	0.5951	0.5883	**0.6272***
MRR	0.5754	0.6154	0.6003	0.5939	**0.6330***

* indicates $p\text{-}value<0.01$

Table 5: Ranking performance on normal click set.

	LogisicReg	Examine	UBM	DBN	BSS
P@1	0.3623	0.3878	0.5316	0.4273	**0.5462+**
P@2	0.3284	0.3058	0.3703	0.3166	**0.3823+**
MAP	0.5981	0.5643	0.6688	0.5908	**0.6804+**
MRR	0.6037	0.5786	0.6838	0.6047	**0.6964+**

+ indicates $p\text{-}value<0.05$

serve in the results, although the counting-based UBM and DBN methods achieved better ranking performance than the simple feature-based models in the normal click set, their performance degraded on the random bucket set, due to the lack of observations. And as we have discussed earlier, by leveraging the feature-based and counting-based relevance estimations, BSS model outperformed all the other baseline methods on both data sets.

5.2.3 Estimated relevance as signals for learning-to-rank algorithm training

In this evaluation, we used the estimated relevance given by a click model as labels to extract ranking preference pairs of documents for training a learning-to-rank algorithm. We employed the pairwise RankSVM [13] as our basic learning-to-rank algorithm.

To stimulate the situation where we have to make prediction over some new documents before we can collect sufficient training clicks for each query, e.g., in news search, we only sampled 30% query log from each day in the normal training click set in this experiment. We estimated the click models on the new training set and generated the click preference pairs according to the predictions of each click model on this set. In particular, we ordered the documents under a given query according to their predicted relevance from a click model, and treated the top ranked document

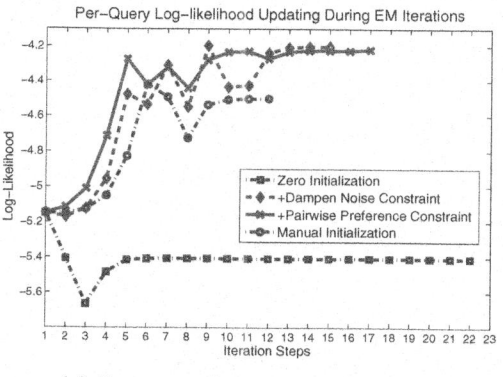
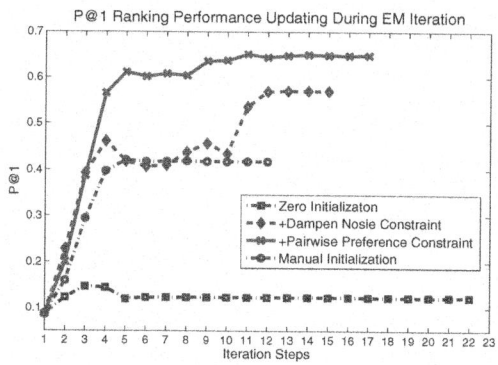

(a) Per-query Log-likelihood updates (b) P@1 ranking performance on training set updates

Figure 4: EM algorithm updating traces with different training settings.

Table 6: RankSVM performance on random bucket click set with different training signals.

	ori. click	UBM	DBN	BSS
P@1	0.3275	0.3823	0.3774	**0.3869**[+]
P@2	0.3081	0.3411	0.3380	0.3411
MAP	0.5724	0.6130	0.6093	**0.6146**[+]
MRR	0.5779	0.6187	0.6151	**0.6206**[+]

[+] indicates $p\text{-}value<0.05$

Table 7: RankSVM performance on editorial judgments with different training signals.

	ori. click	UBM	DBN	BSS
P@1	0.5288	0.6346	0.6250	**0.6442**[+]
P@2	0.4808	0.5313	0.5016	**0.5913**[+]
MAP	0.6173	0.6944	0.6905	**0.7212**[+]
MRR	0.6658	0.7546	0.7545	**0.7719**[+]
NDCG@1	0.4570	0.5902	0.5774	**0.6016**[+]
NDCG@5	0.5731	0.6830	0.6832	**0.7181**[+]

[+] indicates $p\text{-}value<0.05$

as positive and others as negative. The preference pairs are extracted according to this predicted relevance labels under each query and fed into a RankSVM model. In addition, we also included a RankSVM trained on the preference pairs generated by the original clicks with the *skip-above* and *skip-next* click heuristics [14] in this training set as a baseline.

We compared the performance of RankSVM models trained by different relevance signals on both random bucket click set and editorial annotation set. In this experiment, we only included the UBM and DBN as the baseline click models since they performed much better than the simple feature-based Logistic Regression model and Examination Model on the normal click set according to Table 5.

As shown in Table 6 and Table 7, the training signals extracted from click models' output led to much better ranking performance of RankSVM than those extracted based on the simple click heuristics. In addition, though the RankSVM models trained on purely counting-based click models' output have comparable P@1 and NDCG@1 performance as that trained on BSS model's output, their predictions on the lower positions are much worse, e.g., lower MAP and NDCG@5. The main reason is that traditional click models only work in a pointwise way, and they cannot directly optimize the relative order of the predicted relevance; while in the proposed BSS model, we incorporated such ranking-oriented property via the *pairwise preference* constraint, which renders BSS model better capability of distinguishing the relative order among the candidate documents. As a result, the training signals extracted from BSS model's output are more informative for learning to rank algorithm training.

5.3 Effectiveness of Posterior Regularization

We now examine the effectiveness of a key component in the proposed BSS model, i.e., posterior regularization. As discussed in Section 4, there are two motivations for applying posterior regularization: one is to address the problem of "unidentifiability" in the proposed BSS model, and the other is to incorporate pairwise ranking preferences into click modeling. Below we validate the effectiveness of posterior regularization in achieving these two goals.

We first initialized all the model parameters, i.e., $\{w^R, w^C_{R=0}, w^C_{R=1}, w^E_{R=0}, w^E_{R=0}\}$, to be zero in our EM algorithm. We refer to this baseline as "zero initialization". And based on this initialization, we sequentially added the *noise dampening* constraint and *pairwise preference* constraint into the model to obtain two runs of model estimation using posterior regularized EM algorithm. An alternative way for solving the "unidentifiability" problem is to set priors over the model parameters such that we can guide the model to search in a desirable region. However, the difficulty of this approach for our BSS model is that it is unclear how to set proper priors on the model parameters for directly manipulating the probability $P(C|E,R)$, since this probability is defined over a set of different features via a logistic function. Thus to compare with such an approach, we manually set the initial value for the bias term in $w^C_{R=0}$ to be -1 and in $w^C_{R=1}$ to be 1, reflecting the assumption that most of the clicks should be explained by the relevance quality of a document rather than noise. We refer to this baseline as "manual initialization."

We plotted the per-query log-likelihood update trace and the corresponding P@1 ranking performance on the training set during EM iterations for these four different ways of learning our BSS model in Figure 4(a) and 4(b).

Effect of *dampen noise* constraint: as we can clearly observe from the EM update trace that without any specific parameter initialization or posterior regularization, EM failed to find a configuration which could improve the log-likelihood over the all-zero initialized model. Manual initialization helped the model identify better configurations. However, it is not a principled way for achieving so, and the scale of such hard-coded setting will directly bias the learned model. The proposed *dampen noise* constraint serves for the same purpose as manual initialization, but it gives model the freedom to learn such scale from data. As we can find from the updating trace, such constraint successfully led the model to a better configuration for both log-likelihood and P@1 ranking performance than the manual initialization.

Effect of *pairwise preference* constraint: with the *pairwise preference* constraint, which aims to enforce ranking-oriented requirement, the model's ranking capability is further improved, even though the log-likelihood did not gain too much. This is expected: log-likelihood defined in Eq (5) only considers the pointwise relevance estimation of each query-document pair, which does not count the relative order of relevance among the documents under the same query. The *pairwise preference* constraint explores such knowledge, which effectively improves ranking accuracy as shown in Figure 4(b). And we should note that such knowledge can hardly be encoded by manual initialization. Therefore, with the *pairwise preference* constraint, we solved the deficiency of traditional click models that the dependency relation among the clicked/skipped documents is discarded, and we are able to leverage the knowledge about pairwise preferences to further improve the relevance estimation accuracy.

5.4 Understanding User Behaviors with BSS

An interesting additional benefit of the proposed BSS model is that the learned feature weights reveal the influence of different factors on users' click behaviors, which is not available in existing click models. To explore this benefit, we list a subset of learned feature weights in Table 8.

Table 8: Feature weights learned by BSS model.

f^R	age	authority	title match	abs. match
w^R	-0.839	0.017	0.098	0.167
f^C	pos	dis. to last click	query length	bias
$w^C_{R=0}$	-1.133	-0.445	-3.659	-4.654
$w^C_{R=1}$	0.149	0.415	3.707	4.405
f^E	pos	# click	avg cont. sim.	bias
$w^E_{R=0}$	1.807	-0.418	2.947	5.325
$w^E_{R=1}$	-1.381	0.665	-2.237	3.266

The weights learned by our BSS model followed our intuition about their effects in influencing user's click decisions. For example, "age" is an important factor in news search: the most recent document (shorter age) is always preferred. Our BSS model correctly identified this negative correlation and put a relatively large weight over the age feature. The most interesting discovery by our model is the weights learned for the position feature in the click and examine events. In the click event, when the current document is irrelevant (i.e., $R = 0$), the weight for the position feature is quite negative, which indicates that a user is very likely to click on an irrelevant document when its displayed position is on the top, i.e., position-bias. But when the document is relevant (i.e., $R = 1$), the corresponding weight is closer to zero, which means user's click decision is not affected by the displayed positions of relevant documents. And in the examine event, the weight for the position feature is largely positive when the current document is irrelevant, which indicates users tend to further examine lower positions since they have not found satisfactory results. But when the current document is relevant, the weight becomes largely negative, which means users are inclined to stop further examination since their information need has been met by the relevant documents.

6. RELATED WORK

No previous work directly addressed the two deficiencies of existing click models, i.e., ignoring rich information conveyed in the document content when modeling clicks, and failing to exploit the relative order of relevance among the clicked/skipped documents. But there are several studies touched the problem of utilizing features in click modeling.

Richardson et al. [19] were the first to derive a content-based logistic regression model for predicting click throught rate by discounting the bias in lower positions via a position-specific multiplicative factor. However, they treated such discount factor as constant, which was only determined by positions, and thus it was independently estimated without considering the specific displayed documents and the related clicks. In [22], the authors also considered to introduce additional features to model click events; however, they used empirically tuned linear interpolation to combine the estimated relevance by a click model with external signals (e.g., BM25). Our method provides a more principled way for introducing rich descriptive features to formalize the dependency structure for both click and examine events within a query, and learn the optimal combination of those features from the data. Zhu et al. [23] realized the necessity of incorporating features into click models. However, they used the same set of general features (e.g., time and length of URL) to describe both click and examine events without distinguishing their specific effect in these two different events.

7. CONCLUSIONS

Click modeling is an important technique for exploiting search log data and is a crucial component in modern Web search engines. In this work, we proposed a general Bayesian Sequential State (BSS) model for addressing two deficiencies of existing click models, namely failing to utilize document content information for modeling clicks and not being optimized for distinguishing the relative order of relevance among the candidate documents. As our solution, a set of descriptive features and ranking-oriented pairwise preferences are encoded via a probabilistic graphical model, where the dependency relations among a document's relevance quality, examine and click events under a query are automatically captured from the data. Experiments on a large set of news search logs validate the effectiveness of the proposed BSS model comparing to several state-of-the-art click models, where content-based features help BSS model leverage information across different observations when the training set is limited, and pairwise preference constraint gives the model a more accurate estimate of relevance.

As we have shown in the experiment, the proposed BSS model provides an interesting way of understanding user's click behaviors by analyzing the learned weights on different features. With appropriate feature design, our model has the potential to help understand user behavior in various other aspects as well. As our future work, it would be meaningful to incorporate user-related features into our model, i.e., personalized BSS model, where different users will have their own weights over the designed features to reflect their unique search intents.

8. REFERENCES

[1] E. Agichtein, E. Brill, S. Dumais, and R. Ragno. Learning user interaction models for predicting web search result preferences. In *Proceedings of the 29th annual international ACM SIGIR conference on Research and development in information retrieval*, pages 3–10. ACM, 2006.

[2] R. Baeza-Yates and B. Ribeiro-Neto. *Modern information retrieval*, volume 463. ACM press New York, 1999.

[3] D. Bertsekas. *Nonlinear programming*. Athena Scientific, 1999.

[4] O. Chapelle and Y. Zhang. A dynamic bayesian network click model for web search ranking. In *Proceedings of the 18th international conference on World wide web*, pages 1–10. ACM, 2009.

[5] W. Chen, D. Wang, Y. Zhang, Z. Chen, A. Singla, and Q. Yang. A noise-aware click model for web search. In *Proceedings of the fifth ACM international conference on Web search and data mining*, pages 313–322. ACM, 2012.

[6] C. L. Clarke, M. Kolla, G. V. Cormack, O. Vechtomova, A. Ashkan, S. Büttcher, and I. MacKinnon. Novelty and diversity in information retrieval evaluation. In *Proceedings of the 31st annual international ACM SIGIR conference on Research and development in information retrieval*, pages 659–666, 2008.

[7] N. Craswell, O. Zoeter, M. Taylor, and B. Ramsey. An experimental comparison of click position-bias models. In *Proceedings of the international conference on Web search and web data mining*, pages 87–94. ACM, 2008.

[8] G. E. Dupret and B. Piwowarski. A user browsing model to predict search engine click data from past observations. In *Proceedings of the 31st annual international ACM SIGIR conference on Research and development in information retrieval*, pages 331–338. ACM, 2008.

[9] J. Graça, K. Ganchev, and B. Taskar. Expectation maximization and posterior constraints. *Advances in Neural Information Processing Systems*, 20:569–576, 2007.

[10] L. A. Granka, T. Joachims, and G. Gay. Eye-tracking analysis of user behavior in www search. In *Proceedings of the 27th annual international ACM SIGIR conference on Research and development in information retrieval*, pages 478–479. ACM, 2004.

[11] F. Guo, C. Liu, A. Kannan, T. Minka, M. Taylor, Y.-M. Wang, and C. Faloutsos. Click chain model in web search. In *Proceedings of the 18th international conference on World wide web*, pages 11–20. ACM, 2009.

[12] K. Järvelin and J. Kekäläinen. Cumulated gain-based evaluation of ir techniques. *ACM Transactions on Information Systems (TOIS)*, 20(4):422–446, 2002.

[13] T. Joachims. Optimizing search engines using clickthrough data. In *Proceedings of the eighth ACM SIGKDD international conference on Knowledge discovery and data mining*, pages 133–142. ACM, 2002.

[14] T. Joachims, L. Granka, B. Pan, H. Hembrooke, and G. Gay. Accurately interpreting clickthrough data as implicit feedback. In *Proceedings of the 28th annual international ACM SIGIR conference on Research and development in information retrieval*, pages 154–161. ACM, 2005.

[15] D. Koller and N. Friedman. *Probabilistic graphical models: principles and techniques*. The MIT Press, 2009.

[16] L. Li, W. Chu, J. Langford, and X. Wang. Unbiased offline evaluation of contextual-bandit-based news article recommendation algorithms. In *Proceedings of the fourth ACM international conference on Web search and data mining*, pages 297–306. ACM, 2011.

[17] D. C. Liu and J. Nocedal. On the limited memory bfgs method for large scale optimization. *Mathematical programming*, 45(1):503–528, 1989.

[18] R. Neal and G. Hinton. A view of the em algorithm that justifies incremental, sparse, and other variants. *Learning in Graphical Models*, 89:355–368, 1998.

[19] M. Richardson, E. Dominowska, and R. Ragno. Predicting clicks: estimating the click-through rate for new ads. In *Proceedings of the 16th international conference on World Wide Web*, pages 521–530. ACM, 2007.

[20] S. Shen, B. Hu, W. Chen, and Q. Yang. Personalized click model through collaborative filtering. In *Proceedings of the fifth ACM international conference on Web search and data mining*, pages 323–332. ACM, 2012.

[21] Wikipedia. *Standard score*. http://en.wikipedia.org/wiki/Standard_score.

[22] Y. Zhang, D. Wang, G. Wang, W. Chen, Z. Zhang, B. Hu, and L. Zhang. Learning click models via probit bayesian inference. In *Proceedings of the 19th ACM international conference on Information and knowledge management*, pages 439–448. ACM, 2010.

[23] Z. A. Zhu, W. Chen, T. Minka, C. Zhu, and Z. Chen. A novel click model and its applications to online advertising. In *Proceedings of the third ACM international conference on Web search and data mining*, pages 321–330. ACM, 2010.

Is It Time For a Career Switch?

Jian Wang, Yi Zhang
University of California, Santa Cruz
Santa Cruz, CA 95060 USA
{jwang30, yiz}@soe.ucsc.edu

Christian Posse, Anmol Bhasin
LinkedIn Corp
Mountain View, CA 94043 USA
{cposse, abhasin}@linkedin.com

ABSTRACT

Tenure is a critical factor for an individual to consider when making a job transition. For instance, *software engineers* make a job transition to *senior software engineers* in a span of 2 years on average, or it takes for approximately 3 years for *realtors* to switch to *brokers*. While most existing work on recommender systems focuses on finding *what* to recommend to a user, this paper places emphasis on *when* to make appropriate recommendations and its impact on the item selection in the context of a job recommender system. The approach we propose, however, is general and can be applied to any recommendation scenario where the decision-making process is dependent on the tenure (i.e., the time interval) between successive decisions.

Our approach is inspired by the proportional hazards model in statistics. It models the tenure between two successive decisions and related factors. We further extend the model with a hierarchical Bayesian framework to address the problem of data sparsity. The proposed model estimates the likelihood of a user's decision to make a job transition at a certain time, which is denoted as the **tenure-based decision probability**. New and appropriate evaluation metrics are designed to analyze the model's performance on deciding when is the right time to recommend a job to a user. We validate the soundness of our approach by evaluating it with an anonymous job application dataset across 140+ industries on LinkedIn. Experimental results show that the hierarchical proportional hazards model has better predictability of the user's decision time, which in turn helps the recommender system to achieve higher utility/user satisfaction.

Categories and Subject Descriptors

H.3.3 [**Information Storage and Retrieval**]: Information Search and Retrieval

General Terms

Algorithms, Design, Experimentation

Keywords

Recommender System, Hazards Model, Tenure

Copyright is held by the International World Wide Web Conference Committee (IW3C2). IW3C2 reserves the right to provide a hyperlink to the author's site if the Material is used in electronic media.
WWW 2013, May 13–17, 2013, Rio de Janeiro, Brazil.
ACM 978-1-4503-2035-1/13/05.

1. INTRODUCTION

Recommender systems are popular research topics in the information retrieval community. Host of academic and industrial incarnations of recommender systems exists in domains such as movies (Netflix), music (Pandora), e-commerce product recommendations (eBay, Amazon). Traditional research in recommender systems aims to find right item(s) to recommend to a user. For example, a job recommender system would recommend a *senior software engineer* position to a user working in an engineering function in the software domain. This discovery can be powered by content-based models, collaborative filtering, or hybrid systems. In addition to finding the right item to recommend, another key aspect is the timeliness aspect of making the appropriate recommendation. This aspect becomes critical in settings where the decision-making process is dependent on the tenure (i.e., the time interval) between successive decisions, such as in a job transiting scenario. To make recommendations at the right time helps the system to achieve higher utility. Utility is defined as the satisfaction or value a user gets. To motivate the discussion, consider the following question - when should the recommender system recommend a *senior software engineer* position to *software engineers*? The system is likely to achieve positive utility when a *software engineer* who works for 2 years receives such a recommendation. Yet the system might achieve negative utility when a *software engineer* who works for 2 months or 5+ years receives such a recommendation. In this paper, we focus on building models to find the right time to make appropriate recommendations.

We start tackling the problem by assuming that the job transiting process follows the Markov renewal process, i.e. the sequence of making decisions is a Markov chain. In addition the waiting time depends only on the last decision and the current decision. Inspired by the survival model in statistics, waiting time between successive decisions can be modeled by the Weibull distribution. In reality however, the waiting time is not only dependent on the last decision and the current decision, but also dependent on other factors. In the job domain these factors include the user's profile and behavioral characteristics, the nature of the current position and potential job opportunities, the interaction patterns between the user and the job or the functional area, the global economic environment, and a host of other externalities like location, time of the year, etc. To illustrate the point, let us consider the scenario of a potential job from a company with a high reputation. In this case, the user may change to this new job earlier than average. To incorporate these covariates (i.e., factors or features) into the model, we use the proportional hazards model to model the tenure before a job transition. We further extend the model with the hierarchical Bayesian framework to solve the data sparsity issue. The proposed model predicts the probability of a user making a decision at time t, given that the user did not make the decision before time t. We denote this probability as the **tenure-based decision probability**. This could be used by a hybrid recommender system in two ways. To determine whether to present the recommendation at a certain time in the push-based scenario, the system can treat the probability as a threshold in the filtering process. To determine which items to recommend in the pull-based scenario, the system can use the probability as the item's additional feature in the ranking process.

We perform experiments with an anonymous job application dataset from millions of users in 140+ industries from LinkedIn. New evaluation metrics are designed to analyze the hazards model's performance on predicting the tenure-based decision probability. Metrics include the perplexity/likelihood of the model, the accuracy of the estimated decision time/tenure, the utility of the recommender system, etc. Experiments demonstrate that the hierarchical proportional hazards model has the better predictability of the decision time, which in turn improves the utility of the recommender system.

The major contribution of this paper includes the following:

- Analyze the problem of finding the **right time** to make recommendations in the job domain.

- Propose using the **proportional hazards model** to tackle the problem and extend it with a hierarchical Bayesian framework.

- Evaluate the model with a real-world job application data from LinkedIn to demonstrate the better predictability of the proposed model, as well as the effect of the **tenure-based decision probability** in improving the utility of recommender systems.

2. RELATED WORK

A major task of the recommender system is to present recommendations to the user. The task is usually conducted by first predicting a user's ratings for each item and then ranking all items in the descending order. There are two major recommendation approaches: content-based filtering and collaborative filtering. Content-based filtering [16, 19] assumes that descriptive features of an item indicate a user's preferences. Thus, a recommender system makes a decision for a user based on the descriptive features of other items the user likes or dislikes. Usually, the system recommends items that are similar to what the user liked before. Collaborative filtering [9, 25, 10, 15, 27, 18, 8] on the other hand assumes that users with similar tastes on some items may also have similar preferences on other items. Thus, the main idea is to use the behavior history from other like-minded users to provide the current user with good recommendations. Research on collaborative filtering algorithms reached a peak due to the 1 million dollar Netflix movie recommendation competition [1]. Factorization-based collaborative filtering approaches [4, 11, 28, 23], such as the regularized Singular Value Decomposition performed well on this competition, possibly better than Netflix's own well-tuned Pearson correlation coefficient algorithm. A common characteristic of these models is the introduction of user latent factors or/and item latent factors to solve the data sparsity issue.

Factoring time [12, 27, 34, 22, 24, 14, 33, 5, 13, 31, 26] has received much research attention. In the field of recommender systems, one focus is about the drift of the user's preference over time [12, 32, 21]. Koren [12] revamped two popular collaborative filtering methods by modeling the time drifting factor of user preferences. Rendel et. al [21] proposed a factorized personalized model that subsumes both a common Markov chain and the normal matrix factorization model. Compared to their work, our work explicitly models the tenure and the user's interest at each time as a white box. On one hand, the resulting tenure-based decision probability can be used in the hybrid system to find relevant items while on the other, it can be used as a signal to determine when is the right time to recommend an item. Another research focus is modeling the tenure between purchase orders in the e-commerce domain [27, 34]. Wang et. al [27] discovered different post-purchase behavior in different time windows after purchase. Zhao et. al [34] used the purchasing tenure to improve the temporal diversity [21]. The tenure and the corresponding purchase probability is modeled inside the framework of a utility-based recommender system [28]. The hybrid system takes the tenure into consideration when ranking all candidate items. Different from their work, we propose a more generalized model to explicitly predict the tenure-based decision probability. This probability can be leveraged in the filtering process of recommendation items from any system in the domain where the time interval between successive decisions is an important factor.

3. HIERARCHICAL PROPORTIONAL HAZARDS MODEL

3.1 Problem Definition

In this paper, we aim to answer the question: When is the right time to make a job recommendation and how do we leverage it in a job recommender system? The following notations are used in this paper. The relationship between different variables is shown in Figure 1.

- $u = 1, 2, ..., U$: the index of the user.

- $a, b = 1, 2, ..., C$: the index of the item category. In the job domain, it is the title of the job, such as *software engineer*, *realtor*, *lawyer*, etc.

- $j_a = 1_a, 2_a, ..., J_a$: the index of the item in category a. In our setup, an item is a job. This item has metadata like industry, seniority, function, company, etc. For example, a job in category *Software Engineer* belongs to the *computer software* industry, *Information Technology* function, *Google* company, and *Entry* seniority level.

- $m = 1, 2, ..., M$: the index of the decision transition between items in category a to items in category b. If a user with job j_a applies to a job j_b, these two job categories $\{a \rightarrow b\}$ form a decision transition m. Note that horizontal transitions such as $\{a \rightarrow a\}$ is included in the model as well.

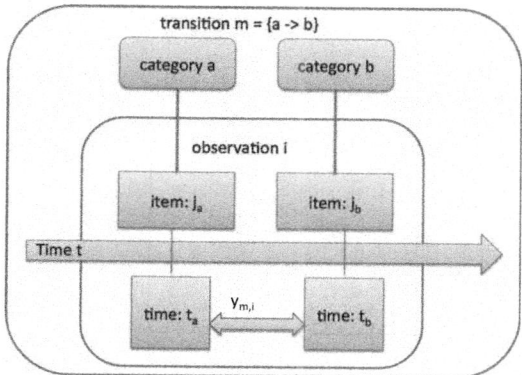

Figure 1: Illustration of the relationship of variables. The user first makes a job decision of item j_a in category a at time t_a and then makes a decision of item j_b in category b at time t_b. This transition from category a to category b is the ith observation in transition $m = \{a \to b\}$. This observation is associated with two parts: 1) tenure $y_{m,i}$ and 2) covariates $\mathbf{x}_{m,i}$ (which is not shown in the plot).

- $D = \{D_1, ..., D_m, ..., D_M\}$: The observed data of all transitions from all users.

- $D_m = \{y_{m,i}, \mathbf{x}_{m,i}\}$: A set of observed data associated with transition m. Each transition m has N_m data observations from all users. Each observation $i = 1, ..., N_m$ in transition m is associated with two parts: the tenure $y_{m,i}$ and covariates $\mathbf{x}_{m,i}$.

- $y_{m,i}$: the tenure with the ith observation in transition m. It is the tenure between the user's decision time t_b of item j_b and the user's decision time t_a of item j_a. $y_{m,i} = t_b - t_a$.

- $\mathbf{x}_{m,i}$: the k-dimensional vector of covariates that associate with the ith observation in transition m. Covariates could be associated with user u who makes the decision transition, the source item j_a, the destination item j_b, the interaction between j_a and j_b, the global environment, etc.

The goal of the model is to predict the probability that a user makes a decision of item j_b at current time t_b, given that she made the last decision of j_a at time t_a and she did not make the transition decision up to time t_b. It is the same as predicting the probability that a user makes a decision of item j_b at tenure $y_{m,i} = t_b - t_a$ with covariates $\mathbf{x}_{m,i}$ being associated with the transition.

3.2 Review of Proportional Hazards Model

Before describing the hierarchical model that we propose, we first briefly review the basic proportional hazards model. In survival analysis, the survival function determines the time of a particular event, often the failure of a machine or the death of a subject. Here we consider *failure* as a user making a decision to transit to a new job. Let $p(y)$ denote the probability density function of such an event. The cumulative distribution function $P(y)$ and survival function $S(y)$ are then given by

$$P(y) = Pr(T \le y) \qquad (1)$$
$$S(y) = Pr(T > y) = 1 - P(y) \qquad (2)$$

where T is a random variable denoting the survival time. In addition, the hazards function is defined as the event rate at tenure y, given that the event does not occur until tenure y or later. $h(y) = \frac{p(y)}{S(y)}$. In the real world, the hazards function is dependent on covariates. Two common approaches to incorporate covariates $\mathbf{x}$ in the hazards model are:

Cox proportional hazards model, which assumes that the covariates are multiplicatively related to the hazards [20]:

$$h(y) = h_0(y) exp(\beta^{\mathbf{T}} \mathbf{x}) \qquad (3)$$

where $h_0(y)$ is the baseline hazards function and β is a vector of parameters.

Accelerated life model, which assumes that the covariates are multiplicatively related to the survival time [30], i.e., $T = T_0 exp\{-\beta^T \mathbf{x}\}$ where T_0 is the baseline survival time. Hence,

$$S(y|\mathbf{x}) = Pr(T > y|\mathbf{x}) \qquad (4)$$
$$= Pr(T_0 exp\{-\beta^T \mathbf{x}\} > y) \qquad (5)$$
$$= Pr(T_0 > y \cdot exp\{\beta^T \mathbf{x}\}) \qquad (6)$$
$$= S_0(y \cdot exp\{\beta^{\mathbf{T}} \mathbf{x}\}) \qquad (7)$$

where $S_0(y)$ is the baseline survival function.

Both approaches coincide if the Weibull distribution is used for $p(y)^1$. Thus, we choose that distribution in this paper, which is given by

$$p(y) = \gamma \theta y^{\gamma - 1} exp\{-\theta y^\gamma\} \qquad (8)$$

where γ is the shape parameter and θ is the scale parameter. The corresponding baseline hazards function becomes:

$$h_0(y) = \gamma \theta y^{\gamma - 1} = \gamma exp(\beta_0) y^{\gamma - 1}. \qquad (9)$$

- If $\gamma > 1$, $h_0(y)$ increases with time.

- If $\gamma < 1$, $h_0(y)$ decreases with time.

- If $\gamma = 1$, $h_0(y)$ is constant.

To incorporate covariates $\mathbf{x} = \{x_1, ..., x_k\}$, we extend θ from $exp(\beta_0)$ to $exp\{\beta_0\} exp\{\beta_1 x_1 + ... + \beta_k x_k\}$, i.e., $exp\{\beta^T \mathbf{x}\}$ where we extend $\beta = \{\beta_0, ..., \beta_k\}$ and $\mathbf{x}$ as $\{x_0 = 1, x_1, ..., x_k\}$. Thus, the probability density function becomes:

$$p(y) = \gamma exp\{\beta^T \mathbf{x}\} y^{\gamma-1} exp\{-exp\{\beta^T \mathbf{x}\} y^\gamma\} \qquad (10)$$

This probability density function represents the basic proportional hazards model that models the tenure before a transition with associated covariates.

---
[1] Mathematical details are in
http://data.princeton.edu/pop509/ParametricSurvival.pdf.
γ in our notation is p in their notation. θ in our notation is λ^p in their notation.

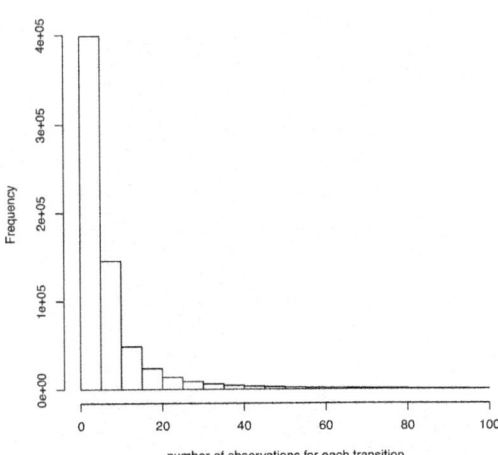

Figure 2: Histogram of number of observations (from 3 to 50) for each job transition $m = \{a \rightarrow b\}$.

3.3 Model Extension with Bayesian Framework

In real use cases, the number of observations for each transition tends to follow the power law distribution. In other words, few transitions are often observed while most transitions are rare events, making it hard to learn parameters of the corresponding hazards model. To illustrate this, we show the histogram of the number of observations for each transition in the job application data in Figure 2. To solve the data sparsity issue, we extend the proportional hazards model with a hierarchical Bayesian framework.

The goal of the hierarchical Bayesian framework is to borrow information from other transitions when learning the parameters for transition m. We derive the following hierarchical model, which is illustrated in Figure 3:

- For each transition m, β_m is sampled from the Gaussian distribution: $\beta_m \sim N(\mu_\beta, \Sigma_\beta)$ and γ_m is sampled from the Gaussian distribution: $\gamma_m \sim N(\mu_\gamma, \sigma_\gamma^2)$. Note that μ_β is a $(k+1)$-dimensional vector and Σ_β is a $(k+1) \times (k+1)$ matrix, where k is the number of covariates in the model. We denote $\phi = (\mu_\beta, \Sigma_\beta, \mu_\gamma, \sigma_\gamma^2)$.

- μ_β and μ_γ are sampled from $N(0, a\mathbf{I})$ and $N(0, b)$, respectively, and Σ_β and σ_γ^2 are sampled from the inverse Wishart Distribution $\mathbf{W}^{-1}(\mathbf{I}, c)$ and the inverse Gamma distribution $\Gamma^{-1}(1, d)$, respectively, where $\mathbf{I}$ is the $(k+1) \times (k+1)$ identity matrix, and $a, b, c, d > 0$.

- For each ith observation of transition m with its covariates $\mathbf{x_{m,i}}$, its tenure $y_{m,i}$ is sampled from the proportional hazards model

$$p(y_{m,i}|\mathbf{x_{m,i}}, \beta_m, \gamma_m) \qquad (11)$$
$$= \gamma_m exp\{\beta_m^T \mathbf{x_{m,i}}\} y_{m,i}^{\gamma_m - 1} exp\{-exp\{\beta_m^T \mathbf{x_{m,i}}\} y_{m,i}^{\gamma_m}\}$$

Let $\sigma = (\phi, \beta_1, \gamma_1, ..., \beta_M, \gamma_M)$ represent parameters that need to be estimated. The joint likelihood for all variables in the probabilistic model is:

$$L(D, \sigma) = p(\phi) \prod_{m=1}^{M} p(\beta_m, \gamma_m|\phi) \prod_{i}^{N_m} p(y_{m,i}|\beta_m, \gamma_m, \mathbf{x_{m,i}}) \quad (12)$$

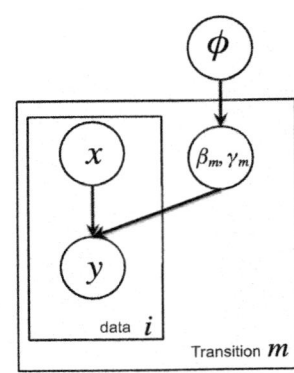

Figure 3: Illustration of dependencies of variables in the hierarchical proportional hazards model. It shows the ith observation of transition m. $y_{m,i}$ is the tenure which is conditioned on covariates $\mathbf{x_{m,i}}$ that are related to this transition and the proportional hazards model. Each transition m has its own parameters of the hazards model β_m, γ_m. Models of each transition share information through the prior, $\phi = (\mu_\beta, \Sigma_\beta, \mu_\gamma, \sigma_\gamma^2)$.

3.4 Parameter Estimation

Our model contains many hidden variables, some of them being high-dimensional vectors (μ_β and all β_m). Hence, the traditional Bayesian method might be too computationally expensive to learn the model. Instead we propose an iterative method with a point estimation in each step. We first introduce constants $c_i, (i = 1, 2, 3, 4)$ to replace functions of $a, b, \Sigma_\beta, \sigma_\gamma^2$, respectively, with the same model effect. They can be viewed as regularization factors to avoid overfitting and can be set by cross-validation in the experiment. The maximum likelihood estimation of the remaining parameters is shown in Equation 13.

$$(\hat{\mu}_\beta, \hat{\mu}_\gamma, \hat{\beta}_1, \hat{\gamma}_1, ..., \hat{\beta}_M, \hat{\gamma}_M) = \arg\max L(D, \sigma) \quad (13)$$
$$= \arg\min\{c_1||\mu_\beta||^2 + c_2\mu_\gamma^2\}$$
$$+ \sum_{m=1}^{M}\{c_3||\beta_m - \mu_\beta||^2 + c_4(\gamma_m - \mu_\gamma)^2\}$$
$$+ \sum_{m=1}^{M}\{\sum_{i=1}^{N_m} -\log(p(y_{m,i}|\beta_m, \gamma_m, \mathbf{x_{m,i}}))\}$$

The steps to solve the previous equation are shown in Algorithm 1. We first initialize μ^0 and update parameters by following steps 3-5 and step 6 iteratively until convergence.

In steps 3-5, the goal is to estimate parameters of the hazards model $\beta_1^n, \gamma_1^n, ..., \beta_M^n, \gamma_M^n$, based on the current estimation of the prior $\mu^n = (\mu_\beta^n, \mu_\gamma^n)$, where n denotes the iteration index. Because the parameters β_m^n, γ_m^n for each transition m are independent from each other, we estimate them one by

Algorithm 1 The parameter learning algorithm
1: Initialize $\mu^0 = \{\mu_\beta^0, \mu_\gamma^0\}, n \leftarrow 0$
2: **repeat**
3:    **for** <m = 1,...,M> **do**
4:       Compute the parameters of the hazards model, β_m^n and γ_m^n, based on μ^n for each transition m.
5:    **end for**
6:    Compute μ^{n+1} based on the hazards model β_m^n, γ_m^n of each transition m with conjugate gradient descent.
7:    $n \leftarrow n + 1$
8: **until** <Convergence>
9: **return** $\mu = \{\mu_\beta, \mu_\gamma\}, \beta_1, \gamma_1, ..., \beta_M, \gamma_M$

one as:

$$(\hat{\beta_m^n}, \hat{\gamma_m^n}) = \arg\min\{c_3||\beta_m - \mu_\beta^n||^2 + c_4(\gamma_m - \mu_\gamma^n)^2\} \\ - \sum_{i=1}^{N_m}\{\log p(y_{m,i}|\beta_m, \gamma_m, \mathbf{x_{m,i}})\} \quad (14)$$

We use the following steps in Algorithm 2 iteratively to estimate β_m^n, γ_m^n.

Algorithm 2 Step 4 in Algorithm 1
1: Initialize $\gamma_m^{n,0}, c \leftarrow 0$
2: **repeat**
3:    Compute $\beta_m^{n,c}$ based on $\gamma_m^{n,c}$ with conjugate gradient descent.
4:    Compute $\gamma_m^{n,c+1}$ based on $\beta_m^{n,c}$ with conjugate gradient descent.
5:    $c \leftarrow c + 1$
6: **until** <Convergence>
7: **return** β_m^n, γ_m^n

4. TENURE-BASED DECISION PROBABILITY

4.1 Definition

The **tenure-based decision probability** of item j_b for user u is defined as: the probability that user u would make a job transition to j_b at time between t_b and $t_b + \Delta t$, given that the user starts her current position j_a at time t_a and she did not make the decision up to time t_b. In other words, it is the probability that the survival time T would be between $y_{m,i}$ and $y_{m,i} + \Delta t$, given that T is not less than $y_{m,i}$. We denote the prediction of the tenure-based decision probability by model q as $q(y_{m,i}, \mathbf{x_{m,i}})$. It is given by

$$q(y_{m,i}, \mathbf{x_{m,i}}) = Pr(y_{m,i} < T \leq y_{m,i} + \Delta t | T > y_{m,i}) \quad (15)$$
$$= \frac{Pr(T \leq y_{m,i} + \Delta t) - Pr(T \leq y_{m,i})}{1 - Pr(T \leq y_{m,i})} \quad (16)$$

where

$$Pr(T \leq y_{m,i}) = 1 - exp\{-y_{m,i}^{\gamma_m} exp\{\beta_m^T \mathbf{x_{m,i}}\}\} \quad (17)$$

and each transition m has its own parameters (β_m, γ_m) in model q.

Table 1: The utility set of the recommender system. There are four types of utilities, depending on whether the system shows the item to the user and whether the user accepts the item.

	show:Y	show:N
accept:Y	u_{TP}	u_{FN}
accept:N	u_{FP}	u_{TN}

4.2 Usage

The major goal of the recommender system is to achieve high utility/user satisfaction. The user satisfaction is dependent on both the relevance and the time of the recommendation. While an irrelevant recommendation results in a negative utility, a relevant item could also lead to a negative utility due to the wrong time. We consider relevant items at the right time as *good* recommendations. On the other hand, we consider irrelevant items or relevant item at the wrong time as *bad* recommendations. We explore how to use this tenure-based decision probability in two scenarios.

Push-based Scenario In this scenario, the recommender system pushes items to the user proactively regardless of whether the user comes to the website. The recommendations could be sent to the user by email or other campaign methods. The challenge is to determine the right time to make relevant recommendations to maximize the user utility/satisfaction.

In Table 1, we show the utility set of the recommender system for different types of recommendation. The utility of model q for a set of recommendation items g is calculated with Equation 18:

$$utility_g(q) = \sum(u_{TP}I_{show,accept} + u_{FP}I_{\overline{show},accept} \\ + u_{FN}I_{show,\overline{accept}} + u_{TN}I_{\overline{show},\overline{accept}}) \quad (18)$$

I_* is the indicator function where $I_* = 1$ if $*$ is true. The recommendation threshold [7] $Thres_{rec}$ is automatically determined as [2]

$$Thres_{rec} = \frac{u_{FP} - u_{TN}}{u_{FP} - u_{TN} + u_{FN} - u_{TP}} \quad (19)$$

where "reasonableness conditions" assume $u_{FP} < u_{TN}$ and $u_{FN} < u_{TP}$. It indicates that the utility of a right label is always higher than the utility of a wrong label.

The system could leverage the tenure-based decision probability as a signal in the process. If the tenure-based decision probability of an item is greater than the threshold $Thres_{rec}$, the recommendation is presented to the user. Otherwise, it is not presented.

Pull-based Scenario In this scenario, the recommender systems selects a set of items to recommend to the user when the user comes to the website. The goal is to select most relevant items to present to the user. A natural approach is to incorporate the tenure-based decision probability of an item for a user as an additional feature in the hybrid recommender system. This feature indicates a user's aspiration to make the job transition to the item at the recommendation time. The hybrid system first ranks all candidate items based on

---
[2]Mathematical details can be referred to the paper [7].

all features that are associated with the user and the item, then selects the top items to present to a user.

5. EVALUATION OF HAZARDS MODEL

In this section, we evaluate the performance of the hierarchical proportional hazards model in predicting the transition time. We first list all research questions that we intend to answer, followed by the experimental setup and performance analysis. Major research questions include:

- How accurate is the tenure-based decision probability that is predicted by the hazards model? Will the model predict a higher probability when the user is likely to transit to new job and a lower probability when the user is not likely to make transitions?

- How accurate is the predicted decision time, compared to the actual decision time in the data?

- Is it important to consider covariates that are associated with the transition? Does the hierarchical proportional hazards model make more accurate prediction by taking covariates into consideration?

5.1 Evaluation Metrics

Determining the right recommendation time is a relatively new research topic. We introduce two metrics to evaluate the accuracy of the tenure-based decision probability and its effect in the recommendation utility.

5.1.1 Perplexity/Likelihood

The first metric is the perplexity of the model. It is widely used in the evaluation of language models and speech recognition [3]. We assume that the testing data is drawn from the same probability distribution as the training data. After a probability model q is trained with the training data, the perplexity reflects how well model q predicts the testing data. The perplexity of the model q is defined as

$$perplexity(q) = \left(\prod_{m=1}^{M} \prod_{i=1}^{N_m} \frac{1}{q(y_{m,i}, \mathbf{x_{m,i}})} \right)^{\frac{1}{\sum_{m=1}^{M} N_m}} \quad (20)$$
$$= 2^{-\sum_{m=1}^{M} \sum_{i=1}^{N_m} \frac{1}{\sum_{m=1}^{M} N_m} log_2 q(y_{m,i}, \mathbf{x_{m,i}})}$$

where $q(y_{m,i}, \mathbf{x}_{m,i})$ is defined in Equation 15. As we can see, perplexity is the inverse of the probability. If model q gives higher data likelihood to transitions in the testing data, the corresponding $perplexity(q)$ would be lower. The lower the perplexity, the better the model.

5.1.2 Estimated Decision Time

The second metric is to compare the estimated decision time and the actual one. It is the same as comparing the estimated tenure $y_{m,i}$ and the actual tenure $\hat{y_{m,i}}$. After model q predicts the distribution of the tenure, we use the mean of the distribution as the estimated tenure $\hat{y}_{m,i}$. The absolute error of the estimation is given by $|\hat{y_{m,i}} - y_{m,i}|$. The mean absolute error (MAE) across all testing data can then be used for analysis and comparison. $MAE(q) = \frac{1}{\sum_{m=1}^{M} N_m} \sum_{m=1}^{M} \sum_{i=1}^{N_m} |\hat{y_{m,i}} - y_{m,i}|$. The smaller the MAE, the better the model.

5.2 Models to Compare

In our experiments, we compare the following models.

H-One is the hazards model that fits a **single** set of parameters with no covariates (i.e., the basic Weibull distribution) to the tenure data. All transitions $m = \{* \to *\}$ share the same parameters, regardless of the transition's source a and destination b.

H-Source is the hazards model that fits **multiple** sets of parameters with no covariates to the tenure data. All transitions $m = \{a \to *\}$ from source a share the same parameters, regardless of the destination b.

H-SourceDest is the hazards model that fits **multiple** sets of parameters with no covariates to the tenure data. All transitions $m = \{a \to b\}$ from source a and destination b share the same parameters. It only uses the tenure information with no covariates.

H-SourceDestCov further incorporates covariates into the hazards model in *H-SourceDest*. In this case, the probability density function and the underlying hazards function change for each user u at time t if values of the associated covariates change. In this paper, we use the following covariates: 1) about the user u: the user's gender, age, number of connections, number of jobs that the user has changed, average months that the user changes a job; 2) about the item j_a or j_b: discretized company size, the company age, i.e., the current year minus the year the company was founded; 3) about the relationship between j_a and j_b: the ratio of the company size, the ratio of the company age; whether j_a and j_b are in the same function, whether they are in the same industry; 4) about the user's aspiration of category b: number of job applications from user u in category b in the last week, last month, last two months, and last three months. We choose these covariates to show the effect of the proportional hazards model. Extensive feature engineering can be applied here to include more useful features/covariates which could be explored in future work.

For all models, we learn parameters for a job transition if the transition is performed by at least k_u unique users in the training data. k_u is set to be 5 in the experiment. If parameters of transitions $m = \{a \to b\}$ are not learned in the training process, average values of parameters of transitions $m = \{a \to *\}$ are used to represent parameters of $m = \{a \to b\}$. If all parameters of transitions $m = \{a \to *\}$ are not learned in the training process, average values of parameters of transitions $m = \{* \to *\}$ are used to represent parameters of $m = \{a \to *\}$. In the prediction step, we smooth the probability estimation $q'(y_{m,i}, \mathbf{x_{m,i}}) = \max(\text{minThres}, q(y_{m,i}, \mathbf{x_{m,i}}))$ to avoid having a probability that is too low. minThres is set as 0.001. $\Delta(t)$ in Equation 15 is set as 3 (i.e., 3 months) for all models during the prediction step.

5.3 Dataset

As positioned earlier in the document, we apply our techniques in the context of a job recommender system and use a real-world dataset from LinkedIn to evaluate our models. We first analyze the user's changing job behavior in recent

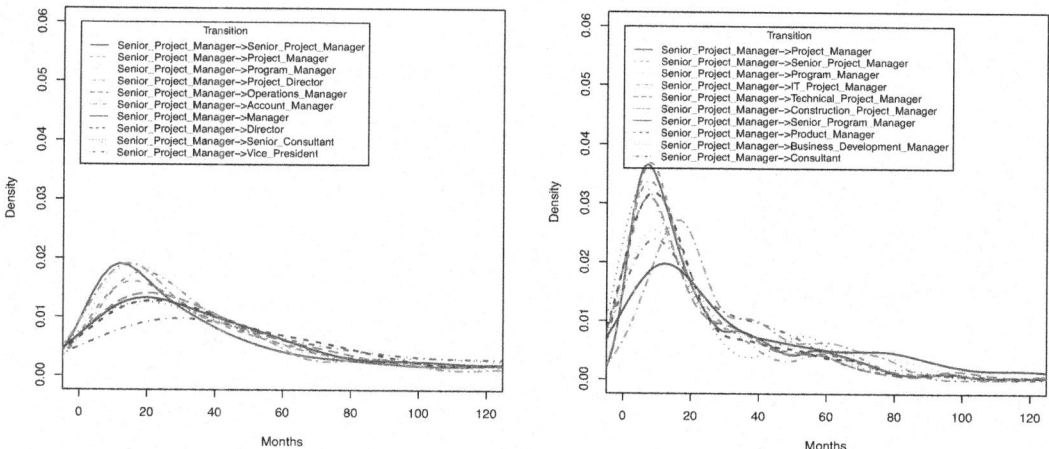

Figure 4: Density plot of the tenure before job transitions from *senior project managers*. (a) tenure before users make the job transition (b) tenure before users start to apply for the new job.

5 years to understand the role of the tenure in the job transiting process. Figure 4 shows the density plot of the tenure before a job transition from *senior project managers*. The first one shows the tenure before users make the transition and start the new job. It is clear that different job transitions usually happen at different tenures. For example, horizontal transitions from *senior project manager* to *senior project manager* are likely to happen at tenures of approximately 18 months while transitions from *senior project manager* to *vice president* are likely to happen at tenures of approximately 30 months. Users tend to transit to a higher position if they stay at the current position longer. The second plot in Figure 4 shows the tenure before users start to apply for new jobs. We notice that different job applications from the same job position also happen at different tenures. This justifies our motivation that we should take the time factor into consideration when making recommendations. The goal of the recommender system is to recommend jobs for users to apply. An actual job transition may or may not happen after a user applies to a job. Thus, we evaluate our models with the job application dataset and not necessarily the actual position transition data (which is also available). The dataset is composed of a sample of 11 million job applications over years. 10-fold cross validation is performed.

5.4 Performance Analysis

5.4.1 Perplexity/Likelihood

Here we compare the perplexity of all models in Section 5.2. As we describe before, the tenure-based decision probability $q(y_{m,i}, \mathbf{x_{m,i}}) = Pr(y_{m,i} < T \leq y_{m,i} + \Delta t | T > y_{m,i})$. The baseline model, *uniform*, assigns the uniform distribution to all tenures. The probability density function is $p(y_{m,i}) = \frac{1}{T_{uniform}}$ where $T_{uniform}$ is the number of tenures to consider. We set $T_{uniform} = 100$, i.e., 100 months.

First, we show the perplexity of all models from the 10-fold cross validation of the job application data in Table 2. In each job application, the user's job before the application and the job that the user applies to are available. It is clear that all hazards models have lower perplexity than the baseline *uniform*. It demonstrates the effect of modeling the tenure with the hazards model. Among all hazards models, *H-SourceDestCov* achieves the lowest perplexity, followed by *H-SourceDest*, *H-Source*, and *H-One*. *H-SourceDestCov* fits the parameters of the proportional hazards model for each $m = \{a \to b\}$ transition and incorporates related covariates. It shows the importance of considering covariates when modeling the tenure before a transition.

Second, we show the perplexity of different degrees of job seekers from a survey data. The data contains 9k LinkedIn users who were surveyed about their job seeking level in December 2011. All users categorized themselves into the following five categories from active job seekers to passive ones. 1) *Aggressively looking*: I'm actively looking for a new job and sharing my resume; 2) *Somewhat looking*: I'm casually looking for a new job 2-3 times per week to see what is available; 3) *Tiptoers*: I'm thinking about changing jobs and have reached out to close associates but am not actively looking; 4) *Explorers*: I'm not looking for a new job, but would discuss an opportunity with a recruiter to see if the job is interesting to me. 5) *Super passive*: I'm completely happy in my current job and am not interested in discussing any new job opportunities. The more passive the user, the lower the tenure-based decision probability. Because the perplexity is the inverse of the likelihood, a good model is expected to have higher perplexity for more passive users. In the survey data, the destination job or the job category that the user looked for is unknown. Thus, *H-SourceDest* and *H-SourceDestCov* that need the information of the destination are not included in the comparison. The perplexity of *H-One* and *H-Source* for different degrees of job seekers is shown in Figure 5. One can see that the perplexity increases for more passive job seekers and this trend is more pronounced with model *H-Source*. The figure also reveals that model *H-Source*, which learns multiple sets of parameters (one for each source category a), has better predictability for both job seekers and non-job seekers, compared to model *H-One*.

Table 2: Perplexity of different hazards models

Uniform	H-One	H-Source	H-SourceDest	H-SourceDestCov
22.47	9.17	8.11	7.27	**5.30**

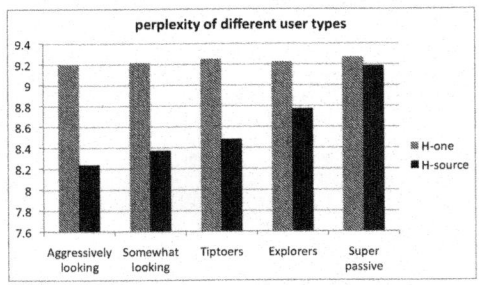

Figure 5: Perplexity of models for different degrees of job seekers.

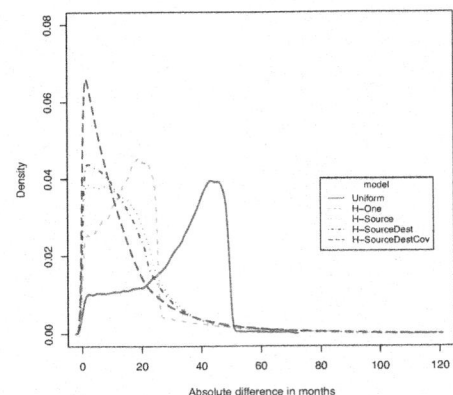

Figure 6: Density plot of the absolute difference between the estimated tenure and the actual tenure

5.4.2 Estimated Decision Time/Tenure

Here we compare the estimated tenure $\hat{y}$ with the actual tenure y before a transition. As before, the basic model *uniform* assigns the uniform distribution to all tenures. $p(y_{m,i}) = \frac{1}{T_{uniform}}$ where $T_{uniform}$ is set as 100 months. Hence, the corresponding estimated tenure is always 50 months.

In Figure 6, we show the density plot of the absolute error between the estimated tenure and the actual tenure, i.e., $|\hat{y} - y|$. The distribution of the absolute error of *H-SourceDestCov* is closest to 0. This is confirmed by Table 3 which reports the MAE between $\hat{y}$ and y. All hazards models perform better than the baseline *uniform* while *H-SourceDestCov* gives the most accurate estimation of the decision time/tenure, followed by *H-SourceDest*, *H-Source*, and *H-One*. In order to get a better estimated decision time, we plan to evaluate other estimators (such as the median) in the future work.

6. EVALUATION OF RECOMMENDATION MODEL

In this section, we incorporate the hazards model into the recommender system and evaluate its contribution in different scenarios.

6.1 In the Push-Based Scenario

6.1.1 Experimental Setup

In the push-based scenario, the goal is to determine the right time to make relevant recommendations to maximize the user utility. We use a sample of 6 million job impression data that were collected after the previous 11 million job application data. The hazards model is trained with the 11 million job application data and predicts the tenure-based decision probability for each impression in the 6 million impression dataset. An impression might lead to a job application or not, which corresponds to a *good* recommendation

Table 3: Mean absolute error (MAE) between the estimated tenure and the actual tenure

Uniform	H-One	H-Source	H-SourceDest	H-SourceDestCov
32.02	17.35	16.07	15.57	**14.25**

or a *bad* one. The impression item is selected by a hybrid recommender system with decent performance. The item is assumed to be relevant to the candidate user. Evaluations with two datasets are presented for each set. One dataset $Impression_{all}$ contains all sets of impressions, regardless of whether users applies to any of the impression in a set. The other dataset $Impression_{app}$ contains sets of impressions with at least one application, i.e., a user applies to at least one job in a set of impressions on that day.

The evaluation metric is the utility of the testing data. The testing data consists of a set of item impressions that the system predicted to be relevant to user u at time t. The user then choose whether to accept the items presented by the system. Assume that there are G sets of impressions in the test data. The average utility $utility(q)$ can be calculated as following: $utility(q) = \frac{\sum_{g=1}^{G} utility_g(q)}{G}$ where $utility_g(q)$ for each set of impressions is calculated by Equation 18. Unlike traditional metrics such as precision@K and recall@K, $utility(q)$ considers both the positive effect for *good* recommendations and the negative effect for different types of *bad* recommendations. The higher the utility, the better the model. In addition, we compare the average number of recommendations and the recommendation coverage after filtering items with $q(y_{m,i}, \mathbf{x_{m,i}}) > Thres_{rec}$. Coverage is the percentage of sets of impressions that contain at least one recommendation. Models that have both high utility and high coverage are preferred.

6.1.2 Performance Analysis

Based on the tenure-based decision probability, the system decides whether or not to present an item (impression) to a user. The baseline model *AlwaysRec* shows all impressions to the user.

In the real world scenario, the customized utility set is determined by the application's usage and the users' tolerance for *bad* recommendations. In Table 4, we show three sets of utility that correspond to different scenarios.

In the first utility set, the utility u_{TP} is set to 20 when the system shows an impression and the user applies to it. When the system shows an impression and the user does not apply to it, the utility u_{FP} is -2. When the system does not show an impression but the user actually applies to it, the utility u_{FN} is set to -2. When the system does not show

Table 4: Utility of the model. $Impression_{all}$ contains all groups of impressions. $Impression_{app}$ contains sets of impressions with at least one application. In each utility set, the *first* line shows the average utility of the model for each set of impressions. The *second* line shows the lift of the model compared to the baseline *AlwaysRec*. The *third* line shows the average number of recommendations. The *fourth* line shows the coverage of recommendations.

	\multicolumn{5}{c}{$u_{TP} = 20, u_{FN} = -2$ $u_{FP} = -2, u_{TN} = 0$ Threshold = 0.083}				
Data	AlwaysRec	H-One	H-Source	H-SourceDest	H-SourceDestCov
$Impression_{all}$	-41.38	-41.38	-37.89	-38.02	-37.97
		(0.00)	**(3.49)**	(3.36)	(3.41)
	(24.12)	(24.12)	(23.11)	(22.79)	(22.62)
	(100%)	(100%)	(91.28%)	(97.20%)	(99.13%)
$Impression_{app}$	-31.45	-31.45	-29.06	-29.15	-29.07
		(0.00)	**(2.39)**	(2.30)	(2.38)
	(25.76)	(25.76)	(24.73)	(24.39)	(24.20)
	(100%)	(100%)	(91.59%)	(97.44%)	(99.23%)
	\multicolumn{5}{c}{$u_{TP} = 20, u_{FN} = -10$ $u_{FP} = -2, u_{TN} = 0$ Threshold = 0.063}				
Data	AlwaysRec	H-One	H-Source	H-SourceDest	H-SourceDestCov
$Impression_{all}$	-41.38	-41.38	-40.67	-40.30	-39.65
		(0.00)	(0.71)	(1.08)	**(1.73)**
	(24.12)	(24.12)	(23.89)	(23.73)	(23.55)
	(100%)	(100%)	(98.06%)	(98.88%)	(99.59%)
$Impression_{app}$	-31.45	-31.45	-31.12	-30.91	-30.51
		(0.00)	(0.33)	(0.54)	**(0.94)**
	(25.76)	(25.76)	(25.54)	(25.37)	(25.18)
	(100%)	(100%)	(98.18%)	(98.95%)	(99.62%)
	\multicolumn{5}{c}{$u_{TP} = 20, u_{FN} = -2$ $u_{FP} = -10, u_{TN} = 0$ Threshold = 0.313}				
Data	AlwaysRec	H-One	H-Source	H-SourceDest	H-SourceDestCov
$Impression_{all}$	-231.83	-0.62	-15.79	-26.81	-71.37
		(231.21)	(216.04)	(205.02)	(160.46)
	(24.12)	(0.00)	(0.78)	(1.43)	(2.91)
	(100%)	(0%)	(6.45%)	(26.47%)	(66.93%)
$Impression_{app}$	-230.24	-1.82	-17.61	-28.90	-73.60
		(228.42)	(212.63)	(201.34)	(156.64)
	(25.76)	(0.00)	(0.87)	(1.59)	(3.21)
	(100%)	(0%)	(6.69%)	(28.15%)	(68.55%)

an impression and the user does not apply to it, the utility u_{TN} is 0. In this case, users are quite tolerant to *bad* recommendations with u_{TP} being much higher than u_{FP}. Model *H-One* achieves the same utility as *AlwaysRec*, while the other three models achieve better utility than the baseline. *H-Source* has a slightly better utility yet it has the lowest coverage. In *H-One*, a single Weibull distribution is fitted to all data from all transitions. The fitted Weibull distribution has shape $\gamma = 0.978$ and scale $\theta = 25.93$. As shown in Equation 3, the hazards function is $h(y) = \gamma \theta y^{\gamma-1}$, which is pretty stable for different tenure values y when $\gamma = 0.978$. In the experiment, Δt is set as 3 months in Equation 15. The resulting tenure-based decision probability of *H-one* is around 0.10 to 0.11 for different tenure values. Given that the recommendation threshold is 0.083 in this utility set, all impressions are therefore shown to the user in model *H-one*. Thus, it performs the same as the baseline model *AlwaysRec*.

In the second utility set, the utility u_{FN} is set to -10, indicating more utility penalization when the system does not show an impression yet the user would actually apply to it. In this scenario, *H-SourceDestCov* wins with the highest recommendation utility and coverage, followed by *H-SourceDest*, *H-Source*, *H-One*, and *AlwaysRec*. This indicates that *H-SourceDestCov* has better predictability of whether the user applies to a job at the recommendation time.

In the third utility set, the utility u_{FP} is set to -10, indicating that the user does not tolerate **bad** recommendations. In this case, the best model does not show any recommendation, as in the case of model *H-one* with coverage of 0%. All other models have higher utility than *AlwaysRec* but less utility than *H-one*. There is a tradeoff between the utility and the recommendation coverage, which can be tuned in a real-world application.

We discover that the overall utility of the best approach is still negative. There are two possible reasons behind it. 1) The ratio between *bad* items and *good* items is highly unbalanced in the impression dataset. It is challenging for the recommender system to keep *good* items while filtering out most *bad* items. 2) It is true that the user's decision to accept a relevant item is not purely dependent on the time. Recommender systems also take related factors [6] into account. A potentially better filtering signal is to combine the tenure-based decision probability with other probabilities, such as the probability of an item being relevant, the probability of an item being in the right location, etc.

6.2 In the Pull-Based Scenario

6.2.1 Experimental Setup

In the pull-based scenario, the goal is to select most relevant items to present to the user when the user comes to the site. The recommendation model is trained with a sample of millions of job application data in one month and tested with a sample of job application data in the following two weeks.

We evaluate the recommender system in the context of a ranking task [4]. For each job application, we first apply a heuristic filter to all open jobs available that day. First, only open jobs that are in the same geographical region as the user, for example, *San Francisco bay area*, are retained. Second, jobs must have a seniority level comparable to the user's current position seniority. In other words, the system won't recommend entry-level jobs to users in a senior position. All potential jobs that remain after the heuristic filter are used in the ranking step. Similar to other work in recommender systems [4, 28, 34], we use the commonly used IR metrics, precision@K of all testing cases, to compare models. The task focus is on evaluating a model's performance on ranking relevant items in top positions while ignoring the negative effect of different types of *bad* recommendations. The number of recommendations is fixed to be K.

In the experiment, **BasicModel** with basic features serves as the baseline. Basic features include similarity-related features between the user profile (including the user's working experience, education information, etc) and the job information (including the job's title, description, etc). The following feature groups are compared to the baseline. **Basic+TranProb** adds the smoothed transition probability in addition to basic features. The smoothed transition probability from j_a to j_b is calculated as following: $P(j_a \rightarrow j_b) = \frac{\# \ j_a \rightarrow j_b + \lambda}{\sum \# \ j_a \rightarrow * + J \cdot \lambda}$. $\# \ j_a \rightarrow j_b$ is the number of transitions from j_a to j_b. $\sum \# \ j_a \rightarrow *$ is the number of all transitions from j_a. J is the number of jobs and λ is the smoothing factor, which is set as 0.1. **Basic+TranProb+Tenure** further adds the pure tenure value (such as 8 for 8 months) as an additional feature. Instead of using the pure tenure value, **Ba-**

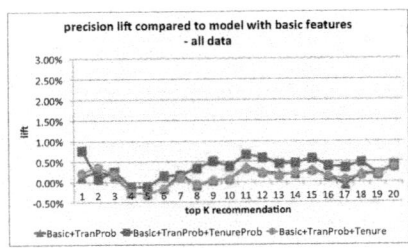 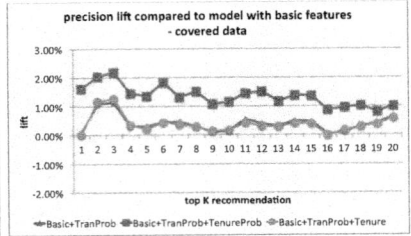 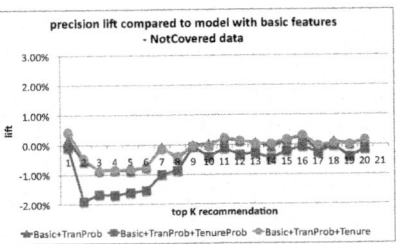

Figure 7: Precision lift of the hybrid recommender system with different feature groups. (a) performance of all testing data (6435 cases) (b) performance of testing cases that are covered by top transitions (47.7% of all cases) (c) performance of testing cases that are not covered by top transitions (52.3% of all cases)

sic+TranProb+TenureProb uses the tenure-based decision probability from hazards model *H-SourceDestCov*.

In practice, there are several mechanisms for building hybrid recommender systems [2, 29] to use. We use logistic regression, which is a common practice in industry [17]. It achieves decent performance with low computational complexity.

6.2.2 Performance Analysis

We compare the precision lift of different feature groups by using **BasicModel** as the baseline in Figure 7. We show the precision lift of all testing cases, cases that are covered by top transitions, and cases that are not covered. Suppose that the testing user is working as j_a and applies to j_b. This testing case is covered by top transitions if more than k_u unique users working with jobs in category a applied to jobs in category b in the training data. k_u is set to be 5. For example, common destinations of *software engineers* include *senior software engineers*, *technical leads*, *consultants*, etc. If a user as *software engineer* does apply to a job in one of these common destinations, the case is covered by the top transitions. Otherwise, it is not covered.

In the first plot in Figure 7, we observe a 0.5% to 1% lift of all testing cases by adding **TranProb** and **TenureProb** features. The difference between the model with basic features and the one with **Basic+TranProb+TenureProb** is significant after the top 9 recommendations ($p \leq 0.05$).

In the second plot in Figure 7 with testing cases that are covered by top transitions, it is clear that the model with **Basic+TranProb+TenureProb** performs the best. The model with **Basic+TranProb** features gives 0.21% lift in precision@5, compared with the baseline **BasicModel**. The model with **Basic+TranProb+TenureProb** gives 1.36% lift in precision@5. The difference between the model with basic features and the one with **Basic+TranProb+Tenure Prob** is significant for all top K positions ($p \leq 0.05$). On the other hand, the model with the pure tenure value **Basic+TranProb+Tenure** does not give further improvement, compared to the model with **Basic+TranProb**. We observe that the pure tenure value is noisy for hybrid systems that do not capture interactions among features. First, it is independent of the source job, which is the user's current job. The same tenure value for users working in different jobs does not indicate the same aspiration of changing jobs. Secondly, it is independent of the destination job. However, the reality is that the same tenure value indicates different level of aspiration for different destination jobs. Thus, it is essential to use the tenure-based decision probability instead of the pure tenure value in hybrid systems such as logistic regression models. If more advanced hybrid systems, such as gradient boosted tree algorithms are used to capture interactions among features, pure tenure values might perform similarly as the tenure-based decision probability.

In the third plot in Figure 7 with testing cases that are not covered by top transitions, we observe that incorporating **TranProb** and **TenureProb** features hurts the performance a little. It is not surprising because the transition probability and tenure-based decision probability reflect transitions that are shared by most users. If a user has her own career plan, such as transiting to be a *novel writer* after working as a *software engineer* for *two* years, it won't be captured by the transition probability or the tenure-based decision probability. Instead, these transitions need to be captured by the user's behavior signals, such as job searches, job clicks, etc. Besides such job applications are more likely to happen after a user proactively searches the system. This is an important problem to analyze and study, but beyond the scope of this paper.

7. CONCLUSION AND FUTURE WORK

We performed research to answer the following question: When is the right time to make a job recommendation and how do we use this inference to improve the utility of a job recommender system? We proposed using the hierarchical proportional hazards model. Experiments with the real-world job application data demonstrated the effectiveness of the hazards model and the importance of considering the time factor in the recommendation process. This was just the first step in exploring the right time to make the recommendation. More interesting models to leverage the tenure information could be studied and compared with the hazards model. We plan to also explore other approaches to use the tenure-based decision probability and evaluate it in other domains beyond job recommendations as well.

Acknowledgments

We would like to thank Ethan Zhang in LinkedIn for his help and comments. Part of this work was funded by National Science Foundation IIS-0953908 and CCF-1101741. Any opinions, findings, conclusions or recommendations expressed in this paper are the authors, and do not necessarily reflect those of the sponsors.

8. REFERENCES

[1] J. Bennett and S. Lanning. The netflix prize. 2007.

[2] R. Burke. Hybrid recommender systems: Survey and experiments. *User Modeling and User-Adapted Interaction*, 12(4):331–370, Nov. 2002.

[3] S. Chen, D. Beeferman, and R. Rosenfeld. Evaluation metrics for language models. In *DARPA Broadcast News Transcription and Understanding Workshop (BNTUW)*, Lansdowne, Virginia, USA, Feb. 1998.

[4] P. Cremonesi, Y. Koren, and R. Turrin. Performance of recommender algorithms on top-n recommendation tasks. In *Proceedings of the fourth ACM RecSys 2010*, pages 39–46, New York, NY, USA, 2010. ACM.

[5] M. Dubinko, R. Kumar, J. Magnani, J. Novak, P. Raghavan, and A. Tomkins. Visualizing tags over time. *ACM Trans. Web*, 1(2), Aug. 2007.

[6] P. Dütting, M. Henzinger, and I. Weber. Maximizing revenue from strategic recommendations under decaying trust. In *Proceedings of the 21st ACM international CIKM'12*.

[7] C. Elkan. The foundations of cost-sensitive learning. In *Proceedings of the 17th IJCAI'01*.

[8] N. Golbandi, Y. Koren, and R. Lempel. Adaptive bootstrapping of recommender systems using decision trees. In *Proceedings of the fourth ACM WSDM'11*.

[9] J. L. Herlocker, J. A. Konstan, A. Borchers, and J. Riedl. An algorithmic framework for performing collaborative filtering. In *Proceedings of the 22nd ACM SIGIR*, pages 230–237, New York, NY, USA, 1999. ACM.

[10] R. Jin, L. Si, C. Zhai, and J. Callan. Collaborative filtering with decoupled models for preferences and ratings. In *Proceedings of the twelfth CIKM*, pages 309–316, New York, NY, USA, 2003. ACM.

[11] Y. Koren. Factorization meets the neighborhood: a multifaceted collaborative filtering model. In *Proceeding of the 14th ACM SIGKDD*, KDD '08, pages 426–434, New York, NY, USA, 2008. ACM.

[12] Y. Koren. Collaborative filtering with temporal dynamics. In *KDD*, 2009.

[13] R. Kumar, P. Raghavan, S. Rajagopalan, and A. Tomkins. Recommendation systems: A probabilistic analysis. In *Proceedings of the 39th Annual Symposium on Foundations of Computer Science*, FOCS '98, pages 664–, Washington, DC, USA, 1998. IEEE Computer Society.

[14] C. Liu, R. W. White, and S. Dumais. Understanding web browsing behaviors through weibull analysis of dwell time. In *Proceedings of the 33rd ACM SIGIR'10*.

[15] B. Marlin and R. S. Zemel. The multiple multiplicative factor model for collaborative filtering. In *Proceedings of the 21st ICML '04*.

[16] R. J. Mooney and L. Roy. Content-based book recommending using learning for text categorization. In *DL '00*, pages 195–204, New York, NY, USA, 2000.

[17] D. Parra, A. Karatzoglou, X. Amatriain, and I. Yavuz. Implicit feedback recommendation via implicit-to-explicit ordinal logistic regression mapping. In *Proceedings of the CARS-2011*, 2011.

[18] D. Parra-Santander and P. Brusilovsky. Improving collaborative filtering in social tagging systems for the recommendation of scientific articles. *Web Intelligence and Intelligent Agent Technology*, 1:136–142, 2010.

[19] M. Pazzani, D. Billsus, S. Michalski, and J. Wnek. Learning and revising user profiles: The identification of interesting web sites. In *Machine Learning*, pages 313–331, 1997.

[20] C. D. R. Regression models and life tables. *Journal of the Royal Statistic Society*, B(34):187–202, 1972.

[21] S. Rendle, C. Freudenthaler, and L. Schmidt-Thieme. Factorizing personalized markov chains for next-basket recommendation. In *Proceedings of the 19th WWW '10*.

[22] E. J. Ruiz, V. Hristidis, C. Castillo, A. Gionis, and A. Jaimes. Correlating financial time series with micro-blogging activity. In *Proceedings of the fifth ACM WSDM '12*.

[23] E. Shmueli, A. Kagian, Y. Koren, and R. Lempel. Care to comment?: recommendations for commenting on news stories. In *Proceedings of the 21st WWW'12*.

[24] M. Shokouhi and K. Radinsky. Time-sensitive query auto-completion. In *Proceedings of the 35th international ACM SIGIR'12*.

[25] L. Si and R. Jin. Flexible mixture model for collaborative filtering. In *Proc. of ICML*, pages 704–711. AAAI Press, 2003.

[26] M. D. Smucker and C. L. A. Clarke. Modeling user variance in time-biased gain. In *Proceedings of the Symposium on Human-Computer Interaction and Information Retrieval*, HCIR '12, pages 3:1–3:10, New York, NY, USA, 2012. ACM.

[27] J. Wang, B. Sarwar, and N. Sundaresan. Utilizing related products for post-purchase recommendation in e-commerce. In *Proceedings of the fifth ACM conference on Recommender systems*, RecSys '11, pages 329–332, New York, NY, USA, 2011. ACM.

[28] J. Wang and Y. Zhang. Utilizing marginal net utility for recommendation in e-commerce. In *Proceedings of the 34th international ACM SIGIR'11*, pages 1003–1012. ACM, 2011.

[29] J. Wang, Y. Zhang, and T. Chen. Unified recommendation and search in e-commerce. In *Information Retrieval Technology*, pages 296–305. Springer Berlin Heidelberg, 2012.

[30] L. J. Wei. The accelerated failure time model: A useful alternative to the cox regression model in survival analysis. *Statistics in Medicine*, 11(14-15):1871–1879, 1992.

[31] R. W. White, P. Bailey, and L. Chen. Predicting user interests from contextual information. In *Proceedings of the 32nd international ACM SIGIR'09*.

[32] L. Xiang, Q. Yuan, S. Zhao, L. Chen, X. Zhang, Q. Yang, and J. Sun. Temporal recommendation on graphs via long- and short-term preference fusion. In *Proceedings of the 16th ACM SIGKDD*, KDD '10, pages 723–732, New York, NY, USA, 2010. ACM.

[33] D. Zhang, J. Lu, R. Mao, and J.-Y. Nie. Time-sensitive language modelling for online term recurrence prediction. In *Proceedings of the 2nd ICTIR '09*.

[34] G. Zhao, M. L. Lee, W. Hsu, and W. Chen. Increasing temporal diversity with purchase intervals. In *Proceedings of the 35th international ACM SIGIR'12*.

Google+ Ripples:
A Native Visualization of Information Flow

Fernanda Viégas	Martin Wattenberg	Jack Hebert	Geoffrey Borggaard
Google, Inc.	Google, Inc.	Google, Inc.	Google, Inc.
viegas@google.com	wattenberg@google.com	jhebert@google.com	geoffreyb@google.com

Alison Cichowlas	Jonathan Feinberg	Jon Orwant	Christopher R. Wren
Google, Inc.	Google, Inc.	Google, Inc.	Google, Inc.
asc@google.com	feinberg@google.com	orwant@google.com	cwren@google.com

ABSTRACT
G+ Ripples is a visualization of information flow that shows users how public posts are shared on Google+. Unlike other social network visualizations, Ripples exists as a "native" visualization: it is directly accessible from public posts on Google+. This unique position leads to both new constraints and new possibilities for design. We describe the visualization technique, which is a new mix of node-and-link and circular treemap metaphors. We then describe user reactions as well as some of the patterns of sharing that are made evident by the Ripples visualization.

Categories and Subject Descriptors
H5.2. Information interfaces and presentation: User Interfaces. Graphical user interfaces.

Keywords
Visualization, social networks, social data analysis.

1. INTRODUCTION
As long as people have been having conversations, news has spread. Opinions on movies, politics, and friends naturally travel as one person talks to another, who then talks to another. But the process has always been a bit of a mystery: If I tell you a piece of juicy gossip, whom will you tell? And whom will they tell, in turn?

With the advent of social networks that keep persistent histories of public conversations, this process is no longer completely opaque. It is possible to trace the paths of information, at least in public channels, as it flows from one person to the next. These paths are interesting from many points of view. For users of a social network, understanding how information travels can lend a better sense of the potential audience of a post; in turn, this understanding can lead to a feeling of control over their online world. For scientists the data is an invaluable tool for analyzing the mechanics of social networks.

There are two significant challenges in helping people understand information flow. First, online networks can generate large cascades of sharing, involving thousands of people. While it is possible to summarize some of this activity in a few data points or simple chart—say, a list of the people who have been quoted the most—any attempts to aggregate the data lose richness and detail. Thus a natural way to present chains of sharing is not with summary statistics, but with a visualization capable of showing a fuller story.

A second challenge, especially relevant for end users, is one of convenience. While it is possible for third-party sites to create visualizations of public social network data, such tools require a significant context switch. A user who wants to see how a post has spread needs to go to a completely different site. Unfortunately, on the web, requiring more than a click can be a significant barrier to adoption.

This paper introduces Google+ Ripples, a tool that addresses both of these challenges. It includes a visualization that can scale to show large information flows. And it does so natively, directly on the site: users of Google+ who find an interesting post can click a link to see, immediately, a picture of how it spread.

1.1 Google+ and sharing behavior
Google+ is an online social network, launched in 2011. Like networks such as Twitter and Facebook, Google+ allows users to create posts that consist of text and images, and may point to other media via URLs. The list of a user's posts is called their stream. Users can also share posts they read, i.e., they create a post in their own stream referencing that post. A share can be as simple as a pointer to the original post, or it can include additional commentary. Users may comment on each other's posts as well, though the current version of Ripples does not include this data.

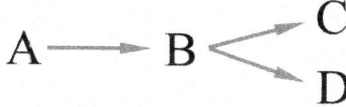

Figure 1. The structure of a simple reshare tree. A: original post; B: reshare of parent; C and D: reshares of B.

An interesting post may be shared and "reshared" in a chain or tree. In other words, Person A might write a post; Person B shares that post with some commentary; then People C and D reshare B's post with some additional commentary. Thus, the flow of dissemination of a post has a natural tree structure (Figure 1) where each post's "parent" is the one that it is resharing. In the example above, A would be the root, and C and D would be leaves.

The temporal aspect of this process is also of interest. Typically the distribution of post dates is bursty. In particular, we observed that for many posts, the vast majority of reshares occur soon after the initial post, with a few occurring much later. This observation echoes that of [10] as well as informal observations on other social networks. As we will see, this uneven distribution turns out to impose design constraints, since using time as a spatial dimension leads to inefficient, hard-to-read layouts.

Finally, it's important to note that not all posts are accessible to all users. A key feature of Google+ is that it enables fine-grained sharing, so that not every user has permission to see every post. It is also possible to share content publicly. As a result, activity on the site is a mix of public and non-public conversation. The Ripples system only displays public posts. While this provides just a partial view of the conversations on the site, it greatly simplifies the task of preserving user privacy.

1.2 Related Work

We discuss several types of related work. First, there is a long history of visualizations of conversations and online sharing. In our review of relevant work, we focus specifically on systems that show disaggregated data; displays of summary statistics alone are numerous but not directly of interest here. Second, there are many visualizations of online social networks that are not native to social platforms, but that depict network structure. Finally, since our system uses a data model that is a collection of trees, it draws on a long line of research into tree visualization. We will discuss this latter stream of work in the context of a detailed description of our visualization technique in Section 3.

There has been extensive work on ways to visualize conversations [5]. Much of this work has been based on "threads," which have a similar structure to the Ripples trees of reshares. There are practical differences, however. For example, a long email thread usually has multiple messages per person, but it is rare (though not impossible) for a user to appear more than once in a reshare tree. Furthermore, the largest Ripples reshare chains easily top 1,000 posts, whereas most email, usenet, or online forum threads are smaller.

One relevant system is Xiong's WebFan [27], which used a radial display of a conversation thread: an initial post in the center, with a subsequent replies branching out. The result was beautifully evocative of a conversation expanding and evolving, but at the same time suffered from crowding at the edges and had difficulty with labeling.

More recently, visualizations based on social network data have appeared. Many of these use data from Twitter: the service is broadly popular and has an open API; furthermore, the public nature of most Twitter posts ("tweets") makes it especially easy to work with. Twitter visualizations tend to fall into two categories. Some ask a user for their login information, and then show a customized view of their own conversations. Others are based on a stored set of public tweets.

Examples of such visualizations are too numerous to review comprehensively here, but we describe some key aspects of such work. Many use node-and-link diagrams to show aggregate patterns of retweeting and conversation, rather than the diffusion of a particular piece of information. An example closer to Ripples comes from SocialFlow [16]. Their technology tracks a specific subject, and appears to show a conversational network (not necessarily a tree) whose geometry is defined via a force-directed layout.

Project Cascade [11] is an installation created by the New York Times for internal analysis of the spread of the newspaper's stories on Twitter. The system runs off of a five-screen video wall controlled by an iPhone, and offers multiple perspectives on information flow. The most detailed of these views uses a 3D polar layout, in which points represent tweets, distance from the origin represents time since the first tweet with a story, and height above the xy plane represents the depth of a retweet chain. The resulting visualizations are beautiful and dramatic, though the use of 3D, and time as a spatial variable, can bring challenges with labels.

All of the systems described above are third-party tools. They exist separately from the social networks they visualize, and a user needs to break context to go from a social network post to its visualization. In a few cases, these third-party tools can be "plugged into" an existing system. For instance, a number of Facebook widgets visualize users' social network; e.g., the Facebook Friends Wheel shows a local view of a user's friends, linking people who know each other [7]. In addition, some blogs include plugins that graph statistics on the blog itself, such as traffic over time [18].

One precedent for what we call *native* visualizations is YouTube Insights [22]. Next to many videos on YouTube there is an icon that, when clicked, displays a dashboard with a graph of viewership over time, a map of viewers' locations, and other data. This immediate, seamless transition from media object to visualization of its history is one of the inspirations for Ripples.

2. THE RIPPLES SYSTEM

Ripples, launched in October 2011, is a feature inside of the Google+ network. That initial version, which we call Ripples V1, was available in the US only and allowed users to track the sharing of an individual Google+ post. A second version, Ripples V2, was launched in March 2012. The V2 edition is internationally available and allows users to track the spread of all posts that contain a specific URL.

2.1 Accessing Ripples

Next to every post on Google+ is a drop-down menu offering a set of relevant user actions. On public posts that have been reshared at least once, this menu includes a "View Ripples" option, which takes the user directly to the Ripples page. The entire page, including the full visualization, usually loads in less than a second, leading to a seamless experience for the user.

2.2 The Ripples page

The Ripples page (Figure 2) is made of several modules that provide information about a given post. At the top is a snippet of the post itself (or the entire post, if it is short), along with instructions. In the center is the main visualization. We describe the visualization in greater detail in Section 3; briefly, Figure 2 shows a collection of posts that mention a particular viral video. Each solid-colored circle represents a tree of reshares. For example, the largest (lavender) circle shows the cascade of reshares of a post originally written by user Chris Pirillo, mentioning the video. To its left is a green circle with the label "Laughing Squid," which shows the tree of reshares of an initial post by user Laughing Squid. Within each circle, arrows and smaller circles show the structure of resharing: e.g., the thick arrow from user "Chris Pirillo" pointing to a circle labelled "Josh Armour" indicates that user Josh Armour reshared Chris Pirillo's post. The smaller circles within the Josh Armour circle indicate further reshares. Note that the visualization scales to relatively large numbers of nodes: Figure 2 depicts a forest of more than 4,500 shares. A final feature of the visualization, introduced in summer of 2012, is that it updates in near real time: within a few seconds of a new post, the visualization will show that post, with a brief "expanding ripples" animation to call attention to the new item.

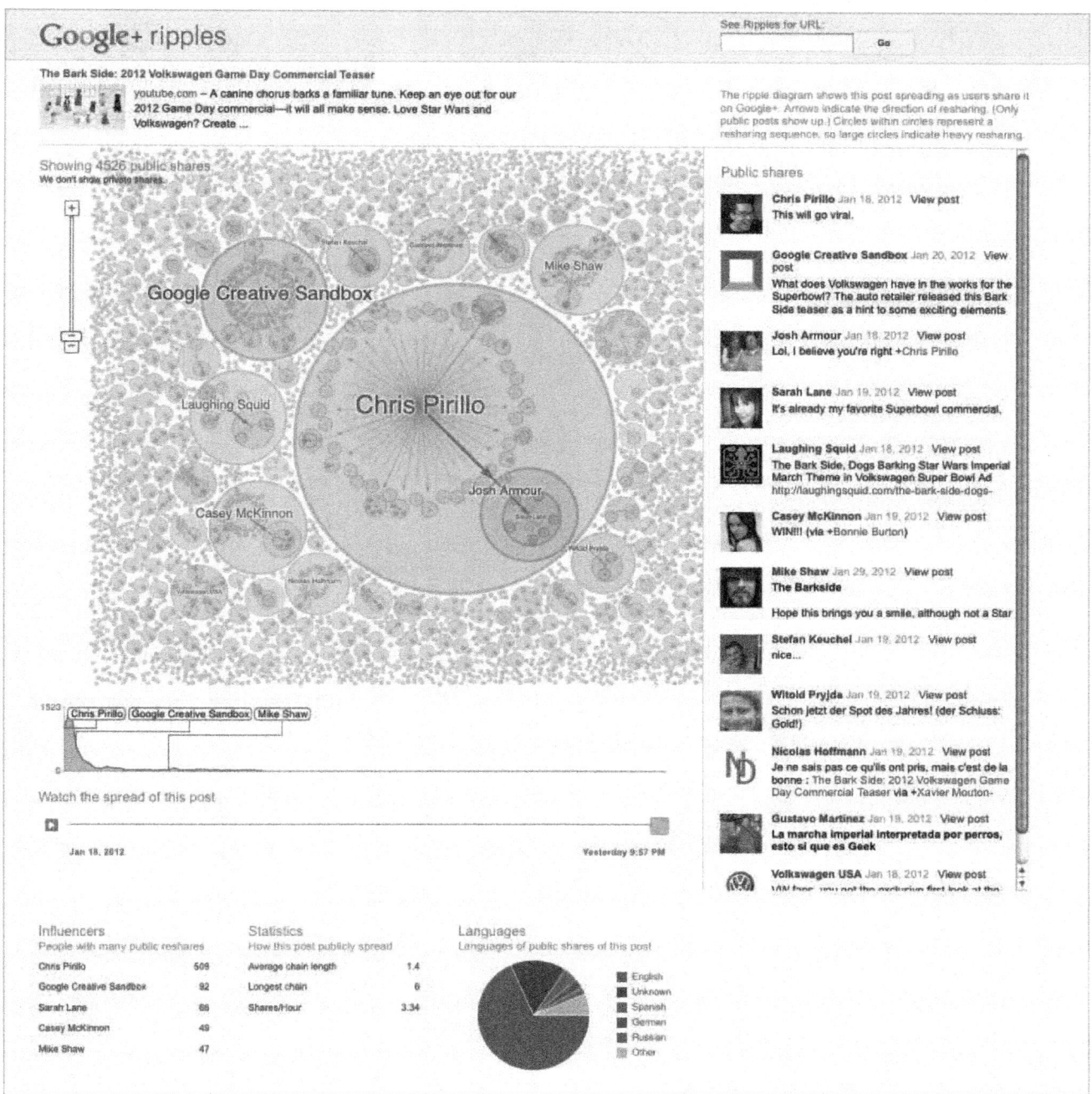

Figure 2. Full Ripples page. At the top of the page is a snippet of the post itself along with instructions. In the center is the main visualization. Below the visualization is a timeline of shares over time and a small table of statistics about the share graph. A sidebar shows the contents of posts made by the most prominent users in view.

Below the visualization is a graph showing the volume of shares over time. As described below, the graph is linked to the visualization, letting users "play back" the sharing history. Underneath the graph is a small table of statistics about the share tree. We include a list of the top "influencers"—that is, the set of people who were individually reshared the most. (For the purposes of this graph, we simply define "influence" as the total number of direct reshares.) The points in time when these people made posts are labeled in the graph as well.

Obviously there are other ways to define influence, and early iterations of the system contained more than one list, corresponding to a variety of metrics. For example, another natural measure of "influence" is the total number of downstream shares, rather than direct shares. In informal user tests, however, we discovered that the use of multiple metrics was often confusing. People often expected a list of influencers ordered by direct reshares, so in the end we used that measure alone.

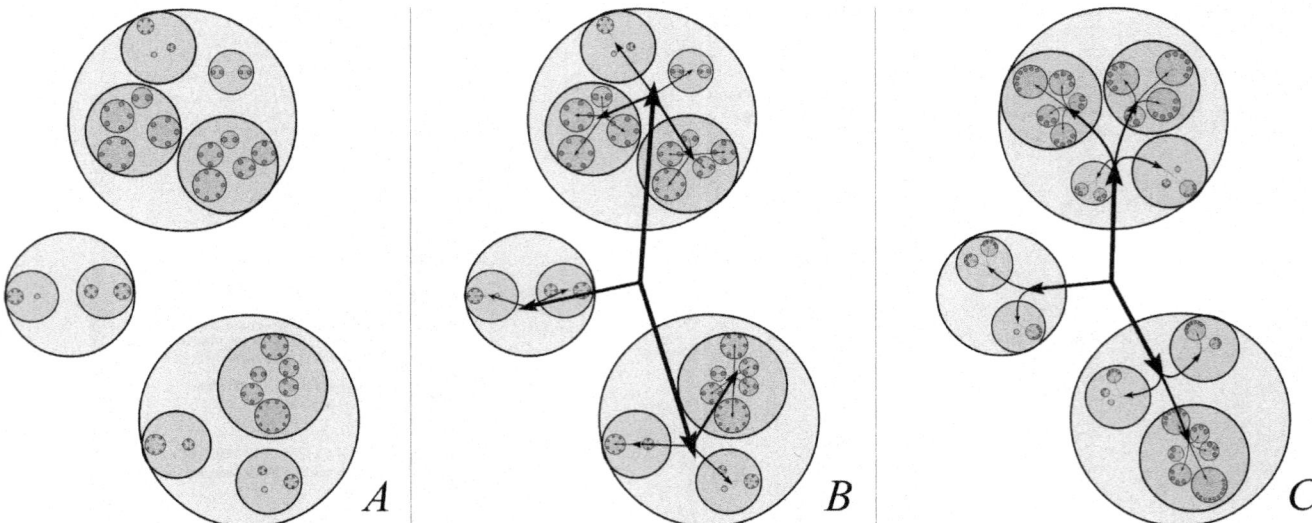

Figure 3. Graphical treatment of directionality. A: no arrows. B: Angular arrows. C: curved arrows along with rotation of circle contents so that the centroid lies opposite the point of entry of an arrow to maximize the appearance of flow.

A second panel provides summary statistics about the share graph itself. We display the average chain length, the length of the deepest chain, and the "shares per hour" for the life of the post. As discussed in section 4, the first two figures seem to reveal information about the type of post and how it was perceived. The "shares per hour" figure—which generally decays over time, after an initial burst—can be useful in identifying "viral" posts. Finally, a third panel shows a pie chart of the distribution of languages of posts. Due to the significant international membership of Google+, this pie chart is helpful in understanding the readership of a given post.

3. VISUALIZATION TECHNIQUE

The centerpiece of the Ripples system is a visualization of share trees. Before going into the details of the visualization, we describe some of the data and design constraints and what we learned from early iterations.

3.1 Design Process

For each public post on Google+, we have access to all of its downstream public reshares, along with a tree structure on those reshares. We also know the timestamp and author of each reshare. In Ripples V1, this constituted the entire data set. Ripples V2, however, displays a forest of trees, showing all posts that mention a given URL (Figure 4). In theory we had more data available to us, including the full text of each reshare, but we could not include all this information in the visualization due to latency and browser memory constraints.

Our first designs were organized temporally. In these views, dots represented posts, the x-axis corresponded to time, and the y-axis corresponded to a depth-first list of tree node. Unfortunately, this approach had multiple problems. Most items see significant sharing early on, and then very little later (e.g. Figure 2 timeline). As a result, basing the x positions of items on time created a crowded view. In a few cases there were multiple "waves" of posts, in which structure could be seen, but these were the exception and not the rule.

We tried several variations on x-axis positioning to avoid the visual overplotting caused by bursts of activity. In one, we set the x position to the order of posting, and in the other we set the x-position of a node to its depth in the sharing tree. While these made the tree structure clearer for small trees, the visualization remained impossible to read for graphs with large branching factors. The basic problem is that there aren't enough pixels vertically to fit thousands of posts.

To solve this problem, we decided we needed a more space-efficient layout. We tried both a standard pivot-by-middle treemap layout [17] and a jigsaw treemap [25]. The irregular arrangement of a jigsaw treemap was immediately deemed unattractive and hard to read. A standard rectangular treemap gave a decent, efficient arrangement of leaf nodes, but finding a natural location for higher-level nodes—usually the most important ones in this context—was problematic.

Most crucially, both methods suffered from a fatal aesthetic drawback. Neither "looked" like flow of information. Understanding the diagrams felt like decoding a complicated message. Connecting shares to their parents with arrows just resulted in an unreadable mess, as the connecting lines collided with other shares beneath them. Given that a native visualization aimed at end users needs to be readily comprehensible, we decided we needed a technique that would allow familiar metaphors to indicate directionality of flow.

3.2 Circle Packing

Our design challenge was to find a visualization technique that could combine the best aspects of these variations. In particular, we wanted a visualization method that met three criteria:

1. Space-efficient layout of leaf nodes, as in a treemap
2. A natural sense of hierarchy, where parents were more prominent than their children
3. Space to overlay arrows from parents to children, to show directionality of flow

To achieve this combination, we used a variant of a circular treemap.

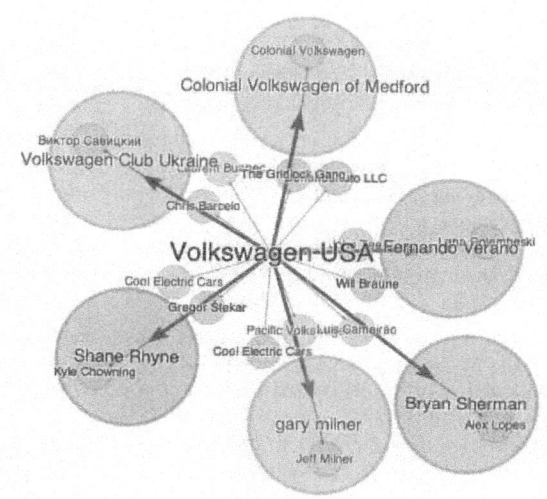
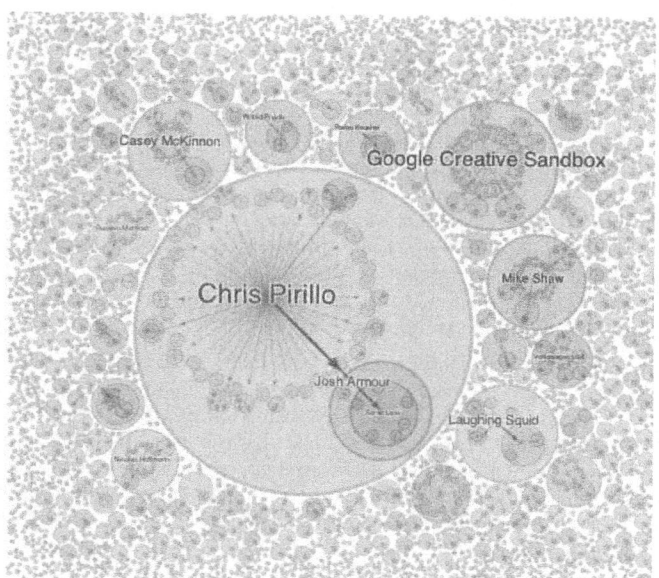

Figure 4: Visualizing the spread of "The Bark Side," a Volkswagen teaser video for the 2012 Super Bowl. *Left*: Ripples V1, showing the spread of the original Volkswagen post (i.e., a single tree). *Right*: Ripples V2, showing all shares of the video (the entire forest). The arrow shows Volkswagen's tree. It is clear that the video spread organically through many channels.

3.2.1 Previous work

Circle-packing visualizations and recursive circular visualizations of trees have been discussed in many contexts. Our technique can be viewed as a hybrid version of previous techniques, which we describe now.

Several systems include visualizations that represent a data set by circles of varying sizes. For example, the "bubble charts" of Many Eyes [20] used this technique. The layout algorithm involved a greedy randomized method with larger items placed toward the center of the screen. More recently, the d3 library [3] provides an interesting layout algorithm that puts circles in a kind of snaking spiral, producing a very different look from the placement algorithm described below.

Hierarchical circle-packing visualizations, also called circular treemaps, have also been proposed [2][6][24][26]. This visualization technique has not become popular, perhaps because the packing is not as space-efficient as rectangular treemaps: circles do not fit snugly together and so leave a significant amount of whitespace. Ironically, in our context this is as much a feature as a bug, since it provides room to overlay connections without creating a visual mess.

Finally, some graph visualization toolkits offer a "balloon layout" for trees [8], in which nodes are arranged in circles around their parents. Balloons offer a natural sense of hierarchy, but not the space efficiency of a treemap-style layout, and for trees with a high branching factor become unreadable.

3.3 The Ripples visualization: a "balloon treemap"

The goal of the Ripples visualization is to combine the relative space-efficiency of a circular treemap with the structural clarity of a balloon graph layout. To do so, we make a set of subtle but important changes to the basic geometry along with careful attention to rendering details. We call this hybrid a *balloon treemap*.

3.3.1 Heterogeneous circle packing geometry

As mentioned before, there are many different ways to pack circles. Existing visualizations typically pick one layout algorithm and use it recursively. After some experimentation, however, we decided that different levels in the share tree hierarchy look best with different layout algorithms.

The layout at the top level depends on whether Ripples is showing the chain of shares for a single post (a network that is a tree) or all posts and shares that mention a particular URL (a forest)—see Figure 4. When placing circles corresponding to the individual trees in a forest, the most natural choice was a layout in which big circles were generally toward the center and small circles could be placed in between large ones if necessary.

At lower levels (or the top level, when showing only a single tree of shares) we discovered that the large-circles-in-center layout suffered from a bad problem with labels: it essentially guaranteed that the label for a node would collide with label for its children. To avoid this problem, for deeper levels of the tree we used the opposite layout algorithm, one in which a "hole" of whitespace was placed at the center, then small circles around that, with the largest ones on the outside.

Our algorithm in both cases is greedy placement of circles, either largest first or smallest first, searching along a spiral [19]. To speed collision detection we use a *kd*-tree structure [12]. As a special case, for large sets of items that are all the same size, we use a golden-ratio spiral to layout instantly, without needing to perform any collision detection calculations, as in [9] and [14]. The resulting algorithm can handle real-world trees of several thousand nodes, all in less than a second.

We also included some special-case layouts for sets consisting of fewer than 10 circles, all of equal size. These simple, special cases were common at the lowest level of hierarchy. In these cases, we simply laid circles out around a 180-degree angle. The reason we used a 180-dgree angle rather than the full 360 degrees relates to the directionality considerations below.

3.3.2 Clarifying Tree Topology

In a circular treemap, the tree topology can be hard to discern. To make a more readable display, we combined the circular layout with the directed arrows typically seen in a traditional graph layout. This is a natural idea, and has been explored in the context of rectangular treemaps by Nguyen and Huang [15]. Our design has a few new elements, however. First, we made sure to use smooth curves, rather than straight lines, to connect items; this helped provide a feel of "flow" from bigger circles to smaller ones. In addition, this technique helped clarify directionality: with polygonal paths we found that direction was ambiguous, so that users would need to carefully read arrows.

Another small but helpful touch was to rotate circle arrangements so they pointed "outward". In other words, we found the centroid of the circles, and rotated the arrangement so it was opposite from the direction of "flow" into the circle. Especially in the case of small sets of items, which were arranged in a half-circle, this resulted in a pleasing, clear sense of directionality. See Figures 3b and 3c, which show example trees with and without these design optimizations.

To help distinguish the different top-level trees (or top-level branches of a single-tree forest) we used a palette of gentle pastels. Each tree/subtree was assigned a unique, mostly transparent color; circles in that tree are then filled with this color. The effect is to convey tree depth with overall darkness (as the mostly transparent colors overlap) and to visually separate neighboring circles. We also tried alternative color schemes—including encoding additional data, such as showing a share's timestamp via color. Unfortunately, it was surprisingly hard to read a graph colored by post time, as the scattered colors ended up looking like a jumble.

3.4 Rendering, Interaction and Animation

The visualization is implemented in JavaScript, and all rendering is performed using the HTML5 Canvas element. For large data sets (more than 1,000 items) rendering in full detail becomes too slow for smooth animations. To avoid choppy motion, during animations we use a level-of-detail calculation to draw only the largest, most prominent visual features. After animations finish, we then draw the full visualization into an offscreen image, and perform a smooth crossfade to draw that image to the screen.

We provide multiple ways of interacting with the main visualization. The primary interface for seeing more details is to zoom and pan. We use essentially the same interface as Google Maps, partly because it seemed like it made sense to users, and partly for consistency between Google properties. However, we also allow users to zoom directly into the "sphere of influence" of a user by clicking on their name or circle.

As the user moves the viewpoint, a sidebar shows the contents of posts made by the most prominent users in view. This is a standard linked view, but an interesting twist arose in the internationalization process. In Ripples V2, the system became available in 60 languages. As a by-product, the internationalization team added logic so that on right-to-left languages (e.g., Hebrew, Arabic) the sidebar switched sides. This is a good example of the kind of flexibility required by native visualizations.

As a user moves the mouse over circles, a "hovercard" appears, displaying post details (Figure 5). The hovercard also includes a "Follow" button, which allows users to add new people/entities to their network. The fact that users can take advantage of the visualization to affect change in their social network is a benefit of a native visualization.

Finally, we wish to show the evolution of the tree over time. Although often share trees grow in a single burst, sometimes there are more interesting patterns. To provide support for exploration of temporal growth, we added an interactive slider to the time graph below the main visualization. Moving the slider, or clicking a "play" button, provides an animated view of the graph, filtering to show only the posts made before or on a given date.

As with zooming and panning, drawing the full graph is too slow to allow smooth motion. In the time animation, however, we can't resort to drawing a low-resolution view—often the appearance of large groups of graphically small leaf nodes is an important aspect of the evolution of a share tree. To provide at least the illusion of interactive behaviour, we used a small trick. As the slider moves forward, from time t_1 to time t_2, we simply draw the shares that appeared between t_1 and t_2. This allows quick animation during forward movement of time, with especially fast drawing when the increment $t_1 - t_2$ is small. When moving the slider backward in time, we redraw the entire graph for that time. This is a slow process, but luckily, it is also uncommon. Thus we achieve smooth motion in the cases when the "play" button is hit and when users move the slider slowly in the forward direction.

A second type of animation occurs when a new post appears and Ripples needs to update the view. In this case, the rendering of the new tree or forest is done in an offscreen image, which is then smoothly blended on top of the existing image. The shifts of layout caused by the insertion of a new node helps call attention to the change, but for large numbers of shares the new node isn't always obvious. To address this problem, we added a short animation of expanding circles (like water ripples) around the new node.

4. PATTERNS OF INFORMATION FLOW

We believe the Ripples visualization brings to light some interesting patterns of social sharing. Both for their intrinsic interest, and because they illustrate how the visualization can illuminate this area of research, we describe them in more detail below.

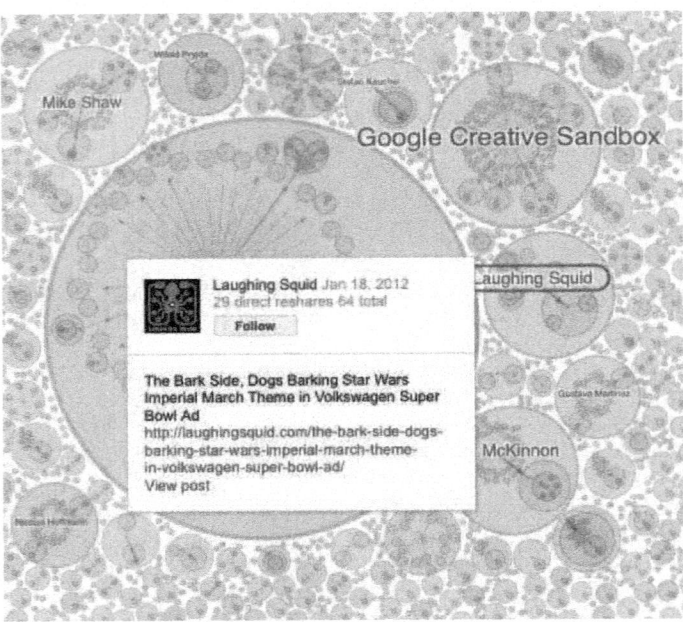

Figure 5: Hovercard showing details of a user's post and a "Follow" button, which may be used to follow the highlighted user directly from the visualization.

4.1 Broad but shallow patterns

A common feature of social networks is the presence of "celebrities," users who have many followers, and whose posts can be highly influential. These celebrities can of course be Hollywood stars, but can also be well known in a particular field, or represent prominent businesses or media outlets. We often observed large share trees when celebrities posted. Yet these trees were notably shallow, with few long reshare chains. Figure 6 (right) shows an example, where Selena Gomez (the well-known teen actress and singer) posted a Valentine's Day message. Many followers shared it, but the spreading rapidly faded out.

We observed this pattern many times, and not just with popular-culture celebrities. Similar effects occur with several technology pundits. An interesting area for future research would be to investigate the significance of these shallow sharing patterns. Are they due to the fact that almost everyone interested in the original post will likely read it at the source? Or perhaps fans overestimate the actual interest of the post when they reshare it?

4.2 Distributed shallow posting

Some URLs seemed to show highly distributed, shallow sharing. That is, there were many initiators of reshare trees, none of which dominate the graph. For example, the image in Figure 6, left, shows the reshare graph for a YouTube video (a viral hit in which a man shoots a gun at his daughter's laptop in a bid to teach her online etiquette). The origin of such evenly distributed sharing would be an interesting subject for future research. One possibility is that no "celebrity" wanted to endorse the video's message. Another possibility is that a celebrity shared the video on another social network or in the mainstream media, and that this pattern reflects the same dynamics as the celebrity pattern of 4.1, but with the celebrity invisible.

4.3 Heterogeneous sharing

Of course, not all posts rely on celebrities to spread. Figure 7, left, shows the Ripples for a classic "viral" YouTube video ("Dollar Shave Club – Our Blades are F**king Great"). The first image shows the full forest of shares, which includes more intricate reshare patterns in bigger circles. Zooming in on the circle indicated by the red arrow (Figure 7, right) reveals further intricate sharing, culminating in a chain that is eight people deep.

This network combines multiple types of sharing. In addition to deep chains, the forest contains many small, shallow share trees. There are also a few people who were very widely reshared; several of these are celebrities within the Google+ network. One might speculate that this heterogeneous collection indicates content that has an unusually broad appeal. Indeed, the Dollar Shave Club video received over three million views, and its rapid spread became the subject of articles in Time Magazine, BusinessWeek, and the Los Angeles Times. An interesting question for future research would be to see if a high level of heterogeneity, detected early after an initial post, could predict future "viral" spread of the post.

Another example of heterogeneous sharing comes from the Ripple of a petition to the White House requiring free access to taxpayer-funded research. The petition URL received around 500 public shares on Google+ (Figure 8), including posts from a number of influential people. As a result the Ripple contains several broad and deep sharing circles. For instance, the Open Science Federation was a strong influencer, as was Tim O'Reilly, a well-known publisher. Separately, writers and scholars—American, Danish and Australian—started their own individual threads. The Ripples visualization shows the diversity of these communities.

An interesting temporal pattern, possibly a reflection of this diversity, is there is no one overwhelming "spike" in the graph of shares over time. Whereas celebrity posts tend to see an initial spike and rapidly fizzle out (e.g. Figure 6, right), here the activity shows multiple peaks over time.

5. REACTIONS TO RIPPLES

A natural way to gauge the efficacy of Ripples was to study reactions in its native environment, the online world. In particular, we wished to investigate two general questions. First, what is the range of usage of Ripples? That is, can we begin to catalogue different ways—common or not—that users have engaged with the visualization in the real world? Second, is there any particular set of people that consistently derives utility from Ripples?

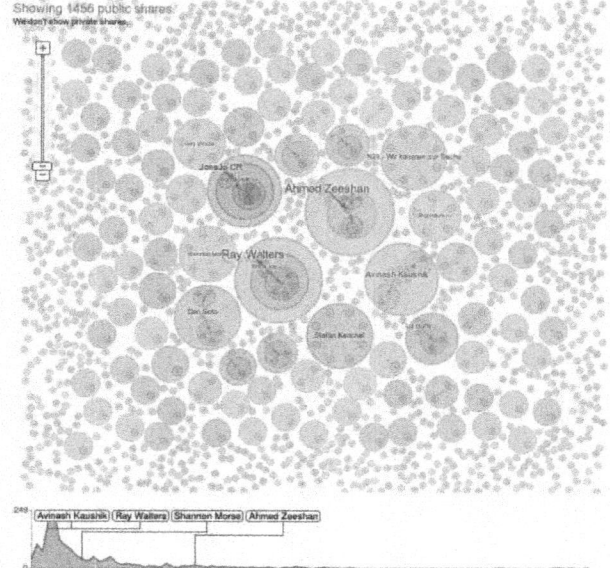
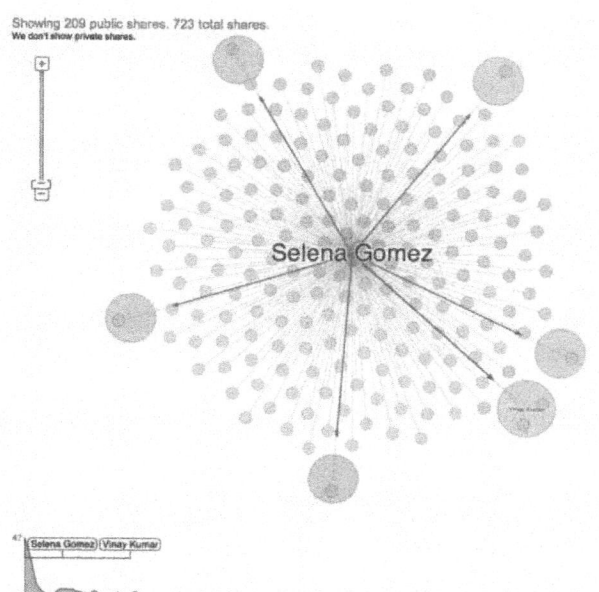

Figure 6. Left: Broad "forest" with deep sharing trees. Right: Celebrity pattern, where sharing action is broad and shallow.

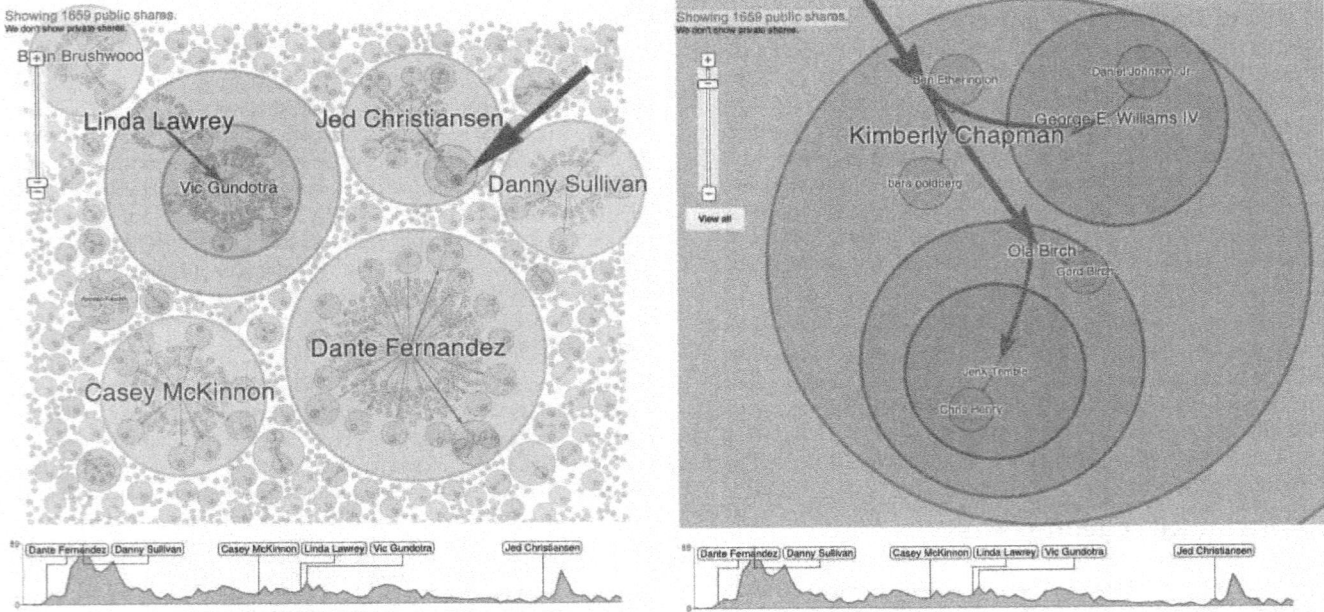

Figure 7. Left: complex share forest of a classic "viral" YouTube video ("Dollar Shave Club – Our Blades are F**king Great"). Right: zooming in on the circle indicated by the red arrow reveals a deep branching structure.

5.1 Data collection

We collected two different samples of data on user reactions, one related to immediate post-launch commentary, and the other looking at later reactions. As one might expect, waves of reactions followed the initial launch of Ripples, as well as the introduction of new features. (Days after the V2 launch, for example, new tweets about Ripples were arriving at the rate of once every 10 seconds.) During the two post-launch periods we looked at as many Ripples-related blogs, articles, and social network posts as we could—sampling on an ad hoc basis—and noted the different ways people reacted to and used Ripples. We call this set of data the "Launch Sample."

These immediate reactions provided useful information on the range of usage scenarios, but they are obviously susceptible to novelty effects and do not provide evidence that the visualization provided sustained utility. To investigate further, a year after the Ripples launch we collected a second sample by performing a Google search for "google plus ripples" and examining the first 100 resulting links. Of these, 36 led to web pages or social media posts that were written in English and provided detailed descriptions of Ripples usage (rather than, for example, simply a link or quote from another site). Within this subset, 17 were written more than a month after the launch of a new feature. We call this subset the "Year Sample."

These online reactions provide an initial probe into how people interact with Ripples in real-world situations. There are, of course, many possible sources of error. To name a few, people who post online are likely to have unusually extreme views; in some situations, people may be more likely to post positive opinions than negative ones. (Then again, online users are traditionally not shy about criticizing products they do not like.) There may also be important use cases and opinions that do not make it online. Nonetheless, the broad themes we uncovered seem like a first step toward understanding the effects of Ripples, and may be a useful guide for future studies of the system.

Usage Scenarios in the Launch Sample

As one would expect, after the initial launch of Ripples there was a wave of reaction on Google+ itself. Comments on Twitter, for instance, were generally positive or interested, ranging from *Google, I'm so glad we are friends. You make such awesome*

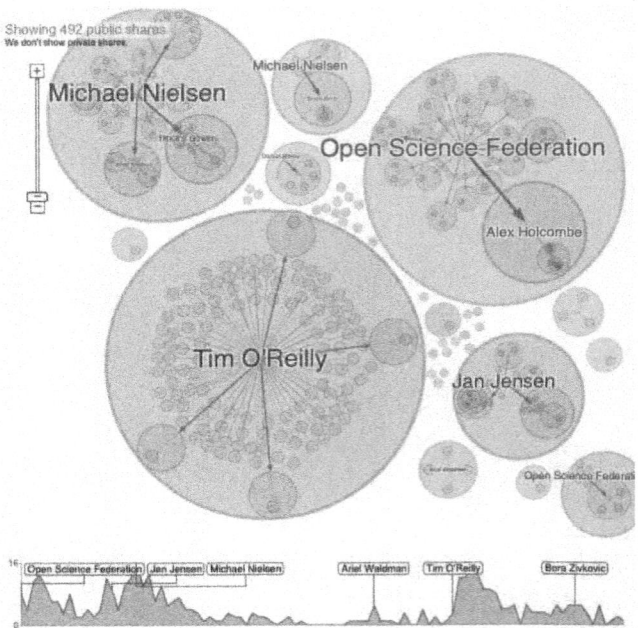

Figure 8. Ripple of a petition to the White House requiring free access to taxpayer-funded research.

"*tools for data scientists*" to "*Google+ Ripples are slicker than snot*". We saw people use the system itself to understand and play with the new feature. For example, several groups of people competed to form the largest share trees. Eventually one Ripple created purely for this purpose grew to more than 4,000 reshares. This playful activity, which as a by-product served to introduce many people to the tool, is reminiscent of some of the games played by users of the Many Eyes system [21].

Users also speculated about the ultimate utility of Ripples. Here the reaction was mixed. A good example is the set of comments in a post from Guy Kawasaki, which asked, "*Other than being interesting, are you finding Ripples actionable?*" Some answers were negative ("*No*" and "*they are neat to look at but I haven't found what they are useful for.*") At the other end of the spectrum, one person said, "*absolutely actionable*," with another providing details: "*definitely actionable… I went to a profile of someone of influence in my space, checked out a popular post (one that was public), checked the Rippled [sic] and I was able to see who shared and re-shared (a/k/a the "ripple") and circled up the "influential" people down the stream.*"

Social media reactions to the launch of Ripples were not confined to Google+. A significant amount of commentary came on Twitter, as well as on blogs. Again, we saw broadly positive reactions, such as "*AMAZEBALLS*" and "*Beautiful. And it just works.*" Several tweets also gave opinions about potential usage, by end users seeking to understand their online world ("*Now I get to be the social webthrologist and peek at the webs we weave*") and by people who analyze social media professionally ("*They've given brands a real-time analytic tool to see how users engage with their content.*") A few users did express confusion with the interface, e.g.,: "*I'm not going to lie, it took me a while to get my head around Google+ Ripples*"

In some cases, people used Ripples to find new individuals to follow. One user, whose post saw over five thousand shares, pointed out that "*you can actually use Ripples to better your experience on Google+ by finding the 'like minded' users who will enhance your engagement.*" Another person used Ripples to "*return favors*" by thanking others for sharing their content. As one blogger put it: "*Should you be so fortunate as to have one of your Google+ posts be reshared enough for it to generate a Ripple, pay attention to the list of people who have publicly shared it. Take a moment to click the "view post" link after each one and leave a brief "Thanks for re-sharing this!" comment…*"

Overall, we saw three main themes in the Launch Sample of reactions. First, "coolness": Many posts described Ripples as cool or innovative. A second reaction—occasionally from the same people—was skepticism about the utility of the visualization. A third consistent theme, utility, usually came from people who identified as professionals in the field of social media marketing; they focused less on "coolness" and aesthetics, and much more on the system's direct practical impact on their work.

5.2 Social Media Analytics: A Common Use Case

Subsequent online reactions provided evidence that Ripples found serious usage in the community of people who analyze social media as part of their business practice. The Year Sample was overwhelmingly made up of posts relating to business uses of Ripples. Of the 17 posts that were made more than a month after launch, 15 described business use cases, all in a positive light. For example, several months after launch, a Guardian article called Ripples "*a stunning visual representation of who within your connections are the most influential, allowing you to reach out to those contacts with targeted messaging.*" [23]. A separate article [4] illustrated a complex reaction to the visualization's aesthetics: "*The technology looks fancy, but it can be quite practical for those really looking to analyze their Google+ presence.*" Interestingly, in this article the "fanciness" of the aesthetics was perceived as a potential negative.

The online reactions cited above give a general sense of excitement over the potential for Ripples as an analysis tool, but how was it actually used in practice? While much analysis happens out of the public eye, social media marketers—perhaps not surprisingly—sometimes work in public as well. To give a sense of how Ripples is used, we describe one blog entry in detail, Tim Moore Online [13]. Moore, according to the blog, decided to "*run a test*" whose "*purpose was simple: To compare the engagement levels by users on Google+ and Facebook.*"

Moore posted the same item to both Google+ and Facebook. He began by looking at engagement metrics, but then to get more detail on how his Google+ post spread, he looked at several views of a Ripples diagram. In each, he annotated his findings. Typical statements were "*Notice Sandra Parlow, Arleen Boyd, Jed Kim and CathiBea Stevenson stand out as the key amplifiers…*" and "*Drilling deeper, you'll see Sandra Parlow as the key amplifier, with 30,108 who have her in circles.*"

The visualization of clear utility to this analyst; as he put it, "*Using Google+ Ripples, was helpful in analyzing 'how' the public posts migrate through the channel*". In addition, the images were a key part of his narrative explaining his results.

5.3 Summary of reactions

Based on the public reaction, it seems that there are two sets of users who express interest in Ripples. First, in the immediate post-launch periods, a highly visible set of people seemed to appreciate the visualization on the basis of aesthetics and novelty. A second more focused group is made of people who routinely analyze social media, typically for purposes of marketing and publicity. Within this group, we saw strong public enthusiasm, along with explanations (blog posts, YouTube videos, etc.) of how they used the system.

Encouragingly for the visualization technique itself, we did not uncover many comments complaining about understanding the diagrams. We saw discussion about the utility of the system, but few negative comments focused on the legibility of the diagrams themselves. Of course, this result could be biased by the self-selected nature of the people who wrote about Ripples; an interesting area for future work would be to verify the legibility of Ripples in a more controlled setting.

6. CONCLUSION AND FUTURE WORK

Google+ Ripples is a visualization of information flow on a social network. Unlike other systems with similar goals, Ripples is a native visualization—that is, it exists as part of the system it visualizes, so that users can access it immediately and seamlessly.

In addition to this unusual position in the user experience, Ripples illustrates a new visualization technique, a hybrid of a circular treemap and a traditional node-and-link tree diagram. This "balloon treemap" makes efficient use of space, while providing an easily understandable metaphor for the diffusion of information.

User reaction to the visualization has been generally positive, with a strong reaction on social media sites. We have seen users invest significant effort in the tool, making many dozens of videos showing it in use, and writing detailed blog entries describing how analysts can gain benefits from it.

We have also seen that the tool has uncovered interesting patterns of information flow. Indeed, one important area for future work would be to use this new visualization technique, likely in conjunction with statistical analysis, to create models for information flow. In particular, it would be good to add quantitative analysis to our informal observations of different patterns. It is possible that these patterns may show how share tree topology can help predict virality of a post, or help classify content.

There is also room for additional research on the visualization technique. A significant amount of work and design went into creating a visualization technique that would scale to large share meanwhile, smaller share trees were sufficiently legible.

Nonetheless, for relatively small trees (say, under 20 shares) the visualization doesn't seem optimal. Indeed, for these situations some of our early designs, which showed very simple traditional tree structures, probably would have been clearer and more pleasing. One could imagine setting a threshold size, below which the simpler visualization is shown, but this could be confusing to users. It would be interesting to develop techniques that would "scale down" smoothly—that is, that would allow the visualization to vary seamlessly between the circular treemap view at large scale, and a traditional tree view at a small one.

Creating a native visualization involves a significant engineering effort. Although there is an obvious advantage in having direct access to data, integrating with an existing system adds a huge layer of complexity to a visualization project. Nonetheless, our experience suggests that creating a native visualization is worthwhile, and that users will welcome even an elaborate visualization if it appears in a familiar, convenient context. Our hope is that in other systems visualization can make a move from an "add-on" to an intrinsic part of the system.

7. ACKNOWLEDGMENTS

Many people contributed to the development of Ripples. Rick Borovoy led product management, along with Julie Farago. Jonathan Terleski provided critical design advice. Bill Strathearn provided technical assistance along with early inspiration. Marshall Gillson created the live version of Ripples. The visualization's smooth transitions owe much to Keith Ito. Alfred Spector's leadership was essential to the project. Many others on the Google+ engineering team helped bring the technology to launch.

8. REFERENCES

[1] B. Bederson and J. Hollan, 1994. Pad++: a zooming graphical interface for exploring alternate interface physics. UIST 1994.

[2] R. Boardman, 2000. "Bubble Trees: The Visualization of Hierarchical Information Structures". Proceedings of CHI 2000.

[3] M. Bostock, V. Ogievetsky, J. Heer, 2011. D3: Data-Driven Documents. IEEE VisWeek 2011.

[4] A. DiSilvestro, 2012. "google+ Ripples Explained," Search Engine Journal. http://www.searchenginejournal.com/google-ripples-explained/48275/ Downloaded Nov. 11, 2012.

[5] J. Donath, K. Karahalios, F. Viégas, 2002. Visualizing Conversation. Hawaii International Conference on Systems Science.

[6] K. Etemad, S. Carpendale, 2009. Shamsehtrees: Providing hierarchical context for nodes of interest. Proceedings of Bridges 2009, 293-300.

[7] Facebook Friend Wheel. http://thomas-fletcher.com/friendwheel/

[8] I. Herman, G. Melancon, M. S. Marshall 2000. "Graph visualization and navigation in information visualization: A survey." IEEE TVCG Jan-Mar. 2000.

[9] Kleiberg, E., van de Wetering, H., J. van Wijk, J., 2001. "Botanical Visualization of Huge Hierarchies," IEEE InfoVis '01.

[10] J. Leskovec, L. Backstrom, J. Kleinberg. Meme-tracking and the dynamics of the news cycle. Proc. 15th ACM SIGKDD Intl. Conf. on Knowledge Discovery and Data Mining, 2009.

[11] J. Thorp and M. Hansen, 2011. Cascade. As described by Suzanne Labarre, "Infographic of the Day: 3D Model Unlocks Secrets of the Twitterverse", Fast Company Online. http://www.fastcodesign.com/1663694/infographic-of-the-day-3-d-model-unlocks-secrets-of-twitterverse-video

[12] A. Moore, 1991. "An introductory tutorial on kd-trees," tech. report Technical Report No. 209, Computer Laboratory, University of Cambridge.

[13] T. Moore. Tim Moore Online, downloaded Feb. 26, 2012. http://timmooreonline.blogspot.com/2012/01/case-study-google-vs-facebook.html

[14] P. Neumann, S. Carpendale, A. Agarawala. 2006 "Phyllotrees: Phyllotactic patterns for tree layout." EUROVIS-Eurographics/IEEE VGTC Symposium on Visualization, 59-66

[15] Q. Nguyen and M. Huang, 2005. "EncCon: an approach to constructing interactive visualization of large hierarchical data," Information Visualization 2005 4, pp. 1-21.

[16] SocialFlow, 2011. http://socialflow.com

[17] B. Shneiderman, M. Wattenberg 2001. "Ordered Treemap Layouts" IEEE Infovis 2001.

[18] A. Vande Moore (downloaded 2012) Information Aesthetics Blog. http://infosthetics.com/

[19] F. Viégas,. M. Wattenberg, J. Feinberg, 2009. "Participatory Visualization with Wordle". IEEE Infovis, 2009.

[20] F. Viégas,. M. Wattenberg, F. van Ham, J. Kriss, M. McKeon, 2007. "Many Eyes: A Site for Visualization at Internet Scale". IEEE Infovis, 2007.

[21] F. Viégas, M. Wattenberg, M. McKeon, F. van Ham, J. Kriss, 2008. "Harry Potter and the Meat-Filled Freezer: A Case Study of Spontaneous Usage of Visualization Tools." Hawaii Int'l Conf. Sys. Sci. (HICSS), 2008.

[22] YouTube Insights. http://www.youtube.com/t/advertising_insight

[23] http://www.guardian.co.uk/media-network/media-network-blog/2012/feb/15/advantages-google-digital-marketing?newsfeed=true

[24] W. Wang, H. Wang, G. Dai, H. Wang, 2006. "Visualization of Large Hierarchical Data by Circle Packing," Proceeding of CHI 2006.

[25] M. Wattenberg, 2005. "A Note on Space-Filling Visualizations and Space-Filling Curves". IEEE InfoVis 2005.

[26] K. Wetzel. "pebbles." http://lip.sourceforge.net/ctreemap.html

[27] R. Xiong and E. Brittain, 1999. LiveWeb: Visualizing live user activities on the Web SIGGRAPH.

From Cookies to Cooks: Insights on Dietary Patterns via Analysis of Web Usage Logs

Robert West[*]
Stanford University
Stanford, California
west@cs.stanford.edu

Ryen W. White
Microsoft Research
Redmond, Washington
ryenw@microsoft.com

Eric Horvitz
Microsoft Research
Redmond, Washington
horvitz@microsoft.com

ABSTRACT

Nutrition is a key factor in people's overall health. Hence, understanding the nature and dynamics of population-wide dietary preferences over time and space can be valuable in public health. To date, studies have leveraged small samples of participants via food intake logs or treatment data. We propose a complementary source of population data on nutrition obtained via Web logs. Our main contribution is a spatiotemporal analysis of population-wide dietary preferences through the lens of logs gathered by a widely distributed Web-browser add-on, using the access volume of recipes that users seek via search as a proxy for actual food consumption. We discover that variation in dietary preferences as expressed via recipe access has two main periodic components, one yearly and the other weekly, and that there exist characteristic regional differences in terms of diet within the United States. In a second study, we identify users who show evidence of having made an acute decision to lose weight. We characterize the shifts in interests that they express in their search queries and focus on changes in their recipe queries in particular. Last, we correlate nutritional time series obtained from recipe queries with time-aligned data on hospital admissions, aimed at understanding how behavioral data captured in Web logs might be harnessed to identify potential relationships between diet and acute health problems. In this preliminary study, we focus on patterns of sodium identified in recipes over time and patterns of admission for congestive heart failure, a chronic illness that can be exacerbated by increases in sodium intake.

Categories and Subject Descriptors: H.2.8 [**Database management**]: Database applications—*Data mining*.
General Terms: Experimentation, Human Factors.
Keywords: log/behavioral analysis, public health, nutrition.

1. INTRODUCTION

Nutrition is a central factor in health and well-being, and poor diets are a major public health concern. The composition of diet has been linked to the risk of acquiring numerous diseases, including cardiovascular disease and diabetes. The economic cost associated with the risks associated with obesity alone is estimated to be $270 billion per year [3].

Addressing the links between nutrition and wellness requires answering challenging questions, such as, *What effects do ingested foods have on health?* Once a causal link is discovered, dangerous foods can be banned or restricted. However, the effectiveness of knowledge about links between diet and health hinges on conscious dietary choices made by informed people. Given the results of research studies, public-health agencies can work to raise this kind of awareness of healthy practices through public-health campaigns. The success of a campaign is vastly increased when it can be tailored to a specific target group [11], but singling out subpopulations particularly at risk is a difficult task in itself, as it requires the answer to yet another hard question: *Who eats what, when, and where?*

Both questions are typically addressed in the fields of medicine, nutritional science, and public health. While much progress has been made, studies of nutrition in the medical community have relied mostly on relatively small cohorts, and often require tedious logging of meals into diaries [10] or focus on specific user groups such as dialysis patients [8].

We study the feasibility of collecting nutritional data from the logging of anonymous user data on the Web. This rich set of data sources provides a means for inferring facts about people and the world on a larger, yet less accurate, scale: logs of search engine use have been studied to identify temporal trends [33, 22] and geographic variations [5], as well as to characterize and predict real-world medical phenomena [24, 13, 37].

We believe that spatiotemporal data mined from Web usage logs can provide signals for large-scale studies in nutrition and public health, and thus contribute to a better understanding of the relationship between nutrition and health, and about dietary patterns within different populations. We pursue three different studies to highlight directions for examining nutrition in populations via the lens of Web usage logs.

First, and most central to this paper, we consider the search and access of recipes over time and space. Previous research [2] analyzed the composition of recipes, providing data on the preparation of dishes, but not on their consumption. We seek connections between large-scale information access behaviors and potential outcomes in the world by aligning shifts in the popularity of meals, using recipes accessed as a proxy for population-wide dietary preferences. We identify and explore recipes that are accessed on the Web. Of course, recipes accessed online cannot be assumed to have been prepared as meals and then ingested. Recipe accesses observed in logs can only provide clues about nutritional interests and consumption patterns at particular times and places. Even when recipes are executed, the resulting meals will typically only represent a portion of a total diet, and we do not understand the background nutritional patterns that are complemented by the pursuit of meals cooked from downloaded recipes. However, we believe that patterns and dynamics of downloading recipes by location and time can suggest nutritional preferences and overall diet.

---

[*]Research done during an internship at Microsoft Research.

Analysis of the volume of recipe downloading at various levels of granularity in terms of nutrients (such as calorie content), as well as ingredients, can reveal systematic population-level variations. We find that the observed variations are predominantly periodic (weekly and annual), but also include nutritional shifts around major holidays. Further, we address the *where* in the above question by exploring regional dietary differences across the United States.

In a second study, we identify users who show evidence of having made a recent commitment to shift their dietary behavior with the goal of reducing their weight. Previous work on dietary change has demonstrated the challenges associated with attempts to alter consumption habits [28, 38]. Via the logs, we identify users who have expressed a strong interest in purchasing a self-help guide on losing weight. Considering this evidence as a landmark representing a commitment to change behavior, we characterize shifts in interests preceding and following the purchase. We examine changes in these users' search queries, with a focus on the changes they make in their recipe queries, and show evidence of regressions to previous dietary habits after only a few weeks.

In a third analysis, we study the potential influence of shifts in diet on acute medical outcomes. Specifically, we explore quantities of sodium in downloaded recipes and compare the time series of recipes with boosts in sodium content with time series of hospital admissions for congestive heart failure (CHF), a costly and dangerous chronic illness that is especially prevalent among the elderly [34]. Patients with CHF must watch their sodium intake carefully. One or more salty meals can kick off an exacerbation, where osmotic shifts lead to water retention and then to pulmonary congestion, necessitating emergency medical treatment. In a preliminary study, we align the admission logs of patients arriving at the emergency department (ED) at a major U.S. hospital with a chief complaint of exacerbation of CHF, demonstrating a strong temporal relationship between the sodium content of recipes and the admissions to the ED with a chief complaint linked to CHF.

Overall, these studies demonstrate the potential value of large-scale log analysis for population-wide nutrition analysis and monitoring. This could have a range of applications from assisting with the timing and location of public-health awareness campaigns, guiding dietary interventions at the level of individual users, and forecasting future health-care utilization. We shall present each of the three case studies in detail and discuss the broader implications of our findings. We first review related work in Section 2. Then, we describe our methodology and data in Section 3, before discussing the three analyses summarized above (Sections 4–7). Finally, we discuss implications, limitations, and potential extensions of our work in Section 8, concluding in Section 9.

2. RELATED WORK

Relevant research includes efforts on (1) mining search logs for insights and associations, (2) studying temporal trends and periodicities in logs, (3) examining seasonal variations in clinical and laboratory variables, (4) studying patterns in food creation and consumption, and (5) understanding changing consumption habits, especially around weight loss. We review each of these areas.

Studies with search logs can provide valuable insights on associations between concepts [23], and previously unknown evidence of associations between nutritional deficiencies and medical conditions can be mined from the medical literature [31, 32]. Researchers have studied trends over short periods of time to learn about the behavior of the querying population at large [4], or clustered terms by temporal frequency to understand daily or weekly variations [9]. Temporal trends and periodicities in longer-term query volume have been leveraged in approaches that aggregate

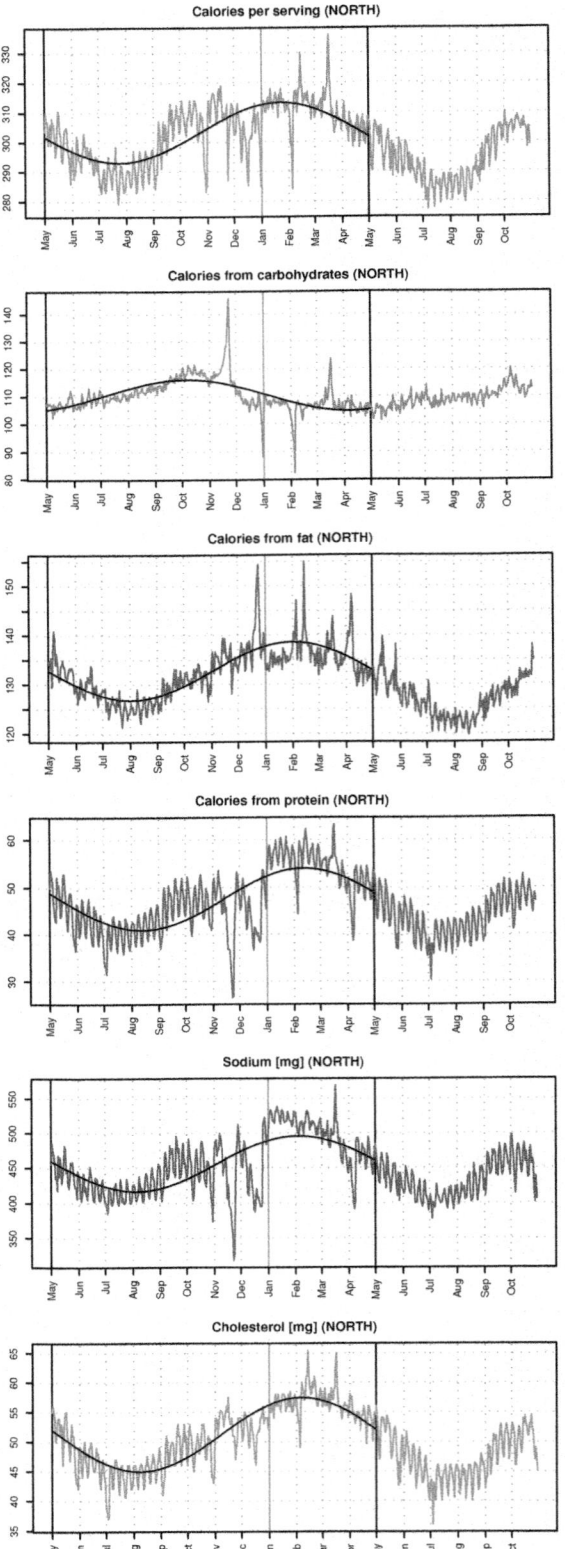

Figure 1: Nutritional contents over the year for several countries in the Northern Hemisphere (USA, Canada, UK, Ireland).

data at the user [24] or the population level [1]. Vlachos et al. [33] proposed methods for discovering semantically similar queries by identifying queries with similar demand patterns over time. More recently, Radinsky et al. [22] predict time-varying user behavior using smoothing and trends and explore other dynamics of Web behaviors, such as the detection of periodicities and surprises. Particularly relevant here is research on the prediction of disease epidemics using logs; e.g., Ginsberg et al. [13] used query logs as a form of surveillance for early detection of influenza. Known seasonal variations in influenza outbreaks also visible in the search logs play an important part in their predictions.

The medical community has a particular interest in studying seasonal variations in a variety of clinical and laboratory variables, including nutrient information such as protein intake and sodium levels. However, the findings pertaining to nutrient intake are inconsistent. Much of the literature suggests that daily total caloric intake does not vary significantly by season [14, 29, 27]. A few studies have provided a more detailed view of the diet, suggesting that the intake of proteins [14, 10] and carbohydrates [14] is also constant throughout the year. Others have proposed that dietary intake of total calories, carbohydrates [10], and fat varies seasonally [10, 27]. For example, de Castro [10] shows that carbohydrate levels are typically higher in the fall and Shahar et al. [27] show that fat, cholesterol, and sodium are higher in winter. Cheung et al. [8] found clear seasonal variations in pre-dialysis blood urea nitrogen levels that could be attributed to variations in protein intake. These studies focus on intake or treatment data, particular cohorts (e.g., dialysis patients, adolescents), and consider fairly small samples of users (of hundreds or low thousands of patients). Search logs provide a view on nutrition through the potentially noisy keyhole of recipe accesses. However, they provide a population-wide lens on dietary interests and can serve as evidence for nutrient intake.

Current food consumption patterns are influenced by a range of factors including an evolved preference for sugar and fat to palatability, nutritional value, culture, ease of production, and climate [25, 12, 18]. Factors such as location and the price of locally produced foods can also affect nutrient intake [20]. Others have mined recipe data from sites such as Allrecipes.com to better understand culinary practice; Ahn et al. [2] introduced the 'flavor network,' capturing the flavor compounds shared by culinary ingredients. This focuses on the creation of dishes (ingredient pairs in recipes) rather than estimating their consumption, something that we believe is possible via logs. Many studies have explored how people attempt to change their consumption habits as part of weight-loss programs [17, 28]. Psychological models, such as the transtheoretical model of change [21], can generalize to dieting [38], and in this realm, too, log-based methods are emerging for analyzing behavior [26].

We extend previous work in several ways. First, rather than studying nutrient intake via intake logs or medical records, which are limited in scope and scale, we propose a complementary method based on log analysis. This enables a new means of probing the nutrition of large and heterogeneous populations. Such large-scale analysis promises to provide more general insights about people's health and well-being than tracking and forecasting nutrition in patients with specific diseases. Also, studying nutrient intake at a variety of locations is costly, whilst geolocation information is readily available in logs, enabling analyses of a broader set of locations at different granularities. Second, we mine logs of recipe accesses to estimate food consumption, rather than crawling recipes only, which characterize content used in the creation of food. In one of our studies, we work to identify users exhibiting evidence of seeking to lose weight and characterize their query dynamics over time.

We believe that such an analysis can help us to better understand people's attempts to change their dietary habits.

3. METHODOLOGY

Web usage logs. The primary source of data for this study is a proprietary data set consisting of the anonymized logs of URLs visited by users who consented to provide interaction data through a widely distributed Web browser add-on provided by Bing search. The data set was gathered over an 18-month period from May 2011 through October 2012 and consists of billions of page views from both Web search (Google, Bing, Yahoo!, etc.) and general browsing episodes, represented as tuples including a unique user identifier, a timestamp for each page view, and the URL of the page visited. We excluded intranet and secure (HTTPS) page visits at the source. Further, we do not consider users' IP addresses but only geographic location information derived from them (city and state, plus latitude and longitude). All log entries resolving to the same town or city were assigned the same latitude and longitude. We leverage this rich behavioral data set in combination with three additional sources of information available on the Web: (1) online recipes with nutritional information, (2) information about diet and weight-loss books that users add to their online shopping carts, and (3) patient admission data from a large U.S. hospital. We now describe in more detail how we leverage each of these data sources.

Online recipes for approximating food popularity. Our goal is to infer from Web usage logs the foods that people ingest. The most basic idea would be to assemble a list of food words and concentrate on queries containing these words. This method, however, has three serious shortcomings. First, it has low precision: for instance, RICE might refer to the grain or the Texan university. Second, this simple approach also suffers from low recall, as it is hard to compile a comprehensive list of food terms. Third, we do not know how food words appearing in queries and content are linked to food ingested by users who query and browse.

We argue that users' typical diet is much more closely reflected in the online recipes they visit. To get an idea whether this intuition is correct, we engaged a random sample of employees at Microsoft to complete a survey. Ninety-nine respondents had recently consulted an online recipe, of whom 68% said they used online recipes at least once a month. Although it is difficult to estimate how well typical recipe users are represented by our sample, the results seem to justify recipe usage as a proxy for diet. Respondents were supposed to recall the last time they had cooked a meal according to an online recipe. Asked if this dish represented what they typically ate, 75% answered yes, and 81% said they had the specific dish in mind when searching for recipes. Further, 77% of users cooked the entire meal or at least the main dish according to the recipe (as opposed to a side dish, desert, etc.). Given these numbers, we concluded that recipe lookups are a good approximation of dietary preferences, at least for users of online recipes (but see Section 8 for a discussion of potential error sources).

Next, there are several options for how to measure recipe popularity. One option is to count the number of clicks a recipe receives across all browse paths. This has the advantage of high recall. Alternatively, we might count only the clicks received by a recipe when displayed on a search engine result page; this results in higher precision, as it does not count clicks received from users casually browsing without the intention of cooking the dish. To find the better method, we asked survey participants how they had found their last recipe, with the result that 76% of respondents clicked directly from a search result page, while only 24% went through browsing a recipe site. This implies that concentrating on the event where a user clicks a recipe from a search result page also gives high recall, in addition to the higher precision, compared to including all clicks. We hence proceed by identifying search queries that result in a click to a recipe page and download a large sample of the recipe pages found this way (additional details available online [36]).

In addition to natural-language content such as ingredient lists, preparation instructions, and reviews, many online recipes contain numeric tables of nutritional information, reminiscent of the 'Nutrition Facts' labels required on most packaged food in many countries. While the text of recipe pages has much rich information that could be mined, these nutrition facts—easily extracted via regular expressions [36]—are concise numeric values and thus give us a direct quantitative handle on people's (approximate) food preferences, without the need for more sophisticated tools from natural-language processing. The set of *nutrients* listed in recipes is not identical across all pages, so we restrict ourselves to extracting six of the most common ones, listed in Table 1.

Nutrient	Unit
Total calories per serving	kcal
Calories from carbohydrates	kcal
Calories from fat	kcal
Calories from protein	kcal
Sodium	mg
Cholesterol	mg

Table 1: Nutrient information extracted from online recipes.

Every recipe can now be represented as a six-dimensional vector of real numbers, which makes it possible to find patterns in recipe use via tools from time series analysis. In particular, we aggregate recipes by day and investigate how the average nutritional content of recipes varies over the 18 months of browser log data analyzed.

Note that we only consider recipes that itemize nutrients *per serving*, which we consider the most principled way of controlling for portion size. We have not analyzed the potential systematic bias that this consideration may have introduced into the recipe data set.

For some analyses, we also consider the ingredients required by recipes. It is much more difficult to transform ingredient quantities to a common representation than it is for nutrients (e.g., How long is a piece of string licorice?), so we approximate recipe contents by 'bags of ingredients:' we extract the ingredient section from the HTML source and give each unique token the same weight.

Finally, we note that 70% of our survey respondents said they had not been considering nutritional facts when using their last online recipes, which we see as an advantage for the sake of analysis, as it means people eat what they would eat in any case, without being skewed by nutritional information.

Pursuit of books on diet and weight loss. We have described our attempt to approximate users' general diets with information about access of recipes. We also attempt to understand the dynamics of intention and access associated with indications that users have decided to change their diets. It is hard to recognize such commitment to change eating habits in browsing logs. One could look for queries involving phrases such as LOSING WEIGHT or HEALTHY EATING; or one could look for visits on certain highly specialized websites such as diet forums. However, neither of these necessarily imply a strong intention to lose weight; e.g., such behavior may be a manifestation of curiosity. Hence, we opt for a third alternative as a proxy for the intention to lose weight, one that requires considerably more commitment on users' behalf. We consider the situation where anonymized users add books from the category DIETS & WEIGHT LOSS to their Amazon shopping carts. We worked to identify such events in our browser logs via characteristic sequences of URL patterns and found that product categories could be obtained by resolving the product number contained in the URL. Although adding a book to the shopping cart does not automatically imply that the user went on to purchase the book, we take it as a strong indicator of a willingness to invest resources in pursuit of the goal of losing weight and/or living a healthier life. We attempt to gain insights into typical behaviors of people showing such a weight-loss intention by analyzing the relevant users' query histories in a window of 100 days each before and after they demonstrate interest in a weight-loss book. Additionally, we investigate the online recipes clicked by these users, to see if and how their dietary patterns change in response to their interest in losing weight.

Hospital-admission records. We use a third additional data set to explore potential relationships between diet and acute health problems. The data set was drawn from the emergency department of the Washington Hospital Center in Washington, D.C., and contains, for each day during the time span of our browser log sample, the number of patients admitted with a diagnosis related to congestive heart failure (CHF). Specifically, for a patient to be counted, the diagnosis must contain at least one of the following terms: CHF, VOLUME OVERLOAD, CONGESTIVE, HEART FAILURE. These counts also constitute a time series and can therefore be correlated with the nutritional time series extracted from recipe queries.

4. NUTRITIONAL TIME SERIES

We start our analysis by analyzing temporal patterns of nutritional variation, asking the question: How do the food preferences of the general population change as a function of time?

Recall from Section 3 that every recipe has a representation as a six-dimensional nutrient vector (cf. Table 1). From each of the six nutrients we obtain a time series as follows: for each day, consider all users who issued at least one recipe query that day; for each user, average the nutrient of interest over all recipes they clicked from a search result page that day; finally, average over all recipe users active that day to obtain the value of the nutrient that day (averages are medians, in order to mitigate the effect of outliers). This effectively gives all active users the same weight on a given day, regardless of how many recipes they clicked, which is important, as we are interested in the average over a population of people, not merely over a set of recipe clicks. The resulting time series are visualized in Fig. 1. We make three immediate observations:

1. There is a low-frequency period of about one year.
2. There is a high-frequency period of much less than a month.
3. Some days deviate heavily from the overall patterns.

Before we discuss each of these three components separately in the next subsections, we decompose the signals in a more principled way by using a standard tool from time series analysis, the discrete Fourier transform (DFT). In a nutshell, the DFT represents a time series as a weighted sum of sinusoidal basis functions of different frequencies. The larger the original signal's amplitude at a given frequency, the larger the weight of the respective sinusoidal will be. The output of a DFT can be visualized in a so-called *spectral-density plot*, which shows frequencies on the *x*-axis and the weights attributed to them on the *y*-axis.

To save space, we display the spectral density for only one specific nutrient (total calories per serving) in Fig. 2(a), but the outcome looks similar across the board. For ease of interpretation, we show wavelength (in days), rather than frequency, on the *x*-axis. Note that there are two clearly discernible peaks, one at 366 days and the other at 7 days. The first peak (366 days) confirms the visual observation that the dominant, low-frequency period is over

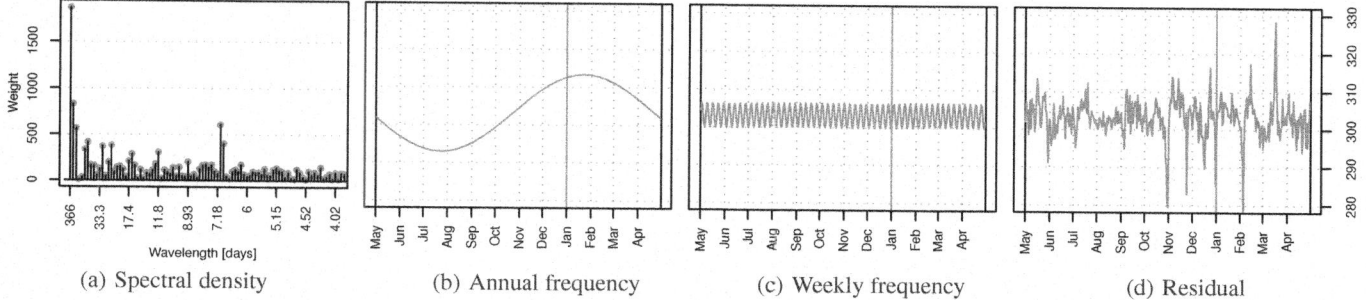

(a) Spectral density (b) Annual frequency (c) Weekly frequency (d) Residual

Figure 2: Result of a discrete Fourier transform (DFT) on the calorie time series (Fig. 1, top): (a) spectral density (shorter wavelengths get small weight and are thus not shown); (b–d) decomposition of the original signal into annual, weekly, and residual components.

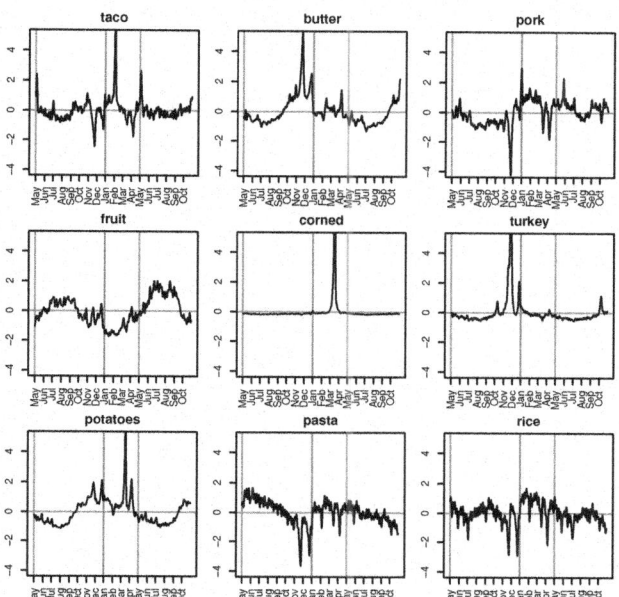

Figure 3: Prevalence of a select number of ingredients over the course of a year (displaying z-scores).

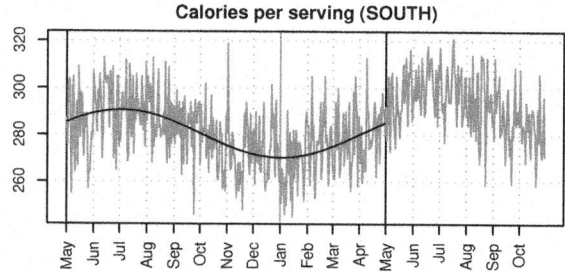

Figure 4: Calorie content over the year for countries in the Southern Hemisphere (Australia, New Zealand, South Africa).

4.1 Annual Period

We now discuss the observed effects in more detail. First, we turn our attention to the strong annual period. For emphasis, we have overlaid the nutrient time series in Fig. 1 with smoothed versions of the curves obtained by low-pass filtering the signal, i.e., by setting to zero all spectral components but the one of wavelength 366 days. These smoothed curves are the equivalents of Fig. 2(b) for each nutrient's time series.

The plot on top of Fig. 1 tells us that overall caloric intake is lowest in summer (July and August) and peaks in fall and winter. The difference among seasons is around 30 kcal per serving (between around 285 and 315), a rather clear ±5% around the annual mean of around 300 kcal. The remaining plots show that calories from protein and fat, as well as sodium and cholesterol, are in phase with total calories, while calories from carbohydrates are out of phase, with a maximum in fall and lower values in winter and spring.

It is interesting to view these findings in the light of some previous medical studies. For instance, Shahar et al. [27] showed (for 94 subjects) that fat, cholesterol, and sodium are typically higher in winter, and de Castro [10] found (for 315 subjects) that overall caloric intake (especially through carbohydrates) is higher in fall, results that are in line with our findings. (In addition to fall, caloric intake is high in winter, too, according to our log data.)

The detected seasonal variation raises the question of its causes. At least two hypotheses come to mind. First, the variation could be directly caused by factors external to the recipe site, such as variation of climatic conditions or availability of ingredients. Second, the effect could be caused (or at least amplified) by site-internal factors, such as different recipes being popular on the sites at different times. The first hypothesis could be directly checked by correlating the nutritional with climatological time series. However, we invoke a less direct argument: Note that Fig. 1 was produced based on

the course of exactly one year. The second peak (7 days) might have been somewhat less obvious from visually inspecting Fig. 1; it implies that the high-frequency period visible in most curves of Fig. 1 fits exactly into one week. We conclude that the nutritional composition of typical meals varies systematically both over the course of a year and over the course of a week.

In addition to these regularities, there are several outliers of large amplitude. To emphasize those, Fig. 2(b–d) breaks the signal for one specific nutrient (again total calories per serving) into three parts: the annual and weekly periods and the residual obtained by subtracting the dominant frequencies from the original signal.

A different, more faceted view is afforded by considering the change in prevalence of ingredients rather than nutrients. We define the value of an ingredient on a given day as the fraction of clicks that are on recipes containing the ingredient (regardless of quantity, cf. Section 3), again weighted such that all active users get the same weight each day. Fig. 3 plots these values for a select number of ingredients. The x-axis is the same as for the nutrient time series; to make different ingredients comparable, the y-axis shows z-scores rather than raw fractions, i.e., differences (in terms of number of standard deviations) from the annual mean of the ingredient.

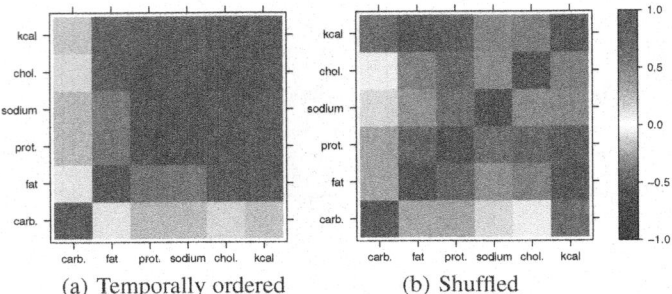

(a) Temporally ordered (b) Shuffled

Figure 5: **Two notions of nutrient correlation.**

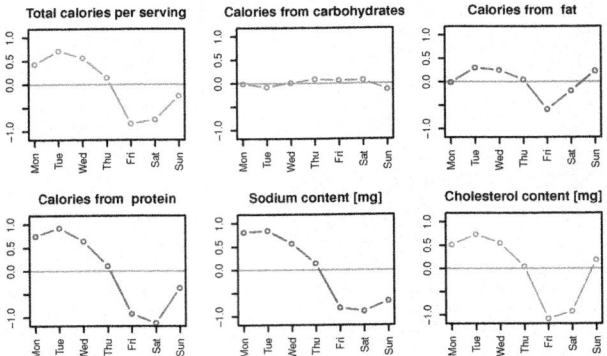

Figure 6: **Nutrients by day of week.** The y-axes show z-scores; standard errors are small and thus omitted.

data including clicks only from users in the Northern Hemisphere. As seasons in the Southern Hemisphere are the reverse of those in the North, we would expect to see a 180-degree phase shift if the nutrient variation is explained by climate. Fig. 4 exposes such a shift. Therefore, since both climatological and dietary patterns are flipped, while site content on the sites we consider (all North American) is presumably identical across hemispheres, we conclude that the observed nutritional periodicity is linked to changes in climate.

We also find it noteworthy that the average caloric intake per serving is significantly lower in the Southern than the Northern Hemisphere, at 285 vs. 300 kcal (a Welch two-sample t-test gives a 95% confidence interval of [14, 17] for the difference of means).

There is a striking overall correlation of all plots in Fig. 1, carbohydrates being the only exception. A simple explanation would be that dishes being rich in one nutrient are typically also rich in the others. For instance, one could fancy a dish such as corned beef, a type of salted, fatty meat or, in other words, sodium-, cholesterol-, and fat-laden protein. To test this hypothesis, we compute two notions of correlation. The first one formalizes the qualitative correlation observed in Fig. 1, and we refer to it as *temporal nutrient correlation:* here, each day constitutes a data point, and we compute Pearson's correlation coefficients for all 36 pairs of daily-nutrient-average vectors. The second notion is that of *shuffled nutrient correlation:* here, we first randomize the temporal order of recipe views (while still mapping all views the same user made the same day to the same shuffled position) before computing the equivalent of temporal nutrient correlation on this shuffled data set. If the 'corned-beef hypothesis' holds, i.e., if the strong correlation of different nutrients over the year is caused by their co-occurrence in the same dishes, then the correlation coefficient would be unaffected by a change in the temporal order of recipe views. However, Fig. 5 shows that this is not the case. While decent positive correlations are in fact to be expected even in a shuffled sequence, i.e., based on ingredient co-occurrence in recipes alone (indicated by the many red cells in Fig. 5(b)), most values are heavily amplified when considering temporal correlation instead, and correlations with carbohydrates are mostly inverted (Fig. 5(a)). Hence, the strongly synchronized time series for five of the six nutrients is not fully explained by mere co-occurrences of nutrients in recipes. Rather, separate dishes, each rich in certain nutrients, must additionally tend to be popular at the same times.

Finally, we take an ingredient- rather than a nutrient-centric perspective on annual dietary fluctuation. Many single ingredients also expose strong annual patterns, and we showcase but a select few in Fig. 3. For instance, fruit is most popular in summer and least in winter, whereas pork and butter follow a roughly opposite annual trend. Indeed, pork and butter are closely aligned with the calorie, fat, protein, sodium, and cholesterol curves of Fig. 1. While this may not be surprising, we want to point out that ingredient time series can in many other cases provide a more faceted view than the very broad nutrient time series. Consider, e.g., the curves for fruit, potatoes, pasta, and rice. While all these ingredients add mostly carbohydrates to dishes, none of them seem overwhelmingly aligned with the overall carbohydrate curve. And even comparing them to each other, we find rather different patterns. This suggests that the concept of ingredient time series adds real value, compared to the bare-bones nutrient time series, which often combine many ingredients of rather different characteristics.

4.2 Weekly Period

We saw that, apart from the annual periodicity, the next most dominant variation of the nutrient time series (Fig. 1) is weekly. In this section, we characterize in more detail how people's dietary preferences change over the course of a typical week, thus essentially zooming in on a typical seven-day period of Fig. 1.

To begin with, we note that online recipes are more frequently accessed on weekends than during the week, with Sundays having on average 18% more unique users than the average day during their respective weeks; the number is 7% for Saturdays. During the week, usage decreases steadily from Monday through Friday.

To characterize a typical week, we proceed as follows. Given a nutrient and a day of the year, compute the z-score of the nutrient on that day with respect to its week, i.e., measure the difference from the weekly mean in standard deviations (mean and standard deviation are defined such that each of the seven days in the target day's week gets the same weight). The rationale behind z-score normalization is to mitigate the effect of anomalous days (e.g., Thanksgiving is always a Thursday).

The emerging weekly 'templates' are displayed in Fig. 6. Maybe surprisingly, caloric intake per serving seems to be higher earlier on in the week (Monday through Thursday) than towards the end (Friday through Sunday). Viewed through this lens, carbohydrates seem to vary much less over the course of a week than the other nutrients, while fat exposes a characteristic dip on Fridays.

To better understand the basis of this weekly pattern, let us again concentrate on a number of representative ingredients and observe how they behave over the course of a typical week. The plots are shown in Fig. 7. In particular, this figure might provide an explanation of why total calories and calories from fat are so low on Fridays: low-fat produce such as lettuce and fruit peak, while fattier ingredients such as steak and pork plummet. This also shows that the carbohydrate pattern in Fig. 6 has to be viewed in a more faceted light: the flat curve seems to be caused by separate carbo-

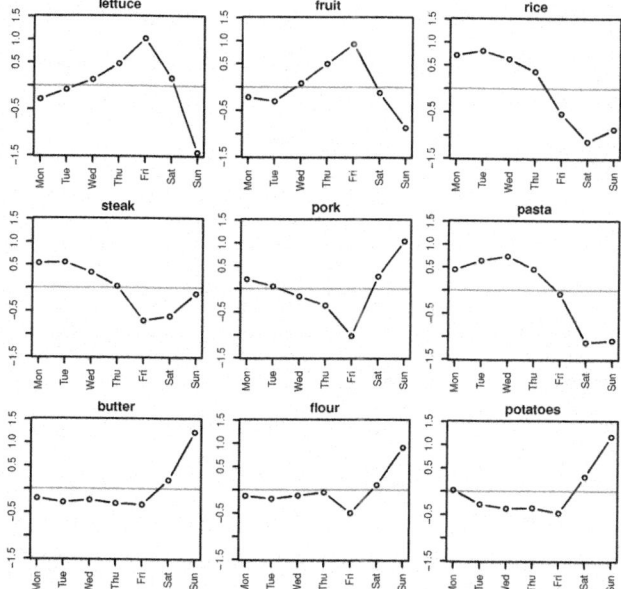

Figure 7: Prevalence of some ingredients by day of week. The y-axes show z-scores; standard errors are small and thus omitted.

hydrate carriers 'canceling out.' Consider, e.g., pasta and potatoes, both rich in carbohydrates but with opposite weekly trends.

4.3 Anomalous Days

The nutritional time series also show a number of sharp peaks and dips that cannot be explained based only on annual and weekly regularities. These are particularly easy to spot in a residual plot such as Fig. 2(d), which is obtained by filtering dominant frequencies from the original time series. At closer inspection, nearly all of the anomalies can be explained by external events of public interest. Here we list but a few, leaving the rest as food for thought to the reader. We point out, from left to right in Fig. 2(d), Memorial Day (5/30/11), Independence Day (7/4/11), Halloween (10/31/11), Super Bowl XLVI (2/5/12), St. Valentine's Day (2/14/12), and St. Patrick's Day (3/17/12).

In addition to such impulse-like anomalies, the annual rhythm is disrupted most in November and December, which contain the two big American feast days, Thanksgiving (11/24/11) and Christmas (12/25/11). While the other anomalies are mostly ephemeral, the holiday season seems to revolve around food for weeks on end.

We conjecture that, while the spikes observed around holidays are useful in helping us determine days with particular dietary customs, the spikes themselves are probably to be taken as qualitative pointers rather than quantitatively exact values corresponding to real consumption. For instance, cookie recipes are popular before Christmas, and while we can infer from this that cookies are more popular at that time than during the rest of the year, it does not imply that people eat predominantly baked goods in December. Conversely, while it is known that people ingest increased amounts of carbohydrates (in the form of alcoholic beverages) on certain days, such as New Year's Eve, we do not observe a corresponding spike for 12/31/11 in the carbohydrate plot of Fig. 1.

5. SPATIOTEMPORAL PATTERNS

Up until now, we have treated the nutritional data predominantly as a temporal signal. Only briefly did we consider geographical information, in Section 4.1, where we divided recipe queries according to their hemisphere of origin. But the log data has much finer spatial granularity, down to the city or town level (cf. Section 3). We now leverage this additional information in an analysis of dietary patterns across the United States.

We again consider nutritional time series such as in Fig. 1, but whereas that figure was based on all queries from the Northern Hemisphere, we now construct a separate set of nutrient time series for each U.S. state. For each time series we compute its frequency spectrum using DFT, thus obtaining a representation like the one in Fig. 2(a). This lets us concisely summarize each state's dietary patterns in two numbers, which we refer to as the *state's spectral coefficients:* (1) the weight of the 366-day wavelength tells us the amplitude of the annual variation of the respective nutrient in the respective state; (2) DFT also gives us a constant offset term, corresponding to the horizontal axis of symmetry in Fig. 2(b–c), capturing the annual mean of the nutrient in the state.

Now consider Fig. 8, a map of the U.S. displaying each state's spectral coefficients for three select nutrients. The top row shows the annual mean of the respective nutrient for each state, the bottom row, the amplitude of annual periodicity. What seems to emerge is a dietary divide between the northern and southern United States. For instance, consider Fig. 8(a), which pertains to total calories per serving and shows that the annual baseline is higher in southern states, while northern states tend to be subject to stronger seasonal fluctuations. The same effect can be observed for cholesterol (Fig. 8(c)) as well as for sodium and calories from fat and protein (not shown). Carbohydrates, once more, play a special role; their baseline tends to be higher in northern than in southern states. Anecdotally, these findings seem to indicate that the South eats richer food[1] and that the North prefers more seasonal variety, possibly due to the rather different climates, but we leave the scientific interpretation to nutritionists.

To conclude the geographical part of our analysis, we briefly turn to a day that deserves particular attention: both total calories and sodium soar to their respective annual maxima on March 17— St. Patrick's Day (Fig. 1). We were interested in knowing whether this spike is a global phenomenon or if it is confined to certain regions. Since St. Patrick is Ireland's national saint, we expected the peak to be particularly salient for regions of strong Irish heritage, such as the New England region centered around Boston, and indeed, Fig. 9 confirms this intuition. The colors in these maps indicate for each state by how many standard deviations its sodium level on St. Patrick's differs from a baseline, with white corresponding to zero, gray tones to negative, and purple tones to positive values. New England stands out both when using the nationwide average on St. Patrick's as the baseline (Fig. 9(a)) and when using each state's own annual average as the baseline (Fig. 9(b)). Looking further into what dishes cause the anomaly, we single out corned beef and cabbage: 13% of all users active on March 17 queried for a corned-beef recipe (cf. Fig. 3). Again, the caveat from Section 4.3 applies: while the popularity of corned beef is vastly increased on St. Patrick's, it is likely amplified in our data, as it is unlikely that 13% of the population consumed corned beef on that day.

6. ONLINE TRACES OF DIET CHANGE

We now seek to enhance our understanding of the typical long-term behavior of users who show evidence of seeking to lose weight, again by leveraging search logs and recipe data.

---

[1] In particular, note that the darkest spot in the calorie-baseline map (Fig. 8(a), top)—Mississippi—coincides with what is usually considered the country's most obese state [30].

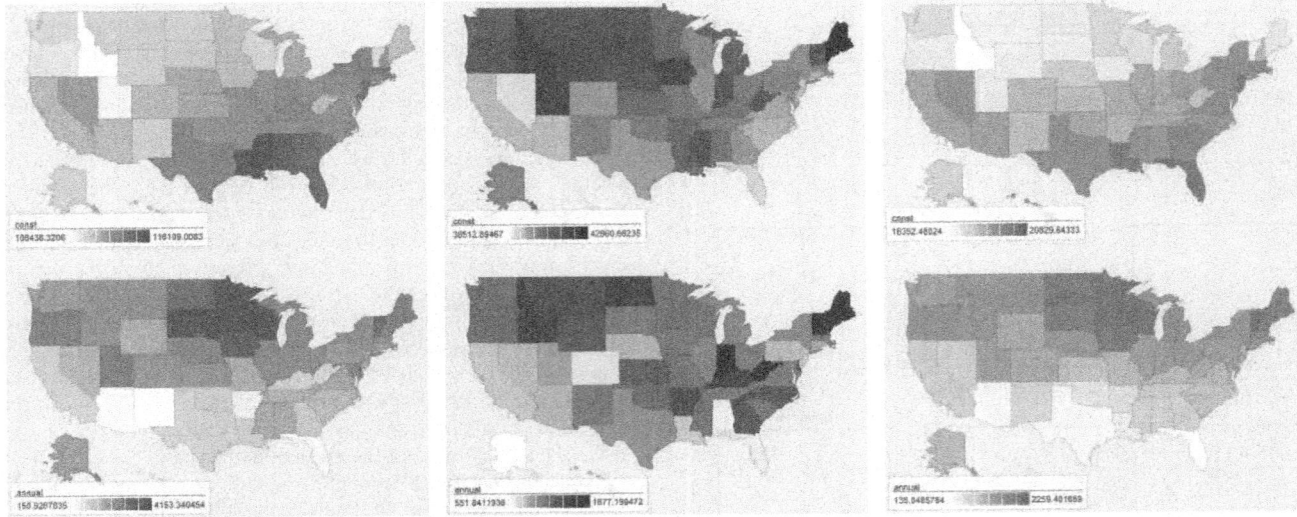

(a) Total calories per serving   (b) Calories from carbohydrates   (c) Cholesterol

Figure 8: **Maps highlighting spatiotemporal nutritional patterns for three nutrients.** *Top:* annual mean (the constant component found via DFT). *Bottom:* amplitude of annual periodicity (the weight of the component with a one-year wavelength found via DFT).

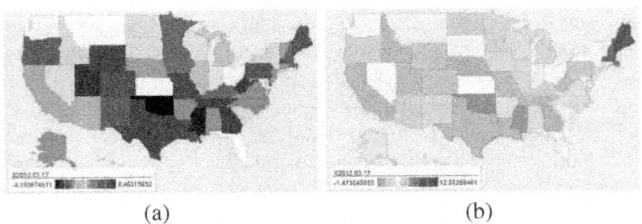

(a)   (b)

Figure 9: **Maps showing that the anomaly on St. Patrick's Day is especially strong in New England:** (a) per-state sodium-level deviation from U.S. average for St. Patrick's; (b) per-state deviation from state average for the entire year (deviation measured in standard deviations, zero mapping to white).

We strive to identify users seeking to lose weight in the logs via the method described in Section 3, by looking for the event where a user adds a book from the category DIETS & WEIGHT LOSS to their Amazon shopping cart. We interpret this event as a stronger signal of determination than, e.g., diet-related search queries or visits to diet fora [26]. For each user, we consider only their first add-to-cart event in our logs, with the rationale of discarding time periods that lie between two such events, as these are part of both a 'before' and an 'after' phase. For the same reason, we also neglect all purchases from our first month of data because we cannot know if the user showed interest in another weight-loss book just before that.

We attempt to make progress regarding two questions: (1) How do users' interests differ before versus after they commit to living a healthier life? (2) How does their diet change at this landmark?

Changes in interest. Given the time that each user adds their first diet book to the cart, we analyze the queries they issue up to 100 days before and after. We refer to days in relative terms, indexing the day of the add-to-cart event with 0, the days before with negative numbers and the days after with positive numbers. Then, we automatically score each query with respect to four dimensions: (1) Is it a recipe query? (2) Does it contain the word DIET or DIETS? (3) What is the probability of the query being about food? (4) What is the probability of the query being about health? The probabilities for the latter two scores are computed using an in-house classifier [6]. For each user–day pair, we compute the average scores of the user over all queries they made that day and finally take the mean over the daily averages of all users to obtain an overall score for each day in the interval $\{-100, \ldots, 100\}$.

The results are presented in Fig. 10(a–d). The gray dots are the per-day means, the black lines are moving averages. Fig. 10(a) shows that interest in diets spikes at day 0, which is not surprising, as users are likely to have arrived on the book product page via a search query. However, zooming in on the gray dots reveals that the spike in the smoothed curve is more than merely an artifact of the impulse at day 0. On average, interest in diets increases smoothly during a period of about a week before the add-to-cart event, then falls of smoothly again. In Fig. 10(b) we see how users' interest in food increases continuously. The intermediate spike on day 0 might well be due to the fact that diet queries are likely to get a high score for the FOOD category, but more important, it seems that the interest in food issues is maintained even after the acute decision to live more healthily. Another slight upward trend is mirrored in the plot showing the fraction of recipe queries (Fig. 10(c)). Finally, user interest in health-related queries exposes the pattern up–spike–down (Fig. 10(d)). Again, the spike is probably caused by diet queries on day 0, but it is interesting that, while food interest is sustained, health interest levels off again after day 0.

Changes in diet. Next, we propose tying the nutritional facts extracted from recipes into the analysis of users with an intention to improve their health. This can complement the observations on users' changing interests, since it gives us a glimpse into how a shift in interests is converted into real-world actions. Consider a fixed user who has signaled an intention to change diet on day 0. We aggregate the user's recipe clicks by week (e.g., week 1 is defined as the seven days following the add-to-cart event), for a period of 15 weeks before and after day 0, and consider the median calories per serving over all recipes the user clicked in a week. Taking medians over all users active in a given week yields the weekly calorie time series shown in Fig. 10(e). The curve fluctuates at the far left and right ends but reaches its minimum in week 3 after day 0, having gone through a decrease over several weeks. After week 3, aver-

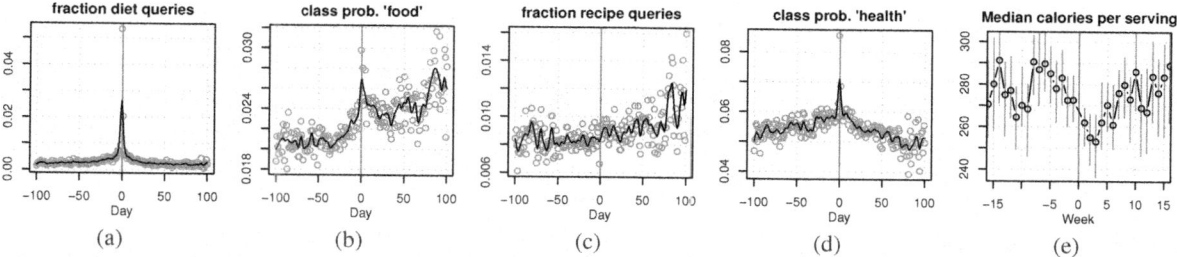

Figure 10: Longitudinal characterization of users seeking to lose weight: (a–d) query properties before and after signaling a weight-loss intention (green line); (e) calories per serving, aggregated by user and week; error bars: bootstrapped 95% confidence intervals.

age caloric intake rebounds to roughly the same level as before the drop. Our research in this area is in an early stage, and future work should strive to draw a more precise picture of the dynamics around day 0, but we report this preliminary result as interesting because it might have connections to a proven phenomenon often encountered during dieting, known commonly as the 'yo-yo effect' [7].

7. FROM RECIPES TO EMERGENCY ROOMS

We have reviewed inferences about the nutrients that people ingest by considering distributions of recipes accessed on the Web over time. Such analyses promise to yield insights about patterns of nutrition and long-term health. The findings also frame questions about the opportunity to harness Web logs as a large-scale sensor network for understanding the influence of shifts in diet on acute medical outcomes. We focus now on the specific and concerning scenario of congestive heart failure (CHF). CHF is a prevalent chronic illness that is believed to affect between six and ten percent of the population over the age of 65. The disease is associated with a high rate of re-hospitalization and annual mortality [34]. CHF is the most common diagnosis for hospitalization by patients reimbursed by Medicare, with total care costs exceeding $35 billion in the U.S. The vitality and longevity of patients diagnosed with CHF frequently depends on maintaining a careful balance of fluids and electrolytes. In particular, the ability of patients with CHF to breathe depends critically on their fluid status. Managing fluids requires careful compliance with diuretic medications and also carefully attending to one's salt and fluid intake. Education and disease management is considered critical in the care of CHF [16, 19]. One or more salty meals consumed by a CHF patient leads to higher sodium levels and an accompanying shift in the amount of water retained by patients. Increasing fluid retention starts a spiral to significant pulmonary congestion, a life-threatening situation that often requires emergency-medical treatment for immediate oxygen therapy and fluid management among other therapies to restore normal respiratory function. Re-admissions for CHF typically involve one to two weeks of careful re-stabilization of the patient. Beyond morbidity and mortality, the therapy provided may cost tens of thousands of dollars. Internists have been known to reflect about additional numbers of elderly patients who arrive in emergency rooms after spending major holidays visiting with families and friends, including speculation that the increased load is founded in ingestion of salty meals, outside the normal regime for the patients [15].

Given the known sensitivity of CHF to sodium intake, and anecdotal evidence of linking the intake of atypically salty meals with hospital admissions for pulmonary congestion, we seek to align the sodium content in downloaded recipes over time and records of admissions of patients arriving at hospitals. We can employ

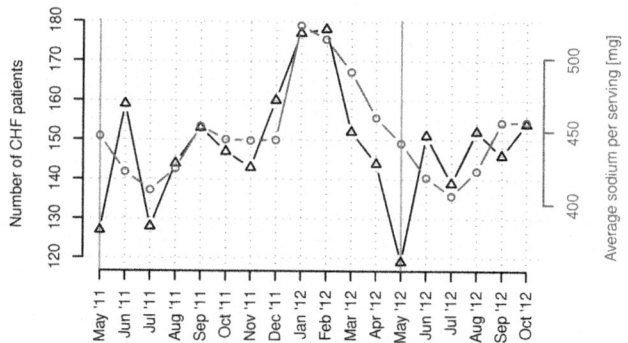

Figure 11: *Black triangles:* number of patients admitted to the emergency department of a major urban hospital in Washington, D.C., with a chief complaint linked to congestive heart failure (CHF). *Purple circles:* average sodium content (per serving) over recipe queries during same time period.

the browsing logs to supply an approximation of population-wide sodium intake via the combination with extracted data from recipes at the focus of attention. We collaborated with a clinician at the Washington Hospital Center (WHC) in Washington, D.C., to gain access to statistics of emergency admissions. WHC is an urban hospital ranked in the top ten hospitals in the U.S. in terms of annual patient densities. The ED data consists of anonymized records of patients admitted to the ED with a chief complaint to acute symptoms of CHF, for the period of our browser log data. We take these numbers as a proxy for the CHF rate in the general population.

To explore the relationship between approximations for sodium intake based on accessed recipes and rates of CHF exacerbation, we align the time series of CHF patients with that of estimated sodium intake per serving (purple circles in Fig. 1) for the same period of time. As patient numbers are generally low (mean 4.9, median 5, per day), we aggregate by month, measuring CHF rate in terms of ED patient count, and sodium in terms of average intake per serving (days weighted equally). If sodium indeed is a causal basis for increases in CHF risk, we might expect to see the two curves following each other closely. Referring to Fig. 11, we observe that this appears to be the case qualitatively. The two y-axes have incomparable units, so the exact y-position and scale are arbitrary, but clearly, the two curves share the same overall trends, reaching their maxima in January and February. The correlation is statistically significant ($r(16) = 0.62$, $p = 0.0028$; after removing the main outlier [May '12], $r(15) = 0.69$, $p = 0.0012$). We cannot confirm a causal relationship in the data; other reasons may explain the alignment we see. Patterns of increases in admissions can be influenced by the details of the demographics of the population of people living in the proximity of a hospital. Rates of admissions also vary by day of week and month of year. Other factors beyond meals may be linked to holidays. For example, there may be more travel and disruption in daily activities leading to loss of compliance with medications. Nevertheless, we present the results as an intriguing direction for ongoing research.

8. DISCUSSION

Although the findings of this work are intriguing and open up a range of possibilities for log-based surveillance and forecasting, we acknowledge several limitations. First, approximating food intake via recipe access might produce false positives: since our study is log-based, we have no way of confirming that a dish that a user searches for is created and consumed. We also do not know if meal preparation and ingestion is the underlying intent of the user at the time of viewing the recipe. Second, false negatives may arise when users eat dishes that differ systematically from their recipe access patterns. For instance, most people will not eat only at home, and their food choices elsewhere may be influenced by several factors (e.g., choices at the company cafeteria, friends' influence when choosing a restaurant, etc.). Also, in many households, there may be a single person cooking and making decisions on the food consumed at home, which would imply that the eating patterns of some people in the household may vary (e.g., one of the spouses may eat corned beef frequently at work, but at home eat greens).

We have attempted to estimate how well recipe access corresponds to recipe users' typical diet by means of a survey (cf. Section 3). The findings suggest that people search for recipes that match what they usually eat, so the type of food and its relationship with general eating habits may be more important than the exact dish itself. However, although these preliminary findings are promising, we cannot rule out the aforementioned error sources, especially since our surveyed user group, comprising exclusively employees at Microsoft, is not likely to be a representative population sample. Thus, further study of the relationship of online recipe access and eating habits is required.

On other limitations, the logs only provide us with insights into what people who visit online recipe sites are interested in. We do not know how this relates to the general population of users, and further studies are needed to understand whether there are any differences in the demographics or locations of these recipe searchers that may bias the signals obtained. For instance, recipe searching might not be a particularly regular occurrence in low-income households, which would introduce a bias, as food consumption patterns depend on income and education levels [35]. The same could apply in certain cultural or regional groups. Finally, logs also offer only a limited lens, and there may be hidden variables that we cannot observe through logs. For example, we identified climate as a possible explanation for the seasonal trends, but there may be other as yet undiscovered explanations that need to be understood.

Beyond the limitations of this research, some key implications emerge. Perhaps the most important relate to public health, especially involving increasing awareness around the effects of dietary choices and initiatives emphasizing prevention over treatment. Using a log-based analysis provides public-health agencies such as the U.S. Public Health Service with real-time sensing capabilities all over the country simultaneously. This supports the real-time tracking of consumption patterns from a large sample of the population at a wide range of locations. Mining weekly and seasonal variations in nutrient intake has a variety of uses, including targeted awareness campaigns in particular regions of the country at different times of the year (e.g., awareness on the risks of high sodium in the days preceding St. Patrick's Day in the Boston area). Our findings can also support dietary awareness among individual users who make the acute decision to change their consumption habits. We have described how we can identify the decision to pursue a change in diet, and can provide cues for intervention if planned lifestyle changes (as observed through interests and online recipe accesses over time) do not appear to be taking hold. The link between trends in querying and health-care utilization also raises the possibility of using search and information access behavior to build forecasting models to assist in real-world planning activities, such as making staff scheduling decisions in medical facilities.

The research paves the way for a number of avenues for future work. One direction is the development of a log-based nutrition surveillance service through which agencies could monitor trends and patterns in nutrient intake at population level and develop targeted awareness campaigns to respond to observed spikes. Work would be needed in partnership with such agencies and others to identify which nutritional information could benefit them most, as well as other key parameters such desired location granularity (city, county, or state) and lag time from the spike occurring to availability of the signal in the service. Given that we can observe potential relapses in diets through the log data, we need to work with users, dietitians, and psychologists to design intervention strategies that could be applied in a respectful and privacy-preserving way to help people get back on track. The link between the logs and hospital admissions data is promising, but in future work we need to confirm the findings at multiple hospitals in different regions of the country. Finally, we need to work directly with people to understand their consumption patterns, including those who do not use online recipes at all, as well as pursue other relevant behavioral signals as a proxy for nutrient intake (e.g., restaurant reservations or online food orders).

9. CONCLUSION

We investigated search and access of recipes over time for different regions of the world. We consider the link, supported by the results of a survey, that recipe accesses observed in logs may provide clues about consumption patterns at particular times and places. In a first analysis, we identify a periodicity in online recipe access patterns suggesting shifting patterns of nutrition, including specific shifts in diet around major holidays. In addition, we found weekly and large-scale annual components in the dietary preferences expressed as accessed recipes. A second study focused on identifying a population of users who exhibit evidence in logs of making a commitment to reduce their weight. We examined changes in these users' search queries, with a focus on the changes they make in their recipe queries, discovering a trend of immediate shift with eventual regression to previous recipe access habits after several weeks. In a third study, we explore links between boosts in sodium content in accessed recipes over time with time series of hospital admissions for congestive heart failure. We find qualitative agreement in sodium in recipes and rates of admissions of patients arriving at the emergency department of a large urban hospital in Washington, D.C. The three studies serve as an initial set of probes into harnessing large-scale logs of Web activity for better understanding nutrition for populations throughout the world.

10. ACKNOWLEDGMENTS

We thank Dr. Justin Gatewood for assistance with providing hospital admission statistics, Dan Liebling for technical support, and Susan Dumais for helpful discussions. We would also like to acknowledge the insightful comments from anonymous reviewers.

11. REFERENCES

[1] Google Trends. Website, 2012. http://www.google.com/trends (accessed Nov. 20, 2012).

[2] Y. Ahn, S. Ahnert, J. Bagrow, and A. Barabási. Flavor network and the principles of food pairing. *Scientific Reports*, 1, 2011.

[3] D. Behan and S. Cox. Obesity and its relation to mortality and morbidity costs. Technical report, Society of Actuaries, 2010.

[4] S. Beitzel, E. Jensen, A. Chowdhury, D. Grossman, and O. Frieder. Hourly analysis of a very large topically categorized Web query log. In *SIGIR'04*, 2004.

[5] P. Bennett, F. Radlinski, R. White, and E. Yilmaz. Inferring and using location metadata to personalize Web search. In *SIGIR'11*, 2011.

[6] P. Bennett, K. Svore, and S. Dumais. Classification-enhanced ranking. In *WWW'10*, 2010.

[7] K. Brownell, M. Greenwood, E. Stellar, and E. Shrager. The effects of repeated cycles of weight loss and regain in rats. *Physiology & Behavior*, 38(4):459–64, 1986.

[8] A. Cheung, G. Yan, T. Greene, J. Daugirdas, J. Dwyer, N. Levin, D. Ornt, G. Schulman, G. Eknoyan, et al. Seasonal variations in clinical and laboratory variables among chronic hemodialysis patients. *J Am Soc Nephrol*, 13(9):2345–52, 2002.

[9] S. Chien and N. Immorlica. Semantic similarity between search engine queries using temporal correlation. In *WWW'05*, 2005.

[10] J. de Castro. Seasonal rhythms of human nutrient intake and meal pattern. *Physiology & Behavior*, 50(1):243–48, 1991.

[11] L. Donohew, E. Ray, and L. Donohew. Public health campaigns: individual message strategies and a model. *Communication and Health: Systems and Applications*, pages 136–52, 1990.

[12] A. Drewnowski and M. Greenwood. Cream and sugar: human preferences for high-fat foods. *Physiology & Behavior*, 30(4):629–33, 1983.

[13] J. Ginsberg, M. Mohebbi, R. Patel, L. Brammer, M. Smolinski, and L. Brilliant. Detecting influenza epidemics using search engine query data. *Nature*, 457(7232):1012–1014, 2008.

[14] A. Hackett, D. Appleton, A. Rugg-Gunn, and J. Eastoe. Some influences on the measurement of food intake during a dietary survey of adolescents. *Hum Nutr Appl Nutr*, 39(3):167–77, 1985.

[15] E. Horvitz. Personal communication, on discussions at the emergency department of the Veterans Administration Hospital, Palo Alto, Calif.

[16] A. Jovicic, J. Holroyd-Leduc, and S. Straus. Effects of self-management intervention on health outcomes of patients with heart failure: a systematic review of randomized controlled trials. *BMC Cardiovasc Disord*, 6:43, 2006.

[17] A. Kendall, D. Levitsky, B. Strupp, and L. Lissner. Weight loss on a low-fat diet: consequence of the imprecision of the control of food intake in humans. *Am J Clin Nutr*, 53(5):1124–9, 1991.

[18] P. Kittler, K. Sucher, and M. Nelms. *Food and Culture*. Wadsworth Publishing Company, 2011.

[19] T. Koelling. Multifaceted outpatient support can improve outcomes for people with heart failure. Commentary. *Evid Based Cardiovasc Med*, 9(2):138–41, 2005.

[20] W. Leonard and R. Thomas. Biosocial responses to seasonal food stress in highland Peru. *Hum Biol*, 61(1):65–85, 1989.

[21] J. Prochaska and W. Velicer. The transtheoretical model of health behavior change. *Am J Health Promotion*, 12(1):38–48, 1997.

[22] K. Radinsky, K. Svore, S. Dumais, J. Teevan, A. Bocharov, and E. Horvitz. Modeling and predicting behavioral dynamics on the Web. In *WWW'12*, 2012.

[23] B. Rey and P. Jhala. Mining associations from Web query logs. In *Proceedings of the Web Mining Workshop*, 2006.

[24] M. Richardson. Learning about the world through long-term query logs. *ACM Transactions on the Web*, 2(4):21–7, 2008.

[25] P. Rozin. The selection of foods by rats, humans, and other animals. *Advances in the Study of Behavior*, pages 21–76, 1976.

[26] M. Schraefel, R. White, P. André, and D. Tan. Investigating Web search strategies and forum use to support diet and weight loss. In *CHI'09*, 2009.

[27] D. Shahar, P. Froom, G. Harari, N. Yerushalmi, F. Lubin, and E. Kristal-Boneh. Changes in dietary intake account for seasonal changes in cardiovascular disease risk factors. *Eur J Clin Nutr*, 53(5):395–400, 1999.

[28] I. Shai, D. Schwarzfuchs, Y. Henkin, D. Shahar, S. Witkow, I. Greenberg, R. Golan, D. Fraser, A. Bolotin, H. Vardi, et al. Weight loss with a low-carbohydrate, Mediterranean, or low-fat diet. *N Engl J Med*, 359(3):229–41, 2008.

[29] A. Subar, C. Frey, L. Harlan, and L. Kahle. Differences in reported food frequency by season of questionnaire administration: the 1987 National Health Interview Survey. *Epidemiology*, 5(2):226–33, 1994.

[30] C. Suddath. Why are Southerners so fat? *Time*, July 9, 2009. http://www.time.com/time/health/article/0,8599,1909406,00.html (accessed Nov. 25, 2012).

[31] D. Swanson. Fish oil, Raynaud's syndrome, and undiscovered public knowledge. *Perspect Biol Med*, 30(1):7–18, 1986.

[32] D. Swanson. Migraine and magnesium: eleven neglected connections. *Perspect Biol Med*, 31(4):526–57, 1988.

[33] M. Vlachos, C. Meek, Z. Vagena, and D. Gunopulos. Identifying similarities, periodicities and bursts for online search queries. In *SIGMOD'04*, 2004.

[34] L. Wang, B. Porter, C. Maynard, C. Bryson, H. Sun, E. Lowy, M. McDonell, K. Frisbee, C. Nielson, and S. Fihn. Predicting risk of hospitalization or death among patients with heart failure in the Veterans Health Administration. *Am J Cardiol*, 10(9):1342–9, 2012.

[35] D. West and D. Price. The effects of income, assets, food programs, and household size on food consumption. *Am J Agricult Econ*, 58(4):725–730, 1976.

[36] R. West. Online supplementary material. Website, 2013. http://ai.stanford.edu/~west1/from-cookies-to-cooks/ (accessed Mar. 7, 2013).

[37] R. White, N. Tatonetti, N. Shah, R. Altman, and E. Horvitz. Web-scale pharmacovigilance: Listening to signals from the crowd. *J Am Med Inform Assoc*, 0:1–5, 2013.

[38] J. Wright, W. Velicer, and J. Prochaska. Testing the predictive power of the transtheoretical model of behavior change applied to dietary fat intake. *Health Education Research*, 24(2):224–36, 2009.

Enhancing Personalized Search by Mining and Modeling Task Behavior

Ryen W. White[1], Wei Chu[2], Ahmed Hassan[1], Xiaodong He[1], Yang Song[1], Hongning Wang[3]

[1] Microsoft Research, Redmond, WA 98052 USA
[2] Microsoft Bing, Bellevue, WA 98004 USA
[3] Department of Computer Science, University of Illinois at Urbana Champaign, Urbana, IL 61801 USA
{ryenw, wechu, hassanam, xiaohe, yangsong}@microsoft.com, wang296@illinois.edu

ABSTRACT
Personalized search systems tailor search results to the current user intent using historic search interactions. This relies on being able to find pertinent information in that user's search history, which can be challenging for unseen queries and for new search scenarios. Building richer models of users' current and historic search *tasks* can help improve the likelihood of finding relevant content and enhance the relevance and coverage of personalization methods. The task-based approach can be applied to the current user's search history, or as we focus on here, all users' search histories as so-called "groupization" (a variant of personalization whereby other users' profiles can be used to personalize the search experience). We describe a method whereby we mine historic search-engine logs to find other users performing similar tasks to the current user and leverage their on-task behavior to identify Web pages to promote in the current ranking. We investigate the effectiveness of this approach versus query-based matching and finding related historic activity from the current user (i.e., group versus individual). As part of our studies we also explore the use of the on-task behavior of particular user cohorts, such as people who are expert in the topic currently being searched, rather than all other users. Our approach yields promising gains in retrieval performance, and has direct implications for improving personalization in search systems.

Categories and Subject Descriptors
H.3.3 [**Information Storage and Retrieval**]: Information Search and Retrieval –*search process, selection process.*

General Terms
Algorithms, Experimentation, Human Factors

Keywords
Task modeling, Task similarity, Personalization, Groupization.

1. INTRODUCTION
Search engines record queries and search-result clicks from their users and leverage that data to enhance result relevance for others issuing the same or similar queries [1,21]. The underlying motivation behind this query-based matching is to find other users with similar information needs, and use their aggregated search behavior to estimate the current user's underlying intent. Historic search interactions from a user over time can be used to personalize search results [37,42], but the focus there is either once again on query-based matching [42] or creating general models of searcher interests across a variety of topics [37]. However, since queries occur in a broader task context, focusing only on query- or topical-interest-matching may be insufficient for effective search-result ranking.

Copyright is held by the International World Wide Web Conference Committee (IW3C2). IW3C2 reserves the right to provide a hyperlink to the author's site if the Material is used in electronic media.
WWW 2013, May 13–17, 2013, Rio de Janeiro, Brazil.
ACM 978-1-4503-2035-1/13/05.

People have been shown to pursue a wide range of different search tasks online [23,31] and inferences about task behavior have been shown to have value in areas such as modeling search satisfaction [20]. There have also been attempts to leverage the on-task behavior of other users to improve retrieval performance. Research on *groupization* [43] showed that extending personalization to groups of users with shared interests could yield relevance gains. However this used information that is typically unavailable to search engines (e.g., length of members' relationships) and is on a small scale. Collaborative filtering attempts to find others with similar interests [13,25], but matches based only on queries [25] or focuses on recommendations and community connectedness not ranking [13].

We believe that by directly modeling task-relevant search behavior as part of personalization we can attain improved search result relevance. In this particular study, we are interested in first modeling users' on-task search behavior, then using the generated task model to find other users attempting similar tasks, identifying the URLs that appear relevant, and then promoting those URLs in the result list for the current query. We answer four questions critical in determining the value of this method: (1) Should matching be performed using task models or is finding other instances of the current query sufficient? (2) How does task-based groupization perform in comparison with task-based personalization? (3) Is in-session task segmentation required to attain performance gains or would an estimation of tasks via search sessions suffice? (4) What is the effect of using specific user cohorts for groupization (e.g., those in a particular geographic location or those with good topic knowledge)? Through empirical analysis we demonstrate that mining and modeling search tasks yields significant gains in retrieval performance.

The remainder of this paper is structured as follows. Section 2 describes related work in task modeling, personalization, and mining task-relevant search behavior. Sections 3 and 4 describe the identification of search tasks and the method for the learning to rank search results by using evidence from similar tasks. Section 5 describes the experiments that we performed to evaluate our methods and Section 6 describes the results. In Section 7 we discuss these findings and their implications, and we conclude in Section 8.

2. RELATED WORK
There are three relevant areas of related work: (1) task modeling, (2) personalization of search engines based on short- and long-term searcher interests, and (3) mining the search behavior of other users to complement and enhance search personalization.

An important part of representing search intent is understanding the various types of search tasks and the different motivations that searchers may have for pursuing their information goals. Previous work has studied the motivation for searching and nature of the search tasks that people perform [14,26]. There has also been research on mining and modeling task-related search behavior from search logs. Jones and Klinkner [22] proposed to classify the query pairs that belong to the same task using, among others, features of query-term overlap and search result similarity. They showed in experiments that their approach attained significant (over 90%) accuracy in segmenting and matching search tasks. Such task models have also been used to predict search success automatically from observed search behavior [18,19,20]. Lucchese et al. [30] identified task-based sessions by combining content (query term edit distance) and semantic (Wikipedia) features. Liao et al. [27] adapt both of the methods described in [19,30] to extract tasks from sessions where a query distance function is learned and used to cluster queries in sessions into tasks. They studied the potential benefit of using tasks for search applications—determining user satisfaction, predicting search interests, and query suggestion—and demonstrate benefit from tasks over sessions or queries. Others have modeled cross-session interests to predict task continuation and resumption [24] or have sought to understand multi-session tasks [31].

Large-scale behavioral data from search engines has been mined extensively to improve search result relevance [1,21]. Radlinski and Joachims [33] proposed the use of query chains comprising connected sequences of queries to learn richer models of relevance that can capitalize on session behavior. However, the basis for the learning is still individual queries, which may not map well to the current user's task. Moving beyond individual queries, Radlinski et al. [34] model intent from queries and clicks in a way that could be directly consumed by Web search engines. Similarly, Downey et al. [12] studied relationships between queries and goals, estimated from the terminal page in the search session. Bilenko and White [7] used signals from aggregated post-query navigation trails to learn better result rankings using search behavior.

Research on personalizing retrieval [35,41] has found that implicitly gathered information such as browser history, query history, and desktop information, can be used to improve the ranking of search results for a given user. Short-term behavior from within the current search session has been used for tasks such as search result ranking [49] or predicting future search interests [45,46]. Teevan et al. [41] found that the performance of the personalization algorithm they studied was improved as more data became available about the target user's interests. Long-term behavior has been used for personalizing search result ranking by building long-terms models of search interests [37], including specifically using previous queries suggesting a pursuit of similar information needs [40]. Other work has focused on personalization based on task-type, including the connection between task type and search behavior [29], and using those signals for personalization [28], although within the same user rather than over many users as we focus on in our method.

When there are insufficient data about the current user, the search behavior of other related users may be beneficial. Teevan et al. [43] explored the similarity of queries, desktop information, and explicit relevance judgments across a small group of 30 work colleagues grouped along two dimensions: (1) the longevity of their relationships, and (2) how explicitly the group is formed. They found that some groupings provide insight into what members consider relevant to queries related to the group focus, but that it can be difficult to identify valuable groups implicitly. We address this challenge directly in this paper, and experiment with different methods for identifying groups to enhance personalization performance at scale.

Collaborative filtering (CF) can be used to find people with similar interests and leverage their activities and preferences to help the current user. There are examples of CF techniques being applied to improve search. Sugiyama et al. [38] addressed sparseness in user term-weight profiles by applying collaborative filtering techniques to provide term weights based on those of users with similar profiles. Similar approaches have used clickthrough data to personalize result rankings and backed off to the clicks of other users [2,39]. Almeida and Almeida [2] used Bayesian algorithms to cluster users of an online bookstore's search service into communities based on links clicked within the site and found that the popularity of links within different communities could be used to customize result rankings. Lee [25] used data mining to uncover patterns in users' queries and browsing to generate recommendations for users with similar queries. All techniques perform matching with other users based on individual queries or URLs, severely limiting their coverage. One way to address this is to use clickthrough behavior. Freyne and Smyth [13] tried to connect different communities based on the degree to which communities' queries and result clicks overlap.

Other methods have been proposed that are query independent. Smyth [36] suggested that clickthrough data from users in the same "search community" (e.g., a group of people who use a special-interest Web portal or who work at the same company) could enhance search result lists. Smyth provided evidence for the existence of search communities by showing that a group of employees from a single company had a higher query similarity threshold than general Web users. Mei and Church [32] found that geographic location might serve as a reasonable proxy for community, since they observed that grouping users based on the similarity of their IP addresses could improve search results. As part of the research presented in this paper, we study the utility of location-based cohorts.

Our research extends previous work in the following ways. First, we model users' tasks and learn from their task-related behavior rather than only using what they do for individual queries or general topical interests. Second, rather than personalizing using the user's own on-task behavior we have developed methods to leverage task models from other users attempting similar tasks. As part of that aspect of our study, we compare the retrieval performance of task-based groupization with task-based personalization. Third, we address the scalability challenges of implicitly modeling task similarity and show gains from leveraging groupization at scale. Finally, we study the effectiveness of using the activities of different cohorts based on location, browser / entry point denoting how users reach the search engine, and high levels of domain expertise.

3. IDENTIFYING TASKS

The first step in applying our method is to identify tasks within search sessions. We now describe the task identification process.

3.1 Log Data

The primary source of data for this study is a proprietary data set comprising anonymized logs of users of the Microsoft Bing search engine. The logs contained a unique user identifier, a search session identifier, the query, the top-10 URLs returned by the search engine for that query, and clicks on the results. We used four weeks of log data gathered from July 2011 to generate features, and to train and evaluate our different ranking models. Logs were collected during A/B tests where other types of personalization support was disabled, so as to not bias our results with other personalization signals. Logs were split into search sessions demarcated with a 30-minute inactivity timeout, such as that used in previous work [12,33].

3.2 Building Task Models

3.2.1 Identifying Tasks in Sessions

To extract tasks from within search sessions, we use the query clustering method QTC [27], which has the advantage of segmenting interleaved tasks within a session. The method works in two steps: first, measure the similarities between query pairs; second, cluster queries into tasks based on their similarity scores.

In order to calculate inter-query similarities, QTC takes a supervised-learning approach. First, human assessors are asked to assign binary labels to a set of randomly-sampled query pairs. A query pair has a positive label if assessors think they are related, e.g., repeated queries [amazon] → [amazon], one query contains narrowing intent of the other [disney] → [disney movies], etc. Otherwise they are assigned a negative label if the queries are unrelated or contain different atomic intentions, e.g., [seattle news] → [space needle]. A logistic regression classifier is then trained with a set of term and temporal features based on the human labels.

Using the learned query similarity function, QTC then builds an undirected graph of queries within each user session, where the vertices of the graph are queries and the edges represent similarities between queries. By dropping the weak edges where the similarities are smaller than a threshold which is determined using cross validation (0.5 in our case), we can extract all connected components of the graph as tasks. See [27] for more on QTC.

3.2.2 Modeling Search Tasks

Now that we have a way to identify the search tasks within sessions, we need to represent searchers' tasks in a way that enables comparisons between them. The two search behaviors that are readily available to us in the logs are queries and search-result clicks. We leverage these two sources to build the following four representations of users' on-task behavior: queries, clicked-result URLs, the Web domains of the clicked results, and topical labels for clicked results from the Open Directory Project (ODP, dmoz.org). Using these four sources, tasks are represented as both sets (for queries, query terms, clicked URLs, clicked URL domains), and as probability distributions across topical category labels assigned to the URLs. For clicked URLs, we only used those with a dwell time exceeding 30 seconds, suggesting that the user was satisfied [14].

The topical labels from ODP were assigned in an automated manner to all URLs in the Bing index using a content-based classifier, described and evaluated in [4]. In turn, this provided us with category information for all search-result clicks. The classifier employs logistic regression to predict the ODP category for a Web page. To lessen the impact of small differences in assigned labels, we use only 219 categories at the top two levels of the ODP hierarchy. The findings in [4] revealed that, when optimized for the score in each category, the content-based classifier has a micro-average F1 of 0.60, which we believed was sufficient for our purposes.

The sources chosen were all available to us at scale and allowed us to compute task similarity along a number of different dimensions. The inter-task similarity features that leverage these representations are described later. Before we discuss these features and how we learn from similar tasks, we present some brief summary statistics on the characteristics of search tasks that we mined from the logs.

3.3 Task Characteristics

In the one-week of log data (from July 1, 2012 to July 8, 2012) used later for feature generation there were more than three million impressions, 1.4 million search sessions, and 1.9 million search tasks. This represented an average of 1.36 tasks per session, 2.52 queries per session, and 1.86 queries per task. Figure 1 illustrates the fraction of sessions containing between one and five search tasks. The figure shows that around 90% of sessions have one or two tasks; 73.3% sessions contain a single task and about 16.0% sessions contain two tasks. This shows that although most sessions comprise a single task, there are still a sizable number of sessions (over 25%) containing multiple tasks. Since using all in-session activity may result in a noisier relevance signal, we may need to consider in-session task boundaries. We explore the effect of using full-session

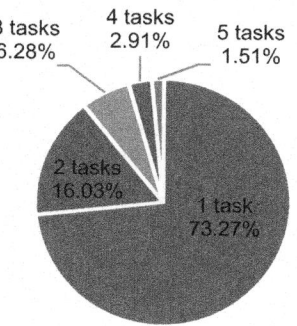

Figure 1. Number of search tasks in search sessions.

search activity versus in-session task activity as part of the ranking experiments described later in the paper.

We now describe the process by which we learn from similar tasks.

4. LEARNING FROM SIMILAR TASKS

Given a user attempting a search task, the goal of our method is to learn from the on-task search behavior of other users. A key part of this process is finding other users attempting the same or similar search tasks. In this section we describe the methods that we use to compute the similarity between pairs of search tasks, how we mine similar tasks, and the features that we generate for ranking.

4.1 Computing Task Similarity

There were a number of ways in which we computed the similarity between a given pair of tasks. These can be grouped together as two similarity features classes: query similarity and result similarity.

4.1.1 Query Similarity

These similarity measures are based on comparing the queries that users issue in both tasks under consideration. Similarity in this case can be based on the exact terminology used in the queries (after normalization) and more generally, on the semantic similarity between the queries. We consider each of these alternatives.

4.1.1.1 Syntactic Similarity

Syntactic similarity describes the string match between the queries. Similarity can be computed based on the overlap between the tasks in terms of: (1) the fraction of queries that are shared between tasks (i.e., the intersection divided by the union), and (2) as the fraction of unique query terms that are shared between tasks.

4.1.1.2 Semantic Similarity

While the queries in two tasks may not have direct term overlap, they may be similar semantically. To address this we also compute the task similarity by measuring the semantic similarity between queries of two tasks. Let $Q = q_1 \ldots q_J$ be one query and $S = s_1 \ldots s_I$ be another, the semantic similarity between these two queries can be measured based on the IBM Model 1 [6,8]. IBM Model 1 was originally proposed to model the probability of translating from one sequence of words in one language to another. Later, the model was applied to various information retrieval (IR) tasks such as query expansion [16] and document ranking [15]. Treating Q and S as two sequences of words, the IBM Model 1-based semantic similarity model is defined as:

$$P(S|Q) = \prod_{i=1}^{I} \sum_{j=1}^{J} P(s_i|q_j) P(q_j|Q) \quad (1)$$

where $P(q|Q)$ is the unigram probability of word q in query Q. The word translation probabilities $P(s|q)$ are estimated on the query-title pairs derived from the clickthrough search logs, assuming that the title terms are likely to be the desired alternation of the paired query. Our method follows the standard training procedure of IBM model 1 as proposed by Brown et al. [8]. Formally, we optimize the model parameters θ, i.e., the set of all word translation probabilities $\{P(s|q)\}$, by maximizing the probability of generating document titles from queries over the entire training corpus:

$$\theta^* = \text{argmax}_\theta \prod_{i=1}^{H} P(S_i|Q_i, \theta) \quad (2)$$

where $P(S|Q, \theta)$ takes the form of IBM Model 1:

$$P(S|Q, \theta) = \frac{\varepsilon}{(J+1)^I} \prod_{i=1}^{I} \sum_{j=1}^{J} P(s_i|q_j) \quad (3)$$

where ε is a constant, I is the token length of S, and J is the token length of Q. The query-title pairs used for model training are sampled from one year of search logs from the Bing search engine, without any overlap with the experiments reported in this paper.

We compute the sematic similarity between two tasks using the average $P(S|Q, \theta)$ across all pairs of queries from the tasks.

4.1.2 Clicked-Result Similarity
The result URLs that are clicked (and have an associated long dwell) provide a different source of information about users' search intent than is available in queries. We compute similarity in three ways: (1) the match between the clicked URLs, (2) the match between the domains of the clicked URLs, and even more generally, (3) the match between the topical categories assigned to the URLs.

4.1.2.1 URL and Domain Similarity
Similarity is computed based on the overlap between the tasks in terms of the fraction of unique clicked URLs shared between them (i.e., the intersection of clicked URLs divided by the union of all clicked URLs), or in terms of the URL domains that are shared between the tasks. Backing off to Web domains provides more opportunity for a match between clicked results, improving coverage while preserving information about the web site of interest.

4.1.2.2 Topical Similarity
Rather than relying on exact matches between particular URLs or their domains, we can also consider matching based on the topicality of the pages described earlier. Given a categorization for each of the clicked URLs for a task t, we can create an ODP category distribution C_t for that task, with a probability for each topical category c (i.e., $P_t(c)$). Given this representation, we can compare the distribution for the current task with the distribution over all other tasks from other users $\{t'\}$. We perform this comparison using both Kullback-Liebler divergence and the cosine similarity. That is,

$$KL(t', t) = \sum_{c \in C} \ln\left(\frac{P_{t'}(c)}{P_t(c)}\right) P_{t'}(c) \quad (4)$$

$$\cos(C_{t'}, C_t) = \frac{C_t \cdot C_{t'}}{\|C_t\| \|C_{t'}\|} \quad (5)$$

Using two measures focused on different aspects of the distributional similarity between tasks: KL computes the information gain and is asymmetric, cosine similarity computes the normalized dot product between the distributions (as vectors) and is symmetric.

4.2 Mining Similar Tasks
Given that we now have a variety of methods for computing the similarity between pairs of search tasks, the next objective is using that information to mine similar tasks and generate ranking features. In this section we describe the procedure that we employ to leverage task similarity in re-ranking the top retrieved results, as well as the different groups from which we can find similar tasks.

4.2.1 Procedure
Recall that the objective of our method is to find other users attempting the same or similar tasks to the current user. During feature generation, we build a representation of the current search task t based on the queries and result clicks of the user in the task so far, including the current query q (but not its clicks). Each task is modeled using the sources described earlier in Section 3.2.2.

Given that we have constructed a model of t, the next objective is to find similar tasks from the search histories of other users. For each of the tasks t' in the set of all tasks observed historically from other users T, we can then compute the similarity between the current task and those tasks $k(t, t')$. For each of the similarity measures in Section 4.1 we can compute a score s_k for a URL u appearing in the top 10 search results for q:

$$s_k(t, u) = \sum_{t' \in T} \left(k(t, t') \cdot w(t', u)\right) \quad (6)$$

Where $w(t', u)$ is a weight reflecting the importance of the URL in a related task. In our case we define $w(t', u)$ as the click frequency on that URL for the related task. Other ways of generating this weight are possible (e.g., the rank position of u in the result list), but we focus on click frequency given its computational simplicity and direct relationship with our goal of learning which URLs are relevant from historic on-task behavior. Although T is primarily composed of all historic tasks from all users, it can come from different groups, including the user's long-term history (for personalization rather than groupization), or specific user cohorts such as those with high levels of expertise in the domain of interest.

Once we have s_k for each of the similarity features described in the previous section, we use those values as additional ranking features for each of the results in the top-10 results for q. We then learn to re-rank those results to generate a new result ordering, which we then evaluate based on user behavior as described later.

4.2.2 Re-ranking Features
The specific features that we use for ranking are listed in Table 1. The functions map to the similarity functions described in this section. The inter-task similarity is computed using $k(t, t')$ which is then multiplied against the click count for each URL in the top-10 (i.e., $w(t', u)$ from Equation 6). The result summed over all tasks in the historic data is used to generate the final feature value.

In addition, we also compute *ClickedTasksCount*, which is the total number of tasks for which a particular URL u is clicked. This measures URL popularity independent of task. Note that since *QueryTranslation* and *CategorySimilarityKL* are asymmetric, we also include reverse variants of these features in our feature set.

4.2.3 Groups
The approach we describe in the paper leverages the on-task behavior of groups comprising the following three sets of users:

- **Individual:** This group comprises only the search behavior of the current user. In this group, the queries and similar search tasks are mined only from the current user's long-term history.
- **Group (Global):** In this group, queries and similar tasks are mined from everyone's search histories.
- **Group (Cohorts):** This group comprises particular subsets of *Global* created based on location, browser and search entry point (i.e., how users reach the engine – more details later),

Table 1. Features used to compute the similarity between two tasks, t and t', in the computation of $k(t, t')$.

Feature name	Definition
FullQueryOverlap	The fraction of all queries in the union of t and t' that the two tasks have in common.
QueryTermOverlap	The fraction of all unique query terms in the union of t and t' that the two tasks have in common.
QueryTranslation	Semantic similarity between the queries in t and the queries in t' ($P(E\|Q, \theta)$ as defined earlier).
ClickedURLOverlap	The fraction of clicked URLs in the union of t and t' that the two tasks have in common.
ClickedDomainOverlap	The fraction of clicked domains in the union of t and t' that the two tasks have in common.
CategorySimilarityKL	The Kullback-Liebler divergence between the ODP category distribution from result clicks in t versus the same distribution from t'.
CategorySimilarityCosine	The cosine similarity between the ODP category distribution from result clicks in t versus the same distribution from t'.

and estimates of topic expertise. The first two are based on information that is readily available in the logs that we used for this study. The latter could be estimated based on patterns of activity, interest on a topic, and success within a topic over time. Queries and similar search tasks in this case are only drawn from the particular cohort (e.g., only from users in the same location as the current searcher) rather than all searchers.

4.2.3.1 Local Cohort
It has been shown that interests can be location specific, e.g., a user querying for [msg] in New York City, NY may be more likely to mean Madison Square Garden than monosodium glutamate [3], and local experts may have better knowledge about the places to select [47]. In this case, we learn our features from users querying from the same location. To identify the user location we use the user's IP address to determine the city and state for every user. We could not use each {city, state} pair as its own cohort because the population of many locations is insufficient. To address this, we use the city for the most populated locations and back-off to state for the less populated ones. Specifically, the location of a given user is his city if they are in one of the largest 200 U.S. cities by population. Otherwise, the location is the state. For example, a user querying from Austin, Texas would be in the "Austin" cohort, whereas a user querying from College Station, TX would be in the "Texas" cohort.

4.2.3.2 Web Browser / Search Entry Point Cohort
We also created groups of users based on the combination of the Web browser(s) that they use (e.g., Internet Explorer, Firefox, Chrome, multiple browsers, etc.) and the entry point(s) that they use to reach Bing (e.g., Bing homepage, MSN.com, browser search box, multiple entry points, etc.). The determination for each user is based on a held out set of log data from before the time period examined for this paper. Our hypothesis was that users using the same Web browser and entry point may have similar search preferences or be similar demographically (as a recent report by ComScore suggests[1]), and demographics can influence search behavior [44].

4.2.3.3 Topic Cohort
Previous work has shown that people with topic knowledge are more efficient and effective in completing their search tasks [50]. We hypothesized that by focusing on the behavior of experts, we could help users target better quality content. As such, in defining the cohorts we limit the tasks to those from users with significant expertise in the topic of interest. This allows us to learn from expert users in particular, versus learning from one's personal history or the set of all users, comprising users of all domain expertise levels.

To identify users with significant expertise in different topics, we had to assign topic labels to different queries. We use one of 25 topics to describe any given query. For each such topic, a set of manually-labeled queries are collected from trained judges and a proprietary text classifier is trained using the labeled data. The classifier is then used to assign topics to other queries. We used a set of binary classifiers, one for each topic, allowing queries to belong to multiple topics. Example topics include: *Entertainment*, *Names*, *Commerce*, *Navigational*, *Travel*, *Technology* and *Sports*.

We use first week of data described in Section 3.1, corresponding to the feature-generation week. A user U is deemed to be an expert in topic P if the following three conditions are satisfied:

1. **Activity:** The number of queries submitted by U is more than the average number of queries per user.
2. **Topic Interest:** The percentage of queries ϵP submitted by U exceeds the average percentage of queries ϵP across all users.
3. **Success:** The task success rate of U on tasks ϵP is greater than the average task success rate of all users on tasks ϵP. Task success is predicted using the method in [18].

Unlike the location and entry-point cohorts, the expertise cohort does not use information about the current user. The intuition here is that experts will select better resources and being pointed to those resources will help all users irrespective of expertise level. Later we show that there is benefit from leveraging particular user cohorts.

4.3 Summary
In this section we have defined methods for computing inter-task similarity, defined the feature generation procedure and the particular features that are assigned to the URLs, and defined the groups from which similar tasks are drawn. We also described each of the cohorts that we investigate. In the next section we describe our experiments to measure the effectiveness of task-based models for personalization, including comparisons with personalization methods and query-based (not task-based) similarity.

5. EXPERIMENTS
Our log-based evaluation method focuses on a re-ranking task, assessing the extent to which the models promote clicked results.

5.1 Baselines
The original ranking from the Bing search engine is our primary baseline. We also setup competitive query-centric baselines:

1. **Query-based Global (QG; same query, all users):** This is a non-personalized approach that finds clicked URLs by matching the current query against previous queries over all users.

---

[1] http://www-cs-faculty.stanford.edu/~eroberts/cs181/projects/firefox-market-dynamics/present.html

2. **Query-based Individual (QI; same query, same user):** This finds clicked URLs by matching the current query with previous queries in the current user's search history. This means that if the current query is observed at some point in the user's search history, then the URLs of interest to them then are likely to be promoted in the re-ranked list now. This is similar to the personalized navigation method in Teevan et al. [42].
3. **Query-based Global and Individual Features (QGI):** This is a strong baseline model combining both QG and QI features.

These are very competitive baselines given that they start with the ranking provided by Bing (which already uses behavior data aggregated at the query level) and then add other signals based on the specific query. We focus on the impact of extracting relevance features in similar tasks, rather than exactly matched queries only.

5.2 Research Questions

We utilize two forms of matching, *query-based* and *task-based*. Query-based matches against historic behavioral data based on the exact (normalized) query string of the current query. Task-based matches against historic behavior using the task models and task similarity functions described earlier in the paper.

To evaluate the benefit of task modeling over query modeling, we trained the following nine models using different features, and then compared their performance on the same test data that comprised over two million queries. The nine models evaluated were the three baselines (Models 1-3) plus the following models:

4. **Task-based Global Features (TG):** Trained with features extracted from all tasks in all search histories;
5. **Task-based Individual Features (TI):** Trained with features from tasks in the individual user's search history only;
6. **Task-based Global and Individual Features (TGI):** This model is trained on both TI and TG features;
7. **Query-based and Task-based Global Features (QTG):** This model is trained on both QG and TG features;
8. **Query-based and Task-based Individual Features (QTI):** This model is trained on both QI and TI features;
9. **QTG and QTI Features (QTGI):** This model is trained on both QTG and QTI features.

The re-ranking models attempt to promote observed *satisfied result clicks* (SAT clicks) toward higher rank positions in the result list. This enables offline evaluation of models performance using judgments personalized to each user. This approach has been used to determine the effectiveness of various re-ranking methods [3,5,37].

As described earlier, we attempt to answer the following research questions with our study (we also include the model comparisons):

RQ1: Does matching based on task models outperform matching using the current query? (Models 1-3 vs. Models 4-6).
RQ2: Does task-based groupization outperform task-based personalization? (Model 4 vs. Model 5 vs. Model 6).
RQ3: Is in-session task segmentation required to attain performance gains or would an estimation of tasks as search sessions suffice? (Models 6 and 9 vs. session-based variants)
RQ4: What is the effect of using specific user cohorts for groupization (e.g., those in a particular location or those with good topic knowledge)? [Model 3 vs. (Model 3 + cohorts)].

Answers to these questions help quantify the potential benefits that they can bring to search engine users. Models 7 and 8 are not assigned to any research questions, but are included for completeness.

5.3 Relevance Judgments

Since we were evaluating personalization methods, we needed a personalized relevance judgment for each result. Obtaining many

Table 2. Statistics of the weekly data for learning/evaluation.

Count	Training	Validation	Test
SAT Clicks	2,086,335	2,062,554	2,082,145
Quickback Clicks	417,432	408,196	413,496
Tasks	1,165,083	1,126,452	1,135,320
Queries per Task	1.678	1.676	1.666

explicit relevance judgments from real users is impractical, and there is no known approach to train expert judges to provide reliable judgments that reflect real user preferences. Hence we obtained these judgments using a log-based methodology inspired by [17] and similar to that used in [3,5,37]. This method infers relevance judgments for query-URL pairs from search-result clicks. We consider three types of clicks in labeling user feedback in the logs: SAT clicks, *quickback* clicks, and no clicks. We define a SAT click in a similar way to previous work [14] as either a click followed by no further clicks for 30 seconds or more, or the last result click in the session. In [14] the authors captured in-situ judgments of satisfaction directly from searchers. This allowed them to determine that a 30-second dwell time was effective in distinguishing satisfaction from dissatisfaction via search behavior alone.

We define the clicks having less than 30 seconds dwelling time as *quickbacks*. We assign one of the three rating labels to each query-URL pair in the top-10. In each impression, if a URL received at least one SAT click, the URL is labeled with a 2; if a URL received only quickback clicks, the URL is labeled with a 1; if a URL was not clicked at all, the URL is labeled with a 0. This gives us a three-level judgment for each top-10 URL for each query. This multi-level labeling allows the ranker to learn more nuanced differences between the results for each query than could be learned with binary labels. In particular, it helps differentiate between cases where the user explored the page but decided that it was not relevant and cases where they did not consider the URL at all. Since our evaluation methodology is personalized to each user, the relevance labels in *impressions* (unique instances) under the same query could be different, since the users who issue the query vary.

5.4 Measures

We measure ranking quality by mean average precision and mean reciprocal rank. In both cases, the mean is calculated over all the impressions in our test set. Mean average precision (MAP) for a set of queries is the mean of the average precision scores for each query. The average precision score is defined as

$$AveragePrecision = \frac{\sum_{k=1}^{n} Precision(k) Rel(k)}{\sum_{k=1}^{n} Rel(k)} \quad (7)$$

where n is the number of URLs in the impression, usually 10, $Rel(k)$ is an indicator function equaling 1 if the URL at rank k is a relevant document, zero otherwise, and $Precision(k)$ is the precision at cut-off k in the ranked list.

Mean reciprocal rank (MRR) for a query set is the average of the reciprocal ranks across all results, which is defined as

$$MRR = \frac{1}{N} \sum_{i=1}^{N} \frac{1}{rank_i} \quad (8)$$

where $rank_i$ is the rank of the first relevant URL in the ranking list, and N is the number of impressions in test.

These measures are complementary in that MRR focuses on the rank of the first relevant document in the top 10, whereas MAP targets the rank of relevant results across the top 10 documents. As

Table 3. MAP/MRR gains on the test data (± SEM). Production ranker is baseline. Query-based baselines highlighted.

Model	Δ MAP(10^{-2})	Δ MRR(10^{-2})	Rerank@1	Coverage	Win	Loss	Cost Rate
QG	**0.0888**±0.0023	**0.1076**±0.0024	0.46%	19.10%	28009	27507	98.21%
QI	**0.1425**±0.0028	**0.1431**±0.0029	0.70%	17.87%	26966	23214	86.09%
QGI	**0.1448**±0.0028	**0.1455**±0.0029	0.71%	19.10%	29259	25097	85.78%
TG	**0.1408**±0.0029	**0.1440**±0.0029	0.88%	67.37%	45866	37668	82.13%
TI	**0.1485**±0.0028	**0.1490**±0.0029	0.71%	19.44%	30932	26586	85.95%
QTI	**0.1691**±0.0030	**0.1695**±0.0030	0.79%	20.23%	30193	25180	83.40%
QTG	**0.1905**±0.0032	**0.1936**±0.0032	1.01%	67.55%	33102	23617	71.35%
TGI	**0.2292**±0.0035	**0.2318**±0.0036	1.22%	67.37%	32753	22292	68.06%
QTGI	**0.2516**±0.0036	**0.2542**±0.0037	1.28%	67.55%	35425	24731	69.81%

such, MAP can also measure performance in queries with multiple clicks. In test, only the URLs that received SAT clicks are considered as relevant, and the URLs received only quickback clicks are not treated as relevant URLs in evaluation. During testing, we wanted to be conservative and only regard results as relevant for which we could be most confident that searchers were satisfied.

In addition to measuring the relevance of the results, we also measure the coverage of the models in two main ways: the fraction of the results at the top-position (rank=1) that are re-ranked by the approach and the fraction of all impressions covered by relevance features. The re-ranking coverage at the most prominent position indicates the extent of the time where the re-ranking signal from the model is extremely strong. Feature coverage indicates fraction of impressions for which a signal is available (e.g., a similar task can be found in all users' search histories).

5.5 Method

We use the four weeks of logs described in Section 3.1 for our experiments. For all of the methods under test, we used the first week of logs for feature generation (i.e., computing the scores (s_k) for the clicked URLs in the first week of data as described earlier in the paper), the second week for model training, the third week for model validation, and the fourth week for testing. Logs were collected from A/B tests where other personalization support was disabled, so as to not bias our results with other personalization signals. Table 2 presents summary statistics on the three data sets used. Each set contains around 2 million impressions, which is less than the 3 million reported earlier since we drop impressions without any SAT clicks. We evaluated the significance of observed differences across all queries in the test week using paired t-tests with the significance level (α) set to $\alpha=0.05$. When performing multiple comparisons, Bonferroni corrections are performed to reduce the likelihood of Type I errors (i.e., incorrectly rejecting a true null hypothesis) by dividing α by the number of pairs under comparison.

Using the described dataset, we trained a ranking model using the LambdaMART learning algorithm [48] for re-ranking the top ten search results. LambdaMART is an extension of LambdaRank [9] based on boosted decision trees. LambdaMART has been shown to be one of the best algorithms for learning to rank. Indeed, an ensemble model in which LambdaMART rankers were the key component won Track 1 of the 2010 Yahoo! *Learning to Rank Challenge* [10]. However, we note the choice of learning algorithm is not central to this work, and any reasonable learning to rank algorithm would likely provide similar results.

6. RESULTS

We now present the results of our analysis, broken out by each of the four research questions described in Section 5.2. Results are primarily reported as averages over the 2 million test queries. Recall that the goal is to re-rank the results *for a given query* using the on-task behavior of the current searcher or other searchers (everyone or particular cohorts of similar users). By varying the model comparisons as suggested in Section 5.2, we can answer each of our research questions. Where appropriate, we analyze the effect of various properties on the results, in particular the number of tokens in the query and the relative position of the query in the search task, supporting the construction of rich interest models. To provide a good sense of the overall impact of the models, we report re-ranking performance across the full set of queries, including many of the queries that have no change in the ranking. Including these queries drove the mean average change in MAP and MRR toward zero, but more fully reflected the overall effect of the models than, say, focusing on the average over queries where metrics changed.

6.1 Task Matching vs. Query Matching

Table 3 reports the MAP/MRR gains of each model versus the baseline (production ranker used in Bing at the time the log data was captured) ± the standard error of the mean (SEM). All differences with that baseline are significant at $p < 2.2\text{e-}16$. As described earlier, the effect of task modeling is measured by comparing the three query-based models (QG, QI, and QGI) with the three task-based variants that use the same sources (TG, TI, and TGI). To test the significance of the observed differences, between models we performed a two-way analysis of variance (ANOVA) with matching method and group as factors. We also computed the effect size of the observed differences using *partial eta squared* (η_p^2), a commonly used measure of effect size in analyses of variance. The main effects of matching method and group were significantly different at $p < 0.001$ ($F_{\text{Matching}}(1,12492864) = 12.94$, $F_{\text{Group}}(2,12492864) = 6.76$). In addition, the matching-group interactions were significant ($F_{\text{Matching} \times \text{Group}}(2,12492864) = 4.82$, $p < 0.01$; Tukey post-hoc testing: all $p < .001$). This was expected given the large sample sizes, but the interaction effect was small in magnitude (i.e., $\eta_p^2 = 0.02$).

Table 3 also presents the feature coverage of each of the nine models, and the win and loss counts in test. The win and loss were determined by the MAP metric. If the re-ranked order results in a positive MAP gain over the baseline model, we count it as a win; it is counted as a loss if the re-ranked order yields negative MAP change against the control model. This helps us to understand the trade-offs between risk and reward in the different methods (i.e., given equal average MAP gains between two models, we would prefer the model with the lower cost rate). Global features yield the largest feature coverage. QTGI (that combines all signals) performs best overall in terms of both MAP and MRR, and the TGI model (combining personalization- and groupization-based task modeling) has the best re-ranking performance in terms of cost rate.

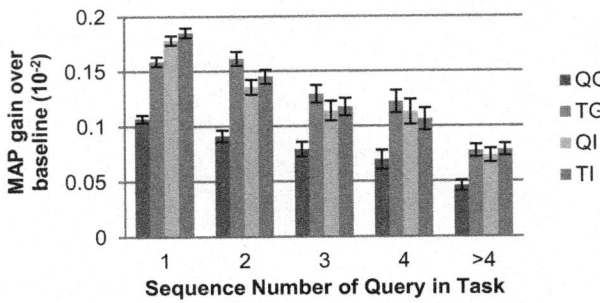

Figure 2. Segment analysis on MAP for queries issued at different points in the task (± SEM).

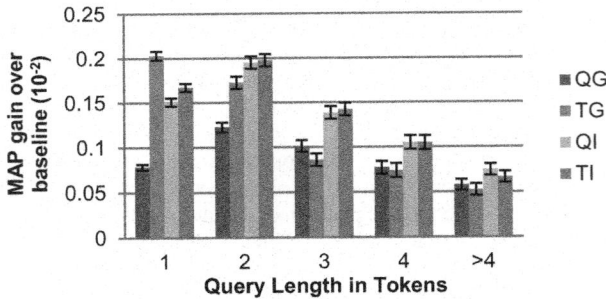

Figure 3. Segment analysis on MAP performance for queries of different lengths (± SEM).

In the next experiment we broke out the experimental results by two conditions, current query length and sequence number of the query in the task. Figure 2 shows that the performance of the two key group variants (group and individual) and the two matching variants (query and task). The figure shows that all models consistently outperform the QG at all points in the search task. The comparison between TG and QG is particularly relevant in this section because it demonstrates the benefit of task-based matching over query-based matching. The three other models are comparable across the range of query positions. The relative drop in MAP over the course of the session is of a similar extent across all queries. The decrease in gain from personalization approaches has been observed in other personalization research [5]; possible explanations include queries becoming more specific as the session proceeds, making the retrieval task more difficult and reducing the potential benefit from personalization, longer tasks being more difficult generally, or that the first query in the session found most of the relevant information.

Figure 3 reports the performance of each of the models as the length of the current query varies. The chart shows once again that TI and QI are comparable across the range of query lengths. TG outperforms QG for queries of length one or two (and the personalized methods QI and TI for queries of length one), and has comparable performance for longer queries (with individual methods performing slightly better). One explanation for this is that for shorter queries, searchers provide specific information that they have searched for before (in which case QI and TI do well) or only providing partial information meaning that identifying resources accessed by others attempting similar tasks might be useful (TG does well).

6.2 Group vs. Individual

An important consideration is the value of the task-based groupization compared to task-based personalization. The next question we considered was the differences in performance between these two methods (i.e., TG vs. TI). We compare re-ranking results using task-based matching against the current user's history (TI) with those of using all history of all users (TG). We also considered how well the methods perform in combination (TGI). Table 4 summarizes the findings, which show that task-based groupization and task-based personalization perform similarly even though the personalized variant is tailored to the current user (TI vs. TG, both $t(2082143) \leq 1.84$, both $p \geq 0.0656$, $\alpha = 0.025$). Therefore, the group-based ranking signal may be a sufficient approximation for personalization and as we show in Table 3, and it has the big advantage of covering many more queries (67% vs. 19%). Interestingly, we also note that the two features cooperate well in the combined model, TGI, leading to significant gains over the baseline.

6.3 Task vs. Session

Another important consideration is the value of segmenting the tasks into sessions, versus simply using the full session. If we could attain similar performance to tasks using temporally-delimited sessions then, for computational simplicity and reduced overhead, we may want to simply use sessions as a proxy for task. To evaluate the benefit of task-based modeling over session modeling, we used the following two comparator models replacing tasks with sessions:

1. **Session-based Global and Individual Features (SGI):** This model is trained on both SI and GI features, which is compared against the TGI model on the same test samples, and;
2. **QGI and SGI Features (QSGI):** This model is trained on both QGI and SGI features, which is compared against the QTGI model on the same test samples.

Table 6 reports the MAP and MRR differences between the TGI model and SGI, directly comparing tasks with sessions. The results of that comparison show that the task-based approach significantly outperforms the session-based method (both $t(2082143) \geq 6.76$, both $p < 1.4e-11$, $\alpha = 0.025$). When we also consider the query-based matching features as part of the comparison (QTGI vs. QSGI) gain observed from the task representation becomes non-significant (both $t(2082143) \leq 1.31$, both $p > 0.1905$, $\alpha = 0.025$). This suggests that much of the gain from the task modeling over the session modeling comes from being able to match based on the same or similar queries, which seems reasonable given that the task modeling generates focused query clusters by design. When query is factored into the model directly (as is the case in moving from TGI to QTGI) then the benefit from using tasks over sessions diminishes.

Table 4. Comparison on the test data. ΔMAP and ΔMRR denote the MAP and MRR difference from the baseline model (TG) respectively (± SEM).

Models	ΔMAP(10^{-2})	ΔMRR(10^{-2})
TI vs. TG	0.0077±0.0033	0.0050±0.0025
TGI vs. TG	0.0884±0.0026	0.0878±0.0031

Table 5. Test results on the test data. ΔMAP and ΔMRR denote the MAP and MRR difference from the baseline model (the original ranking) respectively (± SEM).

Models	ΔMAP(10^{-2})	ΔMRR(10^{-2})	Rerank@1
SGI	0.2134±0.0034	0.2170±0.0035	1.22%
QSGI	0.2497±0.0037	0.2526±0.0037	1.28%

Table 6. Comparison on the test data. ΔMAP and ΔMRR denote the MAP and MRR difference from the baseline models (SGI and QSGI) respectively (± SEM).

Models	ΔMAP(10^{-2})	ΔMRR(10^{-2})
TGI vs. SGI	0.0158±0.0022	0.0147±0.0022
QTGI vs. QSGI	0.0019±0.0021	0.0016±0.0022

Table 7. MAP/MRR gains for cohorts on the test data (± SEM). QGI is baseline.

Models	Δ MAP(10^{-2})	Δ MRR(10^{-2})	Rerank@1	Coverage	Win	Loss	Cost Rate
QGI+Local	**0.0505**±0.0019	**0.0508**±0.0019	0.38%	39.94%	12777	9965	77.99%
QGI+Topic	**0.0851**±0.0024	**0.0872**±0.0024	0.66%	28.40%	38973	33523	86.02%
QGI+Entry	**0.0646**±0.0021	**0.0661**±0.0021	0.48%	23.08%	23018	19453	84.51%

6.4 Effect of User Cohorts

In addition to using the on-task behavior of all users, we also studied the effect of using the three cohorts described earlier in the paper. Our hypothesis was that using the behavior of users who are similar to the current user or who are in some way knowledgeable about the topic of interest would boost retrieval performance. Table 7 summarizes the results when compared against the QGI baseline model. This was our strongest baseline and allowed us to examine the effect of cohorts without conflating task with cohort. All differences with baseline are significant at $p < 2.2e-16$.

The results show clearly that cohorts improve performance over the strong baseline. To directly compare the effect of the different cohorts we used a one-way ANOVA. The results of this analysis show that the differences between the models were significant ($F(2, 6246432) = 15.13$, $p < 0.001$; Tukey post-hoc test: all $p < 0.001$). The best performing cohort model (on average over all queries) was the topic expertise model, suggesting that users may benefit from focusing on the web sites that experts visit. However, the local-cohort model is less risky (lower cost rate) and also covers a larger fraction of the queries. More work is needed to understand the cost-benefit tradeoffs of using cohorts, as well as how cohorts interact.

6.5 Summary

The results of our study show that:

1. Task-based matching to historic data outperforms query-based matching, both in terms of relevance and coverage (RQ1).
2. Task-based groupization has statistically indistinguishable performance from task-based personalization, but has dramatically better coverage (over 3 times greater) (RQ2).
3. Task-based segmentation methods lead to gains in performance over sessions, suggesting that there is value in first grouping session activity into coherent task clusters (RQ3).
4. Leveraging the behavior of particular cohorts rather than all users leads to better performance than a strong baseline (RQ4).

7. DISCUSSION AND IMPLICATIONS

We have presented a study on mining and modeling search tasks to improve search personalization. Our novel approach mines similar tasks from other users and uses them for re-ranking, improving coverage while attaining similar performance gains to traditional personalization methods. However, more detailed analysis of the findings is required to understand exactly when the personalization and groupization approaches are most successful and when to choose between them. Further improvements in performance may well be observed given a broader range of task-oriented features than the modest set employed in this paper. Our main contribution is as the first study to show performance gains via groupization by implicitly modeling all users', and user cohorts', on-task behavior at scale.

Although we showed promising gains with cohort modeling over a strong query-based method, more work is needed to understand how task models can be enhanced using cohort information. Early experiments with TGI + cohort revealed no significant gains over TGI, and it might be the case that cohorts only help when needs are specific. More sophisticated cohort modeling could be employed to leverage other information such a social relationships, available via social networks (e.g., focus on the on-task behavior of friends), or those with similar interests to the current user outside of the current query topic (and hence likely to have similar preferences). The topic cohort focused on finding experts, irrespective of the current user's expertise; modeling *relative* expertise may help.

The success of our approach is dependent on how accurately we can model search tasks. The approach described in this paper was useful to demonstrate the potential value of this method, but more sophisticated models of search tasks could be developed to include signals such as task success [18], e.g., so that we focus on tasks where the outcome was successful or demote unsuccessful tasks. We also focused on behaviors on the search engine (queries and result clicks). However, there may be valuable information in considering search behavior once users click a result and navigate away from the engine [46] or those sites that users target directly without using a search engine, especially for users with domain expertise. The challenge in the latter case is generalizing task modeling to extend beyond search activity and allow a mapping between search tasks and these more general task representations. Richer models could also be developed by considering search and usage behaviors which may not be logged at server side (e.g., document retention events such as printing and bookmarking). In addition, although the current approach focused on re-ranking (mainly necessitated by the need for personalized relevance judgments), the best results may not be available at top positions, and deeper re-ranking or even the injection of non-indexed URLs into the list needs to be considered.

8. CONCLUSIONS

We have studied methods for modeling users' on-task search behavior and using those models to improve personalization methods. We focused on a scenario where by building rich models of the current user's task we can find other users who have performed similar tasks historically, and leverage their on-task behavior to improve personalization performance. We show though extensive experimentation that our methods outperform query-based personalization methods that use the current user's long-term search history, as well as other approaches that match with aggregated behavior of many searchers based on the text of the search query. This clearly demonstrates the value of considering search *tasks* rather than just search *queries* during personalization, as well as the benefit of groupization. Mining on-task behavior from particular cohorts (rather than all users) was also shown to be useful, at least for query-based matching. Future work involves the use of a broader range of cohorts and cohort combinations, and the development of more sophisticated and generalizable models of task behavior that can mine and model task-relevant activity beyond search engine interactions.

REFERENCES

1. Agichtein, E., Brill, E., and Dumais, S. (2006). Improving web search ranking by incorporating user behavior information. *SIGIR*, 19–26.
2. Almeida, R. and Almeida, V. (2004). A community-aware search engine. *WWW*, 413–421.
3. Bennett, P.N., Radlinski, F., White, R.W., and Yilmaz, E. (2011). Inferring and using location metadata to personalize web search. *SIGIR*, 135–144.

4. Bennett, P., Svore, K., and Dumais, S. (2010). Classification-enhanced ranking. *WWW*, 111–120.
5. Bennett, P., White, R.W., Chu, W., Dumais, S., Bailey, P., Borisyuk, F., and Cui, X. (2012). Modeling the impact of short and long-term behavior on search personalization. *SIGIR*, 185–194.
6. Berger, A.L. and Lafferty, J. (1999). Information retrieval as statistical translation. *SIGIR*, 222–229.
7. Bilenko, M. and White, R.W. (2008). Mining the search trails of surfing crowds: identifying relevant websites from user activity. *WWW*, 51–60.
8. Brown, P.F., Della Pietra, S.A., Della Pietra, V.J., and Mercer, R.L. (1993). The mathematics of statistical machine translation: parameter estimation. *Comp. Ling.*, 19(2): 263–311.
9. Burges, C.J.C., Ragno, R., and Le, Q.V. (2006). Learning to rank with non-smooth cost functions. *NIPS*, 193–200.
10. Chapelle, O., Chang, Y., and Liu, T.-Y. (2010). Yahoo! learning to rank challenge. *learningtorankchallenge.yahoo.com*.
11. Dou, Z., Song, R., and Wen, J.R. (2007). A large-scale evaluation and analysis of personalized search strategies. *WWW*, 581–590.
12. Downey, D., Dumais, S.T., Liebling, D., and Horvitz, E. (2008). Understanding the relationship between searchers' queries and information goals. *CIKM*, 449–458.
13. Freyne, J. and Smyth, B. (2006). Cooperating search communities. *AH*, 101–110.
14. Fox, S., Karnawat, K., Mydland, M., Dumais, S.T., and White, T. (2005). Evaluating implicit measures to improve the search experience. *TOIS*, 23(2): 147–168.
15. Gao, J., He, X., and Nie, J.-Y. (2010). Clickthrough-based translation models for web search: from word models to phrase models. *CIKM*, 1139–1148.
16. Gao, J., Xie, S., He, X., and Ali, A. (2012). Learning lexicon models from search logs for query expansion. *EMNLP*.
17. Gao, J., Yuan, W., Li, X., Deng, K., and Nie, J.-Y. (2009). Smoothing clickthrough data for web search ranking. *SIGIR*, 355–362.
18. Hassan, A. (2012). A semi-supervised approach to modeling web search satisfaction. *SIGIR*, 275–284.
19. Hassan, A., Jones, R., and Klinkner, K. (2010) Beyond DCG: user behavior as a predictor of a successful search. *WSDM*, 221–230.
20. Hassan, A., Song, Y., and He, L. (2011). A task-level metric for measuring web search satisfaction and its application on improving relevance estimation. *CIKM*, 125–134.
21. Joachims, T. (2002). Optimizing search engines using clickthrough data. *KDD*, 133–142.
22. Jones, R. and Klinkner, K.L. (2008). Beyond the session timeout: automatic hierarchical segmentation of search topics in query logs. *CIKM*, 699–708.
23. Kellar, M., Watters, C., and Shepherd, M. (2007). A field study characterizing Web-based information-seeking tasks. *JASIST*, 58(7): 999–1018.
24. Kotov, A., Bennett, P.N., White, R.W., Dumais, S.T., and Teevan, J. (2011). Modeling and analysis of cross-session search tasks. *SIGIR*, 5–14.
25. Lee, Y-J. (2005). VizSearch: a collaborative web searching environment. *Computers and Education*, 44(4): 423–439.
26. Li, Y. and Belkin, N.J. (2008). A faceted approach to conceptualizing tasks in information seeking. *IP&M*, 44(6): 1822–1837.
27. Liao, Z., Song, Y., He, L.W., and Huang, Y. (2012). Evaluating the effectiveness of search task trails. *WWW*, 489–498.
28. Liu, J. and Belkin, N.J. (2010). Personalizing information retrieval for multi-session tasks: the roles of task stage and task type. *SIGIR*, 26–33.
29. Liu, J., Cole, M.J., Liu, C., Bierig, R., Gwizdka, J., Belkin, N.J., Zhang, J., and Zhang, X. (2010). Search behavior in different task types. *JCDL*, 69–78.
30. Lucchese, C., Orlando, S., Perego, R., Silvestri, F., and Tolomei, G. (2011). Identifying task-based sessions in search engine query logs. *WSDM*, 277–286.
31. MacKay, B. and Watters, C. (2008). Exploring multi-session web tasks. *SIGCHI*, 1187–1196.
32. Mei, Q. and Church, K. (2008). Entropy of search logs: how hard is search? with personalization? with backoff? *WSDM*, 45–54.
33. Radlinski, F. and Joachims, T. (2005). Query chains: learning to rank from implicit feedback. *KDD*, 239–248.
34. Radlinski, F., Szummer, M. and Craswell, N. (2010). Inferring query intent from reformulations and clicks. *WWW*, 1171–72.
35. Shen, X., Tan, B., and Zhai, C. X. (2005). Implicit user modeling for personalized search. *CIKM*, 824–831.
36. Smyth, B. (2007). A community-based approach to personalizing Web search. *IEEE Computer*, 40(8): 42–50.
37. Sontag, D., Collins-Thompson, K., Bennett, P.N., White, R.W., Dumais, S.T., and Billerbeck, B. (2012). Probabilistic models for personalizing web search. *WSDM*, 433–442.
38. Sugiyama, K., Hatano, K., and Yoshikawa, M. (2004). Adaptive Web search based on user profile constructed without any effort from users. *WWW*, 675–684.
39. Sun, J.-T., Zeng, H.-J., Liu, H., Lu, Y., and Chen, Z. (2005). CubeSVD: a novel approach to personalized web search. *WWW*, 382–390.
40. Tan, B., Shen, X. and Zhai, C. (2006). Mining long-term search history to improve search accuracy. *KDD*, 718–723.
41. Teevan, J., Dumais, S. T., and Horvitz, E. (2005). Personalizing search via automated analysis of interests and activities. *SIGIR*, 449–456.
42. Teevan, J., Liebling, D.J., and Geetha, G.R. (2011). Understanding and predicting personal navigation. *WSDM*, 85–94.
43. Teevan, J., Morris, M.R., and Bush, S. (2009). Discovering and using groups to improve personalized search. *WSDM*, 15–24.
44. Weber, I. and Castillo, C. (2010). The demographics of web search. *SIGIR*, 523–530.
45. White, R.W., Bailey, P. and Chen, L. (2009). Predicting user interests from contextual information. *SIGIR*, 363–370.
46. White, R.W., Bennett, P.N., and Dumais, S.T. (2010). Predicting short-term interests using activity-based search context. *CIKM*, 1009–1018.
47. White, R.W. and Buscher, G. (2012). Characterizing local interests and local knowledge. *SIGCHI*, 1607–1610.
48. Wu, Q., Burges, C.J.C., Svore, K.M., and Gao, J. (2008). Ranking, boosting, and model adaptation. *Microsoft Research Technical Report MSR-TR-2008-10*.
49. Xiang, B., Jiang, D., Pei, J., Sun, X., Chen, E., and Li, H. (2010). Context-aware ranking in web search. *SIGIR*. 451–458.
50. Zhang, X., Anghelescu, H.G.B., and Yuan, X. (2005). Domain knowledge, search behavior, and search effectiveness of engineering and science students. *Inf. Res.*, 10(2): 217.

Inferring Dependency Constraints on Parameters for Web Services

Qian Wu[1], Ling Wu[1], Guangtai Liang[1], Qianxiang Wang[1], Tao Xie[2], Hong Mei[1]

[1]Institute of Software, School of Electronics Engineering and Computer Science
Key Laboratory of High Confidence Software Technologies (Peking University), Ministry of Education
Peking University, Beijing, 100871, China
{wuqian08, wuling07, lianggt08, wqx, meih}@sei.pku.edu.cn

[2]Department of Computer Science, North Carolina State University, Raleigh, NC 27695, USA
xie@csc.ncsu.edu

ABSTRACT

Recently many popular websites such as Twitter and Flickr expose their data through web service APIs, enabling third-party organizations to develop client applications that provide functionalities beyond what the original websites offer. These client applications should follow certain constraints in order to correctly interact with the web services. One common type of such constraints is *Dependency Constraints on Parameters*. Given a web service operation O and its parameters $P_i, P_j,...$, these constraints describe the requirement on one parameter P_i that is dependent on the conditions of some other parameter(s) P_j. For example, when requesting the Twitter operation "GET statuses/user_timeline", a *user_id* parameter must be provided if a *screen_name* parameter is not provided. Violations of such constraints can cause fatal errors or incorrect results in the client applications. However, these constraints are often not formally specified and thus not available for automatic verification of client applications. To address this issue, we propose a novel approach, called *INDICATOR*, to automatically infer *dependency constraints on parameters* for web services, via a hybrid analysis of heterogeneous web service artifacts, including the service documentation, the service SDKs, and the web services themselves. To evaluate our approach, we applied *INDICATOR* to infer dependency constraints for four popular web services. The results showed that *INDICATOR* effectively infers constraints with an average precision of 94.4% and recall of 95.5%.

Categories and Subject Descriptors

D.2.4 [**Software Engineering**]: Software/Program Verification—Programming by contract; D.2.5 [**Software Engineering**]: Testing and Debugging; H.3.5 [**Information Storage and Retrieval**]: Online Information Services—Web-based services

Keywords

Web service; Constraints; Parameters; Testing; Service SDK; Documentation Analysis

1. INTRODUCTION

In recent years, many popular websites expose their data through web service APIs, enabling third-party organizations to develop client applications that provide functionalities beyond what the original websites offer. For example, by making requests to Twitter web services, third-party applications allow users to share movie tastes with their friends, check the comments on a particular restaurant and so on.

These third-party client applications should follow certain constraints in order to correctly interact with the web services. For example, when requesting the Twitter operation[1] "GET statuses/user_timeline", client applications are required to specify either a *user_id* or a *screen_name* parameter. Violations of such constraints can cause fatal errors or incorrect results in the client applications.

These constraints are mainly expressed in natural language in the service documentation. A widely-adopted strategy [7] by developers to build correct client applications is to first read through the service documentation, trying to memorize the constraints, and then develop client applications accordingly. However, conformance to constraints cannot be assured. In fact, a recent study [14] showed that developers may still make mistakes even when they have been rather familiar with the documentation.

Therefore, it is desirable that client applications are formally verified against these constraints, and violations of each constraint are detected as bugs. However, these verification techniques [8, 9, 14] require formally specified constraints, which are often not readily available, due to the large amount of effort needed to manually specify them. For example, it took one of the authors more than 10 hours to only browse the documentation of the Ebay[2] web service operation "AddFixedPriceItem", let alone the time needed to extract and formalize the constraints.

To address the issue, in this paper, we propose a novel approach to automatically infer formal usage constraints for web services. In particular, we focus on one type of constraints that commonly exists in web services, and we call these constraints **Dependency Constraints on Parameters**. We refer to such constraints as dependency constraints in short in the rest of this paper. Given a web-service operation O and its parameters $P_i, P_j,...$, these constraints describe the dependency relationships between parameters: the requirement on the occurrence or the valid value of one parameter P_i depends on the occurrence or the current value of some other parameter(s) P_j. For example, the aforementioned constraint "either a *user_id* or a *screen_name* must be specified" can be interpreted as "when *user_id* is not specified, *screen_name* must be specified, and vice versa". These constraints are beyond type definitions (i.e., requirements on the structure and format of the request message, which are specified in WSDL files for SOAP-based web services), and are currently expressed in only natural language in service documentation. We manually investigated the documentation of four popular web services (Twitter, Flickr,

---

Copyright is held by the International World Wide Web Conference Committee (IW3C2). IW3C2 reserves the right to provide a hyperlink to the author's site if the Material is used in electronic media.
WWW 2013, May 13–17, 2013, Rio de Janeiro, Brazil.
ACM 978-1-4503-2035-1/13/05.

[1] Twitter Web Service: available at https://dev.twitter.com/docs/api/1.
[2] Ebay Services: an online retailing service, available at https://www.x.com/developers/ebay/products/trading-api.

Lastfm[3], and Amazon Product Advertising API (APAA)[4]) and found that an average of 21.9% of their service operations have dependency constraints on their parameters.

Most existing approaches infer usage constraints for web services by testing these web services [2, 5]. These approaches first use the type definitions of the service operations to generate test cases, then execute the test cases by submitting web service requests, and finally infer constraints by observing the responses. A constraint is produced if and only if its satisfying test cases pass and its violating test cases fail. However, two challenges remain unaddressed by these existing approaches.

First, relying on information from only the type definitions would cause an explosion in the number of generated test cases, while very few of them would lead to discovery of real constraints. For example, to find the constraint "either a *user_id* or a *screen_name* must be specified" for the Twitter operation "*GET statuses/user_timeline*" with totally ten parameters, all combinations of every two parameters must be tested, while 44/45 (97.8%) of the test cases contribute to no discovery of constraints. In addition, to save bandwidth and CPU time on the server side, service providers typically limit the rate of clients' requests, making testing web services expensive in either monetary or time cost. For example, the Flickr[5] method "*flickr.activity.userComments*" can be invoked only once an hour by each authenticated user. Therefore, running a large number of generated test cases would not be feasible.

Second, test results may be affected by multiple constraints for one operation, leading to false negatives and false positives. In particular, for a real constraint P, its satisfying test cases could fail due to violations of another constraint Q, which has not been inferred and is unknown to the approach, thus hindering P from being discovered. For example, a Flickr operation "*flickr.places.placesForContacts*" has a constraint that "either *woe_id* or *place_id* must be provided", and the test cases would not pass unless they conform to not only this constraint but also all the other constraints, such as "either *place_type* or *place_type_id* must be provided". Failing to fulfill these latter constraints would prevent the discovery of the former one. If we modify the criterion of producing a constraint to consider only whether its violating test cases fail, a false-positive problem occurs. For a false constraint P, its violating test cases may fail, but due to only violating constraint Q, thus making P a false positive. Taking the same Flickr operation as an example: many false constraints concerning the other optional parameters would be produced, such as "either *threshold* or *contact* must be specified", because all the satisfying and violating test cases fail due to violating the aforementioned two constraints.

To address the preceding two challenges, our approach, called *INDICATOR* (INference of Dependency ConstrAInTs On parameteRs), infers dependency constraints using a hybrid analysis of heterogeneous web service artifacts, including the service documentation, the service SDKs, and the web services themselves. *INDICATOR* consists of two stages: constraint-candidate generation and constraint-candidate validation. In the candidate-generation stage, *INDICATOR* analyzes the service documentation and service SDKs to generate constraint candidates. In the candidate-validation stage, *INDICATOR* validates the candidates through testing: *INDICATOR* invokes the web services with requests satisfying/violating a constraint candidate, and observes the results to determine whether the candidate is a real constraint.

Thanks to the hybrid analysis of heterogeneous artifacts, *INDICATOR* offers two main advantages. First, the candidate-generation stage benefits the candidate-validation stage by not only narrowing down the search space for real constraints, but also reducing the false positives and false negatives of candidate validation. The candidate-generation stage produces multiple constraint candidates for each operation. With these constraint candidates, the candidate-validation stage generates test cases each of which is guaranteed to violate no more than one constraint candidate. Such guided test-case generation enables our approach to validate a constraint candidate without being influenced by any other constraint candidate for the same operation. Second, the candidate-validation stage benefits the candidate-generation stage by refining the generated constraint candidates to reduce false positives.

To evaluate our approach, we applied *INDICATOR* to infer dependency constraints for four popular web services (Twitter, Flickr, Lastfm, and APAA). The results show that *INDICATOR* infers constraints with an average precision of 94.4% and recall of 95.5%. Compared with existing approaches based on only web services themselves, *INDICATOR* improves the precision by 39.4% and recall by 10.3%, while saving 84.7% of the efforts.

In summary, this paper makes the following main contributions:

- An empirical investigation of web service documentation to show the non-trivial presence of dependency constraints on parameters in web services, along with their further classification. We also discuss possible reasons leading to the non-trivial presence of such constraints in web services.

- An effective and efficient approach to inferring dependency constraints of using web services via a hybrid analysis of heterogeneous artifacts, including the service documentation, the service SDKs, and the web services themselves.

The rest of this paper is organized as follows. Section 2 presents the results of the empirical investigation of the distribution and classification of dependency constraints in popular web services. Section 3 gives an overview of our approach. Section 4 describes our approach in detail. Section 5 presents the evaluation results. Section 6 discusses the related work and Section 7 concludes.

2. DEPENDENCY CONSTRAINTS IN WEB SERVICES

In this section, we first show the results of our empirical investigation of dependency constraints in popular web services, and next discuss reasons leading to the non-trivial presence of such constraints in web services.

2.1 Empirical Investigation

We manually investigated the service documentation of four popular web services, and the results are listed in Table 1 (more details of the investigation can be found at http://sa.seforge.org/indicator/). In particular, column "Mashups" lists the number of applications known to be built on each web service (according to the statistics from http://www.programmableweb.com); column "OP" lists the number of operations provided by each web service; column "DC" lists the percentage of operations with dependency constraints. From the statistics, we could observe that a non-trivial percentage (an average of 21.9%) of web service operations have dependency constraints. In addition, hundreds of client applications would benefit from the constraints inferred for a web service.

---

[3] Lastfm: available at http://www.last.fm/api.

[4] Amazon Product Advertising API: available at https://affiliate-program.amazon.com/gp/advertising/api/detail/main.html. API Version: 2011-08-01.

[5] Flickr Service: available at http://www.flickr.com/services/api/.

We further divided these constraints into six categories, as shown in Figure 1. We use "*A*" and "*B*" to denote two different parameters in one operation, and use "*p*" and "*q*" to denote parameter values. The first three categories restrict parameter occurrences. For example, the first category requires "either *A* or *B* (at least one of *A* and *B*) should be specified", which is the most prevalent category. The second category requires "when *A* is included, *B* should (not) be included in the same request". The fourth and fifth categories restrict parameter values. For example, the fourth category requires that "when *B* is specified, *A* must (not) be set to *p* in the same request". Note that the categories shown in Figure 1 are only the most basic constraint categories, from which complex constraints could be composed by using conjunctive or disjunctive connections.

Table 1. Results of empirical investigation of dependency constraints in popular web services.

Subject	Description	#Mashups	#OP	%DC
Twitter	micro-blogging	748	105	38.1
Flickr	photo-sharing	615	186	10.2
Lastfm	online radio	225	130	23.1
APAA	online retailing	416	9	55.6
Total	---	---	430	21.9

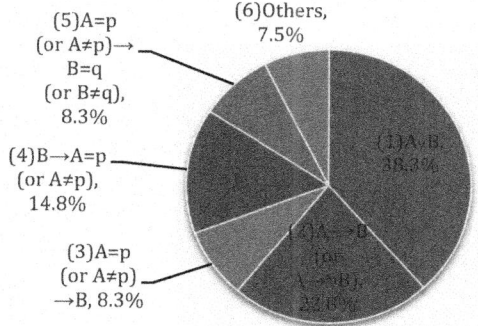

Figure 1. Categories and distribution of dependency constraints in popular web services.

2.2 Reasons of Dependency Constraints

We found empirically that the dependency constraints are much more common in web services, than in local API libraries. We next discuss two main reasons for such phenomenon.

First, parameter values in web services are passed in a much more flexible way. Normally, in local API libraries, the number and order of the parameters for a method are strictly stipulated. In contrast, in web services, parameter values are indexed by only their parameter names, allowing values of any number of parameters being passed in any order. For example, a typical RESTful service request would look like "*https://api.twitter.com/1/statuses/user_timeline.json?screen_name=twitterapi&count=2*". Such a flexible way of passing parameters thus demands additional constraints to restrict whether a parameter should be present.

Second, most web services support parameters only of primitive types. In object-oriented local API libraries, parameters are encapsulated in objects based on their internal relationships, and a proper design could have enforced the constraints between parameters. In contrast, in order to maintain good interoperability, currently most web services (especially RESTful ones) support parameters only of primitive types; in other words, all the parameters hidden in objects for API libraries are flattened to primitive parameters for web services. As a result, to carry the same amount of information as their counterparts in local API libraries, web-service operations require a much larger number of parameters. Meanwhile, the internal relationships between parameters hidden in objects for API libraries have turned into constraints across multiple parameters for web services. For example, the Twitter operation "*POST statuses/update*" requires that the parameters *latitude* and *longitude* should be paired. The code snippet in Figure 2 shows a likely design of encapsulating these two parameters in a *GeoLocation* object in Java local API libraries. It can be observed that this constraint no longer exists in this snippet, because client applications are always enforced to pass both parameters when calling the constructor in Line 4 to create a *GeoLocation* object.

```
1.public class GeoLocation{
2.    private double longitude;
3.    private double latitude;
4.    public GeoLocation(double latitude,double longitude){
5.        this.latitude = latitude;
6.        this.longitude = longitude;
7.    }
8.    public double getLatitude(){return latitude;}
9.    public double getLongitude() {return longitude;}
10.}
```

Figure 2. Example code snippet showing the encapsulation of the parameters *latitude* and *longitude* in OO API libraries.

In general, in order to achieve good interoperability, web services are designed to throw away characteristics that are specific to certain programming languages, such as information hiding via encapsulation in object-oriented languages. Therefore, additional dependency constraints are entailed in order to ensure the correct interaction between client applications and the web services.

3. APPROACH OVERVIEW

In this section, we provide an overview of our general approach through a series of examples.

As Figure 3 shows, our INDICATOR approach infers dependency constraints for web services via a hybrid analysis of three information sources: the service documentation, the service SDK, and the web services themselves. INDICATOR starts with a preparatory analysis, which collects necessary information from the service documentation for subsequent main stages, e.g., type definitions of service operations, descriptions of parameters. The main approach then proceeds in two stages. In the candidate-generation stage, INDICATOR analyzes the service documentation and service SDKs to generate constraint candidates. In the candidate-validation stage, INDICATOR validates the candidates through testing, and outputs only the constraint candidates that have been validated.

In particular, to extract constraint candidates from the service documentation, INDICATOR includes two strategies: the "rigid" and "loose" strategies, to find a potential matching between descriptions in the documentation and predefined constraint templates, e.g., "either parameter *A* or *B* is required". The "rigid" strategy intends to find constraint candidates described by similar words as the templates. While leading to relatively precise results, this strategy is fragile to the word choices of a constraint's description. In other words, false negatives would be produced when a semantically equivalent constraint is described in words not covered by the templates. To alleviate this limitation, INDICATOR includes the "loose" strategy, which generates a constraint candidate when the number of distinct parameters appearing in its describing sentence matches with the number of parameters in a

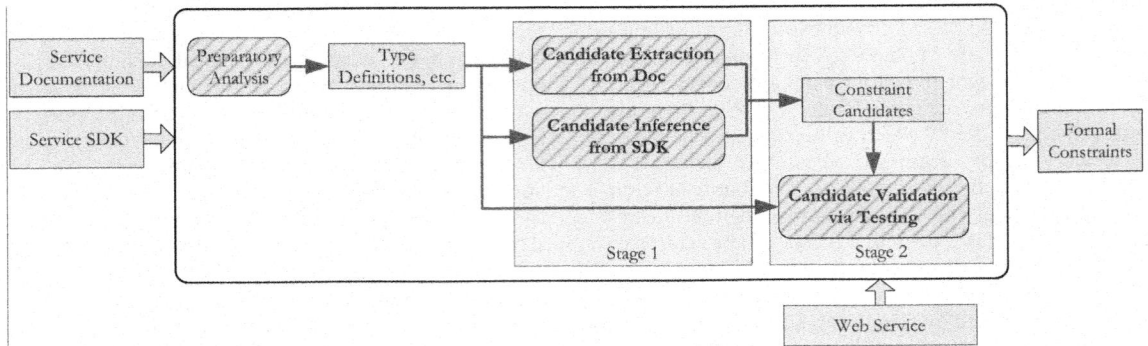

Figure 3. Architecture of *INDICATOR*.

template. Our insight here is that rather than trying very hard to extract the semantics out of sentences, we use only simple and reliable information from the sentences and then rely on testing (to be conducted in the subsequent stage) to figure out the constraint, reflecting a benefit from integrating heterogeneous information sources.

In addition to service documentation, *INDICATOR* also exploits information from service SDKs. For most popular web services, there are SDKs available in various programming languages. Such SDKs wrap interactions with web services, allowing client-application developers to invoke web services as if invoking methods from local API libraries. *INDICATOR* includes a novel technique to infer constraint candidates from service SDKs, based on our insight that SDKs demonstrate legal ways of invoking web services. For example, the code snippet in Figure 4 shows the API method in the Java SDK of the Lastfm web service. Such API method wraps the invocation of the "*artist.getInfo*" operation. The statements in Lines 2-9 collect the parameters, and the statement in Lines 11-12 makes the remote call. As shown in the code snippet, it is ensured that "either an *mbid* or an *artist* is specified", which is actually the constraint for this operation. Our main idea is to identify all possible combinations of parameters included by the SDK to invoke each service operation, and then apply a simple statistical analysis to learn constraints. For the method in Figure 4, there are four distinct paths, making four possible combinations of parameters: {*mbid*, *lang*}, {*artist*, *lang*}, {*mbid*}, and {*artist*}. Then by analyzing the combinations, we notice that either *mbid* or *artist* is present in the set of included parameters, thus leading us to infer the constraint.

Finally, *INDICATOR* validates each constraint candidate through testing. For each candidate, *INDICATOR* generates both satisfying and violating test cases, all of which are ensured to conform to all the other constraint candidates in the same operation. *INDICATOR* considers a constraint candidate to be ***real***, if (1) all its violating test cases fail and at least one of its satisfying test cases passes, or (2) all test cases fail, and the error messages of the violating test cases look alike to the candidate's description. Using these criteria, *INDICATOR* intends to find constraints that are required by correct interactions with the web services. *INDICATOR* reduces false negatives by accommodating occasions when test cases conforming to the constraint candidate fail due to violating other constraints. Meanwhile, *INDICATOR* reduces false positives by exploiting information from the error messages of violating test cases, so that *INDICATOR* confirms that the failure was indeed caused by violating the constraint candidate under validation, but not some other constraints.

```
1.  public Artist getInfo(String artistOrMbid, Locale loc) {
2.    Map<String, String> params = new HashMap<String,
3.  String>();
4.    if(StringUtilities.isMbid(artistOrMbid)){
5.        params.put("mbid", artistOrMbid);}
6.    else{
7.        params.put("artist", artistOrMbid);}
8.    if(loc!=null)
9.        params.put("lang",loc.getLanguage());
10.   ......
11.   Result result = Caller.getInstance().call(
12. "artist.getInfo", params);
13.   return ResponseBuilder.buildItem(result,
14. Artist.class);
15. }
```

Figure 4. Code snippet of the API method *de.umass.lastfm. Artist.getInfo* from the Java SDK of Lastfm web service.

4. APPROACH DETAIL

We next describe the details of our *INDICATOR* approach. In particular, we present the preparatory analysis in Section 4.1. We next present the candidate generation from documentation and SDK in Section 4.2 and Section 4.3, respectively. We finally present the candidate validation through testing in Section 4.4.

4.1 Preparatory Analysis

In preparatory analysis, *INDICATOR* collects various types of information needed by subsequent steps, including (1) the service type definitions, e.g., the available operations names, the list of mandatory and optional parameter names for each operation, and available values for parameters of enumeration types, (2) descriptions for operations and parameters, which might contain usage constraints, and (3) other technical details required to enable automatic invocation of the service operations, e.g., the URL address of the service, the HTTP method to make the request. Unlike SOAP-based web services (most of whose preceding information is available in formal WSDL files), for most currently popular RESTful web services, all the preceding information could be extracted from only the service documents in the form of HTML files. Fortunately, all the information is easy to locate, given user-defined XPath[6] expressions to specify the paths of their corresponding nodes in the HTML files. Only very little manual effort is needed to write the XPath expressions, since documents of different operations in a web service share the same style and structure.

---

[6] XPath: http://www.w3.org/TR/xpath20/.

4.2 Candidate Extraction from Service Documentation

The basic idea to extract constraint candidates from service documentation is to find potential matchings between the descriptions in documentation and the predefined constraint templates. Table 2 shows some typical template sentences, in which "A" and "B" denote two different parameter names, and "p" and "q" denote parameter values. In particular, the first column presents their correspondence with the constraint categories shown in Figure 1. According to our manual investigation, parameter values incorporated in such constraints always belong to enumeration types, and note that all parameter names and available values are already extracted in advance by the preparatory analysis.

INDICATOR includes two strategies to locate the candidate-describing sentences in documentation. The "loose" strategy marks a sentence as describing a constraint candidate when the number of distinct parameters and values appearing in the sentence matches with that in a template. This strategy could identify candidate-describing sentences, even those using completely different words from the templates. However, the number of generated sentences might grow quickly with only a small portion describing real constraints, causing a potential waste of effort in subsequent steps.

Table 2. Example templates of dependency constraints.

Category ID	Template Sentences
(1)	Either A or B must be specified.
(1)	One of A or B is required.
(2)	If providing A, B is also required.
(3)	A is required, when B is set to p.
(5)	When A is set to p, B cannot be set to q.

The "rigid" strategy marks a sentence as describing a constraint candidate when the sentence uses similar words as the template sentences. This strategy computes a *Jaccard Similarity*[7] between the bag of words used in the candidate-describing sentence and a template sentence. Some standard Natural Language Processing (NLP) procedures should be conducted in advance, such as stop-word removing, word stemming, and synonym replacement. In addition, parameter names are also excluded in the similarity computation. Compared with the "loose" strategy, this strategy produces more precise results, but it is sensitive to the word choices of a candidate's description: false negatives would be produced when a real constraint is described in words not covered by the templates. For example, using the first sentence in Table 2 without using the second one would cause the approach to miss constraints described in the second sentence in Table 2, which use different words but share the same semantics.

Our approach provides a way to flexibly choose between the two strategies. It first adopts the "loose" strategy to generate candidate-describing sentences. If the number of the generated sentences is overwhelmingly too many (e.g., beyond a user-defined threshold), it then adopts the "rigid" strategy to further refine the sentences. In this way, INDICATOR could be adaptive to any incoming web services, while maintaining a balance between recall and efficiency.

---

[7] *Jaccard* Similarity$(A, B) = \frac{|A \cap B|}{|A \cup B|}$, where in our approach, A and B represent two sets of words.

Finally, for each candidate-describing sentence, INDICATOR generates the constraint candidate by filling the matched template with the relevant parameter names and values. For templates in which the order of the parameters matters (e.g., the last three templates in Table 2), if the templates contain parameter values, INDICATOR then determines the order of parameters by first identifying the parameter to which the value belongs; otherwise, it simply fills the templates with all possible parameter sequences.

Thanks to integrating information from heterogeneous artifacts, our approach could use only simple information from the documentation, rather than adopting sophisticated NLP techniques: all the constraint candidates are to be (in)validated by means of testing web services in the subsequent stage.

4.3 Candidate Inference from SDK

INDICATOR infers constraint candidates from SDKs based on the observation that the code of the SDK demonstrates legal ways of invoking web services. The main idea of this technique is to identify all combinations of parameters and their values (only values of enumeration types are considered) included by the SDK to invoke each service operation, and then apply a simple statistical analysis to learn the constraints. The technique takes as input the code of the service SDK and the service type definitions (including the operation names and the list of parameter names and values for each operation, which are extracted in advance by the preparatory analysis presented in Section 4.1), and produces as output the inferred constraint candidates.

This technique proceeds in four steps. (1) As a preparatory step, INDICATOR applies a constant propagation [1] to the code of the SDK to replace each String variable with the actual String literal, so that INDICATOR could identify parameter names and values without tracking into the content of their holding variables. In addition, INDICATOR performs an inter-procedural analysis to build the call graph for the whole program. (2) For each operation, INDICATOR searches in the SDK for all the public methods that wrap its invocation, by searching for methods that directly or indirectly access its operation name. For example, for the Lastfm operation "*artist.getInfo*", INDICATOR first locates the method "*getInfo(String, Locale)*", which accesses the operation name in Line 12 as shown in Figure 4, and then searches for all callers of this method based on the call graph. (3) For each SDK method found by Step 2, INDICATOR applies a forward Data Flow Analysis Algorithm [1] to compute all the combinations of parameter names and values included in the method. The formal algorithm of this step is shown in Figure 5, which is explained later. (4) Finally, INDICATOR gathers all the available sets of parameter names and values for each operation, and applies a statistical analysis to learn the constraints.

We next use the SDK method "*artist.getInfo*" as an example to illustrate the algorithm shown in Figure 5. For simplicity, the shown algorithm deals with only parameter names, but the same algorithm could be easily adapted to compute all the encountered parameter-value combinations in each method. Intuitively, this algorithm computes the sets of already encountered parameters by propagating such information from the method entry point along each path of the Control Flow Graph (CFG) to the method exit point. There are three key variables in the propagation process. For each node n (a block of consecutive statements) of the CFG, $IN[n]$ and $OUT[n]$ denote the set of data at the program point before and after the execution of statements in this node, respectively. In particular, each element of $IN[n]$ and $OUT[n]$ is a set of parameter names already encountered along some path leading from the entry point to their corresponding program point. The execution of the statements in the node changes *IN[n]* to *OUT[n]* by including parameter names, which are all recorded in *GEN[n]*. Figure 6 depicts the CFG for the method "*artist.getInfo*", tagged with the computed information at each program point.

Algorithm *computeParamCombinations*
Input *m* the public SDK method wrapping the invocation of *OP*;
  NOP the list of parameter names for *OP*;
Output *NS* {*N* | *N is* a set of parameter names included on each path}
Begin
1. Build a control-flow-graph *CFG* for *m*;
2. **foreach** node *n* in *CFG* **do**
3.   *OUT[n]* = ∅;
4. *OUT[Entry]* = *IN[Entry]* = ∅;
5. *Changed* = {All nodes in *CFG*} − *Entry*;
6.
7. **while** *Changed* ≠ ∅ **do**
8.   choose a node *n* from *Changed*;
9.   *Changed* = *Changed* \ {*n*};
10.
11.   *IN[n]* = ∅;
12.   **foreach** predecessor node *p* of *n* **do**
13.   *IN[n]* = *IN[n]* ⋃ *OUT[p]*;
14.
15.   *GEN[n]* = {*param* | *param* ∈ *NOP* ⋀ *param* visited in *n*}
16.   *OUT[n]* = ∅;
17.   **foreach** element *eleIn* in *IN[n]* **do**
18.   *OUT[n]* = *OUT[n]* ⋃ {*GEN[n]* ⋃ *eleIn*};
19.
20.   **if** (*OUT[n]* changed) **then**
21.   **foreach** successor node *s* of *n* **do**
22.   *Changed* = *Changed* ⋃ {*s*};
23.
24.   **return** *OUT[Exit]*;
End

Figure 5. The algorithm in Step 3 for extracting all the combinations of parameter names for an SDK method.

As Figure 5 shows, INDICATOR starts the algorithm by building a CFG for the given method (Line 1 in Figure 5). In the process, all paths leading to exception-throwing statements are pruned; these paths demonstrate illegal ways of invoking the method or the wrapped operation. After properly initializing the variables (Lines 2-5), INDICATOR iteratively computes the concerned data for each program point until all data converge (Lines 7-22). Once the data *OUT* for a node *n* has been updated, all the *IN* (and hence *OUT*) data for all *n*'s successor nodes must also be recomputed (Lines 20-22). INDICATOR records all the nodes requiring re-computation in the variable *Changed*. In each iteration, INDICATOR randomly selects a node that requires re-computation and computes its *IN* and *OUT* data (Lines 11-22). INDICATOR computes the *IN* data of each node by doing a union of the *OUT* data of all its predecessors (Lines 11-13), so as to gather all possible combinations of parameters encountered so far along each path. For example, for *Node 6* in Figure 6, by doing a union of *OUT[4]* and *OUT[5]*, the *IN[6]* is computed as {{*mbid*}, {*artist*}, {*mbid, lang*}, {*artist, lang*}}, while each element corresponds to the paths (1-2-4-6), (1-3-4-6), (1-2-4-5-6), and (1-3-4-5-6), respectively. INDICATOR next computes the *OUT* data of each node *n* by adding the set of parameter names visited by statements in *n* (Line 15) to each element of the *IN* data (Lines 16-18). Note that the size of *OUT[n]* is equal to that of *IN[n]*, which represents the number of feasible paths leading from the entry to the corresponding point. For example, for *Node 5*, by adding the parameter name "*lang*" to each element of *IN[5]*,

we arrive at *OUT[5]*, which is {{*mbid, lang*}, {*artist, lang*}}, each element corresponding to the paths (1-2-4-5) and (1-3-4-5), respectively. Finally, INDICATOR returns the *OUT* data of the exit point as the final sets of all combinations of parameter names included by the method (Line 24).

Due to space limit, we omit from Figure 5 the details of dealing with method-invocation statements. In fact, for each such statement, the technique would apply an inter-procedural analysis to track the sets of parameters encountered by statements inside the invoked method, and then add all the tracked data into that of the caller method.

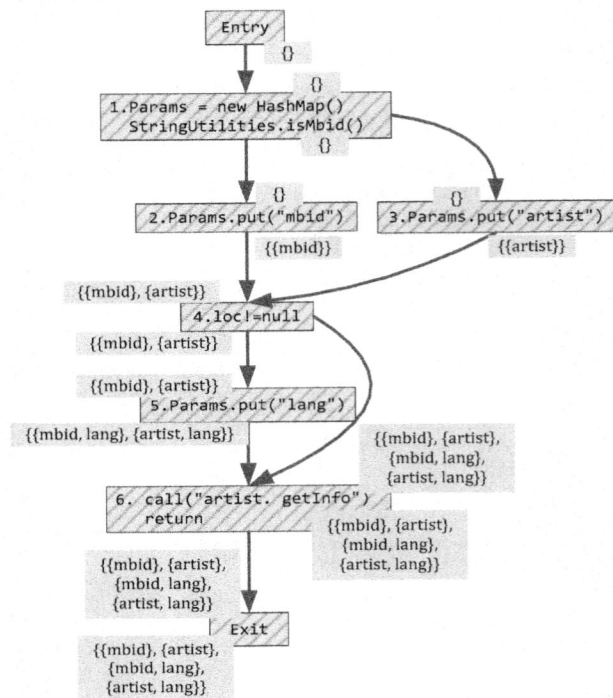

Figure 6. CFG for method "*artist.getInfo*" in Figure 4 along with the *OUT[n]* and *IN[n]* data for each node *n*.

Finally, for each operation *OP*, the technique gathers the computed sets of parameter names and values from all its public wrapping methods in the SDK, and applies a simple statistical analysis to derive the constraints. For example, for the operation "*artist.getInfo*", we found two other public wrapping methods in the SDK, contributing the additional sets of encountered parameter names as follows: {{*mbid, username*}, {*artist, username*}, {*mbid, lang, username*}, {*artist, lang, username*}}. From the total of the eight sets of parameter names, we could learn that each set includes either "*mbid*" or "*artist*", thus leading us to infer the constraint: "either *mbid* or *artist* is required".

4.4 Constraint-Candidate Validation through Testing

The candidate-validation stage determines whether a constraint candidate is real or not via testing.

We consider a constraint as **real**, if it is required to ensure correct interactions with web services. While we cannot prove a constraint to be real, we could observe whether a constraint candidate causes the same consequences on the execution of test cases as a real constraint does. A real constraint typically demonstrates certain observable characteristics: (a) all test cases that violate the constraint would fail (determining test-case failing or passing is elaborated in the end of this section); meanwhile, (b) all test cases that conform to the constraint as well as all the other constraints would pass. Thus the task of candidate validation becomes to first generate test cases according to the requirements in (a) and (b), and to then determine the candidate's likelihood of being real based on the execution outcomes of the test cases. Unfortunately, requirements in (b) may not be fulfilled due to the lack of complete constraints (their presence would obviate the need to infer them in the first place). As a result, false positives/negatives would be produced when test cases violate constraints other than the one under validation, as discussed earlier in Section 1.

Our approach addresses the preceding issue in two ways, attempting to validate a constraint candidate appropriately without the knowledge of complete constraints.

First, *INDICATOR* improves the quality of generated test cases to reduce the possibility of violating other constraints. In the context of web services, the quality of test cases depends on mostly the quality of parameter values. *INDICATOR* collects parameter values from four sources. (1) *INDICATOR* extracts parameter values of enumeration types from the service documentation, as was done by the preparatory analysis. (2) *INDICATOR* caches the responses of executed test cases, in order to provide values for parameters whose values are returned by other operations. For example, in APAA, the only valid value of parameter *CartID* in operation *CartAdd* is returned by operation *CartCreate*. *INDICATOR* identifies such producer-consumer relationships through name and type matching between input and output parameters of different operations. Then *INDICATOR* prioritizes the test cases of operations, so that a parameter is always produced before it is consumed. In this way, errors such as "the cart specified does not belong to you" or "no data found" could be avoided. (3) *INDICATOR* extracts the available example values from service documentation, and these values typically adhere to the syntax requirements and are within the valid range. (4) *INDICATOR* solicits parameter values from users for the remaining parameters if it is feasible to do so.

Table 3. Sample test cases that conform to or violate a given constraint.

Constraint: Either *A* or *B* must be specified.			
Conformance			Violation
Given *A*, no *B*	Given *B*, no *A*	Given *A* and *B*	no *A* no *B*

In addition, with the knowledge of constraint candidates provided by previous steps, our *INDICATOR* approach ensures that each generated test case for one candidate must also conform to all the other constraint candidates of the same operation in a non-conflicting way. The conformance of constraint *A* conflicts with constraint *B*, when the conformance of *A* influences the conformance or violation of *B*. Table 3 shows sample test cases satisfying or violating the constraint "either *A* or *B* must be specified". Note that there is only one way (i.e., including parameter *A* and not *B*) to conform to this constraint without conflicting with another constraint "either *B* or *C* must be specified", because including parameter *B* would coincidentally cause a conformance with the latter constraint.

Second, we adjust the criteria of determining real constraints. *INDICATOR* considers a constraint candidate as **real**, if

a) all the violating test cases fail and at least one of the satisfying test cases passes; **or**

b) all the test cases fail, and the error messages of the violating test cases look alike to the description of the constraint candidate.

Therefore, *INDICATOR* first invalidates a candidate, if some of its violating test cases pass. *INDICATOR* next attempts to validate a candidate by checking whether the execution outcomes of the test cases conform to either of the preceding criteria. Based on the criteria, on one hand, *INDICATOR* reduces false negatives by accommodating occasions when a satisfying test case fails due to violating other constraints. On the other hand, *INDICATOR* reduces false positives by comparing the error messages of the violating test cases with the candidate's description, ensuring to some extent that the failure was indeed caused by violating the candidate under validation, rather than some other constraints. In our evaluation, of the final constraints produced by *INDICATOR*, 86.5% were validated using criterion *a*, while 13.5% were validated using criterion *b*.

In particular, *INDICATOR* determines whether the error messages and the candidate's description are alike, by computing the highest similarity between each pair of the error message and the candidate's description. The same similarity-computation technique presented in Section 4.2 is applicable here. Specifically, for constraint candidates that do not have descriptions (i.e., those generated from SDKs or by the loose strategy from documents), *INDICATOR* uses the template sentences of the relevant constraint category as the candidates' possible descriptions.

In our implementation, we consider a test case to pass or fail based on whether the response is legal or illegal. Such classification is straightforward, since an illegal response would normally contain indications such as an error code or an error message. We did not further examine whether the data contained in a legal response matches with a predefined golden oracle, which would be difficult to specify in the context of web services [10]. The response data for an operation might be changing from time to time. For example, the Twitter operation "*GET statuses/user_timeline*" queries for the recent statuses of a user, for which the response data would change once the user posts new statuses.

4.5 Limitations

We next discuss limitations of our approach in terms of potential false negatives and false positives.

False negatives are produced when a real constraint cannot be generated from either the documentation or the SDK, or its generated candidate cannot be validated by testing. In the step of candidate extraction from documentation, *INDICATOR* would miss real constraints described in words not covered by the given templates, when the rigid strategy is adopted. We have sought to alleviate this issue by introducing the loose strategy. However, the approach is still subject to the quality of the documentation: constraints might be actually missing in the documentation. *INDICATOR* mitigates these issues by including the service SDK as a complement. In the step of candidate inference from SDK, real candidates might not be inferred due to noises in un-pruned infeasible paths. Finally, in the step of candidate validation, *INDICATOR* might not be able to validate a real candidate, when all the test cases fail due to violating some other constraints, and the error messages do not convey similar information as the candidate's description. *INDICATOR* alleviates this issue by ensuring that test cases of a candidate conform to all the other candidates in the same operation.

Table 4. Evaluation results of *INDICATOR*.

Subject	#Real	Final Output			Constraint Candidates							#Exced TC	% Svd TC
		#Ttl	%Pre	%Rec	#Doc	%DP	%DR	#SDK	%SP	%SR	%Flt		
Twitter	40	38	97.4	92.5	113	27.4	77.5	12	100.0	30.0	68.1	221	79.2
Flickr	12	11	100.0	91.7	101	9.9	83.3	1	100.0	8.33	89.2	174	87.3
Lastfm	34	37	91.9	100.0	128	23.4	88.2	23	100.0	67.7	71.1	147	56.0
APAA	2	3	66.7	100.0	9	22.2	100.0	0	100.0	0.0	66.7	12	98.2
Ttl/Avg	88	89	94.4	95.5	351	20.8	82.9	36	100.0	40.9	75.1	554	84.7

False positives are produced when a false candidate is mistakenly validated through testing. Such case happens when the conformance or violation of a candidate causes unintended side effect, which coincidentally leads to the conformance or violation of some other constraints. *INDICATOR* mitigates this issue by making sure that test cases for one candidate are generated without conflicting with the other candidates in the same operation.

Concrete examples of false negatives and false positives observed from our evaluations are further discussed in Section 5.

5. EVALUATION

To evaluate the effectiveness of our *INDICATOR* approach, we applied *INDICATOR* to infer dependency constraints for four web services, i.e., Twitter, Flickr, Lastfm, and APAA. Specifically, this section shows the evaluation results of inferring the most prevalent category of dependency constraints among various categories, i.e., "either parameter A or parameter B must be specified" (we refer to constraints of this category as $(A, B)_{either-or}$ in this section). We applied *INDICATOR* to infer constraint candidates from Java SDKs, namely twitter4j[8] for Twitter, flickrj[9] for Flickr, and lastfm API[10] for Lastfm; there is no Java SDK available for the APAA web service. We solicited parameter values from one researcher in the Institute of Software at Peking University, for only 28 (1.7%) of the involved parameters, while values for all the remaining parameters were collected automatically by *INDICATOR*. We spent two weeks to prepare a golden standard for the web services. We first ran test cases concerning all combinations involving every two parameters for each operation, and then invited two researchers from the institute to manually inspect the results. The golden standard and details of our evaluation results are available at http://sa.seforge.org /indicator/.

Our evaluation addresses the following research questions:

- *RQ1*: How effectively and efficiently can *INDICATOR* infer constraints?
- *RQ2*: How well can information in documentation and SDKs complement each other?
- *RQ3*: How much can the candidate-validation stage benefit the candidate-generation stage?
- *RQ4*: How much can the candidate-generation stage benefit the candidate-validation stage?

The first research question concerns the overall effectiveness and performance of our approach, while the next three ones concern the benefits of integrating information from heterogeneous artifacts. We answer the first three questions in Section 5.1. To answer the last question, we conducted an additional evaluation and present the results in Section 5.2.

5.1 Effectiveness and Efficiency of Constraint Inference

We measure the effectiveness of *INDICATOR* using both precision and recall metrics. We measure the efficiency of *INDICATOR* using the number of executed test cases as the metric, rather than the exact time that *INDICATOR* spent on the web services. The reason is that most (over 95%) of the time was spent on running test cases, and we must control the rate of making requests to avoid exceeding the rate limits imposed by the service providers, e.g., *INDICATOR* slept for 10 seconds after making each authenticated request to Twitter.

The evaluation results are listed in Table 4. Column "Real" lists the number of real constraints used as the golden standard for each web service. For statistics concerning the final output of *INDICATOR*, column "Ttl" lists the total number of constraints produced by *INDICATOR*; and columns "Pre" and "Rec" list the precision and recall, respectively. For statistics concerning the constraint candidates, column "Doc" lists the number of candidates generated from documentation using the loose strategy (we also applied the rigid strategy of extracting candidates from documentation, but the detailed results are omitted due to space limit, instead we will compare their results briefly in the end of this section). Columns "DP" and "DR" list the precision and recall of the candidates generated from documentation, respectively. Column "SDK" lists the number of candidates generated from SDK. Columns "SP" and "SR" list the precision and recall of the candidates generated from SDK, respectively. Column "Flt" lists the percentage of candidates that are filtered (i.e., have not been validated) by testing, and are considered as false candidates by *INDICATOR*. Column "Exced TC" lists the number of distinct test cases executed by *INDICATOR*. Column "Svd TC" lists the percentage of test cases that are exempted from being executed by *INDICATOR*, compared with a brute-force approach of finding the concerned constraints; such brute-force approach tests all combinations involving every two parameters in each operation.

From the results in Table 4, we have the following observations. First, *INDICATOR* achieved high precisions and recalls on these web services, with an average precision of 94.4% and recall of 95.5%. We will later show examples of the false positives and negatives, and analyze the reasons for producing them. Second, compared with documentation, *INDICATOR* inferred much fewer constraint candidates from SDKs, but with much higher precisions. We further depict the percentages of the real constraints covered by each source in Figure 7. In general, 28.4% of the constraints are covered by both sources, while 54.5% come from only documentation, and 12.5% come from only SDKs, indicating that documentation and SDKs complement each other. Third, most (75.1%) of the constraint candidates are filtered in the candidate-validation stage through testing, indicating that testing plays an

---
[8] twitter4j-2.2.5: http://twitter4j.org/.
[9] flickrj-1.2: http://flickrj.sourceforge.net/.
[10] lastfm API: http://www.u-mass.de/lastfm.

important role in improving the quality of the produced constraints. Finally, by integrating information from documentation and SDKs, *INDICATOR* greatly (84.7%) reduced the test cases needed to be executed, compared with a constraint-inference approach in a brute-force manner, which is actually the adopted manner by existing approaches to generate test cases based on only type definitions.

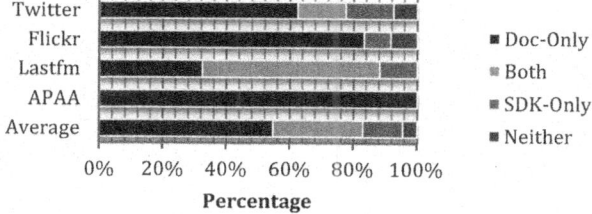

Figure 7. Percentages of the *either-or* constraints covered by different information sources.

We next analyze reasons for producing false positives and negatives. All the five false positives for the four services are caused by coincidental violations and satisfactions of constraints belonging to categories other than the "Either-Or" category. For example, a false positive for Twitter operation "*GET geo/search*" is *(accuracy, lat)either-or*, which was caused by violating/satisfying the constraint that "*lat* and *long* must be paired" (which is described explicitly in the documentation). *INDICATOR* first generated two constraint candidates for this operation, *(accuracy, lat)either-or* and *(lat, long)either-or*. To test the former one, *INDICATOR* avoided violation and conflict of the latter one by including a *long* parameter in all test cases. *INDICATOR* finally considered the former one as a real constraint according to criterion *a* in Section 4.4: all the violating test case failed due to providing *long* but no *lat*, and some of the satisfying test cases passed due to providing both *lat* and *long*.

Another false positive example is *(keywords, title)either-or* for Amazon operation "*ItemSearch*", caused by violating/satisfying the constraint "at least one of its twenty search parameters must be provided". *INDICATOR* first generated *(keywords, title)either-or* as the only candidate for the operation, because no sentences include any two of the other parameters. *INDICATOR* finally considered the candidate as real, because all the violating test case failed due to providing none of the search parameters, and all the satisfying test cases passed due to providing at least one of *keywords* and *title*.

These false positives could be reduced by considering more constraint categories. In theory, they are still unavoidable due to the lack of knowledge of what constraint categories exist in one service. Another way to alleviate the false-positive problem is to apply stricter criteria of validating constraints by additionally requiring the error messages of the violating test cases to be consistent with the candidates' descriptions. However, the stricter criteria would result in a high precision in the price of a low recall: error messages might use different words from the constraint's description to describe the constraint's violation. For example, the error message for violating "*lat* and *long* must be paired" is "Invalid Coordinates".

All the four false negatives of *INDICATOR* are due to that the documentation does not even mention the two parameters in one sentence, indicating inconsistencies between documentation and service implementation: either the documents missed describing some constraints, or the service implemented some requirements that are not necessary.

In addition, seven constraints stated explicitly in the documentation were invalidated by testing, indicating potential bugs in service implementation. For example, the document for Flickr operation "*flickr.places.placesForUser*" states that "you must pass either a *place_id* or a *woe_id*", whereas test cases without neither parameters passed.

Note that all the preceding results were obtained adopting the loose strategy to extract constraint candidates from documentation. To adopt the rigid strategy, *INDICATOR* used the constraint-describing sentences from the other three web services as the template sentences for one web service. Compared with the preceding results, *INDICATOR* produced results with a slightly higher precision (an average of 98.7%) but a lower recall (an average of 84.1%). In addition, the rigid strategy greatly saved the cost of the approach, by producing only 22.9% of the candidates produced by the loose strategy. The lower recall was not only due to that constraints' descriptions use words not covered by the templates, but also due to missing constraints in the documentation. For example, using the loose strategy, *INDICATOR* discovered the real constraint *(user_id, screen_name)either-or* for the Twitter operation "*GET lists/all*", mentioned by the sentence "The user is specified using the *user_id*, or *screen_name* parameters". This sentence is clearly not a constraint-describing sentence, and thus resulted in a false negative for our rigid-strategy-based approach. Details of evaluation results of the rigid strategy are omitted due to space limit.

5.2 Benefit to Candidate Validation from Candidate Generation

The candidate-generation stage from documentation and SDKs benefits the candidate-validation stage in two ways. First, it greatly narrows down the search space for real constraints. *INDICATOR* saved 84.7% of the test cases from being executed, compared with approaches based on only type definitions to generate test cases. Second, it reduces the false positives and negatives for candidate validation, by providing guidance for test-case generation, and ensuring that each test case violates no more than one constraint candidate.

To evaluate the latter benefit, we modified our approach to generate test cases without considering the other constraint candidates in the same operation, and compared the results with those of *INDICATOR*, as shown in Figure 8. In particular, the results for APAA are omitted, for which the modified results remain the same with those of *INDICATOR*. It can be observed that the modified approach resulted in a non-trivial degradation in precision (from the average of 94.4% to 55.1%) and recall (from the average of 95.5% to 85.2%).

Most false positives introduced by the modified approach (not by *INDICATOR*) were due to coincidental violation and satisfaction of another real constraint candidate in the same operation. For example, for the Twitter operation "*GET statuses/oembed*", the modified approach produced three false constraints, *(maxwidth, id)either-or*, *(align, id)either-or*, *(omit_script, id)either-or*, due to violating/satisfying the real constraint candidate, *(url, id)either-or*. These false constraints were produced according to criterion *a* in Section 4.4, because all violating test cases failed, due to providing neither *url* nor *id*, and some of the satisfying test cases passed, due to providing *id*.

All false negatives introduced by the modified approach (not by *INDICATOR*) were due to violation of the other real constraint candidates in the same operation, which contains multiple real constraint candidates. For example, for the Flickr operation "flickr.places.placesForContacts", a false negative *(place_type, place_type_id)*_{either-or} was produced, because all the test cases failed due to violating the other real candidate *(place_id, woe_id)*_{either-or}, with only vague error messages "missing required parameters".

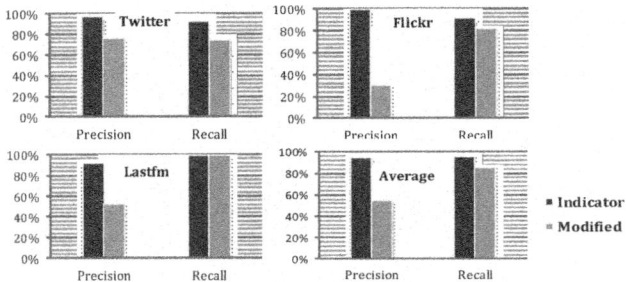

Figure 8. Precisions and recalls of *INDICATOR* and the modified approach.

6. RELATED WORK

To the best of our knowledge, there are only two existing approaches to automatically inferring formal constraints of interacting with web services. Bertolino et al. [2] proposed an approach to synthesize temporal constraints, such as "a *CartCreate* operation should be invoked before a *CartAdd* operation". Their approach first derives these constraints from service type definitions based on data type analysis, and then checks the conformance between the derived constraints and the service implementation by means of testing. Fisher et al. [5] presented an approach also based on testing to discover simple constraints involving single parameters, such as whether a parameter is required. They further applied the discovered constraints to detect imprecision errors in WSDL files, such as declaring a required parameter to be optional. Compared with these two approaches, *INDICATOR* infers a new and important type of constraints, *Dependency Constraints on Parameters*. In addition to testing web services, *INDICATOR* also integrates information from natural-language service documentation and service SDKs to infer constraints effectively and efficiently, addressing the two challenges faced by these approaches, as discussed earlier in Section 1.

All these constraints of interacting with web services could be formally described using service modeling languages such as WSML [3] or OWL-S [11]. To facilitate the automation of service discovering, composing, and invoking, researchers and developers proposed such languages to conceptually model web services. However, according to our investigation, such conceptual descriptions for most popular web services are not readily available. *INDICATOR* could automatically discover these constraints, and might help to build the conceptual models for web services.

Our work is also related to program verification approaches [7-9, 14] that use formally described constraints to detect violations of constraints as bugs in client applications. In particular, Rubinger and Bultan [14] presented their experience on applying the Microsoft Code Contract system to the Facebook API. They provided the system with formal contracts (which are called constraints in this paper) that were manually created according to the Facebook API documentation. The system verified API client applications for contract violations. Their experience indicates that program verification based on contracts enables to build more robust client applications with less effort spent on debugging. Similarly, Hallé et al. [7] conducted a case study on APAA of verifying client applications at runtime against formally described constraints. Both these pieces of work demonstrate the importance of our approach: *INDICATOR* automatically infers formal constraints, thus making these constraint-based verification approaches practical and usable.

We finally present some technically related approaches concerning the constraint inference for local API libraries. According to their inference-data sources, these approaches fall into three categories. The first category of approaches [4, 15] analyzes the source code of API client applications, and infers the frequent API usage patterns as constraints. Although there are also plenty of open source client applications for web services, inferring constraints from these client applications is unlikely to achieve desirable results. The main issue is the low coverage of web service operations: our manual investigation shows that only the several most popular operations are invoked in the available client applications. However, we plan to explore in future work to include client applications as a complementary information source. The second category of approaches [12, 16-18] extracts constraints from API library documentation. In particular, Zhong et al. [18] proposed an approach to infer resource-manipulation constraints from Javadocs. Pandita et al. [12] proposed an approach to infer pre-conditions and post-conditions for invocations of API methods from their method descriptions. Both the two approaches infer constraints by combining sophisticated NLP and machine-learning techniques. In contrast, thanks to integrating heterogeneous information sources, *INDICATOR* uses only simple and reliable information from documentation, and then relies on testing to refine the results. The third category of approaches [6, 13] infers constraints by testing. In particular, Gabel and Su [6] described a framework to automatically validate temporal constraints inferred from client applications by testing. Their framework validates a constraint if all its violating test cases fail. As we earlier discussed in Section 1, using only this criterion would lead to many false positives, when the test cases failed in consequence of violating some other constraints rather than the one under validation. *INDICATOR* avoids these false positives by additionally requiring either that some of the satisfying test cases pass, or that the error messages of the violating test cases are consistent with the constraint's description.

7. CONCLUSION

In this paper, we have proposed a novel approach called *INDICATOR* to automatically inferring *Dependency Constraints on Parameters* for web services. *INDICATOR* infers dependency constraints effectively and efficiently via a hybrid analysis of heterogeneous web service artifacts, including the service documentation, the service SDKs, and the web services themselves. To evaluate our approach, we applied *INDICATOR* to infer dependency constraints for four popular web services. The results show that *INDICATOR* infers constraints with an average precision of 94.4% and recall of 95.5%. Compared with existing approaches based on only web services themselves, *INDICATOR* improves the precision by 39.4% and recall by 10.3%, while saving 84.7% of the efforts.

8. ACKNOWLEDGMENTS

The authors from Peking University are sponsored by the National Basic Research Program of China (Grant No. 2009CB320703), the National Natural Science Foundation of China (Grant No. 61121063 , 61033006), and the High-Tech Research and Development Program of China (Grant No. 2012AA011202). Tao Xie's work is supported in part by NSF grants CCF-0845272, CCF-0915400, CNS-0958235, CNS-1160603, an NSA Science of Security Lablet grant, and a NIST grant.

9. REFERENCES

[1] Aho, A. V., Lam, M. S., Sethi, R. and Ullman, J. D. 1986. *Compilers: Principles, Techniques, and Tools*. Addison Wesley.

[2] Bertolino, A., Inverardi, P., Pelliccione, P. and Tivoli, M. 2009. Automatic synthesis of behavior protocols for composable web-services. In *Proceedings of the 7th Joint Meeting of the European Software Engineering Conference and the ACM SIGSOFT Symposium on the Foundations of Software Engineering (*Amsterdam, The Netherlands, August 24-28, 2009*)*. ESEC/FSE '09. ACM, New York, NY, 141-150.

[3] Bruijn, J. D., Fensel, D., Keller, U., Kifer, M., Lausen, H., Krummenacher, R., Polleres, A. and Predoiu, L. 2005. Web Service Modeling Language (WSML). Available at http://www.w3.org/Submission/WSML/.

[4] Engler, D., Chen, D. Y., Hallem, S., Chou, A. and Chelf, B. 2001. Bugs as deviant behavior: a general approach to inferring errors in systems code. In *Proceedings of the 18th ACM symposium on Operating systems principles* (Chateau Lake Louise, Banff, Canada, October 21-24, 2001). SOSP '01. ACM, New York, NY, 57-72.

[5] Fisher, M., Elbaum, S. and Rothermel, G. 2007. *Automated Refinement and Augmentation of Web Service Description Files*. Technical Report. University of Nebraska - Lincoln.

[6] Gabel, M. and Su, Z. D. 2010. Testing mined specifications. In *Proceedings of the 20th International Symposium on the Foundations of Software Engineering* (Cary, North Carolina, November 11-16, 2012). FSE '12. ACM, New York, NY.

[7] Hallé, S., Bultan, T., Hughes, G., Alkhalaf, M., Villemaire, R. 2010. Runtime verification of web service interface contracts. *Computer*. 43, 3 (March 2010), 59-66.

[8] Havelund, K. and Pressburger, T. 1999. Java PathFinder, a translator from Java to Promela. In *Proceedings of the 5th and 6th International SPIN Workshops on Theoretical and Practical Aspects of SPIN Model Checking* (Trento, Italy, July 5, 1999, Toulouse, France, September 21 and 24, 1999). Springer-Verlag London, UK, 152.

[9] Hovemeyer, D. and Pugh, W. 2004. Finding bugs is easy. *ACM SIGPLAN Notices*. 39, 12 (December 2004), 92-106.

[10] Martin, E., Basu, S. and Xie, T. 2007. Automated testing and response analysis of web services. In *Proceedings of the IEEE International Conference on Web Services, Application Services and Industry Track* (Salt Lake City, Utah, USA, July 9-13, 2007). ICWS '07. 647-654.

[11] Martin, D., Burstein, M., Hobbs, J., Lassila, O., McDermott, D., McIlraith, S., Narayanan, S., Paolucci, M., Parsia, B., Payne, T., Sirin, E., Srinivasan, N. and Sycara, K. 2004. OWL-S: Semantic Markup for Web Services. Available at http://www.w3.org/Submission/OWL-S/.

[12] Pandita, R., Xiao, X. S., Zhong, H., Xie, T., Oney, S. and Paradkar, A. 2012. Inferring method specifications from natural language API descriptions. In *Proceedings of the 34th International Conference on Software Engineering* (Zurich, Switzerland, June 2-9, 2012). ICSE '12. IEEE Press Piscataway, NJ, USA, 815-825.

[13] Pradel, M. and Gross, T. R. 2012. Leveraging test generation and specification mining for automated bug detection without false positives. In *Proceedings of the 34th 2012 International Conference on Software Engineering* (Zurich, Switzerland, June 2-9, 2012). ICSE '12. IEEE Press Piscataway, NJ, USA, 288-298.

[14] Rubinger, B. and Bultan, T. 2010. Contracting the Facebook API. In *Proceedings Fourth International Workshop on Testing, Analysis and Verification of Web Software* (Antwerp, Belgium, September 20-24, 2010). TAV-WEB '10. 63-74.

[15] Weimer, W. and Necula, G. C. 2005. Mining temporal specifications for error detection. In *Proceedings of the 11th International Conference on Tools and Algorithms for the Construction and Analysis of Systems* (Edinburgh, U.K., April 4-8, 2005). TACAS '05. Springer-Verlag, Edinburgh, UK, 461-476.

[16] Wu, Q., Liang, G. T., Wang, Q. X. and Mei, H. 2011. Mining effective temporal specifications from heterogeneous API data. *Journal of Computer Science and Technology*. 26, 6 (November 2011), 1061-1075.

[17] Wu, Q., Liang, G. T., Wang, Q. X., Xie, T. and Mei, H. 2011. Iterative mining of resource-releasing specifications. In *Proceedings of the 26th IEEE/ACM International Conference on Automated Software Engineering* (Lawrence, Kansas, November 6-12, 2011). ASE '11. IEEE Computer Society Washington, DC, USA, 233-242.

[18] Zhong, H., Zhang, L., Xie, T. and Mei, H. 2009. Inferring resource specifications from natural language API documentation. In *Proceedings of the 24th IEEE/ACM International Conference on Automated Software Engineering* (Auckland, New Zealand, November 16-20, 2009). ASE '09. IEEE Computer Society Washington, DC, USA, 307-318.

Predicting Advertiser Bidding Behaviors in Sponsored Search by Rationality Modeling[*]

Haifeng Xu
Centre for Computational
Mathematics in Industry and
Commerce
University of Waterloo
Waterloo, ON, Canada
haifeng.ustc@gmail.com

Bin Gao
Microsoft Research Asia
13F, Bldg 2, No. 5, Danling St
Beijing, 100080, P. R. China
bingao@microsoft.com

Diyi Yang
Dept. of Computer Science
Shanghai Jiao Tong University
Shanghai, 200240, P. R. China
yangdiyi@apex.sjtu.edu.cn

Tie-Yan Liu
Microsoft Research Asia
13F, Bldg 2, No. 5, Danling St
Beijing, 100080, P. R. China
tyliu@microsoft.com

ABSTRACT

We study how an advertiser changes his/her bid prices in sponsored search, by modeling his/her rationality. Predicting the bid changes of advertisers with respect to their campaign performances is a key capability of search engines, since it can be used to improve the offline evaluation of new advertising technologies and the forecast of future revenue of the search engine. Previous work on advertiser behavior modeling heavily relies on the assumption of *perfect* advertiser rationality; however, in most cases, this assumption does not hold in practice. Advertisers may be unwilling, incapable, and/or constrained to achieve their best response. In this paper, we explicitly model these limitations in the rationality of advertisers, and build a probabilistic advertiser behavior model from the perspective of a search engine. We then use the expected payoff to define the objective function for an advertiser to optimize given his/her limited rationality. By solving the optimization problem with Monte Carlo, we get a prediction of mixed bid strategy for each advertiser in the next period of time. We examine the effectiveness of our model both directly using real historical bids and indirectly using revenue prediction and click number prediction. Our experimental results based on the sponsored search logs from a commercial search engine show that the proposed model can provide a more accurate prediction of advertiser bid behaviors than several baseline methods.

Categories and Subject Descriptors

H.3.5 [**Information Systems**]: Information Storage and Retrieval - On-line Information Services

Keywords

Advertiser modeling, rationality, sponsored search, bid prediction.

---

[*]This work was performed when the first and the third authors were interns at Microsoft Research Asia.

Copyright is held by the International World Wide Web Conference Committee (IW3C2). IW3C2 reserves the right to provide a hyperlink to the author's site if the Material is used in electronic media.
WWW 2013, May 13–17, 2013, Rio de Janeiro, Brazil.
ACM 978-1-4503-2035-1/13/05.

1. INTRODUCTION

Sponsored search has become a major means of Internet monetization, and has been the driving power of many commercial search engines. In a sponsored search system, an advertiser creates a number of ads and bids on a set of keywords (with certain bid prices) for each ad. When a user submits a query to the search engine, and if the bid keyword can be matched to the query, the corresponding ad will be selected into an auction process. Currently, the *Generalized Second Price (GSP) auction* [10] is the most commonly used auction mechanism which ranks the ads according to the product of bid price and ad click probability[1] and charges an advertisers if his/her ad wins the auction (i.e., his/her ad is shown in the search result page) and is clicked by users [13].

Generally, an advertiser has his/her goal when creating the ad campaign. For instance, the goal might be to receive 500 clicks on the ad during one week. However, the way of achieving this goal might not be smooth. For example, it is possible that after one day, the ad has only received 10 clicks. In this case, in order to improve the campaign performance, the advertiser may have to increase the bid price in order to increase the opportunity for his/her ad to win future auctions, and thus to increase the chance for the ad to be presented to users and to be clicked.[2]

Predicting how the advertisers change their bid prices is a key capability of a search engine, since it can be used to deal with the so-called second order effect in online advertising [13] when evaluating novel advertising technologies and forecasting future revenue of search engines. For instance, suppose the search engine wants to test a novel algorithm for bid keyword suggestion[3] [7]. Given that the online experiments are costly (e.g., unsuccessful online experiments will lead to revenue loss of the search engine), the algorithm will usually be tested based on the historical logs first to see its ef-

---

[1]Usually a reserve score is set and the ads whose scores are greater than the reserve score are shown.
[2]Note that the advertiser may also choose to revise the ad description, bid extra keywords, and so on. However, among these actions, changing the bid price is the simplest and the most commonly used method by advertisers. Please also note that since GSP is not incentive compatible, advertisers might not bid their true values and changing bid prices is their common behaviors.
[3]The same thing will happen when we evaluate other algorithms like traffic estimation, ad click prediction, and auction mechanism.

fectiveness (a.k.a., offline experiment). However, in many cases, even if the algorithm works quite well in offline experiment, it may perform badly after being deployed online. One of the reasons is that the advertisers might change their bid prices in response to the changes of their campaign performances caused by the deployed new algorithm. Therefore, the experiments based on the historical bid prices will be different from those on online traffic. To tackle this problem, one needs a powerful advertiser behavior model to predict the bid price changes.

In the literature, there have been a number of researches [4] [5] [22] [19] [2] [17] [3] that model how advertisers determine their bid prices, and how their bid strategies influence the equilibrium of the sponsored search system. For example, Varian [19] assumes that the advertisers bid the amount at which their value per click equals the incremental cost per click to maximize their utilities. The authors of [2] and [17] study how to estimate value per click, by assuming advertisers are on the locally envy-free equilibrium, and assuming the distributions of all the advertisers' bids are independent and identically distributed.

Most of the above researches rely highly on the assumptions of *perfect* advertiser rationality and full information access[4], i.e., advertisers have good knowledge about their utilities and are capable of effectively optimizing the utilities (i.e., take the best response). However, as we argue in this paper, this is usually not true in practice. In our opinion, real-world advertisers have limitations in accessing the information about their competitors, and have different levels of rationality. In particular, an advertiser may be *unwilling*, *incapable*, or *constrained* to achieve his/her "best response." As a result, some advertisers frequently adjust the bid prices according to their recent campaign performances, while some other advertisers always keep the bid unchanged regardless of the campaign performances; some advertisers have good sense of choosing the appropriate bid prices (possibly with the help of campaign analysis tools [14] or third-party ad agencies), while some other advertisers choose bid prices at random.

To better describe the above intuition, we explicitly model the rationality of advertisers from the following three aspects:

- **Willingness** represents the *propensity* an advertiser has to optimize his/her utility. Advertisers who care little about their ad campaigns and advertisers who are very serious about the campaign performance will have different levels of willingness.

- **Capability** describes the *ability* of an advertiser to estimate the bid strategies of his/her competitors and take the best-response action on that basis. An experienced advertiser is usually more capable than an inexperienced advertiser; an advertiser who hires professional ad agency is usually more capable than an advertiser who adjusts bid prices by his-self/herself.

- **Constraint** refers to the *constraints* that prevent an advertiser from adopting a bid price even if he/she knows that this bid price is the best response for him/her. The constraint usually (although not only) comes from the lack of remaining budget.

With the above notions, we propose the following model to describe how advertisers change their bid prices, from the perspective of the search engine.[5] First, an advertiser has a certain probability to optimize his/her utility or not, which is modeled by the willingness function. Second, if the advertiser is willing to make changes, he/she will estimate the bid strategies of his/her competitors. Based on the estimation, he/she can compute the expected payoff (or utility) and use it as an objective function to determine his/her next bid price. This process is modeled by the capability function. By simultaneously considering the optimization processes of all the advertisers, we can effectively compute the best bid prices for every advertiser. Third, given the optimal bid price, an advertiser will check whether he/she is able to adopt it according to some constraints. This is modeled by the constraint function.

Please note that the willingness, capability, and constraint functions are all parametric. By fitting the output of our proposed model to the real bid change logs (obtained from commercial search engines), we will be able to learn these parameters, and then use the learned model to predict the bid behavior change in the future. We have tested the effectiveness of the proposed model using real data. The experimental results show that the proposed model can predict the bid changes of advertisers in a more accurate manner than several baseline methods.

To sum up, the contributions of our work are listed as below. First, to the best of our knowledge, this is the first advertiser behavior model in the literature that considers different levels of rationality of advertisers. Second, we model advertiser behaviors using a parametric model, and apply machine learning techniques to learn the parameters in the model. This is a good example of leveraging machine learning in game theory to avoid its unreasonable assumptions. Third, our proposed model leads to very accurate bid prediction. In contrast, as far as we know, most of previous research focuses on estimating value per click, but not predicting bid prices. Therefore, our work has more direct value to search engine, given that bid prediction is a desired ability of search engine as aforementioned.

The rest of the paper is organized as the following. In Section 2, we introduce the notations and describe the willingness, capability, and constraint functions. We present the framework of the bid strategy prediction model in Section 3. In Section 4, we introduce the efficient numerical algorithm of the model. In Section 5, we present the experimental results on real data. We summarize the related work in Section 6, and in the end we conclude the paper and present some insights about future work in Section 7.

2. ADVERTISER RATIONALITY

As mentioned in the introduction, how an advertiser adjusts his/her bid is related to his/her rationality. In our opinion, there are three aspects to be considered when modeling the rationality of an advertiser: *willingness*, *capability*, and *constraint*. In this section, we introduce some notations for sponsored search auctions, and then describe the models for these rationality aspects.

2.1 Notations

We consider the keyword auction in sponsored search. For simplicity, we will not consider connections between different ad campaigns and we assume each advertiser only has one ad and bids on just one keyword for it. That is, the auction participants are the keyword-ad pairs. Advertisers are assumed to be risk-neutral.[6]

---

[4] Please note that some of these works take a Bayesian approach; however, they still assume that the priors of the value distributions are publicly known.

[5] That is, the model is to be used by the search engine to predict advertisers' behavior, but not by the advertisers to guide their bidding strategies.

[6] This assumption will result in a uniform definition of utility functions for all the advertisers. However, our result can be naturally

We use i ($i = 1, \cdots, I$) to index the advertisers, and consider advertiser l as the default advertiser of our interest. Suppose in one auction the advertisers compete for J ad slots. In practice, the search engine usually introduces a reserve score to optimize its revenue. Only those ads whose rank scores are above this reserve score will be shown to users. To ease our discussion, we regard the reserve score r as a virtual advertiser in the auction. We use $a_{i,j}$ to denote the click-through rate (CTR) of advertiser i's ad when it is placed at position j. Similar to the setting in [2][17], we assume $a_{i,j}$ to be separable. That is, $a_{i,j} = \gamma_i \alpha_j$, where γ_i is the ad effect and α_j is the position effect. We let $\alpha_j = 0$ when $j > J$. The sponsored search system will predict the click probability [11] of an ad and use it as a factor to rank the ads in the auction. We use s_i to denote the predicted click probability of advertiser i's ad if it is placed in the first ad slot. Note that both $a_{i,j}$ and s_i are random variables [2], since they may be influenced by many dynamic factors such as the attributes of the query and the user who issues the query.

We assume all the advertisers share the same bid strategy space Ω which consists of B different discrete bid prices denoted by b_i, $i = 1, \cdots, B$. Furthermore, we denote the strategy of advertiser l as $\boldsymbol{\pi}_l = (\pi_{l,1}, \cdots, \pi_{l,B})$, which is a mixed strategy. It means that l will use bid strategy b_i with a probability of $\pi_{l,i}$, $i = 1, \cdots, B$. We assume advertiser l will estimate both the configuration of his/her competitors and their strategies in order to find his/her own best response. We use $\mathbb{S}$ (including l) to indicate the set of advertisers who are regarded by advertiser l as the participates of the auction and use $\mathbb{S}_{-l}$ (excluding l) to indicate the set of competitors of l. We denote $\boldsymbol{\pi}_i^{(l)}$ as l's estimated bid strategy for a competitor i ($i \neq l$), and denote l's own best-response strategy as $\boldsymbol{\pi}_l^{(l)}$.

Note that both $\mathbb{S}$ and $\boldsymbol{\pi}_i^{(l)}$ ($i \neq l$) are random: (i) $\mathbb{S}$ is a random set due to the uncertainty in the auction process: a) the participants of the auction is dynamic [17]; b) in practice l never knows exactly who are competing with him/her since such information is not publicly available. (ii) $\boldsymbol{\pi}_i^{(l)}$ ($i \neq l$) is a random vector due to l's incomplete information and our uncertainty on l's estimation. More intuitions about $\boldsymbol{\pi}_i^{(l)}$ will be explained in the modeling of the capability function (see Section 2.3).

To ease our discussion, we now transform the uncertainty of $\mathbb{S}$ to the uncertainty in bid prices, as shown below. That is, we regard all the other advertisers as the competitors of l and add the zero bid price (denoted by b_0) to extend the bid strategy space. The extended bid strategy space is represented by $\Omega^* = \Omega \bigcup \{b_0\}$. If an advertiser is not a real competitor of l, we regard his/her bid price to be zero. According to the above discussion, $\mathbb{S}$ will be the whole advertiser set with the set size I. Thus, we will only consider the uncertainty of bid prices in the rest of the paper.

2.2 Willingness

Willingness represents the *propensity* an advertiser is willing to optimize his/her utility, which is modeled as a possibility. We model willingness as a logistic regression function $W_l(\boldsymbol{x}_t^{(l)})$. Here the input $\boldsymbol{x}_t^{(l)} = (x_{t,1}^{(l)}, \cdots, x_{t,H}^{(l)})$ is a feature vector (H is the number of features) extracted for advertiser l at period t, and the output is a real number in $[0, 1]$ representing the probability that l will optimize his/her utility.[7] That is, advertiser l with feature vector $\boldsymbol{x}_t^{(l)}$

---

extended to the case where advertisers' different risk preferences are considered.

[7]Note that "willing to optimize" does not always mean a change of bid. Probably, an advertiser attempts to optimize his/her utility, but finally finds that his/her previous bid is already the best choice. In

will have a probability of $W_l(\boldsymbol{x}_t^{(l)})$ to optimize his/her utility, and a probability of $1 - W_l(\boldsymbol{x}_t^{(l)})$ to take no action.

In order to extract the feature vector $\boldsymbol{x}_t^{(l)}$, we split the historical auction logs into T periods (e.g., T days). For each period $t \in T$, $y_t^{(i)}$ indicates whether the bid was changed in period $t+1$. If the bid was changed, $y_t^{(l)} = 1$; otherwise, $y_t^{(l)} = 0$. With this data, the following features are extracted: (i) The number of bid changes before t. The intuition is that an advertiser who changes bid more frequently in the past will also have a higher possibility to make changes in the next period. (ii) The number of periods that an advertiser has kept the bid unchanged until t. Intuitively, an advertiser who has kept the bid unchanged for a long time may have a higher possibility to continue keeping the bid unchanged. (iii) The number of different bid values used before t. The intuition is that an advertiser who has tried more bid values in the past may be regarded as a more active bidder, and we may expect him/her to try more new bid values in the future. (iv) A Boolean value indicating whether there are clicks in t. The intuition is that if there is no click, the advertiser will feel unsatisfied and thus have a higher probability to make changes.

With the above features, we write the willingness function as,

$$W_l(\boldsymbol{x}_t^{(l)}) = \frac{1}{1 + e^{\{\beta_0^{(l)} + \sum_{n=1}^{H} \beta_n^{(l)} x_{t,n}^{(l)}\}}}, \quad (t = 1, \cdots, T).$$

Here $\boldsymbol{\beta}^{(l)} = (\beta_0^{(l)}, \cdots, \beta_H^{(l)})$ is the parameter vector for l.

To learn the parameter vector $\boldsymbol{\beta}^{(l)}$, we minimize the sum of the first-order error $\sum_{t=1}^{T} |y_t^{(l)} - W_l(\boldsymbol{x}_t^{(l)})|$ on the historical data using the classical *Broyden-Fletcher-Goldfarb-Shanno* algorithm (BFGS) [15]. Then we apply the learned parameter $\boldsymbol{\beta}^{(l)}$ to predict i's willingness of change in the future.

2.3 Capability

Capability describes the ability of an advertiser to estimate the bid strategies of his/her competitors and take the best-response action on that basis. A more experienced advertiser may have better capability in at least three aspects: information collection, utility function definition, and utility optimization. Usually, in GSP auctions, a standard utility function is used and the optimal solution is not hard to obtain. Hence, we mainly consider the capability in information collection, i.e., the ability in estimating competitors' bid strategies.

Recalling that l does not have any exact information on his/her competitors' bids, it is a little difficult to model how advertiser l estimates his/her competitors' strategies, because different l has different estimation techniques. Before introducing the detailed model for the capability function, we would like to briefly describe our intuition. It's reasonable to assume that l's estimation on i is based on i's market performance, denoted by $Perf_i$. Then we can write l's estimation as $Est_l(Perf_i)$, which means l applies some specific estimation technique Est_l on $Perf_i$. The market performance $Perf_i$ is decided by all the advertisers' bid profiles due to the auction property. That is, $Perf_i = Perf_{\boldsymbol{\pi}_{-i}^*}(\boldsymbol{\pi}_i^*)$, here $\boldsymbol{\pi}_i^*$ is i's historical bid histogram. Note that we use $\boldsymbol{\pi}_i^*$ and $\boldsymbol{\pi}_{-i}^*$ because we believe the observed market performance $Perf_i$ is based on the auctions during a previous period, while not just one previous auction. However, we are mostly interested in profitable keywords, the auctions of which usually have so many advertisers involved that $\boldsymbol{\pi}_{-i}^*$ can be regarded as a constant environment factor for any i. Therefore, $Perf_i$ only depends on $\boldsymbol{\pi}_i^*$, i.e., $Perf_i = Perf(\boldsymbol{\pi}_i^*)$.

---

this case, he will keep the bid unchanged but we still regard it as "willing to optimize."

Thus, we have $Est_l(Perf_i) = Est_l(Perf(\pi_i^*))$. Till now, the problem becomes much easier: l is blind to π_i^*, but the search engine has all the information of π_i^*. To know $Est_l(Perf_i)$, the search engine only needs to model the function $Est_l(Perf(\cdot))$ given that π_i^* is known.

Specifically, we denote the above $Est_l(Perf(\pi_i^*))$ as our capability function $A_l(\pi_i^*)$. As described in Section 2.1, $A_l(\pi_i^*)$ is denoted by $\pi_i^{(l)}$. The reason that A_l is named as capability function is clear: Est_l, the techniques l uses for estimation, reflects his/her capability. The reason that $\pi_i^{(l)} = A_l(\pi_i^*)$ is modeled to be random is also clear: the search engine does not know what Est_l is, and thus aspired by the concept of "type" in Bayesian Game [12] which is a description of incomplete game setting, we regard Est_l as a "type" of l and model its distribution. For the same π_i^*, different advertisers may have different estimations according to their various capabilities.

To simplify our model, we give the following assumption on $\pi_i^{(l)}$. We assume that l's estimations on other advertisers' bid strategies are all pure strategies. That is, $\pi_i^{(l)}$ is a random Boolean vector with just one element equal to 1.[8]

Given a bid b_n with possibility $\pi_{i,n}^*$ from the historical bid histogram π_i^*, we assume l's estimation has a fluctuation around b_n. The fluctuation can be modeled by a certain probability distribution such as Binomial distribution or Poisson distribution. The parameters of the distribution can be used to indicate l's capability. Here we use Binomial distribution to model the fluctuation due to the following reasons: (i) Theoretically, Binomial distribution can conveniently describe the discrete bids due to its own discrete nature. Furthermore, the two parameters in Binomial distribution can well reflect the capability levels: the trail times N can control the fluctuation range ($N = 0$ means a perfect estimation) and the success possibility $\delta \in (0, 1)$ can control the bias of the estimations. Specifically, if $\delta > 0.5$, it means the estimation is on average larger than the true distribution and *vice versa*. (ii) Experimentally, we have compared Binomial distribution with some other well-known distributions such as Gaussian, Poisson, Beta, and Gamma distributions, and the experiment results show that Binomial distribution performs the best in our model.

For sake of simplicity, we let the fluctuation range be an integer $2N_l \in \Omega$, and the success possibility be $\delta_l \in (0, 1)$. Then (N_l, δ_l) are l's capability parameters. The fluctuation on b_n in π_i^* is modeled by

$$Pr(A_l(b_n)=b_{n+m}) = \pi_{i,n}^* \binom{2N_l}{N_l + m} \delta_l^{(N_l+m)}(1-\delta_l)^{(N_l-m)},$$
$$(m = -N_l, ..., N_l).$$

In the above formula, $i \neq l$; the symbol "=" means the equivalence of strategy; $\binom{2N_l}{N_l+m}$ is the number of $(N_l + m)$-combinations in a set with $2N_l$ integers. Therefore, by considering all the bid values in π_i^*, we have,

$$Pr(\pi_i^{(l)}=b_n) = Pr(A_l(\pi_i^*)=b_n)$$
$$= \sum_{m=-N_l}^{N_l} \pi_{i,n-m}^* \binom{2N_l}{N_l+m} \delta_l^{(N_l+m)}(1-\delta_l)^{(N_l-m)}.$$

2.4 Constraint

Constraint refers to the factor that prevents an advertiser from adopting a bid price even if he/she knows that this bid price is the best response for him/her. In practice, many factors (such as lack of remaining budget and the aggressive/conservative character of the advertiser) may impact advertiser's eventual choices. For example, an advertiser who lacks budget or has conservative character may prefer to bid a lower price than the best response.

We model constraint using a function C_l, which translates the best response (which may be a mixed strategy) to the final strategy with step (a.k.a., difference) $c_t^{(l)}$. That is, if the best bid strategy is $\pi_l^{(l)}$ at period t, then $C_l(\pi_l^{(l)})$ will be $b_n + c_t^{(l)}$ with probability $\pi_{l,n}^{(l)}$. Similar to the proposal in the willingness function, we model the step $c_t^{(l)}$ using a regression model. The difference is that this time we use linear regression since $c_t^{(l)}$ is in nature a translation distance but not a probability. Here we use the remaining budget as the feature $x_t^{(l)}$ and build the following function form:

$$c_t^{(l)} = \beta_{1,l} + \beta_{2,l} \frac{x_t^{(l)} - \overline{x}^{(l)}}{\overline{x}^{(l)}}, \text{ where } \overline{x}^{(l)} = \frac{\sum_{t \in T} x_t^{(l)}}{|T|}.$$

In the above formula, T is the set of periods for training and $x_t^{(l)}$ is l's remaining budget in period t. In the training data, we use $(\sum_{n=1}^{B} b_n \pi_{l,n}^{(l)}) - b_t^{(l)}$ as the label for $c_t^{(l)}$. Here $b_t^{(l)}$ is l's real bid at period t; $\beta_{1,l}$ and $\beta_{2,l}$ are the parameters for the linear regression. Note that $\beta_{1,l}$ is only related to l himself/herself. This parameter reveals l's internal character on whether he/she is aggressive or not. One can intuitively imagine that for aggressive advertisers, $\beta_{1,l}$ will be positive because such advertisers are radical and they would like to overbid. Moreover, we normalize the budget in the formula because the amounts of budget vary largely across different advertisers. The normalization will help to build a uniform model for all advertisers.

3. ADVERTISER BEHAVIOR MODEL

After explaining the advertiser rationality in terms of willingness, capability, and constraint, we introduce a new advertiser behavior model.

Suppose advertiser l has a utility function U_l. The inputs of U_l are l's estimations on his/her competitors' bid strategies, which are given by the capability function A_l. The goal of advertiser l is to find a mixed strategy $\pi_l^{(l)}$ to maximize this utility, i.e.,

$$\arg\max_{\pi_l^{(l)}} U_l(A_l(\pi_i^*), i = 1, \cdots, I)$$
$$= \arg\max_{\pi_l^{(l)}} U_l(\pi_i^{(l)}, i = 1, \cdots, I, i \neq l).$$

If we further consider the changing possibility W_l, the constraint function C_l, and the randomness of A_l, we can get the general advertiser behavior model that explains how advertiser l may determine his/her bid strategy for the next period of time:

$$\pi_l = W_l E_{A_l}(C_l(\arg\max_{\pi_l^{(l)}} U_l(\pi_i^{(l)}, i = 1, \cdots, I, i \neq l))) +$$
$$(1 - W_l)(0, ..0, 1, 0...0)^T, \forall l. \quad (1)$$

Here $(0, ..0, 1, 0...0)$ is the unchanged B-dimension bid strategy where the index of the one (and the only one) equals n if the bid in the previous period is b_n. "arg max" outputs a B-dimension mixed strategy of l; E_{A_l} means the expectation on the randomness of $A_l(\pi_j^*)$; W_l is the possibility that l decides to optimize his/her utility.

We want to emphasis that equation (1) is a general expression under our rationality assumptions. Though we have provided the details of the model in Section 2 about W_l, A_l, C_l and we will

---

[8]Our model can be naturally extended to the mixed strategy cases, with a bit more complicated notations and computing algorithms.

introduce the details about U_l in the next subsection, one can certainly propose any other forms of the model for all these functions.

3.1 Utility Function

To make the above model concrete, we need to define and calculate the utility function U_l for every advertiser.

Recall our assumption that $\pi_i^{(l)} = A_l(\pi_i^*)$ is a pure strategy; that is, only one element in $\pi_i^{(l)}$ is one and all the other elements are zeros. Suppose the bid value that corresponds to the "one" in $\pi_i^{(l)}$ is o_i ($o_i \in \Omega^*$ and $i \neq l$). In this case, the bid configuration is $\boldsymbol{o} = (o_1, \cdots, o_I)$, in which all the advertisers' bids are fixed. Please note that the representations in terms of o_i and the original representations in term of $\pi_i^{(l)}$ are actually equivalent to each other, since they encode exactly the same information and its randomness in the bid strategies of advertisers.

Then we introduce the form of U_l. Based on the bid prices in $\boldsymbol{o}$ and ad quality scores s_i ($i = 1, \cdots, I$), we can determine the ranked list in the auction according to the commonly used ranking rules (i.e., the product of bid price and ad quality score [13]) in sponsored search. Suppose l is ranked in position j and $\hat{l}$ is ranked in position $j+1$. According to the pricing rule in the generalized second price auction (GSP) [10], l should pay $o_{\hat{l}} s_{\hat{l}}/s_l$ for each click. As defined in Section 2.1, the possibility for a user to click l's ad in position j is $a_{lj} = \gamma_l \alpha_j$. Suppose the true value of advertiser l for a click is v_l (which can be estimated using many techniques, e.g., [9]), then we have,

$$U_l = E_{\gamma_l, \alpha_j, s_{\hat{l}}, s_l} \{(\gamma_l \alpha_j (v_l - \frac{o_{\hat{l}} s_{\hat{l}}}{s_l}))\} = \overline{\gamma}_l \overline{\alpha}_j (v_l - \frac{o_{\hat{l}} \overline{s}_{\hat{l}}}{\overline{s}_l}).$$

As explained in Section 2, γ_l, α_j, $s_{\hat{l}}$, s_l are all random variables. Here $\overline{\gamma}_l$, $\overline{\alpha}_j$, $\overline{s}_{\hat{l}}$, and $\overline{s}_l$ are their means. Since U_l is linear and the above four random variables are independent of each other, the outside expectation can be moved inside and substituted by the corresponding means.

3.2 Final Model

With all the above discussions, we are now ready to give the final form of the advertiser model. By denoting $\boldsymbol{o}_{-l} = (o_1, \cdots, o_{l-1}, o_{l+1}, \cdots, o_I)$ as the bid configuration without l's bid, we get the following expression for $l = 1, \cdots, I$:

$$\pi_l = W_l E_{\boldsymbol{o}_{-l}}\{C_l[\arg\max_{\pi_l^{(l)}} (\overline{\gamma}_l \overline{\alpha}_j (v_l - o_{\hat{l}} \overline{s}_{\hat{l}}/\overline{s}_l))]\}$$
$$+ (1 - W_l)(0, ..0, 1, 0...0)^T.$$

Here the randomness of A_l is specifically expressed by the randomness of $\boldsymbol{o}_{-l}$.

Note that $\overline{\gamma}_l$ is a constant for l and it will not affect the result of "arg max". Therefore we can remove it from the above expression to further simplify the final model:

$$\pi_l = W_l E_{\boldsymbol{o}_{-l}}\{C_l[\arg\max_{\pi_l^{(l)}} (\overline{\alpha}_j (v_l - o_{\hat{l}} \overline{s}_{\hat{l}}/\overline{s}_l))]\}$$
$$+ (1 - W_l)(0, ..0, 1, 0...0)^T, \forall l. \quad (2)$$

4. ALGORITHM

In this section we introduce an efficient algorithm to solve the advertiser model proposed in the previous sections. To ease our discussion, we assume that the statistics $\overline{\alpha}_j$, $\overline{s}_{\hat{l}}$, and $\overline{s}_l$ are all known (with sufficient data and knowledge about the market). Furthermore, we assume that the search engine can effectively estimate the true value v_l in (2). Considering the setting of our problem, we choose to use the model in [9] for this purpose.

Table 1: $\mathcal{O}$-simulator

```
initialize o = (o_1, ···, o_I) = (0, 0, ···, 0)
for i = 1, ..., I,
    f = random();
    // random() uniformly outputs a random float number in [0,1].
    sum = 0;
    n = 0;
    while(sum < f)
        sum = sum + P(O_i = b_n);
        n = n + 1;
    end;
    o_i = b_n;
end;
output o;
```

Our discussions in this section will be focused on the computational challenge to obtain the best response for all the cases of bid configurations $\boldsymbol{o}$ (corresponding to $\boldsymbol{o}_{-l}$ in (2)). This is a typical combinatorial explosion problem with a complexity of B^I, which will increase exponentially with the number of advertisers. Therefore, it is hard to solve the problem directly. Our proposal is to adopt a numerical approximation instead of giving an accurate solution to the problem. We can prove that the approximation algorithm can converge to the accurate solution with a small accuracy loss and much less running time.

Our approximation algorithm requires the use of a $\mathcal{O}$-simulator, which is defined as follows.

DEFINITION 1. *($\mathcal{O}$-simulator) Suppose there is a random vector $\mathcal{O} = (O_1, \cdots, O_I) \sim P(\boldsymbol{o})$, i.e., $P(\boldsymbol{o})$ is the distribution of $\mathcal{O}$. Given $\forall \boldsymbol{o} \in \Omega^*$ and $P(\boldsymbol{o})$, an algorithm is called an $\mathcal{O}$-simulator if the algorithm randomly outputs a vector $\boldsymbol{o}$ with the probability $P(\boldsymbol{o})$.*

As described above, $\mathcal{O}$-simulator actually simulates the random vector $\mathcal{O}$ and randomly output its samples. In general, it is difficult to simulate a random vector; however, in our case, all the O_i are independent of each other and they have discrete distributions. Therefore, the simulation becomes feasible. In Table 1 we give a description of $\mathcal{O}$-simulator. Here we assume $\mathcal{O} = (O_1, \cdots, O_I)$ and $O_i \sim P_i(o_i), o_i \in \Omega^*$. Furthermore, $\Omega^* = \{b_0, b_1, \cdots, b_B\}$ is a discrete space shared by all i (like the bid space in our model) and all O_i are independent of each other.

Note that f is a uniformly random number from $[0, 1]$, therefore the possibility that o_i equals b_n is exactly $P(O_i = b_n)$. Thus, the possibility to output $\boldsymbol{o} = (o_1, \cdots, o_I)$ is $\Pi_{i=1}^I P(O_i = o_i)$, which is exactly what we want.

We then give the Monte Carlo Algorithm as shown in Table 2 to calculate $E_{\boldsymbol{o}_{-l}}\{\arg\max_{\pi_l^{(l)}}(\overline{\alpha}_j(v_l - o_{\hat{l}}\overline{s}_{\hat{l}}/\overline{s}_l))\}$ for a certain l. For simplicity, we denote $Pr(\pi_i^{(l)} = b_n)$ as $q_{i,n}^{(l)}$, and thus $q_{i,0}^{(l)}$ is the possibility that i is not in the auction. In this algorithm, the historical bid histogram π_i^* and $q_{i,0}^{(l)}$ are calculated from the auction logs by Maximum Likelihood Estimation. Given rationality parameter δ_l, N_l, and $q_{i,0}^{(l)}$, we initialize $q_{i,0}^{(l)}$ by the capability function. Then with $\boldsymbol{o}_{-l}$ generated by $\mathcal{O}$-simulator, we can calculate which ranked list is optimal for l by solving $\arg\max_{\pi_l^{(l)}}(\overline{\alpha}_j(v_l - o_{\hat{l}}\overline{s}_{\hat{l}}/\overline{s}_l))$. Note that it is possible that different bids may lead to the same optimal ranked list (with the same utility). In this case, the inverse function "$\arg\max_{\pi_l^{(l)}}$" will output a bid set $B_{\boldsymbol{o}_{-l}}$ including all the equally optimal bids. By assuming that advertiser l will take any bid in $B_{\boldsymbol{o}_{-l}}$ with uniform probability, we allocate each bid in $B_{\boldsymbol{o}_{-l}}$ with

Table 2: Monte Carlo Algorithm

```
for i = 0, ..., I,
    initialize π*_i, q^(l)_{i,0}, s̄_i;
end;
for j = 0, ..., J,
    initialize ᾱ_j;
end;
initialize , δ_l, N_l, 1/s̄_l;
π^(l)_{l,n} = 0;
for i = 1, ···, I(l ≠ i) and n = 1, ···, B
    q^(l)_{i,n} = (1 − q^(l)_{i,0}) ×
        ∑_{m=−N_l}^{N_l} π*_{i,n−m} (2N_l choose N_l+m) δ_l^(N_l+m) (1 − δ_l)^(N_l−m);
end;
Build an 𝒪-simulator with P(𝒪 = o_{−l}) = Π^I_{i=1,i≠l} q^(l)_{i,o_i}, ∀o_{−l};
for t = 1, ···, N,
    𝒪-simulator outputs a sample o_{−l};
    Solve arg max_{π^(l)_l} (ᾱ_j (v_l − o_ī s̄_ī/s̄_l)) to get B_{o_{−l}};
    for all b_i ∈ B_{o_{−l}},
        π^(l)_{l,i} = π^(l)_{l,i} + 1/|B_{o_{−l}}|;
    end;
end;
for n = 1, ···, B,
    π^(l)_{l,n} = π^(l)_{l,n}/N.
end;
output π^(l)_{l,n};
```

a weight $\frac{1}{|B_{o_{-l}}|}$ averagely. Finally, we use the simulation times N to normalize the distribution and output it.

For the Monte Carlo Algorithm, we can prove its convergence to the accurate solution, which is shown in the following theorem.

THEOREM 1. *Given π^*_i and $q^{(l)}_{i,0}$, the output of the Monte Carlo Algorithm converges to $E_{o_{-l}}\{\arg\max_{\pi^{(l)}_l}(\bar{\alpha}_j(v_l - o_{\bar{i}}\bar{s}_{\bar{i}}/\bar{s}_l))\}$ as the times of simulation N grows.*

PROOF. We assume that the accurate solution is π^0_l and thus we need to prove $\forall n$ ($n = 1, \cdots, B$), $\pi^{(l)}_{l,n} \to \pi^0_{l,n}$ as $N \to \infty$.

For a certain player l, we construct the following map:

$$M: o_{-l} \to B_{o_{-l}} = \{all\ of\ l's\ best\ bids\ in\ case\ o_{-l}\}, \forall o_{-l}.$$

According to the definition, we know that $\pi^0_{l,n}$ equals to the nth element of $E_{o_{-l}}\{\arg\max_{\pi^{(l)}_l}(\bar{\alpha}_j(v_l - o_{\bar{i}}\bar{s}_{\bar{i}}/\bar{s}_l))\}$, and then

$$\pi^0_{l,n} = \sum_{all\ B_{o_{-l}}\ containing\ b_n} \frac{P(o_{-l})}{|B_{o_{-l}}|}.$$

Here $P(o_{-l})$ is the probability of o_{-l}. In the Monte Carlo algorithm, we initialize $\pi^{(l)}_{l,n} = 0$, and suppose that $\pi^{(l)}_{l,n}$ increases by Δ_t in each step of the loop "for $t = 1, \cdots, N$". Therefore, the value of $\pi^{(l)}_{l,n}$ will finally be $(\sum_{t=1}^N \Delta_t)/N$. However, in each step t, for a sample o_{-l}, the expectation of Δ_t is,

$$E(\Delta_t) = \sum_{all\ B_{o_{-l}}\ containing\ b_n} \frac{P(o_{-l})}{|B_{o_{-l}}|}.$$

Hence, referring to the *Law of Large Number*, $(\sum_{t=1}^N \Delta_t)/N$ will converge to the expectation of Δ_t, which exactly equals $\pi^0_{l,n}$ as N grows. This finishes our proof of Theorem 1. □

Besides the above theorem, we can also prove some properties of the proposed model. We describe the properties in the appendix for the readers who are interested in them.

5. EXPERIMENTAL RESULTS

In this section, we report the experimental results about the prediction accuracy of our proposed model. In particular, we first describe the data sets and the experimental setting. Then we investigate the training accuracy for the willingness, capability, and constraint functions, to show the step-wise results of the proposed method. After that, we test the performance of our model in bid prediction, which is the direct output of the advertiser behavior model. At last, we test the performance of our model in click number prediction and revenue prediction, which are important applications of the advertiser behavior model.

5.1 Data and Setting

In our experiments, we used the advertiser bid history data sampled from the sponsored search log of a commercial search engine. We randomly chose 160 queries from the most profitable 10,000 queries and extracted the related advertisers from the data. We sampled one auction per 30 minutes from the auction log within 90 days (from March 2012 to May 2012)[9], so there are in total 4,320 (90 × 24 × 2) auctions. For each auction, there are up to 14 (4 on mainline and 10 on sidebar) ads displayed. We filtered out the advertisers whose ads have never been displayed during these 4,320 auctions, and eventually kept 5,543 effective advertisers in the experiments.

For the experimental setting, we used the first 3,360 auctions (70 days) for model training, and the last 960 auctions (20 days) as test data for evaluation. In the training period, we used the first 2,400 auctions (50 days) to obtain the historical bid histogram π^*_i ($i = 1, \cdots, I$) and the true value v_l; we then used the rest 960 auctions (20 days) to learn the parameters for the advertiser rationality. For clarity, we list the usage of the data in Table 3. Note that the three periods in the table are abbreviated as P1, P2, and P3.

5.2 Different Aspects of Advertiser Rationality

5.2.1 Willingness

First, we study the logistic regression model for willingness. We train the willingness function using the auctions in P2 according to the description in Section 2.2, and test its performance on actions in P3. In particular, for any auction t in P3, we get the value of $y^{(l)}_t$ according to whether the bid was changed in the time interval $[t-1, t]$, and use it as the ground truth. For the same time period, we apply the regression model to calculate the predicted value $\hat{y}^{(l)}_t \in [0, 1]$ of $y^{(l)}_t$. We find a threshold in $[0, 1]$ such that $\hat{y}^{(l)}_t$ is correspondingly converted to 0 or 1. Then we can calculate the prediction accuracy compared with the ground truth. Figure 1 shows the distribution of different prediction accuracies among advertisers when the threshold is set to 0.15. According to the figure, we can see that the willingness function gets a prediction accuracy of 100% for 39% (2,170 of 5,543) advertisers, and a prediction accuracy over 80% for 68% (3,773 of 5,543) advertisers. In this regard we say the proposed willingness model performs well on predicting whether the advertisers are willing to change their bids.

---
[9] In the search engine, only the latest-90-day data is stored. To deal with the seasonal or holiday effects, we can choose seasonal or holiday data from different years instead of the data in continuous time. We only consider the general cases in our experiments.

Table 3: Data usage in the experiments

Purpose	Training		Test
Period	P1: Day 1 to Day 50	P2: Day 51 to Day 70	P3: Day 71 to Day 90
#auctions	2,400	960	960
Usage	(i) Get historical bid histogram (ii) Learn true value	Learn rationality parameters	Test model
Information required	bid price ad quality score ad position	bid price ad quality score click number budget	bid price ad quality score click number budget pay per click

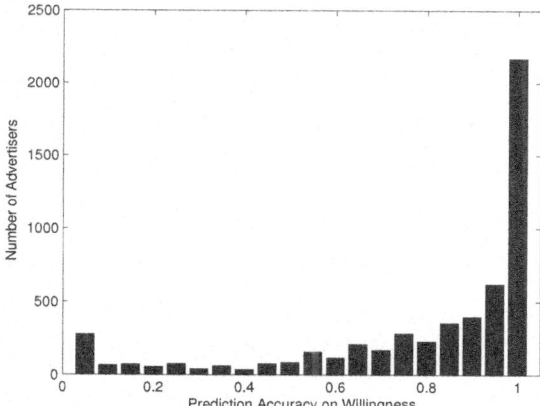

Figure 1: Distribution of the prediction accuracy.

5.2.2 Capability

Second, we investigate the capability function. For this purpose, we set C_l as an identify function, and only consider W_l and A_l. In the capability function A_l, we discretely pick the parameter pair (δ_l, N_l) from the set $\{0, 0.1, \cdots, 0.9, 1.0\} \times \{0, 1, \cdots, 9, 10\}$ and judge which parameter pair is the best using the data in P2 as described in Section 2.3. We call the advertiser model with the learned willingness and capability functions (without considering the constraint function) *Rationality-based Advertiser Behavior model with Willingness and Capability* (or RAB-WC for short). Its performance will be reported and discussed in Section 5.3.

5.2.3 Constraint

Third, the constraint function is implemented with a linear regression model trained on P2, using the remaining budget as the feature, according to the discussions in Section 2.4. By applying the constraint function, we get the complete version of the proposed model. We call it *Rationality-based Advertiser Behavior model with Willingness, Capability, and Constraint* (or RAB-WCC for short). Its performance will be given in Section 5.3.

5.3 Bid Prediction

In this subsection, we compare our proposed advertiser model with six baselines in the task of bid prediction. The predicted bid prices are the direct outputs of the advertiser behavior models. The baselines are listed as follows:

- **Random Bid Model (RBM)** refers to the random method of bid prediction. That is, we will randomly select a bid in the bid strategy space as the prediction.

- **Most Frequent Model (MFM)** refers to an intuitive method for bid prediction, which works as follows. First, we get the historical bid histogram from the bid values in the training period, and then always output the historically most frequently-used bid value for the test period. If there are several bid prices that are equally frequently used, we will randomly select one from them.

- **Best Response Model (BRM)** [5] refers to the model that predicts the bid strategy to be the best response by assuming the advertisers know all the competitors' bids in the previous auction.

- **Regression Model (RM)** [8] refers to the model that predicts the bid strategy using a linear regression function. In our experiments, we used the following 5 features as the input of this function: the average bid change in history, the bid change in the previous time period, click number, remaining budget, and revenue in the previous period.

- **RAB-WC** refers to the model as described in the previous subsection.

- **RAB-WCC-D** refers to the degenerated version of RAB-WCC. That is, we select the bid with the maximum probability in the mixed bid strategy output by RAB-WCC.

We adopt two metrics to evaluate the performances of these advertiser models.

First, we use the likelihood of the test data as the evaluation metric [9]. Specifically, we denote a probabilistic prediction model as $\mathcal{M}$,[10] which outputs a mixed strategy of advertiser l in period t as $\pi_l^{[t]} = (\pi_{l,0}^{[t]}, \cdots, \pi_{l,B}^{[t]})$ in the bid strategy space Ω^0. Suppose the index of the real bid strategy of l in period t is $\omega_l^{[t]}$. Considering a period set $\mathcal{T}$ and an advertiser set $\mathcal{I}$, we define the following likelihood:

$$P_{\mathcal{T},\mathcal{I}}(\mathcal{M}) = \Pi_{t \in \mathcal{T}, l \in \mathcal{I}}(\pi_{l,\omega_l^{[t]}}^{[t]}).$$

$P_{\mathcal{T},\mathcal{I}}(\mathcal{M})$ reflects the probability that model $\mathcal{M}$ produces the real data $\omega_l^{[t]}$ for all $t \in \mathcal{T}$ and all $l \in \mathcal{I}$. To make the metric normalized and positive, we adopt the geometric average and a negative logarithmic function. As a result, we get

$$D_{\mathcal{T},\mathcal{I}}(\mathcal{M}) = -\ln(\sqrt[|\mathcal{T}||\mathcal{I}|]{P_{\mathcal{T},\mathcal{I}(\mathcal{M})}}) = \frac{-\ln P_{\mathcal{T},\mathcal{I}}(\mathcal{M})}{|\mathcal{T}||\mathcal{I}|}.$$

We call it *negative logarithmic likelihood* (NLL). It can be seen that with the same $\mathcal{T}$ and $\mathcal{I}$, the smaller NLL is, the better prediction $\mathcal{M}$ gives.

---

[10] Please note some of the models under investigation are deterministic models. We can still compute the likelihood for them because deterministic models are special cases of probabilistic models.

Second, we use the expected error between the predicted bid strategy and the real bid as the evaluation metric. Specifically, we define the metric as the *aggregated expected error* (AEE) on a period set $\mathcal{T}$ and an advertiser set $\mathcal{I}$, i.e.,

$$\sum_{t\in\mathcal{T}}\sum_{l\in\mathcal{I}}\sum_{i=0}^{B}|\pi_{l,i}^{[t]}(b_i - b_{\omega_l^{[t]}})|. \quad (3)$$

The average NLL and AEE on all the 160 queries of the above algorithms are shown in Table 4. We have the following observations from the table.

- Our proposed RAB-WCC achieves the best performance compared with all the baseline methods.

- RAB-WCC-D performs the second best among these methods, indicating that the bid with the maximum probability in RAB-WCC has been a very good prediction compared with most of the baselines.

- RAB-WC performs the third best among these methods, showing that: a) the proposed rationality-based advertiser model can outperform the commonly used algorithms in bid prediction; b) the introduction of the constraint function to the rationality-based advertiser model can further improve its prediction accuracy.

- RBM performs almost the worst, which is not surprising due to its uniform randomness.

- BRM also performs very bad. Our explanation is as the following. In BRM, we assume the advertisers know all the competitors' bids before selecting the bids for the next auction. However, the real situation is far from this assumption. So the "best response" will not be the real response for most cases.

- MFM model performs better than BRM. This is not difficult to interpret. MFM is a data driven model, without too much unrealistic assumptions. Therefore, it will fit the data better than BRM.

- RM performs better than MFM but worse than RAB-WC, RAB-WCC-D, and RAB-WCC. RM is a machine learning model which leverages several features related to the advertiser behaviors, therefore it can outperform MFM which is simply based on counting. However, RM does not consider the rationality levels in its formulation, and therefore it cannot fit the data as well as our proposed model. This indicates the importance of modeling advertiser rationality when predicting their bid strategy changes.

In addition to the average results, we give some example queries and their corresponding NLL and AEE on the 960th auction in P3 in Table 5 and Table 6. The best scores are blackened in the table. At first glance, we see that RAB-WCC achieves the first positions in most of the example queries, while RAB-WCC-D and RAB-WC achieve the first positions for the rest example queries. In most cases, RBM performs the worst, and RM performs moderately.

To sum up, we can conclude that the proposed RAB-WCC method can predict the advertisers' bid strategies with the best accuracy among all the models under investigation.

5.4 Click and Revenue Prediction

To further test the performance of our model, we apply it to the tasks of click number prediction and revenue prediction.[11] We compare our model with two state-of-the-art models on these tasks. The first baseline model is the Structural Model in Sponsored Search [2], abbreviated as SMSS-1. The second baseline model is the Stochastic Model in Sponsored Search [17], abbreviated as SMSS-2. SMSS-1 calculates the expected number of clicks and the expected expenditure for each advertiser by considering some uncertainty assumptions on sponsored search marketplace. SMSS-2 assumes that all the advertisers' bids are independent and identically distributed and they learn the distribution by mixing all the advertisers' historical bids.

We use the *relative error* and *absolute error* as compared to the real click numbers and revenue in the test period as the evaluation metrics. Specifically, suppose the value output by the model and the ground truth value are ϕ and φ respectively, then the absolute error and the relative error are calculated as $|\phi - \varphi|$ and $|\phi - \varphi|/\varphi$ respectively. The performance of all the models under investigation are listed in Table 7.

According to the table, we can clearly see that RAB-WCC performs better than both SMSS-1 and SMSS-2. The absolute errors on click number and revenue made by SMSS-1 are very large as compared to the other methods. The relative errors made by SMSS-1 are larger than 50% for both click number and revenue prediction, which are not good enough for practical use. The relative error made by SMSS-2 for revenue prediction is even larger than 80%. In contrast, our proposed RAB-WCC method generates relative errors of no more than 20% for both click and revenue prediction (and the absolute errors are also small). Although the results might need further improvements, a 20% prediction error has already provided quite good references for the search engine to make decision.

6. RELATED WORK

Besides the randomized bid strategy and the strategy of selecting the most frequently used bid, there are a number of works on advertiser modeling in the literature. Early work studies some simple cases in sponsored search such as auctions with only two advertisers and auctions in which the advertisers adjust their bids in an alternating manner [1] [21] [18]. Later on, greedy methods were used to model advertiser behaviors. For example, in the random greedy bid strategy [4], an advertiser chooses a bid for the next round of auction that maximizes his/her utility, by assuming that the bids of all the other advertisers in the next round will remain the same as in the previous round. In the locally-envy free bid strategy [10] [16], each advertiser selects the optimal bid price that leads to a certain equilibrium called locally-envy free equilibrium. In [6], the advertiser bid strategies are modeled using the knapsack problem. Competitor-busting greedy bid strategy [22] assumes that an advertiser will bid as high as possible while retaining his/her desired ad slot in order to make the competitors pay as much as possible and thus exhaust their advertising resources. Other similar work includes low-dimensional bid strategy [20], restricted balanced greedy bid strategy [4], and altruistic greedy bid strategy [4]. In [5], a model that predicts the bid strategy to be the best response is proposed by assuming the advertisers know all the competitors' bids in the previous auction. In [8], a linear regression model is used base on a group of advertiser behavior features. In addition, a bid strategy based on incremental cost per click is discussed in [19]

---

[11] After outputting the bid prediction, we simulated the auction process based on those bids and made estimation on the revenue and clicks according to the simulation results.

Table 4: Prediction performance

Model	RBM	MFM	BRM	RM	RAB-WC	RAB-WCC-D	RAB-WCC
NLL	3.939	1.420	2.154	1.289	1.135	1.056	**1.018**
AEE	35.392	34.748	77.526	40.397	14.616	10.553	**8.876**

Table 5: Prediction performance on some example queries (NLL)

Model	RBM	MFM	BRM	RM	RAB-WC	RAB-WCC-D	RAB-WCC
car insurance	3.067	1.198	1.777	2.468	0.995	**0.975**	0.975
disney	2.169	0.541	2.592	0.300	**0.130**	0.140	**0.130**
ipad	4.457	1.288	2.075	0.747	0.315	0.325	**0.310**
jcpenney	2.089	0.511	3.213	0.487	0.263	0.351	**0.262**
medicare	3.649	1.466	1.750	2.866	1.125	1.127	**1.121**
stock market	5.068	1.711	2.100	1.839	1.373	**1.349**	1.362

[2], which proves that an advertiser's utility is maximized when he/she bids the amount at which his/her value per click equals the incremental cost per click.[12]

However, please note that most of the above works assume that the advertisers have the same rationality and intelligence in choosing the best response to optimize their utilities. Therefore they have significant difference from our work. Actually, to the best of our knowledge, there is no work on advertiser behavior modeling that considers different aspects of advertiser rationality.

7. CONCLUSIONS AND FUTURE WORK

In this work, we have proposed a novel advertiser model which explicitly considers different levels of rationality of an advertiser. We have applied the model to the real data from a commercial search engine and obtained better accuracy than the baseline methods, in bid prediction, click number prediction, and revenue prediction.

As for future work, we plan to work on the following aspects.

- First, in Section 2.1, we have assumed that the auctions for different keywords are independent of each other. However, in practice, an advertiser will bid multiple keywords simultaneously and his/her strategies for these keywords may be dependent. We will study this complex setting in the future.

- Second, we will study the equilibrium in the auction given the new advertiser model. Most previous work on equilibrium analysis is based on the assumption of advertiser rationality. When we change this foundation, the equilibrium needs to be re-investigated.

- Third, we will apply the advertiser model in the function modules in sponsored search, such as bid keyword suggestion, ad selection, and click prediction, to make these modules more robust against the second-order effect caused by the advertiser behavior changes.

- Fourth, we will consider the application of the advertiser model in the auction mechanism design. That is, given the advertiser model, we may learn an optimal auction mechanism using a machine learning approach.

8. ACKNOWLEDGMENTS

We thank Wei Chen, Tao Qin, Di He, Wenkui Ding, and Xinxin Yang for their valuable suggestions and comments on this work,

---
[12] Incremental cost per click is defined as the advertiser's average cost of additional clicks received at a better ad slot.

and thank Pingguang Yuan for his help on the data preparation for the experiments.

APPENDIX

In the appendix, we discuss some properties of the proposed model. Firstly, we give a theorem on the relationship of true value and bid. Secondly, we give a theorem related to the estimation accuracy of the true value.

A. RELATIONSHIP

We discuss about the relationship between true value v_l and our predicted bid strategy. Note that we will mainly focus on the results from the capability function because both willingness and compromise functions are not effected by the true value v_l according to their definitions. For this purpose, by setting $W_l = 1$ and C_l as the identity function in π_l, we define:

$$\boldsymbol{F}(v_l) = E_{\sigma_{o_{-l}}}\{\arg\max_{\pi_l^{(l)}}(\overline{\alpha}_j(v_l - o_{\hat{i}}\overline{s}_{\hat{i}}/\overline{s}_l))\}$$

$$E(v_l) = (b_1, b_2, ..., b_B)(\boldsymbol{F}(v_l))^T$$

Here $\boldsymbol{F}(v_l)$ is a B-dimension strategy vector and $E(v_l)$ is the average bid of the strategy $\boldsymbol{F}(v_l)$. Under a very common assumption that ad position effect α_j decreases with the slot index j, Theorem 2 shows that an advertiser with a higher true value will generally set a higher bid to optimize the utility, which is consistent to the intuition. This conclusion shows the consistency of our model in the capability part.

THEOREM 2. *Assume α_j decreases in j, then $E(v_l)$ is monotone nondecreasing in v_l.*

PROOF. To prove $E(v_l)$ is monotone nondecreasing, we only need to prove that $\forall \boldsymbol{o}_{-l}$ and $\forall \Delta > 0$,

$$(b_1, b_2, ..., b_B)(\arg\max_{\pi_l^{(l)}}(\overline{\alpha}_j(v_l(1+\Delta) - o_{\hat{i}}\overline{s}_{\hat{i}}/\overline{s}_l)))$$
$$\geq (b_1, b_2, ..., b_B)(\arg\max_{\pi_l^{(l)}}(\overline{\alpha}_j(v_l - o_{\hat{i}}\overline{s}_{\hat{i}}/\overline{s}_l))), \quad (4)$$

and then the "$\geq$" will keep unchanged in the expectation of $\boldsymbol{o}_{-l}$.

We denote j^{Δ} and j^0 as the best rank of l for the cases that true values are $v_l(1+\Delta)$ and v_l respectively. Here $\boldsymbol{o}_{-l}$ is fixed and "best rank" means the rank that leads to the optimal utility.

Table 6: Prediction performance on some example queries (AEE)

Model	RBM	MFM	BRM	RM	RAB-WC	RAB-WCC-D	RAB-WCC
car insurance	89.459	89.883	305.703	107.335	33.207	22.188	**12.760**
disney	5.019	4.895	9.703	0.217	0.297	0.171	**0.140**
ipad	16.355	15.428	30.856	0.662	0.975	0.458	**0.385**
jcpenney	5.036	5.145	16.337	1.476	1.411	1.165	**0.209**
medicare	98.206	99.014	225.774	111.248	20.221	16.695	**3.744**
stock market	37.576	38.360	72.640	97.035	5.824	4.137	**1.486**

We denote $\hat{l}_\Delta$ and $\hat{l}_0$ as the advertisers who rank at $(j^\Delta + 1)$ and $(j^0 + 1)$ respectively. Note that for a fixed $\boldsymbol{o}_{-l}$, j^Δ and j^0 can be different due to different true value of l. If we are able to prove $j^\Delta \geq j^0$, then the inequality (4) will be valid since a nondecreasing best ranking yields a nondecreasing best bid strategy.

As j^0 is the best rank for the true value v_l, we have,

$$\overline{\alpha}_{j^0}(v_l - o_{\hat{l}_0}\overline{s}_{\hat{l}_0}/\overline{s}_l) \geq \overline{\alpha}_{j^\Delta}(v_l - o_{\hat{l}_\Delta}\overline{s}_{\hat{l}_\Delta}/\overline{s}_l). \quad (5)$$

Assuming $j^\Delta < j^0$, we have,

$$\overline{\alpha}_{j^0} v_l \Delta > \overline{\alpha}_{j^\Delta} v_l \Delta. \quad (6)$$

By adding (3) and (4), we got,

$$\overline{\alpha}_{j^0}(v_l(1+\Delta) - o_{\hat{l}_0}\overline{s}_{\hat{l}_0}/\overline{s}_l) > \overline{\alpha}_{j^\Delta}(v_l(1+\Delta) - o_{\hat{l}_\Delta}\overline{s}_{\hat{l}_\Delta}/\overline{s}_l).$$

This equation reveals that j^0 is a better rank than j^Δ and j^Δ should not be the best rank for the true value $v_l(1 + \Delta)$, which is contradictive to the definition of j^Δ. Therefore, the assumption $j^\Delta < j^0$ is not valid, which also finishes our proof of this theorem. □

B. ESTIMATION ACCURACY

As discussed in Section 4, we choose the model in [9] for the true value prediction. Usually, the estimation is not perfect and there might be some errors. Fortunately, we can prove a theorem which guarantees that the solution of this model will keep accurate if the estimation errors are not very large. This holds true because the payment rule of GSP is discrete and it allows the small-scale vibration of true value.

Before introducing the theorem, we give some notations first. For a fixed $\boldsymbol{o}_{-l}$ and true value v_l, l's best rank is denoted as $BR_{\boldsymbol{o}_{-l}}$ (Best Rank), the optimal utility is denoted as $BU_{\boldsymbol{o}_{-l}}$, and the ranking score of $\hat{l}$ (the one ranked next to l) in the optimal case is denoted $BS_{\boldsymbol{o}_{-l}}$. To describe the theorem, we also denote the second optimal utility as $SU_{\boldsymbol{o}_{-l}}$ (Second Utility), which is the largest utility less than $BU_{\boldsymbol{o}_{-l}}$ in the fixed $\boldsymbol{o}_{-l}$.

THEOREM 3. *We assume that α_j decreases in j and set $\theta = max_{\boldsymbol{o}_{-l}}(\frac{SU_{\boldsymbol{o}_{-l}}}{BU_{\boldsymbol{o}_{-l}}})$, $\rho = max_{\boldsymbol{o}_{-l}}(BR_{\boldsymbol{o}_{-l}})$, and $\omega = max_{\boldsymbol{o}_{-l}}(BS_{\boldsymbol{o}_{-l}})$, $(v_l - \omega/\overline{s}_l > 0)$. Let v_l increase by Δv_l $(\Delta \in R)$, then $F(v_l)$ will keep unchanged if $|\Delta| \leq \frac{\alpha_\rho}{\alpha_1}(1-\theta)(1-\frac{\omega}{\overline{s}_l v_l})$, where α_1 is the CTR at the first position.*

In order to prove the bound of Δ keeps $F(v_l)$ unchanging, we prove the following lemma instead.

LEMMA 1. *If Δ satisfies $|\Delta| \leq \frac{\alpha_\rho}{\alpha_1}(1-\theta)(1-\frac{\omega}{\overline{s}_l v_l})$, then $\forall \boldsymbol{o}_{-l}$ we have, $argmax_{\pi_l^{(l)}} \overline{\alpha}_j(v_l(1+\Delta) - o_{\hat{i}}\overline{s}_{\hat{i}}/\overline{s}_l) = argmax_{\pi_l^{(l)}} \overline{\alpha}_j(v_l - o_{\hat{i}}\overline{s}_{\hat{i}}/\overline{s}_l)$.*

The proof of Theorem 3 will be finished at once after we sum up all the cases of $\boldsymbol{o}_{-l}$ in Lemma 1.

Table 7: Prediction performance in applications

Model	SMSS-1	SMSS-2	RAB-WCC
Relative Error (Click)	0.52	**0.11**	0.19
Absolute Error (Click)	2.02	0.71	**0.23**
Relative Error (Revenue)	0.54	0.83	**0.18**
Absolute Error (Revenue)	659.06	124.80	**25.75**

PROOF. Since a change of "$argmax_{\pi_l^{(l)}}$" is equivalent to a change of "$BR_{\boldsymbol{o}_{-l}}$", we consider the critical point that the increase of Δ makes the best rank transfer exactly from j^0 to j^Δ ($j^0 \neq j^\Delta$).

Thus we have: $\exists j^\Delta(j^\Delta \neq j^0), s.t. j^\Delta, j^0$ maximizes $\overline{\alpha}_j(v_l(1+\Delta) - o_{\hat{i}}\overline{s}_{\hat{i}}/\overline{s}_l)$ simultaneously, and then we can get,

$$\overline{\alpha}_{j^\Delta}(v_l(1+\Delta) - o_{\hat{l}_\Delta}\overline{s}_{\hat{l}_\Delta}/\overline{s}_l) = \overline{\alpha}_{j^0}(v_l(1+\Delta) - o_{\hat{l}_0}\overline{s}_{\hat{l}_0}/\overline{s}_l). \quad (7)$$

From equation (7) we have,

$$\Delta = \frac{\overline{\alpha}_{j^0}(v_l - o_{\hat{l}_0}\overline{s}_{\hat{l}_0}/\overline{s}_l) - \overline{\alpha}_{j^\Delta}(v_l - o_{\hat{l}_\Delta}\overline{s}_{\hat{l}_\Delta}/\overline{s}_l)}{v_l(\alpha_{j^\Delta} - \alpha_{j^0})}. \quad (8)$$

Assume there is a θ_0 such that

$$\overline{\alpha}_{j^\Delta}(v_l - o_{\hat{l}_\Delta}\overline{s}_{\hat{l}_\Delta}/\overline{s}_l) = \theta_0 \overline{\alpha}_{j^0}(v_l - o_{\hat{l}_0}\overline{s}_{\hat{l}_0}/\overline{s}_l). \quad (9)$$

Then equation (8) is transformed as,

$$\Delta = \frac{(1-\theta_0)\overline{\alpha}_{j^0}(v_l - o_{\hat{l}_0}\overline{s}_{\hat{l}_0}/\overline{s}_l)}{v_l(\alpha_{j^\Delta} - \alpha_{j^0})}$$
$$= (1-\theta_0)\frac{\alpha_{j^0}}{\alpha_{j^\Delta} - \alpha_{j^0}}(1 - \frac{o_{\hat{l}_0}\overline{s}_{\hat{l}_0}/\overline{s}_l}{v_l}). \quad (10)$$

Considering j^0 is the best rank, from equation (9) we have,

$$\theta_0 = \frac{\overline{\alpha}_{j^\Delta}(v_l - o_{\hat{l}_\Delta}\overline{s}_{\hat{l}_\Delta}/\overline{s}_l)}{\overline{\alpha}_{j^0}(v_l - o_{\hat{l}_0}\overline{s}_{\hat{l}_0}/\overline{s}_l)} \leq \frac{SU_{\boldsymbol{o}_{-l}}}{BU_{\boldsymbol{o}_{-l}}} \leq \theta < 1. \quad (11)$$

In addition, there holds

$$j^0 \leq max_{\boldsymbol{o}_{-l}}(BR_{\boldsymbol{o}_{-l}}) = \rho,$$
$$\alpha_{j^0} \geq \alpha_\rho, |\frac{\alpha_{j^0}}{\alpha_{j^\Delta} - \alpha_{j^0}}| > \frac{\alpha_\rho}{\alpha_1}, \quad (12)$$

$$o_{\hat{l}_0}\overline{s}_{\hat{l}_0} = BS_{\boldsymbol{o}_{-l}} \leq max_{\boldsymbol{o}_{-l}}(BS_{\boldsymbol{o}_{-l}}) = \omega. \quad (13)$$

According to (10) and (11),(12),(13), we finally have,

$$|\Delta| = |1-\theta_0|\frac{\alpha_{j^0}}{|\alpha_{j^\Delta} - \alpha_{j^0}|}(1 - \frac{o_{\hat{l}_0}\overline{s}_{\hat{l}_0}}{\overline{s}_l v_l}) > \frac{\alpha_\rho}{\alpha_1}(1-\theta)(1-\frac{\omega}{\overline{s}_l v_l}).$$

As Δ is the critical point, for any fixed $\boldsymbol{o}_{-l}$, if $|\Delta| \leq \frac{\alpha_\rho}{\alpha_1}(1-\theta)(1-\frac{\omega}{\overline{s}_l v_l})$, $BR_{\boldsymbol{o}_{-l}}$ and "$argmax_{\pi_l^{(l)}}$" will keep unchanged. This ends our proof of Lemma 1. □

C. REFERENCES

[1] K. Asdemir. Bidding patterns in search engine auctions. In *Second Workshop on Sponsored Search Auctions (2006), ACM Electronic Commerce.* Press., 2006.

[2] S. Athey and D. Nekipelov. A structural model of sponsored search advertising auctions., 2010. Available at `http://groups.haas.berkeley.edu/marketing/sics/pdf_2010/paper_athey.pdf`.

[3] A. Broder, E. Gabrilovich, V. Josifovski, G. Mavromatis, and A. Smola. Bid generation for advanced match in sponsored search. In *Proceedings of the fourth ACM international conference on Web search and data mining*, WSDM '11, pages 515–524, New York, NY, USA, 2011. ACM.

[4] M. Cary, A. Das, B. Edelman, I. Giotis, K. Heimerl, A. R. Karlin, C. Mathieu, and M. Schwarz. Greedy bidding strategies for keyword auctions. In *EC '07 Proceedings of the 8th ACM conference on Electronic commerce.* ACM Press., 2007.

[5] M. Cary, A. Das, B. G. Edelman, I. Giotis, K. Heimerl, A. R. Karlin, C. Mathieu, and M. Schwarz. On best-response bidding in gsp auctions., 2008. Available at `http://www.hbs.edu/research/pdf/08-056.pdf`.

[6] D. Chakrabarty, Y. Zhou, and R. Lukose. Budget constrained bidding in keyword auctions and online knapsack problems. In *WWW '07 Proceedings of the 16th international conference on World Wide Web.* ACM Press., 2007.

[7] Y. Chen, G.-R. Xue, and Y. Yu. Advertising keyword suggestion based on concept hierarchy. In *WSDM '08 Proceedings of the international conference on Web search and web data mining.* ACM Press., 2008.

[8] Y. Cui, R. Zhang, W. Li, and J. Mao. Bid landscape forecasting in online ad exchange marketplace. In *KDD '11 Proceedings of the 17th ACM SIGKDD international conference on Knowledge discovery and data mining.* ACM Press., 2011.

[9] Q. Duong and S. Lahaie. Discrete choice models of bidder behavior in sponsored search. In *Workshop on Internet and Network Economics (WINE).* Press., 2011.

[10] B. Edelman, M. Ostrovsky, and M. Schwarz. Internet advertising and the generalized second-price auction: Selling billions of dollars worth of keywords. In *The American Economic Review.*, 2007.

[11] T. Graepel, J. Q. Candela, T. Borchert, and R. Herbrich. Web-scale bayesian click-through rate prediction for sponsored search advertising in microsoft's bing search engine. In *Proceedings of the 27th International Conference on Machine Learning.* ACM, 2010.

[12] J. C. Harsanyi. Games with incomplete information played by bayesian players, i-iii. In *Management Science.*, 1967/1968.

[13] J. Jansen. *Understanding Sponsored Search: Core Elements of Keyword Advertising.* Cambridge University Press., 2011.

[14] B. Kitts and B. Leblanc. Optimal bidding on keyword auctions. In *Electronic Markets.* Routledge Press., 2004.

[15] D. C. Liu and J. Nocedal. On the limited memory bfgs method for large scale optimization. In *Journal of Mathematical Programming.* Springer-Verlag New York., 1989.

[16] C. Nittala and Y. Narahari. Optimal equilibrium bidding strategies for budget constrained bidders in sponsored search auctions. In *Operational Research: An International Journal.* Springer Press, 2011.

[17] F. Pin and P. Key. Stochasitic variability in sponsored search auctions: Observations and models. In *EC '11 Proceedings of the 12th ACM conference on Electronic commerce.* ACM Press., 2011.

[18] S. S. S. Reddy and Y. Narahari. Bidding dynamics of rational advertisers in sponsored search auctions on the web. In *Proceedings of the International Conference on Advances in Control and Optimization of Dynamical Systems.* Press., 2007.

[19] H. R. Varian. Position auctions. In *International Journal of Industrial Organization*, 2006.

[20] Y. Vorobeychik. Simulation-based game theoretic analysis of keyword auctions with low-dimensional bidding strategies. In *UAI '09 Proceedings of the Twenty-Fifth Conference on Uncertainty in Artificial Intelligence.* AUAI Press., 2009.

[21] X. Zhang and J. Feng. Finding edgeworth cycles in online advertising auctions. In *Proceedings of the 26th International Conference on Information Systems ICIS.* Press., 2006.

[22] Y. Zhou and R. Lukose. Vindictive bidding in keyword auctions. In *ICEC '07 Proceedings of the ninth international conference on Electronic commerce.* ACM Press., 2007.

A Biterm Topic Model for Short Texts

Xiaohui Yan, Jiafeng Guo, Yanyan Lan, Xueqi Cheng
Institute of Computing Technology, CAS
Beijing, China 100190
yanxiaohui@software.ict.ac.cn, {guojiafeng, lanyanyan, cxq}@ict.ac.cn

ABSTRACT

Uncovering the topics within short texts, such as tweets and instant messages, has become an important task for many content analysis applications. However, directly applying conventional topic models (e.g. LDA and PLSA) on such short texts may not work well. The fundamental reason lies in that conventional topic models implicitly capture the document-level word co-occurrence patterns to reveal topics, and thus suffer from the severe data sparsity in short documents. In this paper, we propose a novel way for modeling topics in short texts, referred as *biterm topic model (BTM)*. Specifically, in BTM we learn the topics by directly modeling the generation of word co-occurrence patterns (i.e. biterms) in the whole corpus. The major advantages of BTM are that 1) BTM explicitly models the word co-occurrence patterns to enhance the topic learning; and 2) BTM uses the aggregated patterns in the whole corpus for learning topics to solve the problem of sparse word co-occurrence patterns at document-level. We carry out extensive experiments on real-world short text collections. The results demonstrate that our approach can discover more prominent and coherent topics, and significantly outperform baseline methods on several evaluation metrics. Furthermore, we find that BTM can outperform LDA even on normal texts, showing the potential generality and wider usage of the new topic model.

Categories and Subject Descriptors

H.3.3 [**Information Search and Retrieval**]: Information Search and Retrieval; I.5.3 [**Pattern Recognition**]: Clustering

Keywords

Short Text, Topic Model, Biterm, Content Analysis, document clustering

1. INTRODUCTION

Short texts are prevalent on the Web, no matter in traditional Web sites, e.g. Web page titles, text advertisements and image captions, or in emerging social media, e.g. tweets, status messages, and questions in Q&A websites. Uncovering the topics of such short texts is crucial for a wide range of content analysis tasks, such as content characterizing [26, 35, 14], user interest profiling [32], emerging topic detecting [20] and so on. However, unlike the traditional normal documents (e.g. news articles and academic papers), the lack of rich context in short texts makes the topic modeling a challenging problem.

Conventional topic models, like PLSA [16] and LDA [3], are widely used for uncovering the hidden topics from text corpus. In general, documents are modeled as mixtures of topics, where a topic is a probability distribution over words. Statistical techniques are then utilized to learn the topic components and mixture coefficients of each document. In essence, the conventional topic models reveal the latent topics within the text corpus by implicitly capturing the document-level word co-occurrence patterns [5, 30]. Therefore, directly applying these models on short texts will suffer from the severe data sparsity problem (i.e. the sparse word co-occurrence patterns in each short document) [17]. More specifically, 1) the occurrences of words in short document play less discriminative role compared to lengthy documents where the model has enough word counts to know how words are related [17] ; 2) The limited contexts make it more difficult for topic models to identify the senses of ambiguous words in short documents.

One simple but popular way to alleviate the sparsity problem is to aggregate short texts into lengthy pseudo-documents before training a standard topic model. For example, Weng et al. [32] aggregated the tweets published by individual user into one document before training LDA. Besides the user-based aggregation, Hong et al. [17] also aggregated the tweets containing the same word, and shown that topic models trained on these aggregated messages work better than the regular LDA. However, such heuristic data aggregation methods are highly data-dependent. For example, the user information is not always available in some datasets, like the collection of Web page titles or advertisements. Even if the user information is available, e.g. in tweets data, most users only have few tweets which makes the aggregation less effective.

Another way to deal with the problem is to make stronger assumptions on the data. A typical way is to assume that a short document only covers a single topic. For example, Zhao et al. [35] modeled each tweet in the way of mixture of unigrams [23]. Similar approach can be found in [12], where words in each sentence are assumed to be drawn from the same topic. Compared to LDA and PLSA, the simplified data generation process may help alleviate the sparsity problem in short texts. However, it loses the flexibility to capture different topic ingredients in one document, and suffers from overfitting issues due to the peaked posteriors of topics P(z|d) [3].

Unlike these approaches, in this paper, we propose a novel topic model for short texts to tackle the sparsity problem. The main idea comes from the answers of the following two questions. 1) Since topics are basically groups of correlated words and the correlation is revealed by word co-occurrence patterns in documents, why not explicitly model the word co-occurrence for topic learning? 2) Since topic models on short texts suffer from the problem of severe sparse patterns in short documents, why not use the rich global word co-occurrence patterns for better revealing topics?

Specifically, we propose a generative *biterm topic model (BTM)*, which learns topics over short texts by directly modeling the generation of biterms in the whole corpus. Here, a *biterm* is an unordered word-pair co-occurred in a short context. The data generation process under BTM is that the corpus consist of a mixture of topics, and each biterm is drawn from a specific topic. Compared with conventional topic models, the major differences and advantages of BTM lie in that 1) BTM explicitly models the word co-occurrence patterns (i.e. biterms), rather than documents, to enhance the topic learning; and 2) BTM uses the aggregated patterns in the whole corpus for learning topics to solve the problem of sparse patterns at document-level. By learning BTM, we can obtain the topic components and a global topic distribution of the corpus, except the topic distribution of each individual document as it does not model the document generation process. However, we show that the topic distribution of each document can be naturally derived based on the learned model.

We conduct extensive experiments on two real-world short text collections, i.e. the datasets from Twitter and a Q&A website. Experimental results show that BTM can discover more prominent and coherent topics than the baseline methods. Quantitative evaluations confirm the superiority of BTM on several evaluation metrics. Additionally, we also test our approach on a normal text collection, i.e. 20Newsgroup. It is surprising for us to find that BTM can outperform LDA even on normal texts, showing the potential generality and wider usage of the new topic model.

The rest of the paper is organized as follows: in Section 2, we give a brief review of related works. Section 3 introduces our model for short text topic modeling, and discuss its implementation in Section 4. Experimental results are presented in Section 5. Finally, conclusions are made in the last section.

2. RELATED WORKS

In this section, we briefly summarize the related work from the following two perspectives: topic models on normal texts, and that on short ones.

2.1 Topic Models on Normal texts

Topic models have been proposed to uncover the latent semantic structure from text corpus. The effort of mining semantic structure in a text collection can be dated from latent semantic analysis (LSA) [9], which utilizes the singular value decomposition of the document-term matrix to reveal the major associative words patterns. Probabilistic latent semantic analysis (PLSA) [16] improves LSA with a sounder probabilistic model based on a mixture decomposition derived from a latent class model. In PLSA, a document is presented as a mixture of topics, while a topic is a probability distribution over words. Extending PLSA, Latent Dirichlet Allocation (LDA) [3] adds Dirichlet priors on topic distributions, resulting in a more complete generative model. Due to its nice generalization ability and extensibility, LDA achieves huge success in text mining domain.

In the last decade, topic models have been extensively studied. Many more complicated variants and extensions of LDA and PLSA have been proposed, such as the author-topic model [27], Bayesian nonparametric topic model [29], and supervised topic model [2]. Among them two works close to us are the recently proposed regularized topic model [22] and the generalized Pólya model [21], which also employ word co-occurrence statistics to enhance topic learning. However, both of them utilize word co-occurrences as structure priors for topic-word distribution, rather than directly modeling their generation process. Above all, almost all the models mentioned above deal with normal text without considering the specificity of short texts.

2.2 Topic Models on Short Texts

Early studies mainly focused on exploiting external knowledge to enrich the representation of short texts. For example, Sahami et al.[28] suggested a search-snippet-based similarity measure for short texts. Phan et al.[24] learned hidden topics from large external resources to enrich the representation of short texts. Jin et al.[19] learned topics on short texts via transfer learning from auxiliary long text data. These ways may be helpful in some specific domains, but not general since favorable external dataset might not be always available. Additionally, these approaches and ours are complementary rather than competitive.

With the emergence of social media in recent years, topic models have been utilized for social media content analysis in various tasks, such as content characterizing [26, 35], event tracking [20], content recommendation [25, 8], and influential users prediction [32]. However, due to the lack of specific topic models for short texts, some researchers directly applied conventional (or slightly modified) topic models for analysis [26, 31]. Some others tried to aggregate short texts into lengthy pseudo-documents based on some additional information, and then train conventional topic models [32, 35]. Hong et al. [17] made a comprehensive empirical study of topic modeling in Twitter, and suggested that new topic models for short texts are in demand.

In our previous works, we developed methods based on non-negative matrix factorization for short text clustering [34] and topic learning [33] by exploiting global word co-occurrence information. This work extends them by proposing a more principle approach to model topics over short texts. To the best of our knowledge, the proposed topic model is the first one focusing on general-domain short texts, which does not exploit any external knowledge.

3. OUR APPROACH

Conventional topic models learn topics based on document-level word co-occurrence patterns, whose effectiveness will be highly influenced in short text scenario where the word co-occurrence patterns become very sparse in each document. To tackle this problem, here we propose a novel biterm topic model, which learns topics over short texts by directly modeling the generation of all the biterms (i.e. word co-occurrence patterns) in the whole corpus.

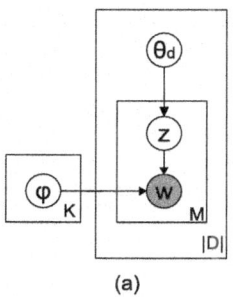 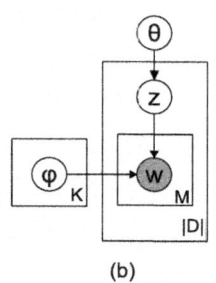 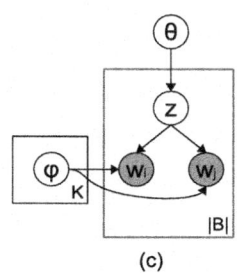

Figure 1: Graphical representation of (a) LDA, (b) mixture of unigrams, and (c) BTM. Different from LDA and mixture of unigrams, BTM models the generation procedure of biterms in a collection, rather than documents. For clarity, the fixed hyperparameters α, β are not presented.

3.1 Biterm Extraction

Without loss of generality, topics are represented as groups of correlated words in topic models, while the correlation is revealed by word co-occurrence patterns in documents. For example, if the words "apple", "iphone", "ipad" and "app" frequently co-occur with each other in the same contexts, we can identify that they belong to a same topic (i.e. apple company and its products). Conventional topic models implicitly capture such word co-occurrence patterns by modeling word generation from the document level. Different from those approaches, our BTM directly models the word co-occurrence patterns based on biterms. A biterm denotes an unordered word-pair co-occurring in a short context (i.e. an instance of word co-occurrence pattern). Here the short context refers to a proper text window containing meaningful word co-occurrences. In short texts, since documents are usually short and specific, we just take each document as an individual context unit. We extract any two distinct words in a short text document as a biterm. For example, in the short text document "I visit apple store.", if we ignoring the stop word "I", there are three biterms, i.e. "visit apple", "visit store", "apple store". The biterms extracted from all the documents in the collection compose the training data of BTM.

3.2 Biterm Topic Model

The key idea of BTM is to learn topics over short texts based on the aggregated biterms in the whole corpus to tackle the sparsity problem in single document. Specifically, we consider that the whole corpus as a mixture of topics, where each biterm is drawn from a specific topic independently[1]. The probability that a biterm drawn from a specific topic is further captured by the chances that both words in the biterm are drawn from the topic. Suppose α and β are the Dirichlet priors. The specific generative process of the corpus in BTM can be described as follows:

1. For each topic z
   (a) draw a topic-specific word distribution $\phi_z \sim \text{Dir}(\beta)$

2. Draw a topic distribution $\theta \sim \text{Dir}(\alpha)$ for the whole collection

3. For each biterm b in the biterm set B
   (a) draw a topic assignment $z \sim \text{Multi}(\theta)$
   (b) draw two words: $w_i, w_j \sim \text{Mulit}(\phi_z)$

Following the above procedure, the joint probability of a biterm $b = (w_i, w_j)$ can be written as:

$$P(b) = \sum_z P(z)P(w_i|z)P(w_j|z).$$
$$= \sum_z \theta_z \phi_{i|z} \phi_{j|z} \quad (1)$$

Thus the likelihood of the whole corpus is:

$$P(B) = \prod_{(i,j)} \sum_z \theta_z \phi_{i|z} \phi_{j|z} \quad (2)$$

We can see that, here we directly model the word co-occurrence pattern, rather than a single word, as an unit conveying semantics of topics. No doubt the co-occurrence of a pair of words can much better reveal the topics than the occurrence of a single word, and then enhance the learning of topics. Moreover, all the biterms from the whole corpus, rather than from a single document, are aggregated together for the topic learning. Therefore, we can fully leverage the rich global word co-occurrence patterns to better reveal the latent topics.

For better understanding the uniqueness of BTM from conventional topic models, here we make a comparison between BTM and two typical models for topic learning, i.e. LDA and mixture of unigrams. Figure 1 illustrates the graphical representation of the three models. We can see, in LDA each document is generated by first drawing a document-level topic distribution θ_d, and then iteratively sampling a topic assignment z for each word w in the document. LDA implicitly captures the document-level word co-occurrence patterns since the topic assignment variable z of each word depends on other words in the same document through sharing the same document-level topic distribution θ_d. Hence, when documents are short, LDA will suffer from the sparsity problem due to its excessive reliance on local observations for the inference of word topic assignment z, which in turn hurts the learning of topics ϕ.

Different from LDA, mixture of unigrams draws the topic assignment z for each document from a corpus-level topic distribution θ. Leveraging the information of the whole corpus, it alleviates the sparsity problem in topic inference,

---
[1]Strictly speaking, two biterms in a document sharing the same word occurrence are not independent. This simplified assumption facilitate the computation by considering BTM as a model built upon a biterm set.

which in turn helps the learning the topic components ϕ. However, mixture of unigrams assumes that all the words in a document are sampled from the same topic. This assumption is so strong that it prevents the model from modeling fine topics in documents. As we can see, even in short texts, there might be multiple topics in one document.

BTM, shown in Figure 1(c), overcomes the data sparsity problem of LDA by drawing topic assignment z from the corpus-level topic distribution θ as mixture of unigrams does. Meanwhile, it also surmounts the disadvantage of mixture of unigrams by breaking documents into biterms. In this way, BTM not only can keep the correlation between words, but also can capture multiple topic gradients in a document, since the topic assignments of different biterms in a document are independent.

3.3 Inferring Topics in a Document

A major difference between BTM and conventional topic models is that BTM does not model the document generation process. Therefore, we cannot directly obtain the topic proportions of documents during the topic learning process. To infer the topics in a document, we assume that the topic proportions of a document equals to the expectation of the topic proportions of biterms generated from the document:

$$P(z|d) = \sum_b P(z|b) P(b|d). \quad (3)$$

In Eq.(3), $P(z|b)$ can be calculated via Bayes' formula based on the parameters estimated in BTM:

$$P(z|b) = \frac{P(z) P(w_i|z) P(w_j|z)}{\sum_z P(z) P(w_i|z) P(w_j|z)},$$

where $P(z) = \theta_z$, and $P(w_i|z) = \phi_{i|z}$. Then the remaining problem is how to obtain $P(b|d)$. Here we simply take the empirical distribution of biterms in the document as the estimation

$$P(b|d) = \frac{n_d(b)}{\sum_b n_d(b)},$$

where $n_d(b)$ is the frequency of the biterm b in the document d. In short texts, $P(b|d)$ is nearly an uniform distribution over all biterms in the document d. Despite of its simplicity, we find this estimation always obtains good results in practice. More sophisticated ways may be studied in the future work.

4. PARAMETERS INFERENCE

In this section, we describe the algorithm to infer the parameters $\{\phi, \theta\}$ in BTM, and compare its complexity with LDA.

4.1 Inference by Gibbs Sampling

Similar as LDA, inference cannot be done exactly in BTM. Hence, we adopt Gibbs sampling to perform approximate inference. Gibbs sampling is a simple and widely applicable Markov chain Monte Carlo algorithm. Compared to other inference methods for latent variable models, like variational inference and maximum posterior estimation, Gibbs sampling has two advantages. First, it is in principal more accurate since it asymptotically approaches the correct distribution. Second, it is more memory-efficient since it only requires to maintain the counters and state variables, mak-

---

Algorithm 1: Gibbs sampling algorithm for BTM

Input: the number of topics K, hyperparameters α, β, biterm set B
Output: multinomial parameter ϕ and θ
initialize topic assignments randomly for all the biterms
for $iter = 1$ to N_{iter} **do**
  for $b \in B$ **do**
    draw z_b from $P(z|\mathbf{z}_{-b}, B, \alpha, \beta)$
    update n_z, $n_{w_i|z}$, and $n_{w_j|z}$

compute the parameters ϕ in Eq.(5) and θ in Eq.(6)

---

ing it preferred for large-scale dataset. More detailed comparison of these methods can be found in [1].

The basic idea of Gibbs sampling is to estimate the parameters alternatively, by replacing the value of one variable by a value drawn from the distribution of that variable conditioned on the values of the remaining variables. In BTM, we need to sample all the three types of latent variables z, ϕ and θ. However, with the technique of collapsed Gibbs sampling [10], ϕ and θ can be integrated out due to the conjugate priors α and β. Consequently, we only have to sample the topic assignment for each biterm from its conditional distribution given the remaining variables.

To perform Gibbs sampling, we first choose initial states for the Markov chain randomly. Then we calculate the conditional distribution $P(z|\mathbf{z}_{-b}, B, \alpha, \beta)$ for each biterm $b = (w_i, w_j)$, where $\mathbf{z}_{-b}$ denotes the topic assignments for all biterms except b, B is the global biterm set. By applying the chain rule on the joint probability of the whole data, we can obtain the conditional probability conveniently:

$$P(z|\mathbf{z}_{-b}, B, \alpha, \beta) \propto (n_z + \alpha) \frac{(n_{w_i|z} + \beta)(n_{w_j|z} + \beta)}{(\sum_w n_{w|z} + M\beta)^2}, \quad (4)$$

where n_z is the number of times of the biterm b assigned to the topic z, and $n_{w|z}$ is the number of times of the word w assigned to the topic z. Following the conventions of LDA, here we use symmetric Dirichlet priors α and β. Note that once a biterm b is assigned to the topic z, the two words w_i and w_j in it will be assigned to the topic simultaneously.

Finally, with the counters of the topic assignments of biterm and word occurrences, we can easily estimate the topic-word distributions ϕ and global topic distribution θ as:

$$\phi_{w|z} = \frac{n_{w|z} + \beta}{\sum_w n_{w|z} + M\beta}, \quad (5)$$

$$\theta_z = \frac{n_z + \alpha}{|B| + K\alpha}, \quad (6)$$

where $|B|$ is the total number of biterms.

An overview of the Gibbs sampling procedure we use is shown in Algorithm 1. Due to space limitation, we omit the detailed derivation of it.

4.2 Complexity Analysis

The major time consuming part in the Gibbs sampling procedure of BTM is evaluating the conditional probability in Eq.(4) for all the biterms, with time complexity $O(K|B|)$. During the entire process, we need to keep the counters n_z, $n_{w|z}$, and the topic assignment z for each biterm, in total of $(K + MK + |B|)$ variables in memory. Note that in LDA, we

Table 1: Time complexity and the number of variables need to be maintained in Gibbs sampling implementation of LDA, mixture of unigrams, and BTM

method	time complexity	#variables
LDA	$O(K|D|\bar{l})$	$|D|K + MK + |D|\bar{l}$
BTM	$O(K|B|)$	$K + MK + |B|$

Table 2: Time cost (seconds) per iteration of BTM and LDA on Tweets2011 collection.

K	50	100	150	200	250
LDA	38.07s	74.38s	108.13s	143.47s	178.66s
BTM	128.64s	250.07s	362.27s	476.19 s	591.24s

Table 3: Memory cost (m) per iteration of BTM and LDA on Tweets2011 collection.

K	50	100	150	200	250
LDA	3177m	5524m	7890m	10218m	12561m
BTM	927m	946m	964m	984m	1002m

need to draw topic assignment for every word occurrence in documents, which costs time $O(K|D|\bar{l})$, where $\bar{l} = \sum_i l_i / |D|$ is the average length of documents in the collection. For memory cost, LDA has to maintain the counters $n_{z|b}$, $n_{w|z}$, and the topic assignment z for each word occurrences[15], in total of $(|D|K + MK + |D|\bar{l})$ variables. Table 1 lists the time complexity and variables required to be maintained in the Gibbs sampling procedure of LDA, and BTM.

To compare the time and memory cost between BTM and LDA, we approximately rewrite $|B|$ as[2]:

$$|B| \approx \frac{|D|\bar{l}(\bar{l} - 1)}{2}.$$

We can see the time complexity of BTM is about $(\bar{l} - 1)/2$ times of LDA. In short texts, the average length of documents are very small, e.g. $\bar{l} = 5.21$ in the Tweets2011 collection, thus the run-time of BTM is still comparable with LDA. However, for very large dataset and a large topic number K, LDA is susceptible to memory problems owing to a huge value of $|D|K$.

Table 2 shows the average run-time (per iteration) of BTM and LDA in our experiments on the Tweets2011 collection. We find the run-time of BTM is always about 3 times of LDA for different topic number K. Table 3 shows the overall memory cost of BTM and LDA in the same collection. We find that memory required by LDA rapidly increases as the topic number K grows, which costs more than 10 times of memory than BTM when K is larger than 200. As opposed to LDA, memory required by BTM grows very slowly. With further investigation, we find the major part of memory in BTM is used to store the biterms in training dataset. Therefore, BTM is a better choice for large dataset and a large topic number K, when the memory cost is a bottleneck.

5. EXPERIMENTS

In this section, we conduct experiments on real-world short text collections to demonstrate the effectiveness of our proposed approach. We take two typical topic models as our baseline methods, namely LDA and mixture of unigrams.

All the experiments were carried on a Linux server with Intel Xeon 2.33 GHz CPU and 16G memory. Both BTM and mixture of unigrams were implemented via C++ code[3]. For LDA, we used the open-source implementation GibbsLDA++[4]. Parameters were tuned via grid search: for LDA, $\alpha = 0.05$ and on short text collections, and $\alpha = 50/K$ on the normal text collection, $\beta = 0.01$; for BTM and mixture of unigrams, $\alpha = 50/K$ and $\beta = 0.01$. In all the methods, Gibbs sampling was run for 1,000 iterations. The results reported are the average over 10 runs.

One typical way for topic model evaluation is to compare the perplexity or marginal likelihood on a held-out test set [3, 11, 12]. However, since BTM not models the generation process of documents, these measures are not available for us. Moreover, these measures do not reflect the topic quality rightly [6]. Therefore, we evaluate the performance of BTM on topic modeling on some other task-dependent metrics.

5.1 Evaluation on Tweets2011 Collection

To verify the effectiveness of BTM on short texts, we carried experiments on a standard short text collection, namely Tweets2011[5]. It was published in TREC 2011 microblog track, which provides approximately 16 million tweets sampled between January 23rd and February 8th, 2011. Besides the complete content of tweets, it also includes an user id, and a timestamp for each tweet. To reduce low-quality tweets, we processed the raw content via the following normalization steps: (a) removing non-Latin characters and stop words; (b) converting letters into lower case; (c) removing words with document frequency less than 10; (d) filtering out tweets with length less than 2; (e) removing duplicate tweets. At last, we left 4,230,578 valid tweets, 98,857 distinct words, and 2,039,877 users. The average document length is 5.21.

We compared BTM with three topic modeling methods on this short texts collection: (a) the standard LDA, which takes each tweet as a document; (b) LDA-U, which aggregates all the tweets from a user to a big psudo-document before training LDA; (c) mixture of unigrams (denoted as Mix), which assumes each tweet only exhibits a single topic. In this collection, we set the number of topics $K = 50$ for all the methods.

5.1.1 Quality of Topics

To investigate the quality of topics discovered by all the test methods, we first sample some topics for visualization. Following [7], we randomly drew two topics shared by the topic sets discovered by the four methods. The selection process is described as follows. Firstly, we collected the top 5 words in each topic into a topical word set for each method individually. Then we randomly chose two terms (i.e., job and snow) from the intersection of the four topical word sets. For each topic, besides the top 20 words, which are

---
[2]For a document with length l, we generate $l(l - 1)/2$ biterms. Here we simply take all the documents as with the same length, since the variance of the length of short documents is not large.

[3]Code of BTM : http://code.google.com/p/btm/
[4]http://gibbslda.sourceforge.net/
[5]http://trec.nist.gov/data/tweets/

most representative for a topic, we also listed 20 non-top words (i.e. ranked from 1001 to 1020) ordered by $P(w|z)$. Ideally, a high quality topic should be coherent as much as possible. Hence, it is expected that the non-top words should be relevant to the top words in the same topic.

Table 4 presents the top words (first row) and non-top words (second row) of the topic selected by the word "job". We find the two words "job" and "jobs" are ranked highest by all the four methods. However, in LDA, some other words, like "web", "website", and "google", are more related to a topic about website, rather than job. The results in LDA-U and mixture of unigrams seem a little better than LDA, but still include a few of less relevant words like "website" and "www". While in BTM, the top 20 words are more prominent and precise about "job". In the non-top words, we find LDA includes the least words about "job", which is hard to connect them to the top words. On the contrary, BTM includes more relevant words about "job" than others, suggesting this topic discovered by BTM is more coherent.

Table 5 presents the top words (first row) and non-top words (second row) of the topic selected by another word "snow". In the first row, again we can see that the top words in LDA are mixed with words about two different subjects "weather" and "car". The results in LDA-U is similar to LDA, but more about "weather". In contrast, the top words in mixture of unigrams and BTM clearly describe weather. In the second row, both LDA and LDA-U list words almost have no connection to "snow", while some of them are related to "car". For mixture of unigrams, it is hard to explain the topic based on these non-top words. In BTM, there are still many words about "weather", like "temperature" and "cyclone". Besides the two topics presented here, we also find similar phenomenon in remaining topics, which suggests that the topics discovered by BTM are is more prominent and coherent than the three baselines.

In order to perform more comprehensive analysis, we utilize an automated metric, namely *coherence score*, proposed by Mimno et al [21] for topic quality evaluation. Given a topic z and its top T words $V^{(z)} = (v_1^{(z)}, ..., v_T^{(z)})$ ordered by $P(w|z)$, the coherence score is defined as:

$$C(z; V^{(z)}) = \sum_{t=2}^{T} \sum_{l=1}^{t} \log \frac{D(v_m^{(z)}, v_l^{(z)}) + 1}{D(v_l^{(z)})},$$

where $D(v)$ is the document frequency of word v, $D(v, v')$ is the number of documents words v and v' co-occurred. The coherence score is based on the idea that words belonging to a single concept will tend to co-occur within the same documents. It is empirically demonstrated that the coherence score is highly correlated with human-judged topic coherence. It must be stressed that the coherence score only is appropriate for measuring frequent words in a topic. Because the frequency of rare words is less reliable.

To evaluate the overall quality of a topic set, we calculated the average coherence score, namely $\frac{1}{K}\sum_k C(z_k; V^{(z_k)})$, for each method. The result is listed in Table 6, where the number of top words T ranges from 5 to 20. We find the result is in agreement with previous qualitative analysis. BTM receives the highest coherence score in all the settings, and the superiority is statistically significant (P-value < 0.01 by T-test). Both LDA-U and mixture of unigrams outperform LDA slightly, but the differences are not significant.

Table 6: Average coherence score on the top T words (ordered by $P(w|z)$) in topics discovered by LDA, LDA-U, mixture of unigrams, and BTM. A larger coherence score means the topics are more coherent. It suggests that BTM outperforms others significantly (P-value < 0.01 by t-test).

T	5	10	20
LDA	-55.0 ± 0.4	-236.4 ± 2.0	-1015.7 ± 5.9
LDA-U	-54.2 ± 0.8	-234.8 ± 1.1	-1009.4 ± 4.4
Mix	-53.8 ± 0.1	-233.0 ± 1.4	-1007.6 ± 6.7
BTM	$\mathbf{-52.4 \pm 0.1}$	$\mathbf{-227.8 \pm 0.3}$	$\mathbf{-990.2 \pm 3.8}$

Table 7: Hashtags used for evaluation, not including the prefix '#'.

jan25 superbowl sotu wheniwaslittle mobsterworld jobs agoodboyfriend bieberfact glee lfc rhoa itunes thegame celebrity tcyasi americanidol cancer socialmedia jerseyshore photography jp6foot7remix factsaboutboys meatschool libra android sagittarius thissummer tnfisherman sagawards ausopen bears weather jaejoongday skins bfgw fashion pandora realestate teamautism travel nba football marketing design oscars food dating kindle snow obama

5.1.2 Quality of Topical Representation of Documents

In the Tweets2011 collection, there is no category information for tweets. Manual labeling might be difficult due to the incomplete and informal content of tweets. Fortunately, some tweets are labeled by their authors with hashtags in the form of "#keyword". By investigating the data, we find there are mainly three types of usage of hashtags: (a) marking events or topics; (b) defining the types of content, like "#ijustsayin", "#quote"; (c) realizing some specified functions, like "#fb" means importing the tweet to Facebook in the meanwhile. In our case, only the first type of hashtags are useful. Therefore, we manually chose 50 frequent hashtags in type (a), listed in Table 7.

Since each hashtag in Table 7 denotes a specific topic labeled by its author, we organized documents with the same hashtag into a cluster. The following evaluation is based on the fact that these clusters should have low intra-cluster distances and high inter-cluster distances.

Considering topic models as a type of dimension reduction methods, each document can be represented by a vector of posterior distribution of topics:

$$d_i = [p(z_1|d_i), ..., p(z_k|d_i)]. \quad (7)$$

Then we can measure the distance of two documents by the Jensen–Shannon divergence:

$$dis(d_i, d_j) = \frac{1}{2} D_{KL}(d_i || m) + \frac{1}{2} D_{KL}(d_j || m),$$

where $m = \frac{1}{2}(d_i + d_j)$, and $D_{KL}(p||q) = \sum_i p_i \ln \frac{p_i}{q_i}$ is the Kullback–Leibler divergence. Given a set of clusters $C = \{C_1, ..., C_K\}$, we introduce two distance scores

Average Intra-Cluster Distance:

$$IntraDis(C) = \frac{1}{K} \sum_{k=1}^{K} \left[\sum_{\substack{d_i, d_j \in C_k \\ i \neq j}} \frac{2 dis(d_i, d_j)}{|C_k||C_k - 1|} \right]$$

Table 4: Topics selected by the word "job" on the Tweets collection. The first row lists the top 20 words, while the second row lists non-top words ranked from 1001 to 1020 based on $P(w|z)$.

LDA	LDA-U	Mixture of unigrams	BTM
job jobs business web website google design online marketing site blog project manager search www company service sales services post	**job** jobs design manager project web website site business service company hiring www support sales services london blog senior engineer	jobs **job** business marketing social media online web design website manager blog project seo internet sales tips company site hiring	jobs **job** manager business sales hiring service services project company senior engineer management marketing nurse office assistant center customer development
nonprofit gallery announced presence published converting select reps requirement mgr territory recruiters power involved announce poster larry dynamics feeds bristol	expertise unemployed med iii host educational fort tags apps assignments labor introduction leads github assurance avon manchester starting automotive table	understand rep industrial sustainability rankings scholarships stay single campus extra cheap 101 vp relationships beginners colorado compliance face winning mechanical	springfield mlm recruit oil req unemployment processing overview awards recruiters ict finish entrepreneur comp assist 1000 alliance locations patent auditor

Table 5: Topics selected by the word "snow" on the Tweets collection. The first row lists the top 20 words, while the second row lists non-top words ranked from 1001 to 1020 based on $P(w|z)$.

LDA	LDA-U	Mixture of unigrams	BTM
snow car weather cold drive storm winter ice road bus driving rain ride traffic cars safe closed due warm train	**snow** weather cold winter ice storm rain stay warm due car closed coming spring drive traffic safe sun blizzard city	**snow** weather cold storm winter ice rain warm degrees stay sun spring safe blizzard coming wind cyclone chicago freezing inches	**snow** cold weather early stay ready ice winter storm hour hours weekend warm late coming spring rain tired sun hot
western dmv covering a4 push pulling milwaukee remains pace idiots 95 commuter buick owner cta transmission cyclist flurries camping tyre	locations sunset drizzle mississippi interstate residents portland students fireplace letting yuck ton counties signal counting blankets pushed 3pm springfield venture	australian thankful station stops groundhogday possibly cleveland traveling sidewalk covering predicting ten grass meant double affect zoo schedule blew causing	temperature cyclone warmth issued colder mood couch snows pre traveling polar outages umbrella filled yawn outage flurries online gloves speed

Average Inter-Cluster Distance:

$$InterDis(C) = \frac{1}{K(K-1)} \sum_{\substack{C_k, C_{k'} \in C \\ k \neq k'}} \left[\sum_{d_i \in C_k} \sum_{d_j \in C_{k'}} \frac{dis(d_i, d_j)}{|C_k||C_{k'}|} \right]$$

The intuition is that if the average inter-cluster distance is small compared to the average intra-cluster distance, the topical representation of documents agrees well with human labeled clusters (via hashtag). Therefore, we calculate the following ratio to evaluate the quality of one topical representation of documents as [4, 13]:

$$H = \frac{IntraDis(C)}{InterDis(C)}.$$

Given a set of different topical representations of documents, the best one is which minimizes the H score.

Table 8 shows the H score for all the test methods. From the results, we can see that BTM preforms significantly better than other three methods (P-value < 0.001). LDA-U outperforms LDA slightly, implying that aggregating tweets for individual users brings moderate benefit. Although LDA dominates mixture of unigrams on normal texts, it is somehow surprising that the performance of mixture of unigrams outperforms LDA and LDA-U substantially in this short text collection. It suggests that the data sparsity problem seriously affects LDA and LDA-U, while less influences mixture of unigrams and BTM. However, the H score of mixture of unigrams is still much worse than BTM. With some further analysis, we find the average intra-cluster distance of mixture of unigrams is extremely large, owing to its peaked posterior distribution of $P(z|d)$. In other words, mixture of

Table 8: H score for different methods on the Tweets2011 collection, smaller value is better. The significant levels(P-value by t-test) are denoted as 0.1*, 0.01**, 0.001***.

Method	H score	Significant differences
LDA	0.576 ± 0.007	
LDA-U	0.564 ± 0.011	>LDA*
Mix	0.503 ± 0.008	>LDA-U**>LDA***
BTM	0.474 ± 0.005	>Mix***>LDA-U***>LDA***

unigrams fails to recognize the resemblance of many documents.

From the above results, we find the improvement of LDA-U over LDA is not so much as shown in [17]. An explanation for this difference is that there are less tweets posted by an user in average in our dataset than theirs. Figure 2 shows the proportions of users who posted certain number of tweets in the Tweets2011 collection, we find 63.3% of users posted one tweet, and only 2.1% of users posted more than 9 tweets. Thus it is not strange that aggregating tweets for individual users has limited affects.

5.2 Evaluation on Question Collection

In order to demonstrate the effectiveness of our approach is domain-independent, we evaluated it on another short text collection, called Question collection. This collection includes 648,514 questions crawled from a popular Chinese Q&A website[6]. Each question has a category label assigned by its questioner, making it convenient for automatic evalu-

---
[6] http://zhidao.baidu.com

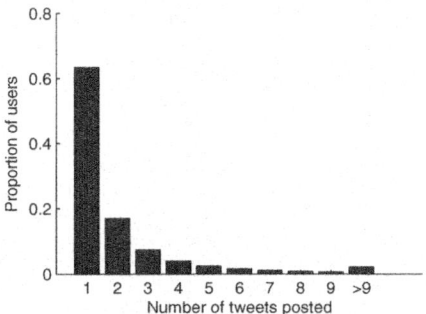

Figure 2: Proportions of users who posted certain number of tweets in the Tweets2011 collection.

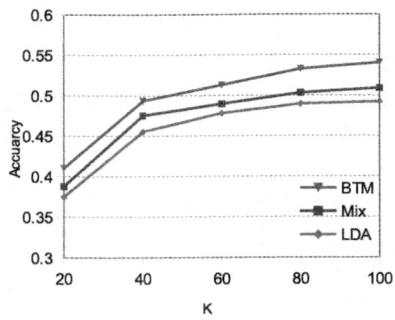

Figure 3: Classification performance of BTM, mixture of unigrams, and LDA on the Question collection.

ation. For pre-process, we removed stop words and low frequency words (i.e. document frequency is less than 3). The final collection contains 189,080 documents, 26,565 distinct words, and 35 categories. The average length of documents is 3.94. Note that in this collection, our baselines do not include LDA-U, since there is few users whole submitted more than one question.

We performed the evaluation based on document classification. Considering topic model as a way for dimensionality reduction, which reduces a document to a fixed set of topical features $P(z|d)$, we would like to see how accurate and discriminative of the topical representation of documents for classification. We randomly split documents into training and test subsets with the ratio 4 : 1, and classified them by the linear SVM classifier LIBLINEAR[7]. We reported the accuracy on 5-fold cross validation in Figure 3.

From the results, we can see that BTM always dominates the two baselines. Moreover, the advantage of BTM becomes more notable as the topic number K grows. That is because when the number of topics is small, topics discovered are usually very general. In such case, a short document is more likely to belong to a single topic, thus the performance of BTM is close to mixture of unigrams. In contrast, with the increase of the topic number K, we will learn more specific topics. However, mixture of unigrams is unable to capture the multiple topics exhibited in a document. Thus the difference between BTM and mixture of unigrams becomes larger. At the same time, a large topic number will aggravate the data sparsity problem of LDA by introducing more parameters, thus the gap between BTM and LDA also increases. Another important finding is that mixture of unigrams outperforms LDA all the time. It suggests that LDA is not a good choice for short texts due to the data sparsity problem.

One may wonder the impact of training data size on these methods. We randomly sampled different proportion of documents, from 0.2 to 1, to train and test these methods separately. The results are shown in Figure 4. We can see when the size of the training data grows, all the methods work better. However, both BTM and mixture of unigrams achieve more improvement than LDA. LDA only get close to mixture of unigrams on small training data. It suggests that increasing the training data will not overcome the data sparsity problem in LDA, since the documents are still short.

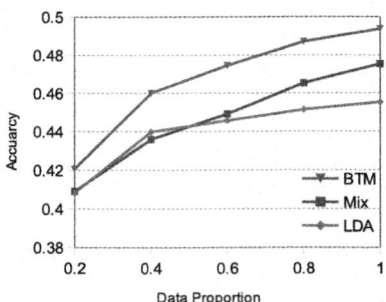

Figure 4: Classification performance comparison with different data proportions on the Questions collection (K=40).

Comparing mixture of unigrams with BTM, we find BTM has stable superiority over mixture of unigrams no matter of the size of the training data.

5.3 Evaluation on Normal Texts

In previous experiments, we have demonstrated the effectiveness of BTM on short texts. Although we propose BTM for the short text scenario, there is no limitation for our model to be applied on normal text collections. Therefore, it is also interesting to see how effective is BTM on normal text. For this purpose, we compared BTM with LDA, one of most popular topic models, on a normal text collection. The experiments were carried out on the 20Newsgroup collection[8], a standard corpora including 18,828 messages harvested from 20 different Usenet newsgroups. Each newsgroup corresponding to a different topic. Table 9 lists the names of these newsgroups. For pre-process, we removed stop words and words with frequency less than 3, but without stemming. Finally, 42697 words are left.

We directly trained LDA on the original documents without any other processing. Note that in BTM, we need to extract biterms from the collection. This process is a little different from that in short texts. Recall that a biterm is defined as a word-pair co-occurred in a short context. It is not appropriate to view a lengthy document as a single short context, since it may involve a wide range of topics. In or-

---

[7]http://www.csie.ntu.edu.tw/~cjlin/liblinear/

[8]http://qwone.com/~jason/20Newsgroups/

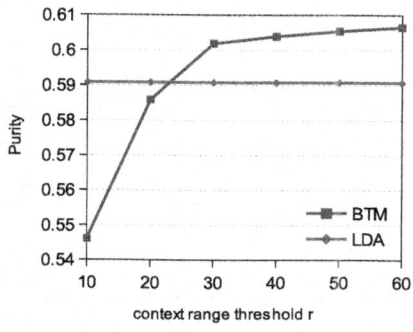 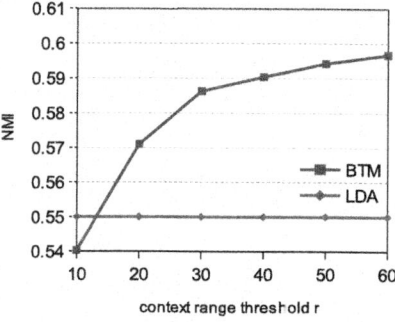 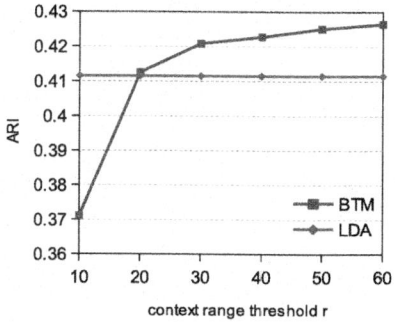

Figure 5: Clustering performance of BTM with different context range thresholds and LDA on the 20 Newsgroups collection ($K = 20$).

Table 9: The newsgroup names in the 20 Newsgroups collection

No.	Newsgroup Name	No.	Newsgroup Name
1	alt.atheism	11	rec.sport.hockey
2	comp.graphics	12	sci.crypt
3	comp.os.ms-windows.misc	13	sci.electronics
4	comp.sys.ibm.pc.hardware	14	sci.med
5	comp.sys.mac.hardware	15	sci.space
6	comp.windows.x	16	soc.religion.christian
7	misc.forsale	17	talk.politics.guns
8	rec.autos	18	talk.politics.mideast
9	rec.motorcycles	19	talk.politics.misc
10	rec.sport.baseball	20	talk.religion.misc

der to reduce meaningless and noise biterms, the biterm set is constructed by extracting any two words co-occur within a context window with range no larger than a predefined threshold r in each document.

5.3.1 Quantitative Evaluation

For quantitative evaluation, we compare the clustering performance of BTM and LDA. Document clustering evaluation is a direct way to measure the effectiveness of a topic model without depending on any extrinsic methods. For document clustering, we take each topic as a cluster, and assign each document d to the topic z with highest value of conditional probability $P(z|d)$. Note that we do not know the optimal context range threshold r ahead, therefore, we tested different values of it, and report their results together.

We adopt three standard metrics in clustering evaluation as follows. Let $\Omega = \{\omega_1, \cdots, \omega_K\}$ be the set of output clusters, and $\mathbb{C} = \{c_1, \cdots, c_P\}$ be P labeled classes of the documents.

- Purity. Suppose documents in each cluster should take the dominant class in the cluster. Purity is the accuracy of this assignment measured by counting the number of correctly assigned documents and divides by the total number of test documents. Formally:

$$\text{purity}(\Omega, \mathbb{C}) = \frac{1}{n} \sum_{i=1}^{K} \max_j |\omega_i \cap c_j|.$$

Note that when all the documents in each cluster are with the same class, purity is highest with value of 1. Conversely, it is close to 0 for bad clustering.

- Normalized Mutual Information(NMI). Let $I(\Omega; \mathbb{C})$ denotes the mutual information between the two partitions Ω and $\mathbb{C}$, NMI penalized $I(\Omega; \mathbb{C})$ by their entropy $H(\Omega)$ and $H(\mathbb{C})$ to avoid the value biasing to large number of clusters. Formally:

$$\text{NMI}(\Omega, \mathbb{C}) = \frac{I(\Omega; \mathbb{C})}{[H(\Omega) + H(\mathbb{C})]/2}$$
$$= \frac{\sum_{i,j} \frac{|\omega_i \cap c_j|}{n} \log \frac{|\omega_i||c_j|}{n|\omega_i \cap c_j|}}{(\sum_i \frac{|\omega_i|}{n} \log \frac{|\omega_i|}{n} + \sum_j \frac{|c_j|}{n} \log \frac{|c_j|}{n})/2}$$

Note that NMI is 1 for perfect match between Ω and $\mathbb{C}$, while 0 if the clustering is random with respect to class membership.

- Adjusted Rand Index(ARI)[18]. Consider documents clustering as a series of pair-wise decisions. If two documents both in the same class and the same cluster, or both in different classes and different clusters, the decision is considered to be correct, else false. Rand index measures the percentage of decisions that are correct. Adjusted Rand index is the corrected-for-chance version of Rand index, whose expected value is 0, while the maximum value is also 1 for exactly match.

$$ARI = \frac{\sum_{i,j} \binom{|\omega_i \cap c_j|}{2} - [\sum_i \binom{|\omega_i|}{2} \sum_j \binom{|c_j|}{2}]/\binom{n}{2}}{\frac{1}{2}[\sum_i \binom{|\omega_i|}{2} + \sum_j \binom{|c_j|}{2}] - [\sum_i \binom{|\omega_i|}{2} \sum_j \binom{|c_j|}{2}]/\binom{n}{2}}$$

The results are shown in Figure 5. On the whole, it is clear that BTM outperforms LDA significantly when the context range threshold r is between 30 and 60, suggesting that BTM also performs very well on normal texts. In particular, we find when $r = 10$, LDA works better than BTM, implying that the context information utilized by BTM is not enough. As the context range threshold r increases, more word co-occurrence patterns are included, which improves the performance of BTM substantially. However, the improvement slows down when the context range threshold r increases from 30 to 60. An explanation for this behavior is that when the distance between two words increasing, they might be less relevant. At this point, the assumption that the two words in a biterm have the same topic will be less credible. Moreover, a larger context range threshold r will generate much more biterms, which increases the training cost. Therefore, for both effectiveness and efficiency consideration, the context range threshold r should not be too small or too large for normal texts in practice.

Table 10: Topics discovered from the 20 Newsgroup collection by BTM and LDA (K=20). "sim" in the last column denotes the cosine similarity of the two topics in a row.

	BTM	LDA	sim
1	ax max g9v b8f a86 1d9 pl 145 3t giz	ax max b8f g9v a86 145 1d9 pl 0t 3t	0.99
2	god jesus christ church bible people lord christian	god jesus bible christian church christ christians paul	0.95
3	key encryption chip clipper keys government system	key encryption chip clipper government keys public	0.95
4	window server display widget set application xterm file	window server set application sun display problem manager	0.93
5	space earth launch mission orbit shuttle system solar	space earth nasa gov time system mission launch	0.91
6	writes article don ca david uk wrote cs org	writes article university uk ca cs michael mail brian	0.90
7	ax 0d cx 145 ah 34u w7 mv scx uw	0d cx ah w7 mv sp 17 uw scx air	0.86
8	people don fbi fire children koresh gun batf	people writes gun fbi fire children article koresh	0.83
9	people don god writes make good point question	people writes true don religion evidence question god	0.82
10	people government president don make time american	president government people state states rights american	0.80
11	disease medical people patients don time writes good	medical health disease drug study drugs men cancer	0.79
12	drive scsi mac bit card apple system monitor problem	windows drive dos card mac system apple scsi disk	0.75
13	image jpeg file graphics images files color data format	file image program files bit jpeg color output line	0.74
14	mail university information fax internet list email	graphics ftp software data mail pub computer	0.62
15	car don writes cars good ve engine time	car cars armenian armenians engine muslims turkish 000	0.62
16	00 year team 10 game 55 play players games 20	writes year play game good ca insurance scott team games	0.61
17	1993 health men number 10 hiv april study homosexual	10 1993 20 15 00 12 93 11 30	0.54
18	windows dos file system files run don os pc program	don people ve time good ll make things thing doesn	0.25
19	armenian armenians people war muslims turkish	information group list book post questions read subject	0.15
20	file entry output program build line printf char info	writes price buy sale problem cost power good interested	0.03

5.3.2 Qualitative Evaluation

Here we study the quality of topics discovered by the two topic models. In practice, a topic model which finds topics with good readability and accurately reflecting the topical structure of data is preferred. Table 10 presents all the topics learned by BTM and LDA, when the number of topics is set to 20. These topics from the two methods are matched based cosine similarity using greedy algorithm. For each topic we list its top words ordered by $P(w|z)$. We can see that the topics 1-16 in BTM and LDA are very similar. Comparison Table 9 and Table 10, we find it is easy to identify the corresponding newsgroup of a topic in topics 1-16, except topic 1 and topic 7. For example, topic 2 is with respect to the newsgroup "soc.religion.christian". It suggests that both BTM and LDA uncover the inherent topical structure of the collection closely.

We also note that topics 17-20 in Table 10 are very different in BTM and LDA. In BTM, we can still identify that topics 17-20 relate to the newsgroups "sci.med", "comp.os.ms-windows.misc", "talk.politics.mideast", "comp.os.ms-windows.misc" respectively. But in LDA, topic 17 is about numeral, topic 18 is a set of common words, while topics 19 and 20 are with poor interpretability. In our view, the differences between the results of the two models are caused by the following reasons. BTM explicitly model the word co-occurrences in local context, it well captures the short-range dependencies between words. Conversely, LDA captures the long-range dependencies in documents [11], which are less specific than short-range ones, resulting in the last four topics more common but less readable.

6. CONCLUSION & FUTURE WORKS

Topic modeling for short texts is an increasingly important task due to the prevalence of short texts on the Web. Compared to normal documents, short texts lack of word frequency and context information, causing severe sparsity problems for conventional topic models. In this paper, we propose a novel probabilistic topic model for short texts, namely biterm topic model (BTM). BTM can well capture the topics within short texts as it explicitly models the word co-occurrence patterns and uses the aggregated patterns in the whole corpus. We carried on experiments on two real-world short text collections and one normal text collection. The results demonstrated that BTM not only can learn higher quality topics, but also more accurately capture the topics of documents than previous methods. Besides, BTM is simple and easy to implement, and also scales up well. All these benefits makes BTM a practicable choice for content analysis on short texts in a wide range of applications.

To the best of our knowledge, we are the first to propose a topic model for general short texts. However, there is still room to improve our work in the future. For example, we would like to find more sophisticated way to estimate the distribution $P(b|d)$, which is uniform in the current work for simplicity. Moreover, it is also interesting to explore the usage of our model in various real-world applications, like content recommendation, event tracking, and short texts retrieval, etc.

7. ACKNOWLEDGEMENTS

This work is funded by the National Natural Science Foundation of China under Grant No. 61202213, 61203298, No. 60933005, No. 61173008, No. 61003166, and 973 Program of China under Grants No. 2012CB316303. We would like to thank the anonymous reviewers for their helpful comments.

8. REFERENCES

[1] A. Asuncion, M. Welling, P. Smyth, and Y. Teh. On smoothing and inference for topic models. In *In Proceedings of the 25th Conference on UAI*, 2009.

[2] D. Blei and J. McAuliffe. Supervised topic models. In J. Platt, D. Koller, Y. Singer, and S. Roweis, editors, *Advances in Neural Information Processing Systems 20*, pages 121–128. MIT Press, Cambridge, MA, 2008.

[3] D. Blei, A. Ng, and M. Jordan. Latent dirichlet allocation. *The Journal of Machine Learning Research*, 3:993–1022, 2003.

[4] I. Bordino, C. Castillo, D. Donato, and A. Gionis. Query similarity by projecting the query-flow graph. In *SIGIR*, pages 515–522. ACM, 2010.

[5] J. Boyd-Graber and D. M. Blei. Syntactic topic models. Technical Report arXiv:1002.4665, Feb 2010.

[6] J. Boyd-Graber, J. Chang, S. Gerrish, C. Wang, and D. Blei. Reading tea leaves: How humans interpret topic models. In *NIPS*, 2009.

[7] D. Cai, Q. Mei, J. Han, and C. Zhai. Modeling hidden topics on document manifold. In *Proceedings of the 17th ACM conference on Information and knowledge management*, pages 911–920. ACM, 2008.

[8] J. Chen, R. Nairn, L. Nelson, M. Bernstein, and E. Chi. Short and tweet: experiments on recommending content from information streams. In *Proceedings of the 28th international conference on Human factors in computing systems*, pages 1185–1194. ACM, 2010.

[9] S. Deerwester, S. Dumais, G. Furnas, T. Landauer, and R. Harshman. Indexing by latent semantic analysis. *Journal of the American society for information science*, 41(6):391–407, 1990.

[10] T. Griffiths and M. Steyvers. Finding scientific topics. *Proceedings of the National Academy of Sciences of the United States of America*, 101(Suppl 1):5228–5235, 2004.

[11] T. Griffiths, M. Steyvers, D. Blei, and J. Tenenbaum. Integrating topics and syntax. *NIPS*, 17:537–544, 2005.

[12] A. Gruber, M. Rosen-Zvi, and Y. Weiss. Hidden topic markov models. *Artificial Intelligence and Statistics (AISTATS)*, 2007.

[13] J. Guo, X. Cheng, G. Xu, and X. Zhu. Intent-aware query similarity. In *Proceedings of the 20th ACM international conference on Information and knowledge management*, pages 259–268. ACM, 2011.

[14] J. Guo, G. Xu, X. Cheng, and H. Li. Named entity recognition in query. In *SIGIR*, pages 267–274. ACM, 2009.

[15] G. Heinrich. Parameter estimation for text analysis. *Technical report*, 2005.

[16] T. Hofmann. Probabilistic latent semantic indexing. In *SIGIR*, pages 50–57. ACM, 1999.

[17] L. Hong and B. Davison. Empirical study of topic modeling in twitter. In *Proceedings of the First Workshop on Social Media Analytics*, pages 80–88. ACM, 2010.

[18] L. Hubert and P. Arabie. Comparing partitions. *Journal of classification*, 2(1):193–218, 1985.

[19] O. Jin, N. Liu, K. Zhao, Y. Yu, and Q. Yang. Transferring topical knowledge from auxiliary long texts for short text clustering. In *Proceedings of the 20th ACM international conference on Information and knowledge management*, pages 775–784. ACM, 2011.

[20] C. X. Lin, B. Zhao, Q. Mei, and J. Han. Pet: a statistical model for popular events tracking in social communities. In *Proceedings of the 16th ACM SIGKDD*, pages 929–938. ACM, 2010.

[21] D. Mimno, H. Wallach, E. Talley, M. Leenders, and A. McCallum. Optimizing semantic coherence in topic models. In *Proceedings of the Conference on Empirical Methods in Natural Language Processing*, pages 262–272. Association for Computational Linguistics, 2011.

[22] D. Newman, E. V. Bonilla, and W. Buntine. Improving topic coherence with regularized topic models. In *Advances in Neural Information Processing Systems 24*, pages 496–504. 2011.

[23] K. Nigam, A. McCallum, S. Thrun, and T. Mitchell. Text classification from labeled and unlabeled documents using em. *Machine learning*, 39(2):103–134, 2000.

[24] X. Phan, L. Nguyen, and S. Horiguchi. Learning to classify short and sparse text & web with hidden topics from large-scale data collections. In *Proceedings of the 17th international conference on World Wide Web*, pages 91–100. ACM, 2008.

[25] O. Phelan, K. McCarthy, and B. Smyth. Using twitter to recommend real-time topical news. In *Proceedings of the third ACM conference on Recommender systems*, pages 385–388, New York, NY, USA, 2009. ACM.

[26] D. Ramage, S. Dumais, and D. Liebling. Characterizing microblogs with topic models. In *International AAAI Conference on Weblogs and Social Media*, volume 5, pages 130–137, 2010.

[27] M. Rosen-Zvi, T. Griffiths, M. Steyvers, and P. Smyth. The author-topic model for authors and documents. In *UAI*, 2004.

[28] M. Sahami and T. Heilman. A web-based kernel function for measuring the similarity of short text snippets. In *Proceedings of the 15th international conference on World Wide Web*, pages 377–386. ACM, 2006.

[29] Y. W. Teh, M. I. Jordan, M. J. Beal, and D. M. Blei. Hierarchical dirichlet processes. *Journal of the American Statistical Association*, 101, 2004.

[30] X. Wang and A. McCallum. Topics over time: a non-markov continuous-time model of topical trends. In *Proceedings of the 12th ACM SIGKDD*, pages 424–433, New York, NY, USA, 2006. ACM.

[31] Y. Wang, E. Agichtein, and M. Benzi. Tm-lda: efficient online modeling of latent topic transitions in social media. In *Proceedings of the 18th ACM SIGKDD*, pages 123–131, New York, NY, USA, 2012. ACM.

[32] J. Weng, E. Lim, J. Jiang, and Q. He. Twitterrank: finding topic-sensitive influential twitterers. In *Proceedings of the third ACM international conference on Web search and data mining*, pages 261–270. ACM, 2010.

[33] X. Yan, J. Guo, S. Liu, X. Cheng, and Y. Wang. Learning topics in short texts by non-negative matrix factorization on term correlation matrix. In *Proceedings of the SIAM International Conference on Data Mining*. SIAM, 2013.

[34] X. Yan, J. Guo, S. Liu, X.-q. Cheng, and Y. Wang. Clustering short text using ncut-weighted non-negative matrix factorization. In *Proceedings of the 20th ACM international conference on Information and knowledge management*, pages 2259–2262, New York, NY, USA, 2012. ACM.

[35] W. Zhao, J. Jiang, J. Weng, J. He, E. Lim, H. Yan, and X. Li. Comparing twitter and traditional media using topic models. *Advances in Information Retrieval*, pages 338–349, 2011.

Unified Entity Search in Social Media Community

Ting Yao
City University of Hong Kong
Kowloon, Hong Kong
tingyao.ustc@gmail.com

Yuan Liu
Ricoh Software Research
Center Co., Ltd.
Beijing, P. R. China
yuanliu.ustc@gmail.com

Chong-Wah Ngo
City University of Hong Kong
Kowloon, Hong Kong
cscwngo@cityu.edu.hk

Tao Mei
Microsoft Research Asia
Beijing, P. R. China
tmei@microsoft.com

ABSTRACT

The search for entities is the most common search behavior on the Web, especially in social media communities where entities (such as images, videos, people, locations, and tags) are highly heterogeneous and correlated. While previous research usually deals with these social media entities separately, we are investigating in this paper a unified, multi-level, and correlative entity graph to represent the unstructured social media data, through which various applications (e.g., friend suggestion, personalized image search, image tagging, etc.) can be realized more effectively in one single framework. We regard the social media objects equally as "entities" and all of these applications as "entity search" problem which searches for entities with different types. We first construct a multi-level graph which organizes the heterogeneous entities into multiple levels, with one type of entities as *vertices* in each level. The *edges* between graphs pairwisely connect the entities weighted by *intra-relations* in the same level and *inter-links* across two different levels distilled from the social behaviors (e.g., tagging, commenting, and joining communities). To infer the strength of intra-relations, we propose a *circular propagation* scheme, which reinforces the mutual exchange of information across different entity types in a cyclic manner. Based on the constructed unified graph, we explicitly formulate entity search as a global optimization problem in a unified Bayesian framework, in which various applications are efficiently realized. Empirically, we validate the effectiveness of our unified entity graph for various social media applications on million-scale real-world dataset.

Categories and Subject Descriptors

H.3.3 [**Information Search and Retrieval**]: Retrieval models

General Terms

Algorithms, Performance, Experimentation.

*This work was performed when Ting Yao was visiting Microsoft Research Asia as a research intern.

Copyright is held by the International World Wide Web Conference Committee (IW3C2). IW3C2 reserves the right to provide a hyperlink to the author's site if the Material is used in electronic media.
WWW'13, May 13-17, Rio de Janeiro, Brazil.
ACM 978-1-4503-2035-1/13/05.

Keywords

Entity search, social media community, friend suggestion, image tagging, personalized image search.

1. INTRODUCTION

The Web is organized by entities. Entity search, that is, returning "object" (e.g., people, media objects, locations, products, organizations, etc.) in response to users' information needs, has received considerable attention recently in various research communities.

In social media communities, such as Flickr, YouTube and Facebook, people are sharing their experiences and interests through substantial amounts of various contents, such as photos, videos, people, tags, geo-locations and documents, which are referred to *entities* in this paper. In addition, these contents are strong correlated by a wide variety of social behaviors, e.g., tagging, commenting, and joining communities. With the large-scale, heterogeneous and correlative sets of data available, there has been increasing expectation for mechanisms that organize and search these entities effectively and efficiently in social networks. To motivate, consider following scenarios, for user Henry who likes taking photographs at the seaside.

Scenario 1 (friend suggestion): Henry wants to find friends who have the similar interests to himself. To begin with, he may use the keywords like "seaside" as the query to find some photos in Flickr, and then he needs to sift through the photostream (all photos shared by a user) of photographers one by one and dig out the interesting ones as his friends. This overall process can be unnecessarily time consuming.

Scenario 2 (image (geo-)tagging): Henry sees a beautiful picture when he browses a webpage and he wants to know where this picture was taken. He may formulate some descriptive words to search similar images via web image search engines and then read through the surrounding words, but it is hard to find the duplicate images in this way due to the sheer volume of Internet images.

Scenario 3 (personalized image search): Henry wants to search photos with sunrise scene. He may use "sunrise" as the query in a web image search engine and many images with sunrise scene are returned. But Henry prefers photos taken by the seaside, to get his expected photos he might have to go through all the images, or formulate the other keywords for hitting promising search images. This could be a very laborious process.

In these scenarios, like every user in many similar situations, Henry is looking for a particular type of *entities* not pages as "relevant documents" to read. This demand has challenged us to face a dilemma: on one hand, the proliferating data on the Internet leads to surge of research activities in social media search, for instance, personalized image search [12][15][19], tag ranking [10], Yahoo people search [20], friend suggestion [8][14][22], and ImageCLEF (Image Retrieval in CLEF) [5]. All of these social media searches are independent and each of them is designed especially for searching a certain type of entities; on the other hand, in real-world social media communities, these existing entities always influence each other in explicit or implicit way. As in scenarios mentioned above, people always look for entities by using the other types of entities; that is to say, the various entity searches are essentially closely related, and the common goal is to discover the relationships among these entities. Therefore, it is more natural and efficient to develop a unified framework which can accomplish these entity searches in a single way, which directly motivates our work in this paper.

Towards this goal, we propose a multi-level graph model to integrate all the entities together. The relevance of an entity for a given query is estimated by the cost of nearest navigated route. As shown in Fig.1(b), the red lines with arrows present a navigated route from query $\mathbf{q}$ to entity v_k^b (will be described in Definition 1) in a three-level graph. The cost comes from two sources, i.e., *intra-relation* between every two same types of entities in each level of graph, and *inter-link* across different types of entities in every two levels of graphs. To leverage the two sources of the route cost, the entity search is formulated from the probabilistic perspective in a Bayesian framework. The intra-relations of entities within the searching pool are modeled as a conditional prior which indicates the ranking score consistency between similar entities; and the inter-links are modeled as a likelihood which reflects the correspondence of the query and entities in searching pool. In the Bayesian framework, the entity search is formulated as maximizing the product of the conditional prior and the likelihood. The foundation of the unified entity search is the proposed *circular propagation* which iteratively refines the intra-relations of entities, through exchanging information across different entity types in a cyclic manner. Instead of exploring similarity metrics used in existing entity search, the procedure encourages interaction among multiple entities to seek for consensus that are useful for entity search. Fig.1 illustrates the unified entity search framework based on the proposed integral multi-level graph.

The main contributions of this work can be summarized as follows:

- We propose to integrate various types of entities in a multi-level graph model, upon which multiple social media applications can be implemented in a single way.

- We propose the circular propagation to exchange information across different entity types in a cyclic manner. In this way, the relationships of various entities are mutually reinforced and refined.

- We explicitly formulate entity search as a global optimization problem in a Bayesian framework, which well leverages the various relationships in social media community.

The remaining sections are organized as follows. Section 2 describes the related work. Section 3 presents the integral multi-level graph construction including circular propagation and its convergence property, while Section 4 formulates the problem of unified entity search and its solution over the integral graph. Section 5 takes a popular photo-sharing site as an example to detail the entity graph constructed from a social media community. Section 6 provides empirical justifications, followed by the conclusions in Section 7.

2. RELATED WORK

We briefly group the related works into two categories: search in social media community and multi-modality fusion. The former draws upon research in searching over extracted entities in social media community, and the later learns the contribution of a modality (entity) in social search applications.

2.1 Search in Social Media Community

There exists rich research on search in social media community, such as friend suggestion (user search), image tagging (tag search) and personalized image search (image search).

Finding potential friends with similar interest will improve photo-sharing and browsing experiences in the social community. Roth *et al.* suggest friends based on an implicit social graph, which is formed by user interaction with contacts and groups of contacts [14]. In another work by Li *et al.* [8], user similarity is firstly mined by using location history and then potential friends are recommended. As an online people search service, Yahoo people search [20] is to find friends and family with whom people have lost touch. People can employ it to search for friends using name and location or phone numbers, or search using email addresses.

Attaching textual or semantic linkage to images will significantly facilitate Web image search and organization. Li *et al.* [7] present a real-time automatic image tagging method. The method takes as input a set of labeled images and tries to learn which low level visual features correspond to higher level semantic labels. The mapping can then be applied to annotate the new unlabeled images. Similar in spirit, Chen *et al.* [1] propose a tag recommendation approach that directly predicts the possible tags with models learned from training data. Therefore, the approach can only recommend the tags from a predefined set. Later in [10], Liu *et al.* first estimate relevance scores for the tags to images based on probability density estimation and then a random walk over a tag similarity graph is performed to refine the relevance. Based on the refined relevance, the associated tags can be ranked in a descending order of their relevance. ImageCLEF (Image Retrieval in CLEF) [5] aims to analyze a collection of Flickr photos in terms of their visual and/or textual features in order to detect the presence of one or more concepts. The detected concepts can then be used for the purpose of automatically annotating the images or for retrieving the best matching images to a given concept-oriented query.

Generating the search results according to the modified user search intents is proved to be an effective mean for enhancing Web search experience. Lu *et al.* [12] utilized a co-clustering method to extract latent interest dimensions, and rerank the images by coming latent interest based user

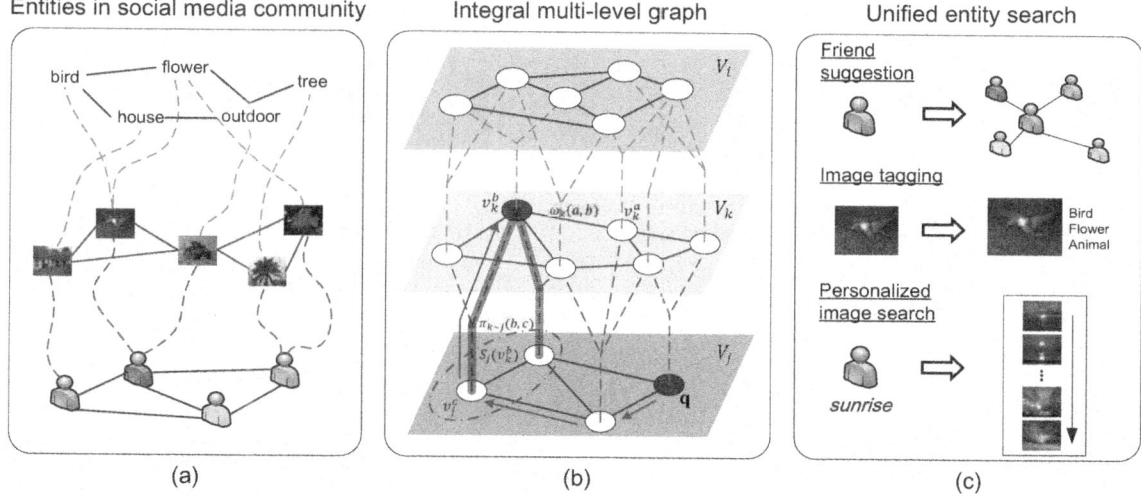

Figure 1: Unified entity search framework (For better viewing, please see original color pdf file). (a) Entities in social media community, such as tags, photos and users. (b) Integral multi-level graph with three types of entity sets, i.e., V_i, V_j and V_k: solid colorful lines in each level of graphs indicate the *intra-relations* of entities of the same types, while dash gray lines indicate the *inter-links* between entities of the different types; black vertex is the query q of entity type j ($\mu_j = 1, \mu_i = 0 (i \neq j)$) and red vertex is the random entity v_k^b to be ranked in the searching pool V_k. Shadow lines denote the links between entity v_k^b and the subset of entities in V_j, enclosed in the purple ellipse. Red lines with arrows present a navigated route from query q to entity v_k^b. (c) Based on the integral multi-level graph, various entity searches can be formulated within a unified framework.

preference and query relevance. Another typical work is performed by Xu *et al.* [19], in which the overall ranking score is not only based on term similarity matching between the query and the documents but also topic similarity matching between the user's interests and the documents' topics.

In short, while these approaches focus on the mining of various entities for different social media search applications, the interaction among entities is not exploited. Our work in this paper contributes by studying not only holistically exploring interaction (or consensus) among all the entities, but also integrating all the social media search applications in a unified framework.

2.2 Multi-modality Fusion

Multi-modality fusion on social media community has been intensively studied in recent years. Sang et al. [15] propose a tensor factorization model that integrates users, images and tags together for annotation prediction. With this, personalized search can be easily formulated by user-specific topic modeling. In [22], Yao et al. characterize the user relationship by combining the visual and geographic information in a contextual graph modeling. Negoescu et al. present to discover hypergroups in Flickr, i.e., communities consisting of groups of Flickr groups, while such hypergroups could serve to enrich Flickr's traditional group search [13]. Zheng *et al.* provide a tensor decomposition-based group recommendation model to combine semantic tags with social relation and to help people more easily engage in group activities [24]. Lin *et al.* model the community discovery through analysis of time-varying and multi-relational data in rich social media community [9]. These approaches, nevertheless, deal with the multiple modalities independently and the interaction among modalities is not exploited. In another work by Zhuang *et al.* [26], social strength is measured in a two-stage learning framework. The first stage is to learn the optimal fusion weights of the multiple proximity graphs for a kernel target alignment; with the learnt kernel, the second stage is to estimate the social strength by a kernel-based learning to rank approach. However, it is still implemented in supervised way, which needs expensive human effort.

3. INTEGRAL MULTI-LEVEL GRAPH

3.1 Notation

To make our formulation more clear, we firstly define a few terms below and some are illustrated in Fig.1(b), an exemplary three-level graph.

DEFINITION 1: Represented by multi-level graph model, the social network $\mathcal{G} = \{G_k : k = 1, 2, \ldots, N\}$ consists of N graphs and each graph is represented by $G_k = (V_k, E_k)$, where k is the entity type id, V_k and E_k are sets of vertices and edges. Specifically, $V_k = \{v_k^1, v_k^2, \ldots, v_k^{Z_k}\}$, where Z_k is the number of entities in V_k; and each edge in E_k connects two vertices, with weight function $w_k : E_k \to \Re^+$ mapping edges to nonnegative real-valued weights, here we call it intra-relation. For instance, $w_k(a,b)$ measures the *intra-relation* strength between entities v_k^a and v_k^b. The affinity matrix $\mathbf{W}_k$ is defined by taking $w_k(a,b)$ as its (a,b)-element.

DEFINITION 2: The link set $\mathcal{L} = \{L_{k \leadsto j} : j, k = 1, 2, \ldots, N\}$ consists of links mutually connecting entities from two levels of graphs. Of entity set V_j, the subset $S_j(v_k^b) = \{v_j^1, v_j^2, \ldots, v_j^M\}$ contains M entities, which are linked to the entity v_k^b in entity set V_k, i.e., $S_j(v_k^b) \subseteq V_j$. The links are weighted by link function $\pi_{k \leadsto j} : L_{k \leadsto j} \to \Re^+$ mapping links to nonnegative real-valued weights and we describe it as *inter-link*. For instance, $\pi_{k \leadsto j}(b,c)$ measures the inter-link strength between entity v_k^b and v_j^c. For self-link, we set $\pi_{k \curvearrowright k}(\cdot,\cdot) = 1$.

3.2 Circular Propagation

To facilitate interaction among different entity relationships, we construct an integral graph, over which the circular propagation is proposed to mutual reinforce each other. Suppose there are N entity types, and thus we can have N views of relationship among these entities by constructing a N-level of affinity graphs. In each level of graphs, the vertices and edges represent the entities and intra-relations of them (w_k), respectively. The entities of different types are mutually linked with inter-link $(\pi_{k \curvearrowright j})$. In this way, N runs of propagations can be conducted separately on each graph to refine the intra-relation of N entity type. The spirit of circular propagation is to encourage entity interaction in a way that an entity starts propagation by using the affinity graph of another entity, while preserving its original estimated intra-relation measures. By arranging the N entities linearly, such that the k-th order entity uses the graph of the $(k-1)$-th order entity, this forms a circular ring that each entity, once completing propagation, will propagate the new result to influence its next linked entities.

Let $w_k(a,b) \equiv w_k^{ab}$, $\pi_{k \curvearrowright j}(b,c) \equiv \pi_{k \curvearrowright j}^{bc}$, the circular propagation is formulated as following:

$$\begin{cases} w_1^{ab(t)} = \theta_1 \sum_{ij} \pi_{1 \curvearrowright N}^{ai} w_N^{ij(t-1)} \pi_{1 \curvearrowright N}^{bj} + (1-\theta_1) w_1^{ab(0)} \\ w_2^{ab(t)} = \theta_2 \sum_{ij} \pi_{2 \curvearrowright 1}^{ai} w_1^{ij(t)} \pi_{2 \curvearrowright 1}^{bj} + (1-\theta_2) w_2^{ab(0)} \\ \cdots \\ w_k^{ab(t)} = \theta_k \sum_{ij} \pi_{k \curvearrowright k-1}^{ai} w_{k-1}^{ij(t)} \pi_{k \curvearrowright k-1}^{bj} + (1-\theta_k) w_k^{ab(0)} \\ \cdots \\ w_{N-1}^{ab(t)} = \theta_{N-1} \sum_{ij} \pi_{N-1 \curvearrowright N-2}^{ai} w_{N-2}^{ij(t)} \pi_{N-1 \curvearrowright N-2}^{bj} + \\ \qquad (1-\theta_{N-1}) w_{N-1}^{ab(0)} \\ w_N^{ab(t)} = \theta_N \sum_{ij} \pi_{N \curvearrowright N-1}^{ai} w_{N-1}^{ij(t)} \pi_{N \curvearrowright N-1}^{bj} + (1-\theta_N) w_N^{ab(0)} \end{cases} \quad (1)$$

where the superscript (t) denotes the iteration, and the tradeoff parameter $\theta_k (0 \leqslant \theta_k \leqslant 1)$ weights the importance of the propagated and initial estimated intra-relations. Note that the first term in each equation represents information exchange from neighboring entity, while the second term is the initial similarity. In this circular propagation, the intra-relations of N entities are produced simultaneously. Instead of estimating the similarity of entities with the same type separately, the circular propagation enforces additional constraint that two entities are similar if the entities of different type which are linked to them are connected strongly.

3.3 Convergence Property

Eq.(1) can be expressed in a matrix form as following,

$$\begin{cases} \mathbf{W}_1^{(t)} = \theta_1 \mathbf{\Pi}_{1 \curvearrowright N} \mathbf{W}_N^{(t-1)} \mathbf{\Pi}_{1 \curvearrowright N}^T + (1-\theta_1) \mathbf{W}_1^{(0)} \\ \mathbf{W}_2^{(t)} = \theta_2 \mathbf{\Pi}_{2 \curvearrowright 1} \mathbf{W}_1^{(t)} \mathbf{\Pi}_{2 \curvearrowright 1}^T + (1-\theta_2) \mathbf{W}_2^{(0)} \\ \cdots \\ \mathbf{W}_k^{(t)} = \theta_k \mathbf{\Pi}_{k \curvearrowright k-1} \mathbf{W}_{k-1}^{(t)} \mathbf{\Pi}_{k \curvearrowright k-1}^T + (1-\theta_k) \mathbf{W}_k^{(0)} \\ \cdots \\ \mathbf{W}_{N-1}^{(t)} = \theta_{N-1} \mathbf{\Pi}_{N-1 \curvearrowright N-2} \mathbf{W}_{N-2}^{(t)} \mathbf{\Pi}_{N-1 \curvearrowright N-2}^T + \\ \qquad (1-\theta_{N-1}) \mathbf{W}_{N-1}^{(0)} \\ \mathbf{W}_N^{(t)} = \theta_N \mathbf{\Pi}_{N \curvearrowright N-1} \mathbf{W}_{N-1}^{(t)} \mathbf{\Pi}_{k \curvearrowright k-1}^T + (1-\theta_N) \mathbf{W}_N^{(0)} \end{cases} \quad (2)$$

where $\mathbf{W}_k = [w_k^{ab}]_{Z_k \times Z_k}$ and $\mathbf{\Pi}_{k \curvearrowright j} = [\pi_{k \curvearrowright j}^{bc}]_{Z_k \times Z_j}$ is affinity and link matrix respectively, correspondingly composed of propagated intra-relations and inter-link. Circular propagation is guaranteed to converge for having the following property:

$$\lim_{t \to \infty} (\mathbf{W}_k^{(t+1)} - \mathbf{W}_k^{(t)}) = 0 \quad (3)$$

Proof:

$$\begin{aligned} &\mathbf{W}_k^{(t+1)} - \mathbf{W}_k^{(t)} \\ &= (\theta_k \mathbf{\Pi}_{k \curvearrowright k-1} \mathbf{W}_{k-1}^{(t+1)} \mathbf{\Pi}_{k \curvearrowright k-1}^T + (1-\theta_k) \mathbf{W}_k^{(0)}) \\ &\quad - (\theta_k \mathbf{\Pi}_{k \curvearrowright k-1} \mathbf{W}_{k-1}^{(t)} \mathbf{\Pi}_{k \curvearrowright k-1}^T + (1-\theta_k) \mathbf{W}_k^{(0)}) \\ &= \theta_k \mathbf{\Pi}_{k \curvearrowright k-1} (\mathbf{W}_{k-1}^{(t+1)} - \mathbf{W}_{k-1}^{(t)}) \mathbf{\Pi}_{k \curvearrowright k-1}^T \\ &= \theta_k \mathbf{\Pi}_{k \curvearrowright k-1} (\theta_{k-1} \mathbf{\Pi}_{k-1 \curvearrowright k-2} \mathbf{W}_{k-2}^{(t+1)} \mathbf{\Pi}_{k-1 \curvearrowright k-2}^T) \mathbf{\Pi}_{k \curvearrowright k-1}^T \\ &\quad - \theta_k \mathbf{\Pi}_{k \curvearrowright k-1} (\theta_{k-1} \mathbf{\Pi}_{k-1 \curvearrowright k-2} \mathbf{W}_{k-2}^{(t)} \mathbf{\Pi}_{k-1 \curvearrowright k-2}^T) \mathbf{\Pi}_{k \curvearrowright k-1}^T \\ &= \theta_k \theta_{k-1} \mathbf{\Pi}_{k \curvearrowright k-1} \mathbf{\Pi}_{k-1 \curvearrowright k-2} (\mathbf{W}_{k-2}^{(t+1)} - \mathbf{W}_{k-2}^{(t)}) \\ &\quad \mathbf{\Pi}_{k-1 \curvearrowright k-2}^T \mathbf{\Pi}_{k \curvearrowright k-1}^T \\ &= \cdots \\ &= \theta_k \ldots \theta_1 \theta_N \ldots \theta_{k+1} \mathbf{\Pi}_{k \curvearrowright k-1} \ldots \mathbf{\Pi}_{1 \curvearrowright N} \mathbf{\Pi}_{N \curvearrowright N-1} \ldots \mathbf{\Pi}_{k+1 \curvearrowright k} \\ &\quad (\mathbf{W}_k^{(t)} - \mathbf{W}_k^{(t-1)}) \mathbf{\Pi}_{k+1 \curvearrowright k}^T \ldots \mathbf{\Pi}_{N \curvearrowright N-1}^T \mathbf{\Pi}_{1 \curvearrowright N}^T \ldots \mathbf{\Pi}_{k \curvearrowright k-1}^T \\ &= (\theta_k \ldots \theta_1 \theta_N \ldots \theta_{k+1} \mathbf{\Pi}_{k \curvearrowright k-1} \ldots \mathbf{\Pi}_{1 \curvearrowright N} \mathbf{\Pi}_{N \curvearrowright N-1} \ldots \mathbf{\Pi}_{k+1 \curvearrowright k})^t \\ &\quad (\mathbf{W}_k^{(1)} - \mathbf{W}_k^{(0)}) (\mathbf{\Pi}_{k+1 \curvearrowright k}^T \ldots \mathbf{\Pi}_{N \curvearrowright N-1}^T \mathbf{\Pi}_{1 \curvearrowright N}^T \ldots \mathbf{\Pi}_{k \curvearrowright k-1}^T)^t \end{aligned} \quad (4)$$

It is easy to see Eq.(3) can be derived when each row of $\mathbf{\Pi}_{k \curvearrowright k-1}$ is normalized to 1, and $0 \leqslant \theta_N, \theta_{N-1}, ..., \theta_1 \leqslant 1$. □

4. UNIFIED ENTITY SEARCH

DEFINITION 3: The query of an entity search is represented by a vector $\mathbf{q} = [v_1^0, v_2^0, \ldots, v_N^0]^T$, which corresponds to another vector $\mathbf{u} = [\mu_1, \mu_2, \ldots, \mu_N]^T$, indicating the importance of different entity types in the query $\mathbf{q}$, $\sum_j \mu_j = 1$.

DEFINITION 4: The objective of an entity search (e.g., searching entities of type k) is to give a ranking score list $\mathbf{r}_k = [r_k^1, r_k^2, \ldots, r_k^{Z_k}]^T$, which is a vector of the ranking scores, corresponding to the entity searching pool V_k, for instance, r_k^b is the ranking score of v_k^b.

DEFINITION 5: An entity search function is defined as follows,

$$\mathbf{r} = f(\mathbf{q}, V_k). \quad (5)$$

Permuting the entities according to this function is called *entity search*. In this paper, we formulate the entity search problem from the probabilistic perspective. Supposing the ranking score list is a random variable, entity search can be regarded as a process to derive the most probable score list given the certain entity query. From the probabilistic perspective, entity search is to derive the optimum $\mathbf{r}^*$ with the maximum a posterior probability given the query $\mathbf{q}$ and entity searching pool V_k,

$$\mathbf{r}_k^* = argmax_{\mathbf{r}_k} \Pr(\mathbf{r}_k|\mathbf{q}, V_k). \quad (6)$$

According to Bayesian formula and the independency assumption of the query $\mathbf{q}$ and entity searching pool V_k, the posterior is proportional to the product of the *conditional prior probability* and the *likelihood*,

$$\Pr(\mathbf{r}_k|\mathbf{q}, V_k) \propto \Pr(\mathbf{r}_k|V_k) \times \Pr(\mathbf{q}|\mathbf{r}_k), \quad (7)$$

where $\Pr(\mathbf{r}_k|V_k)$ is the *conditional prior* of the score list given the entity searching pool V_k. $\Pr(\mathbf{q}|\mathbf{r}_k)$ is the *likelihood*, which expresses how probable the query $\mathbf{q}$ is given the optimal ranking score list $\mathbf{r}_k$. Replacing the posterior in Eq.(6) with Eq.(7), we formulate the entity search as maximizing the product of a conditional prior and a likelihood,

$$\mathbf{r}_k^* = argmax_{\mathbf{r}_k} \Pr(\mathbf{r}_k|V_k) \times \Pr(\mathbf{q}|\mathbf{r}_k). \quad (8)$$

For the *conditional prior* $\Pr(\mathbf{r}_k|V_k)$, we formulate it with a regularization term,

$$\Pr(\mathbf{r}_k|V_k) = \frac{1}{H_1}\exp(-Reg(\mathbf{r}_k, V_k)), \quad (9)$$

where $H_1 = \sum_{\mathbf{r}}\exp(-Reg(\mathbf{r}_k, V_k))$ is a normalizing constant. $Reg(\mathbf{r}_k, V_k)$ is defined as follows following Normalized Laplacian regularizer [25],

$$Reg(\mathbf{r}_k, V_k) = \sum_a \varphi_a(\mathbf{r}_k, V_k), \quad (10)$$

where $\varphi_a(\mathbf{r}_k, V_k)$ defined over entity v_k^a for measuring the visual consistency on its neighbors v_k^b,

$$\varphi_a(\mathbf{r}_k, V_k) = \frac{1}{2}\sum_b w_k(a,b)(\frac{r_k^a}{\sqrt{d_k^a}} - \frac{r_k^b}{\sqrt{d_k^b}})^2, \quad (11)$$

and $d_k^a = \sum_b w_k(a,b)$. Then Eq.(10) can be expressed in a matrix form as following

$$Reg(\mathbf{r}_k, V_k) = \mathbf{r}_k^T \mathbf{S}_k \mathbf{r}_k, \quad (12)$$

where $\mathbf{S}_k = \mathbf{D}_k^{-1/2}\mathbf{W}_k D_k^{-1/2}$ in which $\mathbf{D}_k$ is a diagonal matrix with its (a,a)-element (d_k^a) equal to the sum of the a-th row of $\mathbf{W}_k$.

For the *likelihood* $\Pr(\mathbf{q}|\mathbf{r}_k)$, we formulate it as a *shortest-paths problem* on a weighted graph,

$$\Pr(\mathbf{q}|\mathbf{r}_k) = \frac{1}{H_2}exp(-\rho' \times IR(\mathbf{q}, \mathbf{r}_k)), \quad (13)$$

where $IR(\mathbf{q}, \mathbf{r}_k) = \sum_a (r_k^a - \delta(\mathbf{q}, v_k^b))^2$ measures the degree of the disagreement between the ranking scores and the shortest paths in graph. H_2 is the normalizing constant and $\rho' > 0$ is a scaling parameter.

DEFINITION 6: In a shortest-paths problem, for a weighted graph with entities of the same type j, the weight of path $l = <v_j^m, v_j^{m+1}, \ldots, v_j^{m+n}>$ is the sum of the weights of its constituent edges:

$$\eta_j(l) = \sum_{i=1}^n w_j(m+i-1, m+i). \quad (14)$$

The shortest-part weight from v_j^a to v_j^b is defined by,

$$\delta'(v_j^a, v_j^b) = \begin{cases} \min\{\eta_j(l) : v_j^a \xrightarrow{l} v_j^b\} & if\ \exists v_j^a \to v_j^b \\ \infty & otherwise \end{cases}, \quad (15)$$

where $v_j^a \to v_j^b$ denotes the path from v_j^a to v_j^b. Considering all path weights are nonnegative, we exploit Dijkstra's algorithm to solve the shortest-paths problem in Eq.(13) [17]. When the query type is different from the entities in searching pool, for example, for the path from v_j^d to v_k^b, the shortest-part weight is defined by,

$$\delta'(v_j^d, v_k^b) = \min\{\pi_{k\sim j}(b,c)\delta'(v_j^d, v_j^c) : v_j^c \in S_j(v_k^b)\}. \quad (16)$$

For a query $\mathbf{q}$ with multiple entity types, the shortest part to an entity v_k^b is derived in linear fusion way,

$$\delta(\mathbf{q}, v_k^b) = \sum_j \mu_j \delta'(v_j^0, v_k^b), \quad (17)$$

then we have $IR(\mathbf{q}, \mathbf{r}_k) = \sum_a (r_k^a - \delta(\mathbf{q}, v_k^b))^2$.

Let us further introduce a vector $\mathbf{\Delta}_k$ with its b-th element $\delta(\mathbf{q}, v_k^b)$. With Eq.(9) and Eq.(11), the entity search formulation in Eq.(8) is equivalent to minimizing the following energy function,

$$E(\mathbf{r}_k) = Reg(\mathbf{r}_k, V_k) + \rho \times IR(\mathbf{q}, \mathbf{r}_k), \quad (18)$$

where the two terms on the right-hand side correspond to the conditional prior and the likelihood, respectively. The $\rho = \frac{H_1}{H_2}\rho'$ is a trade-off parameter to the two terms. Given that the energy function in Eq.(18) is quadratic, we minimize $E(\mathbf{r}_k)$ solving $\nabla E(\mathbf{r}_k) = 0$, and have the closed form,

$$\mathbf{r}_k^* = (\mathbf{I} - \rho\mathbf{S}_k)^{-1}\mathbf{\Delta}_k. \quad (19)$$

5. AN EXAMPLE: FLICKR

Without loss of generality, we take the most popular photo sharing site, Flickr, as the social media platform to illustrate our multi-level graph modeling, which mainly has four types of entities, i.e., user (V_u), photo (V_p), tags (V_t) and geo-locations (V_g). It is worth noting that although we take Flickr as an example, the proposed multi-level graph model can be applied to any kind of community, such as Facebook and LinkedIn. Due to the missing and noises of geo-locations for most of photos, we perform the circular propagation by using the entity sets V_u, V_p and V_t as follows, similar to Eq.(2),

$$\begin{cases} \mathbf{W}_t^{(t)} = \theta_t \mathbf{\Pi}_{t\sim u}\mathbf{W}_u^{(t-1)}\mathbf{\Pi}_{t\sim u}^T + (1-\theta_t)\mathbf{W}_t^{(0)} \\ \mathbf{W}_p^{(t)} = \theta_p \mathbf{\Pi}_{p\sim t}\mathbf{W}_t^{(t)}\mathbf{\Pi}_{p\sim t}^T + (1-\theta_p)\mathbf{W}_p^{(0)} \\ \mathbf{W}_u^{(t)} = \theta_u \mathbf{\Pi}_{u\sim p}\mathbf{W}_p^{(t)}\mathbf{\Pi}_{u\sim p}^T + (1-\theta_u)\mathbf{W}_u^{(0)} \end{cases}, \quad (20)$$

where $\mathbf{W}_t^{(t)}$, $\mathbf{W}_p^{(t)}$ and $\mathbf{W}_u^{(t)}$ is the affinity matrix of tags, photos and users at the t-th iteration, respectively. When $t = 0$, the affinity matrixes are initial ones before propagation. $\mathbf{\Pi}_{t\sim u}$, $\mathbf{\Pi}_{p\sim t}$ and $\mathbf{\Pi}_{u\sim p}$ denote the three link matrixes measuring the link strength of the two levels of graphs, i.e., from tag graph to user graph, from photo graph to tag graph, and from user graph to photo graph. θ_t, θ_p and θ_u are tradeoff parameters.

5.1 Initial Intra-relations

- Initial user intra-relation $\mathbf{W}_u^{(0)}$

In a social media community, the initial user similarity is mostly determined by people interaction [18], including explicit interaction (one gives comments to the other's photos or one's photos get comments from others) and implicit interaction (two users simultaneously give comments on the same photos). In addition, photos taken in near locations are often shared by the people with similar interests [3], the intra-relation $w_u^{ab(0)}$ between user v_u^a and user v_u^b is defined as:

$$w_u^{ab(0)} = (f_b(a) + f_a(b) + g(a,b)) \times w_g^{ab}, \quad (21)$$

where $f_a(b)$ denotes the number of the comments given by the user v_u^b on the photos shared by user v_u^a, vice versa. $g(a,b)$ denotes the number of photos on which user v_u^a and v_u^b simultaneously comment. w_g^{ab} is the relation between user v_u^a and v_u^b caused by geo-locations, and it is given by

$$w_g^{ab} = \begin{cases} \pi & min_{gd}(v_u^a, v_u^b) < Th \\ 1 & else \end{cases}, \quad (22)$$

where $min_{gd}(v_u^a, v_u^b)$ is the minimal geo-location distance between photos of user v_u^a and v_u^b, Th is a fixed threshold and π ($\pi > 1$) is a positive number. In this paper, Th is set to $20km$ and π is set to 2.

- Initial photo intra-relation $\mathbf{W}_p^{(0)}$

We follow the approach in [11] and adopt scale-invariant feature transform (SIFT) descriptor with a Difference of Gaussian (DoG) interest point detector for extracting the images' visual patterns. The interest point is referred to as local salient patch, each associated with a 128-dimensional feature vector. We further use K-means to cluster the similar patches into "visual words," and use Bag-of-Word (BoW) to represent each image as it has proven to be effective for object and scene retrieval [6][16][21][23]. Let $\mathbf{f}_a$ and $\mathbf{f}_b$ denote the BoW feature vector of photo v_p^a and v_p^b, respectively, then the initial similarity $w_p^{ab(0)}$ between the two photos is calculated by

$$w_p^{ab(0)} = \exp\left\{-\frac{Ed(\mathbf{f}_a, \mathbf{f}_b)}{2\sigma_1^2}\right\}, \quad (23)$$

where $Ed(\mathbf{f}_a, \mathbf{f}_b)$ denotes the Euclidean distance between $\mathbf{f}_a$ and $\mathbf{f}_b$, σ_1 is the positive radius parameter, and it is estimated by the median value of all the Euclidean distances.

- Initial tag intra-relation $\mathbf{W}_t^{(0)}$

Tags supplied by users describe the content of photos while providing additional contextual modalities about the photos. As a preprocessing step, the standard stemming and stop word removal are firstly applied. The M tags which have highest frequency are selected for computing their similarity.

Analogous to the principle of Google similarity distance [2], we define the tag distance $w_t^{ab(0)}$ between tag v_t^a and v_t^b, as follows:

$$Td(v_t^a, v_t^b) = \frac{\max(\log f(v_t^a), \log f(v_t^b)) - \log f(v_t^a, v_t^b)}{\log G - \min(\log f(v_t^a), \log f(v_t^b))}, \quad (24)$$

where $f(v_t^a)$ and $f(v_t^b)$ are the numbers of photos containing tag v_t^a and v_t^b, respectively. $f(v_t^a, v_t^b)$ is the number of photos containing both tag v_t^a and v_t^b. These numbers can be obtained by performing search on Flickr website using the tags as keywords. The initial tag similarity between tag v_t^a and v_t^b is then given by

$$w_t^{ab(0)} = \exp\left\{-\frac{Td(v_t^a, v_t^b)}{2\sigma_2^2}\right\}. \quad (25)$$

Similar to σ_1, σ_2 is also estimated by the median value of all the tag distances.

5.2 Inter-links

As shown in Eq.(20), there are three types of inter-links, i.e., from tag graph to user graph ($\mathbf{\Pi}_{t\sim u}$), from photo graph to tag graph ($\mathbf{\Pi}_{p\sim t}$), and from user graph to photo graph ($\mathbf{\Pi}_{u\sim p}$). Accordingly, three link matrices are built as follows.

- $\mathbf{\Pi}_{t\sim u} \equiv [\pi_{t\sim u}^{ab}]_{(Z_t \times Z_u)}$: measuring the link strength of entities in tag and user graph. It is defined as:

$$\pi_{t\sim u}^{ab} = \begin{cases} 1/n_{v_t^a} & v_u^b \in v_t^a \\ 0 & else \end{cases}, \quad (26)$$

where $n_{v_t^a}$ denotes the number of users who provide tag v_t^a to a photo, $v_u^b \in v_t^a$ means user v_u^b annotates a photo with tag v_t^a.

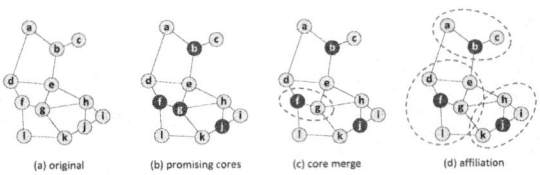

Figure 2: The illustration for building sub-nets.

- $\mathbf{\Pi}_{p\sim t} \equiv [\pi_{p\sim t}^{ab}]_{(Z_p \times Z_t)}$: measuring the link strength of entities in photo and tag graph. It is given by:

$$\pi_{p\sim t}^{ab} = \begin{cases} 1/n_{v_p^a} & v_t^b \in v_p^a \\ 0 & else \end{cases}, \quad (27)$$

where $n_{v_p^a}$ denotes the tag number of visual photo v_p^a, and $v_t^b \in v_p^a$ means tag v_t^b belongs to photo v_p^a.

- $\mathbf{\Pi}_{u\sim p} \equiv [\pi_{u\sim p}^{ab}]_{(Z_u \times Z_p)}$: measuring the link strength of entities in user and photo graph. Similarly, we have:

$$\pi_{u\sim p}^{ab} = \begin{cases} 1/n_{v_u^a} & v_p^b \in v_u^a \\ 0 & else \end{cases}, \quad (28)$$

where $n_{v_u^a}$ denotes the photo number shared by user v_u^a, and $v_p^b \in v_u^a$ means photo v_p^b is shared by user v_u^a.

5.3 Implementations

In practice, it is not necessary to run the multi-level graph propagation as a whole in the social network. Instead, the network itself is usually formed by disconnected sub-nets, and the propagation can be conducted separately on each sub-net. In our implementation, two users are connected if one of the following conditions is met: (1) the maximal initial tag similarity is above an average value; (2) their photos are taken in nearby locations; (3) they comment each other's photos or comment on a photo contributed by a third party. This could result in a number of sub-nets. To make the finding of sub-nets computationally efficient, we first detect the "promising cores" as seeds and then grow the sub-nets from the seeds, by connecting other users fulfilling the aforementioned three conditions. Fig.2 illustrates the procedure of forming social sub-nets.

The "promising core" of a sub-net, intuitively, is the user who has a large number of photos, attracts significant photo views and comments from others, while not connecting to the cores of other sub-nets. Referred to as Fig. 2, we select cores as the users with a minimum of 500 photos, accumulate at least 2,000 comments, and share no more than 20% of similar tags with others. Then the rest of users are selected as the promising cores(Fig. 2(b)). Nearby cores as in Fig. 2(c) may be merged if they have high initial user similarity. Finally, users are connected to the cores based on their initial user similarities. Based on this implementation, taking our experiment as an example, we detect 101 sub-nets from 40,170 Flickr users. Typically, a sub-net contains about 400 users. It is also worth noting that only tags with high frequency will be used in the propagation since tags provided by Flickr users are often imprecise, even containing form and spelling form [10]. We empirically select top 1,000 tags.

6. EXPERIMENTS

In this section, we systematically evaluate the effectiveness of the proposed unified formulation and solution to en-

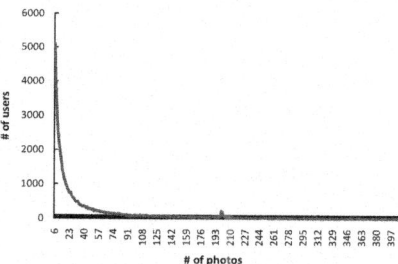

Figure 3: The statistics of photo number owned by users (users owned less than five photos are removed).

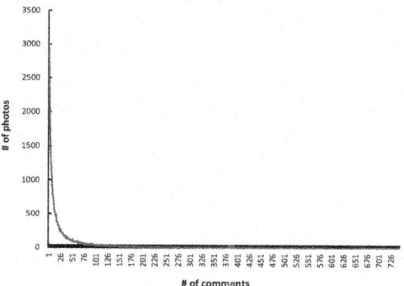

Figure 4: The statistics of comment number given by photos.

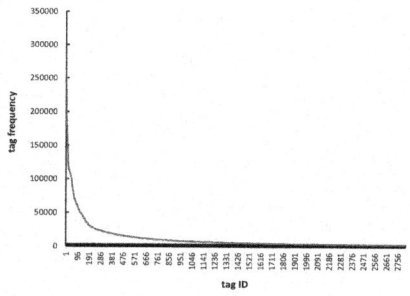

Figure 5: The tag frequency distribution.

tity search in social media community, and report comparative results on three popular entity search tasks, i.e., friend suggestion, image tagging and personalized image search.

6.1 Dataset

We empirically verify the merit of entity search on a dataset crawled from Flickr [4]. The data from Flickr consists of five main elements: users, uploaded photos, the tags associated with each photo, geo-location of each photo, and users who comment on the photo (called "cmt users" for short). We randomly collect 165,558 users and the corresponding photos, tags and comments by using Flickr API. For our experiment, we remove the users who have less than 5 photos, and then the dataset includes 40,170 users (not includes the cmt users), owning about 9 million photos.

Fig.3 shows the number of photos owned by users. The long tail indicates most of users share similar number of photos, and very few users own the extremely large number of photos. In average, a user owns around 200 photos in our experiment. Fig.4 shows the number of comments on photos. The long tail phenomenon also exists, which indicates although the social interaction is complex, the comments on each photo are not too many (13 comments per photo in average). Fig.5 illustrates the tag frequency, where the noise (misspelling words, combination of words and affix variation) and some special words form the long tail.

6.2 Exp-I: Friend Suggestion

Friend suggestion aims to search a list of users, which have similar interests to the given user. Obviously, the entity type of both query and searching pool is "user." Therefore, in this task, the user similarity is mainly explored and a ranking list of users can be obtained according to Eq.(19). We compare our unified framework based friend suggestion (UFS) with the following five methods in both subjective and objective experiments:

- Initial user similarity (IUS). The friends are ranked based on the initial user similarities, which are directly determined by user interaction in photo sharing activities as mentioned in Section 5.1.

- Tag correlations (Tag). A tag correlation measured by the number of common tags on the users' photos. The higher the number of common tags, the more likely to be friends of the two users.

- Visual relationships (Visual). A visual relationship estimated according to the visual similarity of representative photos of users.

- Fusion of user, tag and visual similarity (Fusion). A linear fusion of IUS, Tag and Visual.

- Context-based friend suggestion (Context) [22]. It aims to leverage multiple contexts, including user-contributed photos, their associated tags and geo-locations, as well as user behaviors like viewing and commenting.

6.2.1 Subjective User Study

To evaluate the proposed friend suggestion strategy, we randomly selected 1,000 users as the query users. The similarity of each user pair was manually labeled by three subjects on a scale of 1-3: (1) dissimilar (totally different interest), (2) similar (somewhat relevant interest), and (3) strongly similar (almost same interest). The ground truth similar degree of each pair is the median scale of three evaluations. Considering the pairs with high similarity have especially important for most of applications, we adopted the Normalized Discounted Cumulative Gain (NDCG) as the performance metric. The NDCG score at the depth d in the ranked lists is defined by:

$$NDCG@d = Z_d \sum_{j=1}^{d} \frac{2^{r^j} - 1}{\log(1 + j)} \quad (29)$$

where r^j is the rating of the j-th pair, Z_d is a normalization constant and is chosen so that a perfect ranking's $NDCG@d$ value is 1. After computing the NDCG measure of each query user, we average them to obtain an overall performance evaluation on friend suggestion.

Fig.6 shows the experimental results. Overall, the results across different depth of NDCG consistently indicate that UFS achieves a performance boost compared to IUS, Tag

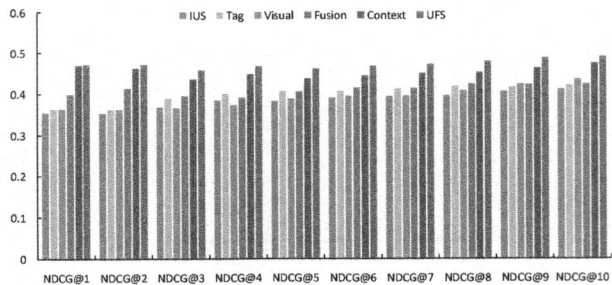

Figure 6: Subjective evaluation on friend suggestion.

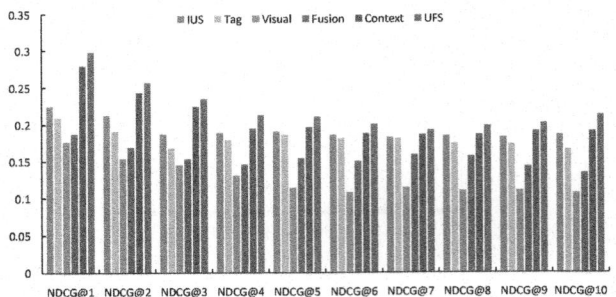

Figure 8: Objective evaluation on friend suggestion.

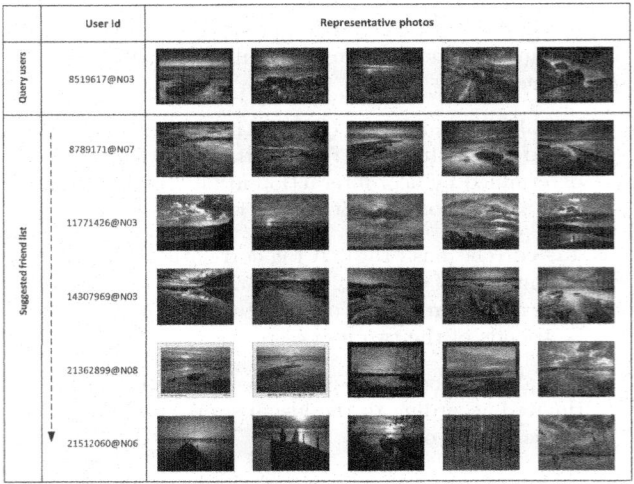

Figure 7: The representative photos of suggested friends for the user Id "8519617@N03."

and Visual which using single entity. Furthermore, in contrast to the linear fusion and context-based method, the superiority of UFS demonstrates that allowing entity interaction can lead to better performance gain. As indicated by our results, the friend suggestion based on our unified entity search framework can better express the user relationship by reinforcing the mutual exchange of information across multiple entities over an integrated graph model.

Fig.7 shows the top five users' representative photos to a query user according to the final user intra-relations. From the representative photos of each user, we can see that these photos are similar with each other. These users are likely to have similar interest and thus are potential candidates for friend suggestion.

6.2.2 Objective Evaluation of Friend Suggestion

The objective evaluation was conducted according to the *contacts* function in Flickr site, which is organized by users themselves. If a user exists in the other user's contact list, we view the two users as friends. We first filtered out the users who have no contacts in Flickr site or in our user set. After filtering, we obtained 2,975 users and took them as the query users. Similar to the subjective user study, the objective comparison as shown in Fig.8 also indicates the strong performance of our proposed UFS in comparison to others.

6.3 Exp-II: Image Tagging

Image tagging is to assign a set of tags to a given image to describe the image content. In our unified entity search framework, the query type is "image" and the type of entities to be searched is "tag." By exploring the affinity matrix $\mathbf{W}_t$, and link matrix $\Pi_{p \sim t}$, the tag ranking list can be obtained by Eq.(19).

We compare our unified framework based image tagging (UIT) with the following two baseline methods.

- Initial image tags in Flickr site (IIT): The tags originally provided by the image owners.

- Tagging ranking (TR). A Random walk is performed over a tag similarity graph to estimate the relevance score of tags for a given image [10].

To demonstrate the effectiveness of the image tagging methods, we randomly select 200 images from our collected Flickr image dataset to perform image tagging. We also invite people to label the tags on a 1-3 scales: (1) "irrelevant," (2) "relevant," and (3) "excellent," and adopt *NDCG* as the performance metric. After computing the *NDCG* score of each image's tag list, we average them to obtain an overall performance evaluation of the image tagging method. Fig.9 shows the experimental results. We can see our proposed unified solution achieves much better performance compared to the other baseline algorithms at different depths of *NDCG*. The improvements demonstrate that UIT can facilitate the relationship and interaction of different entities through mutual reinforcement and all the relationships can be refined.

Fig.10 further illustrates some exemplary images with the top five tags generated by three image tagging methods. We can clearly see that our recommended tags can better characterize the image content.

6.4 Exp-III: Personalized Image Search

Given the large and growing importance of search engines, personalized search has the potential to significantly improve searching experience [15]. Compared with the common image search, in personalized image search, the user-specific information is considered to distinguish the exact intentions of textual queries and rank the images. Formally in our framework, the query types are "user" and "textual tags," while the entities in searching pool are "images." To obtain the image ranking list, we estimate the affinity matrix based on the photo affinity matrix $\mathbf{W}_p$, and link matrixes $\Pi_{u \sim p}$ and $\Pi_{p \sim t}$. According to Eq.(19), we can obtain the image ranking list.

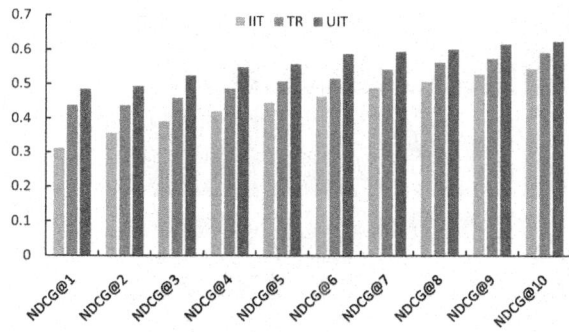

Figure 9: Performance comparison of image tagging methods.

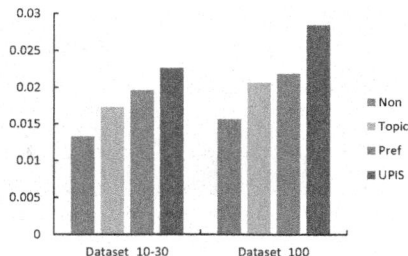

Figure 12: Performance comparison of personalized image search for different methods.

scheme: the commented images are considered relevant for all the test queries. As no query information is involved, for those queries non-relevant with the topic of the commented images, the performance tends to be low. (3) Comparing between the two test scenarios, the average performance of Data_100 also improves over Data_10-30. One possible reason for the improvement is that those users having more comments are active users who are likely to also attend more interest groups and tag more images.

Fig.11 displays exemplary search results for the query "sunrise." The top eight non-personalized results and the personalized results of three users (User A, User B and User C) are shown. We can see that by simultaneously considering query relevance and user information, the unified framework based personalized image search could capture the user's preference under certain topics. From the results, we can see that the top search results for user A mainly focus on sunrise at the seaside, while for user B and user C, the top search results are often co-exist with cloud and plants. For the baseline method (non-personalized) which separate query relevance and user preference, most of the search results are relevant to query, yet may hard to interpret a clear search intent.

Figure 10: Example results of image tagging.

We select the following three state-of-the-art models as the baselines and compare them with our unified framework based method (UPIS).

- Non-personalized (Non). Use the common text-based image search mainly based on *tf-idf* functions [16].

- Topic-based (Topic). It aims to explore folksonomy for personalized search [19].

- Preference-based (Pref). Perform personalized image search by predicting user interests-based preference [12].

Similar to [12], we use *comment*-based evaluation approach, where the images attract comments from user u are treated as relevant when u issues queries. We build two test scenarios for the comment-based evaluation: 1) 50 randomly selected users who gave comments to 10-30 photos, denoted as Dataset_10-30, and 2) 20 users who gave comments to more than 100 photos, denoted as Dataset_100. 15 tags frequently appearing in the tags of commented images are selected as the test queries. The metric of $mMAP$ [15] is utilized to evaluate the performance and the results are demonstrated in Fig.12. From the results, we have the following observations. (1) Our proposed unified solution achieves better performance compared to the other three baseline algorithms. This clearly demonstrates the effectiveness of our proposed unified solution in the personalized image search task. (2) All $mMAP$ values are not very high. This phenomenon reflects the problem of comment-based evaluation

6.5 Complexity Analysis

The complexity of our approach includes offline and online two parts. The offline multi-level graph construction on 40,170 users with their photos, tags and comments can be finished in ten hours on five servers, each having 4GB memories and running four threads. Our online entity search algorithm is extremely efficient. The complexity of the algorithm is $O(|V| \lg |V| + |E|)$, where $|V|$ and $|E|$ represent the number of vertices and edges, respectively. Take 200 images to perform image tagging for example, our algorithm takes less than 60.2 seconds on a regular PC (Intel dual-core 3.33GHz CPU and 4 GB RAM) to complete the whole process. In other words, tagging one image only takes 0.3 seconds. It can be even faster if executed on a more powerful machine with parallel computing capability. Clearly, the speed is efficient and provides almost instant response.

7. CONCLUSIONS

In this paper, we have shown how to integrate various entities in a multi-level graph model, which includes the content from images, tags and geo-locations, as well as the rich context derived from user behaviors. Specifically, the relations between users, images and tags are fully exploited by reinforcing the mutual exchange and propagation of information relevancy across different entities. Upon the model, entity

Figure 11: Example of non-personalized (top) and personalized (second, third and fourth for User A, User B and User C respectively) search results for query "sunrise."

search is explicitly formulated within a unified framework, in which friend suggestion, image tagging and personalized image search can be implemented in one single way. Future work includes the extension to multiple media sharing sites, such as Facebook and LinkedIn. It would be a promising topic to investigate whether these entities are consistent across different social media sharing sites and whether specific factors may impact the way users create, share, use and annotate content.

8. ACKNOWLEDGMENTS

This work was supported in part by a grant from the RGC of the Hong Kong SAR, China (CityU 119610), a grant from the National Natural Science Foundation of China (#61272290), and a grant from Microsoft Research Asia Windows Phone Academic Program (FY12-RES-OPP-107).

9. REFERENCES

[1] H. M. Chen, M. H. Chang, P. C. Chang, M. C. Tien, W. H. Hsu, and J. L. Wu. Sheepdog-group and tag recommendation for flickr photos by automatic search-based learning. In *Proceedings of ACM Multimedia*, 2008.

[2] R. L. Cilibrasi and P. M. Vitanyi. The google similarity distance. *IEEE Trans. on Knowledge and Data Engineering*, 19(3):370–383, 2007.

[3] D. Easley and J. Kleinberg. *Networks and Crowds and Markets: Reasoning About a Highly Connected World*. Cambridge University Press, 2010.

[4] Flickr. http://www.flickr.com/.

[5] ImageClef. http://imageclef.org/.

[6] Y. Jing and S. Baluja. Pagerank for product image search. In *Proceedings of International WWW Conference*, 2008.

[7] J. Li and J. Z. Wang. Real-time computerized annotation of pictures. *IEEE Trans. on Pattern Analysis and Machine Intelligence*, 2008.

[8] Q. Li, Y. Zheng, X. Xie, Y. Chen, W. Liu, and W.-Y. Ma. Mining user similarity based on location history. In *Proceedings of ACM GIS*, 2008.

[9] Y.-R. Lin, J. Sun, P. Castro, R. Konuru, H. Sundaram, and A. Kelliher. Metafac: Community discovery via relational hypergraph factorization. In *Proceedings of ACM KDD*, 2009.

[10] D. Liu, X.-S. Hua, L. Yang, M. Wang, and H.-J. Zhang. Tag ranking. In *Proceedings of International WWW Conference*, 2009.

[11] D. Lowe. Object recognition with informative features and linear classification. In *Proceedings of ICCV*, 2003.

[12] D. Lu and Q. Li. Personalized search on flickr based on searcher's preference prediction. In *Proceedings of International WWW Conference*, 2011.

[13] R.-A. Negoescu, B. Adams, D. Phung, S. Venkatesh, and D. Gatica-Perez. Flickr hypergroups. In *Proceedings of ACM Multimedia*, 2009.

[14] M. Roth, A. David, D. Deutscher, G. Flysher, I. Horn, A. Leichtberg, N. Leiser, Y. Matias, and R. Merom. Suggesting friends using the implicit social graph. In *Proceedings of ACM KDD*, 2010.

[15] J. Sang, C. Xu, and D. Lu. Learn to personalized image search from the photo sharing websites. *IEEE Trans. on Multimedia*, 14(4), 2012.

[16] J. Sivic and A. Zisserman. Video google: A text retrieval approach to object matching in videos. In *Proceedings of IEEE International Conference on Computer Vision*, 2003.

[17] M. Sniedovich. Dijkstra's algorithm revisited: the dynamic programming connexion. *Control and Cybernetics*, 35(3), 2006.

[18] C. Wilson, A. Sala, K. P. N. Puttaswamy, and B. Y. Zhao. Beyond social graphs: User interactions in online social networks and their implications. *ACM Trans. on the Web*, 2012.

[19] S. Xu, S. Bao, B. Fei, Z. Su, and Y. Yu. Exploring folksonomy for personalized search. In *Proceedings of ACM SIGIR*, 2008.

[20] Yahoo. http://people.yahoo.com/.

[21] T. Yao, T. Mei, and C.-W. Ngo. Co-reranking by mutual reinforcement for image search. In *ACM CIVR*, 2010.

[22] T. Yao, C.-W. Ngo, and T. Mei. Context-based friend suggestion in online photo-sharing community. In *Proceedings of ACM Multimedia*, 2011.

[23] T. Yao, C.-W. Ngo, and T. Mei. Circular reranking for visual search. *IEEE Trans. on Image Processing*, 22(4), April 2013.

[24] N. Zheng, Q. Li, S. Liao, and L. Zhang. Flickr group recommendation based on tensor decomposition. In *Proceedings of ACM SIGIR*, 2010.

[25] D. Zhou, O. Bousquet, T. Lal, J. Weston, and B. Schölkopf. Learning with local and global consistency. In *Proceedings of NIPS*, 2003.

[26] J. Zhuang, T. Mei, S. Hoi, X.-S. Hua, and S. Li. Modeling social strength in social media community via kernel-based learning. In *Proceedings of ACM Multimedia*, 2011.

MATRI: A Multi-Aspect and Transitive Trust Inference Model

Yuan Yao
State Key Laboratory for Novel
Software Technology, China
yyao@smail.nju.edu.cn

Hanghang Tong
City College, CUNY, USA
tong@cs.ccny.cuny.edu

Xifeng Yan
University of California at
Santa Barbara, USA
xyan@cs.ucsb.edu

Feng Xu
State Key Laboratory for Novel
Software Technology, China
xf@nju.edu.cn

Jian Lu
State Key Laboratory for Novel
Software Technology, China
lj@nju.edu.cn

ABSTRACT

Trust inference, which is the mechanism to build new pair-wise trustworthiness relationship based on the existing ones, is a fundamental integral part in many real applications, e.g., e-commerce, social networks, peer-to-peer networks, etc. State-of-the-art trust inference approaches mainly employ the *transitivity* property of trust by propagating trust along connected users (a.k.a. trust propagation), but largely ignore other important properties, e.g., prior knowledge, multi-aspect, etc.

In this paper, we propose a multi-aspect trust inference model by exploring an equally important property of trust, i.e., the *multi-aspect* property. The heart of our method is to view the problem as a recommendation problem, and hence opens the door to the rich methodologies in the field of collaborative filtering. The proposed multi-aspect model directly characterizes multiple *latent* factors for each trustor and trustee from the locally-generated trust relationships. Moreover, we extend this model to incorporate the prior knowledge as well as trust propagation to further improve inference accuracy. We conduct extensive experimental evaluations on real data sets, which demonstrate that our method achieves *significant* improvement over several existing benchmark approaches. Overall, the proposed method (MATRI) leads to 26.7% - 40.7% improvement over its best known competitors in prediction accuracy; and up to *7 orders of magnitude* speedup with *linear* scalability.

Categories and Subject Descriptors

H.2.8 [**Database Management**]: Database applications—*Data mining*

Keywords

Trust inference; transitivity property; multi-aspect property; latent factors; prior knowledge

1. INTRODUCTION

Trust is essential to reduce uncertainty and boost collaborations in many real-world applications including social networks [39], e-commerce [11], peer-to-peer networks [12], semantic Web [25], etc. In these applications, trust inference is widely used as the mechanism to build trust among unknown users. Typically, trust inference takes as its input the existing trust ratings that are locally-generated through direct interactions, and outputs an estimated trustworthiness score from a trustor to an unknown trustee. This estimated trustworthiness score indicates to what extent the trustor could expect the trustee to perform a given action.

The basic assumption behind most of the existing trust inference methods is the *transitivity* property of trust [19], which is rooted in the social structural balance theory [4]. This property essentially means that if *Alice* trusts *Bob* and *Bob* trusts *Carol*, *Alice* might also trust *Carol* to some extent. These methods (see Section 6 for a review), referred to as *trust propagation* models as a whole, have been widely studied and successfully applied in many real-world settings [8, 39, 19, 15, 9, 22].

In addition to transitivity, a few trust inference models explore another equally important property, that is, the *multi-aspect* of trust [6, 27]. The basic assumption behind the multi-aspect methods is that trust is the composition of multiple factors, and different users may have different preferences for these factors. For example, in e-commerce, some users might care more about the factor of delivering time, whereas others give a higher weight to the factor of product price. However, the existing multi-aspect trust inference methods [26, 36, 31, 28] require as its input some side information (e.g., the delivering time as well as user's preference for it, etc) in addition to the locally-generated trust ratings, and therefore become infeasible in many trust networks where such side information may not be available.

Another limitation in existing trust inference models is that they tend to ignore some important prior knowledge (e.g., trust bias) during the inference procedure. It was discovered in sociology a long time ago that *trust bias* is an integral part in the final trust decision [30]. Nonetheless, it was not until the very recent years did the computer science community begin to incorporate the trust bias into the inference process. For example, a recent work [23] models trustor bias as the propensity of a trustor to trust others.

In this paper, we aim to integrate all these important properties, including transitivity, multi-aspect and prior knowledge, to maximally boost the inference accuracy. We start by proposing a multi-aspect trust inference model. The heart of our method is to view the problem as a recommendation problem, and hence opens the door to the rich methodologies in the field of collaborative filtering. The proposed multi-aspect model directly characterizes multiple *latent* factors for each trustor and trustee from the locally-generated trust relationships. Based on that, we propose to incorporate the prior knowledge as *specified* aspects and automatically learn the relative weights between latent and specified factors. Finally, we extend this model to incorporate trust propagation to further improve inference accuracy.

To summarize, the main contributions of this paper are as follows:

(1) *Trust Models.* To the best of our knowledge, this is the first work to (a) integrate transitivity, multi-aspect and prior knowledge into one single trust inference model; and (b) directly characterize the multi-aspect trustworthiness relationship solely based on locally-generated trust ratings. It can admit the rich methodologies from collaborative filtering. It is flexible to model the prior knowledge as specified factors and further learn their relative weights.

(2) *Performance Improvements.* We conducted extensive experimental evaluations on two widely used benchmark data sets, and empirically observed significant performance improvements in both effectiveness and efficiency. In terms of prediction accuracy, our MATRI outperforms the best known existing methods by 26.7% - 40.7%. By pre-computation, our MATRI is much faster in terms of on-line response, achieving up to 7 orders of magnitude speedup. Finally, the pre-computation stage itself of the proposed MATRI scales *linearly* wrt the size of the input data set, indicating that it is suitable for large data sets.

The rest of the paper is organized as follows. Section 2 presents the definition of the trust inference problem. Section 3 describes our optimization formulation for the problem defined in the previous section and shows how to incorporate prior knowledge and trust propagation. Section 4 presents the inference algorithm to solve the formulation. Section 5 presents experimental results. Section 6 reviews related work. Section 7 concludes the paper.

2. PROBLEM DEFINITION

In this section, we formally define our trust inference problem. Table 1 lists the main symbols we use throughout the paper.

Table 1: Symbols.

Symbol	Definition and Description
$\mathbf{T}$	the partially observed trust matrix
$\mathbf{F}, \mathbf{G}$	the characterized trustor and trustee matrices
$\mathbf{F}_0, \mathbf{G}_0$	the sub-matrix of $\mathbf{F}$ and $\mathbf{G}$
$\mathbf{T}'$	the transpose of matrix $\mathbf{T}$
$\mathbf{T}(i, j)$	the element at the ith row and j^{th} column of $\mathbf{T}$
$\mathbf{T}(i, :)$	the ith row of matrix $\mathbf{T}$
$\mathcal{K}$	the set of observed trustor-trustee pairs in $\mathbf{T}$
μ	the global bias
$\mathbf{x}$	the vector of trustor bias
$\mathbf{y}$	the vector of trustee bias
$\mathbf{x}(i)$	the ith element of vector $\mathbf{x}$
$\mathbf{z}_{ij}$	the vector of propagation elements for trustor-trustee pair (i, j)
n	the number of users
p, r	the number of bias and latent factors
s	total number of factors, $s = p + r$
t	the maximum propagation step
α_i	the weights/coefficients for bias factors
β_j	the weights/coefficients for propagation elements
u, v	the trustor and the trustee
m	the maximum iteration number
ξ	the threshold to terminate the iteration

Following conventions, we use bold capital letters for matrices, and bold lower case letters for vectors. For example, we use a partially observed matrix $\mathbf{T}$ to model the locally-generated trust relationships, where the existing/observed trust relationships are represented as non-zero trust ratings and non-existing/unobserved relationships are represented as '?'. As for the observed trust rating, we represent it as a real number between 0 and 1 (a higher rating means more trustworthiness). We use calligraphic font $\mathcal{K}$ to denote the set of observed trustor-trustee indices in $\mathbf{T}$. Similar to Matlab, we also denote the ith row of matrix $\mathbf{T}$ as $\mathbf{T}(i,:)$, and the transpose of a matrix with a prime. In addition, we denote the number of users as n and the number of characterized factors as s. Without loss of generality, we assume that the goal of our trust model is to infer the unseen trust relationship from the user u to another user v, where u is the trustor and v is the unknown trustee to u.

Based on these notations, we first define the basic trust inference problem as follows:

PROBLEM 1. *The Basic Trust Inference Problem*

Given: *an $n \times n$ partially observed trust matrix $\mathbf{T}$, a trustor u, and a trustee v, where $1 \leq u, v \leq n$ ($u \neq v$) and $\mathbf{T}(u, v) =$ '?';*

Find: *the estimated trustworthiness score $\hat{\mathbf{T}}(u, v)$.*

In the above problem definition, given a trustor-trustee pair, the only information we need as input is the locally-generated trust ratings (i.e., the partially observed matrix $\mathbf{T}$). The goal of trust inference is to infer the new trust ratings (i.e., unseen/unobserved trustworthiness scores in the partially observed matrix $\mathbf{T}$) by collecting the knowledge from existing trust relationships. In this paper, we assume that we can access such existing trust relationships. For instance, these relationships could be collected by central servers in a centralized environment like eBay, or by individuals in a distributed environment like EigenTrust [12]. How to collect these trust relationships is out of the scope of this work.

As mentioned before, one of our goals is to capture the multi-aspect property of trust. In this paper, we propose a multi-aspect model for such trust inference in Problem 1. That is, we want to infer an $n \times s$ *trustor matrix* $\mathbf{F}$ whose element indicates to what extent the corresponding person trusts others wrt a specific aspect/factor. Similarly, we want to infer another $n \times s$ *trustee matrix* $\mathbf{G}$ whose element indicates to what extent the corresponding person is trusted by others wrt a specific aspect/factor. Such trustor and trustee matrices are in turn used to infer the unseen trustworthiness scores. Based on the basic trust inference problem, we define the multi-aspect trust inference problem as follows:

PROBLEM 2. *The Multi-Aspect Trust Inference Problem*

Given: *an $n \times n$ partially observed trust matrix $\mathbf{T}$, the number of factors s, a trustor u, and a trustee v, where $1 \leq u, v \leq n$ ($u \neq v$) and $\mathbf{T}(u, v) =$ '?';*

Find: *(1) an $n \times s$ trustor matrix $\mathbf{F}$ and an $n \times s$ trustee matrix $\mathbf{G}$; (2) the estimated trustworthiness score $\hat{\mathbf{T}}(u, v)$.*

2.1 An Illustrative Example

To further illustrate our multi-aspect trust inference problem (Problem 2), we give an intuitive example as shown in Fig. 1.

In this example, we observe several locally-generated pair-wise trust relationships between five users (e.g., '*Alice*', '*Bob*', '*Carol*', '*David*', and '*Elva*') as shown in Fig. 1(a). Each observation contains a trustor, a trustee, and a numerical trust rating from the trustor to the trustee. We then model these observations as a 5×5 partially observed matrix $\mathbf{T}$ (see Fig. 1(b)) where $\mathbf{T}(i, j)$ is the trust rating

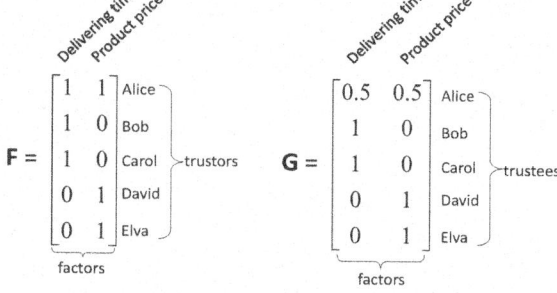

Figure 1: An illustrative example for multi-aspect trust inference problem.

(a) The observed locally-generated pair-wise trust relationships

(b) The partially observed trust matrix **T**

(c) The inferred trustor matrix **F** and trustee matrix **G**

from the ith user to the jth user if the rating is observed and $\mathbf{T}(i, j)$ = '?' otherwise. Notice that we do not consider self-ratings and thus represent the diagonal elements of **T** as '/'. By setting the number of factors $s = 2$, our goal is to infer two 5×2 matrices **F** and **G** (see Fig. 1(c)) from the input matrix **T**. Each row of the two matrices is for the corresponding user, and each column of the matrices represents a certain aspect/factor in trust inference (e.g., 'delivering time', 'product price', etc). For example, we can see that *Alice* trusts others strongly wrt both 'delivering time' and 'product price' (based on **F**), and she is in turn moderately trusted by others wrt these two factors (based on **G**). On the other hand, both *Bob* and *Carol* put more emphasis on the delivering time, while *David* and *Elva* care more about the product price.

Once **F** and **G** are inferred, we can use these two matrices to estimate the unseen trustworthiness scores (i.e., the '?' elements in **T**). For instance, the trustworthiness from *Carol* to *Alice* can be estimated as $\hat{\mathbf{T}}(3, 1) = \mathbf{F}(3, :)\mathbf{G}(1, :)' = 0.5$. This estimation is reasonable because *Carol* has the same preference as *Bob* and the trustworthiness score from *Bob* to *Alice* is also 0.5.

In the next two sections, we will mainly focus on (1) how to infer **F** and **G**; and (2) how to incorporate prior knowledge (i.e., trust bias) and trust transitivity (i.e., trust propagation) based on the partially observed input matrix **T**.

3. THE OPTIMIZATION FORMULATION

In this section, we present our optimization formulation to integrate all the three important properties in trust inference, including multi-aspect, prior knowledge (i.e., trust bias) and trust transitivity (i.e., trust propagation). We start with the basic form to capture the multi-aspect of trust; and then show how to incorporate trust bias and four groups of trust propagation. Finally, we discuss some generalizations of our formulation.

3.1 The Basic Formulation

In this work, we adopt optimization method to solve the trust inference problem defined in the previous section. Formally, Problem 2 can be formulated as the following optimization problem:

$$\min_{\mathbf{F}, \mathbf{G}} \sum_{(i,j) \in \mathcal{K}} (\mathbf{T}(i, j) - \mathbf{F}(i, :)\mathbf{G}(j, :)')^2 + \lambda \|\mathbf{F}\|_{fro}^2 + \lambda \|\mathbf{G}\|_{fro}^2 \quad (1)$$

where λ is a regularization parameter; $\|\mathbf{F}\|_{fro}$ and $\|\mathbf{G}\|_{fro}$ are the Frobenius norm of the trustor and trustee matrices, respectively.

By this formulation, it aims to minimize the squared error on the set of observed trust ratings. Notice that in Eq. (1), we have two additional regularization terms ($\|\mathbf{F}\|_{fro}^2$ and $\|\mathbf{G}\|_{fro}^2$) to improve the solution stability. The parameter $\lambda \geq 0$ controls the amount of such regularization. Based on the resulting **F** and **G** of the above equation, the unseen trustworthiness score $\hat{\mathbf{T}}(u, v)$ can then be estimated by $\mathbf{F}(u, :)$ and $\mathbf{G}(v, :)$ as:

$$\hat{\mathbf{T}}(u, v) = \mathbf{F}(u, :)\mathbf{G}(v, :)' \quad (2)$$

A Collaborative Filtering Metaphor. As mentioned in introduction, we view the trust inference problem as a recommendation problem. To be specific, in the trust matrix **T**, if we treat its rows (i.e., trustors) as 'users'; its columns (i.e., trustees) as 'items'; and its entries (i.e., trustworthiness scores) as 'ratings', the optimization problem in Eq. (1) resembles the same form as that of so-called factorization-based collaborative filtering [13]. This viewpoint opens the door to the rich methodologies in collaborative filtering to capture the multi-aspect of trust.

3.2 Incorporating Trust Bias

The formulation in Eq. (1) can naturally incorporate some prior knowledge such as trust bias into the inference procedure. In this paper, we explicitly consider the following three types of trust bias (i.e., $p = 3$ where p is the number of bias factors): *global bias*, *trustor bias*, and *trustee bias*, although other types of bias can be incorporated in a similar way.

Global bias: The global bias represents the average level of trust in the community. The intuition behind this is that users tend to rate optimistically in some reciprocal environments (e.g., e-commerce) while they are more conservative in others (e.g., security-related applications). As a result, it might be useful to take such global bias into account and we model it as a scalar μ.

Trustor bias: The trustor bias is based on the observation that some trustors tend to generously give higher trust ratings than others. This bias reflects the propensity of a given trustor to trust others, and it may vary a lot among different trustors. Accordingly, we can model the trustor bias as vector **x** with $\mathbf{x}(i)$ indicating the trust propensity of the ith trustor.

Trustee bias: The third type of bias aims to characterize the fact that some trustees might have relatively higher capability in terms of being trusted than others. Similar to the second type of bias, we model this type of bias as vector **y**, where $\mathbf{y}(j)$ indicates the overall capability of the jth trustee compared to the average.

Each of these three types of bias can be represented as a *specified* factor for our model, respectively. By incorporating such bias into

Eq. (1), we have the following formulation:

$$\min_{\mathbf{F},\mathbf{G}} \sum_{(i,j)\in\mathcal{K}} (\mathbf{T}(i,j) - \mathbf{F}(i,:)\mathbf{G}(j,:)')^2 + \lambda\|\mathbf{F}\|^2_{fro} + \lambda\|\mathbf{G}\|^2_{fro}$$

Subject to:
$\mathbf{F}(:,1) = \mu\mathbf{1}$, $\mathbf{G}(:,1) = \alpha_1 \mathbf{1}/\sqrt{n}$ (global bias)
$\mathbf{F}(:,2) = \mathbf{x}$, $\mathbf{G}(:,2) = \alpha_2 \mathbf{1}/\sqrt{n}$ (trustor bias)
$\mathbf{F}(:,3) = \alpha_3 \mathbf{1}/\sqrt{n}$, $\mathbf{G}(:,3) = \mathbf{y}$ (trustee bias) (3)

where α_1, α_2, and α_3 are the weights of bias that we need to estimate based on the existing trust ratings.

In addition to these three specified factors, we refer to the remaining factors in the trustor and trustee matrices as *latent* factors. Let us define two $n \times r$ sub-matrices of $\mathbf{F}$ and $\mathbf{G}$ for the latent factors. That is, we define $\mathbf{F}_0 = \mathbf{F}(:,4:s)$ and $\mathbf{G}_0 = \mathbf{G}(:,4:s)$, where each column of $\mathbf{F}_0$ and $\mathbf{G}_0$ corresponds to one latent factor and r is the number of latent factors. With this notation, we have the following equivalent form of Eq. (3):

$$\min_{\mathbf{F}_0,\mathbf{G}_0,\alpha} \sum_{(i,j)\in\mathcal{K}} (\mathbf{T}(i,j) - (\alpha'[\mu, \mathbf{x}(i), \mathbf{y}(j)]' + \mathbf{F}_0(i,:)\mathbf{G}_0(j,:)'))^2$$
$$+ \lambda\|\mathbf{F}_0\|^2_{fro} + \lambda\|\mathbf{G}_0\|^2_{fro} + \lambda\|\alpha\|^2 \quad (4)$$

where $\alpha = [\alpha_1, \alpha_2, \alpha_3]'$.

Recall that in this paper, we aim to perform trust inference only using the partially observed trust matrix $\mathbf{T}$. Therefore, we estimate the parameters (μ, $\mathbf{x}$ and $\mathbf{y}$) of the trust bias as follows:

$$\begin{cases} \mu = \sum_{(i,j)\in\mathcal{K}} \mathbf{T}(i,j)/|\mathcal{K}| \\ \mathbf{x}(i) = \sum_{j,(i,j)\in\mathcal{K}} \mathbf{T}(i,j)/|row_i| - \mu \\ \mathbf{y}(j) = \sum_{i,(i,j)\in\mathcal{K}} \mathbf{T}(i,j)/|col_j| - \mu \end{cases} \quad (5)$$

where $|row_i|$ is the number of the observed elements in the ith row of $\mathbf{T}$, and $|col_j|$ is the number of the observed elements in the jth column of $\mathbf{T}$.

3.3 Incorporating Trust Propagation

We next describe how to incorporate trust propagation into the model. We consider the following four groups of trust propagation operators defined in [8]: *direct propagation*, *transpose trust*, *co-citation*, and *trust coupling*.

Direct propagation: Direct propagation is probably the most intuitive way to propagate trust as shown in Fig. 2(a). The basic operator in the figure presents the two-step propagation and it can be generalized to multiple steps. We define the first group of $(t-1)$ propagation elements in the matrix form as $\mathbf{T}^2, \mathbf{T}^3, ..., \mathbf{T}^t$, where t is the largest propagation step.

Transpose trust: The second operator is the transpose trust as shown in Fig. 2(b). This operator indicates that user v's trust on user u can cause some level of trust in the opposite direction. This group of t propagation elements can be represented in the matrix form as $\mathbf{T}', (\mathbf{T}')^2, (\mathbf{T}')^3, ..., (\mathbf{T}')^t$.

Co-citation: Co-citation is found to be very powerful to predict trust and distrust in the Epinions website. As shown in Fig. 2(c), co-citation means that if two users u and v are both trusted by another user w, then u might also trust v to some extent. Based on the transitive closure computation, we can represent this group of propagation elements as: $(\mathbf{T}'\mathbf{T}), (\mathbf{T}'\mathbf{T})^2, (\mathbf{T}'\mathbf{T})^3, ..., (\mathbf{T}'\mathbf{T})^t$.

Trust coupling: Fig. 2(d) shows the trust coupling operator, which means that if two users both trust another user, they might also trust each other. Similar to co-citation, we represent the fourth group of propagation elements as $(\mathbf{T}\mathbf{T}'), (\mathbf{T}\mathbf{T}')^2, (\mathbf{T}\mathbf{T}')^3, ..., (\mathbf{T}\mathbf{T}')^t$.

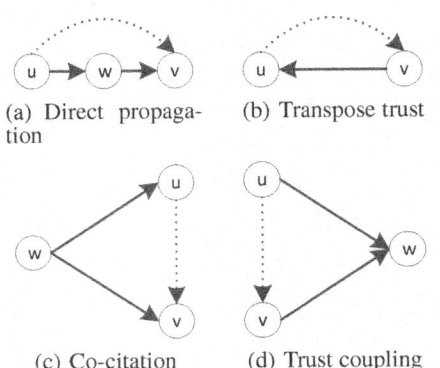

(a) Direct propagation (b) Transpose trust

(c) Co-citation (d) Trust coupling

Figure 2: The four propagation operators. The solid lines indicate existing trust relationships, and the dotted lines indicate propagated trust.

Altogether, we have generated $(4t-1)$ trust propagation matrices, with each corresponding entry measuring one specific trust propagation between the two corresponding users, respectively. For example, $\mathbf{T}^t(i,j)$ measures direct propagation from user i to user j after t steps, and $(\mathbf{T}\mathbf{T}')(i,j)$ quantifies the one-step trust coupling effect between user i and user j, etc. If we further stack all these $(4t-1)$ entries into a propagation vector $\mathbf{z}_{ij}$ for the given user pair (i,j), we have the following form when we incorporate both trust bias and trust propagation into Eq. (1):

$$\min_{\mathbf{F}_0,\mathbf{G}_0,\alpha,\beta} \sum_{(i,j)\in\mathcal{K}} (\mathbf{T}(i,j) - (\alpha'[\mu, \mathbf{x}(i), \mathbf{y}(j)]' + \beta'\mathbf{z}_{ij}$$
$$+ \mathbf{F}_0(i,:)\mathbf{G}_0(j,:)'))^2 + \lambda\|\mathbf{F}_0\|^2_{fro} + \lambda\|\mathbf{G}_0\|^2_{fro}$$
$$+ \lambda\|\alpha\|^2 + \lambda\|\beta\|^2 \quad (6)$$

where $\mathbf{z}_{ij}$ is the vector of propagation elements for the trustor-trustee pair (i,j), $\alpha = [\alpha_1, \alpha_2, \alpha_3]'$ is the weight vector for bias, and $\beta = [\beta_1, \beta_2, ..., \beta_{4t-1}]'$ is the weight vector for trust propagation.

Notice that there is no coefficient before $\mathbf{F}_0(i,:)\mathbf{G}_0(j,:)'$ as it will be automatically absorbed into $\mathbf{F}_0$ and $\mathbf{G}_0$ in our iterative algorithm. Once we have inferred all the parameters (i.e., $\mathbf{F}_0, \mathbf{G}_0, \alpha$, and β) of Eq. (6), the unseen trustworthiness score $\hat{\mathbf{T}}(u,v)$ can be immediately estimated as:

$$\hat{\mathbf{T}}(u,v) = \mathbf{F}_0(u,:)\mathbf{G}_0(v,:)' + \alpha'[\mu, \mathbf{x}(u), \mathbf{y}(v)]' + \beta'\mathbf{z}_{uv} \quad (7)$$

3.4 Discussions and Generalizations

We further present some discussions and generalizations of our optimization formulation.

First, it is worth pointing out that our formulation in Eq. (1) differs from the standard matrix factorization (e.g., SVD) as in the objective function, we try to minimize the square loss *only* on those observed trust pairs. This is because the majority of trust pairs are missing from the input trust matrix $\mathbf{T}$. As mentioned before, our basic problem setting in Eq. (1) is conceptually similar to the standard collaborative filtering, as in both cases, we aim to fill in missing values in a partially observed matrix (trustor-trustee matrix vs. user-item matrix). Indeed, if we fix the coefficients $\alpha_1 = \alpha_2 = \alpha_3 = 1$ and $\beta_1 = \beta_2 = ... = \beta_{4t-1} = 0$ in Eq. (6), it is reduced to the collaborative filtering algorithm in [14]. Our formulation in Eq. (6) goes beyond the standard collaborative filtering by (1) incorporating two other important properties in trust inference (i.e., bias and transitivity); and (2) learning their relative weights (α and β). Our experimental evaluations show that such subtle treatments are crucial and they lead to further performance improvement over these existing techniques.

Second, although our model is a subjective trust inference metric where different trustors may form different opinions on the same trustee [22], as a side product, the proposed model can also be used to infer an objective, unique trustworthiness score for each trustee. For example, this objective trustworthiness score can be computed based on the trustee matrix $\mathbf{G}$. We will compare this feature of the proposed model with a well studied objective trust inference metric EigenTrust [12] in the experimental evaluation section.

Finally, we would like to point out that our formulation is flexible and can be generalized to other settings. For instance, our current formulation adopts the square loss function in the objective function. In other words, we implicitly assume that the residuals of the pair-wise trustworthiness scores follow a Gaussian distribution, and in our experimental evaluations, we found it works well. Nonetheless, our upcoming proposed algorithm can be generalized to *any* Bregman divergence in the objective function. Also, we can naturally incorporate some additional constraints (e.g., non-negativity, sparseness, etc) in the trustor and trustee matrices. After we infer all the parameters (e.g., the coefficients for the bias and propagation, and the trustor and trustee matrices, etc), we use a linear combination to compute the trustworthiness score $\hat{\mathbf{T}}(u, v)$. We can also generalize this linear form to other non-linear combinations, such as the logistic function. For the sake of clarity, we skip the details of such generalizations in the paper.

4. THE PROPOSED MATRI ALGORITHM

In this section, we present the proposed algorithm (MATRI) to solve the trust inference problem in Eq. (6), followed by some effectiveness and efficiency analysis.

4.1 The MATRI Algorithm

Unfortunately, the optimization problem in Eq. (6) is not jointly convex wrt the coefficients (α and β) and the trustor/trustee matrices ($\mathbf{F}_0$ and $\mathbf{G}_0$) due to the coupling between them. Therefore, instead of seeking for a global optimal solution, we try to find a local minima by alternatively updating the coefficients and the trustor/trustee matrices while fixing the other.

4.1.1 Sub-routine 1: updating the trustor/trustee matrices

First, let us consider how to update the trustor/trustee matrices ($\mathbf{F}_0$ and $\mathbf{G}_0$) when we fix the coefficients (α and β). For clarity, we define an $n \times n$ matrix $\mathbf{P}$ as follows:

$$\mathbf{P}(i,j) = \begin{cases} \mathbf{T}(i,j) - (\alpha'[\mu, \mathbf{x}(i), \mathbf{y}(j)]' + \beta' \mathbf{z}_{ij}) & \text{if } (i,j) \in \mathcal{K} \\ \text{``?''} & \text{otherwise} \end{cases} \quad (8)$$

where α and β are some fixed constants, and '?' means the rating is unknown.

Based on the above definition, Eq. (6) can be simplified (by ignoring some constant terms) as:

$$\min_{\mathbf{F}_0, \mathbf{G}_0} \sum_{(i,j) \in \mathcal{K}} (\mathbf{P}(i,j) - \mathbf{F}_0(i,:)\mathbf{G}_0(j,:)')^2 + \lambda \|\mathbf{F}_0\|_{fro}^2 + \lambda \|\mathbf{G}_0\|_{fro}^2 \quad (9)$$

Therefore, updating the trustor/trustee matrices when we fix the coefficients unchanged becomes a standard matrix factorization problem for missing values. Many existing algorithms (e.g., [14, 21, 2]) can be plugged in to solve Eq. (9). In our experiment, we found the so-called alternating strategy, where we recursively update one of the two trustee/trustor matrices while keeping the other matrix fixed, works best and thus recommend it in practice. A brief skeleton of the algorithm is shown in Alg. 1, and the detailed algorithm are presented in our technical report [38].

Algorithm 1 updateMatrix($\mathbf{P}, r$).

Input: The $n \times n$ matrix $\mathbf{P}$, and the latent factor size r
Output: The $n \times r$ trustor matrix $\mathbf{F}_0$, and the $n \times r$ trustee matrix $\mathbf{G}_0$
1: $[\mathbf{F}_0, \mathbf{G}_0] = \text{alternatingFactorization}(\mathbf{P}, r)$;
2: **return** $[\mathbf{F}_0, \mathbf{G}_0]$;

Algorithm 2 computePropagation($\mathbf{T}, l, t$).

Input: The $n \times n$ matrix trust $\mathbf{T}$, the latent factor size l, and the maximum propagation step t
Output: The propagation vector $\mathbf{z}_{ij}$ for all $(i,j) \in \mathcal{K}$
1: $[\mathbf{L}, \mathbf{R}] = \text{updateMatrix}(\mathbf{T}, l)$;
2: **for** each $(i,j) \in \mathcal{K}$ **do**
3:    compute $\mathbf{z}_{ij}$ by Eq. (10);
4: **end for**
5: **return** $[\mathbf{z}_{ij}] \ (i,j) \in \mathcal{K}$;

4.1.2 Sub-routine 2: computing trust propagation

Directly computing the propagation vector $\mathbf{z}_{ij}(i,j) \in \mathcal{K}$ is computationally inefficient as it involves the multiplications of matrices of $n \times n$. To address this issue, we propose the following procedure (Alg. 2) to compute the trust propagation vectors. In Alg. 2, we first factorize the input trust matrix into two low rank matrices $\mathbf{L}, \mathbf{R}$ (step 1); and use them as the base to compute the trust propagation vectors. By doing so, we only need to compute the matrix power or multiplications of $l \times l$, where $l \ll n$.

Notice that in step 1, instead of the standard SVD, we call Alg. 1 to get the two low rank matrices. In this way, we implicitly fill in the missing values in the partially observed matrix $\mathbf{T}$ before performing the propagation. This has the additional advantage to mitigate the sparsity or coverage problem in trust inference [20] where some trustor and trustee might not be connected with each other.

$$\begin{cases} \mathbf{T}^t(i,j) &= \mathbf{L}(i,:)(\mathbf{R}'\mathbf{L})^{t-1}\mathbf{R}(j,:)' \\ (\mathbf{T}')^t(i,j) &= \mathbf{R}(i,:)(\mathbf{L}'\mathbf{R})^{t-1}\mathbf{L}(j,:)' \\ (\mathbf{T}'\mathbf{T})^t(i,j) &= \mathbf{R}(i,:)((\mathbf{L}'\mathbf{L})(\mathbf{R}'\mathbf{R}))^{t-1}(\mathbf{L}'\mathbf{L})\mathbf{R}(j,:)' \\ (\mathbf{T}\mathbf{T}')^t(i,j) &= \mathbf{L}(i,:)((\mathbf{R}'\mathbf{R})(\mathbf{L}'\mathbf{L}))^{t-1}(\mathbf{R}'\mathbf{R})\mathbf{L}(j,:)' \end{cases} \quad (10)$$

4.1.3 Sub-routine 3: updating the coefficients

Here, we consider how to update the coefficients (α and β) when we fix the trustor/trustee matrices.

If we fix the trustor and trustee matrices ($\mathbf{F}_0$ and $\mathbf{G}_0$) and let:

$$\mathbf{P}(i,j) = \begin{cases} \mathbf{T}(i,j) - \mathbf{F}_0(i,:)\mathbf{G}_0(j,:)' & \text{if } (i,j) \in \mathcal{K} \\ \text{``?''} & \text{otherwise} \end{cases} \quad (11)$$

Eq. (6) can then be simplified (by dropping constant terms) as:

$$\min_{\alpha, \beta} \sum_{(i,j) \in \mathcal{K}} (\mathbf{P}(i,j) - (\alpha'[\mu, \mathbf{x}(i), \mathbf{y}(j)]' + \beta' \mathbf{z}_{ij}))^2 + \lambda \|\alpha\|^2 + \lambda \|\beta\|^2 \quad (12)$$

To simplify the description, let us introduce another scalar k to index each pair (i,j) in the observed trustor-trustee pairs $\mathcal{K}$, that is, $(i,j) \in \mathcal{K} \to k = \{1, 2, ..., |\mathcal{K}|\}$. Let $\mathbf{b}$ denote a vector of length $|\mathcal{K}|$ with $\mathbf{b}(k) = \mathbf{P}(i,j)$. We also define a $|\mathcal{K}| \times (4t+2)$ matrix $\mathbf{A}$ as: $\mathbf{A}(k,1) = \mu$, $\mathbf{A}(k,2) = \mathbf{x}(i)$, $\mathbf{A}(k,3) = \mathbf{y}(j)$, $\mathbf{A}(k, 4 : 4t+2) = \mathbf{z}'_{ij}$, $(k = 1, 2, ..., |\mathcal{K}|)$.

Algorithm 3 MATRI(**T**, $\mathcal{K}$, r, l, t, u, v).

Input: The $n \times n$ partially observed trust matrix **T**, the set of observed trustor-trustee pairs $\mathcal{K}$, the latent factor size r, the low rank l for trust propagation, the maximum propagation step t, trustor u, and trustee v

Output: The estimated trustworthiness score $\hat{T}(u,v)$

Pre-computation stage:
1: compute bias: $[\mu, \mathbf{x}, \mathbf{y}] = \text{computeBias}(\mathbf{T})$ by Eq. (5);
2: compute propagation: $\mathbf{z}_{ij} = \text{computePropagation}(\mathbf{T}, l, t)$, $(i,j) \in \mathcal{K}$;
3: initialize $\alpha_1 = \alpha_2 = \alpha_3 = 1, \beta_1 = \beta_2 = ... = \beta_{4t-1} = 0$;
4: **while** not convergent **do**
5:   **for** each $(i,j) \in \mathcal{K}$ **do**
6:     $\mathbf{P}(i,j) = \mathbf{T}(i,j) - (\alpha'[\mu, \mathbf{x}(i), \mathbf{y}(j)]' + \beta' \mathbf{z}_{ij})$;
7:   **end for**
8:   $[\mathbf{F}_0, \mathbf{G}_0] = \text{updateMatrix}(\mathbf{P}, r)$;
9:   **for** each $(i,j) \in \mathcal{K}$ **do**
10:    $\mathbf{P}(i,j) = \mathbf{T}(i,j) - \mathbf{F}_0(i,:)\mathbf{G}_0(j,:)'$;
11:   **end for**
12:   $[\alpha, \beta] = \text{updateCoefficient}(\mathbf{P}, \mu, \mathbf{x}, \mathbf{y}, \mathbf{z}_{ij})$ by Eq. (13);
13: **end while**

On-line query response stage:
14: **return** $\hat{T}(u,v) = \mathbf{F}_0(u,:)\mathbf{G}_0(v,:)' + \alpha'[\mu, \mathbf{x}(u), \mathbf{y}(v)]' + \beta' \mathbf{z}_{uv}$;

Then, the coefficients (α and β) can be updated by solving the following ridge regression problem, which is equivalent to Eq. (12):

$$\gamma = [\alpha; \beta] = \arg\min_\gamma \|\mathbf{b} - \mathbf{A}\gamma\|^2 + \lambda \|\gamma\|^2 \qquad (13)$$

4.1.4 Putting everything together: MATRI

Putting everything together, we propose Alg. 3 for the trust inference problem in Eq. (6). The algorithm first computes trust bias (step 1) and trust propagation (step 2). Next, after an initialization step (step 3), the algorithm begins the alternating procedure (Step 4-13). At each iteration, it first fixes the coefficients (α and β), and updates the trustor matrix $\mathbf{F}_0$ and trustee matrix $\mathbf{G}_0$ (step 5-8). Next, the algorithm fixes $\mathbf{F}_0$ and $\mathbf{G}_0$, and uses ridge regression in Eq. (13) to update the coefficients α and β (step 9-12). We use the following criteria to terminate the alternating procedure: either the L_2 norm between successive estimates of both $\mathbf{F}_0$ and $\mathbf{G}_0$ is below our threshold ξ or the maximum iteration step m is reached. Finally, the algorithm outputs the estimated trustworthiness score from the given trustor u to the trustee v using Eq. (7).

It is worth pointing out that Step 1-13 in the algorithm can be pre-computed and their results (including $\mathbf{F}_0$, $\mathbf{G}_0$, α, β, μ, $\mathbf{x}$, $\mathbf{y}$, $\mathbf{L}, \mathbf{R}, \mathbf{L}'\mathbf{R}, \mathbf{R}'\mathbf{L}, \mathbf{L}'\mathbf{L}$ and $\mathbf{R}'\mathbf{R}$) can be stored in the pre-computational or off-line stage. When an on-line trust inference request arrives, the proposed MATRI only needs to apply Step 14 to return the inference result, which only requires a constant time.

4.2 Algorithm Analysis

Here, we briefly analyze the effectiveness and efficiency of our algorithm.

The effectiveness of the proposed MATRI algorithm can be summarized in Lemma 1, which says that overall, it finds a local minima solution. Given that the original optimization problem in Eq. (6) is not jointly convex wrt the coefficients (α, β) and the trustor/trustee matrices ($\mathbf{F}_0$ and $\mathbf{G}_0$), such a local minima is acceptable in practice.

LEMMA 1. **Effectiveness of MATRI.** *Fixing the propagation vector $\mathbf{z}_{ij}$, Alg. 3 finds a local minima for the optimization problem in Eq. (6).*

PROOF. Omitted for brevity. □

The time complexity of the proposed MATRI is summarized in Lemma 2, which says that MATRI (1) requires *constant* time for on-line query response (step 14) and (2) scales *linearly* wrt the number of users and the number of the observed trustor-trustee pairs in the pre-computational stage (step 1-13).

LEMMA 2. **Time Complexity of MATRI.** *Fixing r, l and t as constants, (P1) Alg. 3 requires $O(nm+|\mathcal{K}|m)$ time for pre-computation, where m is the maximum iteration number in Alg. 3; and (P2) Alg. 3 requires $O(1)$ for on-line query response.*

PROOF. Omitted for brevity. □

The space complexity of MATRI is summarized in Lemma 3, which says that MATRI requires *linear* space wrt the number of users and the number of the observed trustor-trustee pairs.

LEMMA 3. **Space Complexity of MATRI.** *Fixing r, l and t as constants, Alg. 3 requires $O(|\mathcal{K}| + n)$ space.*

PROOF. Omitted for brevity. □

5. EXPERIMENTAL EVALUATION

In this section, we present experimental evaluations, after we introduce the data sets. All the experiments are designed to answer the following questions:

- *Effectiveness*: How accurate is the proposed MATRI for trust inference?

- *Efficiency*: How fast is the proposed MATRI? How does it scale?

5.1 Data Sets Description

Many existing trust inference models design specific simulation studies to verify the underlying assumptions of the corresponding inference models. Here, we focus on two widely used real, benchmark data sets in order to compare the performance of different trust inference models.

The first data set is *advogato*[1]. It is a trust-based social network for open source developers. To allow users to certify each other, the network provides 4 levels of trust assertions, i.e., '*Observer*', '*Apprentice*', '*Journeyer*', and '*Master*'. These assertions can be mapped into real numbers which represent the degree of trust. To be specific, we map '*Observer*', '*Apprentice*', '*Journeyer*', and '*Master*' to 0.1, 0.4, 0.7, and 0.9, respectively (a higher value means more trustworthiness).

The second data set is *PGP* (short for Pretty Good Privacy) [9]. *PGP* adopts the concept of 'web of trust' to establish a decentralized model for data encryption and decryption. Similar to *advogato*, the web of trust in *PGP* data set contains 4 levels of trust as well. In our experiments, we also map them to 0.1, 0.4, 0.7, and 0.9, respectively.

Table 2 summarizes the basic statistics of the two resulting partially observed trust matrices **T**. Notice that for the *advogato* data set, it contains six different snapshots, i.e., *advogato-1*, *advogato-2*,..., *advogato-6*, etc. We use the largest snapshot (i.e., *advogato-6*) in the following unless otherwise stated.

Fig. 3 summarizes the distributions of trustor bias and trustee bias. As we can see, many users in *adovogato* perform averagely

---
[1] http://www.trustlet.org/wiki/Advogato_dataset.

Table 2: High level statistics of *advogato* and *PGP* data sets.

Data set	Nodes	Edges	Avg. degree	Avg. clustering [34]	Avg. diameter [17]	Date
advogato-1	279	2,109	15.1	0.45	4.62	2000-02-05
advogato-2	1,261	12,176	19.3	0.36	4.71	2000-07-18
advogato-3	2,443	22,486	18.4	0.31	4.67	2001-03-06
advogato-4	3,279	32,743	20.0	0.33	4.74	2002-01-14
advogato-5	4,158	41,308	19.9	0.33	4.83	2003-03-04
advogato-6	5,428	51,493	19.0	0.31	4.82	2011-06-23
PGP	38,546	317,979	16.5	0.45	7.70	2008-06-05

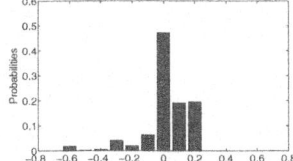

(a) Trustor bias distribution on *advogato*

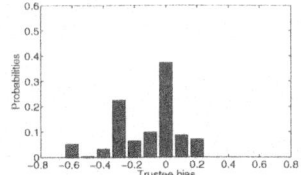

(b) Trustee bias distribution on *advogato*

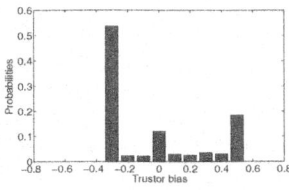

(c) Trustor bias distribution on *PGP*

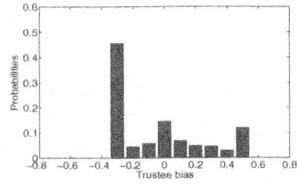

(d) Trustee bias distribution on *PGP*

Figure 3: The distributions of trustor bias and trustee bias.

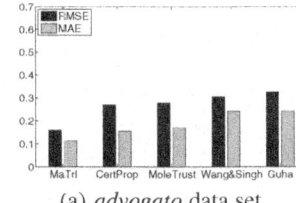

(a) *advogato* data set

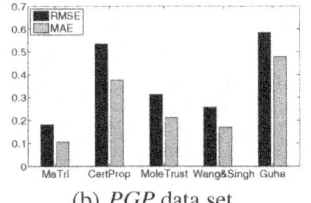

(b) *PGP* data set

Figure 4: Comparisons with subjective trust inference models. Lower is better. The proposed MATRI significantly outperforms all the other existing models wrt both RMSE and MAE on both data sets.

Table 3: Performance gain analysis of MATRI. Smaller is better. Both trust propagation and trust bias further improve trust inference accuracy.

RMSE/MAE	advogato	PGP
Best known competitor	0.269 / 0.155	0.257 / 0.169
Basic form	0.256 / 0.194	0.265 / 0.155
Basic form + propagation	0.174 / 0.124	0.214 / 0.124
Basic form + bias	0.168 / 0.119	0.189 / 0.116
MATRI	0.159 / 0.113	0.181 / 0.105

on trusting others and being trusted by others. On the other hand, a considerable part of *PGP* users are cautiously trusted by others, and even more users tend to rate others conservatively. The global bias for *advogato* (0.668) is much higher than that for *PGP* (0.384). This also suggests that the security-related *PGP* network is a more conservative environment than the developer-based *advogato* network.

5.2 Effectiveness Results

We use both *advogato* (i.e., *advogato-6*) and *PGP* for effectiveness evaluations. For both data sets, we hide a randomly selected sample of 500 observed trustor-trustee pairs as the test set, and apply the proposed MATRI as well as other existing methods on the remaining data set to infer the trustworthiness scores for those hidden pairs. To evaluate and compare the accuracy, we report both the root mean squared error (RMSE) and the mean absolute error (MAE) between the estimated and the true trustworthiness scores. Both RMSE and MAE are measured on the 500 hidden pairs in the test set. We set $r = l = 10$, $m = 10$, and $\xi = 10^{-6}$ in our experiments unless otherwise stated. For the maximum propagation step t, we fix it to 6 due to the "six-degree separation".

(A) Comparisons with Existing Subjective Trust Inference Methods. We first compare the effectiveness of MATRI with several benchmark trust propagation models, including *CertProp* [9], *MoleTrust* [22], *Wang&Singh* [32, 33], and *Guha* [8]. For all these subjective methods, the goal is to infer a pair-wise trustworthiness score (i.e., to what extent the user u trusts another user v).

The result is shown in Fig. 4. We can see that the proposed MATRI significantly outperforms all the other trust inference models wrt both RMSE and MAE on both data sets. For example, on *advogato* data set, our MATRI improves the best existing method (CertProp) by 40.7% in RMSE and by 26.7% in MAE. As for *PGP* data set, the proposed MATRI improves the best existing method (Wang&Singh) by 29.6% in RMSE and by 37.8% in MAE. Overall, the proposed MATRI leads to 26.7% - 40.7% improvement over these best known competitors in prediction accuracy. The results suggest that multi-aspect of trust indeed plays a very important role in the inference process.

(B) Performance Gain Analysis of MATRI. Let us take a close look at where the performance gain of the proposed MATRI comes from. Recall that in the proposed MATRI, we aim to integrate the three important properties of trust, that is, *multi-aspect*, *trust bias* and *trust propagation*. We next analyze how each of these properties improves the trust inference accuracy. The result is shown in Table 3. In Table 3, 'Basic form' only considers multi-aspect of trust by setting the coefficients for trust bias as well as those for trust propagation as 0; 'Basic form + propagation' ignores the trust bias; 'Basic form + bias' ignores the trust propagation; and MATRI is the proposed method that integrates all three properties. We also show the result of the best known competitors, i.e., CertProp for *advogato* and Wang&Singh for *PGP*, in the table for comparison.

As we can see from Table 3, the performance of 'Basic form' which only considers the multi-aspect property is already close to the best known competitors. When trust propagation and trust bias

Table 4: Comparisons with *SVD*, *HCD* [10], and *KBV* [14]. Smaller is better. MATRI performs best.

RMSE/MAE	advogato	PGP
SVD	0.629 / 0.579	0.447 / 0.306
HCD	0.269 / 0.219	0.314 / 0.216
KBV	0.179 / 0.125	0.217 / 0.133
MATRI	0.159 / 0.113	0.181 / 0.105

Table 5: Comparisons with *EigenTrust*. Smaller is better. MATRI is better than EigenTrust wrt both RMSE and MAE on both data sets.

RMSE/MAE	advogato	PGP
EigenTrust	0.700 / 0.653	0.519 / 0.371
MATRI	0.290 / 0.203	0.349 / 0.280

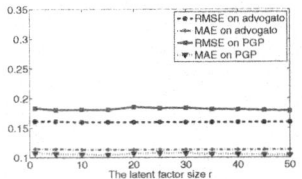
(a) RMSE and MAE of MATRI wrt r. We fix $r = 10$ for both *advogato* and *PGP*.

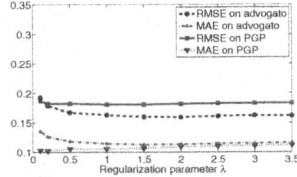
(b) RMSE and MAE of MATRI wrt λ. We fix $\lambda = 0.1$ for *advogato* and $\lambda = 1.0$ for *PGP*.

Figure 5: The sensitivity evaluations. MATRI is robust wrt both parameters.

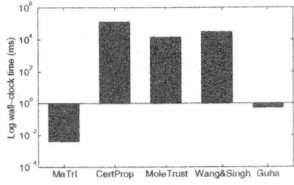
(a) Wall-clock time on *advogato* data set

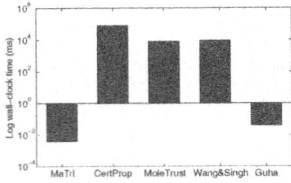
(b) Wall-clock time on *PGP* data set

Figure 6: Speed comparison. MATRI is much faster than all the other methods.

are incorporated, both of them significantly improve trust inference accuracy. For example, on *advogato* data set, trust propagation helps to obtain 32.0% and 36.1% improvements in RMSE and MAE, respectively. Further, trust bias improves RMSE and MAE by 8.6% and 8.9%, respectively. This result confirms our hypothesis that in addition to multi-aspect, both trust propagation and trust bias also play important roles in trust inference.

(C) Comparisons with Existing Matrix Factorization Methods. We also compare MATRI with some existing matrix factorization methods: *SVD*, the low rank approximation algorithm [10] for link sign prediction (referred to as *HCD*), and the collaborative filtering algorithm [14] for recommender systems (referred to as *KBV*).

The result is shown in Table 4. As we can see from the table, MATRI again performs best on both data sets. *SVD* performs poorly as it treats all the unobserved trustor-trustee pairs as zero elements in the trust matrix **T**. MATRI outperforms *HCD* as *HCD* was essentially tailored to predict the *binary* trust/distrust relationship and it ignored the other two important properties (i.e., trust bias and trust propagation). MATRI also outperforms *KBV*. For example, MATRI improves *KBV* by 11.5% in RMSE and by 16.5% in MAE on *PGP* data set. As mentioned before, *KBV* can be viewed as a special case of the proposed MATRI if we (1) fix all the bias coefficients as 1s and (2) ignore the trust propagation. This result indicates that by (1) incorporating the trust propagation and (2) simultaneously learning the relative weights of propagation and trust bias, MATRI leads to further performance improvement.

(D) Sensitivity Evaluations. We also conduct a parametric study for MATRI. The first parameter is the latent factor size r. We can observe from Fig. 5(a) that, in general, both RMSE and MAE stay stable wrt r. The second parameter in MATRI is the regularization coefficient λ. As we can see from Fig. 5(b), both RMSE and MAE stay stable on *advogato*, while they decrease when λ increases up to 1.0 and stay stable after $\lambda > 1.0$ on *PGP*. Based on these results, we conclude that MATRI is robust wrt its parameters. For all the other results we report in the paper, we simply fix $r = 10$, $\lambda = 0.1$ for *advogato*, and $\lambda = 1.0$ for *PGP*.

(E) Comparisons with Existing Objective Trust Inference Methods. Although our MATRI is a subjective trust inference metric, as a side product, it can also be used to infer an objective trustworthiness score for each trustee. To this end, we set $r = 1$ in MATRI algorithm, ignore the trust propagation vectors $\mathbf{z}_{ij}$, and aggregate the resulting trustee matrix/vector $\mathbf{G}_0$ with the bias (the global bias μ and the trustee bias **y**). We compare the result with a widely-cited objective trust inference model *EigenTrust* [12] in Table 5. As we can see, MATRI outperforms EigenTrust in terms of both RMSE and MAE on both data sets. For example, on *advogato* data set, MATRI is 58.6% and 68.9% better than EigenTrust wrt RMSE and MAE, respectively.

5.3 Efficiency Results

For efficiency experiments, we report the average wall-clock time. All the experiments were run on a machine with two 2.4GHz Intel Cores and 4GB memory.

(A) Speed Comparison. We first compare the on-line response of MATRI with *CertProp*, *MoleTrust*, *Wang&Singh*, and *Guha*. Again, we use the *advogato-6* snapshot and *PGP* in this experiment, and the result is shown in Fig. 6. Notice that the y-axis is in the logarithmic scale.

We can see from the figure that the proposed MATRI is much faster than all the alternative methods on both data sets. For example, MATRI is up to 32,000,000x faster than CertProp. This is because once we have inferred the trustor/truestee matrices as well as the coefficients for the bias and propagation, it only takes *constant* time for MATRI to output the trustworthiness score. Among all the alternative methods, Guha is the most efficient. This is because its main workload can also be completed in advance. However, the pre-computation of Guha needs additional $O(n^2)$ space as the model fills nearly all the missing elements in the trust matrix, making it unsuitable for large data sets. In contrast, our MATRI only requires $O(|\mathcal{K}| + n)$ space.

(B) Scalability. Finally, we present the scalability result of MATRI by reporting the wall-clock time of the pre-computational stage (i.e., Step 1-13 in Alg. 3). For *advogato* data set, we directly report the results on all the six snapshots (i.e., *advogato-1*, ..., *advogato-6*). For *PGP*, we use its subsets to study the scalability. The result is shown in Fig. 7, which is consistent with the complexity analysis in Section 4.2. As we can see from the figure, MATRI scales linearly wrt to both n and $|\mathcal{K}|$, indicating that it is suitable for large-scale applications.

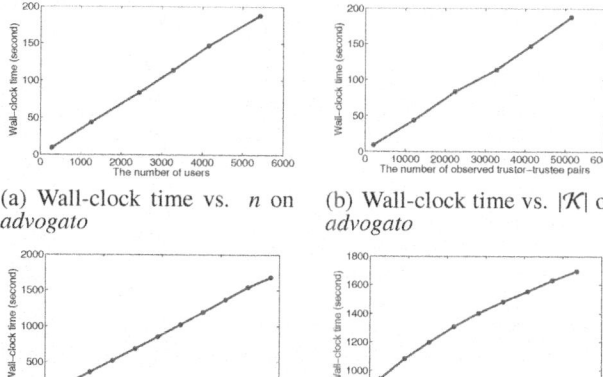

(a) Wall-clock time vs. n on *advogato*

(b) Wall-clock time vs. $|\mathcal{K}|$ on *advogato*

(c) Wall-clock time vs. n on PGP

(d) Wall-clock time vs. $|\mathcal{K}|$ on PGP

Figure 7: Scalability of the proposed MaTrI. MaTrI scales linearly wrt the data size (n and $|\mathcal{K}|$).

6. RELATED WORK

In this section, we briefly review related work, including trust propagation models, multi-aspect trust inference models, etc.

Trust Propagation Models. To date, a large body of trust inference models are based on trust propagation where trust is propagated along connected users in the trust network, i.e., the web of locally-generated trust ratings. Based on the interpretation of trust propagation, we further categorize these models into two classes: *path interpretation* and *component interpretation*.

In the first category of path interpretation, trust is propagated along a path from the trustor to the trustee, and the propagated trust from multiple paths can be combined to form a final trustworthiness score. For example, Wang et al. [32, 33] as well as Hang et al. [9] propose operators to concatenate trust along a path and aggregate trust from multiple paths. Liu et al. [18] argue that not only trust values but social relationships and recommendation role are important for trust inference. In contrast, there is no explicit concept of paths in the second category of component interpretation. Instead, trust is treated as random walks on a graph or on a Markov chain [25]. Examples of this category include [8, 22, 39, 15].

The proposed MaTrI integrates the trust propagation with two other important properties, i.e., the multi-aspect of trust and trust bias. In addition, our multi-aspect model offers a natural way to speed up on-line query response; as well as to mitigate the sparsity or coverage problem in trust inference where some trustor and trustee might not be connected with each other - both are known limitations with the current trust propagation models [37, 20].

Multi-Aspect Trust Inference Models. Social scientists have explored the multi-aspect property of trust for several years [27]. In computer science, there also exist a few trust inference models that *explicitly* explore the multi-aspect property of trust. For example, Xiong and Liu [36] model the value of the transaction in trust inference; Wang and Wu [31] take competence and honesty into consideration; Tang et al. [28] model aspect as a set of products that are similar to each other under product review sites; Sabater and Sierra [26] divide trust in e-commerce environment into three aspects: price, delivering time, and quality.

However, all these existing multi-aspect trust inference methods require some additional side information other than the locally-generated trust ratings, such as the value of transaction, user's preference, product categories, etc. These methods become infeasible when such side information is not available. In contrast, MaTrI directly characterizes the multi-aspect of trust solely based on the locally-generated trust ratings; and therefore it has a broader applicability.

Prior Knowledge in Trust Inference. In sociology, it was discovered a long time ago that certain prior knowledge, e.g., *trust bias*, is an integral part in the final trust decision [30]. Nonetheless, this important aspect has been largely ignored in most of the existing trust inference models. One exception is the work by Nguyen et al. [24], which learns the importance of several trust bias related features derived from a social trust framework. Recently, Mishra et al. [23] propose an iterative algorithm to compute trust bias. Different from these existing works, our focus is to incorporate various types of trust bias as specified factors/aspects to increase the accuracy of trust inference.

Collaborative Filtering vs. Trust Inference. Multi-aspect or low rank approximation methods have been extensively studied in collaborative filtering [1, 14, 21]. These work provides rich methodologies to capture the multi-aspect of trust by viewing the trust inference as a collaborative filtering problem. The proposed MaTrI takes one step further by (1) incorporating trust bias and trust propagation; and (2) learning their relative weights.

On the application side, the goal of collaborative filtering is to predict users' flavors of items. It is interesting to point out that (1) on one hand, trust between users could help to predict the flavors as we may give a higher weight to the recommendations provided by trusted users; (2) on the other hand, trust itself might be affected by the similarity of flavors since users usually trust others with a similar taste [7]. Although out of the scope of this paper, using recommendation to further improve trust inference accuracy might be an interesting topic for future work.

Other Related Work. The concept of stereotype for trust inference is studied by Liu et al. [20] and Burnett et al. [3]. These methods learn the stereotypes from the user profiles of the trustees that the trustor has interacted with, and then use these stereotypes to reflect the trustor's first impression about unknown trustees. Several other work focuses on trust dynamics [29] and the relationship between trust and similarity [7, 35]. There are also some recent work on using link prediction approaches to predict the *binary* trust/distrust relationship [16, 5, 10].

7. CONCLUSION

In this paper, we have proposed an effective trust inference model (MaTrI). The basic idea is to leverage the multi-aspect property of trust by characterizing several aspects/factors for each trustor and trustee based on the existing trust relationships. The proposed MaTrI incorporates the trust propagation and prior knowledge (i.e., trust bias); and further learns their relative weights. By integrating all these important properties, our experimental evaluations on real benchmark data sets show that it leads to significant improvement in prediction accuracy. The proposed MaTrI is also nimble - it is up to 7 orders of magnitude faster than the existing methods in the on-line query response, and in the meanwhile it enjoys the linear scalability for the pre-computational stage in both time and space. Future work includes investigating the capability of MaTrI to address the distrust as well as the trust dynamics.

8. ACKNOWLEDGMENTS

We would like to thank the valuable suggestions from Jiliang Tang as well as the anonymous reviewers. This work is supported by the National Natural Science Foundation of China (No. 61021062,

61073030, 61100037), the National 863 Program of China (No. 2012AA011205), and the National 973 Program of China (No. 2009CB320702). It is partly supported by the Army Research Laboratory under Cooperative Agreement Number W911NF-09-2-0053, the U.S. Defense Advanced Research Projects Agency (DARPA) under Agreement Number W911NF-12-C-0028, and the National Science Foundation under Grant No. IIS-1017415.

9. REFERENCES

[1] R. Bell, Y. Koren, and C. Volinsky. Modeling relationships at multiple scales to improve accuracy of large recommender systems. In *KDD*, pages 95–104. ACM, 2007.

[2] A. Buchanan and A. Fitzgibbon. Damped newton algorithms for matrix factorization with missing data. In *CVPR*, volume 2, pages 316–322, 2005.

[3] C. Burnett, T. Norman, and K. Sycara. Bootstrapping trust evaluations through stereotypes. In *AAMAS*, pages 241–248, 2010.

[4] D. Cartwright and F. Harary. Structural balance: a generalization of heider's theory. *Psychological Review*, 63(5):277–293, 1956.

[5] K. Chiang, N. Natarajan, A. Tewari, and I. Dhillon. Exploiting longer cycles for link prediction in signed networks. In *CIKM*, pages 1157–1162, 2011.

[6] D. Gefen. Reflections on the dimensions of trust and trustworthiness among online consumers. *ACM SIGMIS Database*, 33(3):38–53, 2002.

[7] J. Golbeck. Trust and nuanced profile similarity in online social networks. *ACM Transactions on the Web*, 3(4):12, 2009.

[8] R. Guha, R. Kumar, P. Raghavan, and A. Tomkins. Propagation of trust and distrust. In *WWW*, pages 403–412. ACM, 2004.

[9] C.-W. Hang, Y. Wang, and M. P. Singh. Operators for propagating trust and their evaluation in social networks. In *AAMAS*, pages 1025–1032, 2009.

[10] C. Hsieh, K. Chiang, and I. Dhillon. Low rank modeling of signed networks. In *KDD*, pages 507–515. ACM, 2012.

[11] A. Jøsang and R. Ismail. The Beta reputation system. In *Proc. of the 15th Bled Electronic Commerce Conference*, volume 160, Bled, Slovenia, June 2002.

[12] S. D. Kamvar, M. T. Schlosser, and H. Garcia-Molina. The Eigentrust algorithm for reputation management in p2p networks. In *WWW*, pages 640–651. ACM, 2003.

[13] Y. Koren. Factorization meets the neighborhood: a multifaceted collaborative filtering model. In *KDD*, pages 426–434. ACM, 2008.

[14] Y. Koren, R. Bell, and C. Volinsky. Matrix factorization techniques for recommender systems. *Computer*, 42(8):30–37, 2009.

[15] U. Kuter and J. Golbeck. Sunny: A new algorithm for trust inference in social networks using probabilistic confidence models. In *AAAI*, pages 1377–1382, 2007.

[16] J. Leskovec, D. Huttenlocher, and J. Kleinberg. Predicting positive and negative links in online social networks. In *WWW*, pages 641–650. ACM, 2010.

[17] J. Leskovec, J. Kleinberg, and C. Faloutsos. Graphs over time: densification laws, shrinking diameters and possible explanations. In *KDD*, pages 177–187. ACM, 2005.

[18] G. Liu, Y. Wang, and M. Orgun. Optimal social trust path selection in complex social networks. In *AAAI*, pages 1391–1398, 2010.

[19] G. Liu, Y. Wang, and M. Orgun. Trust transitivity in complex social networks. In *AAAI*, pages 1222–1229, 2011.

[20] X. Liu, A. Datta, K. Rzadca, and E. Lim. Stereotrust: a group based personalized trust model. In *CIKM*, pages 7–16. ACM, 2009.

[21] H. Ma, M. Lyu, and I. King. Learning to recommend with trust and distrust relationships. In *RecSys*, pages 189–196. ACM, 2009.

[22] P. Massa and P. Avesani. Controversial users demand local trust metrics: An experimental study on epinions. com community. In *AAAI*, pages 121–126, 2005.

[23] A. Mishra and A. Bhattacharya. Finding the bias and prestige of nodes in networks based on trust scores. In *WWW*, pages 567–576. ACM, 2011.

[24] V. Nguyen, E. Lim, J. Jiang, and A. Sun. To trust or not to trust? predicting online trusts using trust antecedent framework. In *ICDM*, pages 896–901. IEEE, 2009.

[25] M. Richardson, R. Agrawal, and P. Domingos. Trust management for the Semantic Web. In *ISWC*, pages 351–368. Springer, 2003.

[26] J. Sabater and C. Sierra. Reputation and social network analysis in multi-agent systems. In *AAMAS*, pages 475–482. ACM, 2002.

[27] D. Sirdeshmukh, J. Singh, and B. Sabol. Consumer trust, value, and loyalty in relational exchanges. *The Journal of Marketing*, pages 15–37, 2002.

[28] J. Tang, H. Gao, and H. Liu. mTrust: discerning multi-faceted trust in a connected world. In *WSDM*, pages 93–102. ACM, 2012.

[29] J. Tang, H. Liu, H. Gao, and A. Das Sarmas. etrust: understanding trust evolution in an online world. In *KDD*, pages 253–261. ACM, 2012.

[30] A. Tversky and D. Kahneman. Judgment under uncertainty: Heuristics and biases. *science*, 185(4157):1124–1131, 1974.

[31] G. Wang and J. Wu. Multi-dimensional evidence-based trust management with multi-trusted paths. *Future Generation Computer Systems*, 27(5):529–538, 2011.

[32] Y. Wang and M. P. Singh. Trust representation and aggregation in a distributed agent system. In *AAAI*, pages 1425–1430, 2006.

[33] Y. Wang and M. P. Singh. Formal trust model for multiagent systems. In *IJCAI*, pages 1551–1556, 2007.

[34] D. Watts and S. Strogatz. Collective dynamics of 'small-world' networks. *Nature*, 393(6684):440–442, 1998.

[35] R. Xiang, J. Neville, and M. Rogati. Modeling relationship strength in online social networks. In *WWW*, pages 981–990. ACM, 2010.

[36] L. Xiong and L. Liu. Peertrust: Supporting reputation-based trust for peer-to-peer electronic communities. *IEEE Transactions on Knowledge and Data Engineering*, 16(7):843–857, 2004.

[37] Y. Yao, H. Tong, F. Xu, and J. Lu. Subgraph extraction for trust inference in social networks. In *ASONAM*, pages 163–170, 2012.

[38] Y. Yao, H. Tong, X. Yan, F. Xu, and J. Lu. Matrust: An effective multi-aspect trust inference model. *arXiv preprint arXiv:1211.2041*, 2012.

[39] C. Ziegler and G. Lausen. Propagation models for trust and distrust in social networks. *Information Systems Frontiers*, 7(4):337–358, 2005.

Predicting Positive and Negative Links in Signed Social Networks by Transfer Learning

Jihang Ye   Hong Cheng   Zhe Zhu   Minghua Chen
The Chinese University of Hong Kong
{yjh010, zzhu}@alumni.ie.cuhk.edu.hk, hcheng@se.cuhk.edu.hk,
minghua@ie.cuhk.edu.hk

ABSTRACT

Different from a large body of research on social networks that has focused almost exclusively on positive relationships, we study signed social networks with both positive and negative links. Specifically, we focus on how to reliably and effectively predict the signs of links in a newly formed signed social network (called a *target network*). Since usually only a very small amount of edge sign information is available in such newly formed networks, this small quantity is not adequate to train a good classifier. To address this challenge, we need assistance from an existing, mature signed network (called a *source network*) which has abundant edge sign information. We adopt the transfer learning approach to leverage the edge sign information from the source network, which may have a different yet related joint distribution of the edge instances and their class labels.

As there is no predefined feature vector for the edge instances in a signed network, we construct generalizable features that can transfer the topological knowledge from the source network to the target. With the extracted features, we adopt an AdaBoost-like transfer learning algorithm with instance weighting to utilize more useful training instances in the source network for model learning. Experimental results on three real large signed social networks demonstrate that our transfer learning algorithm can improve the prediction accuracy by 40% over baseline methods.

Categories and Subject Descriptors

H.2.8 [**Database Management**]: Database Applications—*Data mining*

Keywords

Signed Social Network; Sign Prediction; Transfer Learning

1. INTRODUCTION

Online social networks such as Facebook, Twitter and LinkedIn have been gaining increasing popularity in recent years. People usually form links to indicate *friend* or *follow* relationships. But in some other social networks people can form both positive and negative links. Positive links express trust, like or approval attitudes, whereas negative links indicate distrust, dislike or disapproval attitudes. For a given directed link from user u to v in a social network,

Copyright is held by the International World Wide Web Conference Committee (IW3C2). IW3C2 reserves the right to provide a hyperlink to the author's site if the Material is used in electronic media.
WWW 2013, May 13–17, 2013, Rio de Janeiro, Brazil.
ACM 978-1-4503-2035-1/13/05.

we define its *sign* to be positive (or negative) if it expresses a positive (or negative) attitude from u to v. We call such networks with both positive and negative links *signed social networks*. Examples include Epinions[1] whose users can express trust or distrust of others [18], Slashdot[2] whose participants can declare others to be either "friends" or "foes" [11], and Wikipedia[3] whose users can vote for or against the promotion of others to administrator status [2].

In some signed social networks, the attitude of a link can be easily determined based on user rating score, i.e., positive or negative. But in some other cases such as in online forums or BBS, the existence of interactions (i.e., links) between two users can be easily observed while the specific semantic attitudes of these links are not explicitly labeled, since they are usually expressed implicitly by user reviews or comments. As a more general case, hyperlinks between webpages can also indicate agreement or disagreement with the target of the link, but the lack of explicit labels makes it very difficult to determine the attitude over these hyperlinks [20]. Manually analyzing and labeling the signs of links will be very expensive and inefficient. A promising solution is to train a classifier for link sign prediction in the signed networks. However for some signed social networks, especially the newly formed ones, the paucity of available signs makes it difficult to train a good classifier to predict unknown link signs. How to reliably and efficiently predict the signs of links in signed social networks is an important and challenging problem.

Previous research [15] has shown that, the structural information is a powerful and reliable source for the purpose of link prediction in unsigned networks, when applied in a traditional machine learning framework. Some examples of such structural information include the number of common neighbors, or other local neighborhood statistics. As for the signed social networks, a recent work by Leskovec et al. [14] studies the *edge sign prediction problem* using the signed triad features and a logistic regression model. While its major contribution is the connections to theories of balance and status in social psychology, the prediction model makes a very strong assumption on the input network: *the signs of all links except the one to be predicted are known in advance.* This is not very practical in reality as it is very expensive to obtain the signs of all links except one in a large network, especially for newly formed networks.

Thus, in this work we study the edge sign prediction prob-

---
[1] www.epinions.com
[2] slashdot.org
[3] www.wikipedia.org

lem with a more realistic setting as follows. Given a directed signed network, we are interested in predicting the signs of edges whose signs are unknown. We call this network a *target network*. We assume there is a very small amount of edge sign information in the target network as the training data, but the quantity is inadequate to train a good classifier. This assumption holds for many newly formed and fast evolving networks. Thus we consider to leverage another more mature signed social network, called a *source network*, which has abundant edge sign information. The source network may have a different joint distribution of the edge instances and the class labels from the target network, perhaps because the source network is out-dated or is from a different application. But the source network is not completely useless. There still exists a certain degree of similarity, e.g., similar degree distributions and diameters, or common properties, e.g., structural balance and social status [14], between the source and target networks. For example, according to the structural balance theory, many signed networks follow a common principle that "the friend of my friend is my friend" and "the enemy of my friend is my enemy". Thus our task is to leverage the sign information in both the source and target networks to train a good classifier. This approach is known as *transfer learning* [19, 1, 21].

While most existing transfer learning works focus on transactional data [1], image [21] and text [22], in which the data instances are represented in a predefined d-dimensional feature space, a unique challenge in our transfer learning problem across two signed social networks is that there is no predefined feature vector for the edge instances in the networks. Therefore, the first step is to investigate how to construct generalizable features that can transfer knowledge from the source network to the target for edge sign prediction. Specifically, we propose two types of features, i.e., *explicit topological features* which express the manifest properties of edge instances such as degree and triads, and *latent topological features* which capture the common patterns between the source and target networks for knowledge transfer.

With the extracted features, a straightforward solution is to simply combine the source and target training instances and treat them equally to learn a model. However, due to the distributional difference between the two networks, some training instances in the source network are very different from the target network, thus may cause test edges in the target network to be wrongly predicted and degrade the performance. Therefore, we adopt a transfer learning algorithm with instance weighting similar to [3]. This algorithm borrows the AdaBoost learning idea which assigns and iteratively adjusts the weight of each training instance in the source and target networks. This instance weighting mechanism can effectively distinguish the more useful edge instances from the less useful ones in the source network and attach more importance to the former.

Our main contributions are summarized as follows.

- We formulate the problem of edge sign prediction in a signed social network which may have only a very small amount of labeled training instances. We consider to exploit another network, called source network, which has abundant labeled instances. The source and target networks may have different yet related joint distributions. Our task is to leverage the source network instances for feature construction and model learning. To the best of our knowledge, this is the first work on transfer learning across large signed social networks.

- We design the latent topological features which can capture the common structural patterns between the source and target networks, thus are generalizable features across domains. The latent features are obtained by nonnegative matrix tri-factorization [4].

- We adopt an AdaBoost-like transfer learning algorithm with instance weighting to distinguish the more useful training instances from the less useful ones in the source network.

- We conducted extensive experiments on three real large signed networks and demonstrated that our transfer learning algorithm can improve the prediction accuracy by 40% over baseline schemes.

The rest of our paper is organized as follows. We introduce related work in Section 2 and give the problem definition in Section 3. We describe our proposed features for the edge sign prediction problem in Section 4. In Section 5 we propose an AdaBoost-like learning algorithm with instance weighting in the transfer learning framework. Experimental results are presented in Section 6 to show the effectiveness of our features and transfer learning algorithm. Finally, we conclude our work in Section 7.

2. RELATED WORK

In this section we first introduce related studies on signed social networks, and then the state-of-the-art transfer learning research.

Signed social networks have attracted more and more attention since Guha et al. proposed their leading work on trust propagation in signed social networks [6]. Kunegis et al. did spectral analysis on signed networks [11, 12]. They revealed fundamental characteristics of signed networks by evaluating various measures in [11]. They also studied signed spectral clustering methods, signed graph kernels and network visualization methods in signed graphs [12].

For the edge sign prediction problem in signed graphs, existing studies can be categorized into two major approaches: a *matrix kernel* approach [11] and a *machine learning* approach [14]. Kunegis et al. exploited the property of multiplicative transitivity in signed graphs to realize edge sign prediction and their method utilized the node adjacency information only. Leskovec et al. used signed triads as features and constructed a logistic regression model for prediction [14]. While its major contribution is the connections to theories of balance and status in social psychology, the prediction model makes a very strong assumption on the input network: the signs of all links except the one to be predicted are known in advance, which is not very practical in reality.

Transfer learning [19] has been an important research topic and a useful technique in practice. Transfer learning can effectively transfer the information from the source domain to facilitate a different target domain's learning task, where the labeled data in the target domain is very limited [1, 16]. Most existing transfer learning works focus on transactional data [1], image [21] and text [22], in which data instances are represented in a predefined d-dimensional feature space. They typically map data instances from different origins into the same latent domain [21] with sparse coding or other dimension transformation techniques. Some transfer learning methods also use bipartite or tripartite graph as tools to facilitate knowledge transfer [7, 8] by mapping the instances and features to bipartite or tripartite graph nodes. To the best of our knowledge, our work is the first one on transferring topological knowledge across large signed social networks. Specifically, we transfer the knowledge of a source network to the target network for both feature construction and model learning, which have been shown to be very effective.

3. PROBLEM FORMULATION

Let a directed graph $G_t = (V_t, E_t^l, E_t^u, S)$ be the *target graph* for edge sign prediction. Here V_t denotes the set of vertices, E_t^l denotes the set of directed edges with edge sign labels, $S : E_t^l \mapsto \{-1, +1\}$ is the edge sign mapping function that maps an edge $e \in E_t^l$ to a positive label (+1) or a negative label (−1), and E_t^u denotes the set of directed edges whose signs are unknown and need to be predicted. We treat the labeled edges E_t^l as the training data which is an independent and identically distributed (i.i.d.) sample drawn from the target graph. Thus E_t^l has the same distribution as the test edge set E_t^u. However, in many scenarios the quantity of the training edges is inadequate to train a good classifier.

Assume that we have another directed graph $G_s = (V_s, E_s, S)$, called the *source graph*, where V_s denotes the set of vertices, E_s denotes the set of directed edges, and $S : E_s \mapsto \{-1, +1\}$ is the edge sign mapping function that maps an edge $e \in E_s$ to a positive or negative label. The labeled edges E_s are assumed to be abundant, but the distribution of E_s may differ from that of the test edge set in the target graph G_t, perhaps because G_s is out-dated, or is from a different domain. When a classifier trained on E_s is applied to the test edge set E_t^u from G_t, the performance of the classifier may substantially degrade.

However, the labeled edges E_s from the source graph G_s is not entirely useless, because there may still exist a certain degree of similarity or common properties between the source graph G_s and the target graph G_t. Considering the inadequate labeled edges E_t^l from G_t, it is important and beneficial to leverage the labeled edges E_s from G_s to help train a classifier to predict the edge signs of E_t^u in G_t.

Formally, let $T = T_s \cup T_t$ denote the training edge set. $T_s = \{(e_s, S(e_s))\}, \forall e_s \in E_s$, and $T_t = \{(e_t, S(e_t))\}, \forall e_t \in E_t^l$. We denote $|T_s| = n$ and $|T_t| = m$. E_t^u is the unlabeled test edge set. The objective is to learn a classifier $P : E_s \cup E_t^l \mapsto \{-1, +1\}$ that minimizes the prediction error on the test edge set E_t^u.

In the following, we will first study *feature construction* to create useful topological features that are generalizable from the source graph G_s to the target G_t. Then we will study *model learning* that uses an AdaBoost-like method to weigh the training edges from the source graph and the target graph differently, for the transfer learning purpose.

4. FEATURE CONSTRUCTION

In this section, we study how to construct useful features for edge sign prediction. Different from many traditional machine learning or transfer learning problems in which instances are represented in a *predefined* feature vector, there is no predefined feature vector for the edge instances in a signed social network. Therefore the problem is how to construct topological features for the edge instances that are generalizable from the source graph G_s to the target graph G_t. In this work, we propose to create a collection of features from two categories: (1) *explicit topological features* which express manifest properties of the edge instances in the source or target graph; and (2) *latent topological features* which are hidden but express the common patterns between the source graph and the target graph. Such latent topological features are generalizable across domains in principle.

4.1 Explicit Topological Features

For a directed edge $e = (u, v)$, we begin by defining a number of explicit topological features including node degree, betweenness centrality, triad count and edge embeddedness. These features express the connectivity pattern of the edge e and its two end nodes u and v. It is noteworthy that we *do not* include any edge sign information in the features, because we only have a very small amount of edge signs in the target graph G_t. When predicting the sign of an edge $e \in E_t^u$, it is practically infeasible to use the signs of edges in the local neighborhood of e as features, as those signs can be unknown.

Node Degree. For a directed edge $e = (u, v)$, we use $deg_{out}(u)$ and $deg_{in}(v)$ to denote the number of outgoing edges from u and incoming edges to v, respectively. The node degree measures the aggregate connection strength of a node to the rest of a graph.

Betweenness Centrality. Betweenness centrality measures a node's centrality in a graph. For a node $v \in V$, the betweenness centrality $f_{bc}(v)$ is defined as

$$f_{bc}(v) = \sum_{i \neq v \neq j} \frac{\sigma_{i,j}(v)}{\sigma_{i,j}} \quad (1)$$

where $\sigma_{i,j}$ is the number of shortest paths from node i to j and $\sigma_{i,j}(v)$ is the number of shortest paths from node i to j through node v. Here all possible node pairs $i, j \in V$ such that $i \neq v \neq j$ are considered. For a directed edge $e = (u, v)$, we use $f_{bc}(u)$ and $f_{bc}(v)$ as two betweenness centrality features.

Triad Count. Following [14], we also use the triad counts as features. For a directed edge $e = (u, v)$, we consider each triad involving the edge (u, v), consisting of a node w such that w has an edge either to or from u and also an edge either to or from v. Considering that the edge between u (or v) and w can be in either direction, there are $2 \times 2 = 4$ types of triads. For an edge between u and w, we call it a *forward edge* (F) if it points from u to w, or a *backward edge* (B) otherwise. Similarly, for an edge between v and w, we call it a *forward edge* if it points from w to v, or a *backward edge* otherwise. Figure 1 shows the four types of triads involving (u, v). We use four features f_{FF}, f_{FB}, f_{BF} and f_{BB} to record the number of triads of each type that the edge (u, v) is involved in.

Edge Embeddedness. For a directed edge $e = (u, v)$, the edge embeddedness [14] $f_{eb}(e)$ is defined as the number of common neighbors of nodes u and v. $f_{eb}(e)$ is also used as one topological feature.

4.2 Latent Topological Feature

The above explicit topological features, though very intuitive, may not be generalizable from the source graph G_s to the target graph G_t, especially when G_s and G_t have dif-

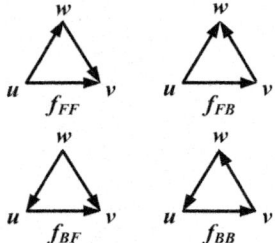

Figure 1: Four Types of Triads

ferent distributions. To better leverage the labeled edges in the source graph, we propose to construct *latent topological features* which can capture the common patterns between G_s and G_t, and thus are generalizable features. Again, it is worth noting that only a very small amount of edge signs are available in the target graph G_t, so it is not practical to include the edge signs in the latent topological features. Therefore, we only use the connectivity information of both graphs without edge signs to construct the latent features.

Specifically, denote the source graph without edge signs as $\overline{G}_s = (V_s, E_s)$ with $|V_s| = M$. Let $A_s \in \{0,1\}^{M \times M}$ denote the $M \times M$ adjacency matrix of $\overline{G}_s$. For a pair of vertices u, v, $A_{s(u,v)} = 1$ iff $(u,v) \in E_s$, and $A_{s(u,v)} = 0$ otherwise. A_s is asymmetric since $\overline{G}_s$ is a directed graph. Similarly, let $A_t \in \{0,1\}^{N \times N}$ denote the $N \times N$ adjacency matrix of the unsigned target graph $\overline{G}_t$ where $|V_t| = N$.

Given A_s and A_t, we propose to use *Nonnegative Matrix Tri-Factorization* (**NMTF**) [4], which originates from Nonnegative Matrix Factorization (**NMF**) [13] and has been widely applied and extended in machine learning [4, 17], to construct latent topological features through factorizing A_s and A_t under the same space. The latent feature space can capture the principal common factors of the original link structures in both G_s and G_t. We formulate the problem of finding the latent feature space as follows:

$$\begin{aligned}
\min \mathcal{J} &= \|A_s - U_s \Sigma_k V_s^T\|_F^2 + \|A_t - U_t \Sigma_k V_t^T\|_F^2 \\
&\quad + \alpha \|\Sigma_k\|_F^2, \\
\text{s.t.} \quad & \sum_{j=1}^k U_{s(\cdot j)} = 1, \quad \sum_{j=1}^k V_{s(\cdot j)} = 1, \\
& \sum_{j=1}^k U_{t(\cdot j)} = 1, \quad \sum_{j=1}^k V_{t(\cdot j)} = 1, \\
& U_s, V_s \in \mathbb{R}_+^{M \times k}, \; U_t, V_t \in \mathbb{R}_+^{N \times k}
\end{aligned} \quad (2)$$

where $\|\cdot\|_F$ is the Frobenius norm. In this formulation, we consider the nonnegative matrix tri-factor decomposition $A_s \approx U_s \Sigma_k V_s^T$ and $A_t \approx U_t \Sigma_k V_t^T$. Matrix $\Sigma_k \in \mathbb{R}_+^{k \times k}$ is the common latent space for both graphs, which ensures that the extracted topological features of both graphs are expressed in the same space. U_s, V_s, U_t, and V_t are four latent topological feature matrices. The ith row of matrix U_s represents the outgoing linkage features of a source graph node i ($i \in V_s$) in the latent space, while the ith row of matrix V_s represents the incoming linkage features of node i in the latent space. Similar interpretations can be derived for matrices U_t and V_t in the target graph G_t. α is the trade-off regularization parameter to weigh the term $\|\Sigma_k\|_F^2$. Since all of our variables are nonnegative, excessively large values in Σ_k will make many entries in U_s, U_t, V_s and V_t approach 0.

As a result, this will cause each node to have nearly indistinguishable latent topological features. Thus it is necessary to constraint the values in Σ_k through a regularization term. In addition, we enforce the constraints that each row in the topological feature matrices is positive and normalized.

By solving the joint NMTF problem in Eq. 2, we obtain four feature matrices U_s, V_s, U_t and V_t for expressing the latent topological (both outgoing and incoming) features for nodes in G_s and G_t in terms of the same latent space Σ_k.

4.2.1 Optimization Algorithm

We develop an iterative update algorithm to minimize $\mathcal{J}$ in Eq. 2. Specifically, we optimize the objective function in Eq. 2 by updating one variable while fixing the other variables. We can rewrite the objective function in Eq. 2 as follows.

$$\begin{aligned}
\mathcal{J} &= \mathbf{tr}(A_s^T A_s - 2 A_s^T U_s \Sigma_k V_s^T + V_s \Sigma_k^T U_s^T U_s \Sigma_k V_s^T) \\
&\quad + \mathbf{tr}(A_t^T A_t - 2 A_t^T U_t \Sigma_k V_t^T + V_t \Sigma_k^T U_t^T U_t \Sigma_k V_t^T) \\
&\quad + \alpha \mathbf{tr}(\Sigma_k^T \Sigma_k)
\end{aligned} \quad (3)$$

Update Rule of U_s: Since we have the constraint $U_s \geq 0$, following the standard constrained optimization theory, we introduce the Lagrangian multiplier $\mathcal{L}_{U_s} \in \mathbb{R}^{M \times k}$ and minimize the Lagrangian function

$$L(U_s) = \mathcal{J} - \mathbf{tr}(\mathcal{L}_{U_s} U_s) \quad (4)$$

We set $\frac{\partial L(U_s)}{\partial U_s} = 0$. Then considering the KKT condition $\mathcal{L}_{U_s(i,j)} U_{s(i,j)} = 0$, we can get

$$(-2 A_s V_s \Sigma_k^T + 2 U_s \Sigma_k V_s^T V_s \Sigma_k^T)_{(i,j)} U_{s(i,j)} = 0 \quad (5)$$

Based on Eq. 5, following a similar approach as in [13], we have the following multiplicative update rule

$$U_{s(i,j)} \leftarrow U_{s(i,j)} \sqrt{\frac{(A_s V_s \Sigma_k^T)_{(i,j)}}{(U_s \Sigma_k V_s^T V_s \Sigma_k^T)_{(i,j)}}} \quad (6)$$

Update Rules of Other Matrices: Similar to the update rule of U_s, the update rules of V_s, U_t, V_t, and Σ_k are

$$V_{s(i,j)} \leftarrow V_{s(i,j)} \sqrt{\frac{(A_s^T U_s \Sigma_k)_{(i,j)}}{(V_s \Sigma_k^T U_s^T U_s \Sigma_k)_{(i,j)}}} \quad (7)$$

$$U_{t(i,j)} \leftarrow U_{t(i,j)} \sqrt{\frac{(A_t V_t \Sigma_k^T)_{(i,j)}}{(U_t \Sigma_k V_t^T V_t \Sigma_k^T)_{(i,j)}}} \quad (8)$$

$$V_{t(i,j)} \leftarrow V_{t(i,j)} \sqrt{\frac{(A_t^T U_t \Sigma_k)_{(i,j)}}{(V_t \Sigma_k^T U_t^T U_t \Sigma_k)_{(i,j)}}} \quad (9)$$

$$\Sigma_{k(i,j)} \leftarrow \Sigma_{k(i,j)} \sqrt{\frac{(U_s^T A_s V_s + U_t^T A_t V_t)_{(i,j)}}{(U_s^T U_s \Sigma_k V_s^T V_s + U_t^T U_t \Sigma_k V_t^T V_t + \alpha \Sigma_k)_{(i,j)}}} \quad (10)$$

Algorithm 1 is the iterative update algorithm that uses the above multiplicative rules for updating each variable matrix to optimize Eq. 2. The convergence criterion is, the gap between any two consecutive objective function values of Eq. 2 is less than a certain threshold.

4.2.2 Convergence Analysis

We now study the convergence property of Algorithm 1. First, we give the following two lemmas from [13, 4].

Algorithm 1: Iterative Update Algorithm for Eq. 2
Data: [Adjacency Matrices A_s, A_t; Regularizer α]
Result: [Latent feature matrices U_s, V_s, U_t, V_t; Latent space Σ_k]
begin
  Initialize $U_s, V_s, U_t, V_t, \Sigma_k$ following [23]
  while *beyond convergence* **do**
    1. Update U_s according to Eq. 6
    2. Update V_s according to Eq. 7
    3. Update U_t according to Eq. 8
    4. Update V_t according to Eq. 9
    5. Update Σ_k according to Eq. 10
    6. Normalize each row of U_s, V_s, U_t, V_t
end

LEMMA 1. *[13] $Aux(h, h')$ is an auxiliary function for $F(h)$ if the conditions $Aux(h, h') \geq F(h)$, $Aux(h, h) = F(h)$ are satisfied. If Aux is an auxiliary function for F, then F is non-increasing under the update*

$$h^{t+1} = \arg\min_h Aux(h, h^t)$$

where h^t is the value of variable h in the tth iteration.

LEMMA 2. *[4] For any matrices $P \in \mathbb{R}_+^{N \times N}$, $Q \in \mathbb{R}_+^{k \times k}$, $S \in \mathbb{R}_+^{N \times k}$, $S' \in \mathbb{R}_+^{N \times k}$, and P and Q are symmetric, the following inequality holds*

$$\sum_{i,j} \frac{(PS'Q)_{i,j} S_{i,j}^2}{S'_{i,j}} \geq \mathbf{tr}(S^T P S Q) \quad (11)$$

THEOREM 1. *Define $\mathcal{J}(U_s)$ according to Eq. 2 as*

$$\mathcal{J}(U_s) = \mathbf{tr}(-2 A_s^T U_s \Sigma_k V_s^T + V_s \Sigma_k^T U_s^T U_s \Sigma_k V_s^T) \quad (12)$$

then the following function

$$Aux(U_s, U_s') = -2 \sum_{i,j} (A_s V_s \Sigma_k^T)_{(i,j)} U'_{s(i,j)} (1 + \ln \frac{U_{s(i,j)}}{U'_{s(i,j)}})$$
$$+ \sum_{i,j} (U_s' \Sigma_k V_s^T V_s \Sigma_k^T)_{(i,j)} \frac{U_{s(i,j)}^2}{U'_{s(i,j)}} \quad (13)$$

is an auxiliary function for $\mathcal{J}(U_s)$. Furthermore, $Aux(U_s, U_s')$ is convex for U_s and its global minimum can be achieved at

$$U_{s(i,j)} = U'_{s(i,j)} \sqrt{\frac{(A_s V_s \Sigma_k^T)_{(i,j)}}{(U_s' \Sigma_k V_s^T V_s \Sigma_k^T)_{(i,j)}}} \quad (14)$$

PROOF. First, in Lemma 2, let $P = I$, $Q = \Sigma_k V_s^T V_s \Sigma_k^T$, $S = U_s$ and $S' = U_s'$. Then we have

$$\mathbf{tr}(S^T P S Q) = \mathbf{tr}(U_s^T \cdot I \cdot U_s \cdot \Sigma_k V_s^T V_s \Sigma_k^T)$$
$$= \mathbf{tr}(U_s^T U_s \Sigma_k V_s^T \cdot V_s \Sigma_k^T)$$
$$\leq \sum_{i,j} (U_s' \Sigma_k V_s^T V_s \Sigma_k^T)_{(i,j)} \frac{U_{s(i,j)}^2}{U'_{s(i,j)}}$$

Based on the property of trace, we have

$$\mathbf{tr}(U_s^T U_s \Sigma_k V_s^T \cdot V_s \Sigma_k^T) = \mathbf{tr}(V_s \Sigma_k^T \cdot U_s^T U_s \Sigma_k V_s^T)$$

Therefore, we can derive

$$\mathbf{tr}(V_s \Sigma_k^T U_s^T U_s \Sigma_k V_s^T) \leq \sum_{i,j} (U_s' \Sigma_k V_s^T V_s \Sigma_k^T)_{(i,j)} \frac{U_{s(i,j)}^2}{U'_{s(i,j)}} \quad (15)$$

Second, since $\forall z > 0$, $z \geq 1 + \ln z$, we have

$$\mathbf{tr}(A_s^T U_s \Sigma_k V_s^T) = \sum_{i,j} (A_s V_s \Sigma_k^T)_{(i,j)} U_{s(i,j)}$$
$$\geq \sum_{i,j} (A_s V_s \Sigma_k^T)_{(i,j)} U'_{s(i,j)} (1 + \ln \frac{U_{s(i,j)}}{U'_{s(i,j)}}) \quad (16)$$

If we multiply both sides of Eq. 16 with -2, we get

$$\mathbf{tr}(-2 A_s^T U_s \Sigma_k V_s^T) \leq -2 \sum_{i,j} (A_s V_s \Sigma_k^T)_{(i,j)} U'_{s(i,j)} (1 + \ln \frac{U_{s(i,j)}}{U'_{s(i,j)}}) \quad (17)$$

When adding Eqs. 15 and 17 on both sides, we have

$$\mathcal{J}(U_s) = \mathbf{tr}(-2 A_s^T U_s \Sigma_k V_s^T + V_s \Sigma_k^T U_s^T U_s \Sigma_k V_s^T)$$
$$\leq -2 \sum_{i,j} (A_s V_s \Sigma_k^T)_{(i,j)} U'_{s(i,j)} (1 + \ln \frac{U_{s(i,j)}}{U'_{s(i,j)}})$$
$$+ \sum_{i,j} (U_s' \Sigma_k V_s^T V_s \Sigma_k^T)_{(i,j)} \frac{U_{s(i,j)}^2}{U'_{s(i,j)}}$$
$$= Aux(U_s, U_s')$$

In addition, it is easy to verify that $Aux(U_s, U_s) = \mathcal{J}(U_s)$. Therefore, we prove $Aux(U_s, U_s')$ defined in Eq. 13 is the auxiliary function for $\mathcal{J}(U_s)$.

Next, if we fix U_s' and minimize $Aux(U_s, U_s')$ w.r.t. each $U_{s(i,j)}$, we get

$$\frac{\partial Aux(U_s, U_s')}{\partial U_{s(i,j)}} = -2(A_s V_s \Sigma_k^T)_{(i,j)} \frac{U'_{s(i,j)}}{U_{s(i,j)}}$$
$$+ 2(U_s' \Sigma_k V_s^T V_s \Sigma_k^T)_{(i,j)} \frac{U_{s(i,j)}}{U'_{s(i,j)}} \quad (18)$$

Moreover, the second partial derivative (*Hessian* matrix) is

$$\frac{\partial^2 Aux(U_s, U_s')}{\partial U_{s(i,j)} \partial U_{s(k,l)}} = \delta_{ik} \delta_{jl} (2(A_s V_s \Sigma_k^T)_{(i,j)} \frac{U'_{s(i,j)}}{U^2_{s(i,j)}}$$
$$+ \frac{2(U_s' \Sigma_k V_s^T V_s \Sigma_k^T)_{(i,j)}}{U'_{s(i,j)}}) \quad (19)$$

We should notice that *Hessian* of $Aux(U_s, U_s')$ w.r.t. U_s is a diagonal matrix with all positive diagonal elements. Thus, $Aux(U_s, U_s')$ is convex over U_s and we can achieve its global minimum through setting Eq. 18 to be 0, which leads to the result in Eq. 14. □

Let $U'_{s(i,j)} = U^t_{s(i,j)}$, then according to the update $h^{t+1} = \arg\min_h Aux(h, h^t)$ in Lemma 1, $U_{s(i,j)}$ defined in Eq. 14 which minimizes $Aux(U_s, U^t_{s(i,j)})$ is exactly $U^{t+1}_{s(i,j)}$. This is essentially our update rule for U_s in Eq. 6. This leads to the following lemma.

LEMMA 3. *Using the update rule in Eq. 6 to update U_s, $\mathcal{J}(U_s)$ in Eq. 12 is monotonically decreasing.*

PROOF. By Lemma 1 and Theorem 1, we have

$$\mathcal{J}(U_s^0) = Aux(U_s^0, U_s^0) \geq Aux(U_s^1, U_s^0) \geq \mathcal{J}(U_s^1) \geq \cdots$$

where U_s^t is the value of matrix U_s in the tth iteration. Therefore, $\mathcal{J}(U_s)$ is monotonically decreasing. □

THEOREM 2. *Using Algorithm 1 to update U_s, V_s, U_t, V_t and Σ_k, the value of the objective function $\mathcal{J}$ will monotonically decrease.*

The proof of Theorem 2 can be similarly achieved through Lemma 3. Since the objective function value $\mathcal{J}$ in Eq. 2 is lower bounded by 0, Algorithm 1 can guarantee convergence by Theorem 2.

Theoretically, the computational complexity of factorizing Eq. 2 is at most $\mathcal{O}(k \cdot \max\{|E_s|, |E_t|\}^2)$ where k is the length of the latent topological feature vector, and $E_t = E_t^l \cup E_t^u$. In practice, due to the sparsity of adjacency matrices A_s and A_t, the exact computational cost can be much lower than the theoretical result.

So far we have constructed both explicit and latent topological features for edge sign prediction. For an edge instance $e = (i, j) \in E_t^l$ with label $S(e)$, we have latent feature vectors $U_{t(i \cdot)}$ and $V_{t(j \cdot)}$ to represent node i's outgoing linkage pattern and node j's incoming linkage pattern. We also have 9 explicit features, including node degrees $deg_{out}(i)$ and $deg_{in}(j)$, betweenness centrality $f_{bc}(i)$ and $f_{bc}(j)$, triad counts $f_{FF}(e)$, $f_{FB}(e)$, $f_{BF}(e)$, $f_{BB}(e)$, and edge embeddedness $f_{eb}(e)$. We can similarly define features for edge instances in E_s. The features are used together, denoted as $F(e)$, for learning an edge sign prediction model.

5. EDGE SIGN PREDICTION BY TRANSFER LEARNING

With the explicit and latent topological features, it is natural to learn a model from the training instances in the target graph, i.e., $T_t = \{(e_t, S(e_t))\}, \forall e_t \in E_t^l$. However, using only the small amount of labeled edge instances for training does not give a classifier with good prediction performance on the target graph.

Fortunately, we still have the full knowledge of the edge signs in the source graph G_s. Thus our task is to learn an edge sign prediction model by leveraging the labeled instances in both the source and target graphs. With our extracted features, the source and target graph edge instances can be represented in the same feature space. A straightforward approach is to simply combine the source and target edge instances and treat them equally to learn a model.

However, since discrepancy always exists between the distribution of source and target graph edges, a classifier learned from this simple combination may not necessarily achieve better performance than the model learned from the target graph edges only. Sometimes the noise in the source graph instances may cause the model to predict wrongly on the test edges from the target graph, thus degrade the performance substantially. Thus we need an effective mechanism to distinguish the more useful edge instances from the less useful ones in the source graph.

5.1 Transfer Learning with Instance Weighting

To address the distributional difference issue, we borrow the AdaBoost idea from Freund and Schapire [5] and Dai et al. [3] for *instance weighting* in our transfer learning framework. That is, we treat the edge instances in $T_s = \{(e_s, S(e_s))\}$, $\forall e_s \in E_s$ and $T_t = \{(e_t, S(e_t))\}$, $\forall e_t \in E_t^l$ differently, by assigning and adjusting the weight of each training instance during model learning. For those edge instances in T_s that are more similar to the target edge instances in T_t, we should give them larger weights to attach more importance to them; conversely, for those edge instances in T_s that are less similar to the target edge instances in T_t, we should give smaller weights to weaken their impacts.

Algorithm 2 shows an iterative algorithm which updates instance weights according to the basic classifier P_t's performance in each round. It is similar to the traditional AdaBoost method where the accuracy of a learner is boosted by carefully adjusting instance weights. We use $w_1, \ldots, w_n$ to denote the weights of edges in T_s, and $w_{n+1}, \ldots, w_{n+m}$ to denote the weights of edges in T_t. It is worth noting the following special instance weighting policy in our transfer learning framework. For an edge e, $P_t(e) \in [-1, 1]$ is the predicted edge sign for e and $S(e)$ is the true edge sign. For any target graph edge $e_t \in E_t^l$, its weight will always get increased by a factor of $\beta_t^{-\frac{|P_t(e_t) - S(e_t)|}{2}} \in [1, +\infty)$, and the weight increment of a wrongly predicted edge is larger than that of a correctly predicted one. In contrast, for any source graph edge $e_s \in E_s$, its weight will always get decreased by a factor of $\beta^{\frac{|P_t(e_s) - S(e_s)|}{2}} \in (0, 1]$, and the weight decrement of a wrongly predicted edge is larger than that of a correctly predicted one, because the wrongly predicted source graph edge may be very dissimilar to the target graph. Therefore, the weights of source graph edges would never increase and are always less than those of target graph edges, which means that the source graph edges will never have a larger influence than the target graph edges in model learning. After K iterations, those source graph edges which are more similar to the target graph edges will have larger weights than the less similar ones to contribute to model learning.

5.2 Training Loss Analysis

We analyze the training loss from both source and target graphs, based on the analysis in Freund and Schapire [5] and Dai et al. [3]. Consider the tth iteration training loss on source graph instances where each instance's normalized loss is defined as $l_t(e_i) = |P_t(e_i) - S(e_i)|/2$, and its overall training loss through K iterations is $\mathcal{L}_i = \sum_{t=1}^{K} l_t(e_i)$, $1 \leq i \leq n$. Thus all source instances' training loss suffered by Algorithm 2 is

$$\Upsilon = \sum_{t=1}^{K} \sum_{i=1}^{n} d_i^t l_t(e_i)$$

where $d_i^t = w_i^t / (\sum_{j=1}^{n} w_j^t)$. We first present the following conclusion.

THEOREM 3. *In Algorithm 2, we have*

$$\frac{\Upsilon}{K} \leq \min_{1 \leq i \leq n} \frac{\mathcal{L}_i}{K} + \sqrt{\frac{2 \ln n}{K}} + \frac{\ln n}{K} \qquad (20)$$

Theorem 3 and its proof can be found in [5]. It can rigidly bound the average training loss of source graph instances through K iterations, which cannot exceed the minimum average training loss of a single instance by more than $\sqrt{\frac{2 \ln n}{K}} + \frac{\ln n}{K}$.

Similar to [3], we have the following theorem.

Algorithm 2: Transfer Learning & Instance Weighting

Data: source edge instances T_s, labeled target edge instances T_t, and the iteration number K
Result: edge sign classifier P
begin

Let $n \leftarrow |T_s|, m \leftarrow |T_t|$
Initialize the weight vector
$\mathbf{w}^1 = (w_1^1, \ldots, w_n^1, w_{n+1}^1, \ldots, w_{n+m}^1)$
for $t = 1, \ldots, K$ **do**

1. $\mathbf{q}^t \leftarrow \mathbf{w}^t / (\sum_{i=1}^{n+m} w_i^t)$
2. Call a basic learner on $T_s \cup T_t$ with $\mathbf{q}^t$ to learn a model $P_t : F(e) \to P_t(e) \in [-1, 1]$
3. Calculate the error of P_t on T_t

$$\epsilon_t = \frac{\sum_{i=n+1}^{n+m} q_i^t \cdot \frac{|P_t(e_i) - S(e_i)|}{2}}{\sum_{i=n+1}^{n+m} q_i^t}$$

4. Set $\beta_t = \frac{\epsilon_t}{1-\epsilon_t}$, $\beta = \frac{1}{1+\sqrt{2\ln n/K}}$
5. Update weight vector $\mathbf{w}^t$

$$w_i^{t+1} = \begin{cases} w_i^t \beta^{\frac{|P_t(e_i) - S(e_i)|}{2}}, & 1 \leq i \leq n \\ w_i^t \beta_t^{-\frac{|P_t(e_i) - S(e_i)|}{2}}, & n+1 \leq i \leq n+m \end{cases}$$

$$P(e) = \begin{cases} 1, & \text{if } \sum_{t=1}^{K} \log \frac{1}{\beta_t} \cdot P_t(e) \geq 0 \\ -1, & \text{otherwise} \end{cases}$$

end

THEOREM 4. *In Algorithm 2, q_i^t denotes the weight of the training instance e_i, which is defined as $\mathbf{q}^t = \mathbf{w}^t / (\sum_{i=1}^{n+m} w_i^t)$. Then,*

$$\lim_{K \to \infty} \frac{\sum_{t=1}^{K} \sum_{i=1}^{n} q_i^t l_t(e_i)}{K} = 0 \quad (21)$$

Theorem 4 shows that the weighted average training loss in the source graph edge instances gradually converges to zero.

Next, according to Step 4 in Algorithm 2, we have the constraint $\epsilon_t \leq 1/2 - \gamma$, for some $\gamma > 0$. Then we have the following bound on the prediction error of the final classifier on the labeled target edge instances.

THEOREM 5. *Let $\mathcal{I} = \{i : P(e_i) \neq S(e_i), e_i \in T_t\}$. Define the error of the final classifier P by Algorithm 2 as $\epsilon = \mathbf{Pr}_{e \in T_t}[P(e) \neq S(e)] = |\mathcal{I}|/|T_t|$ and it is bounded as*

$$\epsilon \leq \exp\{-2 \cdot K\gamma^2\}. \quad (22)$$

Theorem 5 and its proof can be found in [5]. From Theorem 5, we can observe that the final classifier P will reduce the error on target graph labeled instances, when the maximum number of iterations K increases. Therefore Algorithm 2 minimizes both the error on the target graph training instances and the weighted average loss on the source graph training instances simultaneously.

6. EXPERIMENTAL EVALUATION

In this section, we first describe how we prepare data for training and testing. Then we present experimental results to show the effectiveness of our proposed features and the transfer learning algorithm. Studies on the convergence properties of both Algorithms 1 and 2 are also provided.

6.1 Data Preparation

We use three large online social networks *Epinions*, *Slashdot* and *Wikipedia* where each link is explicitly labeled as positive or negative. All three networks are downloaded from Stanford Large Network Dataset Collection[4]. Since the original graphs are too large and sparse, we select 20,000 nodes from Epinions, 16,000 nodes from Slashdot and 7,000 nodes from Wikipedia with the highest degrees, as well as the edges between the selected nodes. There are 13 nodes in Epinions, 1 node in Slashdot and 2 nodes in Wikipedia that are disconnected from the remaining selected nodes. These isolated nodes are removed from the respective network and the remaining ones form a connected component. Table 1 shows the statistics of the three extracted networks.

Table 1: Statistics of Extracted Graphs

	Epinions	Slashdot	Wikipedia
Number of Nodes	19,987	15,999	6,998
Number of Edges	634,215	371,122	121,151
Average Degree	31.731	23.197	17.312
Positive Edges	87.6%	76.5%	71.3%
Average Distance	3.163	3.569	4.014

We can observe that Epinions has the largest number of nodes, edges, average degree and the percentage of positive edges among the three networks, while Wikipedia has the smallest number of nodes, edges, average degree and the percentage of positive edges. The statistics demonstrate that there indeed exists discrepancy in data distribution among the three networks.

As the edge signs in all these networks are overwhelmingly positive, we follow the methodology adopted by both Guha et al. [6] and Leskovec et al. [14], to create a balanced dataset from each signed social network. For every negative edge, we sample a random positive edge to ensure that the number of positive and negative edges is equal. We consider each pair of networks out of the three and use one network as the source and the other as the target for transfer learning, and then reverse the source and the target networks. There are totally $\binom{3}{2} \times 2 = 6$ (*source*, *target*) pairs to test. Moreover, we use 4-fold cross validation for performance evaluation – in each target graph we partition the edge instances into four parts evenly, each having a balanced class distribution. We use one part as the test edge set E_t^u, and randomly sample a small percentage of edge instances in the remaining three parts to form the labeled edge set E_t^l. This small E_t^l and all edges E_s in the source graph form the training set. We run our experiment on the four test edge sets in turn and report the average classification accuracy.

6.2 Evaluation of Transfer Learning with Instance Weighting

Comparison with Other Approaches: We compare the prediction accuracy of the following methods.

---
[4] http://snap.stanford.edu/data/index.html

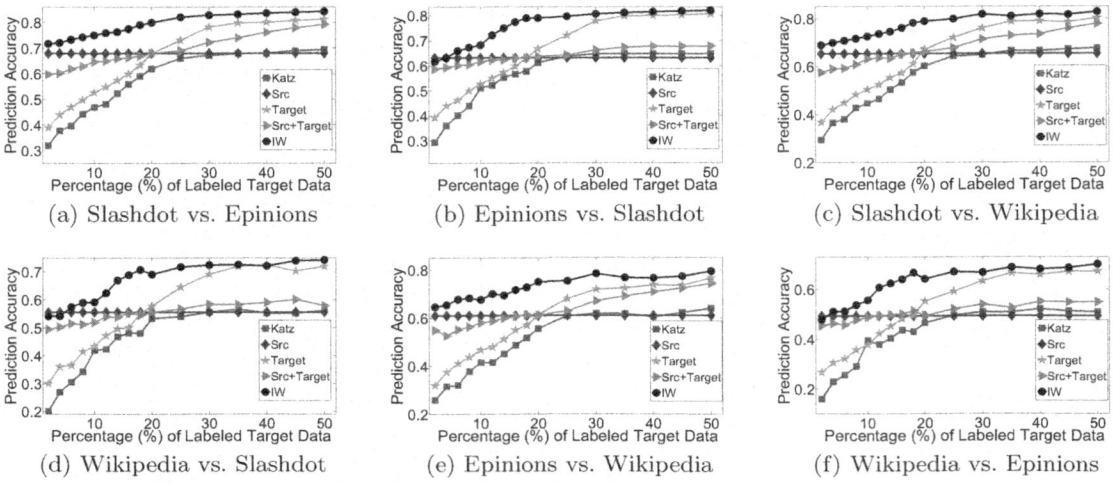

(a) Slashdot vs. Epinions (b) Epinions vs. Slashdot (c) Slashdot vs. Wikipedia
(d) Wikipedia vs. Slashdot (e) Epinions vs. Wikipedia (f) Wikipedia vs. Epinions

Figure 2: Prediction Accuracy by Varying the Percentage of Labeled Target Edge Instances

- *Katz*: Katz kernel [10] is a matrix kernel approach used in [11, 9] for edge sign prediction. It uses the adjacency matrix of labeled edges in the target graph to predict the sign of the test edges.
- *Src*: using all edge instances in the source graph only for training.
- *Target*: using labeled edge instances in the target graph only for training.
- *Src+Target*: using both source graph edges and labeled target graph edges equally for training without instance weighting.
- *IW*: using both source graph edges and labeled target graph edges for training with instance weighting (our Algorithm 2).

For all the above schemes we use SVM as the classification model and use the same test edge set for prediction. All schemes except *Katz* use our proposed explicit and latent topological features. We set $k = 30$ for matrix Σ_k representing the latent feature space.

In the first group of experiment, we use Slashdot as the source and Epinions as the target. We vary the percentage of labeled edge instances in the target graph from 2% to 50% for training and report the classification accuracy. The results are shown in Figure 2(a). We can observe that when the percentage of labeled target edge instances increases, the accuracy of all methods except *Src* increases and gradually saturates. The accuracy of *Target* improves greatly when the percentage increases from 2% to 20% and it outperforms *Src* when the percentage exceeds 20%. The performance of *Src+Target* without instance weighting lies between that of *Src* and *Target*. When the amount of labeled target edge instances is very small, *Src+Target* can improve the accuracy over *Target* by leveraging source graph edge instances; but when the labeled target edge instances are abundant, the source edge instances become less useful, and the noise in the source edge instances may become more obvious, causing *Target* to be better than *Src+Target*. *Katz* performs the worst among all methods. Our proposed method *IW* (Algorithm 2) achieves the highest accuracy in all cases, demonstrating the effectiveness of instance weighting in the transfer learning framework. *IW* consistently outperforms *Target* even if we have 50% labeled target edge instances for training. This result proves that the knowledge transferred from the source graph is beneficial to improve the model's performance, under proper instance weighting.

We can observe similar trends in Figure 2(b) in the second group of experiment when Epinions is the source and Slashdot is the target. But due to the larger number of edges in Epinions, the source edge instances have a larger influence in model learning. This effect causes *Src+Target* to have a very close performance to *Src*.

Similar conclusions can be drawn in Figures 2(c)–2(f) for the other four groups of experiments. Another important observation is that, when the distributional differences between the source and target networks become larger, the transfer learning performance becomes worse. For example, the differences between Wikipedia and Epinions as shown in Table 1 are larger than the differences between Slashdot and Epinions. Consider the case when Epinions is the target network. The prediction accuracy when using Wikipedia as the source (Figure 2(f)) is lower than the accuracy when using Slashdot as the source (Figure 2(a)), due to the larger differences between Wikipedia and Epinions.

Learning Convergence Analysis: It is important to assess the convergence of Algorithm 2 as an iterative algorithm. Besides the theoretical analysis of convergence in Section 5, we also test the learning convergence in all our experiments. Figure 3 shows the prediction accuracy in each iteration on all the $\binom{3}{2} = 3$ pairs of networks. Legend "S vs E-0.02" means using Slashdot as the source and Epinions as the target with 2% labeled target edges for training. We can see that the accuracy gradually increases with more iterations and converges after 30–35 iterations. This result confirms the theoretical analysis on learning convergence.

6.3 Effectiveness of Topological Features

In this experiment, we evaluate the effectiveness of each type of features we propose, including degree, betweenness centrality (BC), triad counts, edge embeddedness (Embed) and latent features constructed by NMTF. We set $k = 30$ in matrix Σ_k for the latent feature space. We use source graph edges and a certain percentage of labeled target graph edges for training; then use our instance weighting algorithm for

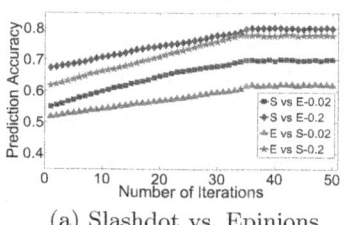
(a) Slashdot vs. Epinions
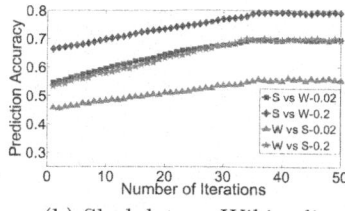
(b) Slashdot vs. Wikipedia
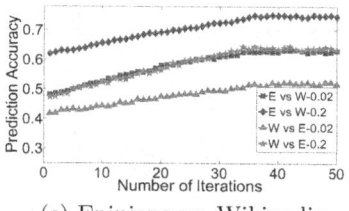
(c) Epinions vs. Wikipedia

Figure 3: Prediction Accuracy by Iteration of Algorithm 2

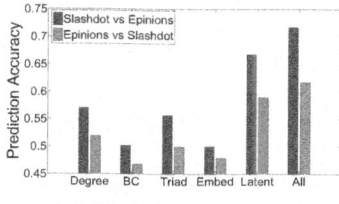
(a) Slashdot vs. Epinions
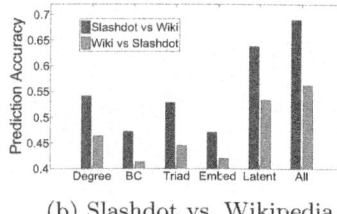
(b) Slashdot vs. Wikipedia
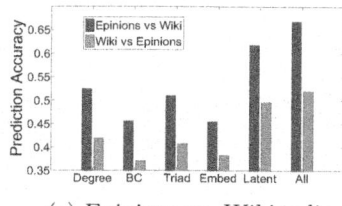
(c) Epinions vs. Wikipedia

Figure 4: Feature Effectiveness Comparison with 2% Target Training Instances

model learning. Only one type of feature is used in each learned model. We also use all these features (All) to learn a model to show their overall performance.

We first use 2% labeled edge instances in the target graph plus all source edge instances for training. Figures 4(a)–4(c) show the prediction accuracy of each feature type on the three network pairs respectively. Among the five types of features, we can see that our latent features always achieve the highest accuracy, followed by Degree, Triad, BC and Embed. This is because the latent features can capture the common structural patterns between the source and target graphs, despite the different distributions between them. Thus the latent features can generalize well from the source graph to the target. In contrast, the other four types of features are not generalizable from the source graph to the target. As the statistics in Table 1 show that the three social networks have different distributions in degree and other dimensions, it is not difficult to understand that a model learned from the source edge instances based on these explicit features cannot generalize well to predict the sign of test edges in the target graph. Finally, the model using all these features achieves the best performance.

When we increase the percentage of labeled target edge instances to 30% for training, the prediction accuracy is shown in Figures 5(a)–5(c). Among the five types of features, Latent still achieves the highest accuracy in most cases, followed by Degree, Triad, BC and Embed. But the performance difference between Latent and Degree/Triad is not as significant. This is because when the amount of labeled target edge instances is much larger, the labeled target instances provide reliable feature values on Degree and Triad. The source graph edges which have a different distribution will have a smaller influence in model learning through instance weighting. Finally, the model using all these features still achieves the best performance.

Tri-Factorization Sensitivity Test: We perform sensitivity test on the dimension of the latent feature space, i.e., k in the $k \times k$ matrix Σ_k computed by matrix tri-factorization. We vary the k value of the latent feature space and report the prediction accuracy in Figures 6(a)–6(c) on the three network pairs respectively. 30% labeled target edge instances plus all source graph edges are used for training. Here legend *Src+Target* means using both source graph edges and labeled target graph edges without instance weighting, and *IW* means our instance weighting method. We can observe that the prediction accuracy increases first when k increases and then becomes stable or even slightly decreases when $k > 30$ for all three groups of experiments. When $k > 30$, we find many entries in the latent feature vector become almost 0, thus contribute little to prediction, or even degrade the performance.

Tri-Factorization Convergence Analysis: We prove the convergence of Algorithm 1 in Section 4.2.2. We report the objective values (in log scale, i.e., $\ln \mathcal{J}$) over 20 iterations under three latent feature dimensions $k = 10, 30, 60$ in Figure 7. Due to the lack of space, we only show the results when Slashdot is the source and Epinions is the target. We can observe that the objective values which measure the difference between the original matrix and the decomposed ones converge very quickly (after 4 iterations) regardless of the feature dimension k. This result confirms our theoretical analysis on the convergence of Algorithm 1.

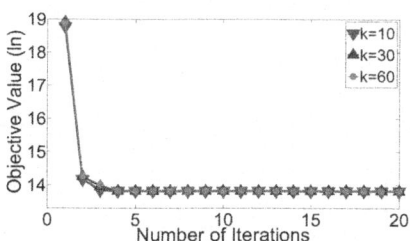

Figure 7: NMTF Convergence

7. CONCLUSIONS

We studied the edge sign prediction problem in signed social networks, which have both positive and negative links. We assume the edge sign information is very scarce in the target network which is very common for newly formed networks. This problem is important because knowing the edge

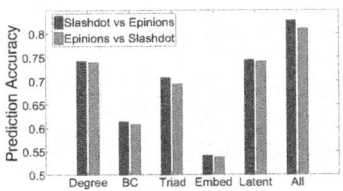 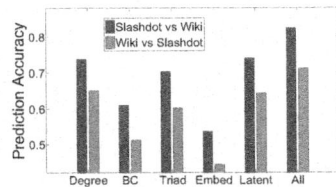 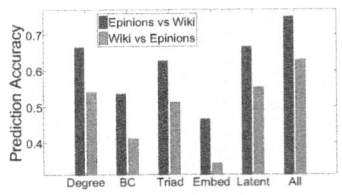

(a) Slashdot vs. Epinions (b) Slashdot vs. Wikipedia (c) Epinions vs. Wikipedia

Figure 5: Feature Effectiveness Comparison with 30% Target Training Instances

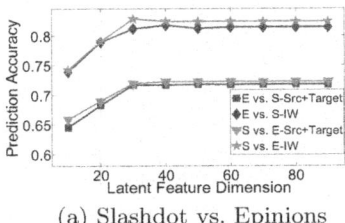 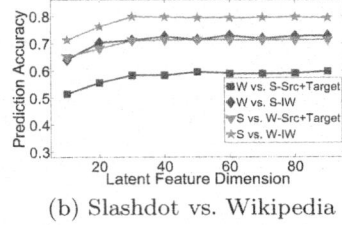 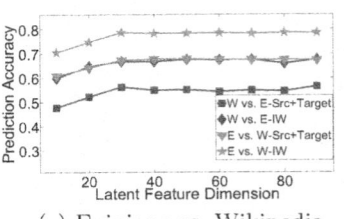

(a) Slashdot vs. Epinions (b) Slashdot vs. Wikipedia (c) Epinions vs. Wikipedia

Figure 6: Sensitivity Test of Latent Feature Dimension

signs will provide us with better understanding of user opinions in a social network. It is challenging due to the inadequate edge signs in the target network and the prohibitive cost of manual labeling. We adopt the transfer learning approach by leveraging a source network with abundant edge sign information but possibly under a different yet related distribution. We propose to construct generalizable latent features through NMTF by considering both the source and target networks, and then adopt an AdaBoost-like algorithm with instance weighting to train a good classifier. Extensive experiments on three real signed networks Epinions, Slashdot and Wikipedia prove the effectiveness of our extracted features and transfer learning algorithm.

8. ACKNOWLEDGMENTS

The work described in this paper was partially supported by two China National 973 projects (grant No. 2012CB315904 and 2013CB336700), several grants from the University Grants Committee of the Hong Kong Special Administrative Region, China (Area of Excellence Project No. AoE/E-02/08 and General Research Fund Project 411211, 411310, 411010 and 411011), and two gift grants from Microsoft and Cisco.

9. REFERENCES

[1] A. Argyriou, T. Evgeniou, and M. Pontil. Multi-task feature learning. In *NIPS*, pages 41–48, 2006.
[2] M. Burke and R. Kraut. Mopping up: Modeling wikipedia promotion decisions. In *CSCW*, pages 27–36, 2008.
[3] W. Dai, Q. Yang, G.-R. Xue, and Y. Yu. Boosting for transfer learning. In *ICML*, pages 193–200, 2007.
[4] C. Ding, T. Li, W. Peng, and H. Park. Orthogonal nonnegative matrix tri-factorizations for clustering. In *KDD*, pages 126–135, 2006.
[5] Y. Freund and R. E. Schapire. A decision-theoretic generalization of on-line learning and an application to boosting. In *EuroCOLT*, pages 23–37, 1995.
[6] R. Guha, R. Kumar, P. Raghavan, and A. Tomkins. Propagation of trust and distrust. In *WWW*, pages 403–412, 2004.
[7] J. He and R. Lawrence. A graph-based framework for multi-task multi-view learning. In *ICML*, pages 25–32, 2011.
[8] J. He, Y. Liu, and R. Lawrence. Graph-based transfer learning. In *CIKM*, pages 937–946, 2009.
[9] T. Ito, M. Shimbo, T. Kudo, and Y. Matsumoto. Application of kernels to link analysis. In *KDD*, pages 586–592, 2005.
[10] E. Katz and P. F. Lazarsfeld. *Personal influence: The part played by people in the flow of mass communications*. Free Press, 1955.
[11] J. Kunegis, A. Lommatzsch, and C. Bauckhage. The slashdot zoo: Mining a social network with negative edges. In *WWW*, pages 741–750, 2009.
[12] J. Kunegis, S. Schmidt, A. Lommatzsch, J. Lerner, E. W. Luca, and S. Albayrak. Spectral analysis of signed graphs for clustering, prediction and visualization. In *SDM*, pages 559–570, 2010.
[13] D. D. Lee and H. S. Seung. Algorithms for non-negative matrix factorization. In *NIPS*, pages 556–562, 2000.
[14] J. Leskovec, D. Huttenlocher, and J. Kleinberg. Predicting positive and negative links in online social networks. In *WWW*, pages 641–650, 2010.
[15] D. Liben-Nowell and J. Kleinberg. The link prediction problem for social networks. In *CIKM*, pages 556–559, 2003.
[16] J. J. Lim, R. Salakhutdinov, and A. Torralba. Transfer learning by borrowing examples for multiclass object detection. In *NIPS*, pages 118–126, 2011.
[17] M. Long, J. Wang, G. Ding, W. Cheng, X. Zhang, and W. Wang. Dual transfer learning. In *SDM*, pages 540–551, 2012.
[18] P. Massa and P. Avesani. Controversial users demand local trust metrics: An experimental study on epinions.com community. In *AAAI*, pages 121–126, 2005.
[19] S. J. Pan and Q. Yang. A survey on transfer learning. *IEEE Transactions on Knowledge and Data Engineering*, 22:1345–1359, 2010.

[20] B. Pang and L. Lee. Opinion mining and sentiment analysis. *Foundations and Trends in Information Retrieval*, 2(1-2):1–135, 2008.

[21] R. Raina, A. Battle, H. Lee, B. Packer, and A. Y. Ng. Self-taught learning: Transfer learning from unlabeled data. In *ICML*, pages 759–766, 2007.

[22] T. Yang, R. Jin, A. K. Jain, Y. Zhou, and W. Tong. Unsupervised transfer classification: Application to text categorization. In *KDD*, pages 1159–1168, 2010.

[23] F. Zhuang, P. Luo, H. Xiong, Q. He, Y. Xiong, and Z. Shi. Exploiting associations between word clusters and document classes for cross-domain text categorization. *Statistical Analysis and Data Mining*, 4(1):100–114, 2011.

Sparse Online Topic Models

Aonan Zhang, Jun Zhu, Bo Zhang
State Key Laboratory of Intelligent Technology and Systems
Tsinghua National Laboratory of Information Science and Technology
Department of Computer Science and Technology
Tsinghua University, Beijing 100084, China
{zan12; dcszj; dcszb}@mail.tsinghua.edu.cn

ABSTRACT

Topic models have shown great promise in discovering latent semantic structures from complex data corpora, ranging from text documents and web news articles to images, videos, and even biological data. In order to deal with massive data collections and dynamic text streams, probabilistic online topic models such as online latent Dirichlet allocation (OLDA) have recently been developed. However, due to normalization constraints, OLDA can be ineffective in controlling the sparsity of discovered representations, a desirable property for learning interpretable semantic patterns, especially when the total number of topics is large. In contrast, sparse topical coding (STC) has been successfully introduced as a non-probabilistic topic model for effectively discovering sparse latent patterns by using sparsity-inducing regularization. But, unfortunately STC cannot scale to very large datasets or deal with online text streams, partly due to its batch learning procedure. In this paper, we present a sparse online topic model, which directly controls the sparsity of latent semantic patterns by imposing sparsity-inducing regularization and learns the topical dictionary by an online algorithm. The online algorithm is efficient and guaranteed to converge. Extensive empirical results of the sparse online topic model as well as its collapsed and supervised extensions on a large-scale Wikipedia dataset and the medium-sized 20Newsgroups dataset demonstrate appealing performance.

Categories and Subject Descriptors

I.5.1 [**Pattern Recognition**]: Models - Statistical

General Terms

Algorithms, Experimentation

Keywords

Large-scale data, Online learning, Topic models, Sparse latent representations

1. INTRODUCTION

Probabilistic topic models, such as probabilistic latent semantic indexing [17] and its fully Bayesian generalization of latent Dirichlet allocation (LDA) [5], have been widely applied to discover latent semantic structures from collections

Copyright is held by the International World Wide Web Conference Committee (IW3C2). IW3C2 reserves the right to provide a hyperlink to the author's site if the Material is used in electronic media.
WWW 2013, May 13–17, 2013, Rio de Janeiro, Brazil.
ACM 978-1-4503-2035-1/13/05.

of data, which can be text documents [5, 3, 6, 4, 9, 28], images [13, 34, 12, 31, 22, 37], and even biological data [1]. Since exact posterior inference is intractable, both variational [5] and Monte Carlo [15] methods have been widely developed for approximate inference, which can normally deal with medium-sized datasets. In order to deal with large-scale data analysis problems, which are not uncommon in many application areas, various techniques have been developed to speed up the inference algorithms, such as the parallel inference algorithms on multiple CPU or GPU cores and multiple machines (please see [40] for a nice summary of existing techniques). Another nice advance is the development of online inference algorithms, which can not only deal with massive data corpora but also can deal with dynamic text streams, where data samples are incoming one-by-one or in small batches. One representative work is the online variational inference method for latent Dirichlet allocation (OLDA) [16]. OLDA and its later extensions, including the online collapsed Gibbs sampling [20] and the hybrid online variational-Gibbs [27] methods have shown a success to scale to corpora containing millions of articles.

However, the above online probabilistic topic models can be ineffective in controlling the sparsity of the discovered representations, partly due to their normalization constraints on the admixing proportions [42]. Sparsity of the representations in a semantic space is a desirable property in text modeling [33] and human vision [29]. For example, we will expect not every topic or sense, but only a few of them that make a non-zero contribution for each document or each word [33]; this is especially important in practice for large scale text mining endeavors such as those undertaken in industry, where it is not uncommon to learn hundreds if not thousands of topics for millions or billions of documents. Without an explicit sparcification procedure, it would be extremely challenging, if not impossible, to nail down the semantic meanings of a document or word.

In this paper, we present an approach to learning sparse online topic models, both to improve time efficiency and to deal with streaming data. Our approach is based on our recent work of sparse topical coding (STC) [42], a hierarchical non-negative matrix factorization (NMF) [23] model using word codes and document codes to represent an article at the individual word level and the whole document level, respectively. By using unnormalized code vectors, STC offers an extra freedom to reconstruct word counts in text using a log-Poisson loss, and it can effectively control the sparsity of latent representations to find compact topical representations by imposing appropriate sparsity-inducing regularization. Such effectiveness has been further demonstrated in the context of learning compact descriptors for images and videos [21, 14, 25]. However, the existing batch dictionary learning algorithm takes a full scan of the corpus at each gradient descent step, which is demanding in terms of both memory and computation; also, the batch algorithm cannot explore the redundancy of large-scale datasets for more effective training. Thus, in the current batch form, STC does not scale up to large-scale datasets and cannot deal with dynamic text streams.

To address the above weakness of STC, we propose a novel sparse online topic model, which is essentially an online algorithm to learn the topical dictionary in STC. Our algorithm, based on the recent success of online stochastic optimization [8, 32], can scale to large data corpora (e.g., the entire Wikipedia corpus containing 6.6M articles) and can cope with dynamic text streams. Our main contributions can be summarised as follows:

- We introduce online sparse topical coding (OSTC), which is efficient for learning online sparse topical representations.

- We provide a theoretical analysis that when using a general setting for the learning rate, our online learning algorithm converges to a stationary point under reasonable conditions.

- We present the collapsed sparse topical coding model as well as its online learning algorithm, and the online learning algorithm for the supervised max-margin sparse topical coding (MedSTC) [42].

- Our empirical results on the medium-sized 20Newsgroups dataset and a large-scale Wikipedia dataset show that 1) online learning algorithms can improve time efficiency, while not sacrificing prediction performance or the perplexity performance of held-out data; 2) online sparse topical coding achieves lower perplexity and higher word code sparsity than probabilistic online LDA.

The rest of the paper is structured as follows. Section 2 summarizes related works. Section 3 briefly overviews STC and its batch learning algorithm. Section 4 presents the online sparse topical coding algorithm, analyzes its convergence, and discusses two extensions for learning collapsed STC and supervised STC. Section 5 presents empirical results on Wikipedia and 20Newsgroups data. Finally, Section 6 concludes.

2. RELATED WORK

Various works have been developed for modeling independent dynamic text streams [39, 20] and dealing with large data corpora using topic models [16, 27, 38]. Online topic models combine these two targets into one objective. It has been shown that these models can easily scale up to a corpus containing a few millions of articles [16, 27] by using proper inference methods.

Another thing we care about is the sparsity of latent representations for the data [23]. Suppose we have an article, we can expect only a few topical meanings in it. In the language of topic models, the latent representations of the article and its words tend to be sparse. Sparsity is also important for large scale text mining endeavors, where it is

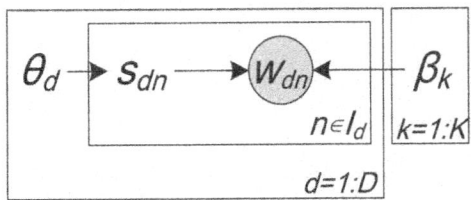

Figure 1: Graphical structure of STC [42].

common to cut down the semantic meaning of a document or word from its topical descriptors learned from millions of articles for storage. Several models aim at faster and more efficient inference procedures [15, 36, 2]. However, the inferred latent representations for these models are very dense. STC is a sparse topic model which relaxes the normalization constraints of the latent representations and explicitly put a sparse-inducing regularization on them. This method has been proved to be more successful to learn a sparse topical representation and its MAP inference is even significantly faster than some probabilistic topic models [42].

Our online model is based on STC. We aim at building a topic model that can scale to a large corpus and can deal with dynamic text streams while simultaneously preserving sparse coding.

3. SPARSE TOPICAL CODING

In this section, we briefly overview sparse topical coding and its existing batch learning algorithm. We also provide a new interpretation for the sparse topic model from the projection point of view.

Let V be a vocabulary with N terms. In a bag-of-words model, a document d is represented as a vector $\mathbf{w}_d = (w_{d1}, \cdots, w_{d|I_d|})^\top$, where I_d is the index set of words that appear and w_{dn} ($n \in I_d$) is the number of appearances of word n in document d. Sparse topical coding is a technique that projects the input $\mathbf{w}_d$ into a linear latent space spanned by a set of automatically learned bases (a basis set is also called a *dictionary*). The combination weights denote a representation of document d in the latent space. STC is a hierarchical non-negative matrix factorization [29], with two-layers of latent representations for words and the entire documents, respectively. For the ease of understanding, it is helpful to start with a probabilistic generating process, which also provides an explicit comparison with LDA.

3.1 A Probabilistic Generating Process

Let $\boldsymbol{\beta}$ denote a dictionary with K bases, of which each row $\boldsymbol{\beta}_k$ is a N dimensional basis. For text documents, $\boldsymbol{\beta}_k$ is a topic, i.e., a unigram distribution over the terms in V. This statement leads to the constraint that $\boldsymbol{\beta}_k \in \mathcal{P}$, where $\mathcal{P}$ is a $(N-1)$-simplex. We will use $\boldsymbol{\beta}_{\cdot n} \in \mathbb{R}^K$ to denote the nth column of $\boldsymbol{\beta}$. Graphically, STC is a hierarchical latent variable model, as shown in Fig. 1, where $\boldsymbol{\theta}_d \in \mathbb{R}^K$ is the *document code* (i.e., the latent representation of a document d) while each $\mathbf{s}_{dn} \in \mathbb{R}^K$ is a *word code* (i.e., latent representation of the individual word n in document d).

Formally, STC assumes that for each document d the word codes $\mathbf{s}_{dn}$ are conditionally independent given its document code $\boldsymbol{\theta}_d$ and the observed word counts w_{dn} are independent given their latent representations $\mathbf{s}_{dn}$. The generative process for each document d is:

1. draw a document code $\boldsymbol{\theta}_d \sim p(\boldsymbol{\theta})$;
2. for each word $n \in I_d$:
   (a) draw a word code $\mathbf{s}_{dn} \sim p(\mathbf{s}|\boldsymbol{\theta}_d)$;
   (b) draw a word count $w_{dn} \sim p(w|\mathbf{s}_{dn}, \boldsymbol{\beta})$.

For the last step of generating word counts, we require the distribution to satisfy the constraint $\mathbb{E}_p[w] = \mathbf{s}_{dn}^\top \boldsymbol{\beta}_{\cdot n} + \epsilon$, where ϵ is a small positive number for avoiding degenerated distributions. One nice choice, as used in STC, is the Poisson distribution

$$p(w_{dn}|\mathbf{s}_{dn}, \boldsymbol{\beta}) = Poisson(w_{dn}; \mathbf{s}_{dn}^\top \boldsymbol{\beta}_{\cdot n} + \epsilon), \quad (1)$$

where the linear combination $\mathbf{s}_{dn}^\top \boldsymbol{\beta}_{\cdot n}$ has been used as the *mean* parameter of a Poisson distribution $Poisson(x; \nu) = \frac{\nu^x e^{-\nu}}{x!}$. This idea of using the linear combination $\mathbf{s}_{dn}^\top \boldsymbol{\beta}_{\cdot n}$ as mean parameters can be generalized to the broad class of exponential family distributions for modeling various types of data. We refer the readers to [42] for more details. But we emphasize one advantage of such a mean parametrization, that is, using the linear combination as mean parameter makes it natural and convenient to constrain the feasible domains (e.g., non-negative domain for modeling word counts) of the word codes in order to have a good interpretation, while it would be reluctant to do so when using the linear combination as natural parameters[1]. As shown in [23], imposing appropriate constraints such as non-negativity constraints could result in significantly sparser and more interpretable patterns.

3.2 STC as a MAP Estimation

The generating procedure defines a joint distribution

$$p(\boldsymbol{\theta}_d, \mathbf{s}_d, \mathbf{w}_d|\boldsymbol{\beta}) = p(\boldsymbol{\theta}_d) \prod_{n \in I_d} p(\mathbf{s}_{dn}|\boldsymbol{\theta}_d) p(w_{dn}|\mathbf{s}_{dn}, \boldsymbol{\beta}), \quad (2)$$

where $\mathbf{s}_d = \{\mathbf{s}_{dn}, n \in I_d\}$. To infer sparse word codes, STC defines $p(\mathbf{s}_{dn}|\boldsymbol{\theta}_d)$ as a product of two component distributions

$$p(\mathbf{s}_{dn}|\boldsymbol{\theta}_d) \propto p(\mathbf{s}_{dn}|\boldsymbol{\theta}_d, \gamma) p(\mathbf{s}_{dn}|\rho) \quad (3)$$

where $p(\mathbf{s}_{dn}|\boldsymbol{\theta}_d, \gamma)$ is an isotropic Gaussian distribution $\mathcal{N}(\boldsymbol{\theta}_d, \gamma^{-1})$ and $p(\mathbf{s}_{dn}|\rho) = Laplace(0, \rho^{-1})$ is a Laplace distribution. This composite distribution is super-Gaussian [19] and the Laplace term will bias towards finding sparse word codes. For $p(\boldsymbol{\theta}_d)$, both the normal prior $p(\boldsymbol{\theta}_d) = \mathcal{N}(0, \lambda^{-1})$ and the Laplace prior $p(\boldsymbol{\theta}_d) = Laplace(0, \lambda^{-1})$ were discussed in [42].

Let $\boldsymbol{\Theta} = \{\boldsymbol{\theta}_d\}, \mathbf{S} = \{\mathbf{s}_d\}$ and $\mathbf{W} = \{\mathbf{w}_d\}$ to denote all the latent document codes, latent word codes and observed word counts in the whole corpus. When $p(\boldsymbol{\theta})$ is normal, STC solves the constrained problem

$$\min_{\boldsymbol{\Theta}, \mathbf{S}, \boldsymbol{\beta}} \ell(\mathbf{S}, \boldsymbol{\beta}) + \lambda \|\boldsymbol{\Theta}\|_2^2 + \frac{\gamma}{2} \sum_{d,n \in I_d} \|\mathbf{s}_{dn} - \boldsymbol{\theta}_d\|_2^2 + \rho \|\mathbf{S}\|_1$$
$$\text{s.t.} : \boldsymbol{\Theta} \geq 0; \ \mathbf{S} \geq 0; \ \boldsymbol{\beta}_k \in \mathcal{P}, \forall k, \quad (4)$$

where the objective function is the negative logarithm of the posterior $p(\boldsymbol{\Theta}, \mathbf{S}, \boldsymbol{\beta}|\mathbf{W})$ with a constant omitted; $\|\boldsymbol{\Theta}\|_2^2 =$

---

[1] For example, the natural parameter of the Poission distribution $Poisson(x; \nu)$ is $\log \nu$. If we use the natural parametrization and let $\log \nu = \mathbf{s}_{dn}^\top \boldsymbol{\beta}_{\cdot n} + \epsilon$, we will have $\nu = \exp(\mathbf{s}_{dn}^\top \boldsymbol{\beta}_{\cdot n} + \epsilon)$. The exponential transformation will make the resulting problem of STC hard to solve.

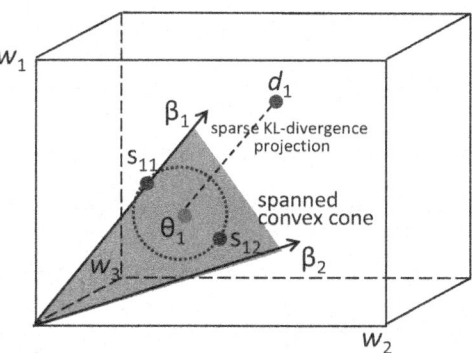

Figure 2: A new projection view of STC with two topical bases over a vocabulary with three terms.

$\sum_d \|\boldsymbol{\theta}_d\|_2^2$ and $\|\mathbf{S}\|_1 = \sum_{d,n} \|\mathbf{s}_{dn}\|_1$. For text, the log-Poisson loss is $\ell(\mathbf{S}, \boldsymbol{\beta}) = \sum_d \ell(\mathbf{s}_d, \boldsymbol{\beta})$, where

$$\ell(\mathbf{s}_d, \boldsymbol{\beta}) = \sum_{n \in I_d} \ell(w_{dn}, \mathbf{s}_{dn}^\top \boldsymbol{\beta}_{\cdot n}) \quad (5)$$

is the log-loss contributed by document d and

$$\ell(w_{dn}, \mathbf{s}_{dn}^\top \boldsymbol{\beta}_{\cdot n}) = -\log Poisson(w_{dn}; \mathbf{s}_{dn}^\top \boldsymbol{\beta}_{\cdot n} + \epsilon) \quad (6)$$

is the loss contributed by the individual word n. Since word counts are non-negative, a negative $\boldsymbol{\theta}$ or $\mathbf{s}$ will lose interpretability. Therefore, STC constrains the code parameters to be non-negative, as in [18]. A non-negative code $\boldsymbol{\theta}$ or $\mathbf{s}$ can be interpreted as representing the relative importance of topics. The parameters (λ, γ, ρ) are non-negative constants and they can be selected via cross-validation.

To help understand the above definition of STC, we also provide a new projection interpretation of STC as illustrated in Fig. 2. Suppose we have two topical bases $\boldsymbol{\beta}_1$ and $\boldsymbol{\beta}_2$ over a vocabulary with three terms $\mathbf{w}_1, \mathbf{w}_2$, and $\mathbf{w}_3$. The document d_1 has two terms, each being projected to a point in the spanned convex cone[2] under a KL-divergence measure[3], and the document code $\boldsymbol{\theta}_1$ is an aggregation of the two word codes $\mathbf{s}_{11}$ and $\mathbf{s}_{12}$. By using appropriate regularization, the projection could be sparse. In this figure we illustrate both sparse and non-sparse cases. For example, the word code $\mathbf{s}_{11}$ is sparse (i.e., on the boundary) while $\mathbf{s}_{12}$ is not.

3.3 Existing Batch Learning Algorithm

Problem (4) is biconvex, i.e., convex over $\boldsymbol{\beta}$ or $(\boldsymbol{\Theta}, \mathbf{S})$ when the other is fixed, but not joint convex over $(\boldsymbol{\Theta}, \mathbf{S}, \boldsymbol{\beta})$. A natural algorithm to solve this biconvex problem for a local optimum is coordinate descent, as used in [42] and sparse coding methods [24]. The algorithm alternately performs the following two steps.

Hierarchical sparse coding: optimizing over $\mathbf{S}$ and $\boldsymbol{\Theta}$. Since documents are i.i.d, we can perform the hierarchical sparse coding for each document separately. For document

---

[2] The combination weight is a word code.
[3] Minimizing the log-Poisson loss in Eq. (6) is equivalent to minimizing the unnormalized KL-divergence between observed word counts w_{dn} and their reconstructions $\mathbf{s}_{dn}^\top \boldsymbol{\beta}_{\cdot n}$ [35].

d, we solve the constrained optimization problem

$$\min_{\boldsymbol{\theta}_d, \mathbf{s}_d} \ell(\mathbf{s}_d, \boldsymbol{\beta}) + \lambda \|\boldsymbol{\theta}_d\|_2^2 + \frac{\gamma}{2} \sum_{n \in I_d} \|\mathbf{s}_{dn} - \boldsymbol{\theta}_d\|_2^2 + \rho \|\mathbf{s}_d\|_1$$
$$\text{s.t.} : \boldsymbol{\theta}_d \geq 0;\ \mathbf{s}_{dn} \geq 0, \forall n \in I_d. \quad (7)$$

As shown in [42], a coordinate descent procedure can be developed with iterative closed-form updates for word codes and document codes. Moreover, this algorithm has the same structure as the variational inference algorithm of the counterpart LDA [5] model. To compare with online LDA [16], which uses variational inference, we adopt the coordinate descent strategy to solve problem (7) in our online sparse topical coding. More formally, the algorithm alternatively solves

Optimize over $\mathbf{s}_d$: when $\boldsymbol{\theta}_d$ is fixed, $\mathbf{s}_{dn}$ are not coupled. For each $\mathbf{s}_{dn}$, the solution is $s_{dn}^k = \max(0, \nu_{dn}^k)$, where ν_{dn}^k is the larger solution of the equation

$$\gamma \beta_{kn}(\nu_{dn}^k)^2 + (\gamma\mu + \beta_{kn}\eta)\nu_{dn}^k + \mu\eta - w_{dn}\beta_{kn} = 0,$$

where $\mu = \sum_{j \neq k} s_{dn}^j \beta_{jn} + \epsilon$ and $\eta = \beta_{kn} + \rho - \gamma \theta_d^k$. This one dimensional problem can be solved in closed-form.

Optimize over $\boldsymbol{\theta}_d$: when $\mathbf{s}_d$ is fixed, the closed-form solution is

$$\forall k,\ \theta_d^k = \frac{\gamma}{\lambda/|I_d| + \gamma} \bar{s}_d^k, \quad (8)$$

where $\bar{s}_d^k = \frac{1}{|I_d|} \sum_{n \in I_d} s_{dn}^k$. If $\lambda \ll \gamma$, the document code $\boldsymbol{\theta}_d$ is close to the *averaging* aggregation of its individual word codes. Another choice is to set $\lambda = \gamma$, and we have $\theta_d^k = \frac{|I_d|}{1+|I_d|} \bar{s}_d^k$, which is again close to the average if $|I_d|$ is large. Following [42], we set $\lambda = \gamma$ since it reduces one parameter to tune. Moreover, if the Laplace prior $p(\boldsymbol{\theta}_d) = \text{Laplace}(0, \lambda^{-1})$ is used, a closed-form solution also exists,

$$\forall k,\ \theta_d^k = \max(0, \bar{s}_d^k - \frac{\lambda}{\gamma|I_d|}), \quad (9)$$

which is a *truncated averaging* strategy for aggregating individual word codes to obtain $\boldsymbol{\theta}_d$.

Dictionary learning: this step involves solving

$$\min_{\boldsymbol{\beta}} \ell(\mathbf{S}, \boldsymbol{\beta}),\ \text{s.t.} : \boldsymbol{\beta}_k \in P, \forall k. \quad (10)$$

STC uses a projected gradient descent method to update $\boldsymbol{\beta}$, where the projection to the ℓ_1-ball can be done efficiently in $O(N)$ time [11]. We will use the public implementation of the batch algorithm as our baseline[4].

4. ONLINE SPARSE TOPICAL CODING

The above algorithm empirically converges faster than the variational inference algorithm of probabilistic LDA by avoiding calls to digamma function [42]. However, it requires a full pass through the corpus at each gradient descent step of learning dictionary. A full pass of a very large dataset would be very expensive in terms of both memory and efficiency. Furthermore, the batch gradient descent for dictionary learning can be inefficient in utilizing the redundance information of a large dataset. To overcome such inefficiency, we propose the online sparse topical coding (OSTC), which uses an online learning algorithm to learn the dictionary $\boldsymbol{\beta}$. Our online algorithm is nearly as simple as the

[4] http://www.ml-thu.net/~jun/stc.html

Algorithm 1 Online Sparse Topical Coding
1: Initialize $\boldsymbol{\beta}^0, \boldsymbol{\theta}_0, s_0$
2: **for** t= 0,1,2,... **do**
3:    read document d^t
4:    $(\boldsymbol{\theta}_t, \mathbf{s}_t) = HierarchicalSparseCoding(d^t)$
5:    let $g^t = \nabla \ell(\boldsymbol{\beta}^t)$ and $\alpha^t = \tau_0/(t+\tau)$
6:    $\boldsymbol{\beta}^{t+1} \leftarrow \Pi_P(\boldsymbol{\beta}^t - \alpha^t g^t)$
7: **end for**

---

batch coordinate descent algorithm for STC, but converges much faster for large datasets, as we shall see.

The online learning algorithm for STC is described in algorithm 1. At each iteration t, we randomly sample a data point $\mathbf{w}_t$ and perform the hierarchical sparse coding step to find the optimal codes $\boldsymbol{\theta}_t$ and $\mathbf{s}_t$, holding the dictionary fixed. Then, we update the dictionary using the information collected from the data $\mathbf{w}_t$ by using the first-order update rule

$$\boldsymbol{\beta}^{t+1} = \Pi_P(\boldsymbol{\beta}^t - \alpha^t \mathbf{g}(\boldsymbol{\beta}^t; \mathbf{w}_t)) \quad (11)$$

where the gradient

$$\mathbf{g}(\boldsymbol{\beta}_t; \mathbf{w}_t) = \nabla \ell(\mathbf{s}_t, \boldsymbol{\beta})|_{\boldsymbol{\beta}^t}$$

and α^t denotes the learning rate. The update rule is in fact the solution of the subproblem

$$\min_{\boldsymbol{\beta}} \ell(\mathbf{s}_t, \boldsymbol{\beta}^t) - \alpha^t \langle \mathbf{g}(\boldsymbol{\beta}^t; \mathbf{w}_t), \boldsymbol{\beta} - \boldsymbol{\beta}^t \rangle + \frac{1}{2} \|\boldsymbol{\beta} - \boldsymbol{\beta}^t\|_2^2$$

under a projection to ensure $\boldsymbol{\beta}$ be a topical dictionary. We have denoted the projection to the simplex P by Π_P.

Mini-batches: A useful technique to reduce noise in stochastic learning is to consider multiple observations per iteration. Suppose we have M data at each iteration. After fitting the sparse codes for each document, the online update rule is

$$\boldsymbol{\beta}^{t+1} = \Pi_P(\boldsymbol{\beta}^t - \alpha^t \frac{1}{M} \sum_{d=1}^{M} \mathbf{g}(\boldsymbol{\beta}_t; \mathbf{w}_t^d)), \quad (12)$$

where $\mathbf{w}_t^d$ is the dth document in mini-batch t. Note that when $M = D$, we recover the batch STC. To provide some intuitive ideas, an illustration of the online learning procedure is shown in Fig. 3, whose detail description will be presented at the end of this section, after we have presented the convergence analysis and extensions.

Comparison with online LDA: Recently efficient online learning algorithms have been proposed for LDA to scale up to large datasets and to deal with dynamic text streams [16, 20, 27]. Our algorithm closely resembles the online variational Bayesian algorithm for LDA [16]. This similarity makes it convenient to compare the two variants of online topic models, including time efficiency and sparsity of word codes, as reported in the experiments.

4.1 Analysis of Convergence

The deterministic formulation of STC allows us to analyze the convergence behavior of the online algorithm. First, we analyze the regularity of the objective function in dictionary learning.

Lemma 1. *The cost function $\ell(\mathbf{s}_t, \boldsymbol{\beta}; \mathbf{w}_t)$ is convex over $\boldsymbol{\beta}$ and bounded from below; and its gradient and Hessian matrix are bounded.*

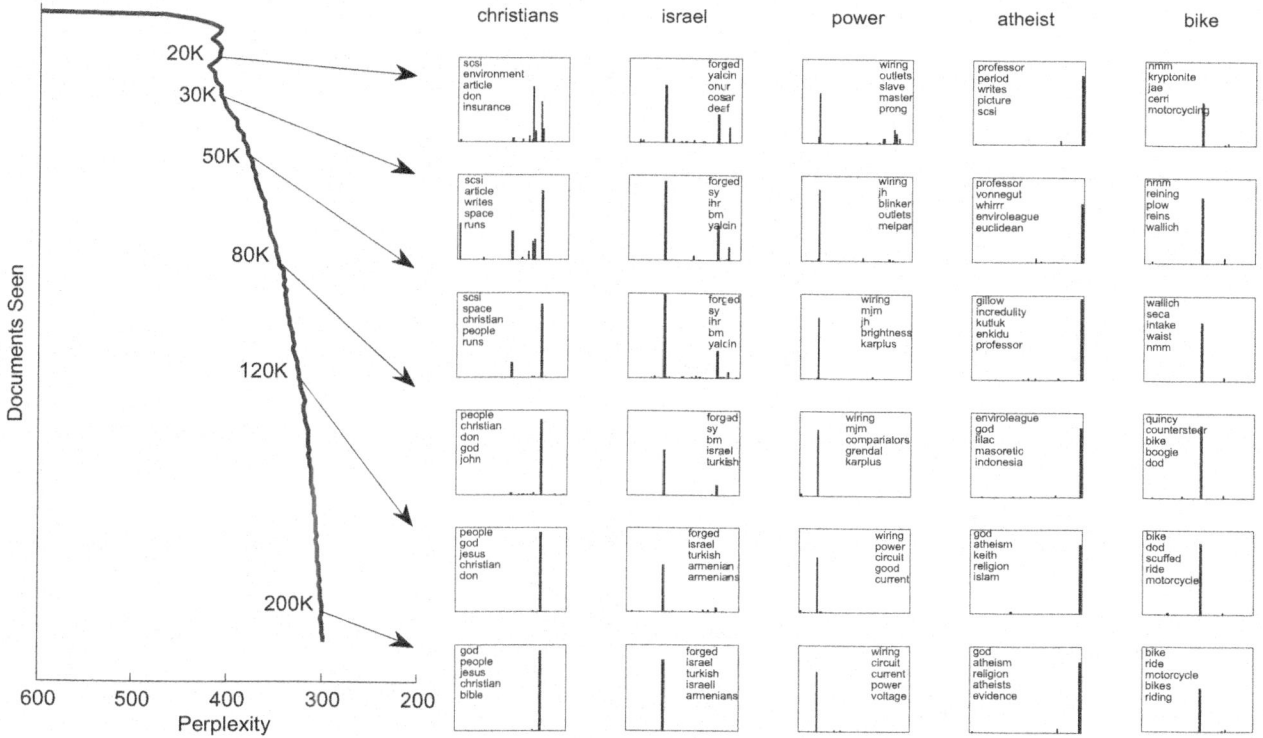

Figure 3: The change of perplexity and average word codes on test documents during the training process of OMedSTC (See section 4.2.2), as the online algorithm scans more articles (see the numbers near the blue curve). From top to bottom, we can see that the held-out perplexity drops down (in the left figure); the average word codes grow sparser (the right five columns); and the semantic meaning of the most salient topics representing the 5 selected words becomes clearer (for each topic, we present the 5 top-ranked terms inside the boxes).

Proof: The first part is obvious for the log-Poisson loss, since we have avoided the degenerated cases by introducing the parameter ϵ and the maximum word count is bounded in real cases. The gradient $\nabla_{\boldsymbol{\beta}_{\cdot n}} \ell(\mathbf{s}_t, \boldsymbol{\beta}; \mathbf{w}_t) = \mathbb{I}(n \in I_t)(1 - \frac{w_{tn}}{\mathbf{s}_{tn}^\top \boldsymbol{\beta}_{\cdot n} + \epsilon})\mathbf{s}_{tn}$ is also bounded for the same reason. For the last part, we directly prove the largest eigenvalue of Hessian matrix is bounded:

$$\lambda_{max} = \sup_{\boldsymbol{\beta} \geq 0} \sup_{\|z\|_2 \leq 1} z^\top \nabla^2_{\boldsymbol{\beta}_{\cdot n}} \ell(\mathbf{s}_t, \boldsymbol{\beta}; \mathbf{w}_t) z$$

$$= \sup_{\boldsymbol{\beta} \geq 0} \sup_{\|z\|_2 \leq 1} z^\top (\sum_{n \in I_t} \frac{\mathbf{s}_{tn} w_{tn} \mathbf{s}_{tn}^\top}{(\mathbf{s}_{tn}^\top \boldsymbol{\beta}_{\cdot n} + \epsilon)^2}) z$$

$$= \sup_{\|z\|_2 \leq 1} z^\top (\sum_{n \in I_t} \frac{\mathbf{s}_{tn} w_{tn} \mathbf{s}_{tn}^\top}{\epsilon^2}) z = \frac{\|\mathbf{s}_t \mathrm{diag}(\mathbf{w}_t) \mathbf{s}_t^\top\|_2}{\epsilon^2}$$

$$\leq \frac{1}{\epsilon^2} \|\mathbf{s}_t\|_2^2 \|\mathrm{diag}(\mathbf{w}_t)\|_2 \leq \frac{w_{t_{max}}}{\epsilon^2} \|\mathbf{s}_t\|_1 \|\mathbf{s}_t\|_\infty.$$

Since $\mathbf{s}_{tn}$ and $\boldsymbol{\beta}_{\cdot n}$ are non-negative, the first supremum is achieved when $\mathbf{s}_{tn}^\top \boldsymbol{\beta}_{\cdot n} = 0$. Then we use the definition of the induced matrix 2-norm to get a more compact expression. Finally, using inequalities of matrix norm and the maximum word count $w_{t_{max}}$, we get the last inequality. Note that $\|\mathbf{s}_t\|_1 = \max_k \sum_n \mathbf{s}_{tn}^k$ was bounded by the number of different words exist in a mini-batch and $\|\mathbf{s}_t\|_\infty = \max_n \sum_k \mathbf{s}_{tn}^k$ relates to the scale of $\mathbf{s}_{tn}$ and was controlled by hyperparameters. So the Hessian matrix of $\ell(\mathbf{s}_t, \boldsymbol{\beta}; \mathbf{w}_t)$ is bounded. □

To analyze the convergence of OSTC, we follow the method used in [16]. Suppose that we sample articles together with their word codes, then we can compute the expected gradient of the cost function. Since STC and OSTC perform MAP estimates and find a single value of each word code, we compute the expectation over $\mathbf{s}$ by using an impulse distribution with our estimate of the codes. Then, we can derive results which are similar as in [7] to ensure that our online algorithm converge to a stationary point, as shown in the following theorem.

Theorem 2. *Assume that the learning rate α^t satisfies $\sum_{t=1}^\infty (\alpha^t)^2 < \infty$, $\sum_{t=1}^\infty \alpha^t = \infty$. Then, OSTC converges.*

Proof: The proof is partly based on [7]. We first define the *Lyapunow sequence* $h^t = \|\boldsymbol{\beta}^t - \boldsymbol{\beta}^*\|^2$ where $\boldsymbol{\beta}^*$ is a stationary point and prove that $\boldsymbol{\beta}^t$ converges based on the convergence of h^t. We denote the previous knowledge (i.e., $\boldsymbol{\beta}^{\hat{t}}, \boldsymbol{\theta}_{\hat{t}}, \mathbf{s}_{\hat{t}}, \forall 0 \leq \hat{t} \leq t$) by P^t. Then

$$\mathbb{E}[h^{t+1} - h^t | P^t] = -2\alpha^t (\boldsymbol{\beta}^t - \boldsymbol{\beta}^*) \mathbb{E}_{\mathbf{w}_t}[\nabla_{\boldsymbol{\beta}} \ell(\mathbf{s}_t, \boldsymbol{\beta}^t; \mathbf{w}_t) | P^t]$$
$$+ (\alpha^t)^2 \mathbb{E}_{\mathbf{w}_t}[(\nabla_{\boldsymbol{\beta}} \ell(\mathbf{s}_t, \boldsymbol{\beta}^t; \mathbf{w}_t))^2 | P^t]$$

Note that the first order derivative is bounded and the second order term was also bounded by $A + B(\boldsymbol{\beta}^t - \boldsymbol{\beta}^*)^2$, where A and B are non-negative values. This is because the eigenvalues of Hessian matrix is bounded and the gradient will not exceed a polynomial threshold. Transforming previous equation we get

$$\mathbb{E}[(h^{t+1} - (1-(\alpha^t)^2 B)h^t | P^t] = \\ -2\alpha^t(\boldsymbol{\beta}^t - \boldsymbol{\beta}^*)\mathbb{E}_{\mathbf{w}_t}[\nabla_{\boldsymbol{\beta}}\ell(\mathbf{s}_t, \boldsymbol{\beta}^t; \mathbf{w}_t)|P^t](\alpha^t)^2 A \quad (13)$$

Using the techniques in [7], if we replace h^t with a scaling term and choose $\alpha^t = \tau_0/(t+\tau)$ where τ and τ_0 are positive constants, we can prove that h^t converges and the infinite sum of the left hand side of Eq. (13) also converges. Therefore, the infinite sum of the right hand side of Eq. (13) also converges, i.e.,

$$\sum_{t=1}^{\infty} \alpha^t (\boldsymbol{\beta}^t - \boldsymbol{\beta}^*) \mathbb{E}_{\mathbf{w}_t}[\nabla_{\boldsymbol{\beta}} \ell(\mathbf{s}_t, \boldsymbol{\beta}^t; \mathbf{w}_t)|P^t] < \infty. \quad (14)$$

Since $\sum_{t=1}^{\infty} \alpha^t = \sum_{t=1}^{\infty} \tau_0/(t+\tau) = \infty$ and the first order derivative is bounded, we must have that $|\boldsymbol{\beta}^t - \boldsymbol{\beta}^*|$ converges to zero. □

In all the experiments, we set $\alpha^t = \tau_0/(t+10)$, which satisfies the assumptions in the above theorem.

4.2 Extensions

Before ending this section, we briefly present two extensions of the online learning algorithm for collapsed sparse topical coding and max-margin supervised dictionary learning.

4.2.1 Online Collapsed STC

STC was intentionally designed as having a hierarchical structure, similar as the hierarchical probabilistic topic models, for easy comparison. But for practical performance, it has been demonstrated in probabilistic topic models that collapsing some parts of the latent variables could potentially improve performance [15]. We take the analogy and develop a collapsed STC (CSTC), and show that our online learning algorithm can be naturally extended for CSTC.

Specifically, as described in Section 3.2, STC is a MAP estimate of a hierarchical Bayesian model. When using a normal prior on $\boldsymbol{\theta}$, we can derive the collapsed STC by marginalizing out $\boldsymbol{\theta}$. For each document d, we have the collapsed distribution

$$p(\mathbf{s}_d, \mathbf{w}_d | \boldsymbol{\beta}) \propto \zeta_d \int_{\boldsymbol{\theta}_d} \exp\left\{ -\lambda \|\boldsymbol{\theta}_d\|_2^2 - \frac{\gamma}{2} \sum_{n \in I_d} \|\mathbf{s}_{dn} - \boldsymbol{\theta}_d\|_2^2 \right\} \\ \propto \zeta_d \exp\left\{ -a \sum_{n \in I_d} \|\mathbf{s}_{dn}\|_2^2 + 2b \sum_{m \neq m'} \mathbf{s}_{dm}^\top \mathbf{s}_{dm'} \right\},$$

where $\zeta_d = \exp\{-\ell(\mathbf{s}_d, \boldsymbol{\beta}) - \rho \|\mathbf{s}_d\|_1\}$ is independent of $\boldsymbol{\theta}_d$, $a = \frac{\gamma}{2} - \frac{\gamma^2}{4(\lambda + \frac{\gamma |I_d|}{2})}$ and $b = \frac{\gamma^2}{4(\lambda + \frac{\gamma |I_d|}{2})}$. Then, by performing MAP estimation, we derive the collapsed STC as solving

$$\min_{\mathbf{S}, \boldsymbol{\beta}} \quad \text{tr}(\mathbf{s}_d^\top \Lambda \mathbf{s}_d) + \ell(\mathbf{s}_d, \boldsymbol{\beta}) + \rho \|\mathbf{s}_d\|_1 \quad (15) \\ \text{s.t.:} \quad \mathbf{S} \geq 0; \ \boldsymbol{\beta}_k. \in P, \forall k,$$

where $\Lambda = (a-b)I + bE$ and $\mathbf{s}_d$ is an $K \times |I_d|$ matrix, of which the column n corresponds to $\mathbf{s}_{dn}$.

The problem is again biconvex, i.e., convex over $\mathbf{S}$ or $\boldsymbol{\beta}$ when the other is fixed. Both batch and online algorithms can be developed to solve Eq. (15), since the dictionary learning step is the same as in STC. The difference is on the sparse coding step, which is now to find the optimal word codes for each document. We can also derive a coordinate descent algorithm, of which each substep has a closed-form solution. Specifically, the optimal solution of s_{dn}^k is $\max(0, \nu_{dn}^k)$, where ν_{dn}^k is the larger solution of the quadratic equation

$$2a\beta_{kn}(\nu_{dn}^k)^2 + c\beta_{kn}\nu_{dn}^k + c\sum_{k' \neq k} s_{dn}^{k'} \beta_{k'n} - w_{dn}\beta_{kn} = 0$$

where $c = \beta_{kn} + \rho + 2b \sum_{m \neq n} s_{dm}^k$.

4.2.2 Online Max-margin STC

Both STC and CSTC learn dictionaries and infer sparse representations of unlabeled samples. But with the increasing availability of free on-line information such as image tags, user ratings, etc., various forms of "side-information" that can potentially offer "free" supervision have lead to a need for new topic models and training schemes that can make an effective use of such information to achieve better results, such as more discriminative latent representations of text contents and more accurate classifiers [4, 41]. In [42], a supervised max-margin STC (MedSTC) was developed to learn predictive representations and a supervised dictionary [26] by exploring the available side-information.

The basic idea of MedSTC is to use document codes as input features for max-margin classifiers, e.g., the multi-class SVM [10]. Formally, MedSTC solves the problem

$$\min_{\boldsymbol{\Theta}, \mathbf{S}, \boldsymbol{\beta}, \boldsymbol{\eta}} f(\boldsymbol{\Theta}, \mathbf{S}, \boldsymbol{\beta}) + C\mathcal{R}(\boldsymbol{\Theta}, \boldsymbol{\eta}) + \frac{1}{2}\|\boldsymbol{\eta}\|_2^2 \quad (16) \\ \text{s.t.}: \quad \boldsymbol{\Theta} \geq 0; \mathbf{S} \geq 0; \boldsymbol{\beta}_k \in P, \forall k,$$

where $f(\boldsymbol{\Theta}, \mathbf{S}, \boldsymbol{\beta})$ is the objective function of STC and

$$\mathcal{R}(\boldsymbol{\Theta}, \boldsymbol{\eta}) = \frac{1}{D} \sum_d \max_y [\Delta(y_d, y) + \boldsymbol{\eta}_y^\top \boldsymbol{\theta}_d - \boldsymbol{\eta}_{y_d}^\top \boldsymbol{\theta}_d]$$

is the multiclass hinge loss with parameters $\boldsymbol{\eta} = [\boldsymbol{\eta}_1; \cdots; \boldsymbol{\eta}_L]$ for L classes, of which each $\boldsymbol{\eta}_l$ is a K-dimensional vector associated with class l. The loss function $\Delta(y_d, y)$ measures the cost of making a prediction y if the ground truth label is y_d. Normally, we assume $\Delta(y, y) = 0$, i.e., no cost for a correct prediction.

The problem is again biconvex, i.e., convex over $(\boldsymbol{\Theta}, \mathbf{S})$ or $(\boldsymbol{\beta}, \boldsymbol{\eta})$ when the other is fixed. In [42], a batch algorithm was developed to alternately solve for $(\boldsymbol{\Theta}, \mathbf{S})$ and $(\boldsymbol{\beta}, \boldsymbol{\eta})$. Since $\boldsymbol{\beta}$ and $\boldsymbol{\eta}$ are not coupled, we can solve for each of them separately. For $\boldsymbol{\eta}$, the subproblem is to learn a linear multi-class SVM. Based on the above online dictionary learning algorithm and the existing high-performance online learning algorithm for SVMs [32], we can develop an online learning algorithm for MedSTC, which is still guaranteed to converge. We denote this method by OMedSTC.

Before presenting all the details of the experiments, we use Fig. 3 to illustrate the change of the perplexity on held-out documents and the word codes along the iterations of online learning. We present the results of OMedSTC with 70 topics on the 20Newsgroup data with a standard train/test split, which will be clear in the next section. Fig. 3 shows the perplexity of the test set and the average word codes of the five popular words, of which each one is from a different category, at different stages of online learning. For each word, we calculate the average word code over the test documents that are from the category as that particular word. For example, the average word code of *bike* is the mean of all the word codes for *bike* in the *rec.motorcycles* category. We can see the held-out perplexity goes down when scanning more articles while at the same time the average word codes for each word grows sparser and at the end of training most words are dominated by a few topics. It is also nice to see that the semantic meanings of the most salient topics describing the selected words become clearer by listing their top words (i.e., words that have highest values in the topic). For example, the average word code for the word *christians* was dominated by some not-clearly-meaningful topics when we scan 20K articles, while at the end of our algorithm it was captured by only one topic that has a very clear topical meaning, with the top five words being *god, people, jesus, christian*, and *bible*, all relating to the target word *christians*.

5. EXPERIMENTS

Now, we present all the details of our empirical results on a dataset with 6.6M articles collected from Wikipedia and the 20Newsgroups dataset to evaluate the effectiveness of online learning algorithms for STC, MedSTC and CSTC. We set the learning rate $\alpha^t = \tau_0/(t+10)$ and tune τ_0 for models with different batch sizes[5]. All the experiments are done on a standard desktop with 2.67GHz processors and 2GB RAM. Note that to reduce the influence of network speed, all the datasets were pre-collected. Thus, the experiments are not really online. But they suffice to evaluate the effectiveness and efficiency of the online learning algorithms.

5.1 Experiments on the Wikipedia Dataset

We first report the results on the unsupervised Wikipedia dataset. We use perplexity as the performance measure, which is defined as the geometric mean of the inverse marginal probability of each word in a held-out set of documents $\mathbf{W}^{test}$. Here, we randomly select 1000 articles as the held-out set. We compare OSTC with the ordinary batch STC and the online LDA (OLDA) using variational inference[6] [16]. We note that other versions of OLDA have been developed by doing hybrid variational inference and Monte Carlo sampling [27], which could improve the time efficiency of OLDA. But since our main focus is on topic sparsity[7], we compare with the variational OLDA, whose procedure is more similar as OSTC. We will discuss the influence of various inference methods for LDA on perplexity later. In the experiments, we set $K = 100$, which is sufficient to fit the data well[8].

Below we first explain the perplexity measure we use for our STC models, which is slightly different from the commonly used perplexity for probabilistic models like LDA.

5.1.1 Perplexity for STC models

---

[5]Since τ_0 may affect the convergence speed, we tune τ_0 for the best performance. Similar as in [16], we set a smaller τ_0 for a larger batch size.

[6]We use the authors' implementation:
http://www.cs.princeton.edu/~blei/downloads/onlineldavb.tar

[7]Although sampling methods for LDA often result in sparse topic representations due to the limited number of samples, both LDA and OLDA are not sparse models. In contrast, both STC and OSTC are sparse due to a soft-thresholding operators as presented in Section 3.3.

[8]We tried K=100, 150, 200 and found no big difference in held-out perplexity.

Perplexity is a common measure of topic models' ability to generalize to test data. It is defined as the geometric mean of word likelihood. For probabilistic models, word likelihood is a marginal of the joint distribution of words and topic assignment, where the topic distribution is inferred from test data. But for STC, since we do not have a distribution of word codes, we then have our perplexity definition different with probabilistic topic models. We now use LDA as an example of probabilistic topic models to explicitly discuss its perplexity definition compared with STC.

For probabilistic topic models, the perplexity was defined as follows. Let n_i^{test} denote all words in a test document i and N_i^{test} is the total word counts in document i. Then the perplexity is the geometric mean of word likelihood in the test set:

$$\text{perplexity} = \exp\left\{-\frac{\sum_i \log p(n_i^{test})}{\sum_i N_i^{test}}\right\}. \quad (17)$$

For LDA and OLDA, since exact inference is intractable, a variational bound was developed to approximate the perplexity [16]. However, this variational bound utilize words in the held-out set and may over-fit the test data. Here we use a 'document completion' method [30] to evaluate the held-out perplexity and this is done by first using half of the test words (denoted by n_{i1}^{test}) to infer document codes for the test documents and then evaluating the held-out perplexity by sampling word code for the other half of words in the test data (denoted by n_{i2}^{test}). This method avoid over-fitting since n_{i2}^{test} was not used for inference. Precisely, the perplexity of LDA is computed as

$$\text{perplexity}_{LDA} \approx \exp\left\{-\frac{\sum_i \log p(n_{i2}^{test}|p(n_{i1}^{test},\alpha,\boldsymbol{\beta})}{\sum_i |N_{i2}^{test}|}\right\}. \quad (18)$$

For STC and OSTC, we do not define a posterior distribution of word codes, which means we can not compute the marginal of the joint distribution of words and topic assignment as in probabilistic topic models. However, in STC we can use a similar strategy as done in LDA by first utilizing half of the test terms (denoted by w_{i1}^{test}) to infer the document codes for the test set and then sample word codes for the other half of terms (denoted by w_{i2}^{test}) to calculate the held-out perplexity as

$$\text{perplexity}_{STC} \approx \exp\left\{-\frac{\sum_i \log p(w_{i2}^{test}|w_{i1}^{test},\boldsymbol{\beta})}{\sum_i |I_{i2}^{test}|}\right\}. \quad (19)$$

From above discussions, we argue that both perplexity definations are proper for their own settings. To further check this, we also provide an 'interchange' experiment in the Appendix. In the following experiments we will use the Eq. (18) to calculate perplexity for LDA models and Eq. (19) for our STC models.

5.1.2 Experiments on 99K subset

To compare with OLDA, we follow the same settings in [16] and randomly choose a 99K subset of the whole Wikipedia data. Fig. 4(a) shows the perplexity of OSTC (with batch size $M = 64$), batch STC and OLDA ($M = 64$). We can see that OSTC converges much faster than batch STC because of its effective exploration of document redundancy. We also observe that OSTC has a lower perplexity than OLDA. The main reason is that STC uses un-normalized word codes, which offer an additional freedom compared to the normalized probability in LDA. This extra freedom could lead to better fitness of the observed data.

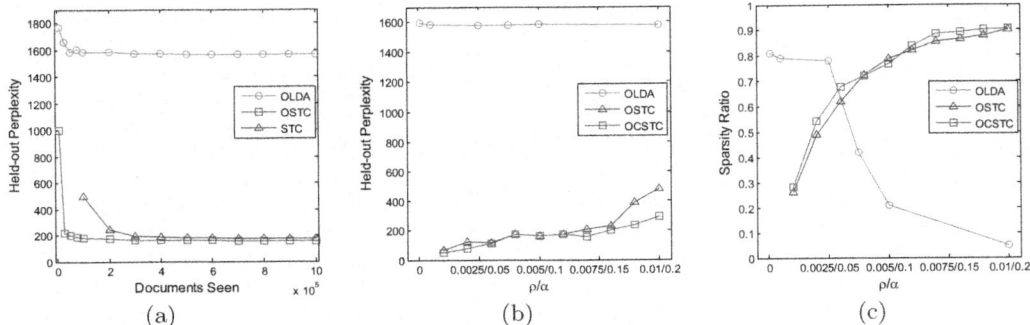

Figure 4: (a) held-out perplexity of STC, online STC and online LDA on the 99K Wikipedia dataset; (b,c) perplexity and sparsity of OSTC and OLDA when the hyper-parameters ρ and α change.

Table 1: Perplexity of LDA, CG-LDA and STC on two datasets.

	LDA	CG-LDA	STC
Wikipedia	1609.16	1503.85	265.37
20Newsgroups	5656.38	4847.65	1588.59

To examine the influence of approximate inference algorithms on perplexity, Table 1 further compares the perplexity of STC with those of the LDA models using variational mean-field as well as the collapsed Gibbs sampling [15]. We denote the LDA using collapsed Gibbs sampling by CG-LDA. We can see that although using collapsed Gibbs sampling can improve the performance of LDA, its perplexity is still significantly higher than that of STC.

Fig. 4(b) and Fig. 4(c) further compare the held-out perplexity and word code sparsity of OSTC and OLDA when their hyper-parameters change. Both models have a single pass on the 99K subset. For OSTC, we fix $\lambda = \gamma = 0.025$ and only change ρ (changing both ρ and γ will lead to even better results), and for OLDA, the hyper-parameter is the Dirichlet parameter α. We can see that for both models, the hyper-parameter affects the word code sparsity much. But for OLDA, the held-out perplexity doesn't change much, all remaining at a level of about 1,600. In contrast, ρ affects much on the perplexity of OSTC. At all points, OSTC obtains a smaller perplexity than OLDA. Moreover, when ρ is set at a relatively large value (e.g., 0.01), OSTC obtains much lower perplexity and higher word code sparsity. Our observations are consistent with those in [42, 21], whose experiments demonstrate the effectiveness of STC on discovering sparse (and interpretable) topical representations.

We also investigate the performance of collapsed STC using online learning. From Fig. 4(b) and Fig. 4(c), we can see that the collapsed OSTC (i.e., OCSTC) outputs slightly sparser word codes and achieves even lower perplexity than OSTC, when both methods using the same hyper-parameters. This performance gain comes from relaxation of conditional independence constraints in the inference step.

5.1.3 Experiments on 6.6M Wikipedia corpus

Now, we use the whole 6.6M Wikipedia dataset to examine the scalability of OSTC. Fig. 5 shows the perplexity of OSTC with different batch sizes, as a function of the running

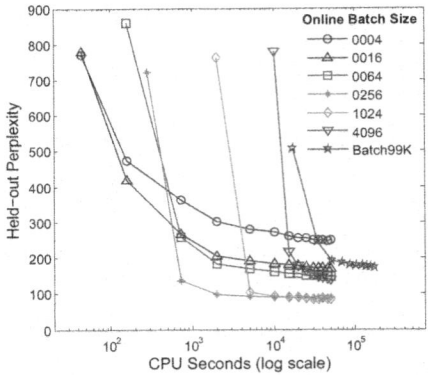

Figure 5: held-out perplexity of online STC using different batch sizes on the whole 6.6M Wikipedia dataset.

time. We can see that the convergence speeds of different algorithms vary[9]. First, since batch algorithm suffers from writing disk operations due to its huge memory cost[10], its performance is much worse than those of the online alternatives. Second, online algorithms with medium batch sizes (e.g., $M = 256$) converge faster than others. When we use a too small batch size (e.g., $M = 4$), it takes a long time to converge because we update the dictionary too frequently in each iteration without enough evidence. Finally, we also note that as the batch size becomes too large (e.g., $M = 4096$), the convergence speed of online algorithm approaches the very slow batch algorithm.

5.2 Experiments on 20Newsgroups Dataset

The 20Newsgroups dataset consists of 18,774 documents from 20 different newsgroups with a standard train/test split[11] of 11,269/7,505. The vocabulary contains 61188 terms, and we remove a standard list of 524 stop words as in [42].

---

[9] Almost all the OSTC models with different batch sizes converge before scanning the whole corpus.

[10] If we use float type and assume each document has on average 100 words, we will need about 4GB memory to store the word codes for the 99K subset when $K = 100$. For the 6.6M dataset, we will need about 250GB.

[11] http://people.csail.mit.edu/jrennie/20Newsgroups/

Table 2: Classification accuracy of LDA, STC and MedSTC on the 20Newsgroups dataset.

batch size	LDA accuracy(%)	LDA time(ks)	STC accuracy(%)	STC time(ks)	MedSTC accuracy(%)	MedSTC time(ks)
1	52.3	61.2	53.1	41.1	65.3	44.4
8	58.3±1.4	17.9	64.7±1.2	7.0	80.0	14.1
16	60.5±0.7	8.5	66.1±0.7	3.9	81.2	12.3
32	**61.7±0.7**	6.2	**66.3±1.0**	2.7	80.5	**8.8**
64	60.9±0.9	**4.0**	65.2±1.6	**2.2**	81.3	10.9
batch	61.4±0.7	8.6	62.7±0.6	4.7	**81.6**	18.4

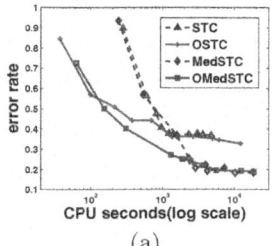
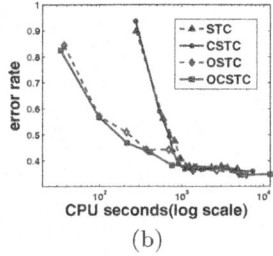

(a)   (b)

Figure 6: (a) error rates of STC and MedSTC as a function of running time; (b) error rates of STC and CSTC as a function of running time.

In these experiments, we focus on comparing both time efficiency and test accuracy between STC and online STC with different batch sizes. The results of other supervised topic models, including MedLDA and sLDA, were reported in [42]. We choose the parameters $K = 60$, $\Delta(y, y') = 3600\mathbb{I}(y \neq y')$, $\rho = 0.1$ and $\lambda = \gamma = 0.01$, which produce good results as shown in [42].

Table 2 presents the classification accuracy of different models with different batch sizes. We can observe that the online STC obtains higher accuracy while with less running time than the online LDA using the same batch size. For STC, online learning algorithms generally improve the time efficiency in order to get a good classification model. For instance, the online STC with a batch size of 32 takes about a half of the running time of the batch STC, and its classification performance is surprisingly much better; for MedSTC, when the batch size is 16, the online MedSTC performs comparably with the batch MedSTC, while taking less running time. We also observe that batch sizes can affect the convergence and classification performance of various online topic models. The reason is that too small batches update β slowly since β is high dimensional, while large batches tend to reach another extreme of being ineffective in exploring data redundancy.

Fig. 6(a) shows the error rates of STC and MedSTC, using both batch and online learning algorithms, as a function of running time. We can see that by cycling on the medium-sized 20Newsgroups dataset, the online algorithms generally reach a good model faster than the batch algorithms. In the unsupervised setting, the online algorithm performs better both in time and classification accuracy. As has been demonstrated on the Wikipedia articles, we can expect large improvements in a much larger and redundant corpus.

Then we report the evaluation of the collapsed STC on the 20Newsgroups dataset for prediction performance, again using both batch and online learning algorithms. Fig. 6(b) presents the error rates as a function of running time. We can see that the online learning algorithms generally converge faster to fairly good results. But the collapsed STC does not shows dramatic improvements compared with STC. This is probably due to the fact that the problem of STC can be solved very well on the this dataset using the coordinate descent algorithm with a hierarchical sparse coding, and the collapsed sparse coding does not help a lot.

Finally, to examine the semantics of the learned topics, Table 3 presents top words (i.e., words that have highest values in the topic) of the most salient topic learned by the online MedSTC for each category (i.e., topic that has highest value in the average document code of each category) on the 20Newsgroups dataset. We can generally see the strong association of the categories and the learned topics.

6. CONCLUSIONS AND DISCUSSIONS

We have presented a sparse online topic model for modeling dynamic text streams and discovering topic representations from large-scale datasets. The online dictionary learning algorithm is efficient and guaranteed to converge. Extensive empirical studies on Wikipedia and 20Newsgroups data have shown appealing performance in terms of held-out perplexity, word code sparsity and prediction accuracy.

For future work, we are interested in various extensions and improvements, including cleverly adjusting the learning rates during learning and dealing with large-scale complex data analysis problems, such as relational network analysis.

7. ACKNOWLEDGMENTS

This work is supported by the National Basic Research Program (973 Program) of China (Nos. 2013CB329403, 2012CB316301), National Natural Science Foundation of China (Nos. 91120011, 61273023), and Tsinghua University Initiative Scientific Research Program (No. 20121088071).

8. APPENDIX

An alternative way to compare STC and LDA

Due to different definitions, more careful analysis should be done on comparing the perplexity between STC and LDA. We now do an interesting 'interchange' experiment. The idea is that although the inference procedure is different between STC and LDA, they both learn normalized topical bases (i.e. the dictionary). So we can turn to test the quality of their bases to see whether one model is strictly better than the other. To do this we first train bases with each model and then calculate the STC held-out perplexity and the LDA held-out perplexity using both bases by Eq. (19) and Eq. (18) separately. For example, we can use STC for training bases (STC bases) and LDA for calculating held-out perplexity (LDA testing). As an upper bound, we

Table 3: Example topics learned by OMedSTC. For each category, we show the most salient topic.

comp.					misc.	talk.			
graphics	ms-windows	ibm.pc	mac	windows.x	forsale	politics.misc	politics.guns	politics.mideast	religion.misc
compass	allocation	dma	gnd	widget	trade	mov	gun	cosmo	incoming
cols	windows	drive	init	entry	msdos	hitler	cranston	power	taoism
rows	yap	aspi	vv	libx	bid	time	guns	erzurum	allocation
graphics	cfg	wires	applelink	xsizehints	toshiba	stephanopoulos	militia	armenian	aleph
rtheta	mywinobj	compaq	mac	libxmu	laptop	viability	people	turks	jesus
ellipse	vb	harddisk	apple	converter	baud	government	weapons	negotiations	bible
sphinx	dos	isa	nubus	accelerators	modem	throws	firearms	turkish	objective
image	file	scsi	backlit	decnet	mpc	chancellor	fire	bayonet	morality
files	bitmap	card	wolves	focus	coupons	president	fbi	labor	christ
color	files	pc	drive	myhint	send	african	law	armenians	christian
sci.				rec.				alt.	soc.
crypt	electronics	med	space	autos	motorcycles	baseball	hockey	atheism	christian
mov	pin	jl	ics	car	gun	roster	pt	contradictory	babylon
nffutils	compass	hiv	incoming	writes	bike	lefthanded	period	rapist	god
maxbyte	tesla	polio	het	tint	zephyr	baseball	switzerland	god	pentecostals
db	hook	oily	space	article	teflon	idle	italy	depression	husband
nist	wire	spect	nasa	carburetor	dog	year	aids	writes	jesus
push	brightness	methanol	launch	lojack	shaft	team	norway	people	senses
offset	doherty	tinnitus	orbit	cars	ride	ball	czech	don	ceremonial
trinomials	power	eye	moon	vw	good	game	austria	allah	people
encryption	blinker	patients	earth	good	hawk	players	qtr	article	christian
key	circuit	msg	shuttle	volvo	back	pitching	game	islam	church

also report the results by using the non-informative uniform basis. Experimental results using different number of topics on the 20Newsgroups dataset are shown below.

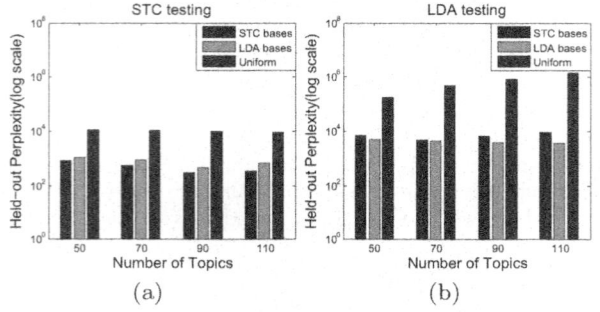

Figure 7: (a) STC testing perplexity for different bases; (b) LDA testing perplexity for different bases.

The left figure shows held-out perplexity by STC using Eq. (19) and the right one shows held-out perplexity by LDA using Eq. (18). Each figure compares among bases learned by both models and the uniform bases (as a baseline). The red bar shows the perplexity calculated by uniform bases as an upper bound. Obviously, both STC and LDA learn meaningful bases and their held-out perplexity is significantly lower than the perplexity produced by the uniform bases (In both figures we use log scale for the perplexity axis.). In the left figure when we calculate held-out perplexity by STC, we achieve a lower perplexity by using STC bases. However, LDA bases get a lower perplexity in the other setting in the right figure. Thus, using the same model for training and testing achieves better results. The bases learned by other models can be useful, but not as accurate as the original one. Finally, we also note that in general, we get lower perplexity when using STC for testing.

9. REFERENCES

[1] E. M. Airoldi, D. M. Blei, S. E. Fienberg, and E. P. Xing. Mixed membership stochastic blockmodels. *Journal of Machine Learning Research*, (9):1981–2014, 2008.

[2] A. Asuncion, M. Welling, P. Smyth, and Y. Teh. On smoothing and inference for topic models. In *Conference on Uncertainty in Artificial Intelligence*, pages 27–34, 2009.

[3] D. Blei and J. Lafferty. Correlated topic models. In *Advances in Neural Information Processing Systems*, pages 147–154, 2005.

[4] D. Blei and J. McAuliffe. Supervised topic models. In *Advances in Neural Information Processing Systems*, pages 121–128, 2007.

[5] D. Blei, A. Ng, and M. Jordan. Latent Dirichlet allocation. *Journal of Machine Learning Research*, (3):993–1022, 2003.

[6] D. M. Blei and J. D. Lafferty. Dynamic topic models. In *International Conference on Machine Learning*, pages 113–120, 2006.

[7] L. Bottou. *Online Learning and Stochastic Approximations*, chapter On-line learning in neural networks. 1998.

[8] L. Bottou and O. Bousquet. The tradeoffs of large scale learning. In *Advances in Neural Information Processing Systems*, pages 161–168, 2008.

[9] J. Boyd-Graber, D. Blei, and X. Zhu. A topic model for word sense disambiguation. In *Conference on Empirical Methods in Natural Language Processing*, pages 1024–1033, 2007.

[10] K. Crammer and Y. Singer. On the algorithmic implementation of multiclass kernel-based vector machines. *Journal of Machine Learning Research*, (2):265–292, 2001.

[11] J. Duchi, S. Shalev-Shwartz, Y. Singer, and T. Chandra. Efficient projections onto the ℓ_1-ball for learning in high dimensions. In *International Conference on Machine Learning*, pages 272–279, 2008.

[12] L. Fei-Fei and P. Perona. A Bayesian hierarchical model for learning natural scene categories. In *IEEE*

Computer Society Conference on Computer Vision and Pattern Recognition, pages 524–531, 2005.

[13] R. Fergus, L. Fei-Fei, P. Perona, and A. Zisserman. Learning object categories from Google's image search. In *IEEE Computer Society Conference on Computer Vision and Pattern Recognition*, pages 1816–1823, 2005.

[14] W. Fu, J. Wang, Z. Li, H. Lu, and S. Ma. Learning semantic motion patterns for dynamic scenes by improved sparse topical coding. In *International Conference on Multimedia and Expo*, pages 296–301, 2012.

[15] T. Griffiths and M. Steyvers. Finding scientific topics. *Proceedings of the National Academy of Sciences*, (101):5228–5235, 2004.

[16] M. Hoffman, D. Blei, and F. Bach. Online learning for latent Dirichlet allocation. In *Advances in Neural Information Processing Systems*, pages 156–164, 2010.

[17] T. Hofmann. Probabilistic latent semantic analysis. In *Uncertainty in Artificial Intelligence*, 1999.

[18] P. Hoyer. Non-negative sparse coding. In *IEEE Workshop on Neural Networks for Signal Processing*, 2002.

[19] A. Hyvarinen. Sparse code shrinkage: Denoising of nongaussian data by maximum likelihood estimation. *Neural Computation*, (11):1739–1768, 1999.

[20] T. Iwata, T. Yamada, Y. Sakurai, and N. Ueda. Online multiscale dynamic topic models. In *Conference on Knowledge Discovery and Data Mining*, pages 663–672, 2010.

[21] R. Ji, L. Duan, J. Chen, and W. Gao. Towards compact topical descriptors. In *Conference on Computer Vision and Pattern Recognition*, pages 2925–2932, 2012.

[22] J. J. Kivinen, E. B. Sudderth, and M. I. Jordan. Learning multiscale representations of natural scenes using Dirichlet processes. In *IEEE International Conference on Computer Vision*, pages 1–8, 2007.

[23] D. Lee and H. Seung. Learning the parts of objects by non-negative matrix factorization. *Nature*, 401:788 – 791, 1999.

[24] H. Lee, R. Raina, A. Teichman, and A. Ng. Exponential family sparse coding with applications to self-taught learning. In *International Joint Conferences on Artificial Intelligence*, pages 1113–1119, 2009.

[25] L.-J. Li, J. Zhu, H. Su, E. Xing, and L. Fei-Fei. Multi-level structured image coding on high-dimensional image representation. In *Asian Conference on Computer Vision*, 2012.

[26] J. Mairal, F. Bach, J. Ponce, G. Sapiro, and A. Zisserman. Supervised dictionary learning. In *Advances in Neural Information Processing Systems*, pages 1033–1040, 2008.

[27] D. Mimno, M. Hoffman, and D. Blei. Sparse stochastic inference for latent Dirichlet allocation. In *International Conference on Machine Learning*, 2012.

[28] D. Mimno, H. Wallach, J. Naradowsky, D. A. Smith, and A. McCallum. Polylingual topic models. In *Conference on Empirical Methods in Natural Language Processing*, pages 880–889, 2009.

[29] B. A. Olshausen and D. J. Field. Emergence of simple-cell receptive field properties by learning a sparse code for natural images. *Nature*, 381(6583):607–609, 1996.

[30] M. Rosen-Zvi, T. Griffiths, M. Steyvers, and P. Smyth. The author-topic model for authors and documents. In *Conference on Uncertainty in Artificial Intelligence*, pages 487–494, 2004.

[31] B. C. Russell, A. A. Efros, J. Sivic, W. T. Freeman, and A. Zisserman. Using multiple segmentations to discover objects and their extent in image collections. In *IEEE Computer Society Conference on Computer Vision and Pattern Recognition*, pages 1605–1614, 2006.

[32] S. Shalev-Shwartz, Y. Singer, and N. Srebro. Pegasos: Primal estimated sub-gradient solver for svm. In *International Conference on Machine Learning*, pages 807–814, 2007.

[33] M. Shashanka, B. Raj, and P. Smaragdis. Sparse overcomplete latent variable decomposition of counts data. In *Advances in Neural Information Processing Systems*, pages 1313–1320, 2007.

[34] J. Sivic, B. C. Russell, A. A. Efros, A. Zisserman, and W. T. Freeman. Discovering objects and their locatioins in images. In *IEEE International Conference on Computer Vision*, pages 370–377, 2005.

[35] S. Sra, D. Kim, and B. Schölkopf. Non-monotonic Poisson likelihood maximization. *Tech. Report, MPI for Biological Cybernetics*, 2008.

[36] Y. W. Teh, D. Newman, and M. Welling. A collapsed variational Bayesian inference algorithm for latent Dirichlet allocation. In *Advances in Neural Information Processing Systems*, pages 1353–1360, 2007.

[37] C. Wang, D. Blei, and L. Fei-Fei. Simultaneous image classification and annotation. In *IEEE Computer Society Conference on Computer Vision and Pattern Recognition*, pages 1903–1910, 2009.

[38] Q. Wang, J. Xu, H. Li, and N. Craswell. Regularized latent semantic indexing. In *Proceedings of the 34th international ACM SIGIR conference on Research and development in Information Retrieval*, pages 685–694, 2011.

[39] L. Yao, D. Mimno, and A. McCallum. Efficient methods for topic model inference on streaming document collections. In *Conference on Knowledge Discovery and Data Mining*, pages 937–946, 2009.

[40] K. Zhai, J. Boyd-Graber, N. Asadi, and M. Alkhouja. Mr. LDA: A flexible large scale topic modeling package using variational inference in MapReduce. In *Proceedings of World Wide Web Conference*, pages 879–888, 2012.

[41] J. Zhu, A. Ahmed, and E. Xing. MedLDA: Maximum margin supervised topic models for regression and classification. In *International Conference on Machine Learning*, pages 1257–1264, 2009.

[42] J. Zhu and E. Xing. Sparse topical coding. In *Conference on Uncertainty in Artificial Intelligence*, pages 831–838, 2011.

TopRec: Domain-Specific Recommendation through Community Topic Mining in Social Network

Xi Zhang, Jian Cheng[*], Ting Yuan, Biao Niu, Hanqing Lu
National Laboratory of Pattern Recognition
Institute of Automation, Chinese Academy of Sciences
Beijing, China
{xi.zhang, jcheng, tyuan, bniu, luhq}@nlpr.ia.ac.cn

ABSTRACT

Traditionally, Collaborative Filtering assumes that similar users have similar responses to similar items. However, human activities exhibit heterogenous features across multiple domains such that users own similar tastes in one domain may behave quite differently in other domains. Moreover, highly sparse data presents crucial challenge in preference prediction. Intuitively, if users' interested domains are captured first, the recommender system is more likely to provide the enjoyed items while filter out those uninterested ones. Therefore, it is necessary to learn preference profiles from the correlated domains instead of the entire user-item matrix. In this paper, we propose a unified framework, TopRec, which detects topical communities to construct interpretable domains for domain-specific collaborative filtering. In order to mine communities as well as the corresponding topics, a semi-supervised probabilistic topic model is utilized by integrating user guidance with social network. Experimental results on real-world data from Epinions and Ciao demonstrate the effectiveness of the proposed framework.

Categories and Subject Descriptors

H.3.3 [**Information Search and Retrieval**]: Information filtering; H.3.5 [**Online Information Services**]: Web-based services

General Terms

Algorithms, Experimentation

Keywords

Recommender Systems, Collaborative Filtering, Social Network, Probabilistic Topic Modeling

1. INTRODUCTION

As electronic commerce becomes increasingly popular, large amounts of available information for products are flooding the Web. To avoid customers inundated with choices, nowadays recommender systems take a central role by selecting the potential enjoyed products and filtering out uninterested ones. Through taking personalized recommendations for products, some famous online shopping websites such as Amazon and Netflix have expanded their marketing successfully [7, 15].

Most of these commercial systems are based on Collaborative Filtering(CF), which is an effective recommendation approach with fundamental assumption that *two users have similar tastes on one item if they have rated other items similarly* [29, 24]. Due to the collaboration effects, CF only relies on users' history behaviors without collecting content information for all users and items. Another benefit of CF is that unexpected products could be recommended to users by mining user-product interactions. Those products are difficult to be discovered by merely analyzing the contents.

Although CF approaches have superior characteristics and have been applied to many real-world systems, there still exist drawbacks which limit their performance. On the one hand, traditional CF considers collaboration effects among users but ignores the variety across different domains. Generally, customers have similar tastes in one domain could not infer that they have similar tastes in other domains. An impressive example is involving Epinions[1], which is one of the largest product review websites with several less-correlated domains such as "Movies", "Music", "Home & Garden", and so on. On the site, two users who love movies of the same type are probably to have totally different preference in "Home & Garden" domain. In this sense, users show heterogenous features across multiple domains. As a consequence, training *domain-specific recommendation* model is more reasonable than training a model on the entire user-item matrix.

On the other hand, recommender systems in practice have to face a main challenge of data sparsity. Typically, there are usually thousands of products on e-commerce websites but most of them are long-tailed. In this case, recommendation based on CF methods is inclined to suggest well-known products rather than those cold ones [19]. Hence, it is quite difficult to predict user preference accurately from the whole item set. To alleviate this problem, an intuitive scheme is to take users' interested topic into account. Considering a scenario that if a user's attitude toward domains is captured first, one who expresses great interest in "Music" would probably receive a recommendation list with more music-related products than popular products in other domains. Compared to prediction in the whole item set, a user's preferred long-tailed items are more likely to be dug out via prediction in the interested domains.

---

[*]corresponding author

Copyright is held by the International World Wide Web Conference Committee (IW3C2). IW3C2 reserves the right to provide a hyperlink to the author's site if the Material is used in electronic media.
WWW 2013, May 13–17, 2013, Rio de Janeiro, Brazil.
ACM 978-1-4503-2035-1/13/05.

[1]http://www.epinions.com

Nevertheless, the information of users' interested topics is absent in most existing consumer review sites. One straightforward solution is to count how many times a user purchased or clicked products in one domain, then whether the user is interested in a domain or not would be inferred by her statistical history reviews. However, users without interest interactions but with social relations in the domain might probably be ignored. Also, since the distribution of review number over users is quite imbalanced, it is unclear how to define a unified criterion to partition users into different domains. Instead, we change our perspective to mining interpretable topics for communities. The process is equivalent to finding user clusters meanwhile align them into the predefined domains, and therefore can be viewed as *community topic mining*.

With all the concerns aforementioned, we develop a novel recommendation framework integrating community topic mining with domain-specific recommendation, which is called *TopRec* for short. As we known, social community detection itself is a very important research task with great challenges in data mining [4, 30]. The crucial difference is, in our TopRec framework, we not only focus on community detection algorithm, but also investigate:(1) *how to align these extracted user communities without explicit topic to the known domains*, and (2) *how to take advantage of the natural social network structure to assist user clustering*. To the best of our knowledge, these issues have not been studied in recommender systems before.

To address above two issues, we propose a unified probabilistic topic model in the context of social network in this paper, by combining semi-supervised methods of user-guided and structure-constrained clustering. Then the accuracy of the top-n recommendation task can be improved by domain-specific CF algorithm. The main contributions of this work are summarized below:

- Proposing a novel recommendation framework, TopRec, for multi-category datasets with trust connections to deal with the limitations of conventional CF methods.

- Introducing user guidance as a sort of prior knowledge in the probabilistic topic model to detect communities and align them with existing domains at the same time.

- Embedding social links as complementary data resource in the probabilistic topic model to satisfy connectivity coherency.

- Employing domain-specific CF approach to formulate heterogenous latent features corresponding to the interested domains for user.

The rest of the paper is organized as follows. A new recommendation framework, TopRec, is introduced in Section 2. A unified probabilistic model for community topic mining is described in Section 3 and a domain-specific CF model for recommendation is presented in Section 4. Then we analyze experimental results on benchmark datasets in Section 5. Finally, we discuss the related work in Section 6 and conclude this work in Section 7.

2. A NEW FRAMEWORK - TOPREC

In this section, we introduce an overview of our recommendation framework, TopRec, and give the problem definition formally.

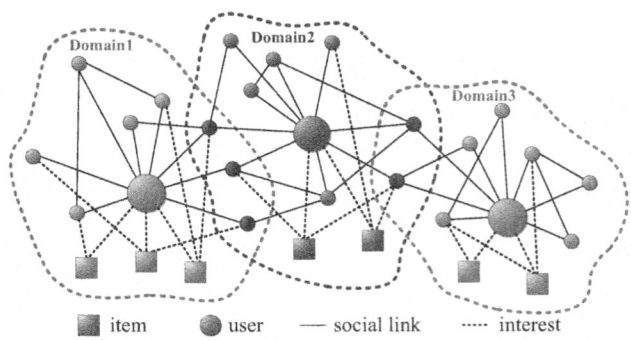

Figure 1: A simple illustration of interest interactions and social network within domains. The larger nodes represent experts in domains.

2.1 Framework Overview

There are three types of data in our framework: the review records and the social network for all users, as well as the category information for all items. Without loss of generality, Figure 1 depicts a typical topology of a heterogeneous graph containing both interest interactions and social network. The essential of our goal is to construct domains by the given data and community topic mining, then conduct domain-specific recommendation, which consists of following two stages:

Stage 1: Community Topic Mining. In this study, we tackle this step with probabilistic topic model for three main considerations. First, individuals in real life are usually multi-faceted. As their interests cannot be captured by one topic, discrete mixed membership models like Probabilistic Latent Semantic Analysis(PLSA) [10] and Latent Dirichlet Allocation(LDA) [1], which can represent objects as distribution over topics, are suitable in our scenario. Second, in consumer review sites such as Epinions, we can always find active users in each domain(the larger node in Figure 1), who can supply prior knowledge of the probabilistic model for topic alignment. Third, probabilistic topic model allows to connect similar users in social relations to enhance community meanwhile indicates why we connect them.

Stage 2: Domain-Specific Collaborative Filtering. After extracting topical communities, users are divided into domains according to their interested topics. To predict user preference, we exploit normal CF in each domain and then return a rank list according to the predicted rating scores. In our case, the particular algorithm utilized is Probabilistic Matrix Factorization(PMF) [21], a state-of-the-art CF approach with promising recommendation results. As a matter of fact, the TopRec is a general framework and has potential to combine other CF methods in practice.

One similar problem has been formulated in Multiclass Co-Clustering(MCoC) model recently [27], which groups users and items into topical subsets to achieve better recommendation results. However, TopRec boosts performance by exploring interpretable domains while the topics in MCoC are implicit.

2.2 Problem Definition

Here we present the notations and definitions to be used in this paper. Suppose there are N users and M items in the given dataset, $\mathcal{U} = \{u_1, \cdots, u_N\}$ denote the user set and $\mathcal{V} = \{v_1, \cdots, v_M\}$ denote the item set. Let $\mathbf{R} = (\mathbf{r}_1, \cdots, \mathbf{r}_N)^T \in \mathbb{R}^{N \times M}$ represent rating matrix, where $\mathbf{r}_i$ is column vector including ratings from user u_i towards item set $\mathcal{V}$. Note that rating vector $\mathbf{r}_i$ can be viewed as feature representation for user u_i. Then a user u_i in collection $\mathcal{U}$ can be denoted by a series of items $\{v_j\}_{j=1}^M$. Let $\mathbf{T} = (\mathbf{t}_1, \cdots, \mathbf{t}_N)^T \in \mathbb{R}^{N \times N}$ denote a binary trust matrix, where $\mathbf{t}_i$ is column vector indicating whether user u_i trust others in user set $\mathcal{U}$. We also model this user-user relationship as a graph $\mathcal{G}$ with adjacency matrix $\mathbf{W}$ to encode this trust relations into community mining model.

Definition 1. **Domain**. Suppose the number of domains is K, a domain $\mathcal{D}_k$ is composed of item subset $\mathcal{V}_k$ and user subset $\mathcal{U}_k$, where $k = 1, \cdots, K$, then we have N_k users and M_k items in each domain. Thus, a set of domain can be represented as $\mathcal{D} = \{\mathcal{D}_1, \cdots, \mathcal{D}_K\}$.

Definition 2. **Problem Definition**. Given review matrix $\mathbf{R}$, social context $\mathbf{T}$ and item-domain information $\mathcal{V}_k = \{v_1, \cdots, v_{M_k}\}$, our goal is: In stage 1, discover domains $\mathcal{D}_k = \{\mathcal{U}_k, \mathcal{V}_k\}$ by mining $\mathcal{U}_k = \{u_1, \cdots, u_{N_k}\}$, where $k = 1, \cdots, K$. In stage 2, for each domain $\mathcal{D}_k$, we train PMF model using the observed ratings of user-item pairs (u_i, v_j), where $u_i \in \mathcal{U}_k$ and $v_j \in \mathcal{V}_k$. Finally, by utilizing the learnt domain-specific latent features in prediction, the personalized rank lists for users in set $\mathcal{U}$ towards the whole item set $\mathcal{V}$ are returned.

3. COMMUNITY TOPIC MINING

In this section, we propose a semi-supervised probabilistic topic model with expert guidance and network structure. By modeling the generative process of user set, the model could explicitly mine their interest topics from both historical ratings and social relationships.

3.1 Basic Idea

Probabilistic generative models such as PLSA have been widely used in many text mining tasks [10, 3, 16], and also play a significant role in recommendation tasks due to their ability in dealing with dyadic data [11, 26]. Following the previous works on probabilistic models, we treat user as a mixture of topics, where each topic is a multinomial distribution over all the items. For instance, a distribution that assigns high probabilities to items such as "iPhone","iPad","Kindle" would suggest that the user loves "Electronics" topic. In order to identify multiple interest topics for user, we model users in a mixture model with K topics and estimate the model parameters so that the likelihood of user collection $\mathcal{U}$ is maximized. In this way, the statistical topic model could capture the co-occurences of items and encourage to group users into communities.

Intuitively, user communities grouped by basic PLSA model can represent interest topics towards item categories. However, these extracted topics are latent variables without explicit meaning and cannot be regarded as the given categories. Thus, simply using PLSA cannot ensure the obtained topic is well-aligned to the specific domains. To overcome this limitation, we introduce user guidance as a priori into the generative clustering process. In reality, most users in consumer review sites are extremely cold. That is, there is little useful information could guide community mining. Fortunately, there exit a few representative and trustable users in each domain, who review and comment frequently meanwhile own a large number of trustors. In this study, we regard these users as *experts* of each community and their rating distribution over items as prior knowledge for clustering.

Another problem is that the social network structure might be neglected. Generally, people not only make interactions with online products but also have trusts relation with other users. Thus only using rating data cannot guarantee that well-connected users are clustered in the same topical community. Besides, more information about cold users can be analyzed from the perspective of their local trusting neighbors. For example, one might do not have enough reviews, while has more trust relations such that mining her interest topic from social view is possible. Accordingly, these linked structures are quite useful in community topic mining.

3.2 Experts-Guided Topic Modeling

To model the user clustering procedure with experts guidance, we introduce a topic variable $z_k \in \{z_1, \cdots, z_K\}$ with each observation of a item $v_j \in \{v_1, \cdots, v_M\}$ is rated by a particular user $u_i \in \{u_1, \cdots, u_N\}$. Each topic z_k is corresponding to the k-th domain. Let $c(u_i, v_j) = R_{ij}$ denote the rating of user u_i giving item v_j to express how much the user like the item.

Given a user collection $\mathcal{U}$, experts-guided topic modeling is to discover topical communities meanwhile label them the known domains, and then users and items with a similar topic could be mapped into the same subgroup. To this end, we take the rating vectors of experts as prior knowledge for each user cluster. To make sure the effect of the guidance, the experts are manually chosen by two criteria:

- **Informative**. The experts should be the persons who contribute a large quantity of reviews in one particular item category, so that their attitude can cover items in the category as more as possible.

- **Reliable**. The experts would better have a great number of followers, which implies their reviews and comments are trustable to some certain extent.

Once the experts are selected, we model such prior as a Dirichlet distribution to enforce the topics to be as close as possible to the predefined domains. Specifically, for each given topic z_k, its probabilistic distribution over items $p(v_j|z_k)$ is assumed to be a multinomial distribution, which is generated from some Dirichlet distribution. We define this Dirichlet prior as $z_k : Dir(\{\sigma_k p(v_j|\bar{u}_k) + 1\}_{v_j \in \mathcal{V}})$, where σ_k is confidence parameter of the prior distribution for topic k, and $\bar{u}_k \in \mathcal{U}$ denote expert corresponding to the topic k.

Similar to PLSA, parameters in our model are $\{p(v_j|z_k), p(z_k|u_i)\}$. We set all the parameters as Θ for succinct in the following paragraph. In general, the prior on the parameters can be presented as

$$P(\Theta) \propto \prod_{k=1}^K \prod_{j=1}^M p(v_j|z_k)^{\sigma_k p(v_j|\bar{u}_k)} \quad (1)$$

where the prior $p(v_j|\bar{u}_k)$ involves the rating distribution of experts over the item set $\mathcal{V}$, and can be obtained by

$$p(v_j|\bar{u}_k) = \frac{c(\bar{u}_k, v_j)}{\sum_{j'=1}^M c(\bar{u}_k, v_{j'})} \quad (2)$$

A large σ_k equals to high confidence on prior of topic k. When $\sigma_k = 0$, the prior of $p(v_j|z_k)$ boils down to a uniform distribution, which means that no guidance is introduced in the clustering process.

In fundamental PLSA model, the log-likelihood of user collection $\mathcal{U}$ is

$$\mathcal{L}(\mathcal{U}) = \log p(\mathcal{U}|\Theta) = \sum_{i=1}^{N}\sum_{j=1}^{M} c(u_i, v_j) \log \sum_{k=1}^{K} p(v_j|z_k)p(z_k|u_i) \quad (3)$$

We may use Bayesian estimation, so the parameter Θ can be estimated by maximizing Eq.(3), which is

$$\hat{\Theta} = \arg\max_{\Theta} \log p(\mathcal{U}|\Theta) \quad (4)$$

With the prior incorporated, Maximum A Posterior (MAP) estimator is used instead of Maximum Likelihood estimator. That is, $\mathcal{L}(\mathcal{U}) = \log(p(\mathcal{U}|\Theta)p(\Theta))$. Therefore, Θ is obtained by

$$\begin{aligned}\hat{\Theta} &= \arg\max_{\Theta} \log(p(\mathcal{U}|\Theta)p(\Theta)) \\ &= \arg\max_{\Theta} \{\sum_{i=1}^{N}\sum_{j=1}^{M} c(u_i, v_j) \log \sum_{k=1}^{K} p(v_j|z_k)p(z_k|u_i) \\ &+ \sum_{k=1}^{K}\sum_{j=1}^{M} \sigma_k p(v_j|\bar{u}_k) \log p(v_j|z_k)\}\end{aligned} \quad (5)$$

3.3 Network-Constrained Topic Modeling

Furthermore, we propose to regularize the user-specific feature space by social network during clustering process. Given a binary trust matrix $\mathbf{T} = (\mathbf{t}_1, \cdots, \mathbf{t}_N)^T \in \mathbb{R}^{N \times N}$, a social graph $\mathcal{G} = (\mathcal{U}, \mathcal{E}, \mathbf{T})$ could be constructed, where $\mathcal{U}$ is a set of N vertices representing users, $\mathcal{E} \subseteq \mathcal{U} \times \mathcal{U}$ is a set of edges representing trust similarity between users in neighborhood, and $\mathbf{T}$ can be regarded as a matrix in which each row corresponds to a vector of feature values of a user. In particular, user relationships are embodied by defining adjacency matrix $\mathbf{W}$ on user graph as

$$W(u_i, u_{i'}) = \begin{cases} sim(u_i, u_{i'}), & \text{if } u_{i'} \in \mathcal{N}(u_i) \text{ or } u_i \in \mathcal{N}(u_{i'}) \\ 0, & \text{otherwise} \end{cases} \quad (6)$$

where $\mathcal{N}(u_i)$ is the k-nearest neighbor of u_i, and $sim(u_i, u_{i'})$ represents the trust similarity measurement. For simplicity, we use cosine distance between vectors $\{\mathbf{t}_i\}_{i=1}^{N}$ here. Though above equation, we transform the original directed trust graph $\mathbf{T}$ to an undirected trust similarity graph $\mathbf{W}$, which is able to formulate into topic model as regularization term directly.

The essential idea of network-constrained user clustering is on the basis of one simple assumption: *users who have a strong connection with each other in social network should have similar preference on topics*. Inspired by this fact, we adopt the following formulation as a constraint for topic model

$$R(\mathcal{U}, \mathcal{G}) = \frac{1}{2} \sum_{\langle u_i, u_{i'} \rangle \in \mathcal{E}} W(u_i, u_{i'}) \sum_{k=1}^{K} (p(z_k|u_i) - p(z_k|u_{i'}))^2 \quad (7)$$

Therefore, our aim is to minimize Eq.(7). Then we utilize this constraint into log-likelihood function generated by PLSA, which means to maximize

$$\mathcal{J}(\mathcal{U}, \mathcal{G}) = \mathcal{L}(\mathcal{U}) - \lambda R(\mathcal{U}, \mathcal{G}) \quad (8)$$

where λ is a regularization parameter which controls the influence of smoothness on topic distribution over network.

3.4 The Unified Model

Combining above two parts of topic modeling, we have a joint objective function with concerning both topical consistency and connectivity coherency at the same time. By substituting the posterior probability formula in Eq.(5) and the regularizer in Eq.(7) into Eq.(8), the final objective function can be written as

$$\begin{aligned}\mathcal{J}(\mathcal{U}, \mathcal{G}) &= \sum_{i=1}^{N}\sum_{j=1}^{M} c(u_i, v_j) \log \sum_{k=1}^{K} p(v_j|z_k)p(z_k|u_i) \\ &+ \sum_{k=1}^{K}\sum_{j=1}^{M} \sigma_k p(v_j|\bar{u}_k) \log p(v_j|z_k) \\ &- \frac{\lambda}{2} \sum_{\langle u_i, u_{i'}\rangle \in \mathcal{E}} W(u_i, u_{i'}) \sum_{k=1}^{K} (p(z_k|u_i) - p(z_k|u_{i'}))^2\end{aligned} \quad (9)$$

3.5 Parameter Estimation

For Maximum Likelihood Estimation (MLE) procedure, the Expectation Maximization (EM) algorithms is commonly used. However, in our MAP case with the combination of regularizer, parameter estimation becomes difficult to handle by the standard EM. Hence, we apply the Generalized Expectation Maximization algorithm (GEM) to estimate the parameter Θ. Parameter in n-th iteration are denoted as Θ_n.

Formally, we conduct a two-step iterative algorithm. In E-step, given all the users' reviews data and parameter Θ_n, the distribution of the topics can be computed simply by the same formula as PLSA

$$p(z_k|u_i, v_j, \Theta_n) = \frac{p_n(v_j|z_k)p_n(z_k|u_i)}{\sum_{k'=1}^{K} p_n(v_j|z_{k'})p_n(z_{k'}|u_i)} \quad (10)$$

In M-step, the algorithm searches better parameters through optimizing Q-function: $\Theta_{n+1} = \arg\max_{\Theta} Q(\Theta; \Theta_n)$, which is present by

$$\begin{aligned}Q(\Theta; \Theta_n) &= \mathcal{J}(\Theta_n) + \sum_{i=1}^{N} \alpha_i(\sum_{k=1}^{K} p(z_k|u_i) - 1) \\ &+ \sum_{k=1}^{K} \alpha_k(\sum_{j=1}^{M} p(v_j|z_k) - 1)\end{aligned} \quad (11)$$

where α_i and α_k are Lagrange multipliers of the constraints $\sum_k p(z_k|u_i) = 1$ for all users and $\sum_j p(v_j|z_k) = 1$ for all topics, respectively.

Computation of $p_n(v_j|z_k)$ To optimize Eq.(11) with respect to $p_n(v_j|z_k)$, we need to consider the original PLSA likelihood function and the user guidance term. By taking partial derivative of $p_n(v_j|z_k)$ to Eq.(11), its updating can be got as

$$p_{n+1}(v_j|z_k) = \frac{\sum_{i=1}^{N} c(u_i, v_j)p(z_k|u_i, v_j, \Theta_n) + \sigma_k p(v_j|\bar{u}_k)}{\sum_{j'=1}^{M}\sum_{i'=1}^{N} c(u_{i'}, v_{j'})p(z_k|u_{i'}, v_{j'}, \Theta_n) + \sigma_k} \quad (12)$$

This formulation can be understood easily. In addition to the data of user collection, the opinions of experts on item distribution over topics are also imposed. Then parameter updating are decided by collaboration of the both factors, which is also consistent with our intuition.

Computation of $p_n(z_k|u_i)$ Optimizing Eq.(11) with respect to $p_n(z_k|u_i)$ directly is more complicated even though it is only related with the terms of data likelihood and network regularization. Similar to [3], we take the strategy in GEM to satisfy $Q(\Theta_{n+1}) \geq Q(\Theta_n)$ in each step, which finds a better Θ rather than finds a globally optimal solution. We apply the normal updating method in standard PLSA to maximize $\mathcal{L}(\mathcal{U})$ in Eq.(8) which can find a start value Θ_{n+1}^1. Then $R(\mathcal{U},\mathcal{G})$ is increased by

$$p_{n+1}^{t+1}(z_k|u_i) = \tau p_{n+1}^t(z_k|u_i) + (1-\tau)\frac{\sum_{i'=1}^N W(u_i,u_{i'})p_{n+1}^t(z_k|u_{i'})}{\sum_{i'=1}^N W(u_i,u_{i'})} \quad (13)$$

where τ is Newton step parameter to limit the effect of smoothness by $R(\mathcal{U},\mathcal{G})$. We repeat this iteration until the Q-function is beginning to drop. Also, we judge the output Θ_{n+1}^t. If $Q(\Theta_{n+1}^t) \geq Q(\Theta_n)$, we adopt the proposal of Θ_{n+1}^t, otherwise, reject it. The E-step and M-step equations are alternated until achieving some termination conditions. In this way, we obtain the estimated parameters $\{p(v_j|z_k), p(z_k|u_i)\}$.

Now, to group each user into more than one topical communities, we set a natural clustering criterion as: *a user u_i is interested in a meaningful topic z_k, if and only if function $f(z_k,u_i)$ is satisfied by $f(z_k,u_i) > \varepsilon$*. Thus, given a user, the function $f(\cdot)$ measures attractiveness of a domain on her, which is defined as

$$f(z_k,u_i) = \sum_{j=1}^M c(u_i,v_j)p(v_j|z_k) \quad (14)$$

Clearly, Eq.(14) could be viewed as a kind of similarity measurement between users and topics.

4. DOMAIN-SPECIFIC COLLABORATIVE FILTERING

In this section, we illustrate domain-specific collaborative filtering in detail. The overall procedure consists of two steps, which are model training and top-n recommendation.

4.1 Model Training

After community topic mining, the observed user-item pairs are allocated into different domains. Let $\mathbf{R}^k \in \mathbb{R}^{N_k \times M_k}$ denote the rating matrix for the k-th domain, where $k = 1,\ldots,K$. M_k and N_k are the number of items and users in each domain respectively. Let $\mathbf{P}^k \in \mathbb{R}^{d \times N_k}$ and $\mathbf{Q}^k \in \mathbb{R}^{d \times M_k}$ denote the latent feature matrices in k-th domain, with column $\mathbf{p}_i^k$ and $\mathbf{q}_j^k$ represent the latent feature vectors of users and items respectively, where d denotes the dimension of latent feature. Adopting PMF model in different domains, the model is trained on rating data by minimizing the square error

$$\frac{1}{2}\sum_{i=1}^{N_k}\sum_{j=1}^{M_k} I_{ij}^k(R_{ij}^k - (\mathbf{p}_i^k)^T\mathbf{q}_j^k)^2 + \frac{\beta}{2}(\sum_{i=1}^{N_k}\|\mathbf{p}_i^k\|^2 + \sum_{j=1}^{M_k}\|\mathbf{q}_j^k\|^2) \quad (15)$$

where I_{ij}^k indicates the training data of user-item pairs belonged to domain k, $\|\cdot\|^2$ denotes the Frobenius norm to make the solution more robust, and β is the regularization coefficient. One important difference between the PMF and our model is that we consider the training process across each domain. Therefore, we have K objective functions in total. The parameters $\mathbf{p}_i^k$ and $\mathbf{q}_j^k$ in Eq.(15) can be minimized by Alternating Least Square(ALS) method, which performs the following two updates alternatively.

First, optimizing Eq.(15) with respect to $\mathbf{p}_i^k$ for $i = 1,2,\ldots,N_k$ in domain k and fixing all $\mathbf{q}_j^k$ leads to

$$\mathbf{p}_i^k = (\sum_{j=1}^{M_k} I_{ij}^k \mathbf{q}_j^k (\mathbf{q}_j^k)^T + \beta \mathbf{I}_d)^{-1}(\sum_{j=1}^{M_k} I_{ij}^k R_{ij}^k \mathbf{q}_j^k) \quad (16)$$

Then, optimizing with respect to $\mathbf{q}_j^k$ for $j = 1,2,\ldots,M_k$ in domain k and fixing all $\mathbf{p}_i^k$ leads to

$$\mathbf{q}_j^k = (\sum_{i=1}^{N_k} I_{ij}^k \mathbf{p}_i^k (\mathbf{p}_i^k)^T + \beta \mathbf{I}_d)^{-1}(\sum_{i=1}^{N_k} I_{ij}^k R_{ij}^k \mathbf{p}_i^k) \quad (17)$$

In order to avoid overfitting on test data, we use the weighted-regularization $\sum_{j=1}^{M_k} m_{v_j}^k \|\mathbf{q}_j^k\|^2$ and $\sum_{i=1}^{N_k} n_{u_i}^k \|\mathbf{p}_i^k\|^2$ instead of the original regularization terms in Eq.(15) in experiment, where $m_{v_j}^k$ and $n_{u_i}^k$ denote the number of ratings of item v_j and user u_i in $\mathcal{D}_k$, respectively.

4.2 Recommendation with Domains

Since top-n recommendation is to produce a ranking list of items with high to low preference, it is necessary to predict ratings for users towards items in each domain first. Corresponding to training process, we consider a two-step filtering to recommend items in the framework of TopRec.

Given a user-item pair (u_i, v_j), the first step is to judge whether the user u_i is interested in the specific domain $\mathcal{D}_k$ where the item v_j belongs to. If she is interested in $\mathcal{D}_k$, the following rating prediction step is implemented using the learnt domain-specific user and item latent feature parameters $\mathbf{p}_i^k$ and $\mathbf{q}_j^k$. Otherwise, we do not predict rating for the user-item pair. In detail, the whole process can be summarized in a unified form

$$\hat{R}_{ij} = \begin{cases} (\mathbf{p}_i^k)^T \mathbf{q}_j^k + r^k & \text{if } u_i \in \mathcal{D}_k \cap v_j \in \mathcal{D}_k \\ 0 & \text{otherwise} \end{cases} \quad (18)$$

where $r^k \in \mathbb{R}$ denotes the global offset of $\mathcal{D}_k$ by averaging observed ratings in the domain. For each node, we sort the predicted rating $\hat{R}_{ij}$ of all the K domains with a decreasing order and then the top-n item list is eventually generated. Basically, TopRec can filter out lots of items for users according to their uninterested domains and then recommend items with high predicted rating score in their interested domains.

5. EXPERIMENTS

In this section, we investigate the performance of TopRec in top-n recommendation task compared to other state-of-the-art algorithms on two real-world datasets. Also, we report the results for different settings of model parameters.

5.1 Datasets

We examine how the TopRec behaves on two multi-domain product review datasets with trust networks: Epinions and Ciao[2]. Both of them are well-known consumer opinion websites where users not only provide reviews to their familiar products but also maintain trust lists of their trusting users.

---
[2] http://www.ciao.co.uk

Table 1: Statistics of the Datasets

	Epinions	Ciao
# of Users	7,475	4,137
# of Items	140,434	72,198
# of Ratings	343,789	194,278
# of Trust Links	143,066	85,877
# of Domains	8	10
Ave Ratings per User	45.99	46.96
Ave Ratings per Item	2.45	2.69
Ave Trusts per User	19.14	20.75
Rating Sparsity	99.97%	99.93%
Trust Network Sparsity	99.74%	99.50%

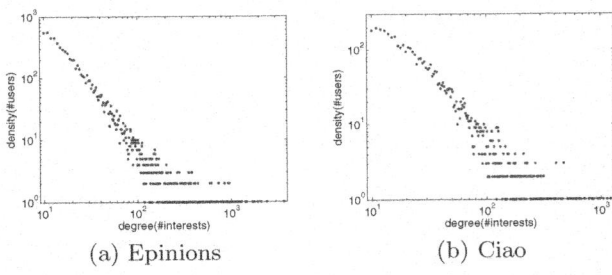

(a) Epinions (b) Ciao

Figure 2: Degree distribution of Epinions and Ciao.

The version of the two datasets[3] used in this study are published by the authors of [25] including data records until May 2011. To evaluate the effects of social network, we first remove users without trust relations. For the purpose of taking each user's top-n recommendation performance into account, we also prune users with fewer than ten reviews to ensure sufficient test data for each user. Then we use eight and ten top popular categories to define the domains for Epinions and Ciao respectively. The detailed statistics of the two datasets are showed in Table 1. Compared to Ciao, Epinions owns more users and products in their most representative categories, which results in more review data and trust links. While the scale of Epinions and Ciao are different, the sparsity of both datasets are comparable. Based on the presented statistics, the high sparsity is fairly noticeable in user-item interaction as well as trust relation. Especially, as we do not sift cold products from the original published datasets, the averaging rating per item is extremely small. Figure 2 shows the degree distribution of the two datasets. As we can see, the datasets are very sparse and suggest power law distribution.

In experiments, we randomly pick 80% of the review data to form the training set and the rest for the test set, and run ten times in each configuration.

5.2 Performance Measures

Because recommender systems in reality normally concerns about personalized ranking of entities but not rating prediction to all products, we analyze performance of each model by comparing the top suggestions in our experiments. For a consistent evaluation with the top-n recommendation literature, three classical measures commonly used are employed: MAP(*Mean Average Precision*), F-measure, and nDCG(*normalized Discounted Cumulative Gain*).

For each user, given a ranked list with n items, we denote $\text{prec}(j)$ as the precision at ranked position j, $\text{pref}(j)$ as a binary preference indicator at position j. AP is defined as

$$AP(u) = \frac{\sum_{j=1}^{n} \text{prec}(j) \times \text{pref}(j)}{\# \text{ of preferred items}} \quad (19)$$

$$MAP = \frac{\sum_{u \in \mathcal{U}} AP(u)}{|\mathcal{U}|} \quad (20)$$

To compute F-measure, let *precision* and *recall* denote the user-oriented averaging precision and recall with top-n list.

$$F1 = \frac{2 \times precision \times recall}{precision + recall} \quad (21)$$

[3]http://www.public.asu.edu/ jtang20/

To obtain nDCG, the preference indicator $\text{pref}(j)$ is also used.

$$\text{nDCG} = \frac{1}{\text{IDCG}} \times \sum_{j=1}^{n} \frac{2^{\text{pref}(j)}-1}{\log_2(j+1)} \quad (22)$$

where IDCG is produced by a perfect ranking algorithm. By this definition, nDCG gives larger credit to top-ranked entities. Higher MAP, F1 and nDCG implies better recommendation result.

5.3 Comparisons

Here we compare three variant methods on the basis of TopRec framework with four baseline methods to demonstrate the effectiveness of each part of our model.

- **TopRec with Single Class (TopRec-S)** In this single class model, we change user clustering criteria as: *a user u_i is interested in topic z_k if and only if $\forall z_{k'}$, $s.t. f(z_k, u_i) > f(z_{k'}, u_i)$.* Thus user membership hypothesis becomes that a user only interested in one topical domain. We set the model as a comparison of users' multi-faceted features assumption. $f(z_k, u_i)$ is still computed by Eq.(14) here.

- **TopRec with Multiple Class (TopRec-M)** The multi-class model based on TopRec framework believes that users are interested in multiple topical domain. Note that both of TopRec-S and TopRec-M are not added social networks.

- **TopRec with Network (TopRec-Net)** As to evaluate the contribution of social network, we embed network-constrained term on the basis of TopRec-M. This model is the unified model described in section 3.4.

- **Probabilistic Matrix Factorization (PMF) [21].** PMF virtually is a low rank matrix factorization model and assumes that a user generates a rating for an item by adding Gaussian noise to the inner product $R_{ij} = (\mathbf{p_i})^T \mathbf{q_j}$, where $\mathbf{p_i} \in \mathbb{R}^d$ and $\mathbf{q_j} \in \mathbb{R}^d$ associate with latent factor vector of user and item.

- **PMF with Domains (PMF-D).** This model takes multiple domains information of items into consideration, so the PMF-D treats different domains independently but has N users in all domains.

- **Multiclass Co-Clustering (MCoC) [27].** This method proposes a framework to extend traditional CF by dividing users and items into multiple subgroups. Different with our framework, it views this allocation procedure as a Multiclass Co-Clustering problem.

Table 2: Performance comparisons of top-n recommendation on Epinions in terms of MAP, F1 and nDCG.

Methods	n=5			n=10			n=15			n=20		
	MAP	F1	nDCG	MAP	F1	nDCG	MAP	F1	nDCG	MAP	F1	nDCG
RANDOM	0.2275	0.1156	0.1357	0.2248	0.1160	0.1109	0.2201	0.1072	0.0957	0.2162	0.0994	0.0855
PMF	0.2896	0.1714	0.1857	0.2911	0.2038	0.1709	0.2835	0.2010	0.1551	0.2759	0.1904	0.1418
PMF-D	0.3666	0.2045	0.2249	0.3593	0.2157	0.1919	0.3467	0.2032	0.1689	0.3360	0.1885	0.1520
MCoC	0.3736	0.1961	0.2492	0.3667	0.1990	0.2017	0.3628	0.1847	0.1714	0.3598	0.1726	0.1518
TopRec-S	0.2951	0.1569	0.1814	0.2904	0.1582	0.1487	0.2844	0.1555	0.1325	0.2779	0.1549	0.1234
TopRec-M	0.3953	0.2169	0.2485	0.3847	0.2206	0.2058	0.3739	0.2041	0.1781	0.3651	0.1882	0.1591
TopRec-Net	**0.4236**	**0.2386**	**0.2710**	**0.4111**	**0.2400**	**0.2235**	**0.3991**	**0.2200**	**0.1927**	**0.3896**	**0.2001**	**0.1709**

- Random Group Model (RANDOM) TopRec divides users into groups with sizes of $\{N_1, \ldots, N_K\}$, so we randomly sample users into K groups with the same sizes of TopRec. The random group model is to create comparison with the process of community topic mining.

To make a fair comparison, we use PMF as the basic CF method either training on user-item domains or entire user-item matrix in all the experiments. For PMF, the latent dimensionality of low rank features is set to be $d = 10$, and the regularization coefficient is set as $\beta = 0.1$.

5.4 Experimental Protocol

To all the comparisons, we utilize the following experimental protocol.

We first notice that both of Epinions and Ciao are employed 5-star rating systems, which refers to user-item interaction are explicit. However, we also find that more than 70% ratings are 4 or 5, which means the rating distribution are fairly imbalanced. This positive ratings phenomenon also appears in many other online consumer rating datasets so that it is inevitably to train overly optimistic estimators by using the observed ratings directly. To address this phenomenon, we adopt a *bias correction* procedure mentioned in [28]. That is to draw uniformly from the set of the unobserved user-item pairs for each user as pseudo-negatives to balance the original training set. The assumption under bias correction is that the unobserved samples are less interested by users compared with observed rating data.

For the evaluation protocol, we follow the evaluation mechanism described in [28, 6]. For each user, as the total number of items is huge in the datasets, while the number of true preferred items is much smaller, it is prohibitive to take all the items as candidates and generate a total ordering of the whole item set. Our test methodology for top-n measure is: for each user, we randomly select S additional items that are not reviewed and mix them with the test data to construct a probe set. Thus we compute the predicted ratings over probe sets to find top-n products. The size of random probes per user is set as $S = 500$ in experiments.

5.5 Results and Analysis

Performance on Epinions. Table 2 shows the experimental results on the Epinions dataset with three different evaluation metrics: MAP, F-measure, nDCG, when we vary the number of returned items $n = 5, 10, 15, 20$. For the three variants of TopRec methods, we pick confidence parameter

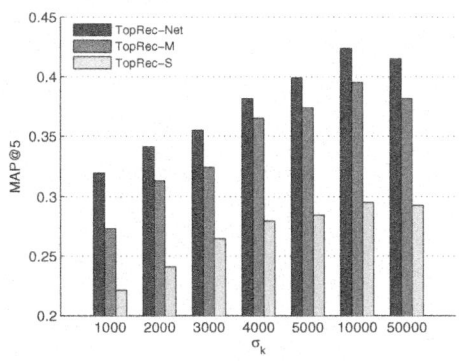

Figure 3: Impact of expert guidance confidence parameter σ_k on MAP@5 performance of Epinions.

$\sigma_k = 10000$, the number of experts 3 for each domain, and the value of regularization parameter $\lambda = 100$. Then we empirically set the number of nearest neighbors as 5, the value of Newton step parameter τ as 0.01.

From Table 2, TopRec-Net yields the best performance under all of the evaluation conditions. By looking at the trend along with the number of returned list n, we can see that all of the performance drops when the returned list n is increasing. This is mainly because that more than half of users only have less than five true interested items in test set. When n becomes large, recall improves while precision declines severely.

Compare models concerned about domain-specific CF (i.e. TopRec variants and PMF-D) with the original PMF, it is clear to conclude that the multiple domains do benefits on recommendation task. TopRec, which allocates users into their interested domains by user clustering and topic mining, outperforms PMF-D, which simply assumes that users are belonged to all the domains. By comparing the three variants of TopRec, we show that TopRec-M and TopRec-Net perform better than TopRec-S, which demonstrates the multi-faceted assumption for online users. Another phenomenon is that TopRec-Net outperforms TopRec-M consistently, which infers that network-constrained topic modeling can bring about performance improvement.

To illustrate the effectiveness of our community topic mining stage, we compare our methods with the state-of-the-art approach MCoC. Both of TopRec and MCoC aim to map users and items into subgroups, but we take advantage of the

Table 3: Performance comparisons of top-n recommendation on Ciao in terms of MAP, F1 and nDCG.

Methods	n=5			n=10			n=15			n=20		
	MAP	F1	nDCG	MAP	F1	nDCG	MAP	F1	nDCG	MAP	F1	nDCG
RANDOM	0.1915	0.0832	0.1139	0.1917	0.0781	0.0872	0.1891	0.0699	0.0727	0.1867	0.0642	0.0638
PMF	0.2296	0.1127	0.1415	0.2357	0.1484	0.1327	0.2312	0.1555	0.1246	0.2258	**0.1534**	0.1169
PMF-D	0.3002	0.1434	0.1760	0.3004	0.1567	0.1508	0.2943	0.1538	0.1339	0.2854	0.1483	0.1224
MCoC	0.3029	0.1265	0.1960	0.2999	0.1418	0.1619	0.2971	0.1329	0.1364	0.2930	0.1233	0.1197
TopRec-S	0.3277	0.1456	0.2011	0.3230	0.1282	0.1488	0.3173	0.1137	0.1231	0.3103	0.1052	0.1083
TopRec-M	0.3839	0.1732	0.2359	0.3787	0.1629	0.1811	0.3706	0.1468	0.1515	0.3634	0.1332	0.1325
TopRec-Net	**0.4025**	**0.1843**	**0.2501**	**0.3963**	**0.1766**	**0.1946**	**0.3878**	**0.1613**	**0.1641**	**0.3878**	0.1479	**0.1431**

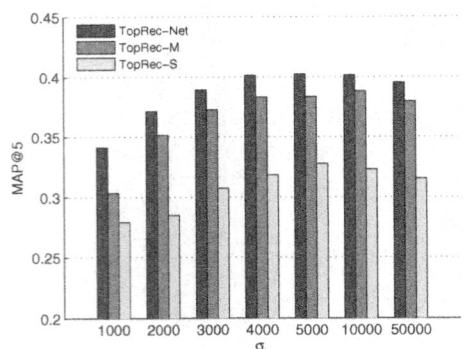

Figure 4: Impact of expert guidance confidence parameter σ_k on MAP@5 performance of Ciao.

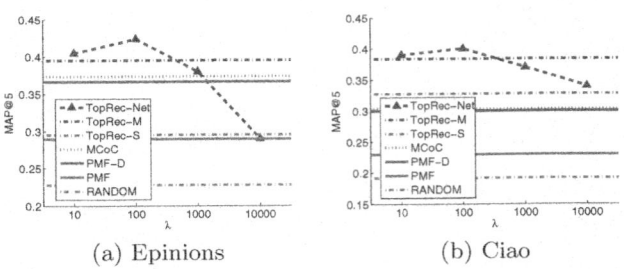

(a) Epinions (b) Ciao

Figure 5: Impact of regularization parameter λ on MAP@5 performance

category relations and employ semi-supervised topic model for user clustering instead of user-item Co-Clustering. The experimental results illustrate that our model works better than MCoC. The reason is as follows. MCoC conducts Co-Clustering only by ratings. However, the user-item rating matrix we faced with is highly sparse, few observed interactions are available for MCoC model. To compensate this, our model combines rating matrix with complementary knowledge of item categories and social networks. At last, we show that user clustering and topic alignment are pivotal for overall recommendation performance by the comparison of TopRec and RANDOM.

Performance on Ciao. Ciao is a smaller dataset with few ratings. We select expert confidence parameter $\sigma_k = 5000$ according to the quantities of observed ratings. Other parameters mentioned above are set the same as Epinions. Experimental results on Ciao are reported in Table 3. It is evident that TopRec-Net outperforms the other methods in almost all cases on this dataset. Different from Epinions data, TopRec-S behaves better than MCoC and PMF-D this time. This is because more users are interested in one domain in the dataset. Similar to Epinions, the number of interested products for majorities is still less than five in test set, which leads to the performance getting worse as the recommended lists expending.

Parameter Study. The TopRec model mainly has two important parameters. We firstly study the effect of confidence parameter σ_k for expert guidance on Epinions and Ciao. The confidence weight of each domain is set from 1000 to 50000. The larger σ_k means the model has more confidence on experts. In Figure 3 and 4, MAP of the top 5 list are plotted as a function of σ_k for Epinions and Ciao respectively. As we increase σ_k, the performance in both Figure first increases and thereafter declines slightly. This observation coincides with the interpretation of experts-guided topic modeling: besides user collection $\mathcal{U}$, we adding a pseudo counts $\sigma_k p(v_j|\bar{u}_k)$ for item v_j, therefore it would be better that σ_k is equivalent to sample size. Yet, if we give a much higher confidence weight to experts, experimental results show that the performance would not raise any more. From the figures, we can see that the trends are quite similar on both of the datasets. According to their sample size, the optimal confidence weight is $\sigma_k = 10000$ for Epinions, and around $\sigma_k = 5000$ for Ciao.

Now, we discuss the second essential parameter of TopRec, λ. Figure 5 shows how the social regularization parameter λ impacts the performance of TopRec-Net. We vary $\lambda \in \{10, 100, 1000, 1000\}$ where larger λ enhance penalty of the disagreement of interest distribution between social neighbors. When λ is small, the unified model TopRec-Net behaves like TopRec-M which does not consider social link. When λ increase, the social regularization term becomes more influential on the model and brings the network information into the community mining. For Epinions and Ciao, the performance reaches the peaks at $\lambda = 100$. Nevertheless, if λ becomes increasingly large, the social smoothness term would overwhelm the rating information which is responsible for community mining, as well as prior knowledge which is in charge of topic alignment. As a result, the performance drops dramatically on the two datasets.

Further Probing on Topic Mining. A key reason for the performance improvement of TopRec is to utilize semi-supervised topic model to mine meaningful topics and align

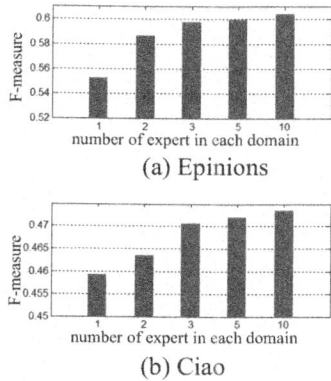

Figure 6: Topic mining results of TopRec-Net under expert guidance.

them with communities. Here we would like to probe further how the topic mining works.

In our framework, community topic mining is posed as an intermediate step and resulting topical communities are used in domain-specific recommendation. The ultimate goal of topic mining for communities is to discover interpretable topics for each user. Yet, it is rather difficult to get a good topical summary for community by a pure unsupervised topic model. Hence, we resort to semi-supervised topic modeling, in which expert guidance is the critical component deciding whether the model can derive desired user clustering results.

To analyze the performance of topic mining, the greatest challenge is we do not know the true topics interested by users. However, the topics in our model could be interpreted by item categories. That is to say, for users, the categories of preferred items in test set are capable to represent their true labels. After topic mining, a series of predicted topics are obtained for users. Then we could evaluate mining results by combining precision and recall with respect to topics. In Figure 6, F-measure on Epinions and Ciao of TopRec-Net is presented as a function of the number of expert. Particularly, the number of experts for each domain is chosen from the range $\{1, 2, 3, 5, 10\}$. In implementation, when there is more than one expert in each domain, their rating distributions over items are added into the vector $c(\bar{u}_k, v_j)$ of Eq.(2). By viewing the tendency of clustering accuracy along with the number of experts in each domain, we can see that, more expert guidance leads to better clustering results.

6. RELATED WORK

In this section, we review related works for recommender systems with collaborative filtering, especially for model-based CF approaches. CF can be classified into two different approaches: memory-based algorithms and model-based algorithms. Memory-based CF algorithm usually search for the similar users or items to produce a prediction or top-n recommendation [22, 9]. Although memory-based approaches are easy implemented and commonly used in reality, they are normally limited by highly sparse data [24], since the similarity cannot be estimated accurately in this case.

In model-based approaches, a compact model employed machine learning and statistical techniques is trained from the known ratings. There are many model-based algorithms proposed, such as latent factor models [11, 23], graphical models [13], clustering models [5, 8], and Bayesian model [2]. One popular latent factor model is low-rank matrix factorization whose premise is that users' preferences are only influenced by a small number of factors, so it uses low-rank latent factors to approximate rating data [21, 14, 20]. From the view of matrix completion, the low-rank factorization models are competent in tasks with a large amount of missing entries. Many evidence have shown that matrix factorization models outperform other CF approaches.

Recently, several approaches resort to trust-aware collaborative filtering [25, 17, 12] where users are no longer treated as independent and identically distributed. All these methods based on common rationale that users are likely to have similar tastes with their trusted friends in social networks. Previous studies manifest that social relations as another form of user information could alleviate sparsity problem and improve recommendation accuracy. Most of the existing social recommendation methods focus on encoding social network in user profile learning. However, many other web mining tasks show that when it comes to mining topics and relationships among objects, network structure are helpful [18, 3]. Our work employ the network-regularized topic modeling into a novel use for user clustering in recommender systems.

Apart from social relations, other relations such as item-category could also been incorporated into recommender systems to make up the lack of rating information. In [32], an extension of the probabilistic matrix factorization to multi-domain case is proposed. Through learning a covariance matrix, rating knowledge is transferred across domains adaptively. Yang et al. [31] model category-specific trust circle from ratings and trust links and formulate multi-faceted trust network into social matrix factorization. Different with [32], they evaluate the model in each domain without given the overall performance.

Clearly, we could take advantage of external information such as user's trust network and item's category to compensate the sparse data. On the other hand, there are more dense patterns or groups in the original rating matrix which can be uncovered though clustering methods. Traditional clustering CF models cluster users based on the items they rated or cluster items based on the users that rated them [5, 24]. However, these models overlook the user-item similarity during clustering procedure. To avoid the shortcomings, co-clustering models are proposed to map user and item into clusters simultaneously, and thus each cluster becomes more dense than the entire rating matrix [8, 27].

In this study, the proposed TopRec model leverages the power of clustering method and external relations to obtain domains with explicit topics. In experiments, we have shown that this combination works well on highly sparse datasets.

7. CONCLUSION

Effectively modeling interest topics for users and accordingly recommending their preferred items are fundamental issues to all recommender systems. In this paper, we propose a novel framework, TopRec, jointly exploiting community topic mining and domain-specific collaborative filtering for top-n recommendation task. To construct domains, we integrate expert guidance with social network to establish a unified probabilistic topic model for community topic mining. Then we utilize the observed user-item ratings across different domains for collaborative filtering. Experimental results on two datasets from real-world consumer review websites have demonstrated that the proposed method produces more accurate recommendation than other competitors.

8. ACKNOWLEDGEMENT

This work was supported in part by the 973 Program under Project 2010CB327905, by the National Natural Science Foundation of China under Grant No. 61170127 and 61070104.

9. REFERENCES

[1] D. M. Blei, A. Y. Ng, and M. I. Jordan. Latent dirichlet allocation. *J. Mach. Learn. Res.*, 3:993–1022, 2003.

[2] J. S. Breese, D. Heckerman, and C. Kadie. Empirical analysis of predictive algorithms for collaborative filtering. In *Proceedings of the Fourteenth conference on Uncertainty in artificial intelligence*, pages 43–52, 1998.

[3] D. Cai, Q. Mei, J. Han, and C. Zhai. Modeling hidden topics on document manifold. In *Proceedings of the 17th ACM conference on Information and knowledge management*, pages 911–920, 2008.

[4] A. Clauset, M. Newman, and C. Moore. Finding community structure in very large networks. *Physical review E*, 70(6), 2004.

[5] M. Connor and J. Herlocker. Clustering items for collaborative filtering. In *SIGIR 2001 Workshop on Recommender Systems*, 2001.

[6] P. Cremonesi, Y. Koren, and R. Turrin. Performance of recommender algorithms on top-n recommendation tasks. In *Proceedings of the fourth ACM conference on Recommender systems*, 2010.

[7] D. M. Fleder and K. Hosanagar. Recommender systems and their impact on sales diversity. In *Proceedings of the 8th ACM conference on Electronic commerce*, pages 192–199, 2007.

[8] T. George and S. Merugu. A scalable collaborative filtering framework based on co-clustering. In *Proceedings of the Fifth IEEE International Conference on Data Mining*, 2005.

[9] J. L. Herlocker, J. A. Konstan, A. Borchers, and J. Riedl. An algorithmic framework for performing collaborative filtering. In *Proceedings of the 22nd annual international ACM SIGIR conference on Research and development in information retrieval*, pages 230–237, 1999.

[10] T. Hofmann. Probabilistic latent semantic indexing. In *Proceedings of the 22nd annual international ACM SIGIR conference on Research and development in information retrieval*, pages 50–57, 1999.

[11] T. Hofmann. Latent semantic models for collaborative filtering. 22(1):89–115, 2004.

[12] M. Jamali and M. Ester. A matrix factorization technique with trust propagation for recommendation in social networks. In *Proceedings of the fourth ACM conference on Recommender systems*, pages 135–142, 2010.

[13] R. Jin, L. Si, and C. Zhai. Preference-based graphic models for collaborative filtering. In *Proceedings of the Nineteenth conference on Uncertainty in Artificial Intelligence*, UAI'03, pages 329–336, 2003.

[14] Y. Koren. Factorization meets the neighborhood: a multifaceted collaborative filtering model. In *Proceedings of the 14th ACM SIGKDD international conference on Knowledge discovery and data mining*, pages 426–434, 2008.

[15] G. Linden, B. Smith, and J. York. Amazon.com recommendations: item-to-item collaborative filtering. *Internet Computing, IEEE*, 7:76–80, 2003.

[16] Y. Lu and C. Zhai. Opinion integration through semi-supervised topic modeling. In *Proceedings of the 17th international conference on World Wide Web*, pages 121–130, 2008.

[17] H. Ma, H. Yang, M. R. Lyu, and I. King. Sorec: social recommendation using probabilistic matrix factorization. In *Proceedings of the 17th ACM conference on Information and knowledge management*, pages 931–940, 2008.

[18] Q. Mei, D. Cai, D. Zhang, and C. Zhai. Topic modeling with network regularization. In *Proceedings of the 17th international conference on World Wide Web*, pages 101–110, 2008.

[19] K. Onuma, H. Tong, and C. Faloutsos. Tangent: a novel, 'surprise me', recommendation algorithm. In *Proceedings of the 15th ACM SIGKDD international conference on Knowledge discovery and data mining*, pages 657–666, 2009.

[20] J. D. M. Rennie and N. Srebro. Fast maximum margin matrix factorization for collaborative prediction. In *Proceedings of the 22nd international conference on Machine learning*, pages 713–719, 2005.

[21] R. Salakhutdinov and A. Mnih. Probabilistic matrix factorization. In *Advances in Neural Information Processing Systems*, 2008.

[22] B. Sarwar, G. Karypis, J. Konstan, and J. Riedl. Item-based collaborative filtering recommendation algorithms. In *Proceedings of the 10th international conference on World Wide Web*, pages 285–295, 2001.

[23] L. Si and R. Jin. Flexible mixture model for collaborative filtering. In *Proceedingins of the 20th international Conference on Machine Learning*, pages 704–711, 2003.

[24] X. Su and T. M. Khoshgoftaar. A survey of collaborative filtering techniques. *Advance in Artificial Intelligence*, pages 4:2–4:2, 2009.

[25] J. Tang, H. Gao, and H. Liu. mtrust: discerning multi-faceted trust in a connected world. In *Proceedings of the fifth ACM international conference on Web search and data mining*, pages 93–102, 2012.

[26] R. Wetzker, W. Umbrath, and A. Said. A hybrid approach to item recommendation in folksonomies. In *Proceedings of the WSDM '09 Workshop on Exploiting Semantic Annotations in Information Retrieval*, pages 25–29, 2009.

[27] B. Xu, J. Bu, C. Chen, and D. Cai. An exploration of improving collaborative recommender systems via user-item subgroups. In *Proceedings of the 21st international conference on World Wide Web*, pages 21–30, 2012.

[28] S.-H. Yang, B. Long, A. Smola, N. Sadagopan, Z. Zheng, and H. Zha. Like like alike: joint friendship and interest propagation in social networks. In *Proceedings of the 20th international conference on World wide web*, pages 537–546, 2011.

[29] S.-H. Yang, B. Long, A. J. Smola, H. Zha, and Z. Zheng. Collaborative competitive filtering: learning recommender using context of user choice. In *Proceedings of the 34th international ACM SIGIR conference on Research and development in Information Retrieval*, pages 295–304, 2011.

[30] T. Yang, R. Jin, Y. Chi, and S. Zhu. Combining link and content for community detection: a discriminative approach. In *Proceedings of the 15th ACM SIGKDD international conference on Knowledge discovery and data mining*, pages 927–936, 2009.

[31] X. Yang, H. Steck, and Y. Liu. Circle-based recommendation in online social networks. In *Proceedings of the 18th ACM SIGKDD international conference on Knowledge discovery and data mining*, pages 1267–1275, 2012.

[32] Y. Zhang, B. Cao, and D.-Y. Yeung. Multi-domain collaborative filtering. In *Proceedings of the Twenty-Sixth conference on Uncertainty in artificial intelligence*, pages 725–732, 2010.

Localized Matrix Factorization for Recommendation based on Matrix Block Diagonal Forms

Yongfeng Zhang   Min Zhang   Yiqun Liu   Shaoping Ma   Shi Feng
State Key Laboratory of Intelligent Technology and Systems
Tsinghua National Laboratory for Information Science and Technology
Department of Computer Science & Technology, Tsinghua University, Beijing, 100084, China
zhangyf07@gmail.com {z-m,yiqunliu,msp}@tsinghua.edu.cn fredfsh@gmail.com

ABSTRACT

Matrix factorization on user-item rating matrices has achieved significant success in collaborative filtering based recommendation tasks. However, it also encounters the problems of data sparsity and scalability when applied in real-world recommender systems. In this paper, we present the *Localized Matrix Factorization (LMF)* framework, which attempts to meet the challenges of sparsity and scalability by factorizing *Block Diagonal Form (BDF)* matrices. In the LMF framework, a large sparse matrix is first transformed into *Recursive Bordered Block Diagonal Form (RBBDF)*, which is an intuitively interpretable structure for user-item rating matrices. Smaller and denser submatrices are then extracted from this RBBDF matrix to construct a BDF matrix for more effective collaborative prediction. We show formally that the LMF framework is suitable for matrix factorization and that any *decomposable* matrix factorization algorithm can be integrated into this framework. It has the potential to improve prediction accuracy by factorizing smaller and denser submatrices independently, which is also suitable for parallelization and contributes to system scalability at the same time. Experimental results based on a number of real-world public-access benchmarks show the effectiveness and efficiency of the proposed LMF framework.

Categories and Subject Descriptors

H.3.3 [**Information Storage and Retrieval**]: Information Filtering; H.3.5 [**Online Information Services**]: Web-based services; G.1.6 [**Mathematics of Computing**]: Optimization

Keywords

Matrix Factorization; Collaborative Filtering; Block Diagonal Form; Graph Partitioning

1. INTRODUCTION

Latent factor model has been one of the most powerful approaches for collaborative filtering. Some of the most successful realizations of latent factor models are based on Matrix Factorization (MF) techniques [17]. The fundamental idea of these approaches is that user preferences can be determined by a relatively small number of latent factors. A variety of matrix factorization methods have been proposed

Copyright is held by the International World Wide Web Conference Committee (IW3C2). IW3C2 reserves the right to provide a hyperlink to the author's site if the Material is used in electronic media.
WWW 2013, May 13–17, 2013, Rio de Janeiro, Brazil.
ACM 978-1-4503-2035-1/13/05.

and applied to various collaborative filtering tasks successfully, such as Singular Value Decomposition (SVD) [17, 33], Non-negative Matrix Factorization (NMF) [18, 19], Max-Margin Matrix Factorization (MMMF) [34, 23] and Probabilistic Matrix Factorization (PMF) [26, 25].

However, MF approaches have also encountered a number of problems in real-world recommender systems, such as data sparsity, frequent model retraining and system scalability. As the number of ratings given by most users is relatively small compared with the total number of items in a typical system, data sparsity usually decreases prediction accuracy and may even lead to over-fitting problems. In addition, new ratings are usually made by users continuously in real-world recommender systems, leading to the need for refactoring rating matrices periodically, which is time consuming for systems with millions or even billions of ratings, and further restricts the scalability of MF approaches.

In this study, we propose a novel MF framework named *Localized Matrix Factorization (LMF)*, which is general and intrinsically compatible with many widely-adopted MF algorithms. Before problem formalization, we would like to use an intuitional example to briefly introduce the matrix structures used in LMF. Figure 1(a) is a sparse matrix where each row/column/cross represents a user/item/rating. By permuting Row4, Row9 and Column7 to 'borders', the remaining part is partitioned into two 'diagonal blocks', which results in a *Bordered Block Diagonal Form (BBDF)* [4] matrix in Figure 1(b). By 'recursively' permuting the first diagonal block, we obtain a *Recursive Bordered Block Diagonal Form (RBBDF)* matrix in Figure 1(c). BBDF and RBBDF structures are generalizations of *Block Diagonal Form (BDF)* structure which has no 'border'.

RBBDF structure is intuitively interpretable in collaborative filtering tasks. Consider movie recommendation as an example. Different users may have different preferences on movie genres, which form different communities, corresponding to the diagonal blocks in the BBDF structure. However, there does exist 'super users' whose interests are relatively broad and thus fall into different communities. This type of user is represented by row borders in the BBDF structure. There are also some classical or hot movies widely known and enjoyed by users from different communities, which are 'super items' making up column borders. The structure may recurse at multiple finer-grained levels in a community, resulting in the generation of RBBDF structures. As different communities may have different rating patterns, it would be better to factorize them independently.

The LMF framework transforms a sparse matrix into RBBDF

structure and further extracts denser submatrices to construct a BDF matrix. Factorization of the BDF matrix is used to approximate the original sparse matrix. The framework brings several attractive benefits to recommender systems: 1) Factorizing extracted dense submatrices instead of the whole sparse matrix improves the prediction accuracy of matrix factorization algorithms. 2) The locality property of LMF makes it possible to refactorize only the recently-updated submatrices rather than the whole matrix. 3) The framework is suitable for parallelization, which further contributes to the scalability of recommender systems.

In summary, the main contributions of this work are:

- The RBBDF structure of rating matrices is investigated, which is intuitively interpretable in CF tasks.
- A density-based algorithm is designed to transform a sparse matrix into RBBDF structure.
- The LMF framework is proposed and its rationality is shown through theoretical analyses.
- Through a comprehensive experimental study on four benchmark datasets, both the efficiency and effectiveness of the LMF framework is verified.

The remainder of this paper will be organized as follows: Section 2 reviews some related work, and Section 3 presents some preliminaries. In Section 4, the LMF framework is introduced and investigated. Experimental results are shown in Section 5. Some discussions will be made in Section 6, and the work is concluded in Section 7.

2. RELATED WORK

Collaborative Filtering (CF) [35] techniques have been known to have several attractive advantages over other recommendation strategies, such as Content-based Filtering [22] in Personalized Recommender Systems [21]. Early CF algorithms mainly focus on memory-based approaches such as User-based [24] and Item-based [29] methods, which calculate the similarities of users or items to make rating predictions [21]. To gain better prediction accuracies and to overcome the shortcomings of memory-based algorithms, model-based approaches have been investigated extensively, which estimate or learn a model on user-item rating matrices to make rating predictions [35, 21].

Latent Factor Models (LFM) based on Matrix Factorization (MF) [36] techniques have been an important research direction in model-based CF methods. Recently, MF approaches have gained great popularity as they usually outperform traditional methods [35, 12] and have achieved state-of-the-art performance, especially on large-scale recommendation tasks [17]. A variety of MF algorithms have been proposed and investigated in different CF settings, such as Principle Component Analysis (PCA) [1], Singular Value Decomposition (SVD) [16, 17, 33], Non-negative Matrix Factorization (NMF) [18, 19], Max-Margin Matrix Factorization (MMMF) [34, 23], and Probabilistic Matrix Factorization (PMF) [26, 25]. They aim at learning latent factors from a matrix, with which to make rating predictions.

According to the unified view of MF in [32], MF algorithms are optimization problems over given loss functions and regularization terms. Different choices of loss functions and regularization terms lead to different MF methods.

However, MF approaches also suffer from a number of problems in real-world recommender systems, such as data

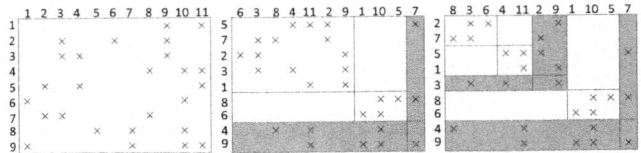

(a) Original matrix (b) BBDF matrix (c) RBBDF matrix

Figure 1: An example of (R)BBDF structure

sparsity, frequent model retraining and system scalability. To overcome the problem of data sparsity, earlier systems rely on imputation to fill in missing ratings and to make the rating matrix dense [28]. However, imputation can be very expensive as it significantly increases the amount of ratings, and inaccurate imputation may distort the data considerably [17]. The problem of frequent model retraining and scalability results from the fact that the total number of users and items is usually very large in practical systems, and new ratings are usually made by users continuously.

Most efforts to improve system scalability focus on matrix clustering techniques [38, 31, 10, 9, 37] or designing incremental and distributed versions of existing MF algorithms [30, 20, 11]. Usually, they can achieve only approximated results compared with factorizing the whole matrix directly, and many of them restrict themselves to one specific MF algorithm. In contrast with these approaches, we demonstrate that the LMF framework on a BDF matrix is theoretically equal to factorizing the whole matrix directly, and that it is compatible with any existing *decomposable* MF algorithm.

Another related research field is graph partitioning, as permuting a sparse matrix into BBDF structure is equivalent to conducting *Graph Partitioning by Vertex Separator (GPVS)* on its corresponding bipartite graph [4]. Graph partitioning is known to be NP-hard [7], but this problem has been investigated extensively, and many efficient and high-quality heuristic-based methods have been proposed [15], such as multilevel methods [14, 6], spectral partitioning [3] and kernel-based methods [2]. It is verified both theoretically and experimentally that multilevel approaches can give both fast execution time and very high quality partitions [27, 4, 14, 6, 15], which guides us to choosing the multilevel graph partitioning approach in this work.

3. PRELIMINARIES

3.1 Matrix Factorization

We take the unified view of MF proposed in [32], which is sufficient to include most of the existing MF algorithms. Let $X \in \mathbb{R}^{m \times n}$ be a sparse matrix, and let $U \in \mathbb{R}^{m \times r}, V \in \mathbb{R}^{n \times r}$ be its factorization. An MF algorithm $\mathcal{P} = (f, \mathcal{D}_W, \mathcal{C}, \mathcal{R})$ can be defined by the following choices:

1. Prediction link $f : \mathbb{R}^{m \times n} \to \mathbb{R}^{m \times n}$.
2. Optional data weights $W \in \mathbb{R}_+^{m \times n}$, which if used must be an argument of the loss function.
3. Loss function $\mathcal{D}_W(X, f(UV^T)) \geq 0$, which is a measure of the error when approximating X with $f(UV^T)$.
4. Hard constraints on factors: $(U, V) \in \mathcal{C}$.
5. Regularization penalty: $\mathcal{R}(U, V) \geq 0$.

For an MF model $X \approx f(UV^T) \triangleq X^*$, we solve:

$$\underset{(U,V) \in \mathcal{C}}{\operatorname{argmin}} \left[\mathcal{D}_W(X, f(UV^T)) + \mathcal{R}(U, V) \right]. \quad (1)$$

The loss $\mathcal{D}(\cdot,\cdot)$ is typically convex in its second argument, and often decomposes into a (weighted) sum over elements of X [32]. For example, the loss function of WSVD [33] is:

$$\mathcal{D}_W(X, f(UV^T)) = \|W \odot (X - UV^T)\|^2_{Fro} \quad (2)$$

where $\odot$ denotes the element-wise product of matrices.

In this paper, we refer to $X = UV^T$ as an Accurate Matrix Factorization of X, and refer to $X \approx f(UV^T) \triangleq X^*$ as an Approximate Matrix Factorization of X.

3.2 BDF, BBDF and RBBDF

We consider permuting the rows and/or columns of a sparse matrix to reform its structure. X is a Block Diagonal Form (BDF) matrix if:

$$X = \begin{bmatrix} D_1 & & & \\ & D_2 & & \\ & & \ddots & \\ & & & D_k \end{bmatrix} \triangleq \mathrm{diag}(D_i) \quad (3)$$

It is not always the case that a sparse matrix can be permuted into BDF, but usually it can be permuted into Bordered Block Diagonal Form (BBDF) [4] shown in (4). Each $D_i (1 \leq i \leq k)$ is a 'diagonal block'. $R_b \triangleq [R_1 \cdots R_k B]$ and $C_b \triangleq [C_1^T \cdots C_k^T B^T]^T$ are row and column 'borders':

$$X = \begin{bmatrix} D & C \\ \hline R & B \end{bmatrix} = \begin{bmatrix} D_1 & & & C_1 \\ & \ddots & & \vdots \\ & & D_k & C_k \\ \hline R_1 & \cdots & R_k & B \end{bmatrix} \quad (4)$$

Any of the k diagonal blocks D_i in (4) may be permuted into BBDF structure recursively, resulting in Recursive Bordered Block Diagonal Form (RBBDF). To avoid notational clutter, we present the following example, where $\mathcal{I}_*$ and $\mathcal{J}_*$ denote the row and column index sets:

$$X = \begin{bmatrix} \mathcal{J}_1 & \mathcal{J}_2 & \mathcal{J}_B \\ D_1 & & C_1 \\ & D_2 & C_2 \\ R_1^T & R_2^T & B \end{bmatrix} \begin{matrix} \mathcal{I}_1 \\ \mathcal{I}_2 \\ \mathcal{I}_B \end{matrix} = \begin{bmatrix} \mathcal{J}_{11} & \mathcal{J}_{12} & \mathcal{J}_{B_1} & \mathcal{J}_2 & \mathcal{J}_B \\ D_{11} & & C_{11} & & C_1^1 \\ & D_{12} & C_{12} & & C_1^2 \\ R_{11} & R_{12} & B_1 & & C_1^3 \\ & & & D_2 & C_2 \\ R_1^1 & R_1^2 & R_1^3 & R_2 & B \end{bmatrix} \begin{matrix} \mathcal{I}_{11} \\ \mathcal{I}_{12} \\ \mathcal{I}_{B_1} \\ \mathcal{I}_2 \\ \mathcal{I}_B \end{matrix} \quad (5)$$

In (5), D_1 is permuted into BBDF recursively. Note that permuting rows and columns related to D_1 affects R_1 and C_1, but it only changes the order of the non-zeros therein. Diagonal blocks D_{11}, D_{12} and D_2 may be further permuted depending on certain stopping rules. This will be introduced in our algorithm for constructing RBBDF structures.

3.3 Graph Partitioning by Vertex Separator

A sparse rating matrix can be equally represented by a bipartite graph. Consider Figure 1(a) and Figure 2(a) as examples. Each row or column of the matrix corresponds to an R-node or a C-node in the bipartite graph.

GPVS partitions a graph into disconnected components by removing a set of vertices (vertex separator) and their incident edges. As demonstrated by [4], permuting a sparse matrix into BBDF structure is equivalent to conducting GPVS on its bipartite graph. For example, removing nodes R_4, R_9 and C_7 in Figure 2(b) corresponds to permuting Row4, Row9 and Column7 to borders in Figure 1(b), and the two resulting disconnected components correspond to two diagonal blocks. GPVS is conducted recursively on the left component, and the RBBDF matrix in Figure 1(c) is constructed.

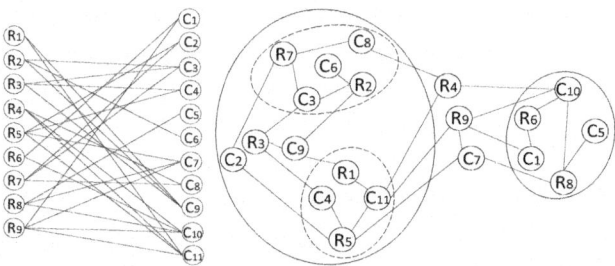

(a) Bipartite graph (b) GPVS on the bipartite graph

Figure 2: The bipartite graph for a sparse matrix and graph partitioning by vertex separator on it.

4. LMF

4.1 Definitions and Theorems

We present some definitions, propositions and theorems in this section, which will be the basis of the LMF framework.

4.1.1 Accurate Matrix Factorization

A matrix in BDF or (R)BBDF structure has some important properties in terms of accurate matrix factorization.

PROPOSITION 1. *For a BDF matrix $X = \mathrm{diag}(D_i)$ in (3), if we have $D_i = U_i V_i^T$ for each diagonal block D_i; we then have $X = \mathrm{diag}(U_i) \cdot \mathrm{diag}(V_i^T)$ as a factorization for X.* □

This proposition shows the independence of diagonal blocks from each other in a BDF matrix in terms of accurate matrix factorization. As stated above, it is not guaranteed that a sparse matrix can be permuted into BDF structure. However, we have the following proposition for a BBDF matrix.

PROPOSITION 2. *For a BBDF matrix X in (4), let:*

$$\tilde{X}_i \triangleq \begin{bmatrix} D_i & C_i \\ R_i & B \end{bmatrix} = U_i V_i^T = \begin{bmatrix} U_{i1} \\ U_{i2} \end{bmatrix} \begin{bmatrix} V_{i1}^T & V_{i2}^T \end{bmatrix} \quad (7)$$

be a factorization of $\tilde{X}_i$; thus, we have:

$$D_i = U_{i1} V_{i1}^T \quad R_i = U_{i2} V_{i1}^T \quad C_i = U_{i1} V_{i2}^T \quad B = U_{i2} V_{i2}^T$$

and let:

$$U = \begin{bmatrix} U_{11} & & & \\ & U_{21} & & \\ & & \ddots & \\ & & & U_{k1} \\ U_{12} & U_{22} & \cdots & U_{k2} \end{bmatrix} \quad V = \begin{bmatrix} V_{11} & & & \\ & V_{21} & & \\ & & \ddots & \\ & & & V_{k1} \\ V_{12} & V_{22} & \cdots & V_{k2} \end{bmatrix}$$

We then have:

$$UV^T = \begin{bmatrix} U_{11}V_{11}^T & & & & U_{11}V_{12}^T \\ & U_{21}V_{21}^T & & & U_{21}V_{22}^T \\ & & \ddots & & \vdots \\ & & & U_{k1}V_{k1}^T & U_{k1}V_{k2}^T \\ U_{12}V_{11}^T & U_{22}V_{21}^T & \cdots & U_{k2}V_{k1}^T & \sum_{i=1}^{k} U_{i2}V_{i2}^T \end{bmatrix} = \begin{bmatrix} D_1 & & & C_1 \\ & \ddots & & \vdots \\ & & D_k & C_k \\ R_1 & \cdots & R_k & kB \end{bmatrix}$$

The only difference between UV^T and X in (4) is that the border cross B in matrix X is multiplied by the number of diagonal blocks k. □

Proposition 2 is in fact factorizing a block diagonal form matrix $\tilde{X} = \mathrm{diag}(\tilde{X}_i) = \mathrm{diag}\left(\begin{bmatrix} D_i & C_i \\ R_i & B \end{bmatrix}\right) (1 \leq i \leq k)$, as denoted in (7). According to Proposition 1, if $\tilde{X}_i = U_i V_i^T$, then we have $\tilde{X} = \mathrm{diag}(U_i) \cdot \mathrm{diag}(V_i^T)$. By averaging the

$$X = \begin{bmatrix} X_1 & & & \\ & X_2 & & \\ & & \ddots & \\ & & & X_k \end{bmatrix} \approx f(UV^T) = f\left(\begin{bmatrix} U_1 \\ U_2 \\ \vdots \\ U_k \end{bmatrix} \begin{bmatrix} V_1^T & V_2^T & \cdots & V_k^T \end{bmatrix}\right) = f\left(\begin{bmatrix} U_1V_1^T & U_1V_2^T & \cdots & U_1V_k^T \\ U_2V_1^T & U_2V_2^T & \cdots & U_2V_k^T \\ \vdots & \vdots & \ddots & \vdots \\ U_kV_1^T & U_kV_2^T & \cdots & U_kV_k^T \end{bmatrix}\right) \quad (6)$$

duplicated submatrices, for example, submatrix B in (4), the original matrix X is reconstructed with the factorizations of $\tilde{X}_i = U_i V_i^T$, where $1 \leq i \leq k$.

This property can be generalized to an RBBDF matrix. To avoid notational clutter, the example in (5) is again used here. To transform X into BDF, diagonal block D_1 is transformed into BDF first, resulting in an intermediate matrix:

$$\tilde{X}_{int.} = \begin{bmatrix} \begin{array}{|cc|} \hline D_{11} & C_{11} \\ R_{11} & B_1 \\ \hline \end{array} & & & C_1^1 & \mathcal{I}_{11} \\ & & & C_1^3 & \mathcal{I}_{B_1} \\ & \begin{array}{|cc|} \hline D_{12} & C_{12} \\ R_{12} & B_1 \\ \hline \end{array} & & C_1^2 & \mathcal{I}_{12} \\ & & & C_1^3 & \mathcal{I}_{B_1} \\ & & \begin{array}{|c|} D_2 \\ \end{array} & C_2 & \mathcal{I}_2 \\ R_1^1 & R_1^3 & R_1^2 & R_1^3 & R_2 & B & \mathcal{I}_B \end{bmatrix} \quad (8)$$

This is a BBDF matrix with 3 diagonal blocks. By conducting the same procedure on $\tilde{X}_{int.}$, it is transformed into a BDF matrix ($\tilde{X}_{ij} = \mathbf{0}$ for $i \neq j$):

$$\tilde{X} = \begin{bmatrix} \begin{array}{|ccc|} \hline D_{11} & C_{11} & C_1^1 \\ R_{11} & B_1 & C_1^3 \\ R_1^1 & R_1^3 & B \\ \hline \end{array} & \tilde{X}_{12} & \tilde{X}_{13} & \mathcal{I}_{11} \\ & & & \mathcal{I}_{B_1} \\ & & & \mathcal{I}_B \\ \tilde{X}_{21} & \begin{array}{|ccc|} \hline D_{12} & C_{12} & C_1^2 \\ R_{12} & B_1 & C_1^3 \\ R_1^2 & R_1^3 & B \\ \hline \end{array} & \tilde{X}_{23} & \mathcal{I}_{12} \\ & & & \mathcal{I}_{B_1} \\ & & & \mathcal{I}_B \\ \tilde{X}_{31} & \tilde{X}_{32} & \begin{array}{|cc|} \hline D_2 & C_2 \\ R_2 & B \\ \hline \end{array} & \mathcal{I}_2 \\ & & & \mathcal{I}_B \end{bmatrix} \quad (9)$$

$$\triangleq \mathrm{diag}(\tilde{X}_1, \tilde{X}_2, \tilde{X}_3)$$

Similarly, $\tilde{X}_1$, $\tilde{X}_2$ and $\tilde{X}_3$ can be factorized independently, and duplicated submatrices are averaged to reconstruct the original matrix X in (5).

In fact, (9) can be derived from (5) directly without constructing intermediate matrices. Each diagonal block $\tilde{X}_i$ in $\tilde{X}$ corresponds to a diagonal block D_i in X. By piecing together D_i with the parts of borders on the right side, down side and right bottom side, $\tilde{X}_i$ can be constructed directly. Additionally, permuting any D_i into BBDF structure recursively in (5) would not affect other block diagonals in $\tilde{X}$.

4.1.2 Approximate Matrix Factorization

In practical applications, approximate matrix factorization algorithms formalized by (1) are used. Consider the BDF matrix $X = \mathrm{diag}(X_i)(1 \leq i \leq k)$ in terms of the approximate matrix factorization denoted by (6). For notational clarity, the superscript 'tilde' of $\tilde{X}$ is removed in this section. Decomposable properties will be investigated in different aspects in detail in this section, as they are of core importance with respect to what types of matrix factorization algorithms the framework can handle.

In the following definitions and theorems, $X_{ij} = \begin{cases} X_i & (i=j) \\ \mathbf{0} & (i \neq j) \end{cases}$ is used to denote submatrices of X in (6), and W_{ij} denotes the weight matrix of X_{ij}. $f(UV^T)_{ij}$ denotes the submatrix in $f(UV^T)$ that approximates X_{ij}, namely, $X_{ij} \approx f(UV^T)_{ij}$. Specifically, $f(UV^T)_i$ is used for $f(UV^T)_{ii}$, and W_i is used for W_{ii} when $i = j$.

DEFINITION 1. **Decomposable prediction link**. A prediction link $f : \mathbb{R}^{m \times n} \to \mathbb{R}^{m \times n}$ is decomposable if:

$$f(UV^T)_{ij} = f(U_i V_j^T) \quad (1 \leq i, j \leq k) \quad (10)$$

A large class of MF algorithms use element-wise prediction links for each pair of element in $Y = f(X)$, namely, $y_{ij} = f(x_{ij})$. For example, the prediction link is $f(x) = x$ in SVD, and in NMF, $f(x) = \log(x)$. Element-wise link functions lead to the decomposable property above naturally.

DEFINITION 2. **Decomposable loss function**. A loss function $\mathcal{D}_W(X, f(UV^T))$ is decomposable if:

$$\mathcal{D}_W(X, f(UV^T)) = \sum_{i=1}^{k} \mathcal{D}_{W_i}(X_i, f(UV^T)_i) \quad (11)$$

This property can be viewed in two aspects here.

First, a substantial number of MF algorithms restrict $\mathcal{D}$ to be expressed as the sum of losses over elements, e.g., SVD[17, 33], NMF[19], MMMF[34] and PMF[26]. Various decomposable regular Bregman divergences are the most commonly used loss functions that satisfy this property [5]. The per-element effect gives the following property:

$$\mathcal{D}_W(X, f(UV^T)) = \sum_{i,j} \mathcal{D}_{W_{ij}}(X_{ij}, f(UV^T)_{ij}) \quad (11.1)$$

Second, rating matrices in CF tasks are usually incomplete and very sparse in practical recommender systems. A 'zero' means only that the user did not make a rating on the corresponding item, rather than rating it zero. As a result, many MF algorithms optimize loss functions on observed ratings. Specifically, $W_{ij} = \mathbf{0}$ ($i \neq j$) in a BDF matrix, and:

$$\mathcal{D}_{W_{ij}}(X_{ij}, f(UV^T)_{ij}) = 0 \quad (i \neq j) \quad (11.2)$$

(11.1) and (11.2) gives the decomposable property of loss functions in Definition 2.

DEFINITION 3. **Decomposable hard constraint**. A hard constraint $\mathcal{C}$ is decomposable if:

$$(U, V) \in \mathcal{C} \quad \text{iff.} \quad (U_i, V_i) \in \mathcal{C} \quad (1 \leq i \leq k) \quad (12)$$

Many MF algorithms do not apply hard constraints to target factorizations, but there are MF methods that require (U, V) to meet some special requirements.

Some commonly used hard constraints are non-negativity (the elements of U,V are non-negative), orthogonality (the columns of U,V are orthogonal), stochasticity (each row of U,V sums to one), sparsity (the row vectors of U,V meet a desired sparseness constraint) and cardinality (the number of non-zeros in each row of U,V satisfies a given constraint).

In this sense, non-negativity, stochasticity, sparsity and cardinality constraints are decomposable hard constraints. For example, each row of (U, V) sums to one if and only if the same property holds for any (U_i, V_i) ($1 \leq i \leq k$). However, orthogonality is not decomposable: the orthogonality in (U, V) does not ensure the orthogonality in each (U_i, V_i). Our primary focus is on decomposable hard constraints.

DEFINITION 4. **Decomposable regularization penalty.**
A regularization penalty $\mathcal{R}(U, V)$ is decomposable if:

$$\mathcal{R}(U, V) = \sum_{i=1}^{k} \mathcal{R}(U_i, V_i) \quad (13)$$

The most commonly used regularization penalty is the ℓ_p-norm regularizer, which is decomposable:

$$\mathcal{R}(U,V) = \lambda_U \|U\|_p^p + \lambda_V \|V\|_p^p$$
$$= \sum_{i=1}^{k} \left(\lambda_U \|U_i\|_p^p + \lambda_V \|V_i\|_p^p \right) = \sum_{i=1}^{k} \mathcal{R}(U_i, V_i)$$

The Frobenius norm is ℓ_p-norm where $p = 2$. The basic MMMF algorithm takes the trace-norm $\|X\|_\Sigma$ (the sum of singular values of X) [34], which is unfortunately not a decomposable regularizer. However, a fast MMMF algorithm based on the equivalence $\|X\|_\Sigma = \min_{X=UV^T} \frac{1}{2}(\|U\|_F^2 + \|V\|_F^2)$ is proposed in [23], which also takes ℓ_p-norm regularizers.

DEFINITION 5. **Decomposable matrix factorization.** A matrix factorization algorithm $\mathcal{P} = (f, \mathcal{D}_W, \mathcal{C}, \mathcal{R})$ is decomposable if $f, \mathcal{D}_W, \mathcal{C}, \mathcal{R}$ are decomposable. Namely, properties (10)~(13) hold. $(U, V) = \mathcal{P}(X, r)$ denotes the factorization of X by $\mathcal{P}$ using r factors.

It is necessary to point out that many commonly used MF algorithms are decomposable, including some of the state-of-the-art techniques, although they are required to satisfy all these four decomposable properties, which seems to be somewhat too strict. Some typical examples are SVD, NMF, PMF, MMMF and their variations, which will be primarily considered and investigated in this work.

THEOREM 1. Suppose X is a BDF matrix in (6), and $\mathcal{P} = (f, \mathcal{D}_W, \mathcal{C}, \mathcal{R})$ is decomposable. Let $(U, V) = \mathcal{P}(X, r)$ and $(U_i, V_i) = \mathcal{P}(X_i, r)(1 \le i \le k)$. We have:
i. $U = [U_1^T U_2^T \cdots U_k^T]^T$, $V = [V_1^T V_2^T \cdots V_k^T]^T$
ii. $X_{ij} \approx f(U_i V_j^T)$ $(1 \le i,j \le k)$

PROOF. i. Consider the optimization problem defined in (1) with decomposable properties of prediction link f, loss function $\mathcal{D}_W$, hard constraint $\mathcal{C}$, and regularizer $\mathcal{R}$; we have:

$$(U, V) = \mathcal{P}(X, r)$$
$$= \underset{(U,V)\in\mathcal{C}}{\operatorname{argmin}} \left[\mathcal{D}_W(X, f(UV^T)) + \mathcal{R}(U, V) \right]$$
$$= \underset{(U,V)\in\mathcal{C}}{\operatorname{argmin}} \sum_{i=1}^{k} \left[\mathcal{D}_{W_i}(X_i, f(UV^T)_i) + \mathcal{R}(U_i, V_i) \right]$$
$$= \underset{(U,V)\in\mathcal{C}}{\operatorname{argmin}} \sum_{i=1}^{k} \left[\mathcal{D}_{W_i}(X_i, f(U_i V_i^T)) + \mathcal{R}(U_i, V_i) \right]$$
$$= \bigwedge_{i=1}^{k} \left\{ \underset{(U_i,V_i)\in\mathcal{C}}{\operatorname{argmin}} \left[\mathcal{D}_{W_i}(X_i, f(U_i V_i^T)) + \mathcal{R}(U_i, V_i) \right] \right\}$$
$$= \bigwedge_{i=1}^{k} \left\{ \mathcal{P}(X_i, r) \right\} = \bigwedge_{i=1}^{k} \left\{ (U_i, V_i) \right\}$$

thus, $U = [U_1^T U_2^T \cdots U_k^T]^T$ and $V = [V_1^T V_2^T \cdots V_k^T]^T$.
ii. This can be derived directly from the decomposable property of prediction link f in (10):

$$X_{ij} \approx f(UV^T)_{ij} = f(U_i V_j^T)$$

and it holds for any $1 \le i,j \le k$, including zero submatrices where $i \ne j$. □

According to Theorem 1, each diagonal block can be factorized independently, and the results can be used directly to approximate not only the non-zero diagonal blocks but also the zero off-diagonal blocks.

4.2 LMF for Collaborative Prediction

Consider predicting the missing values of an incomplete sparse rating matrix through the LMF framework. A sparse rating matrix is permuted into an RBBDF matrix (5) first and further transformed into a BDF matrix (9). LMF is then performed on the resulting BDF matrix to make rating predictions for the original matrix.

Suppose an RBBDF matrix X is transformed into a BDF matrix $\tilde{X} = \operatorname{diag}(\tilde{X}_i)(1 \le i \le k)$. $X_{\mathcal{I}_* \sim \mathcal{J}_*}$ and $\tilde{X}_{\mathcal{I}_* \sim \mathcal{J}_*}$ are used to denote the submatrices in X and $\tilde{X}$ correspondingly. For example, $R_{12} = X_{\mathcal{I}_{B_1} \sim \mathcal{J}_{12}}$ in (5), and it is duplicated twice by $\tilde{X}_{\mathcal{I}_{B_1} \sim \mathcal{J}_{12}}$ in (9). The LMF framework approximates the original matrix X through the approximations of $\tilde{X}$ with three steps:

i. For a decomposable matrix factorization algorithm $\mathcal{P} = (f, \mathcal{D}_W, \mathcal{C}, \mathcal{R})$, obtain the factorization $(U_i, V_i) = \mathcal{P}(\tilde{X}_i, r)$ of each diagonal block $\tilde{X}_i$. Then:

$$\tilde{X}_i \approx f(U_i V_i^T) \triangleq \tilde{X}_i^* \triangleq \tilde{X}_{ii}^* \quad (14)$$

where $\tilde{X}_i^*$ denotes the approximation of $\tilde{X}_i$.

ii. Predict zero blocks $\tilde{X}_{ij}(i \ne j)$ in $\tilde{X}$ using factorizations of $\tilde{X}_i$ and $\tilde{X}_j$:

$$\tilde{X}_{ij} \approx f(U_i V_j^T) \triangleq \tilde{X}_{ij}^* \quad (15)$$

Now $\tilde{X}^* \triangleq \{\tilde{X}_{ij}^* | 1 \le i,j \le k\}$ approximates $\tilde{X}$.

iii. Average duplicated submatrices in $\tilde{X}^*$ to approximate the corresponding submatrix in X.

Suppose that $X_{\mathcal{I}_* \sim \mathcal{J}_*}$ is duplicated k times in $\tilde{X}$, and the tth duplication is in block $\tilde{X}_{i_t j_t}$, whose approximation is $\tilde{X}_{\mathcal{I}_* \sim \mathcal{J}_*}^{*(i_t j_t)}$. Then the approximation of $X_{\mathcal{I}_* \sim \mathcal{J}_*}$ is:

$$X_{\mathcal{I}_* \sim \mathcal{J}_*}^* = \frac{1}{k} \sum_{t=1}^{k} \tilde{X}_{\mathcal{I}_* \sim \mathcal{J}_*}^{*(i_t j_t)} \quad (16)$$

To make it easier to understand, take $R_{12} = X_{\mathcal{I}_{B_1} \sim \mathcal{J}_{12}}$ in (5) as an example. $X_{\mathcal{I}_{B_1} \sim \mathcal{J}_{12}}$ is duplicated twice in (9): one in $\tilde{X}_{12}$ and the other in $\tilde{X}_{22}$. As a result:

$$X_{\mathcal{I}_{B_1} \sim \mathcal{J}_{12}}^* = \frac{1}{2}(\tilde{X}_{\mathcal{I}_{B_1} \sim \mathcal{J}_{12}}^{*(12)} + \tilde{X}_{\mathcal{I}_{B_1} \sim \mathcal{J}_{12}}^{*(22)})$$

Approximation $X_{\mathcal{I}_* \sim \mathcal{J}_*}^*$ is constructed for each submatrix $X_{\mathcal{I}_* \sim \mathcal{J}_*}$ in X. By piecing them together, approximation $X^* = \{X_{\mathcal{I}_* \sim \mathcal{J}_*}^*\}$ is finally achieved for X.

4.3 Algorithm for RBBDF Permutation

As shown in Section 3.3, permuting a matrix into (R)BBDF structure is equivalent to performing GPVS (recursively) on its bipartite graph. In this work, both the performance and efficiency of graph partitioning algorithms are concerned, as the datasets to experiment on are huge[1]. As a result, multilevel graph partitioning approach is chosen. Perhaps the

---
[1] One of the four datasets used is Yahoo! Music from KDDCUP 2011, containing approximately 1m users and 0.6m items, which is the largest in present-day datasets.

most widely known and used package for graph partitioning is Metis [13] by Karypis, which is based on multilevel approach. The core routine for GPVS in Metis is Node-based Bisection, which partitions a graph into two disconnected components by a vertex separator.

A density-based algorithm to permute sparse matrices into RBBDF structure is designed, as dense submatrices or subgraphs are usually interpreted as communities, which is widely used in community detection and graph clustering problems [8]. The density of a matrix X is defined as $\rho(X) = \frac{n(X)}{s(X)}$, where $n(X)$ is the number of non-zeros in X, and $s(X)$ is the area of X. The average density of k matrices $X_1 X_2 \cdots X_k$ is defined as $\bar{\rho}(X_1 X_2 \cdots X_k) = \frac{\sum_{i=1}^{k} n(X_i)}{\sum_{i=1}^{k} s(X_i)}$. Note that the density of a matrix is equal to the density of its corresponding bipartite graph [8].

For an RBBDF matrix X with k diagonal blocks $D_1 D_2 \cdots D_k$ (e.g., the matrix in (5) has 3 diagonal blocks: $D_{11} D_{12}$ and D_2, and the original rating matrix is viewed as a single diagonal block), $\tilde{X} = \text{diag}(\tilde{X}_1 \tilde{X}_2 \cdots \tilde{X}_k)$ is used to denote its corresponding BDF matrix (e.g., the matrix in (9)). Algorithm 1 shows the procedure, followed by more detailed explanations and analyses. RBBDF$(X, \hat{\rho}, 1)$ is called to start the procedure.

Algorithm 1 RBBDF$(X, \hat{\rho}, k)$

Require:
    User-item rating matrix: X
    Average density requirement: $\hat{\rho}$
    Current number of diagonal blocks in X: k

Ensure:
    Matrix X be permuted into RBBDF structure
    BDF matrix $\tilde{X}$ which is constructed from X

1: $\rho \leftarrow \bar{\rho}(\tilde{X}_1 \tilde{X}_2 \cdots \tilde{X}_k)$
2: **if** $\rho \geq \hat{\rho}$ **then**
3:     **return** $\tilde{X}$ ▷ Density requirement has been reached
4: **else**
5:     $[D_{s_1} D_{s_2} \cdots D_{s_k}] \leftarrow \text{Sort}([D_1 D_2 \cdots D_k])$ ▷ Sort diagonal blocks by size in decreasing order
6:     **for** $i \leftarrow 1$ to k **do**
7:       $[D_{s_i}^1, D_{s_i}^2] \leftarrow \text{MetisNodeBisection}(D_{s_i})$ ▷ Partition D_{s_i} into 2 diagonals using core routine of Metis
8:       **if** $\bar{\rho}(\tilde{X}_{s_1} \cdots \tilde{X}_{s_{i-1}} \tilde{X}_{s_i}^1 \tilde{X}_{s_i}^2 \tilde{X}_{s_{i+1}} \cdots \tilde{X}_{s_k}) > \rho$ **then**
9:         $X' \leftarrow$ Permute D_{s_i} into $[D_{s_i}^1, D_{s_i}^2]$ in X
10:        RBBDF$(X', \hat{\rho}, k+1)$ ▷ Recurse
11:        **break** ▷ No need to check the next diagonal
12:       **end if**
13:     **end for**
14:     **return** $\tilde{X}$ ▷ No diagonal improves average density
15: **end if**

Algorithm 1 requires a 'density requirement' $\hat{\rho}$ as input, which is the expected average density of submatrices $\tilde{X}_1 \cdots \tilde{X}_k$ in the final BDF matrix $\tilde{X}$. In each recursion, the algorithm checks each diagonal block D_i of X in decreasing order of matrix areas. If the average density of extracted submatrices can be improved by partitioning a diagonal block, then the algorithm takes the partitioning and recurses, until $\hat{\rho}$ is reached or none of the diagonal blocks can improve the average density any more.

Note that, to gain a high efficiency, a fundamental heuristic is used in this algorithm, which is the area of diagonal blocks, and we explain its rationality here.

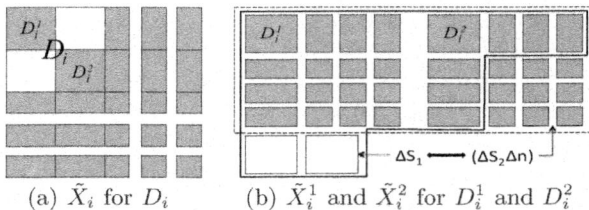

(a) $\tilde{X}_i$ for D_i (b) $\tilde{X}_i^1$ and $\tilde{X}_i^2$ for D_i^1 and D_i^2

Figure 3: Partition a diagonal block, rearrange its corresponding borders, and extract new submatrices. The shaded areas represent non-zero blocks.

Figure 3(a) shows a diagonal block D_i along with its corresponding borders. Note that this figure is, in fact, the submatrix $\tilde{X}_i$ in $\tilde{X}$ corresponding to D_i. Two new submatrices $\tilde{X}_i^1$ and $\tilde{X}_i^2$ are constructed when D_i is partitioned into D_i^1 and D_i^2, which are boxed by dotted lines in Figure 3(b). One can see that the area boxed by solid lines in Figure 3(b) constitutes the original submatrix $\tilde{X}_i$. As a result, transforming $\tilde{X}_i$ to $\tilde{X}_i^1$ and $\tilde{X}_i^2$ is essentially removing the two zero blocks and replacing them with some duplicated non-zero blocks.

Let $s = \sum_{t=1}^{k} s(\tilde{X}_t)$ and $n = \sum_{t=1}^{k} n(\tilde{X}_t)$; let Δs_1 be the total area of removed zero blocks, Δs_2 be the total area of duplicated non-zero blocks, and Δn be the number of nonzeros in Δs_2. The increment of average density after partitioning D_i is:

$$\Delta \rho = \rho' - \rho = \frac{n + \Delta n}{s - \Delta s_1 + \Delta s_2} - \frac{n}{s} = \frac{s \Delta n + n \Delta s}{s(s - \Delta s)} \quad (17)$$

where ρ and ρ' are the average densities of diagonal blocks in $\tilde{X}$ before and after partitioning D_i, and $\Delta s \triangleq \Delta s_1 - \Delta s_2$.

Because $s - \Delta s > 0$, we have the following:

$$\Delta \rho > 0 \leftrightarrow s \Delta n + n \Delta s = s \Delta n + n(\Delta s_1 - \Delta s_2) > 0 \quad (18)$$

If $\Delta s > 0$, then (18) holds naturally. Otherwise, the following is required:

$$\frac{n}{s} < \frac{\Delta n}{\Delta s_2 - \Delta s_1} \quad (19)$$

Although not guaranteed, (19) can usually be satisfied as the following property usually holds:

$$\frac{n}{s} < \frac{\Delta n}{\Delta s_2} < \frac{\Delta n}{\Delta s_2 - \Delta s_1} \quad (20)$$

Intuitively, (20) means that the density of duplicated non-zero blocks after partitioning is usually greater than the original average density of k submatrices $\tilde{X}_1 \tilde{X}_2 \cdots \tilde{X}_k$, as the latter contains many zero blocks. Additionally, a large Δs tends to yield a large density increment $\Delta \rho$ according to (17), which leads to adopting areas of diagonal blocks as heuristics. It will be verified experimentally that this heuristic improves the average density at the first attempt nearly all the time.

The time complexity of Node-based bisection in Metis is $O(n)$, where n is the number of non-zeros in a matrix [14]. Suppose that matrix X is permuted into an RBBDF structure which has k diagonal blocks ($k \ll n$) in the end, and the algorithm chooses the largest diagonal block for partitioning in each recursion; then, the height of the recursion tree will be $O(\lg k)$ and the total computational cost in each level of the tree is $O(n)$. As a result, the time complexity of Algorithm 1 is $O(n \lg k)$.

5. EXPERIMENTS

5.1 Datasets Description

A series of experiments were conducted on four real-world datasets: MovieLens-100K, MovieLens-1M, DianPing and Yahoo!Music. The MovieLens dataset is from GroupLens Research. We also collected a year's data from a famous restaurant rating web site *DianPing*[2] from Jan. 1st to Dec. 31st 2011 and selected those users with 20 or more ratings. The ratings also range from 0 to 5. The Yahoo!Music dataset is from KDD Cup 2011, and its ratings range from 0 to 100. Statistics of these datasets are presented in Table 1.

Table 1: Statistics of four datasets

	ML-100K	ML-1M	DianPing	Yahoo!Music
#users	943	6,040	11,857	1,000,990
#items	1,682	3,952	22,365	624,961
#ratings	100,000	1,000,209	510,551	256,804,235
#ratings/user	106.045	165.598	43.059	256.550
#ratings/item	59.453	253.089	22.828	410.912
average density	0.0630	0.0419	0.00193	0.000411

These datasets are chosen as they have different sizes and densities. Besides, two of them have more users than items, and the others are the opposite. We expect to verify how our framework works on datasets of different sizes and densities.

5.2 Algorithms and Evaluation Metrics

Four popular and state-of-the-art matrix factorization algorithms are the subject of experimentation in this work:
SVD: The Alternating Least Squares (ALS) algorithm in [17] is used for SVD learning.
NMF: The NMF algorithm based on divergence cost in [19] is used. We also use F-norm regularizer, similar to SVD.
PMF: The Bayesian PMF by Markov Chain Monte Carlo method in [25] is used.
MMMF: The fast version of MMMF in [23] is used.

For easier comparison with previous proposed methods in the literature, we use *Root Mean Square Error (RMSE)* to measure the prediction accuracy in this work.

For N rating-prediction pairs $\langle r_i, \hat{r}_i \rangle$:

$$\text{RMSE} = \sqrt{\frac{\sum_{i=1}^{N}(r_i - \hat{r}_i)^2}{N}}$$

Five-fold cross validation is conducted to calculate the average RMSE for MovieLens and DianPing. The Yahoo! Music dataset itself is partitioned into training and validation sets, which are used for training and evaluation, respectively.

5.3 Analyses of RBBDF Algorithm

5.3.1 Number of diagonal blocks

The only parameter to be tuned in the RBBDF algorithm is the average density requirement $\hat{\rho}$. Intuitively, a low density requirement gives less and larger diagonal blocks in $\tilde{X}$, and vice versa. The relationship between the number of diagonal blocks k and the density requirement $\hat{\rho}$ on four datasets is shown by red solid lines in Figure 4.

We see that the number of diagonal blocks increases faster and faster with an increasing density requirement. To investigate the underlying reason, a more straightforward view is given by the relative density increment in Figure 5. Suppose that the current number of diagonal blocks is k; the average density of $\tilde{X}_1 \tilde{X}_2 \cdots \tilde{X}_k$ is $\bar{\rho}_k$, and the average density goes to $\bar{\rho}_{k+1}$ after partitioning a diagonal block. Then, the relative density increment is $\Delta\rho/\rho_1 = (\bar{\rho}_{k+1} - \bar{\rho}_k)/\bar{\rho}_1$, where the constant $\bar{\rho}_1$ is the density of the whole original matrix.

Experimental results show that the relative density increment becomes lower and lower as the number of diagonal blocks increases. As a result, it is relatively easy to improve the average density at the beginning, as partitioning a large diagonal block D_i gains a large density increment $\Delta\rho$. However, this process tends to be more and more difficult when diagonal blocks become small. The experimental result is in accordance with the analysis in (17)~(20). These results partially verify the heuristic used in Algorithm 1.

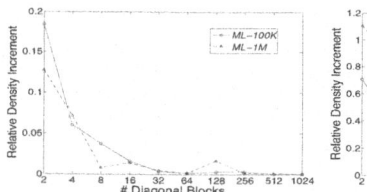 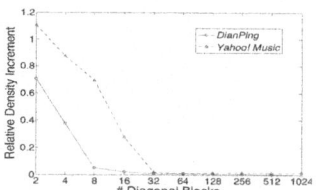

(a) ML-100K & ML-1M (b) DianPing & Yahoo!Music

Figure 5: Relationship between the Relative Density Increment $\Delta\rho/\rho_1$ and the Current number of diagonal blocks k on four datasets.

5.3.2 Verification of heuristic

The *First Choice Hit Rate (FCHR)* is used to verify the heuristic used in the RBBDF algorithm, as we expect the average density to be improved by partitioning the first diagonal block D_{s_1} in the sorted list $[D_{s_1} D_{s_2} \cdots D_{s_k}]$, in which case there is no need to check the remaining diagonal blocks.

$$\text{FCHR} = \frac{\#\ recursions\ where\ D_{s_1}\ is\ chosen}{\#\ recursions\ in\ total}$$

One can see that FCHR = 1 means that average density can always be improved by partitioning the largest diagonal block directly. The relationships between FCHR and density requirement on four datasets are shown by blue dotted lines in Figure 4. On all of the four datasets, FCHR = 1 at the beginning and begins to drop when density requirement is high enough, which is also in accordance with the analysis in Section 4.3. As a result, by taking the areas of diagonal blocks as a heuristic, only one diagonal block is partitioned in each recursion, and there is no redundant computation when an appropriate density requirement is given.

When the density requirement is high, we have FCHR < 1, and redundant computation will be introduced: we might partition a diagonal block without improving the average density. However, we would like to note that it does not matter very much in practice. First, when considering the $O(n)$ complexity of the Node-based Bisection, it will be faster and faster to partition diagonal blocks as they become smaller. Second, there is no need to split a matrix into hundreds or even thousands of diagonal blocks in practice. According to our experiments in the following sections, it is sufficient to gain both high prediction accuracy and computational efficiency by partitioning a matrix into a small number of diagonal blocks, in which case we have FCHR = 1.

5.3.3 Computational Time of RBBDF Algorithm

Experiments were conducted on an 8-core 3.1GHz linux server with 64G RAM. We tuned the density requirement $\hat{\rho}$

---
[2] http://www.dianping.com

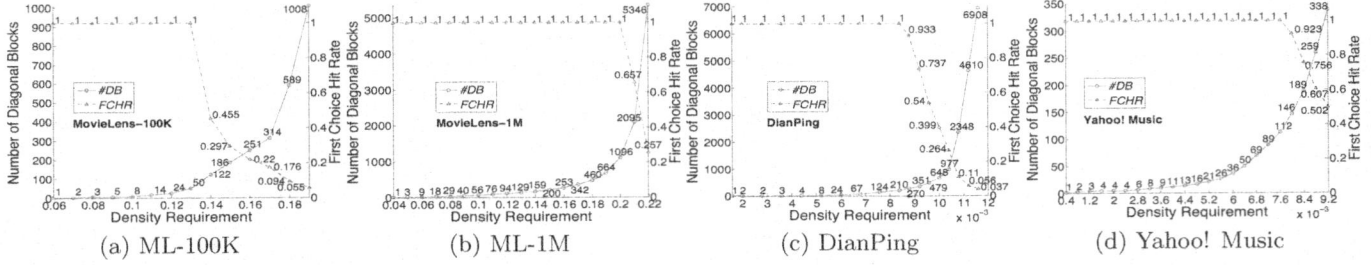

(a) ML-100K (b) ML-1M (c) DianPing (d) Yahoo! Music

Figure 4: Number of Diagonal Blocks (#DB, solid lines) and First Choice Hit Rate (FCHR, dotted lines) under different density requirements $\hat{\rho}$. The tuning steps of $\hat{\rho}$ are 0.01, 0.01, 0.0008 and 0.0004, respectively.

to achieve the expected number of diagonal blocks k. The run time of the RBBDF algorithm is shown in Table 2.

In the experiments, we see that the run time increases along with the number of diagonal blocks, and it takes less time to partition a submatrix as they become smaller. Moreover, the time used by the RBBDF algorithm is much less than that used for training an MF model on matrix X. We will show the results on model training time in Section 5.5.

Table 2: Computational time of the RBBDF algorithm with different numbers of diagonal blocks k.

k	5	10	15	20	50	100	150	200
ML-100K / ms	160	180	196	208	224	340	422	493
ML-1M / s	4.45	5.61	6.25	6.76	8.31	9.51	10.25	10.74
DianPing / s	6.01	9.69	11.61	12.84	14.64	15.06	16.18	16.95
Yahoo! / min	8.03	9.54	10.95	12.08	17.67	21.83	23.35	24.73

5.4 Prediction Accuracy

5.4.1 Number of latent factors

The number of latent factors r plays an important part in MF algorithms. It would be insufficient for approximating a matrix if r is too low, and would be computationally expensive if r is too high. As the diagonal blocks in $\tilde{X}$ and the original matrix X are of different sizes, it's important to investigate how to choose a proper r in practical applications.

We use MovieLens-1M to test the impact of r in the LMF framework. The density requirement is $\hat{\rho} = 0.055$, and matrix X is permuted into an RBBDF structure with 4 diagonal blocks; then, $\tilde{X} = \text{diag}(\tilde{X}_1, \tilde{X}_2, \tilde{X}_3, \tilde{X}_4)$ is constructed. Some statistical information about $\tilde{X}$ is shown in Table 3.

Table 3: Statistics of the four diagonal blocks

	$\tilde{X}_1$	$\tilde{X}_2$	$\tilde{X}_3$	$\tilde{X}_4$
#users	1,507	1,683	1,743	1,150
#items	2,491	3,108	3,616	3,304
#ratings	118,479	259,665	462,586	192,267
density	0.0316	0.0496	0.0734	0.0506

We tuned r from 5 to 100, with a tuning step of 5. It's necessary to note that r is required to be comparable with $\min(m, n)$ in MMMF, where m and n are the numbers of users and items in X. However, it would be time consuming to train a model using thousands or even millions of factors. Fortunately, according to [23], it's sufficient to use much smaller values of r to achieve satisfactory performance in practice ($r = 100$ is used in [23] for ML-1M). As a result, the tuning range of 5 ~ 100 is also used for MMMF.

For each of the four MF algorithms, two sets of experiments were conducted. First, we approximate the original matrix X using r factors directly, and record the RMSE. Second, predictions are made by the LMF framework in Section 4.2 using the four diagonal blocks in $\tilde{X}$, each with r factors. Cross-validation is performed on X to find the best regularization parameters for each MF method. In SVD and NMF, λ is set to 0.065; in PMF, λ_U and λ_V are both 0.002; and in MMMF, the regularization constant C is set to 1.5. RMSE v.s. the number of latent factors r is shown in Figure 7.

Experimental results show that better performance in terms of RMSE can be achieved in the LMF framework. Furthermore, the improvement tends to be more obvious when the number of latent factors r is relatively small. This result could arise because, in such cases, r is not sufficient to approximate the original matrix X, while it is sufficient to approximate relatively small submatrices in $\tilde{X}$. We view this as an advantage of the LMF framework, as better performance can be achieved with fewer factors, which benefits the model complexity and training time.

5.4.2 Different density requirements

The final number of diagonal blocks k in $\tilde{X}$ is different under different density requirements $\hat{\rho}$. We experimented RMSE with different density requirements. The number of latent factors r is set to 60, as we find it sufficient to smooth the performance improvement on the datasets. The regularization coefficients are the same: $\lambda = 0.065$ for SVD and NMF, $\lambda_U = \lambda_V = 0.002$ for PMF, and $C = 1.5$ for MMMF.

The RMSE versus different choices of $\hat{\rho}$ on all of the four datasets are plotted in Figure 6. In each subfigure, the four curves correspond to the four MF methods used, which are SVD, NMF, PMF and MMMF. The density requirement on the first point of each curve is the average density of the corresponding dataset; as a result, RMSE on this point is the baseline performance for the matrix factorization algorithm. Thus, points below the beginning point of a curve indicate an improvement on prediction accuracy, and vice versa.

Experimental results show that our LMF framework helps decomposable MF algorithms to gain better prediction accuracies if appropriate density requirements are given, but might bring negative effects if $\hat{\rho}$ is not appropriately set.

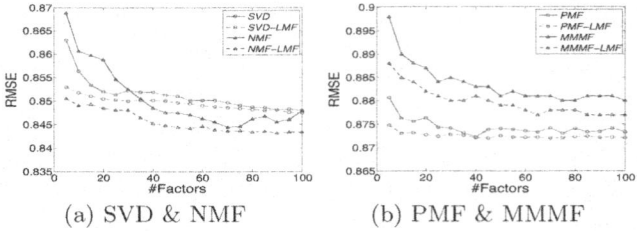

(a) SVD & NMF (b) PMF & MMMF

Figure 7: RMSE v.s. different numbers of latent factors. Solid/dotted lines are results of approximating X directly/through the LMF framework.

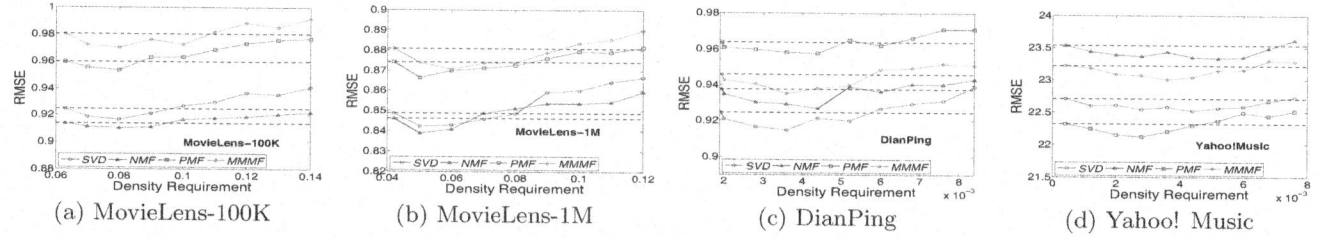

(a) MovieLens-100K (b) MovieLens-1M (c) DianPing (d) Yahoo! Music

Figure 6: RMSE on four datasets using the LMF framework under different density requirements. Dotted lines in each subfigure represent baseline performance of the corresponding matrix factorization algorithm.

Here, by 'appropriate', we mean that $\hat{\rho}$ is not too high. According to the experimental results on four datasets, better prediction accuracies are achieved along with an increasing $\hat{\rho}$ (and also the number of diagonal blocks k) at the beginning, but the performance tends to drop when $\hat{\rho}$ is set too high. In our view, this is not surprising because many small scattered diagonal blocks are extracted when a high density requirement is set, which would bring negative effects to MF algorithms. Table 4 presents the average number of users and items in the diagonal blocks of $\tilde{X}$ under different $\hat{\rho}$ on MovieLens-1M. We see that the average number of users goes to only a hundred or less when $\hat{\rho} \geq 0.1$.

Table 4: Average number of users and items in diagonal blocks of $\tilde{X}$ under different $\hat{\rho}$ on MovieLens-1M.

$\hat{\rho}$	0.045	0.052	0.060	0.069	0.081	0.102	0.129	0.160
k	2	4	8	16	32	64	128	256
Avg #users	3020	1520	779	409	220	128	82	61
Avg #items	3170	3129	3055	3064	3015	3007	3015	3030

However, better performance is achieved given appropriate density requirements. By combining this observation with the experimental results in Section 5.3, it is neither reasonable nor necessary to use high density requirements that result in hundreds or even thousands of diagonal blocks.

Table 5 shows the best RMSE achieved on each dataset for each MF method. To calculate the average RMSE on each dataset, five-fold cross-validation was conducted on MovieLens and DianPing, and experiments were conducted five times on Yahoo! Music. The standard deviations were $\leq$ 0.002 on MovieLens and DianPing, and were $\leq$ 0.01 on Yahoo! Music. We see that, in the best cases, MF algorithms benefit from the LMF framework in terms of RMSE on all of the four datasets. Specifically, the sparser a matrix is, the higher RMSE increment LMF tends to gain.

5.5 Speedup by Parallelization

An important advantage of LMF is that, once the BDF matrix $\tilde{X} = \text{diag}(\tilde{X}_i)$ is constructed, diagonal blocks $\tilde{X}_i$ can be trained in parallel. According to the decomposable property in Theorem 1, sub-problems of learning different (U_i, V_i) are not coupled; as a result, there is no need to implement rather complicated parallel computing algorithms. In fact, simple multi-threading technique is adequate for the task, which contributes to the scalability of recommender systems while, at the same time, keeps system simplicity.

The experiment comprises three stages. In the first stage, X is permuted into an RBBDF structure, and a BDF matrix $\tilde{X} = \text{diag}(\tilde{X}_i)(1 \leq i \leq k)$ is constructed. As we have 8 cores, the density requirement is tuned on each dataset to construct $\tilde{X}$ with 8 diagonal blocks. In the second stage, each diagonal block is factorized independently with a thread, and (U_i, V_i) is achieved. In the last stage, (U_i, V_i) from all of the diagonal blocks are used to approximate the original matrix X by LMF. The computational time consumed in each stage is recorded (in the second stage, the time recorded is the longest among all of the diagonal blocks). Finally, the total time of the three stages is adopted to evaluate the overall efficiency. The number of factors and the regularization coefficients are the same as those in Section 5.4.2. The results are shown in Table 6, where 'Base' represents the computational time of factorizing X directly, 'LMF' is the time used by the LMF framework, and 'Speedup' is 'Base/LMF'.

Table 6: Computational time and speedup by multi-threading with 8 diagonal blocks.

Method	MovieLens-100K			MovieLens-1M		
	Base	LMF	Speedup	Base	LMF	Speedup
SVD	23.9s	7.7s	3.10	184.9s	43.4s	4.26
NMF	8.7s	3.9s	2.23	86.6s	22.1s	3.92
PMF	43.8s	11.6s	3.78	265.1s	60.1s	4.41
MMMF	19.6min	4.71min	4.16	1.73h	21.5min	4.83

Method	DianPing			Yahoo!Music		
	Base	LMF	Speedup	Base	LMF	Speedup
SVD	143.7s	35.7	4.03	6.22h	1.21h	5.14
NMF	64.4s	16.6s	3.88	4.87h	1.05h	4.64
PMF	190.5s	44.1s	4.32	7.91h	1.48h	5.34
MMMF	48.5min	10.2min	4.75	38.8h	6.22h	6.24

Experimental results show that the LMF framework helps to save a substantial amount of model training time through very simple multithreading parallelization techniques. This is especially helpful when learning large magnitude datasets, which is important in real-world recommender systems.

6. DISCUSSIONS

Unlike benchmark datasets, rating matrices in real-world recommender systems usually change dynamically as new ratings are made by users continuously. A typical way to settle this problem in practice is to retrain MF models periodically or when a predefined prediction accuracy threshold (say RMSE) is reached. However, it would be time consuming to refactorize large rating matrices as a whole and to do so frequently. In the LMF framework, however, it is possible to only refactorize those submatrices whose prediction accuracies have reached a predefined threshold, rather than refactorize the whole matrix, which further benefits system scalability. This potential advantage that LMF might bring about will be investigated both by simulation and in practical real-world recommender systems in future work.

7. CONCLUSIONS

In this paper, we explored the BDF, BBDF and RBBDF structures of sparse matrices and their properties in terms of matrix factorization. The LMF framework is proposed, and to explicitly indicate the scope of matrix factorizations

Table 5: Best performance achieved in LMF with corresponding density requirement $\hat{\rho}$ and number of diagonal blocks k. Bold numbers indicate improvements that are ≥ 0.01 on MovieLens and DianPing or ≥ 0.2 on Yahoo!Music. The standard deviations are ≤ 0.002 on MovieLens and DianPing and ≤ 0.01 on Yahoo!Music.

Method	MovieLens-100K				MovieLens-1M				DianPing				Yahoo!Music			
	baseline	$\hat{\rho}$	k	RMSE	baseline	$\hat{\rho}$	k	RMSE	baseline	$\hat{\rho}$	k	RMSE	baseline	$\hat{\rho}$	k	RMSE
SVD	0.9249	0.08	3	0.9165	0.8487	0.05	3	0.8423	0.9244	0.0036	3	0.9145	22.713	0.0044	13	22.519
NMF	0.9138	0.08	3	0.9102	0.8461	0.05	3	0.8388	0.9376	0.0044	4	**0.9267**	23.538	0.0052	21	**23.335**
PMF	0.9598	0.08	3	0.9534	0.8741	0.05	3	0.8664	0.9636	0.0044	4	0.9575	22.312	0.0028	6	22.121
MMMF	0.9807	0.08	3	**0.9703**	0.8810	0.06	9	0.8740	0.9457	0.0036	3	**0.9352**	23.218	0.0036	9	**23.007**

that the framework can handle, decomposable properties of matrix factorization algorithms were investigated in detail. Based on graph partitioning theories, we designed a density-based algorithm to permute sparse matrices into RBBDF structures, and studied its algorithmic properties both formally and experimentally. Experimental results show that LMF helps the matrix factorization algorithms we studied to gain better performance and, at the same time, contributes to system scalability by simple parallelization techniques.

8. ACKNOWLEDGEMENT

The authors thank Jun Zhu for the fruitful discussions and the reviewers for their constructive suggestions. This work was supported by Natural Science Foundation (60903107, 61073071) and National High Technology Research and Development (863) Program (2011AA01A205) of China.

9. REFERENCES

[1] H. Abdi and L. J. Williams. Principal component analysis. *WIREs Comp Stat*, 2:433–459, 2010.
[2] C. Alzate and J. A. Suykens. Multiway spectral clustering with out-of-sample extensions through weighted kernel pca. *PAMI*, 32:335–347, 2010.
[3] B. Arsic et al. Graph spectral techniques in computer sciences. *Appl. Anal. Discrete Math*, 6:1–30, 2012.
[4] C. Aykanat et al. Permuting sparse rectangular matrices into block-diagonal form. *SISC*, 2004.
[5] A. Banerjee, S. Merugu, I. S. Dhillon, and J. Ghosh. Clustering with bregman divergences. *JMLR*, 2005.
[6] E. Boman and M. Wolf. A nested dissection approach to sparse matrix partitioning for parallel computations. *AMM*, 2007.
[7] T. N. Bui and C. Jones. Finding good approximate vertex and edge partitions is np-hard. *IPL*, 1992.
[8] J. Chen and Y. Saad. Dense subgraph extraction with application to community detection. *TKDE*, 2012.
[9] I. S. Dhilon et al. Concept decompositions for large sparse text data using clustering. *JMLR*, 2001.
[10] E. Gallopoulos and D. Zeimpekis. Clsi: A flexible approximation scheme from clustered term-document matrices. *SDM*, 2005.
[11] R. Gemulla et al. Large-scale matrix factorization with distributed stochastic gradient descent. *KDD*, 2011.
[12] J. Herlocker et al. An algorithmic framework for performing collaborative filtering. *SIGIR*, 1999.
[13] G. Karypis. Metis-a software package for partitioning unstructured graphs, meshes, and computing fill reducing orderings of sparse matrices-v5.0. 2011.
[14] G. Karypis et al. A fast and high quality multilevel scheme for partitioning irregular graphs. *SISC*, 1999.
[15] J. Kim, I. Hwang, Y. Kim, et al. Genetic approaches for graph partitioning: A survey. *CECCO*, 2011.
[16] Y. Koren. Factorization meets the neighborhood: a multifaceted collaborative filtering model. *KDD*, 2008.
[17] Y. Koren, R. Bell, et al. Matrix factorization techniques for recommender systems. *Computer*, 2009.
[18] D. Lee and H. Seung. Learning the parts of objects with nonnegative matrix factorization. *Nature*, 1999.
[19] D. Lee and H. Seung. Algorithms for non-negative matrix factorization. *NIPS*, 2001.
[20] C. Liu, H. Yang, J. Fan, L. He, et al. Distributed nonnegative matrix factorization for web-scale dyadic data analysis on mapreduce. *WWW*, 2010.
[21] J. Liu, M. Chen, J. Chen, et al. Recent advances in personal recommender systems. *JISS*, 2009.
[22] M. J. Pazzani and D. Billsus. Content-based recommendation systems. *Adaptive Web LNCS*, 2007.
[23] J. Rennie et al. Fast maximum margin matrix factorization for collaborative prediction. *ICML*, 2005.
[24] P. Resnick et al. Grouplens: An open architecture for collaborative filtering of netnews. *CSCW*, 1994.
[25] R. Salakhutdinov and A. Mnih. Bayesian probabilistic matrix factorization using markov chain monte carlo. *ICML*, 2008.
[26] R. Salakhutdinov and A. Mnih. Probabilistic matrix factorization. *NIPS*, 2008.
[27] P. Sanders and C. Schulz. Engineering multilevel graph partitioning algorithms. *ESA*, 2011.
[28] B. Sarwar et al. Application of dimension reduction in recommender systems - a case study. *WebKDD*, 2000.
[29] B. Sarwar, G. Karypis, et al. Item-based collaborative filtering recommendation algorithms. *WWW*, 2001.
[30] B. Sarwar, G. Karypis, et al. Incremental singular value decomposition algorithms for highly scalable recommender systems. *ICCIT*, 2002.
[31] B. Savas et al. Clustered low rank approximation of graphs in information science applications. *SDM*, 2011.
[32] A. P. Singh and G. J. Gordon. Relational learning via collective matrix factorization. *KDD*, 2008.
[33] N. Srebro and T. Jaakkola. Weighted low-rank approximations. *ICML*, 2003.
[34] N. Srebro, J. Rennie, and T. S. Jaakkola. Maximum-margin matrix factorization. *NIPS*, 2005.
[35] X. Su and T. Khoshgoftaar. A survey of collaborative filtering techniques. *Advances in AI.*, 2009.
[36] G. Takacs, I. Pilaszy, B. Nemeth, and D. Tikk. Investigation of various matrix factorization methods for large recommender systems. *ICDM*, 2008.
[37] B. Xu, J. Bu, and C. Chen. An exploration of improving collaborative recommender systems via user-item subgroups. *WWW*, 2012.
[38] G. Xue, C. Lin, Q. Yang, et al. Scalable collaborative filtering using cluster-based smoothing. *SIGIR*, 2005.

Predicting Purchase Behaviors from Social Media

Yongzheng Zhang
eBay Inc.
2065 Hamilton Ave
San Jose, CA, USA 95125
ytzhang@ebay.com

Marco Pennacchiotti
eBay Inc.
2065 Hamilton Ave
San Jose, CA, USA 95125
mpennacchiotti@ebay.com

ABSTRACT

In the era of social commerce, users often connect from e-commerce websites to social networking venues such as Facebook and Twitter. However, there have been few efforts on understanding the correlations between users' social media profiles and their e-commerce behaviors. This paper presents a system for predicting a user's purchase behaviors on e-commerce websites from the user's social media profile. We specifically aim at understanding if the user's profile information in a social network (for example Facebook) can be leveraged to predict what categories of products the user will buy from (for example eBay Electronics). The paper provides an extensive analysis on how users' Facebook profile information correlates to purchases on eBay, and analyzes the performance of different feature sets and learning algorithms on the task of purchase behavior prediction.

Categories and Subject Descriptors

K.4.4 [**Computers and Society**]: Electronic Commerce; H.3.4 [**Information Storage and Retrieval**]: Systems and Software—*Information networks*; H.3.5 [**Information Storage and Retrieval**]: Online Information Services; I.2.6 [**Artificial Intelligence**]: Learning

Keywords

E-commerce, social networks, social media, social commerce, recommender systems

1. INTRODUCTION

In recent years, many e-commerce companies such as Amazon and eBay have been moving into the social media space by allowing users to connect to social networking sites (e.g. Facebook and Twitter). The main strategic goal for social media interaction is to provide users with a more engaging and social experience, thus increasing user retention and adoption. More importantly, social media is often seen as a means to rejuvenate the user base and attract younger "social-savvy" users. Typical features unlocked by social media include the possibility of sharing purchase activities with friends, and tools such as friends gifting applications and chats.

When users connect from an e-commerce site to social media for the first time, they often agree to share with the e-commerce company basic information such as their demographics and personal interests (e.g. Facebook "likes"). However, e-commerce companies have not fully developed technologies to leverage this information to improve important features such as purchase behavior prediction and product recommendation. Social media information could also help solve the *cold start* problem, i.e., providing an engaging and personalized experience to brand new users. When a new user comes, traditional prediction and recommendation algorithms cannot in fact be applied, as no past information about the user is available.

In this paper we claim that social media information provides sufficient knowledge to predict, to a certain extent, the user's purchase behaviors. For example, a Facebook user who "likes" the Facebook pages of many fashion brands is more likely to purchase fashion products than a user who mostly likes car accessories.

1.1 Problem Statement

We deal with the problem of predicting the purchase behaviors of social media users who have unknown history on an e-commerce website (*cold start*). More in detail, we aim at predicting which product categories (e.g. electronics) the user will buy from by using solely information derived from the social network. Such a predictive system would help in several practical scenarios, including:

- build a *cold start* recommender system, by providing high-level recommendations to social media users who connect for the first time to an e-commerce website;

- improve existing product recommendation engines, by providing category-level priors that can guide the recommender system to find domains of interest for the user;

- provide e-commerce companies with tools for targeted social media campaigns.

We instantiate the problem by choosing Facebook as the social network, and eBay as the e-commerce website[1]. E-commerce companies such as Amazon and eBay ask users to share only a small portion of their personal social media information, in order to protect the privacy of the users and

---
[1]eBay, among many other websites, uses the "Facebook Connect" API to let users connect from eBay to Facebook.

of their friends. For example, both Amazon and eBay do not ask users to share the postings and comments on their social accounts.

In order to keep our task realistic, we therefore focus on the restricted set of Facebook information that users are typically required to share, namely demographic information (age, gender) and the pages that the users have liked on Facebook[2]. In the rest of the paper we will use interchangeably the terms "liked pages" and "likes" to indicate Facebook pages for which a user has expressed a preference by clicking on the *Like* button.

Note that Facebook pages are organized in categories. For example *Beatles* is part of the *Musician/band* category, and *Starbucks* of *Food/beverage*. We will make use of category information throughout the paper. As regards the set of product categories we want to predict, we use the 35 "eBay meta-categories" (or "eBay categories" for brevity) which form the first and most general layer of the eBay product taxonomy. Examples of meta-categories are *Books* and *Home & Garden*. The list of 35 eBay meta-categories and the full taxonomy are available at: http://hub.shop.ebay.com.

This paper has two main goals. The first goal is to explore if users' Facebook information is correlated with the eBay categories from which the users buy. The second goal is to leverage existing correlations to build machine learning algorithms that predict users' purchase behaviors from their Facebook information.

1.2 Main Contributions

This paper provides the following main contributions:

- We provide an extensive analysis of user purchase behaviors and Facebook information over a dataset of 13,619 users. We show that a subset of Facebook features correlates with purchase behaviors with statistical significance.

- We build and evaluate various machine learning models to predict which product categories from which a user will buy, by using Facebook information alone. We show that the prediction task can be successfully solved with promising accuracy.

To our knowledge this is the first study that systematically analyzes the correlations between social media profiles and purchase behaviors on e-commerce websites.

The rest of the paper is organized as follows: Section 2 reviews relevant previous work. Section 3 reports statistics of our dataset. In Section 4 we answer a fundamental question: do users have specific focus when they buy online, or do they exhibit an unpredictable behavior? In Sections 5 and 6, we analyze if specific information from social media, namely demographic data and Facebook likes, correlates to user behaviors on e-commerce websites. In Section 7 we describe and evaluate different algorithms for predicting user purchase behaviors from social media information. Finally, Section 8 concludes our work and describes future research directions.

---

[2]In this study we do not use the list of friends, as this information is not included in the scope of eBay's Facebook Connect.

2. RELATED WORK

2.1 Product Prediction and Recommendation

Recommender systems have been widely studied in the past [26, 5, 27, 16, 8] and applied to various domains. E-commerce is a typical application for these systems, where they are used to predict or recommend product purchases. Two main techniques are most used: collaborative filtering and content-based.

Collaborative Filtering Methods. The underlying assumption of collaborative filtering methods is that users who carry similar characteristics will tend to like similar products. Users are typically represented in a vector space which summarizes their characteristics (e.g. demographics, purchased products, review scores assigned to products). These systems suggest new products to a user by selecting a set of products that similar users have bought or reviewed in the past, but the user has not [30]. Sarwar et al. [28] apply nearest neighbor collaborative filtering for recommending purchases and predicting movie ratings, showing that dimensionality reduction techniques solve scaling issues on large-data without losing accuracy. Some studies [27, 16] have focused on the problem of *sparsity*. In Section 3 we will show the sparsity problem in social media and in the following ones the methods to tackle it.

Item-Item collaborative filtering, on the other hand, makes product recommendations directly based on users' past behaviors on e-commerce websites. Sarwar et al. [29] propose a system that models item to item relationships and demonstrate that such systems deliver good quality recommendations in sparse data situations. The item-item method is also promising for incremental modelling and has big performance gain over user-user modelling.

Content-based Methods. In contrast to collaborative filtering methods, content-based methods often utilize the vast overload of information on the web, such as product reviews, customer opinions, and social media (e.g. blogs, tweets) to directly make product recommendations. In recent years, such systems have become more popular. Wietsma and Ricci [33] propose a system that structures product reviews to help rate and recommend products in a mobile decision aid scenario. Aciar et al. [2] develop a recommender system based on consumer product reviews. The authors apply text mining techniques to extract useful information from review comments and then define an ontology to translate the review information into a form suitable for utilization by a recommendation system. Sen et al. [31] use users' tag preferences to predict movie preferences and demonstrate that such content-based systems are more effective than collaborative filtering methods.

Our system explicitly integrates collaborative filtering techniques in the feature selection phase. Our selection method for Facebook categories/likes/n-grams is inspired by model-based approaches to collaborative filtering discussed among others by Breese et al. [4].

2.2 Recommendation on Social Media

Recommendation on social media is a fairly new topic. Most work focuses on suggesting interesting content items (e.g. URLs, pictures, posts) or new friends. Social media recommender systems differ from classical ones in that they often leverage existing social relations to boost the recommendations. Two main techniques are most used: content-based and community-based.

Content-based methods are most popular even though some interest has focused on collaborative filtering [12]. These systems assume that the content that users share on the social network reflects their own interests, thus recommending new items that are similar to their own shared content [25, 24]. Abel et al. [1] represent users by a frequency vector of the hashtags and entities that they mention in their tweets. A similar vector is built for URLs shared in Twitter by analyzing the content of their links. Users are then recommended URLs whose vector is most similar to theirs. Similarly, Chen et al. [6] represent users with the bag-of-words of all terms of their tweets, and the URLs with the terms of the tweets that mention them. Unlike these methods, in our dataset social content (e.g. Facebook posts) is not available.

Community-based methods make the assumption that the content coming from a user's friends or authoritative users is more likely to be interesting for a user than the rest. This assumption is usually combined with content-based and collaborative filtering approaches. Yan et al. [34] select personalized tweets using random-walks on a graph that joins the user's friends and tweets. The walk is bootstrapped by selecting with higher probability the tweets whose content is similar to what was previously posted by the user. Jamali and Ester [15] also use a random-walk approach, but they integrate collaborative filtering instead of content-based techniques to estimate the probability of a graph transition. Jiang et al. [18] combine user topic preferences and social influence into a probabilistic matrix factorization model, recommending items that are both topically similar to the previous user's preferences and authored by people who are trusted by the user. Community-based systems show better performance with respect to purely content-based and collaborative filtering methods. In our work we cannot use community-based techniques since we do not have access to the social graph of eBay users.

2.3 Social Networks and Purchase Behaviors

Some research has investigated the broader topic of how social network influences users in their purchases. Bhatt et al. [3] empirically demonstrate that a user's friends exercise "peer pressure": if friends widely adopt a product, the user is more likely to buy it. Guo et al. [11] study the trading dynamics on the e-commerce social network Taobao. They show that buyers are more likely to purchase from sellers that friends in their network have already bought from (information passing). They prove that when a buyer has to decide from which seller to buy a product, the social network has a bigger influence on the decision than the sellers' ratings and the price of the product. Similar findings are found in [13, 14].

All these studies assume that the e-commerce site and the social network are integrated into one platform (e.g. Taobao), or that the e-commerce site has holistic access to the social network. To the best of our knowledge, our work is the first to focus on a more practical and common scenario, where the system (e.g. e-commerce companies such as Amazon and eBay) has limited access to social network information.

Table 1: Example of User Information.

Name	Anonymous
Gender	Male
Age group	35-44
Facebook likes (*Category*)	Beatles (*Musician/band*) iPhone 5 (*Electronics*) Starbucks (*Food/beverage*) Walt Disney Studios (*Movie*)
eBay purchases (*Meta-category*)	iPhone 4S (*Electronics*) Beatles T-shirt (*Clothing*) Beatles Mug (*Collectibles*)

Table 2: Statistics of Our Dataset.

Users	13,619
Facebook categories	214
Facebook pages	1,373,984
Facebook likes	4,165,690
eBay categories	35
eBay purchases	628,753

3. FACEBOOK-EBAY DATASET

The dataset we use in this study comes from a database of eBay's "Facebook connect" users. It contains a random sample of 13,619 anonymized eBay users who connected to Facebook between June and August 2012. We excluded users under 18 years of age and those who have no Facebook likes or have not made any purchase on eBay in 2012. For each user, the dataset stores the following information:

- Basic demographic information obtained from Facebook, including age and gender;
- Facebook likes and their categories;
- A list of items purchased on eBay from January to August 2012 (item name and category).

An example of user information collected in our dataset is presented in Table 1.

Basic statistics of our dataset are reported in Table 2.

Figure 1 reports the distribution of gender and age groups in our dataset. We notice a prevalence of women (60% of all users) and people aged between 25 and 44 (55% of all users). In Section 5 we will explore if users in different demographic groups have distinctive purchase behaviors.

Figure 2 reports the distribution of Facebook likes for users, i.e., it indicates how many users have liked a given number of pages. The function is approximately power law with only a few outlier fluctuations, meaning that most users like few Facebook pages, and few users like many pages (the median is 152 likes). While not surprising, this indicates that our task is inherently hard: for most users we have to rely on scarce Facebook information for predicting their purchase behaviors.

Figure 3 reports the distribution of likes for Facebook pages, i.e., it indicates how many pages have a given number of likes. The function follows a perfect power law, showing that the majority of Facebook pages have few likes and only a few pages receive many likes (the median is 1 like). The fact that users' likes are so sparse poses a great challenge for our prediction task when likes are used as features.

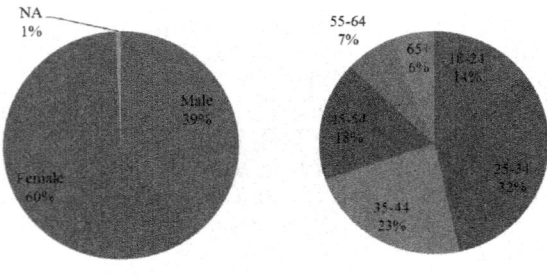

Figure 1: Distribution of user demographics.

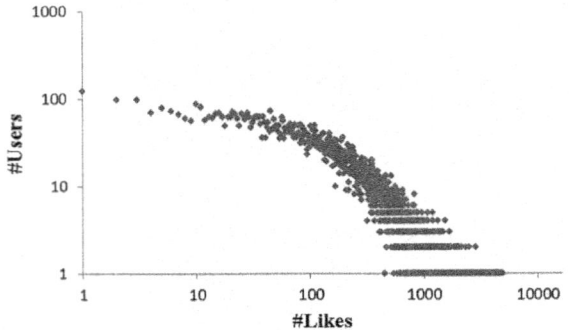

Figure 2: Distribution of likes for users.

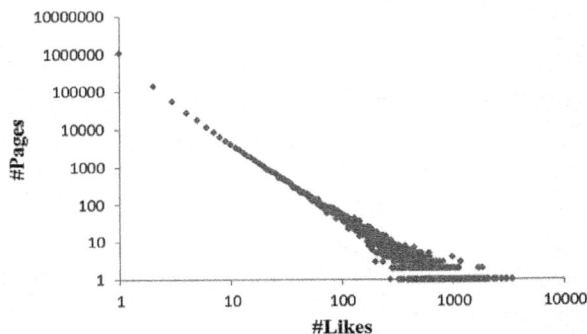

Figure 3: Distribution of likes for pages.

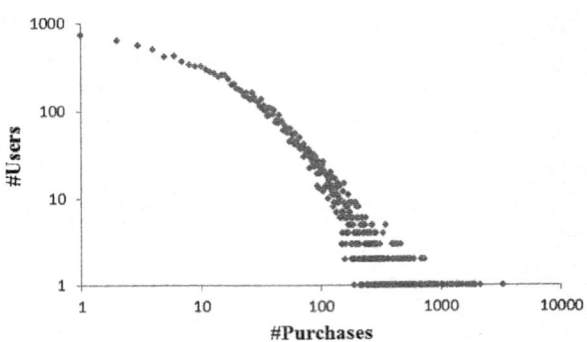

Figure 4: Distribution of purchases for users.

As regards user behaviors on eBay, the distribution of purchased items is also power law, as shown in Figure 4, indicating that most users tend to buy a limited number of items.

Figure 5 reports the distribution of purchases by meta-category. The distribution is highly skewed: more than 50% of all purchases come from the top five meta-categories. The *Clothing, Shoes & Accessories* category alone accounts for 17.5% of all purchases. In the context of our study this means that a system that selects the most popular meta-categories as a prediction of where a user will buy, would achieve a good degree of accuracy. We will have more on this in the experimental section. The median value of purchases per category is 8,316; the average is 17,964.

4. FOCUS ON PURCHASES AND LIKES

The first important question that we want to answer in this study is: are users focused when they buy online? One extreme hypothesis is that a user is completely unfocused, i.e., the user likes to buy randomly across categories. On the other end, the user may have a few favorite categories from which majority purchases are made.

The former hypothesis depicts a chaotic world where it is impossible to predict user behaviors and provide recommendations. In the context of this paper, we hope our world to be more organized than this.

To answer the above question, let us represent with $P(u)_k$ the ranked probability with which a user u buys from the kth favorite category. This rank is obtained by first estimating the probability $P(u, e)$ of a user u buying in each category e, and by successively ranking the probabilities:

$$P(u, e) = \frac{purc(u, e)}{purc(u, E)} \quad (1)$$

where $purc(u, e)$ is the number of purchases of u in category e, and E is the set of all 35 eBay meta-categories. For example if a user buys 3 items from one category and 2 from another, we have: $P(u)_1 = 0.6$ and $P(u)_2 = 0.4$.

To have an estimation of purchase focus we average the $P(u)_k$ across all users U. We thus obtain the probability distribution for the event of an average user buying in the top k ranked category:

$$P(U)_k = \frac{1}{|U|} \cdot \sum_{u \in U} P(u)_k \quad (2)$$

The probability mass function for the distribution is reported in Figure 6, where categories are ordered by rank k.

The hypothesis of a chaotic world where a user buys randomly from different categories would be proved if the distribution was fitted by a uniform distribution. To check the fit, we apply the Kolmogorov-Smirnov (K-S) goodness-of-fit test. The result of the test shows that the hypothesis is rejected. As expected, users do not buy randomly.

We repeat the K-S test to check what continuous distribution best approximates the purchase distribution. The best fit is provided by a Gamma distribution ($\Gamma(0.625, 1.322)$ with the D-statistic of 0.19).

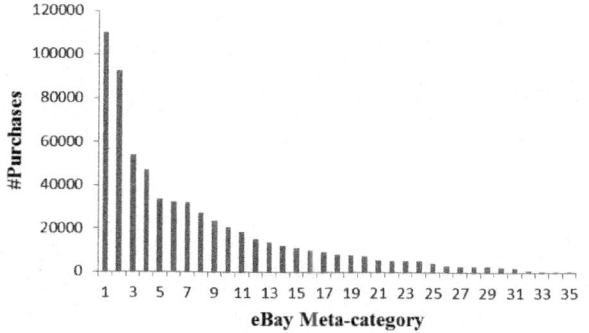

Figure 5: Number of purchases in all eBay meta-categories.

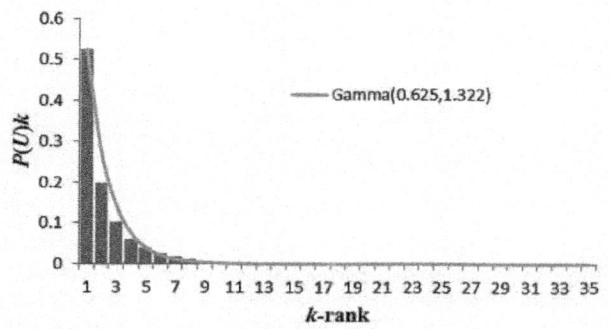

Figure 6: Distribution of purchases in eBay meta-categories.

The shape of the distribution indicates that users are very focused in their purchase behaviors. Figure 6 shows that more than 50% of the times an average user buys from the first preferred category and 20% of the times from the second preferred category. The top 3 categories collectively account for about 85% of a user's purchases.

Another important question is: do users express specific interests on Facebook, i.e., do they like specific categories of pages? Similarly to what we do for eBay categories, we answer this question by checking the hypothesis that Facebook users like pages from random Facebook categories.

We build the probability distribution for the event of an average user liking a Facebook category f using the same procedure used for eBay categories but replacing e with f. The mass function (not reported for space limitation) fits a Gamma distribution that is less steep than the Gamma approximating eBay categories. We again reject the chaotic world hypothesis by running the K-S test on a uniform distribution. On average a Facebook user's most favorite category accounts for 19% of all liked pages, the second about 11%. Facebook likes spread out to more categories with respect to eBay purchases, though users appear to be quite focused also on Facebook.

Overall, the results provided in this section prove that users express strong personal interests on Facebook and are highly focused when purchasing online. One important question remains open. Is there a correlation between interests and purchases, i.e., do users purchase what they like on Facebook? If a correlation exists we could leverage Facebook likes to predict what users will likely purchase. We will answer this question in Section 6.

5. DEMOGRAPHIC DIFFERENCES

This section and the following explore possible correlations between Facebook information and eBay purchases. In Section 7 we will leverage these correlations to build algorithms for predicting purchase behaviors. We start by focusing on demographic information available on Facebook, and later explore the use of the list of liked pages.

A large body of work has studied demographic distinctions in the area of e-commerce. Among others, Garbarino and Strahilevitz [10] and Chiu et al. [7] show that women have a significantly higher sensitivity to risk when buying online. Kau et al. [20] indicate that "on-off shoppers" (people who explore online but buy offline) are prevalently teenagers; "comparative shoppers" (people comparing product features before buying) tend to be males in their twenties; offline shoppers are mostly people over 40. Differences in product adoption across different demographics have been observed, among others, in online movie rentals [21], music downloads and mobile data services [32], though these studies were all limited either in scope or in the size of the data.

Building on previous work, we first analyze if women and men tend to buy from different eBay meta-categories. In order to do so, we compute for both genders the percentage of users who buy in each category. For example about 70% of women in our dataset buy items from the *Clothing, Shoes & Accessories* category, while only 45% of men do so.

For each category, we carry out a t-test between women and men to verify if the difference in percentage is statistically significant. The results of the test show that women buy significantly more than men in 10 categories with a statistical significance of $p = 0.99$. The most female-polarized categories are *Jewelry & Watches*, *Crafts*, and *Clothing, Shoes & Accessories*. Men buy significantly more than women in 16 categories, with the most polarized being *Toys & Hobbies*, *Collectibles* and *Sports Memorabilia*. For the remaining 9 eBay meta-categories we do not observe any significant difference. These results show that purchase behavior strongly varies across genders.

Differences across age groups are less strong. For example, in only 10 categories is there a significant difference between age groups 25-34 and 45-54. In general we observe that young people (25-34) tend to be prevalent in *Fashion*, while older people (45+) are prevalent in *Collectibles* and *Books*.

The overall demographic study suggests that gender and age are important signals for predicting the purchase behaviors of social media users. In the experimental section we will quantitatively analyze their effective value.

For the sake of completeness we also study gender and age differences on Facebook. Similarly to purchase behaviors, we note that different demographic segments tend to like different types of pages. Females are prevalent in liking *Clothing* and *Health/beauty* pages, while males prevail in *Electronics* and *Sports*. Young users like more *Actors & Directors* while older people are prevalent in liking *Politicians*.

It is worth noting that these results refer to our dataset of 13K Facebook-connected eBay users, and may not generalize to the general population of eBay users or to the whole e-commerce spectrum.

Table 3: Examples of Correlated Categories.

eBay Category	Facebook Category	χ
Computers/Tablets	Computers/technology	52.0
Computers/Tablets	Software	51.9
Music	Record label	95.5
Music	Musical Instrument	67.1
Travel	Bags/luggage	7.9
Travel	Book Genre	5.9
Jewelry & Watches	Jewelry/watches	63.6
Jewelry & Watches	Health/beauty	13.4
Cell Phones	Telecommunication	67.2
Cell Phones	Electronics	46.1

6. CORRELATION BETWEEN SOCIAL MEDIA INTERESTS AND PURCHASES

In this section we study the correlation between Facebook categories and eBay meta-categories, and check if there are Facebook categories that are highly predictive of eBay meta-categories. For example we would expect that users who like many *Fashion* pages are likely to buy items in the *Clothing, Shoes & Accessories* meta-category.

Let us define two categorical variables $\mathcal{F}$ and $\mathcal{E}$. $\mathcal{F}$ is defined on the sample space of users, and associates each user to the set of Facebook categories that the user likes at least once. $\mathcal{E}$ associates each user to the eBay meta-categories from which the user has bought at least once.

We compute the correlation between Facebook and eBay categories by applying the Pearson's chi-square test [23] on $\mathcal{E}$ and $\mathcal{F}$. The chi-square test checks if the null-hypothesis that two random variables are independent (i.e. not correlated) is true or not. The result of our test is a strong rejection of the null hypothesis with confidence $p = 0.95$.

This result is encouragingly suggesting that the set of Facebook categories may be predictive of purchase behaviors. However, the test is generic and does not directly indicate which specific Facebook category f is highly correlated to which eBay meta-category e.

We therefore compute the Pearson's chi-square test on single (e, f) events (i.e., we test on a 2×2 contingency table). Table 3 reports the obtained correlations for some eBay meta-categories. For all the pairs reported in the table the null hypothesis that they are independent is rejected with confidence $p=0.99$.

Figure 7 shows the percentage of eBay categories (y-axis) that have a given number of highly correlated (either $p=0.99$ or $p=0.95$) Facebook categories (x-axis). As the figure shows all eBay categories have at least one highly associated Facebook category, while only 15% of eBay categories have 30 or more correlated Facebook categories at $p=0.99$. The median number of correlated Facebook categories across all eBay categories at the $p=0.99$ level is 19. The median number of correlated Facebook categories at the $p=0.95$ level is 35.

These results are very promising. The large number of discovered correlations suggests that eBay categories may be predicted by looking at the Facebook categories liked by the user. However, some eBay categories are inherently hard to predict. For example, *Real Estate*, *Art* and *Everything Else* have respectively only 4, 5 and 6 correlated Facebook categories. This may not be sufficient to correctly support a predictive algorithm for these specific eBay meta-categories. The reason for such low correlations is twofold. First, some

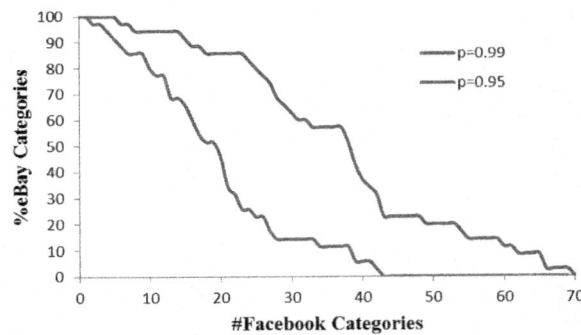

Figure 7: Percentage of eBay categories that have a given number of highly correlated Facebook categories according to the χ^2 statistic.

eBay categories correspond to concepts that are not popularly liked on Facebook (e.g. not many people like Real Estate companies). Second, some categories are too broad and vague to establish correlations (e.g. *Everything Else* and *Art*).

7. PURCHASE BEHAVIOR PREDICTION

In previous sections we have shown that users have focused behaviors when buying online. We have also shown that basic information from Facebook (namely demographics and liked pages) have promising correlation with purchase behaviors. In this section we explore if that information is strong enough to predict purchase behaviors. Specifically, we build and evaluate a variety of machine learning models to solve the following ranking problem.

Problem Statement. Given a social media user u and a set of features derived from the user's social media account, we aim at producing a ranked list of product categories from a category set E, where higher rank is assigned to categories that the user is more likely to buy from.

7.1 Experimental Setup

7.1.1 Gold Standard

As the gold standard dataset for the experiments we use the 13,619 eBay users who connected to Facebook, as described in Section 3. For each user u the gold standard ranks categories by assigning to each category e the ranking score:

$$gsRank(u, e_i) = \frac{purc(u, e_i)}{\sum_{e \in E} purc(u, e)} \quad (3)$$

establishing the rank :

$$e_i \succ e_j \iff gsRank(u, e_i) > gsRank(u, e_j) \quad (4)$$

Categories with the same ranking score are considered ties. For example if a user buys 5 items in *Music*, 3 in *Crafts* and 0 in *Electronics*, the gold-standard ranking for the user will be : *Music* $\succ$ *Crafts* $\succ$ *Electronics*.

The ideal prediction algorithm should provide in output for each user a category ranking equivalent to the gold standard.

7.1.2 Evaluation Measures

To evaluate the prediction models we use the following measures:

Normalized Discounted Cumulative Gain (NDCG). For each user we define Discounted Cumulative Gain (DCG) [17] at position k as:

$$DCG_k = \sum_{i=1}^{k} \frac{w(i)}{\log(i+1)} \quad (5)$$

where $w(i)$ is the relevance weight of the category ranked in position i by the algorithm. We set the relevance weight as follows:

$$w(i) = \frac{purc(e_i)}{\sum_{e \in E} purc(e)} \quad (6)$$

where $purc(e_i)$ is the number of items bought by the user in category e_i. We also define IDCG (ideal DCG) at position k as the DCG of the gold-standard at k. NDCG at position k is defined as $\frac{DCG_k}{IDCG_k}$.

Precision at Rank k (P_k). Given a position k in the predicted ranking for a given user, P_k is defined as:

$$P_k = \frac{\sum_{i=1}^{k} B(e_i)}{k} \quad (7)$$

where $B(e_i)$ equals 1 if the user bought at least one item from category e_i and zero otherwise. We compute P_k for each position, until we reach the position at which the algorithm has retrieved all categories with $B(e_i) = 1$.

Note that we do not use any ranking correlation coefficient for our evaluation (e.g. Spearman or Kendall Tau). Given that we are solving a ranking problem, this choice may seem counterintuitive. However, in our case we are not interested in computing how similar two rankings are as a whole, but just in how good an algorithm is in catching the correct categories as early as possible. In this case, NDCG and precision at rank are more reliable measures.

We evaluate our ranking models using 10-fold cross validation in order to reliably compute statistical significance values. For each fold we use 90% of the users as training and 10% as testing. We compute the above measures for each fold by averaging the measures over all testing users.

7.1.3 Baseline and Learning Models

Baseline. A reasonable system that ranks categories according to their *popularity*, i.e., the number of users in the training set who has bought from the category.

Supervised Mapping. We also experiment with a simple supervised model. In the training phase, we build a bipartite graph where the left side nodes are Facebook categories and the right side nodes are eBay meta-categories. We draw an edge between a Facebook category f and an eBay meta-category e if there exists at least one user who likes a page in f and have bought an item in e. The weight of the edge is computed as:

$$w(f, e) = |f, e| \quad (8)$$

where $|f, e|$ is the number of users who like at least one page in f and have bought from e. In the testing phase, for each user u and eBay meta-category e we compute the ranking score $\sum_{f \in F_u} w(f, e)$, where F_u is the set of Facebook categories that user u likes at least once. The ranking score is used to produce the output ranking for each user.

Naive Bayes (NB) Classification. We use a standard Naive Bayes model which for each user-category pair predicts the probability that the user will purchase from the category. The algorithm returns the ranked list of categories for each user.

Logistic Regression (LR). We use LibLinear [9] to build a regression model for each eBay meta-category e, for a total of 35 models. For training, a user u is represented by a feature vector (features are described in Section 7.1.4), and the label is the ranking score $gsRank(u, e)$. During testing, for each user we collect the predicted scores for each category as produced by the 35 models, and rank the categories accordingly. The $L2$ regularization parameter is optimized on a subset of the training set.

Support Vector Machines (SVM) Classification. We use SVM^{light} [19] to build a SVM classification model for each eBay meta-category e. For training, positive examples are users who buy at least one item in e. An equal number of random negative examples is provided. During testing, for each unknown user SVM returns a confidence score [19] that we use for ranking[3]. SVM parameters are chosen by grid search on a subset of the training sets. We report results for a Radial Basic Function (RBF) kernel. Results for the linear kernel are comparable to or below RBF.

7.1.4 Experimented Features

We apply all our machine learning algorithms (Naive Bayes, Logistic Regression, and SVM classification) using various feature families. We group features in the following four families.

Demographics (D). We have shown in Section 5 that different gender and age groups tend to buy in specific eBay categories. It is therefore natural to use the demographic information as features for the learning algorithms.

We use a total of eight binary features to represent each gender (male or female) and age group (18-24, 25-34, 35-44, 45-54, 55-64, 65+), where the feature value is 1 if the user is of a given gender/age group, 0 otherwise.

Facebook Categories (F). This feature family includes 214 features, one for each Facebook category in the dataset. For each user u and Facebook category f the feature value is computed using TF-IDF [22] as follows:

$$tfidf(u, f) = \frac{like(u, f)}{\max_{f_i \in F} like(u, f_i)} \cdot \log \frac{|U|}{|(U, f)|} \quad (9)$$

where $like(u, f)$ is the number of page likes by user u in category f, and $|(U, f)|$ is the number of users who like at least one page in category f.

---

[3]We also experimented with SVM^{rank}, as it appears to be a natural choice for ranking problems. However, the algorithm did not perform well in our experiment, probably due to the peculiar size of the problem (many users, few categories) and the lack of category-based features. We omit SVM^{rank} results for space reasons.

Facebook Likes (L). In addition to Facebook categories, we also experiment with features derived directly from the liked pages. The intuition is that category features may be too generic to capture useful correlations with the eBay categories that need to be predicted; or even worse, there may be no Facebook categories predictive of an eBay category. In such cases, page-level features may help. The values of these features is computed similarly to Facebook categories, i.e., by computing the $tfidf$ between users and likes.

This feature family includes all the 1.3 million pages liked by users in our dataset. Since the number of irrelevant features may be high, we perform feature selection before feeding the feature vectors to the machine learning algorithms. The feature selection strategy we use is Information Gain, since it has proved to be effective in many learning tasks, e.g. text categorization [35]. Information Gain computes the number of bits of information obtained for the prediction task from a new feature. The information gain of a like l is formally defined as follows:

$$\begin{aligned} IG(l) &= -\sum_{i=1}^{|E|} P(e_i) \log P(e_i) \\ &+ P(l) \sum_{i=|E|}^{l} P(e_i|l) \log P(e_i|l) \\ &+ P(\bar{l}) \sum_{i=1}^{|E|} P(e_i|\bar{l}) \log P(e_i|\bar{l}). \end{aligned} \quad (10)$$

where $|E|$ is the number of eBay categories; $P(e_i)$ is approximated by the fraction of training users who buy from category e_i and $P(l)$ by the fraction of users who like l; $P(e_i|l)$ is approximated by the fraction of users who like l and also buy from category e_i; and $P(\bar{l})$ is approximated by the fraction of users who do not like l.

For each unique like in our dataset, we compute its information gain and remove all likes whose information gain is less than a pre-defined threshold (5% of maximum IG). The underlying reasoning is that likes with high information gain are more useful for category prediction. Hence, the quality of a like feature is proportional to its information gain score, i.e., the higher the $IG(l)$ score, the better the feature is. Each user is represented using a feature vector of $tfidf$ values of top likes.

Using the eBay category *Clothing, Shoes & Accessories* as an example, the top 10 Facebook likes ranked by IG are: *Sephora, Victoria's Secret, Victoria's Secret Pink, Bath & Body Works, JustFab, Macy's, Coach, ShoeDazzle, eBay Fashion, MAC Cosmetics*. As we can see, the top likes are highly related to the *Clothing, Shoes & Accessories* category.

Facebook n-grams (N). We also experiment with n-grams (n=1,2,3) derived from individual Facebook page names, e.g. for the Facebook page *Boston Running Club* we will create a set of candidate n-grams: {*boston, running, club, boston running, running club, boston running club*}. Since we have 1.3 million Facebook pages, the number of derived n-grams will be even larger. We therefore perform feature selection also in this case, to choose the most informative unigrams, bigrams and trigrams. Each user is represented using a feature vector of $tfidf$ values of top n-grams.

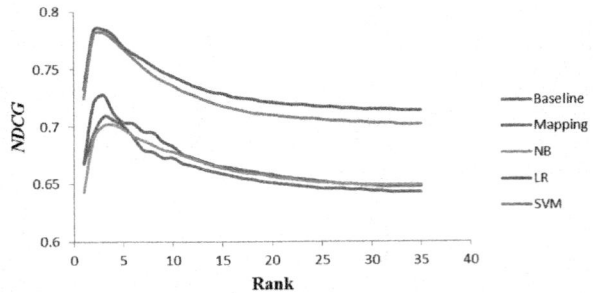

Figure 8: $NDCG_k$ distributions of algorithms using all four feature families.

7.2 Experimental Results

7.2.1 Algorithms

Table 4 reports the results of different algorithms using the complete set of features (demographics, Facebook categories, likes and n-grams) with feature selection. Figure 8 reports the trend of $NDCG$ at different rank levels, for all the experimented algorithms.

Logistic Regression and SVM significantly outperform[4] the baseline system at all rank levels in both precision and $NDCG$. The Mapping system and Naive Bayes show significantly lower accuracy.

In general the Baseline system has good performance. Predicting meta-categories by simply ranking by popularity proves to be a hard baseline to beat, as we would have expected from the statistics reported in Figure 5.

The Mapping algorithm performs slightly better than Baseline, but without statistical significance. Overall, the performances of the two algorithms are very similar. In order to better understand the reason for this behavior, we measure the similarity of the ranking produced by the two algorithms. We do this by computing the Jaccard similarity coefficient J on the set of top 7 ranked categories[5]. We obtain J=0.74, i.e., on average Baseline and Mapping share 5 out of the top 7 predicted categories. The reason for this high correlation is that the weight in Equation 8 promotes eBay categories that are very popular among users, similarly to what Baseline does.

Naive Bayes is the worst performing algorithm, showing performance below or very close to the baseline. A possible explanation is that Naive Bayes assumes feature independence, while the features derived from social media profiles are not necessarily independent of one another. For example, the category *Sports* and *Sport Teams* are highly dependent on each other. The Jaccard coefficient between Naive Bayes and Baseline is $J = 0.52$, showing that the Naive Bayes system is mildly correlated to Baseline, but not as much as Mapping.

The top performing systems, Logistic Regression and SVM, are far apart from all others. The good performance of SVM

---

[4]We calculate the 95% confidence interval for each evaluation measure using the sample obtained from the 10-fold cross validation. If the confidence intervals for two samples do not overlap, then there is a significant difference.

[5]On average the users in our dataset buy from 7 eBay meta-categories.

Table 4: Experimental Results of Different Algorithms Using All Feature Families.

Algorithm	P_1	P_2	P_3	P_5	P_7	$NDCG_1$	$NDCG_2$	$NDCG_3$	$NDCG_5$	$NDCG_7$
Baseline	0.668	0.547	0.513	0.454	0.451	0.668	0.694	0.709	0.701	0.680
Mapping	0.668	0.571	0.524	0.494	0.489	0.668	0.721	0.728	0.704	0.696
NB	0.643	0.560	0.502	0.477	0.469	0.643	0.690	0.701	0.698	0.688
LR	**0.733**†	**0.655**†	**0.628**†	**0.582**†	**0.565**†	**0.733**†	**0.784**†	**0.785**†	**0.770**†	**0.759**†
SVM	0.725†	0.653†	0.622†	0.570†	0.530†	0.725†	0.780†	0.782†	0.768†	0.752†

† indicates statistical significance at 0.95 level with respect to *Baseline*.

is expected. A large volume of previous work has already shown its superior classification power with respect to Naive Bayes and other basic approaches. As for the good performance of Logistic Regression, it indicates that using a regression approach to purchase prediction is a viable, promising direction.

Overall, the results suggest that SVM and Logistic Regression make a much better use of the social features than Mapping and Naive Bayes. These two latter systems appear to be more influenced by the strong meta-category prior probabilities (Figure 5) than by the features themselves.

7.2.2 Feature Analysis

In the previous section we experimented with different algorithms using the full set of features: demographics, Facebook categories, likes and n-grams. In this section we report experimental results for our best performing algorithm, Logistic Regression, with the different feature families described in Section 7.1.4, both in isolation and in combination, in order to analyze how they contribute to the overall task[6].

Table 5 summarizes experimental results for the different feature families.

All feature families taken in isolation outperform the baseline (row 2-5 of Table 5). Demographic features (D) show the smallest improvement. However, results still indicate that simple demographic information easily available on social media, such as age and gender, can help significantly in the purchase prediction task. This is particularly important for those e-commerce applications that do not request social media users to share the complete list of likes.

All other individual feature families, i.e., Facebook categories (F), likes (L) and n-grams (N), significantly outperform D features. This is not surprising because these feature families provide much richer and more relevant information with respect to age and gender. Intuitively, it may often be the case that D features are subsumed by F, L and N. As a matter of fact, we showed at the end of Section 5 that the Facebook categories preferred by a user are usually correlated to the user's gender and age group.

Within the four individual feature families, F performs the best, indicating that social media profiles at the category level convey enough information for predicting users' purchase behaviors on e-commerce sites. However the small difference in performance of F with respect to L and N also suggests that F, L, and N mostly convey the same information. From one side this is expected, since all these three feature families are generated from the same source (the list

of users' likes). From the other side, we would have expected L and N to slightly outperform F, since they carry more fine-grained information. A closer analysis of the L and N feature families reveals that these features are often too sparse, thus limiting their prediction power. On the contrary, F features are general enough to provide generalization power across users. We leave as a future work the exploration of "middle-ground" features that have a degree of generalization in between F and L, such as clusters of likes automatically discovered using topic model techniques or clustering algorithms.

When the best individual feature family F is combined with other feature families (rows 6-12), we see a small additional gain in prediction quality. For example, when Facebook categories and likes are combined, P_1 goes up from 0.708 for F and 0.706 for L to 0.718. In general, the more feature families we use, the greater the gain in prediction quality. However, the gain in performance is very small. As already outlined in the previous paragraph, L and N come from the same source of F but have sparsity problems. Therefore, they do not carry new relevant information with respect to F.

It is finally worth mentioning that the dimensional space of Facebook likes and n-grams is much larger than that of Facebook categories. Hence, when computational cost is concerned, Facebook categories are more favorable.

Feature Selection. All results reported so far use Information Gain for selecting top likes and n-grams. To check the effect of feature selection, we run Naive Bayes and Logistic Regression on the whole set of features but without any feature selection[7]. Results show that both Naive Bayes and Logistic Regression perform worse when feature selection is not performed. For example, P_1 for Naive Bayes goes from 0.643 with feature selection down to 0.376 without feature selection and P_2 goes from 0.560 down to 0.392.

8. CONCLUSIONS

In this paper we study the relations and interactions between social media profiles and purchase behaviors on e-commerce websites. We demonstrate that there are significant correlations between social media information and online purchases. We also develop machine learning algorithms that use different feature families derived from Facebook profiles for solving the task of purchase behavior prediction in a "cold start" setting. Results on a large dataset of eBay users who connected to Facebook show that purchase behaviors can be successfully predicted using social media information alone.

---

[6] Logistic Regression performed better or comparably to other algorithms in all feature combinations. We therefore use only Logistic Regression to illustrate how different feature families perform in the prediction task.

[7] Running SVM with RBF kernel without feature selection would be computationally unfeasible.

Table 5: Experimental Results of Logistic Regression Using Isolate and Combined Feature Families.

Feature Sets	P_1	P_2	P_3	P_4	P_5	$NDCG_1$	$NDCG_2$	$NDCG_3$	$NDCG_5$	$NDCG_7$
Baseline	0.668	0.547	0.513	0.454	0.451	0.668	0.694	0.709	0.701	0.680
D	0.670	0.593	0.565	0.534	0.504	0.670	0.728	0.735	0.721	0.710
F	0.708	0.652	0.621	0.572	0.549	0.708	0.761	0.765	0.749	0.736
L	0.706	0.647	0.613	0.568	0.538	0.706	0.759	0.761	0.748	0.733
N	0.705	0.636	0.605	0.563	0.533	0.705	0.757	0.760	0.745	0.732
F + D	0.715	0.649	0.623	0.575	0.553	0.715	0.766	0.770	0.765	0.753
F + L	0.718	**0.657**	0.625	0.576	0.555	0.718	0.770	0.775	0.768	0.755
F + N	0.717	0.655	0.623	0.578	0.552	0.717	0.769	0.776	0.766	0.752
F + D + L	0.723	0.653	**0.634**	**0.586**	0.559	0.723	0.775	0.782	**0.771**	0.756
F + D + N	0.722	**0.657**	0.624	0.577	0.558	0.721	0.773	0.780	0.770	0.758
F + L + N	0.729	0.656	0.629	0.581	0.563	0.729	0.780	0.778	0.763	0.750
F+D+L+N	**0.733**	0.655	0.628	0.582	**0.565**	**0.733**	**0.784**	**0.785**	0.770	**0.759**

D: Demographics; F: Facebook categories; L: Top Facebook likes; N: Top n-grams(n=1,2,3)

In the future we will explore several research directions, including the following:

- We will go a step further and apply our system to predict behaviors at the subcategory level, e.g., *Women's Handbags* instead of the more generic parent category *Clothing, Shoes & Accessories*. We will go even deeper to verify the feasibility of predicting purchases directly at the product level: this would be considered as a full-fledge recommender system.

- We will extend our feature sets to include other types of features, such as clusters of likes automatically inferred using topic models, and the likes of the user's friends. Even though eBay does not ask users to share the likes of their friends for privacy reasons, these may be provided in other contexts, e.g., at Amazon.com.

- We will experiment with more sophisticated models integrating social graph information, when available.

- We will explore if and how Facebook information can improve existing product recommendation systems that rely on purchase history.

- We will integrate our prediction models into existing products: to offer, for example, a more personalized experience for social media users when they visit an e-commerce website; or to automatically redirect users to the vertical of interest when they access the website.

To the best of our knowledge our study is the first attempt to predict e-commerce behaviors using only social media information. It is our hope that it will help and inspire e-commerce companies to develop better and new recommendation engines that leverage social media features in a time when the issue of monetizing social media information is being more and more debated.

9. ACKNOWLEDGEMENTS

We are thankful to our colleague Pruth Leelaluckanakul for providing the users' Facebook data. We are also grateful to the authors of LibLinear and SVM^{light} for providing great tools for our study.

10. REFERENCES

[1] F. Abel, Q. Gao, G.-J. Houben, and K. Tao. Analyzing temporal dynamics in twitter profiles for personalized recommendations in the social web. In *WebSci'11 Conference Proceedings*, 2011.

[2] S. Aciar, D. Zhang, S. Simoff, and J. Debenham. Recommender system based on consumer product reviews. In *WI'06 Conference Proceedings*, pages 719–723, 2006.

[3] R. Bhatt, V. Chaoji, and R. Parekh. Predicting product adoption in large-scale social networks. In *CIKM'10 Conference Proceedings*, 2010.

[4] J. S. Breese, D. Heckerman, and C. Kadie. Empirical analysis of predictive algorithms for collaborative filtering. In *Proceedings of the 14th Conference on Uncertainty in Artificial Intelligence*, 1998.

[5] R. Burke. Hybrid recommender systems: Survey and experiments. *User Modeling and User-Adapted Interation*, 12(4):331–370, 2002.

[6] J. Chen, R. Nairn, L. Nelson, M. Bernstein, and E. Chi. Short and tweet: experiments on recommending content from information streams. In *CHI'10 Conference Proceedings*, 2010.

[7] Y.-B. Chiu, C.-P. Lin, and L.-L. Tang. Gender differs: assessing a model of online purchase intentions in e-tail service. *International Journal of Service Industry Management*, 16(5):416–435, 2005.

[8] M. D. Ekstrand, J. T. Riedl, and J. A. Konstan. Collaborative filtering recommender systems. *Foundations and Trends in Human-Computer Interaction*, 4(2), 2011.

[9] R.-E. Fan, K.-W. Chang, C.-J. Hsieh, X.-R. Wang, and C.-J. Lin. LIBLINEAR: A library for large linear classification. *Journal of Machine Learning Research*, 9:1871–1874, 2008.

[10] E. Garbarino and M. Strahilevitz. Gender differences in the perceived risk of buying online and the effects of receiving a site recommendation. *Journal of Business Research*, 57(7):768–775, 2004.

[11] S. Guo, M. Wang, and J. Leskovec. The role of social networks in online shopping: information passing, price of trust, and consumer choice. In *ACM EC'11 Conference Proceeding*, pages 157–166, 2011.

[12] J. Hannon, M. Bennett, and B. Smyth. Recommending twitter users to follow using content and collaborative filtering approaches. In *ACM RecSys'10 Conference Proceedings*, pages 199–206, Barcelona, Spain, 2010.

[13] S. Hill, F. Provost, and C. Volinsky. Network-based marketing: Identifying likely adopters via consumer networks. *Statistical Science*, 21(2):256–276, 2006.

[14] R. Iyengar, S. Han, and S. Gupta. Do friends influence purchases in a social network? Working paper, Harvard Business School, 2009.

[15] M. Jamali and M. Ester. Trustwalker: a random walk model for combining trust-based and item-based recommendation. In *KDD'09 Conference Proceedings*, pages 397–406, 2009.

[16] D. Jannach. *Recommender Systems : an Introduction*. Cambridge University Press, 2011.

[17] K. Järvelin and J. Kekäläinen. Cumulated gain-based evaluation of IR techniques. *ACM Transactions on Information Systems*, 20(4):422–446, 2002.

[18] M. Jiang, P. Cui, R. Liu, Q. Yang, F. Wang, W. Zhu, and S. Yang. Social contextual recommendation. In *KDD'12 Conference Proceedings*, pages 45–54, 2012.

[19] T. Joachims. *Learning to Classify Text Using Support Vector Machines*. Dissertation. Kluwer, 2002.

[20] A. K. Kau, Y. E. Tang, and S. Ghose. Typology of online shoppers. *Journal of Consumer Marketing*, 20(2):139–156, 2003.

[21] Y. Koren, R. Bell, and C. Volinsky. Matrix factorization techniques for recommender systems. *Computer*, 42(8):30–37, 2009.

[22] C. D. Manning, P. Raghavan, and H. Schütze. *Introduction to Information Retrieval*. Cambridge University Press, 2008.

[23] M. Nikulin. Chi-squared test for normality. In *Proceedings of the International Vilnius Conference on Probability Theory and Mathematical Statistics*, pages 119–122, 1973.

[24] M. Pennacchiotti and S. Gurumurthy. Investigating topic models for social media user recommendation. In *WWW'11 Conference Proceedings*, 2011.

[25] D. Ramage, S. Dumais, , and D. Liebling. Characterizing microblogs with topic models. In *AAAI ICWSM'10 Conference Proceedings*, 2010.

[26] P. Resnick and H. R. Varian. Recommender systems. *Special Issue of the Communications of the ACM*, 40(3), 1997.

[27] F. Ricci, L. Rokach, B. Shapira, and P. B. Kantor. Recommender systems handbook. *Media*, 54(3):217–253, 2011.

[28] B. Sarwar, G. Karypis, J. Konstan, and J. Riedl. Analysis of recommendation algorithms for e-commerce. In *EC'00 Conference Proceedings*, 2000.

[29] B. Sarwar, G. Karypis, J. Konstan, and J. Riedl. Item-based collaborative filtering recommendation algorithms. In *WWW'01 Conference Proceeding*, 2001.

[30] J. Schafer, J. Konstan, and J. Riedi. Recommender systems in e-commerce. In *ACM EC'99 Conference Proceedings*, 1999.

[31] S. Sen, J. Vig, and J. Riedl. Tagommenders: connecting users to items through tags. In *WWW'09 Conference Proceedings*, pages 671–680, 2009.

[32] W. Shi, P. Wu, W. Zhou, and J. Chen. Gender differences in purchase intention on mobile data services. In *IEEE CSO'09 Conference Proceedings*, pages 773–777, 2009.

[33] R. T. A. Wietsma and F. Ricci. Product reviews in mobile decision aid systems. In *Proceedings of the PERMID*, pages 15–18, Munich, Germany, 2005.

[34] R. Yan, M. Lapata, and X. Li. Tweet recommendation with graph co-ranking. In *ACL'12 Conference Proceedings*, volume 1, 2012.

[35] Y. Yang and J. O. Pedersen. A Comparative Study on Feature Selection in Text Categorization. In *ICML'97 Conference Proceedings*, Nashville, TN, 1997.

Anatomy of a Web-Scale Resale Market: A Data Mining Approach

Yuchen Zhao[†] Neel Sundaresan[‡] Zeqian Shen[‡] Philip S. Yu[†*]

[†]University of Illinois at Chicago, USA [‡]eBay Research Labs, USA [*]King Abdulaziz University, Saudi Arabia
yzhao@cs.uic.edu, {nsundaresan, zeqshen}@ebay.com, psyu@cs.uic.edu

ABSTRACT

Reuse and remarketing of content and products is an integral part of the internet. As E-commerce has grown, online resale and secondary markets form a significant part of the commerce space. The intentions and methods for reselling are diverse. In this paper, we study an instance of such markets that affords interesting data at large scale for mining purposes to understand the properties and patterns of this online market. As part of knowledge discovery of such a market, we first formally propose criteria to reveal unseen resale behaviors by elastic matching identification (**EMI**) based on the *account transfer* and *item similarity* properties of transactions. Then, we present a large-scale system that leverages MapReduce paradigm to mine millions of online resale activities from petabyte scale heterogeneous e-commerce data. With the collected data, we show that the number of resale activities leads to a power law distribution with a 'long tail', where a significant share of users only resell in very low numbers and a large portion of resales come from a small number of highly active resellers. We further conduct a comprehensive empirical study from different aspects of resales, including the temporal, spatial patterns, user demographics, reputation and the content of sale postings. Based on these observations, we explore the features related to "successful" resale transactions and evaluate if they can be predictable. We also discuss uses of this information mining for business insights and user experience on a real-world online marketplace.

Categories and Subject Descriptors

H.2.8 [**Database Management**]: Database Applications - Data Mining; H.3.1 [**Information Storage and Retrieval**]: Content Analysis and Indexing; J.4 [**Social and Behavioral Sciences**]: Sociology, Economics

Keywords

resale market; reseller; MapReduce; big data; e-commerce; eBay; prediction; behavioral analysis

1. INTRODUCTION

Recently there is tremendous republishing of content happening in the internet space and such trend is rapidly growing. While it does not imply copyright violation, marketing groups have studied the importance of "content curation"[1] on websites, e.g., blogs and news. Retweets on Twitter and reclips on Pinterest are other examples of republishing on social networks. In E-commerce, the equivalent of content curation is obtaining inventory for reselling. Given these developments, republishing becomes a key aspect of the internet and resale is a key aspect of electronic commerce. Since reuse and remarketing of content and products is an integral part of the internet, we particularly study the online resale market in this paper.

Resale, which is the selling again of something purchased, is an essential part of a market. There have been many research studies on resale activities in different markets, e.g., tickets [7], real estate [13][6], and automobiles [30]. The previous research is mostly on resale price maintenance [27][22], auctions with resale [12][5], etc. In these existing studies, the resale activities are often conducted by large offline agencies or brokers. However, online resale activities are also a significant part of the resale markets. Therefore, understanding patterns and nature of the e-commerce resale activities is much needed. Since the resellers often purchase and sell items on the same online platform, the data will capture the complete activity from purchase to sale, which is desired for a comprehensive study. Online marketplaces, e.g. eBay, Amazon and Taobao, have been studied in various areas for web mining and modeling, including auction models [4][20][21], bidding and selling strategies [10][26], reputation models [14][23][25] and fraud detection [24]. Although resale is a vital component of online market, there is little research addressing this topic. To the best of our knowledge, this is the first work on empirical studies of resales in a real-world web-scale marketplace.

In this paper, we study the resale market from data obtained from a leading online marketplace vendor, i.e., eBay. There are about 100 million active users on eBay. Among tens of thousands worth of items sold every minute, a large number of the transactions are resales. As discussed above, we focus on those resale activities that occur exclusively at eBay because of the data availability. In other words, the items are bought and sold again both on eBay. Although the data we use throughout the paper is from eBay due to the data availability, the proposed framework in this paper is general and applicable to other online resale markets.

The intentions and methods of reselling can be diverse. In some cases, the items are resold at higher prices, and the resellers make profits from them. In this case, the original sale is considered under-priced. Understanding the reasons for under-priced sales can help us better advise the sellers

Copyright is held by the International World Wide Web Conference Committee (IW3C2). IW3C2 reserves the right to provide a hyperlink to the author's site if the Material is used in electronic media.
WWW 2013, May 13–17, 2013, Rio de Janeiro, Brazil.
ACM 978-1-4503-2035-1/13/05.

to list items more effectively and thus make the marketplace more efficient. In addition, understanding the behaviors of resellers also help build a healthy online platform. Therefore, studying resale activities has tremendous values in suggesting business opportunities and building effective user applications. As part of knowledge discovery of such activities, We summarize the research challenges below:

- Research Challenge #1: How to develop effective criteria to accurately identify resale activities? The connections between the initial purchase and later resale are often not evident due to the nature of e-commerce marketplace. First, it is common that users use different accounts for buying and selling. Linking different accounts from the same person/family is necessary. In addition, many users change item listings (i.e., sale postings) while reselling. In other words, two seemly different listings may actually refer to the same good.

- Research Challenge #2: How to extract resale activities from extremely large-scale data sets? The criteria mentioned in the first challenge need to be applied on petascale transaction data generated on the internet. Furthermore, such data is from multiple sources and heterogeneous in nature. Mining and analysis of such large volume data bring great challenges.

- Research Challenge #3: Can we find some interesting insights from the obtained resale activities? We would like to find similar patterns among the resale activities and understand the motivation for resale. Furthermore, we would like to quantitatively evaluate factors that correlate to profitability. Moreover, can we predict whether a resale transaction is profitable? These are important to understand the nature and dynamics of the resale market.

With these challenges, this paper initiate a study of resale markets at web-scale and makes the following contributions: (1) We formalize the notations and definitions of resale mining as the first known work on this topic. (2) We propose a complete framework to identify and extract resale activities from petabyte-scale data. (3) We qualitatively study and analyze the heterogeneous resale data, and empirically present the answers to the resale prediction task. (4) We propose novel applications of the resale data to get insights. The insights can not only boost the resale market, but can also improve general buying and selling on the online marketplace. In addition, the proposed system can also be extended to analyze other user-to-user web applications.

Further Related Work: Previous research examined the complex networks and graphs, but mostly on one aspect of mining tasks, such as classification[17][34], clustering[9][2][33], outlier detection[3], community detection[19] and social networks applications [16][11][32].

The paper is organized as following. In each section, we will address one research challenge mentioned above. In Section 2, we introduce effective criteria to accurately identify resale activities. Section 3 discusses the large-scale data platform used to extract resale activities. Next, we demonstrate our analysis and prediction of the resale market in Section 4. Deployment and applications to online marketplaces are discussed in Section 5.

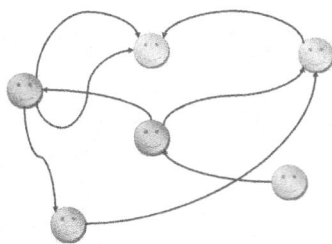

Figure 1: Modeling Transactions as a Massive Graph (Each node represents a user, and directed edges are transactions among users.)

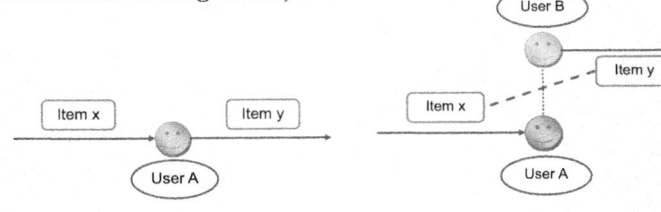

Figure 2: Resale Activity Identification. Figure (b) considers both account linking (blue dotted line) and elastic item matching (red dashed line).

2. IDENTIFYING RESALE ON THE WEB

In this paper, we conduct a systematic study on the resale market, which is a vital component in the internet and e-commerce. In this section, we define the criteria to identify resale activities.

2.1 User-Transaction Network

Modern online marketplace is a complex peer-to-peer network [28]. While we notice that the transactions happen between users, we model the transaction activities as a massive graph among users. In Figure 1, we model the transactions as a graph $G = \{V, E\}$, where V is the set of vertices and E is the set of edges. Each vertex represents a user. The user can both buy and sell, and (s)he can be either an individual or business. Each edge between two vertices is directed, from a user (seller) to another user (buyer). We further note that each edge represents a transaction, which contains information about the items purchased, transaction times, prices, etc.

2.2 An Exact Matching Approach

In order to discover resale, the first step is to set criteria to identify resale activities. In other words, what type of activities can be regarded as reselling? Based on the definition of resale, a resale activity should include the process of selling again of something purchased by an entity. One straightforward approach is to find the activities that satisfy the pattern in Figure 2(a). Formally, we define the resale activity below:

DEFINITION 1 (**Exact Matching Identification**). *A use (User A) bought an item x and sold an item y. The sale activity tuple (x, A, y) is a resale if it satisfies the following constraints:*

(a) Item Constraint: Item x and item y should be in different transactions, but they have to refer to the identical good.

(b) Time Constraint: The purchase time of item x is earlier than the purchase time of item y.

In the above definition, the time constraint (b) is easy to check by comparing the timestamps of two transactions. The problem is how to determine whether the item constraint (a) is satisfied, i.e. if two items from different transactions actually refer to the same good. Although *Universal Product Code (UPC)* is ideal for identifying unique goods, it is not common for items in a real-world e-commerce marketplace to include *UPC*. A straightforward approach is to compare the titles of two items. For example, if the titles of items x and y are the same or use the same set of words, then x and y are the same; otherwise they are different goods.

2.3 Identifying Resale Via Elastic Matching

However, the exact matching identification is clearly not an appropriate criterion. On the one hand, the user A may change the title of item y in order to boost sales. For example, the item x was initially not listed with a suitable title. It is highly likely that item x would be sold at a low price. User A found this fact, and immediately bought this item. (S)he later listed the same product just bought using a more descriptive title, thus had a potential to sell at a higher price and make profits. Therefore, exact matching of item titles will miss a lot of meaningful resale activities. It is much desired that an **elastic matching** of items can be used to accurately identify resales.

On the other hand, the pattern in Figure 2(a) will not capture all resale activities due to the limitation of using the single account matching. A lot of people on a real-world e-commerce marketplace have more than one account. Meanwhile, members of a family might have their own individual accounts. For example, a person can have an account for selling and another account for buying because of privacy. Another scenario might be the husband bought some products online, and later his wife resold again because she did not like them. We call this type of user behavior in reselling as **account transfer**.

Therefore, a more general identification approach is proposed to address the above two issues, which is shown in Figure 2(b). Suppose the accounts of the same person/family are linked together, and the link is illustrated using the blue dotted line; and items referring to the identical goods are linked using the red dashed line. We want to discover the resale activities that satisfy:

DEFINITION 2 (**Elastic Matching Identification [EMI]**). *A user (User A) bought an item x and another user (User B) sold an item y. The sale activity tuple (x, A, B, y) is a resale if it satisfies the following constraints:*

(a) Item Constraint: *Item x and item y should be in different transactions, but they have a similarity score which is greater than a threshold α.*

(b) Time Constraint: *The purchase time of item x is earlier than the purchase time of item y.*

(c) Account Constraint: *User A and User B are linked because they belong to the same person or family (entity).*

The definition of EMI will help identify the case that resellers change the content of listings as well as the resale activities coming through account transfer. In the *Item Constraint*, a similarity function is needed to measure the similarity of two items. On e-commerce marketplaces, there are mainly three attributes to describe items: *Titles*, *Descriptions* and *Photos*. *Descriptions* are noisy which contains many irrelevant content, such as sellers' own stories, refund policies and shipping charges. In the meantime, usually the descriptions are lengthy, thus the computational costs of description similarity matching make it infeasible in a large-scale data environment. For *Photos*, even the state-of-art image comparison techniques cannot achieve satisfactory accuracy, and they are all ineffective for massive data. Considering the above limitations, we use the Jaccard similarity of item *titles* as the similarity function, which provides a good trade-off between accuracy and efficiency. Previous studies [15][29] in a similar context, QA archives, also demonstrate that using titles rather than descriptions for the similarity measure is of highest effectiveness. Let the titles of items x and y are T_x and T_y respectively. The similarity function between items x and y is defined as:

$$similarity(x,y) = \frac{|T_x \bigcap T_y|}{|T_x \bigcup T_y|}$$

where $|T_x \bigcap T_y|$ denotes the number of common words in T_x and T_y, and $|T_x \bigcup T_y|$ denotes the number of unique words in T_x and T_y.

If the similarity score of two items is greater than a given threshold α, the items are considered to be identical. While we understand that for any two random items x and y, even their similarity score is high enough, it is not necessary that they are the identical goods, because they may be different goods but the same type of product. However, considering the account constraint and time constraint, it is required that both items should be bought/sold by the same entity, and the purchase activities are in sequential order. Thus, these ensure that items satisfying above constraints refer to the identical goods.

3. EXTRACTING RESALE ACTIVITIES

In this section, we present how to extract resale activities from large-scale data sets at an e-commerce site given the criteria of resale activity identification in the previous section.

3.1 MapReduce Framework

In order to present how to extract resale activities, we first briefly describe the MapReduce framework. MapReduce [8] is a programming framework to support computation on large-scale data sets in distributed environments. The advantages of MapReduce are (1) the ability to run jobs in parallel (2) automatic management of data replication, transfer, load balancing, etc., and (3) the standardization of Map and Reduce procedures and concepts. MapReduce has been successfully adopted by many companies to handle massive data, including Yahoo, Google, Amazon, eBay, etc.

A typical MapReduce framework mainly contains two steps: Map step and Reduce step. The details of MapReduce can be found in [8] and [18]. Large e-commerce sites usually store multi-petabyte data on distributed machines. Therefore, we use MapReduce paradigm to extract resale activities from large-scale e-commerce transaction data.

3.2 Proposed Algorithms

Based on Definition 2, evaluating whether a transaction is a resale transaction requires to verify the account constraint, time constraint and item constraint. For account constraint, users from the same person/family should be grouped together as a user entity. The grouping policy includes matching of names, gender, addresses and user behaviors. Since

ALGORITHM 1: Account Matching

Input: Account Linking Table: $acc = \{(entity\_id, user\_id)\}$;
Transaction Table: $tran = \{(item\_id, buyer\_id, seller\_id, item)\}$

Account-Matching-Map(Table acc, Table $tran$)
begin
　for each $(entity\_id, user\_id) \in acc$ do
　｜ Output key-value pair $(user\_id, entity\_id)$;
　end
　for each $(item\_id, buyer\_id, seller\_id, item) \in tran$ do
　｜ Output key-value pair $(buyer\_id, (tag:\text{``buy''}, item))$;
　｜ Output key-value pair $(seller\_id, (tag:\text{``sell''}, item))$;
　end
end

Account-Matching-Reduce(Key k, Value $v[1...m]$)
begin
　$output\_key$ = null;
　for each $v \in v[1...m]$ do
　｜ if v is of type ID then
　｜　｜ $output\_key \leftarrow v$; break;
　｜ end
　end
　for each $v \in v[1...m]$ do
　｜ if v is of type $(tag, item)$ then
　｜　｜ Output key-value pair $(output\_key, v)$;
　｜ end
　end
end

ALGORITHM 2: Item Matching

Input: Output from Account Matching

Item-Matching-Map(Key k, Value v)
begin
　｜ Output key-value pair (k, v);
end

Item-Matching-Reduce(Key k, Value $v[1...m]$)
begin
　$buying\_list, selling\_list$ = empty;
　for each $v \in v[1...m]$ do
　｜ if $tag == \text{``buy''}$ then
　｜　｜ add v into $buying\_list$;
　｜ end
　｜ if $tag == \text{``sell''}$ then
　｜　｜ add v into $selling\_list$;
　｜ end
　end
　for each $v \in buying\_list$ do
　｜ for each $v' \in selling\_list$ do
　｜　｜ if $v.timestamp < v'.timestamp$ &&
　｜　｜ $similarity(v, v') > \alpha$ then
　｜　｜　｜ Output resale activity (v, k, v');
　｜　｜ end
　｜ end
　end
end

user grouping is not the focus of this study, we assume the user grouping data are pre-computed. All user entities have unique entity IDs and multiple accounts from the same person/family are linked to the same entity ID. For item constraint, a similarity function is applied to item titles, and the similarity score is used to determine if the two items represent the same good. Usually the transaction data on e-commerce sites are stored in different tables. For the simplicity of algorithm description, we assume all transaction data are stored in one table. This table can be regarded as the join result of a list of transaction related tables.

We propose a two-stage framework to extract resale activities. The first stage is to correlate items with the entity IDs to handle account transfer problem. The second stage is to generate resale transactions bought and sold by the same entity IDs based on elastic item matching and time constraint.

The pseudo code of the first stage is illustrated in Algorithm 1. In the Map step, the inputs are pre-computed account linking table and a table including all transaction data. A pair containing each $user\_id$ and its corresponding $entity\_id$ is sent to the reducer. In order to capture the buying and selling information, each item in transactions is mapped to two key-value pairs, i.e., a pair taking $buyer\_id$ as the key and a pair taking $seller\_id$ as the key. The type information regarding to buying or selling is stored as a tag for future processing. In the Reduce step of account matching, the $entity\_id$ of the user (stored in key k) is first obtained. Then we substitute the $user\_id$ k for the $entity\_id$, and send all items associated with the same user to the next stage. Through the first stage, all items are linked to the entity ID. Thus even transactions from two different accounts belonged to the same person/family, they are aggregated in one place.

In the second stage, the idea is to create two lists of items associated with the same $entity\_id$ using the output of the first stage. For each entity, we collect its all purchased items and add into $buying\_list$. Similarly, we get its all sold items

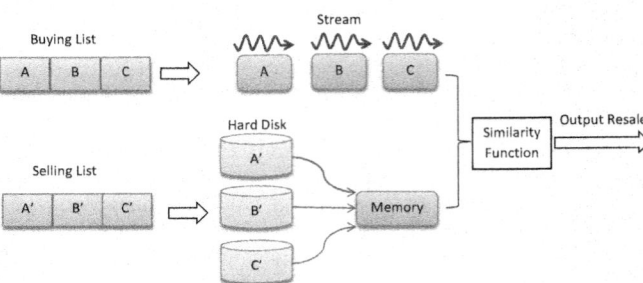

Figure 3: System Illustration: Stream-based Reducer. Lists being partitioned and read sequentially to resolve insufficient memory problem.

and put into $selling\_list$. The tag created in the first stage is used to decide which list a given item should be added into. It is clear that a resale activity must contain one item from $buying\_list$ and one item from $selling\_list$. Thus, we further perform a pair-wise similarity matching of two lists, and if two items satisfy both item constraint and time constraint, they are output as resale activities. The details of the second stage can be found in Algorithm 2. Although the algorithms are described under the resale market context, we note that the proposed algorithms can be easily generalized to different applications which require matching.

3.3 Stream-based Approach

As shown in Algorithm 2, we can see that two item lists have to be stored in the memory. In a global e-commerce marketplace, it is not rare that a single user buys or sells millions of products annually. Therefore, Algorithm 2 becomes infeasible while handling such large-scale data. To make the algorithm work in practice, we extend Algorithm 2 to solve the insufficient memory problem. Inspired by [31], we introduce a stream-based MapReduce approach for Algorithm 2. We note that the proposed stream-based method is interesting in its own right as a general method for reducing memory requirement for large-scale MapReduce tasks, and may be useful for a number of different web-scale applications.

The stream-based reduce step is illustrated in Figure 3. The *buying_list* and *selling_list* in Algorithm 2 are further partitioned into blocks (*buying_list* → (A, B, C) and *selling_list* → (A', B', C')). The size of blocks depends on the actual memory size of local machines. The blocks of one list are stored on the hard disk to prevent insufficient memory. In Figure 3, we store blocks of *selling_list* (A', B', C') on the hard disk. Each block from *selling_list* is read sequentially from the hard disk, and only one block can be stored in the memory at any given time. The blocks from *buying_list* (A, B, C) are sent as streams and match with the block of *selling_list* in the memory. As shown in Figure 3, blocks A', B', C' will be sequentially loaded into memory and match with block A from *buying_list*. After block A has matched with all blocks from *selling_list*, it can be safely removed from the memory, and the next block B from *selling_list* can be streamed in.

4. EXPLORING RESALE MARKET

After resale activities are collected, we explore what can be discovered from the resale market. In order to better understand the market, we apply data mining techniques and address two main problems in this section:

(1) **Observations**: What does the resale market look like? How large is the resale market? Who are doing resales? Why are they doing resales? Do different regional markets show similar patterns?

(2) **Prediction**: What factors lead to a successful (profitable) resale? Given a list of features, can we predict if a resale activity will be profitable?

4.1 Experiment Setup

We use an open source implementation of MapReduce, Hadoop[1], to extract resale activities. The Hadoop cluster stores over 10 petabytes transaction data from the marketplace. For the extracted resale activities satisfying pattern tuple (x, A, B, y) in Figure 2(b), we further obtain a list of attributes associated with users A, B and items x, y from the Hadoop cluster to analyze. As listed in Table 1, 24 attributes of resale activities from multiple sources are captured. Attributes related to x and A are listed in the type *Buying Related*, and attributes related to B and y are listed in the type *Selling Related*. Feedback scores are used to measure the overall rating of users. Generally speaking, a user with high feedback score is often an experienced seller/buyer with good reputation. Each user has two feedback scores: *feedback as seller* and *feedback as buyer*, which represent the user's selling and buying performance, respectively.

4.2 Validation

In order to study the effectiveness of the resale activity identification by elastic matching identification (EMI), we measure the correctness of matched resale activities and test the sensitivity of the parameter of EMI, *i.e.*, the similarity threshold α. We compare our method against the exact matching approach in Section 2.2 as the baseline. Since we do not directly have the ground truth, we use items sold on eBay which are associated with the eBay product catalog[2] as the validation data set. The product information of those items is either manually added by sellers or identified by a

---

[1] http://hadoop.apache.org/
[2] http://pages.ebay.com/help/sell/product-details.html

Table 1: Extracted Attributes Related to Resale That Cover Feedback, Title, Time, Price, Categories, etc.

Type	Attributes
Buying Related	the original seller id, his/her feedback as seller, his/her feedback as buyer, buyer's entity id, user id, his/her feedback as seller, his/her feedback as buyer, item id, item title, purchase date, item price, site id, leaf category name, meta category name
Selling Related	seller's user id, his/her feedback as seller, his/her feedback as buyer, item id, item title, purchase date, item price, site id, leaf category name, meta category name

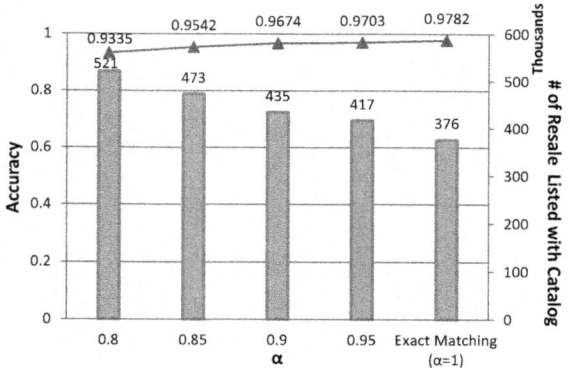

Figure 4: Accuracy Results with Threshold α. The line shows the accuracy scores (left Y-scale) by varying α and the bars represent the corresponding number of resale activities (right Y-scale) in thousands.

combination of UPC, brand, model and ISBN (for books). For each resale activity as tuple (x, A, B, y), we examine if items x and y belong to the same product in the catalog, and calculate the accuracy score to evaluate the proposed elastic matching method. One should note that we do not use the catalog information to obtain resale data due to its limited coverage. We only use the catalog information for evaluation purpose.

The results are reported in Figure 4. The threshold α is illustrated on the X-axis, the accuracy of EMI is illustrated on the left Y-axis and the number of resale activities with catalog information is presented on the right Y-axis. The line shows the accuracy scores by varying α and the bars present the corresponding number of resale activities. α being set to 1 corresponds to the exact matching approach, which is shown as the baseline. From the figure, one can observe that the number of resale activities is 376k for exact matching. For EMI, the number goes up to 521k while setting α to 0.8, which is 36.4% more than that of exact matching. From the effectiveness perspective, the accuracy score of exact matching is 0.9782, because of the noises in the real data set. Some sellers manually typed wrong product information, which causes mismatch even the titles of buying and reselling items are exactly the same. We further notice that the accuracy of EMI is over 93% while setting α is 0.8. This clearly shows the proposed elastic matching approach is highly accurate, and its obtained resale activities are indeed meaningful. We can also observe that the accuracy score further gains with the increase of α, while the number of resale activities decreases. This is quite nat-

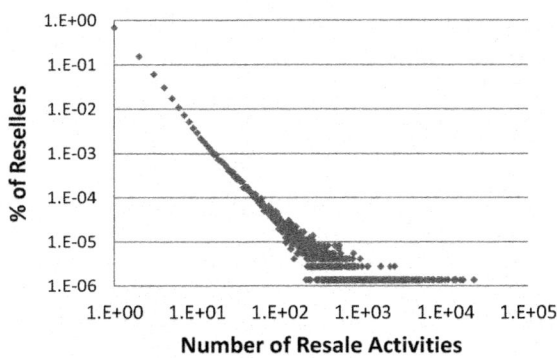

Figure 5: Distribution of the Number of Resale Activities. We note that the number of resale activities follows a power-law distribution with a long tail.

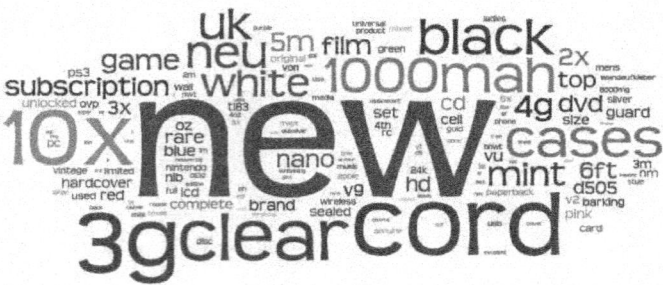

Figure 6: Top Keywords Added to Resale Listings. These frequently added keywords reflect the most common attributes that resellers think users care about.

ural since a tighter constraint on the title similarity reduces the chances of mismatch, but it also misses many reselling. By increasing α from 0.8 to 0.9, the improvement in accuracy is 3.39% but the number of obtained resale activities reduces 16.51%. Considering the tradeoff between accuracy and quantity, we use $\alpha = 0.8$ in the following analyses. Under this setting, we obtain a sample that includes over 13 million resale activities from the Hadoop cluster.

4.3 Observations and Analyses

The sample of resale activities is from over 30 regional sites, which cover 35 meta categories. In the following study, we analyze the resale market from various key perspectives and provide some interesting observations related to online resale.

Who Is Reselling? We first investigate the number of resellers and their resale patterns. We plot the distribution of the number of resale activities in Figure 5 on a log-log scale. The X-axis represents the number of resale activities per user, whereas the Y-axis shows the proportion of resellers who did the corresponding number of resales. From the figure, one can observe that resale follows a heavy-tailed distribution. Interestingly, top 10% resellers contribute 43% of resale activities. 68% of the resellers have only a single resale and they provide 18% of all resale activities. The figure shows that a large portion of users that resell very few times and a significant number of resale activities come from a small group of top highly active resellers. In addition, the trend interestingly follows a power-law distribution:

$$f(x) \propto x^{-\beta}$$

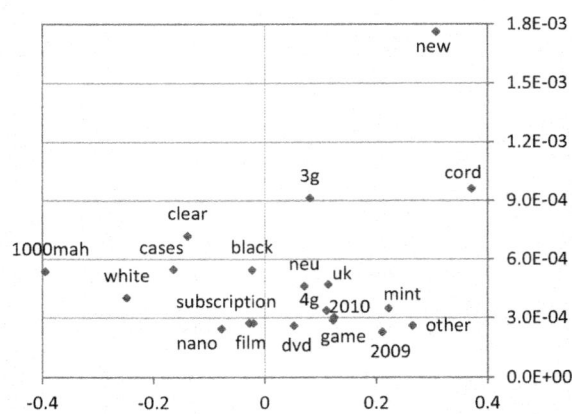

Figure 7: Average Relative Price Difference Versus Word Frequency. Note that X-axis and Y-axis denote the average relative price difference (ARPD) and word frequency, respectively. The higher the ARPD score, the more likely it is for resale to have profits by adding the given keyword.

where x represents the number of resale activities and β is computed to be 2.233.

What Content Do Resellers Change? On e-commerce sites, search results are mostly based on titles. Hence, many experienced sellers optimize titles to achieve better sales. We perform text analysis on the content that resellers added to new listings. For each resale activity, we obtain the added words from the reselling transactions, remove stop words and summarize them into an aggregated word cloud view in Figure 6. We observe that adding the keyword "new" is the most frequent as the largest tag cloud item. In summary, the most common words resellers added are the descriptions of product conditions ((brand) new, sealed, mint, etc.), colors (white, black, pink, etc.), appealing functions (game, dvd, clear, etc.), detailed specifications (1000amh, 3g, 4g, etc.) and years (2009, 2010, etc.). Actually these keywords correspond to the most common attributes that resellers think users care about.

In addition, to study the effectiveness of added words, we present a case study on the top 20 words with their frequencies and *average relative price differences* in Figure 7. The *average relative price difference* (**ARPD**) of a given word w is defined as

$$\frac{\sum_{(x,A,B,y)\in S, w\notin T_x, w\in T_y} \frac{P_y - P_x}{max(P_y, P_x)}}{|\{(x,A,B,y)\} : (x,A,B,y) \in S, w\notin T_x, w\in T_y\}|}$$

where the set S contains all resale activities of the pattern tuple (x, A, B, y). T_x and T_y represent the titles of items x and y, and P_x and P_y denote the corresponding prices. A positive ARPD score means the resale price is greater than the buying price, and vice versa. Clearly, higher ARPD represents greater resale values achieved by adding the word w. From the figure, we observe that "new" is the most frequently added words by resellers, and it is indeed quite effective in terms of resale values. Similarly, "mint" and "neu" (new in German) also have positive effects to increase resale prices. The word "cord" has a very high ARPD score. The reason is that it is usually associated with resales on accessaries such as adapters, cables and power supplies. Many such items were first bought from sellers in China and resold at higher prices to buyers in USA and UK. We further observe that

Table 2: Top 10 Resale Categories. Most significant categories are related to books or electronics.

Category	% of Total Resale
Clothes, Shoes & Accessories	11.1%
Used Books	9.7%
Computers & Networking	7.1%
Consumer Electronics	6.2%
Video Games	5.9%
Phones	5.8%
Home & Garden	4.3%
Cell Phones & PDAs	4.1%
Books	3.3%
Movies	3.0%

Table 3: Resale Activities on Regional Sites and Cross-sites. We observe that resale is an international and cross-border phenomenon.

Description	% of Total Resale
Same Site: USA	37%
Same Site: UK	34%
Same Site: Germany	16%
Same Site: Other	7%
USA ⇒ Other	3%
Other ⇒ USA	1%
Other ⇒ Other	2%

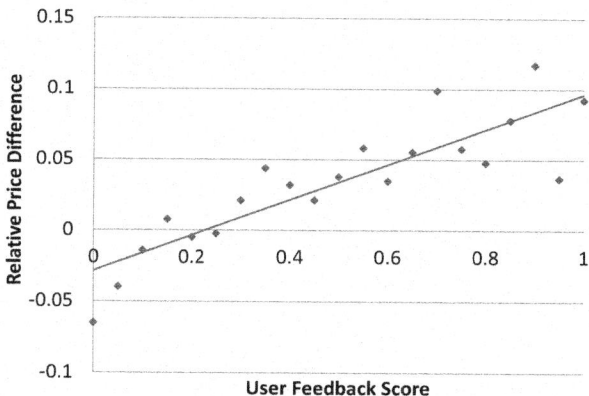

Figure 8: Average Relative Price Difference Versus User Feedback. Users in an online world with higher reputation tend to resell with larger profits. The red line illustrates a linear function that the data roughly fit.

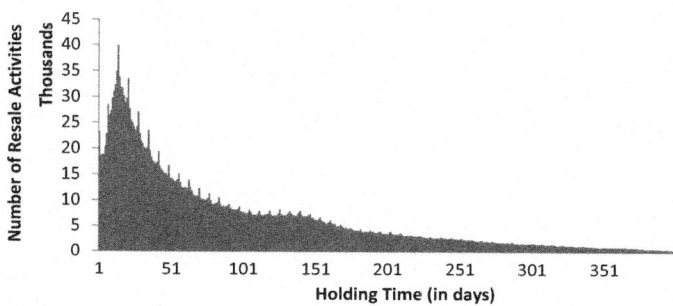

Figure 9: How Long Do Resellers Hold Items Before Resell. We note there is a peak in the range from 10 to 30 days.

some other effective words are related to appealing functions, detailed specifications and years. Interestingly, adding words on colors do not increase resale prices in many cases. We note that "1000mah" especially has a low ARPD score. The reason is that this word is strongly tied with batteries which are considered as consumables, and batteries are priced fairly lower if used.

What Are the Top Categories of Resale? We list the top 10 resale categories in terms of percentile in Table 2. "Clothing, Shoes & Accessories" is the largest category in the resale market, and followed by "Used Books". In the meanwhile, many categories related to electronics appear in the top 10 list, including "Cell Phones & PDAs", "Computers & Networking", "Consumer Electronics", "Phones", etc.

Is Resale an International Activity? Table 3 shows the resale activity distribution on different regional sites. We can learn from the spatial analysis that most resold items are purchased and sold on the same regional sites. The three largest resale markets are USA, UK and Germany, probably because of the popularity of online shopping in these three countries. We also notice cross border resale activities. 5% of resale activities are purchased on one site but resold on another site. 3% of resale activities are bought on the USA site and resold on other sites.

What is the Correlation Between User Reputation and Price? In order to analyze the relationship between reputation and price, we plot the average relative price difference versus user feedback in Figure 8. We normalize the user feedback to range $[0:1]$, and a higher score represents the given user has a more positive rating. The *average relative price difference* with respect to feedback is defined as

$$\frac{\sum_{f(B)\in[r_i,r_{i+1}]}\sum_{(x,A,B,y)\in S}\frac{P_y-P_x}{max(P_y,P_x)}}{|\{(x,A,B,y)\}:(x,A,B,y)\in S, f(B)\in[r_i,r_{i+1}]\}|}$$

where $f(B)$ is the feedback score of user B and $[r_i, r_{i+1}]$ is a given feedback score range. Higher ARPD represents greater profits achieved. There is an obvious trend that users with higher feedback scores achieve larger price increase, mostly because of the positive effects of online trust built in an online world. Although markets are considered stochastic, we can still observe that the data well fit a linear function (R^2 of 0.755).

How Long Do Resellers Hold Items? We show the temporal analysis that resellers hold items before resell in Figure 9. Clearly, most resellers hold items for less than 6 months. In particular, there is a significant peak in the range from 10 to 30 days. This indicates most resale activities happen almost immediately after the buyers receive the merchandise. It can also be concluded that very few resellers hold items for over one year to resell.

4.4 Prediction

As we have found many interesting insights of the resale market from the analysis above, we focus on the fact of successful resales in this subsection. From Figure 8, some resellers are making profits through resale activities, whereas some other users lose money. In order to have a quantitative understanding of what lead to a successful resale, we first analyze the features related to the profitability of resale. Then we use classification models to predict if a resale activity will be profitable given a set of features.

Table 4: Base Features Obtained for the Prediction Task

Type	Feature	Description
Feedback	ORG_SELLER_FDBK_AS_SLR	the *feedback as seller* of the original seller who sells the good to resellers
	ORG_SELLER_FDBK_AS_BYR	the *feedback as buyer* of the original seller
	BUY_FDBK_AS_SLR	the *feedback as seller* of the account reseller used to buy the good
	BUY_FDBK_AS_BYR	the *feedback as buyer* of the account reseller used to buy the good
	SELL_FDBK_AS_SLR	the *feedback as seller* of the account reseller used to resell the good
	SELL_FDBK_AS_BYR	the *feedback as buyer* of the account reseller used to resell the good
Title	BUY_AUCT_TITL	the title in the buying transaction
	SELL_AUCT_TITL	the title in the reselling transaction
Time	BUY_DATE	the purchase date of the buying transaction
	SELL_DATE	the purchase date of the reselling transaction
Site	BUY_SITE_ID	the buying transaction's listed regional site
	SELL_SITE_ID	the reselling transaction's listed regional site
Category	BUY_LEAF_CATEG_ID	the leaf category of the buying transaction
	SELL_LEAF_CATEG_ID	the leaf category of the reselling transaction
	BUY_META_CATEG_ID	the meta category of the buying transaction
	SELL_META_CATEG_ID	the meta category of the reselling transaction
Photo	BUY_PHOTO_COUNT	the number of photos in the buying transaction
	SELL_PHOTO_COUNT	the number of photos in the reselling transaction
Shipping	BUY_SHIPPING_FEE	the shipping fee in the buying transaction
	SELL_SHIPPING_FEE	the shipping fee in the reselling transaction
Quantity	BUY_QUANTITY	the number of items in the buying transaction
	SELL_QUANTITY	the number of items in the reselling transaction
Price	BUY_ITEM_PRICE	the purchase price in the buying transaction

4.4.1 Features Comparison

In order to build the classification models, we obtain a set of related features. For the problems of resale activities classification and prediction, the class labels are set to be binary, which are either *TRUE* (profitable) or *FALSE* (not profitable). For the classification purpose, we have obtained a list of base features from heterogeneous sources including transactions, user profiles, categories, sites, etc. They are listed in Table 4. There are 23 base features in total, which are related to 9 types:

- **Feedback**. The feedback is a score to measure the users performance. Can a user with higher feedback score sell with high profitability? Note that each resale activity is associated with two transactions: a buying transaction and a reselling transaction. Thus, separate features are created for both buying transactions and reselling transactions.

- **Title**. As we have shown in Figures 6 and 7, many resellers changed the listing titles for reselling. Does the length of title affect sale prices? Are titles the longer the better?

- **Time**. Do resale activities vary by seasons? Is there a 'best time' for reselling?

- **Site**. Do different regional markets show similar resale patterns? Which regional market is best for reselling?

- **Category**. We obtain both meta category and leaf category of each item. For example, for an iPod, its meta category is "Consumer Electronics", and its leaf category is "iPod & MP3 Players". Different categories may have different resale performances.

- **Photo**. Does the number of photos affect resale? "A picture is worth a thousand words." Can uploading more photos have a better presentation of products and thus boost sales?

- **Shipping**. The shipping charge is how much consumers need to pay for the shipping of the merchandise. Does free shipping help sales?

- **Quantity**. The number of goods sold in one transaction.

- **Price**. The price of resellers paid to buy the goods. The price of resellers resold is used to generate class labels, hence it is not listed as a feature.

Furthermore, we obtain 12 more features derived from base features. We show them in Table 5. The feature SAME_USER_ID is used to model how account transfer can affect resales. 5 derived features are binary, e.g. SAME_TITL, SAME_SITE, etc, which represent if there are some changes of attributes between buying transactions and reselling transactions. Two features related to the lengths of titles are used to represent the effects of titles. Furthermore, we extract month-of-the-year from date as another type of feature, which helps the model analyze the temporal effects. Other derived features present the numeric differences of attributes, such as time and photo count.

For the 35 features including base features and derived features, it is important to test which features have the most discriminative power in terms of profitability. Hence we measure the importance of features based on three criteria, namely Gain Ratio (GR), Information Gain (IG) and Chi-squared statistic (Chi). The top 15 discriminative features for each criterion are illustrated in Figure 10. The higher GR/IG/Chi score is, the higher discriminative power the corresponding feature has. In addition, we link the same features across different criteria to illustrate the similarities of the outputs.

From the figure, it is clear that the features selected by the three criteria highly overlap. The results on Information Gain and Chi-squared statistic are especially close. We further observe that the feedback scores and leaf categories are the most discriminative features, which are agreed by all three criteria. It is quite natural that feedback scores are important. The reason is that buyers trust sellers with high feedback scores and sellers with high feedback scores are more likely to have good selling skills. The leaf categories are also discriminative. This suggests that products from different categories have different resale potentials. For example, reselling products in Consumer Electronics and Art are easier to get better offers, whereas reselling in Clothing and Shoes is much more difficult to being profitable. Besides feedback scores and categories, TITL_LEN_DIFF and SAME_TITL are also two discriminative features. Clearly it represents a carefully rewritten title will benefit resales. Overall, the most important features are related to category, feedback and title. Besides the features listed in Figure 10, BUY_MONTH and SELL_MONTH are also two interesting features worth to mention. Through our further analysis of data, we find that usually buying in the summer and selling in December and January will make the best profits. The reason might be a lot of people are on vacation during summer time, so it is a low season with fewer buyers and bidders. And December and January are the holiday seasons that bring more people to shop online.

4.4.2 Model Comparison

Next, we investigate the prediction of resale activities using the base and derived features. We construct a number of feature sets corresponding to feature types, and build classifiers for each feature type as baselines. We further compare those classifiers with the classifier built on all features. We split the data into 75% as the training set and 25% as the testing set. SVM is used as the classification model. We evaluate the performance on four metrics: **Precision**, **Recall**, **F-score**, and **ROC**. For all these four measure, the higher scores represent the better performance.

The classification results on various feature sets are illustrated in Table 6. Among all separate feature sets, Category achieves the best performance, with an accuracy score at 65.3%. It suggests the profitability of resale depends largely on what categories the items are listed in. This exactly matches our previous feature analysis in Figure 10. We further discover that the model with all features outperforms the baseline models with separate feature sets. These results demonstrate that different features provide different insights on predictions. Data mining techniques can automatically learn the importance of different feature types and output satisfactory results with all features considered. We further test 4 additional classification models and list the results in Table 7. The overall best classifier we test is the Decision Tree, with an accuracy score of 75.4% and an F-score of 0.826. It gives an 8% improvement over the SVM model and a 17% improvement over the Naïve Bayes model. All the results are clear evidences that the selected base and derived features are indeed essential, and data mining techniques can generate satisfactory performance for resale market predictions.

5. APPLICATIONS

So far, we have analyzed the resale market and studied the prediction on the profitability of resale activities. In this section, we discuss the eBay applications of the findings

Table 6: Effectiveness of Various Feature Sets. The model that combines all features outperforms baselines with standalone feature sets on all measures.

Feature	Accuracy	Precision	Recall	F1	ROC
Feedback	58.2%	0.640	0.582	0.610	0.581
Title	56.6%	0.567	0.566	0.565	0.566
Time	54.6%	0.547	0.546	0.545	0.546
Site	54.3%	0.543	0.543	0.543	0.543
Category	65.3%	0.653	0.653	0.653	0.653
Photo	53.5%	0.564	0.536	0.550	0.537
Shipping	58.4%	0.588	0.584	0.580	0.584
Quantity	51.8%	0.608	0.518	0.559	0.520
All	**69.8%**	**0.755**	**0.668**	**0.709**	**0.686**

in previous sections. We show that, by incorporating the classification results, we can improve the efficiency of the resale market and improve both buyer and seller experience on web marketplaces.

From the classifiers we analyzed in the prediction section, we use the decision tree as the model to demonstrate the application scenarios. The advantages of using the decision tree model are its accuracy and a list of classification rules it can generate. Those rules can be easily interpreted by human beings and thus applied directly as business logics in an e-commerce system. The decision tree model generates over 18,000 rules in total for the resale activity classification task.

Since many rules generated by decision tree are either not statistically significant or not accurate enough for a real-world system, we further set two filters to select highly reliable rules:

- the minimum support of selected rules is S_{min}
- the minimum confidence of select rules is C_{min}

Using these selected highly reliable rules filtered by the minimum support and minimum confidence, we perform instance matching for each resale activity. For each incoming resale activity, if it satisfies one of the rules, the predicted label should be extremely accurate, since all selected rules are filtered based on support and confidence.

In the rest of this section, we give three example scenarios on improving a real production e-commerce system with the deployment of selected rules. We note that all these applications become possible and effective because of the extremely large data set and accurate prediction models.

Improving Reselling: Based on added words shown in Figures 6 and 7, a recommender systems can be applicable to suggest useful keywords according to frequencies and ARPD scores to make the resale title more descriptive. Besides text, we are also able to provide suggestions on category, transaction time, photo, shipping fee, user feedback, etc. Through our study of extracted rules, we find that many of them can be directly incorporated into the system and make resales more effective.

Improving General Buying: The selected reliable rules can not only help resellers, but also improve the experience of online shoppers. For example, when a buyer is browsing an item, the system can match his/her profile and the item with selected rules, and provide more personalized suggestions if the product has a high chance of resale. In general, useful information can be inferred from the classification model and be suggested to users. This feature can

Table 5: Derived Features Created for the Prediction Task

Type	Feature	Description
Account	SAME_USER_ID	binary: if account transfer occurred in the resale activity
Title	BUY_AUCT_TITL_LEN	the length of title in the buying transaction
	SELL_AUCT_TITL_LEN	the length of title in the reselling transaction
	TITL_LEN_DIFF	the difference between buying and selling title lengths
	SAME_TITL	binary: if resellers change the titles
Time	BUY_MONTH	the purchase month of the year in the buying transaction
	SELL_MONTH	the purchase month of the year in the reselling transaction
	TIME_DIFF	the waiting period to resell = reselling time - buying time
Site	SAME_SITE	binary: if the buying and selling transactions are on the same site
Category	SAME_LEAF_CATEG	binary: if resellers change the leaf categories
	SAME_META_CATEG	binary: if resellers change the meta categories
Photo	PHOTO_COUNT_DIFF	the difference between buying and selling photo counts

GR	Feature
0.0257	SELL_FDBK_AS_SLR
0.0233	BUY_LEAF_CATEG_ID
0.0228	SELL_LEAF_CATEG_ID
0.0198	SAME_SITE
0.0197	ORG_SELLER_FDBK_AS_SLR
0.0191	BUY_FDBK_AS_SLR
0.0132	BUY_QUANTITY
0.0116	BUY_ITEM_PRICE
0.0103	SAME_TITL
0.0101	BUY_FDBK_AS_BYR
0.0085	SELL_FDBK_AS_BYR
0.0068	TITL_LEN_DIFF
0.0063	PHOTO_COUNT_DIFF
0.0058	BUY_SHIPPING_FEE
0.0047	SELL_META_CATEG_ID

IG	Feature
0.2333	BUY_LEAF_CATEG_ID
0.2280	SELL_LEAF_CATEG_ID
0.1320	SELL_FDBK_AS_SLR
0.1021	BUY_FDBK_AS_SLR
0.1017	ORG_SELLER_FDBK_AS_SLR
0.0716	BUY_ITEM_PRICE
0.0545	BUY_FDBK_AS_BYR
0.0448	SELL_FDBK_AS_BYR
0.0229	SELL_META_CATEG_ID
0.0220	BUY_META_CATEG_ID
0.0207	BUY_SHIPPING_FEE
0.0134	TITL_LEN_DIFF
0.0133	ORG_SELLER_FDBK_AS_BYR
0.0103	SAME_TITL
0.0087	BUY_QUANTITY

Chi	Feature
34601.15	BUY_LEAF_CATEG_ID
34070.15	SELL_LEAF_CATEG_ID
19950.67	SELL_FDBK_AS_SLR
15656.42	ORG_SELLER_FDBK_AS_SLR
15654.91	BUY_FDBK_AS_SLR
12008.23	BUY_ITEM_PRICE
9406.78	BUY_FDBK_AS_BYR
7708.25	SELL_FDBK_AS_BYR
4096.37	SELL_META_CATEG_ID
3938.31	BUY_META_CATEG_ID
3732.07	BUY_SHIPPING_FEE
2463.13	TITL_LEN_DIFF
2380.58	ORG_SELLER_FDBK_AS_BYR
1913.55	SAME_TITL
1448.55	BUY_QUANTITY

Figure 10: Feature Analysis: Gain Ratio (GR), Information Gain (IG) and Chi-squared statistic (Chi)

Table 7: Effectiveness of Various Models. The decision tree model achieves the best performance on four out of five measures.

Model	Acc.	Pre.	Rec.	F1	ROC
Naïve Bayes	64.6%	0.650	0.646	0.644	0.710
Log Regression	66.7%	0.669	0.667	0.666	0.710
Decision Tree	**75.4%**	**0.753**	**0.914**	**0.826**	0.718
Nearest Neighbor	70.9%	0.709	0.709	0.709	**0.721**

be further integrated with commercial "Trade-in Programs" provided by many online markets[3]. This will also potentially increase the revenue of the whole marketplace.

Improving General Selling: After analyzing the selected rules, we notice that many under-priced sales are due to incorrectly or inappropriately listed categories. To address incorrectly listed items, we may use an accurate classifier to suggest users other possible options. For those items that are listed inappropriately, such as in "Everything Else" or "Other" category, the system may infer the actual categories of the items based on titles, descriptions and photos, and then advise the seller to sell at a more specific category rather than the vague "Everything Else" or "Other" category.

6. CONCLUSIONS AND FUTURE WORK

In this paper, we propose the first systematic framework to mine and analyze a large-scale online resale market. We develop a stream-based MapReduce approach to process peta-scale data, and discover millions of resale activities through elastic matching identification (EMI) with high accuracy ($> 93\%$). We discover that resale activities follow a power law distribution with a 'long tail' phenomenon, where a large portion of them are contributed by a small number of highly active resellers. In the meantime, resale is an international and cross-border behaivor and appears in all different categories of products. We observe that adding useful keywords and building user trust in the online world have positive effects towards resale values. We further utilize data mining models to empirically evaluate a number of features from different sources and predict the profitability of resale activities. Finally we propose three application scenarios to demonstrate how to incorporate the above models to a real-world e-commerce marketplace. It will not only increase revenues in terms of resale but also improve both general buyer and seller experience on web markets.

In our future work, we will consider developing a similarity matching method by incorporating the entities and semantics of listing items that can scale to web-scale data sets. We will also consider applying the proposed system to other user-to-user web applications.

7. ACKNOWLEDGMENT

The first author was a summer intern at eBay Research Labs while this work was done.

---

[3] http://instantsale.ebay.com, http://www.amazon.com/Trade-In, http://www.bestbuy.com/site/Misc/Buy-Back-Program

8. REFERENCES

[1] http://www.kronikmedia.co.uk/blog/content-curation-benefits/4433.

[2] C. C. Aggarwal, Y. Zhao, and P. S. Yu. On clustering graph streams. In *SDM*, pages 478–489, 2010.

[3] C. C. Aggarwal, Y. Zhao, and P. S. Yu. Outlier detection in graph streams. ICDE '11, pages 399–409, 2011.

[4] P. Bajari and A. Hortacsu. The winner's curse, reserve prices, and endogenous entry: empirical insights from ebay auctions. *RAND Journal of Economics*, pages 329–355, 2003.

[5] S. Bukhchandani and C. Huang. Auctions with resale markets: An exploratory model of treasury bill markets. *Review of Financial Studies*, 2(3):311–339, 1989.

[6] P. Chinloy. An empirical model of the market for resale homes. *Journal of Urban Economics*, 7(3):279–292, 1980.

[7] P. Courty. Some economics of ticket resale. *The Journal of Economic Perspectives*, 17(2):85–97, 2003.

[8] J. Dean, S. Ghemawat, and G. Inc. Mapreduce: simplified data processing on large clusters. 2004.

[9] I. Dhillon, Y. Guan, and B. Kulis. A fast kernel-based multilevel algorithm for graph clustering. In *KDD*, pages 629–634, New York, NY, USA, 2005.

[10] Q. Duong, N. Sundaresan, N. Parikh, and Z. Shen. Modeling seller listing strategies. *Agent-Mediated El. Comm*, 2010.

[11] S. Guo, M. Wang, and J. Leskovec. The role of social networks in online shopping: information passing, price of trust, and consumer choice. In Y. Shoham, Y. Chen, and T. Roughgarden, editors, *ACM EC*, pages 157–166, 2011.

[12] P. Haile. Auctions with private uncertainty and resale opportunities. *Journal of Economic Theory*, 108(1):72–110, 2003.

[13] A. Hosios and J. Pesando. Measuring prices in resale housing markets in canada: Evidence and implications*. *Journal of Housing Economics*, 1(4):303–317, 1991.

[14] D. Houser and J. Wooders. Reputation in auctions: Theory, and evidence from ebay. *Journal of Economics & Management Strategy*, 15(2):353–369, 2006.

[15] J. Jeon, W. B. Croft, and J. H. Lee. Finding similar questions in large question and answer archives. CIKM '05, pages 84–90, New York, NY, USA.

[16] H. Kautz, B. Selman, and M. Shah. Referral web: combining social networks and collaborative filtering. *Commun. ACM*, 40:63–65, March 1997.

[17] T. Kudo, E. Maeda, and Y. Matsumoto. An application of boosting to graph classification, 2004.

[18] R. Lämmel. Google's mapreduce programming model - revisited. *Sci. Comput. Program.*, 68:208–237, October 2007.

[19] J. Leskovec, K. J. Lang, and M. Mahoney. Empirical comparison of algorithms for network community detection. WWW, pages 631–640, New York, NY, USA, 2010.

[20] D. Lucking-Reiley. Auctions on the internet: What's being auctioned, and how? *The Journal of Industrial Economics*, 48(3):227–252, 2000.

[21] D. Lucking-Reiley, D. Bryan, N. Prasad, and D. Reeves. Pennies from ebay: The determinants of price in online auctions. *The Journal of Industrial Economics*, 55(2):223–233, 2007.

[22] H. Marvel and S. McCafferty. Resale price maintenance and quality certification. *The RAND Journal of Economics*, pages 346–359, 1984.

[23] M. Melnik and J. Alm. Does a seller's ecommerce reputation matter? evidence from ebay auctions. *The journal of industrial economics*, 50(3):337–349, 2002.

[24] S. Pandit, D. Chau, S. Wang, and C. Faloutsos. Netprobe: a fast and scalable system for fraud detection in online auction networks. In *WWW*, pages 201–210, 2007.

[25] P. Resnick, R. Zeckhauser, J. Swanson, and K. Lockwood. The value of reputation on ebay: A controlled experiment. *Experimental Economics*, 9(2):79–101, 2006.

[26] A. Roth and A. Ockenfels. Last minute bidding and the rules for ending second price auctions: evidence from ebay and amazon auctions on the internet. *American Economic Review*, 92(4):1093–1103, 2002.

[27] G. Shaffer. Slotting allowances and resale price maintenance: a comparison of facilitating practices. *The RAND Journal of Economics*, pages 120–135, 1991.

[28] Z. Shen and N. Sundaresan. ebay: an e-commerce marketplace as a complex network. WSDM '11, pages 655–664, New York, NY, USA, 2011.

[29] A. Shtok, G. Dror, Y. Maarek, and I. Szpektor. Learning from the past: answering new questions with past answers. WWW '12, pages 759–768.

[30] P. Shuchman. Profit on default: An archival study of automobile repossession and resale. *Stan. L. Rev.*, 22:20, 1969.

[31] R. Vernica, M. J. Carey, and C. Li. Efficient parallel set-similarity joins using mapreduce. SIGMOD '10, pages 495–506, New York, NY, USA, 2010.

[32] G. Wang, Y. Zhao, X. Shi, and P. S. Yu. Magnet community identification on social networks. KDD '12, pages 588–596.

[33] Y. Zhao, C. C. Aggarwal, and P. S. Yu. On graph stream clustering with side information. In *SDM*, 2013.

[34] Y. Zhao, X. Kong, and P. S. Yu. Positive and unlabeled learning for graph classification. In *ICDM*, pages 962–971, 2011.

Questions about Questions: An Empirical Analysis of Information Needs on Twitter

Zhe Zhao
Department of EECS
University of Michigan
zhezhao@umich.edu

Qiaozhu Mei
School of Information
University of Michigan
qmei@umich.edu

ABSTRACT

Conventional studies of online information seeking behavior usually focus on the use of search engines or question answering (Q&A) websites. Recently, the fast growth of online social platforms such as Twitter and Facebook has made it possible for people to utilize them for information seeking by asking questions to their friends or followers. We anticipate a better understanding of Web users' information needs by investigating research questions about these questions. How are they distinctive from daily tweeted conversations? How are they related to search queries? Can users' information needs on one platform predict those on the other?

In this study, we take the initiative to extract and analyze information needs from billions of online conversations collected from Twitter. With an automatic text classifier, we can accurately detect real questions in tweets (i.e., tweets conveying real information needs). We then present a comprehensive analysis of the large-scale collection of information needs we extracted. We found that questions being asked on Twitter are substantially different from the topics being tweeted in general. Information needs detected on Twitter have a considerable power of predicting the trends of Google queries. Many interesting signals emerge through longitudinal analysis of the volume, spikes, and entropy of questions on Twitter, which provide insights to the understanding of the impact of real world events and user behavioral patterns in social platforms.

Categories and Subject Descriptors

H.3.3 [**Information Search and Retrieval**]: Text Mining

General Terms

Experimentation, Empirical Studies

Keywords

Information Need, Time Series Analysis, Twitter

1. INTRODUCTION

Recent years have witnessed an explosion of user-generated content in social media. Online social platforms such as Facebook, Twitter, Google+, and YouTube have been complementing and replacing traditional platforms in many daily tasks of Web users, including the creation, seeking, diffusion, and consumption of information. Indeed, a very recent research interest has been shown in understanding how people seek for information through online social networks [26, 8, 29, 28, 21], how this "social information seeking" behavior differs from that through traditional channels such as search engines or online question answering (Q&A) sites, and how the social channel complements these channels [27, 16, 25]. Based on a survey conducted by Morris et al. in 2010, 50.6% of the respondents[1] reported having asked questions through their status updates on social networking sites [26]. The questions they ask involve various needs of recommendations, opinions, factual knowledge, invitations and favor, social connections, and offers. They covered many topics such as technology, entertainment, shopping, and professional affairs [26]. An analysis later by Efron and Winget suggested that 13% of a random sample of tweets (microblogs posted on Twitter.com) were questions [8].

Why is it compelling to understand the questions asked on social platforms? This emerging research interest largely attributes to the importance of understanding the information needs of Web users. Indeed, as the core problem in information retrieval, a correct interpretation of the information needs of the users is the premise of any automatic system that delivers and disseminates relevant information to the users. It is the common belief that the analysis of users' information needs has played a crucial role behind the success of all major Web search engines and other modern information retrieval systems. Better understanding and prediction of users' information needs also provides great opportunities to business providers and advertisers, leading to effective recommender systems and online advertising systems.

Long have Web search engines been the dominating channel of information seeking on the Web. According to recent statistics [2], 4 billion of search queries are submitted to Google every day. The rest of the territory is shared by other channels such as online question answering (Q&A) sites such as Yahoo! Answers. A statistic in 2010 reported a daily volume of 823,966 *questions and answers* [3], in which each question on average earned five to six answers according to [30]. This is much smaller than the number of information needs asked through search engines.

---
[1] Note for the selection bias as all were Microsoft employees.
[2] http://www.comscore.com/Insights/Press_Releases/2012/4/comScore_Releases_March_2012_U.S._Search_Engine_Rankings
[3] http://yanswersblog.com/index.php/archives/2010/05/03/1-billion-answers-served/

The emergence of social platforms seems to be a game-changer. If the ratio reported by Efron and Winget [8] still holds today, there will be over 50 million questions asked through Twitter according to a recent statistic of 400 million tweets posted per day [4]. This number, although still far behind the number of search queries, has already overwhelmed the number of questions in traditional Q&A sites. Moreover, it has been found that people tend to ask different questions to their friends rather than to search engines or to strangers on Q&A sites. In Figure 1, we can see people asking questions in their tweets by either broadcasting so that any of their followers can respond to them, or by targeting the question to particular friends. The results of the survey by Morris et al. suggested that respondents especially prefer social sites over search engines when asking for opinions and recommendations, and they tend to trust the opinions of their friends rather than strangers on Q&A sites [26]. It is reported in [27] that users enjoy the benefits of asking their social networks when they need personalized answers and relevant information that unlikely exists publicly on the Web. It is also reported that information needs through social platforms present a higher coverage of topics related to human interest, entertainment, and technology, compared to search engine queries [29].

Tweets Conveying Information Need	Tweets not Conveying Information Need
Do you know whether there is a roadwork on I94	Man so everybody a frank ocean fan now? Idc I was an original...
Which restaurant nearby has a discount?	Why do I always do this? #hesatool #fml
@someuser u work today???	@someuser how are you?
Can anyone suggest some local restaurants in Beijing?	They're still together, why haven't they broken up yet?!?!
@someuser, do you what I am doing is good?	Umm what? It's already August? Hey Summer, #wheredygo?
What's your favorite summer album to throw on a car stereo?	Im still gone smile! What are you thanking?! Em not
Is my avi cute?	Why won't people understand that?!

Figure 1: Instances of tweets conveying an information need, and those which don't.

All evidence suggests that the questions being asked through social networks present a completely new perspective of online information seeking behaviors. By analyzing this emerging type of behavior, one anticipates to help users effectively fulfill their information needs, to develop a new paradigm of search service that bridges search engines and social networks (e.g., social search [9, 25]), and to predict what the users need in order to strategize information service provision, persuasion campaign, and Internet monetization.

The availability of large scale user-generated content in social network sites has provided a decent platform for this kind of analysis. This revives our memory about the early explorations of analyzing search engine query logs (e.g., [31, 32, 23]). Indeed, the analysis of information needs with large-scale query logs has provided tremendous insights and features to researchers and practitioners, and it has led to a large number of novel and improved tasks including search result ranking [1], query recommendation [2], personalization [33], advertising [4], and various prediction tasks [14, 17]. We believe that a large-scale analysis of information needs on online social platforms will reproduce and complement the success of query log analysis, the results of which will provide valuable insights to the design of novel and better social search and other online information systems.

In this paper, we take the initiative and present the first very large scale and longitudinal study of information needs in Twitter, the leading microblogging site. Questions that convey information needs are extracted from a collection of **billions** of microblogs (i.e., tweets). This is achieved by an automatic text classifier that distinguishes real questions (i.e., tweets conveying real information needs) from tweets with question marks. With this dataset, we are able to present a comprehensive description of the information needs with both the perspectives of content analysis and trend analysis. We find that questions being asked on Twitter are substantially different from the content being tweeted in general. We prove that information needs detected on Twitter have a considerable power of predicting the trends of search engine queries. Through the in-depth analysis of various types of time series, we find many interesting patterns related to the entropy of language and bursts of information needs. These patterns provide valuable insights to the understanding of the impact of bursting events and behavioral patterns in social information seeking.

The rest of the paper is organized as follows. We start by introducing the related work. The setup and dataset of our experiments is presented in Section 3, followed by the description of an automatic classifier of information needs in Section 4. In Section 5, we describe the detailed results and insights drawn from the analysis of the large collection of information needs. We then conclude in Section 6.

2. RELATED WORK

To the best of our knowledge, this is the first work to detect and analyze information needs from billion level, longitudinal collection of tweets. Our work is generally related to the qualitative and quantitative analysis of information seeking through social platforms (e.g., [29, 5, 27]) and temporal analysis of online user behaviors (e.g., [3, 14]).

2.1 Questions on Social Platforms

As described in Section 1, there is a very recent interest in understanding how people ask questions in social networks such as Facebook and Twitter [5, 26, 8, 29, 28, 21]. This body of work, although generally based on surveys or small scale data analysis, provides insights to our large-scale analysis of information needs in Twitter. For example, In [29], the authors labeled 4,140 tweets using Mechanical Turks and analyzed 1,351 of them which were labeled as real questions. They presented a rich characterization of the types and topics in these questions, the responses to these questions, and the effects of the underlying social network. In [26, 27, 36], Morris et al. surveyed whether and how people ask questions through social networks, the differences between these questions and questions asked through search engines, and how different cultures influence the behaviors. Efron and Winget further confirmed this difference with a study of 375,509 tweets. Using a few simple rules, they identified 13% of these tweets as questions. They also provided preliminary findings on how people react to questions.

[4]http://news.cnet.com/8301-1023_3-57448388-93/twitter-hits-400-million-tweets-per-day-mostly-mobile/

More sophisticated methods have been proposed to detect questions in online forums and Q&A sites [6, 35]. A recent work [19] studied the same problem in the context of Twitter, which presented a classifier that achieved 77.5% of accuracy in detecting questions from tweets. A much more accurate classifier is needed, however, to analyze information needs at a very large scale.

It is interesting to see the effort of making use of the understandings of social information seeking. In [16], Morris et al. proposed SearchBuddies, an automatic content recommendation for information seeking behavior. The proposed work finds relevant content based on the content and social context of Facebook status asking for information. Such effort can also be found in work like [9, 27, 34], where a new paradigm of search service, social search, is discussed. These explorations provided good motivations to our effort of large-scale analysis of information needs on social platforms.

2.2 Temporal Analysis of User Activities

The techniques of analysis used in our work is related to the existing work of analyzing user behaviors in general. For example, in [3], the authors proved that sentiment trends in Twitter has a power of predicting the Daw Jones Industrial Average. In their approach, the Granger Causality Test is used to test this predictive power. In [14], the authors used the Google trend related to influenza spread worldwide to detect which stage the flu was at and to predict the trend of the flu. Our analysis provides another important application of these methods. Note that our analysis is also related to the analysis of large scale search engine logs (e.g., [31, 32, 23]). Indeed, we do anticipate the analysis of information needs in social platforms to complement the analysis of information needs through search engines, and provide a totally different perspective and insights to search engine practitioners.

3. EXPERIMENT SETUP

We analyze a longitudinal collection of microblogs (tweets) collected through the Twitter stream API with Gardenhose access, which collects roughly 10% of all public statuses on Twitter. The collection covers a period of 358 days, from July 10th, 2011 to June 31st 2012. A total number of 4,580,153,001 (12.8 million tweets per day) tweets are included in this collection, all of which are self-reported as tweets in English. Every tweet contains a short textual message constrained by 140 characters, based on which we determine whether it conveys an information need. For every tweet, we keep the complete metadata such as the user who posted the tweet, the time stamp at which it was posted, and geographical locations of the user if provided. In the analysis in this paper, we adopt only the time and user information but leave the richer metadata for future analysis.

Note that a tweet may be a retweet of an existing tweet, may mention one or more users by "@" their usernames, and may contain one or more hashtags (user-defined keywords starting with an "#"). In our analysis, we keep the original form of all hashtags, but de-identify all usernames mentioned in the tweets (e.g., substituting all of them with a token "@someuser").

To analyze information needs in these tweets, we focus on tweets that appear to be questions. Specifically, we focus on tweets that contain at least one question mark. Note that this treatment could potentially miss information needs that are presented as statements. According to statistics in [26], 81.5% of information needs asked through social platforms were explicitly phrased as questions and included a question mark. Questions phrased as statements were often preceded by inquisitive phrases like "I wonder," or "I need" [26]. Because there is little foreseeable selection bias, we choose to focus on questions with explicit question marks instead of enumerating these arbitrary patterns in an ad hoc manner. In our collection of tweets, 10.45% of tweets contain explicit appearance of question mark(s).

4. DETECTING INFORMATION NEEDS

Not all tweets with question marks are real questions. In order to detect information needs from tweets collected in Section 3, we need to distinguish tweets that convey a real information need from many false positives such as rhetorical questions, expressions of sentiments/mood, and many other instances. Figure 1 presents examples of tweets that convey real information needs and those which don't.

In this section, we present the task of detecting information needs from tweets which is casted as a text classification problem. Given a tweet that contains one or two question marks, the task is to determine whether it expects an *informational* answer or not. In this section, we first give a formal definition of this problem and rubrics based on which human annotators can accurately classify a tweet. A qualitative content analysis is conducted in order to develop a codebook of classification and generate a set of labeled tweets as training/testing examples. We then introduce a classifier trained with these examples, using the state-of-the-art machine learning algorithms and a comprehensive collection of features. The performance of the text classifier is evaluated and presented in Section 4.5.

4.1 Definition and Rubrics

Given a tweet with question marks, our task is to determine whether this tweet conveys a real information need or not (i.e., real questions). A formal definition is needed to describe what we mean by "a real information need." Inspired by the literature of how people ask questions on Twitter and Facebook [29, 27], we provide the following definition and rubrics of "real questions:"

A tweet conveys an information need, or is a real question, if it expects an informational answer from either the general audience or particular recipients.

Therefore, a tweet conveys an information need if

- **it requests for a piece of factual knowledge, or a confirmation of a piece of factual knowledge.** A piece of factual knowledge can be phrased as a claim that is objective and fact-checkable (e.g., "Barack Obama is the 44th president of the United States").

- **it requests for an opinion, idea, preference, recommendation, or personal plan of the recipient(s), as well as a confirmation of such information.** Here the information been requested is subjective, which is not fact checkable at the present.

A tweet does not convey an information need if it doesn't expect an informational answer. This includes rhetorical questions, expressions of greeting, summary of the content (eye attractors), imperial requests (to be distinguished from invitations), sarcasm, humor, expressions of emotion (complaints, regrets, anger, etc), or conversation starters.

Figure 1 shows some examples of tweets conveying information need and tweets which don't. Using the description we proposed above, a human annotator can easily classify a tweet. In the following subsections, we introduce how we extract features from the tweets, how we select features using the state-of-the-art feature selection techniques, and how we train classifiers using a single type of feature and then combine them using boosting.

4.2 Human Annotation

Based on the rubrics, we developed a codebook[5] and recruited two human annotators to label a random sample of tweets. We sampled 5,000 tweets randomly from our collection, each of which contains at least one question mark and self-reported as English. Finally, 3,119 tweets are labeled as real tweets in English and have same labels by the two coders. Among the 3,119 tweets, 1,595 are labeled as conveying an information need and 1,524 are labeled not conveying an information need. The inter-rater reliability measured by Cohen's kappa score is 0.8350, the proportion of the agreements in all the results is 91.5%. The 3,119 labeled tweets will be used to train and evaluate the classifier of information needs.

4.3 Text Classification

4.3.1 Feature Extraction

The classification of tweets is a particularly challenging because of the extremely short length of content (i.e., a tweet has a limited length of 140 characters). This makes the textual features in an individual tweet extremely sparse. To overcome this challenge, we not only utilize lexical features from the content of the tweets, but also generalize them using the semantic knowledge base WordNet [24, 10]. It is also our intent to include syntactical features as well as metadata features. We extracted four different types of feature from each tweet, i.e., lexical ngrams, synonyms and hypernyms of words (obtained from the WordNet), ngrams of the part-of-speech (POS) tags, and light metadata and statistical features such as the length of the tweet and coverage of vocabulary(i.e., number of different words used in a tweet divided by the number of different words in the whole dataset), etc..

LEXICAL FEATURES

We included unigrams, bigrams, as well as trigrams. The start and end of a tweet are also considered in the ngrams. This gives us great flexibility to capture features that reflects the intuitions from qualitative analysis. For example tweets beginning with the 5Ws (who, when, what, where, and why) are more likely to be real questions. All lexical features are lowercased and stemmed using the Krovetz Stemmer [18]. Hashtags are treated as unique keywords. To eliminate the noise of low frequent words, a feature is dropped if it appears less than 5 times. This resulted in 44,121 lexical features.

WORDNET FEATURES

To deal with the problem of data sparsity, we attempt to generalize the lexical features using the synonyms and the hypernyms of the words in tweets. We hope this approach would connect different features sharing relevant semantics in different tweets. By doing this, our algorithm can also handle words that haven't been seen in the training data, thus is anticipated to achieve a higher performance with limited training data.

In [22], the authors studied how different types of relevant words from WordNet influence the results of text classification. In most cases, using only synonyms and hypernyms can improve classifiers such as Support Vector Machine (SVM) the most. We explored different WordNet features in our task and drew the same conclusion. We therefore adopt only synonyms and hypernyms of words in a tweet as additional features. Note here we actually excluded this semantic generalization for nouns in a tweet. This is because our task is to discover patterns of how people ask questions, instead of what they ask. 23,277 WordNet features are extracted.

PART-OF-SPEECH FEATURES

Compared to a statement, questions present special patterns of syntactic structure. Therefore we attempt to include syntactic features into consideration. Syntactic parsing of billions of tweets appears to be costly and probably unnecessary, since the quality of parsing is compromised given the inaccurate use of language in social media. We thus seek for features that capture light syntactic information. We first obtain part-of-speech of the words in a tweet, and then extract ngrams of these part-of-speech tags. That is, given a tweet with n words, $w_1, w_2, \ldots, w_n$, we extract grams from the part-of-speech sequence of the tweet, is $t_1, t_2, \ldots, t_n$, and then extract unigrams, bigrams and trigrams from this part-of-speech sequence as additional features of the tweet. 3,902 POS features are extracted in total.

META FEATURES

We also include 6 metadata features and simple statistical features of the tweet such as the length of the tweets, the number of words, the coverage of vocabulary, the number of capitalized words, whether or not the tweet contains a URL, and whether or not it mentions other users. We believe these features are possibly indicative of questions.

4.3.2 Feature Selection

The four types of extracted features represent each tweet as a vector with a very large number of dimensions. This is not surprising given the huge and open vocabulary in Twitter. Even though we can reduce the number of features by various heuristics of post-processing, the number of features remaining is still far larger than the number of training examples. Therefore, it is essential to conduct feature selection and further reduce the dimensionality of the data.

In this paper, we adopt the state-of-the-art feature selection method named Bi-Normal Separation (BNS) proposed in [11]. In this work, the author proved that the proposed metric for feature selection outperformed other well-known metric such as Information Gain and Chi-distance. Specifically, let tp and tn be the number of positive cases with and without a given feature, fp and fn be the number of negative cases with and without the feature. Let tpr be the sample true positive ratio (i.e., $tpr = tp/(tp+fn)$) and fpr be the sample false positive ratio (i.e., $fpr = fp/(fp+tn)$).

The BNS metric of a given feature can be calculated by

$$\|F^{-1}(tpr) - F^{-1}(fpr)\|, \qquad (1)$$

where F is the Normal cumulative distribution function.

---

[5]The codebook is made available at http://www-personal.umich.edu/~zhezhao/projects/IN/codebook.html

4.4 Training Classifier

After feature selection, we move forward and train four independent classifiers using the Support Vector Machine (SVM) [7], based on each of the four types of features. We then combine the four classifiers that represent four types of features into one stronger classifier using boosting. This is done through the Adaptive Boosting method called Adaboost [12].

Adaboost is an effective algorithm that trains a strong classifier based on several groups of weak classifiers. Usually Adaboost can obtain one classifier better than any of the weak classifiers. However, when the performances of the weak classifiers are higher than a certain level, it is hard to use this algorithm to generate a better classifier. This situation seems to apply to our scenario, since the SVM classifiers are sufficiently strong. In [20], the authors indicated that the reason why this problem occurs is that after several iterations, when the combination of weak classifiers starts to achieve a higher performance, the diversity inside the combination is getting lower. That says, new weak classifiers are likely to make same predictions as the old ones. To solve this problem, they add a parameter to control for the diversity of the weak learners in each iteration. We aslso adopt this technique to combine the four SVM classifiers.

We define parameter div as the threshold of a minimum diversity of a new weak classifier to be added in each iteration in the Adaboost. The diversity that a new classifier could add in iteration t is defined as follows:

$$div_t = \frac{1}{N} \sum_{i=1}^{N} d_t(x_i) \quad (2)$$

$$d_t(x_i) = \begin{cases} 0 & \exists k, f_k(x_i) = f_t(x_i) \\ 1 & \forall k, f_k(x_i) \neq f_t(x_i) \end{cases} \quad (3)$$

Here $d_t(x_i)$ is the diversity of classifier to be added in iteration t to data point x_i. N is the size of the training set. $f_k(x_i)$ is the predicted result of the classifier in iteration k for data point x_i. Our information need detection algorithm uses this modified Adaboost named AdaboostDIV. The diversity of a classifier represents how much new information it could provide to a group of classifiers that have already been trained in Adaboost. This value will be smaller and smaller when there are more classifiers adopted. In each iteration of AdaboostDIV, we examine the diversity of a new classifier. If the diversity of this classifier is higher than minimal threshold div, we accept this classifier into the group of classifiers. Otherwise we terminate the algorithm.

4.5 Evaluation of the Classifier

We train and evaluate our algorithm using the manually labeled set of 3,119 tweets. 10-fold cross validation and the metric of classification accuracy are adopted to evaluate each candidate classifier.

Before feature selection, there are 44,121 ngram lexical features, 23,277 WordNet features, 3,902 Part-of-Speech features, and 6 meta features. In Table 1, we compare the performance of the four SVM classifiers using each of the four types of features and various feature selection algorithms. The findings are consistent with the conclusions in [11]. Feature selection using the BNS metric outperformed two other metrics, namely accuracy (ACCU) and Information Gain, both of which improved over the classifiers without feature

Feature Type	Lexical	WordNet	POS	Meta
Raw	0.745	0.610	0.668	**0.634**
ACCU	0.790	0.673	0.718	/
Information Gain	0.804	0.676	0.723	/
BNS	**0.856**	**0.702**	**0.745**	/

Table 1: Results of SVM classifiers. Lexical features performed the best. Feature selection improved classification accuracy.

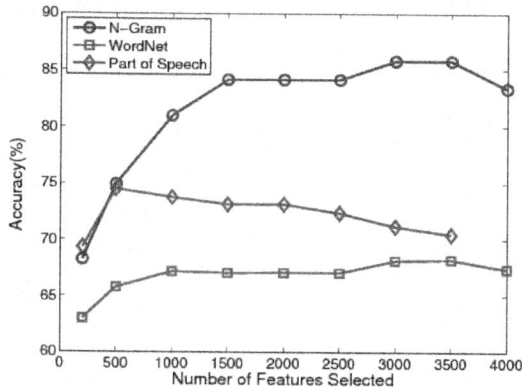

Figure 2: Feature selection using BNS

selection. Among the four types of features alone, ngram lexical features appear to provide the best performance, while the six meta features provide the weakest result which is also far better than random.

Figure 2 shows a fine tuning of the number of features selected using BNS. Clearly, when too few or too many features are selected, the classification performance drops because of insufficient discriminative power and overfitting, respectively. Based on our experiment results, we select 3,795 top ranked lexical features, 3,119 top WordNet features, as well as 505 top Part-of-Speech features.

At last, we combined the four SVM classifiers, representing four types of features, using AdaboostDIV. The accuracy of the classifier (with 10-fold cross validation) improved from 85.6% to 86.6%. The small margin suggests that the lexical features are strong enough in detecting information needs, while other types of features add little to the success. Using Adaboost instead of AdaboostDIV compromised the performance, which is consistent to the findings in [20].

Finally, the best performing classifier (four SVM classifiers combined with AdaboostDIV, with feature selection with BNS) is adopted to classify all the tweets in our collection. In our evaluation, the improvements made by feature selection and AdaboostDIV passed the paired-sample t-test at the 5% significance level.

5. ANALYZING INFORMATION NEEDS

After applying the text classifier above to the entire collection of tweets, we detected 136,841,672 tweets conveying information need between July 10th 2011 to June 31st 2012. This is roughly a proportion of 3% of all tweets, and 28.6% of tweets with question marks. With this large scale collection of real questions on Twitter, we are able to conduct a comprehensive descriptive analysis of user's information

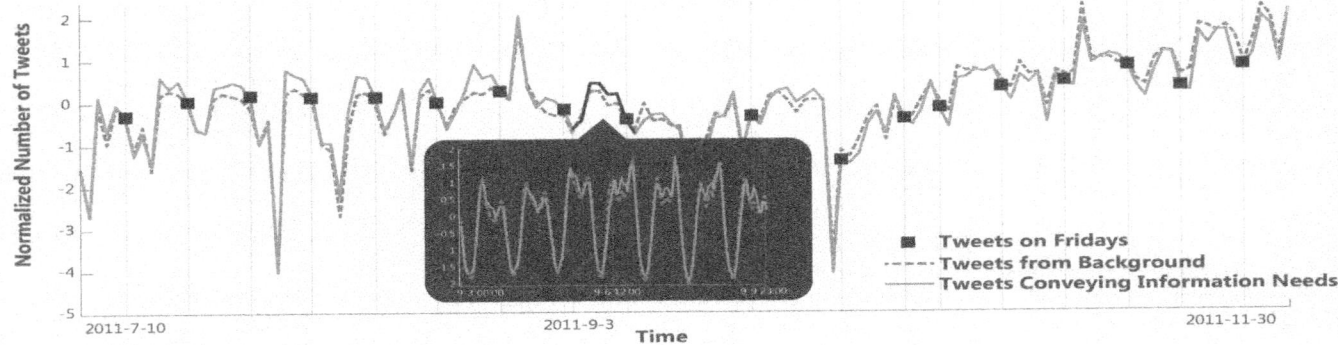

Figure 3: Questions and background tweets over time.

needs. Without ambiguity, we call all the tweets collected as the BACKGROUND tweets, whether they are questions or not. We call tweets that convey information needs as INFORMATION NEEDS (or short as IN), or simply QUESTIONS.

5.1 General Trend

Once we are able to accurately identify real questions (or information needs), the first thing to look at is how many questions are being asked and how they are distributed. Below we present the general trend of the volumes of questions being asked comparing to the total number of tweets in the background. For plotting purposes, we choose to show the trend of the first 5 months from this entire time scope, from July 10th 2011 to November 30th, 2011. Most of the events occurred during this period of time, so plotting the whole year's time series would take more space and cannot be shown distinctly. These 5 months contain a collection of 1,640,850,528 tweets, in which 51,263,378 conveyed an information need. We use this time period for all visualization and time-series analysis below.

Since there is a huge difference between the raw numbers of information needs and the background tweets, we normalize the time series so that the two curves are easier to be aligned on the plot. Specifically, we normalized all the time series using the Z-normalization. That is, for the ith data point valued x_i in the time series, we transform the value by following equation:

$$x'_i = \frac{x_i - \mu}{\sigma} \quad (4)$$

Where μ and σ are the mean and standard deviation of all data points in this time series. This simple normalization doesn't change the trend of the time-series, but allows two series of arbitrary values being aligned to the same range. In the plot, a positive value means the daily count of IN/background tweets is above the average count over time, and a negative value means the count is below the mean. An actual value x on one day indicates that the count of that day is x standard deviations away from the average.

From Figure 3, we observe that both the number of tweets and the number of questions are increasing over time. There are observable but weak days-of-week patterns, which differ search engine logs which present significant weekly patterns (more queries on weekdays than weekends) [23]. The trend is much more sensitive than that of query logs [23], with obvious and irregular spikes and valleys scattered along the time line. This implies that user's information seeking behaviors on Twitter are more sensitive to particular events than the behaviors on search engines. The subfigure presents a strong daily pattern, where both the total number of tweets and information needs peak in late morning and early evening, leaves a valley after noon, and sinks soon after midnight.

In general, the trend of information needs correlates with the trend of the background, which means the information needs on Twitter are likely to be social driven but not information driven. This is not surprising since real world events are likely to stimulate both the demand and supply of information. The more interesting signals in the plot are the noticeable differences between the two curves. On some days there is a significantly overrepresented "demand" of information (i.e., questions) than the "supply" (i.e., background), where there appears a noticeable gap between the two curves. This offers opportunities to analyze what people want, provide better recommendations, and develop propaganda. It is also an interesting observation from the hours-of-day trend that information needs are always overrepresented between the two peaks, before and after noon.

5.2 Keywords

With a sense of the general trend of how people ask, the next question is what people ask. Previous literature has provided insights on the categorization and distribution of topics of questions [26, 29]. Here we are not repeating their efforts, but to provide a finer granularity analysis of the keywords. After removing stopwords from the tweets, we extracted all unigrams and bigrams from tweets classified as conveying information needs. We trim this list of keywords by keeping those appeared every day of our time frame. We believe these keywords that the most representative of the *everyday* information needs of users in Twitter instead of information needs only triggered by particular events. For each of these keywords, we keep the daily count of the number of background tweets containing the keyword and the number of information needs containing the keyword.

With these counts, we can distinguish keywords that appeared frequently in information needs and those appeared frequently in the background. Table 2 lists a subset of keywords that are significantly overrepresented in information needs (i.e., have a much larger frequency in IN than in Background tweets, normalized by the maximum of the two frequencies), compared to the keywords significantly overrep-

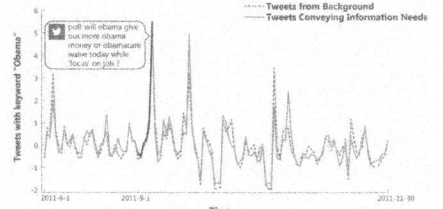 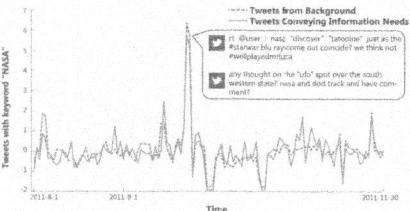 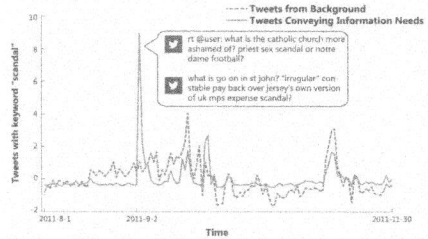

(a) Trend of tweets conveying information need with keyword "obama"   (b) Trend of tweets conveying information need with keyword "nasa"   (c) Trend of tweets conveying information need with keyword "scandal"

Figure 4: Trend of tweets conveying information need with different keywords

Frequent in IN	Frequent in BACKGROUND
noyoutube	http
butterfly fall	user video
pocket camera	follow back
Monday	retweet
skype	beautiful
any suggestion	photo
waterproof phone	good night
any recommend	god bless

Table 2: Overrepresented keywords in information needs and background

resented in the background. One can observe from the table that keywords about technology (e.g., "noyoutube," "pocket camera," "skype," "waterproof phone") and recommendation seeking (e.g., "any suggestion," "any recommend") have a high presence in questions while URLs (e.g., "http"), greetings (e.g., "good night," "god bless") and requests (e.g., "follow back") are more frequent in the background. This finding is consistent with the quantitative analysis in literature [26, 29].

We further dropped the keywords that appeared less than 10 times a day in average, from which we obtained 11,813 keywords. For these keywords, we generated time series that represent the demand of information about these keywords, by counting the number of questions and general tweets containing particular keywords everyday.

Figure 4 presents the trends of information needs and background tweets containing three particular keywords, namely "Obama," "NASA," and "scandal." In Fig. 4(a), we can see that the trend of information needs closely correlates with the background, with several noticeable bursting patterns. These patterns generally correspond to real world events. For example, the largest spike around September 8th was correlated with President Obama's speech about the $450 billion plan to boost jobs. Such types of major events are likely to trigger both questions and discussions in online communities, thus have caused a correlated spike of both information needs and the background.

The trends of the keyword "NASA" present a different pattern. The questions and the background align well around the big spike, but disjoin in other time periods. In general, the trend of information needs is more sensitive than the background discussions, presenting more fluctuation. These smallish spikes are not triggered by major events, but rather reflecting the regular demands of information. The trends of the keyword "scandal" is even more interesting. Even the major spikes don't correlate with questions and with

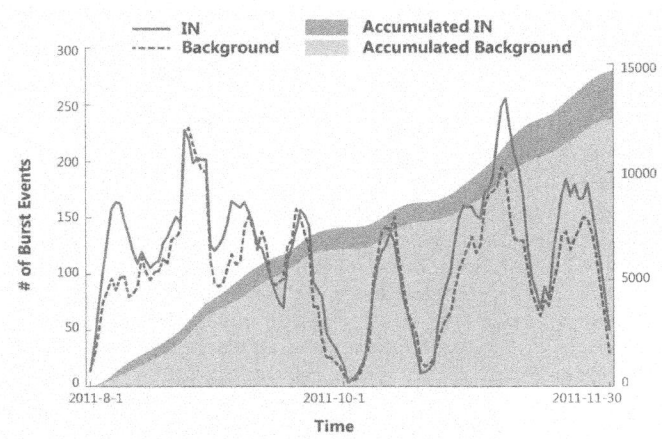

Figure 5: Bursts detected from IN and background

the background. For example, the big spike in information needs was triggered by a widespread cascade of tweets that connects "Priest sex scandal" with "Notre Dame football," which is more like a cascade of persuasion, rumor, or propaganda instead of an real event.

5.3 Burstiness

The anecdotal examples above presented interesting insights in understanding the different roles of bursting patterns in the time series. This is done by comparing individual spikes in information needs with the pattern in the background in the same time period. A different perspective of investigating such bursting patterns is to compare them longitudinally. How many spikes are like the spike caused by Obama's job speech? If a similar bursting pattern can be found among the information needs of a different keyword, that means there is an event that have made a similar impact with the president's speech in terms of triggering the users' behaviors of information seeking.

Literature has thrown light on how to detect real events based on burst detection in social media [38, 37]. In our analysis, we adopt a straightforward solution to detect **similar** burst events in the time series of information needs and the background. Specifically, we select a signature bursting pattern of a real event as a query (e.g., the spike corresponding to Obama's job speech in Figure 4(a)) and retrieve all similar spikes in the time series of other keywords. The

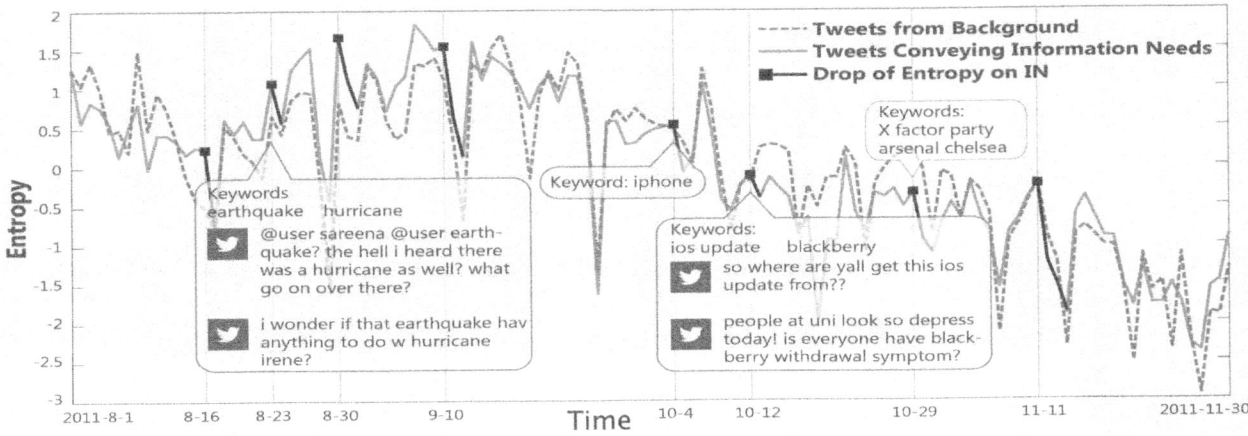

Figure 6: Entropy of word distributions in questions and background

similarity measurement is the Euclidean distance between Z-normalized time series. By doing this, we found 14,640 burst patterns in the time series of information needs and 12,456 burst patterns in the background of all keywords. Figure 5 plots the number of burst events that have a similar impact as the Obama speech, aggregated from the time series of all different keywords. Apparently, there are more such spikes in the time series of information needs rather than in the background, which reassures our finding that the behavior of question asking is more sensitive than the narrative discussions of events. The number of bursting patterns tops in late August and the month of October, which coincides with the two series of events related to "Hurricane Irene" and "Occupy D.C."

5.4 Entropy

The investigation of bursting patterns provides insights about understanding the impact of real events on Twitter users' information seeking behaviors. The impact is featured by the sudden increase of information needs (or background tweets, or both) containing certain keyword. Another way to measure the impact of an event is to look at how it influences the content of information people are tweeting about and asking for. Shannon's Entropy [13] is a powerful tool to measure the level of uncertainty, or unpredictability of a distribution. It is well suited for sizing challenges, compression tasks, as well as the measure of diversity of information. We apply Shannon's entropy to the information needs detected, by measuring the entropy of the word distribution (a.k.a., the language model) in all background tweets and in all questions every day. Clearly, a lower entropy indicates a concentration of discussions on certain topics/keywords, and a higher entropy indicates a spread of discussions on different topics, or a diversified conversation.

Our intuition is that if a major event influences the discussion and information seeking behaviors, the topics in the background or in the questions on that day will concentrate on the topics about that event. Thus we are likely to observe a decreased entropy. Figure 6 plots the entropy of the language models of all information needs, and of all tweets in the background over time. We mark several points in the time series where we observe a sudden drop of entropy on the next day, which indicates a concentration of topics being discussed/asked. We selected these points by the significance of the entropy drop and the differences between the entropy of IN and the entropy of background. We then extract the keywords that are significantly overrepresented in the day after each marked point, which give us a basic idea about the topics that have triggered this concentration. These keywords are good indicators of the actual events that have triggered the concentration (e.g., "the hurricane Irene," "arsenal chelsea" and "the rumor about the release date of iphone 5").

It is especially interesting to notice that on some particular days, entropy drops in information needs but increases in the background. We believe these are very indicative signals for monitoring what the public needs. For example, on October 12th, 2011, there was a sudden drop of entropy in information needs which didn't occur in the background tweets. The discussions concentrated on keywords like "ios," "update," and "blackberry." Indeed, on that day Apple released the new operation system iOS 5, which triggered massive questions about how to get the updates. During the same time, there was a series of outages which caused a shutdown of the Blackberry Internet Service. Such an event has contributed in the concentrations of questions about Blackberry. It is interesting to see that these events about technology indeed had a larger impact in questions instead of the background tweets, which is again consistent with the statistics in literature [26, 29]. Clearly, analyzing the entropy of information needs provides insights on detecting events that have triggered the concentration of information needs. Such discoveries indicate compelling opportunities for search and recommender services, advertising, and rumor detection.

Interestingly, we found entropy analysis not only a powerful tool for macro-level analysis of the impact of events, but also effective in micro-level analysis of the information seeking behaviors of individual users. Indeed, we can also compute the entropy of the distribution of the number of questions that a user asks among different hours of a day. Behaviors of users with a low entropy are more predictable than behaviors of users with a high entropy. Below we show the two behavior patterns from two specific users. One is with high entropy and the other is with low entropy in Figure 7 and 8 respectively. In these two figures, the x-axes represent the 30 days in September, 2011, and the y-axes

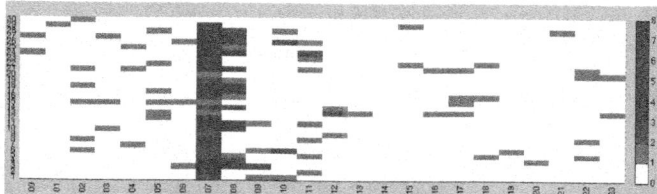

Figure 7: Questions of a user of low entropy.

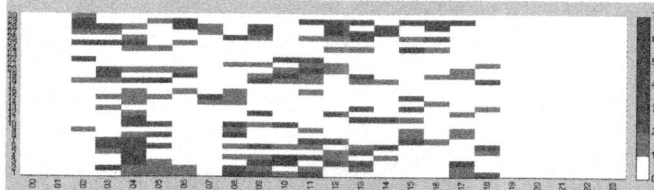

Figure 8: Questions from a user of high entropy.

represent the 24 hours in each day. The different colors in these two figures represent different numbers of posts (the legends are shown on the right side of the figures).

Clearly, the user with low entropy is fairly predictable: he always asks questions at 7am. By looking into his tweets, we found that this is an automatic account that retweets open questions from Yahoo! Answers. The second user is much less predictable, who seemed to be asking questions all over the hours of a day except for the bed time. By looking into his tweets, we found that this is a user who uses Twitter as an instant message platform, who chats with friends whenever he is awake. This user-level analysis on entropy of information needs presents insights on characterizing different individual behaviors.

5.5 Predictive Power

Up to now, we have presented many interesting types of analysis, mostly on the longitudinal patterns of information needs. We see various insights about how to make use of the analysis of information needs in Twitter. Previous literature has visioned the different and complementary roles of social networks and search engines in information seeking. What if we compare the information needs (questions) posted on Twitter and the information needs (queries) submitted to search engines? Is one different from the other? Can one predict the other? If interesting conclusions can be drawn, it will provide insight to the search engine business.

To do this, we compare the trends of information need in Twitter with the trends of Google search queries. Figure 9(a) shows the time series of the Twitter questions containing the keyword "Justin Bieber" and the Google trend of the query "Justin Bieber". We use this query as an example because it is one of the most frequent search queries in Google 2011 and is also contained in a large number of Twitter questions. We can see that information needs in Twitter is more sensitive to bursting events, while the same queries in Google presents a more periodic pattern (e.g., days-of-week pattern).

We then move forward to test whether the information needs from one platform can predict those in the other, using the Granger causality test. The Granger causality test is a statistical hypothesis test for determining whether a time series is useful in forecasting another [15]. In [3], it is used to test whether the sentiment of Twitter users can predict stock market.

Specifically, we selected a subset of keywords and manually downloaded the trends of these keywords as queries submitted to Google [6]. The subset of keywords contains twenty keywords that have a high frequency in background tweets, twenty keywords that have a high frequency in the questions, and twenty keywords from the most popular search queries in Google. To select this subset, we sorted all the keywords by frequency from the three different sources and select the top 20 named entities and nouns. If there is an overlapping keyword from multiple sources, we simply add a new keyword from the source with lower frequency of the overlapping keyword[7]. We then use the Granger causality test to test whether the three trends (Twitter background, Twitter information needs, and Google queries) of each keyword can predict each other. By changing the parameters in Granger causality test, we can test the prediction power of one time series to the other for different lags of time. In this paper, we only show the results with lag of 5 days due to the limitation of space. We obtained similar results with other different lags.

Results show that the trends of information needs in Twitter have a good predictive power in predicting trends of Google queries and are less likely to be predicted by the Google trends. This is measured by *"of how many keywords, one type of time series can predict another type of time series, given certain significance level."* From Figure 9(b), we see that the information needs in Twitter have a better predictive power than the background in predicting Google trends. From Figure 9(c), we see that the information needs in Twitter have a better predictive power in predicting Google trends rather than the other way around. Between information needs in Twitter and Google trends, the questions in Twitter have a stronger predictive power of Google queries, which successfully predicts the Google trends of more than 60% of the keywords with a significance level of 0.05. Among these keywords, 9 of them are from the popular Google queries. This is a promising insight for search engine practitioners to closely watch the questions in Twitter and improve the search results of targeted queries whenever a bursting pattern is observed.

5.6 Implications and Discussion

In this section, we presented various investigations of the questions, or information needs, in Twitter. Most analyses presented are longitudinal, based on the time series of particular statistics and comparisons between the questions and background tweets. The analysis provided interesting implications to social behavior observers, search engine practitioners, and researchers of social search.

To summarize, we confirmed that the behaviors of information seeking (questions) are substantially different from the behaviors of narrative conversations (background) in Twitter. We also find that it differs from behaviors in Web search. Some of the findings reconfirmed the conclusions in literature, such as the overrepresented topics in Twitter

---

[6]Since we don't have access to real search logs, we used the Google trend: http://www.google.com/trends/
[7]The List of the keywords can be found at http://www-personal.umich.edu/~zhezhao/projects/IN/wlist

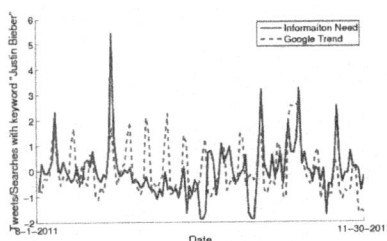
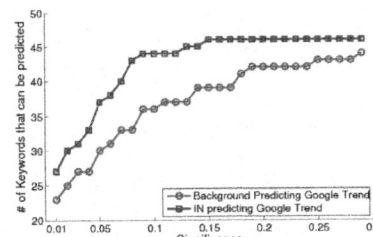

(a) Keyword: Justin Bieber

(b) Background v.s. information needs in predicting Google trends. The higher the better

(c) Information need v.s. Google trends in predicting each other. The higher the better

Figure 9: Twitter information needs can predict search queries.

questions. Interesting patterns emerge when comparing the questions with the background, which implies opportunities for providers of information service. This includes the patterns when the demands (e.g., questions) are significantly higher than the supply (e.g., background), when the information needs concentrate on particular topics, and when the spikes in information needs do not agree with those in the background.

We found that information needs in Twitter are sensitive to real world events (more sensitive than search queries). By comparing the patterns of individual keywords in questions and in the background, we foresee a new and meaningful taxonomy to discriminate the types of information needs. The comparative analysis also provides new ways to differentiate real world events and cascades of persuasion. This implies useful tools to detect propaganda and rumors from social media.

Entropy analysis provided a good way to detect real events and their impact in the topics being asked about in Twitter. It also provided a unique perspective to understand and discriminate the behaviors of individual users. Such analysis implies new tools for business providers and advertisers, which can help them to come up with a better social monetization strategy such as targeted advertising or content recommendation.

With a limited but representative set of keywords and trend information extracted from the Google trend, we found that the information needs in Twitter has a predictive power of search queries in Google. Although this conclusion has to be reevaluated when large-scale query log data is available (which we don't have access to), it implies interesting action moments for search engines. When spikes of information needs are observed in Twitter, the search engine practitioner has time to strategically optimize the search results for the corresponding topics.

Despite the interesting implications, we do see potential limitations of this analysis. For example, all our analysis is done on a **random** sample of tweets. This makes it difficult to answer questions like "*how many questions are answered,*" "*how many questions are distributed (i.e., retweeted),*" or "*consequential user behaviors after information seeking.*" These questions can only be answered with the availability of the complete set of tweets, or subset of tweets sampled in a different way (e.g., all tweets of a sub-network of users). We leave these questions about questions for future work.

6. CONCLUSION

Information needs and information seeking behaviors through social platforms attracted much interest because of its unique properties and complementary role to Web search. In this paper, we present the first large-scale analysis of information needs, or questions, in Twitter. We proposed an automatic classification algorithm that distinguishes real questions from tweets with question marks with an accuracy as high as 86.6%. Our classifier makes use of different types of features with the state-of-the-art feature selection and boosting methods.

We then present a comprehensive analysis of the large-scale collection of information needs we extracted. We found that questions being asked on Twitter are substantially different from the topics being tweeted in general. Information needs detected on Twitter have a considerable power of predicting the trends of Google queries. Many interesting signals emerge through longitudinal analysis of the volume, spikes, and entropy of questions on Twitter, which provide valuable insights to the understanding of the impact of real world events in user's information seeking behaviors, as well as the understanding of individual behavioral patterns in social platforms.

Based on the insights from this analysis, we foresee many potential applications that utilizes the better understanding of what people want to know on Twitter. One possible future work is to develop an effective algorithm to detect and predict what individual users want to know in the future. By doing this one may be able to develop better recommender systems on social network platforms. With the presumption of accessing large scale search query logs, a promising opportunity lies in a large-scale comparison of social and search behaviors in information seeking. On the other hand, improving the classifier to detect tweets with implicit information need such as tweets that is not an explicit question or without a question mark is also a potential future work. Furthermore, it is interesting to do some user-level analysis, such as studying the predictive power of different groups of users to see whether there exists a specific group of users that contributes to predicting the trend most.

Acknowledgement We thank Cliff Lampe, Paul Resnick and Rebecca Gray for the useful discussions. This work is partially supported by the National Science Foundation under grant numbers IIS-0968489, IIS-1054199, and CCF-1048168, and partially supported by the DARPA under award number W911NF-12-1-0037.

7. REFERENCES

[1] E. Agichtein, E. Brill, and S. Dumais. Improving web search ranking by incorporating user behavior information. In *Proceedings of the 29th annual international ACM SIGIR conference on Research and development in information retrieval*, pages 19–26. ACM, 2006.

[2] R. Baeza-Yates, C. Hurtado, and M. Mendoza. Query recommendation using query logs in search engines. In *Current Trends in Database Technology-EDBT 2004 Workshops*, pages 395–397. Springer, 2005.

[3] J. Bollen, H. Mao, and X.-J. Zeng. Twitter mood predicts the stock market. *CoRR*, abs/1010.3003, 2010.

[4] A. Broder, P. Ciccolo, E. Gabrilovich, V. Josifovski, D. Metzler, L. Riedel, and J. Yuan. Online expansion of rare queries for sponsored search. In *Proceedings of the 18th international conference on World wide web*, pages 511–520. ACM, 2009.

[5] E. H. Chi. Information seeking can be social. *Computer*, 42(3):42–46, 2009.

[6] G. Cong, L. Wang, C.-Y. Lin, Y.-I. Song, and Y. Sun. Finding question-answer pairs from online forums. pages 467–474, 2008.

[7] C. Cortes and V. Vapnik. Support-vector networks. *Machine Learning*, 20:273–297, 1995.

[8] M. Efron and M. Winget. Questions are content: a taxonomy of questions in a microblogging environment. *Proceedings of the American Society for Information Science and Technology*, 47(1):1–10, 2010.

[9] B. Evans and E. Chi. Towards a model of understanding social search. In *Proceedings of the 2008 ACM conference on Computer supported cooperative work*, pages 485–494. ACM, 2008.

[10] C. Fellbaum. Wordnet: An electronic lexical database. *Cambridge, MA: MIT Press*, 38(11):39–41, 1998.

[11] G. Forman. An extensive empirical study of feature selection metrics for text classification. *J. Mach. Learn. Res.*, 3:1289–1305, 2003.

[12] Y. Freund and R. E. Schapire. A decision-theoretic generalization of on-line learning and an application to boosting, 1995.

[13] R. Gallager. Claude e. shannon: A retrospective on his life, work, and impact. *Information Theory, IEEE Transactions on*, 47(7):2681–2695, 2001.

[14] J. Ginsberg, M. H. Mohebbi, R. S. Patel, L. Brammer, M. S. Smolinski, and L. Brilliant. Detecting influenza epidemics using search engine query data. *Nature*, 457:1012–1014, February 2009.

[15] C. W. J. Granger. Investigating causal relations by econometric models and cross-spectral methods. *Econometrica*, 37(3):424–38, July 1969.

[16] B. Hecht, J. Teevan, M. R. Morris, and D. Liebling. Searchbuddies: Bringing search engines into the conversation. *ICWSM*, pages 138–145, 2012.

[17] R. Jones, R. Kumar, B. Pang, and A. Tomkins. I know what you did last summer: query logs and user privacy. In *Proceedings of the sixteenth ACM conference on Conference on information and knowledge management*, pages 909–914. ACM, 2007.

[18] R. Krovetz. Viewing morphology as an inference process. *16th ACM SIGIR Conference*, pages 191–202, 1993.

[19] B. Li, X. Si, M. R. Lyu, I. King, and E. Y. Chang. Question identification on twitter. pages 2477–2480, 2011.

[20] X. Li, L. Wang, and E. Sung. Adaboost with svm-based component classifiers. *Eng. Appl. Artif. Intell.*, 21(5):785–795, 2008.

[21] Z. Liu and B. Jansen. Almighty twitter, what are people asking for? *ASIST*, 2012.

[22] T. N. Mansuy and R. J. Hilderman. Evaluating wordnet features in text classification models. In *Proceedings of the Nineteenth International Florida Artificial Intelligence Research Society Conference*, pages 568–573. AAAI Press, 2006.

[23] Q. Mei and K. Church. Entropy of search logs: how hard is search? with personalization? with backoff? In *Proceedings of the international conference on Web search and web data mining*, pages 45–54. ACM, 2008.

[24] G. A. Miller. Wordnet: A lexical database for english. *Communications of the ACM*, 38(11):39–41, 1995.

[25] M. Morris and J. Teevan. Exploring the complementary roles of social networks and search engines. *Human-Computer Interaction Consortium Workshop(HCIC)*, 2012.

[26] M. Morris, J. Teevan, and K. Panovich. What do people ask their social networks, and why?: a survey study of status message q&a behavior. In *Proceedings of the 28th international conference on Human factors in computing systems*, pages 1739–1748. ACM, 2010.

[27] M. R. Morris, J. Teevan, and K. Panovich. A comparison of information seeking using search engines and social networks. *Proceedings of 4th International AAAI Conference on Weblogs and Social Media*, 42(3):291–294, 2010.

[28] J. Nichols and J. Kang. Asking questions of targeted strangers on social networks. In *Proceedings of the ACM 2012 conference on Computer Supported Cooperative Work*, pages 999–1002. ACM, 2012.

[29] S. A. Paul, L. Hong, and E. H. Chi. Is twitter a good place for asking questions? a characterization study. *Proceedings of the 5th International AAAI Conference on Weblogs and Social Media*, 18(11):578–581, 2011.

[30] C. Shah. Measuring effectiveness and user satisfaction in Yahoo! answers. *First Monday*, 16(2-7), 2011.

[31] C. Silverstein, H. Marais, M. Henzinger, and M. Moricz. Analysis of a very large web search engine query log. In *ACm SIGIR Forum*, volume 33, pages 6–12. ACM, 1999.

[32] J. Teevan, E. Adar, R. Jones, and M. Potts. Information re-retrieval: repeat queries in yahoo's logs. In *Proceedings of the 30th annual international ACM SIGIR conference on Research and development in information retrieval*, pages 151–158. ACM, 2007.

[33] J. Teevan, S. Dumais, and D. Liebling. To personalize or not to personalize: modeling queries with variation in user intent. In *Proceedings of the 31st annual international ACM SIGIR conference on Research and development in information retrieval*, pages 163–170. ACM, 2008.

[34] J. Teevan, D. Ramage, and M. Morris. # twittersearch: a comparison of microblog search and web search. In *Proceedings of the fourth ACM international Conference on Web search and Data Mining*, pages 35–44. ACM, 2011.

[35] K. Wang and T.-S. Chua. Exploiting salient patterns for question detection and question retrieval in community-based question answering. pages 1155–1163, 2010.

[36] J. Yang, M. R. Morris, J. Teevan, L. A. Adamic, and M. S. Ackerman. Culture matters: A survey study of social q&a behavior. 2011.

[37] J. Yao, B. Cui, Y. Huang, and X. Jin. Temporal and social context based burst detection from folksonomies. In *AAAI*. AAAI Press, 2010.

[38] J. Yao, B. Cui, Y. Huang, and Y. Zhou. Bursty event detection from collaborative tags. *World Wide Web*, 15(2):171–195, 2012.

Which Vertical Search Engines are Relevant?

Understanding Vertical Relevance Assessments for Web Queries

Ke Zhou
University of Glasgow
Glasgow, United Kingdom
zhouke@dcs.gla.ac.uk

Ronan Cummins
University of Greenwich
London, United Kingdom
r.p.cummins@gre.ac.uk

Mounia Lalmas
Yahoo! Labs
Barcelona, Spain
mounia@acm.org

Joemon M. Jose
University of Glasgow
Glasgow, United Kingdom
jj@dcs.gla.ac.uk

ABSTRACT

Aggregating search results from a variety of heterogeneous sources, so-called verticals, such as news, image and video, into a single interface is a popular paradigm in web search. Current approaches that evaluate the effectiveness of aggregated search systems are based on rewarding systems that return highly *relevant* verticals for a given query, where this *relevance* is assessed under different assumptions. It is difficult to evaluate or compare those systems without fully understanding the relationship between those underlying assumptions. To address this, we present a formal analysis and a set of extensive user studies to investigate the effects of various assumptions made for assessing query vertical *relevance*. A total of more than 20,000 assessments on 44 search tasks across 11 verticals are collected through Amazon Mechanical Turk and subsequently analysed. Our results provide insights into various aspects of query vertical *relevance* and allow us to explain in more depth as well as questioning the evaluation results published in the literature.

Categories and Subject Descriptors: H.3.3 [Information Search and Retrieval]

Keywords: aggregated search, vertical selection, evaluation, user study, relevance assessment

1. INTRODUCTION

Aggregated search originated from federated search [12], which studies the simultaneous retrieval of information from various separate indexes. With the increasing amount of different types of online media (e.g. images, news, video), it is becoming popular for web search engines to present results from a set of specific verticals dispersed throughout the standard 'general web' results, for example, adding image results to the ten blue links for the query "yoga poses". Retrieving and integrating these various information sources into one interface is called *aggregated search* (AS) and has become the de-facto search paradigm in commercial search engines.

A key component of AS is *vertical selection* (VS): *selecting relevant verticals (if any) from which items will be selected to appear on the search result page (SERP)* alongside the *'general web' search results for a given query*. This has been studied in several work [3, 4, 8, 1] and various solutions have been proposed. Evaluating VS approaches [3, 16, 2, 9, 18, 17] is a challenging problem. Much of the research to date assumes that zero to many verticals are pertinent to a particular query, and aims to compare the quality of a set of selected verticals against an annotated set[1]. These type of studies all assume that the annotation set is available and is obtained by either, explicitly collecting labels from assessors [3, 16, 2, 9, 18], or implicitly, by deriving them from user interaction information [9, 5]. Despite the relative success of these evaluation methodologies, the definition of the *relevance* of a vertical, given a query, remains unclear. Different work makes different assumptions when obtaining the assessments for *relevant* verticals across a set of queries.

In this paper, the *relevance* of a vertical for a given query refers to the perceived usefulness of the vertical on a SERP. The underlying assumptions made when assessing the relevance of verticals may have a major effect on the evaluation of a SERP. Consider a user who issues the query "yoga poses" to an AS system that has access to five verticals ('news', 'image', 'video', 'shopping' and 'blog'). Prior to viewing the aggregated results, the user may believe that both the *'image'* and *'video'* vertical might provide more relevant results. If such a pre-retrieval evaluation is conducted, the user might annotate those two verticals as relevant. Conversely, a user who viewed the retrieved results from each vertical might conclude that *'video'* and *'blog'* provided the most relevant results. This may be due to the presence of a blog article that comprehensively describes yoga poses and a highly ranked *'video'* vertical that contains similar information to an *'image'* vertical that appears lower down the ranking. In this case the *'image'* vertical may seem to provide redundant information. These scenarios give us some insight into the complexity of defining the relevance of verticals.

Firstly, pre-retrieval vertical relevance assessments may differ to post-retrieval ones. This could be due to serendipity (finding a surprisingly excellent result from a specific vertical) or to a poorly designed vertical (a poor ranking function within the vertical). In addition, it is possible that making independent vertical relevance assessments does not reflect the characteristics of aggregated search, such as avoiding redundancy (an *'image'* result containing informa-

---

[1] A set of verticals annotated by a user (or users) for a given query.

tion already presented in a *'video'* result). Finally, when AS systems present vertical items embedded within *'general web'* results, it is not clear whether using *'general web'* as a reference for deciding the vertical *relevance* is an appropriate strategy. Understanding these underlying assumptions when assessing the relevance of verticals is important. This is because a different annotation set (i.e. gold standard) will affect the metrics that inform us about the performance of different VS systems.

Although existing work collects assessments (using different processes and assumptions) for evaluating VS, to our knowledge, no work has tried to comprehensively understand and compare those assessment processes and assumptions. This is the focus of this paper. Specifically, we employ all of the various strategies present in the literature, to collect vertical relevance assessments, and investigate three main research questions (RQ):

- **(RQ1)** Are there any differences between the assessments made by users from a pre-retrieval user-need perspective (viewing only vertical labels prior to seeing the final SERP) and the assessments made by users from a post-retrieval user perspective (viewing the vertical results in the final SERP)?

- **(RQ2)** When using *'general web'* results as a reference for making vertical relevance assessments, are these assessments able to predict the users' pairwise preference between *any* two verticals? Does the context (results returned from other verticals) in which vertical results are presented affect a user's perception of the relevance of the vertical of interest?

- **(RQ3)** Is the preference information provided by a population of users able to predict the "perfect" embedding position of a vertical?

To answer these three research questions, we conducted a set of large-scale user studies using the crowd-sourcing platform Amazon Mechanical Turk. In Section 2, we formally outline the problem of vertical selection assessment. Section 3 outlines our experimental design, whereas in Section 4 we present and analyse our results. We conclude the paper in Section 5 by summarising all the findings, discussing the implications of our results and pointing out limitations.

2. VERTICAL RELEVANCE ASSESSMENTS

We start by defining the process involved in collecting vertical relevance assessments. Second, we enumerate the various components within aggregated search that affect vertical relevance assessments and outline their relationships. Thirdly, we review various approaches that derive vertical relevance from the collected assessments. We then present an analysis of the assumptions made in previous work and discuss how they can affect the evaluation of aggregated search systems. We end this section with a summary.

2.1 Assessment Process

Before formally defining the vertical relevance assessment process, we first list the assumptions made for a SERP P. Given a set of verticals $V = \{v_1, v_2, ...v_n\}$, a SERP P can be denoted as $V_p = \{v_{p1}, v_{p2}, ..., v_{pn}\}$ where each v_{pi} indicates the position of the vertical block v_i on the page. For consistency with existing work [9], we assume four positions in which verticals can be embedded into the 'general web'

results: Top of Page (ToP), Middle of Page (MoP), Bottom of Page (BoP), or Not Shown (NS). When we are only interested in a binary scenario (shown or not), it is assumed that it is best to present the vertical at ToP. Note that in V_p, multiple verticals can have the same grade (e.g. two verticals can be simultaneously shown at ToP).

Given a vertical set $V = \{v_1, v_2, ...v_n\}$, the vertical relevance I_t for a search task t is represented by a weighted vector $I_t = \{i_1, i_2, ...i_n\}$, where each value i_k indicates the importance of vertical v_k to search task t. Commonly, I_t is a binary vector [3, 16], where each element indicates whether or not the vertical is *relevant* given the search task. When denoting the best position in which to embed the vertical items in the SERP (ToP, MoP, BoP, NS), a weighted vector I_t can be used [9, 2]. By assigning diminishing weight according to the embedding position[2], each weight $i_k \in I_t$ of vertical v_k is represented by the corresponding assigned weight of v_k's perfect embedding position.

To generate I_t, user studies must be conducted asking an assessor $u_j \in U = \{u_1, u_2, ...u_m\}$ to make decisions $A_j = \{a_{j1}, a_{j2}, ...a_{jl}\}$ over all verticals V. There are generally two types of assessment a_{jk}: absolute assessments ("what is the quality of v_i") and preference-based assessment ("does v_i present better information than v_j"). As AS is concerned with presenting vertical results integrated within 'general web' results, preference assessments [9, 16, 3, 2, 18, 17] have been more widely used. The number of pair-wise assessments l the assessor u_j needs to make for A_j is a matter for research, and may be restricted by the budget of a particular study. Regardless, for each pair-wise preference assessment a_{jk}, there are various factors that influence assessors' decisions. We discuss these in Section 2.2. Ultimately, an $m \times l$ matrix M_t containing all assessments from all users in U for search task t is obtained. A conflation method to derive the final vertical relevance vector I_t from the matrix M_t is used. Different methods have been used to derive this final vector, which we review in Section 2.3.

After I_t is obtained, an aggregated search page P can be evaluated based on this information. Given I_t, we can evaluate the SERP P based on how V_p correlates with I_t. Various metrics can be employed to achieve this. Precision, recall and the f-measure have been used when I_t is treated as a binary decision [3, 16]. Recently, risk has been considered and incorporated into risk-aware VS metrics [18]. When allowing multiple embedding positions within a SERP, the distance between V_p and a perfect page $V_p^{Perfect}$ derived from I_t can be used [2]. The further the distance from the perfect page, the worse the performance of the system that generated that SERP P.

2.2 Making Preference Assessments

This section reviews previous work on making preference assessments for evaluating vertical relevance.

2.2.1 Dependency of Relevance

Current work on determining the preference assessments A can be classified into two categories: *anchor-based* and *inter-dependent* approaches. The former assumes that the quality of the anchoring 'general web' results serve as a reference criteria for deciding vertical relevance (whether an

---
[2]The higher the position, the larger the weight is, i.e. for the four embedding positions used in our work, weight(ToP) > weight(MoP) > weight(BoP) > weight(NS).

assessor believes the vertical results will improve the SERP when added to the 'general web' results). This is achieved by asking assessors to assess each vertical v_i individually, in an independent pair-wise fashion against the 'general web' reference page. A number of work [9, 16, 3] follows this approach. *Inter-dependent* approaches assume that the quality of verticals is relative and dependent on each other. These approaches gather pair-wise preference data over any, and many, possible pairs of verticals v including the '*general web*' w. Arguello et al's work [2] fits into this category. For *anchor-based approaches*, the number of assessments to be made per assessor, l, equals to the number of verticals n. For *inter-dependent approaches*, l will often be much greater than n (e.g. $\frac{1}{2} \cdot (n+1) \cdot n$ in [2]).

2.2.2 Influencing Factors

Various factors can affect a user u_j when assessing a_{jk}, with respect to a specific vertical result v_k:

- **(Result Quality)** the quality of the retrieved results from vertical v_k.
- **(Orientation)** a user's (u_j) orientation (or preference) to information from a vertical v_k.
- **(Aesthetic)** the aesthetic nature of a vertical v_k.

The *result quality* of the retrieved items from a specific vertical depends on both the contents of the vertical v_k and the ranking function of the vertical v_k. For a given search task t, the more topically relevant items contained in the vertical v_k collection, the better the results are likely to be. More importantly, the higher the relevant items are ranked within the vertical, the better the *result quality* is. Either a vertical v_k collection with very few relevant items or a poor ranking function can degrade the user's perception of the quality of the vertical v_k retrieved results.

A user's *orientation* to a vertical v_k reflects the user's (u_j) own perception of the usefulness (utility) of the vertical to the search task t. The user may have his or her own personalised preference over different verticals. As pointed out in [3, 11], it is not only *result quality* that satisfies a user's need, but items from different verticals also satisfy a user's need differently. It is the *type of information* that affects the user's perception of usefulness (i.e. orientation) for an information need.

Vertical *aesthetics* represents the aesthetic nature of the vertical v_k retrieved results. For example, it has been demonstrated in [11, 2] that the visually attractive nature of image results tends to increase users engagement on a SERP, compared to those that do not contain images.

2.3 Deriving Relevance from Assessments

The anchor-based and inter-dependent based approaches use different strategies for deriving vertical relevance (I_t) from the assessments (M_t) for a search task t. For *anchor-based approaches*, most of previous work [16, 3] rank all the verticals of interest based on the percentage of assessors' preference over a 'general web' anchor. Therefore, a majority preference for a particular vertical leads to the most *relevant* vertical for a specific search task. For *inter-dependent approaches*, the Schulze voting method [2, 10] is the most widely used. For two verticals v_i and v_j, if more assessors preferred v_i over v_j than vice versa, then we say that, v_i directly beats v_j. A beatpath from v_i to v_j can be either a direct or an indirect defeat. The strength of an indirect beatpath is the number of votes associated with its weakest direct defeat. Finally, v_i defeats v_j if the strongest (direct or indirect) beatpath from v_i to v_j is stronger than the one from v_j to v_i. All verticals of interest are then ranked by their number of defeats.

2.4 Prior Work

When collecting an assessment a_{jk}, current work makes a number of different assumptions (dependency of relevance, influencing factors) to guide the assessments. Based on the assumptions made, they show the corresponding information to the user for them to make assessments. We formally review and summarize the underlying assumptions made in a number of studies. A short summary is given in Table 1.

Traditionally, in federated search [12, 7] (often known as *distributed* information retrieval), vertical relevance I_t is assumed to solely depend on *result quality*, which is determined by the summation of the number of topically relevant items within a vertical collection. The more topically relevant items the vertical collection contained, the better the given vertical is assumed to be. When evaluating a SERP P, the quality of the page is determined by evaluating the topical relevance of the items returned (and merged from various verticals), based on traditional information retrieval metrics (e.g. precision, MAP). This type of evaluation is heavily focused on topical relevance.

In aggregated search, for example, Zhou et al. [16] assumed that only vertical *orientation* contributes to the usefulness of the page. Therein, the assessors are asked to use the '*general web*' results as an anchor to assess the usefulness of a given vertical (by only showing the vertical label). Without viewing the retrieved results or the vertical collection, only when the assessor thinks that the vertical can potentially provide more appropriate results than the '*general web*', would he/she label it as *relevant*. In that research, four assessors are asked for assessments for each vertical. The vertical relevance I_t is determined in a binary manner (ToP or None), by using a basic assessor preference thresholding approach (e.g. if 75% of the assessors prefer v_i over w, then we label v_i as "ToP", otherwise we label it as "NS"). Finally, VS evaluation is based on the f-measure.

In Arguello et al. [2], although not stated explicitly, it is assumed that the usefulness of the vertical v_k is determined by a combination of *result quality*, *orientation* and *aesthetics*. While viewing results retrieved from each vertical collection using a ranking function unique to the vertical, the assessors are asked to state the preference between any two verticals from $V \bigcup \{w\}$. Four assessors are used for assessing each pair. Different from [16], which uses '*general web*' results as an anchor, the assessments are made between any v_i and v_j pairs and a voting strategy is used to determine I_t, i.e. the perfect position of the vertical to be presented. The quality of the page is then measured by calculating the distance to a reference page (a "perfect" AS page).

In [9, 2], a vertical relevance is assessed by presenting the SERP with the web results and vertical results separately. In Ponnuswami et al. [9], the assessors are asked to rank the vertical relevance on a scale of 0 to 3, indicating whether it should be shown at BoP, MoP or ToP. Only one assessor is used. The differences between [2] and [9] is that, instead of voting across all verticals, the '*general web*' retrieved results are used as an anchor to determine the vertical importance.

Table 1: Summary of Vertical Relevance Assumptions Made in Previous Works.

Work	Relevance Dependency		Influencing Factors			Assessment		# Assessors
	Inter-dependent	Anchor-based	Result Quality	Orientation	Aesthetic	Binary	Graded	
Federated Search [12]	✓		✓			✓		1
Zhou et al. [16]		✓		✓			✓	4
Ponnuswami et al. [9]		✓	✓	✓	✓		✓	1
Arguello et al. [2]	✓		✓	✓	✓	✓		4

2.5 Summary of Aims

We are interested in answering three research questions (RQ1 to RQ3). Given the more formal treatment of the task of aggregated search described in this section, these research questions can be stated as follows:

- **RQ1** deals with comparing the user perspective ([16] and [9] (binary assessment variant)) during the assessment stage (obtaining a_{jk}). When asking assessors to make a_{jk}, are there any differences between the assessments made by only considering *orientation* (pre-retrieval perspective), and the ones that consider a combination of *result quality*, *orientation* and *aesthetics* (post-retrieval perspective)?

- **RQ2** is concerned with comparing the anchor-based approach with an inter-dependent approach ([9] (binary assessment variant) and [2]) during the collection of all assessments A with respect to v_k. We also examine whether the context of other verticals can affect the relevance of the vertical of interest.

- **RQ3** deals with the positioning of vertical results. When asking a set of assessors to make assessments a_{jk} using a binary decision (ToP and NS), is it possible to use the fraction of assessors' preference assessments M_t to derive an accurate graded vertical relevance I_t to indicate the best position for embedding the vertical results (ToP, MoP, BoP and NS)?

3. EXPERIMENTAL DESIGN

This section introduces the methodology for conducting our users studies, followed by a detailed design of each study.

3.1 Methodology

We conducted three studies that follow a similar protocol. All studies consisted of subjects that pair-wisely assessed the quality of two result sets for a series of search tasks. All studies have a similar objective, to investigate the correlation between the vertical *relevance* derived when using one assessment assumption to the vertical *relevance* derived under another assumption.

Figure 1: Flow Diagram Description of Experimental Protocol for Studies 1 to 3.

3.1.1 Protocol

The three studies follow a similar protocol shown in Figure 1. Subjects were given access to an assessment page that consists of a task description, a search task and two search results (tiles), and were asked to make pair-wise preference assessments. Prior to each study, the subjects were presented with a brief instruction, summarizing the experimental protocol and the assessment criteria. They were told to imagine they were performing a natural information search task. Given two search result sets originating from two search engines, the subjects were told to select the result set that would best satisfy the search task. The subjects were then presented with an Assessment Page (ASP) (a screenshot of an ASP is shown in the middle of Figure 2). The experimental manipulation was controlled via each ASP, as discussed in Section 3.1.3.

Following a search query (e.g. "living in India") shown at the top of ASP, the search task description is given in the form of a request for information (e.g. "Find information about living in India."). Under the task description, two search tiles are presented where each tile shows a separate set of search results for the query. Then the subjects made their selection using a "submit" button.

The subjects (assessors) could choose to perform as many tasks as they wished. To avoid learning effects, we ensured that each assessor was not shown the same task more than once. All studies were performed via a crowd-sourcing platform, Amazon Mechanical Turk[3]. The methods employed to collected the data via this platform is described in Section 3.1.4. The result sets shown on each ASP were pre-crawled offline. To lower assessment burden, subjects were unable to browse outside the ASP, i.e. clicking any links within the result page did not redirect them to external web pages. The snippets on the ASP were the sole source of evidence to assess the SERP quality.

3.1.2 Verticals and Search Tasks

In web search, a vertical is associated with content dedicated to either a topic (e.g. "finance"), a media type (e.g. "images") or a genre (e.g. "news")[4]. In this paper, we are mainly concerned with the latter two types, which is less well-studied than the former. We use a number of verticals (listed in Table 2). Those verticals reflect a representative set of vertical engines used in current commercial aggregated web search engines. Instead of constructing verticals from scratch, we use a representative state-of-the-art vertical search engine for each vertical, as listed in Table 2.

Search tasks were chosen to have a varying number and type of relevant verticals. From a preliminary study [16, 15], we collected annotations of users' preferred verticals for 320 search tasks (from the TREC million query and web tracks, originally derived from search engine logs). The preferred verticals reflect the perceived usefulness of a vertical from the user need perspective, without regard to the quality of the vertical results. This is achieved by instructing assessors to make pairwise preference assessments, comparing each

---
[3] https://www.mturk.com
[4] A topic-focused vertical may contain documents of various types, standard web pages, images, reviews, etc.

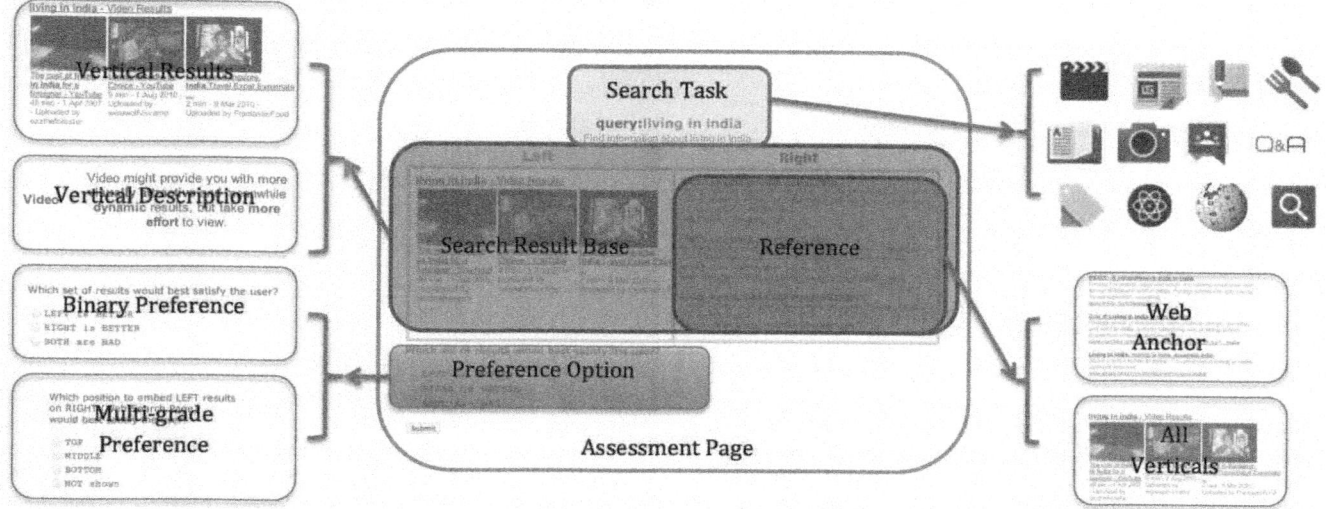

Figure 2: Various Components for Manipulations on Assessment Page of Studies 1 to 3

Table 2: Verticals Used in this Paper.

Vertical	Vertical Engines	Document	Type
Image	Google Image	online images	media
Video	Google Video	online videos	
Recipe	Google Recipe	recipe page	genre
News	Google News	news articles	
Books	Google Books	book review page	
Blog	Yahoo! Blog	blog articles	
Answer	Google Q&A	answers to questions	
Shopping	Google Shopping	product shopping page	
Discussion	Google Forums	discussion thread from forums	
Scholar	Google Scholar	research technical report	
Wiki	wiki.com	encyclopedic entries	
General web	vertical-filtered google.com	standard web pages	

vertical in turn to the reference 'general web' vertical without viewing any vertical results (including the general web). When making assessments, only vertical names/labels were shown and at least four assessors judged each search task.

We then select 44 tasks from those 320 search tasks. The selection is to ensure a wide coverage of information needs with different preferred verticals, including those with no preferred verticals. For each of the 11 verticals, we select 3 search tasks where more than 75% of the assessors preferred the vertical. We also select 11 search tasks where none of the verticals were preferred. For each task description, to avoid any bias, we ensured that it did not contain any vertical-explicit request (e.g. "find images for yoga poses."). Twelve representative example tasks (one per preferred vertical) are shown in Table 3. Although the search task set is not large, it is sufficient to investigate certain aspects of vertical relevance, upon which large-scale user studies can subsequently be carried out.

3.1.3 Assessment Manipulation

To answer our research questions, each ASP has five components that can be manipulated:

- *search task*: the information need (or search task) that assessors encounter;

- *vertical of interest*: the vertical that is presented for assessments;
- *search result base*: the default type of information presented on the SERP for each ASP;
- *assessment reference*: the reference SERP (one of the two result sets on an ASP) against which an assessor will make a preference;
- *preference option level*: the number of options allowed for an assessment (binary or graded) of an ASP.

Search tasks are manipulated to provide a more complete evaluation of AS information needs. *Verticals of interest* are manipulated to provide a comprehensive evaluation of various verticals for AS. *Search result base* refers to the default type of information provided for assessments and in our study was manipulated for two possible options: search engine description or retrieved search results. Those two options reflect on different influencing factors for assessments. The former type reflects on assessors' pre-retrieval user need perspective (orientation) whereas the latter reflects on assessors' post-retrieval user utility perspective (a combination of orientation, result quality and aesthetic). This relates to **RQ1** and a detailed design of this manipulation is described in Study 1. *Assessment reference* deals with which information is used as a reference to make the pair-wise preference assessments for a vertical. It is manipulated to investigate whether there is a dependency between (relevant) verticals. We manipulate this to compare *anchor-based approach* and *inter-dependent approach* for **RQ2** and a detailed design of this can be found in Study 2. Manipulation of the *Preference option level* provides different levels of granularity for assessors to specify their preference based on the quality of two SERPs. A more fine-grained option (multi-graded) provides more details than other simple options (binary). This is manipulated to investigate how much information is lost when assessors are provided with simpler options. This variable relates to **RQ3** and its investigation forms Study 3.

We have five independent variables that can be manipulated within an ASP. However, due to a limited budget, instead of using a full factorial design with all the indepen-

Table 3: Example Search Tasks.

Search Task Description	Preferred Vertical	Query
I am looking for information on the Welch corgi dog.	Image	welch corgi
Find beginners instructions to sewing, both by hand and by machine.	Video	sewing instructions
I am looking for cooking suggestions of turkey leftover.	Recipe	turkey leftover
Find music, tour dates, and information about the musician Neil Young.	News	neil young
Find information on the history of music.	Books	who invented music
Find information about living in India.	Blog	living in india
Find information on how I can lower my heart rate.	Answer	lower heart rate
I am looking for sources for parts for cars, preferably used.	Shopping	used car parts
Find "reasonable" dieting advice, that is not fads or medications but reasonable methods for weight loss.	Discussion	dieting
Find information on obsessive-compulsive disorder.	Scholar	ocd
Find information about the Sun, the star in our Solar System.	Wiki	the sun
Find the homepage of Raffles Hotel in Singapore.	General-web Only	raffles

dent variables, we control four variables when investigating one factor. We set the four variables to their most common setting, in a typical AS scenario, and study the change in the behaviour of our assessors when the test variable (which we are currently testing) changes. Except for *search task* and *vertical of interest*, the three other independent variables in our study represent the RQs that we wish to answer:

- *search result base*: pre-retrieval user need (by showing only vertical descriptions) or post-retrieval user utility (by showing retrieved vertical results).
- *assessment reference*: 'general web' anchor (showing only 'general web') or all verticals (including both 'general web' and all other verticals).
- *preference option*: binary or multi-graded.

To measure the effect of the independent variables on users' vertical relevance assessments, we investigate two dependent variables: the **inter-assessor agreement** (measured by Fleiss' Kappa K_F [6]) and the **vertical relevance correlation** (measured by Spearman correlation). *The inter-assessor agreement* focuses on measuring the ambiguity (or difficulty) of the vertical relevance assessments. This can give us insights on whether it is difficult for assessors to draw agreement on assessing vertical relevance. *The vertical relevance correlation* measures for two assessment processes, whether one agrees with the other for the search task. This can give us insights on comparing different assessment processes and determining which component of the assessment should be controlled more strictly so that it leads to stronger correlations. We report the results of these two dependent variables for all of our studies.

As we are mainly interested in measuring assessor agreement over assessed preference pairs, instead of employing metrics (e.g. overlap measures [14]) to measure inter-assessor agreement on absolute assessments (query-document topical relevance assessment), we used Kappa measure, as prevalently used in previous work [2]. We select Fleiss' Kappa (denoted K_F) to measures the (chance-corrected) inter-assessor agreement between any pair of assessors over a set of triplets. This allows us to ignore the identity of the assessor-pair because it is designed to measure agreement over instances labelled by different (even disjoint) sets of assessors. Specifically, when M_t is available, for all the assessments for a particular assessment a_{jk} or a set of assessments (A_j) for all assessors U, we can calculate the Fleiss' Kappa over all pairs. Therefore, after calculating K_F for both assessment processes, we can compare their assessment agreement, to obtain insights into assessment difficulty and diversity.

We used Spearman's Correlation as our main tool for our data analysis as it is widely used in IR and it is a powerful statistical method to determine the dependency between two variables of interest (two assessment processes in our work). Due to space limitation, more in-depth analysis of the data (e.g. close manual examination) is left for future work.

3.1.4 Crowd-sourcing Data Collection

Our preference assessment data is collected over the Amazon Mechanical Turk crowd-sourcing platform, where each worker was compensated $0.01 for each assessment made. For each ASP, we collect four assessment points. Running user studies on Mechanical Turk requires quality control and we used two approaches for achieving this: "trap" HITs and "trap" search tasks. Both these types of trap are only used to identify careless and/or malicious assessors. Following [13], "trap" HITs are created following a set procedure. Each "trap" HIT consists of a triplet (q, i, j), where either page i or j are taken from a query other than q. We interpreted an assessor preferring the set of extraneous results as evidence of careless assessement. "Trap" search tasks are defined as the search task that contains an explicit reference to a preferred vertical (e.g. "Find information from preferred shopping search results on football tickets"). An assessor who failed to provide preference to an explicitly specified preferred vertical a predefined number of times was treated as careless assessor. Careless assessors were filtered out and all their assessments were discarded. The actual assessments from the traps were also not used in our analysis.

It is objectively difficult to judge whether one assessor is careless since different users might have different vertical preferences for the same search task, and the cost associated with different types of errors (e.g. irrelevant verticals, relevant verticals presented at the bottom of the page or bad retrieved results of relevant verticals), as demonstrated by previous work [17, 2]. As we have two different "trap" approaches and a large percentage of assessments are "traps"[5], we believe that our methodology was able to filter out large percentage of careless assessors.

3.2 Study 1: Comparing User Perspective

Study 1 aims to investigate whether vertical relevance derived from different user perspectives correlate with each other. We controlled the *search reference* to 'general-web' anchor and *preference option* to binary. Therefore, we provide a vertical of interest and '*general web*' together on

---

[5]For example, Study 1 (Section 3.2) contains 18.4% "traps" out of all assessments, which means that approximately for every six assessments made, the assessor encountered one "trap".

an ASP and ask the assessor to provide a binary preference ("left is better" and "right is better"). To avoid overburdening assessors, we also include an option ("both are bad") that captures the scenario where a user is confused due to, for example, poor quality of both SERPs.

For the remaining three independent variables *search task*, *vertical of interest* and *search result base*, we used a full factorial design. We used a total of 44 experimental search tasks that vary in number of preferred verticals, as shown in the upper right in Figure 2. Eleven verticals of interest are used. As specified above, the *search result base* variable manipulated the base information for assessments and had two values: "vertical description" and "vertical results". As shown on the upper left in Figure 2, for "vertical results", the top three items of the vertical search results are returned by the commercial vertical search engine employed. When making assessments, "vertical results" reflects the post-retrieval user utility for each vertical of interest. The "vertical description" did not vary across search tasks. We provided a general description of each vertical that specified the item types provided by the vertical and its unique characteristics (e.g. video results might provide more **visually attractive** and **dynamic** results, but may take **more effort** to view). We aimed to provide an objective description of the typical contents of the vertical to avoid any bias. The vertical relevance assessments derived from "vertical description" reflects a pre-retrieval user need perspective (before retrieving from any verticals, which type of information may satisfy the user needs?).

Study 1 had 968 unique conditions (44 search tasks × 2 search result base × 11 verticals of interest). To ensure the quality of assessments, we manipulated 5 "trap" tasks (randomly selected from 11 "trap" tasks, one per vertical) and 1 "trap" HITs for every search task under each search result base. We collected four data points for each condition and in total we had 3872 assessments (4744 assessments including all "trap" tasks and HITs).

3.3 Study 2: Effects of Context

Study 2 aims to investigate the impact of the context of other verticals to the relevance assessments of a chosen vertical. Study 2 controlled the *preference option* to binary and *search result base* to "vertical results". For the remaining three independent variables *search task*, *vertical of interest* and *search reference*, Study 2 used a full factorial design. The *search reference* had two possible values: "general-web anchor" and "all-verticals", as shown in the lower right of Figure 2. The former used each vertical of interest with 'general web' anchor to form 11 assessment pairs for each search task. The latter used a full possible space of each vertical of interest and all other verticals (including three 'general web' result sets: top-three, top-four-to-six, top-seven-to-ten) to form a total of 91 assessment pairs for each search task. The assessment pairs of the former is a subset of the latter.

Study 2 had 4004 unique conditions (44 search tasks × 91 assessment pairs). We used the same quality control strategy as for study 1. In total we had 16016 assessments (19620 assessments including all "trap" tasks and HITs).

3.4 Study 3: Multi-graded Preference

Study 3 aims to investigate whether it is possible to derive multi-graded preferences using binary preference from a number of users. Study 3 controlled the *search result base* to "vertical results", *vertical reference* to "general-web anchor". We use all of the top-ten 'general web' results as an anchor in this study. This is to be consistent with the multi-graded assessments we aim to investigate as described below. For the remaining three independent variables *search task*, *vertical of interest* and *preference option*, study 2 used a full factorial design. Specifically, the *preference option* is manipulated to be either *binary* or *multi-graded*, as shown in the lower left in Figure 2. Note that this is to compare with the 'general web' results. For the former, assessors were asked for binary assessments (binary preference, i.e. ToP or NS), while for the latter assessors were asked for multi-graded assessments (ToP, MoP, BoP or NS).

Study 2 had 968 unique conditions (44 search tasks × 2 preference options × 11 verticals) using the same quality control strategy as for study 1. We obtained 3872 assessments (4744 assessments including "trap" tasks and HITs).

4. EXPERIMENTAL RESULTS

Our goal is to investigate the correlation of vertical *relevance* when derived from studies with different underlying assumptions. We measure the correlation between two sets of relevance assessments using Spearman's correlation. In each case, we outline whether this correlation is significant[6]. We denote the significance by ▲ (with $p < 0.05$).

4.1 Study 1

We report the results that compare user vertical relevance I_t from different perspectives. Specifically, whether **(1) orientation (pre-retrieval vertical preference)** and the **(2) topical relevance of post-retrieval search results** affect a user's perception of a vertical relevance. For (2), following a standard TREC-style evaluation methodology, we collected graded topical relevance assessments (highly, marginally and not relevant) for the top search results returned from the verticals (including 'general web'). Then for each assessment pair (v_i, w), we use $nDCG(v_i) - nDCG(w)$ to quantify the weighted preference of v_i over w based on topical relevance.

We examined the user agreement when assessing the pairwise preference in both a pre-retrieval and post-retrieval scenario. The Fleiss' Kappa (K_F) obtained for both pre-retrieval and post-retrieval are 0.47 and 0.40, respectively. In both scenarios, the inter-assessor agreement is not high (moderate). This indicates the difficulty (or ambiguity) of AS in general; different users tend to make different decisions regarding the *relevance* of a vertical. A low K_F on a particular query indicates that it is a particularly ambiguous query. Unexpectedly, we observed that there is even more disagreement between assessors when they are allowed to view the results retrieved from each vertical (on each SERP) (post-retrieval setting). In that setting, given that the assessors have more information to make their assessments, one would expect more agreement. However, this is not the case. A number of reasons may cause this. Firstly, it should be noted that as we have only four assessors, the difference in inter-assessor agreement can be substantially affected by one assessor. Secondly, and more importantly, it is possible that providing the search results to each assessor increases the difficulty and ambiguity of the assessment process. This may be due to the fact that the user now has to

---

[6]We determine the significance by using a permutation test.

Table 4: (Study 1) Vertical Relevance using Spearman Correlation with respect to Post-retrieval Approach on a Variety of Influencing Factors (Orientation, Topical Relevance).

Verticals	Image	Video	Recipe	News	Books	Blog	Answer	Shopping	Discussion	Scholar	Wiki	Average
Orientation	0.547▲	0.654▲	0.864▲	0.524▲	0.516▲	0.385▲	0.563▲	0.610▲	0.305▲	0.450▲	0.404▲	0.529
Topical Relevance	0.092	0.205▲	0.637▲	0.301▲	0.187▲	0.429▲	0.354▲	0.264▲	0.571▲	0.393▲	0.484▲	0.356

take more factors into account when making an assessment (pre-retrieval vertical orientation, item relevance, visual attractiveness). These factors may lead to more noisy assessments as each assessor may place different emphasis on these factors. We also calculated the Spearman correlation of the inter-assessor agreement (K_F) between the pre-retrieval and post-retrieval assessments. We found that this correlation is high (0.749), indicating that in both scenarios (pre-retrieval and post-retrieval) the assessors encounter difficulty with the same queries.

Furthermore, we report the Spearman correlation of the two influencing factors (orientation and topical relevance of items) with respect to the post-retrieval vertical relevance for a variety of verticals. The higher the correlation, the more important the factor is in influencing the utility of the search results (from the user point of view). This is shown in Table 4. We can observe that the average Spearman correlation of orientation (pre-retrieval) and topical relevance with respect to post-retrieval vertical relevance over all verticals is 0.529 (moderate) and 0.356 (low), respectively. These correlations are not particularly high (but all are significant) for both influencing factors. Generally, *orientation* is more highly correlated with the utility of a set of search results than *topical relevance*. This demonstrates that neither factor can solely determine the user's perception of the utility of the search results. In addition, in our data, the type of vertical (orientation) is more important for the search result utility than the topical relevance of the search results.[7] When we analyze the *orientation* of each vertical, we observe that some of the verticals obtain comparatively high correlation ('*Video*', '*Recipe*' and '*Shopping*') whereas others obtain comparatively low correlation ('*Blog*' and '*Discussion*'). This suggests that some verticals are inherently more ambiguous in terms of their usefulness for the search task than others.

For *topical relevance*, we observe that the topical relevance of retrieved results for the '*Image*' vertical does not contribute significantly to the search results utility. An in-depth examination showed that this can be explained by the lack of variability of the topical relevance. We observe that most returned image results are topically relevant. Conversely, the topical relevance of the items of other verticals ('*Blog*', '*Discussion*') contributes a larger degree to the utility of a SERP. This is because for those verticals, the results are too similar to '*general web*' results and in this case, topical relevance is the most important aspect for search utility (as in traditional web search). For '*Recipe*', topical relevance correlates highly both with orientation and search utility. This is because '*Recipe*' is more likely to contain relevant results only when user are oriented to that vertical.

Table 5: Overlap of the Top-three Relevant Verticals for Pre-retrieval (Orientation) and Post-retrieval (Search Uutility) for the same Search Tasks.

Overlap	3	2	1	0
Num of Tasks	5	20	14	5
Fraction	11.4%	45.4%	31.8%	11.4%

Thirdly, as we are more concerned with highly relevant verticals, we investigate whether the top relevant verticals are the same for pre- and post-retrieval scenarios. We extract the top-three most preferred verticals from both assessment scenarios and compare them. We calculate the overlap between them and the results are shown in Table 5. There is generally some overlap between vertical relevance for around 90% of the queries. In addition, in 56.8% of the search tasks at least two out of three relevant verticals are in common, when relevance is derived from the different assessment methods (pre- and post-retrieval assessments).

Finally, we investigate whether there is an aesthetic bias for verticals that present more visually salient results ('*Image*', *Video*' and *Shopping*' in our study). We compare the number of occurrences of those verticals that appear within the top-three verticals for various search tasks. Consistent with previous work, we found there is an aesthetic bias in user's perception of the utility of the search results. There are in total 21 occurrences of those verticals appearing within the top-three verticals for all search tasks in the post-retrieval case, compared with 11 occurrences within the pre-retrieval case.

To summarize, Study 1 shows that both *orientation* and *topical relevance* contribute significantly to the search result utility, whereas the impact of *orientation* is more important. In addition, there is an aesthetic bias to user's perception of the search results utility.

4.2 Study 2

In Study 2, we manipulated the assessment reference for each vertical of interest. Again, the reference is manipulated by presenting only general-web anchor results (anchor-based approach) in one approach and all vertical results (interdependent approach) in a separate approach. To derive I_t using assessments M_t obtained for each search task, we used an existing approach. For the *anchor-based approach*, we ranked all the verticals of interest based on the percentage of assessors' preference over 'general web' anchor. For the *inter-dependent approach*, we used Schulze voting method [2]. We report the results comparing user's vertical relevance I_t from both the anchor-based approach and the interdependent approach. For the former, we vary the quality of the 'general web' anchor by using different result sets (Web-1: top 1-3 items, Web-2: top4-6 items or Web-3: top7-10 items). We aim to investigate whether there are significant differences between them.

---

[7] Note that due to our selection of vertical search engines (highly performing verticals) where most vertical search results contain topically relevant items for most of the search tasks, our results are biased to this scenario and might not generalize when vertical search engines perform badly.

Table 6: (Study 2) Spearman Correlation of Vertical Relevance Derived between Anchor-based Approach (using anchors Web-1, Web-2, Web-3) and Inter-dependent Approach.

Anchor	Web-1	Web-2	Web-3	Average
Correlation	0.626▲	0.515▲	0.579▲	0.573

Table 7: Overlap of the Top-three Relevant Vertical for the Anchor-based Approach (Web-1) and the Inter-dependent Approach on same Search Tasks.

Overlap	3	2	1	0
Num of Tasks	12	19	10	3
Fraction	27.3%	43.2%	22.7%	7.8%

We look at the user assessment agreement. The Fleiss' Kappa (K_F) obtained for the anchor-based and inter-dependent approaches are 0.40 and 0.42, respectively. The user assessment agreement is not high (moderate) and, generally, there is not much difference between the assessment agreement of the two approaches. The slight increase of user agreement for assessments in the inter-dependent approach might be due to the comparative ease in assessing some vertical-pairs, over assessing vertical-anchor-pairs.

We show the query-specific Spearman correlation of the anchor-approach using different anchors (Web-1, Web-2, Web-3) with respect to the inter-dependent approach. The results are shown in Table 6. We can observe several important trends. Firstly, the correlation between the anchor-based and inter-dependent approaches is *moderate*. From closer examination, we see many "exchange" between verticals of similar intended level and most of these "exchanges" occur within lowly vertical relevance level. As we are more concerned with highly intended verticals, similarly to Study 1, we report the overlapped top relevant vertical between the two approaches in Table 7. Generally the overlap of the top-three relevant verticals between these two approaches is quite high (more than 70% of the search tasks have the same perception of at least two out of three relevant verticals).

We observe that although there are differences between the approaches that use different anchors, the differences are not large in general (all moderate correlations). Web-1 generally correlates higher than Web-2 and Web-3, and there is not much differences between Web-2 and Web-3. This is quite surprising. We assumed that the change of topical relevance level of the anchor results[8] would result in a change of a user's perception of the results utility. However as this is not the case, we suspect that this can be explained by the finding in Study 1, where when presented with a 'general web' anchor, it is the *type* of information that leads to a more significant impact on the quality of the result set, indeed more so than topical relevance.

Finally, to demonstrate the interaction between verticals, an analysis of the difference between the inter-dependent ranking and anchor-based (Web-1) ranking suggests that context matters, i.e. the relevance of the latter vertical diminishes when the former vertical (context) is shown in advance. We analyse this by finding the most frequent discordant pairs of verticals (v_i, v_j) within the two approaches. All the candidate pairs consist of verticals of interest occurring within the top verticals for at least one approach. We found that most pairs are concordant with each other but there are about 14% of discordant pairs. Specifically, there are several distinct discordant pairs that consistently occur for different number of top results (3 to 6). These pairs are ('Answer', 'Wiki'), ('Books', 'Scholar'), ('Answer', 'Scholar'). For example, ('Answer', 'Wiki') pair means that when 'Answer' is presented before 'Wiki', the relevance of 'Wiki' is diminished. This might be explained by the fact that once a direct answer is available, reading a long wiki article will provide less utility to the user. These results demonstrate that the context of other verticals can diminish the utility of a vertical. This finding requires further examination.

4.3 Study 3

We investigate how various thresholding approaches can be used to accurately derive multi-graded vertical relevance for the anchor-based approaches. We also apply this to the Schulze voting method for the inter-dependent approach [2].

For each search task, based on the multi-graded assessments for each vertical v_i (assessed by four independent assessors), we first derive the ground-truth of the "perfect" embedding position[9] (and corresponding "perfect" page). To achieve this, we assume that there is a continuous range for each grade ([3, 4] for ToP, [2, 3) for MoP, [1, 2) for BoP and [0, 1) for NS). We assign each grade the medium of its corresponding range as its weight (3.5 for ToP, 2.5 for MoP, 1.5 for BoP and 0.5 for NS). Then for four assessors' judged grade, we decide the "perfect" position by calculating the expected assessed grade's weight and finding its corresponding fitted grade range.[10]

For the anchor-based approaches, we use a set of thresholding settings (for binary assessment, this is the fraction of assessors that deem the vertical as relevant) for ToP, MoP, BoP, respectively. For a given vertical, when the fraction of its assessors' assigned "relevant" is larger or equal to the weight assigned for a given grade, we treat that vertical as that specific grade. We vary those thresholding settings for different risk-levels: risk-seeking (0.5, 0.25, 0), risk-medium (0.75, 0.5, 0.25) and risk-averse (1, 0.75, 0.5). As described above, we also use another existing approach (Schulze voting method [2]) for the inter-dependent approach.

Firstly, we look at the user assessment agreement. The Fleiss' Kappa (K_F) obtained for binary and multi-graded approaches are 0.40 and 0.35, respectively. The agreement of multi-graded assessments is not high.[11] From a closer examination, we found that this might result from each assessors' unique preference of verticals and their risk-level [18] (i.e. their willingness to take risk to view more irrelevant verticals). Some of the assessors tend to choose more verticals to be shown at earlier ranking (e.g. ToP, BoP) while oth-

---

[8]We found that the averaged nDCG values satisfy $nDCG(Web\text{-}1) > nDCG(Web\text{-}2) > nDCG(Web\text{-}3)$ based on topical relevance.

[9]Note that this "perfectness" of embedding position and page is likely to be sub-optimal. This is because the multi-grade assessment methodology does not capture the context of other verticals.

[10]For example, when two, one, one and zero assessors assign ToP, MoP, BoP and NS, respectively, we obtain the expected weight of grade $(2 \cdot 3.5 + 1 \cdot 2.5 + 1 \cdot 1.5 + 0)/4 = 2.75$ and therefore its "perfect" embedding position is MoP (as $2.75 \in [2, 3)$).

[11]Note that this K_F agreement is not directly comparable to others as the number of assessment grades changes.

Table 8: (Study 3) Spearman Correlation of Optimal Pages derived from Binary Assessments and Ground-truth Page derived from Multi-grade Assessments, and Precision (for each grade ToP, MoP and BoP).

Binary Approach	risk-seeking	risk-medium	risk-averse	Schulze voting
Correlation	0.135	0.411▲	0.292▲	0.539▲
prec(ToP)	0.30	0.52	0.74	0.67
prec(MoP)	0.18	0.31	0.43	0.25
prec(BoP)	0.09	0.26	0.37	0.39

ers are more careful and select verticals to be shown on the SERP only when they have a high degree of confidence.

Secondly, for each approach used to derive vertical relevance from binary assessment, we obtain its corresponding optimal page (with 'general web' results Web-1, Web-2, Web-3 and verticals that are shown). Then we calculate the Spearman correlation of this page with the ground-truth page derived from the multi-grade assessments. The results are shown in Table 8. As we are concerned with how each binary approach can be used to derive accurate multi-graded assessment, we also calculate the precision of each binary approach with respect to the multi-grade ground-truth.

We notice several important trends. Firstly, most of the binary approaches (risk-medium, risk-averse and Schulze voting) are all significantly correlated with the multi-graded ground-truth. However, the correlations are mostly moderate. It is not surprising that Schulze voting method performs the best, as it uses more assessments (91 assessments) compared with other binary approaches (11 assessments) as well as being more robust to noise. It is also interesting to observe that the risk-medium approach performed second best, which is consistent with our observation that different assessors have different risk-levels. An extreme approach (risk-seeking or risk-averse) is more likely to satisfy only a small subset of assessors while frustrating others. Secondly, when focusing on the precision of each approach for each grade (ToP, MoP and BoP), we can observe that generally, risk-averse performs best, followed by Schulze voting, risk-medium and risk-seeking approaches. This is because the risk-averse approach is more careful when selecting verticals; it only selects verticals (as relevant) when highly confident (large fraction of user's preferences) of this.

5. CONCLUSIONS AND DISCUSSIONS

Our objective was to investigate whether different underlying assumptions made for vertical relevance affects a user's perception of the relevance of verticals. Our results indicate that relevant verticals derived from different assumptions do correlate with each other. However, the correlation is not high (either moderate or low in many cases) as each assumption focuses on different aspects of vertical relevance. With respect to RQ1, both *orientation* (pre-retrieval user need) and *topical relevance* (post-retrieval topical relevance) correlates significantly with the post-retrieval search results utility. The impact of orientation is comparatively more significant (moderate) than topical relevance (low). In addition, there is an aesthetic bias to a user's perception of search results utility. With respect to RQ2, we conclude that the context of other verticals has significant impact on the relevance of a vertical. With respect to RQ3, we found that it is possible to employ a number of binary assessments to predict multi-grade assessments and the correlation of the derived optimal pages is significant (moderate). Using a larger number of assessments (e.g. Schulze voting) contributes to more accurate estimation of multi-grade assessments.

Our results have important implications for aggregated search and in general, evaluation in IR. The moderate correlation between different vertical assessments indicates the need to re-evaluate previous work on vertical selection, based on the assessments (and corresponding assumptions) used. The conclusion drawn from one type of assessments (e.g. VS approach A performed better than B) might not hold for another type of assessments. Researchers need to be careful when drawing conclusions regarding vertical relevance.

Our results have implications for work in vertical selection. As discovered in Study 1, *orientation* has a larger impact on user's perception of the search results utility than topical relevance, which implies that vertical evidence derived from the user need perspective (e.g. query logs) might be more effective at predicting a user's relevant verticals than collection-based estimation (e.g. traditional resource selection methods). In addition, Study 1 implies that for some verticals (e.g. *Video*', *Recipe*' and '*Shopping*'), the VS system generally would have more confidence in returning them as relevant (due to their *orientation*). On the contrary, the VS system should be more careful when returning other verticals (e.g. '*Blog*' and '*Discussion*' results). We are not saying that some verticals ('*Video*') are more useful than others ('*Blog*' and '*Discussion*'); we note that it is easier to *predict* the usefulness of some verticals for an "average" query.

Our results have implications with respect to procuring assessments for aggregated search. In Study 2, we showed that fewer binary assessments (anchor-based approach) correlate moderately with more binary assessments (inter-dependent approach). In Study 3, we showed that moderately correlated multi-graded relevance assessments can be obtained by using a number of binary assessments. As different assessment methodologies involve differing amounts of effort (number of assessments, information load when assessing), there is a need for analyzing both the utility and effort involved in different assessment methodologies so that assessments can be obtained in a more efficient way. In addition, by exploring verticals on aggregated search pages, binary preference of vertical over web results can be obtained/derived by mining query logs [9].

Plans for future work include the following: Firstly, although we have shown that topical relevance has significant impact on user's perception of search results utility, we have not explored how this impact changes according to the different levels of topical relevance, and how it interacts with orientation. Similarly, a comprehensive analysis on aesthetic bias is also needed. Secondly, at the moment we assume a blended presentation strategy, i.e. interleaving vertical results into the web results (ToP, MoP, BoP and NS). Other ways of combining results are possible, for example showing blocks of results on the right side of the page. Finally, the assessments have been obtained by showing only vertical search result snippets to the users, without presenting the actual information items. As the assessment depends solely on snippet, we should examined the impact of this further.

Acknowledgments This work was partially supported by the EU LiMoSINe project (288024).

6. REFERENCES

[1] J. Arguello, F. Diaz, and J. Callan. Learning to aggregate vertical results into web search results. In CIKM 2011, pages 201-210.

[2] J. Arguello, F. Diaz, J. Callan, and B. Carterette. A methodology for evaluating aggregated search results. In ECIR 2011: pages 141-152.

[3] J. Arguello, F. Diaz, J. Callan, and J. Crespo. Sources of evidence for vertical selection. In SIGIR 2009: pages 315-322.

[4] J. Arguello, F. Diaz, and J. Paiement. Vertical selection in the presence of unlabeled verticals. In SIGIR 2010: pages 691-698.

[5] F. Diaz. Integration of news content into web results. In WSDM 2009: pages 182-191.

[6] J. Fleiss. Measuring nominal scale agreement among many raters. Psychological Bulletin, 76(5): pages 378-382, 1971.

[7] D. Hawking and P. Thomas. Server selection methods in hybrid portal search. In SIGIR 2005: pages 75-82.

[8] X. Li, Y. Wang, and A. Acero. Learning query intent from regularized click graphs. In SIGIR 2008: pages 339-346.

[9] A. Ponnuswami, K. Pattabiraman, Q. Wu, R. Gilad-Bachrach, and T. Kanungo. On composition of a federated web search result page: using online users to provide pairwise preference for heterogeneous verticals. In WSDM 2011: pages 715-724.

[10] M. Schulze. A new monotonic, clone-independent, reversal symmetric, and condorcet-consistent single-winner election method. In Social Choice and Welfare, 2010.

[11] S. Sushmita, H. Joho, M. Lalmas, and R. Villa. Factors affecting click-through behavior in aggregated search interfaces. In CIKM 2010: pages 519-528.

[12] M. Shokouhi, and L. Si. Federated Search. Foundations and Trends in Information Retrieval (FTIR) 5(1): pages 1-102, 2011.

[13] M. Sanderson, M. L. Paramita, P. Clough, and E. Kanoulas. Do user preferences and evaluation measures line up? In SIGIR 2010: pages 555-562.

[14] E. M. Voorhees. Variations in relevance judgments and the measurement of retrieval effectiveness. In Information Process Management. 36(5): pages 697-716, 2000.

[15] K. Zhou, R. Cummins, M. Lalmas, and J.M. Jose. Evaluating large-scale distributed vertical search. In CIKM Workshop LSDS-IR 2011.

[16] K. Zhou, R. Cummins, M. Halvey, M. Lalmas, and J. M. Jose. Assessing and predicting vertical intent for web queries. In ECIR 2012: pages 499-502.

[17] K. Zhou, R. Cummins, M. Lalmas, and J. M. Jose. Evaluating aggregated search pages. In SIGIR 2012: pages 115-124.

[18] K. Zhou, R. Cummins, M. Lalmas, and J. M. Jose. Evaluating reward and risk for vertical selection. In CIKM 2012: pages 2631-2634.

Making the Most of your Triple Store: Query Answering in OWL 2 Using an RL Reasoner

Yujiao Zhou
Computer Science Dept.
University of Oxford
yzhou@cs.ox.ac.uk

Bernardo Cuenca Grau
Computer Science Dept.
University of Oxford
berg@cs.ox.ac.uk

Ian Horrocks
Computer Science Dept.
University of Oxford
ian.horrocks@cs.ox.ac.uk

Zhe Wu
Oracle Corporation
alan.wu@oracle.com

Jay Banerjee
Oracle Corporation
jayanta.banerjee@oracle.com

ABSTRACT

Triple stores implementing the RL profile of OWL 2 are becoming increasingly popular. In contrast to unrestricted OWL 2, the RL profile is known to enjoy favourable computational properties for query answering, and state-of-the-art RL reasoners such as OWLim and Oracle's native inference engine of Oracle Spatial and Graph have proved extremely successful in industry-scale applications. The expressive restrictions imposed by OWL 2 RL may, however, be problematical for some applications. In this paper, we propose novel techniques that allow us (in many cases) to compute exact query answers using an off-the-shelf RL reasoner, even when the ontology is outside the RL profile. Furthermore, in the cases where exact query answers cannot be computed, we can still compute both lower and upper bounds on the exact answers. These bounds allow us to estimate the degree of incompleteness of the RL reasoner on the given query, and to optimise the computation of exact answers using a fully-fledged OWL 2 reasoner. A preliminary evaluation using the RDF Semantic Graph feature in Oracle Database has shown very promising results with respect to both scalability and tightness of the bounds.

Categories and Subject Descriptors

I.2.4 [**Knowledge Representation Formalism and Methods**]: Representations (procedural and rule-based); H.4.m [**Information Systems Applications**]: Miscellaneous

Keywords

Semantic Web; Triple Store; Ontologies

1. INTRODUCTION

The success of RDF as a language for representing semi-structured data on the (semantic) Web has led to the proliferation of applications based on large repositories of data stored in RDF format. In these applications, access to data relies on queries formulated in the standard query language SPARQL [28]; additionally, background knowledge required to unambiguously specify the meaning of the data in the context of the application may be captured using the standard ontology language OWL 2 [23].

Efficient management and querying of such large data repositories is a core problem in the development of RDF-based applications. Significant progress has been made in recent years in the design and development of efficient RDF data management systems, and state-of-the-art systems such as Hexastore [33] and RDF-3X [26] have combined highly optimised data structures and query answering algorithms in order to achieve impressive performance. There have also been significant advances in clustering and data partitioning techniques [29, 12, 15], which allow RDF query engines to exploit various forms of parallel architecture. As a result, state-of-the-art RDF management systems are capable of dealing with very large data sets.

When an ontology is used to augment the semantics of the RDF data, query answers need to consider additional triples whose existence is *entailed* by the combination of the ontology and the data. *Materialisation-based* approaches are widely used to extend RDF data management systems to deal with this situation; they work by using forward chaining rules to materialise the entailed triples, and then evaluating queries over the resulting extended data set.

The success in practice of materialisation-based systems led to the development of the RL profile of OWL 2 [22], a large subset of OWL 2 for which query answering is known to be both theoretically tractable (in polynomial time w.r.t. the size of the data), and practically realisable via materialisation. This combination of features has made OWL 2 RL increasingly popular, and state-of-the-art RL reasoners such as OWLim [1] and Oracle's native inference engine of Oracle Spatial and Graph [34, 20] provide robust and scalable support for SPARQL query answering over OWL 2 RL ontologies and RDF data sets.

Although OWL 2 RL captures a substantial fragment of OWL 2, it necessarily restricts expressiveness. OWL 2 RL cannot, for example, capture *disjunctive knowledge* such as that expressed in the following axiom, which states that every student is either an undergraduate or a graduate student:

SubClassOf(Student *ObjectUnionOf*(Grad UnderGrad));

nor can it capture *existentially quantified knowledge* such as that expressed in the following axiom, which states that each

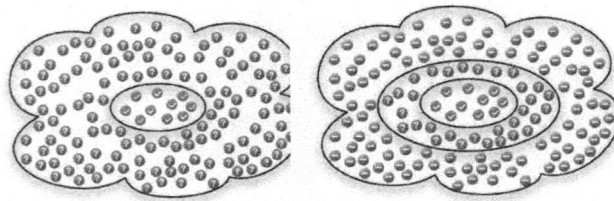

(a) Lower & trivial bound (b) Lower & upper bound

Figure 1: Combination of lower and upper bounds

research assistant works for some research group:

SubClassOf(RA *SomeValuesFrom*(works Group)).

These restrictions limit the applicability of OWL 2 RL in practice since disjunctive and existentially quantified statements abound in OWL ontologies. For example, the NCI Thesaurus contains many disjunctive statements, while ontologies such as SNOMED, FMA, and Fly Anatomy[1] contain thousands of existentially quantified statements.

Although the capabilities of RL reasoners are intrinsically limited, they are flexible enough to process ontologies outside OWL 2 RL on a 'best efforts' basis, as the materialisation rules effectively ignore those (parts of) axioms that are outside the RL profile. In such cases, answers to SPARQL queries are still guaranteed to be sound (the computed answer set includes only valid answer tuples), but may not be complete (the computed answer set may not include all valid answer tuples); thus, the answer set returned by the system can be thought of as a *lower bound* on the exact answers.

To ensure the completeness of query answers in such cases, one could abandon RL reasoners altogether in favour of fully fledged OWL 2 reasoners, such as HermiT [25], Pellet [31] and Racer [10]. However, despite intensive efforts at optimisation, the scalability of such systems falls far short of that exhibited by RL reasoners [19, 11].

In this paper, we propose novel techniques that allow us to (in many cases) to compute sound and complete answers using off-the-shelf RL reasoners, even when the ontology is outside OWL 2 RL. Furthermore, in the cases where exact answers cannot be computed, our techniques allow us to compute an *upper bound* on the exact answers. This upper bound is useful in practice for (at least) two reasons. First, as illustrated in Figure 1(b), it allows us to bound the incompleteness of the RL reasoner by partitioning tuples into three sets: those that are definitely in the answer (marked with '✓'), those that may be in the answer (marked with '?'), and those that are definitely not in the answer (marked with '-'); without the upper bound no tuples can be ruled out, and the status of a potentially huge number of tuples is thus left undetermined (as illustrated in Figure 1(a)). Second, it allows us to optimise the computation of exact answers by checking—e.g., using a fully-fledged OWL 2 reasoner—only the (typically small number of) tuples remaining in the gap between the lower and upper bounds.

Our work is closely related to existing techniques for *theory approximation* [7, 30], where lower and upper bounds to query answers are obtained by transforming the knowledge base (and possibly also the query) into a less expressive language. Systems such as those described in [32, 27, 18], all of which we discuss in detail in Section 6, are able to compute upper bounds to query answers under certain conditions. To the best of our knowledge, however, our approach is the only one that enjoys all of the following desirable properties:

- In contrast to [32] and [27], computation of the upper bound requires only the ontology to be transformed, and is independent of both data and query.

- In contrast to [32], [27], and [18], our transformation increases the size of the ontology only linearly with bounded minimum cardinality constraint values, and can be computed in linear time.

- In contrast to [27] and [18], which approximate the ontology into DL-Lite (i.e., OWL 2 QL), our approach uses OWL 2 RL, which will typically lead to tighter bounds, and allows us to directly exploit an industrial-strength OWL 2 RL reasoner as a "black box".

- In contrast to [32] and [18], our approach is independent of the query language, and hence can be applied not only to SPARQL queries, but also to more general languages such as (unions of) conjunctive queries.

An evaluation of our approach has been performed using the RDF Semantic Graph feature of Oracle Spatial and Graph, a range of test data including both benchmark and realistic ontologies, and a variety of synthetic and realistic queries. The evaluation suggests that the gap between the lower and upper bounds is typically small, indeed often empty, and that the upper bound is usually tight (i.e., it coincides with the exact answers). Moreover, although computing the upper bound increased the cost of materialising the data set, it is still feasible for large scale data sets, and much more efficient than the computation of exact answers using an OWL 2 reasoner; indeed we believe that this is the first time that exact answers have been computed over data sets of this size and w.r.t. an ontology outside any of the OWL 2 profiles.

This paper comes with an online technical report containing all the missing proofs.[2]

2. PRELIMINARIES

We adopt standard notions from first-order logic (FOL) with equality, such as variables, constants, terms, atoms, formulas, sentences, substitutions, satisfiability, unsatisfiability, and entailment (written $\models$). We use the standard notation $t \approx t'$ (an equality atom) to denote equality between terms and the standard abbreviation $t \not\approx t'$ for $\neg t \approx t'$ (an inequality atom). The *falsum* atom, which is evaluated to false in all interpretations, is denoted here as $\bot$, whereas the dual *truth* atom is represented as $\top$.

2.1 Ontologies and Data Sets

We assume basic familiarity with the OWL 2 and OWL 2 RL ontology languages [23, 22], as well as with the syntax and semantics of $\mathcal{SROIQ}$—the description logic (DL) underpinning OWL 2 (see [13] for details).[3]

---

[1] http://obofoundry.org/cgi-bin/detail.cgi?id=fly_anatomy_xp

[2] http://www.cs.ox.ac.uk/isg/tools/UOBMGenerator/TR_paper.pdf

[3] In this paper, we disregard datatypes for simplicity.

In this paper, we exploit the normal form for $\mathcal{SROIQ}$ given in Definition 1. Each $\mathcal{SROIQ}$ TBox can be transformed into this normal form by introducing fresh predicates as needed (see [25] for details on the normalisation algorithm).

DEFINITION 1. *A $\mathcal{SROIQ}$-TBox is normalised if it contains only the following kinds of axioms, where $R_{(i)}$ are either an atomic role or the inverse of an atomic role:*

- *Concept inclusion axioms $\top \sqsubseteq \bigsqcup_{i=1}^{n} C_i$, where each C_i is of the form B, $\{c\}$, $\forall R.B$, $\exists R.\mathsf{Self}$, $\neg \exists R.\mathsf{Self}$, $\geq n\, R.B$, or $\leq n\, R.B$, with B either an atomic concept or the negation of an atomic concept, c an individual, and n a nonnegative integer;*

- *Role axioms $R_1 \sqsubseteq R_2$, $R_1 \circ R_2 \sqsubseteq R_3$, or $R_1 \sqcap R_2 \sqsubseteq \bot$.*

We deviate slightly from the treatment of ontologies given in the W3C specification of OWL 2, where there is no explicit distinction between schema (i.e., TBox) and data (i.e., ABox). It is often convenient, however, to think of the ontology as a TBox (i.e., as containing *only* schema axioms), and to treat the (RDF) data assertions separately; this makes no difference from a semantic point of view. We will, therefore, treat an OWL 2 ontology $\mathcal{O}$ as a $\mathcal{SROIQ}$-TBox, and assume that all assertions are in a separate data set D. W.l.o.g. we restrict ourselves in this paper to data sets consisting only of atoms, including inequalities but excluding $\bot$ and $\top$.

2.2 Queries

A *conjunctive query* (CQ), or simply a *query*, is a first-order formula of the form $Q(\vec{x}) = \exists \vec{y}.\varphi(\vec{x}, \vec{y})$, where Q is a distinguished query predicate and $\varphi(\vec{x}, \vec{y})$ is a conjunction of atoms different from $\bot$ and from an inequality. A tuple of constants $\vec{a}$ is an *answer* to $Q(\vec{x})$ w.r.t. a set $\mathcal{F}$ of first-order sentences and a set of ground atoms D if $\mathcal{F} \cup D \models Q(\vec{a})$. The answer set of $Q(\vec{x})$ w.r.t. $\mathcal{F}$ and D, which we often call the *exact answers* to the query, is denoted as $\mathsf{cert}(Q, \mathcal{F}, D)$, where the free variables of $Q(\vec{x})$ are omitted. SPARQL queries are semantically equivalent to a restricted class of CQs with no existential quantifiers.

2.3 Datalog Languages

The design of OWL 2 RL was inspired by Description Logic Programs [8] — a KR formalism that can be captured using either datalog [6] or DLs. Therefore, there exists a tight connection between datalog rules and OWL 2 RL axioms.

The main difference between OWL 2 and its RL profile is the ability to represent disjunctive and existentially quantified knowledge. Hence, there is a tight connection between OWL 2 and an extension of datalog, which we call datalog$^{\pm,\vee}$, where both existential quantifiers and disjunctions are allowed in the head of rules. The connection between OWL 2 and datalog$^{\pm,\vee}$ is relevant to us, since our approach uses datalog$^{\pm,\vee}$ rules as an intermediate representation of ontology axioms. We next define datalog$^{\pm,\vee}$ and postpone the description of its relationship with OWL 2 until Section 3.1.

A datalog$^{\pm,\vee}$ *rule* r is a first-order sentence of form (1)

$$\forall \vec{x}.[B_1 \wedge ... \wedge B_n] \rightarrow \bigvee_{i=1}^{m} \exists \vec{y}_i.\varphi_i(\vec{x}, \vec{y}_i) \quad (1)$$

$$\mathcal{O} \rightsquigarrow \Sigma_{\mathcal{O}} \rightsquigarrow \Xi(\Sigma_{\mathcal{O}}) \rightsquigarrow \mathcal{O}' \cup D'_{\mathcal{O}}$$
$$\vdots \qquad \vdots \qquad \vdots \qquad \vdots$$
OWL 2   DATALOG$^{\pm,\vee}$ DATALOG   OWL 2 RL

Figure 2: Transformation steps

where each B_j is an atom that is neither $\bot$ nor an inequality atom and whose free variables are contained in $\vec{x}$, and either

- $m = 1$ and $\varphi_1(\vec{x}, \vec{y}_1) = \bot$ (we call such r a $\bot$-rule), or

- $m \geq 1$ and, for each $1 \leq i \leq m$, the formula $\varphi_i(\vec{x}, \vec{y}_i)$ with free variables in $\vec{x} \cup \vec{y}_i$ is a conjunction of atoms different from $\bot$.

The quantifier $\forall \vec{x}$ is left implicit. The *body* of r is the set of atoms $\mathsf{body}(r) = \{B_1, \ldots, B_n\}$, and the *head* of r is the formula $\mathsf{head}(r) = \bigvee_{i=1}^{m} \exists \vec{y}_i.\varphi_i(\vec{x}, \vec{y}_i)$. A datalog$^{\pm,\vee}$ rule r is a datalog$^{\pm}$ rule if $m = 1$ [2], and it is a datalog rule if it is a datalog$^{\pm}$ rule and the head does not contain existentially quantified variables.[4]

For Σ a set of datalog rules and D a set of ground atoms, the *saturation* of Σ w.r.t. D is the set D' of all ground atoms entailed by $\Sigma \cup D$, which can be computed by means of a *forward-chaining* (aka *materialisation-based*) algorithm. The answer set $\mathsf{cert}(Q, \Sigma, D)$ for an arbitrary conjunctive query Q then coincides with $\mathsf{cert}(Q, \emptyset, D')$.

3. CORE TECHNICAL APPROACH

Given an OWL 2 ontology $\mathcal{O}$, our goal is to transform $\mathcal{O}$ into an OWL 2 RL ontology $\mathcal{O}'$ and (possibly) a data set $D'_{\mathcal{O}}$ such that, for any data set D and any query Q:

1. $\mathsf{cert}(Q, \mathcal{O}, D) \subseteq \mathsf{cert}(Q, \mathcal{O}', D \cup D'_{\mathcal{O}})$; and

2. $\mathsf{cert}(Q, \mathcal{O}', D \cup D'_{\mathcal{O}}) \setminus \mathsf{cert}(Q, \mathcal{O}, D)$ is "small".

As we show below, the data set $D'_{\mathcal{O}}$ is only required if $\mathcal{O}$ contains certain kinds of constructs.

There is a tradeoff between the tightness of the upper bound (the size of $\mathsf{cert}(Q, \mathcal{O}', D \cup D'_{\mathcal{O}}) \setminus \mathsf{cert}(Q, \mathcal{O}, D)$) and the efficiency with which $\mathsf{cert}(Q, \mathcal{O}', D \cup D'_{\mathcal{O}})$ can be computed. In our approach, $\mathcal{O}'$ and $D'_{\mathcal{O}}$ are easy to compute (via a linear-time transformation), and $\mathsf{cert}(Q, \mathcal{O}', D \cup D'_{\mathcal{O}})$ can be efficiently computed using an OWL 2 RL reasoner.

To transform the ontology $\mathcal{O}$ into $\mathcal{O}'$ and $D'_{\mathcal{O}}$, we proceed as follows (see Figure 2 for a schematic representation):

1. Transform $\mathcal{O}$ into a set $\Sigma_{\mathcal{O}}$ of datalog$^{\pm,\vee}$ rules such that $\mathsf{cert}(Q, \mathcal{O}, D) = \mathsf{cert}(Q, \Sigma_{\mathcal{O}}, D)$ for any query Q (in the vocabulary of $\mathcal{O}$) and any data set D.

2. Transform $\Sigma_{\mathcal{O}}$ into a set $\Xi(\Sigma_{\mathcal{O}})$ of datalog rules by eliminating disjunctions and existential quantifiers, and such that for every query Q and data set D, we have $\mathsf{cert}(Q, \Sigma_{\mathcal{O}}, D) \subseteq \mathsf{cert}(Q, \Xi(\Sigma_{\mathcal{O}}), D)$.

3. Transform $\Xi(\Sigma_{\mathcal{O}})$ into an OWL 2 RL ontology $\mathcal{O}'$ and a data set $D'_{\mathcal{O}}$ such that, for every query Q and data set D, we have $\mathsf{cert}(Q, \Xi(\Sigma_{\mathcal{O}}), D) \subseteq \mathsf{cert}(Q, \mathcal{O}', D \cup D'_{\mathcal{O}})$.

---
[4] Our definition of datalog allows conjunctions in the head, which is not allowed in the standard, but the rules can be equivalently split into multiple rules with atomic heads.

Step 1 is an answer-preserving transformation from OWL 2 to datalog$^{\pm,\vee}$ rules, which can then be conveniently over-approximated in a weaker logic in the crucial second step. Step 3 is a transformation from datalog to OWL 2 RL which is answer-preserving in most (but not all) cases.

Given that $\mathcal{O}'$ is an OWL 2 RL ontology, we can use any reasoner that is sound for OWL 2 and complete for OWL 2 RL to compute a lower bound answer (using $\mathcal{O}$) and an upper bound answer (using $\mathcal{O}' \cup D'_{\mathcal{O}}$) for any given query Q and data set D. More precisely, if $\mathsf{rl}(Q, \mathcal{O}, D)$ is the query answer computed by such a reasoner, then we have:

$\mathsf{rl}(Q, \mathcal{O}, D) \subseteq \mathsf{cert}(Q, \mathcal{O}, D) \subseteq \mathsf{rl}(Q, \mathcal{O}', D \cup D'_{\mathcal{O}})$ for all Q, D

We next describe the transformations in steps 1–3, and illustrate them with the example ontology $\mathcal{O}_{\mathsf{ex}}$ in Figure 4.

3.1 From OWL 2 to Datalog$^{\pm,\vee}$

The first step is to transform the OWL 2 ontology $\mathcal{O}$ into a set $\Sigma_{\mathcal{O}}$ of datalog$^{\pm,\vee}$ rules. For this, we first transform $\mathcal{O}$ into the normal form given in Definition 1. Let $\mathsf{ar}(R, x, y)$ be defined as follows for each role R occurring in $\mathcal{O}$:

$$\mathsf{ar}(R, x, y) = \begin{cases} S(y, x) & \text{if } R \text{ inverse of the atomic role } S. \\ R(x, y) & \text{if } R \text{ atomic} \end{cases}$$

Then, $\Sigma_{\mathcal{O}}$ contains the following datalog$^{\pm,\vee}$ rules for each axiom in the normalisation of $\mathcal{O}$:

- $\mathsf{lhs}(C) \to \mathsf{rhs}(C)$ for $\top \sqsubseteq C$, where $\mathsf{lhs}(C)$ and $\mathsf{rhs}(C)$ are as given in Figure 3;
- $\mathsf{ar}(R, x, y) \to \mathsf{ar}(S, x, y)$ for $R \sqsubseteq S$;
- $\mathsf{ar}(R, x, y) \wedge \mathsf{ar}(S, y, z) \to \mathsf{ar}(T, x, z)$ for $R \circ S \sqsubseteq T$; and
- $\mathsf{ar}(R, x, y) \wedge \mathsf{ar}(S, x, y) \to \bot$ for $R \sqcap T \sqsubseteq \bot$.

The obtained set $\Sigma_{\mathcal{O}}$ of datalog$^{\pm,\vee}$ rules is equivalent to the normalisation of $\mathcal{O}$, and hence it is a *conservative extension* of $\mathcal{O}$; that is, the models of $\Sigma_{\mathcal{O}}$ are obtained by extending those of $\mathcal{O}$ with the interpretation of any new predicates introduced during normalisation. Thus, $\Sigma_{\mathcal{O}}$ preserves the answers to all queries using the vocabulary of $\mathcal{O}$ [3]. The transformation of our example ontology $\mathcal{O}_{\mathsf{ex}}$ into datalog$^{\pm,\vee}$ rules $\Sigma_{\mathcal{O}_{\mathsf{ex}}}$ is also shown in Figure 4. Note that $\Sigma_{\mathcal{O}_{\mathsf{ex}}}$ is extended with a new unary predicate Aux.

3.2 From Datalog$^{\pm,\vee}$ to Datalog

Next, we transform the datalog$^{\pm,\vee}$ rules $\Sigma_{\mathcal{O}}$ into a set of datalog rules $\Xi(\Sigma_{\mathcal{O}})$ such that $\Xi(\Sigma_{\mathcal{O}}) \models \Sigma_{\mathcal{O}}$, and thus for each query Q and data set D, $\mathsf{cert}(Q, \Sigma_{\mathcal{O}}, D) \subseteq \mathsf{cert}(Q, \Xi(\Sigma_{\mathcal{O}}), D)$. This transformation is performed in two steps:

1) Rewrite each datalog$^{\pm,\vee}$ rule r into a set of datalog$^{\pm}$ rules by transforming disjunctions in the head of r into conjunctions, and splitting the resulting conjunctions into multiple datalog$^{\pm}$ rules. This is a standard "naive" technique for approximating disjunction, and was used, e.g., in the SCREECH reasoner [32]. More sophisticated strategies will be discussed below.

2) Transform the resulting datalog$^{\pm}$ rules into datalog rules by using fresh individuals to Skolemise existentially quantified variables. Our transformation is based on the transformation from datalog$^{\pm}$ into datalog used in recent work for a rather different purpose, namely to check *chase termination* when applied to datalog$^{\pm}$ rules [4].

We next formally define the transformation $\Xi(\cdot)$ for an arbitrary set of datalog$^{\pm,\vee}$ rules; Figure 5 illustrates the application of this transformation to our running example.[5]

DEFINITION 2. *For each datalog$^{\pm,\vee}$ rule r of the form (1) and each $1 \leq i \leq m$, let r_i be the datalog$^{\pm}$ rule*

$$r_i = B_1 \wedge ... \wedge B_n \to \exists \vec{y}_i \varphi_i(\vec{x}, \vec{y}_i)$$

and let $\varphi_i^{\wedge}(\vec{x}, \vec{y}_i)$ be defined as the conjunction of all non-inequality atoms in $\varphi_i(\vec{x}, \vec{y}_i)$.[6]

Finally, for each $1 \leq i \leq m$ and each variable $y_{ij} \in \vec{y}_i$, let c_{ij}^r be a fresh individual unique for y_{ij}, and let θ_i^r be the substitution mapping each variable $y_{ij} \in \vec{y}_i$ to c_{ij}^r. Then, $\Xi(r_i)$ is the following set of datalog rules:

$$\Xi(r_i) = \{B_1 \wedge ... \wedge B_n \to \varphi_i^{\wedge}(\vec{x}, \theta_i^r(\vec{y}_i))\}$$
$$\bigcup \{c_1 \approx c_2 \to \bot \mid c_1 \not\approx c_2 \text{ occurs in } \varphi_i(\vec{x}, \theta_i^r(\vec{y}_i))\} \quad (2)$$

We finally define $\Xi(r) = \bigcup_{i=1}^{m} \Xi(r_i)$ and $\Xi(\Sigma) = \cup_{r \in \Sigma} \Xi(r)$ for Σ a set of datalog$^{\pm,\vee}$ rules.

Note that $\Xi(\Sigma)$ does not contain inequality atoms in rule heads; although such rules are allowed according to our definition of datalog, they cannot (easily) be transformed into equivalent OWL 2 RL axioms, which is our ultimate goal. For instance, the datalog$^{\pm,\vee}$ rule

$$r = B(x) \to R(x, c_1) \wedge A(c_1) \wedge R(x, c_2) \wedge A(c_2) \wedge c_1 \not\approx c_2$$

is transformed as follows, where $c_1 \approx c_2 \to \bot$ is equivalent to an OWL 2 (RL) *DifferentFrom* assertion.

$$\Xi(r) = \{B(x) \to R(x, c_1) \wedge A(c_1) \wedge R(x, c_2) \wedge A(c_2),$$
$$c_1 \approx c_2 \to \bot\}$$

As stated in the following proposition, the proof of which is given in our online technical report, the transformation over-approximates the datalog$^{\pm,\vee}$ rules.

PROPOSITION 1. $\Xi(\Sigma) \models \Sigma$, *for Σ an arbitrary set of datalog$^{\pm,\vee}$ rules.*

Proposition 1 immediately implies

$$\mathsf{cert}(Q, \Sigma_{\mathcal{O}}, D) \subseteq \mathsf{cert}(Q, \Xi(\Sigma_{\mathcal{O}}), D)$$

for an arbitrary query Q and data set D, and hence query answers w.r.t. $\Xi(\Sigma_{\mathcal{O}})$ are an upper bound to those w.r.t. $\Sigma_{\mathcal{O}}$.

Note that when $\Xi(\Sigma_{\mathcal{O}}) \cup D$ is unsatisfiable, the obtained upper bound is the trivial one for all queries, i.e., all tuples of individuals with the appropriate arty. For instance, if we extend $\mathcal{O}_{\mathsf{ex}}$ in Figure 4 with the axiom $\mathsf{Grad} \sqcap \mathsf{UnderGrad} \sqsubseteq \bot$ which states graduate students and undergraduate students are disjoint, we obtain the $\bot$-rule $\mathsf{Grad}(x) \wedge \mathsf{UnderGrad}(x) \to \bot$ in both $\Sigma_{\mathcal{O}_{\mathsf{ex}}}$ and $\Xi(\Sigma_{\mathcal{O}_{\mathsf{ex}}})$. For $D_{\mathsf{ex}} = \{\mathsf{RA}(a)\}$ we have that $\mathcal{O}_{\mathsf{ex}} \cup D_{\mathsf{ex}}$ is satisfiable, but $\Xi(\Sigma_{\mathcal{O}_{\mathsf{ex}}}) \cup D_{\mathsf{ex}}$ is unsatisfiable. In Section 4.1 we discuss how this issue can be dealt with in detail.

---

[5]Note that the size of the transformation is polynomial in minimum cardinality constraint values, but otherwise linear.
[6]Inequality atoms only occur in conjunction with other atoms in $\varphi_i(\vec{x}, \vec{y}_i)$, and hence $\varphi_i^{\wedge}(\vec{x}, \vec{y}_i)$ is well-defined.

C	lhs(C)	rhs(C)
A		$A(x)$
$\neg A$	$A(x)$	
$\{a\}$		$x \approx a$
$\geq n\, R.A$		$\exists y_1,\ldots,y_n \bigwedge_{1\leq i\leq n}[ar(R,x,y_C^i) \wedge A(y_C^i) \wedge \bigwedge_{i<j\leq n} y_C^i \not\approx y_C^j]$
$\geq n\, R.\neg A$		$\exists y_1,\ldots,y_n \bigwedge_{1\leq i\leq n}[ar(R,x,y_C^i) \wedge C_{\neg A}(y_C^i) \wedge \bigwedge_{i<j\leq n} y_C^i \not\approx y_C^j]$
$\exists R.\mathsf{Self}$		$ar(R,x,x)$
$\neg \exists R.\mathsf{Self}$	$ar(R,x,x)$	
$\forall R.A$	$ar(R,x,y_C)$	$A(y_C)$
$\forall R.\neg A$	$ar(R,x,y_C) \wedge A(y_C)$	
$\leq n\, R.A$	$\bigwedge_{1\leq i\leq n+1}[ar(R,x,y_C^i) \wedge A(y_C^i)]$	$\bigvee_{1\leq i<j\leq n+1} y_C^i \approx y_C^j$
$\leq n\, R.\neg A$	$\bigwedge_{1\leq i\leq n+1} ar(R,x,y_C^i)$	$\bigvee_{1\leq i\leq n+1}[A(y_C^i)] \vee \bigvee_{1\leq i<j\leq n+1} y_C^i \approx y_C^j$
$C_1 \sqcup \ldots \sqcup C_n$	$\top$ if lhs(C_i) empty for all $1\leq i\leq n$; $\bigwedge_{i=1}^n$ lhs(C_i) otherwise	$\bot$ if rhs(C_i) empty for all $1\leq i\leq n$; $\bigvee_{i=1}^n$ rhs(C_i) otherwise

Note: $C_{\neg A}$ is a fresh predicate; $A(x) \wedge C_{\neg A}(x) \to \bot$ is added to the datalog$^{\pm,\vee}$ rules in the translation of $\geq n\, R.\neg A$

Figure 3: Translation of Normalised Axioms

Axioms in $\mathcal{O}_{ex}$	Normalised Axioms	Datalog$^{\pm,\vee}$
Student $\sqsubseteq$ Person	$\top \sqsubseteq \neg$Student $\sqcup$ Person	Student(x) $\to$ Person(x)
RA $\sqsubseteq$ Student	$\top \sqsubseteq \neg$RA $\sqcup$ Student	RA(x) $\to$ Student(x)
RA $\sqsubseteq \exists$works.Group	$\top \sqsubseteq \neg$RA $\sqcup \exists$works.Group	RA(x) $\to \exists y[$works$(x,y) \wedge$ Group$(y)]$
Group $\sqsubseteq$ Org	$\top \sqsubseteq \neg$Group $\sqcup$ Org	Group(x) $\to$ Org(x)
	$\top \sqsubseteq \neg$Emp $\sqcup$ Person	Emp(x) $\to$ Person(x)
Emp $\equiv$ Person $\sqcap \exists$works.Org	$\top \sqsubseteq \neg$Emp $\sqcup \exists$works.Org	Emp(x) $\to \exists y[$works$(x,y) \wedge$ Org$(y)]$
	$\top \sqsubseteq$ Emp $\sqcup \neg$Person $\sqcup \forall$works.$\neg$Org	Person(x) $\wedge$ works$(x,y) \wedge$ Org$(y) \to$ Emp(x)
works $\sqsubseteq$ memberOf	works $\sqsubseteq$ memberOf	works$(x,y) \to$ memberOf(x,y)
Student $\sqsubseteq$ Grad $\sqcup$ UnderGrad	$\top \sqsubseteq \neg$Student $\sqcup$ Grad $\sqcup$ UnderGrad	Student(x) $\to$ Grad(x) $\vee$ UnderGrad(x)
func(works)	$\top \sqsubseteq\, \leq 1$ works.$\top$	works$(x,y_1) \wedge$ works$(x,y_2) \to y_1 \approx y_2$
Fellow $\sqsubseteq \exists$works.$\exists$funded.Council	$\top \sqsubseteq \neg$Fellow $\sqcup \exists$works.Aux	Fellow(x) $\to \exists y.[$works$(x,y) \wedge$ Aux$(y)]$
	$\top \sqsubseteq \neg$Aux $\sqcup \exists$funded.Council	Aux(x) $\to \exists y[$funded$(x,y) \wedge$ Council$(y)]$
UnderGrad $\sqsubseteq\, \geq 3$ takes.Course	$\top \sqsubseteq \neg$UnderGrad $\sqcup\, \geq 3$ takes.Course	UnderGrad(x) $\to \exists y_1, y_2, y_3 \bigwedge_i($takes$(x,y_i)$ $\wedge$ Course$(y_i) \wedge \bigwedge_{i<j\leq 3} y_i \not\approx y_j)$

Figure 4: Transforming $\mathcal{O}_{ex}$ into datalog$^{\pm,\vee}$ rules $\Sigma_{\mathcal{O}_{ex}}$

3.3 From Datalog to OWL 2 RL

The last step is to transform $\Xi(\Sigma_{\mathcal{O}})$ into an OWL 2 RL ontology $\mathcal{O}'$ and (possibly) a data set $D'_{\mathcal{O}}$.

Rules in $\Xi(\Sigma_{\mathcal{O}})$ can be of the following types (see Section 3.1, Figure 3 and Definition 2):

R1 Rules originating from (and equivalent to) normalised role axioms $R \sqsubseteq S$, $R \circ S \sqsubseteq T$, or $R \sqcap T \sqsubseteq \bot$.

R2 Rules $c_1 \approx c_2 \to \bot$, with c_1 and c_2 constants.

R3 Rules originating from the transformations applied to normalised axioms of the form $\top \sqsubseteq C$.

Rules of type R1 correspond directly to OWL 2 RL axioms, which will be included in $\mathcal{O}'$. Rules of type R2 correspond to ground atoms of the form $c_1 \not\approx c_2$ (i.e., *DifferentFrom* assertions in OWL 2), which will be included in $D'_{\mathcal{O}}$. Finally, rules of type R3 are of a very specific shape. The variables in the body are arranged in a tree-shape way, with a single root variable x, and branch variables y connected to x by atoms $R(x,y)$ or $R(y,x)$, such that each y occurs in exactly one such atom. Moreover, branch variables only occur in the rule head in atoms of the form $A(y)$ or $y \approx y'$. Rules of this form can be transformed back into OWL 2 axioms by means of the well-known rolling-up technique [14]; for example, the rule Person(x) $\wedge$ works$(x,y) \wedge$ Org$(y) \to$ Emp(x) can be rolled up into the axiom Person $\sqcap \exists$works.Org $\sqsubseteq$ Emp. We formally specify this transformation in the following section.

3.3.1 Rolling up rules into OWL 2 axioms

Given a rule r of type R3, the variables occurring in r are divided into the *root variable* x, and a set of *branch variables* y, such that r satisfies the following properties, where A is a unary predicate, R is a binary predicate, c is a constant, and y, y' are branch variables:

- the body is either $\top$, or a conjunction of atoms of the form $A(x)$, $R(x,x)$, $R(x,y)$, $R(y,x)$, or $A(y)$;

- the head is either $\bot$, or a conjunction of atoms of the form $A(x)$, $R(x,x)$, $x \approx c$, $A(y)$, $A(c)$, $R(x,c)$, $R(c,x)$, and $y \approx y'$;

- each branch variable y occurs in exactly one body atom $R(x,y)$ or $R(y,x)$; also, each constant c occurs in at most one atom $R(x,c)$ or $R(c,x)$; and

- if $y \approx y'$ occurs in the head, then y and y' occur in body atoms $R(x,y)$ or $R(y,x)$ and $R(x,y')$ or $R(y',x)$.

$$
\begin{aligned}
\mathsf{RA}(x) &\to \exists y.[\mathsf{works}(x,y) \wedge \mathsf{Group}(y)] & \leadsto & \quad \mathsf{RA}(x) \to \mathsf{works}(x,c_1) \wedge \mathsf{Group}(c_1) \\
\mathsf{Emp}(x) &\to \exists y.[\mathsf{works}(x,y) \wedge \mathsf{Org}(y)] & \leadsto & \quad \mathsf{Emp}(x) \to \mathsf{works}(x,c_2) \wedge \mathsf{Org}(c_2) \\
\mathsf{Student}(x) &\to \mathsf{Grad}(x) \vee \mathsf{UnderGrad}(x) & \leadsto & \quad \mathsf{Student}(x) \to \mathsf{UnderGrad}(x) \wedge \mathsf{Grad}(x) \\
\mathsf{UnderGrad}(x) &\to \exists y_1, y_2, y_3 \bigwedge_i (\mathsf{takes}(x, y_i) & \leadsto & \quad \mathsf{UnderGrad}(x) \to \bigwedge_{i=3}^{5}(\mathsf{takes}(x, c_i) \wedge \mathsf{Course}(c_i)) \\
& \quad \wedge \bigwedge_{i<j\leq 3} y_i \not\approx y_j) & & \quad c_i \approx c_j \to \bot \text{ for different } i \text{ and } j
\end{aligned}
$$

Note: $c_1, \ldots, c_5$ are fresh individuals

Figure 5: Transforming $\Sigma_{\mathcal{O}_{\mathsf{ex}}}$ into $\Xi(\Sigma_{\mathcal{O}_{\mathsf{ex}}})$. Only the rules that are changed by the transformation are shown.

A rule of this form can be transformed into OWL 2 by exploiting the rolling up technique. There is, however, a technical issue related to the fresh Skolem constants in $\Xi(\Sigma_{\mathcal{O}})$. In particular, the rule $\mathsf{RA}(x) \to \mathsf{works}(x, c_1) \wedge \mathsf{Group}(c_1)$ in our running example does not directly correspond to an OWL 2 axiom. This issue can be addressed by introducing fresh roles; the above rule can be transformed into the following three OWL 2 axioms, where $S^{\mathsf{Group}}_{\mathsf{works}}$ is a fresh role:

$$\mathsf{RA} \sqsubseteq \exists S^{\mathsf{Group}}_{\mathsf{works}}.\{c_1\} \quad \exists (S^{\mathsf{Group}}_{\mathsf{works}})^-.\top \sqsubseteq \mathsf{Group} \quad S^{\mathsf{Group}}_{\mathsf{works}} \sqsubseteq \mathsf{works}$$

We are now ready to define the transformation. Note that, for simplicity, this transformation has been presented in such a way that the axiom might contain redundancies; in practice such redundancies would, of course, be eliminated.

Each atom $\alpha \in \mathsf{body}(r)$ is transformed into a concept C^α as follows, with x the root variable of r, and y a branch variable:

$$
C^\alpha = \begin{cases}
\top & \text{if } \alpha = \top; \\
A & \text{if } \alpha = A(x); \\
\exists R.\mathsf{Self} & \text{if } \alpha = R(x,x); \\
\exists R.\top & \text{if } \alpha = R(x,y); \\
\exists R^-.\top & \text{if } \alpha = R(y,x); \\
\exists R.A & \text{if } \alpha = A(y) \text{ and } R(x,y) \in \mathsf{body}(r); \\
\exists R^-.A & \text{if } \alpha = A(y) \text{ and } R(y,x) \in \mathsf{body}(r);
\end{cases}
$$

Each atom $\beta \in \mathsf{head}(r)$ is transformed into a concept C^β as follows, with x the root variable of r, y and y' branch variables, c a constant, and S^A_R, $S^A_{R^-}$ fresh roles:

$$
C^\beta = \begin{cases}
\bot & \text{if } \beta = \bot; \\
A & \text{if } \beta = A(x); \\
\exists R.\mathsf{Self} & \text{if } \beta = R(x,x); \\
\{c\} & \text{if } \beta = x \approx c; \\
\forall R.A & \text{if } \beta = A(y) \text{ and } R(x,y) \in \mathsf{body}(r); \\
\forall R^-.A & \text{if } \beta = A(y) \text{ and } R(y,x) \in \mathsf{body}(r); \\
\exists S^A_R.\{c\} & \text{if } \beta = A(c) \text{ and } R(x,c) \in \mathsf{head}(r); \text{ or} \\
& \text{if } \beta = R(x,c) \text{ and } A(c) \in \mathsf{head}(r); \\
\exists (S^A_{R^-}).\{c\} & \text{if } \beta = R(c,x) \text{ and } A(c) \in \mathsf{head}(r); \text{ or} \\
& \text{if } \beta = A(c) \text{ and } R(c,x) \in \mathsf{head}(r); \\
\leq 1\, R.A & \text{if } \beta = y \approx y' \text{ and } R(x,y), A(y) \in \mathsf{body}(r) \\
\leq 1\, R^-.A & \text{if } \beta = y \approx y' \text{ and } R(y,x), A(y) \in \mathsf{body}(r)
\end{cases}
$$

We can transform r into an OWL 2 axiom $C(r)$ as follows:

$$C(r) = \prod_{\alpha \in \mathsf{head}(r)} C^\alpha \sqsubseteq \prod_{\beta \in \mathsf{body}(r)} C^\beta$$

We thus obtain an ontology $\mathcal{O}'$ with the following axioms.

- Axioms of the form $R \sqsubseteq S$, $R \circ S \sqsubseteq T$, or $R \sqcap T \sqsubseteq \bot$ obtained from the rules of type R1 in $\Xi(\mathcal{O})$.

- An axiom $C(r)$ for each rule r of type R3 in $\Xi(\mathcal{O})$, and axioms $S^A_R \sqsubseteq R$ and $\exists (S^A_R)^-.\top \sqsubseteq A$ for each fresh role S^A_R introduced in $C(r)$, with R either atomic or an inverse role.

Finally, we obtain a data set $D'_\mathcal{O}$ containing a ground inequality atom for each rule of type R2 in $\Xi(\mathcal{O})$.

Clearly, $\mathcal{O}' \cup D'_\mathcal{O}$ is a conservative extension of $\Xi(\Sigma_\mathcal{O})$, and hence query answers are preserved for arbitrary queries and data sets in the vocabulary of $\Xi(\Sigma_\mathcal{O})$.

3.3.2 Eliminating non-RL axioms

Unfortunately, $\mathcal{O}'$ might not be an OWL 2 RL ontology as it might contain the following kinds of non-RL axioms: *(i)* axioms containing the Self construct; *(ii)* axioms of the form $C \sqsubseteq \{a\}$ for $\{a\}$ a nominal concept; and *(iii)* axioms having $\top$ as the left-hand-side concept.

These kinds of axiom were excluded from OWL 2 RL due to specific design choices, rather than inherent limitations of materialisation-based reasoning techniques; in fact, the OWL 2 RL/RDF rules could be trivially extended to deal with such non-RL axioms. Furthermore, axioms of the kind above are rare in realistic ontologies, and none of the ontologies we used in our evaluation contained any such axiom.

If necessary, however, non-RL axioms can be eliminated by applying to $\mathcal{O}'$ and $D'_\mathcal{O}$ the following sequence of transformations:

1. Replace each occurrence of a concept $\exists R.\mathsf{Self}$ on the l.h.s. of an axiom with $\exists R.\top$; and replace each axiom of the form $C \sqsubseteq \exists R.\mathsf{Self}$ with axioms $C \sqsubseteq \exists S.\{a\}$ and $S \circ S^- \sqsubseteq R$, where a is a fresh individual and S is a fresh role.

2. For each axiom of the form $C \sqsubseteq \{a\}$, define a fresh role P_a as inverse functional; replace the axiom with $C \sqsubseteq \exists P_a.\{a\}$; and extend $D'_\mathcal{O}$ with the assertion $P_a(a,a)$.

3. Replace each axiom of the form $\top \sqsubseteq C$ with $\mathsf{TOP} \sqsubseteq C$, where TOP is a fresh atomic concept; add axioms $A \sqsubseteq \mathsf{TOP}$, $\{a\} \sqsubseteq \mathsf{TOP}$, $\exists R.\top \sqsubseteq \mathsf{TOP}$ and $\exists R^-.\top \sqsubseteq \mathsf{TOP}$ for each atomic concept A, nominal $\{a\}$ and role R in the ontology; and if no nominal occurs in the ontology, add the axiom $\{c\} \sqsubseteq \mathsf{TOP}$, with c a fresh individual.

These transformations could lead to additional answers to certain queries and data sets. For example, if we apply them to $\mathcal{O}' = \{\exists R.\mathsf{Self} \sqsubseteq A\}$ to obtain $\mathcal{O}'' = \{\exists R.\top \sqsubseteq A\}$ and consider $D = \{A(a), R(a,b)\}$ and $Q(x) = A(x)$, we have $\mathsf{cert}(Q, \mathcal{O}', D) = \emptyset$, whereas $\mathsf{cert}(Q, \mathcal{O}'', D) = \{a\}$.

4. ADDITIONAL CONSIDERATIONS

We next discuss some issues related to the second step in our approach, namely the transformation $\Xi(\cdot)$ from datalog$^{\pm,\vee}$ rules into datalog rules.

4.1 Dealing with Unsatisfiability

As mentioned in Section 3.2, the union of a data set D with the rules in $\Xi(\Sigma_\mathcal{O})$ can be unsatisfiable, even when $\Sigma_\mathcal{O} \cup D$ is satisfiable. This issue can be addressed by removing all $\bot$-rules from $\Xi(\Sigma_\mathcal{O})$, which ensures satisfiability for any D.

This is not possible without losing completeness if $\Sigma_\mathcal{O} \cup D$ is unsatisfiable. If $\Sigma_\mathcal{O} \cup D$ is satisfiable, however, $\bot$-rules intuitively do not matter because $\Xi(\cdot)$ strengthens disjunctions in $\Sigma_\mathcal{O}$ into conjunctions; hence, all ground atoms entailed by $\Sigma_\mathcal{O} \cup D$ are also entailed by $\Xi(\Sigma_\mathcal{O}) \cup D$ even after dispensing with the $\bot$-rules. These intuitions are formalised as follows.

THEOREM 1. *Let Σ be a set of datalog$^{\pm,\vee}$ rules, and let $\Xi_\bot(\Sigma)$ be all the $\bot$-rules in $\Xi(\Sigma)$. Then, the following condition holds for each data set D and each query Q: if $\Sigma \cup D$ is satisfiable, then $\mathsf{cert}(Q, \Sigma, D) \subseteq \mathsf{cert}(Q, \Xi(\Sigma) \setminus \Xi_\bot(\Sigma), D)$.*

The proof of the theorem is rather technical, and is deferred to our online appendix. The idea behind the proof is, however, quite simple, and can be explained with an example.

EXAMPLE 1. *Let Σ and D be as follows:*

$$\Sigma = \{A(x) \to B(x) \vee C(x), A(x) \to D(x) \vee E(x),$$
$$B(x) \to \bot, C(x) \wedge D(x) \to \bot\}$$
$$D = \{A(a), C(b)\}$$

Theorem 1 applies because $\Sigma \cup D$ is satisfiable. Given

$$\Xi(\Sigma) \setminus \Xi_\bot(\Sigma) = \{A(x) \to B(x) \wedge C(x),$$
$$A(x) \to D(x) \wedge E(x)\}$$

we need to show that $\mathsf{cert}(Q, \Sigma, D) \subseteq \mathsf{cert}(Q, \Xi(\Sigma) \setminus \Xi_\bot(\Sigma), D)$ for an arbitrary query Q. Because $\Sigma \cup D$ is satisfiable, there exists a (Herbrand) model $\mathcal{J}$ satisfying it, say

$$\mathcal{J} = \{A(a), C(a), E(a), C(b), E(b)\}$$

Pick an arbitrary Q (say, $Q(x) = E(x)$) and an individual (say b) such that $b \notin \mathsf{cert}(Q, \Xi(\Sigma) \setminus \Xi_\bot(\Sigma), D)$. Then, there must exist a (Herbrand) interpretation $\mathcal{I}$ such that

$$\mathcal{I} \models \Xi(\Sigma) \setminus \Xi_\bot(\Sigma) \cup D \quad \text{and} \quad \mathcal{I} \not\models Q(b)$$

In our case, such an interpretation $\mathcal{I}$ could be

$$\mathcal{I} = \{A(a), B(a), C(a), D(a), E(a), C(b)\}$$

Then, we can show that the (Herbrand) interpretation $\mathcal{I} \cap \mathcal{J}$ satisfies $\Sigma \cup D$, but it does not satisfy $Q(b)$, which implies $b \notin \mathsf{cert}(Q, \Xi(\Sigma) \setminus \Xi_\bot(\Sigma), D)$, as required by the theorem.

In practice, checking the satisfiability of $\mathcal{O} \cup D$, which is equisatisfiable with $\Sigma_\mathcal{O} \cup D$, is easier than query answering, and even if it is impractical to check the satisfiability of $\mathcal{O} \cup D$ using an OWL 2 reasoner, e.g., if D is very large, we can still compute an upper bound "modulo satisfiability".

4.2 Transformation of Disjunctions

If $\Xi(\Sigma_\mathcal{O}) \cup D$ is satisfiable for a data set D, we can weaken $\Xi(\Sigma_\mathcal{O})$ from Definition 2 such that $\Sigma_\mathcal{O}$ is still entailed. In particular, when transforming a rule in $\Sigma_\mathcal{O}$ into datalog by replacing disjunction with conjunction, it suffices to keep only one of the conjuncts. For example, given the transformation of $A(x) \to B(x) \vee C(x)$ into $A(x) \to B(x)$ and $A(x) \to C(x)$, we can discard either of the resulting datalog rules in $\Xi(\Sigma_\mathcal{O})$. Each choice might result in a different upper bound. In practice we could use multiple versions of $\mathcal{O}'$ resulting from different choices to try to obtain a tighter bound, or we could make a heuristic choice of rules to retain; e.g., it makes sense to choose the rule with a head predicate that appears least frequently in the bodies of other rules.

Choosing disjuncts instead of taking the conjunction of all of them is, however, incompatible with removing $\bot$-rules, and hence with Theorem 1. Consider Σ and D in Example 1 and $Q(x) = C(x)$; if $A(x) \to B(x) \vee C(x)$ is approximated to $A(x) \to B(x)$, we have $a \in \mathsf{cert}(Q, \Sigma, D)$ but $a \notin \mathsf{cert}(Q, \Xi(\Sigma) \setminus \Xi_\bot(\Sigma), D)$ and query answers are lost.

5. EXPERIMENTS

We have implemented our approach in Java and used Oracle's native OWL 2 RL reasoner in Oracle Database Release 11.2.0.3 as an OWL 2 RL reasoner. The testing machine has a dual quad core (Intel Xeon E5620) CPU, 5 SATA disks, and 40GB RAM with the operating system Linux 2.6.18.

5.1 Test Data

In our experiments, we have used the ontologies and data sets described next. More detailed statistics are given in Table 1.

Lehigh University Benchmark. The Leigh University Benchmark (LUBM) ontology [9] describes the organisation of universities and academic departments. Although the LUBM ontology is quite simple, it is not within the OWL 2 RL profile, as it captures existentially quantified knowledge. LUBM comes with a predefined data set generator, which can be used to test the ability of systems to handle data sets of varying size. We denote with LUBM(n) the LUBM dataset generated for n universities.

University Ontology Benchmark. The University Ontology Benchmark (UOBM) is an extension of LUBM [21] with a more complex ontology, which also contains disjunctive axioms and negation. UOBM provides three different data sets (for one, five and ten universities); in contrast to LUBM, no generator of data sets of varying size is provided for UOBM. To provide a more comprehensive evaluation, we have implemented a data generator for UOBM[7] that replicates the design of LUBM's generator. Data produced by our generator differs in several ways from the default UOBM data. This is because the data in UOBM's default data sets is skewed in what we believe are rather strange ways; for example, students in the UOBM data sets are much more likely to be connected via the isFriendOf relation to faculty members than to other students. Our generator does not replicate this skewing, and thus produces what we believe is more "realistic" data. We denote with GEN-UOBM(n) the generated UOBM data set for n universities.

Fly Anatomy (FLY). This realistic and complex ontology describing the anatomy of flies includes a data set with more than 1,000 manually created individuals. This ontology is rich in existentially quantified knowledge and hence contains a relatively small number of OWL 2 RL axioms.

We have used two kinds of queries in our experiments.

Standard Queries. LUBM and UOBM come with 14 and 15 standard queries, respectively. Since UOBM extends LUBM, we also adapted the 14 LUBM queries to UOBM.

---

[7] http://www.cs.ox.ac.uk/isg/tools/UOBMGenerator/

Table 1: Statistics for data sets

Data	DL	Horn	Existential	Classes	Properties	Axioms	Individuals	Data Set
LUBM(n)	$\mathcal{SHI}$	Yes	8	43	32	93	$1.7 \times 10^4 n$	$10^5 n$
GEN-UOBM(n)	$\mathcal{SHIN}$	No	24	113	44	188	$2.5 \times 10^4 n$	$2 \times 10^5 n$
FLY	$\mathcal{SRI}$	Yes	8,396	7,533	24	144,407	1,606	6,308

Table 2: Synthetic LUBM queries with non-matching bounds. Upper bound is tight in all cases.

Query	Q_3	Q_{51}	Q_{67}	Q_{69}
Lower Bound	540	0	540	0
Upper Bound	1087	547	1087	547

Table 4: Modified LUBM queries for UOBM with non-matching bounds. Lower bound is tight.

Query	Q_1	Q_4	Q_5	Q_9	Q_{12}	Q_{13}
Lower Bound	0	5	648	317	41	991
Upper Bound	1	5,456	687	630	779	1,008

For FLY, we have used 5 realistic queries provided by the biologists who are developing the ontology.

Synthetic Queries. We have used the system SyGENiA [5, 17] to generate synthetic queries for LUBM and UOBM and obtained 78 queries for LUBM, and 198 for UOBM (the larger number reflecting its more complex structure).

5.2 Tightness of the Upper Bound

Results for LUBM(1). Lower and upper bounds coincide for each of the 14 LUBM standard queries and the LUBM(1) data set. This implies that Oracle's reasoner is complete for each of these queries (and the given data set), even if the ontology contains axioms outside OWL 2 RL. As to the synthetic queries, lower and upper bounds coincided in all but 4 cases (see Table 2). For these 4 queries, we used the OWL 2 reasoner HermiT to compute the exact answers, and found the upper bound to be tight in all cases.

Results for GEN-UOBM(1). Lower and upper bounds for the 15 UOBM standard queries and GEN-UOBM(1) are given in Table 3. We found matching bounds for 4 queries. For the remaining ones, the upper bound was significantly smaller than the trivial upper bound; also, by using HermiT, we determined that the lower bound was tight for 9 queries, and in the remaining 2 cases neither of the bounds was tight.

Regarding the 14 LUBM modified queries (see Table 4), we obtained matching bounds for 8 of them. For 5 of the remaining 6 queries, the lower bound was tight and the gap between bounds was typically small. For query Q_4, however, the lower bound is still tight but the gap is much larger. However, the query has a large number of answer variables, and hence a huge trivial upper bound, so the upper bound can still be considered a good approximation.

Finally, concerning the synthetic queries, we obtained matching bounds for 101(51%) of them. Figure 6 illustrates the typical size of the gap between the lower bound (LB) and upper bound (UB) answer sets, relative to the size of LB; it shows the quotient of the number of answer tuples in the gap between bounds over the number of answer tuples in the lower bound, i.e., $\frac{|UB \setminus LB|}{|LB|}$.[8] Quotient values are presented in intervals on the X axis, and the Y axis represents the number of queries that fell within each interval; for example, we can see that for 46 queries, UB\LB contained only 10%–20% of the number of answer tuples in LB. This suggests the potential of our technique as an optimisation that efficiently

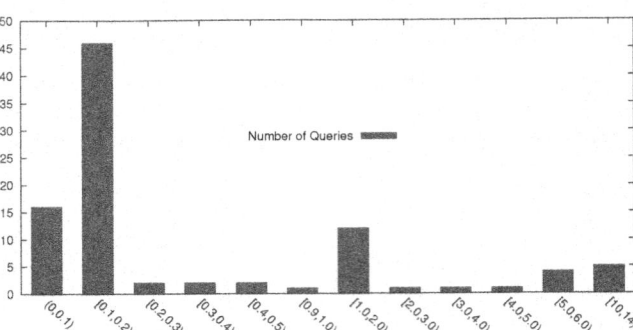

Figure 6: Synthetic UOBM queries. X axis is $\frac{|UB \setminus LB|}{|LB|}$; Y axis is the number of queries falling in each interval on the X axis.

identifies a small number of candidate answer tuples, which can be checked using an OWL 2 reasoner; even in the worst case, where the upper bound is almost 13 times larger than the lower bound, we have ruled out more than 99.9% of the possible answer tuples compared to the trivial upper bound.

Results for FLY. The lower and upper bounds for each of the five realistic queries are presented in Table 5. As can be seen, the lower and upper bounds coincide in Q_3, and the lower bound answers were empty for the remaining four cases. This is because the ontology includes many axioms that are outside the OWL 2 RL profile, and in particular many existential restrictions. We were able to confirm using HermiT that the upper bounds are tight for all these queries.

5.3 Scalability Tests

To test the scalability of upper bound computation using Oracle's reasoner, we have conducted experiments using LUBM and UOBM data sets of increasing size (1, 5, 10, 100 universities for LUBM and UOBM, and 1,000 universities for LUBM). We also report computation times for FLY.

Test for LUBM. Results for all the standard queries and generated queries are summarised in Figure 7(a); in the figure, materialisation time refers to the total time for computing the saturation for each data set and querying time refers to the average query answering time for each query. We can observe that query answering times and scalability behaviour is very similar for lower and upper bound computation. Fully-fledged OWL 2 reasoners are much slower, even for the smallest data sets; for LUBM(1), HermiT required 7,684 seconds to compute the exact answers to one of the queries with matching lower and upper bounds.

---

[8] Excluding three cases where the lower bound is empty and the upper bound non-empty.

Table 3: Standard queries for UOBM

Query	Q_1	Q_2	Q_3	Q_4	Q_5	Q_6	Q_7	Q_8	Q_9	Q_{10}	Q_{11}	Q_{12}	Q_{13}	Q_{14}	Q_{15}
Lower Bound	21	2,465	581	292	235	991	0	376	1,298	8	2,416	50	0	6,271	0
Upper Bound	21	2,465	581	603	235	1,008	50	455	2,528	191	8,852	1,027	455	12,782	455
Gap	0	0	0	311	0	17	50	79	1,230	183	6,436	977	455	6,511	455
Exact Answers	21	2,465	581	292	235	991	0	376	1,298	8	2,416	50	416	6,535	0

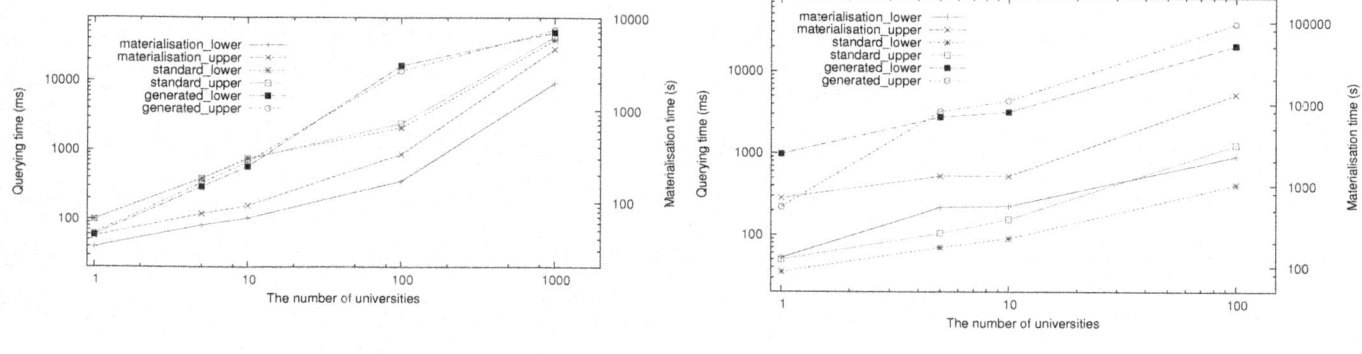

(a) Time for LUBM (b) Time for UOBM

Figure 7: Scalability tests

Table 5: Realistic queries for FLY. Upper bound is tight in all cases.

Query	Q_1	Q_2	Q_3	Q_4	Q_5
Lower Bound	0	0	28	0	0
Upper Bound	803	342	28	25	518

Test for GEN-UOBM. Results for both standard and generated queries are given in Figure 7(b). In this case, the materialisation time is higher for the upper bound than that for the lower bound because of the increased number of materialised triples. The time to answer queries also increases significantly, but is in line with the increased size of the answer. For example, the lower bound for generated Query 195 on UOBM(10) contains 132,411 answer tuples, whereas the upper bound contains 1,961,095 answer tuples. Although less efficient than lower bound computation, upper bound computation significantly outperforms HermiT, and the lower and upper bounds coincide for 9 out of 14 queries. Upper bound computation required less than 2 seconds for *all* standard queries w.r.t. UOBM(1); HermiT, in comparison, failed to compute the answer to one of the standard queries (Query 6)[9], even when given a 24h timeout. We also used HermiT to check tuples in the gap between the lower bound and upper bound for this query, which took only 1 hour. This illustrates the potential of upper and lower bound answers in optimising the computation of exact answers.

Test for FLY. Oracle's reasoner required 164s and 493s respectively to compute the lower and upper bound materialisation, and to answer all queries. The query answering time was negligible compared to materialisation time.

---
[9] $Q(x) \leftarrow \mathsf{hasAlumnus}(\mathsf{Univ0}, x) \wedge \mathsf{Person}(x)$

6. RELATED WORK

Our work is related to *theory approximation*, which was first described in the seminal paper by Kautz and Selman [30]. The idea in theory approximation is to approximate a logical theory $\mathcal{T}$ by two theories $\mathcal{T}_{lb}$ (the *model lower bound*) and $\mathcal{T}_{ub}$ (the *model upper bound*) such that $\mathcal{T}_{lb} \models \mathcal{T} \models \mathcal{T}_{ub}$, both $\mathcal{T}_{lb}$ and $\mathcal{T}_{ub}$ are in a "more tractable" language than $\mathcal{T}$, and $\mathcal{T}_{lb}$ and $\mathcal{T}_{ub}$ are "as close as possible" to $\mathcal{T}$. Kautz and Selman studied this problem for $\mathcal{T}$ in propositional logic and the bounds expressed in its Horn fragment. Del Val [7] studied the problem for first-order logic. This line of research has focused mostly on the computation of the "best" model upper bounds; however, we focus on query answers rather than models and hence our upper bounds correspond to *model lower bounds*, which have received little attention.

The idea of transforming the ontology, data, and/or query to obtain upper bounds to query answers has been already explored in previous work. Table 6 summarises the main differences between our approach and the systems presented in [32, 27, 18], which we next explain in more detail.

The SCREECH system [32] uses KAON2 [16] to transform an ontology into a disjunctive datalog program such that answers to SPARQL queries are preserved, and then approximates the resulting disjunctive program into a datalog program by transforming disjunctions into conjunctions. The transformation of the ontology (which is delegated to KAON2) requires exponential time (and may also be of exponential size) in the size of the input ontology. This exponential blow-up means that, in practice, KAON2 may be unable to process large or complex ontologies; for example, KAON2 was reported to fail on the DOLCE ontology [24]. Finally, due to the dependency on KAON2, SCREECH can only deal with the subset of OWL 2 corresponding to the

Table 6: Comparison between different systems

System	Source	Target	Independence Data	Independence Query	Time	Query
SCREECH [32]	$\mathcal{SHIQ}$	DATALOG	NO	YES	exponential	SPARQL
QUILL [27]	OWL DL	DL-Lite	NO	NO	exponential	CQ
[18]	$\mathcal{SHI}$	DL-Lite	YES	YES	exponential	SPARQL
Ours	OWL 2	OWL 2 RL	YES	YES	polynomial	CQ

$\mathcal{SHIQ}$ DL, and is guaranteed to compute an upper bound only for SPARQL queries; in contrast our approach applies to all of OWL 2 as well as to more general query languages.

The QUILL system transforms both the ontology $\mathcal{O}$ and query Q to compute an upper bound [27]. In this case, the target language for approximation is DL-Lite (a.k.a. OWL 2 QL), instead of OWL 2 RL. QUILL first transforms Q and adds axioms $\mathcal{O}_Q$ to $\mathcal{O}$ based on this transformation. Then, QUILL computes as an approximation OWL 2 QL axioms entailed by $\mathcal{O} \cup \mathcal{O}_Q \cup D$, with D the input data set. Each entailment test requires the use of a fully-fledged OWL reasoner, which can be expensive; also, the required entailments need to be recomputed for each query and each data set.

Kaplunova et al. [18] approximate an ontology $\mathcal{O}$ into an OWL 2 QL ontology $\mathcal{O}'$ to provide an upper bound to queries in SPARQL. Each axiom $C \sqsubseteq D$ in $\mathcal{O}$ is transformed into an OWL 2 QL axiom $C' \sqsubseteq D'$, where C is subsumed by C' and D' is subsumed by D (w.r.t. $\mathcal{O}$). The transformation algorithm, however, is non-deterministic and there can be exponentially many C' and D' satisfying the required properties. Furthermore, as reported in [18], it is often the case that for a given D such that $\mathcal{O} \cup D$ is satisfiable, $\mathcal{O}' \cup D$ is unsatisfiable, regardless of the choices made when computing $\mathcal{O}'$. The large degree of non-determinism means that computing $\mathcal{O}'$ can be expensive, even for small ontologies—it is reported in [18] that "it is very demanding to approximate a TBox with 499 axioms", and that they were unable to compute a coherent approximation "in reasonable time".

7. DISCUSSION

We have proposed novel techniques that allow us to exploit industrial-strength triple stores to answer queries over ontologies that are outside OWL 2 RL, thus "making the most" of state-of-the-art triple store technologies. Our techniques allow us to compute exact answers to queries in many cases. Otherwise, we can still efficiently compute an upper bound to the exact answers, which allows us to estimate the incompleteness of the triple store as well as to optimise OWL 2 reasoners by ruling out many candidate answer tuples.

The results obtained so far open many possibilities for future work. For example, we plan to develop techniques for identifying, during upper bound computation, a (hopefully small) fragment of the ontology and data set that is sufficient for checking whether the answers in the gap between bounds are indeed answers; this fragment can then be used instead of the original ontology when checking answers in the gap using an OWL 2 reasoner.

Acknowledgements. Work supported by the Royal Society, the EU FP7 project OPTIQUE and the EPSRC projects ExODA, and SCORE!.

8. REFERENCES

[1] B. Bishop, A. Kiryakov, D. Ognyanoff, I. Peikov, Z. Tashev, and R. Velkov. OWLim: A family of scalable semantic repositories. *Semantic Web J.*, 2(1):33–42, 2011.

[2] A. Cali, G. Gottlob, T. Lukasiewicz, B. Marnette, and A. Pieris. Datalog+/-: A family of logical knowledge representation and query languages for new applications. In *LICS*, 2010.

[3] B. Cuenca Grau, I. Horrocks, Y. Kazakov, and U. Sattler. Modular reuse of ontologies: Theory and practice. *JAIR*, 31:273–318, 2008.

[4] B. Cuenca Grau, I. Horrocks, M. Krötzsch, C. Kupke, D. Magka, B. Motik, and Z. Wang. Acyclicity conditions and their application to query answering in description logics. In *KR*, 2012.

[5] B. Cuenca Grau and G. Stoilos. What to ask to an incomplete semantic web reasoner? In *IJCAI*, pages 419–476, 2011.

[6] E. Dantsin, T. Eiter, G. Gottlob, and A. Voronkov. Complexity and expressive power of logic programming. *ACM Comput. Surv.*, 33(3):374–425, 2001.

[7] A. Del Val. First order LUB approximations: characterization and algorithms. *Artificial Intelligence*, 162(1-2):7–48, 2005.

[8] B. N. Grosof, I. Horrocks, R. Volz, and S. Decker. Description logic programs: combining logic programs with description logic. In *WWW*, 2003.

[9] Y. Guo, Z. Pan, and J. Heflin. LUBM: A benchmark for OWL knowledge base systems. *J. Web Semantics (JWS)*, 3(2-3):158–182, 2005.

[10] V. Haarslev and R. Möller. RACER system description. *J. of Automated Reasoning (JAR)*, pages 701–705, 2001.

[11] V. Haarslev, R. Möller, and M. Wessel. Querying the semantic web with RACER+NRQL. In *ADL*, 2004.

[12] A. Harth, A. Umbrich, A. Hogan, and S. Decker. Yars2: A federated repository for querying graph structured data from the web. *The Semantic Web*, pages 211–224, 2007.

[13] I. Horrocks, O. Kutz, and U. Sattler. The even more irresistible $\mathcal{SROIQ}$. In *KR*, 2006.

[14] I. Horrocks and S. Tessaris. A conjunctive query language for description logic aboxes. In *AAAI*, 2000.

[15] J. Huang, D. J. Abadi, and K. Ren. Scalable SPARQL querying of large RDF graphs. *PVLDB*, 4(11):1123–1134, 2011.

[16] U. Hustadt, B. Motik, and U. Sattler. Reasoning in description logics by a reduction to disjunctive datalog. *Journal of Automated Reasoning*, 39(3):351–384, 2007.

[17] M. Imprialou, G. Stoilos, and B. Grau. Benchmarking ontology-based query rewriting systems. In *Proceedings of the Twenty-Sixth AAAI Conference on Artificial Intelligence, AAAI*, 2012.

[18] A. Kaplunova, R. Möller, S. Wandelt, and M. Wessel. Towards scalable instance retrieval over ontologies. *Knowledge Science, Engineering and Management*, pages 436–448, 2010.

[19] I. Kollia, B. Glimm, and I. Horrocks. Query answering over SROIQ knowledge bases with SPARQL. In *DL*, 2011.

[20] V. Kolovski, Z. Wu, and G. Eadon. Optimizing enterprise-scale owl 2 rl reasoning in a relational database system. *The Semantic Web–ISWC 2010*, pages 436–452, 2010.

[21] L. Ma, Y. Yang, Z. Qiu, G. Xie, Y. Pan, and S. Liu. Towards a complete OWL ontology benchmark. In *ESWC*, pages 125–139, 2006.

[22] B. Motik, B. Cuenca Grau, I. Horrocks, Z. Wu, A. Fokoue, and C. Lutz. OWL 2 Web Ontology Language Profiles. *W3C Recommendation*, 2009.

[23] B. Motik, P. Patel-Schneider, B. Parsia, C. Bock, A. Fokoue, P. Haase, R. Hoekstra, I. Horrocks, A. Ruttenberg, U. Sattler, et al. OWL 2 Web Ontology Language: Structural Specification and Functional-style Syntax. *W3C recommendation*, 27:17, 2009.

[24] B. Motik and U. Sattler. A comparison of reasoning techniques for querying large description logic aboxes. In *Logic for Programming, Artificial Intelligence, and Reasoning*, pages 227–241. Springer, 2006.

[25] B. Motik, R. Shearer, and I. Horrocks. Hypertableau reasoning for description logics. *J. of Artificial Intelligence Research (JAIR)*, 36(1):165–228, 2009.

[26] T. Neumann and G. Weikum. The RDF-3X engine for scalable management of RDF data. *VLDB J.*, 19(1):91–113, 2010.

[27] J. Pan, E. Thomas, and Y. Zhao. Completeness guaranteed approximations for OWL-DL query answering. *Proc. of DL*, 477, 2009.

[28] J. Pérez, M. Arenas, and C. Gutierrez. Semantics and complexity of SPARQL. *ACM Transactions on Database Systems (TODS)*, 34(3):16, 2009.

[29] K. Rohloff and R. Schantz. High-performance, massively scalable distributed systems using the mapreduce software framework: The shard triple-store. In *Programming Support Innovations for Emerging Distributed Applications*, 2010.

[30] B. Selman and H. Kautz. Knowledge compilation and theory approximation. *J. of the ACM (JACM)*, 43(2):193–224, 1996.

[31] E. Sirin, B. Parsia, B. Cuenca Grau, A. Kalyanpur, and Y. Katz. Pellet: A practical OWL-DL reasoner. *J. Web Semantics (JWS)*, 5(2):51–53, 2007.

[32] T. Tserendorj, S. Rudolph, M. Krötzsch, and P. Hitzler. Approximate OWL-reasoning with screech. In *RR*, number 5341 in LNCS, pages 165–180, 2008.

[33] C. Weiss, P. Karras, and A. Bernstein. Hexastore: sextuple indexing for semantic web data management. *Proceedings of the VLDB Endowment*, 1(1):1008–1019, 2008.

[34] Z. Wu, G. Eadon, S. Das, E. I. Chong, V. Kolovski, M. Annamalai, and J. Srinivasan. Implementing an inference engine for RDFS/OWL constructs and user-defined rules in Oracle. In *ICDE*, pages 1239–1248, 2008.

Security Implications of Password Discretization for Click-based Graphical Passwords*

Bin B. Zhu[1], Dongchen Wei[2], Maowei Yang[3], Jeff Yan[4]
[1] Microsoft Research Asia, Beijing, China
[2,3] Sichuan University, Chengdu, Sichuan, China
[4] Newcastle University, United Kingdom
[1]binzhu@microsoft.com, [2]v-dowe@microsoft.com, [3]djyangmaowei@gmail.com,
[4]jeff.yan@ncl.ac.uk

ABSTRACT

Discretization is a standard technique used in click-based graphical passwords for tolerating input variance so that approximately correct passwords are accepted by the system. In this paper, we show for the first time that two representative discretization schemes leak a significant amount of password information, undermining the security of such graphical passwords. We exploit such information leakage for successful dictionary attacks on Persuasive Cued Click Points (PCCP), which is to date the most secure click-based graphical password scheme and was considered to be *resistant* to such attacks. In our experiments, our purely automated attack successfully guessed 69.2% of the passwords when Centered Discretization was used to implement PCCP, and 39.4% of the passwords when Robust Discretization was used. Each attack dictionary we used was of approximately 2^{35} entries, whereas the full password space was of 2^{43} entries. For Centered Discretization, our attack still successfully guessed 50% of the passwords when the dictionary size was reduced to approximately 2^{30} entries. Our attack is also applicable to common implementations of other click-based graphical password systems such as PassPoints and Cued Click Points – both have been extensively studied in the research communities.

Categories and Subject Descriptors

K.6.5 [**Management of Computing and Information Systems**]: Security and Protection – *Authentication, unauthorized access.*
K.4.4 [**Computers and Society**]: Electronic Commerce – *Security.*

General Terms

Security, Experimentation.

Keywords

Graphical passwords, dictionary attack, discretization, authentication.

1. INTRODUCTION

Passwords have been widely used to authenticate users to remote servers in Web and other applications. Text passwords have been used for a long time. Graphical passwords, introduced by Blonder [1] in 1996, are an alternative to text passwords. In a graphical password, a user interacts with one or more images to create or enter a password. Graphical passwords are intended to capitalize on the promise of better memorability and improved security against guessing attacks. Graphical passwords are particularly suitable for keyboardless devices such as iPads and iPhones whereon inputting a text password is cumbersome. For example, Windows 8 recently released by Microsoft supports graphical password logon. With increasingly popularity of smart phones and slate computers, we expect to see a wider deployment of graphical passwords in Web applications.

Among a large variety of graphical password proposals, click-based graphical passwords have attracted the most attention in both the Human-Computer Interaction (HCI) and security communities. A click-based graphical password consists of a sequence of click-points on one or more images. To log in, a user clicks the same points of her password, in the correct order, on the same image(s). PassPoints [2][3] is a representative click-based graphical password scheme, wherein a password consists of a sequence of points anywhere on an image. Later studies [5]-[11] indicate that PassPoints is vulnerable to dictionary attacks which exploit image hotspots [5][6] (i.e. spots that are more likely to be selected as click-points across users) and patterns of click-points [7]. Purely automated attacks [10][11] detect corner points and centroid points as hotspots, and apply heuristics to select a set of combinations of the detected hotspots to form dictionaries of guessed passwords. The attacks on two representative images used in PassPoints guessed 7-16% of the passwords for dictionaries each with approximately 2^{26} entries, and 48-54% of the passwords for dictionaries each with approximately 2^{35} entries, whereas the full password space contained 2^{43} entries.

Lessons of hotspot-based dictionary attacks on PassPoints led to the design of two improved click-based graphical password schemes, Cued Click Points (CCP) [12] and Persuasive Cued Click Points (PCCP) [13][14]. CCP is a variation of PassPoints with improved security, and PCCP improves the security further. PCCP has been considered robust to all the reported hotspot-based dictionary attacks.

Click-based graphical password schemes such as PassPoints, CCP, and PCCP allow arbitrary click-points in a password. Due to inevitable click inaccuracy, a predefined tolerance distance is used in these schemes that a click is verified correct if it falls in the tolerance region which has a distance to the originally chosen click-point equal to or less than the tolerance distance. This would work well if the password is stored in the clear in the system. For the sake of security, a practical system typically does not store

---

Copyright is held by the International World Wide Web Conference Committee (IW3C2). IW3C2 reserves the right to provide a hyperlink to the author's site if the Material is used in electronic media.
WWW 2013, May 13–17, 2013, Rio de Janeiro, Brazil.
ACM 978-1-4503-2035-1 /13/05.

* Corresponding author: Bin B. Zhu (binzhu@microsoft.com or binzhu@ieee.org). This work was done when Dongchen Wei and Maowei Yang were interns at Microsoft Research Asia.

passwords in the clear. Instead, a password is cryptographically hashed and the hash value is stored in the system. It is impossible for such a system to calculate the distance of a click to the corresponding click-point in the password since a single bit change in the input would result in a completely different hash value. Therefore the system has no way to check if the click is within the tolerance region of the click-point or not. This problem is identified in [15]. A solution is discretization of click-points using grids so that all tolerable clicks of a click-point are inside a single grid cell. A discretization scheme should guarantee a minimum tolerance range of r pixels, i.e., being r-safe: if a clicked point is within r pixels from the desirable point, the same discretization point would always be produced.

Several password discretization schemes have been proposed. Robust Discretization [15] uses three offset grids of grid-square size $6r \times 6r$ to guarantee that for every point in the image, there exists at least one grid whereby the point is r-safe. Centered Discretization [16] determines the grid for a point such that the point is the center of a grid-square of the grid. Its grid-square size is $2r \times 2r$ to maintain that the point is r-safe. Centered Discretization produces a smaller grid-square than Robust Discretization without impacting the usability of the system [16]. Optimal Discretization [17] is the same as Centered Discretization when offset is used, and suffers from the edge problem of discretization (i.e., a small perturbation may result in a wrong grid-square when the click-point is near a grid line) when no offset is used. The edge problem is what the other discretization schemes tried to avoid in their designs. As a consequence, multiple trials of possible grid-squares due to acceptable click-variation are used during authentication to address the edge problem of discretization when offset is not used in Optimal Discretization. Image-dependent discretization is proposed in [18], wherein image features are analyzed and Voronoi polygon tiling is produced that likely click-points are centered within the polygons.

In all these discretization schemes, grid information used for a password is stored in the system in plaintext so that the same grids are used to discretize clicks in authenticating a user. This information may be accessible to adversaries. A natural question arises: what is the security implication of this additional information about a password? It is believed that the additional information of the discretization grids does not lead to weaker security [16]. It has remained for years an open problem whether it is possible for adversaries to exploit such information to their advantage [14][16][19].

In this paper, we for the first time address this open question, which concerns an important aspect of applying click-based graphical password schemes including PassPoints, CCP and PCCP in real applications. Our security analysis on two representative discretization schemes, Robust Discretization and Centered Discretization, indicates that discretization does have significant security implications: it leaks information about password click-points, and thus leads to weaker security. The leaked information can be exploited to mount successful dictionary attacks on click-based graphical password schemes such as PCCP which are otherwise considered robust to the dictionary attacks. Our experimental studies on PCCP show that our purely automatic dictionary attacks using dictionaries each with approximately 2^{35} entries guessed 69.2% of the passwords when Centered Discretization was used, and 39.4% of the passwords when Robust Discretization was used, whereas the full password space was of 2^{43} entries. In addition, for Centered Discretization, our attack still successfully guessed 50% of the passwords when the attack dictionary size was reduced to approximately 2^{30}. Our work sheds light on the future design of secure yet practical discretization schemes.

The remaining paper is organized as follows. Related work is reviewed in Section 2. Technical details of discretization schemes are described in Section 3. We present our security analysis of discretization schemes in Section 4. Our dictionary attacks on PCCP using both Robust Discretization and Centered Discretization are described in Section 5. Discussions are presented in Section 6. The paper concludes in Section 7.

2. RELATED WORK
We briefly review click-based graphical passwords and their dictionary attacks in this section. Details on discretization schemes are provided in Section 3.

2.1 Click-based Graphical Passwords
Since the introduction of the first graphical password scheme by Blonder [1] in 1996, graphical passwords have become an active research topic, and a large number of graphical password schemes have been proposed. Among these schemes, click-based graphical password schemes have attracted the most attention in both HCI and security research communities. They will be briefly described here. For more detailed information of click-based graphical password schemes as well as other types of graphical password schemes, readers are referred to a recent comprehensive review of graphical password schemes [19].

In Blonder's scheme [1], users click on a set of predefined tap regions. Jansen et al. [20] proposed a variation which requires users to click an ordered sequence of visible squares imposed on a background image. The squares are used to help users repeat click-points in subsequent logins. In V-go [21], users click on a sequence of predefined objects in the image. PassPoints [2][3] is the first click-based graphical scheme that allows a user to click anywhere on an image in creating a password. It requires a user to click a sequence of l points anywhere on an image. PassPoints has studied extensively. Studies [2]-[4] indicate that $l = 5$ leads to promising usability. Thus this setting has been widely adopted in the literature. Cued Click Points (CCP) [12] is a variation of PassPoints with improved security. In CCP, a sequence of images is used in entering a password, one click per image, with the next image selected by a deterministic function. The security is further improved with Persuasive Cued Click Points (PCCP) [13][14], which requires a user to select each click-point inside a randomly positioned viewport in creating a password, resulting in more randomly distributed click-points in a password.

2.2 Dictionary Attacks on Click-based Graphical Passwords
Effective dictionary attacks have been conducted on PassPoints-style graphical password schemes by exploiting two weaknesses in human selection of a password: hotspots and patterns. Hotspots [5][6] are spots more likely selected as click-points across users, and patterns [7] are likely click orders and location relationships of click-points in users' passwords. Both are related to predictable preferences in human created passwords.

Image processing techniques have been used to locate hotspots in an image to enable automatic guessing attacks [5][10][11] on click-based graphical passwords. Dirik et al. [5] proposed automatic dictionary attacks on PassPoints, whereby mean-shift image segmentation [22][23] was applied to detect centroids of segments that are not too large or too small, and then grid-squares were sorted according to their probabilities to be in a password, calculated by applying a user attention model, to build attack dictionaries. Experiments on a representative image found 8.45% of the passwords using a dictionary of approximately 2^{31} entries whereas the full password space was of 2^{40} entries [5]. Salehi-Abari et al. [10] proposed an automatic hotspot-based dictionary attack against PassPoints-style graphical passwords, which were subsequently improved by van Oorschot et al. [11]. In these attacks, both corner and centroids are detected to form a set of predicted click-points. This set is too large to build an effective attack dictionary by traversing all combinations of the predicted click-points. Heuristic patterns of click-points in a password and salient regions detected using a visual attention model are used to select likely combinations of the predicted click-points in building attack dictionaries. Experiments using two representative images with a full password space of 2^{43} entries found 7-16% of the passwords using dictionaries each of approximately 2^{26} entries, and 48-54% of the passwords using dictionaries each of approximately 2^{35} entries [11].

In human-seeded attacks [8][9] on PassPoints, click-points from a small set of users are harvested for targeted images, and attack dictionaries are constructed using a first-order Markov model or an independent probability model. In a lab study [8][9] on two representative images with the full password space of 2^{43} entries, the method found 20-36% of the passwords using dictionaries each of 2^{31} to 2^{33} entries built with the independent probability model and 4-10% of the passwords within 100 guesses using the first-order Markov model.

An analysis of user-selected passwords reported in [7] revealed that for CCP, users still tended to select click-points falling within known hotspots, but the patterns of click-points exploited in successful dictionary attacks on PassPoints were eliminated; on the other hand, PCCP had eliminated both common patterns and hotspots. Therefore, PCCP was considered to be robust to all the known dictionary attacks.

3. DISCRETIZATION SCHEMES

We briefly described several discretization schemes in Section 1. Since Optimal Discretization [17] is the same as Centered Discretization [16] when the edge problem of discretization is avoided and the image-dependent discretization scheme [18] lacks detailed information for an actual implantation, our security analysis will focus only on Robust Discretization and Centered Discretization. In the following, we describe these two schemes in detail.

3.1 Robust Discretization

Robust Discretization [15] uses three offset grids to guarantee that for each point in the image, there exists at least one grid in which the point is r-safe. Specifically, each grid $G_k, k \in \{1,2,3\}$ has a grid-square size of $6r \times 6r$, with an offset from each other by a distance of $2r$ in both directions. Figure 1 shows an example of the three grids in Robust Discretization, along with two points A and B, wherein point A is r-safe in grid G_0, and point B is r-safe in both G_1 and G_2. When creating a password, one of the three grids is selected for each click-point. When a click-point is r-safe in more than one grid, a selection algorithm is needed to select one from the candidate grids. An optimal algorithm [16] selects the grid wherein the point is closest to the center of the grid-square in order to minimize the occurrence of false accepts and false rejects of passwords.

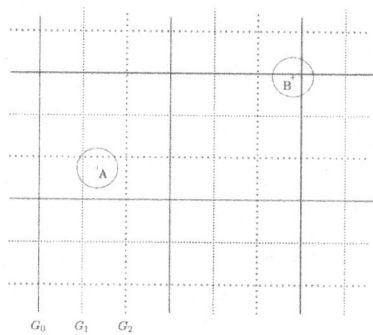

Figure 1. Robust Discretization: Three grids G_0, G_1, and G_2, wherein A is r-safe in G_0 and B is r-safe in both G_1 and G_2 (taken from [15]).

With Robust Discretization, each click-point in a password is associated with an image, a grid selected for the click-point, and a grid-square in the grid where the click-point lies in. Therefore a password can be represented by a sequence of grid-squares in the selected grids with corresponding images associated with the click-points of the password; and a cryptographic hash of the sequence is stored in the system. Identifiers of the selected grids for the password's click-points are also stored in the system but in plaintext. During authentication, the stored grid identifier for each click-point is retrieved to determine the exact grid-square which a user-clicked point actually lie in. The hash of the resulting sequence of the grid-squares with the corresponding images is calculated and compared with the stored hash to determine if authentication is a success or failure.

3.2 Centered Discretization

Centered Discretization [16] finds, for each click-point in a password, a grid wherein the click-point is the center of a grid-square in the grid. This grid can be uniquely determined by an offset to the grid aligned with both x-axis and y-axis. This offset is stored in plaintext in the system, and will be used to reconstruct the grid during authentication. To make the point be r-safe, each grid has a grid-square size of $2r \times 2r$. The grid's offset is For every click-point, Centered Discretization has the same maximal tolerance level of click-variations, which is r pixels on each direction; whereas for click-points at different locations, Robust Discretization has various maximal tolerance levels of click-variations, in the range from r to $3r$. If the click-point is at the center of its grid-square, it can accept click-variations within $3r$ pixels on each direction. That maximal tolerance level reduces gradually to r when the click-point moves from the center towards an edge of the grid-square.

For the same guaranteed tolerance range r of click-variations, a grid-square in Centered Discretization is one third in size of that in Robust Discretization along each direction, resulting in the size of the full password space in Centered Discretization about $9^5 \approx 2^{16}$ times of that in Robust Discretization for passwords of 5 click-points. For the same grid-square size, Centered Discretization has a guaranteed tolerance level three times that Robust Discretization offers, whereas both have the same size for the full password space.

Security of Centered Discretization is compared with that of Robust Discretization in [16] using PassPoints, with the conclusion that both discretization schemes have the same level of security when both have the same size of grid-squares, and that Centered Discretization is more secure when they are both r-safe.

4. A SECURITY ANALYSIS

In this section, we present a security analysis of Robust Discretization and Centered Discretization. We first explain theoretical models assumed in our analysis, and describe key observations that motivated our attacks. Next, we introduce our attack methodology, which consists of two stages. In the first stage, image processing techniques are used to detect potential click-points in each image. In the second stage, discretization information stored in the system is exploited to build attack dictionaries. This security analysis is generic, as it is independent from any specific click-based graphical password scheme.

4.1 Theoretical Models

4.1.1 Threat Model

HTTP Authentication [24] has been widely used in Web applications. It contains two types of authentication protocols, Basic Access Authentication and Digest Access Authentication. The latter is more secure than the former. In Digest Access Authentication, password hash is calculated at the client side. As a consequence, the discretization grid information for each click-point of a password needs to send to client when a discretization scheme is used in Digest Access Authentication, and thus accessible to adversaries. Since discretization grid information is stored in plaintext, it is also accessible to adversaries in offline dictionary attacks. A password guess can be verified with the system for online dictionary attacks or with the stored password hash for offline dictionary attacks. A user ID is frequently stored in a Web browser and thus accessible to adversaries.

In summary, the threat model in our studies is as follows: *Adversaries have access to everything except passwords or the information accessible only with passwords. Particularly, adversaries have access to the discretization information, user IDs, and hash values of passwords stored in the system.*

We note that the above threat model is generic, not necessarily tied with Web applications. For example, the threat model is applicable for offline dictionary attacks whereby adversaries have access to the authentication information stored in the authentication server.

4.1.2 Independent Model of Click-Points

For generality, we assume that click-points are mutually independent. For some click-based graphical password schemes such as PassPoints, there might exist some correlations among the click-points in a password, as exploited by successful dictionary attacks on PassPoints described in Section 2.2. The correlations can be exploited to improve efficiency of the dictionary attacks to be presented in this paper. For example, the heuristic patterns of click-points used in [10][11] or the first-order Markov model used in [8][9] can be applied to improve our dictionary attacks on discretization with PassPoints.

4.2 Key Observations

Our security analysis was motivated with the following two observations. The first is on click-points likely selected in click-based graphical passwords, and the second is on the distribution of human click-variations.

4.2.1 Click-Points of Graphical Passwords

A study [7] reveals that hotspots exist in both PassPoints and CCP, but are eliminated in PCCP, thanks to the requirement that a click-point is selected within a randomly positioned viewport. We conceive that click-points in PCCP are likely salient points in viewports that should be detectable with image processing techniques. That conception led us to using corners and centroids in images to predict click-points for all click-based graphical password schemes.

There are typically too many detected salient points (i.e., corners and centroids) that a dictionary built by traversing all their combinations is too large to mount a meaningful dictionary attack. Patterns of click-points in a password and other techniques such as a user attention model have been used to select only likely salient points and their combinations in dictionary attacks on PassPoints [5][10][11]. These techniques can no longer be used to attack PCCP, as concluded in [7]. With the independent model of click-points assumed in this paper, detected corners and centroids cannot in general mount an effective dictionary attack on a click-based graphical password scheme. We need to reduce the size of dictionaries significantly to mount a meaningful dictionary attack.

4.2.2 Distribution of Human Click Variations

People have different accuracy in re-clicking a point. Figure 2 shows the result of a study by Chiasson et al. [12] with 24 university students on the accuracy that users re-entered click-points for both stages of password confirmation and login. More than 70% of the users had small variations, in the range from 1 to 3 pixels, in re-entering click-points. Click-variations for the remaining users distribute in the long tail in the figure, ranging from 4 to more than 51 pixels.

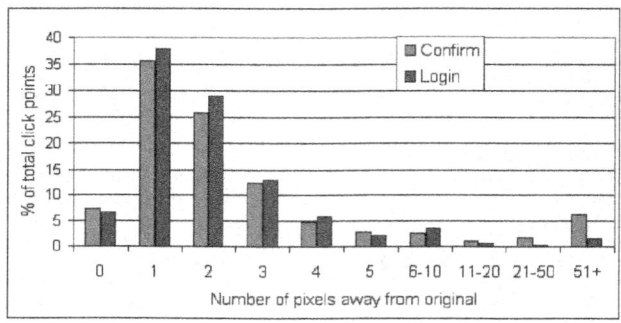

Figure 2. Accuracy in re-entering click-points (taken from [12]).

For acceptable usability, a practical system should select r of a discretization scheme conservatively so that most users should be able to enter their passwords correctly. In other words, r should be selected significantly larger than most users' click-variations. For example r should be 4 pixels or larger from Figure 2. We conceive that the disparity between a large tolerance range of the system and small click-variations for most people can be exploited to remove salient points unlikely related to the click-point currently seeking for: salient points far away from likely locations of the current click-point are removed. Additionally, if the location of a click-point is known within a grid-square as in Centered Discretization or predictable as in the image-dependent discretization scheme [18], salient points can be rank-ordered by their distances to the click-point's locations inside their respective grid-squares: a salient point with a shorter distance is more likely to be the click-point. This conception led to our method to build effective dictionaries from detected salient points by exploiting the location information of a click-point leaked by a discretization scheme, as to be described in Section 4.4.

4.3 Prediction of Click-Points

Like [10][11], corners and centroids are detected with image processing techniques and used as salient points to predict click-points for click-based graphical password schemes such as PCCP, CCP, and PassPoints. A corner is the intersection of two edges, and a centroid is the center point of an object. Corner detection and centroid detection we recommend to use are described as follows.

4.3.1 Corner Detection

Harris corner detection [25] implemented by Kovesi [26] is used to detect corners. Kovesi's implementation contains three parameters, "sigma" (σ), "thresh" (θ), and "radius" (r), where σ is the standard deviation of a smoothing Gaussian filter, θ measures the strength of non-maxima-suppression: all corners with weight lower than θ are suppressed, r is an inhibition radius, measured in pixels around a detected corner. For large θ, Kovesi's detector detects strongly distinctive corners. Weakly distinctive corners can also be detected when the value of θ reduces. The following unique method is applied to detect corners in an image:

1. *Detection of strongly distinctive corners.* Kovesi's detector is applied to the image with the following parameters: $\sigma = 1, \theta = 65, r = 2$. The set of corners detected in this step is denoted by S_1.

2. *Detection of weakly distinctive corners.* Kovesi's detector is applied to the image with the following parameters: $\sigma = 1, \theta = 5, r = 4$. The set of corners detected in this step is denoted by S_2.

3. *Detection of weakly distinctive corners in 2X window.* The image is smoothed using a Gaussian filter with the standard deviation of 1.0, and then down-sampled. Kovesi's detector is applied to the resulting image with the following parameters: $\sigma = 1, \theta = 7, r = 2$. The set of corners detected in this step is denoted as S_3. This is equivalent to using Harris detector with a window twice the size in both directions of the default window used in Kovesi's implementation.

4. *Detection of weakly distinctive corners in both scales.* For each point p in S_2, if there exist a point in S_3 within a distance of 7 pixels from p, then p is kept in S_2. Otherwise p is removed from S_2. The set of survived corners in S_2 is denoted by S_2'.

5. *Detected corners.* The union of S_1 and S_2', $S = S_1 \cup S_2'$, is output as the detected corners of the image.

The detected corners in S are either strongly distinctive corners or weakly distinctive corners of large structures. Figure 3 shows the detected corners for image "pool" which has been widely used in security studies of PassPoints. Each corner is marked by a '+' on the image. Compared to the detected corners of the same image shown in [11], our corner detection produces a slightly smaller number of corners. The major difference between the two corner detection methods is around the tree leaves in the image: weak corners of small structures are suppressed in our corner detection.

4.3.2 Centroid Detection

Centroids are detected with the same method as in [11] except using a different implementation of mean-shift segmentation algorithm [22][23] for our convenience. We use the implementation [27] to segment images with the following values of the three parameters used by the implementation: $sigmaS = 7$, $sigmaR = 9$, and $minRegion = 100$. The last parameter is a threshold for the minimal segment area (in pixels). For the resulting segments, we calculate only the segments with an area of 500 pixels or less. Segments too large or too small are ignored. Only the segments with an area in the range from 100 pixels to 500 pixels are used to calculate centroids.

A segment with an irregular shape may result in a centroid outside the segment. This type of centroid is unlikely selected as a click-point, and thus should be removed. Removing this type of centroid is achieved by checking if the centroid is outside its segment or not. If the centroid is outside the segment, the centroid is removed. Otherwise the centroid is kept. The survived centroids are output as the detected centroids.

Figure 3. Detected corners (each corner is marked by a '+').

4.4 Construction of Dictionaries

For each click-point in a password, once salient points are detected, the discretization information stored in the system is exploited to remove salient points that are unlikely to be the click-point for Robust Discretization, or to rank-order combinations of salient points by their predicted probabilities to be the password for Centered Discretization. This section represents the key insights behind our attacks.

4.4.1 Dictionaries for Centered Discretization

In Centered Discretization, a click-point is the center of some grid-square of the grid associated with the click-point. According to the distribution of click variations shown in Figure 2, a point closer to but not at the center of its grid-square has a higher probability to be the click-point. A password consists of multiple click-points. For each password, we can build a model using distances of salient points to the centers of their grid-squares to predict the probability that a sequence of the salient points is the password.

Before applying the model, we prune salient points so that each grid-square contains at most one salient point. If a grid-square contains more than one salient point, only the salient point closest to the center of the grid-square is kept and all the other salient points in the grid-square are removed. Then one of the following two models is used to build attack dictionaries with entries ordered by their probability to be the password.

Zooming-out Window Model. In this model, we use a series of concentered windows with different sizes to determine the order of grid-squares in constructing a dictionary. More specifically, we place a selecting window W_d of size $2d \times 2d$ at the center of each grid-square, where $0 \leq d \leq r$, and assign a salient point a priority value d if the salient point is in window W_d but not in window W_{d-1}, where we assume that W_{-1} is empty. A salient point with a smaller priority value is closer to the center of its grid-square, and thus considered to be more probably to be the click-point. Salient points not in any selecting window are removed. The priority value of a grid-square is the priority value of the salient point inside the grid-square. Grid-squares containing no salient point are removed. The survived grid-squares are traversed for all possible combinations of grid-squares. Based on the independent model of click-points, the priority value of a sequence of grid-squares is assigned to be the sum of the priority values of the constituent grid-squares. The sequences with priority value s form a set denoted as G_s. A sequence in set G_i is more likely to be the password than a sequence in G_j if $i < j$. A series of dictionaries $\{D_s | s = 0, 1, \cdots\}$ can thus be constructed as follows:

$$D_s = \bigcup_{k=0}^{s} G_k \quad (1)$$

These dictionaries have the following relationship:

$$D_0 \subseteq D_1 \subseteq D_2 \subseteq \cdots \quad (2)$$

Password guesses in a dictionary D_s can therefore be partitioned into a layered order: the guesses in D_0 are ordered as the first layer and tested first; the guesses in D_1 but not in D_0 (i.e., the guesses in G_1) are ordered as the second layer and tested next. This process continues until all the guesses in D_s are ordered and tested. In other words, guesses in a dictionary D_s are tested according to their priority values, from low to high. Guesses with the same priority value can be tested in any order.

Probability Model. If we ignore the value at 0, we can approximate the distribution of user click-variations shown in Figure 2 with a normal distribution

$$f(d) = a \cdot exp(-\frac{d^2}{2\sigma^2}) \quad (3)$$

where a is a normalization coefficient and d ($0 \leq d \leq r$) is the distance of the point to the center of its grid-square. For simplicity, Eq. (3) is also used for the case $d = 0$ in our studies, although $f(d)$ at $d = 0$ deviates considerably from the value shown in Figure 2. We believe that such a deviation will be tolerated by our probability model, as this model is much more accurate than the zooming-out window model. The belief is confirmed true by our experimental results which will be reported later: even the zooming-out window model has produced good results.

For each grid-square containing a salient point, we calculate a probability that the click-point actually lies in the grid-square by using Eq. (3), with d being the distance of the salient point to the center of its grid-square. For every possible password guess constructed from the grid-squares containing salient points, according to the independent model of click-points, we calculate its probability to be the password as multiplication of the probabilities of the constituent grid-squares. These guesses are then sorted by their likelihood of being the password. An attack dictionary can select any number of most probable guesses, and guesses are tested in the order of their probability of being the password.

4.4.2 Dictionaries for Robust Discretization

In Robust Discretization, different schemes can be used to select a grid when more than one grid satisfies the guaranteed tolerance range r. The maximum tolerable range of click-variations runs from r to $3r$, depending on the location of the click-point in its grid-square. To have a good balance between usability and the size of the full password space, it is typical to choose the optimal grid that maximizes the safe distance of the click-point to the edges of the grid-square. This optimal Robust Discretization was used in [16] to study security of Robust Discretization, and has been adopted in our studies too. The optimal Robust Discretization leads to an eligible region that a click-point may lie in. Figure 4 shows the eligible region surrounded by the dashed lines inside the greyed grid-square if grid G_0 is used for the click-point. The eligible region is about 36% of the grid-square. With this information, we remove salient points that are not inside any eligible region. Then we select all the grid-squares that contain at least one salient point, and build a dictionary by traversing all their combinations using the independent model of click-points.

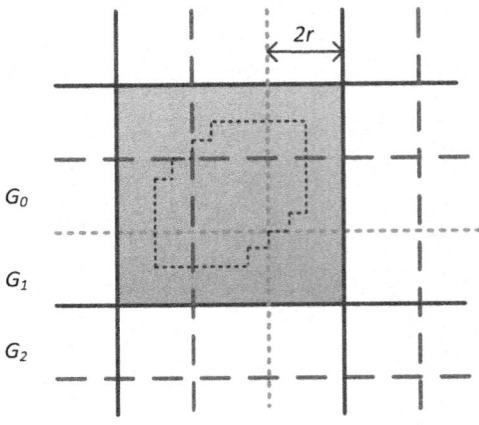

Figure 4. The eligible region that a click-point can lie inside a grid-square for grid G_0.

5. DICTIONARY ATTACKS ON PCCP USING DISCRETIZATION

5.1 Why do We Target PCCP?

PCCP was selected as the click-based graphical password scheme in our studies of the two representative discretization schemes since it was considered the most secure click-based graphical password scheme to date, robust to all the dictionary attacks reported on click-based graphical passwords. It was estimated in [13] that hotspot-based dictionary attacks would guess only 0.03% of PCCP passwords, a percentage that is extremely small as compared to the ratios of passwords guessed by dictionary attacks reported on PassPoints.

For PCCP, next image I_{next} is selected by a deterministic function f of current image I_{curr}, the current tolerance square, and the user ID:

$$I_{next} = f(I_{curr}, gridSquare, userID) \quad (4)$$

Eq. (4) makes PCCP rely on a discretization scheme in selecting a next image so that approximate clicks would result in the same next image. Due to this image selection mechanism, we cannot build a general dictionary to attack all users as in attacking PassPoints. Instead, we need to build personalized attack dictionaries for each individual user, which makes dictionary attacks much more complex than those on PassPoints. Like reported security studies on PassPoints, we assume that each password consists of 5 click-points in our studies.

According to the generic threat model in Section 4.1.1, user IDs are known to adversaries. Once a user ID is known, a single login attempt can obtain the first image used by the account. We also assume that a service is available to adversaries to determine the next image for every input triple consisting of a current image, a clicked grid-square, and a user ID. The generic threat model in Section 4.1 is thus refined as follows for PCCP: *Adversaries have access to everything except passwords or the information accessible only with passwords. Particularly, adversaries have access to the discretization information, user IDs, and hashed password stored in the system. For PCCP, adversaries have access to each user's first image and the image database. The deterministic function is used as an oracle that adversaries can query to get the index of the next image used in entering a password but have no access to and would not try to find the internal logic or parameters of the deterministic function. Adversaries do not have access to any password or any of the remaining images any user uses.*

5.2 Building Personalized Attack Dictionaries

To build personalized attack dictionaries for each participant in our studies, we detected salient points for the first image, processed these points using the grid information associated with the image, as described in Section 4.4, and obtained the grid-squares, $g_k^1 | k = 0, 1, \cdots$, which contain at least one salient point. Each of the grid-squares is a password guess of the first click-point. These grid-square form a set $D^1 = \{g_k^1 | k = 0, 1, \cdots\}$, which comprises of guesses of the user's password up to the first click-point.

Suppose we have finished the construction of set $D^i = \{g_k^i | k = 0, 1, \cdots\}$ comprising of password guesses of the user's password up to i-th click-point, $g_k^i | k = 0, 1, \cdots$, where $i < 5$. We use the following procedure to build the set D^{i+1} comprising of the password guesses of the user's password up to the $(i+1)$-th click-point.

- Initialize D^{i+1} to empty, and a count k to 0.
- For each entry $g_k^i \in D^i$, $k = 0, 1, \cdots$, we obtain the next image by querying the oracle with the current image, the current grid-square, and the user ID. Then we detect and process the salient points of the obtained image in the same way as for the first image. Each of the grid-squares containing at least one salient point for the obtained image is a guess of the $(i+1)$-th click-point of the user's password, and combined with the guess of the preceding click-points of g_k^i. Each resulting guess g_k^{i+1} is inserted into D^{i+1}, with the current value of the count k as the lower index k of the guess. After a guess is inserted into D^{i+1}, the count k is increased by 1.

The above procedure is applied until all the five click-points have been guessed. The resulting set D^5 is the attack dictionary, $D = D^5$, built for the user.

5.3 Experimental Setting

We searched Internet for images with similar complexity as the representative image shown in Figure 3, which has been widely used in security studies on click-based graphical password schemes, and collected 1200 images for our experimental studies on PCCP. These images were cropped to size of 451×331 pixels if necessary. The grid-square sizes in our studies ranged from 9×9 to 19×19. For passwords of 5 click-points, the size of the full password space for an individual user was 2^{43} if the largest grid-square 19×19 was used, or 2^{54} if the smallest grid-square 9×9 was used. The detection algorithms described in Section 4.3 were then applied to each image to detect the salient points in the image. The detected click-points were saved together with the image for later studies. We also implemented PCCP based on the description in [13]. In our implementation, MD5 hash function was used as the deterministic mapping function in Eq. (4) to select the next image, by dividing the resulting hash value by 1200, the total number of images in in our studies. A count starting from 0 was added to the list of parameters of the hash function. The count was increased by 1 when a new image was selected in entering a password, including dropped images as explained next. When the next image selected by the function repeated a preceding image in entering a password, the image was dropped and a new image was selected using the previously clicked grid-square. This process repeated until an image different from all the preceding images was selected. This process would result in a unique sequence of 5 different images for each user and her password.

Since the index of a grid-square depends on the size of the grid-square, Eq. (4) will select a different image and result in a different password for different sizes of grid-squares in our studies even if a user uses the same current image and the same click-point on the image in her password. This would complicate our experiments on different grid-square sizes since a participant would have to create and remember one password for every grid-square size, and we could not rule out interference in memorizing multiple passwords by a participant. To simplify the tasks each participant needed to perform in our studies and to avoid possible interference, we made a minor modification to Eq. (4) as follows:

$$I_{next} = f(I_{curr}, pointCoordinates, userID), \quad (5)$$

where $pointCoordinates$ is the coordinates of the recovered click-point calculated from the user's click. For Centered Discretization, the recovered click-point is the center of the clicked grid-square. For Robust Discretization, the recovered click-point is the point with a given bias from the center of the clicked grid-square, with the bias being the coordinates of the click-point relative to the center of the grid-square it lies in. The bias for each click-point is stored in the oracle to determine the next images for the user. If a user re-clicks the same grid-square in a login attempt, the recovered click-point is the actual click-point, and thus the correct next image is selected by Eq. (5). If a wrong grid-square is clicked, the recovered click-point is different from the actual click-point, and thus a wrong image is selected. Since Eq. (5) depends only on the coordinates of a click-point, which does not change for different grid-square sizes, a participant would create a single password valid for both Centered Discretization and Robust Discretization with different grid-square sizes, greatly simplifying our experiments. Such a modification has no impact on our security studies of the discretization schemes with PCCP when the images in the database are of similar complexity.

5.4 Password Collection

We conducted an in-lab user study with 38 voluntary participants (29 males and 9 females) to collect PCCP passwords. All the participants were engineering students ranging from undergraduate senior to Ph. D. students. All of them were good at using computers and Web browsing but none of them had studied computer or network security, or used the graphical password schemes under study. The participants were trained to get familiar with the experimental tasks in advance. They used Web browsers on their own PCs to create passwords and log into a remote authentication server. Each participant was required to select a password of 5 click-points in length. The selected password was confirmed immediately after creation with all the discretization schemes and configurations under test. Each participant was given up to three trials to pass the confirmation test. If a confirmation login failed three times with any discretization scheme and any configuration, the participant was asked to recreate a new password. This process was repeated until the created password was confirmed successfully. Our experimental results confirmed the distribution of click-variations shown in Figure 2: most participants could pass the confirmation test in a single trial, implying that their re-click variations were 3 pixels or less on each direction from the click-points.

Once a password had been successfully confirmed, the participant was required to pass two login tests, occurred at 24 hours and 7 days, respectively, after creation of the password. In each login test, a participant was required to log in successfully within three trials for each of the discretization schemes and configurations under test. Otherwise the login test was claimed a failure. A participant who failed in either login test was required to re-do the above procedure, only for the failed discretization schemes and configurations, until he or she passed the two login tests successfully for all the discretization schemes and configurations under test. This process was designed to ensure that every participant selected a PCCP password that could be remembered for a reasonably long time. The PCCP passwords which had successfully completed the two login tests were collected.

For each participant, we built personalized dictionaries as described in Section 5.2. Each guess in a personalized dictionary was tested in the following order until the password was found, the dictionary was exhausted, or the termination condition was met: randomly for Robust Discretization; from highest probability to the lowest probability for Centered Discretization using the probability model; or from lowest layer to the highest layer and randomly within the same layer for Centered Discretization using the zooming-out window model. The attack result was recorded.

5.5 Experimental Results

5.5.1 Attack Results for Robust Discretization

For Robust Discretization, only the grid-square size of 19×19, with $r = 3$ pixels, was studied since a smaller grid-square size leads to poor usability according to [16]. For this setting, 15 out of the 38 passwords were found by our attack, with a success rate of 39.4%, and with the attack dictionaries each of approximately 2^{35} entries.

To find out how effectively Robust Discretization has helped reduce dictionary sizes, we constructed the attack dictionaries traversing all combinations of the detected salient points, i.e., without exploiting Robust Discretization. These dictionaries were all of approximately 2^{39} entries. For each user, the individual full search space contains 2^{43} entries for the size of images we used, which is the same size as the full password space for all users in PassPoints. This is because that once the user ID and the first image are determined, each grid-square would select a next image, and there are $391 (= \lfloor 451/19 \rfloor \times \lfloor 331/19 \rfloor)$ grid-squares per image. Therefore, the first click-point has 391 possibilities. For each grid-square in the first image, there are 391 grid-squares in the second image, which contributes 391 possibilities. Therefore the first two click-points contribute $391 \times 391 = 391^2$ possibilities. This procedure repeats until all the five click-points have been taken into consideration, resulting in $391^5 \approx 2^{43}$ possibilities, which is the full search space for an individual user. The prediction of click-points using the corner and centroid detection algorithms described in Section 4.3 has thus effectively reduced the password search space by a factor of 2^4 (= $2^{43} / 2^{39}$), i.e. 4 bits, and Robust Discretization has further reduced the search space by a factor of 2^4 (= $2^{39} / 2^{35}$), i.e., 4 additional bits.

On the other hand, Robust Discretization removes an average of $1.0 - \sqrt[5]{2^{35}/2^{39}} = 42.6\%$ of grid-squares per image when constructing attack dictionaries, which roughly agrees with the 36% area ratio of the eligible region to the grid-square size (see Section 4.4.2).

5.5.2 Attack Results for Centered Discretization

For Centered Discretization, grid-square sizes ranged from 9×9 to 19×19 were used, leading to $r = 4.5, 5.5, ..., 9.5$ pixels. For each r, dictionaries were built respectively with the zooming-out window model using d running from 2 to $\lfloor r \rfloor$, and with the probability model where the size of a dictionary is controlled at the end of the range of an integer power of 2.

Table 1 summarizes our attack results achieved with the zooming-out window model. The leftmost column shows attack success rates (the ratio of the number of guessed passwords to the total number of passwords). Note that for the same d, the success rate remains constant for different grid-square sizes, since a click-point always remains at the center of its grid-square, which is also the center of the selecting window with a size of $2d \times 2d$. When the grid-square size is fixed, the attack success rate is correlated with the dictionary size; the larger dictionaries are used, the higher the attack success rate can be achieved. With attack dictionaries each of approximately 2^{35} entries, our attack successfully guessed 63.2% of the passwords when the grid-square size was 19×19, whereas the full password space was of 2^{43} entries.

Table 1. Attack success rates using the zooming-out window model

Success rate (%)	Dictionary size (bits) per grid-square size					
	19x19	17x17	15x15	13x13	11x11	9x9
76.4	38					
71.1	37	38				
71.1	36	37	39			
63.2	35	36	38	40		
57.9	33	35	37	39	41	
39.5	30	32	34	36	38	41
7.9	27	29	31	33	35	38
2.6	21	23	25	27	30	33

Table 2 summarizes our results achieved with the probability model. The leftmost column is dictionary size (n bits). Attack results for some n values are omitted to avoid an overly lengthy table. When the grid-square size is fixed, the attack success rate is correlated with the dictionary size; the larger dictionaries are used, the higher the success rate can be achieved. For the grid-square size of 19×19, and thus the full search space of 2^{43} entries, the probability model successfully guessed 69.2% of the passwords with attack dictionaries of approximately 2^{35} entries, and guessed 50% of the passwords with attack dictionaries each of approximately 2^{30} entries.

In addition to a better controlled dictionary size, the probability model also produced better success rates than the zooming-out window model did, as we can easily see by comparing Table 1 and Table 2.

Table 2. Attack success rates using the probability model

Dictionary size (bits)	Attack success rate (%) per grid-square size					
	19x19	17x17	15x15	13x13	11x11	9x9
43					65.8	57.9
40		76.3	73.7	71.1	60.5	34.2
39	81.6	76.3	71.1	65.8	52.6	23.7
38	74.4	76.3	71.1	63.2	50	18.4
35	69.2	65.8	52.6	36.9	18.4	7.9
33	63.2	55.3	39.5	18.4	7.9	5.3
32	60.5	50	31.6	10.5	7.9	0
31	52.6	34.2	18.4	7.9	5.3	0
30	50	31.6	10.5	7.9	5.3	0
29	31.6	18.4	7.9	5.3	0	0
28	21.1	10.5	7.9	5.3	0	0
26	10.5	7.9	5.3	0	0	0
23	5.3	2.6	0	0	0	0

Table 3. Full password space and salient point dictionary size for different grid-square sizes

	Grid-square size					
	19x19	17x17	15x15	13x13	11x11	9x9
Salient point dictionary size (bits)	39	40	41	42	43	44
Full password space (bits)	43	44	46	48	51	54

For each grid-square size, we also constructed attack dictionaries using all the detected salient points, but without exploiting any information leaked by Centered Discretization. Table 3 shows the size of each of such dictionaries and the corresponding full password space size. By comparing Table 1 with Table 3 and Table 2 with Table 3, we see how much the information leakage by Centered Discretization has contributed to our attacks, and how much our salient point detection methods have contributed to our attacks, respectively. For example, when the grid-square size was 19×19, our salient point detection reduced the search space by a factor of $2^4 (= 2^{43} / 2^{39})$, i.e. 4 bits, as illustrated in Table 3. When the information leakage by the discretization was exploited, we could further reduce the search space by a factor of $2^9 (= 2^{39} / 2^{30})$, i.e. 9 bits, but still successfully guessed 39.5% of the passwords using the zooming-out window model, and 50% of the passwords using the probability model. This clearly suggests that Centered Discretization can leak a significant amount of password information.

To compare the success rates for both Robust Discretization and Centered Discretization with the same 19×19 grid-square size, our attack on Centered Discretization produced a much higher success rate for similar dictionary sizes or required much smaller dictionaries to achieve similar success rates. This result contradicts the previous conclusion in [16] that they both have the same level of security to dictionary attacks. This contradiction is due to the fact that the information leakage caused by discretization was ignored in [16].

The significantly different success rates between the two discretization schemes for the same grid-square size can be explained by the fact that the discretization schemes leak click-point information at different uncertainty levels: *whether a click-point is in the center of a grid square* in Centered Discretization vs. *whether a click-point is inside an eligible region, i.e. 36% of a grid square* in Robust Discretization. That is, Centered Discretization leaks much more click-point information than Robust Discretization does, and thus the former suffers more from our dictionary attacks.

On the other hand, for the same r, Centered Discretization tends to have a better security than Robust Discretization, as the former allows a much larger theoretical password space. For example, when $r = 3$, our attack guessed 39.4% of the passwords when Robust Discretization (with grid-square size of 19×19) was used, and 7.9% of the passwords when Centered Discretization (with grid-square size of 9×9) was used, both used dictionaries each of approximately 2^{35} entries.

6. DISCUSSIONS

We have not conducted experimental studies on the Image-Dependent Discretization (IDD) scheme [18] due to lack of details to implement the scheme. However, it is possible to apply our ideas for attacking Centered Discretization to mount dictionary attacks on this IDD as well.

In the IDD scheme, image features are analyzed with image processing and computer vision techniques to predict likely click-points, which are then placed at centers of Voronoi polygon tiles. When such prediction is reasonably accurate, we can use the distance of a salient point to the center of a Voronoi polygon tile to model the probability that the salient point is a click-point. In this case, we can actually use the same techniques as we used for Centered Discretization to rank-order sequences of Voronoi polygon tiles that contain salient points. This way, we will be able to achieve a much improved success rate in password guessing than that can be achieved without exploiting click-point information leaked by IDD.

On the other hand, if the prediction of click-points is not very accurate, then the IDD scheme may not be as attractive as other discretization schemes, since a wrong prediction may result in a click-point far away from the center of a Voronoi polygon tile, leading to a significant reduction of the tolerance range of click-variations, and thus may cause unacceptable false accepts and false rejects.

7. CONCLUSION

We have shown that two representative discretization schemes, Robust Discretization and Centered Discretization, both leak information on password click-points, weakening the security of click-based graphical password systems. This is an important issue that had been neglected by researchers and practitioners before our study.

Our purely automated dictionary attacks have successfully exploited click-point information leaked by each of the discretization schemes. In our experiments, our attack successfully guessed 69.2% of the passwords in PCCP when Centered Discretization was used, and 39.4% of the passwords when Robust Discretization was used, with attack dictionaries each of approximately 2^{35} entries whereas the full password space was of 2^{43} entries. In addition, for Centered Discretization, our attack still successfully guessed 50% of the passwords in PCCP when the attack dictionary size was reduced to approximately 2^{30}. These results clearly suggest that both representative discretization schemes leak a significant amount of password information.

PCCP was considered robust to all known dictionary attacks, and thus the most secure click-based graphical password scheme. However, our results for the first time show that PCCP is vulnerable to dictionary attacks when its implementation uses either Centered Discretization or Robust Discretization.

Our attacks are certainly also applicable to other click-based graphical passwords such as PassPoints and CCP. What our attacks have exploited is a fundamental security problem with the underlying discretization mechanisms, and it is straightforward to apply our attacks to PassPoints, CCP or any other click-based graphical passwords. It is worthwhile to highlight that since our attack assumes that password click-points are mutually independent, which is a conservative assumption, our results as reported just indicates a conservative success rate for schemes like PassPoints and CCP (like a lower bound). For example, the heuristic patterns of click-points used in [10][11] or the first-order Markov model used in [8][9] can be applied to significantly boost our attack's success rate on PassPoints. That is, when these attacks are combined with ours, they will lead to a dramatically improved success rate on guessing PassPoints passwords.

As such, our work calls for the design of countermeasures to address our attack, or the design of better discretization schemes or other alternatives. For example, for the sake of security, a discretization scheme should leak as little information as possible. On the other hand, a discretization scheme offering good usability tends to leak click-point information. A good balance between these two contradicting requirements remains a research issue.

This line of exploration is essential for implementing usable and secure click-based graphical passwords in various contexts (including Web applications with increasingly popular keyboardless client devices), and it is our ongoing work.

8. REFERENCES

[1] Blonder, G. 1996. Graphical Passwords. United States Patent 5559961.

[2] Wiedenbeck, S., Waters, J., Birget, J. C., Brodskiy, A., and Memon, N. 2005. Authentication using graphical passwords: Effects of tolerance and image choice. In *Proc. Symp. on Usable Privacy and Security (SOUPS'05)*.

[3] Wiedenbeck, S., Waters, J., Birget, J. C., Brodskiy, A., and Memon, N. 2005. PassPoints: Design and longitudinal evaluation of a graphical password system. *Int. Journal of Human-Computer Studies (Special Issue on HCI Research in Privacy and Security)*. 63, 102–127.

[4] Chiasson, S., van Oorschot, P. C., and Biddle, R. 2007. A second look at the usability of click-based graphical passwords. In *Proc. Symp. on Usable Privacy and Security (SOUPS'07)*.

[5] Dirik, A., Menon, N., and Birget, J. 2007. Modeling user choice in the PassPoints graphical password scheme. In *Proc. Symp. on Usable Privacy and Security (SOUPS'07)*.

[6] Golofit, K. 2007. Click passwords under investigation. In *12th European Symposium on Research in Computer Security (ESORICS'07)*. LNCS vol. 4734 (Sept. 2007).

[7] Chiasson, S., Forget, A., Biddle, R., and van Oorschot, P. C. 2009. User interface design affects security: Patterns in click-based graphical passwords. *Int. Journal of Information Security*. Springer, 8, 6 (2009), 387-398.

[8] Thorpe, J., and van Oorschot, P. C. 2007. Human-seeded attacks and exploiting hot-spots in graphical passwords. In *USENIX Security*.

[9] van Oorschot, P. C., and Thorpe, J. 2011. Exploiting predictability in click-based graphical passwords. *Journal of Computer Security*, 19, 4 (2011), 669-702.

[10] Salehi-Abari, A., Thorpe, J., and van Oorschot, P. C. 2008. On purely automated attacks and click-based graphical passwords. In *Proc. 24th Annual Computer Security Applications Conference (ACSAC)*.

[11] van Oorschot, P. C., Salehi-Abari, A., and Thorpe, J. 2010. Purely automated attacks on PassPoints-style graphical passwords. *IEEE Trans. Information Forensics and Security*. 5, 3 (2010), 393-405.

[12] Chiasson, S., van Oorschot, P. C., and Biddle, R. 2007. Graphical password authentication using cued click Ppoints. In *ESORICS'2007*. LNCS, vol. 4734/2007, 359–374.

[13] Chiasson, S., Forget, A., Biddle, R., and van Oorschot, P. C. 2008. Influencing users towards better passwords: Persuasive cued click-points. In *Proc. of HCI*. British Computer Society.

[14] Chiasson, S., Stobert, E., Forget, A., Biddle, R., and van Oorschot, P. C. 2012. Persuasive cued click-points: Design, implementation, and evaluation of a knowledge-based authentication mechanism. *IEEE Trans. on Dependable and Secure Computing*. 9, 2 (March/April 2012), 222-235.

[15] Birget, J. C., Hong, D., and Memon, N. 2006. Graphical passwords based on robust discretization. *IEEE Trans. Information Forensics and Security*. 1, 3 (2006), 395-399.

[16] Chiasson, S., Srinivasan, J., Biddle, R., and van Oorschot, P. C. 2008. Centered discretization with application to graphical passwords. In *Proc. 1st Conf. on Usability, Psychology, and Security (UPSEC'08)*.

[17] Bicakci, K. 2008. Optimal discretization for high-entropy graphical passwords. In *23rd Int. Symp. on Computer and Information Sciences* (Istanbul, Turkey, 2008).

[18] Kirovski, D., Jojie, N., and Roberts, P. 2006. Click passwords. In *IFIP Int. Federation for Information Processing, vol. 201, Security and Privacy in Dynamic Environments*. 351-363.

[19] Biddle, R., Chiasson, S., and van Oorschot, P. C. 2012. Graphical passwords: Learning from the first twelve years.

ACM Computing Surveys. 44, 4 (August 2012), Article 19, 1-41.

[20] Jansen, W. A. 2003. Authenticating users on handheld devices. In *Proc. of Canadian Information Technology Security Symposium* (2003).

[21] Passlogix. http://www.passlogix.com, site accessed May 6, 2011.

[22] Cheng, Y. 1995. Mean shift, mode seeking, and clustering. *IEEE Trans. on Pattern Analysis and Machine Intelligence.* 17, 8 (1995), 790-799.

[23] Comaniciu, D., and Meer, P. 2002. Mean shift: A robust approach toward feature space analysis. *IEEE Trans. on Pattern Analysis and Machine Intelligence.* 24, 5 (2002), 603-619.

[24] J. Franks, P. Hallam-Baker, J. Hostetler, S. Lawrence, P. Leach, A. Luotonen, and L. Stewart. 1999. HTTP authentication: Basic and digest access authentication, *RFC 2617.*

[25] Harris, C. G., and Stephens, M. J. 1988. A Combined corner and edge detector. In *Proc. of the Fourth Alvey Vision Conference.* 147–151.

[26] Kovesi, P. D. *MATLAB and Octave Functions for Computer Vision and Image Processing.* School of Computer Science & Software Engineering, University of Western Australia. http://www.csse.uwa.edu.au/~pk/research/matlabfns/.

[27] *Edge Detection and Image Segmentation (EDISON) System.* http://coewww.rutgers.edu/riul/research/code/EDISON/doc/segm.html.

Author Index

Abel, Fabian 1273
Aberer, Karl 781
Agarwal, Deepak 571
Aggarwal, Charu C. 1041
Agrawal, Rahul 13
Agrawal, Rakesh 165
Ahmed, Amr 25, 37, 953
Ahn, Hyung-iL 49
Ajmera, Jitendra 49
Akhawe, Devdatta 59
Albrecht, Jeannie 631
Alexandrova, Todorka 803
Almeida, Virgilio 1065
Aly, Mohamed 71
Alzoubi, Hussein A. 83
Amann, Bernhard 59
Amer-Yahia, Sihem 1
Anderson, Ashton 95
Andrews, Matthew 1297
Anyanwu, Kemafor 423
Assunção, Renato 1319
Auer, Sören 1145
Avraham, Uri 515
Backstrom, Lars 1307
Balzarotti, Davide 177
Banerjee, Jay 1569
Banks, Richard 749
Benson, Edward 107
Beutel, Alex 119
Bhasin, Anmol 1377
Bi, Bin 131
Blanco, Roi 561
Borggaard, Geoffrey 1389
Borodin, Allan 141
Borodin, Yevgen 1031
Bozzon, Alessandro 153
Brambilla, Marco 153
Braverman, Mark 141
Bu, Jiajun 1331
Budak, Ceren 165
Bühler, Thomas 1077
Bühmann, Lorenz 977
Cai, Deng 1331
Canali, Davide 177
Cao, Jian 595
Cao, Longbing 595
Caragea, Cornelia 471
Carmel, David 515
Carrascal, Juan Pablo 189

Çatalyürek, Ümit V. 715
Caverlee, James 667
Cecchet, Emmanuel 631
Ceri, Stefano 153
Cha, Meeyoung 827
Chakrabarti, Kaushik ...1261
Chakrabarti, Soumen ...1099
Chandaria, Jigna 965
Chang, Ming-Wei 1353
Chang, Yi 1365
Chen, Chun 1331
Chen, Kuan-Ta 827
Chen, Minghua 1477
Chen, Ying 201
Cheng, Hong 1477
Cheng, Jian 1501
Cheng, Tao 1261
Cheng, Xueqi 1445
Cheng, Zhiyuan 667
Cherubini, Mauro 189
Chi, Ed H. 403
Christin, Nicolas 213
Chu, Wei 1353, 1411
Chuah, Chen-Nee 771
Ciaramita, Massimiliano ...249
Cichowlas, Alison 1389
Contractor, Danish 49
Cook, James 225, 237
Cornolti, Marco 249
Cosley, Dan 1133
Crescenzi, Valter 261
Crowcroft, Jon 965, 1065
Cudré-Mauroux, Philippe 367
Cuevas, Angel 483
Cuevas, Ruben 483
Cummins, Ronan 1557
Czeskis, Alexei 273
Dalvi, Nilesh 285, 295
Danescu-Niculescu-Mizil, Cristian
   307
Das Sarma, Anish 295
Dasgupta, Anirban ...285, 295, 319
Dave, Kushal 331
de Alfaro, Luca 343
de Oliveira, Rodrigo 189
Del Corro, Luciano 355
Demartini, Gianluca 367
Denesuk, Matthew 49
Desmet, Lieven 989

Difallah, Djellel Eddine ...367
Dill, Stephen 49
Dong, Anlei 1365
Dong, Xin Luna 379
Dror, Gideon 391
Dustdar, Schahram 761
Eksombatchai, Chantat ..1237
Erramilli, Vijay 189
Ester, Martin 909
Fabrikant, Alex 237
Faloutsos, Christos ..119, 1319
Faloutsos, Michalis 619
Feinberg, Jonathan 1389
Feng, Shi 1511
Fernquist, Jennifer 403
Ferragina, Paolo 249
Francillon, Aurélien 177
Friedland, Gerald 447
Frossi, Alessandro 861
Fu, Xin 1213
Fuhry, David 1089
Gadiraju, Ujwal 1273
Gaedke, Martin 551
Galárraga, Luis 413
Gao, Bin 1433
Gao, Huiji 607
Gao, Jie 1021
Gao, Sidan 423
Gemulla, Rainer 355
Gerber, Daniel 977
Ghosh, Arpita 319
Gilad, Yossi 435
Giles, C. Lee 471
Gill, Konark 1341
Glaser, Hartmut 0
Gligor, Virgil 679
Goel, Ashish 505
Goga, Oana 447
Goldstein, Daniel G. 459
Gollapalli, Sujatha Das ..471
Gonzalez, Roberto 483
Gorla, Jagadeesh 495
Goyal, Navin 943
Graepel, Thore 131
Grau, Bernardo Cuenca ..1569
Grüneberger, Franz Josef ..551
Gu, Zhiping 595
Guo, Jiafeng 1445
Gupta, Archit 13

Gupta, Pankaj 505	Keegan, Brian 737	Lucier, Brendan 141
Guruswami, Venkatesan 119	Kenthapadi, Krishnaram 225	Lui, John C. S. 849
Guy, Ido 515	Kim, Jong 1191	Lynn, Brian 631
Han, Jiawei 1041	Kim, Tiffany Hyun-Jin 679	Ma, Hao 1201
Hannak, Aniko 527	Kim, Younghoon 691	Ma, Richard T. B. 849
Hardiman, Stephen J. 539	Kleinberg, Jon 95, 1307	Ma, Shaoping 1511
Harth, Andreas 1225	Kliman-Silver, Chloe 919	Maarek, Yoelle 391, 1249
Hassan, Ahmed 1411	Koenigstein, Noam 999	Madhyastha, Harsha V. 619
Hassidim, Avinatan 237	Kohno, Tadayoshi 273	Maggi, Federico 861
Hauff, Claudia 1273	Kolar, Sumanth 331	Mahabadi, Sepideh 1
He, Xiaodong 1353, 1411	Kosinski, Michal 131	Majumder, Anirban 873
He, Xiaofei 1331	Krause, Andreas 1167	Margolin, Drew 737
He, Yeye 1261	Krishnamurthy, Balachander 527	Marshall, Catherine C. 749, 885
Hebert, Jack 1389	Kruegel, Christopher 861	Mauri, Andrea 153
Hein, Matthias 1077	Krushevskaja, Darja 703	McAfee, R. Preston 459
Heinrich, Matthias 551	Küçüktunç, Onur 715	McAuley, Julian 897
Herzberg, Amir 435	Kumar, Ravi 285	Meert, Wannes 989
Hillard, Dustin 1179	Kunegis, Jérôme 727	Mei, Hong 1421
Hollink, Laura 561	Lahaie, Sébastien 1179	Mei, Qiaozhu 1545
Hong, Liangjie 25	Lakshmanan, Laks V. S. 643	Mei, Tao 1457
Horrocks, Ian 1569	Lalmas, Mounia 1557	Mejer, Avihai 391
Horvitz, Eric 1399	Lan, Yanyan 1445	Merialdo, Paolo 261
Hose, Katja 413	Lathia, Neal 495	Mesbah, Ali 815
Houben, Geert-Jan 1273	Laxman, Srivatsan 943	Mika, Peter 561
Hsieh, Cho-Jui 571	Lazer, David 527, 737	Mishra, Nina 225
Hsu, Bo-June (Paul) 583	Lee, Kyumin 667	Mislove, Alan 527, 919
Hu, Liang 595	Lee, Sangho 1191	Misra, Vishal 849
Hu, Xia 607	Lehmann, Jens 977	Mitra, Prasenjit 471
Huang, Lin-Shung 679	Lei, Chin-Laung 827	Mittal, Manas 1157
Huang, Sandy 1237	Lei, Howard 447	Moghaddam, Samaneh 909
Huang, Thomas 1041	Leskovec, Jure ... 95, 307, 897, 1237	Mohanlal, Manish 1341
Huang, Ting-Kai 619	Levine, Brian Neil 631	Molavi Kakhki, Arash 527
Huang, Xinyi (Lisa) 571	Liang, Guangtai 1421	Moon, Sue 0
Hurley, Ryan 631	Liberatore, Marc 631	Moshchuk, Alexander 273
Huttenlocher, Daniel 95	Lin, Jimmy 505	Moshfeghi, Yashar 931
Indyk, Piotr 1	Lin, Yu-Ru 737	Motamedi, Reza 483
Jackson, Collin 679	Lindley, Siân E. 749	Mukherjee, Shibnath 943
Jacovi, Michal 515	Liptchinsky, Vitaliy 761	Nagarajan, Meena 49
Jain, Prateek 943	Liu, Han 771	Nakajima, Tatsuo 803
Jamali, Mohsen 643	Liu, Huan 607	Narayan, Onuttom 1297
Jentzsch, LaDawn 953	Liu, Juan 1021	Narayanamurthy, Shravan 37
Jin, Xiaoran 655	Liu, Tie-Yan 1433	Nath, Abhirup 943
Joosen, Wouter 989	Liu, Xin 781	Navalpakkam, Vidhya 953
Jose, Joemon M. 931, 1557	Liu, Yefeng 803	Nazir, Atif 771
Josifovski, Vanja 37, 71	Liu, Yiqun 1511	Nencioni, Gianfranco 965
Joung, Jinoo 771	Liu, Yuan 1457	Ngo, Chong-Wah 1457
Jurafsky, Dan 307	Lo, James 815	Ngonga Ngomo, Axel-Cyrille ... 977
Kakhki, Arash Molavi 919	Lou, Jing-Kai 827	1145
Kamath, Krishna Y. 667	Lou, Tiancheng 837	Nikiforakis, Nick 989
Karger, David R. 107	Loureiro, Antonio A. F. 1319	Niu, Biao 1501
Katzir, Liran 539	Lu, Hanqing 1501	Oren, Joel 141
Kaya, Kamer 715	Lu, Jian 1467	Orwant, Jon 1389

1593

Ottaviano, Giuseppe 583	Schien, Daniel 1111	Tsiatas, Alexander 1297
Palow, Christopher 119	Schoenebeck, Grant 1123	Ugander, Johan 1307
Pandey, Sandeep 71	Schwabe, Daniel 0	Unger, Christina 977
Paquet, Ulrich 999	Schwagereit, Felix 727	Ur, Sigalit 515
Park, Juyong 827	Sellen, Abigail 749	Vaingankar, Vishal 331
Park, Kunwoo 827	Shabajee, Paul 1111	Vallentin, Matthias 59
Park, Yoonjae 691	Shah, Sam 571	Van Acker, Steven 989
Parthasarathi, Sree Hari Krishnan 447	Sharma, Amit 1133	Varma, Manik 13
Parthasarathy, Srinivasan 1089	Sharma, Aneesh 505	Varma, Vasudeva 331
Pasternack, Jeff 1009	Shavlovsky, Michael 343	Vaz de Melo, Pedro O. S. 1319
Patil, Akshay 1021	Shekarpour, Saeedeh 1145	Verma, Ashish 49
Pelleg, Dan 1249	Shen, Zeqian 1533	Viégas, Fernanda 1389
Pennacchiotti, Marco 1521	Shervashidze, Nino 37	Vigna, Giovanni 861
Perrig, Adrian 679	Shi, Xiaolin 1213	Walls, Robert J. 631
Pesce, João Paulo 1065	Shim, Kyuseok 691	Wang, Beidou 1331
Piessens, Frank 989	Shipman, Frank M. 885	Wang, Can 1331
Posse, Christian 1377	Shokouhi, Milad 131	Wang, Dong 505
Potts, Christopher 307	Shrivastava, Nisheeth 873	Wang, Gang 1341
Prabhu, Yashoteja 13	Singer, Yaron 1157	Wang, Helen J. 273
Preist, Chris 1111	Singla, Adish 1167	Wang, Hongning 1201, 1353
Preusse, Julia 727	Sloan, Marc 655	1365, 1411
Prusty, Swagatika 631	Smola, Alex 25, 953	Wang, Jian 1377
Punera, Kunal 71	Smola, Alexander J. 37	Wang, Jun 495, 655
Puzis, Rami 1031	Sodomka, Eric 1179	Wang, Kuansan 1201
Puzis, Yury 1031	Sommer, Robin 59, 447	Wang, Qianxiang 1421
Qi, Guo-Jun 1041	Song, Jonghyuk 1191	Wattenberg, Martin 1389
Qiu, Disheng 261	Song, Yang 1201, 1213	Wei, Dongchen 1581
Qu, Yan 1053	1353, 1411	West, Robert 307, 1399
Quercia, Daniele 1065	Soroush, Hamed 631	White, Ryen W. 1353, 1399, 1411
Rabinovich, Michael 83	Sosič, Rok 1237	Wilson, Christo 527
Rae, Adam 1285	Spatscheck, Oliver 83	Wohlstadter, Eric 815
Rahman, Md Sazzadur 619	Speiser, Sebastian 1225	Wolak, Janis 631
Ramakrishnan, I.V. 1031	Springer, Thomas 551	Wood, Stephen G. 1111
Rangapuram, Syama 1077	Srivastava, Divesh 379	Wren, Christopher R. 1389
Rastogi, Vibhor 285, 295	Stadtmüller, Steffen 1225	Wu, Ling 1421
Ravi, Sujith 953	Stone-Gross, Brett 861	Wu, Qian 1421
Regan, Tim 749	Stringhini, Gianluca 861	Wu, Zhe 1569
Rejaie, Reza 483	Studer, Rudi 1225	Xie, Tao 1421
Riederer, Christopher 189	Suchanek, Fabian 413	Xu, Feng 1467
Robertson, Stephen 495	Suen, Caroline 1237	Xu, Guandong 595
Ronen, Inbal 515	Sundaresan, Neel 1533	Xu, Haifeng 1433
Roth, Dan 1009	Suri, Siddharth 459	Xu, Heng 201
Ruan, Yiye 1089	Szpektor, Idan 391, 1249	Xu, Wanhong 119
Sandler, Mark 697	Taneva, Bilyana 1261	Yan, Jeff 1581
Saniee, Iraj 1297	Tang, Jie 837	Yan, Xiaohui 1445
Sapieżyński, Piotr 527	Tang, Jiliang 607	Yan, Xifeng 1467
Sarlós, Tamás 295	Tao, Ke 1273	Yang, Diyi 1433
Sastry, Nishanth 965	Teflioudi, Christina 413	Yang, Maowei 1581
Satzger, Benjamin 761	Teixeira, Renata 447	Yao, Ting 1457
Saule, Erik 715	Thomee, Bart 1285	Yao, Yuan 1467
Sawant, Uma 1099	Tiwari, Mitul 571	Ye, Jihang 1477
Sayres, Rory 953	Tong, Hanghang 1467	Yu, Philip S. 1533

Yuan, Ting 1501	Zhang, Wei Vivian 1331	Zhou, Ke 1557
Zabolotnyi, Rostyslav 761	Zhang, Xi 1501	Zhou, Yilu 201
Zadeh, Reza 505	Zhang, Yi 1377	Zhou, Yujiao 1569
Zanero, Stefano 861	Zhang, Yongfeng 1511	Zhu, Bin B. 1581
Zhai, ChengXiang 1365	Zhang, Yongzheng 1521	Zhu, Can 595
Zhang, Aonan 1489	Zhao, Ben Y. 1341	Zhu, Jun 1489
Zhang, Bo 1489	Zhao, Yuchen 1533	Zhu, Sencun 201
Zhang, Jun 1053	Zhao, Zhe 1545	Zhu, Zhe 1477
Zhang, Min 1511	Zheng, Haitao 1341	